American Foreign Relations since *1600*

American Foreign Relations since *1600*

A Guide to the Literature

Second Edition

Volume 1

Robert L. Beisner, Editor

Kurt W. Hanson, Assistant Editor

A B C CLIO

Santa Barbara, California
Denver, Colorado
Oxford, England

Library of Congress Cataloging-in-Publication Data

American Foreign Relations since 1600: a guide to the
literature / edited by Robert L. Beisner. — 2nd ed.
        p. cm.
Rev. ed. of: Guide to American foreign relations
since 1700 / edited by Richard Dean Burns. 1983.

Includes bibliographical references and indexes.
    ISBN: 1-57607-080-8 (acid free paper)
    ISBN: 1-57607-530-3 (e-book)
  1. United States—Foreign relations—bibliography.
I. Beisner, Robert L. II. Guide to Amercan foreign
relations since 1700.

  Z6465.U5G84   2003
  [E183.7]
  016.32773—dc21   2003008684

07 06 05 04 03   10 9 8 7 6 5 4 3 2 1

This book is also available on the World Wide Web
as an e-book. Visit abc-clio.com for details.

ABC-CLIO, Inc.
130 Cremona Drive, P.O. Box 1911
Santa Barbara, California 93116-1911

This book is printed on acid-free paper ∞.
Manufactured in the United States of America

*To the memory of Gerald Bernath,
Myrna Bernath, and Stuart Bernath*

Contents

Preface

In the 1970s, members of the Society for Historians of American Foreign Relations (SHAFR) first conceived the idea of producing an annotated bibliographical guide to the study of the history of U.S. foreign relations. The plan originated in the hope of updating (and superseding) the impressive but by then hopelessly obsolete Samuel Flagg Bemis and Grace Gardner Griffin, eds., *Guide to the Diplomatic History of the United States, 1775–1921* (Washington, DC: Government Printing Office, 1935). SHAFR's ambition bore fruit in a superb new work, Richard Dean Burns, ed., *Guide to American Foreign Relations since 1700* (Santa Barbara, CA: ABC-CLIO, 1983). A collective effort of forty-one contributing editors and ninety-two contributors, the 1983 *Guide* included 9,255 entries that ranged from American Historical Association, *The American Historical Association's Guide to Historical Literature* (New York: Macmillan, 1961) on page 5, to Philip J. Klass, *Secret Spies in Space* (New York: Random House, 1971) on page 1,213.[1] It was organized into forty chapters and included maps and two appendices—one an analytical listing of "Makers of American Foreign Policy," the other a set of biographical sketches of secretaries of state from Robert R. Livingston to George P. Shultz. A substantial historiographical essay preceded each chapter.

This fine compendium of historical scholarship immediately became indispensable to researchers and teachers alike. Like many, I acquired two copies, one for my university office (still bearing the bold, taped-on message, "Do Not Remove from Office") and one for my study at home. Discussing everything from freshman term papers to doctoral dissertations, I referred students to the *Guide* hundreds of times and consulted it for my own work as often. But relevant new publications also appeared by the hundreds each year, and before long SHAFR members began wondering about the possibilities of an update or new edition. The Burns *Guide* had not become obsolete—it remains extremely useful even now—but it became progressively necessary to venture beyond it in bibliographical searches. (The same fate, of course, awaits the present work.) By the mid-nineties, members of the SHAFR Council were actively considering the production of a new *Guide*.

In 1997, I was asked to oversee a new edition. I consulted widely, especially among members of a distinguished advisory board I appointed for the purpose, before making several important decisions. Although the original *Guide* would serve as a general model for its successor, it seemed advisable to depart from its design in a few respects, especially in not including maps or the lists of foreign policy "makers" and biographical sketches of secretaries of state. Most of this information is readily available in other publications, including textbooks and the Internet. Somewhat reluctantly, we also decided against the substantial historiographical essays that introduced each chapter of the original book, judging that although they had added significant intellectual weight to it, they had mostly gone unread. In the current work, brief editors' statements about their selection criteria are included instead; moreover, the editors make historiographical work the focus of a section of each chapter. Influencing these decisions was an awareness that the likely size of the new work (as it turned out, over 16,000 entries compared to 9,000-plus) made it important to save space where we could. The result is that the new volumes are not a *Guide to American Foreign Relations since 1700* but a straightforward annotated bibliography; thus the title, *American Foreign Relations since 1600: A Guide to the Literature.* After making basic organizational decisions, in the spring and summer of 1998 I turned to the sometimes daunting task of recruiting editors for specific chapters, a small number of whom required substitution over the next two years.

Several other decisions shape the character and structure of this work. Lengthy consideration and consultation with the advisory board focused on a possible effort to create some kind of "balance" in coverage among different periods of U.S. history. Having available no magic wand that would tell me *how* to "balance," say, Civil War diplomacy and the early cold war, being concerned that "balance" would produce unproductive excavations to the bottom of the barrel in some fields but a mere skimming of the top soil in others, and from the outset discomfited by the idea of portioning a roughly equal number of entries to each chapter, I decided that market forces should prevail and so advised the chapter editors. The result is readily apparent; just as with the Burns *Guide,* works on the twentieth century—and the post–World War II period—predominate, reflecting U.S. years as a great power and the scholarship such status attracts. The number of entries in particular chapters ranges from 140 to 1,335.

I asked all editors to include helpful works on historiography. That some chapters are relatively bereft of such entries does not reflect any lack of industry on the editors' part but the simple fact that little historiographical attention has been given to certain areas, leaving gaps that the editors of *Diplomatic History,* with their power to commission work, might help fill in the future. I also urged editors to pay more than the usual attention to journal articles and essay collections. To ensure attention to the latter, which often gather dust because scholars or students are unaware of their contents, we have usually specifically identified authors, essay titles, and page numbers in such collections (all authors so identified appear in the Authors and Editors index).

Annotations were to be descriptive but if possible contain pointed guidance about an item's relative importance. In 1997–1998, we "decided" not to include websites, but as time passed some editors viewed this as unduly restrictive, and there are some forty references in the *Guide* to such sites. Although operating on the assumption that we were largely producing a guide to historical literature published in English, I encouraged editors to include works in other languages when they thought them of great importance. Many did so, but chapters vary, depending on editors' judgment about selection and their varying familiarity with foreign-language sources. Dissertations were to be included only when considered high in quality and necessary to fill gaps not addressed by published scholarship—nearly a hundred are listed or mentioned. Publications about other countries were to be included only when they bore heavily on U.S. subject matter.

This work also reflects a commitment to mainstreaming. With the exception of the opening chapters on reference works, overviews, and syntheses, we have eschewed using separate chapters on particular topics, such as economic or military history, or, to point to more recent historical trends, cultural relations or the impact of sex and gender on the conduct of foreign policy.

Since SHAFR owned the copyright to the contents of the 1983 *Guide,* editors were free to use, revise, or exclude old references and annotations and were given digital files from that work, scanned for the purpose. I also shared with them the contents of a diplomatic-military history bibliography of some 17,000 items I had assembled over the years (with due warning about likely inaccuracies in the collection).

The quality of the results is for others to judge. Although the chapters that follow vary in quality, as is inevitable in any collective enterprise, I am personally impressed by the editors' range, expertise, and judgment. Reading every single annotation was like being in graduate school again, and I once more received a fine education, but not enough to succumb to the temptation to pronounce on the "meaning" of the total body of scholarship represented here. Several trends, however, are immediately notable. One is the broadening of scholars' definition of what they mean by the "history of U.S. foreign relations." Brief reference to the editors' use of a keyword system will help make this clear. Part of the substructure of these volumes (though not printed in them) is a uniform set of keywords from which editors drew to attach to every entry. The result shows the growing interest in and attention to "nontraditional" aspects of the field. Of a total of 16,356 entries, editors assigned the keyword "Domestic Society" to 363, "Race and Racism" to 527 (and 269 to "African-Americans"), "Cultural Relations" to 581, and "Sex and Gender" to 201. In light of the decision to regard as a form of "foreign relations" the relations between Native Americans and first the local colonial rulers and later the federal government, 260 entries are associated with the keyword "Indians." The keywords "Religion" or "Religious Groups" are imbedded in 285 entries.

Although many factors influence how much scholarship is produced on different periods and subjects, this bibliography provides a rough measure of where work has and has not been concentrated since 1982, the last year of publication of works mentioned in the 1983 *Guide*. On the average, works published since 1982 comprise almost exactly half of the new *Guide*. As one would expect, the percentage of such works is far higher in the chapters covering the period since 1961 (running, in chapters 25–32, from 78 to 100 percent, except for chapter 30—on U.S.-African relations—where there is a nearly even split between pre- and post-1982 work). The pattern for earlier chapters is not so clear. Not counting the first two, nonchronological, chapters, one can detect a very general rule at work—the farther back in U.S. history, the more listings of pre-1982 publications. But there are notable exceptions, perhaps most dramatically illustrated by chapters 3 and 4. In chapter 3, on the seventeenth century and pre-1776 eighteenth century, 58 percent of listed works were published after 1981. Yet in chapter 4, on the revolutionary years themselves, only 16 percent of listed works date from the last two decades. Chapters 5 through 24 run from a low of 18 percent (chapter 8 on the diplomacy of the Civil War) to a high of 79 percent (chapter 21 on the Eisenhower years).

As many of our colleagues have made a point of declaring in recent years, there is little reason for tearing of hair and gnashing of teeth about the guild's health and vigor. Although many history departments and universities may currently undervalue the field, the quality of the work here recorded and annotated demonstrates that it is not the result of any deficiencies in how contemporary historians of U.S. foreign relations are practicing their profession. As the institutions that normally house such historians return to a sensible appreciation for the importance of the role of power in human affairs and the relations between the nations and peoples of the world, as they surely will, I have little doubt that they will also restore the teaching of the field to its rightful place. (For yet another sign of its continuing health, I also invite readers to note the expanding number of non-American scholars represented in the Authors and Editors index.)

Will someone else be writing a similar preface in another ten, fifteen, or twenty years? Perhaps. Even now, SHAFR is considering how to avoid starting over from scratch in the future. It may be possible, for example, using SHAFR's website to post supplements to this *Guide*. In a few years, those using it might be able to swing from the book to an integrated spot on the Internet in pursuing their bibliographical searches. Because this *Guide* has been prepared in digital form, such supplements, if kept reasonably updated, should greatly simplify the preparation of a later edition of this work, which may also eventually be put online in its entirety.

Some Conventions and Things to Know in Using the Guide

All involved in the production of this work have striven mightily to avoid errors, but we know better than to think we have completely succeeded. Readers who discover such errors would do us a great service (and help in perfecting any supplements or new editions) by reporting full, specific information about them. Instructions on reporting errors can be found on the SHAFR website at http://shafr.history.ohio-state.edu/.

Besides the general table of contents at the beginning of this work, we have also provided a more detailed table of contents at the outset of each chapter, followed as already noted by a brief editor's essay about the criteria used in determining what would appear in the chapter.

A reference item number in boldface identifies each work listed in the Guide. For example, **8:72**, the seventy-second item in chapter 8, identifies Lynn M. Case, *French Opinion on the United States and Mexico, 1860–1867: Extracts from the Reports of the Procureurs Généraux* (New York: D. Appleton-Century Company, 1936). When a work is listed more than once, which is true in hundreds of cases, subsequent references have their own number but are also cross-referenced to the primary citation, with the original reference item number appearing in parentheses after the title. Thus, Joseph W. Alsop, with Adam Platt, *"I've Seen the Best of It": Memoirs* (New York: W. W. Norton, 1992) first appears in chapter 19 and is tagged with the item reference number, **19:372**, but the same work also appears in chapters 21 (**21:210**), 22 (**22:87**), 23 (**23:144**), and 24 (**24:51**), each time listed in a shorter form—Alsop, *"I've Seen the Best of It": Memoirs* (19:372). In some cases, such later references include a distinct annotation, sometimes simply a statement directing the reader to an earlier chapter, and sometimes both. In the case of the Alsop book, each entry is annotated.

Within an annotation, when full publishing data are given for a mentioned book or article, other than the reference item itself, the work will not be otherwise listed as a separate reference item. Thus, in **17:1041**, the passage, "See also Haight's 'France's First War Mission to the United States,' *Airpower History* 11 (January 1964): 11–15 and 'Roosevelt as Friend of France,' *Foreign Affairs* 44 (April 1966): 518–26," signals that these two articles are not separately recorded or annotated. In contrast, when a publication is identified only by the author's last name, title, and date—as in "This account . . . has been largely superseded by Reckner, *Teddy Roosevelt's Great White Fleet* (1982)" (**11:105**)—the item mentioned is itself a *Guide* listing (in this case **11:108**); the reference item number will direct the reader to the first citation of the work.

To ease the reader's ability to navigate the *Guide,* we have provided three separate indexes. The keywords already mentioned were at the core of building these indexes. ("United States" does not appear in an index because of the assumption that virtually all entries concern the United States.) Readers should note that the indexes, while extremely detailed and precise in associating particular references to particular subjects, are not "nested" and do not include names, words, or phrases not used as keywords. (With any future online edition, however, researchers will be able to make simple text, as well as keyword, searches.) Many people appear both in the Individuals and Authors and Editors indexes—in the first case as historical actors and in the second as writers or editors.

In most cases, articles are rendered in the following bibliographical form: (**20:17**) Lester H. Brune, "Recent Scholarship and Findings about the Korean War," *American Studies International* 36 (October 1998): 4–16. When, instead, one finds (**6:260**) Rolf Adamson, "Swedish Iron Exports to the United States, 1783–1860," *Scandinavian Economic History Review* 17, no. 1 (1969): 58–114, the journal in question does not (or did not then) identify issues by month or season.

Where authors have published under different versions of their names—e.g., Rupert Wilson Thomas, R. Wilson Thomas, R. W. Thomas, or Rupert W. Thomas—we have used the same version throughout, usually that used by the authors in their latest, or most recent, publications. The names of Asian and Asian-American scholars, or Asian scholars publishing in western outlets, present a considerable challenge, which I am sure we have not fully solved. In most cases, we have listed their names as the authors themselves do, but since authors of no nationality can control how their names are alphabetized, this was of little help in indexing. I can only say that we tried to be reasonable and did the best we could. Another challenge was rendering a uniform spelling of the names of certain historical actors from cultures not using a Latin alphabet. A notoriously difficult example is the name of the mercurial Iranian nationalist, Mohammed Mosaddeq: even a cursory reading in the field will reveal that western writers have adopted several spellings for both names. In such cases, I have sought and followed the advice of specialists; when other spellings are used in titles or in quoted passages within annotations, of course, we have adhered to the original. Finally, except when it would generate a name with which most Americans are completely unfamiliar, either in the listing of an entry's author or in the indexes, we have stripped titled persons of their titled names (Anthony Eden rather than the Earl of Avon).

Capitalization sometimes presented problems, especially of particular words within the titles of books, articles, and essays. We have tried faithfully to follow the original, but it is sometimes difficult to identify the original, for both title pages and library entries sometimes capitalize words that are clearly not intended to be considered as capitalized (e.g., common prepositions such as "to") or, contrarily, fail to capitalize all but the first word of a title.

Generally, we list reprint editions when issued after 1969, but not if issued almost simultaneously with the original edition and usually not if the original publisher issued the reprint.

Over a hundred microform (usually microfilm or microfiche) works are listed in this *Guide*. We hope we have the correct publisher's information for these but cannot guarantee that the information will long remain accurate, for these collections tend to migrate from the control of one publisher to another. Thus, works first issued by the National Archives or the Congressional Information Service journeyed to University Publications and thence to LexisNexis Academic and Library Solutions. The publication dates of many of these are also often a mystery; sometimes the same collection will have several publication dates yet not be considered as different "editions."

Finally, we have tried to make this *Guide* as current as possible. Where it was too late to ask a contributing editor to write a new entry, I took the liberty to add "see also" notes to the annotations of related items. Thus, in the annotation for 30:368, readers will find: "For an even more recent, related account, see Kate A. Baldwin, *Beyond the Color Line and the Iron Curtain: Reading Encounters between Black and Red, 1922–1963* (Durham, NC: Duke University Press, 2002), which explores the political, social, and intellectual allure—in some cases eventually spurned—of the Soviet Union to Langston Hughes, W. E. B. Du Bois, Claude McKay, and Paul Robeson." All chapters were definitively locked down in October 2002.

Robert L. Beisner

NOTE

1. This edition goes from *The Annals of America* (Chicago: Encyclopaedia Britannica, 1968–1987) to Uri Savir, *The Process: 1,100 Days That Changed the Middle East* (New York: Random House, 1998).

Acknowledgments

Sufficient acknowledgment of the many people (besides the chapter editors themselves) who helped carry out this massive project would take more pages than are available. If only briefly, however, we want to mention those who deserve recognition as important contributors to the production of this bibliography.

This entire venture was sponsored by the Society for Historians of American Foreign Relations (SHAFR), a professional association that owes much of its vigor to the long-standing moral and financial support received from the late Gerald and Myrna Bernath, who in effect adopted—and financially nurtured—SHAFR in memory of their son, Stuart L. Bernath, a fine historian cut down in his youth by cancer. Most of SHAFR's prizes and awards draw on this generosity, as does this bibliographical project, which is dedicated to the Bernaths.

I personally have many people to thank for a variety of kinds of help and encouragement. The president of SHAFR in 1997, Emily S. Rosenberg, whom I did not then know personally, first picked up the telephone to ask me if I would undertake the editing of a new SHAFR guide, did sterling work in the months to follow triangulating the efforts and obligations of SHAFR, ABC-CLIO, and myself, and remained supportive throughout the project. Her immediate successors as president—Arnold O. Offner, Walter LaFeber, Robert D. Schulzinger, and Robert J. McMahon— were also helpful, especially in their apparent confidence that an enterprise that took longer than I first predicted would nonetheless be completed in fairly timely fashion. SHAFR presidents annually come and go, but through most of the history of what we officially called the SHAFR Bibliographical Project, the society's indispensable Executive Secretary-Treasurer Allan B. Spetter smoothed the way through any number of problems and obstacles and offered valuable information about all kinds of matters from his remarkable SHAFR institutional memory. Although the new guide was nearly complete by the time Peter L. Hahn succeeded to the executive secretary-treasurer's post, his assistance, too, was important.

Asked not only to oversee the creation of this work, but also to design its coverage and structure, I asked for help from an advisory board I named for the purpose. Through 1997 and 1998, as the design was decided upon and the editorial work got under way, board members provided excellent advice and, in response to my questions, made many fruitful suggestions about the recruitment of contributing editors. The advisory board consisted of Kinley J. Brauer, Richard Dean Burns (the editor of SHAFR's 1983 *Guide to American Foreign Relations since 1700*), Diane S. Clemens, John Lewis Gaddis, Michael H. Hunt, Diane B. Kunz, Walter LaFeber, Thomas J. Noer, Thomas G. Paterson, Stephen G. Rabe (who later agreed to take on a chapter of his own), Emily Rosenberg, and Betty Miller Unterberger. Tom Paterson was particularly astute in helping to identify those who might be willing to serve as chapter editors.

To the contributing editors themselves, naturally, I owe the most. Asked to master a bibliographical software with which they were unfamiliar and to take on tasks for which the sole reward would be found in a historian's heaven, they accepted my naïve assurances that their work would surely be done within a year and a half. It did not turn out that way, but, in my own view, the editors responded by creating an extraordinary reference work. A few were unable to stay with the project, but a remarkable corps of scholars already laboring on their own chapters took on the orphaned chapters as well, sometimes by combining them with their own. My special thanks, therefore, to James E. Lewis, Jr., Justus D. Doenecke, Chester J. Pach, and Robert D. Schulzinger for their selfless response to my call for help. Doenecke and Pach deserve even more emphatic recognition, the first for taking on the entire period between World Wars I and II, the second for grappling with the massive body of scholarship on the early cold war as well as the burgeoning body of work on the Eisenhower era—their chapters comprise over 20 percent of the entries in the *Guide*. In addition, Chester Pach's enthusiasm and technical expertise made him a kind of unofficial adviser to me throughout the enterprise.

The software referred to above is EndNote (now in version 6.0), a stunningly flexible bibliography program. Except for a few texts like these acknowledgments, we produced the entire new *Guide* on EndNote. Though this was sometimes a cause of despair among chapter editors, most in time ably adapted themselves to it. As the general editor, I found it at times even more valuable in searching for errors than in the original production of chapters, and I want to extend our gratitude to Richard K. Niles, president of ISI ResearchSoft, for donating multiple copies of EndNote to use in producing this work. Technical help of different kinds—imaginative and invaluable—came at the end of the project from ABC-CLIO's Anna Kaltenbach.

The *Guide* builds on the 1983 edition overseen by the redoubtable Richard Dean Burns. Because SHAFR controlled the copyright of the material in that work, when we included works also listed in the 1983 book, editors were free to use the original annotations (or to revise them). Those of us who have assembled this new edition, therefore, owe a mighty debt to those who produced the 1983 work. Our thanks go, first, to 1983's contributing editors (in a few cases to their memory): Edward M. Bennett, Robert S. Bothwell, Albert Hall Bowman, Thomas A. Bryson, Thomas H. Buckley, Richard Dean Burns, Raymond A. Esthus, Robert H. Ferrell, John Lewis Gaddis, Lawrence E. Gelfand, Scott R. Hall, George C. Herring, Jr., Gary R. Hess, Larry D. Hill, Paul S. Holbo, Michael H. Hunt, Akira Iriye, Howard Jones, Lawrence S. Kaplan, Warren F. Kimball, Warren F. Kuehl, Bruce R. Kuniholm, Lester D. Langley, Thomas M. Leonard, Frank J. Merli, Thomas J. Noer, Thomas G. Paterson, Bradford Perkins, David M. Pletcher, Forrest C. Pogue, Armin Rappaport, Gary M. Ross, John H. Schroeder, Martin Sherwin, Joseph M. Siracusa, William C. Stinchcombe, David F. Trask, Roger R. Trask, Russell F. Weigley, Joan Hoff Wilson (Joan Hoff), and Louis Wilson. (Among these, only Howard Jones has returned as an editor.) And, second, to those who helped them: Henry S. Albinski, David L. Anderson, John Duke Anthony, Glen St. John Barclay, Sharon L. Bollinger, Gene M. Brack, Alan S. Brown, Peter H. Buckingham, Richard Dean Burns, John C. Campbell, John Chay, Edward W. Chester, Anthony Cheung, Christopher Chipello, J. Garry Clifford, Bruce Cumings, Calvin D. Davis, Charles DeBenedetti, R. Hrair Dekmejian, Roger V. Dingman, Robert A. Divine, Justus D. Doenecke, Steven Dorr, Carolyn Woods Eisenberg, Thomas H. Etzold, Wilton Fowler, John Gimbel, Mary Gormly, Ross Gregory, Robert Griffith, Fraser J. Harbutt, George Harris, Robert A. Hart, Alan K. Henrikson, Richard Herr, Peter P. Hill, Michael Hudson, James H. Hutson, Richard H. Immerman, Ronald J. Jensen, Howard Jones, William Kamman, Allen H. Kitchens, Marvin W. Kranz, Mary V. Kuebel, Walter LaFeber, David C. Lawson, Melvyn P. Leffler, Ann M. Lesch, Steven I. Levine, David Long, Mark M. Lowenthal, Michael A. Lutzker, William H. Masterson, Robert E. May, Robert L. Messer, Aaron David Miller, Jean-Donald Miller, James A. Nathan, Arthur Ned Newberry, III, Arnold A. Offner, John L. Offner, Alison G. Olson, Gary B. Ostrower, Carl P. Parrini, R. K. Ramazani, James Reardon-Anderson, Bernard Reich, David Reynolds, Barry R. Rigby, Gary M. Ross, Michael Schaller, Mary K. Schenck, Thomas D. Schoonover, Louise Sieminski, William Z. Slany, Ronald H. Spector, Mark A. Stoler, Roland N. Stromberg, Edwin B. Strong, Sandra C. Taylor, Eugene P. Trani, Nancy Bernkopf Tucker, Michael Van Dusen, Robert H. Van Meter, Jr., William O. Walker,

III, Samuel F. Wells, Jr., Mira Wilkins, Lawrence S. Wittner, Lawrence A. Yates, and Marvin R. Zahniser. Of this group, David Anderson, Justus Doenecke, John L. Offner, Mark A. Stoler, and, again, Howard Jones returned to the new project.

I am one of many involved in this undertaking who depended on imaginative and intrepid interlibrary loan librarians, in my case usually to secure copies of (sometimes obscure) essay collections needed to identify accurate information on authors, essay titles, and page numbers. I relied repeatedly on the outstanding work of Rolliette Gooding of American University's Bender Library. E-mails between us sometimes coursed back and forth through the Internet ether several times a day. (Other interlibrary loan librarians are mentioned below in chapter editors' acknowledgments.) Bender Library's circulation department was also immensely helpful. American University's History Department, too, supported the project by paying for a supply of SHAFR Bibliography Project letterheads and envelopes, for which I want to thank my old friend, colleague, and then chair of the department, Allan J. Lichtman.

Another person who offered help whenever asked was Jeremi Suri, who occasionally dropped everything to supply translations of titles from French or German and, even more notably, to read articles in foreign languages and write annotations for them. I also thank John Lewis Gaddis for directing me to Jeremi. Similar help on Japanese texts and the treatment of the names of Asian scholars came from Joseph M. Henning. In addition, dozens of individual scholars and journal editors responded in a timely way to inquiries about various kinds of publication minutiae, especially in journal articles.

Finally, though he is properly recorded as assistant editor of the *Guide,* special thanks are owed to Kurt W. Hanson. Kurt is one of two doctoral students I carried with me into retirement from American University's History Department. At the beginning of the project, I did not yet understand how thoroughly it would become a digital rather than paper affair, but I knew I needed the help of someone whose computer and technical literacy ranked well beyond my own and asked Kurt to take on the job, even though my guilty conscience was clear that the work would impede the progress of his dissertation. There is no way this project could have been completed without his help and creativity. It was he who instantly realized that our editors should be producing digital databases rather than word processing documents, and it was he who importuned Richard Niles to help by contributing copies of EndNote. Then it was also he whose coaching helped make me enough of a master of EndNote to understand what we were doing and to assist editors unable to reach Kurt himself. He walked nearly all the editors through the working of the software and how to exploit its powers, something he did with unusual grace and patience. As the project advanced, the two of us developed an efficient routine: all editors first sent the product of their work to Kurt, who vetted it before sending it to me for further editing. Our strengths in editing were not identical, which was a good thing, for each of us often managed to inspire "Ah ha!" exclamations in the other. Midway through the project, Kurt and his family moved from the suburbs of Washington, D.C., to those of Seattle. Happily, e-mail and its power to transmit massive files back and forth allowed us to continue working as a team. As the editing neared completion, Kurt also took on the primary liaison work with the publisher's technicians. He did all this over the years while also carrying out his large responsibilities as a husband, father of two daughters (one born even as we worked), and son of parents living in his home. Sadly, his father Beverley Hanson, whom I had the good fortune to meet in 1999, attending with him one of the first home games played in Safeco Field, died three years later as we neared the end of our work. When that work was finally finished, Kurt returned his attention to a promising dissertation reinterpreting phases of the late-nineteenth-century American sense of mission.

I must also thank my good spouse, Valerie French, currently chair of the History Department at American University. She was not directly involved in this venture and in fact was careful to maintain a safe distance from it, but its consumption of my own time constantly impeded on her life. Happily, she only rarely raised an eyebrow at how this crimped my time for summer and holiday travel. (In my defense, I record that reaching European shores three times within the five years of the project's life span is not so bad.) Further, I frequently talked aloud with Valerie about this and that challenge or problem entailed by the *Guide's* editing. As she has done for a quarter century, she invariably supplied me with unerringly on-target advice about how to cope with these challenges and problems. As always, I am profoundly grateful to be married to the kind of person who can do this as well as put up with my own foibles.

Returning to Kurt Hanson, he would like to add acknowledgments to Sara Wilson, who originally suggested him to me as an assistant editor, and to Debbie Doyle, another American University graduate student, for many hours spent in converting the 1983 text into digital files, which greatly facilitated the work of our contributing editors. To the editors themselves, he extends his appreciation of their hard work, patience, and flexibility as they graciously accepted new methods and sometimes incomplete instructions in the process of creating this book, and he values the friendships made along the way. He also thanks his parents, Bev and Jean, who did not leave the room when he went on at length about "variable reference elements," "hierarchical label sorting," and other even less charming issues. His daughters, Rosalyn (seven) and Audrey (nearly two), generously allowed him to edit *Guide* data when they thought his time might better be spent playing with them, so long as they were able to climb on him as he did so. He reserves special thanks for his wife, Laurie, who resisted the completely understandable temptation to toss him and his computer out of the house as the eighteen-month project stretched into its fifth year. Such restraint is rare and must be commended. Beyond this there were many friends in the historical profession who listened to Kurt's problems and suggested remedies, especially Elizabeth Stewart, Bernard Unti, and David Winkler, but no one was subjected to more of this than Kenneth Durr, who deserves thanks and apologies in more or less equal measure.

Many of our editors received substantial help from others. In many cases, their contributions are recorded on the title pages of individual chapters, where they are listed along with the names of the contributing editors themselves. In addition to these, Mary Mintz wishes to thank her husband, James P. May as well as Mary Wyche Mintz, Melissa Becher, John Edward, Kent Stevens, and American University. John L. Offner thanks Sylvia L. Hilton of Universidad Complutense de Madrid for her bibliographical advice and assistance in obtaining recent Spanish publications on 1898; something of a bibliographer herself, this historian was very helpful in sorting through Spanish authors writing on the era. Joseph A. Fry thanks Ms. Vicky Hart and Ms. Delores Brownlee in the University of Nevada, Las Vegas Document Delivery Department (interlibrary loan). Nancy Mitchell thanks her colleague Jerry Suhr, who read Russian texts for her. Anne L. Foster thanks Ray Lum and Hilde DeWeerdt, both of Harvard's Yenching Library.

Thomas J. Knock wishes to acknowledge three historians whose contributions made it possible for him to undertake and complete his chapter on the United States and World War I. He could not have found his way without the compass that Lawrence E. Gelfand provided in the form of his original chapter for the 1983 edition. And for guidance of a different sort in another time, he records his personal and professional debt to Arthur S. Link and Arno J. Mayer, authors of multiple works of enduring and monumental significance in this field and, since his first semester of graduate study at Princeton, each in his own inimitable way an ongoing source of inspiration.

Mark A. Stoler thanks the faculty and staff of the University of Vermont and the university library, particularly in the reference, documents, and interlibrary loan departments. Chester J. Pach thanks Richard Dodgson and James Waite for their assistance. Robert D. Schulzinger offers thanks to Anne LeFever. Douglas Little acknowledges the valuable help of the "interlibrary loan folks" at Clark University. And John Stoner thanks the librarians at Columbia University and Skidmore College.

1

Reference Works and Bibliographies

Contributing Editor
MARY MINTZ
American University

With the Assistance of
KURT W. HANSON
American University

Contents

Introduction

Resources by Type

This chapter on reference aids is substantially changed in several ways from that in the 1983 edition. The original 1983 chapter remains useful, particularly for its inclusion of guides to foreign or international repositories of manuscripts and archives as well as for some older reference works, some of them not repeated here. The most essential resources for U.S. diplomatic history, however, are again listed in this edition, though the annotations are largely new or revised. Many additional titles published in the intervening twenty years have also been included.

This chapter reflects the expanding sense of the history of U.S. foreign policy. The growth of specialized resources in specific areas such as peace research, environmental policy, human rights, international development, and terrorism reflect the global issues that increasingly inform international relations. As the concerns of diplomacy have broadened, publication formats have also significantly expanded to include electronic resources, though generally Internet sites are not included here. Electronic resources available through subscription on the World Wide Web are included, though they too are subject to rapid, continuous change, not only in the sense that most of them are regularly updated, but also because their search functions and features and even titles and addresses may change and evolve.

Rather than organizing this chapter according to the traditional genres of reference works (e.g., encyclopedia, government document, bibliography), I have used an arrangement emphasizing the subject or focus of the work whenever possible. Finally, this chapter is selective rather than exhaustive in its coverage of resources for the field. Researchers will find, however, that the reference aids here are comprehensive in the sense that many serve as starting points leading to additional, related resources. For instance, I do not intend to present a comprehensive bibliography on an intergovernmental organization such as the United Nations but have listed a basic introduction to sources useful to the historian who may wish to initiate further research on a UN-related topic. Also, to assist researchers not only in identifying resources, but also in determining the potential value of those resources, this chapter frequently offers annotations that are evaluative rather than merely descriptive.

ARCHIVES, MANUSCRIPTS, AND OTHER DOCUMENTARY RESOURCES

1:1   *The Annals of America.* 21 vols. Chicago: Encyclopedia Britannica, 1968–1987. An expansive documentary history of the United States in twenty-one volumes, this work covers the period 1493–1986 in a popular approach that nevertheless includes important official and unofficial statements about U.S. foreign policy. Each document is preceded by a brief preface. The "Introduction" accompanying the set includes a longish explanatory preface and also functions as a table of contents for the chronologically arranged documents.

1:2   *ArchivesUSA: Integrated Collection and Repository Information.* Web Subscription Resource. Alexandria, VA: Chadwyck-Healey, Inc., 1997–. This is an Internet resource encompassing over 5,400 repositories and 124,400 collections of primary source material across the United States. It absorbs all of the *National Union Catalog of Manuscript Collections* (see 1:6) and a microfiche series, National Inventory of Documentary Sources in the United States. Additional material is submitted from libraries and other repositories on an ongoing basis. Collection descriptions as well as detailed contact information are included, including phone and fax numbers, hours of service, materials solicited, e-mail, and home page URLs when available. The database is thoroughly accessible through keyword searching. See http://archives.chadwyck.com/; and for detailed information on some of this source's contents, http://archives.chadwyck.com/infopage/ausa_abt.htm. See also U.S. National Historical Publications and Records Commission, *Directory of Archives and Manuscript Repositories in the United States,* 2d ed. (Phoenix: Oryx Press, 1988).

1:3   *Guide to Microforms in Print.* Washington, DC: Microcard Review, 1961–. When used with the companion *Subject Guide to Microforms in Print* (Munich: Sauer, 1978–), this title provides access to microform materials including monographs, journals, official records, and other special microfiche sets available for purchase from U.S. publishers. This work also incorporates *International Microforms in Print.*

1:4 *Historic Documents.* Washington, DC: Congressional Quarterly, Inc., 1985–. A competitor to *Vital Speeches of the Day* (see entry 1:129), though it is more limited in scope and depth and lacks the extensive back file that characterizes *Vital Speeches,* this annual compendium of documents (the year is reflected in the title, e.g., *Historical Documents of 1985*) annually covers important texts and events. International events and U.S. involvement abroad receive equal attention along with the domestic events. Summaries sometimes substitute for actual texts, while accompanying explanatory material provides background information. Website addresses are given for many documents. For 2000, a cumulative index for 1996–2000 is included. A separately published volume provides an index for 1972–1995.

1:5 *National Register of Microform Masters.* Washington, DC: Library of Congress, 1965. This annual publication lists and provides locations for the "microform masters," which can be used for making microform copies. Commercial microform masters held by publishers as well as library holdings are represented. All types of materials—books, journals, manuscripts, official records, etc.—are included. Entries are arranged alphabetically.

1:6 *National Union Catalog of Manuscript Collections.* 29 vols. Washington, DC: Library of Congress, 1959–1993. This 29-volume set contains the reported holdings of about 1,400 manuscript repositories in the United States describing approximately 72,300 collections. Indexes by subject, geographic place-name, and personal, family, and corporate name enhance accessibility. Many of the collections indexed consist of personal papers, so the NUCMC is useful for locating documents relating to a wide range of persons, both prominent and otherwise. The thorough indexing includes references to persons who are not necessarily the central focus of a collection but whose correspondence (or other types of references) might be included. The best access to the NUCMC is now through the electronic *ArchivesUSA* (see 1:2), which includes the complete NUCMC.

1:7 *Oral History Index: An International Directory of Oral History Interviews.* Westport, CT: Meckler, 1990. An extensive listing of 30,000 oral histories and their locations in 400 collections in the United States, Canada, Great Britain, and Israel, this work is arranged alphabetically by interviewee. The interview topics range widely, so it is somewhat difficult to determine its overall value for diplomatic historians. Dean Rusk, as an example, has four entries. For the renowned Columbia University oral history collection, see Elizabeth B. Mason and Louis M. Starr, eds., *The Oral History Collection of Columbia University* (New York: Oral History Research Office, 1979), and http://www.columbia.edu/cu/lweb/indiv/oral/.

1:8 Commager, Henry Steele, and Milton Cantor, eds. *Documents of American History.* 2 vols. 10th ed. Englewood Cliffs, NJ: Prentice-Hall, 1988. This convenient, well-established, and carefully selected collection of primary source documents in U.S. history includes diplomatic history. The second volume is updated through 1987 to include excerpts from the congressional reports on the Iran-Contra affair. First published in 1934.

1:9 Janes, Robert W., with Katherine R. Tromble. *Scholars' Guide to Washington, D.C., for Peace and International Security Studies.* Washington, DC: Woodrow Wilson Center Press, 1995. Sponsored by both the Woodrow Wilson International Center for Scholars and the United States Institute of Peace, this book includes extensive information on over 750 collections and organizations in the Washington, D.C., area. Information about the accessibility of the agencies and research institutes in the area is subject to change, but the descriptions of resources remain useful especially since international security studies is broadly defined. U.S. diplomatic historians may find the "Personal Papers Index" particularly useful.

ATLASES, CHRONOLOGIES, AND OTHER MISCELLANEOUS RESOURCES

1:10 *Europa World Year Book.* London: Europa Publications Limited, 1959–. Also published earlier as the *Europa Year Book,* this title has had worldwide coverage since the second year of its publication and is probably the best scholarly handbook available for countries of the world. For each country (or territory), extensive entries include essays, economic and demographic statistics, and directory information for diplomatic representation, government, political parties and organizations, the media, etc. The scholarly essays provide informed overviews of nations' recent histories (including politics, government, and foreign policy) and their current economic situation. A series of related publications, *Africa South of the Sahara, The Far East and Australasia, The Middle East and North Africa, Eastern Europe, Russia and Central Asia, and Western Europe,* offer similarly detailed information in regional groupings. The *Europa Year Book* is also particularly useful for its extensive directory of international organizations that opens each volume. Usually issued in two volumes.

1:11   *Worldmark Yearbook.* Detroit: Gale Group, 2000–. Accessible and similar in structure to the *Europa World Year Book* (see 1:10), *Worldmark* is more general and less scholarly. It provides information about recent history, some of it given through a timeline that, while useful, lacks analytical depth. Economic, directory, and statistical information is also more limited and intended for a more general audience.

1:12   Biger, Gideon, with International Boundaries Research Unit, University of Durham, England, eds. *The Encyclopedia of International Boundaries.* New York: Facts on File, 1995. With its occasional photographs, many maps, and large type, this work may give the appearance of being less than scholarly, but it is—and is uniquely useful. Arranged by country name, a separate entry is given for every boundary shared with another nation. Each boundary is extensively described according to its geography, its historical background, and its "present situation," whether it is in dispute or not, and if in dispute, the causes and history of the dispute.

1:13   Brune, Lester H., ed. *Chronological History of U.S. Foreign Relations.* 3 vols. 2d ed. New York: Routledge, 2002. Another essential reference work for the field of U.S. diplomatic history, this publication goes beyond a mere chronological list of events to provide an explanation or description of each event. Chapters conveniently divide history into eras, but the coverage is year by year from 1776 to the present in three volumes. The index is extensive; the select bibliography fairly brief. First published 1985–1991.

1:14   Cook, Chris, with Whitney Walker, eds. *The Facts on File World Political Almanac: From 1945 to the Present.* 4th ed. New York: Facts on File, 2001. Separate chapters of this work treat international political organizations and movements, heads of state and government, legislatures and constitutions, treaties, alliances and diplomatic agreements, political parties, and elections. Specialized additional chapters cover conflict, the nuclear age, and demographic trends. Two brief dictionaries, one for political terms and events and one for biographical entries, complete this ready reference source. First appeared in 1989.

1:15   Esposito, Vincent J., ed. *The West Point Atlas of American Wars.* First published in 1959. See chapter 5 of this Guide (5:60).

1:16   Urdang, Laurence, ed. *The Timetables of American History.* Updated ed. New York: Simon and Schuster, 1996. Following a successful model also used for a world history publication, this volume provides a chronological recounting of U.S. history with parallel text columns labeled "History and Politics," "The Arts," "Science and Technology," and "Miscellaneous." Coverage begins in 1000. Events in America are matched with those from "Elsewhere" to provide greater historical context. The "History and Politics" section includes basic information about events central to U.S. diplomatic history. First published in 1981.

GENERAL BIBLIOGRAPHICAL RESOURCES

1:17   *Bibliographies in History.* 2 vols. Santa Barbara, CA: ABC-CLIO, 1988. This publication consists of two volumes respectively extracted from *America: History and Life* (1:99) and *Historical Abstracts* (1:103), the two ABC-CLIO indexes and databases. Every journal article and dissertation in those indexes that could be described with either of the keywords, "bibliography" or "bibliographies," is included in the set. Volume 1 on U.S. and Canadian history has fairly brief sections on "foreign relations" and on "military history, strategic studies, and peace research." Volume 2 on world history includes only seven entries on "international history" (one, however, is an interesting article by Gordon Craig about early works on diplomacy). This bibliography of bibliographies is arranged by the same subject and index approach used in the printed indexes. All of this material can now be more easily accessed in the electronic versions of those indexes. The foreword by Eric H. Boehm gives a brief evaluation of the state of bibliography in U.S. history.

1:18   *Reviews in American History.* 1973–. Published quarterly, this journal provides review essays for some of the most important monographs and topics published in the discipline of U.S. history, including diplomatic history.

1:19   American Historical Association. *Writings on American History: 1902–1990.* Edited by Grace Gardner Griffin, James J. Dougherty, and James R. Masterson. Washington, DC, and Millwood, NY: American Historical Association, Kraus-Thomson, and KTO Press, 1904–1978, 1962–1990. This important annual series, though slow in publication, is one of the important resources available to U.S. historians, recently carrying the subtitle, *A Subject Bibliography of Articles.* Former publishers include the Carnegie Institution, American Historical Association, and the House of Representatives. Later, its listings were drawn from the "Recently Published Articles" section of the *American Historical Review.* Originally covering some Canadian and Latin American history, its scope has become more limited to the United States or U.S. relations with those areas. Originally reviews of books were also cited. Recent volumes list books as well as more than 600 journals in a topical subject arrangement, followed by an author index. See chapter 3 of this Guide (3:30).

1:20   Balay, Robert, with Vee Friesner Carrington and Murray S. Martin, eds. *Guide to Reference Books.* 11th ed. Chicago: American Library Association, 1996. Through its various editions (dating from 1902), frequently and informally known by the

editors' names (Mudge, Winchell, Sheehy), this work is the ultimate guide to reference resources. It may be used to supplement this bibliography for additional references and information, particularly for archival and manuscript resources, both domestic and foreign, as well as detailed, historical descriptions of indexes, handbooks, and other guides to history and other relevant disciplines. History and "Area Studies" are covered in separate sections. The forthcoming twelfth edition, edited by Bob Kieft, will be titled *Guide to Reference Sources* to reflect an increasing number of sources available in non-book formats.

1:21   Bemis, Samuel Flagg, and Grace Gardner Griffin, eds. *Guide to the Diplomatic History of the United States, 1775–1921.* Washington, DC: Government Printing Office, 1935. This landmark work is remarkably thorough. Over 5,000 works are cited in what amounts to an extended review of the literature in a mostly essay format and extending to nearly 1,000 pages. Essays in Part I follow a chronological layout from 1775 to 1921, with full attention to printed works, bibliographical aids, and "suggestions" for works in manuscripts; this section concludes with a lengthy annotated list of reference works. Part II is devoted to primary sources and government documents. An astonishing breadth of knowledge and depth of research is evident throughout but particularly here, where the authors describe both domestic and foreign manuscript depositories, the status of government records in various countries, etc.

1:22   Blazek, Ron, and Anna H. Perrault. *United States History: A Selective Guide to Information Sources.* Englewood, CO: Libraries Unlimited, 1994. An excellent comprehensive, well-organized guide to the reference materials for all of U.S. history, this work should be used as a supplement to this chapter, especially for its in-depth coverage of both classic and newer reference works in the discipline of history. For details about library catalogs, government publications, chronologies, bibliographies of U.S. publications from the seventeenth, eighteenth, and nineteenth centuries, and other reference works, consult the first chapter on "Sources of General Importance to U.S. History." Other chapters, topically arranged, include "Diplomatic History and Foreign Affairs," "Politics and Government," and "Military

History." Within chapters, a standardized arrangement by type of resource is used where applicable. Annotations for the nearly 1,000 entries are extensive, substantive, and useful.

1:23   Boehm, Eric H., ed. *Bibliographies on International Relations and World Affairs: An Annotated Directory*. Santa Barbara, CA: Clio Press, 1965. Though now badly outdated, researchers may still find this pioneering work useful. A bibliography of bibliographies, it includes standard works and information about journals on international affairs and library accession lists and is analytical as well as substantive in approach.

1:24   Brown, J. Cudd, with Mark Newman and Murray S. Martin, eds. *Administration of United States Foreign Affairs: A Bibliography*. Rev. ed. University Park: Pennsylvania State University Libraries, 1972. This locally produced bibliography was regarded highly enough to be collected by other libraries. It was part of a series by Brown, who produced several other compilations with coauthors, including *Africa: A Selective Working Bibliography* (University Park: Pennsylvania State University, 1970) and A*merican National Security Policies: A Selective Working Bibliography* (University Park: Pennsylvania State University, 1971), all appearing as inexpensive reproductions in the 1960s or early 1970s. Designed for specific seminars but listing materials that should be widely available in research libraries, the first part of the bibliography is divided into specific subject areas, such as "Decision Making and Foreign Policy," "Diplomacy," and "Military Affairs and Defense." Part 2 is devoted to specific regions. A list of periodicals and a brief bibliography supplement the work. Diplomatic historians seeking comprehensive coverage will wish to consult this work, though many of the unannotated entries for books, articles, and government documents are probably listed elsewhere. First published in 1968 with Michael B. Rieg as coeditor.

1:25   Burns, Richard Dean, ed. *Guide to American Foreign Relations since 1700*. Santa Barbara, CA: ABC-CLIO, 1983. Along with Bemis and Griffin, *Guide to the Diplomatic History of the United States, 1775–1921* (1935) (1:21), the first edition of the volume in hand was the other most significant contribution to the bibliographical literature for U.S. diplomatic history in the twentieth century. Following two

introductory chapters on reference aids and overviews, this work, commonly referred to as the "SHAFR Guide," is arranged chronologically through the cold war. Subsequent chapters sometimes chronologically overlap in their focus on U.S. relations with different areas of the world. Two more thematic chapters on economic and defense issues complete the work, which also has thorough indexing by author, title, and subject as well as an appendix with brief biographical profiles of the secretaries of state. Prepared by scholars in the field, each chapter has a separate table of contents, an introduction, and an arrangement suitable to the period or topic. Annotations are ordinarily succinct but usually evaluative. Monographs, journal articles, and government publications are included.

1:26   Conover, Helen Field, ed. *A Guide to Bibliographic Tools for Research in Foreign Affairs*. 2d ed. Washington, DC: Library of Congress, 1958. Reprint 1970 (Greenwood Press). This early but thorough work describes the reference literature for foreign affairs in 351 entries. The detailed annotations are still useful for establishing the history and contents of the bibliographic literature available at mid-twentieth century. Some of the work's principal value appears in the description of international bibliographies then available. First published in 1956.

1:27   Council on Foreign Relations. *Catalog of the Foreign Relations Library*. 9 vols. Boston: G. K. Hall, 1969. The 148,000 cards listed in this catalog cross-reference some 55,000 books, documents, and pamphlets in western languages. Subject headings generally are those of the Library of Congress. This valuable catalog covers all phases of international relations after 1918.

1:28   Dexter, Byron, with Elizabeth H. Bryant and Janice L. Murray, eds. *The Foreign Affairs 50-Year Bibliography: New Evaluations of Significant Books on International Relations 1920–1970*. New York: R. R. Bowker Co., 1972. Published in part to celebrate the fiftieth anniversary of the journal *Foreign Affairs,* the titles here are drawn from the extensive Langer and Armstrong et al., *Foreign Affairs Bibliography: A Selected and Annotated List of Books on International Relations* (1933–1976) (1:37). About 3,000 "landmark" books were selected; approximately 2,000 are presented with extensive annotations that amount to brief book reviews. Part of the value of this work is the selectivity of the titles and the reappraisals offered by the distinguished contributors.

1:29   Freidel, Frank, with Richard K. Showman, eds., *Harvard Guide to American History*. 2 vols. Rev. ed. Cambridge, MA: Belknap Press of Harvard University Press, 1974. This classic bibliography for U.S. history was originally published in 1954 and 1967 when edited by Oscar Handlin. Volume 1 is primarily topical in its approach. Part 1 opens with essays on the research and writing of history, the care and editing of manuscripts, and the "materials of history." Important chapters on reference aids, public documents, unpublished sources, microforms, and other printed works follow. Part 2 is devoted to biographies; part 3 to area and regional studies; part 4 to the topics or "special subjects." The second volume is arranged chronologically and has an important section on "Foreign Relations since 1945." Though unannotated, mere selection for inclusion in this bibliography is sufficient indication of the value of a journal article or monograph.

1:30   Goehlert, Robert U., and Elizabeth R. Hoffmeister, eds. *The Department of State and American Diplomacy: A Bibliography*. New York: Garland Publishing, 1986. This bibliography is a major contribution to the study of U.S. foreign relations though it has a specialized focus. As the introduction notes, it is the first to focus exclusively on the Department of State and its history, activities, and functions, though the authors also decided to exclude works relating to foreign affairs since coverage of that literature is widely available elsewhere. The emphasis is essentially on the past and present conduct of diplomacy, and the unannotated citations are drawn primarily from the scholarly literature in the disciplines of history, political science, public administration, and law. All citations are to English-language works, most published after 1945. The bibliography is divided into four sections: the Department of State and diplomatic service, the conduct of U.S. foreign policy, geographical studies, and biographies. The latter has two separate sections, for secretaries of state and other diplomats. The introduction also provides an excellent guide to the publications of the State Department and particularly to the literature on treaties, to other government documents, to publications about government documents, and to general and specialized bibliographies.

1:31   Groom, A. J. R., and C. R. Mitchell, eds. *International Relations Theory: A Bibliography*. New York: Nichols Pub. Co., 1978. This collection of bibliographic essays focuses almost entirely on the state of international relations as a discipline with some nods to psychology and anthropology. Its usefulness to historians would be for its primarily theoretical approaches. Individual essays and authors: Michael Nicholson, "The Methodology of International Relations" (13–20); John C. Fahy and Nancy Wilshusen Fahy, "Research Methods in International Relations" (21–26); Frances Pinter, "International Relations Textbooks" (27–32); Mitchell, "Systems Theory and International Relations" (33–47); Richard Little, "International Stratification" (48–68); Anthony V. S. De Reuck, "Theories of Power, Influence and Authority" (69–77); Mitchell, "Conflict and War" (78–103); Groom, "Strategy" (104–27); John W. Burton and Hedda Ramsden, "Order and Change" (128–39); Groom, "Integration" (140–52); Christopher Hill and Margot Light, "Foreign Policy Analysis" (153–71); A. N. Oppenheim, "Psychological Aspects of International Relations" (172–86); De Reuck, "Anthropology and International Relations" (187–94); and Michael H. Banks, "Ways of Analyzing the World Society" (195–215).

1:32   Haines, Gerald K., and J. Samuel Walker, eds. *American Foreign Relations, A Historiographical Review*. Westport, CT: Greenwood Press, 1981. Each essay in this important collection discusses significant scholarly literature in U.S. diplomatic history, much of it published during the 1950s, 1960s, and 1970s. See chapter 2 of this Guide (2:9).

1:33   Hanke, Lewis, ed. *Guide to the Study of United States History Outside the U.S., 1945–1980*. 5 vols. White Plains, NY: Kraus International Publications, 1985. Sponsored by the American Historical Association and the University of Massachusetts at Amherst, this unique publication combines essays and bibliographies on teaching and research about U.S. history in other countries. Following some initial essays by distinguished historians, the first three volumes are devoted to nation-by-nation reports on the study of U.S. history. The content of these reports, written primarily by foreign scholars, ranges widely but often includes specific information about archival resources and degree of accessibility in specific countries. The great importance of these materials to diplomatic historians and the need for accessibility is discussed at length in the introductory remarks. As the editor notes, "scholars abroad concerned with U.S. history usually give considerable attention to comparing their own country with the U.S. and emphasize relations between the two countries." This attention is particularly evident in the last two volumes, which are devoted entirely to an annotated bibliography of over 2,000 works. Though all annotations are in English, much of the literature cited was originally published in other languages and is easily accessible only through this particular bibliography. The arrangement of the bibliographical volume is at first comprehensive and then chronological with many listings given under "Foreign Policy and Foreign Relations" throughout. All types of literature (monographs, journal articles, etc.) are included but not dissertations.

1:34   Harmon, Robert B., ed. *The Art and Practice of Diplomacy: A Selected and Annotated Guide.* Metuchen, NJ: Scarecrow Press, 1971. This briefly annotated list of nearly 900 articles, books, and documents reflects the nature and objectives of modern diplomacy. Included are the historical evolution of diplomacy and the diplomatic and consular services of various nations. Indexes.

1:35   Killen, Linda R., and Richard L. Lael, eds. *Versailles and After: An Annotated Bibliography of American Foreign Relations, 1919–1933.* New York: Garland Pub., 1983. This is an outstanding but, unfortunately, now dated work focusing on the fate of Wilson's vision of a new international order. The introduction gives an overview of the issues and questions faced by the United States. The initial chapters are arranged according to type of source: reference guides, manuscripts and primary sources, and biographical materials. Following a chapter devoted to "broader sources," succeeding chapters are devoted to specific topics, significantly enhancing the value of the bibliography. Chapters focus, for example, on the Paris Peace Conference, economics and diplomacy, and U.S. relations with various countries. Annotations are brief and all materials cited are in English. Users are encouraged to use both the author and subject indexes.

1:36   Lakos, Amos, ed. *International Negotiations: A Bibliography.* Boulder: Westview Press,

1989. Negotiations are the focus of this bibliography, but its treatment is so thorough that the work merits broader usage. Negotiation theory in all its aspects is covered, as are specific historic negotiations of various kinds: multilateral, arms control, summits, and international trade. Diplomacy, Soviet diplomacy, and American diplomacy also have separate sections. Other regions and countries also have individual sections; many of these references are also pertinent to the study of U.S. history. Each section is divided into three parts: books, journals, and "documents and reports." The latter category provides excellent coverage of literature that is often more ephemeral. Subject and author indexes enhance the accessibility of the more than 5,000 unannotated entries.

1:37   Langer, William L., and Hamilton Fish Armstrong et al., eds. *Foreign Affairs Bibliography: A Selected and Annotated List of Books on International Relations.* 5 vols. New York: Harper for the Council on Foreign Relations, 1933–1976. This important bibliography in international relations was prepared under the auspices of the Council on Foreign Relations and derived in part from regular bibliographic listings in the council's journal, *Foreign Affairs.* Historian William L. Langer coedited the first volume, which covered 1919–1932. Thereafter the series followed a pattern of decennial publication with subsequent volumes for 1932–1942, 1942–1952, 1952–1962, and 1962–1972. Editors varied, but each volume was subdivided into topical, historical, and geographical sections. Of particular use is the recurring, extensive section on "The World since 1914." Only books are listed, but each volume averages approximately 10,000 titles, and every entry is annotated, annotations being usually both evaluative and descriptive. First published by Harper, the last volume in the series was published by R. R. Bowker Co.

1:38   Norton, Mary Beth, with Pamela Gerardi, eds. *The American Historical Association's Guide to Historical Literature.* 2 vols. 3d ed. New York: Oxford University Press, 1995. The third edition of this bibliography follows the classic editions of 1931 and 1961, both edited by George M. Dutcher and both still worthy of consultation. Like its predecessors, the 1995 edition is a massive collection of almost 27,000 annotated citations, mostly for English-language works published between 1961 and 1992. Researchers will find forty-eight sections covering world and other national histories, with six chronological sections devoted to U.S. history and two separate sections devoted to international relations. All sections are edited by distinguished scholars who were highly selective in their choices for this important bibliography. Each section is preceded by an introductory essay and usually begins with reference materials.

1:39 Prucha, Francis Paul. *Handbook for Research in American History: A Guide to Bibliographies and Other Reference Works.* 2d ed. Lincoln: University of Nebraska Press, 1994. For a complete list of reference sources for U.S. history, this excellent work should be consulted in addition to the bibliographies in this Guide. Similar in scope and comprehensiveness to Blazek and Perrault, *United States History: A Selective Guide to Information Sources* (1994) (1:22), it includes general and specialized resources. First published in 1987.

1:40 Wright, Moorhead, Jane Davis, and Michael Clarke, eds. *Essay Collections in International Relations: A Classified Bibliography.* New York: Garland Pub., 1977. This bibliography makes essay collections published between 1945 and 1977 more accessible. Though the chapter arrangement reflects a traditionally political science orientation, numerous entries appear under "United States" in the index and suggest its potential usefulness for U.S. diplomatic history. The lack of an update, of course, is a significant limitation.

1:41 Zawodny, J. K., ed. *Guide to the Study of International Relations.* San Francisco: Chandler Pub. Co., 1965. Zawodny's collection is only slightly less dated than Conover, *A Guide to Bibliographic Tools for Research in Foreign Affairs* (1958) (1:26), but remains useful as a baseline bibliography for its time. Compared to Conover, the approach is slightly more contemporary in its division by genre—atlases, biographies, dictionaries, etc.—with less comprehensive annotations.

GENERAL BIOGRAPHICAL RESOURCES

1:42 *Chiefs of State and Cabinet Members of Foreign Governments.* Washington, DC: Central Intelligence Agency, National Foreign Assessment Center, 1974–. Updated monthly in print and weekly on the Internet by the Directorate of Intelligence, this publication provides a continuous record of the heads of state and other high government officials for each nation. This series originated in a 1974 CIA publication titled *Countries of the World.* See http://www.odci.gov/cia/publications/chiefs/.

1:43 *Diplomatic List.* Washington, DC: Department of State, 1909–. The Diplomatic List (of missions in the United States) is prepared by the Office of Protocol of the Department of State. It contains the names of members of the diplomatic staffs (having diplomatic rank) of all missions and their spouses. Asterisks identify those who do not have full immunity under provisions of the Vienna Convention on Diplomatic Relations. Now issued quarterly, the date of origin of this long-standing publication is uncertain, but it apparently appeared as a monthly publication as early as 1909. Since 1997 published online at http://www.state.gov/s/cpr/rls/dpl/.

1:44 *Foreign Representatives in the U.S. Yellow Book: Who's Who in the U.S. Offices of Foreign Corporations, Foreign Nations, the Foreign Press, and Intergovernmental Organizations.* New York: Leadership Directories, Inc., 1996–. Available as part of a subscription database on the web under the title *Leadership Library on the Internet* (see http://www.leadershipdirectories.com/, which also includes information on the print version), this directory is also part of a series of directories known as "yellow books." This particular title is published semiannually and includes representatives of approximately 200 embassies, consulates, and missions in the United States as well as about 200,000 persons involved in the categories described in the subtitle. It is a good source of timely and growing historical information on high-level diplomats, information officers, and U.S. representatives (including public relations firms) for other nations.

1:45 *The International Year Book and Statesmen's Who's Who.* East Grinstead, West Sussex, UK: Kelly's Directories, 1953–. Partially comparable to *The Statesman's Yearbook* (see entry 1:46), this British serial originally published by Burke's Peerage also has entries for many international organizations as well as succinct entries for each nation. Individuals from the United Kingdom and other Commonwealth and European countries seem to predominate in the biographical section.

1:46 *The Statesman's Yearbook.* New York: St. Martin's Press, 1864–. Published since 1864, currently by St. Martin's Press, this British handbook is divided into two parts, one with extensive reference materials on international organizations, and one with expansive entries for each nation. The national entries describe key historical events, basic demographics, recent elections, and information about constitutions, governments, defense, economies, agriculture, industry, international relations, international communications, social institutions, culture, and diplomatic representatives. A brief bibliography closes each entry. Details about political subdivisions are also included for some countries.

1:47 *Who's Who in International Affairs.* 2d ed. London: Europa Publications Ltd., 1998. Entries follow a style similar to who's who publications, providing for each person his or her nationality, education, career, and contact information. Indexes by nationality and by country or organization increase accessibility. First appeared in 1990.

1:48 Bemis, Samuel Flagg, and Robert H. Ferrell, eds. *The American Secretaries of State and Their Diplomacy.* 20 vols. New York; Totowa, NJ: Alfred A. Knopf; Cooper Square Publishers, 1927–. Originally published between 1927 and 1929 as a ten-volume set, this classic work has been expanded over time to include twenty volumes, each devoted to describing the careers of a secretary of state or, especially in the early set, several secretaries, and their impact on U.S. diplomacy. The first volume of the original set contains a lengthy introduction to the office and its historical role by James Brown Scott.

1:49 Boyce, Richard Fyfe, and Katherine Randall Boyce, eds. *American Foreign Service Authors: A Bibliography.* Metuchen, NJ: Scarecrow Press, 1973. A unique resource that does not pretend to be comprehensive, this work nevertheless supplements other available biographical information for 706 persons who served in the U.S. diplomatic corps, many in the twentieth century. Brief biographical information, usually diplomatic assignments, is provided for each individual.

1:50 Garraty, John A., with Mark C. Carnes, eds., *American National Biography.* 24 vols. New York: Oxford University Press, 1999. Published under the auspices of the American Council of Learned Societies, this authoritative work is a significant contribution to biographical and historical research. It includes important figures in U.S. history who were deceased by 1995. The first print supplement was published in 2002 and adds more than 400 new entries to the original 17,500. An electronic version, regularly updated with new entries, is currently accessible for subscription at http://www.anb.org/. The essays are uniformly well written and researched with assessments of each person's significance. The *ANB* replaces and updates the *Dictionary of American Biography* (see entry 1:51). Researchers may wish to consult both titles for differing perspectives on a single person.

1:51 Johnson, Allen, et al., eds. *Dictionary of American Biography.* New York: Charles Scribner's Sons, 1928–1996. This basic authority for biographical information began publication in 1928 and, including ten supplementary volumes, extended through 1996 to incorporate recently deceased figures. Published under the auspices of the American Council of Learned Societies, its editors attracted first-rate scholars to write most of the entries, some many (large) pages long. Brief bibliographies complete each entry. Followed, some would say succeeded, by Garraty and Carnes, *American National Biography* (1999) (1:50).

1:52 Nolan, Cathal J., ed. *Notable U.S. Ambassadors since 1775: A Biographical Dictionary.* Westport, CT: Greenwood Press, 1997. Arranged alphabetically by surname, approximately sixty individuals "who had notable careers in the U.S. Foreign Service" are included in this dictionary. The diplomats were selected because they were major figures who contributed to the development of the diplomatic service, had significant influence, or made significant personal achievements. Some were also chosen because they represent particular historical periods. Each substantive entry is both biographical and historical with brief bibliographies of works by and about the diplomats.

1:53 Parker, Thomas, ed. *America's Foreign Policy, 1945–1976: Its Creators and Critics.* New York:

Facts on File, 1980. Prefaced by an introductory essay on U.S. foreign policy, 1945–1976, this volume concludes with a chronology of events and a bibliography. In between are biographical entries written in an accessible style by various scholars. Though basic biographical information is included with each entry, their greater value lies in extended accounts and assessments of the diplomats and other policymakers' careers. The bibliography primarily lists monographs and is arranged according to presidential administration.

1:54   Plischke, Elmer. "Bibliography on United States Diplomacy: Autobiographies, Biographies, Commentaries, and Memoirs." In *Instruction in Diplomacy: The Liberal Arts Approach,* ed. Smith Simpson, 99–342. Philadelphia: American Academy of Political and Social Science, 1972. This bibliography is a select list of biographical and autobiographical resources for figures connected with U.S. diplomacy. It follows an earlier Plischke publication, *American Diplomacy: A Bibliography of Biographies, Autobiographies, and Commentaries* (College Park: University of Maryland, 1957).

1:55   _____. *United States Diplomats and Their Missions: A Profile of American Diplomatic Emissaries since 1778.* Washington, DC: American Enterprise Institute for Public Policy Research, 1975. Plischke's retrospective study of the diplomatic corps, though not strictly a reference work, summarizes his findings in both text and appended tables. A wide variety of data, ranging from the geographic origins, age, and sex of diplomats to diplomats as authors, is covered. Appointments and other political characteristics are the primary focus of the study, which covers the period from 1780 to 1973. See also his *U.S. Department of State: A Reference History* (1999), also a combination of narrative, analysis, and reference work. For more information on the 1999 work, see chapters 2 and 9 of this Guide (2:197; 9:149).

1:56   Smith, Walter B., II. *America's Diplomats and Consuls of 1776–1865: A Geographic and Biographic Directory of the Foreign Service from the Declaration of Independence to the End of the Civil War.* Washington, DC: Government Printing Office, 1986. This directory is based largely on the appointment records of the Department of State and provides

information that predates U.S. Department of State, *Biographic Register* (1870–). It is an excellent resource for study of the development of the U.S. diplomatic corps.

1:57   Sobel, Robert, ed. *Biographical Directory of the United States Executive Branch, 1774–1989.* New York: Greenwood Press, 1990. All cabinet officers are included; thus all secretaries of state appear. The entries are fairly basic, however, and would be useful only for quick reference. Brief bibliographical notes are also included. First published in 1971.

1:58   U.S. Department of State. *Biographic Register.* Washington, DC: Government Printing Office, 1870–. For nearly the first seventy years of its publication, this title was the *Register of the Department of State* and contained additional information about the foreign service as well as biographical information. Since 1944, it has been primarily biographical and is composed of concise alphabetical entries that rely heavily on abbreviations to describe the careers and provide limited additional biographical information about State Department employees who rank at the equivalent of GS-12 or above, including those appointed to administrative posts and ambassadorships. Personnel from related agencies such as the Agency for International Development are also included.

1:59   U.S. Department of State. Office of the Historian. *Principal Officers of the Department of State and United States Chiefs of Mission, 1778–1990.* Washington, DC: Government Printing Office, 1991. According to the preface, "this volume is the most recent historical listing of principal officers of the Department of State and diplomatic agents of the United States." Earlier versions appeared in 1873, 1937, 1957, 1973, 1986, and 1988. Updates or revisions were provided in each new edition, resulting finally in this outstanding and outstandingly detailed resource. Part I provides comprehensive historical lists of the secretaries of state and all other high-ranking officers at a rank equivalent to assistant secretary, such as director general. Directors of the U.S. Arms Control and Disarmament Agency, the U.S. Information Agency, and the U.S. Trade Representatives are also given, along with the heads of foreign assistance agencies. Entries are extensively researched and detailed with dates of appointment, etc. Part II provides a listing of the chiefs of mission for every nation and for up to thirteen international organizations to which the United States appoints representatives at ambassador level. Part III is an index by person with birth and death dates with references to each qualifying appointment. For online updates, see http://www.state. gov/r/pa/ho/po/.

GENERAL DICTIONARIES AND ENCYCLOPEDIAS

1:60   Adams, James Truslow, ed. *Dictionary of American History.* 8 vols. 3d rev. ed. New York: Charles Scribner's Sons, 1976–1978. The best available "dictionary" of American history is actually a multivolume encyclopedia. Though still carrying the original editor's name—James Truslow Adams—this work was prepared under the auspices of Louise B. Ketz and supersedes the earlier editions; all 7,200 entries are either revised or new, written by scholars and experts. The entries vary in length but often have helpful bibliographical notes. A two-volume supplement was issued in 1996, prepared under the editorship of Joan Hoff (formerly Hoff-Wilson) and Robert H. Ferrell.

1:61   Becker, Carol A., ed. *International Relations Dictionary.* Rev. ed. Washington, DC: Department of State Library, 1981. A resource derived from practical experience, this dictionary was principally written by a librarian at the Department of State Library. The entries are derived from questions received at the library and cover a broad range of terms, organizations, acronyms, etc. Though dated, the *Dictionary* nevertheless has historic value for researchers, particularly in the annotated footnotes that appear with each entry. First published in 1969.

1:62   Berridge, G. R., and Alan James, eds. *A Dictionary of Diplomacy.* New York: Palgrave, 2001. As the preface notes, the terminology of diplomacy has expanded in keeping with the growth of the subject matter of diplomacy. This expansion encompasses economic and legal relations and also reflects the growth of international organizations. Intended for practitioners and for "historians of diplomacy, their close cousins, the diplomatic historians, and all students of international relations." The wit and personal perspective of the preface are sometimes reflected in the entries themselves.

1:63   Boyer, Paul, ed. *The Oxford Companion to United States History.* Oxford: Oxford University Press, 2001. This publication received outstanding reviews and immediately became an essential reference work on U.S. history. While acknowledging the extensive changes in the discipline of history in the last part of the twentieth century, the work also attempts "to give full attention to the political, military, and diplomatic topics that remain crucial to an understanding of the American experience—but within a modern vantage point that placed these events and developments within their larger social context." To that end, a past president of SHAFR, Emily S. Rosenberg, edited the essays on diplomatic and military history. All of the editors are distinguished historians, and the many contributors are also experts in their areas of specialization. The essays are all well written with brief bibliographic notes attached.

1:64   DeConde, Alexander, ed. *Encyclopedia of American Foreign Policy: Studies of the Principal Movements and Ideas.* 3 vols. New York: Scribner, 1978. This highly regarded resource is a collection of scholarly essays by distinguished specialists. Not intended to be comprehensive except in its coverage of broad, important concepts, the encyclopedia's essays are substantive and analytical. All entries are accompanied by brief bibliographical essays or lists of citations, which are excellent resources in their own right. Cross-references also enhance the usefulness of the essays. A major update appeared recently: DeConde, Richard Dean Burns, and Fredrik Logevall, eds., *Encyclopedia of American Foreign Policy,* 2d ed. (3 vols., New York: Charles Scribner's Sons, 2002).

1:65   Elfstrom, Gerard. *International Ethics: A Reference Handbook.* Santa Barbara, CA: ABC-CLIO, 1998. In a different approach to international relations, this work takes into account perceptions of globalism and addresses "issues and responsibilities that stretch across international boundaries." The work is highly personal in that the author makes frequent use of first-person plural and second-person singular, particularly in the defining introductory matter. He briefly identifies and describes key issues in ethics such as human rights, nationalism, refugees, and terrorism. Also included are a chronology, some biographical sketches, a set of significant documents, and bibliographies of print and nonprint resources.

1:66   Findling, John E., ed. *Dictionary of American Diplomatic History.* 2d ed. New York: Greenwood Press, 1989. In its second edition, this single-volume reference on U.S. diplomatic history covers the field from its beginnings through mid-1988. The approximately 1,200 alphabetical entries tend toward brevity but include brief bibliographies for further reading. Half of the entries are biographical with an emphasis on chiefs of mission and others with significant roles in foreign policy (though not all presidents are included). Appendices include a chronology, a list of key personnel arranged by administration, locations of manuscript collections and oral histories, and a list by country of the "Initiation, Suspension, and Termination of Diplomatic Relations." Less essential but interesting is a state-by-state arrangement of birthplaces for those covered in the biographical entries. First published in 1980.

1:67   Finkelman, Paul, and Peter Wallenstein, eds. *The Encyclopedia of American Political History.* Washington, DC: CQ Press, 2001. This basic one-volume encyclopedia seems intended for a more general audience and, as the editors readily acknowledge, as a "starting place" for inquiry. All articles are written by scholars or other specialists. Brief bibliographies accompany each entry.

1:68   Flanders, Stephen A., and Carl N. Flanders, eds. *Dictionary of American Foreign Affairs.* New York: Macmillan, 1993. This one-volume reference on U.S. diplomatic history covers the field from its beginnings through most of the twentieth century and is intended for a broad audience. Using a broad definition of foreign relations, it includes all presidents and secretaries of state, on the one hand, and material relating to environmental and technology matters, on the other. The nearly 1,400 entries are in standard alphabetical order with ample cross-references to related topics in the dictionary. The several useful appendices include a chronology-timeline of events, descriptions of executive branch and congressional organizations dealing with foreign affairs, a list of conferences and summits, a glossary, and a useful, basic bibliography. Cartography by Thomas Nast.

1:69   Freeman, Chas. W., Jr., ed. *The Diplomat's Dictionary.* 2d ed. Washington, DC: United States Institute of Peace Press, 1997. Not intended as a purely scholarly work, this dictionary of quotations informs as it entertains with witty anecdotes and observations from a highly experienced practitioner from the U.S. diplomatic corps with a great deal of multicultural experience. It is historical in the sense that it draws from many eras, from the ancient to the modern. An index increases its accessibility. First published in 1994.

1:70   Greene, Jack P., ed. *Encyclopedia of American Political History: Studies of the Principal Movements and Ideas.* 3 vols. New York: Scribner, 1984. This outstanding encyclopedia is composed of essays by eminent scholars who write about some of the most important issues in U.S. political history. The focus is almost exclusively domestic, however, except where there are underlying international themes or chapters (e.g., "Territories and Statehood," "Pacifism and Peace Movements") that touch more closely on issues related to foreign relations.

1:71   Jentleson, Bruce W., and Thomas G. Paterson, eds. *Encyclopedia of U.S. Foreign Relations.* 4 vols. New York: Oxford University Press, 1997. A more traditional encyclopedia than DeConde, *Encyclopedia of American Foreign Policy: Studies of the Principal Movements and Ideas* (1978) (1:64), this reference work, published and prepared under the auspices of the Council on Foreign Relations, is an essential and important scholarly resource. Written by specialists, most of the 1,000 entries are accompanied by suggestions for further reading. The introduction gives an overview of the history of U.S. foreign policy and its "core goals" over time, while the entries provide the specifics from the historical beginnings through most of the twentieth century. An excellent index and numerous cross-references expand its usefulness; appendices include one of the best chronologies of U.S. foreign relations available, a table with extensive statistical data for countries, and a bibliography listing both general and specific reference works.

1:72   Kutler, Stanley I., with Robert Dallek, David A. Hollinger, Thomas K. McCraw, and Judith Kirkwood, eds. *Encyclopedia of the United States in the Twentieth Century.* 5 vols. New York: Charles Scribner's Sons, 1996. This multivolume work is divided into six parts, including one titled, "Global America." Like the remainder of the work, it provides a group of topical essays by important scholars. The essays cover subjects such as pacifism and arms limitations, foreign policy, the national security state, limited wars, etc. Each essay concludes with sound bibliographical notes. The sections on the economy and on politics also offer at least two essays that may be of use to diplomatic historians. An index and chronology also accompany the encyclopedia.

1:73   Ziring, Lawrence, Jack C. Plano, and Roy Olton, eds. *International Relations: A Political Dictionary.* 5th ed. Santa Barbara, CA: ABC-CLIO, 1995. This general dictionary for international relations is divided into broad subject sections. One section with approximately 100 entries is devoted to U.S. foreign policy. Cross-references and an index give users access to the numbered entries and definitions. First appeared in 1969 as *The International Relations Dictionary.*

DISSERTATION RESOURCES

1:74   *Dissertation Abstracts International.* Ann Arbor: University Microfilms, Inc., 1938–. Published in book form since 1938, this title and several related titles are now accessible in their most comprehensive form through the Internet. All electronic versions provide access to indexing for most U.S. and Canadian dissertations from 1861 to the present. Predecessor print titles include: *Comprehensive Dissertation Index, Dissertation Abstracts, Dissertation Abstracts International,* and *Masters Abstracts.* Many of the dissertations indexed are available for purchase through UMI (now part of ProQuest); some large research libraries also subscribe to a microfiche set of the dissertations indexed. The current web version offers "twenty-four-page previews" in addition to abstracts of the dissertations. See http://wwwlib. umi.com/dissertations/.

1:75   Kuehl, Warren F., ed. *Dissertations in History, 1970–June 1980: An Index to Dissertations Completed in History Departments of United States and Canadian Universities.* Santa Barbara, CA: ABC-CLIO, 1985. This collection lists about 13,500 dissertations by author. A subject index is included.

GENERAL GOVERNMENT RESOURCES

1:76   *American Foreign Policy and Treaty Index.* Bethesda, MD: Congressional Information Service, 1993–1999. Published as the *American Foreign Policy Index* from 1993 to 1995 and the *American Foreign Policy and Treaty Index* from 1996 to 1999, this printed index and its accompanying microfiche set provided access to many government publications dealing with foreign affairs. Highly useful for the duration of its publication, this title was unique in attempting to provide access to government publications related to foreign affairs from the State Department, Congress, and elsewhere. The *AFPTI* also provides all documents related to the treaty ratification process. The printed index is composed of two parts: indexes and related abstracts. The accompanying microfiche set provides full text in two versions for depository and nondepository libraries.

1:77   *Congressional Universe.* Fee-based subscription service. Bethesda, MD: LexisNexis Academic and Library Solutions, 1998–. This commercial resource, now known through a shift in ownership as *LexisNexis Congressional,* provides greater ease of access to government and other publications through a subscription web-based publication. Updated daily, it provides full text of bills since 1989, public laws (1988), committee reports (1990), House and Senate documents (1995), the *Congressional Record* (1985), and *Federal Register* (1980). These documents include many of use to U.S. diplomatic historians, who will also wish to consult a predecessor publication, the *CIS Index* or the *CIS/Index to Publications of the United States Congress,* which continues to be published in print format. An accompanying microfiche set of documents is also available. See http://www. lexisnexis.com/academic/1univ/cong/default.htm.

1:78   *U.S. Government Periodicals Index.* Bethesda, MD: LexisNexis Academic and Library Solutions, 1994–. Now available both in print and as an electronic subscription, this commercially published annual provides access to government magazines and journals including the *Department of State Bulletin, Department of State Dispatch, Army History,* "Background Notes" (see entry 1:95), and *DISAM: Journal of International Security Assistance Management.* Many other military journals are also included, allowing for easy access to articles on space warfare, regional conflicts, and other topics. Indexing is by subject and by personal name such as author. See http://www.lexisnexis.com/academic/1univ/govper/Default.htm.

1:79   Andriot, John L., Donna Andriot, and Donna Batten. *Guide to U.S. Government Publications.* Detroit: Gale Research, 2000–. The items in this work, the successor to John Andriot's *Guide to U.S. Government Serials and Periodicals* and the original *Guide to U.S. Government Publications,* are arranged by SUDOCS (Superintendent of Documents) numbers and therefore by government department or agency. Thoroughly indexed with approximately 36,000 entries by agency, title, and keyword, this publication also has an "agency class chronology" section that can be used to track earlier publications that have ceased or changed titles. It is an excellent resource for those researchers seeking a comprehensive list of publications for the State Department, Agency for International Development, Arms Control and Disarmament Agency, National Archives, Department of Defense, and War Department, among others.

1:80   Boyd, Anne Morris, and Rae Elizabeth Rips, eds. *United States Government Publications.* 3d rev. ed. New York: H. W. Wilson, 1952. This volume includes information on the nature, distribution, and catalogs and indexes of U.S. government publications. It lists and describes important typical publications of the legislative, judicial, and executive branches. Originally published in 1931.

1:81   Gales, Joseph, ed. *The Debates and Proceedings in the Congress of the United States: With an Appendix Containing Important State Papers and Public Documents, and All the Laws of a Public Nature, with a Copious Index; Compiled from Authentic Materials.* See chapter 5 of this Guide (5:25).

1:82   Haines, Gerald K. *A Reference Guide to United States Department of State Special Files.* Westport, CT: Greenwood Press, 1985. This extraordinary work describes the "Lot Files" of the Department of State for the period 1940 to 1959. The Lot Files contain the working papers of various parts of the State Department such as memoranda, correspondence, or position papers. They may also contain duplicates of official records recorded (or cited) in the *Foreign Relations of the United States* series. The files vary as to accessibility, in terms of both restrictions and finding aids, but this guide carefully documents accessibility, location, and any known aids. Haines not only lists the boxes and contents, but has also done exceptional work in describing the files and their individual importance. An extensive index furthers the accessibility of this highly organized work, which is essential for diplomatic historians studying the 1940s and 1950s.

1:83   Hasse, Adelaide R., ed. *Index to United States Documents Relating to Foreign Affairs, 1828–1861.* 3 vols. Washington, DC: Government Printing Office, 1914–1921. Reprint 1965 (Kraus Reprint). This index is essential for locating U.S. documents on foreign affairs from 1828 to 1861, the years surveyed falling between Lowrie and Clarke, *American State Papers: Documents, Legislative and Executive, of the Congress of the United States . . . Selected and Edited under the Authority of Congress* (1832–1861) (5:10) and the *Foreign Relations of the United States* series. The index covers the reports of Congress, *Senate Executive Journal, Opinions of the Attorney General, Statutes-at-Large,* and *Congressional Globe,* and uses place (e.g., Cuba), name (e.g., John Forsyth), and subject (e.g., canals) organization.

1:84   Morehead, Joe, ed. *Introduction to United States Government Information Sources.* 6th ed. Englewood, CO: Libraries Unlimited, 1999. This guide to research and resources is one of the best available introductions to U.S. government documents and can be readily used as a starting point to identify additional resources beyond this bibliography. First published in 1975 as *Introduction to United States Public Documents.*

1:85   Plischke, Elmer, ed. *American Foreign Relations, A Bibliography of Official Sources.* College Park: University of Maryland, 1955. This publication represents an early attempt to list government documents useful for the study of U.S. diplomatic relations.

1:86   U.S. Congress. House Committee on Foreign Affairs and Senate Committee on Foreign Relations. *Legislation on Foreign Relations Through. . . .* Washington, DC: Government Printing Office, 1977–. This annual publication began in 1977, usually appearing in three volumes. The first two contain current legislation and related executive orders, the third, which is revised only as necessary, treaties and related material. The publication is useful because it collects all foreign relations legislation and contains the affected public laws, regardless of date of passage, as amended.

1:87   U.S. Congress. *The Congressional Globe: 23rd Congress to 42nd Congress, Dec. 2, 1833, to March 3, 1873.* 46 vols. in 110. Washington, DC: Printed at the Globe Office, 1834–1873. See entry for the *Congressional Record* (1:88).

1:88   _____. *Congressional Record: Proceedings and Debates of the Congress: 43rd Congress, 4 March 1873–.* Washington, DC: Government Printing Office, 1873–. This, along with *The Debates and Proceedings in the Congress of the United States* (1:81), the *Register of Debates in Congress* (1:89), and *The Congressional Globe* (1:87), contain texts of debates and speeches as well as the details of congressional proceedings that have been reported in official and unofficial publications since 1824.

1:89   _____. *Register of Debates in Congress: 18th–25th Congress, 6 December 1824–16 October 1837.* 14 vols. in 29. Washington, DC: Gales and Seaton, 1825–1937. These cannot be considered either accurate or complete but, along with papers of individual members of Congress, are all the researcher can consult for the contents of congressional debates in these years.

1:90   U.S. Congress. House. Committee on Foreign Affairs. *Congress and Foreign Policy.* Washington, DC: Government Printing Office, 1974–. An annual publication that reflects the most important foreign relations work of Congress conducted in the previous year, this title has occasionally been issued in microfiche. Prepared by the Congressional Research Service, Library of Congress. Early editions reflected the House committee's former name, Committee on International Relations.

1:91   U.S. Congress. Senate. Committee on Foreign Relations. *Background Information on the Committee on Foreign Relations.* 5th rev. ed. Washington, DC: Government Printing Office, 1982. Issued irregularly, this publication always includes a useful bibliographical section in addition to information about the committee and its work. First published in 1966.

1:92   U.S. Department of State. *American Foreign Policy: Current Documents.* Washington, DC: Government Printing Office, 1957–. Under various titles and publication schedules and regimes, the State Department for a half century has been issuing principal messages, addresses, statements, reports, diplomatic notes, and treaties, fairly contemporary with the events they concern. This series is not to be compared, however, with the retrospective *Foreign Relations of the United States* series.

1:93   _____. *Foreign Relations of the United States, 1861–1869.* 20 vols. Washington, DC: Government Printing Office, 1861–1869. The most important government publication for U.S. diplomatic history is an extensive, ongoing set, now numbering several hundred volumes. It contains materials from State Department archival files including correspondence, notes, memoranda, and related documents for each year; volumes for more recent years include documents from other government agencies as well, in addition to papers from private collections. Occasionally, special volumes devoted to a particular country or diplomatic event are published. Compilation for this undertaking is necessarily slow, responding to both legal restrictions and declassification controversies; a gap of thirty years from the event is not uncommon. For an earlier period, see Lowrie and Clarke, *American State Papers: Documents, Legislative and Executive, of the Congress of the United States . . . Selected and Edited under the Authority of Congress* (1832–1861). For details, see chapter 5 of this Guide (5:10).

1:94   _____. *Publications of the Department of State: A Cumulative List from October 1, 1929 to January 1, 1953.* Washington, DC: Government Printing Office, 1954. Supplements published by the Government Printing Office in 1958 and 1961 cover the periods January 1, 1953 to December 31, 1957, and January 1, 1958 to December 31, 1960. Arranged alphabetically by subject, with an index by series. Followed by U.S. Department of State, Historical Office, *Major Publications of the Department of State* (Washington, DC: Department of State, 1966), a seventeen-page pamphlet; and the twenty-seven-page U.S. Department of State, Office of the Historian, *Major Publications of the Department of State: An Annotated Bibliography* (Washington, DC: Department of State

Bureau of Public Affairs, Office of the Historian, 1977). For an ongoing record of contemporary State Department publications, see http://www.state.gov/r/pa/ho/pubs/.

1:95   U.S. Department of State. Office of Media Services. "Background Notes." Washington, DC: Government Printing Office, 1954–1978. This is a pamphlet series written by officers in the Department of State's geographical bureaus. They include information about each country's geography, people, history, government, political conditions, economy, foreign relations, and U.S. policy toward that country. A profile, brief travel notes, and a list of governments are also included. After 1978, the pamphlets have been issued irregularly and since 2000 are available only in an electronic format.

1:96   U.S. Department of State. Office of Public Communication. Bureau of Public Affairs. *Dispatch Magazine.* Washington, DC: Government Printing Office, 1990–. See chapter 25 of this Guide (25:9).

1:97   U.S. President. *Public Papers of the Presidents of the United States.* Washington, DC: Government Printing Office, 1961–. These volumes constitute an official compilation of the public messages, speeches, and statements of the presidents since President Harry Truman. Especially valuable are the recapitulations of presidential press conferences. Each volume is indexed separately, and there are several volumes for each presidency.

1:98   Zwirn, Jerrold, ed. *Congressional Publications and Proceedings.* 2d ed. Englewood, CO: Libraries Unlimited, 1988. One of the best guides available to the U.S. legislative process and its documentation (bills, hearings, committee reports), this work also contains a separate chapter on the treaty-making process and its documentation. Originally published in 1983.

INDEXES, ABSTRACTS, AND ELECTRONIC RESOURCES

1:99   *America: History and Life.* Santa Barbara, CA: ABC-CLIO, 1964–. The primary index for U.S. history is now available in electronic formats, often as part of a university library system (see http://sb2.abc-clio.com:8080/), which offer more ease for searching than the printed version. Though the system has varied, the printed version has an annual index for abstracts or citations, arranged according to publication type (journal articles, book reviews, dissertations, etc.). It is also possible to search by geographic area and by period. Over 2,000 publications are typically indexed, including history journals published outside the United States and Canada.

1:100   *CIAO: Columbia International Affairs Online.* Web-based Subscription Resource. New York: Columbia University, 1997–. Commonly known as CIAO, Columbia International Affairs Online includes research institute working papers, NGO occasional papers, research projects drawing funding from foundations, and conference proceedings published since 1991. Also included are journal abstracts, book information, policy briefs, economic indicators, links to home pages of contributing institutions, and maps and country data. Updates, depending on the kind of information involved, come either weekly or monthly. Researchers can access materials through organization, author, subject, title, or publication format. Materials may be downloaded or printed. See http://www.ciaonet.org/.

1:101   *CSA Political Science & Government.* Bethesda, MD: Cambridge Scientific Abstracts, 1969–. Familiar to researchers from 1969 to 2000 as *ABC Pol Sci* (when published by ABC-CLIO), this title continues to be available in both print and CD-ROM formats. An excellent current awareness service for the scholarly literature in political science, an accumulation of over thirty years enhances its usefulness for historians as well. The indexing is based on the table of contents for each journal covered.

1:102   *Essay and General Literature Index.* New York: H. W. Wilson, 1934–. The original volume of this index covers 1900 to 1933. This reference work has given important coverage for many years to *Festschriften* and other collections of essays that are often not included in discipline-specific indexes. It is particularly useful for locating more limited or esoteric subjects, both biographical and nonbiographical, that would not necessarily have entire monographs devoted to them. It is now available in multiple electronic formats; many university libraries subscribe to H. W. Wilson databases.

1:103 *Historical Abstracts.* Santa Barbara, CA: ABC-CLIO, 1955–. Prior to 1964 when *America: History and Life* began publication, this index also covered the United States (and Canada). Issued in two parts with various indexes (subject, author, geographical) leading to brief abstracts and full citations, it remains the leading index for world history. Now available in electronic formats (often as part of a university library system at http://sb2.abc-clio.com: 8080/), it originated as a continuation of Boehm's *Historical Abstracts, 1775–1945.*

1:104 *Humanities Index.* New York: H. W. Wilson, 1974–. This index, available in electronic formats, covers the most essential scholarly journals in the humanities disciplines, including history. It is a successor to the combined *Social Sciences and Humanities Index* (see entry 1:107). All indexed journals are English-language publications.

1:105 *International Index to Periodicals.* New York: H. W. Wilson, 1907–1965. Beginning as a supplement to H. W. Wilson Company's *Reader's Guide to Periodical Literature* and succeeded by the *Social Sciences and Humanities Index* (1:107), this title was once more international in scope. Before World War II, it indexed some journals published outside the United States.

1:106 *Public Affairs Information Service Bulletin.* New York: Public Affairs Information Service, 1915–. Available as both an electronic resource (see http://www.pais.org/index.stm) and as a print title, this important index covers scholarly literature (monographs and journals), government publications, and other specialized materials. Its focus on public affairs includes relations between the United States and other countries. Retrospective to 1915, it is usually known as PAIS. The separate *Foreign Language Index* began coverage in 1968 and subsequently merged with the original publication in 1991, adding valuable non-English-language material to the index.

1:107 *Social Sciences and Humanities Index.* New York: H. W. Wilson, 1965–1974. The interim index for scholarly literature in the humanities and social sciences disciplines published by H. W. Wilson follows the same system as the familiar *Reader's Guide to Periodical Literature.* The predecessor title was the *International Index to Periodicals* (see entry 1:105). In 1974, the title split into *Social Sciences Index* (see entry 1:108) and *Humanities Index* (see entry 1:104). All indexed journals are English-language journals.

1:108 *Social Sciences Index.* New York: H. W. Wilson, 1974–. This index, available in electronic formats, covers the most essential scholarly journals in the social science disciplines, including political science. It is a successor to the combined *Social Sciences and Humanities Index* (see entry 1:107). All indexed journals are English-language publications.

1:109 U.S. Foreign Broadcast Information Service, and U.S. Joint Publications Research Service. *World News Connection: A Foreign News Service from the U. S. Government.* Web-based subscription resource. Washington, DC: NTIS, 1995–. This important full-text subscription resource accesses vast quantities of news from non-U.S. media, including radio and television broadcasts as well as print sources. All non-English-language material is translated, often within two days of broadcast. Particularly useful for its regional access (e.g., Middle East, Eastern Europe, etc.), it also provides subject access. Printed and microfiche versions of FBIS or "Daily Reports," as this publication has been popularly known, have been available for several decades before the arrival of the web version; start dates vary according to region. Researchers may wish to use the commercially produced print or CD-ROM indexes that have been available for some years. See http://wnc.fedworld.gov.

1:110 University Microfilms International. *Periodical Abstracts.* Subscription web resource. Ann Arbor: University Microfilms International, 1986–. This subscription web resource is an excellent starting place for research since it provides indexing for a large number of general interest and scholarly periodicals, including many in history and political science. Full text or full image is provided for a significant proportion of the periodicals, including some of the peer-reviewed titles. The title has varied but the content remains approximately equivalent to that of four Wilson publications and databases (*Reader's Guide* and the *Humanities, Social Sciences,* and *General Science* indexes). The publisher, UMI, is now part of ProQuest. See http://www.ovid.com/products/databases/database_info.cfm?dbID=61.

RESOURCES FOR INTERNATIONAL ORGANIZATIONS: GENERAL

1:111 *Annual Review of United Nations Affairs.* Dobbs Ferry, NY: Oceana Publications, 1949–. A useful, commercial compilation of significant UN documents for each year, this work typically includes material from the General Assembly, Security Council, Economic and Social Council, International Court of Justice, and Secretariat as well as annual reports from such UN organizations as the Development Programme and High Commission for Refugees. Agendas, resolutions, membership lists, and important speeches are included as appropriate. After 1977, the *Review* was issued in parts.

1:112 *The Directory of EU Information Sources.* 11th rev. ed. Genval, Belgium: Euroconfidentiel, 1990–. Though commercially published, this print directory (with an equivalent electronic version also available) is a very extensive directory of the European Union itself, journalists who cover the EU, consultants and attorneys who specialize in the EU, and organizations and universities with EU-related programs. It includes extensive coverage of EU documents. The complexity of accessing this list of EU publications can be overcome by using the electronic version, but the print version reflects the complex and expansive nature of the EU publication and documentation system. Eleventh edition published in 2000; also known as the *Red Book.* Consult the information at http://www.euroconfidential.com/cgi-bin/virtualshop.pl?config=directories.cfg#redbook.

1:113 *International Information Directory.* Washington, DC: Congressional Quarterly, Inc., 1998–. Similar to the Congressional Quarterly standard *Washington Information Directory* (same publisher, since 1976), this work offers access to domestic, government, and international organizations (and to lists of organizations) through a broad topical arrangement, such as humanitarian affairs, regional affairs, security and arms control, etc. For each organization, directory information such as addresses, phone numbers, fax numbers, and web page addresses is included with a brief description of the organization, its membership, and purview. All organizations are located within the United States. A separate section lists resources by country; another lists U.S. Export Assistance Centers. A detailed index facilitates access. In 1999, the title expanded to *International Information Directory 2000–2001.*

1:114 *United Nations Juridical Yearbook.* New York: United Nations, 1962–. This annual publication is mandated by the General Assembly of the UN to document certain legal materials pertaining to the organization. The arrangement of the yearbook is also mandated and typically includes legislative texts and treaty provisions relating specifically to the UN, a general review of the legal activities of the UN and its related intergovernmental organizations, international treaties made under the auspices of the UN, and a multilanguage bibliography.

1:115 Baer, George W., ed. *International Organizations, 1918–1945: A Guide to Research and Research Materials.* Rev. ed. Wilmington, DE: Scholarly Resources Inc., 1991. Though part of a series on European diplomatic history, this publication is also useful to U.S. diplomatic historians, given American involvement with European nations in the period indicated—many of the 1,724 bibliographic entries directly refer to the United States in their titles. The bibliography is divided into both topical and chronological chapters: "Peace Settlements: The 1920s," for example, follows sections on the founding and history of the League of Nations. All the resources cited are scholarly and though not annotated, chapter prefaces and other texts supply brief but reliable scholarly histories of each era. Manuscript, archival, and documents collections are covered in two other chapters. First published in 1981.

1:116 Birchfield, Mary Eva, ed. *The Complete Reference Guide to United Nations Sales Publications, 1946–1978.* 2 vols. Pleasantville, NY: UNIFO Publishers, 1982. Given the difficulty posed by maintaining bibliographic control over UN publications in its first decades of existence, an actual reference publication of this type was needed. Now it need be consulted only as a last resort for identifying elusive UN documents. Volume 1 is a catalog of UN publications with their document numbers, volume 2 an index by keyword and title. In some cases, the author had to create the document numbers. *UNDOC* (see entry for *United Nations Documents Index* [1:124]) subsequently offers the bibliographic control that was previously lacking.

1:117   Dimitrov, Th. D., ed. *Documents of International Organisations: A Bibliographic Handbook Covering the United Nations and Other Intergovernmental Organisations.* Chicago: American Library Association, 1973. This work begins with a chapter largely intended for librarians who must process materials of international organizations. The material that follows is potentially useful to the researcher in describing various resources for accessing information and publications about international organizations, especially intergovernmental organizations.

1:118   Hajnal, Peter I. *Guide to United Nations Organization, Documentation & Publishing for Students, Researchers, Librarians.* Dobbs Ferry, NY: Oceana Publications, 1978. This earlier reference work on the UN describes the organization and gives the text of a few important documents. Other sections, including the section on how to obtain UN publications, are outdated, but the annotated bibliography of UN documents and secondary sources retains some usefulness for historians.

1:119   Lindbergh, Ernest, ed. *International Law Dictionary.* Cambridge, MA: Kuwer Law and Taxation Publishers, 1993. The purpose of this work is to provide French-, German-, and English-language equivalents for terms used in international law. As a polyglot dictionary it is useful, but researchers should not be misled by the title to expect definitions.

1:120   Matsuura, Kumiko, Joachim W. Müller, and Karl P. Sauvant. *Chronology and Fact Book of the United Nations, 1941–1991.* 8th ed. Dobbs Ferry, NY: Oceana Publications, 1992. A cumulative supplement to a series, *Annual Review of United Nations Affairs* (see entry 1:111), this work covers the period indicated in its title. It includes a year-by-year, month-by-month chronological accounting of UN related activities and events, many involving the United States. Each event is carefully labeled, e.g., "Environment," "Hostages," "Central America." A separate chapter provides background information, such as the membership of various UN councils; another provides a set of basic UN documents.

1:121   Osmanczyk, Edmund Jan, ed. *The Encyclopedia of the United Nations and International Agreements.* 2d ed. Philadelphia: Taylor and Francis, 1990. This encyclopedia provides a basic description and history of the most important intergovernmental organizations. It also includes definitions of relevant terms and excerpts or summaries of more than 1,000 treaties. First published in 1985.

1:122   Schechter, Michael G., ed. *Historical Dictionary of International Organizations.* Lanham, MD: Scarecrow Press, 1998. One of fifteen to thirty planned or published volumes in a series on international organizations, this is probably the most useful thus far for the U.S. diplomatic historian. Entries are brief, informative, and scholarly. Every important organization, person, and concept is covered. The dictionary also features a chronology of events ranging from the Congress of Vienna in 1815 to the 1998 Indian and Pakistani nuclear weapons tests. An excellent bibliography intentionally restricted to recent books with a "variety of ideological perspectives" completes the volume.

1:123   Schraepler, Hans-Albrecht. *Directory of International Organizations.* Washington, DC: Georgetown University Press, 1996. The author's intention for this volume was to provide a "practical and concise" guide to international (mostly intergovernmental) organizations, based in part on his own practical experience with such organizations. He has succeeded with a particularly helpful arrangement of entries that cover the UN and its related organizations, NATO, regional organizations, and a few other organizations of "worldwide relevance." For each organizational entry, he gives purpose, structure, members, activities, financial resources, and other information. This volume provides accessible, reliable, and succinct introductions to international organizations.

1:124   United Nations. *United Nations Documents Index.* New York: United Nations, Dag Hammarskjöld Library, 1950–. This title is the primary successor to *UNDOC, Current Index: United Nations Documents Index* (1979–1997), which was itself formed from the merger of several other UN document index publications, including *UNDEX* (1970–1978). It is the most comprehensive printed index of UN documents available.

RESOURCES FOR RATINGS, RANKINGS, AND STATISTICS

1:125 *Country Forecasts.* Syracuse: Political Risk Services, Frost and Sullivan, 1988–. A semiannual publication since 1988 (under various titles), this serial originally began ca. 1980. Intended primarily for those concerned about "business investments and trade in 100 countries around the world," *Country Forecasts* predicts political, financial, and economic risks, measured with data on political turmoil, gross development product and inflation rates, and other national and international economic indicators. These indicators are presented in a convenient retrospective format for each entry along with other country information. Various ratings and statistics are appended including the status of elections (required, scheduled, etc.) for each country.

1:126 Gibbs, Brian H., and J. David Singer. *Empirical Knowledge on World Politics: A Summary of Quantitative Research, 1970–1991.* Westport, CT: Greenwood Press, 1993. The goal of this book is to provide summaries of all "data-based research" articles relating to world politics and published between 1970 and 1991. The authors chose 1970 because their undertaking was similar to that of a predecessor publication, Singer and Susan D. Jones, *Beyond Conjecture in International Politics: Abstracts of Data-Based Research* (Itasca, IL: F. E. Peacock, 1972), covering the 1956–1969 period. Almost 300 articles, most published in about 40 English-language journals, are described in great detail—including spatial-temporal domain, variables, data sources, data operations, and findings. To be included an article must meet fairly rigorous substantive and methodological criteria described in the introduction. A topical index provides additional access.

1:127 Kurian, George Thomas. *The Illustrated Book of World Rankings.* 5th ed. Armonk, NY: Sharpe Reference, 2001. Now in its fifth edition (which now includes a CD-ROM version), this work is a useful collection of comparative data on countries. Rankings for approximately 300 different national characteristics ranging from population to economic freedom are included. With each new edition, the variety of measurements has expanded.

Resources for Topics in International Relations

GENERAL: DOCUMENTS AND ANALYSES

1:128 *Survey of International Affairs.* 45 vols. New York: Oxford University Press, 1920–1963. A distinguished series of essays—sometimes whole volumes, as in the case of McNeill, *America, Britain and Russia: Their Cooperation and Conflict, 1941–1946* (1953) (18:670)—covers specific aspects of international affairs, written soon after the events described. Together, they provide a valuable detailed narrative of international diplomacy through 1963. Through most of its history, this series was supervised by Arnold J. Toynbee.

1:129 *Vital Speeches of the Day.* New York: City News Publishing Co., 1934–. Published twice per month and widely indexed, this periodical is a useful compendium of important speeches given by notable persons in many fields. Speeches by U.S. presidents and secretaries of state are regularly included as are significant foreign policy addresses by others.

1:130 Council on Foreign Relations, ed. *The United States in World Affairs.* 40 vols. New York: Simon and Schuster, 1931–1971. Originally published from 1928 to 1931 as the *Survey of American Foreign Relations,* after 1971 this title was absorbed in part by two others, *American Foreign Relations: A Documentary Record* and *Documents on American Foreign Policy.* These more recent annual compendiums provide collections of important documents and overviews of U.S. diplomatic relations in each year. The original *Survey* is a narrative that accompanies an annual collection of documents titled *Documents on American Foreign Relations.* Edited over the years by Walter Lippmann, William O. Scroggs, Whitney Hart Shepardson, and Richard P. Stebbins.

1:131 Schlesinger, Arthur M., Jr., ed. *The Dynamics of World Power: A Documentary History of United States Foreign Policy, 1945–1973.* New York:

Chelsea House Publishers, 1973. Reprint 1983 in 10 vols. (Chelsea House). See chapter 19 of this Guide (19:51).

ARMS CONTROL AND DISARMAMENT

1:132 *Arms Control and Disarmament Agreements: Texts and Histories of Negotiations.* Washington, DC: U.S. Arms Control and Disarmament Agency, 1972–. This title has been published irregularly since 1972, though each edition has been retrospective with coverage back to 1959. The subtitle is an appropriate description, though the history is usually a chronological table of signatories, ratifications, etc. An explanatory introduction provides useful background information.

1:133 *The Arms Control Reporter.* Brookline, MA: Institute for Defense and Disarmament Studies, 1982–. This loose-leaf or filing service has been updated monthly in print since 1982 and is also now available in electronic formats (both Internet and CD—see http://www.idds.org/acrindex.html). The cumulative annual is in effect the most highly detailed reporting service available on disarmament and constitutes an important historical record on negotiations and treaties. The primary audience for the service is the "arms control professional," including scholars. The sponsoring institute has the goal of supporting "research and education on ways to minimize the risk of war, reduce the burden of military spending, and promote democratic institutions."

1:134 *The United Nations Disarmament Yearbook.* New York: United Nations, 1976–. Published annually since 1976, this yearbook essentially surveys progress toward disarmament efforts by the UN and is an official publication of that body. In addition to being an annual report, the yearbook contains texts of resolutions and decisions, voting patterns, and the status of agreements. It covers nuclear, chemical, biological, and conventional weapons.

1:135 Ali, Sheikh Rustum, ed. *The Peace and Nuclear War Dictionary.* Santa Barbara, CA: ABC-CLIO, 1989. Intended for an academic audience, this dictionary provides entries for over 300 topics related to nuclear arms control and disarmament, each in-

cluding a separate paragraph on the subject's significance. Also included are many technical terms and other jargon relating to this field of study as well as persons, events, and negotiations.

1:136 Burns, Richard Dean. *Arms Control and Disarmament: A Bibliography.* Santa Barbara, CA: Clio Books, 1977. An exceptionally comprehensive bibliography for its time, this includes a large number of articles. Although its coverage ranges beyond American experiences, and even further distant in time than 1700, it does provide sources for the Rush-Bagot agreement (1817), the Hague conferences (1899, 1907), the interwar treaties and negotiations, and post-1945 efforts. It concentrates on arms control and disarmament themes and negotiations; it also arranges conferences and treaties in chronological order according to type, e.g., arms limitation, demilitarization, outlawing of weapons, arms traffic, and rules of war.

1:137 _____. *Encyclopedia of Arms Control and Disarmament.* 3 vols. New York: Scribner's, 1993. The best and most comprehensive reference work available on arms control and disarmament for the United States and elsewhere, this work opens with an introduction by the editor in chief describing his terminology and placing the major issues and topics in historical perspective. The first two volumes are primarily composed of scholarly essays, which conclude with substantial bibliographies. The three volumes as a whole are divided into national and regional dimensions, themes and institutions, historical dimensions to 1945, and activities since 1945. The third volume consists of treaties or excerpts of treaties and a useful index. The same author also prepared *Arms Control and Disarmament: A Bibliography* (1977) (1:136).

1:138 Elliot, Jeffrey M., and Robert Reginald, eds. *The Arms Control, Disarmament, and Military Security Dictionary.* Santa Barbara, CA: ABC-CLIO, 1989. This scholarly dictionary includes over 250 entries, each given in two helpfully distinct parts: the description or definition and its significance. History is one of the dictionary's emphases.

1:139 Goldblat, Jozef, ed. *Arms Control Agreements: A Handbook.* Rev. ed. New York: Praeger, 1983. This handbook was sponsored by the Stockholm International Peace Research Institute (SIPRI) and is based on a similar work used at a 1982 meeting of the UN General Assembly. Divided into seven chapters, it consists primarily of the texts of treaties and other documents on the regulation of arms and discussion of those texts. An index, a brief bibliography, a good glossary, and various tables, including an extensive one arranged by nation on the status of major multilateral treaties, complete the work.

1:140 McClean, Andrew, ed. *Security, Arms Control, and Conflict Reduction in East Asia and the Pacific: A Bibliography, 1980–1991.* Westport, CT: Greenwood Press, 1993. Though the focus is not on the United States, its involvement in the region is reflected in this bibliography.

1:141 Shepard, Mary G., ed. *Disarmament and Security: A Collection of Documents, 1919–55.* Washington, DC: Government Printing Office, 1956. Also made available as a microform reprint, this committee print compiled for the use of the subcommittee on disarmament of the Senate Committee on Foreign Relations is a convenient, historic compilation of important documents that date from World War I.

1:142 U.S. Arms Control and Disarmament Agency. *World Military Expenditures and Arms Transfers.* Washington, DC: Government Printing Office, 1965–. This important publication records military spending by all nations as well as arms transfers, including trade, among countries. This work is a particularly important resource on the arms race and buildup during the cold war, giving tables with figures such as GNP and population conveniently juxtaposed along with arms suppliers and recipients. Coverage dates back to 1965. Volumes for 1998 and beyond issued by the State Department's Bureau of Verification and Compliance.

ECONOMIC RELATIONS

1:143 *Human Development Report.* New York: Oxford University Press, 1990–. Published since 1990 for the United Nations Development Programme, this annual is similar to the *World Development Report* in that it focuses on a different topic or theme in its essay section each year. With many statistical tables always incorporated in the text, the *Report* is also ex-

tremely useful for its ongoing appended statistical series on the quality of political, social, and economic life for individuals within nations.

1:144 *International Financial Statistics Yearbook.* Washington, DC: International Monetary Fund, 1979–. A retrospective compilation of detailed financial information for each nation, this title is now available in electronic format updated monthly. A monthly print title, *International Financial Statistics,* which has been in publication since 1948, inaugurated this series of country tables, which now form an indispensable historical record of any nation's finances. See http://www.imf.org/external/pubind.htm.

1:145 *The New International Economic Order: A Selective Bibliography.* New York: United Nations, 1980. This bibliography includes citations to journal articles in many languages published between 1974 and 1980. It is representative of a number of bibliographies published during an era when new attention was focused on developing nations and related issues such as technology transfer.

1:146 *World Data.* CD-ROM. Washington, DC: International Bank for Reconstruction and Development, 1994–. This CD-ROM database collects data from several current World Bank–IBRD print publications including the *Social Indicators of Development, World Debt Tables, World Tables,* and *Trends in Developing Economies,* all of which may be consulted separately for their significant and retrospective collections of statistical data for developing countries. A user's guide accompanies this annual publication.

1:147 *World Development Indicators.* CD-ROM. Washington, DC: World Bank, 1997–. Over 500 time-series indicators, covering 1960 through the latest available, are included in this electronic resource (available as an annual CD-ROM). *World Development Indicators* cumulates the data from the annual print versions of the *World Development Report* (see entry 1:148) and from the printed *World Development Indicators* and therefore provides a comprehensive, retrospective statistical survey of economic development throughout the world. Export capabilities and other advanced features enhance its usefulness.

1:148 *World Development Report.* New York: Oxford University Press, 1978–. This publication from the World Bank is essential for any study of developing economies and international economic relations. Each annual volume revolves around a different topical theme, but the annual appendices present a consistent series of important statistics and indicators for world development that are also available for export from the *World Development Indicators* (see entry 1:147).

1:149 *World Investment Report.* New York: United Nations, 1991–. Published annually, each issue of this yearbook has a different theme, but consistent data and information on transnational corporations and foreign direct investment are always included.

1:150 Blake, Michael J., Igor I. Kavass, and Howard A. Hood, eds. *United States Legislation on Foreign Relations and International Commerce: A Chronological and Subject Index of Public Laws and Joint Resolutions of the Congress of the United States.* 5 vols. Buffalo: W. S. Hein, 1977–. Well described by its title, this set is kept up-to-date with a loose-leaf service or "Current Index," which provides coverage from 1980 to date. Relevant legislation, regulations, and treaties are indexed in chronological order with the first volume including the years 1789–1899 and subsequent volumes covering two decades apiece through 1979.

1:151 Fouloy, Christian D. De. *Glossary of NAFTA Terms.* Boston: M. Nijhoff Publishers, 1994. With the premise that NAFTA "should be viewed as a continuation of the post-1945 experience in the Western Hemisphere," this work not only defines terminology associated with it, but provides the text of and interprets the treaty.

1:152 Gorman, G. E., and M. Mahoney, with Lyn Gorman, eds. *Index to Development Studies Literature.* Wokingham, Berkshire: Van Nostrand Reinhold, 1985. Intended to be an annual index to periodical articles in "major development studies journals produced around the world," this title apparently ended after one year and thus provides a stand-alone bibliography for about 400 journals received between 1983 and 1984 by the preparers. Arranged according to an OECD classification scheme, it contains a section on "international relations," but some of the geographic indexing terms have been broadened, which renders it less useful.

1:153 Holbein, James R., and Donald J. Musch, eds. *NAFTA: Final Text, Summary, Legislative History & Implementation Directory.* New York: Oceana Publications, 1994. The subtitle describes the contents of this useful compendium on NAFTA.

1:154 Kurian, George Thomas, ed. *Encyclopedia of the Third World.* 3 vols. 4th ed. New York: Facts on File, 1992. Each edition of this work has a preface defining third world countries and describing their status with respect to each other and to more developed countries. For each developing nation, a separate extended entry provides a specified set of information. Each country is described in such detail that the work can be used as adjunct to the *Europa World Year Book* (see entry 1:10) in the years in which it was published. Additional information includes entries for relevant international organizations and various statistical tables. First published in 1978.

1:155 Zangari, B. J., ed. *NAFTA: Issues, Industry Sector Profiles and Bibliography.* Commack, NY: Nova Science Publishers, 1994. A basic guide to NAFTA, this title is based largely on public documents. It brings together 1) descriptions of major issues such as tariffs, dispute settlements, etc.; 2) descriptions of NAFTA's expected impact on various U.S., Canadian, and Mexican industries; and 3) a simple bibliography with limited scholarly material.

ENVIRONMENTAL RESOURCES

1:156 Nordquist, Joan, ed. *Environmental Issues in the Third World: A Bibliography.* Santa Cruz, CA: Reference and Research Services, 1991. This slight volume deals with the U.S. role in international environmental issues largely by implication. The eight separate sections deal with specific developing countries, with regions, and with specific issues such as deforestation, agriculture, toxic waste dumping, and multinational corporations. Another section lists resources about the role of the World Bank.

1:157 Tolba, Mostafa Kamal, with Iwona Rummel-Bulska. *Global Environmental Diplomacy: Negotiat-*

ing Environmental Agreements for the World, 1973–1992. Cambridge, MA: MIT Press, 1998. While this work primarily focuses on the topic indicated by its title, Tolba also offers a substantive bibliography that includes technical works and studies on international environmental negotiations, many involving the United States.

HUMAN RIGHTS

1:158 *CRITIQUE: Review of the U.S. Department of State's Country Reports on Human Rights Practices.* New York: Lawyers Committee for Human Rights, 1982–. An independent organization for the promotion of human rights, the author-publisher of this work provides an annual critique of the State Department's annual *Country Reports on Human Rights Practices* (see entry 1:178). While acknowledging improvements, this organization typically reports three areas of concerns: State Department failure to hold particular countries responsible for political reasons, failure to apply its procedures consistently (resulting in uneven standards of judgment), and presenting results in a compartmentalized report that can shield government complicity. In addition to an overview, the *CRITIQUE* provides a country-by-country analysis of selected nations on which it judges State Department analyses most inaccurate. This publication draws heavily on the work of many international, regional, and local organizations and is valuable for synthesizing perspectives not readily available even in the other major annual reports from human rights organizations.

1:159 *Freedom in the World: Political Rights and Civil Liberties.* New York: Freedom House, 1978–. Published as a yearbook since 1978, this annual compilation from the Freedom House, a nonpartisan human rights organization that promotes political and economic freedom, is an important survey and analysis of political rights and civil liberties throughout the world. Typically, the yearbook contains an explanation of survey methodology, tables with ratings and rankings ("free," "partly free," and "not free") for individual countries, and a few brief opinion essays. But the bulk of the yearbook is a multipage assessment of every nation and "related territories." The country entries are particularly helpful not only in their details (polity, economy, life expectancy, ethnic groups, etc.) and assessments of contemporary political rights and civil liberties, but also in the overviews, which contain recent political histories for each nation. Predecessor publications were titled *Balance Sheet of Freedom* and *Annual Survey of the Progress of Freedom.*

1:160 Amnesty International. *The Amnesty International Report.* London: Amnesty International Publications, 1976–. The annual publication of Amnesty International, an international voluntary organization that promotes human rights, contains general reports and individual reports for each nation. Very specific details, including individuals' names, are provided in the country reports, which vary according to the contemporary concerns of Amnesty International.

1:161 Andrews, John A., and W. D. Hines. *Keyguide to Information Sources on the International Protection of Human Rights.* New York: Facts on File, 1987. This dated work retains some possible usefulness for historians in its bibliographical chapters, particularly the one describing monographs and essay collections.

1:162 Bennett, James R., ed. *Political Prisoners and Trials: A Worldwide Annotated Bibliography, 1900 through 1993.* Jefferson, NC: McFarland, 1995. A unique reference aid that spans most of the twentieth century, the bibliography is preceded by an essay and other opinion material. Following a section of general resources, lists of annotated citations are arranged by country. Over 2,000 titles are represented, many being personal accounts and memoirs. Political prisoners and the "disappeared" included here have often become a focus of U.S. diplomacy.

1:163 Blaustein, Albert P., Roger S. Clark, and Jay A. Sigler, eds. *Human Rights Sourcebook.* New York: Paragon House, 1987. An extensive and convenient compendium of documents and instruments in the area of human rights, this collection contains UN declarations and conventions grouped into subject categories. UN procedures and comparative constitutional excerpts are also included. UNESCO and International Labor Organization declarations, conventions, and procedures are provided in separate sections. Some other regional organizations are also represented.

1:164 Condé, H. Victor, ed. *A Handbook of International Human Rights Terminology.* Lincoln: University of Nebraska Press, 1999. An important dictionary of human rights terminology, this work is intended primarily for an audience of students and scholars (rather than practitioners). Some legal terms relevant to the study of human rights are also included in a conventional alphabetical arrangement as well as some basic instruments and a succinct but useful bibliography.

1:165 Garling, Marguerite. *The Human Rights Handbook: A Guide to British, American, and International Human Rights Organisations.* New York: Facts on File, 1979. The value of this title is its historical snapshot of American and British human rights organizations and activities in the mid- to late 1970s when human rights concerns were drawing unusual worldwide attention. Divided into British, U.S., and international sections, each is further subdivided into voluntary organizations, professional organizations, and refugee organizations. The entries are evaluative, and sometimes comparative, but always informative.

1:166 Gibson, John S., ed. *Dictionary of International Human Rights Law.* Lanham, MD: Scarecrow Press, 1996. This scholarly work is in effect an encyclopedia of various rights described and categorized in broader groupings (e.g., "collective rights," "declaratory rights," etc.). Each right is described and defined, as is its origins and history under the subheading, "Landmarks." The dictionary includes a brief but useful bibliography and a helpful prefatory essay.

1:167 Gorman, Robert F., and Edward S. Mihalkanin, eds. *Historical Dictionary of Human Rights and Humanitarian Organizations.* Lanham, MD: Scarecrow Press, 1997. This resource contains entries for national and international organizations, both governmental and non-governmental, concerned with human rights. A bibliography and the texts for several major human rights conventions are also included.

1:168 Human Rights Watch, ed. *Human Rights Watch World Report.* New York: Human Rights Watch, 1991–. The third of its kind in the genre of non-governmental annual reports on human rights around the world (joining Amnesty International and Freedom House), the *World Report* of this organiza-

tion is similar in providing a survey arranged by continent and country. A separate section is devoted to special issues and campaigns such as land mines and refugees. A predecessor publisher was Helsinki Watch.

1:169 Humana, Charles, ed. *World Human Rights Guide.* 3d ed. New York: Oxford University Press, 1992. While Amnesty International, Freedom House, and Human Rights Watch all compile annual evaluative guides to human rights on a nation-by-nation basis, yet another rating system is an important addition to the genre. The *World Human Rights Guide* is the basis of the Human Freedom Index used by the UN Development Programme in its *Human Development Report* (1990–). The compiler developed a classification system based on responses to forty questions about nations derived from UN instruments on human rights. An overall world progress report is included in this edition. First published in 1986.

1:170 Langley, Winston, ed. *Encyclopedia of Human Rights Issues since 1945.* Westport, CT: Greenwood Press, 1999. Edited by an international relations specialist, this scholarly reference work includes succinct entries on issues, incidents, events, people, organizations, and instruments connected with human rights. Many entries recommend other texts. A glossary and list of significant dates add to the work's useful material.

1:171 _____. *Human Rights: Sixty Major Global Instruments Introduced, Reprinted, and Indexed.* Jefferson, NC: McFarland, 1992. Well described by its title, this is a useful collection of documents mainly originating as UN declarations or conventions. The editor divides them into subject categories such as "War Crimes and Crimes against Humanity." Each category has a separate introduction, which is occasionally editorial in approach. Additional suggestions for further reading are also presented.

1:172 Lawson, Edward, with Jan K. Dargel and Mary Lou Bertucci, eds. *Encyclopedia of Human Rights.* 2d ed. Washington, DC: Taylor and Francis, 1996. An attempt to bring "together in a single volume everything important to know about the international, regional, and national activities so far undertaken with a view to promoting the enjoyment by everyone of his human rights and fundamental freedoms," this encyclopedia is a substantial and comprehensive work. Probably the most important reference work on human rights, it has a substantive entry on the United States and many other entries relating to U.S. diplomatic history. All relevant UN documents are also included, and many entries have excellent bibliographies for further research. First published in 1991.

1:173 Lewis, James R., and Carl Skutsch, eds. *The Human Rights Encyclopedia.* 3 vols. Armonk, NY: Sharpe Reference, 2001. Approximately 600 entries accompanied by brief bibliographies fill this more general and less scholarly encyclopedia, which also contains photographs and maps. Divided into two alphabetic sections, the first contains an entry for each country with a description of its human rights record; the second includes terminology, events, organizations, and persons.

1:174 Maddex, Robert L., ed. *International Encyclopedia of Human Rights: Freedoms, Abuses, and Remedies.* Washington, DC: CQ Press, 2000. Including approximately 150 concepts, 100 documents, 50 biographies, and many organizations, this creative, accessible encyclopedia offers thorough coverage of human rights at the end of the twentieth century. Relevant organizations are also cited in other entries along with e-mail and web addresses and other directory information. Additional readings are suggested in most entries. Many entries also have brief quotations from related documents. Some photographs and introductions by the UN secretary-general and Bishop Desmond Tutu add to the contemporary quality of this academic resource.

1:175 Redman, Nina, and Lucille Whalen, eds. *Human Rights: A Reference Handbook.* 2d ed. Santa Barbara, CA: ABC-CLIO, 1998. This handbook has some historical value as a collection of resources in human rights. In addition to a compendium of important human rights instruments and other documents still in effect, the editors also include a chronology, a set of brief biographical sketches, a directory of organizations, an annotated bibliography of reference works, and a limited list of media. First published in 1989.

1:176 Simmons, Mary Kate, ed. *Unrepresented Nations and Peoples Organization: Yearbook.* Cambridge, MA: Kluwer Law International, 1995–. With a membership of approximately fifty and headquarters at The Hague, the Unrepresented Nations and Peoples Organization has published at least two yearbooks since its founding in 1991. The yearbooks provide a brief history of the organization and its activities as well as entries describing each of its members and their current situations. Members are "occupied nations, indigenous peoples, minorities, and other disenfranchised peoples," and the entries are given under their preferred names rather than official government names.

1:177 Social and Human Sciences Documentation Centre, UNESCO. *World Directory of Human Rights Research and Training Institutions = Répertoire mondial des institutions de recherche et de formation sur les droits de l'homme = Repertorio mundial de instituciones de investigación y de formación en materia de derechos humanos.* 4th ed. Paris: UNESCO Publishing, 1998. In its fourth edition, this multilingual directory has nearly 500 thoroughly indexed entries for organizations, many of them academic. Of particular value to researchers in the field are the "Recent Publications on Human Rights" given for each institution. The initial title of this publication was *World Directory of Human Rights Teaching and Research Institutions,* published in 1988.

1:178 U.S. Department of State. *Country Reports on Human Rights Practices for. . . .* Washington, DC: Government Printing Office, 1979–. As required by law, this report is annually submitted to the U.S. House Committee on Foreign Affairs and the Senate Committee on Foreign Relations by the Department of State. Now available on the Department of State website, its predecessor title was *Report on Human Rights Practices in Countries Receiving U.S. Aid.* Prefaced by an introductory overview, the reports are arranged by region and within region by country. This report is annually reviewed by *CRITIQUE: Review of the U.S. Department of State's Country Reports on Human Rights Practices* (1982–) (see entry 1:158).

1:179 UNIFO Editorial Staff, ed. *International Human Rights Instruments of the United Nations.* Pleasantville, NY: UNIFO Publishers, 1983. A simple commemorative publication for the thirty-fifth anniversary of the Universal Declaration of Human Rights, this

UN-sponsored publication presents twenty-one declarations and conventions in a chronological arrangement. Its other value lies in a contemporary "chart of acceptances" by member nations, including the United States.

1:180 Verstappen, Berth, ed. *Human Rights Reports: An Annotated Bibliography of Fact-Finding Missions.* New York: H. Zell Publishers, 1987. A unique resource in the field of human rights study, this bibliography lists and annotates public reports of various fact-finding missions, most sponsored by fifty some intergovernmental or non-governmental organizations such as Amnesty International. This valuable work provides descriptions of over 350 reports, most originating between 1970 and 1986 and many of them ephemeral or difficult to obtain. Though "government delegations" are deliberately excluded, many missions describe situations affecting the conduct of U.S. foreign relations.

MILITARY HISTORY
AND ISSUES

1:181 *The Military Balance.* London: International Institute for Strategic Studies, 1966–. An important annual publication since the early 1960s, and published under various titles, this survey provides an important continuing documentary record of the armaments and the military capabilities of each nation. The United States, NATO, and Soviet Union–Russia lead the country-by-country list. Additional comparative tables and maps are occasionally included.

1:182 *Webster's American Military Biographies.* Springfield, MA: G. & C. Merriam Co., 1978. Including more than 1,000 U.S. military and military-related biographies, this dictionary also has a brief chronology of U.S. wars and lists of the secretaries of defense, chiefs of the various armed forces, etc. The biographical entries focus on individuals' importance and contributions as well as provide standard biographical information.

1:183 Borklund, Carl W. *U.S. Defense and Military Fact Book.* Santa Barbara, CA: ABC-CLIO, 1991. An excellent handbook on the contemporary U.S. military with a concentration on public policy and defense issues such as budgets, organizations, and facilities, this publication also has a history section that provides an overview of military affairs from 1946 to 1990.

1:184 Chambers, John Whiteclay, II, ed. *The Oxford Companion to American Military History.* New York: Oxford University Press, 1999. Like the broader Boyer, *The Oxford Companion to United States History* (2001) (1:63), this one-volume encyclopedia brings together the work of many scholars and specialists to provide an excellent resource on U.S. military history. It provides outstanding coverage from the colonial period to the date of publication when, the preface presciently notes, the U.S. military will be increasingly called upon to act against regional threats and to take on duties such as "border security, counter-terrorism, and . . . peacekeeping." Arms limitations and diplomacy associated with U.S. military events are another focus of the more than 1,000 entries. Major relevant articles include the entries on foreign policy, national security, and terrorism and counterterrorism. It is also well indexed, and entries include good bibliographical notes and cross references.

1:185 DeRouen, Karl R., ed. *Historical Encyclopedia of U.S. Presidential Use of Force, 1789–2000.* Westport, CT: Greenwood Press, 2001. This encyclopedia is a collection of scholarly pieces that examine presidential use of force in many contexts—constitutional, relations and obligations to the UN, U.S. military intervention in the Middle East and other regions, etc. A substantive bibliography is also included.

1:186 Dupuy, R. Ernest, and Trevor N. Dupuy, eds. *The Harper Encyclopedia of Military History: From 3500 BC to the Present.* 4th ed. New York: HarperCollins, 1993. The fourth edition of this classic work recounts war (and weaponry) from the "dawn of military history" through the end of the cold war. Extensive indexing makes the chronological and geographical arrangement of the contents more accessible. It remains the consummate reference work on military history. First published in 1970.

1:187 Gallay, Alan, ed. *Colonial Wars of North America, 1512–1763: An Encyclopedia.* New York: Garland, 1996. Through its 700 detailed entries, prepared by scholars and specialists, this encyclopedia constitutes a comprehensive overview on wars and other military actions fought in North America during the years indicated in the title. Coverage is given to individuals, events, and areas associated with the friction among colonists, Native Americans, and rival European nations.

1:188 Higham, Robin, ed. *A Guide to the Sources of United States Military History.* Hamden, CT: Archon Books, 1986. The most comprehensive bibliography available on U.S. military history, it has been revised several times by a corps of scholars since its initial publication in 1975. (See chapter 18 [18:101] of this Guide for details.) Prepared by U.S. historians, each topical chapter provides an introductory overview of predominant issues and literature followed by 300 bibliographic entries. Altogether this series provides outstanding coverage of every period of U.S. military history, during both war and peace.

1:189 Jessup, John E., ed. *A Chronology of Conflict and Resolution, 1945–1985.* New York: Greenwood Press, 1989. The military historian who edited this work readily admits the difficulty of arriving at a definition of conflict that is not arbitrary. Nevertheless, the resulting work is a month-by-month chronology of "conflicts from 1945 to 1985." Many entries appear under "United States" in the index.

1:190 Jessup, John E., and Robert W. Coakley, eds. *A Guide to the Study and Use of Military History.* See chapter 5 of this Guide (5:43).

1:191 Lane, Jack C., ed. *America's Military Past: A Guide to Information Sources.* Detroit: Gale Research Co., 1980. Brief annotations accompany the entries in this bibliography, which focus on land and air operations, though many of the sources are more generally useful, especially those listed in the chapters on America's rise to world power, the world wars, the nuclear age, and "limited wars." Both books and articles are included in the chronologically arranged work from the colonial era to the present.

1:192 Lewis, John Rodney, ed. *Uncertain Judgment: A Bibliography of War Crimes Trials.* Santa Barbara, CA: ABC-CLIO, 1979. This volume is valuable for appropriate nineteenth- and twentieth-century treaties and trials. Extensive coverage is provided for the Nuremburg tribunal, the Far East tribunals, and Vietnam trials and charges.

1:193 Marley, David. *Wars of the Americas: A Chronology of Armed Conflict in the New World, 1492 to the Present.* Santa Barbara, CA: ABC-CLIO, 1998. Covering two continents, this work supplies a precise chronology for conflicts and military actions that occurred between 1492 and 1998. Entries are arranged in chapters, e.g., "Pax Americana" (1898-Present). A brief bibliography is also included.

1:194 Petersen, Neal H., ed. *American Intelligence, 1775–1990: A Bibliographical Guide.* Claremont, CA: Regina Books, 1992. An excellent, comprehensive guide to the history of U.S. intelligence work, this resource offers more than 6,000 unannotated entries. Arranged chronologically, each section and subsection has a brief evaluative introduction. The bibliography covers books, journals, and magazines, and is particularly thorough in the coverage of more elusive literature in the military field.

1:195 Roberts, Adam, and Richard Guelff, eds. *Documents on the Laws of War.* 3d ed. New York: Oxford University Press, 2000. A convenient compendium on the laws of war, this source contains the text of treaties and other relevant documents. The substantive, explanatory introduction provides a scholarly overview, as do the document prefaces added by the editors. First published in 1981.

1:196 Smith, Myron J., Jr., ed. *The Secret Wars: A Guide to Sources in English. Vols. 1–2: Intelligence, Propaganda, and Psychological Warfare. Vol. 1: Resistance Movements, and Secret Operations, 1939–1945. Vol. 2: Covert Operations, 1945–1980. Vol. 3: International Terrorism, 1968–1980.* 3 vols. Santa Barbara, CA: ABC-CLIO, 1980. These volumes, now dated, catalog, without annotation, books, articles, and documents related to intelligence, covert operations, propaganda, psychological warfare, and international terrorism, 1939–1980.

PEACE MOVEMENTS

1:197 Bennett, James R., ed. *Peace Movement Directory: North American Organizations, Programs, Museums, and Memorials.* Jefferson, NC: McFarland, 2001. Not a scholarly work, its entries fit the broad definition of the subtitle and include many small, local organizations.

1:198 Cho, Yong-sik, ed. *World Encyclopedia of Peace.* 8 vols. 2d ed. New York: Oceana Publications, 1999. According to the preface, the second edition of this encyclopedia has undergone a "large-scale revision," adding new articles and updating others and reflecting the end of the cold war, the Gulf War, the Earth Summit in Rio, and other major events occurring after 1986, the date of the first, four-volume edition. The first five volumes are devoted to articles, the sixth to treaties, the seventh to a chronology of peace movements, profiles of UN secretaries-general and Nobel Peace Prize laureates, and the eighth to a bibliography and various indexes, all of which definitely show signs of updating.

1:199 Cook, Blanche Wiesen, ed. *Bibliography on Peace Research in History.* Santa Barbara, CA: ABC-CLIO, 1969. Listing 1,129 archival sources, guides to peace research literature, journals and institutions related to peace studies, monographs, general studies, bibliographical works, dissertations, and works in progress, this was once the most comprehensive (though sometimes not entirely accurate) compilation in the field. Several of the sections deal with materials related to peace groups. Those entries not easily identified by their titles are annotated.

1:200 Day, Alan J., ed. *Peace Movements of the World.* Phoenix: Longman, 1986. The movements described in this directory are organizations that vary a great deal in size from a few members to many. Many were founded in the 1960s, 1970s, and 1980s in response to the arms race of the cold war. The organizations are grouped by region or continent with a separate section on international movements.

1:201 Doenecke, Justus D., ed. *Anti-Intervention: A Bibliographical Introduction to Isolationism and Pacifism from World War I to the Early Cold War.* New York: Garland, 1987. This volume expands upon and updates Doenecke's earlier *The Literature of Isolationism: A Guide to Non-Interventionist Scholarship, 1930–1972* (1972) (1:202).

1:202 _____. *The Literature of Isolationism: A Guide to Non-Interventionist Scholarship, 1930–1972.* Colorado Springs: R. Myles, 1972. This slim volume of bibliographic essays remains important for its thoughtful discussions of the scholarly literature about isolationists from 1939 to 1941 when U.S. entry into World War II was subject to public debate. The dates in the title refer to the publication dates of the literature reviewed.

1:203 International Institute for Peace and Conflict Research. *SIPRI Yearbook of World Armaments and Disarmaments.* Stockholm: Almqvist and Widsell, 1969–. The organizational author of this publication was previously called the Stockholm International Peace Research Institute, which explains the origins of the title. This annual publication provides an extensive report on the arms race and the reduction or increase of conflict in the world during the previous year. Scholarly and analytical, it also includes supporting data, such as information on arms expenditures. The most recent, 2002, edition is titled *Armaments, Disarmament, and International Security,* published by Oxford University Press.

1:204 Josephson, Harold, with Sandi E. Cooper, Solomon Wank, and Lawrence S. Wittner, eds. *Biographical Dictionary of Modern Peace Leaders.* Westport, CT: Greenwood Press, 1985. An international dictionary that includes many U.S. figures, this outstanding and highly scholarly resource includes cross-references to F. Kuehl, ed., *Biographical Dictionary of Internationalists* (17:91). Deceased nineteenth- and twentieth-century persons who fulfill specific criteria are included. Each entry is given in three parts: standard biographical information, peace activities and leadership, and a bibliography, including publicly accessible manuscript collections. The second part receives the most emphasis and attention. The introduction gives a helpful overview of the history of peace movements, particularly in the United States. A list of peace leaders by country and an index complete the volume, which was sponsored by the Council of the Conference on Peace Research in History.

1:205 Woodhouse, T. *The International Peace Directory.* Plymouth, UK: Northcote House, 1988. This directory is divided into several parts: an introductory essay on "Research, Education, and Action for Peace," arranged by country, a bibliography on peace literature, and various indexes to the organizations. This earnest volume is characterized by brevity; historians will find much of the information available elsewhere.

1:206 Yu, Chong-nyol, and Ervin Laszlo, eds. *World Encyclopedia of Peace.* 4 vols. New York: Pergamon Press, 1986. The introductory bibliographic essay on "Encyclopedias of the Past and Present" provides an excellent overview of an emerging genre of resources and should be consulted for additional titles in the field. The articles in this encyclopedia, initiated by the Institute of International Peace Studies at Kyung Hee University and intended to promote peace through education, were largely written by scholars and practitioners. The first two volumes consist of articles on a wide variety of topics, each article concluding with a succinct but helpful bibliography. Volume 3 reproduces the texts of 39 relevant treaties and has a separate section of 77 articles about Nobel Peace Prize recipients from 1901 to 1985, primarily focusing on the contributions of each laureate. The fourth volume is divided into a directory of peace organizations, a bibliography consisting primarily of books arranged in categories, a list of journals in the field arranged in the categories of peace research, peace activism, and international relations, and indexes. Linus Pauling is the honorary editor in chief.

RESOURCES FOR INTERNATIONAL LAW

1:207 *Yearbook—International Court of Justice.* The Hague: International Court of Justice, 1947–. An annual publication since 1947, this yearbook succinctly documents the Court's history with background material such as the UN statute establishing the Court and with contemporary information on the work of the Court, its individual justices, and their biographies. This ongoing historical record also includes a list of Court publications.

1:208 Bernhardt, Rudolf, ed. *Digest of the Decisions of the International Court of Justice, 1959–1975.* 2 vols. New York: Springer-Verlag, 1978. Summaries of International Court decisions are given for the years indicated in the title.

1:209 Bledsoe, Robert L., and Boleslaw Adam Boczek, eds. *The International Law Dictionary.* Santa Barbara, CA: ABC-CLIO, 1987. A sound scholarly dictionary of international law with a topical arrangement, this publication has 368 entries in twelve different subject chapters covering, for example, general international law, human rights, and the laws of war and neutrality. Each entry has a separate section on its significance, and many entries are helpfully cross-referenced.

1:210 Deák, Francis, Frank S. Ruddy, and Bernard D. Reams, eds. *American International Law Cases.* 51 vols. in 3 series. Dobbs Ferry, NY: Oceana Publications, 1971–2001. The extensive set is considered the most complete source on American case law that involves international law or international legal issues.

1:211 Hajnal, Peter I. *International Information: Documents, Publications, and Electronic Information of International Governmental Organizations.* 2d ed. Englewood, CO: Libraries Unlimited, 1997. While perhaps most helpful to information professionals such as librarians, this outstanding reference work is also intended for information users. Researchers may find several chapters particularly valuable, including chapters providing 1) information on the organization of international bodies, 2) intergovernmental organizations as publishers, 3) citation of publications, 4) microform publications, and 5) computer information systems, particularly those of the UN and EEC. In fact, the UN and EEC are the overall focus of the work. Another important chapter is "Reference and Information Work," helpful to anyone attempting to retrieve information from the publications of either organization. First published in 1988.

1:212 Parry, Clive, and John P. Grant, eds. *Parry and Grant Encyclopaedic Dictionary of International Law.* New York: Oceana Publications, 1986. The editors admit in their informally worded introduction that they had some diversity of opinion about the intended genre of their reference work. As the title indicates, an "encyclopaedic dictionary" was the resulting compromise. The entries are sound and formal; a wide range of topics, including international law cases, terms, and participants, are included.

1:213 Rosenne, Shabtai, ed. *Documents on the International Court of Justice = Documents relatifs à la Cour internationale de justice.* 3d ed. Boston: M. Nijhoff Publishers, 1991. This edited collection of documents is a useful companion volume to Rosenne's explanatory *The World Court: What It Is and How It Works* (1995) (1:214). All important documents (to publication date) related to the founding and history of the Court are included. First published in 1974; though officially a third edition, this is the first bilingual edition.

1:214 _____. *The World Court: What It Is and How It Works.* 5th completely rev. ed. Dordrecht: M. Nijhoff, 1995. This useful work describes the International Court of Justice, its founding, history, and judges in an introductory section. Another section covers court jurisdiction, trial procedures, and cases that have come before the court. Discussion of past work of the court includes brief descriptions of cases and more subjective evaluations of the significance of each case. A chapter on assessment of the court shares that same subjectivity. Several documents relating to the establishment, rules, and composition of the court are appended along with statistics on court cases. First published in 1962.

RESOURCES FOR TREATIES

1:215 *Multilateral Treaties Deposited with the Secretary-General.* New York: United Nations, 1982–. Now regularly updated at its Internet site (http://untreaty.un.org/English/treaty.asp), this list of treaties has been published annually since 1982, following a predecessor publication, *Multilateral Treaties in Respect of Which the Secretary-General Performs Depositary Functions.* It is arranged in two parts, the second being a shorter list of League of Nations treaties and the participants to those agreements. Part I lists all the multilateral treaties of the UN (and League treaties amended by the UN) and groups them in such broad categories as disarmament, obscene publications, human rights, refugees and stateless persons, law of the sea, and environment. For each treaty, participants are given as well as any exceptions or reservations made by parties to the treaties. Notes are also included for nations assuming treaty responsibility for other regions or territories.

1:216 *United States Treaties and Other International Agreements.* Washington, DC: Government Printing Office, 1950–. Prior to 1950, treaties to which the United States was a party were published in *Statutes at Large.* Earlier treaties are most accessible in Bevans, *Treaties and Other International Agreements of the United States of America,*

1776–1949 (1968–1976) (1:217). This is the official record of all treaties since that date and is often referred to as *UST,* collecting all treaties issued in the pamphlet series, *Treaties and Other International Acts.*

1:217 Bevans, Charles I., ed. *Treaties and Other International Agreements of the United States of America, 1776–1949.* 13 vols. Washington, DC: Department of State, 1968–1976. This useful compilation of treaties supersedes a similar collection edited by William M. Mallory and issued from 1930 to 1938. The first four volumes provide texts of multilateral treaties in chronological order from 1776 through 1949. Volumes 5 through 12 contain bilateral treaties arranged by country name from Afghanistan to Zanzibar. The final volume is an index.

1:218 Israel, Fred L., with Emanuel Chill, eds. *Major Peace Treaties of Modern History, 1648–1967.* 5 vols. New York: Chelsea House Publishers, 1967–1980. Called the "first comprehensive collection of peace treaties to appear in English," the original four volumes of this title cover the period 1648–1966. Though international in scope, several separate sections are devoted to the United States, in addition to its coverage in such areas as the world wars. Volume 5 is titled *Major Peace Treaties of Modern History, 1967–1979,* again with extensive coverage of areas (South Asia and the Middle East) in which the United States was significantly involved. The first four volumes are prefaced with an introductory essay by Arnold Toynbee, the fifth with an introduction by Hans J. Morgenthau; both are commentaries on the general direction of world affairs. Maps are included in some volumes with indexes in the first and fifth volumes.

1:219 Meyer, Herman H. B., ed. *List of References on the Treaty-Making Power.* Washington, DC: Government Printing Office, 1920. One of the first significant reference works for U.S. diplomatic history, this work seems to have been inspired at least in part by the controversy over the Treaty of Versailles. While the title suggests informality, the book is topically arranged in chapters beginning with general references on the treaty-making power, then the treaty-making power in foreign states, and finally the treaty-making power in the history of the United States dating back to the Confederation. It retains its importance as a reference work because it collects sources, including many primary sources that have not been collated since. Citations to presidential papers, and their accompanying annotations, for instance, reflect quite specific, detailed research. With author and subject indexes for over a thousand works, this is a remarkable early achievement in collecting resources for American foreign relations.

1:220 U.S. Department of State. *Treaties in Force: A List of Treaties and Other International Agreements of the United States in Force as of January 1, 2001.* Washington, DC: Government Printing Office, 2002. The title given is the most recent version of a publication issued annually by the Department of State since 1941 (with earlier versions dating from 1929). It includes those agreements, pending and actual, that are defined as treaties by the U.S. Constitution and other international agreements covered by a broader definition of the term "treaty"; both bilateral and multilateral treaties (with a list of all signatories) are recorded. Part I lists treaties alphabetically by nation and organization, Part II by topic (e.g., "Diplomatic Agents," "Diplomatic Relations," "Polar Bears," "Prisoners of War"). Minimal annotations are included. For all treaties, entry numbers for several other important U.S. document series are given, including the *Treaty Series, United States Treaties and Other International Agreements,* and *Treaties and Other International Acts Series.* Occasionally a treaty is designated as "NP" or not printed in the latter publications. This is the most comprehensive listing of U.S. treaties.

RESOURCES FOR TERRORISM

1:221 Atkins, Stephen E. *Terrorism: A Reference Handbook.* Santa Barbara, CA: ABC-CLIO, 1992. This handbook has a useful variety of information. The introduction provides sound background material on terrorism and various aspects of the issue, and the chronology lists terrorist events occurring between 1894 and 1992. Chapter 3 provides biographical profiles of leading terrorists active between 1945 and 1990. A slender documents section is followed by a directory of terrorist organizations. An excellent annotated bibliography of the "best works" on terrorism, including other reference works, is arranged by

genre. Identifying terrorists and terrorist organizations involves some subjectivity, but the author has achieved some balance by including, for instance, both Israeli and Palestinian leaders when their histories warrant such coverage. Overall, Atkins provides a fine overview of the topic.

1:222 Babkina, A. M., ed. *Terrorism: An Annotated Bibliography.* Commack, NY: Nova Science Publishers, 1998. Soon to appear in a second edition, part 1 of this work covers books and reports, part 2, journal articles. The former is presented in alphabetical order by author, so the subject index is a necessity. Less clear is the order of the journal entries, many taken from the Lexis/Nexis database. Again the subject index is important for access.

1:223 B'nai B'rith Anti-Defamation League. *The . . . Annual on Terrorism.* Boston: M. Nijhoff Publishers, 1986–1988. This short-lived reference work brought a particular perspective to the study of terrorism. Typically, part 1 provides an overview of national and international terrorism for the past year, including a list of events and some data analysis. Part 2 is composed of essays. It was published for approximately three years.

1:224 Lakos, Amos, ed. *International Terrorism: A Bibliography.* Boulder: Westview Press, 1986. This bibliography, along with Lakos, *Terrorism, 1980–1990: A Bibliography* (1991) (1:225), offers comprehensive coverage of three decades of literature from all disciplines, including history. Popular and general interest literature are also extensively represented. The subject arrangement by chapter is similar to that in the later work.

1:225 _____. *Terrorism, 1980–1990: A Bibliography.* Boulder: Westview Press, 1991. This title should be used in conjunction with Lakos, *International Terrorism: A Bibliography* (1986) (1:224). This work adds material from the mid-1960s to the mid-1980s, covered in Lakos's earlier work, and thoroughly covers the rest of the 1980s. Like its predecessor, this bibliography is arranged in subject chapters that cover every aspect of the literature on terrorism from the most general to the most specific, e.g., "civil aviation aspects," "psychological and social aspects," and "counter-measures." Extensive indexing makes the 5,850 unannotated entries more accessible. Researchers should be aware that many of the entries are derived from popular and general as well as scholarly sources, but when used with the earlier work, this constitutes one of the most comprehensive bibliographies on terrorism available. A predecessor, published by the same press in 1980, was Augustus R. Norton and Martin H. Greenberg, eds., *International Terrorism: An Annotated Bibliography and Research Guide.*

1:226 Mickolus, Edward F., with Susan L. Simmons. *Terrorism, 1992–1995: A Chronology of Events and a Selectively Annotated Bibliography.* Westport, CT: Greenwood Press, 1997. In addition to this bibliography, Mickolus has also coauthored several earlier works, including *Terrorism, 1988–1991: A Chronology of Events and a Selectively Annotated Bibliography* (Westport, CT: Greenwood Press, 1993); with Peter A. Flemming, *Terrorism, 1980–1987: A Selectively Annotated Bibliography* (New York: Greenwood Press, 1988); and *Annotated Bibliography on Transnational and International Terrorism* (Washington, DC: CIA, 1976), which taken together provide comprehensive access to a growing body of scholarly and general literature on the subject. Both books and articles are cited. Chronologies of terrorist and related events are also included.

1:227 Rosie, George, with Paul Rosie, eds. *The Directory of International Terrorism.* New York: Paragon House, 1987. This directory is actually a dictionary with entries for people, events, ideas, and organizations. The introduction gives a good overview of the problem for the United States.

1:228 Thackrah, John Richard, ed. *Encyclopedia of Terrorism and Political Violence.* New York: Routledge and Kegan Paul, 1987. In his preface, the editor takes a thoughtful approach to the complications inherent in defining and explaining terrorism. When, for instance, does a terrorist become a fighter in guerrilla warfare? Intended for an academic audience, this work by virtue of its mixture of entries on concepts, theories, events, persons, nations, and movements successfully illustrates the complexities of the topic. Cross-references enhance its value as does a brief bibliography.

Resources for Regions and Nations

AFRICA

1:229 DeLancey, Mark, with Peter Steen and William Cyrus Reed, eds. *African International Relations: An Annotated Bibliography.* 2d ed. Boulder: Westview Press, 1997. This work briefly annotated books, articles, and pamphlets in several languages on African states, their foreign policies (including relations with each other), and African organizations. It contains over 4,000 items, most published since this work appeared in a first edition in 1980, and arranged in eleven broad subject headings, including U.S.-African relations.

1:230 El-Khawas, Mohamed A., and Francis A. Kornegay, Jr., eds. *American–Southern African Relations: Bibliographic Essays.* Westport, CT: Greenwood Press, 1975. A product of its time when U.S. and South African relations were particularly complex, this collection of bibliographic essays is composed by practitioners and covers scholarly and nonscholarly literature. The essays focus on U.S. relations with southern Africa, especially Angola, Mozambique, Zimbabwe, and Namibia. Economic relations receive particularly strong attention. See chapter 30 of this Guide for details on individual essays (30:27).

1:231 Keto, C. Tsehloane, ed. *American–South African Relations, 1784–1980: Review and Select Bibliography.* Athens, OH: Ohio University Center for International Studies, Africa Studies Program, 1985. Published prior to the abolition of apartheid in South Africa, this bibliography reflects that earlier era in its introductory review essay. Two sections, "American-African Relations" and "American Policy," are particularly useful to the diplomatic historian. The entire work, however, especially the duplicative chronological and topical chapters, reflects U.S. and South African interaction throughout American history. All genres—monographs, articles, dissertations—are included among the unannotated entries of sources published in four languages (English, Afrikaans, German, and French).

1:232 Lulat, Y. G.-M., ed. *U.S. Relations with South Africa: An Annotated Bibliography*. 2 vols. Boulder: Westview Press, 1991. This extensive bibliography in two volumes is the most comprehensive on the topic. Volume 1 focuses on "Books, Documents, Reports, and Monographs." Volume 2 concentrates on periodical literature and "sources of current information." For each type of document, the same subject arrangement is used; thus, "U.S. Foreign Policy" appears as a separate chapter title six times. Though perhaps more complex than necessary, especially since chapters also further separate annotated and unannotated entries, the work is comprehensive in coverage of general interest (except newspapers) and scholarly literature. The editor deliberately makes the annotations not evaluative; extensive book annotations summarize the book and sometimes refer to reviews. The indexing is not as detailed, but an essay for users who wish to update their research beyond the publication date of the bibliography is included.

1:233 Shavit, David, ed. *The United States in Africa: A Historical Dictionary*. New York: Greenwood Press, 1989. Another excellent resource with the same approach as Shavit's *The United States in the Middle East: A Historical Dictionary* (1988) (1:261), this dictionary covers Africa south of the Sahara. In addition to numerous biographical entries, many events and organizations also are recorded. A guide to place-names and a chronology are included along with a useful bibliographical essay. As the introduction notes, the United States and Africa have had "relations" dating to the origins of the slave trade in the seventeenth century, and the dictionary amply reflects that history.

1:234 Skurnik, W. A. E., ed. *Sub-Saharan Africa: A Guide to Information Sources*. Detroit: Gale Research Co., 1977. While this pathbreaking bibliography might be more readily categorized as belonging to the disciplines of political science and economics, many of the citations would be useful to the historian. For example, the chapter on "politics and foreign aid" includes a section on U.S. foreign aid. As the introduction and the selected citations make clear, "economic interests are an important dimension of foreign policy." Divided into subject chapters with a final chapter on other reference works, this resource also has subject, title, and author indexes. It is, unfortunately, also dated.

ASIA

1:235 *China: U.S. Policy since 1945*. Washington, DC: Congressional Quarterly, 1980. Using more of a current events rather than a scholarly approach, this work brings together a chronology, a set of biographies, a group of documents, and a narrative of U.S.-Chinese relations between 1945 and 1980.

1:236 Brune, Lester H., and Richard Dean Burns, eds. *America and the Indochina Wars, 1945–1990: A Bibliographical Guide*. Claremont, CA: Regina Books, 1991. This useful bibliography follows and supplements Burns's earlier *The Wars in Vietnam, Cambodia, and Laos, 1945–1982: A Bibliographical Guide* (1984) (23:34) and *The Vietnam Conflict: Its Geographical Dimensions, Political Traumas, & Military Developments* (Santa Barbara, CA: ABC-CLIO, 1973), both with Milton Leitenberg. Approximately 3,500 items, most published since 1990, appear in the newer work. Author and subject indexes provide additional access to the broader topical arrangement of the chapters.

1:237 Clarence, V., ed. *China in World Affairs*. See chapter 28 of this Guide (28:9).

1:238 McCutcheon, James M., ed. *China and America: A Bibliography of Interactions, Foreign and Domestic*. See chapter 5 of this Guide (5:46).

1:239 Morley, James W., ed. *Japan's Foreign Policy, 1868–1941: A Research Guide*. New York: Columbia University Press, 1974. Though now badly dated, this massive volume of mainly Japanese-language research aids, sponsored by the East Asian Institute of Columbia University, remains highly valuable.

1:240 Shavit, David, ed. *The United States in Asia: A Historical Dictionary*. New York: Greenwood Press, 1990. Unlike the other Shavit dictionaries, this is devoted almost entirely to persons. In addition to diplomats, others who played prominent roles such as missionaries and businessmen are also included. Basic biographical information is supplied for each. Additional material includes a chronology, a list of chiefs of mission between 1843 and 1989, and a good bibliographical essay.

CANADA, EUROPE, RUSSIA, AND THE SOVIET UNION

1:241 Cortada, James W., ed. *A Bibliographical Guide to Spanish Diplomatic History, 1460–1977.* Westport, CT: Greenwood Press, 1977. This bibliography does not include information on manuscript materials but does list various guides to the archives. In his introduction, Cortada notes with regret the paucity of general surveys of Spanish diplomacy and of specialized works covering many areas, including the early nineteenth century, but he nonetheless is able to list a substantial number of useful accounts. See chapter 10 of this Guide for information on a spate of recent Spanish scholarship on the war of 1898.

1:242 Hill, Kenneth L., ed. *Cold War Chronology: Soviet-American Relations, 1945–1991.* Washington, DC: Congressional Quarterly, 1993. This chronology, in some 2,000 entries, is a useful month-to-month, year-to-year listing of cold war events from September 1945 through December 1991 (the demise of the Soviet Union). Each event (and its source) is succinctly described. Valuable subject index.

1:243 Kanet, Roger E., ed. *Soviet and East European Foreign Policy: A Bibliography of English and Russian-Language Publications 1967–1971.* Santa Barbara, CA: ABC-CLIO, 1974. Now badly dated itself, this work was intended to update Thomas T. Hammond, ed., *Soviet Foreign Relations and World Communism: A Selected, Annotated Bibliography of 7,000 Books in Thirty Languages* (Princeton: Princeton University Press, 1965). Despite its age, Kanet's work remains useful, containing over 3,000 citations of books and articles on the foreign policy of the USSR and of the eight East European countries. An idiosyncratic organization is a challenger to researchers.

1:244 Lincove, David A., and Gary R. Treadway, eds. *The Anglo-American Relationship: An Annotated Bibliography of Scholarship, 1945–1985.* New York: Greenwood Press, 1988. For this particularly important and useful bibliography, the editors have done an outstanding job of collecting the literature on the "special relationship" between Britain and the United States. The years in the title refer to the scope of the publication dates; the bibliography itself covers the period between 1783 and 1985. The first part

is on "Social and Cultural Interactions" (but including trade and other economic interactions); the second, chronological part is wholly devoted to diplomatic and military relations. With the exception of dissertations, the nearly 2,000 entries are annotated. Books, essays from collections, and journal articles are included. Historical lists of chief diplomatic representatives for each country are appended.

1:245 Manning, William R., ed. *Diplomatic Correspondence of the United States: Canadian Relations, 1784–1860.* 4 vols. Washington, DC: Carnegie Endowment for International Peace, 1940–1945. These volumes contain documents relating to the relations of the United States with Britain and France as well as with British Canada.

1:246 McNenly, Jennifer, and Andrew McGregor, eds. *A Bibliography of Works on Canadian Foreign Relations, 1991–1995.* Toronto: Canadian Institute of International Affairs, 1998. This is the most recent of a distinguished series supplying bibliographical references (usually unannotated) on Canadian foreign relations. It was preceded, starting with the first, by Donald M. Page, ed., *A Bibliography of Works on Canadian Foreign Relations, 1945–1970* (1973); Page, ed., *A Bibliography of Works on Canadian Foreign Relations, 1971–1975* (1977); Jane R. Barrett and Jane Beaumont, eds., *A Bibliography of Works on Canadian Foreign Relations, 1976–1980* (1982); Barrett and Beaumont, eds., *A Bibliography of Works on Canadian Foreign Relations, 1981–1985* (1987); and Staff of the John Holmes Library, ed., *A Bibliography of Works on Canadian Foreign Relations, 1986–1990* (1994), all published by the Canadian Institute of International Affairs. Materials in both English and French are cited; the dates in the titles refer to when the items in question were published, not when events occurred.

1:247 Okinshevich, Leo, ed. *United States History & Historiography in Postwar Soviet Writings, 1945–1970.* Santa Barbara, CA: Clio Books, 1976. A unique reference source, this bibliography describes Soviet literature on the history of the United States, including U.S.-Soviet relations. The introduction discusses at length the issue of bias in the literature itself. The arrangement is largely chronological according to the periods in U.S. history. Additional sections look at Soviet authors' responses to U.S. historians, especially those writing about the Soviet Union. Each entry gives the original Russian title, a translation of the title, and a brief annotation. Both monographs and journal articles are included.

1:248 Shavit, David, ed. *United States Relations with Russia and the Soviet Union: A Historical Dictionary.* Westport, CT: Greenwood Press, 1993. An excellent reference work designed for scholars focusing on U.S. relations with Russia and the Soviet Union, this dictionary includes topical and biographical entries from the eighteenth through twentieth centuries. Many entries relate to the cold war. Supplemental material includes a chronology, a list of U.S. chiefs of mission, and a bibliographical essay that provides an overview of the most important monographic literature.

LATIN AMERICA

1:249 Griffin, Charles C., with J. Benedict Warren, eds. *Latin America: A Guide to the Historical Literature.* Conference on Latin American History for the Conference on Latin American History. Austin: University of Texas Press, 1971. Though now dated, this major historical bibliography for Latin America includes not only sections for specific periods, but also an extensive separate section on "International Relations since 1830," with a subsection, "Relations with the United States." The 7,000 works cited are not limited to English-language publications, and all entries were selected and annotated by scholars in the field.

1:250 Leonard, Thomas M. *Central American and United States Policies, 1820s–1980s: A Guide to Issues and References.* Claremont, CA: Regina Books, 1985. This slim volume includes an overview of the period referred to in the title and a parallel, selective bibliography of approximately 450 titles, most in English. The bibliography is topically arranged with particular attention given not only to history but also to the "contemporary conflict [of the 1980s]" and relations between the United States and Central American countries.

1:251 Library of Congress. Hispanic Division. *Handbook of Latin American Studies.* 57 vols. Austin: University of Texas Press, 1935–2000. This remarkable serial publication is the model of a scholarly bibliography. Beginning in 1964, the *Handbook* began to alternate between the humanities and social sciences for each year. International relations is included in the social sciences volumes; history in the humanities. All annotated entries are written by distinguished scholars. Staff at the Library of Congress provide similar expertise and support for the selection of materials to be included and for editorial work. Each major disciplinary section is prefaced with an overview of developments in the literature for that discipline. Significant journal articles as well as monographs are included. Works in both Spanish and English as well as other languages are included. Volumes 1–60 are available free online at the HLAS website (at the Library of Congress website, http://lcweb2.loc.gov/hlas/); volumes 50–60 may also be searched in the Library of Congress catalog on the web. A CD-ROM version is also available for volumes 1–55.

1:252 Manning, William R., ed. *Diplomatic Correspondence of the United States Concerning the Independence of the Latin-American Nations.* See chapter 5 of this Guide (5:11).

1:253 _____. *The Diplomatic Correspondence of the United States: Inter-American Affairs, 1831–1860.* See chapter 6 of this Guide (6:6).

1:254 Meyer, Michael C., ed. *Supplement to a Bibliography of United States–Latin American Relations since 1810.* Lincoln: University of Nebraska Press, 1979. See the entry for Trask, Meyer, and Trask, *A Bibliography of United States–Latin American Relations since 1810: A Selected List of Eleven Thousand Published References* (1968) (1:257).

1:255 Pérez, Louis A., Jr., ed. *Cuba: An Annotated Bibliography.* New York: Greenwood Press, 1988. As *Choice* noted at the time of publication, "Probably no American scholar is better qualified to prepare a general bibliographic guide to Cuba than Pérez." This is a selective work, "intended for generalists or other scholars working outside their specialty," with an emphasis on English-language works available outside Cuba.

1:256 Tarragó, Rafael E., ed. *Early U.S.-Hispanic Relations, 1776–1860: An Annotated Bibliography.* Metuchen, NJ: Scarecrow Press, 1994. This volume is a significant addition to the literature that should be used to supplement the fundamental Trask and

Meyer bibliographies. Those begin in 1810; Tarragó's overlaps and fills a gap, by covering literature on U.S.-Hispanic relations from the colonial era to 1860. A chronological arrangement follows sections of guides, aids, and general works. Annotations are brief and consistent.

1:257 Trask, David F., Michael C. Meyer, and Roger R. Trask, eds. *A Bibliography of United States–Latin American Relations since 1810: A Selected List of Eleven Thousand Published References.* Lincoln: University of Nebraska Press, 1968. As the subtitle notes, this bibliography contains over 11,000 entries. The 1979 supplement (Meyer, *Supplement to a Bibliography of United States–Latin American Relations since 1810* [1979] [1:254], which follows the same arrangement and updates coverage through the Nixon and Ford administrations) adds over 3,500 citations to this outstanding work, the only major bibliography on Latin America to focus exclusively on the history of its relations with the United States. Works in non-English languages and from many serials are included. After a section on bibliographies, there are two principal divisions: 1) the chronological history of U.S.-Latin American relations; and 2) the individual histories of U.S. relations with specific countries.

1:258 Wilson, Larman C., and David W. Dent, eds. *Historical Dictionary of Inter-American Organizations.* Lanham, MD: Scarecrow Press, 1998. Though this dictionary focuses on inter-American organizations as the title indicates, its usefulness extends to include many entries on important persons, events, treaties, and conferences. Other helpful additions include a chronology of events (beginning with 1804), appendices listing post–World War II inter-American conferences, extensive information about the Organization of American States, and a directory of organizations. A very useful bibliography completes the volume.

MIDDLE EAST
AND NORTH AFRICA

1:259 Bryson, Thomas A., ed. *United States/Middle East Diplomatic Relations, 1784–1978: An Annotated Bibliography.* See chapter 29 of this Guide (29:9).

1:260 Kuniholm, Bruce R. *The Persian Gulf and United States Policy: A Guide to Issues and References.* Claremont, CA: Regina Books, 1984. This overview of the Persian Gulf area and U.S. relations with the region contains a significant bibliography of over 900 unannotated entries, mostly in English and emphasizing "the problem of formulating a U.S. policy toward the region." Divided into subsections, the bibliography also has an author index. Kuniholm also prepared the similar *The Palestinian Problem and United States Policy: A Guide to Issues and References* (Claremont, CA: Regina Books, 1986).

1:261 Shavit, David, ed. *The United States in the Middle East: A Historical Dictionary.* New York: Greenwood Press, 1988. An excellent reference work designed for scholars focusing on U.S. relations with the Middle East, this dictionary includes topical and biographical entries covering the eighteenth through twentieth centuries. Its focus on diplomatic relations is so strong that the author notes in the preface the precise number (seventy-three) of chiefs of diplomatic mission included in the volume. Entries for specific missionaries, archeologists, anthropologists, travelers, and those involved in commercial endeavors reflect their important roles in U.S.-Middle East relations. Supplemental material includes a guide to place-names, a chronology, a complete list of chiefs of mission between 1831 and 1986, and a succinct but helpful bibliographic essay. References are also briefly noted for each entry.

1:262 Silverburg, Sanford R., and Bernard Reich, eds. *U.S. Foreign Relations with the Middle East and North Africa: A Bibliography.* Metuchen, NJ: Scarecrow Press, 1994. This bibliography is the best available for coverage of U.S. relations with North Africa and the Middle East during the twentieth century through the early 1990s. Most materials cited are in English. All genres of books, articles, dissertations, and government documents are included. Over 3,600 unannotated entries are arranged alphabetically; an index supports additional access. The noteworthy introduction defines the region and provides an excellent, extended overview of the history of U.S. interaction with the region. It was followed by *U.S. Foreign Relations with the Middle East and North Africa: A Bibliography, Supplement 1998* (with the same editors) (Lanham, MD: Scarecrow Press, 1999).

2

Overviews and Syntheses

Contributing Editor
JERALD A. COMBS
San Francisco State University

Contributor
JAMES CARTNAL
San Francisco State University

Contents

Introduction

This chapter on "Overviews and Syntheses" in the history of American foreign relations covers:

1. Historiography and the state of studies in the field
2. Theoretical analyses of American foreign policy and its history
3. General histories of American foreign relations, including influential textbooks
4. Studies of domestic influences on the making of U.S. foreign policy
5. Histories organized around specific themes rather than chronological periods
6. General histories of America's bilateral relations with specific nations or areas

The section on "Historiography and the State of the Art" privileges the most recent works.

The section on "Theory" taps into the vast literature on general international relations theory as well as theoretical works concerning the history of American foreign relations. The categories listed here do not mesh as neatly with one another as might be wished but then the debates have not progressed neatly either.

The categories in "U.S. Policy Formation" often overlap with one another. For instance, almost all of the works listed separately as dealing with the concept of national security, national interest, or balance of power inevitably deal with the other concepts as well. Works that study the presidential, congressional, or diplomatic and consular influences on American policy also overlap. Therefore, those seeking works about one or another of these subjects might wish to cast their bibliographical net across several of these categories.

On the other hand, most of the categories listed under "Themes in U.S. Foreign Relations" overlap little with one another. This no doubt reflects the fact that historians often select a theme because they regard it as *sui generis*.

Finally, although the editor looked especially for works on U.S. bilateral relations that covered the full chronological sweep of the relationship, many of the most important and influential works dealt with more limited time periods and so many of those were included as well. Many others, however, appear in other chapters.

Document Collections

2:1   U.S. Department of State. *Foreign Relations of the United States.* This large official series now contains several hundred volumes, since 1861 printing selected materials from the files of the State Department and, in later years, such organizations as the National Security Council, CIA, Department of Defense, and even private papers (1:93).

Historiography and the State of the Art

2:2   Brands, H. W. "Fractal History, or Clio and the Chaotics." *Diplomatic History* 16 (Fall 1992): 495–510. Brands surveys the history of scientific theories and their effects on the assumptions in the discipline of social science to argue that history is art rather than science.

2:3   Buhle, Paul M., and Edward Rice-Maximin. *William Appleman Williams: The Tragedy of Empire.* New York: Routledge, 1995. This is an admiring biography of the dean of the revisionists. It examines his intellectual, political, and personal life in a way that illuminates the historiographical quarrels of the last half century.

2:4   Cohen, Warren I., ed. "Symposium: Responses to Charles S. Maier, 'Marking Time: The Historiography of International Relations.'" *Diplomatic History* 5 (Fall 1981): 353–82. Michael H. Hunt, Akira Iriye, Walter LaFeber, Melvyn Leffler, Robert D. Schulzinger, and Joan Hoff (formerly Joan Hoff-Wilson) respond to the criticisms of the field of diplomatic history made by Charles S. Maier.

2:5   Combs, Jerald A. *American Diplomatic History: Two Centuries of Changing Interpretations.* Berkeley: University of California Press, 1983. This book describes and analyzes conflicting interpretations of the history of American foreign policy from the revolution to the early 1980s. It pays particular attention to the rise of the contemporary nationalist, realist, and revisionist views.

2:6   DeConde, Alexander. *American Diplomatic History in Transformation.* Washington, DC: American Historical Association, 1976. DeConde was one of the earliest of the diplomatic historians who criticized the field for its narrowness in methodology and subject matter. His survey of the literature in this pamphlet is outdated, but his critique of the field helped trigger the subsequent decades of self-criticism in the discipline.

2:7   Gardner, Lloyd C., ed. *Redefining the Past: Essays in Diplomatic History in Honor of William Appleman Williams.* Corvallis, OR: Oregon State University Press, 1986. This book assesses the impact of William Appleman Williams on diplomatic history. It discusses and gives examples of his revisionist "open door" thesis, but also offers essays by some of his students that depart from that view. It includes: William G. Robbins, "William Appleman Williams: 'Doing History Is Best of All. No Regrets'" (3–20); Bradford Perkins, "'The Tragedy of American Diplomacy': Twenty-Five Years After" (21–34); Ivan R. Dee, "Revisionism Revisited" (35–44); David W. Noble, "William Appleman Williams and the Crisis of Public History" (45–62); Carl P. Parrini, "Theories of Imperialism" (65–84); Edward P. Crapol, "The Foreign Policy of Antislavery, 1833–1846" (85–104); Fred Harvey Harrington, "'Europe First' and Its Consequences for the Far Eastern Policy of the United States" (105–20); Walter LaFeber, "The Evolution of the Monroe Doctrine from Monroe to Reagan" (121–42); Patrick J. Hearden, "Herbert C. Hoover and the Dream of Capitalism in One Country" (143–56); Margaret Morley, "Freda Kirchway: Cold War Critic" (157–68); Gardner, "The Atomic Temptation, 1945–1954" (169–94); and Thomas J. McCormick, "'Every System Needs a Center Sometimes': An Essay on Hegemony and Modern American Foreign Policy" (195–220).

2:8   Gilderhus, Mark T. "Founding Father: Samuel Flagg Bemis and the Study of U.S.–Latin American Relations." *Diplomatic History* 21 (Winter 1997): 1–13. This is a brief critical analysis of Samuel Flagg Bemis's contributions to the historiography of U.S.–Latin American relations. It praises Bemis's pioneering multiarchival research and condemns his chauvinistic interpretations.

2:9   Haines, Gerald K., and J. Samuel Walker, eds. *American Foreign Relations, A Historiographical Review.* This is a collection of essays on the state of historiography in particular areas of U.S. diplomatic history as of the beginning of the 1980s. It includes: Jonathan R. Dull, "American Foreign Relations before the Constitution: A Historiographical Wasteland" (3–16); Ronald L. Hatzenbuehler, "The Early National Period, 1789–1815: The Need for Redefinition" (17–32); Lester D. Langley, "American Foreign Policy in an Age of Nationalism, 1812–1840" (33–48); Anna Kasten Nelson, "Destiny and Diplomacy, 1840–1865" (49–64); Hugh De Santis, "The Imperialist Impulse and American Innocence, 1865–1900" (65–90); Paolo E. Coletta, "The Diplomacy of Theodore Roosevelt and William Howard Taft" (91–114); Edith James, "Wilsonian Wartime Diplomacy: The Sense of the Seventies" (115–32); Ernest C. Bolt, Jr., "Isolation, Expansion, and Peace: American Foreign Policy between the Wars" (133–58); Haines, "Roads to War: United States Foreign Policy, 1931–1941" (159–86); Mark A. Stoler, "World War II Diplomacy in Historical Writing: Prelude to Cold War" (187–206); Walker, "Historians and Cold War Origins: The New Consensus" (207–36); Robert J. McMahon, "United States Relations with Asia in the Twentieth Century: Retrospect and Prospect" (237–70); Thomas J. Noer, "'Non-Benign Neglect': The United States and Black Africa in the Twentieth Century" (271–92); Roger R. Trask, "United States Relations with the Middle East in the Twentieth Century: A Developing Area in Historical Literature" (293–310); Richard V. Salisbury, "Good Neighbors? The United States and Latin America in the Twentieth Century" (311–34); and Haines and Walker, "Some Sources and Problems for Diplomatic Historians in the Next Two Decades" (335–54) (1:32).

2:10   Hogan, Michael J., ed. *America in the World: The Historiography of American Foreign Relations since 1941.* New York: Cambridge University Press, 1995. Drawn mostly from the pages of *Diplomatic History,* this series of historiographical essays concentrates on the period after 1941 but includes several on the general state of the field. This volume includes: Hogan, "State of the Art: An Introduction" (3–19); Bruce Cumings, "'Revising Postrevisionism,' Or, the Poverty of Theory in Diplomatic History" (20–62); Melvyn P. Leffler, "New Approaches, Old Interpretations, and Prospective Reconfigurations" (63–92); Michael H. Hunt, "The Long Crisis in U.S. Diplomatic History: Coming to Closure" (93–126); Cumings, Leffler, and Hunt, "Commentaries" (127–58); Hogan, "The Historiography of American Foreign Relations: An Introduction" (159–65); Mark A. Stoler, "A Half-Century of Conflict: Interpretations of U.S. World War II Diplomacy" (166–205); J. Samuel Walker, "The Decision to Use the Bomb: A Historiographical Update" (206–33); Howard Jones and Randall B. Woods, "Origins of the Cold War in Europe and the Near East: Recent Historiography and the National Security Imperative" (234–69); Rosemary Foot, "Making Known the Unknown War: Policy Analysis of the Korean Conflict since the Early 1980s" (270–99); Stephen G. Rabe, "Eisenhower Revisionism: The Scholarly Debate" (300–25); Burton I. Kaufman, "John F. Kennedy as World Leader: A Perspective on the Literature" (326–57); Gary R. Hess, "The Unending Debate: Historians and the Vietnam War" (358–94); Robert D. Schulzinger, "Complaints, Self-Justifications, and Analysis: The Historiography of American Foreign Relations since 1969" (395–423); Mark T. Gilderhus, "An Emerging Synthesis? U.S.–Latin American Relations since the Second World War" (424–61); Douglas Little, "Gideon's Band: America and the Middle East since 1945" (462–500); Robert J. McMahon, "The Cold War in Asia: The Elusive Synthesis" (501–35); Diane B. Kunz, "The Power of Money: The Historiography of American Economic Diplomacy" (536–61); and John Ferris, "Coming in from the Cold War: The Historiography of American Intelligence, 1945–1990" (562–98).

2:11 Hogan, Michael J., and Thomas G. Paterson, eds. *Explaining the History of American Foreign Relations*. New York: Cambridge University Press, 1991. This is an outstanding set of essays on the varying approaches, methodologies, ideologies, and explanations of American foreign relations practiced by contemporary historians. It includes: Robert J. McMahon, "The Study of American Foreign Relations: National History or International History?" (11–23); Emily S. Rosenberg, "Walking the Borders" (24–36); Paterson, "Defining and Doing the History of American Foreign Relations: A Primer" (36–55); Ole R. Holsti, "International Relations Models" (57–89); Thomas J. McCormick, "World Systems" (89–99); Louis A. Pérez, Jr., "Dependency" (99–111); Stephen E. Pelz, "Balance of Power"

(111–41); Richard H. Immerman, "Psychology" (151–64); Melvin Small, "Public Opinion" (165–77); Alan K. Henrikson, "Mental Maps" (177–93); Michael H. Hunt, "Ideology" (193–202); Melvyn P. Leffler, "National Security" (202–14); Akira Iriye, "Culture and International History" (214–26); and Hogan, "Corporatism" (226–37).

2:12 Hunt, Michael H. "The Long Crisis in U.S. Diplomatic History: Coming to Closure." *Diplomatic History* 16 (Winter 1992): 115–40. Hunt argues that U.S. diplomatic history has emerged from an extended period of criticism as an increasingly self-confident field enriched by the dialogue among three contending domains of study—the "realist" domain that deals with the state and key decisionmakers, the "progressive" domain that concentrates on domestic factors in American foreign relations, and the "internationalist" domain that emphasizes the policies and societies with which the United States has relations.

2:13 LaFeber, Walter. *Liberty and Power: U.S. Diplomatic History, 1750–1945.* Revised and Expanded ed. Washington, DC: American Historical Association, 1997. A successor to the AHA historiographical pamphlet of Alexander DeConde (*American Diplomatic History in Transformation,* 1976), LaFeber's examines books that illustrate the ways in which the "new history" has affected even U.S. diplomatic history.

2:14 _____. "The World and the United States." *American Historical Review* 100 (October 1995): 1015–33. LaFeber praises historians of American foreign relations of the past fifty years for attacking the nationalist bias of earlier diplomatic historians, paying more attention to domestic influences on foreign policy, increasing research in foreign archives to create a more international history, and incorporating the work of social historians to broaden concerns beyond elite decisionmakers to the influences of gender, race, and the activities of ordinary people of all nations.

2:15 Leffler, Melvyn P. "New Approaches, Old Interpretations, and Prospective Reconfigurations." *Diplomatic History* 19 (Spring 1995): 173–96. This is a good brief survey of the state of U.S. diplomatic history in the 1990s, especially the relationship of new theoretical work to traditional archival research.

2:16   Leopold, Richard W. "The History of United States Foreign Policy: Past, Present, and Future." In *The Future of History: Essays in the Vanderbilt University Centennial Symposium,* ed. Charles F. Delzell, 231–46. Nashville: Vanderbilt University Press, 1977. Leopold, one of the founding fathers of American diplomatic history and the most knowledgeable about the early practitioners of the discipline, reviews the field as of the mid-1970s.

2:17   Maier, Charles S. "Marking Time: The Historiography of International Relations." In *The Past before Us: Contemporary Historical Writing in the United States,* ed. Michael G. Kammen, 355–87. Ithaca: Cornell University Press, 1980. Maier argues in this highly influential essay that the history of international relations was something of a stepchild in the 1970s because its methodological impoverishment, narrow focus, parochialism, and concentration on elites kept it from being among the pioneering fields. Maier did describe some exceptions to this trend and said that the development of world systems theory offered promise of a greater collective purpose for international historians, but his generally pessimistic tone helped set off more than a decade of soul searching among practitioners of diplomatic history.

2:18   Mastny, Vojtech. "The New History of Cold War Alliances." *Journal of Cold War Studies* 4 (Spring 2002): 55–84. Mastny provides a comprehensive multilingual review of the vast literature focused on the military and political history of NATO and the Warsaw Pact. Much of this literature is very recent and based on documentation that became available after the end of the cold war.

2:19   McCormick, Thomas J. "The State of American Diplomatic History." In *The State of American History,* ed. Herbert J. Bass, 119–41. Chicago: Quadrangle Books, 1970. In this historiographical essay, McCormick surveyed the status of diplomatic history from a nascent world systems viewpoint.

2:20   Rabe, Stephen G. "Marching Ahead (Slowly): The Historiography of Inter-American Relations." *Diplomatic History* 13 (Summer 1989): 297–316. Rabe summarizes the critiques of the field of diplomatic history and counters with illustrations drawn from recent histories of inter-American relations.

2:21   Smith, Geoffrey S., ed. "Diplomatic Historians and Their Impact." *Diplomatic History* 9 (Fall 1985): 293–328. Contemporary historians Gaddis Smith, Raymond G. O'Connor, and Walter LaFeber write on the character and impact of their mentors Samuel Flagg Bemis, Thomas Bailey, and Fred Harvey Harrington. Richard Leopold adds his own recollections and encyclopedic knowledge to these assessments.

Diplomatic Histories

2:22   Bailey, Thomas A. *A Diplomatic History of the American People.* 10th ed. Englewood Cliffs, NJ: Prentice-Hall, 1980. The most popular of the first generation of diplomatic history textbooks, it is detailed, episodic, and witty. Bailey emphasized the problems with a foreign policy that was too beholden to popular opinion. First published in 1940.

2:23   Bartlett, Ruhl J. *Policy and Power: Two Centuries of American Foreign Relations.* New York: Hill and Wang, 1963. This textbook by one of the deans of the profession is learned, insightful, and judicious.

2:24   Bemis, Samuel Flagg. *A Diplomatic History of the United States.* 5th ed. New York: Holt, Rinehart and Winston, 1965. This was the most detailed and authoritative of the first generation of diplomatic history textbooks. It was also one of the most chauvinistic. First published in 1936.

2:25   Carroll, John M., and George C. Herring, Jr., eds. *Modern American Diplomacy.* 2d ed. Wilmington, DE: Scholarly Resources, 1996. This is a series of essays on the critical events and issues of twentieth-century American diplomatic history. It includes: Joseph A. Fry, "In Search of an Orderly World: U.S. Imperialism, 1898–1912"; Melvin Small, "Woodrow Wilson and U.S. Intervention in World War I"; William C. Widenor, "The United States and the Versailles Peace Settlement"; Carroll, "American Diplomacy in the 1920s"; Jane Karoline Vieth, "The Diplomacy of the Depression"; Jonathan G. Utley, "The United States Enters World War II"; Robert L. Messer, "World War II and the Coming of the Cold War"; Mark H. Lytle, "Containment and American Foreign Policy, 1945–1963"; Marc S. Gallicchio, "The Cold War in Asia"; Walter L. Hixson, "Nuclear Weapons and Cold War Diplomacy"; Herring, "The Vietnam War"; Lester D. Langley, "Latin America from Cuba to El Salvador"; James W. Harper, "The Middle East, Oil, and the Third World"; and Herring, "Afterword: Facing a New World Order." The earlier, 1984 edition included Carol Morris Petillo, "The Cold War in Asia" and George T. Mazuzan, "American Nuclear Policy."

2:26   Clarfield, Gerard H. *United States Diplomatic History: From Revolution to Empire.* Vol. 1. 2 vols. Englewood Cliffs, NJ: Prentice-Hall, 1992. This text emphasizes the conflict between America's desire for non-entanglement and its economic interest in expansion.

2:27   _____. *United States Diplomatic History: The Age of Ascendancy.* Vol. 2. 2 vols. Englewood Cliffs, NJ: Prentice-Hall, 1992. This second volume of Clarfield's text argues that the United States resolved the tension between its desire for non-entanglement and its economic needs for expansion with a complete defeat of isolationism after World War II.

2:28   Cohen, Warren I. *America in the Age of Soviet Power, 1945–1991.* Vol. 4. 4 vols. The Cambridge History of American Foreign Relations, ed. Warren I. Cohen. New York: Cambridge University Press, 1993. Cohen attempts a balanced postrevisionist account of the cold war, arguing that the United States and the Soviet Union might have gotten along but for the security dilemma in which actions that increased one side's security automatically threatened the other's. In the end, however, he argues that the United States was correct to resist the vision of Joseph Stalin.

2:29   Cole, Wayne S. *An Interpretive History of American Foreign Relations.* 2d ed. Homewood, IL: Dorsey Press, 1974. In this text, first published in 1968, Cole tried to moderate between contending schools of historiography by self-consciously emphasizing both the domestic and international influences on American foreign policy.

2:30   Combs, Jerald A., with Arthur G. Combs.

The History of American Foreign Policy. 2d ed. New York: McGraw-Hill, 1997. This is a textbook that combines a restrained realist narrative with attention to conflicting issues and historiography. First published in 1986.

2:31   DeConde, Alexander. *A History of American Foreign Policy.* 3d ed. New York: Scribner's, 1978. One of the most detailed texts on American diplomatic history, it is thorough and well written. First issued in 1963.

2:32   Dulles, Foster Rhea. *America's Rise to World Power 1898–1954.* New York: Harper, 1955. This classic textbook depicts the continuing struggle between those forces in the nation that favored and those that opposed taking on international responsibilities.

2:33   Editors of the Foreign Policy Association. *A Cartoon History of United States Foreign Policies, 1776–1976.* New York: William Morrow, 1975. This is a selection of about 200 cartoons drawn from American newspapers with short commentaries to put the cartoons in context.

2:34   Ekirch, Arthur A., Jr. *Ideas, Ideals, and American Diplomacy: A History of Their Growth and Interaction.* New York: Appleton-Century-Crofts, 1966. This is an intellectual history of American foreign policy concentrating on such themes as mission, Manifest Destiny, and overseas expansion.

2:35   Ferrell, Robert H. *American Diplomacy: A History.* 3d ed. New York: Norton, 1975. A classic of the first generation of diplomatic history texts with a fairly conservative political interpretation, this was originally issued in 1959.

2:36   Gardner, Lloyd C., Walter LaFeber, and Thomas J. McCormick. *Creation of the American Empire.* 2d ed. Chicago: Rand-McNally College Pub. Co., 1976. This is a textbook by three of the most prominent revisionist diplomatic historians.

2:37   Iriye, Akira. *The Globalizing of America, 1913–1945.* Vol. 3. 4 vols. The Cambridge History of American Foreign Relations, ed. Warren I. Cohen. New York: Cambridge University Press, 1993. Iriye praises the very international activities of the United

States that Walter LaFeber condemns in the previous volume of this series (*The American Search for Opportunity, 1865–1913,* 1993) (2:40). He traces America's attempt to internationalize economic, security, and cultural affairs both during and between the world wars.

2:38   Jones, Howard. *Quest for Security: A History of U.S. Foreign Relations.* New York: McGraw-Hill, 1996. This text argues that American leaders have almost always followed a foreign policy that, while motivated to some extent by ideals, rarely risked national security in the name of morality.

2:39   LaFeber, Walter. *The American Age: U.S. Foreign Policy at Home and Abroad since 1750.* 2d ed. New York: Norton, 1994. This text takes a revisionist view of the history of American foreign relations. It emphasizes the nation's landed and commercial expansion, the centralization of power in the executive branch, the American desire for a unilateral foreign policy, and the conflict between America's desire for democracy and its devotion to market capitalism.

2:40   _____. *The American Search for Opportunity, 1865–1913.* Vol. 2. 4 vols. The Cambridge History of American Foreign Relations, ed. Warren I. Cohen. New York: Cambridge University Press, 1993. LaFeber argues that American foreign policy in this period was simply the overseas representation of domestic interests, which he characterizes as the iron rule of the new corporation. He sees the resulting American economic and territorial expansionism as terribly destructive for many people both within and outside the United States.

2:41   Leopold, Richard W. *The Growth of American Foreign Policy: A History.* New York: Alfred A. Knopf, 1962. This is another classic of the first generation of diplomatic history textbooks. It is learned and judicious in tone.

2:42   Paterson, Thomas G., J. Garry Clifford, and Kenneth J. Hagan. *American Foreign Relations: A History to 1920.* Vol. 1. 2 vols. 4th ed. Lexington, MA: D. C. Heath, 1995. This text is colorfully written, lavishly illustrated, and mildly revisionist in tone. It emphasizes American expansionism, its opponents, and its victims.

2:43   _____. *American Foreign Relations: A History since 1865.* Vol. 2. 2 vols. 4th ed. Lexington, MA: D. C. Heath, 1995. This volume carries its mildly revisionist analysis of American foreign relations into the Clinton administration. It continues to emphasize American expansionism, its opponents, and its victims.

2:44   Perkins, Bradford. *The Creation of a Republican Empire, 1776–1865.* Vol. 1. 4 vols. The Cambridge History of American Foreign Relations, ed. Warren I. Cohen. New York: Cambridge University Press, 1993. Perkins has written a realist account of early American foreign relations emphasizing the precedents set in this period for later American foreign policy. He praises people like George Washington and John Adams for their moderation in the pursuit of American interests and respect for the balance of power. He regards Thomas Jefferson and James Madison as inept failures for overreaching in pursuit of their ideals and bringing on war. He sees American expansionism as made inevitable by the vacuum of power in North America but argues that expansion could have been achieved by more restrained and peaceful measures than those Madison, Polk, and others adopted.

2:45   Pratt, Julius W., Vincent P. De Santis, and Joseph M. Siracusa. *A History of United States Foreign Policy.* 4th ed. Englewood Cliffs, NJ: Prentice-Hall, 1980. This classic text was first published in 1955 by one of the major early historians of American foreign policy and was updated by two younger historians in 1980.

2:46   Schulzinger, Robert D. *U.S. Diplomacy since 1900.* 5th ed. New York: Oxford University Press, 2002. This is a learned and rather irreverent survey of modern U.S. diplomatic history.

2:47   Van Alstyne, Richard W. *The Rising American Empire.* New York: Oxford University Press, 1960. This book describes American history and foreign policy as a chronicle of unrelenting expansionism until the early twentieth century. Although the theme of the book is compatible with the revisionist view, Van Alstyne's tone and basic assumptions are not.

2:48   Varg, Paul A. *America, from Client State to World Power: Six Major Transitions in United States*

Foreign Relations. Norman: University of Oklahoma Press, 1990. Paul Varg traces American diplomatic history from the colonial period through six major transitions to the beginning of the cold war. He emphasizes throughout the benefits of restraint in U.S. foreign policy.

2:49 Williams, William Appleman. *The Contours of American History.* Cleveland: World Publishing Co., 1961. Reprint 1988 (W. W. Norton). In this book, Williams made a pioneering attempt to provide a general revisionist history of the interaction between domestic and foreign policy throughout American history. He described a capitalist market-driven political economy that he saw as the driving force behind U.S. expansionism and imperialism and which he argued had a deleterious effect not only upon the victims of expansionism but also upon American domestic society itself. A 1973 edition (New York: New Viewpoints) includes a new author's foreword.

Theory

GENERAL

2:50 Bailey, Thomas A. *The Art of Diplomacy: The American Experience.* New York: Appleton-Century-Crofts, 1968. A dean of American diplomatic history develops a series of maxims, based on U.S. experiences, in his renowned witty fashion.

2:51 Dougherty, James E., and Robert L. Pfaltzgraff, Jr. *Contending Theories of International Relations.* 5th ed. New York: Longman, 2001. This is an excellent review of the literature and contending theories of international relations. First published in 1971.

2:52 Doyle, Michael W., and G. John Ikenberry, eds. *New Thinking in International Relations Theory.* Boulder: Westview Press, 1997. After two introductory chapters surveying the recent history of general international relations theory, the remainder of the essays in this book examine the state of a particular aspect of that theory. The volume contains: Doyle and Ikenberry, "Introduction: The End of the Cold War,

the Classical Tradition, and International Change" (1–19); Miles Kahler, "Inventing International Relations: International Relations Theory after 1945" (20–53); James Der Derian, "Post-Theory: The Eternal Return of Ethics in International Relations" (54–76); Jean Bethke Elshtain, "Feminist Inquiry and International Relations" (77–90); Daniel H. Deudney, "Geopolitics and Change" (91–123); James DeNardo, "Complexity, Formal Methods, and Ideology in International Studies" (124–62); Joseph M. Grieco, "Realist International Theory and the Study of World Politics" (163–201); Matthew Evangelista, "Domestic Structure and International Change" (202–28); Steven Weber, "Institutions and Change" (229–65); and Ikenberry and Doyle, "Conclusion: Continuity and Innovation in International Relations Theory" (266–80).

2:53 Evans, Laurence. "The Dangers of Diplomatic History." In *The State of American History,* ed. Herbert J. Bass, 142–56. Chicago: Quadrangle Books, 1970. Evans urges historians to pursue the history of foreign policy rather than diplomatic history or broader histories of general foreign relations because the study of policymaking processes is a matter of survival.

2:54 Gaddis, John Lewis. "New Conceptual Approaches to the Study of American Foreign Relations: Interdisciplinary Perspectives." *Diplomatic History* 14 (Summer 1990): 405–23. Gaddis bemoans what he sees as the methodological impoverishment of diplomatic history and suggests that historians learn from the methodologies of political science and international relations. A brief commentary and critique by Thomas J. McCormick follows the article.

2:55 Harbutt, Fraser J. *The Cold War Era.* Malden, MA: Blackwell Publishers, 2002. Harbutt provides a brief survey of the cold war that incorporates historiographical debates within the narrative and attempts to strike a balance between competing historiographical positions based on recent documentary evidence.

2:56 Holsti, Ole R. "International Relations Models." In *Explaining the History of American Foreign Relations,* ed. Michael J. Hogan and Thomas G. Paterson, 57–88. New York: Cambridge University

Press, 1991. Holsti offers an extraordinarily thoughtful and methodical comparison of three models of the international system—realism, global society, and Marxism (world systems dependency), and three models of internal decisionmaking—bureaucratic politics, group dynamics, and individual decisionmaking.

2:57   Lauren, Paul Gordon, ed. *Diplomacy: New Approaches in History, Theory, and Policy.* New York: Free Press, 1979. Although the essays in this book draw only some of their case studies and examples from the history of U.S. foreign relations, the excellent discussions of varying approaches to the study of international relations have great value for the study of American foreign policy. Contents: Lauren, "Diplomacy: History, Theory, and Policy" (3–21); Gordon A. Craig, "On the Nature of Diplomatic History: The Relevance of Some Old Books" (21–43); Alexander L. George, "Case Studies and Theory Development: The Method of Structured, Focused Comparison" (43–69); Melvin Small, "The Quantification of Diplomatic History" (69–99); Ole R. Holsti, "Theories of Crisis Decision Making" (99–137); Samuel R. Williamson, Jr., "Theories of Organizational Process and Foreign Policy Outcomes" (137–62); Richard Smoke, "Theories of Escalation" (162–83); Lauren, "Theories of Bargaining with Threats of Force: Deterrence and Coercive Diplomacy" (183–212); Robert Jervis, "Systems Theories and Diplomatic History" (212–45); Roger V. Dingman, "Theories of, and Approaches to, Alliance Politics" (245–69); and Samuel F. Wells, Jr., "History and Policy" (269–79).

2:58   Mead, Walter Russell. *Special Providence: American Foreign Policy and How It Changed the World.* New York: Alfred A. Knopf, 2001. Mead argues that American foreign policy, rather than being naïve or sinister as realists and revisionists have maintained, has instead been a beneficent factor in making the United States the richest and most powerful nation in history. American policy has been a healthy if somewhat messy product of debate among four schools of thought: Hamiltonian realistic interventionists, Wilsonian idealistic interventionists, Jeffersonian idealistic quasi-isolationists, and Jacksonian populists who are isolationist when it comes to the interests or human rights of foreigners but ready to fight for total victory when American interests are involved. Mead argues that the tug and haul among

these approaches has generally resulted in a better alignment of U.S. policy with national interests than what could be devised by even the most brilliant individual statesman, especially when there was some agreement between the schools about the American relationship to the international order—between 1823 and World War I, when all generally agreed to work within the world system organized by the British, and after 1947, when all agreed to assume the British role and lead a world coalition against the Soviets. The book is interesting conceptually but not well versed in the details, nuances, or monographic literature of the field and almost entirely ignores revisionist interpretations.

REALIST THESIS

2:59   Combs, Jerald A. "Norman Graebner and the Realist View of American Diplomatic History." *Diplomatic History* 11 (Summer 1987): 251–64. This article surveys the contributions of Norman Graebner to the realist interpretation of U.S. diplomatic history and charts his transition to a softer version of that view. The article concludes that Graebner had not to that date answered many of the revisionist challenges to the realist view.

2:60   Divine, Robert A. *Perpetual War for Perpetual Peace.* College Station: Texas A&M University Press, 2000. Despite borrowing this title from an early isolationist polemic by Harry Elmer Barnes, Robert Divine uses this slim volume to make the case for restrained interventionism. He surveys American wars, especially those of the twentieth century, and argues that while most American presidents prior to the twentieth century fought wars for properly limited goals, presidents in the twentieth century have rallied the nation to back justified wars by setting idealistic goals that exceeded both America's national interests and capabilities.

2:61   Graebner, Norman A. *America as a World Power: A Realist Appraisal from Wilson to Reagan: Essays.* Wilmington, DE: Scholarly Resources, 1984. This is a continuation of the series of essays collected in his *Foundations of American Foreign Policy: A Realist Appraisal from Franklin to McKinley: Essays* (1985) (2:62). Graebner applies his realist analysis to the key episodes and decisionmakers of American foreign policy in the twentieth century. Some of the essays are dated and do not make use of the latest information and monographs on their topics, but his history is still better informed than that used in most of the case studies offered by realist political scientists and strategic thinkers who are not trained historians.

2:62   _____. *Foundations of American Foreign Policy: A Realist Appraisal from Franklin to McKinley: Essays.* Wilmington, DE: Scholarly Resources, 1985. In this series of essays, Graebner explicitly applies a realist analysis to the key episodes and decisionmakers of American foreign policy in the period up to the turn of the twentieth century. Some of the essays were published early in Graebner's career and are therefore somewhat dated.

2:63   Halle, Louis J., Jr. *Dream and Reality: Aspects of American Foreign Policy.* New York: Harper, 1959. Reprint 1973 (Greenwood Press). In this classic statement of the realist interpretation, a former member of the State Department's policy planning staff uses examples from the full range of American history to argue for balancing restrained goals with the power to implement them rather than succumbing to the illusions of popular idealism.

2:64   _____. *The Elements of International Strategy: A Primer for the Nuclear Age.* Lanham, MD: University Press of America, 1984. This is a brief textlike explication of the realist thesis and its applicability to the cold war by one of the theory's most renowned and prolific advocates.

2:65   Kennan, George F. *American Diplomacy, 1900–1950.* Chicago: University of Chicago Press, 1951. In one of the most influential of all essays on American foreign policy, Kennan offered a realist critique of the major events in twentieth-century American diplomatic history. The historical research behind this essay was dated even at the time Kennan wrote his book, but the power of his ideas and the literacy with which he expressed them made an enormous impact on the historical profession. Several times reprinted, including as an "expanded edition" in 1984.

2:66   Kissinger, Henry. *Diplomacy.* New York: Simon and Schuster, 1994. In a grand survey of diplomatic history from Cardinal Richelieu through Woodrow Wilson and Theodore Roosevelt to the present, Kissinger argues that the United States has never appreciated the balance-of-power system that was made necessary in Europe by the presence of several strong nation states. Neither America's ideology of democracy and self-determination nor its diplomatic experience as an imperial power without rivals in the Western Hemisphere and then as a superpower in a bipolar system inclined the nation toward a system that required moderation in the pursuit of its ideals and interests in exchange for stability. Yet, according to Kissinger, the United States will face a multipolar world in the post–cold war era despite the globalizing influences of trade, technology, environmental concerns, and multinational corporations. In the face of several strong nations that do not share America's history and ideological outlook, therefore, the United States and other major powers will have to learn how to operate in a balance-of-power system or face disaster.

2:67   Lippmann, Walter. *U.S. Foreign Policy: Shield of the Republic.* Boston: Little, Brown and Company, 1943. Lippmann's early and highly influential realist tract sketched American diplomatic history to argue that the "solvency" of foreign policy depends on maintaining a balance between national goals and the power to achieve them. Lippmann analyzed world geopolitics to criticize previous American overextensions and to urge concentration on a defense of the "Atlantic Community."

2:68   Liska, George. *Career of Empire: America and Imperial Expansion over Land and Sea.* Baltimore: Johns Hopkins University Press, 1978. Comparing the rise and decline of the American empire to that of Rome and Britain, Liska argues that empires rise first as a response to security threats but continue to expand after the threat has dissipated because of internal economic pressures. They then decline because the costs of expansion exceed the gains to those internal groups seeking a greater empire and because the absence of foreign pressures tempts the political elite to turn inward to self-indulgence. He is particularly interested in the effect of rising empires on the international equilibrium, a theme he traces in more detail in the companion to this volume, *Quest for Equilibrium: America and the Balance of Power on Land and Sea* (1977) (2:69).

2:69 _____. *Quest for Equilibrium: America and the Balance of Power on Land and Sea.* Baltimore: Johns Hopkins University Press, 1977. Liska developed a concept of equilibrium in several previous books on international affairs. Here he examines the roles played by the United States and Great Britain in trying to maintain the equilibrium of the European balance-of-power system in the twentieth century. It is an informed and idiosyncratic book written in complex and convoluted language.

2:70 McDougall, Walter A. *Promised Land, Crusader State: The American Encounter with the World since 1776.* Boston: Houghton Mifflin, 1997. McDougall argues in this survey that eighteenth- and nineteenth-century American foreign policy was wiser than twentieth-century policy because it avoided the crusading spirit that infused modern U.S. diplomacy. McDougall believes that the earlier emphasis on liberty at home, a unilateralist foreign policy, the Monroe Doctrine, and territorial and commercial expansion served the national interest at minimal risk and properly balanced American ideals, interests, and power. The progressive imperialism of Theodore Roosevelt, the liberal internationalism of Wilson, the containment policies of the cold war, and the global meliorism of the post–cold war Clinton policies all partook of an excessive crusading spirit that was arrogant, overreaching, and ultimately futile.

2:71 Morgenthau, Hans J. *Politics among Nations: The Struggle for Power and Peace.* 6th ed. New York: McGraw-Hill, 1985. In this highly influential book, first published in 1948, one of the founders of the realist school uses historical examples to argue that U.S. foreign policy should be based on national interest and the balance of power rather than idealism.

2:72 Osgood, Robert E. *Ideals and Self-Interest in America's Foreign Relations: The Great Transformation of the Twentieth Century.* Chicago: University of Chicago Press, 1953. Osgood's book was a highly influential early statement of the realist thesis in part because the case studies he drew from the history of American foreign policy were more detailed and carefully researched than the brief examples used by other such early realists as Hans J. Morgenthau and Walter Lippmann.

2:73 Rostow, Eugene V. *Toward Managed Peace: The National Security Interests of the United States, 1759 to the Present.* New Haven: Yale University Press, 1993. Rostow surveys the entire history of American diplomacy to argue that the United States, contrary to its fondest myths of isolationism, has always been an integral part of the world's state system. He concludes that America's national interest remains involvement in international affairs to create a functioning world order as a system of peace through the maintenance of a favorable balance of power.

2:74 Whitcomb, Roger S. *The American Approach to Foreign Affairs: An Uncertain Tradition.* Westport, CT: Praeger, 1998. Whitcomb analyzes the historical development of various national traditions relating to American foreign policy and the environmental inducements, moral imperatives, and assumptions about human behavior that produced these sometimes contradictory traditions. He generally approves of the traditions and ideals that emerged but, in the restrained realist tradition, not of the arrogance and intolerance with which America has applied them abroad.

CRITICS OF REALIST THESIS

2:75 Beer, Francis A., and Robert Hariman, eds. *Post-Realism: The Rhetorical Turn in International Relations.* East Lansing: Michigan State University Press, 1996. This series of essays deconstructs the realist views of American history and foreign policy. It includes: Beer and Hariman, "Realism and Rhetoric in International Relations" (1–34); Hariman, "Henry Kissinger: Realism's Rational Actor" (35–54); Robert L. Ivie, "Realism Masking Fear: George F. Kennan's Political Rhetoric" (55–74); James Arnt Aune, "Reinhold Niebuhr and the Rhetoric of Christian Realism" (75–94); Charles Jones, "E. H. Carr: Ambivalent Realist" (95–120); Roger Epp, "Martin Wight: International Relations as Realm of Persuasion" (121–42); G. Thomas Goodnight, "Hans J. Morgenthau, *In Defense of the National Interest:* On Rhetoric, Realism, and the Public Sphere" (143–70); Jean Bethke Elshtain, "Rethinking Sovereignty" (171–92); Paul A. Chilton, "The Meaning of Security" (193–216); Jennifer L. Milliken, "Metaphors of Prestige and Reputation in American Foreign Policy and American Realism" (217–38); Yosef Lapid, "Nationalism and Realist Discourses of International Relations" (239–56); V. Spike Peterson, "The Gender of Rhetoric, Reason, and Realism" (256–76); James Der Derian, "A Reinterpretation of Realism: Genealogy, Semiology, Dromology" (277–308); David J. Sylvan and Stephen J. Majeski, "Rhetorics of Place Characteristics in High-Level U.S. Foreign Policy Making" (309–30); Roxanne Lynn Doty, "The Logic of *Différance* in International Relations: U.S. Colonization of the Philippines" (331–46); Franke Wilmer, "Indigenous Peoples, Marginal Sites, and the Changing Context of World Politics" (347–68); Beer and G. R. Boynton, "Realistic Rhetoric but not Realism: A Senatorial Conversation on Cambodia" (369–86); and Beer and Hariman, "Strategic Intelligence and Discursive Realities" (387–414).

2:76   Katzenstein, Peter J., ed. *The Culture of National Security: Norms and Identity in World Politics.* New York: Columbia University Press, 1996. On the grounds that international relations theorists failed to predict the end of the cold war, these essays argue that traditional international theory, especially neorealism, is sorely lacking. The authors insist especially that the concept of "national interest" is not an objective reality, as the realists assume, but instead is a constructed concept based on the norms, sense of identity, and culture of different nations at different times. Chapters include: Katzenstein, "Introduction" (1–32); Donald L. Jepperson, Alexander Wendt, and Katzenstein, "Norms, Identity, and Culture in National Security" (33–78); Dana P. Eyre and Mark C. Suchman, "Status, Norms, and the Proliferation of Conventional Weapons: An Institutional Theory Approach" (79–113); Richard Price and Nina Tannenwald, "Norms and Deterrence: The Nuclear and Chemical Weapons Taboos" (114–52); Martha Fennemore, "Constructing Norms of Humanitarian Intervention" (153–85); Robert G. Herman, "Identity, Norms, and National Security: The Soviet Foreign Policy Revolution and the End of the Cold War" (271–316); Thomas Risse-Kappen, "Collective Identity in a Democratic Community: The Case of NATO" (357–99); Paul Kowert and Jeffrey Legro, "Norms, Identity, and Their Limits: A Theoretical Reprise" (451–97); and Katzenstein, "Conclusion: National Security in a Changing World" (498–538).

2:77   Keohane, Robert O., and Joseph S. Nye, Jr.

Power and Interdependence. 3d ed. New York: Longman, 2001. Keohane and Nye argue that realist theory overemphasizes the ever-present possibility of war among sovereign states because it takes inadequate account of economic integration and the roles played by international institutions. The authors analyze the international history of monetary and oceanic policy from 1920 through the 1970s along with the history of U.S.-Canadian-Australian relations in the same period to illustrate how economics and international institutions moderated power struggles between nation states. First published in 1977 with the subtitle, *World Politics in Transition.*

2:78   McElroy, Robert W. *Morality and American Foreign Policy: The Role of Ethics in International Affairs.* Princeton: Princeton University Press, 1992. Using case studies of U.S. famine relief to Soviet Russia in 1921, American renunciation of chemical and biological warfare, U.S. policy toward the Panama Canal, and the bombing of Dresden at the end of World War II, McElroy argues that international moral norms accounted for some significant instances of state behavior that traditional realist approaches cannot explain.

2:79   Nye, Joseph S., Jr. "Neorealism and Neoliberalism." *World Politics* 40 (January 1988): 235–51. This short review article does a good job of summarizing the conflicts between realist and liberal theory and argues that there can and should be a substantial synthesis of the two.

2:80   Smith, Michael Joseph. *Realist Thought from Weber to Kissinger.* Baton Rouge: Louisiana State University Press, 1986. After a careful survey of the thought of several prominent realists, Smith argues that the realist view has significant shortcomings. He calls attention especially to its excessive emphasis on the state as a unitary actor, the conflicting prescriptions for contemporary policy to which realist thought has led, and the lack of self-consciousness among realism's progenitors about the ethical values embedded in their thought.

2:81   Tickner, J. Ann. "Hans Morgenthau's Principles of Political Realism: A Feminist Reformulation." In *Gender and International Relations,* ed. Rebecca Grant and Kathleen Newland, 27–40. Bloomington: Indiana University Press, 1991. Tickner revises Morgenthau's six principles of realism. To his unitary definitions of power and national interest, a feminist perspective requires the addition of principles of interdependence and justice.

2:82   Zakaria, Fareed. *From Wealth to Power: The Unusual Origins of America's World Role.* Princeton: Princeton University Press, 1998. Zakaria analyzes the history of the United States to argue that states expand in consonance with their power, not in response to threats. Thus, when the United States was a strong nation but a relatively weak state in the nineteenth century, it expanded less than when it was a strong state in the twentieth century.

LIBERALISM-DEMOCRACY

2:83   Brands, H. W. *What America Owes the World: The Struggle for the Soul of Foreign Policy.* New York: Cambridge University Press, 1998. Brands argues that almost all American policymakers and intellectuals, even those who style themselves realists, have had a strong sense of idealism and mission. The major dispute in American foreign policy, therefore, has not been between realists and idealists, but between "exemplars" (quasi-isolationists) and "vindicators" (quasi-interventionists). Brands uses short intellectual biographies of major figures from Puritan times to the present to illustrate this tension.

2:84   Ninkovich, Frank A. *The Wilsonian Century: U.S. Foreign Policy since 1900.* Chicago: University of Chicago Press, 1999. Ninkovich argues that the liberal democratic ideology behind U.S. foreign policy in the twentieth century did not lead to misperceptions of America's "objective" national interest and thus to tragedy and error, as realists like George Kennan and revisionists like William Appleman Williams both would hold. Instead, Ninkovich takes the postmodernist position that there is no "objective" national interest, and that U.S. ideology has been rather successful in constructing that interest. He defines twentieth-century U.S. foreign policy ideology as alternating between "normal" internationalism, which combined political isolationism with commercial and private transnational activity, and crisis (Wilsonian) internationalism, which called for global U.S. intervention in times of actual or threatened global warfare. He be-

lieves that Wilsonian ideology was indeed appropriate for crisis periods like World War I, World War II, and the cold war, but that "normal" internationalism was and remains more appropriate for less critical times.

2:85   Owen, John M., IV. *Liberal Peace, Liberal War: American Politics and International Security.* Ithaca: Cornell University Press, 1997. This is a major contribution to the debate between realists, who hold that all nations fight over power and interest regardless of their internal ideologies, and those who argue that internal ideology matters to the point that democracies never fight one another. Examining the record from the revolution to the Spanish-American War, Owens argues that, as a liberal (a term he prefers to democratic) state, the United States is less likely to fight a state of similar ideology. Therefore, liberalism matters.

IMPERIALISM

2:86   May, Ernest R. *American Imperialism: A Speculative Essay.* Chicago: Imprint Publications, 1991. This book combines historiographical analysis, questions about the process and timing of expansionism, and insights from social science about public opinion and elite influence to argue that foreign fashions helped cause a shift from anticolonialism to imperialism in the United States. First published in 1968.

2:87   Nearing, Scott, and Joseph Freeman. *Dollar Diplomacy: A Study in American Imperialism.* New York: B. W. Huebsch and Viking Press, 1925. This study is one of the classic radical indictments of U.S. foreign policy, especially U.S. policy toward Latin America.

2:88   Ninkovich, Frank A. *The United States and Imperialism.* Malden, MA: Blackwell Publishers, 2001. In tracing the history of American imperialism, Ninkovich rejects the idea that all expansion, free trade, or globalization is just imperialism in disguise. His primary argument is that America's concern for the third world during the cold war was more geopolitical than economic. See also Mary Ann Heiss, "The Evolution of the Imperial Idea and U.S. National Identity," *Diplomatic History* 26 (Fall 2002): 511–40.

2:89   Parrini, Carl P. "Theories of Imperialism." In *Redefining the Past: Essays in Diplomatic History* *in Honor of William Appleman Williams,* ed. Lloyd C. Gardner, 65–84. Corvallis, OR: Oregon State University Press, 1986. This is a brief but informed and helpful explication of the differences between socialist and nonsocialist interpretations of modern imperialism. Parrini believes that the emotions surrounding the cold war have inhibited the research necessary to demonstrate the validity of the various competing interpretations.

2:90 Pérez, Louis A., Jr. "Dependency." In *Explaining the History of American Foreign Relations,* ed. Michael J. Hogan and Thomas G. Paterson, 99–111. New York: Cambridge University Press, 1991. Louis Pérez describes the rise of dependency theory in the context of U.S.–Latin American relations and sees its emphasis on social and cultural domination as a valuable addition to the almost exclusive concern with economics and politics in the concept of imperialism. He examines some of the conflicts between subscribers to dependency theory but argues that all dependency theorists are united in their critique of liberal capitalism.

2:91 Smith, Tony. *The Pattern of Imperialism: The United States, Great Britain, and the Late-Instrializing World since 1815.* Cambridge, MA: Cambridge University Press, 1981. This is an excellent comparative study of the motivations and forces behind British and American imperialism. It emphasizes as factors in the rise of Anglo-American imperialism the various combinations of economic industrial expansion, political great power rivalries, and the capacity of weaker nations to cope with these forces.

REVISIONIST THESIS (OPEN DOOR IMPERIALISM)

2:92 Craig, Campbell. "The Not-So-Strange Career of Charles Beard." *Diplomatic History* 25 (Spring 2001): 251–74. The author argues that World War II caused Charles A. Beard to abandon his earlier belief that America's extra-continental entanglements and wars had been unnecessary and motivated by the economic interests of a few elite merchants and politicians. The war convinced him that U.S. security could indeed be put at risk by the rage and revenge of militarists abroad who had no particular economic motivation. Consequently, he abandoned

his prewar argument that Rooseveltian interventionism was economically motivated for an indictment of FDR's deceptiveness and unconstitutional actions.

2:93 Kennedy, Thomas C. *Charles A. Beard and American Foreign Policy.* Gainesville: University Presses of Florida, 1975. This is the best full biography of the historian many consider to be the progenitor of the revisionist thesis.

2:94 Mills, C. Wright. *The Power Elite.* New York: Oxford University Press, 1956. A pioneering analysis of what would later become known as the American "establishment," this book has influenced many revisionist critiques of U.S. foreign policy. Mills argued that American society is run by elites (corporate, political, military, and social) who are not representative of the American public generally.

2:95 Williams, William Appleman. *The Great Evasion: An Essay on the Contemporary Relevance of Karl Marx and on the Wisdom of Admitting the Heretic into the Dialogue about America's Future.* Chicago: Quadrangle Books, 1964. Williams offers a critique of the effect of capitalism, markets, and corporations on American foreign and domestic policy and thus makes explicit the philosophical underpinnings of his revisionist historical accounts of U.S. diplomatic history.

2:96 _____. *The Roots of the Modern American Empire: A Study of the Growth and Shaping of Social Consciousness in a Marketplace Society.* New York: Random House, 1969. In elaborating on the revisionist thesis of his earlier works, Williams here emphasizes that the need for overseas markets made American agricultural interests almost as expansionist as commercial and industrial interests in late-nineteenth-century America.

2:97 _____. *The Tragedy of American Diplomacy.* 2d rev. and enl. ed. New York: Dell Publishing Co., 1972. Reprint 1988 (Norton). Although there were earlier socialist and radical histories of American diplomatic history, this is generally regarded as the progenitor of the revisionist school of interpretation. Williams sees the open door as the root of American foreign policy. Thus, American leaders, at least since the turn of the century, shared the conviction that prosperity at home required economic expansion overseas, which in turn restricted the legitimate revolutionary aspirations of other countries. First published in 1959.

CRITICS OF REVISIONIST THESIS

2:98   Becker, William H., and Samuel F. Wells, Jr., eds. *Economics and World Power: An Assessment of American Diplomacy since 1789.* New York: Columbia University Press, 1984. The essays in this book generally accept the importance of economics in American foreign policy but argue that economics' influence varies depending on the period of American history, the relative power of the major states at the time, the compatibility of their economic strategies, and how much economics motivated the other major states. Thus, most essays contradict the revisionist thesis of an ideologically based U.S. consensus on the need for foreign economic expansion to solve domestic economic and social problems. The contents of the volume are: James A. Field, Jr., "1789–1820: All Oeconomists, All Diplomats" (1–54); Kinley J. Brauer, "1821–1860: Economics and the Diplomacy of American Expansionism" (55–118); David M. Pletcher, "1861–1898: Economic Growth and Diplomatic Adjustment" (119–72); Becker, "1899–1920: America Adjusts to World Power" (173–224); Melvyn P. Leffler, "1921–1932: Expansionist Impulses and Domestic Constraints" (225–76); Robert M. Hathaway, "1933–1945: Economic Diplomacy in a Time of Crisis" (277–332); Robert A. Pollard and Wells, "1945–1960: The Era of American Economic Hegemony" (333–90); and David P. Calleo, "Since 1961: American Power in a New World Economy" (391–458).

2:99   Cohen, Benjamin J. *The Question of Imperialism: The Political Economy of Dominance and Dependence.* New York: Basic Books, 1973. Saying he believes that capitalism can be reformed, Cohen skeptically analyzes Marxist and radical theories of imperialism. In the final chapter he suggests an alternative explanation of imperialism based on "the anarchic organization of the international system of states" that drives nations to become preoccupied with national security.

2:100   Field, James A., Jr. "American Imperialism: The Worst Chapter in Almost Any Book." *American Historical Review* 83 (June 1978): 644–83. This article poses a technological explanation for imperialism based on the communications revolution and stresses the role of historical accident. An exchange of opinion follows with Walter LaFeber and Robert L. Beisner.

2:101   Gaddis, John Lewis. "The Emerging Post-Revisionist Synthesis on the Origins of the Cold War." *Diplomatic History* 7 (Summer 1983): 171–90. In a highly influential article, Gaddis argued that there was a postrevisionist synthesis emerging on the study of the cold war that combined the insights of the contending revisionist and orthodox historians. Commentaries by Lloyd C. Gardner, Lawrence S. Kaplan, Warren F. Kimball, and Bruce R. Kuniholm immediately follow. They make clear that although there indeed has been some synthesis between contending views, the quarrel between revisionists and traditionalists would continue over the cold war and other episodes in American diplomatic history.

2:102   Perkins, Bradford. "'The Tragedy of American Diplomacy': Twenty-five Years After." *Reviews in American History* 12 (March 1984): 1–18. Perkins criticizes the work of William Appleman Williams and the "Wisconsin School" of revisionism for its overemphasis on expanding markets as the primary factor in American foreign policy, but concludes that Williams's revisionism has had a profound and largely beneficial effect on the writing of American diplomatic history.

2:103   Siracusa, Joseph M. *New Left Diplomatic Histories and Historians: The American Revisionists.* Updated ed. Claremont, CA: Regina Books, 1993. Despite being revised in 1993 from the 1973 original, this is a fairly dated analysis of the American revisionists. Its primary virtue is an extended survey of William Appleman Williams and his work.

WORLD SYSTEMS

2:104   Cumings, Bruce. "'Revising Postrevisionism,' or, The Poverty of Theory in Diplomatic History." *Diplomatic History* 17 (Fall 1993): 539–69. Cumings deconstructs various orthodox and postrevisionist histories to argue that they wrongly marginalize revisionist histories and suffer from the lack of a consistent theoretical base. He contends that world systems theory offers the best theoretical construct presently available to diplomatic historians.

2:105 McCormick, Thomas J. "'Every System Needs a Center Sometimes': An Essay on Hegemony and Modern American Foreign Policy." In *Redefining the Past: Essays in Diplomatic History in Honor of William Appleman Williams,* ed. Lloyd C. Gardner, 195–220. Corvallis, OR: Oregon State University Press, 1986. McCormick shows how world system theory can be applied to American foreign relations. He argues that by 1950, New York had become the center of an international capitalist system just as Venice had been its center in 1450, Antwerp in 1550, Amsterdam in 1650, and London in 1850.

2:106 _____. "World Systems." In *Explaining the History of American Foreign Relations,* ed. Michael J. Hogan and Thomas G. Paterson, 89–98. New York: Cambridge University Press, 1991. This is a fascinating description and critique of world systems theory by its most important practitioner in the writing of American diplomatic history.

2:107 Ninkovich, Frank A. "The End of Diplomatic History?" *Diplomatic History* 15 (Summer 1991): 439–48. This feature review of Thomas McCormick's *America's Half-Century: United States Foreign Policy in the Cold War* (1989) (19:165) offers a trenchant criticism of world systems theory.

CORPORATISM

2:108 Gaddis, John Lewis. "The Corporatist Synthesis: A Skeptical View." *Diplomatic History* 10 (Fall 1986): 357–62. Gaddis criticizes the corporatist synthesis on the grounds that it fails to take adequate account of geopolitics, idealism, distinctive individuals, and domestic conflict between groups as factors in American foreign policy.

2:109 Hogan, Michael J. "Corporatism." In *Explaining the History of American Foreign Relations,* ed. Michael J. Hogan and Thomas G. Paterson, 226–36. New York: Cambridge University Press, 1991. Hogan defines corporatism as a system in which organized groups such as labor, business, and

agriculture collaborate with the government and public elites to develop a foreign policy that will stabilize and harmonize public and private interests. He then surveys recent work that develops or uses that theory in analyzing the history of American foreign relations.

2:110 _____. "Corporatism: A Positive Appraisal." *Diplomatic History* 10 (Fall 1986): 363–72. Hogan argues that critics of corporatism misunderstand the theory, and that corporatism does cast light on geopolitical, idealistic, domestic, and other factors influencing American foreign policy.

2:111 Wiarda, Howard J. *Corporatism and Comparative Politics: The Other Great "Ism."* Armonk, NY: M. E. Sharpe, 1997. This book places American corporatism and corporatist theory in a comparative context with European and Latin American corporatism. Wiarda considers the rise of corporatist theory in light of tendencies in liberal-pluralist and Marxist theory.

2:112 Zunz, Olivier. *Why the American Century?* Chicago: University of Chicago Press, 1998. This is a sophisticated analysis of a partnership among big business, government, and higher education to engineer and manage a new America and to construct an ideology that could serve as a basis for a Pax Americana. While Zunz concentrates primarily on the shaping of the domestic consensus, he uses the occupation of Japan after World War II as a case study of America's attempt to spread its ideology abroad.

FEMINISM

2:113 Grant, Rebecca. "The Sources of Gender Bias in International Relations Theory." In *Gender and International Relations,* ed. Rebecca Grant and Kathleen Newland, 2–27. Bloomington: Indiana University Press, 1991. Grant argues that international relations theory is gender biased because it relies on concepts like the state of nature, the state, the sovereign man, and the security dilemma that are themselves gender biased. Even critics of neorealist theory like Richard Ashley, who deconstruct concepts such as sovereign man, give insufficient attention to gender bias among the other exclusions and biases they find in international relations theory. Gender-neutral international theory would reduce the distinctions between public and private realms and therefore of national and international politics.

2:114   Steans, Jill. *Gender and International Relations: An Introduction.* New Brunswick: Rutgers University Press, 1998. Steans tries to show how gender concerns and feminist theory challenge and contribute new insights to international relations theory.

2:115   Sylvester, Christine. *Feminist Theory in International Relations in a Postmodern Era.* New York: Cambridge University Press, 1994. Sylvester argues that the three major debates over international relations theory in the past century—realist versus idealist, scientific versus traditional, and modernist versus postmodernist—would all have been greatly altered by feminist theorizing.

2:116   Tickner, J. Ann. *Gender in International Relations: Feminist Perspectives on Achieving Global Security.* New York: Columbia University Press, 1992. Tickner shows how a feminine perspective challenges all of the major international relations theories, including realism, liberalism, economic nationalism, and Marxism.

OTHERS

2:117   Crabb, Cecil V., Jr. *American Diplomacy and the Pragmatic Tradition.* Baton Rouge: Louisiana State University Press, 1989. Crabb argues that pragmatism, as formally defined by William James, better describes customary American viewpoints and conduct in foreign affairs than unitary theories such as realism or idealism.

2:118   Kennedy, Paul. *The Rise and Fall of the Great Powers: Economic Change and Military Conflict from 1500 to 2000.* New York: Random House, 1987. Kennedy examines numerous empires and concludes that they fell because the military expenses of overexpansion ultimately undermined their economies. He examines the history of American foreign policy and expansion and concludes that the United States is following in the same path.

2:119   Klingberg, Frank L. *Positive Expectations of America's World Role: Historical Cycles of Real-istic Idealism.* Lanham, MD: University Press of America, 1996. Klingberg argues that a strain of "realistic idealism" runs through the history of American foreign relations, but that the expression of that strain alters according to cycles of various sorts. The book offers a convoluted description of these, including cycles of introversion (isolationism) versus extroversion (interventionism), cultural political developments, and domestic political developments.

2:120   May, Ernest R. *"Lessons" of the Past: The Use and Misuse of History in American Foreign Policy.* New York: Oxford University Press, 1973. May issues a warning to statesmen and historians about the way in which the use of simplistic historical analogies can lead to mistakes in policy and historical judgment.

2:121   Ninkovich, Frank A. "Interests and Discourse in Diplomatic History." *Diplomatic History* 13 (Spring 1989): 135–61. Ninkovich deconstructs the work of Charles Beard and George Kennan in a postmodernist demonstration that their "radical" and "realist" discourse was often based on arbitrary and culturally determined notions of what constituted the national interest.

2:122   _____. "No Post-Mortems for Postmodernism, Please." *Diplomatic History* 22 (Summer 1998): 451–66. Ninkovich reviews seven works that illustrate the benefits that postmodern approaches can bring to international relations theory.

U.S. Policy Formation

GENERAL DOMESTIC INFLUENCES

2:123   Crabb, Cecil V., Jr. *The Doctrines of American Foreign Policy: Their Meaning, Role, and Future.* Baton Rouge: Louisiana State University Press, 1982. Cecil Crabb examines the many doctrines in American diplomatic history from the Monroe Doctrine to the Carter Doctrine. He argues that the unique importance of doctrines in U.S. foreign policy, which he sees as a way of rallying public opinion to support various presidential policies, has signified a rigid and doctrinaire approach to international affairs. This contrasts with his later books extolling what he came to see as the pragmatic tradition of American foreign policy.

2:124   Fry, Joseph A. *Dixie Looks Abroad: The South and U.S. Foreign Relations, 1789–1973*. Baton Rouge: Louisiana State University Press, 2002. This is an outstanding survey of the influence of the south on American foreign policy from 1789 to the end of the Vietnam War in 1973. Fry argues that the south's dependence on staple agriculture and low-wage industries, racial attitudes, concern for personal and national honor, and devotion to territorial and economic expansion significantly affected U.S. foreign policy until 1973, when changes in the region eroded many of the peculiar characteristics that had formed the basis for Dixie's distinctive response to foreign relations.

2:125   Shoup, Laurence H., and William Minter. *Imperial Brain Trust: The Council on Foreign Relations and United States Foreign Policy*. New York: Monthly Review Press, 1977. Described as a work of "Marxian historical sociology" in the preface, this volume argues that monopoly capitalists on the Council on Foreign Relations led the United States down the imperialist path.

2:126   Small, Melvin. *Democracy & Diplomacy: The Impact of Domestic Politics on U.S. Foreign Policy, 1789–1994*. Baltimore: Johns Hopkins University Press, 1996. Small emphasizes the impact of domestic political as opposed to economic factors on various instances of American diplomacy and argues that such influences were not inimical to an intelligent foreign policy. He finds that American policymakers more often blundered when they operated secretly and ignored public opinion or refused to cooperate with domestic interest groups.

2:127   Trubowitz, Peter. *Defining the National Interest: Conflict and Change in American Foreign Policy*. Chicago: University of Chicago Press, 1998. Trubowitz argues that the economic interests of various sections of the United States significantly affect the politics of U.S. foreign policy formation. He examines three periods of intense conflict over foreign policy: the debate over imperialism in the 1890s, the conflict between isolationism and internationalism in the 1930s, and the fight over cold war internationalism in the 1980s.

IDEOLOGY AND CULTURE

2:128   Booth, Ken, and Moorhead Wright, eds. *American Thinking about Peace and War: New Essays on American Thought and Attitudes*. New York: Barnes and Noble, 1978. This is a stimulating series of essays on American strategic thinking about peace and war. It includes: Booth, "American Strategy: The Myths Revisited" (1–37); Harvey Starr, "Alliances: Tradition and Change in American Views of Foreign Military Entanglements" (37–59); Anatol Rapoport, "Changing Conceptions of War in the United States" (59–83); Edmund Ions, "Vigilant Ambivalence: American Attitudes to Foreign Wars" (83–101); Wright, "The Existential Adventurer and War: Three Case Studies from American Fiction" (101–11); Charles Chatfield, "More than Dovish: Movements and Ideals of Peace in the United States" (111–35); James P. Piscatori, "Law, Peace, and War in American International Legal Thought" (135–59); Kenneth W. Thompson, "The Ethical Dimension in American Thinking about War and Peace" (159–89); Catherine McArdle Kelleher, "In Peace and War: The Institutional Balance Reappraised" (189–207); and Claude L. Inis, Jr., "American Attitudes towards International Organization" (207–23).

2:129   Dallek, Robert. *The American Style of Foreign Policy: Cultural Politics and Foreign Affairs*. New York: Alfred A. Knopf, 1983. In a sort of psychohistory of American foreign policy, Dallek describes the irrational influences and national moods that have affected U.S. diplomacy. While not dismissing material interests or strategic factors, he argues that the United States has often made overseas affairs a vehicle for expressing unresolved internal tensions.

2:130   Heald, Morrell, and Lawrence S. Kaplan. *Culture and Diplomacy: The American Experience*. Westport, CT: Greenwood Press, 1977. This significant study seeks to trace the "cultural setting" of U.S. foreign policy from colonial days to the present, on the assumption that to understand American diplomacy it is necessary to understand the culture within which policy is formed. Heald and Kaplan look at the cultural assumptions of the public at large and at the interests of smaller pressure groups they believe in most eras have had greater effect than the amorphous "public" on American foreign policy.

2:131 Hunt, Michael H. "Ideology." In *Explaining the History of American Foreign Relations,* ed. Michael J. Hogan and Thomas G. Paterson, 193–202. New York: Cambridge University Press, 1991. Hunt bemoans the tendency of Americans to believe that somehow they are free from ideology and analyzes the scholars who have recognized and tried to define the ideology that has influenced American foreign policy.

2:132 _____. *Ideology and U.S. Foreign Policy.* New Haven: Yale University Press, 1987. Informed by anthropological and sociological concepts, Hunt's important work argues that the United States has pursued a foreign policy greatly influenced by a coherent if ethnocentric ideology rooted deeply in the national culture. That ideology measured the worth of other peoples and nations against a racial hierarchy, displayed hostility toward revolutions that diverged from America's own, and based its hopes for national greatness on making the world safe for liberty.

2:133 Iriye, Akira. "Culture and International History." In *Explaining the History of American Foreign Relations,* ed. Michael J. Hogan and Thomas G. Paterson, 214–26. New York: Cambridge University Press, 1991. Iriye describes the various ways in which culture affects the relations between nations and surveys a valuable compendium of books on American foreign relations that take a cultural approach.

2:134 Lent, Ernest S. "American Foreign Policy and the Principle of Self-Determination." *World Affairs* 133 (1971): 293–303. Lent focuses on the consistency with which practice in American diplomacy has conformed to the principle of self-determination. "National self-determination" is applied to nationality groups as in Europe; "colonial self-determination" refers to overseas dependencies of major powers; and "secessionist self-determination" refers to the rights claimed by groups within the borders of independent nations.

2:135 Mayers, David. *Wars and Peace: The Future Americans Envisioned, 1861–1991.* New York: St. Martin's Press, 1998. Mayers analyzes the foundations of U.S. foreign policy since 1861 to see how Americans conceptualized the peacetime eras that would follow major wars. He seeks to relate those concepts to the way Americans are now conceptualizing the end of the cold war.

2:136 Miscamble, Wilson D. "Catholics and American Foreign Policy from McKinley to McCarthy: A Historiographical Survey." *Diplomatic History* (Summer 1980): 223–40. This is a historiographical survey that attempts to assess the influence of Catholics on American foreign policy in the first half of the twentieth century. Miscamble concludes that Catholics had some influence in preventing Roosevelt from lifting the embargo during the Spanish civil war but little in other episodes of this period. Unlike some smaller and better-organized groups like American Jews, Miscamble argues that the Catholic Church was more influenced by U.S. foreign policy than American foreign relations were affected by Catholics.

Psychology

2:137 Immerman, Richard H. "Psychology." In *Explaining the History of American Foreign Relations,* ed. Michael J. Hogan and Thomas G. Paterson, 151–65. New York: Cambridge University Press, 1991. Immerman surveys the ways in which psychological analysis has or should have influenced the writing of histories of American foreign relations. He especially shows its relevance for understanding the individual cognition of decisionmakers in such activities as negotiations, deterrence, and intelligence evaluation.

2:138 Janis, Irving L. *Victims of Groupthink: A Psychological Study of Foreign-Policy Decisions and Fiascoes.* Boston: Houghton Mifflin, 1972. Janis examines the psychology of group dynamics and the effect of what he calls groupthink on American foreign policy decisionmaking based on case studies dealing with Pearl Harbor, the Marshall Plan, Korea, the Bay of Pigs, the Cuban missile crisis, and Vietnam.

PUBLIC OPINION

2:139   Almond, Gabriel Abraham. *The American People and Foreign Policy.* New York: Harcourt, Brace, 1950. This analysis of public opinion and foreign policy, drawing on studies done in the immediate postwar years, constituted a methodological breakthrough. The concepts of elites and moods, which it pioneered, are now part of the political science lexicon; its generalizations about public opinion are of lasting value in understanding American foreign policy.

2:140   Alterman, Eric. *Who Speaks for America? Why Democracy Matters in Foreign Policy.* Ithaca: Cornell University Press, 1998. This is a journalistic but informed history of American foreign policy designed to demonstrate that when American foreign affairs leaders and experts have ignored the popular will, as they have been advised to do by the realists and bribed to do by special interests, they have betrayed both American ideals and true American interests.

2:141   Bailey, Thomas A. *The Man in the Street.* New York: Macmillan, 1948. Bailey examines the power of public opinion in the United States, with examples from the time of the American revolution to the present, although the emphasis is on the twentieth century.

2:142   Hero, Alfred O., Jr. *American Religious Groups View Foreign Policy: Trends in Rank-and-File Opinion, 1937–1969.* Durham, NC: Duke University Press, 1973. This is a model statistical study of the impact of the churches and the public stances of their national and international leadership on church members. Nearly half of the book is taken up with statistical tables.

2:143   _____. *The Southerner and World Affairs.* Baton Rouge: Louisiana State University Press, 1965. This is a model statistical study of one region's views on past foreign policy issues. Hero concludes that the south's view shifted in the period between World War II and the mid-1960s from enthusiasm for international cooperation to measured skepticism.

2:144   Hilderbrand, Robert C. *Power and the People: Executive Management of Public Opinion in*

Foreign Affairs, 1897–1921. Chapel Hill: University of North Carolina Press, 1981. Hilderbrand looks at the attempts of presidential administrations from McKinley through Wilson to respond to and manipulate public opinion. He finds that the White House increasingly sought to be the source and therefore the main interpreter of news about foreign policy issues and describes the procedures, personnel, and institutions that were used in the attempt.

2:145   Holsti, Ole R. *Public Opinion and American Foreign Policy.* Ann Arbor: University of Michigan Press, 1996. Although this book covers only the period after 1945, it is such a sophisticated analysis of American public opinion and foreign affairs that it is a model for understanding that phenomenon throughout American diplomatic history.

2:146   Small, Melvin. "Public Opinion." In *Explaining the History of American Foreign Relations,* ed. Michael J. Hogan and Thomas G. Paterson, 165–77. New York: Cambridge University Press, 1991. Small analyzes the role of public opinion in the making of American foreign policy, cites some of the major works on the subject, and concludes that although it is difficult to measure public opinion's impact on specific decisions, its central role in American diplomatic history is undeniable.

PARTY POLITICS AND ELECTIONS

2:147   Divine, Robert A. *Foreign Policy and U.S. Presidential Elections. Vol. 1: 1940–1948. Vol. 2: 1952–1960.* 2 vols. New York: New Viewpoints, 1974. In a thorough discussion of the role of foreign policy in each of six presidential elections (1940–1960), Divine argues that campaign commitments have generally not significantly affected subsequent diplomacy, but that presidential aspirants have oversimplified foreign policy issues in the interests of getting elected.

2:148   Westerfield, H. Bradford. *Foreign Policy and Party Politics: Pearl Harbor to Korea.* New Haven: Yale University Press, 1955. Reprint 1972 (Octagon Books). Despite its age, this book remains a significant comprehensive analysis of the interaction between foreign policy and party politics. The author concludes that bipartisanship reached its high point with the 1948 election, and declined thereafter.

GENDER

2:149 "Culture, Gender, and Foreign Policy: A Symposium." *Diplomatic History* 18 (Winter 1994): 47–124. These articles and commentaries discuss the relationship of gender and cultural studies to the field of U.S. diplomatic history. They include: Laura McEnaney, "He-Men and Christian Mothers: The America First Movement and the Gendered Meanings of Patriotism and Isolationism" (47–57); Emily S. Rosenberg, "'Foreign Affairs' after World War II: Connecting Sexual and International Politics" (59–70); Elaine Tyler May, "Ideology and Foreign Policy: Culture and Gender in Diplomatic History" (71–78); Geoffrey S. Smith, "Security, Gender, and the Historical Process" (79–90); Susan Jeffords, "Culture and National Identity in U.S. Foreign Policy" (91–96); Amy Kaplan, "Domesticating Foreign Policy" (97–105); Anders Stephanson, "Considerations on Culture and Theory" (107–19); and Bruce Kuklick, "Confessions of an Intransigent Revisionist about Cultural Studies" (121–24).

2:150 Crapol, Edward P., ed. *Women and American Foreign Policy: Lobbyists, Critics, and Insiders.* 2d ed. Wilmington, DE: SR Books, 1992. This is a series of essays on women who had an impact on the making of U.S. foreign policy. Contents: Crapol, "Lydia Maria Child: Abolitionist Critic of American Foreign Policy" (1–19); Robert E. May, "'Plenipotentiary in Petticoats': Jane M. Cazneau and American Foreign Policy in the Mid-Nineteenth Century" (19–45); Janet L. Coryell, "Duty with Delicacy: Anna Ella Carroll of Maryland" (45–67); John M. Craig, "Lucia True Ames Mead: American Publicist for Peace and Internationalism" (67–91); Blanche Wiesen Cook, "Eleanor Roosevelt and Human Rights: The Battle for Peace and Planetary Decency" (91–119); Lynne K. Dunn, "Joining the Boys' Club: The Diplomatic Career of Eleanor Lansing Dulles" (119–37); Jeanne Zeidler, "Speaking Out, Selling Out, Working Out: The Changing Politics of Jane Fonda" (137–53); Judith Ewell, "Barely in the Inner Circle: Jeane Kirkpatrick" (153–73); and Joan Hoff (formerly Joan Hoff-Wilson), "Conclusion: Of Mice and Men" (173–89).

RACE AND ETHNICITY

2:151 Borstelmann, Thomas. *The Cold War and the Color Line: American Race Relations in the Global Arena.* Cambridge, MA: Harvard University Press, 2001. This book analyzes the connection between America's position in the cold war and the civil rights movement. The author argues that the United States generally slowed the decolonization movement before 1960 because it chose to support European mother countries against the Soviet Union in the opening stages of the cold war. But U.S. policy shifted after 1960 toward both decolonization abroad and civil rights at home because cold war conflict shifted toward the third world.

2:152 DeConde, Alexander. *Ethnicity, Race, and American Foreign Policy: A History.* Boston: Northeastern University Press, 1992. This is the best and most complete history of the effect of ethnicity on U.S. foreign policy. It is comprehensive, learned, and suggestive rather than conclusive in measuring the impact of ethnicity on American diplomacy.

2:153 Füredi, Frank. *The Silent War: Imperialism and the Changing Perception of Race.* New Brunswick: Rutgers University Press, 1998. This book analyzes the relationship between Anglo-American racism and imperialism from the late nineteenth century to the 1990s. The author finds that the imperial era began with an Anglo-American racial confidence that degenerated over the years into racial fear.

2:154 Gerson, Louis L. *The Hyphenate in Recent American Politics and Diplomacy.* Lawrence: University of Kansas Press, 1964. This study examines the influence of immigrant Americans on U.S. foreign policy.

2:155 Krenn, Michael L., ed. *Race and U.S. Foreign Policy during the Cold War.* Vol. 4, *Race and U.S. Foreign Policy from the Colonial Period to the Present: A Collection of Essays.* New York: Garland Publishing Inc., 1998. This series is a collection of important articles on race and U.S. foreign policy published in the past fifty years. The contents of this volume include: Robert L. Harris, Jr., "Racial Equality and the United Nations Charter" (2–24); Paul Gordon Lauren, "First Principles of Racial Equality: History and the Politics and Diplomacy of Human

Rights Provisions in the United Nations Charter" (25–50); James William Park, "Latin America and the Discovery of Underdevelopment, 1945–1960" (51–88); Frenise A. Logan, "Racism and Indian-U.S. Relations, 1947–1953: Views in the Indian Press" (89–98); Charles H. Heimsath, "The American Images of India as Factors in U.S. Foreign Policy Making" (99–118); Krenn, "'Outstanding Negroes' and 'Appropriate Countries': Some Facts, Figures, and Thoughts on Black U.S. Ambassadors, 1949–1988" (119–30); Thomas J. Noer, "Truman, Eisenhower, and South Africa: The 'Middle Road' and Apartheid" (131–60); Tilden J. LeMelle, "Race, International Relations, U.S. Foreign Policy, and the African Liberation Struggle" (161–76); Mary L. Dudziak, "Desegregation as a Cold War Imperative" (177–236); Krenn, "'Unfinished Business': Segregation and U.S. Diplomacy at the 1958 World's Fair" (237–59); Harold R. Isaacs, "American Race Relations and the United States Image in World Affairs" (260–74); Hazel Erskine, "The Polls: World Opinions of U.S. Racial Problems" (275–88); Rodolfo O. de la Garza, "Chicanos and U.S. Foreign Policy: The Future of Chicano-Mexican Relations" (289–300); and Steven Metz, "Congress, the Antiapartheid Movement, and Nixon" (301–22).

2:156 _____. *Race and U.S. Foreign Policy from 1900 through World War II.* Vol. 3, *Race and U.S. Foreign Policy from the Colonial Period to the Present: A Collection of Essays.* New York: Garland Publishing Inc., 1998. Krenn gathers a set of key articles on race and U.S. foreign policy published in the last fifty years. This volume's contents include: David H. Burton, "Theodore Roosevelt's Social Darwinism" (1–17); Robert W. Rydell, "The Louisiana Purchase Exposition, Saint Louis, 1904: 'The Coronation of Civilization'" (18–56); Brenda Gayle Plummer, "The Afro-American Response to the Occupation of Haiti, 1915–1934" (57–75); William Jordan, "'The Damnable Dilemma': African-American Accommodation and Protest during World War I" (76–98); Paul Gordon Lauren, "Human Rights in History: Diplomacy and Racial Equality at the Paris Peace Conference" (99–121); Ben F. Rogers, "William E. B. Du Bois, Marcus Garvey, and Pan-Africa" (122–33); William R. Scott, "Black Nationalism and the Italo-Ethiopian Conflict, 1934–1936" (134–51); Robert G. Weisbord, "Black America and the Italian-Ethiopian Crisis: An Episode in Pan-

Negroism" (152–63); Red Ross, "Black Americans and Italo-Ethiopian Relief, 1935–1936" (164–74); David J. Hellwig, "Afro-American Reactions to the Japanese and the Anti-Japanese Movement, 1906–1924" (175–86); Akira Iriye, "The Genesis of American-Japanese Antagonism" (187–214); John W. Dower, "Yellow, Red, and Black Men" (215–56); Christopher Thorne, "Racial Aspects of the Far Eastern War of 1941–1945" (257–306); Richard H. Minear, "Cross-Cultural Perception and World War II: American Japanists of the 1940s and Their Images of Japan" (307–32); Thomas Hachey, "Walter White and the American Negro Soldier in World War II: A Diplomatic Dilemma for Britain" (333–41); and Thorne, "Britain and the Black G.I.s: Racial Issues and Anglo-American Relations in 1942" (342–51).

2:157 _____. *Race and U.S. Foreign Policy from Colonial Times through the Age of Jackson.* Vol. 1, *Race and U.S. Foreign Policy from the Colonial Period to the Present: A Collection of Essays.* New York: Garland Publishing Inc., 1998. This series is a collection of significant articles on race and U.S. foreign policy published in the past fifty years. The contents of this volume include: Paul Seabury, "Racial Problems and American Foreign Policy" (2–20); George W. Shepherd, Jr., "The Study of Race in American Foreign Policy and International Relations" (21–49); Michael H. Hunt, "The Hierarchy of Race" (50–98); Reginald Horsman, "Liberty and the Anglo-Saxons" (99–120); G. E. Thomas, "Puritans, Indians, and the Concept of Race" (121–46); Roy Harvey Pearce, "The Metaphysics of Indian-Hating" (147–60); Gary B. Nash, "Red, White, and Black: The Origins of Racism in Colonial America" (161–87); Richard Drinnon, "The Metaphysics of Empire-Building: American Imperialism in the Age of Jefferson and Monroe" (188–210); Stuart Creighton Miller, "The American Trader's Image of China, 1785–1840" (211–32); Philip Borden, "Found Cumbering the Soil: Manifest Destiny and the Indian in the Nineteenth Century" (233–59); John J. Johnson, "Domestic Factors II: Racial and Ethnic Influences" (260–303); Thomas R. Hietala, "Continentalism and the Color Line" (304–44); and Edward P. Crapol, "The Foreign Policy of Antislavery, 1833–1846" (345–66).

2:158 _____. *Race and U.S. Foreign Policy in the Ages of Territorial and Market Expansion,*

1840–1900. Vol. 2, *Race and U.S. Foreign Policy from the Colonial Period to the Present: A Collection of Essays*. New York: Garland Publishing Inc., 1998. This collection of the major articles on race and U.S. foreign policy published in the past fifty years includes: Albert K. Weinberg, "The White Man's Burden" (1–42); Arnoldo De Leon, "Initial Contacts: Redeeming Texas from Mexicans, 1821–1836" (43–60); Raymund A. Paredes, "The Origins of Anti-Mexican Sentiment in the United States" (61–88); David J. Weber, "'Scarce More than Apes': Historical Roots of Anglo American Stereotypes of Mexicans in the Border Region" (89–102); Gene M. Brack, "Mexican Opinion, American Racism, and the War of 1846" (103–16); Kinley J. Brauer, "The Slavery Problem in the Diplomacy of the American Civil War" (117–48); Luther W. Spoehr, "Sambo and the Heathen Chinee: Californians' Racial Stereotypes in the Late 1870's" (149–68); Merline Pitre, "Frederick Douglass and American Diplomacy in the Caribbean" (169–88); Rubin Francis Weston, "Racism and the Imperialist Campaign" (189–207); Thomas F. Gossett, "Imperialism and the Anglo-Saxon" (208–40); Christopher Lasch, "The Anti-Imperialists, the Philippines, and the Inequality of Man" (241–53); Philip W. Kennedy, "Race and American Expansion in Cuba and Puerto Rico, 1895–1905" (254–65); Kennedy, "The Racial Overtones of Imperialism as a Campaign Issue, 1900" (266–76); Willard B. Gatewood, Jr., "Black Americans and the Quest for Empire, 1898–1903" (277–99); Michael C. Robinson and Frank N. Schubert, "David Fagen: An Afro-American Rebel in the Philippines, 1899–1901" (300–16); Louis R. Harlan, "Booker T. Washington and the White Man's Burden" (317–44); George P. Marks, "Opposition of Negro Newspapers to American Philippine Policy, 1899–1900" (345–70); Stuart Anderson, "Racial Anglo-Saxonism and the American Response to the Boer War" (371–89); and Gatewood, "Black Americans and the Boer War, 1899–1902" (390–408).

2:159 Lauren, Paul Gordon. *Power and Prejudice: The Politics and Diplomacy of Racial Discrimination*. 2d ed. Boulder: Westview Press, 1996. This is an outstanding comprehensive survey of the role of race and ethnicity in world politics and U.S. diplomacy over the past four centuries. First published in 1988.

2:160 Miller, Jake C. *The Black Presence in American Foreign Affairs*. Washington, DC: University Press of America, 1978. Miller briefly surveys black diplomats and ambassadors who served the United States from 1869 to 1976 before devoting the larger part of his book to analyzing the influence of blacks on American foreign policy in the 1970s.

2:161 Plummer, Brenda Gayle. "'Below the Level of Men': African Americans, Race, and the History of U.S. Foreign Relations." *Diplomatic History* 20 (Fall 1996): 639–50. This brief article describes recent work on the impact of African-Americans on U.S. foreign policy. While most of its examples concern the early cold war, Plummer provides a historiography, an intellectual rationale, and an agenda for using race as well as gender and class as lenses through which to view American foreign policy, international relations, and African-American engagement with global issues.

2:162 Smith, Tony. *Foreign Attachments: The Power of Ethnic Groups in the Making of American Foreign Policy*. Cambridge, MA: Harvard University Press, 2000. Smith argues that organized ethnic group influences pushed American foreign policy toward isolationism during the eras of World War I and II and toward intervention during the cold war. Since the cold war, ethnic pressure groups have produced a mixed bag of influences. Smith traces the histories of various ethnic pressure groups throughout American history and generally believes that they often work—inevitably—counter to the national interest of the United States.

CONCEPTS OF NATIONAL SECURITY, NATIONAL INTEREST, AND BALANCE OF POWER

2:163 Beard, Charles A., with G. H. E. Smith. *The Idea of National Interest: An Analytical Study in American Foreign Policy*. New York: Macmillan, 1934. This is an effort to trace the evolution of the idea of national interest throughout American history. In general, Beard sees the national interest as arising out of conflicts among domestic economic interest groups.

2:164 Brands, H. W. "The Idea of the National Interest." *Diplomatic History* 23 (Spring 1999): 239–61. Brands traces the changing concept of American national interest, especially in the twentieth century. He argues that the national interest is composed of three primary factors—national security, prosperity, and democracy—and that U.S. policy has gone awry when one factor has predominated to the point that it disrupted the proper balance among the three.

2:165 Chace, James, and Caleb Carr. *America Invulnerable: The Quest for Absolute Security from 1812 to Star Wars.* New York: Summit Books, 1988. This is an anecdotal realist tract that argues that Americans have been engaged in a doomed search for absolute security since the War Hawks of 1812 abandoned the more restrained policies of the nation's founders. The authors argue that since 1812 the United States has spurned negotiations that would involve compromise and instead has relied on unilateralism and constant military interventions to protect the nation against exaggerated foreign threats. The book concludes with a plea for policies of realistic accommodation that will properly balance America's goals with its capabilities.

2:166 Cohen, Saul B. *Geography and Politics in a World Divided.* 2d ed. New York: Oxford University Press, 1973. A leading political geographer summarizes in introductory fashion the work of Guyot, Ratzel, Mahan, Mackinder, Haushofer, Spykman, de Seversky, and other forerunners. Focusing on major "power cores"—the United States, the Soviet Union, and maritime Europe—he applies geopolitical concepts to the cold war. Appendix on theoretical approaches to international relations. Bibliography. First issued in 1963.

2:167 Ekirch, Arthur A., Jr. "Charles A. Beard and Reinhold Niebuhr: Contrasting Conceptions of National Interest in American Foreign Policy." *Mid-America* 59 (April-July 1977): 103–16. Beard believed that the United States should confine itself to the defense of the Western Hemisphere to preserve the national interest. Niebuhr concluded that realism demanded American intervention in world affairs.

2:168 Gelfand, Lawrence E. "Hemispheric Regionalism to Global Universalism: The Changing Face of United States National Interests." *Mid-America* 76 (Fall 1994): 187–204. Gelfand traces the changing definition of American national interests from one that emphasized interests within the Western Hemisphere to one that encompassed worldwide interests. He argues that the transition has been marred by too much inconsistency and that the alternation between hemispheric and universal values has hampered American foreign policy.

2:169 Johansen, Robert C. *The National Interest and the Human Interest: An Analysis of U.S. Foreign Policy.* Princeton: Princeton University Press, 1980. Johansen uses case studies of the Vladivostok Arms agreement, U.S. aid to India, U.S. policy toward human rights in Chile, and the U.S. position on marine pollution to illustrate the disparities between the pious rhetoric and actual policies of the United States toward the building of a humane world community.

2:170 Leffler, Melvyn P. "National Security." In *Explaining the History of American Foreign Relations,* ed. Michael J. Hogan and Thomas G. Paterson, 202–13. New York: Cambridge University Press, 1991. Leffler argues that the concept of national security in American or any other national foreign policy is designed not only to protect the nation against real threats but also against perceived threats to national core values. He illustrates his thesis with examples drawn primarily from twentieth-century American foreign relations.

2:171 Mahan, Alfred T. *The Interest of America in Sea Power, Present and Future.* Boston: Little, Brown and Company, 1897. This collection of Mahan's more popular writings—on the strategic importance to the United States of Hawaii, the Isthmus of Darien, and the islands of the Caribbean, among other subjects—provides a good introduction to this most influential of all American strategic thinkers.

2:172 Pelz, Stephen E. "Balance of Power." In *Explaining the History of American Foreign Relations,* ed. Michael J. Hogan and Thomas G. Paterson, 111–40. New York: Cambridge University Press, 1991. Pelz provides a rigorous analysis of the concept of the balance of power and how it can and should be used by realist theorists. He surveys the history of American foreign relations to describe the nature of the balance-of-power system at various times and the impact each system has had on the policies of the United States and the other major powers. He identifies a multipolar system (System I) from 1776 to 1793 and from 1815 to 1892; a bipolar revolutionary-counterrevolutionary system (System II) from 1793 to 1815 and from 1917 to 1945; a nationalistic bipolar balance-of-power system from 1892 to 1914 (System III); and a nuclear revolutionary bipolar system from 1945 to 1964 (System IV).

2:173   Wolfers, Arnold. "'National Security' as an Ambiguous Symbol." *Political Science Quarterly* 47 (December 1952): 481–502. Wolfers argues that when political formulas such as national interest or national security gain popularity, they need to be scrutinized with particular care. They may not mean the same things to different people; they may not have any precise meaning at all.

DECISIONMAKING MODELS

2:174   Clifford, J. Garry. "Bureaucratic Politics." In *Explaining the History of American Foreign Relations,* ed. Michael J. Hogan and Thomas G. Paterson, 141–50. New York: Cambridge University Press, 1991. Clifford describes the major studies using the bureaucratic politics model, many of them fostered by the Harvard Faculty Study Group on Bureaucracy, Politics, and Policy that began in the 1960s.

2:175   Halperin, Morton H., with Priscilla Clapp and Arnold Kanter. *Bureaucratic Politics and Foreign Policy.* Washington, DC: Brookings Institution, 1974. This is a classic work on the impact of bureaucracies on foreign policy designed to illustrate how "where you stand depends on where you sit." It argues that the behavior of states cannot be understood apart from the interests of the bureaucracies charged with implementing it.

2:176   Walker, William O., III. "Decision-Making Theory and Narcotic Foreign Policy: Implications for Historical Analysis." *Diplomatic History* 15 (Winter 1991): 31–45. Walker uses case studies drawn from his work on the history of U.S. drug policy to illustrate the benefits of decisionmaking theory, especially bureaucratic and psychological models.

PRESIDENTIAL ROLE

2:177   DeConde, Alexander. *Presidential Machismo: Executive Authority, Military Intervention, and Foreign Relations.* Boston: Northeastern University Press, 2000. This is an anecdotal and irreverent gloss on the concept of the imperial presidency. After a brief survey of the ways in which early presidents used and misused the constitutional power of their office to give wide sway to their belligerence, DeConde concentrates on the middle and late twentieth century to argue that American presidents are habitually macho and that the academic and electoral publics reward them for it.

2:178   Margolis, Lawrence. *Executive Agreements and Presidential Power in Foreign Policy.* New York: Praeger, 1986. Margolis analyzes the history, frequency, and desirability of executive agreements. He concludes that American presidents have rarely used executive agreements to circumvent senatorial views, but that somewhat greater congressional control of presidential power in the making of foreign policy would be beneficial.

2:179   Neustadt, Richard E. *Presidential Power and the Modern Presidents: The Politics of Leadership from Roosevelt to Reagan.* New York: Free Press, 1990. This classic analysis of the nature of presidential power has important implications for foreign policy. The main point is that the president's power is more that of persuasion than command, even within the executive branch of the government, and that much depends on the avidity with which the president seizes and wields the reins of power. First published in 1960 as *Presidential Power: The Politics of Leadership.*

2:180   Schlesinger, Arthur M., Jr. *The Imperial Presidency.* Boston: Houghton Mifflin, 1973. In this very influential book written in the wake of Vietnam, Schlesinger surveyed the history of the American presidency to argue that postwar presidents have assumed far more power in the conduct of foreign affairs than was intended in the Constitution.

2:181   Wriston, Henry M. *Executive Agents in American Foreign Relations.* Baltimore: Johns Hopkins Press, 1929. This 1929 work remains the primary compendium of executive agents used as diplomats by the president in place of formal State Department representatives.

CONGRESSIONAL ROLE

2:182   Holt, W. Stull. *Treaties Defeated by the Senate: A Study of the Struggle between President and Senate over the Conduct of Foreign Relations.* Baltimore: Johns Hopkins Press, 1933. This pioneering monograph assesses the Senate's ratification votes on treaties negotiated between the adoption of the Constitution and the Versailles Treaty. Holt criticizes the Senate for excessive partisanship in many of these votes and warns that American foreign policy is endangered by conflicts between the Senate and the president.

2:183   Johnson, Robert David. "Congress and the Cold War." *Journal of Cold War Studies* 3 (Spring 2001): 76–100. This is an outstanding survey of the literature and historiography surrounding the relationship between Congress and American foreign policy. It concentrates on the cold war period but includes much information on earlier eras as well. It also goes well beyond the usual simplistic formulation that Congress had little influence on the cold war until the War Powers Act wrested power from the imperial presidency.

2:184   Silbey, Joel H., ed. *To Advise and Consent: The United States Congress and Foreign Policy in the Twentieth Century.* Vol. 1, *The Congress of the United States, 1789–1989.* Brooklyn: Carlson, 1991. This is an outstanding collection of articles about the congressional role in many of the most important twentieth-century events of U.S. diplomatic history. Volume I includes: Barton J. Bernstein and Franklin A. Leib, "Progressive Republican Senators and American Imperialism, 1898–1916: A Reappraisal" (1–44); Howard W. Allen, "Republican Reformers and Foreign Policy, 1913–1917" (45–52); Robert D. Grinder, "Progressives, Conservatives and Imperialism: Another Look at the Senate Republicans, 1913–1917" (53–64); Walter A. Sutton, "Republican Progressive Senators and Preparedness, 1915–1916" (65–86); Philip R. Vander Meer, "Congressional Decision-Making and World War I: A Case Study of Illinois Congressional Opponents" (87–108); Dewey W. Grantham, Jr. "The Southern Senators and the

League of Nations, 1918–1920" (109–28); Jolyon P. Girard, "Congress and Presidential Military Policy: The Occupation of Germany, 1919–1923" (129–38); Herbert F. Margulies, "The Senate and the World Court" (139–54); John M. Carroll, "Henry Cabot Lodge's Contribution to the Shaping of Republican European Diplomacy, 1920–1924" (155–68); Thomas N. Guinsburg, "Victory in Defeat: The Senatorial Isolationists and the Four-Power Treaty" (169–82); Richard F. Grimmett, "Who Were the Senate Isolationists?" (183–202); James T. Patterson, "Eating Humble Pie: A Note on Roosevelt, Congress, and Neutrality Revision in 1939" (203–10); Philip J. Briggs, "Congress and Collective Security: The Resolutions of 1943" (211–24); Thomas G. Paterson, "Presidential Foreign Policy, Public Opinion, and Congress: The Truman Years" (225–42); Henry W. Berger, "A Conservative Critique of Containment: Senator Taft on the Early Cold War Program" (243–58); Mary W. Atwell, "A Conservative Response to the Cold War" (259–72); and Gary W. Reichard, "Divisions and Dissent: Democrats and Foreign Policy, 1952–1956" (273–94).

2:185   _____. *To Advise and Consent: The United States Congress and Foreign Policy in the Twentieth Century.* Vol. 2, *The Congress of the United States, 1789–1989.* Brooklyn: Carlson, 1991. This is an outstanding collection of articles about the congressional role in many of the most important twentieth-century events of American diplomatic history. This volume includes: Annette Baker Fox, "NATO and Congress" (295–314); Arnold Kanter, "Congress and the Defense Budget, 1960–1970" (315–30); Alton Frye and Jack Sullivan, "Congress and Vietnam: The Fruits of Anguish" (331–52); James McCormick and Michael Black, "Ideology and Senate Voting on the Panama Canal Treaties" (353–72); James McCormick, "The Changing Role of the House Foreign Affairs Committee in the 1970s and 1980s" (373–92); Fred Kaiser, "Oversight of Foreign Policy: The U.S. House Committee on International Relations" (393–418); Doyle W. Buckwalter, "The Congressional Concurrent Resolution: A Search for Foreign Policy Influence" (419–44); Barry Bozeman and Thomas E. James, "Toward a Comprehensive Model of Foreign Policy Voting in the U.S. Senate" (445–64); Robert A. Bernstein and William W. Anthony, "The ABM Issue in the Senate, 1968–1970: The Importance of Ideology" (465–74);

Neil Heighberger, "Representatives' Constituency and National Security" (475–86); and Charles M. Tidmarch and Charles M. Sabatt, "Presidential Leadership Change and Foreign Policy Roll-Call Voting in the U.S. Senate" (487–500).

STATE DEPARTMENT AND DIPLOMATIC OFFICIALS

2:186   Barnes, William, and John Heath Morgan. *The Foreign Service of the United States: Origins, Development, and Functions.* Washington, DC: U.S. Department of State, 1961. Reprint 1979 (Greenwood Press). This is an official history of the U.S. foreign service published by the State Department.

2:187   Bemis, Samuel Flagg, ed. *The American Secretaries of State and Their Diplomacy.* 20 vols. Vols. 1–10. New York: Alfred A. Knopf, 1927–1929. These classic volumes contain dated but useful biographies of American secretaries of state from the time of the American revolution to 1925. Authors include M. L. Bonham, Jr., Bemis, D. R. Anderson, H. J. Ford, A. J. Montague, C. E. Hill, Charles C. Tansill, Julius W. Pratt, Dexter Perkins, Theodore E. Burton, John Spencer Bassett, F. Rawle, Eugene I. McCormac, C. A. Duniway, R. G. Adams, St. George L. Sioussat, Mary W. Williams, Foster Stearns, H. B. Learned, Lewis Einstein, Roy F. Nichols, Henry W. Temple, Louis Martin Sears, Philip M. Brown, William Castle, Jr., Montgomery Schuyler, Joseph V. Fuller, Claude G. Bowers and Helen D. Reid, Joseph B. Lockey, Lester B. Shippee, Royal B. Way, Alfred L. P. Denis, James Brown Scott, H. F. Wright, J. Spargo, and Charles C. Hyde (1:48).

2:188   Bemis, Samuel Flagg, and Robert H. Ferrell, eds. *The American Secretaries of State and Their Diplomacy.* 20 vols. New series. Vols. 11–19. New York: Cooper Square Publishers, 1963–1980. These volumes contain excellent biographies of American secretaries of state from 1925 through 1968. Authors include Ferrell, Julius W. Pratt, Richard L. Walker, George Curry, Gaddis Smith, Louis L. Gerson, G. Bernard Noble, Warren I. Cohen, and David S. McLellan (1:48).

2:189   De Santis, Hugh. *The Diplomacy of Silence: The American Foreign Service, the Soviet Union, and the Cold War, 1933–1947.* Chicago: University of Chicago Press, 1980. This is a "psycho-social" analysis of the influence of professional foreign service officers on the course of America's Soviet relations from recognition to the Truman Doctrine. The author makes extensive use of interviews with former officers and State Department records, and concludes that foreign service officers contributed significantly to the disintegration of American-Soviet postwar relations. New author's preface to 1983 paper edition.

2:190   DeConde, Alexander. *The American Secretary of State: An Interpretation.* New York: Praeger, 1962. DeConde uses historical examples to argue that the role of the secretary of state depends less on the constitutional status of the office than on the personal relations between the secretary and the president.

2:191   Garthoff, Raymond L. *A Journey through the Cold War: A Memoir of Containment and Coexistence.* Washington, DC: Brookings Institution Press, 2001. This is a memoir by a CIA and State Department professional who participated in major analyses of Soviet military and nuclear strength and had a close view of such critical cold war episodes as the Cuban missile crisis, disarmament negotiations, and the end of the cold war. He argues that the cold war ended because the Soviet Union gave up its view of inevitable conflict between irreconcilable systems, not because of the Reagan arms buildup.

2:192   Graebner, Norman A., ed. *An Uncertain Tradition: American Secretaries of State in the Twentieth Century.* New York: McGraw-Hill, 1961. This volume contains brief biographies of the secretaries of state who served between 1900 and 1959, omitting only three short-serving incumbents. It contains: Graebner, "The Year of Transition, 1898" (1–21); Foster Rhea Dulles, "John Hay, 1898–1905" (21–39); Charles W. Toth, "Elihu Root, 1905–1909" (40–58); Walter V. Scholes, "Philander C. Knox, 1909–1913" (59–78); Richard D. Challener, "William Jennings Bryan, 1913–1915" (79–101); Daniel M. Smith, "Robert Lansing, 1915–1920" (101–27); J. Chal Vinson, "Charles Evans Hughes, 1921–1925" (128–48); L. Ethan Ellis, "Frank B. Kellogg, 1925–1929" (149–67); Richard N. Current, "Henry L. Stimson, 1929–1933" (168–83); Donald F. Drummond, "Cordell Hull, 1933–1944" (184–209); Walter Johnson, "Edward R. Stettinius, Jr., 1944–1945" (210–22);

Richard D. Burns, "James F. Byrnes, 1945–1947" (223–44); Alexander DeConde, "George Catlett Marshall, 1947–1949" (245–66); Graebner, "Dean G. Acheson, 1949–1953" (267–88); and Hans J. Morgenthau, "John Foster Dulles, 1953–1959" (289–308).

2:193 Kennedy, Charles Stuart. *The American Consul: A History of the United States Consular Service, 1776–1914.* New York: Greenwood Press, 1990. This is a brief survey of the history of Americans serving as foreign consuls that discusses their various functions, contributions, and problems.

2:194 Merli, Frank J., and Theodore A. Wilson, eds. *Makers of American Diplomacy. Vol. 1: From Benjamin Franklin to Alfred Thayer Mahan.* New York: Scribner, 1974. This is a set of biographical essays that includes some presidents and secretaries of state but also some second-echelon makers of diplomacy. The essays include: Cecil B. Currey, "Ben Franklin in France: A Maker of American Diplomacy" (1–26); Ian Mugridge, "Alexander Hamilton and the Diplomacy of Influence" (27–52); Lawrence S. Kaplan, "Thomas Jefferson: The Idealist as Realist" (53–80); Patrick C. T. White, "From Independence to War: James Madison and American Foreign Policy" (81–104); Norman A. Graebner, "John Quincy Adams: Empiricism and Empire" (105–34); Geoffrey S. Smith, "Charles Wilkes and the Growth of American Naval Diplomacy" (135–64); David M. Pletcher, "James K. Polk and the Rewards of Rashness" (165–94); Gordon H. Warren, "Imperial Dreamer: William Henry Seward and American Destiny" (195–222); James B. Chapin, "Hamilton Fish and American Expansion" (223–52); Lester D. Langley, "James Gillespie Blaine: The Ideologue as Diplomatist" (253–78); and Kenneth J. Hagan, "Alfred Thayer Mahan: Turning America Back to the Sea" (279–304). The first of a two-volume set; also published in a single volume.

2:195 _____. *Makers of American Diplomacy. Vol. 2: From Theodore Roosevelt to Henry Kissinger.* New York: Scribner, 1974. This is a set of biographical essays that includes some presidents and secretaries of state but also some second-echelon makers of diplomacy. The essays include: Eugene P. Trani, "Cautious Warrior: Theodore Roosevelt and the Diplomacy of Activism" (1–28); Helen Dodson

Kahn, "Willard D. Straight and the Great Game of Empire" (29–54); Ross Gregory, "To Do Good in the World: Woodrow Wilson and America's Mission" (55–80); Charles DeBenedetti, "Peace Was His Profession: James T. Shotwell and American Internationalism" (81–102); William Kamman, "Henry L. Stimson: Republican Internationalist" (103–26); Russell D. Buhite, "The Open Door in Perspective: Stanley K. Hornbeck and American Far Eastern Policy" (127–54); Wilson and Richard D. McKinzie, "The Masks of Power: Franklin D. Roosevelt and the Conduct of American Diplomacy" (155–88); John Lewis Gaddis, "Harry S. Truman and the Origins of Containment" (189–218); Robert H. Ferrell and David McLellan, "Dean Acheson: Architect of a Manageable World Order" (219–48); Thomas G. Paterson, "The Search for Meaning: George F. Kennan and American Foreign Policy" (249–84); Herbert S. Parmet, "Power and Reality: John Foster Dulles and Political Diplomacy" (285–316); Robert A. Divine, "The Education of John F. Kennedy" (317–44); David F. Trask, "The Congress as Classroom: J. William Fulbright and the Crisis of American Power" (345–72); and Michael Roskin, "An American Metternich: Henry A. Kissinger and the Global Balance of Power" (373–96). The second of a two-volume set; also published in a single volume.

2:196 Nolan, Cathal J., ed. *Notable U.S. Ambassadors since 1775: A Biographical Dictionary.* This volume contains short biographies of nearly sixty American ambassadors who had notable careers in the U.S. foreign service. The selection is very arbitrary, but this is a handy reference for those ambassadors it includes (1:52).

2:197 Plischke, Elmer. *U.S. Department of State: A Reference History.* Westport, CT: Greenwood Press, 1999. This enormous but very traditional volume covers the history of the State Department's functions and activities from the American revolution through the Clinton administration. It includes numerous tables and figures listing treaties, officers of the department, administrative charts, and the like, living up to the volume's subtitle. Over thirty pages of bibliography.

2:198 Schulzinger, Robert D. *The Making of the Diplomatic Mind: The Training, Outlook, and Style of United States Foreign Service Officers, 1908–*

1931. Middletown, CT: Wesleyan University Press, 1975. This is one of the most important historical analyses of the shaping of the modern Department of State and the influence of the department on American foreign policy. Schulzinger argues that the professionalization of the State Department reflected the enlarged role of the United States in world politics as well as aspirations and anxieties of professional diplomats.

2:199 Weil, Martin. *A Pretty Good Club: The Founding Fathers of the U.S. Foreign Service.* New York: Norton, 1978. This book surveys the impact on American foreign policy of the clubby elite of career diplomats who shaped the State Department from the 1920s through the cold war.

2:200 Werking, Richard Hume. *The Master Architects: Building the United States Foreign Service, 1890–1913.* Lexington: University Press of Kentucky, 1977. This important work on the development of the U.S. Department of State analyzes the bureaucratic determinants of American foreign policy. The thesis is that young, aggressive, ambitious officials in the department, abetted by businessmen and reformers, used the argument of foreign trade expansion to develop and reform the foreign service and especially the consular service. They enjoyed little success before 1898.

INTELLIGENCE AND COVERT ACTIVITIES

2:201 Bamford, James. *Body of Secrets: Anatomy of the Ultra-Secret National Security Agency: From the Cold War through the Dawn of a New Century.* New York: Doubleday, 2001. This is a lively history of the National Security Agency from the cold war to the twenty-first century. It recounts much surprising information derived from America's satellite and eavesdropping capabilities.

2:202 Jeffreys-Jones, Rhodri. *Cloak and Dollar: A History of American Secret Intelligence.* New Haven: Yale University Press, 2002. This is a critical survey of American intelligence from the revolution to the present. Jeffreys-Jones argues that U.S. intelligence agencies and individuals exaggerated both foreign threats and their own accomplishments to improve their positions and budgets.

2:203 Knott, Stephen F. *Secret and Sanctioned: Covert Operations and the American Presidency.* New York: Oxford University Press, 1996. This book traces the extensive role of covert operations in presidential policy from Washington to the present. It emphasizes the period up to 1882 in an attempt to show that contemporary intelligence activities are simply an extension of a long American tradition.

2:204 Matthias, Willard C. *America's Strategic Blunders: Intelligence Analysis and National Security Policy, 1936–1991.* University Park: Pennsylvania State University Press, 2001. A former CIA official who was responsible for the periodic "Estimate of the World Situation" argues that the United States has often blundered by ignoring the analysis of State Department and CIA civilians in favor of more alarmist analyses by Defense intelligence officials. Because government officials failed to heed the CIA and State Department understanding that the Soviets sought expansion by nonmilitary means, the author believes Washington fought unnecessary wars in Korea and Vietnam. Moreover, when anticommunist hardliners blamed CIA and State for the decline of America's status in the 1970s, ousted Richard Helms as CIA director, and abolished the Board of National Estimates, the Reagan administration was able to accelerate an unnecessary and dangerous arms race.

2:205 O'Toole, G. J. A. *Honorable Treachery: A History of U.S. Intelligence, Espionage, and Covert Action from the American Revolution to the CIA.* New York: Atlantic Monthly Press, 1991. This is an extensive, well-informed, and well-written popular history of the role of intelligence in American foreign policy from the time of the American revolution to the 1990s. O'Toole punctures the myth that the United States until recently was innocent in the ways of espionage and covert activities. He is generally favorable toward the uses to which Washington has put such activities but not entirely uncritical.

Themes in U.S. Foreign Relations

INTERNATIONAL ECONOMICS AND TRADE

2:206   Ellings, Richard J. *Embargoes and World Power: Lessons from American Foreign Policy.* Boulder: Westview Press, 1985. Ellings surveys European and U.S. history from the sixteenth century to the present to demonstrate that the use of strategic embargoes is not just a recent phenomenon. He then analyzes the use of economic sanctions for strategic purposes in the cold war era to argue that the ability of the United States to coerce adversaries with such measures has been steadily declining, but that Washington has continued to rely on them for at least symbolic and signaling purposes.

2:207   Gill, William J. *Trade Wars against America: A History of United States Trade and Monetary Policy.* New York: Praeger, 1990. This is a journalistic history of the contest between protectionism and free trade in the United States by an ardent advocate of protectionism and national self-sufficiency.

2:208   Goldstein, Judith. *Ideas, Interests, and American Trade Policy.* Ithaca: Cornell University Press, 1993. Goldstein argues that the history of U.S. commercial policy contains too many inconsistencies to be explained completely by a structural realist analysis of U.S. economic and political interests or a bureaucratic-political analysis of domestic interest group activities. She sees ideas and beliefs as important causal factors in the choices American leaders made for protectionism between 1816 and 1933 and for free trade between 1934 and the present.

PEACE MOVEMENTS

2:209   Howlett, Charles F., and Glen Zeitzer. *The American Peace Movement: History and Historiography.* AHA Pamphlets. Washington, DC: American Historical Association, 1985. This is a brief history of the American peace movement followed by a critical

historiographical essay on the subject. It is a good guide through the date of its publication.

2:210   Stomfay-Stitz, Aline M. *Peace Education in America, 1828–1990: Sourcebook for Education and Research.* Metuchen, NJ: Scarecrow Press, 1993. This book traces what the author calls "the hidden strand of America's intellectual history," the attempts by some educators to teach peace in the nation's schools. In addition to a historical narrative of these attempts, this book contains a list of resources valuable to peace educators.

2:211   Wittner, Lawrence S. "Peace Movements and Foreign Policy: The Challenge to Diplomatic Historians." *Diplomatic History* 11 (Fall 1987): 355–70. This short bibliographical essay surveys the state of the field of peace studies and the literature on peace movements.

INTERNATIONALISM AND INTERNATIONAL ORGANIZATIONS

2:212   Ball, Howard. *Prosecuting War Crimes and Genocide: The Twentieth-Century Experience.* Lawrence: University Press of Kansas, 1999. This book traces the history of genocide and war crimes in the twentieth century, including the invasion of Belgium and the killing of the Armenians in World War I, the Nazi and Japanese atrocities in World War II, and the more recent genocidal crimes in Cambodia, Rwanda, and the Balkans. The book also discusses the various attempts to bring the perpetrators of these crimes before international tribunals. It concludes with an analysis of the UN negotiations that drafted the Rome Statute of 1998 creating a Permanent International Criminal Court and critiques the opposition of the United States to much of that statute.

2:213   Inis, Claude L., Jr. "International Organization." In *Encyclopedia of American Foreign Policy: Studies of the Principal Movements and Ideas,* ed. Alexander DeConde, 2: 473–81. New York: Scribner, 1978. This essay emphasizes conceptual developments rather than concrete bodies, showing the tendency of the United States to be supportive of ideas and organizations despite isolationist tendencies. It also contains a valuable elaboration on sovereignty. Bibliography.

2:214 Kuehl, Warren F. *Seeking World Order: The United States and International Organization to 1920.* Nashville: Vanderbilt University Press, 1969. This is the standard work on the history of internationalism in the United States until 1920. It is learned and judicious.

2:215 Moore, John Allphin, Jr., and Jerry Pubantz. *To Create a New World? American Presidents and the United Nations.* New York: Peter Lang, 1999. Drawn from secondary sources, this is a good survey of the attitudes and actions of America's presidents toward the UN. The authors see American presidents as oscillating between a more realistic view, which tended to downgrade the importance of the UN, and a more idealistic view, which emphasized the importance of world opinion and humanitarian goals. The authors argue that a proper policy is one that combines the two tendencies with the realization that the UN is an important political arena.

2:216 Ostrower, Gary B. *The United Nations and the United States.* New York: Twayne Publishers, 1998. This book traces the history of U.S. interactions with the United Nations from the founding of the international body through much of the Clinton administration. It is a colorful narrative history that includes some trenchant analysis of events and the ups and downs of America's relationship with the international organization.

ISOLATIONISM

2:217 Billington, Ray Allen. "The Origins of Middle Western Isolationism." *Political Science Quarterly* 60 (March 1945): 44–64. Changing socioeconomic conditions and the turbulent politics of the 1890s help to account for the shift to isolationism in the middle west in the twentieth century. Republican midwesterners mistrusted the expansionism of Democratic presidents, eastern bankers, and large corporations, preferring instead to advocate a continuation of the isolationist tradition.

2:218 Rieselbach, Leroy N. *The Roots of Isolationism: Congressional Voting and Presidential*

Leadership in Foreign Policy. Indianapolis: Bobbs-Merrill, 1966. This study of congressional voting tries to find the root causes of isolationist sentiment in the United States and to prioritize the importance of such factors as party affiliation, geography, constituent opinions, and demographics. It surveys the isolationist impulse from the founding of the nation to World War II but concentrates on congressional votes taken between 1939 and 1958.

MANIFEST DESTINY

2:219 LaFeber, Walter. "The Evolution of the Monroe Doctrine from Monroe to Reagan." In *Redefining the Past: Essays in Diplomatic History in Honor of William Appleman Williams,* ed. Lloyd C. Gardner, 121–41. Corvallis, OR: Oregon State University Press, 1986. LaFeber argues that the Monroe Doctrine was originally intended to support an open door policy but was transformed between 1895 and 1905 into an ideological justification for a separate if usually soft sphere of influence.

2:220 Merk, Frederick, with Lois Bannister Merk. *Manifest Destiny and Mission in American History: A Reinterpretation.* New York: Alfred A. Knopf, 1963. Reprint 1995 (Harvard University Press). In a survey of American expansionism, Merk argued that there were two concepts that lay behind expansionism in the nineteenth century—mission, which involved the spread of American ideals by example, and Manifest Destiny, which was the extension of those ideals by force. Therefore, mission, which underlays most of American expansion, was idealistic, self-denying, and properly American. The Manifest Destiny of the Mexican and Spanish-American Wars, however, was oppressive, aggressive, and un-American.

2:221 Schulte Nordholt, Jan Willem. *The Myth of the West: America as the Last Empire.* Translated by Herbert H. Rowen. Grand Rapids, MI: William B. Eerdmans Publishing Company, 1995. A European writer uses poetic expressions of the "heliotropic myth," the idea that human beings and their civilization are involved in the movement of the sun from east to west, to plumb the motivations for Europe's movement to the New World and America's movement westward.

2:222 Stephanson, Anders. *Manifest Destiny: American Expansionism and the Empire of Right.* New York: Hill and Wang, 1995. Stephanson argues that the belief in their own exceptional virtue has predominated throughout Americans' history. This belief in exceptionalism has most often led the United States to separate itself from the corrupt and fallen world, the author contends, but here he focuses on the periods in which, embodied in a tradition of Manifest Destiny, Americans justified expansion and intervention.

2:223 Weinberg, Albert K. *Manifest Destiny: A Study of Nationalist Expansionism in American History.* Baltimore: Johns Hopkins Press, 1935. Reprint 1979 (AMS Press). This is a classic and caustic analysis of the rationales Americans put forward to justify their westward expansion, especially Manifest Destiny. Weinberg insists that Americans sincerely believed these rationales and that the story of U.S. expansionism was "perhaps the most cheerful record of such perilous ambitions that one can find," but his portrait of Manifest Destiny is devastating nonetheless.

CONSTITUTION

2:224 Adler, David Gray, and Larry N. George, eds. *The Constitution and the Conduct of American Foreign Policy.* Lawrence: University Press of Kansas, 1996. Arguing that the balance between the constitutionally mandated partnership between the president and Congress in making American foreign policy is more a political than a legal question, the essays in this book examine the historical development of that constitutional relationship. Contents: Adler, "Court, Constitution, and Foreign Affairs" (19–56); George, "Democratic Theory and the Conduct of American Foreign Policy" (57–82); Robert J. Spitzer, "The President, Congress, and the Fulcrum of Foreign Policy" (85–113); Donald L. Robinson, "Presidential Prerogative and the Spirit of American Constitutionalism" (114–32); Harold Hongju Koh, "Why the President Almost Always Wins in Foreign Affairs" (158–80); Adler, "The Constitution and Presidential Warmaking" (183–226); Louis Fisher, "The Spending Power" (227–40); Edward Keynes, "The War Powers Resolution and the Persian Gulf War" (241–56); Gerhard Casper, "The Washington Administration, Congress, and Algiers" (259–73); Dean Alfange, Jr., "The

Quasi-War and Presidential Warmaking" (274–90); Daniel N. Hoffman, "Secrecy and Constitutional Controls in the Federalist Period" (291–312); Fisher, "The Barbary Wars: Legal Precedent for Invading Haiti?" (313–19); and Fisher, "Truman in Korea" (320–34).

2:225 Cox, Henry Bartholomew. *War, Foreign Affairs, and Constitutional Power. Vol. 2: 1829–1901.* Cambridge, MA: Ballinger Pub. Co., 1984. This is the second volume of a series sponsored by the American Bar Association to analyze the conflict over the constitutional role of the president and Congress in making foreign policy and war. Continuing the theme of Abraham Sofaer's first volume, *War, Foreign Affairs and Constitutional Power. Vol. 1: The Origins* (1976) (2:229), Cox's work is based on case studies drawn from the Jacksonian period, the era of Manifest Destiny, the Civil War, and the latter half of the nineteenth century.

2:226 Glennon, Michael J. *Constitutional Diplomacy.* Princeton: Princeton University Press, 1990. Glennon provides an informed historical and legal treatise on the development of constitutional law regarding American diplomacy. He argues that the United States would benefit from a closer adherence to the constitutional limits on the president and the proper role of Congress in making war, conducting foreign policy, and controlling intelligence agencies.

2:227 Henkin, Louis. *Foreign Affairs and the United States Constitution.* 2d ed. New York: Oxford University Press, 1996. This is the authoritative guide to the development and status of constitutional law regarding American diplomacy. Henkin does not attempt to prove a thesis. He is more interested in explaining the complexity and uncertainty of constitutional law as it tries to regulate the relationships among Congress, the courts, and the president; among the federal government, the states, and individuals; and among the United States, foreign governments, and international organizations in making and implementing American foreign policy. First published in 1972 as *Foreign Affairs and the Constitution.*

2:228 LaFeber, Walter. "The Constitution and United States Foreign Policy: An Interpretation." *Journal of American History* 74 (December 1987): 695–717. LaFeber argues that until World War II, Congress and the president paid a good deal of attention to constitutional restraints on U.S. foreign policy even if they quarreled over the nature and extent of those restraints. Since that time, however, the Congress, courts, and executive branch have ignored the constitutional restrictions on the making of foreign policy except for a brief spate of activity in the 1970s that resulted in the War Powers Act.

2:229 Sofaer, Abraham D. *War, Foreign Affairs, and Constitutional Power. Vol. 1: The Origins.* Cambridge, MA: Ballinger Pub. Co., 1976. Here in the first of a two-volume study (see Cox, *War, Foreign Affairs, and Constitutional Power. Vol. 2: 1829–1901,* 1984 [2:225], for the second) a legal historian examines presidential powers through a series of events ranging from the Louisiana Purchase to the War of 1812.

GEOGRAPHY AND GEOPOLITICS

2:230 Henrikson, Alan K. "Mental Maps." In *Explaining the History of American Foreign Relations,* ed. Michael J. Hogan and Thomas G. Paterson, 177–93. New York: Cambridge University Press, 1991. Henrikson uses examples from the history of American foreign relations to illustrate the effect of mental maps or concepts of geography and geopolitics on decisionmaking.

2:231 Logan, John Arthur. *No Transfer: An American Security Principle.* New Haven: Yale University Press, 1961. From the beginning of the nation, Logan believes, Americans opposed the transfer of colonial possessions in the Western Hemisphere from one European power to another (stronger) one. This principle was closely allied to the Monroe Doctrine although not at first formally connected to it.

2:232 Mackinder, Halford J. *Democratic Ideals and Reality. With Additional Papers.* Rev. ed. New York: Norton, 1962. This classic of political geography, remembered mainly for its simple formula that control of East Europe brought command of the heartland, world-island, and world, is a work of complexity, imagination, and power. It repays careful reading, especially in light of Mackinder's own reconsiderations (1942) included in this volume. Edited with an introduction by Anthony J. Pearce. First pub-

lished in 1919 as *Democratic Ideals and Reality: A Study in the Politics of Reconstruction.*

2:233 Spykman, Nicholas J. *America's Strategy in World Politics: The United States and the Balance of Power.* New York: Harcourt, Brace and Company, 1942. In this early treatise of foreign policy realism, Spykman stresses the dependence of American security on the balance of power, especially in Europe. Additionally, he analyzes the history of U.S. foreign relations with reference to the American geographical position.

2:234 Whitaker, Arthur Preston. *The Western Hemisphere Idea: Its Rise and Decline.* Ithaca: Cornell University Press, 1954. Whitaker traces the development of the idea of the Western Hemisphere from its origins in Europe through its development in the history of the United States up to the 1950s. He argues that the idea has exerted a very strong influence on American foreign policy from the beginnings of the nation, but that there was always substantial dissent from it, particularly in the more recent period.

MISSIONARIES

2:235 Fairbank, John K., ed. *The Missionary Enterprise in China and America.* Cambridge, MA: Harvard University Press, 1974. This set of studies deals with the impact of American Protestant missionaries on both China and the United States, including: Fairbank, "Introduction: The Many Faces of Protestant Missions in China and the United States" (1–22); James A. Field, Jr., "Near East Notes and Far East Queries" (23–55); Valentin H. Rabe, "Evangelical Logistics: Mission Support and Resources to 1920" (56–90); Clifton J. Phillips, "The Student Volunteer Movement and Its Role in China Missions, 1886–1920" (91–109); William R. Hutchison, "Modernism and Missions: The Liberal Search for an Exportable Christianity, 1875–1935" (110–34); M. Searle Bates, "The Theology of American Missionaries in China, 1900–1950" (135–58); Adrian A. Bennett and Kwang-Ching Liu, "Christianity in the Chinese Idiom: Young J. Allen and the Early Chiao-hui hsin-pao, 1868–1870" (159–96); Paul A. Cohen, "Littoral and Hinterland in Nineteenth Century China: The 'Christian' Reformers" (197–225); Philip West, "Christianity and Nationalism: The Career of

Wu Lei-ch'uan at Yenching University" (226–48); Stuart Creighton Miller, "Ends and Means: Missionary Justification of Force in Nineteenth Century China" (249–82); Shirley Stone Garrett, "Why They Stayed: American Church Politics and Chinese Nationalism in the Twenties" (283–310); Paul A. Varg, "The Missionary Response to the Nationalist Revolution" (311–35); and Arthur M. Schlesinger, Jr., "The Missionary Enterprise and Theories of Imperialism" (336–75).

2:236   Hunter, Jane. *The Gospel of Gentility: American Women Missionaries in Turn-of-the-Century China.* New Haven: Yale University Press, 1984. This is an outstanding example of a study of foreign relations rather than foreign policy. It captures the conflict of American and Chinese culture more graphically than the works by Varg (*Missionaries, Chinese, and Diplomats: The American Protestant Missionary Movement in China, 1890–1952*, 1958 [2:239]) and Fairbank (*The Missionary Enterprise in China and America*, 1974 [2:235]) on American missionaries in China.

2:237   Lutz, Jessie G. *China and the Christian Colleges, 1850–1950.* Ithaca: Cornell University Press, 1971. This study evaluates the role of the Christian colleges in the development of modern, revolutionary, and nationalistic China. The author concludes that the educational endeavor of the missionaries had a much greater impact on China than did the evangelical endeavor.

2:238   Phillips, Clifton J. *Protestant America and the Pagan World: The First Half Century of the American Board of Commissioners for Foreign Missions, 1810–1860.* Cambridge, MA: East Asian Research Center, Harvard University, 1969. The ABCFM was founded by New England Congregationalists but also represented for a time the Presbyterian and Dutch Reformed churches. The study recounts its activities in the Middle East, Africa, South Asia, East Asia, and the Pacific.

2:239   Varg, Paul A. *Missionaries, Chinese, and Diplomats: The American Protestant Missionary Movement in China, 1890–1952.* Princeton: Princeton University Press, 1958. This is a classic history of American missionaries and their effect on U.S. policy at a time most American missionary efforts con-

centrated on China. Varg has a favorable view of these missionary efforts but admits they were largely failures. Thus, he counsels caution in attempts to spread American views of religion or politics to vastly different cultures.

ECOLOGY

2:240   Lytle, Mark H. "An Environmental Approach to American Diplomatic History." *Diplomatic History* 20 (Spring 1996): 279–300. Lytle describes the ways in which a study of environmentalism is vital to understanding U.S. foreign relations and international history. He provides a working bibliography of major works on ecology and suggests avenues of research for international historians.

2:241   Tucker, Richard P. *Insatiable Appetite: The United States and the Ecological Degradation of the Tropical World.* Berkeley: University of California Press, 2000. This book traces the history of America's participation in the economic and ecological transformation of the tropics. With the support of the U.S. government and navy, American speculators built economic empires based on sugar, bananas, coffee, rubber, beef, and timber. Such exploitation resulted in a drastic decline in the biodiversity of the Caribbean, Central and South America, the Pacific, Southeast Asia, and West Africa.

OTHERS

2:242   Basiuk, Victor. *Technology, World Politics & American Policy.* New York: Columbia University Press, 1977. This book suggests the impact of technology on international relations and societies for the next seventy-five years, and speculates on what changes will result.

2:243   Boot, Max. *The Savage Wars of Peace: Small Wars and the Rise of American Power.* New York: Basic Books, 2002. Although 80 percent of this book is devoted to a basic narrative of U.S. "small wars," from those off the Barbary coasts to the early-twentieth-century interventions in the Caribbean and Central America, Boot's purpose is to argue for the efficacy of using such force in the twenty-first century. The United States should abjure the "Powell

Doctrine" and be willing to use force on behalf of the goals of a beneficent hegemon, and, Boot holds, its historical experience demonstrates that it can do so successfully.

2:244   Buhite, Russell D. *Lives at Risk: Hostages and Victims in American Foreign Policy.* Wilmington, DE: Scholarly Resources, 1995. With his interest piqued by the Iran hostage crisis and Ronald Reagan's rigid rhetorical response to such terrorism, Buhite surveys responses to hostage-taking throughout American history, from the Barbary pirates to the Reagan administration. He finds that the United States was more aggressive in hostage crises during the nineteenth century, when racism made it easier for Americans to justify harsh measures against supposedly barbarous people who took hostages, than in the twentieth century, when national interest more often prevailed over the claims of national honor.

2:245   Green, Fitzhugh. *American Propaganda Abroad.* New York: Hippocrene Books, 1988. As an introduction to a history and analysis of the United States Information Agency, a former officer of the USIA surveys in the space of forty pages the history of America's use of propaganda from the revolution to the time of Jimmy Carter.

2:246   Iriye, Akira. *Cultural Internationalism and World Order.* Baltimore: Johns Hopkins University Press, 1997. Iriye describes instances in the period between 1900 and the cold war in which individuals and groups of people from different lands sought to develop an alternative community of nations and peoples on the basis of their cultural interchanges. See also his *Global Community: The Role of International Organizations in the Making of the Contemporary World* (Berkeley: University of California Press, 2002).

2:247   McAllister, William B. *Drug Diplomacy in the Twentieth Century: An International History.* New York: Routledge, 2000. Deeply researched in English-language sources of the United States, Canada, Great Britain (including the India Office), the League of Nations, United Nations, and World Health Organization, this book analyzes the development of international drug laws and institutions in the twentieth century. It traces how these institutions and laws, because they were based on western attitudes, privileged alcohol and manufactured drugs over opiate and coca derivatives and regulated supply more than consumption.

2:248   Nielson, Jonathan M., ed. *Paths Not Taken: Speculations on American Foreign Policy and Diplomatic History, Interests, Ideals, and Power.* Westport, CT: Praeger, 2000. This is a set of historiographically informed essays examining significant decisions taken during the history of American foreign policy to see if alternatives were available and the likely consequences had they been chosen. Contents: Alexander DeConde, "John Adams: Peace at a Price?" (13–29); Nielson, "1917: What If the United States Had Not Intervened?" (31–65); Brian J. C. McKercher, "Lost Opportunities: The Diplomacy of the 1930s" (67–107); Kyle Longley, "When Nationalism Confronted Hegemony: The U.S. Challenge to the Cuban Revolution, 1959–1961" (109–29); Antonio Donno and Daniele De Luca, "Eisenhower, Dulles, and U.S. Policy toward Israel and the Middle East Crisis at Suez, 1956" (131–59); James F. Goode, "A Liberal Iran: Casualty of the Cold War" (161–73); and Mitchell Lerner, "Lyndon Johnson and America's Military Intervention in Southeast Asia" (175–207).

2:249   Power, Samantha. *"A Problem from Hell": America and the Age of Genocide.* New York: Basic Books, 2002. This is an extensive journalistic account of America's response to instances of genocide in Armenia, Nazi Europe, Cambodia, Iraq, Rwanda, and Bosnia. The author is highly critical of U.S. failure to intervene earlier and more decisively in these cases, which she blames primarily on ignorance, indifference, and a failure of imagination on the part of both the U.S. government and people.

2:250   Ryan, David, and Victor Pungong, eds. *The United States and Decolonization: Power and Freedom.* New York: St. Martin's Press, 2000. These essays examine the conflicting strains within American policy toward decolonization, including racism, economic interest, anticolonial ideology, and cold war imperatives. Individual essays are Ryan, "By Way of Introduction: The United States, Decolonization and the World System" (1–23); Walter LaFeber, "The American View of Decolonization, 1776–1920: An Ironic Legacy" (24–40); Laurie Johnston, "The Road to Our America: The United States in Latin America and the Caribbean" (41–62); Paul Orders, "'Adjusting to a New Period in World History': Franklin Roosevelt and European Colonialism" (63–84); Pungong, "The United States and the International Trusteeship System" (85–101); Dennis Merrill, "The Ironies of History: The United States and the Decolonization of India" (102–20); Lloyd C. Gardner, "How We 'Lost' Vietnam, 1940–54" (121–39); Scott Lucas, "The Limits of Ideology: US Foreign Policy and Arab Nationalism in the Early Cold War" (140–67); John Kent, "The United States and the Decolonization of Black Africa, 1945–63" (168–87); A. J. Stockwell, "The United States and Britain's Decolonization of Malaya, 1942–57" (188–206); Michael H. Hunt, "Conclusions: The Decolonization Puzzle in US Policy: Promise versus Performance" (207–29); and Cary Fraser, "Afterword" (230–32).

2:251   Small, Melvin. *Was War Necessary? National Security and U.S. Entry into War.* Beverly Hills, CA: Sage Publications, 1980. Small argues that American entry into the nation's six major international wars was unnecessary because U.S. national security was not threatened sufficiently in any of them to justify the call to arms.

2:252   Walker, William O., III. "Drug Control and National Security." *Diplomatic History* 12 (Spring 1988): 187–99. Walker traces the impact of drugs on American foreign policy. Briefly mentioning the China opium trade of the nineteenth century, he concentrates on the U.S. government drug war of the 1930s as the precedent for contemporary drug policies.

Regional Studies and American Bilateral Relations

AFRICA

General

2:253   Chester, Edward W. *Clash of Titans: Africa and U.S. Foreign Policy.* Maryknoll, NY: Orbis

Books, 1974. This is the first comprehensive survey (1783–1974) of the subject. It touches on economic, religious, and cultural as well as political contacts. All of the pertinent material in the *Foreign Relations* series has been examined and included. The volume is valuable for the years from 1783 to 1945. Indexes, tables, and extensive bibliography.

2:254   Curtin, Philip D., with Steven Feierman. *African History: From Earliest Times to Independence.* 2d ed. New York and London: Longman, 1995. This brief survey, from prehistory to postcolonial decades, is a good starting point for those interested in white contacts with the continent. First published in 1978.

2:255   Duignan, Peter, and L. H. Gann. *The United States and Africa: A History.* New York: Cambridge University Press, 1984. This full survey examines American relations with Africa from the time of the American revolution to the early 1980s. Bibliography.

2:256   Fage, J. D., and Roland Oliver, eds. *The Cambridge History of Africa.* 8 vols. New York: Cambridge University Press, 1975–1986. This outstanding eight-volume series provides a detailed summary of African history, incorporating important recent scholarship. Volume 1 begins from the earliest times to circa 500 B.C.E. Volumes 6 through 8 cover the periods 1870–1905, 1905–1940, and 1940–1975, respectively. Includes bibliographies and indexes.

2:257   McCarthy, Michael. *Dark Continent: Africa as Seen by Americans.* Westport, CT: Greenwood Press, 1983. This work deals with the image of the black in western thought. It examines how Africa and Africans—both the land and its people—were seen by Americans in Africa and how their descriptions shaped American ideas and created a language of discourse about the continent. Bibliography.

2:258   Schraeder, Peter J. *United States Foreign Policy toward Africa: Incrementalism, Crisis, and Change.* New York: Cambridge University Press, 1994. This is a comprehensive analysis of foreign policy toward Africa from the 1940s to the 1990s that explains continuity and change in U.S. policies. This work also examines the U.S. policymaking establishment. Bibliography.

North Africa

Algeria-Morocco-Tunisia

2:259   Gallagher, Charles F. *The United States and North Africa: Morocco, Algeria, and Tunisia.* Cambridge, MA: Harvard University Press, 1963. This is a useful and succinct analysis of North Africa's prehistory and history as well as a sound overview of U.S.–North African relations (1784–1963) by a perceptive and often sympathetic observer. Bibliography.

2:260   Hall, Luella J. *The United States and Morocco, 1776–1956.* Metuchen, NJ: Scarecrow Press, 1971. The author contends that America's relations with Morocco were more extensive than is commonly realized, and that this relationship should be viewed against a growing Moroccan nationalism. Extensive bibliography.

Libya

2:261   Davis, Brian L. *Qaddafi, Terrorism, and the Origins of the U.S. Attack on Libya.* New York: Praeger, 1990. This work examines American-Libyan relations in the period beginning with Qaddafi's rule through the 1986 American air strike against Libya. The book concludes with an analysis of the international reaction to the air strikes and explores the consequences and lessons of these actions. Bibliographical essay.

2:262   ElWarfally, Mahmoud G. *Imagery and Ideology in U.S. Policy toward Libya, 1969–1982.* Pittsburgh: University of Pittsburgh Press, 1988. In this highly theoretical and method-driven study, the author analyzes the prevailing U.S. official image of Libya from 1969 to 1982. The author explores the degree to which image and U.S. policy toward Libya were congruent.

Sub-Saharan Africa

Nigeria

2:263   Ate, Bassey E. *Decolonization and Dependence: The Development of Nigerian-U.S. Relations, 1960–1984.* Boulder: Westview Press, 1987. This book explores how the United States emerged as the most important country in determining postcolonial Nigerian foreign, economic, and political policies.

The author analyzes U.S.-Nigerian relations within the context of both the decolonization movement and Nigeria's dependence on the capitalist world economy, contending that American policy in Nigeria sought to preserve the colonial order as a means of thwarting Soviet attempts to challenge western domination in Africa. Bibliography.

2:264   Shepard, Robert B. *Nigeria, Africa, and the United States: From Kennedy to Reagan.* Bloomington: Indiana University Press, 1991. The author explicitly eschews writing a chronicle of the diplomatic relations between the two nations, attempting instead to offer an analytical history of the factors that shaped American thinking about Nigeria. Discussion of the actual relationship of these two countries comprises only part of each chapter, with the greater focus on the larger context in which that relationship operated, providing the reader with background to U.S. policy toward the entire continent of Africa. Bibliography.

South Africa

2:265   Hull, Richard W. *American Enterprise in South Africa: Historical Dimensions of Engagement and Disengagement.* New York: New York University Press, 1990. This survey examines three centuries of American entrepreneurial activity in South Africa, spanning the period from the late 1600s to 1988. The author argues that American involvement in South Africa extends far into the past and has been marked by cycles of engagement and disengagement that were influenced as much by the economic policies of the United States as by the actions of Great Britain and South Africa. Extensive bibliography.

2:266   Minter, William. *King Solomon's Mines Revisited: Western Interests and the Burdened History of Southern Africa.* New York: Basic Books, 1986. This book examines the relationship between the west, largely Great Britain and the United States, and southern Africa, from the late nineteenth century to the early 1980s. This survey links two levels of analysis most commonly considered separately: the political economy of the interests of classes, nations, and ethnic groups, and the political practice of foreign policymaking. The author seeks to isolate the perceived and actual interests in southern Africa of western ruling circles, to determine their views of appropriate local allies, and to show the consequences of their actions for the people of southern Africa. Extensive bibliography.

West Africa

Liberia

2:267   Harris, Katherine. *African and American Values: Liberia and West Africa*. Lanham, MD: University Press of America, 1985. This work analyzes nineteenth-century U.S.-Liberian diplomacy, claiming that these relations can be divided into two phases. The first phase covered the period from 1820 to 1862, the second after the 1862 U.S. recognition of the African republic and continued throughout the nineteenth century. The author seeks to place early American-Liberian relations in the context of the political and social foundation of Jacksonian America. Bibliographical essay.

2:268   Sisay, Hassan B. *Big Powers and Small Nations: A Case Study of United States–Liberian Relations*. Lanham, MD: University Press of America, 1985. This work examines American-Liberian relations from the 1820s to the late 1970s. The author maintains that the Liberian production of rubber led to a number of internal problems in that nation and produced an international scandal that placed the United States in the position of supporting an oppressive regime to further its financial interests in Liberia. U.S. support for these economic interests strained relations between the two countries. Bibliography.

Others

2:269   Cooper, Allan D. *U.S. Economic Power and Political Influence in Namibia, 1700–1982*. Boulder: Westview Press, 1982. This work examines how economic interests have influenced American foreign policy toward Namibia. The book is organized into four chapters. Chapter 1 analyzes U.S. trade with Namibia from a historical perspective and documents the American contribution to colonialism in Namibia. Chapter 2 traces U.S. foreign policy toward Namibia since 1920; the third explores American corporate activity in Namibia along with the official policies of the U.S. government; and the final chapter examines key U.S. financial leaders who influenced Washington's policy toward Namibia. Bibliography.

2:270   Lefebvre, Jeffrey A. *Arms for the Horn: U.S. Security Policy in Ethiopia and Somalia, 1953–1991*. Pittsburgh: University of Pittsburgh Press, 1991. This work traces four decades of superpower action and confrontation in the Horn of Africa. It employs a theoretical framework that studies influence and how it is used in a great-power-supplier and small-power-recipient relationship.

ASIA AND THE PACIFIC

General

2:271   Dudden, Arthur Power. *The American Pacific: From the Old China Trade to the Present*. New York: Oxford University Press, 1992. This work of synthesis, based on published sources, attempts to direct attention away from a European, Atlantic, and hemispheric context of traditional diplomatic histories toward one focused on Asia and the Pacific. The work covers the period 1784 through the 1980s and tells the story of how the American Pacific became the American empire.

2:272   Isaacs, Harold R. *Images of Asia: American Views of China and India*. New York: Harper, 1972. This is a valuable study of American images and ideas of China and India (1700s–1957) based on books and popular literature but mainly on intensive interviews of a selected group of 181 persons conducted in the mid-1950s. The author describes a wide spectrum of impressions, attitudes, and feelings, tracing their sources within individual experience as well as the related historical background. Originally published as *Scratches on Our Minds: American Images of China and India* (1958); the 1972 edition includes a new preface.

2:273   May, Ernest R., and James C. Thomson, Jr., eds. *American–East Asian Relations: A Survey*. Cambridge, MA: Harvard University Press, 1972. This chronological survey of American diplomatic, commercial, and military relations with East Asia, with emphasis on China and Japan, consists of seventeen essays organized in four periods: eighteenth and nineteenth centuries, 1900–1922, 1922–1941, and 1941–1969. A general work itself, it offers a stimulating basis for further studies and research in the field. Individual chapters and contributors: Edward D. Graham, "Early American–East Asian Relations" (3–18); John K. Fairbank, "America and China: The Mid-Nineteenth Century" (19–33); Kwang-Ching Liu, "America and China: The Late Nineteenth Century" (34–96); Robert S. Schwantes, "America and Japan" (97–128); Marilyn B. Young, "The Quest for Empire" (131–42); Raymond A. Esthus, "1901–1906" (143–54); Charles E. Neu, "1906–1913"; Burton F. Beers, "1913–1917" (173–89); Roger V. Dingman, "1917–1922" (190–218); Akira Iriye, "1922–1931" (221–42); Waldo H. Heinrichs, "1931–1937" (243–59); Louis Morton, "1937–1941" (260–90); Peter W. Stanley, "The Forgotten Philippines, 1790–1946" (291–316); Jim Peck, "America and the Chinese Revolution, 1942–1946: An Interpretation" (319–55); Robert Dallek, "The Truman Era" (356–76); Morton H. Halperin, "The Eisenhower Years" (377–89); and Thomson, "The Nineteen Sixties as History: A Preliminary Overview" (390–409).

2:274 Thomson, James C., Jr., Peter W. Stanley, and John Curtis Perry. *Sentimental Imperialists: The American Experience in East Asia.* New York: Harper and Row, 1981. This is a good, reliable general survey of the multicultural complexity of American–East Asian relations (including several particular countries) from the late eighteenth century to the late 1970s. The authors contend that U.S. failings in East Asia have been due to American difficulty understanding distant East Asian societies and cultures that come from a separate historical tradition. Foreword by John K. Fairbank.

China

2:275 Chen Jian. *Mao's China and the Cold War.* Chapel Hill: University of North Carolina Press, 2001. Writing from recently released documents and memoirs, Chen Jian analyzes key episodes in Chinese-American relations and argues that Mao's foreign policy reflected his ideological ambition to revolutionize China while restoring it to a central place in world affairs. Thus, he sees little chance that a more moderate U.S. policy toward China would have made much difference.

2:276 Cohen, Warren I. *America's Response to China: A History of Sino-American Relations.* 4th ed. New York: Columbia University Press, 2000. This work examines Chinese-American relations over the course of two centuries, beginning in the mid-nineteenth century and continuing through the late 1990s. The author focuses on the American response to China, emphasizing the statesmen who have attempted to create an East Asian policy consistent with the ideals and interests of the American people. This work attempts to place Chinese-American relations within a larger geopolitical context that influenced this bilateral relationship. Bibliographical essay. First published in 1971.

2:277 Etzold, Thomas H., ed. *Aspects of Sino-American Relations since 1784.* New York: New Viewpoints, 1978. The authors generally find American policy toward Asia and particularly China to be ambiguous and hazy. The essays are arranged chronologically. William Brinker surveys the first century of Sino-American cultural relations; Frederick Hoyt and Eugene Trani examine nineteenth-century Chinese immigration to the United States; Raymond Esthus discusses the open door policy (1899–1922); David Trask and Etzold, respectively, deal with American policy at the 1919 Paris Peace Conference and U.S. Asian strategy, 1948–1951. In the last chapter, Jerome Holloway and Etzold describe America's relations with Chinese communist leaders since the 1920s. Bibliographies.

2:278 Fairbank, John K. *The United States and China.* 4th ed. Cambridge, MA: Harvard University Press, 1983. Until recently this was the standard text on U.S.-China relations. The bulk of this study is an analysis of China's history and culture, although two chapters deal directly with U.S. China policy and provide a thoughtful commentary on the nature of that policy in the nineteenth and twentieth centuries. Bibliography. Originally published in 1948.

2:279 Hunt, Michael H. *The Making of a Special Relationship: The United States and China to 1914.* New York: Columbia University Press, 1983. This work examines the evolution of Sino-American relations from the late eighteenth to the early twentieth centuries. The author claims that a special relationship developed between the United States and China through a process of economic, diplomatic, and cultural interaction among a large and diverse group of Chinese and Americans. By the early twentieth century, that relationship between two countries widely separated by culture and geography was notable for its breadth, complexity, and instability. A bibliographical essay precedes the footnotes of each chapter.

2:280 Iriye, Akira. *Across the Pacific: An Inner History of American–East Asian Relations.* Rev. ed. Chicago: Imprint Publications, 1992. This study examines the images that Americans, Chinese, and Japanese have had of one another (1780–1963). While giving new estimates of the leaders and diplomats and their policies, the author attempts to penetrate the surface of diplomacy to analyze the misperceptions and misunderstandings resulting from the differing cultural milieus of those leaders and statesmen. First published in 1967. Bibliography.

2:281 Jiang, Arnold Xiangze. *The United States and China.* Chicago: University of Chicago Press, 1988. This survey examines U.S.-Chinese relations from the late eighteenth century through the U.S. recognition of the People's Republic of China in 1978, emphasizing the Chinese perspective. Three themes emerge: that between the two goals of American policy toward China, friendship and self-interest, the latter has dominated; that the United States consistently supported corrupt, unpopular, and repressive regimes in China; and that as a result of pursuing its policy of friendship and self-interest, the United States became involved in contradictions and unrealities.

2:282 Spence, Jonathan. *The China Helpers: Western Advisers in China, 1620–1960.* London: Bodley Head, 1969. Of the sixteen advisers dealt with in this study, eight are American. They are Peter Parker, commissioner to China; Frederick Townsend Ward, commander of the Ever Victorious Army; W. A. P. Martin, missionary and educator; Edward Hume, head of Yale in China; O. J. Todd, an engineer; and the American generals Claire Chennault, Joseph Stilwell, and Albert Wedemeyer. The analyses are perceptive but based entirely on published sources.

Japan

2:283 Ibe, Hideo. *Japan, Thrice Opened: An Analysis of Relations between Japan and the United States.* Translated by Lynne E. Riggs and Manabu Takechi. New York: Praeger, 1992. This work examines Japanese-American relations since 1850, also exploring the process of Japanese modernization and westernization. Bibliography.

2:284 LaFeber, Walter. *The Clash: A History of U.S.-Japan Relations.* New York: W. W. Norton, 1997. This work explores three themes in U.S.-Japanese relations since the mid-nineteenth century. First, although the United States and Japan have largely worked together in most East Asian affairs, the relationship has endured numerous clashes over the past 150 years. The source of these clashes has been the two nations' different economic and social systems. The third theme focuses on how China has been at the center of Japanese-American conflict. Excellent bibliography.

2:285 Nester, William R. *Power across the Pacific: A Diplomatic History of American Relations with Japan.* Washington Square: New York University Press, 1996. This work analyzes Japanese-American relations from the mid-nineteenth century to the mid-1990s. The author identifies two great cycles in U.S.-Japanese relations: one geopolitical, covering the years 1853–1945, the other geoeconomic, spanning the period 1945 to the mid-1990s. Excellent bibliography.

2:286 Neu, Charles E. *The Troubled Encounter: The United States and Japan.* New York: Wiley, 1975. In this work, Neu examines U.S.-Japanese relations over the course of the nineteenth and twentieth centuries, focusing on the period of 1890 to 1941. The author seeks to explain the many facets of each government's policy and examines the intellectual assumptions, bureaucratic perspectives, domestic political currents, and national aspirations that influenced the formation of official policy. Bibliographical essay.

2:287 Nish, Ian. *Japanese Foreign Policy, 1869–1942: Kasumigaseki to Miyakezaka.* Boston: Routledge and Kegan Paul, 1977. Basing his biographical approach on documents heretofore unavailable in English, a leading authority on Anglo-Japanese relations probes the motives and ideas of the Japanese foreign ministry. Bibliography.

2:288 Reischauer, Edwin O. *The United States and Japan.* 3d ed. Cambridge, MA: Harvard University Press, 1965. This classic work focuses on what the author considers the most important phase of Japanese-American relations, the U.S. occupation of Japan from 1945 to 1952. Originally published in 1950. Appendices and short bibliographical essay.

Korea

2:289 Cumings, Bruce. *The Origins of the Korean War. Vol. 1: Liberation and the Emergence of Separate Regimes, 1945–1947.* Princeton: Princeton University Press, 1981. In this indispensable study, the author argues that the origins of the Korean War are found in the period 1945–1950; the opening of conventional war in the summer of 1950 continued by other means a conflict that was civil and revolutionary in character. The work, which is highly critical of U.S. policy, is organized into three sections. The first examines Korea during the colonial period; the second explores Korean and international politics in 1945–1947; and the third focuses on Korean and American actions in Korea from 1945 to 1947. Excellent bibliography.

2:290 _____. *The Origins of the Korean War. Vol. 2: The Roaring of the Cataract, 1947–1950.* Princeton: Princeton University Press, 1990. This is the second volume of Cumings's authoritative works on the origins of the Korean War. The book is organized into four sections. The first focuses on U.S. relations with the world in the late 1940s; the second examines Korea in the 1947–1950 period; the third analyzes the period leading up to the outbreak of hostilities. The last section is an epilogue where the author develops his claim that the Korean War was a civil and revolutionary war. This book was written before the publication of the records of Stalin's discussions with Kim Il Sung and Mao Zedong that cast considerably more light on this issue. Excellent bibliography.

2:291 Lee, Yur-Bok, and Wayne Patterson, eds. *One Hundred Years of Korean-American Relations, 1882–1982.* University: University of Alabama Press, 1986. This edited collection of essays is based on papers presented at the annual meeting of the American Historical Association or that of the Association for Asian Studies in 1982. The essay topics include "Duality and Dominance: A Century of Korean-American Relations" (Patterson and Hilary Conroy, 1–11); "Korean-American Diplomatic Relations, 1882–1905" (Lee, 12–45); "An American View of Korean-American Relations, 1882–1905" (Fred H. Harrington, 46–67); "Relations between the Japanese Colonial Government and the American Missionary Community in the Postwar Period" (Wi Jo Kang, 68–85); "Transition and Continuity in American-Korean Relations in the Postwar Period" (Robert T. Oliver, 86–107); and "The Security Relationship between Korea and the United States, 1960–1984" (Tae-Hwan Kwak and Patterson, 108–26). Bibliography.

2:292 Lone, Stewart, and Gavan McCormack. *Korea since 1850.* New York: St. Martin's Press, 1993. This work surveys Korean history in the modern period from monarchy, to colony, to the division of Korea into two republics. Korean-American relations are explored in the last three chapters, covering the post–World War II period. Extensive bibliography.

India

2:293 Brands, H. W. *India and the United States: The Cold Peace.* Boston: Twayne Publishers, 1990. This work examines American-Indian relations since Indian independence in 1947 and suggests that these relations can best be characterized as both tumultuous and idealistic. The author emphasizes the personalities involved in forming and maintaining these emotionally charged relations. This book places American-Indian relations within a context of U.S. interaction with Asia and the third world. Bibliographical essay.

2:294 Gould, Harold A., and Sumit Ganguly, eds. *The Hope and the Reality: U.S.-Indian Relations from Roosevelt to Reagan.* Boulder: Westview Press, 1992. This collection of essays reveals a dominant theme: relations with India and the United States after Indian independence have been far from ideal, never reaching the concord that many in both countries anticipated. The chapters of the book examine public opinion studies of both the United States and

India, analyze congressional attitudes toward India, and explore the Indian policies of presidential administrations from Roosevelt to Reagan: Gould and Ganguly, "Introduction: The Strained Relationship" (1–16); Gould, "U.S.-Indian Relations: The Early Phase" (17–42); Jane S. Wilson, "The Kennedy Administration and India" (43–64); Walter K. Anderson, "U.S.-Indian Relations, 1961–1963: Good Intentions and Uncertain Results" (65–80); Thomas P. Thornton, "U.S.-Indian Relations in the Nixon and Ford Years" (91–120); Robert F. Goheen, "U.S. Policy toward India during the Carter Presidency" (121–38); Stephen Philip Cohen, "The Reagan Administration and India" (139–54); Arthur G. Rubinoff, "Congressional Attitudes toward India" (155–78); Elizabeth Crump Hanson, "Public Opinion and Policy Choices in U.S. Relations with India" (179–98); and William L. Richter, "Long-Term Trends and Patterns in Indian Public Opinion toward the United States" (199–217).

2:295 Palmer, Norman D. *The United States and India: The Dimensions of Influence.* New York: Praeger, 1984. This work examines Indo-American relations from the period of Indian independence to the early 1980s. The author argues that these relations have been highly competitive, troubled, and characterized by misperceptions and misunderstandings. Bibliography.

Philippines

2:296 Brands, H. W. *Bound to Empire: The United States and the Philippines.* New York: Oxford University Press, 1992. This work is a study in power, focusing on the power that bound the United States and the Philippines together from the late nineteenth century to the early 1990s. The author contends that U.S.-Filipino relations provide a useful case study with which to understand American international relations generally. Bibliography.

2:297 Stanley, Peter W. *A Nation in the Making: The Philippines and the United States, 1899–1921.* Cambridge, MA: Harvard University Press, 1974. This readable and detailed work recounts the efforts by the Americans to win over the Philippine elite and the relationship of these efforts to the development and modernization of the islands and their eventual

independence. It is an excellent survey of U.S.-Philippine relations. Bibliography.

2:298 _____, ed. *Reappraising an Empire: New Perspectives on Philippine-American History.* Cambridge, MA: Harvard University Press, 1984. This volume examines the political, economic, and cultural interactions between the United States and the Philippines from the mid-nineteenth century to the early 1970s. The work reevaluates the notion that a special relationship existed between the two countries, arguing that it is a hubristic illusion for Americans to imagine that they modernized, liberalized, or exploited the Philippines in any lasting way. Individual chapters include Richard E. Welch, Jr., "America's Philippine Policy in the Quirino Years (1948–1953): A Study in Patron-Client Diplomacy" (286–306); Stuart Creighton Miller, "The American Soldier and the Conquest of the Philippines" (13–34); and Bonifacio S. Salamanca, "The Negotiation and Disposition of the Philippine War Damage Claims: A Study in Philippine-American Diplomacy, 1951–1972" (263–83).

Others

2:299 Gardner, Paul F. *Shared Hopes, Separate Fears: Fifty Years of U.S.-Indonesian Relations.* Boulder: Westview Press, 1997. This work examines U.S.-Indonesian relations from 1945 to 1995. The author argues that interaction between the two countries was made difficult by geographic, cultural, and historical factors. The first twenty-five years, covering the formative period of discovery, misadventure, and crisis, receive the most attention in this account.

2:300 Harper, Norman D. *A Great and Powerful Friend: A Study of Australian American Relations between 1900 and 1975.* New York: University of Queensland Press, 1987. This work traces the development of closer diplomatic relations between Australia and the United States in the twentieth century. Australia's interest in closer ties came after independence from the British empire left it with a need for a new great and powerful friend. This study also examines the problem of relations between junior and senior partners in the U.S.-Australian alliance. Bibliography.

2:301 Tahir-Kheli, Shirin R. *The United States and Pakistan: The Evolution of an Influence Relationship.* New York: Praeger, 1982. This book examines U.S.-Pakistani relations in the postwar period, focusing on the events of the 1970s. The author explores the relationship between a superpower and a third world country as they seek to influence one another on a variety of issues of national and international concern. Bibliography.

CANADA

2:302 Craig, Gerald M. *The United States and Canada.* Cambridge, MA: Harvard University Press, 1968. Craig surveys U.S.-Canadian relations from the early seventeenth century to the 1960s and argues that one of the biggest problems in those relations has been American unwillingness to show more than mild concern for Canadian interests. Extensive bibliography.

2:303 Eldridge, C. C., ed. *Kith and Kin: Canada, Britain, and the United States from the Revolution to the Cold War.* Cardiff: University of Wales Press, 1997. This collection of essays examines the history of the North Atlantic triangle largely from a British perspective. Broad in chronological sweep, the collection begins with an essay on British developments in North America leading up to the War of 1812 and concludes with an essay on the diplomacy of the period 1947–1949. The chapters include "The political persistence of British North America, 1763–1815," by Peter Marshall; "Making British North America British, 1815–1860," by P. A. Buckner; "Maps and Boundaries: Canada in Anglo-American Relations," by Muriel E. Chamberlain; "'Our Advices from Canada Are Unimportant': The Times and British North America, 1841–1861," by Ged Martin; "Learning about Oneself: The Making of Canadian Nationalism, 1867–1914," by James Sturgis; "Partners and Rivals: Britain, Canada, the United States, and the Impact of the First World War," by Keith Robbins; "The Political Economy of the North Atlantic Triangle in the 1930's," by Tim Rooth; "Canada, Britain, the United States and the Policy of 'Appeasement,'" by Ritchie Ovendale; and "Ernest Bevin, George C. Marshall and Lester B. Pearson, January 1947 to January 1949: A North Atlantic Triangle?" by M. Thornton.

2:304 Granatstein, J. L., and Norman Hillmer. *For Better or for Worse: Canada and the United States to the 1990s.* Toronto: Copp Clark Pitman, 1991. This work traces the evolution of Canadian-American relations from 1860 through the 1990s. The authors argue that the relationship between the two countries is characterized by a continued tension between conflict and cooperation. Canada has had little freedom to maneuver in its interaction with the United States, but has used the freedom it has with skill and determination. Bibliography.

2:305 Stewart, Gordon T. *The American Response to Canada since 1776.* East Lansing: Michigan State University Press, 1992. This survey of the period from 1776 to the 1980s seeks to correct the dearth of U.S. analyses of American-Canadian relations. The author argues that Canada has had to adjust its policies to the fact of U.S. dominance of the continent and that Canadian leaders have always viewed a collaborative relationship with the United States as essential to Canada's national well-being. Bibliography.

2:306 Thompson, John Herd, and Stephen J. Randall. *Canada and the United States: Ambivalent Allies.* 3d ed. Athens, GA: University of Georgia Press, 2002. This work traces U.S.-Canadian relations from the late eighteenth century to the early 1990s. Over the two centuries there have been substantial conflicts, bilateral and multilateral institution building, tranquillity, and turbulence. Studies that emphasize the special relationship between Washington and Ottawa belie the dissonance of the nineteenth century and exaggerate the harmony of the twentieth. First issued in 1994. Bibliographical essay.

EUROPE

Central Europe

Germany

2:307 Gatzke, Hans W. *Germany and the United States, a "Special Relationship"?* Cambridge, MA: Harvard University Press, 1980. This excellent survey examines German-American relations between the late eighteenth century and the 1970s. The author argues that no special relationship existed between the two countries. Bibliography.

2:308   Jonas, Manfred. *The United States and Germany: A Diplomatic History.* Ithaca: Cornell University Press, 1984. This book is a full survey of German-American relations covering the period from the late eighteenth century to the late 1970s. The author explores how German-American relations were influenced by mutual perceptions and misperceptions rooted in the historical experiences of each country. Bibliographical essay.

Eastern Europe

Russia (Soviet Union)

2:309   Gaddis, John Lewis. *Russia, the Soviet Union, and the United States: An Interpretive History.* 2d ed. New York: McGraw-Hill Pub. Co., 1990. This excellent survey examines relations between the United States and Russia and the Soviet Union from the late eighteenth century to the late 1980s, focusing on relations with the Soviet Union from the Bolshevik revolution to the Gorbachev era. Extensive bibliographical essay. First published in 1978.

2:310   Saul, Norman E. *Distant Friends: The United States and Russia, 1763–1867.* Lawrence: University Press of Kansas, 1991. Conceived as the first volume in a three-volume study covering American-Russian relations, this survey examines the period from the late eighteenth century to the purchase of Alaska. The author contends that relations were largely friendly, brought about by the geopolitical circumstances of the age, which drew the nations together in a quasi-alliance. Friendly relations were fueled by a common sense of destiny and a kindred psychological makeup. Extensive bibliography. Followed in 1996 by *Concord and Conflict: The United States and Russia, 1867–1914* (9:349) and in 2001 by *War and Revolution: The United States and Russia, 1914–1921* (same publisher).

2:311   Shavit, David, ed. *United States Relations with Russia and the Soviet Union: A Historical Dictionary.* This well-organized reference work covers all American relations with Russia and the Soviet Union to the early 1980s. It includes entries on events, policies, summit meetings, treaties, individuals, institutions, organizations, and businesses involved in U.S.-Russian relations. Bibliographical essay (1:248).

2:312   Sivachev, Nikolai V., and Nikolai N. Yakovlev. *Russia and the United States.* Translated by Olga Adler Titelbaum. Chicago: University of Chicago Press, 1979. This book interprets and summarizes relations from 1776 to the present. Based on Marxist methodology as well as American and Soviet unpublished and published materials, it is extraordinarily interesting.

2:313   Ulam, Adam B. *Expansion and Coexistence: Soviet Foreign Policy, 1917–73.* 2d ed. New York: Praeger, 1974. This work is a classic survey of Soviet foreign policy. The revised second edition includes two chapters analyzing the late 1960s and early 1970s. Ulam contends that 1971–1972 marked the beginning of a new phase, a departure in Soviet foreign policy as important as that occurring after Stalin's death in 1953. First published in 1968.

2:314   Williams, William Appleman. *American-Russian Relations, 1781–1947.* New York: Rinehart, 1952. Reprint 1971 (Octagon Books). In this classic work, Williams anticipated the revisionist writings now so much a part of Soviet-American historiography. Its appearance early in the cold war caused a mild sensation because of its critique of the policy of containment, its suggestion that American leaders of the 1920s, 1930s, and the war years mishandled relations, and its contention that Soviet-American antagonism had long roots in pre-revolutionary relations. Extensive bibliography.

Yugoslavia

2:315   Lampe, John R., Russell O. Prickett, and Ljubisa Adamovic. *Yugoslav-American Economic Relations since World War II.* Durham, NC: Duke University Press, 1990. This study surveys economic relations between Yugoslavia and the United States since World War II. The authors contend that the economic and commercial relations between the two countries have functioned well in the postwar period after overcoming some initial tension. Selected bibliography.

2:316   Lees, Lorraine M. *Keeping Tito Afloat: The United States, Yugoslavia, and the Cold War.* University Park: Pennsylvania State University Press, 1997. This study explores the U.S.-Yugoslav relationship from the hostility of the immediate postwar period, to the decision to assist Yugoslavia against the Soviet

Union, to the hopes for a Yugoslav association with NATO. The book focuses on the period 1945–1960.

Western Europe

France

2:317   Blumenthal, Henry. *France and the United States: Their Diplomatic Relation, 1789–1914.* Chapel Hill: University of North Carolina Press, 1970. This diplomatic survey concentrates on the policy development in Franco-American relations rather than public attitudes in the two nations toward one another. The judgments are clear, thoughtful, and moderate. Bibliography.

2:318   _____. *Illusion and Reality in Franco-American Diplomacy, 1914–1945.* Baton Rouge: Louisiana State University Press, 1986. This work argues that Franco-American relations, characterized in the nineteenth century as friendly though at times strained, remained largely unchanged up to 1939. After World War II, the failure of each country to realistically estimate its own power produced increased friction in Franco-American relations. Bibliography.

2:319   Duroselle, Jean-Baptiste. *France and the United States from the Beginnings to the Present.* Translated by Derek Coltman. Chicago: University of Chicago Press, 1978. This work examines Franco-American relations from a French perspective. The author contends that while there has not been a "special relationship" between France and the United States in the diplomatic, strategic, economic, and intellectual spheres, powerful ties of sentiment have drawn the two nations closer together through the nineteenth and twentieth centuries. Bibliography.

2:320   Levenstein, Harvey A. *Seductive Journey: American Tourists in France from Jefferson to the Jazz Age.* Chicago: University of Chicago Press, 1998. This work traces the rise of the mass tourist industry from the revolutionary period to the 1930s, exploring how a trip to France changed from an activity of the very wealthy to one in which an increasing number of middle-class Americans participated. The study also examines how travel to France crossed gender and racial lines in the country's first 150 years.

2:321   Zahniser, Marvin R. *Uncertain Friendship: American-French Diplomatic Relations through the Cold War.* New York: Wiley, 1975. In this excellent survey, the author examines the uneven course of Franco-American relations by focusing on the persistent conflict between the vital interests of these two countries. Zahniser argues that they have often needed each other; they have grown closer on occasion but have never developed the trust and confidence of full-fledged allies or certain friends. Bibliographical essay.

United Kingdom

2:322   Allen, H. C. *Great Britain and the United States: A History of Anglo-American Relations (1783–1952).* New York: St. Martin's Press, 1955. This general survey describes the vagaries of the transatlantic connection between the United States and Great Britain. Allen argues that social, political, and economic factors prevailed over the issues threatening the Atlantic relationship. He maintains that, because "there was no deep, inherent antagonism" between the nations after the War of 1812, "Anglo-American cordiality" developed quickly after 1814. The work is organized into four sections. Section 1 traces the broad outline of the relationship. The remaining sections examine the history of Anglo-American diplomatic relations. Bibliography.

2:323   Brebner, John Bartlet. *North Atlantic Triangle: The Interplay of Canada, the United States and Great Britain.* New Haven: Yale University Press for the Carnegie Endowment for International Peace, 1945. Reprint 1970 (Russell and Russell). Brebner discusses the major factors involved in American-British-Canadian relations in North America from the 1490s through the 1940s. Extensive bibliography.

2:324   Campbell, Charles Soutter. *From Revolution to Rapprochement: The United States and Great Britain, 1783–1900.* New York: Wiley, 1974. In this brief survey, the author contends that a real Anglo-American rapprochement was not realized until the end of the nineteenth century. Bibliography.

2:325   Dimbleby, David, and David Reynolds. *An Ocean Apart: The Relationship between Britain and America in the Twentieth Century.* New York: Random House, 1988. Informed by the BBC TV and KCET Los Angeles television series of the same name, this work traces the complex relationship between Great Britain and the United States, focusing on the twentieth century, but includes treatment of the period beginning in the early seventeenth century. The authors contend that contact between Britons and Americans has always been easy at every level, diplomatic, military, personal, and political. Extensive collection of historical cartoons and maps. Bibliography.

2:326   Dobson, Alan P. *Anglo-American Relations in the Twentieth Century: Of Friendship, Conflict and the Rise and Decline of Superpowers.* New York: Routledge, 1995. This work analyzes the development of Anglo-American relations since 1895 and argues that the relationship between the two countries was more interdependent than has been previously recognized. The author explores various conflicts between the two countries, examines how these conflicts were resolved, and speculates on the future of Anglo-American relations. Bibliography.

2:327   Nicholas, H. G. *The United States and Britain.* Chicago: University of Chicago Press, 1975. The author argues that a shared language and a common historical inheritance created a set of mutually acceptable habits of thought and behavior that led to the formation of common policies and a common cast of mind. Though differences of opinion existed in the U.S.-British relationship, they were mitigated by the interpenetration of the two cultures, economies, and social structures. Bibliographical essay.

2:328   Watt, Donald Cameron. *Succeeding John Bull: America in Britain's Place, 1900–1975: A Study of the Anglo-American Relationship and World Politics in the Context of British and American Foreign-Policy-Making in the Twentieth Century.* New York: Cambridge University Press, 1984. This work examines how foreign policymakers of each country perceived the process by which the United States came to replace Great Britain as the primary world and naval power. Bibliography.

Ireland

2:329   Akenson, Donald Harman. *The United States and Ireland.* Cambridge, MA: Harvard University Press, 1973. This book covers Irish history, but concentrates on the twentieth century and the 1960s in particular. This is a useful starting point for students. Extensive bibliography.

2:330   Cronin, Seán. *Washington's Irish Policy, 1916–1986: Independence, Partition, and Neutrality.* St. Paul, MN: Irish Books and Media, 1987. This popular history surveys American-Irish relations beginning in 1916. The author argues that the United States subordinated its Irish policy to other geopolitical concerns designed to protect and advance its status as a world power.

Italy

2:331   Hughes, H. Stuart. *The United States and Italy.* 3d ed. Cambridge, MA: Harvard University Press, 1979. This account remains a basic starting point for studying U.S.-Italian relations. As Hughes has noted, most Americans think they are very familiar with Italy when in fact they know very little. First published in 1953. Bibliography.

2:332   Wollemborg, Leo J. *Stars, Stripes, and Italian Tricolor: The United States and Italy, 1946–1989.* New York: Praeger, 1990. The author argues that unlike relations with France, Germany, and the United Kingdom, American-Italian relations have been dominated by questions of domestic Italian politics rather than foreign policy issues. The book focuses on two decisive turning points in postwar Italian politics: the opening to the left in the early 1960s and the failure of the Italian Communist Party to form a compromise government with the Christian Democrats in 1977–1978. Foreword by Richard N. Gardner. Bibliography.

Scandinavia

2:333   Chester, Edward W. *The United States and Six Atlantic Outposts: The Military and Economic Considerations.* Port Washington, NY: Kennikat Press, 1980. This account reviews American contacts with Iceland, Greenland, the Azores, Bermuda, Jamaica, and the Bahamas. By World War II, both U.S. merchants and investors had shown an interest in these Atlantic outposts; military activities date from the 1770s. Extensive bibliography.

2:334   Cole, Wayne S. *Norway and the United States, 1905–1955: Two Democracies in Peace and War.* Ames, IA: Iowa State University Press, 1989. This work examines U.S.-Norwegian relations starting with Norway's independence from Sweden and extending into the mid-1950s. Focusing on the periods of the two world wars and the early cold war,

Cole explores the processes by which two democratic countries with long-standing traditions of neutrality and noninvolvement in European wars turned away from those policies to embrace a system of collective security. Bibliography.

2:335   Hanhimäki, Jussi M. *Scandinavia and the United States: An Insecure Friendship*. New York: Twayne Publishers, 1997. This study examines the complex web of relationships that connected Denmark, Finland, Iceland, Norway, and Sweden to the United States during and after the cold war. The work demonstrates that the Nordic countries acted as intermediaries between the two cold war blocs and shows how the Scandinavian middle way provided a challenge to economic and political systems of the superpowers. Bibliographical essay.

2:336   Scott, Franklin D. *Scandinavia*. Rev. and enl. ed. Cambridge, MA: Harvard University Press, 1975. This volume is an excellent starting point for the American student and covers all the Scandinavian countries. First published in 1950 as *The United States and Scandinavia*. Bibliography.

Spain

2:337   Botero, Rodrigo. *Ambivalent Embrace: America's Troubled Relations with Spain from the Revolutionary War to the Cold War*. Westport, CT: Greenwood Press, 2001. This is a solid and sober survey of relations between the United States and Spain, including the nineteenth-century rivalry over the Spanish empire in North America, three decades of indifference until the Spanish civil war, ambivalent relations with Franco, and finally cooperation with a democratic Spain that is part of the European Union. The author is a historian who once served as finance minister of Colombia.

2:338   Cortada, James W. *Two Nations over Time: Spain and the United States, 1776–1977*. Westport, CT: Greenwood Press, 1978. The author analyzes Spanish-American relations by examining economic, cultural, and domestic political factors of both countries. Bibliography.

Switzerland

2:339   Meier, Heinz K. *Friendship under Stress: U.S.-Swiss Relations 1900–1950*. Bern: Herbert Lang, 1970. If nothing else, this book demonstrates the paucity of literature dealing with prewar diplomacy between the United States and Switzerland. The author focuses on U.S.-Swiss relations during the two world wars, exploring economic relations and Switzerland's importance as a neutral nation. Bibliography.

2:340   _____. *The United States and Switzerland, in the Nineteenth Century*. The Hague: Mouton, 1963. This study traces the generally friendly relations that existed between these two nations to the outbreak of World War I. Bibliography.

Others

2:341   Stearns, Monteagle. *Entangled Allies: U.S. Policy toward Greece, Turkey, and Cyprus*. New York: Council on Foreign Relations Press, 1992. This work examines U.S. policy toward Greece, Turkey, and Cyprus in the period after World War II and suggests that the United States, with more imaginative diplomacy and greater attention to the political realities in the region, can play a larger role in improving the relations between Greece and Turkey.

2:342   Vitas, Robert A. *The United States and Lithuania: The Stimson Doctrine of Nonrecognition*. New York: Praeger, 1990. This work examines the American policy of nonrecognition from World War II to the 1990s. Following the Soviet occupation of Lithuania, the U.S. government froze Lithuanian assets and property, blocking the Soviet Union's attempt to claim them. The author contends that the policy of nonrecognition became a moral and practical tool in condemning illegal Soviet aggression. Bibliography.

2:343   Wandycz, Piotr S. *The United States and Poland*. Cambridge, MA: Harvard University Press, 1979. This work is essentially a history of Poland that incorporates an analysis of its bilateral relationship with the United States, including an examination of cultural contacts and the attitudes that Americans and Poles held toward each other. Appendices and bibliographical essay.

LATIN AMERICA

General

2:344   Aguilar Monteverde, Alonso. *Pan-Americanism from Monroe to the Present: A View from the Other Side.* Translated by Asa Zatz. Rev. English ed. New York: MR Press, 1968. This revised English edition presents a sweeping view of U.S.–Latin American relations. The author sees U.S. policy in various eras as designed to promote weak and dependable allies in the Western Hemisphere and to exploit Latin America. Bibliography referring to other critical works.

2:345   Bemis, Samuel Flagg. *The Latin American Policy of the United States: An Historical Interpretation.* New York: Harcourt, Brace and Company, 1943. Reprint 1971 (Norton). This classic account of U.S.–Latin American relations does not reflect recent research and interpretations. Bibliography.

2:346   Bethell, Leslie, ed. *The Cambridge History of Latin America.* 11 vols. New York: Cambridge University Press, 1984–1995. This outstanding eleven-volume series provides a detailed summary of Latin American history, incorporating important recent scholarship. Includes bibliographies and indexes.

2:347   Connell-Smith, Gordon. *The Inter-American System.* New York: Oxford University Press, 1966. This study by an English scholar is of special value because it provides a view from outside the Western Hemisphere. The author is adept in pointing out the gap between the exaggerated claims made by the United States for the success of the system and its modest achievements. Extensive bibliography.

2:348   _____. *The United States and Latin America: An Historical Analysis of Inter-American Relations.* New York: Wiley, 1974. This analysis by a prominent British Latin Americanist, generally critical of U.S. policy, aims to counterbalance the orthodox account of Samuel Flagg Bemis. Modestly footnoted, with no formal bibliography.

2:349   Gardner, James A. *Legal Imperialism: American Lawyers and Foreign Aid in Latin America.* Madison: University of Wisconsin Press, 1980. This book offers a scholarly and carefully documented history of the role of American lawyers in legal assistance for Latin America, and an analysis of the American legal models that informed and were carried abroad as part of this process.

2:350   Langley, Lester D. *America and the Americas: The United States in the Western Hemisphere.* Athens, GA: University of Georgia Press, 1989. This work is the introductory volume of the outstanding series *The United States and the Americas.* The author examines the interaction of the politics, economics, and culture of the United States in the Americas and explores bilateral issues in detail only when they have affected U.S. policy toward the entire region. Bibliographical essay.

2:351   Perkins, Dexter. *A History of the Monroe Doctrine.* Rev. ed. Boston: Little, Brown, 1963. In the classic survey of the history of the Monroe Doctrine, Perkins ranges from the doctrine's origins during the colonial and revolutionary periods through the first decade of the post–World War II era. Originally published in 1941 as *Hands Off: A History of the Monroe Doctrine.*

2:352   Stuart, Graham H., and James L. Tigner. *Latin America and the United States.* 6th ed. Englewood Cliffs, NJ: Prentice-Hall, 1975. A comprehensive textbook, arranged by topics and by countries, it is useful for basic information. First published, with Stuart as sole author, in 1922. Bibliography.

Central America

General

2:353   Findling, John E. *Close Neighbors, Distant Friends: United States–Central American Relations.* New York: Greenwood Press, 1987. This study examines U.S. relations with Guatemala, Honduras, El Salvador, Nicaragua, and Costa Rica from 1800 to the 1980s. Bibliographical essay.

2:354   Karnes, Thomas L. *The Failure of Union: Central America, 1824–1975.* Rev. ed. Tempe, AZ: Center for Latin American Studies, Arizona State University, 1976. Using Central American archives, the author traces the ill-fated attempts at union in the region. The work's strength is in the post-1871 period.

First published in 1961 as *The Failure of Union: Central America, 1824–1960*. Extensive bibliography.

2:355   LaFeber, Walter. *Inevitable Revolutions: The United States in Central America*. 2d ed. New York: W. W. Norton, 1993. This work examines the relations between the United States and Central America from the early nineteenth century to the 1980s. The author explores how the application of the American system—a confidence in capitalism, willingness to use military force, a fear of foreign influence—has led to great revolutionary instability in the region. First published in 1983. Bibliography.

2:356   Leonard, Thomas M. *Central America and the United States: The Search for Stability*. Athens, GA: University of Georgia Press, 1991. This work examines the history of the relations between the United States and Central America from 1820 to the Reagan administration. The author contends that three distinct time periods can be observed in the history of U.S.–Central American relations: 1820–1903, 1903–1948, and 1948 to the Reagan administration. The book seeks to explain how American policies toward Central America in the 1980s were rooted in a complex past shaped by nearly two centuries of interaction. Bibliographic essay.

Panama

2:357   Anguizola, G. A. *The Panama Canal: Isthmian Political Instability from 1821 to 1977*. 2d ed. Washington, DC: University Press of America, 1977. A Panamanian scholar, employing Panamanian documents, adds a different dimension to the discussion of the U.S. construction and operation of the Canal. Bibliography.

2:358   Conniff, Michael L. *Panama and the United States: The Forced Alliance*. 2d ed. Athens, GA: University of Georgia Press, 2001. This work explores U.S.-Panamanian relations over the past 170 years, emphasizing the forced nature of the relations between the two countries. The author argues that they needed each other to fulfill basic national aspirations and that the relationship between them has been unequal. Bibliographical essay. First published in 1992.

2:359   Ealy, Lawrence O. *Yanqui Politics and the Isthmian Canal*. University Park: Pennsylvania State University Press, 1971. Ealy discusses U.S. Canal politics from the 1840s to the 1970s. The book is arranged chronologically to 1914 and topically thereafter. It is a broad study that is informative on political debates in the United States. Bibliography.

2:360   LaFeber, Walter. *The Panama Canal: The Crisis in Historical Perspective*. Updated ed. New York: Oxford University Press, 1989. After describing pre-1903 Panamanian nationalism, the author discusses the 1903 Panamanian revolution and U.S.-Panama relations in the ensuing seventy-five years, emphasizing the forces of the past that influenced the treaty negotiations of the mid-1970s. LaFeber sees the 1978 treaties as a "diplomatic triumph" for the United States. First published in 1978. Excellent bibliographical essay.

2:361   Major, John. *Prize Possession: The United States and the Panama Canal, 1903–1979*. New York: Cambridge University Press, 1993. This study focuses on five important themes: the Canal's defense and its place in American strategy, the Zone's system of government, its segregated labor force, its commercial development at the expense of Panama, and the controversial issue of U.S. intervention in Panamanian politics. Extensive bibliography.

Others

2:362   Bermann, Karl. *Under the Big Stick: Nicaragua and the United States since 1848*. Boston: South End Press, 1986. This examination of 130 years of American intervention in the affairs of Nicaragua was written in part to provide background to the U.S. attempt to put down the Sandinista revolution, which, the author contends, was itself the result of past American involvement in Nicaragua.

2:363   Bonner, Raymond. *Weakness and Deceit: U.S. Policy and El Salvador*. New York: Times Books, 1984. This is an examination of the revolution in El Salvador with an analysis of the American response. It is written by a *New York Times* staff writer and based on his personal experience in El Salvador as well as on interviews with leading U.S. foreign policy specialists. Bibliography.

Caribbean

General

2:364   Langley, Lester D. *Struggle for the American Mediterranean: United States–European Rivalry in the Gulf-Caribbean, 1776–1904.* Athens, GA: University of Georgia Press, 1976. This is a synthesis of the international history of the Caribbean in the nineteenth century that deals with various episodes of American-European rivalry. The author concludes that twentieth-century U.S. interventionist policy was deeply rooted in the nineteenth century. Bibliography.

2:365   _____. *The United States and the Caribbean in the Twentieth Century.* 4th ed. Athens, GA: University of Georgia Press, 1989. This volume continues the synthesis of the international history of the Caribbean begun in Langley's *Struggle for the American Mediterranean: United States–European Rivalry in the Gulf-Caribbean, 1776–1904* (1976) (2:364). In the fourth edition, the author explains that U.S.-Caribbean relations have been complicated by the modern character of the relationship, brought about by the penetration of the American economy and culture into highly structured Caribbean polities and societies. The relations between the United States and the Caribbean have been further strained by the unappreciated impact of Caribbean immigration on the American economy. First published in 1980. Extensive bibliographical essay.

2:366   Maingot, Anthony P. *The United States and the Caribbean: Challenges of an Asymmetrical Relationship.* Boulder: Westview Press, 1994. This study examines U.S.-Caribbean relations from 1823 to the early 1990s. The author describes U.S.-Caribbean relations as one of complex interdependence involving three characteristics: the societies in the region have been connected through multiple channels, there has been no hierarchy in the agenda of U.S.-Caribbean relations, and military force has receded in importance in direct relationship to the growth of a complex interdependence. Bibliography.

2:367   Perkins, Dexter. *The United States and the Caribbean.* Rev. ed. Cambridge, MA: Harvard University Press, 1966. In this classic work, Perkins explores twentieth-century U.S.-Caribbean relations. The second edition includes an examination of eco-nomic interests. The author contends that changing conditions make maintenance of good relations much more difficult. First published in 1947. Bibliography.

Cuba

2:368   Benjamin, Jules R. *The United States and the Origins of the Cuban Revolution: An Empire of Liberty in an Age of National Liberation.* Princeton: Princeton University Press, 1990. This work traces American-Cuban relations beginning in the early nineteenth century, emphasizing the period between 1898 and 1961. The author explores how fundamental elements in American institutions and culture influenced the use of U.S. power against Cuba with lasting and damaging structural results. Bibliography.

2:369   Langley, Lester D. *The Cuban Policy of the United States: A Brief History.* New York: Wiley, 1968. This is a general survey of U.S. policy toward Cuba (1776–1962) with two chapters on the years 1808–1861, one on the Ten Years' War (1868–1878), one on the war with Spain, one on the protectorate era (1898–1934), and the final chapter on the United States and Batista and Castro. The theme of the book is that Castro fulfilled U.S. dreams of a "progressive" Cuba but did so in a socialist, anti-U.S. framework. Bibliography.

2:370   Pérez, Louis A., Jr. *Cuba and the United States: Ties of Singular Intimacy.* 2d ed. Athens, GA: University of Georgia Press, 1997. This work explores how Cuba's relations with the United States shaped and influenced its history, values, attitudes, and behavior. It also examines the various ways Cubans influenced the social, economic, political, and cultural life in the United States while tracing Cuban-American relations from colonial times through the Cuban revolution. First published in 1990. Bibliographical essay.

2:371   Thomas, Hugh. *Cuba, or, The Pursuit of Freedom.* Updated ed. New York: Da Capo Press, 1998. This is a monumental work covering Cuban society, economics, politics, and especially the island's international history (1762–1968). The theme of the twentieth century is the failure of the republic created after the Spanish-American War. The work contains information on the Cuban economy. First published in 1971. Extensive bibliography.

Grenada

2:372   Heine, Jorge, ed. *A Revolution Aborted: The Lessons of Grenada.* Pittsburgh: University of Pittsburgh Press, 1990. This collection of essays is the product of the Caribbean Institute and Study Center for Latin America at the Inter-American University of Puerto Rico, San Germán, and analyzes the Peoples' Revolutionary Government (PRG) in Grenada. The book is organized into four sections: the domestic record of the PRG, international affairs, crisis and aftermath, and a comparative assessment of the politics of Grenada. The section on international affairs examines the foreign policy of the PRG and the PRG's economic policies with the Soviet bloc as well as the cause of the American invasion. Essays of special pertinence to U.S. historians include Robert A. Pastor, "The United States and the Grenada Revolution: Who Pushed First and Why?" (181–214); and Vaughan Lewis, "Small States, Eastern Caribbean Security, and the Grenada Intervention" (257–64). Bibliographical essay.

2:373   Lewis, Gordon K. *Grenada: The Jewel Despoiled.* Baltimore: Johns Hopkins University Press, 1987. This work covers the period from the early 1950s through the middle of the 1980s. It examines the sociopolitical history of Grenada including the rise of the New Jewel Movement, the American invasion, and its aftermath.

Puerto Rico

2:374   Carr, Raymond. *Puerto Rico, a Colonial Experiment.* New York: New York University Press, 1984. This extensive survey examines American–Puerto Rican relations from the late nineteenth century to the early 1980s. The book is organized into five sections. The first section explores the history of American–Puerto Rican relations, with each of the later sections focusing on a particular aspect of the troubled relationship. Bibliographical essay.

2:375   Fernandez, Ronald. *The Disenchanted Island: Puerto Rico and the United States in the Twentieth Century.* 2d ed. Westport, CT: Praeger, 1996. This work examines the evolution of American colonialism in Puerto Rico and explores the cynicism, economic pretensions, racism, and denial of democratic rights that have often characterized the relations between the United States and its colony. The work covers the period from the late nineteenth century to the early 1990s. Brief bibliography. First issued in 1992.

Santo Domingo (Dominican Republic and Haiti)

2:376   Atkins, G. Pope, and Larman C. Wilson. *The Dominican Republic and the United States: From Imperialism to Transnationalism.* Athens, GA: University of Georgia Press, 1998. An outstanding survey of American-Dominican political, economic, social, and cultural relations, this work covers the period beginning in the middle of the nineteenth century and continuing up to the mid-1990s. The book analyzes this bilateral relationship from both the Dominican and U.S. perspectives. Bibliographical essay.

2:377   _____. *The United States and the Trujillo Regime.* New Brunswick: Rutgers University Press, 1971. In this excellent survey of U.S.–Dominican Republic relations (1904–1960s), with an emphasis on the Trujillo era, the authors conclude that the United States should recognize that democracy cannot be imposed from the outside. Bibliography.

2:378   Clausner, Marlin D. *Rural Santo Domingo: Settled, Unsettled, and Resettled.* Philadelphia: Temple University Press, 1973. This general survey treats the agrarian situation and its impact on the politics of the Dominican Republic (1850–1960). Bibliography.

2:379   Heinl, Robert Debs, Jr., Nancy Gordon Heinl, and Michael Heinl. *Written in Blood: The Story of the Haitian People, 1492–1995.* 2d ed. Lanham, MD: University Press of America, 1996. This work traces the history of Haiti from the period of European discovery to the mid-1990s, focusing on political and military history and with considerable reference to U.S.-Haitian relations. A chronological index provides a summary of important dates in Haitian history. Extensive bibliography. First published in 1978.

2:380   Logan, Rayford W. *Haiti and the Dominican Republic.* New York: Oxford University Press, 1968. This general introduction to the history of the Dominican Republic (1750–1960) emphasizes its troubled relations with Haiti. Bibliography.

Virgin Islands

2:381   Boyer, William W. *America's Virgin Islands: A History of Human Rights and Wrongs.*

Durham, NC: Carolina Academic Press, 1983. This survey, organized into three sections, explores the history of the U.S. Virgin Islands from the time of discovery by Columbus to the early 1980s. It is a broadly conceived history of the struggle of slaves, serfs, and citizens to gain control of their own destinies, a story of human rights and wrongs. The first section focuses on the period 1492–1917, the second examines the freedom struggle, 1917–1954, and the third focuses on the tourism syndrome, 1954–1980. Bibliography.

Mexico

2:382　　Cline, Howard F. *The United States and Mexico.* Rev. enl. ed. New York: Atheneum, 1963. A classic survey of U.S.-Mexican relations, this work is organized into four parts. The first section examines the history of Mexico before the Mexican revolution, including discussion of culture, race, and class in Mexico; the second focuses on the Mexican revolution, with the third part exploring Mexican resurgence and World War II. The concluding section covers the period of institutional revolution in Mexico, 1946–1952, and includes an epilogue that brings the analysis up to the 1960s. Bibliographical essay and updated bibliography for the revised edition. First published in 1953.

2:383　　Hart, John M. *Empire and Revolution: The Americans in Mexico since the Civil War.* Berkeley: University of California Press, 2002. This is a profound and detailed study of the economic, political, and personal interactions between Americans in Mexico, especially elite groups of financiers and industrialists, and the Mexicans themselves. The author sees these relationships as the precursors to America's role in much of the developing world during the march toward globalization. He argues that elite economic interests have dominated U.S. policy toward Mexico, in part because most other American citizens have remained indifferent. An exception has been those middle-class American residents and retirees in Mexico, who have promoted a somewhat more democratic vision of the American dream.

2:384　　Raat, W. Dirk. *Mexico and the United States: Ambivalent Vistas.* 2d ed. Athens, GA: University of Georgia Press, 1996. This work examines Mexico's history in the context of its relationship with the United States and the world economy, paying particular attention to the manner in which the latter affected Mexican history and influenced its values, attitudes, and conditions. This book is also a study of comparative civilizations: the western culture of Protestant North America and the Native American-Hispanic society of Catholic Mexico. First published in 1992. Extensive bibliography.

2:385　　Schmitt, Karl M. *Mexico and the United States, 1821–1973: Conflict and Coexistence.* New York: Wiley, 1974. This work explores the interaction of the two nations, focusing on the growing power differential that became the main source of tension in their relations as they moved from rivalry and conflict to respect for each other's distinctive position in the international community. Bibliographical essay.

2:386　　Vázquez, Josefina Zoraida, and Lorenzo Meyer. *The United States and Mexico.* Chicago: University of Chicago Press, 1985. This survey analyzes United States–Mexican relations since the Mexican-American War. Written from a contemporary Mexican perspective, the book focuses, first, on the nineteenth century and, in a second part, on the twentieth. Bibliography.

South America

General

2:387　　Pike, Fredrick B. *The United States and the Andean Republics: Peru, Bolivia, and Ecuador.* Cambridge, MA: Harvard University Press, 1977. A synthesis based primarily on secondary works, this volume provides an analysis of the political and economic developments in Peru, Ecuador, and Bolivia that have taken place under the patronage of the United States. Pike demonstrates that U.S. leaders, stressing such principles as competitive independence, have never fully comprehended the Andean culture, which emphasizes corporate (patron-client) value systems. Extensive bibliography.

2:388　　Whitaker, Arthur Preston. *The United States and the Southern Cone: Argentina, Chile, and Uruguay.* Cambridge, MA: Harvard University Press, 1976. This history stresses the twentieth century and argues that U.S. imperialism, earlier restricted to the

Caribbean, was gradually extended to the Southern Cone nations. Extensive bibliographical essay.

Argentina

2:389   Peterson, Harold F. *Argentina and the United States, 1810–1960*. Albany: State University of New York Press, 1964. This work contains considerable information on the diplomatic relationship between two antagonists in the inter-American system. Peterson emphasizes the misunderstandings and misperceptions between Argentina and the United States and is especially detailed in covering the Falkland Islands dispute (1830s), Argentina's opposition to the United States in the Pan-American system, and the Perón era. Extensive bibliography.

2:390   Tulchin, Joseph S. *Argentina and the United States: A Conflicted Relationship*. Boston: Twayne, 1990. This work examines U.S.-Argentine relations from the late eighteenth century to the late 1980s and describes the long and often contentious history between the two countries. Bibliographic essay.

2:391   Whitaker, Arthur Preston. *The United States and Argentina*. Cambridge, MA: Harvard University Press, 1954. This is a short overall survey by one of the pioneers in the history of U.S. dealings with Latin America.

Brazil

2:392   Burns, E. Bradford. *A History of Brazil*. 3d ed. New York: Columbia University Press, 1993. Burns has prepared an excellent scholarly history of Brazil; it covers a wide array of topics, including discussion of European discovery, the Brazilian colonial experience, the process of nation-building, democratization, and military dictatorship. Appendices provide the reader with a chronology of important dates in Brazilian history as well as a list of Brazilian chiefs of state. The third edition (the first was published in 1970) covers up through the early 1990s. Bibliographical essay.

2:393   Fontaine, Roger W. *Brazil and the United States: Toward a Maturing Relationship*. Washington, DC: American Enterprise Institute for Public Policy Research, 1974. This study examines the strains imposed on the traditional relationship of the two countries when Brazil became the "other major

power" in the Western Hemisphere. The author maintains that two issues—development of the Amazon Basin and Brazil's ambitious nuclear energy program—will dominate relations in the future.

Chile

2:394   Pike, Fredrick B. *Chile and the United States, 1880–1962: The Emergence of Chile's Social Crisis and the Challenge to United States Diplomacy*. Notre Dame, IN: University of Notre Dame Press, 1963. This is a detailed analysis of the development of social problems in Chile and their effects on relations with the United States. The author argues that the United States typically supported the upper classes in Chile. Bibliography.

2:395   Sater, William F. *Chile and the United States: Empires in Conflict*. Athens, GA: University of Georgia Press, 1990. This work surveys the history of American-Chilean relations from the early 1800s to the 1990s. The author contends that Chileans have developed a complicated scenario of betrayal to explain their nation's domestic discord and its fall from power in international affairs. Chileans of both the right and left attribute their country's political and economic decline to capitalism and its driving force, the United States. This book explores how these two nations and cultures arrived at this point in the relationship. Extensive bibliographical essay.

Colombia

2:396   Parks, E. Taylor. *Colombia and the United States, 1765–1934*. Durham, NC: Duke University Press, 1935. Reprint 1970 (Arno Press). This general survey of American-Colombian diplomatic relations provides a good account of Colombian political history. The emphasis is on American canal policy in the nineteenth century. Bibliography.

2:397   Randall, Stephen J. *Colombia and the United States: Hegemony and Interdependence*. Athens, GA: University of Georgia Press, 1992. Focusing on the period since 1890, this study notes several levels of U.S.-Colombian relations during the past two centuries. The first is the formal diplomatic level of treaties and power, the second of connections between the private sectors of each country, and a third of relations in the realm of popular culture. The author argues that the United States in its interaction with Colombia has failed to recognize that Colombians and their political representatives have not seen themselves as a weak, unimportant, third world country. Bibliographical essay.

Peru

2:398 Carey, James C. *Peru and the United States, 1900–1962*. Notre Dame, IN: University of Notre Dame Press, 1964. This is a reliable account of U.S.-Peruvian relations that emphasizes private business and financial affairs. Also included in this work are a comprehensive treatment of U.S. aid programs and an excellent analysis of Vice-President Nixon's 1958 misadventures in Lima.

2:399 Pike, Fredrick B. *The Modern History of Peru*. New York: Praeger, 1967. A readable, concise history of Peru since independence, it stresses political considerations. It is useful for background information.

Venezuela

2:400 Ewell, Judith. *Venezuela and the United States: From Monroe's Hemisphere to Petroleum's Empire*. Athens, GA: University of Georgia Press, 1996. This work explores U.S.-Venezuelan relations from the late eighteenth century to the 1990s. The author claims that Venezuela has avoided suffering major American military, diplomatic, or economic sanctions by relying on the counterweight of British trade and presence in the late nineteenth century, by enforcing an orderly domestic peace in the first half of the twentieth century, by using multilateral alliances and the forum of U.S. and international public opinion in the post–World War II period to further its own interests, and by exploiting weakness and division within U.S. political institutions. Bibliographical essay.

2:401 Liss, Sheldon B. *Diplomacy & Dependency: Venezuela, the United States, and the Americas*. Salisbury, NC: Documentary Publications, 1978. This is a detailed survey of bilateral relations (1810–1977); despite the title, there is little treatment of inter-American relations. Although the author's purpose was to test dependency theory, most of the account is orthodox diplomatic history. Yet the author is convincing in demonstrating that the United States has had considerable impact on Venezuela's economic growth, political liberalism, and maldistribution of wealth, especially after the early days of petroleum development. Extensive bibliography.

MIDDLE EAST

General

2:402 Brands, H. W. *Into the Labyrinth: The United States and the Middle East, 1945–1993*. New York: McGraw-Hill, 1994. Three important factors drew American attention to the Middle East: oil, the Soviet Union, and Israel. American involvement in the region was reactive, based largely on ad hoc responses to a half century of regional crises. This work tells the story of how the Middle East came to occupy a position of central importance in U.S. foreign policy. Extensive bibliographical essay.

2:403 Bryson, Thomas A. *American Diplomatic Relations with the Middle East, 1784–1975: A Survey*. Metuchen, NJ: Scarecrow Press, 1977. Bryson surveys U.S. relations with Middle Eastern states and discusses the growth of commercial intercourse and missionary activities in shaping U.S. policy. The author suggests that American officials pursued policy that followed certain guiding principles and the concept of the national interest. The work is based on English-language sources. Bibliography.

2:404 _____. *Tars, Turks, and Tankers: The Role of the United States Navy in the Middle East, 1800–1979*. Metuchen, NJ: Scarecrow Press, 1980. The author treats the role of the U.S. navy in supporting American foreign policy objectives in the Middle East. While the bulk of this work deals with the era following World War II, the period prior to the war is given ample treatment. Bibliography.

2:405 Lenczowski, George. *American Presidents and the Middle East*. Durham, NC: Duke University Press, 1990. This work explores the attitudes and actions of American presidents toward the Middle East from Truman to Reagan. The author examines how the presidents perceived the issues with which they were confronted and how these perceptions influenced their foreign policy decisions toward the region. Extensive bibliography.

2:406 Shavit, David, ed. *The United States in the Middle East: A Historical Dictionary*. This historical dictionary provides useful information about the persons, institutions, and events that influenced the relationship between the United States and the region of the Middle East. Bibliographical essay (1:261).

2:407 Tillman, Seth P. *The United States in the Middle East, Interests and Obstacles.* Bloomington: Indiana University Press, 1982. This survey is organized into seven chapters. The first provides a broad overview of the region since ancient times. The second focuses on U.S. interests in the Middle East, and subsequent chapters cover Israeli, Saudi Arabian, Palestinian, and Soviet interests in the region. In the concluding chapter, the author assesses how peace could be attained in the Middle East.

Iran

2:408 Bill, James A. *The Eagle and the Lion: The Tragedy of American-Iranian Relations.* New Haven: Yale University Press, 1988. This work analyzes U.S.-Iranian relations from the early 1940s to 1979. The author argues that American policy toward Iran was flawed, confused, and based largely on ignorance, bureaucratic conflict, and Soviet-centricity. The relations between the two countries were further strained after the Iranian revolution by an inexperienced, beleaguered, and paranoid leadership in the Islamic Republic that created policy based on its own misunderstandings of the United States. Bibliography.

2:409 Cottam, Richard W. *Iran and the United States: A Cold War Case Study.* Pittsburgh: University of Pittsburgh Press, 1988. This book explores how, in little more than a generation, Iranians altered their view of the United States from support to hatred. The work focuses on the sociopolitical circumstances inside Iran, beginning with a survey of nineteenth-century American policy toward Iran and how this policy over time influenced change within that nation.

2:410 Ramazani, R. K. *The Foreign Policy of Iran: A Developing Nation in World Affairs, 1500–1941.* Charlottesville: University Press of Virginia, 1966. The author surveys Iranian diplomacy from the sixteenth century to World War II. He asserts that the Persians wanted the United States to serve as a counterweight to the British and Russians. Bibliography.

2:411 Ramazani, R. K. *Iran's Foreign Policy, 1941–1973: A Study of Foreign Policy in Moderniz-*

ing Nations. Charlottesville: University Press of Virginia, 1975. This comprehensive analysis draws on primary sources as well as extensive field research and observation to provide the best single volume on Iran's foreign policy in the postwar period. Extensive bibliography.

2:412 Rubin, Barry. *Paved with Good Intentions: The American Experience and Iran.* New York: Oxford University Press, 1980. This book examines U.S.-Iranian relations from the early twentieth century to the Iranian hostage crisis. The author argues that American policies toward Iran were directed toward reasonable and rational goals, but ultimately failed because they did not take into account the currents of Iranian or Middle East politics. Excellent bibliography.

2:413 Samii, Kuross A. *Involvement by Invitation: American Strategies of Containment in Iran.* University Park: Pennsylvania State University Press, 1987. This work examines U.S.-Iranian relations from 1911 to 1980, the author identifying two distinct historical periods in their involvement: from 1911 to 1954 and from the Shah's ascendancy in 1954 to the American hostage crisis. The key difference between the two periods lies in the perceptions of the Iranian people, whose image of the United States changed from benevolence to antipathy. Bibliography.

Israel

2:414 Ball, George W., and Douglas B. Ball. *The Passionate Attachment: America's Involvement with Israel, 1947 to the Present.* New York: W. W. Norton, 1992. This work by a long-time and influential member of the Department of State analyzes how the United States developed a passionate attachment to Israel that has distorted American relations with both Israel and the Arab nations and resulted in diminishing American authority in the region, preventing development of an effective U.S. policy for the Middle East.

2:415 Reich, Bernard. *The United States and Israel: Influence in the Special Relationship.* New York: Praeger, 1984. This book analyzes the evolution and dynamics of the U.S.-Israeli relationship after the United States assumed a preeminent position in Israel's security in 1967. Reich examines the relationship in terms of influence, arguing that each state at different times has been successful in shaping the other's behavior through a multiplicity of techniques. Bibliography.

2:416 Rubenberg, Cheryl A. *Israel and the American National Interest: A Critical Examination.* Urbana: University of Illinois Press, 1986. This work argues that the United States has shown an extraordinary amount of support for Israel, even though Israel has not served Washington's interests in the Middle East. The work focuses particularly on the partition of Palestine, the Sinai-Suez crisis of 1956, the Six Day War of 1967, the October War of 1973, the Camp David Accords, and the Israeli invasion and occupation of Lebanon in 1982.

2:417 Schoenbaum, David. *The United States and the State of Israel.* New York: Oxford University Press, 1993. This work explores American-Israeli relations since 1948, which the author characterizes as a product of often ambiguous, untidy, and fortuitous places, times, and circumstances. Three premises have defined and propelled the relationship—the moral and psychic legacy of the Holocaust, common belief in Judeo-Christian values, and the cold war. Bibliography.

Lebanon

2:418 Friedman, Thomas L. *From Beirut to Jerusalem.* Updated with a new chapter. New York: Doubleday, 1995. Written by a *New York Times* correspondent, this popular and informed history recounts U.S. relations with Israel and its Arab neighbors in the post–World War II era. First published in 1989.

2:419 Hiro, Dilip. *Lebanon: Fire and Embers: A History of the Lebanese Civil War.* New York: St. Martin's Press, 1993. This work examines the Lebanese civil war during the period 1975–1990. The main body of the book is divided into two sections: one centers on the period before the June 1982 Israeli invasion of Lebanon, the other on the period after the invasion. The limitations of Israeli-American efforts in Lebanon are explored in chapter 5. Bibliography.

Palestine

2:420 Neff, Donald. *Fallen Pillars: U.S. Policy towards Palestine and Israel since 1945.* Washington, DC: Institute for Palestine Studies, 1995. This work explores the changing nature of U.S. policy toward Palestine. The author contends that in the first half of the twentieth century, American policymakers debated whether the United States should support the formation of a Jewish homeland. In the second half of the century, they supported the formation of the Israeli state. The evolution of policy has brought the United States closer to Israel while pushing it further from the Palestinians. Bibliography.

2:421 Shadid, Mohammed K. *The United States and the Palestinians.* New York: St. Martin's Press, 1981. The author argues that U.S. policy toward the Palestinian people went through three stages of development. The United States dealt with the Palestinian people as refugees, participants in international terrorism, and, lastly, as a political entity. This work tells the story of America's long string of failures to resolve the Palestine issue, resulting from failures of both policy and understanding. American domination of the Middle East was accountable for the powder keg that threatened to destroy the entire region. Bibliography.

Saudi Arabia

2:422 Emerson, Steven. *The American House of Saud: The Secret Petrodollar Connection.* New York: F. Watts, 1985. This book attempts to show how Saudi lobbying initiatives have affected the political process in the United States. The author explores how Saudi Arabia and its corporate supporters have altered U.S. foreign policy, manipulated the American public, and produced an impact on American society.

2:423 Long, David E. *The United States and Saudi Arabia: Ambivalent Allies.* Boulder: Westview Press, 1985. American-Saudi relations have been characterized by ambivalence since their beginning over seventy-five years ago. The Arab-Israeli conflict, the superpower–small state dichotomy, the separation of cultures, traditions, and perceptions, and the division between buyer and seller of petroleum products have all added to the anomalies that have characterized the relationship between the two countries. This work explores the economic, commercial, military, and political issues that have complicated this bilateral relationship. Selected bibliography.

centuries and that commercial and strategic interests and political and religious expectations combined to form a distinctive policy that can be characterized as self-interested, pragmatic, and naïve. Extensive bibliography.

Yemen

2:424   Almadhagi, Ahmed Noman Kassim. *Yemen and the United States: A Study of a Small Power and Super-State Relationship, 1962–1994.* New York: I. B. Tauris Publishers, 1996. This work examines the U.S. relationship with the former Yemen Arab Republic during the period between the 1962 North Yemeni revolution and the unification of the two Yemens in May 1990 and with the reunited Yemen between 1990 and 1994. Bibliography.

2:425   Halliday, Fred. *Revolution and Foreign Policy: The Case of South Yemen, 1967–1987.* New York: Cambridge University Press, 1990. This study examines the foreign policy of South Yemen from the time of its independence from Great Britain in 1967 until 1987. It traces its relations with the west, including the United States, and with the Soviet Union and China. The work also includes analysis of South Yemen's conflicts with its neighbors, North Yemen, Saudi Arabia, and Oman. Bibliography.

Others

2:426   Howard, Harry N. *Turkey, the Straits, and U.S. Policy.* Baltimore: Johns Hopkins University Press, 1974. The former State Department official and university professor traces American interest in the Turkish Straits beginning in the nineteenth century, when U.S. sailing vessels began to pass regularly through the Bosphorus and Dardanelles. The "basic consistency" in American policy has been the continuing insistence on freedom for commercial traffic and keeping the Black Sea an open area. Extensive bibliography.

2:427   Palmer, Michael A. *Guardians of the Gulf: A History of America's Expanding Role in the Persian Gulf, 1833–1992.* New York: Free Press, 1992. The author argues that American involvement in the Persian Gulf has developed over the course of two

Native Americans

2:428   Bolt, Christine. *American Indian Policy and American Reform: Case Studies of the Campaign to Assimilate the American Indians.* Boston: Allen and Unwin, 1987. Through a series of case studies, this book explores important aspects of Indian policy and reform in the context of ethnic conflict and the American reform tradition. Organized into two sections, it covers the period from colonial times to the 1970s. Bibliography.

2:429   Gallay, Alan, ed. *Colonial Wars of North America, 1512–1763: An Encyclopedia.* This is a useful reference guide for those interested in the study of Native Americans during the colonial period. The book provides reference citations on a variety of historical issues, peoples, and events, and includes nearly 700 essays on such topics as forts, locales, conflicts, treaties, warfare, and intercultural relationships. Bibliographic references are found throughout the volume (1:187).

2:430   Nobles, Gregory H. *American Frontiers: Cultural Encounters and Continental Conquest.* New York: Hill and Wang, 1997. This is a work of historical synthesis, bringing together the frontier histories of the east and west. This book emphasizes the role of the imperial or national governments in promoting state-planned programs of expansion and settlement. This work covers European, American, and Native American relations over a period of four centuries. Excellent bibliographical essay.

2:431   Prucha, Francis Paul. *The Great Father: The United States Government and the American Indians.* 2 vols. Lincoln: University of Nebraska Press, 1984. This two-volume work surveys the course of U.S. Indian policy development and implementation from the American revolution to the 1980s. The same press also published an abridged edition in 1986. Appendices and substantial bibliographical essay.

2:432   Weeks, Philip. *Farewell, My Nation: The American Indian and the United States, 1820–1890.* Arlington Heights, IL: Harlan Davidson, 1990. This book is an excellent introduction to the topic. It explores the variety of policies that the federal government pursued in search of a lasting solution to the Indian during the period 1820–1890. During this period the U.S. federal government pursued three fundamental policies: separation, concentration, and Americanization. Very good bibliographical essay.

3

The Seventeenth and Eighteenth Centuries before the Revolution

Contributing Editor
ROGER H. BROWN
American University

With the Assistance of
JAMES HUSTON
Library of Congress
LAWRENCE S. KAPLAN
Kent State University
ALISON OLSON
University of Maryland, College Park

Contents

Introduction

Except for a few pre-1983 references of exceptional, continuing utility, this chapter identifies recent scholarly works in the field of colonial and imperial foreign relations published in the last two decades. Owing to major shifts of emphasis within the field and the appearance of a large corpus of new work, I decided that this chapter should identify important new work rather than repeat older references noted in the 1983 *Guide.* Those interested in older publications or in a full roster of old and new references are advised to consult the 1983 *Guide* in conjunction with this chapter.

My criteria for inclusion in current listings are somewhat broader than those of the 1983 *Guide.* They call for important scholarly publications that bear on, or have implications for, colonial foreign relations, broadly conceived, meaning especially the formal and informal dealings among different governments and peoples, and emphasizing, but not limited to, diplomacy and war. Most of the categories are similar to those used in the 1983 *Guide,* but, in response to new trends in scholarship, my chapter includes sections on "British Diplomatic History"; "Military and Naval Action and Affairs"; "Growth of Colonial Statecraft: Transatlantic Lobbies and Politicians"; "Indian-White Relations and Diplomacy"; "Slave Trade and Slavery"; and "British-American Cultural Relations and Attitudes."

Published Primary Sources

3:1   Abbot, W. W., and Dorothy Twohig, with Philander D. Chase, Beverly H. Runge, and Frederick Hall Schmidt, eds. *The Papers of George Washington: Colonial Series.* Vol. 1–10. Charlottesville: University of Virginia Press, 1983–1995. During the Seven Years War, the young man George Washington was actively engaged in various military roles including service as an agent to warn the French out of Ohio, an officer at Braddock's defeat, and a colonel of a Virginia regiment. Later he was increasingly concerned about the direction of British imperial policy toward the colonies. This expertly edited collection of Washington's papers is a valuable source for study of Virginia's role in the Seven Years War, relations between whites and Indians, and colonial attitudes toward British and colonial troops, Indians, the French, and the British government.

3:2   Bailyn, Bernard, with Jane N. Garrett, eds. *Pamphlets of the American Revolution, 1750–1776.* Cambridge, MA: Belknap Press of Harvard University Press, 1965. The first of four projected volumes of pamphlets relating to the Anglo-American revolutionary struggle, this volume provides the text of selected pamphlets published between 1750 and 1765. The project includes bibliographical references and an index of future volumes. The author's introduction forms the basis for his important *Ideological Origins of the American Revolution* (1967) (3:262).

3:3   Boehm, Randolph, Linda Womaski, Great Britain. Public Record Office, Great Britain. Colonial Office and Library of Congress. Manuscript Division. *Records of the British Colonial Office, Class 5.* Microfilm. Frederick, MD: University Publications of America, 1983. The materials reproduced in this 5-part, 53-reel microfilm project have been selected from Records of the British Colonial Office transcripts and microforms in the Manuscript Reading Room of the Library of Congress. Part 1, "Westward Expansion," includes Indian-white relations and diplomacy, Anglo-French and Anglo-Spanish relations, and reports of royal governors. Part 2, "The Board of Trade, 1660–1782," includes instructions to imperial officials, petitions and letters, and reports on conditions in the colonies. Part 3, "The French and Indian War, 1754–1763," includes military correspondence and reports, colonial contributions to the war, and reports and correspondence relating to the French, Spanish, and Indians. Part 4, "Royal Instructions and Commissions to Colonial Officials, 1702–1784," has instructions to royal governors of British mainland and West Indian colonies. Part 5, "The American Revolution, 1772–1784," includes military correspondence of General Thomas Gage and reports and correspondence among British ministerial officials regarding America. Printed guides to these series are available from University Publications of America. A more complete set of Colonial Office 5 materials is available, with a finding aid, on 235 microfilm reels in the Manuscript Reading Room of the Library of Congress.

3:4   Bonwick, Colin, and Thomas R. Adams. *British Pamphlets Relating to the American Revolution.* Microfilm. East Ardsley, Wakefield, Yorkshire: Microform Ltd., 1982. This project makes available, on forty-nine microfilm reels, 1,161 pamphlets, broadsides, and controversial books published in Great Britain between 1764 and 1783 and related to the American revolution. Selections are made from the listings in Thomas R. Adams, *The American Controversy: A Bibliographical Study of the British Pamphlets about the American Disputes, 1764–1783* (1980) (3:28). A guide, published in 1982 under the same title, supplies keys to the films.

3:5   Boyd, Julian P., and Robert J. Taylor, eds. *The Susquehannah Company Papers.* 11 vols. Ithaca: Cornell University Press for Wyoming Historical and Geological Society, Wilkes-Barre, PA, 1931–1971. By claiming jurisdiction over and establishing settlements in the Wyoming Valley of northeastern Pennsylvania in the 1750s and 1760s, the Connecticut-based Susquehannah Land Company touched off a dangerous conflict among rival groups of claimants and settlers, Iroquois and Delaware Indians, two colonial governments, the British crown, and eventually the Continental Congress. Jurisdiction and ownership were not resolved until after the revolution. These documents illustrate the intercolonial, interracial, and imperial dimensions of this jurisdictional property dispute.

3:6   Davenport, Frances Gardiner, and Charles O. Paullin, eds. *European Treaties Bearing on the History of the United States and Its Dependencies.* 4 vols. Washington, DC: Carnegie Institution of Washington, 1917–1937. This is a useful collection of European treaties, agreements, truces, papal bulls, contracts, and other official diplomatic documents that relate to U.S. colonial history. Although a few documents involve colonial signatories, most concern agreements between and among the major powers of Europe. Each document is preceded by an editor's introduction and a brief bibliography; foreign-language texts are in both the original and English. Chronological coverage is as follows: Vol. 1. To 1648; 2. 1680–1697; 3. 1716–1815; 4. 1716–1815.

3:7   Donnan, Elizabeth, ed. *Documents Illustrative of the History of the Slave Trade to America.* 4 vols. Washington, DC: Carnegie Institution of Washington, 1930–1935. This four-volume collection of nearly 1,300 documents is selective but provides broad and varied coverage illustrating the Atlantic slave trade to the thirteen colonies, the West Indies, and Spanish America. Among the themes illustrated are European trade rivalries on the west coast of Africa; the Anglo-French contest for control of the trade; the *assiento* in European diplomacy; and the increasing involvement of colonial merchants and planters in the Atlantic slave trade. Printed and manuscript sources from depositories in Great Britain, Spain, and the United States have been utilized. Vol. I. 1441–1700. II. The eighteenth century. III. New England and the middle colonies. IV. The border colonies and the southern colonies.

3:8   Dunn, Richard S., and Mary Maples Dunn, with Richard A. Ryerson, Scott M. Wilds, and Jean R. Soderlund, eds. *The Papers of William Penn.* 5 vols. Philadelphia: University of Pennsylvania Press, 1981. Impeccably edited and introduced, these volumes provide nearly 700 documents relating to William Penn, his life as a Quaker, and his Pennsylvania proprietary colony. The items illustrate such subjects as Penn's negotiations for a royal charter, dealings with the Delaware Indians, and boundary disputes with Lord Baltimore. In addition, they cover his lobbying in London to save his colony, action against piracy, illegal trade, customs evasions, and dealings with neighboring colonies over boundary and other issues. The five volumes include bibliographies and indexes and are arranged as follows: v. 1, 1644–1679; v. 2, 1680–1684; v. 3, 1685–1700; v. 4, 1701–1718; and v. 5, William Penn's Published Writings, 1660–1726: An Interpretive Bibliography. The William Penn papers, originally filmed by the Historical Society of Pennsylvania, are commercially available on microfilm from Bell and Howell, University Microfilms International.

3:9   Great Britain. Board of Trade. *Journals of the Commissioners for Trade and Plantations . . . Preserved in the Public Record Office.* Vol. 1–14. London: H. M. Stationery Office, 1920–1938. The Board of Trade played an important advisory role in administrative and political relations between the American colonies and London. The published journals of the Board of Trade provide insight into imperial views and policies and the efforts of colonial and English lobbyists, claimants, and petitioners to influence the imperial government. Volumes 1–148 of the Board of Trade papers are also available on microfilm in the Manuscript Reading Room of the Library of Congress.

3:10   Great Britain. Parliament, Richard C. Simmons, and Peter D. G. Thomas, eds. *Proceedings and Debates of the British Parliaments Respecting North America 1754–1783.* 5 vols. to date. Millwood, NY: Kraus International Publications, 1982–. When completed, this series will provide an authoritative compilation of known primary texts of debates in British Parliaments, regarding North America, from 1754 to 1783. The editors have included material from various sources including the official printed journals of the two houses of Parliament, diaries, correspondence, and reports of debates in contemporary magazines, pamphlets, and newspapers. Each volume includes a bibliography and index. To date, the following have been published: v. 1. 1754–1764; v. 2. 1765–1768; v. 3. 1768–1773; v. 4. January to May, 1774; v. 5. June 1774 to March 1775.

3:11   Great Britain. Parliament, and Leo F. Stock, eds. *Proceedings and Debates of the British Parliaments Respecting North America.* 4 vols. Washington, DC: Carnegie Institution of Washington, 1924–1937. This compilation of parliamentary debates relating to North America between 1600 and 1740 draws on parliamentary journals and other less official sources where debate was recorded. Parliamentary debate ranged widely and covered many subjects including North American colonial trade and commerce, the navigation acts, and England's commercial and colonial competition with Spain, the Netherlands, and France. The volumes cover the following years: v. 1. 1542–1688; v. 2. 1688–1702: v. 3. 1702–1727; v. 4. 1728–1739.

3:12   Great Britain. Privy Council, William Lawson Grant, James Munro, and Almeric William FitzRoy, eds. *Acts of the Privy Council of England. Colonial Series.* 6 vols. London: His Majesty's Stationery Office, 1908–1912. The Privy Council advised the crown and exercised formal authority over the colonies until the revolution. This published collection makes available the manuscript record of the council's many decisions on colonial matters including review of colonial laws and judicial decisions, receipt of petitions from colonial agents, referrals to the

Board of Trade, and approval of instructions to colonial governors. The collection is also commercially available on microfiche from Brookhaven Press.

3:13   Greene, Jack P., ed. *Colonies to Nation: 1763–1789.* New York: McGraw-Hill, 1975. Reprint 1975 (Norton). A highly useful one-volume assemblage of sources relating to the history of the American revolution, this collection makes accessible a wide range of important documents with expert editorial comment. Nearly half is devoted to documents relating to the genesis of the revolution and includes major British imperial initiatives as well as examples of colonial protest and resistance.

3:14   _____. *Settlements to Society: 1584–1763.* New York: McGraw-Hill, 1966. Reprint 1975 (Norton). The best one-volume assemblage of sources relating to the history of colonial America, this collection makes accessible a wide selection of documents with expert editorial comment. Many of the documents deal with internal colonial developments, but included also are documents relating to foreign relations including royal charters, the Navigation Acts, British imperial reforms, Indian relations, intercolonial affairs, maritime commerce, and colonists' views of themselves as British citizens.

3:15   Hall, Michael G., Lawrence H. Leder, and Michael G. Kammen, eds. *The Glorious Revolution in America: Documents on the Colonial Crisis of 1689.* Chapel Hill: University of North Carolina Press for the Institute of Early American History and Culture, 1964. The Glorious Revolution in England touched off a series of mini-revolutions in colonial Massachusetts, New York, and Maryland that overturned the Dominion of New England and led to a new relationship with the metropolitan center. These documents, expertly introduced and selected, illuminate the character of these upheavals and of the new imperial relationship that endured until the American revolution.

3:16   Jennings, Francis, and William N. Fenton, with Mary A. Druke and David R. Miller. *Iroquois Indians: A Documentary History of the Diplomacy of the Six Nations and Their League.* Microfilm. Woodbridge, CT: Research Publications, 1984. Assembled from a wide variety of depositories and sources, this collection of reports, letters, treaties, and other written materials relating to the foreign relations of the Six Nations forms a definitive archive of Iroquoian diplomacy. Presented in fifty microfilm reels, with an introduction by Mary A. Druke, the material is arranged chronologically from 1613 to the 1980s with most from the eighteenth century. A printed guide keys the films: *Iroquois Indians: A Documentary History of the Diplomacy of the Six Nations and Their League: Guide to the Microfilm Collection* (1985).

3:17   Jensen, Merrill, ed. *American Colonial Documents to 1776.* Vol. 9. New York: Oxford University Press, 1955. This useful volume presents a reliable, comprehensive collection of important documents related to the internal development of the American mainland colonies, their relations with Great Britain, and the genesis of the American revolution. The collection does not include documents that pertain to intercolonial relations or to relations between the colonies and the French, Spanish, or Indians. The volume includes an expert historical overview and a select bibliography.

3:18   Kavenagh, W. Keith, ed. *Foundations of Colonial America: A Documentary History.* 3 vols. New York: Chelsea House, 1973. Reprint 1983 (Chelsea House). This is a comprehensive collection of basic documents relating to the chartering, founding, and internal development of the thirteen North American mainland colonies from 1606 to 1761. Although the documents focus more on the institutional, social, and economic development of the New England, middle, and southern colonies than on foreign and intercolonial relations, the volumes include the Navigation Acts and other acts of Parliament relating to the colonies, royal proclamations, the Albany Plan of Union, and the proceedings of the Albany congress in 1754. The volumes are cumulatively indexed and include extensive references to other document collections. Foreword by Richard B. Morris.

3:19   Labaree, Leonard Woods, ed. *Royal Instructions to British Colonial Governors, 1670–1776.* 2 vols. New York: D. Appleton-Century Company, 1935. This important collection makes available selected instructions to British royal governors in colonial North America between 1670 and the American revolution. Approved by the Privy Council, the instructions were drafted by the Board of Trade, which often consulted colonial agents, merchants, and other government officials. The instructions are an important source for British colonial policy and imperial relations with the colonies, and deal not only with legislative, financial, military, and naval matters, but Indians, trade, and relations with other colonies and nearby French and Spanish colonies. The selections have been chosen for their topical representativeness; for a complete listing of instructions see Charles M. Andrews, "List of Commissions, Instructions, and Additional Instructions Issued to the Royal Governors and Others in America," *The Annual Report of the American Historical Association for the Year 1911,* pp. 393–528.

3:20   Labaree, Leonard Woods, Whitfield J. Bell, Jr., William B. Willcox, Claude-Anne Lopez, and Barbara B. Oberg, eds. *The Papers of Benjamin Franklin.* 35 vols. to date. New Haven: Yale University Press, 1959–. This magisterial edition of Franklin's private and public writings now extends to 1781. Included in the volumes for the 1760s and 1770s is Franklin's extensive correspondence in his first two missions to London. While serving as agent for Pennsylvania during the second mission, Franklin met with George Grenville about the proposed Stamp and Quartering Acts, unsuccessfully arguing against their enactment. Vols. 15–26 are edited by W. B. Willcox; vol. 27 by Claude-Anne Lopez; and vols. 28–34 by Barbara B. Oberg. The volumes include bibliographical references and indexes.

3:21   Lincoln, Charles Henry, ed. *Correspondence of William Shirley, Governor of Massachusetts and Military Commander in America, 1731–1760.* 2 vols. New York: Macmillan Company, 1912. Reprint 1974 (AMS Press). The England-born William Shirley was royal governor of colonial Massachusetts during King George's War and the early years of the Seven Years War, playing major roles in organizing the successful expedition against French-held Louisbourg (1745) and as temporary supreme commander of British land forces after Braddock's defeat (1755–1756). Although also an Anglo-American politician, his correspondence emphasizes his military activities. Among the subjects covered are efforts to raise colonial troops and supplies, his correspondence with Sir William Johnson about Indian negotiations, and his response to the popular anti-impressment riots in Boston (1747).

3:22 O'Callaghan, E. B., ed. *The Documentary History of the State of New-York.* Vol. 1–4. Albany: Weed Parsons & Co., Public Printers, 1850–1851. Although a miscellaneous hodgepodge of various sources, these volumes preserve and make available many otherwise inaccessible or destroyed primary documents, including papers relating to the Iroquois and other Indians, the French on the Canada–New York frontier, the Anglo-Dutch wars, Leisler's Rebellion, the Palatine Germans, and the Albany conference of 1754. The entire collection is available on microfilm from Bell and Howell, Wooster, Ohio.

3:23 Quinn, David B., with Alison M. Quinn and Susan Hillier, eds. *New American World: A Documentary History of North America to 1612.* 5 vols. New York: Arno Press, 1979. These five volumes provide an expert, comprehensive collection of documents relating to European discovery, exploration, colonization, and rivalry in North America to 1612. Documents relate to Viking, Spanish, Portuguese, French, Dutch, and English enterprise in North America, ending with the establishment of English Virginia and Spanish New Mexico. Expert commentary, references, and an extensive bibliography and index in volume 5 add further value. The volumes include the following topics: 1. America from concept to discovery; early exploration of North America. 2. Major Spanish searches in earlier North America; the Franco-Spanish clash in Florida; the beginning of Spanish Florida. 3. English plans for North America; the Roanoke voyages; New England ventures. 4. Newfoundland from fishery to colony; Northwest Passage searches. 5. The extension of settlement in Florida, Virginia, and the Spanish southwest.

3:24 Sheridan, Eugene R., ed. *The Papers of Lewis Morris.* Collections of the New Jersey Historical Society. 3 vols. Newark: New Jersey Historical Society, 1991–1993. Lewis Morris was a wealthy Anglo-American politician who held high offices in the New York and New Jersey colonial governments. His papers provide an important source for colonial domestic politics but also throw light on colonial-imperial relations.

3:25 Van Horne, John C., and George Reese, eds. *The Letter Book of James Abercromby, Colonial Agent 1751–1773.* Richmond: Virginia State Library and Archives, 1991. James Abercromby's letter book is a valuable collection of official and semiofficial documents written by a Scottish barrister and member of Parliament who served as colonial agent for North Carolina and Virginia. An ardent advocate of supreme imperial administration, Abercromby "worked tirelessly" to represent his clients' interests before the Board of Trade, the Privy Council, the Treasury, and the principal officers of state. This publication affords insight into the quasi-diplomatic nature and workings of the colonial agency.

3:26 Vaughan, Alden T., ed. *Early American Indian Documents: Treaties, and Laws, 1607–1789.* 18 vols. to date. Washington, DC: University Publications of America, 1979–. These volumes are an indispensable source for the study of colonial-Indian relations and diplomacy. Organized chronologically by colony, each volume presents the texts of treaties, reports of council meetings, colonial laws, proclamations, minutes, contemporary correspondence, and other Indian-related published and unpublished documents. Under the general editorship of Alden T. Vaughan, they have been compiled and edited by specialists and include valuable general and chapter introductions and brief bibliographies. Volumes published to date include: v. 1, Pennsylvania and Delaware Treaties, 1629–1737, edited by Donald H. Kent; v. 2, Pennsylvania Treaties, 1737–1756, edited by Kent; v. 4, Virginia Treaties, 1607–1722, edited by W. Stitt Robinson; v. 5, Virginia Treaties, 1723–1775, edited by Robinson; v. 6, Maryland Treaties, 1762–1775, edited by Robinson; v. 7, New York and New Jersey Treaties, 1609–1682, edited by Barbara Graymont; v. 8, New York and New Jersey Treaties, 1683–1713, edited by Graymont; v. 9, New York and New Jersey Treaties, 1714–1753, edited by Graymont; v. 11, Georgia Treaties, 1733–1763, edited by John T. Juricek; v. 15, Maryland and Maryland Laws, edited by Vaughan and Deborah A. Rosen; v. 16, Carolina and Georgia Laws, edited by Vaughan and Rosen; and v. 18, Revolution and Confederation, edited by Colin G. Calloway. Volumes are planned for all thirteen mainland colonies; volumes 3, 10, 12, 13, 14, 17 are still to be published. Volumes 5–6 were published by University Publications of America at Frederick, MD; volumes 8, 9, 15, 16, and 18 were published at Bethesda, MD.

Research Aids and Bibliographies

3:27   *Guide to Microforms in Print: Author/ Title; Guide to Microforms in Print: Subject.* 2 vols. Munich: K. G. Sauer, 1999. This annually published guide lists microform collections currently in print and available commercially. Among items associated with colonial foreign relations and identified by *Microforms Guide* as commercially available on film are the following manuscript collections: Sir Jeffrey Amherst, Jonathan Belcher, William Blathwayt, Iroquois Indians, Louisbourg, Thomas Penn, William Penn, and William Pepperell; also, Colonial Office records, class 5, Colonial Office records on Early American history and affairs, and papers of the United Society for the Propagation of the Gospel. The listings for the 1999 *Microforms Guide* are not entirely complete: e.g., the papers of George Grenville, Duke of Newcastle, and Lord North, housed in the British Library, on microfilm in the Manuscript Reading Room of the Library of Congress, and commercially available from Harvester Press, U.K., are not listed. Many films are also available in the Manuscript Reading Room of the Library of Congress and in the microform reading rooms of certain research libraries such as the Firestone Library at Princeton.

3:28   Adams, Thomas R., ed. *The American Controversy: A Bibliographical Study of the British Pamphlets about the American Disputes, 1764–1783.* 2 vols. Providence, RI: Brown University Press, 1980. This bibliography lists some 1,400 titles of pamphlets, broadsides, and controversial books published in Great Britain between 1764 and 1783 that relate to controversies involving the American colonies. The titles reflect controversies over taxation, trade, administration, and other issues and include American and continental titles later reprinted in Great Britain. The work identifies locations of each title; most titles can be found in the microfilm *British Pamphlets Relating to the American Revolution, 1764–1783* (Wakefield, West Yorkshire, UK: Microform Imaging Ltd., 1982).

3:29   _____. *American Independence: The Growth of an Idea: A Bibliographic Study of the American Political Pamphlets Printed between 1764 and 1776 Dealing with the Dispute between Great Britain and Her Colonies.* Providence, RI: Brown University Press, 1965. Reprint 1980 (Jenkins and Reese). This study presents a selective list of American political pamphlets, published between 1764 and 1776, relating to issues or events connected to the coming of the revolution and independence. Depository locations of each item are identified. Microfiche copies of these same pamphlets may be found in the monumental collection, *Early American Imprints,* first series, published by the Readex Corporation in cooperation with the American Antiquarian Society. Each pamphlet in *Early American Imprints,* in turn, can be located through the numbering system established in Charles Evans, *American Bibliography: A Chronological Dictionary of All Books, Pamphlets and Periodical Publications Printed in the United States of America, 1639–1800* (Chicago: privately printed for the author by Blakely Press, 14 vols., 1903–1959). These identification numbers can be more conveniently located through the index in Clifford Kenyon Shipton, James E. Mooney, and Roger P. Bristol, eds., *National Index of American Imprints through 1800: The Short-Title Evans* (Wooster, MA: American Antiquarian Society, 2 vols., 1969).

3:30   American Historical Association. *Writings on American History: 1902–1990.* Edited by Grace Gardner Griffin, James J. Dougherty, and James R. Masterson. Washington, DC, and Millwood, NY: American Historical Association, Kraus-Thomson, and KTO Press, 1904–1990. Published until 1990 in annual and occasionally longer cumulations, these volumes have been a standard research tool. Early volumes were compiled by Grace Gardner Griffin, later volumes by James J. Dougherty and James R. Masterson. Works relating to colonial foreign relations are found in sections arranged by chronology, by geographic region, and by diplomatic history, foreign policy, and foreign relations. A cumulative *Index to the Writings on American History, 1902–1940,* David M. Matteson, editor, was published in 1956. The first series of *Writings on American History* included both books and articles and, except for 1904–1905 and 1941–1947, covered each year through 1961 (1:19). For the years 1962 and after, a second series was issued as *Writings on American History: A Subject Bibliography of Articles* (1962–1973, 1989–1990), James M. Dougherty, compiler, and *Writings on American History, 1962–1973: A Subject Bibliography of Books and Monographs Based on a Compilation by James R. Masterson* (1:19).

3:31   Ammerman, David L., and Philip D. Morgan, eds. *Books about Early America: 2001 Titles.* Williamsburg: Institute of Early American History and Culture, 1989. This is a selective list of 2,001 important recent titles in the field of early American history from the colonial period to 1815. It takes a broad perspective and includes both traditional and nontraditional titles. Besides narrative works in the colonial and revolution periods, titles in such thematic categories as politics and society, African-Americans and slavery, Indians, imperial relations, military studies, and cultural works are listed as well as important reference works, biographies, and source collections.

3:32   Andrews, Charles M., ed. *Guide to the Materials for American History, to 1783, in the Public Record Office of Great Britain.* 2 vols. Washington, DC: Carnegie Institution of Washington, 1912–1914. An essential guide to America-related manuscripts in London's Public Record Office, this lists a vast array of materials relating to the colonial and revolutionary periods. Subjects range from colonial governors' reports on conditions in the colonies, to Board of Trade letters about relations with French and Dutch settlements, to British treasury lists of gift expenditures, to various Indian peoples. Materials are organized according to British government civil and military administrative units and pertain both to relations between Britain and the American colonies and to Britain and Europe.

3:33   _____. "List of Commissions, Instructions, and Additional Instructions Issued to the Royal Governors and Others in America." In *The Annual Report of the American Historical Association for the Year 1911* 1: 393–528. Washington, DC: American Historical Association, 1913. This is a comprehensive list of commissions, instructions, circular instructions, and additional instructions issued to governors of royal colonies, proprietary colonies, and corporate colonies from 1670 through the revolution. Arranged by colony and by governor, the list briefly identifies each document, notes its most important contents, and cites its location. Royal (and occasion-

ally proprietary) and corporate governors received official instruction from the Privy Council, but the list includes instructions from proprietors to their governors as well. These instructions throw light on many aspects of the British government's dealings with the colonies including trade, politics, internal economic affairs, constitutional issues, and relations with Indian peoples and with the colonial possessions of the European powers.

3:34   Andrews, Charles M., and Frances Gardiner Davenport, eds. *Guide to the Manuscript Materials for the History of the United States to 1783, in the British Museum, in Minor London Archives, and in the Libraries of Oxford and Cambridge.* Washington, DC: Carnegie Institution of Washington, 1908. This is an indispensable guide to manuscript materials relating to colonial America held by the British Museum, the libraries of Oxford and Cambridge, and other smaller libraries such as the House of Lords and Fulham Palace. Subjects range widely and relate to colonial political, diplomatic, economic, missionary, military, and Indian affairs.

3:35   Beers, Henry Putney, ed. *Bibliographies in American History, 1942–1978: Guide to Materials for Research.* 2 vols. Woodbridge, CT: Research Publications, 1982. This compilation carries the author's 1942 edition forward to 1978. The categories conform to the same format as those in the 1942 (rev. in 1959) edition (*Bibliographies in American History: Guide to Materials for Research* [3:36]).

3:36   _____. *Bibliographies in American History: Guide to Materials for Research.* Rev. ed. Paterson, NJ: Pageant Books, 1959. Although outdated, this bibliography of bibliographies still has utility for the history of colonial foreign relations. Chapter 2 on the Colonial, Revolution, and Confederation periods lists bibliographies of primary and secondary sources relating to the Spanish, French, and English in North America and to the several mainland colonies. First published in 1942.

3:37   _____. *The French & British in the Old Northwest: A Bibliographical Guide to Archive and Manuscript Sources.* Detroit: Wayne State University Press, 1964. This is a useful guide to bibliographic and unpublished and published source materials (including document reproductions from foreign archives) relating to the French and British regimes in the Old Northwest. Listings include Indian-white relations, the fur trade, exploration, military and diplomatic affairs, and missionaries.

3:38 _____. *French and Spanish Records of Louisiana: A Bibliographical Guide to Archive and Manuscript Sources.* Baton Rouge: Louisiana State University Press, 1989. This is a comprehensive listing of unpublished and published sources relating to colonial Louisiana under French and Spanish ownership. Many citations refer to Indian-white relations, exploration, military affairs, and diplomatic relations with Great Britain, the United States, Spain, and France.

3:39 _____. *The French in North America: A Bibliographical Guide to French Archives, Reproductions, and Research Missions.* Baton Rouge: Louisiana State University Press, 1957. This descriptive guide to primary source materials relating to the French in Canada, Louisiana, and the Old Northwest identifies the holdings of archives located mainly in France but also in the United States and Canada. Especially useful is the identification of document compilations, transcripts, and reproductions in the United States and Canada generated by researchers in French archives.

3:40 _____. *Spanish and Mexican Records of the American Southwest: A Bibliographical Guide to Archive and Manuscript Sources.* Tucson: University of Arizona Press, 1979. Emphasizing later records from the post-Spanish Mexican era in the southwest and California, this guide also identifies unpublished and published source materials and their location from the earlier Spanish era. Coverage includes correspondence of Spanish officials, Indian-white relations, military affairs, and missions and missionaries.

3:41 Coker, William S., and Jack D. L. Holmes. "Sources for the History of the Spanish Borderlands." *Florida Historical Quarterly* 49 (April 1971): 380–93. This article describes the abundance of source materials—published, microcopied, and manuscript—located in Spain, France, and the United States, relating particularly to Spanish Florida and Spanish Louisiana.

3:42 Crick, B. R., and Miriam Alman, eds. *A Guide to Manuscripts Relating to America in Great Britain and Ireland.* London: Oxford University Press for the British Association for American Studies, 1961. This important reference identifies and describes manuscript holdings that relate to colonial America in numerous archives, libraries, and other depositories in Great Britain and Ireland. Including many public and private county and local depositories, the work describes in detail the important holdings relating to colonial America in the Public Record Office and British Library. Raimo, *A Guide to Manuscripts Relating to America in Great Britain and Ireland: A Revision of the Guide Edited in 1961 by B. R. Crick and Miriam Alman* (1979) (3:53) should also be consulted.

3:43 Davies, Godfrey, and Mary Frear Keeler, eds. *Bibliography of British History: Stuart Period, 1603–1714.* 2d ed. Oxford: Clarendon Press, 1970. A highly detailed, comprehensive bibliography of Stuart England, this work includes sections on England's foreign relations (including primary and secondary sources) and on the overseas colonies. First published in 1928.

3:44 Gallay, Alan, ed. *Colonial Wars of North America, 1512–1763: An Encyclopedia.* More than a strictly military history reference, this encyclopedia provides nearly 700 essays by 135 specialists on a broad variety of traditional and nontraditional subjects ranging in time from the Spanish conquistadors to Pontiac's 1763 war, and in space from the Atlantic coast to the Spanish southwest and Russian Alaska. Essays and bibliographical references concern groups, colonies, individuals, forts, locales, conflicts, treaties, and intercultural relationships (1:187).

3:45 Gephart, Ronald M., ed. *Revolutionary America, 1763–1789: A Bibliography.* 2 vols. Washington, DC: Library of Congress, 1984. Although confined to the era of the revolution, this bibliography of research aids and of primary and secondary sources is a gold mine, with many useful references having a bearing on foreign relations. Included are sections on the British empire (including the Old Colonial System and colonial agents), the colonies on the eve of revolution (including political ideology and constitutional thought), the genesis of the revolution, relations with Indians, and the west.

3:46 Gipson, Lawrence Henry. *The British Empire before the American Revolution. Vol. 14: A*

Bibliographical Guide to the History of the British Empire, 1748–1776. New York: Alfred A. Knopf, 1968. Comprehensive and judicious, this work identifies published primary and secondary works relating to mid-eighteenth-century Britain and its worldwide possessions. Diplomatic, military, and naval sources are included, with especially helpful listings on the trans-Appalachian west, Indian relations, and French and Spanish rivalry.

3:47 _____. *The British Empire before the American Revolution. Vol. 15: A Guide to Manuscripts Relating to the History of the British Empire, 1748–1776.* New York: Alfred A. Knopf, 1970. This work presents a highly useful descriptive guide to manuscripts relating to Britain and its global possessions in the period 1748–1776. The work identifies the manuscript holdings of depositories in England and Scotland, France, Spain, and the United States on a variety of subjects including diplomatic, naval, military, and Indian affairs.

3:48 Greene, Jack P., with Edward C. Papenfuse, Jr., comps. *The American Colonies in the Eighteenth Century.* New York: Appleton-Century Crofts, 1969. This older but still useful bibliography includes sections on European imperial rivalries, diplomatic relations, relations between Britain and the mainland colonies, colonial agents, English colonial policy and administration, European and colonial military and naval conflict, and Indian-white relations.

3:49 Griffin, Grace Gardner, ed. *A Guide to Manuscripts Relating to American History in British Depositories Reproduced for the Division of Manuscripts in the Library of Congress.* Washington, DC: Library of Congress, 1946. This guide outlines the extensive collection of transcripts and photocopied documents relating to British-American relations from the seventeenth to the twentieth centuries copied from originals in various British depositories and located in the Manuscript Division of the Library of Congress. The bulk of these copied materials are from the eighteenth century. Especially useful are transcribed and photocopied documents from the Colonial Office 5 series, the Board of Trade papers, the Lord Jeffrey Amherst papers, and the Privy Council Office papers in the Public Record Office, London; from the Newcastle, Grenville, and North papers in the British Museum; and from the papers of the

United Society for the Propagation of the Gospel in Foreign Parts in Lambeth Palace. Under the library's copying program, new material has been added since the publication of Griffin's *Guide*. Listings of new acquisitions are to be found in the folder located in the Manuscript Division labeled "Foreign Copying Program: Great Britain" and in the file drawers containing individual accession folders.

3:50 McCusker, John J. "New Guides to Primary Sources on the History of Early British America." *William and Mary Quarterly* 3d ser. 41 (April 1984): 277–95. This is an invaluable listing, updating, and description of new and old guides to primary sources on the history of British America emphasizing manuscript sources in British and European repositories. Beginning with the early Carnegie Institution manuals, McCusker identifies many newer guides, manuals, calendars, and indexes to the manuscript and microform holdings of British, French, and other European repositories as well as archives, libraries, and historical societies in the United States and Canada. Also identified are guides to newspapers and other early printed records. The same essay, updated and revised again, appears in McCusker, *Essays in the Economic History of the Atlantic World* (New York: Routledge, 1997).

3:51 Pargellis, Stanley, and D. J. Medley, eds. *Bibliography of British History: The Eighteenth Century, 1714–1789.* Oxford: Oxford University Press, 1951. Reprint 1971 (Rowman and Littlefield). This is a splendid bibliography of primary, secondary, and bibliographic sources relating to eighteenth-century British history, broadly construed, with comprehensive sections listing works on British foreign affairs and diplomacy, wars, and relations with Britain's overseas colonies. The last includes annotated listings of works on British colonial policy and administration, the North American mainland colonies, Indians, French and British Canada, the West Indies, Florida, and Africa.

3:52 Raimo, John W., ed. *Biographical Directory of American Colonial and Revolutionary Governors, 1607–1789.* Westport, CT: Meckler Books, 1980. This biographical directory of some 370 colonial and revolutionary governors, lieutenant governors, and acting governors provides basic personal information but little political or diplomatic analysis or interpretation. Brief bibliographies list relevant primary and secondary references at each entry.

3:53 _____. *A Guide to Manuscripts Relating to America in Great Britain and Ireland: A Revision of the Guide Edited in 1961 by B. R. Crick and Miriam Alman.* Westport, CT: Meckler Books for the British Association for American Studies, 1979. The most recent update and revision of the highly important 1961 Crick and Alman, *A Guide to Manuscripts Relating to America* (3:42), this reference includes newly accessioned material organized according to county and local location. Unless they have been recently acquired, the guide refers to, but does not describe, the extensive manuscript holdings deposited in the Public Record Office and British Museum. For this, see the 1961 Crick and Alman *Guide* and Andrews, *Guide to the Materials for American History, to 1783, in the Public Record Office of Great Britain* (1912–1914) (3:32).

3:54 Read, Conyers, ed. *Bibliography of British History: Tudor Period, 1485–1603.* 2d ed. Oxford: Oxford University Press, 1959. This comprehensive bibliography focuses on internal aspects of Tudor England but includes sections on foreign affairs, discovery, and early colonization. First published in 1933.

3:55 Vaughan, Alden T., ed. *The American Colonies in the Seventeenth Century.* New York: Appleton-Century Crofts, 1971. Emphasizing the founding and early development of Britain's mainland colonies, this selective bibliography, now thirty years old, includes still-useful sections on the imperial matrix, seventeenth-century colonial conflict, Indian-white relations, slavery and the slave trade, early French and Spanish settlements, and international disputes.

3:56 Washburn, Wilcomb E., ed. *Handbook of North American Indians. Vol. 4: History of Indian-White Relations.* Washington, DC: Smithsonian Institution, 1988. Part of a massive, multivolume project, this is a basic reference work on the history of interactions in North America between Indians on the one hand and Europeans and Africans on the other. Historical chapters by contributors for the colonial period include British Indian policies to 1763; Dutch, Swedish, French, and Spanish Indian policies; colonial Indian wars; British colonial Indian treaties; colonial government agencies that dealt with Indians; the fur trade in the colonial northeast; economic relations in the southeast until 1783; missions to the Indians; and white conceptions of the Indians. An extensive bibliography is also included.

Historiography

3:57 Axtell, James. "Columbian Encounters: 1992–1995." *William and Mary Quarterly* 3d ser. 52 (October 1995): 649–96. Surveying the surge of scholarship generated by the 1992 Columbus quincentenary, Axtell expertly summarizes important contributions to a wide range of Columbian-encounter subjects. Most notable are new studies of Columbus's intellectual world; fifteenth-century Spanish culture and society; exploration, conquest, and colonization in the Americas by Spanish, Portuguese, French, and English; Indian and European cultural brokers as mediators of Indian-white relations; and the many human, biological, and cultural exchanges between America's natives and European newcomers.

3:58 Black, Jeremy. "British Foreign Policy in the Eighteenth Century: A Survey." *Journal of British Studies* 26 (January 1987): 26–53. Describing recent works of scholarship on the history of eighteenth-century British foreign policy, this article calls for less attention to diplomats and their doings and more emphasis on public opinion, king, and Parliament. The article questions the utility of such concepts as "balance of power" and "natural interest" in British policymaking, and challenges the conventional wisdom that eighteenth-century British foreign policymakers were inflexible and uncreative.

3:59 Carp, E. Wayne. "Early American Military History: A Review of Recent Work." *Virginia Magazine of History and Biography* 94 (July 1996): 259–84. This essay discusses important contributions made to colonial military history, broadly construed, in the 1970s and 1980s. Highlighted is new work on the nature of Indian-white warfare, the character and organization of colonial militias, the role of colonial militias and privateers in the imperial wars of the eighteenth century, and the impact of imperial wars on colonial life and attitudes.

3:60   Higginbotham, Don. "The Early American Way of War: Reconnaissance and Appraisal." *William and Mary Quarterly* 3d ser. 44 (April 1987): 230–73. This is an authoritative evaluation of new scholarship on military-related themes and issues in colonial and revolutionary history, including military and diplomatic relations with Indians, colonial dealings with British military forces sent to America, the debate over whether England's imperial administration was basically military or commercial, relations between local colonial populations and the royal navy, and the role played by colonial anti-army sentiment in the coming of the revolution. Also discussed is how colonial Americans regarded war, whether as a limited and rational instrument of diplomacy or an all-out crusade designed to obliterate the adversary.

3:61   Johnson, Richard R. "Charles McLean Andrews and the Invention of Colonial History." *William and Mary Quarterly* 3d ser. 43 (October 1986): 519–41. This article assesses the important contributions made by the imperial historian Charles McLean Andrews to the study of the colonies and their growth within an imperial framework and their formal administration by Britain. The author identifies and describes a growing body of post-Andrews scholarship that is informed by the same transatlantic perspective, but that puts more emphasis on social and cultural and other less formal interactions across the Atlantic.

3:62   _____. "The Imperial Webb: The Thesis of Garrison Government in Early America Considered." *William and Mary Quarterly* 3d ser. 43 (July 1986): 408–30. A detailed critique of Stephen Saunders Webb's "garrison government" thesis (*The Governors-General: The English Army and the Definition of the Empire, 1569–1681*, 1979) (3:82), this article examines and evaluates Webb's contention that an ethic of militant military imperialism drove English empire-building in America during the seventeenth century. Citing Webb's various writings, the author holds that, in the first century of British colonial imperialism, commerce and revenue were more important guides to policy than military expansion

and control. Webb's extended rejoinder is printed in the same issue.

3:63   Speck, W. A. "The International and Imperial Context." In *Colonial British America: Essays in the New History of the Early Modern Era,* ed. Jack P. Greene and J. R. Pole, 384–407. Baltimore: Johns Hopkins University Press, 1984. This essay critically analyzes current literature on issues such as whether "mercantilism" guided England's navigation system or a coherent philosophy her imperial policy, and whether the chief objectives of England's empire were commercial, fiscal, or military. The essay also evaluates works that explore the diplomacy of colonial agents in London and discern important turning points in Anglo-colonial relations.

3:64   Steele, Ian K. "Exploding Colonial American History: Amerindian, Atlantic, and Global Perspectives." *Reviews in American History* 26 (March 1998): 70–95. Describing a broad pattern of trends in new writing about colonial history, this essay briefly discusses recent works in the subject areas of Indian-white relations and diplomacy; cultural, economic, and political relations within Britain's Atlantic empire; the international slave trade; non-British colonial populations; and colonial relations with populations in French Illinois and Louisiana and in Spanish Florida and the Spanish southwest.

3:65   Washburn, Wilcomb E., and Bruce G. Trigger. "Native Peoples in Euro-American Historiography." In *The Cambridge History of the Native Peoples of the Americas. Vol. 1: North America,* ed. Bruce G. Trigger and Wilcomb E. Washburn, 61–124. New York: Cambridge University Press, 1996. An important general discussion of historical, anthropological, ethnohistorical, and other writings about Indians, this essay helpfully discusses recent historiographical trends and lists up-to-date bibliographical references.

3:66   West, Delno. "Christopher Columbus and His Enterprise to the Indies: Scholarship of the Last Quarter Century." *William and Mary Quarterly* 3d ser. 49 (April 1992): 254–77. This article describes new scholarship on Columbus and on technological, geographical, religious, and international aspects of his world. While the Columbian project of reaching the Orient by sailing west remains a central concern of this scholarship, the millennial, messianic, and prophetic dimensions of Columbus's ambitions have also received fresh attention. The article also reports on major source collections, repositories, and edited documents.

Overviews: Colonial-Imperial Experience

3:67   Andrews, Charles M. *The Colonial Period of American History.* 4 vols. New Haven: Yale University Press, 1934–1938. These magisterial volumes survey the founding and development of England's mainland colonies and the creation of an imperial system of administration from an institutional perspective. Although now largely superseded, Andrews's work broke new paths in concept and method and still has utility.

3:68   Barrow, Thomas C. *Trade and Empire: The British Customs Service in Colonial America, 1660–1775.* Cambridge, MA: Harvard University Press, 1967. This book describes the origins, development, and administration of the British colonial customs service in the colonies between 1673 and 1775. Responsible for collecting duties on colonial commerce and enforcing the Navigation Acts, the colonial customs administration was ineffective. The author describes this ineffectiveness and the administrative reforms of the 1760s, which helped set the stage for revolution.

3:69   Canny, Nicholas, ed. *The Oxford History of the British Empire. Vol. 1: The Origins of Empire.* New York: Oxford University Press, 1998. This collaborative work, assembling twenty-one essays reflecting the newest trends in scholarship, authoritatively treats a wide range of subjects relating to Britain and the colonies in the seventeenth century. The essays address early English colonizing in America, early trade with West Africa and the Far East, Anglo-Indian encounters, the Glorious Revolution and America, seventeenth-century trade and empire, and other topics. Individual essays include Canny, "The Origins of Empire: An Introduction" (1–33); Anthony Pagden, "The Struggle for Legitimacy and the Image of Empire in the Atlantic to c.1700"

(34–54); John C. Appleby, "War, Politics, and Colonization, 1558–1625" (55–78), N. A. M. Rodger, "Guns and Sails in the First Phase of English Colonization, 1500–1650" (79–98); Canny, "England's New World and the Old, 1480s–1630s" (148–69); Hilary McD. Beckles, "The 'Hub of Empire': The Caribbean and Britain in the Seventeenth Century" (218–40); Michael J. Braddick, "The English Government, War, Trade, and Settlement, 1625–1688" (286–308); Peter C. Mancall, "Native Americans and Europeans in English America, 1500–1700" (328–50); Naula Zahedieh, "Overseas Expansion and Trade in the Seventeenth Century" (398–422); Jonathan I. Israel, "The Emerging Empire: The Continental Perspective, 1650–1713" (423–44); Richard S. Dunn, "The Glorious Revolution and America" (445–66); and G. E. Aylmer, "Navy, State, Trade, and Empire" (467–80). Chronology. For a detailed summary and evaluation, see the essay review by Bernard Bailyn in *William and Mary Quarterly* 3d ser. 57 (July 2000): 647–60.

3:70   Gipson, Lawrence Henry. *The British Empire before the American Revolution.* 15 vols. New York: Alfred A. Knopf, 1958–1970. This magisterial series authoritatively surveys the history of Great Britain, the empire, and the colonies from 1748 to the outbreak of the American revolution. Celebrating Britain's enlightened imperial rule, the author judges colonial Americans as the "freest, most enlightened, most prosperous, and most politically experienced of all colonials in the world of the eighteenth century." Volumes 1–3 describe conditions at mid-century in England, Ireland, the southern colonies, and the northern colonies; volumes 4–5 the imperial rivalries among the British, French, and Spanish empires in the New World and the Far East; volumes 6–8 the conduct, management, and outcome of the Seven Years War including the Albany congress and colonial military contributions; and volumes 9–12 the genesis and outbreak of the American revolution. Volume 13 summarizes Gipson's judgments and includes discussion and assessment of other historians and their work. Volume 14 (3:46) is a bibliographical guide to the history of the British empire and volume 15 (3:47) is a guide to manuscripts relating to the history of the British empire. These volumes were first published in 1936 with the first three volumes having the imprint Caxton Printers, Caldwell, Idaho. Knopf published revised editions of volumes 1–3 in 1939 and again in 1949. Between 1958 and 1970, Knopf issued a completely revised edition in fifteen volumes.

3:71   Greene, Jack P. *Peripheries and Center: Constitutional Development in the Extended Politics of the British Empire and the United States, 1607–1788.* Athens, GA: University of Georgia Press, 1986. This book presents a highly valuable survey of recurring constitutional controversies between the English metropolitan center and the American colonies over the terms and dimensions of imperial power. The work is especially helpful in showing the persistence of colonial claims to rights of self-government within the empire and of repeated English attempts to reduce the colonies to stricter control.

3:72   Kammen, Michael G. *Empire and Interest: The American Colonies and the Politics of Mercantilism.* Philadelphia: Lippincott, 1970. This concise inquiry investigates the comparative impact of mercantilist thinking and interest group pressure on the administration of Britain's first colonial empire. The author holds that British imperial policymaking changed in the third quarter of the eighteenth century from a national politics of mercantilism to a narrow politics of special interest advantage. More exploratory than definitive, this suggestive book is indispensable to any study of Anglo-American imperial relations.

3:73   Marshall, P. J., ed. *The Oxford History of the British Empire. Vol. 2: The Eighteenth Century.* New York: Oxford University Press, 1998. Comprising twenty-six chapters by leading specialists, this collaborative work authoritatively summarizes and interprets the existing state of knowledge about the eighteenth-century British empire and its colonial dependencies. Subjects include imperial expansion, the imperial economy, governance, the American revolution, Anglo-Indian relations, the slave trade, African-Americans in the empire, and the empire and colonial identity. Individual chapters include Patrick K. O'Brien, "Inseparable Connections: Trade, Economy, Fiscal State, and the Expansion of Empire, 1688–1815" (53–77); Jacob M. Price, "The Imperial Economy, 1700–1776" (78–104); Ian K. Steele, "The Anointed, the Appointed, and the Elected: Governance of the British Empire, 1689–1784" (105–27); Bruce P. Lenman,

"Colonial Wars and Imperial Instability, 1688–1793" (151–68); N. A. M. Rodger, "Sea-Power and Empire, 1688–1793" (169–83); Jack P. Greene, "Empire and Identity from the Glorious Revolution to the American Revolution" (208–30); Richard Drayton, "Knowledge and Empire" (231–52); Richard R. Johnson, "Growth and Mastery: British North America, 1690–1748" (276–99); John Shy, "The American Colonies in War and Revolution, 1748–1783" (300–24); Stephen Conway, "Britain and the Revolutionary Crisis, 1763–1791" (325–46); Daniel K. Richter, "Native Peoples of North America and the Eighteenth-Century British Empire" (347–71); Peter Marshall, "British North America, 1760–1815" (372–93); David Richardson, "The British Empire and the Atlantic Slave Trade, 1660–1807" (440–64); and Marshall, "Britain without America—A Second Empire?" (576–95). For a detailed summary and evaluation, see the essay review by Bernard Bailyn, *The William and Mary Quarterly* 3d ser. 57 (July 2000): 647–60.

3:74   McCusker, John J., and Russell R. Menard. *The Economy of British America, 1607–1789.* Chapel Hill: University of North Carolina Press for the Institute of Early American History and Culture, 1985. Modestly billed as a survey of the state of the art, this work critically and expertly synthesizes an extensive theoretical and descriptive literature about the economic growth and development of British North America. Emphasizing the importance of colonial commerce with England, the book discusses mercantilism, the navigation system, the centrality of maritime trade and staple exports, the costs and benefits of empire, and increasing economic integration among the colonies. The book advances an economic explanation for the genesis of the American revolution and holds that the robust economic growth of the mainland colonies made independence "thinkable" by the 1770s.

3:75   Middleton, Richard. *Colonial America: A History, 1607–1760.* 2d ed. Cambridge, MA: Blackwell, 1996. This one-volume history of colonial America briefly surveys colonial development and pays special attention to themes in the scholarship of the past thirty years. Among its subject areas are the slave trade and slavery, imperial political and cultural relations, the new social history, and the new Indian history. Although short on analysis, the book provides a useful topical bibliography of recent books and articles. Originally published in 1992.

3:76 Olson, Alison Gilbert. "Relations with the Parent Country: The British Colonies." In *Encyclopedia of the North American Colonies,* ed. Jacob Ernest Cooke and William J. Eccles, 1: 330–38. New York: C. Scribner's Sons, 1993. Brief and authoritative, this essay sketches the development of Anglo-American imperial relations and argues that Britain's first colonial empire did work, partly because of effective colonial lobbying and partly because of *de facto* colonial self-government. Once British administrative and policy reforms removed these advantages, the colonists moved toward independence.

3:77 Parry, J. H. *The Discovery of the Sea.* New York: Dial Press, 1974. This book synthesizes the best scholarship on the Portuguese and Spanish voyages of the fifteenth century that climaxed with Columbus and Magellan. The work masterfully describes sailing and navigational technology, geographical knowledge, and the sea-route-to-Asia project that inspired Columbus and his contemporaries to link inhabited known and unknown areas of the world with usable sea routes.

3:78 Quinn, David B. "Colonies in the Beginning, Examples from North America." In *Explorers and Colonies: America, 1500–1625,* ed. David B. Quinn, 127–50. Ronceverte, WV: Hambledon Press, 1990. This essay explores early Spanish, French, and English colony-building in North America. As such, it suggests explanations for such interpretive problems as the different pace and timing of each nation's involvement in the imperial project, the role of strategic competition among the powers, and the comparative effectiveness of each nation's early colony-building.

3:79 _____. "Exploration and the Expansion of Europe." In *Explorers and Colonies: America, 1500–1625,* ed. David B. Quinn, 127–50. Ronceverte, WV: Hambledon Press, 1990. This essay analyzes the rise of a vigorous multinational literature of European exploration and expansion. A prime vehicle for disseminating knowledge about Africa, the Far East, and America throughout Europe, this literature helped promote further exploration and expansion. Early European expansion was highly competitive, and the literature of expansion had not only humanistic but promotional and propagandistic objectives.

3:80 Russell, Elmer Beecher. *The Review of American Colonial Legislation by the King in Council.* Vol. 64, no. 2, Studies in History, Economics and Public Law. New York: Columbia University, 1915. Reprint 1981 (W. S. Hein). This study describes how the English Privy Council exercised an effective check on colonial legislation through much of the colonial period. Of 8,563 pieces of legislation submitted by the continental colonies for council review, 5.5 percent were disallowed. The book describes the various criteria used in disallowing colonial laws, outlines the procedures by which the council made its decisions, and concludes that until shortly before the American revolution, disallowance did not constitute a serious burden for the colonies.

3:81 Simmons, Richard C. *The American Colonies: From Settlement to Independence.* London: Longman, 1976. Although more than twenty years old, this detailed account by an English historian summarizes a vast literature and contains an extremely useful bibliography. The book emphasizes colonial settlement and social development, but has chapters on imperial conflicts and wars, imperial trade, the workings of the empire, and the genesis of the revolution.

3:82 Webb, Stephen Saunders. *The Governors-General: The English Army and the Definition of the Empire, 1569–1681.* Chapel Hill: University of North Carolina Press for the Institute of Early American History and Culture, 1979. A major challenge to Charles M. Andrews's views about the commercial nature of English colonial policy, this book argues that militarism, centralization, and imperialism, not commerce and trade, guided the direction, staffing, and administration of England's empire in Virginia and the West Indies in the seventeenth century. In a sweeping claim, the author holds that "garrison government" prevailed throughout the history of England's first colonial empire with Walpole's policy of "salutary neglect" providing a brief interlude.

Overviews: Origins of American Diplomacy

3:83   Gilbert, Felix. *To the Farewell Address: Ideas of Early American Foreign Policy.* Princeton: Princeton University Press, 1961. In his famous farewell address, Washington recommended ideas about a proper American foreign policy that expressed both realism and idealism. This book finds the origins of these two American diplomatic traditions in earlier British debates over the "Continental connexion," the free trade ideas of the French *philosophes,* Paine's *Common Sense,* and the ideas of continental writers about the "permanent interests" of nation states.

3:84   Greene, Jack P. *The Intellectual Construction of America: Exceptionalism and Identity from 1492 to 1800.* Chapel Hill: University of North Carolina Press, 1993. Examining a variety of definitions of the special meaning of America from Columbus through the revolution, these published lectures by a preeminent colonial historian center on themes of American exceptionalism. Acknowledging that colonial Americans shared much with Britain and Europe, he holds that "in one form or another, a notion of distinctiveness was a significant component in intellectual constructs of America from the beginning." The author also holds that Americans' experience in winning the revolution further fostered this sense of exceptionalism to the point that it became a highly important ingredient in American relations with native peoples and the rest of the world.

3:85   Hutson, James H. "Intellectual Foundations of Early American Diplomacy." *Diplomatic History* 1 (Winter 1977): 1–19. This article challenges Felix Gilbert's contention in *To the Farewell Address* (1961) (3:83) that America's first diplomatic statesmen were primarily idealists who espoused an internationalist foreign policy based on free trade. On the contrary, the essay argues, revolutionary leaders were realists, well schooled by their colonial experience in mercantilist notions of national wealth and power, in a balance-of-power approach to international relations, and in a belief in the deterrent effect of a strong military force.

3:86   Savelle, Max. "The American Balance of Power and European Diplomacy, 1713–1778." In *The Era of the American Revolution: Studies Inscribed to Evarts Boutell Greene,* ed. Richard B. Morris, 140–69. New York: Columbia University Press, 1939. This essay explores the increasing importance of American colonial possessions in eighteenth-century European balance-of-power calculations. By 1775, the balance of European power was assumed to depend on possessions held in America.

3:87   _____. "Colonial Origins of American Diplomatic Principles." *Pacific Historical Review* 3 (September 1934): 334–50. This article finds the roots of the American diplomatic doctrines of abstention from Europe, freedom of the seas, the open door, assertive neutral rights, and other principles in the words and actions of British, European, and American colonial leaders and writers of the seventeenth and eighteenth centuries.

3:88   _____. "The International Approach to Early American History." In *The Reinterpretation of Early American History: Essays in Honor of John E. Pomfret,* ed. Ray Allen Billington, 201–29. San Marino, CA: Huntington Library, 1966. A distillation of themes developed in the author's book *The Origins of American Diplomacy: The International History of Angloamerica, 1492–1763* (1967) (3:89), this essay summarizes basic patterns and subject matter of intercolonial, Anglo-colonial, and Anglo-European diplomacy in the seventeenth and eighteenth centuries through the Seven Years War.

3:89   Savelle, Max, with Margaret Anne Fisher. *The Origins of American Diplomacy: The International History of Angloamerica, 1492–1763.* New York: Macmillan, 1967. An ambitious synthesis, this narrative concentrates on the diplomatic history of the European powers and their statecraft as they relate both to the American mainland and Caribbean colonies. Savelle also treats colonial governments and their intercolonial relations. The author concludes that this experience, and the attitudes, policies, and principles fostered by it, formed "the foundations for the established diplomatic policies of the American nation in later centuries."

Overviews: British Diplomatic History

3:90   Baugh, Daniel A. "Maritime Strength and Atlantic Commerce: The Uses of a 'Grand Marine Empire.'" In *An Imperial State at War: Britain from 1689 to 1815,* ed. Lawrence Stone, 185–223. New York: Routledge, 1994. This essay takes a fresh look at Britain's Atlantic empire and its maritime-imperial objectives from 1650 to 1783. Before 1750, British imperial policy promoted commerce, naval power, and revenue to acquire the sinews of war needed in Europe and European seas. After 1750, however, the imperial conflict with France required that priority be placed on defending colonial territories and tightening imperial control from the center.

3:91   Black, Jeremy. "Foreign Policy and the British State, 1742–1793." In *British Politics and Society from Walpole to Pitt, 1742–1789,* ed. Jeremy Black, 147–75. New York: St. Martin's Press, 1990. This essay summarizes major themes in the conduct of British foreign policy from 1742 to 1793 including the roles of the king, Parliament, and public opinion. Noting that diplomacy after 1760 left Britain without any major European ally, the author defends the policies of peace and retrenchment that saw it retreat from European great power politics after the costly Seven Years War. Nevertheless, when France and Spain joined the American War of Independence against the British, Britain was diplomatically and militarily isolated.

3:92   _____. *A System of Ambition? British Foreign Policy, 1660–1793.* 2d ed. Stroud, UK: Sutton, 2000. This compact, up-to-date history effectively relates British foreign policy from 1660 to 1793 to the domestic context, emphasizing the role played in shaping policy by king, Parliament, lobbies, and public opinion. Magisterial in his judgments, Black holds that policy was more reactive than purposeful, more concerned with avoiding war than preparing for it, and more preoccupied with the vulnerability of the home island and overseas possessions than with pursuing a coherent blueprint of continental or colonial hegemony. A complete bibliography is appended. Originally published in 1991.

3:93   Dull, Jonathan R. *A Diplomatic History of the American Revolution.* New Haven: Yale University Press, 1985. This compact introduction to the diplomacy of the American revolution begins with four chapters that set the background for the French decision to support the rebellious colonies in the revolution. These include chapters on the prehistory of American diplomacy (colonial agents), the European balance of power in 1763, the failure of British diplomacy to end Britain's isolation during the interwar years, and the objectives of French diplomacy after the Seven Years War. The book contains a useful annotated bibliography.

3:94   Scott, H. M. *British Foreign Policy in the Age of the American Revolution.* New York: Oxford University Press, 1990. Although Britain's diplomatic isolation during the American revolution did not alone determine its outcome, it contributed to Britain's defeat. Covering 1763–1783, this book stresses the failure of Britain's diplomacy to enlist a single continental power on its side during the revolution.

3:95   Steele, Ian K. "The European Contest for North America." In *Encyclopedia of the North American Colonies,* ed. Jacob Ernest Cooke and William J. Eccles, 2: 271–88. New York: C. Scribner's Sons, 1993. Emphasizing events in Europe, this essay expertly describes changes in power relations among the European states and their impact on the European military and diplomatic contest for North America during the colonial era. Major Anglo-Dutch, Anglo-Spanish, and Anglo-French wars and diplomacy are briefly surveyed.

3:96   Symcox, Geoffrey. *War, Diplomacy, and Imperialism, 1618–1763.* New York: Walker, 1974. This book takes a long look at the role of colonial possessions in European diplomacy, war, and empire-building in the seventeenth and eighteenth centuries. For most of the seventeenth century, Europe's overseas colonies formed a separate political and military sphere, but the War of Spanish Succession (Queen Anne's War) "first set the pattern for the wars of the eighteenth century in which the rivalries of the European Powers were fought out on a global scale." Selected representative documents illustrate this and other themes such as the nature of European diplomacy, of land and sea warfare, of imperial competition on the West African coast and in the Far East and

Caribbean, and the growing importance to both England and France of colonial commerce.

3:97   Wilson, Kathleen. "Empire of Virtue: The Imperial Project and Hanoverian Culture, c.1720–1785." In *An Imperial State at War: Britain from 1689 to 1815,* ed. Lawrence Stone, 128–64. New York: Routledge, 1994. This essay explores the relatively new subject of eighteenth-century English popular support for empire. Examining newspapers, theater, and political discourse, the author shows how these media coaxed, focused, and reflected middle-class support for the imperial project. Among several popular notions that valorized empire was the idea that empire-building was manly and virtue-building.

3:98   _____. "Empire, Trade, and Popular Politics in Mid-Hanoverian Britain: The Case of Admiral Vernon." *Past and Present,* no. 121 (November 1988): 74–109. Focusing on the celebrations of Vice-Admiral Edward Vernon's naval victories in the Caribbean in the Anglo-Spanish War of Jenkins Ear, this article examines British imperial greatness as a theme in mid-Hanoverian popular politics. Imperial expansion was a stirring popular issue in George II's England; its agitation by various politicians and interest groups not only helped bring on the Spanish war but eventually drove Walpole from power.

Biographical Studies

BENJAMIN FRANKLIN

3:99   Morgan, David T. *The Devious Dr. Franklin, Colonial Agent: Benjamin Franklin's Years in London.* Macon, GA: Mercer University Press, 1996. This book concentrates on Franklin's years in London from 1757 to 1775 when he was colonial agent for Pennsylvania, Georgia, New Jersey, and Massachusetts. He lobbied for a royal charter for Pennsylvania, pursued schemes for a private colony in the Illinois Country, and tried to defuse the imperial crisis occasioned by parliamentary taxation. The book details his resourcefulness as agent, lobbyist, propagandist, and advocate but sharply criticizes his alleged deceptions and self-promotion.

3:100   Stourzh, Gerald. *Benjamin Franklin and American Foreign Policy.* 2d ed. Chicago: University of Chicago Press, 1969. This is an inquiry into Benjamin Franklin's thinking about international politics. While much of the book deals with the revolution and post-revolution periods, Stourzh also relates Franklin's foreign policy ideas at a time he remained emotionally and culturally an Englishman, arguing that he had a coherent policy for colonial America that included maintaining a modified mercantile empire with Britain, an intercolonial confederation, and a protective imperialism that incorporated western lands and Canada into the empire. First published in 1954.

3:101   Van Doren, Carl. *Benjamin Franklin.* New York: Viking Press, 1938. For over sixty years this detailed, comprehensive, full-length biography by a famous literary historian and critic has been a classic. Well stocked with aptly chosen quotations, suggestive leads for further research, and interesting information about both the public and private sides of Franklin's life and career, it remains indispensable.

3:102   Wright, Esmond. *Franklin of Philadelphia.* Cambridge, MA: Belknap Press of Harvard University Press, 1986. This authoritative biography of Franklin effectively describes the multidimensional life of the day's most famous colonial American. Drawing on a wide range of sources, the book offers accurate descriptions, useful insights, and balanced judgments not only about Franklin as scientist, inventor, journalist, and publisher, but Indian commissioner, author of the Albany Plan of Union, Anglo-American politician, colonial agent in London, press campaigner for colonial rights, and champion of colonial dominion status.

OTHERS

3:103   Batinski, Michael C. *Jonathan Belcher, Colonial Governor.* Lexington: University Press of Kentucky, 1996. Jonathan Belcher, son of a wealthy Boston merchant, was at various times royal governor of Massachusetts, New Hampshire, and New Jersey. This book describes his political career as colonial governor and transatlantic politician, and analyzes the local and imperial factors that made for his successes and failures.

3:104   Ross, J. S. Hoffman. *Edmund Burke, New York Agent, with His Letters to the New York Assembly and Intimate Correspondence with Charles O'Hara, 1761–1776.* Vol. 41, Memoirs of the American Philosophical Society. Philadelphia: American Philosophical Society, 1956. Edmund Burke, Rockingham Whig, member of Parliament, and opponent of its taxation of the colonies, was appointed colonial agent by the New York provincial assembly in 1770. Although he believed that Britain's American policy was mistaken, his representation of the American side of the controversy was halfhearted. The volume contains a large number of Burke's letters.

3:105   Brooke, John. *King George III.* New York: McGraw-Hill, 1972. This magisterial biography of the "Last king of America" treats its subject with warm sympathy and humanistic appreciation. Perhaps Britain's most cultured monarch, George III was thoroughly a man of his times in his stubborn defense of Parliament's claim to supremacy over the resisting colonies. The book covers many aspects of the king's life and contains a fine chapter on his mainly supportive role in British policymaking.

3:106   Lawson, Philip. *George Grenville, a Political Life.* New York: Oxford University Press, 1984. This balanced biography concentrates on the public career of the man most responsible for the fateful trade regulations and taxes that Parliament imposed on the colonies in 1764 and 1765. Even as he believed that Parliament must "revitalize a ramshackle imperial system operating to the detriment of the mother country," he was more prudent, flexible, and moderate than he is often credited. His chief failure was not to foresee, understand, or respond to the fierce resistance that these measures generated in America.

3:107   Lustig, Mary Lou. *Robert Hunter, 1666–1734: New York's Augustan Statesman.* Syracuse: Syracuse University Press, 1983. Royal governor of New York and New Jersey (1709–1720), the military veteran Colonel Robert Hunter was a highly successful Anglo-American politician. Aided by his Whig patrons at Whitehall, this adroit figure proved highly effective in dealing with recalcitrant provincial legislatures by mixing soldierly firmness, personal erudition, and well-placed political appointments, emoluments, and favors.

3:108   Webb, Stephen Saunders. "The Strange Career of Francis Nicholson." *William and Mary Quarterly* 3d ser. 23 (October 1966): 513–48. Francis Nicholson, an English military officer and veteran, served in five colonial governorships in the late seventeenth and early eighteenth centuries when royal administrators were trying to tighten the bonds of empire. This article describes him as an authoritarian soldier-governor whose methods and attitudes were thoroughly attuned to the impulse of strong imperialist control.

3:109   Hall, Michael G. *Edward Randolph and the American Colonies, 1676–1703.* Chapel Hill: University of North Carolina Press for the Institute of Early American History and Culture, 1960. In 1676, Edward Randolph, an ambitious royal administrator, was sent to Boston to persuade the recalcitrant colony of Puritan Massachusetts to accept the full sovereignty and rule of the English king. This study traces the career of an important if minor figure whose service to the crown, along with that of other civil servants, helped shape the structure and administration of England's first colonial empire.

3:110   Schutz, John A. *William Shirley, King's Governor of Massachusetts.* Chapel Hill: University of North Carolina Press for the Institute of Early American History and Culture, 1961. William Shirley, English gentleman and lawyer, was arguably the most effective royal governor in the history of colonial Massachusetts. This book examines Shirley's success as governor (1741–1756), which derived from his skilled distribution of contracts and offices in Massachusetts and the personal backing of crown officials in London.

3:111   Nelson, Paul David. *William Tryon and the Course of Empire: A Life in British Imperial Service.* Chapel Hill: University of North Carolina Press, 1990. William Tryon was the imperious royal governor of North Carolina and New York on the eve of the American revolution. This book describes his unsuccessful attempts to enforce imperial tax, land, and ecclesiastical policies, his quelling of the North Carolina Regulation, and his failed effort to settle the dispute between New Hampshire and New York claimants to lands in Vermont.

3:112   Wilderson, Paul. *Governor John Wentworth and the American Revolution: The English Connec-*

tion. Hanover, NH: University Press of New England, 1994. This comprehensive biography describes the improving policies, transatlantic connections, and political trials of the last royal governor of New Hampshire, the wealthy America-born Portsmouth merchant and landowner, John Wentworth.

3:113   Dunn, Richard S. *Puritans and Yankees: The Winthrop Dynasty of New England, 1630–1717.* Princeton: Princeton University Press, 1962. This study describes the important political and diplomatic roles played by three generations of Winthrops within both their own colonies of Massachusetts and Connecticut and the British empire. The book contains much valuable material on such matters as English schemes for imperial centralization, relations with the Dutch and French, lobbying at Whitehall, and the abortive Dominion of New England.

Rival Colonial Empires

ANGLO-DUTCH RELATIONS

3:114   Boxer, C. R. *The Dutch Seaborne Empire, 1600–1800.* New York: Alfred A. Knopf, 1965. This detailed study provides an authoritative background for Dutch empire-building in the Americas, Africa, and Far East in the seventeenth and eighteenth centuries. Foreign relations with European rivals receive some attention, but the main emphasis is on internal social, commercial, religious, and economic themes and their relation to Dutch overseas enterprise.

3:115   Jones, J. R. *The Anglo-Dutch Wars of the Seventeenth Century.* New York: Longman, 1996. This book provides a fresh narrative of the three mid-seventeenth-century Anglo-Dutch wars. Written from a naval historian's perspective, the book emphasizes the maritime dimension, provides equal weight to both Dutch and English protagonists, and advances a revisionist thesis holding Stuart political ambitions responsible for the second and third wars. In this view, war against the Dutch was the means by which the crown could release itself from financial dependence on Parliament.

3:116   Pincus, Steven C. A. *Protestantism and Patriotism: Ideologies and the Making of English Foreign Policy, 1650–1668.* New York: Cambridge University Press, 1996. This detailed, deeply researched study challenges the classic mercantilist-commercial interpretation and advances a political-ideological account of Anglo-Dutch wars and foreign relations in the 1650s and 1660s. Linking the changing fortunes of the Orangist and Republican Parties within the United Provinces to English foreign policy, the book holds that domestic concerns over possible threats posed by these parties to the security of their regimes within England guided both Commonwealth and Anglican warmakers.

3:117   Schmidt, Benjamin. "Mapping an Empire: Cartographic and Colonial Rivalry in Seventeenth-Century Dutch and English North America." *William and Mary Quarterly* 3d ser. 54 (July 1997): 549–78. This article explores the use of maps by Dutch and English empire-builders in the imperial contest over rival claims to New England and Maryland. Although English seizure of New York determined the outcome, Dutch mapmakers and designers, the author concludes, won the cartographic war.

3:118   Wilson, Charles H. *Profit and Power: A Study of England and the Dutch Wars.* New York: Longmans, Green, 1957. This influential book locates the causes of the three Anglo-Dutch wars of the mid-seventeenth century in England's worldwide mercantilist rivalry with the seafaring Dutch in the Baltic and North Seas, American colonies, and West Africa. The book emphasizes the influence of mercantilist writers like Thomas Mun, the Navigation Acts, pressures from England's mercantile community, and popular resentment over England's loss to the Dutch of commercial and financial wealth.

ANGLO-SPANISH RELATIONS

3:119   Andrews, Kenneth R. *Trade, Plunder and Settlement: Maritime Enterprise and the Genesis of the British Empire, 1480–1630.* New York: Cambridge University Press, 1984. This book expertly synthesizes recent scholarship on sixteenth-century English maritime expansion. Emphasizing that the Atlantic was a sideshow of enterprise during this period compared with Russia, the Levant, and the Orient,

Andrews describes the developing rivalry with Spain, emphasizing the role played by piracy and privateering in the short-term, treasure-centered policy of Tudor monarchs toward the Spanish.

3:120   Cook, Warren L. *Flood Tide of Empire: Spain and the Pacific Northwest, 1543–1819*. New Haven: Yale University Press, 1973. Although mostly dealing with the post-revolutionary period, three chapters of this book describe seventeenth- and eighteenth-century Spanish exploration and imperial rivalry with British and Russian claimants in the Pacific northwest.

3:121   Gibson, Charles. *Spain in America*. New York: Harper and Row, 1966. A useful background for the study of Spanish empire-building in the Americas, this work has a chapter titled "The Borderlands" summarizing Spain's conflicts with France and Great Britain in the southern and southwest borderlands. Although somewhat dated, the bibliography is still helpful.

3:122   Pares, Richard. *War and Trade in the West Indies, 1739–1763*. London: F. Cass, 1963. This model study emphasizes the commercial and naval dimensions of British, French, and Spanish imperial rivalry in the Caribbean and West Indies. As trading partners with the foreign sugar islands, the mainland American colonies were substantially affected by events in the Caribbean, but more important was Britain's strategic decision to oust France from Canada and the trans-Appalachian west after the Seven Years War.

3:123   Parry, J. H. *The Spanish Seaborne Empire*. New York: Alfred A. Knopf, 1966. This is a general history of the rise and decline of Spain's American empire that treats such topics as the means and motives of conquest, patterns of administration and government, the benefits and costs of empire, and Creole revolts. Later chapters discuss the intensifying British, French, and Dutch military and diplomatic pressure on Spain's holdings.

3:124   Quinn, David B. "James I and the Beginning of Empire in America." In *Explorers and Colonies: America, 1500–1625,* ed. David B. Quinn, 321–39. Ronceverte, WV: Hambledon Press, 1990. This previously published essay describes Anglo-

Spanish diplomacy at the onset of English commerce- and colony-building activity in the Caribbean and Virginia. Quinn concludes that naval weakness and preoccupation with the rebellious United Provinces defeated Spain's ability to contest the English presence.

3:125   Wright, J. Leitch, Jr. *Anglo-Spanish Rivalry in North America*. Athens, GA: University of Georgia Press, 1971. Although the West Indies saw more extensive Anglo-Spanish military and naval action, from 1670 to 1763 the Florida-Carolina borderland was also a zone of friction. This book chronicles Anglo-Spanish military and diplomatic conflict along the Georgia-Florida border from the first English forays into Carolina through the American revolution. A detailed bibliography lists many primary and secondary sources.

ANGLO-FRENCH RELATIONS

3:126   Anderson, Fred. *Crucible of War: The Seven Years' War and the Fate of Empire in British North America, 1754–1766*. New York: Alfred A. Knopf, 2000. This wide-ranging synthesis provides a highly detailed, comprehensive narrative of the many military, political, and diplomatic events and themes of the Anglo-French Seven Years War. The book not only describes major campaigns and battles in America and Europe, but argues for the crucial contribution to Britain's victory in America made by colonial troops and Indian allies. The author holds that a major lesson of the war was the colonies' basic loyalty to the empire, provided that their commercial prosperity, local self-government, and voluntary noncoerced participation were respected by British leaders.

3:127   Dorn, Walter L. *Competition for Empire: 1740–1763*. New York: Harper and Brothers, 1940. Although over sixty years old, this survey of European nation states in an age of intensifying competition on the continent and overseas is still useful. Such topics as mercantilism, concern for the balance of power, the psychology of war, the professional army, and the rise of state bureaucracies are highly informative. Similarly, the European diplomatic revolution of 1756, the worldwide contest for commerce and colonies between Great Britain and France, and the events of the Seven Years War are well treated.

3:128   Eccles, William J. *Canada under Louis XIV, 1663–1701.* New York: Oxford University Press, 1964. This monograph concentrates on the efforts of Louis XIV and his ministers to build French Canada into a strong, self-sustaining royal province, treating in detail how the French crown constructed alliances with the Hurons and other Indians to counter Indian and English threats from both south and north.

3:129   _____. *France in America.* Rev. ed. East Lansing: Michigan State University Press, 1990. An updated work, this study authoritatively treats French colony-building and administration in Canada, Louisiana, and the West Indies. Major emphasis is placed on the French-English wars for control of North America. An updated critical bibliography of both primary and secondary sources is also provided. First published in 1972.

3:130   _____. "The Fur Trade and Eighteenth-Century Imperialism." *William and Mary Quarterly* 3d ser. 40 (July 1983): 341–62. This is a useful general discussion of Anglo-French rivalry in the trans-Appalachian west and of the role played by the fur trade and Indian alliances in this rivalry.

3:131   Middleton, Richard. *The Bells of Victory: The Pitt-Newcastle Ministry and the Conduct of the Seven Years' War, 1757–1762.* New York: Cambridge University Press, 1985. This is the best study of the roles played by William Pitt and the Duke of Newcastle in the Seven Years War. Frankly revisionist, it concludes that the strength of British finances, Spanish neutrality, and French failure to fortify colonial and maritime possessions were far more important to Britain's victory than Pitt's strategic foresight or organizational genius. The Great Commoner's managerial, organizational, and strategic abilities have been greatly overrated.

3:132   Stanley, George Francis Gilman. *New France: The Last Phase, 1744–1760.* Toronto: McClelland and Stewart, 1968. Beginning with the 1745 capture of Louisbourg, this book narrates the final military phases of the struggle for Canada and the Old Northwest between French and Anglo-American forces, relating such events as Washington's surrender at Fort Necessity, the deportation of the Acadians, and the fall of Quebec. It assigns ultimate responsibility for the fall of New France to the failure of the French Court to grasp Canada's potential as a colonial possession.

3:133   Usner, Daniel H., Jr. *Indians, Settlers, and Slaves in a Frontier Exchange Economy: The Lower Mississippi Valley before 1783.* Chapel Hill: University of North Carolina Press for the Institute of Early American History and Culture, 1992. Primarily an economic and cultural study of interactions among French and African slaves in the lower Mississippi valley, this book also includes a diplomatic chapter ("The Indian Alliance Network") describing how French empire-builders used Indian proxies and the fur trade.

Indian-White Relations and Diplomacy

3:134   Axtell, James. *Beyond 1492: Encounters in Colonial North America.* New York: Oxford University Press, 1992. Eleven essays and lectures illustrate the strengths of ethnohistory as applied to the history of colonial Indian-white relations. Among the most notable pieces are discussions of moral judgmentalism; the Indian consumer revolution; initial Indian and European reactions to each other's presence; textbook portrayals of Indians; and Indian strategies of resistance to the European invasion.

3:135   _____. *The European and the Indian: Essays in the Ethnohistory of Colonial North America.* New York: Oxford University Press, 1981. Taking an ethnohistorical approach in these ten essays, Axtell expertly explores cultural themes related to the Anglo-French invasion of North America and ensuing European-Indian interactions. Included are discussions of ethnohistory and its methods, the European cultural invasion of America, precontact Indian scalping practices, English missionary efforts to convert Indians, the white Indians of colonial America, and the cultural impact of Indians on Europeans and vice versa.

3:136   _____. *The Invasion Within: The Contest of Cultures in Colonial North America.* New York: Oxford University Press, 1985. This book describes the Anglo-French contest for colonial North America as an aggressive quest for Indian conversion conducted by Puritan and Jesuit missionaries. Emphasizing the three-sided nature of the relationship, Axtell demonstrates the tenacity of the Indians' cultural practices and ability to resist and survive.

3:137   Berkhofer, Robert F. "White Conceptions of Indians." In *Handbook of North American Indians. Vol. 4: History of Indian-White Relations,* ed. Wilcomb E. Washburn, 522–47. Washington, DC: Smithsonian Institution, 1988. This essay discusses how Europeans in the colonial period defined Indians as "others" and held them to be intellectually, culturally, and morally deficient. The author argues that this "description by deficiency" holds the key to "the conceptual categories, classificatory schemes, explanatory frameworks, and moral criteria, by which past and present Whites perceived, observed, evaluated, and interpreted Indians as others."

3:138   Bitterli, Urs. *Cultures in Conflict: Encounters between European and Non-European Cultures, 1492–1800.* Translated by Ritchie Robertson. Stanford, CA: Stanford University Press, 1989. This book by a distinguished Swiss historian contains a case study, "Cultural Relations as 'Holy Experiment': The English in Pennsylvania," examining early relations between the English Quakers in Pennsylvania and the indigenous Delaware Indians. Sensitive to cultural and psychological dimensions, the author concludes that the Quaker experiment in mutual tolerance between the races was bound to fail because of inherently contradictory cultural values, objectives, and technologies.

3:139   Calloway, Colin G. *New Worlds for All: Indians, Europeans, and the Making of Early America.* Baltimore: Johns Hopkins University Press, 1997. Organized by theme, this extended essay by a leading expert discusses cultural, biological, diplomatic, religious, technological, and military aspects of encounters between Indians and Europeans in North America to 1800. Stressing "creative adaptation" on both sides, the book summarizes current knowledge, discusses "New World Diplomacy and New World Foreign Relations," and provides an up-to-date, highly useful bibliographical essay.

3:140   Cave, Alfred A. *The Pequot War.* Amherst:

University of Massachusetts Press, 1996. This study of New England's first Anglo-Indian war offers a revisionist perspective on a crucial turning point in Puritan-Indian relations. Based on published sources, the book discusses previous interpretations of the war, identifies Massachusetts Puritans as the aggressors, and sees the war through Puritan eyes as a holy crusade against Satan's agents.

3:141   Crane, Verner W. *The Southern Frontier, 1670–1732.* Durham, NC: Duke University Press, 1928. Reprint 1981 (Norton). This is a classic study of diplomatic and military conflict between colonial Anglo-Americans and their Spanish, French, and Indian adversaries in the borderland from South Carolina to the Mississippi. The book emphasizes the key role played by Indians and the fur trade in this struggle for dominance.

3:142   Dennis, Matthew. *Cultivating a Landscape of Peace: Iroquois-European Encounters in Seventeenth-Century America.* Ithaca: Cornell University Press, 1993. This book describes the history of seventeenth-century Iroquois, Dutch, and French contact and interaction before the English conquest of New York in 1664. The book emphasizes Iroquois aspirations for a peaceful system of interracial kinship and reciprocity with the Europeans, an ideal that the imperatives of the white man's diseases, culture, and expansionist impulses made unattainable.

3:143   Dowd, Gregory Evans. *A Spirited Resistance: The North American Indian Struggle for Unity, 1745–1815.* Baltimore: Johns Hopkins University Press, 1992. This book describes the rise and fall of pan-Indian movements for unity beginning in the second half of the eighteenth century and ending in the military defeats of the War of 1812. The movement was spurred by Indian prophets who preached moral and cultural reform, nativist identity, and unified resistance against white culture and settlement. The author concentrates on the Delaware, Shawnee, Cherokee, and Creeks and shows how the cause of Indian unity was fatally undermined by Indian accommodationists.

3:144   Fenton, William N. *The Great Law and the Longhouse: A Political History of the Iroquois Confederacy.* Norman: University of Oklahoma Press, 1998. This narrative by a distinguished ethnologist tells the story of the Iroquois Confederacy in the seventeenth and eighteenth centuries. Drawing on both recent scholarship and contemporary Iroquois sources, he constructs a chronology of Iroquois history that is especially strong on myth, tradition, and attitudes.

3:145   Hinderaker, Eric. *Elusive Empires: Constructing Colonialism in the Ohio Valley, 1673–1800.* New York: Cambridge University Press, 1997. A highly original synthesis of recent scholarship, this describes changing patterns of European-Indian relations in the Ohio Valley between 1673 and 1800. Emphasizing cultural, diplomatic, and commercial interactions, the author posits three different kinds of empire (commerce, land, and liberty) and investigates the differential impact of each on native populations.

3:146   Hudson, Charles, and Carmen Chaves Tesser, eds. *The Forgotten Centuries: Indians and Europeans in the American South, 1521–1704.* Athens, GA: University of Georgia Press, 1994. This collection concentrates on the changing world of Indian peoples of southeastern North America in the sixteenth and seventeenth centuries. Multidisciplinary in nature, the papers, written by various specialists, address the social and economic structures of Indian chiefdoms in the early contact period and discuss comparatively the impact on Indian life of contact with Spanish explorers and missionaries and English fur and slave traders.

3:147   Jennings, Francis. "Brother Miquon: Good Lord!" In *The World of William Penn,* ed. Richard S. Dunn and Mary Maples Dunn, 195–214. Philadelphia: University of Pennsylvania Press, 1986. This essay describes the Indian land and treaty dealings of the founder and proprietor of Pennsylvania, the Quaker William Penn. A rarity among the Europeans in North America, Penn took pains to pay the Indians a fair price for land cessions and treated them as equals. Penn's successors were not so accommodating.

3:148   _____. *The Invasion of America: Indians, Colonialism, and the Cant of Conquest.* Chapel Hill: University of North Carolina Press for the Institute of Early American History and Culture, 1975. This work sweepingly indicts the European invasion

of Indian America as a story of unremitting duplicity, aggression, and injustice toward Indian peoples. The author holds that from the very beginning European colonists intended to dispossess and exterminate the Indian. Part II applies this formula to Puritan-Indian relations.

3:149   Jennings, Francis, William N. Fenton, Mary A. Druke, and David R. Miller, eds. *The History and Culture of Iroquois Diplomacy: An Interdisciplinary Guide to the Treaties of the Six Nations and Their League.* Syracuse: Syracuse University Press, 1985. The seven essays in this volume provide an interdisciplinary introduction to the methods, rituals, and functioning of Iroquois forest diplomacy during the seventeenth and eighteenth centuries, paying major attention to the protocols and symbols of Iroquois treaty-making. Anthropologist William N. Fenton introduces the collection with an analysis of change and continuity in Iroquois treaty-making. Ethnohistorian Francis Jennings traces the history and significance of Iroquois alliances in American history, while Robert J. Surtees, Mary A. Druke, and Michael K. Foster discuss the Iroquois in Canada, common forms of Iroquois treaties, and the function of wampum in Iroquois-white treaty-making. The book includes a glossary of Iroquoian diplomatic terms and symbols, a descriptive calendar of Iroquoian treaties (1613–1913), a list of participants in Iroquoian diplomacy, and a bibliography.

3:150   John, Elizabeth A. H. *Storms Brewed in Other Men's Worlds: The Confrontation of Indians, Spanish, and French in the Southwest, 1540–1795.* 2d ed. Norman: University of Oklahoma Press, 1996. This pioneering synthesis tells the story of encounters between the Spanish and Indians in New Mexico and the French and Indians in Texas between 1540 and 1795. Based on archival and secondary sources, the work emphasizes European imperial rivalries in America and examines the impact of these encounters on Indian life and culture. Originally published in 1975.

3:151   Jones, Dorothy V. *License for Empire: Colonialism by Treaty in Early America.* Chicago: University of Chicago Press, 1982. This study traces the brief life of a mutually advantageous "treaty system" negotiated between Indian peoples and British authorities in the Old Northwest during the 1760s.

Built on mutual accommodation rather than domination, the system broke down in the early 1770s owing to white expansion, the onset of the revolution, and intra-Indian rivalries.

3:152 Kupperman, Karen Ordahl. "Presentment of Civility: English Reading of American Self-Preservation in the Early Years of Colonization." *William and Mary Quarterly* 3d ser. 54 (January 1997): 193–228. This article explores early English attitudes about Indians and race in North America. Initially, English colonizers regarded Indians as akin to English and culturally improvable, but when Indians proved unwilling to assimilate, English observers concluded that they were racially inferior.

3:153 _____. *Settling with the Indians: The Meeting of English and Indian Cultures in America, 1580–1640.* Totowa, NJ: Rowman and Littlefield, 1980. This revisionist study examines the ideas of the first English colonizers and settlers of Virginia and Massachusetts about Indians and Indian culture. Rather than view Indians as inherently inferior by race, the first English saw them as "younger brothers" who could be civilized, Christianized, and assimilated into English society. Not until relations broke down and the Indians became formidable adversaries did the settlers begin to think of them as racially inferior and candidates for expropriation and enslavement.

3:154 Lurie, Nancy O. "Indian Cultural Adjustment to European Civilization." In *Seventeenth-Century America: Essays in Colonial History,* ed. James Morton Smith, 33–60. Chapel Hill: University of North Carolina Press for the Institute of Early American History and Culture, 1959. An important bellwether of the new Indian history and its methods, this case study of early Jamestown describes the political goals and diplomatic interactions of Indians and whites from both their points of view.

3:155 Martin, Joel W. "Southeastern Indians and the English Trade in Skins and Slaves." In *The Forgotten Centuries: Indians and Europeans in the American South, 1521–1704,* ed. Charles Hudson and Carmen Chaves Tesser, 304–24. Athens, GA: University of Georgia Press, 1994. This essay discusses the development and impact of the English trade in slaves and animal skins with Indian peoples of the interior southeast in the seventeenth and eighteenth centuries. Using ruthless tactics, exploitative English traders from Virginia and Carolina obtained thousands of Indian slaves and hundreds of thousands of animal skins and in the process undermined Indians' ability to resist English cultural and political domination.

3:156 McConnell, Michael N. *A Country Between: The Upper Ohio Valley and Its Peoples, 1724–1774.* Lincoln: University of Nebraska Press, 1992. This is a detailed account of diplomatic, military, and cultural interplay among Ohio Valley Indians (Delaware, Seneca, Shawnee) and French, British, and Anglo-American officials, traders, and border settlers in the mid-eighteenth century. Like the Iroquois, the Ohio Indians used the "play-off" system to check French and British imperial-colonial expansion only to find it unavailing once France ceded Canada. This book is the indispensable work on Indian-white diplomacy and politics in this most important "zone of international friction" before the American revolution.

3:157 Merrell, James H. "'The Customes of Our Countrey': Indians and Colonists in Colonial America." In *Strangers within the Realm: Cultural Margins of the First British Empire,* ed. Bernard Bailyn and Philip D. Morgan, 117–56. Chapel Hill: University of North Carolina Press for the Institute of Early American History and Culture, 1991. Drawing on a wide range of recent scholarship, this essay discusses patterns of encounter between Indians and Europeans in the colonial era, including the terms of interaction (war, disease, and settlement), and the protocols, language, and methods of both formal Indian diplomacy and informal personal contact.

3:158 _____. *Into the American Woods: Negotiators on the Pennsylvania Frontier.* New York: W. W. Norton, 1999. This book investigates the role of white and Indian "go-betweens" in forest diplomacy between the two cultures on the Pennsylvania frontier from the 1720s to the 1760s. It describes the special intercultural, linguistic, and behavioral qualifications required for the effective mediation of conflicts that were constantly occurring between Indians and Anglo-Americans whose visions of life and values were so sharply at odds.

3:159   Milanich, Jerald T. "Franciscan Missions and Native Peoples in Spanish Florida." In *The Forgotten Centuries: Indians and Europeans in the American South, 1521–1704,* ed. Charles Hudson and Carmen Chaves Tesser, 276–303. Athens, GA: University of Georgia Press, 1994. This essay discusses the history and role of Franciscan missions in Spanish Florida and Georgia in the seventeenth century. Backed by the Spanish crown as agents of empire, the 130 Franciscan missions founded during the century were shaken by repeated Indian uprisings and decisively destroyed by English-Indian military expeditions from Carolina during Queen Anne's War.

3:160   Morrison, Kenneth M. *The Embattled Northeast: The Elusive Ideal of Alliance in Abenaki-Euramerican Relations.* Berkeley: University of California Press, 1984. This book describes Abenaki Indian diplomatic and cultural relations with English and French authorities, missionaries, and settlers in the contested ground of northern New England and Nova Scotia. The work discusses Abenaki and European cultural and religious attitudes and traces the failed Abenaki effort to construct neutral partnerships with the French and English.

3:161   Oberg, Michael Leroy. *Dominion and Civility: English Imperialism and Native America, 1585–1685.* Ithaca: Cornell University Press, 1999. This detailed and balanced narrative of relations between the English and Indians in seventeenth-century Virginia and New England contends that English metropolitan elites pursued benevolent programs of Indian civilizing, Christianizing, and integration but invariably failed because of white settlers' racism, land hunger, and unwillingness to create an inclusive empire.

3:162   Reid, John Phillip. *A Better Kind of Hatchet: Law, Trade, and Diplomacy in the Cherokee Nation during the Early Years of European Contact.* University Park: Pennsylvania State University Press, 1976. This study investigates trade and diplomatic relations between Anglo-American South Carolinians and the Cherokee Indian towns of the southern mountain interior. The author describes Charles Town's use of a "trade diplomacy" strategy to bind to it Cherokee and other Indians and shows how the Cherokee became increasingly dependent on British

cloth, firearms, and tools after siding with Charles Town in the Yamasee War against the Creeks.

3:163   Richter, Daniel K. "Indian-Colonial Conflicts and Alliances." In *Encyclopedia of the North American Colonies,* ed. Jacob Ernest Cooke and William J. Eccles, 2: 223–36. New York: C. Scribner's Sons, 1993. This essay by a specialist provides a brief, authoritative account of colonial-Indian relations in the Chesapeake, New England, Pennsylvania, New York, and the Carolinas from first encounters until the revolution. The author's analysis of the contrasting cultural imperatives that guided English and Indian modes of conducting war and diplomacy is especially useful.

3:164   _____. *The Ordeal of the Longhouse: The Peoples of the Iroquois League in the Era of European Colonization.* Chapel Hill: University of North Carolina Press for the Institute of Early American History and Culture, 1992. A study of the Iroquois League in the seventeenth and eighteenth centuries, this important book concentrates on the nature and workings of Iroquois culture and society but discusses Iroquois politics and diplomacy as well. Richter emphasizes internal division and conflict within Indian clans and shows how these impeded the League's ability to organize united and sustained diplomatic and military responses to Euro-American imperial expansion.

3:165   Richter, Daniel K., and James H. Merrell, eds. *Beyond the Covenant Chain: The Iroquois and Their Neighbors in Indian North America, 1600–1800.* Syracuse: Syracuse University Press, 1987. These state-of-the-art essays by leading ethnohistorians treat the nature of Iroquois foreign relations and diplomacy in the seventeenth and eighteenth centuries. Focusing on whether an eighteenth-century Iroquois Covenant Chain alliance system actually existed, Daniel K. Richter and Richard L. Hahn see Iroquois relations with other peoples as decentralized, with abundant factionalism and divided councils. Other essays by Mary A. Druke, Neal Salisbury, Francis Jennings, Michael McConnell, James H. Merrell, Theda Perdue, and Douglass Boyce explore related issues, including Iroquois relations with the English, Algonquians, Delaware, Ohio Indians, Catawba, Cherokee, and the Tuscarora. Foreword by Wilcomb E. Washburn.

3:166   Rountree, Helen C. "The Powhatans and the English: A Case of Multiple Conflicting Agendas." In *Powhatan Foreign Relations, 1500–1722*, ed. Helen C. Rountree, 173–205. Charlottesville: University of Virginia Press, 1993. Emphasizing wide cultural differences between the Powhatans and Jamestown settlers, ethnohistorian Rountree relates the breakdown in their relations, the three ensuing tidewater wars, and the achievement of English military and cultural supremacy. In the same volume, essays by Jeffrey Hantman, Thomas Davidson, and Charlotte Gradie describe Powatan relations with the Piedmont Monacans, Eastern Shore Indians, and the Spanish.

3:167   Salisbury, Neal. "The Indians' Old World: Native Americans and the Coming of Europeans." *William and Mary Quarterly* 3d ser. 53 (July 1996): 435–58. This important article advances a conceptual framework for understanding the impact of Europeans on long-term patterns and processes of North American Indian life and culture. Prior to contact with Europeans, Indian societies had engaged in extensive indigenous trade and exchange; formed rivalries, alliances, and networks; and had concentrated and dispersed in large and small population centers. The first Europeans tended to accommodate to these patterns through trade, diplomacy, and forming of alliances, with Indians heavily influencing the form and content of these exchanges. But by the mid-eighteenth century, disease, war, and settlement had worked such devastation that remnant Indians had either retreated across the Mississippi or settled into politically powerless enclaves. Case studies of the Iroquois, Creeks, and Pueblo Indians document these generalizations.

3:168   _____. *Manitou and Providence: Indians, Europeans, and the Making of New England, 1500–1643*. New York: Oxford University Press, 1982. This study describes early contacts and interaction between English Puritans and Indian tribal groups in New England and traces ensuing changes in their perceptions and behavior from coexistence to hostility. The book emphasizes the actions and attitudes of both Puritans and Indians.

3:169   _____. "Native People and European Settlers in Eastern North America, 1600–1783." In *The Cambridge History of the Native Peoples of the Americas. Vol. 1: North America*, ed. Bruce G. Trigger and Wilcomb E. Washburn, 399–460. New York: Cambridge University Press, 1996. A synthesis of recent scholarship, this essay outlines the ever-changing kaleidoscope of rivalries, alliances, contests, and warfare among Indians and English, French, and Spanish colonials from 1607 through the American revolution. The author also discusses the various diplomatic strategies used by Indians to advance their interests and protect their autonomy. The essay concludes with a useful up-to-date bibliography.

3:170   Shannon, Timothy J. "Dressing for Success on the Mohawk Frontier: Henrick, William Johnson, and the Indian Fashion." *William and Mary Quarterly* 3d ser. 53 (January 1996): 13–42. This article explores the use by Indians and Europeans of each other's dress fashions in intercultural diplomacy on the New York–Indian frontier. Not only did Indian and Anglo-American diplomats achieve success by donning European and Indian clothing, but gifts of clothing also reflected its importance in forest diplomacy.

3:171   Trigger, Bruce G., and William R. Swagerty. "Entertaining Strangers: North America in the Sixteenth Century." In *The Cambridge History of the Native Peoples of the Americas. Vol. 1: North America*, ed. Bruce G. Trigger and Wilcomb E. Washburn, 325–98. New York: Cambridge University Press, 1996. This is a useful summary of early Spanish and French encounters and diplomatic relations with Indians in the West Indies and North America and includes an excellent bibliography.

3:172   Usner, Daniel H., Jr. "American Indians of the East." In *Encyclopedia of American Social History*, ed. Mary Kupiec Cayton, Elliot J. Gorn, and Peter W. Williams, 2: 657–65. New York: Charles Scribner's Sons, 1993. This essay discusses recent themes in the new scholarship of Indian-white relations in colonial America, discerning a trend away from geopolitical events and international conflicts to an emphasis on the complex ways that Indians related and responded to white settlement, especially through strategies of adaptation and resistance.

3:173   Vaughan, Alden T. *New England Frontier: Puritans and Indians, 1620–1675*. 3d ed. Norman: University of Oklahoma Press, 1995. This book describes contact, interaction, and adjustment between Puritans and Indians in seventeenth-century New England, emphasizing the Puritan viewpoint and Puritan agency. Topics include diplomatic contacts, missionary efforts, the United Colonies of New England, and the Pequot and King Phillip's Wars. First published in 1965.

3:174 Washburn, Wilcomb E. "Seventeenth-Century Indian Wars." In *Handbook of North American Indians. Vol. 15: Northeast,* ed. Bruce G. Trigger, 89–100. Washington, DC: Smithsonian Institution, 1978. Challenging the idea that the Europeans invaded the American continent determined to exterminate native peoples, Washburn proposes an accommodation-breakdown thesis to explain Indian-white conflict. "The history of European contact with the Indians of the East Coast, while often compared with the establishment of a military beachhead, was in fact a slower, less abrupt process of cautious feeling out of each party by the other, mutual accommodation according to what each had to offer the other, and eventual military confrontation over issues that are often obscure in their origin."

3:175 Weber, David J. *The Spanish Frontier in North America.* New Haven: Yale University Press, 1992. This is a broad, detailed, expert synthesis of scholarship on important phases of European-Indian contact in the borderlands from Florida to California. Although emphasizing social, cultural, and diplomatic interaction between Spanish and Indians, Weber also treats physical contacts and conflicts among Spanish, French, English, and Indians. He adds an excellent bibliography of primary and secondary sources.

3:176 White, Richard. *The Middle Ground: Indians, Empires, and Republics in the Great Lakes Region, 1650–1815.* New York: Cambridge University Press, 1991. This book traces the changing fortunes of a "middle ground" system of cultural, social, diplomatic, and political accommodation among French, British, and Indians in the Great Lakes region of North America in the mid-eighteenth century. By accommodation, adaptation, and negotiation, diverse ethnic groups and peoples coexisted in relative security and peace until the coercive and paternalistic policies of the new American republic upset this equilibrium.

3:177 Williams, Robert A. *Linking Arms Together: American Indian Treaty Visions of Law and Peace, 1600–1800.* New York: Oxford University Press, 1997. An extended essay by a legal historian, this book argues that an idealistic vision of multicultural harmony and coexistence guided the diplomacy of eastern woodland Indians between 1600 and 1800. Inferring from Indian treaty-making protocols, rituals, and rhetoric, the author holds that eastern Indians sought values of mutual trust, sharing, harmony, law, and peace in their treaty-making with English, and that these values can today constructively guide multiculturalism.

Slave Trade and Slavery

3:178 Blackburn, Robin. "The Old World Background to European Colonial Slavery." *William and Mary Quarterly* 3d ser. 54 (January 1997): 65–102. This article traces the history of European slavery from multiethnic Roman slavery to its medieval decline to its revival as African plantation slavery in the Americas. Based on a larger book-length study (*The Making of New World Slavery: From the Baroque to the Modern 1492–1800,* London: Verso, 1997), the article highlights colonial expansion, capitalist sugar production, and racial stigmatization as the driving forces behind slavery's revitalization.

3:179 Coughtry, Jay. *The Notorious Triangle: Rhode Island and the African Slave Trade, 1700–1807.* Philadelphia: Temple University Press, 1981. As the principal colonial carriers of slaves in the Atlantic system, eighteenth-century Rhode Island merchant captains conducted nearly a thousand voyages to West Africa. This book describes various facets of this slave trade including methods of negotiation with African slave rulers and merchants.

3:180 Davies, Kenneth Gordon. *The Royal African Company.* New York: Longmans, Green, 1957. Reprint 1975 (Octagon Books). This study describes the history of the Royal African Company (1672–1752) chartered by the English crown to trade with West Africa for gold, ivory, and slaves. The book also describes the fierce scramble among the

European powers on the West African coast for forts, allies, and slave sellers.

3:181   Davis, David Brion. "Constructing Race: A Reflection." *William and Mary Quarterly* 3d ser. 54 (January 1997): 7–18. Written by a leading scholar of slavery in western society, this essay forms a useful introduction to the theme of constructing race and racism. Not only does it incisively discuss recent historiographical trends about whether slavery created racism or vice versa, but offers insightful observations on such matters as differing European racial reactions to Africans and Indians, the flexibility and variability of early European racial attitudes, and Europeans' tendency to apply bestial stereotyping to a wide variety of class, religious, and racial "outsiders."

3:182   Klein, Herbert S. *The Atlantic Slave Trade.* New York: Cambridge University Press, 1999. The best recent synthesis, this book authoritatively discusses the Atlantic slave trade in its various transatlantic aspects including the mutual but complex nature of the relations between Africans and Europeans operating in the African marketplace. An especially useful chapter describes the fierce imperial competition among the European colonial powers for control of the trade. The book includes an excellent and comprehensive bibliographic essay.

3:183   Law, Robin. "West Africa in the Atlantic Community: The Case of the Slave Coast." *William and Mary Quarterly* 3d ser. 56 (April 1999): 307–34. This article explores interracial, intercultural, and diplomatic aspects of an "Atlantic community" of Africans and Europeans mutually involved in the transatlantic slave trade. Not only did African rulers repeatedly send diplomatic envoys to England, France, and Portuguese Brazil to encourage and regularize commercial exchanges in slaves, but, the authors hold, the trade generated such extensive interracial networks of traders and intermediaries and such intense cultural and social linkages across racial and national boundaries as to constitute a genuine Atlantic "community."

3:184   McGowan, Winston. "African Resistance to the Atlantic Slave Trade in West Africa." *Slavery and Abolition* 2, no. 1 (1990): 5–29. Drawing on recent secondary literature in his discussion of African resistance to the European slave trade in the Atlantic slave trade era, McGowan, a University of Guyana scholar, argues that African rulers' resistance was "relatively rare and was in striking contrast to the frequent resistance displayed by the captives themselves." He analyzes both how the trade operated in its African setting and how and why African rulers usually supported but occasionally resisted the trade.

3:185   Miller, Joseph C. "The Slave Trade." In *Encyclopedia of the North American Colonies,* ed. Jacob Ernest Cooke and William J. Eccles, 2: 45–66. New York: C. Scribner's Sons, 1993. This essay focuses on the international dimensions of the competition among the European imperial powers for access to African sources of slaves and to American and Caribbean markets. This competition intensified diplomatic, naval, and military rivalries and conflicts in both Europe and the Americas.

3:186   Morgan, Philip D. "African Migration." In *Encyclopedia of American Social History,* ed. Mary Kupiec Cayton, Elliot J. Gorn, and Peter W. Williams, 2: 795–809. New York: Charles Scribner's Sons, 1993. An excellent background synthesis of new scholarship, this essay by a leading specialist discusses slavery in Africa, the impact on the world of the Atlantic slave trade, the experience of transit, and issues of numbers, destinations, and cultural transmission. The essay includes a useful bibliography.

3:187   _____. "British Encounters with Africans and African-Americans, circa 1600–1700." In *Strangers within the Realm: Cultural Margins of the First British Empire,* ed. Bernard Bailyn and Philip D. Morgan, 157–219. Chapel Hill: University of North Carolina Press for the Institute of Early American History and Culture, 1991. Drawing on and identifying recent scholarship, the author discusses patterns of social and cultural interaction between whites and blacks in the several slave and slave-owning societies of England's Atlantic world. The essay also touches on diplomatic relations between English and West African rulers in the slave trade and on English and maroon communities in the colonies.

3:188   Rawley, James A. *The Transatlantic Slave Trade: A History.* New York: Norton, 1981. This is a useful synthesis of old and new scholarship that analyzes the transatlantic slave trade from the standpoint of the major European participants. The book describes English, European, and colonial slave merchants and their operations and explains how white slave captains negotiated access to slaves at waterside in West Africa. The international role played by the trade in the several imperial contests between Great Britain and her European commercial rivals is also described.

3:189   Reynolds, Edward. *Stand the Storm: A History of the Atlantic Slave Trade.* London: Allison and Busby, 1985. This is a compact, balanced introduction to the rise, working, demise, and impact on Africa of the Atlantic slave trade. The book shows the complexity of Africans' response to the slave trade and their difficulty in stopping it once it had gathered momentum.

3:190   Sweet, James H. "The Iberian Roots of American Racist Thought." *William and Mary Quarterly* 3d ser. 54 (January 1997): 143–66. This revisionist study argues the presence of strongly pejorative racial thinking about Africans on the part of Iberian Muslims, Portuguese, and Spanish well before the establishment of African plantation slavery in Latin America. Racial stigmatization, the author contends, was a necessary precondition for the rapid rise of plantation slavery in Portuguese Brazil and the Spanish West Indies.

3:191   Thornton, John. *Africa and Africans in the Making of the Atlantic World, 1400–1680.* New York: Cambridge University Press, 1992. This important study of the slave trade, emphasizing the role played by Africans as well as Europeans in the rise and operations of the Atlantic system, focuses on Africans as active participants in both the slave trade itself and in the slave and the slave-owning societies of North and South America.

Military and Naval Action and Affairs

3:192   Anderson, Fred. *A People's Army: Massachusetts Soldiers and Society in the Seven Years' War.* Chapel Hill: University of North Carolina Press for the Institute of Early American History and Culture, 1984. This book describes the formative experiences of Massachusetts provincial militiamen in the British-led campaigns of the Seven Years War. The book argues that the brutality of British army discipline and arrogance of the officer class toward American militia laid the basis for the province's hostile response to the arrival of British army units in Boston in 1768.

3:193   Brewer, John. *The Sinews of Power: War, Money, and the English State, 1688–1783.* New York: Alfred A. Knopf, 1989. This important book describes the rise of Britain's "fiscal-military state," which played a central role in its emergence as a great power. The author challenges prevailing notions of a weak, decentralized eighteenth-century state, holding that the excise, funding, and an efficient bureaucracy provided indispensable support for imperial Britain's century-long contest with France.

3:194   Gwyn, Julian. "British Government Spending and the North American Colonies, 1740–1755." In *The British Atlantic Empire before the American Revolution,* ed. Peter Marshall and Glyndwr Williams, 74–84. Totowa, NJ: Frank Cass, 1980. This chapter helps document the substantial contributions of men and supplies made by northern and middle colonies to Britain's war effort in America during King George's and the Seven Years Wars. In addition to large outlays of direct spending by British forces in America, Parliament provided for direct reimbursement to colonies that contributed, conveying £1,544,000 to the colonies as compensation for men and supplies between 1749 and 1763.

3:195   Lane, Kris E. *Pillaging the Empire: Piracy in the Americas, 1500–1750.* Armonk, NY: M. E. Sharpe, 1998. This overview narrative briskly describes the rise and fall of maritime predation from 1500 to the early eighteenth century. Focusing on the Spanish empire and the Caribbean, the book describes piracy and privateering as practiced by French, English, and Dutch captains and seamen until Great Britain decided that the ocean must be made safe for British commerce.

3:196   Lax, John, and William Pencak. "The Knowles Riot and the Crisis of the 1740's in Massachusetts." *Perspectives in American History* 10

(1976): 163–214. This essay analyzes the popular resistance to British impressment of colonial seamen for the royal navy that erupted in Boston in 1747. The article holds that impressment, a recurring practice, not only provoked crowd action against royal officers, but fostered an ideology of resistance that invoked the use of popular force in defense of fundamental rights.

3:197　　Leach, Douglas Edward. *Arms for Empire: A Military History of the British Colonies in North America, 1607–1763.* New York: Macmillan, 1973. This book begins by surveying the colonial Indian wars of the seventeenth century, but puts major emphasis on the four Anglo-French wars fought in North America between 1689 and 1763. The work pays special attention to campaigns, battles, and guerrilla warfare, to the role of European naval and military power, and to friction between British and provincial forces.

3:198　　_____. *Roots of Conflict: British Armed Forces and Colonial Americans, 1677–1763.* Chapel Hill: University of North Carolina Press, 1986. This study of relations between American publics and British military and naval forces during the eighteenth-century colonial wars stresses the negative impact of the latter on colonial attitudes. Quarrels between American provincial forces and British troops, abusive British recruiting and impressment, imperious behavior by British officers, and the brutality of British martial law were among the irritants that degraded relations. The book contends that these incidents alienated colonial publics from Great Britain and prepared them psychologically for revolution and independence.

3:199　　Peckham, Howard H. *The Colonial Wars 1689–1762.* Chicago: University of Chicago Press, 1964. This is a summary account of the wars waged by Anglo-Americans against France, Spain, and various Indian adversaries in eastern North America. Despite their distance from Europe, the American colonies were quickly embroiled in all the European wars, to which they contributed soldiers, ships, and supplies.

3:200　　Rediker, Marcus. *Between the Devil and the Deep Blue Sea: Merchant Seamen, Pirates, and the Anglo-American Maritime World, 1700–1750.*

New York: Cambridge University Press, 1987. Although mainly concerned with class, labor, and culture in the seafaring life of English and colonial seamen, this book also explores piracy, impressment, anti-impressment riots, and the African slave trade. Footnotes to these topics are especially useful.

3:201　　Ritchie, Robert C. *Captain Kidd and the War against the Pirates.* Cambridge, MA: Harvard University Press, 1986. The Scotland-born, sometime New York captain William Kidd operated as a privateer and pirate in the Caribbean and Indian Ocean in the 1690s. This book describes his piratical activities and represents his arrest, trial, and execution by imperial authorities as an important stage in a new British determination to make the maritime world safe for lawful commerce.

3:202　　Selesky, Harold E. *War and Society in Colonial Connecticut.* New Haven: Yale University Press, 1990. This study examines Connecticut's participation in Anglo-colonial wars and military expeditions between 1690 and 1762. Using cash bounties backed by impressment, the Connecticut assembly raised sizable contingents of militia volunteers for intercolonial expeditions that took Louisburg, invaded Canada, and captured Spanish strongholds in the Caribbean. In 1775, the confidence of Connecticut leaders in their military capability encouraged them to take up arms against the British empire.

3:203　　Shy, John W. *Toward Lexington: The Role of the British Army in the Coming of the American Revolution.* Princeton: Princeton University Press, 1965. This classic study shows how deployment of the British army in the mainland colonies affected the coming of the American revolution. The book authoritatively analyzes the fateful decision to station 10,000 troops, supported by colonial taxation, in North America and describes the ensuing train of incidents, disputes, and clashes between local civilians and British forces that fostered the breakdown of relations.

3:204　　Steele, Ian K. *Warpaths: Invasions of North America.* New York: Oxford University Press, 1994. A work of both synthesis and interpretation, this book describes the invasion of North America by the Spanish, French, Dutch, and English, the responses of Indian peoples to these "invasions," and their impact on Indian life and culture. Attention is paid to the roles of European regular and colonial military forces, the shifting patterns of Indian allies and adversaries, and the effect of these wars on both Indians and colonial Europeans.

3:205   Stout, Neil R. *The Royal Navy in America, 1760–1775: A Study of Enforcement of British Colonial Policy in the Era of the American Revolution.* Annapolis: Naval Institute Press, 1973. In 1763, the British admiralty ordered a squadron of twenty-one royal navy vessels to American waters to enforce British trade and tax regulations. This study describes the history of this naval phase of the new trade and taxing program and how the navy's operations (including the impressment of colonial sailors) fostered colonial resentment, resistance, and finally revolution.

3:206   Swanson, Carl E. "American Privateering and Imperial Warfare, 1739–1748." *William and Mary Quarterly* 3d ser. 42 (July 1985): 357–82. Colonial privateers played an important role during the Anglo-Spanish and Anglo-French wars of the 1740s. The mainland colonies contributed 30,000 seamen and more than 100 privateers to the maritime phase of the war against France and Spain.

3:207   _____. *Predators and Prizes: American Privateering and Imperial Warfare, 1739–1748.* Columbia: University of South Carolina Press, 1991. This study expands the author's earlier article, "American Privateering and Imperial Warfare, 1739–1748" (1985) (3:206), on colonial privateering and its role in the Anglo-Spanish-French War of Jenkins' Ear and King George's War (1739–1748), describing the nature of eighteenth-century privateering and giving valuable comparative data on numbers of colonial, English, Spanish, and French privateers engaged, prizes taken, sailors participating, and financial gains and losses. The study concludes that privateering "played the leading role in America's war effort in the 1740s."

Growth of Colonial Statecraft

VIEW FROM AMERICA

3:208   Hinderaker, Eric. "The 'Four Indian Kings' and the Imaginative Construction of the First British Empire." *William and Mary Quarterly* 3d ser. 53 (July 1996): 487–526. This article explores the stage-managed diplomatic visit to London in 1710 of four Iroquois "kings." Orchestrated by colonial leaders to drum up English support for an invasion of French Canada, the visit inspired not only official support for an Anglo-American expedition in 1711, but elicited a new popular patriotic enthusiasm for empire in the British public.

3:209   Johnson, Richard R. *Adjustment to Empire: The New England Colonies, 1675–1715.* New Brunswick: Rutgers University Press, 1981. This detailed study traces the adjustment to empire of the four New England colonies of Massachusetts, New Hampshire, Connecticut, and Rhode Island. Eschewing former tactics of obstructionism and resistance, New England leaders after the Glorious Revolution accepted a measure of control from Whitehall, learned to accommodate to the new imperial order, mastered transatlantic lobbying, and turned the opportunities of empire to their own advantage.

3:210   Lovejoy, David S. *The Glorious Revolution in America.* New York: Harper and Row, 1972. Reprint 1987 (Wesleyan University Press). This is a valuable study of the first major intercolonial protest against imperial centralization. The work shows the depth of the colonies' aspirations for guaranteed self-government within the empire and the early use of transatlantic lobbying, constitutional claims, and civil disobedience.

3:211   Newbold, Robert C. *The Albany Congress and Plan of Union of 1754.* New York: Vantage Press, 1955. This is a narrative history of the summer 1754 Albany congress, which met at the initiative of the Board of Trade to repair relations with the Iroquois. Instead of Indian affairs, however, the book emphasizes the plan for a permanent confederation, proposed by Benjamin Franklin, to be headed by a grand council of elected delegates and a president-general chosen by the British king. Intended to bolster the colonies' security against the French in Canada, the Albany plan failed to muster support from any colonial legislature or the British government.

3:212   Olson, Alison Gilbert. "The British Government and Colonial Union, 1754." *William and Mary Quarterly* 3d ser. 17 (January 1960): 22–34. This article examines the British government's failure to endorse the plan for a permanent confederation recommended by the Albany congress in 1754. Although the Board of Trade had proposed a similar plan for colonial union, the article suggests that a major factor in Britain's indifference was concern that a confederation would encourage colonial independence from Great Britain.

3:213   Pencak, William. *War, Politics, & Revolution in Provincial Massachusetts.* Boston: Northeastern University Press, 1981. Pencak holds that between 1690 and 1763, Massachusetts was called on by Britain to support her American military campaigns against France and that the colony "proved far more diligent" in supplying both men and money than other colonies. Describing these contributions in detail, he further contends that the colony's resistance to British tax policies in the 1760s and 1770s resulted in part from resentment at Britain's apparent lack of appreciation.

3:214   Ritchie, Robert C. *The Duke's Province: A Study of New York Politics and Society, 1664–1691.* Chapel Hill: University of North Carolina Press, 1977. Concentrating on internal domestic development, this book discusses international and intercolonial diplomatic relations as well. Seventeenth-century English New York was subject to chronic ethnic and factional conflict, land and sea attacks, and fears of internal conspiracy and enemy invasion. Unhappy with the Dominion of New England, New York remained in turmoil until the more accommodating royal charter of 1691 established a firmer basis for stability.

3:215   Shannon, Timothy J. *Indians and Colonists at the Crossroads of Empire: The Albany Congress of 1754.* Ithaca: Cornell University Press, 2000. A revisionist study of the Anglo-Indian-colonial congress held in Albany, New York, in 1754, this book emphasizes the conference as a chapter in British empire-building rather than nascent state-making or federalism. Although the colonial delegates accepted Franklin's plan for an intercolonial union, their main business was treaty-making and diplomacy with the Iroquois against a background of impending Anglo-French war in the Ohio Country. The book contains an extensive, up-to-date bibliography.

3:216   Sosin, Jack M. *English America and Imperial Inconstancy: The Rise of Provincial Autonomy, 1696–1715.* Lincoln: University of Nebraska Press, 1985. This is a political study of relations between Britain and the mainland colonies from 1696 to 1715 at a time when the colonies' autonomy was still at risk. Although royal officials wanted stronger imperial controls over the colonies, they were thwarted by distance, ministerial instability, changes in the Board of Trade, and especially the decision to make royal governors financially dependent on colonial assemblies. The book overlooks, however, the development of an effective system of transatlantic lobbying, patrons, and interest groups through which colonial political leaders won concessions, resolved local disputes, and made the empire work.

3:217   Ward, Harry M. *"Unite or Die": Intercolony Relations, 1690–1763.* Port Washington, NY: Kennikat Press, 1971. This is a useful introduction to political, military, and diplomatic cooperation among the British mainland colonies between 1690 and 1763. Topics include early ideas of political union, intercolonial war planning conferences and military operations, and joint boundary commissions. The colonies often did not work together effectively and frequently appealed to the English crown for help in resolving disputes and for financial and military aid.

TRANSATLANTIC LOBBIES AND POLITICIANS

3:218   Dickerson, Oliver M. *American Colonial Government, 1696–1765: A Study of the British Board of Trade in Its Relation to the American Colonies, Political, Industrial, and Administrative.* Cleveland: Arthur H. Clark Company, 1912. This classic study describes the methods, responsibilities, and dealings of the British Board of Trade in relation to the American colonies and other major departments and officers of Britain's imperial administration. With only an advisory role in most colonial matters, the board's members were nonetheless constantly sought after by colonial agents, lobbyists, claimants, and petitioners who wanted favorable treatment by British authorities.

3:219 Henretta, James A. *"Salutary Neglect": Colonial Administration under the Duke of Newcastle.* Princeton: Princeton University Press, 1972. This book analyzes the politics of "salutary neglect" that English imperial officials pursued from 1720 to 1750. Guided by expediency, patronage, constitutional legalism, and bureaucratic inertia, "salutary neglect" was an improvised, haphazard policy that rejected constructive proposals for administrative reform and encouraged aggressive colonial claims to legislative and fiscal autonomy within the empire.

3:220 Hutson, James H. "Benjamin Franklin and the Parliamentary Grant for 1758." *William and Mary Quarterly* 3d ser. 23 (October 1966): 575–95. Benjamin Franklin was actively engaged as the Pennsylvania assembly's agent in London during much of the Seven Years War. This article describes his successful lobbying of the British government for reimbursement to Pennsylvania for troops and money contributed to the British war effort. Franklin invested this money in public securities, which subsequently depreciated owing to Pitt's resignation and the war's continuation.

3:221 Kammen, Michael G. *A Rope of Sand: The Colonial Agents, British Politics, and the American Revolution.* Ithaca: Cornell University Press, 1968. The most detailed, comprehensive study of the colonial agency, this book analyzes the methods, resources, and effectiveness of Anglo-American colonial agents at Westminster and Whitehall. Numerous American and English agents served throughout the colonial period as quasi-diplomatic emissaries and lobbyists for the American colonies that employed them. Compiling a mixed record, by the late 1760s and early 1770s colonial agents had lost much of their ability to influence British policy as the terms of the Anglo-colonial constitutional dispute hardened. The book contains valuable biographical and bibliographical data.

3:222 Katz, Stanley Nider. *Newcastle's New York: Anglo-American Politics, 1732–1753.* Cambridge, MA: Belknap Press of Harvard University Press, 1968. This work uses the province of New York in a detailed case study of Anglo-American colonial politics from 1732 to 1752. The book demonstrates the haphazard nature of English colonial policy, the poor quality of royal governors, and the importance of political influence at Whitehall for both royal governors and their colonial political adversaries.

3:223 Lonn, Ella. *The Colonial Agents of the Southern Colonies.* Chapel Hill: University of North Carolina Press, 1945. This pioneering study of the rise and activities of colonial agents who represented the southern mainland colonies in London still has value. Although superseded in many respects by Kammen's *A Rope of Sand: The Colonial Agents, British Politics, and the American Revolution* (1968) (3:221), the book is well researched, offers useful descriptive information, and has an extensive bibliography.

3:224 Olson, Alison Gilbert. *Anglo-American Politics 1660–1775: The Relationship between Parties in England and Colonial America.* New York: Oxford University Press, 1973. This study usefully describes how colonial agents, transatlantic lobby groups, and colonial officials influenced English policymaking and appointments in the early and middle decades of the eighteenth century. Olson also traces the decline of this policymaking system in the 1750s, 1760s, and 1770s.

3:225 _____. *Making the Empire Work: London and American Interest Groups, 1690–1790.* Cambridge, MA: Harvard University Press, 1992. The product of a lifetime of research, this study analyzes the operation of the transatlantic system of politics and influence that kept the British empire working relatively well in the half century before the American revolution. Strong transatlantic mercantile, ecclesiastical, and ethnic lobbies proved effective in getting British agencies (including Parliament) to act favorably on desired imperial and colonial legislation and to block or disallow local legislation considered offensive. As a result, colonial America grew accustomed to a responsive and restrained imperial London government. The book ends with an insightful discussion of why this system collapsed in revolution.

3:226 _____. "The Virginia Merchants of London: A Study in Eighteenth-Century Interest Group Politics." *William and Mary Quarterly* 3d ser. 40 (July 1983): 363–88. This article shows the role played by informal transatlantic lobbies in the working of the British empire before 1763.

3:227 Olson, Alison Gilbert, and Richard Maxwell Brown, eds. *Anglo-American Political Relations, 1675–1775.* New Brunswick: Rutgers University Press, 1970. The eleven essays in this volume represent examples of the new Anglo-American history, emphasizing informal modes of Anglo-American political and diplomatic interaction in the colonial era. Most notable are Richard S. Dunn's analysis of the different reactions by local leaders in Massachusetts and Jamaica to imperial centralization in the 1680s, Stanley N. Katz's discussion of how Anglo-American politician James DeLancey used his London connections to political advantage in provincial New York, and Alison G. Olson's investigation of the commissaries of the Bishop of London and their use of London church connections.

3:228 Price, Jacob M. "Who Cared about the Colonies? The Impact of the Thirteen Colonies on British Society and Politics, circa 1714–1775." In *Strangers within the Realm: Cultural Margins of the First British Empire,* ed. Bernard Bailyn and Philip D. Morgan, 395–436. Chapel Hill: University of North Carolina Press for the Institute of Early American History and Culture, 1991. This exploratory survey identifies groups and classes of people within England connected to the colonies and assesses how they influenced decisionmaking through office holding, lobbying, and agitation. Price also discusses the economic, fiscal, and administrative burdens of empire and the role of colonial trade in the English economy.

3:229 Sosin, Jack M. *Agents and Merchants: British Colonial Policy and the Origins of the American Revolution, 1763–1775.* Lincoln: University of Nebraska Press, 1965. This is a detailed study of attempts by colonial agents and British merchants to head off confrontation between Britain and the mainland colonies over new imperial policies and Parliament's claim to supreme sovereignty. While their lobbying at Whitehall and Westminster achieved some success, they could not resolve the constitutional issue between Britain and the colonies' claim to home rule.

3:230 _____. *Whitehall and the Wilderness: The Middle West in British Colonial Policy, 1760–1775.* Lincoln: University of Nebraska Press, 1961. Still the best treatment of British management of the trans-Allegheny middle west between 1760 and 1775, this book describes the failure of British authorities to protect Indians by regulating colonial fur traders and holding back white settlers and the heavy lobbying of British officials at Whitehall by the agents of colonial land companies seeking crown approval of wilderness claims. Based on extensive archival research, it includes an extensive bibliographic essay and listings.

3:231 Steele, Ian K. "The Board of Trade, the Quakers, and Resumption of Colonial Charters, 1699–1702." *William and Mary Quarterly* 3d ser. 23 (October 1966): 596–619. Intermittently during the late seventeenth and early eighteenth centuries, imperial officials like William Blathwayt pressed for the repeal of corporate and proprietary charters in their quest for greater administrative control over English colonies. This article describes how lobbying by English Quakers, activated by William Penn, blocked a Reunion Bill of 1701 that would have royalized Pennsylvania and other private and corporate colonies.

3:232 _____. *Politics of Colonial Policy: The Board of Trade in Colonial Administration 1696–1720.* Oxford: Clarendon Press, 1968. This detailed study investigates the composition, administration, and policies of the Board of Trade from its creation in 1696 through the reign of Queen Anne, when it tried to increase English trade and revenues by tightening imperial control of the colonies, unsuccessfully urging that Parliament replace corporate and proprietary charters with royal government. Lobbying by William Penn, other English Quakers, and colonial agents helped defeat the proposal.

British-American Cultural Relations and Attitudes

3:233　Bonomi, Patricia U. *The Lord Cornbury Scandal: The Politics of Reputation in British America.* Chapel Hill: University of North Carolina Press for the Omohundro Institute of Early American History and Culture, 1998. Edward Hyde, Lord Cornbury, was an army officer, Tory royalist, cousin of Queen Anne, and royal governor of New York and New Jersey from 1702 to 1710. This revisionist study demolishes the conventional view of Cornbury as a grafter, voluptuary, and cross-dresser while describing his governorship in terms of British empire-building and the highly partisan, changeful transatlantic politics of the early empire.

3:234　Botein, Stephen. "The Anglo-American Book Trade before 1776: Personnel and Strategies." In *Printing and Society in Early America,* ed. William L. Joyce, David D. Hall, Richard D. Brown, and John B. Hench, 48–82. Worcester, MA: American Antiquarian Society, 1983. This essay establishes a useful framework for viewing the transatlantic Anglo-colonial book trade as "a mechanism for cultural transmission." Examining such themes as categories of books imported, business strategies, and changing book-buying habits, the essay underscores the fact of a dramatic growth in English book imports in the three decades before the revolution.

3:235　Bowen, H. V. *Elites, Enterprise, and the Making of the British Overseas Empire, 1688–1775.* New York: St. Martin's Press, 1996. This synthesis of recent scholarship explores the forces that made for the integration and unity of Britain's overseas empire in the first two-thirds of the eighteenth century. Emphasizing commercial, social, and cultural developments in Britain and her colonies in North America, the West Indies, and India, the author describes this eighteenth-century empire as a "commercial, cultural, and social body of reasonably sharp definition which had its roots very firmly planted in metropolitan society." The book discusses recent historiographical trends and provides important bibliographical and footnote references.

3:236　Breen, T. H. "'Baubles of Britain': The American and Consumer Revolutions of the Eighteenth Century." In *Of Consuming Interests: The Style of Life in the Eighteenth Century,* ed. Cary Carson, Ronald Hoffman, and Peter J. Albert, 444–82. Charlottesville: University Press of Virginia for the United States Capitol Historical Society, 1994. This essay finds the origins of American nationalism in a colonial reaction against a surge of imported "baubles from Britain" that supplied the "consumer revolution" of the mid-eighteenth century. Originally vehicles of Anglicization, consumer goods imported into the colonies from Britain stirred an emergent national consciousness, then translated into a shared commitment to collective action. Frankly speculative, this important essay was first published in *Past and Present* (no. 119, 1988): 73–104.

3:237　_____. "An Empire of Goods: The Anglicization of Colonial America, 1690–1776." *Journal of British Studies* 25 (October 1986): 467–99. Emphasizing the influx of British imports into the mainland colonies after 1740, this book holds that growing consumption of British-made consumer goods made for greater integration of each mainland colony not only with Britain but other colonies. The author further argues that this development meant that "on the eve of the American Revolution, Americans were more English than they had been in the past since the first years of the colonies."

3:238　_____. "Ideology and Nationalism on the Eve of the American Revolution: Revisions Once More in Need of Revising." *Journal of American History* 84 (June 1997): 13–39. Citing new scholarship on mid-eighteenth-century English state-building, nationalism, and popular enthusiasm for empire, this essay breaks new ground by suggesting a relationship between these trends and colonial resistance to Britain's imperial measures of the 1760s and 1770s. Proud of being part of a free, prosperous, and glorious imperial community, patriotic colonial Americans resented their exclusion from the empire's full rights and benefits to which they felt they had an equal claim. The essay also summarizes recent historiographical trends.

3:239　Clark, Charles E. *The Public Prints: The Newspaper in Anglo-American Culture, 1665–1740.* New York: Oxford University Press, 1993. This detailed study emphasizes the cultural importance of colonial newspapers both as agents of Anglicization and of intercolonial awareness. Heavily weighted toward English and European subject matter but including a small but growing amount of American news, colonial newspapers fostered not only British patriotism and "a sense of Englishness," but "a sense of kinship with colonials elsewhere."

3:240   Clark, Charles E., and Charles Wetherell. "The Measure of Maturity: The Pennsylvania Gazette, 1728–1765." *William and Mary Quarterly* 3d ser. 46 (April 1989): 279–303. Based on a content analysis of the *Pennsylvania Gazette,* this article demonstrates that Franklin's weekly newspaper presented its readers with a Eurocentric world preoccupied with military and diplomatic news. Reports of military, naval, and diplomatic subjects, copied from British, European, and colonial newspapers, dominated the *Gazette*'s pages, especially during war years. Challenged by the imperial crisis over taxation in the 1760s, the *Gazette* and other newspapers changed from "provincial mirrors of English culture and imperial authority to active combatants in the political wars," and local American subjects now dominated their news.

3:241   Colley, Linda. *Britons: Forging the Nation, 1707–1837.* New Haven: Yale University Press, 1992. This important work provides a rich analysis of the rise of popular British nationalism during the long series of eighteenth- and early-nineteenth-century imperial and continental wars with France. Defined as a sense of "imagined political community," British nationalism developed in the context of these wars and carried a special sense of identity that was largely forged in reaction against the Other. Colonial Americans belonged to this same "imagined political community" until they broke with Britain over their claims to its full and equal rights and benefits.

3:242   Gould, Eliga H. *The Persistence of Empire: British Political Culture in the Age of the American Revolution.* Chapel Hill: University of North Carolina Press for the Omohundro Institute of Early American History and Culture, 2000. This book addresses the question of the nature of British public support for the government's efforts to establish parliamentary supremacy over North America in the face of the colonies' insistence on setting their own constitutional terms. The work holds that ministerial backing for post-1760 tax and regulation colonial policies rested on a broad popular base of enthusiasm for empire and a conviction that the colonies were morally bound to contribute financially to help protect, police, and preserve the hard-won gains of the Seven Years War. The book also considers public support for the "bluewater" policy of colonial expansion that replaced the Europe-centered strategic focus of the pre-1750 decades.

3:243   Greene, Jack P. *Pursuits of Happiness: The Social Development of Early Modern British Colonies and the Formation of American Culture.* Chapel Hill: University of North Carolina Press, 1988. This highly informative work of both synthesis and interpretation places the mainland colonies in a broader framework of British-American social and cultural development. The book identifies salient behaviors and values of an emerging American society centering on "the notion of an America as a place peculiarly favored for the quest of the good life, defined as the pursuit of individual happiness and material achievement."

3:244   Hancock, David. *Citizens of the World: London Merchants and the Integration of the British Atlantic Community, 1735–1785.* New York: Cambridge University Press, 1995. A penetrating study of twenty-three London merchants who traded with Africa, the West Indies, India, and mainland English America in an age of imperial expansion, this book explores how they managed the business of empire, expanded and settled imperial holdings, improved the infrastructure of Atlantic commercial and cultural integration, and spread the ideas and practices of the practical Enlightenment.

3:245   Landsman, Ned C. "The Provinces and the Empire: Scotland, the American colonies, and the Development of British Provincial Identity." In *An Imperial State at War: Britain from 1689 to 1815,* ed. Lawrence Stone, 258–87. New York: Routledge, 1994. This essay investigates mid-eighteenth-century commercial and cultural relations between Scotland and the American colonies and posits the development of a distinct consciousness in each. Both dependencies celebrated a common British citizenship in an empire of British constitutional liberty but also viewed the free, burgeoning American colonies as the empire's moral center and most dynamic sector. This consciousness provided an important basis for the American revolutionary challenge to British authority.

3:246 Reilly, Elizabeth Carroll. "The Wages of Piety: The Boston Book Trade of Jeremy Condy." In *Printing and Society in Early America,* ed. William L. Joyce, David D. Hall, Richard D. Brown, and John B. Hench, 83–131. Worcester, MA: American Antiquarian Society, 1983. Drawing on the credit records and estate inventory of Boston bookseller Jeremy Condy, Reilly sheds valuable light on the process of Anglo-colonial cultural transmission on the eve of the revolution, analyzing the occupations and locations of Condy's New England customers. Included is a detailed inventory of English book and periodical publications in stock at the time of his death in 1768.

3:247 Sachse, William L. *The Colonial American in Britain.* Madison: University of Wisconsin Press, 1956. This book explores the experience of colonial students, merchants, clergy, educators, agents, lobbyists, politicians, and tourists who crossed the Atlantic to visit England during the colonial period. While these colonial Americans found much in English society and culture to admire, by the 1760s many also felt disenchantment.

3:248 Shields, David S. *Oracles of Empire: Poetry, Politics, and Commerce in British America, 1690–1750.* Chicago: University of Chicago Press, 1990. Drawing on many little-known print and manuscript texts, this study demonstrates the existence of a strong Anglo-American literature of imperial celebration in the first half of the eighteenth century, the direct impact of British politico-literary traditions on colonial culture, and the close attention colonial writers paid to British and American commercial and imperial successes. It also explores an emerging colonial literature affirmative of colonial rights and critical of royal governors.

3:249 Smith, Mark M. "Culture, Commerce, and Calendar Reform in Colonial America." *William and Mary Quarterly* 3d ser. 60 (October 1998): 557–84. This article suggestively explores the implications of the Parliament-imposed Gregorian calendar reform of 1752 as it affected England and the colonies. Immediately accepted without dissent by the colonies, calendar reform not only confirmed the reality of an

Anglo-colonial identity but laid a necessary basis for the eventual construction of an American national consciousness.

3:250 Steele, Ian K. *The English Atlantic, 1675–1740: An Exploration of Communication and Community.* New York: Oxford University Press, 1986. This book describes the growth of transatlantic shipping and communication from 1690 to 1740 as well as its impact on Anglo-American relations. Such developments as increased shipping, books, newspapers, mail, and periodicals made for closer economic, cultural, and political ties, at least for literate elites, and promoted a truly integrated transatlantic community.

Anglo-American Confrontation

FIRST PHASE: 1763–1768

3:251 Bullion, John L. "British Ministers and American Resistance to the Stamp Act, October-December 1765." *William and Mary Quarterly* 3d ser. 49 (January 1992): 89–107. This detailed examination of British ministerial responses to the Stamp Act riots sheds new light on political-military calculations by the Rockingham cabinet and lobbying by British merchants trading with America.

3:252 _____. *A Great and Necessary Measure: George Grenville and the Genesis of the Stamp Act, 1763–1765.* Columbia: University of Missouri Press, 1982. This work is a searching inquiry into the purposes behind Treasury Lord George Grenville's fateful Sugar and Stamp Acts. The study holds that these tax and regulation measures were guided as much by a perceived need to reduce the colonies to obedient subordination as to raise revenue for the new burdens of empire.

3:253 _____. "Security and Economy: The Bute Administration's Plan for the American Army and Revenue, 1762–1763." *William and Mary Quarterly* 3d ser. 45 (July 1988): 499–509. This article sheds fresh light on the thinking of George III and Lord Bute as they weighed how to manage Britain's new possessions in Canada and the west. Needing military forces for defense and the funds to pay for them, they committed the power and prestige of the government to raising revenue in America, thus forcing Bute's successors to experiment with stamp and sugar duties.

3:254 Clark, Dora Mae. *The Rise of the British Treasury: Colonial Administration in the Eighteenth Century.* New Haven: Yale University Press, 1960. This book provides the standard account of the rise of the British Treasury as a major force in eighteenth-century imperial administration and policymaking. Early in the century Walpole and the Pelhams accepted the necessity of a laxly administered empire, but by 1758 increasing expenditures occasioned by outlays for Nova Scotia and Georgia and the Seven Years War forced the Treasury to begin fiscal reforms. In 1763, the aggressive George Grenville as First Treasury Lord launched a fateful program of new colonial taxes and imperial tightening.

3:255 Marshall, P. J. "The Eighteenth Century Empire." In *British Politics and Society from Walpole to Pitt, 1742–1789,* ed. Jeremy Black, 177–200. New York: St. Martin's Press, 1990. A compact discussion of the theme of change and continuity in Britain's developing eighteenth-century empire, this essay not only summarizes current scholarship on Britain's world empire, but usefully restates the prevailing view of historians about the origins of the American revolution. "A new sense of empire" and a "new determination to enforce old policies " took form during the Seven Years War, which, in turn, led to a series of "piecemeal and incoherent" parliamentary measures aimed at a greater imperial control.

3:256 Morgan, Edmund S., and Helen M. Morgan. *The Stamp Act Crisis: Prologue to Revolution.* Chapel Hill: University of North Carolina Press for the Institute of Early American History and Culture, 1995. This classic study describes the anatomy of colonial resistance to the Sugar and Stamp Acts, which were George Grenville's measures for raising money and establishing authority in America. The book examines the attempts by colonial agents in London to head these measures off and assesses the impact of the crisis on the genesis of the revolution. Earlier editions were published in 1953 and 1963. The 1995 edition contains a new author's preface and bibliographical references.

3:257 O'Shaughnessy, Andrew Jackson. "The Stamp Act Crisis in the British Caribbean." *William and Mary Quarterly* 3d ser. 51 (April 1994): 203–26. Although sharing the same adverse views of parliamentary taxation, the British West Indies did not join the thirteen mainland colonies in a revolutionary opposition. This article describes popular resistance to the Stamp Act on the islands of St. Kitts and Nevis, but acknowledges that, unlike the mainland colonists, colonial islanders as a whole were deeply concerned about "their domestic military strength and the danger of local slave rebellions."

3:258 Thomas, Peter D. G. *British Politics and the Stamp Act Crisis: The First Phase of the American Revolution, 1763–1767.* Oxford: Clarendon Press, 1975. The first of three volumes that treat Britain's failed attempt to establish effective parliamentary supremacy over the empire, this book focuses on the early British policies and constitutional claims that set the stage for revolution. Although problems associated with the American west and Indians had some importance, the author emphasizes British concern over the colonies' growing maturity and defiance of trade laws.

3:259 _____. *The Townshend Duties Crisis: The Second Phase of the American Revolution.* Oxford: Clarendon Press, 1987. This book authoritatively treats the revival of the constitutional controversy between Great Britain and the colonies over the claim that Britain's sovereignty centered in, and should be exercised through, Parliament. The second of three volumes that pursues this theme, the book treats the Townshend Acts crisis up to the Tea Act of 1773 and emphasizes British policymaking.

3:260 Tucker, Robert W., and David C. Hendrickson. *The Fall of the First British Empire: Origins of the War of American Independence.* Baltimore: Johns Hopkins University Press, 1982. This expert synthesis by two political scientists productively reassesses a large literature and makes the case for the American revolution as the result of problems at the colonial periphery rather than a basic change of attitude at the imperial center. Analyzing the program of imperial reform adopted at the end of the Seven Years War, they stress not only its basic continuity with long-standing imperial objectives but the intractable contradiction between Britain and the mainland colonies in terms of what each expected and could accept in the imperial-colonial relationship.

SECOND PHASE: 1768–1775

3:261   Ammerman, David L. *In the Common Cause: American Response to the Coercive Acts of 1774.* Charlottesville: University Press of Virginia, 1974. This book examines the anatomy of intercolonial resistance that developed in the wake of the Coercive Acts enacted by Parliament in 1774. Aimed at Massachusetts alone, the acts galvanized protest, organization, and resistance that crossed colonial lines, encompassing all thirteen colonies and culminating in the First Continental Congress.

3:262   Bailyn, Bernard. *The Ideological Origins of the American Revolution.* Cambridge, MA: Belknap Press of Harvard University Press, 1967. Based heavily on pamphlets and other writings of the revolutionary generation's literate elite, this book holds that the revolution was primarily an ideological-constitutional struggle. The book emphasizes the determinative importance of a received British Radical Whig tradition, relates this tradition to the emerging British-colonial struggle, and effectively describes its transforming effect on Americans' sense of themselves as a people uniquely positioned to construct a new and better polity. The book is a slightly modified version of the general introduction to vol. 1 of his *Pamphlets of the American Revolution, 1750–1776* (1965) (3:2).

3:263   Donoughue, Bernard. *British Politics and the American Revolution: The Path to War, 1773–75.* London: Macmillan, 1964. This is a detailed, balanced discussion of the last stages of the confrontation between the British government and the colonies over the issue of parliamentary supremacy. After the Tea Act provoked renewed colonial resistance, the North ministry could not let such a blatant challenge to British imperial authority go unpunished. British coercion of Boston, in turn, led to new tests of strength, dooming last-ditch attempts by colonial agent Benjamin Franklin and colonial secretary Lord Dartmouth to negotiate reconciliation. The book also describes the important role of a resolute and determined king, and concludes by doubting whether any compromise or concession could have saved the empire.

3:264   Labaree, Benjamin Woods. *The Boston Tea Party.* New York: Oxford University Press, 1964. The Boston Tea Party, intended to foil a perceived ministerial stratagem to trap colonial Americans into paying the Townshend tax on imported tea, triggered a cycle of action and reaction that led directly to revolution. This classic account describes the genesis of this event and persuasively explains why the British ministry and Boston leaders adamantly refused to yield.

3:265   O'Shaughnessy, Andrew Jackson. *An Empire Divided: The American Revolution and the British Caribbean.* Philadelphia: University of Pennsylvania Press, 2000. A broad synthesis of secondary and primary sources, this work addresses why Anglo-Americans in the British West Indies remained loyal to the British crown while their counterparts on the mainland engaged in resistance and revolution. Acknowledging the force of such considerations as racial and military security, the book holds that whites in the West Indies were too dependent socially and culturally on Britain to embrace revolution.

3:266   Reid, John Phillip. *Constitutional History of the American Revolution. Vol. 1: The Authority of Rights. Vol. 2: The Authority to Tax. Vol. 3: The Authority to Legislate. Vol. 4: The Authority of Law.* Madison: University of Wisconsin Press, 1986–1993. These four volumes learnedly examine issues of the revolutionary era from a legal-constitutional standpoint. Reid argues that legal and constitutional issues, not political, ideological, economic, or nationalistic differences, dominated the controversy between Parliament and the colonies, finally precipitating revolution. The books stress the English origins of the colonies' constitutional claims and emphasize the legalistic constitutionalism of the American Whig mind. The volumes yield much information about American and British constitutional thinking and claims on the eve of revolution. A one-volume abridged edition published in 1995 restates these arguments.

3:267   Sainsbury, John. *Disaffected Patriots: London Supporters of Revolutionary America, 1769–1782.* Kingston, Ontario: McGill-Queen's University Press, 1987. This book describes the political activities of a small English opposition that identified with the colonists' cause during the American revolution.

Championing similar anti-authoritarian constitutional principles, this opposition, centered on London tradesmen and their hero John Wilkes, registered strong dissent against the policies that led to war but were too weak to force change until military defeat and war weariness altered the political balance.

3:268   Thomas, Peter D. G. *Tea Party to Independence: The Third Phase of the American Revolution, 1773–1776.* New York: Oxford University Press, 1991. Emphasizing the anatomy of British policy-making more than the colonial response, Thomas an-

alyzes the final breakdown of relations between Britain and the colonies following American defiance of the Tea Act. Detached and authoritative, the study describes the unavailing attempts by the North ministry to maintain parliamentary supremacy over the colonies in the face of their determination to set their own terms for participation in the empire. Acknowledging that mistakes, misunderstandings, and paranoia played a part in the coming of the revolution, the author nevertheless concludes that the "root cause" of the revolution was "the question whether or not Parliament was the legislature for the British Empire."

4

The Diplomacy of the American Revolution

Contributing Editor
MARY A. GIUNTA
National Historical Publications and Records Commission

With the Assistance of
CLAIRE BETTAG

Contents

Introduction

The entries of this chapter provide a basic list of publications for the understanding of U.S. diplomacy during the American revolution. Most are appropriate for undergraduate-level research and writing. All are appropriate for teaching at the undergraduate and graduate levels and, when used in conjunction with an expanded manuscripts base, for the preparation of studies and monographs.

From the very beginning of the War for Independence, American leaders recognized the importance of foreign assistance as critical to success. By July of 1776, U.S. foreign relations were being established, though on a limited footing. With the signing of the French treaties in 1778, U.S. diplomats secured in a formal manner the help necessary to a possible defeat of Great Britain. When the U.S. ministers signed the Treaty of Paris of 1783 with British negotiators, the efforts of American leaders to secure independence were at last successful. Accordingly, many of the entries focus on these subjects, actions, and events. Other subjects covered include relations with Spain, the Netherlands, Russia, Native Americans, and the role of naval and military strategy and action in diplomatic affairs.

To prepare this chapter, a comprehensive search was conducted for articles, monographs, and collected documentary editions on U.S. foreign relations for the period published since 1980. This search was made easier by an extensive bibliographical list prepared by the general editor of this volume during his years of teaching diplomatic history. The search also included selections of Spanish- and French-language works dealing with U.S.-Spanish and U.S.-French foreign relations that were not in the first edition. The use of these latter materials is essential to a fuller realization and a better understanding of the events during the American revolution. In addition, modern documentary editions significant to understanding the period have been included. These cover (through letters and writings) the actions of many of the individuals involved including Benjamin Franklin and John Adams. Most were published since 1980.

For all new entries and for some previously included in the earlier bibliography, new notes were written or updated. No attempt was made to account for publications of lesser distinction or for those that reworked or summarized the works of others.

Published Primary Materials

4:1　　Burnett, Edmund C., ed. *Letters of Members of the Continental Congress.* 8 vols. Washington, DC: Carnegie Institution of Washington, 1921–1936. Burnett has long been a standard source. His decision to print a letter depended on whether the member was attending Congress at the time. Because of space limitations, he excerpts many letters and inevitably omits information critical to scholars. This reference has been largely replaced by Smith, *Letters of Delegates to Congress, 1774–1789* (1976–2000) (4:15).

4:2　　Butler, John P., ed. *Index, The Papers of the Continental Congress, 1774–1789.* 5 vols. Washington, DC: National Archives and Records Service, 1978. This is an exhaustive alphabetical and chronological index to all of the papers of the Continental Congress. All items refer to microfilm series and reel numbers for convenient use. Used with the *Index: Journals of Continental Congress, 1774–1789* (Washington, DC: National Archives and Records Service, 1976), any document of the Continental Congress can be quickly located.

4:3　　Chinard, Gilbert, ed. *The Treaties of 1778, and Allied Documents.* Baltimore: Johns Hopkins Press, 1928. This is a complete edition of the treaties of alliance in both English and French. The accompanying documents are selective but well chosen. Introduction by James Brown Scott.

4:4　　Clark, William Bell, and William J. Morgan. *Naval Documents of the American Revolution.* 10 vols., ed. Michael J. Crawford. Washington, DC: Government Printing Office, 1964–1996. This compilation provides information often unobtainable elsewhere, but the absence of a consistent editorial policy and occasional failure to consult original documents have been justly criticized. A useful but not thorough documentation of the navy's role in the American revolution.

4:5　　Doniol, Henri, ed. *Histoire de la participation de la France à l'établissement des États-Unis d'Amérique: Correspondance diplomatique et docu-*

ments [*History of the French Role in United States Independence: Diplomatic Correspondence and Documents*]. 5 vols. Paris: Imprimerie nationale, 1886–1892. This massive compilation of documents from many ministries charts the increased French involvement with the Americans. This work should be used with caution since, for example, omissions in the documents appear without notice. Doniol sought to prove the closeness of the two nations. In French.

4:6   Ford, Worthington C., Gaillard Hunt, John C. Fitzpatrick, and Roscoe R. Hill, eds. *The Journals of the Continental Congress, 1774–1789: Edited from the Original Records in the Library of Congress.* 34 vols. Washington, DC: Government Printing Office, 1904–1937. This soundly edited work includes the debates for which sources were available, resolutions, and roll call votes. Although not totally complete, this is a reliable guide to the actions of Congress.

4:7   Giunta, Mary A., with J. Dane Hartgrove, eds. *Documents of the Emerging Nation: U.S. Foreign Relations, 1775–1789.* Wilmington, DE: Scholarly Resources, Inc., 1998. This is a primary source reader of the early foreign relations of the United States, complementing other history publications, including classroom texts. Documents are drawn primarily from the same sources used for the National Historical Publications and Records Commission's *The Emerging Nation: A Documentary History of the Foreign Relations of the United States under the Articles of Confederation, 1780–1789* (ed. Giunta, 1996) (4:8). Foreign documents are translated into English for ease of use.

4:8   Giunta, Mary A., with J. Dane Hartgrove and Mary-Jane M. Dowd, eds. *The Emerging Nation: A Documentary History of the Foreign Relations of the United States under the Articles of Confederation, 1780–1789.* 3 vols. Washington, DC: National Historical Publications and Records Commission, 1996. This is the place to begin study of early U.S. diplomacy. The work's value lies in the selected nature of the documents, the translation of foreign-language documents into English, and the headnotes that provide context for the documents. Documentary materials come from collections in universities, libraries, historical societies, private organizations, and government archival sources, including the Na-

tional Archives and Records Administration, the Library of Congress, the Public Record Office of Great Britain, and the Archives du Ministère des Affaires Étrangeres of France. See also Giunta, *Documents of the Emerging Nation: U.S. Foreign Relations, 1775–1789* (1998) (4:7).

4:9   Great Britain. Historical Manuscripts Commission. *A Report on American Manuscripts in the Royal Institution of Great Britain.* 4 vols. London: Mackie and Co. for His Majesty's Stationery Office, 1904–1909. Reprint 1972 (Gregg Press). These documents focus on British military reports and letters regarding the conduct of the war in the colonies. The work's value is somewhat limited except for the logistics of military planning and execution.

4:10   Kinnaird, Lawrence, ed. *Spain in the Mississippi Valley, 1765–1794. Part 1: The Revolutionary Period, 1765–1781. Part 2: Post War Decade, 1782–1791. Part 3: Problems of Frontier Defense, 1792–1794.* 3 vols. Vols. 2–4, The Annual Report of the American Historical Association for the Year 1945. Washington, DC: Government Printing Office, 1946–1949. These translations of French and Spanish documents from Spanish governmental files for Louisiana and West Florida are deposited at the Bancroft Library. Although incomplete, these volumes offer material not frequently used, including many letters of New Orleans merchant and land speculator Oliver Pollock.

4:11   Murdoch, David H., ed. *Rebellion in America: A Contemporary British Viewpoint, 1765–1783.* Santa Barbara, CA: Clio Books, 1978. This collection has over 900 facsimile pages from Burke's *Annual Register,* coupled with identification of key people and editorial commentary.

4:12   Paullin, Charles O., ed. *Out-Letters of the Continental Marine Committee and Board of Admiralty, August, 1776–September, 1780.* 2 vols. New York: De Vinne Press for the Naval History Society, 1914. This is a good source but of somewhat limited value for diplomatic history; his editing is careful but without elaborate annotation.

4:13   Rice, Howard C., Jr., and Anne S. K. Brown, eds. *The American Campaigns of Rochambeau's*

Army, 1780, 1781, 1782, 1783. 2 vols. Princeton: Princeton University Press, 1972. The journals of three French officers, the Comte de Clermont-Crevecoeur, Jean B. P. A. de Verger, and Louis-Alexandre Berthier, give some idea of how French officers viewed the revolution and the alliance. The second volume includes many reproductions of French maps and views of the United States. The editing by Rice and Brown, who also translated, is impeccable. Bibliography.

4:14 Rodney, George Brydges. *Letter-Books and Order-Book of George, Lord Rodney, Admiral of the White Squadron, 1780–1782.* 2 vols. New York: New York Historical Society for the Naval History Society, 1932. This is a good source for the West Indian campaign of 1782, with a preface containing a good description of other Rodney papers at the British Public Record Office. Superb index.

4:15 Smith, Paul H., with Gerard W. Gawalt, Rosemary Fry Plakas, and Eugene R. Sheridan, eds. *Letters of Delegates to Congress, 1774–1789.* 26 vols. Washington, DC: Library of Congress, 1976–2000. This is a comprehensive edition of official and personal letters of the members of the Continental Congress, gathered from the holdings of the Library of Congress, the National Archives, and other repositories around the world. It more than doubles the number of letters printed in Burnett, *Letters of Members of the Continental Congress* (1921–1936) (4:1). It is annotated lightly but with sure scholarship. Completed in twenty-six volumes, the last of which includes a cumulative index. Available as a set and also available on CD-ROM.

4:16 Stevens, Benjamin Franklin, ed. *B. F. Stevens's Facsimiles of Manuscripts in European Archives Relating to America, 1773–1783: With Descriptions, Editorial Notes, Collations, References and Translations.* 25 vols. London: Photographed and Printed by Malby and Sons, 1889–1898. Reprint 1970 (Mellifont Press). The wide variety of documents from British, French, and Spanish archives, and their exact reproduction, make this series an invaluable source. It is incomplete, but the editor has demonstrated care and intelligence in his selection.

4:17 Wharton, Francis, ed. *The Revolutionary Diplomatic Correspondence of the United States.* 6

vols. Washington, DC: Government Printing Office, 1889. Wharton is the standard collection of American diplomatic correspondence for the revolution. He omits some documents and others are only printed in part, because Wharton did not decode the letters. The complete editions of the Adams, Franklin, and Laurens papers, along with the microfilm of the Lee Family Papers, will fill in most of the missing documents. The editor's hostile attitude toward the Lee Family lessens the value of the work but it remains useful. See also Giunta, *The Emerging Nation: A Documentary History of the Foreign Relations of the United States under the Articles of Confederation, 1780–1789* (1996) (4:8).

4:18 Whitaker, Arthur Preston, ed. *Documents Relating to the Commercial Policy of Spain in the Floridas, with Incidental Reference to Louisiana.* De-Land, FL: Florida State Historical Society, 1931. In this collection, covering 1778–1808, Whitaker translated and presented thirty documents, mostly from the *Archivo General de las Indias;* they reveal the special commercial problems facing the Spanish crown in a revolutionary era and the concessions Spain made to trade between Pensacola and New Orleans and France, Great Britain, and the United States.

Bibliographies and Other Reference Works

BIBLIOGRAPHIES

4:19 *Bibliographie annuelle de l'histoire de France du cinquième siècle à 1939 [Annual Bibliography on the History of France from the Fifth Century to 1939].* 10 vols. Paris: Éditions du Centre national de la recherche scientifique, 1953–1963. This convenient guide to French scholarship was restarted in 1964 under the title *Bibliographie annuelle de l'histoire de France du cinquième siècle à 1945,* 11 vols. (1964–1974), first by the Comité français des sciences historiques (1964–1971) and then by the Centre national de la recherche scientifique, Centre de documentation Sciences humaines (1972–1974).

4:20 Beers, Henry Putney, ed. *The French & British in the Old Northwest: A Bibliographical Guide to Archive and Manuscript Sources.* Although not specifically on the revolutionary war, this guide lists published and unpublished primary sources for American and Canadian participation in the American midwest and Upper Canada during the revolution (3:37).

4:21 _____. *The French in North America: A Bibliographical Guide to French Archives, Reproductions, and Research Missions.* Beers describes works by American and Canadian historians (and institutions) in the French archives, including documentary compilations and reproductions. A particularly interesting chapter, "Historians of American Diplomacy," begins with Jared Sparks's initial investigations. Lists materials for 1775 to 1783 (3:39).

4:22 Coker, William S., and Jack D. L. Holmes. "Sources for the History of the Spanish Borderlands." This article describes the abundance of source materials (published, microcopied, and in manuscript) located in Spain, France, and various U.S. collections, relating particularly to Spanish Florida and Spanish Louisiana (3:41).

4:23 Cortada, James W., ed. *A Bibliographical Guide to Spanish Diplomatic History, 1460–1977.* This bibliography does not include information on manuscript materials, although it does list various guides to the archives. In his introduction, Cortada notes with regret the paucity of general surveys of Spanish diplomacy and of specialized works covering many areas, including the early nineteenth century, but he nevertheless is able to list a substantial number of useful accounts. The work lists more than fifty Spanish works on the American revolution (1:241).

4:24 Dippel, Horst, ed. *Americana Germanica, 1770–1800: Bibliographie deutscher Amerikaliteratur [German Works on the United States, 1770–1800].* Stuttgart: J. B. Metzler, 1976. This is a precise and exacting companion volume to the author's work *Germany and the American Revolution* (1977) (4:256). It reveals that German interest in the revolution was much more extensive than previously believed.

4:25 Gipson, Lawrence Henry. *The British Em-pire before the American Revolution.* Vol. 14: *A Bibliographical Guide to the History of the British Empire, 1748–1776.* See Gipson, *The British Empire before the American Revolution. Vol. 15: A Guide to Manuscripts Relating to the History of the British Empire, 1748–1776* (1970) (3:46).

4:26 _____. *The British Empire before the American Revolution. Vol. 15: A Guide to Manuscripts Relating to the History of the British Empire, 1748–1776.* These last two volumes (14 and 15) of the author's history of the British empire reflect the prodigious work that went into the first thirteen volumes of his opus. Although these are most useful for the period before the revolution, many of the materials that Gipson used are relevant for the entire war. These volumes were first published in 1936 with the first three volumes having the imprint Caxton Printers, Caldwell, Idaho. Knopf published revised editions of volumes 1–3 in 1939 and again in 1949. Between 1958 and 1970, Knopf issued completely revised editions of all fifteen volumes (3:47).

4:27 Library of Congress. Division of Bibliography, and Appleton P. C. Griffin, eds. *List of Works Relating to the French Alliance in the American Revolution.* Washington, DC: Government Printing Office, 1907. Now badly out of date, the remaining value of this forty-page booklet is its listing of articles and documents published in obscure and now nonexistent American periodicals.

4:28 Library of Congress. General Reference and Bibliography Division, and Stefan M. Harrow, eds. *The American Revolution: A Selected Reading List.* Washington, DC: Government Printing Office, 1968. A general reading list aimed at the undergraduate, it covers all phases of the American revolution, including many works on diplomacy, but is less than forty pages long.

4:29 Lincove, David A., and Gary R. Treadway, eds. *The Anglo-American Relationship: An Annotated Bibliography of Scholarship, 1945–1985.* Intended as a "starting point for research on Anglo-American topics," this bibliography of scholarly works includes books, essays, journal articles, and doctoral dissertations that focus on the Anglo-American relationship. It is divided into two parts, one first listing works on essentially nondiplomatic areas and then on diplomatic interactions between the United States and Great Britain. Part 2 is arranged chronologically, beginning with the signing of the Treaty of Peace (1783) and continuing through the post–World War II period. A basic reference work (1:244).

4:30   Monaghan, Frank, ed. *French Travellers in the United States, 1765–1932: A Bibliography: With Supplement by Samuel J. Marino.* New York: Antiquarian Press, 1961. An annotated list of 1,800 published accounts of French, Belgian, Swiss, and French-Canadian travelers in the United States, this does not include accounts in journals and newspapers. Items are arranged alphabetically by author, with appropriate cross-references, and a note where the account is located. An indispensable guide. Originally published in 1933 by the New York Public Library.

4:31   Pargellis, Stanley, and D. J. Medley, eds. *Bibliography of British History: The Eighteenth Century, 1714–1789.* In addition to materials on foreign relations, this includes a special section on the American colonies and sections on the political, economic, and military history of the revolutionary period. Some citations annotated. Issued under the direction of the American Historical Association and the Royal Historical Society of Great Britain (3:51).

4:32   Shy, John W., ed. *The American Revolution.* Northbrook, IL: AHM, 1973. Shy lists books, essays, and other items on a wide range of topics relating to the revolution.

4:33   Smith, Myron J., Jr., ed. *Navies in the American Revolution: A Bibliography.* Metuchen, NJ: Scarecrow Press, 1973. This is a sound guide that features naval affairs but includes items relevant to revolutionary war diplomacy. The work emphasizes American and English sources and is very lightly annotated.

4:34   Thomas, Daniel H., and Lynn M. Case, eds. *Guide to the Diplomatic Archives of Western Europe.* Philadelphia: University of Pennsylvania Press, 1959. Combined with the same editors' *The New Guide to the Diplomatic Archives of Western Europe* (Philadelphia: University of Pennsylvania Press, 1975), these volumes in separate articles provide descriptions of the archival collections of Western Europe and some international organizations from the

eighteenth century to the near mid-twentieth century. The 1975 edition revises and enlarges on that published in 1959. Appended to each chapter are lists of printed documentary materials and guides to manuscripts. Between the two books, coverage extends to Austria (Arthur James May and M. L. Brown), Belgium (Thomas), Denmark (Waldemar Westergaard and E. Anderson), France (Vincent Confer), Germany (Raymond J. Sontag and Fritz T. Epstein), Great Britain (Keith Eubank), Italy (Mary Lucille Shay and Vincent Ilardi), the Netherlands (Dirk Petrus Marius Graswinckel and Willard A. Fletcher), Norway and Sweden (F. J. Sherriff and Raymond E. Lindgren), Portugal (Manoel Da Silveira Cardozo), Spain (Lino Gómez Canedo), Switzerland (Case), Vatican City (N. Summers and R. L. Cummings), Bavaria (Oron J. Hale), Finland (K. Forster), Greece (D. Visvizi-Dontas), Luxembourg (Fletcher), League of Nations and United Nations (Robert Claus and Yves Pérotin), International Labor Organization (Y. Pérotin), International Telecommunication Union (G. Pérotin), UNESCO (Richard H. Heindel and Luther Harris Evans), and Public Opinion (J. J. Mathews and Case). A good place to start.

OTHER REFERENCE WORKS

4:35   Boatner, Mark M., III, ed. *Encyclopedia of the American Revolution.* 2d ed. New York: D. McKay, 1974. This handy, well-organized reference work includes entries on major persons, battles, and political events. First published in 1966.

4:36   Brune, Lester H., ed. *Chronological History of U.S. Foreign Relations.* This basic chronology for the reference shelf includes brief summaries of events and actions and is helpful to student, researcher, and teacher alike (1:13). First published 1985–1991.

4:37   Cappon, Lester J., ed., with Barbara B. Petchenik, cartographic ed., and John Hamilton Long, assistant ed. *Atlas of Early American History: The Revolutionary Era, 1760–1790.* Princeton: Princeton University Press for the Newberry Library and the Institute of Early American History and Culture, 1976. This well-researched and elaborately produced work covers many phases of the revolution, including revolutionary-era city maps for different periods, population maps for 1760 and 1790, economic patterns, and cultural activity. It also has detailed military and alliance maps for different periods of the war, including of the Spanish borderlands and West Indies. Extensive bibliography.

4:38 Clark, David Sanders, ed. *Index to Maps of the American Revolution in Books and Periodicals: Illustrating the Revolutionary War and Other Events of the Period, 1763–1789.* Westport, CT: Greenwood Press, 1974. The sources are clearly indicated and the coverage is extensive and careful. The index is superb, a great asset in reference books of this kind. Military, naval, state, and population maps are among those indexed.

4:39 Marshall, Douglas W., and Howard H. Peckham, eds. *Campaigns of the American Revolution: An Atlas of Manuscript Maps.* Ann Arbor: University of Michigan Press, 1976. This atlas of fifty-eight battle maps (1775–1781) is drawn primarily from the Sir Henry Clinton Papers. They are clearly reproduced as originally drawn. The research and notes on sources are concise and scholarly.

4:40 Wheat, James Clements, and Christian F. Brun, eds. *Maps and Charts Published in America before 1800: A Bibliography.* Rev. ed. New York: R. B. Arkway, 1978. This listing notes locations, whether printed or in manuscript collections, of over 900 maps identified as having been produced in the United States before 1800. Many military maps made during the American revolution are not included. First published in 1969.

Historiography

4:41 Ben-Atar, Doron S. "Nationalism, Neo-Mercantilism, and Diplomacy: Rethinking the Franklin Mission." *Diplomatic History* 22 (Winter 1998): 101–14. Ben-Atar argues that the founding fathers, including Franklin, espoused and believed in republican principles but encouraged strong commercial nationalism as the basis for the success of the United States as a new nation. This article also touches on the decline in the number of writings in revolutionary war diplomacy.

4:42 Bowling, Kenneth R. "An Extraordinary Man: A Review Essay on George Washington." *Wisconsin Magazine of History* 73 (Summer 1990): 287–93. This is an evaluation of thirteen biographies and document collections on George Washington. While an interesting, well-thought-out piece, it does not include information on George Washington as a diplomat.

4:43 DeConde, Alexander. "Historians, the War of American Independence, and the Persistence of the Exceptionalist Ideal." *International History Review* 5 (August 1983): 399–430. This comprehensive review essay of the international significance of the revolutionary war written by historians and others in monographs, essays, and documentary collections is an excellent starting point on the subject for the basic literature prior to 1983. A well-researched piece.

4:44 Kaplan, Lawrence S. "The American Revolution in an International Perspective: Views from Bicentennial Symposia." *International History Review* 1 (July 1979): 408–26. Diplomatic historian Lawrence S. Kaplan summarizes papers given at meetings between 1975 and 1978 to honor the bicentennial of the American revolution. He considers the influence of the revolution on other countries, Anglo-American relations after the revolution, and the French-American alliance.

4:45 _____. "The Treaty of Paris 1783: A Historiographical Challenge." *International History Review* 5 (August 1983): 431–42. This well-written bibliographical essay on the Treaty of Paris by one of the deans of early U.S. diplomatic history can be considered a basic starting point for an understanding of most major writings on the subject through the time of writing.

4:46 McDermott, John Francis, ed. *The Spanish in the Mississippi Valley, 1762–1804.* Urbana: University of Illinois Press, 1974. Three of these essays are of a bibliographical nature useful to the diplomatic historian: Charles Edwards O'Neill, "The State of Studies on Spanish Colonial Louisiana" (16–25); A. Otis Hébert, "Resources in Louisiana Repositories for the Study of Spanish Activities in Louisiana" (26–37); and C. Harvey Gardiner, "The Mexican Archives and the Historiography of the Mississippi Valley in the Spanish Period" (38–50); see especially

Gardiner's extensive footnotes. See also Robert L. Gold, "Governor Bernardo de Gálvez and Spanish Espionage in Pensacola, 1777" (87–99); and Carl H. Chapman, "The Indomitable Osage in the Spanish Illinois (Upper Louisiana), 1763–1804" (287–313).

4:47 Weeks, William Earl. "New Directions in the Study of Early American Foreign Relations." *Diplomatic History* 17 (Winter 1993): 73–96. This general examination of recent works on U.S. foreign relations for the period 1787–1828 is well written and researched, providing and commenting on many and varied references that are the backbone for a study of the period.

Overviews

4:48 Barrow, Thomas C. "The American Revolution as a Colonial War for Independence." *William and Mary Quarterly* 3d ser. 25 (October 1968): 452–64. Historians' comparisons of the American revolution with the later French and Russian revolutions have not produced a better understanding of the first. The drive for independence and autonomy makes the American revolution different from classical revolutions. While challenging, the author's thesis does not answer Palmer's in *The Challenge,* Vol. I in *The Age of the Democratic Revolution: A Political History of Europe and America, 1760–1800* (1959) (4:69).

4:49 Bemis, Samuel Flagg. *American Foreign Policy and the Blessings of Liberty, and Other Essays.* New Haven: Yale University Press, 1962. Of value for the revolution are "The British Secret Service and the French-American Alliance," "The Rayneval Memoranda of 1782 on Western Boundaries and Some Comments on the French Historian Doniol," and "Canada and the Peace Settlement of 1782–1783." Based on extensive research, these articles by one of the foremost diplomatic historians have not been surpassed in their total contribution.

4:50 _____. *The Diplomacy of the American Revolution.* New York: D. Appleton-Century, 1935. Reprint 1983 (Greenwood Press). In the best summary of the diplomacy of the American revolution in Europe (originally published in 1935 by D. Appleton-

Century), Bemis skillfully exploits archives in offering a whig interpretation of an innocent America dealing with corrupt Europe. The interpretation has been challenged but not the coverage and detailed analysis.

4:51 Bourguignon, Henry J. *The First Federal Court: The Federal Appellate Prize Court of the American Revolution, 1775–1787.* Philadelphia: American Philosophical Society, 1977. This first satisfactory study of American prize courts during the revolution is deserving of an important place in the historiography of international law. Extensive bibliography.

4:52 Burnett, Edmund C. *The Continental Congress.* New York: Macmillan Company, 1941. This general work on Congress is by the original editor of the *Letters of Members of the Continental Congress* (1921–1936) (4:1). Although challenged in subsequent literature, it remains the best book for studying how the Congress functioned and for evaluating its limited success.

4:53 Burrows, Edwin G., and Michael Wallace. "The American Revolution: The Ideology and Psychology of National Liberation." *Perspectives in American History* 6 (1972): 167–305. The emphasis is on psychology rather than ideology and comparisons are drawn to twentieth-century national liberation struggles. The mother-child analogy is heavily used, and the authors conclude that Americans came to equate national liberation with personal liberation.

4:54 Dull, Jonathan R. *A Diplomatic History of the American Revolution.* Aimed at graduate and undergraduate students, teachers, historians, and general readers, what may be the best one-volume treatment of the subject reevaluates various aspects of American diplomacy during the revolution. He considers relations with Great Britain, France, Spain, the Netherlands, and others, including Russia. Extensive annotated bibliography (3:93).

4:55 Field, James A., Jr. *America and the Mediterranean World, 1776–1882.* Princeton: Princeton University Press, 1969. Reprint 1991 (Imprint Publications). Although including little on the revolutionary war period, this is an interesting approach to U.S. ties, many unofficial, with the states and societies bordering on the Mediterranean. The 1991 reprint is titled *From Gibraltar to the Middle East: America and the Mediterranean World, 1776–1882.*

4:56   Gilbert, Felix. *To the Farewell Address: Ideas of Early American Foreign Policy.* Gilbert analyzes the intellectual origins of American foreign policy from the Model Treaty to the farewell address (3:83).

4:57   Goodwin, Albert, ed. *New Cambridge Modern History. Vol. 8: The American and French Revolutions, 1763–93.* Cambridge, UK: Cambridge University Press, 1965. The most valuable chapters for students of foreign relations are Robert R. Palmer, "Social and Psychological Foundations of the Revolutionary Era" (421–47) and Esmond Wright, "American Independence in Its American Context: Social and Political Aspects: Western Expansion" (509–36). See also Christopher Lloyd, "Navies" (174–89); J. R. Western, "Armies" (190–217); M. S. Anderson, "European Diplomatic Relations, 1763–1790" (252–78); R. A. Humphreys, "The Development of the American Communities outside British Rule" (397–420); and Maldwyn A. Jones, "American Independence in Its Imperial, Strategic and Diplomatic Aspects" (480–508).

4:58   Greene, Jack P., ed. *The American Revolution: Its Character and Limits.* New York: New York University Press, 1987. This volume of essays stemming from a public symposium focuses on problems raised but not solved by the American revolution. Of greatest interest to diplomatic historians are "The Ambiguities of Power" by J. R. Pole (124–30), "Two Republics in a Hostile World: The United States and the Netherlands in 1780s" by Jonathan R. Dull (149–63), and "Declaration of Independence: Indian-White Relations in the New Nation" by James H. Merrell (197–223). See also John W. Shy, "Force, Order, and Democracy in the American Revolution" (75–79), and Don Higginbotham, "The American Republic in a Wider World" (164–70).

4:59   Horsman, Reginald. "The Dimensions of an 'Empire for Liberty': Expansion and Republicanism, 1775–1825." *Journal of the Early Republic* 9 (Spring 1989): 1–20. How big could a country become before it could not sustain a republican form of government? The arguments between Federalists and

anti-Federalists over this issue during the 1780s and 1790s are presented here as well as similar concerns created by the Louisiana Purchase. The article covers the period from the Constitutional Convention into the nineteenth century with two brief paragraphs on the revolutionary era.

4:60   _____. *The Diplomacy of the New Republic, 1776–1815.* Arlington Heights, IL: Harlan Davidson, 1985. Professor Horsman's little (153 pages) volume is an excellent introduction to the history of early U.S. diplomacy. The bibliographical essay covers the most significant secondary sources on the 1776–1815 period available at the time of publication. The volume is part of the American History Series, edited by John Hope Franklin and Abraham S. Eisenstadt. A good undergraduate—and for some classes, a graduate—reading list item.

4:61   Hutson, James H. "Early American Diplomacy: A Reappraisal." *Quarterly Journal of the Library of Congress* 33 (July 1976): 183–98. This is what the author considers a correction to the "misconceptions" about early U.S. foreign policy created by Felix Gilbert's *To the Farewell Address: Ideas of Early American Foreign Policy* (1961) (3:83). Read Gilbert first, then Hutson's article, to fully appreciate this author's approach.

4:62   _____. "The Partition Treaty and the Declaration of American Independence." *Journal of American History* 58 (September 1972): 877–96. The timing of the Declaration of Independence is related to many reports suggesting a partitioning of the New World between England and France, which would allow England an unfettered hand in crushing the rebellion. This careful analysis shows a more sensitive reaction by members of the Continental Congress to the international arena than previously believed.

4:63   Kaplan, Lawrence S., ed. *The American Revolution and "A Candid World."* Kent, OH: Kent State University Press, 1977. This valuable collection covers diverse diplomatic topics, including the reasons for the failure of reconciliation by the North cabinet, appraisals of the Model Treaty, Catherine the Great's shrewd appraisal of the American revolution and the British government, the location of the American revolution in the law of nations, and the movement toward isolation after 1775: Carl B. Cone,

"George III—America's Unknown King" (1–16); Alan S. Brown, "The Impossible Dream: The North Ministry, the Structure of Politics, and Conciliation" (17–39); James H. Hutson, "Early American Diplomacy: A Reappraisal" (40–68); William C. Stinchcombe, "John Adams and the Model Treaty" (69–84); David M. Griffiths, "Catherine the Great, the British Opposition, and the American Revolution" (85–110); Gregg L. Lint, "The Law of Nations and the American Revolution" (111–33); and Kaplan, "Toward Isolationism: The Rise and Fall of the Franco-American Alliance, 1775–1801" (134–60).

4:64 _____. *Colonies into Nation: American Diplomacy, 1763–1801*. New York: Macmillan, 1972. Kaplan incorporates recent contributions in this synthesis of early American diplomacy, one of the few surveys to place its origins in the colonial period. He sees the colonial agent as the precursor of the American diplomat. Biographical essay.

4:65 Ketcham, Ralph L. "France and American Politics, 1763–1793." *Political Science Quarterly* 78 (June 1963): 198–223. Although James Madison and many of his political allies could be considered pro-French, the author rightly argues that many of them considered France the only counterweight to Britain, particularly after the Declaration of Independence. The same considerations affected foreign policy long after the revolution.

4:66 Lint, Gregg L. "The Law of Nations and the American Revolution." *Diplomatic History* 1 (Winter 1977): 20–34. This is a very useful assessment of the American interest in the law of nations during the revolution (1776–1783).

4:67 Mackesy, Piers. *The War for America, 1775–1783*. Cambridge, MA: Harvard University Press, 1964. Reprint 1993 (University of Nebraska Press). This is perhaps the finest description of British military objectives and successes. Based on massive research, the work presents the complicated struggle among France, Spain, and Great Britain in the West Indies, where, the author holds, the war was ultimately lost, leading to Yorktown as a result. Bibliography.

4:68 Middlekauff, Robert. *The Glorious Cause: The American Revolution, 1763–1789*. New York:

Oxford University Press, 1982. A general history of the American revolution covering some diplomatic subjects, this work does not dig deeply into foreign relations issues.

4:69 Palmer, Robert R. *The Age of the Democratic Revolution: A Political History of Europe and America, 1760–1800. Vol. 1: The Challenge*. Princeton: Princeton University Press, 1959. In perhaps the most influential intellectual and political history of the last generation, the author posits a widespread democratic movement in Europe, of which the United States was a part and to which Americans made their own distinct contributions. The scope, research, and analysis of this volume make it an appropriate book with which to begin a study of the diplomacy of the revolution.

4:70 Patterson, David S. "The Department of State: The Formative Years 1775–1800." *Prologue* 21 (Winter 1989): 315–29. This is the best general account of the beginnings of U.S. foreign relations, first under the Continental Congress, 1774–1789, and then under the Constitution. Patterson briefly recounts the establishment of the Committee of Secret Correspondence in November 1775, its successors, and the appointment of the first secretary of foreign affairs, Robert R. Livingston, in 1781. He also covers the establishment of consular appointments, U.S.-French relations during the French revolution, and early homes of the Department of State.

4:71 Perkins, Bradford. *The Creation of a Republican Empire, 1776–1865*. This is an able synthesis by one of the masters of the early history of U.S. foreign relations, the first volume of a well-planned series (2:44).

4:72 Sagnac, Philippe. *La fin de l'ancien régime et la révolution américaine (1763–1789) [The end of the Old Regime and the American Revolution (1763–1789)]*. 3d ed. Paris: Presses universitaires de France, 1952. This is a wide-ranging, integrated study that reveals several critical differences in the study of history by French scholars as compared to American. Sagnac seeks to cover changes in secular life and material conditions as well as political and diplomatic developments. First published in 1941.

4:73 Stinchcombe, William C. *The American*

Revolution and the French Alliance. Syracuse: Syracuse University Press, 1969. The author analyzes the domestic reaction to the French alliance in the United States. Americans clearly realized the advantages of the alliance and suspended their traditional anti-French and anti-Catholic beliefs to make it a success. Extensive bibliography.

4:74 Stuart, Reginald C. *United States Expansionism and British North America, 1775–1871.* Chapel Hill: University of North Carolina Press, 1988. According to the Canadian author, this volume "explores the cultural dynamics behind America's external relations with a particular group of foreigners—British North Americans, both French and Anglo-Saxon—on the northern frontier of the United States." About twenty pages cover the revolutionary war period.

4:75 Van Alstyne, Richard W. *Empire and Independence: The International History of the American Revolution.* New York: John Wiley, 1965. Based on bountiful primary sources and contemporary books printed at the time of the revolution, including parliamentary and congressional debates, the author presents a multifaceted story, incorporating a good dose of domestic and international factors and influences. Anticipating later scholars, Van Alstyne insists that international history is not the same as "diplomatic" history.

4:76 Varg, Paul A. *Foreign Policies of the Founding Fathers.* East Lansing: Michigan State University Press, 1964. In a work that includes two chapters on the revolutionary period, Varg holds that an understanding of the foreign relations of the new nation, 1774–1812, offers guidance to understanding policies after World War II.

4:77 Weeks, William Earl. *Building the Continental Empire: American Expansion from the Revolution to the Civil War.* Chicago: Ivan R. Dee, 1996. Weeks treats the revolutionary period mainly as background for a work focusing on the period from 1815 to 1861.

4:78 Williams, William Appleman. "The Age of Mercantilism: An Interpretation of the American Political Economy, 1763–1828." *William and Mary Quarterly* 3d ser. 15 (October 1958): 419–37.

Williams argues that a better understanding of the "nature and practice" of mercantilism as practiced in the United States from 1763 to 1828 offers a clearer picture of American society and the forces—including expansionism and the early development of the federal government—influencing the country's growth and later ability to withstand economic crises and civil war.

ECONOMIC AFFAIRS

4:79 Godechot, Jacques. "Les Relations Economiques entre la France et les États-Unis de 1779 à 1789 [Economic Relations between France and the United States, 1779–1789]." *French Historical Studies* 1, no. 1 (1958): 26–39. This article on economic relations updates the traditional view that the United States and France did not have complementary trade relations. Though generally sound, the article underplays the importance of Bordeaux in the American trade and understates the amount of trade between the French West Indies and the United States. Godechot also emphasizes France's failure to achieve its own commercial and political objectives through trade with the United States.

4:80 Griffiths, David M. "American Commercial Diplomacy in Russia: 1780–1783." *William and Mary Quarterly* 3d ser. 27 (July 1970): 379–410. The best-researched piece on relations with Russia, it additionally provides more information about the mysterious but important role of Stephen Sayre in American diplomacy. Catherine would not alienate Great Britain because of problems with Turkey; thus, commercial diplomacy failed because of overriding Russian concerns, not because of the anti-U.S. policies of the British and French ambassadors in Russia.

4:81 Lüthy, Herbert. *La banque protestante en France, de la révocation de l'Édit de Nantes à la Révolution [The Protestant Bank in France from the Revocation of the Edict of Nantes to the Revolution].* 2 vols. Paris: S. E. V. P. E. N., 1959. The second volume of this wide-ranging and excellent work has many details on the effects of the American revolution on the financial situation in Europe. The author traces interconnected banking families and their involvement in all aspects of trade and politics, including the financing of American loans and French credit policy.

4:82   Martin, Gaston. "Commercial Relations between Nantes and the American Colonies." *Journal of Economic and Business History* 4 (August 1932): 812–29. The author has extensively mined the records of the important port of Nantes. Trade with the United States increased from 1775 to 1778, but with French intervention and subsequent British blockade, it declined rapidly. Bordeaux remained the most important port for French-American commerce.

4:83   Price, Jacob M. *France and the Chesapeake: A History of the French Tobacco Monopoly, 1694–1791, and of Its Relationship to the British and American Tobacco Trades.* 2 vols. Ann Arbor: University of Michigan Press, 1973. This is a superb economic and political history of the tobacco trade. In his well-written and extensively researched work, Price covers the important role of Scottish merchants as intermediaries in selling American tobacco to the monopolistic French Farmers General. Extensive bibliography.

4:84   Setser, Vernon G. *The Commercial Reciprocity Policy of the United States, 1774–1829.* Philadelphia: University of Pennsylvania Press, 1937. The author follows American efforts to institute new, liberal commercial programs upon independence. All failed, owing to the closed imperial economic systems maintained by European powers. Bibliography.

4:85   Tarrade, Jean. *Le commerce colonial de la France à la fin de l'Ancien Régime: l'évolution du régime de l'Exclusif de 1763 à 1789 [French Colonial Commerce at the End of the Old Regime, 1763–1789].* 2 vols. Paris: Presses universitaires de France, 1972. In a meticulous account of France's relaxation of its mercantilist policy in its West Indian colonies, the author shows the political difficulties in gaining the consent of French merchants. The war caused an ever-increasing colonial demand for foodstuffs, which allowed local officials to relax the ban against American traders. Bibliography.

4:86   Ubbelohde, Carl. *The Vice-Admiralty Courts and the American Revolution.* Chapel Hill: University of North Carolina Press for the Institute of Early American History and Culture, 1960. This essential work stresses the role these juryless courts played after 1763 in causing friction between British officials and colonial Americans. Extensive bibliography.

4:87   Winter, Pieter Jan van, with James C. Riley. *American Finance and Dutch Investment, 1780–1805, with an Epilogue to 1840.* Translated by C. M. Geyl and I. Clephane. 2 vols. New York: Arno Press, 1977. A revised, updated, and translated version of Winter's *Het aandeel van den Amsterdamschen handel aan den opbouw van het Amerikaansche gemeenebest* (1927–1933) and adapted for English publication by James C. Riley, this work investigates Dutch investment in the United States (trade, government loans, Bank of the United States, canal-building, and unsettled land). The research in Dutch and American sources is prodigious, and the work is the finest treatment of the subject in print, examining in minute and exacting fashion the commercial and financial connections between the United States and the Netherlands during the war. Extensive bibliography.

THE AMERICAN WEST IN THE REVOLUTION

4:88   Abernethy, Thomas Perkins. *Western Lands and the American Revolution.* New York: D. Appleton-Century, 1937. The role of speculators and the development of congressional policy toward the frontier are the subjects of this richly researched study written in the mode of the Progressive era. This is the best study available of the national and international connections of the Indiana, Vandalia, Illinois, and Wabash land companies. Extensive bibliography.

4:89   Bannon, John Francis. *The Spanish Borderlands Frontier, 1513–1821.* New York: Holt, Rinehart and Winston, 1970. Bannon ranges across the continent as he explores the economic, political, religious, and military impact of Spain's tenuous and always defensive presence in North America. He concludes that the Spanish borderlanders were also pioneers, whose achievements in opening the frontier have too long been overlooked. The author's outstanding bibliography merits the attention of any scholar working in Spanish-American relations in the pre-1821 period.

4:90 Caughey, John Walton. *Bernardo de Gálvez in Louisiana, 1776–1783*. Berkeley: University of California Press, 1934. Reprint 1972 (Pelican). This impressive piece of research remains one of the best monographs available in English on the Spanish efforts in the lower Mississippi valley during the revolution. The author puts in perspective the genuine Spanish contributions to the victory in the American west. Bibliography.

4:91 Lyon, E. Wilson. *Louisiana in French Diplomacy, 1759–1804*. Norman: University of Oklahoma Press, 1934. Before publication of DeConde, *This Affair of Louisiana* (1976) (5:481), this study and Whitaker, *The Mississippi Question, 1795–1803: A Study in Trade, Politics, and Diplomacy* (1934) (5:490), were the most important contributions to the history of the Louisiana Purchase. Both still retain great value, and they are complementary rather than rival studies, each stressing different aspects of the Louisiana affair. Lyon's emphasis is on the formulation of French policy, including a discussion of the motives, which impelled Napoleon to abandon his Louisiana project. Lyon relies on the now questionable assumption that France continued to desire Louisiana after cession to Spain in 1763.

4:92 Nasatir, Abraham P. *Borderland in Retreat: From Spanish Louisiana to the Far Southwest*. Albuquerque: University of New Mexico Press, 1976. Though not diplomatic history as such, Nasatir's study focuses on Spain's defensive posture in coping with British, French, and American pressures on six separate frontiers, 1762–1822. Bibliography.

4:93 Phillips, Paul C. *The West in the Diplomacy of the American Revolution*. Urbana: University of Illinois Press, 1913. The struggle for the Mississippi valley during the revolution is viewed from Philadelphia and Paris. Using Doniol and Stevens extensively but failing to exploit appropriate Spanish sources, the author depicts Spain as grasping, while the United States sought only what rightfully belonged to it.

4:94 Sosin, Jack M. *The Revolutionary Frontier, 1763–1783*. New York: Holt, Rinehart and Winston, 1967. Sosin's succinct, clear account challenges the Turner thesis on the frontier's leveling tendency and points out that established institutions were critical to

the region's development. He also presents a clear account of the role of Indians during the revolution. Extensive bibliography.

4:95 Starr, J. Barton. *Tories, Dons, and Rebels: The American Revolution in British West Florida*. Gainesville: University Presses of Florida, 1976. This is largely a military history of campaigns in West Florida (1776–1783). The British chose to garrison the area, thus using troops that might have been employed elsewhere. A good source on the subject.

MILITARY HISTORY

4:96 Allen, Gardner Weld. *A Naval History of the American Revolution*. 2 vols. Boston: Houghton Mifflin, 1913. This is an old but still eminently useful account of American naval activities during the revolution. Battles and exploits are stressed, so this work should be used in conjunction with others dealing more directly with diplomatic aspects.

4:97 Clark, William Bell. *Ben Franklin's Privateers: A Naval Epic of the American Revolution*. Baton Rouge: Louisiana State University Press, 1956. Clark describes the American privateers in French ports before and after the alliance was signed with France. Franklin had nominal control of the legalized pirate raids against the British. This work should be used in conjunction with the Deane and Lee papers, however, because Franklin was not involved as much as many other Americans in the operations.

4:98 Dull, Jonathan R. "Mahan, Sea Power, and the War for American Independence." *International History Review* 10 (February 1988): 59–67. The author, an authority on U.S.-French relations and Benjamin Franklin, uses the American revolution in a critical examination of Alfred Thayer Mahan's understanding of sea power, an excellent source for those interested in naval history and sea power as well as diplomatic history.

4:99 Hertzog, Keith P. "Naval Operations in West Africa and the Disruption of the Slave Trade during the American Revolution." *American Neptune* 55 (Winter 1995): 42–48. Hertzog explores how the American revolution practically provided "an experiment in the abolition of the slave trade" and how this affected that issue in later years, illustrating some of the wider ramifications of the war.

4:100   Higginbotham, Don. *The War of American Independence: Military Attitudes, Policies, and Practices, 1763–1789.* New York: Macmillan, 1971. Reprint 1983 (Northeastern University Press). This excellent, well-written survey of the military history of the revolution is based on substantial primary sources as well as a prodigious amount of secondary literature. The author succeeds in widening the scope of traditional military history. Extensive bibliography.

4:101   James, W. M. *The British Navy in Adversity: A Study of the War of American Independence.* New York: Longmans, Green and Co., 1926. Reprint 1970 (Russell and Russell). This work, based on extensive work in British archives, gives a sustained narrative of all major encounters of the British navy. The appendices contain lists of the ships of all sides in important battles. Still a worthwhile source, it can be supplemented by the Sandwich and Rodney papers.

4:102   Johnson, Ruth Y. "American Privateers in French Ports, 1776–1778." *Pennsylvania Magazine of History and Biography* 53 (December 1929): 352–74. This account of privateers, up to the French-American alliance in 1778, is useful but not comprehensive. The author covers the political side of the question between England and France but not the financial implications for Americans or the implications for British shipping.

4:103   Kite, Elizabeth S. *Brigadier-General Louis Lebègue Duportail, Commandant of Engineers in the Continental Army, 1777–1783.* Baltimore: Johns Hopkins Press, 1933. Duportail was recruited because of his engineering background, and throughout the revolution the Americans had to rely on such French assistance to sustain their campaigns. Vergennes secured approval for a number of French-paid officers, including DeKalb and Duportail, to help the Americans.

4:104   Lacour-Gayet, Georges. *La marine militaire de la France sous le règne de Louis XVI [The French Navy in the Reign of Louis XVI].* Paris: H. Champion, 1905. The author has mined the French archives effectively, and this edition, unlike a later

1910 edition, contains a number of pertinent documents. A useful summary of French naval participation in the war, but it is superseded by Dull, *The French Navy and American Independence: A Study of Arms and Diplomacy, 1774–1787* (1976) (4:219).

4:105   Lawrence, Alexander A. *Storm over Savannah: The Story of Count d'Estaing and the Siege of the Town in 1779.* Athens, GA: University of Georgia Press, 1951. Count d'Estaing attempted two joint ventures with the Americans, and both ended in military and political failure. The first was at Newport in 1778; the next was an effort to dislodge the British from Savannah. This work is a well-written and documented study of that campaign, although wider strategic ramifications are ignored.

4:106   Patterson, A. Temple. *The Other Armada: The Franco-Spanish Attempt to Invade Britain in 1779.* Manchester, UK: Manchester University Press, 1960. The work adequately explains the failure but does not probe deeply into French policy. Because Spain insisted on this invasion, no substantial aid was given to the Americans in 1779, which in turn affected British strategy. This study has been superseded by Dull, *The French Navy and American Independence: A Study of Arms and Diplomacy, 1774–1787* (1976) (4:219).

4:107   Smith, Paul H. *Loyalists and Redcoats: A Study in the British Revolutionary Policy.* Chapel Hill: University of North Carolina Press for the Institute of Early American History and Culture, 1964. After the defeat at Saratoga, the British increasingly relied on loyalists to maintain British forces in the colonies. This well-researched study is a model of policy analysis and the best place to begin a study of the complicated problem of the loyalists.

4:108   Syrett, David. *Shipping and the American War 1775–83: A Study of British Transport Organization.* London: Athlone Press, 1970. Syrett offers a study of the Naval Board and the multitude of problems that it faced. After 1779, it was responsible for all supplies to America and other theaters of war. The author is judicious, and his careful study draws primarily from the British Public Record Office.

4:109 Tracy, Nicholas. *Navies, Deterrence, and American Independence: Britain and Seapower in the 1760s and 1770s.* Vancouver: University of British Columbia Press, 1988. Tracy focuses on Britain's defense policy between 1763 and 1778, using its navy as an instrument of coercion over other foreign governments, especially France. The volume should be read and used in conjunction with other publications on the influence of naval power on diplomacy, particularly Dull's *The French Navy and American Independence: A Study of Arms and Diplomacy, 1774–1787* (1976) (4:219). Based primarily on British Admiralty and State papers.

INDIANS

4:110 Graymont, Barbara. *The Iroquois in the American Revolution.* Syracuse: Syracuse University Press, 1972. White settlers split the Six Nations, as some tribes supported the British and others the Americans. The Iroquois backed the British and paid dearly when they lost. A well-written, adequately researched book that concludes the Iroquois were doomed, whichever side they chose, but that a British victory would have slowed the process.

4:111 O'Donnell, James H., III. *Southern Indians in the American Revolution.* Knoxville: University of Tennessee Press, 1973. O'Donnell examines British and American policies toward the southern Indians, particularly the Cherokees. The United States sought through friendship or, more often, war to ensure the Indians did not side with the British. This concise work shows the decline of British influence and the ascendancy of American settlers.

4:112 Schaaf, Gregory. *Wampum Belts & Peace Trees: George Morgan, Native Americans, and Revolutionary Diplomacy.* Golden, CO: Fulcrum Publishing, 1990. Based on privately held and other papers of George Morgan, land speculator and Indian agent for the Continental Congress, this volume—an interesting source on early U.S.-Indian relations—recounts his role in dealing with indigenous peoples before and after adoption of the Declaration of Independence.

PEACE NEGOTIATIONS

4:113 Bemis, Samuel Flagg. "Canada and the Peace Settlement of 1782–3." *Canadian Historical Review* 14 (September 1933): 265–84. Bemis suggests that the United States did not gain more of Canada during the Paris discussions because Britain knew that both Spain and France opposed America's westward expansion and because Americans placed more value on the Mississippi valley.

4:114 Brown, Marvin L., ed. and translator. *American Independence through Prussian Eyes: A Neutral View of the Peace Negotiations of 1782–1783: Selections from the Prussian Diplomatic Correspondence.* Durham, NC: Duke University Press, 1959. These excerpts from materials by Prussian diplomats on the progress and success of the peace negotiations are soundly edited. Not much new information is added, as the Prussians were as surprised as the French at how much the Americans achieved.

4:115 Conn, Stetson. *Gibraltar in British Diplomacy in the Eighteenth Century.* New Haven: Yale University Press, 1942. Spain made repeated attempts to regain Gibraltar from 1776 to 1779, first by peaceful means and later, after Spain entered the war, through military force. After 1782, the British did not seriously consider ceding Gibraltar to Spain.

4:116 Harlow, Vincent T. *The Founding of the Second British Empire, 1763–1793. Vol. 1: Discovery and Revolution.* New York: Longmans, Green, 1952. Backed by massive research, the author argues convincingly that Great Britain started to pursue a new colonial policy when the loss of the American colonies became apparent. Harlow's book is important because it makes the strongest and best case for Shelburne's agency in envisioning a future of closer U.S.-British relations. For a different view, see Charles R. Ritcheson, "The Earl of Shelburne and Peace with America, 1782–1783: Vision and Reality," *International History Review* 5 (August 1983): 322–45, and his chapter in Hoffman and Albert, *Peace and the Peacemakers: The Treaty of 1783* (1986) (4:117).

4:117 Hoffman, Ronald, and Peter J. Albert, eds. *Peace and the Peacemakers: The Treaty of 1783.* Charlottesville: University Press of Virginia for the

United States Capitol Historical Society, 1986. This collection of essays on the Treaty of Peace of 1783 by a corps of renowned scholars offers a multifaceted approach to the circumstances surrounding the treaty giving the United States its formal independence. Individual chapters: Esmond Wright, "The British Objectives, 1780–1783: 'If Not Dominion Then Trade'"; Gregg L. Lint, "Preparing for Peace: The Objectives of the United States, France, and Spain in the War of the American Revolution"; James H. Hutson, "The American Negotiators: The Diplomacy of Jealousy"; Charles R. Ritcheson, "Britain's Peacemakers, 1782–1783: 'To an Astonishing Degree Unfit for the Task?'"; Jonathan R. Dull, "Vergennes, Rayneval, and the Diplomacy of Trust"; Marcus Cunliffe, "'They Will All Speak English': Some Cultural Consequences of Independence"; Samuel F. Scott, "Military Nationalism in the Aftermath of the American Revolution"; Bradford Perkins, "The Peace of Paris: Patterns and Legacies"; and Richard B. Morris, "The Durable Significance of the Treaty of 1783." The papers were originally presented at the United States Capitol Historical Society and published as part of the Society's Perspectives on the American Revolution.

4:118   Klingelhofer, Herbert E. "Mathew Ridley's Diary during the Peace Negotiations of 1782." *William and Mary Quarterly* 3d ser. 20 (January 1963): 95–133. An American merchant in Paris, Ridley had close contacts with John Adams and John Jay. This important, well-informed diary, carrying the gossip of the day, offers a distinctive picture of American negotiations.

4:119   Morris, Richard B. "The Great Peace of 1783." *Proceedings of the Massachusetts Historical Society* 95 (1983): 29–51. The paper explores the political and diplomatic circumstances surrounding the negotiations leading to the signing of the Treaty of Paris in 1783 at Versailles. Discussion focuses on how complex political struggles among European powers at the time played into the treaty negotiations. See also Morris's *The Peacemakers: The Great Powers and American Independence* (1965) (4:120).

4:120   _____. *The Peacemakers: The Great Powers and American Independence.* New York: Harper and Row, 1965. Reprint 1983 (Northeastern

University Press). This is the standard account of Henry Laurens, John Adams, Benjamin Franklin, and particularly John Jay in negotiating the peace with Great Britain in 1782. This well-researched work is marred by the author's excessive distrust of Vergennes and Europeans in general.

4:121   Murphy, Orville T. "The Comte de Vergennes, the Newfoundland Fisheries and the Peace Negotiations of 1783: A Reappraisal." *Canadian Historical Review* 46 (March 1965): 32–46. Examining the issue of the fisheries and later historians' charges that Vergennes sought to exclude the Americans, Murphy shows convincingly that he was far more concerned with maintaining French rights and sought to make sure that England and the United States would not exclude France. See also Murphy's *Charles Gravier, Comte de Vergennes: French Diplomacy in the Age of Revolution, 1719–1787* (1982) (4:222).

4:122   Ritcheson, Charles R. "The Earl of Shelburne and Peace with America, 1782–1783: Vision and Reality." *International History Review* 5 (August 1983): 322–45. At the beginning of peace negotiations, Shelburne's advocacy of free trade with the United States promised a new relationship with England. The Fox-North coalition, however, shelved the plan and reaffirmed Britain's long-established practice of mercantile monopoly. Shelburne's historical reputation as politician and statesman must be viewed in terms of his private character. This excellent article provides the basis for viewing him as "a friend" of the United States after the revolution. Ritcheson's *Aftermath of Revolution: British Policy toward the United States, 1783–1795* (1969) (5:603) is an excellent source on postwar British policy.

4:123   Smith, Paul H. "Sir Guy Carleton, Peace Negotiations, and the Evacuation of New York." *Canadian Historical Review* 50 (September 1969): 245–64. Carleton, who succeeded Clinton as commander of the British forces in North America in 1782, deliberately sought to undermine the peace talks in Paris by delaying the evacuation of New York. The article demonstrates the British commander's stubbornness and the new administration's determination to abide by parliamentary resolutions and peace agreements.

Biographical Studies

AMERICAN

John Adams

4:124   Butterfield, Lyman H., ed., with Leonard C. Faber and Wendell D. Garrett, assistant eds. *The Adams Papers. Ser. 1, Diaries: Diary and Autobiography of John Adams.* 5 vols. Cambridge, MA: Belknap Press of Harvard University Press, 1961–1966. John Adams's diary (1755–1804) offers a great deal of material on the revolution and diplomacy. The autobiography shows Adams trying to rewrite the history of the revolution, as in his treatment of the Model Treaty. The editing is beyond reproach, and, in addition to biographical information, the notes offer a commentary on scholars' interpretations.

4:125   Butterfield, Lyman H., Marc Friedlaender, and Richard Alan Ryerson, eds., with Wendell D. Garrett, associate ed., and Marjorie E. Sprague, assistant ed. *The Adams Papers. Ser. 2, Adams Family Correspondence.* 6 vols. Cambridge, MA: Belknap Press of Harvard University Press, 1963–1993. The letters among the members of the Adams family are of equal importance to the diary, particularly John Adams's description of his two missions to France, negotiations in the Netherlands, and part in the peace negotiations of 1782.

4:126   Taylor, Robert J., Mary-Jo Kline, and Gregg L. Lint, eds. *Papers of John Adams. Series 3: General Correspondence and Other Papers of the Adams Statesmen.* 10 vols. Cambridge, MA: Harvard University Press, 1977–1996. This comprehensive edition of the correspondence of John Adams is well edited with scholarly annotations and the best source for Adams in a printed edition.

4:127   Cappon, Lester J., ed. *The Adams-Jefferson Letters: The Complete Correspondence between Thomas Jefferson and Abigail and John Adams.* 2 vols. Chapel Hill: University of North Carolina Press for the Institute of Early American History and Culture, 1959. This well-edited and astutely annotated edition is more useful for diplomacy of the later period when both men served in Europe, yet their views and those of Abigail Adams are important. In the latter part of their lives, both men reviewed the meaning and significance of the American revolution.

4:128   Hutson, James H., ed. *Letters from a Distinguished American: Twelve Essays by John Adams on American Foreign Policy, 1780.* Washington, DC: Library of Congress, 1978. Hutson presents twelve previously unreprinted essays by Adams, ten originally published in a British newspaper in 1782. They refuted arguments of loyalist Joseph Galloway in the latter's pamphlet (published in London), *Cool Thoughts on the Consequences to Great Britain of American Independence.* Adams's essays embody sentiments later incorporated into the Provisional Peace Treaty of November 1782.

4:129   _____. *John Adams and the Diplomacy of the American Revolution.* Lexington: University Press of Kentucky, 1980. Hutson argues that Adams's erratic and often contradictory and self-defeating actions stemmed from a paranoia that caused him to view all those he encountered, colleagues and adversaries alike, as involved in conspiracies against him. The volume should be considered as a beginning point to the understanding of Adams as a diplomat. Sources include both printed document and manuscript collections in U.S. and foreign archives as well as significant secondary publications.

4:130   Shaw, Peter. *The Character of John Adams.* Chapel Hill: University of North Carolina Press for the Institute of Early American History and Culture, 1976. Shaw's superior study analyzes Adams's actions in times of stress, such as in his argument with Vergennes in 1781, and in clarifying what Adams said about his role in the American revolution.

4:131   Smith, Page. *John Adams.* 2 vols. Garden City, NY: Doubleday, 1962–1963. While other biographies compete, Page Smith's two-volume edition must be considered a standard by which to measure the others. The first volume covers the period from 1735 to 1784, including Adams's services as commissioner to France, member of the peace delegation, and minister to the Netherlands.

Silas Deane

4:132   *The Deane Papers: Correspondence between Silas Deane, His Brothers and Their Business and Political Associates, 1771–1795*. Hartford, CT: Connecticut Historical Society, 1930. Really a supplement to the New York Historical Society's volumes (Isham, *The Deane Papers . . . 1774–1790*, 1887–1890) (4:133), this edition includes political letters but mostly deals with Deane's business affairs. This should be used with other printed Deane papers and important documents still in manuscript collections.

4:133   Isham, Charles, ed. *The Deane Papers . . . 1774–1790*. 5 vols. New York: New York Historical Society, 1887–1890. Very useful for Deane's activities up to the signing of the French alliance in 1778, the papers also cover his attempts at exoneration by the Continental Congress, which recalled him under unclear circumstances. They are also useful for Deane's extensive business activities for the government and his own private interest.

4:134   James, Coy Hilton. *Silas Deane, Patriot or Traitor?* East Lansing: Michigan State University Press, 1975. This short book places Deane on that fine line between public and private interest, especially ill-defined in eighteenth-century America. The passage of time and the author's efforts at explanation do not lift the shadow over Deane but do provide an interesting perspective on the general distrust of merchants at the time and their danger in having close ties with British officials during the revolutionary war. James shed little new light on Arthur Lee's role.

Benjamin Franklin

4:135   Labaree, Leonard Woods, Whitfield J. Bell, Jr., William B. Willcox, Claude-Anne Lopez, and Barbara B. Oberg, eds. *The Papers of Benjamin Franklin*. This is the authoritative and comprehensive edition of the papers and correspondence of the scientist and statesman. Of the thirty-five volumes already published, fourteen are relevant to the time period: volumes 21–34 cover 1774–1780. To be completed in fifty volumes. Earlier volumes (1–14) and autobiography edited by Leonard W. Labaree and Whitfield J. Bell, Jr. (3:20).

4:136   Aldridge, Alfred Owen. *Franklin and His French Contemporaries*. New York: New York University Press, 1957. Franklin's reputation as a scientist was already widely known in Paris before his arrival, and he exploited this fame to win converts to the American cause.

4:137   Brands, H. W. *The First American: The Life and Times of Benjamin Franklin*. New York: Doubleday, 2000. Beginning with Franklin's boyhood, Brands traces the life of one of the most important figures of American history. Franklin's experiences in England before the outbreak of the American revolution, his return as one of its leaders, his crucial contributions to the formation of the new republic, and his diplomatic endeavors are all aptly detailed. Brands paints the picture of a man of genius and a patriot who helped win independence and whose diplomatic efforts contributed greatly to guaranteeing the future of a new nation.

4:138   Currey, Cecil B. *Code Number 72/Benjamin Franklin, Patriot or Spy?* Englewood Cliffs, NJ: Prentice-Hall, 1972. The author presents a suggestive and not conclusive case that Benjamin Franklin spied for the British while American minister to France. There was a gray area in which men acted as intermediaries for all powers during the revolution. Franklin was lax about protecting secrets and had around him a number of men who combined the role of spy and intermediary.

4:139   Dull, Jonathan R. *Franklin the Diplomat: The French Mission*. Philadelphia: American Philosophical Society, 1982. An editor of the papers of Benjamin Franklin at Yale University and published by Yale University Press, Dull presents a lengthy scholarly essay on Franklin's performance as a diplomat, an excellent piece by a first-rate Franklin scholar. This is vol. 72, part 1 of the *Transactions of the American Philosophical Society.*

4:140   Hawke, David Freeman. *Franklin*. New York: Harper and Row, 1976. Late in this well-written book, the author quotes Franklin's famous unsent July 1775 letter to William Strahan, ending, "You are now my enemy,—and I am yours, B. Franklin." Hawke primarily covers Franklin's life up to the break with Great Britain.

4:141 Henderson, H. James. "Congressional Factionalism and the Attempt to Recall Benjamin Franklin." *William and Mary Quarterly* 3d ser. 27 (April 1970): 246–67. Congressional—and essentially sectional—politics nearly led to Franklin's recall in 1779. Henderson's analysis is sound but perhaps emphasizes sectional voting too much, overlooking the continuing skepticism about Franklin held by many members of Congress.

4:142 Lemay, J. A. Leo, ed. *Reappraising Benjamin Franklin: A Bicentennial Perspective.* Cranbury, NJ: Associated University Presses, 1993. This is a Franklin gem, a group of essays on the many-faceted Benjamin Franklin. It will stand as one of the basic sources, alongside his papers, for understanding the man. The 480-page collection includes essays on Franklin as journalist and printer, scientist, and philosopher; it contains a chronology, brief biographies of contributors, and an extensive bibliography. A short introduction (19–29) by Lemay provides good context. Other chapters include Claude-Anne Lopez, "Was Franklin Too French?" (143–53), and Esmond Wright, "The Peace Treaties of 1782 and 1783: Diplomacy by Affection" (154–74).

4:143 Lopez, Claude-Anne. *Mon Cher Papa, Franklin and the Ladies of Paris.* New Haven: Yale University Press, 1966. See Lopez and Herbert, *The Private Franklin: The Man and His Family* (1975) (4:144).

4:144 Lopez, Claude-Anne, and Eugenia W. Herbert. *The Private Franklin: The Man and His Family.* New York: Norton, 1975. Franklin was the most important American diplomat of the revolution. The previous editions of his writings will be superseded by the Yale edition, Willcox et al., *The Papers of Benjamin Franklin* (1959–1998) (3:20). These two works by Lopez (and Herbert) contain new information pertaining to diplomacy, showing more convincingly than previously Franklin's deep hostility toward Great Britain, as highlighted in his relationship with his Tory son, William Franklin. Bibliographies.

4:145 Middlekauff, Robert. *Benjamin Franklin and His Enemies.* Berkeley: University of California Press, 1996. Historian Robert Middlekauff gives readers a different view of Franklin and others around him "in crisis." The author views him under pressures of enemies and the influences of passions—love, friendship, hatred, anger, scorn—as forces in history. This volume should be read along with Lemay, ed., *Reappraising Benjamin Franklin: A Bicentennial Perspective* (1993) (4:142) and biographical accounts of John Adams, a Franklin enemy.

4:146 Stourzh, Gerald. *Benjamin Franklin and American Foreign Policy.* This is a sound, penetrating analysis of the intellectual origins of Franklin's thoughts about foreign policy. Despite overtones of the cold war realist school, this is the best book on Franklin and foreign policy and a good source for both graduate student and trained scholar. First issued in 1954 (3:100).

4:147 Van Doren, Carl. *Benjamin Franklin.* This is a book for the general history reader as well as the historian and remains an excellent biography of Franklin (3:101).

Alexander Hamilton

4:148 Flexner, James T. *The Young Hamilton: A Biography.* Boston: Little, Brown, 1978. Although dealing with only the first half of Hamilton's life, the author ranges widely to support his thesis that his subject's career was prefigured by young manhood. This is the most perceptive and unbiased of Hamilton biographies.

4:149 Mitchell, Broadus. *Alexander Hamilton. Vol. 1: Youth to Maturity, 1755–1788.* 2 vols. New York: Macmillan, 1957. The first volume of this masterly biography finds the precocious Hamilton not only involved in politics as Washington's aide, but also acting independently during the revolution. Although largely tangential to diplomacy, this is the best place to begin studying Hamilton's role. Extensive bibliography.

John Jay

4:150 Johnston, Henry P., ed. *The Correspondence and Public Papers of John Jay.* 4 vols. New York: G. P. Putnam's Sons, 1890–1893. Reprint 1970 (B. Franklin). This still valuable nineteenth-century edition includes papers related to Jay as first chief justice of the United States, member and president of the Continental Congress, minister to Spain, member of the commission to negotiate a treaty of independence, envoy to Great Britain, and governor of New York. Should be used along with Morris, *John Jay* (1975–1980) (4:151).

4:151   Morris, Richard B., ed. *John Jay. Vol. 1: The Making of a Revolutionary: Unpublished Papers, 1745–1780. Vol. 2: The Winning of the Peace: Unpublished Papers, 1780–1784.* 2 vols. New York: Harper and Row, 1975–1980. This is an edition of the previously unpublished papers of John Jay, president of the Continental Congress, minister plenipotentiary to Spain and peace commissioner at Paris, secretary for foreign affairs, first chief justice of the Supreme Court, and negotiator of Jay's Treaty. It contains some previously published materials from Johnston's *Correspondence and Public Papers of John Jay,* (1890–1893) (4:150). To be completed with the publication of one additional volume.

4:152   Monaghan, Frank. *John Jay, Defender of Liberty against Kings & Peoples, Author of the Constitution & Governor of New York, President of the Continental Congress, Co-author of the Federalist, Negotiator of the Peace of 1783 & the Jay Treaty of 1794, First Chief Justice of the United States.* Indianapolis: Bobbs-Merrill, 1935. Reprint 1972 (AMS Press). In the only full-length biography of Jay (1745–1829), Monaghan favorably views his diplomacy (1780s-1790s) as secretary of foreign affairs and minister to England. Monaghan used Jay papers not included in Johnston, ed., *The Correspondence and Public Papers of John Jay* (1890–1893) (4:150).

Thomas Jefferson

4:153   Boyd, Julian P., Lyman H. Butterfield, Charles T. Cullen, and John Catanzariti, eds. *The Papers of Thomas Jefferson.* 29 vols. to date. Princeton: Princeton University Press, 1950–. Twenty-eight volumes (to be completed in eighty-three) of the definitive edition of Jefferson's papers take the story to February 1796. The first six of Series I concern the period from 1760 to 1784. Scholars who rely on printed materials must continue to use older editions, such as Lipscomb and Bergh, *The Writings of Thomas Jefferson* (1903– 1904) (5:190), and *Thomas Jeffer-*

son Correspondence, Printed from the Originals in the Collections of William K. Bixby, notes by Worthington C. Ford (Boston: Privately printed, 1916), for the period after 1796. Lipscomb and Bergh is now available online on the Internet. The papers show Jefferson's concern about Alexander Hamilton's manipulations. Supplemented by three "temporary" indexes covering vols. 1–6, 7–12, and 13–18, compiled by Elizabeth J. Sherwood and Ida T. Hopper (published in 1954–1973). Beginning with vol. 21, permanent cumulative indexes will appear after each decimal volume; vol. 21 itself indexes the first twenty volumes, replacing the earlier "temporary" indexes.

4:154   Kaplan, Lawrence S. *Jefferson and France: An Essay on Politics and Political Ideas.* New Haven: Yale University Press, 1967. Reprint 1980 (Greenwood Press). This modest volume attempts to reevaluate Jefferson's complex relationship with the French and the underlying philosophy that influenced it, examining whether his attachment to France and his policies ultimately better served France or his own country, and more specifically, whether his endeavors lent support to the French revolution, and later, to Napoleon. In short chapters, the work discusses Jefferson's roles in the American revolution, and then as a diplomat, statesman, politician, and national leader. A final section looks at the aged Jefferson's reflections on France.

4:155   Malone, Dumas. *Jefferson the Virginian.* Boston: Little, Brown, 1948. Malone's extensively researched and well-written volume, the first in his biography of Jefferson, describes his intellectual background, sporadic interest in foreign affairs, and appointment as a peace commissioner. The treatment of the intellectual influences and Jefferson's role in drafting the Declaration of Independence have been superseded by Garry Wills's *Inventing America: Jefferson's Declaration of Independence* (Garden City, NY: Doubleday, 1978). Still, this is the best biography for Jefferson's entire revolutionary career.

Henry and John Laurens

4:156   "Correspondence between Hon. Henry Laurens and His Son, John, 1777–1780." *South Carolina Historical and Genealogical Magazine* 6 (1905): January 1905 (3–11), April 1905 (47–52), July 1905 (103–10), and October 1905 (137–60).

This correspondence covers Henry Laurens as president of the Continental Congress until his resignation in the Deane-Lee controversy. Father and son expressed their minds about a great number of national and international issues. This work will be replaced by *The Papers of Henry Laurens* (Columbia: University of South Carolina Press, 1968– [14 vols. to date]). See also Marquis de Lafayette, "Letters from Marquis de Lafayette to Hon. Henry Laurens, 1777–1780" (1906–1908) (4:206).

4:157   "The Mission of Col. John Laurens to Europe in 1781." *South Carolina Historical and Genealogical Magazine* 1–2 (1900–1901): January 1900 (13–40), April 1900 (136–50), July 1900 (213–22), October 1900 (311–22); January 1901 (27–43), April 1901 (108–25). John Laurens was sent to France in 1781 to press for increased military and financial aid. These articles include all of the important documents, but they fail to cover French reaction or Franklin's dismay at young Laurens's style. Laurens successfully returned with the necessary money and promise of supplies just before Yorktown.

4:158   Wallace, David D. *The Life of Henry Laurens, with a Sketch of the Life of Lieutenant-Colonel John Laurens.* New York: G. P. Putnam's Sons, 1915. This biography is still the best work on Laurens as president of the Continental Congress, his subsequent capture and imprisonment in London, and his token participation in the 1782 peace negotiations. The microfilm edition of the Laurens Papers and the limited letterpress edition of his letters, however, allow for a new assessment.

James Madison

4:159   Hutchinson, William T., William M. E. Rachal, and Robert Allen Rutland, eds. *The Papers of James Madison: Congressional Series.* 17 vols. Chicago and Charlottesville: University of Chicago Press (vols. 1–10); University Press of Virginia (vols. 11–17), 1962–1989. Madison's papers offer the finest record of a politically active congressman. Volumes 1–7 deal with the period in question, going from March 1751 to February 1784. The French understood Madison's attachment to them and cultivated him carefully. Best documentary source on Madison and associates.

4:160   Brant, Irving. *James Madison: The Nationalist, 1780–1787.* Indianapolis: Bobbs-Merrill, 1948. This volume by Madison's best-known modern biographer delves deeply into Madison's career in Congress. Madison participated in many of the formal and informal decisions on foreign policy during the last years of the war, gaining his lifelong reputation of being pro-French.

John Sullivan

4:161   Hammond, Otis G., ed. *Letters and Papers of Major-General John Sullivan, Continental Army.* 3 vols. Concord, NH: New Hampshire Historical Society, 1930–1939. After inflaming French-American relations by his ill-chosen remarks following the failure at Newport, Sullivan later, while in the Continental Congress, became a paid agent of the French minister, Luzerne. Though useful and carefully edited, these volumes do not contain all of Sullivan's papers.

4:162   Whittemore, Charles Park. *A General of the Revolution, John Sullivan of New Hampshire.* New York: Columbia University Press, 1961. This is a well-researched biography of the controversial general known for his swagger and conceit. Sullivan was deeply involved in French-American relations. Although the author minimizes his activities as a paid agent of the French in the Continental Congress, he is otherwise objective in treating Sullivan's performance and failings. Bibliography.

George Washington

4:163   Chase, Philander D., Dorothy Twohig, and Frank E. Grizzard, Jr., eds. *The Papers of George Washington: Revolutionary War Series.* 11 vols. Charlottesville: University Press of Virginia, 1985–2000. Within *The Papers of George Washington,* the *Revolutionary War Series* is one of three series containing Washington's correspondence. It is the first comprehensive edition of his papers covering the period from June 1775 to December 1783, when he served as commander in chief of the Continental army. The series documents his role in winning the war and includes his wartime correspondence with military and civilian leaders, letters to and from family members and private individuals, general orders, special instructions, addresses, proclamations, and the minutes of his councils of war. This is of general interest to diplomatic historians. See also Institut français de Washington, *Correspondence of General Washington and Comte de Grasse* (1931) (4:165).

4:164 Fitzpatrick, John C., ed. *The Writings of George Washington from the Original Manuscript Sources, 1745–1799: Prepared under the Direction of the United States George Washington Bicentennial Commission and Published by Authority of Congress.* 39 vols. Washington, DC: Government Printing Office, 1931–1944. The standard edition of Washington's letters is done with skill, but since it does not print Washington's incoming letters, the Library of Congress microfilm edition should be consulted along with the new, comprehensive edition of Washington's papers published by the University of Virginia (e.g., Chase et al., *The Papers of George Washington: Revolutionary War Series,* 1985–2000) (4:163). Washington had many contacts with Frenchmen and with members of Congress, which makes his papers an exceptionally good source.

4:165 Institut français de Washington, ed. *Correspondence of General Washington and Comte de Grasse, 1781, August 17–November 4. With Supplementary Documents from the Washington Papers in the Manuscripts Division of the Library of Congress.* Washington, DC: Government Printing Office, 1931. De Grasse and Washington letters cover the Yorktown campaign (August 17–November 4, 1781). In contrast to many wartime allied contacts, de Grasse cooperated fully with both Washington and Rochambeau. See also Chase et al., *The Papers of George Washington: Revolutionary War Series* (1985–2000) (4:163).

4:166 Flexner, James T. *George Washington: In the American Revolution, 1775–1783.* Boston: Little, Brown, 1968. The second volume of a well-written four-volume biography presents much more analysis of Washington's motives, politics, and pride than Freeman, *Leader of the Revolution* (1951) (4:167). Using his evidence carefully, the author presents a different picture of Washington's personality than available elsewhere. The research is adequate.

4:167 Freeman, Douglas Southall. *George Washington, A Biography. Vol. 4: Leader of the Revolution.*

New York: Charles Scribner's Sons, 1951. See Freeman, *George Washington, A Biography. Vol. 5: Victory with the Help of France* (1952) (4:168).

4:168 _____. *George Washington, A Biography. Vol. 5: Victory with the Help of France.* New York: Charles Scribner's Sons, 1952. Volumes 4 and 5 (of seven) of Freeman's biography detail Washington's military exploits and dealings with the French and British. The scholarship is first-rate, with extensive research, but Freeman is hesitant in analyzing Washington's political actions. Even so, these volumes remain the best biography for this period.

Others

4:169 Alberts, Robert C. *The Golden Voyage: The Life and Times of William Bingham, 1752–1804.* Boston: Houghton Mifflin, 1969. The opening chapters of this well-written work cover Bingham's rise as a wealthy merchant during the revolution. As congressional agent in Martinique, he enriched himself and his business partners while fulfilling his public duties. The biography is soundly based on the Bingham Papers but thin in analysis. Bibliography.

4:170 Coe, Samuel Gwynn. *The Mission of William Carmichael to Spain.* Baltimore: Johns Hopkins Press, 1928. This is the best available work on the minor diplomat. It does not cover Carmichael's earlier activities, which were as important as the mission. Carmichael was involved in the Silas Deane controversy and later in Spain broke with John Jay. We probably will not learn more about Carmichael than is available here because his papers were apparently destroyed.

4:171 James, James Alton. *The Life of George Rogers Clark.* Chicago: University of Chicago Press, 1928. This is the best biography of the mediocre general credited with winning the Old Northwest. The author, who edited Clark's papers for the revolutionary period, has extensively researched his dealings with Spanish and French officials, but tends to excuse Clark's faults. This work, together with Clark's papers, is the best place to begin a study of the Mississippi valley during the revolution.

4:172   Cresson, William P. *Francis Dana, a Puritan Diplomat at the Court of Catherine the Great.* New York: Dial Press, 1930. This is an undistinguished biography of the U.S. minister to Russia, who earlier served as John Adams's secretary in Europe. The section on Russian politics and diplomacy is superficial, yet this is the only work on Dana himself that is worthy of note. See Griffiths, "American Commercial Diplomacy in Russia: 1780–1783" (1970) (4:80).

4:173   Showman, Richard K., with Margaret Cobb and Robert E. McCarthy, eds. *The Papers of General Nathanael Greene.* 11 vols. to date. Chapel Hill: University of North Carolina Press for the Rhode Island Historical Society, 1976–. One of Washington's most trusted aides, Greene had many contacts with Frenchmen, which will make this series valuable for the study of diplomacy. Greene worked to mend Franco-American differences after their joint failure at Newport in 1778. The editing and notes are exemplary. To be completed in thirteen volumes.

4:174   Morison, Samuel Eliot. *John Paul Jones: A Sailor's Biography.* Boston: Little, Brown, 1959. The research is thorough, the author knows his subject and the sea, and he writes with grace and verve. Morison does not dwell on the political and financial aspects of the American navy in France, but this is a minor quibble about the best biography of John Paul Jones.

4:175   Ballagh, James Curtis, ed. *The Letters of Richard Henry Lee.* 2 vols. New York: Macmillan Company, 1911–1914. Reprint 1970 (Da Capo). Lee's letters are critical because of his extensive interest in foreign affairs, as reflected in his correspondence with his brothers in Europe and with Massachusetts figures. While this edition is fairly complete, it should be used in conjunction with the Lee Family Papers (microfilm).

4:176   Ford, Worthington C., ed. *Letters of William Lee, Sheriff and Alderman of London, Commercial Agent of the Continental Congress in France, and Minister to the Courts of Vienna and Berlin, 1766–1783.* 3 vols. Brooklyn: Historical Printing Club, 1891. Reprint 1971 *(New York Times).* These papers of one of four politically active brothers include materials on Lee's trips to Prussia and on the divisive Lee-Deane quarrel. The Lee Family Papers (microfilm) includes a few items not printed here, but this work retains its value. The 1971 reprint is titled *Letters of William Lee, 1766–1783.*

4:177   Dangerfield, George. *Chancellor Robert R. Livingston of New York, 1746–1813.* New York: Harcourt, Brace, 1960. As secretary of foreign affairs from 1781 to 1784, Livingston was not reticent about giving instructions to American diplomats. His pro-French proclivities are fairly treated and his position clearly presented. The writing is excellent and the research faultless. Extensive bibliographical notes.

4:178   Ferguson, E. James, John Catanzariti, Elizabeth M. Nuxoll, and Mary A. Gallagher, eds. *The Papers of Robert Morris, 1781–1784.* 9 vols. Pittsburgh: University of Pittsburgh Press, 1973–1988. This is the definitive printed edition of the diary, correspondence, and official papers of Morris during his period of service as Superintendent of Finance and Agent of Marine, 1781–1784. His activities included arranging European loans and handling the disintegrating American finances. Morris was as deeply involved in foreign policy as was Robert R. Livingston. The editing and notes are first-rate.

4:179   Foner, Philip S., ed. *The Complete Writings of Thomas Paine.* 2 vols. New York: Citadel Press, 1945. In addition to strongly stating his views on foreign policy in *Common Sense* in 1776, Paine served as secretary of the congressional committee handling foreign affairs and became involved in the Deane-Lee controversy in 1778–1779. The editor has succeeded in bringing together the works and letters of this important man.

4:180   Butterfield, Lyman H., ed. *The Letters of Benjamin Rush.* 2 vols. Princeton: Princeton University Press for the American Philosophical Society, 1951. Rush was not only involved in many events touching on foreign affairs, he entertained opinions on every happening. He argued with New England delegates over the ultimatum to be included in the peace commissioners' instructions, urged a larger American navy, and later reflected a moderate's view of the French alliance. Well edited.

4:181   Shackelford, George Green. "William Short: Diplomat in Revolutionary France, 1785–1793."

Proceedings of the American Philosophical Society 102 (December 1958): 596–612. Diplomat Short was in Europe from 1785 to 1792, first as Thomas Jefferson's private secretary and later as chargé d'affaires in France, and then as minister resident at the Hague. He kept company with the French *philosophes* and communicated his observations about the French revolution in correspondence, much of it with Jefferson, with whom he maintained a close connection. His enthusiasm during the early phase of the French revolution waned and turned to alarm around 1792, when he saw that a constitutional monarchy, the avenue he thought best for a liberal government, would not prevail.

BRITISH

Edmund Burke

4:182   *The Correspondence of Edmund Burke.* Vols. 3–5. 10 vols. Chicago: University of Chicago Press, 1958–1978. One of the most prominent members of the opposition to Lord North's American policy, Burke grew more reticent as violence erupted. He was as interested in showing that the American War of Independence demonstrated the North coalition's inability to govern as in discerning the nature of the revolution. Well edited by successive editors.

4:183   Cone, Carl B. *Burke and the Nature of Politics. Vol. 1: The Age of the American Revolution.* Lexington: University Press of Kentucky, 1957. Indirectly the author gives an excellent sense of the nature of American policy in British politics. This first volume, which goes to the downfall of the North cabinet in 1782, shows Burke to be a pragmatic politician believing in reconciliation with the United States but maintaining the supremacy of Parliament.

Lord Carlisle

4:184   Selwyn, George Augustus, George James Howard Carlisle, R. E. G. Kirk, and Great Britain Historical Manuscripts Commission, eds. *The Manuscripts of the Earl of Carlisle, Preserved at Castle Howard.* London: Eyre and Spottiswoode for His Majesty's Stationery Office, 1897. As the head of the

commission for negotiations with the United States in 1778, offered in response to the French alliance, Carlisle quickly became disillusioned with the possibility of success. This volume reveals some of the problems the British had in seriously considering accommodation after 1776.

4:185   Brown, Weldon A. *Empire or Independence: A Study in the Failure of Reconciliation, 1774–1783.* Baton Rouge: Louisiana State University Press, 1941. This careful study of ill-fated British negotiations with the colonies concentrates on the Carlisle Commission in 1778. The author points out that Great Britain offered compromises only when forced to do so, and then too little and too late. Bibliography. See Gruber's *The Howe Brothers and the American Revolution* (1972) (4:194) and Lord Carlisle's papers, Great Britain, Historical Manuscripts Commission, *The Manuscripts of the Earl of Carlisle, Fifteenth Report, Appendix VI* (1897) (4:184).

Sir Henry Clinton

4:186   Willcox, William B., ed. *The American Rebellion: Sir Henry Clinton's Narrative of His Campaigns, 1775–1782, with an Appendix of Original Documents.* New Haven: Yale University Press, 1954. After the Yorktown disaster, Clinton was dismissed, and his request for a parliamentary inquiry was refused. Clinton wrote a long defense of his role as head of the British forces. The document, although repetitive, is interesting and valuable.

4:187   _____. *Portrait of a General: Sir Henry Clinton in the War of Independence.* New York: Alfred A. Knopf, 1964. In this finest biography of any British military leader or minister during the revolution, the author analyzes his subject's personality, war leadership, and ultimate failure, drawing a perceptive psychological portrait. This work is a good place to begin in understanding the British position in the American revolution.

George III

4:188   Fortescue, John, ed. *The Correspondence of King George the Third from 1760 to December*

1783, Printed from the Original Papers in the Royal Archives at Windsor Castle. 6 vols. London: Macmillan, 1927. Reprint 1971 (Da Capo). The exchanges between Lord North and George III cover many areas, including English spies in France and military efforts against the Americans. The king encouraged compromise and accommodation in 1778 at the time of the Carlisle Commission and reluctantly acknowledged American independence in 1782. A well-edited and informative source.

4:189   Brooke, John. *King George III.* In a work based on extensive research, Brooke correctly depicts George III as a good Whig king who accepts the limitations placed upon him by the British political system. But he also persistently refused to compromise and fought the recognition of American independence to the very last (3:105).

Others

4:190   Wickwire, Franklin, and Mary Wickwire. *Cornwallis: The American Adventure.* Boston: Houghton Mifflin, 1970. A sound work covering the most talented and aggressive British general, it is particularly good on the southern campaigns leading to the Yorktown debacle. The writing is graceful and the research solid, but Cornwallis's attitudes toward the revolution's political issues remain elusive.

4:191   Oliver, Andrew, ed. *The Journal of Samuel Curwen, Loyalist.* 2 vols. Cambridge, MA: Harvard University Press for the Essex Institute, 1972. This diary of a loyalist exile in Great Britain during the war traces the optimism and more often the pessimism loyalists felt toward the North government. Curwen offers interesting observations about American leaders. He did not have a government position as did Thomas Hutchinson, so his diary is even more valuable. The editing and introduction are first-rate.

4:192   Reid, Loren. *Charles James Fox: A Man for the People.* Columbia: University of Missouri Press, 1969. This is an acceptable biography of the leader of the opposition to the king and Lord North in the House of Commons. The subtitle to the contrary, Fox, like many eighteenth-century Whigs, did not believe in the cause of the people or in democracy. In foreign policy he remained more concerned about the

European balance of power than the war in America. Bibliography.

4:193   Brown, Gerald S. *The American Secretary: The Colonial Period of Lord George Germain, 1775–1778.* Ann Arbor: University of Michigan Press, 1963. Germain has deservedly had the reputation for being stubborn and less than brilliant. The author does very well in placing him within the eighteenth-century context and in clearly depicting the frustrations and eventual failure of Germain's American policy.

4:194   Gruber, Ira D. *The Howe Brothers and the American Revolution.* New York: Atheneum for the Institute of Early American History and Culture, 1972. The not entirely convincing but provocative argument of this work, based on all available Howe material, is that the ambiguity caused by the Howes' dual commission to plan the war and make peace with the Americans led to their failure.

4:195   Bellot, Leland J. *William Knox: The Life & Thought of an Eighteenth-Century Imperialist.* Austin: University of Texas Press, 1977. A colonial agent for Georgia and undersecretary of state in the American Department under Lord North, Knox was a central figure in the transformation of the Navigation Acts after the French and Indian War. He appears as a consistent supporter of imperial government over the colonies but a subordinate rather than a policymaker. The work adds new details on his contributions during the peace negotiations and dealings with the Earl of Shelburne. This sensible book on a career civil servant reflects adequate research in the William Knox Papers. Bibliography.

4:196   Valentine, Alan. *Lord North.* 2 vols. Norman: University of Oklahoma Press, 1967. Although short on analysis of the relationship between politics in the House of Commons and the issues of the war, this biography gives a fine account of the partnership between Lord North and the king. North was more inclined to compromise, while the king remained intransigent toward the Americans.

4:197   Hoffman, Ross J. S. *The Marquis: A Study of Lord Rockingham, 1730–1782.* New York: Fordham University Press, 1973. This is a study of Rockingham as a pillar of the Old Whigs and their defense of the British Constitution against Tory encroachment and, without ignoring Rockingham's deficiencies as a leader, an examination of the leader of the opposition to Lord North during the war. The author shows a mastery of parliamentary politics and British manuscript sources and defines the entire problem in terms of English politics. Bibliography.

4:198   Barnes, George Reginald, and John Owen, eds. *The Private Papers of John, Earl of Sandwich, First Lord of the Admiralty, 1771–1782.* 4 vols. London: Navy Records Society, 1932–1938. The editors argue that Sandwich, the ineffective and often criticized first lord of the admiralty during the American revolution, has been unjustly criticized by Whig historians, but in recent years non-Whig scholars have been just as harsh. The editing is sparse; the work should be used in conjunction with Mackesy, *The War for America, 1775–1783* (1964) (4:67).

4:199   Norris, John M. *Shelburne and Reform.* New York: St. Martin's Press, 1963. This good monograph, including a chapter on the Shelburne ministry, examines one of the most puzzling and distrusted British political leaders in the era of the American revolution. An appendix clearly explains the complicated vote on the peace treaty.

FRENCH

Francois Barbe-Marbois

4:200   Chase, Eugene P., ed. and translator. *Our Revolutionary Forefathers: Letters of Francois Marquis de Barbe-Marbois, during His Residence in the United States as Secretary of the French Legation, 1779–1785.* New York: Duffield and Co., 1929. The diary of Barbe-Marbois, first secretary to the French minister, Chevalier de la Luzerne (1779– 1785), is an interesting document. Barbe-Marbois certainly edited it later in his life, and parts were omitted at his family's request. The diary reflects more on the mores of American society than on the revolution's politics.

4:201   Lyon, E. Wilson. *The Man Who Sold Louisiana: The Career of Francois Barbe-Marbois.* Norman: University of Oklahoma Press, 1942. This biography is by one of the foremost students of the

Louisiana question in French-American diplomacy. The research has not been superseded, and the author shows that the American revolution made the careers of men such as Barbe-Marbois just as it did for their American counterparts.

Conrad Alexandre Gerard

4:202   Meng, John J., ed. *Despatches and Instructions of Conrad Alexandre Gerard, 1778–1780: Correspondence of the First French Minister to the United States with the Comte de Vergennes.* Baltimore: Johns Hopkins Press, 1939. The correspondence of Gerard, first French minister to the United States (July 1778– October 1779), with Vergennes, French minister of foreign affairs, sheds light on the diplomatic negotiations in Philadelphia just after independence was won. This edition of Gerard's original correspondence, together with other manuscript and printed sources and carefully selected secondary works, constitutes the definitive printing of his texts, greatly expanding previously published selections of his correspondence. The work includes a ninety-page historical introduction sketching Gerard's diplomatic endeavors. Contains documents in French and English.

4:203   Hudson, Ruth Strong. *The Minister from France: Conrad-Alexandre Gerard, 1729–1790.* Euclid, OH: Lutz, 1994. This book profiles the life and career of Conrad Alexandre Gerard, the first foreign diplomatic representative accredited to the United States. Prepared for the job by his dealings with the American agents in Paris, and with Benjamin Franklin, Silas Deane, and Arthur Lee, Gerard came to Philadelphia just after the American revolution. Though he became entangled in the Lee-Deane controversy, he won the respect of most American political leaders. Until now most writings have focused on Gerard, the diplomat. Hudson delves into the available primary and selected secondary sources to give a more complete picture of Gerard the man, beginning with his origins in Alsace, then covers his service in Versailles, Philadelphia, and Strasbourg. Good bibliography.

Comte de Grasse

4:204   Lewis, Charles L. *Admiral de Grasse and American Independence.* Annapolis: United States

Naval Institute, 1945. Reprint 1980 (Arno Press). This biography of de Grasse strives mightily to exonerate him from his disgrace in 1782 but is not altogether successful. For material on de Grasse during the revolutionary era, the author relies far too heavily on Doniol (4:218).

4:205 Scott, James Brown. *De Grasse à Yorktown [De Grasse at Yorktown].* Baltimore: Johns Hopkins Press for the Institut français de Washington, 1931. The author, who relied excessively on Doniol (4:218) and the old edition of Lafayette's *Memoires,* now superseded by a new edition, is enamored of the idea of close French-American relations, detracting from his assessment of de Grasse and the motives underlying allied actions.

Marquis de Lafayette

4:206 "Letters from Marquis de Lafayette to Hon. Henry Laurens." *South Carolina Historical and Genealogical Magazine* 7–9 (1906–1908): January 1906 (3–11), April 1906 (53–68), July 1906 (115–29), October 1906 (179–93); January 1907 (3–18), April 1907 (57–68), July 1907 (123–31), October 1907 (181–88); January 1908 (3–8), April 1908 (59–66), July 1908 (109–14), October 1908 (173–80). Lafayette was an incorrigible patronage seeker for his friends, and many of the letters in this work concern this issue. The letters are from the Laurens Papers, and will be superseded with the publication of the Lafayette Papers and Laurens Papers.

4:207 Burnett, Edmund C., and Waldo G. Leland. "Letters from Lafayette to Luzerne, 1780–1782." *American Historical Review* 20 (January, April 1915): 341–76, 577–612. More often than not, Lafayette urged the French to be more active in supporting the Americans. Luzerne sought to control his often impetuous countryman and allow decisions by the commander of the French forces in the United States, General Rochambeau (see also entries for la Luzerne). This is a useful source but see the modern edition of Lafayette's papers in Idzerda et al., *Lafayette in the Age of the American Revolution: Selected Letters and Papers, 1776–1790* (1977–1983) (4:209).

4:208 Gottschalk, Louis R., and Shirley A. Bill, eds. *The Letters of Lafayette to Washington:* 1777–1799. 2d ed. Philadelphia: American Philosophical Society, 1976. An edition of the complete correspondence between the two men, it is important for Lafayette's role at Newport in 1778 and in Virginia in 1781. Well edited, but users should consult modern editions of the George Washington and Marquis de Lafayette papers. Originally published in 1944 in a private edition.

4:209 Idzerda, Stanley J., Roger E. Smith, Linda J. Pike, and Mary Ann Quinn, eds. *Lafayette in the Age of the American Revolution: Selected Letters and Papers, 1776–1790.* 5 vols. Ithaca: Cornell University Press, 1977–1983. This is a limited edition of the more important documents on Lafayette's role in the American revolution. It supersedes any other source, particularly Lafayette's multivolume memoirs as well as the articles containing Lafayette's letters to Luzerne and Henry Laurens. To be completed in six volumes.

4:210 Gottschalk, Louis R. *Lafayette and the Close of the American Revolution.* Chicago: University of Chicago Press, 1942. This is the outstanding biography of Lafayette by the acknowledged authority on the subject. The range of research, level of analysis, and detachment with which the author views the subject and the issues all make this a first-rate biography. In the popular mind as well as in official circles, Lafayette was the foremost Frenchman in the American revolution. The Gottschalk volumes are the place to begin any study of Lafayette, French-American relations, the Battle of Newport, and the campaign leading to Yorktown.

4:211 Gottschalk, Louis R. *Lafayette Comes to America.* Chicago: University of Chicago Press, 1935. See Gottschalk, *Lafayette and the Close of the American Revolution* (1942) (4:210).

4:212 _____. *Lafayette Joins the American Army.* Chicago: University of Chicago Press, 1937. See Gottschalk, *Lafayette and the Close of the American Revolution* (1942) (4:210).

Chevalier de la Luzerne

4:213 O'Donnell, William Emmett. *The Chevalier de La Luzerne, French Minister to the United States, 1779–1784.* Bruges: Desclée de Brouwer,

1938. O'Donnell was given access to the Luzerne Papers while they were still in private hands, and he skillfully exploits this source. Because the author is the only scholar to see this entire collection, his work on Luzerne should be consulted.

4:214   Sioussat, St. George L. "The Chevalier de la Luzerne and the Ratification of the Articles of Confederation in Maryland, 1780–1781." *Pennsylvania Magazine of History and Biography* 60 (October 1936): 391–418. Luzerne and Barbe-Marbois intervened to assure Maryland's ratification of the Articles of Confederation. Financial and military inducements caused several opponents of ratification to be absent from the critical vote. Accompanying documents validate the author's thesis.

Comte de Rochambeau

4:215   Kennett, Lee. *The French Forces in America, 1780–1783.* Westport, CT: Greenwood Press, 1977. The finest account of Rochambeau's army in the United States, Kennett's book examines the interactions of French and American cultures during the revolution. The research is excellent, the conclusions just and reasonable. The professional behavior exhibited by French officers offered a contrast to British and American performance.

4:216   Rochambeau, Jean-Baptiste-Donatien de Vimeur. *Memoirs of the Marshall Count de Rochambeau, Relative to the War of Independence of the United States.* Translated by M. W. E. Wright. Paris: Belin and Co., 1838. Reprint 1971 *(New York Times)*. The memoirs of the general who commanded the French army at Yorktown have the flaws of many memoirs written long after the event, but they do show Rochambeau's appreciation of Washington and the sacrifices Americans were willing to make to defeat the British. They also reveal Rochambeau's ability to work in harmony with Americans in difficult situations. Drawn from the original memoirs in French, published in 1809.

Comte de Vergennes

4:217   Hardman, John, and Munro Price, eds. *Louis XVI and the Comte de Vergennes: Correspondence,*

1774–1787. Oxford: Voltaire Foundation, 1998. This work publishes an extensive portion of the extant personal correspondence between Louis XVI and his long-serving foreign minister, Charles Gravier, Comte de Vergennes. Selections of the king's letters from the Vergennes archives, most published for the first time, and the foreign minister's letters from the *Archives nationales* are complemented by many additional primary and secondary source citations and a substantial introductory essay. Altogether, they provide insights on central themes of French foreign policy from 1774 to 1787, the American War for Independence chief among them. The letters are in French; introductory essay and explanatory notes are in English.

4:218   Doniol, Henri. "Le Ministère des Affaires Étrangères de France sous le Comte de Vergennes [The French Ministry of Foreign Affairs under Count de Vergennes]." *Revue d'Histoire Diplomatique* 7 (1893): 528–60. This description of the office of foreign affairs under Count de Vergennes includes an account of his assistants carrying out his American policy. Though this article offers a good way to summarize Doniol's many years of labor in French-American relations, Murphy, *Charles Gravier, Comte de Vergennes: French Diplomacy in the Age of Revolution, 1719–1787* (1982) (4:222) supersedes his work.

4:219   Dull, Jonathan R. *The French Navy and American Independence: A Study of Arms and Diplomacy, 1774–1787.* Princeton: Princeton University Press, 1975. From exacting research in French archives, Dull contends that Vergennes set French policy and guided Louis XVI and the cabinet. If the author overemphasizes the naval buildup's role in the 1778 intervention, he nonetheless has written one of the finest political-military studies of French intervention. Extensive bibliography.

4:220   Faÿ, Bernard. "Portrait de Comte de Vergennes [Portrait of Count of Vergennes]." *Franco-American Review* 1, no. 3 (1936): 143–48. This very brief sketch is by a renowned scholar on the influence of the American revolution on France. Faÿ is not uncritical of Vergennes, but the reader should also consult Orville T. Murphy's *Charles Gravier, Comte de Vergennes: French Diplomacy in the Age of Revolution, 1719–1787* (1982) (4:222) for a more up-to-date analysis.

4:221   Murphy, Orville T. "Charles Gravier de Vergennes: Profile of an Old Regime Diplomat." *Political Science Quarterly* 83 (September 1968): 400–18. Murphy astutely examines the foreign minister's motives and personality, arguing that Vergennes's commitment to duty, discipline, and honor distinguishes him more than intellectual ability or insight in French-American affairs. This is a necessary corrective to the portrait of Vergennes as a cynical, realpolitik diplomat.

4:222   _____. *Charles Gravier, Comte de Vergennes: French Diplomacy in the Age of Revolution, 1719–1787.* Albany: State University of New York Press, 1982. This is a very good and possibly the best biography of Vergennes. Based on primary sources, it is full and extensive, covering European, colonial, and early U.S. diplomacy. A solid piece of research and writing.

Others

4:223   Morton, Brian N., and Donald C. Spinelli, eds. *Correspondance [de] Beaumarchais [Correspondence of Beaumarchais].* 4 vols. Paris: A.-G. Nizet, 1969. The first three volumes deal with Beaumarchais's controversial intermediary service between Americans in France and the French government before the French-American alliance, a role that diminished greatly after 1778. This is one of the best sources for French involvement with the United States before 1778.

4:224   Chastellux, François Jean. *Travels in North America, in the Years 1780, 1781, 1782.* Translated by Howard C. Rice, Jr. 2 vols. Chapel Hill: University of North Carolina Press for the Institute of Early American History and Culture, 1963. Second in command of the French army in the United States, Chastellux traveled throughout the country during the winter season. His comments are usually intelligent, but he overrates the simplicity and republican nature of the United States. This edition includes the notes of the original translator, George Grieve, who also toured the United States during the revolution; thus, the reader gains both Chastellux and Grieve's views. A well-edited work with exceptionally informative notes by Howard C. Rice, Jr., who also provides an introduction and the revised translation.

Originally published in 1827 as *Voyages dans l'Amérique septentrionale.*

4:225   Schaeper, Thomas J. *France and America in the Revolutionary Era: the Life of Jacques-Donatien Leray de Chaumont, 1725–1803.* Providence, RI: Berghahn Books, 1995. This first comprehensive biography of Jacques-Donatien Leray de Chaumont clarifies his contribution to the American revolutionary cause. Though known primarily as Benjamin Franklin's landlord in Passy (1777–1785), Chaumont played a much more important role in France's involvement in the American conflict. Working largely behind the scenes, he dealt as a businessman with such essentials as procurement of arms and clothing, negotiating bills of exchange, and similar business matters. These dealings brought him in contact not only with Franklin, but with other prominent leaders of both countries as well, including John Adams, Silas Deane, John Paul Jones, Beaumarchais, Lafayette, and Vergennes. The work is based largely on archival sources in almost thirty American and French repositories and numerous published primary sources. Good bibliography.

4:226   Acomb, Evelyn M., ed. *The Revolutionary Journal of Baron Ludwig Von Closen, 1780–1783.* Chapel Hill: University of North Carolina Press for the Institute of Early American History and Culture, 1958. Von Closen offered many descriptions of American officials and soldiers whom he met, and he also reported Rochambeau's reactions to events. An excellent biographical directory supplements this fine and complete journal; the translating (also by Acomb) and editing are superb.

Europe and the American Revolution

FRANCE

4:227   Aulard, Albert. "La Dette Americaine envers la France [The American Debt to France]." *Revue de Paris* 32 (May-June 1925): 319–38, 524–50. Obviously inspired by the controversy over World War I allied debts to the United States, the author analyzed French loans to the United States during and after the American revolution and their repayment. He emphasized French patience and generosity, noting that the debt constituted the only tangible connection between the two countries.

4:228   Corwin, Edward S. *French Policy and the American Alliance of 1778*. Princeton: Princeton University Press, 1916. Reprint 1970 (B. Franklin). Though a sound account of the reasons for French intervention set in a European framework, this has been superseded by Dull, *The French Navy and American Independence: A Study of Arms and Diplomacy, 1774–1787* (1975) (4:219). Vergennes's demand for a more assertive French role to redress British preponderance is now widely accepted as a result of this work.

4:229   Dull, Jonathan R. "Lafayette, Franklin, and the Coming of Rochambeau's Army." *Proceedings of the Annual Meeting of the Washington Association of New Jersey* (1980): 15–24. This address given to an annual meeting of New Jersey's Washington Association uses primary and secondary sources to trace the discussions leading to foreign troops coming to America in 1780.

4:230   Echeverria, Durand. *Mirage in the West: A History of the French Image of American Society to 1815*. Princeton: Princeton University Press, 1957. This intriguing book suggests that the French saw in the United States the kind of society that they desired for their own nation. The revolutionary period abounds in comments by Frenchman and French visitors to the United States, who often wrote from little knowledge. The research is exquisite, but it is the subtle analysis of both French and American reactions that makes the work a significant contribution.

4:231   Faÿ, Bernard. *The Revolutionary Spirit in France and America: A Study of Moral and Intellectual Relations between France and the United States at the End of the Eighteenth Century*. New York: Harcourt, Brace, 1927. A well-researched intellectual history of the Enlightenment's influence on eighteenth-century revolutions by a recognized scholar of American influence on France, this volume does not explore the economic aspects of the revolution and their effects on France or American influence outside the intellectual elite. Bibliography.

4:232   Godechot, Jacques. *France and the Atlantic Revolution of the Eighteenth Century, 1770–1799*. Translated by Herbert H. Rowen. New York: Free Press, 1965. This work sees the American and, in part, French revolutions in the larger context of a late-eighteenth-century Atlantic revolution, including the rapid development of such French ports as Nantes and Bordeaux to accommodate expanding commerce from the West Indies. Godechot's thesis is provocative and his comments on the American revolution shrewd although not supported by elaborate research.

4:233   Hill, Peter P. *French Perceptions of the Early American Republic, 1783–1793*. Philadelphia: American Philosophical Society, 1988. In a series of essays the author discusses the deterioration of French-American relations just after the American revolution and the factors leading to the outbreak of hostilities in 1793. The research is based on French consular records of the period—reports, dispatches, memoranda written by consuls, vice-consuls, and agents posted all along the eastern seaboard. In those documents the French officials express their deep disappointment with the fragility of the Franco-American relationship and the "neutral" American policies favoring Britain, despite their country's contribution to the War for American Independence. Good bibliography.

4:234   Hoffman, Ronald, and Peter J. Albert, eds. *Diplomacy and Revolution: The Franco-American Alliance of 1778*. Charlottesville: University Press of Virginia for the United States Capitol Historical Society, 1981. Five interpretative essays offer views about the Franco-American alliance of 1778: Alexander DeConde, "The French Alliance in Historical Speculation"; William C. Stinchcombe, "Americans Celebrate the Birth of the Dauphin"; Jonathan R. Dull, "France and the American Revolution Seen as Tragedy"; Orville T. Murphy, "The View from Versailles: Charles Gravier Comte de Vergennes' Perceptions of the American Revolution"; and Lawrence S. Kaplan, "The Treaties of Paris and Washington, 1778 and 1949: Reflections on Entangling Alliances." Among the themes explored are the influences motivating French policy from 1763 to 1778; French impact on post-revolutionary American diplomacy; American attitudes toward the alliance; European influences shaping French policy toward the American revolution; and a comparative study of the Franco-

American relationship during the alliances of 1778 and 1949. This is a good starting point for the study of the Franco-American Alliance of 1778.

4:235 Jones, Howard Mumford. *America and French Culture, 1750–1848.* Chapel Hill: University of North Carolina Press, 1927. Jones presents detailed information on how French culture influenced American society and concludes that religious and other differences hindered its acceptance. Bibliography.

4:236 Meng, John J. "French Diplomacy in Philadelphia, 1778–1779." *Catholic Historical Review* 24 (April 1938): 39–57. After he had negotiated the alliance with the United States, Gerard was instructed to maintain it and assure French rights to the Newfoundland fishery, which he accomplished with ease. The author downplays the hostility to Gerard and to France because of his 1779 intervention on behalf of Silas Deane.

4:237 Murphy, Orville T. "The Battle of Germantown and the Franco-American Alliance of 1778." *Pennsylvania Magazine of History and Biography* 82 (January 1958): 55–64. The author, contending that historians have overlooked this battle as a precipitating cause of French intervention, hopes to redress the balance. Germantown demonstrated that Washington's army could not be annihilated; combined with the victory at Saratoga and the possibility of American-British negotiations, these events prompted Vergennes to recognize the United States.

4:238 Rakove, Jack N. "French Diplomacy and American Politics: The First Crisis, 1779." *Mid-America* 60, Supplement (1978): 27–36. Rakove discusses Franco-American diplomacy just after the American revolution and how it affected evolving American politics. The framers of the Constitution, studying foreign policy issues like fishing rights, commercial treaties between America and European countries, and navigational rights on the Mississippi River, saw that giving broad diplomatic prerogatives to Congress risked continuing the kinds of divisive debates that had occurred in 1779. Instead, they assigned increased diplomatic responsibility to the executive branch.

4:239 Van Tyne, Claude H. "French Aid before the Alliance of 1778." *American Historical Review* 31 (October 1925): 20–40. The research and the thesis of this article on French supplies before 1778 have stood the test of subsequent scholarship. The supplies and particularly the gunpowder from the Netherlands and France were invaluable to the American armies. A more detailed explanation is now available; see Morton's *Correspondance [de] Beaumarchais* (1969) (4:223) and Dull's *The French Navy and American Independence: A Study of Arms and Diplomacy, 1774–1787* (1975) (4:219).

4:240 _____. "Influences Which Determined the French Government to Make the Treaty with America, 1778." *American Historical Review* 21 (April 1916): 528–41. Though nearly a century old, this article about why the French allied with the United States in 1778 remains interesting, if superseded by much more recent scholarship. France, the author holds, faced a dilemma: fighting against Great Britain when it was the latter that could give America its independence and after Saratoga became inclined to do so.

4:241 Willson, Beckles. *America's Ambassadors to France (1777–1927): A Narrative of Franco-American Diplomatic Relations.* New York: Frederick A. Stokes Company, 1928. Reprint 1984 (Core Collection Micropublications) Microfiche. Willson recounts the careers of thirty-seven U.S. ministers and ambassadors, including Franklin in his first chapter. Though dated, this volume remains a good source for U.S. relations with France and is well written besides. Prepared to celebrate the 150th anniversary of the U.S.-French Treaty of 1778.

GREAT BRITAIN

4:242 Bemis, Samuel Flagg. *The Hussey-Cumberland Mission and American Independence: An Essay in the Diplomacy of the American Revolution.* Princeton: Princeton University Press, 1931. This is the best account in English of British efforts, never seriously pursued, to reach separate peace terms with Spain without Spanish recognition of U.S. independence. The author's research is extensive, but his anti-European bias leads to a number of overstated conclusions about Spain and European diplomacy.

4:243 Bonwick, Colin. *English Radicals and the American Revolution.* Chapel Hill: University of

North Carolina Press, 1977. Bonwick studies the small group of English radicals concentrated in dissenter groups who came to see the American revolution as vital to the cause of preserving liberties in Britain. This group, however, did not penetrate the upper or lower classes and had only minimal effects on policy. Bibliography.

4:244   Brebner, John Bartlet. *North Atlantic Triangle: The Interplay of Canada, the United States and Great Britain.* This general survey of the relations among the three countries, including the American revolutionary period, is somewhat dated but still a good narrative of events (2:323).

4:245   Christie, Ian R. *The End of North's Ministry, 1780–1782.* New York: St. Martin's Press, 1958. A well-researched account of the last years of the North ministry, this is an astute analysis of the 1780 parliamentary election and its relationship to the growth of party. The competition among the king, ministers, and shifting factions in the House of Commons is well presented.

4:246   Clark, Dora Mae. "British Opinion of Franco-American Relations: 1775–1795." *William and Mary Quarterly* 3d ser. 4 (July 1947): 305–16. This article, based on English newspapers during and after the revolution, found the British so convinced of the virtues of their form of government and religion that they could not believe the Americans would betray them by signing an alliance with France. The author is unable to determine how deeply the opinions expressed in the newspapers penetrated the British middle class or influenced the ruling class.

4:247   Norton, Mary Beth. *The British Americans: The Loyalist Exiles in England, 1774–1789.* Boston: Little, Brown, 1972. A well-researched account of loyalists who chose exile in England, this work nicely complements Smith, *Loyalists and Redcoats: A Study in the British Revolutionary Policy* (1964) (4:107). While her analysis of the American community and its influence on British policy is sound, Norton may understate the problem of merchants who chose exile to maintain their commercial position.

4:248   O'Shaughnessy, Andrew Jackson. *An Empire Divided: The American Revolution and the British Caribbean.* The author examines why the

British colonies in the Caribbean did not side with their mainland counterparts in the revolution. He also weighs the influences of the British West Indies on colonial policy exercised in North America and the islands' role before and during the revolution. An exploration of the revolution's effects on subjects in the British islands rounds out this new look at the subject (3:265).

4:249   Scott, H. M. *British Foreign Policy in the Age of the American Revolution.* The opening chapters of this well-documented approach to Britain's position in world affairs provide a historical and bibliographical context in defining the author's goals. Later chapters recount Britain's policy and position within European diplomacy, the role of France in contributing to that position, and the impact of domestic politics on British diplomacy. This is one of the best recent works on British foreign policy (3:94).

NETHERLANDS

4:250   Boxer, C. R. *The Dutch Seaborne Empire, 1600–1800.* Dutch policy necessarily steered between a preoccupation with European trade and preoccupation with colonial quarrels that sucked European powers into wars. There is very little here on the colonies themselves. Bibliography (3:114).

4:251   Edler, Friedrich. *The Dutch Republic and the American Revolution.* Baltimore: Johns Hopkins Press, 1911. Reprint 1971 (AMS Press). Although the conclusions of this political account of the role of the Netherlands in the American revolution have not been challenged, the work has been superseded by Winter, *American Finance and Dutch Investment, 1780–1805, with an Epilogue to 1840* (1977) (4:87) and Schama, *Patriots and Liberators: Revolution in the Netherlands, 1780–1813* (1977) (4:253).

4:252   Jameson, J. Franklin. "St. Eustatius in the American Revolution." *American Historical Review* 8 (July 1903): 683–703. This article demonstrates the value of neutrality in wartime. St. Eustatius, a Dutch possession, was an entrepôt for Dutch and French powder and other war supplies to reach the United States. After the French entry into the war, the role of St. Eustatius declined, and it was finally destroyed by Admiral Rodney when the Dutch entered the war in 1780.

4:253   Schama, Simon. *Patriots and Liberators: Revolution in the Netherlands, 1780–1813.* New York: Alfred A. Knopf, 1977. Although this social and political history of the Netherlands extends beyond the revolution, the author's opening chapters add new material on its impact on the Patriot Party in the Netherlands. He finds the influence of John Adams (1781–1782) to be as profound as Adams proclaimed it to be. A first-rate analysis treating both internal Dutch affairs and international politics, it should be combined with Winter's *American Finance and Dutch Investment, 1780–1805, with an Epilogue to 1840* (1977) (4:87). Extensive bibliography.

4:254   Schulte Nordholt, Jan Willem. *The Dutch Republic and American Independence.* Chapel Hill: University of North Carolina Press, 1982. This covers U.S.-Dutch relations, examines the actions of Dutch leaders, provides a general description of Dutch government policy, treats John Adams's actions and reactions to them, and explores Dutch policies toward other nations. Chapter 18 covers Pieter Johan van Berckel, the first Dutch representative to the U.S. government, along with other Dutch who sailed for America.

PRUSSIA

4:255   Adams, Henry Mason. *Prussian-American Relations, 1775–1871.* Cleveland: Press of Western Reserve University, 1960. Reprint 1980 (Greenwood Press). Part 1 of this small volume, though little more than an introduction to the subject, includes a general description of Prussian-American relations from the revolutionary war period to 1800. The author used printed sources and substantive quotes from documents. The bibliography refers only to printed sources.

4:256   Dippel, Horst. *Germany and the American Revolution, 1770–1800: A Sociohistorical Investigation of Late Eighteenth-Century Political Thinking.* Translated by Bernhard A. Uhlendorf. Chapel Hill: University of North Carolina Press for the Institute of Early American History and Culture, 1977. The research is deep but the analysis is not always clear. This exhaustive study does show that the influence of the American revolution was far greater in Germany than previously believed even though Prussia, and to a lesser extent Austria, pursued a policy of neutrality and showed little sympathy for Americans. Extensive bibliography; foreword by Robert R. Palmer.

RUSSIA

4:257   Bailey, Thomas A. *America Faces Russia: Russian-American Relations from Early Times to Our Day.* Ithaca: Cornell University Press, 1950. Bailey's highly anecdotal survey dwells thematically on the superficial nature of American-Russian "friendship" and on the historical continuity of diplomatic problems between the two nations. Bibliography.

4:258   Bashkina, Nina N., et al., eds. *The United States and Russia: The Beginning of Relations, 1765–1815.* Washington, DC: Government Printing Office, 1980. The modern documentary edition of early U.S.-Russian diplomatic relations prepared as a joint publication of the U.S. State Department, the National Archives and Records Administration, and major Russian contributors for the early period, this is also available in a Russian edition. This is the starting place for the subject.

4:259   Bolkhovitinov, Nikolai N. *The Beginnings of Russian-American Relations, 1775–1815.* Translated by Elena Levin. Cambridge, MA: Harvard University Press, 1975. See Bashkina et al., *The United States and Russia: The Beginning of Relations, 1765–1815* (1980) (4:258).

4:260   _____. *Russia and the American Revolution.* Translated by C. Jay Smith. Tallahassee: Diplomatic Press, 1976. The author, a Russian specialist, emphasizes the ambiguity of Catherine's response to America because of Russian interests in Turkey. Bolkhovitinov has used a wide variety of Russian and American sources, and his footnotes and bibliographical essay illustrate current Russian research on the American revolution, but Griffiths, "American Commercial Diplomacy in Russia: 1780–1783" (1970) (4:80) provides better insight into the interplay between the United States and Russia.

4:261   Dulles, Foster Rhea. *The Road to Teheran: The Story of Russia and America, 1781–1943.* Princeton: Princeton University Press, 1944. This volume traces relations between the United States and Russia from 1776 to the 1940s. It is a general, pre–cold war introduction to the subject.

4:262   Madariaga, Isabel de. *Britain, Russia, and the Armed Neutrality of 1780: Sir James Harris's Mission to St. Petersburg during the American Revolution.* New Haven: Yale University Press, 1962. This is an excellent study of the League of Armed Neutrality under the guidance of Catherine and supported by France. The research is outstanding and conclusions fair, though perhaps unduly emphasizing Harris's role to the detriment of the indigenous Russian pressure for continued trade with all belligerents. Foreword by Samuel Flagg Bemis.

4:263   Saul, Norman E. *Distant Friends: The United States and Russia, 1763–1867.* The first volume of Saul's studies of U.S.-Russian relations is a must for its exploration of the two nation's early ties in the revolutionary era. It is based on major manuscript sources, primarily American, but including British and Russian as well (2:310).

SPAIN

4:264   Beerman, Eric. *España y la independencia de Estados Unidos [Spain and the Independence of the United States].* Madrid: Editorial MAPFRE, 1992. Beerman contends that Spain played a vital, though unrecognized, role in helping win American independence. The 1779 treaty between Spain and France, which gave Spain a more open role in the War for Independence, assigned military responsibilities in North America to France, while Spain was responsible for the Caribbean, Central America, and Europe, and for providing supplies to the French forces at Yorktown. This strategy of territorial division forced Great Britain to confront forces in many parts of the world as it tried subduing the rebellious colonies in North America. Beerman argues that Spanish military and naval operations were central to American success, and that Spanish soldiers fighting in Nicaragua or Gibraltar were as important for the cause as those fighting at Yorktown. Part 1 covers the Spanish campaign in North America, part 2 the Caribbean front, and part 3 covers the Spanish in Europe. Annotated bibliography.

4:265   Chavez, Thomas E. *Spain and the Independence of the United States: An Intrinsic Gift.* Albuquerque: University of New Mexico Press, 2002. Chavez researched Spanish archives to produce a work that corrects the general notion that any Spanish help for American revolutionaries was grudging at best. Spain not only supplied money and supplies, but many soldiers fought the British on American soil, recruited from throughout the Spanish empire. This work furthers the transition from "diplomatic" to international history.

4:266   Cummins, Light Townsend. *Spanish Observers and the American Revolution, 1775–1783.* Baton Rouge: Louisiana State University Press, 1991. Cummins relates the story of Spanish espionage agents and observers in North America and the Caribbean who provided information and developed contacts with the U.S. government both before and after Spain's entry in the war against Great Britain. Despite the title, the author carries the story to 1786. A very good narrative, it will encourage more research and writing on the subject in general and especially on British and French agents during the period.

4:267   Yela Utrilla, Juan F. *España ante la independencia de los Estados Unidos [Spain before United States Independence].* 2 vols. Lérida: Gráficos Academia Mariana, 1925. This sound interpretation of Spain's contributions to U.S. independence contains an accurate listing of Spanish aid. The title is so worded because Spain did not recognize the United States until after Great Britain accepted the Treaty of Paris in 1783. Volume 2 prints a number of important documents from Spanish archives dealing with American, French, and Spanish diplomacy.

OTHER NATIONS

4:268   Fogdall, Soren J. M. P. *Danish-American Diplomacy, 1776–1920.* Iowa City: The University, 1922. This work generally covers U.S.-Danish diplomatic relations from the revolution to the end of the nineteenth century with an added chapter on the U.S. purchase of the Danish West Indies. The first chapter covers the period 1776–1800, including brief accounts of the "Bergen Prizes" incident of 1779–1780 and American correspondence with the Danish premier and minister of foreign affairs.

4:269   Libiszowska, Zofia. "L'Opinion polonaise et la Revolution americaine au XVIIIe siecle [Polish Opinion of the American Revolution in the Eighteenth Century]." *Revue d'Histoire Moderne et Contemporaine* 17 (October-December 1970): 984–98. After the partition of Poland in 1773, the Poles were responsive to the influences of the American revolution. In addition to their own anti-Russian nationalism, the Poles adapted from the revolution a desire for political reforms based on parliamentary practices. This good study does not supersede Palmer's treatment in *The Challenge,* Vol. 1 in *The Age of the Democratic Revolution: A Political History of Europe and America, 1760–1800* (1959) (4:69).

4:270   Barton, H. Arnold. "Sweden and the War of American Independence." *William and Mary Quarterly* 3d ser. 23 (July 1966): 408–30. The author finds in this reexamination of the role of Sweden, particularly of Swedish soldiers who fought in the American revolution, that, contrary to previous findings, more Swedish soldiers enlisted in the British army and navy than in the American; the next largest contingent served in the French forces.

5

From the Confederation through the Jeffersonian Era

Contributing Editor
JAMES E. LEWIS, JR.
Kalamazoo College

Contributor
S. HEATH MITTON
Louisiana State University

Contents

Introduction

This chapter combines what were two complete chapters (on 1783 to 1801 and 1801 to 1815) and part of a third chapter (on the Floridas, Texas, and the beginnings of the Spanish-American revolutions) from the previous edition. In revising and updating this chapter, the editors decided to broaden the focus by adding works on a variety of topics that are, perhaps, more widely recognized as aspects of "foreign relations" than was the case two decades ago. Relations with Indian nations comprise one significant addition in this vein; studies of backcountry and frontier regions, particularly those that focus on actual or potential separatist movements, make up another. Another new addition is the inclusion of works representing exciting new perspectives on early American nationalism. An effort was also made to broaden the coverage of the Confederation era and the Constitution to include not only background works, but also studies that address the possibility that the American states would interact with each other as foreign nations. Finally, it provides more depth on the international aspects of early exploration, particularly the Lewis and Clark Expedition and on the Burr Conspiracy.

In contrast, less emphasis was placed on adding what are essentially background works in European history. For one thing, other reference works can be used to access those sources; for another, diplomatic history has been a relatively neglected field of European history for this period during the last few decades. A sampling of the most recent work in European diplomatic history for this period can be found in the published proceedings of the annual meeting of the Consortium on Revolutionary Europe, 1750–1850.

Published Primary Materials

GENERAL

5:1   Adams, Henry, ed. *Documents Relating to New-England Federalism, 1800–1815*. Boston: Little, Brown, and Company, 1877. The product of a newspaper war between then-president John Quincy Adams and some of the last survivors of the Hartford Convention, this book is anything but an impartial collection of letters and documents. Still, it is valuable for what it helps illumine about New England's place in American foreign affairs at the time of the Louisiana Purchase, the Embargo, and the War of 1812.

5:2   Bennett, Norman R., and George E. Brooks, Jr., eds. *New England Merchants in Africa: A History through Documents, 1802 to 1865*. Boston: Boston University Press, 1965. The documents in this collection—which were selected primarily for the light they throw on the African scene—have been drawn from a wide variety of sources.

5:3   Bevans, Charles I., ed. *Treaties and Other International Agreements of the United States of America, 1776–1949*. This work is the definitive compilation of U.S. treaties concluded prior to 1950. The first four volumes are for multilateral treaties; thereafter, bilateral treaties are organized alphabetically by country (1:217).

5:4   Cochran, Thomas Childs, ed. *The New American State Papers*. 195 vols. Wilmington, DE: Scholarly Resources, 1972–1981. This tremendously valuable collection of original documents, printed in facsimile, includes thousands of papers from the National Archives and Library of Congress organized into thirteen separate series, each with its own editor. Of particular value are the series on Commerce and Navigation, Exploration, Indian Affairs, Military Affairs, and Naval Affairs.

5:5   Giunta, Mary A., with J. Dane Hartgrove and Mary-Jane M. Dowd, eds. *The Emerging Nation: A Documentary History of the Foreign Relations of the United States under the Articles of Confederation, 1780–1789*. This collection, with its immense number of documents from a wide variety of sources, is an invaluable resource for the study of the Confederation period. The periodization and organization are a little odd at times, but the volumes are well indexed and easy to use (4:8). For a partial compilation of these documents, intended for classroom use, see Giunta, *Documents of the Emerging Nation: U.S. Foreign Relations, 1775–1789* (1998) (4:7).

5:6   Hackworth, Green Haywood, ed. *Digest of International Law.* 8 vols. Washington, DC: Government Printing Office, 1940–1944. Hackworth, as a legal adviser of the State Department, compiled this series as a supplement to Moore's eight-volume *Digest of International Law . . .* (1906) (5:14). It contains excerpts of diplomatic exchanges, rulings, treaties, and other material on recognition, expansion, neutrality, intervention, the Monroe Doctrine, extradition, nationality, and diplomatic codes (1789–1940). Volume 8 is an index. Succeeding Hackworth's compilation is Marjorie Millace Whiteman, ed., *Digest of International Law,* 15 vols. (Washington, DC: U.S. Department of State, 1963–1973).

5:7   Jackson, Donald, ed. *The Journals of Zebulon Montgomery Pike, with Letters and Related Documents.* 2 vols. Norman: University of Oklahoma Press, 1966. This collection brings together the journal, instructions, and other important letters relating to the Pike Expedition of 1806–1807. This expedition, which went into the hotly disputed southwestern portion of the Louisiana Purchase and was captured by Spanish forces, produced a far more explosive diplomatic issue than that of Lewis and Clark.

5:8   _____. *Letters of the Lewis and Clark Expedition with Related Documents, 1783–1854.* 2 vols. 2d ed. Urbana: University of Illinois Press, 1978. This collection is far more useful than Gary E. Moulton, ed., *The Journals of the Lewis and Clark Expedition,* 13 vols. (Lincoln: University of Nebraska Press, 1983–2001) for understanding the diplomatic complications with Spain created by the expedition; the *Journals,* however, remain more valuable for investigating relations with western Indians. First published in 1962.

5:9   Jensen, Merrill, et al., eds. *The Documentary History of the Ratification of the Constitution.* 18 vols. Madison: State Historical Society of Wisconsin, 1976–1997. As a number of books and articles have shown, foreign affairs, in various guises, was an important issue during the founding. This collection reprints newspaper and pamphlet material from the ratification battle as well as the proceedings of the different state conventions. It is projected to run twenty-three volumes.

5:10   Lowrie, Walter, and Matthew St. Clair Clarke, eds. *American State Papers: Documents, Legislative and Executive, of the Congress of the United States . . . Selected and Edited under the Authority of Congress.* 38 vols. Washington, DC: Gales and Seaton, 1832–1861. Reprint 1998 (W. S. Hein). These volumes, published by direction of Congress, contain a mass of documentary material bearing on the early history of the United States. Of the various subseries, the six volumes of *Class I: Foreign Relations* are, of course, most directly useful to diplomatic historians, but others, notably *Class II: Indian Affairs* and *Class IV: Commerce and Navigation,* also repay examination. Unfortunately, the editing is not just careless, but actually deliberately distorted, so that the volumes must be used with extreme care.

5:11   Manning, William R., ed. *Diplomatic Correspondence of the United States Concerning the Independence of the Latin-American Nations.* 3 vols. New York: Oxford University Press, 1925. The selections in these volumes (1809–1830) are arranged first by country and then chronologically. They include correspondence with European countries regarding Latin America as well as exchanges between the Department of State and Latin American and U.S. diplomats.

5:12   _____. *Diplomatic Correspondence of the United States: Canadian Relations, 1784–1860.* These volumes contain documents pertaining to the relations of the United States with British Canada that cover a wide variety of topics (1:245).

5:13   Marcus, Maeva, and James R. Perry et al., eds. *The Documentary History of the Supreme Court of the United States, 1789–1800.* 6 vols. to date. New York: Columbia University Press, 1985–. Enough cases in the Supreme Court's early years dealt with international issues to make this a worthwhile collection. Of particular value, thus far, are volumes 5, concerning suits against states, and 6, including the court's cases from 1790 to 1795.

5:14   Moore, John Bassett, ed. *A Digest of International Law: As Embodied in Diplomatic Discussions, Treaties and Other International Agreements, International Awards, the Decisions of Municipal Courts, and the Writings of Jurists.* 8 vols. Washington, DC: Government Printing Office, 1906. These volumes cover law as revealed through discussions, treaties, agreements, awards, precedents, and policies enunciated by government officials. The emphasis is on the U.S. role. See also Hackworth, *Digest of International Law* (1940–1944) (5:6).

5:15   Richardson, James D., ed. *A Compilation of the Messages and Papers of the Presidents, 1789–1897.* 10 vols. Washington, DC: Government Printing Office, 1897–1899. There are numerous versions of these volumes containing the official papers of the eighteenth- and nineteenth-century presidents that differ only in publication information and coverage.

5:16   Storing, Herbert J., with Murray Dry, eds. *The Complete Anti-Federalist.* 7 vols. Chicago: University of Chicago Press, 1981. After a provocative essay on "What the Anti-Federalists Were For," these volumes collect and reprint essays published in opposition to the Constitution. International (or even interstate) relations are surely not central to all of these essays, but what the anti-Federalists said about these issues, and where they differed from the Federalists, are significant.

5:17   U.S. Office of Naval Records and Library, ed. *Naval Documents Related to the Quasi-War between the United States and France: Naval Operations . . . February 1797–December 1801.* 7 vols. Washington, DC: Government Printing Office, 1935–1938. This collection includes diplomatic, commercial, and military documents from February 1797 through December 1801. These materials relate to the establishment of the Navy Department, American armed merchant vessels, and encounters between American and French vessels. Editing supervised by navy captain Dudley W. Knox.

5:18   _____. *Naval Documents Related to the United States Wars with the Barbary Powers . . . Naval Operations Including Diplomatic Background.* 6 vols. Washington, DC: Government Printing Office, 1939–1944. These volumes compile a thorough collection related to American naval and diplomatic relations with the Barbary powers (1794–1817). Editing supervised by navy captain Dudley W. Knox.

CONGRESS

5:19   Burnett, Edmund C., ed. *Letters of Members of the Continental Congress.* See chapter 4 of this Guide (4:1).

5:20   Butler, John P., ed. *Index, The Papers of the Continental Congress, 1774–1789.* See chapter 4 of this Guide (4:2).

5:21   Claussen, Martin P., ed. *The Journal of the House of Representatives.* The National State Papers of the United States: Texts of Documents (1789–1817), Part 1. 33 vols. Wilmington, DE: Michael Glazier, 1977. This collection and the corresponding *Journal of the Senate* (32 vols.) reprint the full texts of the House and Senate journals. The collections are oddly organized, with the numbering of the volumes restarting with each presidential administration from Washington to Madison.

5:22   Cunningham, Noble E., Jr., with Dorothy Hagberg Cappel, eds. *Circular Letters of Congressmen to Their Constituents, 1789–1829.* 3 vols. Chapel Hill: University of North Carolina Press, 1978. This valuable collection, mostly comprised of letters from representatives from the southern and western states, contains a wealth of information on national concerns as expressed in congressional debates. The editor notes that "from the First Congress to the end of the War of 1812, the most striking feature of the circulars as a group is the emphasis given to foreign affairs." Well indexed.

5:23   De Pauw, Linda Grant, et al., eds. *Documentary History of the First Federal Congress of the United States of America, March 4, 1789–March 3, 1791.* 14 vols. to date. Baltimore: Johns Hopkins University Press, 1972–. This wide-ranging collection of documents—private diaries and letters as well as official records—is invaluable for understanding a Congress whose laws and precedents influenced the workings of American diplomacy for years.

5:24   Ford, Worthington C., Gaillard Hunt, John C. Fitzpatrick, and Roscoe R. Hill, eds. *The Journals of the Continental Congress, 1774–1789: Edited from the Original Records in the Library of Congress.* See chapter 4 of this Guide (4:6).

5:25   Gales, Joseph, ed. *The Debates and Proceedings in the Congress of the United States: With an Appendix Containing Important State Papers and Public Documents, and All the Laws of a Public Nature, with a Copious Index; Compiled from Authentic Materials.* 42 vols. Washington, DC: Gales and Seaton, 1834–1856. This series, usually called and often footnoted as the *Annals of Congress,* is neither complete nor invariably accurate. Nevertheless, there is no substitute to which one can turn for accounts of congressional debates in this period.

5:26   Smith, Paul H., with Gerard W. Gawalt, Rosemary Fry Plakas, and Eugene R. Sheridan, eds. *Letters of Delegates to Congress, 1774–1789.* The definitive edition of these letters, this collection more than doubles the number of letters printed in Burnett, *Letters of Members of the Continental Congress* (1921–1936) (4:1). It is annotated lightly but with sure scholarship (4:15).

BRITISH

5:27   Great Britain, ed. *British and Foreign State Papers.* 166 vols. London: H. M. Stationery Office, 1812–1962. Compiled and indexed by the librarian and keeper of the papers in the British Foreign Office, these annual papers include correspondence between Great Britain and the United States after 1812. The series continued as Great Britain, *Foreign and Commonwealth Office. British and Foreign State Papers.*

5:28   Mayo, Bernard, ed. *Instructions to the British Ministers to the United States, 1791–1812.* Vol. 3, The Annual Report of the American Historical Association for the Year 1936. Washington, DC: Government Printing Office, 1941. This volume reproduces with scrupulous accuracy every one of the instructions from the foreign secretaries and their deputies to British representatives in the American capital. Mayo's editorial contributions include content footnotes that identify personalities, summarize reports and developments, and sometimes point to the location of other important materials.

5:29   Webster, C. K., ed. *Britain and the Independence of Latin America, 1812–1830: Select Documents from the Foreign Office Archives.* 2 vols. New York: Oxford University Press, 1938. Reprint 1970 (Octagon Books). This superb collection is introduced by a summary of the policies of Castlereagh and Canning toward Latin America. Volume 1 contains communications between London and Latin American governments; volume 2, communications between London and European governments and the United States.

5:30   _____. *British Diplomacy, 1813–1815: Select Documents Dealing with the Reconstruction of Europe.* London: G. Bell and Sons, 1921. This collection of official British documents thoroughly covers Castlereagh's efforts to restore a balance of power in Europe during and after the Napoleonic Wars. Even though documents relating to the contemporaneous negotiations with the United States at Ghent are omitted, this volume provides valuable background. The lack of an index, however, makes it somewhat difficult to use.

OTHER

5:31   Bashkina, Nina N., et al., eds. *The United States and Russia: The Beginning of Relations, 1765–1815.* This selection of documents by a joint Soviet-American team covers a broad range of topics — trade, diplomacy, cultural relations, and territorial issues. Arranged chronologically, it is a critical resource for the Russian side of early relations (4:258).

5:32   Turner, Frederick Jackson, ed. *Correspondence of the French Ministers to the United States, 1791–1797.* The Annual Report of the American Historical Association for the Year 1903. Vol. 2. Washington, DC: Government Printing Office, 1904. Turner conveniently collects the correspondence between the French ministers in Philadelphia (including Genet and Fauchet) and Paris during a period of often tense French-American relations.

Bibliographies and Other Reference Works

BIBLIOGRAPHIES

5:33　Albion, Robert G., ed. *Naval & Maritime History: An Annotated Bibliography.* 4th ed. Mystic, CT: Munson Institute of American Maritime History, 1972. This book lists works, some unpublished, on all aspects of naval affairs. The sections that touch upon the early national period are thin, but still useful.

5:34　Ammon, Harry, ed. *James Monroe: A Bibliography.* Westport, CT: Meckler, 1991. This annotated bibliography does a terrific job of pulling together the primary sources, published and manuscript, and secondary works for the entirety of Monroe's career. It provides the best starting place for research on Monroe.

5:35　Bemis, Samuel Flagg, and Grace Gardner Griffin, eds. *Guide to the Diplomatic History of the United States, 1775–1921.* A predecessor to the present volume, it is still indispensable for eighteenth- and nineteenth-century printed and manuscript materials (1:21).

5:36　Carr, James A., ed. *American Foreign Policy during the French Revolution: Napoleonic Era, 1789–1815, a Bibliography.* New York: Garland Publishing, 1994. This unannotated bibliography is fairly comprehensive, but its usefulness is compromised by the extraordinary number of typographical errors included in it.

5:37　Coletta, Paolo E., ed. *A Bibliography of American Naval History.* Annapolis: Naval Institute Press, 1981. This bibliography is fairly comprehensive and well organized but is not annotated.

5:38　Crawford, Michael J., and Christine F. Hughes. *The Reestablishment of the Navy, 1787–1801: Historical Overview and Select Bibliography.* Washington, DC: Naval Historical Center, 1995. After a brief historical overview of naval developments between the Constitutional Convention and the end of Adams's presidency, the authors provide a mostly unannotated, fairly limited (only about 200 entries) bibliography. They include, however, many key works on standard topics and individuals.

5:39　Ferguson, E. James, ed. *Confederation, Constitution, and Early National Period, 1781–1815.* Northbrook, IL: AHM Publishing Corp., 1975. This volume provides an unannotated listing of published books and articles on the period (1781–1815). There are sections devoted to foreign affairs in each of the major parts of the book.

5:40　Ferling, John E., ed. *John Adams: A Bibliography.* Westport, CT: Greenwood Press, 1994. This bibliography thoroughly covers the entirety of Adams's life, listing both primary and secondary sources. It is only lightly annotated, however, particularly in comparison to some of the other volumes in this series.

5:41　Fredriksen, John C., comp. *Shield of Republic, Sword of Empire: A Bibliography of United States Military Affairs, 1783–1846.* Westport, CT: Greenwood Press, 1990. This bibliography of military affairs is thorough and well organized, with chronological and topical sections. It includes published primary and secondary sources.

5:42　Graebner, Norman A., ed. *American Diplomatic History before 1900.* Arlington Heights, IL: AHM Publishing Corp., 1978. This collection of judiciously chosen items includes some not cited in this Guide.

5:43　Jessup, John E., and Robert W. Coakley, eds. *A Guide to the Study and Use of Military History.* Washington, DC: Center of Military History, United States Army, 1979. This is an indispensable bibliography of world military history, with emphasis on the United States. In addition to the bibliography, chapters by both U.S. army historians and civilian academics treat the history of the writing of military history. The bibliography lists relevant journals.

5:44　Kinnell, Susan K., ed. *Military History of the United States: An Annotated Bibliography.* Santa Barbara, CA: ABC-CLIO, 1986. This annotated bibliography is fairly comprehensive, but its organization in chronological sections covering relatively long periods (1787–1860, for example) makes it a bit cumbersome to use.

5:45　　Krewson, Margrit B., ed. *German-American Relations: A Selective Bibliography*. Washington, DC: Library of Congress, 1995. This bibliography covers the seventeenth through the twentieth centuries. It is especially rich in German-language books and articles.

5:46　　McCutcheon, James M., ed. *China and America: A Bibliography of Interactions, Foreign and Domestic*. Honolulu: University Press of Hawaii, 1972. This is a highly selective bibliography of secondary literature in English on Sino-American interactions from the eighteenth century to the present. It includes books, articles, and dissertations arranged by subjects such as foreign policy, public opinion, economics, missionaries, and immigration.

5:47　　Meyer, Michael C., ed. *Supplement to a Bibliography of United States–Latin American Relations since 1810*. Meyer follows the organization of Trask, Meyer, and Trask, *A Bibliography of United States–Latin American Relations since 1810: A Selected List of Eleven Thousand Published References* (1968) (1:257), with a few new subsections reflecting new trends and events; it essentially adds material published since 1967, plus additional older materials (1:254).

5:48　　Monaghan, Frank, ed. *French Travellers in the United States, 1765–1932: A Bibliography: With Supplement by Samuel J. Marino*. See chapter 4 of this Guide (4:30).

5:49　　Mugridge, Ian, ed. *United States Foreign Relations under Washington and Adams: A Guide to the Literature and Sources*. New York: Garland Publishing, 1982. This work is a useful annotated bibliography of some of the most important primary (published and unpublished) and secondary sources on this topic. It is quite brief, numbering barely 400 entries.

5:50　　Parsons, Lynn Hudson, ed. *John Quincy Adams: A Bibliography*. Westport, CT: Greenwood Press, 1993. The best starting place for research on Adams, this annotated bibliography compiles key primary sources, published and manuscript, and a wide range of secondary works for Adams's whole career.

5:51　　Prucha, Francis Paul, ed. *A Bibliographical Guide to the History of Indian-White Relations in the United States*. Chicago: University of Chicago Press, 1977. This comprehensive, but unannotated, bibliography is organized by subject and easily searched using the table of contents and index. Prucha published a supplement covering five more years of publications as *Indian-White Relations in the United States: A Bibliography of Works Published, 1975–1980* (Chicago: University of Chicago Press, 1982).

5:52　　Shuffleton, Frank, ed. *Thomas Jefferson: A Comprehensive, Annotated Bibliography of Writings about Him (1826–1980)*. New York: Garland Publishing, 1983. Given the unceasing torrent of work on Jefferson, this work is already dated. It also suffers from being excessively comprehensive and poorly organized, with the nearly 3,500 entries divided into just five chapters. When the Jefferson volume of Meckler's "Bibliographies of the Presidents of the United States" series is published, it should supplant this work for most purposes. Shuffleton followed this work with *Thomas Jefferson: A Comprehensive, Annotated Bibliography* (Garland Publishing, 1992) and then, online, *Thomas Jefferson: A Comprehensive, Annotated Bibliography of Writings about Him, 1826–1997*, which in 2002 could be found at http://etext.lib.virginia.edu/jefferson/bibliog/.

5:53　　Smith, Dwight L., ed. *Indians of the United States and Canada: A Bibliography*. Santa Barbara, CA: ABC-CLIO, 1974. This volume should be of assistance to those who are looking into U.S.-Indian relationships during the early national period; it is less comprehensive, however, than the two volumes by Francis Paul Prucha (5:51).

5:54　　_____. *The War of 1812: An Annotated Bibliography*. New York: Garland Publishing, 1985. This extremely valuable annotated bibliography includes close to 1,400 separate entries, primary and secondary. It covers not only the military aspects of the war, but also the tensions that led up to it, the negotiations that ended it, and the domestic political context that shaped it.

5:55　　Smith, Dwight L., and Terry A. Simmerman, eds. *Era of the American Revolution: A Bibliography*. Santa Barbara, CA: ABC-CLIO, 1975. Sections on diplomacy and foreign affairs are thin in this annotated bibliography (1763–1789), but the introduction to the entire subject is good.

5:56   Smith, Myron J., Jr., ed. *The American Navy, 1789–1860: A Bibliography.* Metuchen, NJ: Scarecrow Press, 1974. Smith's bibliography deals largely with naval matters, but there are items referring to the Quasi-War and other incidents that affected diplomacy.

5:57   Trask, David F., Michael C. Meyer, and Roger R. Trask, eds. *A Bibliography of United States–Latin American Relations since 1810: A Selected List of Eleven Thousand Published References.* This is the only comprehensive guide to publications in English, Spanish, Portuguese, French, and other languages in the field of U.S.–Latin American relations. It is organized chronologically and topically, with country chapters (1:257). See also Meyer, *Supplement to a Bibliography of United States–Latin American Relations since 1810* (1979) (1:254).

ATLASES

5:58   Cappon, Lester J., ed., with Barbara B. Petchenik, cartographic ed., and John Hamilton Long, assistant ed. *Atlas of Early American History: The Revolutionary Era, 1760–1790.* See chapter 4 of this Guide (4:37).

5:59   Clark, David Sanders, ed. *Index to Maps of the American Revolution in Books and Periodicals: Illustrating the Revolutionary War and Other Events of the Period, 1763–1789.* See chapter 4 of this Guide (4:38).

5:60   Esposito, Vincent J., ed. *The West Point Atlas of American Wars.* These volumes contain battlefield and strategic maps as well as accompanying text (1:15). First published in 1959.

5:61   Prucha, Francis Paul, ed. *Atlas of American Indian Affairs.* Lincoln: University of Nebraska Press, 1990. This thorough collection of maps covers a wide range of topics, including land cessions, wars, and the locations of government factories, agencies, and military posts. Some of the maps, however, are less precise than could be wished.

5:62   Tanner, Helen Hornbeck, ed. *Atlas of Great Lakes Indian History.* Norman: University of Oklahoma Press, 1987. This elegantly produced collection of maps is an invaluable resource for studying Indian-white interactions in the Great Lakes region during the critical decades from the end of the revolution through the War of 1812. Extensive bibliography.

5:63   Wheat, James Clements, and Christian F. Brun, eds. *Maps and Charts Published in America before 1800: A Bibliography.* See chapter 4 of this Guide (4:40).

OTHER REFERENCE WORKS

5:64   DeConde, Alexander, ed. *Encyclopedia of American Foreign Policy: Studies of the Principal Movements and Ideas.* This huge, selective reference work contains ninety-five topical essays providing conceptual analysis of themes of American foreign policy by diplomatic historians and other specialists. Many of the essays deal with themes covering the whole span of American foreign policy; titles include "Alliances, Coalitions, and Ententes," "Armed Neutralities," and "Isolationism." Others deal with more traditional episodes, such as "King Cotton Diplomacy" or "Truman Doctrine" (1:64). For a critical review, see Bradford Perkins, "Rating DeConde's Stable of Diplomatic Historians," *Diplomatic History* 3 (Fall 1979): 439–42 (1:64). A major update appeared recently: DeConde, Richard Dean Burns, and Fredrik Logevall, eds., *Encyclopedia of American Foreign Policy,* 2d ed. (3 vols., New York: Charles Scribner's Sons, 2002).

5:65   Garraty, John A., and Mark C. Carnes, eds. *American National Biography.* This immense undertaking, totaling about 23,000 pages, contains biographies of nearly 17,500 famous and lesser-known individuals. The quality of the entries and the bibliographies that follow each entry make it a valuable tool for scholars. While it does not include every individual in the *Dictionary of American Biography* (1928–1946) (1:51), it should supplant it for most purposes (1:50).

5:66   Heidler, David S., and Jeanne T. Heidler, eds. *Encyclopedia of the War of 1812.* Santa Barbara,

CA: ABC-CLIO, 1997. The emphasis of this encyclopedia is heavily weighted toward military matters but does cover some diplomatic and domestic issues.

Historiography

5:67　　Egan, Clifford L. "The Origins of the War of 1812: Three Decades of Historical Writing." *Military Affairs* 38 (April 1974): 72–75. This short article seeks to update Goodman, "The Origins of the War of 1812: A Survey of Changing Interpretations" (1941) (5:69). The text discusses only a limited number of works, and the comments are often brisk. The footnotes, as lengthy as the article itself, provide a good guide to works published between 1940 and 1973.

5:68　　Gilbert, Arthur N. "The American Indian and United States Diplomatic History." *History Teacher* 8 (February 1975): 229–41. Gilbert offers an early and persuasive argument for the need to incorporate Indian relations into diplomatic history, particularly for the late eighteenth and early nineteenth centuries.

5:69　　Goodman, Warren H. "The Origins of the War of 1812: A Survey of Changing Interpretations." *Mississippi Valley Historical Review* 28 (September 1941): 171–86. This able historiographical article, often considered a model, thoughtfully assesses the material available to 1941. Goodman's judgments are deft, and his suggestions for further work and speculations as to its likely outcome are impressive, especially since many have come true.

5:70　　Haines, Gerald K., and J. Samuel Walker, eds. *American Foreign Relations, A Historiographical Review.* See chapters 1 and 2 of this Guide (1:32; 2:9)).

5:71　　Hatzenbuehler, Ronald L. "The Early National Period, 1789–1815: The Need for Redefinition." In *American Foreign Relations, A Historiographical Review,* ed. Gerald K. Haines and J. Samuel Walker, 17–32. Westport, CT: Greenwood Press, 1981. This now somewhat dated essay discusses the historiography of a period that Hatzenbuehler argues needs to be redefined and synthesized.

5:72　　Hickey, Donald R. "The War of 1812: Still a Forgotten Conflict?" *Journal of Military History* 65 (July 2001): 741–69. In this straightforward historiographical essay, Hickey surveys recent work on the War of 1812, with a focus on military history. He highlights works published in the 1990s, which he describes as "the most prolific decade ever for 1812 studies."

5:73　　Higginbotham, Don. "The Early American Way of War: Reconnaissance and Appraisal." This article provides a thorough, though now slightly dated, review of the "new military history," with its emphasis on who fought and why. It covers the period from the Seven Years War to the War of 1812 (3:60).

5:74　　Horsman, Reginald. "The War of 1812 Revisited." *Diplomatic History* 15 (Winter 1991): 115–24. Ostensibly a review of Hickey, *The War of 1812: A Forgotten Conflict* (1989) (5:684), this article is more nearly an updating of the historiographical essays, Goodman, "The Origins of the War of 1812: A Survey of Changing Interpretations" (1941) (5:69), and Egan, "The Origins of the War of 1812: Three Decades of Historical Writing" (1974) (5:67). Horsman provides a valuable survey of the main points of controversy and principal arguments of works published in the previous three decades.

5:75　　Hull, James P. "From Many, Two: A Bibliographic History of Canadian-American Relations." *American Studies International* 36 (June 1998): 4–22. This historiography of Canadian-American relations addresses the entire period from the revolution to the present. As such, its coverage of the late eighteenth and early nineteenth centuries is fairly brief, but still useful.

5:76　　Perkins, Bradford. "Early American Foreign Relations: Opportunities and Challenges." *Diplomatic History* 22 (Winter 1998): 115–20. The conclusion to a symposium on early U.S. foreign relations, this brief essay by one of the elder statesmen of the field combines an overview of the historiography with a suggestion of opportunities for future scholarship.

5:77　　Trask, Roger R. "Inter-American Relations." In *Latin American Scholarship since World*

War II: Trends in History, Political Science, Literature, Geography, and Economics, ed. Roberto Esquenazi-Mayo and Michael C. Meyer, 203–21. Lincoln: University of Nebraska Press, 1971. This bibliographical essay reviews the historiography of inter-American relations. Schools of historians are categorized and described. The additional bibliography alone makes this piece worthwhile.

5:78   Weeks, William Earl. "New Directions in the Study of Early American Foreign Relations." This extremely valuable article thoroughly canvasses the state of the field of early American diplomatic history (1787–1828). Weeks includes as well numerous suggestions for new lines of inquiry (4:47).

Overviews

5:79   Abernethy, Thomas Perkins. *The South in the New Nation, 1789–1816.* Baton Rouge: Louisiana State University Press, 1961. Abernethy's account of the Burr Conspiracy is more concise and somewhat different from his earlier monograph on that subject, *The Burr Conspiracy* (1954) (5:494). His treatment of the West Florida rebellion is extremely well done, and his examination of southern attitudes toward the War of 1812 is helpful. The "Critical Essay on Authorities" is a superb guide to material of all types.

5:80   Adams, Henry. *History of the United States during the Administrations of Jefferson and Madison.* 9 vols. New York: Scribner's, 1889–1891. This classic work is, unfortunately, more often praised than read. Adams includes masses of detail, but sometimes mishandles his sources. These shortcomings are far outweighed by the breadth of his research, the vigor of his prose, and his often provocative judgments. For a sophisticated critique, see Merrill D. Peterson, "Henry Adams on Jefferson the President," *Virginia Quarterly Review* 39 (Spring 1963): 187–201.

5:81   Belohlavek, John M. "Economic Interest Groups and the Formation of Foreign Policy in the Early Republic." *Journal of the Early Republic* 14 (Winter 1994): 476–84. In this brief, but sweeping,

essay, Belohlavek encourages all historians of the early republic, not merely those of diplomacy, to pay greater attention to the interrelationship of economics and foreign policy.

5:82   Bemis, Samuel Flagg, ed. *The American Secretaries of State and Their Diplomacy.* These dated but still useful sketches, prepared by different historians, cover each secretary of state. Volume 1 includes the secretaries who served under the Confederation government, Robert R. Livingston and John Jay; volume 2 treats those of the Federalist era, Thomas Jefferson, Edmund Randolph, Timothy Pickering, and John Marshall; volume 3 covers James Madison, Robert Smith, and James Monroe (1:48).

5:83   Cunliffe, Marcus. *Soldiers & Civilians: The Martial Spirit in America, 1775–1865.* Boston: Little, Brown, 1968. Cunliffe, an English historian, permits us to see a major part of the American military past as others see it. American distrust of professional soldiers notwithstanding, Cunliffe perceives Americans as fascinated by military affairs and the panoply of war. He sets the history of American professional and citizen-soldiers alike in a social and intellectual context. Bibliography.

5:84   Davis, David Brion. *Revolutions: Reflections on American Equality and Foreign Liberations.* Cambridge, MA: Harvard University Press, 1990. This extended essay—a series of lectures delivered by Davis at Harvard—examines changing American attitudes toward foreign revolutions, particularly those in France and Haiti. A précis of Davis's argument appeared as "American Equality and Foreign Revolutions," *Journal of American History* 76 (December 1989): 729–52.

5:85   Field, James A., Jr. "1789–1820: All Œconomists, All Diplomats." In *Economics and World Power: An Assessment of American Diplomacy since 1789,* ed. William H. Becker and Samuel F. Wells, Jr., 1–54. New York: Columbia University Press, 1984. Field argues that the "central aim of foreign policy" during these decades "was to extend commercial relations while avoiding political entanglements." He takes a broad view of commercial relations in this overview of early American foreign policy.

5:86   Goodwin, Albert, ed. *New Cambridge Modern History. Vol. 8: The American and French Revolutions, 1763–93.* This wide-ranging collection of essays covers the period of the American and French revolutions from a variety of perspectives, political, social, cultural, economic, and diplomatic. American affairs receive reasonably full coverage (4:57).

5:87   Graebner, Norman A. *Foundations of American Foreign Policy: A Realist Appraisal from Franklin to McKinley: Essays.* This collection of essays and papers by one of the deans of American diplomatic history covers much ground, including Jefferson's mission to France in the 1780s, American neutrality in the 1790s, and Madison's decisions leading to the War of 1812 (2:62).

5:88   Greene, Jack P., ed. *The American Revolution: Its Character and Limits.* This collection of essays examines developments in a variety of economic, social, political, military, and diplomatic areas during the post-revolutionary era. It includes papers by E. Wayne Carp on the army (14–50), Jack N. Rakove on federalism (80–103), Drew R. McCoy on foreign trade (131–48), Jonathan R. Dull on relations with the Netherlands (149–63), Peter S. Onuf on western expansion (171–96), and James H. Merrell on Indian affairs (197–223) (4:58).

5:89   Heald, Morrell, and Lawrence S. Kaplan. *Culture and Diplomacy: The American Experience.* This significant study seeks to trace the "cultural setting" of U.S. foreign policy from the colonial period to the present, on the assumption that to understand American diplomacy it is necessary to understand the culture within which policy is formed. Of particular value for this period are essays on the "neocolonial impulse" that continued to bind some Americans to Britain between 1783 and 1820, on relations between the United States and France, and on the American "ambivalence" to the Latin American revolutions (2:130).

5:90   Horsman, Reginald. "The Dimensions of an 'Empire for Liberty': Expansion and Republicanism, 1775–1825." Horsman traces the debates over the appropriate size for a republican government from the American revolution to the 1820s. This de-

bate peaked with the Constitutional Convention, the Louisiana Purchase, and the Hartford Convention (4:59).

5:91   _____. *The Diplomacy of the New Republic, 1776–1815.* This work is a broad and brief overview of American diplomatic history between the revolution and the War of 1812. Horsman's coverage and judgments are sensible, but the most valuable part of this book may be the extensive bibliographical essay (4:60).

5:92   Hutson, James H. "Intellectual Foundations of Early American Diplomacy." Differing sharply with Felix Gilbert, the author contends that Americans of the revolutionary generation (1776–1796) acted according to the same assumptions of power politics that dominated contemporary European statecraft. American ideas derived from English opposition ideology rather than from the French *philosophes* (3:85).

5:93   Kaplan, Lawrence S., ed. *The American Revolution and "A Candid World."* This is a good series of articles on diverse topics of diplomacy. For the period after the Treaty of Paris, the most useful essays are on the location of the American revolution in the law of nations and the movement toward isolation from 1775 to 1801 in the context of the French-American alliance. See chapter 4 of this Guide (4:63).

5:94   _____. *Colonies into Nation: American Diplomacy, 1763–1801.* See chapter 4 of this Guide (4:64).

5:95   _____. *Entangling Alliances with None: American Foreign Policy in the Age of Jefferson.* Kent, OH: Kent State University Press, 1987. This book collects many of Kaplan's articles and essays on the foreign policies of the early republic. Common topics include: idealism and realism, French-American relations, Jefferson, the War of 1812, and the historiography of early American foreign policy. For a thoughtful examination of Kaplan's contribution to this historiography, see Alexander DeConde's essay in Scott L. Bills and E. Timothy Smith, eds., *The Romance of History: Essays in Honor of Lawrence S. Kaplan* (Kent, OH: Kent State University Press, 1997).

5:96　　Krenn, Michael L., ed. *Race and U.S. Foreign Policy from Colonial Times through the Age of Jackson. Vol. 1, Race and U.S. Foreign Policy from the Colonial Period to the Present: A Collection of Essays.* This book reprints articles and book chapters examining the intersection of race and American foreign policy from the colonial period through the 1840s. With everything in the volume available elsewhere, its value lies in its convenience. Chapters relevant to the late eighteenth and early nineteenth centuries, many about Indians, are by Reginald Horsman, G. E. Thomas, Roy Harvey Pearce, Gary B. Nash, Richard Drinnon, and Stuart Creighton Miller. See chapter 2 of this Guide for more details (2:157).

5:97　　LaFeber, Walter. "Foreign Policies of a New Nation: Franklin, Madison, and the 'Dream of a New Land to Fulfill with People in Self-Control,' 1750–1804." In *From Colony to Empire: Essays in the History of American Foreign Relations,* ed. William Appleman Williams, 9–37. New York: John Wiley, 1972. Focusing on Franklin and Madison, LaFeber argues that a commitment to expanding the territorial and commercial reach of a rapidly expanding population of independent citizens operated from the very beginnings of the new nation.

5:98　　Lang, Daniel G. *Foreign Policy in the Early Republic: The Law of Nations and the Balance of Power.* Baton Rouge: Louisiana State University Press, 1985. This book, which focuses on the diplomacy of the 1780s and 1790s, examines the influence of international law on the founders, particularly Vattel's thinking on the balance of power and the law of nations. This thinking provided significant common ground for Hamilton, Jefferson, and Madison, though the last sought to broaden the law of nations. Bibliography.

5:99　　Langley, Lester D. *The Americas in the Age of Revolution, 1750–1850.* New Haven: Yale University Press, 1996. Langley's comparative study discusses three revolutions: American, Haitian, and Spanish-American. He focuses on the differences between the revolutions as a way to explain the differences in post-revolutionary political and social developments in each region.

5:100　　McCoy, Drew R. *The Elusive Republic: Political Economy in Jeffersonian America.* Chapel Hill: University of North Carolina Press, 1980. McCoy's book is a critical effort to link specific foreign and domestic policies to republican ideology. His discussion of the place of territorial and commercial expansion in evolving republican thought includes new insights into issues as diverse as the Constitutional Convention, the Louisiana Purchase, and the War of 1812.

5:101　　Merli, Frank J., and Theodore A. Wilson, eds. *Makers of American Diplomacy. Vol. 1: From Benjamin Franklin to Alfred Thayer Mahan.* See chapter 2 of this Guide (2:194).

5:102　　Murrin, John M. "The Jeffersonian Triumph and American Exceptionalism." *Journal of the Early Republic* 20 (Spring 2000): 1–25. Originally delivered as the author's presidential address to the Society for Historians of the Early American Republic, this article provides an interpretative overview of early American foreign policy. Murrin argues that the Jeffersonians largely succeeded in combining territorial expansion, hemispheric hegemony, and limited government during the first decades of the new government.

5:103　　Nelson, John R., Jr. *Liberty and Property: Political Economy and Policymaking in the New Nation, 1789–1812.* Baltimore: Johns Hopkins University Press, 1987. This study performs the same function for liberalism that McCoy, *The Elusive Republic: Political Economy in Jeffersonian America* (1980) (5:100) does for republicanism—linking it to specific domestic and foreign policies. It is stronger on the Federalist era than on the Jefferson and Madison presidencies. Some of Nelson's key insights regarding Hamilton's tariff policy appeared earlier in his "Alexander Hamilton and American Manufacturing: A Reexamination," *Journal of American History* 65 (March 1979): 971–95.

5:104　　Onuf, Peter S. "A Declaration of Independence for Diplomatic Historians." *Diplomatic History* 22 (Winter 1998): 71–83. This essay, part of a symposium on early U.S. foreign relations, urges diplomatic historians to examine the ways in which the founding of the American union represented an effort to deal with the traditional problems of complex state systems and, in doing so, to recognize the centrality of their scholarly interests to early American political development.

5:105   Onuf, Peter S., and Nicholas Onuf. *Federal Union, Modern World: The Law of Nations in an Age of Revolution, 1776–1814.* Madison: Madison House, 1993. Coauthored by a political theorist and historian, this book is at times an unsteady mix. But it includes valuable insights on the evolving view of the balance of power, the law of nations, and federalism in the context of the American revolution and the wars of the French revolution.

5:106   Palmer, Robert R. *The Age of the Democratic Revolution: A Political History of Europe and America, 1760–1800.* See chapter 4 of this Guide (4:69).

5:107   Pelz, Stephen E. "Changing International Systems, the World Balance of Power, and the United States, 1776–1976." *Diplomatic History* 15 (Winter 1991): 47–81. In this long-term modeling of changes in the international states' system, Pelz sees a shift in 1793 from a balance-of-power to a revolutionary-counterrevolutionary system. Ole R. Holsti's comments appear as "International Systems, System Change, and Foreign Policy: Commentary on 'Changing International Systems,'" 83–89.

5:108   Perkins, Bradford. *The Creation of a Republican Empire, 1776–1865.* This broad survey of early American foreign policy distinguishes realist, though anglophilic, Federalists from more idealist, and expansionist, Republicans. Bibliographic essay (2:44).

5:109   _____. "Interests, Values, and the Prism: The Sources of American Foreign Policy." *Journal of the Early Republic* 14 (Winter 1994): 458–66. This essay, a part of a special issue on early American foreign policy, contains a précis of the argument about the sources of foreign policymaking that Perkins develops in full in *The Creation of a Republican Empire, 1776–1865* (1993) (5:108).

5:110   Setser, Vernon G. *The Commercial Reciprocity Policy of the United States, 1774–1829.* See chapter 4 of this Guide (4:84).

5:111   Van Alstyne, Richard W. "The American Empire Makes Its Bow on the World Stage, 1803–1845." In *From Colony to Empire: Essays in the History of American Foreign Relations,* ed. William Appleman Williams, 39–81. New York: John Wiley, 1972. Van Alstyne emphasizes the growth of the American territorial empire in his general survey of the foreign policies of the early and mid-nineteenth century.

5:112   Varg, Paul A. *Foreign Policies of the Founding Fathers.* Varg's basic theme is useful; the interplay of ideals and reality, especially economic reality, is the reason this extended essay is sometimes a stimulating book. As a work of interpretation, the study understandably rests almost entirely on secondary works; more serious is the apparent failure to consult many important historical studies (4:76).

5:113   _____. *New England and Foreign Relations, 1789–1850.* Hanover, NH: University Press of New England, 1983. This book does less than it might have with an intriguing topic. Varg includes an interesting discussion of the Embargo and War of 1812, but says relatively little about New England's reaction to the Louisiana Purchase, which included a short-lived separatist movement. The emphasis throughout is on commercial, rather than political, sources for New England's distinctiveness in foreign affairs. Bibliography.

5:114   Weeks, William Earl. "American Nationalism, American Imperialism: An Interpretation of United States Political Economy, 1789–1861." *Journal of the Early Republic* 14 (Winter 1994): 485–95. Part of a special issue on early American foreign policy, this essay offers a brief statement of the argument about the close links among nationalism, expansionism, and imperialism that Weeks fully develops in *Building the Continental Empire: American Expansion from the Revolution to the Civil War* (1996) (5:115).

5:115   _____. *Building the Continental Empire: American Expansion from the Revolution to the Civil War.* This brief survey of American expansion has an intriguing thesis: that nationalism grew alongside territorial and commercial empire. But the real focus of this book is on Texas, Oregon, and the Mexican War, with only one chapter on the period before 1815 (4:77).

5:116   Williams, William Appleman. *The Contours of American History.* Part 1 of this broad overview of American history expands on Williams's well-known "The Age of Mercantilism: An Interpretation of the American Political Economy, 1763–1828" (1958) (2:49).

NATIONALISM

5:117   Bruce, Dickson D., Jr. "National Identity and African American Colonization, 1773–1817." *Historian* 58 (Autumn 1995): 15–28. An interesting counterpart to Onuf, "'To Declare Them a Free and Independent People': Race, Slavery, and National Identity in Jefferson's Thought" (1998) (5:122), Bruce's essay looks at the separate nationalism of African-Americans, which was encouraged by the rhetoric of pro-colonization arguments. Of particular interest to Bruce is Paul Cuffe, the leading black spokesman of African colonization in the early national period.

5:118   Curti, Merle E. *The Roots of American Loyalty.* New York: Columbia University Press, 1946. The early chapters are informative on the development of American national consciousness, what Curti calls "the beginnings of American patriotism." Bibliography.

5:119   Millican, Edward. *One United People: The Federalist Papers and the National Idea.* Lexington: University Press of Kentucky, 1990. According to Millican, the authors of *The Federalist*—Hamilton, Madison, and Jay—hoped that the Constitution, and their lengthy exposition of it, would help create a single nation state and a sense of national feeling. Bibliography.

5:120   Nagel, Paul C. *This Sacred Trust: American Nationality, 1798–1898.* New York: Oxford University Press, 1971. This older study starts with a different notion of nationalism than the recent works of Simon P. Newman (5:121), Len Travers (5:123), and David Waldstreicher (5:124). Nagel places the beginnings of American nationalism in times of distress, particularly the Quasi-War and the War of 1812.

5:121   Newman, Simon P. *Parades and the Politics of the Street: Festive Culture in the Early American Republic.* Philadelphia: University of Pennsylvania Press, 1997. Newman argues that early festive culture, which responded to and was influenced by the French revolution, played a crucial role in replacing loyalty to state or region with loyalty to nation. Bibliography.

5:122   Onuf, Peter S. "'To Declare Them a Free and Independent People': Race, Slavery, and National Identity in Jefferson's Thought." *Journal of the Early Republic* 18 (Spring 1998): 1–46. In a pathbreaking essay, Onuf argues that, from the Declaration of Independence to the end of his life, Jefferson viewed slaves as a distinct nation within the American nation who, because of race, could never join that nation. In Jefferson's view, a state of war, or at least incipient war, existed between these two nations that only slavery (or colonization) could keep in check.

5:123   Travers, Len. *Celebrating the Fourth: Independence Day and the Rites of Nationalism in the Early Republic.* Amherst: University of Massachusetts Press, 1997. One of a spate of books on nationalism and festive culture in the early national period, Travers's study focuses on Fourth of July celebrations in Boston, Charleston, and Philadelphia. Such celebrations, and the political competition that surrounded them, acted to validate and maintain nationalism. Bibliography.

5:124   Waldstreicher, David. *In the Midst of Perpetual Fetes: The Making of American Nationalism, 1776–1820.* Chapel Hill: University of North Carolina Press for the Omohundro Institute of Early American History and Culture, 1997. The most theoretically sophisticated of the recent works on festive culture and nationalism, this work shows how nationalistic celebrations fueled both consensus and conflict and stresses the role of print media. A key period for Waldstreicher, as for Simon P. Newman and Len Travers (5:121; 5:123), is the 1790s, and a key subject is the French revolution and the official and unofficial American response to it.

THE PROCESS OF DIPLOMACY

5:125   Davis, Robert R., Jr. "Diplomatic Plumage: American Court Dress in the Early National Period." *American Quarterly* 20 (Summer 1968): 164–79. Davis surveys the dilemma that American diplomats faced regarding the wearing of court attire in foreign countries.

5:126   _____. "Republican Simplicity: The Diplomatic Costume Question, 1789–1867." *Civil War History* 15 (March 1969): 19–29. This article traces the evolution of formal dress for American diplomats from 1789 to 1867. After an initial period of generally conforming to European practices, a movement toward simple, "democratic" dress began under President Jackson.

5:127   Ilchman, Warren Frederick. *Professional Diplomacy in the United States, 1779–1939: A Study in Administrative History.* Chicago: University of Chicago Press, 1961. This study of the administrative history of the American diplomatic corps focuses on the development of professionalism in the foreign service. The period from 1779 to 1888 is covered in just one chapter, however. Bibliography.

5:128   Kennedy, Charles Stuart. *The American Consul: A History of the United States Consular Service, 1776–1914.* Kennedy provides a helpful account of the birth and early use of the consular service. Of particular value for the early national period are his discussions of the reliance on consuls in the Barbary states and consuls' efforts in Europe and the Caribbean to protect American seamen and commercial access during Europe's wars. Bibliography (2:193).

5:129   Knott, Stephen F. *Secret and Sanctioned: Covert Operations and the American Presidency.* With one eye clearly fixed on the controversial status of the CIA and post–World War II covert operations, Knott examines the presidential use of secret agents over roughly the first century of American independence. In his effort to root recent and contemporary activities in the founding, however, he frequently misunderstands or misrepresents late-eighteenth- and early-nineteenth-century practices. Bibliography (2:203).

5:130   Long, David F. *Gold Braid and Foreign Relations: Diplomatic Activities of U.S. Naval Officers, 1798–1883.* Annapolis: Naval Institute Press, 1988. Though the practice of using naval officers for diplomatic negotiations became more common in the mid-nineteenth century, Long includes valuable chapters on such activity in the Quasi-War, the Barbary wars, and the Spanish-American revolutions. This work essentially supplants Charles O. Paullin, *Diplomatic Negotiations of American Naval Officers, 1778–1883* (Baltimore: Johns Hopkins Press, 1912).

5:131   Wriston, Henry M. *Executive Agents in American Foreign Relations.* This massive volume surveys the American practice and logic of using executive agents for various purposes. The book includes chapters on the use of executive agents to open diplomatic relations, to negotiate with unrecognized governments, to communicate with colonial states, and to deal with governments which had terminated formal diplomatic relations (2:181).

Biographical Studies

COLLECTIVE

5:132   Cappon, Lester J., ed. *The Adams-Jefferson Letters: The Complete Correspondence between Thomas Jefferson and Abigail and John Adams.* Late in their lives, Adams and Jefferson resumed their past correspondence on both current and historical events (4:127).

5:133   Kennedy, Roger G. *Burr, Hamilton, and Jefferson: A Study in Character.* New York: Oxford University Press, 2000. Burr is clearly the central figure, and the Burr Conspiracy is one of the central events, in this idiosyncratic study of three of the most intriguing men of the early republic. Relying on questionable assumptions and frequently mishandled evidence, Kennedy defends Burr and damns Hamilton and, especially, Jefferson. Bibliography.

5:134   Smith, James Morton, ed. *The Republic of Letters: The Correspondence between Thomas Jefferson and James Madison, 1776–1826.* 3 vols. New York: Norton, 1995. With both Jefferson and Madison the subject of comprehensive papers projects, the value of this book is somewhat limited for scholars. Already, the letters from more than half of the period that it covers (through mid-May 1803 and from March 1809 to July 1812) are easily available elsewhere. For the time being, however, it remains the best-edited, most accessible source for letters and other documents exchanged between these two prominent figures during the remainder of this period.

AMERICAN

John Adams

5:135 Adams, Charles Francis, ed. *The Works of John Adams, Second President of the United States: With a Life of Author, Notes and Illustrations.* 10 vols. Boston: Little, Brown and Company, 1850–1856. Long a standard reference for Adams materials (1735–1826), the usefulness of this set has been diminished by publication of Butterfield, *The Adams Papers. Ser. 2: Adams Family Correspondence* (1963–) (4:125), and by the microfilming of the Adams Papers at the Massachusetts Historical Society, now available on 608 reels.

5:136 Butterfield, Lyman H., ed., with Leonard C. Faber and Wendell D. Garrett, assistant eds. *The Adams Papers. Ser. 1, Diaries: Diary and Autobiography of John Adams.* John Adams's diary (1755–1804) is very thin after 1790 or so. The editing is beyond reproach, and, in addition to biographical information, the notes offer commentary on scholars' interpretations (4:124).

5:137 Butterfield, Lyman H., Marc Friedlaender, and Richard Alan Ryerson, eds., with Wendell D. Garrett, associate ed., and Marjorie E. Sprague, assistant ed. *The Adams Papers. Ser. 2: Adams Family Correspondence.* The letters among the members of the Adams family are of great value, though all of the Adamses wrote so frequently to people outside the family that the use of the Massachusetts Historical Society's microfilm collection of Adams Papers is essential. At present, this collection extends only through 1785, with volumes 5 and 6 covering the period after the revolution (4:125).

5:138 Clarfield, Gerard H. "John Adams: The Marketplace and American Foreign Policy." *New England Quarterly* 52 (September 1979): 345–57. In this brief and broad survey of Adams's presidential foreign policies, Clarfield argues that they were driven by economic concerns, especially foreign trade.

5:139 Ferling, John E. *John Adams: A Life.* Knoxville: University of Tennessee Press, 1992. Ferling's biography covers both the public and private side of Adams's life. Ferling finds Adams more successful as both diplomat and president than have contemporaries and other historians.

5:140 Smith, Page. *John Adams.* Adams's career as peace commissioner to negotiate an end to the revolutionary war, as minister to England during the Confederation, and as vice-president and president are recounted in volume 2. Smith treats Adams's presidential term sympathetically, including his negotiating strategy with France, but almost no foreign research materials are used. Bibliography (4:131).

John Quincy Adams

5:141 Adams, Charles Francis, ed. "A Collection of Unpublished Letters from John Quincy Adams to Thomas Boylston Adams." *Proceedings of the Massachusetts Historical Society* 2d ser. 10 (December 1895): 374–92. All of the letters in this collection were written while John Quincy Adams was serving as minister to Russia. Adams's concerns about deteriorating relations with Great Britain and dismay at the course of the War of 1812, more than his Russian diplomacy, fill this correspondence. For another collection of Adams letters from the same period, see Charles Francis Adams, ed., "Correspondence of John Quincy Adams, 1811–1814," *Proceedings of the American Antiquarian Society* new ser. 23 (April 1913): 110–69.

5:142 Adams, Charles Francis, ed. *Memoirs of John Quincy Adams, Comprising Portions of His Diary from 1795 to 1848.* 12 vols. Philadelphia: J. B. Lippincott & Co., 1874–1877. The first three volumes of this collection cover Adams's activities during the Federalist era, when he served as minister to the Netherlands and Prussia; his role during the Jefferson and Madison administrations (as senator from Massachusetts repudiated by his constituency because he refused to follow the Federalist line); as envoy to Russia; and as peace commissioner to Ghent. Passages describing the Ghent negotiations are particularly important, but Adams's nature (and his politics) frequently colored his understanding of the behavior of others.

5:143   Allen, David Grayson, et al., eds. *Diary of John Quincy Adams.* 2 vols. to date. Cambridge, MA: Belknap Press of Harvard University Press, 1981–. The new edition of Adams's diary is well edited and includes much material missing from the version edited by his grandson over a century ago. Unfortunately, the project thus far extends only to 1788 and has moved at an incredibly slow pace.

5:144   Ford, Worthington C., ed. *Writings of John Quincy Adams.* 7 vols. New York: Macmillan Company, 1913–1917. Ford was selective rather than comprehensive, but the editing is sensible. This incomplete edition stops at 1823. Both official and private correspondence are included; among the latter are a series of marvelous letters to Adams's parents. The first two volumes cover the period through the end of the Federalist era; volume 5 contains nearly 250 pages on the negotiations that brought the War of 1812 to a close.

5:145   Bemis, Samuel Flagg. *John Quincy Adams and the Foundations of American Foreign Policy.* New York: Alfred A. Knopf, 1949. Reprint 1973 (Norton). This sturdy volume is particularly important because of Bemis's use of the previously closed Adams manuscripts. The views are somewhat nationalistic, and John Quincy Adams (here covered from 1767 to 1829) is pictured as a heroic figure. But Bemis is far too good a scholar to toy with the evidence or to conceal his own preconceptions.

5:146   Parsons, Lynn Hudson. *John Quincy Adams.* Madison: Madison House, 1998. The best of the recent, one-volume biographies of Adams, Parson's work includes some discussion of his diplomatic service in the Netherlands and Prussia during the Washington and Adams administrations and a thorough treatment of his transformation from a Federalist to a Republican while serving in the Senate under Jefferson and during his mission to Russia for Madison.

5:147   Russell, Greg. *John Quincy Adams and the Public Virtues of Diplomacy.* Columbia: University

of Missouri Press, 1995. Russell examines the role of ethics and ideals in Adams's statecraft throughout his career. Because this book is organized thematically rather than chronologically, it requires some effort to assemble Adams's thinking on any one event, though there is a solid chapter on Adams's upbringing and training as a statesmen. The basic argument previously appeared in Daniel G. Lang and Greg Russell, "The Ethics of Power in American Diplomacy: The Statecraft of John Quincy Adams," *Review of Politics* 52 (Winter 1990): 3–31. Bibliography.

5:148   Thompson, Robert R. "John Quincy Adams, Apostate: From 'Outrageous Federalist' to 'Republican Exile,' 1801–1809." *Journal of the Early Republic* 11 (Summer 1991): 161–83. Thompson places Adams's shift from Federalist to Republican in the context of American foreign policy, particularly the struggle with Great Britain over neutral rights and impressment. It was in response to the *Chesapeake* Affair and the Embargo that Adams completed the break with the party of his youth.

James A. Bayard

5:149   Donnan, Elizabeth, ed. *Papers of James A. Bayard, 1796–1815.* The Annual Report of the American Historical Association for the Year 1913. Vol. 2. Washington, DC: Government Printing Office, 1915. Reprint 1971 (Da Capo Press). The main interest in Bayard's correspondence derives from his leadership of moderate southern Federalists and participation in the Ghent negotiations.

5:150   Borden, Morton. *The Federalism of James A. Bayard.* New York: Columbia University Press, 1955. Borden's biography provides a useful, cool analysis of the behavior and attitudes of the Federalist congressman and senator from Delaware. Perhaps even more than Rufus King, Bayard may have represented moderate opinion within the party. Borden provides no discussion of his small role as commissioner at Ghent. Extensive bibliography.

William Blount

5:151   Masterson, William H. *William Blount.* Baton Rouge: Louisiana State University Press, 1954.

Despite its limitations, this work is the only full-length biography of Blount, a key figure in the early west. Masterson portrays Blount as a businessman in all of his activities, including his conspiracy. Bibliographic essay.

5:152 Melton, Buckner F., Jr. *The First Impeachment: The Constitution's Framers and the Case of Senator William Blount.* Macon, GA: Mercer University Press, 1998. Melton's emphasis, to a much greater degree than in Masterson, *William Blount* (1954) (5:151), is on Congress's handling of Blount and the constitutional basis of impeachment, though he provides a useful account of the Blount Conspiracy. Extensive bibliography.

Aaron Burr

5:153 Kline, Mary-Jo, with Joanne Wood Ryan et al., eds. *Political Correspondence and Public Papers of Aaron Burr.* 2 vols. Princeton: Princeton University Press, 1983. Though not a complete collection of Burr's papers (which are available in a microfilm edition compiled by the same editors), these volumes provide most of Burr's surviving incoming and outgoing correspondence on political matters. The editorial notes are extremely valuable for clarifying some of the confusion surrounding the Burr Conspiracy.

5:154 Lomask, Milton. *Aaron Burr.* 2 vols. New York: Farrar, Straus and Giroux, 1979–1982. These two volumes, which divide with the end of Burr's term as vice-president in March 1805, form the most recent, complete biography of the controversial figure. Volume 2 includes most of the material of interest to diplomatic historians, including the Burr Conspiracy and Burr's subsequent activities in Great Britain and France aimed at revolutionizing the Spanish colonies. Bibliography.

5:155 Schachner, Nathan. *Aaron Burr, A Biography.* New York: Frederick A. Stokes Company, 1937. Though old, this biography remains one of the most interesting and most useful studies of Burr. Schachner conceals few of Burr's many faults, but his interpretation tends to be favorable—and, therefore, provocative. Extensive bibliography.

William C. C. Claiborne

5:156 Rowland, Dunbar, ed. *Official Letter Books of W. C. C. Claiborne, 1801–1816.* Vol. 6. Jackson, MS: State Department of Archives and History, 1917. Reprint 1972 (AMS Press). The governor of Mississippi and Orleans Territory and, later, the state of Louisiana, Claiborne, despite his often questioned abilities, was one of Jefferson and Madison's top men on the southern frontier for fifteen years. This collection of documents, though lacking the hallmarks of modern editorial methods, is an invaluable resource for the Burr Conspiracy, Indian affairs, border tensions with Spain over Florida and Texas, and the War of 1812.

5:157 Bradley, Jared W. "W. C. C. Claiborne and Spain: Foreign Affairs under Jefferson and Madison, 1801–1811." *Louisiana History* 12 (Fall 1971): 287–314; 13 (Winter 1972): 5–26. Bradley's two-part article deals with the unremitting efforts of Claiborne, governor of two American territories contiguous to the Spanish empire, to shape a more forceful policy.

5:158 Hatfield, Joseph T. *William Claiborne: Jeffersonian Centurion in the American Southwest.* Lafayette: University of Southwestern Louisiana Press, 1976. Claiborne was an important lieutenant of Jefferson and an unvarying expansionist. This biography contributes to an understanding of the acquisition of Louisiana and West Florida, the Burr Conspiracy, and the coming of the War of 1812.

Henry Clay

5:159 Hopkins, James F., with Mary W. M. Hargreaves, eds. *The Papers of Henry Clay.* 10 vols. and Supplement. Lexington: University Press of Kentucky, 1959–1992. The definitive edition of Clay's papers, these volumes include material from numerous repositories and full editorial notes. Of particular interest is volume 1, which covers Clay's role in the Burr Conspiracy, actions in Congress on the eve of and during the War of 1812, and participation in the Ghent negotiations.

5:160 Mayo, Bernard. *Henry Clay: Spokesman of the New West.* Boston: Houghton Mifflin Company,

1937. This extremely lively, readable study stresses Clay's importance and especially highlights the dramatics of the war session. Despite impressive research, Mayo does not appear to have been able to question traditional interpretations of the coming of war in 1812. Extensive bibliography.

5:161   Remini, Robert V. *Henry Clay: Statesman for the Union.* New York: W. W. Norton, 1991. The work of a long-time Jackson biographer, this most recent biography of Clay as frequently presents the interpretations of Clay's critics and opponents as of Clay himself. It deals with the period through the Ghent negotiations fairly quickly. Bibliographic essay.

Benjamin Franklin

5:162   Hawke, David Freeman. *Franklin.* This is a good modern political biography of Franklin, whose most significant activities following the Treaty of Paris included his participation in the Constitutional Convention (4:140).

5:163   Stourzh, Gerald. *Benjamin Franklin and American Foreign Policy.* See chapter 3 of this Guide (3:100).

Albert Gallatin

5:164   Adams, Henry, ed. *The Writings of Albert Gallatin.* 3 vols. Philadelphia: J. B. Lippincott & Co., 1879. This work offers the most complete printed collection of Gallatin's incoming and outgoing correspondence, though it lacks modern editorial apparatus. But it should be used in conjunction with Barbara B. Oberg, ed., *The Papers of Albert Gallatin: A Microfilm Supplement* (Wilmington, DE: Scholarly Resources, 1985).

5:165   Walters, Ray. *Albert Gallatin: Jeffersonian Financier and Diplomat.* New York: Macmillan, 1957. This biography is very favorable to its subject, whose papers the author was the first to use since Henry Adams's *The Writings of Albert Gallatin* (Philadelphia: Lippincott, 1879) (5:164). The work is particularly useful for the treatment of Republican styles of government, the problems posed by the Embargo, and the enervating effect of factionalism. The account of the Ghent negotiations is less satisfactory. Extensive bibliography.

Elbridge Gerry

5:166   Gerry, Elbridge. *Letterbook, Paris, 1797–1798.* Salem, MA: Essex Institute Press, 1966. Gerry's letters, mostly to his wife, during his mission to France are reprinted. Edited by Russell W. Knight.

5:167   Billias, George A. *Elbridge Gerry, Founding Father and Republican Statesman.* New York: McGraw-Hill, 1976. Gerry, one of the XYZ diplomats, has received harsh treatment from historians. Rather than viewing him as a political chameleon, Billias sees him as a man constantly guided by principle. This study focuses on Gerry in the American revolution, at the federal Constitutional Convention, and in the administrations of Washington and Adams. Based on widely scattered materials, this volume is now the standard account of Gerry's life. Bibliography.

Alexander Hamilton

5:168   Syrett, Harold C., with Jacob Ernest Cooke, eds. *The Papers of Alexander Hamilton.* 27 vols. New York: Columbia University Press, 1961–1987. This definitive edition of Hamilton's papers (1768–1804) supersedes John C. Hamilton, ed., *The Works of Alexander Hamilton: Comprising his Correspondence, and His Political and Official Writings, Exclusive of the Federalist, Civil and Military,* 7 vols. (New York: C. S. Francis & Company, 1851), and Henry Cabot Lodge, ed., *The Works of Alexander Hamilton,* 12 vols. (New York: G. P. Putnam's Sons, 1904). Notes are generally economical, revealing editorial balance and great erudition.

5:169   Hendrickson, Robert. *Hamilton.* 2 vols. New York: Mason/Charter, 1976. This detailed biography is highly favorable to Hamilton, but John C. Miller's older *Alexander Hamilton: Portrait in Paradox* (New York: Harper, 1959) is briefer and better balanced. Forrest McDonald's *Alexander Hamilton: A Biography* (New York: Norton, 1979) is frankly partisan, but is especially good on the background of Hamilton's financial policies.

5:170   Kaplan, Lawrence S. *Alexander Hamilton: Ambivalent Anglophile.* Wilmington, DE: Scholarly Resources, 2002. This brief biography by the doyen of the Hamiltonian-Jeffersonian era measures the effects on the foreign policy of the Washington and Adams administrations of this aristocratic anglophile. While the analysis of Hamilton's foreign policy views and maneuvers reveals nothing unexpected, Kaplan makes the interesting point that the unpopularity of his pro-British attitudes obscured the credit he should have received for his opposition to slavery.

5:171   Lycan, Gilbert L. *Alexander Hamilton & American Foreign Policy: A Design for Greatness.* Norman: University of Oklahoma Press, 1970. This volume lauds Hamilton's excursions into foreign policy and denounces his critics. The tone is adulatory, but not entirely uncritical. Bibliography.

5:172   Mitchell, Broadus. *Alexander Hamilton.* 2 vols. New York: Macmillan, 1957–1962. Mitchell's masterly biography covers Hamilton's involvement in the movement for a new constitution, in volume 1, and his activities as Washington's secretary of the treasury and leader of the Federalist Party, in volume 2.

5:173   Rosen, Stephen Peter. "Alexander Hamilton and the Domestic Uses of International Law." *Diplomatic History* 5 (Summer 1981): 183–202. According to Rosen, Hamilton hoped to use the law of nations to extend federal, especially executive, power over the people on international issues as a means of promoting realism in the policymaking of the new nation.

5:174   Stourzh, Gerald. *Alexander Hamilton and the Idea of Republican Government.* Stanford, CA: Stanford University Press, 1970. The author concludes that Hamilton considered himself the founder of an empire. He differed from his American contemporaries in rejecting the philosophy of Locke in favor of Hume and Hobbes and the political economy of Adam Smith. His foreign policy was directed toward the power and the glory of the state, based on an aristocratic society and a partnership with Britain.

5:175   Walling, Karl-Friedrich. *Republican Empire: Alexander Hamilton on War and Free Government.* Lawrence: University Press of Kansas, 1999. Walling attempts to rebut the frequent portrayal of Hamilton as a militarist, arguing instead that he sought to integrate military power with self-government, personal liberty, and restraint.

Benjamin Hawkins

5:176   Grant, C. L., ed. *Letters, Journals, and Writings of Benjamin Hawkins.* 2 vols. Savannah, GA: Beehive Press, 1980. The various papers of Hawkins, the federal agent with the Creeks from the mid-1790s through the War of 1812, are an essential source for understanding the interactions among British, Spanish, Indians, and Americans on the southern frontier over a period of nearly two decades.

5:177   Henri, Florette. *The Southern Indians and Benjamin Hawkins, 1796–1816.* Norman: University of Oklahoma Press, 1986. This book offers a fairly comprehensive account of Hawkins's activities as federal Indian agent with the Creeks, emphasizing his efforts on behalf of the government's "civilization program." It includes useful discussions of the Blount Conspiracy, the Creek War, and the War of 1812.

5:178   Pound, Merritt B. *Benjamin Hawkins: Indian Agent.* Athens, GA: University of Georgia Press, 1951. Older but in some ways more scholarly than Henri, *The Southern Indians and Benjamin Hawkins, 1796–1816* (1986) (5:177), this work focuses on Hawkins's activities in the Creek agency, which Pound generally considers laudable. Bibliography.

Andrew Jackson

5:179   Bassett, John Spencer, ed. *Correspondence of Andrew Jackson.* 7 vols. Washington, DC: Carnegie Institution of Washington, 1926–1935. This edition provides a useful collection of Jackson's personal correspondence. While it is far from complete, it has not been entirely superseded by the University of Tennessee Press edition (*The Papers of Andrew Jackson,* 1980–) (5:181) and includes letters omitted from the more recent version. Volume 7 is an extensive index.

5:180   Moser, Harold D., et al. *The Papers of Andrew Jackson, 1770–1845: A Microfilm Supplement.* 39 rolls. Microfilm. Wilmington, DE: Scholarly Resources, 1987. This microfilm publication provides documents from repositories and private holdings throughout the world, with the exception of those at the Library of Congress. The accompanying guide and index makes it easy to work with this collection.

5:181   Smith, Sam B., et al., eds. *The Papers of Andrew Jackson.* 5 vols. to date. Knoxville: University of Tennessee Press, 1980–. This modern edition of Jackson's incoming and outgoing correspondence is not comprehensive; in fact, it excludes some letters and other documents that are published in Bassett, *Correspondence of Andrew Jackson* (1926–1935) (5:179). Each volume, however, includes an extremely helpful calendar of Jackson's correspondence.

5:182   James, Marquis. *Andrew Jackson, the Border Captain.* Indianapolis: Bobbs-Merrill Company, 1933. James has written a powerful historical narrative with rich detail on Jackson's early years.

5:183   Remini, Robert V. *Andrew Jackson and the Course of American Empire, 1767–1821.* 3 vols. New York: Harper and Row, 1977. This is the first volume of a three-volume biography. One of its major themes is that Jackson's view of, and role in, American expansion virtually determined the course of American empire. Extensive bibliography.

5:184   Rogin, Michael Paul. *Fathers and Children: Andrew Jackson and the Subjugation of the American Indian.* New York: Alfred A. Knopf, 1975. Rogin combines a Marxian analysis with Freudian psychology to argue that Jackson persecuted the Indians (1813–1837) to prove his manliness and to provide new cotton lands for agrarian capitalists.

John Jay

5:185   Johnston, Henry P., ed. *The Correspondence and Public Papers of John Jay.* A leading Federalist, collaborator on the Federalist Papers with Hamilton and Madison, chief justice of the United States, and governor of New York, Jay is mainly important during the Federalist era for Jay's Treaty. A

new edition of Jay's writings, edited by Richard B. Morris, has reached only the early 1780s (4:150).

5:186   Monaghan, Frank. *John Jay, Defender of Liberty against Kings & Peoples, Author of the Constitution & Governor of New York, President of the Continental Congress, Co-author of the Federalist, Negotiator of the Peace of 1783 & the Jay Treaty of 1794, First Chief Justice of the United States.* In the only, modern full-length biography of Jay (1745–1829), Monaghan favorably views Jay's diplomacy (1780s–1790s) as secretary of foreign affairs and minister to England (4:152). Monaghan used Jay papers not included in Johnston, *The Correspondence and Public Papers of John Jay* (1890–1893) (4:150). Bibliography.

5:187   Morris, Richard B. *John Jay: The Nation, and the Court.* Boston: Boston University Press, 1967. This brief work, composed of essays originally delivered as a series of lectures, highlights Jay's term as chief justice of the Supreme Court, particularly his decisions that touched on sovereignty issues.

Thomas Jefferson

5:188   Boyd, Julian P., Lyman H. Butterfield, Charles T. Cullen, and John Catanzariti, eds. *The Papers of Thomas Jefferson.* Only twenty-seven volumes of the definitive edition of Jefferson's papers have thus far appeared, taking the story to the end of his term in the State Department. Scholars who rely on printed materials must continue to use older editions of his writings, such as Lipscomb and Bergh, *The Writings of Thomas Jefferson* (1903–1904) (5:190), and Ford, *The Writings of Thomas Jefferson* (1892–1899) (5:189). This edition is superbly edited (4:153).

5:189   Ford, Paul Leicester, ed. *The Writings of Thomas Jefferson.* 10 vols. New York: G. P. Putnam's Sons, 1892–1899. Ford uses very little modern editorial apparatus, making understanding sometimes difficult. In addition, he chose to omit an even higher proportion of Jefferson's writings while president than he did for earlier periods (volumes 9 to 11 contain material on 1801 to 1815). This and all other editions of Jefferson's writings will eventually be rendered totally obsolete by Julian P. Boyd's edition. At present, however, it remains the only published source for some of Jefferson's letters from the late 1790s.

5:190   Lipscomb, Andrew A., and Albert E. Bergh, eds. *The Writings of Thomas Jefferson.* 20 vols. Washington, DC: Thomas Jefferson Memorial Association, 1903–1904. Volumes 10 to 14 reproduce Jefferson's letters from the years 1801 to 1815, although later volumes include additional letters and some retrospective observations on that period. It is more complete but less accurate than Ford, *The Writings of Thomas Jefferson* (1892–1899) (5:189), though each includes some letters missing in the other.

5:191   Adams, William Howard. *The Paris Years of Thomas Jefferson.* New Haven: Yale University Press, 1997. While not especially scholarly, this lavishly illustrated book does include one chapter on Jefferson's French diplomacy and another on his initial reactions to and involvement in the French revolution. Bibliography. Also interesting is George Green Shackelford, *Thomas Jefferson's Travels in Europe, 1784–1789* (Baltimore: Johns Hopkins University Press, 1995).

5:192   Ben-Atar, Doron S. *The Origins of Jeffersonian Commercial Policy and Diplomacy.* New York: St. Martin's Press, 1993. Ben-Atar examines Jefferson's views and policies regarding foreign commerce, economic coercion, and international relations from the imperial crisis with Great Britain in the 1770s through his presidency. By placing Jefferson's thought in the context of republicanism, he attempts to get beyond the realism versus idealism debate.

5:193   Jackson, Donald. *Thomas Jefferson & the Stony Mountains: Exploring the West from Monticello.* Urbana: University of Illinois Press, 1981. Jackson assigns Jefferson a key role in westward expansion in the early national period, which derived from his early interest in the west and support for scientific exploration. Bibliography.

5:194   Johnstone, Robert M., Jr. *Jefferson and the Presidency: Leadership in the Young Republic.* Ithaca: Cornell University Press, 1978. This examination of Jefferson's leadership, employing approaches adapted from political science, concludes that he was an effective leader, in large part through his astute use of informal modes of influence. (The sole cited exception is the Embargo.) The author's grasp of diplomacy is limited, and the research base is too insubstantial to give confidence to all his findings, although many of them are shared by other scholars.

5:195   Kaplan, Lawrence S. *Jefferson and France: An Essay on Politics and Political Ideas.* Jefferson is presented as an ardent nationalist, yet a Francophile who wanted strong national connections with France and on occasion took questionable steps to ensure the bond. The work is well argued and based on primary sources, but at variance with recent Jefferson biographies. Bibliography (4:154).

5:196   _____. *Thomas Jefferson: Westward the Course of Empire.* Wilmington, DE: SR Books, 1999. In this brief survey, Kaplan assembles and expands upon a lifetime of work on Jeffersonian and early national foreign policy. His general account of Jefferson's ideas about and role in foreign policy includes chapters on his Paris mission, term as secretary of state, and presidency. Bibliographic essay.

5:197   LaFeber, Walter. "Jefferson and an American Foreign Policy." In *Jeffersonian Legacies,* ed. Peter S. Onuf, 370–91. Charlottesville: University Press of Virginia, 1993. LaFeber depicts Jeffersonian foreign policy as committed to agrarian expansion as a means of preserving republicanism. One result, traceable to the Louisiana Purchase in particular, was the expansion of federal and, especially, presidential power.

5:198   Malone, Dumas. *Jefferson and His Time.* 6 vols. Boston: Little, Brown, 1948–1981. The second volume of this magisterial biography covers Jefferson's years in Paris and term as secretary of state. The third details Jefferson's actions during the years of Federalist ascendancy and describes the election of 1800. The fourth and fifth cover the two terms of Jefferson's presidency, but, except for material on the Louisiana Purchase, the former has relatively little on diplomacy; volume 5, in contrast, includes the effort to acquire Florida, the Burr Conspiracy, the deepening conflict with Britain, and the Embargo. Malone's treatment is at once respectful and critical, yet not free from bias either, and at various points vulnerable to contradiction or dispute. Extensive bibliography.

5:199   O'Brien, Conor Cruise. *The Long Affair: Thomas Jefferson and the French Revolution, 1785–1800.* Chicago: University of Chicago Press, 1996. O'Brien offers a scathing indictment of Jefferson, the historians who have written about him, and his place in modern memory. O'Brien argues that Jefferson's hostility to the slave revolt in Haiti finally cooled his excessive ardor for the revolution in France.

5:200   Onuf, Peter S. *Jefferson's Empire: The Language of American Nationhood.* Charlottesville: University Press of Virginia, 2000. With the addition of a new introduction and epilogue, Onuf repackages five essays (two previously unpublished in English) into a fascinating and provocative meditation on Jefferson's understanding of nation, empire, union, and race. Equally provocative is Onuf and Leonard J. Sadosky, *Jeffersonian America* (Malden, MA: Blackwell Publishers, 2002).

5:201   Peterson, Merrill D. *The Jefferson Image in the American Mind.* New York: Oxford University Press, 1960. This masterful work evaluates American views of Jefferson, from 1826 to 1956, tracing the ups and downs of his reputation among scholars and others. There is sufficient reference to Jefferson's diplomacy to make the volume a useful introduction. Extensive bibliography.

5:202   _____. "Thomas Jefferson and Commercial Policy, 1783–1793." *William and Mary Quarterly* 3d ser. 22 (October 1965): 584–610. Jefferson's attempts in the 1780s to weaken links with Great Britain, chiefly through encouragement of trade with France, were unsuccessful. French commercial nationalism, Hamilton's orientation of American trade policy toward England, and Genet's mission combined to wreck Jefferson's commercial plan.

5:203   _____. *Thomas Jefferson and the New Nation: A Biography.* New York: Oxford University Press, 1970. By far the best one-volume biography of the third president, Peterson's work is insightful, well written, and comprehensive, interweaving treatments of Jefferson's thought and actions. The judgments are on the whole favorable to Jefferson,

although Peterson is quite critical of some policies and often incorporates, while refuting, negative assessments. Essentially, this is a work of high-quality synthesis based on a nearly exhaustive reading of earlier scholarly work, although at various points primary research strengthens the study and fills in gaps.

5:204   Risjord, Norman K. *Thomas Jefferson.* Madison: Madison House, 1994. Another entry in the apparently endless stream of Jefferson studies, Risjord's work at least has the benefit of his solid grounding in the domestic and foreign policies of the early republic. This brief sketch focuses on Jefferson's evolving political and economic thought.

5:205   Ronda, James P., ed. *Thomas Jefferson and the Changing West: From Conquest to Conservation.* Albuquerque: University of New Mexico Press, 1997. This wide-ranging collection of essays provides a valuable addition, and at times counterpoint, to Jackson, *Thomas Jefferson & the Stony Mountains: Exploring the West from Monticello* (1981) (5:193). Of particular interest are Anthony F. C. Wallace, "'The Obtaining Lands': Thomas Jefferson and the Native Americans" (25–41), and Peter S. Onuf, "Thomas Jefferson, Missouri, and the 'Empire for Liberty'" (111–53).

5:206   Sofka, James R. "The Jeffersonian Idea of National Security: Commerce, the Atlantic Balance of Power, and the Barbary War, 1786–1805." *Diplomatic History* 21 (Fall 1997): 519–44. With a commitment to foreign commerce, in various forms, as a central national interest, Jefferson, Sofka argues, acted as a realist, setting policies that would have been familiar to Europe's great powers. While the Barbary wars offer the prime example in support of this argument, Sofka sees evidence of the same commitment in Jefferson's policies toward Europe in the 1790s.

5:207   Stuart, Reginald C. *The Half-Way Pacifist: Thomas Jefferson's View of War.* Toronto: University of Toronto Press, 1978. This short, trenchant discussion of Jefferson's attitude toward war concludes that he was no pacifist and instead saw war as a legitimate instrument of policy. It criticizes him for failing to understand political and military realities that developed during his lifetime.

5:208 Tucker, Robert W., and David C. Hendrickson. *Empire of Liberty: The Statecraft of Thomas Jefferson.* New York: Oxford University Press, 1990. The entirety of Jefferson's career in foreign policy is addressed in this frequently critical account. Generally inspired by Henry Adams's interpretations, the authors argue that Jefferson often blundered into his successes, abandoned his ideals, and adopted measures that violated his principles. A present-mindedness and an insistence on viewing Jefferson through the lens of realism-idealism weaken the argument. Bibliography.

Rufus King

5:209 King, Charles R., ed. *The Life and Correspondence of Rufus King: Comprising His Letters, Private and Official, His Public Documents, and His Speeches.* 6 vols. New York: G. P. Putnam's Sons, 1894–1900. A close friend and confidant of Alexander Hamilton, King was sent as minister to Great Britain in 1796 and was so effective that Jefferson retained him at that post after 1801. His quoted correspondence (1755–1827), far more useful than the connecting narrative, provides essential information on Anglo-American relations, as well as on the thinking of Federalist leaders.

5:210 Ernst, Robert. *Rufus King, American Federalist.* Chapel Hill: University of North Carolina Press for the Institute of Early American History and Culture, 1968. This detailed narrative is particularly important for its treatment of King's mission to London, which included the first few years of the Jefferson administration. However, there is also helpful information on national and especially Federalist politics thereafter.

Robert R. Livingston

5:211 Parsons, Edward Alexander, ed. "The Letters of Robert R. Livingston: The Diplomatic Story of the Louisiana Purchase." *Proceedings of the American Antiquarian Society* new ser. 52 (October 1942): 363–407. This useful collection is made up primarily of excerpts of letters exchanged between Livingston, in Paris, and Rufus King, in London, during the period of the Louisiana Purchase.

5:212 Dangerfield, George. *Chancellor Robert R. Livingston of New York, 1746–1813.* As Jefferson's minister to France, Livingston would help to negotiate the Louisiana Purchase. Extensive bibliographical notes (4:177).

James Madison

5:213 Brugger, Robert J., et al., eds. *The Papers of James Madison: Secretary of State Series.* 5 vols. to date. Charlottesville: University Press of Virginia, 1986–. Once completed, this well-edited, comprehensive collection of Madison's incoming and outgoing correspondence will replace all earlier editions of his writings. At present, however, it extends only through October 1803. Still, it includes crucial material on Barbary affairs, the Haitian revolution, and Louisiana.

5:214 Hunt, Gaillard, ed. *The Writings of James Madison, Comprising His Public Papers and His Private Correspondence, Including Numerous Letters and Documents Now for the First Time Printed.* 9 vols. New York: G. P. Putnam's Sons, 1900–1910. Until the completion of the two series of the University Press of Virginia's edition covering these years, Hunt's edition remains useful. Still, it has important drawbacks: fewer than four volumes (6–9) cover the period from 1801 to 1815, and much important material is omitted. There is no editorial apparatus to clarify the context in which Madison's letters are written.

5:215 Hutchinson, William T., William M. E. Rachal, and Robert Allen Rutland, eds. *The Papers of James Madison: Congressional Series.* Madison's papers offer the finest record of a politically active congressman and key figure in the formation of the Republican Party. The series is excessively annotated, sometimes losing Madison but illuminating many obscure incidents and figures (4:159).

5:216 Rives, William C., and Philip R. Fendall, eds. *Letters and Other Writings of James Madison, Fourth President of the United States.* 4 vols. Philadelphia: J. B. Lippincott & Co., 1865. In time, these old volumes will be completely superseded by the modern edition of Madison's writings. Now, however, they need to be used in conjunction with

Hunt, *The Writings of James Madison, Comprising His Public Papers and His Private Correspondence, Including Numerous Letters and Documents Now for the First Time Printed* (1900–1910) (5:214) and the microfilm series from the Library of Congress. Rives and Fendall are particularly strong on the period of Madison's retirement.

5:217 Rutland, Robert Allen, et al., eds. *The Papers of James Madison: Presidential Series.* 4 vols. to date. Charlottesville: University Press of Virginia, 1984–. Once complete, this comprehensive, effectively edited collection of Madison's incoming and outgoing correspondence will supersede all earlier versions. At present, however, it extends only to early July 1812.

5:218 Brant, Irving. *James Madison.* 6 vols. Indianapolis: Bobbs-Merrill, 1941–1961. In this six-volume biography, written almost entirely from original sources, the author attempts with considerable success to revise the traditional perception of Madison as a pale reflection of Jefferson. Of particular interest here are the second, third, and fourth volumes: *James Madison: The Nationalist, 1780–1787, James Madison: Father of the Constitution, 1787–1800,* and *James Madison: Secretary of State, 1800–1809.* The final two volumes treat his years as president (1809–1817) and beyond.

5:219 Ketcham, Ralph L. *James Madison: A Biography.* New York: Macmillan, 1971. This recent biography of Madison admits a great debt to Irving Brant, but Ketcham has also derived assistance from other students of the period. A lengthy, one-volume biography, it has utility, but the judgments tend to be conventional.

5:220 Russell, Greg. "Madison's Realism and the Role of Domestic Ideals in Foreign Affairs." *Presidential Studies Quarterly* 25 (Fall 1995): 711–23. In this brief article, Russell finds a blending of idealism and realism in Madison's foreign policymaking.

John Marshall

5:221 Johnson, Herbert A., with Charles T. Cullen, Nancy G. Harris et al., eds. *The Papers of John Marshall.* 10 vols. to date. Chapel Hill: University of North Carolina Press, 1974–. Published volumes cover Marshall's mission to France and the XYZ affair as well as his brief service as secretary of state under President Adams. Though the editing is superb, little of Marshall's private correspondence has survived for some periods.

5:222 Baker, Leonard. *John Marshall: A Life in Law.* New York: Macmillan, 1974. "Book Three: Diplomat" relates the experiences of Marshall and his colleagues during the XYZ affair in Paris in 1797. Although based on manuscript collections, French sources are not among them. Although a highly favorable treatment, this work revises Beveridge, *The Life of John Marshall* (1916–1919) (5:223), in many particulars and is less admiring of Marshall. Bibliography.

5:223 Beveridge, Albert J. *The Life of John Marshall.* 4 vols. Boston: Houghton Mifflin Company, 1916–1919. Volume 2 (1789–1801) covers Marshall's part in the XYZ mission and his service as secretary of state. Volume 3 covers the first part of Marshall's years on the Supreme Court, with ample attention to such issues as the Burr trial and a variety of cases that touched upon international law. Bibliography. Also laudatory of Marshall is Andrew J. Montague's study of Marshall in volume 2 of Samuel Flagg Bemis, ed., *The American Secretaries of State and Their Diplomacy* (1:48).

5:224 Rudko, Frances Howell. *John Marshall and International Law: Statesman and Chief Justice.* New York: Greenwood Press, 1991. Rudko focuses on 1793 to 1801, using Marshall's experiences as minister to France and secretary of state to make sense of his later decisions as chief justice on a variety of international law questions. It is an intriguing, if not entirely successful, approach. Bibliography.

5:225 Smith, Jean Edward. *John Marshall: Definer of a Nation.* New York: H. Holt and Co., 1996. This recent, comprehensive biography includes a judicious account of Marshall's actions in France at the time of the XYZ affair and of his brief service as secretary of state as well as offering a positive assessment of Marshall's service as chief justice of the Supreme Court. Extensive bibliography.

Alexander McGillivray

5:226   Caughey, John Walton. *McGillivray of the Creeks.* Norman: University of Oklahoma Press, 1938. This work remains the major study of Alexander McGillivray, the Creek leader whose diplomacy played a key role in U.S. and Spanish efforts to gain political ascendancy in the Old Southwest. A 60-page biography is followed by 214 reproduced letters to and from McGillivray spanning the years from 1783 until his death in 1793.

5:227   Whitaker, Arthur Preston. "Alexander McGillivray, 1783–1793." *North Carolina Historical Review* 5 (April 1928; July 1928): 181–203; 289–309. This two-part article, which divides at 1789, covers the period of McGillivray's ascendancy among the Creeks, highlighting his efforts to use Spanish power to check American expansion.

5:228   Wright, J. Leitch, Jr. "Creek-American Treaty of 1790: Alexander McGillivray and the Diplomacy of the Old Southwest." *Georgia Historical Quarterly* 51 (December 1967): 379–400. The author untangles the commercial and territorial interests of Britain, Spain, the state of Georgia, and several Indian factions as he explains what McGillivray hoped to accomplish by the treaty of New York and why he failed.

James Monroe

5:229   Garrison, Curtis W. *James Monroe Papers in Virginia Repositories.* 13 rolls. Microfilm. Charlottesville: University of Virginia Library, 1969. This microfilm publication provides a useful supplement both to Monroe's published papers and to the more easily accessible manuscript collections at the Library of Congress and the New York Public Library. Most of the material, however, covers his years in Virginia's state government.

5:230   Hamilton, Stanislaus Murray, ed. *The Writings of James Monroe, Including a Collection of His Public and Private Papers and Correspondence Now for the first Time Printed.* 7 vols. New York: G. P. Putnam's Sons, 1898–1903. Though a modern edition of Monroe's papers is promised in the future, scholars must now work with this collection. Hamil-

ton omitted a large proportion even of Monroe's outgoing correspondence and public papers. This work suffers as well from occasional inaccuracies, generally due to the editor's misreading of what may have been the most difficult handwriting of any early American statesman.

5:231   Brown, Stuart G., with Donald G. Baker, eds. *The Autobiography of James Monroe.* Syracuse: Syracuse University Press, 1959. An introduction and notes are supplied by the editor to long fragments of this unfinished autobiography. Written between 1827 and 1830, they reflect a faulty memory and the mellowing of old age. Monroe deals with his missions to France, 1794–1797 and 1803; the account ends with his mission to Britain in 1806.

5:232   Ammon, Harry. *James Monroe: The Quest for National Identity.* New York: McGraw-Hill, 1971. Reprint 1990 (University Press of Virginia). Monroe is depicted as very political in his judgments, shrewd, and sensitive to criticism. His missions to France and England are treated with maturity and balance. Now the definitive Monroe biography, this is based on manuscript collections, most of which are on microfilm. Extensive bibliography.

Gouverneur Morris

5:233   Davenport, Beatrix Cary, ed. *A Diary of the French Revolution, by Gouverneur Morris, 1752–1816.* 2 vols. Boston: Houghton Mifflin, 1939. Morris's account describes his European wanderings from the beginning of the French revolution through the end of his first eight months as minister to France in January 1793.

5:234   Mintz, Max M. *Gouverneur Morris and the American Revolution.* Norman: University of Oklahoma Press, 1970. This sound but brief and somewhat episodic biography is more reliable than Howard Swiggett's *The Extraordinary Mr. Morris* (Garden City, NY: Doubleday, 1952). Extensive bibliography.

Timothy Pickering

5:235   Clarfield, Gerard H. *Timothy Pickering and American Diplomacy, 1795–1800.* Columbia:

University of Missouri Press, 1969. Secretary of State Pickering's hatred of the French revolution is depicted, as is his preference by 1798 for an Anglo-American military alliance. The author somewhat modifies the harsh views of Pickering in most recent scholarship. Still useful is Edward H. Phillips, "The Public Career of Timothy Pickering, Federalist, 1745–1802" (Ph.D. diss., Harvard University, 1950).

5:236 _____. *Timothy Pickering and the American Republic.* Pittsburgh: University of Pittsburgh Press, 1980. This general biography of Pickering's life in politics provides a valuable supplement to the same author's earlier account of his term as secretary of state (*Timothy Pickering and American Diplomacy, 1795–1800,* 1969 [5:235]). Of particular value is his account of Pickering's life before entering the State Department, including his brief service as secretary of war. Also valuable is his discussion of Pickering's activities as a prominent New England Federalist at the time of the Louisiana Purchase, the Embargo, and the War of 1812. Though dated, Hervey Putnam Prentiss, *Timothy Pickering as the Leader of New England Federalism, 1800–1815* (Salem, MA: Essex Institute Press, 1934), also includes some useful material.

5:237 Pickering, Octavius, and Charles Wentworth Upham, eds. *The Life of Timothy Pickering.* 4 vols. Boston: Little, Brown, and Company, 1867–1873. These volumes print the correspondence of Timothy Pickering (1745–1829), with particular attention to his career as secretary of state and later as U.S. senator. The major collection of Pickering papers, at the Massachusetts Historical Society, has been microfilmed.

Edmund Randolph

5:238 Brant, Irving. "Edmund Randolph, Not Guilty!" *William and Mary Quarterly* 3d ser. 7 (April 1950): 179–98. This is a definitive exoneration of the secretary of state (1794–1795), whom the author shows to have been the victim of his cabinet colleagues, Pickering and Wolcott, and of the intermeddling of the British government.

5:239 Reardon, John J. *Edmund Randolph: A Biography.* New York: Macmillan, 1974. In this solid

biography sympathetic to Randolph (1753–1813), the author agrees with the judgment of James Madison: "His best friend can't save him from the self-condemnation of his political career, as explained by himself." Extensive bibliography.

5:240 Tachau, Mary K. Bonsteel. "George Washington and the Reputation of Edmund Randolph." *Journal of American History* 73 (June 1986): 15–34. Tachau defends Randolph and slights Washington for allowing his reputation to suffer despite his innocence, but, ultimately, argues that Randolph doomed himself by publishing a pamphlet attacking the president.

William Short

5:241 Boyce, Myrna. "The Diplomatic Career of William Short." *Journal of Modern History* 15 (June 1943): 97–119. This concise sketch examines all major aspects of Short's diplomatic career (1786–1798). Most fully treated are his functions as legation secretary to Jefferson and later as chargé d'affaires in Paris.

5:242 Shackelford, George Green. *Jefferson's Adoptive Son: The Life of William Short, 1759–1848.* Lexington: University Press of Kentucky, 1993. This biography details the life and career of William Short, a relatively minor diplomat, but a close friend and confidant of Jefferson, who served in Spain and Russia. Short also worked to arrange loans for the federal government in Antwerp and Amsterdam. Bibliography. See also his "William Short: Diplomat in Revolutionary France, 1785–1793," *Proceedings of the American Philosophical Society* 102, no. 6 (1958): 596–612.

Samuel Smith

5:243 Cassell, Frank A. *Merchant Congressman in the Young Republic: Samuel Smith of Maryland, 1752–1839.* Madison: University of Wisconsin Press, 1971. This solidly researched volume traces the career of an important Republican of the second rank, a factional leader who often caused difficulty for Jefferson and Madison. Because Smith was also an important commercial figure, the volume also provides insights into the relationship between business interests and the formulation of foreign policy.

5:244   Pancake, John S. *Samuel Smith and the Politics of Business: 1752–1839.* University: University of Alabama Press, 1972. Pancake's biography covers much the same ground as Cassell, *Merchant Congressman in the Young Republic: Samuel Smith of Maryland, 1752–1839* (1971) (5:243), highlighting Smith's far-flung commercial interests and his use of his political influence as a congressmen and brother of a cabinet minister in the Jefferson-Madison years to advance them. Bibliography.

Tecumseh

5:245   Edmunds, R. David. *Tecumseh and the Quest for Indian Leadership.* Boston: Little, Brown, 1984. This brief, but thorough, biography of Tecumseh presents him as a forceful spokesman of pan-Indianism who was independent of the British but willing to use them to achieve his goals. It is very nearly a double biography of Tecumseh and Tenskwatawa, whose story is told more fully by Edmunds in *The Shawnee Prophet* (Lincoln: University of Nebraska Press, 1983). Bibliographic essay.

5:246   Sugden, John. *Tecumseh: A Life.* New York: Henry Holt and Co., 1998. Sugden's work is the first comprehensive, scholarly biography of the important Shawnee leader and is based on multi-archival research. Sugden emphasizes Tecumseh's pan-Indian vision and military activities. Bibliography. A less scholarly, but still useful, work is Bil Gilbert, *God Gave Us This Country: Tekamthi and the First American Civil War* (New York: Atheneum, 1989).

George Washington

5:247   Abbot, W. W., and Dorothy Twohig, with Philander D. Chase, Beverly H. Runge, Beverly S. Kirsch, and Debra B. Kessler, eds. *The Papers of George Washington: Confederation Series.* 6 vols. Charlottesville: University Press of Virginia, 1992–1997. This completed series of the Washington papers covers the period from January 1784 through September 1788. For these years, this well-edited

collection, which includes both incoming and outgoing correspondence, supersedes all earlier editions.

5:248   Abbot, W. W., and Dorothy Twohig, with Mark A. Mastromarino, Philander D. Chase, and Beverly H. Runge, eds. *The Papers of George Washington: Presidential Series.* 9 vols. to date. Charlottesville: University Press of Virginia, 1987–. This series of Washington's papers currently extends from September 1788 through September 1791. For this period, this well-edited, complete edition of the first president's incoming and outgoing correspondence replaces earlier collections.

5:249   Fitzpatrick, John C., ed. *The Writings of George Washington from the Original Manuscript Sources, 1745–1799: Prepared under the Direction of the United States George Washington Bicentennial Commission and Published by Authority of Congress.* See chapter 4 of this Guide (4:164).

5:250   Jackson, Donald, with Dorothy Twohig, eds. *The Diaries of George Washington.* 6 vols. Charlottesville: University Press of Virginia, 1976–1979. Whether acting as a central figure in American politics, such as during the decade that began with the Constitutional Convention and ended with his retirement from the presidency, or playing a more peripheral role, Washington remained attentive to political and diplomatic developments. As such, this modern edition of his diaries is a valuable resource, though the diaries are very thin after July 1791.

5:251   Twohig, Dorothy, et al., eds. *The Papers of George Washington: Retirement Series.* 4 vols. Charlottesville: University Press of Virginia, 1998–1999. This well-edited collection of Washington's incoming and outgoing correspondence covers from March 1797 through Washington's death. His correspondence with Hamilton about the Quasi-War and the army makes this valuable.

5:252   Flexner, James T. *George Washington.* 4 vols. Boston: Little, Brown, 1965–1972. The third and fourth volumes of this gracefully written, interpretive biography cover Washington's career from the Treaty of Paris of 1783 until his death.

5:253   Freeman, Douglas Southall, with John Alexander Carroll and Mary Wells Ashworth. *George*

Washington, A Biography. 7 vols. New York: Scribner, 1948–1957. This magisterial biography contains every known fact concerning Washington (1732–1799). Volume 6, *Patriot and President* (1954), traces Washington's career from the Peace of 1783 to the end of his first term as president; volume 7, *First in Peace* (1957), was written from Freeman's voluminous notes by John A. Carroll and Mary W. Ashworth. The book is long on detail and short on interpretation but remains an indispensable resource. Extensive bibliography.

Anthony Wayne

5:254   Knopf, Richard C., ed. *Anthony Wayne, A Name in Arms: Soldier, Diplomat, Defender of Expansion Westward of a Nation: The Wayne-Knox-Pickering-McHenry Correspondence.* Pittsburgh: University of Pittsburgh Press, 1959. Knopf publishes the correspondence between General "Mad" Anthony Wayne and Washington's three secretaries of war from 1792 to 1796. During this period, Wayne directed the prosecution of the Indian war in the Old Northwest, negotiated the Treaty of Greenville, and helped enact the frontier provisions of the Jay Treaty.

5:255   Nelson, Paul David. *Anthony Wayne, Soldier of the Early Republic.* Bloomington: Indiana University Press, 1985. This biography of a key figure in the Indian wars in the Northwest Territory ably shows that "Mad" Anthony Wayne was prudent and careful despite his reputation. Bibliography.

James Wilkinson

5:256   Cox, Isaac Joslin. "General Wilkinson and His Later Intrigues with the Spaniards." *American Historical Review* 19 (July 1914): 794–812. Cox details Wilkinson's continuing intrigues with the Spanish government in the years after the transfer of Louisiana in 1804, particularly in the context of the Burr Conspiracy.

5:257   Hay, Thomas Robson, and Morris Robert Werner. *The Admirable Trumpeter: A Biography of General James Wilkinson.* Garden City, NY: Doubleday Doran and Company, 1941. Hay and Werner suggest that Wilkinson found no incongruity between self-interest and national interest and was an expansionist ahead of his time. The authors point out that the general deceived Spanish officials as readily as he did Americans.

5:258   Jacobs, James Ripley. *Tarnished Warrior, Major General James Wilkinson.* New York: Macmillan Company, 1938. Probably the least damning of the general's biographers, Jacobs portrays Wilkinson (1757–1825) not unsympathetically as a frontier extrovert who gave major impetus to Kentucky's separatist intrigues with Spain in the late 1780s and early 1790s. Although this study is more narrative than analytical, readers will find it adequately documented. Bibliography. Also useful is Royal Ornan Shreve, *The Finished Scoundrel: General James Wilkinson, Sometime Commander-in-Chief of the Army of the United States, Who Made Intrigue a Trade and Treason a Profession* (Indianapolis: Bobbs-Merrill, 1933).

Others

5:259   Nichols, Roy F. *Advance Agents of American Destiny.* Philadelphia: University of Pennsylvania Press, 1956. This work, a collection of ten essays, focuses on promoters of American overseas trade from the revolution to the Civil War. A prominent subject is William Shaler, consul in Cuba and semi-official observer of an early attempt to revolutionize Texas. Nichols also discussed Shaler in "William Shaler: New England Apostle of Rational Liberty," *New England Quarterly* 9 (March 1936): 71–96.

5:260   Edmunds, R. David, ed. *American Indian Leaders: Studies in Diversity.* Lincoln: University of Nebraska Press, 1980. This collection of biographical essays on prominent Indian leaders includes discussions of the most significant northern (James O'Donnell, "Joseph Brant," 21–40) and southern (Michael Green, "Alexander McGillivray," 41–63) figures of the immediate post-revolutionary era.

5:261   Allgor, Catherine. "'A Republican in a Monarchy': Louisa Catherine Adams in Russia." *Diplomatic History* 21 (Winter 1997): 15–43. In this intriguing but not entirely successful article, Allgor uses Louisa Catherine Adams's experiences while in Russia with her husband John Quincy Adams to explore the usefulness of gender for diplomatic historians. She finds that Louisa Catherine was crucial to John Quincy's success because Russia's court society relied so heavily on social interaction.

5:262   Duffy, John J., ed. *Ethan Allen and His Kin: Correspondence, 1772–1819.* 2 vols. Hanover, NH: University Press of New England, 1998. Since Vermont was effectively an independent nation between 1777 and 1791, the letters of Allen and other Vermont leaders are valuable sources for the triangular diplomacy among the United States, Great Britain, and Vermont in the 1780s. Ira Allen's efforts to arrange French support for an invasion of Canada in the late 1790s is also documented (see Graffagnino, "'Twenty Thousand Muskets!!!': Ira Allen and the *Olive Branch* Affair, 1796–1800" [1991] [5:455] and Ojala, "Ira Allen and the French Directory, 1796: Plans for the Creation of the Republic of United Columbia" [1979] [5:457]).

5:263   Skeen, C. Edward. *John Armstrong, Jr., 1758–1843: A Biography.* Syracuse: Syracuse University Press, 1981. This book is the only biography of Armstrong, who served as minister to France from 1804 to 1810, went to Spain to negotiate on the Floridas and the Louisiana boundary, and acted as secretary of war from early 1813 through the burning of Washington. Unfortunately, the destruction of Armstrong's papers by fire limits what Skeen can say in this still valuable study. Bibliographic essay.

5:264   Haeger, John Denis. *John Jacob Astor: Business and Finance in the Early Republic.* Detroit: Wayne State University Press, 1991. Haeger's focus is clearly on Astor's entrepreneurial skills and business methods. But he provides solid coverage of Astoria, Astor's fur trading outpost at the mouth of the Columbia River between 1807 and 1814, emphasizing its role in international commerce. Bibliography. A newer, popular account is available in Axel Madsen, *John Jacob Astor: America's First Multimillionaire* (New York: John Wiley, 2001).

5:265   Brant, Irving. "Joel Barlow, Madison's Stubborn Minister." *William and Mary Quarterly* 3d ser. 15 (October 1958): 438–52. This article describes Barlow as a vigorous, perceptive representative in France at a difficult time (1810–1812), when Napoleon's tortuous but also neglectful policy to-

ward the United States created difficulty for Madison's administration. Brant's article renders obsolete the brief treatment of this episode in the standard biography, James Leslie Woodress, *A Yankee's Odyssey: The Life of James Barlow* (Philadelphia: Lippincott, 1958).

5:266   Sugden, John. *Blue Jacket: Warrior of the Shawnees.* Lincoln: University of Nebraska Press, 2000. Sugden goes far toward rehabilitating the reputation of Blue Jacket, one of the most significant Shawnee war leaders of the late eighteenth century. In many ways the prototype for Tecumseh, Blue Jacket envisioned and assembled a multitribal coalition of Indians in the Upper Ohio Valley to resist American expansion between the American revolution and the Battle of Fallen Timbers (1794). Bibliography.

5:267   Kelsay, Isabel Thompson. *Joseph Brant, 1743–1807, Man of Two Worlds.* Syracuse: Syracuse University Press, 1984. Kelsay's general biography of one of the most important Iroquois leaders provides extensive coverage of his post-revolutionary efforts to preserve Iroquois land and power by securing British support. Kelsay portrays Brant as an early and important voice for pan-Indian cooperation. Bibliography.

5:268   Wiltse, Charles M. *John C. Calhoun. Vol. 1: Nationalist, 1782–1828.* 3 vols. Indianapolis: Bobbs-Merrill Co., 1944. Calhoun, according to Wiltse, was the "one true nationalist" of the era (1812–1828). This first of three volumes contains much information on Calhoun's role in the movement toward war in 1812. Extensive bibliography.

5:269   Coe, Samuel Gwynn. *The Mission of William Carmichael to Spain.* See chapter 4 of this Guide (4:170).

5:270   James, James Alton. *The Life of George Rogers Clark.* This is the best biography of a key figure in the early west. The author, who edited Clark's papers for the revolutionary period, has extensively researched his dealings with Spanish and French officials, but tends to excuse his faults. This work, together with Clark's papers, is the best place to begin a study of the Mississippi valley in this period (4:171).

5:271 Steffen, Jerome O. *William Clark: Jeffersonian Man on the Frontier.* Norman: University of Oklahoma Press, 1977. Steffen's biography provides a useful account of a key federal agent in the early-nineteenth-century west. After the Lewis and Clark Expedition, Clark served as governor of the Louisiana (later Missouri) Territory, playing important roles in both Indian affairs and the War of 1812 in the upper Mississippi valley. Bibliography.

5:272 Robinson, Blackwell P. *William R. Davie.* Chapel Hill: University of North Carolina Press, 1957. A prominent North Carolina Federalist, Davie, together with Oliver Ellsworth and William Vans Murray, followed the XYZ mission and concluded the Treaty of Mortfontaine. Robinson's analysis of the mission, although based on manuscript sources, adds little information or insight. Davie's role in the negotiation remains unclear. Bibliography.

5:273 Edwards, Samuel. *Barbary General: The Life of William H. Eaton.* Englewood Cliffs, NJ: Prentice-Hall, 1968. While William Eaton, a key figure in the Barbary wars of the Jefferson administration, still awaits a scholarly biography, this work is more useful than Francis Rennell Rudd, *General William Eaton: The Failure of an Idea* (New York: Minton, Balch, 1932).

5:274 Cleaves, Freeman. *Old Tippecanoe: William Henry Harrison and His Time.* New York: C. Scribner's, 1939. Cleaves's well-researched biography of Harrison (1773–1841), American commander on the western front during the War of 1812, traces the gradual development of American military power, culminating in the battles of Lake Erie and the Thames. Earlier portions of this work show the rising tensions on the frontier. Bibliography.

5:275 Steiner, Bernard C., ed. *The Life and Correspondence of James McHenry, Secretary of War under Washington and Adams.* Cleveland: Burrows Brothers Company, 1907. Reprint 1979 (Arno Press). Despite a sympathetic editor, the contemporary and historical judgment concerning McHenry's incompetence is amply illustrated. Alexander Hamilton's most slavish follower, McHenry was eventually dismissed by President Adams for disloyalty. Bibliography.

5:276 Ferguson, E. James, John Catanzariti, Elizabeth M. Nuxoll, and Mary A. Gallagher, eds. *The Papers of Robert Morris, 1781–1784.* See chapter 4 of this Guide (4:178).

5:277 Morison, Samuel Eliot. *The Life and Letters of Harrison Gray Otis, Federalist, 1765–1848.* 2 vols. Boston: Houghton Mifflin Company, 1913. A leading Massachusetts Federalist of the second generation, Otis was generally more moderate than most of his elders. Morison adopts a generally sympathetic but not uncritical attitude toward his ancestor; his narrative and extensive selections from Otis's correspondence are presented separately.

5:278 Zahniser, Marvin R. *Charles Cotesworth Pinckney, Founding Father.* Chapel Hill: University of North Carolina Press for the Institute of Early American History and Culture, 1967. Pinckney, minister to France succeeding Monroe, was originally sympathetic to the French revolution, but his experiences as minister and XYZ commissioner embittered him toward France and the revolution. He used his powerful family and state connections to ensure South Carolina's support of the Adams administration in the Quasi-War. Bibliography.

5:279 Brown, Everett Somerville, ed. *William Plumer's Memorandum of Proceedings in the United States Senate, 1803–1807.* New York: Macmillan Company, 1923. Plumer's diary provides an invaluable resource for studying congressional involvement in and reaction to policymaking from the fall of 1803 through the spring of 1807. The Louisiana Purchase, the efforts to acquire the Floridas from Spain, the conflict over neutral rights and impressment with Britain, and the Burr Conspiracy were key issues for the Senate in these years.

5:280 Bruce, William Cabell. *John Randolph of Roanoke, 1773–1833: A Biography Based Largely on New Material.* 2 vols. New York: Putnam's, 1922. Reprint 1970 (Octagon Books). This tedious biography provides the most useful sketch of the life and political career of its subject. Randolph was an important, highly individualistic figure, who increasingly opposed the foreign policies of Jefferson and Madison; Bruce quotes much of his vigorous criticism.

5:281 Densmore, Christopher. *Red Jacket: Iroquois Diplomat and Orator.* Syracuse: Syracuse University Press, 1999. With this brief biography, Densmore provides a rich account of the Seneca leader who rose to prominence in the early 1790s as a voice of peace and accommodation. As such, he emerged as a competitor to the other great Iroquois leader of the post-revolutionary era, Joseph Brant. Red Jacket's oratorical powers, displayed in frequent tours of American cities, won him acclaim and respect. Bibliography.

5:282 Armstrong, Thom M. *Politics, Diplomacy and Intrigue in the Early Republic: The Cabinet Career of Robert Smith, 1801–1811.* Dubuque, IA: Kendall/Hunt Publishing, 1991. This biography attempts to redeem the reputation of Smith, whose brief career as secretary of state ended when Madison discharged him in early 1811. While this effort is not entirely successful, Armstrong does well to recall the achievements of Smith's service as secretary of the navy for eight years under Jefferson. He also provides a helpful account of some of the factionalism and intrigue within the Republican Party. Bibliography.

5:283 Rogers, George C. *Evolution of a Federalist: William Loughton Smith of Charleston (1758–1812).* Columbia: University of South Carolina Press, 1962. For loyally supporting Hamiltonian causes in Congress, Smith was appointed minister to Lisbon in 1797. Chapter 13 describes his four years as an observer of the XYZ affair, the advent of Bonaparte, and the Ellsworth mission; he also played a small part in U.S. diplomacy with the Barbary powers. Bibliography.

BRITISH

Phineas Bond

5:284 Jameson, J. Franklin, ed. "Letters of Phineas Bond, British Consul at Philadelphia, to the Foreign Office of Great Britain, 1787–1789." In *The Annual Report of the American Historical Association for the Year 1896,* 513–659. Washington, DC: Government Printing Office, 1897. For much of the period of these letters, Bond was the most important British official at the most important city in the new

United States. This collection certainly has a commercial focus, tracking the impact of rising tensions over the war in Europe and neutral rights, but Bond's observations are wide-ranging. The letters are continued for the period 1790–1794 in *The Annual Report of the American Historical Association for the Year 1897* (1898), 454–568.

5:285 Neel, Joanne Loewe. *Phineas Bond: A Study in Anglo-American Relations, 1786–1812.* Philadelphia: University of Pennsylvania Press, 1968. Bond was a loyalist who fled to England during the American revolution and returned as British consul at New York (1786–1812). Always devoted to the British empire, he disliked the United States and was fearful of its growing power. Bibliography.

George Canning

5:286 Hinde, Wendy. *George Canning.* London: Collins, 1973. Reprint 1989 (Blackwell). This work has very little on American affairs. The personal characteristics that colored Canning's American policy are clearly shown not to have been aberrations; the main objectives of his policy, which largely determined his attitude toward the United States while at the Foreign Office (1807–1809), are made clear. Even less attention to American affairs is paid in Peter Dixon, *Canning, Politician and Statesman* (London: Weidenfeld and Nicolson, 1976).

5:287 Temperley, Harold. *Life of Canning.* London: J. Finch and Co. Ltd., 1905. Reprint 1970 (Greenwood Press). This dated, essentially uncritical study of Canning's public career devotes only one chapter to his tenure at the Foreign Office (1807–1809), which does not delve into relations with the United States. The book, although considered a classic work, is useful to historians of American diplomacy only in providing background information.

Lord Castlereagh

5:288 Vane, Charles William, ed. *Correspondence, Despatches, and Other Papers of Viscount Castlereagh, Second Marquess of Londonderry.* 12 vols. London: Henry Colburn, 1848–1853. Volumes 9 and 10, which include letters to and from

Castlereagh, include some material dealing with the negotiations at Ghent in 1814. Although useful, the selections do not fully elucidate British policy during the negotiations. These were published interruptedly from 1848 through 1853 by three publishers, William Shorberl and John Murray being the latter two; the latter volumes carried the subtitle *Correspondence, Despatches, and Other Papers.*

5:289   Bartlett, C. J. *Castlereagh.* New York: Scribner, 1967. The shortcomings of this biography are obvious: it does not rest on research in primary materials. Its merits are briskness, clarity, and judgment. Castlereagh's general outlook, the setting in which he worked, and the impact of his larger problems on relations with the United States are made clear. Bibliographical note.

Robert Liston

5:290   Perkins, Bradford, ed. "A Diplomat's Wife in Philadelphia: Letters of Henrietta Liston, 1796–1800." *William and Mary Quarterly* 3d ser. 11 (October 1954): 592–632. These letters, written from New York and Philadelphia, provide, in Perkins's view, interesting "sidelights" on domestic politics during Adams's presidency.

5:291   Kyte, George W. "Robert Liston and Anglo-American Cooperation, 1796–1800." *Proceedings of the American Philosophical Society* 93, no. 3 (1949): 259–66. The author credits Liston with the high degree of Anglo-American cooperation, but "the temporary Anglo-American accord of 1796–1800" deteriorated because of the British government's refusal to change its policies toward neutrals, President Adams's successful policy with France, and Liston's succession by less able ministers.

5:292   Wright, Esmond. "Robert Liston, Second British Minister to the United States." *History Today* 11 (February 1961): 118–27. Liston was "a model diplomat of the old school," who returned to England at the end of 1800 with Anglo-American relations much more cordial than they had been on his arrival five years before.

Others

5:293   Reuter, Frank T. "'Petty Spy' or Effective Diplomat: The Role of George Beckwith." *Journal of the Early Republic* 10 (Winter 1990): 471–92. Beckwith, a British secret service agent, reported from the United States during the early 1780s and again during the early years of Washington's presidency. The information he provided was often slanted and not always followed.

5:294   Menk, Patricia Holbert, ed. "D. M. Erskine: Letters from America, 1798–1799." *William and Mary Quarterly* 3d ser. 6 (April 1949): 251–84. The young Erskine had been sent to America by his father. His letters contain some shrewd comments about Americans and their generally hostile attitudes toward England. Erskine returned to the United States as British minister in 1806.

5:295   Reid, Loren. *Charles James Fox: A Man for the People.* Fox's death on the eve of the Monroe-Pinkney negotiations in 1806 was viewed, probably incorrectly, as a missed opportunity. Bibliography (4:192).

5:296   Nelson, Larry L. *A Man of Distinction among Them: Alexander McKee and British-Indian Affairs along the Ohio Country Frontier, 1754–1799.* Kent, OH: Kent State University Press, 1999. Nelson provides a helpful account of a crucial British Indian agent in the post-revolutionary Ohio Valley. A minor figure in the Indian Office as early as the 1750s, McKee remained loyal to the crown and to the Shawnees, among whom he had been raised and continued to trade, during and after the revolution. Bibliography.

5:297   Lester, Malcolm. *Anthony Merry Redivivus: A Reappraisal of the British Minister to the United States, 1803–6.* Charlottesville: University Press of Virginia, 1978. This effort to restore the reputation of Merry, who was universally excoriated by previous historians, is vigorous and provocative, if not entirely successful. Bibliography.

5:298   Gray, Denis. *Spencer Perceval: The Evangelical Prime Minister, 1762–1812.* Manchester, UK: Manchester University Press, 1963. This turgid yet impressive biography emphasizes that portion of

Perceval's career (1807–1812) most important for American diplomatic historians. No other work more comprehensively deals with British factional politics, and there is extended treatment of the 1807 order-in-council. However, Gray's limited knowledge of American developments leads to some errors. Extensive bibliography.

5:299   Rose, J. Holland. *William Pitt and the Great War.* London: G. Bell, 1911. Reprint 1971 (Greenwood Press). Rose's treatment of Pitt's role (1789–1806) during the Anglo-French wars will remain the standard work only until John Ehrman completes his *The Younger Pitt,* 3 vols. to date (London: Constable, 1969–). There is little bearing directly upon the United States in Rose's detailed, nationalistic account.

FRENCH

Napoleon Bonaparte

5:300   Bonaparte, Napoleon. *Correspondance de Napoléon Ier publiée par ordre de l'empéreur Napoléon III [Correspondence of Napoleon I Published by Order of the Emperor Napoleon III].* 32 vols. Paris: Plon et Dumaine, 1858–1870. Reprint 1974 (AMS Press). This collection includes a very useful table of contents ("Table des Pièces") that lists all items by number, gives the date of all documents, indicates for whom the item was intended, and gives a brief summary of contents.

5:301   Castelot, André. *Napoleon.* Translated by Guy Daniels. New York: Harper and Row, 1971. This popular biography of Napoleon includes no notes and is thus of limited utility for scholars.

5:302   Lefebvre, Georges. *Napoleon, from 18 Brumaire to Tilsit, 1799–1807.* Translated by Henry F. Stockhold. 2 vols. New York: Columbia University Press, 1969. This two-volume work, which covers from 1799 to 1815 and divides at 1807, is a translation of portions of Lefebvre's classic study, *Napoléon,* first published in 1935. Lefebvre's research is prodigious although somewhat unobtrusive since there are no footnotes. The scope is broad, both geographically and topically; this is the study of an

age even more than a biography. Bibliography of printed materials. Reprinted by the same publisher in 1990.

5:303   Schom, Alan. *Napoleon Bonaparte.* New York: HarperCollins, 1997. This recent work provides a good, general biography of Napoleon; it includes relatively little on the United States, however. Bibliography.

Marquis de Lafayette

5:304   Gottschalk, Louis R., and Shirley A. Bill, eds. *The Letters of Lafayette to Washington: 1777–1799.* An edition of the complete correspondence between the two men, it is useful for their respective views of the French revolution. Well edited. The original edition was privately printed in 1944 (4:208).

5:305   Gottschalk, Louis R. *Lafayette between the American and the French Revolutions (1783–1789).* Chicago: University of Chicago Press, 1950. Gottschalk argues that American men and ideas had significance for French revolutionary developments. This volume (1783–1789) is particularly useful in explaining French-American commercial problems and the commercial policy of Vergennes. Gottschalk's multivolume biography (1935–1969), of which this is part, is the most satisfying account available. Extensive bibliography.

Prince Talleyrand

5:306   Orieux, Jean. *Talleyrand: The Art of Survival.* Translated by Patricia Wolf. New York: Alfred A. Knopf, 1974. This biography of Talleyrand, like all the others, gives scant space to American affairs. Extensive bibliography. The most complete biography is Georges Lacour-Gayet, *Talleyrand, 1754–1838,* 4 vols. (Paris: Payot, 1928–1934), but it has not been translated. Others in English include Crane Brinton, *The Lives of Talleyrand* (New York: W. W. Norton & Company, 1936), and J. F. Bernard, *Talleyrand: A Biography* (New York: Putnam, 1973).

5:307   Pallain, Georges, ed. *Le Ministère de Talleyrand sous le Directoire [The Ministry of Talleyrand*

SPANISH

under the Directory]. Paris: Plon, Nourrit, 1891. The editor provides an introduction to selections of Talleyrand's correspondence as foreign minister (1797–1799). Talleyrand's reports consistently urged reconciliation with the United States.

5:308 Stinchcombe, William C., ed. "A Neglected Memoir by Talleyrand on French-American Relations, 1793–1797." *Proceedings of the American Philosophical Society* 121, no. 3 (1977): 195–208. This is a translation of a long overlooked memoir by Talleyrand of October 1797 intended to formulate the French position for negotiations with American commissioners John Marshall, Charles Cotesworth Pinckney, and Elbridge Gerry in 1797. Because of the vindictive attitude of the directory toward the United States, however, it had little impact.

Others

5:309 Conlin, Michael F. "The American Mission of Citizen Pierre-Auguste Adet: Revolutionary Chemistry and Diplomacy in the Early Republic." *Pennsylvania Magazine of History and Biography* 74 (October 2000): 489–520. This thin, but intriguing, article demonstrates that Adet, the French minister to the United States in the mid-1790s, used his reputation as a scientist to strengthen his position in Philadelphia, particularly with the Republican opposition.

5:310 Lyon, E. Wilson. *The Man Who Sold Louisiana: The Career of Francois Barbe-Marbois.* See chapter 4 of this Guide (4:201).

5:311 Fauchet, Joseph. "Mémoire sur les États Unis d'Amérique par Joseph Fauchet [Memoir Concerning the United States of America by Joseph Fauchet]." In *The Annual Report of the American Historical Association for the Year 1936,* ed. Carl L. Lokke, 1: 83–123. Washington, DC: Government Printing Office, 1938. Fauchet succeeded Genet as minister to America, serving from February 1794 to June 1795. In the second part of this memoir, he recounts his extensive efforts to defeat the Jay Treaty, whose purpose, he states, might be frustrated if France played a skillful political game in America.

Manuel Luis Gayoso de Lemos

5:312 Holmes, Jack D. L. *Gayoso: The Life of a Spanish Governor in the Mississippi Valley, 1789–1799.* Baton Rouge: Louisiana State University Press for the Louisiana Historical Association, 1965. This biography of the first Spanish governor of the Natchez District complements any study of Spanish affairs during the Federalist era. Gayoso negotiated the Indian treaties of Natchez (1792) and Nogales (1793) and ably provided for the defense of the Lower Mississippi. Extensive bibliography.

Manuel de Godoy

5:313 Chastenet, Jacques. *Godoy, Master of Spain 1792–1808.* Translated by J. F. Huntington. London: Batchworth Press, 1953. Reprint 1972 (Kennikat Press). Manuel de Godoy, Spanish premier (1792–1798, 1801–1808), is portrayed as a well-meaning, occasionally skillful statesman. Although Chastenet dwells too much on court intrigue, this work accurately explains the fluctuating relations between Spain and France, which in turn help to explain U.S. relations with both powers. The 1972 reprint lacks footnotes and bibliography.

Estéban Miro

5:314 Burson, Caroline M. *The Stewardship of Don Esteban Miro, 1782–1792: A Study of Louisiana Based Largely on the Documents in New Orleans.* New Orleans: American Printing Co., 1940. Although this work treats internal developments, the diplomatic historian may profit from the author's analysis of the governor's efforts to befriend the southwest tribes as a barrier to American encroachment, and from the account of Miro's colonization efforts, principally at New Madrid, and his dealings with Wilkinson and Gardoqui. Bibliography.

Others

5:315   Almaráz, Félix D., Jr. *Tragic Cavalier: Governor Manuel Salcedo of Texas, 1808–1813.* Austin: University of Texas Press, 1971. This work is a useful biography of the Spanish governor of Texas at a time of increased revolutionary turmoil and filibustering activity, including the Gutiérrez-Magee Expedition. Salcedo was ultimately executed by revolutionaries after surrendering to the expedition's leaders. Bibliography.

LATIN AMERICAN

Francisco de Miranda

5:316   Robertson, William Spence. "Francisco de Miranda and the Revolutionizing of Spanish America." In *The Annual Report of the American Historical Association for the Year 1907,* ed. William Spence Robertson, 1: 189–550. Washington, DC: Government Printing Office, 1908. This correspondence covers Miranda's career: his intrigues with both France and Great Britain to obtain aid in overthrowing Spanish rule in South America and his relations with Rufus King and other Americans in London in 1798.

5:317   _____. *The Life of Miranda.* 2 vols. Chapel Hill: University of North Carolina Press, 1929. This biography, although old, is still the most useful life of the first important Latin American revolutionary. Francisco de Miranda (1750–1816) had many contacts with Americans and drew support from them, particularly for his 1806 filibustering expedition. Robertson's research is impressive, although it concentrates rather narrowly on Miranda rather than on the setting in which he operated. Bibliography.

Confederation Era

5:318   Allen, Michael. "The Mississippi River Debate, 1785–1787." *Tennessee Historical Quarterly* 36 (Winter 1977): 447–67. Allen shows that the debates in the Confederation Congress over the Jay-Gardoqui negotiations and the closing of the Mississippi River to American trade fueled sectional tensions between the northeast and the south and west.

5:319   Burnett, Edmund C. *The Continental Congress.* See chapter 4 of this Guide (4:52).

5:320   Davis, Joseph L. *Sectionalism in American Politics, 1774–1787.* Madison: University of Wisconsin Press, 1977. This brief book includes two chapters of particular value for understanding the diplomacy of the Confederation era. One discusses the problems of international trade and attempts at commercial reform; the other examines the conflict in Congress over the Jay-Gardoqui negotiations and the Mississippi River.

5:321   Jensen, Merrill. *The New Nation: A History of the United States during the Confederation, 1781–1789.* New York: Alfred A. Knopf, 1950. This is a standard work on the Confederation, written from the viewpoint of the progressive school of historiography. The author rejects the traditional "critical period" interpretation of the Confederation.

5:322   _____. "The Sovereign States: Their Antagonisms and Rivalries and Some Consequences." In *Sovereign States in an Age of Uncertainty,* ed. Ronald Hoffman and Peter J. Albert, 226–50. Charlottesville: University Press of Virginia, 1981. Jensen examines internal rivalries within the Confederation during the 1780s, emphasizing sectional above state divisions.

5:323   Marks, Frederick W., III. *Independence on Trial: Foreign Affairs and the Making of the Constitution.* 2d ed. Wilmington, DE: Scholarly Resources, 1986. In the only diplomatic survey of the Confederation period (1781–1789), Marks argues that anxiety about foreign affairs, particularly British trade restrictions, and the ineffectiveness of the Confederation government were important factors in demands for a new constitution. John Jay's diplomacy is treated sympathetically. Extensive bibliography. First published in 1973.

5:324   _____. "Power, Pride, and Purse: Diplomatic Origins of the Constitution." *Diplomatic*

History 11 (Fall 1987): 303–19. In this article, Marks elaborates and extends his arguments from *Independence on Trial: Foreign Affairs and the Making of the Constitution* (1986) (5:323). In terms of foreign commerce, Indian affairs, and separatist movements, the crisis of the Confederation government accelerated in 1785 and 1786.

5:325   Matson, Cathy D., and Peter S. Onuf. *A Union of Interests: Political and Economic Thought in Revolutionary America.* Lawrence: University Press of Kansas, 1990. This intriguing book looks at the intersection of political ideology and economic interests in a number of contexts between the Declaration of Independence and the ratification of the Constitution. A brief version of this argument appeared earlier as "Toward a Republican Empire: Interest and Ideology in Revolutionary America," *American Quarterly* 37 (Fall 1985): 496–531. Bibliography.

5:326   Merritt, Eli. "Sectional Conflict and Secret Compromise: The Mississippi River Question and the United States Constitution." *American Journal of Legal History* 35 (April 1991): 117–71. This article is overly long and not very clearly written, but offers a complete account of the impact of the Jay-Gardoqui negotiations on the Constitution. Too often, however, Merritt exaggerates the impact of this issue, which he links to a variety of constitutional debates and clauses.

5:327   Morris, Richard B. *The Forging of the Union, 1781–1789.* New York: Harper and Row, 1987. Written by a long-time scholar of the period, this general overview of the Confederation era thoroughly covers the impact of foreign affairs on the movement for a stronger government, including interstate tensions as well as foreign trade, the Jay-Gardoqui negotiations, and European diplomacy. Bibliographic essay.

5:328   Onuf, Peter S. *Statehood and Union: A History of the Northwest Ordinance.* Bloomington: Indiana University Press, 1987. This work offers a brilliant analysis of the ideas behind the initial provisions of government for the Northwest Territory in the 1780s and, thus, in some ways, for all later expansion into areas that were to be incorporated into the union as states.

5:329   Rakove, Jack N. *The Beginnings of National Politics: An Interpretive History of the Continental Congress.* New York: Alfred A. Knopf, 1979. Reprint 1982 (Johns Hopkins University Press). The subtitle reveals the scope of a book that touches in many places on foreign affairs. The author studies the Continental Congress as an institution and the rise of politics as a profession, in contrast to Edmund C. Burnett's treatment of debates, bills, and finances in *The Continental Congress* (1941) (4:52).

5:330   Rowe, G. S., and Alexander W. Knott. "The Longchamps Affair (1784–86), the Law of Nations, and the Shaping of Early American Foreign Policy." *Diplomatic History* 10 (Summer 1986): 199–220. By examining a case involving the protection of the persons and property of foreign diplomats, the authors address whether the Confederation government had the intention and capability of enforcing the law of nations on the state governments. The struggle over the Longchamps affair, they find, helped to produce a clear statement of federal supremacy on such matters in the Constitution. See also the same authors' "Power, Justice, and Foreign Relations in the Confederation Period: The Marbois-Longchamps Affair, 1784–1786," *Pennsylvania Magazine of History and Biography* 104 (July 1980): 275–307.

CONSTITUTION

5:331   Adler, David Gray, and Larry N. George, eds. *The Constitution and the Conduct of American Foreign Policy.* This collection includes a number of general essays, generally on executive-legislative disputes, and a small group of more focused essays on the 1790s. For details, see chapter 2 of this Guide (2:224).

5:332   Ball, Terence, and J. G. A. Pocock, eds. *Conceptual Change and the Constitution.* Lawrence: University Press of Kansas, 1988. This collection includes two essays of particular value: Pocock's "States, Republics, and Empires: The American Founding in Early Modern Perspective" (55–77) and Peter S. Onuf's "State Sovereignty and the Making of the Constitution" (78–98). These essays examine the contemporary, and changing, meaning of such crucial concepts as "state," "republic," "empire," and "sovereignty."

5:333　Beeman, Richard, Stephen Botein, and Edward C. Carter, II, eds. *Beyond Confederation: Origins of the Constitution and American National Identity.* Chapel Hill: University of North Carolina Press for the Institute of Early American History and Culture, 1987. This book is one of the best of the many collections of essays generated by the bicentennial of the Constitution. The most useful papers include Lance Banning's "The Practicable Sphere of a Republic: James Madison, the Constitutional Convention, and the Emergence of Revolutionary Federalism" (162–87), Drew R. McCoy's "James Madison and Visions of American Nationality in the Confederation Period: A Regional Perspective" (226–58), and John M. Murrin's "A Roof without Walls: The Dilemma of American National Identity" (333–48).

5:334　Deudney, Daniel H. "The Philadelphian System: Sovereignty, Arms Control, and Balance of Power in the American States-Union, circa 1787–1861." *International Organization* 49 (Spring 1995): 191–228. Deudney, a political scientist, argues that the United States was neither a unified state nor a state system, but a hybrid of the two, between the Constitutional Convention and the Civil War. Such a "Philadelphian system" could address contemporary, and future, problems by checking state sovereignty, reducing tensions, and preserving state independence better than a balance-of-power system.

5:335　Goldwin, Robert A., and Robert A. Licht, eds. *Foreign Policy and the Constitution.* Washington, DC: AEI Press, 1990. This collection of essays draws on an eclectic collection of political scientists, historians, politicians, and others. Of particular value are Jack N. Rakove's "Making Foreign Policy—The View from 1787" (1–19) and Nathan Tarcov's "Principle, Prudence, and the Constitutional Division of Foreign Policy" (20–39).

5:336　Graebner, Norman A. "Isolationism and Antifederalism: The Ratification Debates." *Diplomatic History* 11 (Fall 1987): 337–53. In Graebner's view, "essentially the debates on the ratification of the U.S. Constitution turned on two competing conceptions of the external world and the presumed requirements for successful coexistence with it." The Federalists, in this view, were realistic internationalists; the anti-Federalists were idealistic isolationists.

5:337　Henkin, Louis. *Foreign Affairs and the United States Constitution.* This work is one of the best analyses of the connections between the provisions of the Constitution and the conduct of foreign policy (1789–1972). It is also important for its discussion of the American approach to international law (2:227). First published in 1972 as *Foreign Affairs and the Constitution.*

5:338　Kaplan, Lawrence S. "Jefferson and the Constitution: The View from Paris, 1786–1789." *Diplomatic History* 11 (Fall 1987): 321–35. Kaplan discovers in Jefferson an intense concern with what the French, and other Europeans, thought of him, the Convention, and the new Constitution.

5:339　Moore, John Allphin, Jr. "Empire, Republicanism, and Reason: Foreign Affairs as Viewed by the Founders of the Constitution." *History Teacher* 26 (May 1993): 297–315. Relying heavily on *The Federalist,* Moore argues that, despite their desire for territorial and commercial expansion, the founders designed a somewhat cumbersome foreign policy process to protect republicanism and liberty.

5:340　Onuf, Peter S. "Anarchy and the Crisis of the Union." In *To Form a More Perfect Union: The Critical Ideas of the Constitution,* ed. Herman Belz, Ronald Hoffman, and Peter J. Albert, 272–302. Charlottesville: University Press of Virginia for the United States Capitol Historical Society, 1992. Onuf demonstrates that growing interstate tensions during the Confederation era led many proponents of a stronger central government to fear that a dissolution of the union would permit the emergence of a European-style state system in North America.

5:341　Onuf, Peter S. *The Origins of the Federal Republic: Jurisdictional Controversies in the United States, 1775–1787.* Philadelphia: University of Pennsylvania Press, 1983. This work provides a valuable reminder that the line between interstate and international relations was often hazy during a period when the states could legitimately claim a significant degree of sovereignty and when new states, such as Vermont and the planned state of Franklin, existed outside the union.

5:342　_____. "Reflections on the Founding: Constitutional Historiography in Bicentennial

Perspective." *William and Mary Quarterly* 3d ser. 46 (April 1989): 341–75. This fairly recent historiographical overview of the founding of the Constitution discusses much of the flood of work unleashed by the bicentennial in 1787.

5:343 Powell, H. Jefferson. "The Founders and the President's Authority over Foreign Affairs." *William and Mary Law Review* 40 (May 1999): 1471–1537. Though the author's principal concern is with contemporary debates over presidential power in foreign affairs, he provides a useful discussion of the thinking of the founders about this issue. By examining six early incidents (primarily from 1790 to 1800), Powell shows that the founders expected the executive branch to take the lead in most foreign policy matters.

Federalist Era

5:344 Bemis, Samuel Flagg. *American Foreign Policy and the Blessings of Liberty, and Other Essays.* This collection of some of Bemis's essays and articles includes a number that address events and individuals of the Federalist era, such as Thomas Pinkney's London mission, the foreign policies of Hamilton and Washington, and various aspects of the Jay Treaty. Bibliography of Bemis's work (4:49).

5:345 Ben-Atar, Doron S., and Barbara B. Oberg, eds. *Federalists Reconsidered.* Charlottesville: University Press of Virginia, 1998. This wide-ranging collection of essays examines the twelve years of Federalist rule from various perspectives. Of particular value are Ben-Atar, "Alexander Hamilton's Alternative: Technology Piracy and the Report on Manufactures," and Andrew R. L. Cayton, "Radicals in the 'Western World': The Federalist Conquest of Trans-Appalachian North America."

5:346 Bowman, Albert H. "Jefferson, Hamilton, and American Foreign Policy." *Political Science Quarterly* 71 (March 1956): 18–41. After examining American foreign policy contests (1790–1794), Bowman concludes, contrary to the realist school, that Jefferson rather than Hamilton had the truer vision of U.S. interests.

5:347 Brown, Ralph A. *The Presidency of John Adams.* Lawrence: University Press of Kansas, 1975. This book offers a favorable assessment of John Adams as president and concludes that he had greater popular support in 1800 than in 1796. Bibliography.

5:348 Casto, William R. "The Origins of Federal Admiralty Jurisdiction in an Age of Privateers, Smugglers, and Pirates." *American Journal of Legal History* 37 (April 1993): 117–57. Casto's primary goal seems to be to remind lawyers that American admiralty law, which is now mostly private and civil, began in the 1790s as mostly public and criminal. This work is useful for elaborating the sovereignty issues that were central to at least one aspect of the Judiciary Act of 1790.

5:349 DeConde, Alexander. *Entangling Alliance: Politics & Diplomacy under George Washington.* Durham, NC: Duke University Press, 1958. Alexander Hamilton is presented as the major figure in shaping foreign policy, with Washington serving as a useful figurehead. Washington's diplomacy (1789–1797) was shaped by the needs of foreign trade, the strength of the British navy, and the requirements of the Hamiltonian fiscal system. The farewell address is depicted as a partisan political document, devised by Hamilton to help Federalists win the election of 1796. Bibliography.

5:350 Elkins, Stanley, and Eric McKitrick. *The Age of Federalism.* New York: Oxford University Press, 1993. This book provides a comprehensive, general overview of the Federalist era in a manner generally more favorable to the Washington and Adams administrations than to the opposition party. Elkins and McKitrick's wide-ranging study includes character sketches of many of the major and minor public figures of the decade.

5:351 Goebel, Julius. *History of the Supreme Court of the United States. Vol. 1: Antecedents and Beginnings to 1801.* New York: Macmillan, 1971. This volume is perhaps less valuable for scholars of American foreign relations than most in this series. It is heavily weighted toward the "antecedents" of the Supreme Court, with over half of its roughly 800 pages covering the period before the Judiciary Act of 1789. In its final three chapters, however, it examines many of the international law and sovereignty cases of the Federalist era. Bibliography.

5:352   Hoffman, Ronald, and Peter J. Albert, eds. *Launching the "Extended Republic": The Federalist Era.* Charlottesville: University Press of Virginia for the United States Capitol Historical Society, 1996. This strong collection of essays on the era of Federalist rule in the 1790s ranges across a variety of political, cultural, and social topics. Of particular value are Andrew R. L. Cayton's "'When Shall We Cease to Have Judases?': The Blount Conspiracy and the Limits of the 'Extended Republic'" (156–89) and Bernard W. Sheehan's "The Indian Problem in the Northwest: From Conquest to Philanthropy" (190–222). See also Thomas P. Slaughter, "'The King of Crimes': Early American Treason Law, 1787–1860."

5:353   Howe, John R., Jr. "Republican Thought and the Political Violence of the 1790s." *American Quarterly* 19 (Summer 1967): 147–65. Howe traces the violent political culture of the 1790s to republican principles shared by both Federalists and Republicans.

5:354   Kurtz, Stephen G. *The Presidency of John Adams: The Collapse of Federalism, 1795–1800.* Philadelphia: University of Pennsylvania Press, 1957. This standard account of the Adams presidency is favorable to Adams and his decision to defy Federalist leaders in seeking peace with France, but Adams's actions, particularly his nomination of envoys to France in 1799, remain controversial.

5:355   McDonald, Forrest. *The Presidency of George Washington.* Lawrence: University Press of Kansas, 1974. In this imaginative, provocative tour de force, the author confronts the "Washington myth" and concludes that the first president (1789–1797) was "indispensable, but only for what he was, not for what he did." Bibliography.

5:356   Newman, Paul Douglas. "The Federalists' Cold War: The Fries Rebellion, National Security, and the State, 1787–1800." *Pennsylvania History* 67 (Winter 2000): 63–104. Newman highlights cold war parallels to show how the Federalists of the Washington and Adams administrations tried to build a "national security state" that could meet both foreign and domestic threats to the new nation.

5:357   Reuter, Frank T. *Trials and Triumphs: George Washington's Foreign Policy.* Fort Worth: Texas Christian University Press, 1983. This work examines the contribution of Washington (and his advisers) to the American foreign policy tradition. It lacks footnotes, but includes a long and valuable bibliographic essay.

5:358   Sharp, James Roger. *American Politics in the Early Republic: The New Nation in Crisis.* New Haven: Yale University Press, 1993. This work is an excellent general overview of the 1790s. Briefer than Elkins and McKitrick, *The Age of Federalism* (1993) (5:350), this book does a better job of emphasizing the fragility of the union throughout the 1790s and, especially, during the period leading to the election of 1800. Bibliography.

5:359   Smelser, Marshall. "The Federalist Period as an Age of Passion." *American Quarterly* 10 (Winter 1958): 391–419. The author shows that the Federalist era, especially after 1793, was characterized by obsessive political passions: Federalists saw Jacobin plots everywhere, and Republicans believed that the Federalists intended to crush republicanism. In "The Jacobin Phrenzy: The Menace of Monarchy, Plutocracy, and Anglophilia, 1789–1798," *Review of Politics* 21 (April 1959): 239–58, he concentrates on Republican obsessions; see also his "The Jacobin Phrenzy: Federalism and the Menace of Liberty, Equality, and Fraternity," ibid. 13 (July 1951): 457–82.

5:360   White, Leonard D. *The Federalists: A Study in Administrative History.* New York: Macmillan Company, 1948. Reprint 1978 (Greenwood Press). Dated and occasionally mistaken in its political inferences, this book is useful on the workings of the State Department (1789–1801) and on Hamilton's interference with Jefferson's conduct of foreign affairs. The author makes it clear that President Washington controlled his administration, while President Adams did not.

POLITICAL PARTIES

5:361   Appleby, Joyce. *Capitalism and a New Social Order: The Republican Vision of the 1790s.* New York: New York University Press, 1984. This book is the most important work for the liberal interpretation of Jeffersonian Republicanism. The author's understanding of the 1790s and the Republicans highlights the importance of foreign commerce, particularly in the form of neutral trade during the wars of the French revolution.

5:362 Banning, Lance. *The Jeffersonian Persuasion: Evolution of a Party Ideology.* Ithaca: Cornell University Press, 1978. Banning's study of the origins of political parties in the 1790s places the Jeffersonian Republicans squarely in the classical republican tradition. Key events in the emergence of political parties for Banning include the French revolution, the Quasi-War, and the Alien and Sedition Acts.

5:363 Cunningham, Noble E., Jr. *The Jeffersonian Republicans: The Formation of Party Organization, 1789–1801.* Chapel Hill: University of North Carolina Press for the Institute of Early American History and Culture, 1957. This standard work on the early Republican Party is especially useful on the influence of the French revolution and the Anglo-French war on party development in the United States. Bibliography.

5:364 Dauer, Manning J. *The Adams Federalists.* Baltimore: Johns Hopkins Press, 1953. President Adams is portrayed as an able political leader whose pursuit of a moderate course, recognizing the claims of both the agrarian and mercantile interests, isolated the Hamiltonians and provided continuity in American domestic and foreign policies. Extensive bibliography.

5:365 Durey, Michael. *Transatlantic Radicals and the Early American Republic.* Lawrence: University Press of Kansas, 1997. Durey traces the careers of a number of political refugees who were driven from the British Isles in the 1790s, went to the United States, and became newspaper editors and writers. Fiercely egalitarian and anti-British, most of them became Jeffersonians. Despite the Alien and Sedition Acts that largely targeted them, they reached their peak of influence in the late 1790s and helped Jefferson win the election of 1800. Extensive bibliography. Of interest as well is David A. Wilson, *United Irishmen, United States: Immigrant Radicals in the Early Republic* (Ithaca: Cornell University Press, 1998).

5:366 Hofstadter, Richard. *The Idea of a Party System: The Rise of Legitimate Opposition in the United States, 1780–1840.* Berkeley: University of California Press, 1969. This thoughtful study, by highlighting the persistence of antiparty sentiment, is a useful corrective to the tendency to view politics in the early national period as a contest between clearly defined Republican and Federalist Parties. From a different angle, it makes somewhat the same point as Young's *The Washington Community, 1800–1828* (1966) (5:400).

MILITARY POLICY

5:367 Cress, Lawrence Delbert. *Citizens in Arms: The Army and the Militia in American Society to the War of 1812.* Chapel Hill: University of North Carolina Press, 1982. This book examines the ideal of the citizen-soldier in republican ideology and finds it indicative less of antimilitary sentiment than of a hostility to central authority and power. Cress argues that this ideal changed in the decades after the revolution. Bibliography.

5:368 Hagan, Kenneth J., and William R. Roberts, eds. *Against All Enemies: Interpretations of American Military History from Colonial Times to the Present.* Westport, CT: Greenwood Press, 1986. This collection includes two essays of particular value for scholars of early national military policy: Lawrence Delbert Cress's "Reassessing American Military Requirements, 1783–1807" (49–69) and Harry L. Coles's "From Peaceable Coercion to Balanced Forces, 1807–1815" (71–89).

5:369 Jacobs, James Ripley. *The Beginning of the U.S. Army, 1783–1812.* Princeton: Princeton University Press, 1947. Although largely concerned with Indian campaigns, this volume is the fullest history of the founding of the regular army. The evolution of tactical and administrative organization is well handled. Bibliography.

5:370 Kohn, Richard H. *Eagle and Sword: The Federalists and the Creation of the Military Establishment in America, 1783–1802.* New York: Free Press, 1975. If Alexander Hamilton had his way, the U.S. army might have become active in domestic politics and would also have been designed for international adventures. Kohn's is the standard political-military history of the army's most politicized period. Extensive bibliography.

5:371 Koistinen, Paul A. C. *Beating Plowshares into Swords: The Political Economy of American Warfare, 1606–1865.* Lawrence: University Press of Kansas, 1996. Koistinen covers the period through the War of 1812 relatively quickly. He argues that "political disorganization" throughout this era consistently undermined military power by making it harder to harness the economy to military production.

5:372 Nichols, Roger L. "From the Revolution to the Mexican War." In *A Guide to the Sources of United States Military History,* ed. Robin Higham, 125–51. Hamden, CT: Archon Books, 1975. This essay contains a few items on the Quasi-War, but it is most valuable on the establishment of the peacetime army after the revolution.

5:373 Smelser, Marshall. *The Congress Founds the Navy, 1787–1798.* Notre Dame, IN: University of Notre Dame Press, 1959. Smelser reviews the congressional debates about the navy and treats equally those who championed naval power and those who viewed it with reluctance. Bibliography.

5:374 Stuart, Reginald C. *War and American Thought: From the Revolution to the Monroe Doctrine.* Kent, OH: Kent State University Press, 1982. Stuart tracks evolving attitudes toward war among the politicians and policymakers of the revolutionary generation between the 1770s and the 1820s. Looking at the Constitutional Convention, the disputes between Federalists and Republicans, and the War of 1812, he explores the links between military and foreign policy. Bibliographic essay.

5:375 Symonds, Craig L. *Navalists and Anti-navalists: The Naval Policy Debate in the United States, 1785–1827.* Newark: University of Delaware Press, 1980. In this study of the origins of the navy, Symonds contradicts the conventional wisdom by downplaying party divisions and arguing that those who wanted a navy large enough to affect the European balance of power were unrealistic. Bibliography.

5:376 Ward, Harry M. *The Department of War, 1781–1795.* Pittsburgh: University of Pittsburgh Press, 1962. Reprint 1981 (Greenwood Press). The development of the War Department and the army under the Confederation progressed far enough, notwithstanding lack of funds, to lend some support to the thesis that the Confederation might in time have evolved into an effective government; the Washington administration built on an established foundation. See also Jacobs, *The Beginning of the U.S. Army, 1783–1812* (1947) (5:369).

NEUTRALITY

5:377 Adams, Donald R., Jr. "American Neutrality and Prosperity, 1793–1808: A Reconsideration." *Journal of Economic History* 40 (December 1980): 713–37. Adams finds that the only real benefits of neutrality for the American economy were to the re-export trade and, thus, were highly concentrated among already wealthy eastern merchants. Otherwise, he contends, economic growth between the onset of the European wars and the Embargo was consistent with long-term trends.

5:378 Bukovansky, Mlada. "American Identity and Neutral Rights from Independence to the War of 1812." *International Organization* 51 (Spring 1997): 209–43. The author, a political scientist, advances a constructionist argument about the American commitment to neutral rights, seeing it as a key to American self-identity. A liberal view of neutral rights was thus a critical American interest, even though the United States was not strong enough to enforce it at the time.

5:379 Clauder, Anna Cornelia. *American Commerce as Affected by the Wars of the French Revolution and Napoleon, 1793–1810.* Philadelphia: University of Pennsylvania, 1932. Reprint 1972 (A. M. Kelley). This work attempts only to weigh the impact on American trade of European restrictions, not to understand the origins of those restrictions. Because the scene shifted so frequently, few clear and persistent themes emerge, but the data presented are important for understanding the period. Bibliography.

5:380 Curtis, Roy Emerson. "The Law of Hostile Military Expeditions as Applied by the United States." *American Journal of International Law* 8 (January 1914, April 1914): 1–37, 224–55. Curtis provides a useful legal background for understanding the federal government's efforts to prevent incursions by American citizens into neighboring countries.

Unfortunately, he makes no effort to show the chronological development of these laws, opting instead to treat the period from the 1780s to the 1910s as a unit.

5:381   Forbes, John D. "European Wars and Boston Trade, 1783–1815." *New England Quarterly* 11 (December 1938): 709–30. Forbes chronicles the ebb and flow of Boston's foreign trade in response to external (European wars) and internal (economic sanctions and warfare) developments.

5:382   Goldin, Claudia D., and Frank D. Lewis. "The Role of Exports in American Economic Growth during the Napoleonic Wars, 1793 to 1807." *Explorations in Economic History* 17 (January 1980): 6–25. Like Adams, "American Neutrality and Prosperity, 1793–1808: A Reconsideration" (1980) (5:377), this article downplays the economic benefits of the European wars for the American economy between 1793 and the Embargo. By tracking changes in per capita income, the authors find little spillover from the shipping and export sectors to the general economy.

FAREWELL ADDRESS

5:383   Bemis, Samuel Flagg. "Washington's Farewell Address: A Foreign Policy of Independence." *American Historical Review* 39 (January 1934): 250–68. Although long the standard treatment, the author's claim that the address has "ever since [been] a polestar of American foreign policy" has increasingly been questioned in recent years.

5:384   DeConde, Alexander. "Washington's Farewell, the French Alliance, and the Election of 1796." *Mississippi Valley Historical Review* 43 (March 1957): 641–58. The farewell address is viewed as a partisan campaign document shaped largely by Hamilton to influence the 1796 election. Washington's famous warnings were directed against the Republican opposition and the French alliance.

5:385   Fry, Joseph A. "Washington's Farewell Address and American Commerce." *West Virginia History* 37 (July 1976): 281–90. The author maintains that Alexander Hamilton was solely responsible for the section of the address devoted to foreign commerce, which sought to guarantee close commercial ties with Great Britain.

5:386   Kaufman, Burton I., ed. *Washington's Farewell Address: The View from the 20th Century.* Chicago: Quadrangle Books, 1969. This collection of essays on the farewell address published from 1899 to 1969 provides a useful survey of changing interpretations. Individual essays: Robert Ellis Jones, "Washington's Farewell Address and Its Applications" (35–52); Roland G. Usher, "Washington and Entangling Alliances" (53–62); St. George Leakin Sioussat, "The Farewell Address in the Twentieth Century" (67–81); J. G. Randall, "George Washington and 'Entangling Alliances'" (82–88); Samuel Flagg Bemis, "Washington's Farewell Address: A Foreign Policy of Independence" (89–110); Alexander DeConde, "Washington's Farewell, the French Alliance, and the Election of 1796" (116–36); Nathan Schachner, "Washington's Farewell" (137–50); Felix Gilbert, "The Farewell Address" (151–68); and Kaufman, "Washington's Farewell Address: A Statement of Empire" (169–87). Bibliography.

5:387   Markovitz, Arthur A. "Washington's Farewell Address and the Historians: A Critical Review." *Pennsylvania Magazine of History and Biography* 44 (April 1970): 173–91. This essay reviews the historiography of the address and concludes: "Only a person lacking historical insight into the period would argue that Washington's valedictory was a noble and disinterested legacy to the nation."

5:388   Paltsits, Victor H., ed. *Washington's Farewell Address: In Facsimile, with Transliterations of All the Drafts of Washington, Madison, & Hamilton Together with Their Correspondence and Other Supporting Documents.* New York: New York Public Library, 1935. This work contains successive drafts of the address by Washington, Madison, and Hamilton, together with their correspondence and other supporting documents. Extensive bibliography.

5:389   Pessen, Edward. "George Washington's Farewell Address, the Cold War, and the Timeless National Interest." *Journal of the Early Republic* 7 (Spring 1987): 1–27. This essay, Pessen's presidential address to the Society of Historians of the Early American Republic, argues that Washington's analysis of world politics and American interests still had value in the cold war era.

5:390   Rossignol, Marie-Jeanne. "Early Isolationism Revisited: Neutrality and Beyond in the 1790s." *Journal of American Studies* 29 (August 1995): 215–27. By insisting on the importance of viewing Washington's farewell address in the context of domestic and foreign limits to American action, Rossignol demonstrates that it was a "realistic appeal to caution" far more than an idealistic statement of an eternal "isolationist" principle. Rossignol's interesting views of early American foreign policy are developed more fully in *Le ferment nationaliste: Aux origines de la politique extérieure des États-Unis, 1789–1812* (Paris: Belin, 1994).

5:391   Spalding, Matthew, and Patrick J. Garrity. *A Sacred Union of Citizens: George Washington's Farewell Address and the American Character.* Lanham, MD: Rowman and Littlefield, 1996. This recent study of Washington's valedictory emphasizes the first president's desire to shape a national character that was suited to a republican government as well as the subsequent impact of the address.

Jeffersonian Era

5:392   Cunningham, Noble E., Jr. *The Process of Government under Jefferson.* Princeton: Princeton University Press, 1978. This detailed study examines the administrative processes of the executive and legislative branches of government during Jefferson's administrations. While there is very little that bears directly on American diplomacy, the volume is useful because it explores such things as the relationship between the president and his lieutenants and the locations of influence in Congress. Bibliography.

5:393   Graber, Doris A. *Public Opinion, the President, and Foreign Policy: Four Case Studies from the Formative Years.* New York: Holt, Rinehart and Winston, 1968. While pointing out that the early presidents' concepts of public sentiment varied a good deal, Graber suggests that in the cases under review (including Louisiana and the war decision of 1812) the influence of public opinion was small. Interesting for methodology, the study suffers from a paucity of research and a lack of historical sophistication.

5:394   Haskins, George Lee, and Herbert A. Johnson. *History of the Supreme Court of the United States. Vol. 2: Foundations of Power: John Marshall, 1801–15.* New York: Macmillan Publishing Co., 1981. Though oddly organized, this book provides a comprehensive account of the first fifteen years of the Marshall Court. During this period, the Court ruled on a variety of issues that touched on American foreign relations, including Embargo violations and other forms of smuggling, prize law and other matters of international law, and questions raised by the Burr Conspiracy.

5:395   McDonald, Forrest. *The Presidency of Thomas Jefferson.* Lawrence: University Press of Kansas, 1976. McDonald's generally critical account of Jefferson's presidency includes both domestic and foreign affairs, with a slight tilt in favor of the latter. It is valuable as a brief counterweight to the pertinent volumes of Dumas Malone's more favorable biography. Bibliographic essay.

5:396   Rutland, Robert Allen. *The Presidency of James Madison.* Lawrence: University Press of Kansas, 1990. Rutland's broad survey of Madison's presidency focuses, not surprisingly, on diplomatic and military issues. It is generally balanced and commends Madison for accepting constitutional limits that make him look ineffective from a modern perspective. Bibliographic essay.

5:397   Smelser, Marshall. *The Democratic Republic, 1801–1815.* New York: Harper and Row, 1968. Essentially a work of synthesis, this study sometimes seems to meld rather than compare or evaluate contradictory interpretations, and on other occasions it follows rather than builds on standard accounts. All things considered, however, this now dated work remains a useful introduction to American politics and diplomacy in this period. Extensive bibliography and useful footnotes.

5:398   Sofaer, Abraham D. *War, Foreign Affairs, and Constitutional Power. Vol. 1: The Origins.* This groundbreaking study by a legal historian explores the extent of the president's diplomatic and war powers. It discusses such issues as the Louisiana Purchase, the West Florida annexation, the Embargo, and the War of 1812. The first of a two-volume study (2:229).

5:399 White, Leonard D. *The Jeffersonians: A Study in Administrative History, 1801–1829.* New York: Macmillan, 1951. Jefferson's managerial style, the methods of conducting diplomacy, and Gallatin's difficulties in enforcing the Embargo are among the topics examined by White.

5:400 Young, James Sterling. *The Washington Community, 1800–1828.* New York: Columbia University Press, 1966. Young offers an intriguing account of the physical conditions of governance in the new national capital and their impact on the process of government. This often intricate, occasionally overstated study argues that, after a brief period of successful leadership by Jefferson, presidents lost control of Congress, in part because the Republican Party was composed of uncontrollable blocs with little loyalty to its leaders or its policies.

DOMESTIC POLITICS

5:401 Banner, James M., Jr. *To the Hartford Convention: The Federalists and the Origins of Party Politics in Massachusetts, 1789–1815.* New York: Alfred A. Knopf, 1970. This thoroughly researched and forcefully argued study sheds much light on the setting for diplomacy. Banner not only exposes Federalist errors and inconsistencies, he makes their positions understandable and goes far to explain their rise and fall. Bibliography.

5:402 Cunningham, Noble E., Jr. *The Jeffersonian Republicans in Power: Party Operations, 1801–1809.* Chapel Hill: University of North Carolina Press for the Institute of Early American History and Culture, 1963. This sequel to *The Jeffersonian Republicans: The Formation of Party Organization, 1789–1801* (1957) (5:363) concentrates in perhaps excessive detail on organization and operation. Among its strengths are an exposure of the differences between states and an examination of the congressional caucus as an instrument of leadership. Bibliographical note.

5:403 Fischer, David Hackett. *The Revolution of American Conservatism: The Federalist Party in the Era of Jeffersonian Democracy.* New York: Harper and Row, 1965. In this stimulating study of patterns of party behavior, Fischer argues that Federalists, if reluctantly and defensively, abandoned their deferential view of politics and embraced a majoritarian one.

5:404 Kerber, Linda K. *Federalists in Dissent: Imagery and Ideology in Jeffersonian America.* Ithaca: Cornell University Press, 1970. Kerber's interest is in ideology far more than either domestic or foreign politics, but she provides a thought-provoking analysis of articulate Federalists during the era of Jeffersonian ascendancy. Bibliographic essay.

5:405 Mason, Matthew E. "Slavery Overshadowed: Congress Debates Prohibiting the Atlantic Slave Trade to the United States, 1806–1807." *Journal of the Early Republic* 20 (Spring 2000): 59–81. Mason's analysis of the congressional debates over the prohibition of the Atlantic slave trade demonstrates that they took place with relatively little press or public attention, due in large part to the overshadowing presence of the Burr Conspiracy and rising tensions with Great Britain. During the congressional debates, however, arguments were aired and positions taken that foreshadowed later crises over slavery.

5:406 Risjord, Norman K. *The Old Republicans: Southern Conservatism in the Age of Jefferson.* New York: Columbia University Press, 1965. Although Risjord's primary purpose is to identify the "Old Republicans," a faction led by John Randolph that resisted nationalizing tendencies, his discussion of Republican schisms, the nature of presidential leadership, and the decision for war in 1812 sheds broad light on the period. Extensive bibliography.

MILITARY POLICY

5:407 Crackel, Theodore J. *Mr. Jefferson's Army: Political and Social Reform of the Military Establishment, 1801–1809.* New York: New York University Press, 1987. In this valuable book, Crackel demonstrates that Jefferson did not, as is often supposed and as Jefferson himself sometimes claimed, slash the size of the armed forces and the defense budget. Instead, he adopted far more subtle means of breaking the army's ties to the Federalists and harnessing it to republican government. Bibliography. For a précis of this argument, see "Jefferson, Politics, and the Army: An Examination of the Military Peace Establishment

Act of 1802," *Journal of the Early Republic* 2 (April 1982): 21–38.

5:408 MacLeod, Julia H. "Jefferson and the Navy: A Defense." *Huntington Library Quarterly* 8 (February 1945): 153–84. MacLeod seeks to correct the impression that Jefferson was entirely hostile to the development of a navy. Jefferson advocated the use of force against the Barbary pirates, believing it less costly than the payment of tribute. But he opposed an untimely naval expansion before the country's economic resources could support it.

5:409 Smith, Gene A. *"For the Purposes of Defense": The Politics of the Jeffersonian Gunboat Program.* Newark: University of Delaware Press, 1995. Smith examines the ideological and political considerations that led to Jefferson's heavy reliance on the often criticized gunboats. Bibliography. For a different perspective, which highlights the actual use of these ships during the Embargo and War of 1812, see Spencer C. Tucker, *The Jeffersonian Gunboat Navy* (Columbia: University of South Carolina Press, 1993).

Regions

NORTH AMERICA

5:410 Adelman, Jeremy, and Stephen Aron. "From Borderlands to Borders: Empires, Nation-States, and the Peoples in Between in North American History." *American Historical Review* 104 (June 1999): 814–41. Building on the framework of Herbert Bolton, the authors attempt to erect a synthesis of North American history by focusing on intercultural relations on frontiers. They contend that independent nations, particularly the United States, demanded far more exclusive borders and far more restricted interactions than had the colonial powers.

5:411 Chevigny, Hector. *Russian America: The Great Alaskan Venture, 1741–1867.* New York: Viking Press, 1965. Reprint 1979 (Binford and Mort). This history surveys the exploration and settlement of Alaska. It provides useful background for one of the issues addressed by John Quincy Adams as

the first American minister to Russia between 1809 and 1814. Bibliography.

5:412 Clark, Thomas D., and John D. W. Guice. *Frontiers in Conflict: The Old Southwest, 1795–1830.* Albuquerque: University of New Mexico Press, 1989. Reprint 1996 (University of Oklahoma Press). This work provides a solid overview of developments in the area that would become the states of Mississippi and Alabama. Clark and Guice are generally successful in their effort to integrate social, economic, political, diplomatic, and military issues; they provide rich accounts of boundary disputes, filibustering, the War of 1812, and the Creek War. Bibliography.

5:413 Gibson, James R. *Imperial Russia in Frontier America: The Changing Geography of Supply of Russian America, 1784–1867.* New York: Oxford University Press, 1976. Gibson recounts the supply problems that the Russian-American Company never fully overcame. Although this study deals principally with the company, its bibliography includes nearly all secondary works, published in Russian, English, and French prior to 1976, relating to Russian colonization in North America.

5:414 Kushner, Howard I. *Conflict on the Northwest Coast: American-Russian Rivalry in the Pacific Northwest, 1790–1867.* Westport, CT: Greenwood Press, 1975. Kushner's emphasis is on American-Russian relations leading to the Alaska purchase. But he includes details on American commercial expansion into the Pacific northwest in the context of the fur trade with China. Bibliography.

5:415 Ronda, James P. *Astoria & Empire.* Lincoln: University of Nebraska Press, 1990. Ronda provides a thorough account of John Jacob Astor's fur trading outpost at the mouth of the Columbia River. He situates it within both its commercial and diplomatic contexts, discussing its relations with Indians and Europeans, particularly the British, and describing its expected role in linking the fur trade and the China trade. Bibliography.

5:416 Wright, J. Leitch, Jr. *Britain and the American Frontier, 1783–1815.* Athens, GA: University of Georgia Press, 1975. The author omits no important interface among Great Britain, Spain, France, the United States, and the Indians. Wright clearly understands the dynamics of frontier encounters, whether in East and West Florida or in the Old Northwest during the 1790–1794 Anglo-American crisis brought about by the Nootka Sound incident. Extensive bibliography.

Frontier and Backcountry

5:417   Allen, Michael. "The Federalists and the West, 1783–1803." *Western Pennsylvania Historical Magazine* 61 (October 1978): 315–32. In a wide-ranging discussion of ideas and policies regarding the early west, Allen shows the Federalists to have been, at best, reluctant expansionists in the two decades before the Louisiana Purchase. He examines the approach of men such as John Jay, Rufus King, and Timothy Pickering to such western interests as land policy, Indian affairs, statehood, and the opening of the Mississippi River to American trade.

5:418   Bemis, Samuel Flagg. "Relations between the Vermont Separatists and Great Britain, 1789–1791." *American Historical Review* 21 (April 1916): 547–60. Bemis introduces and reprints six documents on negotiations between leading Vermonters and British officials in both Canada and London concerning the future of the then independent nation.

5:419   Cayton, Andrew R. L. "'Separate Interests' and the Nation-State: The Washington Administration and the Origins of Regionalism in the Trans-Appalachian West." *Journal of American History* 79 (June 1992): 39–67. Cayton sees the Washington administration's contrasting policies toward the Indians north and south of the Ohio River as an important basis for regional differentiation within the west.

5:420   Farnham, Thomas J. "Kentucky and Washington's Mississippi Policy of Patience and Persuasion." *Register of the Kentucky Historical Society* 64 (January 1966): 14–28. In the mid-1790s, Kentuckians supported more forcible measures against Spain than the Washington administration regarding the Mississippi River. Following the abortive Genet-Clark invasion of Louisiana, Kentuckians continued their pressure, helping to force the negotiations that resulted in Pinckney's Treaty.

5:421   Green, Thomas Marshall. *The Spanish Conspiracy: A Review of Early Spanish Movements in the South-West. Containing Proofs of the Intrigues of James Wilkinson and John Brown; of the Complicity Therewith of Judges Sebastian, Wallace, and Innes; the Early Struggles of Kentucky for Autonomy; the Intrigues of Sebastian in 1795–7, and the Legislative Investigation of His Corruption.* Cincinnati: Robert Clarke and Co., 1891. Written by a grandson of Humphrey Marshall, the most prominent Federalist in early Kentucky and the most inveterate foe of the alleged conspirators, this book barely pretends to be an impartial history. Still, it is essential, though difficult, reading for anyone interested in this curious episode in early American foreign affairs.

5:422   Horsman, Reginald. *The Frontier in the Formative Years, 1783–1815.* New York: Holt, Rinehart and Winston, 1970. Working with a fairly Turnerian idea of the frontier as the leading edge of white settlement, Horsman sees these decades as a tragic period for the Indians, and often for the settlers as well. The emphasis in this book is on the process of settlement rather than on policymaking and diplomacy. Bibliographic essay.

5:423   Nobles, Gregory H. "Breaking into the Backcountry: New Approaches to the Early American Frontier, 1750–1800." *William and Mary Quarterly* 3d ser. 46 (October 1989): 641–70. Though more interested in the political and social than the diplomatic history of the early frontier, this historiographical essay provides a useful overview of recent work, highlighting the similarities between various frontier and backcountry areas and their differences from eastern urban centers and farm districts.

5:424   Onuf, Peter S. "State-Making in Revolutionary America: Independent Vermont as a Case Study." *Journal of American History* 67 (March 1981): 797–815. As an independent nation outside the union between 1777 and 1791, Vermont's existence was intolerable to many Americans for a combination of reasons, including diplomatic ones, since its independence encouraged British overtures and interference.

5:425   Rohrbough, Malcolm J. *The Trans-Appalachian Frontier: People, Societies, and Institutions, 1775–1850.* New York: Oxford University

Press, 1978. Rohrbough provides a solid overview of the history of the trans-Appalachian west, covering political, economic, and social developments. The first two (of six) parts address the period to the end of the War of 1812. Bibliography.

5:426 Shepherd, William R. "Wilkinson and the Beginnings of the Spanish Conspiracy." *American Historical Review* 9 (April 1909): 490–506. Relying on documents in the Spanish archives, this early article demonstrates that James Wilkinson, rather than Spanish officials in New Orleans, suggested a political connection with the west.

5:427 Slaughter, Thomas P. *The Whiskey Rebellion: Frontier Epilogue to the American Revolution.* New York: Oxford University Press, 1986. Unlike most accounts of the Whiskey Rebellion, Slaughter's makes clear the concerns over foreign involvement—particularly Spanish or British—and western separatism. He depicts a struggle between "friends of liberty" (the rebels and their supporters) and "friends of order" (Washington, Hamilton, and the Federalists).

5:428 Tachau, Mary K. Bonsteel. *Federal Courts in the Early Republic: Kentucky, 1789–1816.* Princeton: Princeton University Press, 1978. This book is both broader and narrower than its title suggests. In the early period, it closely follows the life and career of federal judge Harry Innes. But Innes was a central figure in the Spanish Conspiracy and subsequent western separatism; Tachau also has much to say about the Whiskey Rebellion and the Burr Conspiracy in Kentucky. Bibliography. Also helpful is her article on "The Whiskey Rebellion in Kentucky: A Forgotten Episode of Civil Disobedience," *Journal of the Early Republic* 2 (Fall 1982): 239–59.

5:429 Turner, Frederick Jackson, ed. "Documents on the Blount Conspiracy, 1795–1797." *American Historical Review* 10 (April 1905): 574–606. Records are printed from the British Public Record Office, the Department of State, and the Archives du Ministère des Affaires Etrangères to illustrate the plan for frontiersmen, Indians, and a British expedition from Canada to seize Louisiana and the Floridas from Spain before France did so.

5:430 Warren, Elizabeth. "Senator John Brown's Role in the Kentucky Spanish Conspiracy." *Filson Club Historical Quarterly* 36 (April 1962): 158–76. Warren clears John Brown of any serious complicity in General James Wilkinson's Spanish Conspiracy (1787–1792), contending that historians have read too much into Brown's conversations with Diego de Gardoqui and given too much credence to Wilkinson's readiness to identify Brown as an enthusiastic separatist.

5:431 Watlington, Patricia. *The Partisan Spirit: Kentucky Politics, 1779–1792.* New York: Atheneum, 1972. Watlington's account of early Kentucky includes a solid account of the Spanish Conspiracy, which she views as fairly limited in scope. See also her "John Brown and the Spanish Conspiracy," *Virginia Magazine of History and Biography* 75 (January 1967): 52–68. Bibliography.

5:432 Williams, Samuel Cole. *History of the Lost State of Franklin.* Johnson City, TN: Watauga Press, 1924. This work provides a detailed account of the Franklin movement in western Virginia and North Carolina between 1784 and 1788, linking it to Spain's closure of the Mississippi River among other factors. It includes brief biographies of the key figures as well as some key documents. Bibliography.

Indian Affairs

5:433 Allen, Robert S. *His Majesty's Indian Allies: British Indian Policy in the Defence of Canada, 1774–1815.* Toronto: Dundurn Press, 1992. Allen provides a more chronological, policy-oriented approach to British-Indian relations in the Great Lakes region leading up to the War of 1812 than Calloway, *Crown and Calumet: British-Indian Relations, 1783–1815* (1987) (5:434). As such, it makes a useful counterpart to Horsman, *Expansion and American Indian Policy, 1783–1812* (1967) (5:439). Bibliography.

5:434 Calloway, Colin G. *Crown and Calumet: British-Indian Relations, 1783–1815.* Norman: University of Oklahoma Press, 1987. Calloway presents less a chronological account than a study of how the British and Indians viewed and understood each other. He suggests that their respective assessments were based on commerce and military ability rather than race. Extensive bibliography.

5:435 Cayton, Andrew R. L. "'Noble Actors' upon 'the Theatre of Honour': Power and Civility in the Treaty of Greenville." In *Contact Points: American Frontiers from the Mohawk Valley to the Mississippi, 1750–1830*, ed. Andrew R. L. Cayton and Fredrika J. Teute, 235–69. Chapel Hill: University of North Carolina Press, 1998. Cayton examines the commonalities and conflicts in the differing views of diplomacy and treaty-making at the conference that produced the Treaty of Greenville that temporarily ended the Indian wars in the Northwest Territory in 1795.

5:436 Dowd, Gregory Evans. *A Spirited Resistance: The North American Indian Struggle for Unity, 1745–1815.* This work tracks the rise and fall of a succession of efforts to develop pan-Indian sensibility and cooperation, frequently grounded in prophetic visions, in the trans-Appalachian west. The years between the revolution and the Treaty of Greenville marked one of the high points of coordinated action, as did the cooperation of northern Shawnees, led by Tecumseh, and southern Creeks in the period before and during the War of 1812 (3:143).

5:437 Griffith, Benjamin W., Jr. *McIntosh and Weatherford, Creek Indian Leaders.* Tuscaloosa: University of Alabama Press, 1988. This book is an intriguing joint biography of two Creek leaders of the Jeffersonian era, William McIntosh and William Weatherford. By the time of the Creek War, their paths had diverged so fully that McIntosh cooperated with Andrew Jackson, and Weatherford led the anti-American Red Stick faction. Bibliography.

5:438 Horsman, Reginald. "British Indian Policy in the Northwest, 1807–1812." *Mississippi Valley Historical Review* 45 (June 1958): 51–66. Horsman demonstrates that British Indian policy was essentially negative, precautionary, and defensive in purpose. Still, the acquisitiveness of Americans, the consequent Indian resistance, and the overzealousness of British agents created an explosive situation. Horsman elaborates on these themes in *Matthew Elliott, British Indian Agent* (Detroit: Wayne State University Press, 1964).

5:439 _____. *Expansion and American Indian Policy, 1783–1812.* East Lansing: Michigan State University Press, 1967. Reprint 1992 (University of Oklahoma Press). The author describes the tension between expansionist pressures and the belief that the Indian tribes should be fairly treated; he also explains the emerging difficulties in the trans-Appalachian west leading to the War of 1812. The author focuses substantially on the lingering warfare between the end of the revolution and the Treaty of Greenville.

5:440 McLoughlin, William G. *Cherokee Renascence in the New Republic.* Princeton: Princeton University Press, 1986. With this informative and provocative book, McLoughlin does a much better job than in most studies of Cherokee removal of describing the emergence of the Cherokee nation and its interactions with the federal and state governments over the full course of the early national period. The Cherokees formed the most important test of Jeffersonian Indian policies. Bibliography.

5:441 Prucha, Francis Paul. *American Indian Policy in the Formative Years: The Indian Trade and Intercourse Acts, 1790–1834.* Cambridge, MA: Harvard University Press, 1962. Reprint 1998 (W. S. Hein). Prucha offers a thorough account of the key statement of early federal Indian policy, the Trade and Intercourse Acts, as they were first set up by Washington and Henry Knox in the early 1790s and later modified by Jefferson and Henry Dearborn. The goal was to regulate trade and remove intruders from Indian lands to preserve the peace; the problem was that the government either could not or would not enforce the acts. Bibliographic essay.

5:442 _____. *American Indian Treaties: The History of a Political Anomaly.* Berkeley: University of California Press, 1994. In this fascinating work, Prucha explores in depth the logic and illogic of Indian treaties. The federal government negotiated treaties with the Indians as with European powers, but did not acknowledge the full sovereignty of Indian nations. Bibliography.

5:443 _____. *The Great Father: The United States Government and the American Indians.* This broad survey of federal Indian policy covers warfare, trade, and diplomacy. The last of four parts in the first volume spans the period from the end of the revolution until removal (2:431).

5:444   Sheehan, Bernard W. *Seeds of Extinction: Jeffersonian Philanthropy and the American Indian.* Chapel Hill: University of North Carolina Press for the Institute of Early American History and Culture, 1973. This intellectual history of early American Indian policy sets up the ideas about the Indian, civilization, and savagery available to the first generation of policymakers, including Washington, Knox, and Jefferson. A commitment to "civilizing" the Indians provided a basic consistency between Federalists and Republicans, who wanted what they believed was best for the Indians, but were limited by "a failure of the intellect."

5:445   Smith, Dwight L. "A North American Neutral Indian Zone: Persistence of a British Idea." *Northwest Ohio Quarterly* 61 (Spring-Summer-Autumn 1989): 46–63. Smith traces the British idea of an Indian buffer state in the upper Ohio Valley and Great Lakes region from the 1750s until its final appearance as a proposal during the Ghent negotiations of 1814.

5:446   Smith, F. Todd. *The Caddo Indians: Tribes at the Convergence of Empires, 1542–1854.* College Station: Texas A&M Press, 1995. Smith situates the Caddos between Spain and the United States, recognizing that they were "a key to the diplomacy of the region" in the early years after the Louisiana Purchase. Only one chapter covers the period from 1803 to 1815; it was previously published as "The Kadohadacho Indians and the Louisiana-Texas Frontier, 1803–1815," *Southwestern Historical Quarterly* 95 (October 1991): 177–204. Bibliography.

5:447   Sugden, John. "The Southern Indians in the War of 1812: The Closing Phase." *Florida Historical Quarterly* 60 (January 1982): 273–312. Sugden shows that British designs on the Gulf Coast in the final months of the War of 1812 helped reinvigorate the hostility of Creeks and Seminoles, who had essentially stopped fighting after the Battle of Horseshoe Bend. This article is particularly useful for setting up the conditions that led to the First Seminole War in 1817–1818.

5:448   Sword, Wiley. *President Washington's Indian War: The Struggle for the Old Northwest, 1790–1795.* Norman: University of Oklahoma Press, 1985. This is the first comprehensive history of the Indian war in the Old Northwest from 1790 to 1795. Fairly workmanlike, it is with few exceptions narrow in focus and chronologically organized. Bibliography.

5:449   Wallace, Anthony F. C. *Jefferson and the Indians: The Tragic Fate of the First Americans.* Cambridge, MA: Belknap Press of Harvard University Press, 1999. Wallace examines Jefferson's attitudes, beliefs, and policies and finds them to have been often hypocritical and duplicitous. The unintended consequences of Jefferson's policies were often catastrophic for the Indians.

5:450   White, Richard. *The Middle Ground: Indians, Empires, and Republics in the Great Lakes Region, 1650–1815.* One of the most important works on Indian-white interactions of the last quarter century, this book's account of the "middle ground" has had a tremendous impact on historical views of the frontier. While most of this book focuses on the period before 1765, it ends with strong chapters on the impact of the American revolution and the post-revolutionary era on the Old Northwest (3:176).

5:451   Wright, J. Leitch, Jr. *Creeks & Seminoles: The Destruction and Regeneration of the Muscogulge People.* Lincoln: University of Nebraska Press, 1986. Wright offers a wide-ranging, ethnohistorical account of the Creek and Seminole Indians. Included are thorough discussions of their complex relations with the British, Spanish, and with Americans and the Creek War. Bibliography.

British Canada

5:452   Brebner, John Bartlet. *North Atlantic Triangle: The Interplay of Canada, the United States and Great Britain.* See chapter 2 of this Guide (2:323).

5:453   Burt, Alfred L. *The United States, Great Britain, and British North America from the Revolution to the Establishment of Peace after the War of 1812.* New Haven: Yale University Press, 1940. This long standard work's discussion of the Jay Treaty highlights the often neglected Canadian aspects. It deals much more with the coming of the War of 1812 than with the Ghent negotiations. Particularly noteworthy is his challenge, unusual for its time, to the emphasis on western ambitions as the major cause of the War of 1812. Burt relies chiefly on published government documents, rather than archival material, although he incorporates the work of other scholars.

5:454   Errington, Jane. *The Lion, the Eagle, and Upper Canada: A Developing Colonial Ideology.* Kingston, Ontario: McGill-Queen's University Press, 1987. Errington provides a useful counterpart to Stuart, "Special Interests and National Authority in Foreign Policy: American-British Provincial Links during the Embargo and the War of 1812" (1984) (5:459) by examining the tangled and divided loyalties of the upper St. Lawrence valley and lower Great Lakes region during the Embargo and War of 1812 from the Canadian side. Bibliography.

5:455   Graffagnino, J. Kevin. "'Twenty Thousand Muskets!!!': Ira Allen and the *Olive Branch* Affair, 1796–1800." *William and Mary Quarterly* 3d ser. 48 (July 1991): 409–31. In 1796, Ethan Allen's brother, Ira, went to France to secure support for a joint French-American invasion of Canada in the hope of founding an independent United Columbia centered on the Champlain Valley.

5:456   Jones, Howard. *To the Webster-Ashburton Treaty: A Study in Anglo-American Relations, 1783–1843.* Chapel Hill: University of North Carolina Press, 1977. Jones traces the origins of the northeastern boundary dispute from the vague provisions of the Treaty of Paris of 1783 through the various Anglo-American attempts to effect a settlement. Besides chronicling the diplomatic aspects of the question, Jones emphasizes how American domestic politics and deep-rooted anglophobia continually defeated the negotiators' efforts to mark the North American boundary. Bibliography.

5:457   Ojala, Jeanne A. "Ira Allen and the French Directory, 1796: Plans for the Creation of the Republic of United Columbia." *William and Mary Quarterly* 3d ser. 36 (July 1979): 436–48. Ojala discusses and publishes Allen's proposal to the French government to support a rebellion against British authority in Quebec that looked to the creation of an independent government outside the United States.

5:458   Sheppard, George. *Plunder, Profit, and Paroles: A Social History of the War of 1812 in Up-per Canada.* Montreal: McGill-Queen's University Press, 1994. This study of the impact of the war in Upper Canada provides a valuable counterpoint to Errington, *The Lion, the Eagle, and Upper Canada: A Developing Colonial Ideology* (1987) (5:454) and an interesting supplement to Stuart, "Special Interests and National Authority in Foreign Policy: American-British Provincial Links during the Embargo and the War of 1812" (1984) (5:459). Sheppard highlights the divisions and uncertainties in the province about fighting trading partners and, in some cases, family members on the other side of Lake Erie. Bibliography.

5:459   Stuart, Reginald C. "Special Interests and National Authority in Foreign Policy: American-British Provincial Links during the Embargo and the War of 1812." *Diplomatic History* 8 (Fall 1984): 311–28. Stuart shows that on the northern frontier from western New York to Maine, social and economic ties between American citizens and Canadian subjects often outweighed the diplomatic conflicts between their governments. Neither government enjoyed much power or authority in the region, with the result that trade, in the form of smuggling, continued almost unabated despite various forms of economic coercion and, even, war.

5:460   _____. *United States Expansionism and British North America, 1775–1871.* Stuart provides much more comprehensive coverage of the period from 1783 to 1815 than most general surveys of Canadian-American relations. He pays attention to cultural, economic, and social, as well as diplomatic, contacts during a period he describes as an "era of defensive expansion" for the United States. Extensive bibliography (4:74).

5:461   Taylor, Alan. "The Divided Ground: Upper Canada, New York, and the Iroquois Six Nations, 1783–1815." *Journal of the Early Republic* 22 (Spring 2002): 55–75. In this article, Taylor shows how American efforts to realize the northern boundary established by the Treaty of Paris (1783) faced intense Iroquois opposition, often supported by British policymakers in London or officials in Upper Canada. For the Iroquois, and to some extent for white settlers, the northern boundary seemed unnatural, dividing peoples who were connected by blood, marriage, and trade.

Spanish Louisiana and Florida

5:462 Bannon, John Francis. *The Spanish Borderlands Frontier, 1513–1821.* See chapter 4 of this Guide (4:89).

5:463 Din, Gilbert C., ed. *The Louisiana Purchase Bicentennial Series in Louisiana History. Vol. 2: The Spanish Presence in Louisiana, 1763–1803.* Lafayette: Center for Louisiana Studies, University of Southwestern Louisiana, 1996. This collection of essays—most of them previously published, many of them long ago—covers the full range of the Spanish experience in Louisiana.

5:464 Fletcher, Mildred Stahl. "Louisiana as a Factor in French Diplomacy from 1763 to 1800." *Mississippi Valley Historical Review* 17 (December 1930): 367–76. In this brief article, Fletcher finds little French interest in recovering Louisiana from Spain between 1763 and the 1790s; contrary to other accounts, she sees a pronounced change in French policy toward the former colony after 1796, when reacquiring it from Spain became a high priority.

5:465 Gaspar, David Barry, and David Patrick Geggus, eds. *A Turbulent Time: The French Revolution and the Greater Caribbean.* Bloomington: Indiana University Press, 1997. This collection of essays provides useful background material on the impact of the French revolution in the Western Hemisphere, including, but going beyond, Saint Domingue. Of particular interest are Jane G. Landers's "Rebellion and Royalism in Spanish Florida: The French Revolution on Spain's Northern Colonial Frontier" (156–77), Kimberly S. Hanger's "Conflicting Loyalties: The French Revolution and Free People of Color in Spanish New Orleans" (178–203), and Robert L. Paquette's "Revolutionary Saint Domingue in the Making of Territorial Louisiana" (204–25).

5:466 Nasatir, Abraham P. *Borderland in Retreat: From Spanish Louisiana to the Far Southwest.* See chapter 4 of this Guide (4:92).

5:467 Turner, Frederick Jackson. "The Policy of France toward the Mississippi Valley in the Period of Washington and Adams." *American Historical Review* 10 (January 1905): 249–79. Turner demonstrates France's deep, continuing interest in controlling the Mississippi valley to limit English influence, to have a granary for the French West Indies, to influence American policies, and to undercut Spain's New World influence.

5:468 Weber, David J. *The Spanish Frontier in North America.* Weber provides a comprehensive survey of the social, cultural, economic, and diplomatic issues surrounding the northern frontier of Spain's American empire from exploration to the present. The British-French-American-Spanish rivalry for trade and territory receives significant attention. Extensive bibliography (3:175).

5:469 Whitaker, Arthur Preston. *The Spanish American Frontier, 1783–1795: The Westward Movement and the Spanish Retreat in the Mississippi Valley.* Boston: Houghton Mifflin Company, 1927. Whitaker maintains that Charles Pinckney's diplomatic triumph stemmed not so much from European events (the Bemis thesis) as from Madrid's realization "that it had failed, and knew that it had failed, in its frontier conflict with the United States."

5:470 Wright, J. Leitch, Jr. *Anglo-Spanish Rivalry in North America.* Wright argues that between 1492 and 1821 Spain saw its North American colonies, especially Florida and Louisiana, as buffers to protect Mexico and to safeguard strategic sailing routes. Most of the book covers the period before 1763. Extensive bibliography (3:125).

Nootka Sound Affair

5:471 Cook, Warren L. *Flood Tide of Empire: Spain and the Pacific Northwest, 1543–1819.* The author details the Spanish interaction with British, Russian, American, and Indian interests on the Pacific northwest coast that culminated in the Nootka Sound controversy (1790–1794). More than half of this historical-anthropological study centers on the events at Nootka, but the outcome was decided in Europe and the United States. Extensive bibliography (3:120).

5:472 Manning, William R. "The Nootka Sound Controversy." In *The Annual Report of the American Historical Association for the Year 1904,* 279–478.

Washington, DC: Government Printing Office, 1905. This classic study of the Anglo-Spanish conflict on the Pacific northwest coast provides a detailed account of events that had repercussions in Madrid and London and raised serious questions for the Washington administration. This publication is *The Annual Report of the American Historical Association for the Year 1904.* Bibliography.

Louisiana Purchase

5:473   "Despatches from the United States Consulate in New Orleans, 1801–1803." *American Historical Review* 32, 33 (July 1927, January 1928): 801–24, 331–59. These despatches are valuable not only for tracking American commercial activity in New Orleans, but also for understanding American fears about the transfer of Louisiana and the closure of the Mississippi during the crisis that ended with the Louisiana Purchase.

5:474   Balleck, Barry J. "When the Ends Justify the Means: Thomas Jefferson and the Louisiana Purchase." *Presidential Studies Quarterly* 22 (Fall 1992): 679–96. Balleck defends Jefferson's actions at the time of the Louisiana Purchase, admitting that, while he did violate his constitutional principles, he did so to serve his larger goals.

5:475   Bowman, Albert H. "Pichon, the United States and Louisiana." *Diplomatic History* 1 (Summer 1977): 257–70. Bowman highlights the role of Louis Pichon, the French chargé in Washington, in the Louisiana Purchase, arguing that by reporting intense American hostility and warning that the province could not be defended against an American force, he helped influence Napoleon to abandon his dream of American empire.

5:476   Brown, Everett Somerville. *The Constitutional History of the Louisiana Purchase, 1803–1812.* Berkeley: University of California Press, 1920. Reprint 2000 (Lawbook Exchange). Brown examines the multifaceted constitutional issues raised by the Louisiana Purchase and the necessity of establishing a government for the new territory. This remains a useful work even though each of the issues addressed has been examined in more recent works. Bibliography.

5:477   Carson, David A. "Blank Paper of the Constitution: The Louisiana Purchase Debates." *Historian* 54 (Spring 1992): 477–90. Carson sees the reversal of both Federalists and Republicans on the matter of constitutional construction at the time of the Louisiana Purchase as evidence of a shift in ideology, not merely a case of political expediency.

5:478   _____. "The Role of Congress in the Acquisition of the Louisiana Territory." *Louisiana History* 26 (Fall 1985): 369–83. Carson emphasizes the role of the resolution proposed by Federalist Senator James Ross, which called for the immediate seizure of New Orleans, in leading Bonaparte to sell the entire province. Unfortunately, he misses the fact that news of the resolution arrived in Paris only after Bonaparte's decision to sell.

5:479   Currie, David P. "The Constitution in Congress: Jefferson and the West, 1801–1809." *William and Mary Law Review* 39 (May 1998): 1441–1503. This lengthy article shows that key Republicans in Congress and the administration, rather than the Federalists who controlled the judiciary, took the leading role in broadly interpreting federal powers relative to western expansion. Currie discusses debates over Ohio statehood and the Cumberland Road as well as the Louisiana Purchase.

5:480   Dargo, George. *Jefferson's Louisiana: Politics and the Clash of Legal Traditions.* Cambridge, MA: Harvard University Press, 1975. On the surface, Dargo's book is a study of the conflict between the French civil law and American common law traditions in early Louisiana. In reality, it offers a much broader analysis of the "problems of colonial rule" and how to incorporate a different population and extensive territory into the American union. Bibliographic essay.

5:481   DeConde, Alexander. *This Affair of Louisiana.* New York: Scribner, 1976. This volume, now the standard, full-length treatment of the Louisiana cession, rests on extensive research. Although DeConde discusses and often incorporates the judgments of others, his emphasis is on the drive for Louisiana as part of an expansionist, even imperialist, American tradition. Extensive bibliographical essay.

5:482   Farnham, Thomas J. "The Federal-State Issue and the Louisiana Purchase." *Louisiana History* 6

(Winter 1965): 5–25. This article focuses on the intense opposition of New England Federalists to the Louisiana Purchase, particularly as evidenced by the actions of the Massachusetts General Court rather than of Federalist congressmen in Washington.

5:483   Gannon, Kevin M. "Escaping 'Mr. Jefferson's Plan of Destruction': New England Federalists and the Idea of a Northern Confederacy, 1803–1804." *Journal of the Early Republic* 21 (Fall 2001): 413–43. Gannon offers a fairly thorough account of the flurry of disunionist planning among New England Federalists in response to the Louisiana Purchase. This article brings new attention to an incident that has been almost entirely neglected since Charles Raymond Brown's *The Northern Confederacy According to the Plans of the "Essex Junto," 1796–1814* (Princeton: Princeton University Press, 1915).

5:484   Kastor, Peter J. "'Motives of Peculiar Urgency': Local Diplomacy in Louisiana, 1803–1821." *William and Mary Quarterly* 3d ser. 58 (October 2001): 819–48. Less about the Louisiana Purchase than its aftermath, this article examines the complex interactions of a variety of parties—Indian, Spanish, and American—regarding the future of the lower Mississippi valley. Kastor is especially good at developing the interplay among private citizens, federal officials in Louisiana, and the administration in Washington.

5:485   Labbé, Dolores Egger, ed. *The Louisiana Purchase and Its Aftermath, 1800–1830.* Lafayette: Center for Louisiana Studies, University of Southwestern Louisiana, 1998. This collection reprints essays, articles, and book chapters, many of which are quite old, covering every aspect of the Louisiana Purchase. It is a useful starting place for studying this issue.

5:486   LaFeber, Walter. "An Expansionist's Dilemma." *Constitution* 5 (Fall 1993): 4–13. LaFeber argues that Jefferson set aside his strict constructionist principles in the Louisiana Purchase to preserve an agrarian republic. In doing so, he helped transform the Constitution in ways that encouraged later "imperial" presidents.

5:487   Lyon, E. Wilson. *Louisiana in French Diplomacy, 1759–1804.* See chapter 4 of this Guide (4:91).

5:488   Onuf, Peter S. "The Expanding Union." In *Devising Liberty: Preserving and Creating Freedom in the New American Republic,* ed. David Thomas Konig, 50–80. Stanford, CA: Stanford University Press, 1995. This thought-provoking article sets the Louisiana Purchase into the context of Republican thinking about expansion, the west, and the union.

5:489   Smith, Ronald D. "Napoleon and Louisiana: Failure of the Proposed Expedition to Occupy and Defend Louisiana, 1801–1803." *Louisiana History* 12 (Winter 1971): 21–40. Smith gracefully reviews the factors underlying Napoleon's policies toward Louisiana. His conclusion, the result of a careful study of French official documents, is that a combination of circumstances led the emperor to order the sale to the United States.

5:490   Whitaker, Arthur Preston. *The Mississippi Question, 1795–1803: A Study in Trade, Politics, and Diplomacy.* New York: Appleton-Century, 1934. Whitaker still provides the most complete study of the growth of American trade and interest in the area; he also offers a less intensive but thoughtful treatment of French and Spanish policy.

Lewis and Clark Expedition

5:491   Allen, John Logan. *Passage through the Garden: Lewis and Clark and the Image of the American Northwest.* Urbana: University of Illinois Press, 1975. Focusing on the expedition itself, Allen's cultural study looks at how the myth and symbol of the "passage" and the "garden" were transformed by the Lewis and Clark Expedition. Bibliography.

5:492   Ronda, James P. "Exploring the American West in the Age of Jefferson." In *North American Exploration. Vol. 3: A Continent Comprehended,* ed. John Logan Allen, 9–74. Lincoln: University of Nebraska Press, 1997. Ronda's essay provides an overview of exploration in North America from the 1790s to the 1820s. He emphasizes the competition between the United States and various European powers at a time when territorial claims remained largely unfixed. Bibliography.

5:493   _____. *Lewis and Clark among the Indians.* Lincoln: University of Nebraska Press, 1984.

Ronda concentrates on the relations between the "corps of discovery" and the Indian tribes and villages along its route. But he also discusses Jefferson's plans for the diplomatic and economic relations between the United States and the western Indians.

Burr Conspiracy

5:494   Abernethy, Thomas Perkins. *The Burr Conspiracy.* New York: Oxford University Press, 1954. This extensively researched account emphasizes the threat to the union posed by the Burr Conspiracy (1803–1808). Although the author concentrates on domestic ramifications, including Burr's trial for treason, he also closely examines Spanish and British connections with the leading actors, notably Burr and General James Wilkinson. Extensive bibliography.

5:495   Cox, Isaac Joslin. "Hispanic-American Phases of the 'Burr Conspiracy.'" *Hispanic American Historical Review* 12 (May 1932): 145–75. Cox sets Burr and Wilkinson's planning and recruiting in the context of Spanish-American revolutionary activity, particularly that of Francisco de Miranda, and American interest in the liberation of Spanish America, particularly Mexico.

5:496   Mohl, Raymond A. "Britain and the Aaron Burr Conspiracy." *History Today* 21 (June 1971): 391–98. Mohl discusses the links between British officials in the United States, particularly Anthony Merry and Charles Williamson, and the Burr Conspiracy, which he considers an "early expression of the spirit of 'Manifest Destiny.'"

5:497   Szászdi, Adam. "Governor Folch and the Burr Conspiracy." *Florida Historical Quarterly* 38 (January 1960): 239–51. In this brief article, Szászdi examines the Burr Conspiracy from the perspective of Vicente Folch, the Spanish governor of West Florida.

Florida and Texas

5:498   Coker, William S., and Thomas D. Watson. *Indian Traders of the Southeastern Spanish Borderlands: Panton, Leslie & Company and John Forbes &* *Company, 1783–1847.* Pensacola: University of West Florida Press, 1986. This work provides a thorough study of two Scottish trading firms. Coker and Watson do a good job of tracing the political effects of their changing connections to the Indians, the Spanish, and the United States. Bibliography.

5:499   Cox, Isaac Joslin. "The Border Missions of General George Mathews." *Mississippi Valley Historical Review* 12 (December 1925): 309–33. Cox provides a brief biographical sketch of George Mathews, the ex-governor of Georgia, who seized East Florida in 1812. He argues, moreover, that Mathews served a "covetous and vacillating administration" in Washington.

5:500   _____. "The Louisiana-Texas Frontier: Part II—The American Occupation of the Louisiana-Texas Frontier." *Southwestern Historical Quarterly* 17 (July 1913, October 1913): 1–42, 140–87. In this article, Cox recounts the exploration and occupation of the newly acquired lands in the immediate aftermath of the Louisiana Purchase. He also discusses some of the early disputes and negotiations over the Louisiana-Texas boundary.

5:501   Cox, Isaac Joslin. *The West Florida Controversy, 1798–1813: A Study in American Diplomacy.* Baltimore: Johns Hopkins Press, 1918. This lengthy, even tedious, study comes to life only in Cox's frequent criticisms of almost every American leader involved in this affair, above all Jefferson. The research in American and Spanish governmental archives is exemplary, but the French side is neglected, although during Jefferson's administration Paris was almost as important as Madrid.

5:502   Egan, Clifford L. "The United States, France and West Florida, 1803–1807." *Florida Historical Quarterly* 47 (January 1969): 227–53. Egan's article supplements Cox, *The West Florida Controversy, 1798–1813: A Study in American Diplomacy* (1918) (5:501), particularly as a consequence of his close examination of French archives. Nicely written, it tells as much about this aspect of the controversy as readers will want to know. Jefferson emerges very badly, primarily because his reading of developments in France was blindly optimistic.

5:503   Gronet, Richard W. "The United States and

the Invasion of Texas, 1810–1814." *Americas* 25 (January 1969): 281–306. Despite exaggerating the level of government involvement, this article remains a useful account of American activity in Texas during this period. Gronet presents the Gutiérrez-Magee Expedition as a "United States sponsored scheme to aid the Mexican Revolution."

5:504   Haggard, J. Villasana. "The Neutral Ground between Louisiana and Texas, 1806–1821." *Louisiana Historical Quarterly* 28 (October 1945): 1001–28. This long article provides exhaustive coverage of the tensions between Spain and the United States over the "neutral ground" established by Gen. James Wilkinson to prevent collisions on the uncertain border between Texas and Louisiana.

5:505   Holmes, Jack D. L. "Showdown on the Sabine: General James Wilkinson vs. Lieutenant-Colonel Simón de Herrera." *Louisiana Studies* 3 (Spring 1964): 46–76. This article describes the growing war crisis that developed on the still undefined border between Louisiana and Texas during Jefferson's second term and the tense negotiations on the spot between Wilkinson and Herrera that produced the informal "neutral ground" agreement in the fall of 1806.

5:506   Logan, John Arthur. *No Transfer: An American Security Principle.* From the beginning of the nation, Logan contends, Americans opposed the transfer of colonial possessions in the Western Hemisphere from one European power to another, particularly from Spain to a stronger nation. This principle was first formally expressed with regard to East Florida in 1811 (2:231).

5:507   Owsley, Frank L., Jr., and Gene A. Smith. *Filibusters and Expansionists: Jeffersonian Manifest Destiny, 1800–1821.* Tuscaloosa: University of Alabama Press, 1997. This work draws together the many and varied signs of American territorial interest in the Gulf Coast, from Florida to Texas, over the course of two decades. Its emphasis is on the period after 1810, including the Gutiérrez-Magee Expedition into Texas and the Patriot War in East Florida. The authors may be too quick to see official complicity in or encouragement of private filibustering efforts. Bibliography.

5:508   Stagg, J. C. A. "The Madison Administration and Mexico: Reinterpreting the Gutiérrez-Magee Raid of 1812–1813." *William and Mary Quarterly* 3d ser. 59 (April 2002): 449–80. Balanced judgment and thorough research, particularly in the papers of William Shaler, make this article a valuable corrective to much of the recent work on the southwestern borderlands in the 1810s. As a special bonus, an associated website (at http://www.wm.edu/oieahc/WMQ/Apr02/stagg.htm) includes six fascinating essays written by Shaler and edited by Stagg.

5:509   Waciuma, Wanjohi. *Intervention in Spanish Floridas, 1801–1813: A Study in Jeffersonian Foreign Policy.* Boston: Branden Press, 1976. This highly critical work reviews American pressure against Spanish Florida from Jefferson's inaugural to the intervention of 1813. It covers the absorption of West Florida (1810–1813), the Mathews invasion of East Florida, and Mitchell's mission to Florida. Both Jefferson and Madison are portrayed as men of intrigue and duplicity in their efforts to acquire the Spanish colony.

5:510   Warren, Harris Gaylord. *The Sword Was Their Passport: A History of American Filibustering in the Mexican Revolution.* Baton Rouge: Louisiana State University Press, 1943. Despite its somewhat lurid title, this work is in fact the most thorough, scholarly account of the many filibustering expeditions that set out from the United States to help revolutionize Mexico between 1810 and 1820. Bibliography.

5:511   White, David H. "The Forbes Company in Spanish Florida, 1801–1806." *Florida Historical Quarterly* 52 (January 1974): 274–85. The Forbes company assumed the trading interests of a British company holding a monopoly on the Indian trade in Spanish Florida. Spanish nationals complained that the Forbes company evaded Spanish trade regulations, but the company continued to operate until 1819.

5:512   Wyllys, Rufus Kay. "The East Florida Revolution of 1812–1814." *Hispanic American Historical Review* 9 (November 1929): 415–45. The various filibustering projects from American territory into East Florida during the War of 1812 are assessed. Wyllys argues that the United States did not profit by these invasions immediately, but did learn the technique of pressuring the Spanish to relinquish Florida.

CARIBBEAN

5:513   Coatsworth, John H. "American Trade with European Colonies in the Caribbean and South America, 1790–1812." *William and Mary Quarterly* 3d ser. 24 (April 1967): 243–66. This study describes the growth, distribution, and composition of American exports to the Caribbean and South American possessions of Britain, France, and Spain.

5:514   Langley, Lester D. *Struggle for the American Mediterranean: United States-European Rivalry in the Gulf-Caribbean, 1776–1904.* This synthesis of the international history of the Caribbean deals with various episodes of American-European rivalry, primarily in the nineteenth century. Bibliography (2:364).

5:515   Nichols, Roy F. "Trade Relations and the Establishment of the United States Consulates in Spanish America, 1779–1809." *Hispanic American Historical Review* 13 (August 1933): 289–313. Nichols deals almost exclusively with U.S. "consuls" at Havana, who enjoyed greatest success whenever Cuba's need for American commodities and carriers reached a peak, usually when Spain and Britain were at war. The author draws on both Spanish and U.S. archival sources.

5:516   Toth, Charles W. "Anglo-American Diplomacy and the British West Indies (1783–1789)." *Americas* 32 (January 1976): 418–36. American leaders in the peace negotiations, and consistently thereafter, sought commercial access to the British West Indies. Little was achieved until after the outbreak of war in Europe in 1793.

Haitian Revolution

5:517   "Letters of Toussaint Louverture and of Edward Stevens, 1798–1800." *American Historical Review* 16 (October 1910): 64–101. This useful collection of consular documents includes numerous reports from John Adams's man on the ground in St. Domingue during a critical period of the Haitian revolution.

5:518   Hickey, Donald R. "America's Response to the Slave Revolt in Haiti, 1791–1806." *Journal of the Early Republic* 2 (Winter 1982): 361–79. Hickey attributes the fluctuations in policy toward the Haitian revolution to tensions between commercial interests, which were generally favored by Federalists, and slavery concerns, which were generally dominant with Republicans. He argues, contrary to the prevailing wisdom, that party divisions outweighed those of section.

5:519   Hunt, Alfred N. *Haiti's Influence on Antebellum America: Slumbering Volcano in the Caribbean.* Baton Rouge: Louisiana State University Press, 1988. This book is not really a work of diplomatic history but a wide-ranging account of the complex and varied ways in which Haitian independence was experienced in the United States in the decades before the Civil War. Of particular importance for the early nineteenth century was the influx of white refugees, often with slaves, who emigrated to the United States and the deepening of southern fears of slave insurrection and of the "contagion" of rebelliousness in the Caribbean.

5:520   Logan, Rayford W. *The Diplomatic Relations of the United States with Haiti, 1776–1891.* Chapel Hill: University of North Carolina Press, 1941. Though old, this work remains a standard monograph on U.S. diplomacy toward the Haitian revolution. It should, however, be read in conjunction with recent essays and articles by Donald R. Hickey (5:518), Timothy Matthewson (5:521), and Michael Zuckerman (5:525). Extensive bibliography. The first three chapters offer a comprehensive treatment of U.S. relations with Haiti in the late eighteenth century. Logan includes the text of the Maitland Convention, but overlooks the formal role of American diplomacy in the Anglo-American-Haitian commercial arrangement. Extensive bibliography.

5:521   Matthewson, Timothy M. "George Washington's Policy toward the Haitian Revolution." *Diplomatic History* 3 (Summer 1979): 321–36. According to Matthewson, the Washington administration "played a major role in efforts to check this foreign slave insurrection" by providing funds and selling arms to French planters. The slave rebellion on St. Domingue posed a multifaceted threat powerful enough to unite Washington's chief advisers, Hamilton and Jefferson, behind a single policy.

5:522 _____. "Jefferson and Haiti." *Journal of Southern History* 61 (May 1995): 209–48. Focusing on his presidency, Matthewson argues that Jefferson's hostility to the Haitian revolution, particularly after the Louisiana Purchase, reflected his desire to secure French support to acquire the Floridas and his identification with southern planters, who feared that the Haitian "contagion" would spread to their slaves. For a similar argument, see Matthewson's later "Jefferson and the Nonrecognition of Haiti," *Proceedings of the American Philosophical Society* 140 (March 1996): 22–48.

5:523 Montague, Ludwell Lee. *Haiti and the United States, 1714–1938.* Durham, NC: Duke University Press, 1940. This concise, analytical book remains valuable, though much of it is devoted to the late nineteenth and early twentieth centuries.

5:524 Ott, Thomas O. *The Haitian Revolution, 1789–1804.* Knoxville: University of Tennessee Press, 1973. Toussaint L'Ouverture, through the upheavals caused by the French revolution, international war, domestic rebellion, and occupation by the British, vanquished all his rivals and enemies save one: Napoleon Bonaparte.

5:525 Zuckerman, Michael. "The Power of Blackness: Thomas Jefferson and the Revolution in St. Domingue." In *Almost Chosen People: Oblique Biographies in the American Grain,* ed. Michael Zuckerman, 175–218. Berkeley: University of California Press, 1993. Zuckerman sees the American response to the revolution in St. Domingue (Haiti), particularly during the Jefferson administration, as the most poignant example of the abandonment of the ideals of the American revolution. Racism kept many Americans from living up to their professed beliefs, with Jefferson foremost among them.

SOUTH AMERICA

5:526 Bernstein, Harry. *Origins of Inter-American Interest, 1700–1812.* Philadelphia: University of Pennsylvania Press, 1945. Chapter 3 docu-

ments the growing commerce between the United States and Spanish America in the late eighteenth century. Later chapters explore the cultural exchanges and the formation of "political ties" that antedated Latin American independence. Extensive bibliography.

5:527 Bierck, Harold A., Jr. "The First Instance of U.S. Foreign Aid: Venezuelan Relief in 1812." *Inter-American Economic Affairs* 9 (Summer 1955): 47–59. In 1812, the United States provided $50,000 worth of foodstuffs in relief following an earthquake in the pro-independence areas of Venezuela. The misuse of the funds and the onset of the War of 1812 prevented this aid from leading to the improved commercial opportunities that many of its advocates predicted.

5:528 Chandler, Charles Lyon. "United States Merchant Ships in the Rio de la Plata (1801–1808), as Shown by Early Newspapers." *Hispanic American Historical Review* 2 (February 1919): 26–54. This article—and the same author's "United States Shipping in the La Plata Region, 1809–1810," *Hispanic American Historical Review* 3 (May 1920): 159–76—tries to track the ebb and flow of American commerce in a critical part of South America in the decade before revolution wracked the region.

5:529 Pike, Fredrick B. *The United States and Latin America: Myths and Stereotypes of Civilization and Nature.* Austin: University of Texas Press, 1992. Though only a relatively small part of this book is specifically about the period covered by this chapter, the work as a whole provides valuable background on how the people of the United States viewed Latin Americans. Drawing a dichotomy between a civilized United States and a primitive or natural Latin America, Anglo-Americans were skeptical of the ability of Latin Americans to govern themselves.

5:530 Shurbutt, T. Ray, ed. *United States–Latin American Relations, 1800–1850: The Formative Generations.* Tuscaloosa: University of Alabama Press, 1991. The essays in this work are organized by nation. The emphasis throughout is heavily on the period after Latin American independence. Wesley P. Newton's "Origins of United States–Latin American Relations" (1–24) provides useful background. The essays on Brazil (by Phil Brian Johnson and Robert Kim Stevens, 86–101), Chile (by Shurbutt,

228–60), and Mexico (by Edward H. Moseley, 122–96) also include some coverage of the pre-1815 period. Bibliography.

5:531   Smelser, Marshall. "George Washington Declines the Part of El Libertador." *William and Mary Quarterly* 3d ser. 11 (January 1954): 42–51. Smelser recounts the 1797–1799 scheme, developed by Francisco de Miranda and Rufus King, and subsequently supported by Alexander Hamilton, to liberate Spanish America. George Washington, as titular commander of the American army, declined to countenance it.

Spanish-American Revolutions

5:532   Bemis, Samuel Flagg. "Early Diplomatic Missions from Buenos Aires to the United States, 1811–1824." *Proceedings of the American Antiquarian Society* new ser. 49 (April 1939): 11–101. This highly factual account argues that the United States contributed more than Britain to the cause of Argentine independence.

5:533   Bethell, Leslie, ed. *The Cambridge History of Latin America. Vol. 3: From Independence to c. 1870.* New York: Cambridge University Press, 1985. This collection of essays covers the independence movements in Spanish and, later, Portuguese America from various angles, making it an essential background work. Of particular value are John Lynch, "The Origins of Spanish American Independence" (3–50); Timothy E. Anna, "The Independence of Mexico and Central America" (51–94); David Bushnell, "The Independence of Spanish South America" (95–156); Bethell, "The Independence of Brazil" (157–96); and D. A. G. Waddell, "International Politics and Latin American Independence" (197–228). Bibliographic essays.

5:534   Costeloe, Michael P. *Response to Revolution: Imperial Spain and the Spanish American Revolutions, 1810–1840.* New York: Cambridge University Press, 1986. This study examines the Spanish-American revolutions from the Spanish, rather than the colonial, perspective. Costeloe provides a valuable account of how Spain reacted to the dissolution of its New World empire. Bibliography.

5:535   Cox, Isaac Joslin. "The Pan-American Policy of Jefferson and Wilkinson." *Mississippi Valley Historical Review* 1 (September 1914): 212–39. Cox describes Jefferson's response to the earliest news of the political upheaval in Spain that ultimately triggered the Spanish-American revolutions. Intrigued about the potential impact on Cuba and the Floridas, Jefferson enlisted Gen. James Wilkinson to monitor and, if possible, shape developments.

5:536   Domínguez, Jorge I. *Insurrection or Loyalty: The Breakdown of the Spanish American Empire.* Cambridge, MA: Harvard University Press, 1980. By applying a political science approach, this work attempts to explain why the process of revolution played out so differently in Spain's different colonies. Focusing on Chile, Cuba, Mexico, and Venezuela, Domínguez emphasizes the role of internal forces that were distinct to each province.

5:537   Griffin, Charles C. *The United States and the Disruption of the Spanish Empire, 1810–1822: A Study of the Relations of the United States with Spain and the Rebel Spanish Colonies.* New York: Columbia University Press, 1937. Reprint 1974 (Octagon Books). In this standard work, based on multiarchival research, the author examines both the American response to the revolutions in the Spanish-American colonies and the American pressure upon Texas and Florida. Extensive bibliography.

5:538   Kaufmann, William W. *British Policy and the Independence of Latin America, 1804–1828.* New Haven: Yale University Press, 1951. In a solid, traditional diplomatic history, Kaufmann assesses British actions and motives in the Latin American struggle for independence. Bibliography.

5:539   Lockey, Joseph Byrne, ed. "An Early Pan-American Scheme." *Pacific Historical Review* 2 (December 1933): 439–47. Lockey publishes a memorandum written by American consul and special agent William Shaler for Secretary of State James Monroe in the summer of 1812. Responding to the emergence of revolutionary movements in some of the Spanish colonies, Shaler proposed a joint Anglo-American effort to organize the Americas into five nations south of the United States, which in his plan would have acquired the Floridas, Canada, and Cuba.

5:540　Lockey, Joseph Byrne. *Pan-Americanism: Its Beginnings.* New York: Macmillan Company, 1920. Reprint 1970 (Arno Press). This is a thorough study, based on printed sources, which surveys the U.S. reaction to the independence movements in Latin America (1810–1860). Extensive bibliography.

5:541　Lynch, John. *The Spanish-American Revolutions, 1808–1826.* 2d ed. New York: Norton, 1986. An informative and well-researched synthesis of Latin America's struggle for independence (1808–1826), it demonstrates how the revolutions created new nations but did not change the basic social structure. Extensive bibliography. First published in 1973.

5:542　Rippy, J. Fred. *Rivalry of the United States and Great Britain over Latin America (1808–1830).* Baltimore: Johns Hopkins Press, 1929. Reprint 1972 (Octagon Books). Rippy's focus is on economic and political issues in assessing the antagonism of the United States and Britain over Spanish Florida, Texas, Cuba, and South American commerce. He used archives in Britain and the United States.

5:543　Robertson, William Spence. *France and Latin-American Independence.* Baltimore: Johns Hopkins Press, 1939. An extensively researched study, it shows how Napoleon, perhaps unintentionally, furthered the independence movement by his actions in Spain in 1808. Later, Napoleon realized that the independence of Latin America was inevitable. Extensive bibliography.

5:544　Rodríguez O., Jaime E. *The Independence of Spanish America.* New York: Cambridge University Press, 1998. Emphasizing political and cultural elements, this account argues that the revolutions in Spanish America were less an anticolonial movement than an aspect of the contemporary revolution within Spain itself. Bibliography.

5:545　Wellborn, Alfred Toledano. "The Relations between New Orleans and Latin America, 1810–1824." *Louisiana Historical Quarterly* 22 (July 1939): 710–94. This long article develops in full the connections between New Orleans and the Spanish and Portuguese colonies to its south during the revolutions of the 1810s and 1820s. Of particular interest to Wellborn is New Orleans's role in launching and outfitting filibustering and privateer-ing expeditions.

5:546　Whitaker, Arthur Preston. *The United States and the Independence of Latin America, 1800–1830.* Baltimore: Johns Hopkins Press, 1941. The first three chapters of this classic account describe the early development of commercial contacts, the dispatch of commercial agents to Latin America, and the "Large Policy of 1808"—Jefferson's dreams of expansion. Bibliographical note.

EUROPE

5:547　Brinton, Crane. *A Decade of Revolution, 1789–1799.* New York: Harper and Brothers, 1934. Given the importance of European affairs to this period of American history, this volume provides a useful overview. A more recent survey is George Rudé, *Revolutionary Europe, 1783–1815,* rev. ed. (Malden, MA: Blackwell, 2000, originally published in 1964). Bibliography.

5:548　Crawley, C. W., ed. *New Cambridge Modern History. Vol. 9: War and Peace in an Age of Upheaval, 1793–1830.* Cambridge, UK: Cambridge University Press, 1965. This cooperative work in European history contains chapters of very uneven merit. Still, it provides a useful, wide-ranging study of the background of diplomacy as well as of diplomacy itself. The most pertinent chapters are Norman Gibbs and C. C. Lloyd, "Armed Forces and the Art of War" (60–90); Geoffrey Bruun, "The Balance of Power during the Wars, 1793–1814" (250–74); Felix Markham, "The Napoleonic Adventure" (307–36); Frank Thistlethwaite, "The United States and the Old World, 1794–1828" (591–611); and R. A. Humphreys, "The Emancipation of Latin America" (612–38).

5:549　Godechot, Jacques. *L'Europe et l'Amérique à l'époque napoléonienne [Europe and America in the age of Napoleon].* Paris: Presses universitaires de France, 1967. American historians are likely to find this book both rewarding and irritating. The portions on the Western Hemisphere are cursory and simplistic, but the treatment of the age is broad and imaginative. It is a fine introduction to the diplomacy of the period. The lengthy bibliographical essay includes a very capable discussion of French materials.

5:550   Kissinger, Henry. *A World Restored: Metternich, Castlereagh and the Problems of Peace, 1812–1822.* Boston: Houghton Mifflin, 1957. This classic study, by a future U.S. secretary of state, includes a lengthy account of the wartime alliance against Napoleon and the postwar reconstruction of Europe's balance of power at the Congress of Vienna. Bibliography.

5:551   McKay, Derek, and H. M. Scott. *The Rise of the Great Powers, 1648–1815.* New York: Longman, 1983. This general survey of European diplomatic history covers nearly two centuries. Bibliographic essay.

5:552   Ross, Steven T. *European Diplomatic History, 1789–1815: France against Europe.* Garden City, NY: Anchor Books, 1969. Reprint 1981 (Krieger). Though somewhat dated, this book provides a fairly detailed account, heavily centered on France, of European diplomacy and warfare during the French revolution and Napoleonic era.

France

5:553   Bowman, Albert H. *The Struggle for Neutrality: Franco-American Diplomacy during the Federalist Era.* Knoxville: University of Tennessee Press, 1974. Federalist diplomacy (1789–1801) is viewed as not neutral toward France, a point highlighted by the Jay Treaty. Bowman makes a valuable contribution by showing how American policy was viewed by members of the French foreign office. French desire to involve America in the European war is outlined, as are the views of Talleyrand.

5:554   Childs, Frances Sergeant. *French Refugee Life in America, 1790–1800: An American Chapter of the French Revolution.* Baltimore: Johns Hopkins Press, 1940. This book deals with French refugees who fled the French West Indies, Saint-Domingue (Santo Domingo) in particular, during the revolutionary upheavals there. Mostly destitute and torn by factional disputes, they were a constant source of trouble to successive French ministers and American authorities. Bibliography.

5:555   Connelly, Owen. *The French Revolution and Napoleonic Era.* 2d ed. Fort Worth: Holt Rinehart and Winston, 1991. This work provides a solid overview of Europe in general and France in particular during the revolutionary and Napoleonic eras, though it tends to emphasize military affairs. Bibliography. For a somewhat broader coverage of this period, see Martyn Lyons, *Napoleon Bonaparte and the Legacy of the French Revolution* (New York: St. Martin's Press, 1994).

5:556   Echeverria, Durand. *Mirage in the West: A History of the French Image of American Society to 1815.* See chapter 4 of this Guide (4:230).

5:557   Egan, Clifford L. *Neither Peace nor War: Franco-American Relations, 1803–1812.* Baton Rouge: Louisiana State University Press, 1983. Egan covers the full range of diplomatic relations between the United States and France, examining both the territorial issues created by the Louisiana Purchase and American desire for the Floridas and the commercial problems raised by French and British efforts to shape American neutrality to their own interests. Bibliography.

5:558   Hill, Peter P. *French Perceptions of the Early American Republic, 1783–1793.* Hill finds that, long before the Jay Treaty, French officials were struck by American ingratitude and concerned by American indifference. The failure to arrange commercial reciprocity or a consular convention, the smuggling in the French West Indies, and the disappointments of French-American trade showed the limits to the wartime friendship. Bibliography (4:233).

5:559   Jones, Howard Mumford. *America and French Culture, 1750–1848.* See chapter 4 of this Guide (4:235).

5:560   Kennedy, Roger G. *Orders from France: The Americans and the French in a Revolutionary World, 1780–1820.* New York: Alfred A. Knopf, 1989. This quirky book takes a broad view of cultural exchanges between France and the United States, highlighting architecture, but covering as well commercial, political, and intellectual matters. While Kennedy draws some intriguing connections, he fails to inspire much confidence in his command of the material, describing his chronological parameters, for example, as "the Declaration of Independence of 1775 [sic] and the Monroe Doctrine in 1818 [sic]." Bibliography.

5:561 Ketcham, Ralph L. "France and American Politics, 1763–1793." See chapter 4 of this Guide (4:65).

5:562 Levenstein, Harvey A. *Seductive Journey: American Tourists in France from Jefferson to the Jazz Age.* The first of four parts of this wide-ranging study of American tourism in and cultural relations with France covers the period from 1786 to 1848 (2:320).

5:563 Price, Jacob M. *France and the Chesapeake: A History of the French Tobacco Monopoly, 1694–1791, and of Its Relationship to the British and American Tobacco Trades.* See chapter 4 of this Guide (4:83).

5:564 Stover, John F. "French-American Trade during the Confederation, 1781–1789." *North Carolina Historical Review* 35 (October 1958): 399–414. French-American commerce failed to reach its potential as direct trade favored America by a ratio of approximately five to one. From 1784 to 1790, French exports to the United States totaled less than 5 percent of British exports to the United States. See the earlier work of Edmund Buron, "Statistics on Franco-American Trade, 1788–1806," *Journal of Economic and Business History* 4 (1931–1932): 571–80.

French Revolution

5:565 Appleby, Joyce. "America as a Model for the Radical French Reformers of 1789." *William and Mary Quarterly* 3d ser. 28 (April 1971): 267–86. Here is a discussion of the debate among French reformers over the relative merits of the American and British political systems as models for France.

5:566 Banning, Lance. "Jeffersonian Ideology and the French Revolution: A Question of Liberticide at Home." *Studies in Burke and His Time* 17 (Winter 1976): 5–26. Following intellectual and psychological interpretations of the revolutionary era advanced by Bernard Bailyn, Gordon S. Wood, and others, the author explains what he calls the emotional response in America to the French revolution and the European war.

5:567 Doyle, William. *The Oxford History of the French Revolution.* New York: Oxford University Press, 1989. Doyle provides a solid, recent overview of France from the Old Regime through the revolution, ending in 1802. He treats this period broadly, providing useful background material but including little on the United States. Bibliographic essay.

5:568 Godechot, Jacques. *France and the Atlantic Revolution of the Eighteenth Century, 1770–1799.* Translated by Herbert H. Rowen. See chapter 4 of this Guide (4:232).

5:569 Hazen, Charles D. *Contemporary American Opinion of the French Revolution.* Baltimore: Johns Hopkins Press, 1897. This work is divided into two sections—the opinions of Americans abroad, primarily those of Gouverneur Morris, Monroe, and Jefferson, and the opinions of Americans at home—and provides an excellent analysis of an unfavorable American reaction setting in as atheism and terrorism marked the French revolution.

5:570 Lefebvre, Georges. *The French Revolution.* Translated by Elizabeth Moss Evanson, John Hall Stewart, and James Friguglietti. 2 vols. New York: Columbia University Press, 1962–1964. Lefebvre's works are indispensable guides to the social and political setting of the French revolution. These two volumes, which divide at 1793, along with his *The Thermidorian & the Directory: Two Phases of the French Revolution,* trans., Robert Baldick (New York: Random House, 1964), present both overview and synthesis. Bibliography.

Genet Affair

5:571 Ammon, Harry. *The Genet Mission.* New York: Norton, 1973. Ammon concludes that Genet was unsuccessful mainly because of his ignorance of the American political system and his unusual capacity for self-deception. The work is based primarily on printed documents and a skillful use of secondary literature. Bibliography. Still useful are two doctoral dissertations: Maude H. Woodfin, "Citizen Genêt and His Mission" (Chicago: University of Chicago, 1928), and William F. Keller, "American Politics and the Genêt Mission, 1793–1794" (Pittsburgh: University of Pittsburgh, 1951).

5:572   Coulter, E. Merton. "The Efforts of the Democratic Societies of the West to Open the Navigation of the Mississippi River." *Mississippi Valley Historical Review* 11 (December 1924): 376–89. Coulter describes the machinations of western Republicans against Spanish control of the Mississippi River in 1793–1794. He finds that the scheming continued even after the initial failure of the plans of Edmond Charles Genet and George Rogers Clark.

5:573   Minnigerode, Meade. *Jefferson, Friend of France, 1793: The Career of Edmond Charles Genet, Minister Plenipotentiary from the French Republic to the United States, as Revealed by His Private Papers, 1763–1843.* New York: G. P. Putnam's Sons, 1928. The title is ironic: the book is a biography of Genet, with an emphasis on his 1793 mission. Written from Genet's private papers, it portrays Jefferson as the principal author of "a tale of perfidy" directed against Genet. It provides virtually the only defense of Genet's conduct.

5:574   Sheridan, Eugene R. "The Recall of Edmond Charles Genet: A Study in Transatlantic Politics and Diplomacy." *Diplomatic History* 18 (Fall 1994): 463–88. This article provides an in-depth examination of the Washington administration's decision to ask the French government to recall Genet and the French acceptance of this request. It adds nuance to earlier portrayals.

5:575   Turner, Frederick Jackson, ed. "Documents on the Relations of France to Louisiana, 1792–1795." *American Historical Review* 3 (April 1898): 490–516. These documents from the Archives du Ministère des Affaires Etrangères demonstrate Genet's attempts to take Louisiana in 1793 and 1794. Turner also includes various analyses of Louisiana, its value to France, and plans to take it, and a description of Genet's conduct and reception in the United States.

5:576   _____. "The Mangourit Correspondence in Respect to Genêt's Projected Attack upon the Floridas, 1793–94." In *The Annual Report of the American Historical Association for the Year 1897,* 569–679. Washington, DC: Government Printing Of-

fice, 1898. Michel Ange Bernard de Mangourit, Minister Genet, and others were involved in the plan to incite revolts and seize the Floridas and Louisiana. Documents also include an interesting analysis of the Genet mission by Minister Adet.

5:577   _____. "The Origins of Genet's Projected Attack on Louisiana and the Floridas." *American Historical Review* 3 (July 1898): 650–71. This article recounts the plans of the Girondist regime in France to extend the French empire of liberty in North America. The Spanish-American revolutionary, Francisco de Miranda, George Rogers Clark, and others were involved in the elaborate schemes.

5:578   _____. "Selections from the Draper Collection in the Possession of the State Historical Society of Wisconsin, to Elucidate the Proposed French Expedition under George Rogers Clark against Louisiana in the Years 1793–94." In *The Annual Report of the American Historical Association for the Year 1896,* 1: 930–1107. Washington, DC: Government Printing Office, 1897. This selection includes the Clark-Genet correspondence as well as correspondence copied from the Spanish archives showing Spanish awareness of the French scheme against Louisiana and the Floridas. A brief historical introduction and a chronological index to documents related to the Clark-Genet venture also appear.

Quasi-War

5:579   Allen, Gardner Weld. *Our Naval War with France.* Boston: Houghton Mifflin, 1909. This is the standard, if old, account of the naval operations of the undeclared war with France.

5:580   Anderson, William G. "John Adams, the Navy, and the Quasi-War with France." *American Neptune* 30 (April 1970): 117–32. This article presents a relatively brief, fairly basic, and generally favorable overview of Adams's policy in the Quasi-War.

5:581   DeConde, Alexander. *The Quasi-War: The Politics and Diplomacy of the Undeclared War with France 1797–1801.* New York: Scribner, 1966. DeConde demonstrates that peace was never beyond the reach of reasonable statesmen. Adams is depicted as wavering, while Talleyrand is viewed as persistently moving toward a peaceful resolution. Extensive bibliography.

5:582   Hill, Peter P. "Prologue to the Quasi-War: Stresses in Franco-American Commercial Relations, 1793–1796." *Journal of Modern History* 49 (March 1977): 1039–69. Drawing upon French naval records, Hill shows that, at least from the French perspective, Franco-American commercial relations were strained by both structural and diplomatic factors in the years leading up to the Quasi-War.

5:583   Tolles, Frederick B. "Unofficial Ambassador: George Logan's Mission to France, 1798." *William and Mary Quarterly* 3d ser. 7 (January 1950): 3–25. After he had left the presidency, John Adams gave some of the credit for his decision in 1799 to send a new mission to France to the information on French conciliation reported by Logan. The congressional response to Logan's personal mission was the Logan Act. For a full biography, see Tolles's *George Logan of Philadelphia* (New York: Oxford University Press, 1953).

XYZ Affair

5:584   Ford, Worthington C., ed. "Letters of William Vans Murray to John Quincy Adams, 1797–1803." In *The Annual Report of the American Historical Association for the Year 1912,* 341–715. Washington, DC: Government Printing Office, 1914. The letters in this compilation are drawn from the Adams Papers, Pickering Papers, and Murray Papers in the Pennsylvania Historical Society, the Morgan Library in New York, and the Library of Congress as well as Murray's official dispatches in the Department of State. They are helpful in understanding Murray's role as a peacemaker following the XYZ affair.

5:585   Hill, Peter P. *William Vans Murray, Federalist Diplomat: The Shaping of Peace with France, 1797–1801.* Syracuse: Syracuse University Press, 1971. Murray, a Federalist congressman from Maryland, was appointed U.S. minister to the Batavian Republic (Netherlands) in 1797. Although the author focuses principally on Murray's role in ending the Quasi-War, his mission found him reporting the frequent upheavals in Dutch revolutionary politics and the problems of Dutch-American commerce. Bibliography.

5:586   Kramer, Eugene. "John Adams, Elbridge Gerry, and the Origins of the XYZ Affair." *Essex Institute Historical Collections* 94 (January 1958): 57–68. Kramer shows in this critical evaluation of President Adams's appointment of Gerry to the commission to France with John Marshall and Charles Cotesworth Pinckney that he had no prior contact with the State Department or with his colleagues on the objects of the mission and entertained incompatible views.

5:587   Ray, Thomas M. "'Not One Cent for Tribute': The Public Addresses and American Popular Reaction to the XYZ Affair, 1798–1799." *Journal of the Early Republic* 3 (Winter 1983): 389–412. By examining petitions and addresses submitted to the federal government or published in newspapers, Ray finds that the wave of anti-French sentiment generated by the XYZ affair crossed party and sectional lines. This unity did not last long, in part due to the Alien and Sedition Acts, but it did serve to dispel what Ray describes as an "unhealthy" Francophilia.

5:588   Stinchcombe, William C. *The XYZ Affair.* Westport, CT: Greenwood Press, 1981. For the first time, the full story is told, using new materials. The author reviews not only foreign policy conflicts between Federalists and Republicans, but also differences within Adams's own cabinet. Even more important, French policies are fully explored and the role of Talleyrand and the French agents are fully developed.

Convention of 1800

5:589   Cooke, Jacob Ernest. "Country above Party: John Adams and the 1799 Mission to France." In *Fame and the Founding Fathers,* ed. Edmund P. Wills, 53–77. Bethlehem, PA: Moravian College, 1967. This is a highly critical analysis of President Adams's decision in 1799 to send a new mission to France, a decision, the author says, that unnecessarily and irreparably divided the Federalist Party. A demurring "Comment" by Stephen G. Kurtz follows, pp. 78–79.

5:590   Kurtz, Stephen G. "The French Mission of 1799–1800: Concluding Chapter in the Statecraft of John Adams." *Political Science Quarterly* 80 (December 1965): 543–57. Adams's positive response to

Talleyrand's peace overtures was governed by his desire to maintain peace, defuse domestic tensions, and squelch Federalist militarist adventurers. His leisurely appointment of negotiators was deliberate; Adams wished to strengthen the Caribbean fleet before negotiating.

5:591　Lyon, E. Wilson. "The Franco-American Convention of 1800." *Journal of Modern History* 12 (September 1940): 305–34. This is a standard work on the convention.

5:592　Rohrs, Richard C. "The Federalist Party and the Convention of 1800." *Diplomatic History* 12 (Summer 1988): 237–60. As a vehicle for studying John Adams and Alexander Hamilton's success as party leaders, this article examines the reception of the Convention of 1800 by the Federalist-dominated Senate. Rohrs finds that most Federalists rejected the advice of Adams and Hamilton to ratify the convention unconditionally.

Napoleonic Era

5:593　Horward, Donald D. "American Opinion on Napoleon's Downfall." *History Today* 16 (December 1966): 832–40. This brief article shows that American opinion, as expressed in newspapers and correspondence, was highly skeptical about Napoleon's defeat at Waterloo. When this skepticism finally gave way, it was replaced by a sense of shock.

5:594　Lovie, Jacques, and André Palluel-Guillard. *L'épisode napoléonien, 1799–1815. v 2: Aspects extérieurs [The Napoleonic Period, 1799–1815. Vol. 2: Foreign Developments]*. Paris: Editions de Seuil, 1972. This work is an able, if brief, work of synthesis, much of which is devoted to military campaigns. The treatment of diplomacy and particularly the Continental system—often critical of Napoleon—helps explain his American diplomacy.

Great Britain

5:595　Campbell, Charles Soutter. *From Revolution to Rapprochement: The United States and Great Britain, 1783–1900*. The thesis of this brief survey is that a real Anglo-American rapprochement was not realized until the end of the nineteenth century. The

period through the War of 1812 is covered in two chapters (of twelve). Bibliography (2:324).

5:596　Christie, Ian R. *Wars and Revolutions: Britain 1760–1815*. Cambridge, MA: Harvard University Press, 1982. This work provides a useful overview of British foreign policy from before the American revolution to the end of the Napoleonic era. It is best used for background, though there is some effort to include Anglo-American affairs after the revolution. Bibliographic essay.

5:597　Cross, Jack L. *London Mission: The First Critical Years*. East Lansing: Michigan State University Press, 1968. The author finds more accomplishments in Thomas Pinckney's mission (1794–1796) than does Bemis. Pinckney "swallowed his injured pride" and aided John Jay and, additionally, is credited with securing the repeal of the obnoxious order of November 8, 1793, barring American trade with the West Indies. The argument is not altogether convincing. Bibliography.

5:598　Hickey, Donald R. "The Monroe-Pinkney Treaty of 1806: A Reappraisal." *William and Mary Quarterly* 3d ser. 44 (January 1987): 65–88. Hickey compares the Monroe-Pinkney Treaty to the Jay Treaty and finds it preferable in terms of both trade and neutral rights. As such, he considers Jefferson's refusal to submit it to Congress a missed opportunity for an accommodation with Great Britain.

5:599　Marshall, P. J., ed. *The Oxford History of the British Empire. Vol. 2: The Eighteenth Century.* This collection of twenty-six essays examines various aspects of the British empire during the "long eighteenth century" (1688–1815). Most of the essays focus on economic and political relations within the empire, but others address emigration, religion, and warfare. The geographical coverage includes Asia, India, Ireland, and the Caribbean as well as the North American mainland. Although mostly concerned with the period up to the American revolution, the essays also include Patrick K. O'Brien, "Inseparable Connections: Trade, Economy, Fiscal State, and the Expansion of Empire, 1688–1815" (53–77); N. A. M. Rodger, "Sea-Power and Empire, 1688–1793" (169–83); Stephen Conway, "Britain and the Revolutionary Crisis, 1763–1791" (325–46); Peter Marshall, "British North America, 1760–1815" (372–93);

David Richardson, "The British Empire and the Atlantic Slave Trade, 1660–1807" (440–64); and Marshall, "Britain without America—A Second Empire?" (576–95) (3:73).

5:600 Perkins, Bradford. *Castlereagh and Adams: England and the United States, 1812–1823.* Berkeley: University of California Press, 1964. The last of a trilogy on Anglo-American relations from 1795 to 1823, this volume includes the most recent, extended discussion of the Ghent negotiations. Perkins's analysis often revises traditional interpretations, most generally by arguing that the settlement owed at least as much to British weakness of purpose as to the firmness and talents of the American negotiators.

5:601 _____. *The First Rapprochement: England and the United States, 1795–1805.* Philadelphia: University of Pennsylvania Press, 1955. The early chapters of this fine book examine the improvement in Anglo-American relations made possible by the ratification of the Jay Treaty and the election of John Adams. The last five chapters deal with Jefferson's first administration, with particular attention to England's role during the Louisiana controversy and to the growing tension after 1803. Extensive bibliography.

5:602 _____. *Prologue to War: England and the United States, 1805–1812.* Berkeley: University of California Press, 1961. In this comprehensive treatment of the road to the War of 1812, Perkins is very critical of the leadership of Jefferson and Madison and perhaps excessively understanding of some British figures. He ascribes the coming of the war primarily to maritime issues, as much for their psychological as material impact, and downplays sectionalism as a factor.

5:603 Ritcheson, Charles R. *Aftermath of Revolution: British Policy toward the United States, 1783–1795.* Dallas: Southern Methodist University Press, 1969. This important study forcefully presents the case for Great Britain's American policy. The view is from Whitehall. Extensive bibliography.

5:604 Ward, A. W., and G. P. Gooch, eds. *The Cambridge History of British Foreign Policy, 1783–1919. Vol. 1: 1783–1815.* New York: Macmillan Company, 1922. Reprint 1971 (Greenwood Press). Though now quite dated, this volume is still the best survey of its subject. The chapter on Anglo-American relations—C. K. Webster, "The American War and the Treaty of Ghent, 1812–1824" (522–42)—is thin, but other chapters develop British policies toward Europe in ways that make policy toward the United States more understandable.

5:605 Watson, John Steven. *The Reign of George III, 1760–1815.* Oxford: Clarendon Press, 1960. Like others in this section, this book is valuable essentially for the background it provides. Internal politics in Great Britain and the problems of the French war, two matters of great importance for relations with the United States, are covered, the first more satisfactorily than the second. Bibliography.

5:606 Webster, C. K. *The Foreign Policy of Castlereagh, 1812–1815, Britain and the Reconstruction of Europe.* Vol. 1. 2 vols. 2d ed. London: G. Bell, 1931. Although there is almost no mention of the United States, this volume provides the best understanding of Britain's position at the time of the Ghent negotiations. More than most background works, it should not be ignored. First published in 1925.

Jay Treaty

5:607 Bemis, Samuel Flagg. *Jay's Treaty: A Study in Commerce and Diplomacy.* Rev. ed. New Haven: Yale University Press, 1962. Reprint 1975 (Greenwood Press). The author concludes, in this still standard work, that the treaty would have been more acceptable without Alexander Hamilton's intervention; nevertheless, the treaty probably prevented war between the United States and Great Britain. Originally published in 1923.

5:608 Combs, Jerald A. *The Jay Treaty: Political Battleground of the Founding Fathers.* Berkeley: University of California Press, 1970. In this useful work, the struggle over the Jay Treaty is explained in terms of perceptions of power: Federalists saw their nation as weak and vulnerable and therefore feared provoking Great Britain; Republicans viewed the country as strong and geographically secure and so opposed compromising American principles.

5:609 Estes, Todd. "Shaping the Politics of Public Opinion: Federalists and the Jay Treaty Debate." *Journal of the Early Republic* 20 (Fall 2000): 393–422. Estes uses the debates over the Jay Treaty—in Congress, the press, and the streets—to examine Federalist ambivalence about mobilizing the public in support of specific policies. Federalists skillfully shaped public opinion in support of the treaty, despite their usual reluctance about involving the people in this manner. For a more narrowly focused essay on the same topic, see his "'The Most Bewitching Piece of Parliamentary Oratory': Fisher Ames' Jay Treaty Speech Reconsidered," *Historical Journal of Massachusetts* 28 (Winter 2000): 1–22.

5:610 Farnham, Thomas J. "The Virginia Amendments of 1795: An Episode in the Opposition to Jay's Treaty." *Virginia Magazine of History and Biography* 75 (January 1967): 75–88. Republicans in Virginia passed a petition in opposition to the Jay Treaty; though circulated to the other states, it received no support.

The Netherlands

5:611 Schama, Simon. *Patriots and Liberators: Revolution in the Netherlands, 1780–1813*. See chapter 4 of this Guide (4:253).

5:612 Westermann, Johannes Cornelis. *The Netherlands and the United States: Their Relations in the Beginning of the Nineteenth Century*. The Hague: M. Nijhoff, 1935. One of few treatments exclusively focusing on early Dutch-American relations (1780–1821), this study examines the Treaty of 1782. Bibliography.

5:613 Winter, Pieter Jan van, with James C. Riley. *American Finance and Dutch Investment, 1780–1805, with an Epilogue to 1840*. Translated by C. M. Geyl and I. Clephane. See chapter 4 of this Guide (4:87).

Russia

5:614 Bolkhovitinov, Nikolai N. *The Beginnings of Russian-American Relations, 1775–1815*. Translated by Elena Levin. Bolkhovitinov, a Soviet scholar, paints a broad picture of Russian-American relations that includes commerce, cultural contacts, politics, and diplomacy in Europe and North America (4:259).

5:615 Crosby, Alfred W. *America, Russia, Hemp, and Napoleon: American Trade with Russia and the Baltic, 1783–1812*. Columbus: Ohio State University Press, 1965. While this book provides few insights into Russian diplomacy, it does depict the nature of American trade with Russia and the economic warfare being conducted in Europe. Bibliographies.

5:616 McFadden, David W. "John Quincy Adams, American Commercial Diplomacy, and Russia, 1809–1825." *New England Quarterly* 66 (December 1993): 613–29. As minister to Russia and secretary of state, Adams sought to expand American trade with Russia, both in Europe and on the northwest coast of North America, according to McFadden. The article is thin, however, on the context created for Adams's efforts by the Napoleonic Wars.

5:617 Saul, Norman E. *Distant Friends: The United States and Russia, 1763–1867*. This work offers a thorough overview of early Russian-American relations, which were at a low ebb, at least in diplomatic terms, for a quarter century after the revolution. The book includes a long chapter on the critical diplomatic and commercial relations at the time of the Napoleonic Wars and the War of 1812. Extensive bibliography (2:310).

5:618 Schlafly, Daniel L., Jr. "The First Russian Diplomat in America: Andrei Dashkov on the New Republic." *Historian* 60 (Fall 1997): 39–57. Dashkov arrived in the United States in July 1809 and remained until 1819. Schlafly is more interested in a report on American society that Dashkov prepared after returning to Russia than in his activities while at his post.

Pinckney's Treaty

5:619 Bemis, Samuel Flagg. *Pinckney's Treaty: A Study of America's Advantage from Europe's Distress, 1783–1800*. Baltimore: Johns Hopkins Press, 1926. Bemis's still valid thesis, borrowed from Jefferson, is that European quarrels in this era could be relied upon to advance the purposes of American foreign policy. The author contends that the Treaty of San Lorenzo, highly acceptable to the United States, resulted from Spain's distress at the prospect of a French invasion and at possible implications of the Jay Treaty. Bibliography.

5:620   Whitaker, Arthur Preston. "New Light on the Treaty of San Lorenzo: An Essay in Historical Criticism." *Mississippi Valley Historical Review* 15 (March 1929): 435–54. Based on his study on multi-archival research, Whitaker downplays the importance of developments in France and Great Britain (including the Jay Treaty) on Spain as factors leading to Pinckney's Treaty.

5:621   Young, Raymond A. "Pinckney's Treaty: A New Perspective." *Hispanic American Historical Review* 43 (November 1963): 526–35. While ascribing Pinckney's success partly to Godoy's alarm at the implications of the Jay Treaty and partly to the certainty that London would resent Spain's exit from the First Coalition, the author insists on the critical importance of Pinckney's role as negotiator.

Germany-Prussia

5:622   Adams, Henry Mason. *Prussian-American Relations, 1775–1871.* Using German and English sources, Adams explains why Prussia, tenaciously neutral during the American revolution, was moved to conclude the "liberal" commercial treaty with Adams in 1785. Bibliography (4:255).

5:623   Barclay, David E., and Elisabeth Glaser-Schmidt, eds. *Transatlantic Images and Perceptions: Germany and America since 1776.* New York: Cambridge University Press, 1997. Two articles in this collection are useful for the early national period: A. Gregg Roeber, "'Through a Glass Darkly': Changing German Ideas of American Freedom, 1776–1806," and Hermann Wellenreuther, "'Germans Make Cows and Women Work': American Perceptions of Germans as Reported in American Travel Books, 1800–1840."

5:624   Dippel, Horst. *Germany and the American Revolution, 1770–1800: A Sociohistorical Investigation of Late Eighteenth-Century Political Thinking.*

Translated by Bernhard A. Uhlendorf. See chapter 4 of this Guide (4:256).

5:625   Reeves, Jesse S. "The Prussian-American Treaties." *American Journal of International Law* 11 (July 1917): 475–510. Reeves analyzes the Treaty of 1785, which Benjamin Franklin negotiated with Frederick the Great, and its several renewals. The 1785 treaty was "acclaimed at the time as setting a new standard of international conduct, realizing to the fullest extent the humanitarian aspirations of the eighteenth century."

AFRICA AND ASIA

5:626   Allison, Robert J. *The Crescent Obscured: The United States and the Muslim World, 1776–1815.* New York: Oxford University Press, 1995. While Allison discusses the Barbary wars of the late eighteenth and early nineteenth centuries, his focus is actually on American, especially governmental, views of Islam and the Muslim world. He looks, in particular, at the subjects that stood out in American assessments—politics, gender roles, and slavery.

5:627   Bradley, Harold W. *The American Frontier in Hawaii: The Pioneers, 1789–1843.* Stanford, CA: Stanford University Press, 1942. Bradley emphasizes the narrowly commercial nature of early contacts, seeing them as "the harbinger of permanent ties to follow." This study is well researched, but only from English-language sources.

5:628   Brooks, George E., Jr. *Yankee Traders, Old Coasters & African Middlemen: A History of American Legitimate Trade with West Africa in the Nineteenth Century.* Boston: Boston University Press, 1970. This monograph seeks to describe the growth and organization of legitimate American trade with West Africa from the 1790s until the 1870s, and to relate American commerce to that of European, African, and Eurafrican traders. Extensive bibliography.

5:629   Clendenen, Clarence C., and Peter Duignan. *Americans in Black Africa up to 1865.* Stanford, CA: Hoover Institution on War, Revolution, and Peace, 1964. The three major sections of this brief monograph deal with American traders, missionaries and colonization societies, and explorers and frontiersmen. Bibliography.

5:630 Field, James A., Jr. *America and the Mediterranean World, 1776–1882.* This elegantly written account treats the full range of American contacts with the various peoples and nations of North Africa and the Middle East, including trade, missionary, educational, naval, and diplomatic interchange. The 1991 reprint is titled *From Gibraltar to the Middle East: America and the Mediterranean World, 1776–1882.* Extensive bibliography (4:55).

5:631 Furber, Holden. "The Beginnings of American Trade with India, 1784–1812." *New England Quarterly* 11 (June 1938): 235–65. Prior to 1792–1793, U.S. trade with such ports as Madras, Calcutta, and Bombay appeared to be merely ancillary to the China trade. The loose wording and lax enforcement of article 13 of the Jay Treaty gave Americans greater access to Indian markets than the company would otherwise have permitted.

5:632 Levi, Werner. "The Earliest Relations between the United States of America and Australia." *Pacific Historical Review* 12 (December 1943): 351–61. Levi explains that prevailing winds made Australia a convenient port of call for Canton-bound American merchantmen, touching at New South Wales (1792–1812) shortly after the first colonists were settled there.

Barbary States

5:633 Baepler, Paul, ed. *White Slaves, African Masters: An Anthology of American Barbary Captivity Narratives.* Chicago: University of Chicago Press, 1999. This volume reprints excerpts from nine narratives of Americans held in captivity in the Barbary states. Seven of the nine recount captivities during the period from the 1780s through the 1810s. Baepler's lengthy introduction helps to place the narratives in a variety of contexts. The book includes a bibliography, and publication history, of all American works of this type.

5:634 Barnby, H. G. *The Prisoners of Algiers: An Account of the Forgotten American-Algerian War 1785–1797.* New York: Oxford University Press,

1966. This work is easily the best account of the war with Algiers. It is rendered in good narrative style, with interpretive analysis that relates domestic and foreign policy, demonstrates the force of the Boston shipping lobby in shaping policy, and criticizes American diplomacy. Barnby also includes material on consular officials Joel Barlow, David Humphreys, James Cathcart, and Richard O'Brien. Bibliography.

5:635 Cantor, Milton. "A Connecticut Yankee in a Barbary Court: Joel Barlow's Algerian Letters to His Wife." *William and Mary Quarterly* 3d ser. 19 (January 1962): 86–109. These personal letters, mostly from 1796, show Barlow's role in Algerian diplomacy and include his observations on Algerian society.

5:636 _____. "Joel Barlow's Mission to Algiers." *Historian* 25 (February 1963): 172–94. During his Paris mission (1796–1797), James Monroe asked Joel Barlow to go to Algiers to expedite the release of American seamen. Cantor details Barlow's expensive but ultimately successful ransoming efforts, depicting him as the most skillful of several American diplomats engaged in this drawn-out negotiation. Cantor also examines Barlow's dealing with Tunis and Tripoli.

5:637 Carr, James A. "John Adams and the Barbary Problem: The Myth and the Record." *American Neptune* 26 (October 1966): 231–57. The "myth" the author finds repeated is that Adams, unlike Jefferson, preferred paying tribute to taking naval action. Carr maintains that Adams was less unwilling than unable to take strong action, hindered as he was by antinavy Republicans in Congress and preoccupied with using what navy he had to prosecute the Quasi-War with France.

5:638 Irwin, Ray W. *The Diplomatic Relations of the United States with the Barbary Powers, 1776–1816.* Chapel Hill: University of North Carolina Press, 1931. Reprint 1970 (Russell and Russell). Still useful to scholars, this early study of U.S. relations with Algiers, Morocco, Tripoli, and Tunis is drawn largely from U.S. consular correspondence and published works. Bibliography.

5:639 Kitzen, Michael L. S. *Tripoli and the United States at War: A History of American Rela-*

tions with the Barbary States, 1785–1805. Jefferson, NC: McFarland and Co., 1993. Relying almost entirely on the documents collected by Dudley W. Knox (see U.S. Office of Naval Records and Library, *Naval Documents Related to the United States Wars with the Barbary Powers . . . Naval Operations Including Diplomatic Background* [1939–1944] [5:18]), this work emphasizes "facts" rather than interpretation in telling the story of American diplomacy with the Barbary states. The "best of ideals and intentions become clouded by politics and political ineptitude," according to Kitzen.

5:640 Tucker, Glenn. *Dawn Like Thunder: The Barbary Wars and the Birth of the U.S. Navy.* Indianapolis: Bobbs-Merrill, 1963. This account of the Barbary wars focuses very closely on the navy, which admittedly had a diplomatic role in this matter. It is fairly comprehensive, but lacks documentation. Bibliography.

5:641 Wilson, Gary E. "American Hostages in Moslem Nations, 1784–1796: The Public Response." *Journal of the Early Republic* 2 (Summer 1982): 123–41. Wilson charts the early failures of the U.S. government to handle the problem of Barbary piracy and the concomitant growth of private interest in this issue. By the mid-1790s, public opinion had become a critical force in pressing a weak government to act, even as private philanthropic groups provided monetary support for American captives.

5:642 _____. "The First American Hostages in Moslem Nations, 1784–1789." *American Neptune* 41 (July 1981): 208–23. Wilson provides a general account of an early period in the American struggle with Barbary piracy, particularly in Morocco and Algiers. Jefferson, in Paris, and Adams, in London, played key roles.

5:643 Wright, Louis B., and Julia H. MacLeod. *The First Americans in North Africa: William Eaton's Struggle for a Vigorous Policy against the Barbary Pirates, 1799–1805.* Princeton: Princeton University Press, 1945. This critical study of early American diplomatic efforts with the Barbary states focuses on the career of William Eaton. The authors relate American Barbary policy to the Boston shipping lobby that favored an aggressive commercial policy in the Mediterranean. Timothy Pickering is portrayed

as a staunch advocate of an aggressive policy toward Barbary. Bibliography.

The War of 1812

GENERAL

5:644 Horsman, Reginald. *The Causes of the War of 1812.* Philadelphia: University of Pennsylvania Press, 1962. Horsman stresses the importance of maritime issues, reaching the rather commonsensical conclusion that, had there been no European conflict and thus no assault on American neutral rights, there would have been no war between the United States and Britain. His critical examination of the importance of the Indian problem and the presumed desire to conquer Canada is particularly impressive. Bibliography.

5:645 Stagg, J. C. A. *Mr. Madison's War: Politics, Diplomacy, and Warfare in the Early American Republic, 1783–1830.* Princeton: Princeton University Press, 1983. Probably the most significant work on the War of 1812 of the last three decades, this book provides a comprehensive account of the political, diplomatic, and military history of the war. Stagg offers new explanations of the role of Canada and the place of divisions within the Republican Party in the movement toward war. His discussion of the war itself emphasizes the structural problems within the federal government, in general, and the War Department and army, in particular, that undermined American efforts.

5:646 Watts, Steven. *The Republic Reborn: War and the Making of Liberal America, 1790–1820.* Baltimore: Johns Hopkins University Press, 1987. In this intriguing, if not always convincing, work, Watts locates the War of 1812 at a crucial point in the transition of the United States from a republican to a liberal capitalist order. The war helped ease this transformation, according to Watts, by providing a way to vent anxieties. He argues that the same group of men took the lead in advancing liberal ideals and in moving the nation toward war; the capsule biographies that he includes, however, discuss an odd mix of people—the authors Charles Brockden Brown, Mason Locke Weems, and Hugh Henry

Brackenridge—and generally omit key policymakers, such as Madison and Monroe.

SOURCES OF CONTROVERSY

European Restrictions on Commerce

5:647   Crouzet, François. *L'économie britannique et le blocus continental, 1806–1813 [The British Economy and the Continental System, 1806–1813].* 2 vols. Paris: Presses universitaires de France, 1958. Reprint 1993 (E. Elgar). This study is essential to an understanding of economic conditions in Britain and of the effectiveness of French policy toward commerce. It cannot be ignored by the student of Anglo-American relations, although only a small part deals directly with American commerce. The bibliography contains exhaustive lists of British government archives and the manuscripts of business figures and commercial houses.

Impressment

5:648   Gaines, Edwin M. "The *Chesapeake* Affair: Virginians Mobilize to Defend National Honor." *Virginia Magazine of History and Biography* 64 (April 1956): 131–42. In this article, Gaines shows that the Virginia militia was called out as much to maintain order in a population that had responded to rumors of a British invasion with rioting and panic as to defend against the British. He also does well to show the constant tension between the federal and state governments during this crisis.

5:649   McKee, Christopher. "Foreign Seamen in the United States Navy: A Census of 1808." *William and Mary Quarterly* 3d ser. 42 (July 1985): 383–93. Using evidence from the New York station, McKee is able to attach some hard numbers to what was a hotly contested issue between the United States and Great Britain in the aftermath of the *Chesapeake* Affair—the number of British subjects in the U.S. navy. McKee finds that about half of the seamen in the navy were foreign nationals, about three-quarters of whom were from the British Isles.

5:650   Steel, Anthony. "Impressment in the Monroe-Pinkney Negotiations, 1806–1807." *American Historical Review* 57 (January 1952): 352–69. Steel argues that impressment was vital to British security and indeed survival in the face of the Napoleonic challenge but, for the Americans, an essentially minor issue to be exploited or not, as politics suggested.

5:651   Tucker, Spencer C., and Frank T. Reuter. *Injured Honor: The Chesapeake-Leopard Affair, June 22, 1807.* Annapolis: Naval Institute Press, 1996. In this relatively brief book, Tucker and Reuter provide a full account of the encounter between the *Chesapeake* and the *Leopard* and discuss its multifaceted diplomatic and political consequences. Bibliography.

5:652   Zimmerman, James F. *Impressment of American Seamen.* New York: Columbia University Studies in History, Economics and Public Law, 1925. The only monograph solely devoted to impressment, Zimmerman's work deserves examination. It is very much dated and it fails to place the issue in a broad context. However, this work provides a chronology and seeks to solve the vexing (perhaps insoluble) problem of the number of men taken by the Royal Navy.

Economic Coercion

5:653   Frankel, Jeffrey A. "The 1807–1809 Embargo against Great Britain." *Journal of Economic History* 42 (June 1982): 291–308. Frankel employs economic data to weigh the impact of the Embargo on the United States and Great Britain. While both nations' economies were effectively reduced to autarky, that of the British was harder hit, according to Frankel, in terms of the relative price increase of products that were interdicted by the Embargo.

5:654   Heaton, Herbert. "Non-Importation, 1806–1812." *Journal of Economic History* 1 (November 1941): 178–98. Heaton's study demonstrates that the Embargo and other legislation restricting American commerce left open far more trade than has often been assumed. He thus casts a negative light on the effectiveness of economic coercion as a means to procure satisfaction from the European powers.

5:655   Higham, Robin. "The Port of Boston and the Embargo of 1807–1809." *American Neptune* 16

(July 1956): 189–210. This useful article shows that, at least in Boston, the Embargo did not mean the death of commerce. An upsurge in coastal trade made the decline in overseas commerce less painful, and there were evasions and violations of the Embargo whose magnitude cannot be established.

5:656   Jones, Douglas Lamar. "'The Caprice of Juries': The Enforcement of the Jeffersonian Embargo in Massachusetts." *American Journal of Legal History* 24 (October 1980): 307–30. By focusing on the courts, Jones provides a compelling study of the failure of the Embargo in Massachusetts. He documents the impact of hostile public opinion, as expressed by juries in smuggling cases, in effectively nullifying the Embargo in Boston and recounts the successful, if ultimately meaningless, effort to have the Embargo declared unconstitutional in the state courts.

5:657   Mannix, Richard. "Gallatin, Jefferson, and the Embargo of 1808." *Diplomatic History* 3 (Spring 1979): 151–72. Mannix provides an essential perspective on the Embargo by highlighting the smuggling that undermined it and the inability of the government to enforce it. Increasingly, Mannix shows, Jefferson passed the burden to Gallatin and the Treasury Department, distancing himself from the details even as he urged more and more repressive steps to prevent smuggling.

5:658   Muller, H. N., III. "Smuggling into Canada: How the Champlain Valley Defied Jefferson's Embargo." *Vermont History* 38 (Winter 1970): 5–21. Even though Vermont generally supported Jefferson, it became a hotbed of smuggling after the Embargo was extended to nonmaritime trade in May 1808. The refusal of Vermonters to abandon their accustomed trade into Canada and their resistance of federal customs officials ultimately resulted in a presidential proclamation.

5:659   Pancake, John S. "Baltimore and the Embargo, 1807–1809." *Maryland Historical Magazine* 47 (September 1952): 173–87. Baltimore, Pancake argues, was hard hit by the Embargo, which gave new energy to the minority Federalist Party. The dominant Republicans continued to support the measure publicly, even as they petitioned for relief and helped to bring about a repeal in Congress in early 1809.

5:660   Sears, Louis Martin. *Jefferson and the Embargo.* Durham, NC: Duke University Press, 1927. Reprint 1978 (Octagon Books). With Walter W. Jennings, *The American Embargo, 1807–1809, with Particular Reference to Its Effect on Industry* (Iowa City: University of Iowa Studies in the Social Sciences, 1921), and Spivak, *Jefferson's English Crisis: Commerce, Embargo, and the Republican Revolution* (1979) (5:661), this is one of the essential works on the great Jeffersonian experiment (1807–1809). The underlying hypothesis—that Jefferson, a pacifist, sought to preserve peace by adopting the Embargo—is open to question. But Sears presents an argument that deserves to be considered.

5:661   Spivak, Burton I. *Jefferson's English Crisis: Commerce, Embargo, and the Republican Revolution.* Charlottesville: University Press of Virginia, 1979. This is the most satisfactory monograph on Jefferson's thinking on the Embargo. According to Spivak, Jefferson first conceived of it as a precautionary withdrawal from the ocean but subsequently came to hope that it would have a coercive impact on Europe, especially Britain, and finally hoped that a cessation of foreign trade would help America turn away from "English" commercialism, which had a deleterious impact on the nation's social and political mores. Bibliography.

5:662   Stagg, J. C. A. "James Madison and the Coercion of Great Britain: Canada, the West Indies, and the War of 1812." *William and Mary Quarterly* 3d ser. 38 (January 1981): 3–34. This article adds a new dimension to the discussion of American reasons for attacking Canada. Stagg argues that Madison sought its conquest to deprive the British empire, especially the West Indies, of goods exported (often illegally) through Canada from the United States and also of the increasing exports of Canada itself. Otherwise, Madison feared, his preferred policy of commercial restriction would be fatally undermined.

5:663   Strum, Harvey. "Rhode Island and the Embargo of 1807." *Rhode Island History* 52 (May 1994): 59–67. This brief article shows that hostility to the Embargo in Rhode Island was manifested in extensive smuggling and a revitalization of the Federalists. Strum's state-by-state study of the Embargo continues in "New Jersey and the Embargo, 1807–1809," *New Jersey History* 116 (Fall-Winter 1998): 16–47.

5:664 _____. "Smuggling in Maine during the Embargo and the War of 1812." *Colby Library Quarterly* 19 (June 1983): 90–97. In this brief article, Strum shows that the restrictions on commerce resulting from the Embargo, the Non-Intercourse Act, and the War of 1812 resulted in widespread hardship in Maine that made them unpopular and led to smuggling.

5:665 Stuart, Reginald C. "James Madison and the Militants: Republican Disunity and Replacing the Embargo." *Diplomatic History* 6 (Spring 1982): 145–67. Stuart argues that, in the winter of 1808–1809, a loose coalition of Republicans wanted to replace the Embargo not with the weaker measures that were eventually adopted, but with limited military reprisals. They were encouraged in this end by President-elect Madison. But the opposition of Quids, Federalists, and other Republicans prompted Madison and the "militants" to back down. Still, Stuart sees them as having taken "the first major step on the road to the War of 1812" during this period.

5:666 Ward, Christopher. "The Commerce of East Florida during the Embargo, 1806–1812: The Role of Amelia Island." *Florida Historical Quarterly* 68 (October 1989): 160–79. By tracking the growing trade through Amelia Island, Ward shows the extensive smuggling between Georgia and Spanish East Florida during the years of the Embargo and Non-Intercourse Act. This traffic — in slaves, cotton, turpentine, barrel staves, and other goods — provided many products that were badly needed by the British empire.

THE DECISION FOR WAR

State and Local Opinion

5:667 Barlow, William R. "The Coming of the War of 1812 in Michigan Territory." *Michigan History* 53 (Summer 1969): 91–107. As early as 1807, Barlow argues, Michiganders were resigned to war with England. However, in an explicit refutation of the thesis of Pratt, *The Expansionists of 1812* (1925) (5:672), Barlow maintains that, far from seeking war as a solution to Indian problems, Michiganders feared that a conflict with England would touch off an Indian war for which they were unprepared.

5:668 _____. "Ohio's Congressmen and the War of 1812." *Ohio History* 72 (Summer 1963): 175–94. Barlow shows that Ohio and its representatives in Washington were by no means unanimously for war in 1812; Canada was a target of opportunity rather than a war aim.

5:669 Haynes, Robert V. "The Southwest and the War of 1812." *Louisiana History* 5 (Winter 1964): 41–51. This brief examination of developments in the Mississippi and Orleans territories applies the interpretation of western sentiment advanced in Taylor, "Agrarian Discontent in the Mississippi Valley Preceding the War of 1812" (1931) (5:673). Southwesterners also had their eyes on the Floridas, since Spain's possession of those provinces impeded their access to the sea.

5:670 Latimer, Margaret K. "South Carolina — A Protagonist of the War of 1812." *American Historical Review* 60 (July 1956): 914–29. This article convincingly extends to South Carolina, and by implication to the entire south and perhaps even to all areas producing agricultural goods for export, the thesis of Taylor, "Agrarian Discontent in the Mississippi Valley Preceding the War of 1812" (1931) (5:673). Many in South Carolina, suffering economically, blamed their problems on European interference with trade and concluded that war with Britain was the solution to their problems.

5:671 Stagg, J. C. A. "Between Black Rock and a Hard Place: Peter B. Porter's Plan for an American Invasion of Canada in 1812." *Journal of the Early Republic* 19 (Fall 1999): 385–422. Stagg uses a lengthy memorandum prepared by New York Congressman Porter in the spring of 1812 for someone high in the administration to elucidate the tensions between private and public interests and the place of Canada in the calculations that ended in a divisive declaration of war. The article includes the complete memorandum.

Western Issues

5:672 Pratt, Julius W. *Expansionists of 1812.* New York: Macmillan Company, 1925. Without question the most influential study of the coming of the War of 1812, this work argues that, at the behest of the west and the south, the United States went to war in an effort to conquer Canada and Florida. Westerners sought to eradicate Indian interference, southerners to acquire territory and to open trade routes. Much recent scholarship suggests corrections, but many textbooks still follow his interpretation. Bibliography.

5:673   Taylor, George Rogers. "Agrarian Discontent in the Mississippi Valley Preceding the War of 1812." *Journal of Political Economy* 39 (August 1931): 471–505. After an unstable boom, Taylor argues, the Mississippi valley suffered a sharp series of economic setbacks after 1806. Ascribing depressed agricultural prices solely, but erroneously, to European interference with trade, westerners supported the Embargo to coerce Europe; when that failed, they endorsed war as an alternative. Taylor introduces a new element into the discussion of the west's war spirit, but does not seek to assay the west's responsibility for the War of 1812.

The War Session

5:674   Bell, Rudolph M. "Mr. Madison's War and Long-Term Congressional Voting Behavior." *William and Mary Quarterly* 3d ser. 36 (July 1979): 373–95. Based upon his analysis of some 600 roll call votes from 1789 to 1812 that demonstrate the strength of party loyalty, Bell concludes that Madison could have reasonably counted on the support of Congress in a declaration of war when he asked for one. Such a focus on long-term trends, however, might miss the growing fragmentation of the Republican Party and could give an incorrect impression of Madison's confidence in the spring of 1812.

5:675   Brown, Roger H. *The Republic in Peril: 1812.* New York: Columbia University Press, 1964. Reprint 1971 (W. W. Norton). This important contribution stresses partisan as opposed to sectional considerations in the vote for war in 1812. Brown downplays the differences within the Republican Party, denying, for example, that there were any real War Hawks. His study of Republican actions and attitudes in 1811–1812 is unmatched. Extensive bibliography.

5:676   Fritz, Harry W. "The War Hawks of 1812:

Party Leadership in the Twelfth Congress." *Capitol Studies* 5 (Spring 1977): 25–42. This article seeks to restore, in a more sophisticated form, the War Hawk interpretation. Although important, Fritz argues that partisan interest and Republican ideology would have been insufficient to produce a declaration of war but for the leadership of the War Hawks. The argument is certainly worth considering.

5:677   Hatzenbuehler, Ronald L., and Robert L. Ivie. *Congress Declares War: Rhetoric, Leadership, and Partisanship in the Early Republic.* Kent, OH: Kent State University Press, 1983. Looking at the relative importance of rhetoric, partisanship, and leadership, Hatzenbuehler and Ivie develop a model of decisionmaking that can explain why war was declared in 1812 and not in either 1798 or 1807. They conclude that, despite the Constitution's delegation of the war power to Congress, a presidential request for a declaration of war was essential. Bibliographic essay.

5:678   _____. "Justifying the War of 1812: Toward a Model of Congressional Behavior in Early War Crises." *Social Sciences History* 4 (Fall 1980): 453–77. This article suggests that there were enough Republican votes in Congress for a declaration of war against Great Britain well before June 1812. What was lacking was a rhetoric that could justify war to the public and to the congressmen themselves.

5:679   Hickey, Donald R. "The Federalists and the Coming of War, 1811–1812." *Indiana Magazine of History* 75 (March 1979): 70–81. Hickey argues that, in the period leading up to the declaration of war against Great Britain, the Federalists acted with increasing unity regardless of regional differences. In his view, they were not simply obstructionists, but men acting upon reasoned policy considerations and long-standing party positions.

5:680   Horsman, Reginald, Roger H. Brown, Alexander DeConde, and Norman K. Risjord. "The War Hawks and the War of 1812." *Indiana Magazine of History* 60 (June 1964): 119–58. In this symposium, Horsman and Brown reiterate arguments, respectively, for and against the existence of a War Hawk faction in the Congress of 1811–1812. DeConde and Risjord comment. Taken together, the contributions summarize the controversy.

5:681 Johnson, Leland R. "The Suspense Was Hell: The Senate Vote for the War of 1812." *Indiana Magazine of History* 65 (December 1969): 247–67. A detailed examination of the Senate during the war session, this article argues that the outcome in the upper chamber was even more problematical than in the House. Republican factionalism made a majority for war seem almost impossible, but party loyalty eked out a victory.

5:682 Morison, Samuel Eliot. "The Henry-Crillon Affair of 1812." *Proceedings of the Massachusetts Historical Society* 3d ser. 69 (December 1949): 207–31. This article is a lively, scholarly treatment of a British secret agent, who was later a turncoat. Madison sought to use Henry's disclosures to influence the move toward war in 1812. The entire affair reflects little credit on anyone involved, least of all the president. (Morison's article adds much to E. A. Cruikshank, *The Political Adventures of John Henry: The Record of an International Imbroglio* [Toronto: Macmillan, 1936].)

5:683 Risjord, Norman K. "1812: Conservatives, War Hawks, and the Nation's Honor." *William and Mary Quarterly* 3d ser. 18 (April 1961): 196–210. Risjord argues that, faced with the alternatives of submission or war, Americans chose the latter as the only means to preserve the nation's honor. He downplays the importance of material factors such as ship seizures, economic depression, and expansionism

.

THE WAR OF 1812 AND THE TREATY OF GHENT

Military Aspects

5:684 Hickey, Donald R. *The War of 1812: A Forgotten Conflict.* Urbana: University of Illinois Press, 1989. Hickey's study of the War of 1812 focuses primarily on the military conflict itself, though it provides substantial attention to domestic politics and economics. While it advances few new arguments and says little about the origins of the war, this book is somewhat broader than Harry L. Coles's *The War of 1812* (Chicago: University of Chicago Press, 1965).

5:685 Horsman, Reginald. "On to Canada: Manifest Destiny and United States Strategy in the War of 1812." *Michigan Historical Review* 13 (Fall 1987): 1–24. Without adopting the view that a desire for Canada led the United States, or even the trans-Appalachian west, to seek war in 1812, Horsman argues that annexation of the provinces was a hoped for, and even expected, collateral benefit of the war for many Americans. Canada had long been viewed as a threat to American security and a reminder of British power.

5:686 _____. *The War of 1812.* New York: Alfred A. Knopf, 1969. This skillful narrative is particularly strong in reconstructing British policy and organization, although the interpretations tend to confirm rather than alter previous ones. The plan of the volume precludes much attention to diplomacy. Bibliographical note.

5:687 Kastor, Peter J. "Toward 'the Maritime War Only': The Question of Naval Mobilization, 1811–1812." *Journal of Military History* 61 (July 1997): 455–80. Kastor tries to discern the factors that led the Madison administration to commit an unprepared American fleet to a war against the largest navy on earth without having made any advance preparations or begun any new construction. He finds the explanation at the "intersection of military strategy, political economy, and political process."

5:688 Owsley, Frank L., Jr. *Struggle for the Gulf Borderlands: The Creek War and the Battle of New Orleans, 1812–1815.* Gainesville: University Presses of Florida, 1981. This book is primarily a military history of the War of 1812 in the south, and the associated Creek War, in which the key figure is Andrew Jackson. But Owsley is well aware of the diplomatic aspects of this warfare and does a solid job, based on multiarchival research, of establishing the links among the British, Spanish, and Indians in the region. Bibliography.

5:689 Skeen, C. Edward. *Citizen Soldiers in the War of 1812.* Lexington: University Press of Kentucky, 1999. Skeen focuses on the use of the state militias by the federal government during the War of 1812, surveying their performance, reviewing the operations, and examining their shortcomings. In his opinion, the militia failed because the Constitution divided the responsibility for them between federal and state governments. Bibliographic essay.

5:690   Stagg, J. C. A. "Enlisted Men in the United States Army, 1812–1815: A Preliminary Survey." *William and Mary Quarterly* 3d ser. 43 (October 1986): 615–45. This article is essentially a prospectus, with some initial results, for a "new military history" of the War of 1812 that tries to answer such questions as who served and why. One of Stagg's most interesting conclusions is that the army had actually enlisted far more men than the administration ever realized; administration strategy was, therefore, needlessly limited by an undercounting of its available forces.

Internal Aspects

5:691   Brynn, Edward. "Patterns of Dissent: Vermont's Opposition to the War of 1812." *Vermont History* 40 (Winter 1972): 10–27. Brynn examines smuggling, newspapers, and voting during the Embargo and War of 1812 as evidence of Vermont's dissent from administration policies. He relates this dissent to the social, economic, and political transformation that was ongoing in the state.

5:692   Buckley, William E., ed. "Letters of Connecticut Federalists, 1814–1815." *New England Quarterly* 3 (April 1930): 316–31. These letters, written by a number of Connecticut Federalists, provide an interesting insight into Federalist thinking on the eve of and during the Hartford Convention.

5:693   Cassell, Frank A. "The Great Baltimore Riot of 1812." *Maryland Historical Magazine* 70 (Fall 1975): 241–59. In this intriguing examination of the interaction of domestic politics and foreign affairs in a single city, Cassell discusses the origins of the pro-war, anti-Federalist riot and shows how the backlash against the Republican mob gave the Federalists enough power to cripple the war effort in Maryland.

5:694   Everest, Allan S. *The War of 1812 in the Champlain Valley.* Syracuse: Syracuse University Press, 1981. Covering the period from the Embargo through the War of 1812, Everest shows how the commercial ties that tied the Champlain valley region

of Vermont and New York more closely to British Canada than to the United States undermined American policy.

5:695   Gribbin, William. *The Churches Militant: The War of 1812 and American Religion.* New Haven: Yale University Press, 1973. Both opponents and supporters of the war found justification for their positions in the Bible. The nation as a whole, however, believed that the successful conclusion of the war showed God's continued faith in the United States. Bibliography.

5:696   Hammack, James Wallace. *Kentucky and the Second American Revolution: The War of 1812.* Lexington: University Press of Kentucky, 1976. This brief book combines an account of the military activities of Kentuckians in the War of 1812 with a discussion of the changing attitudes and conditions within the state during the war. Bibliographic essay.

5:697   Hickey, Donald R. "American Trade Restrictions during the War of 1812." *Journal of American History* 68 (December 1981): 517–38. Hickey demonstrates that wartime restrictions on American trade were no more successful than those in place from 1807 to 1812, even though much of the smuggling now involved trading with the enemy.

5:698   _____. "New England's Defense Problem and the Genesis of the Hartford Convention." *New England Quarterly* 50 (December 1977): 587–604. Hickey sees the origins of the Hartford Convention not in New England separatism or Federalist obstructionism, but in a real concern that the federal government was incompetent to defend the nation against a British invasion. Rather than meeting the threat in a state-by-state fashion, as even loyal Republican states were doing, the small New England states hoped to assemble a regional defense force.

5:699   Lemmon, Sarah McCulloh. *Frustrated Patriots: North Carolina and the War of 1812.* Chapel Hill: University of North Carolina Press, 1973. This extremely intensive study examines North Carolina's attitudes toward the declaration of war and the war itself. There was significant opposition between 1812 and 1815. Lemmon emphasizes the importance of the national honor theme, downplaying the contributions of expansionism, fear of the Indians, and commercial depression. Bibliography.

5:700   Morison, Samuel Eliot. "Dissent in the War of 1812." In *Dissent in Three American Wars,* ed. Samuel Eliot Morison, Frederick Merk, and Frank Freidel, 3–31. Cambridge, MA: Harvard University Press, 1970. Morison's graceful essay contends that this was America's most unpopular war and suggests that civil war might have broken out in 1815 had the Ghent negotiations not succeeded.

5:701   Morison, Samuel Eliot, ed. "Two Letters of Harrison Gray Otis on the Hartford Convention, 1814–1815." *Proceedings of the Massachusetts Historical Society* 3d ser. 60 (November 1926): 24–31. Morison prints two letters written by Otis about the Hartford Convention but missing from his *The Life and Letters of Harrison Gray Otis, Federalist, 1765–1848* (1913) (5:277). In the letters, Otis makes clear that he opposes New England's secession from the union but hopes that the states will be able to take over federal resources for their own defense.

5:702   Muller, H. N., III. "A 'Traitorous and Diabolical Traffic': The Commerce of the Champlain-Richelieu Corridor during the War of 1812." *Vermont History* 44 (Spring 1976): 78–96. Despite the outbreak of war, Vermonters continued to trade with British Canada, just as earlier during the Embargo. In Muller's view, the "trade exhibited signs of being impervious to national boundaries." In time, the administration agreed to permit some trade into Canada (in nonmilitary goods) to prevent an open revolt in the region.

5:703   Pitcavage, Mark. "'Burthened in Defense of our Rights': Opposition to Military Service in Ohio during the War of 1812." *Ohio History* 104 (Summer-Autumn 1995): 142–62. Pitcavage argues that the reluctance of Ohioans to join the army emerged from military rather than political considerations. Their exposure to frequent Indian attacks led them to believe that they were already bearing the brunt of the war and leaving home to join the army would only expose their communities and families to new raids.

5:704   Sapio, Victor A. *Pennsylvania & the War of 1812.* Lexington: University of Kentucky Press,

1970. This monograph confirms the recent emphasis on party considerations in the coming of the War of 1812. Outraged by British attacks on American rights and convinced that peaceful coercion had failed, but not economically in distress, Pennsylvania Republicans supported war as an undesirable imperative.

5:705   Strum, Harvey. "The Politics of the New York Antiwar Campaign, 1812–1815." *Peace and Change* 8 (Spring 1982): 7–18. Activity against the War of 1812 in New York included the first attempt to form a nonpartisan peace party. While this wartime effort failed, it did fuel the creation of the postwar New York Peace Society.

5:706   _____. "Smuggling in the War of 1812." *History Today* 29 (August 1979): 532–37. This essay concisely discusses smuggling from New York and Vermont into Canada during the Embargo and War of 1812.

5:707   Wehtje, Myron F. "Opposition in Virginia to the War of 1812." *Virginia Magazine of History and Biography* 78 (January 1970): 65–86. Wehtje shows that the opposition to the war in Virginia was mostly confined to Federalist strongholds in the Tidewater district. Although it included relatively few people in a relatively small area, the antiwar sentiment was intense.

The Treaty of Ghent

5:708   Carr, James A. "The Battle of New Orleans and the Treaty of Ghent." *Diplomatic History* 3 (Summer 1979): 273–82. This brief essay systematically examines and rejects the thesis that the British would have abandoned the Treaty of Ghent in favor of U.S. territorial cessions in the west if they had won at New Orleans.

5:709   Dangerfield, George. *The Era of Good Feelings.* New York: Harcourt, Brace, 1952. Despite its title, this book contains an extended discussion of the negotiations at Ghent and a shorter section dealing with the causes of the War of 1812. Dangerfield's judgments are not, in any real sense, revisionist, but they are so forcefully and colorfully presented as to reward the reader.

5:710 Gates, Charles M. "The West in American Diplomacy, 1812–1815." *Mississippi Valley Historical Review* 26 (March 1940): 499–510. Gates traces both American and British policy toward the west, showing in particular the rise and fall at Ghent of London's Indian barrier state project.

5:711 Golder, Frank A. "The Russian Offer of Mediation in the War of 1812." *Political Science Quarterly* 31 (September 1916): 380–91. Because of Golder's work in Russian archives, this old article is still the best account of the episode. He makes clear the tangle of conflicting motives behind the Russian offer to mediate between the United States and Russia's ally, Great Britain. The offer, embraced by the Americans, was rejected by the British.

5:712 Updyke, Frank A. *The Diplomacy of the War of 1812.* Baltimore: Johns Hopkins Press, 1915. Although dated, this study is the most detailed account of the Ghent negotiations. Updyke used American and, to a lesser degree, British primary sources, but much more has become available, and many of his judgments are now questioned.

6

United States Relations with Europe, the Caribbean, Africa, and the Middle East, 1815–1860

Contributing Editor
JOHN M. BELOHLAVEK
University of South Florida

Contents

Introduction

Within the past decade historians have called for a new synthesis and for new directions in the study of American foreign policy in the antebellum era. Even so, economic, gender, cultural, and political integration remain generally absent or low profile in the most recent historiography. Of the 400-plus entries cited, only 25 percent have been written in the past twenty years. To facilitate the examination of all the items, the chapter has been divided into the following sections: "Published Primary Material"; "Bibliographies and Other Reference Works"; "Historiography"; "Overviews and General Works"; "Biographical Studies"; "Bilateral Relations with Other Nations (Europe, the Middle East, Africa, Latin America and the Caribbean)"; "Northeast and Northwest"; and "Expansion and Imperialism."

The major personalities of the era have been reexamined within the past generation, and numerous biographies and presidential studies explore their contributions. The most recent works on European-American relations continue to focus on Great Britain, with an emphasis on issues relating to the Canadian Rebellion or Oregon. Several new books deal with Russia (the Crimean War) or Greece (the War of Independence). A few of these volumes range into cultural, economic, or intellectual areas. For example, several studies examine French revolutionary ideology or British travel literature. The Caribbean has received only limited attention, generally directed at Cuba and the subject of the filibustering expeditions of the 1850s. Neither Africa nor the Middle East is well represented; a handful of scholars investigate Liberia and the slave trade and a similar number discuss the Holy Land, especially the interaction of missionaries with the culture.

Published Primary Material

6:1   Bevans, Charles I., ed. *Treaties and Other International Agreements of the United States of America, 1776–1949.* This invaluable tool presents texts of important treaties (arranged by country) with the major European powers that relate to boundaries and trade as well as those concerning the expanding role of the United States in the Western Hemisphere, especially with Mexico (1:217). This work supersedes Malloy et al., *Treaties, Conventions, International Acts, Protocols, and Agreements between the United States and Other Powers, 1776–1937* (1910–1938) (8:5).

6:2   Catterall, Helen Tunnicliff, ed. *Judicial Cases Concerning American Slavery and the Negro.* 5 vols. Washington, DC: Carnegie Institution of Washington, 1926–1937. Reprint 1998 (W. S. Hein) with additional material. These volumes contain material on the legal questions involved in the domestic slave trade and other cases relating to slavery. The documents show that the question of slavery became so intricately involved in Anglo-American difficulties that it threatened settlement of seemingly unrelated matters such as the U.S.-Canadian boundary.

6:3   Hasse, Adelaide R., ed. *Index to United States Documents Relating to Foreign Affairs, 1828–1861.* Essential for locating documents for the 1828–1861 period not covered by either the *American State Papers* or *Foreign Relations* series, this work identifies remarks by congressmen and senators on numerous issues and is especially valuable for the boundary controversies in both the northeast and northwest (1:83).

6:4   Lowrie, Walter, and Matthew St. Clair Clarke, eds. *American State Papers: Documents, Legislative and Executive, of the Congress of the United States . . . Selected and Edited under the Authority of Congress.* This exceptional collection of documents, Class 1 covering foreign affairs, also covers Indian, military, and naval affairs. It is a vital primary source for any scholar in the field (5:10).

6:5   Manning, William R., ed. *Diplomatic Correspondence of the United States: Canadian Relations, 1784–1860.* This is an exceptional primary source for the key issues of the early nineteenth century, especially relating to the boundary questions and Canadian rebellion (1:245).

6:6   _____. *The Diplomatic Correspondence of the United States: Inter-American Affairs, 1831–1860.* 12 vols. Washington, DC: Carnegie Endowment for International Peace, 1932–1939. These volumes, by a famous scholar of hemispheric relations, are an indispensable source for State Department material on inter-American affairs in the mid-nineteenth century. The organization of the volumes is by country, and Manning favors coverage of the more important hemispheric nations (Argentina, Brazil, Chile, and Mexico) and slights the less important, for example, Bolivia.

6:7   Richardson, James D., ed. *Messages and Papers of the Presidents.* 20 vols. New York: Bureau of National Literature, 1897–1925. This series is a critical starting point for White House views on foreign affairs since it contains a variety of presidential letters and statements—including the annual messages to Congress. See also (5:15).

6:8   Stock, Leo F., ed. *United States Ministers to the Papal States: Instructions and Despatches, 1848–1868.* Washington, DC: Catholic University Press, 1933. This volume is an excellent source for examining U.S. goals, problems, and issues in dealing with the papacy during a time of European revolution and American Civil War.

6:9   Wiley, Bell I., ed. *Slaves No More: Letters from Liberia, 1833–1869.* Lexington: University Press of Kentucky, 1980. Wiley offers a series of 270 letters from recently emancipated slaves who had emigrated to Liberia in the antebellum era. The letters reflect their impressions of and experiences in Africa, including their negative views of the local population. Overall, the volume projects an optimistic, confident tone that is pro-Liberia.

6:10   Adams, Charles Francis, ed. *Memoirs of John Quincy Adams, Comprising Portions of His Diary from 1795 to 1848.* This is the multivolume Adams memoir and diary; an abbreviated version has been compiled by Allan Nevins, *The Diary of John Quincy Adams, 1794–1845: American Diplomacy, and Political, Social, and Intellectual Life from Washington to Polk* (New York: Ungar, 1928). The material in this complete edition offers insights from Adams's blunt perspective into most of the major issues of foreign policy in the Jacksonian era (5:142).

6:11   Ford, Worthington C., ed. *Writings of John Quincy Adams.* These volumes contain an excellent collection of Adams letters to domestic politicians and international figures, but also some fascinating family missives to wife, Abigail, and father, John. Volumes 6 and 7, covering Adams's tenure as secretary of state, are especially worthwhile (5:144).

6:12   Belmont, August. *Letters, Speeches and Addresses of August Belmont.* New York: Privately printed, 1890. This is a collection of materials relating to a leading banker, diplomat, and Democratic Party operative of the era. Belmont served as U.S. consul in Austria under James K. Polk and as minister to the Netherlands under Franklin Pierce.

6:13   Buchanan, James. *James Buchanan's Mission to Russia, 1831–1833: His Speeches, State Papers, and Private Correspondence.* New York: Arno Press, 1970. Originally published in the second volume of Moore, *Works of James Buchanan: Comprising His Speeches, State Papers, and Private Correspondence* (1908–1911) (6:14), this interesting volume provides information on his treaty negotiations in 1832 and a diary that largely discusses his travels. Some letters to Secretary of State Edward Livingston are included.

6:14   Moore, John Bassett, ed. *Works of James Buchanan: Comprising His Speeches, State Papers, and Private Correspondence.* 12 vols. Philadelphia: J. B. Lippincott Company, 1908–1911. Although old and incomplete, this edition of Buchanan's papers remains the best available and is useful for students of American diplomacy. There are a large number of significant speeches, personal letters, and state papers from his career as diplomat, secretary of state, and president. The collection contains marvelous revelations of Buchanan as minister to Russia (vol. 2), secretary of state (vols. 6 and 7), and minister to Great Britain (vols. 9 and 10).

6:15   Meriwether, Robert Lee, W. Edwin Hemphill, Clyde N. Wilson, and Shirley Bright Cook, eds. *The Papers of John C. Calhoun.* 26 vols. Columbia: University of South Carolina Press, 1959–. A forty-year project that approaches completion, this extensive compilation of the Calhoun papers has particular value for issues involving his tenure as secretary of state (vols. 17–20) and the Mexican War (vols. 24–25).

6:16   Colton, Calvin, ed. *The Works of Henry Clay: Comprising His Life, Correspondence and Speeches.* 6 vols. New York: A. S. Barnes and Burr, 1857. Colton's work is a memorial to Clay, who died in 1852. While still valuable for the variety of primary documents included, it has been largely superseded by the eleven volumes of Hopkins, *The Papers of Henry Clay* (1959–1992) (6:17).

6:17   Hopkins, James F., with Mary W. M. Hargreaves, eds. *The Papers of Henry Clay.* The definitive edition of Clay's papers, these volumes include material collected from numerous sources and are accompanied by full editorial notes. Of particular interest here are volumes 4 and 5, which cover Clay's first twenty-two months as secretary of state (1825–1826) (5:159).

6:18   Dallas, Julia, ed. *George M. Dallas, Letters from London, 1856–1860.* London: Richard Bentley, 1870. This volume is an excellent primary source for examining Anglo-American relations in the late 1850s from the perspective of the American minister. Major problems revolved around the Caribbean, British expansion, and the slave trade.

6:19   Dallas, Susan, ed. *Diary of George Mifflin Dallas, While United States Minister to Russia 1837–1839, and to England 1856 to 1861.* Philadelphia: J. B. Lippincott Company, 1892. Reprint 1970 (Arno Press). This significant volume provides insights into commercial negotiations and court lifestyles in Russia during the reign of Nicholas I and the varied problems with Great Britain over the Caribbean and the slave trade in the 1850s.

6:20   Bassett, John Spencer, ed. *Correspondence of Andrew Jackson.* This edition provides an excellent collection of Jackson's personal correspondence but is not complete and tends to focus on domestic politics (5:179). Volume 7 is an extensive index by David Maydole Matteson.

6:21   Hamilton, Stanislaus Murray, ed. *The Writings of James Monroe, Including a Collection of His Public and Private Papers and Correspondence now for the First Time Printed.* This is a worthwhile collection of Monroe letters, especially volumes 6 and 7, which cover the presidential years. It includes correspondence to various individuals about critical events involving Great Britain, Florida, and Latin America (5:230).

6:22   Nevins, Allan, ed. *Polk: The Diary of a President, 1845–1849, Covering the Mexican War, the Acquisition of Oregon, and the Conquest of California and the Southwest.* New York: Longmans, Green, 1929. This is the brief, abridged version of a rare presidential diary. Polk is often candid about his views on politics, Oregon, and the Mexican War.

6:23   Rush, Richard. *Memoranda of a Residency at the Court of London, 1819–1825, Comprising Incidents Official and Personal from 1819–1825. Including Negotiations on the Oregon Question, and Other Unsettled Questions between the United States and Great Britain.* 2 vols. Philadelphia: Lea and Blanchard, 1845. Rush, American minister to Britain in the Monroe era (1817–1825), was an anglophile. He published this lengthy, detailed diary in an era of Anglo-American antagonism to calm relations. A slightly different version first published in 1833.

6:24   Tyler, Lyon Gardiner, ed. *The Letters and Times of the Tylers.* 3 vols. Richmond: Whittet and Shepperson, 1884–1896. Reprint 1970 (Da Capo Press). Microform. This collection is valuable because most of Tyler's papers were destroyed in 1865. The compiler, the president's son, wrote his father's correspondents and secured copies of letters to and from the former president.

6:25   Shewmaker, Kenneth E., ed., with Kenneth R. Stevens and Anita McGurn, assistant eds. *The Papers of Daniel Webster. Series 3. Diplomatic Papers. Vol. 1: 1841–1843. Vol. 2: 1850–1852.* Hanover, NH: University Press of New England, 1983–1987. These volumes are an invaluable source in exploring Webster's views and policies in his two terms as secretary of state. Included are his activities on the *Amistad* and *Creole* affairs, the *Caroline* and Canadian boundary disputes, and later problems with Austria over the 1848 revolutions and in the Caribbean over filibustering and British expansion.

6:26   Barnes, James J., and Patience P. Barnes, eds. *Private and Confidential: Letters from British Ministers in Washington to the Foreign Secretaries in London, 1844–67.* Selinsgrove, PA: Susquehanna University Press, 1993. This is a valuable collection of letters that reveals the perceptions of British diplomats at mid-century on a number of Anglo-American issues including the Oregon dispute, the Crimean recruitment issue, Cuba, Central America, and the slave trade.

6:27 Irish University Press Series on British Parliamentary Papers. *Slave Trade.* 95 vols. Shannon: Irish University Press, 1968–1971. This extensive collection consists of reprinted nineteenth-century British diplomatic correspondence, naval officers' reports, findings of mixed commissions in cases trying captured slavers, select committee reports, antislavery treaties, and much more material. Volume 24 contains correspondence dealing with the *Creole* case, while volumes 11, 14, 15, 20, 25, 39, 41, 43–48, and 50 are rich in correspondence on British efforts to gain U.S. agreement to antislavery treaties and joint patrol issues.

6:28 Gooch, G. P., ed. *The Later Correspondence of Lord John Russell, 1840–1878.* 2 vols. New York: Longmans, Green, 1925. Gooch has provided a good and representative selection of the correspondence of the British foreign secretary. While these volumes contain much that is valuable, they must be supplemented with the unpublished material in the British Public Record Office.

Bibliographies and Other Reference Works

6:29 Albion, Robert G. *Naval & Maritime History: An Annotated Bibliography.* 4th ed. Mystic, CT: Munson Institute of American Maritime History, 1972. This dated but still valuable bibliography has noteworthy citations on Africa and the slave trade, commerce with Europe, international law, and the evolution of the U.S. navy and merchant marine.

6:30 Bradley, Phillips, ed. *A Bibliography of the Monroe Doctrine, 1919–1929.* London: London School of Economics, 1929. Though dated, this short reference work is still worth examining for the English perspective on sources relating to the Monroe Doctrine.

6:31 Bryson, Thomas A., ed. *United States/Middle East Diplomatic Relations, 1784–1978: An Annotated Bibliography.* This bibliography is not particularly strong in the antebellum period but does have some citations relating to Turkey, Egypt, Syria, the Barbary states, and the Greek revolution (1:259).

6:32 Goehlert, Robert U., and Elizabeth R. Hoffmeister, eds. *The Department of State and American Diplomacy: A Bibliography.* A good source for State Department and foreign service listings, this includes dissertations and articles in nonhistorical journals. The volume covers geographical areas and individual biographical citations (1:30).

6:33 Hanham, H. J., ed. *Bibliography of British History, 1851–1914.* Oxford: Clarendon Press, 1976. This mammoth compilation lists the major works that a scholar is likely to consult and is comprehensive through 1973. It includes a section on contemporary printed materials and a selection of biographies and autobiographies.

6:34 Lincove, David A., and Gary R. Treadway, eds. *The Anglo-American Relationship: An Annotated Bibliography of Scholarship, 1945–1985.* This excellent annotated bibliography includes a thirty-page chapter on the 1815–1861 period. The title, "Diplomatic Conflict and Compromise," indicates the chapter's themes, which revolve largely around North American boundary issues, the slave trade, and Latin America (1:244).

6:35 Ragatz, Lowell Joseph, ed. *A Guide for the Study of British Caribbean History, 1763–1834, Including the Abolition and Emancipation Movements.* Vol. 3, The Annual Report of the American Historical Association for the Year 1930. This annotated bibliography, a major reference, includes manuscripts and official records of Great Britain, the United States, and the British West Indies as well as secondary works.

6:36 Silverburg, Sanford R., and Bernard Reich, eds. *U.S. Foreign Relations with the Middle East and North Africa: A Bibliography.* This volume focuses largely on the twentieth century but includes nineteenth-century references to philanthropy, missions, churches, and education (1:262).

Historiography

6:37   Brauer, Kinley J. "The Great American Desert Revisited: Recent Literature and the Prospects for the Study of American Foreign Relations, 1815–1861." *Diplomatic History* 13 (Summer 1989): 395–417. Brauer does an excellent job of discussing the reasons for the decline of interest in the middle period by diplomatic scholars and urges the incorporation of cultural, women's, and African-American history in the study of foreign affairs.

6:38   _____. "The Need for a Synthesis of American Foreign Relations, 1815–1861." *Journal of the Early Republic* 14 (Winter 1994): 467–76. With the involvement of special interests and self-conscious communities, Brauer argues for a corporatist analysis of nineteenth-century American foreign relations.

6:39   Carroll, Francis M. "The Passionate Canadians: The Historical Debate about the Eastern Canadian-American Boundary." *New England Quarterly* 70 (March 1997): 83–101. Carroll offers a historiographical discussion of the Canadian border issue in the late nineteenth and early twentieth centuries from a Canadian-British perspective and evaluates whether the 1842 treaty was a good compromise for Canada.

6:40   Kenny, Stephen. "The Canadian Rebellions and the Limits of Historical Perspective." *Vermont History* 58 (Summer 1990): 179–98. The article examines how historians on both sides of the border have treated the U.S. repercussions of the Canadian rebellion of the 1830s. Kenny notes that this is a neglected subject and that scholars generally limit themselves to their side of the border.

6:41   Perkins, Bradford. "Interests, Values, and the Prism: The Sources of American Foreign Policy." Perkins notes the impact of forces such as individualism and republicanism on American foreign affairs. A limited vision of revolution, a strong sense of isolation, and a fear of contamination also drove U.S. perceptions (5:109).

Overviews and General Works

6:42   Haines, Charles Grove, and Foster H. Sherwood. *The Role of the Supreme Court in American Government and Politics. Vol. 2: 1835–1864.* Berkeley: University of California Press, 1957. The authors analyze the legal and constitutional differences between the *Amistad* and *Creole* cases.

6:43   Varg, Paul A. *New England and Foreign Relations, 1789–1850.* In this fine regional study examining New England's commercial and industrial development and its tariff policies, Varg also deals with advocates and opponents of territorial and commercial expansion in Maine, Texas, and Oregon, explores the burgeoning China trade, and assesses the problems raised by the Mexican War and political divisions caused by expansion, particularly within the Whig Party (5:113).

6:44   _____. *United States Foreign Relations, 1820–1860.* East Lansing: Michigan State University Press, 1979. Varg relates U.S. foreign policy to Europe and Asia as well as to its expansionist concerns in North America. Commercial goals were vital, but numerous elements entered into the American decisionmaking process. By 1860, the United States dominated North America and, though seriously threatened by the divisive issue of slavery, had taken great steps toward becoming a world power.

6:45   Weeks, William Earl. "American Nationalism, American Imperialism: An Interpretation of United States Political Economy, 1789–1861." Weeks urges a redefinition of both nationalism and imperialism, suggesting both have often been seen by scholars as antithetical or discrete phenomena. American commerce was linked to nationalism, and federal policy in the era promoted both commerce and westward expansion (5:114).

DIPLOMATS AND NAVAL DIPLOMATS

6:46   Davis, Robert R., Jr. "Diplomatic Plumage: American Court Dress in the Early National Period."

Davis illustrates the movement toward republican simplicity in diplomatic dress that emerged in the Jacksonian era and culminated in the costume circular under William Marcy in 1853 (5:125).

6:47 _____. "Republican Simplicity: The Diplomatic Costume Question, 1789–1867." Davis deals with the issue of court costume especially in the 1840s and 1850s and focuses on William L. Marcy's generally well-received costume circular of 1853 that simplified and "republicanized" American court dress (5:126). This piece is similar to his "Diplomatic Plumage: American Court Dress in the Early National Period" (1968) (6:46).

6:48 Long, David F. *Gold Braid and Foreign Relations: Diplomatic Activities of U.S. Naval Officers, 1798–1883*. This fine synthetic study of the activities of naval officers in the nineteenth century updates Paullin, *Diplomatic Negotiations of American Naval Officers, 1778–1883* (1912) (6:49). Long examines naval diplomacy worldwide (including chapters on the Middle East and Hawaii), noting circumstances in which officers acted where there was no other official U.S. representative present (5:130).

6:49 Paullin, Charles O. *Diplomatic Negotiations of American Naval Officers, 1778–1883*. Baltimore: Johns Hopkins Press, 1912. This older study of the diplomatic activity of U.S. navy officers focuses on the promotion of American interests largely in the Middle East and North Africa. It has been superseded by Long, *Gold Braid and Foreign Relations: Diplomatic Activities of U.S. Naval Officers, 1798–1883* (1988) (6:48).

6:50 Schroeder, John H. *Shaping a Maritime Empire: The Commercial and Diplomatic Role of the American Navy, 1829–1861*. Westport, CT: Greenwood Press, 1985. This excellent study examines the relationship between the enlarged U.S. navy and its role as protector of American commerce and, surprisingly often, its officers as diplomatic agents. Schroeder includes a particularly fine chapter on activities in the Caribbean.

ECONOMICS

6:51 Belohlavek, John M. "Economic Interest

Groups and the Formation of Foreign Policy in the Early Republic." The author contends that commerce and business interests must be more seriously considered in examining the formulation of foreign policy in the early republic (5:81).

6:52 North, Douglass C. *The Economic Growth of the United States, 1790–1860*. Englewood Cliffs, NJ: Prentice-Hall, 1961. The book contains several useful chapters on the role international trade played in the growth of the American economy in the antebellum era.

6:53 Taylor, George Rogers. *The Transportation Revolution, 1815–1860*. New York: Holt, Rinehart and Winston, 1951. This economic history of American business and commerce provides a detailed background for commercial relations in the period and includes chapters on foreign trade and the American merchant marine.

6:54 Willett, Thomas D. "International Specie Flows and American Monetary Stability, 1834–1860." *Journal of Economic History* 28 (March 1968): 28–50. This article concludes that the international movement of specie played a significant role in America's monetary disturbances.

TRANSATLANTIC COMMERCE

6:55 Albion, Robert G., with Jennie Barnes Pope. *The Rise of New York Port, 1815–1860*. New York: C. Scribner's Sons, 1939. Albion's detailed study, based on exhaustive research, traces the rise of New York as the chief American seaport. The book contains thirty-one appendices of commercial information and statistics and has an extensive bibliography.

6:56 Albion, Robert G. *Square-Riggers on Schedule: The New York Sailing Packets to England, France, and the Cotton Ports*. Princeton: Princeton University Press, 1938. Based on extensive primary research, this book is a fine study of this aspect of American commerce with England and France.

6:57 Cutler, Carl C. *Greyhounds of the Sea: The Story of the American Clipper Ship*. New York: Halcyon House, 1930. For the nonspecialist, this narrative offers a general account of the commercial ventures of the majestic clipper ships. Foreword by Charles Francis Adams; 117 illustrations.

6:58   Homans, Isaac Smith, ed. *An Historical and Statistical Account of the Foreign Commerce of the United States, 1820–1856.* New York: G. P. Putnam and Co., 1857. Reprint 1976 (Arno Press). This mid-nineteenth-century volume includes a brief summary of American commerce with individual nations and geographic areas of the world with a useful statistical chart included for each.

6:59   Johnson, Emory R., et al. *History of Domestic and Foreign Commerce of the United States.* 2 vols. in 1. Washington, DC: Carnegie Institution of Washington, 1915. Although outdated in many respects, this work contains a useful narrative on aspects of American commerce as well as a wealth of statistical information.

6:60   Morison, Samuel Eliot. *The Maritime History of Massachusetts, 1783–1860.* Boston: Houghton Mifflin Company, 1921. This volume remains the classic history of maritime activity in Massachusetts. Thoroughly researched and well written, the study provides an insightful treatment of maritime activity in the state.

6:61   Porter, Kenneth W. *The Jacksons and the Lees: Two Generations of Massachusetts Merchants, 1765–1844.* 2 vols. Cambridge, MA: Harvard University Press, 1937. This documentary study includes a narrative of the commercial activities of the two families and an extensive collection of correspondence from each family.

6:62   Tyler, David B. *Steam Conquers the Atlantic.* New York: Appleton-Century, 1939. Reprint 1972 (Arno Press). Although dated, this narrative history provides a solid account for the nonspecialist of the rise and development of the Atlantic steamship in trade, mail service, and passenger service in the nineteenth century.

SECTIONAL ISSUES

6:63   Crapol, Edward P. "The Foreign Policy of Antislavery, 1833–1846." In *Redefining the Past: Essays in Diplomatic History in Honor of William Ap-*pleman Williams, ed. Lloyd C. Gardner, 85–104. Corvallis, OR: Oregon State University Press, 1986. Crapol develops an antislavery critique of American foreign policy through the eyes of Lydia Maria Child, who was pro-Haitian recognition, anti-Texas, and antislave power, and of Joshua Leavitt, who hoped to use an anti-Corn Law strategy to influence British policymakers.

6:64   Eaton, Clement. *The Freedom-of-Thought Struggle in the Old South.* New York: Harper and Row, 1964. Many times, especially during the 1830s, the lower south experienced great anxiety over the possibility of slave revolts. Though Eaton does not argue it, one can infer from his findings that this state of fear influenced southerners to oppose any tampering with slavery—especially when British interference with the institution seemed imminent. A revised and enlarged edition of his 1940 book, *Freedom of Thought in the Old South.*

6:65   Potter, David. *The Impending Crisis, 1848–1861.* New York: Harper and Row, 1976. Potter's detailed survey of the coming of the Civil War includes excellent material on American diplomacy in the 1850s. It is a masterful work that manages to see old subjects in a new light. Completed and edited by Don E. Fehrenbacher.

6:66   Wish, Harvey. "American Slave Insurrections before 1861." *Journal of Negro History* 22 (July 1937): 299–320. The *Creole* revolt was one of at least fifty-five insurrections at sea from 1699 to the 1840s. The result, Wish believes, was a "conspiracy of silence" in the south on the incidence of slave revolts, a strategy designed to stop their spread.

YOUNG AMERICA

6:67   Curti, Merle E. "Young America." *American Historical Review* 32 (October 1926): 34–49. Although this article was written seventy-five years ago, it still provides a good introduction and insights into the Young America movement.

6:68   Danborn, David B. "The Young America Movement." *Journal of the Illinois State Historical Society* 67 (June 1974): 294–306. Danborn provides a summary of the Young America movement, its composition, and attitudes on American foreign policy in the 1850s.

Biographical Studies

JOHN QUINCY ADAMS

6:69   Bemis, Samuel Flagg. *John Quincy Adams and the Foundations of American Foreign Policy.* This classic study of Adams comes from a historian who helped establish his reputation as a preeminent secretary of state. This volume explores Adams's views and actions on both the Oregon and Maine boundaries as well as problems with fishing disputes and the slave trade (5:145).

6:70   _____. *John Quincy Adams and the Union.* New York: Alfred A. Knopf, 1956. The second of a two-volume biography, this book treats the years from 1829 to 1848 in great detail. Because Adams served almost all of this time in the House, the study concentrates primarily on domestic political issues; however, Bemis does discuss Adams's positions on the *Amistad* and *Creole* controversies.

6:71   Hargreaves, Mary W. M. *The Presidency of John Quincy Adams.* Lawrence: University Press of Kansas, 1985. This sympathetic study deals with traditional subjects such as the Panama Congress and the frustrating West Indian trade. The author argues for significant gains by the administration that benefited merchants and producers. She is critical, however, of Adams's faults as both administrator and politician.

6:72   Lewis, James E., Jr. *John Quincy Adams: Policymaker for the Union.* Wilmington, DE: SR Books, 2001. Part of a series of brief biographies of leaders in American foreign policy, this volume focuses on J. Q. Adams as secretary of state and president, emphasizing his advocacy of union and federal power as well as the interlocking of foreign and domestic issues. The author tends to be more critical than many biographers, stressing his subject's failures as a policymaker as well as his successes.

6:73   Nagel, Paul C. *John Quincy Adams: A Public Life, A Private Life.* New York: Alfred A. Knopf,

1997. This is a psychological edged full biography that critically analyzes Adams. In what many scholars might deem a speculative approach, Nagel perceives his subject driven by his neuroses—depression, self doubt, and failure—while ably discussing his extensive diplomatic career in Europe and America.

6:74   Russell, Greg. *John Quincy Adams and the Public Virtues of Diplomacy.* Russell, a political scientist, aims his study at scholars of international affairs. This is a volume on Adams's philosophical foundations and how his ideas played out in the public and diplomatic spheres. Largely theoretical rather than event oriented, the work relies little on recent historiography (5:147).

6:75   Weeks, William Earl. *John Quincy Adams and American Global Empire.* Lexington: University Press of Kentucky, 1992. This thoughtful study advances the notion that the devious and resourceful Adams set the United States on the course of global empire with the negotiation of the Transcontinental Treaty. While Florida remains the focus of the volume, it also discusses other topics, including western boundaries. Adams emerges as a personally troubled and tormented individual, but a complex visionary who pursued a successful policy.

GEORGE BANCROFT

6:76   Handlin, Lilian. *George Bancroft: The Intellectual as Democrat.* New York: Harper and Row, 1984. Handlin, in the most recent study of Bancroft, focuses more on his academic endeavors and politics than his foreign missions to Great Britain or Germany.

6:77   Howe, M. A. De Wolfe, ed. *Life and Letters of George Bancroft.* 2 vols. New York: Charles Scribner's Sons, 1908. Reprint 1971 (Kennikat). Volume 2 of this traditional study contains a number of important letters written while Bancroft was U.S. minister to Great Britain in the 1840s and Prussia in the 1860s.

6:78   Nye, Russel B. *George Bancroft: Brahmin Rebel.* New York: Alfred A. Knopf, 1944. Based primarily on the voluminous collection of Bancroft manuscripts, this study remains the standard biography of this historian, politician, and diplomat. Bancroft's career included service as minister to Great Britain (1846–1849) and Germany (1867–1874).

JAMES BUCHANAN

6:79   Binder, Frederick Moore. *James Buchanan and the American Empire.* Selinsgrove, PA: Susquehanna University Press, 1994. Binder gives us a generally positive examination of Buchanan's views and involvement with foreign affairs from the 1830s through the end of his presidency. A nationalist and expansionist, Buchanan eagerly embraced Manifest Destiny. He served credibly as minister to Russia in the 1830s and with less success to Great Britain in the 1850s as well as secretary of state to James K. Polk. Buchanan was an anglophobe who tempered his views with ambition for high political office.

6:80   Horton, Rushmore G. *The Life and Public Services of James Buchanan: Late Minister to England and Formerly Minister to Russia . . . and Secretary of State, Including the Most Important of His State Papers.* New York: Derby and Jackson, 1856. Reprint 1971 (Kennikat). Part of the campaign literature for Buchanan in 1856, this volume extols his diplomatic virtues and experience by citing key documents from his role as minister and secretary of state. It is nonetheless valuable for the ready access to such items.

6:81   Klein, Philip S. *President James Buchanan: A Biography.* University Park: Pennsylvania State University Press, 1962. Klein's comprehensive scholarly biography of Buchanan includes detailed information on his service as secretary of state, minister to Russia, and minister to England as well as his one term as president.

6:82   Smith, Elbert B. *The Presidency of James Buchanan.* Lawrence: University Press of Kansas, 1975. This straightforward and scholarly account of Buchanan's presidency, while focusing on the domestic political crisis, also includes pertinent information about American foreign policy.

LEWIS CASS

6:83   Klunder, Willard Carl. *Lewis Cass and the Politics of Moderation.* Kent, OH: Kent State Uni-

versity Press, 1996. An intelligent, dispassionate, and balanced biography of Cass that will likely be definitive for a generation, Klunder's well-researched study, which includes Cass's tenure as minister to France and secretary of state under James Buchanan, reveals his subject as both expansionist and anglophobe.

6:84   Spencer, Donald S. "Lewis Cass and Symbolic Intervention: 1848–1852." *Michigan History* 53 (Spring 1969): 1–17. This article analyzes the precise content and specific meaning of Lewis Cass's pleas for the United States to assume a more aggressive role in supporting the democratic revolutionary movements in Europe between 1848 and 1852. For Cass, emotionalism, idealism, anglophobia, and political opportunism dovetailed into a posture of symbolic intervention into European affairs. Cass appealed, however, for moral censure and did not urge the use of military force.

6:85   Woodford, Frank B. *Lewis Cass: The Last Jeffersonian.* New Brunswick: Rutgers University Press, 1950. Although the best biography is Klunder, *Lewis Cass and the Politics of Moderation* (1996) (6:83), this study provides a solid survey of the Michigan politician and diplomat as minister to France (1836–1842) and as secretary of state (1857–1860). Woodford explains Cass's long-time opposition to British search policies in the suppression of the slave trade.

6:86   Young, William T. *Sketch of the Life and Public Services of General Lewis Cass: With the Pamphlet on the Right of Search, and Some of His Speeches on the Great Political Questions of the Day.* 2d ed. Detroit: Markham and Elwood, 1852. This old account includes the correspondence of the American minister to France with leaders of the Tyler administration as well as a reprint of Cass's anonymously written pamphlet opposing the British search policy as a step leading to impressment and thus to destruction of American honor.

HENRY CLAY

6:87   Remini, Robert V. *Henry Clay: Statesman for the Union.* This excellent and lengthy biography of Clay contains two brief chapters on the office of secretary of state (1825–1829) and policies of the department under the auspices of the Kentuckian (5:161).

6:88   Van Deusen, Glyndon G. *The Life of Henry Clay*. Boston: Little, Brown and Company, 1937. This favorable biography sums up Clay's role in foreign affairs. It discusses Clay as a War Hawk from 1810 to 1812, a delegate to the Ghent negotiations, a proponent of an active Latin American policy, and secretary of state (1825–1829).

GEORGE DALLAS

6:89   Ambacher, Bruce. "George M. Dallas, Cuba, and the Elections of 1856." *Pennsylvania Magazine of History and Biography* 97 (July 1973): 318–32. Dallas was a critic of the Pierce administration's efforts to acquire Cuba. He was appointed minister to Great Britain in 1856 to remove him from the United States.

6:90   Belohlavek, John M. *George Mifflin Dallas: Jacksonian Patrician*. University Park: Pennsylvania State University Press, 1977. This account is a traditional biography of a Jacksonian politician and diplomat who served as a senator and vice-president as well as American minister to Russia (1837–1839) and Great Britain (1856–1861).

EDWARD EVERETT

6:91   Frothingham, Paul Revere. *Edward Everett, Orator and Statesman*. Boston: Houghton Mifflin Company, 1925. Reprint 1971 (Kennikat Press). This study is the only full account of Everett's long public career. It is based on the voluminous Everett manuscript collections and contains an adequate account of Everett's terms as minister to England (1841–1845) and secretary of state (1852–1853). His correspondence with Secretary of State Webster may be found in the microfilm edition of Webster's papers.

6:92   Varg, Paul A. *Edward Everett: The Intellectual in the Turmoil of Politics*. Selinsgrove, PA: Susquehanna University Press, 1992. Varg offers the most recent examination of the lengthy public career

of this Whig politician and diplomat who served as both Tyler's minister to England and Fillmore's secretary of state.

ALBERT GALLATIN

6:93   Kuppenheimer, L. B. *Albert Gallatin's Vision of Democratic Stability: An Interpretive Profile*. Westport, CT: Praeger, 1996. This interesting interpretive study of Gallatin as visionary includes two chapters on foreign affairs: diplomacy through compromise and through "vivacity of intellect."

6:94   Walters, Ray. *Albert Gallatin: Jeffersonian Financier and Diplomat*. Walters's study remains the best biography of Gallatin. The work deals with Gallatin in Paris and London and his activities in fostering resolution of both the Maine and Oregon boundary disputes (5:165).

ANDREW JACKSON

6:95   Belohlavek, John M. *Let the Eagle Soar: The Foreign Policy of Andrew Jackson*. Lincoln: University of Nebraska Press, 1985. In the only full-length study of Jackson's diplomacy, the author contends that "Old Hickory" was aggressive and proactive in foreign affairs. He was guided by a conscious desire to promote American commerce around the world and foster territorial growth and American nationalism.

6:96   Cole, Donald B. *The Presidency of Andrew Jackson*. Lawrence: University Press of Kansas, 1993. Cole offers a fine critical study of the Jackson presidency that incorporates analysis of his generally successful foreign policy. He views "Old Hickory" as a prideful and insecure president who was often controlled by, rather than controlling, the turbulent events around him.

6:97   Remini, Robert V. *Andrew Jackson and the Course of American Democracy, 1833–1845*. Vol. 3. 3 vols. New York: Harper and Row, 1984. This third volume of the Remini trilogy on Jackson focuses on his second administration. French spoliations and the Texas question commanded most of the president's attention in foreign affairs—the conduct of which Remini dubs "extraordinarily successful." The author is critical, however, of some of Jackson's appointments.

6:98 _____. *Andrew Jackson and the Course of American Freedom, 1822–1832*. Vol. 2. 3 vols. New York: Harper and Row, 1981. This is the second volume of Remini's comprehensive and sympathetic three-volume biography of Jackson. Although the author devotes only a small number of pages to foreign affairs, he views "Old Hickory" as proactive in his approaches to boundary and spoliations issues and discusses a number of trade treaties.

THOMAS JEFFERSON

6:99 Kaplan, Lawrence S. "Jefferson as Anglophile: Sagacity or Senility in the Era of Good Feeling?" *Diplomatic History* 16 (Summer 1992): 487–94. Kaplan asks why Jefferson, after decades as an anglophobe, called for an entangling alliance with Britain in 1823. The answer rests not with the Virginian's sudden anglophilia, but rather his view that the British were now serving U.S. interests after the Napoleonic Wars. He consequently adopted a more benign view of the crown.

6:100 Moss, Sidney Phil, and Carolyn J. Moss. "The Jefferson Miscegenation Legend in British Travel Books." *Journal of the Early Republic* 7 (Fall 1987): 253–74. The authors examine the Jefferson miscegenation "legend" as viewed from British travel books from 1806 into the mid-nineteenth century. Most of the books, beginning with Frances Trollope's, attacked the Virginian; few, including Frances Wright, defended him.

LORD PALMERSTON

6:101 Bulwer, Henry Lytton, and Evelyn Ashley. *The Life of Henry John Temple, Viscount Palmerston: With Selections from His Diaries and Correspondence*. 3 vols. Philadelphia: J. B. Lippincott, 1870–1876. A continuation of Evelyn Ashley, *The Life of Henry John Temple, Viscount Palmerston, 1846–1865. With Selections from His Speeches and Correspondence*, 2 vols. (London: R. Bentley and Sons, 1876), this volume added some letters and speeches from the period 1835–1847. But this "au-

thorized" life leaves much to be desired in the way of standards of historical editing.

6:102 Guedalla, Philip. *Palmerston, 1784–1865*. New York: G. P. Putnam's Sons, 1927. Perhaps the most vividly written of the Palmerston biographies, this was one of the first to appreciate and utilize the private papers at Broadlands. Whatever its defects—and professors and pedants have found many—this is biography as art, more interested in personality than politics or policies.

6:103 Ridley, Jasper Godwin. *Lord Palmerston*. London: Constable, 1970. Despite this highly laudable and very readable attempt, Palmerston (1784–1865) still awaits a biographer who can do justice to both the man and his measures.

6:104 Southgate, Donald. *"The Most English Minister. . .": The Policies and Politics of Palmerston*. New York: St. Martin's Press, 1966. Not quite a biography, this study slights American affairs (and gets one or two things wrong when mentioning them) but has many acute observations about Palmerstonian statecraft.

FRANKLIN PIERCE

6:105 Gara, Larry. *The Presidency of Franklin Pierce*. Lawrence: University Press of Kansas, 1991. This solid study of the presidency of Franklin Pierce devotes some attention to his Spanish affairs, including efforts to acquire Cuba and the "Black Warrior" incident as well as problems with Great Britain in Central America.

6:106 Nichols, Roy F. *Franklin Pierce: Young Hickory of the Granite Hills*. 2d ed. Philadelphia: University of Pennsylvania Press, 1964. This full and traditional biography includes a sound account of foreign policy questions—including problems with Spain over Cuba—during the presidency of Pierce. First published in 1958.

JAMES K. POLK

6:107 Bergeron, Paul H. *The Presidency of James K. Polk*. Lawrence: University Press of Kansas, 1987.

This generally positive study of the Polk presidency gives its subject high marks for his handling of foreign affairs in Texas, Oregon, and the Mexican War. Bergeron is less complimentary when dealing with Polk's domestic political strategies and policies.

6:108 Haynes, Sam W. *James K. Polk and the Expansionist Impulse.* New York: Longman, 1997. This is a fine, brief, interpretive study largely intended for an undergraduate audience. Haynes portrays Polk as an activist president in both foreign and domestic policy. While admiring his leadership, the author criticizes his unquestioning arrogance and cultural nationalism.

6:109 McCormac, Eugene I. *James K. Polk: A Political Biography.* Berkeley: University of California Press, 1922. McCormac offers a traditional political biography of Polk that does little with his personal life. Although the study touches on topics such as Oregon, it is superseded by Sellers, *James K. Polk, Continentalist, 1843–1846* (1966) (6:110), and Bergeron, *The Presidency of James K. Polk* (1987) (6:107).

6:110 Sellers, Charles Grier. *James K. Polk, Continentalist, 1843–1846.* Princeton: Princeton University Press, 1966. This is the well-executed second volume of Sellers's biography of Polk. It focuses on his run for the White House and the first year of his presidency, including a fine examination of the Oregon question.

ZACHARY TAYLOR

6:111 Bauer, K. Jack. *Zachary Taylor: Soldier, Planter, Statesman of the Old Southwest.* Baton Rouge: Louisiana State University Press, 1985. This is a fine one-volume study that devotes a chapter to the policies of Taylor and John Clayton in Central America and the Caribbean.

6:112 Hamilton, Holman. *Zachary Taylor.* 2 vols. Indianapolis: Bobbs-Merrill, 1941–1951. The second volume of the biography, which commences in 1847, focuses on the Taylor presidency and includes John M. Clayton's activities in dealing with problems in Central America and the Caribbean.

6:113 Smith, Elbert B. *The Presidencies of Zachary Taylor & Millard Fillmore.* Lawrence: University Press of Kansas, 1988. This sympathetic study of the Taylor-Fillmore presidencies focuses on domestic issues but does deal with the Clayton-Bulwer Treaty and issues involving trade, expansion, and filibustering in Latin America.

JOHN TYLER

6:114 Crapol, Edward P. "John Tyler and the Pursuit of National Destiny." *Journal of the Early Republic* 17 (Fall 1997): 467–91. Crapol rejects the notion that Tyler was a narrow sectionalist and claims he argued for a broad national expansionist agenda. He promoted this vision of national destiny—including to the Pacific and beyond—in large part to preserve the union.

6:115 Morgan, Robert J. *A Whig Embattled: The Presidency under John Tyler.* Lincoln: University of Nebraska Press, 1954. Reprint 1974 (Archon Books) with new author's preface. This is an older study of the Tyler presidency that should be supplemented with Peterson's more recent *The Presidencies of William Henry Harrison & John Tyler* (1989) (6:116). Topics of importance include the efforts to obtain Texas and the resolution of the northeastern boundary.

6:116 Peterson, Norma Lois. *The Presidencies of William Henry Harrison & John Tyler.* Lawrence: University Press of Kansas, 1989. Peterson is sympathetic to the president without a party. Tyler is depicted as an executive of courage and conviction who pursued a series of successful diplomatic initiatives in North America and Asia.

6:117 Seager, Robert, II. *And Tyler Too: A Biography of John & Julia Gardiner Tyler.* New York: McGraw-Hill, 1963. Seager offers a lengthy, well-crafted personal study of the lives of Tyler and his second wife that also incorporates material on the issues of Oregon and the northeastern border.

MARTIN VAN BUREN

6:118 Curtis, James C. *The Fox at Bay: Martin Van Buren and the Presidency, 1837–1841.* Lexington: University Press of Kentucky, 1970. Based on extensive research, this volume concentrates on Van Buren's presidency, including problems with Great Britain over the Canadian rebellion and the northeastern boundary. It also includes a useful summary of Van Buren's career before his election in 1836.

6:119 Fitzpatrick, John C., ed. *Autobiography of Martin Van Buren.* Washington, DC: Government Printing Office, 1920. This detailed autobiography focuses on domestic politics while also providing insights into Van Buren's tenure as secretary of state. Unfortunately, the work concludes during the Jackson presidency.

6:120 Niven, John. *Martin Van Buren: The Romantic Age of American Politics.* New York: Oxford University Press, 1983. This fine comprehensive biography focuses on domestic politics but also deals with Van Buren as secretary of state and the various Canadian boundary problems with Great Britain he faced as president. Some attention is also paid to Texas and the *Amistad* affair.

6:121 Wilson, Major L. *The Presidency of Martin Van Buren.* Lawrence: University Press of Kansas, 1984. This excellent study of the Van Buren White House deals with issues relating to the annexation of Texas and problems with Great Britain relating to Canada. Van Buren emerges as strong party advocate guided by principles. He is more of an activist president than many historians have perceived him.

DANIEL WEBSTER

6:122 Bartlett, Irving H. *Daniel Webster.* New York: Norton, 1978. Bartlett offers a balanced, well-researched biography of Webster that focuses largely on his political career. Not as ambitious as Remini, *Daniel Webster: The Man and His Time* (1997) (6:125), this volume provides a fine introduction to Webster and foreign affairs, emphasizing his first stint in the State Department under John Tyler.

6:123 Fuess, Claude Moore. *Daniel Webster.* 2 vols. Boston: Little, Brown and Company, 1930. This is an early, lengthy, and sympathetic study of Webster by a scholar who approaches the work with narrative more in mind than interpretation. Fuess did

a thorough job of scrutinizing the extensive Webster papers.

6:124 Graebner, Norman A., ed. *Traditions and Values: American Diplomacy, 1790–1865. Vol. 7: American Values Projected Abroad.* Lanham, MD: University Press of America, 1985. A chapter in this collection, Kenneth E. Shewmaker, "Daniel Webster and American Conservatism," appraises Webster's activities rather than assessing his thought. He is seen as a pragmatist who generally advocated commercial rather than territorial expansion and pioneered work for U.S. interests in the Pacific. Shewmaker also focuses on Anglo-American relations, particularly involving the northeastern border.

6:125 Remini, Robert V. *Daniel Webster: The Man and His Time.* New York: W. W. Norton & Co., 1997. Arguably the finest biography of Webster, this volume does a credible job with "Black Dan's" tour as secretary of state under John Tyler but is more superficial in examining his stint in the early 1850s.

6:126 Shewmaker, Kenneth E. "Congress Can Only Declare War and the President Is Commander in Chief: Daniel Webster and the War Power." *Diplomatic History* 12 (Fall 1988): 383–410. Shewmaker deals with Webster's evolving view of federal authority. Webster was firm that the federal government had warmaking power and that the president and secretary of state could make policy. The author uses Webster's activities in the State Department, especially his "gunboat diplomacy," as examples.

6:127 _____. "Daniel Webster and the Politics of Foreign Policy, 1850–1852." *Journal of American History* 63 (September 1976): 303–15. The author argues that Webster accepted the appointment as secretary of state (1850–1852) primarily to promote the Compromise of 1850 and national unity. The article contends that Webster used the Hulsemann affair to this end, not as a device to advance his chances for the presidency in 1852.

OTHERS

6:128 Gregory, Frances W. *Nathan Appleton, Merchant and Entrepreneur, 1779–1861.* Charlottesville: University Press of Virginia, 1975. Gregory's detailed biography focuses on the business and commercial practices of an extremely successful nineteenth-century American entrepreneur.

6:129　　Argyll, George Douglas Campbell. *Autobiography and Memoirs.* 2 vols. London: John Murray, 1906. A politician and economic and social reformer, the duke was a key member of Palmerston's cabinet in the 1850s and adviser on foreign affairs. His views on Anglo-American relations, free trade, and the Crimea are especially worth examining. Edited by Ina Erskine Campbell Argyll.

6:130　　Porter, Kenneth W. *John Jacob Astor: Business Man.* 2 vols. Cambridge, MA: Harvard University Press, 1931. Based on extensive research, this volume is the most complete account of Astor's life. The successful merchant and fur trader was arguably also Jeffersonian America's wealthiest man.

6:131　　Davis, Hugh. *Leonard Bacon: New England Reformer and Antislavery Moderate.* Baton Rouge: Louisiana State University Press, 1998. Davis offers an excellent full-length biography of the Connecticut minister who was a leading advocate for colonization in the antebellum era.

6:132　　Benton, Thomas Hart. *Thirty Years' View: Or, a History of the Workings of the American Government for Thirty Years, from 1820 to 1850.* 2 vols. New York: D. Appleton and Co., 1854. The perceptions of the legendary Missouri Jacksonian on issues such as Oregon and Canada—including his speeches—make volume 2 of his memoir especially well worth examining.

6:133　　Long, David F. *Sailor-Diplomat: A Biography of Commodore James Biddle, 1783–1848.* Boston: Northeastern University Press, 1983. Long presents a well-written biography of a naval officer who spent his post-1815 years protecting American interests and commerce in the Oregon country, the West Indies, South America, and the Mediterranean. By the 1840s, he commanded the East Indian Squadron and attempted to treat with the Chinese and Japanese.

6:134　　Fladeland, Betty. *James Gillespie Birney: Slaveholder to Abolitionist.* Ithaca: Cornell University Press, 1955. Birney was an antislavery editor and presidential candidate of the Liberty Party. He was active in presenting legal arguments during the *Creole* affair as well as protesting the gag rule in the House of Representatives.

6:135　　Wiltse, Charles M. *John C. Calhoun. Vol. 3: Sectionalist, 1840–1850.* Indianapolis: Bobbs-Merrill, 1951. This is the third in a three-volume biography of Calhoun and includes detailed treatment of Calhoun's term as secretary of state from 1844 to 1845.

6:136　　Nelson, Anna K. "Jane Storms Cazneau: Disciple of Manifest Destiny." *Prologue* 18 (Spring 1986): 25–40. Nelson presents a detailed account of Cazneau's activities as a champion of Cuban and Dominican annexation to the United States in the mid-nineteenth century.

6:137　　Oeste, George I. *John Randolph Clay: America's First Career Diplomat.* Philadelphia: University of Pennsylvania Press, 1966. Oeste's scholarly biography of Clay traces his career as a diplomatic representative of the United States from 1836 to the late 1860s.

6:138　　Williams, Mary W. "John Middleton Clayton." In *The American Secretaries of State and Their Diplomacy,* ed. Samuel Flagg Bemis, 6: 1–74. New York: Alfred A. Knopf, 1928. Williams provides an old but still valuable examination of Zachary Taylor's secretary of state. The study merits attention especially for matters related to Central America and the Caribbean.

6:139　　Rayback, Robert J. *Millard Fillmore: Biography of a President.* Buffalo: H. Stewart for Buffalo Historical Society, 1959. This remains the only modern scholarly biography of Fillmore and his public career.

6:140　　Duckett, Alvin Laroy. *John Forsyth: Political Tactician.* Athens, GA: University of Georgia Press, 1962. Forsyth was minister to Spain (1819–1823) and secretary of state (1834–1841). This detailed scholarly biography summarizes the Georgian's career.

6:141　　Maxwell, Herbert. *The Life and Letters of George William Frederick, Fourth Earl of Clarendon,*

K. G., G. C. B. 2 vols. London: E. Arnold, 1913. If little known in America, Lord Clarendon's influence on Anglo-American affairs, though muted, was often very strong. This standard life may be supplemented with his grandson's more intimate, private biography: George Villiers, *A Vanished Victorian: Being the Life of George Villiers, Fourth Earl of Clarendon, 1800–1870* (London: Eyre and Spottiswoode, 1938).

6:142   McMaster, John Bach. *The Life and Times of Stephen Girard, Mariner and Merchant.* 2 vols. Philadelphia: Lippincott, 1918. This traditional life and times biography of Girard examines the career of the wealthy and powerful Philadelphia banker and merchant between the 1770s and 1820s.

6:143   Hatcher, William B. *Edward Livingston, Jeffersonian Republican and Jacksonian Democrat.* University: Louisiana State University Press, 1940. Reprint 1970 (Peter Smith). Livingston served as secretary of state (1831–1833) and minister to France (1833–1835). This is a detailed scholarly treatment of his life and public career.

6:144   Spencer, Ivor D. *The Victor and the Spoils: A Life of William L. Marcy.* Providence, RI: Brown University Press, 1959. Based on the large collection of Marcy papers, this scholarly study presents a traditional account of Marcy's political career, including a summary of his term as secretary of state from 1853 to 1857.

6:145   Lowenthal, David. *George Perkins Marsh: Versatile Vermonter.* New York: Columbia University Press, 1958. A thoroughly researched traditional biography, this volume provides a detailed account of the intellectual as well as diplomatic facets of Marsh's career, which included ministerial sojourns in Turkey in the early 1850s and Italy in the 1860s and 1870s. Revised, enlarged, and published under the title, *George Perkins Marsh, Prophet of Conservation* (Seattle: University of Washington Press, 2000).

6:146   Cunningham, Noble E., Jr. *The Presidency of James Monroe.* Lawrence: University Press of Kansas, 1996. Cunningham presents a sympathetic account of Monroe that shows him as an adept politician and statesman: a good president with a clear vision. Monroe is a team leader who recognizes and takes advantage of the wisdom of capable subordinates such as John Quincy Adams and John C. Calhoun. The volume includes material on Jackson in Florida and the Monroe Doctrine.

6:147   Seaburg, Carl, and Stanley Paterson. *Merchant Prince of Boston: Colonel T. H. Perkins, 1764–1854.* Cambridge, MA: Harvard University Press, 1971. This clearly written and well-documented study focuses on the business and investment activities of Colonel Thomas Handasyd Perkins, the Boston merchant who made a fortune in the China trade.

6:148   Long, David F. *Nothing Too Daring: A Biography of Commodore David Porter, 1780–1843.* Annapolis: U.S. Naval Institute, 1970. This is a fascinating biography of the colorful naval officer who served in the Quasi-War, Barbary wars, and War of 1812 before commanding the West India Squadron in 1823. Court-martialed and forced out of the service, he became the U.S. consul to Algiers and later chargé to Turkey in the 1830s.

6:149   May, Robert E. *John A. Quitman: Old South Crusader.* Baton Rouge: Louisiana State University Press, 1985. This excellent biography portrays a southern nullifier who supported the Texas revolution, the Mexican War, and expansion into Cuba. This Mississippi politician (governor, congressman, senator) turned filibuster and attempted to organize an expedition against Cuba during the Pierce administration.

6:150   Langley, Harold D. "The Tragic Career of H. G. Rogers, Pennsylvania Politician and Jacksonian Diplomat." *Pennsylvania History* 31 (January 1964): 30–61. Langley explores the career of a Pennsylvania Democrat who becomes a diplomat in Sardinia in 1840–1841.

6:151   Powell, John H. *Richard Rush, Republican Diplomat, 1780–1859.* Philadelphia: University of Pennsylvania Press, 1942. A son of Dr. Benjamin Rush, Richard Rush served as comptroller of the U.S. Treasury (1811–1814), attorney general (1814–1817), secretary of state ad interim (1817), and secretary of the treasury (1825–1829). This scholarly treatment is his standard biography, including his important mission as minister to Great Britain

(1817–1825) when the Monroe Doctrine was formulated. Anthony M. Brescia has edited *The Letters and Papers of Richard Rush* (microfilm), which contains correspondence with most of the important figures of the first five decades of the nineteenth century.

6:152   Walpole, Spencer. *The Life of Lord John Russell.* 2 vols. London: Longmans, Green, 1889. As much as possible, the author intended to let Lord John (1792–1878) speak for himself and to quote documents not published elsewhere. Of course, Gooch, *The Later Correspondence of Lord John Russell, 1840–1878* (1925) (6:28), should be consulted.

6:153   Curti, Merle E. "George N. Sanders—American Patriot of the Fifties." *South Atlantic Quarterly* 27 (January 1928): 79–87. This article provides a summary of the life and career of one of the most aggressive proponents of the Young America doctrines. The revolutionary outbursts of 1848 in Europe stimulated some American idealists who inaugurated the Young America movement, which had as one of its goals active intervention against European despotisms.

6:154   Sharrow, Walter G. "William Henry Seward and the Basis for American Empire, 1850–1860." *Pacific Historical Review* 36 (August 1967): 325–42. Seward, a U.S. senator from 1849 to 1861, had a conceptual base for his vision of inevitable American empire. The article focuses on his land policy in the west and his pro-settlement, pro-homestead views.

6:155   Wayland, Francis F. *Andrew Stevenson, Democrat and Diplomat, 1785–1857.* Philadelphia: University of Pennsylvania Press, 1949. This extensively researched biography examines Stevenson's career as speaker of the House of Representatives (1827–1834) and minister to England (1836–1841). He was able to maintain amicable relations with England while upholding the American position on a series of sensitive issues, especially the search controversy in the slave trade suppression dispute.

6:156   Hall, Claude Hampton. *Abel Parker Upshur, Conservative Virginian, 1790–1844.* Madison: State Historical Society of Wisconsin, 1964. This traditional biography presents a detailed description of Upshur's life and public career, which included a sig-

nificant term as secretary of the navy (1841–1843) and a brief tenure as secretary of state (1843–1844).

6:157   Baker, Elizabeth F. *Henry Wheaton, 1785–1848.* Philadelphia: University of Pennsylvania Press, 1937. This is the only biography of the famed Rhode Island lawyer who served as chargé to Denmark from 1827 to 1833 (settling shipping claims) and then as minister to Prussia in 1835–1846.

Bilateral Relations with Other Nations

EUROPE: GENERAL

6:158   Murphy, Thomas K. *A Land without Castles: The Changing Image of America in Europe, 1780–1830.* Lanham, MD: Lexington Books, 2001. The author examines the shifting images of the United States through perceptions of social and political institutions in England and France. He explores the spoken and impressionistic transatlantic dialogue to determine the "sense" of America in the continental mind. The role of early American diplomats is considered as is contemporary travel literature.

6:159   Strout, Cushing. *The American Image of the Old World.* New York: Harper and Row, 1963. Based on writings of American political and intellectual figures, this study provides an intellectual history of American images of Europe. The primary value of the book rests with its combination of historical and literary sources.

Belgium

6:160   Laurent, Pierre-Henri. "Belgium's Relations with Texas and the United States, 1839–1844." *Southwestern Historical Quarterly* 68 (October 1964): 220–36. This article summarizes commercial negotiations between Texas and Belgium and the attempt to establish a Belgian settlement in Texas, which the author believes stimulated U.S. expansionism by provoking a reaction against European interference in North America.

6:161   Rooney, John W. *Belgian-American Diplomatic and Consular Relationships, 1830–1850: A Study in American Foreign Policy in the Mid-Nineteenth Century.* Louvain: Bureaux du Recueil, Bibliothèque de l'Université, 1969. A detailed and thoroughly researched study traces the continuous efforts by the United States and Belgium to develop mutually advantageous trade relations and to strengthen them through treaty provisions.

6:162   _____. "The Diplomatic Mission of Henry Washington Hilliard to Belgium, 1842–1844." *Alabama Historical Quarterly* 30 (Spring 1968): 19–31. This article summarizes Hilliard's rather uneventful mission to Belgium. His main contribution was to stress the need for a commercial treaty between the two nations.

6:163   Wagner, Jonathan E. "Beaumont in Brussels: An American Response to the Revolution of 1830." *Studies in History and Society* 6 (February 1975): 46–59. The article summarizes the observations and criticism of the Belgian revolution of 1830 by a doctrinaire, anti-British liberal who was born in Connecticut but had settled in Jamaica.

Britain

6:164   Barnes, James J. *Authors, Publishers, and Politicians: The Quest for an Anglo-American Copyright Agreement, 1815–1854.* Columbus: Ohio State University Press, 1974. Barnes examines the struggle for a copyright law, an often neglected divisive factor in Anglo-American relations.

6:165   Bourne, Kenneth. *Britain and the Balance of Power in North America, 1815–1908.* Berkeley: University of California Press, 1967. Based on extensive research in British archives, this study examines the problems raised by the possibility of a future war with the United States and "their influence on official British policy toward the United States." The volume usefully concentrates on Anglo-American hostility in contrast to those studies that stress the cordial relations in the period.

6:166   _____. *The Foreign Policy of Victorian England, 1830–1902.* Oxford: Clarendon Press, 1970. The author's mastery of all facets of British diplomacy allows him to stress the interconnectedness of American and European affairs. The few items devoted to America in the documents section help convey the point that, to London, Europe and other parts of the world demanded more attention than the United States.

6:167   Brauer, Kinley J. "The United States and British Imperial Expansion, 1815–1860." *Diplomatic History* 12 (Winter 1988): 19–38. Examining Britain's policy and actions in the period, Brauer seeks to determine whether the United States sought to halt or contain its commercial expansion. He contends that the Americans did try to respond but, especially with the race issue present, were reluctant to annex distant colonies and were too divided to create an informal empire. These internal problems facilitated the continuance of the British empire.

6:168   Buck, Norman Sydney. *The Development of the Organisation of Anglo-American Trade, 1800–1850.* New Haven: Yale University Press, 1925. This topic-by-topic monograph examines in detail the "methods of buying and selling goods" between the United States and Great Britain. The volume concentrates on American cotton and English manufacturing goods.

6:169   Connor, Charles P. "Archbishop Hughes and the Question of Ireland, 1829–1862." *Records of the American Catholic Historical Society of Philadelphia* 95 (March-December 1984): 15–26. The article discusses the efforts of New York archbishop John Hughes to Americanize the Irish immigrant and deal with the ongoing problems of secret Irish societies and their activities in the United States.

6:170   Crawford, Martin. *The Anglo-American Crisis of the Mid-Nineteenth Century: The Times and America, 1850–1862.* Athens, GA: University of Georgia Press, 1987. A solid examination of the leading British paper's attitude toward Anglo-American relations in the 1850s, this focuses on major debates over the Caribbean and Central America, the slave trade, and the Crimean War.

6:171   Crook, D. P. *American Democracy in English Politics, 1815–1850.* Oxford: Clarendon Press, 1965. In this fine study exploring the debate over American democracy in British politics, Crook deals with the Whig-Tory struggle, highlighted by views of Jeremy Bentham and John Stuart Mill. The discussion reveals how British opinion about the United States was formed, ultimately affecting Anglo-American relations.

6:172 Donovan, Theresa A. "Difficulties of a Diplomat: George Mifflin Dallas in London." *Pennsylvania Magazine of History and Biography* 92 (October 1968): 421–40. This well-written article explores the problems Dallas encountered as minister to Britain in the late 1850s, especially over the international slave trade and Anglo-American rivalry in Central America and the Caribbean.

6:173 _____. "President Pierce's Ministers at the Court of St. James." *Pennsylvania Magazine of History and Biography* 91 (October 1967): 457–70. This essay traces the services of James Buchanan and George M. Dallas as ministers and their efforts to interpret American policy to England and to reduce ill feeling toward the United States.

6:174 Fladeland, Betty. *Men and Brothers: Anglo-American Antislavery Cooperation.* Urbana: University of Illinois Press, 1972. Fladeland shows the effect of slavery and the African slave trade on Anglo-American relations from 1830 to 1860. She examines the *Creole* affair within the context of international law and the African slave trade controversy and also includes a discussion of the *Amistad* case.

6:175 Geiger, John O. "A Scholar Meets John Bull: Edward Everett as United States Minister to England, 1841–1845." *New England Quarterly* 49 (December 1976): 577–95. Geiger summarizes and praises Everett's role as minister to Great Britain under President Tyler.

6:176 Hidy, Ralph W. *The House of Baring in American Trade and Finance: English Merchant Bankers at Work, 1763–1861.* Cambridge, MA: Harvard University Press, 1949. This masterful exercise in business history traces the affairs, down to 1861, of what came to be the English banking house most heavily involved in American trade and finance. The research is exemplary, wide-ranging, and deep, although primary reliance is understandably on the records of the House of Baring itself.

6:177 Jones, Howard. *To the Webster-Ashburton Treaty: A Study in Anglo-American Relations, 1783–1843.* Jones offers an excellent synthesis of Anglo-American controversies resulting from the revolution, including discussions of expansion, focusing on the Oregon and Maine boundaries as well as issues involving commerce, tariffs, and the slave trade (5:456).

6:178 Jones, Wilbur D. *The American Problem in British Diplomacy, 1841–1861.* Athens, GA: University of Georgia Press, 1974. Jones examines British policy toward the United States by placing the topic in the context of British domestic politics, imperial problems, and relations with other nations. Particularly useful for American historians, it explains how British leaders viewed the United States and the tactics they used.

6:179 _____. *Lord Aberdeen and the Americas.* Athens, GA: University of Georgia Press, 1958. Based largely on the Aberdeen Papers, this volume focuses on Lord Aberdeen's diplomacy toward the United States from 1841 to 1846 and centers on four problems: the Webster-Ashburton Treaty, British plans in Texas, Anglo-French intervention in La Plata, and the Oregon question.

6:180 Kaplan, Lawrence S. "The Brahmin as Diplomat in Nineteenth Century America: Everett, Bancroft, Motley, Lowell." *Civil War History* 19 (March 1973): 5–28. Kaplan examines the role and significance of these four well-qualified ministers to the Court of St. James. He concludes that despite their considerable talents, the role of diplomatic ministers "mattered little or not at all" to U.S. foreign policy in the nineteenth century.

6:181 Kelley, Robert. *The Transatlantic Persuasion: The Liberal-Democratic Mind in the Age of Gladstone.* New York: Alfred A. Knopf, 1969. Although this intellectual history concentrates on the age of Gladstone, it contains excellent chapters on the ideas and influence of Adam Smith, Edmund Burke, and Thomas Jefferson. Accordingly, it provides appropriate background material for an understanding of Anglo-American relations before the Civil War.

6:182 Killick, John. "Bolton Ogden and Company: A Case Study in Anglo-American Trade, 1790–1850." *Business History Review* 48 (Winter 1974): 501–19. The author concludes that many functions discharged by general merchants in 1800 had been divided among specialists such as shipowners, manufacturers, bankers, speculators, and stockbrokers by the 1840s. This allowed vast increases in commerce, but caused such traditional firms as Bolton Ogden and Company to decline.

6:183   Laurent, Pierre-Henri. "Anglo-American Diplomacy and the Belgian Indemnities Controversy, 1836–1842." *Historical Journal* 10, no. 2 (1967): 197–217. Laurent traces Anglo-American cooperation in the indemnities controversy that arose from the revolution of 1830.

6:184   Lingelback, Anna L. "William Huskisson as President of the Board of Trade." *American Historical Review* 43 (July 1938): 759–74. This article summarizes Huskisson's term as president of the British Board of Trade from 1823 to 1827 and his role in setting a commercial policy directly affecting the United States.

6:185   Maisch, Christian J. "The Falkland/Malvinas Islands Clash of 1831–1832: U.S. and British Diplomacy in the South Atlantic." *Diplomatic History* 24 (Spring 2000): 185–209. This effort revisits the U.S. role in the British takeover of the Falklands, focusing on Anglo-American diplomacy. The author concludes that there was no U.K.-U.S. conspiracy to support a British occupation, but Washington did oppose Argentine control of the islands out of economic self-interest.

6:186   Martin, Kingsley. *The Triumph of Lord Palmerston: A Study of Public Opinion in England before the Crimean War.* New and rev. ed. London: Hutchinson, 1963. Originally published in 1924, this engaging little book has much to say about two subjects necessary to understand the Crimean War's international dimension: Lord Palmerston and public opinion.

6:187   Martin, Thomas P. "Cotton and Wheat in Anglo-American Trade and Politics, 1846–1852." *Journal of Southern History* 1 (August 1935): 293–319. Martin summarizes the importance of American cotton and wheat to Great Britain between

1846 and 1852 and describes the effect this trade had on English policy toward the United States.

6:188   _____. "The Upper Mississippi Valley in Anglo-American Anti-Slavery and Free Trade Relations: 1837–1842." *Mississippi Valley Historical Review* 15 (September 1928): 204–20. Martin traces the alliance of antislavery forces and wheat farmers in the upper Mississippi valley to pressure England to reduce its restrictive Corn Laws.

6:189   Merk, Frederick. "The British Corn Crisis of 1845–46 and the Oregon Treaty." *Agricultural History* 8 (July 1934): 95–123. Merk focuses on the British food crisis of the mid-1840s, noting that imported American cornmeal was not well received in the British Isles and that supplies of U.S. wheat were less than those brought in from the Baltic or Mediterranean. Thus, even though food was not a critical component in forcing British concessions on Oregon in 1846, the crisis created a political environment in Britain that made the treaty possible.

6:190   Mulvey, Christopher. *Anglo-American Landscapes: A Study of Nineteenth-Century Anglo-American Travel Literature.* Cambridge, UK: Cambridge University Press, 1983. This is an examination of approaches taken in travel literature by both Americans and Britons to the cultures they encountered. Many travelers who took the "grand tour" had romantic expectations. British tourists had little understanding of the United States and were often struck by the rawness of its life and society. The volume has clear philosophical insights and adds new and valuable dimensions to the subject of travel literature.

6:191   _____. *Transatlantic Manners: Social Patterns in Nineteenth-Century Anglo-American Travel Literature.* Cambridge, UK: Cambridge University Press, 1990. An English scholar examines writers on both sides of the Atlantic, including Hawthorne, Emerson, Fuller, Martineau, and Bryce. In this quality study he examines class, race, democracy, and aristocracy, but creates no definitive national portrait.

6:192   Perkins, Bradford. *Castlereagh and Adams: England and the United States, 1812–1823.* This is a fine study of Anglo-American relations that deals with the War of 1812 and postwar issues such as the Rush-Bagot agreement, the Convention of 1818, and the Monroe Doctrine (5:600).

6:193   Ritcheson, Charles R. "Van Buren's Mission to London, 1831–1832." *International History Review* 8 (May 1986): 190–213. The domestic political motives for the appointment of Martin Van Buren as minister to Britain in 1831 are examined as well as his success in representing the United States in London. Ritcheson points out that the interruption of his mission prohibited solving any of the outstanding Anglo-American problems, especially the impressment issue.

6:194   Roeckell, Lelia M. "Bonds over Bondage: British Opposition to the Annexation of Texas." *Journal of the Early Republic* 19 (Summer 1999): 257–78. Roeckell examines British policy toward Texas through the lens of British-Mexican relations, viewing the extent and limits of the crown's political and economic influence in Mexico. Britain's priorities were to maintain its economic interests in the area and preserve Mexican stability. Ultimately, it did not "lose" Texas, a territory over which it had minimal influence.

6:195   Sandberg, Lars G. "A Note on British Cotton Cloth Exports to the United States: 1815–1860." *Explorations in Economic History* 9 (Summer 1972): 427–29. This brief note presents the value and volume of British cotton cloth exports to the United States from 1815 to 1860, showing the sharp decline following the Panic of 1837 and the similarly dramatic rise following the Walker tariff reductions of 1846, which continued through 1860.

6:196   Thistlethwaite, Frank. *The Anglo-American Connection in the Early Nineteenth Century.* Philadelphia: University of Pennsylvania Press, 1959. These six lectures explore the types and extent of "communication" between the United States and Great Britain in the early nineteenth century. They provide an especially useful background to diplomatic and commercial relations between the two nations.

6:197   Van Alstyne, Richard W. "John Crampton, Conspirator or Dupe?" *American Historical Review* 41 (April 1936): 492–503. Van Alstyne examines the activities in the United States of British Minister John Crampton in 1855–1856 in recruiting soldiers for the British army in the Crimean War. The author

concludes that Crampton was "a loyal servant" who blundered badly and paid the price when Secretary of State William Marcy handed him and his consuls their credentials in May 1856.

6:198   Webster, C. K. *The Foreign Policy of Castlereagh, 1815–1822, Britain and the European Alliance.* Vol. 2. 2 vols. 2d ed. London: G. Bell, 1934. This is the definitive study of Castlereagh's foreign policy. Unfortunately, the New World is slighted in the author's portrayal of Castlereagh as a European statesman striving to restore the balance of power to a shattered continent. Originally published in 1931.

6:199   _____. *The Foreign Policy of Palmerston, 1830–1841: Britain, the Liberal Movement, and the Eastern Question.* 2 vols. London: G. Bell, 1951. By design, this masterwork omits American affairs, but it is required reading for any consideration of Palmerstonian statecraft. There is no reason to question that he disliked Yankees or distrusted the French, but occasionally he could subordinate distaste and distrust to the pursuit of British national interests, which he regarded as eternal.

6:200   White, Laura A. "The United States in the 1850's as Seen by British Consuls." *Mississippi Valley Historical Review* 19 (March 1933): 509–36. This article summarizes the observations made by British consuls to the British Foreign Office on political and social conditions in the United States.

6:201   Willson, Beckles. *America's Ambassadors to England (1785–1929): A Narrative of Anglo-American Diplomatic Relations.* New York: Frederick A. Stokes Company, 1929. The companion volume to Willson's *America's Ambassadors to France (1777–1927): A Narrative of Franco-American Diplomatic Relations* (1928) (6:214), this work offers an undocumented, but worthwhile, survey of U.S. representatives to the Court of St. James, including Richard Rush, Albert Gallatin, Andrew Stevenson, Edward Everett, George Bancroft, James Buchanan, and George M. Dallas.

France

6:202   Barker, Nancy Nichols. *Distaff Diplomacy: The Empress Eugénie and the Foreign Policy of the*

Second Empire. Austin: University of Texas Press, 1967. This book provides one of the rare glimpses of the influence of women on diplomacy (1850–1870) at the French court of Napoleon III.

6:203   Blumenthal, Henry. *American and French Culture, 1800–1900: Interchanges in Art, Science, Literature, and Society.* Baton Rouge: Louisiana State University Press, 1975. Blumenthal offers an impressive examination of the cultural impact rendered on both sides of the Atlantic in religion, art, sculpture, literature, theater, music, dance, painting, and science.

6:204   _____. *France and the United States: Their Diplomatic Relation, 1789–1914.* Although this is a survey, the author devotes considerable space to the issues of revolution in France, the spoliations claims, Napoleon III, Cuba, and the Crimean War (2:317).

6:205   _____. *A Reappraisal of Franco-American Relations, 1830–1871.* Chapel Hill: University of North Carolina Press, 1959. Blumenthal challenges the traditional assumption that Franco-American relations were friendly and cordial during this period. Instead, he concludes that relations were clouded by hostility, distrust, and misunderstanding.

6:206   Carosso, Vincent P., and Lawrence H. Leder. "Edward Livingston and Jacksonian Diplomacy." *Louisiana History* 7 (Summer 1966): 241–48. This piece summarizes the French claims episode and reprints a letter from Livingston to Secretary of State John Forsyth dated June 21, 1835.

6:207   Curtis, Eugene N. "American Opinion of the French Nineteenth Century Revolutions." *American Historical Review* 29 (January 1924): 249–70. Curtis surveys the opinion of the American press and leading politicians toward the French revolutions of 1830, 1848, and 1870.

6:208   Gray, Walter D. *Interpreting American Democracy in France: The Career of Édouard Laboulaye, 1811–1883.* Newark: University of Delaware Press, 1994. Gray draws a portrait of a French law professor who wrote a history of the United States in 1855. A scholar and a liberal, Laboulaye raised sensitive issues of political and religious liberty based in part on his study of the United States.

6:209   McLemore, Richard A. *Franco-American Diplomatic Relations, 1816–1836.* Baton Rouge: Louisiana State University Press, 1941. Reprint 1972 (Kennikat Press). This study traces the rise and development of the "aggressive nationalism" manifested in American policy toward France during the spoliations claims controversy.

6:210   Neely, Sylvia. "The Politics of Liberty in the Old World and the New: Lafayette's Return to America in 1824." *Journal of the Early Republic* 6 (Summer 1986): 151–71. Lafayette came to America with his political fortunes at a low ebb in France. For Americans he was less an individual than a symbol of an increasingly lost revolutionary generation of Spartan values and sacrifice in an increasingly materialistic world. His promotion of Greek and Latin American independence was aligned with the views of many in the Monroe administration.

6:211   Rémond, René. *Les Etats-Unis devant l'opinion française, 1815–1852 [The United States in French Opinion, 1815–1852].* 2 vols. Paris: A. Colin, 1962. These volumes contain an exhaustive study of the evolution of French attitudes toward the United States in the first half of the nineteenth century, including coverage of Franco-American diplomatic relations.

6:212   Rohrs, Richard C. "American Critics of the French Revolution of 1848." *Journal of the Early Republic* 14 (Fall 1994): 359–77. Most Americans supported the revolution of 1848, but a significant minority was concerned about the overthrow of government and the accompanying violence. Their fear of radicalism and skepticism were based on the results of earlier revolutions in France.

6:213   Thomas, Robert C. "Andrew Jackson versus France: American Policy toward France, 1834–1836." *Tennessee Historical Quarterly* 35 (Spring 1976): 51–64. Thomas summarizes Jackson's policy toward France in the spoliations crisis of 1834 to 1836. The author concludes that the lack of a strong, constructive domestic opposition permitted Jackson to pursue a dangerous policy that threatened a needless war.

6:214   Willson, Beckles. *America's Ambassadors to France (1777–1927): A Narrative of Franco-*

American Diplomatic Relations. Willson offers an undocumented but still useful survey of the characters who served the United States in Paris in the nineteenth century, including Albert Gallatin, William Rives, Edward Livingston, Lewis Cass, Richard Rush, and John Y. Mason (4:241).

Italy

6:215   Bárány, George. "A Note on the Prehistory of American Diplomatic Relations with the Papal States." *Catholic Historical Review* 47 (January 1962): 508–13. This article details the visit of American diplomat Daniel Jenifer to the Papal States in 1844. His positive report led to the establishment of formal diplomatic relations between the United States and the Papal States under Polk.

6:216   DeConde, Alexander. *Half Bitter, Half Sweet: An Excursion into Italian-American History.* New York: Scribner, 1971. DeConde includes a brief summary of early contacts between the United States and the Italian people. Substantial bibliography.

6:217   Fry, Joseph A. "Eyewitness by Proxy: Nelson M. Beckwith's Evaluation of Garibaldi, September 1861." *Civil War History* 28 (March 1982): 65–71. Fry recounts an unflattering appraisal of Garibaldi by an American businessman who claimed to accompany Henry S. Sanford to Italy in 1861. Sanford's mission was to offer the Italian revolutionary a military command in the Union army.

6:218   Humphreys, Sexson E. "United States Recognition of the Kingdom of Italy." *Historian* 21 (May 1959): 296–312. The article focuses on the 1860–1861 period, discussing American support for the unification of Italy and competition for the post of first minister to the new nation, which was wisely given to George P. Marsh by the Lincoln administration.

6:219   Marraro, Howard Rosario. *American Opinion on the Unification of Italy, 1846–1861.* New York: Columbia University Press, 1932. Marraro traces American opinion and diplomatic response toward the events leading to the unification of Italy.

6:220   Pagano, Luigi A. "Comunicazioni: Sicilia e Stati Uniti di America nel Risorgimento [Sicily and the United States of America during the Risorgimento]." *Rassegna Storica del Risorgimento* 41 (April-September 1954): 484–93. Pagano focuses on the friendly attitudes existing in 1848–1849 and 1860 between the Sicilian revolutionary government and American diplomats and naval commanders.

6:221   Stock, Leo F. "American Consuls to the Papal States, 1797–1867." *Catholic Historical Review* 15 (October 1929): 233–51. This is a brief summary of various American consuls and their activities in promoting commercial and diplomatic relations with the papacy in the early nineteenth century.

Spain

6:222   Chadwick, French Ensor. *The Relations of the United States and Spain: Diplomacy.* New York: C. Scribner's Sons, 1909. This book is a detailed diplomatic history based on traditional archival sources. Approximately one-quarter of the book deals with the period from 1815 to 1860 and includes discussions of the Holy Alliance, Cuba, filibustering, and the "Black Warrior" incident.

6:223   Ettinger, Amos A. *The Mission to Spain of Pierre Soulé, 1853–1855: A Study in the Cuban Diplomacy of the United States.* New Haven: Yale University Press, 1932. An exhaustive study, based on American and European (but not Spanish) sources, this work examines the Pierce administration's effort to purchase Cuba and argues that Soulé represented those southern slave interests wanting Cuban annexation.

6:224   Robertson, William Spence. "The United States and Spain in 1822." *American Historical Review* 20 (July 1915): 781–800. Robertson deals with Spanish anticipation of the Monroe Doctrine and their warnings to Britain and the other European powers about the potential dangers of a republican political system.

Netherlands

6:225   Hoekstra, Peter. "Thirty-Seven Years of Holland-American Relations, 1803–1840." Ph.D. dissertation, University of Pennsylvania, 1916. This study provides a traditional survey of commercial relations and negotiations between the United States and Holland during these four decades.

6:226   Minnen, Cornelis A. van. *American Diplomats in the Netherlands, 1815–50.* New York: St. Martin's Press, 1993. A translation of a Dutch dissertation, this study presents the perceptions of American diplomats such as Alexander Hill Everett, Christopher Hughes, William Pitt Preble, and Auguste Davezac of the Netherlands. Minnen goes beyond the traditional financial-commercial ties to explore the ministers' changing views as their focus shifted from king and court to the maneuvering of an increasingly powerful parliament.

6:227   Westermann, Johannes Cornelis. *The Netherlands and the United States: Their Relations in the Beginning of the Nineteenth Century.* Westermann, a Dutch scholar who uses a wide range of sources, exhausts the subjects of reciprocity and commerce between the Netherlands and the United States following the liberation from Napoleonic conquest (5:612).

Germany

6:228   Adams, Henry Mason. *Prussian-American Relations, 1775–1871.* This slim volume of less than 100 pages of text surveys the intellectual and educational influences of Germans on the United States and explores Prussian-American trade, especially in tobacco (4:255).

6:229   Beutin, Ludwig. *Bremen und Amerika [Bremen and America].* Bremen: C. Schünemann, 1953. This thorough study focuses on commercial relations between the United States and Bremen from 1800 to 1939 and explains how the economic life of Bremen was changed by its relations with the United States.

6:230   Gazley, John Gerow. *American Opinion of German Unification, 1848–1871.* New York: Columbia University Press Studies in History, Economics and Public Law, 1926. Gazley's detailed survey is based primarily on U.S. press opinion and the writings of American political and intellectual figures.

Russia

6:231   Bergquist, Harold E., Jr. "Russo-American Economic Relations in the 1820's: Henry Middleton as a Protector of American Interests in Russia and Turkey." *East European Quarterly* 11 (Spring 1977): 27–41. The article summarizes Middleton's activities as American minister to Russia in the 1820s on behalf of American commercial interests and his important role in negotiating the 1830 treaty with Turkey.

6:232   Dowty, Alan. *The Limits of American Isolation: The United States and the Crimean War.* New York: New York University Press, 1971. Dowty examines opinion and policy toward the Crimean crisis to demonstrate that the United States played the role of an active neutral during this conflict rather than the role of an isolationist power. Foreword by Hans J. Morgenthau.

6:233   Dvoichenko-Markov, Eufrosina. "Americans in the Crimean War." *Russian Review* 13 (April 1954): 137–45. This is a brief summary of those few Americans in the Crimean War who actively participated on the Russian side.

6:234   Golder, Frank A. "Russian-American Relations during the Crimean War." *American Historical Review* 31 (April 1926): 462–76. Based on Russian archival sources, this article examines Russian motivation for seeking U.S. support and the reasons for American sympathy for Russia during the Crimean War.

6:235   Henderson, Galvin. "The Diplomatic Revolution of 1854." *American Historical Review* 43 (October 1937): 22–50. This article provides excellent background for understanding the Crimean War, and U.S. marginal connections to it, by focusing on the crisis of 1854 and the breakdown of the European powers system created in 1815.

6:236   Hildt, John C. *Early Diplomatic Negotiations of the United States with Russia.* Baltimore: Johns Hopkins Press, 1906. The author concludes with a chapter on the Treaty of 1824 in this traditional study of Russo-American relations that begins with the American revolution and focuses on the period prior to 1815.

6:237 Jones, Horace P. "Southern Opinion on the Crimean War." *Journal of Mississippi History* 29 (May 1967): 95–117. Jones surveys the response of a large number of southern newspapers and periodicals to the Crimean War. The author concludes that the region's deep hostility to England resulted in a large majority of southern newspapers being pro-Russia during the crisis.

6:238 Kirchner, Walther. *Studies in Russian-American Commerce, 1820–1860.* Leiden: Brill, 1975. This volume includes a considerable amount of statistical detail as well as information on how trade between the two nations was organized. The author finds no indication of "colonial exploitation" of Russia by the United States.

6:239 Langley, Lester D. "Two Jacksonian Diplomats in Czarist Russia." *Research Studies* 45 (June 1977): 92–99. This article summarizes the diplomatic activities of Andrew Jackson's two appointees as minister to Russia: John Randolph and James Buchanan. The author emphasizes the importance of commercial rather than political relations.

6:240 Laserson, Max M. *The American Impact on Russia, Diplomatic and Ideological, 1784–1917.* New York: Macmillan, 1950. Laserson focuses on the post–Civil War era, but devotes about seventy-five pages to the 1815–1860 period, with highlights including the impact of Jeffersonian ideals on the Russians, the Decembrist movement, and the Crimean War.

6:241 McFadden, David W. "John Quincy Adams, American Commercial Diplomacy, and Russia, 1809–1825." McFadden discusses the consistency of John Quincy Adams's support for commerce with Russia as both minister to St. Petersburg and as secretary of state (5:616).

6:242 Nolan, Cathal J. "Detachment from Despotism: U.S. Responses to Tsarism, 1776–1865." *Review of International Studies* 19 (October 1993): 349–68. Commerce and geopolitics helped create a generally amicable Russo-American relationship in the last half of the nineteenth century. American isolationism and strong negative reactions to tsarist despotism, however, blocked a more intimate bond.

6:243 Oliva, L. Jay. "America Meets Russia: 1854." *Journalism Quarterly* 40 (Winter 1963): 65–69. This article surveys American press opinion at the outset of the Crimean War and finds that it was predominantly anti-Russian, while public opinion was sympathetic to Russia.

6:244 Saul, Norman E. *Distant Friends: The United States and Russia, 1763–1867.* This is the best recent account of Russian-American relations in English. Saul notes the two nations grew closer despite important ideological differences. He cites the importance of Russian trade to the United States and a strong literary impact in the cultural sphere. Russian-American friendship flourished even when real tensions existed over territorial issues in the Pacific northwest (2:310).

6:245 Saul, Norman E., and Richard D. McKinzie, eds. *Russian-American Dialogue on Cultural Relations, 1776–1914.* Columbia: University of Missouri Press, 1997. This edited collection of eleven chapters of Russian scholarship includes commentary by American historians. Of particular interest is the chapter by I. A. Ivanchenko on the "Development of Culture and Literacy in the USA during Jacksonian Democracy in the Assessment of Russian Periodicals."

6:246 Thomas, Benjamin P. *Russo-American Relations, 1815–1867.* Baltimore: Johns Hopkins Press, 1930. Reprint 1970 (Da Capo Press). This early work contains a traditional survey of diplomatic relations between the United States and Russia but is based only on American sources.

Greece

6:247 Cline, Myrtle A. "American Attitude toward the Greek War of Independence, 1821–1828." Ph.D. dissertation, Columbia University, 1930. The most detailed account of the U.S. reaction to the Greek revolution against the Turks, this work demonstrates the growth of public and congressional support for U.S. intervention. American commercial interests were among the opponents of an activist position.

6:248 Dakin, Douglas. *The Greek Struggle for Independence, 1821–1833.* Berkeley: University of California Press, 1973. This study provides a thorough examination of the movement for Greek independence. Although the author does not relate the Greek struggle to U.S. diplomacy, his book offers an excellent background.

6:249   Earle, Edward Mead. "American Interest in the Greek Cause, 1821–1827." *American Historical Review* 33 (October 1927): 44–63. Earle demonstrates that American concern for the Greek cause—including providing men, supplies, and money—could have had detrimental effects on U.S.-Turkish relations leading up to the negotiation of the 1830 U.S.-Turkish treaty.

6:250   Kaplan, Lawrence S. "The Monroe Doctrine and the Truman Doctrine: The Case of Greece." *Journal of the Early Republic* 13 (Spring 1993): 1–22. Kaplan compares isolationism toward Greece in the 1820s with the interventionist view of the 1940s. He focuses on John Quincy Adams's opposition to intervention despite the "Greek fever" among politicians and intellectuals. Congress chose not to act on resolutions to recognize Greece but put forth the view that the Greeks were Europeans—and the United States would stay out of the Old World if the Europeans would refrain from interfering in the New.

6:251   Larrabee, Stephen A. *Hellas Observed: The American Experience of Greece, 1775–1865.* New York: New York University Press, 1957. Based on English-language sources, this volume traces the extensive American interest in Greece and Americans' image of the country.

6:252   Pappas, Paul C. *The United States and the Greek War for Independence, 1821–1828.* New York: Columbia University Press, 1985. This is the only monograph in English based on Greek manuscript materials. The author documents the U.S. government's shift from nonintervention to benevolent neutrality and treats the secret American collaboration with Greek agents to build ships. There are minor flaws in the book resulting from poor editing and some factual errors.

Austria-Hungary

6:253   Curti, Merle E. "Austria and the United States, 1848–1852, A Study in Diplomatic Rela-

tions." In *Smith College Studies in History,* 11: 141–206. Northampton, MA: Department of History of Smith College, 1926. This study is a traditional account of the diplomatic relations between the United States and Austria from the revolutions of 1848 through the Kossuth affair of 1851–1852.

6:254   Deák, István. *The Lawful Revolution: Louis Kossuth and the Hungarians, 1848–1849.* New York: Columbia University Press, 1979. Deák provides the fullest account in English of the 1848 Hungarian revolution. The author focuses on Kossuth as a symbol of liberalism in America and elsewhere.

6:255   Efroyinson, Clarence. "An Austrian Diplomat in America, 1840." *American Historical Review* 41 (April 1936): 503–14. The article relates the travels of Austrian Secretary of Legation (and later chargé) Johann Van Hulsemann as he tours the northeast, upper midwest, and Canada in the summer of 1840 and relates his impressions to his superiors.

6:256   Komlos, John H. *Louis Kossuth in America, 1851–1852.* Buffalo: East European Institute, 1973. This monograph provides a summary of Kossuth's life, his 1851–1852 visit to the United States, and his career beforehand.

6:257   Oliver, John W. "Louis Kossuth's Appeal to the Middle West, 1852." *Mississippi Valley Historical Review* 14 (March 1928): 481–95. Oliver provides a description of Kossuth's travels in the middle west and a useful summary of the region's reaction to the Hungarian revolutionary leader.

6:258   Spencer, Donald S. *Louis Kossuth and Young America: A Study of Sectionalism and Foreign Policy, 1848–1852.* Columbia: University of Missouri Press, 1977. Spencer describes Kossuth's visit to the United States in 1851–1852 and examines his appeals for American intervention in Europe as well as the subsequent decline in support for his cause among a variety of groups.

6:259   Szilassy, Sandor. "America and the Hungarian Revolution of 1848–1849." *Slavonic and East European Review* 44 (January 1966): 180–96. The article traces the activities of William Stiles, the pro-revolutionary American chargé, who mediated for the Hungarian rebels with the Austrians. It also contrasts the parallel role of Austrian chargé, C. Hulsemann, in Washington and explores the Kossuth visit to the United States and American attitudes toward the Hungarian exiles in Turkey.

Scandinavia

6:260   Adamson, Rolf. "Swedish Iron Exports to the United States, 1783–1860." *Scandinavian Economic History Review* 17, no. 1 (1969): 58–114. Containing detailed charts, maps, and tables, this article summarizes the trade that flourished in the 1830s before declining significantly in the 1840s and 1850s.

6:261   Carlson, Knute Emil. *Relations of the United States with Sweden.* Allentown, PA: H. R. Haas and Co., 1921. In this very brief study that concludes in 1830 the author devotes two chapters to the settlement of shipping claims from the Napoleonic Wars and the negotiation of a new commercial treaty.

6:262   Dunham, Chester Gray. "A Nineteenth Century Baltimore Diplomat: Christopher Hughes Goes to Sweden." *Maryland Historical Magazine* 72 (Fall 1977): 387–401. Dunham focuses on the activities of a Maryland merchant who served as chargé in both Sweden and the Netherlands in a long diplomatic career. This article discusses his role in finalizing a commercial treaty with Sweden between 1816 and 1818 as well as resolving numerous problems with shipping claims.

6:263   Fogdall, Soren J. M. P. *Danish-American Diplomacy, 1776–1920.* This reliable but uninspired study includes a discussion of Henry Wheaton and the settlement of American merchant claims against Denmark resulting from the Napoleonic Wars (4:268).

6:264   Frederickson, J. William. "American Shipping in the Trade with Northern Europe, 1783–1860." *Scandinavian Economic History Review* 4, no. 2 (1956): 109–25. The author examines the comparatively small amount of U.S. trade with Russia and Scandinavia and analyzes the economic and political factors that affected that trade.

6:265   Hovde, Brynjolf Jakob. *Diplomatic Relations of the United States with Sweden and Norway,*
1814–1905. Iowa City: University of Iowa Studies in the Social Sciences, 1920. Based entirely on American sources, this brief study summarizes U.S. diplomatic relations with Sweden and Norway in the nineteenth century.

Others

6:266   Bearss, Sara B. "Henry Clay and the American Claims against Portugal, 1850." *Journal of the Early Republic* 7 (Summer 1987): 167–80. Bearss discusses the relationship between Clay's support for the Taylor administration in 1849–1850 and his son's (James B. Clay) ultimately unsuccessful negotiations to settle shipping violations claims against Portugal.

6:267   Lerski, Jerzy J. *A Polish Chapter in Jacksonian America: The United States and the Polish Exiles of 1831.* Madison: University of Wisconsin Press, 1958. Lerski describes the plight of the Polish exiles who emigrated to the United States in 1831.

6:268   May, Arthur J. "Contemporary American Opinion of the Mid-Century Revolutions in Central Europe." Ph.D. dissertation, University of Pennsylvania, 1927. May's survey, based on newspapers, magazines, and political correspondence, summarizes, but does not analyze, the positive American response to the revolutions.

6:269   Meier, Heinz K. *The United States and Switzerland, in the Nineteenth Century.* The study focuses on Swiss-American relations commencing with the Treaty of 1850 and emphasizing the role of the first U.S. diplomatic agent, Theodore Fay (2:340).

6:270   Webster, C. K. "British Mediation between France and the United States, 1834–1836." *English Historical Review* 42 (January 1927): 58–78. Although England was never an official mediator in this Franco-American dispute, Lord Palmerston played an important role in helping to resolve the crisis. Palmerston feared a French conflict with the United States, which might have minimized Paris's role in a future struggle against Russia—a more vital geopolitical contest.

MIDDLE EAST

6:271   Bryson, Thomas A. *An American Consular Officer in the Middle East in the Jacksonian Era: A Biography of William Brown Hodgson, 1801–1871.* Atlanta: Resurgens Publications, 1979. John Quincy Adams sent Hodgson to Algiers as a consul in 1826. This volume is an unusual look at an American who remained in the Middle East until 1842, traveling widely (including in Egypt and Turkey) and sharing his observations.

6:272   Daniel, Robert L. *American Philanthropy in the Near East, 1820–1960.* Athens, OH: Ohio University Press, 1970. An excellent study, this largely focuses on Christian missionaries' role in philanthropic efforts in Syria, Malta, and Turkey. There is also coverage of efforts to assist the Greeks during the 1820s revolution.

6:273   Earle, Edward Mead. "Early American Policy Concerning Ottoman Minorities." *Political Science Quarterly* 42 (September 1927): 337–67. This short account demonstrates the conflict (1821–1828) between popular sentiment and the national interest in relationship to the Greek revolution. The precedent of nonintervention set the course for later U.S. reaction to the pleas of Ottoman minorities.

6:274   Field, James A., Jr. *America and the Mediterranean World, 1776–1882.* This volume is a fine survey of commercial, naval, and missionary activity in the Middle East, focusing on Turkey and the Levant (4:55). The 1991 reprint is titled *From Gibraltar to the Middle East: America and the Mediterranean World, 1776–1882.*

6:275   Finnie, David H. *Pioneers East: The Early American Experience in the Middle East.* Cambridge, MA: Harvard University Press, 1967. This fine study deals largely with nonpolitical activity (commerce, science, missionary work) in Turkey, Persia, Syria, Palestine, and Mesopotamia in the 1830s and 1840s.

6:276   Langley, Lester D. "Jacksonian America and the Ottoman Empire." *Muslim World* 68 (January 1978): 46–56. Langley surveys early U.S. relations with the Ottoman empire in the 1830s, including

David Porter's mission to Turkey, William Hodgson in Egypt (see Bryson, *An American Consular Officer in the Middle East in the Jacksonian Era: A Biography of William Brown Hodgson, 1801–1871* [1979] [6:271]), and commercial and missionary activities through North Africa.

6:277   Porter, David. *Constantinople and Its Environs in a Series of Letters, Exhibiting the Actual State of the Manners, Customs, and Habits of the Turks, Armenians, Jews, and Greeks.* 2 vols. New York: Harper, 1835. This is a valuable account of the experiences of a former naval officer who became consul for Algiers and then chargé to Turkey. First issued as written "by an American, long resident at Constantinople."

6:278   Serpell, David R. "American Consular Activities in Egypt, 1849–1863." *Journal of Modern History* 10 (September 1938): 344–63. Serpell explains why the United States failed to penetrate the Egyptian market, dominated by Great Britain, in the mid-nineteenth century, placing much of the blame on the small U.S. economic stake in the region and an indifferent State Department that appointed consuls on an irregular and interrupted basis.

6:279   Sha'ban, Fuad. *Islam and Arabs in Early American Thought: Roots of Orientalism in America.* Durham, NC: Acorn Press, 1991. Presenting American perceptions of the Islamic world, the author treats the Barbary Wars, missionaries and travelers, and romantic views as reflected in literature and the imagination.

6:280   Tibawi, A. L. *American Interests in Syria, 1800–1901: A Study of Educational, Literary and Religious Work.* Oxford: Clarendon Press, 1966. Tibawi devotes approximately 150 pages to the examination of American interests in Syria prior to 1860. He focuses on trade, missionary activity (including mission schools), and schools for young women.

6:281   Vogel, Lester I. *To See a Promised Land: Americans and the Holy Land in the Nineteenth Century.* University Park: Pennsylvania State University Press, 1993. Vogel examines the cultural attachment of American Protestants to the Holy Land. His focus is post-1865, but settlers, archaeologists, traders, and diplomats (the United States established a consulate in Jerusalem by 1856) in the pre–Civil War era are also discussed.

6:282 Wright, Lenoir Chambers. *United States Policy toward Egypt, 1831–1914.* New York: Exposition Press, 1969. An examination of American involvement in Egypt focuses on the post–Civil War era but provides some insights into earlier missionary activity in the Middle East.

AFRICA

General

6:283 Booth, Alan R. *The United States Experience in South Africa, 1784–1870.* Cape Town: A. A. Balkema, 1976. Booth offers a fine study of the New England traders who exchanged foodstuffs for building supplies, hides, and wool in the antebellum era. He also discussed the American Zulu mission in Natal that adopted an unpopular (among the whites) sympathy for the native population and their landholding rights.

6:284 Clendenen, Clarence C. *Americans in Black Africa up to 1865.* Stanford, CA: Hoover Institution on War, Revolution, and Peace, Stanford University, 1964. This is a slim, narrow study that focuses on Liberia and deals with traders and missionaries. The bibliography is limited and there is unfortunately no index.

6:285 Stevens, Kenneth R. "Of Whaling Ships and Kings: The Johanna Bombardment of 1851." *Prologue* 18 (Winter 1986): 241–49. Stevens discusses an incident of gunboat diplomacy involving the naval bombardment of the tiny island kingdom of Johanna off the East Africa coast. An American whaling captain had been temporarily imprisoned and national honor offended, and violence was the remedy of first choice against a nonwestern people.

Colonization Movement and Liberia

6:286 Beyan, Amos Jones. *The American Colonization Society and the Creation of the Liberian State: A Historical Perspective, 1822–1900.* Lanham, MD: University Press of America, 1991. Beyan offers a study of the impact of the American Colonization Society on Liberia in determining the political culture and economic structure of the nation. While the role of whites seems strong in these areas, the colonists seem to have determined their own religion. The author sees the ACS as heavily influenced by southern slave owners.

6:287 Davis, Hugh. "Northern Colonizationists and Free Blacks, 1823–1837: A Case Study of Leonard Bacon." *Journal of the Early Republic* 17 (Winter 1997): 651–75. Davis examines the attitudes of New England cleric Leonard Bacon, who believed that colonization would benefit not only black and white Americans, but also Africans. Bacon, who was antiabolitionist and not pro-equality, felt that blacks could economically have their best chance for success in Africa.

6:288 Gatewood, Willard B., Jr. "To Be Truly Free: Louis Sheridan and the Colonization of Liberia." *Civil War History* 29 (December 1983): 332–48. Gatewood recounts the story of a well-respected free black slave owner and merchant in North Carolina who supported colonization in Liberia in the 1840s.

6:289 Harris, Katherine. *African and American Values: Liberia and West Africa.* This is a brief narrative that focuses on U.S.-Liberian relations between 1820 and 1850. It emphasizes the government's informal colonization efforts, with Washington transferring control to the states and voluntary societies. Clear and well written, almost half the volume is devoted to notes and bibliography (2:267).

6:290 Moses, Wilson Jeremiah, ed. *Liberian Dreams: Back-to-Africa Narratives from the 1850s.* University Park: Pennsylvania State University Press, 1998. This work takes a fascinating look at Liberia through the letters of four men—two of whom were clergymen—on the problems of colonization and everyday life in Africa in the 1850s.

6:291 Sherwood, H. N. "The Formation of the American Colonization Society." *Journal of Negro History* 2 (July 1917): 209–28. In this older study exploring the motives of the founders of the American Colonization Society in 1815–1816, the author notes the humanitarian motives, including the cessation of the slave trade.

6:292   Slaughter, Philip. *Virginian History of African Colonization.* Richmond: MacFarlane and Fergusson, 1855. Reprint 1970 (Books for Libraries Press). This is an interesting primary study of the activities of the Virginia Colonization Society, written by an involved cleric, in promoting the resettlement of free blacks and of the group's role in Liberia.

6:293   Staudenraus, P. J. *The African Colonization Movement, 1816–1865.* New York: Columbia University Press, 1961. This work is the major study of the movement to establish Liberia as a haven for free blacks after the War of 1812 and the problems inherent in the project both in the United States and Africa.

Slave Trade and Efforts against It

6:294   Booth, Alan R. "The United States African Squadron, 1843–1861." *Boston University Papers in African History* 1 (1964): 77–117. Booth discusses the ineffectiveness of the joint-squadron idea and concludes that the attitudes of U.S. secretaries of the navy, mostly southerners or southern sympathizers, made the arrangement impossible. Instead of suppressing the slave trade, they sought to build American commerce along the African coast, encourage inadequate congressional funding of the plan, and authorize the use of unseaworthy ships.

6:295   Du Bois, William E. B. *The Suppression of the African Slave-Trade to the United States of America, 1638–1870.* New York: Longmans, Green, 1896. Reprint 1986 (Viking Press). Du Bois reviews the efforts made by Americans to limit and suppress the slave trade. He also discusses the slavers' illegal use of the American flag to avoid the British slave patrol, a matter of serious dispute in Anglo-American relations from the 1820s to the 1860s.

6:296   Duignan, Peter, and Clarence C. Clendenen. *The United States and the African Slave Trade, 1619–1862.* Stanford, CA: Hoover Institution on War, Revolution, and Peace, Stanford University, 1963. A brief history of U.S. involvement in the slave trade, it clearly illustrates the ineffectual use of

the joint-squadron plan established by the Webster-Ashburton Treaty.

6:297   Foote, Andrew H. *Africa and the American Flag.* New York: D. Appleton and Co., 1854. Reprint 1970 (Dawsons). This narrative, first published in 1854, is the reflection of a U.S. naval officer who served off the coast of West Africa in 1850–1851. He presents fascinating observations of Liberia, the slave trade, and the role of the navy in dealing with the problem.

6:298   Howard, Warren S. *American Slavers and the Federal Law, 1837–1862.* Berkeley: University of California Press, 1963. Reprint 1976 (Greenwood Press). This study contains information on the Webster-Ashburton Treaty's joint-cruising arrangement.

6:299   Mathieson, William Law. *Great Britain and the Slave Trade, 1839–1865.* London: Longmans, Green, 1929. Mathieson provides a detailed analysis of British attempts to stamp out the slave trade and induce other nations, especially the United States, to cooperate in the venture. The book refers incidentally to the Lyons-Seward Treaty of 1862 for suppression of the trade.

6:300   Milne, A. Taylor. "The Slave Trade and Anglo-American Relations, 1807–1862." *Bulletin of the Institute of Historical Research* 9 (November 1931): 126–29. This brief piece, a synopsis of the author's thesis, sees slavery and the slave trade as a major factor in the "uneasy relationship" of the United States and Great Britain before the Civil War. Milne argues that American failure to suppress the slave trade antagonized influential people in England and slowed British efforts to eradicate the odious business.

6:301   Soulsby, Hugh G. *The Right of Search and the Slave Trade in Anglo-American Relations, 1814–1862.* Baltimore: Johns Hopkins University Studies in Historical and Political Science, 1933. The right-of-search and African slave trade questions intertwined to pose great problems for the Webster-Ashburton negotiations and other issues in Anglo-American relations.

6:302   Takaki, Ronald T. *A Pro-Slavery Crusade: The Agitation to Reopen the African Slave Trade.*

New York: Free Press, 1971. Takaki examines the move in the American south in the 1850s to reopen the African slave trade. He attributes the activity in part to rising internal social tensions.

6:303   Van Alstyne, Richard W. "The British Right of Search and the African Slave Trade." *Journal of Modern History* 2 (March 1930): 37–47. This essay emphasizes how the right-of-search question was involved in the African slave trade debate, and admits to a theoretical distinction between the alleged right of "search" and the right of "visit," just as the Peel ministry claimed. The search controversy did not end until Britain and the United States adopted mutual search policies during America's Civil War.

6:304   Wish, Harvey. "The Revival of the African Slave Trade with the U.S., 1856–1860." *Mississippi Valley Historical Review* 27 (March 1941): 569–88. This discusses the efforts of South Carolinian L. W. Spratt and others to legally reinstitute the African slave trade into the south—a commerce that had illegally continued in spite of the 1807 prohibition.

Amistad Mutiny

6:305   Jones, Howard. *Mutiny on the* Amistad: *The Saga of a Slave Revolt and Its Impact on American Abolition, Law, and Diplomacy.* New York: Oxford University Press, 1987. This fine study is a marked improvement over previous examinations of the subject. Jones excels at discussion of the legal entanglements, especially the quagmire of problems with Spain.

6:306   McClendon, R. Earl. "The *Amistad* Claims: Inconsistencies of Policy." *Political Science Quarterly* 48 (September 1933): 386–412. The article briefly explores the *Amistad* affair while focusing on the lengthy legal battle waged by the Spanish government to obtain claims for the confiscated ship and slave cargo. The contest in court and Congress lasted until 1861 when, embroiled in a climate of antislavery sentiment, Secretary of State William H. Seward simply refused to pay.

6:307   Noonan, John T., Jr. *The Antelope: The Ordeal of the Recaptured Africans in the Administrations of James Monroe and John Quincy Adams.* Berkeley: University of California Press, 1977. Noo-

nan examines the plight of a cargo of slaves captured off the Florida coast in 1820 by a U.S. revenue cutter. The controversial case involved two presidential administrations and took years before it was resolved by the Marshall Court.

LATIN AMERICA AND THE CARIBBEAN

6:308   Benns, F. Lee. *The American Struggle for the British West India Carrying-Trade, 1815–1830.* Bloomington: Indiana University Studies, 1923. This thoroughly researched study details the American drive to win trade concessions from Great Britain in the West Indies, which culminated with the Reciprocity Treaty of 1830.

6:309   Foner, Philip S. *A History of Cuba and Its Relations with the United States. Vol. 1: From the Conquest of Cuba to La Escalera.* New York: International Publishers, 1962. This is the first in a multivolume series based on Cuban and U.S. sources. Writing from a perspective sympathetic to Castro, Foner argues that expansion of slavery was the motivating force in U.S. policy toward Cuba from the 1820s to the 1840s.

6:310   Langley, Lester D. *The Cuban Policy of the United States: A Brief History.* This is a good brief study of U.S. policy toward Cuba from Jefferson through Kennedy that includes a chapter on the filibustering-annexationist efforts of the 1840s and 1850s (2:369).

6:311   Logan, Rayford W. *The Diplomatic Relations of the United States with Haiti, 1776–1891.* Logan wrote a fine, detailed study relating how the existence of Haiti created nettlesome problems for the United States in reaching a consistent and logical foreign and domestic policy in the antebellum era (5:520).

6:312   Martinez-Fernández, Luis. "Caudillos, Annexationism, and the Rivalry between Empires in the Dominican Republic, 1844–1874." *Diplomatic History* 17 (Fall 1993): 571–98. This article explains the motivations of the caudillos for Dominican annexation in the nineteenth century. Pedro Santana and Buenaventura Baez were self-serving strongmen but not the only Dominicans who promoted absorption.

The fever peaked at the period of imperial rivalry over the republic. The caudillos' annexationist preferences were dictated by geopolitical circumstances beyond their control. The French, British, and Americans all struggled for influence in a region the United States came to dominate by the 1870s.

6:313   Rauch, Basil. *American Interest in Cuba: 1848–1855.* New York: Columbia University Press Studies in History, Economics and Public Law, 1948. While this volume thoroughly covers the annexationist schemes of the era, the author used no works in Spanish. Unfortunately, the book does contain some errors.

6:314   Tansill, Charles Callan. *The United States and Santo Domingo, 1798–1873: A Chapter in Caribbean Diplomacy.* Baltimore: Johns Hopkins Press, 1938. This is a classic study of bilateral relations with a strong overlay of race. U.S. policy toward Santo Domingo and Haiti, issues of trade, recognition, and separation are dealt with in both a political and diplomatic context.

6:315   Wesley, Charles H. "The Struggle for the Recognition of Haiti and Liberia as Independent Republics." *Journal of Negro History* 2 (October 1917): 369–83. The article traces the congressional debate over the (largely) southern opposition to the recognition of Haiti between 1819 and 1862 and Liberia in the 1850s and early 1860s.

Northeast and Northwest

6:316   Reeves, Jesse S. *American Diplomacy under Tyler and Polk.* Baltimore: Johns Hopkins Press, 1907. This older study still has value in examining ongoing problems with both the northeastern and northwestern boundaries and general concerns with Great Britain in the 1840s.

NORTHEAST

6:317   Adams, Ephraim D. "Lord Ashburton and the Treaty of Washington." *American Historical Re-* view 17 (July 1912): 764–82. This is an examination of the Webster-Ashburton negotiations (not only the Maine boundary) from an English point of view with the author giving high praise to the English diplomat for a "mission of distinguished success."

6:318   Arndt, Christopher. "Maine in the Northeastern Boundary Controversy: States' Rights in Antebellum New England." *New England Quarterly* 62 (June 1989): 205–23. This fine article focuses on the domestic political issues (especially in Maine) surrounding the northeastern border dispute in the 1830s.

6:319   Burrage, Henry S. *Maine in the Northeastern Boundary Controversy.* Portland, ME: State of Maine, 1919. This is the classic study of the northeastern boundary controversy. Burrage provides a good deal of information on the evolution of the problem, but could have been more analytical.

6:320   Callahan, James M. *American Foreign Policy in Canadian Relations.* New York: Cooper Square Publishers, 1967. Originally published in 1937, this work ably surveys major issues like the Oregon and Maine boundary disputes, the Great Lakes, and questions of trade and reciprocity.

6:321   Calloway, Colin G. "The End of an Era: British-Indian Relations in the Great Lakes Region after the War of 1812." *Michigan Historical Review* 12 (Fall 1986): 21–44. Calloway examines the strained relationship between British officials in Canada and the increasingly disillusioned Indians of the upper midwest in the period 1815–1830.

6:322   Carroll, Francis M. *A Good and Wise Measure: The Search for the Canadian-American Boundary, 1783–1842.* Toronto: University of Toronto Press, 2001. This work examines attempts to settle the Canadian-American boundary from the Treaty of Paris through the Webster-Ashburton Treaty. While paying attention to politics and diplomacy, Carroll also looks at the various surveys and surveying crews. There is special emphasis on the movement from arbitration in the 1830s to reasonable compromise in the 1840s. This work excellently complements various works of Howard Jones.

6:323   _____. "Kings and Crises: Arbitrating the Canadian-American Boundary Dispute and the

Belgian Crisis of 1830–1831." *New England Quarterly* 73 (June 2000): 179–210. The author argues the importance of the Belgian revolution and the attached role of Britain in obscuring for Americans the merits of King William's arbitration proposal. The inability of the Americans to overcome their bias resulted in the delay of the Maine boundary solution for another decade.

6:324   Corey, Albert B. *The Crisis of 1830–1842 in Canadian-American Relations.* New Haven: Yale University Press, 1941. This good examination of the border disputes, especially along the Canadian frontier in the 1830s and 1840s, has been largely superseded by the more recent Stevens, *Border Diplomacy: The Caroline and McLeod Affairs in Anglo-American-Canadian Relations, 1837–1842* (1989) (6:346). The author includes an account of the Patriot Wars and the Webster-Ashburton Treaty.

6:325   Dent, John C. *The Story of the Upper Canadian Rebellion: Largely Derived from Original Sources and Documents.* 2 vols. Toronto: C. B. Robinson, 1885. This nineteenth-century account relies heavily on a journalistic approach to the Canadian rebellion.

6:326   Gill, George J. "Edward Everett and the Northeastern Boundary Controversy." *New England Quarterly* 42 (June 1969): 201–13. Gill offers an examination of the views and contributions of Edward Everett as minister to Great Britain in the early 1840s as the Maine boundary was resolved in the Webster-Ashburton Treaty. Everett favored a negotiated settlement and spent considerable time poring over maps trying to prove the American position.

6:327   Guillet, Edwin C. *Lives and Times of the Patriots: An Account of the Rebellion in Upper Canada, 1837–1838, and of the Patriot Agitation in the United States, 1837–1842.* Toronto: University of Toronto Press, 1938. This unevenly documented study of the Canadian rebellion of 1837–1838 covers the actions and fate of the U.S. "Patriot Hunters."

6:328   Harris, Marc. "The Meaning of Patriot: The Canadian Rebellion and American Republicanism, 1837–1839." *Michigan Historical Review* 23 (Spring 1997): 33–69. The article examines the notion of republicanism in the Canadian rebellion of 1837 and

why the "patriots" received American public support. It is an excellent summary of events that includes a discussion of the ruthless and autocratic rule of the British governors.

6:329   Haydon, Roger, ed. *Upstate Travels: British Views of Nineteenth-Century New York.* Syracuse: Syracuse University Press, 1982. The editor offers forty-two excerpts from the writings of Britons who traveled in New York between 1815 and 1845. The genteel tourists were impressed by New York's economic growth and rendered a wide range of impressions on topics including agriculture, politics, and the weather.

6:330   Hembree, Michael F. "The Question of 'Begging': Fugitive Slave Relief in Canada, 1830–1865." *Civil War History* 37 (December 1991): 314–27. Hembree discusses the problems of providing aid and relief to the tens of thousands of blacks, often fugitive slaves, who fled to Vancouver and Upper Canada in the wake of the Fugitive Slave Law of 1850. Many came as families, most unprepared for the Canadian climate and culture.

6:331   Hitsman, J. Mackay. *Safeguarding Canada, 1763–1871.* Toronto: University of Toronto Press, 1968. This is an excellent study of the British strategy to defend Canada in war and peace through the eighteenth and nineteenth centuries. Approximately half the book deals with the post–War of 1812 era and includes discussions of border problems, the Canadian rebellion, and the Fenians.

6:332   Jones, Howard. "Anglophobia and the Aroostook War." *New England Quarterly* 48 (December 1975): 519–39. Jones emphasizes events along the northeastern border between Maine and New Brunswick between 1837 and 1839. Although Maine farmers engaged their Canadian neighbors in the short-lived "Aroostook War," the Van Buren administration struggled to keep the peace with Great Britain.

6:333   _____. "The *Caroline* Affair." *Historian* 38 (May 1976): 485–502. Focusing on the period 1837–1842, Jones explains how leaders in London and Washington prevented the inflammatory border incident on the Niagara River (the burning of the vessel *Caroline* in U.S. waters) from igniting a broader Anglo-American conflict.

6:334   _____. "The Peculiar Institution and National Honor: The Case of the *Creole* Slave Revolt." *Civil War History* 21 (March 1975): 28–50. The insurrection on board the *Creole* affected the settlement of Maine's boundary (1841–1842), as the question of national honor threatened to elevate the revolt into an Anglo-American crisis. Not only did the emotional slavery issue pose a threat, but the lack of an Anglo-American extradition agreement forced Webster to appeal for return of the escaped slaves on the principle of comity.

6:335   Jones, Wilbur D. "The Influence of Slavery on the Webster-Ashburton Negotiations." *Journal of Southern History* 22 (February 1956): 48–58. Jones emphasizes the importance of the *Creole* affair and issue of extradition of slaves, a sore spot for British abolitionists. The broader question of the African slave trade was discussed and although provisions were made in the treaty, the results proved less than satisfactory from a British vantage point.

6:336   Le Duc, Thomas. "The Maine Frontier and the Northeastern Boundary Controversy." *American Historical Review* 53 (October 1947): 30–41. Le Duc surveys the boundary problems between Maine and New Brunswick, emphasizing the period 1837–1839 and the Aroostook War.

6:337   _____. "The Webster-Ashburton Treaty and the Minnesota Iron Ranges." *Journal of American History* 51 (December 1964): 476–81. Did Daniel Webster and Lord Ashburton know about the iron deposits in the Mesabi and other Minnesota ranges as they negotiated their treaty in 1842? The author claims they did not, indicating the first published revelation of the deposits appeared in the early 1850s.

6:338   McEwen, Alec C. "Alden Partridge and the United States–Canadian Boundary." *Vermont History* 59 (Spring 1991): 97–110. This article contains the diary of Alden Partridge, the chief U.S. surveyor to the boundary commission, in the summer of 1819 as he surveyed in northern Maine.

6:339   Merk, Frederick, with Lois Bannister Merk. *Fruits of Propaganda in the Tyler Administration.* Cambridge, MA: Harvard University Press, 1971. Merk offers an interesting exploration of the activities of the Tyler administration in its efforts to acquire Texas and resolve the northeastern border issue. The volume is highlighted by an extensive collection of documents related to these topics.

6:340   Officer, Lawrence H., and Lawrence B. Smith. "The Canadian-American Reciprocity Treaty of 1855 to 1866." *Journal of Economic History* 28 (December 1968): 598–623. The treaty provided for free trade in natural products, free fishing access for the United States in Atlantic waters, and use of the St. Lawrence for U.S. vessels at low rates. The authors challenge the classic interpretation that the agreement ushered in a new era of Canadian prosperity.

6:341   Rakestraw, Donald A., and Howard Jones. *Prologue to Manifest Destiny: Anglo-American Relations in the 1840s.* Wilmington, DE: SR Books, 1997. This detailed study of Anglo-American relations focuses on the Maine and Oregon boundary disputes and shows how both sides were driven by national honor. Daniel Webster emerges as the hero in this well-done examination of a rivalry tempered by economic considerations.

6:342   Rosentreter, Roger. "Liberating Canada: Michigan and the Patriot War." *Michigan History* 67 (March-April 1983): 32–34. The article explores the role played by the "Patriot Hunters" along the Michigan frontier in the 1830s.

6:343   Shewmaker, Kenneth E. "Hook and Line, and Bob and Sinker: Daniel Webster and the Fisheries Dispute of 1852." *Diplomatic History* 9 (Spring 1985): 113–29. While the surface issue in 1852 seemed to focus on the action of the British navy in preventing the encroachment of American fishermen in the North Atlantic, Shewmaker argues the real dispute involved a deliberate effort by the crown to create a crisis and resolve the trade reciprocity issue. The situation, from the American side, was sadly mismanaged by an ill and dispirited Daniel Webster.

6:344   Shortridge, Wilson P. "The Canadian-American Frontier during the Rebellion of 1837–1838." *Canadian Historical Review* 7 (March 1926): 13–26. In this fine survey of Patriot-Hunter lodges and their activities in 1837–1838, the author examines the hotbeds of western New York, northern Ohio, and eastern Michigan. He contends that the Americans were motivated by both perceived injustices to the Canadians and by personal gain.

6:345 Stacey, Charles P. "The Myth of the Unguarded Frontier, 1815–1871." *American Historical Review* 56 (October 1950): 1–18. Stacey argues that the impact of the Rush-Bagot agreement was greatly exaggerated. With an Anglo-American war still a possibility after 1815, the Canadian border was defended and fortifications erected. The situation only changed dramatically after the negotiation of the Treaty of Washington in 1871.

6:346 Stevens, Kenneth R. *Border Diplomacy: The Caroline and McLeod Affairs in Anglo-American-Canadian Relations, 1837–1842.* Tuscaloosa: University of Alabama Press, 1989. This thoughtful and balanced study examines the escalation of a border incident into near Anglo-American conflict. Finally resolved by calmer heads exercising restraint, the *Caroline* and *McLeod* affairs affected international law and federal-state relations.

6:347 _____. "James Grogan and the Crisis in Canadian-American Relations, 1837–1842." *Vermont History* 50 (Fall 1982): 219–26. The article relates the adventures of a border raider who burned farmhouses in Canada and was kidnapped and imprisoned by the British. It demonstrates the efforts at compromise made by both sides to attain his release and keep the peace.

6:348 Stuart, Reginald C. "United States Expansionism and the British North American Provinces, 1783–1871." In *Arms at Rest: Peacemaking and Peacekeeping in American History,* ed. Joan R. Challinor and Robert L. Beisner, 101–32. Westport, CT: Greenwood Press, 1987. Stuart examines ideology, politics, trade, and boundary issues as he explores why Canada escaped the tentacles of U.S. expansion in the nineteenth century.

6:349 Tansill, Charles Callan. *The Canadian Reciprocity Treaty of 1854.* Baltimore: Johns Hopkins Press, 1922. Tansill offers the authoritative account of a treaty intended to provide a commercial breakthrough between the United States and Canada but that lasted only a decade and produced mixed results.

6:350 Warner, Donald F. *The Idea of Continental Union: Agitation for the Annexation of Canada to the United States, 1849–1893.* Lexington: University of Kentucky Press, 1960. Warner briefly deals with the pre–Civil War period, noting the approach-avoidance attitude of Canadians to annexation to the United States. This option was heightened by the positively received Reciprocity Treaty of 1854.

6:351 Watson, Samuel J. "United States Army Officers Fight the Patriot War: Responses to Filibustering on the Canadian Border, 1837–1839." *Journal of the Early Republic* 18 (Fall 1998): 485–519. Watson focuses on the increased professionalism of U.S. army officers on the border as they attempted to enforce the administration's policy of neutrality and halt filibustering perceived to endanger national security. Officers also sought to advance their social status and stable employment.

NORTHWEST

6:352 Anderson, Stuart. "British Threats and the Settlement of the Oregon Boundary Dispute." *Pacific Northwest Quarterly* 66 (October 1975): 153–60. Anderson looks at the interpretive poles of Julius Pratt ("James K. Polk and John Bull," 1943 [6:382]) and Frederick Merk (*The Oregon Question: Essays in Anglo-American Diplomacy and Politics,* 1967) (6:378) regarding the impact of the British navy on Anglo-American relations. He contends the navy was a factor (but not a decisive one) in clearing the path for a final agreement between Polk and Peel on Oregon.

6:353 Bolkhovitinov, Nikolai N. "The Crimean War and the Emergence of Proposals for the Sale of Russian America, 1853–1861." *Pacific Historical Review* 59 (February 1990): 15–49. This article examines the evolution of Russian thinking on the possible sale of Alaska to the United States after the Crimean debacle. Russian authorities became insecure about their ability to retain Alaska against an increasingly imperial United States.

6:354 _____. "Russia and the Declaration of the Non-Colonization Principle: New Archival Evidence." *Oregon Historical Quarterly* 72 (June 1971): 101–26. This article, by a Soviet historian who has written extensively on Russian-American relations and the Monroe Doctrine, argues that the noncolonization principle of Monroe's message of 1823 originated in American expansionist ambitions in the Pacific northwest. The famous Ukase of 1821 was only a pretext used by John Quincy Adams to justify the noncolonization principle, which was aimed primarily against the British. Translated by Basil Dmytryshyn.

6:355 _____. *Russko-Amerikanskie Othosheniia i Prodazha Aliaski, 1834–1867 [Russian-American Relations and the Sale of Alaska, 1834–1867].* Translated by Richard A. Pierce. Moscow: Academy of Sciences of the USSR, 1990. Bolkhovitinov, the leading Russian scholar in the field, examines nineteenth-century U.S.-Russian relations and the background of the purchase of Alaska. English edition published in 1996 by Limestone Press, Fairbanks, Alaska.

6:356 Carson, Gerald. "Fifty-Four Forty or Fight: The Oregon Crisis." *Timeline* 7 (June-July 1990): 2–16. Carson presents a good popular summary of the unsuccessful movement to acquire all of Oregon in the mid-1840s. The article offers valuable cartoons and photographs from the period.

6:357 Commager, Henry Steele. "England and the Oregon Treaty of 1846." *Oregon Historical Quarterly* 28 (March 1927): 18–38. Commager discusses the Oregon negotiations from the English vantage point, drawing a picture of an astute Peel and a cautious Aberdeen. Both talented politicians, they were not bluffed by Polk on the Oregon question but recognized that war with the United States would ill serve Britain, which had little reason to protect the Hudson's Bay Company's interests.

6:358 Dawson, Will. *The War That Was Never Fought.* Princeton: Auerbach Publishers, 1971. This slim volume studies the controversy between the United States and Great Britain over the San Juan Islands after the Treaty of 1846 that almost resulted in armed conflict in the late 1850s.

6:359 Dykstra, David L. *The Shifting Balance of Power: American-British Diplomacy in North America, 1842–1848.* Lanham, MD: University Press of America, 1999. Dykstra examines the British shift away from North America and the movement of the United States to assume power on the continent. The Americans, driven by land hunger, stirred problems between the two nations, but compromises to preserve the status quo averted war. Nevertheless, the United States soon became the dominant power in the Western Hemisphere.

6:360 Farrar, Victor J. "Background to the Purchase of Alaska." *Washington Historical Quarterly* 13, no. 2 (April 1922): 93–104. Farrar traces Alaska's place in Russian-American relations (1820–1850), especially the fishing rights conflict and other issues raised by Russian presence in Alaska.

6:361 Fish, Andrew. "The Last Phase of the Oregon Boundary Question: The Struggle for San Juan Island." *Oregon Historical Quarterly* 22 (September 1921): 161–224. This lengthy study of the problem of the disposition of San Juan Island focuses on the problems between the United States and Great Britain generated by the military occupation of U.S. General William Harney in 1859.

6:362 Galbraith, John S. "France as a Factor in the Oregon Negotiations." *Pacific Northwest Quarterly* 44 (April 1953): 69–73. The British, fearful of the French and the advantage they might take of the crown's involvement in a North American war, weighed the "French factor" seriously in seeking to reach a peaceful accord with the United States over Oregon.

6:363 _____. *The Hudson's Bay Company as an Imperial Factor, 1821–1869.* Berkeley: University of California Press, 1957. Galbraith relates the growth and decline of the British firm's fur trade to the political and diplomatic history of the period.

6:364 Graebner, Norman A. "Politics and the Oregon Compromise." *Pacific Northwest Quarterly* 52 (January 1961): 7–14. Graebner analyzes the Whig-Democratic strategies and maneuvering in the great debate over an Oregon settlement in 1846; both parties were seeking political advantage more than a reasonable diplomatic solution.

6:365 Howe, Daniel Wait. "The Mississippi Valley in the Movement for Fifty-Four Forty or Fight." *Proceedings of the Mississippi Valley Historical Association for the Year 1911–1912* (1912): 99–116.

Howe discusses the strong pressure in the midwest for the "all Oregon" movement in the 1840s.

6:366 Husband, Michael B. "Senator Lewis F. Linn and the Oregon Question." *Missouri Historical Review* 66 (October 1971): 1–19. Lewis Linn of Missouri was the major force in the Senate in advocating the American cause in Oregon from 1837 until his death in 1843. This piece recounts his activities and speeches on behalf of U.S. expansion.

6:367 Hutsuliak, Mykhailo. *When Russia Was in America: The Alaska Boundary Treaty Negotiations, 1824–25, and the Role of Pierre de Poletica.* Vancouver: Mitchell Press, 1971. Negotiations arose from the ukase promulgated in St. Petersburg in 1821, which endorsed broad Russian territorial claims. The United States and Great Britain rejected these claims, and the resulting agreement restricted Russia to the Alaska region.

6:368 Jones, Wilbur D., and J. Chal Vinson. "British Preparedness and the Oregon Settlement." *Pacific Historical Review* 22 (November 1953): 353–64. Lord Aberdeen successfully prepared the British public and his political opposition for compromise in 1846 on Oregon. He attained many of his goals on the issue and viewed the result as a diplomatic triumph.

6:369 Kushner, Howard I. *Conflict on the Northwest Coast: American-Russian Rivalry in the Pacific Northwest, 1790–1867.* Kushner shows that American traders in the 1790s sought the pelts of the sea otter to further their commercial interests in China. See chapter 5 of this Guide (5:414).

6:370 Long, John W., Jr. "The Origin and Development of the San Juan Island Water Boundary Controversy." *Pacific Northwest Quarterly* 43 (July 1952): 187–213. The Anglo-American treaty of 1846 resolving the Oregon boundary in 1846 left possession of San Juan Island in doubt. Long traces the struggle over this unlikely hot spot from the 1840s through the provocative occupation by U.S. General William Harney in 1859.

6:371 Manning, Clarence A. *Russian Influence on Early America.* New York: Library Publishers, 1953. By focusing on the theme of expansionism, this volume traces Russia's advance along the northwest coast of North America and subsequent attempts to preserve its interests in the area to 1867.

6:372 Mazour, Anatole G. "The Russian-American and Anglo-Russian Conventions, 1824–1825: An Interpretation." *Pacific Historical Review* 14 (September 1945): 303–10. This article analyzes why Russia was so lenient in negotiations of 1824 and 1825, concluding that Russia was more concerned with its rivalry in the Near East with Great Britain than in its claims on the remote northwest coast of North America.

6:373 McCabe, James O. "Arbitration and the Oregon Question." *Canadian Historical Review* 41 (December 1960): 308–27. The British under Lord Aberdeen embraced the concept of arbitration in the 1840s to resolve the Oregon issue, since it was an issue of low importance for them. In contrast, the Americans opposed arbitration because the loss of Oregon would have devastated U.S. expansionists and raised political havoc.

6:374 _____. *The San Juan Water Boundary Question.* Toronto: University of Toronto Press, 1964. This slim volume examines the controversy over San Juan Island from the unclear approach to the problem in the Anglo-American Treaty of 1846 to its resolution in 1871.

6:375 Merk, Frederick. *Albert Gallatin and the Oregon Problem: A Study in Anglo-American Diplomacy.* Cambridge, MA: Harvard University Press, 1950. In this brief study, Merk focuses on the failed efforts of peacemaker Albert Gallatin to effect a permanent settlement to the boundary dispute in the Pacific northwest in 1826–1827.

6:376 _____. "British Government Propaganda and the Oregon Treaty." *American Historical Review* 40 (October 1934): 38–62. Merk praises Lord Aberdeen for his handling of the Oregon crisis of 1845–1846, a situation in which he manipulated the British press and public to his viewpoint.

6:377 _____. "The Oregon Question in the Webster-Ashburton Negotiations." *Mississippi Valley Historical Review* 43 (December 1956): 379–404. Oregon had been a long-standing issue when Webster and Ashburton met to discuss the northeastern boundary and other questions in 1842. Unfortunately, Ashburton's instructions made a settlement virtually impossible, prompting a postponement of a settlement. Merk notes that Webster remained skeptical that Oregon would or should become a part of the United States and saw it more likely as an independent country.

6:378 _____. *The Oregon Question: Essays in Anglo-American Diplomacy and Politics.* Cambridge, MA: Harvard University Press, 1967. Merk presents a comprehensive treatment of the Oregon question commencing with the 1790s. He illustrates why negotiations to resolve the boundary failed for over a generation and how the forces of moderation came together on both side of the Atlantic to produce a compromise settlement.

6:379 Miles, Edwin A. "'Fifty-Four Forty or Fight'—An American Political Legend." *Mississippi Valley Historical Review* 44 (September 1957): 291–309. Miles reveals that, contrary to political legend, the cry of "54 40 or fight" in reference to claims to all of the Oregon country was not used in the Democratic campaign of 1844, but rather a year later. Texas, not Oregon, was the major issue for most Americans in 1844.

6:380 Murray, Keith A. *The Pig War.* Tacoma, WA: Washington State Historical Society, 1968. Murray offers a brief pamphlet on the "war" that was almost fought in the northwest between Great Britain and the United States over the San Juan Islands in 1859—territory that had been left in dispute by the Treaty of 1846.

6:381 Nichols, Irby C., Jr. "The Russian Ukase and the Monroe Doctrine: A Reevaluation." *Pacific Historical Review* 36 (February 1967): 13–26. Nichols examines the Russian decree of 1821, closing off Alaskan waters to foreign commerce, and argues that the ukase was issued for internal political reasons rather than as an assertion of Russian imperialism.

6:382 Pratt, Julius W. "James K. Polk and John Bull." *Canadian Historical Review* 24 (December 1943): 341–49. Pratt examines how firm James K. Polk was in challenging Great Britain over the Oregon boundary and argues that, alarmed by the

prospect of war with the crown, he did make concessions.

6:383 Rakestraw, Donald A. *For Honor or Destiny: The Anglo-American Crisis over the Oregon Territory.* New York: Peter Lang, 1995. Rakestraw presents the most comprehensive examination of the background and negotiations of the Oregon dispute of the 1840s since Merk's *The Oregon Question: Essays in Anglo-American Diplomacy and Politics* (1967) (6:378).

6:384 Ross, Frank E. "The Retreat of the Hudson's Bay Company in the Pacific North-West." *Canadian Historical Review* 18 (September 1937): 262–80. Ross relates the efforts of the Hudson's Bay Company to resist the gradual infiltration of Americans into the northwest in the 1837–1860 period. As the number of settlers increased, so did Yankee determination to push the company out of the region.

6:385 Sage, Walter N. "The Oregon Treaty of 1846." *Canadian Historical Review* 27 (December 1946): 349–67. Sage presents an overview of the treaty and contends that both sides ultimately compromised, producing a satisfactory settlement.

6:386 Schafer, Joseph. "The British Attitude toward the Oregon Question, 1815–1846." *American Historical Review* 16 (January 1911): 273–99. Schafer contends that the British were concerned about U.S. threats over Oregon and wanted to settle the issue without a conflict. However, to placate domestic opposition, the ministry was obliged to finesse the abandonment of the 49th parallel.

6:387 Schuyler, Robert L. "Polk and the Oregon Compromise of 1846." *Political Science Quarterly* 26 (September 1911): 443–61. Schuyler was one of the first scholars to use the Polk diary to explain the president's position on Oregon. Polk took a tough stand, and Schuyler credits Peel for averting hostilities and negotiating the best terms possible.

6:388 Scott, Leslie M. "Influence of American Settlement upon the Oregon Boundary Treaty of 1846." *Oregon Historical Quarterly* 29 (March 1928): 1–19. Scott explains the role of the more than 13,000 American settlers (by 1850) in the northwest in fostering U.S. dominance over the Hudson's Bay Company.

6:389 Shewmaker, Kenneth E. "Daniel Webster and the Oregon Question." *Pacific Historical Review* 51 (May 1982): 195–201. The author attempts to correct the misinterpretation of Webster's position on Oregon, arguing that he had no intention of sacrificing U.S. national interests in the region. His top priority was San Francisco, however, and he hoped to attain it through the negotiation of a tripartite pact with Great Britain and Mexico, which, of course, failed.

6:390 Shippee, Lester B. "Federal Relations of Oregon." *Oregon Historical Quarterly* 19 (June, September 1918): 89–133, 189–230. The two-part article is a traditional examination of discussions in the federal government, especially the Congress, involving the Oregon Territory between 1819 and 1842.

6:391 Stacey, Charles P. "The Hudson's Bay Company and Anglo-American Military Rivalries during the Oregon Dispute." *Canadian Historical Review* 18 (September 1937): 281–300. This article focuses on the 1840s and both Washington and London's efforts to fortify the northwest militarily to protect their political and economic interests.

6:392 Stuart, Reginald C. *United States Expansionism and British North America, 1775–1871.* In a work well grounded in primary sources, Stuart presents an examination of Canadian-American diplomatic, commercial, political, and cultural relations and the evolving issue of annexation. This thoughtful and valuable work shows that Americans were driven by fears of encirclement and enticements of economic opportunity (4:74).

6:393 Van Alstyne, Richard W. "International Rivalries in the Pacific Northwest." *Oregon Historical Quarterly* 46 (September 1945): 185–218. Van Alstyne traces the international rivalry that adopted both "sea" and "land" approaches to involvement in the Oregon country. Over a century (1770–1870), Spain, Russia, Great Britain, and the United States became major economic players in the region.

6:394 Wheeler, Mary E. "Empires in Conflict and Cooperation: The 'Bostonians' and the Russian-American Company." *Pacific Historical Review* 40 (November 1971): 419–41. This article analyzes the development of competition and cooperation between the Russian-American Company and the shippers of Boston along the northwest coast in the two decades prior to 1825.

Expansion and Imperialism

6:395 Brown, Charles H. *Agents of Manifest Destiny: The Lives and Times of the Filibusters.* Chapel Hill: University of North Carolina Press, 1980. A well-written narrative of the filibusters of the 1850s, this work focuses on American participation in the Cuban revolutionary expeditions of Narciso López and on William Walker's two great expeditions, to Mexico and Nicaragua. The filibusters of the fifties, the author concludes, dreamed of a tropical empire.

6:396 Chaffin, Tom. *Fatal Glory: Narciso López and the First Clandestine U.S. War against Cuba.* Charlottesville: University Press of Virginia, 1996. Chaffin offers a revisionist view of the Cuban filibuster that perceives him as a symbol of the Young America movement and as an advocate of American territorial and republican goals, rather than as an agent of slave interests. The author emphasizes the national support in the United States that López received as he organized his ill-fated campaigns.

6:397 _____. "Sons of Washington: Narciso Lopez, Filibustering, and U.S. Nationalism, 1848–1851." *Journal of the Early Republic* 15 (Spring 1995): 79–108. Chaffin offers a different viewpoint on filibustering by detailing the broad national base of support for López. Filibustering embodied U.S. patriotism and republican values and was not an agent of southern nationalism and sectionalism.

6:398 Crapol, Edward P., ed. *Women and American Foreign Policy: Lobbyists, Critics, and Insiders.* This far-ranging work on women in foreign policy includes chapters on Jane Cazneau, who championed American annexation of Cuba and the Dominican Republic, and on Ella Carroll, who was a pro-Union expansionist in the 1850s. See chapter 2 of this Guide for details (2:150).

6:399   de la Cova, Antonio R. "Filibusters and Freemasons: The Sworn Obligation." *Journal of the Early Republic* 17 (Spring 1997): 95–120. This is a revealing examination of the relationship between freemasons in Cuba and the United States and their role in promoting filibustering and the Cuban independence movement in the 1840s and early 1850s.

6:400   Graebner, Norman A. *Empire on the Pacific: A Study in American Continental Expansion.* New York: Ronald Press, 1955. This is a classic study of American expansionism under Polk that treats the issue of Oregon as well as the Mexican War.

6:401   Haynes, Sam W., and Christopher Morris, eds. *Manifest Destiny and Empire: American Antebellum Expansionism.* College Station: Published for the University of Texas at Arlington by Texas A&M University Press, 1997. This work offers a collection of six essays on antebellum expansion: Robert W. Johannsen on the meaning of Manifest Destiny (7–20); John M. Belohlavek on the imperial views of Caleb Cushing (21–47); Thomas R. Hietala on painter George Catlin and Native Americans (48–67); Samuel J. Watson on army officers' views of Manifest Destiny (68–114); Sam W. Haynes on the annexation of Texas and anglophobia (115–45); and Robert E. May on filibusters (146–79).

6:402   Hietala, Thomas R. *Manifest Design: Anxious Aggrandizement in Late Jacksonian America.* Ithaca: Cornell University Press, 1985. In this challenging interpretive study about the motives behind antebellum expansion, Hietala concentrates on the southwest, although he does deal with Oregon.

6:403   Katz, Irving. "August Belmont's Cuban Acquisition Scheme." *Mid-America* 50 (January 1968): 52–63. Belmont was a Democratic Party chieftain who continually intrigued in schemes for purchasing Cuba in the 1850s. The author argues that Belmont played an important role in the origins of the Ostend Manifesto.

6:404   Langley, Lester D. "The Whigs and the López Expeditions to Cuba, 1849–1851: A Chapter in Frustrating Diplomacy." *Revista de Historia de América* 71 (January-June 1971): 9–22. Based mostly on U.S. State Department material, the article focuses on the troubles of the Taylor-Fillmore ad-

ministration in enforcing the neutrality laws against filibustering expeditions to Cuba (1849–1851).

6:405   May, Robert E. *The Southern Dream of Caribbean Empire, 1854–1861.* Baton Rouge: Louisiana State University Press, 1973. Reprint 2002 (University Press of Florida). May offers a first-rate account of southern efforts to keep Manifest Destiny alive in the 1850s by expansion into the Caribbean and Central America. While William Walker in Nicaragua is the logical focal point, May includes other areas of interest such as Cuba.

6:406   Merk, Frederick, with Lois Bannister Merk. *Manifest Destiny and Mission in American History: A Reinterpretation.* This volume joins Weinberg's *Manifest Destiny: A Study of Nationalist Expansionism in American History* (1935) (2:223) as a classic study of Manifest Destiny. While emphasizing the distinction between benign "Manifest Destiny" thinking and imperialism, Merk explores the motivations and agencies that promoted expansion in North America and the Caribbean, including the press, political parties, and sectional goals (2:220).

6:407   _____. *The Monroe Doctrine and American Expansionism, 1843–1849.* New York: Alfred A. Knopf, 1966. Merk's study of the Monroe Doctrine includes an examination of the real or perceived British threats to Oregon, California, and Cuba in the 1840s.

6:408   Nichols, Roy F. *Advance Agents of American Destiny.* Five of the chapters relate to Latin America. See chapter 5 of this Guide (5:259).

6:409   Pletcher, David M. *The Diplomacy of Annexation: Texas, Oregon, and the Mexican War.* Columbia: University of Missouri Press, 1973. This lengthy, detailed study focuses on Texas and the Mexican War, but Pletcher also offers worthwhile insights on American expansion in the northwest.

6:410   Portell-Vilá, Hermínio. *Narciso López y su época [Narciso Lopez and His Era].* 3 vols. Havana: Compailia Editora de Libros y Folletos, 1930–1958. A major work in Cuban history, this multivolume study is based on an amazing amount of source material. The author forcefully argues that López was neither an annexationist nor a dupe of southern expansionists.

6:411 Stephanson, Anders. *Manifest Destiny: American Expansionism and the Empire of Right.* This conceptual approach to Manifest Destiny explores American expansion from the colonial period through 1990 and includes a lengthy chapter on the antebellum era. The focus is on dynamic capitalism, westward expansion, and sectionalism versus nationalism (2:222).

6:412 Urban, C. Stanley. "The Africanization of Cuba Scare, 1853–1855." *Hispanic American Historical Review* 37 (February 1957): 29–45. The liberal policy of the Cuban governor-general, under British influence, convinced American southerners that Cuban slavery would be abolished. This led to American efforts to purchase the island and, those failing, to the Ostend Manifesto, which advocated seizure of Cuba.

6:413 Weeks, William Earl. *Building the Continental Empire: American Expansion from the Revolution to the Civil War.* This brief synthesis covers the period from the 1770s to the 1860s, but focuses on the antebellum era after 1815. Uneven in coverage, it is a valuable introductory work that incorporates much recent historiography on American expansion (4:77).

6:414 Weinberg, Albert K. *Manifest Destiny: A Study of Nationalist Expansionism in American History.* The volume remains a worthwhile and provocative study of the motivations of U.S. Manifest Destiny, including freedom, geography, regeneration, economics, divine intervention, politics, self-defense, and race (2:223).

7

Expansion into the Americas, Asia, and the Pacific, 1815–1861

Contributing Editor
WILLIAM EARL WEEKS
Frostburg, Maryland

Contributors
KURT W. HANSON
American University

ROBERT L. BEISNER
American University

LEILA ROECKELL
Molloy College

Contents

Introduction

This chapter, with considerable revisions, draws in large part on six chapters (7, 9, 17, 32, 39, and 40) of the 1983 edition. This version emphasizes the central role of territorial, commercial, and ideological expansionism in defining the foreign policy of the era and highlights the global nature of that expansionism. Integrating the traditional emphases on the western frontier and Europe (covered in chapter 6) in a global context illuminates fields of study such as isthmian diplomacy, Hawaii, and China, whose significance during the era has hitherto been underestimated.

This chapter also differs fundamentally from the 1983 edition in its new emphasis on social, cultural, racial, economic, military, and gender issues that have augmented the traditional focus on diplomatic and political topics. Thus, U.S. relations with Native Americans is included as a topic of study and examined from a range of new perspectives. The role of women, missionaries, whaling, and the overseas narratives of "average" Americans are given new importance as part of the resuscitation of a field declared dead by some. These changes are in keeping with widespread calls for the profession to broaden its approach and is reflective of a newfound faith that insight into the larger trends of American foreign policy may be gleaned from the details of individual experience.

The chapter retains a substantial number of citations from the 1983 edition on the grounds that historical knowledge is evolutionary and from the conviction that it is mistaken to assume that newer works necessarily supersede their predecessors. Space considerations have kept article citations to a minimum. In sum, a field that seemed exhausted in 1983 has, with the application of new techniques and approaches, shown a surprising fertility.

Published Primary Materials

7:1　　　　Alcaraz, Ramón, et al. *Apuntes para la historia de la guerra entre Mexico y los Estados-Unidos [Notes for the History of the War between Mexico*

and the United States]. Mexico, DF: Tipográfica de M. Payno (Hijo), 1848. This account contains partially eyewitness accounts by journalists, politicians, and other publicists. English translation published in the United States (New York: J. Wiley, 1850), edited by Albert C. Ramsey.

7:2　　　　Beasley, W. G., ed. *Select Documents on Japanese Foreign Policy, 1853–1868.* New York: Oxford University Press, 1955. This is a translation of documents on the Perry Treaty of 1854, the Harris Treaty of 1858, the expulsion order of 1863, the Shimonoseki indemnity issue of 1863–1864, the imperial ratification of the treaties in 1865, and the opening of Hyogo in 1867. When Beasley (who also translated the documents) published this book, the documents in the *Dai Nihon Komonjo: Bakumatsu Gaikoku Kankei Monjo* reached only to 1859; he draws the documents for 1860 to 1868 from other Japanese sources. Extensive bibliography.

7:3　　　　Bosch García, Carlos, ed. *Material para la historia diplomática de México: México y los Estados Unidos, 1820–1848 [Material for the Diplomatic History of Mexico: Mexico and the United States, 1820–1848].* Mexico, DF: Universidad Nacional Autónoma de México, Escuela Nacional de Ciencias Políticas y Sociales, 1957. This collection of diplomatic documents, mostly Spanish translations of U.S. State Department communications, contains few documents from the Mexican archives.

7:4　　　　Clyde, Paul Hibbert, ed. *United States Policy toward China: Diplomatic and Public Documents, 1839–1939.* See chapter 13 of this Guide (13:19).

7:5　　　　Fay, George E., ed. *Treaties between the Tribes of the Great Plains and the United States of America: Comanche and Kiowa, Arikara, Gros Ventre and Mandan, 1835–1891.* Greeley, CO: University of Northern Colorado, Museum of Anthropology, 1982. Though less than a hundred pages, this is a useful compilation of primary documents on the treaties in question. Fay edited a series of such volumes, the others being *Treaties between the Menominee Indians and the United States of America, 1817–1856* (Oshkosh, WI: Wisconsin State University, Museum of Anthropology, 1965); *Treaties between the Oneida Indians and the United States of America, 1784–1838* (Greeley, CO: University of

Northern Colorado, Museum of Anthropology, 1978); *Treaties between the Potawatomi Tribe of Indians and the United States of America, 1789–1867* (same publisher, 1971); *Treaties between the Stockbridge-Munsee Tribe(s) of Indians and the United States of America, 1805–1871* (same publisher, 1970); *Treaties between the Tribes of the Great Plains and the United States of America, Cheyenne and Arapaho, 1825–1900 &c.* (same publisher, 1977); and *Treaties between the Winnebago Indians and the United States of America, 1817–1856* (same publisher, 1967).

7:6   Garrison, George P., ed. *Diplomatic Correspondence of the Republic of Texas.* The Annual Report of the American Historical Association for the Years 1907, 1908. 3 vols. Washington, DC: Government Printing Office, 1908–1911. This standard source for the diplomatic correspondence of Texas (1836–1845) contains all of the important materials from the manuscript archives. It is divided into sections on correspondence with the United States, Mexico, Yucatán, and European states.

7:7   Gayón Córdova, María, ed. *La ocupación yanqui de la Ciudad de México, 1847–1848 [The Yankee Occupation of Mexico City, 1847–1848].* Córdoba: Instituto Nacional de Antropología e Historia, 1997. This is a rich and diverse compilation of documents on the U.S. occupation of Mexico City. Arranged in chronological order from the wartime defensive preparations through the occupation's end in June 1848, Gayón Córdova presents a collection of American and Mexican documents culled from memoirs, diaries, letters, and newspapers that illuminates the political and social life of occupied Mexico.

7:8   Gullick, Charles Adams, et al., eds. *The Papers of Mirabeau Buonaparte Lamar.* 6 vols. in 7. Austin, TX: A. C. Baldwin and Sons, 1921–1927. These are the papers of a prominent figure in Texas expansionism and president of the Texas Republic, 1838–1841, succeeding Sam Houston. He opposed annexation by the United States but fought in Zachary Taylor's army in the Mexican War.

7:9   Hammond, George P., ed. *The Larkin Papers: Personal, Business and Official Correspondence of Thomas Oliver Larkin, Merchant and United States Consul in California.* 10 vols. Berkeley: University of California Press for the Bancroft

Library, 1951–1968. This collection includes Larkin's correspondence with all of the salient figures in the California theater of the Mexican War, including Mexican officials. The researcher will also find extensive documentation on Larkin's many business interests. Letters and documents in Spanish do not have accompanying translations. The tenth volume is an index published in 1968.

7:10   Hopkins, James F., with Mary W. M. Hargreaves, eds. *The Papers of Henry Clay.* See chapters 5 and 6 of this Guide (5:159; 6:17).

7:11   LaFeber, Walter, ed. *John Quincy Adams and American Continental Empire: Letters, Papers and Speeches.* Chicago: Quadrangle Books, 1965. This is a valuable collection of Adams's writings that reveals the diverse aspects of his thinking, particularly about expansionist projects.

7:12   Lowrie, Walter, and Matthew St. Clair Clarke, eds. *American State Papers: Documents, Legislative and Executive, of the Congress of the United States . . . Selected and Edited under the Authority of Congress.* See chapter 5 of this Guide (5:10).

7:13   Manning, William R., ed. *Diplomatic Correspondence of the United States Concerning the Independence of the Latin-American Nations.* See chapters 1 and 5 of this Guide (1:252; 5:11).

7:14   _____. *The Diplomatic Correspondence of the United States: Inter-American Affairs, 1831–1860.* See chapters 1 and 6 of this Guide (1:253; 6:6).

7:15   McAfee, Ward, and J. Cordell Robinson, eds. *Origins of the Mexican War: A Documentary Source Book.* 2 vols. Salisbury, NC: Documentary Publications, 1982. This is a useful compilation of documents on the Mexican War and includes documents translated from Spanish. Bibliography. See also McAfee's "A Reconsideration of the Origins of the Mexican-American War," *Southern California Quarterly* 62 (Spring 1980): 49–65.

7:16   México. Secretaría de Relaciones Exteriores and Enrique Santibañez. *La Diplomacia Mexicana [Mexican Diplomacy].* 3 vols. Mexico, DF: T. Artistica, 1910–1913. This is roughly the equivalent for Mexico of Manning, *Diplomatic Correspondence of the United States Concerning the Independence of the Latin-American Nations* (1925) (7:13) and includes the first Mexican mission to the United States in the 1820s.

7:17   Miller, David Hunter. "Translations of 12 Interviews of Harris with Inouye Shinano no Kami and Iwase Higo no Kami." In *Treaties and Other International Acts of the United States of America, 1776–1863,* 7: 638–48, 1089–1170. Washington, DC: Government Printing Office, 1942. Provided here are the Japanese minutes of the talks between Harris and Japanese officials during the negotiations for the 1858 treaty.

7:18   Moore, John Bassett, ed. *Works of James Buchanan: Comprising His Speeches, State Papers, and Private Correspondence.* Although old and incomplete, this edition of Buchanan's papers is still very useful for students of American diplomacy. There are a large number of significant speeches, personal letters, and state papers from his career as diplomat, secretary of state, and president (6:14).

7:19   Nevins, Allan, ed. *Polk: The Diary of a President, 1845–1849, covering the Mexican War, the Acquisition of Oregon, and the Conquest of California and the Southwest.* While this volume contains only part of the Polk diary, it includes most of the important entries concerning diplomacy and the Mexican War. Also, Nevins has added a long introduction, analyzing Polk and the principal members of his government with much perceptiveness (6:22).

7:20   Quaife, Milo Milton, ed. *The Diary of James K. Polk during His Presidency, 1845 to 1849, Now First Printed from the Original Manuscript in the Collections of the Chicago Historical Society.* 4 vols. Chicago: A. C. McClurg and Co., 1910. These volumes present a complete transcript of Polk's detailed and very revealing diary, beginning in August 1845 and covering nearly all his presidency. A considerable amount of the diary concerns foreign relations, the Oregon question, the settlement of Texas annexation, and the Mexican War.

7:21   Sakanishi, Shiho, ed. *A Private Journal of John Glendy Sproston, U.S.N.* Tokyo: Sophia University, 1940. This journal by a midshipman on the

Macedonian was not used by Hawks in compiling the official narrative (Hawks, *Narrative of the Expedition of an American Squadron to the China Seas and Japan, Performed in the Years 1852, 1853, and 1854 under the Command of Commodore M. C. Perry, United States Navy* [1856–1858] [7:473]). The writer was part of Perry's second visit to Japan.

7:22   _____. *Some Unpublished Letters of Townsend Harris.* New York: Japan Reference Library, 1941. Most of these long, descriptive letters from Harris in Japan were written to Catherine Ann Drinker, a young girl in a family that Harris met in Hong Kong.

7:23   Temperley, Harold. "Documents Illustrating the Reception and Interpretation of the Monroe Doctrine in Europe, 1823–4." *English Historical Review* 39 (October 1924): 590–93. Temperley offers several documents showing that Monroe's message met with more concern in Europe than has been otherwise believed.

7:24   U.S. Congress (19th Cong., 1st Sess., 1825–1826). Senate. *The Executive Proceedings of the Senate of the United States on the Subject of the Mission to the Congress at Panama: Together with the Messages and Documents Relating Thereto.* Washington, DC: Gales and Seaton, 1826. This is a valuable primary source on early U.S. policies toward Latin America.

7:25   U.S. President. *Message of the President of the United States Transmitting a report of the Secretary of the Navy, in Compliance with a Resolution of the Senate of December 6, 1854, Calling for Correspondence, &c., Relative to the Naval Expedition to Japan.* Washington, DC: Gales and Seaton, 1855. This collection includes correspondence between Perry and the Navy Department and records of the negotiations at Kanagawa. This is Senate Executive Document 34, 33d Cong., 2d Sess.

7:26   U.S. Senate. *Correspondence between the Commander of the East India Squadron and Foreign Powers.* Washington, DC: Gales and Seaton, 1846. This document (which is Senate Document 139, 29th Cong., 1st Sess.) includes the exchange between Lawrence Kearny and the governor at Canton concerning American trading privileges in China.

7:27 _____. *Correspondence of the Late Commissioners in China.* 2 vols. Washington, DC: Gales and Seaton, 1859. These volumes (Senate Executive Document 22, 35th Cong., 2d Sess.) contain the diplomatic correspondence of Commissioners Robert McLane and Peter Parker, 1854–1857.

7:28 _____. *Correspondence Relating to the Treaty with the Ta Tsing Empire.* Washington, DC: Gales and Seaton, 1845. The Senate document (Senate Documents 58 and 67, 28th Cong., 2d Sess.) includes almost all of the diplomatic correspondence relative to the Cushing mission.

7:29 _____. *Instructions to and Dispatches from the Late and Present Ministers in China.* Washington, DC: Gales and Seaton, 1860. This volume contains the diplomatic correspondence of Minister William B. Reed and Minister John E. Ward, 1857–1859, the period that included the negotiation and ratification of the Treaty of Tientsin. This is Senate Executive Document 30, 36th Cong., 1st Sess. See also Foster M. Farley, "William B. Reed: President Buchanan's Minister to China 1857–1858," *Pennsylvania History* 37 (July 1970): 269–80.

7:30 Wilkes, Charles. *Narrative of the United States Exploring Expeditions during the Years 1838, 1839, 1840, 1841, 1842.* 5 vols. and atlas. Philadelphia: Lea and Blanchard, 1845. These volumes cover the U.S. South Seas Surveying and Exploring Expedition, detailing observations on natural history, anthropology, geology, and hydrology of the area as well as history and politics. Volumes 2 and 3 cover Australia and New Zealand, the rest primarily Oceania.

Bibliographies and Other Reference Works

7:31 Beers, Henry Putney, ed. *Spanish and Mexican Records of the American Southwest: A Bibliographical Guide to Archive and Manuscript Sources.* This invaluable guide covers the whole sweep of history from Spanish rule to the present. There are four main geographical sections (New Mexico, Texas, California, and Arizona), each of which includes provincial and legal records, archival reproductions, documentary publications, manuscript collections, and land and ecclesiastical records. Each section is preceded by an account of history and government (3:40).

7:32 Frazier, Donald S., ed. *The United States and Mexico at War: Nineteenth-Century Expansionism and Conflict.* New York: Macmillan Reference USA, 1998. This is an easy-to-read and nicely illustrated reference work on the Mexican War and events leading to it.

7:33 Irick, Robert L., Ying-shih Yü, and Kwang-Ching Liu, eds. *American-Chinese Relations, 1784–1941: A Survey of Chinese-Language Materials at Harvard.* Cambridge, MA: Committee on American Far Eastern Policy Studies, Dept. of History, Harvard University, 1960. This listing includes entries on reference works, document collections, libraries, and archives in the United States and East Asia, economic and cultural relations, Christian missions, education, social reform, immigration, and diplomatic relations.

7:34 Moseley, Edward H., and Paul Coe Clark, Jr., eds. *Historical Dictionary of the United States–Mexican War.* Lanham, MD: Scarecrow Press, 1997. This excellent reference work provides the essential facts, figures, and background to the Mexican War. It includes numerous entries on the participants (statesmen, generals, and ordinary persons who merit mention) as well as descriptions of battles, battle sites, and other places of interest. In addition to narrative summaries of the origins and conclusions of the war, the editors included an extensive chronology, unannotated bibliography, and maps.

7:35 Rabe, Valentin H., and Harvard University Library, eds. *American-Chinese Relations, 1784–1941: Books and Pamphlets Extracted from the Shelf Lists of Widener Library.* Cambridge, MA: Committee on American Far Eastern Policy Studies, Dept. of History, Harvard University, 1960. This brief volume list contains over 1,000 items in the Widener Library, plus materials in other Harvard University libraries.

7:36   Snoke, Elizabeth R., ed. *The Mexican War: A Bibliography of MHRC [Military History Research Collection] Holdings for the Period 1835–1850.* Carlisle Barracks, PA: U.S. Military History Research Collection, 1973. Although pertaining to a single collection, this is a convenient guide to secondary sources and printed primary sources on the war.

7:37   Tutorow, Norman E., ed. *The Mexican-American War: An Annotated Bibliography.* Westport, CT: Greenwood Press, 1981. An extensively annotated bibliography, this reference aid is still an essential guide to sources (both printed and archival). Its eight appendices include a chronology, tables, graphs, and war maps; also included is a listing of military organizations, prominent politicians, and naval vessels.

7:38   University of Texas at Arlington Libraries, Jenkins Garrett, and Katherine R. Goodwin. *The Mexican-American War of 1846–1848: A Bibliography of the Holdings of the Libraries, the University of Texas at Arlington.* College Station: Texas A&M University Press for the University of Texas at Arlington, 1995. This is both a finding aid and a description of the massive holdings on the Mexican War at the University of Texas. It includes secondary publications, but also an impressive array of primary data including contemporary fiction, congressional speeches, manuscripts, sermons, sheet music, and newspapers. Its 2,500 entries are divided into nineteen chapters and a seven-part appendix, which includes the speeches recorded in the *Congressional Globe* relevant to Mexican-American relations.

7:39   Weber, David J. "Mexico's Far Northern Border, 1821–1845: A Critical Bibliography." *Arizona and the West* 19 (Autumn 1977): 225–66. In this guide to literature on Texas, New Mexico, Arizona, and California before the Mexican War, some cited works relate indirectly to U.S.-Mexican diplomacy.

Historiography

7:40   Brauer, Kinley J. "The Great American Desert Revisited: Recent Literature and Prospects for the Study of American Foreign Relations, 1815–61." Assessing recent work on the period, Brauer concludes that American foreign policy was both more activist and wider ranging than previously believed (6:37).

7:41   Gilbert, Arthur N. "The American Indian and United States Diplomatic History." This is one of the first articles to argue for the necessity of including American Indian policy as a part of American foreign relations (5:68).

7:42   Harstad, Peter T., and Richard W. Resh. "The Causes of the Mexican War: A Note on Changing Interpretations." *Arizona and the West* 6 (Winter 1964): 289–302. This is a roughly chronological study of how interpretations have changed over the decades and how they relate to one another. The most significant change over a long period is the decline of the controversy over the "slaveocracy" interpretation of the Mexican War, succeeded by arguments made in the context of the history of U.S. expansionism. For a more recent estimate, see Thomas Benjamin, "Recent Historiography of the Origins of the Mexican War," *New Mexico Historical Review* 54 (July 1979): 169–82.

7:43   Limerick, Patricia Nelson, Clyde A. Milner, II, and Charles E. Rankin, eds. *Trails: Toward a New Western History.* Lawrence: University Press of Kansas, 1991. This collection presents various perspectives on the history of the west by leading practitioners of the "new" western history. Those most related to this chapter are Limerick, "What on Earth Is the New Western History?" (81–88); Gerald Thompson, "Another Look at Frontier/Western Historiography" (89–96); Michael P. Malone, "The 'New Western History,' an Assessment" (97–102); Elliott West, "A Longer, Grimmer, but More Interesting Story" (103–11); Brian W. Dippie, "American Wests: Historiographical Perspectives" (112–37); Malone, "Beyond the Last Frontier: Toward a New Approach to Western American History" (139–60); and William G. Robbins, "Laying Siege to Western History: The Emergence of New Paradigms" (182–214).

7:44   Nichols, Roger L., ed. *American Frontier and Western Issues: A Historiographical Review.* Westport, CT: Greenwood Press, 1986. This collection focuses on the frontier experience in its entirety as it moved westward across the continent. The emphasis of each chapter is the relationship between "issues of settlement and local development." Of particular interest to diplomatic historians is Robert Schulzinger's chapter on "Foreign Affairs and Expansion," separately treated; John Opie, "The Environment and the Frontier" (7–26); John D. Haeger, "Economic Development of the American West" (27–50); Nichols, "Historians and Indians" (149–78); and Paul A. Hutton, "The Frontier Army" (253–74).

7:45   Schulzinger, Robert D. "Foreign Affairs and Expansion." In *American Frontiers and Western Issues: A Historiographical Review*, ed. Roger L. Nichols, 217–34. Westport, CT: Greenwood Press, 1986. Schulzinger surveys the literature written between 1920 and 1984 on the western expansion of the United States during the nineteenth century. He discusses in detail the War of 1812, the Monroe Doctrine, and the Mexican War and its aftermath, noting that recent literature is influenced by the controversies surrounding the Vietnam War as well as by recent ideas of domination and dependency. This essay appeared before the flood of works exploring the new western history was published after 1986. The groundwork for the later literature was laid, however, in the reevaluation of American history that began in the 1970s and that is the central focus of this essay.

7:46   Weeks, William Earl. "New Directions in the Study of Early American Foreign Relations." See chapter 4 of this Guide (4:47).

Overviews and General Works

7:47   Becker, William H., and Samuel F. Wells, Jr., eds. *Economics and World Power: An Assessment of American Diplomacy since 1789*. See chapter 2 of this Guide (2:98) for details on this collection of provocative essays of varying lengths on the economic dimension of American foreign relations, which includes Kinley J. Brauer, "1821–1860: Economics and the Diplomacy of American Expansionism" (55–118).

7:48   Cunliffe, Marcus. *Soldiers & Civilians: The Martial Spirit in America, 1775–1865*. See chapter 5 of this Guide (5:83).

7:49   Eckes, Alfred E., Jr. *Opening America's Market: U.S. Foreign Trade Policy since 1776*. Chapel Hill: University of North Carolina Press, 1995. Although devoted primarily to the post–Civil War era, early chapters provide an illuminating discussion of federal trade policy by one of the foremost scholars in the field.

7:50   Johnson, Emory R., et al. *History of Domestic and Foreign Commerce of the United States*. See chapter 6 of this Guide (6:59).

7:51   Langley, Harold D. *Social Reform in the United States Navy, 1798–1862*. Urbana: University of Illinois Press, 1967. This history of efforts to alleviate the harsh life of the seaman ties naval history to the currents of nineteenth-century reforms. It also provides details about the navy that showed the flag and guarded commerce in places as distant as Constantinople and the South China Sea. Extensive bibliography.

7:52   Long, David F. *Gold Braid and Foreign Relations: Diplomatic Activities of U.S. Naval Officers, 1798–1883*. See chapter 5 of this Guide (5:130).

7:53   Morison, Samuel Eliot. *The Maritime History of Massachusetts, 1783–1860*. See chapter 6 of this Guide (6:60).

7:54   North, Douglass C. *The Economic Growth of the United States, 1790–1860*. See chapter 6 of this Guide (6:52).

7:55   Reeves, Jesse S. *American Diplomacy under Tyler and Polk*. Although published nearly 100 years ago, Reeves's book remains interesting for historiographical reasons. Notes (6:316).

7:56   Sprout, Harold, and Margaret Sprout. *The Rise of American Naval Power, 1776–1918*. Rev. ed. Princeton: Princeton University Press, 1942. Reprint 1990 (Naval Institute Press). Though it is concerned with naval policy and strategy at the places where the navy and the civilian executive and legislature intersect, rather than with the development of policy and strategy, this book remains the nearest approach to a satisfactory history of the navy. Bibliography. Originally published in 1939.

7:57 Taylor, George Rogers. *The Transportation Revolution, 1815–1860*. See chapter 6 of this Guide (6:53).

7:58 Varg, Paul A. *United States Foreign Relations, 1820–1860*. See chapter 6 of this Guide (6:44). See also Perkins, *The Creation of a Republican Empire, 1776–1865* (1993) (2:44).

Biographical Studies

JOHN QUINCY ADAMS

7:59 Bemis, Samuel Flagg. *John Quincy Adams and the Union*. See chapter 6 of this Guide (6:70).

7:60 Hargreaves, Mary W. M. *The Presidency of John Quincy Adams*. This comprehensive and learned assessment of the Adams presidency is particularly illuminating on Adams's foreign policy, including the Panama Congress and trade issues in the Caribbean. Hargreaves follows others in seeing the president as an inept politician (6:71).

7:61 Lewis, James E., Jr. *John Quincy Adams: Policymaker for the Union*. See chapter 6 of this Guide (6:72). See also Lewis's *The American Union and the Problem of Neighborhood: The United States and the Collapse of the Spanish Empire, 1783–1829* (Chapel Hill: University of North Carolina Press, 1998), which is also an important source on the Monroe Doctrine, and Russell, *John Quincy Adams and the Public Virtues of Diplomacy* (1995) (5:147).

7:62 Parsons, Lynn Hudson. *John Quincy Adams*. See chapter 5 of this Guide (5:146).

7:63 _____, ed. *John Quincy Adams: A Bibliography*. This is a valuable reference work by a long-time Adams scholar (5:50).

7:64 Richards, Leonard L. *The Life and Times of Congressman John Quincy Adams*. New York: Oxford University Press, 1986. This is a sympathetic view of Adams's "second career" as a congressional foe of slavery and the slave trade.

JAMES BUCHANAN

7:65 Binder, Frederick Moore. *James Buchanan and the American Empire*. This perceptive study illuminates Buchanan's lifelong commitment to American nationalism and expansion (6:79).

7:66 Smith, Elbert B. *The Presidency of James Buchanan*. This book provides a straightforward scholarly account of Buchanan's presidency. Although it focuses on the domestic political crisis, the volume includes an adequate treatment of Buchanan's hands-on but unsuccessful efforts to promote U.S. expansion. Bibliography (6:82).

JAMES K. POLK

7:67 Haynes, Sam W. *James K. Polk and the Expansionist Impulse*. 2d ed. New York: Longman, 2002. In this brief (as designed) volume, Haynes portrays Polk as part of a grassroots expansionist movement that aimed to strengthen the country but instead contributed to its collapse in civil war. First published in 1997.

7:68 McCormac, Eugene I. *James K. Polk: A Political Biography*. This classic political biography casts Polk as utterly humorless, devoid of charm, lacking imagination despite possessing a grand vision, and absolutely successful in attaining his political goals, not the least of which was the acquisition of the northern half of his southern neighbor (6:109).

7:69 Sellers, Charles Grier. *James K. Polk, Continentalist, 1843–1846*. This is the second volume of a projected three-volume biography. It is primarily political, but Sellers also devotes attention to diplomacy with Mexico and Britain. Polk's personal life, well developed in the first volume, is subordinated here. Extensive bibliography (6:110).

FRANKLIN PIERCE

7:70   Gara, Larry. *The Presidency of Franklin Pierce.* This is one of the only works available on this expansionist president, but it focuses far more on the internal American sectional conflict than foreign policy (6:105).

7:71   Nichols, Roy F. *Franklin Pierce: Young Hickory of the Granite Hills.* A detailed, traditional biography, this includes a sound account of foreign policy questions during the presidency of Pierce. Bibliography (6:106). First published in 1931.

WINFIELD SCOTT

7:72   Eisenhower, John S. D. *Agent of Destiny: The Life and Times of General Winfield Scott.* New York: Free Press, 1997. Written by a retired general, and son of the thirty-fourth president, this is a reliable and compelling popular history. Eisenhower, however, did not make use of archival materials or recent secondary literature; consequently, his work does not supersede Charles Winslow Elliott, *Winfield Scott, The Soldier and the Man* (New York: Macmillan, 1937; 1979 reprint, Arno Press), which devotes several chapters to the Mexican War.

7:73   Johnson, Timothy D. *Winfield Scott: The Quest for Military Glory.* Lawrence: University Press of Kansas, 1998. This biography counters the traditional image of "Old Fuss and Feathers," depicting Scott as a complex man and a military genius. Johnson argues that, as one of the first U.S. officers to study European military theory and history, Scott employed what he learned in the Mexican campaign and brought a new sense of professionalism to the nineteenth-century U.S. army.

OTHERS

7:74   Porter, Kenneth W. *John Jacob Astor: Business Man.* Based on extensive research, this detailed account of Astor's life and business activities remains the most complete treatment of this topic (6:130).

7:75   Méndez Pereira, Octavio. *Bolivar y las rela-* *ciones interamericanas [Bolivar and Inter-American Relations].* Panamá: Imprenta Nacional, 1960. Méndez Pereira presents an interpretive study of inter-American relations and the influence of Bolivar's thought. Bibliography.

7:76   Wiltse, Charles M. *John C. Calhoun. Vol. 3: Sectionalist, 1840–1850.* See chapter 6 of this Guide (6:135).

7:77   Van Deusen, Glyndon G. *The Life of Henry Clay.* See chapter 6 of this Guide (6:88).

7:78   Nevins, Allan. *Fremont, Pathmarker of the West.* 2 vols. New York: Ungar, 1955. Nevins's second biography of Frémont (1813–1890) represents more up-to-date research than *Frémont, the World's Greatest Adventurer, etc.* (2 vols., New York: Harper and Brothers, 1928) and offers some revised conclusions. The enlarged 1955 edition deals with Frémont's activities in California. Bibliography.

7:79   Grant, Ulysses. *Memoirs and Selected Letters: Personal Memoirs of U.S. Grant, Selected Letters 1839–1865.* 2 vols. in one. New York: Library of America, 1990. This publication combines important letters pertaining to Grant's service in the Mexican War along with his remarkable memoirs. The latter are forthright and well written, describing his military career. Of particular interest here is his experience in, and candid appraisal of, the war against Mexico, which he considered an illegal aggression against a troubled neighbor.

7:80   Joerger, Pauline King. *A Political Biography of David Lawrence Gregg, American Diplomat and Hawaiian Official.* New York: Arno Press, 1982. This is the only work detailing the political career of an important American diplomat in Hawaii in the 1850s.

7:81   Bassett, John Spencer. *The Life of Andrew Jackson.* 2 vols. Garden City, NY: Doubleday, Page, 1911. In an exhaustive, ponderously written narrative based on primary sources, Bassett discusses the Florida question in detail. He argues that Monroe was correct about the Rhea letter, which allegedly proved Jackson's claim that he was ordered into Spanish Florida.

7:82   Porter, Kenneth W. *The Jacksons and the Lees: Two Generations of Massachusetts Merchants, 1765–1844.* This book is a documentary study that includes a narrative of the commercial activities of the two families and an extensive collection of correspondence from each family (6:61).

7:83   Copeland, Fayette. *Kendall of the Picayune: Being His Adventures in New Orleans, on the Texan Santa Fé Expedition, in the Mexican War, and in the Colonization of the Texas Frontier.* Norman: University of Oklahoma Press, 1943. This biography covers the career of one of the foremost editorial promoters of westward expansion, who became America's first war correspondent when he accompanied U.S. forces invading Mexico in 1846. A 1997 reprint issued by the same publisher includes a foreword by Robert W. Johannsen.

7:84   Seaburg, Carl, and Stanley Paterson. *Merchant Prince of Boston: Colonel T. H. Perkins, 1764–1854.* This is a clearly written and well-documented study that focuses on the business, investment, and trading activities of Colonel Thomas Handasyd Perkins. Bibliography (6:147).

7:85   Rippy, J. Fred. *Joel R. Poinsett, Versatile American.* Durham, NC: Duke University Press, 1935. Reprint 1970 (Scholarly Press). Rippy's biography, very pro-Poinsett, is a readable account of this diplomat and secretary of war (1779–1851).

7:86   Bauer, K. Jack. *Zachary Taylor: Soldier, Planter, Statesman of the Old Southwest.* This is a comprehensive and sympathetic view of a neglected historical figure by a respected scholar (6:111).

7:87   Crapol, Edward P. "John Tyler and the Pursuit of National Destiny." Crapol portrays Tyler as a nationalist and an expansionist in addition to being proslavery, and possessed of a vision of global U.S. commercial and territorial expansion (6:114).

7:88   Shewmaker, Kenneth E. "Daniel Webster and the Politics of Foreign Policy, 1850–1852." The author argues that Webster accepted his appointment and used his position as secretary of state (1850–1852) primarily to promote the Compromise of 1850 and national unity. The article contends that Webster used the Hulsemann affair to this end, not as a device

to advance his chances for the presidency in 1852 (6:127). See also Remini, *Daniel Webster: The Man and His Time* (1997) (6:125).

Monroe Doctrine

7:89   Alvarez, Alejandro. *The Monroe Doctrine: Its Importance in the International Life of the States of the New World.* New York: Oxford University Press, 1924. This collection combines narrative of the history of the Monroe Doctrine, original texts of documents, mostly Latin American, and a section titled "Declarations of Statesmen and Opinions of Publicists of Latin America and the United States in Regard to the Monroe Doctrine": eleven Latin American states are represented by the former and nineteen Americans (from John Barrett to Woodrow Wilson) by the latter.

7:90   Bingham, Hiram. *The Monroe Doctrine: An Obsolete Shibboleth.* New Haven: Yale University Press, 1913. This classic account condemned the use of the Monroe Doctrine to justify American expansion.

7:91   Bolkhovitinov, Nikolai N. "Russia and the Declaration of the Noncolonization Principle: New Archival Evidence." *Oregon Historical Quarterly* 72 (June 1971): 101–26. This article, by a Soviet historian who had written extensively on Russian-American relations and the Monroe Doctrine, argues that the noncolonization principle of Monroe's message of 1823 originated in American expansionist ambitions in the Pacific northwest. The famous Ukase of 1821 was only a pretext used by John Quincy Adams to justify the noncolonization principle, which was aimed primarily against the British. Translated by Basil Dmytryshyn.

7:92   Bornholdt, Laura. "The Abbé de Pradt and the Monroe Doctrine." *Hispanic American Historical Review* 24 (May 1944): 201–21. The author refutes the theory that Napoleon's aide influenced Jefferson's thinking on the concept of the two spheres, an integral part of the Monroe Doctrine.

7:93 Brauer, Kinley J. "The United States and British Imperial Expansion, 1815–1860." Brauer examines limitations on U.S. action in competing for territory with the British. Conflicts over slavery were a significant impediment (6:167).

7:94 Crapol, Edward P. "John Quincy Adams and the Monroe Doctrine: Some New Evidence." *Pacific Historical Review* 48 (August 1979): 413–18. Based on a recently discovered letter from Adams to Rush, Crapol concludes that the noncolonization clause of the Monroe Doctrine was aimed at both British and Russian expansionism in the Western Hemisphere.

7:95 Craven, W. R., Jr. "The Risk of the Monroe Doctrine." *Hispanic American Historical Review* 7 (August 1927): 320–33. Craven concludes that there was little danger of European intervention (1823–1824) in Spanish America and that Adams shrewdly recognized that British interests would thwart any interventionist plans.

7:96 Cunningham, Noble E., Jr. *The Presidency of James Monroe.* Cunningham portrays Monroe as both a staunch nationalist and ardent expansionist whose achievements as president have been underestimated (6:146).

7:97 Davis, Thomas B., Jr. "Carlos de Alvear and James Monroe: New Light on the Origin of the Monroe Doctrine." *Hispanic American Historical Review* 23 (November 1943): 632–49. Davis assesses the impressions of the Monroe Doctrine on Argentina's first minister to the United States, who believed the doctrine pledged the United States to protection of South America.

7:98 Ford, Worthington C. "John Quincy Adams and the Monroe Doctrine." *American Historical Review* 7 (July 1902): 676–96. The author uses extensive quotations from Adams's writings to illustrate his decisive influence on the making of the Monroe Doctrine in the critical four months of 1823 before the message was delivered. Ford was an excellent scholar, and this is still worth reading despite its being superseded by a century of scholarship.

7:99 Manning, William R. "Statements, Interpretations, and Applications of the Monroe Doctrine and of More or Less Allied Doctrines: From 1823–1845." *Proceedings of the American Society of International Law* 8 (1914): 34–58. This essay is a handy reference on the evolution of the Monroe Doctrine from Monroe to Polk. This entire issue of the *Proceedings* is devoted to the evolution of the doctrine to 1914. Other authors who address the origins and early years of the Monroe Doctrine include Charles Francis Adams and Dexter Perkins.

7:100 May, Ernest R. *The Making of the Monroe Doctrine.* Cambridge, MA: Belknap Press of Harvard University Press, 1975. May argues that the origin of the message lay in the domestic political situation and the jockeying for position in the upcoming election of 1824. John Quincy Adams was motivated in large part by political opportunism and his realization that a stern warning in Monroe's message would enhance his presidential ambitions. Extensive bibliography.

7:101 McGee, Gale W. "The Monroe Doctrine—A Stopgap Measure." *Mississippi Valley Historical Review* 38 (September 1951): 233–50. According to McGee, Canning's proposal to Rush for a joint statement on Latin America was in fact an American idea, and Monroe's message of December 1823 anticipated further Anglo-American cooperation.

7:102 Merk, Frederick, with Lois Bannister Merk. *The Monroe Doctrine and American Expansionism, 1843–1849.* In his "study in the psychology of expansionism," Merk examined the American belief that European interference in North America retarded the nation's Manifest Destiny. American leaders worried about European pressures because of public support for expansionism (6:407).

7:103 Perkins, Dexter. "Europe, Spanish America, and the Monroe Doctrine." *American Historical Review* 27 (January 1922): 207–18. Perkins argues that European powers, in 1823–1824, never had a practical policy for reconquest of Spanish America. Monroe's message did not readily affect their policy. Timothy E. Anna, *Spain & the Loss of America* (Lincoln: University of Nebraska Press, 1983).

7:104 _____. *The Monroe Doctrine, 1823–1826.* Cambridge, MA: Harvard University Press, 1927. Perkins concludes, in this standard work on the doctrine, that it embodied two principles: noncolonization and noninterference. After an exhaustive study of European archives, he holds that there was no real threat to Spanish America by the continental powers. Extensive bibliography.

7:105 _____. *The Monroe Doctrine, 1826–1867*. Baltimore: Johns Hopkins Press, 1933. In the sequel to *The Monroe Doctrine, 1823–1826* (1927) (7:104), the author uses a vast array of published and unpublished sources to trace the evolution of the doctrine: forgotten in the 1830s, revived in the 1840s, exploited in the 1850s, and championed in the 1860s. Extensive bibliography.

7:106 _____. "Russia and the Spanish Colonies, 1817–1818." *American Historical Review* 28 (July 1923): 656–72. Perkins argues that the Russian czar sympathized with Spain about the loss of its New World empire, but he was unwilling to act without British approval. The Holy Alliance, then, was no threat to the republics.

7:107 Powell, John H. *Richard Rush, Republican Diplomat, 1780–1859*. See chapter 6 of this Guide (6:151).

7:108 Robertson, William Spence. "South America and the Monroe Doctrine, 1824–1828." *Political Science Quarterly* 30 (March 1915): 82–105. The author evaluates South America's reception of the Monroe Doctrine.

7:109 Schellenberg, Thomas R. "Jeffersonian Origins of the Monroe Doctrine." *Hispanic American Historical Review* 14 (February 1934): 1–32. In this intellectual analysis of Jefferson's contribution to the Monroe Doctrine, the author argues that the concept of two spheres, implicit in Monroe's messages, comes from Jefferson's philosophy of the New World.

7:110 Tatum, Edward Howland, Jr. *The United States and Europe, 1815–1823: A Study in the Background of the Monroe Doctrine*. Berkeley: University of California Press, 1936. Tatum argues, from published sources, that the Monroe Doctrine was aimed at Great Britain to prevent possible British seizure of Spanish Cuba. He also offers an account of European impressions of the United States after 1815. Bibliography.

Manifest Destiny

7:111 Boucher, Chauncey W. "In Re That Aggressive Slaveocracy." *Mississippi Valley Historical Review* 8 (June-September 1921): 13–79. This is the classic article in which Boucher concluded that there was no aggressive slaveocracy. It remains controversial.

7:112 Chaffin, Tom. "Sons of Washington: Narciso López, Filibustering, and U.S. Nationalism, 1848–1851." This article (6:397) outlines in brief compass the men, motives, and methods behind the U.S.-based effort to topple the Spanish colonial regime in Cuba, which Chaffin has further developed in his book, *Fatal Glory: Narciso López and the First Clandestine U.S. War against Cuba* (Charlottesville: University Press of Virginia, 1996), which describes the four expeditions López launched against the Spanish colony (all opposed by Washington) but is based on thin archival research.

7:113 Curti, Merle E. "George N. Sanders—American Patriot of the Fifties." This article provides a summary of the life and career of one of the most aggressive proponents of the Young America doctrines. The revolutionary outbursts of 1848 in Europe stimulated some American idealists who inaugurated the Young America movement, which had as one of its goals active intervention against European despotisms (6:153).

7:114 _____. "Young America." See chapter 6 of this Guide (6:67).

7:115 Dangerfield, George. *The Awakening of American Nationalism, 1815–1828*. New York: Harper and Row, 1965. This is a well-written interpretation of America during the Monroe and Adams presidencies. The chapters on foreign affairs contain considerable insights on British reaction to the Florida dispute and the Monroe Doctrine. Bibliography.

7:116 Drinnon, Richard. *Facing West: The Metaphysics of Indian-Hating and Empire Building*. Minneapolis: University of Minnesota Press, 1980. Reprint 1997 (University of Oklahoma Press). In this loosely knit work covering racism in America from the seventeenth century through most of the twentieth, Drinnon argues that U.S. expansion, or empire-building, was inherently racist. Borrowing themes of repression from Freud, and ascetic imprisonment from Max Weber, Drinnon sees U.S. racism as an outgrowth of psychic and sexual repression.

7:117   Eckert, Allan W. *Twilight of Empire: A Narrative.* Boston: Little, Brown, 1988. This volume chronicles the rise of Black Hawk and ensuing war. A narrative, it includes several biographical sketches.

7:118   Gibson, Joe. "A. Butler: 'What a Scamp!'" *Journal of the West* 11 (April 1972): 235–47. Gibson details Butler's efforts to exploit the troubled Mexican political situation (1832–1835) to the advantage of the United States, especially in the purchase of Texas. Butler was Joel Poinsett's successor as minister to Mexico and a close friend of Andrew Jackson.

7:119   Goetzmann, William H. "The United States–Mexican Boundary Survey, 1848–1853." *Southwestern Historical Quarterly* 62 (October 1958): 164–90. This key early work by a noted historian details border surveys leading to the Gadsden purchase.

7:120   _____. *When the Eagle Screamed: The Romantic Horizon in American Diplomacy 1800–1860.* New York: Wiley, 1966. The author provides a brief interpretation of American expansionist diplomacy from 1800 to 1850, arguing that the primary impulse for American expansion stemmed from European ideas, particularly the romantic and global ideas of grandeur and destiny.

7:121   Grant, Susan-Mary. *North over South: Northern Nationalism and American Identity in the Antebellum Era.* Lawrence: University Press of Kansas, 2000. The author argues that divisions over meanings and applications of American nationalism were a crucial factor in precipitating the Civil War.

7:122   Haynes, Sam W., and Christopher Morris, eds. *Manifest Destiny and Empire: American Antebellum Expansionism.* This is an accomplished collection of essays on various aspects of Manifest Destiny by noted scholars in the field: Robert W. Johannsen, "The Meaning of Manifest Destiny" (7–20); John M. Belohlavek, "Race, Progress, and

Destiny: Caleb Cushing and the Quest for American Empire" (21–47); Thomas R. Hietala, "'This Splendid Juggernaut': Westward a Nation and Its People" (48–67); Samuel J. Watson, "The Uncertain Road to Manifest Destiny: Army Officers and the Course of American Territorial Expansionism, 1815–1846" (68–114); Haynes, "Anglophobia and the Annexation of Texas: The Quest for National Security" (115–45); and Robert E. May, "Manifest Destiny's Filibusters" (146–79) (6:401).

7:123   Hietala, Thomas R. *Manifest Design: Anxious Aggrandizement in Late Jacksonian America.* Hietala emphasizes the insecurities—real and imagined—of American politicians and pundits as a motive force for expansion. One chapter is devoted to "The Myths of Manifest Destiny" (6:402).

7:124   Horsman, Reginald. *Race and Manifest Destiny: The Origins of American Racial Anglo-Saxonism.* Cambridge, MA: Harvard University Press, 1981. Horsman wrote the landmark analysis of the pivotal role of race and racism in the era of Manifest Destiny. But readers should not neglect Weinberg's mordant *Manifest Destiny: A Study of Nationalist Expansionism in American History* (1935) (2:223) either.

7:125   Jehlen, Myra. *American Incarnation: The Individual, the Nation, and the Continent.* Cambridge, MA: Harvard University Press, 1986. In this nuanced discussion of the role of expansionism in the making of a national identity, Jehlen examines three texts (Emerson's *Nature,* Hawthorne's *The Marble Faun,* and Melville's *Pierre*) to show that American notions of liberal individualism were "grounded, literally, in the American soil." This, in turn, is the central organizing principle of American ideology. Historians who do not accept Puritan New England as the model of American settlement will find fault with this work.

7:126   Kolodny, Annette. *The Land before Her: Fantasy and Experience of the American Frontiers, 1630–1860.* Chapel Hill: University of North Carolina Press, 1984. This innovative analysis explores how responses to the frontier and frontier conditions depended in part on gender. The frontier was not only a space but a venue for multicultural encounters.

7:127   Krenn, Michael L., ed. *Race and U.S. Foreign Policy in the Ages of Territorial and Market*

Expansion, 1840–1900. This provocative collection argues for the centrality of race and racism in the expansionist process (2:158).

7:128   Kushner, Howard I. *Conflict on the Northwest Coast: American-Russian Rivalry in the Pacific Northwest, 1790–1867.* See chapters 5 and 6 of this Guide (5:414; 6:369).

7:129   Leckie, Robert. *From Sea to Shining Sea: From the War of 1812 to the Mexican War, the Saga of America's Expansion.* New York: HarperCollins, 1993. This is a vividly written, popular overview of the expansionist process by a prolific historian.

7:130   Limerick, Patricia Nelson. *The Legacy of Conquest: The Unbroken Past of the American West.* New York: Norton, 1987. This is a scathing indictment of U.S. expansionism by a leading practitioner of the "new" western history.

7:131   May, Robert E. "Young American Males and Filibustering in the Age of Manifest Destiny: The United States Army as a Cultural Mirror." *Journal of American History* 78 (December 1991): 857–86. May infers that enlistees in filibuster expeditions came from all classes and backgrounds, and that federal efforts—army officers took a dim view of filibusters—to suppress them were both lax and ineffectual.

7:132   Merk, Frederick, with Lois Bannister Merk. *Manifest Destiny and Mission in American History: A Reinterpretation.* This classic work argues that the aggressive spirit of the age of Manifest Destiny in the 1840s was sharply distinguished from the more benevolent "mission" spirit of 1898 (2:220).

7:133   Morrison, Michael A. *Slavery and the American West: The Eclipse of Manifest Destiny and the Coming of the Civil War.* Chapel Hill: University of North Carolina Press, 1997. This is a richly researched text that argues that, prior to 1848, divisions over slavery had a minimal impact on the expansionist impulse.

7:134   Nelson, Anna K. "Jane Storms Cazneau: Disciple of Manifest Destiny." Nelson details Cazneau's role as a somewhat unsung figure of Manifest Destiny who corresponded with the likes of Polk, Buchanan, Burr, George Bancroft, and other notable American political figures (6:136).

7:135   Nichols, Roy F. *Advance Agents of American Destiny.* This work, a collection of ten essays, focuses on promoters of American overseas trade from the revolution to the Civil War. Five of the chapters relate to Latin America. A prominent subject is William Shaler, American consul in North Africa and Havana. Two chapters deal with the "guano" promoters of the 1850s. Bibliography (5:259).

7:136   Onuf, Peter S. *Jefferson's Empire: The Language of American Nationhood.* Onuf argues that Jefferson's vision of empire was essentially a consensual, republican adaptation of the British model, and that he conceived of his egalitarianism within an imperial context. Race was a significant limitation because he saw both Indians and blacks as unassimilable (5:200).

7:137   Pletcher, David M. *The Diplomacy of Annexation: Texas, Oregon, and the Mexican War.* This study relates the three issues mentioned in the title from 1815 to 1848, emphasizing choices open to policymakers. Employing American, Texan, Mexican, British, French, and Spanish sources, Pletcher suggests that Polk might have avoided the Mexican War but chose an aggressive style of diplomacy that brought about steady escalation of peacetime enmity and then fighting. Extensive bibliography (6:409).

7:138   Rézé, Michel, and Ralph Henry Bowen. *The American West: History, Myth and the National Identity.* Paris: Armand Colin, 1998. This work presents a cultural studies approach to the meaning of the "west" for Americans and the ideology of expansionism, the authors discussing captivity and pastoral myths, popular and serious fiction, Wild West shows, and histories. Among particular American figures discussed are Daniel Boone, Davey Crockett, Kit Carson, Thomas Jefferson, James Fenimore Cooper, William F. Cody (Buffalo Bill), Francis Parkman, Theodore Roosevelt, John Muir, Nathaniel Hawthorne, Herman Melville, Henry David Thoreau, Walt Whitman, and Mark Twain.

7:139   Shewmaker, Kenneth E., ed., with Kenneth R. Stevens and Anita McGurn, assistant eds. *The Papers of Daniel Webster. Series 3. Diplomatic Papers.*

Vol. 2: 1850–1852. 2 vols. Hanover, NH: University Press of New England, 1987. This is the annotated version of the public papers of Webster as secretary of state by his foremost modern student.

7:140   Slotkin, Richard. *The Fatal Environment: The Myth of the Frontier in the Age of Industrialization, 1800–1890.* New York: Atheneum, 1985. Reprint 1998 (University of Oklahoma Press). This is a complicated, sometimes powerful argument about the effects of the frontier on national development. Supported by a diverse collection of sources, Slotkin contends that the "dominant themes of the Frontier Myth are those that center on the conception of American history as a heroic-scale Indian war, pitting race against race; and the central concern of the mythmakers is with the problem of reaching the 'end of the Frontier.' Both of these themes are brought together in the 'Last Stand' legend, which is the central fable of the industrial or 'revised' Myth of the Frontier."

7:141   Smith, Gene A. *Thomas Ap Catesby Jones: Commodore of Manifest Destiny.* Annapolis: Naval Institute Press, 2000. This recent biography relates the story of a naval officer whose career spanned nearly fifty years but was most famous for his mistaken seizure of Monterey, California, in 1842, four years before the war with Mexico. Smith covers Jones's encounters with smugglers, slave traders, the British at the Battle of New Orleans as well as his 1820 assignment to Hawaii and efforts to bring California into the union. He concludes that Jones was the "embodiment of the nationalistic spirit that gripped the United States following the War of 1812."

7:142   Smith, Geoffrey S. "The Navy before Darwinism: Science, Exploration, and Diplomacy in Antebellum America." *American Quarterly* 28 (Spring 1976): 41–55. This article describes the critical role of the navy in contributing to the sum of scientific knowledge and in creating the scientific foundations for commercial expansionism.

7:143   Stephanson, Anders. *Manifest Destiny: American Expansionism and the Empire of Right.* The early chapters of this short book discuss the pre–Civil War roots of the religion-based mission ideology the author thinks pervades American history (2:222).

7:144   Van Every, Dale. *The Final Challenge: The American Frontier, 1804–1845.* New York: Morrow, 1964. Reprint 1988 (Quill). This is the last installment of Van Every's four-volume series on eighteenth- and nineteenth-century westward expansion. The author, a novelist and journalist before turning to history, presents a vivid narrative, which is not supported by archival research. He covers essentially the same material as Theodore Roosevelt's *The Winning of the West* (4 vols., New York: G. P. Putnam's Sons, 1894–1896), especially his focus on "the frontier people," who, like Roosevelt's "frontier folk," became a distinctive American who hated both the Indian and governmental authority.

7:145   Weeks, William Earl. "American Nationalism, American Imperialism: An Interpretation of United States Political Economy, 1789–1861." See chapters 5 and 6 of this Guide (5:114; 6:45).

7:146   _____. *Building the Continental Empire: American Expansion from the Revolution to the Civil War.* See chapters 4–6 of this Guide (4:77; 5:115; 6:413).

7:147   Wexler, Alan, ed. *Atlas of Westward Expansion.* New York: Facts on File, 1995. This atlas condenses 150 years of U.S. diplomatic, military, and social history into a graphic presentation of westward expansion. It is supplemented with a well-written historical text, two appendices, a three-page bibliography, and subject and name indexes.

7:148   Wilgus, A. Curtis. "Official Expression of Manifest Destiny Sentiment Concerning Hispanic America, 1848–1871." *Louisiana Historical Quarterly* 15 (July 1932): 486–506. This is largely a string of quotations from Congress and the press.

THE FILIBUSTERS

7:149   Bridges, C. A. "The Knights of the Golden Circle: A Filibustering Fantasy." *Southwestern Historical Quarterly* 44 (January 1941): 287–302. The Knights were an ultraexpansionist southern organization (1855–1865) focused on expansion into Mexico.

7:150   Brown, Charles H. *Agents of Manifest Destiny: The Lives and Times of the Filibusters.* A well-written narrative of the filibusters of the 1850s, this work focuses on American participation in the Cuban revolutionary expeditions of Narciso López and on William Walker's two great expeditions to Mexico and Nicaragua. The filibusters of the fifties, the author concludes, dreamed of a tropical empire. Bibliography (6:395).

7:151   Carr, Albert H. Z. *The World and William Walker.* New York: Harper and Row, 1963. Carr has written a psychological portrait of Walker, who ruled Nicaragua with his filibusters in the 1850s.

7:152   Dunn, Roy Sylvan. "The KGC in Texas, 1860–1861." *Southwestern Historical Quarterly* 70 (April 1967): 543–73. This essay focuses on the strength and activities of the filibustering Knights of the Golden Circle in the principal Texas areas of settlement.

7:153   Feipel, Louis N. "The Navy and Filibustering in the Fifties." *U.S. Naval Institute Proceedings* 44 (April–September 1918): 767–80, 1009–29, 1219–40, 1527–46, 1837–48, 2063–86. A serialized account of the navy's efforts to deal with isthmian filibustering in the 1850s, this work includes considerable material on the burning of Greytown in 1854.

7:154   Fornell, Earl W. "Texans and Filibusters in the 1850's." *Southwestern Historical Quarterly* 59 (April 1956): 411–28. Fornell comes to much the same conclusions as other writers about filibusters' motives: money and adventure. He adds the desire for cheap labor and the slave trade.

7:155   Greene, Laurence. *The Filibuster: The Career of William Walker.* Indianapolis: Bobbs-Merrill Company, 1937. In a narrative account based heavily on Scroggs, *Filibusters and Financiers: The Story of William Walker and His Associates* (1916) (7:158), Greene argues that Walker was courageous but lacked the qualities of a statesman.

7:156   May, Robert E. *Manifest Destiny's Underworld: Filibustering in Antebellum America.* Chapel Hill: University of North Carolina Press, 2002. May considers the many antebellum filibustering expeditions, and the thousands of Americans who participated in them, through a survey of popular culture, journalism, and advertising literature. He concludes

that not only did filibustering damage U.S.–Latin American relations but also contributed to sectional conflict within the United States.

7:157   Owsley, Frank L., Jr., and Gene A. Smith. *Filibusters and Expansionists: Jeffersonian Manifest Destiny, 1800–1821.* Owsley and Smith skillfully synthesize the existing literature—and bolster their arguments with primary source material where appropriate—to sort out the cast of characters in early-nineteenth-century expansion, from the White House to the Gulf Coast. Rejecting the idea that Manifest Destiny was a product of mid-nineteenth-century romantic nationalism (contra Merk and Belohlavek), Owsley and Smith find its roots in the colonial era and see it as an underlying theme in U.S. history (5:507).

7:158   Scroggs, William O. *Filibusters and Financiers: The Story of William Walker and His Associates.* New York: Macmillan Company, 1916. This biography of William Walker presents a dated account of filibustering in the 1850s. Scroggs denies that Walker was spreading slavery, though he contemplated conquest of Cuba and eventual union of Central America and Cuba with the southern states.

7:159   Stout, Joseph A., Jr. *The Liberators: Filibustering Expeditions into Mexico, 1848–1862, and the Last Thrust of Manifest Destiny.* Los Angeles: Westernlore Press, 1973. This is a good synthesis on filibustering, both American and French, from California into Mexico. Stout argues that filibusters were motivated by the desire for adventure and for economic gain, and shows the efforts of the U.S. government to intercept filibusters. See also Stout's more recent *Schemers & Dreamers: Filibustering in Mexico, 1848–1921* (Fort Worth: Texas Christian University Press, 2002).

7:160   TePaske, John J. "Appleton Oaksmith, Filibuster Agent." *North Carolina Historical Review* 35 (October 1958): 427–47. Oaksmith served with Walker in Nicaragua and became Walker's representative to the United States, promoting Nicaraguan securities in this country.

7:161   Walker, William. *The War in Nicaragua. Written by Gen'l William Walker.* Mobile, AL: S. H. Goetzel and Co., 1860. Reprint 1971 (Blaine

Ethridge Books). This is Walker's own self-serving account of his Nicaraguan campaign.

7:162   Wyllys, Rufus Kay. "Henry A. Crabb—A Tragedy of the Sonora Frontier." *Pacific Historical Review* 9 (June 1940): 183–94. This 1857 episode discouraged the California sport of filibustering until long after the Civil War and created a nationalistic legend for the people of the Sonoran borderlands.

7:163   _____. "The Republic of Lower California, 1853–1854." *Pacific Historical Review* 2 (June 1933): 194–213. This account examines William Walker's abortive effort to detach Baja California from Mexico.

North America (Excluding Oregon and Canada)

7:164   Adelman, Jeremy, and Stephen Aron. "From Borderlands to Borders: Empires, Nation-States, and the Peoples in Between in North American History." The authors discuss the changing conceptualization employed by historians from "frontier" to "borderlands." Rather than an open or closed frontier, "borderlands" illuminates the intercultural process of "mixing and accommodation as opposed to unambiguous triumph" (5:410).

7:165   Albion, Robert G., with Jennie Barnes Pope. *The Rise of New York Port, 1815–1860.* See chapter 6 of this Guide (6:55).

7:166   Graebner, Norman A. *Empire on the Pacific: A Study in American Continental Expansion.* Graebner's study of American expansionism in both California and Oregon (1820–1848) emphasizes the maritime aspects of American expansion into California. Bibliography (6:400).

7:167   Hosen, Frederick E. *Unfolding Westward in Treaty and Law: Land Documents in United States History from the Appalachians to the Pacific, 1783–1934.* Jefferson, NC: McFarland, 1988. Hosen has compiled full texts of treaties and laws legitimating the acquisition of lands and organization of territories west of the Appalachians.

7:168   Miller, Angela L. *The Empire of the Eye: Landscape Representation and American Cultural Politics, 1825–1875.* Ithaca: Cornell University Press, 1993. Working mainly from landscape paintings, Miller writes on the relationship between the aesthetic and the political in the support of nationalism and national identity in the face of the centrifugal forces of expansionism. This is a multidisciplinary work that employs literary criticism, culture, and political theory. She argues that the moral dilemmas of "imperialistic behavior" are reflected in the art of the era.

7:169   Remini, Robert V. *Andrew Jackson & His Indian Wars.* New York: Viking, 2001. Jackson's preeminent biographer, demonstrating Jackson's belief that "Indians had to be shunted to one side or removed to make the land safe for white people to cultivate and settle," argues that removal was both inevitable and in the long-term best interest of the Indians, in that, remaining in the east, they might have been virtually liquidated.

7:170   Turner, Frederick Jackson. *History, Frontier, and Section: Three Essays.* Albuquerque: University of New Mexico Press, 1993. These are reprints of Turner's most noteworthy essays—"The Significance of History" (1891), "The Significance of the Frontier in American History" (1893), and "The Significance of Section in American History" (1925)—which remain important contributions to the study of American nationalism and expansionism. Edited by Martin Ridge.

THE FLORIDAS

7:171   Baker, Maury. "The Spanish War Scare of 1816." *Mid-America* 45 (April 1963): 67–78. U.S.-Spanish antagonism over Florida boundary, and the assault on an American ship, helped persuade Spain to sign the Transcontinental Treaty of 1819.

7:172   Bécker, Jerónimo. *Historia de las relaciones exteriores de la España durante el siglo XIX [History of the Foreign Relations of Spain during the*

Nineteenth Century]. 3 vols. Madrid: Estab. tip. de J. Ratés, 1924–1926. Bécker was archivist of the Spanish Foreign Office and based this history, considered a classic, on material from the Spanish archives.

7:173   Bisceglis, Louis R. "The Florida Treaty and the Gallatin-Vives Misunderstanding." *Florida Historical Quarterly* 48 (January 1970): 247–63. The author deals with the mission of General Dionisio Vives to the United States in 1820 to discuss the misunderstandings arising over the Florida treaty. Vives indicated to Albert Gallatin that Florida could be transferred immediately if the United States pledged a policy of neutrality toward the Spanish rebellion.

7:174   Bowman, Charles H., Jr. "Vicente Pazos and the Amelia Island Affair, 1817." *Florida Historical Quarterly* 53 (January 1975): 273–95. This essay chronicles the efforts of Pazos, an Argentine exile, to establish a "republic of Florida" on Amelia Island in 1817.

7:175   Brooks, Philip C. *Diplomacy and the Borderlands: The Adams-Onís Treaty of 1819.* Berkeley: University of California Press, 1939. Reprint 1970 (Octagon Books). This is a meticulously researched if at times hard-to-follow account of the negotiations leading to the Transcontinental (Adams-Onís) Treaty. Samuel Flagg Bemis is said to have relied extensively upon it in writing his biography of John Quincy Adams.

7:176   Fuentes Mares, José. *Génesis del expansionismo norteamericano [Genesis of American Expansionism].* 2d ed. Mexico, DF: El Colegio de México, 1984. This is an astute analysis of U.S. relations with Spain in the first quarter of the nineteenth century by a respected historian.

7:177   James, Marquis. *Andrew Jackson, the Border Captain.* James's narrative biography includes rich detail on the Florida raid of 1818 and Jackson's governorship (5:182). This is still worth reading, though superseded by Remini, *Andrew Jackson & His Indian Wars* (2001) (7:169).

7:178   Weeks, William Earl. *John Quincy Adams and American Global Empire.* See chapter 6 of this Guide (6:75).

7:179   _____. "John Quincy Adams's 'Great Gun' and the Rhetoric of American Empire." *Diplomatic History* 14 (Winter 1990): 25–42. This is a detailed analysis of the context and content of one of Adams's most noteworthy diplomatic communiqués.

TEXAS AND
THE SOUTHWEST

7:180   Adams, Ephraim D. *British Interests and Activities in Texas, 1838–1846.* Baltimore: Johns Hopkins Press, 1910. While entirely based on Foreign Office correspondence, Adams's account is still largely the accepted version of Anglo-Texan political relations, although others have added materials on British economic interests.

7:181   Argüello, Silvia, and Raúl Figueroa. *El Intento de México por Retener Texas [The Intention of Mexico to Retain Texas].* Mexico, DF: Fondo de Cultura Económica, 1982. This is a thematic treatment of U.S.-Mexican relations, the last two chapters of which cover the Mexican attempts to retain Texas. The first three chapters describe the U.S.-Mexican relationship and "ideological" differences from 1821 to 1845, including descriptions of the Mexican government and its denunciations of Manifest Destiny. The remaining four chapters detail the life and mission of the Mexican consul in New Orleans, don Francisco de Paula de Arrangoiz, through whom Mexican efforts in the United States were executed.

7:182   Ashford, Gerald. "Jacksonian Liberalism and Spanish Law in Early Texas." *Southwestern Historical Quarterly* 57 (July 1953): 1–37. Ashford provides the background for some of the unrest in Texas in 1835–1836.

7:183   Bancroft, Hubert H., Henry Lebbeus Oak, William Nemos, and J. J. Peatfield. *History of the North Mexican States and Texas.* 2 vols. San Francisco: A. L. Bancroft and Company, 1884–1889. Volume 2 has a detailed account of Texas-Mexican relations, the revolution of 1836, and events leading to Texas annexation, and is based on extensive use of American and Mexican archival sources. Later historians have revised some of its conclusions. Elaborate notes.

7:184   Barker, Eugene C. "The Annexation of Texas." *Southwestern Historical Quarterly* 50 (July 1946): 49–74. This is a brief outline and overview of Texas's path to annexation, 1836 to 1844. Originally written for publication in Texas newspapers to commemorate the centennial of Texas statehood, it is a useful introduction to the issues of the day, including British opposition to U.S. aggrandizement.

7:185   _____. "Land Speculation as a Cause of the Texas Revolution." *Texas Historical Quarterly* 10 (July 1906): 76–95. Barker minimizes the importance of land speculation as a reason for American enlistment in the Texas army but admits its significance as a contributing cause of settlement and friction with Mexico (1821–1836).

7:186   _____. "President Jackson and the Texas Revolution." *American Historical Review* 12 (July 1907): 788–809. Barker denies that Jackson (1829–1836) intrigued with Houston or anyone else to bring on the revolution.

7:187   Binkley, William C. *The Texas Revolution.* Baton Rouge: University of Louisiana Press, 1952. An interpretive essay, this places immediate responsibility for the revolution (1835–1836) on the Mexican government while recognizing the underlying divergence between Texas and Mexico.

7:188   Garrison, George P. "The First Stage of the Movement for the Annexation of Texas." *American Historical Review* 10 (October 1904): 72–96. Many details have been added, but this early account, based largely on U.S. and Texan diplomatic sources, is still a useful summary of the efforts.

7:189   Hartnett, Stephen. "Senator Robert Walker's 1844 Letter on Texas Annexation: The Rhetorical 'Logic' of Imperialism." *American Studies* 38 (Spring 1997): 27–54. This is a cultural studies piece that employs textual analysis to help determine the significance of Walker's famous argument for expansion. Hartnett argues that the "Letter" is an example "of a rapidly modernizing nation struggling to comprehend and rationalize its ascendancy as one of the world's dominant imperialist powers."

7:190   Howren, Alleine. "Causes and Origin of the Decree of April 6, 1830." *Southwestern Histori-* *cal Quarterly* 16 (April 1913): 378–422. The 1830 decree was a Mexican effort to avert the American threat to Texas by forbidding immigration and constructing a chain of forts.

7:191   Hutchinson, C. Alan. "Mexican Federalists in New Orleans and the Texas Revolution." *Louisiana Historical Quarterly* 39 (January 1956): 1–47. Hutchinson analyzes relations between a group of Mexican Federalist (i.e., anti–Santa Anna) exiles in New Orleans and Texans discontented with Mexican rule. The Federalists were interested only in opposing the centralist organization of Mexico, while Texans moved toward outright independence.

7:192   Lowrie, Samuel H. *Culture Conflict in Texas, 1821–1835.* New York: Columbia University Press, 1932. Lowrie attributes the Texas revolution primarily to cultural differences between Americans and Mexicans, arising from misunderstandings and centering on questions about religion, slavery, and politics, the last of which finally precipitated the revolution. Bibliography.

7:193   McClendon, R. Earl. "Daniel Webster and Mexican Relations: The Santa Fe Prisoners." *Southwestern Historical Quarterly* 36 (April 1933): 288–311. Webster worked with eventual success for the release of Texans (1842–1843) captured during an ill-advised attack on Santa Fe and kept in Perote and other central Mexican prisons.

7:194   McElhannon, Joseph Carl. "Imperial Mexico and Texas, 1821–1823." *Southwestern Historical Quarterly* 53 (October 1949): 117–50. The author discusses the political relations between Agustín de Iturbide (emperor of Mexico) and the early settlements of Texas.

7:195   Middleton, Annie. "Donelson's Mission to Texas in Behalf of Annexation." *Southwestern Historical Quarterly* 24 (April 1921): 247–91. Donelson, Polk's representative (and Andrew Jackson's nephew), joined several private propagandists and played a more vital role in annexation than Commodore Robert F. Stockton, whom he restrained. This article largely contradicts the conspiracy thesis developed by Stenberg ("The Texas Schemes of Jackson and Houston" [1934] and other cited works) and Price (*Origins of the War with Mexico:*

The Polk-Stockton Intrigue [1967] [7:321]) regarding the annexation.

7:196   Morrison, Michael A. "Martin Van Buren, the Democracy, and the Partisan Politics of Texas Annexation." *Journal of Southern History* 61 (November 1995): 695–724. Morrison argues that Van Buren's chances for the 1844 Democratic nomination for president were seriously weakened by his opposition to Texas annexation. The Democrats generally saw Texas as a unifying issue rather than a matter of slavery or antislavery.

7:197   _____. "Westward the Curse of Empire: Texas Annexation and the American Whig Party." *Journal of the Early Republic* 10 (Summer 1990): 221–49. Morrison concludes that the Democrats' ability to equate Texas annexation with the expansion of individual freedom rather than the extension of slavery was crucial to their victory in 1844.

7:198   Park, Joseph F. "The Apaches in Mexican-American Relations, 1843–1861: A Footnote to the Gadsden Treaty." *Arizona and the West* 3 (Summer 1961): 129–46. Park deals largely with actions on the American side of the border and uses mostly published sources.

7:199   Renda, Lex. "Retrospective Voting and the Presidential Election of 1844: The Texas Issue Revisited." *Presidential Studies Quarterly* 24 (Fall 1994): 837–54. Generalizing his findings for Connecticut to other northern states, Renda argues that Clay's position on Texas annexation helped rather than hurt him in the north.

7:200   Roeckell, Leila M. "Bonds over Bondage: British Opposition to the Annexation of Texas." The author claims that British policy in Mexico was influenced chiefly by its commercial interests in the country, not the fear of U.S. expansionism in the region (6:194).

7:201   Schwartz, Rosalie. *Across the Rio to Freedom: U.S. Negroes in Mexico.* El Paso: Texas Western Press, University of Texas at El Paso, 1975. This pamphlet effectively traces the fugitive slave problem that complicated U.S.-Mexican relations (1820–1860).

7:202   Smith, Justin H. *The Annexation of Texas.* New York: Barnes and Noble, 1941. Reprint 1971 (AMS Press). This is a straightforward account, based on extensive research, which emphasizes the negotiation of the annexation treaty and its discussion by the American public and Congress. Though superseded in some areas, this is still a major work. Bibliography.

7:203   Spell, Lota M. "Gorostiza and Texas." *Hispanic American Historical Review* 37 (November 1957): 425–62. Manuel de Gorostiza, Mexican minister to Washington during part of the Texan annexation movement, confronted the State Department impotently on the subject, foreshadowing the later major crisis of 1845–1846.

7:204   Stenberg, Richard R. "Jackson, Anthony Butler, and Texas." *Southwestern Social Science Quarterly* 13 (December 1932): 264–86. Here Stenberg extends his plot thesis concerning U.S.-Mexican relations, accusing Jackson of intending from the beginning of his administration to acquire Texas and of using Butler as his agent; the accusations against Butler are the more convincing of the two.

7:205   _____. "The Texas Schemes of Jackson and Houston, 1829–1836." *Southwestern Social Science Quarterly* 15 (December 1934): 229–50. Stenberg's sequel to his "Jackson, Anthony Butler, and Texas" (1932) (7:204) develops the plot between Jackson and Houston (1829–1837) to split Texas from Mexico.

CALIFORNIA

7:206   Bancroft, Hubert H. *History of California.* 7 vols. San Francisco: The History Company, 1884–1890. Volumes 3 to 5 have a detailed account of events of 1825 to 1848, leading to American occupation of California; scholars have subsequently revised some of its conclusions. Extensive use of American and Mexican archival sources, as identified in copious footnotes, makes this work still valuable.

7:207   Brooke, George M., Jr. "The Vest Pocket War of Commodore Jones." *Pacific Historical Review* 31 (August 1962): 217–33. This is a carefully documented account of Commodore Thomas Ap Catesby Jones's occupation of California in 1842.

7:208   Chamberlin, Eugene Keith. "Baja California after Walker: The Zerman Enterprise." *Hispanic American Historical Review* 34 (May 1954): 175–89. Chamberlin concludes that Juan Napoleón Zerman, active in Baja California in the 1850s and 1860s, was not a filibuster but was viewed as such because of Walker's earlier invasion.

7:209   Cleland, Robert Glass. "The Early Sentiment for the Annexation of California: An Account of the Growth of American Interest in California, 1835–1846." *Southwestern Historical Quarterly* 18 (January, July 1914): 1–40, 231–60. In this two-part article, Cleland describes the events and the publications in the eastern United States, as well as in California itself, that supported annexation.

7:210   Coughlin, Magdalen, C.S.J. "California Ports: A Key to Diplomacy for the West Coast, 1820–1845." *Journal of the West* 5 (April 1966): 153–72. Coughlin basically agrees with Graebner, *Empire on the Pacific: A Study in American Continental Expansion* (1955) (7:166), in emphasizing commercial motivations for the desire to annex California.

7:211   Fox, John. *Macnamara's Irish Colony and the United States Taking of California in 1846.* Jefferson, NC: McFarland, 2000. This is a lively and largely sympathetic account of a little-known effort to counter U.S. interests in Mexican California. Fox recounts the fascinating story of a priest's efforts to save California for Mexico and Catholicism.

7:212   Hague, Harlan, and David J. Langum. *Thomas O. Larkin: A Life of Patriotism and Profit in Old California.* Norman: University of Oklahoma Press, 1990. The authors present a detailed and nuanced view of Larkin as both Old California merchant and covert Bear Flag revolutionist. He was the U.S. consul (and secret agent) during the "Americanizing" years before the Mexican War began.

7:213   Harlow, Neal. *California Conquered: The Annexation of a Mexican Province, 1846–1850.* Berkeley: University of California Press, 1989. Harlow deftly examines the cultural, economic, and political aspects of the U.S. conquest and occupation of California. For the foreseeable future, this will be the definitive treatment of the end of the Mexican era in California.

7:214   Hawgood, John, ed. *First and Last Consul: Thomas Oliver Larkin and the Americanization of California: A Selection of Letters.* San Marino, CA: Huntington Library, 1962. Larkin was the U.S. consul at Monterey, California, during the Mexican period. This volume is important for the background and events that led to the Bear Flag revolt. Larkin later eased the shift from Mexican to American control of California.

7:215   _____. "The Pattern of Yankee Infiltration in Mexican Alta California, 1821–1846." *Pacific Historical Review* 27 (February 1958): 27–37. This account discusses the role of Thomas O. Larkin, U.S. consul at Monterey, California, in the American penetration of California and the events leading to the Bear Flag revolt.

7:216   Holliday, J. S. *The World Rushed In: The California Gold Rush Experience.* New York: Simon and Schuster, 1981. Holliday provides both an intimate portrait of the gold miners, especially William Swain (upon whose journals this work is based), as well as a general history of the California gold rush. The most recent treatment is H. W. Brands, *The Age of Gold: The California Gold Rush and the New American Dream* (New York: Doubleday, 2002).

7:217   Hussey, John Adam. "The Origin of the Gillespie Mission." *California Historical Society Quarterly* 19 (March 1940): 43–58. Hussey traces the inception of the secret mission (1845–1846) to Larkin and Frémont from Polk's reception of Larkin's alarmist dispatch to Gillespie's departure.

7:218   Jones, Oakah L., Jr. "The Pacific Squadron and the Conquest of California, 1846–1847." *Journal of the West* 5 (April 1966): 187–202. Jones traces the movements of Sloat's squadron during the crisis leading up to the occupation of California and the Bear Flag revolution and reviews accounts by other writers concerning the myth of the British intentions to occupy California.

7:219   Kearney, Thomas. "The Mexican War and the Conquest of California—Stockton or Kearny

Conqueror and First Governor?" *California Historical Society Quarterly* 8 (September 1929): 251–61. This study tries to settle the long-standing debate about the credit for establishing American rule firmly in California after Sloat's original proclamation of occupation (1846–1847); the author favors Kearny.

7:220   Kelsey, Rayner Wickersham. "The United States Consulate in California." *Academy of Pacific Coast History Publications* 1, no. 5 (1910): 161–267. This extended essay concentrates on activities of Thomas O. Larkin, 1840 to 1847.

7:221   Knapp, Frank A., Jr. "The Mexican Fear of Manifest Destiny in California." In *Essays in Mexican History,* ed. Thomas E. Cotner and Carlos Eduardo Castañeda, 192–208. Austin: University of Texas Institute of Latin American Studies, 1958. Reprint 1972 (Greenwood Press). Knapp analyzes the rising concern for California (1838–1847) in the Mexican press and Congress, and Mexican inability to do anything effective to resist the threat.

7:222   Marti, Werner Herman. *Messenger of Destiny: The California Adventures, 1846–1847, of Archibald Gillespie, U.S. Marine Corps.* San Francisco: J. Howell Books, 1960. This is a detailed account of Gillespie's secret mission to John C. Frémont, 1846, and the ensuing Bear Flag revolution in California; Marti defends Frémont.

7:223   Moyano Pahissa, Angela. *La resistencia de las Californias a la invasión norteamericana (1846–1848) [The Resistance of the Californias to the North American Invasion].* Mexico, DF: Consejo Nacional para la Cultura y las Artes, 1992. This work details both resistance to and collaboration with the U.S. forces in California. Moyano Pahissa sheds light on the tenuous connection between Californian Mexicans and the national government.

7:224   Phillips, George Harwood. *Indians and Intruders in Central California, 1769–1849.* Norman: University of Oklahoma Press, 1993. Phillips, a leader in the field, recounts the story of the European invasion of California from the Native American point of view. He sees them as active participants in their lives rather than mere victims.

7:225   Stenberg, Richard R. "Polk and Fremont,

1845–1846." *Pacific Historical Review* 7 (September 1938): 211–27. Stenberg argues that Polk's secret instructions to Frémont authorized him to seize California.

7:226   Tays, George. "Fremont Had No Secret Instructions." *Pacific Historical Review* 9 (June 1940): 157–72. In essence, this is a reply to Stenberg, "Polk and Fremont, 1845–1846" (1938) (7:225). Although it is generally considered impossible to prove a negative proposition, Tays presents strong evidence.

7:227   Terrazas y Basante, María Marcela. *En busca de una nueva frontera: Baja California en los proyectos expansionistas norteamericanos, 1846–1853 [In Search of a New Frontier: Baja California and North American Expansionist Projects, 1846–1853].* Mexico, DF: Universidad Nacional Autónoma de México, 1995. Terrazas y Basante analyzes the role of Baja California in U.S.-Mexican relations during the war and its aftermath, focusing on the ideology of American expansionism, Mexican political instability, and the disruptive effect of American filibustering expeditions. Noting that many Mexicans openly advocated the annexation of Baja California to the United States, she finds that they were mostly wealthy Mexicans, while the church, Spanish-Mexicans, and the lower strata opposed U.S. rule.

7:228   Walker, Dale L. *Bear Flag Rising: The Conquest of California, 1846.* New York: Forge, 1999. This well-documented history of the U.S. seizure of California builds its narrative on a series of biographical capsules, including the U.S. military leaders in California: Commodores Robert Field Stockton, General Watts Kearny, and, of course, John Charles Frémont.

7:229   Wiltsee, Ernest A. *The Truth about Frémont: An Inquiry.* San Francisco: J. H. Nash, 1936. This pamphlet-size account argues that Frémont's plan to revolutionize California (1845–1847) was part of a plot developed by Polk.

WESTERN FRONTIER

7:230   Antelyes, Peter. *Tales of Adventurous Enterprise: Washington Irving and the Poetics of Western*

Expansion. New York: Columbia University Press, 1990. Antelyes compares the theme of adventure in Irving's western writings to economic expansion and entrepreneurialism in the west, writing that, while Irving promoted expansion, he did so with a view to enlisting "self-interest in the communal interest of American expansion" as opposed to simple greed. The works under consideration are *A Tour on the Prairies* (1835), *Astoria: or, Anecdotes of an Enterprise beyond the Rocky Mountains* (1835), and *The Adventures of Captain Bonneville U.S.A., in the Rocky Mountains and the Far West* (1837).

7:231   Billington, Ray Allen. *The Far Western Frontier, 1830–1860.* New York: Harper, 1956. Reprint 1995 (University of New Mexico Press). This is Billington's classic synthesis of westward expansion, which draws heavily on primary materials. The first part of the book deals extensively with the Spanish borderlands and the fur trade, while the middle half of the book deals with expansionist themes, culminating with the Mexican War. Thereafter he synthesizes the literature on postwar expansion, especially the railroad boom. The sense of the book is captured in its closing sentence: "Man had begun his battle against nature with only his hands and his brawn to aid him; man was to continue that battle with such efficient tools that only thirty years later the continent had been conquered and all the Far West subjected to the elevating forces of civilization."

7:232   Billington, Ray Allen, and Martin Ridge. *Westward Expansion: A History of the American Frontier.* 6th ed. Albuquerque: University of New Mexico Press, 2001. This is a durable work of history that remains a significant part of the historiography of westward expansionism. First published in 1949 with the collaboration of James Blaine Hedges.

7:233   Binder, Wolfgang, ed. *Westward Expansion in America (1803–1860).* Erlangen: Verlag Palm and Enke Erlangen, 1987. This is an edited collection of the papers given at the first Franco-German Colloquium on Nineteenth-Century America, held at Erlangen, July 3–4, 1987. Those most closely related to the history of expansionism are Yves Carlet, "Emerson as Expansionist" (65–78); Jean-Pierre Martin, "Southern Expansionism Exposed: A British Analysis" (181–92); Simone Vauthier, "*Mexico Versus*

Texas: Remarks on the First Texian Novel" (213–36); and Binder, "Romances of the War with Mexico: Variations of and Responses to Expansionist Discourse" (237–66).

7:234   Cayton, Andrew R. L., and Fredrika J. Teute, eds. *Contact Points: American Frontiers from the Mohawk Valley to the Mississippi, 1750–1830.* Chapel Hill: University of North Carolina Press, 1998. This is an uneven collection of essays on the multiplicity of interpretive frontiers that historians have discovered since abandoning Frederick Jackson Turner's monolithic interpretation. The editors and contributors hold that race relations are key to understanding the west. Among the essays relevant for this chapter are Lucy Eldersveld Murphy, "To Live among Us: Accommodation, Gender, and Conflict in the Western Great Lakes Region, 1760–1832," and John Mack Faragher, "'More Motley than Mackinaw': From Ethnic Mixing to Ethnic Cleansing on the Frontier of the Lower Missouri, 1783–1833."

7:235   Georgi-Findlay, Brigitte. *The Frontiers of Women's Writing: Women's Narratives and the Rhetoric of Westward Expansion.* Tucson: University of Arizona Press, 1996. Georgi-Findlay uses a broad range of documents to challenge assumptions about the masculine myth of empire-building in the west. Her sources include diaries of the overland trails, letters and journals of military wives, professional travel writing, and missionary correspondence. She suggests that feminist historians have, in their focus on gender issues, "tended to overlook the racial politics that prompted the pastoral myth, in which the white self was defined against racial others—a quest in which white women were enlisted as much as . . . white men."

7:236   Goetzmann, William H. *New Lands, New Men: America and the Second Great Age of Discovery.* New York: Viking, 1986. Reprint 1995 (Texas State Historical Association). Goetzmann, a Pulitzer Prize–winning historian who presents a compelling narrative of the worldwide explosion of exploration following the Enlightenment and scientific revolution, includes an analysis of U.S. participation in the advance of knowledge through the Lewis and Clark Expedition and later exploration of the Pacific and Antarctica.

7:237   Gordon-McCutchan, R. C., ed. *Kit Carson: Indian Fighter or Indian Killer?* Boulder: University Press of Colorado, 1996. This collection of essays seeks, for the most part, to rehabilitate the tainted reputation of one of America's erstwhile frontier heroes: Darlis A. Miller, "Kit Carson and Dime Novels: The Making of a Legend"; Gordon-McCutchan, "'Rope Thrower' and the Navajo"; Lawrence C. Kelly, "The Historiography of the Navajo Roundup"; Marc S. Simmons, "Kit and the Indians"; and Robert M. Utley, "An Indian before Breakfast: Kit Carson Then and Now."

7:238   Limerick, Patricia Nelson. *Something in the Soil: Legacies and Reckonings in the New West.* New York: W. W. Norton, 2000. This is a collection of essays from the leading multiculturalist historian of the American west. She largely focuses on interethnic relations and conflict and includes a historiographical critique of textbooks.

7:239   Rhody, Kurt, and Rob Reilly. *Rendezvous: Reliving the Fur Trade Era, 1825 to 1840.* Mariposa, CA: Sierra Press, 1996. This is an illustrated history of the waning days of the North American fur trade. Text and photographs by Rhody; edited by Rob Reilly.

7:240   Truettner, William H., ed. *The West as America: Reinterpreting Images of the Frontier, 1820–1920.* Washington, DC: Published for the National Museum of American Art by the Smithsonian Institution Press, 1991. This collection presents a vigorous and controversial analysis of both the rhetoric and reality of westward expansionism. In addition to a foreword by Elizabeth Broun, contents include Howard R. Lamar, "An Overview of Westward Expansion" (1–26); Truettner, "Ideology and Image: Justifying Westward Expansion" (27–54) and "Prelude to Expansion: Repainting the Past" (55–96); Patricia Hills, "Picturing Progress in the Era of Westward Expansion" (97–148); Julie Schimmel "Inventing 'the Indian'" (149–90); Elizabeth Johns, "Settlement and Development: Claiming the West" (191–236); Nancy K. Anderson, "'The Kiss of Enterprise': The Western Landscape as Symbol and Resource" (237–84); Alex Nemerov, "Doing the 'Old America': The Image of the American West, 1880–1920" (285–344); and Joni Louise Kinsey, "Artist Biographies" (345–72).

7:241   Turner, Frederick Jackson. *The Frontier in American History.* New York: H. Holt and Company, 1920. Reprint 1986 (University of Arizona Press). This collection of Turner's essays includes both his seminal 1893 essay, "The Significance of the Frontier in American History," his later refinements on the subject, and the beginning of his growing interest in the role of sections in influencing the course of American history.

7:242   Wall, James T. *The Boundless Frontier: America from Christopher Columbus to Abraham Lincoln.* Lanham, MD: University Press of America, 1999. This is a broad overview of the record of western expansionism from Columbus to Lincoln.

7:243   White, Richard. *"It's Your Misfortune and None of My Own": A History of the American West.* Norman: University of Oklahoma Press, 1991. An acerbic view of U.S. expansionism in North America, this is a good representation of the multiculturalist new western history, which long ago abandoned anything like discussion of Turnerian frontiers. The west, White insists, should be defined more by people and history than geography and environment. His emphasis is on the central role of the federal government in the formation and maintenance of the west and the states' rights–inclined westerners' ambivalence about the federal role.

Native American Relations

7:244   Abel, Annie Heloise, ed. *Chardon's Journal at Fort Clark, 1834–1839: Descriptive of Life on the Upper Missouri; of a Fur Trader's Experiences among the Mandans, Gros Ventres and Their Neighbors; of the Ravages of the Small-Pox Epidemic of 1837.* Pierre, SD: Dept. of History, State of South Dakota, 1932. Reprint 1997 (University of Nebraska Press). This is the journal that Chardon, a Philadelphian, kept during his command of Fort Clark, a main post of the American Fur Company on the upper Missouri River. His journal presents his observances of the daily life of the Mandan Indians as well as many interesting characters in the fur trade such as Charbonneau and James Dickson. Abel's introduction sets the journal in its historical context.

7:245   Abert, J. W., and H. Bailey Carroll. *Expedition to the Southwest: An 1845 Reconnaissance of Colorado, New Mexico, Texas, and Oklahoma.* Lincoln: University of Nebraska Press, 1999. Expanded to include a bibliography and index, this is the report of Lieutenant Abert of his reconnaissance on the upper Arkansas River, given to the president in 1846, when it was originally published. Introduction by John Miller Morris.

7:246   Calloway, Colin G., ed. *Our Hearts Fell to the Ground: Plains Indian Views of How the West Was Lost.* Boston: Bedford Books of St. Martin's Press, 1996. This is a moving collection of original documents on the theme of Indian dispossession.

7:247   Jablow, Joseph. *The Cheyenne in Plains Indian Trade Relations, 1795–1840.* New York: J. J. Augustin, 1951. Reprint 1994 (University of Nebraska Press). Analyzing the reaction of the Cheyennes to the evolving commercial environment on the Great Plains in the first half of the nineteenth century, Jablow traces their development transitions from horticulturists, to nomadic hunters, to shrewd traders and crucial middlemen in the expanding economic network connecting the various tribes with each other as well as the whites.

7:248   Peyer, Bernd C. *The Tutor'd Mind: Indian Missionary-Writers in Antebellum America.* Amherst: University of Massachusetts Press, 1997. The author examines a mix of biography, literature, history, missionary influences, and U.S. Indian policy, tracing the transitions in American Indian literature from salvationism and assimilationism through removal and modernity by analyzing the work of four main writers: Samson Occom, William Apess, Elias Boudinot, and George Copway.

7:249   Phillips, George Harwood. *Indians and Indian Agents: The Origins of the Reservation System in California, 1849–1852.* Norman: University of Oklahoma Press, 1997. This is a detailed and candid study of the early days of the reservation system.

7:250   Rogin, Michael Paul. *Fathers and Children: Andrew Jackson and the Subjugation of the American Indians.* New York: Alfred A. Knopf, 1975. Rogin combines a Marxian analysis with Freudian psychology to argue that Jackson persecuted the Indians (1813–1837) to prove his manliness and to provide new cotton lands for agricultural capitalists.

7:251   Scheckel, Susan. *The Insistence of the Indian: Race and Nationalism in Nineteenth-Century American Culture.* Princeton: Princeton University Press, 1998. Scheckel, a professor of English, examines how white American ideas about Indians shaped the "American National Character." Focusing on the years of removal, Scheckel argues that "American attempts to define the meaning of the nation . . . became intertwined with efforts to define the status and rights of Indians." To this end, she analyzes contemporary texts (novels, legal opinions, etc.) for "interconnected projects of self-definition."

7:252   Unrau, William E. *White Man's Wicked Water: The Alcohol Trade and Prohibition in Indian Country, 1802–1892.* Lawrence: University Press of Kansas, 1996. While offering a devastating portrait of the role of alcohol in the winning of the west, Unrau deprecates the notion that whites deliberately aimed at ruining the Indians with alcohol sales.

7:253   Utley, Robert M. *Frontiersmen in Blue: The United States Army and the Indian, 1848–1865.* New York: Macmillan, 1967. This work is useful not only for its discussions of military organization and enduring patterns of administration, but also for its detailing of the influence of the problem of defending the west on strategic thought. Extensive bibliography.

7:254   Walker, Cheryl. *Indian Nation: Native American Literature and Nineteenth-Century Nationalisms.* Durham, NC: Duke University Press, 1997. Walker examines the texts of five Indian writers (William Apess, Black Hawk, Sarah Winnemucca, George Copway, and John Ridge). She labels their work as either transpositional or subjugated discourse, the former of which "emphasizes the essential parity of Indians with whites," while the latter accentuates "differences . . . of power, prestige, and purpose."

REMOVAL POLICY

7:255   Debo, Angie. *And Still the Waters Run: The Betrayal of the Five Civilized Tribes.* Princeton: Princeton University Press, 1940. This classic work on the white man's lawless seizure of Indian lands and resources has been reissued by the original publisher as recently as 1991.

7:256   Foreman, Grant. *Indian Removal: The Emigration of the Five Civilized Tribes of Indians.* New ed. Norman: University of Oklahoma Press, 1957. Written in five books, one for each tribe, the author described this work as "a picture of that interesting and tragic enterprise as revealed by an uncolored day-by-day recital of events." Foreman used painstaking and extensive primary research to present a vastly detailed account of the removal experiences of these tribes that is completely devoid of analysis or interpretation, as the author intended it. Originally published in 1953, this remains a significant work.

BY TRIBE AND CONFLICT

Native America

7:257   Debo, Angie. *A History of the Indians of the United States.* Norman: University of Oklahoma Press, 1970. This is a major, and sympathetic, account of the "Five Civilized Tribes" and their relations with the United States. See also Washburn, *Handbook of North American Indians. Vol. 4: History of Indian-White Relations* (1988) (3:56).

Black Hawk

7:258   Eby, Cecil. *"That Disgraceful Affair," the Black Hawk War.* New York: Norton, 1973. In this analysis of the tensions leading up to the four-month war, Eby argues that the real perpetrators were not the professional soldiers or Indians but the "people": squatters, businessmen, frontiersmen, and politicians. The "mass hysteria" and "racial hatred" that spread among the white population of the Old Northwest after the Sauk and Fox Indians returned to the Iowa territory under Chief Black Hawk in 1832, according to Eby, gave rise to a series of aggressions that left the Native Americans no alternative but to make war.

7:259   Nichols, Roger L. *Black Hawk and the Warrior's Path.* Arlington Heights, IL: Harlan Davidson, 1992. Nichols's biography of the Sauk chief (1767–1838) focuses on communication problems as an impediment to peaceful U.S.-Indian relations. He argues that this was a major factor in the failure to establish mutually satisfactory treaty arrangements and contributed to the loss of Indian lives.

7:260   _____. *Black Hawk's Autobiography.* Ames, IA: Iowa State University Press, 1999. Originally published in 1834 (as *Life of Ma-ka-tai-me-she-kia-kiak or Black Hawk*), this brief autobiography (ninety-five pages of text) offers the vantage point of the Sauk chief, born in 1767, to the European and American expansion on the continent as well as attendant conflicts and negotiations. Nichols includes a chronology, maps of Illinois, Iowa, and Wisconsin where Black Hawk fought, and an extensive index.

7:261   Whitney, Ellen M., ed. *The Black Hawk War, 1831–1832.* 2 vols. in 4. Springfield, IL: Illinois State Historical Library, 1970. This is a collection of primary sources on the Black Hawk War, covering both the settlers' and Indians' sides of the story. The first volume includes a lengthy introduction by the anthropologist Anthony F. C. Wallace.

Cherokees

7:262   Anderson, William L., ed. *Cherokee Removal: Before and After.* Athens, GA: University of Georgia Press, 1991. The most infamous of the tribal removals as seen from political, demographic, social, and cultural perspectives by leaders in the field: Douglas C. Wilms, "Cherokee Land Use in Georgia before Removal" (1–28); Ronald N. Satz, "Rhetoric versus Reality: The Indian Policy of Andrew Jackson" (29–54); Theda Perdue, "The Conflict Within: Cherokees and Removal" (55–74); Russell Thornton, "The Demography of the Trail of Tears Period: A New Estimate of Cherokee Population Losses" (75–95); John R. Finger, "The Impact of Removal on the North Carolina Cherokees" (96–111); Rennard Strickland and William M. Strickland, "Beyond the

Trail of Tears: One Hundred Years of Cherokee Survival" (112–38); and Anderson, "Bibliographical Essay" (139–47).

7:263   Carter, Samuel. *Cherokee Sunset: A Nation Betrayed: A Narrative of Travail and Triumph, Persecution and Exile.* Garden City, NY: Doubleday, 1976. This is a well-written, succinct, popular narrative. Written entirely from secondary sources, it is most valuable as an introduction to the story of removal.

7:264   Clarke, Mary Whatley. *Chief Bowles and the Texas Cherokees.* Norman: University of Oklahoma Press, 1971. This biography of the Texas Cherokee, Chief Bowles, also known as Duwali, covers his efforts to negotiate territorial agreements with Mexico and eventually independent Texas, which ultimately failed. He died in the final battle between whites and Cherokees in Texas, the Battle of the Neches, fighting forced expulsion from the republic.

7:265   Ehle, John. *Trail of Tears: The Rise and Fall of the Cherokee Nation.* New York: Doubleday, 1988. This is a popular history of the removal of the Cherokees from Georgia that outlines the arguments and factions on both sides of the debate, in both white and Cherokee camps. Ehle focuses on the irony in removing the most Europeanized of all Native Americans.

7:266   Everett, Dianna. *The Texas Cherokees: A People between Two Fires, 1819–1840.* Norman: University of Oklahoma Press, 1990. Based on the author's dissertation, this work documents the failed diplomatic efforts of the Texas Cherokees, and policymaking within their own councils, as they sought an agreement with Mexico and then Texas to secure land. It is a well-researched and thoroughly documented work.

7:267   Gregory, Jack, and Rennard Strickland. *Sam Houston with the Cherokees, 1829–1833.* Austin: University of Texas Press, 1967. Reprint 1996 (University of Oklahoma Press). The authors argue that Houston's disappearance into western Cherokee country, 1829–1833, was not due to the traditional explanation of drunken melancholy. Rather, Houston was aware of political opportunities in Texas as well as recruitment possibilities among the Cherokees, which he pursued at this time.

7:268   McLoughlin, William G. *After the Trail of Tears: The Cherokees' Struggle for Sovereignty, 1839–1880.* Chapel Hill: University of North Carolina Press, 1993. McLoughlin writes that the Cherokees survived removal with their national identity intact, and were able to withstand factional conflict between mixed-bloods and full-bloods as well as sectional conflict during the Civil War. They were, however, unable to resist pressures of westward expansion, especially from the railroads, that ultimately opened their new homeland to settlement.

7:269   _____. *Cherokee Renascence in the New Republic.* This is a densely researched and effectively argued story of oppression and survival, taken up to the Trail of Tears and focusing on both internecine conflict and conflict with the federal government (5:440).

7:270   Perdue, Theda, ed. *Cherokee Editor: The Writings of Elias Boudinot.* Knoxville: University of Tennessee Press, 1983. Reprint 1996 (University of Georgia Press). Purdue's editing and in-depth annotations establish the context for these documents, which reveal the tensions Cherokees faced as the desire to remain in their southeast home conflicted with the "inevitability" of removal. The collection of Boudinot's writings includes personal correspondence, articles, editorials, and pamphlets that show the evolution of his opinion from opposition to acceptance of removal.

7:271   Phillips, Joyce B., and Paul Gary Phillips, eds. *The Brainerd Journal: A Mission to the Cherokees, 1817–1823.* Lincoln: University of Nebraska Press, 1998. This is the annotated transcription of a missionary journal documenting efforts to "civilize" the Cherokees.

Choctaw

7:272   Carson, James Taylor. *Searching for the Bright Path: The Mississippi Choctaws from Prehistory to Removal.* Lincoln: University of Nebraska Press, 1999. Carson examines the evolution of Choctaw culture from its Mississippian origins within the context of European and, eventually, American imperialism. He employs a Geertzian conception of culture as ideology in interpreting the Choctaws' response to American expansion.

7:273   Coleman, Michael C. *Presbyterian Missionary Attitudes toward American Indians, 1837–1893.* Jackson, MS: University Press of Mississippi, 1985. Coleman presents a scathing indictment of missionary ethnocentrism and "cultural intolerance." He uses the correspondence of the missionaries to show how they sought to substitute Calvinist individualism for tribal communalism, which he credits with the ultimate breakdown of tribal life among the groups he studied, the Choctaws in Oklahoma and the Nez Perce in Idaho. Other scholars suggest that a radically changed environment resulting from white settlement is a more important factor.

7:274   Cushman, H. B. *History of the Choctaw, Chickasaw, and Natchez Indians.* Norman: University of Oklahoma Press, 1999. In a work first published in 1899, Cushman presents a sympathetic history that is leavened with his personal observations. As the son of missionaries, Cushman witnessed the Choctaw removal from Mississippi, 1831–1833, and continued his association with the Choctaws and Chickasaws in Texas thereafter. Angie Debo's abridgment of the original (appearing first in 1962) removes several repetitions and adds a valuable foreword.

7:275   Debo, Angie. *The Rise and Fall of the Choctaw Republic.* 2d ed. Norman: University of Oklahoma Press, 1961. A detailed and candid narrative of the Choctaw struggle for survival through the tribe's forced removal from its ancestral lands. First published in 1934.

7:276   Kidwell, Clara Sue. *Choctaws and Missionaries in Mississippi, 1818–1918.* Norman: University of Oklahoma Press, 1995. Dealing primarily with the period 1818–1830, Kidwell demonstrates that the Choctaw's sincere efforts to adopt the ways of American civilization proved no barrier to their removal.

Comanches

7:277   Chalfant, William Y. *Without Quarter: The Wichita Expedition and the Fight on Crooked Creek.* Norman: University of Oklahoma Press, 1991. In this

story of an aggressive military campaign that ultimately destroyed the former lords of the southwest plains, Chalfant focuses on one phase of a larger effort to pacify the Comanches in southern Kansas, a surprise attack in 1859 on a Comanche village.

7:278   Fehrenbach, T. R. *Comanches: The Destruction of a People.* New York: Alfred A. Knopf, 1974. Reprint 1994 (Da Capo Press). Fehrenbach focuses on the ferocity of the Comanches as warriors, who ruled the Comancheria as a privileged sanctuary into which neither Spaniard nor Anglo ventured successfully. The military tide turned forever in 1840, but Fehrenbach argues that besides warfare, the Comanche power was eventually destroyed by the decimation of the buffalo herds, smallpox, and cholera.

Creeks

7:279   Debo, Angie. *The Road to Disappearance.* Norman: University of Oklahoma Press, 1941. This is the best source on the removal of the Creek Indians by one of the giants in the field. Later printings included the subtitle, *A History of the Creek Indians.*

7:280   Wright, J. Leitch, Jr. *Creeks & Seminoles: The Destruction and Regeneration of the Muscogulge People.* This is a basic work in the literature of Indian removal by one of the leaders in the field (5:451).

Latin America

7:281   Auchmuty, James Johnston. *The United States Government and Latin American Independence, 1810–1830.* London: P. S. King and Son, Ltd., 1937. The author argues that the United States failed to make friends among the republics. It is based on material in Manning, *Diplomatic Correspondence of the United States Concerning the Independence of the Latin-American Nations* (1925) (7:13), but contains errors of fact.

7:282   Bernstein, Harry. *Making an Inter-American Mind.* Gainesville: University of Florida Press, 1961.

A sequel (1812–1900) to the author's *Origins of Inter-American Interest, 1700–1812* (1945) (5:526), this volume deals with the interplay among scientists, intellectuals, and scholars in the United States and their colleagues in Latin America and Iberia. Bibliography.

7:283 Clay, Henry. *Spanish America.* London: Wilson, 1829. This brief account focuses on Poinsett's mission to Mexico and relations generally with Latin America (1823–1828).

7:284 Griffin, Charles C. *The United States and the Disruption of the Spanish Empire, 1810–1822: A Study of the Relations of the United States with Spain and the Rebel Spanish Colonies.* Griffin argues that impetus for recognition of the republics derived mostly from the prospect of commercial gain. See chapter 5 of this Guide (5:537).

7:285 Harrison, John P. "Science and Politics: Origins and Objectives of Mid-Nineteenth Century Government Expeditions to Latin America." *Hispanic American Historical Review* 35 (May 1955): 175–202. Harrison discusses the U.S. Exploring Expedition (1838–1842); the Naval Astronomical Expedition to the Southern Hemisphere (1849–1852); the Amazon Exploration (1851–1852); and the Expedition to Rio de la Plata (1853–1856). These expeditions, he argues, were inspired as much by Manifest Destiny as by science.

7:286 Hoskins, H. L. "The Hispanic American Policy of Henry Clay, 1816–1828." *Hispanic American Historical Review* 7 (November 1927): 460–78. According to Hoskins, Clay's interest in, and promotion of, hemispheric understanding derived naturally from his "western" ideals.

7:287 Kaufmann, William W. *British Policy and the Independence of Latin America, 1804–1828.* In a solid, traditional diplomatic history, Kaufmann assesses British actions and motives in the Latin American struggle for independence. Bibliography (5:538).

7:288 Langley, Lester D. "The Jacksonians and the Origins of Inter-American Distrust." *Inter-American Economic Affairs* 30 (Winter 1976): 3–21. Langley deals with the Jacksonian push for commercial treaties and economic concessions from Latin American republics. In negotiating with the republics, Jacksonian diplomats created considerable ill will.

7:289 Lockey, Joseph Byrne. *Pan-Americanism: Its Beginnings.* This is a thorough study, based on printed sources, which surveys the U.S. reaction to the independence movements in Latin America (1810–1860). Extensive bibliography (5:540).

7:290 Lynch, John. *The Spanish-American Revolutions, 1808–1826.* See chapter 5 of this Guide (5:541).

7:291 Madariaga, Salvador de. *The Fall of the Spanish American Empire.* New rev. ed. New York: Collier Books, 1963. This is an intellectual and psychological portrait of an empire in decline (1776–1824) by a noted Spanish historian. Bibliography. First published in 1948.

7:292 Rippy, J. Fred. *Rivalry of the United States and Great Britain over Latin America, 1808–1830.* Rippy's focus is on economic and political issues in assessing antagonism of the United States and Britain over Spanish Florida, Texas, Cuba, and commercial rivalry in South America. He used archives in Britain and the United States (5:542).

7:293 Robertson, William Spence. "The First Legations of the United States in Latin America." *Mississippi Valley Historical Review* 2 (September 1915): 183–212. From 1822 to 1827, the United States accredited diplomatic missions to six Latin American governments. Robertson argues that the main efforts of these missions were commercial, with little emphasis on political connection; yet he believes such efforts laid the basis for Pan-Americanism.

7:294 _____. "The Recognition of the Hispanic American Nations by the United States." *Hispanic American Historical Review* 1 (August 1918): 239–69. A detailed study, this argues that recognition occurred (1821–1826) because of congressional pressure and presidential expedience.

Mexico

MEXICAN-U.S. PREWAR RELATIONS, 1821–1846

7:295   Alessio Robles, Vito. *Coahuila y Texas, desde la consumación de la independencia hasta el tratado de paz de Guadalupe Hidalgo [Coahuila and Texas, from the Completion of Independence to the Peace Treaty of Guadalupe Hidalgo].* 2 vols. Mexico, DF: n.p., 1945–1946. Reprint 1979 (Editorial Porréua). Thoroughly researched in archival and secondary sources of both Mexico and the United States, this account concentrates on the diplomatic and military aspects of border rivalries (1821–1848). Extensive bibliography.

7:296   Blaisdell, Lowell L. "The Santangelo Case: A Claim Preceding the Mexican War." *Journal of the West* 11 (April 1972): 248–59. This is a well-written and fascinating case study of a claims case that complicated U.S.-Mexican relations in the decade before the Mexican War.

7:297   Bosch García, Carlos. *Historia de las relaciones entre Mexico y los Estados Unidos, 1819–1848 [History of Relations between Mexico and the United States, 1819–1848].* Mexico, DF: Escuela Nacional de Ciencias Politicas y Sociales, 1961. Useful primarily for the Mexican viewpoint of diplomatic problems, this account is based largely on American archival sources, with some use of Mexican documents and secondary works. His bibliography includes interesting comments on principal secondary works.

7:298   _____. *Problemas diplomáticas del México independiente [Diplomatic Problems of Independent Mexico].* Mexico, DF: El Colegio de México, 1947. This account deals with foreign recognition of independent Mexico and related problems of the 1820s but provides little on the Texas question. The emphasis is heavily political and diplomatic, based on Mexican archival documents and, for the United States, Manning's *Diplomatic Correspondence of the United States Concerning the Independence of the Latin-American Nations* (1925) (7:13)

and *The Diplomatic Correspondence of the United States: Inter-American Affairs, 1831–1860* (1932–1939) (7:14). Bibliography.

7:299   Brack, Gene M. *Mexico Views Manifest Destiny, 1821–1846: An Essay on the Origins of the Mexican War.* Albuquerque: University of New Mexico Press, 1975. Brack provides a useful account of rising Mexican suspicions of the United States. He suggests that few Mexicans desired war and especially refutes Justin Smith on this point. The most important sources used are Mexican newspapers and pamphlets. Extensive bibliography.

7:300   Engelson, Lester D. "Proposals for Colonization of California by England in Connection with the Mexican Debt to British Bondholders, 1837– 1846." *California Historical Society Quarterly* 18 (June 1939): 136–48. Whereas John Quincy Adams established that England never seriously planned intervention, this article details the proposals made by private parties to the British Foreign Office.

7:301   Fuentes Mares, José. *Poinsett, historia de una gran intriga [Poinsett, History of a Great Intrigue].* 5th ed. Mexico, DF: Editorial Jus, 1975. This account uses the Poinsett Papers and the published State Department correspondence to develop the Mexican case against Poinsett as the spearhead of American imperialism (1821–1829).

7:302   Graebner, Norman A. "United States Gulf Commerce with Mexico, 1822–1848." *Inter-American Economic Affairs* 5 (Summer 1951): 36–51. Graebner provides a good account of early economic ties based on published original and secondary sources.

7:303   MacCorkle, Stuart Alexander. *American Policy of Recognition towards Mexico.* Baltimore: Johns Hopkins Press, 1933. This comprehensive study remains an important part of the historiography of U.S.-Mexican relations in the 1820s.

7:304   Manning, William R. *Early Diplomatic Relations between the United States and Mexico.* Baltimore: Johns Hopkins Press, 1916. This account extends to the end of Poinsett's mission (1821–1829) and provides a straightforward account of diplomacy based on State Department archives. Bibliography.

7:305 Rives, George Lockhart. *The United States and Mexico, 1821–1848: History of the Relations between the Two Countries from the Independence of Mexico to the Close of the War with the United States.* 2 vols. New York: C. Scribner's Sons, 1913. Rives's work is based on published sources and some State Department manuscripts. More conventional and less colorful than Justin Smith's volumes, it is still both readable and reliable, although modem research has added details and new interpretations. Extensive notes. See also Schmitt, *Mexico and the United States, 1821–1973: Conflict and Coexistence* (1974) (2:385).

7:306 Smith, Ralph A. "Indians in American-Mexican Relations before the War of 1846." *Hispanic American Historical Review* 43 (February 1963): 34–64. Smith describes how Indian raids multiplied Mexico's problems. Developments on both sides of the Rio Grande encouraged the Apache, Navajos, Utes, Comanche, and Kiowas in making raids. Bibliographical notes.

7:307 Warren, Harris Gaylord. *The Sword Was Their Passport: A History of American Filibustering in the Mexican Revolution.* This is the first comprehensive account of the filibustering campaigns against Spanish power in Texas. Warren depicts these early filibusters as a diverse group that included Mexican revolutionaries, French pirates, and land-hungry Anglos, concluding that the most important contribution the United States made to revolutionary Mexico was "its failure to enforce neutrality" (5:510).

7:308 Weber, Ralph E. "Joel R. Poinsett's Secret Mexican Dispatch Twenty." *South Carolina Historical Magazine* 75 (April 1974): 67–76. Weber deals with Poinsett's suspicions of a threatened European invasion against Mexican independence and particularly of French designs.

MEXICAN-AMERICAN WAR AND AFTERMATH

Overviews

7:309 Bauer, K. Jack. *The Mexican War, 1846–1848.* New York: Macmillan, 1974. Reprint 1993 (University of Nebraska Press). A leader in the field writes one of the standard modern accounts of the Mexican War. Introduction to the reprint edition by Robert W. Johannsen.

7:310 Christensen, Carol, and Thomas Christensen. *The U.S.-Mexican War.* San Francisco: Bay Books, 1998. This is the companion text to the Public Television series, "The U.S.-Mexican War, 1846–1848."

7:311 Dodd, William E. "The West and the War with Mexico." *Journal of the Illinois State Historical Society* 5 (July 1912): 159–72. Dodd finds that an alliance of south and west was responsible for the prosecution of the war. He blames Trist for his failure to take all of Mexico.

7:312 Engstrand, Iris H. W., Richard Griswold del Castillo, and Elena Poniatowska. *Culture y Cultura: Consequences of the U.S.-Mexican War, 1846–1848.* Los Angeles: Autry Museum of Western Heritage, 1998. This is the companion volume to the exhibit at the Autry Museum of Western Heritage. A candid and provocative assessment of the legacy of the treaty ending the Mexican War, it includes both essays and the text of the Treaty of Guadalupe Hidalgo in both English and Spanish. Those in English are Engstrand's "The Impact of the U.S.-Mexican War on the Spanish Southwest" (12–31); Richard Griswold del Castillo's "The U.S.-Mexican War: Contemporary Implications for Mexican American Civil and International Rights" (76–85); and Poniatowska's "Afterword: Interior Frontiers" (107–10). Bibliography

7:313 Francaviglia, Richard V., and Douglas W. Richmond, eds. *Dueling Eagles: Reinterpreting the U.S.-Mexican War, 1846–1848.* Fort Worth: Texas Christian University Press, 2000. This collection from a 1996 symposium at the University of Texas, Arlington, includes work from Mexican and U.S. historians on the Mexican War. The essays examine such issues as the influence of Great Britain, the role and reception of war journalism in both countries, and the reasons behind Mexican collaboration with U.S. troops. Contents include Francaviglia, "The Geographic and Cartographic Legacy of the U.S.-Mexican War" (1–18); Sam W. Haynes, "'But What Will England Say?'—Great Britain, the United States, and the War with Mexico" (19–40); Josefina Zoraida Vázquez, "Causes of the War with the United

States" (41–66); Richard Bruce Winders, "'Will the Regiment Stand It?' The 1st North Carolina Mutinies at Buena Vista" (67–90); Miguel A. González Quiroga, "The War between the United States and Mexico" (91–102); Mitchel Roth, "Journalism and the U.S.-Mexican War" (103–26); Richmond, "A View of the Periphery: Regional Factors and Collaboration during the U.S.-Mexico Conflict, 1845–1848" (127–54); and Robert W. Johannsen, "Young America and the War with Mexico" (155–76).

7:314   Mahin, Dean B. *Olive Branch and Sword: The United States and Mexico, 1845–1848*. Jefferson, NC: McFarland, 1997. This is a concise overview of the U.S.-Mexican conflict. See also Robert W. Johannsen, *To the Halls of the Montezumas: The Mexican War in the American Imagination* (New York: Oxford University Press, 1985).

7:315   Smith, Justin H. *The War with Mexico*. 2 vols. New York: Macmillan, 1919. Awarded a Pulitzer Prize in 1920, this work dominated American attitudes toward the Mexican War for a half century. Its account of the causes of the war is now recognized to be unduly biased against Mexico, and its military narrative has been superseded by several works. Based on exhaustive research and written in a lively style. Extensive bibliography.

7:316   Spell, Lota M. "The Anglo-Saxon Press in Mexico, 1846–1848." *American Historical Review* 38 (October 1932): 20–31. Spell deals with the newspapers sponsored by the American army, which achieved modest success and became the foundation of the press in the postwar American southwest.

7:317   Tyler, Ronnie C. "The Mexican War: A Lithographic Record." *Southwestern Historical Quarterly* 77 (July 1973): 1–84. This is a collection of contemporary lithographs of American military forces and Mexican scenes during the war, with brief accompanying text comparing the pictorial record of the war with that of other nineteenth-century wars.

Origins

7:318   De Voto, Bernard. *The Year of Decision, 1846*. Boston: Little, Brown and Company, 1943. Reprint 2000 (St. Martin's Press). Along with two other works in what amounted to a trilogy on the subject of mid-nineteenth-century American expansionism—*Across the Wide Missouri* (Boston: Houghton Mifflin, 1952) and *The Course of Empire* (Boston: Houghton Mifflin, 1952)—this work describes the spread of America's institutions and culture and the gradual development of the concept of federal union. De Voto illustrates the effect pioneers had on the acquisition of Oregon by 1846 and carries the story to the fall of Mexico City in 1847.

7:319   Kohl, Clayton Charles. *Claims as a Cause of the Mexican War*. New York: New York University Press, 1914. A thorough treatment of a narrow subject (1821–1848), this brief work remains the standard study of a factor that loomed large in Polk's war message but was deprecated by his opponents and by most subsequent writers.

7:320   Mullins, William H. "The British Press and the Mexican War: Justin Smith Revised." *New Mexico Historical Review* 52 (July 1977): 207–27. Mullins writes that Smith, in his 1919 book *The War with Mexico* (7:315), was wrong to think that the British press encouraged the Mexicans to fight. The British, to be sure, disliked the United States but respected its strength.

7:321   Price, Glenn W. *Origins of the War with Mexico: The Polk-Stockton Intrigue*. Austin: University of Texas Press, 1967. Price provides the fullest available exposition of the plot thesis—that Polk tried to provoke a war with Mexico in the spring of 1845, using Robert F. Stockton as his principal agent provocateur and the protection of Texas during the annexation process as his "cover." It is based on extensive research but relies considerably on surmise. Extensive bibliography. For a broader view, see also Norman A. Graebner, "The Mexican War: A Study in Causation," *Pacific Historical Review* 49 (August 1980): 405–26.

7:322   Stenberg, Richard R. "The Failure of Polk's Mexican War Intrigue of 1845." *Pacific Historical Review* 4 (March 1935): 39–68. This is the first full statement of the plot thesis of the causes of the Mexican War; later revived and amplified by Price, *Origins of the War with Mexico: The Polk-Stockton Intrigue* (1967) (7:321), with the addition of new material on Robert F. Stockton.

7:323   Vázquez, Josefina Zoraida. *Mexicanos y Norteamericanos ante la guerra del 47 [Mexicans and Americans before the War of '47].* Mexico, DF: Sep Setenta, 1972. This is a 50-page interpretive and synthetic essay followed by 225 pages of contemporary and secondary accounts interpreting the causes of the Mexican War (1845–1846). See also Vázquez and Meyer, *The United States and Mexico* (1985) (2:386).

The Home Front

7:324   Borit, Gabor S. "Lincoln's Opposition to the Mexican War." *Journal of the Illinois State Historical Society* 67 (February 1974): 79–100. As a Whig member of the House of Representatives, Lincoln offered partisan opposition in 1847 to the war. His stand would be worth, at most, no more than a paragraph but for his later career.

7:325   Collins, John R. "The Mexican War: A Study in Fragmentation." *Journal of the West* 11 (April 1972): 225–34. This study of congressional voting on war issues (1846–1848) shows partisan and sectional fragmentation.

7:326   Connor, Seymour V., and Odie B. Faulk. *North America Divided: The Mexican War, 1846–1848.* New York: Oxford University Press, 1971. A short, popular account, this echoes Justin Smith, *The War with Mexico* (1919) (7:315), in explaining the causes of the war. Extensive bibliography.

7:327   De Armond, Louis. "Justo Sierra O'Reilly and Yucatecan–United States Relations, 1847–1848." *Hispanic American Historical Review* 31 (August 1951): 420–36. O'Reilly bore an invitation for U.S. annexation of Yucatán at the end of the Mexican War, which precipitated an argument in Congress but led to no action.

7:328   Ellsworth, Clayton Sumner. "The American Churches and the Mexican War." *American Historical Review* 45 (January 1940): 301–26. Ellsworth writes that most religious groups supported the war, with the exception of many Catholics and most New England denominations.

7:329   Fuller, John Douglas Pitts. *The Movement for the Acquisition of All Mexico, 1846–1848.* Baltimore: Johns Hopkins Press, 1936. Reprint 1971 (Scholarly Press). This study of press and congressional opinion in the United States, with some consideration of its influence on Polk, is still worth examination. Bibliography.

7:330   Goldin, Gurston. "Business Sentiment and the Mexican War, with Particular Emphasis on the New York Businessman." *New York History* 33 (January 1952): 54–70. Golden argued that many business leaders opposed the war, both because they disliked the disturbance it caused and because they feared it would encourage abolitionism and harm their profitable ties with the south.

7:331   Graebner, Norman A. "Lessons of the Mexican War." *Pacific Historical Review* 47 (August 1978): 325–42. The title is deceptive, for the essay deals with the dilemma facing Polk in late 1847 and early 1848, after the occupation of Mexico City, when he was caught between Whigs and other opponents of the war and the developing all-Mexico movement.

7:332   Haun, Cheryl. "The Whig Abolitionists' Attitude toward the Mexican War." *Journal of the West* 11 (April 1972): 260–72. Haun analyzes the most determined opposition group. Setting their face against their own party's view, the Whig abolitionists joined in the formation of the Free Soil Party.

7:333   Hinckley, Ted C. "American Anti-Catholicism during the Mexican War." *Pacific Historical Review* 31 (May 1962): 121–37. This essay established that the forces of American nationalism, the traditions of religious tolerance, and the presence of a substantial antiwar movement prevented passions over the Mexican War from being transformed into an anti-Catholic movement, either in Mexico or at home.

7:334   Lambert, Paul F. "The Movement for the Acquisition of All Mexico." *Journal of the West* 11 (April 1972): 317–27. Lambert suggests that American peace sentiment might have prevailed on Polk to end the war even if Trist had not opportunely negotiated an acceptable treaty.

7:335   Lander, Ernest M., Jr. *Reluctant Imperialists: Calhoun, the South Carolinians, and the Mexi-*

can War. Baton Rouge: Louisiana State University Press, 1979. Senator John C. Calhoun of South Carolina was against sending American troops deep into Mexico and was a severe critic of President Polk's war policy. South Carolinians had mixed feelings about the war and, like other southerners, were worried about the danger to slavery if additional territory were wrestled from Mexico. Extensive bibliography.

7:336   Merk, Frederick. "Dissent in the Mexican War." In *Dissent in Three American Wars,* ed. Samuel Eliot Morison, Frederick Merk, and Frank Freidel, 35–63. Cambridge, MA: Harvard University Press, 1970. Mainly a review of antiwar newspapers, Merk's essay serves as a useful supplement to Schroeder, *Mr. Polk's War: American Opposition and Dissent, 1846–1848* (1973) (7:337).

7:337   Schroeder, John H. *Mr. Polk's War: American Opposition and Dissent, 1846–1848.* Madison: University of Wisconsin Press, 1973. Schroeder's work covers some of the same ground as Merk, "Dissent in the Mexican War" (1970) (7:336), but offers a more detailed study of the types and growth of American opposition to the war. Bibliography.

7:338   Streeby, Shelley. *American Sensations: Class, Empire, and the Production of Popular Culture.* Berkeley: University of California Press, 2002. Streeby, a professor of literature, analyzes the influence of the Mexican War on American perceptions through popular literature, journalism, and political tracts, mining these sources for both self-image and images of the Latino in the American mind. The author concludes that the 1840s, not the 1860s, should be seen as the critical period in nineteenth-century American history.

7:339   Tutorow, Norman E. *Texas Annexation and the Mexican War: A Political Study of the Old Northwest.* Palo Alto: Chadwick House, 1978. This quantitative study of voting and editorial opinion (1843–1848) is limited to the states of Ohio, Indiana, Illinois, and Michigan. Extensive bibliography.

Military History and Eyewitness Accounts

7:340   Amon Carter Museum of Western Art, Martha A. Sandweiss, Rick Stewart, and Ben W. Huseman, eds. *Eyewitness to War: Prints and Daguerreotypes of the Mexican War, 1846–1848.* Washington, DC: Smithsonian Institution Press, 1989. This riveting collection of images provides an indispensable view of the American invasion of Mexico.

7:341   Bravo Ugarte, José. "La misión confidencial de Moses Y. Beach en 1847, y el clero Mexicano [The Confidential Mission of Moses Y. Beach in 1847 and the Mexican Clergy]." *Ábside* 12 (octubre-diciembre 1948): 476–96. This article, which complements Nelson's "Mission to Mexico: Moses Y. Beach, Secret Agent" (1975) (7:354), relies largely on Mexican sources and emphasizes Beach's machinations with the pro-clerical rebels.

7:342   Caruso, A. Brooke. *The Mexican Spy Company: United States Covert Operations in Mexico, 1845–1848.* Jefferson, NC: McFarland, 1991. This concise and revealing report on an often overlooked aspect of the war shows that Polk launched covert operations (and paid bribes) to make sure that Texans voted for U.S. annexation and that they would be fighting Mexico at the same time the United States was. Agents worked in Cuba as well as Texas and Mexico itself. The "Company" named in the title consisted of Mexican bandits used by the Americans as what would a century later be called fifth columnists within Mexico itself.

7:343   Castañeda, Carlos Eduardo. "Relations of General Scott with Santa Anna." *Hispanic American Historical Review* 29 (November 1949): 455–73. Scott unsuccessfully sought in 1847 to avoid an attack on the Valley of Mexico by negotiating.

7:344   Chalfant, William Y. *Dangerous Passage: The Santa Fe Trail and the Mexican War.* Norman: University of Oklahoma Press, 1994. Chalfant's narrative recounts the guerrilla warfare between the United States and the Native Americans along the Santa Fe Trail during the Mexican War. He analyzes how increased commercial traffic, new small battalion tactics, and rapid-fire carbines led to the settlement of the New Mexico Territory and the end of a way of life for the Cheyennes, Arapahos, Kiowas, Comanches, and Apaches.

7:345　　Clayton, Lawrence R., and Joseph E. Chance, eds. *The March to Monterrey: The Diary of Lieutenant Rankin Dilworth, U.S. Army: A Narrative of Troop Movements and Observations on Daily Life with General Zachary Taylor's Army during the Invasion of Mexico.* El Paso: Texas Western Press, 1996. This is a valuable text that sheds light on the social and military aspects of the U.S. invasion of Mexico.

7:346　　Davies, Thomas J., Jr. "Assessments during the Mexican War: An Exercise in Futility." *New Mexico Historical Review* 41 (July 1966): 197–216. The assessments or taxes were U.S.-forced contributions on the Mexican authorities during the occupation. Davies discusses the origins of the policy and obstacles to its implementation.

7:347　　Drumm, Stella M., ed. *Down the Santa Fe Trail and into Mexico: The Diary of Susan Shelby Magoffin, 1846–1847.* New Haven: Yale University Press, 1962. Reprint 1982 (University of Nebraska Press). These are the daily observations of a contemporary woman on the Santa Fe Trail during the Mexican War.

7:348　　Foos, Paul. *A Short, Offhand, Killing Affair: Soldiers and Social Conflict during the Mexican-American War.* Chapel Hill: University of North Carolina Press, 2002. Foos holds that harsh army discipline and other frustrations and disappointments experienced by American soldiers turned some of them toward a murderous and looting approach to the Mexican population and others to desertion, resulting in a tarnished vision of Manifest Destiny.

7:349　　Gardner, Mark L., and Marc S. Simmons, eds. *The Mexican War Correspondence of Richard Smith Elliott.* Norman: University of Oklahoma Press, 1997. This is valuable reportage from the front written by an army lieutenant (as "John Brown") for a St. Louis newspaper.

7:350　　Gerhard, Peter. "Baja California in the Mexican War, 1846–1848." *Pacific Historical Review* 14 (December 1945): 418–24. This is a detailed history of events based on original sources.

7:351　　Hogan, Michael. *The Irish Soldiers of Mexico.* Guadalajara, Mexico: Fondo Editorial Universitario, 1997. This is a vigorously written and well-researched narrative that is largely sympathetic to the San Patricios Irish, who fought for Mexico against the predominantly Protestant United States. Hogan draws heavily on sources in Mexico, where the book is far better known than in the United States.

7:352　　Howell, H. Grady, Jr., ed. *A Southern Lacrimosa: The Mexican War Journal.* Madison, MS: Chickasaw Bayou Press, 1995. Thomas Neely Love's journal offers a look at the Mexican War from the point of view of a surgeon with the 2d Mississippi Volunteers. It is more about medicine than either Mexico or Mexicans.

7:353　　McCaffrey, James M., ed. *Surrounded by Dangers of All Kinds: The Mexican War Letters of Lieutenant Theodore Laidley.* Denton, TX: University of North Texas Press, 1997. This is another in a recent series of Mexican War narratives by American soldiers. See also McCaffrey's *Army of Manifest Destiny: The American Soldier in the Mexican War, 1846–1848* (New York: New York University Press, 1992).

7:354　　Nelson, Anna K. "Mission to Mexico: Moses Y. Beach, Secret Agent." *New York Historical Society Quarterly* 59 (July 1975): 227–45. This is an account of Beach's unsuccessful effort in 1847 to negotiate peace and his efforts to exploit the pro-clerical revolt in Mexico City for his purposes.

7:355　　Pacheco, José Emilio, and Andrés Reséndez, with José Manuel Villalpando César. *Crónica del 47 [Chronicle of '47].* Mexico, DF: Clío, 1997. In this brief, heavily illustrated work, Pacheco gives an account of the U.S. military operations in Mexico, the divisions between the military and political leadership, and an analysis of how the North Americans were able to occupy Mexico City.

7:356　　Peskin, Allan, ed. *Volunteers: The Mexican War Journals of Private Richard Coulter and Sergeant Thomas Barclay, Company E, Second Pennsylvania Infantry.* Kent, OH: Kent State University Press, 1991. These journals present the enlisted man's view of the U.S. invasion of Mexico.

7:357　　Pohl, James W. "The Influence of Antoine

Henri de Jomini on Winfield Scott's Campaign in the Mexican War." *Southwestern Historical Quarterly* 77 (July 1973): 85–110. Jomini's writings on Napoleonic strategy and tactics influenced several generations of American military leaders; Scott, who was a great student of the subject, furnishes one of the best examples of the influence.

7:358   Sachsen-Altenburg, Hans von, and Laura Gabiger, eds. *Winning the West: General Stephen Watts Kearny's Letter Book 1846–1847*. Booneville, MO: Pekitanoui, 1998. This collection of the general's letters includes an introduction by Stephanie Kearny and bibliographical references.

7:359   Winders, Richard Bruce. *Mr. Polk's Army: The American Military Experience in the Mexican War*. College Station: Texas A&M University Press, 1997. This is a synthesis of recent work on the Mexican War, but Winders supports his arguments with primary source material where appropriate, especially on military life.

7:360   Wynn, Dennis J. *The San Patricio Soldiers: Mexico's Foreign Legion*. El Paso: Texas Western Press, University of Texas at El Paso, 1984. This brief (fifty-four pages) narrative recalls the ill-fated Mexican Legion of St. Patrick, which was composed mostly of Irish deserters from the U.S. army. Most were killed during the war, but some fifty more were captured, tried, and executed as deserters. Wynn also discusses the Partricios' counterpart in the U.S. army, the Spy Company.

The Treaty of Guadalupe Hidalgo

7:361   Johnson, Kenneth M. "Baja California and the Treaty of Guadalupe Hidalgo." *Journal of the West* 11 (April 1972): 328–47. Johnson exonerates Trist for not securing the annexation of Baja California in the treaty.

7:362   Nortrup, Jack. "Nicholas Trist's Mission to Mexico: A Reinterpretation." *Southwestern Historical Quarterly* 71 (January 1968): 321–46. Nortrup faults Trist for not carrying out his instructions. The result was a treaty that satisfied neither president nor Congress.

7:363   Ohrt, Wallace. *Defiant Peacemaker: Nicholas Trist in the Mexican War*. College Station: Texas A&M University Press, 1997. This is a short biography that attempts to redeem Trist's historical reputation.

7:364   Sears, Louis Martin. "Nicholas P. Trist, A Diplomat with Ideals." *Mississippi Valley Historical Review* 11 (June 1924): 85–98. This is an early, sympathetic view of Trist by a distinguished historian.

The War and Its Aftermath in Mexico

7:365   Berge, Dennis E. "A Mexican Dilemma: The Mexico City Ayuntamiento and the Question of Loyalty, 1846–1848." *Hispanic American Historical Review* 50 (May 1970): 229–56. Berge's study is one of a very few scholarly treatments that discuss the Mexican side of a Mexican War episode.

7:366   Chavezmontes, Julio. *Heridas que no cierran [Wounds That Do Not Close]*. Política mexicana. Mexico, DF: Grijalbo, 1988. This is a passionate indictment of the still not fully healed wounds opened by the Mexican War.

7:367   Figueroa, Raúl. *La guerra de corso de México durante la invasión norteamericana, 1845–1848 [The Mexican Cruiser Warfare during the North American Invasion, 1845–1848]*. Mexico, DF: Instituto Tecnológico Autónomo de México, 1996. The author describes the Mexican program of outfitting privateers to disrupt American merchant shipping, its ultimate ineffectiveness, and the complications that it created for Spain, where the Mexican ships were armed.

7:368   Hale, Charles A. "The War with the United States and the Crisis in Mexican Thought." *Americas* 14 (October 1957): 153–74. This is a penetrating study of Mexican liberalism before and during the war that draws from extensive Mexican sources and shows understanding of the dilemma facing liberals, who had formerly admired American institutions and could not repudiate them suddenly.

7:369   Herrera Serna, Laura, ed. *México en guerra, 1846–1848: perspectivas regionales [Mexico* *at War, 1846–1848: Regional Perspectives].* Mexico, DF: Consejo Nacional para la Cultura y las Artes: Museo Nacional de las Intervenciones, 1997. This collection of papers from the first Congreso de Historia de las Intervenciones, held in November 1994, considers the complexity of the "Mexican" perception of the war.

7:370   Keller, Gary D., and Cordelia Candelaria, eds. *The Legacy of the Mexican and Spanish-American Wars: Legal, Literary, and Historical Perspectives.* Tempe, AZ: Bilingual Review/Press, 2000. This is a collection of selected papers from the Transhistoric Thresholds Conference (Arizona State University, 1998). As the title implies, these papers cover the two wars from a number of different disciplines and methods. Those relevant to this chapter include Christopher David Ruiz Cameron, "One Hundred Fifty Years of Solitude: Reflections on the End of the History Academy's Dominance of Scholarship on the Treaty of Guadalupe Hidalgo" (1–22); Kevin R. Johnson, "Immigration, Citizenship, and U.S./Mexico Relations: The Tale of Two Treaties" (23–38); George A. Martínez, "Dispute Resolution and the Treaty of Guadalupe Hidalgo: Parallels and Possible Lessons for Dispute Resolution under NAFTA" (39–62); and Rosemary King, "Border Crossings in the Mexican American War" (63–86).

7:371   Santoni, Pedro. *Mexicans at Arms: Puro Federalists and the Politics of War, 1845–1848.* Fort Worth: Texas Christian University Press, 1996. Santoni brings coherence to the dizzying array of conspiracies, factional struggles, and governments in Mexico during its war with the United States. He delineates four main parties: the radical liberals *(puros)*, moderate liberals *(moderados),* conservatives, and *santanistas.* Antonio Lopez de Santa Anna, for whom the last party is named, was courted by each group, but loyal to none. This is the first work to fully chronicle this period in Mexican national politics.

7:372   Valadés, José C. *México, Santa Anna y la Guerra de Texas [Mexico, Santa Anna and the Texas War].* 3d ed. Mexico, DF: Editores Mexicanos Unidos, 1965. First published in 1936, this is a reasonably dispassionate, even resigned, study of the loss of Texas from the Mexican viewpoint. Bibliography.

7:373   Velasco Martínez, Jesús. *La Guerrade 47 y la opinión pública [The War of 1847 and Public Opinion].* Mexico, DF: Secretaria de Educación Pública, 1975. This account supplements Brack, *Mexico Views Manifest Destiny, 1821–1846: An Essay on the Origins of the Mexican War* (1975) (7:299), using some of the same sources, and extends into the postwar period.

7:374   Velázquez, María del Carmen. *Establecimiento y pérdida del septentrión de Nueva España [The Establishment and Loss of Northern New Spain].* Mexico, DF: Colegio de México, 1974. Velázquez details the political disposition and administration of the northern territories of New Spain and Mexico from their discovery to 1848. She includes considerable detail on the relationship between the indigenous populations and the Europeans in the international rivalries among Spain, France, and Britain. The last two chapters discuss the loss of Texas and the rest of northern Mexico.

7:375   Williams, Mary W. "Secessionist Diplomacy of Yucatan." *Hispanic American Historical Review* 9 (May 1929): 132–43. Williams traces the efforts of a local regime in Yucatán to end a caste (actually race) war (1847–1848) with the Indians through secession from Mexico and annexation to the United States. The mission of O'Reilly, described in De Armond, "Justo Sierra O'Reilly and Yucatecan–United States Relations, 1847–1848" (1951) (7:327), was the result.

MEXICAN-AMERICAN POSTWAR RELATIONS

7:376   Fuentes Mares, José. *Juárez y los Estados Unidos [Juárez and the United States].* Mexico, DF: Libro Mex Editores, 1960. This work includes an account of the negotiations leading to the McLane-Ocampo Treaty (1857–1860). Bibliography.

7:377   Garber, Paul N. *The Gadsden Treaty.* Philadelphia: University of Pennsylvania Press, 1923. This has long been the standard work on the subject, but it is now considerably dated. Extensive bibliography.

7:378   Meyer, Lorenzo. "Mexico and the United

States: The Historical Structure of Their Conflict." *Journal of International Affairs* 43 (Winter 1990): 251–71. Meyer roots contemporary problems in Mexican-American relations to patterns established early on in the relationship. Long after its defeat in war with the United States, Mexico found itself harassed and pressured by its northern neighbor. See also Richard Griswold del Castillo, *The Treaty of Guadalupe Hidalgo: A Legacy of Conflict* (Norman: University of Oklahoma Press, 1990).

7:379   Moseley, Edward H. "Indians from the Eastern United States and the Defense of Northeastern Mexico: 1855–1864." *Southwestern Social Science Quarterly* 46 (December 1965): 273–80. Spanish-ruled Mexico was long able to contain the power of Indians pushed into its northeast from the United States; later, with the encouragement of Governor Santiago Vidaurri, Seminoles and Kickapoos who had migrated into Mexico fought with it in the war against the United States.

7:380   Pletcher, David M. "A Prospecting Expedition across Central Mexico, 1856–1857." *Pacific Historical Review* 21 (February 1952): 21–41. Led by Edward Lee Plumb, an important U.S-Mexican agent and promoter during the 1860s and 1870s, the expedition sought and found exploitable iron deposits, but their supporting company lacked capital for development.

7:381   Porter, Kenneth W. "The Seminole in Mexico, 1850–1861." *Hispanic American Historical Review* 31 (February 1951): 1–36. Seminoles voluntarily migrated from the Indian Territory because they opposed having the Creeks as neighbors. They and their black slaves fought for Mexico on the frontier.

7:382   Rippy, J. Fred. "Diplomacy of the United States and Mexico Regarding the Isthmus of Tehuántepec, 1848–1860." *Mississippi Valley Historical Review* 6 (March 1920): 503–21. Rippy has prepared a detailed account of treaty discussions and American entrepreneurs interested in developing the Tehuántepec route.

7:383   Tamayo, Jorge L. "El Tratado McLane-Ocampo [The McLane-Ocampo Treaty]." *Historia Mexicana* 21 (abril-junio 1972): 573–613. After a lengthy background, this is primarily a diplomatic

account (1848–1859). From the few notes, the author has apparently used only published sources.

Central America and the Isthmian Canal

7:384   Bourne, Kenneth. "The Clayton-Bulwer Treaty and the Decline of British Opposition to the Territorial Expansion of the United States, 1857–1860." *Journal of Modern History* 33 (September 1961): 287–91. This article describes how the United States became resentful of the Clayton-Bulwer Treaty and insisted on greater prerogative in Central America. Britain finally acquiesced.

7:385   Folkman, David I., Jr. *The Nicaragua Route.* Salt Lake City: University of Utah Press, 1972. This is an account of the intense commercial rivalry between promoters of the Nicaraguan and Panamanian routes (1850–1868) across the isthmus. The author emphasizes business concerns in the Nicaragua route, especially those of Cornelius Vanderbilt. The "route" referred to in the title was to the California goldfields. Bibliography.

7:386   Hackett, Charles W. "The Development of John Quincy Adams's Policy with Respect to an American Confederation and the Panama Congress, 1822–1825." *Hispanic American Historical Review* 8 (November 1928): 496–526. This detailed assessment of Adams's thought on hemispheric confederation is based heavily on Manning, *Diplomatic Correspondence of the United States Concerning the Independence of the Latin-American Nations* (1925) (7:13).

7:387   Howe, George F. "The Clayton-Bulwer Treaty: An Unofficial Interpretation of Article VIII in 1869." *American Historical Review* 42 (April 1937): 484–90. Howe offers a brief interpretation of article 8 of the Clayton-Bulwer Treaty, dealing with Anglo-American protection of isthmian routes. Britain refused Colombia a guarantee of sovereignty over Panama.

7:388   LaFeber, Walter. *Inevitable Revolutions: The United States in Central America.* An overview of the record of U.S. relations with Central America by a leading authority. Early chapters deal with the cultural, economic, and political origins of U.S. policy in the region. See chapter 2 of this Guide (2:355). First published in 1983.

7:389   Leonard, Thomas M. *Central American and United States Policies, 1820s–1980s: A Guide to Issues and References*. See chapter 1 of this Guide (1:250).

7:390   Lockey, Joseph Byrne. "Diplomatic Futility." *Hispanic American Historical Review* 10 (August 1930): 265–94. This informative and entertaining article describes U.S. missions to Central America from 1824 to 1849 and demonstrates the ineptness of American policy before 1845.

7:391   Lockey, Joseph Byrne. "A Neglected Aspect of Isthmian Diplomacy." *American Historical Review* 41 (January 1936): 295–305. Lockey examines the origins of the 1846 treaty with New Granada (Colombia) and traces the history of treaty negotiations with Colombia from 1824 to 1846. Colombia feared British pretensions in the isthmus and chose American guarantees.

7:392   Munro, Dana G. *The Five Republics of Central America: Their Political and Economic Development and Their Relations with the United States*. New York: Oxford University Press, 1918. This is a dated treatment of U.S.–Central American relations by a noted historian and diplomat.

7:393   Naylor, Robert A. "The British Role in Central America Prior to the Clayton-Bulwer Treaty of 1850." *Hispanic American Historical Review* 40 (August 1960): 361–82. Naylor argues that the British role was commercially opportunistic despite the fact that Britain did not recognize the Central American federation or establish normal diplomatic relations.

7:394   Reinhold, Frances L. "New Research on the First Pan American Congress Held at Panama in 1826." *Hispanic American Historical Review* 18 (August 1938): 342–63. Reinhold discusses northern press reaction to the Panama Congress and compares editorial judgments with attitudes of policymakers and congressional leaders. The press was eager for involvement, largely for commercial reasons.

7:395   Schoonover, Thomas D. *The French in Central America: Culture and Commerce, 1820–1930*. Wilmington, DE: Scholarly Resources, 1999. Schoonover writes on an overlooked chapter in the international competition of nineteenth-century diplomacy, the French attempt to establish a sphere of influence in Central America. This brought them, rather unsuccessfully, into competition with British, U.S., and German interests. Schoonover examines the French tactic of establishing cultural bonds through education, religious orders, and military missions, combining as a program of social imperialism.

7:396   Schott, Joseph L. *Rails across Panama: The Story of the Building of the Panama Railroad, 1849–1855*. Indianapolis: Bobbs-Merrill, 1967. This vividly written popular history re-creates many of the now debunked legends of the building of the railroad.

7:397   Stansifer, Charles L. "E. George Squier and the Honduras Interoceanic Railroad Project." *Hispanic American Historical Review* 46 (February 1966): 1–27. In the early 1850s, Squier, Zachary Taylor's emissary to Central America in 1849, negotiated a contract with the Honduran government to construct a railroad. Later, the contract was sold to British investors and led to a series of poor loans contracted by Honduras.

7:398   Williams, Alfred. *The Inter-Oceanic Canal and the Monroe Doctrine*. New York: G. P. Putnam's Sons, 1880. Reprint 1999 (Gaunt). This old work includes a chronological list of the efforts to secure interoceanic transits across the isthmus or the continent of Central America.

South America

7:399   Billingsley, Edward B. *In Defense of Neutral Rights: The United States Navy and the Wars of Independence in Chile and Peru*. Chapel Hill: University of North Carolina Press, 1967. U.S. naval officers (1815–1824), though sympathetic to the Latin American revolutionaries, protected American commercial rights and opposed paper blockades.

Naturally, the rebels sometimes resented such actions. Bibliography.

7:400 Nolan, Louis C. "The Relations of the United States and Peru with Respect to Claims, 1822–1870." *Hispanic American Historical Review* 17 (February 1937): 30–66. Nolan writes that the United States was insistent on Peru's admission of its obligation to pay claims advanced by private American citizens.

7:401 Nuerinberger, Gustave A. "The Continental Treaties of 1856: An American Union Exclusive of the United States." *Hispanic American Historical Review* 20 (February 1940): 32–55. Latin Americans, fearful of U.S. commercial expansion, failed to agree among themselves on a defensive federation, despite Chilean efforts.

7:402 Pratt, Edwin J. "Anglo-American Commercial and Political Rivalry in the Plata, 1820–1830." *Hispanic American Historical Review* 11 (August 1931): 302–35. The shrewdness of British diplomats paved the way for Uruguayan independence under British protection. The British did not want a confrontation with the United States in the La Plata region in the 1820s. The American minister to Argentina (J. M. Forbes) advanced American interests, but his British counterpart was clearly his superior in dealing with the Argentineans and Brazilians. Based on British and American archival sources.

7:403 Rippy, J. Fred. "Bolivar as Viewed by Contemporary Diplomats of the United States." *Hispanic American Historical Review* 15 (August 1935): 287–97. Rippy argues that diplomats sent to Gran Colombia (1820–1830) had preconceptions about Latin American leaders, and thus misunderstood Bolivar.

7:404 Stewart, Watt. "The South American Commission, 1817–1818." *Hispanic American Historical Review* 9 (February 1929): 31–59. The U.S. commission visited Rio de Janeiro, Buenos Aires, and Santiago de Chile. Inspiration came from the public's desire for information and, most important, from a presidential wish to stall the revolutionary governments in their quest for U.S. recognition. The commission's report argued for recognition of Buenos Aires and Chile.

ARGENTINA

7:405 Bemis, Samuel Flagg. "Early Diplomatic Missions from Buenos Aires to the United States, 1811–1824." This highly factual account argues that the United States contributed more than Great Britain to the cause of Latin American independence (5:532).

7:406 Cady, John F. *Foreign Intervention in the Rio de la Plata, 1838–50: A Study of French, British, and American Policy in Relation to the Dictator Juan Manuel Rosas.* Philadelphia: University of Pennsylvania Press, 1929. Cady covers the foreign rivalries of French, British, and American governments in the La Plata region during the era of Juan Manuel de Rosas, dictator of Argentina (1828–1852). Bibliography.

7:407 Currier, Theodore S. *Los Corsarios del Rio de la Plata [Pirates of the Rio de la Plata].* Buenos Aires: Impr. de la Universidad, 1929. This is an important account of a key aspect of relations with the United States in Argentina's first years of independence.

7:408 Davis, Thomas Brabson. *Carlos de Alvear, Man of Revolution: The Diplomatic Career of Argentina's First Minister to the United States.* Durham, NC: Duke University Press, 1955. This biography of the colorful career of the Argentine soldier and diplomat, who possessed an ability to alter his political views to advance his own circumstances, includes his years as the diplomatic representative to the United States, 1838 to 1852. In this capacity he sought fruitlessly to gain U.S. support for Argentina in its opposition to French and British intervention in La Plata and opposed U.S. expansion during the Mexican War.

7:409 Dusenberry, William. "Juan Manuel de Rosas as Viewed by Contemporary American Diplomats." *Hispanic American Historical Review* 41 (November 1961): 495–514. Dusenberry writes that American diplomats who served in Argentina during the era of the dictator, or caudillo, Juan Manuel de Rosas (1830–1851), gradually become more critical of his regime. This work is based mostly on State Department material.

7:410 Goebel, Julius. *The Struggle for the Falkland Islands: A Study in Legal and Diplomatic*

History. New Haven: Yale University Press, 1927. In this exhaustive study, Goebel emphasizes the U.S.-Argentine squabble (1783–1835) caused by seizure of an American fishing vessel in the Falklands in 1831. Extensive bibliography. See also Maisch, "The Falkland/Malvinas Islands Clash of 1831–1832: U.S. and British Diplomacy in the South Atlantic" (2000) (6:185), and Paul D. Dickens, "The Falkland Islands Dispute between the United States and Argentina," *Hispanic American Historical Review* 9 (November 1929): 471–87.

7:411　Keen, Benjamin. *David Curtis DeForest and the Revolution of Buenos Aires.* New Haven: Yale University Press, 1947. Reprint 1970 (Greenwood Press). This is a biography of an early inter-Americanist who promoted American commercial interests in Argentina and the latter's cause at home.

7:412　Palomeque, Alberto. *Oríjenes de la diplomacia arjentina, misión Aguirre á Norte América [Origins of Argentinean Diplomacy: Aguirre's Mission to North America].* 2 vols. Buenos Aires: Estab. gráfico Robles & cia, 1905. Based on primary materials from the Argentine foreign ministry as well as memoirs and biographies of many of the participants, this is one of the first scholarly treatments of the revolutionary generation in Argentina, 1810–1830. Palomeque, who was far more generous in his estimation of U.S. intentions than later generations of South American scholars, saw the United States as an inspiration to the revolutionaries and a cautious ally in South American independence.

COLOMBIA

7:413　Bowman, Charles H., Jr. "The Activities of Manuel Torres as Purchasing Agent, 1820–1821." *Hispanic American Historical Review* 48 (May 1968): 234–45. Bowman explores the role of Torres as revolutionary agent in the United States before his acceptance as the first minister of Colombia to this country. The author exploits both American and Colombian sources.

7:414　Vivian, James F. "The Paloma Claim in United States and Venezuelan-Colombian Relations, 1818–1826." *Caribbean Studies* 14 (January 1975): 57–72. Vivian explores the claims of American prop-

erty owners against privateers acting ostensibly on behalf of rebel governments. He shows that Adams held out for strict accountability, while Monroe inclined toward flexibility, in U.S. settlement of such cases.

7:415　Winn, Wilkins B. "The Issue of Religious Liberty in the United States Commercial Treaty with Colombia, 1824." *Americas* 26 (January 1970): 291–301. The author suggests that article 11 of the 1824 treaty with Colombia served as a model for American treaties with other Latin American governments. It provided that non-Catholic U.S. citizens would not be forced to worship according to the Roman Catholic religion.

PARAGUAY

7:416　Flickema, Thomas O. "'Sam Ward's Bargain': A Tentative Reconsideration." *Hispanic American Historical Review* 50 (August 1970): 538–42. This brief article deals with the American naval expedition in Paraguay (1858–1859), controversies with Paraguay, and the role of Samuel Ward, who had been secretary to the expedition, in the arbitral settlement of 1860.

7:417　_____. "The Settlement of the Paraguayan-American Controversy of 1859: A Reappraisal." *Americas* 25 (July 1968): 49–69. In 1858–1859, an impressive American naval force entered the Rio de la Plata to deal with claims against Paraguay. The author contends that the conciliatory approach of American commissioner James Bowlin and Paraguayan president Carlos Antonio Lopez was significant in settling the issues.

CHILE

7:418　Goebel, Dorothy Burne. "British-American Rivalry in the Chilean Trade, 1817–1820." *Journal of Economic History* 2 (November 1942): 190–202. American traders in Chile during these years suffered from royalist harassment, rebel hostility, and British competition. This is a still valuable contribution to the literature.

7:419　Neumann, William L. "United States Aid

to the Chilean Wars of Independence." *Hispanic American Historical Review* 27 (May 1947): 204–19. In this account of commercial and naval assistance from 1815 to 1820, supplied by individual Americans, the author deemphasizes the British role in Chile's war of independence.

7:420   Worcester, Donald Emmet. *Seapower and Chilean Independence.* Gainesville: University of Florida Press, 1962. This short study, based mostly on published sources, extends beyond Chile's independence struggle (1815–1820) in its significance; it also provides information on Peru.

VENEZUELA

7:421   Ewell, Judith. *Venezuela and the United States: From Monroe's Hemisphere to Petroleum's Empire.* Ewell employs a diverse array of source material to show both sides of the U.S.-Venezuelan relationship, which she says is a microcosm of U.S.–Latin American relations. The early and enduring impediment to better relations, writes Ewell, was the U.S. sense of moral and political superiority (2:400).

7:422   Gray, William H. "American Diplomacy in Venezuela, 1835–1865." *Hispanic American Historical Review* 20 (November 1940): 551–74. Using Venezuelan and American sources, the author concentrates on major diplomatic issues: nonintervention, Pan-Americanism, naturalization problems, commerce, maritime questions, and claims. Though Venezuela was suspicious of American motives during the Mexican War, the two countries had forged a friendly relationship by 1865.

Asia

7:423   Gould, James W. "American Imperialism in Southeast Asia before 1898." *Journal of Southeast Asian Studies* 3 (September 1972): 306–14. Gould divides American activity in Southeast Asia before 1898 into three main periods: 1784 to 1831, 1832 to 1871, and 1872 to 1898. Although all three periods are

marked by intense activity, only the middle period, according to Gould, can be described as imperialistic.

7:424   Hutchison, William R. *Errand to the World: American Protestant Thought and Foreign Missions.* Chicago: University of Chicago Press, 1987. Hutchison details the ways in which Protestant missionary thought complemented the ideology of American nationalist expansionism.

7:425   Johnston, James D. *China and Japan: Being a Narrative of the Cruise of the U.S. Steam Frigate Powhatan, in the Years 1857, '58, '59, and '60. Including an Account of the Japanese Embassy to the United States.* Philadelphia: Charles Desilver, 1861. The author was executive officer of the *Powhatan* and accompanied the first Japanese embassy to the United States.

7:426   Livermore, Seward W. "Early Commercial and Consular Relations with the East Indies." *Pacific Historical Review* 15 (March 1946): 31–58. This recounts early consular appointments to Batavia, Bombay, Calcutta, Manila, Rangoon, and Singapore and the largely unsuccessful efforts to secure recognition of consuls in colonial ports (1784–1856).

7:427   Spector, Ronald H. "The American Image of Southeast Asia, 1790–1865: A Preliminary Assessment." *Journal of Southeast Asian Studies* 3 (September 1972): 299–305. Spector concludes that Americans saw the people of the area as backward, treacherous, and rapacious and believed that Christianity and western civilization would be immensely beneficial to the Asians.

CHINA

7:428   Banno, Masataka. *China and the West, 1858–1861: The Origins of the Tsungli Yamen.* Cambridge, MA: Harvard University Press, 1964. This monograph describes the creation, and explains the methods, of China's first modern Foreign Office. Based on Chinese sources, it helps clarify the Chinese side of Sino-western relations. Extensive bibliography.

7:429   Boardman, Eugene Powers. *Christian Influence upon the Ideology of the Taiping Rebellion,*

1851–1864. Madison: University of Wisconsin Press, 1952. This study focuses on the Taiping ideology in 1851–1854, the first three years of the rebellion. It discusses what the Taipings took, and failed to take, from Christianity and evaluates the role the Christian element played in the final outcome of the rebellion. Extensive bibliography.

7:430   Chang, Hsin-pao. *Commissioner Lin and the Opium War.* Cambridge, MA: Harvard University Press, 1964. This book focuses on Tse-hsü Lin (1785–1850), the leading Chinese official who helped precipitate the Opium War, and on the English with whom he had to deal. Chang sees other westerners in this crisis as merely subordinates of the English, a perception derived from research in Chinese sources. Extensive bibliography.

7:431   Cohen, Warren I. *America's Response to China: A History of Sino-American Relations.* This is a classic overview of the record of Sino-American ties, although it emphasizes the twentieth rather than nineteenth century (2:276).

7:432   Curti, Merle E., and John Stalker. "'The Flowery Flag Devils'—The American Image in China 1840–1900." *Proceedings of the American Philosophical Society* 96 (December 1952): 663–90. Americans attempted to present to the Chinese an image of the United States as a peaceful, commercial nation with qualities that distinguished it from Europe. The Chinese accepted this impression but remained skeptical; by the end of the nineteenth century, the Chinese viewed Americans with a mixture of fear and admiration.

7:433   Danton, George H. *The Culture Contacts of the United States and China: The Earliest Sino-American Culture Contacts, 1784–1844.* New York: Columbia University Press, 1931. Reprint 1974 (Octagon Books). This book draws attention to a facet of Sino-American relations that emerged along with commercial contacts. Especially valuable is the author's discussion of the philanthropic societies at Canton aimed at aiding the Chinese through education, medicine, etc. Bibliography.

7:434   Downs, Jacques M. "American Merchants and the China Opium Trade, 1800–1840." *Business History Review* 42 (Winter 1968): 418–42. This ar-

ticle argues that the opium trade was significant to the commercial success of many Americans in the China trade. The author has synthesized earlier material and added new evidence to offer a thorough account of American participation in the illegal trade.

7:435   _____. *The Golden Ghetto: The American Commercial Community at Canton and the Shaping of American China Policy, 1784–1844.* Bethlehem, PA: Lehigh University Press, 1997. This landmark study of the origins of American economic, cultural, and political influence in nineteenth-century China is impressively researched and engagingly written. Though focused on American merchants in China, Downs's book also thoroughly develops Caleb Cushing's mission to China, culminating in the 1844 Treaty of Wanghia.

7:436   Drake, Fred W. "A Nineteenth-Century View of the United States of America from Hsu Chi-yu's *Ying-huan chih-lüeh*." *Papers on China* 19 (December 1965): 30–54. Hsü Chi-yü was governor of Fukien. In 1848, he published *Ying-huan chih-lüeh* [*Brief Description of the Oceans Roundabout*], which served as a guide for China's nineteenth-century new-style diplomats. The material on America, mostly descriptive, was favorable and naive.

7:437   Dulles, Foster Rhea. *The Old China Trade.* New York: Houghton Mifflin Company, 1930. Reprint 1970 (AMS Press). This is a well-written description of Yankee traders and merchants and their adventures on the high seas and at Canton during the early decades of the China trade. This book has a precise bibliography of manuscript collections, journals, ships' logs, etc., important to research in the period 1784 to 1844.

7:438   Fairbank, John K. *Trade and Diplomacy on the China Coast: The Opening of the Treaty Ports, 1842–1854.* 2 vols. Cambridge, MA: Harvard University Press, 1953–1956. The author argues that national distinctions among westerners are an ineffective means of understanding this period, since the Chinese viewed all westerners as similar in attitude and behavior. Thus, Sino-American relations became merely a subordinate facet of overall Sino-western relations, which were determined by the more powerful British. Extensive bibliography.

7:439 _____. *The United States and China.* This is the fourth edition of a groundbreaking 1948 work by a pioneer in Asian scholarship. Although the book is much more about China than about Sino-American relations, Fairbank details and critiques traditional U.S. China policy and specifies "deadly sins in our thinking," in what was originally an effort to encourage cold war analysts to perceive China on its own terms (2:278).

7:440 Fay, Peter W. "The Protestant Mission and the Opium War." *Pacific Historical Review* 40 (May 1971): 145–61. This relates the views of Protestant missionaries toward the Chinese and toward the Opium War (1834–1842). American missionaries in China at this time included Coleman Bridgman, Ira Tracy, David Abeel, Peter Parker, I. J. Roberts, J. Lewis, and Samuel R. Brown.

7:441 Goldstein, Jonathan. *Philadelphia and the China Trade, 1682–1846: Commercial, Cultural, and Attitudinal Effects.* University Park: Pennsylvania State University Press, 1978. Philadelphia controlled about a third of America's China trade from 1783 to 1846. The author seeks to analyze this trade, its role in stimulating the economy of Philadelphia, and the cultural impact of China on Philadelphia. He argues that Philadelphians had a generally positive image of China and its merchants.

7:442 Griffin, Eldon. *Clippers and Consuls: American Consular and Commercial Relations with Eastern Asia, 1845–1860.* Ann Arbor: Edwards Bros., 1938. Reprint 1972 (Scholarly Resources). A digest rather than an analysis, this book offers a wealth of information concerning American consuls in China as well as American shipping in the treaty ports.

7:443 Gulick, Edward V. *Peter Parker and the Opening of China.* Cambridge, MA: Harvard University Press, 1973. This biography, based on missionary and diplomatic records, traces Parker's career as missionary doctor at Canton and then U.S. commissioner to China (1855–1857). The author finds that Parker's achievements as a pioneer medical missionary in China greatly exceeded his accomplishments as a diplomat.

7:444 Harris, Paul W. "Cultural Imperialism and American Protestant Missionaries: Collaboration and Dependency in Mid-Nineteenth-Century China." *Pacific Historical Review* 60 (August 1991): 309–38. Harris portrays Protestant missionaries in China as dedicated to the propagation of both American nationalism and of Christianity.

7:445 Henson, Curtis T., Jr. *Commissioners and Commodores: The East India Squadron and American Diplomacy in China.* University: University of Alabama Press, 1982. Henson describes the origins of the use of naval power for commercial ends in Asia. Merchants, who earlier had preferred the more benign status of neutrals among the powers, appreciated the military diplomacy that secured most-favored-nation treatment for them in the 1840s. See also Johnson, *Far China Station: The U.S. Navy in Asian Waters, 1800–1898* (1979) (9:252).

7:446 _____. "The U.S. Navy and the Taiping Rebellion." *American Neptune* 38 (January 1978): 28–40. Henson narrates the activities of the American East India squadron on the China coast (1850–1861) and analyzes the problems resulting from the lack of cooperation between American naval and diplomatic officials during the Taiping Rebellion. Trying simultaneously to handle ramifications of the rebellion and "open" Japan put severe strains on the squadron.

7:447 Hunt, Michael H. *The Making of a Special Relationship: The United States and China to 1914.* Hunt expertly dismantles the myth of the special relationship in a book that set a new standard for works on U.S.-Chinese relations. The extensive, and balanced, primary research on both Chinese and U.S. foreign policy reveals the complexity and fragmentation of policy formation on both sides. Hunt shows that decisionmaking was not subject to monolithic interests (such as markets) on either side. This is also the first work to integrate Chinese immigration into a study of U.S. foreign policy (2:279).

7:448 Latourette, Kenneth Scott. *A History of Christian Missions in China.* New York: Macmillan Company, 1929. See chapter 13 of this Guide (13:199) on this account of early U.S. missions to China.

7:449 Layton, Thomas N. *The Voyage of the "Frolic": New England Merchants and the Opium*

Trade. Stanford, CA: Stanford University Press, 1997. After discovering Chinese porcelain in northern California, an archaeologist reconstructs the story of the merchant ship that foundered after a brief career in the Chinese trade, involving silks and opium as well as porcelain. A stellar example of the social and economic aspect of American foreign relations.

7:450 Lockwood, Stephen Chapman. *Augustine Heard and Company, 1858–1862: American Merchants in China.* Cambridge, MA: East Asian Research Center, Harvard University, 1971. Along with Russell and Company, Augustine Heard and Company was one of the biggest American commission houses on the China coast. The company's development reached its peak from 1858 to 1862.

7:451 Miller, Stuart Creighton. "The American Trader's Image of China, 1785–1840." *Pacific Historical Review* 36 (November 1967): 375–95. This article argues that from the beginning of America's trade with China, Americans had negative attitudes and opinions about the Chinese. Compare with Goldstein, *Philadelphia and the China Trade, 1682–1846: Commercial, Cultural, and Attitudinal Effects* (1978) (7:441).

7:452 Ross, Frank E. "American Adventures in the Early Marine Fur Trade with China." *Chinese Social and Political Science Review* 21, no. 2 (1937): 221–67. Based on journal accounts, this article details the early encounters (1787–1812) between American fur traders and their Spanish and Russian counterparts on the Pacific coast.

7:453 Rubinstein, Murray A. *The Origins of the Anglo-American Missionary Enterprise in China, 1807–1840.* Lanham, MD: Scarecrow Press, 1996. This book shows how British and American missionaries worked together to form an influential missionary community in south China. Rubinstein discusses the cultural and political background of the missionaries.

7:454 Schneider, Laurence A. "Humphrey Marshall, Commissioner to China, 1853–1854." *Kentucky Historical Society Register* 63 (April 1965): 97–120. Marshall's role as commissioner to China was hampered by difficulties from all quarters, the Chinese government, the British and the French, and even the U.S. navy.

7:455 Stelle, Charles C. "American Trade in Opium to China, 1821–1839." *Pacific Historical Review* 10 (March 1941): 57–74. This article discusses the innovations American merchants used to monopolize the trade in Turkish opium. They were able to increase their profits from the drug even though their major competitors, the English, possessed all the advantages of a vast and powerful commercial empire.

7:456 _____. "American Trade in Opium to China, Prior to 1820." *Pacific Historical Review* 9 (November 1940): 425–44. The first recorded participation of Americans in the opium trade came two decades after the opening of trade in 1784. Prohibited by the English from trading with India, the drug's major source, they developed a profitable and competitive trade in Turkish opium.

7:457 Swisher, Earl. *China's Management of the American Barbarians: A Study of Sino-American Relations, 1841–1861, with Documents.* New Haven: Yale University Press for the Far Eastern Association, 1953. Reprint 1972 (Octagon Books). The author analyzes official Chinese attitudes and policies toward foreigners in general and Americans in particular. Seven hundred pages of translated documents support the author's argument that the Chinese perceived all westerners as similar and thus based their relations with Americans on precedents set by Sino-English contacts. Extensive bibliography and a glossary of Chinese names and places.

7:458 Teng, Ssü-yu. *The Taiping Rebellion and the Western Powers: A Comprehensive Survey.* Oxford: Clarendon Press, 1971. In this survey of all western nations regarding the Taiping rebels, the author suggests that American policy, nominally one of neutrality, followed the whims of various individuals from attempted intervention to passive nonaction, yet, whatever its course, the United States did not follow English leadership. Extensive bibliography.

7:459 Teng, Ssü-yu, and John K. Fairbank. *China's Response to the West: A Documentary Survey, 1839–1923.* See chapter 13 of this Guide (13:17).

7:460 Teng, Yuan-chung. "Reverend Issachar Jacox Roberts and the Taiping Rebellion." *Journal of Asian Studies* 23 (November 1963): 55–67. Teng analyzes the influence of Roberts (1837–1862) on the future leader of the Taiping rebels, Hung Hsiu-ch'üan, as a result of Hung's study with him in Canton. He also recounts the later visits of Roberts to the Taiping capital and his final assessment of Hung as a "crazy man." See also Teng's *Americans and the Taiping Rebellion: A Study of American-Chinese Relationship, 1847–1864* (Taipei: China Academy, 1982).

7:461   Tong, Te-kong. *United States Diplomacy in China, 1844–60.* Seattle: University of Washington Press, 1964. The author perceives the 1840s and 1850s as a period of flux in which the Chinese and Americans adjusted to the new treaty system. He argues that American diplomats concluded that the only feasible U.S. policy was that which later became known as the open door principle. Extensive bibliography.

7:462   Welch, Richard E., Jr. "Caleb Cushing's Chinese Mission and the Treaty of Wanghia: A Review." *Oregon Historical Quarterly* 58 (December 1957): 328–57. Welch discusses Cushing's attitudes, his negotiations with the Chinese, and the final Sino-American treaty. The article not only lauds Cushing's mission as a protection of American interests in China but argues that mercantile interests were as crucial a component of Manifest Destiny as were agrarian interests. See also the older Ping Chia Kuo, "Caleb Cushing and the Treaty of Wanghia, 1844," *Journal of Modern History* 5 (March 1933): 34–54, which concludes that Cushing's success came less from his ability than Chinese inexperience in dealing with westerners. And see William J. Donahue, "The Caleb Cushing Mission," *Modern Asian Studies* 16 (April 1982): 193–216, and Claude Moore Fuess, *The Life of Caleb Cushing* (2 vols., New York: Harcourt, Brace and Company, 1923).

JAPAN

7:463   America-Japan Society, ed. *The First Japanese Embassy to the United States of America, Sent to Washington in 1860 as the First of the Series of Embassies Specially Sent Abroad by the Tokugawa Shogunate.* Tokyo: American-Japan Society, 1920. This is mainly the diary of vice-ambassador Muragaki Awaji-no-kami (translated by Shigehiko Miyoshi), along with other contemporary Japanese

and American observations on the embassy. Muragaki's diary was also published as a series in Japan in the 1950s.

7:464   Bain, Chester A. "Commodore Matthew Perry, Humphrey Marshall, and the Taiping Rebellion." *Far Eastern Quarterly* 10 (May 1951): 258–70. This article details the controversy (1853–1854) between Perry and Marshall that resulted from Perry's refusal to make warships available to Marshall for the commissioner's transportation to north China and for the protection of American lives and property threatened by the Taiping rebels.

7:465   Bartlett, Merrill L. "Commodore James Biddle and the First Naval Mission to Japan, 1845–1846." *American Neptune* 41 (January 1981): 25–35. Bartlett suggests that the lessons of Biddle's perceived failure to engage the Japanese during his 1845–1846 expedition guided the actions of Matthew C. Perry when he "opened" Japan to American interests in 1854.

7:466   Cole, Allan B. "Japan's First Embassy to the United States, 1860." *Pacific Northwest Quarterly* 32 (April 1941): 131–66. This is a thorough account of the mission.

7:467   _____. *A Scientist with Perry in Japan: The Journal of Dr. James Morrow.* Chapel Hill: University of North Carolina Press, 1947. As agriculturalist with the Perry mission, Morrow spent more time on shore and met more Japanese than any other member of the expedition.

7:468   _____. *With Perry in Japan: The Diary of Edward Yorke McCauley.* Princeton: Princeton University Press, 1942. McCauley was an acting master's mate on the *Powhatan*. His diary recounts Perry's second voyage to Japan.

7:469   _____. *Yankee Surveyors in the Shogun's Seas: Records of the U.S. Surveying Expedition to the North Pacific Ocean, 1853–1856.* Princeton: Princeton University Press, 1947. This is the report of the brash naval officers who landed armed men at will along the coast of Japan and surveyed Japan's inland waters in violation of the Perry treaty.

7:470   Consenza, Mario Emilio, ed. *The Complete Journal of Townsend Harris, First American Consul General and Minister to Japan.* Rutland, VT: C. E. Tuttle, 1959. This is the major published source on Townsend Harris. The journal covers the period to June 18, 1858, and thus does not extend into the period when Harris served as minister at Edo. First published in 1930.

7:471   Dulles, Foster Rhea. *Yankees and Samurai: America's Role in the Emergence of Modern Japan, 1791–1900.* New York: Harper and Row, 1965. This is probably Dulles's best book. America's role in the emergence of modem Japan is broadly examined. The emphasis is not upon trade and diplomacy but rather on important cultural relations—the experiment in development in Hokkaido, Ernest Fenollosa, Lafcadio Hearn, William Elliot Griffis, American visitors to Japan, etc. The focus is on individuals, both Americans and Japanese, who provided a bridge between the two cultures. Extensive bibliography.

7:472   Graff, Henry F., ed. *Bluejackets with Perry in Japan.* New York: New York Public Library, 1952. This is a day-by-day account of Master's Mate John R. C. Lewis of the *Macedonian* and Cabin Boy William B. Allen of the *Vandalia* in Perry's historic voyage opening up Japan.

7:473   Hawks, Francis L. *Narrative of the Expedition of an American Squadron to the China Seas and Japan, Performed in the Years 1852, 1853, and 1854 under the Command of Commodore M. C. Perry, United States Navy.* 3 vols. Washington, DC: A. O. P. Nicholson, 1856–1858. Volume 1 of this detailed official narrative report is based primarily on the journal of Commodore Perry but also incorporates material from the journals and reports of Fleet Captain Henry A. Adams, Flag Lieutenants Silas Bent and John Contee, Captain Joel Abbot, Commander Franklin Buchanan, Surgeons Daniel S. Green and Charles F. Fahs, Chaplain George Jones, Bayard Taylor, and others. Volume 2 contains various scientific reports, and volume 3 is a report on zodiacal light observations. In 1980, a microfilm edition was made available by Research Publications of Woodbridge, Connecticut.

7:474   Heusken, Henry C. J. *Japan Journal, 1855–1861.* New Brunswick: Rutgers University Press, 1964. This is the journal of Townsend Harris's Dutch secretary and interpreter, who recorded the events from October 1855 to June 1858. He resumed the journal in January 1861, just two weeks before being assassinated by an anti-foreign Japanese ronin. Translated and edited by Jeannette C. van der Corput and Robert A. Wilson.

7:475   Miyoshi, Masao. *As We Saw Them: The First Japanese Embassy to the United States (1860).* Berkeley: University of California Press, 1979. Reprint 1994 (Kodansha International). Written by a specialist in comparative literature, this book examines the diaries kept by members of the 1860 Japanese mission to the United States, describing how the first visitors to America reacted to new situations and comparing them with the diary of Townsend Harris. See also Lewis W. Bush, *77 Samurai: Japan's First Embassy to America* (Palo Alto: Kodansha International, 1968), based on a work by the Japanese author, Itsuro Hattori.

7:476   Morison, Samuel Eliot. *"Old Bruin": Commodore Matthew C. Perry, 1794–1858, The American Naval Officer Who Helped Found Liberia, Hunted Pirates in the West Indies, Practised Diplomacy with the Sultan of Turkey and the King of the Two Sicilies; Commanded the Gulf Squadron in the Mexican War, Promoted the Steam Navy and the Shell Gun, and Conducted the Naval Expedition Which Opened Japan.* Boston: Little, Brown, 1967. Perry's role in the opening of Japan to American commerce makes him a conspicuous example of the military man involved in foreign policy. Perry was a sailor-diplomat not only in Japan, but also in Liberia, the West Indies, the Ottoman empire, and the Kingdom of the Two Sicilies. Bibliography.

7:477   Nester, William R. *Power across the Pacific: A Diplomatic History of American Relations with Japan.* See chapter 2 of this Guide (2:285). For an early study of the first years of what became a troublesome element in U.S.-Japanese relations, see F. C. Jones, *Extraterritoriality in Japan and the Diplomatic Relations Resulting in Its Abolition, 1853–1899* (New Haven: Yale University Press, 1931; reprint 1970, AMS Press).

7:478   Pineau, Roger, ed. *The Japan Expedition, 1852–1854: The Personal Journal of Commodore Matthew C. Perry.* Washington, DC: Smithsonian Institution Press, 1968. Perry dictated this journal during the voyage. It was the most significant source for the official narrative, but Hawks, *Narrative of the Expedition of an American Squadron to the China Seas and Japan, Performed in the Years 1852, 1853, and 1854 under the Command of Commodore M. C. Perry, United States Navy* (1856–1858) (7:473), did not include everything from it. Bibliography. Introduction by Samuel Eliot Morison.

7:479   Preble, George H. *The Opening of Japan: A Diary of Discovery in the Far East, 1853–1856.* Norman: University of Oklahoma Press, 1962. As a lieutenant on the *Macedonian,* Preble was a close observer of events, including the negotiations at Kanagawa. Like many others, he refused to obey Perry's order to turn over his diary to the navy for use in compiling the official narrative. Edited by Boleslaw Szczesniak.

7:480   Sakamaki, Shunzo. *Japan and the United States, 1790–1853.* Tokyo: Asiatic Society of Japan, 1939. Reprint 1973 (Scholarly Resources). This study, based on Japanese and English-language sources, is especially useful for information on American voyages to Japan in the 1830s and 1840s.

7:481   Schroeder, John H. *Matthew Calbraith Perry: Antebellum Sailor and Diplomat.* Annapolis: Naval Institute Press, 2001. This is the first major biography of Perry since Morison's *"Old Bruin": Commodore Matthew C. Perry, 1794–1858, . . .* (1967) (7:476), about half of which concerns his historic voyages to Japan in the early 1850s. Schroeder is balanced in his assessment of "the preeminent naval officer of the antebellum generation."

7:482   Spalding, J. W. *The Japan Expedition: Japan and around the World: An Account of Three Visits to the Japanese Empire, with Sketches of Madeira, St. Helena, Cape of Good Hope, Mauritius, Ceylon, Singapore, China, and Loo-Choo.* New York: Redfield, 1855. The author was the captain's clerk on the *Mississippi,* the flagship of the squadron. Though he states that he did not keep a journal—which by Perry's order he would have been required to surrender to the navy—he gives a detailed day-by-day account of both voyages of Perry to Japan.

7:483   Statler, Oliver. *Shimoda Story.* New York:

Random House, 1969. The book is written with literary grace and, as the author states, with some liberty in filling out events where the evidence is scanty. The bulk of the volume relates to the experiences of Townsend Harris in Shimoda. Two final chapters relate the negotiations at Edo in 1858 and the subsequent residence of Harris in Edo. Extensive bibliography. Another popular account is Carl Crow, *He Opened the Door of Japan: Townsend Harris and the Story of His Amazing Adventures in Establishing American Relations with the Far East* (New York: Harper and Brothers, 1939; reprint 1974, Greenwood Press).

7:484   Vernon, Manfred C. "The Dutch and the Opening of Japan by the United States." *Pacific Historical Review* 28 (February 1959): 39–48. Though the Dutch were uneasy about the Perry Expedition and expected it to fail, the governor-general of Java sent instructions to the Dutch foreman at Nagasaki to give support to the objective of opening Japan.

7:485   Walworth, Arthur. *Black Ships off Japan: The Study of Commodore Perry's Expedition.* New York: Alfred A. Knopf, 1946. Walworth was the first writer to use sources, such as the records of Williams, Spalding, and Preble, that were not incorporated in the official narrative.

7:486   Warinner, Emily V. *Voyager to Destiny: The Amazing Adventure of Manjiro, the Man Who Changed Worlds Twice.* Indianapolis: Bobbs-Merrill, 1956. A popular, entertaining, but thoroughly researched account of the Japanese fisherman who was shipwrecked, rescued by an American ship, and educated in New England, and who returned to Japan in 1850.

7:487   Wiley, Peter Booth, with Korogi Ichiro. *Yankees in the Land of the Gods: Commodore Perry and the Opening of Japan.* New York: Viking, 1990. This is an effective retelling of the famous meeting in Tokyo, documented by an abundance of both American and Japanese sources.

7:488   Williams, S. Wells. *A Journal of the Perry Expedition to Japan (1853–1854).* Yokohama: Kelly and Walsh, 1910. Reprint 1973 (Scholarly Resources). Williams's journal was not used in the compilation of the official narrative. It gives the most extensive coverage of any of the private journals. Edited by his son, Frederick Wells Williams.

7:489   Wood, William Maxwell. *Fankwei: Or, the San Jacinto in the Seas of India, China, and Japan.* New York: Harper and Brothers, 1859. This long account, written by the surgeon of the fleet, covers the voyage of Harris to Siam, China, and Japan and the landing of Harris at Shimoda.

INDIA

7:490   Barpujari, H. K. *The American Missionaries and North-East India, 1836–1900 A.D.: A Documentary Study.* Guwahati: Spectrum Publishers, 1986. Based primarily on missionary correspondence, this work is a rich source for impressions of India through American eyes. The lengthy introduction provides a summary of missionary activity in India, 1836–1900, and the book includes biographical notes on the missionaries and several Indian national leaders who facilitated their mission. The author served as the area secretary for Baptist Missions.

7:491   Misra, Panchananda. "Indo-American Trade Relations: The Period of Growth, 1784–1850." *Journal of Indian History* 42 (December 1964): 833–46. This is a useful summary of the development of Indo-American trade and of the activities of early American diplomats in India. See also G. Bhaghat, *Americans in India, 1784–1860* (New York: New York University Press, 1970).

THAILAND (SIAM)

7:492   Lord, Donald C. "Missionaries, Thai, and Diplomats." *Pacific Historical Review* 35 (November 1966): 413–31. Lord recounts the role of American missionaries in Siam as advisers to both the Thai government and as American diplomats during the reigns of Nang Klao (1824–1851) and Mongkut (1851–1868).

7:493   _____. *Mo Bradley and Thailand.* Grand Rapids, MI: Eerdmans, 1969. Dan Beach (Mo) Bradley was a close friend, adviser, and physician to King Mongkut. He made few converts but introduced surgery, the printing press, vaccination, and modern

obstetrics to Siam. Lord notes that American missionaries played a constructive role as advisers and interpreters for the Siamese government. Bibliography.

7:494   Roberts, Edmund. *Embassy to the Eastern Courts of Cochin-China, Siam and Muscat: In the U.S. Sloop-of-War Peacock, David Geisinger, Commander, during the Years 1832–3–4.* New York: Harper and Brothers, 1837. Reprint 1972 (Scholarly Resources). Roberts was one of the pioneer American diplomats in Southeast Asia. He negotiated the first American treaty with Siam in 1833 and unsuccessfully attempted to negotiate a treaty with Cochin-China (Vietnam).

7:495   Ruschenberger, W. S. W. *A Voyage round the World: Including an Embassy to Siam and Muscat in 1835, 1836, and 1837.* Philadelphia: Carey, Lea and Blanchard, 1838. Ruschenberger, a naval surgeon, accompanied Edmund Roberts on his second mission to Southeast Asia in 1835–1836 to exchange ratifications of the treaty with Siam and make another attempt at negotiations with Annam (Vietnam).

SUMATRA

7:496   Gould, James W. *Americans in Sumatra.* The Hague: M. Nijhoff, 1961. Gould traces the development of American commercial, scientific, humanitarian, and political activities in Sumatra from the Atjeh War in 1873 to 1940. Of special interest is the discussion of the role of Americans in the development of the oil and rubber industries. Bibliography.

7:497   _____. "Sumatra—America's Pepperpot, 1784–1873, Part I, Part II, Part III." *Historical Collections of the Essex Institute* 92 (January-October 1956): 83–153, 203–52, 295–349. This is a thorough account that throws light on American activities in the rest of Southeast Asia as well. Gould demonstrates that Americans had a substantial impact on the economic life of Sumatra and also influenced the policies of European powers.

7:498   Long, David F. "'Martial Thunder': The First Official American Armed Intervention in Asia." *Pacific Historical Review* 42 (May 1973): 143–62.

This is an account of the attack on the Sumatran town of Quala Batu by the U.S. frigate *Potomac* in 1832 in reprisal for the robbery of the Salem merchant ship *Friendship*. The *Potomac*'s action raised a national argument over the wisdom of the attack and a constitutional debate over the right of the president to commit the nation to hostilities without a declaration of war.

7:499   Taylor, Fitch W. *The Flag Ship: Or a Voyage around the World in the United States Frigate Columbia: Attended by Her Consort the Sloop of War John Adams: And Bearing the Broad Pennant of Commodore George C. Read.* 2 vols. New York: D. Appleton and Co., 1840. Taylor sailed in the *Columbia* on its punitive expedition to the north coast of Sumatra to punish a local raja for the robbery of the American ship *Eclipse* in 1838. (Much of the cargo stolen was apparently opium.)

OTHERS

7:500   Ahmat, Sharom. "American Trade with Singapore, 1819–65." *Journal of the Malaysian Branch Royal Asiatic Society* 38 (1965): 241–57. This article discusses the growth of the American trade with Singapore and details the ways in which the barriers to it were gradually overcome.

7:501   _____. "Rhode Island Traders in Java, 1799–1836." *Journal of Southeast Asian History* 6 (March 1965): 94–107. Rhode Island merchants enjoyed a brief period of prosperity trading in Javanese coffee. Jefferson's embargo hurt the trade badly, and after 1817, the Rhode Islanders faced British and Dutch commercial restrictions as well as the threat of piracy.

Pacific

7:502   Dulles, Foster Rhea. *America in the Pacific: A Century of Expansion.* 2d ed. Boston: Houghton Mifflin Company, 1938. This survey of the historical background of U.S. interests in the Pacific covers the western expansion of the continent, early relations with China and Japan, and the acquisition of

Samoa, Hawaii, and the Philippines. Bibliography. First published in 1932.

7:503   Fredman, Lionel E. *The United States Enters the Pacific.* Sydney: Angus and Robertson, 1969. In this brief sketch of American expansionism, Fredman, a well-known Australian Americanist, provides an excellent chapter in American-Australian relations, from the earliest beginnings to 1968. Not unlike many other commentators on the relationship, the author concludes the American alliance will continue to be a cardinal feature of Australian foreign policy. Bibliography.

7:504   Grattan, C. Hartley. *The Southwest Pacific to 1900: A Modern History: Australia, New Zealand, the Islands, Antarctica.* Ann Arbor: University of Michigan Press, 1963. This is a broad survey of Pacific history concentrating on international rivalry. Bibliography.

7:505   _____. *The United States and the Southwest Pacific.* Cambridge, MA: Harvard University Press, 1961. In this study Grattan deals with American-Australian relations from the long-term historical perspective. This is a significant book by a leading American Australianist. Bibliography.

7:506   Shewmaker, Kenneth E. "Forging the 'Great Chain': Daniel Webster and the Origins of American Foreign Policy toward East Asia and the Pacific, 1841–1852." *Proceedings of the American Philosophical Society* 129 (September 1985): 225–59. Shewmaker emphasizes Webster's role in encouraging antebellum East Asian expansionism, especially of a commercial nature.

7:507   Swisher, Earl. "Commodore Perry's Imperialism in Relation to America's Present-Day Position in the Pacific." *Pacific Historical Review* 16 (February 1947): 30–40. Swisher discusses Perry's proposal for U.S. control of Hawaii, the Bonin Islands, Okinawa, and Formosa.

HAWAII

7:508   King, Pauline, ed. *The Diaries of David Lawrence Gregg: An American Diplomat in Hawaii, 1853–1858.* Honolulu: Hawaiian Historical Society,

1982. This is a valuable collection of the correspondence of an early and influential American diplomat in Hawaii. The author is elsewhere in this chapter called Pauline King Joerger (7:80). See also W. Patrick Strauss, "Pioneer American Diplomats in Polynesia, 1820–1840," *Pacific Historical Review* 31 (February 1962): 21–30.

7:509 Merry, Sally Engle. *Colonizing Hawai'i: The Cultural Power of Law.* Princeton: Princeton University Press, 2000. This is a landmark study that traces how American notions of law and American legal institutions effectively colonized Hawaii decades before annexation. See also Harold W. Bradley, *The American Frontier in Hawaii: The Pioneers, 1789–1843* (1942) (5:627).

7:510 Rolle, Andrew F. "California Filibustering and the Hawaiian Kingdom." *Pacific Historical Review* 19 (August 1950): 251–63. This is a key early source in a little-known chapter of Hawaiian history.

GUAM

7:511 Ballendorf, Dirk Anthony, and William L. Wuerch. "Captain Samuel J. Masters, U.S. Consul to Guam, 1854–56: Harbinger of American Pacific Expansion." *Diplomacy & Statecraft* 2 (November 1991): 306–26. This work recounts the tenure of Masters as an unrecognized and unwelcome consul to Spanish-controlled Guam.

AUSTRALIA AND NEW ZEALAND

7:512 Greenwood, Gordon. *Early American-Australian Relations from the Arrival of the Spaniards in America to the Close of 1830.* Melbourne: Melbourne University Press, 1944. In one of the earliest works on the subject, the author traces Australian-American relations from the first settlement in New South Wales to the time of the gold fever in Victoria. The work also takes into consideration relations with South America. Bibliography.

7:513 Levi, Werner. *American-Australian Relations.* Minneapolis: University of Minnesota Press, 1947. In an early work on the subject, the author

traces the growth and development of American-Australian relations from the late eighteenth century to the aftermath of World War II. Levi concludes that despite their differences, the United States and Australia will continue to be important to each other. Extensive bibliography.

7:514 Lissington, Margaret P. *New Zealand and the United States, 1840–1944.* Wellington, NZ: A. R. Shearer, Govt. Printer, 1972. A cursory but very well documented survey, this slim volume has the additional merit of being the only one of its kind. Extensive bibliography.

7:515 Potts, E. Daniel, and Annette Potts. *Young America and Australian Gold: Americans and the Gold Rush of the 1850's.* St. Lucia: University of Queensland Press, 1974. This study examines American migration to Australia during the gold rush of the 1850s. Although few Americans in Australia were associated with the Young America movement, "most would have shared their beliefs in capitalistic progress and romantic individualism." Bibliography.

Whaling

7:516 Bennett, Frederick Debell. *Narrative of a Whaling Voyage round the Globe, from the Year 1833 to 1836: Comprising Sketches of Polynesia, California, the Indian Archipelago, etc. with an Account of Southern Whales, the Sperm Whale Fishery, and the Natural History of the Climates Visited.* 2 vols. London: R. Bentley, 1840. Reprint 1970 (Da Capo Press). This is a classic account of American whaling in the Pacific and a major source for Herman Melville's *Moby Dick* (1851).

7:517 Bradley, Henry, Thomas H. Bennett, and Washington Chase. *A Voyage from the United States to South America, Performed during the Years 1821, 1822, & 1823: Embracing a Description of the City of Rio Janeiro in Brazil, of Every Port of Importance in Chili, of Several in Lower Peru, and of an Eighteen Months Cruise in a Nantucket Whaleship: The Whole Interspersed with a Variety of Original Anecdotes.* Newburyport, MA: Herald Press, 1823. This is a valuable primary source on early South American relations.

7:518　　Creighton, Margaret S. *Rites and Passages: The Experience of American Whaling, 1830–1870.* New York: Cambridge University Press, 1995. This valuable contribution illuminates the social history of American economic expansionism. See also the Creighton and Lisa Norling edited collection, *Iron Men, Wooden Women: Gender and Seafaring in the Atlantic World, 1700–1920* (Baltimore: Johns Hopkins University Press, 1996).

7:519　　Davis, Lance Edwin, Robert E. Gallman, and Karin Gleiter. *In Pursuit of Leviathan: Technology, Institutions, Productivity, and Profits in American Whaling, 1816–1906.* Chicago: University of Chicago Press, 1997. This is an impressively researched and persuasively argued text on a critical aspect of American economic expansionism. By the 1840s, Americans had the largest whaling industry in the world, but it began a long decline in the next decade, hit by competition from petroleum and growing difficulty manning its ships.

7:520　　Lofstrom, William Lee. *Paita, Outpost of Empire: The Impact of the New England Whaling Fleet on the Socioeconomic Development of Northern Peru, 1832–1865.* Mystic, CT: Mystic Seaport Museum, 1996. The author uses the concept of *espacio económico* as a tool for understanding the relationship among the local social, political, and economic lives of a Peruvian whaling entrepôt and the wider world with which it interacts. This work is es-

sentially a core-periphery analysis but is not burdened by the determinism of the dependency school.

7:521　　Seward, William. *Commerce in the Pacific Ocean.* Washington, DC: Buell and Blanchard, 1852. This fourteen-page pamphlet prints a speech, given July 29, 1852, that was a significant statement of American global economic destiny by one of the leading policymakers of the nineteenth century.

7:522　　Stackpole, Edouard A. *The Sea-Hunters: The New England Whalemen during Two Centuries, 1635–1835.* New York: Bonanza Books, 1953. This is a classic work by one of the early leaders in the field.

7:523　　_____. *Whales & Destiny: The Rivalry between America, France, and Britain for Control of the Southern Whale Fishery, 1785–1825.* Amherst: University of Massachusetts Press, 1972. Though focused only on whaling, this is a prototype analysis of economics as the basis of great power rivalries.

7:524　　Starbuck, Alexander. *History of the American Whale Fishery, from Its Earliest Inception to the Year 1876.* Washington, DC: Government Printing Office, 1878. Reprint 1989 (Castle). This is a pioneer narrative of the U.S. whaling enterprise, replete with voyage statistics and economic data. Other works followed, both to update and correct Starbuck, especially Reginald B. Hegarty, *Returns of Whaling Vessels Sailing from American Ports: A Continuation of Alexander Starbuck's "History of the American Whale Fishery," 1876–1928* (New Bedford, MA: Old Dartmouth Historical Society and Whaling Museum, 1959).

The Diplomacy of the Civil War

Contributing Editors

HOWARD JONES
University of Alabama

DONALD A. RAKESTRAW
Georgia Southern University

Contents

Introduction

Research for this project involved conventional and electronic methodology. The conventional research began with the titles retrieved from Frank J. Merli's "Civil War" chapter in the first edition of the *Guide to American Foreign Relations since 1700*, the catalogs of the Library of Congress and the British Library, both general and specific bibliographies on the period, and such well-known aids as *America: History and Life* and *Historical Abstracts*. The bibliographies of post-1983 monographs and other secondary sources helped to flesh out the list, as did various published bibliographies and indices. As with all research of this nature, the list expanded as one article or book after another led to additional works.

The electronic research revealed numerous online resources. Online access to the various library catalogs such as those of the Library of Congress, the British Library, and the many university libraries proved extremely valuable in ferreting out sources. Also useful was a variety of Civil War websites. As expected, most of these focused on the military or domestic aspects of the war, but some sites nevertheless provided references to materials relating to international matters. The best starting point for this topic is the "Index of Civil War Information Available on the Internet," found at http://www.cwc.lsu.edu/civlink.htm. Perhaps the most important source for current titles is ABC-CLIO's electronic versions of *America: History and Life* and *Historical Abstracts* at http://serials.abc-clio.com. Beyond scanning the various databases supported by the University of Georgia's "Galileo" system at http://www.galileo.usg.edu., other sites contributing to the process included http://sunsite.utk.edu/civil-war/warweb.html.

Published Primary Materials

UNION

8:1   *Digest of the United States Supreme Court Reports: U.S. vols. 207–244.* Vols. 5–8. Rochester, NY: Lawyers' Co-operative Publishing Company, 1918. This set remains a highly useful work in analyzing the legal issues involved in a civil war.

8:2   Bevans, Charles I., ed. *Treaties and Other International Agreements of the United States of America, 1776–1949* (5:3). These volumes supersede Malloy et al., *Treaties, Conventions, International Acts, Protocols, and Agreements between the United States and Other Powers, 1776–1937* (1910–1938) (8:5).

8:3   Catterall, Helen Tunnicliff, ed. *Judicial Cases Concerning American Slavery and the Negro.* This is a valuable collection of primary materials relating to slavery and the slave trade, emphasizing court cases in many states of the union, both north and south, as well as Canada and Jamaica (6:2).

8:4   Harrington, Fred H. "A Peace Mission of 1863." *American Historical Review* 46 (October 1940): 76–86. This is primarily a collection of documents showing Lincoln's abortive peace effort of 1863 that involved sending a spy to discuss terms with the Confederate cabinet in Richmond. The failure showed how hard the lines were separating north and south.

8:5   Malloy, William M., et al., eds. *Treaties, Conventions, International Acts, Protocols, and Agreements between the United States and Other Powers, 1776–1937.* 4 vols. Washington, DC: Government Printing Office, 1910–1938. These volumes remain useful but are superseded by Bevans, *Treaties and Other International Agreements of the United States of America, 1776–1949* (1968–1974) (8:2).

8:6   Miller, David Hunter, ed. *Treaties and Other International Acts of the United States of America, 1776–1863.* 8 vols. Washington, DC: Government Printing Office, 1931–1948. This collection is dated but still useful.

8:7   U.S. Congress. *The Congressional Globe: 23rd Congress to 42nd Congress, Dec. 2, 1833, to March 3, 1873.* Most of the speeches contain more rhetoric than substance, but this official record is useful in fleshing out American public opinion along with some of the foreign relations issues during the Civil War. Subtitles vary on the title pages (1:87).

8:8   U.S. Department of State, ed. *Correspondence Concerning Claims against Great Britain, Transmitted to the Senate of the United States in Answer to the Resolutions of December 4 and 10, 1867, and of May 27, 1868.* 7 vols. Washington, DC: Government Printing Office, 1869–1871. This collection, although difficult to use, contains valuable materials on Civil War diplomacy. Especially important are the official documents on the postwar Alabama claims dispute.

8:9   _____. *Foreign Relations of the United States, 1861–1869.* These rich volumes contain items from the State Department, including correspondence, notes, memoranda, and documents on all issues affecting foreign relations during and immediately following the Civil War (1:93).

8:10   U.S. War Department. *The War of the Rebellion: A Compilation of the Official Records of the Union and Confederate Armies.* 70 vols. in 128. Washington, DC: Government Printing Office, 1880–1901. Reprint 1985 (National Historical Society). This mammoth collection remains the most important source of primary materials on the military history of the war.

8:11   Wheaton, Henry. *Elements of International Law.* Boston: Little, Brown and Company, 1866. This is a highly useful examination of international law by the foremost American legal theorist of the early nineteenth century. It touches on many issues that would surface during the Civil War, including Russell's reasons for recognizing Confederate belligerency, the role of the Declaration of Paris of 1856 in the war's deliberations, and the Confederate shipbuilding controversy. First published in 1836.

Personal Papers and Diaries

8:12   Ford, Worthington C., ed. *A Cycle of Adams Letters, 1861–1865.* 2 vols. Boston: Houghton Mifflin Company, 1920. Filled with astute and often biting comment on a wide variety of subjects, these volumes bear the imprint of their famous correspondents, the son and two grandsons of John Quincy Adams. They contain valuable insights by Union minister Charles Francis Adams into En-

gland's attitude toward the war, including such topics as slavery, the blockade, recognition of the Confederacy, the *Trent* crisis, the Emancipation Proclamation, and numerous other issues affecting the diplomacy of the war. Most striking is the lack of trust between the Union and England.

8:13   Levenson, J. C., et al., eds. *The Letters of Henry Adams.* 6 vols. Cambridge, MA: Belknap Press of Harvard University Press, 1982–1988. This collection contains numerous insights into the Union's diplomacy as well as Britain's reaction to the war. Dissolution of the Union, many British observers believed, was unavoidable—a reality that they thought the Lincoln administration must accept.

8:14   Silver, Arthur W., ed. "Henry Adams' 'Diary of a Visit to Manchester.'" *American Historical Review* 51 (October 1945): 74–89. Among other pieces of useful information, Adams learned from merchants in Manchester that by the spring of 1862 a cotton shortage could develop that might cause growing pressure to lift the Union blockade and recognize the south.

8:15   Beale, Howard K., ed. *The Diary of Edward Bates, 1859–1866.* Washington, DC: Government Printing Office, 1933. This diary of Lincoln's attorney general contains entries relating to the administration's concern about British and French intervention in the war. Bates also emphasized the necessity of conducting the war in a way that would not encourage slave insurrections. This is volume 4 of *The Annual Report of the American Historical Association for the Year 1930.*

8:16   Pease, Theodore Calvin, and James G. Randall, eds. *The Diary of Orville Hickman Browning.* 2 vols. Springfield, IL: Trustees of the Illinois State Historical Library, 1925–1933. This is the diary of one of Lincoln's closest confidants, for a year and a half the successor to the Senate seat of Illinois's Stephen Douglas. It contains useful information on the president's move toward antislavery as well as his concern over foreign intervention in the war and other international issues.

8:17   Dobson, Samuel H., and George S. Denison, eds. *Diary and Correspondence of Salmon P. Chase.* 2 vols. Washington, DC: Government Printing

Office, 1903. Reprint 1971 (Da Capo Press). This diary and papers provide some information on the Lincoln administration's move toward antislavery. Published as the sixth report of the Historical Manuscripts Commission.

8:18   Donald, David Herbert, ed. *Inside Lincoln's Cabinet: The Civil War Diaries of Salmon P. Chase.* New York: Longmans, Green, 1954. Reprint 1970 (Kraus Reprint). This diary helps to show the inner workings of the Lincoln administration as it moved toward antislavery.

8:19   Thompson, Robert Means, and Richard Wainwright, eds. *Confidential Correspondence of Gustavus Vasa Fox, Assistant Secretary of the Navy, 1861–1865.* 2 vols. New York: Naval History Society, 1918–1919. Reprint 1972 (Books for Libraries Press). Though this set (vols. 9–10 of the *Publications of the Naval History Society*) is disappointing on foreign affairs, it is extremely good on matters of technological innovation in naval war.

8:20   Dennett, Tyler, ed. *Lincoln and the Civil War in the Diaries and Letters of John Hay.* New York: Dodd, Mead and Company, 1939. Reprint 1988 (Da Capo Press). This collection is useful in exploring Lincoln's evolving ideas about slavery and antislavery.

8:21   Basler, Roy P., with Marion Dolores Pratt and Lloyd A. Dunlap, eds. *The Collected Works of Abraham Lincoln.* 9 vols. New Brunswick: Rutgers University Press, 1953–1955. These rich volumes demonstrate the eloquence of Lincoln as well as his understanding of the intricate relationship between domestic and foreign policy and the growing importance of antislavery in constructing a new and improved Union. Lincoln confronted the dilemma of slavery's standing as a legal right and a moral wrong, leading him as a Republican to oppose its extension into new territories while promising to leave it alone in areas where it already existed. As the war went on, however, he realized that slavery had to end for a new birth of freedom for the republic. In 1974, Greenwood Press published *The Collected Works of Abraham Lincoln: First Supplement, 1832–1865* (reprinted in 1990 by Rutgers University Press); see also Basler and Christian O. Basler, eds., *The Collected Works of Abraham Lincoln: Second Supplement,* *1848–1865* (New Brunswick: Rutgers University Press, 1990).

8:22   Sears, Stephen W., ed. *The Civil War Papers of George B. McClellan: Selected Correspondence, 1860–1865.* New York: Ticknor and Fields, 1989. Reprint 1992 (Da Capo Press). This selection of correspondence is revealing on McClellan's thoughts about Lincoln and the antislavery issue.

8:23   Wallace, Sarah Agnes, and Frances Elma Gillespie, eds. *The Journal of Benjamin Moran, 1857–1865.* 2 vols. Chicago: University of Chicago Press, 1948–1949. This invaluable source provides an inside view of Civil War diplomacy as seen by Union minister Charles Francis Adams's assistant secretary of the London legation. Moran was a shrewd and waspish commentator and highly critical of the British. His colorful, acerbic, and insightful memoir is useful for social as well as diplomatic history.

8:24   Curtis, George William, ed. *The Correspondence of John Lothrop Motley.* 2 vols. New York: Harper and Brothers, 1889. This collection of papers of the Union's minister to Austria contains several important elements, including an observation on the legalities affecting the *Trent.*

8:25   Baker, George E., ed. *The Works of William H. Seward.* 5 vols. New York: Redfield, 1853–1884. Reprint 1972 (AMS Press). This collection remains useful in analyzing the thinking of Lincoln's secretary of state.

8:26   _____. *The Works of William H. Seward.* Vol. 5: *The Diplomatic History of the War for the Union.* Boston: Houghton Mifflin and Company, 1884. The fifth volume in this set is sometimes cited separately as *The Diplomatic History of the War for the Union.* It contains some useful information on Seward's thinking.

8:27   Palmer, Beverly W., ed. *The Selected Letters of Charles Sumner.* 2 vols. Boston: Northeastern University Press, 1990. Section 5 of volume 2 covers the period 1859–1865 and contains useful material on the British reaction to the Civil War. Sumner's correspondents include British members of Parliament John Bright and Richard Cobden.

8:28 Pierce, Edward L., ed. "Bright-Sumner Letters, 1861–1872." *Proceedings of the Massachusetts Historical Society* 46 (October 1912): 93–164. This collection of letters from John Bright to Charles Sumner illuminates Bright's position not just on the war but also on the crisis over the *Alabama* claims after the war. The letters provide insight into British sentiment toward the war, slavery, and international law.

8:29 _____. "Letters of Richard Cobden to Charles Sumner, 1862–1865." *American Historical Review* 2 (January 1897): 306–19. This collection of letters demonstrates the British belief that disunion was a fait accompli and that Europe would need cotton by the end of 1862. Cobden felt confident that the Union's emancipation policy in 1863 would prevent the British government from extending recognition to the slaveholding Confederacy. He also underlined the British policy of neutrality by noting Russell's anger over the *Alabama*'s escape from British shipyards.

8:30 Pierce, Edward L., ed. *Memoir and Letters of Charles Sumner.* 4 vols. Boston: Roberts Brothers, 1878–1893. Volume 4 covers the period 1860–1874 and contains useful correspondence relating to the Union's relations with Great Britain during the Civil War. Sumner's correspondents include parliamentary members John Bright and Richard Cobden, and among the topics discussed in their letters are the *Trent* affair, slavery, and possible British intervention in the war.

8:31 Beale, Howard K., ed. *Diary of Gideon Welles: Secretary of the Navy under Lincoln and Johnson.* 3 vols. New York: W. W. Norton and Company, 1960. This collection demonstrates Lincoln's changing views toward antislavery as he prepared to issue the Emancipation Proclamation. It also contains valuable information relating to maritime issues during the war, including Confederate raiders.

CONFEDERACY

8:32 Confederate States of America. Congress. *Journal of the Congress of the Confederate States of America, 1861–1865.* 7 vols. Washington, DC: Government Printing Office, 1904–1905. These volumes contain some useful information relating to King Cotton diplomacy.

8:33 Merli, Frank J., guest ed. *Journal of Confederate History: Special Commemorative Naval Issue on CSS Alabama.* Brentwood, TN: Southern Heritage Press, 1989. This special issue of the *Journal of Confederate History* contains a collection of essays dealing with the CSS *Alabama* from the last two years of the Civil War through five years after the discovery of its wreckage off Cherbourg in late 1984. The volume also contains an annotated bibliography of primary and secondary materials on the subject.

8:34 Pecquet du Bellet, Paul. *The Diplomacy of the Confederate Cabinet of Richmond and Its Agents Abroad: Being Memorandum Notes Taken in Paris during the Rebellion of the Southern States from 1861 to 1865.* Tuscaloosa: Confederate Publishers, 1963. This primary source recounts the activities and observations of Confederate operatives in Europe. It must be used with caution, however, for it is a reprint of a transcription that came to the Library of Congress via a circuitous route rather than from the long missing original. Edited, with an introduction, by William Stanley Hoole.

8:35 Richardson, James D., ed. *A Compilation of the Messages and Papers of the Confederacy, Including the Diplomatic Correspondence, 1861–1865.* 2 vols. Nashville: United States Publishing Co., 1905. Volume 1 contains the papers of Jefferson Davis, while volume 2 has the diplomatic correspondence.

Personal Papers and Diaries

8:36 Hoole, W. Stanley, ed. *Confederate Foreign Agent: The European Diary of Major Edward C. Anderson.* University: Confederate Publishing Co., 1976. This diary furnishes a daily summary of Confederate Maj. Gen. Edward C. Anderson's purchasing efforts in England and France from May to November 1861.

8:37 Woodward, C. Vann, ed. *Mary Chesnut's Civil War.* New Haven: Yale University Press, 1981. This is a superb republication and editing of one of the best southern diaries of the Civil War, first published in 1905 as *Diary from Dixie.* Then, in 1984, Woodward, along with Elisabeth Muhlenfeld, published the famous southern diarist's writings as she composed them during the war in *Private Mary Chesnut: The Unpublished Civil War Diaries* (New York: Oxford University Press).

8:38 Monroe, Haskell M., James T. McIntosh, and Lynda Lasswell Crist, et al., eds. *The Papers of Jefferson Davis*. 10 vols. Baton Rouge: Louisiana State University Press, 1971–. This series, now reaching August 1864, promises to be definitive in a projected fifteen volumes. Some of the earlier volumes have been revised and reissued (e.g., vols. 1, 2, and 5, originally published in 1971, 1975, and 1985 and revised, respectively, in 1991, 1987, and 2000).

8:39 Roland, Dunbar, ed. *Jefferson Davis, Constitutionalist: His Letters, Papers, and Speeches*. 10 vols. Jackson, MS: Mississippi Department of Archives and History, 1923. Reprint 1973 (AMS Press). This collection remains useful in providing some insights into the president of the Confederacy.

8:40 Mason, Virginia. *The Public Life and Diplomatic Correspondence of James M. Mason: With Some Personal History*. Roanoke, VA: Stone Printing Co., 1903. This collection of Mason's papers by his wife contains useful insights into Confederate diplomacy.

8:41 Hoole, W. Stanley, ed. "Notes and Documents: William L. Yancey's European Diary, March–June 1861." *Alabama Review* 25 (April 1972): 134–42. This is a disappointing collection of materials. On speaking of his meetings with Lord Russell on May 3 and 9, 1861, Yancey called the foreign minister "cautious and non-committal."

BRITAIN

8:42 Austin, John. *The Province of Jurisprudence Determined*. London: J. Murray, 1832. Reprint 2000 (Prometheus Books). Austin was the British legal theorist whose work of 1832 pointed to the difficulties in determining when to extend diplomatic recognition to a self-professed "nation" attempting to achieve independence. British foreign secretary Lord John Russell used Austin's writings along with others to justify intervention in the American war. British secretary for war George Cornewall Lewis, however, used the same work to argue against recognition of the Confederacy.

8:43 Barnes, James J., and Patience P. Barnes, eds. *Private and Confidential: Letters from British Ministers in Washington to the Foreign Secretaries in London, 1844–67*. This volume contains letters from Lord Lyons, British minister in Washington during the Civil War, touching on various aspects of politics and society in America. Six chapters focus on several issues during the Civil War, in particular those relating to British neutrality. The editors have also incorporated helpful remarks about the diplomatic records along with a biographical section on 101 persons during the period (6:26).

8:44 Bourne, Kenneth, Donald Cameron Watt, and Great Britain Foreign Office, eds. *British Documents on Foreign Affairs—Reports and Papers from the Foreign Office Confidential Print. Part I: From the Mid-Nineteenth Century to the First World War. Series C: North America, 1837–1914. Vol. 5: The Civil War Years, 1859–1861. Vol. 6: The Civil War Years, 1862–1865*. Bethesda, MD: University Publications of America, 1986. This huge collection contains many useful items relating to British policy toward North America and the American Civil War.

8:45 Brigg, Mary, ed. *The Journals of a Lancashire Weaver, 1856–60, 1860–64, 1872–75*. Liverpool: Record Society for Lancashire and Cheshire, 1982. The first journal, covering 1856–1860, reveals a time of prosperity in Lancashire and Cheshire, while the second, for 1860–1864, demonstrates the negative effects of strikes and the cotton famine.

8:46 Great Britain. Foreign Office. *British and Foreign State Papers*. Vols. 51–57, 61. London: H. M. Stationery Office, 1812–1925. These rich volumes contain information from the British Foreign Office on all major issues that affected Anglo-American relations during the Civil War. British neutrality becomes clear from this collection of documents.

8:47 Great Britain. Parliament. *The Parliamentary Debates*. 356 vols. Edited by T. C. Hansard. London: Wyman, 1830–1891. These remain the standard volumes for following the debates in Parliament over what members called "the American War."

8:48   Great Britain. Parliament. House of Commons. *British Sessional Papers, 1801–1900.* Microfiche. New York: Readex Microprint, 1960–. These materials include correspondence among officials in England, Canada, and the United States.

8:49   _____, ed. *Irish University Press Area Studies Series, British Parliamentary Papers: United States of America.* 60 vols. Shannon, UK: Irish University Press, 1971. This is a valuable collection of official British "sessional and command" papers relating to diplomatic correspondence, negotiations, treaties, and economic issues. Volumes of particular relevance here are 16: *Correspondence and Other Papers Relating to the American Civil War, 1861–1862; 17: Correspondence and Other Papers Relating to the American Civil War, 1863–1864; 18: Correspondence and Other Papers Respecting the American Civil War and Civil War Claims, 1864–1870; 24: Papers Relating to Canada, 1861–63; 46: Correspondence and Other Papers Relating to Fugitive Criminals and the Slave Trade, 1842–1890;* and 91: *Papers Relating to the Slave Trade, 1861–74.*

8:50   Jones, Robert H. "The American Civil War in the British Sessional Papers: Catalogue and Commentary." *Proceedings of the American Philosophical Society* 107 (October 1963): 415–26. These documents are helpful primarily on the period 1861–1862 but weak on the final years of the war. They demonstrate Britain's consistent neutrality and realistic view of the war, which was in sharp contrast with contemporary public and press accounts.

Personal Papers and Diaries

8:51   Connell, Brian, ed. *Regina vs. Palmerston: The Correspondence between Queen Victoria and Her Foreign and Prime Minister, 1837–1865.* Garden City, NY: Doubleday, 1961. This collection has only a few references to the *Trent* and the Civil War.

8:52   Guedalla, Philip, ed. *Gladstone and Palmerston: Being the Correspondence of Lord Palmerston with Mr. Gladstone, 1851–1865.* London: Victor Gollancz, 1928. Reprint 1971 (Books for Libraries Press). This collection includes a memorandum by Gladstone of July 1862, which offered the suggestions of a "Southern Gentleman" on how to draw a postwar border between the "Northern and Southern Republics."

8:53   Pearson, M., ed. "Letters of the Duke and Duchess of Argyll to Charles Sumner." *Proceedings of the Massachusetts Historical Society* 47 (December 1913): 66–107. Pearson develops commentary on an insightful collection of letters to Charles Sumner from George and Elizabeth Douglas Campbell, the Duke and Duchess of Argyle, into a loose narrative. The duke served in Palmerston's cabinet during the American Civil War and, with the duchess, argued the British position to their American friend. The article is useful in showing the British cabinet's attitude toward the American conflict.

8:54   Bright, John. *Speeches of John Bright, M.P., on the American Question.* Boston: Little, Brown & Company, 1865. Reprint 1970 (Kraus Reprint). This source is particularly useful for understanding the conviction with which member of Parliament John Bright viewed the American war, regarding it as right versus wrong and a contest for the survival of slavery as an immoral labor system. Bright's speeches demonstrate his zeal in countering British sympathizers for the southern cause.

8:55   Gwin, Stanford P. "Slavery and English Polarity: The Persuasive Campaign of John Bright against English Recognition of the Confederate States of America." *Southern Speech Communication Journal* 49 (Summer 1984): 406–19. Gwin argues that John Bright's efforts to make slavery the central issue of the Civil War helped to shape British popular sentiment toward American events and thereby encouraged the crown to withhold recognition from the Confederacy.

8:56   Walling, R. A. J., ed. *The Diaries of John Bright.* New York: W. Morrow and Company, 1931. Reprint 1971 (Kraus Reprint). Though disappointing for consideration of the American war, this includes Bright's remark in March 1862 relating to Lord John Russell's House of Commons declaration that the north should accept southern separation. It was, Bright indignantly recorded, a "monstrous proposition from an 'impartial spectator.'"

8:57   Lankford, Nelson D., ed. *An Irishman in Dixie: Thomas Conolly's Diary of the Fall of the Confederacy.* Columbia: University of South Carolina Press, 1988. This diary of a member of Parliament who visited the south in early 1865 is of little value in understanding the British view of the war, largely because Conolly looked only to satisfy his own personal pleasures without attempting to understand the last days of the Confederacy.

8:58   Corsan, W. C. *Two Months in the Confederate States: An Englishman's Travels through the South.* Baton Rouge: Louisiana State University Press, 1996. In the fall of 1862, while the Palmerston ministry in London considered a joint intervention in the American Civil War, English businessman W. C. Corsan traveled throughout the south. Shortly after his return home, he published an account (*Two Months in the Confederate States: Including a Visit to New Orleans, under the Domination of General Butler* [London: R. Bentley, 1863]) that summarized his views on the war. The Union could not win, he insisted; the south was engaged in a war against northern oppression and not for slavery. It is impossible to be sure how much his views might have affected the British government's thinking, but they would have at least confirmed its stated position on the war. Edited with an introduction by Benjamin H. Trask.

8:59   Ashmore, Owen, ed. "The Diary of James Garnett of Low Moor, Clitheroe, 1858–65. Vol. 1: Years of Prosperity, 1858–60." *Transactions of the Historical Society of Lancashire and Cheshire for the Year 1969* 121 (1970): 77–98. This part of the diary shows the years of prosperity for the area's cotton mills from 1858 to 1860.

8:60   _____. "The Diary of James Garnett of Low Moor, Clitheroe, 1858–65. Vol. 2: The American Civil War and the Cotton Famine, 1861–65." *Transactions of the Historical Society of Lancashire and Cheshire for the Year 1971* 123 (1972): 105–43. This part of the diary demonstrates the great changes in the area's cotton mills brought on by increased shortages in cotton and rising prices—marketing problems resulting from overproduction.

8:61   Matthew, H. C. G., ed. *The Gladstone Diaries. Vol. 6: 1861–1868.* Oxford: Clarendon Press, 1978. This volume covers the war years and includes

useful information on the British mediation issue, Gladstone's Newcastle speech, and the pressure for recognition of the Confederacy.

8:62   [Harcourt, William], ed. *Letters by Historicus on Some Questions of International Law: Reprinted from "The Times" with Considerable Additions.* London: Macmillan and Co., 1863. "Historicus" (a pseudonym for William Harcourt, stepson-in-law of British secretary for war George Cornewall Lewis) wrote these letters in collaboration with Lewis to warn that premature recognition of the Confederacy would be tantamount to signing a treaty with that government and declaring war on the Union. Recognition could come only when the Confederacy had proved its claim to nationhood.

8:63   Lewis, Gilbert Frankland, ed. *Letters of the Right Hon. Sir George Cornewall Lewis, Bart., to Various Friends.* London: Longmans, Green, 1870. This is a collection of correspondence of the British secretary for war who presented the clinching argument against intervention in the Civil War.

8:64   Palmer, Roundell. *Memorials. Part I, Vols. 1–2: Family and Personal, 1776–1865.* New York: Macmillan Co., 1896. Palmer, the Earl of Selborne, was Queen Victoria's solicitor-general in the Civil War years, and his signature appears on nearly all legal opinions given to the government during the war. Volume 2 of this work contains a number of useful chapters on international law, belligerent rights, the *Trent,* the cruisers, the rams, and the case of the *Alexandra.*

8:65   Gooch, G. P., ed. *The Later Correspondence of Lord John Russell, 1840–1878.* This correspondence touches on a wide range of issues, including British neutrality, Mexico, the *Trent* affair, the blockade, mediation, Russell's belief in the inevitability of separation between north and south, his differences with Secretary for War George Cornewall Lewis over Napoleon III's arbitration plan, and Confederate shipbuilding efforts (6:28).

8:66   MacCarthy, Desmond, and Agatha Russell, eds. *Lady John Russell: A Memoir with Selections from Her Diaries and Correspondence.* New York: John Lane Company, 1911. Correspondence from William Vernon Harcourt focused on Lord John Russell's ability to stay out of the American war, and that from Gladstone praised his moral fiber. Lady John Russell noted her husband's relief at the *Trent* crisis's ending.

8:67   Crawford, Martin. "William Howard Russell and the Confederacy." *Journal of American Studies* 15 (August 1981): 191–210. Crawford examines how Russell's writings on the American war confirmed the early belief of the London *Times* that Lincoln could not preserve the Union. According to the author, Russell's comments on the Confederacy's determination and its commitment to King Cotton diplomacy provided the chief means for attracting British and French intervention in the war. Russell's writings had major influence on British public and governmental opinion in that they constituted the first independent coverage of southern views since Lincoln's election in 1860.

8:68   _____. *William Howard Russell's Civil War: Private Diary and Letters, 1861–1862*. Athens, GA: University of Georgia Press, 1992. This volume covers the private record of British correspondent for the London *Times,* William Howard Russell, during the first part of the American Civil War. His diary contains little information not already found in his account published in 1863, *My Diary North and South* (8:69). But his private letters reveal a contemporary's view that the Confederacy was considerably weaker than the north and would have to rely on defensive capabilities to win the war. Indeed, his secret hatred for slavery and favoritism for the Union became plain to the south, while his straightforward account of the Union's debacle at Bull Run in July 1861 made him unwelcome in the north as well. Like the published diary, this work is useful in explaining how British views developed about the Civil War.

8:69   Russell, William Howard. *My Diary North and South.* New York: O. S. Felt, 1863. Reprint 1988 (Temple University Press). This diary by the London *Times* correspondent in the United States during the first two years of the Civil War reveals how the British came to believe the Union had no chance of subjugating the Confederacy. His realistic coverage of the First Battle of Bull Run, in particular, which he described as a rout affirming the south's drive for independence, enraged northerners. The 1988 reprint, edited, with a new introduction by Eugene H.

Berwanger, stems from an older edition of Russell's correspondence.

8:70   Buckle, George E., ed. *The Letters of Queen Victoria: Second Series. A Selection from Her Majesty's Correspondence and Journal between the Years 1862 and 1878.* 2 vols. New York: Longmans, Green, 1926. These letters focus primarily on European questions, but they prove helpful in showing a British preoccupation with continental affairs that further dictated neutrality toward the American war. The *Trent* crisis attracted the queen's concern.

8:71   Esher, Reginald Baliol Brett, and Arthur Christopher Benson, eds. *The Letters of Queen Victoria, 1837–1861: A Selection from Her Majesty's Correspondence between the Years 1837 and 1861.* 3 vols. New York: Longmans Green and Co., 1907. There are some items of interest in the third volume relating to early British reactions to the American Civil War.

FRANCE

8:72   Case, Lynn M., ed. *French Opinion on the United States and Mexico, 1860–1867: Extracts from the Reports of the Procureurs Généraux.* New York: D. Appleton-Century Company, 1936. These French documents contain reports from Napoleon's legal agents in the twenty-eight districts, allowing examination of public opinion of the American Civil War and intervention in Mexico.

8:73   France. Ministère des Affaires Estrangères. *Documents diplomatique (livres jaunes) [Diplomatic Documents (Yellow Books)].* 13 vols. Paris: Imprimerie Impériale, 1860–1869. This is a highly useful reference to sources for continental and French materials.

8:74   Vattel, Emerrich de. *The Law of Nations, or, Principles of the Law of Nature Applied to the Conduct and Affairs of Nations and Sovereigns.* New York: Samuel Campbell, 1796. This translation of the French-language original is an invaluable explication of international law by the renowned Swiss theorist (1714–1767), first published in 1758. It is strong on nearly all the legal issues that related to the Civil War and America's relations with other countries.

Personal Papers and Diaries

8:75　　Ferri-Pisani, Camille. *Prince Napoleon in America, 1861: Letters from His Aide-de-Camp.* Translated by Georges J. Joyaux. Bloomington: Indiana University Press, 1959. Reprint 1973 (Kennikat Press). Ferri-Pisani's letters, originally published in 1862, provide a unique view of the United States during Prince Napoleon's visit in the early months of the Civil War.

8:76　　Wellesley, Victor, and Robert Sencourt, eds. *Conversations with Napoleon III: A Collection of Documents Mostly Unpublished and Almost Entirely Diplomatic.* London: E. Benn, 1934. This volume contains conversations between Napoleon III and First Earl Cowley, Henry Richard Charles.

8:77　　Cowley, Henry Richard Charles Wellesley, and Frederick Arthur Wellesley, eds. *Secrets of the Second Empire: Private Letters from the Paris Embassy: Selections from the Papers of Henry Richard Charles Wellesley, 1st Earl of Cowley, Ambassador at Paris, 1852–1867.* New York: Harper and Brothers, 1929. Although only a small portion of this work treats American affairs, the selections from letters of Britain's ambassador in Paris, Henry Richard Charles Wellesley, 1st Earl of Cowley, contain many references to London's mistrust of France and fear of unsettled conditions on the continent, factors that largely shaped the British response to the American war. Even when Napoleon III supported England, as in the *Trent* affair, British officials remained suspicious of his motives.

GENERAL AND MISCELLANEOUS

8:78　　Adamov, E. A., ed. "Documents Relating to Russian Policy during the American Civil War." *Journal of Modern History* 2 (December 1930): 603–11. The title is descriptive but the collection disappointing.

8:79　　Baxter, James Phinney. "Papers Relating to Belligerent and Neutral Rights, 1861–1865." *American Historical Review* 34 (October 1928): 77–91. This is a collection of documents from the State Department in Washington, the Public Record Office in London, and the Archives de la Marine in Paris, and is essentially an appendix to the author's article, "The British Government and Neutral Rights, 1861–1865," which appeared in the same issue of the *American Historical Review.*

8:80　　U.S. Naval War Records Office. *Official Records of the Union and Confederate Navies in the War of the Rebellion.* 30 vols. Washington, DC: Government Printing Office, 1894–1922. These are the records of the Naval War Records Office during the Civil War, which are strong on Confederate diplomatic correspondence. The *ORN,* as this set is commonly called, is a valuable source of naval affairs during the war. In addition to day-to-day naval operations, the set contains large amounts of diplomatic correspondence. The *ORN* should be used in conjunction with its more ponderous companion set, the *ORA,* the official records of the Union and Confederate armies. Most recently, the naval records have been issued as *The Civil War CD-ROM II: Official Records of the Union and Confederate Navies in the War of the Rebellion* (Carmel, IN: Guild Press of Indiana, 1999).

8:81　　U.S. Navy Department, and U.S. Naval War Records Office. *Official Records of the Union and Confederate Navies in the War of the Rebellion: General Index.* New York: Antiquarian Press, 1961. This is an exact photocopy of a 1927 edition. In addition, Philip Van Doren Stern has furnished an introduction that gives a capsule history of the publication of these volumes, offers advice on their use, and summarizes material in the *ORN* volumes. Edited by Dudley W. Knox.

Bibliographies and Other Reference Works

8:82　　Aimone, Alan C. "Official Data Gold Mine: The Official Records of the Civil War." *Lincoln Herald* 74 (Winter 1972): 192–202. This bibliographic essay or guide to one of the major resources of Civil War history provides a much needed service. The author traces the history of the set, points out some of the difficulties in using it, suggests remedies for them, and mentions some recent reference aids. Aimone, with Barbara A. Aimone, is also coauthor of *A User's Guide to the Official Records of the American Civil War* (Shippensburg, PA: White Mane Pub. Co., 1993).

8:83   Beers, Henry Putney. *Guide to the Archives of the Government of the Confederate States of America.* Washington, DC: National Archives and Records Service, 1968. This volume is a companion to Munden and Beers, *Guide to Federal Archives Relating to the Civil War* (1962) (8:93). In addition to describing archival materials, the editor provides in each section "bibliographical references, notations of finding aids, documentary publications, and other pertinent information." The sections on the Navy and State Departments are the most useful.

8:84   Bemis, Samuel Flagg, and Grace Gardner Griffin, eds. *Guide to the Diplomatic History of the United States, 1775–1921.* Although dated, chapter 13 of this volume remains indispensable in citing printed and manuscript materials relating to the Civil War (1:21).

8:85   Echard, William E., ed. *Foreign Policy of the French Second Empire: A Bibliography.* New York: Greenwood Press, 1988. Chapter 18 contains nearly 200 references to the Civil War, including those relating to French interest in these events in America.

8:86   Ferris, Norman B. "Diplomacy." In *Civil War Books: A Critical Bibliography,* ed. Allan Nevins, James I. Robertson, Jr., and Bell I. Wiley, 1: 241–78. Baton Rouge: Louisiana State University Press, 1967. Reprint 1996 (Broodfoot Pub. Co.). This collection contains annotations of nearly 400 items dealing with international aspects of the American Civil War. The list includes German, Austrian, and French works.

8:87   Graebner, Norman A., ed. *American Diplomatic History before 1900.* This slim volume contains items relating to the Civil War (5:42).

8:88   Hanham, H. J., ed. *Bibliography of British History, 1851–1914.* This compilation contains a short section on Anglo-American relations during the Civil War (6:33).

8:89   Jentleson, Bruce W., and Thomas G. Paterson, eds. *Encyclopedia of U.S. Foreign Relations.* This prize-winning set of essays by numerous authors was prepared under the auspices of the Council on Foreign Relations and is invaluable for its many articles relating to the American Civil War (1:71).

8:90   Lincove, David A., and Gary R. Treadway, eds. *The Anglo-American Relationship: An Annotated Bibliography of Scholarship, 1945–1985.* This useful annotated bibliography offers a section on British policy and public opinion and a section on American policy—north and south—toward the crown. The chapter on the Civil War includes an examination of postwar relations through Reconstruction (1:244).

8:91   Mitchell, B. R. *European Historical Statistics, 1750–1970.* New York: Columbia University Press, 1975. This is a valuable reference work, particularly on the impact of the Civil War on the availability of American cotton in Europe.

8:92   Moore, John Bassett, ed. *A Digest of International Law: As Embodied in Diplomatic Discussions, Treaties and Other International Agreements, International Awards, the Decisions of Municipal Courts, and the Writings of Jurists.* These volumes provide valuable materials on the relationship between international law and the American Civil War (5:14).

8:93   Munden, Kenneth W., and Henry Putney Beers. *Guide to Federal Archives Relating to the Civil War.* Washington, DC: National Archives and Records Service, 1962. A 1986 reprint is titled *The Union: Guide to Federal Archives Relating to the Civil War.* Although primarily a guide to documentary sources, this work, like its companion volume on Confederate archives, Beers, *Guide to the Archives of the Government of the Confederate States of America* (1968) (8:83), contains a useful commentary on the literature. The sections on the State Department and naval affairs will prove helpful to students of diplomacy. The editors have not restricted themselves to the war years but have included material on claims and other matters that stretched into the postwar years.

8:94   Nevins, Allan, James I. Robertson, Jr., and Bell I. Wiley, eds. *Civil War Books: A Critical Bibliography.* 2 vols. Baton Rouge: Louisiana State University Press, 1967–1969. Reprint 1996 (Broadfoot Pub. Co.). In addition to covering the domestic aspects of the war, this edited work contains a section entitled "The Navies," by Thomas Henderson Wells (vol. 1, pp. 217–39). Of the estimated 50,000 to 60,000 items relating to the Civil War, the Nevins bibliography attempts to evaluate some 5,000 to 6,000.

8:95   Poore, Ben Perley, ed. *A Descriptive Catalogue of the Government Publications of the United States, September 5, 1774–March 4, 1881.* Washington, DC: Government Printing Office, 1885. Reprint 1970 (Johnson Reprint Corp.). This highly useful volume contains descriptions of the House, Senate, and executive branch documents found in the *United States Congressional Serial Set* (documents of the Congress, not including the *Congressional Record*), all in chronological order.

8:96   Smith, Myron J., Jr., ed. *American Civil War Navies: A Bibliography.* Metuchen, NJ: Scarecrow Press, 1972. This work is a valuable collection of nearly 4,000 alphabetized works on Union and Confederate naval history.

8:97   Stoflet, Ada M., and Earl M. Rogers. "A Bibliography of Civil War Articles, 1972." *Civil War History* 19 (September 1973): 238–76. This bibliographical essay contains materials on foreign affairs as well as naval and military matters. Similar articles by Stoflet appear in *Civil War History* in 1964, 1965, and 1973.

8:98   U.S. Naval History Division. *Civil War Naval Chronology, 1861–1865.* Washington, DC: Government Printing Office, 1971. This is a day-by-day summary of naval activity, replete with illustrative material that includes battle scenes, extracts from letters, and contemporary paintings and drawings.

8:99   Woodworth, Steven E., ed. *The American Civil War: A Handbook of Literature and Research.* Westport, CT: Greenwood Press, 1996. This large

volume indicates manuscript and documentary collections as well as other primary and secondary sources. Two chapters focus on the war's diplomacy, one on the Union and the other on the Confederacy.

Overviews and General Works

8:100   Barker, Alan. *The Civil War in America.* Garden City, NY: Doubleday, 1961. This brief but thought-provoking book provides an introduction for both the general reader and the college student. Written by an Englishman, it offers a foreign perspective.

8:101   Catton, Bruce. *The Centennial History of the Civil War.* 3 vols. Garden City, NY: Doubleday, 1961–1965. This is one of the best general accounts of the war. E. B. Long served as director of research.

8:102   Foote, Shelby. *The Civil War, A Narrative.* 3 vols. New York: Random House, 1958–1974. Foote's work provides a narrative history of the war with some brief sections on international affairs.

8:103   Hyman, Harold M., ed. *Heard round the World: The Impact Abroad of the Civil War.* New York: Alfred A. Knopf, 1969. Essays in this collection trace the impact of the war on Britain, France, Central Europe, Russia, Canada, and Latin America in an early attempt to widen the scope of scholarship on the international dimensions of the war. The notes give a good introduction to the literature as of 1969. The individual essays are H. C. Allen, "Civil War, Reconstruction, and Great Britain" (3–96); David H. Pinkney, "France and the Civil War" (97–144); John Hawgood, "The Civil War and Central Europe" (145–76); Hans Rogger, "Russia and the Civil War" (177–256); John A. Williams, "Canada and the Civil War" (257–98); and Harry Bernstein, "The Civil War and Latin America" (299–326).

8:104   Jones, Robert H. *Disrupted Decades: The Civil War and Reconstruction Years.* New York: Scribner, 1973. Chapters 13 and 14 of this work, essentially a text for college courses, deal with foreign affairs.

8:105 Kelly, Alfred H., Winfred A. Harbison, and Herman Belz. *The American Constitution: Its Origins and Development.* 2 vols. 7th ed. New York: Norton, 1991. This survey provides important information pertaining to the legal issues that arose during the Civil War. First published in 1948 by Kelly and Harbison.

8:106 Lauterpacht, Hersch. *Recognition in International Law.* Cambridge, UK: Cambridge University Press, 1947. Reprint 1978 (AMS Press). This volume contains useful information on the legal issues connected to the diplomatic recognition of new countries.

8:107 Mahin, Dean B. *One War at a Time: The International Dimensions of the American Civil War.* Washington, DC: Brassey's, 1999. This book claims to be both a comprehensive treatment of Civil War diplomacy and a corrective toward establishing Lincoln as master of his administration's foreign policy. Resting mainly on published sources, the work falters on both propositions—it is neither comprehensive nor convincing. It does, however, offer a somewhat useful survey of foreign relations during the war. Students should not rely exclusively on the work since it also contains occasional factual errors.

8:108 May, Robert E., ed. *The Union, the Confederacy, and the Atlantic Rim.* West Lafayette, IN: Purdue University Press, 1995. This collection of essays by four historians focusing on the international dimensions of the American Civil War originates in the 1994 Louis Martin Sears Lecture series at Purdue University. Robert E. May's essay, "History and Mythology: The Crisis over British Intervention in the Civil War," introduces the volume. Essays by R. J. M. Blackett (8:353), Howard Jones (8:300), James M. McPherson (8:115), and Thomas D. Schoonover (8:279) are listed and annotated separately in this chapter.

8:109 McPherson, James M. *Abraham Lincoln and the Second American Revolution.* New York: Oxford University Press, 1990. This collection of essays is useful in analyzing Lincoln's views toward the interrelationship of the Union, liberty, and emancipation. The "Second American Revolution," McPherson argues, was a complex combination of the abolition of slavery, the destruction of the Old South, and the shift in power toward the north.

8:110 _____. *Battle Cry of Freedom: The Civil War Era.* New York: Oxford University Press, 1988. This is a splendid survey of the Civil War, rich not only in domestic matters but in recognizing the importance of foreign affairs to its outcome. McPherson weaves together diplomatic events with all the expected themes of the period, resulting in a magisterial coverage characterized by a finely written narrative style.

8:111 _____. *Drawn with the Sword: Reflections on the American Civil War.* New York: Oxford University Press, 1996. This study contains important material on Lincoln's antislavery policies, by implication providing helpful information on his use of such ideas in shaping foreign affairs.

8:112 _____. *For Cause and Comrades: Why Men Fought in the Civil War.* New York: Oxford University Press, 1997. Using the letters and diaries of soldiers on both sides in the Civil War, McPherson shows the ideological bases of their fight for liberty, with the term defined by the Union as the demise of slavery and by the Confederacy as the right to own slaves. A sense of honor and duty permeated both sides as patriotism, religious beliefs, and love of family underwrote their drive. The Union soldiers' growing emphasis on emancipation provided further justification for Lincoln's own increasing focus on the subject as both a domestic and foreign weapon that proved crucial to the war's outcome.

8:113 _____. *Ordeal by Fire: The Civil War and Reconstruction.* 3d ed. Boston: McGraw-Hill, 2000. This is a sweeping survey of the entire period that includes much useful information on the foreign relations aspects of the Civil War. First published in 1982.

8:114 _____. *What They Fought For, 1861–1865.* Baton Rouge: Louisiana State University Press, 1994. This small book (the Walter Lynwood Fleming Lectures in Southern History at Louisiana State University) explores the ideological reasons for fighting the war. After analyzing soldiers' diaries and letters from both sides, McPherson concludes that Union and Confederate soldiers sought the same ideals of liberty, except that the former wanted to preserve the nation of 1861, while the latter fought for freedom from alleged northern oppression. As Lincoln's views of slavery evolved and he altered his strategy in foreign relations, so did the Union soldiers' attitude toward abolition change when they saw the integral relationship between emancipation and preservation of the Union. Confederates, however, focused on racial issues and emphasized the need to protect their freedom to own slaves as a property right guaranteed by the Constitution.

8:115 _____. "'The Whole Family of Man': Lincoln and the Last Best Hope Abroad." In *The Union, the Confederacy, and the Atlantic Rim,* ed. Robert E. May, 131–58. West Lafayette, IN: Purdue University Press, 1995. In this essay, McPherson examines the understanding of the Civil War among peoples abroad, particularly those in Europe and Latin America. Reform groups supported Lincoln's move to end slavery and saw the Union as the model of democracy while others criticized democracy and supported the Union's breakup. Russia, McPherson shows, exemplified both views. British reformers, Spanish republicans, and Brazilian and Cuban abolitionists drew inspiration from the Union's efforts.

8:116 Nevins, Allan. *The Statesmanship of the Civil War.* New, enl. ed. New York: Collier Books, 1962. Nevins views Lincoln as a realist who regarded slavery as a moral wrong but protected by law, and more than a statesman in seeing the Civil War as part of a long historical process leading to a grander vision of humanity set out by Washington and others before him. First published in 1953.

8:117 _____. *The War for the Union.* 4 vols. New York: Scribner, 1959–1971. This masterful work covers the military, technical, political, and diplomatic aspects of the war. Had the British recognized the Confederacy, Nevins declares, the move would have changed the course of history.

8:118 Parish, Peter J. *The American Civil War.* New York: Holmes and Meier Publishers, 1975. This history of the war devotes two chapters to diplomatic history that detail all significant issues and incidents from foreign opinion to Napoleon III's final bid for mediation. It is most useful for its treatment of maritime matters.

8:119 Perkins, Bradford. *The Creation of a Republican Empire, 1776–1865.* This synthesis contains

a brief section on the international dimensions of the Civil War (2:44).

8:120 Potter, David. *The South and the Sectional Conflict.* Baton Rouge: Louisiana State University Press, 1968. This collection of essays contains some of the author's best efforts to grapple with the enigmas of southern history from 1800 to 1865. Most helpful are the two final essays, "Jefferson Davis and the Political Factors in Confederate Defeat" and "The Civil War in the History of the Modern World: A Comparative View."

8:121 Rakestraw, Donald A. "Foreign Relations: The Civil War." In *Encyclopedia of the United States in the Nineteenth Century,* ed. Paul Finkelman, 1: 508–12. New York: Charles Scribner's Sons, 2001. This piece offers a brief but sound survey of all pertinent aspects of U.S. and Confederate foreign relations associated with the Civil War.

8:122 Randall, James G. *Constitutional Problems under Lincoln.* Rev. ed. Urbana: University of Illinois Press, 1951. This volume is especially valuable in exploring Lincoln's legal problems regarding slavery and other issues. First published in 1926.

8:123 Randall, James G., and David Herbert Donald. *The Civil War and Reconstruction.* 2d ed. Lexington, MA: D. C. Heath, 1969. This volume is rich in information, including recognition of the importance of foreign relations in the outcome of the Civil War. First published by Randall alone in 1937.

8:124 St. Clair, Sadie Daniel. "Slavery as a Diplomatic Factor in Anglo-American Relations during the Civil War." *Journal of Negro History* 30 (July 1945): 260–75. The author argues that the British public was not informed enough to know how domestic politics restricted Lincoln's actions regarding slavery. The Emancipation Proclamation set off a "battle for democracy" in England as well as America.

UNION BLOCKADE

8:125 Anderson, Bern. *By Sea and by River: The Naval History of the Civil War.* New York: Alfred A. Knopf, 1962. In this work, Anderson suggests that writers have exaggerated the success of the south's blockade runners.

8:126   Anderson, Stuart. "1861: Blockade vs. Closing the Confederate Ports." *Military Affairs* 41 (December 1977): 190–94. This brief but useful article focuses on Welles's support for an alternative to a naval blockade of the southern coast that was, he thought, of dubious legality. His proposal would have closed southern ports instead. Anderson contends that Britain and France would have rejected such port closures while accepting a Union blockade that showed due respect to neutrals.

8:127   Blume, Kenneth J. "The Flight from the Flag: The American Government, the British Caribbean, and the American Merchant Marine, 1861–1865." *Civil War History* 32 (March 1986): 44–55. The American merchant marine drastically declined during the Civil War, attributable in part to the work of Confederate raiders and cruisers, but primarily to Union naval policies aimed at denying goods to the Confederacy. According to the author, hundreds of thousands of tons of American goods were sold to foreign shippers—mainly British—so that they could reach the Caribbean under the safety of Britain's neutral flag—hence, "the flight from the flag."

8:128   Browning, Robert M., Jr. *From Cape Charles to Cape Fear: The North Atlantic Blockading Squadron during the Civil War.* Tuscaloosa: University of Alabama Press, 1993. This work is an encyclopedic description, with little analysis, of the role of the Union navy in blockading the coastal and inland waters of North Carolina and Virginia.

8:129   Coddington, Edwin B. "The Civil War Blockade Reconsidered." In *Essays in History and International Relations, in Honor of George Hubbard Blakeslee,* ed. Dwight E. Lee and George E. McReynolds, 284–305. Worcester, MA: Clark University, 1949. The author examines the effectiveness of the Union blockade and the pragmatic approach taken by the British in acquiescing to its principles.

8:130   Courtemanche, Regis A. *No Need of Glory: The British Navy in American Waters, 1860–1864.* Annapolis: Naval Institute Press, 1977. Largely based on the private papers of Vice-Admiral Sir Alexander Milne, the British commander of the Royal Navy's North American and West Indian station, this small monograph shows how carefully Britain monitored events in America, particularly the Union's enforcement of the blockade of the Confederate coast.

8:131   Hanna, Kathryn Abbey. "Incidents of the Confederate Blockade." *Journal of Southern History* 11 (May 1945): 214–29. The author relates both international and national issues involved in the Union's efforts to blockade the Confederacy. The drama and complexity of these events become clear in her examination of the *Peterhoff* case and others.

8:132   Johnson, Ludwell H., III. "Abraham Lincoln and the Development of Presidential War-Making Powers: *Prize* Cases (1863) Revisited." *Civil War History* 35 (September 1989): 208–24. The author focuses on Lincoln's proclamation of a blockade and the *Prize* cases of 1863 to demonstrate how he greatly augmented the warmaking powers of his office. Today, Johnson argues, the issue of peace or war rests on what the president perceives as a threat to national security—the "dangerous legacy" of Lincoln's victory in the courts.

8:133   Johnson, Robert Erwin. "Investment by Sea: The Civil War Blockade." *American Neptune* 32 (January 1972): 45–57. The author argues that the Union's blockade did not mark any new departures in warfare but was an adaptation of well-established principles of naval war to the special circumstances of the Civil War. He stresses the unprecedented extent of its limits and the unusual feature of the use of this weapon in a "domestic disturbance."

8:134   Jones, Virgil Carrington. *The Civil War at Sea.* 3 vols. New York: Holt, Rinehart and Winston, 1960–1962. Though primarily aimed at the general reader, this work includes a good treatment of the blockade and the efforts of the south's commerce raiders to combat it.

8:135   Laas, Virginia Jeans. "'Sleepless Sentinels': The North Atlantic Blockading Squadron, 1862–1864." *Civil War History* 31 (March 1985): 24–38. This article contains useful material on the problems confronting the Union's attempts to blockade the North Atlantic during two crucial years of the war.

8:136 Lebergott, Stanley. "Through the Blockade: The Profitability and Extent of Cotton Smuggling, 1861–1865." *Journal of Economic History* 41 (December 1981): 867–88. In this article, the author discusses a curiosity of the Union blockade: on the one hand, Confederate blockade runners made significant profits from cotton smuggling, but, on the other, they were reluctant to continue the practice. Lebergott argues that even with an annual profit of 40 percent, the element of risk dissuaded hundreds of ship captains from making a second run.

8:137 Neely, Mark E., Jr. "The Perils of Running the Blockade: The Influence of International Law in an Era of Total War." *Civil War History* 32 (June 1986): 101–18. The author demonstrates how the Union blockade was not as dangerous to either the Union or the Confederacy as usually depicted, and that international law and uncertain Union policies kept the practice in the category of limited rather than total war.

8:138 Pelzer, John, and Linda Pelzer. "'Cotton, Cotton, Everywhere!': Running the Blockade through Nassau." *Civil War Times Illustrated* 19 (January 1981): 10–17. This is a colorful account of blockade running through Nassau, which became a chief link between the Confederacy and the outside world. The Union's blockade of the Confederate coast revived Nassau's fortunes because of its geographical and climatic advantages over Bermuda and Havana.

8:139 Symonds, Craig L. *Charleston Blockade: The Journals of John B. Marchand, U.S. Navy, 1861–1862.* Microfiche. Newport, RI: Naval War College Press, 1976. This work provides a look at the monotony of blockade duty. The commentary woven through the notes calls attention to related matters. Distributed to depository libraries in microfiche.

8:140 Taylor, Thomas E. *Running the Blockade: A Personal Narrative of Adventures, Risks, and Escapes during the American Civil War.* 3d ed. London: John Murray, 1896. Reprint 1995 (Naval Institute Press). This is a firsthand account of blockade running by a participant in the events he describes. He also provides useful information on the British attitude toward the technicalities of the blockade.

8:141 Vandiver, Frank E., ed. *Confederate Blockade Running through Bermuda, 1861–1865: Letters and Cargo Manifests.* Austin: University of Texas Press, 1947. Reprint 1970 (Kraus). The documents contained in this slim volume are important sources for the activities of southern commercial interests in Bermuda.

8:142 Wise, Stephen R. *Lifeline of the Confederacy: Blockade Running during the Civil War.* Columbia: University of South Carolina Press, 1988. In this work, the first to analyze the entire issue of the Union blockade, the author concludes that Confederate blockade runners were highly successful in importing over half of the south's arms and numerous other goods important to the war effort. Had the Richmond government supported the enterprise from the outset of the fighting, Wise argues, it would have secured even more materiel. Instead, Confederate leaders left the matter to private concerns until 1864, hurting themselves in the process but not enough to have made a difference in the war's outcome.

NAVAL AFFAIRS

8:143 Baxter, James Phinney. *The Introduction of the Ironclad Warship.* Cambridge, MA: Harvard University Press, 1933. This work remains highly useful in showing new directions in the study of technology and naval affairs from the 1850s through 1870.

8:144 Booth, Alan R. "*Alabama* at the Cape, 1863." *American Neptune* 26 (April 1966): 96–108. The author fits the *Alabama*'s visits at the Cape of South Africa in August 1863 and March 1864 within the context of its captain's wish to raid commercial vessels working in and out of the Far East. People at the Cape, Booth shows, were strongly pro-Confederate.

8:145 Boykin, Edward Carrington. *Sea Devil of the Confederacy: The Story of the Florida and Her Captain, John Newland Maffitt.* New York: Funk and Wagnalls, 1959. This sprightly account focuses on the career of the famous blockade runner and cruiser commander but lacks footnotes, is a bit overwritten, and rests on standard secondary sources.

8:146 Dalzell, George W. *The Flight from the Flag: The Continuing Effect of the Civil War upon the American Carrying Trade.* Chapel Hill: University of

North Carolina Press, 1940. This book focuses on the destruction of the American merchant marine by the Confederate cruisers.

8:147 Horn, Stanley F. *Gallant Rebel: The Fabulous Cruise of the C.S.S.* Shenandoah. New Brunswick: Rutgers University Press, 1947. This is an extended treatment of the last Confederate raider's activities.

8:148 Marvel, William. *The* Alabama *& the* Kearsarge: *The Sailor's Civil War.* Chapel Hill: University of North Carolina Press, 1996. Although focusing on the sailor's life in the Civil War, this readable volume provides some useful information on Confederate shipbuilding efforts in England.

8:149 Maynard, Douglas H. "The Confederacy's Super—*Alabama.*" *Civil War History* 5 (March 1959): 80–95. This article provides a good introduction to one of the south's lesser-known warships (1862–1864). The work is one of several articles by the author on the general topic of Confederate naval affairs in Europe.

8:150 Merli, Frank J. "The Confederate Navy, 1861–1865." In *In Peace and War: Interpretations of American Naval History, 1775–1978,* ed. Kenneth J. Hagan, 126–44. Westport, CT: Greenwood Press, 1978. The author attempts an assessment of the unique circumstances of Confederate naval affairs and tries to relate those experiences to the larger experience of American naval history.

8:151 Nash, Howard Pervear. *A Naval History of the Civil War.* South Brunswick, NJ: A. S. Barnes, 1972. The author attempts to synthesize the wide-ranging naval dimensions of the war and offers a helpful section on Confederate cruisers.

8:152 Owsley, Frank L., Jr. *The C.S.S. Florida: Her Building and Operations.* Philadelphia: University of Pennsylvania Press, 1965. Reprint 1987 (University of Alabama Press). This work provides a detailed, scholarly history of the career of one of the most famous Confederate raiders.

8:153 Reed, Rowena. *Combined Operations in the Civil War.* Annapolis: Naval Institute Press, 1978. This book is a study of combined military and naval operations in the Civil War. The author claims that "the first six months of the Civil War might be regarded, from the standpoint of strategy and operations, as a continuation in greatly expanded proportion of the Mexican War."

8:154 Roland, Charles P. *An American Iliad: The Story of the Civil War.* Lexington: University Press of Kentucky, 1991. This survey includes a discussion of the role of both the Union and Confederate navies in foreign affairs.

8:155 Scharf, J. Thomas. *History of the Confederate States Navy from Its Organization to the Surrender of Its Last Vessel: Its Stupendous Struggle with the Great Navy of the United States, the Engagements Fought in the Rivers and Harbors of the South, and upon the High Seas, Blockade-Running, First Use of Iron-Clads and Torpedoes, and Privateer History.* New York: Rogers and Sherwood, 1887. Reprint 1996 (Gramercy Books). This is a detailed history of the Confederate navy that remains of some use.

8:156 Spencer, Warren F. *The Confederate Navy in Europe.* University: University of Alabama Press, 1983. Southern naval activities in Europe, whether to build a navy or engage in various other operations, threatened to end British and French neutrality during the Civil War. Spencer examines the problems that Confederate agents encountered in these maritime enterprises, in the process showing the impact of external factors on the outcome of the war. Both Britain and France, he argues, hampered the Confederacy's shipbuilding efforts because of their consistent neutrality built primarily on self-interest.

8:157 Still, William N., Jr. "Confederate Naval Policy and the Ironclad." *Civil War History* 9 (June 1963): 145–56. Though this article stresses domestic naval affairs, it demonstrates the centrality of ironclads to southern naval policy.

8:158 Strong, Edwin, Thomas H. Buckley, and Annetta St. Clair. "The Odyssey of the CSS *Stonewall.*" *Civil War History* 30 (December 1984): 306–23. Despite the Confederacy's attempts to acquire ironclad rams in Europe, it succeeded only once—in securing the CSS *Stonewall* from a French firm in Bordeaux. The ill-fated vessel, however, arrived a few days after the war had ended and had no impact on the outcome. The real story lay in the period of the building process. Not only did the controversy raise questions about French neutrality but involved Denmark, Spain, and Portugal as well. The authors conclude that because of design and construction problems, the rams could not have changed the course of the war even had they arrived earlier.

8:159 Summersell, Charles Grayson. *The Cruise of C.S.S. Stanter.* Tuscaloosa: Confederate Pub. Co., 1965. This work is useful in describing the early career of Raphael Semmes and illustrating the difficulties the Confederacy had in creating a navy.

8:160 Wells, Thomas Henderson. *The Confederate Navy: A Study in Organization.* University: University of Alabama Press, 1971. This book has a chapter on naval administration in Europe as well as appendices that furnish information not available elsewhere.

8:161 West, Richard S., Jr. *Mr. Lincoln's Navy.* New York: Longmans, Green, 1957. Though relying primarily on printed sources, this work includes chapters on the Union blockade and the war on the high seas as well as one on Wilkes and the *Trent* affair. It is a good introduction to Union naval strategy and to Welles's part in formulating it.

8:162 Wilson, H. W. *Ironclads in Action: A Sketch of Naval Warfare from 1855 to 1895, with Some Account of the Development of the Battleship in England.* 2 vols. London: Sampson, Low, Marston and Company, 1896. Though rarely cited in the literature of the American Civil War, this work provides a unique history of the war's naval aspects. Nine of the fifteen chapters in the first volume focus on the Civil War, and the tenth contains an account of the 1866 Battle of Lissa, the only real test of the ramming principle revived by the application of steam to naval war. Alfred T. Mahan wrote the introduction.

Biographical Studies

AMERICAN

Charles Francis Adams

8:163 Adams, Charles Francis, Jr. *Charles Francis Adams, 1835–1915: An Autobiography.* Boston: Houghton Mifflin Company, 1916. Reprint 1973 (Greenwood Press). Among other attributes, this work explains the personal reasons for Charles Francis Adams's delay in reaching London as the Union's minister, unfortunately timing his arrival to coincide with the British proclamation of neutrality that infuriated northerners.

8:164 _____. *Charles Francis Adams, by his Son, Charles Francis Adams.* Boston: Houghton Mifflin and Company, 1900. Reprint 1980 (Chelsea House). This work, long outdated, retains its utility for Adams's view of Civil War diplomacy.

8:165 Duberman, Martin B. *Charles Francis Adams, 1807–1886.* Boston: Houghton Mifflin, 1961. This first-rate biography of the Union's minister to England during the Civil War is a balanced and judicious work that establishes the war's international dimension by covering the myriad problems in Anglo-American relations. Adams emerges as a major moderating influence in this relationship.

John Bigelow

8:166 Bigelow, John. *Retrospections of an Active Life.* 5 vols. New York: Baker and Taylor Co., 1909–1913. These autobiographical volumes constitute a mine of information about the American consul and minister in Paris during the war and retain the imprint of their author's personality and strong opinions. Vols. 4–5 published by Doubleday, Page and Company.

8:167 Bigelow, Poultney. "John Bigelow and Napoleon III." *New York History* 13 (April 1932): 154–65. The descendant of John Bigelow, Union minister to Paris late in the war, praises him for blocking Napoleon III's efforts to equip and arm Confederate cruisers.

8:168   Clapp, Margaret. *Forgotten First Citizen: John Bigelow.* Boston: Little, Brown, 1947. Although the author did not use French sources, she still presents a good account of the Union consul's role in Paris during the war.

Abraham Lincoln

8:169   Anastaplo, George. *Abraham Lincoln: A Constitutional Biography.* Lanham, MD: Rowman and Littlefield Publishers, 1999. In this work, the author examines the legal and constitutional bases of Lincoln's views toward slavery.

8:170   Boritt, Gabor S., ed. *Lincoln, The War President: The Gettysburg Lectures.* New York: Oxford University Press, 1992. This collection of essays highlights numerous aspects of Lincoln's presidency, including his views on emancipation as a basis for "a new birth of freedom" that had an important impact on foreign affairs. See especially James M. McPherson, "Lincoln and the Strategy of Unconditional Surrender" (29–62); David Brion Davis, "The Emancipation Moment" (63–88); Kenneth M. Stampp, "One Alone? The United States and Self-Determination" (121–44); and Boritt, "War Opponent and War President" (179–212).

8:171   Cox, LaWanda. *Lincoln and Black Freedom: A Study in Presidential Leadership.* Columbia: University of South Carolina Press, 1981. Focusing on Lincoln's views toward race, slavery, and freedom, Cox argues that he based them on moral principle and expanded his call for emancipation into a push for equal rights. His antislavery position was consistent, restrained only by the practical political realities of the time. The implications of this argument bear heavily on Lincoln's tying the end of slavery to the development of an improved Union that he could use to ward off foreign intervention in the Civil War.

8:172   Diggins, John P. *On Hallowed Ground: Abraham Lincoln and the Foundations of American History.* New Haven: Yale University Press, 2000. In this work, the author analyzes Lincoln's search for a philosophical basis for his views toward liberty and his growing opposition to slavery.

8:173   Donald, David Herbert. *Lincoln.* New York: Simon and Schuster, 1995. This biography examines events from Lincoln's perspective.

8:174   Fehrenbacher, Don E. "Only His Stepchildren: Lincoln and the Negro." *Civil War History* 20 (December 1974): 293–310. This article is useful in examining Lincoln's views toward slavery.

8:175   _____. *Prelude to Greatness: Lincoln in the 1850's.* Stanford, CA: Stanford University Press, 1962. This standard work on Lincoln in the 1850s promotes an understanding of his evolving views on slavery, which rested on social, political, moral, and legal considerations. Lincoln was eminently practical, thinking slavery morally wrong but protected by law.

8:176   Fredrickson, George M. "A Man but Not a Brother: Abraham Lincoln and Racial Equality." *Journal of Southern History* 41 (February 1975): 39–58. The author demonstrates that Lincoln was not anti-black and yet did not favor racial equality. One must judge the president within the context of his times in understanding that he distinguished between slavery and white supremacy by insisting that the former violated the natural rights doctrine of the Declaration of Independence, while the denial of political and social equality fit the era's conception of citizenship rights. Blacks could become free only by leaving the United States. Lincoln's pragmatic approach to the issue led him to consider the black "a man but not a brother."

8:177   Guelzo, Allen C. *Abraham Lincoln: Redeemer President.* Grand Rapids, MI: W. B. Eerdmans Pub. Co., 1999. In this "intellectual biography," Guelzo links Lincoln's opposition to racism and slavery as violations of his Whiggish views toward self-government and liberal economics. He then shows the moral bases of Lincoln's stand against slavery.

8:178   Jaffa, Harry V. *A New Birth of Freedom: Abraham Lincoln and the Coming of the Civil War.* Lanham, MD: Rowman and Littlefield Publishers, 2000. In this study, the author offers a useful examination of Lincoln's emphasis on preserving the Union as the means for ending slavery.

8:179 Johannsen, Robert W. *Lincoln, the South, and Slavery: The Political Dimension.* Baton Rouge: Louisiana State University Press, 1991. In this volume, the author attempts to view Lincoln in his prepresidential years through the eyes of his contemporaries. Lincoln in the 1850s emerges, not surprisingly, as a politician and, perhaps surprisingly, one with moral convictions. Using this narrow approach, Johannsen examines how Lincoln's attitude toward slavery evolved from one of little active concern to that of a politician having to deal with the issue during the Illinois debates with Stephen A. Douglas. He formulated the "ultimate extinction" and "house divided" ideas, both out of political expediency, albeit with a moral base. Not so convincingly, Johannsen insists that Lincoln had virtually become an abolitionist by the end of the decade. The book, however, is useful in tracing his ever-developing approach to slavery through the Civil War.

8:180 Johnson, Ludwell H., III. "Lincoln's Solution to the Problem of Peace Terms, 1864–1865." *Journal of Southern History* 34 (November 1968): 576–86. According to the author, Lincoln at first hoped to return to the Union of 1861, with slavery dying only incidentally with the rush of war. But the sheer force of the war soon carried him and the Union far beyond the original objective to the point that he supported emancipation in an effort to fulfill the Republican Party platform and maintain leadership of the party into the Reconstruction period.

8:181 Jones, Howard. *Abraham Lincoln and a New Birth of Freedom: The Union and Slavery in the Diplomacy of the Civil War.* Lincoln: University of Nebraska Press, 1999. Lincoln, according to the author, implemented a new birth of freedom in the United States by tying the end of slavery to the beginning of a new and improved Union far different from the one he had hoped to preserve at the outset of the Civil War. A conflict had developed between the natural rights of freedom guaranteed by the Declaration of Independence and the rights to property in slaves protected by the Constitution. By the time of the Gettysburg Address, Lincoln had become convinced that slavery's abolition was integral to the universal advance of freedom. Through the war itself, he used the slavery issue to prevent European intervention on behalf of the south but, ironically, in announcing the preliminary Emancipation Proclamation in September 1862 after the Union's razor-thin victory at Antietam, infuriated the British by leaving the impression of attempting to incite slave revolts as a way to salvage an unwinnable war. By the time the Proclamation went into effect on January 1, 1863, however, most British observers recognized that the document had started the momentum toward an end to slavery.

8:182 Monaghan, Jay. *Diplomat in Carpet Slippers: Abraham Lincoln Deals with Foreign Affairs.* Indianapolis: Bobbs-Merrill Company, 1945. Reprint 1997 (University of Nebraska Press). This highly readable account rests solely on American sources and exaggerates Lincoln's role in diplomacy at the expense of Seward but remains useful in understanding how foreign affairs helped determine the war's outcome. The 1997 reprint reverses title and subtitle and contains an introductory essay by Howard Jones.

8:183 Oates, Stephen B. "'The Man of Our Redemption': Abraham Lincoln and the Emancipation of the Slaves." *Presidential Studies Quarterly* 9 (Winter 1979): 15–25. According to Oates, the real Lincoln was neither the Great Emancipator nor a racist. The president confronted the great "moral paradox" of slavery existing in a country built on the Declaration of Independence. The war gave him the opportunity to end slavery. But he faced the dilemma of having to hold on to the support of northern Democrats and border states while removing slavery as the cause of the war, keeping the British out of the conflict, and putting down the rebellion. His solution was to confine the institution to a slow death in the south while colonizing free blacks outside the country. Gradual emancipation and colonization finally changed to military action when the border states refused these halfway measures.

8:184 _____. *Our Fiery Trial: Abraham Lincoln, John Brown, and the Civil War Era.* Amherst: University of Massachusetts Press, 1979. The author provides information on Lincoln's decision for emancipation.

8:185 _____. *With Malice toward None: The Life of Abraham Lincoln.* New York: Harper and Row, 1977. This biography contains useful information on Lincoln's views toward slavery and its relation to the diplomacy of the Civil War.

8:186   Paludan, Phillip Shaw. *"A People's Contest": The Union and Civil War, 1861–1865.* 2d ed. Lawrence: University Press of Kansas, 1996. This study contains a superb analysis of Lincoln's thinking on slavery and thus offers insight into his views of how issues of slavery and the Union affected foreign relations during the interventionist crisis of 1862. First published in 1988.

8:187   _____. *The Presidency of Abraham Lincoln.* Lawrence: University Press of Kansas, 1994. The author shows how Lincoln related the slavery issue to all aspects of the Civil War, including international relations, and demonstrates the intricate ties between emancipation and both preserving and improving the Union. Lincoln's policies rested on the natural rights guaranteed in the Declaration of Independence, an objective he sought to accomplish by achieving equal rights for everyone. As he underwent his transition to an increasingly active role in ending slavery, so did he recognize the need for both blacks and whites to make the adjustment from slavery to freedom.

8:188   Randall, James G. *Lincoln the President.* 4 vols. New York: Dodd, Mead, 1945–1955. This detailed life touches only lightly on foreign affairs (mostly in volume 3) but includes perceptive comments on the war's international dimension as well as Lincoln's views on slavery.

8:189   Rawley, James A. *Abraham Lincoln and a Nation Worth Fighting For.* Wheeling, IL: Harlan Davidson, 1996. This book provides valuable insights into Lincoln's evolving emphasis on a form of republicanism that rested more on the egalitarian principles of the Declaration of Independence than on the property rights in slavery guaranteed by the Constitution. The nation Lincoln sought to preserve became clear in the Gettysburg Address, the result of a new birth of freedom that necessitated the end of slavery. Although not part of this book, the implications of Lincoln's thinking bore heavily on his attempt to ward off foreign intervention in the Civil War.

8:190   Thomas, Benjamin P. *Abraham Lincoln: A Biography.* New York: Alfred A. Knopf, 1952. This work, perhaps the best of the one-volume lives of Lincoln, has little of value on foreign affairs, but it may serve as a prelude to more detailed treatments of the Civil War president.

8:191   Welles, Gideon. *Lincoln and Seward: Remarks upon the Memorial Address of Chas. Francis Adams, on the late William H. Seward, with Incidents and Comments Illustrative of the Measures and Policy of the Administration of Abraham Lincoln. And Views as to the Relative Positions of the Late President and Secretary of State.* New York: Sheldon and Company, 1874. In response to Charles Francis Adams's 1873 public criticisms of Abraham Lincoln, wartime Secretary of the Navy Welles thought the president superior to Secretary of State William Seward in intellect and in understanding the meaning of the war. He includes a few copies of correspondence. This book is an elaboration on articles first appearing in *Galaxy* in 1873.

8:192   Wills, Garry. *Lincoln at Gettysburg: The Words That Remade America.* New York: Simon and Schuster, 1992. In this wonderfully written analysis of Lincoln's Gettysburg Address, Wills emphasizes how the Emancipation Proclamation was a brilliant combination of the ideal and the real. Given the political circumstances of the time, Lincoln went as far as he could in undermining slavery. The ramifications of Wills's analysis bear directly on Lincoln's handling of the foreign interventionist question during the Civil War.

Thomas Dudley

8:193   Dyer, Brainerd. "Thomas H. Dudley." *Civil War History* 1 (December 1955): 401–13. This unfootnoted article provides a good starting place for a study of Dudley, who tried to thwart Confederate shipbuilding in England as the Union's consul in Liverpool.

8:194   Potts, William John. *Biographical Sketch of the Late Hon. Thomas H. Dudley.* Philadelphia: Press of MacCalla and Co., 1895. This detailed (but only thirty-page) biographical sketch of Dudley, the Union's consul in Liverpool, also contains some useful documents. This was reprinted from vol. 34 of the *Proceedings of the American Philosophical Society,* June 4, 1895.

William Seward

8:195   Bancroft, Frederic. *The Life of William H. Seward.* 2 vols. New York: Harper and Brothers, 1900. This early biography of Seward contains substantial material on the Civil War years. Eleven of the nineteen chapters in the second volume treat the secretary of state's participation in everything from the design of Lincoln's foreign policy to the Union's reaction to French intervention in Mexico.

8:196   Ferris, Norman B. "William H. Seward and the Faith of a Nation." In *Traditions and Values: American Diplomacy, 1790–1865,* ed. Norman A. Graebner, 153–77. Lanham, MD: University Press of America, 1985. In this piece, Ferris argues that Seward was most effective in reminding the European powers they could best serve their interests by not moving past recognizing the Confederacy's belligerency to granting it diplomatic recognition.

8:197   Sowle, Patrick. "A Reappraisal of Seward's Memorandum of April 1, 1861, to Lincoln." *Journal of Southern History* 33 (May 1967): 234–39. In this article, the author refutes the traditional view that Seward's memorandum to Lincoln was a private matter by quoting from a letter suggesting that the secretary of state intended to publish the proposals along with the president's expected approval. The move would show Seward's statesmanship and cultivate southern Unionist sentiment for a peaceful reunification. Lincoln, however, rejected the memo.

8:198   Taylor, John M. *William Henry Seward: Lincoln's Right Hand.* New York: HarperCollins, 1991. Based primarily on secondary sources, this volume is nonetheless useful in examining Seward's policies toward the *Trent,* the interventionist crisis, and the problems with French involvement in Mexico.

8:199   Temple, Henry W. "William H. Seward." In *The American Secretaries of State and Their Diplomacy,* 7: 3–115. New York: Alfred A. Knopf, 1928. This chronicle of Seward's tenure in the State Department focuses almost exclusively on the Civil War. The first chapter deals briefly with the political atmosphere in which he received his appointment, and the last of nine chapters examines the Union reaction to the French intervention in Mexico and the U.S. acquisition of Alaska. Temple's study shows the complications that confronted the Lincoln administration as it attempted to ward off foreign intervention in the Civil War.

8:200   Van Deusen, Glyndon G. *William Henry Seward.* New York: Oxford University Press, 1967. This volume remains the standard biography of Seward. It is particularly strong on showing the secretary of state's emphasis on preserving America's rights and his close relationship with Lincoln. Seward, according to the author, kept Lincoln informed on foreign affairs, although the president exercised greater control during crises.

8:201   Warren, Gordon H. "Imperial Dreamer: William Henry Seward and American Destiny." In *Makers of American Diplomacy. Vol. 1: From Benjamin Franklin to Alfred Thayer Mahan,* ed. Frank J. Merli and Theodore A. Wilson, 195–221. New York: Scribner, 1974. In this essay, Warren stresses the work of the statesman and diplomat as well as the expansionist and politician with dreams of American empire.

Charles Wilkes

8:202   Henderson, Daniel. *The Hidden Coasts: A Biography of Admiral Charles Wilkes.* New York: William Sloane, 1953. Reprint 1971 (Greenwood Press). This is an exceedingly positive appraisal of the Union naval captain who brought on the *Trent* crisis.

8:203   Jeffries, William W. "The Civil War Career of Charles Wilkes." *Journal of Southern History* 11 (August 1945): 324–48. Jeffries explores Wilkes's career after the *Trent* affair, noting that he continued to ignore the rules when to his advantage and that he had an "abnormal persecution complex." Less than a year after the *Trent,* he became commander in the West Indies, infuriating the British and French with his heavy-handed naval policies. Recalled in June 1863, he underwent a general court-martial that found him guilty of violating orders and resulted in his suspension from the navy. He eventually received a commission as rear admiral on the retired list.

8:204   Smith, Geoffrey S. "Charles Wilkes and the Growth of American Naval Diplomacy." In *Makers of American Diplomacy. Vol. 1: From Benjamin*

Franklin to Alfred Thayer Mahan, ed. Frank J. Merli and Theodore A. Wilson, 135–63. New York: Scribner, 1974. Wilkes's career—which included more than the *Trent* imbroglio—demonstrates the way in which naval officers were in fact "the sharp cutting edge of diplomacy."

8:205 Wilkes, Charles. *Autobiography of Rear Admiral Charles Wilkes, U.S. Navy, 1798–1877.* Washington, DC: Naval History Division, Department of the Navy, 1978. This autobiography reveals its author's driving ambition and egotism but also contains valuable commentary on nineteenth-century politics, naval affairs, and science. Edited by William J. Morgan et al.

Others

8:206 Adams, Henry. *The Education of Henry Adams: An Autobiography.* Boston: Houghton Mifflin Co., 1918. Reprint 2000 (1st Mariner Books, Houghton Mifflin). This autobiography contains a useful contemporary perspective on the British attitude toward the Civil War from the office of the Union's minister to London, Charles Francis Adams. His son Henry devotes five chapters to the interactions of many of the pivotal characters involved in critical Anglo-American issues. Originally printed privately in 1906.

8:207 Cain, Marvin R. *Lincoln's Attorney General, Edward Bates of Missouri.* Columbia: University of Missouri Press, 1965. Chapter 9 of this biography addresses the constitutional and legal issues involved in the Civil War. Despite an appreciation of his own weakness in international law, Bates accepted his responsibility of counseling the president on matters such as the naval blockade, the commissioning of privateers, and the adjudication of prize cases. Cain shows the cabinet's influence on Lincoln's foreign policy and the legal technicalities and ramifications involved in prosecuting a domestic conflict in an international context.

8:208 Crawford, Martin. "Anglo-American Perspectives: J. C. Bancroft Davis, New York Correspondent of *The Times,* 1854–1861." *New York Historical Society Quarterly* 62 (July 1978): 190–217. In trying to explain the sometimes incongruous British attitude toward the Civil War, Crawford shows the pro-northern sentiments of the London *Times* correspondent in New York, J. C. Bancroft Davis, who submitted his pieces to London editors who were increasingly sympathetic to the Confederacy.

8:209 Frothingham, Paul Revere. *Edward Everett, Orator and Statesman.* The final chapter of this dated biography of a prominent political figure and ardent wartime advocate of the Union includes numerous excerpts of his correspondence with such pivotal figures as Charles Francis Adams and William Seward. Everett offers an assessment of America's foreign policy (6:91).

8:210 Freidel, Frank. *Francis Lieber: Nineteenth-Century Liberal.* Baton Rouge: Louisiana State University Press, 1947. This work contains an assessment of Lieber's key role in codifying the rules of land warfare during the Civil War as well as some commentary on his interest in international law.

8:211 Owsley, Harriet Chappell. "Henry Shelton Sanford and Federal Surveillance Abroad, 1861–1865." *Mississippi Valley Historical Review* 48 (September 1961): 211–28. The author argues that the Union's overseas intelligence network—federal surveillance abroad—played an important part in the Union's success.

8:212 Seward, Frederick William. *Reminiscences of a War-Time Statesman and Diplomat, 1830–1915.* New York: G. P. Putnam's Sons, 1916. The secretary of state's son and secretary provides useful commentary on wartime Washington and is perhaps best in his private appraisals of men and events. His work also contains numerous insights into the administration's concern over foreign intervention in the war.

8:213 Thomas, Benjamin P., and Harold M. Hyman. *Stanton: The Life and Times of Lincoln's Secretary of War.* New York: Alfred A. Knopf, 1962. The is a useful biography of Lincoln's secretary of war, who thought the president too careful on the black issue and wanted to use blacks in the Union army as a "military necessity" and a natural result of emancipation.

8:214 Donald, David Herbert. *Charles Sumner and the Rights of Man.* New York: Alfred A. Knopf, 1970. Reprint 1996 (Da Capo Press). This study stresses Sumner's impact on foreign affairs (1861–1871), his role in the Senate Foreign Relations Committee, his attitudes toward England, and his part in the resolution of the *Trent* affair. The 1996 reprint also includes the volume's predecessor, *Charles Sumner and the Coming of the Civil War* (New York: Alfred A. Knopf, 1960).

8:215   Niven, John. *Gideon Welles: Lincoln's Secretary of the Navy.* New York: Oxford University Press, 1973. Reprint 1994 (Louisiana State University Press). This work provides a detailed, analytical assessment of the Union navy's role in thwarting southern independence and of Welles's key role in implementing the strategy that helped defeat the south.

CONFEDERATE

Judah P. Benjamin

8:216   Evans, Eli N. *Judah P. Benjamin, The Jewish Confederate.* New York: Free Press, 1988. This biography lightly surveys the activities and observations of the Confederacy's secretary of state.

8:217   Meade, Robert D. *Judah P. Benjamin, Confederate Statesman.* New York: Oxford University Press, 1943. Reprint 1975 (Arno Press). This work argues for Benjamin's important role as secretary of state for the Confederacy.

8:218   _____. "The Relations between Judah P. Benjamin and Jefferson Davis: Some New Light on the Working of the Confederate Machine." *Journal of Southern History* 5 (November 1939): 468–78. Meade sees Davis relying more on Benjamin, in his three years as secretary of state, than on any other person. Benjamin was highly practical, even breaking from King Cotton diplomacy to support emancipation in an abortive effort to win British recognition. He was "one of the coolest and most dangerous revolutionists whom the North had to face."

Jefferson Davis

8:219   Davis, Varina. *Jefferson Davis, Ex-President of the Confederate States of America: A Memoir by His Wife.* 2 vols. New York: Belford, 1890. This memoir by Jefferson Davis's wife provides some interesting insights into the president of the Confederacy.

8:220   Eaton, Clement. *Jefferson Davis.* New York: Free Press, 1977. Chapter 17 of this biography shows that the president of the Confederacy had such a legalistic mind that he could not fathom why the foreign powers placed more emphasis on national interests than international law. Furthermore, Davis was so preoccupied with military matters that he relied almost exclusively in foreign affairs on his secretary of state, Judah P. Benjamin. King Cotton diplomacy failed for a number of reasons, including a cotton glut in Britain, the Palmerston ministry's refusal to risk war with the Union over the recognition issue, and the south's defeats on the battlefield.

8:221   Hendrick, Burton J. *Statesmen of the Lost Cause: Jefferson Davis and His Cabinet.* Boston: Little, Brown and Company, 1939. This work, though dated, contains useful information on the Union blockade and Confederate diplomacy relating to Europe and Mexico.

8:222   Patrick, Rembert W. *Jefferson Davis and His Cabinet.* Baton Rouge: Louisiana State University Press, 1944. In this study, the author provides short sketches of Confederate cabinet members.

8:223   Whitridge, Arnold. "Jefferson Davis and the Collapse of the Confederacy." *History Today* 11 (February 1961): 79–89. This popular piece by a distinguished British journalist-historian is critical of Davis. It is one of several articles published in *History Today* on the general topic of Britain and the American Civil War during its centennial.

Stephen Mallory

8:224   Durkin, Joseph T. *Stephen R. Mallory: Confederate Navy Chief.* Chapel Hill: University of North Carolina Press, 1954. This is a major source for the study of southern naval strategy from 1861 to 1865 and Mallory's part in it as secretary of the navy.

8:225   Melvin, Philip. "Steven Russell Mallory, Southern Naval Statesman." *Journal of Southern History* 10 (May 1944): 137–60. After tracing Mallory's pre–Civil War career, the author focuses on his efforts while Confederate secretary of navy to break the Union blockade by the use of commerce destroyers and ironclads. Mallory sent Bulloch to England to purchase or build six ships, and he pioneered the building of submarine mines and torpedoes.

Mason and Slidell

8:226 Sears, Louis Martin. "A Confederate Diplomat at the Court of Napoleon III." *American Historical Review* 26 (January 1921): 255–81. The author relies almost entirely on the James Mason papers in the Library of Congress (because of the destruction of the John Slidell papers) to show that Slidell came away from a one-hour meeting with Napoleon III fully convinced that France would intervene in the Civil War on the side of the south even if England remained neutral. Napoleon expressed sympathy for the Confederacy and thought he had made a mistake in recognizing a Union blockade that had not been effective for at least six months. The British, according to the emperor, had not fully appreciated French support during the *Trent* crisis. In an 1864 statement that revealed southern disenchantment over failure to win either French or British support, Slidell declared, "A plague I say on both your houses."

8:227 _____. *John Slidell*. Durham, NC: Duke University Press, 1925. This biography is heavier on Slidell's domestic activities than on his mission to Paris.

8:228 Willson, Beckles. *John Slidell and the Confederates in Paris (1862–65)*. New York: Minton Balch and Company, 1932. Reprint 1970 (AMS Press). The author mixes gossip with secondary accounts to concoct a tale of intrigue at the highest level of international diplomacy and finance.

8:229 Young, Robert W. *Senator James Murray Mason: Defender of the Old South*. Knoxville: University of Tennessee Press, 1998. This biography, the first full-scale work on Mason, includes coverage of his role in foreign affairs, from the 1850s while he was in the Senate, to the Civil War, when he served as Confederate envoy to London.

Raphael Semmes

8:230 Semmes, Raphael. *Memoirs of Service Afloat, during the War between the States*. Vol. 1869. Baltimore: Kelly, Piet and Co., 1869. Reprint 1996 (Louisiana State University Press). This memoir by the captain of the CSS *Alabama* provides a fairly accurate account of the commerce-raiding activities of the *Sumter* and *Alabama*. The 1996 reprint includes a new introduction and notes by John M. Taylor and the original engravings.

8:231 Spencer, Warren F. *Raphael Semmes: The Philosophical Mariner*. Tuscaloosa: University of Alabama Press, 1997. This biography provides useful information on the multifaceted interests of the commander of the Confederate raider *Alabama* during the Civil War.

8:232 Taylor, John M. *Confederate Raider: Raphael Semmes of the Alabama*. Washington, DC: Brassey's Inc., 1994. This is a solid biography of the commander of the CSS *Sumter,* who later captained the most famous commerce raider of the Civil War, the CSS *Alabama.*

Others

8:233 Oates, Stephen B. "Henry Hotze: Confederate Agent Abroad." *Historian* 27 (February 1965): 131–54. Relying mostly on secondary American sources and the papers of Henry Hotze, this article sheds light only on the relatively narrow subject of Confederate propaganda efforts. The author is not clear which British leaders, if any, came under Hotze's influence.

8:234 Delaney, Norman C. *John McIntosh Kell of the Raider Alabama*. University: University of Alabama Press, 1973. This study of the career of the *Alabama*'s first mate contains a superb reconstruction of the duel of the *Alabama* and the *Kearsarge* in the English Channel off Cherbourg in June 1864.

8:235 Freeman, Douglas Southall. *R. E. Lee, A Biography*. 4 vols. New York: C. Scribner's Sons, 1934–1935. Freeman's work remains the most complete biography of the Confederate general.

8:236 Williams, Frances L. *Matthew Fontaine Maury: Scientist of the Sea.* New Brunswick: Rutgers University Press, 1963. This is a solid biography of one of the south's internationally recognized citizens. Few observers question the importance of Maury's scientific work in oceanography, but some critics have reservations about his performance as a purchasing agent for the Confederate navy.

8:237 Davis, Charles Shepard. *Colin J. McRae: Confederate Financial Agent.* Tuscaloosa: Confederate Pub. Co., 1961. This brief work provides an introduction to the south's problems in financing its operations overseas.

BRITISH

John Bright

8:238 Ausubel, Herman. *John Bright, Victorian Reformer.* New York: Wiley, 1966. This is a biography of one of the chief members of Parliament who thought slavery lay at the basis of the American war.

8:239 Trevelyan, George Macaulay. *The Life of John Bright.* Boston: Houghton Mifflin Company, 1913. Reprint 1971 (Greenwood Press). Chapter 14 of this work focuses on the American Civil War and contains useful excerpts from letters and speeches by John Bright prodding British leaders to sympathize with the Union cause.

8:240 Zorn, Roman J. "John Bright and the British Attitude to the American Civil War." *Mid-America* 38 (July 1956): 131–45. John Bright, according to the author, was strongly pro-Union because of its emphasis on freedom, and worked to convince industrial workers that their freedom depended on the north's ability to end slavery.

William E. Gladstone

8:241 Collyer, C. "Gladstone and the American Civil War." *Philosophical and Literary Society Proceedings* 6, no. 8 (1951): 583–94. Collyer provides a minor assessment of the Civil War's impact on British politics and politicians, and especially notes

Gladstone's ambivalent reactions to transatlantic affairs.

8:242 Magnus, Philip. *Gladstone, A Biography.* New York: Dutton, 1954. This biography contains a brief section highlighting Gladstone's wish to mediate the American conflict out of concern over the war's atrocities and the hardships of his people in Lancashire suffering from the growing cotton shortage.

8:243 Matthew, H. C. G. *Gladstone, 1809–1874.* New York: Oxford University Press, 1986. The author argues that Gladstone's Newcastle speech proved an embarrassment to the Palmerston ministry, whether or not he sought recognition of the Confederacy. The ideas expressed in the address were not new.

8:244 Morley, John. *The Life of William Ewart Gladstone.* 3 vols. New York: Macmillan Company, 1903. Reprint 1972 (Scholarly Press). Chapter 5 in Book 5 of volume 2 contains some useful information on the British reaction to the American Civil War.

Lord Palmerston

8:245 Bell, Herbert C. F. *Lord Palmerston.* 2 vols. New York: Longmans, Green, 1936. Volume 2 of this standard biography shows how Palmerston found measured satisfaction in the breakup of the United States because of Seward's republicanism and American boldness, the criticisms of England by Irish journalists in America, and concern about protecting Canada from U.S. encroachments. The prime minister considered mediation, however, not out of favor to the south—mediation, he thought at the outset of the American troubles, would provide recognition of the south in exchange for a treaty against the African slave trade. He gave up this plan by the summer of 1861 once he realized that staying out of the conflict was advisable and that neutrality was the wisest approach. There is considerable valuable information on numerous foreign relations issues, including the Robert Bunch affair (see Bonham, *The British Consuls in the Confederacy* [1911] [8:469]), the blockade, *Trent* crisis, Mexico, and Confederate shipbuilding efforts.

8:246 Chamberlain, Muriel E. *Lord Palmerston.* Washington, DC: Catholic University of America Press, 1987. This slim biography is sketchy on American affairs.

8:247 Ridley, Jasper Godwin. *Lord Palmerston.* This biography of the British prime minister shows his belief that dissolution of the Union was a fait accompli and argues, questionably, that the sympathies of Palmerston, Russell, and Gladstone lay with the south. In early 1861, Palmerston feared that north and south would resolve their differences and invade Canada, thereby necessitating his order to reinforce British North America (6:103).

8:248 Russell, John. *Recollections and Suggestions, 1813–1873.* Boston: Roberts Brothers, 1875. This volume contains Russell's thoughts on the American war, in particular his views on the *Trent,* neutrality, and Confederate shipbuilding efforts.

Lord John Russell

8:249 Scherer, Paul H. "Partner or Puppet? Lord John Russell at the Foreign Office, 1859–1862." *Albion* 19 (Fall 1987): 347–71. Here the author tries to restore Russell's reputation as foreign secretary under Palmerston. Although focusing on European matters, Scherer reveals much about Palmerston's willingness to follow Russell's lead in foreign affairs. "They were a true partnership."

8:250 Tilby, A. Wyatt. *Lord John Russell, A Study in Civil and Religious Liberty.* New York: Richard R. Smith, 1931. This volume contains a useful analysis of Russell's thinking about movements for independence, helping explain his attitude toward the south in the American Civil War. Both north and south spoke of freedom, the former for the individual and the latter for the state. Russell opposed slavery, but his Whig philosophy favored independence over empire. Thus, when Lincoln declared that the war concerned the preservation of the Union (and hence not slavery), Russell sympathized with the Confederate cause.

8:251 Walpole, Spencer. *The Life of Lord John Russell.* Chapter 29 focuses on Russell's reaction to the American Civil War and includes a number of excerpts from primary sources (6:152).

Others

8:252 Churchman, Michael. "Walter Bagehot and the American Civil War." *Dublin Review* 239 (Winter 1965): 377–93. In examining the attitude of the British press toward the Civil War, the author focuses on the perspective of the influential editor of the *Economist,* Walter Bagehot, who slowly turned from an acceptance of the inevitability of southern independence to an appreciation of Lincoln's determination to preserve the Union.

8:253 Weinberg, Adelaide. *John Elliot Cairnes and the American Civil War: A Study in Anglo-American Relations.* London: Kingswood, 1970. This work addresses a major problem of the British response to the Civil War—the relationship of slavery to the disruption of the Union. Cairnes wrote an influential antislavery book that helped to educate and shape British public opinion toward the north.

8:254 Cook, Edward. *Delane of the Times.* New York: H. Holt and Company, 1916. Though this work probably gives too much credit to the editor of the London *Times* for creating the public image of Palmerston, it hints at an important truth about public relations in this period. Palmerston showed a keen awareness of public opinion in his responses to crisis diplomacy.

8:255 Campbell, Ina Erskine McNeill, ed. *Autobiography and Memoirs: George Douglas, Eighth Duke of Argyll.* 2 vols. London: J. Murray, 1906. Volume 2 shows that Argyll was pro-north because of his hatred of slavery and favor for "unionist" political ideas. Secession, he asserted, was anarchy. The war would bring an end to slavery, "a fact so evident . . . that I cannot understand its being questioned."

8:256 Reid, T. Wemyss. *Life of the Right Honourable William Edward Forster.* 2 vols. London: Chapman and Hall, 1888. Reprint 1970 (Adams and Dart). This is a life and times biography of one of the Union's strongest supporters in Parliament. Forster was strongly antislavery, a stand derived from his father's profession as Quaker missionary and the campaigns against slavery carried out by his uncle, Thomas Fowell Buxton. The American war was about slavery and abolition, according to Forster.

8:257 Maxwell, Herbert. *The Life and Letters of George William Frederick, Fourth Earl of Clarendon, K. G., G. C. B.* Volume 2 focuses on the Civil War years, particularly British interest in stopping the fighting in the name of civilization. Clarendon thought southern independence "a fait accompli" but was especially concerned about Palmerston's "meddling proclivities" (6:141).

8:258 Petty-Fitzmaurice, Edmond-George. *The Life of Granville George Leveson Gower, Second Earl Granville, K. G., 1815–1891.* 2 vols. New York: Longmans, Green, 1905. Volume 1 contains valuable information on British interest in mediation growing from a concern to stop a war that was not only atrocious to humanity, but injurious to British trade and manufacturing. British public opinion criticized *both* north and south on the slavery issue.

8:259 Jenkins, Brian. "William Gregory: Champion of the Confederacy." *History Today* 28 (May 1978): 322–30. The author argues that William Gregory, a member of Parliament who was one of the most vocal proponents of the Confederacy in the first two years of the war, feared that the disruption of the southern system would hurt British industry.

8:260 Gardiner, A. G. *The Life of Sir William Harcourt.* 2 vols. New York: George H. Doran, 1923. Harcourt was the coauthor, with Secretary for War George Cornewall Lewis, of the long memorandum to the British cabinet arguing against intervention in the American war largely because such a step could lead to a third Anglo-American conflict. Harcourt was also Lewis's stepson-in-law.

8:261 Jenkins, Brian. "Frank Lawley and the Confederacy." *Civil War History* 23 (June 1977): 144–60. Frank Lawley, London *Times* correspondent in the south from the autumn of 1862 to the end of the Civil War, accompanied Gen. Robert E. Lee and other Confederate commanders on numerous campaigns. His firsthand accounts greatly molded the British view toward American events. Fearing an ultimate war between England and the United States, he supported the Confederacy's bid for independence as a way of weakening America and helping his own country. England must therefore extend recognition to the south, a belief coloring his early stories published in the *Times*. Even though the Union held the

field at Antietam, Lawley argued that the massive destruction of the war presented conclusive evidence of its pointlessness and the need for the Union to recognize it could not subjugate the south. Not until the end of the war did he realize that the Union would win.

8:262 Hoole, W. Stanley, ed. *Four Years in the Confederate Navy: The Career of Captain John Low on the C. S. S. Fingal, Florida, Alabama, Tuscaloosa, and Ajax.* Athens, GA: University of Georgia Press, 1964. This brief work focuses on Captain Low, who served on the *Alabama* under the command of Raphael Semmes.

8:263 Newton, Thomas Wodehouse Legh. *Lord Lyons: A Record of British Diplomacy.* 2 vols. London: Edward Arnold, 1913. Volume 1 overly praises the British minister to the Union but includes important insight into his fears of Seward's aggressive diplomacy. Lyons opposed British intervention and thought a slave uprising possible that might lead to the deaths of British subjects as well as Americans. The volume also contains extensive quotes from Lyons's private papers.

8:264 Leader, Robert Eadon. *Life and Letters of John Arthur Roebuck . . . with Chapters of Autobiography.* New York: Edward Arnold, 1897. This life and times biography furnishes useful information on the M.P. who worked with colleague William Lindsay in pushing for British (and French) recognition of the Confederacy. A divided America, which Roebuck considered inevitable, would help England. "The North will never be our friends," he told Palmerston. "Of the South," he added, "you can make friends. They are Englishmen. They are not the scum and refuse of Europe."

8:265 Atkins, John B. *The Life of Sir William Howard Russell: The First Special Correspondent.* 2 vols. New York: E. P. Dutton, 1911. The author argues that London *Times* news correspondent William H. Russell helped to persuade the British that the Union was right. In a highly debatable statement, he calls Palmerston, Russell (the British foreign secretary), and Gladstone "opponents of the North." Russell the correspondent perhaps caused more than a few of his countrymen to hesitate about helping the south when he told his editor, John T. Delane, that some northerners warned of war with any European nation that extended recognition to the Confederacy.

8:266   Woodham-Smith, Cecil. *Queen Victoria: From Her Birth to the Death of the Prince Consort.* New York: Alfred A. Knopf, 1972. American affairs do not loom large in this work, but it contains a vivid account of the death of the prince at the time of the *Trent* crisis. The materials used in writing this book help in reconstructing the prince's role in drafting the British note to America at the time of that crisis.

U.S. Foreign Relations with Other Countries and Areas

EUROPE: GENERAL AND MISCELLANEOUS

8:267   Adams, Charles Francis, Jr. "The Crisis of Foreign Intervention in the War of Secession, September-November, 1862." *Proceedings of the Massachusetts Historical Society* 47 (1914): 372–424. In this work, the son of the Union minister to England discusses a wide range of issues that led to the crisis over foreign intervention in the war. Included are insights into John Slidell, the French involvement in American and Mexican affairs, British interest in mediation, and the final decision by the Palmerston ministry against intervention. According to the author, the Emancipation Proclamation marked the pivotal point in making the British realize that slavery was an issue in the war and that a Union victory meant the end of slavery.

8:268   _____. "The Negotiations of 1861 Relating to the Declaration of Paris of 1856." *Proceedings of the Massachusetts Historical Society* 46 (1912): 23–84. This article draws heavily from the diaries of Gideon Welles and William H. Russell in reexamining Seward's European policy from Fort Sumter to First Bull Run. Focusing on the directives to his father as the Union minister in England to revisit the Declaration of Paris with the Palmerston government, Adams considers these negotiations ill considered, based on the notion that the American

conflict was or was not a war depending on which approach best served U.S. interests under shifting circumstances. Seward's policy in the first three months of the war rested on a "misapprehension" of affairs in America, Europe, and the south.

8:269   Brauer, Kinley J. "Seward's 'Foreign War Panacea': An Interpretation." *New York History* 55 (April 1974): 133–57. According to the author, Seward had both foreign and domestic objectives in sending his famous April 1861 memo to the president calling for him to order Spain out of Santo Domingo and warn Europeans against interfering in the Western Hemisphere and U.S. domestic affairs. The secretary of state's goal was to ward off foreign intervention in the Civil War while perhaps reunifying Americans against outside intruders.

8:270   _____. "The Slavery Problem in the Diplomacy of the American Civil War." *Pacific Historical Review* 46 (August 1977): 439–69. The author argues that Seward opposed immediate abolition as destructive to the world economy and urged gradual emancipation to give the south a chance to adjust to a free labor system. The slavery issue, he thought, would block all attempts at north-south reconciliation, undermine the American economy and empire, and invite European involvement in the war.

8:271   Crook, D. P. *Diplomacy during the American Civil War.* New York: Wiley, 1975. This able synthesis is an abridged edition, more useful in the classroom, of his earlier work, *The North, the South, and the Powers, 1861–1865* (1974) (8:272).

8:272   _____. *The North, the South, and the Powers, 1861–1865.* New York: Wiley, 1974. This work provides useful information on foreign relations during the war by fitting the American issues within worldwide diplomacy. The Emancipation Proclamation improved the Union's image in Europe but was not the most critical element in warding off foreign intervention in the American war. More important were the realistic warnings of war with the Union, which Secretary of War George Cornewall Lewis raised in a pivotal November 1862 cabinet meeting. Lord Palmerston, therefore, opted against intervention.

8:273   Ferris, Norman B. *Desperate Diplomacy: William H. Seward's Foreign Policy, 1861.* Knoxville: University of Tennessee Press, 1976. This detailed work demonstrates Seward's aggressive diplomacy, all designed to discourage foreign intervention on the side of the Confederacy. Any thought of recognition of the south, the secretary of state made clear to European nations, could lead to war with the Union.

8:274 _____. "Transatlantic Misunderstanding: William Henry Seward and the Declaration of Paris Negotiation, 1861." In *Rank and File: Civil War Essays in Honor of Bell Irvin Wiley,* ed. James I. Robertson, Jr. and Richard M. McMurry, 55–78. San Rafael, CA: Presidio Press, 1976. Ferris questions the assumption that Britain's early determination to treat Seward with suspicion developed from his intentionally provocative "foreign war panacea." Examining the failed negotiations in 1861 over the Union's position on the Declaration of Paris of 1856, Ferris finds Seward staunchly defending his government and yet conciliatory throughout his tenure in office. British and French diplomats set the belligerent tone of the Union's relations with Europe.

8:275 Graebner, Norman A. "European Interventionism and the Crisis of 1862." *Journal of the Illinois State Historical Society* 69 (February 1976): 35–45. This article describes some of the tensions that developed in diplomatic circles on the subjects of military stalemate, slavery, foreign sympathy for the Confederacy, and European distrust of the Lincoln administration.

8:276 _____. "Northern Diplomacy and European Neutrality." In *Why the North Won the Civil War,* ed. David Herbert Donald, 49–75. Baton Rouge: Louisiana State University Press, 1960. Reprint 1996 (Simon and Schuster). The author argues that any level of European support for the south could have changed the outcome of the war. England was the key, providing the critical element in the world balance of power between the Old and New Worlds. Only Russia, Graebner insists, favored the Union's preservation. In the end, however, the British and French decisions not to intervene rested on their fear of alienating the Union and hurting their own territorial and commercial interests in the New World. The outcome vindicated Seward's threats of retaliation against any interventionist power.

8:277 Jordan, Donaldson, and Edwin J. Pratt. *Europe and the American Civil War.* Boston: Houghton Mifflin Company, 1931. This study of European public opinion and the war argues that British bourgeois and nonconformist opinion strongly supported the Union.

8:278 Landry, Harral E. "Slavery and the Slave Trade in Atlantic Diplomacy, 1850–1861." *Journal of Southern History* 27 (May 1961): 184–207. This article provides useful background information for understanding Seward's April 1, 1861, memorandum to Lincoln. In examining Seward's Senate career in the 1850s, Landry shows that U.S. relations with England and Spain over the slavery issue were no longer dangerous by 1860, and that Seward as secretary of state under Lincoln sought to revive the controversy by uniting north and south against a common threat from the outside by again subordinating slavery to the forces of nationalism.

8:279 Schoonover, Thomas D. "Napoleon Is Coming! Maximilian Is Coming? The International History of the Civil War in the Caribbean Basin." In *The Union, the Confederacy, and the Atlantic Rim,* ed. Robert E. May, 101–30. West Lafayette, IN: Purdue University Press, 1995. Using Immanuel Wallerstein's world systems theory as his point of reference, Schoonover fits the Civil War into long-standing American and European rivalry for the Gulf-Caribbean region. The Union's economic strength, he argues, gave it an advantage over the Confederacy in this multinational contest. French intervention in Mexico, he insists, would probably have taken place even without the Civil War. The main objective there and elsewhere was a type of social imperialism in which the imperial country sought to improve domestic conditions by expansionist activities abroad.

8:280 Sideman, Belle Becker, and Lillian Friedman, eds. *Europe Looks at the Civil War.* New York: Orion Press, 1960. The editors use this far-ranging set of excerpts from published materials to capture the human interest appeal and a sense of excitement. For American students, perhaps the most useful portions of the work are those providing translations from contemporary French writings on the Civil War.

8:281 Stern, Philip Van Doren. *When the Guns Roared: World Aspects of the American Civil War.*

Garden City, NY: Doubleday, 1965. Though this work, much of which focuses on England and France, is a "popular" history, the author has done an impressive amount of work in out-of-the-way archives.

8:282 Tyrner-Tyrnauer, A. R. *Lincoln and the Emperors.* New York: Harcourt, Brace and World, 1962. In this work, the author examines Lincoln's efforts to ward off European intervention in North America, particularly Napoleon III's installation of an Austrian monarch in Mexico.

BRITAIN

8:283 Adams, Charles Francis, Jr. *Before and after the Treaty of Washington: The American Civil War and the War in the Transvaal.* New York: Printed for the [New York Historical] Society, 1902. The son of the Union minister to London explores the numerous issues involved in the Lincoln administration's relations with England, particularly its anger over British neutrality and Confederate shipbuilding efforts in England.

8:284 _____. "The British Proclamation of May, 1861." *Proceedings of the Massachusetts Historical Society* 48 (1915): 190–241. This article relies on diaries and correspondence, both public and private, of many key participants whose papers were not then readily accessible to historians. Adams argues that the British neutrality proclamation resulted from practical considerations rather than motives intended to insult the Union. He includes several lengthy excerpts from the documents.

8:285 Adams, Ephraim D. *Great Britain and the American Civil War.* 2 vols. New York: Longmans, Green and Co., 1925. Although dated and pro-British, these volumes remain a standard survey of Anglo-American relations during the Civil War. The author is particularly strong on the British response to the war.

8:286 Adams, Henry. *The Great Secession Winter of 1860–61 and Other Essays.* New York: Sagamore Press, 1958. Henry Adams was fascinated all his life by the duel he had witnessed between his father and the British foreign secretary during the

years he served as his father's secretary in London. He details this in his chapter on "The Declaration of Paris, 1861" (361–90) and elsewhere in the volume. In *The Education of Henry Adams: An Autobiography* (1918) (8:206), he bitterly referred to the "double-dyed rascality and duplicity of Lord Russell." Edited, with an introduction, by George Hochfield.

8:287 _____. "Why Did Not England Recognize the Confederacy?" *Proceedings of the Massachusetts Historical Society* 66 (1942): 204–22. This article examines Britain's consideration of Confederate recognition in the fall of 1862. It rests on a number of documents, including those of Union minister to England Charles Francis Adams and his son Henry, and concludes that only a small minority in Palmerston's cabinet supported mediation. Even then, according to the author, the British intended to remain neutral at least until the south first demonstrated success on the battlefield.

8:288 Baxter, James Phinney. "The British Government and Neutral Rights, 1861–1865." *American Historical Review* 34 (October 1928): 9–29. The author demonstrates Britain's concern over precedents and maintaining neutrality in the American Civil War, but its maritime interests dictated a policy that favored the north.

8:289 Beloff, Max. "Historical Revision No. CXVIII: Great Britain and the American Civil War." *History* 37 (February 1952): 40–48. The author argues that British neutrality was sincere in light of Palmerston's concerns about a European war, Canada's defenselessness, and his fear of conflict with the Union. The interventionist threat came to an end in November 1862.

8:290 Bernard, Mountague. *A Historical Account of the Neutrality of Great Britain during the American Civil War.* London: Longmans, Green, Reader and Dyer, 1870. Although still necessary for understanding the British defense of their actions during the Civil War, this should be used with caution. The author's interpretation of British neutrality seems slanted toward Whitehall.

8:291 Blume, Kenneth J. "Coal and Diplomacy in the British Caribbean during the Civil War." *Civil*

War History 41 (June 1995): 116–41. Both the Union and Confederate navies tried throughout the Civil War to secure coal from the British West Indies, a competition that revealed numerous insights into British neutrality as well as north-south naval troubles. The Bahamas became a hot spot of blockade runners as Union and Confederate vessels made their way into the Caribbean for coal. British neutrality hampered Union efforts to acquire the product, driving home the U.S. need to have a naval outpost in the Caribbean. Ironically, Britain's effective enforcement of neutrality helped to upset the balance of power in the hemisphere by demonstrating the need for the United States to expand its holdings in the Caribbean and the Pacific.

8:292   Bourne, Kenneth. *Britain and the Balance of Power in North America, 1815–1908.* Bourne provides the British perspective on the American Civil War, showing that the struggle fitted within the longtime Anglo-American struggle for hegemony in North America. A balance of power was the key to peace, although relations between the Atlantic nations remained raw into the 1860s, particularly exacerbated by the war scare over the *Trent* affair in 1861. Bourne's theme is Britain's military weakness (6:165).

8:293   _____. *The Foreign Policy of Victorian England, 1830–1902.* This survey contains useful material on British foreign policy during the American Civil War (6:166).

8:294   Brauer, Kinley J. "British Mediation and the American Civil War: A Reconsideration." *Journal of Southern History* 38 (February 1972): 49–64. The author focuses on the intervention crisis in the fall of 1862, arguing that the battle of Antietam confirmed the British belief that neither side could win and led several spokesmen, including Russell and Gladstone, to support a joint mediation to end the war. Palmerston, however, adhered to the advice of Granville and Lewis against intervention and opted to wait for the war to render its own verdict.

8:295   Burn, W. L. *The Age of Equipoise: A Study of the Mid-Victorian Generation.* London: George Allen and Unwin, 1964. In covering the period 1852 to 1867, the author plays down politics but demonstrates how the political milieu circumscribed governmental initiatives. Norton published the work in the United States in 1965.

8:296   Ellsworth, Edward W. "Anglo-American Affairs in October of 1862." *Lincoln Herald* 66 (Summer 1964): 89–96. The author argues that Lord John Russell's mediation plan was a sincere attempt to end the American Civil War, and that the British government was divided over the issue but primarily neutral. Ellsworth recounts Secretary for War George Cornewall Lewis's arguments against mediation but does not give him much credit for warding off the call for intervention.

8:297   Gough, Barry M. *The Royal Navy and the Northwest Coast of North America, 1810–1914: A Study of British Maritime Ascendancy.* Vancouver: University of British Columbia Press, 1971. Chapter 9 provides a useful examination of Anglo-American tensions during the Civil War from the perspective of the Royal Navy. Focusing on the Pacific northwest, Gough reports on the security concerns and neutrality issues that affected British interests in the Pacific and the crown's response to those issues. Although the British navy made only minor additions to its Pacific squadron, its contingency plans included the blockading of San Francisco and indicated the seriousness with which the London government viewed the problems arising from the war.

8:298   Jenkins, Brian. *Britain & the War for the Union.* Vol. 1. 2 vols. Montreal: McGill-Queen's University Press, 1974. This is the first of a two-volume survey of Britain's reaction to the Civil War, covering Anglo-American relations from November 1860 to spring 1862. British neutrality, Jenkins argues, rested on self-interest and apprehension over hostilities with the Union. Most British observers, though divided in their reasons for neutrality, considered southern independence a fait accompli and feared that a prolonged war would hurt international trade. The author includes considerable information on Canadian-American relations as well as the public battle between the pro-Union and pro-Confederate forces in Britain.

8:299   _____. *Britain & the War for the Union.* Vol. 2. 2 vols. Montreal: McGill-Queen's University Press, 1980. This volume completes the author's two-volume survey of Britain's reaction to the Civil War. Starting with the spring of 1862, Jenkins provides an especially detailed record of the critical period from that spring to the end of 1862.

8:300   Jones, Howard. "History and Mythology: The Crisis over British Intervention in the Civil War." In *The Union, the Confederacy, and the Atlantic Rim,* ed. Robert E. May, 29–67. West Lafayette, IN: Purdue University Press, 1995. This essay focuses on the possibility of British intervention in the Civil War, highlighting the warnings contained in Secretary for War George Cornewall Lewis's memorandum to the cabinet about the certainty of war with the Union if the Palmerston ministry did so. The controversy again demonstrates the international dimension of the American Civil War.

8:301   Jones, Robert H. "Anglo-American Relations, 1861–1865, Reconsidered." *Mid-America* 45 (January 1963): 36–49. Based largely on the British Sessional Papers, this article demonstrates the sincerity of British neutrality in the Civil War by showing Palmerston's primary concern over a European war and his realization that Canada was vulnerable. Jones also argues that British workers' support for the Union had little influence on the prime minister's policy because they had no members in Parliament. British neutrality, he concludes, worked to the north's benefit because commercial avenues remained open.

8:302   Jones, Wilbur D. *The American Problem in British Diplomacy, 1841–1861.* The author provides helpful information on Anglo-American issues during the two decades preceding the Civil War, many of which reappeared during the war (6:178).

8:303   Krein, David F. *The Last Palmerston Government: Foreign Policy, Domestic Politics, and the Genesis of "Splendid Isolation."* Ames, IA: Iowa State University Press, 1978. This survey of Palmerston's final years as prime minister includes useful information on the British reaction to the American Civil War. One chapter focuses on the Mexican intervention, and another centers on the *Trent* crisis and the interventionist controversy of 1862.

8:304   Owsley, Frank L. "America and the Freedom of the Seas, 1861–65." In *Essays in Honor of William E. Dodd, by His Former Students at the University of Chicago,* ed. Avery Craven, 194–256.

Chicago: University of Chicago Press, 1935. In this essay, the author stresses expediency's victory over principle in tracing the Union's shift from its rigid adherence to neutral rights in wartime. Owsley touches on several issues that arose during the conflict, including the paper blockade, contraband, illegal searches and seizures, questionable prize claims, and neutral port closures.

8:305   Reid, Robert L., ed. "William E. Gladstone's 'Insincere Neutrality' during the Civil War." *Civil War History* 15 (December 1969): 293–307. Reid argues that Gladstone's Newcastle speech of October 1862 did not derive from southern sympathy but from his humanitarian interest in stopping the war. The north, Gladstone insisted, should let the south go. Reid focuses on an 1872 letter from Gladstone to the American minister in Britain in which he attempts to reconcile his seemingly pro-south comments made during the Civil War with his insistence that he had always supported the Union.

8:306   Thomas, Mary Elizabeth. "Jamaica and the U.S. Civil War." *Américas* 24 (January 1972): 25–32. This brief article demonstrates the problems of British neutrality during the Civil War by addressing the precarious position of the British colony of Jamaica, whose ports became havens for Confederate blockade runners.

8:307   Ward, A. W., and G. P. Gooch, eds. *The Cambridge History of British Foreign Policy, 1783–1919. Vol. 2: 1815–1866.* New York: Macmillan Company, 1923. Chapter 12 of this volume, written by A. P. Newton and titled "Anglo-American Relations during the Civil War, 1860–1865," presents the British perspective on the war, emphasizing the sincerity of British neutrality.

8:308   Whitridge, Arnold. "The Peaceable Ambassadors." *American Heritage* 8 (April 1957): 40–43, 98–103. This brief article examines the work of Charles Francis Adams, the Union minister in London, and Lord Lyons, the British minister in Washington, in maintaining peaceful Anglo-American relations during the Civil War.

8:309   Willson, Beckles. *America's Ambassadors to England (1785–1929): A Narrative of Anglo-American Diplomatic Relations.* Chapter 16 focuses on the Union minister to England during the Civil War, Charles Francis Adams, and covers the numerous crises in Anglo-American relations during those four tumultuous years (6:201).

8:310   Winks, Robin W. *Canada and the United States: The Civil War Years.* Baltimore: Johns Hopkins University Press, 1960. Reprint 1988 (University Press of America). This work examines nearly every aspect of Canadian-American relations during the American Civil War from Canadian opinion to the impact of the war on Canadian union and the need for an Anglo-American rapprochement. Winks supplies a new preface to the 1988 reprint.

The Trent Affair

8:311   Adams, Charles Francis, Jr. "The Trent Affair." *American Historical Review* 17 (April 1912): 540–62. Adams argues that the Lincoln administration missed an opportunity to set precedents in international law by not immediately renouncing Wilkes's removal of Mason and Slidell from the *Trent* as a violation of neutral rights and thus establishing America's credibility in the world. Such a move would have tied the British and the Confederacy to the right of search and possibly eased the threat of recognition of the south.

8:312   _____. "The *Trent* Affair." *Proceedings of the Massachusetts Historical Society* 45 (November 1911): 35–148. The minister's son was one of the first to begin exploiting his father's papers, and this early assessment of the *Trent* was a prime example of their contents. The same issue of the *Proceedings* contains a piece by R. H. Dana, "The *Trent* Affair: An Aftermath," pp. 508–22, and a rejoinder by Adams, pp. 522–30.

8:313   Bourne, Kenneth. "British Preparations for War with the North, 1861–1862." *English Historical Review* 76 (October 1961): 600–32. The author shows how close England and the United States came to war over the *Trent.* Although British defenses in North America were weak, the Union was at war with the Confederacy, and the French had offered assurances of support, alleviating the Palmerston ministry's fear that they might move aggressively in Europe or elsewhere while London was at war.

8:314   Cohen, Victor H. "Charles Sumner and the *Trent* Affair." *Journal of Southern History* 22 (May 1956): 205–19. The author shows that Sumner as head of the Senate Foreign Relations Committee had letters from British members of Parliament John Bright and Richard Cobden warning of war if James Mason and John Slidell of the *Trent* did not go free. Sumner, who discerned a relationship between the *Trent* and impressment, revealed this warning to Lincoln's cabinet at its December 25, 1861, meeting, suggesting the senator's peacekeeping role.

8:315   Drake, Frederick C. "The Cuban Background of the Trent Affair." *Civil War History* 19 (March 1973): 29–49. This article adds a new dimension to the context of this diplomatic crisis. The author emphasizes the role of the Union's consul in Cuba, Robert W. Shufeldt, in the events preceding the capture of Mason and Slidell.

8:316   Ferris, Norman B. "The Prince Consort, *The Times,* and the *Trent* Affair." *Civil War History* 6 (June 1960): 152–56. Ferris shows that the Prince Consort's push for a milder tone in the British official reaction to the *Trent* affair echoed the sentiments of the *Times* of London, which favored conciliation.

8:317   _____. *The Trent Affair: A Diplomatic Crisis.* Knoxville: University of Tennessee Press, 1977. This detailed study examines one of the most famous of diplomatic crises of the Civil War. In late 1861, Union naval Captain Charles Wilkes ignited talk of an Anglo-American war by his illegal and unauthorized removal of Confederate agents James Mason and John Slidell as contraband from the British mail packet *Trent.* Ferris uses U.S., British, and French materials to show how the Lincoln administration gave in to British demands for the two men's release, covering its retreat with the confusing and erroneous argument that it had won British admission to neutral rights.

8:318   Hancock, Harold B., and Norman B. Wilkinson. "'The Devil to Pay!': Saltpeter and the *Trent* Affair." *Civil War History* 10 (March 1964): 20–32. The author relates the story of the Union's efforts to secure saltpeter (essential to manufacturing gunpowder) from Great Britain in the wake of the *Trent* crisis. At one point, Palmerston considered banning the sale of arms, gunpowder, and saltpeter but finally decided against doing so. The French likewise considered such a ban but followed Britain's lead.

8:319   Harris, Thomas L. *The Trent Affair, Including a Review of English and American Relations at the Beginning of the Civil War.* Indianapolis: Bobbs-Merrill, 1896. Though long outdated, this work long remained the best on the subject and continues to be useful.

8:320   Long, John Sherman. "Glory-Hunting off Havana: Wilkes and the *Trent* Affair." *Civil War History* 9 (June 1963): 133–44. Long shows that Union navy captain Charles Wilkes, the chief architect of the *Trent* crisis, had an "insatiable thirst for naval glory" that contributed to his seizure of Mason and Slidell. The *Trent* affair promoted southern defeat by making European governments, already involved in their own troubles, wary of dealing with either north or south.

8:321   O'Rourke, Alice. "The Law Officers of the Crown and the *Trent* Affair." *Mid-America* 54 (July 1972): 157–71. This article traces the evolution of the views of British legal advisers about the law of the *Trent,* and concludes that Seward's defense — or apology — had been substantially foreshadowed.

8:322   Rawley, James A. *Turning Points of the Civil War.* Lincoln: University of Nebraska Press, 1966. This volume contains a useful chapter on the *Trent* crisis.

8:323   Warren, Gordon H. *Fountain of Discontent: The Trent Affair and Freedom of the Seas.* Boston: Northeastern University Press, 1981. This work contains a thorough discussion of the impact of international law on the *Trent* affair.

8:324   Welles, Gideon. "The Capture and Release of Mason and Slidell." *Galaxy* (May 1873): 640–51. The Union's secretary of the navy, Gideon Welles, offers a good summary of the legalities involved in the Lincoln administration's decision to release Mason and Slidell after Wilkes's unauthorized seizure of the *Trent.* Welles attributed much of the strong British and French reaction to their antidemocratic sentiment and concern over the rising power of the American republic.

8:325   Wheeler-Bennett, John. "The *Trent* Affair." *History Today* 11 (December 1961): 805–16. This is a popular account of the *Trent* affair that is noteworthy for its inclusion of rare archival materials.

8:326   Whitridge, Arnold. "The *Trent* Affair 1861." *History Today* 4 (June 1954): 394–402. This brief article surveys the crisis resulting from the Union's removal of southern envoys James Mason and John Slidell from the British mail steamer *Trent* in November 1861. The resulting emotional storm produced excitement in the north over a rare success in the first year of the war and outraged Britain as an affront to national honor and neutral rights. Lincoln calmed matters by capitulating in the release of his two Confederate prizes.

Other Prize Cases

8:327   Bernath, Stuart L. "British Neutrality and the Civil War Prize Cases." *Civil War History* 15 (December 1969): 320–31. In a concise and comprehensive survey of British mercantile press reactions to American interpretations of maritime law, the author surveys the attitudes (and motives) of parliamentary critics of government policy and traces the implementation of that policy by the British minister in Washington and commander of Royal Naval units in American waters.

8:328   _____. *Squall across the Atlantic: American Civil War Prize Cases and Diplomacy.* Berkeley: University of California Press, 1970. The author illuminates large questions by his detailed analysis of a highly technical topic, showing the intricate relationship between international law and national self-interest. The book's superb bibliography demonstrates the value of an interdisciplinary approach to diplomatic history. Students of legal aspects of the war will pay particular attention to those works cited on international maritime law.

8:329   _____. "Squall across the Atlantic: The *Peterhoff* Episode." *Journal of Southern History* 34 (August 1968): 382–401. This article contains a fine summary of the complexities of the doctrine of continuous voyage in maritime law that were such a point of contention between England and the United States during the Civil War.

Alabama Claims

8:330   Cook, Adrian. *The* Alabama *Claims: American Politics and Anglo-American Relations, 1865–1872.* Ithaca: Cornell University Press, 1975. This remains the standard work on the Alabama claims dispute between the United States and England that culminated in the Treaty of Washington of 1871.

8:331   Dashew, Doris W. "The Story of an Illusion: The Plan to Trade the 'Alabama' Claims for Canada." *Civil War History* 15 (December 1969): 332–48. The Civil War, according to the author, revived U.S. expansionist hopes northward into Canada. Some Americans, including Hamilton Fish, used Union bitterness against Britain from the war to press a surrender of monetary claims to gain Canada instead. Not until October 1870 did this plan die.

8:332   Ek, Richard A. "Charles Sumner's Address at Cooper Union." *Southern Speech Journal* 32 (Spring 1967): 169–79. This article centers on a fall 1863 speech delivered by Charles Sumner, chair of the Senate Committee on Foreign Relations, who detailed the numerous British efforts benefiting the Confederacy, chastised the crown for awarding belligerent status to the south, and warned against intervention. Sumner's influence on Anglo-American relations extended to the *Alabama* claims dispute in the postwar years.

8:333   Hollett, David. *The Alabama Affair: The British Shipyards Conspiracy in the American Civil War.* Cheshire, UK: Sigma Press, 1993. Based primarily on secondary and published documentary sources, this is a useful history of Confederate shipbuilding efforts in England, with particular emphasis on the *Alabama* and the charge of conspiracy leveled against the British companies.

8:334   MacChesney, Brunson. "The *Alabama* and the Queen's Advocate—A Mystery of History." *Northwestern University Law Review* 62 (September-October 1967): 568–85. In this article, the author examines the legal issues impeding the efforts of Charles Francis Adams as Union minister and the British Foreign Office to block the departure of #290 (CSS *Alabama*) from British shipyards. The vessel escaped British waters more from legal entanglements, resulting delays, and the untimely illness of Sir John Harding, the Queen's Advocate, than from the lack of a good-faith effort by Lord John Russell in the Foreign Office.

8:335   Maynard, Douglas H. "Plotting the Escape of the *Alabama*." *Journal of Southern History* 20 (May 1954): 197–209. This article examines James Bulloch's efforts to procure ships for a Confederate navy from British shipyards.

8:336   _____. "Union Efforts to Prevent the Escape of the *Alabama*." *Mississippi Valley Historical Review* 41 (June 1954): 41–60. This article shows the diplomatic efforts by the Union's emissaries in Great Britain to block the deployment of the CSS *Alabama* from British shipyards. See also Maynard, "Plotting the Escape of the *Alabama*" (1954) (8:335).

8:337   Robinson, Charles M., III. *Shark of the Confederacy: The Story of the CSS Alabama.* Annapolis: Naval Institute Press, 1995. This is a well-written narrative that rests mainly on primary sources and provides rich detail on the *Alabama*'s operations from its construction to its fatal encounter with the *Kearsarge*.

Confederate Shipbuilding

8:338   Adams, Brooks. "The Seizure of the Laird Rams." *Proceedings of the Massachusetts Historical Society* 45 (1911–1912): 243–333. This long account of the Laird rams crisis provides useful information on Charles Francis Adams's diplomacy. Lord John Russell's decision in 1863 to detain the rams came without much pressure from Adams.

8:339   Jones, Wilbur D. *The Confederate Rams at Birkenhead: A Chapter in Anglo-American Relations.* Tuscaloosa: Confederate Pub. Co., 1961. Jones's work remains an essential source for any study of southern efforts to contract with British shipbuilders for the construction of a Confederate navy and the dilemma faced by the Palmerston ministry in trying to balance neutrality and maritime law against the long-term interests of the crown. Among the many special features of this study is the detailed analysis of British policy in the decision to seize the Laird rams in 1863. Equally impressive is the author's careful investigation of efforts to build a case against those vessels.

8:340 Krein, David F. "Russell's Decision to Detain the Laird Rams." *Civil War History* 22, no. 2 (June 1976): 158–63. According to the author, Russell finally decided in 1863 that he had enough evidence to call the rams vessels of war that were going to the enemy of a country friendly to Great Britain. Ships built in England and ending up in the Confederate navy, the foreign secretary determined, demonstrated a "hostile neutrality" by the British. Although he lacked evidence of the rams' final destination, he knew that Egypt denied making any deal for the ships and that there was sufficient suspicion for him to go beyond international law to demonstrate his neutrality. The author uses the papers of the British undersecretary of state, Austin H. Layard, to trace the evolution of this decision and plays down the importance of Charles Francis Adams's note to Russell on September 5, 1863.

8:341 Maynard, Douglas H. "The Escape of the *Florida*." *Pennsylvania Magazine of History and Biography* 77 (April 1953): 181–97. In this article, the author examines the efforts of Union emissaries in Great Britain, particularly the consul in Liverpool, Thomas H. Dudley, to block the departure of the *Oreto* from British shipyards. The ship, commissioned by Confederate agent James Bulloch, cleared port as the CSS *Florida* and threatened Anglo-American relations as it damaged Union shipping.

8:342 Merli, Frank J. "Crown versus Cruiser: The Curious Case of the *Alexandra*." *Civil War History* 9 (June 1963): 167–77. Based on a wide variety of British sources, this work points out the legal difficulties facing the British government as it attempted to define the limits of neutrality.

8:343 _____. *Great Britain and the Confederate Navy, 1861–1865*. Bloomington: Indiana University Press, 1970. By focusing on the narrow theme of Confederate naval construction in Great Britain, the author illuminates many aspects of the larger dimensions of Britain's response to the American Civil War.

8:344 Merli, Frank J., et al. "The South's Scottish Sea Monster." *American Neptune* 29 (January 1969): 5–29. The authors show how British neutrality complicated Confederate attempts to acquire the so-called Scottish sea monster (an ironclad frigate), reportedly a state-of-the-art warship.

8:345 Merli, Frank J., and Thomas W. Green. "Great Britain and the Confederate Navy, 1861–1865." *History Today* 14 (October 1964): 687–95. This article scrutinizes the Confederacy's effort to recruit British shipbuilders to help produce a navy capable of breaking the Union blockade of southern ports. The authors question the likelihood of success even had Confederate designs gone unimpeded. They point out, however, that this scenario was never put to the test because the Palmerston ministry resisted legal challenges and ultimately blocked Confederate ship procurement.

8:346 Smith, John David. "Yankee Ironclads at Birkenhead? A Note on Gideon Welles, John Laird, and Gustavus V. Fox." *Mariner's Mirror* 67 (February 1981): 77–81. This brief piece examines the allegation by British shipbuilder John Laird that the Union, while railing against his firm for violating neutrality by supplying ships to the Confederacy, actually approached him about building ships for the Union. Although the Union's secretary of the navy, Gideon Welles, denied making such a request, Smith shows that Welles's assistant secretary, Gustavus V. Fox, did indeed approach Laird about the prospects of supplying the Union navy.

8:347 Thomas, Mary Elizabeth. "The CSS *Tallahassee*: A Factor in Anglo-American Relations, 1864–1866." *Civil War History* 21 (June 1975): 148–59. One night in early August 1864, this Confederate raider slipped past the Union blockade at Wilmington, North Carolina, and moved northward to the waters off New York harbor, where it captured, damaged, or sank perhaps fifty merchant vessels in a span of six days. When it then left that area and entered Nova Scotia, the Union consul in Halifax made it an international issue that brought into question the sincerity of British neutrality. After the war, the Union consul in Liverpool filed suit for the *Tallahassee* (now under the guise of a merchant vessel named the *Chameleon*) and in 1866 gained possession of it as a ship that once belonged to Confederate rebels.

British Reaction to the Civil War

8:348   Baxter, James Phinney. "Some British Opinions as to Neutral Rights, 1861 to 1865." *American Journal of International Law* 23 (July 1929): 517–37. Baxter argues that the crown's lawyers tried to stay neutral in the Civil War, but British neutrality leaned toward the Union.

8:349   Beckett, Ian F. W. *The War Correspondents: The American Civil War.* Dover, NH: Alan Sutton, 1993. Beckett examines the influential newspapers in London that covered the American war and argues that the personal views of their correspondents—William Howard Russell, Antonio Gallenga, Charles Mackay, and Francis Lawley—produced a confusing picture of the conflict that misled the British public. For the American—at least Union—side, see Bernard A. Weisberger, *Reporters for the Union* (Boston: Little, Brown, 1953).

8:350   Bellows, Donald. "A Study of British Conservative Reaction to the American Civil War." *Journal of Southern History* 51 (November 1985): 505–26. According to the author, British conservatives considered secession a democratic right and therefore thought the Union repressive in resisting the move. They dismissed the moral issue of slavery, arguing that antislavery advocates had exaggerated its evils and that Union imperialism and not slavery had been the crucial cause of the war. Secession, they added, would help the north by ridding it of slavery. Conservatives concluded that democracy itself had bred both anarchy and despotism, leading to secession and civil war.

8:351   Berwanger, Eugene H. *The British Foreign Service and the American Civil War.* Lexington: University Press of Kentucky, 1994. This work covers the British foreign service's relations with both sides during the American Civil War but does not convincingly demonstrate whether the consuls had a major impact on their home government's policies. Consuls, after all, focused on commercial matters and safeguarding the rights of British nationals. Since Britain's twenty-two consuls (in nine Union and six Confederate cities) were on the American scene, however, they were in the position to forward much useful information to their superiors in London.

Berwanger shows that those in the north were more open to its arguments than those in the south were sympathetic to the Confederacy.

8:352   Blackett, R. J. M. *Divided Hearts: Britain and the American Civil War.* Baton Rouge: Louisiana State University Press, 2001. In this impressive work, Blackett examines British sympathies toward the American Civil War, concluding that the country was deeply divided but that the majority of workers supported the Union. His analysis of pro-Union and pro-Confederate societies in England reveals that their publications rested on propaganda, making them unreliable guides in determining British attitudes. He also shows that racism helped to mold British feelings. More than forty African-Americans traveled throughout England, trying to stir up weakened abolition sentiment and win support for the Union. According to Blackett, the British believed slavery lay at the heart of the southern attempt to secede from the Union.

8:353   _____. "Pressure from Without: African Americans, British Public Opinion, and Civil War Diplomacy." In *The Union, the Confederacy, and the Atlantic Rim,* ed. Robert E. May, 69–100. West Lafayette, IN: Purdue University Press, 1995. In this essay, the author examines the impact of British public opinion on the issue of intervention in the American Civil War. Included in his analysis is the role of about forty African-Americans who delivered pro-Union lectures in England that helped to undermine Confederate sympathizers' attempts to demonstrate a strong wave of southern support among British textile workers. Both sides in the controversy succeeded only in exposing deep divisions among workers to the Palmerston ministry.

8:354   Brook, Michael. "Confederate Sympathies in North-East Lancashire, 1862–1864." *Lancashire and Cheshire Antiquarian Society* 75–76 (1977): 211–17. The author demonstrates Confederate support in British Lancashire and Cheshire.

8:355   Carpenter, John A. "The New York International Relief Committee: A Chapter in the Diplomatic History of the Civil War." *New York Historical Society Quarterly* 56 (July 1972): 239–52. The author shows how New York businessmen and philanthropists established this committee near the end of 1862 in an effort to feed unemployed textile workers in Lancashire, thus easing Anglo-Union relations when the interventionist threat was high. In the six months of the committee's existence, the Palmerston ministry became aware of the close relationship between English workers and the American republic as well as their hostility to slavery and the Confederacy.

8:356   Crawford, Martin. "The Anglo-American Crisis of the Early 1860's: A Framework for Revision." *South Atlantic Quarterly* 82 (Autumn 1983): 406–23. Crawford focuses on how a generally positive relationship between the Washington and London governments turned so abruptly toward crisis at the outbreak of the Civil War. Among the factors was an atmosphere in which northern sensitivities that attributed hostile motives to British neutrality met with sharp Britons' criticisms of what they deemed an inept federal government. The south, Crawford contends, was "immunized" by secession, with Britain laying the blame for the disruption on a foundering U.S. government.

8:357   _____. *The Anglo-American Crisis of the Mid-Nineteenth Century: The Times and America, 1850–1862.* This book focuses on the reaction by the London *Times* to the turbulent 1850s in the United States and the first year of the Civil War. The author shows how the British failed to understand the issues behind slavery and the war as well as the Union blockade and Confederate naval policies. In mid-1864, following three years of anti-Union invective, the *Times* announced support for recognition of the Confederacy even though the Palmerston ministry did not (6:170).

8:358   Crook, D. P. "Portents of War: English Opinion on Secession." *Journal of American Studies* 4 (February 1971): 163–79. Crook argues that pro-Union sentiment was strong among British labor groups. Most Englishmen, however, thought that the north and south should separate because of irreconcilable differences. British expressions of pacifism and humanitarianism, he insists, were real—especially when these feelings coincided with the national interest.

8:359   Daniel, W. Harrison. "The Response of the Church of England to the Civil War and Reconstruction in America." *Historical Magazine of the Protes-*

tant Episcopal Church 47 (March 1978): 51–72. The author suggests that the Anglican church agreed with other British clerics in abhorring slavery but remained generally sympathetic to the south.

8:360   Ellison, Mary. *Support for Secession: Lancashire and the American Civil War.* Chicago: University of Chicago Press, 1972. This study examines one of the Civil War's major issues affecting diplomacy: whether British workers favored the Union. Ellison argues that Britain's cotton interests supported an independent south. Epilogue by Peter d'A. Jones.

8:361   Foner, Philip S. *British Labor and the American Civil War.* New York: Holmes and Meier, 1981. Foner holds that British workers supported the Union because of their opposition to slavery, making the Emancipation Proclamation an important consideration in preventing British recognition of the Confederacy.

8:362   Hernon, Joseph M., Jr. "British Sympathies in the American Civil War: A Reconsideration." *Journal of Southern History* 33 (August 1967): 356–67. The author declares that British opinion toward the American Civil War was highly complex, although upper-class hatred of democracy was the biggest reason for its favoring the south. Recognition did not follow because of Lord Palmerston's caution. The Emancipation Proclamation had no impact on British abolitionists such as Lord Brougham, who supported the south's drive for self-determination. Perhaps a majority of British workers, Hernon believes, favored southern independence.

8:363   _____. *Celts, Catholics & Copperheads: Ireland Views the American Civil War.* Columbus: Ohio State University Press, 1968. The author relates the struggle for independence in the American south to the question of home rule in Ireland in a study of what he calls "the texture of opinion."

8:364   _____. "Irish Religious Opinion on the American Civil War." *Catholic Historical Review* 49 (January 1964): 508–23. In examining the Irish clergy's attitude toward the American Civil War, Hernon concludes that even though these religious leaders opposed slavery, they wanted the Union to end the bloodshed by conceding Confederate independence. Catholic leaders believed that Union discrimination and exploitation constituted a threat to Catholicism in the United States and therefore worked for peace through avenues that would deliver a Confederate victory.

8:365　　　Jones, Wilbur D. "Blyden, Gladstone and the War." *Journal of Negro History* 49 (January 1964): 56–61. This brief piece contains three letters from Edward Wilmot Blyden, the black diplomat from Liberia, to William E. Gladstone, Chancellor of the Exchequer in the Palmerston ministry, which help to focus both men's views toward the American war. Blyden denounced the racism that permeated both north and south and praised the British for maintaining a neutrality policy that helped push the Union into making the war into a moral crusade that Gladstone and others could support.

8:366　　　_____. "The British Conservatives and the American Civil War." *American Historical Review* 58 (April 1953): 527–43. The author focuses on the traditional belief that the British Conservative Party favored a Confederate victory in the Civil War and concludes that most members were less interested in the American conflict than Poland and Denmark, helping persuade them of the wisdom of neutrality in the American war. No party member called for a permanently divided United States, and no one advocated southern victory as the chief means for destroying republicanism. In one of the best articles on the British response to the war, the author also concludes that in Conservative circles sympathy for the south was far less than commonly believed.

8:367　　　Joyce, Davis D. "Pro-Confederate Sympathy in the British Parliament." *Social Science* 44 (April 1969): 95–100. This brief article focuses on three of the most influential pro-southern members of Parliament—William Gregory, William Lindsey, and John Arthur Roebuck.

8:368　　　Klinefelter, Lee M. "Lampooned in London." *Civil War Times Illustrated* 20 (February 1982): 28–35. This article shows the generally pro-southern position taken by the London *Punch* toward the American Civil War.

8:369　　　Logan, Kevin J. "The *Bee-Hive* Newspaper and British Working Class Attitudes toward the American Civil War." *Civil War History* 22 (December 1976): 337–48. The author focuses on the traditional argument that the British aristocracy supported the south and the workers favored the north in the American Civil War. The *Bee-Hive*, a London weekly newspaper, was the official spokesman of the London Trades Council and therefore was not as economically involved in the war's outcome as were other working groups. Early in the war, it was moderately pro-south in calling for peaceful separation and an end to the fighting; by the fall of 1862, however, many workers urged the British government to support the north because of its opposition to slavery. Logan admits to inconclusive evidence and calls for more research into the matter.

8:370　　　Macdonald, Helen G. *Canadian Public Opinion on the American Civil War.* New York: Columbia University Press, 1926. Reprint 1974 (Octagon Books). The author surveys British North American newspapers to examine Canadian sentiment toward the U.S. Civil War and to show how the war affected the Canadian confederation movement. According to her findings, Canadian liberals aligned with the Union and conservatives with the Confederacy. The Canadian provinces remained apprehensive about the likelihood of becoming the battleground if war erupted between the Union and Britain.

8:371　　　Maurer, Oscar. "*Punch* on Slavery and Civil War in America, 1841–1865." *Victorian Studies* 1 (September 1957): 5–28. The author shows that London's *Punch* magazine changed from its "radical-humanitarian, anti-aristocratic, anti-clerical" position into a more conservative stance by the 1860s.

8:372　　　Maynard, Douglas H. "Civil War 'Care': The Mission of the '*George Griswold.*'" *New England Quarterly* 34 (September 1961): 291–310. Maynard examines the efforts of Americans to extend food to families of British textile workers whose hardships resulted in part from the Union blockade on southern ports. The mission of the American ship *George Griswold* to feed the people of Lancashire encouraged pro-northern sentiment during the Civil War.

8:373　　　Merli, Frank J., and Theodore A. Wilson. "The British Cabinet and the Confederacy: Autumn 1862." *Maryland Historical Magazine* 65 (Fall 1970): 239–62. In the fall of 1862, the authors argue, the British came close to intervention but did not proceed because the prime minister, Lord Palmerston, was less bellicose than usually depicted, and Secretary for War George Cornewall Lewis warned of war with the Union.

8:374 Park, Joseph H. "The English Workingmen and the American Civil War." *Political Science Quarterly* 39 (September 1924): 432–57. The author argues that English workers hated slavery and supported the north because of its emphasis on democracy and free labor. Their interest in political and economic freedoms outweighed the damage caused by the Union blockade.

8:375 Shippee, Lester B. *Canadian-American Relations, 1849–1874.* New Haven: Yale University Press, 1939. Chapters 6 through 8 of this work are useful in assessing Canadian opinion on the war. They show irritation over Union recruiting practices across the border and over Confederate harassment of Union ships on the upper lakes. The author also addresses complications in Union-Canadian reciprocity stemming from the U.S. Congress's perception of the Canadians' lack of adequate sympathy for the Union cause.

8:376 Vanauken, Sheldon. *The Glittering Illusion: English Sympathy for the Southern Confederacy.* Washington, DC: Regnery Gateway, 1989. The author argues, questionably, that British sympathies for the Confederacy were strong because of the "glittering illusion" of southern gentility and military superiority. Although the publication date is fairly recent, this work is actually an unrevised version (with an added epilogue) of the author's thesis at Oxford University in 1957.

8:377 Whitridge, Arnold. "British Liberals and the American Civil War." *History Today* 12 (October 1962): 688–95. The author argues that Liberals were poorly informed on the meaning of the American Civil War and never grasped the ramifications of Lincoln's policy. Some hated slavery and considered the Union a protector of democracy, while others remained neutral though both opposed to slavery and appalled by the war.

8:378 Wright, D. G. "Bradford and the American Civil War." *Journal of British Studies* 8 (May 1969):

69–85. The author declares the industrial city of Bradford as clearly pro-Union, even though prosouthern feeling among the middle and working classes was stronger than previously thought. Bradford's own W. E. Forster, son of a Quaker preacher and nephew of antislavery spokesman Thomas Fowell Buxton, won election to Parliament in February 1861 as a Liberal and argued that the Civil War was essentially a battle between freedom and slavery. Bradford's stance contributed to the British government's neutrality during the Civil War.

8:379 _____. "English Opinion on Secession: a Note." *Journal of American Studies* 5 (August 1971): 151–54. In showing the wide range of British opinion on southern secession, Wright suggests the difficulty in determining the country's sympathies toward the American war. All kinds of journals expressed differing views, regardless of their size and circulation. But the general sentiment backed a British neutrality that in reality favored the north.

Slavery and the Slave Trade

8:380 Adams, Neal Monroe. "Northern Negrophobia during the Civil War: As Reported by the London *Times*." *Negro History Bulletin* 28 (October 1964): 7–8. This short piece examines the London *Times'* views of the Union's rationale for war. Contrary to the Union argument that the war centered on slavery, the *Times* contended that the north's major concern was to maintain its economic advantages over the south.

8:381 Fladeland, Betty. *Men and Brothers: Anglo-American Antislavery Cooperation.* This standard work focuses on the antislavery connection between Great Britain and the United States (6:174).

8:382 Greenleaf, Richard. "British Labor against American Slavery." *Science and Society* 17 (Winter 1953): 42–58. The author focuses on British labor unions in arguing that workers opposed slavery and helped prevent Palmerston from intervening in the American Civil War.

8:383 Harrison, Royden. "British Labour and American Slavery." *Science and Society* 25 (December 1961): 291–319. Harrison argues that at the outset of the Civil War, British labor strongly opposed American slavery but that workers hated the north so much they liked the south. After the close of 1862, however, most workers were pro-north because of its democratic principles, the solidarity of labor, and family ties.

8:384   Henderson, Conway W. "The Anglo-American Treaty of 1862 in Civil War Diplomacy." *Civil War History* 15 (December 1969): 308–19. Henderson argues that the Lincoln administration hoped to draw British support in the Civil War by signing the treaty of 1862 authorizing Anglo-American cooperation in suppressing the African slave trade.

8:385   Jones, Howard. *To the Webster-Ashburton Treaty: A Study in Anglo-American Relations, 1783–1843.* The author provides information on the African slave trade and search issues, both emerging during the Civil War (5:456).

8:386   Lennon, E. James. "The Pro-Northern Movement in England, 1861–1865." *Quarterly Journal of Speech* 41 (February 1955): 27–37. This article examines the activities of the London Emancipation Society and associated pro-northern orators led by John Bright, Richard Cobden, and Thomas Bayley Potter.

8:387   Lorimer, Douglas A. "The Role of Anti-Slavery Sentiment in English Reactions to the American Civil War." *Historical Journal* 19 (June 1976): 405–20. According to the author, the British were almost totally antislavery and thought the American Civil War lacked moral justification when the north denied that slavery lay at the heart of the conflict. With either a northern victory or southern secession, the British believed, slavery would die. Lord John Russell, foreign minister, agreed with the common view that an independent Confederacy would have to free its slaves because of world pressure.

8:388   McPherson, James M. *The Negro's Civil War: How American Negroes Felt and Acted during the War for the Union.* New York: Pantheon Books, 1965. Reprint 1991 (Ballantine Books). McPherson shows the importance of the "Negro Question" to the Civil War by letting blacks express their feelings in their own words.

8:389   Milne, A. Taylor. "The Lyons-Seward Treaty of 1862." *American Historical Review* 38 (April 1933): 511–25. Milne shows that one of the reasons for the Lyons-Seward Treaty was to attract British sentiment for the Union by establishing a mutual effort to suppress the African slave trade.

8:390   Thistlethwaite, Frank. *The Anglo-American Connection in the Early Nineteenth Century.* This rich volume provides valuable information on the social, economic, and cultural connections between the Atlantic nations in the years before the Civil War. The author is strong on the growing antislavery connection between the English-speaking peoples (6:196).

Emancipation Proclamation

8:391   Franklin, John Hope. *The Emancipation Proclamation.* Garden City, NY: Doubleday, 1963. This is Franklin's classic account of Lincoln's move to emancipation, including an analysis of his understanding of its impact on foreign policy during the Civil War.

8:392   Heckman, Richard A. "British Press Reaction to the Emancipation Proclamation." *Lincoln Herald* 71 (Winter 1969): 150–53. The author cites liberal, independent, and conservative newspapers in Britain in showing the widespread hostility toward the Emancipation Proclamation as a hypocritical effort by Lincoln to incite slave rebellions and salvage victory in a lost war.

8:393   Jones, Howard. *Union in Peril: The Crisis over British Intervention in the Civil War.* Chapel Hill: University of North Carolina Press, 1992. Contrary to the traditional interpretation, the Union's victory at Antietam followed by the Emancipation Proclamation did not end the possibility of British intervention in the Civil War. At various points in the war, the British (and French) considered a mediation that entailed recognition of the south's independence. Though Lincoln issued the Emancipation Proclamation confident that it would stop all talk of intervention, the British considered the move a hypocritical effort to win the war by stirring up slave rebellions. France's proposal for a five-power intervention resting on arbitration and an implied use of force to bring the war to a close was rejected in London for fear of war with the

Union. By the close of 1863, England, coming to realize that the Emancipation Proclamation would ultimately kill slavery, decided to maintain its neutrality.

8:394 McConnell, Roland C. "From Preliminary to Final Emancipation Proclamation: The First Hundred Days." *Journal of Negro History* 48 (October 1963): 260–76. In focusing on the hundred days between the preliminary and final Emancipation Proclamation, the author shows how the final paper omitted passages misinterpreted by many as a call for slave insurrections as well as those referring to colonization and compensated emancipation.

8:395 Trefousse, Hans L. *Lincoln's Decision for Emancipation.* Philadelphia: Lippincott, 1975. This short volume provides some useful information on Lincoln's view toward slavery and emancipation.

8:396 Welles, Gideon. "The History of Emancipation." *Galaxy* (December 1872): 838–51. The Union's secretary of the navy, Gideon Welles, shows the Lincoln administration's legal and constitutional problems in dealing with the slavery issue. Fear of foreign recognition of the Confederacy helped determine the president's move toward emancipation.

Cotton and Trade

8:397 Brady, Eugene A. "A Reconsideration of the Lancashire 'Cotton Famine.'" *Agricultural History* 37 (July 1963): 156–62. Brady shows that contemporary writings demonstrate that the so-called 1861–1862 cotton famine in Lancashire was a myth—that there was no shortage of raw cotton, and that there was an excess of cotton yarn and textiles caused by overproduction from 1858 to 1861.

8:398 Broadbridge, Stanley. "The Lancashire Cotton 'Famine,' 1861–1865." In *The Luddites, and Other Essays,* ed. Lionel M. Munby, 143–60. London: Michael Katanka, Ltd., 1971. This essay stresses the anti-south attitude prevalent within British labor and the broader impact of this opposition on the evolution of the labor movement in Great Britain as leaders rallied workers against the Confederate cause. Broadbridge contends that British industry suffered more from overproduction than from the effects of the Civil War.

8:399 Claussen, Martin P. "Peace Factors in Anglo-American Relations, 1861–1865." *Mississippi Valley Historical Review* 26 (March 1940): 511–22. According to the author, England and the United States came close to war because of the Palmerston ministry's neutrality policy, which actually benefited the Confederacy. The chief factor in preventing British intervention in the Civil War was the pressure from commercial groups (not just those using cotton) interested in maintaining peace.

8:400 Earle, Edward Mead. "Egyptian Cotton and the American Civil War." *Political Science Quarterly* 41 (December 1926): 520–45. The author asserts that India's failure to provide high-quality cotton for the British turned them to Egypt, which furnished a type of cotton as good as that from the south, save for its Sea Island produce, and thereby took them a major step toward modernity. Indeed, Britain's increased reliance on Egyptian cotton perhaps influenced its decision to occupy Egypt.

8:401 Ginzberg, Eli. "The Economics of British Neutrality during the American Civil War." *Agricultural History* 10 (October 1936): 147–56. The author dismisses wheat as an important element in British neutrality during the Civil War.

8:402 Harnetty, Peter. "The Imperialism of Free Trade: Lancashire, India, and the Cotton Supply Question, 1861–1865." *Journal of British Studies* 6 (November 1966): 70–96. Harnetty examines the British government's attempts, prodded by Lancashire cotton interests, to find alternatives to southern cotton in India. British cotton merchants at home were less than enthusiastic because of their belief that the ultimate return of southern cotton's availability would make any investment in lower-quality Indian cotton a net loss.

8:403 Henderson, W. O. *The Lancashire Cotton Famine, 1861–1865.* Manchester, UK: Manchester University Press, 1934. This work centers on the impact of the so-called cotton famine on the approximately 500,000 Lancashire employees associated with the industry and the government's efforts to alleviate these conditions.

8:404 Jones, Robert H. "Long Live the King?" *Agricultural History* 37 (July 1963): 166–69. Relying on the British Sessional Papers for his statistics, Jones argues that neither wheat nor cotton was short in British supply and therefore had no impact on preventing British intervention in the Civil War.

8:405   Khasigian, Amos. "Economic Factors and British Neutrality, 1861–1865." *Historian* 25 (August 1963): 451–65. The author argues that no outside nation ever felt sufficient economic need to warrant intervening in the Civil War. The need for wheat, he insists, balanced off the interest in cotton, creating a complicated mixture of economic factors that benefited Britain while keeping it neutral.

8:406   Logan, Frenise A. "India—Britain's Substitute for American Cotton, 1861–1865." *Journal of Southern History* 24 (November 1958): 472–80. The author demonstrates that Britain's import of Indian cotton so grew that by 1864 it provided 67 percent of the home supply. By war's end, India had furnished more than 55 percent of Britain's cotton.

8:407   O'Connor, Thomas H. "Lincoln and the Cotton Trade." *Civil War History* 7 (March 1961): 20–35. In this article, the author shows Lincoln's problems during the war over cotton vis-à-vis England and France, but also with the border states wanting to maintain a cotton trade with the south and the cotton textile manufacturers in the north who also needed the product. Squeezed between the demands to blockade the Confederacy and the pressure to furnish cotton to England and France to ward off intervention, the Lincoln administration finally adopted the policy of commerce following the flag—that areas in Union hands were open to the cotton trade.

8:408   Pelzer, John. "Liverpool and the American Civil War." *History Today* 40 (March 1990): 46–52. In this brief piece, the author shows the economic, ideological, and sentimental connections among Liverpool, England, and the south during the Civil War. The chances for profit had a great impact on Liverpool's cotton trade.

8:409   Pomeroy, Earl S. "French Substitutes for American Cotton, 1861–1865." *Journal of Southern History* 9 (November 1943): 555–60. This brief article examines France's disorganized efforts to find substitutes for southern cotton in places such as North Africa, Central America, Mexico, Italy, Haiti,

Cambodia, Cyprus, and Syria. The Paris government's lack of a policy yielded no real successes but for that very reason benefited the south's attempts to revive its cotton trade in the postwar era.

8:410   Potter, J. "Atlantic Economy, 1815–1860: The U.S.A. and the Industrial Revolution in Britain." In *Essays in American Economic History,* ed. A. W. Coats and Ross M. Robertson, 14–48. New York: Barnes and Noble, 1969. In addition to making a useful contribution to transatlantic history and the economic history of the Anglo-American world, the author provides background information for the Civil War by evaluating the place of corn (wheat) and cotton in the British economy in the mid-nineteenth century.

8:411   Reclus, Elisée. "Le coton et la crise américaine [Cotton and the American Crisis]." *Revue des deux mondes* 37 (January 1862): 176–208. This is a useful primary source on the French concerns about the disruption of their American cotton supply and the prospects for alternative sources.

8:412   Schmidt, Louis B. "The Influence of Wheat and Cotton on Anglo-American Relations during the Civil War." *Iowa Journal of History and Politics* 16 (July 1918): 400–39. According to the author, northern wheat was a central factor in balancing off Britain's need for cotton and preventing its recognition of the south.

8:413   Woodman, Harold D. *King Cotton & His Retainers: Financing & Marketing the Cotton Crop of the South, 1800–1925.* Lexington: University of Kentucky Press, 1968. This is a detailed examination of cotton culture and its place in the world economic system, including a section on the south's scramble to market its crop on the eve of and during the Civil War.

FRANCE

8:414   Bernstein, Samuel. *Essays in Political and Intellectual History.* New York: Paine-Whitman Publishers, 1955. In a chapter on "French Diplomacy and the American Civil War," Bernstein investigates the internal struggle in France between labor groups and Napoleon III over the government's inclination to help the south. French labor, Bernstein shows, strongly objected to the emperor's proslavery position.

8:415 Berwanger, Eugene H. "Union and Confederate Reaction to French Threats against Texas." *Journal of Confederate History* 7 (1991): 97–111. Students examining the ramifications of Napoleon III's Mexican adventure on the Civil War will find this article useful. Berwanger investigates the postures taken by both the Lincoln and Davis governments toward the French pressure on Texas.

8:416 Bigelow, John. *France and the Confederate Navy, 1862–1868: An International Episode.* New York: Harper and Brothers, 1888. Reprint 1973 (Books for Libraries). This book provides an interesting look into the confused French response to the war. The information that Bigelow received of Confederate naval construction in France enabled the Americans to impede and finally to stop such activity.

8:417 Blackburn, George M. *French Newspaper Opinion on the American Civil War.* Westport, CT: Greenwood Press, 1997. This survey of French press opinion provides useful information on why the Paris government, which followed popular sentiment fairly closely, did not intervene in the American Civil War. Ideological persuasion, according to the author, was more important than wartime events in determining attitude.

8:418 Blumenthal, Henry. *A Reappraisal of Franco-American Relations, 1830–1871.* This survey provides a brief but useful analysis of Franco-American relations during the Civil War (6:205).

8:419 Bock, Carl H. *Prelude to Tragedy: The Negotiation and Breakdown of the Tripartite Convention of London, October 31, 1861.* Philadelphia: University of Pennsylvania Press, 1966. This long work traces the Anglo-French-Spanish intervention in Mexico that started as a joint effort to secure debt payments but ended with the British and Spanish withdrawal, leaving the French to continue the interventionist efforts that resulted in their placing Archduke Maximilian on the Mexican throne.

8:420 Carroll, Daniel B. *Henri Mercier and the American Civil War.* Princeton: Princeton University Press, 1971. This work covers the French minister's opinion of the Union and explores his relationship with Seward. Carroll exonerates Mercier of excessive partisanship for the south while demonstrating his belief, like the British, that southern independence was a fait accompli.

8:421 Case, Lynn M., and Warren F. Spencer. *The United States and France: Civil War Diplomacy.* Philadelphia: University of Pennsylvania Press, 1970. This mammoth work rests on a solid foundation of sources, including private documents used to flesh out the official records. The authors give their book a European orientation, rather than the traditional view from London or Washington. Besides presenting important information relating to Napoleon III's Mexican venture, they are particularly strong in explaining the differing views on diplomacy between the emperor and his ministers on the possibility of intervening in the American Civil War.

8:422 Crook, Carland Elaine. "Benjamin Théron and the French Designs in Texas during the Civil War." *Southwestern Historical Quarterly* 68 (April 1965): 432–54. Examining the Confederate reaction to two letters from Benjamin Théron, a French consular agent and vice-consul for Spain in Galveston, intimating a desire to detach Texas from the Confederacy, Crook demonstrates French Civil War intrigue involving designs on Mexico and the American southwest.

8:423 Gavronsky, Serge. "American Slavery and the French Liberals: An Interpretation of the Role of Slavery in French Politics during the Second Empire." *Journal of Negro History* 51 (January 1966): 36–52. This article focuses more on French politics than diplomacy, examining the co-opting of the slavery issue by the French liberal opposition as much for its own domestic purposes as to deter French intrusion in the Civil War. The author provides useful information in investigating the domestic impediments to Napoleon III's consideration of intervention.

8:424 _____. *The French Liberal Opposition and the American Civil War.* New York: Humanities Press, 1968. This work shows how the American war impinged on the policies of French liberalism.

8:425 Leary, William M., Jr. "*Alabama* versus

Kearsarge: A Diplomatic View." *American Neptune* 29 (July 1969): 167–73. This short article focuses on the attempts of the Union's minister to France, William L. Dayton, to block French aid to the Confederacy. He urged the Paris government to refuse sanctuary for the Confederate ship *Alabama* and then moved to end all French assistance.

8:426 Spencer, Warren F. "French Tobacco in Richmond during the Civil War." *Virginia Magazine of History and Biography* 71 (April 1963): 185–202. The author shows the difficulties over neutrality faced by the French consul in Richmond, Alfred Paul, in dealing with both Judah Benjamin and William Seward as he tried moving a huge supply of French tobacco out of Virginia from October 1862 to the end of the war. In the process, Paul was among a minority of French observers who came to believe that the south could not win the war because of insufficient manpower and economic resources. Not until the end of the war was he able to move the tobacco to France.

8:427 _____. "The Jewett-Greeley Affair: A Private Scheme for French Mediation in the American Civil War." *New York History* 51 (April 1970): 238–68. In early January 1863, Horace Greeley, editor of the *New York Tribune,* and William C. Jewett, a private American citizen known for his adventurist activities, engaged in unofficial mediation talks with the French minister to the United States, Henri Mercier. The discussions had no relation to the official French efforts of late October 1862 except that both proved fruitless.

8:428 Valone, Stephen J. "'Weakness Offers Temptation': William H. Seward and the Reassertion of the Monroe Doctrine." *Diplomatic History* 19 (Fall 1995): 583–99. Although this article focuses on Seward's efforts after the Civil War to deal with Napoleon III's intervention in Mexico, it contains insights into that crisis during the war years.

8:429 West, W. Reed. *Contemporary French Opinion on the American Civil War.* Baltimore: Johns Hopkins Press, 1924. This work attempts to evaluate French public opinion and the role of propaganda during the war.

8:430 Willson, Beckles. *America's Ambassadors*

to France (1777–1927): A Narrative of Franco-American Diplomatic Relations. Chapters 15 and 16 cover the Union's wartime ministers to France, William Dayton and John Bigelow, with particular focus on French relations with America over the interventionist issue and the Mexican question (4:241).

8:431 Wright, Gordon. "Economic Conditions in the Confederacy as Seen by the French Consuls." *Journal of Southern History* 7 (May 1941): 195–214. According to the author, the French consuls in Richmond, Charleston, and New Orleans, along with the vice-consuls and consular agents in other places, became especially important in reporting the south's economic situation after it expelled the British consuls in 1863. The consuls found that the Union blockade badly hurt the Confederacy, that staple crops had all but disappeared by the end of the war, that Confederate leaders had helped to create a state of financial disruption not conducive to French investors, and that Confederate morale suffered a devastating blow from high prices and food shortages.

ITALY

8:432 Alvarez, David J. "The Papacy in the Diplomacy of the American Civil War." *Catholic Historical Review* 69 (April 1983): 227–48. The author investigates the interaction of the north and south with Rome, suggesting a pragmatic Vatican approach to the Civil War that favored neither side. It assessed each issue on its own merits, keeping in mind the interests of the church.

8:433 Amundson, R. J. "Sanford and Garibaldi." *Civil War History* 14 (March 1968): 40–45. Drawing on the Sanford papers, this piece sketches the attempts by Henry S. Sanford, Lincoln's minister to Belgium, to persuade the Italian military leader, Giuseppe Garibaldi, to assist the Union's military forces at the beginning of the war.

8:434 Zettl, Herbert, ed. "Garibaldi and the American Civil War." *Civil War History* 22 (March 1976): 70–76. The document (1861) provides an unusual view of an unusual man confronting a most unusual proposal. The prospect of Garibaldi in command of the Union armed forces, empowered "to declare emancipation if he judged it necessary," as he demanded if he were to help the north, conjures up strange visions indeed.

POLAND

8:435   Fischer, LeRoy H. *Lincoln's Gadfly, Adam Gurowski.* Norman: University of Oklahoma Press, 1964. This work rests largely on the diary of Polish Count Adam Gurowski and offers the perspective of a foreign critic of the Lincoln administration who traveled in Washington's inner political circles during the Civil War. Chapter 10 contains Gurowski's views on Civil War events and diplomacy.

8:436   Kutolowski, John. "The Effect of the Polish Insurrection of 1863 on American Civil War Diplomacy." *Historian* 27 (August 1965): 560–77. This essay examines the relationship between the American Civil War and continental affairs in the 1860s, showing how the Polish uprising of 1863 impinged on the fortunes of the Confederates and Unionists in Europe.

8:437   Orzell, Laurence J. "A 'Favorable Interval': The Polish Insurrection in Civil War Diplomacy, 1863." *Civil War History* 24 (December 1978): 332–50. The Polish insurrection of 1863 exerted a great negative influence on Confederate efforts to win European recognition of its independence. Throughout that year, England and France focused on the Polish uprising against the Russians, joining Austria in threatening to intervene on behalf of the Poles in view of Russia's harsh rule. But doing so, the three powers knew, might inspire a Russo-American alliance. The Union profited from this preoccupation, just as the Confederacy suffered. Events in Poland pushed the Union and Russia closer together—they both confronted potential enemies in England and France and both encountered domestic rebellions that seeded the ground for foreign intervention. When Russian ships arrived in America in the autumn of 1863, they left the impression of a growing Russian-American friendship that helped to dissuade Europeans from intervening in the American war.

RUSSIA

8:438   Adamov, E. A. "Russia and the United States at the Time of the Civil War." *Journal of Mod-* ern *History* 2 (December 1930): 586–602. The author emphasizes Russian friendliness toward the United States by showing no sympathy for separation and a refusal to participate in any form of foreign intervention. Translated by R. P. Churchill. This article should be read in conjunction with Golder, "The American Civil War through the Eyes of a Russian Diplomat" (1921) (8:439).

8:439   Golder, Frank A. "The American Civil War through the Eyes of a Russian Diplomat." *American Historical Review* 26 (April 1921): 454–63. The author shows that the Russian minister in Washington, Edward de Stoeckl, did not consider slavery the cause of the Civil War but did think that democracy had opened the door to demagogues who promoted disorder and destruction of the Union.

8:440   Higham, Robin. "The Russian Fleet on the Eastern Seaboard, 1863–1864: A Maritime Chronology." *American Neptune* 20 (January 1960): 49–61. After dismissing the argument that the Russian fleet's appearance was attributable to sympathy for the Union, the author ties the visit to European events and then relates the maritime story. The fleet's presence, however, raised Union morale while depressing that of the south. Its ability to avoid entrapment in frozen waters also contributed to Britain and France's backing down on the Polish issue. Indeed, if war had broken out, the Russian ships would have been in the position to scout British and French colonies and trade routes.

8:441   Kushner, Howard I. "The Russian Fleet and the American Civil War: Another View." *Historian* 34 (August 1972): 633–49. The author argues that the Lincoln administration realized that winter conditions in the Baltic and ongoing problems with Britain and France over Poland lay behind the visit of the Russian fleet in 1863, but that the president and secretary of state skillfully exploited its presence as a demonstration of Russian support for the Union in the Civil War.

8:442   Nagengast, William E. "The Visit of the Russian Fleet to the United States: Were Americans Deceived?" *Russian Review* 8 (January 1949): 46–55. According to the author, the sole objective of the Russian fleet's visit to the United States in 1863 was to avoid what happened in the Crimean War of the 1850s—being blockaded in European waters by British and French vessels. The contemporary press in both north and south realized the visit resulted from European problems over the Polish question and did not relate to the Civil War.

8:443 Pomeroy, Earl S. "The Myth after the Russian Fleet, 1863." *New York History* 31 (April 1950): 169–76. Pomeroy points out that contemporary American newspapers recognized in 1863 that the arrival of the Russian fleet did not signal either love of the Union or hatred of slavery. The Russians did not want to be entrapped again as in the Crimean War, when the British blockaded the Russian fleet at Cronstadt while Anglo-French naval forces entered the Black Sea to approach Sebastopol.

8:444 Saul, Norman E. *Distant Friends: The United States and Russia, 1763–1867.* In this work, the author argues that the Russian minister to the United States, Edward de Stoeckl, privately supported a French initiative aimed at mediating the war because of his own government's noninterventionist stance along with his belief that the Union would reject any British offer. A Franco-Russian proposal seemed acceptable, but only when *both* north and south were ready to negotiate. All chances for such a joint mediation disappeared when the Polish rebellion broke out in 1863 and the Union refused to support the insurgents, placing it in the Russian camp. The visit of the Russian fleet, Saul insists, resulted from several considerations, one of which was to demonstrate friendship with the Union. Many Russians supported the outcome of the Civil War and the prospect of American support against the British (2:310).

8:445 Thomas, Benjamin P. *Russo-American Relations, 1815–1867.* Chapter 8 of this work deals with Union-Russian relations during the Civil War. Although it provides a useful survey of events, it draws entirely from U.S. and British sources and is written from an exclusively western perspective (6:246).

8:446 Woldman, Albert A. *Lincoln and the Russians.* Cleveland: World Pub. Co., 1952. This disappointing work provides mostly extracts from the papers and dispatches of the Russian minister in Washington. It is not very helpful or detailed on Russo-American relations.

SPAIN

8:447 Brauer, Kinley J. "The Appointment of Carl Schurz as Minister to Spain." *Mid-America* 56 (April 1974): 75–84. This is an evaluation of efforts to head off a crisis in Spanish-American relations in 1861 over the appointment of the "revolutionary" Schurz as the Union's minister to Madrid. Brauer has some useful things to say about Cuba's role in the efforts of the south.

8:448 _____. "Gabriel García y Tassara and the American Civil War: A Spanish Perspective." *Civil War History* 21 (March 1975): 5–27. Brauer's article on the Spanish minister in Washington, virtually the only study on its special subject, uses sources in Madrid to trace Spain's response to the war, a reaction the author calls "a strange combination of daring new ventures and excessive caution."

8:449 Cortada, James W. "Florida's Relations with Cuba during the Civil War." *Florida Historical Quarterly* 59 (July 1980): 42–52. This article examines Spain's concern about Cuba's security as it tried to maintain a balance between its official neutrality during the Civil War and its trade with the Confederacy through Florida. The Spanish followed a cautious policy of trading with the south in nonmilitary goods until the outcome of the American conflict became clear.

8:450 _____. *Spain and the American Civil War: Relations at Mid-Century, 1855–1868.* Philadelphia: American Philosophical Society, 1980. The Union's wartime relations with Spain occupy approximately a third of this volume. Cortada suggests that relations between the nations during the Civil War revolved around two central questions: the Union's transgressions of international law affecting neutrality, the blockade, and Spanish property, and the more critical issue of Spanish recognition of the Confederacy. Cortada's work is useful for understanding Spain's unique problems in trying to navigate relations with both the Union and the Confederacy.

OTHER EUROPEAN STATES

8:451 Blumberg, Arnold. "United States and the Role of Belgium in Mexico, 1863–1867." *Historian*

26 (February 1964): 206–27. The author shows that the Belgian government granted leaves of absence to regimental members who wished to accompany French and Austrian forces to Mexico. Belgium was caught between the expansionist French and the imperialist Prussians and became an auxiliary to Napoleon III. Its leaders immediately extended recognition to the new Mexican government because, they declared, the republic had ceased to exist.

8:452 Homan, Gerlof D. "Netherlands-American Relations during the Civil War." *Civil War History* 31 (December 1985): 353–64. This article explores the difficulties between the Union and the Netherlands over neutrality during the Civil War. According to the author, the Lincoln administration protested anything it thought a concession to the Confederacy but always sought an accommodation out of concern that the Netherlands government might extend belligerent rights to the south. The Civil War concerned few people in the Netherlands but attracted the interest of Amsterdam's financiers, who bought American securities and thereby helped the Union.

Mexico

8:453 Barker, Nancy Nichols. "France, Austria, and the Mexican Venture, 1861–1864." *French Historical Studies* 3 (Fall 1963): 224–45. Barker shows the relationship between Napoleon III's Mexican venture and his ongoing interests in Europe. Offering the Mexican throne to Maximilian grew out of Napoleon's plans for an Austrian alliance that would lead to the cession of Venetia and cooperation on the Polish issue. Failure to secure such an alliance by 1863 left Maximilian on his own in Mexico.

8:454 Hanna, Alfred Jackson, and Kathryn Abbey Hanna. *Napoleon III and Mexico: American Triumph over Monarchy.* Chapel Hill: University of North Carolina Press, 1971. This is the most complete account of Napoleon III's attempt to implement his "Grand Design" in Mexico, which was to mark the beginning of his attempt to end republicanism throughout the Americas and build a French empire in the Western Hemisphere.

8:455 Schoonover, Thomas D. *Dollars over Dominion: The Triumph of Liberalism in Mexican-United States Relations, 1861–1867.* Baton Rouge: Louisiana State University Press, 1978. This is a well-researched work that examines Union and Confederate relations with Mexico during the American Civil War and a short period afterward. Schoonover argues that the Republicans in Washington shared some common ideological tenets with the Liberal Party in Mexico, which prompted the two sets of leaders to view their problems and solutions as interrelated. According to the author, this attitude relieved stress between the Union and Mexico.

8:456 _____. "Mexican Cotton and the American Civil War." *Americas* 30 (April 1974): 429–47. The author examines the impact of the Civil War on trade with Mexico and the rise of its cotton culture. Although Schoonover admits to the inconclusive nature of the data concerning the expansion of Mexican cotton, he provides valuable information on Mexico's relations with both sides during the American war.

8:457 _____, ed. *Mexican Lobby: Matías Romero in Washington, 1861–1867.* Lexington: University Press of Kentucky, 1986. In this edited and translated book, Schoonover presents the dispatches of Matías Romero in highlighting his tenure as Mexico's envoy in Washington during the Civil War and Reconstruction. Particularly noteworthy was Romero's role in securing a limited amount of American assistance for Benito Juarez's struggle against the French-sponsored regime of Emperor Maximilian. Seward, for reasons not explained in the volume, was the chief impediment to Romero's success. Assisted by Ebba Wesener Schoonover.

8:458 _____. *A Mexican View of America in the 1860's: A Foreign Diplomat Describes the Civil War and Reconstruction.* Rutherford, NJ: Fairleigh Dickinson University Press, 1991. In this volume, Schoonover has translated and edited a collection of letters and dispatches from Matías Romero, the Mexican chargé and minister to America during the Civil War and early Reconstruction period, that will facilitate inquiries into the relationship between domestic and foreign policy.

8:459 _____. "Misconstrued Mission: Expansionism and Black Colonization in Mexico and

Central America during the Civil War." *Pacific Historical Review* 49 (November 1980): 607–20. Schoonover uses Mexican and Central American archival materials to flesh out the story of black colonization efforts by the United States. According to the author, Americans used black migration to extend their nation's territorial boundaries and political, economic, and cultural influence. Not only did they seek to establish a home for free blacks, but they wanted to prevent European domination of strategic areas while facilitating U.S. commercial expansion into the Caribbean. Mexico and Central America blocked U.S. efforts because they feared a domestic intervention that would leave them no voice in planning.

8:460   Tyler, Ronnie C. "An Auspicious Agreement between a Confederate Secret Agent and a Governor of Northern Mexico." *American West* 9 (January 1972): 38–43, 63. Students of Mexico's role in the Civil War will find this article along with the author's more exhaustive *Santiago Vidaurri and the Southern Confederacy* (1973) (8:461) useful. Here Tyler chronicles the efforts of Confederate secret agent Jose A. Quintero to develop relations with Governor Santiago Vidaurri in northern Mexico, expediting the war effort of Confederate operatives in Texas.

8:461   _____. *Santiago Vidaurri and the Southern Confederacy.* Austin: Texas State Historical Association, 1973. This book addresses the narrow topic of Mexican regional leader Santiago Vidaurri's establishment of a virtual entente between the Confederacy and the area he controlled in northeastern Mexico. In 1862–1863, his association with the Confederacy provided a means for the south to circumvent the Union blockade.

Confederate Foreign Relations

8:462   "The Confederacy and the Declaration of Paris." *American Historical Review* 23 (July 1918): 826–35. Trescot, assistant secretary of state until his home state of South Carolina announced secession in December 1860, dealt as a private citizen with the British and French consuls' entreaties from Charles-

ton in July 1861 to persuade the Confederacy to adhere to the Declaration of Paris of 1856, which concerned rules of maritime war. The issue became entangled with questions of recognition of the Confederacy when Trescot pointed out that the Declaration spoke of "the powers" who adhered to its principles. Even though the consuls would only say that acceptance would ultimately lead to recognition, Jefferson Davis and the Confederate Congress agreed to the declaration because its principles were part of international law and, they claimed, the Confederacy was a nation. Provided to the *American Historical Review* by Trescot's son, Edward A. Trescot.

8:463   Andreano, Ralph Louis. "A Theory of Confederate Finance." *Civil War History* 2 (December 1956): 21–28. This analytical article contains an extensive footnote review of the literature on a technical subject. See also Andreano, ed., *The Economic Impact of the American Civil War,* 2d ed. (Cambridge, MA: Schenkman Pub. Co., 1967), for a wider view.

8:464   Ball, Douglas B. *Financial Failure and Confederate Defeat.* Urbana: University of Illinois Press, 1991. The Confederacy's poor management of financial and economic matters, according to the author, constituted the biggest reason for its Civil War defeat. The south ignored economic theory to engage in self-destructive programs that included alienating Europeans with "King Cotton Diplomacy," failing to float bonds or establish a centralized purchasing mechanism on the continent, opposing the creation of a steamship line to England and the West Indies, and maintaining a laissez-faire policy toward business.

8:465   Bauer, Craig A. "The Last Effort: The Secret Mission of the Confederate Diplomat, Duncan F. Kenner." *Louisiana History* 22 (Winter 1981): 67–95. This article describes the mission to Europe by the Louisiana congressman in early 1865 in which he instructed commissioners James Mason and John Slidell to offer emancipation in exchange for British and French recognition. Napoleon would not act without Britain's lead, and Palmerston promptly discarded the idea.

8:466   _____. *A Leader among Peers: The Life and Times of Duncan Farrar Kenner.* Lafayette: Center for Louisiana Studies, University of Southwestern Louisiana, 1993. Here Bauer demonstrates the Confederacy's desperate effort to win European recognition late in the war. Finally convinced by late 1864 that the only avenue for survival lay in emancipation, Jefferson Davis authorized a secret diplomatic mission headed by Kenner to trade emancipation for recognition, but Palmerston refused the offer. Bauer contends that battlefield victories and not emancipation provided the means for recognition.

8:467 Blumenthal, Henry. "Confederate Diplomacy: Popular Notions and International Realities." *Journal of Southern History* 32 (May 1966): 151–71. Blumenthal demonstrates the naïveté of Confederate diplomacy, including failing to understand the importance of offering commercial gains in exchange for a European alliance to assist in building a war machine. Recognition, the south insisted, would come as an "act of justice." Instead, it should have argued that the Union blockade was effective rather than ineffective to establish a stronger claim for outside help. Its efforts to withhold cotton further showed its capacity to delude itself into believing that European nations would act out of sympathy for the south rather than out of self-interest.

8:468 Boaz, Thomas. *Guns for Cotton: England Arms the Confederacy.* Shippensburg, PA: Burd Street Press, 1996. This short work focuses on the Confederacy's attempts to secure arms in Great Britain. According to the author, the south was more successful than traditionally argued.

8:469 Bonham, Milledge L., Jr. *The British Consuls in the Confederacy.* New York: Columbia University, Longmans, Green and Co., Agents, 1911. This work remains virtually the only treatment of its special subject. The author shows the difficulties faced by the British consuls from 1861 to 1863 and explains the rising southern sentiment for their expulsion. The chapter on Robert Bunch is especially helpful since, from his post in Charleston, he was present at the time of secession and concerned about the status of the Declaration of Paris of 1856.

8:470 _____. "The French Consuls in the Confederate States." In *Studies in Southern History and Politics,* 83–104. New York: Columbia University Press, 1914. In this essay, one of several inscribed by students to William A. Dunning, former professor of history and political philosophy at Co-lumbia University, Bonham argues that French consular agents in seventeen southern cities in 1861 were basically friendly toward the Confederacy but rarely did anything to evade the Union blockade. Only on occasion did the consuls depart from neutrality in favor of the south.

8:471 Bulloch, James D. *The Secret Service of the Confederate States in Europe: Or, How the Confederate Cruisers Were Equipped.* 2 vols. New York: G. P. Putnam's Sons, 1884. Reprint 2001 (Modern Library). This is Confederate agent James Bulloch's account of the Confederacy's efforts to compensate for its lack of naval power. It contains extensive extracts from his official correspondence.

8:472 Callahan, James M. *Diplomatic History of the Southern Confederacy.* Baltimore: Johns Hopkins Press, 1901. This work includes an account of the acquisition of the so-called Pickett Papers, a major collection of documents on diplomatic and naval affairs in the south.

8:473 _____. "Diplomatic Relations of the Confederate States with England, 1861–1865." In *The Annual Report of the American Historical Association for the Year 1898,* 267–83. Washington, DC: Government Printing Office, 1899. This brief piece draws from a manuscript collection of Confederate documents to sketch the efforts to negotiate British recognition from the dispatch of the Confederate commissioners to London in early spring 1861 to the futile Duncan Kenner mission at the end of the war.

8:474 Coulter, E. Merton. *The Confederate States of America, 1861–1865.* Baton Rouge: Louisiana State University Press, 1950. This still useful study is heavier on fact than interpretation. Chapter 9, "Diplomacy," is an adequate summary, though much outdated.

8:475 Cullop, Charles P. *Confederate Propaganda in Europe, 1861–1865.* Coral Gables: University of Miami Press, 1969. This study of propaganda focuses on Henry Hotze, the chief Confederate agent, but offers little analysis of the impact of the south's message on leaders of British public opinion.

8:476 Daddysman, James W. *The Matamoros Trade: Confederate Commerce, Diplomacy, and In-*

trigue. Newark: University of Delaware Press, 1984. The Union blockade of southern ports made the city of Matamoros on the Mexican side of the Rio Grande River a port for the passage of Confederate import-export goods. Neither the north nor south devoted much attention to the port, however, considering it of secondary importance compared to other matters.

8:477   Davis, Jefferson. *The Rise and Fall of the Confederate Government.* 2 vols. New York: D. Appleton and Co., 1881. This is Davis's own account of the Confederacy.

8:478   Delaney, Norman C. "The Strange Occupation of James Bulloch: When Can You Start?" *Civil War Times Illustrated* 21 (March 1982): 18–27. This brief article describes Confederate agent James Bulloch's attempts to circumvent British laws to secure private contracts for the building of a navy.

8:479   Eaton, Clement. *A History of the Southern Confederacy.* New York: Macmillan, 1954. Chapter 4 of this standard history of the Confederacy focuses on diplomacy. Eaton argues that the south fell under the illusion of King Cotton diplomacy, believing that economic pressure could force recognition, thus failing to understand the importance of securing treaties and foreign loans. Simple recognition could not forcefully break the Union blockade and permit the huge influx of economic and military materiel needed to win the war.

8:480   Farley, Foster M. "Confederate Financier George Trenholm: 'The Manners of a Prince.'" *Civil War Times Illustrated* 21 (December 1982): 18–25. This short article focuses on the efforts of Charleston financier and treasurer of the Confederacy, George Trenholm, to run the Union blockade. According to the author, Trenholm put his ships under British registry and sent cotton to England in exchange for arms and munitions that came into southern ports through his offices in Liverpool and Nassau.

8:481   Gentry, Judith Fenner. "A Confederate Success in Europe: The Erlanger Loan." *Journal of Southern History* 36 (May 1970): 157–88. The author argues that the Erlanger loan, the only foreign loan in the Civil War, was a success in securing arms, materiel, and ships for the Confederacy through 1863 and early 1864.

8:482   Hanna, Kathryn Abbey. "The Roles of the South in the French Intervention in Mexico." *Journal of Southern History* 20 (February 1954): 3–21. In this article, the author reveals the complexities of the French intervention in Mexico. The south initially welcomed the move in an effort to block Union troops from crossing northern Mexico to attack Texas. While European nations generally sought to stop the growth of the United States, Napoleon III's objective was to establish a monarchy in Mexico. He exploited the north-south split to facilitate his Grand Design, held out the possibility of Confederate recognition to strengthen the new empire, and allowed Confederate migration into Mexico near the end of the French involvement following the American Civil War.

8:483   Hubbard, Charles M. *The Burden of Confederate Diplomacy.* Knoxville: University of Tennessee Press, 1998. The author focuses on the Confederacy's effort to win recognition in Europe as well as its negotiations with the Union during the war. Confederate diplomacy was ineffective, not only because of inept and inexperienced representatives, but also because of the burdens of slavery, cotton, and reactionary ideology. Failure to achieve recognition, Hubbard argues, strongly undermined the south's drive for independence.

8:484   Huse, Caleb. *The Supplies for the Confederate Army: How They Were Obtained and How Paid For.* Boston: Press of T. R. Marvin and Son, 1904. This is a brief and sketchy personal reminiscence by one of the most determined and successful procurers of arms and supplies from British businesses for the Confederate army.

8:485   Johnson, Ludwell H., III. "Contraband Trade during the Last Year of the Civil War." *Mississippi Valley Historical Review* 49 (March 1963): 635–52. Johnson focuses on the lucrative contraband trade between north and south during the Civil War by showing the northern businessmen's need for southern cotton and the southern need for northern products. Cotton would protect the Union's declining gold reserves, and the more cotton on the market, the less chance of British and French intervention in the war. According to the author, the Lincoln administration's move toward free trade with the south probably prolonged the war. Not until afterward did the U.S.

Supreme Court rule that war halts trade with the enemy unless a law specifically authorized such trade.

8:486 _____. "Trading with the Union: The Evolution of Confederate Policy." *Virginia Magazine of History and Biography* 78 (July 1970): 308–25. According to the author, the Confederacy acted wisely in refusing to prohibit contraband trade with the Union during the war. Indeed, the Confederacy should have established a consistent and regulated trade that might have better facilitated the sale of cotton as the basis for securing loans. But the south held on to King Cotton diplomacy, hoping to end the Union blockade and open trade with the entire world rather than just the Union.

8:487 Lebergott, Stanley. "Why the South Lost: Commercial Purpose in the Confederacy, 1861–1865." *Journal of American History* 70 (June 1983): 58–74. The south lost the war, Lebergott argues, because it refused to devote sufficient resources to the fighting and chose instead to focus on commercial objectives. Thus, a ban on the exportation of cotton might have forced Great Britain and France to come to its aid, but such a move also endangered the South's monopoly on cotton by encouraging Europeans to seek the product elsewhere. Consequently, the south permitted its planters to make cotton available to blockade runners, keeping the profits down and spread out while bringing in little revenue to the government. It, therefore, could not market sufficient quantities of bonds, removing the capacity to attract foreign resources and helping to ensure its own defeat.

8:488 Lester, Richard I. "An Aspect of Confederate Finance during the American Civil War: The Erlanger Loan and the Plan of 1864." *Business History* 16 (July 1974): 130–44. The author examines the impact of the so-called cotton loan negotiated on behalf of the Confederacy by John Slidell with Emile Erlanger and Company of France. Heralded at its inception as "a financial recognition" of Confederate independence, the loan faltered in parallel with Confederate setbacks on the battlefield. The Confederate Congress took control of cotton commerce in 1864 in a tardy attempt to put the crop to work for the government, but, according to Lester, the Davis government could not overcome four years of inept financial and procurement policies.

8:489 _____. *Confederate Finance and Purchasing in Great Britain.* Charlottesville: University Press of Virginia, 1975. Lester's book is a highly detailed analysis of a complex subject containing useful technical data on shipbuilding, finance, and ordnance. Its appendices are a mine of information.

8:490 Owsley, Frank L. *King Cotton Diplomacy: Foreign Relations of the Confederate States of America.* 2d ed., rev. Harriet Chappell Owsley. Chicago: University of Chicago Press, 1959. A pioneering work of research and synthesis, this book is sympathetic to the south and stresses the economic factors prompting British responses. First published in 1931, this remains a basic source for the study of the international dimension of the American Civil War.

8:491 Ramsdell, Charles W. *Behind the Lines in the Southern Confederacy.* Baton Rouge: Louisiana State University Press, 1944. Ramsdell's work provides a good overview of the southern economy during wartime. Edited with a foreword by Wendell H. Stephenson.

8:492 Roberts, William P. "James Dunwoody Bulloch and the Confederate Navy." *North Carolina Historical Review* 24 (July 1947): 315–66. In this article, the author shows Bulloch's efforts in Europe to establish a Confederate navy in the face of insurmountable obstacles.

8:493 Schwab, John Cristopher. *The Confederate States of America, 1861–1865: A Financial and Industrial History of the South during the Civil War.* New York: C. Scribner's Sons, 1901. This work focuses on Confederate economic history during the war.

8:494 Thomas, Emory M. *The Confederate Nation, 1861–1865.* New York: Harper and Row, 1979. Thomas shows the south's naïveté in believing that foreign recognition would come simply because of the righteousness of its cause and the dictates of King Cotton diplomacy.

8:495 Thompson, Samuel Bernard. *Confederate Purchasing Operations Abroad.* Chapel Hill: University of North Carolina Press, 1935. Though researching no materials in foreign archives, the author provides useful information on imports into the Confederacy.

8:496 Warren, Gordon H. "The King Cotton Theory." In *Encyclopedia of American Foreign Policy: Studies of the Principal Movements and Ideas,* ed. Alexander DeConde, 2: 515–20. New York: Scribner, 1978. Warren shows how the south relied too heavily on the potential coercive power of cotton to achieve its diplomatic ends. Europe's economic well-being, he insists, did not rest on southern cotton. Confederate leaders badly miscalculated in deciding to withhold cotton in an effort to win foreign intervention by forcing England and France to break the Union blockade. Rather, the Confederacy should have exported cotton to build credit abroad that could have underwritten the acquisition of military and naval materiel.

Native Americans

8:497 Gaines, W. Craig. *The Confederate Cherokees: John Drew's Regiment of Mounted Rifles.* Baton Rouge: Louisiana State University Press, 1989. At the outset of the American Civil War, the Cherokee nation (in today's Oklahoma) found itself in territories and states divided between Union and Confederate loyalties. The Cherokees themselves were divided—many owned slaves and sympathized with the south, while others hated the south as land hungry and thus dangerous to their future. Confederate leaders exploited the former sentiment to negotiate a treaty with the Cherokees and recruited two military units that fought in the Civil War despite bitter internal squabbles. Within the first year of its existence, however, Col. John Drew's regiment became the only regiment to desert the Confederacy and join the Union side.

8:498 Nichols, David A. *Lincoln and the Indians: Civil War Policy and Politics.* Columbia: University of Missouri Press, 1978. Reprint 2000 (University of Illinois Press). According to the author, the Lincoln administration's preoccupation with the Civil War encouraged governmental neglect of Native Americans, causing them to suffer from long-standing corruption in Washington's Indian Affairs division. The Navajos and other western tribes became victims of military pressure, the onslaught of gold miners, and the hardship of drought. The American movement west slowed during the war, but it continued to force the widespread uprooting of Native Americans who, according to many contemporaries, obstructed the spread of civilization.

8:499 Perdue, Theda, ed. *Nations Remembered: An Oral History of the Five Civilized Tribes, 1865–1907.* Westport, CT: Greenwood Press, 1980. Reprint 1993 (University of Oklahoma Press). From the 112-volume WPA collection of "Indian-Pioneer" oral history, the author focuses on the Cherokee, Chickasaw, Choctaw, Creek, and Seminole nations to cover the period from 1861 to 1907. Troubles among the five tribes occurred during the American Civil War period and continued into the twentieth century. The 1993 reprint is titled *Nations Remembered: An Oral History of the Cherokees, Chickasaws, Choctaws, Creeks, and Seminoles in Oklahoma, 1865–1907.*

Expansion and Diplomacy after the Civil War, 1865–1889

Contributing Editor

JOYCE S. GOLDBERG
University of Texas at Arlington

With the Assistance of

ROBERT L. BEISNER
American University

Contents

Introduction

The organization of this chapter closely follows that of the original *Guide to American Foreign Relations since 1700,* emphasizing a narrative of major historical events, episodes, and diplomatic incidents. It also continues the format of a separate biographical category for major makers and implementers of U.S. diplomacy, although often the role or impact of an individual's actions compels inclusion within the narrative category.

This chapter substantially increases the number of what once might have been labeled as merely peripheral topics, with special emphasis on broad regional studies, specific economic developments, and some significant military issues. Reflecting contemporary trends and a more inclusive understanding of the nature of U.S. foreign relations, this chapter includes a considerable number of nontraditional studies such as the efforts of specific religious, cultural, social, or ethnic groups to influence the formulation and execution of foreign policy. It also includes recent scholarship investigating the cultural ramifications of diplomacy, for example, the social or intellectual impact upon foreign relations experts or U.S. foreign relations of journalists, missionaries, tourists, athletes, art collectors, world's fairs and expositions, and ideas of gender and race.

In the interests of space, this chapter excludes most sources from the original *Guide* published before the twentieth century yet also includes a number of important sources unaccountably excluded from the 1983 publication. It also gives significant attention to previously neglected journal articles, single chapters within edited books, and multiauthored collections of essays. Nonetheless, the emphasis of this revised chapter remains with monographs, based on an assumption that good monographic bibliographies will direct readers to more obscure primary or secondary sources.

Published Primary Materials

9:1   U.S. Department of State. *Foreign Relations of the United States.* This essential series of official documents was just under way in this era, usually with one volume published each calendar year for the diplomacy of the previous year. Though selective and then drawn exclusively from State Department documents, these fifty some volumes for the 1865–1898 period are vital to any researcher (1:93).

9:2   Clyde, Paul Hibbert, ed. *United States Policy toward China: Diplomatic and Public Documents, 1839–1939.* Topics covered by these documents include the open door, Tientsin Massacre, Chinese immigration, taxation issues, foreign trade, railroads, missionaries, and protection of foreigners. Clyde reproduces treaties as well as diplomatic correspondence, and brief introductions place the documents in context. List of U.S. diplomatic representatives in China included (7:4).

9:3   McCune, George M., John A. Harrison, Spencer J. Palmer, and Scott S. Burnett, eds. *Korean-American Relations: Documents Pertaining to the Far Eastern Diplomacy of the United States.* Vol. 3. Berkeley: University of California Press, 1951–1963. Reprint 1971 (Kraus). These documents reveal how all the major world powers of the era were actively involved in Korea's destiny. The United States saw its relationship to Korea as subordinate to its other commitments and interests in the Far East. Nor was it "willing to support Korean independence, if that meant opposing one of the other interested parties." The third volume published by the University of Hawaii Press.

9:4   Simon, John Y., ed. *The Papers of Ulysses S. Grant.* 24 vols. Carbondale: Southern Illinois University Press, 1967–1998. This carefully edited collection is of considerable value for the study of Grant's foreign relations ideas and actions.

9:5   Bergeron, Paul H., LeRoy P. Graf, and Ralph W. Haskins, eds. *The Papers of Andrew Johnson.* 16 vols. Knoxville: University of Tennessee Press, 1967–2000. Volumes 10–16, edited by Bergeron, cover the period from February 1866 to July 1875 and include veto messages, speeches, presidential proclamations, executive orders, and other administrative documents relevant to Johnson's presidency. The dominant subject matter is not foreign policy but the end of the Civil War, Johnson's war with Congress, and the impeachment crisis and trial. The papers reveal that he was politically bankrupt by the end of the summer of 1867.

9:6   Seager, Robert, II, and Doris D. Maguire, eds. *Letters and Papers of Alfred Thayer Mahan.* 3 vols. Annapolis: Naval Institute Press, 1975. These 2,000 pages of letters and papers demonstrate that Mahan's influence on the pre–World War I generation was impressive. Although he was not the only outspoken naval officer linking the protection of vital American exports with the need for a new battleship fleet to protect those exports and provide badly needed jobs and status for naval officers, these letters and papers demonstrate his effective articulation of these ideas.

9:7   Morison, Elting E., with John Morton Blum, eds. *The Letters of Theodore Roosevelt.* 8 vols. Cambridge, MA: Harvard University Press, 1951–1954. The first two volumes, *The Years of Preparation, 1868–1898* and *1898–1900,* cover Roosevelt's life from the first available letter of an uncertain youth through his energetic campaign for the vice-presidency. Letters reflecting TR's years as New York police commissioner, assistant secretary of the navy, Rough Rider, and governor of New York are especially interesting.

9:8   Volwiler, Albert T., ed. *The Correspondence between Benjamin Harrison and James G. Blaine, 1882–1893.* Philadelphia: American Philosophical Society, 1940. This extensive set of letters reveals the problematic relationship of the two men and their sometimes corresponding, sometimes conflicting ideas about politics and diplomacy.

9:9   Foner, Philip S., and Richard C. Winchester, eds. *The Anti-Imperialist Reader: A Documentary History of Anti-Imperialism in the United States. Vol. 1: From the Mexican War to the Election of 1900.* New York: Holmes and Meier, 1984. This excellent collection includes contemporary critiques and comments on U.S. expansionism at the end of the century, focusing on Hawaii, Cuba, and the Philippines.

9:10   Fisher, Raymond H., ed. *Records of the Russian-American Company, 1802, 1817–1867.* Microfilm. Washington, DC: U.S. National Archives and Records Service, 1971. This is an annotated listing of the records of the Russian-American Company, which had economic and political control over Alaska before the U.S. purchase in 1867. One document from 1802 and the rest for the period 1817–1867 are in Russian longhand. National Archives microfilm publications M-11; 77 rolls.

9:11   Barnes, James J., and Patience P. Barnes, eds. *Private and Confidential: Letters from British Ministers in Washington to the Foreign Secretaries in London, 1844–67.* British diplomatic correspondence in the nineteenth century took the form of official or "public" dispatches, which Parliament had the right to call for, debate, and eventually publish. British ministers in Washington sent almost 300 dispatches per year. Two chapters cover dispatches from April 1865 to September 1867 in which ministers commented on the American preoccupation with Reconstruction and domestic affairs (6:26).

Bibliographies and Other Reference Works

9:12   Brune, Lester H., ed. *Chronological History of U.S. Foreign Relations.* Though a reference source, this work also provides straightforward descriptions and explanations of specific events of U.S. diplomacy (1:13). Volume 1 covers 1776–1898. First published 1985–199.

9:13   Bryson, Thomas A., ed. *United States/Middle East Diplomatic Relations, 1784–1978: An Annotated Bibliography.* This is a bibliographic guide to books, articles, documents, and dissertations that relate to the American diplomatic experience in the Middle East. Only the first few short chapters concern the nineteenth century, and fewer still treat the 1865–1900 era (1:259).

9:14   De Santis, Vincent P., ed. *The Gilded Age, 1877–1896.* Arlington Heights, IL: AHM, 1973. Though now rather dated, this remains a useful bibliography, emphasizing politics and foreign affairs.

9:15 Goehlert, Robert U., and Elizabeth R. Hoffmeister, eds. *The Department of State and American Diplomacy: A Bibliography.* This unannotated bibliography of over 3,800 titles on the State Department and foreign service (recruitment, functions, organization, structure, protocol, and procedures) lists sources pertaining to the conduct of foreign policy (including theoretical studies of decisionmaking and policy formulation) and relations between foreign affairs and the presidency, Congress, and the military. Biographical material on secretaries of state (1:30).

9:16 Kaplan, Stephen S. "The Use of Military Force Abroad by the United States since 1798: An Annotated Bibliography of Unclassified Lists of Incidents Prepared by the U.S. Government." *Journal of Conflict Resolution* 19 (December 1975): 708–12. This is a short annotated bibliography of interventionist episodes prepared by the U.S. government.

9:17 Keto, C. Tsehloane, ed. *American–South African Relations, 1784–1980: Review and Select Bibliography.* This short, unannotated bibliography of American-African relations includes reference works, bibliographies, newspapers, periodicals, and journals and is divided into chronological and subject categories (1:231).

9:18 Leonard, Thomas M. *Central American and United States Policies, 1820s–1980s: A Guide to Issues and References.* Forty pages of bibliography follow an eighty-page survey that "seeks to place the problems of the region and their implications for U.S. foreign policy in historical perspective" (with chapter 2 tracing the evolution of U.S. policy toward Central America by focusing on the fundamental objectives of keeping Europe out and maintaining order and stability) (1:250).

9:19 Lincove, David A., and Gary R. Treadway, eds. *The Anglo-American Relationship: An Annotated Bibliography of Scholarship, 1945–1985.* This bibliography includes monographs, essays, journal articles, and doctoral dissertations concentrating on Anglo-American interaction between 1783 and 1945. Each annotation includes the author's thesis and descriptive information about the issues or events discussed (1:244).

9:20 Nolan, Cathal J., ed. *Notable U.S. Ambas-sadors since 1775: A Biographical Dictionary.* This book contains fifty-eight brief historical biographies, from Madeleine K. Albright to Andrew Young, Jr., with a few late-nineteenth-century figures included, such as George Bancroft, Townsend Harris, and Andrew Dickson White (1:52).

9:21 Norton, Mary Beth, with Pamela Gerardi, eds. *The American Historical Association's Guide to Historical Literature.* Covering mainly works published from the early 1960s to the early 1990s, this mammoth work includes nearly 27,000 annotated items, including old standards and classics in the history of U.S. foreign relations. Sections 42 and 43 cover the period from 1815 to 1920 (1:38).

9:22 Petersen, Neal H., ed. *American Intelligence, 1775–1990: A Bibliographical Guide.* This is a comprehensive but unannotated bibliography of books and articles on the general subjects of intelligence, counterintelligence, and internal security covering all federal intelligence agencies and federal intelligence policy since 1775 (1:194).

9:23 Silverburg, Sanford R., and Bernard Reich, eds. *U.S. Foreign Relations with the Middle East and North Africa: A Bibliography.* This is a well-organized bibliography that covers many facets of the relations between the United States and the Middle East and North Africa. It includes works on significant persons, places, events, institutions, and issues but contains only a few sources for the period 1865–1900 (1:262).

9:24 Smith, Myron J., Jr., ed. *The American Navy, 1865–1918: A Bibliography.* Metuchen, NJ: Scarecrow Press, 1974. While it focuses on naval matters, this work lists many references of value for the diplomatic historian.

9:25 Trask, David F., Michael C. Meyer, and Roger R. Trask, eds. *A Bibliography of United States–Latin American Relations since 1810: A Selected List of Eleven Thousand Published References.* This is a comprehensive bibliographical guide to the literature of U.S.–Latin American relations containing an extensive listing of published sources in a wide variety of languages, and includes guides to manuscript collections (1:257). See also Meyer, *Supplement to a Bibliography of United States–Latin American Relations since 1810* (1979) (9:26).

9:26 Meyer, Michael C., ed. *Supplement to a Bibliography of United States–Latin American Relations since 1810.* This is a companion volume to Trask, Meyer, and Trask, *A Bibliography of United States–Latin American Relations since 1810: A Selected List of Eleven Thousand Published References* (1968) (9:25). A few supplementary chapter subsections accommodate important new hemispheric trends and diplomatic events. References embrace studies of multinational corporations, dependency theory, and inter-American law of the sea (1:254).

9:27 U.S. Department of State. *Foreign Travels of the Secretaries of State, 1866–1990.* Washington, DC: Department of State, 1990. This book details foreign visits of the secretaries of state.

9:28 _____. Office of the Historian. *Principal Officers of the Department of State and United States Chiefs of Mission, 1778–1990.* This book lists State Department officials and its ministers and ambassadors abroad (1:59).

Historiography

9:29 Becker, William H. "American Manufacturers and Foreign Markets, 1870–1900: Business Historians and the 'New Economic Determinists.'" *Business History Review* 47 (Winter 1973): 466–81. This article draws from economic history to refute the thesis about overproduction and a business consensus on the need for foreign markets. Most producers with excess capacity created pools and trusts and limited output by mergers. Those who sought foreign trade did not suffer overproduction but were relatively innovative (such as Eastman and Singer), had economic advantages, and possessed effective sales organizations. Foreign demand and prices were most important.

9:30 Becker, William H., and Howard B. Schonberger. "An Exchange of Opinion: Foreign Markets for Iron and Steel, 1893–1913: A New Perspective on the Williams School of Diplomatic History." *Pacific Historical Review* 44 (May 1975): 233–62. Becker challenges the open door thesis with attention to the pivotal iron and steel industries, arguing that steel

men addressed their problems by action at home, not by seeking foreign markets with government aid. Howard B. Schonberger provides a rebuttal.

9:31 Cohen, Warren I. "The History of American–East Asian Relations: Cutting Edge of the Historical Profession." *Diplomatic History* 9 (Spring 1985): 101–12. This is a brief but useful historiographical essay on some of the important historical scholarship of the 1980s. Cohen contends that historians who study U.S.–East Asian relations have produced some of the most exciting, important, and readable work written by historians generally. A SHAFR presidential address.

9:32 Crapol, Edward P. "Coming to Terms with Empire: The Historiography of Late-Nineteenth-Century American Foreign Relations." *Diplomatic History* 16 (Fall 1992): 573–97. Crapol concludes that while it would be wrong to suggest late-nineteenth-century historiography has undergone a transformation comparable to work on World War II and the cold war, a number of new directions have influenced and revitalized the scholarship of the 1865–1900 era, such as the role of gender, missionary activities, cultural imperialism, and social history in the exercise of state power.

9:33 Fry, Joseph A. "From Open Door to World Systems: Economic Interpretations of Late Nineteenth Century American Foreign Relations." *Pacific Historical Review* 65 (May 1996): 277–303. Fry gauges the ongoing influence of economic considerations in the interpretation of late-nineteenth-century American foreign relations. This article evaluates the centrality of economic influences and dependency theory.

9:34 Healy, David F. *Modern Imperialism: Changing Styles in Historical Interpretation.* Washington, DC: Service Center for Teachers of History, 1967. This twenty-nine-page historiographical essay emphasizes the late nineteenth century. It is both interpretive and an important guide to earlier works.

9:35 Holbo, Paul S. "Economics, Emotion, and Expansion: An Emerging Foreign Policy?" In *The Gilded Age.* Rev. and enl. ed. Ed. H. Wayne Morgan, 199–221. Syracuse: Syracuse University Press, 1970. This essay criticizes the arguments and evidence of earlier interpretations, especially those stressing foreign markets, Social Darwinism, and foreign example. Holbo instead emphasizes emotional and irrational elements but contends that McKinley basically conducted policy firmly and conservatively.

9:36 LaFeber, Walter. "The World and the United States." LaFeber surveys the work of several generations of writers on U.S. diplomatic history and assesses their contributions, concluding that the recent inclusion of social, economic, and nontraditional approaches has made the field of U.S. foreign relations one of the most comprehensive fields of historical studies (2:14).

9:37 Randall, Stephen J. "Ideology, National Security, and the Corporate State: The Historiography of U.S.–Latin American Relations." *Latin American Research Review* 27, no. 1 (1991): 205–17. Randall examines Latin American historiography and international relations theory through a collective review of recent books. Noting that most authors are critical of U.S. policies, he expresses disappointment in their general failure to develop the Latin American side of their accounts.

9:38 Thompson, John A. "William Appleman Williams and the 'American Empire.'" *Journal of American Studies* 7 (April 1973): 91–104. This theoretical appraisal of the Williams school criticizes the loose use of words such as "expansion" and "empire," the elusiveness of some arguments, the lack of evidence for interest groups' influence, the assumption of the primacy of economic ideas, the emphasis on consensus, and the conception of trade as inherently imperialistic.

the turn of the century. Crapol examines Blaine's goal of achieving global economic supremacy through energetic government action, explains his desire to displace Britain from the Western Hemisphere in pursuit of U.S. economic nationalism, and concludes that in the late nineteenth century he was the most important architect of American empire and most able and popular political leader.

9:40 Healy, David F. *James G. Blaine and Latin America.* Columbia: University of Missouri Press, 2001. The brilliant and imaginative Blaine, leader of the Republican Party and perennial presidential prospect, "believed that the United States was destined to be a great power and wanted it to begin acting like one." To that end, he tried to make the United States supreme in the Western Hemisphere, mainly by displacing Britain's economic and diplomatic dominance in the region. Healy sets out to examine Blaine's vision for America, focusing on his Latin American policy. He concludes that he "brought a new and faster tempo to U.S. foreign relations, which would never return to the limited and reactive pace of the past. His clearly articulated vision of national greatness and his vigorous nationalist rhetoric helped prepare the ground for his country's emergence as a great power only a few years after his death." He was "a terminal figure in a foreign policy age of comparative innocence."

9:41 Tyler, Alice Felt. *The Foreign Policy of James G. Blaine.* Minneapolis: University of Minnesota Press, 1927. Tyler's thesis in this good introduction to the subject is that Blaine's stance was transitional between Seward's expansionism and later economic penetration, and that he had greater grasp and vision than any other secretary of his era.

Biographical Studies

JAMES G. BLAINE

9:39 Crapol, Edward P. *James G. Blaine: Architect of Empire.* Wilmington, DE: Scholarly Resources, 2000. This biography assesses Blaine's pivotal role in shaping American foreign relations near

GROVER CLEVELAND

9:42 Dulebohn, George Roscoe. "Principles of Foreign Policy under the Cleveland Administrations." Ph.D. dissertation, University of Pennsylvania, 1941. This work treats Cleveland as a conservative in foreign policy who meant to preserve national security, avoid entanglement in power politics, and settle disputes by peaceful means. The author argues that he was an archfoe of imperialism.

9:43 Merrill, Horace Samuel. *Bourbon Leader: Grover Cleveland and the Democratic Party.* Boston: Little, Brown, 1957. Merrill treats Cleveland as an honest but plodding conservative and generally inactive president. The brief sections on foreign policy emphasize the influence of Olney and Cleveland's political isolation and irritability.

9:44 Nevins, Allan. *Grover Cleveland: A Study in Courage.* New York: Dodd, Mead and Company, 1932. This admiring biography treats Cleveland as careful, honest, patient, and an unyielding opponent of imperialism. The major focus in foreign policy is on Venezuela, where Cleveland's unfortunate message awakened the public to accept the Monroe Doctrine, and Hawaii, where policy went awry.

9:45 Welch, Richard E., Jr. *The Presidencies of Grover Cleveland.* Lawrence: University Press of Kansas, 1988. This book disputes the traditional identification of Cleveland with outmoded politics and negative political philosophy. Despite his ambivalent political philosophy and mixed record, Welch finds a believer in popular government aware of the new problems posed by industrialization. While not a great man, Cleveland's tenure reinvigorated the presidency and provided an essential step toward its modern evolution.

SANFORD B. DOLE

9:46 Damon, Ethel M. *Sanford Ballard Dole and His Hawaii. With an Analysis of Justice Dole's Legal Opinions.* Palo Alto: Pacific Books for the Hawaiian Historical Society, 1957. An important member of the Hawaiian government, Dole became the first president of the provisional government established after the revolution of 1893 and retained that post after the formation of the Republic of Hawaii in 1894. He later became the first territorial governor after annexation of the islands to the United States. Notes by Samuel B. Kemp.

9:47 Dole, Sanford B. *Memoirs of the Hawaiian Revolution.* Honolulu: Advertiser Publishing, 1936. This is the personal account of the Hawaiian revolution of 1893 by one of Hawaii's most important figures. Dole argued that the revolution would not have happened in 1893 but for the knowledge that U.S.

Minister to Hawaii John L. Stevens was in sympathy with it. Edited by Andrew Farrell.

WILLIAM M. EVARTS

9:48 Barrows, Chester L. *William M. Evarts, Lawyer, Diplomat, Statesman.* Chapel Hill: University of North Carolina Press, 1941. Barrows finds Secretary of State Evarts less serious than Fish and less spectacular than Blaine. An old-fashioned diplomat (1877–1881), he was never hurried, flustered, or bored by routine. The most useful section is on the Monroe Doctrine and the isthmian canal.

9:49 Dyer, Brainerd. *The Public Career of William M. Evarts.* Berkeley: University of California Press, 1933. Two chapters of this biography deal with Evarts's term as secretary of state. Dyer notes Evarts's procrastination and criticizes his Latin American policies, marked by aggressiveness (but not personal profiteering) and reversals over Mexico, the use of amateur diplomats, and failure to consummate a Canal treaty.

HAMILTON FISH

9:50 Chapin, James B. "Hamilton Fish and American Expansion." In *Makers of American Diplomacy. Vol. 1: From Benjamin Franklin to Alfred Thayer Mahan,* ed. Frank J. Merli and Theodore A. Wilson, 223–51. New York: Scribner, 1974. This is a provocative essay, notable for its sharply critical view. Chapin portrays Fish as a wealthy, upper-class conservative who survived in the Grant administration by shifting allegiance to the Stalwarts, a subtle, conscious expansionist who believed in protectorates and "informal empire."

9:51 Nevins, Allan. *Hamilton Fish: The Inner History of the Grant Administration.* New York: Dodd, Mead and Company, 1936. This biography must be used with care because of Nevins's protective treatment of Fish and hostile view of other members of the Grant administration. The narrative is often quite dramatic and the interpretation worthy of note if used with care.

JOHN W. FOSTER

9:52   Devine, Michael J. "John W. Foster and the Struggle for the Annexation of Hawaii." *Pacific Historical Review* 46 (February 1977): 29–50. In this account of the Hawaiian annexation issue, Devine demonstrates Foster's determination and sense of mission and describes some of the political machinations in Honolulu and Washington.

9:53   _____. *John W. Foster: Politics and Diplomacy in the Imperial Era, 1873–1917*. Athens, OH: Ohio University Press, 1981. Devine sees Foster as among the most capable and experienced diplomats in the late nineteenth century, whose record reflected a large continuity in the evolution of U.S. foreign policy from Grant to Wilson.

9:54   Foster, John W. *Diplomatic Memoirs*. 2 vols. Boston: Houghton Mifflin Company, 1909. These anecdotal volumes, which do not follow strict chronological order, contain useful details on Foster's important diplomatic service, notably his several foreign missions, negotiations for reciprocity, and work for other governments. Foster also offers many candid comments on presidents, secretaries of state, and foreign envoys.

JAMES A. GARFIELD

9:55   Brown, Harry J., and Frederick D. Williams, eds. *The Diary of James A. Garfield*. 4 vols. East Lansing: Michigan State University Press, 1967–1981. This carefully edited series is of value for the study of foreign affairs in the short Garfield presidency.

9:56   Peskin, Allan. *Garfield: A Biography*. Kent, OH: Kent State University Press, 1978. Filled with observations on personalities and politics, this lengthy biography devotes a few pages to foreign policy, in which Garfield is credited for the major ventures of his short-lived administration.

9:57   Pletcher, David M. *The Awkward Years: American Foreign Relations under Garfield and Arthur*. Columbia: University of Missouri Press, 1962. This study of a neglected period contends that the Garfield and Arthur administrations set the stage

for later expansionism. They were "a preparation and crude testing in response to impulses which, though strong, were still vaguely formed and not clearly understood." Even though awkward and nonproductive, the Garfield-Arthur diplomacy "made possible greater self-confidence and seemingly spontaneous determination a few years later."

ULYSSES S. GRANT

9:58   Carpenter, John A. *Ulysses S. Grant*. New York: Twayne Publishers, 1970. This work depicts Grant's developing relationship with and dependence on Hamilton Fish, who is described as fully informed about and supportive of the Dominican annexation plan. Carpenter also discusses Cuba, several arbitration efforts, and Santo Domingo.

9:59   Coolidge, Louis A. *Ulysses S. Grant*. Boston: Houghton Mifflin Company, 1917. Reprint 1972 (AMS Press). This dated biography provides a sympathetic view of Grant's character, stressing his determination and honesty. It includes chapters on arbitration and Santo Domingo.

9:60   Hesseltine, William B. *Ulysses S. Grant, Politician*. New York: Dodd, Mead and Company, 1935. This book refutes charges that Grant was stupid or corrupt but accuses him of ignorance of the Constitution and of a lack of vision. Hesseltine treats Fish as the restraining force in foreign affairs, especially on Cuba, and finds unscrupulous persons behind Dominican policy.

9:61   McFeely, William S. *Grant: A Biography*. New York: Norton, 1981. This is an outstanding portrait of a man whose talents brought him military success but who proved inadequate in the White House. It is thoroughly researched, sensitively written, and compelling.

WALTER Q. GRESHAM

9:62   Calhoun, Charles W. *Gilded Age Cato: The Life of Walter Q. Gresham*. Lexington: University Press of Kentucky, 1988. This biography describes Gresham as a complex and enigmatic public figure whose career combined both successes and frustrations. Imbued with a strong sense of duty and justice, he carried his desire to restore the nation's lost virtue into the State Department, where he attempted to moderate nationalistic or jingoistic tendencies and stem the rising tide of imperialism.

9:63 Gresham, Matilda. *Life of Walter Quintin Gresham, 1832–1895.* 2 vols. Chicago: Rand, McNally and Company, 1919. Five chapters in the second volume concern Gresham's service as secretary of state, including the Bering Sea arbitrations, Hawaii, and Latin America. The book's chief virtues are its vignettes and anecdotes, the clues to political alignments, and its revelations of Gresham's moral values.

BENJAMIN HARRISON

9:64 Sievers, Harry J. *Benjamin Harrison. Vol. 3: Hoosier President: The White House and After.* 2d ed. Indianapolis: Bobbs-Merrill, 1968. Sievers contends that Harrison steered foreign policy to achieve national strength and noninterference from European powers. The treatment of the important Hawaiian episode is brief and not analytical.

9:65 Socolofsky, Homer E., and Allan B. Spetter. *The Presidency of Benjamin Harrison.* Lawrence: University Press of Kansas, 1987. This is an important analysis of one of the least-understood presidents of the nineteenth century, whose first two years in office produced some landmark domestic legislation and whose last two years pointed out a new direction for U.S. foreign policy.

9:66 Spetter, Allan B. "Harrison and Blaine: Foreign Policy, 1889–1893." *Indiana Magazine of History* 65 (Spring 1969): 215–27. Spetter argues that Harrison was determined to assume charge of foreign policy and that Blaine's frequent illnesses in 1890 diminished his influence. Harrison not only was aggressive, utilizing naval power, but supported a "large policy."

RUTHERFORD B. HAYES

9:67 Barnard, Harry. *Rutherford B. Hayes, and His America.* Indianapolis: Bobbs-Merrill, 1954. This work contains information on Hayes's foreign policy views toward Mexico as well as many scattered references to his hostile relations with Blaine.

9:68 Davison, Kenneth E. *The Presidency of Rutherford B. Hayes.* Westport, CT: Greenwood Press, 1972. This balanced study of the Hayes-Evarts administration considers promotion of trade (through better consular reporting) their foremost achievement. Davison discusses improved relations with Mexico and argues that Hayes extended the Monroe Doctrine to Panama. Policies toward Europe and Canada were less successful.

9:69 Hoogenboom, Ari. *The Presidency of Rutherford B. Hayes.* Lawrence: University Press of Kansas, 1988. Hoogenboom views Hayes as a decent human being, an apt and effective politician, and an able president. He was hampered by a hostile Congress and restrained by the large number of people convinced he had been elected by fraud. Diligent and conscientious, he embraced reform and took modest steps on the road to the modern presidency.

9:70 _____. *Rutherford B. Hayes: Warrior and President.* Lawrence: University Press of Kansas, 1995. This biography reveals a complex man and subtle leader whose limited options constrained his performance but who nonetheless served his country well. Hoogenboom portrays Hayes as honest, decent, hardworking, empathetic, ambitious, determined, principled, and self-confident.

9:71 Williams, T. Harry, ed. *Hayes: The Diary of a President, 1875–1881, Covering the Disputed Election, the End of Reconstruction, and the Beginning of Civil Service.* New York: D. McKay Co., 1964. The diary focuses heavily on ceremonial life and domestic politics but also contains passing references to policy toward Mexico, an isthmian canal, Chinese immigration, and diplomatic appointments.

GEORGE F. HOAR

9:72 Hoar, George F. *Autobiography of Seventy Years.* 2 vols. New York: C. Scribner's Sons, 1903. The chief value of this book, except for sections concerned with his anti-imperialism at the time of the Spanish-American War, are Hoar's accounts of the Treaty of Washington, the fisheries question, and his strong opposition to discriminatory treatment of Chinese immigrants and the annexation of Hawaii.

9:73 Welch, Richard E., Jr. *George Frisbie Hoar and the Half-Breed Republicans*. Cambridge, MA: Harvard University Press, 1971. This biography portrays Senator Hoar as a highly partisan Free Soil and Half-Breed Republican who was an ardent protectionist, advocate of increasing trade, supporter of executive power in foreign affairs (except by Cleveland), and opponent of expansion who caused a stir within his own party by questioning the annexation of Hawaii.

ALFRED T. MAHAN

9:74 Crowl, Philip A. "Alfred Thayer Mahan: The Naval Historian." In *Makers of Modern Strategy: From Machiavelli to the Nuclear Age,* ed. Peter Paret, with Gordon A. Craig and Felix Gilbert, 444–77. Princeton: Princeton University Press, 1986. Crowl describes Mahan's transformation from naval misfit to international guru as historian, strategist, imperialist, and navalist who influenced presidents, world leaders, and navalists around the world. He concludes that many of Mahan's questions are still relevant: the meaning of national interest, the moral dimensions of military force, the responsibilities of world power, and the uses of navies as instruments of national policy.

9:75 Mahan, Alfred T. *From Sail to Steam: Recollections of Naval Life*. New York: Harper, 1907. Mahan's memoirs offer a summary of his major strategic ideas and are also useful for his own account of their genesis.

9:76 Seager, Robert, II. *Alfred Thayer Mahan: The Man and His Letters*. Annapolis: Naval Institute Press, 1977. This biography of Mahan examines his controversial naval career, emergence as a historian, origins of his economic ideas, and his political influence in the last part of the nineteenth century. Seager assesses Mahan's understanding of the power of militarism and nationalism, the role of force in international relations, and the fragile nature of the European balance of power.

WILLIAM MCKINLEY

9:77 Coletta, Paolo E. "Prologue: William McKinley and the Conduct of United States Foreign Relations." In *Threshold to American Internationalism: Essays on the Foreign Policies of William McKinley,* ed. Paolo E. Coletta, 11–33. New York: Exposition Press, 1970. This chapter partakes of both an older, more critical view and a newer, more favorable view of McKinley as politician, statesman, and foreign policy implementer.

9:78 Dobson, John M. *Reticent Expansionism: The Foreign Policy of William McKinley*. Pittsburgh: Duquesne University Press, 1988. Dobson thinks McKinley had "no sustained, cohesive foreign policy" but instead followed "the path of least resistance," remaining a "reactive . . . rather than an active" president. He acted more from a sense of "democratic mission," "morality," or desire to defuse crises than from any coherent vision of commercial empire, and his policies were marked by irresolution, ambiguity, lethargy, and expedience.

9:79 Morgan, H. Wayne. *William McKinley and His America*. Syracuse: Syracuse University Press, 1963. This solidly researched biography views McKinley as a shrewd politician and a strong, modern, activist president.

JOHN TYLER MORGAN

9:80 Fry, Joseph A. *John Tyler Morgan and the Search for Southern Autonomy*. Knoxville: University of Tennessee Press, 1992. This is a biography of a southern nationalist, devoted to Alabama and the south, who was a dominant political figure and important representative of the Gilded Age south. His foreign policy views derived from his perceptions of the southern condition after the Civil War, especially the belief that economic and territorial expansion could help rescue the south from its colonial position.

9:81 _____. "John Tyler Morgan's Southern Expansionism." *Diplomatic History* 9 (Fall 1985): 329–46. This article analyzes the influential southern expansionist's agenda as a member of the Senate Foreign Relations Committee, 1878–1907. Morgan embraced the national government's expansionist projects by advocating aggressive commercial expansion, an interoceanic canal, an enlarged merchant marine and navy, and acquisition of Hawaii, Puerto Rico, the Philippines, and Cuba. Fry suggests Morgan was the south's most prominent expansionist.

WHITELAW REID

9:82   Contosta, David R. "Whitelaw Reid and the Inadvertent Empire." *Old Northwest* 12 (Spring 1986): 27–40. Contosta describes Whitelaw Reid as a "mild expansionist," who opposed many aspects of U.S. interventionism abroad—even war with Spain at first—but once the nation undertook overseas adventures, he was willing to have it accept the consequences of imperialism and embrace new responsibilities.

9:83   Contosta, David R., and Jessica R. Hawthorne, eds. *Rise to World Power: Selected Letters of Whitelaw Reid, 1895–1912*. Philadelphia: American Philosophical Society, 1986. This selection of letters from the microfilm edition of the Whitelaw Reid Papers illuminates the conduct and formulation of U.S. diplomacy, reveals Reid's own role, and demonstrates his attempts to manipulate public opinion about U.S. foreign policy. Only fifteen pages of letters predate the Spanish-American War. This is vol. 76, pt. 2 of the *Transactions of the American Philosophical Society*.

THEODORE ROOSEVELT

9:84   Beale, Howard K. *Theodore Roosevelt and the Rise of America to World Power*. Baltimore: Johns Hopkins Press, 1956. Chapter 1 of this thorough account of Roosevelt's attempt to establish U.S. influence throughout the world deals with his background, professional career, and diplomatic attitudes before he became president.

9:85   Collin, Richard H. *Theodore Roosevelt, Culture, Diplomacy, and Expansion: A New View of American Imperialism*. Baton Rouge: Louisiana State University Press, 1985. Collin contends that the diplomacy of the Roosevelt era was the product of America's "coming of age." Cultural growth and independence—from a new national museum and a refurbished White House to a sophisticated presi-

dent whose circles included writers and artists as well as politicians and heads of state—emphasized America's modernization. This book stresses the recognition by TR and others of the need to establish and maintain a balance of power among the United States, Japan, Germany, and Britain for security reasons and to prove America was neither provincial nor weak, but a worthy adversary or a valuable ally.

9:86   Lodge, Henry Cabot, Sr., and Charles F. Redmond, eds. *Selections from the Correspondence of Theodore Roosevelt and Henry Cabot Lodge, 1884–1918*. 2 vols. New York: Da Capo Press, 1971. The Roosevelt-Lodge correspondence reproduced here deals with topics ranging from family and friends to literature and life, including in the first volume (1884–1902) little discussion of foreign relations until the McKinley administration, when the subject of the Cuban revolution looms large. Originally published in 1925.

9:87   Turk, Richard W. *The Ambiguous Relationship: Theodore Roosevelt and Alfred Thayer Mahan*. New York: Greenwood Press, 1987. Turk argues that Roosevelt and Mahan were anything but close friends who conspired with others to launch and popularize the "Large Policy" approach to American imperialism. This book contains all known Roosevelt-Mahan correspondence and demonstrates that they frequently clashed on issues.

WILLIAM SEWARD

9:88   Bancroft, Frederic. *The Life of William H. Seward*. The second volume covers Seward's years as secretary of state, including his role in Reconstruction, aspirations for territorial expansion, and the *Alabama* claims negotiations (8:195).

9:89   Paolino, Ernest N. *The Foundations of the American Empire: William Henry Seward and U.S. Foreign Policy*. Ithaca: Cornell University Press, 1973. The author emphasizes the economic nature of Seward's expansionist perspective (connecting his outlook to the mercantile ideology of John Quincy Adams) and discusses commercial ideology, the gold supply, technological advances in communication, and literary propaganda in support of expansion.

9:90　Taylor, John M. *William Henry Seward: Lincoln's Right Hand.* This is a biography of one of the more complex figures in American political history. Taylor also sees Seward as an occasionally devious person but one of the political giants of his generation and deserving of more recognition (8:198).

9:91　Valone, Stephen J. "'Weakness Offers Temptation': William H. Seward and the Reassertion of the Monroe Doctrine." Valone analyzes Seward's actions as secretary of state when in 1866 he learned that Austrian soldiers might replace the French in Mexico. While Seward patiently endured the lengthy French occupation of Mexico, the prospect of an Austrian occupation elicited a bellicose response. Seward exploited Austria's European distresses to reassert the Monroe Doctrine in dramatic fashion and to reap domestic political gains for himself and President Andrew Johnson (8:428).

CLAUS SPRECKELS

9:92　Adler, Jacob. *Claus Spreckels' Rise and Fall in Hawaii with Emphasis on the London Loan of 1886.* Honolulu: Hawaiian Historical Society, 1959. Spreckels became the head of the California sugar trust and gained a strong voice in the affairs of Hawaii under King Kalakaua. This is the 67th Annual Report of the Hawaiian Historical Society.

9:93　————. *Claus Spreckels: The Sugar King in Hawaii.* Honolulu: University of Hawaii Press, 1966. Adler argues that Spreckels dominated the Hawaiian sugar industry. He was involved in Hawaiian politics (1876–1908), first in dealings with King Kalakaua and later in attempting to restore Queen Liliuokalani following the revolution of 1893.

OTHERS

9:94　Williams, William Appleman. "Brooks Adams and American Expansion." *New England Quarterly* 25 (June 1952): 217–32. This is an analysis of Adams's views on expansionism and of America's international role, chiefly as related to Asia. He supposedly exerted considerable influence on the proponents of the "large policy" during the Spanish-American War.

9:95　Duberman, Martin B. *Charles Francis Adams, 1807–1886.* Two-thirds of the chapters of this enormous and judicious biography cover Adams's life and work before the Civil War, but the latter part of the work explores Adams's role in settling the *Alabama* claims (8:165).

9:96　DeNovo, John A. "The Enigmatic Alvey A. Adee and American Foreign Relations, 1870–1924." *Prologue* 7 (Summer 1975): 69–80. This is one of the few studies of the contributions of this important bureaucrat, who served in important capacities for more than forty years. He was a skilled craftsman of dispatches and treaties with an encyclopedic knowledge of U.S. diplomatic practices and precedents and international law. DeNovo presents an analysis of a faithful and witty bureaucrat, who tutored many diplomats, State Department officials, and presidents.

9:97　Reeves, Thomas C. *Gentleman Boss: The Life of Chester Alan Arthur.* New York: Alfred A. Knopf, 1975. This is a sympathetic biography based on a few newly discovered sources but still heavily reliant on previous studies. Contending that Arthur's precarious health problems precluded a reelection bid in 1884, Reeves asserts that he deserves credit for a reasonable record of accomplishment in the time he did serve. The biography relates much of the standard story of late-nineteenth-century American politics.

9:98　Nye, Russel B. *George Bancroft: Brahmin Rebel.* This New England aristocrat, who both made and wrote history, represented Washington as a minister to both Great Britain and Germany. His histories "caught the spirit of his age best." The last three chapters cover 1860–1891 (6:78).

9:99　Harrington, Fred H. *Fighting Politician: Major General N. P. Banks.* Philadelphia: University of Pennsylvania Press, 1948. Reprint 1970 (Greenwood Press). This biography is valuable because of the extended treatment of Banks's role in shaping foreign policy and pressing for expansion. The scattered Banks manuscripts were consolidated following publication of this book, but it remains an interesting source.

9:100　Prisco, Salvatore, III. *John Barrett, Progressive Era Diplomat: A Study of a Commercial Ex-*

pansionist, 1887–1920. University: University of Alabama Press, 1973. This is a short biography of a commercial evangelist and former minister in Latin America who helped promote closer commercial ties in the hemisphere. Barrett lobbied small businessmen who did not usually think in terms of foreign trade and eagerly sought to make the Pan American Union an important agency of hemispheric trade.

9:101 Wynes, Charles E. "Ebenezer Don Carlos Bassett, America's First Black Diplomat." *Pennsylvania History* 51 (July 1984): 232–40. Wynes examines Bassett's role as minister to Haiti during the Grant administration, 1869–1877.

9:102 Tansill, Charles Callan. *The Foreign Policy of Thomas F. Bayard, 1885–1897.* New York: Fordham University Press, 1940. This massive, immensely detailed biography focuses entirely on Bayard's diplomatic service, especially as secretary of state. The author praises his concern for good relations with England and criticizes Olney, Cleveland, Blaine, and most Republicans.

9:103 Peterson, Harold F. *Diplomat of the Americas: A Biography of William I. Buchanan (1852–1909).* Albany: State University of New York Press, 1977. This biography of an effective though obscure U.S. minister and troubleshooter, who helped strengthen hemispheric relations through diplomatic skill and talent, sees him as a commercial expansionist who helped promote inter-American goodwill through success in several sensitive assignments.

9:104 Coletta, Paolo E. "French Ensor Chadwick: The First American Naval Attache, 1882–1889." *American Neptune* 39 (April 1979): 126–41. The Navy Department's Office of Naval Intelligence sent its first naval attachés abroad to collect, classify, and disseminate intelligence about the growth and progress of foreign navies in materials, construction, personnel, technology, harbor fortifications, and anything else deemed valuable. Chadwick was assigned to London where for six years he obtained information about shipbuilding, ordnance, and the naval educational system. Due to his personal charm, tact, judgment, and extraordinary abilities he was able to obtain classified information, much of it scientific in nature.

9:105 Richardson, Leon B. *William E. Chandler, Republican.* New York: Dodd, Mead, 1940. This is a balanced account of the inexperienced but energetic secretary of the navy's management of complex naval politics, patronage (1882–1885), and oversight of the early new navy. Richardson presents a lively discussion of political disputes over the navy's first steel ships.

9:106 McFeely, William S. *Frederick Douglass.* New York: Norton, 1991. This biography of one of the foremost champions of freedom and racial equality contends that Douglass was negligent in his post as minister to Haiti and easily manipulated by Secretary of State James G. Blaine.

9:107 Goldberg, Joyce S. "Patrick Egan: An Irish-American Minister to Chile." *Eire-Ireland* 14 (Fall 1979): 83–95. Goldberg assesses the contribution to the transformation of American foreign policy at the end of the nineteenth century of Patrick Egan, minister to Chile from 1889 to 1893. Possibly appointed to contest British commercial dominance of South America, Egan became embroiled in America's bungling policy during the Chilean civil war and subsequent crisis known as the *Baltimore* affair. Forgotten today, Egan was a prudent and politically astute agent of America's changing foreign policy.

9:108 Armstrong, William M. *E. L. Godkin and American Foreign Policy, 1865–1900.* New York: Bookman Associates, 1957. Reprint 1974 (State University of New York Press). Godkin, born in Britain, was editor of *The Nation* from 1865 and of the *New York Evening Post* after 1881. Anglo-American relations received his editorial commentary frequently, as did U.S. relations with other European nations.

9:109 Clymer, Kenton J. *John Hay: The Gentleman as Diplomat.* Ann Arbor: University of Michigan Press, 1975. This volume contains valuable information about diplomatic appointments during the McKinley administration and the evolution of Hay's foreign policy views from ardent young Republican to unsentimental Anglo-American.

9:110 Castel, Albert. *The Presidency of Andrew Johnson.* Lawrence: Regents Press of Kansas, 1979. Castel seeks to revise the view of Johnson as a stubborn blunderer and racist who interfered with the Republican Party's objectives of racial justice. Johnson failed as president, not because of his racial views, but because of his inept use of power.

9:111   Younger, Edward. *John A. Kasson: Politics and Diplomacy from Lincoln to McKinley.* Iowa City: State Historical Society of Iowa, 1955. This is a biography of a notable Iowa politician who served his state and country for most of the second half of the nineteenth century. As minister to Austria-Hungary, 1877–1881, he dealt most notably with issues of tainted pork imports and tariffs; in Germany, from 1884 to 1888, he had important dealings with Bismarck, participated in the Berlin conference, and helped negotiate an end to the Samoan controversy.

9:112   Travis, Frederick F. *George Kennan and the American-Russian Relationship, 1865–1924.* Athens, OH: Ohio University Press, 1990. This work explores how Kennan (uncle of George F.) achieved his status as "the most renowned American interpreter of Russian life" between 1865 and 1924. Until the 1880s, he vigorously defended Russian expansion into central and eastern Asia, then reversed himself and emerged as an unbending critic of Russian autocracy. Travis sees no evidence that Kennan had a direct impact on U.S. policy or U.S. diplomatic relations with Russia.

9:113   Garraty, John A. *Henry Cabot Lodge: A Biography.* New York: Alfred A. Knopf, 1953. This comprehensive and sympathetic appraisal of Henry Cabot Lodge is based on his private papers, to which Garraty was given unrestricted access. Almost half of the book deals with pre-1900 issues, but only one chapter is devoted to Lodge and foreign policy, focusing primarily on his position on the Venezuela boundary dispute.

9:114   Craig, John M. *Lucia Ames Mead (1856–1936) and the American Peace Movement.* Lewiston, NY: E. Mellen Press, 1990. This is a study of one of the most prominent, neglected American female pacifists of her day, a leader of the peace reform and anti-imperialist movements. Craig devotes the first chapter and a half to her views prior to the Spanish-American War.

9:115   Carosso, Vincent P., with Rose C. Carosso. *The Morgans: Private International Bankers,* *1854–1913.* Cambridge, MA: Harvard University Press, 1987. In a massive work, the Carossos trace the rise of three Morgan family members: Junius S., Pierpont, and Jack. They emphasize how bankers of relatively modest means achieved great international financial power in an age of colossal fortunes, eclipsing men who wielded much greater resources. This work details Morgan family loans to Chile, Argentina, China, Manchuria, Russia, Mexico, Canada, and other nations.

9:116   Eggert, Gerald G. *Richard Olney: Evolution of a Statesman.* University Park: Pennsylvania State University Press, 1974. This extensively researched biography graphically reveals Olney's harsh personality and his generally responsible positions in foreign policy. The author refutes the theories of open door imperialism as applied to the second Cleveland administration (1893–1897) and includes a valuable discussion of arbitration.

9:117   Mowat, R. B. *The Life of Lord Pauncefote, First Ambassador to the United States.* Boston: Houghton Mifflin Co., 1929. Mowat write sympathetically about an indefatigable worker who arrived in the United States in 1889, felt at home, enjoyed Washington life, yet remained a thoroughgoing Englishman who typified the spirit of the Foreign Office. Pauncefote "moved with ease and unaffected enjoyment in that somewhat formal and recondite world of Continental high officials and masters of the diplomatic profession."

9:118   Fry, Joseph A. *Henry S. Sanford: Diplomacy and Business in Nineteenth-Century America.* Reno: University of Nevada Press, 1982. This is a comprehensive study of an important figure in business and diplomacy who played an active role in nineteenth-century diplomacy as chargé d'affaires in Paris, minister to Belgium, and a central figure in the evolution of U.S. policies in Africa. As a businessman, he also promoted economic and territorial expansion in Latin America. Fry believes his diplomatic activities influenced trends in late-nineteenth-century U.S. foreign policy, although he never attained much fame for all his accomplishments.

9:119   Drake, Frederick C. *The Empire of the Seas: A Biography of Rear Admiral Robert Wilson Shufeldt, USN.* Honolulu: University of Hawaii

Press, 1984. Drake demonstrates how Admiral Shufeldt's career typified the links between the continental expansion of the antebellum period and the post–Civil War drive for commercial expansion. He also notes Shufeldt's passion for African and Asian markets.

9:120 Muller, Dorothea R. "Josiah Strong and American Nationalism: A Reevaluation." *Journal of American History* 53 (December 1966): 487–503. This article corrects earlier arguments that Strong was a Darwinian, advocate of Anglo-Saxon supremacy, and territorial expansionist before 1898.

9:121 Dahl, Victor C. "Granville Stuart in Latin America: A Montana Pioneer's Diplomatic Career." *Montana Magazine of Western History* 21 (Summer 1971): 18–33. Dahl describes Stuart's life in Montana as miner, cattleman, and frontiersman as well as his imprint on diplomacy when he served as minister to Uruguay and Paraguay, 1894–1898. Hoping to find the fortune that eluded him at home, Stuart expected that his talents, astute reports, and dignified countenance would lead to a new, important position in life. Though this did not occur, he fulfilled his mission at a time the United States was emerging as a global power. His career is also recorded in Paul C. Phillips, ed., *Forty Years on the Frontier as Seen in the Journals and Reminiscences of Granville Stuart, Gold-Miner, Trader, Merchant, Rancher and Politician* (2 vols., Cleveland: Arthur H. Clarke Company, 1925).

9:122 Cooling, Benjamin Franklin. *Benjamin Franklin Tracy: Father of the Modern American Fighting Navy.* Hamden, CT: Archon Books, 1973. One of the most important and influential secretaries of the navy, Tracy espoused the idea of sea power, nickel armor, and a balanced battle fleet. He was a skilled politician who revived the Naval War College, introduced the merit system in the navy yards, and proved to be an important influence on Benjamin Harrison and James G. Blaine.

9:123 Shenton, James P. *Robert John Walker, a Politician from Jackson to Lincoln.* New York: Columbia University Press, 1961. Shenton's biography traces Walker's expansionist beliefs (1850–1870), association with other promoters of the Alaskan cession, and his lobbying activities for the Alaska ap-

propriation.

9:124 Van Deusen, Glyndon G. *Thurlow Weed, Wizard of the Lobby.* Boston: Little, Brown and Company, 1947. Good detail about organizational and factional politics enhance this biography, which also contains information relevant to foreign policy after the Civil War.

9:125 Kaplan, Lawrence S. "The Brahmin as Diplomat in Nineteenth Century America: Everett, Bancroft, Motley, Lowell." This article, examining complaints of post–Civil War eastern intellectuals and reformers about the quality of U.S. diplomats—focusing on their ignorance of social skills, lack of professionalism, and incompetence in performing diplomatic duties—contends that in Edward Everett, George Bancroft, John Lothrop Motley, and James Russell Lowell, the nation had exactly what the reformers wanted. These "Boston Brahmins" were refined, well educated, well traveled, and linguistically talented, and comprised a clearly identifiable group of distinguished gentlemen who met the "highest possible standard of excellence . . . with personal qualifications few professional diplomats could command." Ultimately, however, "they all retired from office with an exaggerated sense of their own importance," unable to accept their own mistakes while painfully aware of being unappreciated (6:180).

Overviews and General Works

9:126 Beisner, Robert L. *From the Old Diplomacy to the New, 1865–1900.* 2d ed. Arlington Heights, IL: Harlan Davidson, 1986. An indispensable introduction to U.S. diplomacy after the Civil War, this work assesses scholarly views of the period, identifies the chief issues, and offers a credible interpretation. Instead of emphasizing economic influences or imperialism as an explanation for U.S. diplomacy after the Civil War, Beisner stresses a shift from a passive, reactive, ad hoc diplomacy to a more systematic, deliberative, formal diplomacy brought about by a combination of political, economic, military, and cultural issues that led Americans to a sense of national insecurity and military vulnerability. First published in 1975.

9:127 _____. "Thirty Years before Manila: E. L. Godkin, Carl Schurz, and Anti-Imperialism in the Gilded Age." *Historian* 30 (August 1968): 561–77. Anti-imperialists found expression for their fears about expansion long before the Spanish-American War. For over thirty years, holds the author, such anti-imperialists as E. L. Godkin and Carl Schurz "waged verbal warfare against American imperialism" and "remained in the forefront of public opposition to any government policy of expansion. In 1898, they and others mounted a major campaign against imperialism, a campaign built on foundations that had been laid in the Gilded Age."

9:128 Buhite, Russell D. *Lives at Risk: Hostages and Victims in American Foreign Policy.* Buhite examines how the U.S. government dealt with the holding of its citizens as hostages on foreign territory and how it responded to cases in which Americans were victimized while living or conducting business abroad. Chapter 2 has case studies from the nineteenth century (2:244).

9:129 Campbell, Charles Soutter. *The Transformation of American Foreign Relations, 1865–1900.* New York: Harper and Row, 1976. This comprehensive survey is an essential volume for the study of American foreign relations after 1865. It focuses on the transformation of America's international position and especially on changes in Anglo-American relations. It deemphasizes the importance of economic considerations in explaining U.S. diplomatic activities.

9:130 Darby, Phillip. *Three Faces of Imperialism: British and American Approaches to Asia and Africa, 1870–1970.* New Haven: Yale University Press, 1987. This useful comparative study focuses more on Britain than America in the late nineteenth century. Darby views each nation's approach to Asia and Africa in terms of "Power," "Moral Responsibility," and "Economic Interest."

9:131 Dobson, John M. *America's Ascent: The United States Becomes a Great Power, 1880–1914.* DeKalb: Northern Illinois University Press, 1978. Dobson contends that efforts to expand commerce,

obtain colonies and protectorates, and assert American moral superiority underlay the appearance of the United States as a world power. The book synthesizes revisionist and orthodox interpretations to demonstrate that economic expansion combined with political aggrandizement and moral assertiveness in a drive for prestige and power.

9:132 Dulles, Foster Rhea. *Prelude to World Power: American Diplomatic History, 1860–1900.* New York: Macmillan, 1965. Reprint 1971 (Collier Books). Dulles portrays American policy as active until 1867 and at low ebb through the 1880s as Americans were absorbed in domestic activities. Intellectual, journalistic, commercial, and naval influences caused the nation to look outward and led to revived nationalism, war, and empire.

9:133 Fry, Joseph A. "Phases of Empire: Late Nineteenth-Century U.S. Foreign Relations." In *The Gilded Age: Essays on the Origins of Modern America,* ed. Charles W. Calhoun, 261–88. Wilmington, DE: Scholarly Resources, 1996. Fry finds that the motivations, processes, and imperial results of the era demonstrate continuity rather than change in the history of U.S. foreign relations. He stresses the remarkable economic growth that became critical to the formulation of diplomacy. Considerations of national security, national greatness (based on race), and mission justified expansion along with the belief in the necessity of enlarging overseas markets to sustain national prosperity and growth.

9:134 Gelfand, Lawrence E. "Hemispheric Regionalism to Global Universalism: The Changing Face of United States National Interests." Gelfand describes how U.S. foreign policy veered from an emphasis on hemispheric regionalism to the Wilsonian concept of universalism, concluding that cyclical movements proved detrimental to the maintenance of a coherent diplomacy (2:168).

9:135 Graebner, Norman A. *Foundations of American Foreign Policy: A Realist Appraisal from Franklin to McKinley: Essays.* Graebner believes U.S. foreign policymakers realistically pursued U.S. national interests. Turn-of-the-century diplomatic successes were not accidental because foreign policymakers balanced means and ends, national interests and ideals, and personal ambitions and national needs (2:62).

9:136   Grenville, J. A. S., and George Berkeley Young. *Politics, Strategy, and American Diplomacy: Studies in Foreign Policy, 1873–1917.* New Haven: Yale University Press, 1966. This book provides sharply etched and skillfully connected studies of navalists, politicians, lobbyists, and statesmen. The essays on Luce, Harrison, Cleveland, and Lodge are noteworthy interpretations, as are the analyses of specific diplomatic episodes and naval developments.

9:137   Healy, David F. *US Expansionism: The Imperialist Urge in the 1890s.* Madison: University of Wisconsin Press, 1970. This book looks at the background and consequences of expansion in the 1890s, including a fresh examination of the thinking both major and secondary political figures held about foreign policy. The treatment of American interest in Canada and Cuba is particularly sophisticated, as is the recognition of the duality of expediency and morality in expansionist thought.

9:138   Hunt, Michael H. *Ideology and U.S. Foreign Policy.* Hunt argues that three factors have combined to produce the ideology that has shaped American foreign relations from the late eighteenth century to the present—the conception of national mission and duty to promote liberty abroad; the belief in a racial hierarchy handed down from the founding fathers; and the hostility toward revolutions that are not made in the image of America's own conservative revolution (2:132).

9:139   Kennedy, Charles Stuart. *The American Consul: A History of the United States Consular Service, 1776–1914.* This is a compilation of short biographies and anecdotes about U.S. consuls and their adventures abroad. Kennedy observes that until 1917 the consular service was both larger and more important than the foreign service and finds that most consuls conducted the principal business of the State Department with competence and success, promoting trade, helping U.S. citizens abroad, and protecting or disciplining U.S. seamen (2:193).

9:140   LaFeber, Walter. *The American Search for Opportunity, 1865–1913.* This book traces the U.S. search for order in foreign policy in the face of the eruption of revolutions (Mexico, China, Russia, Cuba, Philippines, Hawaii, Panama, Nicaragua) and America's rise to world power, which necessitated the development of a naval force to protect commerce. LaFeber argues that the struggle for markets drove U.S. foreign policy more than did global pacification or a search for order (2:40).

9:141   _____. *The New Empire: An Interpretation of American Expansion, 1860–1898.* Rev. ed. Ithaca: Cornell University Press, 1998. This book offers an economic-determinist interpretation of American overseas expansion, holding that expansionism resulted from the aggressive efforts of politicians, intellectuals, navalists, and business interests to obtain overseas markets and investments as a consequence of the industrial revolution and especially the Depression of 1893. "Spurred by a fantastic industrial revolution, which produced ever larger quantities of surplus goods, depressions, and violence, and warned by a growing radical literature that the system was not functioning properly, the United States prepared to solve its dilemmas with foreign expansion." This edition carries a new author's preface; the original edition appeared in 1963.

9:142   Martel, Gordon, ed. *American Foreign Relations Reconsidered, 1890–1993.* New York: Routledge, 1994. This collection gathers essays by distinguished diplomatic historians summarizing important themes or eras, explaining controversies, and exploring specific questions. Four essays are pertinent: Michael H. Hunt, "Traditions of American Diplomacy: From Colony to Great Power" (1–20); J. Garry Clifford, "Institutions of American Diplomacy and the Policy Process" (21–36); Emily S. Rosenberg, "Economic Interest and United States Foreign Policy" (37–51); and Joseph A. Fry, "Imperialism, American Style, 1890–1916" (52–70).

9:143   May, Ernest R. *Imperial Democracy: The Emergence of America as a Great Power.* New York: Harcourt, Brace and World, 1961. Reprint 1973 (Harper and Row). This broad-ranging study takes the view that Americans were concerned with domestic events, that their leadership was weak, and that world power was thrust on the United States. The book's value lies in its portrayal of the perception and reaction by foreign powers to America's emergence.

9:144   McDougall, Walter A. *Promised Land, Crusader State: The American Encounter with the World since 1776.* This is an interpretive narrative of

American relations with the external world. McDougall suggests that none of the historic traditions of American foreign policy ever died. The nation's leaders from 1776 to 1898 imagined the nation as a New Jerusalem in the Promised Land, destined to enjoy the blessings of liberty if the nation did not go abroad in search of monsters to destroy. He dismisses the realist-idealist dichotomy as an inadequate, ahistorical explanation of American foreign policy traditions (2:70).

9:145 Morgan, H. Wayne. *Unity and Culture: The United States, 1877–1900.* Baltimore: Penguin Books, 1971. This concise volume is a good introduction to the patterns of politics, economic growth, art and literature, and foreign policy in the late nineteenth century.

9:146 Pelz, Stephen E. "Changing International Systems, the World Balance of Power, and the United States, 1776–1976." Pelz uses political science theory revolving around the "realist approach," stressing the importance of international balances of power, to sketch the effect of those systems on U.S. policymakers. The world in which they made policy in the late nineteenth century was dominated by a revolutionary-counterrevolutionary system. Ole R. Holsti's comments appear as "International Systems, System Change, and Foreign Policy: Commentary on 'Changing International Systems,'" 83–89 (5:107).

9:147 Perkins, Dexter. *The Monroe Doctrine, 1867–1907.* Baltimore: Johns Hopkins Press, 1937. Perkins describes the "remarkable extension of the Doctrine and of a variety of new applications" from the no-transfer principle to the canal question, Venezuela boundary dispute, blockade of Venezuela in 1902, and other interventions in Latin America.

9:148 Plesur, Milton. *America's Outward Thrust: Approaches to Foreign Affairs, 1865–1890.* DeKalb: Northern Illinois University Press, 1971. This book is an introductory survey of American international contacts in the Gilded Age. The author quarrels with the old assumption that the era was dull, boring, and scandal-ridden. The chapters on cultural and popular interactions between the United States and other lands are the most interesting and unusual at the time of publication.

9:149 Plischke, Elmer. *U.S. Department of State: A Reference History.* This is a history of the organization and functions of the Department of State, a single-volume reference history of the agency responsible for the conduct of foreign policy. Chapter 5, "The Road to Becoming a Great World Power," describes the State Department between 1861 and 1913 (2:197).

9:150 Richardson, James L. *Crisis Diplomacy: The Great Powers since the Mid-Nineteenth Century.* New York: Cambridge University Press, 1994. This massive study seeks to distinguish between the underlying structural issues that make international conflict likely and the part played by crisis diplomacy during the course of a confrontation.

9:151 Rosenberg, Emily S. *Spreading the American Dream: American Economic and Cultural Expansion, 1890–1945.* New York: Hill and Wang, 1982. This work studies governmental-cultural interactions and cultural imperialism. Rosenberg suggests that from the 1890s policymakers took great interest in what Americans did abroad and even sought to direct their activities to promote national interests, especially to create an environment conducive to the extension of American trade and investment.

9:152 Stephanson, Anders. *Manifest Destiny: American Expansionism and the Empire of Right.* This brief book traces the evolution of a single ideology from its religious sources in Puritanism through an era of massive secular change. Stephanson defines Manifest Destiny broadly as a "national ideology" that has functioned since the early seventeenth century. In the chapter on the period from 1865 to 1914, he discusses the use of the term by ideologues to justify overseas colonial imperialism and commercial expansion (2:222).

9:153 Varg, Paul A. *America, from Client State to World Power: Six Major Transitions in United States Foreign Relations.* This book presents a conceptual framework consisting of six major foreign policy transitions, reflecting the relationship of the United States to the rest of the world. Varg identifies a shift in the 1890s to the acquisition of noncontiguous territory, which invariably led to greater and different involvement with the rest of the world (2:48).

9:154 Vevier, Charles. "American Continentalism: An Idea of Expansion, 1845–1910." *American Historical Review* 65 (January 1960): 323–35. Vevier examines the intellectual basis of American expansionism, arguing that the ideology of continentalism expressed American national values, domestic accomplishments, and international goals. The doctrine of geopolitical centrism was the conceptual instrument that projected American continentalism onto the world scene and anticipated its use by the expansionists of 1898.

9:155 Werking, Richard Hume. *The Master Architects: Building the United States Foreign Service, 1890–1913.* By 1913, "after sixteen years of Republican rule, the foundations and framework of the modern United States foreign service had appeared." The success in making State an efficient agency for promoting U.S. national interest owed much to a group of capable, assertive, and sophisticated young public bureaucrats—"master architects"—who sought to advance their own careers while promoting the national interest (2:200).

9:156 White, Leonard D., with Jean Schneider. *The Republican Era: A Study in Administrative History.* New York: Macmillan, 1958. In this last of a four-volume series, White studies important administrative institutions and the men who operated them. Behind them were basic ideas and ideals that endured through economic transformations, political convulsions, and even wars. Congressional-executive relations and the battle for reform dominated the late nineteenth century, years that "marked the culmination of Jacksonian theory and practice, with all their strengths and weaknesses. Federalist doctrine, long in disrepute, again made itself felt, but in a new partnership with democratic ideas."

9:157 Wiebe, Robert H. *The Search for Order, 1877–1920.* New York: Hill and Wang, 1967. Wiebe argues that America was transformed from a splintered society with small-town values to a unified society with new values of management and middle-class rationality. The change affected the manner of dealing with all public issues, including foreign affairs.

SOCIAL AND CULTURAL FACTORS

9:158 Alonso, Harriet Hyman. *Peace as a Women's Issue: A History of the U.S. Movement for World Peace and Women's Rights.* Syracuse: Syracuse University Press, 1993. Alonso analyzes many women's peace organizations from their origins in the early nineteenth century to the present. She emphasizes the Women's International League for Peace and Freedom and the notion of peace as a special woman's issue, and examines doctrines, policies, activities, and organizational structures, while including brief sketches of major leaders.

9:159 Bederman, Gail. *Manliness & Civilization: A Cultural History of Gender and Race in the United States, 1880–1917.* Chicago: University of Chicago Press, 1995. Bederman contends that "civilization" at the turn of the century was explicitly understood as a racial and gendered concept because Americans were obsessed with the connections among manhood, race, and civilization. The most advanced, "civilized" races had evolved the most perfect "manliness" and "womanliness"—the Anglo-Saxon races. Bederman also discusses the changing historical meanings of such words as "manliness" and "masculinity" for leaders such as Theodore Roosevelt.

9:160 Blondheim, Menahem. *News over the Wires: The Telegraph and the Flow of Public Information in America, 1844–1897.* Cambridge, MA: Harvard University Press, 1994. Blondheim argues that newspapers cooperated in telegraphic news gathering not to reduce transmission costs but to manage a complex process and maximize the use of the wires. This work delineates the causes and consequences of the information monopoly established by the telegraph and news services and underscores the political consequences of these arrangements.

9:161 Boyd, Nancy. *Emissaries: The Overseas Work of the American YWCA, 1895–1970.* New York: Woman's Press, 1986. This book examines the overseas work of the American YWCA in three periods: 1895–1920, 1920–1940, and 1940–1970. Boyd discusses the motivations and leadership styles of some individual American YWCA secretaries posted abroad, demonstrates the women's commitment to an egalitarian style of leadership that encouraged group decision and consensus, and challenges the portrayal of women missionaries as agents of cultural imperialism.

9:162   Cassell, Frank A. "The Columbian Exposition of 1893 and United States Diplomacy in Latin America." *Mid-America* 67 (October 1985): 109–24. This article examines the connection between U.S. foreign policy goals in Latin America and the Chicago World's Fair of 1893. Cassell claims Harrison and Blaine were attempting to advance their economic and political goals in Latin America, specifically reorienting it more toward the United States and away from Europe. The World's Fair added a new dimension to U.S. policy.

9:163   Cohen, Warren I. *East Asian Art and American Culture: A Study in International Relations.* New York: Columbia University Press, 1992. This work intertwines diplomatic and cultural history, exploring how the volume and flow of Asian art reflected political and economic power relations. Cohen shows how Japan and China used art as an instrument of foreign policy and discusses the U.S. reception of Chinese and Japanese fine arts from the 1780s to the 1980s, focusing on those who collected it, exhibited it, and wrote about or taught it.

9:164   Conn, Steven. "An Epistemology for Empire: The Philadelphia Commercial Museum, 1893–1926." *Diplomatic History* 22 (Fall 1998): 533–63. This is a study of the Philadelphia Commercial Museum, which sought to encourage U.S. economic expansion overseas through exhibits and extensive publication of information. By providing advice, expertise, and education, the museum tried to persuade the public that commercial conquest was a worthy objective and that "commercial expansion could bring the benefits of imperialism without any of its attendant perils."

9:165   Crapol, Edward P., ed. *Women and American Foreign Policy: Lobbyists, Critics, and Insiders.* This work attempts to integrate women's history and issues of gender into studies of U.S. foreign relations. Crapol argues that many women, through the power of their ideas and the force of their actions, attempted to influence the course of American foreign relations. The only relevant chapter, however, is John M. Craig, "Lucia True Ames Mead: American Publicist for Peace and Internationalism" (67–91) (2:150). See also Craig's *Lucia Ames Mead (1856–1936) and the American Peace Movement* (1990) (9:114).

9:166   Crunden, Robert M. *American Salons: Encounters with European Modernism, 1885–1917.* New York: Oxford University Press, 1993. This is an interesting survey of the relations among some of the founding figures of modernism. Crunden assesses the critiques of nineteenth-century canons and conventions that prepared the way for the social and cultural transformation that followed.

9:167   DeConde, Alexander. *Ethnicity, Race, and American Foreign Policy: A History.* This work explores the important roles of ethnic and racial groups in U.S. foreign relations. DeConde assesses the perceived and actual influence of Americans of African, Asian, European, Hispanic, and Middle Eastern descent and contends that foreign policy has been shaped largely by Anglo-Saxon racism and ethnocentrism. Ethnic and racial considerations have often taken priority over morality, ideology, or other factors in the making of American policy (2:152).

9:168   Endy, Christopher. "Travel and World Power: Americans in Europe, 1890–1917." *Diplomatic History* 22 (Fall 1998): 565–94. This article demonstrates how private travel contributed to the international perspective of affluent Americans (businessmen, tourists, cultural critics, policymakers, women) between 1890 and 1914; travel "formed a cultural or ideological foundation for imperialism" and helped contribute to the U.S. decision to intervene on behalf of the Allied powers in 1917. "Transatlantic travel and the popular commentary it inspired influenced conceptions of national identity and formed part of a public debate about how the United States should behave in the world."

9:169   Gyory, Andrew. *Closing the Gate: Race, Politics, and the Chinese Exclusion Act.* Chapel Hill: University of North Carolina Press, 1998. This work traces the origins of the Chinese Exclusion Act of 1882, which was the first federal law banning a group of immigrants solely on the basis of race or nationality and set a precedent for future restrictions against immigrants. Gyory contends that politicians sought a safe, non-ideological solution to the nation's industrial crisis and latched onto Chinese exclusion. "In all senses of the term, Chinese exclusion was a 'political' act." While rejecting standard views of a racist and bigoted labor movement, Gyory concludes that the act sanctioned, perpetuated, and legitimized racist actions at every level of society.

9:170 Harris, Paul W. "Cultural Imperialism and American Protestant Missionaries: Collaboration and Dependency in Mid-Nineteenth-Century China." After defining cultural imperialism, Harris analyzes missionary efforts in the context of the deeper, cultural forces that shaped missionary behavior. Harris uses dependency theory to study missionary history, especially American Protestant missionaries in China in the mid-nineteenth century (7:444).

9:171 Hill, Patricia R. *The World Their Household: The American Woman's Foreign Mission Movement and Cultural Transformation, 1870–1920.* Ann Arbor: University of Michigan Press, 1985. This is a careful analysis of the women's foreign mission movement and how it promoted cultural imperialism in the nonwestern world and reflected changing cultural paradigms of ideal womanhood in the United States.

9:172 Hofstadter, Richard. *Social Darwinism in American Thought.* Rev. ed. Boston: Beacon Press, 1955. This is a brilliant exposition of the development and influence of Darwinism in American intellectual and political life and in foreign affairs. Originally published in 1944 as *Social Darwinism in American Thought, 1860–1915.*

9:173 Hutchison, William R. *Errand to the World: American Protestant Thought and Foreign Missions.* This book analyzes the evolution of foreign mission thought and reassesses the history of the American missionary enterprise. Hutchison reconstructs the intellectual principles and theological doctrines that underlay the missionary spirit (7:424).

9:174 Jacobson, Matthew Frye. *Barbarian Virtues: The United States Encounters Foreign Peoples at Home and Abroad, 1876–1917.* New York: Hill and Wang, 2000. Jacobson demonstrates how white, native-born Americans encountered foreign peoples at home and abroad and provided a context within which the former forged a national identity. Considering how "dominant notions of national des-

tiny and of proper Americanism draw upon charged encounters with disparaged peoples whose presence is as reviled in the political sphere as it is inevitable in the economic," the author calls for integration between economic and cultural approaches to American imperialism.

9:175 Kleppner, Paul. *The Cross of Culture: A Social Analysis of Midwestern Politics, 1850–1900.* 2d ed. New York: Free Press, 1970. This is a quantitative, value-oriented political history, stressing religious values rather than economic forces in the transformation of the Republican Party to a party of prosperity. The broad political analysis is useful, as is the study of the tariff.

9:176 Papachristou, Judith. "American Women and Foreign Policy, 1898–1905: Exploring Gender in Diplomatic History." *Diplomatic History* 14 (Fall 1990): 493–509. This article discusses the Gilded Age and Progressive era involvement of women in foreign policy, especially the deliberate effort of some to interest women's organizations in international issues and thus form a distinct female foreign policy constituency. Papachristou claims women developed a unique female perspective on foreign policy.

9:177 Ricard, Serge, ed. *An American Empire: Expansionist Cultures and Policies, 1881–1917.* Aix-en-Provence: Université de Provence, 1990. This book contains essays on the rhetoric of expansionism and imperialism in painting, fiction, poetry, language, law, and anthropology in the late nineteenth century: Heinz Ickstadt, "The Rhetoric of Expansionism in Painting and Fiction (1880–1901)"; Friedrich W. Horlacher, "The Language of Late Nineteenth-Century American Expansionism"; Jean-Pierre Martin, "American Imperialism and the Anthropological Bric-a-Brac"; Ricard, "Expansionists and Anti-Expansionists of 1898: The Unfinished Debate"; Liliane Kerjan, "Acquisition of Domain in International Law: American Reports"; Wolfgang Binder, "The Tropical Garden and the Mahanesque Resting-Place in the Caribbean: Remarks on the Early Incorporation of Puerto Rico by the United States of America"; Hubert Perrier, "The U.S. Left on War and Empire, 1880–1920"; Yves-Charles Grandjeat, "Capital Ventures and Dime Novels: U.S.-Mexican Relations during the Porfiriana"; Walter Grünzweig, "Noble Ethics and Loving Aggressiveness: The Imperialist Walt Whitman"; Hans-Joachim Lang, "Course of Empire: Four Harvard Perspectives on Imperialism"; Hélène Christol, "The Pacifist Warrior: William James and His 'Moral Equivalent of War'"; Alfred Hornung, "Evolution and Expansion in Jack London's Personal Accounts: The Road and John Barleycorn"; Manfred Pütz, "Mark Twain and the Idea of American Superiority at the End of the Nineteenth Century"; and Daniel Royot, "The Fantastic Record of a Maniac: King Leopold's Soliloquy Revisited."

9:178   Rupp, Leila J. "Constructing Internationalism: The Case of Transnational Women's Organizations, 1888–1945." *American Historical Review* 99 (December 1994): 1571–1600. Through a comparative discussion of the International Council of Women, International Alliance of Women, and Women's International League for Peace and Freedom, Rupp finds that forging bonds among women across national boundaries was not easy before 1945. She describes reactions of women of different nations, races, and classes to issues of colonialism, imperialism, and war, and finds deep divisions among them.

9:179   _____. *Worlds of Women: The Making of an International Women's Movement*. Princeton: Princeton University Press, 1997. This book studies the International Council of Women, International Alliance of Women, and Women's International League for Peace and Freedom to tell the story of the international women's movement. Rupp analyzes what drew women together into an international sisterhood, points out the movement's flaws and the limits of the women's vision, and focuses on the remarkable bonds that women forged across national boundaries, languages, and cultures.

9:180   Rydell, Robert W. *All the World's a Fair: Visions of Empire at American International Expositions, 1876–1916*. Chicago: University of Chicago Press, 1984. Rydell argues that the expositions held in the United States between 1876 and 1916—transparently ideological events—all contained specific social agendas. Organized, directed, and controlled by local and national elites, they projected a ruling-class vision in response to class conflict at home and imperial designs overseas. They were "triumphs of hegemony as well as symbolic edifices."

9:181   Schott, Marshall E. "The South and American Foreign Policy, 1894–1900: New South Prophets and the Challenge of Regional Values." *Southern Studies* 4 (Fall 1993): 295–308. The south's debate over foreign policy objectives, especially overseas expansion, occurred in the context of the region's understanding of its own history and the white south's concerns over the expanding power of the central government. While a small group of progressive southerners articulated a vision of an economically diversified, prosperous south, they were opposed by the vast majority of whites, who consistently expressed anxieties about a more outward-looking foreign policy, fearing that intervention abroad might greatly enlarge the power of the national government.

9:182   Smith, Shannon. "From Relief to Revolution: American Women and the Russian-American Relationship, 1890–1917." *Diplomatic History* 19 (Fall 1995): 601–16. This article illustrates through the careers of Clara Barton and Alice Stone Blackwell the expanding role of women in American society, in foreign relations, and especially in the gradual disintegration of a cordial diplomatic relationship between the United States and czarist Russia. Progressivism exercised a strong influence on U.S. foreign relations, and American women played growing roles in both.

9:183   Tucker, Robert W., Charles B. Keely, and Linda Wrigley, eds. *Immigration and U.S. Foreign Policy*. Boulder: Westview Press, 1990. Historians, sociologists, and political commentators consider immigration and foreign policy. The most pertinent essays are Tucker, "Immigration and Foreign Policy: General Considerations"; Oscar Handlin, "The Nineteenth-Century Immigration"; Aristide R. Zolberg, "The Roots of U.S. Refugee Policy"; Robert L. Bach, "Immigration and U.S. Foreign Policy in Latin America and the Caribbean"; Jorge I. Domínguez, "Immigration as Foreign Policy in U.S.–Latin American Relations"; and Myron Weiner, "Asian Immigrants and U.S. Foreign Policy."

9:184   Tyrrell, Ian. *Woman's World/Woman's Empire: The Woman's Christian Temperance Union in International Perspective, 1880–1930*. Chapel Hill: University of North Carolina Press, 1991. This is a study of the many women who contributed to the missionary impulse of the WCTU from the 1870s to the 1930s. Tyrrell contends that its international efforts were far more extensive and more indicative of the scope and limits of reform than any other part of the women's movement except for the vast foreign missionary endeavors. He also discusses feminism's international aspirations.

ECONOMIC ISSUES AND FACTORS

9:185   Beard, Charles A., and Mary R. Beard. *The Rise of American Civilization.* 2 vols. Rev. and enl. ed. New York: Macmillan Company, 1933. Volume 2 of this classic established the basis for the economic determinist interpretation of U.S. foreign relations and depicts the development of American imperialism during the Gilded Age through that prism. First published in 1927.

9:186   Becker, William H. *The Dynamics of Business-Government Relations: Industry & Exports, 1893–1921.* Chicago: University of Chicago Press, 1982. This book describes and analyzes business-government cooperation in developing export markets, although the results were often disappointing to both bureaucrats and private traders. Becker concludes that plans for cooperation were often frustrated by rival factions in the business community, government preoccupation with other matters, obstructionists in Congress, bureaucratic divisions in the executive branch, or general business distrust of the federal government.

9:187   Clark, William, and Charles Turner. "International Trade and the Evolution of the American Capital Market, 1888–1911." *Journal of Economic History* 45 (June 1985): 405–10. This is a brief analysis of the relationship between international trade and regional American credit markets. Clark suggests foreign payment flows had a significant effect on the level of interest rates in specific regions of the country.

9:188   Clayton, Lawrence A. *Grace: W. R. Grace & Co., The Formative Years, 1850–1930.* Ottawa, IL: Jameson Books, 1985. This is a biographical and institutional history that emphasizes the W. R. Grace and Company's positive role in sugar, rubber,

cable communications, and coal exporting. Clayton finds no incompatibility between the private interests of Grace entrepreneurs and the public welfare of Peruvians.

9:189   Davies, Robert B. "'Peacefully Working to Conquer the World': The Singer Manufacturing Company in Foreign Markets, 1854–1889." *Business History Review* 43 (Autumn 1969): 299–325. Davies contends that Singer was not affected by domestic business cycles and built an international sales and marketing organization without government aid.

9:190   Frieden, Jeffry A. "The Economics of Intervention: American Overseas Investments and Relations with Underdeveloped Areas, 1890–1950." *Comparative Studies in Society and History* 31 (January 1989): 55–80. Frieden connects changes in the goals and tactics of American policies toward less developed countries to changes in the domestic economies at both ends of the exchange.

9:191   Hearden, Patrick J. *Independence & Empire: The New South's Cotton Mill Campaign, 1865–1901.* DeKalb: Northern Illinois University Press, 1982. Hearden examines some of the key impulses behind southern economic expansionism.

9:192   Paterson, Thomas G. "American Businessmen and Consular Service Reform, 1890's to 1906." *Business History Review* 40 (Spring 1966): 77–97. Paterson emphasizes the domestic pressures of businessmen on foreign policy, arguing that the need to recover from the Depression of 1893 and the lure of growing U.S. economic power impelled reform.

9:193   Pletcher, David M. "1861–1898: Economic Growth and Diplomatic Adjustment." In *Economics and World Power: An Assessment of American Diplomacy since 1789,* ed. William H. Becker and Samuel F. Wells, Jr., 119–71. New York: Columbia University Press, 1984. Pletcher expresses ambivalence about the successes of American imperial expansion and the nature of empire in the last half of the nineteenth century.

9:194   _____. *The Diplomacy of Trade and Investment: American Economic Expansion in the Hemisphere, 1865–1900.* Columbia: University of Missouri Press, 1998. This book appraises the potential for U.S. economic expansion and assesses actual U.S. business undertakings, revealing a failure to devise a single overarching policy to cover all expansionist thought or action. Pletcher demonstrates that late-nineteenth-century U.S. economic expansion was usually ill defined, improvised, and reactive. Heated congressional debates often resulted in defeat for expansionist measures, businessmen's divisiveness prevented unified programs, and the presidency, State Department, and consular services did not prove to be determined allies of the expansionists.

9:195 _____. "Rhetoric and Results: A Pragmatic View of American Economic Expansionism, 1865–98." *Diplomatic History* 5 (Spring 1981): 93–106. This is an important and provocative analysis of U.S. economic expansion suggesting that business was less than successful in promoting an expansionist foreign policy in the latter part of the nineteenth century.

9:196 Rosenberg, Emily S. "Foundations of United States International Financial Power: Gold Standard Diplomacy, 1900–1905." *Business History Review* 59 (Summer 1985): 169–202. Describing the gold standard diplomacy worked out by the U.S. government along with a small group of experts who sought to establish a foreign financial policy, Rosenberg suggests such efforts reflected America's growing economic power, increasing stake in a stable international order, the emergence of a new profession of foreign financial advisers, and Washington's hope to play a leading role in international currency matters. The late nineteenth century was a period in which Americans "reformulated institutions and attitudes."

9:197 _____. "Revisiting Dollar Diplomacy: Narratives of Money and Manliness." *Diplomatic History* 22 (Spring 1998): 155–76. A SHAFR presidential address adapted from the author's then upcoming book, *Financial Missionaries to the World: The Politics and Culture of Dollar Diplomacy, 1900–1930* (1999) (11:91), this article analyzes the politics of America's early-twentieth-century foreign lending policies.

9:198 Rosenberg, Emily S., and Norman L. Rosenberg. "From Colonialism to Professionalism: The Public-Private Dynamic in United States Foreign Financial Advising, 1898–1929." *Journal of*

American History 74 (June 1987): 59–82. Focusing on Latin America, this essay "analyzes the forms that United States foreign financial advising took during the transitional period from 1898 to 1930, after territorial colonialism had ceased to seem a viable way of imposing financial arrangements, but before the advent of post–World War II international financial institutions."

9:199 Schonberger, Howard B. *Transportation to the Seaboard: The "Communication Revolution" and American Foreign Policy, 1860–1900.* Westport, CT: Greenwood Press, 1971. Farm surpluses formed an important part of the modern American empire, and farmers acted as businessmen with an expansionist mentality in the post–Civil War period. Schonberger analyzes the relationships among debates over internal improvements, railroad regulation, and the search for foreign markets.

9:200 Verdier, Daniel. *Democracy and International Trade: Britain, France, and the United States, 1860–1990.* Princeton: Princeton University Press, 1994. This is a comparative study of the historical development of American, British, and French trade policy aimed at testing a general theory of political behavior. Using social science theory and vocabulary, complex charts and tables, the author contends that trade policy, especially tariffs, is a function of the electoral process. For a contrasting view, see Lake, *Power, Protection, and Free Trade: International Sources of U.S. Commercial Strategy, 1887–1939* (1988) (9:208).

9:201 Wilkins, Mira. *The History of Foreign Investment in the United States to 1914.* Cambridge, MA: Harvard University Press, 1989. In this weighty book, Wilkins concludes that by 1913 the European capital invested in the United States had provided benefits that "far surpassed the costs." It also played an enormous part in making the United States a great industrial power. This work surveys long-term foreign investment in the United States to World War I.

9:202 Yergin, Daniel. *The Prize: The Epic Quest for Oil, Money, and Power.* New York: Simon and Schuster, 1991. This is an account of the history of oil as the critical factor in both "high" and "low" politics of states.

9:203   Zingg, Paul J. "To the Shores of Barbary: The Ideology and Pursuit of American Commercial Expansion, 1816–1906." *South Atlantic Quarterly* 79 (Autumn 1980): 408–24. The naval presence in North Africa following the Algerian-American peace treaty of 1816 and the pacific role attached to it enhanced the commercially opportunistic policies that American diplomats and traders abroad pursued afterward. Zingg devotes most attention to the period before the Civil War.

Tariffs and Trade

9:204   Eckes, Alfred E., Jr. *Opening America's Market: U.S. Foreign Trade Policy since 1776.* Eckes challenges the free trade doctrine and the diplomatic, rather than economic, rationale behind commercial liberalism (7:49).

9:205   Goldstein, Judith. *Ideas, Interests, and American Trade Policy.* This is a concise history of American trade policy from 1789 that emphasizes the shared ideas and beliefs influencing decisionmakers, constraining options, and shaping responses in the nation's trade policy (2:208).

9:206   Kaplan, Edward S., and Thomas W. Ryley. *Prelude to Trade Wars: American Tariff Policy, 1890–1922.* Westport, CT: Greenwood Press, 1994. This work contains a legislative biography of North Dakota's Porter J. McCumber integrated into summaries of the tariff acts and major international issues of the period.

9:207   Kenkel, Joseph F. *Progressives and Protection: The Search for a Tariff Policy, 1866–1936.* Lanham, MD: University Press of America, 1983. Kenkel describes how businessmen, politicians, farmers, and "others of a progressive mind" worked to develop a reasonable tariff policy to "promote the common good." Although they failed, their efforts reveal much about progressivism and U.S. politics.

9:208   Lake, David A. *Power, Protection, and Free Trade: International Sources of U.S. Commercial Strategy, 1887–1939.* Ithaca: Cornell University Press, 1988. Lake advances a revisionist argument that the commercial policy of the United States arose not from conflicts between interest groups or politi-

cal parties, but from the constraints and opportunities within the international economy.

9:209   Reitano, Joanne R. *The Tariff Question in the Gilded Age: The Great Debate of 1888.* University Park: Pennsylvania State University Press, 1994. Reitano focuses on the Mills Bill of 1888, a deeply partisan tariff proposal that damaged the Democratic Party as well as Grover Cleveland's chances for reelection. She analyzes the heated debate it caused and the role of government in management of economic affairs.

9:210   Stanwood, Edward. *American Tariff Controversies in the Nineteenth Century.* 2 vols. Boston: Houghton Mifflin, 1903. Reprint 1974 (Garland Publishing). Stanwood, who favored the protective tariff, also supported Blaine's reciprocity program. These volumes, while moderate in their treatment of Cleveland, provide a detailed political analysis from Blaine's point of view.

9:211   Tarbell, Ida M. *The Tariff in Our Times.* New York: Macmillan, 1911. Tarbell believed that protective tariffs in the late nineteenth century controverted the public will and involved unprincipled bargaining. This volume contains a number of revelations designed to support this view and to stress the importance of the tariff issue.

9:212   Taussig, Frank W. *Some Aspects of the Tariff Question: An Examination of the Development of American Industries under Protection.* 3d enl. ed. Cambridge, MA: Harvard University Press, 1934. Taussig analyzes tariffs according to the product, such as sugar, wool, and copper. Originally published in 1915.

9:213   Terrill, Tom E. *The Tariff, Politics, and American Foreign Policy, 1874–1901.* Westport, CT: Greenwood Press, 1973. Terrill's thesis, approaching economic determinism, is that the tariff was an instrument for overseas economic expansion. The author treats the Harrison-Blaine administration as an important prelude to later developments and the two political parties as differing merely over tactics. There is an abbreviated discussion of reciprocity and its fate.

9:214   Wolman, Paul. *Most Favored Nation: The Republican Revisionists and U.S. Tariff Policy,*

1897–1912. Chapel Hill: University of North Carolina Press, 1992. This book describes changes in Republican tariff policy from the Dingley Tariff Act of 1897 through implementation of the Payne-Aldrich Tariff Act of 1909. Wolman places these policies within the context of the rapidly changing role of the United States in the international economy.

POLITICAL ISSUES AND FACTORS

9:215   Dobson, John M. *Politics in the Gilded Age: A New Perspective on Reform.* New York: Praeger Publishers, 1972. This is an even-handed comparison of the morals and motives of politicians and reformers, focusing on the election of 1884. Dobson underplays the importance of the tariff, and foreign policy receives scant attention.

9:216   Doenecke, Justus D. *The Presidencies of James A. Garfield & Chester A. Arthur.* Lawrence: Regents Press of Kansas, 1981. Doenecke interprets Garfield and Arthur as "transitional figures" who occupied the presidency during a period of national turmoil and uncertainty. They were men of "considerable ability," although in politics they apparently failed more often than they succeeded.

9:217   Dozer, Donald M. "Anti-Expansionism during the Johnson Administration." *Pacific Historical Review* 12 (September 1943): 253–75. Dozer sketches expansionist efforts (1865–1869), measuring their strength by the reactions of Congress and the press, in a primarily descriptive article.

9:218   Faulkner, Harold U. *Politics, Reform, and Expansion, 1890–1900.* New York: Harper, 1959. The 1890s appear as a time of new intellectual awareness about changes in American life—the frontier, expansion, the city, immigration, and economic developments. The author often minimizes the impact of economic influences on foreign policy.

9:219   Hilderbrand, Robert C. *Power and the People: Executive Management of Public Opinion in Foreign Affairs, 1897–1921.* This history of presidential exploitation of the news media from McKinley to Wilson begins with McKinley's acute awareness of the potential of the press and his use of it. The author

also explores the early development of presidential press relations staff and State Department press relations and contends that the growth of presidential "manipulation" of the press came at the expense of the "public's voice in making foreign policy" (2:144).

9:220   Keller, Morton. *Affairs of State: Public Life in Late Nineteenth Century America.* Cambridge, MA: Harvard University Press, 1977. Keller's study describes the values and organizational patterns of American public life, treating foreign policy within the context of the changes and tensions resulting from industrial policies.

9:221   Kleppner, Paul. *The Third Electoral System, 1853–1892: Parties, Voters, and Political Cultures.* Chapel Hill: University of North Carolina Press, 1979. Combining quantitative and verbal analysis with documentary study, this volume emphasizes ethno-religious perspectives in shaping national politics and challenges the liberal-rational analysis of political behavior.

9:222   LaFeber, Walter. "The Constitution and United States Foreign Policy: An Interpretation." LaFeber discusses the historic and changing relationship between the Constitution and U.S. foreign policy, raising debates about the president's powers in the global arena, arguments over the proper balance between extending power abroad and maintaining liberty at home, and doubts about the ability of the traditional constitutional system to deal with the global issues of the cold war (2:228).

9:223   Leuchtenburg, William E. "Progressivism and Imperialism: The Progressive Movement and American Foreign Policy, 1898–1916." *Mississippi Valley Historical Review* 39 (December 1952): 483–504. Leuchtenburg argues that progressives, despite their primary concern for domestic reform, favored imperialism, a thesis that still stirs historical controversy.

9:224   Mattox, Henry E. *The Twilight of Amateur Diplomacy: The American Foreign Service and Its Senior Officers in the 1890s.* Kent, OH: Kent State University Press, 1989. Here a foreign service officer investigates the roles of senior-level U.S. diplomats in the 1890s, including their preparation, aptitude, and general competence, concluding that the senior diplomatic officer corps represented the United States abroad in a manner adequate to the needs of the day.

9:225　　Morgan, H. Wayne. *From Hayes to McKinley: National Party Politics, 1877–1896.* Syracuse: Syracuse University Press, 1969. Morgan successfully evokes the spirit of party politics in the Gilded Age. The forging of a national party system was led by forward-looking Republicans who were also inclined to develop more forceful approaches to foreign policy.

9:226　　_____, ed. *The Gilded Age.* Rev. and enl. ed. Syracuse: Syracuse University Press, 1970. This collection includes Morgan, "Toward National Unity"; John Tipple, "Big Businessmen and a New Economy"; and Paul S. Holbo, "Economics, Emotion, and Expansion: An Emerging Foreign Policy?" First published in 1963.

9:227　　Nichols, Jeannette P. "The United States Congress and Imperialism, 1861–1897." *Journal of Economic History* 21 (December 1961): 526–38. Nichols stresses groups opposed to imperialism, centering on domestic politics, costs and wealth, and negative attitudes toward foreigners, especially the British. She found changes in the 1880s, but concludes that attitudes in the 1861–1897 period were erratic.

9:228　　Small, Melvin. *Democracy & Diplomacy: The Impact of Domestic Politics on U.S. Foreign Policy, 1789–1994.* Small studies how domestic politics have affected U.S. diplomacy throughout American history, holding that "the central role of domestic politics in determining American foreign policy has changed little since Washington's day . . . and, if anything, has increased in potency and complexity" (2:126).

9:229　　Summers, Mark Wahlgren. *The Gilded Age, or, The Hazard of New Functions.* Upper Saddle River, NJ: Prentice-Hall, 1997. Emphasizing domestic over foreign issues, this revisionist account examines the men and women who tried to confront the challenges facing the nation in the Gilded Age. The label "the age of energy" better fits the era, Summers believes, and he tries to restore politics to its "right-

ful place" as the major shaping force in people's lives. Instead of a dark time of injustice, complacency, and shallow thinking, he finds a nation of creativity and idealism.

9:230　　Williams, R. Hal. *Years of Decision: American Politics in the 1890s.* New York: Wiley, 1978. This study of national politics synthesizes research on election patterns and presents the Republicans as activists who governed and the Democrats as negative.

Military Studies

OVERVIEWS

9:231　　Boemeke, Manfred F., Roger Chickering, and Stig Förster, eds. *Anticipating Total War: The German and American Experiences, 1871–1914.* New York: Cambridge University Press, 1999. This large collection of essays offers varied discussions of thoughts about warfare in the United States and Germany between 1871 and 1914, all pointing toward the protracted and cataclysmic wars to come and focusing on "the massive impact of changes in technology and social organization on the conduct of war as well as the impact of warfare on broader social, political, and cultural developments in the two lands." Most pertinent are Irmgard Steinisch, "Different Path to War: A Comparative Study of Militarism and Imperialism in the United States and Imperial Germany, 1871–1914"; Paul A. C. Koistinen, "Political Economy of Warfare in America, 1865–1914"; Bruce White, "War Preparations and Ethnic and Racial Relations in the United States"; David I. MacLeod, "Socializing American Youth to Be Citizen-Soldiers"; John Whiteclay Chambers II, "American Debate over Modern War, 1871–1914"; David F. Trask, "Military Imagination in the United States, 1815–1917"; and Robert M. Utley, "Total War on the American Indian Frontier."

9:232　　Hassler, Warren W., Jr. *With Shield and Sword: American Military Affairs, Colonial Times to the Present.* Ames, IA: Iowa State University Press, 1982. This is a comprehensive narrative of military operations, policy, and policymakers from colonial times to the contemporary era. Hassler emphasizes the persistent military unpreparedness of the United States and the unique ability of the nation to improvise for whatever exigency required military force.

9:233   Koistinen, Paul A. C. *Mobilizing for Modern War: The Political Economy of American Warfare, 1865–1919*. Lawrence: University Press of Kansas, 1997. The first third of this book traces late-nineteenth-century developments in the army and navy through the Spanish-American War. Koistinen believes the navy adjusted better than the army to the new era of industrial warfare and professionalization.

THE ARMY

9:234   Coffman, Edward M. *The Old Army: A Portrait of the American Army in Peacetime, 1784–1898*. New York: Oxford University Press, 1986. This is a comprehensive study of the U.S. army in the peacetime intervals between 1784 and 1898 and the experiences of the people who made up the various Old Armies. Coffman traces the army's evolution from its days of limited resources to the modern military age that began with the Spanish-American War.

9:235   Cooper, Jerry. *The Rise of the National Guard: The Evolution of the American Militia, 1865–1920*. Lincoln: University of Nebraska Press, 1997. This book explains the varied responses of guardsmen to the growing tension between the Guard's old social emphasis and the new demands of American foreign policy.

9:236   Hagan, Kenneth J., and William R. Roberts, eds. *Against All Enemies: Interpretations of American Military History from Colonial Times to the Present*. This is a useful series of essays covering American army history from colonial times to the post-Vietnam era. Two articles are pertinent for the last half of the nineteenth century: Jerry Cooper, "The Army's Search for a Mission, 1865–1890," and Roberts, "Reform and Revitalization, 1890–1903" (5:368).

9:237   Janda, Lance. "Shutting the Gates of Mercy: The American Origins of Total War, 1860–1880." *Journal of Military History* 59 (January 1995): 7–26. Seeing the doctrine of total warfare as revolutionary and anathema to codes of behavior developed during the Enlightenment, Janda argues that rather than originating in the Civil War it emerged as a weapon of choice on the western frontier in dealing with Native Americans. By 1880, total war dominated the mainstream of American military thought.

9:238   Reardon, Carol. *Soldiers and Scholars: The U.S. Army and the Uses of Military History, 1865–1920*. Lawrence: University Press of Kansas, 1990. Reardon focuses on the currents of professionalism that influenced the military after the Civil War, analyzing the rise of military education, army efforts to institutionalize the study of military history, and the relationship of officers to the handful of academics who showed interest in military history.

THE NAVY

9:239   Apt, Benjamin L. "Mahan's Forebears: The Debate over Maritime Strategy, 1868–1883." *Naval War College Review* 50 (Summer 1997): 86–111. Apt contends that by the time national politicians, the press, and corporations called for more U.S. assertiveness overseas, the "imperialist view" had already taken hold among advocates of the new navy. Through articles, lectures, debates, and formal organizations, navalists analyzed, praised, debated, and built on one another's arguments. Interest in technology was the leading impetus behind the lobbying efforts for an enlarged navy.

9:240   Bradford, James C., ed. *Admirals of the New Steel Navy: Makers of the American Naval Tradition, 1880–1930*. Annapolis: Naval Institute Press, 1990. This collection of biographical essays describes the important shapers of the new navy, the most significant naval builders of the new empire, and the most important contributors to the construction of a navy second to none. Most relevant are John B. Hattendorf, "Stephen B. Luce: Intellectual Leader of the New Navy" (3–23); Robert Seager II, "Alfred Thayer Mahan: Christian Expansionist, Navalist, and Historian" (24–72); Malcolm Muir, Jr., "French Ensor Chadwick: Reformer, Historian, and Outcast" (97–119); Benjamin Franklin Cooling, "Bradley Allen Fiske: Inventor and Reformer in Uniform" (120–45); Joseph G. Dawson III,

"William T. Sampson: Progressive Technologist as Naval Commander" (149–79); Harold D. Langley, "Winfield Scott Schley: The Confident Commander" (180–221); and Vernon L. Williams, "George Dewey: Admiral of the Navy" (222–49). Bibliography.

9:241 _____. *Captains of the Old Steam Navy: Makers of the American Naval Tradition, 1840–1880.* Annapolis: Naval Institute Press, 1986. This book contains biographical essays on prominent naval officers whose professional lives and collected careers sum up the diversity, vitality, and torpidity of the U.S. navy in the early, transitional age of steam. For the post–Civil War years, see Robert Erwin Johnson, "John Rodgers: The Quintessential Nineteenth Century Naval Officer" (253–74); Frederick C. Drake, "Robert Wilson Shufeldt: The Naval Officer as Commercial Expansionist and Diplomat" (275–300); and Dean C. Allard, "Benjamin Franklin Isherwood: Father of the Modern Steam Navy" (301–22).

9:242 Braisted, William Reynolds. "The Navy in the Early Twentieth Century, 1890–1941." In *A Guide to the Sources of United States Military History,* ed. Robin Higham, 344–77. Hamden, CT: Archon Books, 1975. Braisted focuses largely on politics and naval affairs, especially on the rationale for the new navy.

9:243 Buhl, Lance C. "Maintaining 'An American Navy,' 1865–1889." In *In Peace and War: Interpretations of American Naval History, 1775–1978,* ed. Kenneth J. Hagan, 145–73. Westport, CT: Greenwood Press, 1978. The post–Civil War navy, third-rate but more effective than many historians have admitted, was adequate for its defensive continental mission and its traditional aim of advancing commerce. Focusing narrowly on naval bills, the author demonstrates that Congress justifiably placed the navy toward the bottom of national priorities. This essay is unavailable in the second (1984) edition of this work.

9:244 Coletta, Paolo E. "The 'Nerves' of the New Navy." *American Neptune* 38 (April 1978): 122–30. Coletta considers communications developments in the modernizing navy between the 1870s and 1900.

9:245 Cooling, Benjamin Franklin. *Gray Steel and Blue Water Navy: The Formative Years of Amer-* ica's Military-Industrial Complex, 1881–1917. Hamden, CT: Archon Books, 1979. Cooling contends that the building of a modern navy initiated the institutional interaction that led to the military-industrial complex of today. He also argues that the requirements of the nation's new fleet were instrumental in the emergence of the steel industry. Contending that the symbiotic connection between private contractors and the navy developed impetus even earlier than Cooling believes is Kurt Hackemer, in *The U.S. Navy and the Origins of the Military-Industrial Complex, 1847–1883* (Annapolis: Naval Institute Press, 2001).

9:246 Dorwart, Jeffery M. *The Office of Naval Intelligence: The Birth of America's First Intelligence Agency, 1865–1918.* Annapolis: Naval Institute Press, 1979. This is a modest account of one important facet of the naval revolution of the late nineteenth century, demonstrating the navy's interest in more serious and professional capabilities.

9:247 Hagan, Kenneth J. *American Gunboat Diplomacy and the Old Navy, 1877–1889.* Westport, CT: Greenwood Press, 1973. This book argues that a well-established naval policy existed from the late 1870s. Global gunboat diplomacy by a navy consisting of commerce raiders, used to expand commerce as an index of national greatness, proved fundamental to nineteenth-century U.S. diplomacy. Hagan includes useful descriptions of technical issues and the ideas of officers such as Luce, Porter, and Shufeldt.

9:248 _____. *This People's Navy: The Making of American Sea Power.* New York: Free Press, 1991. This history covers 200 years of naval power, tracing the interaction of many variables that shaped the American people's navy. Chapter 6 surveys the post–Civil War years in which the navy seemed divided against itself, and chapter 7 the rise of the new navy.

9:249 Hattendorf, John B. "Luce's Idea of the Naval War College." *Naval War College Review* 37 (September-October 1984): 35–43. This article presents an overview of Luce's views on professional naval education. He insisted that a naval officer, more than just perform a job, carry out his work as a highly educated, trained specialist, with established procedures and ethical standards; he should use a highly developed body of theoretical knowledge and have a strong feeling of group identity.

9:250 _____, ed. *Mahan on Naval Strategy: Selections from the Writings of Rear Admiral Alfred Thayer Mahan.* Annapolis: Naval Institute Press, 1991. This is a selection of the key pieces in which Mahan presented his philosophy and basic arguments, including his initial attempt to form naval theory by linking it with military theory.

9:251   Herrick, Walter R., Jr. *The American Naval Revolution.* Baton Rouge: Louisiana State University Press, 1967. A revolution in naval doctrine and administration occurred around the early 1890s, after the appearance of the steel cruisers, which by 1898 transformed the weak postwar navy into a unified battle fleet. This book emphasizes the stewardship of Benjamin F. Tracy, due, in part, to his friendship with Benjamin Harrison.

9:252   Johnson, Robert Erwin. *Far China Station: The U.S. Navy in Asian Waters, 1800–1898.* Annapolis: Naval Institute Press, 1979. In this chronicle of the navy's multifarious activities in the eastern seas from 1819 to 1898 Johnson argues that most U.S. diplomatic achievements were the products of "jackal diplomacy" in which it simply claimed for itself what Britain or France had won by fighting. Initially Washington dispatched ships to Asia primarily to protect American merchants or transport its own diplomats. After 1860, the navy increasingly responded to missionaries' appeals as they moved further inland and away from more secure treaty ports.

9:253   Karsten, Peter. "The Nature of 'Influence': Roosevelt, Mahan, and the Concept of Sea Power." *American Quarterly* 23 (October 1971): 585–600. This careful analysis successfully challenges the accepted notion that Alfred T. Mahan significantly influenced Theodore Roosevelt, whose writings advocating naval preparedness antedated Mahan's—he "used" Mahan, and each had a role to play. The Young Turk navalists championed Mahan's work because it supported their views. In short, navalistic ideas were already circulating and influencing diplomats, politicians, and the navy itself.

9:254   Long, David F. *Gold Braid and Foreign Relations: Diplomatic Activities of U.S. Naval Officers, 1798–1883.* Long comprehensively chronicles all activities of U.S. naval officers influencing U.S. foreign relations from 1798 to 1883 (and succeeds Paullin, *Diplomatic Negotiations of American Naval Officers, 1778–1883* [1912] [6:49]) either as direct agents of the president or as decisionmakers who assumed authority in the absence of timely communication with government officials. He finds that sometimes patience and tact ruled the day, but all too often, arrogance, indiscretion, force, or the threat of force ruled (5:130).

9:255   Nicolosi, Anthony S. "The Founding of the Newport Naval Training Station, 1878–1883: An Exercise in Naval Politics." *American Neptune* 49 (Fall 1989): 291–304. Nicolosi discusses the founding of a naval training station at Newport, Rhode Island, which the author contends was a watershed in navy-government and navy–Rhode Island relations. Officers concerned with the sorry state of the navy and interested in modernization through a formal training system in the best possible location lobbied for a naval training station at Newport.

9:256   O'Connell, Robert L. *Sacred Vessels: The Cult of the Battleship and the Rise of the U.S. Navy.* Boulder: Westview Press, 1991. Reprint 1993 (Oxford University Press). This is a critical history of the modern battleship and its place in U.S. history. O'Connell concludes that battleships have never been the most effective naval weapon, but the early chapters show how they captured the hearts of the military and the imaginations of the public beginning in the 1880s.

9:257   Seager, Robert, II. "Ten Years before Mahan: The Unofficial Case for the New Navy, 1880–1890." *Mississippi Valley Historical Review* 40 (December 1953): 491–512. This important article analyzes the ideological concepts and contemporary political arguments used to remedy the navy's extreme weakness and describes efforts as early as the Hayes and Arthur administrations for naval development. Seager sees Mahan and Benjamin F. Tracy not as innovators but codifiers of ideas already current.

9:258   Shulimson, Jack. *The Marine Corps' Search for a Mission, 1880–1898.* Lawrence: University Press of Kansas, 1993. This is a study of the marine corps' connection to post–Civil War army concerns, the birth of the new navy, technological developments, partisan politics, and a changing foreign policy. Shulimson probes the connection between the corps and the search for order and rationality marking U.S. society in the late nineteenth century and examines the transformation of the corps from a structural anomaly to a modern organization with all the trappings of professionalism.

9:259 _____. "Military Professionalism: The Case of U.S. Marine Office Corps, 1880–1898." *Journal of Military History* 60 (April 1996): 231–42. The U.S. marine corps was an organizational anomaly in disarray in 1880. Reform-minded officers called for its resuscitation, and between 1880 and 1898 the marine corps underwent a metamorphosis from almost moribund to nearly professional. After a period of discord, marine officers eventually accommodated themselves to the challenges of the "new professionalism."

9:260 Shulman, Mark Russell. *Navalism and the Emergence of American Sea Power, 1882–1893.* Annapolis: Naval Institute Press, 1995. Examining the era of "the first major American peacetime military buildup," when the navy experienced fundamental changes in technology and doctrine, Shulman analyzes how navalists turned their efforts to "selling the navy" to the American public by stressing the heroic role it could play. He focuses on shifts in strategic doctrine and the political culture of modernization, concluding that officers of the new navy were more imperialistic and militant than their predecessors.

9:261 Spector, Ronald H. "The Triumph of Professional Ideology: The U.S. Navy in the 1890s." In *In Peace and War: Interpretations of American Naval History, 1775–1978*, ed. Kenneth J. Hagan, 174–85. Westport, CT: Greenwood Press, 1978. The 1890s saw a vindication of advocates of the battleship and command-of-the-sea strategy. The author discusses the impact of the ideas of Tracy, Luce, and Mahan, and of the new British battleship and a possible canal. Navy planners focused on defense against Britain to mid-1897, although Spain and Japan also received attention.

9:262 Sprout, Harold, and Margaret Sprout. *The Rise of American Naval Power, 1776–1918.* The Sprouts deal with the beginnings of the new navy,

providing a detailed analysis of the political setting, especially the situation in Congress. A third chapter puts Mahan in the context of the new Manifest Destiny. Originally published in 1939 (7:56).

9:263 Still, William N., Jr. *American Sea Power in the Old World: The United States Navy in European and Near Eastern Waters, 1865–1917.* Westport, CT: Greenwood Press, 1980. Still describes the activities of the European Squadron as well as provides biographical sketches of all its commanders.

9:264 Thiesen, William H. "Professionalization and American Naval Modernization in the 1880s." *Naval War College Review* 49 (Spring 1996): 33–49. Thiesen sees the 1880s as a turning point for the American navy—an end to the "dark ages" and the beginning of the "New Navy." The decade heralded the end of the commerce-raiding approach of the post–Civil War era and the beginning of open ocean fleet tactics. It also saw the professionalization of the officer and engineer corps and the rapid development of naval technology.

The Alaska Purchase

ALASKAN HISTORIES

9:265 Chevigny, Hector. *Russian America: The Great Alaskan Venture, 1741–1867.* This history surveys the exploration and settlement of Alaska, centers on the political and economic development of the Russian-American Company, and concludes with an analysis of Russian motives for ceding the territory (5:265).

9:266 Sherwood, Morgan B., ed. *Alaska and Its History.* Seattle: University of Washington Press, 1967. This collection of twenty-five previously published journal articles (most separately cited in this chapter) includes eight on the annexation period as well as articles on the era of Russian occupation and American settlement. Those of greatest interest deal with postpurchase matters: Ted C. Hinckley, "Sheldon Jackson and Benjamin Harrison" (293–314); Charles Soutter Campbell, "The Anglo-American

Crisis in the Bering Sea, 1890–1891" (315–42); Jeannette P. Nichols, "Advertising and the Klondike" (343–52); and L. H. Carlson, "The Discovery of Gold at Nome, Alaska" (353–82).

9:267   Tompkins, Stuart Ramsay. *Alaska, Promyshlennik and Sourdough.* Norman: University of Oklahoma Press, 1945. Tompkins's history of Alaska describes Russian and American efforts to exploit the resources of the territory. The short chapter on purchase negotiations stresses mutual economic advantages the treaty would bring to both nations.

THE ALASKA PURCHASE

9:268   Bailey, Thomas A. "Why the United States Purchased Alaska." *Pacific Historical Review* 3 (March 1934): 39–49. Bailey's analysis, resting on a survey of newspapers and congressional speeches, asserts that Americans' feeling of obligation to Russia for support during the Civil War aided passage of the Alaska treaty.

9:269   Bolkhovitinov, Nikolai N. "How It Was Decided to Sell Alaska." *International Affairs* (August 1988): 116–26. Claiming that the story of the sale of Alaska still awaits serious, unemotional, well-considered examination, the author relates the events of December 16, 1866, the day the Russians decided to sell Russian possessions in North America at a "special conference." All participants pronounced themselves unreservedly in favor of selling, and in "ceding its American possessions to the United States, Russia became the first European power to renounce its overseas colonies voluntarily."

9:270   Dunning, William A. "Paying for Alaska." *Political Science Quarterly* 27 (September 1912): 385–98. Dunning reopened speculation about the use of bribery to facilitate the Alaska appropriation, basing his article on the Andrew Johnson Papers.

9:271   Farrar, Victor J. *The Annexation of Russian America to the United States.* Washington, DC: W. F. Roberts Co., 1937. Farrar narrates but does little to analyze the negotiation process (1854–1868) that resulted in the Alaska cession.

9:272   Golder, Frank A. "The Purchase of Alaska." *American Historical Review* 25 (April 1920): 411–25. In this first study of the purchase based on Russian archival sources, Golder concludes that cordial Russian-American relations before 1867 greatly influenced the negotiation for Alaska.

9:273   Holbo, Paul S. *Tarnished Expansion: The Alaska Scandal, the Press, and Congress, 1867–1871.* Knoxville: University of Tennessee Press, 1983. Holbo describes the original investigations of the scandal by the press and Congress, claiming that the reaction to the Alaska scandal was even more important than the wrongdoing itself. The issue of corruption in the appropriation for Alaska tarnished the expansionists' efforts and placed substantial roadblocks in the path to imperialism.

9:274   Jensen, Ronald J. *The Alaska Purchase and Russian-American Relations.* Seattle: University of Washington Press, 1975. Jensen examines cession negotiations from their tentative beginnings in 1854 through the congressional appropriation debate of 1868. He analyzes the motives of both powers in the context of mid-nineteenth-century diplomacy and concludes that strategic interests in China and the North Pacific determined the actions of policymakers in Russia and the United States.

9:275   Keithahn, Edward L. "Alaska Ice, Inc." *Pacific Northwest Quarterly* 36 (April 1945): 121–32. Keithahn outlines the activities of the American Russian Commercial Company of San Francisco (1850–1869) and concludes that its profitable ice contracts with the Russians contributed to the pressure for cession, at least in California.

9:276   Luthin, Reinhard H. "The Sale of Alaska." *Slavonic and East European Review* 16 (Winter 1937): 168–82. Luthin traces the congressional appropriation for Alaska, rather than the cession itself, and gives special attention to the lobbying efforts of Robert J. Walker and to rumors of bribery.

9:277   Mazour, Anatole G. "The Prelude to Russia's Departure from America." *Pacific Historical Review* 10 (September 1941): 311–19. This interpretive essay emphasizes Russia's interest in devoting more attention to continental Asia as a prime factor in the decision to cede Alaska.

9:278 Reid, Virginia Hancock. *The Purchase of Alaska: Contemporary Opinion.* Long Beach, CA: Press-Telegram Printers, 1939. Reid surveys public opinion, primarily as expressed in contemporary American newspapers, and concludes that the purchase of Alaska was popular at the time despite the well-publicized references to "Seward's Folly."

9:279 Sherwood, Morgan B. "George Davidson and the Acquisition of Alaska." *Pacific Historical Review* 28 (May 1959): 141–54. Davidson explored Alaska for the U.S. government immediately after the treaty was signed. Although his report was intended to influence congressional passage of the Alaska appropriation, Sherwood finds its impact limited.

9:280 Shiels, Archibald Williamson. *The Purchase of Alaska.* College, AK: University of Alaska Press, 1967. The excerpts from documents, newspaper articles, and journals contained in this volume are loosely connected by the compiler's commentary. Created for centennial celebrations of the purchase.

9:281 Welch, Richard E., Jr. "American Public Opinion and the Purchase of Russian America." *American Slavic and East European Review* 17 (December 1958): 481–94. Welch surveys forty-eight newspapers across the United States published between April 1867 and July 1868 and concludes that press opinion supported the Alaskan cession, largely for economic reasons.

U.S. Foreign Relations with Other Countries and Areas

AFRICA

9:282 Duignan, Peter, and L. H. Gann. *The United States and Africa: A History.* Duignan and Gann examine the role of whalers, explorers, soldiers, miners, hunters, scientists, merchants, and missionaries through much of the southern part of the African continent and include brief discussions of early U.S. diplomatic contacts (2:255).

9:283 Franklin, John Hope. *George Washington Williams: A Biography.* Chicago: University of Chicago Press, 1985. Reprint 1988 (Duke University Press). This is an engaging biography of the often neglected nineteenth-century patriarch of African-American history. Franklin describes Williams's efforts to Christianize Africa and his devastating critique of Belgian imperialism in the Congo, which Franklin sees as a turning point in U.S.-African relations.

9:284 Jacobs, Sylvia M. *The African Nexus: Black American Perspectives on the European Partitioning of Africa, 1880–1920.* Westport, CT: Greenwood Press, 1981. Jacobs focuses on the attitude of American black intellectuals toward the European dismemberment of Africa. This opposition to European imperialism, according to the author, nurtured Pan-Africanism in America and a movement toward black cultural nationalism.

9:285 _____, ed. *Black Americans and the Missionary Movement in Africa.* Westport, CT: Greenwood Press, 1982. This book contains several essays related to the late nineteenth century: Sandy Dwayne Martin, "Black Baptists, Foreign Missions, and African Colonization, 1814–1882" (63–76); Walter L. Williams, "William Henry Sheppard, Afro-American Missionary in the Congo, 1890–1910" (135–54); Jacobs, "The Impact of Black American Missionaries in Africa" (219–25); and Jacobs, "Black Americans and the Missionary Movement in Africa: A Bibliography" (229–37).

9:286 Kennedy, Pagan. *Black Livingstone: A True Tale of Adventure in the Nineteenth-Century Congo.* New York: Viking, 2002. Kennedy describes the experiences and impressions of an African-American Presbyterian missionary, William Sheppard, who traveled in the Congo in the late nineteenth century. More devoted to improving lives than saving souls, he collected graphic evidence of the ghastly atrocities orchestrated by the Belgium colonial administration in pursuit of the Congo's rubber riches. His most significant contributions were the images of Africa he communicated at home in the United States, emphasizing Africa's cultural richness and the complexity of its societies to church members, anthropologists, big-game hunters, and politicians.

9:287 Meyer, Lysle E. *The Farther Frontier: Six*

Case Studies of Americans and Africa, 1848–1936. Selinsgrove, PA: Susquehanna University Press, 1992. Meyer examines six Americans who played important roles in Africa between 1848 and 1936, a missionary, explorer and writer, soldier-explorer, diplomat-lobbyist, mining engineer, and a taxidermist-naturalist. These biographical studies expand the picture of American activities in Africa and help explain the developing American image of Africa.

9:288 Pierson, Gerald J. "U.S. Consuls in Zanzibar and the Slave Trade, 1870–1890." *Historian* 55 (Autumn 1992): 53–68. Americans protested but did little to stop Zanzibar's slave trade because U.S. consuls, who were primarily businessmen, saw their primary duty as representing New England commercial houses, which wished to maintain and expand trade with eastern Africa. While the goods Zanzibar sold to the United States were produced by slaves, U.S. consuls feared that tampering with slavery might interfere with trade and profits. Antislavery efforts in Europe they saw as proof of efforts to squeeze out U.S. competition and British opposition to slavery as motivated more by commercial than humanitarian sentiments.

9:289 Skinner, Elliott P. *African Americans and U.S. Policy toward Africa, 1850–1924: In Defense of Black Nationality.* Washington, DC: Howard University Press, 1992. Written by a former U.S. ambassador, this monograph demonstrates that although African-Americans had "very limited power and prestige" with which to influence U.S. diplomacy, they used a variety of "formal and symbolic means" to shape policy toward Africa. Skinner focuses on Booker T. Washington, W. E. B. Du Bois, and Marcus Garvey and their educational, emigrationist, and religious movements.

MIDDLE AND NEAR EAST

9:290 Bryson, Thomas A. *American Diplomatic Relations with the Middle East, 1784–1975: A Survey.* See chapter 2 of this Guide (2:403).

9:291 _____. *Tars, Turks, and Tankers: The Role of the United States Navy in the Middle East, 1800–1979.* Bryson emphasizes the peacekeeping mission of the navy in diplomatic dealings with Arab states. While the bulk of this work deals with the era following World War II, the early chapters recount the navy's response to problems in the Mediterranean before the twentieth century (2:404).

9:292 Daniel, Robert L. *American Philanthropy in the Near East, 1820–1960.* In the context of an Arab cultural awakening, Daniel depicts U.S. experiences (including numerous hardships) in missionary activity, education, medicine, agriculture, technology, printing, and publishing from Albania and Bulgaria to central Persia. Nationalism sometimes deterred and sometimes stimulated American proselytizing and westernizing (6:272).

9:293 Goode, James F. "A Good Start: The First American Mission to Iran, 1883–1885." *Muslim World* 74 (April 1984): 100–18. Religious considerations inspired the establishment of diplomatic relations between the United States and Iran in 1883. However, America's first minister to Iran, Samuel Greene Wheeler Benjamin, envisioned more than merely protecting American missionaries. He encouraged understanding of Iranian society and culture, but he hoped most of all to expand U.S. commerce into Central Asia. Unfortunately, his open-minded views were ahead of their time.

9:294 Gordon, Leland James. *American Relations with Turkey, 1830–1930: An Economic Interpretation.* Philadelphia: University of Pennsylvania Press, 1932. This is a most important study of U.S.-Turkish relations as well as a pioneer study in U.S.–Middle East relations. While concentrating on economic relations, Gordon recognizes the missionary influence on policymaking.

9:295 Grabill, Joseph L. *Protestant Diplomacy and the Near East: Missionary Influence on American Policy, 1810–1927.* Minneapolis: University of Minnesota Press, 1971. Primarily concerned with the Wilson administration, Grabill discusses the vigorous missionary effort that by the late nineteenth century had created sizable evangelical and educational establishments in Turkey, Bulgaria, and Persia. He demonstrates how missionaries and their supporters tried to influence U.S. policy in the wake of local resistance or even attacks on missionaries. Extensive bibliography.

9:296 Kark, Ruth. *American Consuls in the Holy Land, 1832–1914.* Detroit: Wayne State University Press, 1994. Kark describes the economic and social transformation of Palestine as it changed from a place of secondary importance in the Ottoman empire to the focus of Europeans' attention, noting the increasingly influential role of U.S. consuls stemming from a significant growth in American trade. The U.S. agents established an American presence beyond humanitarian and philanthropic endeavors. Idealism and moralism determined the direction of policy and motivated the conduct of consuls in Jerusalem; U.S. support of a Jewish return to the Holy Land is deeply rooted in the nineteenth century.

9:297 Kuklick, Bruce. *Puritans in Babylon: The Ancient Near East and American Intellectual Life, 1880–1930.* Princeton: Princeton University Press, 1996. This book tells the complex story of the beginnings of American archaeology in the Near East. Kuklick explains how expeditions stimulated a struggle among wealthy sponsors, individual experts, museum directors, and university administrators.

9:298 Palmer, Michael A. *Guardians of the Gulf: A History of America's Expanding Role in the Persian Gulf, 1833–1992.* Palmer analyzes the roots of U.S. commitments to Persian Gulf security and identifies the milestones along the road to U.S. supremacy in the Gulf (2:427).

9:299 Sha'ban, Fuad. *Islam and Arabs in Early American Thought: Roots of Orientalism in America.* Sha'ban contends that the commitments and assumptions of nineteenth-century American intellectuals, derived from religion and literature, helped shape U.S. attitudes. The evolution of America's cultural attitudes corresponded to its growth as a commercial power with contacts in the Mediterranean and Islamic worlds (6:279).

9:300 Vogel, Lester I. *To See a Promised Land: Americans and the Holy Land in the Nineteenth Century.* In a book about Americans and the Holy Land, Vogel focuses on "five recurrent points of American contact . . . American tourists/pilgrims, American missionaries, American settlers/colonists, American explorers/archaeologists/biblical scholars, and American diplomats." Extensive bibliography (6:281).

EUROPE AND CANADA

Great Britain and Ireland

9:301 Anderson, Stuart. *Race and Rapprochement: Anglo-Saxonism and Anglo-American Relations, 1895–1904.* Rutherford, NJ: Fairleigh Dickinson University Press, 1981. This attempts to isolate Anglo-Saxonism as the most crucial rationale and force for the diplomatic rapprochement between Great Britain and the United States at the close of the nineteenth century. Anderson concludes that without the shared acceptance of this doctrine, an easing of tensions and an Anglo-American accord could not have occurred.

9:302 Blake, Nelson M. "The Olney-Pauncefote Treaty of 1897." *American Historical Review* 50 (January 1945): 228–43. This essay describes the origins of a pioneering agreement to submit controversies between Britain and the United States to arbitration. This search for a substitute for force in international relations was defeated by "agrarians suspicious of the intrigues of Wall Street, Anglophobes, and legislators jealous of senatorial power."

9:303 Brown, Thomas M. *Irish-American Nationalism, 1870–1890.* Philadelphia: Lippincott, 1966. Synthesizing the history of home rule and the Land League, Brown focuses on the importance of the American milieu in shaping Irish-American political behavior. Of the two most important forces in Irish-American history, Irish nationalism and the search for social justice, he concludes that the former was the more powerful force.

9:304 Campbell, Charles Soutter. "The Anglo-American Crisis in the Bering Sea, 1890–1891." *Mississippi Valley Historical Review* 48 (December 1961): 393–414. In analyzing the steps to the modus vivendi reached by Blaine and Salisbury in 1891, Campbell emphasizes the influence of Henry W. Elliott, an American naturalist.

9:305 _____. "The Dismissal of Lord Sackville." *Mississippi Valley Historical Review* 44 (March 1958): 635–48. In this thorough study of the decision by Cleveland's administration to dismiss the British minister in 1888, Campbell finds the hastiness of the dismissal discreditable, for which he blames Edward Phelps, the U.S. minister in London.

9:306   Cook, Adrian. *The Alabama Claims: American Politics and Anglo-American Relations, 1865–1872.* Cook examines the settlement of the *Alabama* claims as well as several other problems plaguing Anglo-American relations in the post–Civil War period. Secretary of State Hamilton Fish's reputation, he holds, cannot be based on his performance in the *Alabama* claims negotiations; U.S. success owed more to luck or Britain's desire to settle the issue than to astute diplomacy (8:302).

9:307   Crapol, Edward P. *America for Americans: Economic Nationalism and Anglophobia in the Late Nineteenth Century.* Westport, CT: Greenwood Press, 1973. Crapol contends that anglophobia in late-nineteenth-century America originated in economic competition and that the U.S. search for markets induced strident anti-British feelings and policy.

9:308   Dashew, Doris W. "The Story of an Illusion: The Plan to Trade the '*Alabama*' Claims for Canada." As a spirit of "Manifest Destiny" resurfaced after the Civil War, most expansionist attention focused on acquiring Canada, causing the idea of its annexation in exchange for the monetary claims resulting from British actions during the war for Canada to take seed and grow, precluding consideration of other modes of settlement. This idea was only abandoned when domestic and international concerns made amiable reconciliation with Great Britain necessary (8:303).

9:309   Davis, J. C. Bancroft. *Mr. Fish and the Alabama Claims: A Chapter in Diplomatic History.* Boston: Houghton Mifflin, 1893. Davis, the assistant secretary of state under Fish, contends in this brief narrative of the negotiations and arbitration of the *Alabama* claims that approval of the U.S. initial, gigantic claims for indemnity would have proved dangerous to it as a neutral in the future.

9:310   DeRosier, Arthur H., Jr. "The Settlement of the San Juan Controversy." *Southern Quarterly* 4 (October 1965): 74–88. The author, tracing the dispute from its origins in the Oregon Treaty of 1846 through its settlement by German arbitration in 1872, shows that this was the only U.S. boundary matter

ever resolved by a disinterested party. It also signified the growth of Anglo-American friendship and an increased sense of maturity in the Department of State.

9:311   Edwards, Owen Dudley. "American Diplomats and Irish Coercion, 1880–1883." *Journal of American Studies* 1 (October 1967): 213–32. Edwards presents U.S. views of the Anglo-Irish crisis through the reactions of its diplomats in the 1880s. Soon Charles Stewart Parnell would begin holding mass meetings in the United States to rally financial and moral support from Irish-Americans for his crusade against the prevailing Irish land system.

9:312   Grenville, J. A. S. *Lord Salisbury and Foreign Policy: The Close of the Nineteenth Century.* London: University of London, Athlone Press, 1964. This account of the diplomatic history of the years of Lord Salisbury's last administration as prime minister and foreign minister, 1895–1902, features many of the most serious Anglo-American misunderstandings, primarily the Venezuela boundary dispute.

9:313   Libby, Justin H. "Hamilton Fish and the Origins of Anglo-American Solidarity." *Mid-America* 76 (Fall 1994): 205–26. Hamilton Fish as diplomat illustrates the maxim that "some men have greatness thrust upon them." Libby demonstrates that his intellectual and diplomatic growth, patience, resolve, and attention to detail brought about a reconciliation between the United States and Britain by settling the *Alabama* claims; he lauds Fish for creating Anglo-American cordiality in a quiet, conciliatory way.

9:314   McCabe, James O. *The San Juan Water Boundary Question.* British officials in the Washington negotiations unnecessarily sacrificed a strong Canadian claim by agreeing to exclude from the discussions the "Middle Channel," an area that could have been included because of the ambiguity of the Oregon Treaty of 1846 (6:374).

9:315   Orde, Anne. *The Eclipse of Great Britain: The United States and British Imperial Decline, 1895–1956.* New York: St. Martin's Press, 1996. Orde links the global ascent of the United States and the decline of Britain as a world power. This is a study of the process of the replacement of the one power by the other and how this transformation was perceived at the time on both sides of the Atlantic.

9:316   Robson, Maureen M. "The *"Alabama"* Claims and the Anglo-American Reconciliation, 1865–71." *Canadian Historical Review* 42 (March 1961): 1–22. Robson contends the conflict over Confederate cruisers encompassed more than the issues of law on which a settlement was based. The *Alabama* claims involved every dispute between Britain and the United States between 1862 and 1872, and thus settlement by arbitration at Geneva closed a difficult period in Anglo-American relations. British diplomats and politicians considered settlement in light of wider pressures and concluded that more was at stake than merely points of law or national prestige.

9:317   Sewell, Mike. "'All the English-Speaking Race Is in Mourning': The Assassination of President Garfield and Anglo-American Relations." *Historical Journal* 34 (September 1991): 665–86. This article explains how public rituals reveal and dramatize solidarities or tensions in international relationships. Sewell suggests that analysis of public ceremonies can yield valuable insights for diplomatic historians, seeing in the outpouring of British sentiment about Garfield's death an emerging sense of cordiality in Anglo-American relations.

9:318   _____. "Political Rhetoric and Policy-Making: James G. Blaine and Britain." *Journal of American Studies* 24 (April 1990): 61–84. Sewell finds gaps between Blaine's reputation as an anglophobe and his failure to act like one when in office and between his rhetoric and practice as secretary of state in 1881. For Blaine and many contemporary politicians, public twisting of the lion's tail was instinctive, yet too many historians have failed to understand that Blaine's antagonistic rhetoric did not result in violently anti-British policies. Strong anglophobic rhetoric coexisted with strategic pressures for cooperation.

9:319   Smith, Goldwin. *The Treaty of Washington 1871: A Study in Imperial History.* Ithaca: Cornell University Press, 1941. In this scholarly study—especially useful for British and Canadian viewpoints on the treaty—arbitration, reciprocity, boundaries, and fisheries all receive full treatment.

9:320   Tate, Merze. "British Opposition to the Cession of Pearl Harbor." *Pacific Historical Review* 29 (November 1960): 381–94. The British admiralty believed the harbor was the only suitable one in case of war. The 1887 revolution in Hawaii cleared the way for American ownership of Pearl Harbor, but by then London was no longer concerned with the matter.

9:321   Willson, Beckles. *America's Ambassadors to England (1785–1929): A Narrative of Anglo-American Diplomatic Relations.* This contains portraits of forty official representatives to Great Britain since independence. In attitude, contacts, and experiences, the author sees them as a breed apart from the rest of the diplomatic corps—five became president and ten became secretaries of state, and all were "practical men" (6:201).

9:322   _____. *Friendly Relations: A Narrative of Britain's Ministers and Ambassadors to America (1791–1930).* Boston: Little, Brown, and Company, 1934. Using transcriptions from Foreign Office correspondence, this volume describes thirty eminent diplomatic representatives from Britain to the United States. Willson believes each acquitted himself according to his temper, instructions, and the peculiar circumstances of the time, and each personified Britain in America.

France

9:323   Blumenthal, Henry. *American and French Culture, 1800–1900: Interchanges in Art, Science, Literature, and Society.* This interdisciplinary study—with chapters covering literature, theater, music, dance, painting, sculpture, architecture, medicine, science, religion, and philosophy—provides an "overall picture of the social and cultural contacts and interactions of Americans and Frenchmen throughout the nineteenth century," contending that such contacts were a vital part of the U.S.-French connection (6:203).

9:324   _____. *France and the United States: Their Diplomatic Relation, 1789–1914.* This survey of U.S.-French relations contends that the idea of their historic friendship embodies both myth and reality. "In spite of many frictions and controversies, France and the United States have always managed to restore the kind of harmony and understanding characteristic of close members of an occasionally quar-relling family" (2:317).

9:325 _____. *A Reappraisal of Franco-American Relations, 1830–1871.* This study of mid-nineteenth-century Franco-American relations holds that "contrary to popular notions, the relations between the two countries were not friendly." Ideo-logical and religious differences, conflicts concern-ing the balance of power, ramifications of industri-alization, and factors beyond anyone's control "led to a growing estrangement between Paris and Wash-ington." The last three chapters cover the Civil War, the Maximilian affair, and Franco-Prussian War (6:205).

9:326 Clifford, Dale. "Elihu Benjamin Wash-burne: An American Diplomat in Paris, 1870–71." *Prologue* 2 (Winter 1970): 161–74. This article inves-tigates the efforts of the U.S. minister to France dur-ing a volatile period of French history, even though he had sought the post primarily because of its lack of activity. Unfortunately, the Franco-Prussian War and the Paris Commune of 1871 both interfered with a leisurely posting. The article relates Washburne's pro-German sentiment, his general success in protecting American citizens and property, and his inability to analyze the French political environment.

9:327 Dougherty, Patricia. *American Diplomats and the Franco-Prussian War: Perceptions from Paris and Berlin.* Washington, DC: Institute for the Study of Diplomacy, Georgetown University, 1980. This is a brief account of U.S. diplomats' perceptions of the conflict between France and Prussia.

9:328 Gould, Lewis L. "Diplomats in the Lobby: Franco-American Relations and the Dingley Tariff of 1897." *Historian* 39 (August 1977): 659–80. This ar-ticle, based on multiarchival research, demonstrates the connection between bimetallism and tariff mak-ing. Intense negotiations occurred between French diplomats and American senators, who used reci-procity to obtain French cooperation on bimetallism. A search for foreign markets was only a secondary factor behind reciprocity in 1897. The author also finds considerable French interest and involvement in the McKinley and Wilson-Gorman tariffs.

9:329 Gray, Walter D. *Interpreting American*

Democracy in France: The Career of Édouard Laboulaye, 1811–1883. This is a biography of France's leading historian and exponent of American ideals and institutions after Alexis de Tocqueville. He favored the Union during the Civil War, attacked the institution of slavery, supported women's rights, and led the drive for the Statue of Liberty (6:208).

9:330 Levenstein, Harvey A. *Seductive Journey: American Tourists in France from Jefferson to the Jazz Age.* Levenstein demonstrates that being a tourist is not necessarily the best way to understand foreign people since tourists are looking mostly to their own improvement. This book shows why and how American tourists came to constitute the bulk of tourism in France (2:320).

9:331 Portes, Jacques. *Fascination and Misgiv-ings: The United States in French Opinion, 1870–1914.* Translated by Elborg Forster. New York: Cambridge University Press, 2000. Through the views of French travelers and French studies of North Amer-ica, the United States "became increasingly present in French opinion" and achieved a pivotal place in its consciousness by the second half of the nineteenth century. The French saw an economic power emerg-ing on the international stage, found attractive models in U.S. schools and universities, and hoped to emulate the development of a middle class and the indepen-dence of women. By World War I, the United States had a large place in French public opinion.

9:332 Washburne, Elihu B. *Recollections of a Minister to France, 1869–1877.* 2 vols. New York: C. Scribner's Sons, 1887. With Volume 1 covering the years 1869 to 1871 and Volume 2, 1869 to 1877, Washburne recounts his eight years as minister to France. He details his personal experiences and minis-terial duties involved in the declaration of the Franco-Prussian War, expulsion of Germans from France, fall of the Bonaparte dynasty, declaration of the French Republic, U.S. recognition of the new French govern-ment, the armistice ending the war, rise of the Paris commune, political instability and anarchy, restoration of peace, and Washburne's return to the United States.

9:333 Willson, Beckles. *America's Ambassadors to France (1777–1927): A Narrative of Franco-American Diplomatic Relations.* Willson provides short biographical and character sketches of each

American minister and ambassador to France, suggesting they were selected for their character and ability, service to their party, favorable inclination toward France, and wealth and social class. While many proved to be distinguished envoys, they were rarely professionals (4:241).

Spain

9:334   Cortada, James W. "Diplomatic Rivalry between Spain and the United States over Chile and Peru, 1864–1871." *Inter-American Economic Affairs* 27 (Spring 1974): 47–57. Secretary of State Seward endeavored to get his diplomats in Europe and Latin America to work toward peaceful resolution of crises in Chile and Peru, but Spain rejected Washington's mediation efforts. Many Latin Americans were embittered when the United States failed to help the Chileans defend the port of Valparaiso against a Spanish bombardment in 1866.

9:335   _____. *Spain and the American Civil War: Relations at Mid-Century, 1855–1868.* Cortada contends that "friendlier relations between Madrid and Washington . . . were an impossible dream" because both "competed for dominance in the New World and each wanted to govern Cuba." This is volume 70, pt. 4 of the *Transactions of the American Philosophical Society* (8:450).

9:336   _____. *Two Nations over Time: Spain and the United States, 1776–1977.* Cortada describes the important cultural and diplomatic relationship between the United States and Spain. This book contains two chapters on cultural relations, a useful list of envoys sent by each nation to the other, and a helpful bibliographic essay. It is a valuable review of the importance of the bilateral relationship, prejudices and misconceptions included (2:338).

Germany

9:337   Herwig, Holger H. *Politics of Frustration: The United States in German Naval Planning, 1889–1941.* Boston: Little, Brown, 1976. This work examines the basis for an impending German-American naval war through the eyes of German naval planners.

9:338   Jonas, Manfred. *The United States and Germany: A Diplomatic History.* This is an overview of German-American relations (2:308).

9:339   Rinke, Stefan H. "The German Ambassador Hermann Speck von Sternburg and Theodore Roosevelt, 1889–1908." *Theodore Roosevelt Association Journal* 17 (Winter 1991): 2–12. This extremely brief summary provides background information about Sternburg's life and career and explores some of the reasons why friendship with Roosevelt was possible.

9:340   Schieber, Clara Eve. *The Transformation of American Sentiment toward Germany, 1870–1914.* Boston: Cornhill Publishing Company, 1923. The U.S. government and American public opinion were sympathetic toward Germany during the Franco-Prussian conflict of 1870–1871, and Schieber examines how this sympathy changed to hostility by 1917.

9:341   Stolberg-Wernigerode, Otto. *Germany and the United States of America during the Era of Bismarck.* Translated by Otto E. Lessing. Reading, PA: Henry Janssen Foundation, 1937. This survey reconstructs German-American relations during their rise as world powers. It attributes the rising tension between them to competitive economic expansion.

9:342   Vagts, Alfred. "Hopes and Fears of an American-German War, 1870–1915 I." *Political Science Quarterly* 54 (December 1939): 514–35. This extended essay, in two parts, is an illuminating discussion of naval leaders' thoughts on both sides of the Atlantic. See also "Hopes and Fears of an American-German War, 1870–1915 II" (1940) (9:343).

9:343   _____. "Hopes and Fears of an American-German War, 1870–1915 II." *Political Science Quarterly* 55 (March 1940): 53–76. See Vagts, "Hopes and Fears of an American-German War, 1870–1915 I" (1939) (9:342) for annotation.

Russia

9:344   Carstensen, Fred V. *American Enterprise in Foreign Markets: Studies of Singer and International Harvester in Imperial Russia.* Chapel Hill: University of North Carolina Press, 1984. This book presents an organizational history of management procedures, labor relations, and marketing strategies within the Singer and International Harvester companies operating in Russia under the last czars.

9:345   Griffin, Frederick C. "Protesting Despotism: American Opposition to the U.S.-Russian Extradition Treaty of 1887." *Mid-America* 70 (April-July 1988): 91–99. This article contends that Americans became highly critical of czarist despotism by the late 1880s, reflected in widespread protests directed against an extradition treaty concluded in 1887. Americans were most offended by the treaty's definitions of political offenses and political crimes.

9:346   Healy, Ann E. "Tsarist Anti-Semitism and Russian-American Relations." *Slavic Review* 42 (Fall 1983): 408–25. Czarist policies toward Jews were the major irritant in otherwise comparatively harmonious U.S. relations with Russia. Recurring diplomatic disputes over Jewish issues centered largely on individual Russian acts of discrimination against Americans, many naturalized citizens of Russian origin and mostly Jews. Healy concludes that U.S. responses were motivated not only by humanitarian matters, but also concern about how Jewish immigrants affected the U.S. labor market, wages, urban poverty, and domestic antisemitism.

9:347   Jensen, Ronald J. "The Politics of Discrimination: America, Russia and the Jewish Question, 1869–1872." *American Jewish History* 75 (March 1986): 280–95. Jensen counters the view that failure in its first attempts to change Russian policy toward Jews caused Washington later to protest only in response to a rising tide of Jewish immigration. The Grant administration twice tried ending religious persecution, provoking angry reactions from the Russian government. Although Grant's actions failed to help Jews in Russia, they reveal much about the emerging role of Jews in American politics and attitudes of American policymakers toward them.

9:348   Saul, Norman E. *Concord and Conflict: The United States and Russia, 1867–1914.* Lawrence: University Press of Kansas, 1996. Saul covers the period from the sale of Alaska to the beginning of World War I, exploring the flow and fluctuation of bilateral economic, diplomatic, social, and cultural re-

lations as well as the evolution of each nation's perceptions of the other. He recounts the historic turn from friendship to hostility in Russian-American relations that began in the 1890s.

9:349   _____. *Distant Friends: The United States and Russia, 1763–1867.* This study surveys Russian-American relations from the earliest contact to the transfer of Alaska, describing commercial intercourse, cultural exchange, international politics, and diplomacy. Saul concludes that an absence of conflicting vital interests and common feelings of Manifest Destiny and anglophobia promoted harmonious relations (2:310).

9:350   Saul, Norman E., and Richard D. McKinzie, eds. *Russian-American Dialogue on Cultural Relations, 1776–1914.* Essays here mainly explore U.S.-Russian cultural and intellectual relations from the American revolution to World War I, including G. P. Kuropiatnik, "Russians in the United States: Social, Cultural, and Scientific Contacts in the 1870s" (with a comment by Ronald J. Jensen); I. P. Dement'ev, "Leo Tolstoy and Social Critics in the United States at the Turn of the Century"; and A. F. Tsvirkun, "Some Questions on American Foreign Policy in 1898–1914 in the Russian Bourgeois Press" (with comment by Saul) (6:245).

9:351   Vevier, Charles. "The Collins Overland Line and American Continentalism." *Pacific Historical Review* 28 (August 1959): 237–53. Vevier describes the efforts of Perry McDonough Collins to establish a telegraph line between the United States and Russia via Russian America. The line failed but the enterprise called American attention to the strategic value of Alaska as a commercial link to Asia.

9:352   Willis, James F. "An Arkansan in St. Petersburg: Clifton Rodes Breckinridge, Minister to Russia, 1894–1897." *Arkansas Historical Quarterly* 38 (Spring 1979): 3–31. Willis finds the only Arkansan ever to represent the United States as minister at a major nineteenth-century European capital, Clifton Rodes Breckinridge, was "one of the ablest American diplomats of his era." A thoughtful reporter and observer, he analyzed U.S. interests within the context of European rivalries, recognized the beginning of a fundamental shift in American-Russian relations, and urged appropriate adjustments in policy.

Central and Eastern Europe

9:353 Best, Gary Dean. *To Free a People: American Jewish Leaders and the Jewish Problem in Eastern Europe, 1890–1914.* Westport, CT: Greenwood Press, 1982. Best describes the efforts of the Jewish lobby to improve conditions for Jews in Eastern Europe and preserve America as a haven for refugees. He uncovers a connection between prominent American Jewish leaders and the makers of U.S. foreign policy in the formation of immigration policy as well as attempts to alleviate oppressive political and economic conditions for Jews in Russia and Romania.

9:354 Jensen, Ronald J. "Eugene Schuyler and the Balkan Crisis." *Diplomatic History* 5 (Winter 1981): 23–37. This article assesses the role of one of America's first Russian experts, a legation secretary, linguist, scholar, and journalist who helped shape the diplomacy of the Eastern Question in 1876 and whose actions "resulted in a significant contribution toward developing European diplomacy." Schuyler intervened in a political campaign in Britain, promoted the nationalist movement in Bulgaria, helped implement Russia's Balkan policy, and participated in an international summit conference.

9:355 Moss, Kenneth. "The United States and Central Europe, 1861–1871: Some American Approaches to National Development and the Balance of Power." *Historian* 39 (February 1977): 248–69. American policymakers used antebellum ideas about the U.S. role in international affairs as a point of reference in developing policies toward Central Europe, with U.S. diplomats working primarily to get Europeans to recognize U.S. interests.

9:356 Petrovich, Michael B. "Eugene Schuyler and Bulgaria, 1876–1878." *Bulgarian Historical Review* 7 (Fall 1979): 51–69. This article describes the actions of the experienced U.S. consul-general at Istanbul during the nine-month uprising of Bulgarians, October 1878–June 1879. Motivated by sincere sympathy for Bulgaria and hope for its "resurrection," Schuyler collaborated with his friendly Russian counterpart to expose Turkish atrocities, draft a proposed constitution for an autonomous Bulgaria, and draw attention to and win support for the Bulgarian movement for national and social liberation. Unsur-

prisingly, his actions caused problems for U.S. relations with Turkey, which cited the Monroe Doctrine in an effort to embarrass Schuyler and his government. The enmity of the Ottomans ultimately cost him his diplomatic career.

Canada

9:357 Bogue, Margaret Beattie. "To Save the Fish: Canada, the United States, the Great Lakes, and the Joint Commission of 1892." *Journal of American History* 79 (March 1993): 1429–54. This article focuses on the activities of a joint Anglo-American commission, acting on behalf of conservation-conscious Canadians and Americans, that investigated the fisheries in the contiguous waters of the two nations and after four years recommended regulations to save the fish of all Canadian-U.S. waters, especially those of the Great Lakes. Neither of the North American governments responded positively, but the Joint Commission of 1892 illuminates early efforts to conserve shared natural resources in the western world.

9:358 Bothwell, Robert. *Canada and the United States: The Politics of Partnership.* New York: Twayne Publishers, 1992. This book offers fresh insights on the complex and highly developed U.S.-Canada relationship. Bothwell reviews nineteenth-century diplomacy but provides an especially impressive study of the decades after 1945.

9:359 Brown, Robert C. *Canada's National Policy, 1883–1900: A Study in Canadian-American Relations.* Princeton: Princeton University Press, 1964. The fisheries, pelagic sealing, and Alaska boundary disputes are thoroughly canvassed in this study, which rests on exhaustive investigation of archives and printed documents. Brown finds Canadian nationalism maturing during this period of British-American negotiations over Canadian questions. Extensive bibliography.

9:360 Busch, Briton Cooper. *The War against the Seals: A History of the North American Seal Fishery.* Kingston, Ontario: McGill-Queen's University Press, 1985. This work documents the quest for profits and the slaughters by North American sealers who hunted in the world's oceans and seas. Busch aims to understand and analyze the growth and development of the industry and its impact. He deals with the curbing of pelagic sealing in the late nineteenth century.

9:361 Campbell, Charles Soutter. "American Tariff Interests and the Northeastern Fisheries, 1883–1888." *Canadian Historical Review* 45 (September 1964): 212–28. Campbell praises the Cleveland administration, even though "burdened by a presidential election year, harassed by the forces of protection," for overcoming "a dangerous state of affairs in the cold waters of the northeastern fisheries." Protracted negotiations to establish a joint commission led to agreement in 1887, but prospects for its success were not bright since Congress was hostile.

9:362 DeRosier, Arthur H., Jr. "Importance in Failure: The Fenian Raids of 1866–1871." *Southern Quarterly* 3 (April 1965): 181–97. During the late 1860s, Fenian activities in Canada increased problems for those trying to resolve the *Alabama* claims dispute, fisheries' matter, San Juan question, and Manitoba-Dakota boundary issue. The Fenians also stirred up Canadian annexationists in the United States, which ironically heightened Canadian nationalism.

9:363 Gay, James Thomas. *American Fur Seal Diplomacy: The Alaskan Fur Seal Controversy.* New York: Peter Lang, 1987. This book deals with the diplomacy of the Alaskan fur seal arbitration.

9:364 Gluek, Alvin C., Jr. *Minnesota and the Manifest Destiny of the Canadian Northwest: A Study in Canadian-American Relations.* Toronto: University of Toronto Press, 1965. This regional study focuses on the Red River Valley as the economic and physical link between the two nations (1821–1870).

9:365 _____. "The Riel Rebellion and Canadian-American Relations." *Canadian Historical Review* 36 (September 1955): 199–221. Gluek describes and analyzes the U.S. reaction to an insurrection in Rupert's Land, which Americans chose to interpret as a sign of disaffection within the dominion. Expansionists' hopes to detach the Canadian northwest through the uprising proved stronger than Canadian dissatisfaction with British North American rule.

9:366 Jenkins, Brian. *Fenians and Anglo-American Relations during Reconstruction.* Ithaca: Cornell University Press, 1969. The second half of this detailed narrative of British and Canadian diplomatic reactions to Fenian plots focuses on the activities of the Irish-American nationalist organization known as the Fenian Brotherhood, including during Reconstruction. The British government thought the United States should do more to restrain the Irish "Dynamiters"—especially when many of the Fenians' plots seemed to have been formulated in New York. Despite heightened emotions, both nations' determination to avert war prevailed, and by 1871 "Fenianism was obviously a spent force."

9:367 Martin, Lawrence. *The Presidents and the Prime Ministers: Washington and Ottawa Face to Face: The Myth of Bilateral Bliss, 1867–1982.* Garden City, NY: Doubleday, 1982. The author, a former Washington correspondent, has isolated distinguishable eras in the history of U.S.-Canadian bilateral interaction, contending that it has been characterized by American imperiousness and indifference, threats and contempt, and Canadian ingratitude caused by incapacity to appreciate the benefits of living so close to the United States.

9:368 Preston, Richard A. *The Defence of the Undefended Border: Planning for War in North America, 1867–1939.* Montreal: McGill-Queen's University Press, 1977. Preston catalogs the politicians and journalists who joined army officers in thinking about and planning for war across the Canadian-American border after the Treaty of Washington, studying invasion plans and the unlikely prospects of success in case of war. Considerations of military resources, problems of distance and the climate, questions about public support, and the possibility of British intervention "probably suggested to thoughtful people . . . that war would be a very uncertain means of achieving political objectives."

9:369 Senior, Hereward. *The Last Invasion of Canada: The Fenian Raids, 1866–1870.* Toronto: Dundurn Press, 1991. Senior provides an account of the Fenian border incursions into Canada between 1866 and 1870. The Fenians hoped to use conquered territory to pressure England out of Ireland, and Senior holds that most Fenian soldiers were discharged Irish-American veterans of the Civil War.

9:370 Shi, David E. "Seward's Attempt to Annex British Columbia, 1865–1869." *Pacific Historical Review* 47 (May 1978): 217–38. This careful analytical treatment of Seward's attempt to annex British Columbia confirms his commercial orientation and offers a connection to the Alaska purchase and *Alabama* claims negotiations. While Seward responded to the unstable political situation in British Columbia, he ultimately concluded that most Americans were too preoccupied with Reconstruction to consider territorial expansion. He also underestimated the vitality of Canadian nationalism.

9:371 Shippee, Lester B. *Canadian-American Relations, 1849–1874.* This basic study of Canadian-American relations describes the decision by Canadians and Americans to pursue separate yet friendly ways and national destinies. Shippee examines how Canadians assumed greater independence toward both the United States and Great Britain (8:347).

9:372 Stuart, Reginald C. *United States Expansionism and British North America, 1775–1871.* This work describes "the cultural dynamics behind America's external relations with . . . British North Americans on the northern frontier of the United States." Seeing U.S. expansionism as "a broad phenomenon with cultural, demographic, diplomatic, economic, ideological, political, and territorial ramifications," Stuart covers the creation and growth of the borderlands area as well as popular attitudes toward the possible acquisition of British North America by the United States (4:74).

9:373 Tansill, Charles Callan. *Canadian-American Relations, 1875–1911.* New Haven: Yale University Press, 1943. Tansill examines a series of difficult controversies and seemingly unsolvable problems involving international law—fisheries, fur-seal hunting, the Alaskan boundary—and the tariff and other commercial arrangements. Settlement of these long-standing disputes laid the foundation for cordial relations between the United States and Canada.

9:374 Tate, Merze. "Canada's Interest in the Trade and Sovereignty of Hawaii." *Canadian Historical Review* 44 (March 1963): 20–42. With the completion of the Canadian Pacific Railroad, the islands were an ideal link in a Liverpool to Australia route

and would serve as a good landing area for a cable between the two regions.

9:375 Thompson, John Herd, and Stephen J. Randall. *Canada and the United States: Ambivalent Allies.* The authors balance traditional diplomatic, military, and economic aspects of the generally amiable and complex Canadian-American relationship with attention to cultural, demographic, and environmental issues (2:306). First published in 1994.

9:376 Warner, Donald F. *The Idea of Continental Union: Agitation for the Annexation of Canada to the United States, 1849–1893.* This monograph attempts to assess the strength of the continental union movement in Canada from its "real beginnings" in the 1840s to 1893, when persistent failure and growing Canadian nationalism finally "settled the question." U.S. efforts at annexation are relegated to a supporting role (6:350).

Others

9:377 Bowman, Larry W. "The United States and Mauritius, 1794–1994: A Bicentennial Retrospective." *American Neptune* 56 (Spring 1996): 145–62. Bowman surveys the duties of consuls on this island in the Indian Ocean, and concludes they maintained generally amicable diplomatic relations with trade issues dominating.

9:378 Meier, Heinz K. *The United States and Switzerland, in the Nineteenth Century.* This study traces the generally friendly relations that existed between these two nations to the outbreak of World War I (2:340).

9:379 Smith, David A. "From the Mississippi to the Mediterranean: The 1891 New Orleans Lynching and Its Effects on United States Diplomacy and the American Navy." *Southern Historian* 19 (Spring 1998): 60–85. Smith recounts the repercussions of nativist tensions, mob violence, and vigilante justice in New Orleans's Italian community in 1891. The lynching of eleven men found not guilty of murdering the police superintendent "directly created much new agitation for a great and fast increase in naval strength and better military readiness for the United States." The messy contretemps between Washington and the

Italian government stemmed from Secretary of State Blaine's illness and President Harrison's indifference, but "the real and lasting importance of the war scare" was its exposure of U.S. naval weakness; "it took a war scare to make the average American awaken from the slumber of over two decades of peace."

LATIN AMERICA AND THE CARIBBEAN

9:380 Bostert, Russell H. "Diplomatic Reversal: Frelinghuysen's Opposition to Blaine's Pan American Policy in 1882." *Mississippi Valley Historical Review* 42 (March 1956): 653–71. The author notes that Frelinghuysen favored a less active policy than Blaine, and that one factor in the cancellation of the Pan-American conference was its identification with Blaine's interest in increasing trade between the United States and Latin America.

9:381 _____. "A New Approach to the Origins of Blaine's Pan American Policy." *Hispanic American Historical Review* 39 (August 1959): 375–412. Bostert shows that Blaine's record before 1881 reveals no serious interest in foreign policy and that he came to the State Department with no "formula for dealing with Latin America." Pan-Americanism attracted him as a way to bring about peace in a hemisphere troubled by wars, threats of war, boundary disputes, territorial rivalries, and inept diplomacy. "Troubled by the blunders of his ministers and the consequences of his own negligent policy, caught in the whirlwind of suspicion and mistrust," he attempted to save his Latin American policy through an inter-American conference.

9:382 Dahl, Victor C. "A Montana Pioneer Abroad: Granville Stuart in South America." *Journal of the West* 4 (July 1965): 345–66. This brief biography of Granville Stuart and the development of talents deemed necessary to survive and prosper in the American west includes a description of his short career as a diplomat in South America, where he "made no enormous impact."

9:383 Fifer, J. Valerie. *United States Perceptions of Latin America, 1850–1930: A "New West" South of Capricorn?* New York: Manchester University Press, 1991. Fifer contends that in the late nineteenth century, Americans looked abroad to replicate the frontier development of the United States. The book traces the evolving U.S. perceptions of temperate South America, particularly Argentina and Chile, which originally seemed progressive and prosperous and evoked comparisons with the United States. Ultimately, however, travelers, geographers, journalists, entrepreneurs, and diplomats concluded a "new west" was not to be found in South America.

9:384 Gilderhus, Mark T. *The Second Century: U.S.–Latin American Relations since 1889.* Wilmington, DE: Scholarly Resources, 2000. Starting with the Pan-American conference in 1889, Gilderhus provides a concise narrative of modern U.S.–Latin American relations, including the contest between U.S. hegemony and Latin American nationalism, clashes between rival ideologies, debates among ambitious implementers of policy, and geopolitical interests. The first chapter deals with U.S. expansion in 1889–1913.

9:385 Joseph, Gilbert M., Catherine C. LeGrand, and Ricardo D. Salvatore, eds. *Close Encounters of Empire: Writing the Cultural History of U.S.–Latin American Relations.* Durham, NC: Duke University Press, 1998. This collection on U.S.–Latin American relations investigates the intersection of culture and power, examining a wide range of imperial encounters through the lens of recent developments in social theory. Those most pertinent for this chapter are Joseph, "Close Encounters: Toward a New Cultural History of U.S.–Latin American Relations"; Steven J. Stern, "The Decentered Center and the Expansionist Periphery: The Paradoxes of Foreign-Local Encounters"; Salvatore, "The Enterprise of Knowledge: Representational Machines of Informal Empire"; Deborah Poole, "Landscape and the Imperial Subject: U.S. Images of the Andes, 1859–1930"; Eileen J. Findlay, "Love in the Tropics: Marriage, Divorce, and the Construction of Benevolent Colonialism in Puerto Rico, 1898–1910"; Steven C. Topik, "Mercenaries in the Theater of War: Publicity, Technology, and the Illusion of Power during the Brazilian Naval Revolt of 1893"; and Emily S. Rosenberg, "Turning to Culture."

9:386 Langley, Lester D. *America and the Americas: The United States in the Western Hemisphere.* Langley surveys U.S.–Latin American relations from independence to the presidency of Ronald Reagan through the analytical framework of contrasting themes: the idea of U.S. hegemony and the idea of Latin America as a distinct culture not always amenable to the imposition of U.S. institutions and values (2:350).

9:387   Leonard, Thomas M., ed. *United States–Latin American Relations, 1850–1903: Establishing a Relationship.* Tuscaloosa: University of Alabama Press, 1999. This collection includes essays on U.S. relations with particular countries: Don M. Coerver, "Mexico: Conflicting Self-Interests"; Louis A. Pérez, Jr., "Cuba: Sugar and Independence"; Helen Delpar, "Colombia: Troubled Friendship"; Leonard, "Central America: The Search for Economic Development"; William L. Harris, "Venezuela: Wars, Claims, and the Cry for a Stronger Monroe Doctrine"; Lawrence A. Clayton, "Peru: Dominance of Private Businessmen"; Joseph S. Tulchin, "Argentina: Clash of Global Visions I"; William F. Sater, "Chile: Clash of Global Visions II"; Joseph Smith, "Brazil: On the Periphery I"; and José B. Fernández and Jennifer M. Zimnoch, "Paraguay and Uruguay: On the Periphery II."

9:388   Millington, Herbert. *American Diplomacy and the War of the Pacific.* New York: Columbia University Press, 1948. This short monograph focusing on a neglected chapter in U.S. diplomacy, the 1879–1883 War of the Pacific between Chile and the alliance of Peru and Bolivia, finds U.S. "meddling and muddling" in its attempt to mediate. The State Department did not set down a realistic policy at the outset of the war, did not pursue its agenda with tact, and did not have men of ability, energy, or skill on the scene. American intervention "represents one of the lost opportunities" of U.S. diplomacy.

9:389   Mitchell, Nancy. *The Danger of Dreams: German and American Imperialism in Latin America.* Chapel Hill: University of North Carolina Press, 1999. Based on three case studies from the early twentieth century (Venezuela, Brazil, and Mexico), the author contends that U.S. leaders consistently overrated German ambitions in the Western Hemisphere. In spite of a host of rhetorical excesses, German policies were actually cautious and accommodating to U.S. interests since Germany lacked both the will and the means to be otherwise.

9:390   Park, James William. *Latin American Underdevelopment: A History of Perspectives in the United States, 1870–1965.* Baton Rouge: Louisiana State University Press, 1995. Park examines the consensus of travel writers, essayists, journalists, and educators who analyzed Latin American underdevelopment beginning in the 1870s. They exhibited "a consistent and enduring pattern of disdain toward the peoples and cultures of Latin America" and judged the continent politically unstable, technologically backward, and culturally barren.

9:391   Pike, Fredrick B. *The United States and Latin America: Myths and Stereotypes of Civilization and Nature.* This work presents a unique perspective on the history of U.S.–Latin American relations, using concepts of "nature" and "civilization" as an analytical framework. Pike contends that whether due to religious, cultural, or racial weaknesses, Latin Americans have been seen in the United States as lacking the requisite fortitude to dominate or subjugate nature (5:529).

9:392   Pletcher, David M. "Reciprocity and Latin America in the Early 1890s: A Foretaste of Dollar Diplomacy." *Pacific Historical Review* 47 (February 1978): 53–89. Describing a series of reciprocity agreements negotiated with Latin American nations under provisions of the McKinley Tariff, the author finds that economic interventions through such piecemeal measures often brought unintended results but nonetheless were significant as precursors to dollar diplomacy.

9:393   Schoultz, Lars. *Beneath the United States: A History of U.S. Policy toward Latin America.* Cambridge, MA: Harvard University Press, 1998. This is an overview of the policies the United States has developed to protect its interests in and hegemony over Latin America. What still endures, Schoultz argues, is the idea that Latin America is fundamentally inferior, stubbornly underdeveloped, and persistently incapable of managing its own affairs. A pervasive conviction about Latin American inferiority has been the fundamental principle of U.S. policy for over two centuries. The book includes two chapters on 1865–1898.

9:394   Skaggs, Jimmy M. *The Great Guano Rush: Entrepreneurs and American Overseas Expansion.*

New York: St. Martin's Press, 1994. Skaggs attempts to demonstrate the "myth of laissez faire" by showing how the U.S. government made guano available to farmers facing declining productivity and prices. The book concludes that "the ponderous machinery of the United States government was nudged into motion, inexorably toward empire" by the search for guano on Peruvian offshore islands.

9:395   Smith, Joseph. *Illusions of Conflict: Anglo-American Diplomacy toward Latin America, 1865–1896.* Pittsburgh: University of Pittsburgh Press, 1979. Smith contends the British never developed a plan to exploit Latin America, an area of peripheral interest, because of Foreign Office prejudice. Britain sought only to protect its commercial interests in contrast to America's drive for preeminence in the area. In most cases, the former was content to accept the U.S. view that in Latin America its fiat was law.

Mexico

9:396   Berbusse, Edward J. "General Rosecrans' Forthright Diplomacy with Juarez's Mexico, 1868–1869." *Americas* 36 (April 1980): 499–514. Berbusse traces U.S. minister William S. Rosecrans's blunt criticism of the Juarez administration for its "dictatorial power." With Secretary of State Seward expressing a new U.S. emphasis on investments in Mexico rather than territorial expansion, Rosecrans advised Juarez to "change for the benefit of Mexico."

9:397   Burnside, William H. "Powell Clayton: Ambassador to Mexico, 1897–1905." *Arkansas Historical Quarterly* 38 (Winter 1979): 328–44. Powell Clayton was an admirable, dignified, restrained, efficient, energetic, and determined envoy who encouraged Mexican neutrality during the Spanish-American War.

9:398   Cosío Villegas, Daniel. *The United States versus Porfirio Díaz.* Translated by Nettie Lee Benson. Lincoln: University of Nebraska Press, 1963. This is a well-documented account of the two-year struggle (1876–1878) of the Diaz government for recognition by the United States.

9:399   Gregg, Robert D. *The Influence of Border

Troubles on Relations between the United States and Mexico, 1876–1910. Baltimore: Johns Hopkins Press, 1937. Reprint 1970 (Da Capo Press). This specialized study focuses on one of the most durable and irritating problems between the two nations during the *Porfiriato*.

9:400   Griswold del Castillo, Richard. *The Treaty of Guadalupe Hidalgo: A Legacy of Conflict.* Norman: University of Oklahoma Press, 1990. This book traces the history of the Treaty of Guadalupe Hidalgo, identifying conflicting interpretations given to its provisions by officials, commissions, legislatures, and courts in the United States since its ratification. The author concludes that many provisions have been interpreted in ways violating both the treaty's letter and spirit.

9:401   Hanna, Alfred Jackson, and Kathryn Abbey Hanna. *Napoleon III and Mexico: American Triumph over Monarchy.* The authors see sharply contrasting ideologies at the root of the confrontation between the United States and France. "European monarchs, in particular Napoleon III, feared American republican ideas would subvert their systems and traditions." Thus, Napoleon endeavored to establish on the southern front of the United States a strong monarchy as a buffer against further U.S. expansion, hoping to convert other Latin American republics into French-style monarchies. The first part of the book deals with the French background of the intervention, the second with Seward's diplomacy leading to the French departure from Mexico (8:454).

9:402   Pastor, Robert A., and Jorge G. Castañeda. *Limits to Friendship: The United States and Mexico.* New York: Alfred A. Knopf, 1988. This is a collection of essays and debates by an American and a Mexican political scientist, the latter a future Mexican foreign minister. They contend that "the tensions, conflicts, and misconceptions which have always characterized the U.S.-Mexican relationship are rooted in history, asymmetry, and changes in each of the countries."

9:403   Pletcher, David M. *Rails, Mines, and Progress: Seven American Promoters in Mexico, 1867–1911.* Ithaca: Cornell University Press, 1958. Pletcher describes the expansion of U.S. economic influence in Mexico during the late nineteenth century, examining several promoters to determine what they intended to do, how they went about accomplishing their goals, and whether they succeeded or failed. He also addresses whether the dollars invested in Mexico really worked for the best interests of Mexicans and how much they profited American investors.

9:404   Sayles, Stephen. "The Romero-Frelinghuysen Convention: A Milestone in Border Relations." *New Mexico Historical Review* 51 (October 1976): 295–311. Beginning in 1877, the U.S. government came under heavy pressure to deal with problems of border violence. Successive administrations tried to establish friendly relations with Mexico through railroads and steamboats, preventing border raids and providing greater military defense capabilities along the Rio Grande. "Railroads and border stabilization became inextricably linked in American foreign policy." In the Romero-Frelinghuysen Convention, Mexico received a great influx of U.S. capital and railroad construction, and the United States secured the desired border stability and a new market for investment capital.

9:405   Schmitt, Karl M. "American Protestant Missionaries and the Díaz Regime in Mexico: 1876–1911." *Journal of Church and State* 25 (Spring 1983): 253–77. Schmitt discusses the concerted efforts of Protestant missionaries to penetrate Mexico with the final triumph of the Liberal government of Benito Juárez, who began to enforce reform laws, including guaranteed protection for all religious beliefs. By 1910 and the end of the Diaz dictatorship, seventeen American Protestant societies were engaged in missionary work in Mexico.

9:406   _____. *Mexico and the United States, 1821–1973: Conflict and Coexistence.* This synthesis focuses on Mexico's responses to encounters with the United States and the mechanisms it created to defend itself against its northern neighbor. Schmitt emphasizes Mexico's economic dependency, U.S. economic penetration, and the power differential that became a main source of tension between the two countries. Chapter 4 covers 1850–1910 (2:385).

9:407   Schoonover, Thomas D., ed. *Mexican Lobby: Matías Romero in Washington, 1861–1867.* Matías Romero served the Juárez administration in Washington between 1861 and 1867, attaching him-

self to the Radical Republicans in the hope of precipitating a forceful implementation of the Monroe Doctrine in Mexico. The author selected, translated, and edited 125 of Romero's dispatches to the Mexican government, most concerned with schemes to obtain economic aid for Mexico and remove French troops supporting Maximilian. Translated by Schoonover; assisted by Ebba Wesener Schoonover (8:457).

9:408   Vázquez, Josefina Zoraida, and Lorenzo Meyer. *The United States and Mexico.* This book sets forth many important themes in U.S.-Mexico relations from a Mexican perspective. Vázquez and Meyer describe the legacies of the nineteenth century, most notably U.S. territorial expansion, control of natural resources, and the evolution of Mexican nationalism (2:386).

The Caribbean

9:409   Koht, Halvdan. "The Origin of Seward's Plan to Purchase the Danish West Indies." *American Historical Review* 50 (July 1945): 762–67. Tracing the origins of Seward's attempt to acquire the Danish West Indies, Koht contends that his West Indies policies, often thought expansionist, were "of a purely defensive character." Austria became interested in the islands after Germany defeated Denmark, seeing them as a connection to Maximilian's Mexico. Rumors also surfaced about a swap with Germany for part of Schleswig.

9:410   Langley, Lester D. *Struggle for the American Mediterranean: United States–European Rivalry in the Gulf-Caribbean, 1776–1904.* This is a readable survey of U.S.-European rivalry in the Caribbean and Mexico that briefly analyzes U.S. motives and ideals. It contains good sections on the background to the Clayton-Bulwer Treaty, the French intervention in Mexico, and the European background to the Spanish-American War (2:364).

9:411   May, Robert E. "Lobbyists for Commercial Empire: Jane Cazneau, William Cazneau, and U.S. Caribbean Policy, 1846–1878." *Pacific Historical Review* 48 (August 1979): 383–412. May describes the entrepreneurial and diplomatic activities of the Cazneaus in Cuba, Mexico, Nicaragua, and the Dominican Republic to show how U.S. expansionists were induced to redirect their thinking from territorial imperialism to commercial expansionism. May also comments on the significance of Jane Cazneau's career because her work departed from accepted norms of female behavior.

9:412   McWilliams, Tennant S. "The Lure of Empire: Southern Interest in the Caribbean, 1877–1900." *Mississippi Quarterly* 29 (Winter 1975–1976): 43–63. This article focuses on the south and foreign policy; McWilliams appraises the region's interest in penetrating the Caribbean in the late nineteenth century.

9:413   Smith, Robert Freeman. *The Caribbean World and the United States: Mixing Rum and Coca-Cola.* New York: Twayne Publishers, 1994. Smith argues that U.S. policy never had imperialist designs but was based on the perceived need to keep the Europeans—the British in the nineteenth century, the Germans and Soviets in the twentieth—out of the Caribbean basin. He emphasizes the humanitarianism accompanying America's penetration of the Caribbean, and concludes that its benevolence has never been sufficiently acknowledged.

9:414   Tansill, Charles Callan. *The Purchase of the Danish West Indies.* Baltimore: Johns Hopkins Press, 1932. This is a detailed study based on multi-archival research.

Cuba

9:415   Benjamin, Jules R. *The United States & Cuba: Hegemony and Dependent Development, 1880–1934.* Pittsburgh: University of Pittsburgh Press, 1977. Though emphasizing the twentieth century, Benjamin discusses the U.S. economic presence in Cuba from the 1880s onward, emphasizing Cuba's increasing dependency. Chapter 1 deals with the origins of American hegemony on the island until 1902.

9:416   Bradford, Richard H. *The Virginius Affair.* Boulder: Colorado Associated University Press, 1980. This work focuses on the diplomatic crisis of 1873 that erupted when Spanish officials in Cuba seized the *Virginius* and executed many of its American crew on the grounds that they were pirates who supported Cuban revolutionaries. Bradford uncovers

domestic interest groups, corruption, and bureaucratic wrangling while presenting a complex portrayal of Secretary of State Hamilton Fish's statecraft. He underscores the emerging international forces that helped shape U.S. diplomacy in the 1870s and the pivotal diplomatic role of Great Britain, which led to the Grant administration's decision not to intervene in Cuba in 1873. Foreword by Walter LaFeber.

9:417   Foner, Philip S. *A History of Cuba and Its Relations with the United States. Vol. 2: 1845–1895: From the Era of Annexationism to the Outbreak of the Second War for Independence.* New York: International Publishers, 1962. This volume discusses the Cuban revolution and provides a useful, if economic-determinist, background (1845–1895) to U.S. interests in Cuba. Overall, Foner indicts American policy. Bibliography.

9:418   Hernández, José M. *Cuba and the United States: Intervention and Militarism, 1868–1933.* Austin: University of Texas Press, 1993. Hernández describes the origins and evolution of Cuban militarism. Contrary to the view that the United States imposed a militaristic tradition on the country, he sees Washington only incidentally abetting the militarists' cause against other Cuban revolutionaries who wanted an independent Cuba with a military subservient to civilian authority. The author contends that Cuba's liberators coveted power as much as had the Spanish military.

9:419   McWilliams, Tennant S. "Procrastination Diplomacy: Hannis Taylor and the Cuban Business Disputes, 1893–1897." *Diplomatic History* 2 (Winter 1978): 63–80. This article demonstrates how the relatively unknown U.S. minister to Spain, Hannis Taylor, was plagued by Spanish politics before 1898, sometimes over issues unrelated to Cuba. Tensions, disagreements, and friction between the United States and Spain had been developing for years, and U.S. policymakers were frustrated with Spain long before Cuban issues erupted. Taylor contributed through reporting home his unfavorable impressions of the government and views of Spanish ineptitude.

9:420   Pérez, Louis A., Jr. "Between Baseball and Bullfighting: The Quest for Nationality in Cuba, 1868–1898." *Journal of American History* 81 (September 1994): 493–517. This article discusses the ideological implications of Cuba's appropriation of baseball as an expression of Cuban nationalism, vindication of its revolution, and metaphor for nationhood. Pérez analyzes baseball as a sport, state of mind, and statement of national identity in Cuba's search for independence.

9:421 _____. *Cuba and the United States: Ties of Singular Intimacy.* This book explains the rise of radical nationalism in Cuba. Pérez emphasizes the cultural relations and personal contacts that have tied the two nations together since the eighteenth century, focusing on the pervasive and often decisive influence of the United States. He analyzes the Cuban groups that sought to emulate and those that sought to repudiate the United States (2:370). First published in 1990.

9:422 _____. *Cuba between Empires, 1878–1902.* Pittsburgh: University of Pittsburgh Press, 1983. Pérez demonstrates the importance of the U.S. government's hostility to the Cuban revolution.

9:423 Poyo, Gerald E. *With All, and for the Good of All: The Emergence of Popular Nationalism in the Cuban Communities of the United States, 1848–1898.* Durham, NC: Duke University Press, 1989. This book analyzes the development of popular nationalism among Cubans living in the United States between 1848 and 1898. Poyo explores the evolution of ideological divisions over a future autonomous Cuba that divided the emigre settlements of New York, New Orleans, and Florida.

Dominican Republic and Haiti

9:424 Logan, Rayford W. *The Diplomatic Relations of the United States with Haiti, 1776–1891.* This is the standard diplomatic study of Haitian relations with the United States, with the first three chapters focusing on the late eighteenth century. Logan pays little attention to Anglo-American-Haitian commercial relations but contributed significantly with his analysis of the impact of racial factors in the Haitian-American relationship. Extensive bibliography (5:520).

9:425 Martinez-Fernández, Luis. "Caudillos, Annexationism, and the Rivalry between Empires in

the Dominican Republic, 1844–1874." Martinez-Fernández seeks to explain the motivations behind the caudillos' seemingly chronic annexationism from 1844 to 1874 in the context of imperial rivalry over the Dominican Republic. Annexationist preferences, the author holds, were dictated by geopolitical circumstances beyond the caudillos' control (6:312).

9:426 Montague, Ludwell Lee. *Haiti and the United States, 1714–1938.* This is a concise, analytical book that includes a valuable discussion of the quiet twenty years after 1871, with useful appraisals of the differing stances of Seward, Fish, Evarts, and Frelinghuysen (5:523).

9:427 Nelson, William Javier. *Almost a Territory: America's Attempt to Annex the Dominican Republic.* Newark: University of Delaware Press, 1990. Nelson studies the struggle over the annexation of the Dominican Republic as an illustration of Dominican helplessness in the face of U.S. strength, recounting the sequence of events leading to the island state's request for absorption by the United States and the efforts of men like Charles Sumner and Carl Schurz to prevent it.

9:428 Pitre, Merline. "Frederick Douglass and the Annexation of Santo Domingo." *Journal of Negro History* 62 (October 1977): 390–400. Douglass's fidelity to the Republican Party is exemplified in the position he took on the U.S. efforts to acquire Santo Domingo. He was so concerned with projecting U.S. institutions abroad that he found himself in conflict with Charles Sumner, who opposed annexation. Ultimately, Douglass confused a short-range objective (ascendancy of the Republican Party) with a long-range goal (elevation and liberation of blacks).

9:429 Plummer, Brenda Gayle. *Haiti and the United States: The Psychological Moment.* Athens, GA: University of Georgia Press, 1992. This is a survey of the complex and odd relationship between the United States and Haiti. Few Americans realize, Plummer shows, how important Haiti has been to the United States and how deeply intertwined relations between these two nations have been.

9:430 Tansill, Charles Callan. *The United States and Santo Domingo, 1798–1873: A Chapter in Caribbean Diplomacy.* This is a standard, early work on the evolution of U.S. interest in the island, especially the lure of the West Indian commercial market and the strategic worth of Samana Bay (6:314).

9:431 Welles, Sumner. *Naboth's Vineyard: The Dominican Republic, 1844–1924.* 2 vols. New York: Payson and Clarke, 1928. Reprint 1972 (Arno Press). This comprehensive account of U.S.-Dominican relations covers the state's origins, the early years of independence to the dictatorship of Ulises Heureaux, the liberal reaction against him, and negotiations for annexation to the United States before proceeding to twentieth-century issues.

Argentina

9:432 McGann, Thomas F. "Argentina at the First Pan-American Conference." *Inter-American Economic Affairs* 1 (Summer 1947): 21–53. The author discusses the four main issues at the 1889–1890 conference: organization and procedure; a monetary union; an arbitration agreement; and a customs union. He concludes that Argentina's consistent differences with the United States meant that the new Pan-American Union "was born with a South as well as a North Pole."

9:433 _____. *Argentina, the United States, and the Inter-American System, 1880–1914.* Cambridge, MA: Harvard University Press, 1957. The author studies Argentina's European orientation beginning in the 1880s and the U.S.-Argentina competition for hemispheric leadership.

9:434 Peterson, Harold F. *Argentina and the United States, 1810–1960.* This important study of the two oldest independent states in the hemisphere and their first timid diplomatic steps toward one another contends that they found themselves in comparable situations in 1810, protecting independence, ensuring freedom from entangling alliances, seeking commercial agreements, and managing issues of contiguous territories. Peterson also traces the evolution of inter-American misunderstandings and misperceptions that "form the central theme of Argentine-American diplomatic relations in the twentieth century" (2:389).

9:435 Tulchin, Joseph S. *Argentina and the United States: A Conflicted Relationship.* In this survey, Tulchin describes the U.S.-Argentine relationship as conflicted, due in part to both countries' being arrogant and expansionist with hemispheric, and then global, visions that infringed on each other (2:390).

Brazil

9:436 Calhoun, Charles W. "American Policy toward the Brazilian Naval Revolt of 1893–94: A Reexamination." *Diplomatic History* 4 (Winter 1980): 39–56. This reassessment of U.S. policy during the Brazilian naval officers' 1893 revolt discounts economic motivation and contends that "although Gresham was not indifferent to the prospects for increased trade with Brazil, neither those prospects nor a determination to save reciprocity dictated his policy toward the revolt." He relied on diplomatic traditions and international law to frame U.S. policy. "The essential feature of the American position throughout the revolt was not aggressiveness against the insurgents, but 'watchfulness' . . . in the interests of legitimate American trade and against possible European intervention."

9:437 Smith, Joseph. *Unequal Giants: Diplomatic Relations between the United States and Brazil, 1889–1930.* Pittsburgh: University of Pittsburgh Press, 1991. This work suggests that the images Brazilians and Americans have toward each other have changed little over time, as is also true of policy patterns and trends. Chapter 1 covers 1889–1901. Good bibliographical essay.

9:438 Topik, Steven C. *Trade and Gunboats: The United States and Brazil in the Age of Empire.* Stanford, CA: Stanford University Press, 1996. This book details the first commercial agreement between the United States and Brazil, the Blaine-Mendonca Treaty, and the U.S. intervention in the Brazilian naval revolt of 1893–1894. Topik focuses on Secretary of State James G. Blaine, who never thought in terms of military or naval power but expansionist economic policies. The result was a more aggressive U.S. foreign policy by the end of the nineteenth century.

9:439 Vivian, James F. "United States Policy during the Brazilian Naval Revolt, 1893–94: The Case for American Neutrality." *American Neptune* 41 (October 1981): 245–61. President Cleveland insisted that during the Brazilian naval revolt U.S. neutrality would be maintained, yet many observers thought Washington then moved to active intervention, which Vivian sees as a departure in nineteenth-century U.S. diplomacy and an important precedent for the Venezuelan and Cuban crises to follow.

Chile

9:440 Blakemore, Harold. *British Nitrates and Chilean Politics, 1886–1898: Balmaceda and North.* London: Athlone Press for the Institute of Latin American Studies, 1974. This volume assesses British economic influence in Chile, especially in the rapidly expanding nitrate industry. It is a well-written, astute evaluation of British and American economic interests in Chile during the presidency of Jose Manuel Balmaceda and the constitutional and political crisis that led to revolution in 1891. Blakemore presents a detailed study of British financier John Thomas North—the Nitrate King—and his role in Chile. He also includes the U.S. reaction to British influence in Chile.

9:441 Goldberg, Joyce S. *The "Baltimore" Affair.* Lincoln: University of Nebraska Press, 1986. This is a detailed analysis of U.S. and Chilean diplomatic maneuvering in the wake of the *Baltimore* incident, which served as an important prelude to the more aggressive U.S. diplomatic and military policy of 1898.

9:442 _____. "Consent to Ascent: The '*Baltimore*' Affair and the U.S. Rise to World Power Status." *Americas* 41 (July 1984): 21–35. This article analyzes the *Baltimore* affair of 1891 in Chile as a pivotal step in the rise of America to world power status.

9:443 Pike, Fredrick B. *Chile and the United States, 1880–1962: The Emergence of Chile's Social Crisis and the Challenge to United States Diplomacy.* Pike describes the internal social, political, and economic development of Chile to show how its diplomacy grew from its values, attitudes, and experiences. The book includes a detailed analysis of the

development of specific social problems in Chile and their effects on relations with the United States. Two chapters cover U.S.-Chilean relations from 1880 to 1920, marked by chronic tensions (2:394).

9:444 Sater, William F. *Chile and the United States: Empires in Conflict.* Sater describes the U.S.-Chilean relationship as historically antagonistic because the two countries were rival expanding empires in the nineteenth century, each believing in its own sense of destiny and greatness, relying on racism to justify their imperial impulses, and competing for markets as exporters. Two chapters cover 1865–1898 (2:395).

9:445 _____. *Chile and the War of the Pacific.* Lincoln: University of Nebraska Press, 1986. Sater describes Chile's attitude toward U.S. intervention in the War of the Pacific.

9:446 Sherman, William Roderick. *The Diplomatic and Commercial Relations of the United States and Chile, 1820–1914.* Boston: R. G. Badger, 1926. This work is mostly useful for its attention to commercial relations.

Peru

9:447 Bishel, William V. "Fall from Grace: U.S. Business Interests versus U.S. Diplomatic Interests in Peru, 1885–1890." *Diplomatic History* 20 (Spring 1996): 163–83. This article examines the battle waged between W. R. Grace and Company and the U.S. minister in Peru, Charles W. Buck, mainly over the best way to protect U.S. citizens' economic interests in the face of Grace and Company's negotiations with the Peruvian government on the issue of Peru's enormous foreign debt.

9:448 Clayton, Lawrence A. *Peru and the United States: The Condor and the Eagle.* Athens, GA: University of Georgia Press, 1999. This work delineates economic, political, and cultural connections between Peru and the United States. Clayton emphasizes economic and trade relations with New England whalers in the eighteenth century, farmers seeking guano and nitrates for fertilizers in the nineteenth, mining and railroad investments in the late nineteenth century, and further economic penetration in the twentieth, including contemporary narcotrafficking issues.

9:449   Secada, C. Alexander G. de. "Arms, Guano, and Shipping: The W. R. Grace Interests in Peru, 1865–1885." *Business History Review* 59 (Winter 1985): 597–621. This article analyzes the origins of W. R. Grace and Co. and its rise as a dominant actor in Peru's economic history. Secada attributes the company's ascendancy to the arms trade Grace carried out for Peru during the War of the Pacific. Its ability to manipulate this trade made it one of the first truly inter-American commercial enterprises.

Venezuela

9:450   Blake, Nelson M. "Background of Cleveland's Venezuela Policy." *American Historical Review* 47 (January 1942): 259–77. Grover Cleveland, a man naturally inclined toward caution in foreign affairs, supported by Secretary of State Walter Q. Gresham and Ambassador Thomas F. Bayard, "challenged Britain on the Venezuela issue only after he became personally convinced that the Monroe Doctrine was at stake and that it was his duty to maintain it."

9:451   Ewell, Judith. *Venezuela and the United States: From Monroe's Hemisphere to Petroleum's Empire.* Emphasizing conflicting interests and purposes, Ewell demonstrates that U.S.-Venezuelan relations reflected all the core issues of inter-American relations generally: racism, distrust of revolution, the American mission, and U.S. assumptions of superiority. Chapter 3 covers 1866–1896 (2:400).

9:452   Hood, Miriam. *Gunboat Diplomacy 1895–1905: Great Power Pressure in Venezuela.* 2d ed. Boston: Allen and Unwin, 1983. A short monograph describing Venezuelan history and the role of Anglo-American relations in the country's history, Hood's work summarizes domestic developments, including the rise of Venezuelan nationalism. Two chapters describe the Venezuelan boundary dispute from Venezuela's perspective and the foreign relations issues of the Cipriano Castro years, including the blockade. First published in 1975.

9:453   Mathews, Joseph J. "Informal Diplomacy in the Venezuelan Crisis of 1896." *Mississippi Valley Historical Review* 50 (September 1963): 195–212. Semiofficial diplomacy proved useful in the Anglo-American crisis arising from the Venezuelan boundary dispute. While "it would be incorrect to conclude that informal diplomacy solved the Venezuela controversy, . . . the evidence does indicate that unofficial negotiations were more significant than has been recognized." Individuals outside the regular diplomatic service "met needs for which the regular machinery was inadequate."

Others

9:454   Dahl, Victor C. "Uruguay under Juan Idiarte Borda: An American Diplomat's Observations." *Hispanic American Historical Review* 46 (February 1966): 66–77. U.S. minister to Uruguay in the second Cleveland administration, Granville Stuart closely observed the activities of Juan Idiarte Borda from his inauguration as president to his 1897 assassination. Meeting the diplomatic challenges of a turbulent time, he reported on the threats of an Argentine-Chilean boundary war that involved Brazil and Uruguay and the growing internal unrest in Uruguay that erupted into revolution and civil war in 1897.

9:455   Randall, Stephen J. *Colombia and the United States: Hegemony and Interdependence.* Randall stresses the degree of equality that characterized U.S.-Colombian relations at the time of independence, compares the eras of nation-building and civil war in the two countries, and analyzes the half century of rivalry between the United States and Britain for regional, commercial, and strategic hegemony (2:397).

Central America

9:456   Chomsky, Aviva. *West Indian Workers and the United Fruit Company of Costa Rica, 1870–1940.* Baton Rouge: Louisiana State University Press, 1996. Chomsky sets out to explore the social, economic, and cultural complexities of Costa Rica's coastal banana plantation society. This book exposes a history of racial conflict and exploitation by the United Fruit Company, which imported black laborers, mostly from Jamaica, to create its tropical enterprise on Costa Rica's Atlantic coast and forced them to work under conditions reminiscent of nineteenth-century slave plantations.

9:457   Clayton, Lawrence A. "The Nicaragua Canal in the Nineteenth Century: Prelude to American Empire in the Caribbean." *Journal of Latin American Studies* 19 (November 1987): 323–52. Clayton sees the Nicaraguan canal as one of the great American dreams of the nineteenth century and a magnet that drew U.S. attention for the first time to Central America.

9:458   Coatsworth, John H. *Central America and the United States: The Clients and the Colossus.* New York: Twayne Publishers, 1994. This book demonstrates the impact of domestic considerations on foreign policy decisions both in the United States and abroad. Coatsworth concludes that the long-time subordination of the Central American republics to client status is the major factor contributing to the local elite's historic resistance to change and argues that the U.S. policymakers' goal of regional stability and keeping Europeans out denied them a realistic understanding of Central America's domestic dynamics.

9:459   Crowell, Jackson. "The United States and a Central American Canal, 1869–1877." *Hispanic American Historical Review* 49 (February 1969): 27–52. Crowell describes U.S. efforts between 1869 and 1877 to locate a route and begin constructing an isthmian waterway in Central America. Grant came into office convinced of the military importance of an interoceanic canal route and ordered exploration and survey of possible routes. His hopes for construction were shattered because of the complex technical problems involved and because Washington could not find a way to modify or abrogate the Clayton-Bulwer Treaty to give the United States exclusive control.

9:460   Dozier, Craig L. *Nicaragua's Mosquito Shore: The Years of British and American Presence.* University: University of Alabama Press, 1985. This is a case study of Anglo-American competition for trade and influence.

9:461   Findling, John E. *Close Neighbors, Distant Friends: United States–Central American Relations.* Findling emphasizes the U.S. impact on Central America, describing its interventionism and widespread economic penetration. He also profiles many diplomatic envoys (2:353).

9:462   Heinrichs, Waldo H. "The Panama Canal in History, Policy, and Caricature." *Latin American Research Review* 17, no. 2 (1982): 247–61. This review essay of six monographs published in the late 1970s on the Canal from its creation to the controversy surrounding ratification of the treaty returning it to Panamanian authority contends that an "air of unreality pervades" the literature and that the "canal and its host nation tend to get lost in symbolism and hyperbole."

9:463   Langley, Lester D., and Thomas D. Schoonover. *The Banana Men: American Mercenaries and Entrepreneurs in Central America, 1880–1930.* Lexington: University Press of Kentucky, 1995. Using world systems and dependency analysis, the authors assert that the United States—an emerging metropole state with superior industrial, financial, and military power—forced a nonindustrialized Central America into its informal empire in the belief that this would ameliorate domestic social woes. This work highlights the activities of individual entrepreneurs and adventurers who established a beachhead for U.S. interests in Central America and who were crucial to the construction of an American empire.

9:464   Schoonover, Thomas D. *Germany in Central America: Competitive Imperialism, 1821–1929.* Tuscaloosa: University of Alabama Press, 1998. This book analyzes the relationship between Germany and Central America within the framework of imperial rivalries. Two chapters cover 1871–1898 and consider the U.S. reaction to the German presence in Central America.

9:465   _____. *The United States in Central America, 1860–1911: Episodes of Social Imperialism and Imperial Rivalry in the World System.* Durham, NC: Duke University Press, 1991. This is a study of U.S. foreign relations in Central America as part of international history, guided by the theoretical framework of world systems. Schoonover contends that in its relations with Central America, the United States exercised social imperialism, pursuing a policy of expanding foreign markets to relieve domestic economic and social crises. The first five chapters cover 1869–1900.

9:466 Wicks, Daniel H. "Dress Rehearsal: United States Intervention on the Isthmus of Panama, 1885." *Pacific Historical Review* 49 (November 1980): 581–605. The landing force of 1,200 men sent ashore to assume responsibility for maintaining order in Panama in 1885 served as a dress rehearsal for the more famous U.S. intervention of 1903.

HAWAII

Labor, Immigration, and Economic Factors

9:467 Conroy, Hilary. *The Japanese Frontier in Hawaii, 1868–1898.* Berkeley: University of California Press, 1953. This is a scholarly study based largely on Hawaiian archival materials that considers the diplomatic problems the United States saw in the rising Japanese immigration to Hawaii.

9:468 Davis, Eleanor H. *The Norse Migration: Norwegian Labor in Hawaii.* Honolulu: Hawaiian Historical Society, 1962. In 1881 the first shipload of Norwegian contract laborers arrived in Hawaii to work the sugar fields. Conditions were not as good as the immigrants had expected, and many demanded improvements or release from their contracts. Eventually the plantation owners turned to what they hoped would be more docile Asian labor. This is the 71st Annual Report of the Hawaiian Historical Society.

9:469 Dozer, Donald M. "The Opposition to Hawaiian Reciprocity, 1876–1888." *Pacific Historical Review* 14 (June 1945): 157–83. The reciprocity treaties between the United States and Hawaii were opposed especially by American sugar cane and beet sugar producers and by those believing the treaties unjust in conferring one-sided benefits on Hawaii. The anti-imperialist wing of the Democratic Party opposed the Pearl Harbor amendment.

9:470 Okihiro, Gary Y. *Cane Fires: The Anti-Japanese Movement in Hawaii, 1865–1945.* Philadelphia: Temple University Press, 1991. In this study of Hawaiian anti-Japanese movements, Okihiro refutes the contention that Hawaii was a land of racial harmony where Asian immigrants were neither oppressed nor harassed. Workers were forced to labor under oppressive conditions with the full backing of the law. Virulent anti-Japanese attitudes prevailed, with most political or social problems viewed in terms of the "Yellow Peril" or the "Japanese Menace."

9:471 Patterson, John. "The United States and Hawaiian Reciprocity, 1867–1870." *Pacific Historical Review* 7 (March 1938): 14–26. Patterson focuses on the unsuccessful effort in 1867 to obtain a reciprocity treaty. Political motives were mixed; some opponents feared reciprocity would prevent annexation.

9:472 Russ, William Adam. "Hawaiian Labor and Immigration Problems before Annexation." *Journal of Modern History* 15 (March-December 1943): 207–22. Russ explains the massive labor shortage Hawaiian industry faced in the 1850s and 1860s. Because the native Hawaiian population was decimated from repeated battles with disease, it became necessary to import labor from Europe and the Pacific. Russ supplies data on the relative importation costs that sugar planters faced in bringing various ethnic groups to the islands.

9:473 Tate, Merze. *Hawaii: Reciprocity or Annexation.* East Lansing: Michigan State University Press, 1968. Tate concentrates on the arguments surrounding the issue of reciprocity treaties between the United States and Hawaii while supplying a detailed account of the motivations of Americans and Hawaiians during the 1876 treaty discussions and the important issue of the Pearl Harbor clause in the 1887 treaty.

Revolution of 1893

9:474 Andrade, Ernest, Jr. "Great Britain and the Hawaiian Revolution and Republic, 1893–1898." *Hawaiian Journal of History* 24 (Winter 1990): 91–116. Andrade analyzes Britain's long but unsuccessful effort to prevent U.S. acquisition of Hawaii, having decided by mid-century that "Hawaii's absorption by the United States was merely a matter of time," especially after the Reciprocity Treaty of 1875 and, then, the overthrow of the Hawaiian monarchy. Only the

1895 insurrection, which might have restored the monarchy, gave the United Kingdom new hope, but only briefly and, even then, it understood, only temporarily.

9:475 Baker, George W., Jr. "Benjamin Harrison and Hawaiian Annexation: A Reinterpretation." *Pacific Historical Review* 33 (August 1964): 295–309. Harrison, unlike Blaine, was not an expansionist until 1893 and then was cautious, inward-looking, and determined to be proper and avoid imputations of imperialism.

9:476 Calhoun, Charles W. "Morality and Spite: Walter Q. Gresham and U.S. Relations with Hawaii." *Pacific Historical Review* 52 (August 1983): 292–311. This article examines the motives behind the Cleveland administration's decision to reverse President Harrison's policy of negotiating a treaty for the annexation of Hawaii. Calhoun describes how Cleveland and Gresham proposed to reinstate the queen, who had surrendered in the face of a revolution engineered by a group of non-native, American-descended businessmen, lawyers, and planters. The wrangling over Hawaii in Congress and the press was a dress rehearsal for the debates over expansion at the end of the decade.

9:477 Castle, Alfred L. "Tentative Empire: Walter Q. Gresham, U.S. Foreign Policy, and Hawai'i, 1893–1895." *Hawaiian Journal of History* 29 (Fall 1995): 83–96. Contrary to assessments of U.S. support for the overthrow of Queen Liliuokalani that emphasize economic and geostrategic motives, Castle emphasizes Secretary of State Walter Q. Gresham's opposition to annexation and "the impact his principled opposition to the Provisional Government had on events in Hawai'i from 1893 to 1895." His "rather astonishing independent actions to undo the overthrow of the queen reminds us how tentative, even contradictory, U.S. foreign policy was with respect to Hawai'i in the period 1893–1895." While he failed to prevent annexation, he delayed it, but his anti-imperialism and desire for revenge against congressional opponents "weakened his influence in the Democratic party, embarrassed Cleveland on several occasions, and gave Republicans like Henry Cabot Lodge and Theodore Roosevelt issues to exploit." The result was to discredit anti-imperialism.

9:478 Hammett, Hugh B. "The Cleveland Administration and Anglo-American Naval Friction in Hawaii, 1893–1894." *Military Affairs* 40 (February 1976): 27–31. The Cleveland administration was opposed to annexation but still wished to block foreign moves into the islands. Actions of American naval officers in Honolulu complicated Cleveland's task by appearing to back the provisional government, or by offending British naval officers or officials.

9:479 Hodges, William C. *The Passing of Liliuokalani.* Honolulu: Honolulu Star Bulletin, 1918. This short biography of the last monarch of Hawaii covers her life from childhood to her overthrow in the revolution of 1893 as well as the annexation of the islands in 1898.

9:480 Joesting, Edward. *Hawaii: An Uncommon History.* New York: Norton, 1972. Focusing on selected episodes, the author has written a very human history. The instances covered include the effect of the gold rush, the impact of meddling by American, French, and British consuls, the problems of the monarchy, and the revolution of 1893.

9:481 Kuykendall, Ralph S., and A. Grove Day. *Hawaii: A History, from Polynesian Kingdom to American State.* Rev. ed. Englewood Cliffs, NJ: Prentice-Hall, 1961. The authors provide much important information on the U.S.-Hawaiian reciprocity treaties, the revolution of 1893, and the annexation of the Hawaiian islands in 1898. Originally published in 1948.

9:482 Lanier, Osmos, Jr. "'Paramount' Blount: Special Commissioner to Investigate the Hawaiian Coup, 1893." *West Georgia College Studies in the Social Sciences* 11 (Fall 1972): 45–55. Blount went to Hawaii at the request of the president, who was interested in the role played by American forces. His report led directly to Cleveland's attempted restoration of Hawaiian Queen Liliuokalani in December 1893.

9:483 Loomis, Albertine. *For Whom Are the Stars?* Honolulu: University of Hawaii Press, 1976. Although more concerned with the events that occurred after the revolution of 1893, Loomis describes the Republic of Hawaii, the 1893 revolution and 1895 counterrevolution as well as James Blount's special mission to the islands.

9:484   Russ, William Adam. *The Hawaiian Revolution, 1893–94.* Selinsgrove, PA: Susquehanna University Press, 1959. Russ finds that Minister Stevens made it clear to the revolutionaries that he was in sympathy with them before they acted. The greater menace in their minds was not the monarchy but the Japanese and Japanese-Hawaiians. The landing of American troops by Stevens made it impossible for the monarchy to defend itself.

9:485   _____. "The Role of Sugar in Hawaiian Annexation." *Pacific Historical Review* 12 (December 1943): 339–50. Although Russ demonstrated that Spreckels was opposed to annexation, as were many other prominent sugar men, sugar's role in the revolution of 1893 was its creation of a demand for cheap Asian labor in Hawaii.

9:486   Stevens, Sylvester K. *American Expansion in Hawaii, 1842–1898.* Harrisburg, PA: Archives Publishing Company of Pennsylvania, 1945. This is a traditional account of the steady growth of U.S. influence in Hawaii up to the time of annexation.

9:487   Tate, Merze. *The United States and the Hawaiian Kingdom: A Political History.* New Haven: Yale University Press, 1965. This is a thorough study of American influence in the islands from the missionary beginnings to annexation in 1898. Tate argues that the U.S. minister encouraged the rebels who ousted the queen in 1893, and that the revolution of 1893 was caused by the determination of the propertied class (mostly American) to control the government. Bibliography.

9:488   Thurston, Lorrin A. *Memoirs of the Hawaiian Revolution.* Honolulu: Advertiser Publishing, 1936. Thurston, son of a missionary couple who was instrumental in carrying off the Hawaiian revolution of 1893 and opening the way for American annexation, argues that the actions of Minister Stevens were not the deciding factor in the success of the action. Edited by Andrew Farrell.

9:489   Weigle, Richard D. "Sugar and the Hawaiian Revolution." *Pacific Historical Review* 16 (February 1947): 41–58. Spreckels opposed annexation of Hawaii to the United States since it might cut off the flow of cheap Asian labor to the islands. The revolutionists, however, were more concerned with secu-

rity. Weigle counters the view that the 1893 revolution was brought about by the sugar industry to gain benefits secured by American producers.

Annexation of 1898

9:490   Appel, John C. "American Labor and the Annexation of Hawaii: A Study in Logic and Economic Interest." *Pacific Historical Review* 23 (February 1954): 1–18. American labor opposed the annexation of the Hawaiian islands, believing the move imperialistic and designed to save the purses of the upper class. Skilled labor saw few openings in the agriculturally based Hawaiian economy and feared that Asian laborers in Hawaii might come to the United States to compete for jobs.

9:491   Armstrong, William N. *Around the World with a King.* New York: F. A. Stokes Company, 1904. Reprint 2000 (Kegan Paul International). Armstrong, a member of Kalakaua's cabinet, accompanied the last king on his circumnavigation of the world in 1881. The final chapter includes a study of the last days of the monarchy, the growth of American influence in the islands, and annexation to the United States.

9:492   Bailey, Thomas A. "Japan's Protest against the Annexation of Hawaii." *Journal of Modern History* 3 (March 1931): 46–61. Bailey argues that Hawaiian efforts to stem Japanese immigration provoked a controversy, and Japan's protest added impetus to the annexation of Hawaii.

9:493   _____. "The United States and Hawaii during the Spanish-American War." *American Historical Review* 36 (April 1931): 552–60. Rather than exercising neutrality during the Spanish-American War, the Hawaiian government aided the American war effort even before Dewey's victory at Manila. Bailey argues that Hawaii was not needed for successful prosecution of the war.

9:494   Daws, Gavan. *Shoal of Time: A History of the Hawaiian Islands.* New York: Macmillan Company, 1968. Reprint 1982 (University of Hawaii Press). This is a detailed history of the Hawaiian islands, covering the growth of American influence, Asian immigration, the end of the monarchy, and annexation.

9:495 Day, A. Grove. *Hawaii and Its People.* Rev. ed. New York: Meredith Press, 1968. Day's work covers Hawaiian history from the arrival of Captain Cook in 1778 to statehood in 1959. Although the study is oriented more toward a study of life on the islands, it includes information on the growth of American influence and the annexation of 1898. First published in 1955.

9:496 McWilliams, Tennant S. "James H. Blount, the South, and Hawaiian Annexation." *Pacific Historical Review* 57 (February 1988): 25–46. McWilliams describes how the short diplomatic career of Georgian James H. Blount helps elucidate the story of the New South leaders and their hopes to modernize the region without turning to economic expansion or international conflict. Cleveland sent Blount to Hawaii to investigate the events leading to the revolution of 1893. Blount concluded that Hawaiian natives opposed the coup while the U.S. capitalists supported it, and that U.S. capitalists and revolutionary leaders dethroned the queen with the aid of the U.S. minister.

9:497 _____. *The New South Faces the World: Foreign Affairs and the Southern Sense of Self, 1877–1950.* Baton Rouge: Louisiana State University Press, 1988. McWilliams explores late-nineteenth-century southern attitudes toward expansion and includes an account of James Blount's mission to Hawaii.

9:498 Morgan, William Michael. "The Anti-Japanese Origins of the Hawaiian Annexation Treaty of 1897." *Diplomatic History* 6 (Winter 1982): 23–44. Morgan restudies the annexation of Hawaii outside the events of the war with Spain and concludes that annexation was intended "as a powerful hands-off warning to Japan, which the McKinley administration believed was about to overthrow or subvert the Hawaiian government."

9:499 Osborne, Thomas J. *"Empire Can Wait": American Opposition to Hawaiian Annexation, 1893–1898.* Kent, OH: Kent State University Press, 1981. Osborne analyzes the resistance to Hawaiian annexation and Cleveland's abandonment of the proposal as well as the importance of the Hawaiian question for establishing a precedent for empire building.

9:500 _____. "The Main Reason for Hawaiian Annexation in July 1898." *Oregon Historical Quarterly* 71 (June 1970): 161–78. Osborne argues that the main reason for the annexation of Hawaii in 1898 was the lure of commercial interests in Asia.

9:501 _____. "Trade or War? America's Annexation of Hawaii Reconsidered." *Pacific Historical Review* 50 (August 1981): 285–307. Osborne sees the expansion of U.S. trade with the Far East as the primary reason for annexing Hawaii and that too much attention has been attached to a military interpretation of annexation. Few senators viewed the action as essential to U.S. coastal defense or military strategy.

9:502 Pearce, George. "Assessing Public Opinion: Editorial Comment and the Annexation of Hawaii: A Case Study." *Pacific Historical Review* 43 (August 1974): 324–41. Pearce argues that accounts of a massive wave of public opinion backing annexation of Hawaii are myths. Moreover, public opinion had little if any influence on decisionmakers.

9:503 Pratt, Julius W. *Expansionists of 1898: The Acquisition of Hawaii and the Spanish Islands.* Baltimore: Johns Hopkins Press, 1936. This imaginative, influential work boldly challenges the economic interpretation of American policy and blends the study of intellectual and diplomatic history. The author stresses Darwinian ideas and gives considerable attention to public opinion.

9:504 Russ, William Adam. *The Hawaiian Republic, 1894–98, and Its Struggle to Win Annexation.* Selinsgrove, PA: Susquehanna University Press, 1961. The Spanish-American War finally made annexation of Hawaii possible. In 1893, the islands were not needed, but in 1898 they were wanted. Many in the islands saw annexation to the United States as the only way to counter the oriental threat or, in case Asian immigration ended, economic ruin.

9:505 Tate, Merze. "Great Britain and the Sovereignty of Hawaii." *Pacific Historical Review* 31 (November 1962): 327–48. In 1854, Britain's official policy was to stop annexation, and in 1873 it opposed the cession of Pearl Harbor to the United States. By 1893, however, it showed no concern over the possibility of annexation, while Russia wanted American control of the islands and Japan looked to three-party control of the strategic area. By 1898, Britain desired American ownership to stop German moves.

9:506   _____. "Hawaii: A Symbol of Anglo-American Rapprochement." *Political Science Quarterly* 79 (December 1964): 555–75. This is primarily a study of changing British views over a half century. The British were interested in some type of position in the Hawaiian islands in the 1850s but gradually reduced their interest until in the 1890s they were urging the United States to annex them.

9:507   _____. "The Myth of Hawaii's Swing toward Australasia and Canada." *Pacific Historical Review* 33 (August 1964): 273–93. Tate argues that Hawaiian politicians often used the threat of a swing toward Australia and Canada as a prod to the American Congress to get a reciprocity treaty passed. Such a move, however, was impossible, for the markets needed by the Hawaiian sugar industry could be found only in the United States.

9:508   _____. "Twisting the Lion's Tail over Hawaii." *Pacific Historical Review* 36 (February 1967): 27–46. The study covers the changes in British policy toward American annexation of Hawaii from 1854 to 1898. British control of the islands would have been a threat to the United States in light of the coming isthmian canal. By 1898, London no longer opposed American ownership of Hawaii, an indication of an Anglo-American rapprochement.

SAMOA

9:509   Anderson, Stuart. "'Pacific Destiny' and American Policy in Samoa, 1872–1899." *Hawaiian Journal of History* 12 (1978): 45–60. This overview presents the hypothesis that the persistent interest of the United States in Samoa derived from the idea of an American "Manifest Destiny" in the Pacific.

9:510   Brookes, Jean I. *International Rivalry in the Pacific Islands, 1800–1875.* Berkeley: University of California Press, 1941. Brookes's general narrative of the emergence of the Pacific as an arena of international rivalry devotes one chapter to the Steinberger episode in Samoa.

9:511   Calhoun, Charles W. "Rehearsal for Anti-Imperialism: The Second Cleveland Administration's Attempt to Withdraw from Samoa, 1893–1895." *Historian* 48 (February 1986): 209–24. Calhoun examines the arguments against U.S. involvement in Samoa and their backers. Doubts peaked during Cleveland's second administration when Secretary of State Walter Q. Gresham sought to cut off American participation in a joint protectorate over the islands. While he failed in this, he articulated an elaborate case against interference in other nations' affairs and the difficulties inherent in territorial acquisition or informal empire.

9:512   Churchward, L. G. "American Enterprise: The Foundations of the Pacific Mail Service." *Historical Studies* 3 (November 1947): 217–24. Churchward outlines the American attempt to win control over Pacific commerce through government subsidies and a Samoan coaling station.

9:513   Davidson, James Wightman. "Lauaki Namulau'ulu Mamoe: A Traditionalist in Samoan Politics." In *Pacific Islands Portraits,* ed. James Wightman Davidson and Deryck Scarr, 267–99. Canberra: Australian National University Press, 1970. Davidson's essay examines the foreign competition over Samoa through the eyes of a Samoan opponent of foreign political control.

9:514   Ellison, Joseph Waldo. *Opening and Penetration of Foreign Influence in Samoa to 1880.* Corvallis, OR: Oregon State College, 1938. This is a brief outline of the beginnings of international rivalry in Samoa.

9:515   _____. "The Partition of Samoa: A Study in Imperialism and Diplomacy." *Pacific Historical Review* 8 (September 1939): 259–88. Ellison's account deals with how competing American, German, and British claims to Samoa were settled in 1899.

9:516   Gilson, Richard P. *Samoa 1830 to 1900: The Politics of a Multi-Cultural Community.* New York: Oxford University Press, 1970. The author's anthropological training and his painstaking research make this an important work for any study of American relations with Samoa. Published posthumously; completed and introduced by J. W. Davidson.

9:517 Gray, John A. C. *Amerika Samoa: A History of American Samoa and Its United States Naval Administration*. Annapolis: United States Naval Institute, 1960. This is the official naval history of American Samoa with material on the background to annexation, including a chapter on the 1889 crisis.

9:518 Hoyt, Edwin P. *The Typhoon That Stopped a War*. New York: D. McKay Co., 1968. Hoyt's narrative is a minimalist account of the 1889 crisis. It especially neglects much of the Samoan background for the drama.

9:519 Kennedy, Paul. *The Samoan Tangle: A Study in Anglo-German-American Relations, 1878–1900*. New York: Barnes and Noble, 1974. Kennedy discusses Samoa in relation to broader questions of Anglo-German-American diplomacy and politics. In scope and depth, this book is first-rate international history, a requirement for assessing the changing relations of the great powers in the late nineteenth century.

9:520 Masterman, Sylvia. *The Origins of International Rivalry in Samoa, 1845–1884*. Stanford, CA: Stanford University Press, 1934. This brief study shows how the United States, Britain, and Germany became involved in Samoa.

9:521 Rigby, Barry R. "The Origins of American Expansion in Hawaii and Samoa, 1865–1900." *International History Review* 10 (May 1988): 221–37. This article emphasizes the importance of "men on the spot" as agents of U.S. expansion in Hawaii and Samoa. Rigby believes historians, overlooking the decisive accomplishments of these agents in the 1870s, have erroneously concluded that U.S. expansion did not begin in earnest until the 1890s. In fact, agents on the islands were giving it momentum and direction two decades earlier.

9:522 _____. "Private Interests and the Origins of American Involvement in Samoa 1872–1877." *Journal of Pacific History* 8 (1973): 75–87. This brief analysis focuses on the importance of backstairs influence and land speculation in establishing the American stake in Samoa in the 1870s.

9:523 Stevenson, Robert L. *Footnote to History: Eight Years of Trouble in Samoa*. New York: Charles Scribner's Sons, 1892. Reprint 1996 (University of Hawaii Press). This intriguing narrative includes some vivid personal sketches and an especially memorable description of the 1889 crisis.

ASIA

Overviews

9:524 Hart, Robert A. *The Eccentric Tradition: American Diplomacy in the Far East*. New York: Scribner, 1976. This is a journalistic, interpretive history of U.S. relations with Asia.

9:525 Iriye, Akira. *Across the Pacific: An Inner History of American–East Asian Relations*. This is the revised edition (with two new chapters) of a most important work examining the history of U.S. relations with East Asia. Iriye delves into the intellectual, emotional, and psychological sources of the people and leaders of Asian nations as they dealt with their counterparts abroad, presenting a cross-cultural perspective on international history. Originally published in 1967; extensive bibliographical essay (2:280).

9:526 Perry, John Curtis. *Facing West: Americans and the Opening of the Pacific*. Westport, CT: Praeger, 1994. Perry traces the American eagerness to expand westward to the Pacific from the origins of the nation to the presidency of Ronald Reagan, focusing mainly on the ideology and methods behind the extension of the U.S. sphere of influence.

9:527 Thomson, James C., Jr., Peter W. Stanley, and John Curtis Perry. *Sentimental Imperialists: The American Experience in East Asia*. This synthesis covers the history of American–East Asian affairs since initial contacts in the eighteenth century. The authors trace the often troubled encounter between the United States and the countries of East Asia, emphasizing nationalism, ethnocentrism, intolerance, and America's sense of mission and obsession with China. Foreword by John K. Fairbank (2:274).

Korea

9:528 Lee, Yur-Bok. *Diplomatic Relations between the United States and Korea, 1866–1887*. New

York: Humanities Press, 1970. This study of the first years of formal American-Korean diplomatic and cultural relations focuses on Korea's attempt to strengthen itself with U.S. assistance in the face of strong opposition from China, suggesting that by the middle of the nineteenth century the "western order" proved superior in science, technology, military, and political matters.

China

9:529   Anderson, David L. *Imperialism and Idealism: American Diplomats in China, 1861–1898.* Bloomington: Indiana University Press, 1985. This study, focusing on the lives, careers, and policies of the first U.S. diplomats in China, attempts to explain late-nineteenth-century contradictions in Washington's China policies that resulted from the tension between altruistic American ideals (fairness, justice, self-determination, cooperation, mutual respect) and self-interest (exploitation of unequal treaties, protection and expansion of economic interests). Anderson concludes that "American expressions of altruism often appeared more self-serving than self-evident."

9:530   Clyde, Paul Hibbert. "Attitudes and Policies of George F. Seward, American Minister at Peking, 1876–1880: Some Phases of the Cooperative Policy." *Pacific Historical Review* 2 (November 1933): 387–404. Clyde does not rank Seward highly among American diplomats in nineteenth-century China, but his lengthy dispatches to Washington contain much information on questions of treaty revision and interpretation, especially on judicial proceedings, extraterritoriality, and tariffs.

9:531   _____. "The China Policy of J. Ross Browne, American Minister at Peking, 1868–1869." *Pacific Historical Review* 1 (August 1932): 312–33. According to Clyde, Browne was accurate when he described his predecessor, Burlingame, as a sentimentalist who refused to acknowledge the antagonism of Chinese officials toward foreigners. Browne contended that the only realistic western policy was to force China to obey the treaties, especially the commercial provisions.

9:532   _____. "Frederick F. Low and the Tientsin Massacre." *Pacific Historical Review* 2

(February 1933): 100–08. Clyde characterizes Low, who served as U.S. minister to Peking from 1870 to 1874, as a "careful observer" and provides numerous excerpts from his reports to Washington on the diplomatically troublesome issues occasioned by western missionary activity in China.

9:533   Cohen, Warren I. *America's Response to China: A History of Sino-American Relations.* This is an incisive analysis of Chinese-American relations, emphasizing the gap between America's romantic yearnings, based on a naïve racism, and the relative unimportance of China in the broad range of American national interests. Cohen contends that as an Atlantic-centered nation, the United States consistently subordinated its China policies to more pressing demands in Latin America and Europe. Twenty-five pages deal with the late nineteenth century (2:276). First published in 1971.

9:534   _____. "Art Collecting as International Relations: Chinese Art and American Culture." *Journal of American–East Asian Relations* 1 (Winter 1992): 409–34. The collecting of East Asian art in the nineteenth century affected American perceptions of China and Japan. U.S. admiration for Asian art was politically significant and proved to be an important form of intercultural relations. American collectors often misunderstood but respected East Asian art, a step, Cohen contends, toward accepting East Asians as real people capable of sophistication, skill, and genius.

9:535   Dennett, Tyler. *Americans in Eastern Asia: A Critical Study of the Policy of the United States with Reference to China, Japan and Korea in the 19th Century.* New York: Macmillan Company, 1922. This pioneering and still rewarding work studies the origins and development of U.S. policies in China, Japan, Korea, Siam, India, and the Pacific Ocean. Dennett uses and reproduces many documents.

9:536   Dorwart, Jeffery M. *The Pigtail War: American Involvement in the Sino-Japanese War of 1894–1895.* Amherst: University of Massachusetts Press, 1975. Dorwart traces the U.S. reaction to and involvement in the Sino-Japanese conflict of 1894–1895, seeing in Secretary Gresham's moralistic posture and concept of progress a harbinger of later administrations' policies. He also illustrates U.S. reliance on amateurs to run foreign policy and the problems created by petty bureaucratic rivalries.

9:537 Dudden, Arthur Power. *The American Pacific: From the Old China Trade to the Present.* Dudden provides an overview of two centuries of American encounters with the diverse peoples and cultures of the Pacific. The book blends events in domestic politics, missionary activities, military campaigns, and diplomatic maneuvers and offers portraits of key individuals who shaped history in the Pacific (2:271).

9:538 Fairbank, John K. *The Great Chinese Revolution, 1800–1985.* New York: Harper and Row, 1986. This is a narrative of historical events and a synthesis summarizing trends, patterns, issues, and individuals. The book emphasizes the high level of Chinese cultural, institutional, and intellectual achievements before the impact of westernization. The Chinese were slow to adopt western ways because indigenous institutions worked so well that there seemed little need to change them.

9:539 Flynt, Wayne, and Gerald W. Berkley. *Taking Christianity to China: Alabama Missionaries in the Middle Kingdom, 1850–1950.* Tuscaloosa: University of Alabama Press, 1997. Flynt provides details about forty-seven Alabamians who helped shape American opinion about China through the talks they gave while at home, by writing for church, local, and statewide newspapers, and by hosting visiting American opinion makers who visited with them while traveling in China.

9:540 Hammersmith, Jack L. "American Attempts to Prevent a War over 'Vietnam': The Experience of John Russell Young, 1882–85." *Historian* 38 (February 1976): 253–67. The State Department and its minister to China, John Russell Young, sought to mediate a Sino-French dispute over Tonkin, which led to the Black Flags war and the French conquest of northern Vietnam.

9:541 Henson, Curtis T., Jr. *Commissioners and Commodores: The East India Squadron and American Diplomacy in China.* In this analysis of the origins and early use of naval power as a tool in furthering U.S. objectives in China, Henson emphasizes the ad hoc nature of U.S. diplomacy and details the actions and maneuvers of various naval officers (7:445).

9:542 Hunt, Michael H. *The Making of a Special Relationship: The United States and China to 1914.* Using multiarchival sources and a cultural perspective, the author assesses the Chinese role in influencing Sino-American relations. Important cross-cultural bibliographic essay (2:279).

9:543 Hunter, Jane. *The Gospel of Gentility: American Women Missionaries in Turn-of-the-Century China.* Hunter explores the feminization of missions in China and the concept of religion as a necessary accompaniment to or justification for expansion. This sociological study links women's search for productive careers in late-nineteenth-century America to overseas expansion (2:236).

9:544 Jiang, Arnold Xiangze. *The United States and China.* This is a short, interpretive analysis that seeks to provide a framework for understanding 150 years of bilateral relations. Jiang argues that after 1844 "United States aggression and Chinese resistance defined the Sino-American relationship" (2:281).

9:545 Kehoe, Barbara B. "William Patterson Jones: American Consul in China, 1862–1868." *Journal of the Illinois State Historical Society* 73 (Spring 1980): 45–52. Kehoe describes an early, Illinois "old China hand," who spent six years in China in the 1860s and retained a deep appreciation for it as an ancient and worthy civilization. Jones was greatly attracted to the Chinese people, admired their merchants, praised their respect for education, and blamed most of China's problems on greedy westerners.

9:546 Kessler, Lawrence D. *The Jiangyin Mission Station: An American Missionary Community in China, 1895–1951.* Chapel Hill: University of North Carolina Press, 1996. This work tracks a specific American Presbyterian mission and its inhabitants from the anti-Christian riots of the 1890s through the communist triumph in 1949. Kessler argues for the importance of the Social Gospel movement that took hold of foreign missions at the end of the nineteenth century and emphasized social transformation through secular good works rather than individual conversion.

9:547 McClellan, Robert. *The Heathen Chinee: A Study of American Attitudes toward China, 1890–1905.* Columbus: Ohio State University Press, 1971.

This study evaluates public opinion as expressed in contemporary periodical literature, the author finding the collective American opinion ambivalent, reflecting both a sympathetic interest in Chinese culture and a strong antipathy to Chinese immigration.

9:548 McCormick, Thomas J. *China Market: America's Quest for Informal Empire, 1893–1901.* Chicago: Quadrangle Books, 1967. McCormick explores the origins of the nineties commitment to marketplace expansionism, contending that U.S. proponents of expansion into the China market, having discovered the causes of U.S. social instability in production surpluses, sought a solution in the form of "overseas mercantile expansion." Many of this view rejected colonialism as undesirable and unnecessary, but their efforts to sell agricultural and manufacturers' surpluses led to an effort to acquire the China market.

9:549 Miller, Stuart Creighton. *The Unwelcome Immigrant: The American Image of the Chinese, 1785–1882.* Berkeley: University of California Press, 1969. Anti-Chinese sentiment was not confined to western states but present from the time of first contacts throughout the United States. Nationwide support for exclusion came from traders, diplomats, and missionaries, whose arguments were broadly disseminated by both the eastern and western press.

9:550 Neils, Patricia, ed. *United States Attitudes and Policies toward China: The Impact of American Missionaries.* Armonk, NY: M. E. Sharpe, 1990. This book contains chapters on Baptist educational work in the nineteenth century, the popularization of China missions in the United States in the early 1800s, domestic support for foreign missions in the nineteenth century, and popular images of China in missionary and secular presses late in the century. See, for example, Charles W. Weber, "Conflicting Cultural Traditions in China: Baptist Educational Work in the Nineteenth Century" (25–45).

9:551 Paulsen, George E. "The Abrogation of the Gresham-Yang Treaty." *Pacific Historical Review* 40 (November 1971): 457–77. The author uses the voluminous correspondence of the ten-year life of the Gresham-Yang Treaty to explain China's grievances over enforcement and violations of the U.S. exclusion laws. China considered the discriminatory im-

migration policy insulting and condemned the United States for not carrying out its treaty obligations. The record shows that before 1904 "neither the McKinley nor Roosevelt administrations showed any great concern over China's repeated protests and warnings."

9:552 _____. "The Gresham-Yang Treaty." *Pacific Historical Review* 37 (August 1968): 281–97. The Sino-American treaty of 1894 suspended immigration of Chinese laborers for a period of ten years, an arrangement acceptable to China only because the alternative was even harsher U.S. restrictions.

9:553 _____. "Secretary Gresham, Senator Lodge, and American Good Offices in China, 1894." *Pacific Historical Review* 36 (May 1967): 123–42. During the Sino-Japanese War, the U.S. consul at Shanghai turned over to China two alleged Japanese spies who were quickly executed by Chinese authorities, drawing sharp criticism from Senator Henry Cabot Lodge.

9:554 _____. "The Szechwan Riots of 1895 and American Missionary Diplomacy." *Journal of Asian Studies* 28 (February 1969): 285–98. Examining U.S. policy dealing with antimissionary riots in Chengtu and Kutien, Paulsen concludes that although America's strong stand and close cooperation with the British brought the degradation of the Szechwan viceroy, the policy failed to prevent new outrages in subsequent years.

9:555 Tsai, Shih-shan Henry. *China and the Overseas Chinese in the United States, 1868–1911.* Fayetteville: University of Arkansas Press, 1983. Tsai contends that Chinese government weakness and ambiguous U.S. policy helped kindle Chinese nationalism.

Japan

9:556 Beasley, W. G. *Japan Encounters the Barbarian: Japanese Travellers in America and Europe.* New Haven: Yale University Press, 1995. This work describes the groups of Japanese diplomats and students who traveled abroad in the 1860s and 1870s to initiate direct study of the western world. Beasley emphasizes the role of the Japanese government in acquiring western military skills and technology by means of overseas study missions. Annotated bibliography.

9:557   Cosenza, Mario Emilio, ed. *The Complete Journal of Townsend Harris, First American Consul and Minister to Japan.* 2d ed. Garden City, NY: Doubleday, Doran and Company, 1930. This collection contains important first perspectives and impressions of Americans in Japan. Notes and introduction by the editor.

9:558   Davidann, Jon Thares. "The American YMCA in Meiji Japan: God's Work Gone Awry." *Journal of World History* 6 (Spring 1995): 107–25. Davidann uses the theoretical perspective of the new cultural history to evaluate missionary history. Looking not only at the missionaries and the society they inhabited, but examining the converts in relation to each other, he demonstrates the dramatic success of Christianity in Japan during the first two decades of the Meiji period and finds Japan highly vulnerable to conversion, though the converts adamantly refused to have their Christianity dictated to them by foreign missionaries.

9:559   _____. *A World of Crisis and Progress: The American YMCA in Japan, 1890–1930.* Bethlehem, PA: Lehigh University Press, 1998. This history of the YMCA in Japan emphasizes the impact of American Protestant outreach on Japanese youth, contending that the missionary zeal of American Christians in Japan spawned a nationalistic form of Christianity that ultimately challenged and marginalized the American Christian enterprise. The dual goals of the YMCA—developing indigenous leadership and maintaining a commitment to evangelism—turned out to be incompatible. Japanese Christians asserted their own leadership over the association and abandoned evangelism for a more liberal theology.

9:560   Dorwart, Jeffery M. "The Independent Minister: John M. B. Sill and the Struggle against Japanese Expansion in Korea, 1894–1897." *Pacific Historical Review* 44 (November 1975): 485–502. Sill, U.S. minister in Korea between 1894 and 1897, informed his government of irreconcilable Japanese-American differences long before the Russo-Japanese War. He labored to block Japanese expansion in Korea, which would close it to American trade, travel, and missionary enterprise, and tried to uphold American treaty rights. He advocated a formal open door policy several years before the State Department adopted such a program. His bent for independence and controversial decisions, and criticisms of timid naval officers and remote government bureaucrats, did nothing to "alter American policies or attitudes toward Japan. He never convinced his government of the dangers to American interests in East Asia posed by increased Japanese power."

9:561   Earns, Lane. "The Foreign Settlement in Nagasaki, 1859–1869." *Historian* 56 (Spring 1994): 483–500. When Nagasaki was opened to foreign trade and settlement in 1859, western missionaries, merchants, and diplomatic envoys poured into the city, making it a premier port in Japan.

9:562   Fujita, Fumiko. *American Pioneers and the Japanese Frontier: American Experts in Nineteenth-Century Japan.* Westport, CT: Greenwood Press, 1994. This is a case study of fifty Americans employed from 1871 to 1882 by the Meiji regime to help develop and transform Hokkaido. Fujita describes the ideas and attitudes Americans carried into their work, their reactions to the Japanese with whom they worked, and the ideas about Japan they took home. The book relates how key Japanese officials directed the work and what they thought of Americans, and concludes that, on the whole, collaboration succeeded.

9:563   Henning, Joseph M. *Outposts of Civilization: Race, Religion, and the Formative Years of American-Japanese Relations.* New York: New York University Press, 2000. This work reveals how Gilded Era Americans grappled with the challenge Japan posed to their belief in white, Christian superiority. Rather than abandon this conviction, Henning argues, many important experts found a new position for Japan within it—they adopted the Japanese as a white race that was Christian at heart.

9:564   LaFeber, Walter. *The Clash: A History of U.S.-Japan Relations.* This work highlights the highly dangerous clashes—stemming from two different and competing forms of capitalism and each nation's relationship to China—that have been the historical norm in the relationship between the United States and Japan since 1853 and that set them on a collision course from the first. Chapter 2 covers 1868–1900, when parallel progress, accommodation, and coincidental interests helped postpone the inevitable military clash (2:284).

9:565 Moriyama, Alan Takeo. *Imingaisha: Japanese Emigration Companies and Hawaii, 1894–1908.* Honolulu: University of Hawaii Press, 1985. The author reviews conditions making emigration to Hawaii attractive for over 125,000 Japanese between 1894 and 1908 and describes the companies that expedited the movement, discussing the entrepreneurs who set them up, their sources of capital, their agents and how they worked, and the companies' relations with government officials, shipping firms, and boardinghouses near ports. Moriyama also outlines the immigrants' socioeconomic background and how they financed their journeys, describes life and work on Hawaiian plantations, and demonstrates how much of the money the immigrants saved filtered back to Japan.

9:566 Notehelfer, F. G. *American Samurai: Captain L. L. Janes and Japan.* Princeton: Princeton University Press, 1985. This is a biography of a nineteenth-century agent of modernist transformation who is deemed by the author to be "the most successful missionary in Japan." Janes's ambition, self-aggrandizement, piousness, and self-righteousness led him to the leadership of a Japanese school devoted to preparing young samurai for a new society.

9:567 _____, ed. *Japan through American Eyes: The Journal of Francis Hall, Kanagawa and Yokohama, 1859–1866.* Princeton: Princeton University Press, 1992. Reprint 2001 (Westview Press). This book contains a brief biographical sketch of Francis Hall, active in consular affairs in Japan, 1859–1866, plus his journal, transcribed and annotated. Hall, who also wrote articles for the New York press, proved to be a sensitive and objective observer of Japan as well as the western community there.

9:568 Roden, Donald. "Baseball and the Quest for National Dignity in Meiji Japan." *American Historical Review* 85 (June 1980): 511–34. Roden describes how baseball "rose from oblivion to embody the Social Darwinist spirit of competition and vigor that swept Japan in the 1890s, how it heralded a new chapter in Japanese-American relations, and how it ultimately enhanced both the social image of a student-elite and the geopolitical image of a nation that was just breaking free from the shackles of unequal treaties." Japanese enthusiasm for the game helped spread the western Victorian ideology of manliness and duty.

9:569 Rosenstone, Robert A. *Mirror in the Shrine: American Encounters with Meiji Japan.* Cambridge, MA: Harvard University Press, 1988. Rosenstone describes the experiences of an American missionary, scientist, and novelist who found in nineteenth-century Japan an outlet for their energies and an environment that permitted them psychological satisfaction.

9:570 Sawada, Mitziko. "Culprits and Gentlemen: Meiji Japan's Restrictions of Emigrants to the United States, 1891–1909." *Pacific Historical Review* 60 (August 1991): 339–59. This article sees Japan's actions on emigration to the United States as contradicting the "victimization" assumption so often used to explain its response to America. Japan's actions on emigration represent not acquiescence to U.S. dictates but a keen sense of independence and timing as well as a wish to convey a positive self-image to the west.

9:571 Shankman, Arnold. "'Asiatic Ogre' or 'Desirable Citizen'? The Image of Japanese Americans in the Afro-American Press, 1867–1933." *Pacific Historical Review* 46 (November 1977): 567–87. Shankman examines the image of Japanese-Americans in the black press between 1867 and 1933. Topics include black fears of competition for jobs, Japanese business practices, and assimilation problems.

9:572 Strauss, David. "The 'Far East' in the American Mind, 1883–1894: Percival Lowell's Decisive Impact." *Journal of American–East Asian Relations* 2 (Fall 1993): 217–41. This article explores the cultural significance of an investor, Asian hand, and astronomer who portrayed Japan as an arrested civilization incapable of stimulating the imagination. But Lowell also admired Japanese art, architecture, gardens, and other artistic achievements. An important interpreter of Japanese life to the American reading public, he solidified the idea of western superiority to the Orient.

9:573 Taylor, Sandra C. "The Ineffectual Voice: Japanese Missionaries and American Foreign Policy,

1870–1941." *Pacific Historical Review* 53 (February 1984): 20–38. American missionaries, a large and cohesive interest group who viewed the Japanese positively as a people with a right to determine their own destiny, were nonetheless unable to counter the negative image of Japan as an imperialistic, militaristic threat to U.S. interests or of the Japanese as aggressive, hostile, and an object of fear.

9:574   Treat, Payson J. *Diplomatic Relations between the United States and Japan, 1853–1905.* 3 vols. Stanford, CA: Stanford University Press, 1932–1938. Written by the pioneer scholar of Japanese-American diplomatic relations, the first two volumes, covering the period 1853 to 1895, are the most valuable. All three focus exclusively on diplomatic relations, recounting in detail even minor diplomatic issues.

Korea

9:575   Chay, Jongsuk. *Diplomacy of Asymmetry: Korean-American Relations to 1910.* Honolulu: University of Hawaii Press, 1990. This work presents the ideas and roles of presidents, secretaries of state, and diplomatic agents who influenced the course of U.S. relations with Korea. Chay contends that Korean-American relations before 1910 were characterized by "asymmetry," an imbalance between Korean faith in and expectations of U.S. commitments to Korea and Washington's limited interests in the small, distant East Asian peninsula.

9:576   Davies, Daniel M. "The Impact of Christianity upon Korea, 1884–1910: Six Key American and Korean Figures." *Journal of Church and State* 36 (Autumn 1994): 795–820. Between 1600 and the 1940s, Korea experienced two phases of Christian influence—Catholic (1600–1876) and Protestant (1876–1940), and Davies finds the impact on political and social life of Protestantism the greater. Christians generally held Shamanism, Buddhism, and Confucianism responsible for Korea's political and social corruption. The article includes brief sketches of six Protestant missionaries and their work—three Americans and three Korean converts.

9:577   Deuchler, Martina. *Confucian Gentlemen and Barbarian Envoys: The Opening of Korea, 1875–1885.* Seattle: University of Washington Press,

1977. A diplomatic history emphasizing Korea's relations with Japan, China, and the west between 1877 and 1885, especially the creation of treaty ports and the development of international trade, Deuchler's book describes political, intellectual, and economic changes as well as Korean diplomatic developments.

9:578   Harrington, Fred H. "An American View of Korean-American Relations, 1882–1905." In *One Hundred Years of Korean-American Relations, 1882–1982,* ed. Yur-Bok Lee and Wayne Patterson, 46–67. University: University of Alabama Press, 1986. Harrington describes U.S. diplomacy in Korea from 1882 to 1905 as "inconsistent, indifferent, unconcerned, and thus hardly reliable."

9:579   _____. *God, Mammon and the Japanese: Dr. Horace N. Allen and Korean-American Relations, 1884–1905.* Madison: University of Wisconsin Press, 1944. Although this book centers on Horace N. Allen, the most important individual in American-Korean relations until 1905, it is a comprehensive and readable work on the subject of American-Korean relations for the pre–World War I period, describing the diplomatic, commercial, and missionary relationships between the two nations. Extensive bibliography.

9:580   Lee, Yur-Bok, and Wayne Patterson, eds. *One Hundred Years of Korean-American Relations, 1882–1982.* See chapter 2 of this Guide (2:291).

9:581   Ryu, Dae Young. "An Odd Relationship: The State Department, Its Representatives, and American Protestant Missionaries in Korea, 1882–1905." *Journal of American–East Asian Relations* 6 (Winter 1997): 261–87. While Korea seemed so poor it promised little in the way of importance when the U.S. Congress ratified the Shufeldt Treaty in 1882, it proved to be the "only country on the Asian continent where American influence, among Western powers, predominated." The key factor explaining the discrepancy between Washington's apathy and America's great influence over Korea was the missionaries. The State Department's strategic indifference and the missionaries' religious successes seemed contradictory, producing an "odd relationship."

9:582   Swartout, Robert R., Jr. *Mandarins, Gunboats, and Power Politics: Owen Nickerson Denny*

and the International Rivalries in Korea. Honolulu: Asian Studies Program, University of Hawaii, 1980. Swartout focuses on the role played by an American adviser to the Korean monarchy from 1886 to 1890.

Native Americans

9:583   Berkhofer, Robert F. *The White Man's Indian: Images of the American Indian from Columbus to the Present.* New York: Alfred A. Knopf, 1978. This work seeks to present a comprehensive account of what white people have thought about Native Americans across the generations by focusing on images, ideas, values, and policies and showing how little these themes have varied over time. Berkhofer contends the dual image of the Indian as the "noble savage" has had the firmest hold on the white mind.

9:584   Drinnon, Richard. *Facing West: The Metaphysics of Indian-Hating and Empire Building.* While the first half of this book concerns racism and Native Americans from the 1630s to the 1840s, Drinnon afterward discusses aspects of American expansionist theory and practice in the late nineteenth and twentieth centuries. Throughout, he emphasizes the racism and repression involved in American empire-building (7:116).

9:585   Gilbert, Arthur N. "The American Indian and United States Diplomatic History." Examining the Native American's position in law as a "domestic dependent nation," Gilbert describes how the U.S. government until 1871 continued to conclude treaties with them as they did with any foreign power, the only difference being Indian weakness and proximity vis-à-vis the United States (5:68).

9:586   Prucha, Francis Paul. *American Indian Treaties: The History of a Political Anomaly.* This large book examines the development and meaning of Indian treaties as political and legal documents. Prucha describes the odd political reality of treaty-making: how Indian treaties varied from those with European nations, rested on the concept of Indians as quasi-sovereign nations, protected yet impinged on Indian sovereignty, and how the Indians' growing economic dependence and erosion of tribal sovereignty created by federal policies slowly undercut the legal relevance of the treaties (5:442).

9:587   St. Germain, Jill. *Indian Treaty-Making Policy in the United States and Canada, 1867–1877.* Lincoln: University of Nebraska Press, 2001. The author compares treaties negotiated by the United States with the Cheyenne, Comanche, Kiowa, and Sioux Indians with those Canada negotiated with the Blackfoot, Cree, and Ojibwa. Canadian dealings with native peoples were as problematic and political as those of the United States.

9:588   Viola, Herman J. *Diplomats in Buckskins: A History of Indian Delegations in Washington City.* Washington, DC: Smithsonian Institution Press, 1981. Reprint 1995 (Rivilo Books). This book traces the evolution of tribal delegations to Washington, D.C., invited because U.S. government officials assumed it easier to make treaties there than in the field. Viola describes ceremonial features, White House receptions, exchanges of presents, and bureaucratic encounters with the Bureau of Indian Affairs. The work focuses on the nineteenth century.

9:589   Wooster, Robert. *The Military and United States Indian Policy, 1865–1903.* New Haven: Yale University Press, 1988. Reprint 1995 (University of Nebraska Press). Probing the army's role on the Indian frontier after the Civil War, Wooster discusses the split between military and federal authorities about Indian policy and concludes that the War Department and army had no real strategy or policy for dealing with Indians and no institutional mechanism for formulating a strategy or policy. Military and civilian authorities reacted in an ad hoc manner to each crisis as it occurred.

10

The Spanish-Cuban-American War and Turn-of-the-Century Imperialism

Contributing Editors

JOHN L. OFFNER
Shippensburg University

JOSEPH A. FRY
University of Nevada, Las Vegas

Contents

Introduction

Since the publication of the 1983 *Guide to American Foreign Relations since 1700,* the field of diplomatic history has greatly expanded writings on social and cultural affairs. Chapter 10, when compared to the 1983 *Guide,* reflects the changing nature of the discipline. Responding to the new cultural directions, this chapter has added topics on missionaries and gender, and it has increased the number of entries on race. Many of these entries go beyond the traditional economic and political diplomatic history approaches. In the more customary political and economic areas there is a greater emphasis on sectionalism and ideology as a backdrop to foreign policy formulation.

The chapter also includes many non-American authors and foreign-language publications, an area of scholarship largely overlooked in the 1983 edition. The bibliography was created during the centennial years of the 1898 war and its aftermath, which saw an outpouring of Spanish, Cuban, and Puerto Rican conference papers and publications. Accordingly, there is a large amount of centennial scholarship, much of it in Spanish. Though extensive, the international entries are not comprehensive. Many conference papers were excluded because the authors simply summarized their earlier work. An international emphasis also appears in the increased number of entries of foreign document collections.

Document Collections and Published Primary Materials

10:1   U.S. Department of State. *Foreign Relations of the United States.* Washington, DC: Government Printing Office, 1896–1902. Annual volumes for 1895 through 1901 (eight volumes in all) are of great value in examining the diplomacy of the Spanish-American-Cuban-Philippine War and acquisition of an empire (1:93).

10:2   U.S. Congress. House of Representatives. *Message of the President of the United States, Communicated to the Two Houses of Congress, on the Re-* lations of the United States to Spain by Reason of Warfare in the Island of Cuba. 55th Cong. 2d Sess., House Doc. 405. Washington, DC: Government Printing Office, 1898. McKinley's April 11, 1898, message to Congress reviews Spanish-Cuban-American relations and provides a rationale for Congress to authorize intervention in Cuba.

10:3   U.S. Congress. Senate. *Papers Relating to the Treaty with Spain.* 56th Cong., 2d Sess., Sen. Doc. 148. Washington, DC: Government Printing Office, 1901. This compilation of documents covers the Paris Peace Conference negotiations that led to the 1898 Treaty of Paris.

10:4   _____. *Treaty of Peace between the United States and Spain and Accompanying Papers: Message from the President of the United States.* 55th Cong., 3rd Sess., Sen. Doc. 63. Washington, DC: Government Printing Office, 1899. This publication contains the diplomatic exchanges between the United States and Spain that culminated in the 1899 Treaty of Paris.

10:5   U.S. War Department. Office of Adjutant General. *Correspondence Relating to the War with Spain and Conditions Growing Out of the Same, Including the Insurrection in the Philippine Islands and the China Relief Expedition, between the Adjutant-General of the Army and Military Commanders in the United States, Cuba, Porto Rico, China and the Philippine Islands, from April 15, 1898 to July 30, 1902.* 2 vols. Washington, DC: Government Printing Office, 1902. The U.S. military documents contain exchanges between U.S. authorities and Spanish, Cuban, and Filipino leaders. Several directives to field commanders spell out McKinley's policies.

10:6   U.S. Congress. Senate. *Communications between the Executive Departments of the Government and Aguinaldo, etc. Message from the President of the United States Transmitting in Response to Resolution of the Senate of January 17, 1900 Copies of Communications between the Executive Departments of the Government and Aguinaldo or Other Persons Undertaking to Represent the People in Arms against the United States in the Philippine Islands, Together with other Official Documents Relating to the Philippine Islands.* 56th Cong., 1st Sess., Sen. Doc. 208. Washington, DC: Government Printing Office, 1900.

This compilation of documents contains exchanges between U.S. officers and Emilio Aguinaldo.

10:7 U.S. National Archives and Records Service. *History of the Philippine Insurrection against the United States, 1899–1903; and Documents Relating to the War Department Project for Publishing the History.* Microfilm. 9 rolls. Washington, DC: n.d. These are nine rolls of microfilm on the Philippine war.

10:8 _____. *Philippine Insurgent Records, 1896–1901; with Associated Records of the U.S. War Department, 1900–1906.* Microfilm. 643 rolls. Washington, DC: n.d. These microfilm records concern Filipino nationalism, the Philippine government, the war, and the U.S. army. Many records are in Spanish, and some have been translated into English. There are finding aids.

10:9 Taylor, John R. M., ed. *The Philippine Insurrection against the United States: A Compilation of Original Documents with Notes and Introduction.* 5 vols. Pasay City, Philippines: Eugenio Lopez Foundation, 1971. Taylor compiled and translated five volumes of Filipino documents from captured records. In 1906, the U.S. War Department made ten copies of galley proofs but never published this valuable collection of Filipino records. Taylor's introduction to the documents provides a justification for U.S. military action and imperial control of the Philippines.

10:10 Spain. Ministerio de Estado, ed. *Spanish Diplomatic Correspondence and Documents, 1896–1900: Presented to the Cortes by the Minister of State.* Washington, DC: Government Printing Office, 1905. This is an English translation of two Red Books issued by Praxedes Mateo Sagasta's government that contain Spanish diplomatic documents associated with the origins of the Spanish-Cuban-American War and the 1898 Paris Peace Conference.

10:11 Dawes, Charles G., ed. *A Journal of the McKinley Years.* Chicago: Lakeside Press, 1950. This account, edited by Bascom N. Timmons, contains the comptroller of the currency's perceptive observations on McKinley and his administration.

10:12 Mayo, Lawrence S., ed. *America of Yesterday, as Reflected in the Journal of John D. Long.*

Boston: Atlantic Monthly Press, 1923. Long's journal provides a day-by-day account of cabinet meetings and his reactions to events; compare with Gardner Weld Allen, ed., *The Papers of John Davis Long, 1897–1904* (Boston: Massachusetts Historical Society, 1939).

10:13 Seager, Robert, II, and Doris D. Maguire, eds. *Letters and Papers of Alfred Thayer Mahan.* See chapter 9 of this Guide (9:6).

10:14 Hattendorf, John B., ed. *Mahan on Naval Strategy: Selections from the Writings of Rear Admiral Alfred Thayer Mahan.* Following an introduction to Mahan's writings are selections arranged by strategic and organizational topics. Most come from Mahan's twentieth-century publications (9:250).

10:15 Contosta, David R., and Jessica R. Hawthorne, eds. *Rise to World Power: Selected Letters of Whitelaw Reid, 1895–1912.* This collection of Reid letters focuses on the Spanish-Cuban-American War, negotiating the 1898 Treaty of Paris, and improving Anglo-American relations (9:83).

10:16 Brands, H. W., ed. *The Selected Letters of Theodore Roosevelt.* New York: Cooper Square Press, 2001. This useful volume of letters provides good coverage of Roosevelt's views and actions as assistant secretary of the navy during the period leading to war with Spain and of his adventures in Cuba. Subsequent U.S. policy in the Philippines receives comparatively little attention.

10:17 Partido Revolucionario Cubano. *Correspondencia diplomática de la delegación cubana en Nueva York durante la guerra de independencia de 1895 á 1898 [Diplomatic Correspondence of the Cuban Delegation in New York during the War of Independence, 1895–1898].* 5 vols. La Habana: Talleres del Archivo Nacional, 1943–1946. This is the published diplomatic record of the Cuban revolutionary party in New York City, which was headed by Tomas Estrada Palma. See Primelles, *La revolución del 95 según la correspondencia de la delegación cubana en Nueva York* (1932–1937) (10:18), for five additional edited volumes of Cuban diplomatic correspondence.

10:18 Primelles, León, ed. *La revolución del 95 según la correspondencia de la delegación cubana en*

Nueva York [The Revolution of '95 as Reflected in the Correspondence of the Cuban Delegation in New York]. 5 vols. Vedado, Habana: Editorial Habanera, 1932–1937. These are published papers of the Cuban Junta, a primary source on Cuban diplomacy. See Partido Revolucionario Cubano, *Correspondencia diplomática de la delegación cubana en Nueva York durante la guerra de independencia de 1895 á 1898* (1943–1946) (10:17), for five additional volumes of diplomatic correspondence.

10:19   Ojeda Reyes, Félix, ed. *La manigua en París: correspondencia diplomática de Betances [The Thicket in Paris: Diplomatic Correspondence of Betances].* San Juan de Puerto Rico: Centro de Estudios Avanzados de Puerto Rico y El Caribe en colaboración con el Centro de Estudios Puertorriqueños, Hunter College, City University of New York, 1984. Although a Puerto Rican, Ramón Emeterio Betances headed the Cuban efforts in Paris to achieve independence. This collection of correspondence comes principally from Cuban archives. There is also an explanatory essay.

10:20   Martí, José. *Our America: Writings on Latin America and the Struggle for Independence.* Translated by Elinor Randall, with Juan de Onis and Roslyn Held Foner. New York: Monthly Review Press, 1977. A lengthy introduction by Philip S. Foner precedes this collection of Martí's translated documents.

Bibliographies and Other Reference Works

10:21   Beede, Benjamin R., ed. *The War of 1898 and U.S. Interventions, 1898–1934: An Encyclopedia.* New York: Garland, 1994. Composed of 608 pages of text and another 96 pages of maps and appendices, this encyclopedia gives primary emphasis to the war of 1898 while also examining other U.S. interventions through 1934. The coverage of 1898 includes the U.S. intervention, land and naval operations, peace negotiations, and postwar occupations.

10:22   Berner, Brad K., ed. *The Spanish-American War: A Historical Dictionary.* Lanham, MD: Scarecrow Press, 1998. This volume provides a compact and useful reference for studying the war and its aftermath in Cuba, Guam, Hawaii, the Philippines, and Puerto Rico.

10:23   Braisted, William Reynolds. "The Navy in the Early Twentieth Century, 1890–1941." In *A Guide to the Sources of United States Military History,* ed. Robin Higham, 344–77. This essay includes important references for the war of 1898, in both the Caribbean and the Pacific (9:242).

10:24   Castillo Ramírez, Yanelet, ed. *Bibliografías de historia de España. Num. 8. La crisis del 98 [Bibliographies of the History of Spain. No. 8: The Crisis of '98].* Madrid: Centro de Información y Documentación Científica, 1998. This Spanish bibliography covering from the start of the insurrection in 1895 through the conclusion of the Paris Peace Conference contains 2,094 references.

10:25   Centro de Información y Documentación Científica (Spain), ed. *En Torno al 98: Cuba, Puerto Rico y Filipinas, 1880–1910 [Around '98: Cuba, Puerto Rico and the Philippines, 1880–1910].* Madrid: Centro de Información y Documentación Científica, 1995. This Spanish bibliography contains 401 references with brief descriptive annotations.

10:26   Cortada, James W., ed. *A Bibliographical Guide to Spanish Diplomatic History, 1460–1977.* This volume gives relatively little attention to the war of 1898 (1:241).

10:27   Crawford, Michael J., Mark L. Hayes, and Michael D. Sessions, eds. *The Spanish-American War: Historical Overview and Select Bibliography.* Washington, DC: Naval Historical Center, Dept. of the Navy, 1998. Following a twenty-six-page historical overview and commentary on topics in need of further research, this volume provides 590 briefly annotated entries.

10:28   Dyal, Donald H., with Brian B. Carpenter and Mark A. Thomas, eds. *Historical Dictionary of the Spanish American War.* Westport, CT: Greenwood Press, 1996. Following a brief historiographical, bibliographic introduction, the war is covered in a functional, straightforward manner.

10:29 Ellis, Richard N. "Civil-Military Relations, Operations, and the Army, 1865–1917." In *A Guide to the Sources of United States Military History,* ed. Robin Higham, 247–68. Hamden, CT: Archon Books, 1975. Ellis provides references to military-diplomatic episodes during the war of 1898 in both the Caribbean and the Pacific.

10:30 García Carranza, Araceli, ed. *Bibliografía de la guerra de la independencia (1895–1898) [Bibliography of the War of Independence (1895–1898)].* La Habana: Editorial Orbe, 1976. This is a comprehensive, annotated list of books and other materials that are in the Biblioteca Nacional de Cuba.

10:31 Geary, James W. "Afro-American Soldiers and American Imperialism, 1898–1902: A Select Annotated Bibliography." *Bulletin of Bibliography* 48 (December 1991): 189–93. This is a very useful list of sources with informative annotations. It provides excellent access to citations on Willard B. Gatewood, Jr.'s extensive work on this topic, including a number of state studies.

10:32 Gould, Lewis L., and Craig H. Roell, eds. *William McKinley: A Bibliography.* Westport, CT: Meckler, 1988. This useful bibliography provides an extensive listing of sources (some annotated) on McKinley's life and career, including the war of 1898 and its aftermath. There is also a chapter on other persons in the McKinley administration.

10:33 Hilton, Sylvia L. "Democracy Goes Imperial: Spanish Views of American Policy in 1898." In *Reflections on American Exceptionalism,* ed. David K. Adams and Cornelis A. van Minnen, 97–128. Staffordshire, UK: Ryburn Pub., 1994. This English-language bibliography of over 100 works published between 1981 and 1993 of Spanish literature on the Spanish-Cuban-American War is an essential starting point for analysis of contemporary Spanish authors.

10:34 Petersen, Neal H., ed. *American Intelligence, 1775–1990: A Bibliographical Guide.* The section on the Spanish-Cuban-American War lists twenty unannotated entries (1:194).

10:35 Rosario Natal, Carmelo. *El 1898 Puertorriqueño en la historiografía: ensayo y bibliografía crítica [Puerto Rico in the Historiography of 1898:*

Essay and Annotated Bibliography]. San Juan: Academia Puertorriqueña de la Historia, 1997. This well-organized bibliography is a valuable tool for studying Puerto Rico as it exchanged Spanish for American rule. The author provides a sketch of Puerto Rican history, changing historiographical interpretations, and extensive bibliographic annotations that stress Puerto Rican events. He includes a category for U.S. military government of Puerto Rico.

10:36 Saito, Shiro, ed. *Philippine-American Relations: A Guide to Manuscript Sources in the United States.* Westport, CT: Greenwood Press, 1982. This volume provides good descriptions of the records and is a valuable research tool for locating American manuscripts and other records housed in the United States.

10:37 Stubbs, Jean, Lila Haines, and Meic F. Haines, eds. *Cuba.* Edited by Robert G. Neville. Vol. 75, World Bibliographical Series. Santa Barbara, CA: Clio Press, 1996. The historical section of this annotated bibliography devotes only four pages and eighteen entries to 1898–1902.

10:38 Venzon, Anne Cipriano, ed. *The Spanish-American War: An Annotated Bibliography.* Vol. 11, Wars of the United States Series. New York: Garland, 1990. This volume contains 860 annotated entries describing nonfiction materials and 320 unannotated references to works of fiction and music.

Historiography

10:39 Clymer, Kenton J. "Not So Benevolent Assimilation: The Philippine-American War." *Reviews in American History* 11 (December 1983): 547–52. Although the primary focus of this review is on Miller, *"Benevolent Assimilation": The American Conquest of the Philippines, 1899–1903* (1982) (10:449), the author provides an excellent historiographical summary of the principal work published after 1906 on the Philippine-American War.

10:40 Combs, Jerald A. *American Diplomatic History: Two Centuries of Changing Interpretations.* This excellent work examines the evolving historiographical interpretations from the time of the war through the early 1970s. These interpretations are set against the backdrop of influential events in the nation's history (2:5).

10:41   Crapol, Edward P. "Coming to Terms with Empire: The Historiography of Late-Nineteenth-Century American Foreign Relations." In this perceptive essay, the author concentrates on materials written after 1980, responds to criticisms of the field of the history of U.S. foreign relations, and contends that imperial history provides the most promising analytical framework for understanding the era (9:32).

10:42   De Santis, Hugh. "The Imperialist Impulse and American Innocence, 1865–1900." In *American Foreign Relations, A Historiographical Review,* ed. Gerald K. Haines and J. Samuel Walker, 65–90. Westport, CT: Greenwood Press, 1981. The article reviews the major interpretive schools from the first decade of the century through the late 1970s. The author asserts that a modernist synthesis giving greater emphasis to social and cultural influences was emerging in 1981 as the most engaging perspective.

10:43   Elizalde Pérez-Grueso, María Dolores. "La historiografía norteamericana ante la dimensión oriental de la guerra hispano-norteamericana de 1898 [North American Historiography in Light of the Far Eastern Dimension of the Spanish-American War of 1898]." *Revista Española de Estudios Norteamericanos* 7, no. 11 (1996): 87–127. This Spanish essay examines American historiography of the Spanish-Cuban-American War related to East Asian expansionism. It takes up economic and political interest in expansionism and McKinley's decisions, covering the Hawaiian islands, Philippines, and the China market.

10:44   _____. "La lucha por el Pacífico en 1898. Interpretaciones en torno a la dimensión oriental de la guerra hispano-norteamericana [The Struggle for the Pacific in 1898: Interpretations around the Eastern Dimension of the Spanish-American War]." In *Las relaciones internacionales en el Pacífico (siglos XVIII–XIX): colonización, descolonización y encuentro cultural [International Relations in the Pacific in the 18th and 19th Centuries: Colonization, Decolonization, and Cultural Encounters],* ed. María Dolores Elizalde Pérez-Grueso, 291–315. Madrid: Consejo Superior de Investigaciones Científicas,

1997. This article sketches international interests in the Pacific in 1898 and provides brief treatments of American, British, German, and French historiography of the subject before a fuller treatment of Spanish historiography, stressing the influence of Jesús Pabón and José María Jover Zamora.

10:45   Field, James A., Jr. "American Imperialism: The Worst Chapter in Almost Any Book." Field criticizes historical treatments of the late nineteenth century for being too rational and ethnocentric, for ignoring elements of cost, technology, and distance, for confusing rhetoric with intentions and capabilities, and for asking the wrong questions. Included with Field's provocative essay are responses by Robert L. Beisner and Walter LaFeber (2:100).

10:46   Fry, Joseph A. "From Open Door to World Systems: Economic Interpretations of Late Nineteenth Century American Foreign Relations." Fry recounts and assesses the work of both the proponents and critics of economic interpretations of Gilded Age U.S. foreign relations. He concludes that the advocates of a broadly conceived economic perspective continue to set the terms of debate (9:33).

10:47   _____. "Imperialism, American Style, 1890–1916." In *American Foreign Relations Reconsidered, 1890–1993,* ed. Gordon Martel, 52–70. New York: Routledge, 1994. This article defines imperialism and assesses the writing of U.S. historians on both the domestic bases and international impact of American expansion. The author concludes that U.S. imperialism at the turn of the century followed logically from prior U.S. foreign policy and was neither so innocent nor so accidental as sometimes portrayed.

10:48   _____. "William McKinley and the Coming of the Spanish-American War: A Study in the Besmirching and Redemption of an Historical Image." *Diplomatic History* 3 (Winter 1979): 77–97. This article carefully reviews the McKinley scholarship through the mid-1970s. The McKinley who emerges is much stronger personally, more astute politically, and more in command of his administration and foreign policy than the figure most often presented prior to the late 1950s.

10:49   Gould, Lewis L. "Chocolate Eclair or Mandarin Manipulator? William McKinley, the Spanish-

American War, and the Philippines: A Review Essay." *Ohio History* 94 (Summer-Autumn 1985): 182–87. While reviewing two works on the period, the author argues that McKinley rather than Theodore Roosevelt controlled policy and that the president deserves to have his actions assessed fairly and accurately.

10:50   Healy, David F. *Modern Imperialism: Changing Styles in Historical Interpretation.* In this pamphlet, Healy provides an excellent assessment of the literature and offers suggestions for further inquiry (9:34).

10:51   Hilton, Sylvia L. "Democracy Beats the 'Disaster' Complex: Spanish Interpretations of the Colonial Crises." *OAH Magazine of History* 12 (Spring 1998): 11–17. This is an informative overview of the Spanish historiographical treatment of the war of 1898 from the immediate aftermath through the 1990s. The author demonstrates how this treatment has evolved from a narrow, exceptionalist context finding blame for the national disaster to much broader domestic and international perspectives.

10:52   Hilton, Sylvia L., and Steve J. S. Ickringill. "William McKinley and the Pacific: Spanish and British Interpretations, an Essay in Comparative History." In *Las relaciones internacionales en el Pacífico (siglos XVIII–XIX): colonización, descolonización y encuentro cultural [International Relations in the Pacific in the 18th and 19th Centuries: Colonization, Decolonization, and Cultural Encounters],* ed. María Dolores Elizalde Pérez-Grueso, 317–55. Madrid: Consejo Superior de Investigaciones Científicas, 1997. This careful review of Spanish and British historiography compares the different explanations that British and Spanish authors have given for U.S. expansion in the Philippines. Spanish historians, having little knowledge of American politics and stressing domestic Spanish considerations, have provided a superficial analysis of McKinley's actions. British historians have placed McKinley's imperialism within the broader context of Britain's East Asian interests.

10:53   Holbo, Paul S. "Perspectives on American Foreign Policy, 1890–1916: Expansion and World Power." *Social Studies* 58 (November 1967): 246–56. The author explores the varying explana-

tions of the U.S. rise to world power and summarizes the historiography.

10:54   Hugo, Markus M. "La Guerra de 1898 y su contexto internacional. Tendencias historiográficas y publicaciones con motivo del Centenario [The War of 1898 and Its International Context: Historiographical Tendencies and Publications Motivated by the Centenary]." *Notas* 6, no. 2 (1999): 2–16. Hugo counts at least fifty-eight academic conferences, symposia, and congresses that celebrated or commemorated the 1898 centennial. These events produced several major collections of papers, and Hugo examines some of these, commenting on historiographical trends.

10:55   Paterson, Thomas G. "United States Intervention in Cuba, 1898: Interpretations of the Spanish-American-Cuban-Filipino War." *History Teacher* 29 (May 1996): 341–61. Drawing primarily on materials written since 1980, the author identifies four levels of analysis: international, regional, national, and individual. These analytical constructs allow for the incorporation of geopolitical, domestic political, economic, ideological, and social-psychological influences. See also, Paterson, "U.S. Intervention in Cuba, 1898: Interpreting the Spanish-American-Cuban-Filipino War," *OAH Magazine of History* 12 (Spring 1998): 5–10.

10:56   Pérez, Louis A., Jr. "Cuba-U.S. Relations: A Survey of Twentieth Century Historiography." *Review of Inter-American Bibliography* 39 (July-September 1989): 311–28. This broad-ranging essay includes attention to both U.S. and Cuban publications treating the 1895–1902 period.

10:57   _____. "The Meaning of the *Maine:* Causation and the Historiography of the Spanish-American War." *Pacific Historical Review* 58 (August 1989): 293–322. This article examines the historiographical treatment of the destruction of the *Maine,* its relation to public opinion and the coming of war, and McKinley's performance as president. The author contends that by focusing on the *Maine,* U.S. historians have portrayed the war as coming by chance and for idealistic ends rather than by choice for and imperial objectives.

10:58   _____. *The War of 1898: The United States and Cuba in History and Historiography.*

Chapel Hill: University of North Carolina Press, 1998. This provocative and forcefully argued book provides both the U.S. and Cuban historiographical perspectives on the war and its meaning. The author criticizes North American writings for failing to draw on Cuban sources, to acknowledge the Cuban role in the war, or to admit America's interested and imperialistic actions.

10:59   Schlesinger, Arthur M., Jr. *The Cycles of American History.* Boston: Houghton Mifflin, 1986. In chapter 7, the author reviews the various theoretical explanations of imperialism, examines the U.S. imperial experience, and criticizes economic theories and their application to American history.

10:60   Shenton, James P. "Imperialism and Racism." In *Essays in American Historiography: Papers Presented in Honor of Allan Nevins,* ed. Donald H. Sheehan and Harold C. Syrett, 230–50. New York: Columbia University Press, 1960. The author contends that turn-of-the-century imperialism and the underlying racism were continuations of earlier U.S. actions and attitudes.

10:61   Siracusa, Joseph M. "Progressivism, Imperialism, and the Leuchtenburg Thesis, 1952–1974: An Historiographical Appraisal." *Australian Journal of Politics and History* 20 (December 1974): 312–25. This is a useful historiographical essay tracing the course, impact, and validity of the Leuchtenburg thesis, with which Siracusa is sympathetic.

10:62   Smith, Ephraim K. "William McKinley's Enduring Legacy: The Historiographical Debate on the Taking of the Philippine Islands." In *Crucible of Empire: The Spanish-American War and Its Aftermath,* ed. James C. Bradford, 205–49. Annapolis: Naval Institute Press, 1993. This article provides a comprehensive and judicious evaluation of the historical debate over McKinley's decision to annex the Philippines. Based on this assessment and memoranda from Chandler P. Anderson and Major General Francis V. Greene, Smith contends that McKinley was a hesitant and reluctant expansionist who acted principally from political motives and a belief in U.S. destiny.

10:63   Trask, David F. "U.S. Historians and the War of 1895–1898: The Influence of International Politics on Scholarship." In *1898: enfoques y per-*

spectivas [1898: Focal Points and Perspectives], ed. Luis E. González Vales, 97–108. San Juan: Academia Puertorriqueña de la Historia, 1997. The author divides a century of historiography into four major categories: progressive, power realist, new left, and eclectic. All authors were influenced by the international power politics of their day. For a similar analysis in Spanish, see David F. Trask, "La guerra cubano-hispano-americana durante el año 1898: análisis historiográfico," in *1898: entre la continuidad y la ruptura,* edited by María del Rosario Rodríguez Díaz (Morelia, Mexico: Universidad Michoacana de San Nicolás de Hidalgo, 1997), 66–97.

10:64   Winks, Robin W. "The American Struggle with 'Imperialism': How Words Frighten." In *The American Identity: Fusion and Fragmentation,* ed. Rob Kroes, 143–77. Amsterdam: Amerika Instituut Universiteit Van Amsterdam, 1980. This essay criticizes both traditional and revisionist diplomatic historians for failing to place the U.S. experience in an international context and for portraying this experience as exceptional. Imperialism is defined as the inevitable domination of high-technology cultures over other less developed ones, and the author urges American historians to examine the process in unemotional terms.

Overviews and General Works

SYNTHESES AND MISCELLANEOUS

10:65   Beisner, Robert L. *From the Old Diplomacy to the New, 1865–1900.* Chapter 5 provides an excellent synthesis and interpretation of the coming of the war and its imperial results. McKinley is portrayed as a strong leader who controlled his administration and U.S. policy (9:126). First published in 1975.

10:66   Campbell, Charles Soutter. *The Transformation of American Foreign Relations, 1865–1900.* Campbell presents an excellent overview of the period, the coming of the war with Spain, and the imperial aftermath. His overall treatment of McKinley is positive, but he criticizes him for imprecise diplomacy and poor appointments (9:129).

10:67   Cazemajou, Jean. *American Expansionism and Foreign Policy (1885–1908)*. Paris: Armand Colin Longman, 1988. This is a broad-ranging overview based on secondary sources.

10:68   Dennis, Alfred L. P. *Adventures in American Diplomacy, 1896–1906 (From Unpublished Documents)*. New York: E. P. Dutton and Company, 1928. Dennis concludes that the war was unnecessary, but inevitable given U.S. public opinion, domestic politics, and economic interests.

10:69   Dobson, John M. *America's Ascent: The United States Becomes a Great Power, 1880–1914*. This study argues that expansion at the turn of the century resulted naturally from economic, strategic, and ideological influences originating in the 1880s (9:131).

10:70   Dulles, Foster Rhea. *The Imperial Years*. New York: Crowell, 1956. Dulles portrays McKinley as having been pushed into war and the acquisition of the Philippines by Congress, the press, public opinion, and the proponents of the "large policy."

10:71   Fry, Joseph A. "Phases of Empire: Late Nineteenth-Century U.S. Foreign Relations." In *The Gilded Age: Essays on the Origins of Modern America*, ed. Charles W. Calhoun, 261–88. This article asserts that late-nineteenth-century U.S. foreign relations should be viewed from an imperial perspective and that turn-of-the-century expansion followed naturally from long-accepted ideology and previous interactions with Native Americans, Hawaiians, and Cubans (9:133).

10:72   Graebner, Norman A. *Foundations of American Foreign Policy: A Realist Appraisal from Franklin to McKinley: Essays*. In chapter 13, titled, "World Power: The McKinley Years," the author argues that the United States went to war in 1898 and thereafter acquired an empire in the name of humanity rather than because of a deliberate weighing of interests or the capacity to obtain them. In so doing the country broke with the careful balancing of ends and

means that had led to consistent success in the eighteenth and nineteenth centuries (2:62).

10:73   Grenville, J. A. S., and George Berkeley Young. *Politics, Strategy, and American Diplomacy: Studies in Foreign Policy, 1873–1917*. The authors conclude that McKinley's diplomatic policy was consistent, patient, and pacific; he went to war only when that course appeared to be the only way to obtain Cuban independence (9:136).

10:74   Healy, David F. *US Expansionism: The Imperialist Urge in the 1890s*. In this graceful and broad-ranging analysis, Healy examines the U.S. imperialist impulse against the backdrop of European colonialism. Healy incorporates the U.S. sense of national destiny, economic objectives, missionary endeavors, and concern for the nation's moral fiber and traditional values. He also provides an incisive synopsis of the imperialist/anti-imperialist debate (9:137).

10:75   LaFeber, Walter. *The American Search for Opportunity, 1865–1913*. In this significant overview, the author contends that the United States persistently and primarily sought economic but also missionary and strategic opportunities abroad—often at the expense of order. Disorder was repeatedly the price of opportunity, and the wars in Cuba and the Philippines were prime examples. McKinley is viewed as exercising clear executive authority in pursuit of U.S. interests and as the first modern president (2:40).

10:76   _____. *The New Empire: An Interpretation of American Expansion, 1860–1898*. In the eighteen-page preface to this edition, the author assesses the arguments he made in the original 1963 edition in view of subsequent work on the period from 1865 to 1898. Although he notes some second thoughts, his primary regret is not having argued the principal themes in the original study more strongly. Economic influences and a positive portrayal of McKinley's ability (if not his policies) remain central (9:141).

10:77   Langer, William L. *The Diplomacy of Imperialism, 1890–1902*. 2d ed. New York: Alfred A. Knopf, 1951. Originally published in 1935, this classic account of the diplomacy of the European powers provides an indispensable backdrop to America's role at the turn of the century.

10:78   May, Ernest R. *Imperial Democracy: The Emergence of America as a Great Power.* This study is valuable for its portrayal of the European reaction to the U.S. emergence as a great power. The war of 1898 resulted from domestic pressures, and McKinley was a weak leader who capitulated to public hysteria (9:143).

10:79   Merk, Frederick, with Lois Bannister Merk. *Manifest Destiny and Mission in American History: A Reinterpretation.* The authors contrast the expansion of the 1840s, which they believe sought to elevate neighboring peoples, to the selfish, nationalistic impulses in the 1890s. McKinley is viewed as a weak leader who took the country into a needless war. The 1995 reprint edition includes a new foreword by John Mack Faragher (2:220).

10:80   Ninkovich, Frank A. *The United States and Imperialism.* Ninkovich interprets imperialism as part of the modernizing process and gives primary weight to the liberal U.S. desire to promote civilization and development. From this perspective, imperialism, anti-imperialism, and later globalization all derived from the same worldview. The author applies this perspective to war with Spain in 1898 and U.S. involvement in the Caribbean, Philippines, and China (primarily from the 1890s forward) (2:88).

10:81   Nugent, Walter T. "Frontiers and Empires in the Late Nineteenth Century." *Western Historical Quarterly* 20 (November 1989): 393–408. In this comparison of European (including American) empires and stock frontiers, the author concludes that clear distinctions between the two are difficult to draw in terms of either motives or impact on indigenous peoples.

10:82   Ricard, Serge, and James Bolner, Sr., eds. *La république impérialiste: l'expansionnisme et la politique extérieure des États-Unis, 1885–1909: études et documents [The Imperial Republic: Expansionism and the Foreign Policy of the United States, 1885–1909: Studies and Documents].* Aix-en-Provence: Université de Provence, 1987. This volume contains thirteen essays and 139 pages of relevant documents. Like other Ricard-edited works based on meetings of the Groupe de Recherte et d'Etudes Nord-Americaines, this collection provides an insightful variety of U.S. and European scholarly perspectives. The essays most useful in understanding the Spanish-Cuban-American War and its aftermath are: Ricard, "The Advent of the Imperial Republic: An Introduction"; Richard H. Bradford, "Rumors of War: The Spanish Problem in American Politics 1868–1898"; John L. Offner, "United States Expansionism: The McKinley Administration"; Göran Rystad, "Republic or Empire? The Philippine-American War and American Expansionism at the Turn of the Century"; Bolner, "The Supreme Court, the *Insular Cases,* and American Expansionism"; and Alexander E. Campbell, "Expansionism and Imperialism." Other contributors examine the U.S. imperial rationale, strategic considerations, the role of U.S. presidents, the American press, the American Federation of Labor, Theodore Roosevelt, and George Washington Cable.

10:83   Ricard, Serge, and Hélène Christol, eds. *Anglo-Saxonism in U.S. Foreign Policy: The Diplomacy of Imperialism, 1899–1919.* Aix-en-Provence: Publications de l'Université de Provence, 1991. In this collection, although the overall theme of Anglo-Saxonism is illusive, one can profitably examine Göran Rystad, "The Constitution and the Flag: Aspects of American Expansionism at the Turn of the Century," and Rhodri Jeffreys-Jones, "Massachusetts Labor, Henry Cabot Lodge, and the Abortion of Empire." Other essays on events or persons include Christol, "Du Bois and Expansionism: A Black Man's View of Empire," and Ricard, "The Anglo-German Intervention in Venezuela and Theodore Roosevelt's Ultimatum to the Kaiser: Taking a Fresh Look at an Old Enigma."

10:84   Rystad, Göran. *Ambiguous Imperialism: American Foreign Policy and Domestic Politics at the Turn of the Century.* Stockholm: Esselte Studium, 1975. Rystad provides a historiographical discussion of U.S. expansionism and an analysis of the interaction of politics and foreign affairs as reflected in the election of 1900.

10:85   Stephanson, Anders. *Manifest Destiny: American Expansionism and the Empire of Right.* The author concludes that the war was largely unnecessary since Spain had essentially capitulated to U.S. demands. Chapter 3 provides an overview and analysis of the arguments for and against imperial expansion (2:222).

10:86   Vevier, Charles. "American Continentalism: An Idea of Expansion, 1845–1910." The author ties the expansionism of the 1890s to the previous landed expansion across the continent; therefore, imperialism at the turn of the century demonstrated continuity in U.S. foreign policy rather than an aberration (9:154).

10:87   Wiebe, Robert H. *The Search for Order, 1877–1920.* The author argues that turn-of-the-century U.S. involvement abroad consisted of a series of incidents rather than a "policy" and that the nature of this involvement derived from domestic influences rather than an assessment of external reality. U.S. entry into war in 1898 was just another such item, rather than a well-conceived action (9:157).

POLITICS AND IDEOLOGY

10:88   Bailey, Thomas A. "Was the Presidential Election of 1900 a Mandate on Imperialism?" *Mississippi Valley Historical Review* 24 (June 1937): 43–52. The issues were too numerous and confusing to isolate one as primary.

10:89   Cooper, John Milton, Jr. "Progressivism and American Foreign Policy: A Reconsideration." *Mid-America* 51 (October 1969): 260–77. Cooper distinguishes among three groups of Progressives: the Roosevelt-Lodge "Imperial Progressives," the Bryanite "Agrarian Isolationists," and the Wilsonian "Liberal Internationalists."

10:90   Hunt, Michael H. *Ideology and U.S. Foreign Policy.* The war of 1898 in Cuba and subsequent repression of the Filipinos provide examples of U.S. policy based on an ideology emphasizing the pursuit of national greatness, assuming the inferiority of non-whites, and fearing genuine social revolution. McKinley subscribed to these beliefs and employed them to explain his actions (2:132).

10:91   Markowitz, Gerald E. "Progressivism and Imperialism: A Return to First Principles." *Historian* 37 (February 1975): 257–75. Between 1898 and 1917, progressives favored imperialism. They agreed on the U.S. mission to elevate inferior peoples, the need to impose order abroad, and the necessity of securing foreign markets. The latter were needed to avoid depression and social strife at home.

10:92   Merrill, Horace Samuel, and Marian Galbraith Merrill. *The Republican Command, 1897–1913.* Lexington: University Press of Kentucky, 1971. The authors provide an account of important Republican leaders, such as William B. Allison, Stephen B. Elkins, Orville Platt, and John Spooner, and their relations with the McKinley administration.

ECONOMICS AND TRADE

10:93   Becker, William H. *The Dynamics of Business-Government Relations: Industry & Exports, 1893–1921.* The author cautions against an overemphasis on coordinated government-business actions. The largest producers and exporters of manufactured goods did so without significant government assistance; smaller producers were more solicitous of and dependent on government aid. Business responded to surplus production primarily through mergers and price-fixing and secondarily through "dumping" products abroad (9:186).

10:94   Lake, David A. *Power, Protection, and Free Trade: International Sources of U.S. Commercial Strategy, 1887–1939.* The author asserts that the United States pursued protectionism at home and free trade abroad from 1887 through 1997. During the 1897–1912 period, the United States maintained protectionism at home and expanded the practice of bilateral bargaining abroad. Strategies during both periods were predicated on British hegemony, which tolerated this dichotomy in U.S. policy (9:208).

SOCIETY AND CULTURE

10:95   Lears, T. J. Jackson. *No Place of Grace: Antimodernism and the Transformation of American Culture, 1880–1920.* New York: Pantheon Books, 1981. The author contends that the assertion of the martial ideal as an antimodern antidote to materialism, positivism, and overcivilization provided an important endorsement of turn-of-the-century imperialism, especially among northeastern bourgeoisie.

10:96   McConnell, Stuart. *Glorious Contentment: The Grand Army of the Republic, 1865–1900.* Chapel Hill: University of North Carolina Press,

1992. This cultural and social history of the Grand Army of the Republic examines the organization as a lobby not only for political and economic objectives but also for ways to interpret the nation's history and for a particular brand of nationalism. This patriotic nationalistic crusade contributed to the jingoistic tone of the 1890s and culminated in the war of 1898.

10:97   Ricard, Serge, ed. *An American Empire: Expansionist Cultures and Policies, 1881–1917.* See chapter 9 of this Guide (9:177).

10:98   Rosenberg, Emily S. *Spreading the American Dream: American Economic and Cultural Expansion, 1890–1945.* This book examines U.S. foreign relations generally and turn-of-the-century U.S. imperialism specifically against the ideological backdrop of liberal internationalism, which emphasized free enterprise, open trade and investment, free flow of information and culture, and the presumption that other states could follow the U.S. example. Individual business persons, missionaries, philanthropists, and entertainers as well as an increasingly active state advanced this American ideology and accompanying interests (9:151).

10:99   Rydell, Robert W. *All the World's a Fair: Visions of Empire at American International Expositions, 1876–1916.* The author demonstrates how international expositions presented images of U.S. economic progress and white racial superiority and in so doing mitigated domestic class conflict and provided a nationalistic ideological rationale for empire abroad (9:180).

10:100   Schott, Marshall E. "The South and American Foreign Policy, 1894–1900: New South Prophets and the Challenge of Regional Values." New South prophets, such as John T. Morgan and Hernando de Soto Money, helped form a southern consensus in favor of a Nicaragua canal and economic expansion. These leaders also favored intervention in Cuba and the acquisition of an insular empire, but the majority of southerners opposed imperial expansion. They feared a strengthened central government and military that might intervene in the south, compared suppression of native Hawaiians and Filipinos to Reconstruction, and worried that war and imperialism would divert funds from domestic

needs and benefit northern bondholders and financial interests (9:181).

10:101   Spurr, David. *The Rhetoric of Empire: Colonial Discourse in Journalism, Travel Writing, and Imperial Administration.* Durham, NC: Duke University Press, 1993. The author draws on nineteenth- and twentieth-century British, French, and American writing in this accessible and useful volume, but there are only a few brief references to Cuba or the Philippines.

THE NAVY

10:102   Cooling, Benjamin Franklin. *Gray Steel and Blue Water Navy: The Formative Years of America's Military-Industrial Complex, 1881–1917.* The book examines the formation of an alliance between the government and the steel industry, and chapter 6 traces the government procurement of armor from 1897 through 1902 (9:245). See also Kurt Hackemer, in *The U.S. Navy and the Origins of the Military-Industrial Complex, 1847–1883* (Annapolis: Naval Institute Press, 2001).

10:103   Hagan, Kenneth J. *This People's Navy: The Making of American Sea Power.* The 1890s, the Spanish-Cuban-American War, and subsequent fighting in the Philippines were crucial to a profound change in U.S. naval strategy, as the United States abandoned its traditional strategy of commerce raiding and coastal operations in favor of the Mahanian theory of battleships, fleet engagements, and command of the seas (9:248).

LATIN AMERICA AND THE CARIBBEAN

10:104   Bemis, Samuel Flagg. *The Latin American Policy of the United States: An Historical Interpretation.* This study argues that the war was avoidable and resulted from the pressure of public opinion. Subsequent relations with Cuba are characterized as generous and benevolent (2:345).

10:105   Bergquist, Charles W. *Labor and the Course of American Democracy: US History in Latin American Perspective.* New York: Verso, 1996. In examining the social origins of U.S. expansionism and the war of 1898, the author emphasizes the role of labor unrest in motivating elites to pursue imperialism as a means to quell domestic discord.

10:106 Healy, David F. *Drive to Hegemony: The United States in the Caribbean, 1898–1917.* Madison: University of Wisconsin Press, 1988. In the book's first four chapters, the author examines the economic, strategic, and racial assumptions behind U.S. intervention in Cuba and Puerto Rico and turn-of-the-century imperialism. McKinley is portrayed as forced into war against his wishes, but also as following a conscious policy of enhancing U.S. influence in the Caribbean, Pacific, and East Asia.

10:107 Langley, Lester D. *The Banana Wars: United States Intervention in the Caribbean, 1898–1934.* Rev. ed. Lexington: University Press of Kentucky, 1985. Reprint 2002 (SR Books). Chapter 1 provides a brief overview of the U.S. military, political, and economic occupation of Cuba from 1898 to 1902. Originally published in 1983.

10:108 _____. *Struggle for the American Mediterranean: United States–European Rivalry in the Gulf-Caribbean, 1776–1904.* Langley places the war of 1898 in the context of U.S.-European strategic rivalries and U.S. security concerns (2:364).

10:109 Perkins, Dexter. *The Monroe Doctrine, 1867–1907.* McKinley and his contemporaries did not employ the Monroe Doctrine to explain intervention in Cuba. Perkins finds that although the doctrine did not justify U.S. actions, legitimate security concerns were involved (9:147).

COLONIES AND DEPENDENCIES

10:110 Perkins, Whitney T. *Constraint of Empire: The United States and Caribbean Interventions.* Westport, CT: Greenwood Press, 1981. The author focuses on Cuba, Nicaragua, the Dominican Republic, and Haiti from 1898 through the 1960s. He concludes that the United States intervened largely for idealistic reasons and argues that the interventions were doomed to fail both because of U.S. domestic opposition to empire and because the United States

was inevitably drawn into and impeded by the politics of the peripheral dependencies.

10:111 _____. *Denial of Empire: The United States and Its Dependencies.* Leyden: A. W. Sythoff, 1962. Perkins acknowledges the existence of U.S. empire but argues that American motives were beneficent rather than cynical and tempered by the safety valve of seeking to promote self-government. Uncomfortable with the contradiction between this professed goal and the domination of others, the United States deemed colonial rule only temporary. Efforts to extend U.S. institutions to other cultures sought the impossible and most often failed.

10:112 Pratt, Julius W. *America's Colonial Experiment: How the United States Gained, Governed and in Part Gave Away a Colonial Empire.* New York: Prentice-Hall, 1950. The first two chapters cover the background and process of imperial expansion.

Biographical Studies

AMERICAN

Albert J. Beveridge

10:113 Bowers, Claude G. *Beveridge and the Progressive Era.* Boston: Houghton Mifflin Company, 1932. This is a dated, but still useful biography of one of the Republican Party's most fervent expansionists.

10:114 Braeman, John. *Albert J. Beveridge: American Nationalist.* Chicago: University of Chicago Press, 1971. This is the most recent and best biography.

William Jennings Bryan

10:115 Ashby, LeRoy. *William Jennings Bryan: Champion of Democracy.* Boston: Twayne Publishers, 1987. Bryan opposed a coercive foreign policy and annexing the Philippines, but was similar to the imperialists in his nationalism, patriotism, racial views, and support for commercial expansion and previous territorial acquisitions.

10:116   Cherny, Robert W. *A Righteous Cause: The Life of William Jennings Bryan.* Boston: Little, Brown, 1985. The examination of Bryan's anti-imperialism, decision to support ratification of the Treaty of Paris, and the election of 1900 is brief and standard in interpretation.

10:117   Coletta, Paolo E. *William Jennings Bryan. Vol. 1: Political Evangelist, 1860–1908. Vol. 2: Progressive Politician and Moral Statesman, 1909–1915. Vol. 3: Political Puritan, 1915–1925.* 3 vols. Lincoln: University of Nebraska Press, 1964–1969. In this biography, the author offers a standard interpretation of Bryan supporting the Treaty of Paris of 1899 while opposing imperialism.

10:118   Koenig, Louis W. *Bryan: A Political Biography of William Jennings Bryan.* New York: Putnam, 1971. The author emphasizes Bryan's political calculations in responding to war in 1898. After calling for intervention in March, he volunteered for service, only to be constrained politically by being held in the military until December. Bryan declared against imperialism while still in the army, but his strategies for opposition were ineffective both in the fight over the annexation of the Philippines and the presidential campaign of 1900.

William R. Day

10:119   McLean, Joseph E. *William Rufus Day: Supreme Court Justice from Ohio.* Baltimore: Johns Hopkins Press, 1946. McLean describes Day's important role in McKinley's foreign policy formation and implementation. The author credits public opinion with forcing both McKinley and Day to war in 1898.

10:120   Shippee, Lester B., and Royal B. Way. "William Rufus Day." In *The American Secretaries of State and Their Diplomacy,* ed. Samuel Flagg Bemis, 9: 27–112. New York: Alfred A. Knopf, 1929. Skeptical of Spanish actions in Cuba, Day turned earlier than McKinley to intervention. He subsequently supported annexation of the Philippines.

George Dewey

10:121   Dewey, George. *Autobiography of George Dewey, Admiral of the Navy.* New York: Scribner, 1913. Dewey tells his story of the victory at Manila Bay and interactions with the Filipinos.

10:122   Healy, Laurin Hall, and Luis Kutner. *The Admiral.* New York: Ziff-Davis Publishing Co., 1944. This is a comprehensive life of Dewey that thoroughly recounts his service at Manila Bay.

10:123   Nicholson, Philip V. "George Dewey and the Expansionists of 1898." *Vermont History* 42 (Summer 1974): 214–27. This article examines Dewey's expansionist views and the role of Redfield Proctor and Theodore Roosevelt in his appointment as commander of the Far Eastern Squadron in 1897.

10:124   Spector, Ronald H. *Admiral of the New Empire: The Life and Career of George Dewey.* Baton Rouge: Louisiana State University Press, 1974. Based on solid research, this is the most recent and best biography of Dewey.

Edwin L. Godkin

10:125   Armstrong, William M. *E. L. Godkin and American Foreign Policy, 1865–1900.* The editor of the *Nation* and the *New York Post,* Godkin opposed war with Spain and the acquisition of colonies (9:108).

10:126   _____. *E. L. Godkin: A Biography.* Albany: State University of New York Press, 1978. The book's final chapter examines Godkin's views on late-nineteenth-century foreign policy. Godkin denounced national chauvinism, the new navy, yellow journalism, McKinley, war with Spain, and imperial expansion.

John Hay

10:127   Clymer, Kenton J. *John Hay: The Gentleman as Diplomat.* This important study provides useful information on McKinley's diplomatic appointments, on Hay's views and actions regarding turn-of-the-century U.S. foreign relations, and on Anglo-American relations (9:109).

10:128 Dennett, Tyler. *John Hay: From Poetry to Politics.* New York: Dodd, Mead and Company, 1933. This is an older but still useful account that is stronger on detail than analysis.

10:129 Dulles, Foster Rhea. "John Hay (1898–1905)." In *An Uncertain Tradition: American Secretaries of State in the Twentieth Century,* ed. Norman A. Graebner, 22–39. New York: McGraw-Hill, 1961. An internationalist, anglophile, and talented diplomat and compromiser, Hay lacked a genuine understanding of the realities of international politics but conducted diplomacy skillfully and was an excellent spokesman for U.S. interests.

10:130 Kushner, Howard I., and Anne Hummel Sherrill. *John Milton Hay: The Union of Poetry and Politics.* New York: Twayne Publishers, 1977. This biography gives greater attention to Hay's childhood, youth, and relationship with Lincoln than to turn-of-the-century foreign relations.

10:131 Sears, Louis Martin. "John Hay in London, 1897–1898." *Ohio Historical Quarterly* 65 (October 1956): 356–75. Sears describes Hay's year as ambassador.

10:132 Thayer, William Roscoe. *The Life and Letters of John Hay.* 2 vols. Boston: Houghton Mifflin Company, 1915. This is an old but excellent life that includes Hay letters as well as extensive information on his career.

William Randolph Hearst

10:133 Mugridge, Ian. *The View from Xanadu: William Randolph Hearst and United States Foreign Policy.* Montreal: McGill-Queen's University Press, 1995. This balanced study examines Hearst's views and influence on U.S. policy from the 1890s through the 1940s. The treatment of the war of 1898 is brief and concludes that the press had an important but not a decisive influence on the coming of the war and that Hearst established the prototype for the newspaper campaigns he would wage over the subsequent forty years.

10:134 Nasaw, David. *The Chief: The Life of William Randolph Hearst.* Boston: Houghton Mifflin, 2000. The author provides a lively treatment of Hearst's coverage of the war, his efforts to have one of his yachts commissioned for use by the U.S. navy, and his service as a war correspondent. Drawing on Walter LaFeber and John Offner, Nasaw concludes that the yellow press did not drive McKinley to war; larger strategic, economic, and political forces were decisive. See also his "How Do You Like the Journal's War?" *Biblion* 7 (Spring 1999): 33–64.

10:135 Procter, Ben. *William Randolph Hearst: The Early Years, 1863–1910.* New York: Oxford University Press, 1998. In chapters 6 and 7 Proctor carefully traces Hearst's motives and actions, including his brief tenure as a war correspondent in Cuba. Although the assertions regarding press influence are cautious, Hearst certainly deemed the conflict the *Journal*'s war, and the author portrays McKinley as being driven to war by public opinion.

10:136 Swanberg, W. A. *Citizen Hearst: A Biography of William Randolph Hearst.* New York: Scribner, 1961. Reprint 1986 (Collier Books). In this stimulating, prize-winning biography, the author traces Hearst's circulation battle with Joseph Pulitzer and the inflammatory coverage of events in Cuba.

10:137 Winkler, John Kennedy. *William Randolph Hearst, a New Appraisal.* New York: Hastings House, 1955. This work traces the influence of Hearst and the *Journal* on public opinion and foreign policy decisions in the months leading to intervention in Cuba in 1898.

George F. Hoar

10:138 Welch, Richard E., Jr. *George Frisbie Hoar and the Half-Breed Republicans.* This intelligent biography examines Hoar's support for the acquisition of Hawaii and opposition to the annexation of the Philippines. Hoar's anti-imperialism is tied to his fear that expansionism would harm American institutions (9:73).

10:139 _____. "Opponents and Colleagues: George Frisbie Hoar and Henry Cabot Lodge,

1898–1904." *New England Quarterly* (June 1966): 182–209. Although opponents on the issue of expansionism, they avoided a rupture in their private lives.

Henry Cabot Lodge

10:140   Garraty, John A. *Henry Cabot Lodge: A Biography*. Garraty provides an astute and sympathetic appraisal of Lodge's views and role in policymaking (9:113).

10:141   Widenor, William C. *Henry Cabot Lodge and the Search for an American Foreign Policy*. Berkeley: University of California Press, 1980. In this intellectual biography examining Lodge's relation to U.S. foreign policy from the 1870s into the 1920s, Widenor carefully and thoughtfully assesses the senator's jingoistic nationalism and support for imperialism in the 1890s. He considers his devotion to realpolitik, the influence of strategic and economic considerations, and the relation of foreign policy to desired domestic social changes.

Alfred Thayer Mahan

10:142   Hagan, Kenneth J. "Alfred Thayer Mahan: Turning America Back to the Sea." In *Makers of American Diplomacy. Vol. 1: From Benjamin Franklin to Alfred Thayer Mahan*, ed. Frank J. Merli and Theodore A. Wilson, 279–304. New York: Scribner, 1974. Hagan focuses on Mahan's thought and identifies precursors for most of his ideas. Mahan had limited influence on policy but was a successful propagandist.

10:143   LaFeber, Walter. "A Note on the 'Mercantilistic Imperialism' of Alfred Thayer Mahan." *Journal of American History* 48 (March 1962): 674–85. In this analysis of the philosophic bases of Mahan's writings, LaFeber argues that he believed in commercial rather than landed expansion, a strong navy but not necessarily a strong merchant marine, and an open door approach rather than formal colonialism.

10:144   Livezey, William E. *Mahan on Sea Power*. Rev. ed. Norman: University of Oklahoma Press, 1980. This summary and analysis of Mahan's ideas also contains a useful bibliography of his writings.

The author finds Mahan less influential with his peers than Luce or Sims. Originally published in 1947.

10:145   Mahan, Alfred T. *From Sail to Steam: Recollections of Naval Life*. This (9:75) is a better place to get a view of Mahan's most important ideas about strategy than in his most famous book, *The Influence of Sea Power upon History, 1660–1783* (Boston: Little, Brown and Company, 1890).

10:146   Pratt, Julius W. "Alfred Thayer Mahan." In *The Marcus W. Jernegan Essays in American Historiography, by His Former Students at the University of Chicago*, ed. William T. Hutchinson, 207–26. Chicago: University of Chicago Press, 1937. Pratt provides a useful analysis of Mahan as a historian, propagandist, and prophet.

10:147   Puleston, William D. *Mahan: The Life and Work of Captain Alfred Thayer Mahan*. New Haven: Yale University Press, 1939. This is a solid biography that remains worthy of consultation.

10:148   _____. "A Re-examination of Mahan's Concept of Sea Power." *U.S. Naval Institute Proceedings* 66 (1940): 1229–36. Puleston argues that Mahan was cognizant of technological change in formulating his strategic principles.

10:149   Seager, Robert, II. *Alfred Thayer Mahan: The Man and His Letters*. In this solid biography and assessment of Mahan's intellectual contributions, Seager recounts his role in the war of 1898, which was confined to advising the government on strategy (9:76).

10:150   Sumida, Jon Tetsuro. "Alfred Thayer Mahan, Geopolitician." *Journal of Strategic Studies* 32 (June-September 1999): 39–62. Based on a thorough reading of Mahan's voluminous works, Sumida argues that his importance extends well beyond his influence on contemporary imperial thought and action. Mahan deemed political and military decision-making as crucial as geographical factors, believed naval superiority would result from a transnational consortium, and perceived global free trade as the ideal system.

10:151   _____. *Inventing Grand Strategy and*

Teaching Command: The Classic Works of Alfred Thayer Mahan Reconsidered. Baltimore: Johns Hopkins University Press, 1997. Sumida argues that Mahan's thought was far more complex than previously acknowledged. Mahan believed that national security and protection of international trade in the twentieth century would depend on a transnational consortium of naval power. In teaching command, he went beyond instructional principles and sought to create naval officers with incisive intelligence, sound character, and ability to make good decisions based on incomplete or even misleading information.

William McKinley

10:152   Dobson, John M. *Reticent Expansionism: The Foreign Policy of William McKinley.* This volume portrays McKinley as lacking clear vision and following a reactive, irresolute, and expedient course. Still, he retained control of his administration's policy during the coming, fighting, and aftermath of the war of 1898, recruited able subordinates, and resolved the issues created by the conflict (9:78).

10:153   Gould, Lewis L. *The Presidency of William McKinley.* Lawrence: Regents Press of Kansas, 1980. In this important study, the author argues that McKinley was the first modern president, greatly strengthening and expanding executive powers, with his handling of foreign relations a crucial component of this process. He exercised coherent and courageous leadership in the coming of the war in 1898, as commander in chief, and in the annexation and administration of the island empire. See also Gould, "Thoroughly Modern McKinley: Presidential Power at the Turn of the Century," *Culturefront* 7 (Spring 1998): 55–58.

10:154   Holbo, Paul S. "Presidential Leadership in Foreign Affairs: William McKinley and the Turpie-Foraker Amendment." *American Historical Review* 72 (August 1967): 1321–35. Holbo asserts convincingly that McKinley exercised strong presidential leadership in preventing Congress from recognizing Cuban belligerency.

10:155   Johnson, Lyman L. "Presidential Leadership in Foreign Affairs: McKinley's Role in the Spanish-American War." *Boletín Americanista* 28

(1986): 55–74. Focusing on the decisionmaking process that led to the acquisition of the U.S. island empire, the author argues that McKinley understood the executive's ability to initiate political change, skillfully used the powers and prerogatives of his office to direct foreign affairs, and was responsible for enacting the "Large Policy."

10:156   Latcham, John S. "President McKinley's Active-Positive Character: A Comparative Revision with Barber's Typology." *Presidential Studies Quarterly* 12 (Fall 1982): 491–521. Latcham concludes that McKinley possessed the active character trait and left presidential power in a stronger state than any chief executive since Lincoln. McKinley's foreign policy decisions comprised a key component of the evidence for this assessment.

10:157   Leech, Margaret. *In the Days of McKinley.* New York: Harper, 1959. Leech's account was an important corrective to the portrayal of McKinley as a weak, unprincipled leader. Still, while viewing the president as personally stoic and courageous, she criticizes him for failing to restrain Congress and the public as the nation went to war in 1898.

10:158   McDonald, Timothy G. "McKinley and the Coming of War with Spain." *Midwest Quarterly* 7 (April 1966): 225–39. The author correctly portrays McKinley as understanding the potential economic and strategic value of the Philippines but goes beyond his evidence in speculating that the president delayed war so he could seize the islands.

10:159   Morgan, H. Wayne. *William McKinley and His America.* In this groundbreaking study, Morgan portrays McKinley as a strong leader and a shrewd manager of men who controlled his administration. His decision for war was a logical extension of previous policies rather than the result of pressure from the public or Congress (9:79).

10:160   _____. "William McKinley as a Political Leader." *Review of Politics* 28 (October 1966): 417–32. Morgan provides a perceptive analysis of McKinley's political acumen and tactics in party affairs.

10:161   Olcott, Charles S. *The Life of William McKinley.* 2 vols. Boston: Houghton Mifflin Company, 1916. This study anticipates several of the themes later presented by Morgan, Leech, and Gould. McKinley is viewed as a strong, perceptive leader who controlled his administration and went to war only after exhausting all other viable options.

10:162   Smith, Ephraim K. "'A Question from Which We Could Not Escape': William McKinley and the Decision to Acquire the Philippine Islands." *Diplomatic History* 9 (Fall 1985): 363–75. Drawing particularly on a memorandum written by Charles P. Anderson immediately following his meeting with McKinley on November 19, 1998, this article argues that the president was an unenthusiastic expansionist and that retaining the archipelago occurred more by accident than design. This careful analysis examines McKinley's explanations to several visitors about annexing the Philippine Islands.

10:163   Welch, Richard E., Jr. "William McKinley: Reluctant Warrior, Cautious Imperialist." In *Traditions and Values: American Diplomacy, 1865–1945. Vol. 8: American Values Projected Abroad,* ed. Norman A. Graebner, 29–52. Lanham, MD: University Press of America, 1985. This balanced assessment of McKinley's foreign policy falls into the revisionist category that portrays him as a competent president who controlled his administration and achieved many foreign policy successes. Neither his ideas nor policies were as consistent as his critics or supporters have asserted, and he erred most seriously in annexing the Philippines.

John Tyler Morgan

10:164   Burnette, O. Lawrence. "John Tyler Morgan and Expansionist Sentiment in the New South." *Alabama Review* 18 (July 1965): 163–82. This is a useful summary of Morgan's advocacy of territorial and economic expansionism and the construction of an isthmian canal.

10:165   Fry, Joseph A. *John Tyler Morgan and the Search for Southern Autonomy.* The south's most aggressive economic and territorial expansionist, Morgan favored recognition of Cuban belligerence and annexation, U.S. intervention, and the acquisition of Hawaii, Puerto Rico, and the Philippines. He hoped to acquire both additional southern markets and

states (9:80). See also Fry, "John Tyler Morgan's Southern Expansionism," *Diplomatic History* 9 (Fall 1985): 329–46.

Whitelaw Reid

10:166   Cortissoz, Royal. *The Life of Whitelaw Reid.* 2 vols. New York: Charles Scribner's Sons, 1921. This is an older, but still reliable treatment of Reid, who was an important member of the U.S. commission to negotiate the peace agreement with Spain in 1898.

10:167   Duncan, Bingham. *Whitelaw Reid: Journalist, Politician, Diplomat.* Athens, GA: University of Georgia Press, 1975. About one-third of this book is devoted to Reid's diplomatic career as the minister to France, member of the peace commission following war in 1898, and minister to Great Britain. This biography supersedes all others in terms of both interpretation and coverage.

Frederic Remington

10:168   Allen, Douglas. *Frederic Remington and the Spanish-American War.* New York: Crown, 1971. This study contains Remington reports, illustrations, and pictures from Cuba.

10:169   Vorpahl, Ben M. "A Splendid Little War: Frederic Remington's Reaction to the 1898 Cuban Crisis as Revealed through His Letters to Owen Wister." *American West* 9 (April 1972): 25–35. Remington saw the war as an exciting adventure much like the winning of the west.

Theodore Roosevelt

10:170   Collin, Richard H. *Theodore Roosevelt, Culture, Diplomacy, and Expansion: A New View of American Imperialism.* The author argues that the term and concept of imperialism does not apply to turn-of-the-century U.S. actions. He emphasizes instead modernism and American dynamism in the cultural, economic, artistic, technological, and diplomatic spheres. Collin stresses Roosevelt's complexity, dismisses the anti-imperialists as mere racists, ascribes the war in the Philippines to cultural misunderstanding, and portrays the U.S. presence there as a matter of duty and necessity (9:85).

10:171 Gerstle, Gary. "Theodore Roosevelt and the Divided Character of American Nationalism." *Journal of American History* 86 (December 1999): 1280–1307. Gerstle uses Roosevelt as a vehicle to examine the contradictory character of American nationalism. Roosevelt simultaneously promoted a racial ideology that endorsed the subjugation of allegedly savage people while celebrating the United States as a country welcoming all peoples willing to contribute to the common good. His foreign policy positions on the war of 1898 and its imperial aftermath illustrated the first of these inclinations.

10:172 Jeffers, H. Paul. *Colonel Roosevelt: Theodore Roosevelt Goes to War, 1897–1898.* New York: John Wiley and Sons, 1996. This study traces and synthesizes existing material on Roosevelt's attitudes and actions regarding foreign relations prior to war in 1898.

10:173 Morris, Edmund. *The Rise of Theodore Roosevelt.* New York: Coward, McCann and Geoghegan, 1979. Focusing on Roosevelt's life through 1901, this book devotes far greater attention to his ambitions for political advancement and military glory and his military service than to his attitudes and influence on foreign policy.

10:174 _____. *Theodore Rex.* New York: Random House, 2001. Morris treats U.S. involvement in the Philippines principally within the context of Roosevelt's domestic political calculations and maneuvers.

10:175 Turk, Richard W. *The Ambiguous Relationship: Theodore Roosevelt and Alfred Thayer Mahan.* This slim volume traces the collaboration and tensions in the Roosevelt-Mahan relationship from the late 1880s through 1914. For the 1898–1902 period, the relationship helped mobilize American opinion for expansion and stimulate use of the navy to accomplish foreign policy goals. The book also includes sixty-three pages of Roosevelt-Mahan correspondence (9:87).

Leonard Wood

10:176 Hagedorn, Hermann. *Leonard Wood, A Biography.* 2 vols. New York: Harper and Brothers, 1931. Hagedorn examines Wood's role as military leader during the war and governor-general of Cuba during the subsequent occupation.

10:177 Hitchman, James H. *Leonard Wood and Cuban Independence, 1898–1902.* The Hague: Nijhoff, 1971. The author justifies American occupation on the grounds that only the United States could provide the necessary preparation for Cuban independence.

10:178 Lane, Jack C. *Armed Progressive: General Leonard Wood.* San Rafael, CA: Presidio Press, 1978. This solid study examines Wood's long career: he was a Rough Rider, military governor of Cuba from 1899 to 1902, and governor of Moro Province in the Philippines, 1903–1904.

Others

10:179 Bradford, James C., ed. *Admirals of the New Steel Navy: Makers of the American Naval Tradition, 1880–1930.* See chapter 9 of this Guide (9:240).

10:180 West, Richard S., Jr. *Admirals of the American Empire: The Combined Story of George Dewey, Alfred Thayer Mahan, Winfield Scott Schley and William Thomas Sampson.* Indianapolis: Bobbs-Merrill Co., 1948. Reprint 1971 (Greenwood Press). This volume includes biographies of several career naval officers in the war of 1898, including Schley, Sampson, Dewey, and Mahan.

10:181 Sage, Leland L. *William Boyd Allison: A Study in Practical Politics.* Iowa City: State Historical Society of Iowa, 1956. Allison was an important Republican leader in the Senate during the Cuban crisis.

10:182 Nevins, Allan. *Grover Cleveland: A Study in Courage.* Nevins portrays Cleveland as a strong and principled leader who resisted an unnecessary war with Spain and opposed imperial annexations. This book set the tone for subsequent scholarship that treated Cleveland much more sympathetically than McKinley (9:44).

10:183   Lubow, Arthur. *The Reporter Who Would Be King: A Biography of Richard Harding Davis.* New York: Scribner, 1992. The author recounts Davis's trip to Cuba in December 1896–December 1897 on behalf of the *New York World* and his subsequent coverage of the war and especially Theodore Roosevelt and the Rough Riders.

10:184   Devine, Michael J. *John W. Foster: Politics and Diplomacy in the Imperial Era, 1873–1917.* As an international lawyer, diplomat, secretary of state, and policy adviser, Foster played an active role in U.S. foreign relations for four decades. He favored economic expansion and the acquisition of Hawaii but opposed the annexation of the Philippines and Puerto Rico (9:53).

10:185   Schlup, Leonard. "Quiet Imperialist: Henry C. Hansbrough and the Question of Expansion." *North Dakota History* 45 (Spring 1978): 26–31. A Republican senator from North Dakota from 1891 to 1909, Hansbrough made no important speeches but consistently supported McKinley's expansionist policies.

10:186   Meyerhuber, Carl I., Jr. "Henry Lee Higginson and the New Imperialism, 1890–1900." *Mid-America* 56 (July 1974): 182–99. This article traces how Higginson, a Boston banker, moved from opposition to war and expansionism to the support of colonial acquisitions.

10:187   O'Connell, Marvin R. *John Ireland and the American Catholic Church.* St. Paul, MN: Minnesota Historical Society Press, 1988. The author devotes a chapter to the Vatican's perceptions of the war of 1898, to church politics, and to Ireland's efforts to prevent the U.S.-Spanish conflict.

10:188   Kennedy, Padraic C. "La Follette's Imperialist Flirtation." *Pacific Historical Review* 29 (February 1960): 131–44. Although generally viewed as a pacifist and isolationist, La Follette supported the war in 1898 and territorial expansion.

10:189   Garrett, Wendell D. "John Davis Long, Secretary of the Navy, 1898–1902: A Study in Changing Political Alignments." *New England Quarterly* 31 (March 1958): 291–311. Long is portrayed as a firm and able administrator; although not a jin-

goist, he was concerned with bringing the navy to combat strength and efficiency.

10:190   Bacevich, A. J. *Diplomat in Khaki: Major General Frank Ross McCoy and American Foreign Policy, 1898–1949.* Lawrence: University Press of Kansas, 1989. This thoroughly researched biography examines McCoy's long military-diplomatic career including service in Cuba and the Philippines. The author concentrates on McCoy's diplomatic service between wars and the influence of military elites on foreign policy formation.

10:191   Schlup, Leonard. "Hernando De Soto Money: War Advocate and Anti-Imperialist, 1898–1900." *Journal of Mississippi History* 60 (Winter 1998): 315–39. Money, a U.S. senator from Mississippi, favored intervention in Cuba on humanitarian, economic, and strategic grounds and endorsed the annexation of Cuba and Hawaii with an eye toward their subsequent incorporation as states. He opposed the acquisition of the Philippines, a noncontiguous colony, as imperialism.

10:192   Coolidge, Louis A. *An Old-Fashioned Senator: Orville H. Platt of Connecticut: The Story of a Life Unselfishly Devoted to the Public Service.* New York: G. P. Putnam's Sons, 1910. Reprint 1971 (Kennikat Press). Platt was one of the influential Republican senators close to the McKinley administration during the Cuban crisis.

10:193   Swanberg, W. A. *Pulitzer.* New York: Scribner, 1967. This excellent biography of Pulitzer sees his *New York World* as both reflecting and provoking the public excitement against Spain.

10:194   Robinson, William A. *Thomas B. Reed, Parliamentarian.* New York: Dodd, Mead and Company, 1930. Although a Republican and Speaker of the House, Reed opposed war and annexation of new territories.

10:195   Trefousse, Hans L. *Carl Schurz, a Biography.* 2d ed. New York: Fordham University Press, 1998. One chapter provides a careful examination of Schurz's opposition to war in 1898 and to the annexation of Hawaii, Puerto Rico, and the Philippines. First published in 1982.

10:196 McWilliams, Tennant S. *Hannis Taylor: The New Southerner as American.* University: University of Alabama Press, 1978. Taylor, who served as U.S. minister to Spain from 1893 to 1897, favored U.S. intervention in Cuba, retention of the island as American territory, military control of Puerto Rico, and retention of the Philippines as a protectorate. See also McWilliams, "'No Sterile Monster': Hannis Taylor, the New South, and American Expansion," *Alabama Review* 30 (January 1977): 34–50.

SPANISH, CUBAN, FILIPINO AND PUERTO RICAN LEADERS

10:197 Estrade, Paul, and Félix Ojeda Reyes. *Ramón Emeterio Betances: el anciano maravilloso [Ramón Emeterio Betances: The Old Marvel].* Río Piedras, PR: Instituto de Estudios del Caribe, Comité del Centenario de 1898 Universidad de Puerto Rico, 1995. This life of Betances focuses on his leading role in Paris as head of the Cuban–Puerto Rican community working for independence from Spain. Betances, a Puerto Rican, counseled fellow Puerto Ricans to cooperate with the U.S. invasion of the island but also to reject U.S. annexation or a protectorate in favor of complete independence.

10:198 Buznego Rodríguez, Enrique. *Mayor general Máximo Gómez Báez: sus campañas militares [Maj. General Máximo Gómez Báez: His Military Campaigns].* 2 vols. La Habana: Editora Política, 1986. This biography, commemorating the 150th anniversary of the birth of Máximo Gómez, focuses on his military career.

10:199 Fernández Almagro, Melchor. *Cánovas, su vida y su política [Cánovas, His Life and Politics].* Madrid: Ediciones Ambos Mundos, 1951. Reprint 1972 (Ediciones Giner). This well-written biography of Antonio Cánovas del Castillo provides insight into Spain's relations with the Cleveland administration.

10:200 Foner, Philip S. *Antonio Maceo: The "Bronze Titan" of Cuba's Struggle for Independence.* New York: Monthly Review Press, 1977. An African Cuban, General Antonio Maceo y Grajales symbolized the hopes of black Cubans as he fought for racial equality as well as Cuban independence.

10:201 Gray, Richard B. *José Martí: Cuban Patriot.* Gainesville: University of Florida Press, 1962. This biographical account of Martí's life and times describes his contribution to the development of Cuban nationalism.

10:202 Pascual, Ricardo R. *The Philosophy of Rizal.* Manila: P. B. Ayuda, 1962. Rizal's writings exemplified rising Filipino nationalism.

10:203 Cepeda Adán, José. *Sagasta: el político de las horas difíciles [Sagasta: A Politician of Difficult Times].* Madrid: Fundación Universitaria Española, 1995. This brief political biography adds little to understanding Spanish-American diplomatic relations in 1898 but is one of the few available biographies of Sagasta and provides a Spanish nationalistic perspective that supported war with the United States in 1898.

10:204 Weyler, Valerià. *Mi mando en Cuba (10 febrero 1896 á 31 octubre 1897); historia militar y política de la última guerra separatista durante dicho mando [My Command in Cuba (10 February 1896–31 October 1897): Military and Political History of the Last Separatist War during My Command].* 5 vols. Madrid: F. González Rojas, 1910. The Spanish commander in Cuba and the creator of the "reconcentration" order justifies his policies in Cuba.

U.S. Intervention

POLITICAL CAUSES

10:205 Dallek, Robert. *The American Style of Foreign Policy: Cultural Politics and Foreign Affairs.* In the book's first chapter, Dallek argues that U.S. involvement in the war of 1898 resulted primarily from the national desire to relieve the social and economic tensions that accompanied modernization in the late nineteenth century. The resulting public pressure pushed McKinley to war, and the nation turned to imperialism as a purposeful alternative to the frustration and psychic tensions of the 1890s (2:129). See also Dallek, "National Mood and American Foreign Policy: A Suggestive Essay," *American Quarterly* 34 (Fall 1982): 339–61.

10:206   Foster, Gaines M. *Ghosts of the Confederacy: Defeat, the Lost Cause, and the Emergence of the New South, 1865 to 1913.* New York: Oxford University Press, 1987. In chapter 16, the author examines how the participation of southerners in the war of 1898 and the Philippines enabled the south to demonstrate its patriotism and loyalty to the Union and secure northern recognition of the honorable course of the Confederacy. This chapter discusses the south's positions prior to 1898, participation in these conflicts, and responses to imperialism.

10:207   Hofstadter, Richard. "Manifest Destiny and the Philippines." In *America in Crisis: Fourteen Crucial Episodes in American History,* ed. Daniel Aaron, 173–203. New York: Alfred A. Knopf, 1952. Hofstadter views the outbreak of war and subsequent expansion from a social history perspective and posits the existence of a "psychic crisis," in which the United States converted domestic social tensions into both belligerent and humanitarian impulses abroad. Reprinted in his *The Paranoid Style in American Politics* (New York: Vintage, 1967), 147–87.

10:208   Holbo, Paul S. "The Convergence of Moods and the Cuban Bond 'Conspiracy' of 1898." *Journal of American History* 55 (June 1968): 54–72. Politicians, particularly Populists and Democrats who distrusted bankers and wanted war against Spain and the freeing of Cuba, accused McKinley of resisting because of the pressure of the holders of Cuban bonds issued by Spain.

10:209   Leuchtenburg, William E. "The Needless War with Spain." *American Heritage* 8 (February 1957): 33–41, 95. The author concludes that McKinley surrendered to public opinion against his own wishes and the advice of important segments of his party.

10:210   Offner, John L. "La política norteamericana y la guerra hispano-cubana [U.S. Politics and the Spanish-Cuban War]." In *Vísperas del 98. Orígenes y antecedentes de la crisis del 98 [On the Eve of '98: Origins and Antecedents of the 1898 Crisis],* ed. Juan Pablo Fusi Aizpurúa and Antonio Niño Rodríguez, 195–203. Madrid: Biblioteca Nueva, 1997. This article examines domestic politics from 1895 to 1898, describing the political factors that influenced Republican Party legislators to pressure McKinley to enter the Spanish-Cuban conflict.

10:211   _____. "United States Politics and the 1898 War over Cuba." In *The Crisis of 1898: Colonial Redistribution and Nationalist Mobilization,* ed. Angel Smith and Emma Dávila-Cox, 18–44. New York: St. Martin's Press, 1998. While providing both a historiographical and historical analysis of the coming of the war and subsequent U.S. acquisition of the Philippines, the author assesses the roles of ideology, economics, and politics. He deems the latter decisive in the coming of the war, citing the number and timing of persons writing to McKinley and the geographic base of insurgent Republicans. See also Offner, "Why Did the United States Fight Spain in 1898?" *OAH Magazine of History* 12 (Spring 1998): 19–23.

10:212   Pratt, Julius W. *Expansionists of 1898: The Acquisition of Hawaii and the Spanish Islands.* Pratt argues against an economic interpretation of the war and its aftermath; he posits instead the formative influence of Social Darwinism and public opinion (9:503).

10:213   _____. "The 'Large Policy' of 1898." *Mississippi Valley Historical Review* 19 (September 1932): 219–42. Pratt cites a group of influential imperialists, including Mahan, Roosevelt, Beveridge, Lodge, and Brooks Adams, as viewing U.S. expansion more from strategic than economic perspectives and as being more responsible for policy implementation than McKinley.

10:214   Rippy, J. Fred. "Enthusiasms of 1898." *South Atlantic Quarterly* 37 (April 1938): 139–49. Rippy cites feelings of destiny and belief in the white man's burden as primarily responsible for U.S. imperial expansion.

ECONOMIC CAUSES AND ARGUMENTS

10:215   Becker, William H. "1899–1920: America Adjusts to World Power." In *Economics and World Power: An Assessment of American Diplomacy since 1789,* ed. William H. Becker and Samuel F. Wells, Jr., 173–233. New York: Columbia University Press, 1984. Becker argues that economic interests were not the principal consideration for the most important

U.S. policymakers. Among U.S. businesses, the largest and most successful exporters did not seek or benefit from significant government assistance; smaller producers were more solicitous of and dependent on government aid.

10:216 Casellas, Salvador E. "Causas y Antecedentes diplomaticos de la Guerra hispano-americana [Causes and Diplomatic Antecedents to the Spanish-American War]." *Revista de Ciencias Sociales* 9 (March 1965): 55–75. The author finds that U.S. financial and commercial interests caused intervention in Cuba and war with Spain.

10:217 Etherington, Norman. "The Capitalist Theory of Capitalist Imperialism." *History of Political Economy* 15 (Spring 1983): 38–62. This essay examines the origins of the theory of economic imperialism and highlights H. Gaylord Wilshire, an American Marxist, as an important forerunner of both Hobson and Lenin.

10:218 _____. *Theories of Imperialism: War, Conquest, and Capital*. Totowa, NJ: Barnes and Noble Books, 1984. This examination of the explanations of imperialism running from the 1890s through the 1970s gives particular attention to the American origins of capitalist theories of imperialism and to H. Gaylord Wilshire's writings and influence on John A. Hobson.

10:219 Foner, Philip S. "Why the United States Went to War with Spain in 1898." *Science and Society* 32 (Winter 1968): 39–65. Foner concludes that intervention in Cuba was caused by the need for new markets and was prompted by U.S. trusts.

10:220 Hearden, Patrick J. *Independence & Empire: The New South's Cotton Mill Campaign, 1865–1901*. Hearden contends that late-nineteenth-century southerners sought to escape northern economic domination by building cotton mills and selling their products abroad. By 1898, northern and southern producers agreed on the need for markets, which provided a crucial backdrop to war and helped lay the basis for U.S. empire (9:191).

10:221 LaFeber, Walter. "That 'Splendid Little War' in Historical Perspective." *Texas Quarterly* 11 (Winter 1968): 89–98. The author argues that the war

resulted from the collision of three chains of causes: the domestic economic crisis of the 1890s, commercial opportunities in the Caribbean and Pacific, and the growing partnership between business and government. For a more recent LaFeber comment, see "The White Whale of the Caribbean: The War of 1898, Cuba, and U.S. Foreign Policy," *Culturefront* 7 (Spring 1998): 4–8, 75.

10:222 McCormick, Thomas J. "The 1890s as a Watershed Decade." In *Safeguarding the Republic: Essays and Documents in American Foreign Relations, 1890–1991*, ed. Howard Jones, 1–18. New York: McGraw-Hill, 1992. In the brief introductory essay, the author outlines the international and domestic conditions underlying U.S. imperialism and emphasizes the nation's preference for informal empire. The majority of the accompanying documents are drawn from the 1898–1902 period.

10:223 _____. *China Market: America's Quest for Informal Empire, 1893–1901*. In this important revisionist study, the author emphasizes the decisive influence of the business community and its political and intellectual allies. Pressured by domestic overproduction and depression and the threat of exclusion from export markets in China, the McKinley administration's attention to East Asian developments was second only to its focus on Cuba in the spring of 1898. This combination of economic need at home and potential economic opportunity abroad led to the acquisition of Hawaii, Guam, Wake, and the Philippines not as traditional territorial acquisitions but as stepping stones to the China market (9:548). See also his "Insular Imperialism and the Open Door: The China Market and the Spanish-American War" (1963) (10:224).

10:224 _____. "Insular Imperialism and the Open Door: The China Market and the Spanish-American War." *Pacific Historical Review* 32 (May 1963): 155–69. McCormick emphasizes the quest for markets in Asia and the preference for informal empire as the essential backdrops to war in Cuba. The subsequent island acquisitions were seen as stepping stones to trade in China.

10:225 McWilliams, Tennant S. "Petition for Expansion: Mobile Businessmen and the Cuban Crisis, 1898." *Alabama Review* 28 (January 1975): 58–63.

Mobile business interests favored intervention to restore peace and safeguard their markets.

10:226   Parrini, Carl P. "The Age of Ultraimperialism." *Radical History Review* 57 (Fall 1993): 7–20. This essay focuses on economic issues and places the McKinley administration's imperial activities within an overall assessment of U.S. imperialism in the twentieth century.

10:227   _____. "Theories of Imperialism." In *Redefining the Past: Essays in Diplomatic History in Honor of William Appleman Williams*, ed. Lloyd C. Gardner, 65–83. While examining the differences and similarities between socialist and nonsocialist interpretations of imperialism, this article gives extensive attention to Charles Conant and the influence of his theories during the 1890s and early twentieth century (2:89).

10:228   Parrini, Carl P., and Martin J. Sklar. "New Thinking about the Market, 1896–1904: Some Economists on Investment and the Theory of Surplus Capital." *Journal of Economic History* 48 (September 1983): 559–78. This article concentrates on the economic arguments of Arthur Twining Hadley, Jeremiah W. Jenks, and Charles A. Conant; they formulated the concepts of a business cycle, oversaving, and the need for global investment and monetary policy. The McKinley administration acted on these concepts in the Philippines, Mexico, Nicaragua, and China.

10:229   Pletcher, David M. "1861–1898: Economic Growth and Diplomatic Adjustment." In *Economics and World Power: An Assessment of American Diplomacy since 1789*, ed. William H. Becker and Samuel F. Wells, Jr., 119–71. The author argues against the coherent, consistent, and aggressive pursuit of foreign markets by either U.S. business leaders or policymakers. There was much pro-trade rhetoric and many discrete efforts, but no official policy prior to 1898. The conflict with Spain did not result primarily from economic pressures or objectives, although key businessmen came to favor U.S. intervention (9:193).

10:230   _____. *The Diplomacy of Trade and Investment: American Economic Expansion in the Hemisphere, 1865–1900*. In this meticulously researched and richly detailed study, the author examines U.S. economic expansion in both Canada and Latin America. He argues in opposition to revisionist themes and emphasizes the tentative, experimental, improvised, and inconsistent nature of economic expansion and government policy. Economic and noneconomic motivations were conflicting and business opinion undecided prior to war in 1898. McKinley viewed economic factors as deterrents to be removed before intervening rather than as positive incentives to action (9:194).

10:231   _____. "Rhetoric and Results: A Pragmatic View of American Economic Expansionism, 1865–98." The author argues in opposition to scholars who have emphasized the influence of business and economic considerations on U.S. foreign relations. He asserts that they have exaggerated the deliberate, systematic nature of policy by emphasizing words over deeds. The more appropriate description would portray the period as one of education, experimentation, and preparation in the economic realm (9:195).

10:232   Pratt, Julius W. "American Business and the Spanish-American War." *Hispanic American Historical Review* 14 (May 1934): 163–201. Pratt contends that U.S. financial and commercial interests opposed war. They feared that the disruption of normal channels of trade and the weakening of the currency would harm the domestic economy.

10:233   Rosenberg, Emily S. "Foundations of United States International Financial Power: Gold Standard Diplomacy, 1900–1905." Rosenberg demonstrates how the promotion of a gold standard exchange by Charles Conant, Jeremiah Jenks, and Edwin Kemmerer coincided with U.S. economic and strategic expansion and provided the basis for financial policies in the Philippines, Puerto Rico, and then more generally in the twentieth century (9:196).

10:234   Schoonover, Thomas D. "Columbus, the Spanish-Cuban-American War, and the Advance of U.S. Liberal Capitalism in the Caribbean and Pacific Region." In *1898: su significado para Centroamérica y el Caribe ¿Cesura, Cambio, Continuidad? [1898: Its Meaning for Central America and the Caribbean: Pause, Change, or Continuity?]*, ed. Walther L. Bernecker, 61–75. Frankfurt am Main: Vervuert, 1998.

The author links the war to 400 years of capitalist desire to enter and control trade with Asia.

10:235   Schott, Marshall E. "Louisiana Sugar and the Cuban Crisis, 1895–1898." *Louisiana History* 31 (Summer 1990): 265–72. Louisiana sugar interests were generally more concerned with protective tariff legislation and improving the efficiency of their operations than developments in Cuba. There were different responses depending on geographic region and political affiliation, but all groups feared the possibility of incorporating Cuba under the U.S. tariff umbrella.

10:236   Sklar, Martin J. "The NAM and Foreign Markets on the Eve of the Spanish-American War." *Science and Society* 23 (Spring 1959): 133–62. Finding the National Association of Manufacturers deeply involved in efforts to secure overseas markets on the eve of the war, Sklar suggests a reappraisal of Pratt's thesis that business opposed the conflict.

10:237   Trubowitz, Peter. *Defining the National Interest: Conflict and Change in American Foreign Policy.* Trubowitz contends that domestic regional conflicts deriving from different degrees of economic development have been the decisive influence in the formation of U.S. foreign policy. The author focuses on the 1880s, 1890s, and 1930s. In the first period, the imperialist northeast contested with the anti-imperialist south, and the west served as a swing vote (2:127).

10:238   Voltes Bou, Pedro. "Nuevo análisis de los antecedentes de la guerra de 1898 [A New Analysis of the Origins of the War of 1898]." *Cuadernos de Economía* 11 (May-August 1983): 313–53. The author asserts that conflicting American and Spanish economic interests in Cuba made the war inevitable.

10:239   Williams, William Appleman. *The Roots of the Modern American Empire: A Study of the Growth and Shaping of Social Consciousness in a Marketplace Society.* In a variation on his previous arguments, Williams argues that agricultural interests rather than metropolitan businessmen provided the primary economic impetus to the U.S. search for markets and in so doing provided the principal backdrop to the war of 1898 and imperial expansion (2:96).

10:240   _____. *The Tragedy of American Diplomacy.* In perhaps the most influential single volume written on U.S. foreign relations (first published in 1959), the author asserts that the pursuit of foreign markets to dispose of surplus domestic production and thereby alleviate internal social and political tensions drove American foreign policy. This policy in turn curtailed indigenous revolutions abroad. Both the motives and the effects were evident in the war of 1898 (2:97).

PRESS AND PUBLIC OPINION

10:241   Abrams, Jeanne. "Remembering the *Maine:* The Jewish Attitude toward the Spanish American War as Reflected in *The American Israelite.*" *American Jewish History* 76 (June 1987): 439–55. The *American Israelite* was prowar and favored annexing Hawaii, but opposed acquiring Guam, Puerto Rico, and the Philippines. Its editors also used the war as an opportunity to emphasize Jewish patriotism and integration into American society.

10:242   Appel, John C. "The Unionization of Florida Cigar Makers and the Coming of the War with Spain." *Hispanic American Historical Review* 36 (February 1956): 38–49. Labor sympathized with the Cubans, many of whom were cigar makers and unionists, and favored war with Spain.

10:243   Bailey, Harris Moore, Jr. "The Splendid Little Forgotten War: The Mobilization of South Carolina for the War with Spain." *South Carolina Historical Magazine* 92 (July 1991): 189–209. This article concentrates on the recruitment and mobilization of military companies and provides useful material on the responses of black South Carolinians. The difficulty recruiters encountered contradicts the image of a particularly martial south.

10:244   Bouvier, Virginia M. "Imperial Humor: U.S. Political Cartoons and the War of 1898." *Colonial Latin American Historical Review* 8 (Winter 1999): 5–41. This article analyzes more than 140 cartoons published by Charles Nelan in the *New York Herald.* Nelan supported U.S. economic expansion, was ambivalent about the coming of war, largely ignored the Cubans and their role, and portrayed the

United States as culturally superior to the other participants in the war and as a generous and benevolent colonial ruler.

10:245   Collomp, Catherine. "L'American Federation of Labor et la politique extérieures des États-Unis: de l'anti-impérialisme à la coopération idéologique [The American Federation of Labor and U.S. Foreign Policy: From Anti-Imperialism to Ideological Cooperation]." In *La république impérialiste: l'expansionnisme et la politique extérieure des États-Unis, 1885–1909: études et documents [The Imperial Republic: Expansionism and the Foreign Policy of the United States, 1885–1909: Studies and Documents]*, ed. Serge Ricard and James Bolner, Sr., 181–93. Aix-en-Provence: Université de Provence, 1987. The author explains the rationale of the AFL's support of Cuba Libre and opposition to U.S. imperialism.

10:246   Davis, Michelle B., and Robin W. Quimby. "Senator Proctor's Cuban Speech: Speculations on a Cause of the Spanish-American War." *Quarterly Journal of Speech* 55 (May 1969): 131–41. Proctor's report on his trip to Cuba reinforced both the prevailing view of conditions there and the need for U.S. intervention.

10:247   DeTemple, Jill. "Singing the *Maine*: The Popular Image of Cuba in Sheet Music of the Spanish-American War." *Historian* 63 (Summer 2001): 715–29. By 1898, sheet music was big business, and the activities of songwriters, promoters, and entertainers may have surpassed those of the national press. This music condemned Spanish treachery, reinforced national unity between the north and south, and called on Americans to avenge the murdered sailors, redress the attack on U.S. national sovereignty, and establish the nation as a world power.

10:248   Doyle, David Noel. *Irish Americans: Native Rights and National Empire: The Structure, Divisions, and Attitudes of the Catholic Minority in the Decade of Expansion, 1890–1901*. New York: Arno Press, 1976. Doyle argues that the majority of Catholics were pro-Cuban but antiwar prior to April 1898; they supported the war once it came but were uneasy at the prospect of an Anglo-American entente and opposed imperialism.

10:249   Gibson, George H. "Attitudes in North Carolina Regarding the Independence of Cuba, 1868–1898." *North Carolina Historical Review* 43 (January 1966): 43–65. During the 1870s, North Carolinians favored Cuban independence but opposed U.S. intervention or annexation. Similarly, in the 1890s, North Carolina residents moved toward war reluctantly and with reservations about the costs and the prospects of increased central authority.

10:250   Hilderbrand, Robert C. *Power and the People: Executive Management of Public Opinion in Foreign Affairs, 1897–1921*. In chapters 1 and 2 the author contends that McKinley was the first president to demonstrate clear understanding of the advantages of good press relations. His efforts to centralize and control the flow of information, initiate and carry on systematic relations with the press, and set the parameters of public debate embodied the beginning of presidential management of public opinion in the foreign policy realm (2:144).

10:251   Johnson, J. R. "Imperialism in Nebraska, 1898–1904." *Nebraska History* 44 (September 1963): 141–66. The author traces Nebraska's response to turn-of-the-century U.S. imperialism by examining the views of political leaders, farmers, labor, women, hyphenated-Americans, and the press.

10:252   King, G. Wayne. "Conservative Attitudes in the United States toward Cuba." *Proceedings of the South Carolina Historical Association* (1973): 94–104. King argues that conservative congressional leaders, businessmen, and press opposed propaganda favoring war and delayed intervention.

10:253   Leffler, John J. "The Paradox of Patriotism: Texans in the Spanish-American War." *Hayes Historical Journal* 8 (Spring 1989): 24–48. Leffler finds that the reactions of Texans to the diplomatic crisis and war were more rational and calculated than the idea of a psychic crisis would suggest. Texans balanced the dangers against the prospects for self-improvement both in terms of character and economic standing.

10:254   Lemons, J. Stanley. "Cuban Crisis of 1895–1898." *Missouri Historical Review* 60 (October 1965): 63–74. Based on an examination of forty-two papers from county-seat towns and three others reflecting a Populist, independent, and nonpolitical perspective, Lemons concludes that the Missouri press practiced virtually no yellow journalism. The great bulk of the papers were Democratic, pro-silver, critical of both Cleveland and McKinley, and suspicious that both were influenced by gold forces, Britain, and Jewish bankers.

10:255   Marotta, Gary. "The Academic Mind and the Rise of U.S. Imperialism: Historians and Economists as Publicists for Ideas of Colonial Expansion." *American Journal of Economics and Sociology* 42 (April 1983): 217–34. The American Historical Association, American Economic Association, and American Academy of Political and Social Science supported U.S. imperial acquisitions and endorsed an activist state seeking to promote commercial expansion.

10:256   McNeil, W. D. "'We'll Make the Spanish Grunt': Popular Songs about the Sinking of the '*Maine.*'" *Journal of Popular Culture* 2 (Spring 1968): 537–51. The article considers some forty songs about the sinking of the *Maine* that aroused sentiment for war by blaming the Spanish for the disaster.

10:257   McWilliams, Tennant S. *The New South Faces the World: Foreign Affairs and the Southern Sense of Self, 1877–1950.* This informative book develops the general theme of sectional responses to and influences on U.S. policy and has a specific chapter on the *Mobile Register* and the war of 1898. Ambivalent about the prospect of war, the *Register* fell in line in February 1898 largely to demonstrate southern patriotism. The paper feared that war would threaten the gold standard and disrupt southern trade and race relations (9:497).

10:258   Quint, Howard H. "American Socialists and the Spanish-American War." *American Quarterly* 10 (Summer 1958): 132–54. Although the party opposed the war, some individuals broke ranks and supported the conflict out of humanitarian considerations or the passion of the moment. The party solidly opposed expansion.

10:259   Rosenberg, Morton M., and Thomas P. Ruff. *Indiana and the Coming of the Spanish-American War.* Muncie, IN: Ball State University, 1976. This pamphlet-length monograph examines press opinion on the issues leading to war.

10:260   Schellings, William J. "Florida and the Cuban Revolution, 1895–1898." *Florida Historical Quarterly* 39 (October 1960): 175–86. Florida was the only state in which all the major newspapers opposed war. Opposition derived from the fear of Spanish attack and the threat of business disruption and competition if Cuba were annexed. Opposition declined after the Teller Amendment eliminated this possibility.

10:261   Wilkerson, Marcus M. *Public-Opinion and the Spanish-American War: A Study in War Propaganda.* Baton Rouge: Louisiana State University Press, 1932. This is a useful book that provides a broad compilation of newspaper quotations, but lacks strong analysis.

Press and Reporters

10:262   Auxier, George W. "Middle Western Newspapers and the Spanish-American War, 1895–1898." *Mississippi Valley Historical Review* 26 (March 1940): 523–34. Based on a sampling of forty papers, Democratic, Republican, and Populist, Auxier concludes that the press contributed to the coming of war by emphasizing issues in dispute with Spain rather than through sensationalism.

10:263   Berg, Meredith William, and David M. Berg. "The Rhetoric of War Preparation: The New York Press in 1898." *Journalism Quarterly* 45 (Winter 1968): 653–60. The authors examine the treatment of the events of 1898 in the *World, Journal,* and *Times.*

10:264   Boles, David C. "Editorial Opinion in Oklahoma and Indian Territory on the Cuban Insurrection, 1895–1898." *Chronicles of Oklahoma* 47 (August 1969): 258–67. The press was lukewarm about Cuba until the sinking of the *Maine,* after which it supported intervention and the annexation of Cuba.

10:265   Brown, Charles H. "Press Censorship in the Spanish-American War." *Journalism Quarterly* 42 (Autumn 1965): 581–90. The U.S. government and military censured the mail going to Spanish possessions, seized telegraph lines and cable stations, and threatened to revoke press credentials. This censorship was not generally effective, and correspondents periodically demonstrated a marked lack of responsibility in the strategic and military information they published.

10:266   Fry, Joseph A. "Silver and Sentiment: The Nevada Press and the Coming of the Spanish-American War." *Nevada Historical Society Quarterly* 20 (Winter 1977): 222–39. Fry analyzes editorials in twenty-five Nevada newspapers, all of which criticized Spanish rule in Cuba and most of which disagreed with McKinley's Cuban policies. Papers supporting free silver resorted to sensationalism and advocated war out of a desire to improve Nevada's economy.

10:267   Gatewood, Willard B., Jr. "A Black Editor on American Imperialism: Edward E. Cooper of the *Colored American,* 1898–1901." *Mid-America* 57 (January 1975): 3–19. Cooper supported McKinley, the Republican Party, and imperialism in hopes of strengthening the federal government and thereby weakening the states and diminishing their ability to enforce segregation.

10:268   Gullason, Thomas A. "Stephen Crane's Private War on Yellow Journalism." *Huntington Library Quarterly* 22 (Summer 1959): 201–8. Crane, a correspondent in Cuba, attacked the unscrupulous demands of editors and newspaper owners for sensational news.

10:269   Harrington, Peter. "'You Supply the Pictures, I'll Supply the War.'" *MHQ: The Quarterly Journal of Military History* 10 (Summer 1998): 52–65. In this pictorial essay, Harrington argues that the artists who went to the front during the war of 1898 depicted what they saw in realistic, rather than jingoist, terms.

10:270   Hilton, Sylvia L. "The Spanish-American War of 1898: Queries into the Relationship between the Press, Public Opinion and Politics." *Revista Española de Estudios Norteamericanos* 5, no. 7 (1994): 71–87. This article examines the contribution the press made to the war spirit in both the United States and Spain. It provides more coverage to the Spanish press and contains an excellent bibliography on Spanish public opinion and the Spanish government's decision to go to war.

10:271   Lande, Nathaniel. *Dispatches from the Front: News Accounts of American Wars, 1776–1991.* New York: H. Holt, 1995. The chapter on the war of 1898 includes dispatches dating from January 1897 through May 1899. They provide insight into the coming and fighting of the war and the impressions conveyed to the American public. Republished in 1998 by Oxford University Press under the title *Dispatches from the Front: A History of the American War Correspondent.*

10:272   Lopez-Briones, Carmen Gonzalez. "The Indiana Press and the Coming of the Spanish-American War, 1895–1898." *Atlantis* 12 (June 1990): 165–76. Based on an analysis of six papers, the author concludes that the Indiana press did not promote U.S. entry into war through sensationalism. The papers emphasized U.S. interests, Manifest Destiny, and Spanish misdeeds and thereby prepared their readers for war.

10:273   Mander, Mary J. "Pen and Sword: Problems of Reporting the Spanish-American War." *Journalism History* 9 (Spring 1982): 2–9, 28. The author distinguishes between the literary stars, such as Richard Harding Davis and Stephen Crane, and successful journalists, such as Christopher Michaelson. She argues that the reporters, who had no blind faith in the military, should be assessed within the context of their times.

10:274   Milton, Joyce. *The Yellow Kids: Foreign Correspondents in the Heyday of Yellow Journalism.* New York: Harper and Row, 1989. Milton traces the activities of such reporters as Richard Harding Davis, Sylvester Scovel, and George Brown Rea, but provides no sustained argument about the relation of the press or public opinion to foreign relations.

10:275   Olasky, Marvin. "Hawks or Doves? Texas Press and Spanish-American War." *Journalism Quarterly* 64 (Spring 1987): 205–8. This essay examines the contents of fifteen Texas papers from February 15 through April 21, 1898. Over the first month, they were highly critical of the yellow press. Following the *Maine* Commission's report, the Texas press called for war.

10:276   Ponder, Stephen. "The President Makes News: William McKinley and the First Presidential Press Corps, 1897–1901." *Presidential Studies Quar-*

terly 24 (Fall 1994): 823–36. This article examines McKinley's innovative initiatives in managing the Washington press corps and anticipating and shaping the coverage of himself and his administration. These initiatives made press relations more predictable and routine and anticipated Theodore Roosevelt's subsequent activities.

10:277   Simundson, Daniel. "The Yellow Press on the Prairie: South Dakota Daily Newspaper Editorials Prior to the Spanish-American War." *South Dakota History* 2 (Summer 1972): 210–29. Based on an examination of the editorials in thirteen daily papers from March 1897 through April 11, 1898, this essay concludes that the South Dakota press was more restrained than eastern metropolitan dailies; nevertheless, McKinley was pushed toward war by both pro- and antiadministration papers.

10:278   Stevens, John D. *Sensationalism and the New York Press.* New York: Columbia University Press, 1991. Chapter 9 of this book, which runs from the 1830s through the 1920s, examines the sensational press coverage of the war of 1898 as part of the Pulitzer-Hearst competition, but contends that larger social and economic tensions more than the newspapers were responsible for U.S. bellicosity.

10:279   Sylvester, Harold J. "The Kansas Press and the Coming of the Spanish-American War." *Historian* 31 (February 1969): 251–67. The press supported the war after McKinley declared it necessary.

10:280   Welter, Mark M. "The 1895–98 Cuban Crisis in Minnesota Newspapers: Testing the 'Yellow Journalism' Theory." *Journalism Quarterly* 47 (Winter 1970): 719–24. Based on an examination of eight papers, the author asserts that Minnesota papers did not adopt or imitate the sensational practices of the New York press. They were more balanced and objective and criticized the lack of professionalism evidenced by the yellow press.

10:281   Wisan, Joseph E. *The Cuban Crisis as Reflected in the New York Press (1895–1898).* New York: Columbia University Press, 1934. This account draws primarily on the *Journal* and *World* and has been widely cited because of the assumption that these papers played a major role in creating the public demand for war.

10:282   Zobrist, Benedict K. "How Victor Lawson's Newspapers Covered the Cuban War of 1898." *Journalism Quarterly* 38 (Summer 1961): 323–31. Lawson's Chicago papers, the *Record* and *Daily News,* refrained from sensational reporting. Their correspondents in Cuba wrote factual reports.

The Churches

10:283   Hudson, Winthrop S. "Protestant Clergy Debate the Nation's Vocation, 1898–1899." *Church History* 42 (March 1973): 110–18. Hudson situates the Protestant clergy, such as Lyman Abbott and Washington Gladden, as opinion leaders. The clergy resisted intervention in Cuba until March 1898, reluctantly supported acquisition of the Philippines, and coalesced in opposition to imperialism when faced with the Philippine resistance.

10:284   Johnke, James. "Kansas Mennonites during the Spanish-American War." *Mennonite Life* 26, no. 2 (June 1971): 70–82. Mennonites initially supported the war but opposed expansion. During the war, they acted in noncombatant capacities.

10:285   MacKenzie, Kenneth M. *The Robe and the Sword: The Methodist Church and the Rise of American Imperialism.* Washington, DC: Public Affairs Press, 1961. The church did not propagate imperialism directly, but it did develop a rationale that made expansionism more palatable to those who might have been critical.

10:286   Quinn, D. Michael. "The Mormon Church and the Spanish-American War: An End to Selective Pacifism." *Pacific Historical Review* 43 (August 1974): 342–66. Brigham Young, Jr. opposed the war, but other church leaders argued that Mormons had a duty to support national policy. This essay has been reprinted in *Dialogue* 17 (Winter 1984): 10–30.

10:287   Reuter, Frank T. *Catholic Influence on American Colonial Policies, 1898–1904.* Austin: University of Texas Press, 1967. This book examines the relationship of Catholics to U.S. imperialism in Cuba, Puerto Rico, Guam, and the Philippines.

European Views

10:288   Hilton, Sylvia L. "La "nueva" Doctrina Monroe de 1895 y sus implicaciones para el Caribe español: algunas interpretaciones coetáneas españolas [The "New" Monroe Doctrine of 1895 and Its Implications for the Spanish Caribbean: Some Contemporary Spanish Interpretations]." *Anuario de Estudios Americanos* 55 (January-June 1998): 125–51. The author notes how Spain associated Cleveland's use of the Monroe Doctrine during the Venezuela crisis with McKinley's 1898 interventionist policy toward Cuba. Although the American press rarely mentioned the Monroe Doctrine, the Spanish press often linked U.S. actions to the Monroe Doctrine.

10:289   _____. "The United States through Spanish Republican Eyes in the Colonial Crisis of 1895–1898." In *European Perceptions of the Spanish-American War of 1898,* ed. Sylvia L. Hilton and Steve J. S. Ickringill, 53–70. Bern: Peter Lang, 1999. Spain's republican press was divided by its support for republican ideals (associated with the United States) and opposition to American intervention in Cuba. Besides plumbing the Spanish republican dilemma, this article describes Spain's overall press reaction to the United States.

10:290   Hilton, Sylvia L., and Steve J. S. Ickringill, eds. *European Perceptions of the Spanish-American War of 1898.* Bern: Lang, 1999. The introduction and articles in this book provide new information about how the European press and some government officials viewed the Spanish-American conflict. Many European analysts used the foreign conflict to comment on national political and economic issues, such as ongoing debates pitting republican liberal reformism against monarchical and conservative principles. The individual chapters are Nico A. Bootsma, "Reactions to the Spanish-American War in the Netherlands and in the Dutch East Indies" (35–52); Hilton, "The United States through Spanish Republican Eyes in the Colonial Crisis of 1895–1898" (53–70); Markus M. Hugo, "'Uncle Sam I Cannot Stand, for Spain I Have No Sympathy': An Analysis of Discourse about the Spanish-American War in Imperial Germany, 1898–1899" (71–94); Ickringill, "Silence and Celebration: Ulster, William McKinley, and the Spanish-American War" (95–110); Ludmila N. Pop-

kova, "Russian Press Coverage of American Intervention in the Spanish-Cuban War" (111–32); Serge Ricard, "The French Press and Brother Jonathan: Editorializing the Spanish-American Conflict" (133–50); Augustín R. Rodríguez, "Portugal and the Spanish Colonial Crisis of 1898" (151–66); Daniela Rossini, "The American Peril: Italian Catholics and the Spanish-American War, 1898" (167–80); Nicole Slupetzky, "Austria and the Spanish-American War" (181–94); and Joseph Smith, "British War Correspondents and the Spanish-American War, April-July 1898" (195–209).

CUBAN JUNTA ACTIVITIES

10:291   Auxier, George W. "The Propaganda Activities of the Cuban Junta in Precipitating the Spanish-American War, 1895–1898." *Hispanic American Historical Review* 19 (August 1939): 286–305. This is a useful analysis of the junta's organization, methods, and efforts to influence public opinion—especially as reflected in the editorials of forty midwestern newspapers.

10:292   Detter, Raymond A. "The Cuban Junta and Michigan, 1895–1898." *Michigan History* 48 (March 1964): 35–46. Detter uses Michigan as an example of the interference of Cuban exiles in the U.S. political process.

10:293   Poyo, Gerald E. *With All, and for the Good of All: The Emergence of Popular Nationalism in the Cuban Communities of the United States, 1848–1898.* This study focuses on the Cuban communities in the United States as a laboratory for examining the evolution of the popular nationalism that underlay the insurrection beginning in 1895. Two chapters are devoted to the 1890s (9:423).

10:294   Proctor, Samuel. "Filibustering Aboard the 'Three Friends.'" *Mid-America* 38 (April 1956): 84–100. This is an account of American efforts to ship arms and other materiel to Cuba between 1895 and 1898.

10:295   Rubens, Horatio S. *Liberty: The Story of Cuba.* New York: Brewer, Warren and Putnam, 1932. Reprint 1970 (Arno Press). Rubens served as the legal adviser to the Cuban junta.

THE *MAINE*

10:296 Blow, Michael. *A Ship to Remember: The Maine and the Spanish-American War.* New York: Morrow, 1992. This is a readable history of the Spanish-Cuban-American War. The author, whose grandfather died in the *Maine,* focuses on the cause of the explosion. After examining many theories, he concludes that no explanation is completely convincing; thus, the destruction of the ship remains a mystery.

10:297 Bradford, Richard H. "From the *Virginius* to the *Maine:* Two Crises of the Gilded Age." *Journal of the West Virginia Historical Association* 5 (1981): 27–39. This article compares the American response to these two foreign policy crises. Among the issues considered are domestic economic, social, and political milieus; the context of U.S.-Spanish relations; and U.S. leadership—especially Hamilton Fish versus William McKinley.

10:298 Calleja Leal, Guillermo G. "La voladura del *Maine* [The Explosion of the *Maine*]." *Revista de Historia Militar* 69 (1990): 163–96. This article reviews various American, Spanish, and Cuban explanations for the sinking of the *Maine.* With limited documentation, Calleja concludes that Federico Blume, a Peruvian bomb expert, and Cubans associated with the New York junta exploded a bomb under the ship to embarrass Spain. Instead of producing a minor explosion, they sank the ship.

10:299 Feuer, A. B. *The Spanish-American War at Sea: Naval Action in the Atlantic.* Westport, CT: Praeger, 1995. In the first chapter, the author recounts the destruction of the *Maine,* concludes that the explosion resulted from spontaneous combustion, and argues that its sinking and resulting newspaper furor were central to the coming of the war.

10:300 Rickover, Hyman G. *How the Battleship Maine Was Destroyed.* Washington, DC: Naval History Division, U.S. Department of the Navy, 1976. Reprint 1994 (Naval Institute Press). Rickover concludes that an internal explosion destroyed the *Maine.*

10:301 Weems, John Edward. *The Fate of the Maine.* New York: Holt, 1958. This popular history

covers the *Maine* from its commissioning to its destruction.

Spanish-American Diplomacy, 1895–1898

10:302 Almuiña, Celso. "España dentro del complejo contexto internacional finisecular, 1898 [Spain within the Complex International Context at the End of the Century, 1898]." In *1895: la guerra en Cuba y la España de la restauración [1895: The Cuban War and Restoration Spain],* ed. Emilio de Diego, 119–43. Madrid: Universidad Complutense, 1996. This essay, based largely on secondary sources, provides a standard Spanish view of Spain's international relations on the eve of the 1898 war. It includes a foreign affairs overview, relations with the United States, the positions of the European powers, and internal press opinion.

10:303 Alvarez Gutiérrez, Luis. "El contexto internacional del noventa y ocho [The International Context of '98]." In *La nación soñada: Cuba, Puerto Rico y Filipinas ante el 98: actas del congreso internacional celebrado en Aranjuez del 24 al 28 de abril de 1995 [The Dreamed Nation: Cuba, Puerto Rico, and the Philippines before '98: Transactions of the International Congress Held at Aranjuez, 24–28 April 1995],* ed. Consuelo Naranjo Orovio, Miguel Ángel Puig-Samper, and Luis Miguel García Mora, 713–28. Aranjuez (Madrid): Doce Calles, 1996. This article places the Spanish conflict with the United States over Cuba in the context of European great power politics. It reflects the changing viewpoint of Spanish diplomatic historians that has taken place during the last twenty years.

10:304 _____. "Los imperios centrales ante el progresivo deterioro de las relaciones entre España y los Estados Unidos [The Central Powers before the Progressive Deterioration of Relations between Spain and the United States]." *Hispania (Spain)* 57 (May-August 1997): 435–78. Based on research in Austrian, German, Russian, and Spanish diplomatic archives, the author examines the role Germany and

Austria-Hungary played in the growing crisis between Spain and the United States. In March 1898, Austria-Hungary agreed to provide greater diplomatic support for Spain.

10:305   Bécker, Jerónimo. *Historia de las relaciones exteriores de España durante el siglo XIX [History of Spanish Foreign Relations in the Nineteenth Century].* 3 vols. Madrid: Editorial Voluntad, 1924. Written by the archivist of the Spanish foreign office, this work is based on Spanish diplomatic archives. It is a starting point for studying Spanish foreign affairs.

10:306   Benton, Elbert J. *International Law and Diplomacy of the Spanish-American War.* Baltimore: Johns Hopkins Press, 1908. Based on U.S. diplomatic documents, this is a legalistic study of U.S. foreign policy from 1895 to the signing of the Paris peace treaty.

10:307   Bridge, Francis Roy. "Great Britain, Austria-Hungary, and the Concert of Europe on the Eve of the Spanish-American War." *Mitteilungen des Österreichischen Staatsarchivs* 44 (1996): 87–108. Drawing on Austrian, German, and British archives, Bridge describes the efforts of the European powers to prevent the Spanish-American War through a diplomatic démarche in Washington. The author focuses also on a failed attempt in mid-April to organize a second European démarche, concluding that Germany was largely responsible for restraining Austria-Hungary.

10:308   Chadwick, French Ensor. *The Relations of the United States and Spain: Diplomacy.* A participant in the war, Chadwick provides a traditional diplomatic account that justifies U.S. policies (6:222).

10:309   Clymer, Kenton J. "Checking the Sources: John Hay and Spanish Possessions in the Pacific." *Historian* 48 (November 1985): 82–87. Correcting misinformation, Clymer points out that in a February 1898 letter to McKinley, Hay opposes war with Spain and does not suggest that a war would furnish an occasion to seize Spanish colonies.

10:310   Coletta, Paolo E. "McKinley, the Peace Negotiations, and the Acquisition of the Philippines." *Pacific Historical Review* 30 (November 1961): 341–50. The author believes that McKinley set out to annex the Philippines.

10:311   Companys Monclús, Julián. "La carta de Dupuy de Lôme [The Dupuy de Lôme Letter]." *Boletín de la Real Academia de la Historia* 184 (September-December 1987): 465–81. Largely based on U.S. sources, this is a traditional account of the Dupuy de Lôme letter. The author notes that Woodford's candid descriptions of Spanish government figures were as critical as Dupuy de Lôme's depiction of McKinley. He asserts that Spain's loss of Cánovas, Weyler, and Dupuy de Lôme favored the insurgent cause.

10:312   _____. "La reina regente y los intentos de paz antes del 98 [The Queen Regent and the Efforts at Peace in 1898]." In *Antes del "desastre": Orígenes y antecedentes de la crisis del 98 [Before the "Disaster": Origins and Antecedents of the 1898 Crisis],* ed. Juan Pablo Fusi Aizpurúa and Antonio Niño Rodríguez, 289–96. Madrid: Universidad Complutense de Madrid Departamento de Historia Contemporánea, 1996. The author recounts the Spanish Queen Regent's efforts to enlist the Austro-Hungarian, English, and Russian monarchs in preventing American intervention in the Cuban war.

10:313   Diego, Emilio de, ed. *Hacia el 98. La España de la restauración y la crisis colonial 1895–1898 [Towards '98: Restoration Spain and the Colonial Crisis of 1895–1898].* Madrid: Ministerio de Asuntos Exteriores Escuela Diplomática, 1997. This volume consists of speeches of diplomats and scholars delivered at a 1996 conference sponsored by the Foreign Ministry. There are no footnotes or bibliography. Jesús Pabón y Suárez de Urbina gave the principal speech on the diplomatic situation in 1898. It accords with his 1952 dissertation entitled "El 98: acontecimiento internacional." The published papers reflect Spanish views of 1898 one century later.

10:314   Eggert, Gerald G. "Our Man in Havana: Fitzhugh Lee." *Hispanic American Historical Review* 47 (November 1967): 463–85. Lee, the U.S. consul-general in Havana, urged U.S. intervention in Cuba and annexation of the island.

10:315   Elizalde Pérez-Grueso, María Dolores. "Las grandes potencias y el Pacífico español: los intentos de los paises hegemónicos en la colonia de las Islas Carolinas [The Great Powers and the Spanish Pacific: The Intentions of the Hegemonic Powers toward the Caroline Islands]." *Revista de Estudios del Pacífico* 1 (July-December 1991): 65–82. The author believes that the United States and Britain allowed Germany to acquire the Caroline Islands as compensation for having received nothing in the Philippines.

10:316   Farrell, John T. "Archbishop Ireland and Manifest Destiny." *Catholic Historical Review* 33 (October 1947): 269–301. Pope Leo XIII used Archbishop Ireland to attempt to prevent war between the United States and Spain.

10:317   Ferrara, Orestes. *The Last Spanish War: Revelations in "Diplomacy."* Translated by William E. Shea. New York: Paisley Press, Inc., 1937. A Cuban diplomat examines Spain's efforts to involve the European powers in the Spanish-Cuban conflict.

10:318   Fusi Aizpurúa, Juan Pablo, and Antonio Niño Rodríguez, eds. *Vísperas del 98: orígenes y antecedentes de la crisis del 98 [On the Eve of '98: Origins and Antecedents of the 1898 Crisis].* Madrid: Biblioteca Nueva, 1997. This volume, containing nineteen papers, resulted from an international conference held in 1995 by Complutense Universidad de Madrid. A companion volume, also edited by Fusi and Niño, *Antes del "desastre": orígenes y antecedentes de la crisis del 98,* contains thirty-eight additional papers. Authors of some of the more relevant papers represented in the two works are Steve J. S. Ickringill and Sylvia L. Hilton, Julián Companys Monclús, John L. Offner, and Rosario de la Torre del Río.

10:319   Hilton, Sylvia L., and Steve J. S. Ickringill. "'Americana en letra y espíritu': la Doctrina Monroe y el presidente McKinley en 1898 ['American in Letter and Spirit': The Monroe Doctrine and President McKinley in 1898]." *Cuadernos de Historia Contemporánea* 20 (1998): 205–19. The authors argue that McKinley did not invoke the Monroe Doctrine to justify intervention in Cuba because that would have narrowed his expansionistic options and also was likely to create opposition in Great Britain and the United States.

10:320   Ickringill, Steve J. S., and Sylvia L. Hilton. "Cleveland and the Anglo-Venezuelan Dispute in

1895: A Prelude to McKinley's Intervention in the Spanish-Cuban War." In *Antes del "desastre": Orígenes y antecedentes de la crisis del 98 [Before the "Disaster": Origins and Antecedents of the 1898 Crisis],* ed. Juan Pablo Fusi Aizpurúa and Antonio Niño Rodríguez, 337–58. Madrid: Universidad Complutense de Madrid Departamento de Historia Contemporánea, 1996. The authors contend that Cleveland's aggressive Venezuelan policy in 1895 influenced McKinley's diplomacy. Learning from Cleveland's mistakes, McKinley pursued a reluctant, cautious intervention in Cuba that was politically successful at home, and by not invoking the Monroe Doctrine, McKinley minimized Latin American antagonism.

10:321   Kwiecien, Zbigniew. "The Far Eastern Issues in the American-Spanish Peace Negotiations in Paris in 1898." *American Studies (Poland)* 9 (1990): 37–58. Relying solely on U.S. documents and monographs, the author develops U.S.-Spanish negotiations that led to the 1898 Treaty of Paris.

10:322   Liberati, Luigi Bruti. *La Santa Sede e le origini dell'imperio americano: la guerra del 1898 [The Holy See and the Origin of U.S. Imperialism: The War of 1898].* Milano: Edizioni Unicopli, 1985. Based on Vatican archives, this slim book describes the Holy See's relations with the U.S. and Spanish governments and with U.S. bishops. It covers papal mediation in April 1898 and the efforts by the Holy See to preserve Catholic Church authority and property in Puerto Rico and the Philippines.

10:323   Michael, M. A. "Middle Man for Peace: Senator Stephen B. Elkins and the Spanish-American War." *West Virginia History* 57 (June 1998): 46–61. This brief account of Spanish-American diplomacy is based on the Elkins diary of events.

10:324   Morgan, H. Wayne. "The De Lôme Letter: A New Appraisal." *Historian* 26 (November 1963): 36–49. Morgan believes the De Lôme letter was important because it destroyed American confidence in Spain's honesty.

10:325   Naranjo Orovio, Consuelo, Miguel Ángel Puig-Samper, and Luis Miguel García Mora, eds. *La nación soñada: Cuba, Puerto Rico y Filipinas ante el 98: actas del congreso internacional celebrado en Aranjuez del 24 al 28 de abril de 1995 [The Dreamed*

Nation: Cuba, Puerto Rico, and the Philippines before '98: Transactions of the International Congress Held at Aranjuez, 24–28 April 1995]. Aranjuez (Madrid): Doce Calles, 1996. These fifty-nine articles, contributed to a 1995 congress at Aranjuez, are about political, economic, and social aspects of Spain's colonial empire prior to 1898. Of eight articles on international relations, three relating closely to the United States are cited separately: see Luis Álvarez Gutiérrez, María Dolores Elizalde Pérez-Grueso, and Cristóbal Robles Muñoz.

10:326   Offner, John L. "The DeLôme Letter: A Spanish and Cuban Perspective." In *MACLAS Latin American Essays: Selected Papers Presented at the 11th Annual Conference of the Middle Atlantic Council of Latin American Studies, Rutgers University, April 1990,* ed. Robert J. Alexander, Juan Espadas, and Vincent Peloso, 79–87. Collegeville, PA: Ursinus College, 1990. This article places the Dupuy de Lôme letter in the context of Cuban, Spanish, and American foreign affairs. The letter was a serious blunder that the Spanish government sought to overcome as quickly as possible. Publication of the letter irritated McKinley and adversely affected his relations with the Cuban Junta.

10:327   _____. "The Philippine Settlement: The United States, Spain, and Great Britain in 1898." In *1898: enfoques y perspectivas [1898: Focal Points and Perspectives],* ed. Luis E. González Vales, 353–70. San Juan: Academia Puertorriqueña de la Historia, 1997. Based on U.S., British, and Spanish diplomatic archives, the author explains the role Great Britain played in Spanish deliberations as the 1898 settlement was under negotiation at Paris. Faced by growing British threats over Gibraltar and declining military power in the Philippines, Spain reluctantly accepted a U.S. ultimatum.

10:328   _____. "President McKinley's Final Attempt to Avoid War with Spain." *Ohio History* 94 (Summer-Autumn 1985): 125–38. This article describes McKinley's efforts during the first ten days of April 1898 to prevent war with Spain.

10:329   _____. *An Unwanted War: The Diplomacy of the United States and Spain over Cuba, 1895–1898.* Chapel Hill: University of North Carolina Press, 1992. In this model of multiarchival re-search and international history, the author places primary emphasis on domestic politics and the American public's sympathy for the Cuban people in convincing McKinley to opt for war. The yellow press, economic considerations, and national security were less influential.

10:330   Pereira Castañares, Juan Carlos. "Aislamiento internacional y crisis finisecular: argumentos para una reinterpretación de la historia de la política exterior española [International Isolation and Crisis at the End of the Century: Arguments for a Reinterpretation of the History of Spanish Foreign Relations]." In *Los significados del 98. La sociedad española en la génesis del siglo XX [The Significance of '98: Spanish Society at the Beginning of the 20th Century],* ed. Octavio Ruiz-Manjón Cabeza and María Alicia Langa Laorga, 101–18. Madrid: Fundación ICO, Biblioteca Nueva Universidad Complutense de Madrid, 1999. The author contends that Spanish diplomatic historians have misinterpreted Spanish diplomatic isolation in 1898. The Spanish government played an active role in international politics before 1898, and there was nothing more that it could have done in Europe to prevent a conflict with the United States.

10:331   Robles Muñoz, Cristóbal. "1898: la batalla por la paz: la mediación de León XIII entre España y Estados Unidos [The Fight for Peace in 1898: Pope Leo XIII's Mediation between Spain and the United States]." *Revista de Indias* 46 (January-June 1986): 247–96. The author examines Spain's attempt to use the Vatican to prevent war between the United States and Spain.

10:332   _____. "España y Europa durante la crisis cubana (1896–1897) [Spain and Europe during the Cuban Crisis (1896–1897)]." In *La nación soñada: Cuba, Puerto Rico y Filipinas ante el 98: actas del congreso internacional celebrado en Aranjuez del 24 al 28 de abril de 1995 [The Dreamed Nation: Cuba, Puerto Rico, and the Philippines before '98: Transactions of the International Congress Held at Aranjuez, 24–28 April 1995],* ed. Consuelo Naranjo Orovio, Miguel Ángel Puig-Samper, and Luis Miguel García Mora, 729–54. Aranjuez (Madrid): Doce Calles, 1996. Grounded in Spanish, French, Italian, and Vatican diplomatic archives, this article examines the development of Spanish foreign policy by Antonio Cánovas del Castillo toward other European powers as the Cleveland administration grew more interested in the Cuban conflict.

10:333 _____. "La oposición al activismo independentista cubano [Opposition to Cuban Efforts for Independence]." *Hispania (Spain)* 48 (January-April 1988): 227–88. From 1878 to 1898, Spain sought to keep Cubans from using the United States as a base of operations. Its attempts to enlist the United States in its efforts had some success, but Spain believed Washington allowed illegal support for the Cubans. Thus, Spain had a moral commitment and just cause in resisting U.S. diplomatic steps to acquire Cuba.

10:334 _____. "Negociar la paz en Cuba (1896–1897) [To Negotiate Peace in Cuba (1896–1897)]." *Revista de Indias* 53 (May-August 1993): 493–527. Based on Spanish diplomatic archives, Robles Muñoz examines Spain's efforts to negotiate a solution to the Cuban colonial revolt. Spain failed to enlist sufficient support in the Cleveland administration and it did not win over the Cuban insurgents. Thus, the McKinley administration faced a deteriorating Spanish colonial situation.

10:335 Ruiz-Manjón Cabeza, Octavio, and María Alicia Langa Laorga, eds. *Los significados del 98. La sociedad española en la génesis del siglo XX [The Significance of '98: Spanish Society at the Beginning of the 20th Century]*. Madrid: Biblioteca Nueva, 1999. The Universidad Complutense de Madrid sponsored this volume of fifty-nine articles commemorating the events of 1898 and their significance for Spanish history. The articles are grouped into sections on political life, society and economy, intellectual life, and general reflections. Three articles are listed separately in this chapter: see Aline Helg, Markus M. Hugo, and Juan Carlos Pereira Castañares.

10:336 Serrano, Carlos. *Final del imperio: España, 1895–1898 [The End of Empire: Spain, 1895–1898]*. Madrid: Siglo Veintiuno de España Editores, 1984. The author believes that Cuba was moving toward independence, and therefore the United States played a secondary role in freeing Cuba from Spanish rule. To solve domestic political problems caused by the colonial conflict, Spain accepted war with the United States.

10:337 Togores Sánchez, Luis Eugenio. "España y la expansión de los Estados Unidos en el Pacífico. (De la guerra hispano-americana de 1898, y la pérdida de Filipinas, al pleito por Sibutú y Cagayán de Joló) [Spain and U.S. Expansion in the Pacific (From the Spanish-American War of 1898, and the Loss of the Philippines, to the Dispute over Sibutu and Cagayan Sulu]." In *Estudios históricos. Homenaje a los profesores José María Jover Zamora y Vicente Palacio Atard [Historical Studies in Honor of Professors José María Jover Zamora and Vicente Palacio Atard]*, ed. Universidad Complutense de Madrid. Departamento de Historia Contemporánea, 1: 655–76. Madrid: Departamento de Historia Contemporánea Facultad de Geografía e Historia Universidad Complutense, 1990. The author believes the United States acquired the Philippines because it wanted a string of islands stretching across the Pacific Ocean that would facilitate trade with China. Great Britain encouraged U.S. annexation of the Philippines to get support for an open door for trade in China and to limit German influence in East Asia.

10:338 Torre del Río, Rosario de la. "1895–1898: Inglaterra y la búsqueda de un compromiso internacional para frenar la intervención norteamericana en Cuba [1895–1898: England and the Search for an International Compromise to Restrain U.S. Intervention in Cuba]." *Hispania (Spain)* 57 (May-August 1997): 515–49. Drawing on British and Spanish diplomatic archives, the author places British-Spanish relations in a larger 1890s context before focusing on the Cuban crisis. The article culminates in the April 7 great power note delivered in Washington and its aftermath.

10:339 _____. "La situación internacional de los años 90 y la política exterior española [The International Situation of the '90s and Spanish Foreign Policy]." In *Vísperas del 98. Orígenes y antecedentes de la crisis del 98 [On the Eve of '98: Origins and Antecedents of the 1898 Crisis]*, ed. Juan Pablo Fusi Aizpurúa and Antonio Niño Rodríguez, 173–93. Madrid: Biblioteca Nueva, 1997. The author provides a broad view of Spain's 1890s foreign policy problems, leading to its failure from 1896 to 1898 to secure European support against the United States.

Spanish-Cuban-American War

10:340   Bradford, James C., ed. *Crucible of Empire: The Spanish-American War and Its Aftermath.* Annapolis: Naval Institute Press, 1993. This edited book focuses largely on naval topics. Ephraim K. Smith, "William McKinley's Enduring Legacy: The Historiographical Debate on the Taking of the Philippine Islands" (205–50), offers a helpful historiographical appraisal. Diane E. Cooper's essay, "Diplomat and Naval Intelligence Officer: The Duties of Lt. George L. Dyer, U.S. Naval Attaché to Spain" (1–22), based on Dyer's papers and U.S. naval documents, describes the personnel and work procedures of the Madrid legation during Stewart L. Woodford's 1897–1898 mission but offers little information about U.S. or Spanish policy. In David F. Trask, "American Intelligence during the Spanish-American War" (23–46), the author describes U.S. intelligence operations before and during the war and assesses how much intelligence gathering influenced U.S. diplomatic and military decisions.

10:341   Braisted, William Reynolds. "The Philippine Naval Base Problem, 1898–1909." *Mississippi Valley Historical Review* 41 (March 1954): 21–40. This article describes the debate within the Navy Department over the value of Subic Bay as a naval base.

10:342   Brown, Charles H. *The Correspondents' War: Journalists in the Spanish-American War.* New York: Scribner, 1967. This study covers the exploits of newspaper correspondents during the war.

10:343   Caudill, Edward. *Darwinian Myths: The Legends and Misuses of a Theory.* Knoxville: University of Tennessee Press, 1997. In chapter 5, devoted to the war of 1898, the author argues that Social Darwinism and science were decidedly less important as justifications for the conflict than arguments based on economics, race, strategic calculations, and ideas of U.S. mission.

10:344   Chadwick, French Ensor. *The Relations of the United States and Spain: The Spanish-American War.* 2 vols. New York: Charles Scribner's Sons,

1911. A naval officer during the war, Chadwick provides a detailed description of the land and sea battles.

10:345   Cosmas, Graham A. *An Army for Empire: The United States Army in the Spanish-American War, 1898–1899.* Columbia: University of Missouri Press, 1971. This examines the War Department and army structure, composition, and administration. Cosmas concludes that policymakers were not responsible for the army's failures.

10:346   Craib, Raymond B., and D. Graham Burnett. "Insular Visions: Cartographic Imagery and the Spanish-American War." *Historian* 61 (Fall 1998): 101–18. This article, including illustrative maps, demonstrates how the insular acquisitions and protectorates were incorporated both visually and ideologically into the American empire.

10:347   Davis, Richard Harding. *The Cuban and Puerto Rican Campaigns.* New York: Charles Scribner's Sons, 1898. Davis, a newspaper correspondent, provides an eyewitness account of the war.

10:348   Dierks, Jack. *A Leap to Arms: The Cuban Campaign of 1898.* Philadelphia: Lippincott, 1970. Dierks analyzes the military and naval operations at Santiago de Cuba.

10:349   Elorza, Antonio, and Elena Hernández Sandoica. *La guerra de Cuba, 1895–1898: Historia política de una derrota colonial [The Cuban War, 1895–1898: The Political History of a Colonial Defeat].* Madrid: Alianza Editorial, 1998. This study places the war in the context of Spanish politics and the unfavorable foreign developments that led to the loss of Spain's colonies. The authors depict the McKinley administration as relentless and devious in its imperial expansion.

10:350   Freidel, Frank. *The Splendid Little War.* Boston: Little, Brown, 1958. This study treats the war seriously, emphasizing the human costs of the fighting.

10:351   Gatewood, Willard B., Jr., ed. *"Smoked Yankees" and the Struggle for Empire: Letters from Negro Soldiers, 1898–1902.* Urbana: University of Illinois Press, 1971. These letters appeared in newspapers and revealed the experiences and attitudes of black servicemen in Cuba, the Philippines, and the United States.

10:352   Gould, Lewis L. *The Spanish-American War and President McKinley.* Lawrence: University Press of Kansas, 1982. This slim book contains three chapters from the author's pathbreaking *The Presidency of William McKinley* (1980) (10:153). To this material Gould has added an opening and closing chapter. Overall, Gould provides a favorable view of McKinley's political, diplomatic, and military leadership.

10:353   _____. "William McKinley: 'The Man at the Helm.'" In *Commanders in Chief: Presidential Leadership in Modern Wars,* ed. Joseph G. Dawson III, 49–64. Lawrence: University Press of Kansas, 1993. The author argues that McKinley used the constitutional war power to expand presidential leadership in foreign affairs and colonial rule. He also used modern communications to improve presidential decision-making in key military and diplomatic developments.

10:354   Grenville, J. A. S. "American Naval Preparations for War with Spain, 1896–1898." *Journal of American Studies* 2 (April 1968): 33–47. The author traces the development of naval plans in preparation for war with Spain.

10:355   Harrington, Peter, and Frederic A. Sharf. *"A Splendid Little War": The Spanish-American War, 1898: The Artists' Perspective.* Mechanicsburg, PA: Stackpole Books, 1998. In this catalog for an exhibition of forty-five images of the wars in Cuba and the Philippines, the authors have supplied artistic context, biographical information on artists, and excellent reproductions of contemporary pictures.

10:356   Hunt, Michael H. "1898: The Onset of America's Troubled Asian Century." *OAH Magazine of History* 12 (Spring 1998): 30–36. Hunt provides an interpretive overview of the motives for U.S. actions in 1898 and the implications for the American presence in Asia through the 1990s.

10:357   Jeffreys-Jones, Rhodri. "The Montreal Spy Ring of 1898 and the Origins of 'Domestic' Surveillance in the United States." *Canadian Review of American Studies* 5 (Fall 1974): 119–34. Jeffreys-Jones examines the specially organized section of the Treasury Department's Secret Service and its coun-

terintelligence activities against alleged Spanish agents in the United States and Canada. He contends that the doubtful constitutionality of both the agency and its activities established dubious precedents for subsequent U.S. intelligence policies and actions.

10:358   Leckie, Robert. *The Wars of America.* New and updated ed. New York: HarperCollins Publishers, 1992. Part 6 describes the land and sea operations of the war with Spain. First published in 1967.

10:359   Leonard, Thomas C. "The Uncensored War." *Culturefront* 7 (Spring 1998): 59–62. The author emphasizes the role of correspondents from smaller papers who were assigned to cover units from their states and localities. In an era before the U.S. government managed the news, these writers had much greater freedom and showed slight regard for military orthodoxy or potentially privileged information.

10:360   Linderman, Gerald F. *The Mirror of War: American Society and the Spanish-American War.* Ann Arbor: University of Michigan Press, 1974. This book is a social history of the American people at war.

10:361   Lukacs, John. "The Meaning of '98." *American Heritage* 49 (May-June 1998): 72–83. This broad-ranging essay presents a traditional, weak McKinley, emphasizes the force of U.S. public opinion, argues for the comparative benevolence of U.S. imperialism, and dates the American century from 1898.

10:362   Mahan, Alfred T. *Lessons of the War with Spain: And Other Articles.* Boston: Little, Brown and Co., 1899. Reprint 1970 (Books for Libraries Press). Mahan reviews the strategic and tactical naval decisions of the war.

10:363   Millis, Walter. *The Martial Spirit: A Study of Our War with Spain.* Boston: Houghton Mifflin Company, 1931. Reprint 1989 (I. R. Dee). The author criticizes national sentiment on the eve of the war, concluding that public passion pressured a weak president to enter an unnecessary war.

10:364   Morgan, H. Wayne. *America's Road to Empire: The War with Spain and Overseas Expansion.*

New York: Wiley, 1965. Spain's failure to carry out colonial reforms in Cuba provoked the United States to enter the war. Subsequent expansion was a conscious exercise of America's new military power.

10:365   Mount, Graeme S. "The Secret Operation of Spanish Consular Officials within Canada during the Spanish-American War." In *North American Spies: New Revisionist Essays,* ed. Rhodri Jeffreys-Jones and Andrew Lownie, 31–48. Lawrence: University Press of Kansas, 1991. Drawing on Spanish, American, and Canadian sources, the essay examines Spanish and U.S. intelligence efforts in Canada.

10:366   Musicant, Ivan. *Empire by Default: The Spanish-American War and the Dawn of the American Century.* New York: H. Holt, 1998. This is a well-written, detailed, narrative account of the war from an American perspective. It also covers the diplomatic and political origins and conclusion of the war.

10:367   O'Toole, G. J. A. *The Spanish War: An American Epic, 1898.* New York: Norton, 1984. The author provides a journalistic, impressionistic, and nonanalytical account of a heroic war, with Theodore Roosevelt often taking center stage.

10:368   Ransom, Edward. "Baronet on the Battlefield: Sir Bryan Leighton in Cuba." *Journal of American Studies* 9 (April 1975): 3–20. A British observer criticizes the U.S. army in Cuba.

10:369   _____. "British Military and Naval Observers in the Spanish-American War." *Journal of American Studies* 3 (April 1969): 33–56. This article describes British criticisms of U.S. army officers and the chaotic conditions at Santiago.

10:370   Rodríguez González, Agustín R. "Balances navales, estrategias y decisiones políticas en la guerra de 1898 [Naval Balances: Strategies and Political Decisions in the War of 1898]." In *Estudios históricos. Homenaje a los profesores José María Jover Zamora y Vincente Palacio Atard [Historical Studies in Honor of Professors José María Jover Zamora and Vincente Palacio Atard],* ed. Universidad Complutense de Madrid. Departamento de Historia Contemporánea, 1: 633–53. Madrid: Departamento de Historia Contemporánea Facultad de Geografía e Historia Universidad Complutense,

1990. This article counters the argument that Spain entered a short naval war to lose Cuba to the United States as preferable to risking civil unrest that would have resulted from withdrawing from the island without offering a fight. The author notes that before the war both navies were untested and that many ranked them as equals. Moreover, Spanish naval experts and the informed Madrid press believed the Spanish navy would give a good account of itself.

10:371   Roosevelt, Theodore. *The Rough Riders.* New York: Collier, 1899. Reprint 1990 (Da Capo Press). Roosevelt's vivid account reveals his attitudes toward war and his penchant for self-promotion.

10:372   Rosenfeld, Harvey. *Diary of a Dirty Little War: The Spanish-American War of 1898.* Westport, CT: Praeger, 2000. The diary of events begins on April 10, 1898, and ends on August 12, 1898. The book consists of a daily noting of items, mostly drawn from newspapers and memoirs, especially the *New York Times* and Carl Sandburg. The format results in a choppy recitation of events with little integration. The book title refers to Sandburg's description of the war in contrast to John Hay's reference to a splendid war.

10:373   Samuels, Peggy, and Harold Samuels. *Teddy Roosevelt at San Juan: The Making of a President.* College Station: Texas A&M University Press, 1997. This is a biography of Roosevelt up to 1898, focusing on the part he played in the military campaign in Cuba. The authors are critical of the press and Roosevelt for exaggerating his role in fighting the Spanish.

10:374   Sargent, Herbert Howland. *The Campaign of Santiago de Cuba.* 3 vols. Chicago: A. C. McClurg, 1907. Reprint 1970 (Books for Libraries Press). This account is dated but detailed enough to retain some usefulness.

10:375   Saum, Lewis O. "The Western Volunteer and the 'New Empire.'" *Pacific Northwest Quarterly* 57 (January 1966): 18–27. Western soldiers fought for patriotic and moral reasons, not for economic motives.

10:376   Schellings, William J. "The Advent of the Spanish-American War in Florida, 1898." *Florida*

Historical Quarterly 39 (April 1961): 311–29. The author examines Florida's energetic pursuit of defense spending and its impact on the state's economy.

10:377 Schurman, Rob. "'Remember the *Maine*,' Boys, and the Price of this Suit." *Historian* 61 (Fall 1998): 119–34. This article examines how advertising and clothing styles embodied patriotism and nationalism in 1898 and in so doing elucidated concepts of citizenship and national identity.

10:378 Smith, Joseph. "The American Image of the Cuban Insurgents in 1898." *Zeitschrift für Anglistik und Amerikanistik* 40 (1992): 319–29. This article contrasts the favorable view that North Americans had of the Cuban insurgents before U.S. intervention with the change in attitude toward the insurgents after the U.S. army invaded Cuba.

10:379 _____. "British War Correspondents and the Spanish-American War, April-July 1898." In *European Perceptions of the Spanish-American War of 1898,* ed. Sylvia L. Hilton and Steve J. S. Ickringill, 193–209. Bern: Peter Lang, 1999. This article covers the reporting of English war correspondents, primarily John Black Atkins of *The Manchester Guardian* and Charles E. Hands of *The Daily Mail.* The English reporters favored the American soldiers and their exploits.

10:380 _____. *The Spanish-American War: Conflict in the Caribbean and the Pacific, 1895–1902.* New York: Longman, 1994. Although the title refers to the 1895–1902 period, the author writes almost entirely on the Spanish-American naval conflict of 1898. Favorable to the United States, Smith blames Spanish politicians and military leaders for Spain's national disaster.

10:381 _____. "The 'Splendid Little War' of 1898: A Reappraisal." *History* 80 (February 1995): 22–37. The author contrasts the concept of a "splendid little war" with the reality of inept administrative and military decisions that resulted in imperialism. Smith concludes that the war demonstrates the continuing division between myth and reality in American foreign policy.

10:382 Spector, Ronald H. "Who Planned the Attack on Manila Bay?" *Mid-America* 53 (April 1971):

94–102. This article diminishes the role Roosevelt played in ordering Dewey's attack on Manila.

10:383 Sternlicht, Sanford. *McKinley's Bulldog: The Battleship Oregon.* Chicago: Nelson-Hall, 1977. This author describes the part the *Oregon* played in the war, including the trip around South America that convinced many of the need for an isthmian canal.

10:384 Stromberg, Joseph R. "The Spanish-American War as Trial Run, or Empire as Its Own Justification." In *The Costs of War: America's Pyrrhic Victories,* ed. John V. Denson, 169–201. New Brunswick: Transaction Publishers, 1997. This essay emphasizes the costs of U.S. empire both to those abroad such as the Cubans and Filipinos and to Americans at home. Among domestic abuses cited are heightened executive power, bureaucratization, growth of central government at the expense of the states, militarism, social regimentation, decreased public honesty, and retarded domestic development.

10:385 Trask, David F. *The War with Spain in 1898.* New York: Macmillan, 1981. Reprint 1996 (University of Nebraska Press). This is the best monograph on the war. A balanced account, it covers both American and Spanish military, political, and diplomatic events. Trask favorably regards McKinley's wartime leadership yet criticizes the territorial expansionism that followed the war.

10:386 Walker, Leslie W. "Guam's Seizure by the United States in 1898." *Pacific Historical Review* 14 (March 1945): 1–12. This article describes the U.S. navy seizure of Guam.

Cuba and Puerto Rico, 1898–1902

CUBA

10:387 Benjamin, Jules R. *The United States & Cuba: Hegemony and Dependent Development, 1880–1934.* See chapter 9 of this Guide (9:415).

10:388 _____. *The United States and the Origins of the Cuban Revolution: An Empire of Liberty in an Age of National Liberation.* Although the author's focus is twentieth-century U.S.-Cuban relations culminating in the Castro regime, he provides a lengthy criticism of the imposition of U.S. hegemony over Cuba in 1898 (2:368).

10:389 Chapman, Charles E. *A History of the Cuban Republic: A Study in Hispanic American Politics.* New York: Macmillan Company, 1927. Chapman offers a standard account of Cuban developments from 1868 to 1900.

10:390 Crouch, Thomas W. *A Yankee Guerrillero: Frederick Funston and the Cuban Insurrection, 1896–1897.* Memphis: Memphis State University Press, 1975. Funston fought with the Cuban insurgents against Spain.

10:391 Deere, Carmen Diana. "Here Come the Yankees! The Rise and Decline of the United States Colonies in Cuba, 1898–1930." *Hispanic American Historical Review* 78 (November 1998): 729–65. This article describes American attempts to colonize Cuba with the intent of annexation. The U.S. military in Cuba and the government in Washington adopted land and trade polices that encouraged American colonization, particularly on the Isle of Pines. American colonization, except for the Isle of Pines, declined rapidly after 1917.

10:392 Epstein, Erwin H. "The Peril of Paternalism: The Imposition of Education on Cuba by the United States." *American Journal of Education* 96 (November 1987): 1–23. Leonard Wood sought to establish American values in Cuba by expanding the educational system to include the masses. Initial public school enrollments jumped, but Wood's goal was not achieved, as educational enrollment became elitist.

10:393 Estrade, Paul. *La colonia cubana de París, 1895–1898: el combate patriótico de Betances y la solidaridad de los revolucionarios franceses [The Cuban Colony in Paris, 1895–1898: Betances's Patriotic Struggle and the Solidarity of the French Revolutionaries].* La Habana: Editorial de Ciencias Sociales, 1984. Estrade details the efforts of the Cuban exile community in Paris to gain Cuban independence from Spain. Ramón Emeterio Betances, a Puerto Rican physician who directed this struggle, had some diplomatic exchanges with Spanish agents and Tomas Estrada Palma, who directed the Cuban junta in New York City.

10:394 Foner, Philip S. *A History of Cuba and Its Relations with the United States.* 2 vols. New York: International Publishers, 1962–1963. This work provides an economic determinist and pro-Cuban account of U.S.-Cuban relations to 1895.

10:395 _____. *The Spanish-Cuban-American War and the Birth of American Imperialism, 1895–1902.* 2 vols. New York: Monthly Review Press, 1972. Foner takes the Cuban viewpoint that U.S. intervention was not necessary to secure Cuban independence and that the United States was counterrevolutionary.

10:396 Helg, Aline. "Cuba después del 98: ni con todos, ni para el bien de todos [Cuba after 1898: Neither for All, nor for the Good of All]." In *Los significados del 98. La sociedad española en la génesis del siglo XX [The Significance of '98: Spanish Society at the Beginning of the 20th Century]*, ed. Octavio Ruiz-Manjón Cabeza and María Alicia Langa Laorga, 51–65. Madrid: Fundación ICO, Biblioteca Nueva Universidad Complutense de Madrid, 1999. This article examines the Spanish roots of racism in Cuba, the U.S. military government's contribution to insular racism, and after the United States ended its military rule, the continuation during the following decade of racism on the island.

10:397 Hernández, José M. *Cuba and the United States: Intervention and Militarism, 1868–1933.* This political-military history of Cuba explores the relationships among the Cuban army, the Cuban revolutionary government, and the U.S. invading army that gained control of the island (9:418).

10:398 Ibarra, Jorge. *Cuba: 1898–1921: partidos políticos y clases sociales [Cuba, 1898–1921: Political Parties and Social Classes].* La Habana: Editorial de Ciencias Sociales, 1992. The author provides a contemporary Cuban perspective of U.S. imperialism that accords with that of Emilio Roig de Leuchsenring's classic condemnation of U.S. imperialism imposed needlessly on Cuba.

10:399　Maza Miquel, Manuel. *Entre la ideología y la compasión: guerra y paz en Cuba, 1895–1903: testimonios de los archivos vaticanos [Between Ideology and Compassion: War and Peace in Cuba, 1895–1903: Testimonials from the Vatican Archives].* Santo Domingo: Instituto Pedro Francisco Bonó, 1997. Maza provides a carefully researched, long view of papal relations with Cuba. He portrays the Pope's overall diplomatic goals, the role of the Holy See in Spain, the Pope's attempt to stave off U.S. intervention, and Cuban efforts to obtain indigenous bishops.

10:400　Navarro García, Luis. *La independencia de Cuba [Cuban Independence].* Madrid: Editorial MAPFRE, 1992. This account stresses the role of the Cuban insurrectionists in determining the outcome of 1898. The Cuban insurgent insistence on independence ended any chance for autonomy, and the fierce war in Cuba drew in the United States, compromising the insurgent goal of complete independence.

10:401　Pérez, Louis A., Jr. "Between Meanings and Memories of 1898." *Orbis* 42 (Fall 1998): 501–16. This article is a summary of the author's views of U.S. imperialism in Cuba in 1898 and its effects on contemporary Cuban-American relations.

10:402　_____. *Cuba and the United States: Ties of Singular Intimacy.* This work covers nearly two centuries of United States–Cuban relations, emphasizing the Cuban point of view. It relates Cuban economic developments to the United States (2:370). First published in 1990.

10:403　_____. *Cuba between Empires, 1878–1902.* The author asserts that the United States had coveted Cuba for decades. To block Cuban independence, it ended Spanish rule and established a pro-American government under a protectorate (9:422).

10:404　_____. "The Imperial Design: Politics and Pedagogy in Occupied Cuba, 1899–1902." *Cuban Studies* 12 (July 1982): 1–19. The author contends that the United States intended to annex Cuba through voluntary association. To achieve this, it sought to educate Cubans in American values. U.S. authorities created a school curriculum based on the English language, law, and American history. North American schools trained Cuban teachers, and the U.S. curriculum persisted in Cuba long after 1902.

10:405　_____. "Incurring a Debt of Gratitude: 1898 and the Moral Sources of United States Hegemony in Cuba." *American Historical Review* 104 (April 1999): 356–98. The author contrasts the Cuban and North American views of U.S. intervention in 1898. Having defeated Spain, many North Americans believed they were responsible for good governance on the island and that Cubans should be grateful. Many Cubans, however, believed that they had defeated Spain and that the United States had prevented insular independence until Fidel Castro's revolution.

10:406　_____. *On Becoming Cuban: Identity, Nationality, and Culture.* Chapel Hill: University of North Carolina Press, 1999. In this broad-ranging and sophisticated study, Pérez carefully weighs the role of U.S. hegemony in the growth of Cuban identity and nationalism in the century after the 1850s. While U.S. political and military control was crucial to this hegemony, it was secondary to the cultural dominance that resulted in Cubans drawing on North American values as their normative system.

10:407　_____. "The Pursuit of Pacification: Banditry and the United States' Occupation of Cuba, 1898–1902." *Journal of Latin American Studies* 18 (November 1986): 313–32. Pérez explains the causes of banditry after the 1898 war and the American use of Cuban rural guards to kill bandits without judicial safeguards. He believes Leonard Wood was largely responsible for this policy in eastern Cuba and that the long-term effect was a Cuban police guard that lacked judicial restraint.

10:408　Perez-Stable, Marifeli. "The Forgotten Legacy of Cuba Libre." *Culturefront* 7 (Spring 1998): 9–13. The author ties Castro's ascent and subsequent rule to the Cuban belief that the United States had frustrated their nation's pursuit of freedom in 1898.

10:409　Portell-Vilá, Hermínio. *Historia de Cuba en sus relaciones con los Estados Unidos y España [History of Cuba in Its Relations with the United States and Spain].* 4 vols. La Habana: J. Montero, 1938–1941. Carefully documented, this is a critical account of U.S. relations with Cuba and basic to understanding the Cuban perspective.

10:410 _____. *Historia de la Guerra de Cuba y los Estados Unidos contra España [History of the War of Cuba and the United States against Spain].* La Habana: Administracion del Alcalde Sr. N. Castellanos Rivero, 1949. This is a critical account of U.S. intervention in the Cuban war for independence.

10:411 Roig de Leuchsenring, Emilio. *Cuba no debe su independencia a los Estados Unidos [Cuba Does Not Owe Its Independence to the United States].* 5th ed. Santiago de Cuba: Editorial Oriente, 1975. This basic Cuban criticism of the United States argues that the Cuban people won their independence solely by their own efforts and that the United States was the enemy of their independence. Originally published in 1950.

10:412 Tarragó, Rafael E. "The Thwarting of Cuban Autonomy." *Orbis* 42 (Fall 1998): 517–31. The author believes that Cuba, under Spanish rule, was moving toward political, social, and economic reform that would have resulted eventually in insular autonomy and independence. The Cuban insurgents of 1895 halted this evolutionary progress. They destroyed the island's economy and invited U.S. military occupation. The result was U.S. political and economic control of the island leading eventually to Castro's revolution.

10:413 Zeuske, Michael. "1898: Cuba, entre cambio social, transformación y transición. Interpretaciones, comentarios y perspectivas [1898: Cuba between Social Change, Transformation, and Transition: Interpretations, Commentary, and Perspectives]." In *1898: entre la continuidad y la ruptura [1898: Between Continuity and Rupture],* ed. Rodríguez Díaz and María del Rosario, 129–63. Morelia, Michoacán, México: Universidad Michoacana de San Nicolás de Hidalgo Instituto de Investigaciones Históricas Departamento de Historia Latinoamericana, 1997. Although this article is primarily about Cuban political and economic developments, it also contains information about German interests in the West Indies and Cuba as well as an account of U.S. control over the island.

PUERTO RICO

10:414 Berbusse, Edward J. *The United States in Puerto Rico, 1898–1900.* Chapel Hill: University of North Carolina Press, 1966. This is a comprehensive study of Puerto Rico's transition from Spanish to U.S. rule.

10:415 Bolner, James, Sr. "The Supreme Court, the Insular Cases, and American Expansionism." In *La république impérialiste: l'expansionnisme et la politique extérieure des États-Unis, 1885–1909: études et documents [The Imperial Republic: Expansionism and the Foreign Policy of the United States, 1885–1909: Studies and Documents],* ed. Serge Ricard and James Bolner, Sr., 159–80. Aix-en-Provence: Université de Provence, 1987. The author examines the constitutional cases brought before the Supreme Court as a result of U.S. imperialism. He concludes that the justices pursued pragmatic considerations rather than constitutional principles.

10:416 Cabán, Pedro A. "El aparato colonial y el cambio económico en Puerto Rico, 1898–1917 [The Colonial Apparatus and Economic Change in Puerto Rico, 1898–1917]." *Revista de Ciencias Sociales* 27 (March-June 1988): 53–88. The author reasons that U.S. military rule until 1900 followed by governance under the Foraker Act resulted in three major forces controlling Puerto Rico: U.S. geopolitical interests, American capitalistic sectors, and fragmented Puerto Rican economic elites. He holds that these three elements still dominate Puerto Rico.

10:417 Chiles, Paul Nelson. *The Puerto Rican Press Reaction to the United States, 1888–1898.* New York: Arno Press, 1975. The Puerto Rican press commented on political, economic, and cultural aspects of U.S. relations.

10:418 Dávila-Cox, Emma. "Puerto Rico in the Hispanic-Cuban-American War: Re-assessing 'the Picnic.'" In *The Crisis of 1898: Colonial Redistribution and Nationalist Mobilization,* ed. Angel Smith and Emma Dávila-Cox, 96–127. New York: St. Martin's Press, 1999. This article examines Puerto Rico's mild reaction to the change from Spanish to American colonial rule. It considers economic and political factors in 1898 that accounted for a lack of insular nationalism. The author includes some of the views of British and American consuls.

10:419 Estades Font, María Eugenia. *La presencia militar de Estados Unidos en Puerto Rico, 1898–1918: intereses estratégicos y dominación colonial [The U.S. Military Presence in Puerto Rico, 1898–1918: Strategic Interests and Colonial Domination].* Río Piedras, PR: Ediciones Huracán, 1988. The author states that Mahan's strategic designs for the Caribbean shaped U.S. military policies toward Puerto Rico. U.S. military rule created a political-economic system that established twentieth-century capitalistic ways.

10:420 _____. "Los intereses estratégico-militares de los Estados Unidos en Puerto Rico a principios del siglo XX [The Strategic and Military Interests of the United States in Puerto Rico at the Beginning of the 20th Century]." *Op. Cit.: Boletín del Centro de Investigaciones Históricas* 3 (1987–1988): 175–87. The author examines U.S. naval strategic thinking during the final decades of the nineteenth century and concludes that U.S. military necessity was a major reason for establishing U.S. colonial rule over Puerto Rico.

10:421 Fernández Aponte, Irene. *El cambio de soberanía en Puerto Rico. Otro '98 [The Change of Sovereignty in Puerto Rico: The Other '98].* Madrid: Editorial MAPFRE, 1992. The author examines the political, economic, and social disruption—riots, strikes, religious disputes, and educational changes—that followed the U.S. occupation of Puerto Rico.

10:422 García, Gervasio Luis. "I Am the Other: Puerto Rico in the Eyes of North Americans, 1898." *Journal of American History* 87 (June 2000): 39–64. Reflecting on the words of Elihu Root and Salvador Brau, a Puerto Rican literary figure and political essayist, the author considers Puerto Rico in 1898 in terms of its search for autonomy, liberation from Spain, and domination by the United States. The author's Spanish-language treatment of these same themes is in "El otro es uno: Puerto Rico en la mirada norteamericana de 1898," *Revista de Indias* 57 (September-December 1997): 729–59.

10:423 _____. "Strangers in Paradise? Puerto Rico en la correspondencia de los cónsules norteam-

ericanos (1869–1900) [Strangers in Paradise? Puerto Rico in the Correspondence of U.S. Consuls (1869–1900)]." In *Op. Cit.: Revista del Centro de Investigaciones Históricas, no. 9, edición extraordinaria. El Caribe entre imperios (Coloquio de Princeton) [Op. Cit.: Review of the Center of Historical Studies, no. 9, Special Edition: The Caribbean between Empires (Princeton Colloquium)],* ed. Arcadio Díaz Quiñones, 27–55. Río Piedras, PR: Universidad de Puerto Rico, 1997. In 1898, Americans described annexation of Puerto Rico as a sideshow resulting from the war with Spain. The author, however, delineates four decades of growing American economic and political interest in Puerto Rico. Well before 1898, some U.S. consuls and island residents favored annexation.

10:424 Guthunz, Ute. "The Year 1898 in Puerto Rico: Caesura, Change, Continuation." In *1898: su significado para Centroamérica y el Caribe ¿Cesura, Cambio, Continuidad? [1898: Its Meaning for Central America and the Caribbean: Pause, Change, or Continuity?],* ed. Walther L. Bernecker, 171–92. Frankfurt am Main: Vervuert, 1998. The author delineates extensive social, economic, and political changes resulting from Spain's replacement by the United States in Puerto Rico. Despite efforts to "Americanize" Puerto Ricans, much of the Spanish way of life persisted, contributing to a distinct Puerto Rican identity.

10:425 Kerr, James Edward. *The Insular Cases: The Role of the Judiciary in American Expansionism.* Port Washington, NY: Kennikat Press, 1982. This book describes the constitutional and legal status given by the Supreme Court and Congress to the Philippines and Puerto Rico that legally justified U.S. territorial expansionism.

10:426 Libby, Justin H. "'Our Plain Duty': Senator Joseph B. Foraker and the First Civil Government of Puerto Rico." *Mid-America* 69 (January 1987): 39–56. The author traces the House and Senate debates over tariff legislation and the establishment of government for Puerto Rico. The Foraker Act was a legislative compromise that dissatisfied many people, especially Puerto Ricans.

10:427 Luque de Sánchez, María Dolores. "Las franquicias: instrumento de penetración económica en Puerto Rico, 1900–1905 [Franchises: Instrument of Economic Penetration in Puerto Rico, 1900–1905]." In *Politics, Society, and Culture in the Caribbean: Selected Papers of the XIV Conference of Caribbean Historians,* ed. Blanca G. Silvestrini, 147–68. San Juan: Universidad de Puerto Rico, 1983. The author compares the economic condition of Puerto Rico before 1898 to that of the early American occupation, showing that U.S. control resulted in the island's becoming increasingly dependent on foreign capital and markets.

10:428 Picó, Fernando. *1898—la guerra después de la guerra [1898: The War after the War].* Río Piedras, PR: Ediciones Huracán, 1987. Picó argues against the view that Puerto Ricans welcomed U.S. annexation. He examines the social conflict and resistance to American imperialism and details the U.S. military efforts to establish order.

10:429 _____. *Cada Guaraguao: galería de oficiales norteamericanos en Puerto Rico (1898–1899) [Each Bird of Prey: A Gallery of North American Officials in Puerto Rico (1898–1899)].* Río Piedras, PR: Ediciones Huracán, 1998. This short account examines the arrival of the U.S. army in Puerto Rico and establishment of military rule of the island. It focuses on the actions of seven military officers. ("Guaraguao" is a Tainos Indian word describing a bird that preys on other birds or small animals.)

10:430 _____. "El impacto de la invasión americana en la zona cafetalera de Puerto Rico: el caso de Utuado [The Impact of the U.S. Invasion on Puerto Rico's Coffee Zone: The Case of the Utuado]." In *Politics, Society, and Culture in the Caribbean: Selected Papers of the XIV Conference of Caribbean Historians,* ed. Blanca G. Silvestrini, 133–44. San Juan: Universidad de Puerto Rico, 1983. This essay describes the gradual decline of importance in Puerto Rican coffee production as a result of the U.S. annexation of the island. The case study is Utuado, the most important Puerto Rican coffee production site before 1898.

10:431 Silva Gotay, Samuel. "La Iglesia Protestante como agente de americanización en Puerto Rico, 1898–1917 [The Protestant Church as Agent of Americanization in Puerto Rico, 1898–1917]." In *Politics, Society, and Culture in the Caribbean: Se-* lected Papers of the XIV Conference of Caribbean Historians, ed. Blanca G. Silvestrini, 39–66. San Juan: Universidad de Puerto Rico, 1983. This essay describes a political and economic struggle within Puerto Rico with Protestants favoring annexation and Catholics supporting autonomy and independence.

10:432 Silvestrini, Blanca G. "El impacto de la política de salud pública de los Estados Unidos en Puerto Rico, 1898–1913: Consecuencias en el proceso de americanización [The Impact of U.S. Public Health Policies in Puerto Rico, 1898–1913: Consequences of Americanization]." In *Politics, Society, and Culture in the Caribbean: Selected Papers of the XIV Conference of Caribbean Historians,* ed. Blanca G. Silvestrini, 69–83. San Juan: Universidad de Puerto Rico, 1983. The attempts by the United States to improve public health in Puerto Rico suffered delays from cultural misunderstandings and inept U.S. administrators who overlooked Puerto Rican resources.

Philippine Annexation and the U.S.-Philippine War, 1898–1902

THE PHILIPPINE WAR

10:433 Anderson, Warwick. "Immunities of Empire: Race, Disease, and the New Tropical Medicine, 1900–1920." *Bulletin of the History of Medicine* 70 (Spring 1996): 94–118. Focusing on the Philippines, the author examines evolving theories of tropical medicine. Racial explanations for disease liability remained central throughout the period even as the focus on microbes and hygiene developed. With greater concentration on the latter came ceaseless inspection and regulation of the Filipinos.

10:434 Bolton, Grania. "Military Diplomacy and National Liberation: Insurgent-American Relations after the Fall of Manila." *Military Affairs* 36 (October 1972): 99–104. The author believes that lack of instructions from Washington led to the decline in relations between Aguinaldo and the U.S. army command.

10:435　De Bevoise, Ken. *Agents of Apocalypse: Epidemic Disease in Colonial Philippines.* Princeton: Princeton University Press, 1995. The author examines the large loss of Filipino life from epidemics and poor diet during the late nineteenth century, including 1896 to 1903. He concludes that Spanish colonial developments, such as improved transportation and communication, increased the possibility of epidemics. In explaining the Spanish role, the author diminishes the responsibility of American imperialism for epidemics after 1898.

10:436　Gates, John M. "Philippine Guerrillas, American Anti-Imperialism, and the Election of 1900." *Pacific Historical Review* 46 (February 1977): 51–64. Anti-imperialism in the United States encouraged Philippine guerrilla resistance, and Filipino nationalists hoped the 1900 election would lead to McKinley's defeat and the reversal of his policies.

10:437　_____. *Schoolbooks and Krags: The United States Army in the Philippines, 1898–1902.* Westport, CT: Greenwood Press, 1973. This is a favorable view of the role of the U.S. army in the Philippines.

10:438　_____. "War-Related Deaths in the Philippines, 1898–1902." *Pacific Historical Review* 53 (August 1984): 367–78. The author explains that data on war-related deaths is poor. He contends that anti-imperialist estimates of war-related deaths are unrealistically high in light of the 1903 census; the annual rate of births and deaths also argues for many fewer war-related deaths.

10:439　Gillett, Mary C. "U.S. Army Medical Officers and Public Health in the Philippines in the Wake of the Spanish-American War, 1898–1905." *Bulletin of the History of Medicine* 64 (Winter 1990): 567–87. From 1898 to 1905, U.S. army officers were in charge of Filipino public health. During these years there were epidemics of bubonic plague, smallpox, and cholera. In attempting to improve sanitation and to limit epidemics, army doctors had little cooperation from Filipinos.

10:440　Ileto, Reynaldo. "Cholera and the Origins of the American Sanitary Order in the Philippines." In *Imperial Medicine and Indigenous Societies,* ed. David Arnold, 125–48. New York: St. Martin's Press,

1988. This article links a transition in 1902 of U.S. military attacks against Filipinos to a U.S. military deployment against cholera. Many Filipinos did not respond to the change. The author ascribes some of the loss of life during the epidemic to American military methods that engendered Filipino resistance.

10:441　Karnow, Stanley. *In Our Image: America's Empire in the Philippines.* New York: Random House, 1989. Based on secondary sources, this uneven narrative history is highly critical of McKinley, his administration, and U.S. policy. It favors Aguinaldo and the Philippine resistance to U.S. imperialism.

10:442　Linn, Brian McAllister. *The Philippine War, 1899–1902.* Lawrence: University of Kansas Press, 2000. This is a detailed military history of the American side of the war. The author contends that superior U.S. military leadership and equipment and basic civic reforms led to U.S. victory, with Filipino political and military mistakes contributing to its success.

10:443　_____. *The U.S. Army and Counterinsurgency in the Philippine War, 1899–1902.* Chapel Hill: University of North Carolina Press, 1989. This is a careful study of U.S. army efforts to end Filipino resistance in four military districts in Luzon. Having defeated the Filipino army in standard combat, the army faced local resistance of varying size and seriousness. Military officers succeeded largely because they operated flexibly in response to local conditions.

10:444　May, Glenn Anthony. "150,000 Missing Filipinos: A Demographic Crisis in Batangas, 1887–1903." *Annales de Démographie Historique* (1985): 215–43. A careful examination of data and other evidence from 1887 to 1903 leads May to conclude that all extant population records are flawed. Nevertheless, he concludes that several epidemics caused much larger losses of life in Batangas than did the Philippine-American War.

10:445　_____. *Battle for Batangas: A Philippine Province at War.* New Haven: Yale University Press, 1991. In a seminal study of one Tagalog province during the Philippine war, the author provides fresh analysis and suggests new interpretations of several enduring issues about the war: the role of the elites and lower classes in supporting the Philippine revolution, the conduct of U.S. troops, and the cause of large population losses during the war.

10:446 _____. *A Past Recovered.* Quezon City: New Day Publishers, 1987. This is a collection of nine previously published essays, some having been rewritten. They cover the Spanish heritage, the Philippine-American War, and criticism of interpretations of both nationalistic Filipino and American authors.

10:447 _____. "Why the United States Won the Philippine-American War, 1899–1902." *Pacific Historical Review* 52 (November 1983): 353–77. May compares the results of the Philippine and Vietnam Wars. He argues that the United States won the Philippine war in part because of poor Filipino military leadership and weak Filipino public support.

10:448 Miller, Stuart Creighton. "The American Soldier and the Conquest of the Philippines." In *Reappraising an Empire: New Perspectives on Philippine-American History,* ed. Peter W. Stanley, 13–34. Cambridge, MA: Harvard University Press, 1984. This article, largely based on private letters and contemporary newspaper interviews, exposes the racism, inhumanity, and willful destruction U.S. soldiers directed at Filipino soldiers and civilians.

10:449 _____. *"Benevolent Assimilation": The American Conquest of the Philippines, 1899–1903.* New Haven: Yale University Press, 1982. This well-researched account of the American side of the Philippine-American War is highly critical of the McKinley administration, the senior U.S. military officers in the Philippines, and the conduct of the war.

10:450 Robinson, Michael C., and Frank N. Schubert. "David Fagen: An African-American Rebel in the Philippines, 1899–1901." *Pacific Historical Review* 44 (February 1975): 68–83. Fagen led some disillusioned African-American soldiers in desertion during the Philippine war.

10:451 Smythe, Donald. *Guerrilla Warrior: The Early Life of John J. Pershing.* New York: Scribner, 1973. Smythe discusses Pershing's role in the suppression of the Filipinos.

10:452 Tomblin, Barbara B. "The United States Navy and the Philippine Insurrection." *American Neptune* 35 (July 1975): 183–96. This article describes the role of the navy in supporting land operations and capturing islands.

10:453 Welch, Richard E., Jr. "American Atrocities in the Philippines: The Indictment and the Response." *Pacific Historical Review* 43 (May 1974): 233–53. The author found limited outrage in the United States in response to reports of atrocities. Patriotism, racism, and the idea of American mission took precedence.

10:454 Wolff, Leon. *Little Brown Brother: How the United States Purchased and Pacified the Philippine Islands at the Century's Turn.* New York: Doubleday, 1961. Reprint 1970 (Kraus Reprint Co.). This is a harsh account of U.S. imperial conduct during the Philippine war. 1970 reprint titled *Little Brown Brother: America's Forgotten Bid for Empire Which Cost 250,000 Lives.*

THE AMERICAN MISSION AND MISSIONARIES IN THE PHILIPPINES

10:455 Achútegui, Pedro S. de, S.J., and Miguel A. Bernad, S.J. *Religious Revolution in the Philippines.* 3 vols. Manila: Ateneo de Manila, 1960–1971. These volumes describe a religious revolution aimed at replacing Spanish bishops and priests with Filipinos.

10:456 Clymer, Kenton J. "Protestant Missionaries and American Colonialism in the Philippines, 1899–1916: Attitudes, Perceptions, Involvement." In *Reappraising an Empire: New Perspectives on Philippine-American History,* ed. Peter W. Stanley, 143–70. Cambridge, MA: Harvard University Press, 1984. American Protestant missionary societies supported U.S. acquisition of the Philippines and the war required to subdue the Filipinos. Missionaries generally favored U.S. imperialism and the government's efforts to stamp an American image on Filipino society.

10:457 _____. *Protestant Missionaries in the Philippines, 1898–1916: An Inquiry into the American Colonial Mentality.* Urbana: University of Illinois Press, 1986. The author describes missionary ideals, the attempts to change Filipino culture, the clash with Roman Catholicism, and skepticism toward Filipino nationalism. He questions the long-run significance of the missionary movement, yet suggests that some important residues remain in contemporary Filipino culture.

10:458   Ezzell, William Edward. "Secular Missionaries: The Early American Teachers in the Philippines." *Proceedings and Papers of the Georgia Association of Historians* 6 (1985): 96–107. This critical evaluation of American education in the Philippines begins with initial U.S. army schools and extends to 1913. The author concludes that American teachers were poorly prepared. Often moved by humanitarianism, they also exhibited racism and ethnocentrism. Seeking to educate the Filipino masses, the U.S.-sponsored school system failed to do so.

10:459   Kwantes, Anne C. *Presbyterian Missionaries in the Philippines: Conduits of Social Change (1899–1910).* Quezon City: New Day Publishers, 1989. In this generally positive assessment of the missionary movement, the author explains the motivation, methods, successes, and failures of Presbyterian missionaries in the Philippines.

10:460   Margold, Jane A. "Egalitarian Ideals and Exclusionary Practices: U.S. Pedagogy in the Colonial Philippines." *Journal of Historical Sociology* 8 (December 1995): 375–94. This article sets forth the social and political educational objectives of the United States in the Philippines and notes the failure of American teachers to achieve these ends.

10:461   Rafael, Vicente L. "Colonial Domesticity: White Women and United States Rule in the Philippines." *American Literature* 67 (December 1995): 639–66. This essay examines American women's writings on the Philippines from 1899 through 1910 and concentrates on the concept of domesticity in the construction of U.S. imperial ideology and practice.

10:462   Stanley, Peter W. "'The Voice of Worcester Is the Voice of God': How One American Found Fulfillment in the Philippines." In *Reappraising an Empire: New Perspectives on Philippine-American History,* ed. Peter W. Stanley, 117–41. Cambridge, MA: Harvard University Press, 1984. The author sets forth

Dean C. Worcester's motivations and importance as a U.S. colonial administrator for fourteen years in the Philippines.

10:463   Sullivan, Rodney J. *Exemplar of Americanism: The Philippine Career of Dean C. Worcester.* Ann Arbor: Center for South and Southeast Asian Studies, University of Michigan, 1991. Worcester believed that Filipinos were inferior people who needed America's civilized guidance. In 1898, he influenced the McKinley administration and until 1913 helped to shape and direct U.S. colonial policies in the Philippines.

10:464   Welch, Richard E., Jr. "Organized Religion and the Philippine-American War, 1899–1902." *Mid-America* 55 (July 1973): 184–206. Catholics and Protestants divided over Philippine issues such as the conduct of the war and independence for the islands.

AMERICAN IMPERIALISM AND THE PHILIPPINES

10:465   Alfonso, Oscar M. *Theodore Roosevelt and the Philippines, 1897–1909.* Quezon City: University of the Philippines Press, 1970. The author seeks to understand why Roosevelt opposed Filipino self-government.

10:466   Brands, H. W. *Bound to Empire: The United States and the Philippines.* This volume covers a century of U.S. imperialism in the Philippines, including causes of 1890s imperialism, acquisition of the Philippines, fluctuating U.S. colonial policies, and recent U.S.-Philippine relations. The author delineates the power relationships that bound the United States to the Philippines. He shows that colonialism illuminates U.S. foreign relations throughout the twentieth century (2:296).

10:467   Campomanes, Oscar V. "1898 and the Nature of the New Empire." *Radical History Review* 73 (Winter 1999): 130–46. Despite the U.S. rhetoric of natural growth and exceptionalism, Campomanes rejects the contention that the new empire of 1898 was an aberration from previous U.S. practices. He also deems subsequent American informal empire the embodiment of neocolonialism.

10:468 Coletta, Paolo E. "Bryan, McKinley, and the Treaty of Paris." *Pacific Historical Review* 26 (May 1957): 131–46. Bryan supported the treaty to remove the Spanish, to clear the way for congressional authorization for Philippine independence, and to allow the Democrats to concentrate on domestic matters. He did not press for ratification to make Philippine annexation an issue in the 1900 election.

10:469 Contosta, David R. "Whitelaw Reid and the Inadvertent Empire." Contosta provides Whitelaw Reid's views on imperialism during the 1890s, including his analysis of the importance of the Philippines and his efforts to influence their acquisition (9:82).

10:470 Damiani, Brian P. *Advocates of Empire: William McKinley, the Senate, and American Expansion, 1898–1899.* New York: Garland Publishing, 1987. Focusing on McKinley and the expansionist wing of the Republican Party, the author traces the president's decisions and the Senate's responses during the making of peace with Spain and the acquisition of the Philippines. Damiani argues that McKinley and his party were hesitant expansionists, were primarily influenced by considerations of duty, patriotism, and party politics rather than economics, and possessed no coherent imperial perspective.

10:471 Elizalde Pérez-Grueso, María Dolores. "1898: The Coordinates of the Spanish Crisis in the Pacific." In *The Crisis of 1898: Colonial Redistribution and Nationalist Mobilization,* ed. Angel Smith and Emma Dávila-Cox, 128–51. New York: St. Martin's Press, 1999. The author develops pre-1898 Spanish administration of the Philippines and the trade ties of Spain, Great Britain, and the United States to the islands. French, German, Japanese, and Chinese interests are noted. Once the war began, Spain tried to salvage what it could in the Pacific. Elizalde assesses the U.S. decision to annex the islands in light of British, French, German, Russian, and Japanese concerns.

10:472 _____. "De nación a imperio: la expansión de los Estados Unidos por el Pacífico durante la guerra hispano-norteamericana de 1898 [From Nation to Empire: U.S. Expansion in the Pacific during the Spanish-American War of 1898]." *Hispania (Spain)* 57 (May-August 1997): 551–88. Based solely on American primary and secondary sources, Elizalde traces the U.S. acquisition of the Philippines. She reviews American historical interpretations of imperialism in the Pacific and then follows the steps the McKinley administration took in deciding to acquire the islands.

10:473 _____. "Valor internacional de Filipinas en 1898: la perspectiva norteamericana [The International Value of the Philippines in 1898: The North American Perspective]." In *La nación soñada: Cuba, Puerto Rico y Filipinas ante el 98: actas del congreso internacional celebrado en Aranjuez del 24 al 28 de abril de 1995 [The Dreamed Nation: Cuba, Puerto Rico, and the Philippines before '98: Transactions of the International Congress Held at Aranjuez, 24–28 April 1995],* ed. Consuelo Naranjo Orovio, Miguel Ángel Puig-Samper, and Luis Miguel García Mora, 767–84. Aranjuez (Madrid): Doce Calles, 1996. This article traces a century of changing views of American historians toward annexation of the Philippines. After reviewing the most recent American historical literature, the author provides a broad view of the causes of annexation.

10:474 Halle, Louis J., Jr. *The United States Acquires the Philippines: Consensus vs. Reality.* Lanham, MD: University Press of America, 1985. This realist interpretation, in a fifty-seven-page pamphlet, presents a weak McKinley and depicts an unthinking policy of drift leading both to war and acquisition of the Philippines. The author also explores the elements of destiny and reality in a series of counterfactual speculations.

10:475 Hankins, Barry. "Manifest Destiny in the Midwest: Selected Kansans and the Philippine Question." *Kansas History* 8 (Spring 1985): 54–66. This article examines the imperialist and anti-imperialist positions in Kansas, where the arguments corresponded to those propounded nationally.

10:476 Heald, Morrell, and Lawrence S. Kaplan. *Culture and Diplomacy: The American Experience.* Chapter 6 analyzes the U.S. "imperialist impulse" in the Philippines. The authors conclude that the basic American cultural imperatives of democracy and opportunity and the national conscience softened the racism and paternalism inherent in colonialism and foreshadowed the nation's ongoing ambivalent cultural relations with Asia (2:130).

10:477   Hendrickson, Kenneth E., Jr. "Reluctant Expansionist: Jacob Gould Schurman and the Philippine Question." *Pacific Historical Review* 36 (November 1967): 405–21. Schurman disagreed with a commission he led to assess conditions in the Philippines; he favored direct negotiations with Aguinaldo and temporary rule of the islands rather than permanent ownership.

10:478   Kramer, Paul A. "Empires, Exceptions, and Anglo-Saxons: Race and Rule between the British and United States Empires, 1880–1910." *Journal of American History* 88 (March 2002): 1315–53. Focusing particularly on the Philippines, Kramer argues that U.S. imperial projects must be examined in a transnational framework with an eye to interimperial crossings. He asserts that Americans used a shared Anglo-Saxonism with the British to legitimate U.S. colonialism, but that arguments for national exceptionalism and the spread of republican institutions regained dominance in the American brief for imperialism in the first five years of the twentieth century.

10:479   _____. "Making Concessions: Race and Empire Revisited at the Philippine Exposition, St. Louis, 1901–1905." *Radical History Review* 73 (Winter 1999): 74–114. This broad-ranging essay questions many previous assumptions about the interconnections of international expositions and U.S. empire. It asserts that the fairs were as fractured as empires themselves, often conveyed contradictory messages, and were productions of the colonial subjects as well as the metropole imperialists.

10:480   Lindgren, James M. "The Apostasy of a Southern Anti-Imperialist: Joseph Bryan, the Spanish-American War, and Business Expansion." *Southern Studies* 2 (Summer 1991): 151–78. The editor of the *Richmond Times*, Bryan initially opposed intervention in Cuba and imperial acquisitions out of a fear of domestic class conflict and a possible threat to the gold standard. Influenced by the prospects of commercial expansion, he altered his position and came to favor retention of the Philippines by late 1898.

10:481   May, Ernest R. *American Imperialism: A Speculative Essay.* In the original 1968 edition of this

provocative volume (2:86), the author tied the decision to acquire the Philippines to the influence of European imperial examples and to the U.S. foreign policy establishment. In the new introduction to this 1991 reprint, he assesses the literature that has appeared in the interim and concludes that he would alter few of the conclusions offered in 1967 or in *Imperial Democracy: The Emergence of America as a Great Power* (1961) (10:78).

10:482   Morgan, H. Wayne, ed. *Making Peace with Spain: The Diary of Whitelaw Reid, September-December, 1898.* Austin: University of Texas Press, 1965. This is an important insider's view of the peace conference.

10:483   Offner, John L. "Imperialism by International Consensus: The United States and the Philippine Islands." In *From Theodore Roosevelt to FDR: Internationalism and Isolationism in American Foreign Policy,* ed. Daniela Rossini, 45–54. Staffordshire, UK: Keele University Press, 1995. By late 1898, the major interested powers—Great Britain, Germany, France, Russia, and Japan—came to agree that the United States should annex all of the Philippines.

10:484   Parrini, Carl P. "Charles A. Conant, Economic Crises and Foreign Policy, 1896–1903." In *Behind the Throne: Servants of Power to Imperial Presidents, 1898–1968,* ed. Thomas J. McCormick and Walter LaFeber, 35–66. Madison: University of Wisconsin Press, 1993. Parrini examines Conant's critique of classical economic theory, his arguments for finding international outlets for surplus capital, and his attempts to apply his theories in the Philippines.

10:485   Pomeroy, William J. *American Neo-Colonialism: Its Emergence in the Philippines and Asia.* New York: International Publishers, 1970. The author holds that the United States stopped the Filipino agrarian revolution to obtain a base for the China trade.

10:486   Ricard, Serge. "Reluctant Imperialism? The Acquisition of the Philippines Reconsidered." *Annales du Monde Anglophone* 1 (April 1995): 9–19. The author notes that at the start of the Spanish-Cuban-American War the United States had no interest in annexing the Philippines. This changed primarily because of

American racial attitudes that deprecated the ability of the Filipinos to govern themselves.

10:487   Rystad, Göran. "The Philippine Struggle for Independence and Its Effects on American Expansionism at the Turn of the Century." *Revue Internationale d'Histoire Militaire* 70 (1988): 107–29. The author concludes that the bitter, costly Philippine war strengthened American anti-imperialist opinion and weakened expansionist sentiment; as a result the U.S. tide of territorial annexation receded.

10:488   _____. "Republic or Empire? The Philippine-American War and American Expansionism at the Turn of the Century." In *La république impérialiste: l'expansionnisme et la politique extérieure des États-Unis, 1885–1909: études et documents [The Imperial Republic: Expansionism and the Foreign Policy of the United States, 1885–1909: Studies and Documents]*, ed. Serge Ricard and James Bolner, Sr., 131–58. Aix-en-Provence: Université de Provence, 1987. The author examines several roots of American imperialism: military, economic, duty and destiny, racism, and missionary zeal. He concludes that the difficult Filipino war blunted U.S. imperial interests and fostered anti-imperialism.

10:489   Schlup, Leonard. "Reluctant Expansionist: Adlai E. Stevenson and the Campaign against Imperialism in 1900." *Indiana Social Studies Quarterly* 29 (Summer 1976): 32–42. This article describes Stevenson's position on Philippine annexation during the 1900 election.

10:490   Thompson, Winfred Lee. *The Introduction of American Law in the Philippines and Puerto Rico, 1898–1905.* Fayetteville: University of Arkansas Press, 1989. This monograph focuses on the extension of U.S. law to the Philippines. Puerto Rico and the insular cases are of secondary interest and have importance largely as they affect U.S. law in the Philippines.

10:491   Torre del Río, Rosario de la. "Filipinas y el reparto de Extremo Oriente en la crisis de 1898 [The Philippines and the Distribution of the Far East in the Crisis of 1898]." In *Extremo Oriente ibérico: investigaciones históricas: metodología y estado de la cuestión [The Iberian Far East: Historical Studies: Methodology and the State of the Question]*, ed.

Francisco de Solano, Florentino Rodao García, and Luis Eugenio Togores Sánchez, 509–21. Madrid: Agencia Española de Cooperación Internacional en colaboración con el Centro de Estudios Históricos Departamento de Historia de América CSIC, 1989. This is a pithy, thoughtful exposition of Spanish and European interests—England, France, and Germany—in the U.S. decision to acquire the Philippine Islands. Set within José María Jover Zamora's theoretical framework of colonial redistribution at the turn of the century, Torre del Río provides a global context for evaluating American imperialism.

10:492   Tuason, Julie A. "The Ideology of Empire in *National Geographic Magazine*'s Coverage of the Philippines, 1898–1908." *Geographical Review* 89 (January 1999): 34–53. The author relates thirty *National Geographic Magazine* articles on the Philippines to the development of U.S. imperialism and colonial administration. Early magazine articles focused on economic exploitation of Filipino land and labor. Later articles emphasized America's moral responsibility to benefit the Filipino people through scientific and civic progress.

10:493   Van Ells, Mark D. "Assuming the White Man's Burden: The Seizure of the Philippines, 1898–1902." *Philippine Studies* 43 (Fourth Quarter 1995): 607–22. The author contends that racism, embedded in a history of slavery and extermination of Native Americans, was behind U.S. imperialism in the Philippines. It led to the cruelty and barbarity of American soldiers in the Philippines and the unwillingness of the U.S. government to admit that Filipinos could govern themselves.

10:494   Vaughan, Christopher A. "The 'Discovery' of the Philippines by the U.S. Press, 1898–1902." *Historian* 57 (Winter 1995): 303–14. This article concentrates on the depiction of the Filipinos as inferior "others," children, and savages, through the use of racial stereotypes, often drawn from previous wars and mythology, and on efforts to reconcile Filipino suppression with professed U.S. principles.

10:495   Vergara, Benito M., Jr. *Displaying Filipinos: Photography and Colonialism in Early 20th Century Philippines.* Quezon City: University of the Philippines Press, 1995. This monograph relates photography to imperialism. The colonialist mindsets of photographers resulted in stereotyped pictures of Filipinos that in turn demonstrated to American viewers the need for U.S. imperialism.

10:496 Rafael, Vicente L. "The Undead: Photographs from the Filipino-American War." *Culture-front* 7 (Spring 1998): 25–29. Rafael employs photographs taken by J. D. Givens, a California photographer, to probe the issues of genocide, the trauma of empire, and the challenges of narrating historical truths.

10:497 Welch, Richard E., Jr. "The 'Philippine Insurrection' and the American Press." *Historian* 36 (November 1973): 35–41. A study of 180 newspapers found 122 for annexation and 58 against. The debate among them centered on emotional, nonmaterial issues.

10:498 _____. *Response to Imperialism: The United States and the Philippine-American War, 1899–1902.* Chapel Hill: University of North Carolina Press, 1978. This is an excellent account of the impact of the Filipino war on American society and the U.S. government.

10:499 Werking, Richard Hume. "Senator Henry Cabot Lodge and the Philippines: A Note on American Territorial Expansion." *Pacific Historical Review* 42 (May 1973): 234–40. A letter from Lodge to Secretary of State Day places Lodge squarely in the expansionist camp and refutes the views of some scholars that he was not greatly interested in colonialism.

10:500 Williams, Walter L. "United States Indian Policy and the Debate over Philippine Annexation: Implications for the Origins of American Imperialism." *Journal of American History* 66 (March 1980): 810–31. By comparing nineteenth-century Indian policy to turn-of-the-century imperialism, this significant essay demonstrates that the United States had a long tradition of holding nonwhites in colonial bondage.

10:501 Zimmerman, James A. "The Chicago Liberty and Loyalty Meetings, 1899: Public Attitudes toward the Philippine-American War." *North Dakota Quarterly* 43 (Autumn 1975): 29–37. This essay examines two public meetings, one opposing the war and one supporting the McKinley administration, in April and May 1899, as a means of assessing the debate over U.S. imperialism.

U.S. Anti-Imperialism and Peace Movement

10:502 Baron, Harold. "Anti-Imperialism and the Democrats." *Science and Society* 21 (Summer 1957): 222–39. Although considered the party of anti-imperialism, the Democrats were divided on this issue in the congressional and state elections of 1898. Bryan made imperialism central in 1900, but by 1906 it was no longer a primary party concern.

10:503 Bedford, Joseph. "Samuel Gompers and the Caribbean: The AFL, Cuba, and Puerto Rico, 1898–1906." *Labor's Heritage* 6 (Spring 1995): 4–25. The essay examines Gompers's support for Cuban independence, opposition to the annexation of Hawaii, and relations with the Cuban and Puerto Rican labor movements.

10:504 Beisner, Robert L. "1898 and 1968: The Anti-Imperialists and the Doves." *Political Science Quarterly* 85 (Summer 1970): 186–216. Beisner provides an interesting comparison of the two anti-movements in terms of composition, motives, and activities.

10:505 _____. "Thirty Years before Manila: E. L. Godkin, Carl Schurz, and Anti-Imperialism in the Gilded Age." The author examines these two consistent anti-imperialists and the arguments they made during the late nineteenth century (9:127).

10:506 _____. *Twelve against Empire: The Anti-Imperialists, 1898–1900.* Chicago: Imprint Publications, 1992. Focusing on twelve representative Republicans and Mugwumps, the author analyzes the failure of the anti-imperialist movement. While age and elitism, parochialism, racism, disunity, and a lack of viable alternatives were primarily responsible for their failure, they were also contending against a well-established U.S. imperial tradition and practice. Originally published in 1968, this printing has new explanatory forewords written in both 1985 and 1992.

10:507   Bernstein, Barton J., and Franklin A. Leib. "Progressive Republican Senators and American Imperialism, 1898–1916: A Re-appraisal." *Mid-America* 50 (July 1968): 163–205. In response to William Leuchtenburg's 1952 article, the authors assert that most progressive Republican senators opposed aggressive expansionism.

10:508   Cherny, Robert W. "Anti-Imperialism on the Middle Border, 1898–1900." *Midwest Review* 1 (Spring 1979): 19–34. Focusing on Kansas, Nebraska, and South Dakota, Cherny contends that silver advocates (Populists, Bryanite Democrats, and silver Republicans) constituted the principal anti-imperialist forces. This contrasted with the east in which dissident Republicans and gold Democrats led the anti-imperialist movement.

10:509   Craig, John M. "Lucia True Ames Mead: American Publicist for Peace and Internationalism." In *Women and American Foreign Policy: Lobbyists, Critics, and Insiders,* ed. Edward P. Crapol, 67–91. Wilmington, DE: SR Books, 1992. Concentrating on Mead's important pacifist activities from 1898 through 1918, this essay explains how this cause became her principal vocation at the turn of the century.

10:510   Davis, Horace B. "American Labor." *Science and Society* 27 (Spring 1963): 70–76. Labor opposed territorial expansion, fearing low-wage competition.

10:511   Dement'ev, I. P. *USA, Imperialists and Anti-Imperialists: (The Great Foreign Policy Debate at the Turn of the Century).* Translated by David Skvirsky. Moscow: Progress Publishers, 1979. This is a serious work of scholarship. It is grounded in extensive research and examines the traditional topics associated with U.S. expansion at the turn of the century. The author writes from a socialist ideological perspective and gives special attention to the American Anti-Imperialist League, labor, and the socialist press.

10:512   Foner, Philip S. "Literary Anti-Imperialism in the United States at the Turn of the Twentieth Century." *Wissenschaftliche Zeitschrift der Humbolt-Universiteat Berlin* 33 (1984): 349–55. This essay, which is excerpted from volume 2 of Foner and Winchester, *The Anti-Imperialist Reader: A Documen-*

tary History of Anti-Imperialism in the United States (1984) (10:513), examines anti-imperialist poetry and satire. The author concludes that the writers did not influence policymakers but did help expose the hypocrisy of U.S. actions in the Philippines.

10:513   Foner, Philip S., and Richard C. Winchester, eds. *The Anti-Imperialist Reader: A Documentary History of Anti-Imperialism in the United States.* These two volumes provide a rich collection of contemporary commentaries on U.S. expansion at the turn of the century. After an introductory section on U.S. anti-imperialism from 1846 to 1872, the remainder of volume 1 concentrates on U.S. expansion in Hawaii, Cuba, and the Philippines. Among the voices are the middle class, soldiers, blacks, labor, and the Anti-Imperialist League. Volume 2 provides an extended introduction on literary anti-imperialism and excerpts, including those of Peter Finley Dunne, Mark Twain, William Dean Howells, Ambrose Bierce, Ernest Howard Crosby, and Raymond L. Bridgman (9:9).

10:514   Freidel, Frank. "Dissent in the Spanish-American War and the Philippine Insurrection." *Proceedings of the Massachusetts Historical Society* 81 (1969): 167–84. Although there was little dissent during the war against Spain, there was a great deal of opposition to the war in the Philippines. This opposition centered in New England. This essay is also available in Samuel Eliot Morison, Frederick Merk, and Frank Freidel, *Dissent in Three American Wars* (Cambridge, MA: Harvard University Press, 1970).

10:515   Gatewood, Willard B., Jr. "A Negro Editor on Imperialism: John Mitchell, 1898–1901." *Journalism Quarterly* 49 (Spring 1972): 43–50. Mitchell strongly opposed imperialism.

10:516   Gibson, William. "Mark Twain and Howells: Anti-Imperialists." *New England Quarterly* 20 (March 1947): 435–70. Howells was opposed to imperialism from the start; Twain adopted this perspective later after recognizing the adverse effects of expansionism on U.S. democracy. Compare this account to Samuel Stillen, "Dooley, Twain, and Imperialism," *Masses and Mainstream* 1 (December 1948): 6–13, and Fred H. Harrington, "Literary Aspects of Anti-Imperialism," *New England Quarterly* 10 (December 1937): 650–67.

10:517 Harrington, Fred H. "The Anti-Imperialist Movement in the United States, 1898–1900." *Mississippi Valley Historical Review* 22 (September 1935): 211–30. This classic account is particularly valuable for its analysis of the Anti-Imperialist League.

10:518 Hazard, Elizabeth (Wendy). "The *Maine* Remembered: Responses to the Spanish-American War in the Pine Tree State." *Maine History* 37 (Spring 1998): 162–93. Hazard traces Maine's response to the war of 1898, giving particular attention to powerful Republican opponents of war and empire: Speaker of the House Thomas B. Reed, Congressmen Nelson Dingley and Charles Boutelle, Senator Eugene Hale, and feminist Hannah Bailey.

10:519 Lasch, Christopher. "The Anti-Imperialists, the Philippines, and the Inequality of Man." *Journal of Southern History* 24 (August 1958): 319–31. Lasch argues that the anti-imperialists opposed annexation of the Philippines because they did not want to bring inferior races into the American body politic or empire.

10:520 Loy, Edward H. "Editorial Opinion and American Imperialism: Two Northwest Newspapers." *Oregon Historical Quarterly* 72 (September 1971): 209–24. An examination of two newspapers reveals that interest in acquisition of territory declined rapidly after 1899 and practically disappeared by 1903.

10:521 Marks, George P., ed. *The Black Press Views American Imperialism (1898–1900).* New York: Arno Press, 1971. Marks provides a useful selection of excerpts from the black press.

10:522 McKee, Delber L. "Samuel Gompers, the A. F. of L. and Imperialism, 1895–1900." *Historian* 21 (Winter 1959): 187–99. This basically descriptive essay traces Gompers and the AFL's support for the recognition of Cuban belligerency, ambivalence over the coming of the war of 1898, and opposition to territorial expansion.

10:523 McMahon, Dalton E. "Richard Pettigrew's Opposition to Imperialism." *Midwest Review* 8 (1986): 26–39. A Democratic senator from South Dakota, Pettigrew opposed the annexation of Hawaii and the Philippines. He believed that imperialism threatened U.S. democracy and would augment central governmental power.

10:524 Pickens, Donald. "William Graham Sumner as a Critic of the Spanish American War." *Continuity* 11 (Fall 1987): 75–92. This essay analyzes the intellectual bases of Sumner's critique of U.S. imperialism. The author contends that the most important facets of Sumner's thought were Scottish Common Sense philosophy and republicanism rather than Social Darwinism.

10:525 Radosh, Ronald. "American Labor and the Anti-Imperialist Movement." *Science and Society* 28 (Spring 1964): 91–100. Gompers and the AFL favored economic expansion, but opposed military conquests and formal colonialism.

10:526 Schirmer, Daniel B. *Republic or Empire: American Resistance to the Philippine War.* Cambridge, MA: Schenkman Publishing Co., 1972. This account of anti-imperialism in Boston argues that old mercantile families opposed imperialist bankers. Gerald E. Markowitz, "A Note on the Anti-Imperialist Movement of the 1890's," *Science and Society* 37 (Fall 1973): 342–45, critiques this study. Preface by Howard Zinn.

10:527 Schlup, Leonard. "Imperialist Dissenter: William B. Bate and the Battle against Territorial Acquisitions, 1898–1900." *Southern Studies* 6 (Summer 1995): 61–84. A Democratic senator from Tennessee, Bate endorsed a free and independent Cuba and the acquisition of Puerto Rico, but opposed annexing Hawaii and the Philippines.

10:528 Scott, Carole E. "Racism and Southern Anti-Imperialists: The Blounts of Georgia." *Atlanta History* 31 (Fall 1987): 24–29. The author asserts that the anti-imperialist views of James H. Blount, Sr. and James H. Blount, Jr. derived from more than racially based opposition to incorporating Hawaiians or Filipinos into the United States. Both were more influenced by isolationism, a southern empathy for those being subjected to outside oppression, and devotion to self-government.

10:529 Tompkins, E. Berkeley. *Anti-Imperialism in the United States: The Great Debate, 1890–1920.* Philadelphia: University of Pennsylvania Press,

1970. The anti-imperialists had deep roots in a variety of political and ethical concepts and provided a service by alerting the American people to the dangers of overseas empire.

10:530 _____. "The Old Guard: A Study of the Anti-Imperialist Leadership." *Historian* 30 (May 1968): 366–88. This is a useful analysis of the leadership in terms of age, profession, political affiliation, and other personal characteristics.

10:531 _____. "Scylla and Charybdis: The Anti-Imperialist Dilemma in the Election of 1900." *Pacific Historical Review* 36 (May 1967): 143–61. Anti-imperialists were uncomfortable being associated with Bryan's financial positions and did not regard the outcome of the election as a defeat for their cause.

10:532 Welch, Richard E., Jr. "Motives and Policy Objectives of Anti-Imperialists, 1898." *Mid-America* 51 (April 1969): 119–29. This important analysis of twenty-five anti-imperialist leaders during the 1898 debate on the Philippines finds that they believed in white superiority but accepted people of color as capable and favored economic penetration of the islands while opposing political control.

10:533 _____. "Senator George Frisbie Hoar and the Defeat of Anti-Imperialism, 1898–1900." *Historian* 26 (May 1964): 362–80. Welch analyzes a plan by Hoar and Carl Schurz to establish a protectorate over the Philippines. The plan failed because of division among the anti-imperialists.

10:534 Whittaker, William G. "Samuel Gompers: Anti-Imperialist." *Pacific Historical Review* 38 (November 1969): 429–45. Gompers believed that imperialism threatened the American worker, and he helped found the Anti-Imperialist League. See also Delber L. McKee, "Samuel Gompers, the A. F. of L., and Imperialism, 1895–1900," *Historian* 21 (February 1959): 187–99.

10:535 Zimmerman, James A. "Who Were the Anti-Imperialists and the Expansionists of 1893 and 1898: A Chicago Perspective." *Pacific Historical Review* 46 (November 1977): 589–601. The author disputes the contention that the anti-imperialists were aged and conservative. He finds the Chicago leadership to have been drawn from many ideological backgrounds and to have been no older, and in many cases younger, than the imperialists.

Race, Gender, and U.S. Imperialism

RACE

10:536 Duke, Cathy. "The Idea of Race: The Cultural Impact of American Intervention in Cuba, 1898–1912." In *Politics, Society, and Culture in the Caribbean: Selected Papers of the XIV Conference of Caribbean Historians,* ed. Blanca G. Silvestrini, 87–109. San Juan: Universidad de Puerto Rico, 1983. Duke argues that the United States exported its prejudice toward nonwhites and institutionalized racism to Cuba. The resulting racial animosities contributed significantly to internal conflict on the island.

10:537 Ferrer, Ada. "Cuba, 1898: Rethinking Race, Nation, and Empire." *Radical History Review* 73 (Winter 1999): 22–46. Ferrer examines the U.S. intervention in the Cuban revolution and the requirements that the North Americans set to gain their withdrawal. The author asserts that demands for order and stability or rapprochement with Spaniards ran counter to the thirty-year Cuban effort to achieve independence, and the U.S. assumptions of racial hierarchy contradicted Cubans' emphasis on racelessness in their struggle.

10:538 Gatewood, Willard B., Jr. "Black Americans and the Quest for Empire, 1893–1903." *Journal of Southern History* 38 (November 1972): 545–66. Blacks found racists on both sides of the issues associated with imperialism. Thus, while African-American attitudes were mixed, blacks consistently pointed out the inconsistency of a policy that advocated uplift abroad while practicing oppression at home.

10:539 _____. *Black Americans and the White Man's Burden, 1898–1903.* Urbana: University of Illinois Press, 1975. This is the best overall treatment of African-American responses to the wars in Cuba and the Philippines and to U.S. imperialism. Blacks sympathized with Cubans and Filipinos and cited American hypocrisy in allegedly fighting for the white man's burden abroad while practicing discrimination at home. African-Americans also fought valiantly in both wars out of a sense of national duty and the hope that loyal service would improve their chances for equitable citizenship. See also Gatewood, *"Smoked Yankees" and the Struggle for Empire: Letters from Negro Soldiers, 1898–1902* (1971) (10:351).

10:540   Gianakos, Perry E. "The Spanish-American War and the Double Paradox of the Negro American." *Phylon* 26 (Spring 1965): 34–50. The paradox was the U.S. sympathy for beleaguered Cubans and the lack of sympathy for African-Americans.

10:541   Gleijeses, Piero. "African Americans and the War against Spain." *North Carolina Historical Review* 78 (April 1996): 184–214. Focusing primarily on two African-American papers in Washington, D.C., and secondarily on six other papers from around the nation, the article traces black responses to the war of 1898 and U.S. imperialism. The principal theme is an exploration of how African-Americans responded as oppressed people to the white majority and U.S. government that discriminated against them.

10:542   Kennedy, Philip W. "Race and American Expansion in Cuba and Puerto Rico, 1895–1905." *Journal of Black Studies* 1 (March 1971): 306–16. Assumptions of Latin inferiority and Anglo-Saxon superiority influenced U.S. acquisition and governance of its colonies.

10:543   _____. "The Racial Overtones of Imperialism as a Campaign Issue, 1900." *Mid-America* 48 (July 1966): 196–205. Democrats opposed annexation of the Philippines and the acquisition of an alleged race problem; Republicans who opposed domestic slavery now favored colonial control of nonwhites.

10:544   Linn, Brian McAllister. "Taking Up 'The White Man's Burden': U.S. Troop Conduct in the Philippine War, 1899–1902." In *1898: enfoques y perspectivas [1898: Focal Points and Perspectives]*, ed. Luis E. González Vales, 111–42. San Juan: Academia Puertorriqueña de la Historia, 1997. The author

examines the charges of military atrocities that anti-imperialist writers claim stem from racism. Although ample evidence of ethnocentrism exists, there are many other factors that account for military atrocities, which were far fewer than critics contend.

10:545   Little, Lawrence S. *Disciples of Liberty: The African Methodist Episcopal Church in the Age of Imperialism, 1884–1916*. Knoxville: University of Tennessee Press, 2000. Little illustrates the dilemmas confronting the AME leaders and the variety and complexity of their responses to American imperialism. Concerned primarily with domestic issues, closely allied with the Republican Party, subscribing to the ideology of American greatness, and sponsoring an extensive missionary effort, AME responses ranged from support for the extension of U.S. institutions abroad to denunciation of imperialism and its racist foundations.

10:546   Merriman, Allen H. "Racism in the Expansionist Controversy of 1898–1900." *Phylon* 39 (December 1978): 369–80. Both imperialists and anti-imperialists employed racist arguments. The author cites Albert J. Beveridge, Theodore Roosevelt, and Josiah Strong as representative imperialists and Andrew Carnegie, Carl Schurz, and David Starr Jordan as anti-imperialists.

10:547   Nalty, Bernard C. *Strength for the Fight: A History of Black Americans in the Military*. New York: Free Press, 1986. Chapter 5 provides an overview of black responses to the Cuban crisis and Philippine insurrection and of black service in both theaters. The author concludes that this service had little discernible effect on the status of African-Americans in American society.

10:548   Park, James William. *Latin American Underdevelopment: A History of Perspectives in the United States, 1870–1965*. Chapters 2 and 3 examine the period 1870–1921. Relatively fixed negative U.S. images of Latin America as an area inhabited by racially inferior people, who were restricted by authoritarian Spanish culture and a tropical climate, provided the backdrop to U.S. intervention and domination (9:390).

10:549   Payne, James Robert. "Afro-American Literature of the Spanish-American War." *Melus* 10

(Fall 1983): 19–32. Focusing on the work of Charles Frederick White, Sutton E. Griggs, Paul Laurence Dunbar, and James Weldon Johnson, this article explores the themes of innocence, idealism, and disillusionment among black writers.

10:550 Salvatore, Ricardo D. "The Enterprise of Knowledge: Representational Machines of Informal Empire." In *Close Encounters of Empire: Writing the Cultural History of U.S.–Latin American Relations,* ed. Gilbert M. Joseph, Catherine C. LeGrand, and Ricardo D. Salvatore, 69–104. Durham, NC: Duke University Press, 1998. Salvatore explores imagery, representations, and constructions as essential parts of imperial discourse and the establishment of informal U.S. empire.

GENDER

10:551 Apple, Lindsey. "The Evolution of a Family: Gendered 'Spheres' and the Spanish-American War." *Register of the Kentucky Historical Society* 94 (Fall 1996): 363–95. This essay examines the relationship between Lt. Charles D. Clay and his wife Mariah Pepper Clay during the Cuban and Philippine wars, in which Charles served. Both struggled with traditional gender roles and expectations, and changes were gradual and incremental rather than abrupt or extensive.

10:552 Bederman, Gail. *Manliness & Civilization: A Cultural History of Gender and Race in the United States, 1880–1917.* Viewing gender as an ideological process, the author examines the strategies for remaking American manhood at the turn of the century. One chapter focuses on Theodore Roosevelt's crucial role in this process and the implications for U.S. imperialism (9:159).

10:553 Hill, Patricia R. *The World Their Household: The American Woman's Foreign Mission Movement and Cultural Transformation, 1870–1920.* Foreign missionary societies comprised the largest nineteenth-century U.S. women's movement. The foreign mission crusade provided an outlet for the energies and talents of American women and, by seeking to uplift heathen women abroad, served as a medium for the transmission of U.S. cultural values (9:171).

10:554 Hoganson, Kristin L. *Fighting for American Manhood: How Gender Politics Provoked the Spanish-American and Philippine-American Wars.* New Haven: Yale University Press, 1998. This well-researched and argued book contends that a full understanding of these wars requires seeing gender as the central motivating ideology in the United States. This analytical construct places concern for American manhood and the manly American political system at the forefront of explanations for U.S. actions.

10:555 Kaplan, Amy. "Romancing the Empire: The Embodiment of American Masculinity in the Popular Historical Novel of the 1890s." *American Literary History* 2 (Winter 1990): 659–90. The author argues that popular romance novels offer insight into the imperial culture and discourse that provided the bases for the transition from continental to insular and informal empire.

10:556 Papachristou, Judith. "American Women and Foreign Policy, 1898–1905: Exploring Gender in Diplomatic History." The article argues that the 1898–1905 period witnessed a theretofore unprecedented activism and involvement of women in foreign policy issues. The activist organizers and their followers in women's clubs and organizations developed a distinct female culture separate from male values. This women's culture emphasized anti-imperialism, peace, and Christian values (9:176).

10:557 Pettegrew, John. "'The Soldier's Faith': Turn of the Century Memory of the Civil War and the Emergence of Modern American Nationalism." *Journal of Contemporary History* 31 (January 1996): 49–73. This article asserts that the shared memory of the Civil War and expressions of masculinity provided the foundation for turn-of-the-century nationalism and war in Cuba and the Philippines. The author looks especially at how this shared memory and ideology was conveyed through Memorial Day celebrations and veterans' reminiscences.

10:558 Santiago-Valles, Kelvin A. "'Higher Womanhood' Among the 'Lower Races': Julia McNair Henry in Puerto Rico and the 'Burden' of 1898." *Radical History Review* 73 (Winter 1999): 47–73. Through the writings and actions of Julia McNair Henry, this article demonstrates the portrayal of the Puerto Rican colonial subjects as feminine, infantile, brown-skinned, and needing the white civilizing mission provided by U.S. men and women.

10:559   Silber, Nina. *The Romance of Reunion: Northerners and the South, 1865–1900.* Chapel Hill: University of North Carolina Press, 1993. This study analyzes the romantic perspective of middle- and upper-class northerners that helped promote reunion and reconciliation with the south. The final chapter examines the place of the new southern man in the militaristic, patriotic culture that both promoted and resulted from the war of 1898.

10:560   Sneider, Allison L. "The Impact of Empire on the North American Woman Suffrage Movement: Suffrage Racism in an Imperial Context." *UCLA Historical Journal* 14 (1994): 14–32. Focusing on Susan B. Anthony and the imperial acquisition of Hawaii and the Philippines, this essay examines the change of turn-of-the-century suffragism from a rationale based on equal rights to one featuring Anglo-Saxon superiority and racial hierarchy.

10:561   Tyrrell, Ian. *Woman's World/Woman's Empire: The Woman's Christian Temperance Union in International Perspective, 1880–1930.* This book examines the World Woman's Christian Temperance Union and its promotion of temperance, peace, Christianity, and female emancipation. The U.S. branch of the WCTU was the dominant one, and its work provided new careers and opportunities for turn-of-the-century women while also conveying western American values and institutions via cultural imperialism (9:184).

10:562   Wexler, Laura. *Tender Violence: Domestic Visions in an Age of U.S. Imperialism.* Chapel Hill: University of North Carolina Press, 2000. Wexler argues that photographs taken by white female photojournalists provided racial images reinforcing the Anglo-Saxon ideology of whiteness, helping provide the foundation for U.S. imperialism at the turn of the twentieth century. She includes more than 150 photographs taken between 1898 and 1904. Chapters 1, analyzing pictures taken aboard Admiral George Dewey's ship *Olympia,* and 4, examining the 1904 St. Louis World's Fair, intersect most directly with American foreign policy.

Reaction of Great Britain and Boer War

10:563   Anderson, Stuart. *Race and Rapprochement: Anglo-Saxonism and Anglo-American Relations, 1895–1904.* This book argues that Anglo-Saxonism as an intellectual belief and racial conception was crucial, together with strategic and economic considerations, to rapprochement at the turn of the century. Racial affinity was important to mutual Anglo-American support during the Spanish-Cuban-American and Boer Wars (9:301). See also Anderson, "Racial Anglo-Saxonism and the American Response to the Boer War," *Diplomatic History* 2 (Summer 1978): 219–36.

10:564   Blake, Nelson M. "England and the United States, 1897–1899." In *Essays in History and International Relations, in Honor of George Hubbard Blakeslee,* ed. Dwight E. Lee and George E. McReynolds, 257–83. Worcester, MA: Clark University, 1949. This essay describes the origins of Anglo-American cordiality and cooperation during the war with Spain.

10:565   Campbell, Alexander E. *Great Britain and the United States, 1895–1903.* London: Longmans, 1960. Reprint 1974 (Greenwood Press). This British author chronicles the growing Anglo-American cordiality and British sympathy for the United States in the war of 1898. See also his *Anglo-American Understanding, 1893–1903* (Baltimore: Johns Hopkins University Press, 1957).

10:566   Campbell, Charles Soutter. *Anglo-American Understanding, 1898–1903.* Baltimore: Johns Hopkins Press, 1957. In chapter 2, the author examines British support for U.S. war with Spain and subsequent imperial expansion as a vital precursor to successful negotiations over the isthmian canal and Alaska boundary.

10:567   Einstein, Lewis. "British Diplomacy in the Spanish-American War." *Proceedings of the Massachusetts Historical Society* 76 (1964): 30–54. This essay examines British ambassador to the United States Sir Julian Pauncefote's effort to organize a unified

European protest following McKinley's war message of April 11, 1898. Arthur James Balfour, the First Lord of the Treasury, blocked this initiative.

10:568　Ferguson, John H. *American Diplomacy and the Boer War.* Philadelphia: University of Pennsylvania Press, 1939. Ferguson found the U.S. consular service in South Africa inadequate and incompetent, but the United States remained neutral while protecting its rights and interests. Boer attempts to enlist support in the United States were counterproductive.

10:569　Gatewood, Willard B., Jr. "Black Americans and the Boer War, 1899–1902." *South Atlantic Quarterly* 75 (Spring 1976): 226–44. Blacks initially viewed the war as merely a struggle between white men, but as the war progressed and African-Americans learned more about the Boers and their treatment of people of color, they came to favor the British, who seemed to act more liberally toward black Africans.

10:570　Gelber, Lionel M. *The Rise of Anglo-American Friendship: A Study in World Politics, 1898–1906.* New York: Oxford University Press, 1938. This pioneer and stylish study has been largely superseded by the work of Charles Soutter Campbell.

10:571　Hammond, John Hays. *The Autobiography of John Hays Hammond.* 2 vols. New York: Farrar and Rinehart, 1935. An American engineer-capitalist, Hammond was in South Africa during the Boer War and attempted to define and defend U.S. interests.

10:572　Heindel, Richard Heathcote. *The American Impact on Great Britain, 1898–1914: A Study of the United States in World History.* Philadelphia: University of Pennsylvania Press, 1940. Chapters 4 and 5 examine British responses to the war of 1898 and its aftermath. The British welcomed U.S. imperialism, if not all its manifestations, anticipated a united front favoring Anglo-Saxonism and British interests, and criticized U.S. colonial policy. In an interesting forecast of work to come, the author asserts that proper international history goes beyond diplomatic issues to consider economic, social, educational, and political influences.

10:573　Keto, C. Tsehloane. "The Aftermath of the Jameson Raid and American Decision Making in Foreign Affairs, 1896." *Transactions of the American Philosophical Society* 70, part 8 (1980): 1–49. This extended essay examines the arrest of seven American engineers involved in the Johannesburg plot of 1895, the response of the U.S. public and government, and the long-term influence on U.S. policies toward South Africa.

10:574　Knee, Stuart E. "Anglo-American Understanding and the Boer War." *Australian Journal of Politics and History* 30, no. 2 (1984): 196–208. This article examines the bases for U.S. benevolent neutrality and effective support of Great Britain in the Boer War. Mutual interests and objectives are emphasized over race or kinship.

10:575　Mulanax, Richard B. *The Boer War in American Politics and Diplomacy.* Lanham, MD: University Press of America, 1994. This book focuses on how the Boer War affected U.S. diplomacy rather than how U.S. policy affected the war. The author compliments Secretary of State Hay's diplomatic skill in preserving the emerging U.S.-British rapprochement and cites international geopolitical considerations as more responsible for U.S. policy than economics.

10:576　Neale, R. G. *Great Britain and United States Expansion: 1898–1900.* East Lansing: Michigan State University Press, 1966. Neale contends that Anglo-American rapprochement has been exaggerated and that it was not significant in deterring European mediation. See also his "British-American Relations during the Spanish-American War: Some Problems," *Historical Studies: Australia and New Zealand* 6 (November 1953): 72–89.

10:577　Noer, Thomas J. *Briton, Boer, and Yankee: The United States and South Africa, 1870–1914.* Kent, OH: Kent State University Press, 1978. In chapter 4, treating the Boer War, Noer argues that the promotion of U.S. interests explains the McKinley administration's support for Great Britain. American business eyed economic gains; missionaries anticipated converts; and pro-British spokesmen emphasized the racial and governmental benefits of an English victory and control.

10:578 Olasky, Marvin. "Social Darwinism on the Editorial Page: American Newspapers and the Boer War." *Journalism Quarterly* 65 (Summer 1988): 420–24. Based on an examination of seven newspapers, the author determines that the U.S. press expressed some sympathy for the plight and aspirations of the Boers, but the editors concluded that international politics, Anglo-Saxonism, economics, and the promotion of civilization argued against opposing the British.

10:579 Orde, Anne. *The Eclipse of Great Britain: The United States and British Imperial Decline, 1895–1956.* Chapter 1 (1895–1914) of this study examines the beginning of the process in which Britain receded from and the United States rose to the status of world power. During this period, the British made concessions but did not see the U.S. ascent as a serious challenge in vital areas such as trade or imperial possessions (9:315).

10:580 Perkins, Bradford. *The Great Rapprochement: England and the United States, 1895–1914.* New York: Atheneum, 1968. Perkins provides a graceful and nicely detailed account of the evolution of closer Anglo-American relations.

10:581 Reuter, Bertha A. *Anglo-American Relations during the Spanish-American War.* New York: Macmillan Company, 1924. This is an older but still worthwhile work.

10:582 Seed, Geoffrey. "British Reactions to American Imperialism Reflected in Journals of Opinion, 1898–1900." *Political Science Quarterly* 73 (June 1958): 254–72. British opinion supported the United States because of racial affinity, the idea of the white man's burden, and U.S. support for British in China.

10:583 _____. "British Views of American Policy in the Philippines Reflected in Journals of Opinion, 1898–1907." *Journal of American Studies* 2 (April 1968): 49–64. British journals approved of U.S. acquisition of the islands but criticized American colonial management.

10:584 Torre del Río, Rosario de la. "En torno al 98. Ingleses y españoles en el Pacifico [Around '98: The English and Spanish in the Pacific]." In *Las rela-* *ciones internacionales en la España contemporánea [International Relations of Contemporary Spain]*, ed. Luis Alvarez Gutiérrez and Juan Bautista Vilar, 211–22. Murcia: Secretariado de Publicaciones de la Universidad de Murcia, 1989. Using only Spanish diplomatic archives, the author thoughtfully analyzes Spain's relations with Great Britain in Asia in the 1890s, including the 1896 Filipino insurrection and the 1898 U.S.-Spanish negotiations over the future of the Philippines.

10:585 _____. *Inglaterra y España en 1898 [England and Spain in 1898]*. Madrid: Eudema, 1988. Relying on extensive archival research, this is a detailed account of Spanish-British relations in 1898. Spanish-British friction eventually focused on Gibraltar, an issue that was not resolved until after the conclusion of U.S.-Spanish negotiations in Paris.

Reaction of Germany and Samoan Settlement

10:586 Alvarez Gutiérrez, Luis. "La diplomacia alemana ante el conflicto hispano-norteamericano de 1897–1898: primeras tomas de posicion [German Diplomacy before the Spanish-American Conflict of 1897–1898: First Assumptions of Position]." *Hispania (Spain)* 54 (January-April 1994): 201–56. Using German and Spanish diplomatic archives and focusing largely on 1897, the author shows William II's interest in taking Spain's side in the growing controversy with the United States. William's ministers successfully restrained his impulsiveness.

10:587 Bailey, Thomas A. "Dewey and the Germans at Manila Bay." *American Historical Review* 45 (October 1939): 59–81. The author corrects Dewey's view that the German fleet deliberately sought to hinder the U.S. blockade of Manila.

10:588 Doerries, Reinhard R. "1898: A New Beginning or Historical Continuity." In *1898: su significado para Centroamérica y el Caribe ¿Cesura, Cambio, Continuidad? [1898: Its Meaning for Central America and the Caribbean: Pause, Change, or Con-*

tinuity?], ed. Walther L. Bernecker, 37–46. Frankfurt am Main: Vervuert, 1998. The author places the 1898 war with Spain in the context of a German-American competition for influence in the Pacific and Caribbean that foreshadows the political decisions of World War I.

10:589 Elizalde Pérez-Grueso, María Dolores. *España en el Pacífico, la colonia de las Islas Carolinas (1885–1899): un modelo colonial en el contexto internacional del imperialismo [Spain in the Pacific: The Colony of the Caroline Islands (1885–1899): A Colonial Model in the International Context of Imperialism].* Madrid: Consejo Superior de Investigaciones Cientíticas, Instituto de Cooperación para el Desarrollo, 1992. Based heavily on archival sources, this is a detailed account of the Caroline Islands in international politics. The author explains the foreign polices of Spain, Great Britain, the United States, and Japan related to the islands and their ultimate sale to Germany in 1899. A briefer account is printed in: "La proyección de España en al Pacífico durante la época del imperialismo," *Hispania (Spain)* 53 (January-April 1993): 277–95.

10:590 _____. "La venta de las Islas Carolinas, un nuevo hito en el 98 español [The Sale of the Caroline Islands: A New Discovery for Spain of '98]." In *Estudios históricos. Homenaje a los profesores José María Jover Zamora y Vincente Palacio Atard [Historical Studies in Honor of Professors José María Jover Zamora and Vincente Palacio Atard]*, ed. Universidad Complutense de Madrid, Departamento de Historia Contemporánea, 1: 361–80. Madrid: Departamento de Historia Contemporánea Facultad de Geografía e Historia Universidad Complutense, 1990. The author examines Spanish, German, British, American, and Japanese interests in the Caroline Islands prior to the 1898 war. She concludes that at the end of the war Germany obtained the islands in a colonial redistribution of Spanish spoils that British and Americans approved.

10:591 Farmer, Tristram E. "Too Little, Too Late: The Fight for the Carolines, 1898." *Naval History* 3 (Winter 1989): 20–25. The author believes that the United States failed to foresee the military importance of the Caroline Islands. Through political inexperience and administrative confusion, the McKinley administration allowed Germany to acquire them.

10:592 Hardach, Gerd. "Bausteine für ein grosseres Deutschland: Die annexation der Karolinen und Marianen, 1898–1899 [Foundation for a Greater Germany: The Annexation of the Carolines and Marianas, 1898–1899]." *Zeitschrift für Unternehmengeschichte* 33, no. 1 (1988): 1–21. This article explains German interests in the Caroline Islands and Berlin's diplomatic policies that led to their purchase.

10:593 Hugo, Markus M. "'Manila tiene que ser nuestra!' La guerra de 1898 en la política y el público del Imperio Alemán ['Manila Should Be Ours!': The 1898 War in the Politics and Public View of Imperial Germany]." In *Los significados del 98. La sociedad española en la génesis del siglo XX [The Significance of '98: Spanish Society at the Beginning of the 20th Century]*, ed. Octavio Ruiz-Manjón Cabeza and María Alicia Langa Laorga, 175–88. Madrid: Fundación ICO, Biblioteca Nueva Universidad Complutense de Madrid, 1999. This essay describes Germany's diplomatic interests in the Spanish-Cuban-American War. The author focuses on German-Spanish relations, especially German attempts to gain colonial compensation in the Pacific.

10:594 _____. "'Uncle Sam I Cannot Stand, for Spain I Have No Sympathy': An Analysis of Discourse about the Spanish-American War in Imperial Germany, 1898–1899." In *European Perceptions of the Spanish-American War of 1898,* ed. Sylvia L. Hilton and Steve J. S. Ickringill, 71–93. Bern: Peter Lang, 1999. This careful analysis of German newspaper publications relates German interpretations of the war to domestic prejudices and stereotypes. Germans cared little for Spain and were critical of an American interventionism and imperialism that foreshadowed greater German-American rivalry.

10:595 Quinn, Pearl E. "Diplomatic Struggle for the Carolines, 1898." *Pacific Historical Review* 14 (September 1945): 290–302. This article examines the German-American wrangling over the fate of the Carolines.

10:596 Rigby, Barry R. "The Origins of American Expansion in Hawaii and Samoa, 1865–1900." The author argues that imperialism in Samoa was based on the actions of people in the field rather than decisions made in Washington. After the Civil War, land and commodity speculators sought economic opportunity in Samoa. U.S. naval officers helped them. These early interests eventually culminated in U.S. annexation (9:521).

10:597 Rippy, J. Fred. "The European Powers and the Spanish-American War." *James Sprunt Historical Studies* 19 (1927): 12–52. This article focuses on Germany's diplomacy.

10:598 Shippee, Lester B. "Germany and the Spanish-American War." *American Historical Review* 30 (July 1925): 754–77. The author believes that Germany coveted the Philippines and possibly would have gotten them if the United States had not annexed them.

Other Nations

10:599 Belfiglio, Valentine J. "L'Italia e la guerra ispano-americana [Italy and the Spanish-American War]." *Rivista Marittima* 118 (May 1985): 75–87. The author states that of the continental great powers, Italy was the most favorable toward the United States. Preceding the war there was a large Italian emigration to the United States, and many Italian-Americans volunteered to fight in the U.S. army.

10:600 Bootsma, Nico A. "Reactions to the Spanish-American War in the Netherlands and in the Dutch East Indies." In *European Perceptions of the Spanish-American War of 1898,* ed. Sylvia L. Hilton and Steve J. S. Ickringill, 35–52. Bern: Peter Lang, 1999. This article examines Dutch neutrality during the war and Dutch newspaper responses to the war, both in the Netherlands and in the East Indies. The Netherlands had minor territorial disputes with Spain over East Indian islands that posed a potential problem. The Dutch press criticized Spanish colonial misrule and U.S. imperialism.

10:601 Brown, Robert C. "Goldwin Smith and Anti-Imperialism." *Canadian Historical Review* 43 (June 1962): 93–101. This article concludes that Canadians supported the United States during the war and the territorial expansion that followed.

10:602 Eyre, James K., Jr. "Japan and the Ameri-

can Acquisition of the Philippines." *Pacific Historical Review* 11 (March 1942): 55–71. Japan opposed German acquisition of the Philippines and therefore supported American annexation.

10:603 _____. "Russia and the American Acquisition of the Philippines." *Mississippi Valley Historical Review* 28 (March 1942): 539–62. Eyre believes that Russia's interest in the islands spurred the U.S. decision to acquire them.

10:604 Gilmore, N. Ray. "Mexico and the Spanish-American War." *Hispanic American Historical Review* 43 (November 1963): 511–25. Although Mexico was neutral during the war, it sympathized with Spain.

10:605 Ickringill, Steve J. S. "Silence and Celebration: Ulster, William McKinley and the Spanish-American War." In *European Perceptions of the Spanish-American War of 1898,* ed. Sylvia L. Hilton and Steve J. S. Ickringill, 95–110. Bern: Peter Lang, 1999. This article examines Irish nationalist and unionist newspaper views on McKinley and the war. Local politics shaped newspaper editorials toward McKinley, who was of Scotch-Irish descent, and U.S. intervention in Cuba. Irish immigrants in the United States resulted in a strong pro-American bias during the war, but nationalists and unionists divided over the possibility of an Anglo-Saxon alliance.

10:606 Leynseele, H. Va. "Leopold II et les Philippines en 1898 [Leopold II and the Philippines in 1898]." *Bulletin des Séances l'Académie Royale des Sciences Coloniales* 2, no. 6 (1956): 923–37. When the United States hesitated to take the Philippines, Leopold was keenly interested in acquiring them.

10:607 MacDonald, J. Frederic. "Jules Cambon et la menace de l'impérialisme américain (1898–1899) [Jules Cambon and the Menace of American Imperialism (1898–1899)]." *Revue d'Histoire Diplomatique* 86 (August-September 1986): 247–55. Based on Jules Cambon's diplomatic reports, this article reveals the French diplomat's many concerns about menacing U.S. imperialistic ambitions that threatened European interests as the United States entered various world arenas.

10:608 Mount, Graeme S. "Friendly Liberator or Predatory Aggressor? Some Canadian Impressions of the United States during the Spanish-American War." *Canadian Journal of Latin American and Caribbean Studies* 11, no. 22 (1986): 59–70. This article examines views of some of the Canadian press, public officials, and business interests toward the Spanish-Cuban-American War. Canadians were largely anti-Spanish and pro-American and apparently did not fear the effect that an American victory might have on Canadian-U.S. relations.

10:609 Offner, John L. "The United States and France: Ending the Spanish-American War." *Diplomatic History* 7 (Winter 1983): 1–21. The author details the role France took in ending the war. France wanted an early end to the war to limit American expansionism. McKinley conducted U.S. diplomacy, making the key U.S. decisions on ending the war.

10:610 _____. "Washington Mission: Archbishop Ireland on the Eve of the Spanish-American War." *Catholic Historical Review* 73 (October 1987): 562–75. The Vatican sought through the diplomatic efforts of Archbishop John Ireland to prevent a war between the United States and Spain. Although Ireland's efforts led to the modification of U.S. and Spanish positions, Ireland's mission failed as the Cubans refused to cooperate and Congress demanded U.S. intervention.

10:611 Popkova, Ludmila N. "Russian Press Coverage of American Intervention in the Spanish-Cuban War." In *European Perceptions of the Spanish-American War of 1898,* ed. Sylvia L. Hilton and Steve J. S. Ickringill, 110–32. Bern: Peter Lang, 1999. This article about the Russian press includes Russian diplomatic correspondence and provides the editorial views of the state-subsidized press. The pro-American liberal press was restricted. The Russian government sought good relations with the United States but worried about U.S. imperialism, particularly in Asia.

10:612 Ricard, Serge. "The French Press and Brother Jonathan: Editorializing the Spanish-American Conflict." In *European Perceptions of the Spanish-American War of 1898,* ed. Sylvia L. Hilton and Steve J. S. Ickringill, 131–49. Bern: Peter Lang,

1999. The French press was critical of U.S. diplomacy, intervention in Cuba, and imperial expansionism at the conclusion of the war. The French press also worried about a growing American friendship with Great Britain and the emergence of the United States as a world power.

10:613 Rossini, Daniela. "The American Peril: Italian Catholics and the Spanish-American War, 1898." In *European Perceptions of the Spanish-American War of 1898,* ed. Sylvia L. Hilton and Steve J. S. Ickringill, 167–79. Bern: Peter Lang, 1999. Italy was in turmoil in 1898, and the American intervention in Cuba was seen through Italian domestic politics. Italian Catholics divided over the role of church and state. Conservatives condemned the separation of church and state in the United States, while liberals favored "Americanism." This article focuses on the conservative Catholic press and Vatican politics.

10:614 Sears, Louis Martin. "French Opinion of the Spanish-American War." *Hispanic American Historical Review* 7 (February 1927): 25–44. French newspapers were sharply critical of U.S. policies toward Spain.

10:615 Shelby, Charmion C. "Mexico and the Spanish-American War: Some Contemporary Expressions of Opinion." In *Essays in Mexican History,* ed. Thomas E. Cotner, Carlos Eduardo Castañeda, and Charles W. Hackett, 209–28. Austin: University of Texas Institute of Latin American Studies, 1958. Reprint 1972 (Greenwood Press). Although sympathetic to Spain, Mexico remained neutral because of economic dependency and fear of a U.S. invasion.

10:616 Slupetzky, Nicole. "Austria and the Spanish-American War." In *European Perceptions of the Spanish-American War of 1898,* ed. Sylvia L. Hilton and Steve J. S. Ickringill, 181–94. Bern: Peter Lang, 1999. Relying on diplomatic archives, this article examines Austria-Hungary's foreign policy concerning European attempts to prevent American intervention in Cuba, wartime neutrality, and concerns about U.S. imperialism. Slupetzky also describes Austrian newspaper editorials about Vienna's foreign policies.

The United States and Europe, 1900–1914

Contributing Editor

NANCY MITCHELL
North Carolina State University

Contents

Introduction

Hindsight makes the study of U.S.-European relations from 1900 to 1914 unsettling. We know that within a few years American soldiers would be fighting in Europe. We expect foreshadowing. There is none.

I have tried to systematically read the literature in English, German, French, Italian, Spanish, and Portuguese. (The citations in Danish, Russian, and Afrikaans are incidental.) The lack of interest in U.S. relations with Europe in the years immediately preceding World War I cuts across time and space. The most respected studies of Italian, French, and German foreign policy in the early years of the twentieth century and the published collections of these countries' diplomatic documents barely mention the United States. Likewise, studies of American foreign relations in these years barely mention Europe and the selections on European countries in *FRUS* are overwhelmingly concerned with petty crime, passports, and festivities.

Yes, there are some areas of intersection, but they all concern extra-European affairs. Britain and the United States wrestle with the Panama Canal, Mexico, and Canadian issues—fish, seals, borders. Germany and the United States tussle over Latin America, particularly in Venezuela and Brazil. In the early years of the century, Spain and the United States are still mopping up some of the residue of their recent war. Belgium garners moderate interest in the Congo, American Jews are exercised about Tsarist antisemitism, and Washington continues to wrangle with Copenhagen over the Danish West Indies. Teddy Roosevelt has a major role at Portsmouth, the United States is a player at Algeciras, and the European powers and the United States spar and cooperate in China.

This grab bag of incidents exists amid an almost total lack of interest in the core U.S.-European relationship, with the exception of a substantial body of literature on the growth of Anglo-American cooperation. While trade links were increasing across the Atlantic, they have not attracted extensive attention. Diplomatic historians have recently turned their attention to cultural relations, an important and fertile field, but I have not tried to systematically include studies of European-American cultural exchange for fear the porous borders of this pursuit would open the floodgates. I have tried instead to compile a comprehensive bibliography of U.S.-European relations, 1900–1914, with an emphasis on diplomatic, economic, and political affairs.

Though generally the *Guide* does not pretend to record Ph.D. scholarship, I have cited thirty-two dissertations in this chapter, some not in English, because they often supply information and analyses otherwise unavailable.

Published Primary Materials

11:1   Yale Law School. *The Avalon Project: 20th Century Documents.* New Haven: Yale University, 2001–. Website. This excellent collection of treaties includes all the inaugural speeches of the presidents; the Hague conventions, 1899 and 1907; the Hay-Bunau-Varilla Treaty, 1903; the copyright proclamation with Austria-Hungary, 1907; and the arbitration convention between the United States and Austria-Hungary, 1909. See at http://www.yale.edu/lawweb/avalon/avalon.htm.

11:2   Alaskan Boundary Tribunal, United States, and Great Britain. *Proceedings of the Alaskan Boundary Tribunal, Convened at London, under the Treaty between the United States of America and Great Britain, Concluded at Washington, January 24, 1903, for the Settlement of Questions . . . with Respect to the Boundary Line between the Territory of Alaska and the British Possessions in North America.* 7 vols. Washington, DC: Government Printing Office, 1904. This is the final report, plus appendices, of the 1903 Alaska boundary tribunal.

11:3   International Boundary Commission. *Joint Report upon the Survey and Demarcation of the Boundary between Canada and the United States from Tongass Passage to Mount St. Elias.* Ottawa and Washington: International Boundary Commissioners, 1952. This is a key source on the U.S.-Canadian boundary dispute. It includes the text of the 1903 convention, detailed maps, and letters, clarifications, and agreements pursuant to it.

11:4   Higgins, A. Pearce, ed. *The Hague Peace Conferences and Other International Conferences Concerning the Laws and Usages of War: Texts of Conventions with Commentaries.* Cambridge, UK: Cambridge University Press, 1909. This useful volume includes texts of peace conventions from 1899 to 1907 and commentaries on them.

11:5   Scott, James Brown. *The Hague Peace Conferences of 1899 and 1907.* 2 vols. Baltimore: Johns Hopkins Press, 1909. The essays in volume 1 comprehensively describe and assess the declarations, conventions, and resolutions passed at both conferences. The second volume is a collection of the relevant primary documents: the instructions to the U.S. delegates; their official reports and diplomatic correspondence; and the texts of the laws developed at the conferences.

11:6   U.S. Department of State. *Foreign Relations of the United States, 1900–1914.* 17 vols. Washington, DC: Government Printing Office, 1902–1922. The volumes covering 1900–1914 include correspondence relating to commercial and consular matters in Austria-Hungary, Belgium, Bulgaria, Denmark, France, Germany, Great Britain, Greece, Italy, Luxembourg, Montenegro, Netherlands, Norway, Portugal, Romania, Russia, Spain, Sweden, and Switzerland. (Some volumes omit one or more of these countries.) In addition, several volumes include more extensive correspondence on particular issues. "1902, Appendix 1" is about whaling and sealing claims against Russia; "1903" discusses the Venezuela crisis and the Alaskan boundary; "1904" continues the boundary debate and adds fisheries concerns; it also deals with the beginning of the Russo-Japanese War; "1905" continues with the war and also has a brief correspondence with Germany about commercial treaties; discussions with London about Canada continue; "1906, part 1" continues the discussions with Berlin and London; "1906, part 2" includes extensive papers on the Algeciras conference, the Geneva (Red Cross) conference of 1906, and the second Hague peace conference; "1907, part 1" continues commercial discussions with Germany and Canadian disputes with England; "1907, part 2" includes documents on the Portsmouth treaty and the second Hague conference; "1908" adds correspondence with various European powers about arbitration conventions and the investigation of affairs in

the Belgian Congo, and continues discussions of Canadian issues with London; "1909" continues the concerns of the previous volume and adds papers on the Third International Conference on Maritime Law, in Brussels; "1910" continues all the concerns of the previous year and adds the proclamation of conventions of the second Hague conference; "1911" continues the routine commercial, consular, and arbitration matters; "1912" adds a few documents on the wreck of the *Titanic;* "1913" (which does not mention Germany) includes correspondence with London about the tolls dispute and with various European powers about the Radiotelegraph convention; "1914" deals with the coming of war (1:93).

11:7   _____. *Foreign Travels of the Secretaries of State, 1866–1990.* Elihu Root traveled to Newfoundland in 1905 to gather information on the fisheries question and went on an official visit to Canada in 1907. Philander Knox went to St. Thomas in 1912 to converse with Danish officials about the purchase of the islands (9:27).

11:8   Root, Elihu. *North Atlantic Coast Fisheries Arbitration at the Hague: Argument on Behalf of the United States.* Cambridge, MA: Harvard University Press, 1917. This volume, edited by Robert Bacon and James Brown Scott, has an extensive foreword laying out the history of the fisheries dispute and the essence of Root's argument before the Hague. It then offers a verbatim transcript of his thorough and detailed treatment of the subject, with maps.

11:9   Bourne, Kenneth, Donald Cameron Watt, and Great Britain, Foreign Office, eds. *British Documents on Foreign Affairs—Reports and Papers from the Foreign Office Confidential Print. Part I: From the Mid-Nineteenth Century to the First World War. Series C: North America, 1837–1914.* 15 vols. Bethesda, MD: University Publications of America, 1986. Volumes 9–11 of this collection deal with controversies concerning Alaska, the Panama Canal, the Philippines, and Hawaii from 1877 to 1905. Volumes 12–15 deal with trade disputes, the Panama Canal, Canada, and the Mexican revolution. They also include observations on U.S. society, culture, labor, women's suffrage, race, and immigration. This is available on microfilm from the Congressional Information Service Publications and University Publications of America Research Collections.

11:10   Gooch, G. P., and Harold Temperley, eds. *British Documents on the Origins of the War, 1898–1914.* 11 vols. London: H.M.S.O., 1926–1938. This British collection, like its German and French counterparts, focuses primarily on European international rivalries, but it does contain materials relating to U.S. diplomacy.

11:11   France. Commission de publications des document relatifs aux origines de la guerre de 1914. *Documents diplomatiques français (1871–1914) [French Diplomatic Documents, 1871–1914].* 41 vols. Paris: Imprimerie Nationale, 1929–1959. The documents in this basic French collection are arranged chronologically, but each volume has a list of documents arranged by subject. A small number deal with relations with the United States. In series 2 (1901–1911), volumes 4–6 deal with the Russo-Japanese War, the Far East, China, and Morocco; volume 7 includes the Treaty of Portsmouth; volumes 9 and 10 make passing reference to the United States at Algeciras and the second Hague conference.

11:12   Germany, Auswärtiges Amt, Johannes Lepsius, Albrecht Mendelssohn-Bartholdy, and Friedrich Thimme, eds. *Die grosse Politik der europäischen Kabinette, 1871–1914 [The Great Policy of the European Cabinets, 1871–1914].* 40 vols. Berlin: Deutsche Verlagsgesellschaft für Politik und Geschichte, 1922–1927. This is the essential first source for German diplomatic documents of the period. While relations with the United States are marginal, issues that involve correspondence with Washington are included, including the Spanish-American War (vol. 15), Boer War (vol. 16), Venezuela crisis (vol. 17), Russo-Japanese War (vol. 19), Moroccan crises (vol. 20), Algeciras conference (vol. 21), second Hague conference (vol. 23), German-American Chinese entente (vol. 25), and concerns about the integrity of China and the Manchurian railway (vol. 32).

11:13   Dugdale, E. T. S., ed. *German Diplomatic Documents, 1871–1914.* 4 vols. New York: Harper, 1928–1931. These four volumes draw from documents earlier published in *Die grosse Politik der europäischen Kabinette, 1871–1914,* edited by Johannes Lepsius, Albrecht Mendelssohn-Bartholdy, and Friederich Wilhelm Karl Thimme. Volumes 3 and 4 contain references to U.S.-German relations

from 1900 to 1914, but the selection is so partial as to be virtually useless.

11:14   Italy, Commissione per la pubblicazione dei documenti diplomatici [Commission for the Publication of Diplomatic Documents]. *I documenti diplomatici italiani [Italian Diplomatic Documents].* Rome: Libreria dello Stato, 1952. Volumes 4–6 of the third series of these volumes culled from the Italian diplomatic archives briefly mention commercial and ceremonial relations with the United States.

11:15   Basenko, IU. V., V. I. Zhuravleva, and Evgenii IUr'evich Sergeev, eds. *Rossiëiïa i SShA—diplomaticheskie otnosheniëiïa 1900–1917 [Russia and USA—diplomatic relations 1900–1917].* Moscow: MFD, 1999. This useful collection of documents includes memos, reports, and letters detailing the major issues that affected U.S.-Russian relations from 1900 to 1917. It is particularly strong on the Far East.

11:16   Bodnar, John, ed. *Voices from Ellis Island: An Oral History of American Immigration.* Microfiche. Bethesda, MD: LexisNexis Academic and Library Solutions, 1987. These 185 pages of microfiche, with a printed guide, include 200 interviews with immigrants, most from Europe, who passed through Ellis Island from 1892 to 1924.

11:17   Vecoli, Rudolph J., ed. *American Immigrant Autobiographies. Part 1: Manuscript Autobiographies from the Immigration History Research Center, University of Minnesota.* Bethesda, MD: LexisNexis Academic and Library Solutions, 1988. These seven microfilm reels with a printed guide include primary documents about European immigrants to the United States in the early twentieth century.

11:18   Yans-McLaughlin, Virginia, ed. *Records of the Immigration and Naturalization Service. Series A: Subject Correspondence Files. Part 3: Ellis Island, 1900–1933.* Microfilm. Bethesda, MD: LexisNexis Academic and Library Solutions, 1992–1995. These eighteen reels of microfilm with a printed guide are drawn from the main subject file of the commissioner-general of immigration from 1900 to 1933. They detail virtually every aspect of immigration, from health to deportation.

11:19 _____. *Records of the Immigration and Naturalization Service. Series A: Subject Correspondence Files. Part 4: European Investigations, 1898–1936.* Microfilm. Bethesda, MD: LexisNexis Academic and Library Solutions, 1992–1995. These ten reels of microfilm with a printed guide bring together the many investigative reports made of conditions in Europe, including health, the activities of emigration societies, and the role of steamship companies 1898–1917, and include a diverse array of primary sources, including advertisements. Alan M. Kraut, editorial adviser.

11:20 Gibson, Hugh. *A Journal from our Legation in Belgium.* Garden City, NY: Doubleday, Page and Company, 1917. Gibson, who was secretary of the U.S. legation in Brussels, kept a diary from July through December 1914. It is long-winded and chatty but manages to give a good sense of an American's impressions of Belgium in the first months of the war.

11:21 Grew, Joseph C. *Turbulent Era: A Diplomatic Record of Forty Years, 1904–1945.* 2 vols. Boston: Houghton Mifflin, 1940. Reprint 1970 (Books for Libraries Press). In this lively and astute diary, which includes excerpts from his letters, Joseph Grew includes brief descriptions of his early years in Russia as 3d secretary at the U.S. embassy (1907–1908), as 2d secretary in Berlin (1908–1919), and as 1st secretary in Vienna (1911–1912) and Berlin (1912–1914). He also comments on the professionalism of the service. Edited by Walter Johnson, with Nancy Harvison Hooker.

11:22 Hay, John, ed. *Letters of John Hay and Extracts from Diary.* 3 vols. New York: Gordion Press, 1969. These letters, originally compiled (by Henry Adams and Clara Louise Hay) in a 1908 private edition, include comments on U.S. relations with Europe, but they are highly edited and include no index.

11:23 Seymour, Charles, ed. *The Intimate Papers of Colonel House Arranged as a Narrative by Charles Seymour.* 4 vols. Boston: Houghton Mifflin Company, 1926–1928. This highly edited selection from the diary and papers of Edward House, Woodrow Wilson's adviser, includes accounts of his frequent talks with European leaders and reveals his antipathy for the kaiser. The original, which is much more reliable, is at Yale.

11:24 Seager, Robert, II, and Doris D. Maguire, eds. *Letters and Papers of Alfred Thayer Mahan.* These well-edited volumes provide insight into Mahan's views of U.S. international relations and are particularly important in showing the evolution of his view of the German naval threat. The third volume covers the 1902–1914 period (9:6).

11:25 Moore, John Bassett. *The Collected Papers of John Bassett Moore.* 7 vols. New Haven: Yale University Press, 1944. Moore's long and illustrious career included stints as a member of the Permanent Court of Arbitration in the Hague (1912–1938) and counselor to the Department of State (1913–1914). This seven-volume collection of his writings includes articles on international law, touching on issues concerning U.S. relations with Europe, such as the Hay-Pauncefote Treaty and second Hague conference.

11:26 Contosta, David R., and Jessica R. Hawthorne, eds. *Rise to World Power: Selected Letters of Whitelaw Reid, 1895–1912.* This slim volume includes a selection of letters of Whitelaw Reid (1837–1912), best known as owner of the *New York Tribune,* from his years as ambassador to London (1905–1912) when, despite the growing warmth between the United States and England, he had to douse several fires, especially those fanned by the Newfoundland fishermen's imposition of restrictions on U.S. fishermen in violation of U.S. treaty rights. These letters also include trenchant comments about international affairs (9:83).

11:27 Lodge, Henry Cabot, Sr., and Charles F. Redmond, eds. *Selections from the Correspondence of Theodore Roosevelt and Henry Cabot Lodge, 1884–1918.* This selection is particularly useful in revealing the evolution of Roosevelt's perception of the German threat. While Lodge remained adamant that the German navy posed a serious threat to the United States, Roosevelt began to backpedal after he assumed the presidency in 1901. Originally published in 1925 (9:86).

11:28 Morison, Elting E., with John Morton Blum, eds. *The Letters of Theodore Roosevelt.* This beautifully edited selection of Roosevelt's letters includes many revealing and pithy comments on the president's evolving views on relations with the key European powers (9:7).

11:29   Root, Elihu. *Addresses on International Subjects*. Cambridge, MA: Harvard University Press, 1916. This volume, compiled and edited by Robert Bacon and James Brown Scott, includes speeches on the Panama Canal tolls dispute, international law, the 1907 Hague conference, and the termination of the 1832 treaty with Russia.

11:30   Gwynn, Stephen, ed. *The Letters and Friendships of Sir Cecil Spring-Rice: A Record*. 2 vols. Boston: Houghton Mifflin Company, 1929. Correspondence with Woodrow Wilson, Henry Adams, Theodore Roosevelt, Lord Grey, and Balfour is provided in this annotated collection of letters of the British ambassador to America, including discussions of Spring-Rice's friendship with Roosevelt and of his tenure as ambassador in Washington (1913–1918).

11:31   Nevins, Allan, ed. *The Letters and Journal of Brand Whitlock*. 2 vols. New York: D. Appleton-Century Company, 1936. Brand Whitlock (1869–1934), newspaperman, writer, lawyer, and progressive mayor of Toledo, was the U.S. minister to Belgium (1913–1922), where he had an uneventful time until the German occupation, which led him to help organize the Commission for Relief in Belgium. Nevins provides a biographical introduction.

11:32   Ogden, Robert Morris, ed. *The Diaries of Andrew D. White*. Ithaca: Cornell University Library, 1959. The very brief diary entries from White's time as U.S. ambassador at Berlin (1897–1903) give a good sense of the daily round at an important European embassy.

11:33   Link, Arthur S., et al., eds. *The Papers of Woodrow Wilson*. 69 vols. Princeton: Princeton University Press, 1966–1994. Although this meticulously edited selection reveals Wilson's lack of interest in Europe before the outbreak of the war, it remains an indispensable source for understanding U.S.-European relations during his presidency. Volumes 27–31 cover the years 1913 and 1914.

Bibliographies and Other Reference Works

11:34   Howlett, Charles F., ed. *The American Peace Movement: References and Resources*. Boston: G. K. Hall, 1991. This impressive annotated bibliography includes a very useful chapter on international peace movements. See also Howlett's useful essay, *The American Peace Movement: History and Historiography* (Washington: American Historical Association, 1985).

11:35   Pommerin, Reiner, and Michael Frohlich, eds. *Quellen zu der deutsch-amerikanischen Beziehungen, 1776–1917 [Sources on German-American Relations, 1776–1917]*. Darmstadt: Droste, 1996. This volume includes both bibliographies and documents. Roughly sixty pages of documents relate to the 1900–1915 period.

Historiography

11:36   Coletta, Paolo E. "The Diplomacy of Theodore Roosevelt and William Howard Taft." In *American Foreign Relations, A Historiographical Review*, ed. Gerald K. Haines and J. Samuel Walker, 91–113. Westport, CT: Greenwood Press, 1981. In this useful historiographical essay, Coletta refers to TR's relations with Europe, particularly Great Britain and Germany, his role at Portsmouth and Algeciras, and to Taft's negotiations with London about Canadian and Latin American issues.

11:37   Collin, Richard H. "Symbiosis versus Hegemony: New Directions in the Foreign Relations Historiography of Theodore Roosevelt and William Howard Taft." *Diplomatic History* 19 (Summer 1995): 473–97. This bibliographic essay deals at length with changing interpretations of U.S. imperialism in Latin America and briefly discusses U.S. cultural imperialism in Europe.

11:38 Combs, Jerald A. *American Diplomatic History: Two Centuries of Changing Interpretations.* Combs's nuanced description of the changing tides in the analysis of U.S. foreign relations deals, in passing, with the evolution of U.S. attitudes toward the European powers (2:5).

11:39 Grantham, Dewey W. "Theodore Roosevelt in American Historical Writing, 1945–1960." *Mid-America* 43 (January 1961): 3–35. This lucid and useful survey of the historiography of Theodore Roosevelt pays particular homage to Beale, *Theodore Roosevelt and the Rise of America to World Power* (1956) (9:84).

11:40 Holbo, Paul S. "Perspectives on American Foreign Policy, 1890–1916: Expansion and World Power." This survey deals almost exclusively with the 1890s but provides some useful guideposts for the study of the subsequent decades (10:53).

11:41 Hull, James P. "From Many, Two: A Bibliographic History of Canadian-American Relations." This is an excellent, comprehensive, and analytical overview of the historiography of U.S.-Canadian relations (5:75).

11:42 Leopold, Richard W. "The Mississippi Valley and American Foreign Policy, 1890–1941: An Assessment and an Appeal." *Mississippi Valley Historical Review* 37 (March 1951): 625–42. Leopold's appeal for more research on regional attitudes toward U.S. foreign policy remains relevant a half century after it was written. He laments that scholars had not yet investigated the Mississippi valley's attitudes toward the great powers at the beginning of the twentieth century.

11:43 Leuchtenburg, William E. "Progressivism and Imperialism: The Progressive Movement and American Foreign Policy, 1898–1916." In this important article, Leuchtenburg asserts that the progressives' domestic goals and support for imperialism stemmed from the same roots: a tendency to judge actions by their results rather than their means and "an almost religious faith in the democratic mission of America" (9:223). See Siracusa, "Progressivism, Imperialism, and the Leuchtenburg Thesis, 1952–1974: An Historiographical Appraisal" (1974) (10:61).

11:44 Saveth, Edward Norman. *American Historians and European Immigrants, 1875–1925.* New York: Columbia University Press, 1948. This rather dated book remains a useful survey of the often implicit attitudes of U.S. historians in the early years of the twentieth century toward European immigrants, especially those not from England.

Overviews

11:45 Askew, William C., and J. Fred Rippy. "The United States and Europe's Strife, 1908–1913." *Journal of Politics* 4 (February 1942): 68–79. From the Bosnian crisis of 1908–1909, through the Agadir crisis, the Turco-Italian war (1911–1912), and the two Balkan wars (1912–1913), the U.S. government maintained a largely disinterested reserve.

11:46 Cashman, Sean Dennis. *America in the Age of the Titans: The Progressive Era and World War I.* New York: New York University Press, 1988. This overview includes a chapter discussing the relationship between American and European art and literature of the day.

11:47 Coolidge, Archibald Cary. *The United States as a World Power.* New York: Macmillan Company, 1908. Coolidge offers interesting and still valuable information on relations with Germany, Russia, France, and Britain in the late nineteenth and very early twentieth centuries.

11:48 Dennis, Alfred L. P. *Adventures in American Diplomacy, 1896–1906 (From Unpublished Documents).* This early work contains some still valuable chapters on Anglo-American relations, the isthmian question, East Asia, including the Russo-Japanese War, the Jewish question in Eastern Europe, African concerns, the Hague conferences, and the Algeciras conference (10:68).

11:49 Dobson, John M. *America's Ascent: The United States Becomes a Great Power, 1880–1914.* Three chapters on U.S. policy in the Far East and Latin America deal with U.S.-European relations in passing (9:131).

11:50   Esthus, Raymond A. "Isolationism and World Power." *Diplomatic History* 2 (Spring 1978): 117–29. In this excellent article, Esthus asks, "How did the United States' new-found world power status at the beginning of the 20th century affect its foreign policy?" He then examines U.S. relations with Europe and notes "the persistence of traditional attitudes and practices": the United States remained isolationist in terms of involvement in European politics despite occasional limited forays under TR during the first Moroccan crisis and the Russo-Japanese War (which stand in sharp contrast with the absence of U.S. involvement in the second Moroccan crisis and the Balkan wars).

11:51   Fiebig-von Hase, Ragnhild. "Amerikanische Friedensbemühungen in Europa, 1905–1914 [American Peace Initiatives in Europe, 1905–1914]." In *Liberalitas: Festschrift für Erich Angermann zum 65 Geburtstag [Liberalitas: Essays in Honor of Erich Angermann on his 65th Birthday]*, ed. Norbert Finzsch and Hermann Wellenreuther, 285–318. Stuttgart: Franz Steiner, 1992. Fiebig-von Hase analyzes the much discussed role of Theodore Roosevelt, and the all but forgotten role of William Howard Taft, in the Morocco crises.

11:52   Gardner, Lloyd C. "American Foreign Policy, 1900–1921: A Second Look at the Realist Critique of American Diplomacy." In *Towards a New Past: Dissenting Essays in American History*, ed. Barton J. Bernstein, 202–31. New York: Pantheon Books, 1968. In this critique of the realist explanation of U.S. foreign policy, Gardner stresses the role of the arbitration and peace movements in the early years of the twentieth century.

11:53   Iriye, Akira. *From Nationalism to Internationalism: US Foreign Policy to 1914.* Boston: Routledge and Kegan Paul, 1977. Iriye focuses on U.S. expansion but also analyzes the adjustment of the European powers to America's achievement of great power status after the Spanish-American War, stressing London's currying of Washington's favor. This volume includes a selection of seventy-nine key documents on U.S. foreign affairs.

11:54   Kuehl, Warren F. *Seeking World Order: The United States and International Organization to 1920.* This volume includes a good discussion of the 1907 Hague conference (2:214).

11:55   LaFeber, Walter. *The American Search for Opportunity, 1865–1913.* This excellent overview focuses on U.S. policies toward Latin America and Asia; its treatment of Washington's changing relationships with the European powers is brief but deft (2:40). See also LaFeber's "The 'Lion in the Path': The U.S. Emergence as a World Power," *Constitution Magazine* 3 (Spring-Summer 1991): 14–23.

11:56   Langer, William L. *The Diplomacy of Imperialism, 1890–1902.* See chapter 10 of this Guide (10:77). Originally published in 1935.

11:57   Ninkovich, Frank A. *Modernity and Power: A History of the Domino Theory in the Twentieth Century.* Chicago: University of Chicago Press, 1994. This provocative extended essay analyzes the attitudes of Roosevelt, Taft, and Wilson toward the emergence of the United States as a great power at the beginning of the twentieth century.

11:58   _____. *The Wilsonian Century: U.S. Foreign Policy since 1900.* This stimulating rethinking of the Wilsonian paradigm emphasizes the power of "myths" or ideologies in the construction of twentieth-century U.S. foreign policy. Ninkovich gives a broad overview of U.S. relations with Europe at the beginning of the century (2:84).

11:59   Nouailhat, Yves-Henri. *Les États-Unis: l'avènement d'une puissance mondiale, 1898–1933 [The United States: The Emergence of a World Power, 1898–1933].* Paris: Editions Richelieu, 1973. This excellent textbook includes only a brief section on U.S. relations with Europe in the early twentieth century, focusing on the Alaska boundary dispute, the Algeciras conference, and the first and second Hague conferences.

11:60   Perkins, Dexter. *The Monroe Doctrine, 1867–1907.* This volume (9:147) includes a detailed examination of the 1902–1903 Anglo-German-Italian blockade of Venezuela based on a limited array of U.S. and British documents and on Vagts, *Deutschland und die Vereinigten Staaten in der Weltpolitik* (1935) (11:230).

11:61   Powaski, Ronald E. *Toward an Entangling Alliance: American Isolationism, Internationalism, and Europe, 1901–1950.* Westport, CT: Greenwood

Press, 1991. This text includes a concise survey of U.S.-European relations in the decade before World War I.

11:62 Pratt, Julius W. *Challenge and Rejection: America and World Leadership, 1900–1921.* New York: Macmillan, 1967. This overview of U.S. foreign policy in the first decades of the twentieth century deals only in passing with U.S.-European relations prior to World War I.

11:63 Ricard, Serge, and James Bolner, Sr., eds. *La république impérialiste: l'expansionnisme et la politique extérieure des États-Unis, 1885–1909: études et documents [The Imperial Republic: Expansionism and the Foreign Policy of the United States, 1885–1909: Studies and Documents].* This collection of essays by American and European scholars touches only marginally on U.S.-European relations from 1900 to 1915. While most of the essays concern the Spanish-American War, Ricard's own "Theodore Roosevelt: The Right Man in the Right Place" (205–14) is pertinent to this chapter (10:82).

11:64 Taylor, A. J. P. *The Struggle for Mastery in Europe, 1848–1918.* Oxford: Clarendon Press, 1954. Taylor's international history of nineteenth- and early-twentieth-century Europe discusses several U.S. connections.

11:65 Wells, Samuel F., Jr. *The Challenges of Power: American Policy, 1900–1921.* Lanham, MD: University Press of America, 1990. This concise survey includes a brief, pithy chapter on U.S.-European relations. Wells notes that "American diplomatists before 1914 paid markedly less attention to European developments than to those in Latin America and Asia. A century of American isolation from European political rivalries had created a diplomatic tradition that statesmen refused to violate for anything short of a major threat to the nation." (Originally published as a portion of *The Ordeal of World Power: American Diplomacy since 1900,* by Samuel F. Wells, Jr., Robert H. Ferrell, and David F. Trask [Boston: Little, Brown, 1975].)

11:66 Wiebe, Robert H. *The Search for Order, 1877–1920.* Wiebe's discussion of how the transformation undergone by the United States affected foreign policy is brief and focuses more on U.S. rela-

tions with Latin America and Asia than with Europe, a region Americans considered "old and tired and declining." See chapter 9 of this Guide (9:157).

11:67 Williams, William Appleman. *The Tragedy of American Diplomacy.* Williams's analysis of U.S. imperialism in the 1890s and early twentieth century offers an influential backdrop to the understanding of U.S.-European relations in the period (2:97). First published in 1959.

11:68 Zakaria, Fareed. *From Wealth to Power: The Unusual Origins of America's World Role.* This analysis of the U.S. rise to world power includes brief discussions of Washington's changing relations with London and Berlin at the turn of the century. Zakaria argues that despite its great wealth, the United States was hindered in its rise by its weak central government (2:82).

STATE DEPARTMENT AND SECRETARIES OF STATE

11:69 Bemis, Samuel Flagg, ed. *The American Secretaries of State and Their Diplomacy.* 20 vols. Vol. 9. The essays on John Hay by Alfred L. P. Dennis and on Elihu Root by James Brown Scott cover all the major U.S.-European issues of their tenure as secretaries of state (1:48).

11:70 Graebner, Norman A., ed. *An Uncertain Tradition: American Secretaries of State in the Twentieth Century.* See chapter 2 of this Guide for information on the essays useful to an examination of U.S.-European relations of the period (2:192).

11:71 Werking, Richard Hume. *The Master Architects: Building the United States Foreign Service, 1890–1913.* This thorough bureaucratic history of the U.S. Department of State at the turn of the century deals in passing with U.S. relations with Europe (2:200).

11:72 _____. "Selling the Foreign Service: Bureaucratic Rivalry and Foreign-Trade Promotion, 1903–1912." *Pacific Historical Review* 45 (May 1976): 185–207. Werking details the early efforts of the federal government to promote trade, particularly through the consular service and the Department of

Commerce and Labor, and, in so doing, deals with U.S.-European relations in passing. See also his "Bureaucrats, Businessmen, and Foreign Trade: The Origins of the United States Chamber of Commerce," *Business History Review* 52 (Autumn 1978): 321–41.

11:73　West, Rachel. *The Department of State on the Eve of the First World War.* Athens, GA: University of Georgia Press, 1978. In this largely bureaucratic analysis of the failure of the Department of State to predict the outbreak of war in Europe, West strongly criticizes Washington's neglect of European affairs.

PRESIDENTS

11:74　Beale, Howard K. *Theodore Roosevelt and the Rise of America to World Power.* Beale is mainly concerned with Roosevelt's efforts to establish an American presence in world politics. He emphasizes U.S. relations with European powers over Morocco, Latin America, China, the Philippines, and the Hague conference of 1907 (9:84).

11:75　Collin, Richard H. *Theodore Roosevelt, Culture, Diplomacy, and Expansion: A New View of American Imperialism.* This wide-ranging discussion of American cultural and political imperialism includes a detailed analysis of U.S.-British relations and of the Alaskan boundary dispute (9:85).

11:76　Esthus, Raymond A. *Theodore Roosevelt and the International Rivalries.* Waltham, MA: Ginn-Blaisdell, 1970. Reprint 1982 (Regina Books). This is a useful, concise survey of Roosevelt's diplomacy toward East Asia and Europe, with particular emphasis on the first Morocco crisis and the Algeciras conference. Esthus relies primarily but not exclusively on U.S. documents.

11:77　Marks, Frederick W., III. "Morality as a Drive Wheel in the Diplomacy of Theodore Roosevelt." *Diplomatic History* 2 (Winter 1978): 43–62. Marks argues that Theodore Roosevelt had a moralistic approach to international relations, namely that nations were bound by the same moral code as individuals. To prove his point, he examines three case studies: Panama, the Alaska boundary settlement, and the 1906 "Gentleman's Agreement" with Japan.

11:78　_____. *Velvet on Iron: The Diplomacy of Theodore Roosevelt.* Lincoln: University of Nebraska Press, 1979. Marks seeks to correct the myths and misconceptions that have arisen concerning Roosevelt's seemingly contradictory personality and policies.

11:79　Scholes, Walter V., and Marie V. Scholes. *The Foreign Policies of the Taft Administration.* Columbia: University of Missouri Press, 1970. In analyzing U.S. relations with Latin America and the Far East, the Scholeses briefly discuss U.S. relations with Europe during the Taft administration. Their view of Taft is critical, and their discussion of his policy in the Far East is more penetrating than their analysis of Latin American affairs.

11:80　Link, Arthur S. *The Higher Realism of Woodrow Wilson, and Other Essays.* Nashville: Vanderbilt University Press, 1971. Most of the essays in this volume deal with domestic issues but several treat Anglo-American relations during the Wilson presidency.

ECONOMICS AND TRADE

11:81　Becker, William H. *The Dynamics of Business-Government Relations: Industry & Exports, 1893–1921.* This is a detailed examination of the legislation, bureaucracy, and patterns of U.S. foreign trade from 1893 to 1921. Its subject relates intimately to U.S.-European relations, but Becker explicitly mentions Europe only in passing (9:186).

11:82　_____. "Foreign Markets for Iron and Steel, 1893–1913: A New Perspective on the Williams School of Diplomatic History." *Pacific Historical Review* 44 (May 1975): 233–48. Becker questions the validity of the thesis that trade expansion was a necessary condition for the economic well-being of the United States from the 1890s to World War I. See also the rejoinder in the same issue (249–55) by Howard B. Schonberger, "William H. Becker and the New Left Revisionists: A Rebuttal," Becker's rejoinder (255–63), and Schonberger's last word (264).

11:83　Bruchey, Stuart. *Enterprise: The Dynamic Economy of a Free People.* Cambridge, MA: Harvard

University Press, 1990. Bruchey's survey of the development of American capitalism includes a wide-ranging, well-documented chapter on the expansion of U.S. trade and banking abroad at the beginning of the twentieth century.

11:84   Goodhart, C. A. E. *The New York Money Market and the Finance of Trade, 1900–1913*. Cambridge, MA: Harvard University Press, 1969. In a technical book dealing with the relationship between capital flows and foreign trade, Goodhart describes how offsetting capital flows prior to the inception of the Federal Reserve System kept the American economy more stable. If Goodhart is right—he admits that the data on capital flows are inconclusive—then seasonal fluctuations in agricultural trade were not as economically disruptive as previously believed. He concludes that the New York money market was prepared to manage the nation's monetary policy after 1913.

11:85   Hannigan, Robert E. "Dollars and Diplomacy: United States Foreign Policy, 1909–1913." Ph.D. dissertation, Princeton University, 1978. Hannigan argues that Taft's foreign policy was a coherent and fairly sophisticated attempt to respond to the early trends of the twentieth century. He focuses on commercial policy and includes discussions of the disputes with Canada.

11:86   Isaacs, Asher. *International Trade, Tariff and Commercial Policies*. Chicago: Richard D. Irwin, Inc., 1948. This admirably clear text summarizes the history of U.S. and European tariff policy.

11:87   Kaplan, Edward S., and Thomas W. Ryley. *Prelude to Trade Wars: American Tariff Policy, 1890–1922*. This is a rather pedestrian survey of tariff history (9:206).

11:88   Kaufman, Burton I. "The Organizational Dimension of United States Economic Foreign Policy, 1900–1920." *Business History Review* 46 (Spring 1972): 17–44. U.S. foreign trade and investment from 1900 to 1920 united business and banking interests with the federal government to promote expansion. What emerged, Kaufman concludes, was an integrated, efficient organizational structure, which facilitated commercial and financial expansion, especially through modification of the nation's antitrust laws.

11:89   Lake, David A. *Power, Protection, and Free Trade: International Sources of U.S. Commercial Strategy, 1887–1939*. In this clear examination of U.S. commercial strategy, Lake details British decline and U.S. opportunism from the Dingley Act of 1897 to the Underwood Act of 1913, stressing the relationship between U.S. policy and the international economic environment (9:208). See also his "Export, Die, or Subsidize: The International Political Economy of American Agriculture, 1875–1940," *Comparative Studies in Social History* 31 (January 1989): 81–105.

11:90   Novack, David, and Matthew Simon. "Some Dimensions of the American Commercial Invasion of Europe, 1871–1914: An Introductory Essay." *Journal of Economic History* 24 (December 1964): 591–605. This analysis shows the complexity of the American trade invasion of Europe in the half century prior to World War I, contending that the European market for U.S. exports, though important, fell continuously between 1871 and 1914. The authors outline the composition of American export trade to Europe and delineate several "stages" of the trade.

11:91   Rosenberg, Emily S. *Financial Missionaries to the World: The Politics and Culture of Dollar Diplomacy, 1900–1930*. Cambridge, MA: Harvard University Press, 1999. Rosenberg moves beyond traditional diplomatic history to incorporate cultural, intellectual, and social history to shed light on the complex and often contradictory forces that shaped U.S. global capitalism in the twentieth century. While her study concentrates on U.S. policies toward Latin America and Asia, it has ramifications for the understanding of U.S. policies toward the European powers before World War I.

11:92   _____. "Foundations of United States International Financial Power: Gold Standard Diplomacy, 1900–1905." Rosenberg examines the U.S. government's attempt to bring nations onto a gold exchange standard to stabilize exchange rates and promote the nation's growing economic power. These reforms laid the basis for Washington's eventual challenge to London's financial supremacy (9:196).

11:93   Taussig, Frank W. *The Tariff History of the United States*. 8th ed. New York: G. P. Putnam's Sons,

1931. This remains a useful discussion of key tariff legislation. First published in 1888 and periodically updated thereafter to cover new tariff legislation.

11:94   Vanderlip, Frank A. "The American 'Commercial Invasion' of Europe: Second Paper—Italy, Austria, Germany; Third Paper—England, France and Russia." *Scribner's Magazine,* January-March 1902, 3–22; 194–213; 287–306. This three-part article by prominent New York banker and former assistant secretary of the treasury, Frank Vanderlip, is a thorough and glowing assessment of American economic penetration of Europe.

11:95   Verdier, Daniel. *Democracy and International Trade: Britain, France, and the United States, 1860–1990.* This theoretical and factual account includes a long chapter on British-French-American trade from 1887 to 1913. Verdier argues that trade at the time became a divisive issue in Britain and the United States, while in France it remained in the realm of consensus politics (9:200).

11:96   Wilkins, Mira. "An American Enterprise Abroad: American Radiator Company in Europe, 1895–1914." *Business History Review* 43 (Fall 1969): 326–46. The American Radiator Company, spurred by domestic conditions, developed gradually, without planning. It only sought government aid on one occasion, and that for information. This was not a typical case.

11:97   _____. *The Emergence of Multinational Enterprise: American Business Abroad from the Colonial Era to 1914.* Cambridge, MA: Harvard University Press, 1970. Wilkins traces the vigorous and broad-based spread of U.S. direct investment abroad, focusing on 1870–1914. While she devotes more space to a discussion of the Western Hemisphere (including an excellent chapter on Canada), her treatment of U.S. companies' penetration of the European market is new and insightful. She shows that the presumption that most direct investment was in the extractive industries and utilities is a canard, looking at not only copper, oil, aluminum, and electric companies but also gunpowder, tobacco, automobile, and insurance companies.

11:98   _____. *The History of Foreign Investment in the United States to 1914.* This very careful analysis includes a discussion of the response of the U.S. public to foreign investments (9:201).

11:99   Wolman, Paul. *Most Favored Nation: The Republican Revisionists and U.S. Tariff Policy, 1897–1912.* In this detailed and readable book, Wolman argues that the McKinley, Roosevelt, and Taft administrations turned away from traditional Republican protectionism to a regime of tariff reduction and reciprocity, especially with Germany, France, and Canada. His analysis of U.S.-German trade tensions is particularly insightful (9:214).

MILITARY HISTORY AND ARMS LIMITATION

11:100   Braisted, William Reynolds. "The Navy in the Early Twentieth Century, 1890–1941." In *A Guide to the Sources of United States Military History,* ed. Robin Higham, 344–77. This essay concisely explains the rationale for the new navy, a subject with profound effects on U.S.-European relations (9:242).

11:101   Challener, Richard D. *Admirals, Generals, and American Foreign Policy, 1898–1914.* Princeton: Princeton University Press, 1973. This wide-ranging study of the development of the U.S. navy touches on U.S. relations with Europe, particularly concerning crises in Latin America and Asia.

11:102   Dorwart, Jeffery M. *The Office of Naval Intelligence: The Birth of America's First Intelligence Agency, 1865–1918.* This crisp and able account shows the quickening interest in more serious and professional capabilities, not only in the Office of Naval Intelligence but in the navy at large. Dorwart includes an interesting chapter on U.S. fears of Germany in the first years of the twentieth century (9:246).

11:103   Grenville, J. A. S. "Diplomacy and War Plans in the United States, 1890–1917." *Transactions of the Royal Historical Society* ser. 5, 11 (1961): 1–21. Grenville's trenchant discussion of the European complications of U.S. policy in the Far East remains useful. See also his "American Naval Preparations for War with Spain, 1896–1898," *Journal of American Studies* 2 (April 1968): 33–47.

11:104   Grenville, J. A. S., and George Berkeley Young. *Politics, Strategy, and American Diplomacy: Studies in Foreign Policy, 1873–1917.* See chapter 9 of this Guide (9:136).

11:105   Hart, Robert A. *The Great White Fleet: Its Voyage around the World, 1907–1909.* Boston: Little, Brown, 1965. This account of Theodore Roosevelt's dispatch of the American fleet on a global tour reflects America's growing power in world affairs. It has been largely superseded by Reckner, *Teddy Roosevelt's Great White Fleet* (1982) (11:108).

11:106   Leiner, Frederick C. "The Unknown Effort: Theodore Roosevelt's Battleship Plan and International Arms Limitation Talks, 1906–1907." *Military Affairs* 48 (October 1984): 174–79. Leiner argues that Theodore Roosevelt's plan for limiting battleship size in 1906, in response to the development of the dreadnought, was "serious and sincere."

11:107   O'Brien, Phillips Payson. *British and American Naval Power: Politics and Policy, 1900–1936.* Westport, CT: Praeger, 1998. O'Brien argues that the differences in British and American naval development in the early twentieth century reflected differences in their national strategies.

11:108   Reckner, James R. *Teddy Roosevelt's Great White Fleet.* Annapolis: Naval Institute Press, 1982. The Great White Fleet docked in Mediterranean ports in 1909. Reckner describes its welcome in Italy, subdued because of the recent earthquake in Sicily and Calabria, and its brief shore leave in Greece, France, and Gibraltar.

11:109   Safford, Jeffrey J. *Wilsonian Maritime Diplomacy, 1913–1921.* New Brunswick: Rutgers University Press, 1978. This competent overview emphasizes the domestic debates surrounding Wilson's maritime policy. It deals with 1913–1915 in a summary fashion.

11:110   Spector, Ronald H. *Professors of War: The Naval War College and the Development of the Naval Profession.* Newport, RI: Naval War College Press, 1977. This lively volume includes a discussion of the U.S. navy's use of war games and war plans to counter the threat it believed the German navy presented.

11:111   Sprout, Harold, and Margaret Sprout. *The Rise of American Naval Power, 1776–1918.* This classic study provides useful background to understanding U.S.-German-British naval competition at the beginning of the twentieth century (7:56). First published in 1939.

11:112   Still, William N., Jr. *American Sea Power in the Old World: The United States Navy in European and Near Eastern Waters, 1865–1917.* This overview includes a useful chapter on the navy and European powers, 1898–1910 (9:263).

11:113   Tate, Merze. *The Disarmament Illusion: The Movement for a Limitation of Armaments to 1907.* New York: Macmillan Company, 1942. Reprint 1971 (Russell and Russell). Tate focuses on the 1899 Hague conference, emphasizing that disarmament is a political problem.

CULTURE, RACE, TECHNOLOGY, AND MEDIA

11:114   Anderson, Emmet H. "Appraisal of American Life by French Travelers (1860–1914)." Ph.D. dissertation, University of Virginia, 1963. This solid dissertation is an interesting analysis of French travelers' views of U.S. society, politics, religion, education, and press, based on extensive reading of French travel literature and memoirs. It includes observations on the travelers' perceptions of the status of women and minorities in the United States.

11:115   Crunden, Robert M. *American Salons: Encounters with European Modernism, 1885–1917.* This study of international cultural exchange at the beginning of the twentieth century discusses American artists in London and Paris as well as European artists in New York (9:166).

11:116   Endy, Christopher. "Travel and World Power: Americans in Europe, 1890–1917." This nuanced study discusses the wide-ranging political and social impact of the growth of American travel in Europe in the early twentieth century. Endy pays particular attention to the effect of tourism on U.S. relations with Britain, France, and Germany (9:168).

11:117   Fischer, Diane P., ed. *Paris 1900: The*

"American School" at the Universal Exposition. New Brunswick: Rutgers University Press, 1999. The essays by Linda J. Docherty ("Why Not a National Art? Affirmative Responses in the 1890s"), Robert W. Rydell ("Gateway to the 'American Century': The American Representation at the Paris Universal Exposition of 1900"), Gail Stavitsky ("The Legacy of the 'American School': 1901–1938"), and Gabriel P. Weisberg ("The French Reception of American Art at the Universal Exposition of 1900") examine the deliberate construction of a distinctively American school at this important international exhibition.

11:118 Headrick, Daniel R. *The Invisible Weapon: Telecommunications and International Politics, 1851–1945.* New York: Oxford University Press, 1991. Headrick discusses the competition in cable and radio between the United States and the major European powers from 1900 to 1914.

11:119 Heald, Morrell. *Transatlantic Vistas: American Journalists in Europe, 1900–1940.* Kent, OH: Kent State University Press, 1988. This history of foreign correspondents includes an interesting section on the "first wave" of American journalists abroad (1900–1920). Heald focuses on three journalists from the *Chicago Daily News:* Edward Price Bell, posted to London in 1899; Paul Scott Mowrer, to Paris in 1910; and Raymond Swing, who went to Berlin in the same year.

11:120 Iriye, Akira. *Cultural Internationalism and World Order.* In a penetrating and wide-ranging chapter, Iriye analyzes prewar internationalism (2:246).

11:121 Lea, Homer. *The Day of the Saxon.* New York: Harper and Brothers, 1912. In this book, the idiosyncratic American author, Homer Lea (who also wrote *The Valor of Ignorance* [New York: Harper and Brothers, 1909]), predicts and bemoans the collapse of the British empire due to the excessive materialism of the British people.

11:122 Levenstein, Harvey A. *Seductive Journey: American Tourists in France from Jefferson to the Jazz Age.* Levenstein includes five chapters on U.S. travelers in France from 1870 to 1914, discussing both luxury and middle-class travel, detailing the mechanics and the destinations, but paying little attention to either French or American perceptions. The

work includes an interesting discussion of the differences between male and female travelers (2:320).

11:123 Rapson, Richard L. *Britons View America: Travel Commentary, 1860–1935.* Seattle: University of Washington Press, 1971. This survey of British travelers' impressions of the United States is organized topically, with sections on American character, culture, youth, women, education, religion, and politics.

11:124 Rosenberg, Emily S. *Spreading the American Dream: American Economic and Cultural Expansion, 1890–1945.* The first three chapters of this seminal, wide-ranging book deal with U.S. expansion at the turn of the century not just in terms of the high diplomacy of the period, but also with respect to economic, cultural, and scientific affairs (9:151).

11:125 Rydell, Robert W. *All the World's a Fair: Visions of Empire at American International Expositions, 1876–1916.* While Rydell focuses on representations of empire at world fairs, his stimulating book includes discussions of the European participation in the Pan-American Exposition in Buffalo, 1901, where French entrepreneurs built the African village, and in the Louisiana Purchase Exposition in St. Louis, 1904, which included a Boer War exhibit (9:180).

11:126 Schaeper, Thomas J., and Kathleen Schaeper. *Cowboys into Gentlemen: Rhodes Scholars, Oxford, and the Creation of an American Elite.* New York: Berghahn Books, 1998. This history of the Rhodes scholarship program (1902–) provides an interesting window on U.S.-British cultural exchange before World War I.

11:127 Strout, Cushing. *The American Image of the Old World.* This wide-ranging history relies on U.S. literary and travel writing about Europe at the turn of the century as well as a broad array of magazine articles and politicians' letters to describe the changing American view of Europe (6:159).

11:128 Trommler, Frank. "Inventing the Enemy: German-American Cultural Relations, 1900–1917." In *Confrontation and Cooperation: Germany and the United States in the Era of World War I, 1900–1924,* ed. Hans-Jürgen Schröder, 99–125. Providence, RI:

Berg Publishers, 1993. Trommler argues that the growing animosity between Germany and the United States, which culminated in the declaration of war in 1917, was preceded by two decades of cultural alienation so intense that even the most skeptical contemporaries were alarmed. See also Elliott Shore, "The *Kultur* Club," in this volume (127–33).

PEACE MOVEMENTS

11:129   Beales, A. C. F. *The History of Peace: A Short Account of the Organised Movements for International Peace.* London: G. Bell, 1931. This volume includes a good summary of international peace movements before World War I.

11:130   Brock, Peter. *Pacifism in the United States, from the Colonial Era to the First World War.* Princeton: Princeton University Press, 1968. This massive survey includes extended discussions of U.S. peace movements at the beginning of the twentieth century, with particular emphasis on the influence of church-based groups, although Brock also covers nonsectarian groups as well. He indicates the internationalist efforts of these pacifists to establish, for example, an international court, and the influence of Europeans, such as Leo Tolstoy, on their thinking.

11:131   Chambers, John Whiteclay, II, ed. *The Eagle and the Dove: The American Peace Movement and United States Foreign Policy, 1900–1922.* Syracuse: Syracuse University Press, 1991. This volume includes over twenty contemporary sources on the U.S. peace movement from 1900 to 1914. Subjects include the second Hague conference and the arbitration treaties. First published in 1976.

11:132   Chatfield, Charles, with Robert Kleidman. *The American Peace Movement: Ideals and Activism.* New York: Twayne Publishers, 1992. This well-written survey includes a chapter on the "first century of peace reform" in the United States, which touches on transnational movements in the early twentieth century.

11:133   Herman, Sondra R. *Eleven against War: Studies in American Internationalist Thought, 1898–1921.* Stanford, CA: Hoover Institution Press, Stanford University, 1969. This fascinating study of the thought of U.S. internationalists at the beginning of the twentieth century sheds light on the transnational nature of the movement. The U.S. pacifist movement was distinguished from its European counterparts mainly by its diversity. Among Herman's subjects are Elihu Root, Nicholas Murray Butler, Hamilton Holt, Josiah Royce, Jane Addams, Thorstein Veblen, Theodore Marburg, and Woodrow Wilson.

11:134   Johnson, Robert David. *The Peace Progressives and American Foreign Relations.* Cambridge, MA: Harvard University Press, 1995. Johnson includes a chapter on the precursors to the peace progressives of the 1920s. He focuses on congressional politics but mentions some foreign issues, such as reciprocity with Canada (1911) and the Panama tolls controversy (1914).

11:135   Kuehl, Warren F. *The Library of World Peace Studies.* Microfiche. New York: Clearwater Publishing, 1978. This collection of 1,253 microfiche reproduces selections from twenty-three peace periodicals, most of which are from the United States, with a few each from England, Switzerland, and France. Although it spans the nineteenth and twentieth centuries, it thoroughly covers the early years of the twentieth century, a time of activism in the international peace movement. Reissued by University Publications of America Research Collections.

11:136   Lutzker, Michael A. "The Formation of the Carnegie Endowment for International Peace: A Study of the Establishment Centered Peace Movement, 1910–1914." In *Building the Organizational Society: Essays on Associational Activities in Modern America,* ed. Jerry Israel, 143–62. New York: Free Press, 1972. This competent overview of the formation of the Carnegie Endowment includes a discussion of the arbitration treaties with Britain and France.

11:137   _____. "The Pacifist as Militarist: A Critique of the American Peace Movement, 1898–1914." *Societas* 5 (Spring 1975): 87–104. In this examination of the diversity of opinion about the proper role of the military in the U.S. peace movement in the early years of the twentieth century, Lutzker discusses the importance of Anglo-American rapprochement to many peace advocates.

11:138 _____. "Themes and Contradictions in the American Peace Movement, 1895–1917." In *The Pacifist Impulse in Historical Perspective*, ed. Harvey L. Dyck, 320–40. Toronto: University of Toronto Press, 1996. This essay considers the reactions of several key leaders of the U.S. peace movement to the signs of impending war in Europe.

11:139 Marchand, C. Roland. *The American Peace Movement and Social Reform, 1898–1918*. Princeton: Princeton University Press, 1973. This remains the classic study of U.S. peace movements. It traces their growth and fluctuations in strength in the early decades of the twentieth century and discusses their intersection with European movements.

11:140 Papachristou, Judith. "American Women and Foreign Policy, 1898–1905: Exploring Gender in Diplomatic History." Papachristou focuses on the role of women in those early-twentieth-century peace movement in the United States rooted in temperance, suffrage, and abolition movements (9:176).

11:141 Patterson, David S. "Andrew Carnegie's Quest for World Peace." *Proceedings of the American Philosophical Society* 114 (October 1970): 371–83. This admirably concise and readable account of the foundation of the Carnegie Endowment for International Peace (1910) summarizes Andrew Carnegie's views on world affairs, his attitude toward England, and his anxieties about the arms race in Europe.

11:142 _____. "An Interpretation of the American Peace Movement, 1898–1914." In *Peace Movements in America*, ed. Charles Chatfield, 20–38. New York: Schocken Books, 1973. This brief analysis of the diverse leaders of the peace movement notes that their naïveté toward world politics, elitism, and failure to unite weakened the movement before World War I.

11:143 _____. *Toward a Warless World: The Travail of the American Peace Movement, 1887–1914*. Bloomington: Indiana University Press, 1976. This survey of the diverse U.S. peace movement before World War I includes a detailed discussion of the arbitration treaties with France and England.

11:144 Tyrrell, Ian. *Woman's World/Woman's Empire: The Woman's Christian Temperance Union in International Perspective, 1880–1930*. This fascinating study analyzes the International Temperance Union as an example of a transnational messianic movement that bridged Europe and the United States (and many other parts of the world) in the early twentieth century (9:184).

U.S. Foreign Relations with Other Nations and Regions

STUDIES INVOLVING TWO OR MORE OTHER STATES

11:145 Bailey, Thomas A. "The North Pacific Sealing Convention of 1911." *Pacific Historical Review* 4, no. 1 (1935): 1–14. The North Pacific sealing convention of 1911 was an important conservation treaty among the United States, Russia, Japan, and Great Britain (representing Canadian interests) that saved the seals on the Pribilof Islands from extinction. It serves as an excellent case study of U.S. initiative in securing international cooperation. Negotiations for this treaty were begun during the Roosevelt administration and concluded under Taft.

11:146 Beede, Benjamin R. "Foreign Influences on American Progressivism." *Historian* 45 (Summer 1983): 529–49. Before World War I, American progressives were strongly influenced by European ideas and political models because they believed the European powers were coping better than the United States with the impact of industrialization.

11:147 Blake, Nelson M. "Ambassadors at the Court of Theodore Roosevelt." *Mississippi Valley Historical Review* 42 (September 1955): 179–206. This analysis of Theodore Roosevelt's "personal diplomacy" focuses on his relationships with the German, French, and British ambassadors in Washington and includes discussions of the major incidents in their countries' relations with the United States.

Blake contrasts Roosevelt's close relations with Baron Hermann Speck von Sternburg (German ambassador, 1903–1908) and Jean Jules Jusserand (French ambassador, 1903–1924) with his cooler relations with the British ambassadors, particularly Sir Michael Herbert (1902–1906).

11:148   Buehrig, Edward H. *Woodrow Wilson and the Balance of Power.* Bloomington: Indiana University Press, 1955. Based largely on secondary sources, this volume includes a useful, if breezy, overview of U.S. relations with Germany and England on the eve of World War I.

11:149   Campbell, John P. "Taft, Roosevelt, and the Arbitration Treaties of 1911." *Journal of American History* 53 (September 1966): 279–98. This lively and wide-ranging essay about the arbitration treaties of 1911, "an outstanding example of slovenly drafting and bumbling political management," includes discussions of the peace movement in the first decade of the twentieth century, Theodore Roosevelt's crusty contempt for it, and the debate about whether the Anglo-American arbitration treaty could serve as a model for others.

11:150   Child, Richard Washburn. *A Diplomat Looks at Europe.* New York: Duffield and Company, 1925. An ambassador to Italy from 1921 to 1924 provides his impressions of the evolution of U.S. policy toward Europe earlier in the twentieth century.

11:151   Choate, Joseph H. *The Two Hague Conferences.* Princeton: Princeton University Press, 1913. Joseph Choate, who was U.S. ambassador to Britain (1899–1905), represented the United States at the second Hague peace conference (1907). In this volume he summarizes the accomplishments of the two conferences.

11:152   Davis, Calvin DeArmond. *The United States and the Second Peace Conference: American Diplomacy and International Organization, 1899–1914.* Durham, NC: Duke University Press, 1976. This in-depth study of the world system that was emerging before World War I analyzes the U.S. role in the Hague peace conferences and includes a chapter on the Alaska boundary tribunal of 1903 that resolved the last outstanding controversy in U.S.-British relations.

11:153   Dülffer, Jost. *Regeln gegen den Krieg? Die Haager Friedenskonferenzen von 1899 und 1907 in der internationalen Politik [Rules against War? The Hague Peace Conferences of 1899 and 1907 in International Politics].* Berlin: Ullstein, 1981. In discussing the first two Hague peace conferences (1899, 1907) and their aftermath, Dülffer devotes some attention to the role of the United States, particularly its efforts to strengthen the right of arbitration after the second conference. Considered in greater detail are Germany, England, and France.

11:154   Fogelson, Nancy. "The Tip of the Iceberg: The United States and International Rivalry for the Arctic, 1900–1925." *Diplomatic History* 9 (Spring 1985): 131–48. Between 1900 and 1925, the United States negotiated with other countries to keep the Arctic open for American commerce and was party to a dispute with Norway over its failure to invite the United States to a 1908 international conference on the Spitsbergen archipelago (the conference finally met in 1914). For a broader look at the impact of Arctic disputes on the Canadian-American relationship, see her *Arctic Exploration & International Relations, 1900–1932: A Period of Expanding Interests* (1992) (17:704).

11:155   Freytag, Dierk. *Die Vereinigten Staaten auf dem Weg zur Intervention: Studien zur amerikanischen Aussenpolitik, 1910–1914 [The United States on the Road to Intervention: Essays on American Foreign Policy, 1910–1914].* Heidelberg: Carl Winter Universitätsverlag, 1971. This study includes a chapter on the 1911 arbitration treaties that the United States negotiated with France and England.

11:156   Gay, James Thomas. *American Fur Seal Diplomacy: The Alaskan Fur Seal Controversy.* This comprehensive account of the fur seal controversy, based largely on U.S. documents, includes a thorough discussion of the 1911 North Pacific sealing convention signed by the United States, Russia, Japan, and Great Britain (representing Canadian interests) (9:363).

11:157   Gignilliat, John L. "Pigs, Politics and Protection: The European Boycott of American Pork, 1879–1891." *Agricultural History* 35 (January 1961): 3–12. The fear in Europe that American pork products were infected with trichinae triggered a general European boycott of American pork, approximately 10 percent of America's export trade. By 1890, the United States countered these boycotts through retaliation, raising U.S. tariffs, and by ordering government inspections of pork exports. This story provides essential background to the trade tensions between the United States and Germany at the beginning of the twentieth century.

11:158 Kennedy, Paul. "British and German Reactions to the Rise of American Power." In *Ideas into Politics: Aspects of European History 1880–1950,* ed. R. J. Bullen, H. Pogge von Strandmann, and A. B. Polonsky, 15–24. London: Croom Helm, 1984. The growth of U.S. power in the last decade of the nineteenth and the first decade of the twentieth century caused rising anxieties in Germany while it stimulated London to seek rapprochement with Washington.

11:159 _____. *The Samoan Tangle: A Study in Anglo-German-American Relations, 1878–1900.* This definitive account of Anglo-German-American rivalry over Samoa from 1878 to 1900 includes a discussion of the triangular relationship from 1900 to 1914. Kennedy discusses Samoa in relation to broader questions of Anglo-German-American diplomacy and politics (9:519).

11:160 Lammersdorf, Raimund. *Anfänge einer Weltmacht: Theodore Roosevelt und die transatlantischen Beziehungen der USA, 1901–1909 [The Beginnings of World Power: Theodore Roosevelt and US Transatlantic Relations, 1901–1909].* Berlin: Akademie Verlag, 1994. Lammersdorf's study, which is based on U.S. and German archives and the Roosevelt papers, is the most comprehensive analysis of U.S.-European relations, especially German, British, and French, in the Roosevelt years. While the United States was a commercial giant before 1898, its victory in the Spanish-American War rendered it a great power that Europe tried to cultivate. For a brief moment in the Roosevelt presidency, the United States intervened in European power politics, particularly at Portsmouth and Algeciras, two subjects Lammersdorf discusses at length. He analyzes the reaction of Britain to this new state of affairs, stressing its great efforts to cultivate the Americans, despite irritations with TR's intransigence on Canadian issues. On the other hand, the closeness of the Anglo-American relationship was totally absent in German-American affairs, in large part due to Berlin's refusal to bow, publicly, to the

Monroe Doctrine. In a futile attempt to drive a wedge between Washington and London, Berlin courted the United States in East Asia, but failed.

Algeciras Conference, 1906

11:161 Anderson, Eugene N. *The First Moroccan Crisis, 1904–1906.* Chicago: University of Chicago Press, 1930. This monograph includes a brief, useful discussion of U.S.-German relations and of the U.S. role at the Algeciras conference.

11:162 Larsen, Peter. "Theodore Roosevelt and the Moroccan Crisis, 1904–1906." Ph.D. dissertation, Princeton University, 1984. This comprehensive study of the Moroccan crisis, based on the Roosevelt papers, *Congressional Record,* and U.S., French, and German archives, includes a good chapter on the U.S. public's reaction to Roosevelt's policy at Algeciras.

11:163 Lewis, Thomas T. "Franco-American Relations during the First Moroccan Crisis." *Mid-America* 55 (January 1973): 21–36. During the 1904–1906 Moroccan crisis, Theodore Roosevelt departed from the tradition of U.S. noninvolvement in European controversies. His primary motivation was to help prevent a European war; he also hoped that a settlement of the crisis would protect U.S. commercial interests. Overall, his position supported France rather than Germany. Roosevelt's influence on the settlement, while significant, has been exaggerated.

11:164 Ricard, Serge. "Theodore Roosevelt and the First Moroccan Crisis: The Diplomacy of Righteousness." *Theodore Roosevelt Association Journal* 12 (Winter 1986): 14–17. This description of Roosevelt's diplomacy during the final Moroccan crisis is based on French documents. See also the chapter on the crisis in his *Théodore Roosevelt et la justification de l'impérialisme* (Aix-en-Provence: Université de Provence, 1986).

Venezuela Crisis, 1902–1903

11:165 Anderson, Kevin M. "The Venezuelan Claims Controversy at The Hague, 1903." *Historian* 57 (Spring 1995): 525–36. Anderson argues that

Theodore Roosevelt's contribution to the arbitration of German, British, Italian, and American claims against Venezuela at the Hague has been overstated.

11:166 Angermann, Erich. "Ein Wendepunkt in der Geschichte der Monroe-Doktrin und der deutsch-amerikanischen Beziehungen: Die Venezuelakrise von 1902/03 im Spiegel der amerikanischen Tagespresse [A Turning Point in the History of the Monroe Doctrine and of German-American Relations: The Venezuela Crisis of 1902–1903 as Reflected in the Daily American Press]." In *Jahrbuch für Amerikastudien [German Yearbook of American Studies]*, ed. Walther Fischer, 3: 22–58. Heidelberg: Carl Winter Universitätsverlag, 1958. Angermann looks at the 1902–1903 Venezuela crisis through the lens of the U.S. press.

11:167 Guthrie, Wayne L. "The Anglo-German Intervention in Venezuela, 1902–03." Ph.D. dissertation, University of California, San Diego, 1983. This dissertation includes a particularly detailed discussion of the Venezuela claims case at the Hague.

11:168 Hendrickson, Embert J. "Roosevelt's Second Venezuelan Controversy." *Hispanic American Historical Review* 50 (August 1970): 482–98. This essay covers the years 1904 to 1908—in the aftermath of the Anglo-German-Italian blockade of Venezuela—when U.S. claims went unsettled because of President Cipriano Castro's opposition.

11:169 Herwig, Holger H. *Germany's Vision of Empire in Venezuela, 1871–1914*. Princeton: Princeton University Press, 1986. This complex study of German policy in Venezuela, based largely on German sources, contributes to the debate about the seriousness of Germany's threat to the Monroe Doctrine.

11:170 Herwig, Holger H., and J. León Helguera. *Alemania y el bloqueo internacional de Venezuela 1902/03 [Germany and the International Blockade of Venezuela, 1902–1903]*. Caracas: Editorial Arte, 1977. This is a detailed study, based largely on German sources, of Germany's participation in the blockade of Venezuela, an action that soured its relationship with the United States. The substantive part of the book is in English by Herwig "with the assistance of Helguera." See also Herwig, "German Imperialism in South America before the First World War: The Venezuelan Case, 1902/03," in *Russland-Deutschland-Amerika: Festschrift für Fritz T. Epstein zum 80. Geburtstag,* edited by Alexander Fischer, Günter Moltmann, and Klaus Schwabe (Wiesbaden: Franz Steiner, 1978): 117–30.

11:171 Holbo, Paul S. "Perilous Obscurity: Public Diplomacy and the Press in the Venezuelan Crisis, 1902–1903." *Historian* 32 (May 1970): 428–48. Holbo discusses the views of various historians on whether Roosevelt issued an ultimatum to Germany in 1902 and concludes that the evidence is not available to resolve the question. He assesses Roosevelt's use of the press in this crisis as an instrument of U.S. public diplomacy.

11:172 Hood, Miriam. *Gunboat Diplomacy, 1895–1905: Great Power Pressure in Venezuela.* This study presents a Venezuelan perspective on the Anglo-German blockade of Venezuela, an event that colored U.S. relations with Germany for at least a decade (9:452). First published in 1977.

11:173 Livermore, Seward W. "Theodore Roosevelt, the American Navy, and the Venezuelan Crisis of 1902–1903." *American Historical Review* 51 (April 1946): 452–71. After an examination of U.S. naval movements in the Caribbean during the crisis, the author concludes that Roosevelt's account of his ultimatum to the Germans, although embellished, is essentially correct.

11:174 Morris, Edmund. "'A Few Pregnant Days': Theodore Roosevelt and the Venezuelan Crisis of 1902." *Theodore Roosevelt Association Journal* 15 (Winter 1989): 2–13. Morris argues that Roosevelt was telling the truth when he asserted that he had brought the Venezuela crisis to a close by threatening the kaiser with Admiral Dewey's fleet.

11:175 Parsons, Edward B. "The German-American Crisis of 1902–1903." *Historian* 33 (May 1971): 436–52. Parsons maintains that Roosevelt's account of his actions in the Venezuela controversy was essentially correct and that he did play the major role in forcing the kaiser's hand. The author also recounts the historiography of the controversy.

11:176 Platt, D. C. M. "The Allied Coercion of Venezuela, 1902–1903: A Reassessment." *Inter-*

American Economic Affairs 15 (Spring 1962): 3–28. Platt refutes the argument that the English, German, and Italian intervention was on behalf of their bondholders; rather, it was the customary response of nations protecting its citizens whose rights had been compromised.

11:177 Ricard, Serge. "The Anglo-German Intervention in Venezuela and Theodore Roosevelt's Ultimatum to the Kaiser: Taking a Fresh Look at an Old Enigma." In *Anglo-Saxonism in U.S. Foreign Policy: The Diplomacy of Imperialism, 1899–1919,* ed. Serge Ricard and Hélène Christol, 65–77. Aix-en-Provence: Publications de Université de Provence, 1991. Ricard argues that Roosevelt delivered an ultimatum to the kaiser near the end of the Venezuela crisis (1902–1903).

11:178 Rippy, J. Fred. "The Venezuelan Claims Settlements of 1903–1905." *Inter-American Economic Affairs* 7 (March 1954): 65–77. This essay reviews the claims presented by Europeans and Americans to the Mixed Claims Commission.

11:179 Spector, Ronald H. "Roosevelt, the Navy, and the Venezuela Controversy: 1902–1903." *American Neptune* 32 (October 1972): 257–63. This analysis of Roosevelt's alleged threat to the kaiser during the second Venezuela crisis is based on a careful analysis of the movements of the U.S. fleet under Admiral George Dewey.

FRANCE

11:180 Blumenthal, Henry. *France and the United States: Their Diplomatic Relation, 1789–1914.* A brief chapter gives an overview of U.S.-French relations from 1901 to 1914, focusing on economic affairs, the Russo-Japanese War, and the Morocco crises (2:317).

11:181 Brooks, Charles W. *America in France's Hopes and Fears, 1890–1920.* 2 vols. New York: Garland Publishing, 1987. The author details France's ambivalent attitude toward U.S. intellectual imperialism on the cusp of the twentieth century, arguing that France both feared and admired U.S. culture.

11:182 Carroll, E. Malcolm. *French Public Opin-*

ion and Foreign Affairs, 1870–1914. New York: Century Company, 1931. This book indicates, by default, the lack of importance France attributed to the United States in the first decades of the twentieth century. It is comprehensive and well researched but includes not one word about the United States.

11:183 Chambers, Samuel Tinsley. "Franco-American Relations, 1897–1914." Ph.D. dissertation, Georgetown University, 1951. This dissertation focuses on U.S.-French diplomatic relations concerning the Spanish-American War, expansion in China, and imperialism in Africa; on economic relations; and on social and cultural relations.

11:184 Forsberg, Aaron. "Ambassador J. J. Jusserand, Theodore Roosevelt, and Franco-American Relations, 1903–1909." In *Theodore Roosevelt—Many-Sided American,* ed. Natalie A. Naylor, Douglas Brinkley, and John Allen Gable, 329–40. Interlaken, NY: Heart of the Lakes, 1992. Forsberg notes that the importance of Jean Jules Jusserand (French ambassador to the United States, 1903–1924) rested on Roosevelt's highly personal approach to diplomacy and to the shared intellectual interests and worldview of the two men. From 1903 to 1908, there was a "high degree of diplomatic cooperation between France and the United States."

11:185 Lewis, Thomas T. "Franco-American Diplomatic Relations 1898–1907." Ph.D. dissertation, University of Oklahoma, 1971. A comprehensive survey of Franco-American relations emphasizing diplomats, economic questions, imperial aspirations, and cultural relations, this is based mainly on American sources. Lewis sees a Franco-American convergence in such areas as China, Liberia, Venezuela, and at the Algeciras conference of 1906.

11:186 Portes, Jacques. *Fascination and Misgivings: The United States in French Opinion, 1870–1914.* Translated by Elborg Forster. Portes presents an overview of French public opinion toward U.S. society, foreign policy, and politics based on a survey of the contemporary literature and a limited selection of the press (9:331). First published, in French, in 1987.

11:187 Skinner, James M. *France and Panama:*

The Unknown Years, 1894–1908. New York: Peter Lang, 1989. This history of La Compagnie Nouvelle du Canal de Panama describes the attempts of the French owners to attract the interest of the U.S. government in their struggling concern and their company's role in the 1903 rebellion in Panama. The French government did not identify with or support the company, and the United States held all the good cards.

11:188　Tardieu, André. *Notes sur les États-Unis: la société—la politique—la diplomatie [Notes on the United States: Society, Politics, and Diplomacy].* Paris: Calmann-Lévy, 1908. Tardieu was a member of the French Chamber of Deputies and an army officer. His study of U.S. society and politics paints an upbeat picture of Franco-American social, intellectual, and political relations. Tardieu explains U.S. perceptions of some international events, including the first Morocco crisis, and discusses U.S. relations with the European powers and Japan.

11:189　White, Elizabeth Brett. *American Opinion of France from Lafayette to Poincaré.* New York: Alfred A. Knopf, 1927. The dearth of other sources on U.S.-French relations from 1900 to 1915 makes this study based largely on the U.S. popular press useful, though dated and brief. White describes educational, intellectual, literary, and artistic exchanges between the two countries; recounts the experiences of travelers in both; and explains the tensions caused in 1894–1906 by the Dreyfus affair and in 1908–1910 by French pressure on Liberia.

11:190　Whitehead, James Louis. "French Reaction to American Imperialism, 1895–1908." Ph.D. dissertation, University of Pennsylvania, 1942. On the basis of a study of the French press, Whitehead concludes that fear of American economic strength and of the ramifications of the Monroe Doctrine formed the root of French fears of U.S. imperialism from 1895 to 1908. He looks at tensions over the isthmian canal, Venezuela, and possessions in the Pacific.

11:191　Willson, Beckles. *America's Ambassadors to France (1777–1927): A Narrative of Franco-American Diplomatic Relations.* This old-fashioned book includes portraits of U.S. ambassadors to France: Horace Porter (1897–1905), Robert Sanderson McCormick (1905–1907), Henry White (1907–

1909), Robert Bacon (1910–1912), Myron T. Herrick (1912–1914), and William Graves Sharp (1914–1919). Despite its age it is useful because there is so little written on the subject (4:241).

11:192　Zahniser, Marvin R. *Uncertain Friendship: American-French Diplomatic Relations through the Cold War.* This brief survey includes a chapter on Franco-American relations from 1867 to 1913, years that saw no major irritants and an important growth of mutual understanding (2:321).

GERMANY

11:193　Beale, Howard K. "Theodore Roosevelt, Wilhelm II. und die deutsch-amerikanischen Beziehungen [Theodore Roosevelt, Wilhelm II, and German-American Relations]." *Welt als Geschichte [Germany]* 15, nos. 3–4 (1955): 155–87. Beale examines the relationship between Theodore Roosevelt and Kaiser Wilhelm II as a factor in German-American relations.

11:194　Deicke, Gertrud. "Das Amerikabild der deutschen öffentlichen Meinung von 1898–1914 [The Image of America in German Public Opinion, 1898–1914]." Ph.D. dissertation, University of Hamburg, 1956. This thesis includes useful observations about German attitudes toward Theodore Roosevelt, the Panama Canal, Pan-Americanism, U.S. policy toward Mexico, and U.S.-German relations.

11:195　Doerries, Reinhard R. "Empire and Republic: German-American Relations before 1917." In *America and the Germans: An Assessment of a Three-Hundred-Year History. Vol. 2: The Relationship in the Twentieth Century,* ed. Frank Trommler and Joseph McVeigh, 3–17. Philadelphia: University of Pennsylvania Press, 1985. This is a very brief overview of U.S.-German relations before U.S. entry in World War I written by an expert in the field.

11:196　_____. *Imperial Challenge: Ambassador Count Bernstorff and German-American Relations, 1908–1917.* Translated by Christa D. Shannon. Chapel Hill: University of North Carolina Press, 1989. A translation and revision of *Washington-Berlin 1908/1917* (Düsseldorf: Schwann, 1975), this is a well-written account, based on research in German, U.S., and British archives, of Bernstorff's increasingly demanding job as the German ambassador in Washington. Doerries's analysis takes off after 1914; it is somewhat less reliable for the preceding years.

11:197 Drexler, Wolfgang J. M. *Andrew D. White in Deutschland: der Vertreter der USA in Berlin, 1879–1881 und 1897–1902 [Andrew D. White in Germany: The Representative of the USA in Berlin, 1879–1881 and 1897–1902].* Stuttgart: Hans-Dieter Heinz, 1987. Using U.S. archives and published German sources, Drexler traces Andrew White's career as minister (1879–1881) and then ambassador (1897–1902) to Germany. He discusses the Boxer revolt and first Hague conference.

11:198 Fiebig-von Hase, Ragnhild. "The United States and Germany in the World Arena, 1900–1917." In *Confrontation and Cooperation: Germany and the United States in the Era of World War I, 1900–1924,* ed. Hans-Jürgen Schröder, 2: 33–68. Providence, RI: Berg Publishers, 1993. Fiebig-von Hase argues that Eurocentrism and a belief in U.S. isolationism have clouded scholars' perceptions of the world system in 1900, which consisted of centers of power not only in Europe but also in the Western Hemisphere and East Asia. The United States and Germany were world powers intent on restructuring the world system, the former by economic means, the latter by both economic and military means.

11:199 Gatzke, Hans W. "The United States and Germany on the Eve of World War I." In *Deutschland in der Weltpolitik des 19. und 20. Jahrhunderts [Germany in World Politics in the 19th and 20th Centuries],* ed. Imanuel Geiss and Bernd Jürgen Wendt, 271–86. Düsseldorf: Bertelsmann Universitätsverlag, 1973. Gatzke begins with a useful and astute survey of the literature on U.S.-German relations at the beginning of the twentieth century before moving to an analysis of these relations based on research in the German archives. He stresses the British-German-American diplomatic triangle. See also his shorter treatment of the subject in his *Germany and the United States: A "Special Relationship"?* (Cambridge, MA: Harvard University Press, 1980).

11:200 Gerhards, Josef Werner. "Theodore Roosevelt im Urteil der deutschen öffentlichen Meinung

(1901–1919) [Theodore Roosevelt in the Judgment of German Public Opinion (1901–1919)]." Ph.D. dissertation, Johannes-Guttenberg-Universität zu Mainz, 1962. The major contribution of this slim thesis is the author's use of the German press to elucidate the German public's attitude toward Theodore Roosevelt.

11:201 Hall, Luella J. "The Abortive German-American-Chinese Entente of 1907–08." *Journal of Modern History* 1 (June 1929): 219–35. The author provides an account of Germany's attempt to force an American-German-Chinese entente in the face of increasingly strong British and French opposition in East Asia. Roosevelt rejected the entente after a year of negotiations because he realized that the American position, even with the support of Germany, was untenable in China vis-à-vis Japan.

11:202 _____. "A Partnership in Peacemaking: Theodore Roosevelt and Wilhelm II." *Pacific Historical Review* 13 (December 1944): 390–411. Hall traces Theodore Roosevelt's attempts during the Russo-Japanese War to persuade Germany to help safeguard U.S. interests in the Pacific, while Berlin sought Washington's cooperation in Morocco.

11:203 Hildebrand, Klaus. *Das vergangene Reich: Deutsche Aussenpolitik von Bismarck bis Hitler, 1871–1945 [The Bygone Empire: German Foreign Policy from Bismarck through Hitler, 1871–1945].* Stuttgart: Deutsche Verlags-Anstalt, 1995. This massive volume includes two chapters on the 1900–1914 period that are noteworthy for their almost complete absence of interest in relations with the United States.

11:204 Johnson, Charles Thomas. *Culture at Twilight: The National German-American Alliance, 1901–1918.* New York: Peter Lang, 1999. From 1901 to 1918, the National German-American Alliance sought to preserve and promote aspects of German culture in America. Johnson presents its rise and fall, with scant attention to its impact on or reflection of relations between Berlin and Washington.

11:205 Jonas, Manfred. "The Major Powers and the United States, 1898–1910: The Case of Germany." In *Perspectives in American Foreign Policy: Essays on Europe, Latin America, China, and the Cold War: Papers Selected from the Society for His-*

torians of American Foreign Relations' First National Meeting, Held at Georgetown University, August 15–16, 1975, ed. Jules Davids, 30–77. New York: Arno Press, 1976. This is a straightforward, concise, and accurate description of U.S.-German relations from 1898 to 1910.

11:206 _____. *The United States and Germany: A Diplomatic History*. This concise volume includes the best summary of U.S.-German relations in the early twentieth century (2:308).

11:207 Junker, Detlef. *The Manichaean Trap: American Perceptions of the German Empire, 1871–1945*. Washington, DC: German Historical Institute, 1995. This elegant booklet-sized essay deals briefly with U.S. images of Germany before World War I, arguing that it was above all the U.S. assessment of the German political scene that shaped Americans' image of Germany, an image that deteriorated markedly during the Wilhelmine period. Introduction by Klaus Hildebrand and comment by Paul W. Schroeder.

11:208 Keim, Jeannette. *Forty Years of German-American Political Relations*. Philadelphia: William J. Dornan, 1919. This comprehensive analysis of U.S.-German relations deals with the following controversies of the early twentieth century: tariff disputes, the open door in China, and the Monroe Doctrine. While dated and based on limited resources, it remains useful.

11:209 Kortmann, Bernhard. "Präsident Theodore Roosevelt und Deutschland." Inaugural dissertation, University of Münster, 1933. In this dated but thorough study of Roosevelt's diplomacy toward Germany, based largely on *Die Grosse Politik* and a narrow selection of the German press, Kortmann discusses the Venezuela crisis, Russo-Japanese War, Moroccan crises, and the Algeciras conference.

11:210 Kreider, John K. "Diplomatic Relations between Germany and the United States 1906–1913." Ph.D. dissertation, Pennsylvania State University, 1969. The study focuses on the Algeciras conference, tariff arrangements and trade, and converging interests of the two nations in Africa and Asia. The author emphasizes the cleavage between a pro-British Washington and the anti-British policies in Berlin.

11:211 Kremp, Werner. *In Deutschland liegt unser Amerika: Das sozialdemokratische Amerikabild von den Anfängen der SPD bis zur Weimarer Republik [In Germany Is Our America: The Social Democrats' Image of America from the Beginnings of the SPD to the Weimer Republic]*. Münster: Lit Verlag, 1993. Using a wide array of social-democratic newspapers, memoirs, and party documents, Kremp analyzes, in great detail, the Social Democrats' views of the United States in the early twentieth century.

11:212 Lammersdorf, Raimund. *Amerika und der Kaiser [America and the Kaiser]*. Berlin: Akademie Verlag, 1994. In this well-researched study, Lammersdorf argues that the U.S. misperception that Wilhelm II totally determined German policy led both Washington and the U.S. public to exaggerate the importance of his militant and belligerent personality. See also his "Amerika und der Kaiser: Zur Perzeption Wilhelms II in den Vereinigten Staaten, 1888–1909," *Amerikastuden* 31, no. 3 (1986): 295–302.

11:213 Leab, Daniel J. "Screen Images of the 'Other' in Wilhelmine Germany and the United States, 1890–1918." *Film History* 9, no. 1 (1997): 49–70. Leab compares the images of Germans and German-Americans in early U.S. movies, which were largely negative even before the outbreak of war in Europe, with the more mixed images—from crass materialists to enlightened democrats—of the Americans in German movies made before 1919.

11:214 Leusser, Hermann. *Ein Jahrzehnt deutsch-amerikanischer Politik 1897–1906 [A Decade of German-American Politics, 1897–1906]*. Munich: R. Oldenbourg, 1928. This remains a useful, albeit dated, study of political relations between Germany and the United States at the turn of the century.

11:215 Mehnert, Ute. "Deutschland, Amerika und die 'Gelbe Gefahr': Zur Karriere eines Schlagworts in der grossen Politik, 1905–1917 [Germany, America, and the 'Yellow Peril': The Development of a Catchphrase in the Great Policy, 1905–1917]." Ph.D. dissertation, University of Stuttgart, 1995. This well-researched and penetrating study includes a chapter comparing U.S. and German perceptions of the "yellow peril" and shows how Germany tried to use U.S. fears of Japan to leverage a rapprochement with the United States in 1906. See also her "German *Welt-*

politik and the American Two-Front Dilemma: The 'Japanese Peril' in German-American Relations, 1904–1917," *Journal of American History* 82 (March 1996): 1452–77.

11:216 Menning, Ralph R., and Carol Bresnahan Menning. "'Baseless Allegations': Wilhelm II and the Hale Interview of 1908." *Central European History* 16 (December 1983): 368–97. In July 1908, Kaiser Wilhelm II granted an interview to William Bayard Hale, an ordained minister, respected journalist, and literary editor of the *New York Times,* in which he launched into a bitter attack against England. The Mennings argue, based on extensive research in British and German archives, that although the interview was never published, it became a matter of lively concern in high diplomatic circles— American, British, German, French, Japanese, and Swedish.

11:217 Meyer, Luciana R. W. "German-American Migration and the Bancroft Naturalization Treaties 1868–1910." Ph.D. dissertation, City University of New York, 1970. This study emphasizes the difficulties in administering the treaties regulating emigration between Germany and the United States, particularly in demonstrating the right of people to change nationality voluntarily and then return to their country of origin.

11:218 Peters, Evelene H. T. "Roosevelt und der Kaiser: Ein Beitrag zur Geschichte der deutsche-amerikanischen Beziehungen 1895–1906 [Roosevelt and the Kaiser: A Contribution to the History of German-American Relations, 1895–1906]." Ph.D. dissertation, University of Berlin, 1936. Peters concludes that the reports of a friendship between Theodore Roosevelt and Kaiser Wilhelm II were exaggerations.

11:219 Pommerin, Reiner. *Der Kaiser und Amerika. Die USA in der Politik der Reichsleitung 1890–1917 [The Kaiser and America: The USA in the Policy of the Leadership of the Reich, 1890–1917].* Cologne: Böhlau, 1986. This is the only comprehensive overview of U.S.-German relations during the Wilhelmine period. Using U.S. and German sources, Pommerin discusses U.S.-German commercial, military, cultural, and diplomatic relations. He analyzes conflicts in the Pacific, the Far East, China, Samoa, and Latin America; he discusses the Venezuela and Morocco crises and the Russo-Japanese War.

11:220 Rinke, Stefan H. "A Misperception of Reality: The Futile German Attempts at an Entente with the United States, 1907–1908." In *Theodore Roosevelt—Many-Sided American,* ed. Natalie A. Naylor, Douglas Brinkley, and John Allen Gable, 369–82. Interlaken, NY: Heart of the Lakes, 1992. Rinke describes the futile German attempt in 1907–1908 to reach some kind of alliance with the United States to guarantee the integrity of China. Clumsily and unsuccessfully, the Germans tried to play on American fears of "the yellow peril" and anti-Japanese sentiment.

11:221 Schieber, Clara Eve. *The Transformation of American Sentiment toward Germany, 1870–1914.* This dated account of U.S.-German relations, which relies primarily on the popular U.S. press, is noteworthy for its anti-German tone. Schieber argues that despite German attempts to garner America's favor, U.S. sentiment toward Germany deteriorated from 1870 to 1914 due to fears of *Weltpolitik,* particularly in the Western Hemisphere (9:340).

11:222 Schottelius, Ursula. "Das Amerikabild der deutschen Regierung in der Ära Bülow, 1897–1909 [The German Government's Image of America in the Bülow Era, 1897–1909]." Ph.D. dissertation, University of Hamburg, 1956. This survey includes useful material about the German government's perception of U.S. policy toward East Asia, the Monroe Doctrine, the Anglo-American relationship, and U.S.-German economic relations. Based on German archives.

11:223 Schröder, Hans-Jürgen. *Deutschland und Amerika in der Epoche des Ersten Weltkriegs, 1900–1924 [Germany and America in the Epoch of the First World War, 1900–1924].* Stuttgart: Franz Steiner, 1993. This survey contains a brief chapter on U.S.-German relations before World War I that is largely a commentary on the author's edited volume, *Confrontation and Cooperation: Germany and the United States in the Era of World War I: 1890–1924* (1993).

11:224 Shepardson, Donald E. "Theodore Roosevelt and William II: The New Struggle for Atlantic

Supremacy." In *Problems in European History*, ed. Harold Talbot Parker, 165–76. Durham, NC: Moore Publications, 1979. This article reviews German-American relations from the accession of Wilhelm II (1888) to the funeral of Edward VII (1910), with special emphasis on the relationship between Wilhelm and Theodore Roosevelt.

11:225 Shippee, Lester B. "German-American Relations, 1890–1914." *Journal of Modern History* 8 (December 1936): 479–88. This review of Alfred Vagts's *Deutschland und die Vereinigten Staaten in der Weltpolitik* (1935) (11:230) retains its usefulness since Vagts's magnum opus has never been translated into English.

11:226 Small, Melvin. "The American Image of Germany, 1906–1914." Ph.D. dissertation, University of Michigan, 1965. Small's nuanced argument, based on a close reading of the popular U.S. press, is that Americans' image of Germany on the eve of World War I was ambivalent.

11:227 Sondermann, Fred A. "The Wilson Administration's Image of Germany." Ph.D. dissertation, Yale University, 1953. This is a study of selected U.S. officials' views of Germany on the eve of World War I. Sondermann finds that official Washington had a generally positive view of Kaiser Wilhelm II and the German government, but was suspicious of German military leaders.

11:228 Turk, Eleanor L. "Prince Henry's Royal Welcome: German-American Response to the Visit of the Kaiser's Brother, 1902." *Yearbook of German-American Studies* 33 (1998): 127–38. Turk recounts Prince Henry's goodwill visit to the United States, a manifestation of the effort of his brother, Kaiser Wilhelm II, to curry American goodwill.

11:229 Ullrich, Volker. *Die nervöse Grossmacht: Aufstieg und Untergang des deutschen Kaiserreichs 1871–1918 [The Nervous Great Power: The Rise and Fall of the German Empire, 1871–1918]*. Frankfurt: Fischer Verlag, 1997. In his discussion of German foreign policy from 1897 to 1914, Ullrich mentions the United States only in passing.

11:230 Vagts, Alfred. *Deutschland und die Vereinigten Staaten in der Weltpolitik [Germany and the*

United States in the World Arena]. 2 vols. New York: Macmillan Company, 1935. This magisterial work retains significance because Vagts used German documents that were lost during World War II. He deals at length with German-American tensions in the Far East and Latin America and discusses the 1902–1903 Venezuela crisis and first Moroccan crisis. See also his "Hopes and Fears of an American-German War, 1870–1915," parts I and II (December 1939 and March 1940) (9:342; 9:343).

11:231 _____. "Die Juden im amerikanisch-deutschen imperialistischen Konflikt vor 1917 [Jews in the American-German Imperial Conflict before 1917]." *Amerikastudien* 24 (1979): 56–71. Before World War I, Jews in the United States and Germany felt a sense of solidarity against the hated Tsarist Russia. Vagts explores the economic and financial ties between German and American Jews and the attempts by prominent individuals to improve relations between the two communities.

11:232 Wehler, Hans Ulrich. *Der Aufstieg des amerikanischen Imperialismus: Studien zur Entwicklung des Imperium Americanum 1865–1900 [The Rise of American Imperialism: Studies on the Development of the Imperium Americanum, 1865–1900]*. Göttingen: Vandenhoeck and Ruprecht, 1974. Although concentrating on the broad sweep of American expansion, this work includes an important section on Samoa and a remarkable fifty-eight-page bibliography.

11:233 Wiegand, Wayne A. "Ambassador in Absentia: George Meyer, William II, and Theodore Roosevelt." *Mid-America* 56 (January 1974): 3–15. This article describes the close personal relationship existing between Kaiser William II and George Meyer (ambassador to Russia, 1905–1907).

Germany, Latin America, and the Monroe Doctrine

11:234 Arnold, William Thomas. *German Ambitions as They Affect Britain and the United States of America*. New York: G. P. Putnam's Sons, 1903. This is a good example of an alarmist British explanation of the pan-Germans' designs on the Monroe Doctrine. It first appeared in a series of articles under the pseudonym, "Vigilans sed Aequus."

11:235 Baecker, Thomas. "The Arms of the '*Ypiranga*': The German Side." *Americas* 30 (July 1973): 1–17. Baecker argues that the German government was unaware that the Hamburg-American Line's *Ypiranga* was carrying a shipment of arms for the Mexican government of Victoriano Huerta. U.S. forces seized Veracruz to prevent these arms from reaching Huerta, whose government the Wilson administration had refused to recognize.

11:236 _____. *Die deutsche Mexikopolitik, 1913/1914 [Germany's Policy toward Mexico, 1913–1914].* Berlin: Colloquium Verlag, 1971. This thorough study of German policy in Mexico, based largely on German sources, includes a discussion of Berlin's response to Woodrow Wilson's policy toward the Mexican revolution. See also his "Los intereses militares del imperio alemán en México: 1913–1914 [Imperial Germany's Military Interests in Mexico, 1913–1914]," *Historia Mexicana* 20 (January-March 1972): 347–62.

11:237 Brunn, Gerhard. *Deutschland und Brasilien (1889–1914) [Germany and Brazil, 1889–1914].* Cologne: Böhlau, 1971. Relying primarily on German sources, Brunn analyzes the full range of German-Brazilian relations before World War I: economic (trade and finance), demographic (emigration), security (military missions), and diplomatic (the Panther incident). This book provides essential background to assessing the U.S. reaction to the alleged German threat to the Monroe Doctrine in Brazil.

11:238 Clifford, J. Garry. "Admiral Dewey and the Germans, 1903: A New Perspective." *Mid-America* 49 (July 1967): 214–20. In this brief article, Clifford examines the influence of Admiral George Dewey's strongly anti-German views on the Roosevelt administration's response to the 1902–1903 Venezuela crisis.

11:239 Fiebig-von Hase, Ragnhild. "Die Rolle Kaiser Wilhelms II. in den deutsch-amerikanischen Beziehungen, 1890–1914 [The Role of Kaiser Wilhelm II in German-American Relations, 1890–1914]." In *Der Ort Kaiser Wilhelms II. in den deutschen Geschichte [The Place of Kaiser Wilhelm II in German History]*, ed. John C. G. Röhl, 223–57. Munich: Oldenbourg, 1991. In this article, Fiebig-

von Hase extends the analysis of U.S.-German relations she set forth in her *Lateinamerika als Konfliktherd der deutsch-amerikanischen Beziehungen 1890–1903: vom Beginn der Panamerikapolitik bis zur Venezuelakrise von 1902/03* (1986) (11:240) to the beginning of World War I.

11:240 _____. *Lateinamerika als Konfliktherd der deutsch-amerikanischen Beziehungen, 1890–1903: vom Beginn der Panamerikapolitik bis zur Venezuelakrise von 1902/03 [Latin America in the Context of German-American Relations, 1890–1903: From the Start of Pan-Americanism to the Venezuela Crisis of 1902–03].* 2 vols. Göttingen: Vandenhoeck and Ruprecht, 1986. This massive study, based largely on research in the German archives, asserts that Wilhelm II's Germany posed a serious threat to the Monroe Doctrine at the beginning of the twentieth century. See also her "Großmachtkonflikte in der Westlichen Hemisphäre: Das Beispiel der Venezuelakrise vom Winter 1902/03," in R. Fiebig-von Hase, J. Dülffler, M. Kröger, and R.-H. W. Wippich, eds., *Vermiedene Kriege: Deeskalation von Konflikten der Großmächte zwischen Krimkrieg und Erstem Weltkrieg, 1865–1914* (Munich: Oldenbourg, 1997): 527–78.

11:241 Harrison, Austin. *The Pan-Germanic Doctrine. Being a Study of German Political Aims and Aspirations.* New York: Harper, 1904. This is a good example of alarmist British commentary on the aims of the pan-Germans that helped sour U.S.-German relations. It includes a chapter on their ambitions in Latin America.

11:242 Hell, Jürgen. "Der Griff nach Südbrasilien: Die Politik des deutschen Reiches zur Verwandlung der drei brasilianischen Südstaaten in ein überseeisches Neudeutschland (1890 bis 1914) [The Grab for Southern Brazil: The Policy of the German Empire to Transform the Three Southern Brazilian States into an Overseas New Germany, 1890–1914]." Ph.D. dissertation, University of Rostock, 1966. Due to Hell's impressive research in German archives, his study of German policy in south Brazil provides useful background to an analysis of U.S. fears of a German threat to the Monroe Doctrine despite the fact that he, an East German scholar, promotes the thesis—not credibly supported by his evidence—that Wilhelmine Germany was behaving in an aggressive imperial manner in Brazil. See also his "Das 'südbrasilianis-che Neudeutschland.' Der annexationistische Grundzug der wilhelminischen und nazistischen Brasilienpolitik (1895 bis 1938)," in *Der deutsche Faschismus in Lateinamerika, 1933–1943* (Berlin: Humbolt-Universität zu Berlin, 1966): 103–10.

11:243 Herwig, Holger H. *Politics of Frustration: The United States in German Naval Planning, 1889–1941.* The first third of this volume is an overview, based on multiarchival research, of U.S.-German naval tensions in the Far East and Latin America before World War I. Herwig contends that the Germans did pose a threat to the Monroe Doctrine (9:337).

11:244 Joffily, José. *O Caso Panther [The Panther Incident].* Rio de Janeiro: Paz e Terra, 1988. This is the only full-length study of a diplomatic incident between Germany and Brazil that helped foster the budding U.S.-Brazilian friendship and sour U.S. relations with Germany. Joffily, a Brazilian scholar, uses Brazilian sources.

11:245 Meyer, Michael C. "The Arms of the *Ypiranga*." *Hispanic American Historical Review* 50 (August 1970): 543–56. Meyer argues that the arms carried to Mexico by the *Ypiranga* in April 1914, precipitating Woodrow Wilson's occupation of Veracruz, had been purchased in the United States by German agents and that they provided Wilson with an excuse for the final effort to oust General Victoriano Huerta.

11:246 Mitchell, Nancy. *The Danger of Dreams: German and American Imperialism in Latin America.* Mitchell argues that at the end of the nineteenth and beginning of the twentieth century, Washington exaggerated the German threat to the Monroe Doctrine. Based on extensive research in U.S., German, and British archives, she shows that the war plans of both navies were academic exercises and that Berlin went to great pains to accommodate U.S. policy during the second Venezuela crisis and the Mexican revolution through 1914. The large German community in southern Brazil posed no threat to U.S. interests (9:389). See also her "Germans in the Backyard: *Weltpolitik* versus Protective Imperialism" (1992) (12:49); "The Height of the German Challenge: The Venezuela Blockade, 1902–3" (1996) (12:350); and

"Protective Imperialism versus *Weltpolitik* in Brazil: Part One: Pan-German Vision and Mahanian Response" and "Part Two: Settlement, Trade and Opportunity" (1996) (12:329; 12:330).

11:247 Rinke, Stefan H. *Zwischen Weltpolitik und Monroe Doktrin: Botschafter Speck von Sternburg und die deutsch-amerikanischen Beziehungen, 1898–1908 [Between Weltpolitik and the Monroe Doctrine: Ambassador Speck von Sternburg and German-American Relations, 1898–1908].* Stuttgart: Hans-Dieter Heinz, 1992. This well-researched and insightful study of Speck von Sternburg traces his involvement in U.S.-German relations from the beginnings of his friendship with Theodore Roosevelt through his tenure as German ambassador to the United States (1903–1908). It covers crises in Samoa, South Africa, Venezuela, Morocco, and East Asia. See also his "The German Ambassador Hermann Speck von Sternburg and Theodore Roosevelt, 1889–1908," *Theodore Roosevelt Association Journal* 17 (Winter 1991): 2–12, and "A Diplomat's Dilemma: Ambassador von Sternburg and the Moroccan Crisis, 1905–1906," *Mid-America* 75 (April-July 1993): 165–96.

11:248 Schoonover, Thomas D. *Germany in Central America: Competitive Imperialism, 1821–1929.* Schoonover's wide-ranging study includes two chapters on the success of German economic penetration in Central America from 1898 to 1914, the apogee of German influence in the hemisphere (9:464).

11:249 Small, Melvin. "The United States and the German 'Threat' to the Hemisphere, 1905–1914." *Americas* 28 (January 1972): 252–70. Using U.S. documents and published sources, Small argues that the Germans posed no military or political threat to Latin America after the Venezuela controversy of 1902–1903. The Germans after 1903 fully recognized the Monroe Doctrine and its corollaries, and would not seek to contravene them, nor could they, since events in the Old World were commanding their full attention.

11:250 Tonnelat, Ernest. *L'expansion allemande hors d'Europe [German Expansion beyond Europe].* Paris: Librairie Armand Colin, 1908. Tonnelat, a French journalist, discusses, inter alia, German immigrants in Brazil and the United States.

German Naval Policy

11:251 Baecker, Thomas. "Blau gegen Schwarz. Der amerikanische Kriegsplan von 1913 für einen deutsch-amerikanischen Krieg [Blue versus Black: The American War Plans of 1913 for a German-American War]." *Marine-Rundschau* 69 (June 1972): 347–60. Baecker argues that the U.S. navy's war plan against Germany was based on an international scenario that had an unrealistically pessimistic projection of the U.S. position in the world. He concludes that the image of Germany as an enemy was useful to the U.S. navy.

11:252 _____. "Das deutsche Feindbild in der amerikanischen Marine, 1900–1914 [The American Navy's Image of the German as an Enemy, 1900–1914]." *Marine-Rundschau* 70 (February 1973): 65–84. Baecker argues, using U.S. documents, that the U.S. navy continued to view Germany as the most serious threat to the United States until 1914, despite the fact that after 1905–1906 a number of naval officers, including members of the navy's General Board, expressed doubts about the gravity of the threat.

11:253 Diederichs, Otto von. "Darstellung der Vorgänge vor Manila von Mai bis August 1898 [Description of the Events off Manila, May to August 1898]." *Marine-Rundschau* 25 (March 1914): 253–79. The author asserts that the reports that his fleet inconvenienced U.S. Admiral George Dewey in Manila Bay during the Spanish-American War are inaccurate. This detailed and defensive account reveals the continuing salience of the issue immediately before the outbreak of World War I.

11:254 Edelsheim, Franz. *Operations upon the Sea: A Study.* New York: Outdoor Press, 1914. This slim volume caused a sensation when first published in German in 1901, describing the German navy's detailed war plans against England and the United States at the turn of the century. The war plan against the United States, an academic study, was shelved by 1905.

11:255 Forstmeier, Friedrich. "Deutsche Invasionspläne gegen die USA um 1900 [German Invasion Plans against the USA in 1900]." *Marine-Rundschau* 68 (June 1971): 344–51. Forstmeier argues that Her-

wig and Trask, "Naval Operations Plans between Germany and the United States of America, 1898–1913: A Study of Strategic Planning in the Age of Imperialism" (1970) (11:256), exaggerated the importance of the German war plans against the United States.

11:256 Herwig, Holger H., and David F. Trask. "Naval Operations Plans between Germany and the United States of America, 1898–1913: A Study of Strategic Planning in the Age of Imperialism." *Militärgeschichtliche Mitteilungen* 2 (February 1970): 5–32. This important article was the first detailed analysis of the German navy's war planning against the United States at the beginning of the twentieth century. Also available in Paul M. Kennedy, ed., *The War Plans of the Great Powers, 1880–1914* (Boston: Allen and Unwin, 1979).

11:257 Maurer, John. "American Naval Concentration and the German Battle Fleet, 1900–1918." *Journal of Strategic Studies* 6 (June 1983): 147–81. In this important article, Maurer meticulously traces how the U.S. navy's fear of Germany influenced its strategy in the early years of the twentieth century.

11:258 Overlack, Peter. "German War Plans in the Pacific, 1900–1914." *Historian* 60 (Spring 1998): 578–93. Overlack argues that in the first decade of the twentieth century the German navy tried to counter the success of U.S. imperialism in the Philippines and Hawaii and prepared for war in the Pacific.

German-American Commercial Relations

11:259 Berg, Manfred. *Gustav Stresemann und die Vereinigten Staaten von Amerika: Weltwirtschaftliche Verflechtung und Revisionspolitik, 1907–1929 [Gustav Stresemann and the United States of America: International Economic Ties and the Policy of Revisionism, 1907–1929].* Baden-Baden: Nomos, 1990. This biography of the foreign minister of the Weimar Republic includes a chapter on Stresemann's 1912 trip to the United States, which provides a good example of the German bourgeoisie's ambivalence toward America—both condescending and impressed.

11:260 Blaich, Fritz. *Amerikanische Firmen in Deutschland 1890–1914: US-Direktinvestitionen im* deutschen Maschinenbau [*American Firms in Germany, 1890–1914: U.S. Direct Investment in German Construction Equipment*]. Wiesbaden: F. Steiner, 1984. This is a detailed study of U.S. direct investment in factory tools in Germany. It is based on extensive research in German archives.

11:261 Crouse, Janet K. Wellhousen. "The Decline of German-American Friendship: Beef, Pork, and Politics, 1890–1906." Ph.D. dissertation, University of Delaware, 1980. This excellent dissertation shows that the deterioration in German-American relations at the beginning of the twentieth century was not caused just by high policy differences—such as German defiance of the Monroe Doctrine and the shadow of German militarism—but also by down-to-earth commercial rivalry: Germany restricted U.S. meat exports in response to American tariff rates. Tensions and frustrations accumulated.

11:262 Fiebig-von Hase, Ragnhild. "Die deutsch-amerikanischen Wirtschaftsbeziehungen, 1890–1914 [German-American Economic Relations, 1890–1914]." *Amerikastudien* 33 (June 1988): 329–57. Fiebig-von Hase argues that U.S.-German trade was important to both countries, that both were highly protectionist, and that their economic rivalry created resentment on both sides. However, because Germany was more vulnerable to U.S. tariffs than vice versa, it felt particularly threatened and frustrated.

11:263 Fisk, George M. "German-American Diplomatic and Commercial Relations, Historically Considered." *Review of Reviews* 25 (January-June 1902): 323–28. This article remains of value because its description of commercial, naturalization, and extradition treaties, industrial relations, and the Samoan question sheds light on German-American relations not only in the late nineteenth century, when Fisk was a U.S. consul in Berlin, but also in the early years of the twentieth century.

11:264 Kabisch, Thomas R. *Deutsches Kapital in den USA: Von der Reichsgründung bis zur Sequestrierung (1917) und Freigabe [German Capital in the USA: From the Establishment of the Empire to the Freeze (1917) and Release]*. Stuttgart: Klett-Cotta, 1982. This detailed and well-researched study uses company archives and the contemporary German press to trace the transfer of capital from Germany to German businesses in the United States from 1871 to 1914. Of particular interest is Kabisch's discussion of the attitudes of Germans toward capital investment abroad.

11:265 McClure, Wallace. "German-American Commercial Relations." *American Journal of International Law* 19 (October 1925): 689–701. This article traces the history of the American most-favored-nation clause in treaties with the German states to the treaty of 1923.

11:266 Stone, N. I. "Commercial Relations between Germany and the United States." *North American Review* 182 (March 1906): 433–45. This clear and thorough analysis of the debate over granting MFN to Germany in the Roosevelt administration includes a good history of German-American tariff negotiations. See also his "The International Aspect of Our Tariff Situation," *North American Review* 180 (March 1905): 381–93, and "The New German Customs Tariff," *North American Review* 181 (September 1905): 392–406.

GREAT BRITAIN

11:267 Allen, H. C. *Great Britain and the United States: A History of Anglo-American Relations (1783–1952)*. Allen includes a brief but useful survey of Roosevelt's policy toward Britain (2:322).

11:268 Anderson, Stuart. *Race and Rapprochement: Anglo-Saxonism and Anglo-American Relations, 1895–1904*. Anderson includes chapters dealing with the Anglo-American response to the Boer War and to Russian expansion in the Far East (9:301). See also his "Racial Anglo-Saxonism and the American Response to the Boer War," *Diplomatic History* 2 (Summer 1978): 219–36.

11:269 Bax, Emily. *Miss Bax of the Embassy*. Boston: Houghton Mifflin, 1939. Bax, a Briton, has written a chatty description of life at the U.S. embassy in London where she was a secretary from 1902 to 1913.

11:270 Beloff, Max. *The Great Powers: Essays in Twentieth Century Politics*. London: George Allen and Unwin, 1959. This collection includes a brief and insightful essay on Theodore Roosevelt and the British empire.

11:271 Bevir, Mark. "British Socialism and American Romanticism." *English Historical Review* 110 (September 1995): 878–901. Bevir traces the influence of U.S. romantics, especially Ralph Waldo Emerson and Henry David Thoreau, on the ethical socialism of Britain's Independent Labor Party at the turn of the century.

11:272 Burton, David H. "Theodore Roosevelt and the 'Special Relationship' with Great Britain." *History Today* 23 (August 1973): 527–35. This thorough, accessible article argues that Theodore Roosevelt deserves credit for laying the foundation of the "special relationship" in the twentieth century. Although a consistent anglophile, Roosevelt asserted U.S. interests in disputes with England over the Canadian boundary and the Panama Canal; London acceded to American wishes. His diplomacy in the Russo-Japanese War and Morocco crises furthered the rapprochement. See also his "Theodore Roosevelt and His English Correspondents: The Intellectual Roots of the Anglo-American Alliance," *Mid-America* 53 (January 1971): 12–34, and "Theodore Roosevelt and His English Correspondents: A Special Relationship of Friends," *Transactions of the American Philosophical Society,* New Series 63, no. 2 (1973): 3–70.

11:273 Campbell, Alexander E. *Great Britain and the United States, 1895–1903.* See chapter 10 of this Guide (10:565), and see also Campbell's "Great Britain and the United States in the Far East, 1895–1903," *Historical Journal* 1, no. 2 (1958–1959): 154–75.

11:274 Campbell, Charles Soutter. "Anglo-American Relations, 1897–1901." In *Threshold to American Internationalism: Essays on the Foreign Policies of William McKinley,* ed. Paolo E. Coletta, 221–51. Campbell emphasizes the fragile or "hothouse" quality of the Anglo-American rapprochement.

11:275 _____. *Anglo-American Understanding, 1898–1903.* A painstaking and balanced investigation of the diplomatic negotiations over the isthmian canal and the Alaska boundary during John

Hay's tenure as secretary of state, this book makes exhaustive use of State Department and Foreign Office archives (10:566). It overlaps with Perkins, *The Great Rapprochement: England and the United States, 1895–1914* (1968) (10:580), but remains useful.

11:276 Conyne, G. R. *Woodrow Wilson: British Perspectives, 1912–21.* New York: St. Martin's Press, 1992. This discussion of portraits of Woodrow Wilson limned by prominent Britons contains a chapter on views of the president before the war, which provides Conyne an opportunity to write a concise survey of the key issues troubling U.S.-British relations from 1912 to 1914.

11:277 Coogan, John W. *The End of Neutrality: The United States, Britain, and Maritime Rights, 1899–1915.* Ithaca: Cornell University Press, 1981. Coogan argues that U.S. entry in World War I had its roots not in the discussion of neutral rights in 1914 but rather the longer history of negotiations about maritime rights between London and Washington beginning after the Spanish-American War.

11:278 Crapol, Edward P. "From Anglophobia to Fragile Rapprochement: Anglo-American Relations in the Early Twentieth Century." In *Confrontation and Cooperation: Germany and the United States in the Era of World War I, 1900–1924,* ed. Hans-Jürgen Schröder, 13–31. Providence, RI: Berg Publishers, 1993. This highly condensed and subtle analysis of the growing cooperation between the United States and England at the beginning of the twentieth century highlights London's courtship of Washington in a "lopsided . . . workable, if fragile, rapprochement."

11:279 Dobson, Alan P. *Anglo-American Relations in the Twentieth Century: Of Friendship, Conflict and the Rise and Decline of Superpowers.* This brief survey includes a useful chapter on Anglo-American relations from 1900 to 1919 (2:326).

11:280 Edelstein, Michael. "The Determinants of U.K. Investment Abroad, 1870–1913: The U.S. Case." *Journal of Economic History* 34 (December 1974): 980–1007. Calculations of supply and demand elasticities show that the United States was among several beneficiaries of a demand for high-return, medium-risk assets that accompanied the growth of wealth in Great Britain. "Pull" forces strengthened from 1895 to 1913, but "push" forces dominated British investment in American railway securities.

11:281 Friedberg, Aaron L. *The Weary Titan: Britain and the Experience of Relative Decline, 1895–1905.* Princeton: Princeton University Press, 1988. This elegant volume, based on extensive and perceptive research in the British archives, provides essential background to understanding U.S.-British relations at the time.

11:282 Gelber, Lionel M. *The Rise of Anglo-American Friendship: A Study in World Politics, 1898–1906.* Gelber emphasizes the importance of the rapprochement between Washington and London at the beginning of the twentieth century (10:570). Though still an excellent read, this has been largely superseded by Campbell, *Anglo-American Understanding, 1898–1903* (1957) (10:566) and Perkins, *The Great Rapprochement: England and the United States, 1895–1914* (1968) (10:580).

11:283 Gollin, Alfred. "The Wright Brothers and the British Authorities, 1902–1909." *English Historical Review* 95 (April 1980): 293–320. Gollin traces the British government's early interest in the discoveries of the Wright brothers.

11:284 Heindel, Richard Heathcote. *The American Impact on Great Britain, 1898–1914: A Study of the United States in World History.* This is an early, and pioneering, study of the relations between the two powers as they moved from hostility to friendship and understanding (10:572).

11:285 Hindman, E. James. "The General Arbitration Treaties of William Howard Taft." *Historian* 36 (November 1973): 52–65. This article concentrates on the negotiation of and reaction to the arbitration treaty with England in 1911–1912.

11:286 Kennedy, Paul. *Strategy and Diplomacy, 1870–1945: Eight Studies.* Boston: Allen and Unwin, 1984. This volume includes an interesting essay on Alfred Thayer Mahan's influence on the development of the Royal Navy at the turn of the century.

11:287 Larsen, Peter. "Sir Mortimer Durand in Washington: A Study in Anglo-American Relations in the Era of Theodore Roosevelt." *Mid-America* 66 (April-July 1984): 65–78. Larsen argues that the "Durand affair" of 1906—in which the British ambassador to Washington, Sir Mortimer Durand, was replaced—reflected not only Theodore Roosevelt's dissatisfaction with him but also underlying tensions in the Anglo-American relationship, exacerbated by disagreements over the Russo-Japanese War and the Moroccan crisis.

11:288 McGeoch, Lyle A. "Lord Lansdowne and the American Impact on British Diplomacy, 1900–1905." *Theodore Roosevelt Association Journal* 7 (Fall 1981): 13–18. Lansdowne, British foreign secretary from 1900 to 1905, led his country's policy toward the United States with a sage and steady hand. He preserved British interests, and placated the Americans, in the disputes over Panama, Canada, and Venezuela.

11:289 Monger, George W. *The End of Isolation: British Foreign Policy, 1900–1907.* New York: T. Nelson, 1963. Although this classic account mentions the United States only in passing, it provides essential background to understanding U.S. policy toward Europe.

11:290 Neale, R. G. *Great Britain and United States Expansion: 1898–1900.* Neale includes a thoughtful chapter on the impact of the Spanish-American War on U.S.-British relations (10:576).

11:291 Orde, Anne. *The Eclipse of Great Britain: The United States and British Imperial Decline, 1895–1956.* This cursory study reviews the state of Anglo-American relations in the early years of the twentieth century, focusing mostly on Latin American issues (9:315).

11:292 Pelling, Henry. *America and the British Left: From Bright to Bevan.* New York: New York University Press, 1957. Pelling includes a chapter examining the impact of labor troubles and the growth of monopolies in the United States on the development of the British Labour Party at the beginning of the twentieth century.

11:293 Perkins, Bradford. *The Great Rapproche-*

ment: England and the United States, 1895–1914. This able account of the efforts by the two governments to bring the countries closer together remains useful (10:580).

11:294 Perren, Richard. "The North American Beef and Cattle Trade with Great Britain, 1870–1914." *Economic History Review* 2d ser. 24 (August 1971): 430–44. The shipment of live cattle from North America to the United Kingdom began in 1868 and became important about 1875. Despite restrictions imposed on American cattle by the Contagious Disease Animals Act in 1878, and on Canadian cattle in 1893, and despite humane legislation regulating conditions of transportation, the commerce expanded until about 1900.

11:295 Rippy, J. Fred. "Europe and Hispanic America: The British Bondholders and the Roosevelt Corollary of the Monroe Doctrine." *Political Science Quarterly* 49 (June 1934): 195–207. Rippy presents a careful analysis of the influence of British bondholders with interests in the Dominican Republic on Theodore Roosevelt's formulation of his "corollary" to the Monroe Doctrine (1904) and of their reaction to it. This essay is based on U.S. sources.

11:296 Rothstein, Morton. "America in the International Rivalry for the British Wheat Market, 1860–1914." *Mississippi Valley Historical Review* 47 (December 1960): 401–18. Following repeal of the English corn laws (1846), American wheat production became dependent on the English market. Conversely, Great Britain came to regard the United States as her most dependable source of breadstuffs. By 1900, as rivals adopted American farming and marketing techniques, the United States lost its leadership in the wheat export trade, with disastrous results in the 1920s.

11:297 Seed, Geoffrey. "British Reactions to American Imperialism Reflected in Journals of Opinion, 1898–1900." British opinion supported American expansionism because of racial affinity, the idea of the white man's burden, and American support for the British in China (10:582).

11:298 _____. "British Views of American Policy in the Philippines Reflected in Journals of

Opinion, 1898–1907." See chapter 10 of this Guide (10:583).

11:299 Tilchin, William N. *Theodore Roosevelt and the British Empire: A Study in Presidential Statecraft.* New York: St. Martin's Press, 1997. This study of Theodore Roosevelt's policy toward Britain includes an extended essay on the Jamaica incident, a topic that has received little attention elsewhere. TR personally intervened to resolve the incident that arose when the British governor of Jamaica, J. Alexander Swettenham, rudely addressed a U.S. admiral who was conducting a relief mission on the island following the disastrous earthquake of 1907. The incident is a useful gauge of the growing Anglo-American friendship. See also his "Theodore Roosevelt, Anglo-American Relations and the Jamaica Incident of 1907," *Diplomatic History* 19 (Summer 1995): 385–405, and "The U.S. Navy, the Royal Navy, and Anglo-American Relations during the Presidency of Theodore Roosevelt," *Theodore Roosevelt Association Journal* 22 (Fall 1997): 3–9.

11:300 Ward, Alan J. *Ireland and Anglo-American Relations, 1899–1921.* Toronto: University of Toronto Press, 1969. This case study of the impact of domestic politics on foreign affairs looks at the impact of Britain's "Irish problem" on Anglo-American relations. Ward stresses the displeasure of Irish-Americans at the growing Anglo-American rapprochement.

11:301 Watt, Donald Cameron. "America and the British Foreign-Policy-Making Elite, from Joseph Chamberlain to Anthony Eden, 1895–1956." In *Personalities and Policies: Studies in the Formulation of British Foreign Policy in the Twentieth Century,* ed. Donald Cameron Watt, 19–52. Notre Dame, IN: University of Notre Dame Press, 1965. A suggestive rather than definitive consideration of elites in policy formulation, Watt's hypothesis is that the rapprochement of 1898 to 1906 rested "very much" on the accident that policymakers in both countries belonged to social groups of similar outlooks.

11:302 Willson, Beckles. *America's Ambassadors to England (1785–1929): A Narrative of Anglo-American Diplomatic Relations.* This old-fashioned book includes portraits of John Hay, Joseph H. Choate, Whitelaw Reid, and Walter H. Page, U.S. ambassadors to London, 1898–1918 (6:201).

11:303 _____. *Friendly Relations: A Narrative of Britain's Ministers and Ambassadors to America (1791–1930).* This old-fashioned book includes portraits of Mortimer Durand, James Bryce, and Cecil Spring-Rice, British ambassadors to Washington, 1903–1918 (9:322).

Canada, Alaska, and Fisheries

11:304 Bailey, Thomas A. "Theodore Roosevelt and the Alaska Boundary Settlement." *Canadian Historical Review* 18 (June 1937): 123–35. This essay provides a balanced assessment of the Alaska boundary dispute from the U.S. point of view.

11:305 Baker, W. M. "A Case Study of Anti-Americanism in English-Speaking Canada: The Election Campaign of 1911." *Canadian Historical Review* 51 (December 1970): 426–49. Baker traces the potency of anti-Americanism in the Canadian election of 1911 in which the Conservatives swept to victory after a campaign emphasizing the dangers of the reciprocity agreement the Liberals had negotiated with the United States. Playing on fears of Americanization and annexation, the Conservatives succeeded in killing the agreement. Baker notes that the almost 500,000 U.S. citizens who had emigrated to Canada between 1901 and 1910 gave rise to anti-Americanism, especially in Alberta, where they formed the largest minority. A nuanced conclusion weighs the relative importance of anti-Americanism and of party disorganization in the defeat of the Liberals.

11:306 Bourne, Kenneth. *Britain and the Balance of Power in North America, 1815–1908.* This dense and useful study includes chapters on the rapprochement of 1895–1901 and the tensions in the western Atlantic and Great Lakes in 1901–1908 (6:165).

11:307 Brebner, John Bartlet. *North Atlantic Triangle: The Interplay of Canada, the United States and Great Britain.* This survey includes a chapter on the period when the North Atlantic triangle was formed, 1880–1917 (2:323).

11:308 Carroll, Francis M. "Robert Lansing and the Alaskan Boundary Settlement." *International History Review* 9 (May 1987): 270–90. This is a reprint, with an extended introduction, of an address that Robert Lansing (who participated in the tribunal as a young lawyer) gave in 1904 in which he vividly describes the Alaska boundary negotiations and offers his opinion that while the U.S. case was solid, the Canadian objections were not spurious.

11:309 Clements, Kendrick A. "Manifest Destiny and Canadian Reciprocity in 1911." *Pacific Historical Review* 42 (February 1973): 32–52. Clements argues that the reciprocity agreement of 1911 posed little danger to Canada.

11:310 Dorsey, Kurkpatrick. *The Dawn of Conservation Diplomacy: U.S.-Canadian Wildlife Protection Treaties in the Progressive Era.* Seattle: University of Washington Press, 1998. This is the first full-scale scholarly study of three key treaty negotiations between the United States and Canada: the Inland Fisheries Treaty (1908), North Pacific Fur Seal Convention (1911), and Migratory Bird Treaty (1916). Attacking the issue from a conservationist's viewpoint rather than a strictly diplomatic one, Dorsey analyzes why the fisheries treaty failed to conserve fish stocks, while the seal convention proved to be a great success. See also his "Scientists, Citizens, and Statesmen: U.S.-Canadian Wildlife Protection Treaties in the Progressive Era," *Diplomatic History* 19 (Summer 1995): 407–29.

11:311 Ellis, L. Ethan. *Reciprocity 1911: A Study in Canadian-American Relations.* New Haven: Yale University Press, 1939. This careful and detailed analysis emphasizes the role of political concerns in the 1911 negotiations on reciprocity between the United States and Canada.

11:312 Fisher, Robin. "Duff and George Go West: A Tale of Two Frontiers." *Canadian Historical Review* 68 (December 1987): 501–28. This tale of two brothers born in Ontario in the 1870s who ventured westward in the 1890s, one in the U.S. west, the other in Canada, is a lively comparison of the two frontiers at the beginning of the twentieth century.

11:313 Fraser, Allan M. "Fisheries Negotiations with the United States, 1783–1910." In *Newfoundland: Economic, Diplomatic, and Strategic Studies,* ed. R. A. Mackay, 333–410. Toronto: Oxford University Press, 1946. Reprint 1979 (AMS Press). In 1905,

Newfoundland, irritated by the U.S. refusal to ratify the Bond-Hay Convention, declared that the United States could not fish in the bays and harbors of Newfoundland. Fraser describes the ensuing controversy, and its submission to the Hague in 1910, in two insightful and detailed chapters.

11:314   Gluek, Alvin C., Jr. "Programmed Diplomacy: The Settlement of the North Atlantic Fisheries Question, 1907–1912." *Acadiensis* 6 (Autumn 1976): 43–70. In this comprehensive analysis of the North Atlantic fisheries question, Gluek asserts that the 1910 Hague decision was cryptic and subtle, leading Canadian authors to interpret it as pro-Canadian, while Americans have seen it as pro-American. In fact, its intent was unclear until 1912, when a second treaty, clearly favoring American interests, was struck.

11:315   Granatstein, J. L. *How Britain's Weakness Forced Canada into the Arms of the United States.* Toronto: University of Toronto Press, 1989. This slim volume of essays by a Canadian historian includes a brief analysis of the 1911 reciprocity negotiations.

11:316   Granatstein, J. L., and Norman Hillmer. *For Better or For Worse: Canada and the United States to the 1990s.* This breezy, journalistic survey covers the disputes over Alaska, fisheries, and reciprocity (2:304).

11:317   Green, Lewis. *The Boundary Hunters: Surveying the 141st Meridian and the Alaskan Panhandle.* Vancouver: University of British Columbia Press, 1982. This detailed study of the Alaskan boundary dispute (1825–1913) by a Canadian geologist concentrates on the surveyors but does not ignore the politicians. Green is critical of America's strong-arm tactics and Britain's flaccidity at the Alaska boundary tribunal in 1903.

11:318   Hannigan, Robert E. "Reciprocity 1911: Continentalism and American *Weltpolitik.*" *Diplomatic History* 4 (Winter 1980): 1–18. In 1910 and 1911, the Taft administration sought to negotiate a reciprocal tariff agreement with Canada to pave the way toward the economic annexation of Canada, to block imperial preferences, and to bring Canada into a commercial union with the United States. The agreement was popular with many export firms in

the United States but was defeated by Canadian conservatives backed by British protectionists. See also his "Continentalism and *Mitteleuropa* as Points of Departure for a Comparison of American and German Foreign Relations in the Early Twentieth Century," in Schröder, *Confrontation and Cooperation: Germany and the United States in the Era of World War I, 1900–1924* (Providence, RI: Berg, 1993): 33–68.

11:319   Keenleyside, Hugh L. *Canada and the United States: Some Aspects of Their Historical Relations.* Rev. and enl. ed. New York: Alfred A. Knopf, 1952. Reprint 1971 (Kennikat Press). This study is important for boundary and fishing controversies. Originally published in 1929 as *Canada and the United States: Some Aspects of the History of the Republic and the Dominion.*

11:320   Martin, Lawrence. *The Presidents and the Prime Ministers: Washington and Ottawa Face to Face: The Myth of Bilateral Bliss, 1867–1982.* This is a journalistic survey of U.S.-Canadian relations, including three chapters dealing with the 1900–1914 period (9:367).

11:321   Neary, Peter. "Grey, Bryce, and the Settlement of Canadian-American Differences, 1905–1911." *Canadian Historical Review* 49 (December 1968): 357–80. Neary looks beyond the mundane disputes (fisheries, fur seals) to the transformations in U.S.-Canadian-British relations from the 1903 Alaska tribunal to the 1911 defeat of reciprocity and fall of the Laurier government.

11:322   Penlington, Norman. *The Alaska Boundary Dispute: A Critical Reappraisal.* Toronto: McGraw-Hill Ryerson, 1972. Penlington offers a bitter Canadian perspective on the Alaskan boundary dispute between the United States and Canada from 1896 to 1903.

11:323   Preston, Richard A. *The Defence of the Undefended Border: Planning for War in North America, 1867–1939.* This study of the military factor in Canadian-American relations investigates war planning in Canada, the United States, and Britain. Acknowledging that much planning for a North American war was primarily for training purposes, and keeping his conclusions modest, Preston nevertheless brings to light an important and little studied aspect of the triangular relationship. In his investigation of official and unofficial thinking in Canada and the United States about the problems of fighting such a war, Preston shows that the improved war planning abilities of the U.S. army revealed that the conquest of Canada would be difficult, despite British withdrawal and increasing U.S. strength (9:368).

11:324 Sarty, Roger. "Canada and the Great Rapprochement, 1902–1914." In *The North Atlantic Triangle in a Changing World: Anglo-American-Canadian Relations, 1902–1956,* ed. Brian J. C. McKercher and Lawrence Aronsen, 12–47. Toronto: University of Toronto Press, 1996. This essay is a useful overview of how Canada's land and maritime defense policies affected—and were affected by—its relations with Britain and the United States from 1902 to 1914.

11:325 Scheinberg, Stephen. "Invitation to Empire: Tariffs and American Economic Expansion in Canada." *Business History Review* 47 (Summer 1973): 218–38. Scheinberg forces U.S.-Canadian economic history into "a banana republic mold," arguing that the United States consciously sought economic conquest of Canada, and Canadians consciously welcomed it, in the final decades of the nineteenth century and the first decades of the twentieth.

11:326 Shields, R. A. "Imperial Policy and Canadian-American Commercial Relations, 1880–1911." *Bulletin of the Institute of Historical Research* 59 (May 1986): 108–21. This is an admirably concise description of the "hostile and abrasive Canadian-American commercial relations" in the thirty years preceding the 1911 reciprocity agreement.

11:327 Stacey, Charles P. *Canada and the Age of Conflict: A History of Canadian External Policies. Vol. 1: 1867–1921.* Toronto: Macmillan of Canada, 1977. In this clear, comprehensive, and solidly researched account, Stacey deals at length with the shifting U.S.-Canadian-British triangle from 1896 to 1914. He predictably stresses the Alaska issue and the reciprocity treaty but also adds an interesting discussion of the problem of Asian immigration in U.S.-Canadian relations.

11:328 Stewart, Gordon T. *The American Response to Canada since 1776.* This ambitious study includes an interesting chapter on U.S.-Canadian trade relations in the early years of the twentieth century (2:305). See also his "'A Special Contiguous Country Economic Regime': An Overview of America's Canadian Policy," *Diplomatic History* 6 (Fall 1982): 339–58.

11:329 Tansill, Charles Callan. *Canadian-American Relations, 1875–1911.* This is the most comprehensive source on the Alaska boundary settlement from the U.S. point of view. Fisheries are also dealt with in detail and arbitral tribunals and commissions described carefully (9:373).

11:330 Thompson, John Herd, and Stephen J. Randall. *Canada and the United States: Ambivalent Allies.* This survey of U.S.-Canadian relations includes one chapter describing the state of affairs at the beginning of the twentieth century when Canada and the United States were on the verge of establishing a bilateral relationship independent of Great Britain. First issued in 1994 (2:306).

The Boer War

11:331 Changuion, Louis J. S. "Arbitration or Mediation? The Role Played by the U.S.A. in the Anglo-Boer War, 1899–1902." Ph.D. dissertation, University of South Africa, 1982. During the Boer War, American public opinion was pro-Boer and anti-British, but the McKinley and Roosevelt administrations successfully protected the growing rapprochement with Great Britain. Particularly important was the role of Roosevelt's secretary of state, John Hay. This dissertation is written in Afrikaans.

11:332 Ferguson, John H. *American Diplomacy and the Boer War.* See chapter 10 of this Guide (10:568).

11:333 Gatewood, Willard B., Jr. "Black Americans and the Boer War, 1899–1902." Many African-Americans lent support to the British cause during the Boer War and were disappointed that the settlement imposed conditions on Africans that resembled the conditions of blacks in the American south (10:569).

11:334 Knee, Stuart E. "Anglo-American Understanding and the Boer War." This competent overview argues that the U.S. assertion of neutral rights in the Boer War in fact tilted Washington toward London, thereby provoking controversy in the United States and also paving the way for deepening Anglo-American friendship (10:574).

11:335 Mulanax, Richard B. "South Africa and the United States at the End of the 19th Century: The Boer War in American Politics and Diplomacy." Ph.D. dissertation, Florida State University, 1992. American concern for South Africa during the Boer War focused on how the war affected wider American interests, and especially the budding rapprochement with Britain. Guided by Secretary of State John Hay, the United States emerged from this diplomatic cauldron unscathed. Hay was accused of subordinating the interests of his country to Britain but in reality consistently pressed Britain for concessions, which the British made to garner American diplomatic support.

11:336 Noer, Thomas J. *Briton, Boer, and Yankee: The United States and South Africa, 1870–1914.* This competent study deals at some length with the U.S. response to the Boer War and with U.S. interest in South Africa after the war, and therefore touches on U.S.-British relations at the turn of the century (10:577).

11:337 Sands, W. H. "The American and African Civil Wars." *Contemporary Review* 79 (May 1901): 664–70. This is an interesting comparative examination of the American and Boer civil wars, separated by a generation in time and by the Atlantic Ocean.

Great Britain and Latin America

11:338 Adams, William. "Strategy, Diplomacy, and Isthmian Canal Security, 1880–1917." Ph.D. dissertation, Florida State University, 1974. Adams includes a competent discussion of isthmian security and U.S. relations with Britain during the Theodore Roosevelt presidency.

11:339 Calvert, Peter. "Great Britain and the New World, 1905–1914." In *British Foreign Policy under Sir Edward Grey,* ed. F. H. Hinsley, 382–94. New York: Cambridge University Press, 1977. Calvert provides a useful overview of U.S.-British relations and an astute discussion of London and Washington's policies toward Latin America, particularly Mexico. (Other chapters in this edited volume include passing references to Grey's policy toward the United States.)

11:340 _____. *The Mexican Revolution, 1910–1914: The Diplomacy of Anglo-American Conflict.* Cambridge, UK: Cambridge University Press, 1968. This excellent book, based on extensive research in the British archives, examines Anglo-American conflict and eventual agreement on Mexican policy. The relationship between British and American oil companies in Mexico and how this relationship affected British and U.S. diplomatic action is given some emphasis.

11:341 Coker, William S. "The Panama Canal Tolls Controversy: A Different Perspective." *Journal of American History* 55 (December 1968): 555–64. Coker discusses the canal tolls controversy within the context of the terms of the Anglo-American arbitration treaty of 1908 and the British desire to submit the dispute to arbitration. After this treaty was renewed in 1914, Wilson pushed for repeal of the discriminatory tolls law.

11:342 Grenville, J. A. S. "Great Britain and the Isthmian Canal, 1898–1901." *American Historical Review* 61 (October 1955): 48–69. Grenville argues, persuasively, that the Hay-Pauncefote Treaty of 1901 marked Britain's conscious recognition of U.S. preeminence in the Western Hemisphere.

11:343 Kaplan, Edward S. "William Jennings Bryan and the Panama Tolls Controversy." *Mid-America* 56 (April 1974): 100–08. Kaplan seeks to redress the neglect of William Jennings Bryan's pivotal role in the resolution of the Panama tolls controversy. He stresses the importance of Bryan's contribution to the passage of the Sims Act, which repealed the exemption clause in the Panama Canal Act of 1912.

11:344 Kneer, Warren G. *Great Britain and the Caribbean, 1901–1913: A Study in Anglo-American Relations.* East Lansing: Michigan State University Press, 1975. In this excellent study, the author argues that Great Britain conceded political hegemony to the United States in the Caribbean area after the Spanish-American War of 1898 but insisted on an economic open door and equal opportunity in financial and commercial matters.

11:345   Scholes, Walter V., and Marie V. Scholes. "Wilson, Grey, and Huerta." *Pacific Historical Review* 37 (May 1968): 151–58. Using British documents, the authors show that Sir Edward Grey thought Wilson's policy in Mexico was unwise and tried to change Wilson's attitudes toward Huerta.

11:346   Wells, Samuel F., Jr. "British Strategic Withdrawal from the Western Hemisphere, 1904–1906." *Canadian Historical Review* 49 (December 1968): 335–56. This very good analysis of the thinking behind the British decision to withdraw the bulk of its fleet from the Western Hemisphere and to rely on U.S. friendship is based on a close reading of British documents.

ITALY AND THE VATICAN

11:347   Aicardi, Cinzia Maria, and Alessandra Cavaterra, eds. *I fondi archivistici della Legazione Sarda e delle Rappresentanze Diplomatiche Italiane negli U.S.A. (1848–1901) [The Archives of the Sardinian Legation and of Italian Diplomatic Posts in the United States (1848–1901)].* Rome: Instituto Poligrafico e Zecca dello Stato, 1988. This volume provides useful background to an understanding of U.S.-Italian relations from 1900 to 1914.

11:348   Albònico, Aldo, and Gianfausto Rosoli. *Italia y América [Italy and America].* Madrid: Editorial MAPFRE, 1994. This survey includes a competent, if brief, overview of U.S.-Italian relations from 1900 to 1915, focusing on immigration, the dominant issue between the two countries. Beginning in the 1880s, large numbers of Italians, most from the south and illiterate, emigrated to the United States where they faced virulent anti-Italian prejudice, culminating in several well-publicized lynchings.

11:349   Alvarez, David J. "Purely a Business Matter: The Taft Mission to the Vatican." *Diplomatic History* 16 (Summer 1992): 357–69. In 1902, William Howard Taft, then governor of the Philip-

pines, led a U.S. delegation to persuade the Holy See to dispose of the friars' lands in the Philippines. The U.S. government believed the hostility of the local population toward the friars was complicating its task of pacification and wanted, ultimately, to expel the religious orders. While the mission failed, it represented a new awareness on the part of both the Vatican and the United States that relations between the two were not irrelevant.

11:350   Bosworth, R. J. B. *Italy, the Least of the Great Powers: Italian Foreign Policy before the First World War.* New York: Cambridge University Press, 1979. After noting that the United States was important to Italy both as the destination of choice for emigrants and its third largest trading partner, Bosworth makes the relevant point that "Italian diplomatists, even more than their other European counterparts, continued to underestimate or simply ignore the growing might of the United States."

11:351   Caroli, Betty Boyd. *Italian Repatriation from the United States, 1890–1914.* New York: Center for Migration Studies, 1973. Caroli's comprehensive study includes a chapter on the reaction of the Italian government to emigration to and repatriation from the United States.

11:352   Ciuffoletti, Zeffiro. *L'emigrazione nella storia d'Italia dal 1868 al 1914: Storia e documenti [Emigration in Italian History from 1868–1914: History and Documents].* Firenze: Vallecchi, 1978. Ciuffoletti, whose useful volume includes Italian documents dealing with emigration, discusses the Italian government's alarm at the measures debated in the United States in 1897, 1902, 1907, and 1913 to restrict the immigration of illiterates, a category that included the majority of Italians emigrating to the United States. The Italian authorities were concerned that such restrictions could have had serious repercussions on internal stability in Italy.

11:353   Draper, William F. *Recollections of a Varied Career.* Boston: Little, Brown and Company, 1908. This memoir includes several chapters on Draper's experiences as U.S. ambassador to Italy (1897–1900), when the principal concerns were murders of Italians in the United States, immigration, and commercial agreements. Draper adds trenchant reflections on the U.S. diplomatic corps at the time.

11:354　Farrell, John T. "Background of the Taft Mission to Rome." *Catholic Historical Review* 37 (April 1951): 1–22. This article, which includes certain relevant documents, explains the background to the negotiations for the American purchase of the friar lands in the Philippines.

11:355　Fogarty, Gerald P. *The Vatican and the American Hierarchy from 1870–1965.* Stuttgart: Anton Hiersemann, 1982. Reprint 1985 (Liturgical Press). This bureaucratic survey contains a few pages on relations between the Vatican and the U.S. church in the early decades of the twentieth century, a time of the Romanization of the U.S. hierarchy.

11:356　Lowe, C. J., and F. Marzari. *Italian Foreign Policy, 1870–1940.* London: Routledge and Paul, 1975. This competent survey is noteworthy only because it typifies the lack of attention paid to Italian-U.S. relations. Lowe and Marzari do not mention the United States until after covering World War I.

11:357　Mangione, Jerre, and Ben Morreale. *La Storia: Five Centuries of the Italian American Experience.* New York: HarperCollins Publishers, 1992. This superb study of the Italian experience in America is wide-ranging but places particular emphasis on the 1880–1924 period, the years of the great migration. It describes what the immigrants left behind in Italy, what motivated them to leave, and what greeted them in the United States. It does not deal with U.S.-Italian diplomatic relations.

11:358　Vernassa, Maurizio. *Emigrazione, diplomazia e cannoniere. L'intervento italiano in Venezuela, 1902–1903 [Emigration, Diplomacy, and Gunboats: Italy's Intervention in Venezuela, 1902–1903].* Livorno: Editrice Stella, 1980. Vernassa deals with a forgotten aspect of what is often called the Anglo-German blockade of Venezuela (1902–1903): Italy was also a blockading power. He discusses the muted U.S. reaction to Italian participation. This book is based largely on Italian sources and includes a selection of relevant documents.

11:359　Villari, Luigi. *Gli Stati Uniti d'America e l'emigrazione italiana [The United States of America and Italian Emigration].* Milano: Fratelli Treves Editori, 1912. Reprint 1975 (Arno Press). Villari devotes most of his book to a description of the United States, but he also includes a detailed, dispassionate description of the Italian communities therein at the turn of the century. He does not treat diplomatic issues.

RUSSIA

11:360　Allen, Robert V. *Russia Looks at America: The View to 1917.* Washington, DC: Library of Congress, 1988. Although Allen deals briefly with diplomatic relations between Russia and the United States from 1900 to 1914, his most interesting chapters on the period describe Russian reactions to U.S. literature, film, technology, and education. He also compares U.S. and Russian agricultural practices.

11:361　Bailey, Thomas A. *America Faces Russia: Russian-American Relations from Early Times to Our Day.* Bailey's readable descriptions of the impact of the Russo-Japanese War and the Russian persecution of Jews on U.S.-Russian relations in the early years of the twentieth century remain useful (4:257).

11:362　Dement'ev, I. P. "Leo Tolstoy and Social Critics in the United States at the Turn of the Century." In *Russian-American Dialogue on Cultural Relations, 1776–1914,* ed. Norman E. Saul and Richard D. McKinzie, 170–91. Columbia: University of Missouri Press, 1997. After 1885, Tolstoy's works began to receive attention in the United States, where he was frequently perceived as both a moral and political teacher. In turn, Tolstoy criticized U.S. monopolistic capitalism and praised America's respect for freedom of expression.

11:363　Gaddis, John Lewis. *Russia, the Soviet Union, and the United States: An Interpretive History.* This respected text includes one chapter on U.S.-Russian relations at the turn of the century, focusing, correctly, on the two controversial issues: the Far East and the treatment of Jews in Russia (2:309). First published in 1978.

11:364　Lincoln, A. "Theodore Roosevelt and the First Russian-American Crisis." *Southern California Quarterly* 45 (December 1963): 323–36. Lincoln focuses on U.S.-Russian relations in 1903, a time when relations between the two countries became increasingly tense over increasing Russian domination of China, especially Manchuria.

11:365   Minger, Ralph Eldin. "William Howard Taft's Forgotten Visit to Russia." *Russian Review* 22 (April 1963): 149–56. Relying on the Taft papers, correspondence and contemporary memoirs, Minger describes Taft's visit to Russia in 1907 as secretary of war. "He was now far more disposed to view Russia in a friendly light," Minger argues.

11:366   Saul, Norman E. *Concord and Conflict: The United States and Russia, 1867–1914.* This is the most authoritative source on U.S.-Russian relations from the end of the U.S. Civil War to World War I. Saul examines diplomatic, cultural, and economic ties using Russian and American archives, the press, memoirs, and extensive secondary sources in Russian and English. His command of detail is impressive and at times overwhelming (9:348).

11:367   Schimmelpenninck van der Oye, David. "From Cooperation to Confrontation? Reflections on the Russian-American Encounter on the Pacific." *Itinerario [Netherlands]* 22, no. 3 (1998): 39–50. Senator Albert Beveridge, a close ally of Theodore Roosevelt, wrote a best-selling book about the Russian Far East in 1901 following his tour of the area. At a time when most American leaders were turning against Russia, Beveridge enthusiastically described its expansion and compared it favorably to traditional imperial powers like Britain and France.

11:368   Smith, Shannon. "From Relief to Revolution: American Women and the Russian-American Relationship, 1890–1917." Clara Barton, president of American Red Cross, was involved in famine relief; Alice Stone Blackwell, a leading suffragist, helped shape the anticzarist movement. Both represent the reformist impulse in the United States (9:182).

11:369   Thompson, Arthur W., and Robert A. Hart. *The Uncertain Crusade: America and the Russian Revolution of 1905.* Amherst: University of Massachusetts Press, 1970. This study examines the rapid shifts in the response of the U.S. press to the 1905 Russian revolution from enthusiasm to doubt, disillusionment, and downright hostility.

11:370   Trani, Eugene P. "Russia in 1905. The View from the American Embassy." *Review of Politics* 31 (January 1969): 48–63. Trani describes the diplomatic reporting provided by the U.S. ambassador, George von Lengerke Meyer (1905–1907), pertaining to the abortive revolution of 1905 and Russo-Japanese peace moves. He concludes that much of Meyer's reporting was distorted, missing the essence of Russian political discontent due to his limited, upper-class Russian sources.

11:371   Travis, Frederick F. *George Kennan and the American-Russian Relationship, 1865–1924.* Travis contends that George Kennan, a leading U.S. expert on Russia from 1865 until his death in 1924, had a decisive influence on U.S. public opinion. By 1886, he had turned from admirer to critic of St. Petersburg, and through his many popular publications and lectures brought U.S. public opinion with him. He exercised less influence on the U.S. government's perception of Russia (9:112).

11:372   Tsvirkun, A. F. "Some Questions on American Foreign Policy in 1898–1914 in the Russian Bourgeois Press." In *Russian-American Dialogue on Cultural Relations, 1776–1914,* ed. Norman E. Saul and Richard D. McKinzie, 227–40. Columbia: University of Missouri Press, 1997. Three bourgeois liberal monthlies *(Vestnik Evropy, Mir Bozhii, Russkaia Mysl)* provided extensive coverage of U.S. foreign policy and society in the early years of the twentieth century. They focused on the peace and arbitration movements, and, while impressed by American democracy, tended to be critical of U.S. expansionism. See also the comment by Norman E. Saul (241–42).

11:373   Viatkin, M. P., ed. *Iz istorii imperializma v Rossii [From the History of Imperialism in Russia].* Leningrad: Izdatel'stvo Akademii Nauk SSSR, 1959. As a product of the Soviet Academy of Sciences Institute of History's talented and less ideological Leningrad branch, this collection includes articles by several of the best Soviet scholars. On U.S.-Russian relations at the beginning of the twentieth century, see especially Alexander A. Fursenko, "From the History of Russian-American Relations at the Turn of the 19th Century" (219–69). See also L. E. Shepelev, "The Establishment of Joint-Stock Companies in Russia" (134–82); B. V. Anan'ich, "The Russian Autocracy and Foreign Loans in 1898–1902" (183–

218); and R. Sh. Ganelin, "Financial-Economic Relations of Russia and the USA after the Beginning of the First World War (August 1914–November 1915)" (270–308).

11:374   Williams, William Appleman. *American-Russian Relations, 1781–1947*. This lively and opinionated study remains useful. In a concise chapter, Williams traces the "disintegration of American-Russian relations" from 1898 to 1905, focusing on conflicts over Tsarist treatment of the Jews (2:314).

11:375   Zabriskie, Edward H. *American-Russian Rivalry in the Far East: A Study in Diplomacy and Power Politics, 1894–1914*. Philadelphia: University of Pennsylvania Press, 1946. Reprint 1973 (Greenwood Press). This remains a useful study of U.S.-Russian tensions in Manchuria and of U.S.-Russian relations during the Russo-Japanese War (1904–1905). Zabriskie argues that TR had to assume personal control of the negotiations after his aides failed him. Based largely on U.S. documents.

Russo-Japanese War

11:376   Best, Gary Dean. "Financing a Foreign War: Jacob H. Schiff and Japan, 1904–05." *American Jewish Historical Quarterly* 61 (June 1972): 313–24. Close to 25 percent of the total foreign loans Japan received during its war against Russia were raised in the United States. Jacob H. Schiff (1847–1920), outraged by Russia's persecution of the Jews, played a leading role in these efforts.

11:377   Brodskii, Roman Mikhailovich. "K Voprosu o pozitii S.Sh.A. v russko-iaponskoi voine i portsmutskikh peregovorakh [On the Position of the U.S.A. in the Russo-Japanese War and the Portsmouth Treaties]." *Voprosy istorii [Problems of History]* 2 (February 1959): 144–55. In this critique of U.S. historiography on the Russo-Japanese War and the Portsmouth treaty, Brodskii argues that American "ruling circles" miscalculated in thinking their tilt toward Japan during the war and the subsequent negotiations would benefit U.S. economic penetration of China.

11:378   Dennett, Tyler. *Roosevelt and the Russo-Japanese War: A Critical Study of American Policy in Eastern Asia, 1902–5, Based Primarily upon the Private Papers of Theodore Roosevelt*. Garden City, NY: Doubleday, Page and Company, 1925. This comprehensive study uses the Roosevelt papers to describe U.S. relations with Russia and Germany during the Russo-Japanese War. Dennett asserts that Roosevelt greatly helped the Japanese attain a favorable outcome at Portsmouth.

11:379   Dobrov, Aleksandr Solomonovich. *Dal'nevostochnaia politika S.Sh.A. v period russko-iaponskoi voiny [The Far Eastern Policy of the U.S.A. in the Period of the Russo-Japanese War]*. Moscow: Gosudarstvennoe izdatel'stvo politicheskoi literatury, 1952. This standard work is a full-dress indictment of the American imperialists' role in the Russo-Japanese War and in the Far East in general at the beginning of the twentieth century. See Ernest May's comments, "The Far Eastern Policy of the United States in the Period of the Russo-Japanese War: A Russian View," *American Historical Review* 62 (January 1957): 345–51.

11:380   Esthus, Raymond A. *Double Eagle and Rising Sun: The Russians and Japanese at Portsmouth in 1905*. Durham, NC: Duke University Press, 1988. This excellent study, which relies on U.S., Japanese, and Russian sources, focuses on the Russo-Japanese peace negotiations at Portsmouth and therefore includes extensive discussion of U.S.-Russian relations.

11:381   _____. "Roosevelt, Russia, and Peacemaking 1905." In *Perspectives in American Foreign Policy: Essays on Europe, Latin America, China, and the Cold War: Papers Selected from the Society for Historians of American Foreign Relations' First National Meeting, Held at Georgetown University, August 15–16, 1975*, ed. Jules Davids, 2–29. New York: Arno Press, 1976. Esthus challenges the belief that Theodore Roosevelt deserves primary credit for the success of the Portsmouth conference and emphasizes, instead, the contribution of the Russian delegate, Count Witte.

11:382   _____. *Theodore Roosevelt and Japan*. Seattle: University of Washington Press, 1967. This authoritative book about U.S. relations with Japan touches on U.S.-Russian relations, particularly during the 1905 Portsmouth conference.

11:383   Gal'perin, A. L. "Diplomaticheskaia podgotovka Portsmutskoi mirnoi konferentsii Iapono-anglo-amerikanskim blokom [The Diplomatic Preparation of the Treaty of Portsmouth through the Anglo-American-Japanese Bloc]." *Istoricheskie zapiski* 50 (1955): 169–223. This presents the Soviet perception of America's role in the Russo-Japanese War, based on U.S. primary sources.

11:384   _____. "Iz Istorii Iaponskoi i Amerkano-angliiskoi diplomatii vo vremia Russko-iaponskoi voiny 1904–1905 [From the History of Japanese and Anglo-American Diplomacy during the Russo-Japanese War 1904–1905]." In *Sbornik statei po istorii stran dal'nego vostoka [Collected Articles on the History of the Countries of the Far East]*, ed. L. V. Simonovskaia and M. F. Iur'ev, 191–202. Moscow: Izdatel'stvo Moskovskogo universiteta, 1952. Gal'perin, a serious scholar from the University of Moscow, uses Russian, English, and Japanese sources to support the contention that during the Russo-Japanese War Russia was somehow victimized by the imperialists, i.e., the United States, Great Britain, and Japan.

11:385   Greenwood, John Thomas. "The American Military Observers of the Russo-Japanese War (1904–1905)." Ph.D. dissertation, Kansas State University, 1971. This voluminous military history of the war sheds some light on U.S.-Russian relations.

11:386   Johnson, Paul W. "The Journalist as Diplomat: E. J. Dillon and the Portsmouth Peace Conference." *Journalism Quarterly* 53 (Winter 1976): 689–93. Dr. Emile Joseph Dillon (1854–1953), the St. Petersburg correspondent for the London *Daily Telegraph* during the Russo-Japanese War (1904–1905), led the public relations campaign in the American press on behalf of the Russian negotiator, Sergei Witte.

11:387   Parsons, Edward B. "Roosevelt's Containment of the Russo-Japanese War." *Pacific Historical Review* 38 (February 1969): 21–44. This article examines Roosevelt's claim that he cautioned Germany not to align with Russia against Japan in 1904–1905 and concludes that Roosevelt did indeed warn the Germans to back off. The article includes a historiographical treatment of Roosevelt's attempt to use Japan as the lever for an open door in China.

11:388   Thorson, Winston B. "American Public Opinion and the Portsmouth Peace Conference." *American Historical Review* 53 (April 1948): 439–64. This article seeks to overturn the notion that Japan's supposedly harsh peace terms made Americans more cognizant of growing Japanese domination in East Asia. The author concludes that the peace of Portsmouth did not sway American opinion away from Japan and cannot be considered a significant turning point in American-Japanese relations.

11:389   Trani, Eugene P. *The Treaty of Portsmouth: An Adventure in American Diplomacy.* Lexington: University Press of Kentucky, 1969. This book, based on multiarchival research, gives Roosevelt the greater share of credit for ending the Russo-Japanese War. Roosevelt persuaded the Japanese to limit their demands, while at the same time convincing the Russians to cut their losses.

11:390   Ueda, Toshio. "The Russo-Japanese War and the Attitude of the United States." In *Japan-American Diplomatic Relations in the Meiji-Taisho Era,* ed. Hikomotsu Kamikawa, 195–264. Tokyo: Pan-Pacific Press, 1958. This discussion of the U.S. response to the Russo-Japanese War presents the Japanese point of view systematically, quoting Japanese and American officials, but provides no footnotes or indication of its sources.

11:391   White, John Albert. *The Diplomacy of the Russo-Japanese War.* Princeton: Princeton University Press, 1964. Using sources that were not available to Dennett when he wrote his standard account of the war, *Roosevelt and the Russo-Japanese War: A Critical Study of American Policy in Eastern Asia, 1902–5, Based Primarily upon the Private Papers of Theodore Roosevelt* (1925) (11:378), White expands rather than supplants Dennett's argument by presenting an international and carefully balanced point of view. He focuses on the diplomatic rather than the military side of the war and includes a comprehensive discussion of the Portsmouth conference.

Jews and Russian Antisemitism

11:392   Adler, Cyrus, and Aaron M. Margalith. *With Firmness in the Right: American Diplomatic*

Action Affecting Jews, 1840–1945. New York: American Jewish Committee, 1946. Reprint 1977 (Arno Press). This study, arranged by country and chronologically, includes an extended discussion of U.S. diplomacy on behalf of Jews in Russia, 1864–1933.

11:393   Best, Gary Dean. *To Free a People: American Jewish Leaders and the Jewish Problem in Eastern Europe, 1890–1914.* Best examines the reaction of U.S. Jews to the persecution of Jews in Russia and Romania, describes the lobbying efforts of U.S. Jewish leaders on their behalf, and explains the deleterious effect of this persecution on U.S.-Russian relations. He also describes the important role U.S. Jewish financiers played in the Russo-Japanese War by raising loans on behalf of Japan (9:353).

11:394   Healy, Ann E. "Tsarist Anti-Semitism and Russian-American Relations." Healy describes how Tsarist mistreatment of Jews hurt U.S.-Russian relations. In 1906, Jewish leaders in the United States formed the American Jewish Committee to pressure the White House and State Department to protest Russia's antisemitic policies (9:346).

11:395   Knee, Stuart E. "The Diplomacy of Neutrality: Theodore Roosevelt and the Russian Pogroms of 1903–1906." *Presidential Studies Quarterly* 19 (Winter 1989): 71–78. Knee discusses how Russian antisemitism affected relations with the United States during the Roosevelt administration.

11:396   Kuznets, Simon. "Immigration of Russian Jews to the United States: Background and Structure." *Perspectives in American History* 9 (1975): 35–124. From 1881 to 1914, 13 million Russian Jews emigrated to the United States, motivated by the pressures of industrialization and new technology, the dislocation of people from the land, and rising antisemitism in Russia.

11:397   Nolan, Cathal J. "The United States and Tsarist Anti-Semitism, 1865–1914." *Diplomacy & Statecraft* 3 (November 1992): 438–67. This competent overview traces the "long, slow deterioration in the overall relationship" between Russia and the United States due to czarist antisemitism.

11:398   Schoenberg, Philip Ernest. "The American Reaction to the Kishinev Pogrom of 1903." *American Jewish Historical Quarterly* 63 (March 1974): 262–83. In 1903, U.S. Jewish leaders convinced Theodore Roosevelt to present a petition to the czar protesting the pogrom against the Jews of Kishinev. Although the Russian government refused to accept the petition, the publicity it had garnered in the U.S. press had already made its point. Furthermore, it set a precedent of U.S. governmental protest against the violation of human rights by governments within their own borders.

11:399   Shankman, Arnold. "Brothers across the Sea: Afro-Americans on the Persecution of Russian Jews, 1881–1917." *Jewish Social Studies* 37 (Spring 1975): 114–21. From 1881 to 1917, African-Americans joined European and American liberals in attacking Russian antisemitism. Unlike other protesters, however, they emphasized the parallel between czarist oppressions of the Jews and white America's persecution of blacks.

11:400   Stults, Taylor. "Roosevelt, Russian Persecution of Jews, and American Public Opinion." *Jewish Social Studies* 33 (January 1971): 13–22. Stults traces the reaction of the U.S. Jewish community to the 1903 pogrom in Kishinev, Russia. In addition to holding protest meetings, Jews tried to obtain an official statement from the U.S. government, which led to correspondence between Theodore Roosevelt and Secretary of State John Hay on the matter.

11:401   Szajkowski, Zosa. "The European Aspect of the American-Russian Passport Question." *Publications of the American Jewish Historical Society* 46 (December 1956): 86–100. In 1911, President William Howard Taft abrogated the American-Russian treaty of 1832 because of Russia's refusal to treat American Jews traveling in Russia on the same basis as other American nationals. Most European governments took a less definite stand on the discrimination of their Jewish nationals because of considerations of "high policy."

Business and Economics

11:402   Carstensen, Fred V. *American Enterprise in Foreign Markets: Studies of Singer and International Harvester in Imperial Russia.* This book is a detailed investigation into the archives of Singer and International Harvester, whose subsidiaries were the largest companies, domestic or foreign, operating in Russia in 1914 (9:344). See also the author's dissertation, "American Multinational Corporations in Imperial Russia: Chapters in Foreign Enterprise and Russian Economic Development" (Yale, 1976) and that of Elizabeth Cowan Pickering, "The International Harvester Company in Russia: A Case Study of a Foreign Corporation in Russia from the 1860's to the 1930's" (Princeton, 1974).

11:403   Owen, Gail L. "Dollar Diplomacy in Default: The Economies of Russian-American Relations, 1910–1917." *Historical Journal* 13 (June 1970): 251–72. Efforts to apply dollar diplomacy to the imperial Russian domain were initially blocked in Manchuria and Persia by czarist obstruction and in Russia proper by the Jewish-inspired U.S. denunciation of the Russian-American trade agreement. World War I, however, forced the Russians to turn primarily to the United States for needed materiel.

11:404   Queen, George Sherman. *The United States and the Material Advance in Russia, 1881–1906.* New York: Arno Press, 1976. This reprint of the author's 1941 University of Illinois dissertation examines the impact of U.S. ideas on the development of Russia at the beginning of the twentieth century. Based on U.S. sources, it is limited, but may remain useful because it covers terrain that remains relatively untilled.

SPAIN

11:405   Collier, William Miller. *At the Court of His Catholic Majesty.* Chicago: A. C. McClurg and Co., 1912. Collier describes the social and ceremonial aspects of his job as U.S. minister to Spain (1905–1909).

11:406   Cortada, James W. *Two Nations over Time: Spain and the United States, 1776–1977.* This survey includes a brief section on U.S.-Spanish relations in the years immediately following the Spanish-American War. The controversy over the sinking of the *Maine* continued to dominate public debate on both sides of the Atlantic, Americans blaming Spain, and the Spanish indignantly denying any responsibility. Simmering tensions also occurred over economic

and cultural competition in Latin America. Madrid viewed U.S. promotion of Pan-Americanism as a thinly disguised attempt to reduce Spanish influence in the hemisphere (2:338).

11:407   Flannigan, Alice Pierce. "The Role of Joseph Willard as American Ambassador to Spain (1913–1921)." Ph.D. dissertation, University of South Carolina, 1991. While the focus of this dissertation is on the period after the outbreak of World War I, it includes some information on Willard's first year, all the more useful because of the poverty of the literature. Throughout his tenure, Willard won high praise from his colleagues for his sensitivity and goodwill. His reports include valuable information on the internal situation in Spain.

11:408   Jackson, Shirley Fulton. "The United States and Spain 1898–1918." Ph.D. dissertation, Florida State University, 1967. This account, based on U.S. and Spanish sources, considers Spanish-American relations in the two decades following the war of 1898. Problems considered include the American indemnity claims against Spain, negotiation of a supplementary treaty for the cession of two overlooked islands in the Philippines, and reopening of the investigation into the *Maine* disaster. Commercial relations were important in these years, as were concerns over the events accompanying the Mexican revolution.

CENTRAL AND EASTERN EUROPE

11:409   Challener, Richard D. "Montenegro and the United States: A Balkan Fantasy." *Journal of Central European Affairs* 17 (October 1957): 236–42. Challener discusses the Montenegrin government's curious offers, in 1909 and 1911, of naval bases to the United States. On the first occasion, the U.S. minister to Greece and Montenegro was enthusiastic about the offer, in contrast to President Taft, the navy, and Department of State.

11:410   Dyrud, Keith P. "The Rusin Question in Eastern Europe and in America, 1890–World War I." Ph.D. dissertation, University of Minnesota, 1976. This study includes a discussion of the difficulties of adjustment that the Rusins, an ethnic group from within the Austro-Hungarian empire, faced when significant numbers of them emigrated to the United States at the turn of the century.

11:411 Meier, Heinz K. *Friendship under Stress: U.S.-Swiss Relations 1900–1950.* The first chapter describes the "calm years" in U.S.-Swiss relations before World War I. U.S. scholars were interested in Swiss political institutions, particularly the referendum and initiative and universal military training, while the diplomats representing either country carried on the routine business of diplomacy, interrupted only occasionally by unusual matters such as the request to stock Yellowstone National Park with chamois from the Swiss Alps or the negotiation of an arbitration treaty in 1914 (2:339).

11:412 Nestorova, Tatyana. *American Missionaries among the Bulgarians, 1858–1912.* Boulder: East European Monographs, Distributed by Columbia University Press, 1987. This diligent monograph about the American Board's proselytizing in Bulgaria asserts that the Bulgarians overwhelmingly rejected the religious message of the missionaries but accepted some of their cultural innovations, particularly in education and literature. The missionaries' views of the Bulgarians were ambivalent.

11:413 Schulte Nordholt, Jan Willem, and Robert P. Swierenga, eds. *A Bilateral Bicentennial: A History of Dutch-American Relations, 1782–1982.* New York: Octagon Books, 1982. Robert P. Swierenga ("Exodus Netherlands, Promised Land America: Dutch Immigration and Settlement in the United States," 127–48) details Dutch settlement in the United States from 1820 to 1920, which was small in relative and absolute terms. According to the author, the Dutch never contracted "America fever." Frank Freidel ("The Dutchness of the Roosevelts," 149–67) challenges Theodore and Franklin Delano's proud claims to Dutch ancestry. "Both Roosevelts were Dutch more in name and in tradition than in origins."

11:414 Wandycz, Piotr S. *The United States and Poland.* This overview includes ten pages on the period from 1900 to 1915. It is worthy of note because there is such a dearth of secondary literature on U.S.-Polish relations in the period (2:343).

SCANDINAVIA

11:415 Cole, Wayne S. *Norway and the United States, 1905–1955: Two Democracies in Peace and War.* This excellent introduction to the diplomatic relations between Norway and the United States begins with a chapter on the "tranquil beginnings" before World War I. Trade and immigration linked the two countries long before formal diplomatic relations were established upon Norway's independence in 1905. In 1914, Norway signed an arbitration agreement with the United States (2:334).

11:416 Dybdahl, Vagn. "Dansk Industri og de Store Udstillinger 1889–1914 [Danish Industry and the Great Exhibitions]." *Erhvervshistorisk Årbog [Denmark]* 12 (1960): 7–26. Danish industry reluctantly participated in World's Fairs from 1889 through 1914 and only when subsidized by the government. This study includes an analysis of Denmark's role in the St. Louis Fair of 1904.

11:417 Fogdall, Soren J. M. P. *Danish-American Diplomacy, 1776–1920.* This extended and dated essay has a brief section on U.S.-Danish relations from 1900 to 1920 that remains useful due to the absence of other sources. Fogdall lists outstanding issues between the two countries, including copyright law, Danish claims at Samoa, the arbitration treaty signed in 1914, and, foremost, the purchase of the Danish West Indies. This is vol. 8, no. 2, in the University of Iowa Studies in the Social Sciences (4:268).

11:418 Nørregaard, Georg. *Vore Gamle Tropekolonier. vol. 4: Dansk Vestindien 1880–1917 [Our Colonies in the Tropics. Vol. 4: The Danish West Indies 1880–1917].* Copenhagen: Fremad, 1966. This provides the most detailed study of the on-again, off-again negotiations between Denmark and the United States for the sale of the Danish West Indies.

11:419 Pendleton, Leila Amos. "Our New Possessions: The Danish West Indies." *Journal of Negro History* 2 (July 1917): 267–88. This well-researched article surveys the history of the Danish West Indies (which became the U.S. Virgin Islands in 1917), with an emphasis on race relations in the islands and U.S. negotiations to purchase the island group from Denmark.

11:420 Tansill, Charles Callan. *The Purchase of the Danish West Indies.* Relying on multiarchival research, Tansill gives a thorough examination to the intermittent U.S.-Danish negotiations concerning the West Indies (9:414).

11:421 Tilberg, Frederick. *The Development of Commerce between the United States and Sweden, 1870–1925.* Rock Island, IL: Augustana Library Publications, 1929. Tracing the origins of American-Swedish trade to the late eighteenth century, this work emphasizes the half century after 1870. Tilberg discusses the treaties, tariffs, and changing nature of the commodities being traded.

AFRICA

11:422 Duignan, Peter, and L. H. Gann. *The United States and Africa: A History.* Through their discussion of U.S. relations with South Africa, the Congo, and Liberia, Duignan and Gann deal with U.S. relations at the turn of the century with Belgium, England, and, to a very minor extent, France. This rather uninspired survey is arranged thematically, dealing in turn with Washington, interest groups, preachers, teachers, and African-Americans (2:255).

11:423 Hochschild, Adam. *King Leopold's Ghost: A Story of Greed, Terror, and Heroism in Colonial Africa.* New York: Houghton Mifflin, 1998. This elegant history includes a brief, interesting, and accurate description of the Theodore Roosevelt administration's reluctant involvement in the international controversy over the rule of King Leopold of Belgium in the Congo Free State.

11:424 Jacobs, Sylvia M. *The African Nexus: Black American Perspectives on the European Partitioning of Africa, 1880–1920.* This well-researched study describes the reactions of African-Americans to the European partitioning of Africa and includes a discussion of their attempts to influence U.S. policy, particularly on Liberia (9:284).

11:425 McStallworth, Paul. "The United States and the Congo Question, 1884–1914." Ph.D. dissertation, Ohio State University, 1954. This dissertation, which is based on the U.S. press, *Congressional Record,* and diplomatic archives, is the most detailed study of U.S. relations with the Congo—and in connection with this, Belgium and England—at the turn of the century.

11:426 Pakenham, Thomas. *The Scramble for Africa: White Man's Conquest of the Dark Continent from 1876 to 1912.* New York: Random House, 1991. This sweeping overview deals briefly with the international crusade against King Leopold's policy in the Congo, and in so doing touches on U.S. relations with Belgium during the Theodore Roosevelt administration. Pakenham describes how the lobbying effort included strange bedfellows—from humanitarians to the powerful Senator John T. Morgan, who hoped someday to ship African-Americans to a stable Congo.

11:427 Rosenberg, Emily S. "The Invisible Protectorate: The United States, Liberia, and the Evolution of Neocolonialism, 1909–1940." *Diplomatic History* 9 (Summer 1985): 191–214. In this interesting article, Rosenberg touches on U.S. relations with France, Germany, and England.

11:428 Skinner, Elliott P. *African Americans and U.S. Policy toward Africa, 1850–1924: In Defense of Black Nationality.* This well-written and well-researched book deals extensively with U.S. policy toward Africa from 1900 to 1914, and in so doing examines U.S. policy toward the European colonial powers. While its focus is on African-Americans, it provides useful insight into U.S. policy, particularly toward the Congo Free State, Boer War, and Liberia (whose independence was threatened by French and British encroachment). Skinner ably documents how African-Americans pushed a reluctant Theodore Roosevelt to take a stand against Belgium's policy in the Congo Free State (9:289).

LATIN AMERICA

11:429 Baker, George W., Jr. "The Woodrow Wilson Administration and Guatemalan Relations." *Historian* 27 (February 1965): 155–69. Baker deals in passing with Secretary of State William Jennings Bryan's intervention, at the request of the Guatemalan president, Manuel Estrada Cabrera, in a dispute between Guatemala and Great Britain over unpaid loans.

11:430 Blasier, Cole. "The United States and Madero." *Journal of Latin American Studies* 4 (November 1972): 207–31. Blasier uses the diary of the German minister to Mexico to show that he cooperated with the U.S. minister, Henry Lane Wilson, to overthrow Mexican President Francisco Madero in 1913.

11:431 Collin, Richard H. *Theodore Roosevelt's Caribbean: The Panama Canal, the Monroe Doctrine, and the Latin American Context.* Baton Rouge: Louisiana State University Press, 1990. This political and cultural history of U.S.-Latin American relations in the Roosevelt years includes discussions of the European dimension. See also his "The Big Stick as *Weltpolitik*: Europe and Latin America in Theodore Roosevelt's Foreign Policy," in Natalie A. Naylor, Douglas Brinkley, and John Allen Gable, eds., *Theodore Roosevelt—Many-Sided American* (Interlaken, NY: Heart of the Lakes, 1992): 295–316.

11:432 Deitl, Ralph. *USA und Mittelamerika: Die Aussenpolitik von William J. Bryan, 1913–1915 [The USA and Central America: The Foreign Policy of William J. Bryan, 1913–1915].* Stuttgart: Franz Steiner, 1996. This detailed study of U.S. policy in the Caribbean, Central America, and Mexico from 1913 to 1915 focuses on the role of Secretary of State William Jennings Bryan and includes discussions of relations with the European powers, especially Great Britain. It is based on extensive research in U.S. and U.K. archives.

11:433 McCullough, David. *The Path between the Seas: The Creation of the Panama Canal, 1870–1914.* New York: Simon and Schuster, 1977. This popular history of the canal includes discussions of early French interest in a canal and of the Hay-Pauncefote treaties, which contributed to the rapprochement between England and the United States.

11:434 Munro, Dana G. *Intervention and Dollar Diplomacy in the Caribbean, 1900–1921.* Princeton: Princeton University Press, 1964. In this comprehensive study, Munro deals with how matters in the Dominican Republic, Haiti, Nicaragua, Cuba, and Panama caused complications in U.S. relations with the European powers.

11:435 Plummer, Brenda Gayle. *Haiti and the Great Powers, 1902–1915.* Baton Rouge: Louisiana

State University Press, 1988. Using a sweeping, holistic approach, Plummer describes how, despite their chronic instability, the Haitian governments were able to keep French, American, and German ambitions toward Haiti at bay from 1902 until the U.S. occupation of 1915. This monograph provides a good example of great power competition in the Caribbean. See also Plummer, "Black and White in the Caribbean: Haitian-American Relations, 1902–1934," Ph.D. dissertation, Cornell University, 1981.

11:436 Schoonover, Thomas D. *The United States in Central America, 1860–1911: Episodes of Social Imperialism and Imperial Rivalry in the World System.* Using a world systems approach and multiarchival research, Schoonover analyzes U.S. competition with the European powers for trade and influence in Central America (9:465).

Biographical Studies

JOHANN H. VON BERNSTORFF

11:437 Bernstorff, Johann H. von. *Memoirs of Count Bernstorff.* Translated by Eric Sutton. New York: Random House, 1936. Bernstorff devotes one chapter to his experiences as ambassador in Washington (1908–1917), focusing on his attempts to prevent U.S. entry in the war and including observations about America and U.S.-German relations in the preceding years. Many of the most interesting passages are culled from letters he wrote to friends at the time.

11:438 _____. *My Three Years in America.* New York: Scribner, 1920. This memoir includes a chapter surveying U.S.-German relations before the war in which Bernstorff analyzes "mutual misunderstandings" and discusses the importance of public opinion in America.

WILLIAM JENNINGS BRYAN

11:439 Coletta, Paolo E. *William Jennings Bryan.* 3 vols. In volume 2 of this comprehensive biography,

Coletta includes some brief comments on Bryan's handling of the European powers during the Mexican revolution (10:117).

11:440   Curti, Merle E. "Bryan and World Peace." *Smith College Studies in History* 16 (April-July 1931): 113–262. This is a dated and hagiographic study of William Jennings Bryan's attempts to implement pacifist policies, but it remains useful due to its careful attention to detail.

11:441   Ogle, Arthur Bud. "Above the World: William Jennings Bryan's View of the American Nation in International Affairs." *Nebraska History* 61 (Summer 1980): 152–71. Ogle includes a brief discussion of the worldview and vision of Europe of Woodrow Wilson's first secretary of state, William Jennings Bryan.

JAMES BRYCE

11:442   Fisher, H. A. L. *James Bryce (Viscount Bryce of Dechmont, O.M.).* 2 vols. New York: Macmillan Company, 1927. When Bryce was British ambassador to Washington (1907–1913), the main diplomatic issues in U.S.-British relations concerned Canada and the Panama Canal.

11:443   Ions, Edmund. *James Bryce and American Democracy 1870–1922.* London: Macmillan, 1968. This study of James Bryce, the British ambassador to Washington (1907–1913), includes discussions of U.S.-Canadian-British relations and of the approach of war, based largely on secondary sources with some British documents.

JOSEPH HODGES CHOATE

11:444   Martin, Edward Sandford. *Life of Joseph Hodges Choate as Gathered Chiefly from His Letters, Including His Own Story of His Boyhood and Youth.* 2 vols. New York: Scribner's, 1927. Reprint 1989 (Fred B. Rothman) Microfiche. This book, which is almost a memoir, includes a long, chatty chapter on Joseph Choate's tenure as U.S. ambassador to Britain (1899–1905). It deals, in passing, with Anglo-American tensions concerning the Boer War, Samoa, the Far East, Panama, and Alaska.

11:445   Strong, Theron G. *Joseph H. Choate: New Englander, New Yorker, Lawyer, Ambassador.* New York: Dodd, Mead, 1917. Reprint 1991 (Fred B. Rothman) Microfiche. This laudatory, breezy, and old-fashioned biography of the U.S. ambassador to the United Kingdom (1899–1901) mentions the major issues in U.S.-U.K. relations, including the Alaska boundary disputes and relations with China.

JOHN W. FOSTER

11:446   Devine, Michael J. *John W. Foster: Politics and Diplomacy in the Imperial Era, 1873–1917.* Foster, who was known to his contemporaries as "America's first professional diplomat," early advocated an enlarged American presence abroad. After his stint as secretary of state he remained an influential adviser and helped negotiate several disputes between the United States and Canada in the first decade of the twentieth century (9:53).

11:447   Foster, John W. *Diplomatic Memoirs.* There is material here on Foster's work on European relations 1900–1919, negotiations with Canada 1891–1903, the Alaskan boundary settlement of 1903, and the Second Hague Peace Conference of 1907. See chapter 9 of this Guide (9:54).

JAMES GERARD

11:448   Barthold, Theodore R. "Assignment to Berlin: The Embassy of James W. Gerard, 1913–1917." Ph.D. dissertation, Temple University, 1981. Based on extensive primary sources, this is the definitive study of Gerard's tenure in Berlin, illustrating the character of German-American relations. Gerard's ambassadorial tasks before August 1914 were minimal as relations between Germany and the United States were calm. The major issue between the two countries was Germany's concern over Wilson's Mexican policy, about which Berlin refrained from voicing its irritation too loudly to preserve amity with Washington.

11:449   Gerard, James W. *Face to Face with Kaiserism.* New York: George H. Doran Company, 1918. This expands on the author's *My Four Years in Germany* (1917) (11:451), with an added degree of alarm about the German threat to the United States.

11:450 _____. *My First Eighty-three Years in America: The Memoirs of James W. Gerard.* Garden City, NY: Doubleday, 1951. This memoir includes recollections of Gerard's experiences as U.S. ambassador to Germany (1913–1917), touching briefly on Bryan's peace treaties, negotiations with Standard Oil, and, of course, the war.

11:451 _____. *My Four Years in Germany.* New York: George H. Doran Company, 1917. Gerard, who was U.S. ambassador to Germany (1913–1917), writes a chatty and informative memoir, which focuses on the war years but also includes useful comments on Germany's response to Wilson's policy in Mexico. Gerard's anti-Germanism becomes more pronounced as the memoir proceeds. This book was made into a virulently anti-German film in 1918.

11:452 Troisi, James Lawrence. "Ambassador Gerard and American-German Relations, 1913–1917." Ph.D. dissertation, Syracuse State University, 1978. This detailed study of Gerard's years as U.S. ambassador in Berlin (1913–1917) devotes one chapter to the prewar years. It emphasizes the social side of the post but also includes a discussion of Germany's perception of Wilson's policy toward the Mexican revolution.

JOHN HAY

11:453 Clymer, Kenton J. *John Hay: The Gentleman as Diplomat.* This volume contains valuable information about the evolution of Hay's foreign policy views (9:109).

11:454 Dennett, Tyler. *John Hay: From Poetry to Politics.* This old account of McKinley's ambassador to Great Britain and Theodore Roosevelt's secretary of state remains a useful source. Though short on analysis, its narrative of Hay's eventful life in public affairs is complete (10:128).

11:455 Kushner, Howard I., and Anne Hummel Sherrill. *John Milton Hay: The Union of Poetry and Politics.* A concise chapter on the Hay-Pauncefote treaty emphasizes the importance of the Canal for the

Americans and the connections between these negotiations and those involving disputes with Canada (10:130).

11:456 Thayer, William Roscoe. *The Life and Letters of John Hay.* This old-fashioned biography of John Hay (secretary of state, 1898–1904) by a friend and confidant remains important because it includes the widely cited account of Theodore Roosevelt's ultimatum to the kaiser during the Venezuela crisis of 1901–1903. It also discusses the Hay-Pauncefote treaties and the "German menace" (10:132).

HENRY CABOT LODGE

11:457 Garraty, John A. *Henry Cabot Lodge, A Biography.* The standard biography of one of the leading expansionists, this is an astute and sympathetic appraisal of the senator from the U.S. point of view. It includes an extended discussion of the Alaskan boundary negotiations of 1903 (9:113). See also his "Henry Cabot Lodge and the Alaskan Boundary Tribunal," *New England Quarterly* 24 (December 1951): 469–94.

11:458 Widenor, William C. *Henry Cabot Lodge and the Search for an American Foreign Policy.* This intellectual biography focuses on the development of Henry Cabot Lodge's thought on questions of foreign policy. It is centrally concerned with Lodge's views on imperialism and his jingoism, but deals as well with his ideas on U.S. relations with the European powers (10:141).

ALFRED THAYER MAHAN

11:459 Baecker, Thomas. "Mahan über Deutschland [Mahan on Germany]." *Marine-Rundschau* 73 (January, February 1976): 10–19; 86–102. Baecker argues that Mahan's influence over both Roosevelt and Wilhelm II has been exaggerated: Mahan simply stated what both leaders already wanted to hear. Baecker then contrasts Mahan's Germanophobia with his anglophilia.

11:460 LaFeber, Walter. "A Note on the 'Mercantilistic Imperialism' of Alfred Thayer Mahan." This article on the philosophic basis of Mahan's writings concludes that his views differed from traditional (seventeenth- and eighteenth-century) mercantilism in several important ways: he believed in commercial rather than landed imperialism; he emphasized the need for a strong navy but not necessarily a strong merchant marine; and he advocated an open door approach rather than the formation of a colonial empire. LaFeber argues that Mahan, therefore, adapted his mercantilistic views to the needs of the day (10:143).

11:461   Turk, Richard W. *The Ambiguous Relationship: Theodore Roosevelt and Alfred Thayer Mahan.* This slim volume, which includes selections from the correspondence of Mahan and Roosevelt, sheds light on both men's changing views of Great Britain and Germany (9:87).

GEORGE VON LENGERKE MEYER

11:462   Howe, M. A. De Wolfe. *George von Lengerke Meyer: His Life and Public Services.* New York: Dodd, Mead and Company, 1920. This biography includes a brief chapter on Meyer's stint as U.S. ambassador to Italy (1901–1905) and a very long section on his tenure as ambassador to Russia, (1905–1907), when he dealt with questions arising from the Russo-Japanese War. It has been largely superseded by Wiegand, *Patrician in the Progressive Era: A Biography of George Von Lengerke Meyer* (1988) (11:463).

11:463   Wiegand, Wayne A. *Patrician in the Progressive Era: A Biography of George Von Lengerke Meyer.* New York: Garland, 1988. This biography of George Meyer, a politician from Massachusetts who became ambassador to Italy in 1901 and to Russia in 1905, provides a brief and all-too-rare glimpse into U.S. relations with both countries. When Meyer arrived in Rome, public opinion (already affected by U.S. ill treatment of Italian immigrants) was inflamed against the United States because it had just been disclosed that the plot to kill King Humbert I had been organized in America. Wiegand describes a series of other minor irritants, all of which Meyer successfully soothed, while never neglecting the social rounds of this secondary post that Theodore Roosevelt called "a glorified pink tea party." In Russia, Meyer reported on the confused domestic situa-

tion and the role the United States played at the treaty of Portsmouth.

WHITELAW REID

11:464   Cortissoz, Royal. *The Life of Whitelaw Reid.* This is a dated yet useful biography of Whitelaw Reid, who was the U.S. ambassador to the United Kingdom, 1905–1912 (10:166).

11:465   Duncan, Bingham. *Whitelaw Reid: Journalist, Politician, Diplomat.* This biography of Whitelaw Reid (1837–1912) focuses on his role as the editor of the *New York Tribune* but also includes a brief discussion of his years as U.S. ambassador to London (1905–1912). This was a "dull" period in Anglo-American relations, with the most important source of tension, the Newfoundland fisheries dispute, handled largely in Washington (10:167).

THEODORE ROOSEVELT

11:466   Brands, H. W. *T.R.: The Last Romantic.* New York: Basic Books, 1997. This readable biography relies principally on Roosevelt's voluminous correspondence. Brands briefly covers the key moments in TR's handling of the Europeans and puts particular stress on the perceived German threat to Latin America.

11:467   Cooper, John Milton, Jr. *The Warrior and the Priest: Woodrow Wilson and Theodore Roosevelt.* Cambridge, MA: Belknap Press of Harvard University Press, 1983. This stimulating and accessible comparative study of Theodore Roosevelt and Woodrow Wilson makes passing reference to U.S. policy toward Europe before World War I.

11:468   Gould, Lewis L. *The Presidency of Theodore Roosevelt.* Lawrence: University Press of Kansas, 1991. This concise history includes an overview of Theodore Roosevelt's foreign policies.

11:469   Harbaugh, William H. *Power and Responsibility: The Life and Times of Theodore Roosevelt.* New York: Farrar, Straus and Cudahy, 1961. An intelligent examination of Roosevelt's thoughts and actions, this one-volume biography includes extended discussions of his role at Portsmouth and in the 1905–1906 Morocco crisis.

11:470 Miller, Nathan. *Theodore Roosevelt: A Life.* New York: Morrow, 1992. This solid, accessible biography of Theodore Roosevelt, based on secondary sources and the president's letters, puts his dealings with the European powers in the overall context of his presidency.

11:471 Ninkovich, Frank A. "Theodore Roosevelt: Civilization as Ideology." *Diplomatic History* 10 (Summer 1986): 221–45. This fascinating article relates Roosevelt's foreign policy to an ideology of civilization and includes a perceptive analysis of Roosevelt's policy toward the Russo-Japanese War.

11:472 Olson, William C. "Theodore Roosevelt's Conception of an International League." *World Affairs Quarterly* 29 (January 1959): 329–53. Olson traces Theodore Roosevelt's early advocacy of an international league.

11:473 Pringle, Henry F. *Theodore Roosevelt: A Biography.* Rev. ed. New York: Harcourt, Brace and World, 1956. This old-fashioned biography covers Roosevelt's policy toward the key European powers, especially Germany. First published in 1931.

11:474 Roosevelt, Theodore. *The Autobiography of Theodore Roosevelt.* New York: Macmillan, 1913. Reprint 1985 (Da Capo Press). While this self-congratulatory autobiography is mainly devoted to domestic issues, it includes some references to relations with European powers, in particular to Roosevelt's role in the settlement of the Russo-Japanese War.

ELIHU ROOT

11:475 Jessup, Philip C. *Elihu Root.* 2 vols. New York: Dodd, Mead and Company, 1938. This detailed biography covers all the major U.S.-European tensions (including those concerning Alaska) during Elihu Root's long career of government service.

11:476 Scott, James Brown. "Elihu Root's Services to International Law." In *International Conciliation: Documents for the Year 1925,* 25–78. New York: Carnegie Endowment for International Peace,

1925. This comprehensive essay covers Root's thinking on international law and on certain aspects of U.S.-British relations.

JACOB SCHIFF

11:477 Adler, Cyrus. *Jacob H. Schiff: His Life and Letters.* 2 vols. Garden City, NY: Doubleday, Doran, 1928. Jacob Henry Schiff (1847–1920) led the movement in the United States to raise loans for the Japanese in their war against Russia (1904–1905). This hagiographic biography has been largely superseded by Cohen, *Jacob H. Schiff: A Study in American Jewish Leadership* (1999) (11:478).

11:478 Cohen, Naomi W. *Jacob H. Schiff: A Study in American Jewish Leadership.* Hanover, NH: University Press of New England for Brandeis University Press, 1999. This well-crafted biography, based on extensive primary sources, discusses Schiff's role in the Russo-Japanese War and U.S. relations with Russia.

WILLIAM HOWARD TAFT

11:479 Coletta, Paolo E. *The Presidency of William Howard Taft.* Lawrence: University Press of Kansas, 1973. This survey of the Taft presidency deals with Europe only in passing but includes a brief chapter on tariff reciprocity with Canada.

11:480 Minger, Ralph Eldin. *William Howard Taft and United States Foreign Policy: The Apprenticeship Years, 1900–1908.* Urbana: University of Illinois Press, 1975. This study briefly touches on Taft's 1907 trip through Russia.

11:481 Pringle, Henry F. *The Life and Times of William Howard Taft: A Biography.* 2 vols. New York: Farrar and Rinehart, 1939. This broadly descriptive biography deals at length with foreign affairs during the first three decades of the twentieth century.

11:482 Rowe, Joseph M., Jr. "William Howard Taft: Diplomatic Trouble-Shooter." Ph.D. dissertation, Texas A&M University, 1977. Rowe's laudatory study of Taft's diplomacy includes an analysis of his mission to the Vatican in 1902 when he was Roosevelt's secretary of war and most trusted adviser.

ANDREW WHITE

11:483   Altschuler, Glenn C. *Andrew D. White, Educator, Historian, Diplomat.* Ithaca: Cornell University Press, 1979. This comprehensive biography based on primary sources includes two chapters on White's time as U.S. ambassador in Berlin (1897–1903).

11:484   White, Andrew Dickson. *Autobiography of Andrew Dickson White.* 2 vols. New York: Century Company, 1905. A historian by training and profession, White was ambassador to Germany (1897–1903) and chairman of the U.S. delegation to the Hague conference (1899). His memoirs include valuable, spirited, and idiosyncratic accounts of U.S.-German relations at the time and pungent comments on the U.S. role at the Hague.

HENRY WHITE

11:485   Kostandarithes, Danton P. "The Diplomatic Career of Henry White, 1883–1919." Ph.D. dissertation, Tulane University, 1992. This study uses American, British, and French diplomatic documents and manuscript collections to trace the long, influential career of Henry White, one of the first U.S. eminent career diplomats. By the time of his retirement in 1919, he had served as first secretary at the American Ministry (and later embassy) in Britain and as ambassador in Italy and France, and had represented the United States at the 1906 Algeciras conference. A lifelong friend of Theodore Roosevelt, White became one of his most trusted diplomats.

11:486   Nevins, Allan. *Henry White: Thirty Years of American Diplomacy.* New York: Harper and Brothers, 1930. This biography of arguably America's premier diplomat between the Civil War and World War I considers American relations with the principal European states and Canada. Although the research was limited mainly to the White collection, the volume merits a careful reading.

OTHERS

11:487   DeNovo, John A. "The Enigmatic Alvey A. Adee and American Foreign Relations, 1870–1924." Adee was particularly influential around the turn of the century. See chapter 9 of this Guide (9:96).

11:488   Anderson, Isabel, ed. *Larz Anderson: Letters and Journals of a Diplomat.* New York: Fleming H. Revell, 1940. This memoir, written in the form of a diary, includes a brief chapter on Anderson's days as U.S. ambassador to Belgium, 1911–1912. Although frothy, it is useful because there is so little else available on U.S.-Belgian relations at the time.

11:489   Scott, James Brown. *Robert Bacon: Life and Letters.* Garden City, NY: Doubleday, Page and Company, 1923. Bacon was the U.S. ambassador to France, 1910–1912, a languid period in Franco-American relations. "There was nothing eventful in Mr. Bacon's ambassadorship," Scott notes. Introduction by Elihu Root.

11:490   Bowers, Claude G. *Beveridge and the Progressive Era.* This old-fashioned biography includes an interesting, gossipy chapter on Beveridge's trip to Russia in 1901 (10:113).

11:491   Tabouis, Geneviève. *The Life of Jules Cambon.* Translated by C. F. Atkinson. London: J. Cape, 1938. Tabouis provides a chatty discussion of Cambon's years as ambassador in Washington, 1897–1902. Cambon's reports and letters discuss U.S.-French relations in passing and provide a lively commentary on U.S. domestic politics, with particularly incisive remarks on the situation of American blacks.

11:492   Wall, Joseph Frazier. *Andrew Carnegie.* New York: Oxford University Press, 1970. This comprehensive biography includes an extended description of Carnegie's international peace activism.

11:493   Spector, Ronald H. *Admiral of the New Empire: The Life and Career of George Dewey.* This excellent life of Dewey is based on solid research and includes an interesting analysis of the admiral's views of Germany (10:124).

11:494 Sykes, Percy. *The Right Honourable Sir Mortimer Durand, P.C., O.C., M.G., K.C., S.L., K.C., I.E.: A Biography.* London: Cassell and Company, 1926. This old-fashioned biography includes four chapters about Durand's tenure as British ambassador in Washington, 1903–1906. It quotes extensively from his letters, giving his impressions of American leaders, particularly Theodore Roosevelt, and of the diplomacy of the Russo-Japanese War; includes an extended discussion of the Alaska boundary and the Newfoundland fisheries disputes; and describes Durand's reaction to his recall, a "staggering" blow, due, Sykes asserts, to Roosevelt's desire to have his friend Cecil Spring-Rice in the post.

11:495 Egan, Maurice Francis. *Recollections of a Happy Life.* New York: George H. Doran Company, 1924. This interesting memoir covers Egan's tenure as U.S. minister in Copenhagen (1907–1918). His recollections describe the social and cultural whirl, the European political scene, World War I, and the U.S. purchase of the Danish West Indies.

11:496 Einstein, Lewis. *A Diplomat Looks Back.* New Haven: Yale University Press, 1968. This memoir was written toward the end of his career by a highly perceptive and active American observer whose experiences in diplomacy extended from the Algeciras conference to stints in Turkey, China, Costa Rica, and the Balkans prior to 1915. Einstein urged Washington to adopt a more active approach to Europe. Edited by Lawrence E. Gelfand.

11:497 Heinrichs, Waldo H. *American Ambassador: Joseph C. Grew and the Development of the United States Diplomatic Tradition.* Boston: Little, Brown, 1966. This excellent study of Grew's long career includes a short section on his early days as a diplomatic secretary in the U.S. embassy in Berlin (1908–1917), years of "humdrum diplomacy" until the war began.

11:498 Grey, Edward. *Twenty-Five Years, 1892–1916.* 2 vols. New York: Frederick A. Stokes Co., 1925. In these memoirs, Sir Edward Grey, British foreign secretary from 1905 to 1916, includes very little on relations with the United States, explaining: "In the years from 1905 to 1912 there was not much in the handling of public affairs between the government of the United States and ourselves that retains sufficient interest to be described here."

11:499 Harper, Samuel N. *The Russia I Believe In: The Memoirs of Samuel N. Harper, 1902–1941.* Chicago: University of Chicago Press, 1945. In this intelligent and lively memoir, Harper describes his studies in the University of Moscow in 1904–1906 and his subsequent almost annual trips through Russia. His observations of daily life, culture, and politics in those turbulent years are penetrating. Edited by Paul V. Harper, with Ronald Thompson.

11:500 Mott, T. Bentley. *Myron T. Herrick: Friend of France: An Autobiographical Biography.* Garden City, NY: Doubleday, Doran and Company, 1930. This sympathetic biography of the Cleveland banker who served as President Taft's ambassador to France, remaining in Paris until the onset of the European war, briefly considers Herrick's views of the controversy over the Panama Canal and describes his activities as ambassador through 1914.

11:501 Parkman, Aubrey. *David Jayne Hill and the Problem of World Peace.* Lewisburg, PA: Bucknell University Press, 1975. David Hill, an academic and diplomat, was U.S. envoy to Switzerland (1903–1905), the Hague (1905–1908), and Germany (1908–1911). This biography treats diplomatic issues lightly but includes an interesting account of Hill's stormy tenure in Berlin, beginning with the "Hill incident," in which the kaiser made it clear that he was not a welcome appointment, and ending with the "Potash incident," in which Hill took a hard line on behalf of U.S. exporters—when Washington changed its policy, he believed he had been set up to take the fall.

11:502 Jusserand, J. J. *What Me Befell: The Reminiscences of J. J. Jusserand.* Boston: Houghton Mifflin Company, 1933. This memoir by Jean Jules Jusserand (French ambassador to the United States, 1903–1924), covering only the Roosevelt years, includes chatty recollections of his friend Theodore Roosevelt, the Washington social scene, American domestic politics and of the 1902 Venezuela crisis, Panama affair, Russo-Japanese War, Algeciras conference, and journey of the Great White Fleet.

11:503 Weeks, Charles J., Jr. *An American Naval Diplomat in Revolutionary Russia: The Life and Times of Vice Admiral Newton A. McCully, 1867–1951.* Annapolis: Naval Institute Press, 1993. This interesting account of Newton A. McCully, a

U.S. naval officer stationed in Russia from 1904 to 1921, asserts that although he was one of the most competent U.S. observers of Russian affairs, the U.S. government and particularly the Wilson administration failed to make effective use of his timely and accurate information.

11:504   Mott, T. Bentley. *Twenty Years as Military Attaché.* New York: Oxford University Press, 1937. This memoir includes detailed descriptions of the U.S. embassy in Paris in 1900 and 1909, emphasizing the social swirl, and of the embassy in St. Petersburg during the Russo-Japanese War. While not penetrating, Mott's recollections do convey a glimpse of life of a mid-level member of U.S. delegations to Europe in the early decades of the twentieth century.

11:505   Gregory, Ross. *Walter Hines Page: Ambassador to the Court of St. James's.* Lexington: University Press of Kentucky, 1970. Walter Hines Page, U.S. ambassador to Great Britain (1913–1918), struggled ably to improve U.S.-British relations on the eve of World War I. Gregory pays scant heed to the Mexico and Panama tolls crises and focuses on the war years, especially on the gap between Page's conviction that it was in America's interest to intervene on behalf of the Allies and Wilson's determination to preserve neutrality.

11:506   Mowat, R. B. *The Life of Lord Pauncefote, First Ambassador to the United States.* This biography ends with a straightforward discussion of the Hay-Pauncefote treaties (1900, 1901) (9:117).

11:507   Owens, Richard H. "Peaceful Warrior: Horace Porter (1837–1921) and United States Foreign Relations." Ph.D. dissertation, University of Maryland, 1988. From 1897 to 1905, Porter served as U.S. ambassador to France. By the time he resigned his post, Franco-American relations had improved considerably. In 1907, he was a delegate to the second Hague Peace Conference.

11:508   Swanberg, W. A. *Pulitzer.* While primarily concerned with domestic issues, Joseph Pulitzer (1847–1911), editor of the *New York World,* also focused on U.S.-British relations (10:193).

11:509   Burton, David H. *Cecil Spring Rice: A Diplomat's Life.* Rutherford, NJ: Fairleigh Dickinson University Press, 1990. Cecil Spring-Rice served as British ambassador to Washington from 1913 to 1918, but his importance in American affairs began much earlier, when he struck up a friendship with Theodore Roosevelt in 1886. This slim biography emphasizes his wartime career in Washington while deftly fleshing out his relationship with Roosevelt and his circle.

11:510   Rosen, Roman Romanovich. *Forty Years of Diplomacy.* 2 vols. New York: Alfred A. Knopf, 1922. In this memoir, Rosen, the Russian ambassador to the United States (1905–1911), mentions Roosevelt's role at the Portsmouth conference but does not dwell on it.

11:511   Smalley, George W. *Anglo-American Memories.* New York: G. P. Putnam's Sons, 1911. Smalley, the *Times*'s famous American correspondent, writes trenchant and gossipy commentary on the Anglo-American scene at the turn of the century.

11:512   Wilson, F. M. Huntington. *Memoirs of an Ex-Diplomat.* Boston: Bruce Humphries, Inc., 1945. Huntington Wilson includes chatty and informative accounts of the diplomatic service under Roosevelt and Taft, when he was assistant secretary of state for Latin America. While he focuses on bureaucratic affairs and U.S. relations with Latin America, he also provides insight into U.S. relations with Germany, despite, or perhaps because of, his virulent anti-German sentiments.

11:513   Wilson, Henry Lane. *Diplomatic Episodes in Mexico, Belgium and Chile.* Garden City, NY: Doubleday, Page and Company, 1927. Henry Lane Wilson (who became notorious for his involvement in the coup against Mexican President Francisco Madero) was U.S. minister to Belgium, 1905–1909. This chatty and self-serving memoir offers a rare glimpse of the U.S. legation in Brussels and briefly discusses U.S. concerns about King Leopold's Congo policy and Belgian interest in the Manchurian railway.

11:514   Wilson, Hugh R. *The Education of a Diplomat.* New York: Longmans, Green and Co., 1938. These recollections and impressions cover the early phase of Wilson's diplomatic career and are particularly useful for the few pages they contain about his days in Lisbon in 1911, when a series of unstable governments followed the overthrow of the monarchy. The volume ends with his impressions of Berlin on the eve of U.S. entry into World War I.

11:515 Vitte, Sergei Iul Evich (Count Witte). *The Memoirs of Count Witte.* Translated by Sidney Harcave. Armonk, NY: M. E. Sharpe, 1990. Harcave's new translation is based on a different and allegedly more authoritative version of Witte's memoirs than Abraham Yarmolinsky's translation (Garden City, NY: Doubleday, Page and Company, 1921). Like the earlier edition, it includes a discussion of the Portsmouth peace talks during the Russo-Japanese War, at which Witte was the principal Russian delegate and over which Theodore Roosevelt presided. Witte comments on the U.S. role, on U.S. public opinion, and on his contacts with Jewish banking leaders during the negotiations.

The United States, Latin America, and the Caribbean, 1898–1919

Contributing Editor
Mark T. Gilderhus
Texas Christian University

Contents

Introduction

This bibliographical compilation of published works pertains to an era in United States–Latin American relations dating from 1899 through 1921, that is, from the immediate aftermath of the war with Spain until the Republican restoration following World War I. The selections include seven types of references: 1) printed primary sources; 2) bibliographies; 3) historiographical accounts; 4) overviews and general works; 5) biographical studies; 6) scholarly works on U.S. relations with Mexico, Central America, and the Caribbean; and 7) scholarly work on U.S. relations with the countries of South America. The dominating themes concern the expansion of U.S. hegemony in the Western Hemisphere and the various responses, including resistance, among Latin Americans.

These books and articles take into account the consequences of the Spanish-American-Cuban-Filipino War; the role of intervention in the Caribbean region under Roosevelt, Taft, and Wilson; the establishment of protectorates; the effects of the Mexican revolution; and the impact of World War I on the nations of the Western Hemisphere. The studies chosen for inclusion are primarily by historians from the United States, though not exclusively. Some reside in Latin America and Europe. These works represent the best of contemporary scholarship on the subject. They incorporate rigorous methodologies, illuminating research, and discerning analyses presented from diverse points of view. Taken together, this rich body of scholarly literature draws readers into an ongoing debate among historians over the structure, meaning, and significance of international relations in the Western Hemisphere during the first two decades of the twentieth century.

Published Primary Materials

12:1 U.S. Department of State. *Foreign Relations of the United States, 1898–1919.* 31 vols. Wash-

ington, DC: Government Printing Office, 1901–1947. Materials on Mexico, Central and South America, and the Caribbean appear throughout the thirty-plus volumes of the official record of diplomatic papers, spanning from McKinley to Wilson (1:93).

12:2 _____. *Foreign Relations of the United States: The Lansing Papers, 1914–1920.* 2 vols. Washington, DC: Government Printing Office, 1939–1940. These volumes contain important state papers of Secretary of State Robert Lansing.

12:3 Fabela, Isidro, ed. *Documentos Históricos de la Revolución Mexicana. Vol. 3: Revolución y Régimen Constitucionalista: Carranza, Wilson y el ABC [Historical Documents of the Mexican Revolution. Vol. 3: The Constitutionalist Revolution and Regime: Wilson, Carranza, and the ABC Powers].* México, DF: Fondo de Cultura Económica, 1962. This collection, edited by Mexican scholar-diplomat Isidro Fabela, presents indispensable documents from the Mexican side.

12:4 _____, ed. *Documentos Históricos de la Revolución Mexicana. Vol. 20: Las Relaciones Internacionales en la Revolución y Régimen Constitucionalista y la Cuestión Petrolera. 1913–1919 [Historical Documents of the Mexican Revolution: International Relations in the Constitutionalist Revolution and Regime and the Petroleum Question, 1913–1919].* México, DF: Editorial Jus, S.A., 1971. See Fabela, *Documentos Históricos de la Revolución Mexicana. Vol. 3: Revolución y Régimen Constitucionalista: Carranza, Wilson y el ABC* (1962) (12:3).

12:5 _____, ed. *Expedición Punitiva [The Punitive Expedition].* 27 vols. Vols. 12–13, Documentos Históricos de la Revolución Mexicana [Historical Documents of the Mexican Revolution]. México, DF: Editorial Jus, S.A., 1967. See Fabela, *Documentos Históricos de la Revolución Mexicana. Vol. 3: Revolución y Régimen Constitucionalista: Carranza, Wilson y el ABC* (1962) (12:3).

12:6 _____. *Historia Diplomática de la Revolución Mexicana (1912–1917) [Diplomatic History of the Mexican Revolution, 1912–1917].* 2 vols. México, DF: Fondo De Cultura Económica, 1958–1959. Reprint 1985 (Comisión Nacional para las Celebraciones del 175 Aniversario de la Independencia Nacional y 75 Aniversario de la Revolución Mexicana). This indispensable work by Mexican scholar-diplomat Isidro Fabela tells the story of diplomatic relations with the United States from a Carrancista point of view, using Mexican documents drawn from his personal archive, many of which are reprinted. This work emphasizes the importance of Mexican nationalism.

12:7 Bunau-Varilla, Philippe. *Panama: The Creation, Destruction, and Resurrection.* New York: McBride, Nast and Company, 1914. This memoir is Bunau-Varilla's personal, somewhat self-aggrandizing account of the Panama affair.

12:8 Cronon, E. David, ed. *The Cabinet Diaries of Josephus Daniels, 1913–1921.* Lincoln: University of Nebraska Press, 1963. The cabinet diaries of Josephus Daniels, the secretary of the navy under Wilson, contain significant information on U.S. policy toward Mexico and the rest of Latin America.

12:9 Seymour, Charles, ed. *The Intimate Papers of Colonel House Arranged as a Narrative by Charles Seymour.* These excerpts from the House Papers at Yale University bear significantly on issues concerning Latin America, the Mexican revolution, Pan-Americanism, and World War I (11:23).

12:10 Brands, H. W., ed. *The Selected Letters of Theodore Roosevelt.* This wonderful collection underscores Roosevelt's intellectual vitality. In his lifetime, he corresponded regularly with his children and many distinguished figures, and his letters demonstrate his many interests and strong viewpoints. Only a few concern Latin America, emphasizing his understanding of the Monroe Doctrine and defenses of his administration's policies in Panama and Cuba (10:16).

12:11 Morison, Elting E., with John Morton Blum, eds. *The Letters of Theodore Roosevelt.* Volumes 5–6 in this standard collection focus on foreign affairs, including Latin American and Caribbean issues (9:7).

12:12 Lodge, Henry Cabot, Sr., and Charles F. Redmond, eds. *Selections from the Correspondence of Theodore Roosevelt and Henry Cabot Lodge, 1884–1918.* These letters address many issues in foreign relations, including those in Latin America. Originally published in 1925 (9:86).

12:13 Bacon, Robert, and James Brown Scott, eds. *Latin America and the United States: Addresses by Elihu Root.* Cambridge, MA: Harvard University Press, 1917. According to the editors, these addresses, most of which Secretary of State Elihu Root delivered during trips to South America and Mexico in 1906, set forth a new Root doctrine, emphasizing the importance of goodwill, kindly consideration, honorable obligation, and a common destiny among all inhabitants of the Western Hemisphere.

12:14 _____, eds. *The Military and Colonial Policy of the United States: Addresses and Reports by Elihu Root.* Cambridge, MA: Harvard University Press, 1916. Reprint 1970 (AMS Press). These addresses on military and colonial policy by Secretary of War Elihu Root trace the origins of U.S. policies toward Cuba, the Philippines, and Puerto Rico and his understanding of the reasons behind them.

12:15 Wilson, Henry Lane. *Diplomatic Episodes in Mexico, Belgium and Chile.* This diplomatic memoir contains Ambassador Henry Lane Wilson's defense of his actions in support of General Victoriano Huerta against Mexican President Francisco Madero during the coup d'état of February 1913 (11:513).

12:16 Baker, Ray Stannard, and William E. Dodd, eds. *The Public Papers of Woodrow Wilson.* 6 vols. New York: Harper and Brothers, 1925–1927. Reprint 1970 (Kraus Co.). This basic documentary collection has been superseded by Arthur S. Link's compilation of the Wilson papers.

12:17 Link, Arthur S., et al., eds. *The Papers of Woodrow Wilson.* This magnificent collection of primary materials supersedes all previous collections of Wilson papers. It is indispensable (11:33).

Bibliographies and Other Reference Works

12:18 Beede, Benjamin R., ed. *Intervention and Counterinsurgency: An Annotated Bibliography of the Small Wars of the United States, 1898–1984.* New

York: Garland Publishing, 1985. This compilation provides a useful aid to researchers.

12:19　Britton, John A., ed. *The United States and Latin America: A Select Bibliography.* Lanham, MD: Scarecrow Press, 1997. This useful annotated bibliography provides a roster of important works and some historiographical commentary.

12:20　Buckingham, Peter H., ed. *Woodrow Wilson: A Bibliography of His Times and Presidency.* Wilmington, DE: Scholarly Resources, 1990. This finding aid provides a useful means of tracking down material on the Wilson presidency.

12:21　Coletta, Paolo E., ed. *William Howard Taft: A Bibliography.* Westport, CT: Meckler, 1989. This volume is a useful aid for finding materials on William Howard Taft.

12:22　Dent, David W. *The Legacy of the Monroe Doctrine: A Reference Guide to U.S. Involvement in Latin America and the Caribbean.* Westport, CT: Greenwood Press, 1999. This reference work by a political scientist provides a synthesis of the major themes in the history of U.S. involvement with Latin America and the Caribbean since independence and focuses especially on the Monroe Doctrine. It contains an introduction and twenty-four country-by-country chapters.

12:23　Meyer, Michael C., ed. *Supplement to a Bibliography of United States–Latin American Relations since 1810* (1:254). This volume updates the original volume by Trask, Meyer, and Trask, *A Bibliography of United States–Latin American Relations since 1810: A Selected List of Eleven Thousand Published References* (1968) (1:257).

12:24　Trask, David F., Michael C. Meyer, and Roger R. Trask, eds. *A Bibliography of United States–Latin American Relations since 1810: A Selected List of Eleven Thousand Published References.* A massive undertaking at its time, this bibliographical work is still a place to begin any search into the literature of U.S.–Latin American relations (1:257). See also Meyer, *Supplement to a Bibliography of United States–Latin American Relations since 1810* (1979) (1:254).

Historiography

12:25　Abrams, Richard M. "United States Intervention Abroad: The First Quarter Century." *American Historical Review* 79 (February 1974): 72–102. This review essay discusses the current writing by historians on U.S. intervention abroad during the early twentieth century and criticizes the adherents of the so-called "Wisconsin school" for overemphasizing economic motivations.

12:26　Berger, Mark T. *Under Northern Eyes: Latin American Studies and U.S. Hegemony in the Americas, 1898–1990.* Bloomington: Indiana University Press, 1995. This ambitious and illuminating work uses the techniques of the new cultural history to appraise historical "discourses" in the United States on Central America and traces the historiographical tendencies since the turn of the century. Following Michel Foucault's lead, the author identifies power with knowledge and sees Latin American studies in the United States as an adjunct of hegemony.

12:27　Collin, Richard H. "Symbiosis versus Hegemony: New Directions in the Foreign Relations Historiography of Theodore Roosevelt and William Howard Taft." While reviewing the historiography of the Roosevelt and Taft administrations, this essay argues in favor of an explanatory model based on "the symbiosis framework" instead of "the hegemony framework." According to the author, an appreciation of international symbiosis, by which he means an association of mutual benefit or dependence, allows more fully for the analysis of interactive relations among nations, peoples, and cultures (11:37).

12:28　Cooper, John Milton, Jr. "Progressivism and American Foreign Policy: A Reconsideration." The author argues that imperialist and anti-imperialist viewpoints toward the Caribbean and elsewhere corresponded with two distinct wings of the progressive movement. The first, exemplified by Theodore Roosevelt, was urban and Republican; the other, identified with William Jennings Bryan, was rural, Democratic, and descended from Populism (10:89).

12:29　Cummins, Lejeune. "The Formation of the 'Platt' Amendment." *Americas* 23 (April 1967):

370–89. This essay explores the historiographical debate over the authorship and intent of the Platt Amendment. The author argues that Secretary of War Elihu Root and General Leonard Wood coauthored the document and that it had a strategic purpose to defend national security by maintaining order in Cuba.

12:30   Hitchman, James H. "The Platt Amendment Revisited: A Bibliographical Survey." *Americas* 23 (April 1967): 343–69. This essay provides a useful survey of the views of Cuban and U.S. writers on the Platt Amendment during the period 1901–1967.

12:31   White, E. Bruce. "The Muddied Waters of Columbus, New Mexico." *Americas* 32 (July 1975): 72–98. This historiographical essay reviews the points at issue in the much discussed controversy over Pancho Villa's motives for attacking Columbus, New Mexico, in 1916. Did Villa seek to obtain revenge against the United States to embarrass the Carranza government, or to serve German interests in embroiling the United States and Mexico in a war?

Overviews and General Works

12:32   Bemis, Samuel Flagg. *The Latin American Policy of the United States: An Historical Interpretation.* This classic work, now out of date, looks on U.S. imperialism at the turn of the century as an aberration and emphasizes the importance of security interests in explaining U.S. interventions in and around the Caribbean basin (2:345).

12:33   Benjamin, Jules R. "The Framework of U.S. Relations with Latin America in the Twentieth Century: An Interpretive Essay." *Diplomatic History* 11 (Spring 1987): 91–112. A complex and abstract analysis, this essay argues the case that the history of U.S. relations with Latin America illustrates the way in which expansion has been adapted to the requirements of cultural, political, and economic changes in the United States.

12:34   Challener, Richard D. *Admirals, Generals, and American Foreign Policy, 1898–1914.* This astute study of civilian-military relations after the war with Spain shows how U.S. policy in the Caribbean centered on the construction and defense of the Panama Canal, the exclusion of European powers, and the maintenance of stability for purposes of order and trade (11:101).

12:35   Chenetier, Marc, and Rob Kroes, eds. *Impressions of a Gilded Age: The American Fin de Siècle.* Amsterdam: Amerika Instituut, Unversiteit Van Amsterdam, 1983. This collection of essays presented by European and American scholars at a meeting of the European Association for American Studies deals with issues of culture and imperialism at the turn of the twentieth century. Part 4, "Faces of Imperialism," connects most directly with foreign policy and includes "Progressive Concepts of World Order" by Alexander E. Campbell; "Monroe Revisited: The Roosevelt Doctrine, 1901–1909" by Serge Ricard; "Ambiguous Anti-Imperialism: American Expansionism and Its Critics at the Turn of the Century" by Göran Rystad; and "The French Perception of American Anti-Imperialism" by J. Portee.

12:36   Coerver, Don M., and Linda B. Hall. *Tangled Destinies: Latin America and the United States.* Albuquerque: University of New Mexico Press, 1999. Chapter 3 considers such prime issues as the Panama question and Venezuela crisis under Roosevelt, Taft's "dollar diplomacy," and Wilson's efforts to reconcile his internationalist idealism with the requirements of capitalist enterprise in and around the Caribbean.

12:37   Connell-Smith, Gordon. *The United States and Latin America: An Historical Analysis of Inter-American Relations.* In this work, the author criticizes the classic Bemis, *The Latin American Policy of the United States: An Historical Interpretation* (1943) (12:32) as a self-congratulatory romance. Connell-Smith, a British scholar, intends a more realistic presentation, taking into account the impact of economic and strategic considerations. Chapter 2 considers the period from 1899 to 1919 (2:348).

12:38   Dobson, John M. *America's Ascent: The United States Becomes a Great Power, 1880–1914.* Chapter 6 of this survey reviews the role of the United States as a great power in the Western Hemisphere after the war with Spain (9:131).

12:39   Drake, Paul W. "From Good Men to Good Neighbors, 1912–1932." In *Exporting Democracy: The United States and Latin America: Themes and Issues,* ed. Abraham F. Lowenthal, 3–40. Baltimore: Johns Hopkins University Press, 1991. This essay examines the first efforts by the United States to promote democracy in Latin America, paradoxically by means of intervention.

12:40   Fifer, J. Valerie. *United States Perceptions of Latin America, 1850–1930: A "New West" South of Capricorn?* This interpretive volume argues that U.S. observers looked upon the temperate zones in Latin America as a new frontier equivalent for the American west (9:383).

12:41   Gardner, Lloyd C. *Safe for Democracy: The Anglo-American Response to Revolution, 1913–1923.* New York: Oxford University Press, 1984. The section on Mexico emphasizes President Wilson's opposition to special interests, the competition with Great Britain, and his efforts to head off the development of some version of state socialism in Mexico.

12:42   Gilderhus, Mark T. *The Second Century: U.S.–Latin American Relations since 1889.* The first two chapters consider the 1899–1919 period and emphasize U.S. efforts to integrate the Western Hemisphere politically and economically under U.S. leadership and supervision (9:384).

12:43   LaFeber, Walter. *The American Search for Opportunity, 1865–1913.* The concluding portions of this book examine the consequences for Latin America of the U.S. war with Spain; the book emphasizes the quest for commercial opportunity (2:40).

12:44   Langley, Lester D. *America and the Americas: The United States in the Western Hemisphere.* This inaugural volume in the Langley series for the University of Georgia Press examines in general terms the role of the United States in the Western Hemisphere. Following Arthur P. Whitaker's lead, Langley is especially interested in shared values among the nations, especially *the idea* of the Western Hemisphere, that is, a kind of unity of values, practices, and political experiences among the inhabitants of the region (2:350).

12:45   Lieuwen, Edwin. *U.S. Policy in Latin America: A Short History.* New York: Praeger, 1965. This concise, somewhat dated rendition emphasizes a mixture of ideological, strategic, and economic motives as the main determinants of U.S. policy.

12:46   Martin, Percy Alvin. *Latin America and the War.* Baltimore: Johns Hopkins Press, 1925. First delivered as the Albert Shaw Lectures on Diplomatic History at Johns Hopkins University in 1921, this book explains why eight of the countries of Latin America declared war on the Central Powers in support of the United States, five severed relations, and seven remained neutral. It emphasizes the role of public opinion in each of the various nations.

12:47   Mecham, J. Lloyd. *The United States and Inter-American Security, 1889–1960.* Austin: University of Texas Press, 1961. This ambitious survey, now dated, focuses on evolving Pan-American mechanisms to promote international cooperation and stresses the promotion of U.S. national security as the principal incentive.

12:48   Mitchell, Nancy. *The Danger of Dreams: German and American Imperialism in Latin America.* This subtle work, described by the author as "a study of threat perception," examines specific cases of an alleged German imperial threat in Venezuela, Brazil, and Mexico in the first two decades of the twentieth century and concludes that no such danger existed. U.S. leaders misperceived German intentions. Nevertheless, the construction of a German menace served U.S. interests by legitimating the exercise of hegemonic influence (9:389).

12:49   _____. "Germans in the Backyard: *Weltpolitik* versus Protective Imperialism." *Prologue* 24 (Summer 1992): 174–83. Based on German sources, this essay argues that apprehensions in the United States over German designs on the Western Hemisphere were much exaggerated.

12:50   Park, James William. *Latin American Underdevelopment: A History of Perspectives in the United States, 1870–1965.* This illuminating work attributes the characteristic disdain for Latin American peoples by observers in the United States to racist perceptions, holding that Latin Americans constituted an inferior people, handicapped by an authoritarian and medieval cultural legacy and by a tropical setting inimical to progress. Ignorance, misinformation, and ethnocentrism also contributed to U.S. attitudes (9:390).

12:51   Pike, Fredrick B. *The United States and Latin America: Myths and Stereotypes of Civilization and Nature.* This daringly innovative study presents a cultural analysis, arguing that U.S. attitudes toward Latin America are rooted in ambivalent myths and stereotypes about civilization and nature and about supposed Latin American deficiencies in each area. At the turn of the century, U.S. perceptions, always tinged with racism, called for the expansion of the western frontier into parts of Latin America and for the uplift of native peoples (5:529).

12:52   Robertson, William Spence. *Hispanic-American Relations with the United States.* New York: Oxford University Press, 1923. Robertson, a skilled historian, traveled in Latin America for a year at the end of World War I under the auspices of the Carnegie Endowment for International Peace and compiled the materials necessary for this remarkable study. Much of it covers nineteenth-century issues. The remainder perceptively deals with an array of contemporary concerns, such as trade, education, the Mexican revolution, the Panama Canal, and Pan-Americanism.

12:53   Schoultz, Lars. *Beneath the United States: A History of U.S. Policy toward Latin America.* This emphatic and persuasive work underscores the importance of racism and condescension in U.S. policy toward Latin Americans. Chapters 9–14 cover the administrations of Theodore Roosevelt, William Howard Taft, and Woodrow Wilson (9:393).

12:54   Smith, Peter H. *Talons of the Eagle: Dynamics of U.S.–Latin American Relations.* 2d ed. New York: Oxford University Press, 2000. This volume by a political scientist conceptualizes U.S.–Latin American relations as a subsystem within a larger global system, subject to "tacit codes of behavior." Part I concerns "The Imperial Era." First published in 1996.

12:55   Tulchin, Joseph S. *The Aftermath of War: World War I and U.S. Policy toward Latin America.* New York: New York University Press, 1971. After

World War I, the United States tried to end its dependency on foreign powers for petroleum, capital, and cables, to consolidate its position in Latin America, and to rely less on protectorates as a means of upholding its interests.

12:56   West, Rachel. *The Department of State on the Eve of the First World War.* This illuminating and insightful study examines the personnel and the practices of the U.S. State Department in 1913–1914 and consequently has direct application to the study of Latin American policy (11:73).

THE MCKINLEY AND ROOSEVELT ADMINISTRATIONS

12:57   Beale, Howard K. *Theodore Roosevelt and the Rise of America to World Power.* This classic work, an expansion of the Albert Shaw Lectures at the Johns Hopkins University, describes Roosevelt as a nationalist and a realist who understood the workings of power. In these lectures, the author tries to present world affairs as Roosevelt understood them and to evaluate the significance of his role (9:84).

12:58   Collin, Richard H. *Theodore Roosevelt, Culture, Diplomacy, and Expansion: A New View of American Imperialism.* Cultural and diplomatic changes produced for the United States a new leadership role in a world already teetering on the brink of chaos, war, and revolution. Strategic necessity, not imperialistic avarice, brought about U.S. interventions in the Philippines, Panama, and elsewhere (9:85).

12:59   Gould, Lewis L. *The Presidency of Theodore Roosevelt.* This study depicts President Theodore Roosevelt as a strong, vigorous, and determined leader who insisted on keeping the European great powers out of the Western Hemisphere (11:468).

12:60   _____. *The Presidency of William McKinley.* This presidential study contains an account of the aftermath of the war with Spain, focusing on relations with Cuba and the formulation of the Platt Amendment (10:153).

12:61   Tilchin, William N. *Theodore Roosevelt and the British Empire: A Study in Presidential Statecraft.* This broadly gauged work examines President Roosevelt's techniques for managing relations with Great Britain and its worldwide empire. It has some bearing on Western Hemisphere issues, notably Anglo-American political and economic competition that outlasted British decisions to yield preeminence to the United States (11:299).

THE TAFT ADMINISTRATION

12:62   Coletta, Paolo E. *The Presidency of William Howard Taft.* This general account describes the Taft administration's wary response to the Mexican revolution and other efforts involving "dollar diplomacy" in Central America (11:479).

12:63   Scholes, Walter V., and Marie V. Scholes. *The Foreign Policies of the Taft Administration.* President Taft and his secretary of state, Philander C. Knox, hoped to develop policies in the Western Hemisphere that would benefit the United States and the countries of Latin America by promoting stability and economic growth. Usually referred to as "dollar diplomacy," administration practices called for infusions of money and U.S. administrative expertise and typically failed. The chapters dealing with Latin America focus on "dollar diplomacy" in the Dominican Republic, Nicaragua, Honduras, and Guatemala and responses to the impending revolution in Mexico (11:79).

THE WILSON ADMINISTRATION

12:64   Bell, Sidney. *Righteous Conquest: Woodrow Wilson and the Evolution of the New Diplomacy.* Port Washington, NY: Kennikat Press, 1972. This book follows the lead of Charles A. Beard, William A. Williams, and Frederick Jackson Turner by arguing that Wilson believed in the necessity of forming a new consensus around a charismatic leader who could create a sense of national purpose and an overseas economic empire to compensate for the closing of the frontier. Emphasizing political economy, three chapters deal with Latin America.

12:65   Calhoun, Frederick S. *Power and Principle: Armed Intervention in Wilsonian Foreign Policy.* Kent, OH: Kent State University Press, 1986. This perceptive work argues that Wilson used controlled force under presidential authority to promote American ideology, enforce international law, and encourage international cooperation with his interventions in Mexico, Haiti, the Dominican Republic, and elsewhere.

12:66   _____. *Uses of Force and Wilsonian Foreign Policy.* Kent, OH: Kent State University Press, 1993. This book examines in specific terms the uses to which Wilson used armed force during his various interventions, including those in Mexico, Haiti, and the Dominican Republic.

12:67   Clements, Kendrick A. *The Presidency of Woodrow Wilson.* Lawrence: University Press of Kansas, 1992. This excellent book regards as a great myth the view that Woodrow Wilson was uninterested in foreign relations and unprepared to conduct diplomacy when he became the president. To the contrary, he exercised more personal control over foreign relations than any other aspect of his administration in his efforts to advance freedom and democracy.

12:68   Gilderhus, Mark T. *Pan American Visions: Woodrow Wilson in the Western Hemisphere, 1913–1921.* Tucson: University of Arizona Press, 1986. This work explores Woodrow Wilson's pursuit of a Pan-American vision, seeking to promote political and economic integration in the Western Hemisphere under the leadership and supervision of the United States.

12:69   _____. "Pan-American Initiatives: The Wilson Presidency and 'Regional Integration,' 1914–17." *Diplomatic History* 4 (Fall 1980): 409–23. This essay explores President Wilson's efforts to coordinate political and economic initiatives to achieve closer relations with the countries of Latin America during the neutrality period before entry into World War I.

12:70   Kaufman, Burton I. "United States Trade and Latin America: The Wilson Years." *Journal of American History* 58 (September 1971): 342–63. This essay examines the techniques used by business leaders and government officials in World War I to capitalize on new opportunities for expanding trade.

12:71   Link, Arthur S. *Wilson the Diplomatist: A Look at His Major Foreign Policies.* Baltimore: Johns Hopkins Press, 1957. First presented as the Albert Shaw Lectures on Diplomatic History at the Johns Hopkins University in December 1956, these essays contain little about Latin America, except to say that Wilson's emphasis on idealism and high principles sometimes caused problems when the president tried to apply them in concrete situations.

12:72   _____. *Woodrow Wilson: Revolution, War, and Peace.* Arlington Heights, IL: AHM Pub. Corp., 1979. This revised version of Link's earlier *Wilson the Diplomatist: A Look at His Major Foreign Policies* (1957) (12:71) takes into account subsequent publications and emphasizes Wilson's commitment to democratic and religious principles as the first anti-imperialist statesman of the twentieth century. In Latin America, Wilson had trouble reconciling high principle with political reality.

12:73   Livermore, Seward W. "'Deserving Democrats': The Foreign Service under Woodrow Wilson." *South Atlantic Quarterly* 69 (Winter 1970): 144–60. The author describes the working of the patronage system during the Wilson presidency as administration leaders tried to find jobs for "deserving Democrats" in the diplomatic corps, sometimes in Latin America.

12:74   Mock, James R. "The Creel Committee in Latin America." *Hispanic American Historical Review* 22 (May 1942): 262–79. This essay, still the standard account, tells how George Creel's Committee on Public Information in 1917–1918 tried to combat German propaganda in Latin America and persuade Latin Americans to endorse U.S. war aims.

12:75   Vivian, James F. "Wilson, Bryan, and the American Delegation to the Abortive Fifth Pan American Conference, 1914." *Nebraska History* 59 (Spring 1978): 56–69. The author reviews the process for choosing U.S. delegates to a proposed Pan-American conference in Santiago, Chile, subsequently cancelled because of the onset of World War I. A willingness to defend Wilson's Latin American policies was a main criterion.

PAN-AMERICANISM AND THE MONROE DOCTRINE

12:76   Aguilar Monteverde, Alonso. *Pan-Americanism from Monroe to the Present: A View from the Other Side.* Translated by Asa Zatz. This radical view employs a Latin American Marxist perspective, depicting Pan-Americanism as a means of U.S. political and economic domination (2:344).

12:77   Alén Lascano, Luis C. *Yrigoyen, Sandino y el panamericanismo [Yrigoyen, Sandino, and Pan Americanism].* Buenos Aires: Centro Editor de América Latina, 1986. This account, something of an Argentine polemic, extols those political leaders, such as Hipólito Yrigoyen and Augusto Sandino, who opposed U.S. hegemony and stood up for Latin American prerogatives.

12:78   Bingham, Hiram. *The Monroe Doctrine: An Obsolete Shibboleth.* This book-length rendition sets forth Bingham's condemnation of the Monroe Doctrine as a paternalistic and antiquated notion unacceptable to Latin Americans. Later during World War I, Bingham, a Yale University history professor, repudiated these views (7:90).

12:79   Caicedo Castilla, José Joaquín. *El Panamericanismo [Pan Americanism].* Buenos Aires: Roque Depalma, 1961. This book presents an account of Pan-American activities, including the conferences before 1919, from the viewpoint of an Argentine international lawyer.

12:80   Casey, Clifford B. "The Creation and Development of the Pan American Union." *Hispanic American Historical Review* 13 (November 1933): 437–56. This still useful article traces the origins of an organizational entity known by 1910 as the Pan American Union, a voluntary association, based in Washington, D.C., and designed to disseminate information, advance commerce, and promote cooperation between the United States and the countries of Latin America.

12:81   Gil, Enrique. *Evolución del Panamericanismo: El Credo de Wilson y el Panamericanismo [Evolution of Pan Americanism: Wilson's Creed and Pan Americanism].* Buenos Aires: J. Menéndez, 1933. This classic work presents an enthusiastic endorsement of Woodrow Wilson's definition of Pan-Americanism by an Argentine expert on international law. Gil sees Wilson as an apostle of peace and democracy.

12:82 Perkins, Dexter. *A History of the Monroe Doctrine*. This now dated classic examines the role of the Monroe Doctrine in U.S. foreign relations, its various interpretations, and how it was implemented. The author emphasizes the importance of security considerations during the early twentieth century (2:351). Originally published in 1941 as *Hands Off: A History of the Monroe Doctrine*.

ECONOMICS AND TRADE

12:83 Drake, Paul W., ed. *Money Doctors, Foreign Debts, and Economic Reforms in Latin America from the 1890s to the Present*. Wilmington, DE: SR Books, 1994. This collective work contains essays on the activities of "money doctors" in the 1899–1921 period, emphasizing the distribution of U.S. loans in Latin America, Haitian protectorates, and dollar diplomacy generally. Particular chapters include "Introduction: The Political Economy of Foreign Advisers and Lenders in Latin America" by Drake; "Dollar Diplomacy" by Scott Nearing and Joseph Freeman; "Occupied Haiti" by Paul H. Douglas; "Haiti under American Control, 1915–1930" by Arthur C. Millspaugh; and "From Colonialism to Professionalism: The Public-Private Dynamic in United States Foreign Financial Advising, 1898–1929" by Emily S. Rosenberg and Norman L. Rosenberg.

12:84 Foner, Philip S. *U.S. Labor Movement and Latin America: A History of Workers' Response to Intervention. Vol. 1: 1846–1919*. South Hadley, MA: Bergin and Garvey, 1988. This book presents an extensive treatment of relations between labor unions in the United States and Latin America, especially during the Mexican revolution, emphasizing U.S. support for nonradical organizations.

12:85 Kaufman, Burton I. *Efficiency and Expansion: Foreign Trade Organization in the Wilson Administration, 1913–1921*. Westport, CT: Greenwood Press, 1974. This book examines the organizational innovations undertaken by business leaders and government officials during the Wilson presidency to expand U.S. trade in Latin America and elsewhere, seeking thereby to take advantage of new opportunities during World War I.

12:86 _____. "Organization for Foreign Trade Expansion in the Mississippi Valley, 1900–1920." *Business History Review* 46 (Winter 1972): 444–65. This article describes organizational efforts among business leaders and government officials in the Mississippi valley to take advantage of the Panama Canal and extend commerce more efficiently into Latin America.

12:87 _____. "The Organizational Dimension of United States Economic Foreign Policy, 1900–1920." This article examines the development of an elaborate organizational structure in the United States to support commercial expansion in Latin America and elsewhere, emphasizing the German model as a means to achieve efficiency (11:88).

12:88 Krenn, Michael L. *U.S. Policy toward Economic Nationalism in Latin America, 1917–1929*. Wilmington, DE: SR Books, 1990. In this broadly comparative work, Krenn examines U.S. opposition to manifestations of economic nationalism in various Latin American countries, including Mexico, and attributes it to the role of economic self-interest, anti-communism, and racism. Since Latin Americans were seen stereotypically as lazy and ignorant, U.S. leaders were flabbergasted when they tried to run their own economies.

12:89 Levenstein, Harvey A. *Labor Organizations in the United States and Mexico: A History of Their Relations*. Westport, CT: Greenwood Press, 1971. This book explores relations between the American Federation of Labor under Samuel Gompers and Mexican labor organizations during the era of the Mexican revolution and argues that the AFL sought closer relations both to promote international solidarity among workers and to exercise a constraining influence over Mexican radicals.

12:90 Nearing, Scott, and Joseph Freeman. *Dollar Diplomacy: A Study in American Imperialism*. Incorporating a radical point of view, this classic work examines the growth of U.S. economic interests abroad during the early decades of the twentieth century and also the diplomatic and military support accorded them by the U.S. government. Chapters 4, 5, and 6 deal with Latin American and Caribbean issues (2:87).

12:91   O'Brien, Thomas F. *The Revolutionary Mission: American Enterprise in Latin America, 1900–1945.* New York: Cambridge University Press, 1996. This ambitious and challenging book argues that U.S. corporations in Latin America had revolutionary potential when they tried to inculcate values of materialism, work, and individuality, which ran counter to Latin American traditions stressing family, community, and mutuality. As a consequence of complex interactions, far-reaching effects took place in the development of Latin American society and in relations with the United States.

12:92   Rosenberg, Emily S. "The Exercise of Emergency Controls over Foreign Commerce: Economic Pressure on Latin America." *Inter-American Economic Affairs* 31 (Spring 1978): 81–96. The author provides a historical overview of the increase of presidential direction in economic foreign policy and analyzes the various ways in which the executive branch under Woodrow Wilson used its authority to enhance diplomatic leverage with Latin America during World War I.

12:93   _____. *Financial Missionaries to the World: The Politics and Culture of Dollar Diplomacy, 1900–1930.* This important and innovative work takes a new look at dollar diplomacy by moving beyond traditional approaches and connecting the subject with cultural history and political economy. Rosenberg argues that dollar diplomacy was "intertwined with cultural contexts that fostered the growth of professionalism, of scientific theories that accentuated racial and gender differences, and of the mass media's emphasis on the attractions and repulsions of primitivism." The effects, often unanticipated by the experts, elicited resistance among foreign peoples, the supposed beneficiaries, and anti-imperialists. This work also includes important information on economist Edwin Kemmerer, who advised various Latin American countries on finances in the 1910s and 1920s (11:91).

12:94   _____. "Foundations of United States International Financial Power: Gold Standard Diplomacy, 1900–1905." In the view of business and po-

litical leaders at the turn of the century, the new U.S. role as a global power required the development of a new financial strategy, based on stable exchange rates, to spread the international gold standard and enhance the position of New York banks. To such ends, the United States tried to reform the silver and bimetallic currency systems of seven colonies or countries by converting them to the gold standard. These endeavors included Mexico, Puerto Rico, Cuba, and the Dominican Republic (9:196).

12:95   _____. *Spreading the American Dream: American Economic and Cultural Expansion, 1890–1945.* In this illuminating interpretive work, the author argues that the American dream of high technology and mass consumption obtained both support and legitimization from an ideology characterized as "liberal-developmentalism," which included a belief system emphasizing private enterprise, free trade, the unhindered flow of information and culture, and the applicability of the U.S. developmental model to other countries. Such views typically guided U.S. activities in Latin America between 1899 and 1919 (9:151).

12:96   Rosenberg, Emily S., and Norman L. Rosenberg. "From Colonialism to Professionalism: The Public-Private Dynamic in United States Foreign Financial Advising, 1898–1929." This essay analyzes the forms taken by U.S. financial advising during the transitional period from 1898 to 1930, that is, after colonialism had ceased to function as a viable way of imposing financial arrangements but before the advent of post–World War II financial institutions. The essay focuses on Latin America and develops a structural framework for understanding the different relationships from which U.S. financial missions drew authority and legitimacy. According to the authors, four mechanisms forming a continuum provided the environment in which advisers operated: colonialism, treaty arrangements, legal contracts, and finally professionalism, that is, a set of prerogatives derived supposedly from expertise (9:198).

IMPERIALISM AND ANTI-IMPERIALISM

12:97   Beisner, Robert L. *Twelve against Empire: The Anti-Imperialists, 1898–1900.* This standard work examines the views of twelve men who opposed the acquisition of a colonial empire after the war with Spain and bears to some extent on Latin American issues, especially Cuba and Puerto Rico. Originally published in 1968, this printing has new explanatory forewords written in both 1985 and 1992 (10:506).

12:98   Dement'ev, I. P. *USA, Imperialists and Anti-Imperialists: (The Great Foreign Policy Debate at the Turn of the Century).* Translated by David Skvirsky. This Marxist appraisal presents the debate between anti-imperialists and imperialists as a contest between the forces of progress and the forces of reaction; it describes Pan-Americanism as a sinister U.S. design by which to dominate Latin America economically (10:511).

12:99   Joseph, Gilbert M., Catherine C. LeGrand, and Ricardo D. Salvatore, eds. *Close Encounters of Empire: Writing the Cultural History of U.S.–Latin American Relations.* This ambitious and significant collection of essays by leading scholars uses the techniques of cultural historical analysis. Using various approaches, typically microcosmic in nature, the authors explore the "encounter" between the inhabitants of the United States and Latin America as a complex interaction among unequal actors, illuminating in new ways their modes of cooperation, subjection, and resistance under changing historical conditions. Only one essay, Steven Palmer, "Central American Encounters with Rockefeller Public Health, 1914–1921," directly concerns U.S.–Latin American relations between 1898 and 1921. In addition, see Ricardo D. Salvatore, "The Enterprise of Knowledge: Representational Machines of Informal Empire"; Deborah Poole, "Landscape and the Imperial Subject: U.S. Images of the Andes, 1859–1930"; and William Roseberry, "Social Fields and Cultural Encounters." See chapter 9 of this Guide for further information (9:385).

12:100   Langley, Lester D. *The Banana Wars: United States Intervention in the Caribbean, 1898–1934.* This useful synthesis of warfare in and around the Caribbean rejects economic explanations of U.S. actions and argues instead that Americans resorted to intervention to deal with what they perceived as uncivilized behavior. A political motive to instill order among lesser peoples became a dominant incentive. Originally published in 1983 (10:107).

12:101   Musicant, Ivan. *The Banana Wars: A History of United States Military Intervention in Latin America from the Spanish-American War to the Invasion of Panama.* New York: Macmillan, 1990. This valuable work takes into account various social, political, racial, and economic factors but regards the strategic imperative of keeping the Europeans out of the Western Hemisphere the overriding consideration in accounting for U.S. policy. "Grenada" rather than "Panama" appears as the last word of the title of some printings.

12:102   Ricard, Serge, and Hélène Christol, eds. *Anglo-Saxonism in U.S. Foreign Policy: The Diplomacy of Imperialism, 1899–1919.* This brief volume consists of five essays by European scholars first presented at the biennial meeting of the European Association for American Studies in London in 1990. The essays emphasize the importance of an ideology characterized as "Anglo-Saxonism," that is, a worldview based on a sense of joint civilizing mission, common culture, and shared heritage between Britons and Americans. Serge Ricard's "The Anglo-American Intervention in Venezuela and Theodore Roosevelt's Ultimatum to the Kaiser: Taking a Fresh Look at an Old Enigma" is the only piece dealing directly with Latin America (10:83).

12:103   Tompkins, E. Berkeley. *Anti-Imperialism in the United States: The Great Debate, 1890–1920.* This standard work examines the debate over expansionism and imperialism, specifically the activities of anti-imperialists who believed that the violation of the principle of self-determination abroad ultimately would destroy it at home, in other words, that the costs would exceed the gains (10:529).

12:104   Weston, Rubin Francis. *Racism in U.S. Imperialism: The Influence of Racial Assumptions on American Foreign Policy, 1893–1946.* Columbia: University of South Carolina Press, 1972. This provocative and illuminating work depicts racism as an essential part of U.S. imperialism, arguing that racial views made an imperialist compromise possible, allowing the flag to advance into insular regions while denying that the Constitution should follow the flag.

Biographical Studies

COLLECTIVE

12:105   Cooper, John Milton, Jr. *The Warrior and the Priest: Woodrow Wilson and Theodore Roosevelt*. In this work, Cooper develops a comparative perspective based on a distinction drawn from Nietzsche. The depiction of Roosevelt as a warrior and Wilson as a priest has many implications for explaining the behavior of each president toward Latin America, notably the aggressive combativeness of the former and the missionary zeal of the latter (11:467).

JOHN BARRETT

12:106   Prisco, Salvatore, III. *John Barrett, Progressive Era Diplomat: A Study of a Commercial Expansionist, 1887–1920*. This work examines the career of John Barrett, a diplomat with experience in Asia and Latin America who also served as director-general of the Pan American Union during the Taft and Wilson presidencies. As an advocate of Pan-Americanism and a commercial expansionist, Barrett favored multilateral approaches to Latin America as a means to extend U.S. trade (9:100).

12:107   _____. "John Barrett's Plan to Mediate the Mexican Revolution." *Americas* 27 (April 1971): 413–25. John Barrett, the director-general of the Pan American Union, proposed in February 1913 that an international commission under the auspices of the Pan American Union mediate among the various contending Mexican factions. But he botched the plan. As an advocate of Pan-American cooperation in the Western Hemisphere and a tireless self-promoter, he announced his intention to the press before obtaining consent from U.S. authorities. He consequently alienated President Taft, President-elect Wilson, and the State Department, thereby destroying any hope for success.

WILLIAM JENNINGS BRYAN

12:108   Clements, Kendrick A. *William Jennings Bryan: Missionary Isolationist*. Knoxville: University of Tennessee Press, 1982. This book describes Bryan's attitudes toward foreign policy as balanced precariously between traditional isolationism and a deep conviction that Christianity required service to others. Chapter 5 applies the theme to Latin America.

12:109   Coletta, Paolo E. *William Jennings Bryan. Vol. 2: Progressive Politician and Moral Statesman, 1909–1915*. Lincoln: University of Nebraska Press, 1969. Still a useful source, this biography depicts William Jennings Bryan as a moralist who performed adequately as secretary of state. In Mexico, he favored arbitration, not intervention. In the Caribbean, he had difficulty reconciling his anti-imperialist preferences with strategic needs to maintain order and keep out the Europeans (10:117).

12:110   Kaplan, Edward S. *U.S. Imperialism in Latin America: Bryan's Challenges and Contributions, 1900–1920*. Westport, CT: Greenwood Press, 1998. This work tries to explain the inconsistencies in Bryan's policies toward Latin America, specifically his opposition to imperialism before he became secretary of state in 1913 and his selective endorsement of interventionist activity afterward. According to the author, Bryan never understood the inconsistency and never defined what he meant by moral obligation to other peoples.

THEODORE ROOSEVELT

12:111   Brands, H. W. *T.R.: The Last Romantic*. This biography by a prolific scholar develops the argument that Roosevelt, a committed romantic, believed that wrongs existed to be righted. As president, he worried most about the threat of German expansion into the Caribbean (11:466).

12:112   Burton, David H. *Theodore Roosevelt: Confident Imperialist*. Philadelphia: University of Pennsylvania Press, 1968. Roosevelt's understanding of imperialism took into account some of the costs but affirmed nevertheless that humankind would benefit from the expansion of western civilization, particularly when spread by the United States. More good than harm would come about, and the lesser races would experience uplift.

12:113　Marks, Frederick W., III. "Morality as a Drive Wheel in the Diplomacy of Theodore Roosevelt." This article argues that Roosevelt's conception of morality influenced his statecraft, even in dealings with Cuba, Panama, and Colombia (11:77).

12:114　_____. *Velvet on Iron: The Diplomacy of Theodore Roosevelt.* According to the author's statement of purpose, this book seeks to establish a conceptual framework capable of accommodating Roosevelt's diplomatic record while revealing his underlying strategy and technique. Marks devises a compelling case, emphasizing the president's understanding of the uses of power, his commitment to his conceptions of morality, and his fear of German intrusions in the Western Hemisphere (11:78).

12:115　Morris, Edmund. *Theodore Rex.* In this volume devoted to Roosevelt's presidency, Morris's coverage of Latin American concerns is sporadic and conventional. Roosevelt was irrepressible in his behavior, moralistic in his views, and realistic in his assessments. He worried about German intrusions in the Western Hemisphere and expressed disparaging attitudes toward Latin Americans (10:174).

12:116　Roosevelt, Theodore. *The Autobiography of Theodore Roosevelt.* In chapter 14, "The Monroe Doctrine and the Panama Canal," Roosevelt exuberantly defends his actions and his use of preventative police power in the Caribbean region. A 1975 edition, edited by Wayne Andrews, is condensed but supplemented by letters, speeches, and other writings (11:474).

12:117　Trani, Eugene P. "Cautious Warrior: Theodore Roosevelt and the Diplomacy of Activism." In *Makers of American Diplomacy. Vol. 2: From Theodore Roosevelt to Henry Kissinger,* ed. Frank J. Merli and Theodore A. Wilson, 1–28. New York: Scribner, 1974. This short essay presents a perceptive overview, emphasizing Roosevelt's infatuation with foreign affairs, his eagerness to advance what he defined as national interests, and his willingness to stretch executive power to the limit. Such themes apply in Latin America.

WOODROW WILSON

12:118　Baker, Ray Stannard, ed. *Woodrow Wilson: Life and Letters.* 8 vols. Garden City, NY: Doubleday, Page and Co., 1927–1939. This basic documentary collection as well as its biographical content has now been superseded by Arthur S. Link's biography and compilation of the Wilson papers.

12:119　Clements, Kendrick A. *Woodrow Wilson, World Statesman.* Boston: Twayne, 1987. In chapter 8 of this fine biography, the author characterizes Wilson's policies toward Latin America as "a paradoxical combination of idealistic commitment to self-determination and intervention."

12:120　Gregory, Ross. "To Do Good in the World: Woodrow Wilson and America's Mission." In *Makers of American Diplomacy. Vol. 2: From Theodore Roosevelt to Henry Kissinger,* ed. Frank J. Merli and Theodore A. Wilson, 55–79. New York: Scribner, 1974. This perceptive short essay argues that President Wilson lacked a systematic philosophy of foreign relations. Hence, he tried to act in accord with his philosophy of life and made diplomacy an extension of his thoughts about humankind, the United States, and himself. Above all, he wanted to make the United States an instrument of global reform, in Latin America by means of intervention when necessary.

12:121　Link, Arthur S. *Wilson. Vol. 2: The New Freedom.* Princeton: Princeton University Press, 1956. This volume of Link's magisterial biography centers on the nature of Wilson's high ideals concerning the New Freedom and Pan-Americanism in support of democracy and constitutionality and the difficulty of applying them in actual circumstances. When New Freedom diplomacy could not uphold the security of the United States, Wilson resorted to interventionist methods.

12:122　_____. *Wilson. Vol. 3: The Struggle for Neutrality, 1914–1915.* Princeton: Princeton University Press, 1960. In this volume of Link's biography, four chapters consider Latin American concerns, specifically responses to the Mexican revolution and the move toward intervention in Haiti and the Dominican Republic. Link emphasizes the difficulty of reconciling high principles with harsh political realities.

12:123 _____. *Wilson. Vol. 4: Confusions and Crises, 1915–1916.* Vol. 4. 5 vols. Princeton: Princeton University Press, 1964. In this volume of Link's authoritative biography, two chapters deal with Mexican issues, specifically Pancho Villa's attack on Columbus, New Mexico, in 1916, the subsequent Pershing punitive expedition into Mexico, and the ensuing possibility of war between the two countries.

12:124 _____. *Wilson. Vol. 5: Campaigns for Progressivism and Peace, 1916–1917.* Vol. 5. 5 vols. Princeton: Princeton University Press, 1965. This volume of Link's Wilson biography considers the activities of the Joint High Commission to place U.S.-Mexican relations on a more regular basis, specifically by finding a way of getting the Pershing punitive expedition out of Mexico; it also considers the impact of the Zimmermann telegram.

OTHERS

12:125 Karnes, Thomas L. "Hiram Bingham and His Obsolete Shibboleth." *Diplomatic History* 3 (Winter 1979): 39–57. Hiram Bingham, a Yale University history professor, obtained a measure of notoriety in 1913 by publicly repudiating the Monroe Doctrine as an "obsolete shibboleth." This essay examines the circumstances, the reactions to Bingham's views, and his own change of heart during World War I.

12:126 Peterson, Harold F. *Diplomat of the Americas: A Biography of William I. Buchanan (1852–1909).* Buchanan was a diplomatic troubleshooter from 1894 to 1909 in Panama and Venezuela (9:103).

12:127 Schmidt, Hans. *Maverick Marine: General Smedley D. Butler and the Contradictions of American Military History.* Lexington: University Press of Kentucky, 1987. This fascinating biography tells the story of Smedley D. Butler, a true warrior who rose to the rank of major-general in the U.S. marine corps. He served in a variety of places in Asia, Europe, and Latin America, including Cuba, Haiti, Honduras, Mexico, and Nicaragua, and helped make the protectorates safe for U.S. interests. Later he rejected his past and claimed that he had been a soldier in service to the interests of big business and Wall Street.

12:128 Richmond, Douglas W. *Venustiano Carranza's Nationalist Struggle, 1893–1920.* Lincoln: University of Nebraska Press, 1983. Based on primary Mexican sources, this work sets forth the theme suggested by the title and also explores Carranza's foreign policies.

12:129 La Botz, Dan. *Edward L. Doheny: Petroleum, Power, and Politics in the United States and Mexico.* New York: Praeger, 1991. This biography depicts Doheny as a leading Yankee entrepreneur in the Mexican oil industry and active lobbyist who sought to influence U.S. foreign policy; it seeks to set straight some of the myths perpetuated by Doheny about himself.

12:130 MacLachlan, Colin M. *Anarchism and the Mexican Revolution: The Political Trials of Ricardo Flores Magón in the United States.* Berkeley: University of California Press, 1991. This work reviews the activities of the Mexican anarchist Ricardo Flores Magón and shows how he posed a threat not only to Mexican authority but to U.S. conceptions of law and order in the borderlands. As a consequence, he spent a great deal of time in U.S. prisons.

12:131 Esposito, David M. "Imagined Power: The Secret Life of Colonel House." *Historian* 60 (Summer 1998): 741–56. The author argues that House was duplicitous, often motivated more by self-importance than by loyalty to President Wilson. House played a behind-the-scenes role in the development of Latin American policy, especially in regard to the Pan-Americanism.

12:132 Meyer, Michael C. *Huerta: A Political Portrait.* Lincoln: University of Nebraska Press, 1972. Based on an array of primary Mexican sources, this biography places Victoriano Huerta's regime in the context of the Mexican revolution and also covers his diplomatic relations with the United States.

12:133 Gibbs, William E. "James Weldon Johnson: A Black Perspective on 'Big Stick' Diplomacy." *Diplomatic History* 8 (Fall 1984): 329–47. This essay presents an intriguing study of Johnson, an African-American, a Republican, and a consular official, who became a critic of the racism underlying Woodrow Wilson's policies in Latin America.

12:134 Hill, Larry D. "The Progressive Politician as a Diplomat: The Case of John Lind in Mexico." *Americas* 27 (April 1971): 355–72. John Lind, a one-term Democratic governor of Minnesota and novice diplomat who knew no Spanish, went to Mexico in August 1913 as Woodrow Wilson's special executive agent and stayed until April 1914. His partisan reports, fiercely critical of Victoriano Huerta, advocated U.S. intervention and reinforced the president's proclivity to get tough.

12:135 Bacevich, A. J. *Diplomat in Khaki: Major General Frank Ross McCoy and American Foreign Policy, 1898–1949.* This work uses biography as a way to examine the relationship between American military and political elites and assess the contribution of the U.S. army to foreign policy. McCoy's extraordinarily diverse career spanned nine administrations from McKinley to Truman. Two chapters deal with his role in the Cuban occupation and the Mexican problem between 1898 and 1919 (10:190).

12:136 Phillips, William. *Ventures in Diplomacy.* Boston: Beacon Press, 1953. These unpretentious memoirs by an assistant secretary of state during the Wilson presidency set forth vivid portraits of leading personalities, an impression of the administration's handling of the Mexican question, and an account of the impact of World War I.

12:137 Minger, Ralph Eldin. *William Howard Taft and United States Foreign Policy: The Apprenticeship Years, 1900–1908.* This monograph covers Taft's involvement with the protectorates, Cuba and Panama, during his tenure as secretary of war (11:480).

12:138 Katz, Friedrich. *The Life and Times of Pancho Villa.* Stanford, CA: Stanford University Press, 1998. This massive biography of a central figure in the Mexican revolution presents as thorough an analysis as scholars are likely to get. It concentrates attention on Villa's dealings with the United States, Great Britain, and Germany. When undertaking the attack against Columbus, New Mexico, Villa believed that President Carranza had sold out Mexican independence to the United States.

12:139 Wilson, F. M. Huntington. *Memoirs of an Ex-Diplomat.* An appeal for realism in foreign policy, these engaging memoirs by a high-ranking State De-

partment official during the Taft administration present an insider's view of relations with Central America, described as "the Balkans" of the Western Hemisphere. They also contain a sympathetic portrait of South America and its people during the author's trip into the region in 1914 (11:512).

U.S. Foreign Relations with Other Countries and Regions

MEXICO

12:140 Buchenau, Jürgen. "Counter-Intervention against Uncle Sam: Mexico's Support for Nicaraguan Nationalism, 1903–1910." *Americas* 50 (October 1993): 207–32. This thoughtful, well-researched essay argues that Mexican President Porfirio Diaz tried to play a major role in Central America to keep U.S. influence at a minimum, and by so doing may have offended leaders in the Taft administration to such an extent they would not support him against Francisco Madero in 1910.

12:141 _____. *In the Shadow of the Giant: The Making of Mexico's Central American Policy, 1876–1930.* Tuscaloosa: University of Alabama Press, 1996. This book breaks with the usual practice of focusing on U.S. actions and emphasizes instead Mexican efforts to play an active role in Central America, seeking thereby to constrain the activity of the United States in the region.

12:142 Cline, Howard F. *The United States and Mexico.* Originally published in 1953, this classic work surveys the course of U.S.-Mexican relations, emphasizing the era of the Mexican revolution, 1910–1920 (2:382).

12:143 Gilderhus, Mark T. "Senator Albert B. Fall and the 'Plot against Mexico.'" *New Mexico Historical Review* 48 (October 1973): 299–311. This article considers the 1919 crisis in U.S.-Mexican relations and Senator Fall's attempt to overturn the Carranza regime by precipitating a conservative revolution against it.

12:144   Grieb, Kenneth J. "Sir Lionel Carden and the Anglo-American Confrontation in Mexico: 1913–1914." *Ibero-Amerikanisches Archiv* 1 (1975): 201–16. Grieb argues that the British need for Mexican oil to sustain the Royal Navy was the main motive for supporting Huerta and confronting the United States. Sir Lionel Carden, the British ambassador to Mexico, had close ties to Lord Cowdray, a big investor in Mexican petroleum.

12:145   Joseph, Gilbert M. *Revolution from Without: Yucatán, Mexico, and the United States, 1880–1924.* New York: Cambridge University Press, 1982. This unique work depicts the impact of the Mexican revolution on a peripheral area, Yucatán, as an imposition from the outside and also explores the implications for relations with the United States, specifically Mexican economic dependency upon henequen production and the International Harvester Company.

12:146   Knight, Alan. *U.S.-Mexican Relations, 1910–1940: An Interpretation.* La Jolla: Center for U.S.-Mexican Studies, University of California, San Diego, 1987. An interpretive synthesis by a noted British historian of Mexico, this brief work perceptively analyzes the causes and effects of U.S. intervention in Mexico between 1910 and 1920 and a long-term tendency toward accommodation between the two countries.

12:147   Meyer, Lorenzo. "The United States and Mexico: The Historical Structure of Their Conflict." *Journal of International Affairs* 43 (Winter 1990): 251–71. This brief overview by a noted Mexican historian emphasizes the era of the Mexican revolution, 1910–1920, as a critical period and the factors of disparities of power, wealth, and influence in influencing the shape of relations between the United States and Mexico.

12:148   Nugent, Daniel, ed. *Rural Revolt in Mexico: U.S. Intervention and the Domain of Subaltern Politics.* Durham, NC: Duke University Press, 1998. This set of interdisciplinary essays by leading historians and anthropologists seeks to establish a context for understanding rural revolts in Mexico by taking into account popular nationalism and anti-imperialism, the role of social class and ethnicity, and the relationship with U.S. intervention. Most relevant for the period 1898–1921 in U.S.-Mexican relations are Alan Knight, "United States and the Mexican Peasantry, circa 1880–1940"; John H. Coatsworth, "Measuring Influence: The United States and Mexican Peasantry"; John Mason Hart, "Social Unrest, Nationalism, and American Capital in the Mexican Countryside, 1876–1920"; Gilbert M. Joseph, "The United States, Feuding Elites, and Rural Revolt in Yucatán, 1836–1915"; Ana María Alonso, "U.S. Military Intervention, Revolutionary Mobilization, and Popular Ideology in the Chihuahua Sierra, 1916– 1917"; and Friedrich Katz, "From Alliance to Dependency: The Formation and Deformation of an Alliance between Francisco Villa and the United States." First published in 1988 as *Rural Revolt in Mexico and U.S. Intervention.*

12:149   Raat, W. Dirk. *Mexico and the United States: Ambivalent Vistas.* This succinct, provocative book examines the span of U.S.-Mexican relations within the context of "world systems analysis." It argues that the era of World War I functioned as a catalyst for nationalist and anticolonial change, for example, in Mexico where a nationalist revolution took place (2:384). First published in 1992.

12:150   Riguzzi, Paolo. "México, Estados Unidos, y Gran Bretaña, 1867–1910: Una difícil relación triangular [Mexico, the United States, and Great Britain, 1867–1910: A Difficult Triangular Relationship]." *Historia Mexicana* 41 (enero-marzo 1992): 365–437. This essay provides a richly detailed study of the intense competition between the United States and Great Britain for economic advantage and political influence during the presidency of Porfirio Diaz in Mexico.

12:151   Schmitt, Karl M. "American Protestant Missionaries and the Díaz Regime in Mexico: 1876–1911." This essay presents the case that Protestant missionaries in Mexico looked on President Diaz as a kind of protector but subsequently found it relatively easy to shift loyalties when the revolution got under way (9:405).

12:152   Trow, Clifford W. "'Tired of Waiting': Senator Albert B. Fall's Alternative to Woodrow Wilson's Mexican Policies, 1920–1921." *New Mexico Historical Review* 57 (April 1982): 159–82. Senator Albert B. Fall, a leading Republican critic of President Wilson's Mexican policies, tried in various ways to force a showdown, overturn the Mexican Constitution of 1917, and compel a settlement of foreign rights on U.S. terms. This essay describes his machinations.

12:153 Turner, Frederick C. "Anti-Americanism in Mexico, 1910–1913." *Hispanic American Historical Review* 47 (November 1967): 502–18. The author of this essay argues provocatively that deep-seated anti-Americanism in Mexico prepared Mexicans to resist Woodrow Wilson's interventions and fueled burgeoning Mexican nationalism.

12:154 Vázquez, Josefina Zoraida, and Lorenzo Meyer. *The United States and Mexico.* This brief survey by two notable Mexican scholars presents an interpretation from a Mexican viewpoint, emphasizing inequality, asymmetry, and dependency. The Mexican revolution, among other things, represented an attempt to break free from U.S. dominance (2:386).

The Mexican Revolution

The Mexican Revolution: General

12:155 Blaisdell, Lowell L. *The Desert Revolution: Baja California, 1911.* Madison: University of Wisconsin Press, 1962. This book describes a Mexican anarchist invasion of Baja California led by Ricardo Flores Magón and the ensuing complexities in U.S.-Mexican relations.

12:156 Blasier, Cole. "The United States and Madero." This detailed account criticizes the behavior of U.S. Ambassador Henry Lane Wilson during the ten tragic days in February 1913 when Mexican rebels rose in opposition to President Francisco Madero. Without express authorization from the Taft administration, Wilson threatened U.S. intervention, tried to arrange Madero's resignation, and encouraged General Victoriano Huerta to seize power (11:430).

12:157 Britton, John A. *Revolution and Ideology: Images of the Mexican Revolution in the United States.* Lexington: University Press of Kentucky,

1995. This insightful book analyzes responses to the Mexican revolution by observers in the United States, including a wide range of political commentators, academics, journalists, creative writers, politicians, businessmen, ministers, and diplomats.

12:158 Calvert, Peter. *The Mexican Revolution, 1910–1914: The Diplomacy of Anglo-American Conflict.* This work by a British historian examines the competition between the United States and Great Britain in Mexico between 1910 and 1913 after the collapse of the Diaz regime. It argues that the defense of concrete interests figured prominently in British diplomacy and criticizes Wilson for failing to understand British aims (11:340).

12:159 Durán, Esperanza. *Guerra y revolución: las grandes potencias y méxico, 1914–1918 [War and Revolution: The Great Powers and Mexico, 1914–1918].* México, DF: El Colegio de México, Centro de Estudios Internacionales, 1985. This fine work by a Mexican scholar is based on multiarchival research; it explores great power competition in Mexico during the era of the Mexican revolution and World War I, focusing especially on the interventionist activities of the United States.

12:160 Escobar, Edward J. "Mexican Revolutionaries and the Los Angeles Policy: Harassment of the Partido Liberal Mexicano, 1907–1910." *Aztlán* 17 (Spring 1986): 1–46. This long article calls attention to the extralegal and illegal means used by U.S. officials against Mexican anarchists, members of the *partido liberal mexicano,* who hatched conspiracies against President Porfirio Diaz, using Los Angeles as a base.

12:161 Hall, Linda B., and Don M. Coerver. *Revolution on the Border: The United States and Mexico, 1910–1920.* Albuquerque: University of New Mexico Press, 1988. The authors examine the social and economic impact of the Mexican revolution on the border regions and also the effects of the struggle on political and military relations between the two countries.

12:162 _____. *Texas and the Mexican Revolution: A Study in State and National Border Policy, 1910–1920.* San Antonio: Trinity University Press, 1984. This book is a study of the conflicts and confusions among local, state, and federal officials in the

United States in response to border problems during the Mexican revolution.

12:163   Harris, Charles H., III, and Louis R. Sadler. *The Border and the Revolution.* 2d ed. Silver City, NM: High-Lonesome Books, 1990. This collection of essays authored by Harris and Sadler, most of which have appeared in scholarly journals, focuses on the clandestine activities of spies, mercenaries, and gunrunners in the making of the Mexican revolution and also includes discussions of revolutionary conspiracies, the Plan of San Diego, Pancho Villa's Columbus raid, and German intrigues along the Mexican border in 1917–1918. First published in 1988.

12:164   _____. "The Plan of San Diego and the Mexican–United States War Crisis of 1916: A Reexamination." *Hispanic American Historical Review* 58 (August 1978): 381–408. In 1915, the Plan of San Diego called upon Mexicans in the borderlands to rise in rebellion against the Anglos. According to this essay, Carranza tried to speed the process of obtaining *de facto* diplomatic recognition by presenting himself as the only one who could control a disorderly situation, and then when he could not, the outcome almost precipitated a war.

12:165   Katz, Friedrich. *The Secret War in Mexico: Europe, the United States, and the Mexican Revolution.* Translated by Loren Goldner. Chicago: University of Chicago Press, 1981. An exceptionally thorough work based on extensive research in primary sources, this book explores in abundant detail the economic competition among the European powers and the United States over Mexican resources, especially oil, and the ensuing efforts to support Mexican conservatives against Mexican radicals.

12:166   López de Roux, María Eugenia. "Relaciones Mexicana-Norteamericana (1917–1918) [Mexican–North American Relations, 1917–1918]." *Historia Mexicana* 14 (enero-marzo 1965): 445–66. This discerning essay by a Mexican scholar employs Mexican sources and shows the effects of World War I, the Mexican Constitution, and the threat of U.S. intervention on U.S.-Mexican relations.

12:167   McKnight, Gerald. "Republican Leadership and the Mexican Question, 1913–1916: A Failed Bid for Party Resurgence." *Mid-America* 62 (April-

July 1980): 105–22. This essay examines Republican efforts to capitalize on President Wilson's difficulties with Mexico, hoping to use them as a means of winning back the presidency in 1916.

12:168   Raat, W. Dirk. "The Diplomacy of Suppression: *Los Revoltosos,* Mexico, and the United States, 1906–1911." *Hispanic American Historical Review* 56 (November 1976): 529–50. This article shows how U.S. authorities under Presidents Roosevelt and Taft kept the activities of Mexican anarchists in the United States under close surveillance and often subjected them to legal harassment.

12:169   _____. *Revoltosos: Mexico's Rebels in the United States, 1903–1923.* College Station: Texas A&M University Press, 1981. This work recounts how U.S. authorities upheld neutrality laws by cracking down on the activities of Mexican rebels in the United States, notably those of Ricardo Flores Magón and the Partido Liberal Mexicano.

12:170   Sandos, James A. *Rebellion in the Borderlands: Anarchism and the Plan of San Diego, 1904–1923.* Norman: University of Oklahoma Press, 1992. This book explores the activities of radical anarchists, notably Ricardo Flores Magón, in Mexico and the United States and argues that the Magonistas originated the Plan of San Diego, a call for Mexicans in Texas in 1915 to rise in rebellion against their Anglo overlords. The latter claim is controversial. Another view holds that no such connection existed with the Magonistas and that the Plan of San Diego was indigenous to south Texas.

12:171   Sloan, John W. "United States Policy Responses to the Mexican Revolution: A Partial Application of the Bureaucratic Political Model." *Journal of Latin American Studies* 10 (November 1978): 283–308. This article tests the "bureaucratic politics" model of explanation and concludes that it has applicability in the case of Mexico. It argues that competition within the U.S. foreign policy establishment had important effects in shaping responses to the Mexican revolution between 1911 and 1941.

12:172   Smith, Robert Freeman. *The United States and Revolutionary Nationalism in Mexico, 1916–1932.* Chicago: University of Chicago Press, 1972. This well-conceived book examines the challenge posed by Mexican revolutionary nationalism to the established world order dominated by industrial and capitalist nations, represented in the Western Hemisphere by the United States. Consequently, the Mexican Constitution of 1917 offended foreigners by affirming an authority to limit property rights and control mineral resources. In response, successive administrations in the United States employed a variety of strategies to turn back such claims, significantly, according to Smith, without resorting to the use of force after the withdrawal of the Pershing punitive expedition in 1917.

12:173   Ulloa, Berta. *La revolución intervenida: Relaciones diplomáticas entre México y Estados Unidos, 1910–1914 [The revolution and intervention: diplomatic relations between Mexico and the United States, 1910–1914].* 2d ed. México, DF: El Colegio de México, 1976. This well-documented, multiarchival study by a Mexican scholar emphasizes the competition between the United States and Great Britain over Mexico and suggests that the United States used the Tampico incident as a pretext for intervention in Mexico in the spring of 1914. First published in 1971.

The Revolution and the Taft Administration

12:174   Cosío Villegas, Daniel. "Sobre Henry Lane Wilson [About Henry Lane Wilson]." *Memoria del Colegio Nacional* 4 (septiembre 1961): 39–55. This account by one of Mexico's most distinguished historians is critical of U.S. Ambassador Henry Lane Wilson's role in the overthrow of Francisco Madero by Victoriano Huerta in February 1913.

12:175   Haley, P. Edward. *Revolution and Intervention: The Diplomacy of Taft and Wilson with Mexico, 1910–1917.* Cambridge, MA: M.I.T. Press, 1970. This work by a political scientist seeks to obtain guidance for responding to revolutionary phenomena in the future by determining how the Taft and Wilson administrations reacted to the Mexican revolution in the past.

12:176   Prida, Ramón. *La culpa de Lane Wilson, embajador de los E. U. A. en la tragedia mexicana de 1913 [The Guilt of Lane Wilson, U.S. Ambassador, in*

the Mexican Tragedy of 1913]. México, DF: Ediciones Botas, 1962. This venerable polemic from a Mexican viewpoint castigates U.S. Ambassador Henry Lane Wilson for bringing down Madero and facilitating the rise of Huerta.

12:177   Shoemaker, Raymond L. "Henry Lane Wilson and Republican Policy toward Mexico, 1913–1920." *Indiana Magazine of History* 76 (June 1980): 103–22. Former Ambassador Henry Lane Wilson left Mexico after Victoriano Huerta took power, widely regarded as a kind of accomplice. He then campaigned in favor of Republican positions and against Woodrow Wilson's policies, which he depicted as weak and vacillating.

The Revolution and the Wilson Administration

12:178   Clements, Kendrick A. "Emissary from a Revolution: Luis Cabrera and Woodrow Wilson." *Americas* 35 (January 1979): 353–72. This essay argues that Cabrera, a diplomatic emissary from Carranza, played a significant role by influencing Wilson's view of the Mexican revolution and moderating the president's interventionist tendencies.

12:179   _____. "'A Kindness to Carranza': William Jennings Bryan, International Harvester, and Intervention in Yucatán." *Nebraska History* 57 (Winter 1976): 479–90. This essay explores a little-known but revealing episode during the Mexican revolution in 1915 in which Secretary of State William Jennings Bryan's moralistic proclivities clashed with political realities. As a kindness to Carranza, Bryan threatened military intervention against rebel factions and supported the International Harvester Company, a major economic presence in Yucatán.

12:180   _____. "Woodrow Wilson's Mexican Policy, 1913–1915." *Diplomatic History* 4 (Spring 1980): 113–36. This essay argues that Wilson wanted to use American power to break the grip of foreign economic interests in Mexico and at the same time avoid dictating to the Mexican people the form and the role of their government.

12:181   Cumberland, Charles C. "The Jenkins Case and Mexican-American Relations." *Hispanic Ameri-*

can *Historical Review* 31 (November 1951): 586–607. This article shows how the abduction of William O. Jenkins, a U.S. consul in Puebla, Mexico, by anti-Carranza rebels brought the two countries to the brink of war.

12:182   Gardner, Lloyd C. "Woodrow Wilson and the Mexican Revolution." In *Woodrow Wilson and a Revolutionary World, 1913–1921,* ed. Arthur S. Link, 2–48. Chapel Hill: University of North Carolina Press, 1982. In this broadly interpretive essay, the author shows Wilson's difficulty in reconciling democratic principles with capitalist imperatives.

12:183   Gilderhus, Mark T. *Diplomacy and Revolution: U.S.-Mexican Relations under Wilson and Carranza.* Tucson: University of Arizona Press, 1977. This monograph argues that President Wilson repeatedly tried to circumscribe the Mexican revolution by containing it within the ideological confines of liberal capitalism.

12:184   _____. "Henry P. Fletcher in Mexico, 1917–1920: An Ambassador's Response to Revolution." *Rocky Mountain Social Science Journal* 10 (October 1973): 61–70. This article examines Ambassador Fletcher's growing disenchantment with the anti-foreign aspects of the Mexican revolution and his insistence on tough policies in response.

12:185   _____. "The United States and Carranza, 1917: The Question of De Jure Recognition." *Americas* 29 (October 1972): 214–31. This essay considers the circumstances leading to the *de jure* recognition of the Carranza regime following the withdrawal of the Pershing punitive expedition and the break in relations with Germany prior to entering World War I.

12:186   _____. "Wilson, Carranza, and the Monroe Doctrine: A Question in Regional Organization." *Diplomatic History* 7 (Spring 1983): 103–15. This essay discusses President Wilson's efforts to give multilateral meaning to the Monroe Doctrine in conjunction with his Pan-American policy and Carranza's efforts to destroy it as an egotistical affront to all Latin Americans.

12:187   Glaser, David. "1919: William Jenkins, Robert Lansing, and the Mexican Interlude." *South-*

western *Historical Quarterly* 74 (January 1971): 337–57. The 1919 crisis in U.S. relations with Mexico resulted from an accumulation of grievances over the Mexican Constitution of 1917, Mexican neutrality in World War I, and the kidnapping of U.S. consular agent William O. Jenkins. Because of Woodrow Wilson's illness, Secretary of State Robert Lansing took charge, assumed a tough position, and ran afoul of the president, who later fired him.

12:188   Grieb, Kenneth J. *The United States and Huerta.* Lincoln: University of Nebraska Press, 1969. In this critical account, Grieb argues that Wilson unwisely abandoned the traditional U.S. policy of extending diplomatic recognition to *de facto* governments and ended up committing a moral transgression in search of moral rectitude by intervening militarily in 1914 to rid Mexico of a despotic tyrant.

12:189   Harper, James W. "The El Paso-Juárez Conference of 1916." *Arizona and the West* 20 (Autumn 1978): 231–44. According to the author's argument, the Scott-Obregón meeting resulted in no formal agreements on border questions but had the effect of reducing tensions and buying time for President Wilson to deal with the Germans.

12:190   _____. "Hugh Lenox Scott y la diplomacia de los Estados Unidos hacia la Revolución Mexicana [Hugh Lenox Scott and the United States Diplomacy toward the Mexican Revolution]." *Historia Mexicana* 27 (enero-marzo 1978): 427–55. This essay describes Scott as the "old soldier of the frontier" and examines his role as a diplomat, seeking to keep the peace during difficult times in relations between the United States and Mexico.

12:191   Harrison, Benjamin T. "Chandler Anderson and the Business Interests in Mexico, 1913–1920: When Business Interests Failed to Alter U.S. Foreign Policy." *Inter-American Economic Affairs* 33 (Winter 1979): 3–23. Harrison argues that in the case of Mexico, Chandler Anderson, a lobbyist, failed to influence U.S. policy in favor of business interests.

12:192   Henderson, Peter V. N. "Woodrow Wilson, Victoriano Huerta, and the Recognition Issue in Mexico." *Americas* 41 (October 1984): 151–76. This author, trained both as historian and lawyer, analyzes the manner in which Woodrow Wilson used the law of recognition in his efforts to unseat the Mexican dictator, Victoriano Huerta.

12:193   Hill, Larry D. *Emissaries to a Revolution: Woodrow Wilson's Executive Agents in Mexico.* Baton Rouge: Louisiana State University Press, 1974. This useful work explores the diplomatic activities of eleven men sent by Woodrow Wilson into Mexico as special executive agents during the era of the revolution between 1913 and 1915. It examines their influence on Wilson's policies and the reactions of Mexican leaders to them. The book concludes with the diplomatic recognition of Venustiano Carranza in October 1915.

12:194   Kahle, Louis G. "Robert Lansing and the Recognition of Venustiano Carranza." *Hispanic American Historical Review* 38 (August 1958): 353–72. Secretary of State Lansing promoted U.S. recognition of the Carranza government as a stabilizing influence because of his concern that Germany might take advantage of the ongoing disorder in Mexico.

12:195   Lazo, Dimitri D. "Lansing, Wilson, and the Jenkins Incident." *Diplomatic History* 22 (Spring 1998): 177–98. In this provocative article, the author argues that Secretary of State Lansing tried to capitalize on the uproar over the kidnapping in Mexico of a U.S. consular official, William O. Jenkins, by forcing President Wilson out of office following his physical collapse in September 1919.

12:196   Machado, Manuel A., Jr., and James T. Judge. "Tempest in a Teapot? The Mexican–United States Intervention Crisis of 1919." *Southwestern Historical Quarterly* 74 (July 1970): 1–23. This essay examines the crisis in U.S.-Mexican relations during the fall of 1919, when an accumulation of grievances over the Mexican Constitution of 1917, Mexican neutrality in World War I, and President Carranza's supposed obduracy over the kidnapping of U.S. Consul William O. Jenkins brought about a war scare.

12:197   Mock, James R., and Cedric Larson. "Activities of the Mexico Section of the Creel Committee, 1917–1918." *Journalism Quarterly* 16 (June 1939): 136–50. The Mexico Section of the Creel Committee tried to combat anti-U.S. sentiments and cultivate opinion in support of the Allies.

12:198   O'Brien, Dennis J. "Petróleo e Interven-

ción: Relaciones entre Estados Unidos y México, 1917–1918 [Petroleum and Intervention: Relations between the United States and Mexico, 1917–1918]." *Historia Mexicana* 27 (julio-septiembre 1977): 103–40. This article argues convincingly that Mexican petroleum had vital importance to the United States and the Allies during World War I and that a cutoff might have persuaded President Wilson to abandon the policy of nonintervention.

12:199   O'Shaughnessy, Edith, ed. *Diplomatic Days.* New York: Harper and Brothers, 1917. As the wife of Nelson O'Shaughnessy, a U.S. diplomat attached to the embassy in Mexico City, Edith O'Shaughnessy wrote vivid, sometimes discerning letters published in this volume, describing the diplomatic life and her impressions of Mexico under President Madero.

12:200   _____. *A Diplomat's Wife in Mexico: Letters from the American Embassy at Mexico City, Covering the Dramatic Period between October 8th, 1913, and the Breaking Off of Diplomatic Relations on April 23rd, 1914, Together with an Account of the Occupation of Vera Cruz.* New York: Harper and Brothers, 1916. Reprint 1970 (Arno Press). This firsthand account by the wife of Nelson O'Shaughnessy, the U.S. chargé d'affaires in Mexico in 1913–1914, favors Huerta as a stabilizing force and criticizes President Wilson for the intervention against him.

12:201   _____. *Intimate Pages of Mexican History.* New York: George H. Doran, 1920. This memoir by Edith O'Shaughnessy, wife of Nelson O'Shaughnessy, a U.S. diplomat in Mexico, offers a personal account of events in the first three years of the Mexican revolution; it favors Huerta and criticizes President Wilson for trying to bring him down.

12:202   Quirk, Robert E. *An Affair of Honor: Woodrow Wilson and the Occupation of Veracruz.* Lexington: University of Kentucky Press, 1962. Still an important account, this book underscores the irony that idealistic proclivities compelled President Wilson to use force against the Mexican people during the 1914 intervention at Veracruz and subsequently produced a threat of war.

12:203   Rausch, George J., Jr. "Poison-Pen Diplomacy: Mexico, 1913." *Americas* 24 (January 1968): 272–80. The reports from such special executive agents in Mexico as John Lind reinforced President Woodrow Wilson's biases by strongly criticizing Victoriano Huerta as a drunken, illegitimate tyrant.

12:204   Rosenberg, Emily S. "World War I and 'Continental Solidarity.'" *Americas* 31 (January 1975): 313–34. Rosenberg discusses countervailing tendencies in the Western Hemisphere during World War I, specifically Wilson's efforts to promote "continental solidarity" under U.S. leadership and reactions against it in Mexico under Carranza and in Argentina under Yrigoyen.

12:205   Sweetman, Jack. *The Landing at Veracruz: 1914, The First Complete Chronicle of a Strange Encounter in April, 1914, When the United States Navy Captured the City of Veracruz, Mexico*. Annapolis: U.S. Naval Institute, 1968. This book presents an operational history of the U.S. intervention at Veracruz in April 1914, using firsthand information obtained from surviving participants.

12:206   Trow, Clifford W. "Woodrow Wilson and the Mexican Interventionist Movement of 1919." *Journal of American History* 58 (June 1971): 46–72. In 1919, critics of the Mexican revolution under the leadership of Senator Albert B. Fall of New Mexico promoted U.S. intervention as a way to oust Venustiano Carranza. President Wilson foiled the plan.

Pancho Villa and the Pershing Expedition

12:207   Clendenen, Clarence C. *Blood on the Border: The United States Army and the Mexican Irregulars*. New York: Macmillan, 1969. This volume recounts the efforts of the U.S. army to police the borderlands between the United States and Mexico, especially during the era of the Mexican revolution between 1910 and 1920.

12:208   _____. *The United States and Pancho Villa: A Study in Unconventional Diplomacy*. Ithaca: Cornell University Press, 1961. Reprint 1972 (Kennikat Press). This standard account, based mainly on U.S. sources, argues that Villa was a friend of the United States until the Wilson administration extended *de facto* recognition to the Carranza regime; then Villa became an enemy and a scourge.

12:209   Hall, Linda B., and Don M. Coerver. "Woodrow Wilson, Public Opinion, and the Punitive Expedition: A Re-assessment." *New Mexico Historical Review* 72 (April 1997): 171–94. Wilson's decision to send the Pershing punitive expedition into Mexico, neither hasty nor capricious, was an effort to cope with an assortment of domestic and international problems, especially to win reelection and to encourage military preparedness.

12:210   Harris, Charles H., III, and Louis R. Sadler. "Pancho Villa and the Columbus Raid: The Missing Documents." *New Mexico Historical Review* 50 (October 1975): 335–46. These lost documents, presumably dropped by Villistas during the Columbus raid, have turned up in the records of the U.S. Department of War, the Adjutant General's Office. They convey more information about Villa's plan of attack but do not reveal his motives for undertaking the raid.

12:211   Katz, Friedrich. "Pancho Villa and the Attack on Columbus, New Mexico." *American Historical Review* 83 (February 1978): 101–30. According to Katz, Villa's primary motive in undertaking the Columbus raid was his belief that President Carranza had sold out Mexican independence to the United States.

12:212   Lerner, Victoria. "Espías mexicanas en tierras norteamericanas (1914–1915) [Mexican Spies in North American Territory, 1914–1915]." *New Mexico Historical Review* 69 (July 1994): 230–48. This essay focuses on the activities of Villa supporters along the border who acted on behalf of the cause by recruiting allies and seeking to uncover conspiracies and machinations among Carrancistas, Huertistas, and others.

12:213   Meyer, Michael C. "Felix Sommerfeld and the Columbus Raid." *Arizona and the West* 25 (Autumn 1983): 213–28. This intriguing excursion into conspiracy theory examines the claim that Felix Sommerfeld, allegedly a German agent, somehow encouraged Villa to attack Columbus, New Mexico, to divert the Wilson administration from Europe. Meyer, a careful scholar, finds no convincing proof.

12:214   Sandos, James A. "Pancho Villa and American Security: Woodrow Wilson's Mexican Diplomacy Reconsidered." *Journal of Latin American*

Studies 13 (November 1981): 292–311. This essay suggests that Wilson's aims in pursuing Villa ran parallel with his goals at the end of World War I. In each case, the president sought to incorporate, first, Mexico and, then, Germany into a new non-revolutionary community of liberal nation states and, at the same time, to ward off threats of revolution.

12:215　Stout, Joseph A., Jr. *Border Conflict: Villistas, Carrancistas, and the Punitive Expedition, 1915–1920.* Fort Worth: Texas Christian University Press, 1999. Based on Mexican primary sources, this intriguing work is a study of the military activities of Venustiano Carranza's Constitutionalist army during the Pershing punitive expedition. It argues that Carranza worried more about Villa's insurgency than the presence of U.S. troops in Mexico and that his army played an active role in fighting Villa.

12:216　Tate, Michael L. "Pershing's Punitive Expedition: Pursuit of Bandits or Presidential Panacea?" *Americas* 32 (July 1975): 46–71. This essay argues that President Wilson initially intended the Pershing expedition in 1916 to eliminate the bandit threat along the border but later significantly expanded its purpose to obtain leverage over the Mexican revolution. In the end, Wilson failed in his effort to make military withdrawal contingent on Mexican concessions over the future course of the revolution.

12:217　Vanderwood, Paul J., and Frank N. Samponaro. *Border Fury: A Picture Postcard Record of Mexico's Revolution and U.S. War Preparations, 1910–1917.* Albuquerque: University of New Mexico Press, 1988. This fascinating pictorial account with an accompanying narrative uses images of the Mexican revolution derived from postcards; it includes a vivid section on the Pershing punitive expedition.

12:218　Wilson, Christopher P. "Plotting the Border: John Reed, Pancho Villa and *Insurgent Mexico.*" In *Cultures of United States Imperialism,* ed. Amy Kaplan and Donald E. Pease, 340–61. Durham, NC: Duke University Press, 1993. Using the techniques of cultural history, this short piece shows how John Reed employed the established conventions of war correspondents in his book, *Insurgent Mexico* (New York and London: D. Appleton and Company, 1914), to depict Pancho Villa as an exotic and unpredictable character capable of great savagery.

12:219　Yockelson, Mitchell. "The United States Armed Forces and the Mexican Punitive Expedition, Part 1." *Prologue* 29 (Fall 1997): 256–62. This brief essay provides an introduction to the subject by describing the background and the course of events during the Pershing punitive expedition.

12:220　_____. "The United States Armed Forces and the Mexican Punitive Expedition, Part 2." *Prologue* 30 (Winter 1997): 334–43. This brief essay describes pertinent Record Groups in the National Archives, Washington D.C., with information on the Pershing punitive expedition.

The German Threat

12:221　Baecker, Thomas. "The Arms of the '*Ypiranga*': The German Side." This essay explains the German side of the episode that precipitated the U.S. intervention at Veracruz in 1914; it emphasizes German caution and prudence while dealing with the Wilson administration (11:235).

12:222　_____. *Die deutsche Mexikopolitik, 1913/1914 [Germany's Policy toward Mexico, 1913–1914].* This work by a German historian shows that German policy in Mexico proceeded opportunistically and that the plan resulting in the Zimmermann telegram did not originate in the Huerta presidency (11:236).

12:223　_____. "Los Intereses Militares del Imperio Alemán in México, 1913–1914 [The Military Interests of the German Empire in Mexico, 1913–1914]." *Historia Mexicana* 22 (enero-marzo 1973): 347–62. This essay characterizes German interests in Mexico as opportunistic and denies any link between policy toward Huerta and the subsequent Zimmermann telegram.

12:224　Katz, Friedrich. "Alemania y Francisco Villa [Germany and Francisco Villa]." *Historia Mexicana* 12 (julio-septiembre 1962): 88–102. According to Katz, Germany undoubtedly wanted to provoke a war between Mexico and the United States after 1914, but no proof exists to show that Villa was operating as a German agent when he attacked Columbus, New Mexico, on March 9, 1916.

12:225   Meyer, Michael C. "The Arms of the *Ypiranga.*" In this essay, the author details the story of Huerta's efforts to buy guns and ammunition, the arrival of which aboard the German commercial vessel *Ypiranga* triggered the U.S. decision to intervene at Veracruz in 1914 (11:245).

12:226   _____. "The Mexican-German Conspiracy of 1915." *Americas* 23 (July 1966): 76–89. Meyer discusses German activity in Mexico and its role in the decision of the United States to recognize Carranza in 1915. The Wilson administration hoped for a stable regime in Mexico, capable of resisting German temptations.

12:227   _____. "Villa, Sommerfeld, Columbus y los alemanes [Villa, Sommerfeld, Columbus, and the Germans]." *Historia Mexicana* 28 (abril/junio 1979): 546–66. In this essay, an earlier version of Meyer's "Felix Sommerfeld and the Columbus Raid" (1983) (12:213), he examines the claim that Felix Sommerfeld, supposedly a German agent, somehow prompted Villa's attack on Columbus, New Mexico. Meyer rejects the claim for lack of proof.

12:228   Sandos, James A. "German Involvement in Northern Mexico, 1915–1916: A New Look at the Columbus Raid." *Hispanic American Historical Review* 50 (February 1970): 70–88. Based on circumstantial evidence, this essay gives credence to the view that German agents might have encouraged Pancho Villa to attack Columbus, New Mexico, in 1915.

12:229   Tuchman, Barbara W. *The Zimmermann Telegram.* New York: Viking Press, 1958. Reprint 1985 (Ballantine Books). This popular work tells the story of the Zimmerman telegram, the inception of the German plan, the interception of the transmission by British intelligence, and the effects on decision-making in the Wilson administration. It has been superseded by Katz, *The Secret War in Mexico: Europe, the United States, and the Mexican Revolution* (1981) (12:165).

Economics and Trade

12:230   Andrews, Gregg. *Shoulder to Shoulder? The American Federation of Labor, the United States,* and the Mexican Revolution, 1910–1924. Berkeley: University of California Press, 1991. This book argues that the American Federation of Labor developed a conception of Pan-Americanism largely in response to the Mexican revolution. The head, Samuel Gompers, embraced the Mexican labor movement during this era of upheaval but also functioned as something of a conservative influence to constrain radical impulses.

12:231   Bell, Samuel E., and James M. Smallwood. "Zona Libre: Trade and Diplomacy on the Mexican Border, 1858–1905." *Arizona and the West* 24 (Summer 1982): 119–52. By exploring the protracted conflict over the free zone along the border between the United States and Mexico, this article illustrates the complexity of political and economic affairs in the region and the cumbersome diplomatic machinery used to resolve disputes.

12:232   Brown, Jonathan C. *Oil and Revolution in Mexico.* Berkeley: University of California Press, 1993. The author focuses on the activities of foreign-owned oil companies in Mexico and argues that the exercise of governmental control over them was part of a complex process of revolutionary state making.

12:233   Hall, Linda B. *Oil, Banks, and Politics: The United States and Postrevolutionary Mexico, 1917–1924.* Austin: University of Texas Press, 1995. This insightful book, based on thorough research in Mexico and the United States, explains the interactions among politicians, finance capitalists, and oil men, particularly in response to the nationalistic provisions of the Mexican Constitution of 1917.

12:234   Meyer, Lorenzo. *Mexico and the United States in the Oil Controversy, 1917–1942.* Translated by Muriel Vasconcellos. Austin: University of Texas Press, 1977. This fine work by a leading Mexican historian places the oil controversy within the framework of economic dependency. Successive Mexican governments tried to break free by controlling the exploitation of petroleum, culminating with the oil expropriation in 1938.

12:235   Paulsen, George E. "Fraud, Honor, and Trade: The United States–Mexico Dispute over the Claim of La Abra Company, 1875–1902." *Pacific Historical Review* 52 (May 1983): 175–90. This case study shows changing attitudes toward investment opportunities in Mexico over a period of twenty years and emphasizes the recklessness of many speculators in the United States.

12:236 Pletcher, David M. "An American Mining Company in the Mexican Revolutions of 1911–1920." *Journal of Modern History* 20 (March 1948): 19–26. Using the example of the Chicago Exploration Company, a silver and copper mining operation in northern Mexico, Pletcher demonstrates the disastrous effects of the revolution on some foreign enterprises.

12:237 _____. "The Fall of Silver in Mexico, 1870–1910, and Its Effect on American Investments." *Journal of Economic History* 18 (March 1958): 33–55. While Mexico was a tempting field for U.S. investors in the late nineteenth century, the Mexican economic situation, and especially the decline in the value of silver, caused some of the investments to be unprofitable, especially in railroads.

12:238 _____. *Rails, Mines, and Progress: Seven American Promoters in Mexico, 1867–1911.* Pletcher considers the activities of seven U.S. investors in Mexico, while describing the expansion of U.S. economic influence in Mexico during the late nineteenth century (9:403).

12:239 Rosenberg, Emily S. "Economic Pressures in Anglo-American Diplomacy in Mexico, 1917–1918." *Journal of Interamerican Studies and World Affairs* 17 (May 1975): 123–52. The United States and Britain undertook efforts (not always cooperative) to get Carranza to end threats to oil fields and other investments in Mexico. The author argues that U.S. and British policy was not dictated by their oil interests.

12:240 Schell, William, Jr. "American Investment in Tropical Mexico: Rubber Plantations, Fraud, and Dollar Diplomacy, 1897–1913." *Business History Review* 64 (Summer 1990): 217–54. This article examines U.S. investment patterns in Mexico at the turn of the century, focusing on the tropical plantation companies, and challenges the usual conclusion that U.S. economic penetration drained away Mexican wealth and undermined political sovereignty. According to this author, each claim is dubious. He calls

for more subtle evaluation of the impact of U.S. investment in Mexico.

12:241 Wasserman, Mark. *Capitalists, Caciques, and Revolution: The Native Elite and Foreign Enterprise in Chihuahua, Mexico, 1854–1911.* Chapel Hill: University of North Carolina Press, 1984. This book reviews the impact of foreign investment and shows how northern Mexico became linked to world economic cycles, which contributed to the onset of revolution in 1910.

CENTRAL AMERICA AND THE CARIBBEAN

General

12:242 Adler, Selig. "Bryan and Wilsonian Caribbean Penetration." *Hispanic American Historical Review* 20 (May 1940): 198–226. This classic article describes the process by which Bryan underwent a transformation from opposing U.S. imperialism to advocating Caribbean expansion.

12:243 Collin, Richard H. "The Caribbean Theater Transformed: Britain, France, Germany, and the U.S., 1900–1906." *American Neptune* 52 (Spring 1992): 102–12. According to this analysis, Presidents McKinley and Roosevelt regarded as a top priority keeping European influences out of the Caribbean and winning European recognition of U.S. hegemony. Germany appeared as the principal adversary.

12:244 Healy, David F. *Drive to Hegemony: The United States in the Caribbean, 1898–1917.* This sophisticated book examines the techniques developed by the United States to exercise hegemony over the small sovereign states of the Caribbean, the reasons why U.S. leaders desired such hegemony, and some of the effects resulting from it (10:106).

12:245 Kennedy, Philip W. "Race and American Expansion in Cuba and Puerto Rico, 1895–1905." The author argues that racist perceptions of Cubans and Puerto Ricans provided U.S. officials with a justification for expansionist practices by emphasizing the need to uplift supposedly lesser peoples (10:542).

12:246 Kneer, Warren G. *Great Britain and the Caribbean, 1901–1913: A Study in Anglo-American Relations.* This book emphasizes the ambivalence in British policy toward the United States over Caribbean issues; British leaders recognized the need to seek accommodation with the United States but displayed reluctance to give up too much (11:344).

12:247 Langley, Lester D. *The United States and the Caribbean in the Twentieth Century.* In the twentieth century, the United States established an empire in the Caribbean but without colonies. Langley's interpretation is balanced, noting a mixture of selfish and unselfish motives calling for political order, economic tutelage, and civic morality. First issued in 1982 (2:365).

12:248 Langley, Lester D., and Thomas D. Schoonover. *The Banana Men: American Mercenaries and Entrepreneurs in Central America, 1880–1930.* In this intriguing collaborative effort, Langley provides details and specifics about the activities of the "banana men" and Schoonover the theoretical apparatus derived from "world systems analysis." The book considers Central America an arena for competing imperialisms emanating from the United States and Europe and examines the costs and the gains (9:463).

12:249 Leonard, Thomas M. *Central America and the United States: The Search for Stability.* The subtitle of this work states the theme. Above all else, the United States desired stability in Central America. The decision to construct the Panama Canal assured the primacy of strategic considerations in U.S. policy (2:356).

12:250 Munro, Dana G. *Intervention and Dollar Diplomacy in the Caribbean, 1900–1921.* This now somewhat dated classic argues that conditions of economic backwardness and political instability in and round the Caribbean basin compelled U.S. intervention for security reasons to guard against European threats (11:434).

12:251 Perkins, Whitney T. *Constraint of Empire: The United States and Caribbean Interventions.* This book presents a controversial case, holding that the United States intervened militarily in Cuba, Nicaragua, the Dominican Republic, and Haiti for

idealistic reasons and, paradoxically, to advance the cause of self-government in and around the Caribbean basin (10:110).

12:252 Schoonover, Thomas D. *The French in Central America: Culture and Commerce, 1820–1930.* This useful book fills a gap in the scholarly literature by exploring France's role in a circumstance of complex international rivalry over Central America. It uses a theoretical approach based on world systems analysis and argues in favor of the utility of dependency theory. Driven by the imperatives of "social imperialism," France tried to relieve stresses at home by acquiring markets and resources overseas (7:395).

12:253 _____. *Germany in Central America: Competitive Imperialism, 1821–1929.* Using an approach based on "world systems analysis," this study places German imperialism in Central America within the larger context of great power competition around the world. German aims included security and economic well-being. The author discusses the impact on Central American countries and also the implications of German intrusions for the United States (9:464).

12:254 _____. *The United States in Central America, 1860–1911: Episodes of Social Imperialism and Imperial Rivalry in the World System.* Using an approach based on "world systems analysis," the author argues that U.S. policymakers tried to relieve social and economic stresses at home by exploiting the resources and dominating the markets of peripheral regions, such as Central America (9:465).

12:255 Smith, Robert Freeman, ed. *The United States and the Latin American Sphere of Influence. Vol. 1: Era of Caribbean Intervention: 1890–1930.* Malabar, FL: Krieger Pub. Co., 1981. This set of essays, mostly excerpts from works originally published elsewhere, presents different points of view and interpretations of U.S. actions in and around the Caribbean basin early in the twentieth century. Among the historians represented are John H. Latané, Albert K. Weinberg, Howard C. Hill, Frederick W. Marks, III, Wilfrid H. Callcott, Hans Schmidt, David F. Healy, Kenneth J. Grieb, and Smith himself.

12:256 Yerxa, Donald A. *Admirals and Empire: The United States Navy and the Caribbean, 1898–1945.* Columbia: University of South Carolina Press,

1991. This book characterizes the U.S. position in the Caribbean region as that of a "maritime empire" in which commerce, overseas dependencies, and naval forces assumed great importance, not merely to defend against other powers but also to keep vital sea lanes open and maintain regional stability. Naval leaders regarded instability within their sphere of influence as anathema.

Costa Rica

12:257   Baker, George W., Jr. "Woodrow Wilson's Use of the Non-Recognition Policy in Costa Rica." *Americas* 22 (July 1965): 3–21. According to the author, Wilson's ill-conceived application of the nonrecognition policy impaired relations with the regime of Federico Tinoco Granados and harmed U.S. interests.

12:258   Salisbury, Richard V. "United States Intervention in Nicaragua: The Costa Rican Role." *Prologue* 9 (Winter 1977): 209–17. This article shows that in 1912 Costa Rica encouraged U.S. intervention in Nicaragua to obtain a stabilizing effect in the region.

El Salvador

12:259   Baker, George W., Jr. "The Woodrow Wilson Administration and El Salvadoran Relations, 1913–1921." *Social Studies* 56 (March 1965): 97–102. This short piece addresses the shift from idealistic toward more realistic policy formulations and considerations during World War I.

12:260   Schoonover, Thomas D. "A United States Dilemma: Economic Opportunity and Anti-Americanism in El Salvador, 1901–1911." *Pacific Historical Review* 58 (November 1989): 403–28. This essay emphasizes the inconsistency and contradiction in U.S. policy toward El Salvador, specifically the inability to reconcile the defense of economic interests with the promotion of democratic idealism.

Guatemala

12:261   Baker, George W., Jr. "The Woodrow Wilson Administration and Guatemalan Relations." An

extended account of U.S. efforts to curry the favor of Guatemalan dictator Manuel Estrada Cabrera, this essay concludes that the courtship accomplished little (11:429).

12:262   Dinwoodie, David H. "Dollar Diplomacy in Light of the Guatemalan Loan Project, 1909–1913." *Americas* 26 (January 1970): 237–53. The essay explores the working of "dollar diplomacy" by examining one of Secretary of State Philander Knox's loan projects, the Guatemalan refunding scheme.

12:263   Dosal, Paul J. *Doing Business with the Dictators: A Political History of United Fruit in Guatemala, 1899–1944.* Wilmington, DE: SR Books, 1993. Without engaging in the usual polemics, this book surveys the formative years of the United Fruit Company in Guatemala and shows how company agents obtained lucrative concessions allowing for monopoly control of the railroad network and the banana business.

Honduras

12:264   Baker, George W., Jr. "Ideas and Realities in the Wilson Administration's Relations with Honduras." *Americas* 21 (July 1964): 3–19. Wilson's policies toward Honduras illustrate how the demands of practicality caused his thinking to evolve from idealism toward realism.

Nicaragua

12:265   _____. "The Wilson Administration and Nicaragua, 1913–1921." *Americas* 22 (April 1965): 339–76. This essay describes Wilson's efforts to solve Nicaraguan financial problems, the negotiation of the Bryan-Chamorro treaty, and other episodes. In this instance, Wilson's interventionism aimed at stabilizing Nicaragua and cementing more intimate ties to assure U.S. control of an alternate canal route.

12:266   Harrison, Benjamin T. *Dollar Diplomat: Chandler Anderson and American Diplomacy in Mexico and Nicaragua, 1913–1928.* Pullman: Washington State University Press, 1988. In the Mexican and Nicaraguan cases, Harrison argues, Chandler Anderson, a lobbyist, failed to influence U.S. policy in favor of business interests. Ideological and religious convictions and notions about isolationism had more importance in the formulation of policy.

12:267 Munro, Dana G. "Dollar Diplomacy in Nicaragua, 1909–1913." *Hispanic American Historical Review* 38 (May 1958): 209–34. This venerable essay is a detailed account of a classic example of dollar diplomacy during the Taft administration, emphasizing the quest for security as a main goal in U.S. policy.

12:268 Salisbury, Richard V. "Great Britain, the United States, and the 1909–1910 Nicaraguan Crisis." *Americas* 53 (January 1997): 379–94. The author examines the competition between Great Britain and the United States in Central America and the efforts of the Taft administration to get rid of a government headed by José Santos Zelaya, who was regarded as an unacceptable troublemaker.

Panama and the Panama Canal

12:269 Ameringer, Charles D. "The Panama Canal Lobby of Philippe Bunau-Varilla and William Nelson Cromwell." *American Historical Review* 68 (January 1963): 346–63. This article clears up confusion over rival and conflicting accounts and shows that Bunau-Varilla and Cromwell worked amicably together in promoting the Panamanian revolution against Colombia and the subsequent arrangements with the United States for a Canal Zone.

12:270 _____. "Philippe Bunau-Varilla: New Light on the Panama Canal Treaty." *Hispanic American Historical Review* 46 (February 1966): 28–52. The author argues that Bunau-Varilla played an important role in fomenting the Panamanian revolution against Colombia and in influencing U.S. policy. He concludes that Bunau-Varilla negotiated a bad treaty for Panama and adversely complicated the future of U.S.-Panamanian relations.

12:271 Baker, George W., Jr. "The Wilson Administration and Panama, 1913–1921." *Journal of Interamerican Studies and World Affairs* 8 (April 1966):

279–93. This essay presents a detailed examination of U.S. efforts to uphold strategic imperatives during World War I by guaranteeing peace and stability in the Panama Canal Zone.

12:272 Coker, William S. "The Panama Canal Tolls Controversy: A Different Perspective." This essay emphasizes British perceptions during the controversy over Panama Canal tolls in 1913–1914 and argues that Wilson's readiness to repeal the exemption for U.S. coastal shipping on ethical grounds was an early manifestation of moral purpose in his foreign policy (11:341).

12:273 Collin, Richard H. *Theodore Roosevelt's Caribbean: The Panama Canal, the Monroe Doctrine, and the Latin American Context.* This work emphasizes historical context as an explanatory device, holding that fear of European intrusions, not a desire to suppress Latin Americans, accounted for TR's actions in the Western Hemisphere (11:431).

12:274 Conniff, Michael L. *Panama and the United States: The Forced Alliance.* This broadly gauged survey takes into account diplomacy, economics, politics, and culture; it also emphasizes the idea of a "forced" and unequal alliance between the United States and its weaker partner (2:358). First published in 1992.

12:275 Friedlander, Robert A. "A Reassessment of Roosevelt's Role in the Panamanian Revolution of 1903." *Western Political Quarterly* 14 (June 1961): 535–43. The author defends President Roosevelt's handling of the Panama episode in 1903, claiming that it was consistent with national honor, morality, and law.

12:276 Hogan, J. Michael. "Theodore Roosevelt and the Heroes of Panama." *Presidential Studies Quarterly* 19 (Winter 1989): 79–94. This essay examines the story of the Panama Canal as told by Theodore Roosevelt and his enthusiasts, who sought to make it an inspirational tale of U.S. power, ingenuity, and perseverance.

12:277 LaFeber, Walter. *The Panama Canal: The Crisis in Historical Perspective.* This significant survey seeks to comprehend the crisis over the Panama Canal in the 1970s by placing the issue in historical perspective. The first three chapters deal with the period from 1899 to 1919 and highlight commercial and strategic considerations (2:360). First published in 1978.

12:278 Major, John. *Prize Possession: The United States and the Panama Canal, 1903–1979*. This fine, comprehensive survey by a British historian, which examines U.S. policy toward the Panama Canal from 1903 to 1979, concentrates on strategic designs for defending the Canal; the Zone's regimental system of government and strictly segregated labor force; the system of commercial development working to the disadvantage of Panama; and the equally controversial issue of U.S. intervention in Panamanian politics (2:361).

12:279 _____. "Who Wrote the Hay-Bunau-Varilla Convention?" *Diplomatic History* 8 (Spring 1984): 115–23. This essay demonstrates the error of Philippe Bunau-Varilla's claim to have written the treaty by showing the contributions of others, notably Secretary of State John Hay and Senator John Tyler Morgan of Alabama.

12:280 McCullough, David. *The Path between the Seas: The Creation of the Panama Canal, 1870–1914*. This fine work tells the story of the building of the Panama Canal. The epic tale had momentous international implications as well as being an unprecedented feat in the history of engineering and the history of medicine (11:433).

12:281 Mellander, G. A. *The United States in Panamanian Politics, the Intriguing Formative Years*. Danville, IL: Interstate, 1967. Bunau-Varilla is credited with organizing the 1903 Panamanian revolt. The author also shows how U.S. interest in and control of the Canal Zone influenced Panamanian politics (1903–1908).

12:282 Ricard, Serge. "Theodore Roosevelt et l'affaire du canal de Panama (1901–1903) [Theodore Roosevelt and the Panama Canal Affair (1901–1903)]." *Revue d'histoire diplomatique* 99, nos. 1–2 (1985): 69–86. This essay by a French scholar depicts Roosevelt's handling of the Panama episode as a prime example of his utilization of the techniques of realpolitik.

12:283 Roosevelt, Theodore. "How the United States Acquired the Right to Dig the Panama Canal." *Outlook* 99 (October 7, 1911): 314–18. TR's account defends his policy and action during the U.S. acquisition of the Canal Zone (1901–1903), calling it the most "honorable chapter" in the history of the United States.

12:284 Vivian, James F. "The 'Taking' of the Panama Canal Zone: Myth and Reality." *Diplomatic History* 4 (Winter 1980): 95–100. This essay raises the question whether Theodore Roosevelt ever really uttered the quotation so often attributed to him about "taking" the Panama Canal Zone and letting the Congress debate. It concludes probably not.

Cuba

12:285 Abel, Christopher A. "Controlling the Big Stick: Theodore Roosevelt and the Cuban Crisis of 1906." *Naval War College Review* 40 (Summer 1987): 88–98. The author argues that TR intervened reluctantly when compelled by an out-of-control navy working at cross-purposes with his administration's best efforts.

12:286 Baker, George W., Jr. "The Wilson Administration and Cuba, 1913–1921." *Mid-America* 46 (January 1964): 48–63. Much as his predecessors, Wilson wanted the United States to play a paternalistic role until Cuba was ready for independence but could not in this case achieve his idealistic ambitions.

12:287 Benjamin, Jules R. *The United States & Cuba: Hegemony and Dependent Development, 1880–1934*. This study shows the overwhelming influence exercised by the United States over Cuba and depicts tactical flexibility as the primary means for maintaining hegemony (9:415).

12:288 Cosmas, Graham A. "Securing the Fruits of Victory: The United States Army Occupies Cuba, 1898–1899." *Military Affairs* 38 (July 1974): 85–91. The author lauds the U.S. army of occupation as well organized, well administered, and working for Cuba's improvement.

12:289 Deere, Carmen Diana. "Here Come the Yankees! The Rise and Decline of the United States

Colonies in Cuba, 1898–1930." This essay focuses on the activities of U.S. immigrants in Cuba after 1898. Mainly farmers, they grew citrus and winter vegetables for sale in the U.S. market. The author shows their economic and social impart on Cuba and argues that their presence kept the annexation movement alive in the United States until about 1917 (10:391).

12:290   Fernández Sosa, Miriam, and Concepción Planos. "Cuba: La aplicación de la enmienda platt en 1906 y su impacto en el pensameinto cubano [Cuba: The Application of the Platt Amendment in 1906 and Its Impact on Cuban Thought]." *Baluarte (Cadiz, Spain)* 1 (1995): 149–61. This essay emphasizes the growth of Cuban nationalism and resistance.

12:291   Gillette, Howard, Jr. "The Military Occupation of Cuba, 1899–1902: Workshop for American Progressivism." *American Quarterly* 25 (October 1973): 410–25. The author depicts the Cuban occupation as an initial attempt through the use of administrative expertise to reform society by means of education, businesslike efficiency, and executive leadership. Success in Cuba supposedly stimulated the growing progressive reform movement in the United States.

12:292   Healy, David F. *The United States in Cuba 1898–1902: Generals, Politicians, and the Search for Policy.* Madison: University of Wisconsin Press, 1963. This monograph discusses the different views of Americans during the occupation period on the U.S. role in Cuba and the future of the island. Ultimately, U.S. policy took form as established by the Platt Amendment and the Reciprocity Treaty of 1902. According to Healy, U.S. soldiers, politicians, and civil servants made the decisions, not the business interests.

12:293   Hernández, José M. *Cuba and the United States: Intervention and Militarism, 1868–1933.* Based on extensive primary sources, this work shows the impact of U.S. interventions on governing Cuban elites and the army during the years 1898–1902 and 1906–1909. The author tries to deal with the issues dispassionately while avoiding nationalistic and rhetorical excesses (9:418).

12:294   Hitchman, James H. "The American Touch in Imperial Administration: Leonard Wood in Cuba,

1898–1902." *Americas* 24 (April 1968): 394–403. This essay presents a traditional defense for the U.S. occupation of Cuba, claiming that Leonard Wood understood the need to prepare Cuba for independence and effectively carried out that role.

12:295   _____. *Leonard Wood and Cuban Independence, 1898–1902.* Here (10:177) Hitchman confirms and elaborates on his arguments in "The American Touch in Imperial Administration: Leonard Wood in Cuba, 1898–1902" (1968) (12:294).

12:296   Millett, Allan R. *The Politics of Intervention: The Military Occupation of Cuba, 1906–1909.* Columbus: Ohio State University Press, 1968. This study of the second Cuban intervention from 1906 to 1909 stresses the use of U.S. armed forces in Cuba and the role of military officers in the policymaking process.

12:297   Pérez, Louis A., Jr. "Capital, Bureaucrats, and Policy: The Economic Contours of United States–Cuban Relations, 1916–1921." *Inter-American Economic Affairs* 29 (Summer 1975): 65–80. According to the author, U.S. policy in Cuba between 1916 and 1921 conformed closely to the requirements of expanding investment capital. Consequently, nonmilitary intervention in all its forms increased in direct proportion to the expansion of U.S. economic interests in Cuba.

12:298   _____. *Cuba and the United States: Ties of Singular Intimacy.* This fine, synthetic work uses the framework of dependency theory, arguing that U.S. hegemony exerted overwhelming influence over the Cuban experience in the twentieth century. It takes into account the various dimensions of the U.S.-Cuban relationship, political, economic, social, and cultural (2:370). First published in 1990.

12:299   _____. "Cuba between Empires, 1898–1899." *Pacific Historical Review* 48 (November 1979): 473–500. The author recounts the process leading to U.S. military occupation and the debate among Cubans over whether to accept a special relationship with the United States.

12:300   _____. *Cuba under the Platt Amendment, 1902–1934.* Pittsburgh: University of Pittsburgh Press, 1986. This theoretically sophisticated work argues that U.S. hegemony over Cuba sought both as a means and an end the defense of U.S. capital interests, the very cornerstone of policy, and ironically ended up galvanizing the forces it sought to contain: nationalism and revolution.

12:301 _____. *Intervention, Revolution, and Politics in Cuba, 1913–1921.* Pittsburgh: University of Pittsburgh Press, 1978. The Platt Amendment made Washington the focal point of Cuban politics, indeed, the most important audience Cuban politicians had to satisfy (and for whom they had to perform). U.S. policy became an integral part of Cuban politics and one of the most active components of the national system.

12:302 _____. *On Becoming Cuban: Identity, Nationality, and Culture.* This big and engrossing volume, largely concerned with the twentieth century, explores non-governmental interactions between the peoples of Cuba and the United States and shows how the cultural forms of the latter have shaped and influenced the sense of identity, nationality, and modernity for the former. Broadly gauged in conception, it provides a subtle and convincing analysis, showing how the standards and norms of U.S. capitalist enterprise took hold in Cuba before Castro (10:406).

12:303 _____. "Supervision of a Protectorate: The United States and the Cuban Army, 1898–1908." *Hispanic American Historical Review* 52 (May 1972): 250–71. This essay recounts U.S. efforts to make the Cuban army a force for stability in the years after 1898.

12:304 Roig de Leuchsenring, Emilio. *Historia de la Enmienda Platt: una interpretación de la realidad cubana [History of the Platt Amendment: An Interpretation of the Cuban Reality].* 3d ed. Vedado, La Habana: Ediciones de Ciencias Sociales, Instituto del Libro, 1973. This is a critical account of the history of the Platt Amendment (1901–1935) by a prominent Cuban scholar. First published in 1935.

12:305 _____. "La Enmienda Platt, su interpretación primitiva y sus applicaciones posteriores [The Platt Amendment, Its Initial Interpretation and Its Later Applications]." *Anuario de la Sociedad Cubana de Derecho Internacional* 5 (1922): 323–462. This very critical account presents an analysis from a Cuban point of view.

12:306 Smith, Robert Freeman. "Cuba: Laboratory for Dollar Diplomacy, 1898–1917." *Historian* 28 (August 1966): 586–609. The United States used Cuba as a laboratory for developing the basic tactics of dollar diplomacy. The results destabilized Cuba and contributed to intense Yankeephobia.

Dominican Republic

12:307 Atkins, G. Pope, and Larman C. Wilson. *The Dominican Republic and the United States: From Imperialism to Transnationalism.* This volume considers official diplomatic relations, focused on political, economic, and military issues, and also the unofficial aspects of cultural exchanges. The authors describe a patron-client dependency relationship but one that is neither simple nor completely lopsided. Chapter 2 deals with "United States imperialism" in the Caribbean between 1900 and 1920 (2:376).

12:308 Calder, Bruce J. "Caudillos and *Gavilleros* versus the United States Marines: Guerrilla Insurgency during the Dominican Intervention, 1916–1924." *Hispanic American Historical Review* 58 (November 1978): 649–75. This essay examines a little-known episode, the guerrilla war between U.S. marines and Dominican rebels after 1916. It explains the program of the occupation government and the reactions of the inhabitants, including the motives of the dissidents *(gavilleros)* who resorted to war.

12:309 _____. *The Impact of Intervention: The Dominican Republic during the U.S. Occupation of 1916–1924.* Austin: University of Texas Press, 1984. This discerning work explains what Calder sees as a complex mixture of strategic and economic causes for the U.S. intervention in the Dominican Republic in 1916. He also explains the impact of the military occupation on the country and Dominican responses, including a resort to guerrilla war.

12:310 Collin, Richard H. "The 1904 *Detroit* Compact: U.S. Naval Diplomacy and the Dominican Revolutions." *Historian* 52 (May 1990): 432–52. This article provides a detailed account of U.S. efforts to mediate between rebel leaders and government officials in a sequence of attempts to restore peace in the Dominican Republic.

Haiti

12:311 Healy, David F. *Gunboat Diplomacy in the Wilson Era: The U.S. Navy in Haiti, 1915–1916.* Madison: University of Wisconsin Press, 1976. This book emphasizes the multiple facets of U.S. interventionism, especially strategic fears about the security of the Panama Canal during World War I; other concerns included economic progress and democratic uplift.

12:312 Millspaugh, Arthur C. *Haiti under American Control, 1915–1930.* Boston: World Peace Foundation, 1931. Reprint 1970 (Negro Universities Press). The author, an economist and financial expert, served in Haiti for part of the period studied. Though somewhat dated, this is a firsthand account.

12:313 Plummer, Brenda Gayle. "The Afro-American Response to the Occupation of Haiti, 1915–1934." *Phylon* 43 (June 1982): 125–43. The author detects little reaction at first among African-Americans and then mounting opposition among civil rights activists and black nationalists.

12:314 _____. *Haiti and the Great Powers, 1902–1915.* This work uses a variety of Haitian sources and presents an intriguing analysis of the interplay among the external actors, the great powers (France, Germany, Great Britain, and the United States), and the internal ones, that is, the Haitian political elite and the foreign merchant community. The author wants to go beyond official diplomacy to include the full range of social, intellectual, and economic exchange among peoples and to highlight the experiences of the relatively powerless (11:435).

12:315 _____. *Haiti and the United States: The Psychological Moment.* A significant survey, this book shows the interplay of diplomacy, race relations, immigration, private philanthropy, and business activity. It emphasizes the U.S. determination to uphold stability in Haiti during World War I (9:429).

12:316 Renda, Mary A. *Taking Haiti: Military Occupation and the Culture of U.S. Imperialism,*

1915–1940. Chapel Hill: University of North Carolina Press, 2001. This compelling work uses cultural analysis to elucidate the various meanings of the U.S. intervention and subsequent occupation of Haiti. The author argues that discourses emphasizing paternalism and employing hierarchies based on class, gender, and race provided an ideological framework justifying U.S. imperialism. Renda focuses on the attitudes and perceptions of U.S. marines who made up the occupying forces and establishes explicit connections between paternalistic assumptions and proclivities toward violence. She also scrutinizes depictions of Haiti derived from popular culture, notably pulp magazines, novels, movies, and travel literature.

12:317 Schmidt, Hans. *The United States Occupation of Haiti, 1915–1934.* New Brunswick: Rutgers University Press, 1971. Unlike other regions outside the Western Hemisphere in which the United States sought an open door, in Haiti the policymakers desired a closed, spheres-of-influence approach to keep out potentially hostile powers, such as Germany. The author also emphasizes the importance of racism in dealings with Haitians.

Jamaica and Puerto Rico

12:318 González-Cruz, Michael. "The U.S. Invasion of Puerto Rico: Occupation and Resistance to the Colonial State, 1898 to the Present." *Latin American Perspectives* 25 (September 1998): 7–26. This article examines how the hegemonic agenda of the United States in Puerto Rico has shaped the formation of the state. Beginning with the military occupation in 1898, the U.S. systematically created structures to promote dependency and economic exploitation. The author also shows how such repression elicited resistance from Puerto Rican nationalists.

12:319 Tilchin, William N. "Theodore Roosevelt, Anglo-American Relations, and the Jamaica Incident of 1907." *Diplomatic History* 19 (Summer 1995): 385–405. When British authorities appeared to insult U.S. national honor by rejecting an offer of help following an earthquake at Kingston, Jamaica, important questions arose about President Roosevelt's conception of Anglo-American friendship. According to this author, his commitment to friendship was strong and passed the test.

SOUTH AMERICA

General

12:320   Albert, Bill, with Paul Henderson. *South America and the First World War: The Impact of the War on Brazil, Argentina, Peru, and Chile.* New York: Cambridge University Press, 1988. This book by a British scholar explores the various effects of World War I on Brazil, Argentina, Peru, and Chile, underscoring in each case the growing economic dominance of the United States in South America.

12:321   Healy, David F. "Admiral William B. Caperton and United States Naval Diplomacy in South America, 1917–1919." *Journal of Latin American Studies* 8 (November 1976): 297–323. Admiral William B. Caperton of the U.S. navy took a south Atlantic patrol squadron to Brazil in May 1917 and during the next two years performed effectively in a diplomatic role, working with civilians, and seeking to ensure maximum U.S. influence in South America.

12:322   Livermore, Seward W. "Battleship Diplomacy in South America: 1905–1925." *Journal of Modern History* 16 (August 1944): 31–48. This venerable but still useful account records the efforts of the United States, Germany, and Great Britain to sell battleships and other naval vessels to Argentina, Brazil, and Chile, especially in the years before World War I, thereby feeding international rivalry in the Southern Cone.

Argentina

12:323   McGann, Thomas F. *Argentina, the United States, and the Inter-American System, 1880–1914.* The author emphasizes U.S.-Argentine competition for leadership within the Western Hemisphere, the U.S. concern for security, and the Argentine preference for a pro-Europe orientation (9:433).

12:324   Peterson, Harold F. *Argentina and the United States, 1810–1960.* This standard survey emphasizes the competition between the United States and Argentina for leadership in the Western Hemisphere, for example, during the era of World War I

when President Hipólito Yrigoyen resisted the Wilson administration's initiatives (2:389).

12:325   Sheinin, David. *Searching for Authority: Pan Americanism, Diplomacy and Politics in United States–Argentine Relations, 1910–1930.* New Orleans: University Press of the South, 1998. According to this revealing work based on extensive use of Argentine sources, the United States and Argentina agreed on the need for stability to promote international trade and finance. At the same time, each sought authority to advance national goals. U.S. leaders wanted larger commercial and investment opportunities in Argentina; the Argentines aspired to a position of regional leadership in South America. The competition became acute during World War I.

12:326   Tulchin, Joseph S. *Argentina and the United States: A Conflicted Relationship.* This fine survey emphasizes the theme that misunderstanding, tension, and missed opportunities for cooperation and friendship have characterized the history of U.S.-Argentine relations. Chapters 2 and 3 consider the differences between the two countries during World War I (2:390).

Brazil

12:327   Abranches, C. D. de. *Rio Branco e a política exterior do Brasil, 1902–1912 [Rio Branco and the Foreign Policy of Brazil, 1902–1912].* 2 vols. Rio de Janeiro: Jornal do Brasil, 1945. This detailed account from a Brazilian point of view emphasizes the importance of winning U.S. support as a counterweight against Argentina and Chile.

12:328   Burns, E. Bradford. *The Unwritten Alliance: Rio Branco and Brazilian-American Relations.* New York: Columbia University Press, 1966. This enduring work explores the role of the Brazilian foreign minister, the Baron of Rio Branco, in forging a special relationship with the United States during his tenure in office from 1902 to 1912. "The unwritten alliance" in his view should function as a way to gain an edge in dealings with rivals in the Southern Cone, notably Argentina and Chile.

12:329   Mitchell, Nancy. "Protective Imperialism versus *Weltpolitik* in Brazil: Part One: Pan-German

Vision and Mahanian Response." *International History Review* 18 (May 1996): 253–78. Inflated expansionist rhetoric created exaggerated anti-German fears in the United States and elicited defensive responses conceived in the context of Alfred Thayer Mahan's theories of seapower.

12:330 _____. "Protective Imperialism versus *Weltpolitik* in Brazil: Part Two: Settlement, Trade and Opportunity." *International History Review* 18 (August 1996): 546–72. Despite efforts to acquire influence in Brazil, Germany possessed scant means by which to challenge U.S. dominance in the Western Hemisphere. Inflated fears of Germany, nevertheless, provided U.S. leaders with a cover for their own expansionist ambitions by enabling them to invoke the Monroe Doctrine, presumably for defensive purposes.

12:331 Rosenberg, Emily S. "Anglo-American Economic Rivalry in Brazil during World War I." *Diplomatic History* 2 (Spring 1978): 131–52. In Brazil, the era of World War I marked a shift in economic power away from Great Britain and toward the United States. During the neutrality period from 1914 to 1917, U.S. opportunities for trade and investment increased substantially. The war drastically curtailed European exports, investment capital, and shipping in the Western Hemisphere. When faced with a crisis, Brazil turned to the United States for markets, money, and supplies.

12:332 Smith, Joseph. "American Diplomacy and the Naval Mission to Brazil, 1917–1930." *Inter-American Economic Affairs* 35 (Summer 1981): 73–91. According to this assessment, the U.S. naval mission to Brazil during World War I signified rising levels of prestige for the United States but otherwise had little strategic or economic importance.

12:333 _____. *Unequal Giants: Diplomatic Relations between the United States and Brazil, 1889–1930.* Based on the diplomatic archives of Brazil, Great Britain, and the United States, this discerning study is a conventional diplomatic history during the era of the "Old Republic," concentrating on Brazil's "unwritten alliance" with the United States (especially during World War I), trade issues, and other maneuvers involving its main rivals, Argentina and Chile. The title reflects the author's emphasis on the disparity of power and influence between the United States and Brazil. In the view of Brazilian leaders, close affiliation with the United States could best advance their country's interests (9:437).

12:334 _____. "United States Diplomacy toward Political Revolt in Brazil, 1889–1930." *Inter-American Economic Affairs* 37 (Autumn 1983): 3–21. This essay examines U.S. policy toward a sequence of Brazilian revolts, some of which succeeded, and concludes that U.S. diplomats neither understood much about nor exercised much control over Brazilian politics.

Colombia

12:335 Coletta, Paolo E. "William Jennings Bryan and the United States–Colombian Impasse, 1903–1921." *Hispanic American Historical Review* 47 (November 1967): 486–501. This article discusses the fight over the negotiation and subsequent ratification of the Thomson-Urrutia treaty to compensate Colombia for the loss of Panama in 1903. As secretary of state and later as a private citizen, Bryan consistently upheld the treaty and defended Colombia's point of view.

12:336 Lael, Richard L. *Arrogant Diplomacy: U.S. Policy toward Colombia, 1903–1922.* Wilmington, DE: Scholarly Resources, 1987. A highly critical account of U.S. dealings with Colombia, this book attributes the "arrogant diplomacy" of the Roosevelt administration to strategic rather than economic considerations and recounts a variety of adverse long-term effects stemming from the decision to take the Panama Canal.

12:337 _____. "Dilemma over Panama: Negotiation of the Thomson-Urrutia Treaty." *Mid-America* 61 (January 1979): 35–45. The author traces the contentious process by which Woodrow Wilson tried to make amends with Colombia over the Panama episode and thereby to make good on his promise to seek the friendship of Latin Americans.

12:338 _____. "Struggle for Ratification: Wilson, Lodge, and the Thomson-Urrutia Treaty." *Diplomatic History* 2 (Winter 1978): 81–102. This article examines attempts by the Wilson administration to assuage Colombia's sense of victimization over the loss of Panama and at the same time to win over Republican support in the U.S. Senate.

12:339 Randall, Stephen J. *Colombia and the United States: Hegemony and Interdependence.* A balanced treatment of both Colombian and U.S. concerns, this book seeks a holistic analysis, taking into account the complete range of relationships, political, economic, and cultural. It emphasizes the disparity of power and influence between the two countries and Colombian efforts to retain dignity and independence, for example, during and after the Panamanian revolt in 1903. Chapter 3 deals with that episode (2:397).

Ecuador and Chile

12:340 Rosenberg, Emily S. "Dollar Diplomacy under Wilson: An Ecuadorian Case." *Inter-American Economic Affairs* 25 (Autumn 1971): 47–53. President Wilson's reluctance to support American economic interests in Mexico was not typical of his policy elsewhere in Latin America. This article explains how the Wilson administration put pressure on Ecuador on behalf of U.S. and English railroad bondholders in that country.

12:341 Sater, William F. *Chile and the United States: Empires in Conflict.* This useful survey emphasizes the importance of asymmetries and inequalities of wealth, power, and prestige in relations between the United States and Chile. It emphasizes Chilean mistrust of U.S. intentions during World War I (2:395).

Venezuela

12:342 Carreras, Charles. *United State Economic Penetration of Venezuela and Its Effects on Diplomacy, 1895–1906.* New York: Garland Publishing, 1987. This book presents a series of case studies showing how U.S. enterprise initially went awry in Venezuela when greedy and aggressive U.S. investors engaged Venezuelan authorities in complicated wrangles over land and concessions. In later years Venezuela became more susceptible to U.S.

economic expansion when oil profits provided powerful incentives.

12:343 Ewell, Judith. *Venezuela and the United States: From Monroe's Hemisphere to Petroleum's Empire.* This useful survey emphasizes the importance of petroleum and argues that relations with Venezuela reveal in microcosm the fundamental aims and priorities of the United States in Latin America, notably the support of stability and the need for resources. Two chapters deal with the 1899–1919 period, showing Venezuelan reactions to U.S. interventionism, the impact of World War I, and the importance of oil (2:400).

12:344 Hendrickson, Embert J. "Roosevelt's Second Venezuelan Controversy." This essay reviews Theodore Roosevelt's tough but prudent stand in support of various foreign claims against Cipriano Castro's Venezuelan government after the more famous episode in 1903 (11:168).

12:345 _____. "Root's Watchful Waiting and the Venezuela Controversy." *Americas* 23 (October 1966): 115–29. As secretary of state from 1905 to 1909, Elihu Root advocated peace and understanding in the Western Hemisphere and employed "watchful waiting techniques" while dealing with the Venezuelan troublemaker, Cipriano Castro. By subtle, noncoercive means, according to this author, Root achieved his goal of promoting goodwill.

12:346 Herwig, Holger H. *Germany's Vision of Empire in Venezuela, 1871–1914.* This circumspect study of German imperialist policy, centering on the blockade of Venezuela undertaken by Germany, Great Britain, and Italy in 1902–1903, rejects theories of economic motivation and emphasizes instead emotional and irrational factors such as pride, prestige, and national honor (11:169).

12:347 Holbo, Paul S. "Perilous Obscurity: Public Diplomacy and the Press in the Venezuelan Crisis, 1902–1903." See chapter 11 of this Guide (11:171).

12:348 Hood, Miriam. *Gunboat Diplomacy, 1895–1905: Great Power Pressure in Venezuela.* This book by a Venezuelan from the distinguished Blanco-Fombonas family presents a Venezuelan point of view. It argues that European pressure on Venezuela, especially the German-British blockade of 1902–1903, compelled the United States to exercise hegemony in the Caribbean region under authority of the Roosevelt Corollary (9:452). First published in 1977.

12:349   Livermore, Seward W. "Theodore Roosevelt, the American Navy, and the Venezuelan Crisis of 1902–1903." See chapter 11 of this Guide (11:173).

12:350   Mitchell, Nancy. "The Height of the German Challenge: The Venezuela Blockade, 1902–3." *Diplomatic History* 20 (Spring 1996): 185–209. Based on German sources, this work disparages the notion that any sort of a German threat existed in the Western Hemisphere. The author regards such apprehensions as the product of German bombast and U.S. paranoia.

12:351   Morris, Edmund. "'A Few Pregnant Days': Theodore Roosevelt and the Venezuelan Crisis of 1902." This speculative essay examines Roosevelt's subsequent claim in 1916 that as president he had faced down the Germans over Venezuela by "talking softly and carrying a big stick." No documentary proof exists of any such threat of war. Nonetheless, Morris concludes that the episode might have happened the way TR told it (11:174).

12:352   Parsons, Edward B. "The German-American Crisis of 1902–1903." This article upholds the essentials of Theodore Roosevelt's subsequent claim that behind-the-scenes pressure forced Germany to back down during the Venezuela crisis (11:175).

12:353   Platt, D. C. M. "The Allied Coercion of Venezuela, 1902–1903: A Reassessment." This revisionist essay argues against sensationalizing the interventionist activities of Germany and Great Britain against Venezuela, since such measures then had legitimacy under international law as a means of defending the rights of aliens (11:176).

The United States, Asia, the Pacific, the Middle East, and Africa, 1899–1919

Contributing Editor

ANNE L. FOSTER
Indiana State University

Contents

Introduction

The broad geographical scope of this chapter did create some particular challenges. Not surprisingly, Japan and China have attracted the most scholarly attention of all countries in this chapter. The scholarship included here therefore tends to be newer and had to meet more selective criteria for inclusion. This would be particularly true for popular topics such as the open door and missionaries, although in these cases I have attempted to include classical works. In selecting studies about the United States and the Philippines, I have considered the colonial relationship an aspect of foreign relations in including some of the exciting, relatively new literature about U.S. colonialism. Works about the Spanish-American War and the acquisition of the Philippines are generally not found in this chapter though, because of their inclusion in chapter 10. The other areas of the world covered in this chapter have attracted little scholarship. In these areas, a desire for maximum, broad coverage supplied the main criteria for inclusion, with attention as well to materials that might suggest possibilities for future research. An important topic in this chapter, generally, is imperialism. Works about imperialism and the struggle against it have been included in the "General Works" section if they are general or comparative, but in the geographical divisions if related to only one country or region. Other than published primary sources, few foreign-language materials have been included in this chapter, although they might appear in web supplements to the Guide.

Document Collections

13:1   U.S. Department of State. *Foreign Relations of the United States.* Washington, DC: Government Printing Office, 1901–1934. Twenty-four volumes of this vital compilation of U.S. diplomatic documents concern Asia, the Pacific, the Middle East, and Africa from 1899 to 1919 (1:93).

13:2   Bacon, Robert, and James Brown Scott, eds. *The Military and Colonial Policy of the United States: Addresses and Reports by Elihu Root.* These

excerpts from speeches by Root and War Department reports focus on two important themes from Root's tenure: formulation of colonial policy and reorganization of the military. This collection remains a useful place to begin research (12:14).

13:3   Link, Arthur S., with Manfred F. Boemke, eds. *The Deliberations of the Council of Four (March 24–June 28, 1919): Notes of the Official Interpreter, Paul Mantoux.* 2 vols. Princeton: Princeton University Press, 1992. These useful volumes publish the only complete account of the deliberations at Versailles. They should not be relied on as the only source, however, since Mantoux did not use shorthand. Volume 2 contains a useful index.

AFRICA

13:4   Throup, David, Kenneth Bourne, Donald Cameron Watt, and Michael Partridge, eds. *British Documents on Foreign Affairs—Reports and Papers from the Foreign Office Confidential Print. Part I: From the Mid-Nineteenth Century to the First World War. Series G: Africa, 1848–1914.* 25 vols. Bethesda, MD: University Publications of America, 1995–1997. This collection includes photocopied documents from the British Foreign Office Confidential Print, the most heavily used portion of Foreign Office records, and therefore is invaluable for scholars. As is true in other portions of this collection listed in this chapter, the work tends to be even more comprehensive than its counterpart, the U.S. series *Foreign Relations of the United States,* especially for these early years. In this section, volumes 1–12 focus on southern Africa, particularly South Africa. Volumes 13–18 cover East Africa, and volumes 19–25 cover West Africa.

13:5   Woodward, Peter, Kenneth Bourne, and Donald Cameron Watt, eds. *British Documents on Foreign Affairs—Reports and Papers from the Foreign Office Confidential Print. Part I: From the Mid-Nineteenth Century to the First World War. Series G: Africa, 1914–1939.* 30 vols. Bethesda, MD: University Publications of America, 1994–1997. See statement for Throup et al. (13:4). Volumes 1–10 cover Egypt and Sudan to the end of the 1920s, emphasizing especially issues related to the Suez Canal. Volumes 11–20 continue that story to 1939, while volume 21 is dedicated to the Suez Canal. Volumes

23–25 cover Morocco, and volumes 26–30 cover the rest of Africa, but mostly Tunisia and Liberia since other parts of sub-Saharan Africa were primarily the responsibility of the Colonial Office.

ASIA

13:6   U.S. Department of State. *Records of the Department of State Relating to Political Relations between the United States and Japan, 1910–1929.* Microfilm. Washington, DC: National Archives and Records Service, 1963. This microfilm collection contains material from the decimal files of the Department of State, Record Group 59, in the U.S. National Archives. These files pertain only to political relations; commercial and cultural relations are not well represented.

13:7   _____. *Records of the U.S. Department of State Relating to Commercial Relations between the United States and Japan, 1910–1929.* Microfilm. Wilmington, DE: Scholarly Resources, 1987. This microfilm collection contains material from the U.S. Department of State decimal file relating to U.S. commercial relations with Japan, specifically documents in the decimal file classifications 611.94 and 694.11.

13:8   Nish, Ian, Kenneth Bourne, Donald Cameron Watt, and Michael Partridge, eds. *British Documents on Foreign Affairs—Reports and Papers from the Foreign Office Confidential Print. Part I: From the Mid-Nineteenth Century to the First World War. Series E: Asia, 1860–1914.* 30 vols. Bethesda, MD: University Publications of America, 1989–1995. See statement for Throup et al. (13:4). Volumes 1–10 cover Japan and Korea, volumes 11–25 cover China, and volumes 26–30 cover Southeast Asia and the Pacific islands.

13:9   Trotter, Ann, Kenneth Bourne, and Donald Cameron Watt, eds. *British Documents on Foreign Affairs—Reports and Papers from the Foreign Office Confidential Print. Part I: From the Mid-Nineteenth Century to the First World War. Series E: Asia, 1914–1939.* 50 vols. Bethesda, MD: University Publications of America, 1991–1997. See statement for Throup et al. (13:4). Volumes 1–18 cover Japan from 1914 through 1939 but include the most material on

Japan's ambitions in China during the 1920s, volumes 19–38 cover China, while volumes 39–48 focus explicitly on Sino-Japanese disputes of the 1930s. Volumes 49 and 50 cover Southeast Asia, with most attention to Thailand.

13:10   Great Britain. Foreign Office. *Great Britain: A Selection of Public Records Foreign Office, General Correspondence before 1906, China, 1815–1905.* Microfilm. Millwood, NY: Kraus-Thomson Organization, 1972–1977. This extensive collection contains 568 microfilm reels of documents from the British Foreign Office on relations with China. A twenty-three-page index has also been published to assist researchers in finding relevant documents.

13:11   Kesaris, Paul, and Great Britain. Foreign Office. *Confidential British Foreign Office Political Correspondence. China, Series 1, 1906–1919.* Microfilm. Bethesda, MD: University Publications of America, 1994–1997. This microfilm collection contains material on British relations with China during the critical years at the beginning of the twentieth century. The material comes from class FO566 and FO371 of the Public Record Office in Britain. 106 reels.

13:12   Great Britain. Foreign Office. *British Foreign Office, Japan Correspondence, 1856–1905: Indexes and Guides to the Scholarly Resources Microfilm Edition of the Public Record Office Collection.* Microfilm. Wilmington, DE: Scholarly Resources, 1975. This microfilm collection contains 240 reels, primarily from FO371, the most heavily used section of Foreign Office files. Reels 1–50 cover 1856–1867; reels 54–227 cover 1868–1890; reels 228–240 cover 1891–1905. The accompanying guide provides information also about FO46, 802, and 566.

13:13   _____. *British Foreign Office: Japan Correspondence, 1906–1913: Dominance of the Genro.* Microfilm. Wilmington, DE: Scholarly Resources, 1988. This microfilm collection contains material from class FO371 of the British Public Record Office, the class most heavily used for research in foreign relations. Material from 1906 covers five reels; from 1907, eight reels; from 1908, five reels; from 1909, five reels; from 1910, five reels; from 1911, seven reels; from 1912, five reels; and from 1913, seven reels.

13:14 _____. *British Foreign Office: Japan Correspondence, 1914–1923: Emergence of Japan as a Pacific Power.* Microfilm. Wilmington, DE: Scholarly Resources, 1988. This microfilm collection contains material from British Public Record Office class FO371, the most heavily used record group for foreign relations. Material for 1914 takes up nine reels; for 1915, nine reels; for 1916, eight reels; for 1917, seven reels; for 1918, six reels; for 1919, six reels; for 1920, seven reels; for 1921, thirteen reels; for 1922, four reels; and for 1923, four reels.

13:15 _____. *Foreign Office Files for Japan and the Far East. Series One, Embassy and Consular Archives.* Microfilm. Calcot, Reading, UK: Adam Matthews, 1991–1996. This microfilm collection, covering the period 1905–1940, contains material from the British Public Record Office class FO262. Reels 1–18 cover 1905–1920; reels 19–62 cover 1921–1923; reels 63–106 cover 1924–1926; reels 107–150 cover 1927–1929; reels 151–175 cover 1930–1933; reels 176–188 cover 1934–1940. The publisher has also provided a printed guide to the collection.

13:16 Wang, Liang, and Yen-wei Wang, eds. *Jingji waijiao shi liao [Historical Material on Foreign Relations in the Latter Part of the Qing Dynasty].* 9 vols. Taibei: Wenhai chubanshe, 1932–1935. The basic documentary source on China's foreign relations in the period between 1875 and 1911, this includes 218 chapters in six volumes on the Kuang-hsu period (1875–1908) and 24 chapters in two volumes on the Hsuan-tung period (1908–1911). The final volume provides an index and maps for the other eight volumes.

13:17 Teng, Ssü-yu, and John K. Fairbank, eds. *China's Response to the West: A Documentary Survey, 1839–1923.* Cambridge, MA: Harvard University Press, 1954. This collection reveals the efforts of Chinese leaders to understand the alien western civilization and to respond to it in a way that would preserve their own culture and institutions. It includes writings by such Chinese leaders as Lin Tse-Hsü, Ch'i-ying, Feng Kuei-fen, Tseng Kuo-fan, Li Hung-chang, Chang Chih-tung, K'ang Yu-wei, Liang Ch'i-ch'ao, and Yüan Shih-k'ai. Though a mere introduction to Chinese thought on these issues, the collection is accessible and well translated. Includes reference notes, discussion of sources, and a bibliography of western, Chinese, and Japanese works. A companion volume, *A Research Guide for China's Response to the West: A Documentary Survey, 1839–1923* (Cambridge, MA: Harvard University Press, 1954), was published separately.

13:18 Fairbank, John K., ed. *Ch'ing Documents: An Introductory Syllabus.* 2 vols. 3d ed. Cambridge, MA: East Asia Research Center, Harvard University, 1965. Volume 1 is a study aid for American scholars wishing to do research in late Ch'ing documents, particularly those relating to China's foreign relations. It deals with problems of translation and lists reference works and major collections of documents; it also contains notes on selected documents. Volume 2 consists of the Chinese texts of these documents.

13:19 Clyde, Paul Hibbert, ed. *United States Policy toward China: Diplomatic and Public Documents, 1839–1939.* Durham, NC: Duke University Press, 1940. This collection of 128 documents, primarily treaties and diplomatic correspondence, serves as a reference work and documentary history of the first century of official U.S.-China relations. Clyde's brief introduction places the items in context and includes a list of American diplomatic representatives in China.

13:20 Gaimusho [Japan Foreign Ministry]. *Dai Nihon gaiko bunsho [Documents on Japanese Foreign Policy].* Tokyo: Nihon Kokusai Kyokai, 1868–. This collection issued by the Japanese Foreign Ministry compares to the *Foreign Relations of the United States* and is a beginning point for research in Japanese foreign policy. The documents appear in their original language, whether Japanese, English, French, or German.

13:21 Gaimusho. Japan. *Nihon gaiko bunsho. Pari Kowa Kaigi keika gaiyo [Documents on Japanese Foreign Policy. Summaries of the Proceedings of the Paris Peace Conference].* Tokyo: Gaimusho [Japanese Foreign Ministry], 1971. This collection includes the official diplomacy of Japan at the Paris Peace Conference. It was originally issued as a confidential document.

13:22 Uyehara, Cecil H., and Gaimusho [Japan Foreign Ministry]. *Archives in the Japanese Ministry of Foreign Affairs, Tokyo, 1868–1945.* Microfilm.

Washington, DC: Library of Congress Photoduplication Service: U.S. Department of State, 1949–1951. This microfilm of over 2 million pages (2,116 reels) is housed in the Library of Congress. An index was published by the Library of Congress (1954), *Checklist of Archives in the Japanese Ministry of Foreign Affairs, Tokyo, Japan, 1868–1945,* compiled by Uyehara. Especially valuable is the Telegram Series listed on pages 155–56 of this checklist.

13:23   Burnett, Scott S., ed. *Korean-American Relations: Documents Pertaining to the Far Eastern Diplomacy of the United States. Vol. 3: The Period of Diminishing Influence, 1896–1905.* Honolulu: University of Hawaii Press, 1989. Although in no way a substitute for the more extensive publication of documents on U.S.-Korean relations during these years to be found in the microfilms of the U.S. National Archives, these carefully selected documents in the third volume of a three-volume set usefully supplement the *Foreign Relations* series. Beginning students will especially appreciate the chronology, index, and list of both American and Korean diplomatic personnel.

MIDDLE EAST

13:24   Hurewitz, J. C., ed. *The Middle East and North Africa in World Politics: A Documentary Record.* 3 vols. 2d rev. ed. New Haven: Yale University Press, 1975–1979. The documents are arranged chronologically, virtually all pertaining to European relations with the area, although U.S. involvement is reflected, especially in the 1920s–1940s. The first volume covers the period of European expansion from 1535 to 1914, while the second covers the period of British and French supremacy during the years 1914 to 1945. Originally published in 1956 under the title *Diplomacy in the Near and Middle East.* Bibliography.

13:25   Sarafian, Ara, ed. *United States Official Documents on the Armenian Genocide. Vol. 1: The Lower Euphrates. Vol. 2: The Peripheries. Vol. 3: The Central Lands.* 3 vols. Watertown, MA: Armenian Review, 1993. This published set of documents is drawn from U.S. Department of State records and the papers of Henry Morgenthau, Sr. Although both are also available on microfilm, the special value of

these volumes lies in their selection from the larger collections, reorganization to be more accessible, and the editor's introduction, maps, document list, and index.

13:26   Davis, Leslie A. *The Slaughterhouse Province: An American Diplomat's Report on the Armenian Genocide, 1915–1917.* New Rochelle, NY: A. D. Caratzas, 1989. After returning to Washington, Davis, the U.S. consul in Harput, Turkey, wrote his report on the conditions there and the oppression of the Armenians. Appendices include some of his dispatches as well as poor reproductions of his photographs. Edited with an introduction and notes by Susan K. Blair.

13:27   Bidwell, Robin Leonard, Kenneth Bourne, and Donald Cameron Watt, eds. *British Documents on Foreign Affairs—Reports and Papers from the Foreign Office Confidential Print. Part II: From the First to the Second World War. Series B: Turkey, Iran, and the Middle East, 1918–1939.* 35 vols. Bethesda, MD: University Publications of America, 1985. See statement for Throup et al. (13:4). Volumes 1–5 cover the end of World War I as well as postwar politics in Turkey, Saudi Arabia, and Syria. Volumes 6–13 provide chronological coverage of Middle Eastern affairs generally. Volume 14 treats the reign of Ibn Saud, while volume 15 is a supplement to volumes 6–13. Volumes 16–28 cover Persia chronologically from 1919 to 1939. Volumes 29–35 cover Turkey chronologically from 1919 to 1939.

13:28   Gillard, David, Kenneth Bourne, and Donald Cameron Watt, eds. *British Documents on Foreign Affairs—Reports and Papers from the Foreign Office Confidential Print. Part I: From the Mid-Nineteenth Century to the First World War. Series B: The Near and Middle East, 1856–1914.* 20 vols. Bethesda, MD: University Publications of America, 1984–1985. See statement for Throup et al. (13:4). Volumes 1–9 cover the Ottoman empire and British understandings of Ottoman policy toward the Balkans, Russia, Asia, and North Africa. Volume 10 covers Persia, volumes 11–12, Russia and Central Asia, and volumes 13–14, Russia and Persia. Volume 15 concerns Egypt and Sudan, volumes 16–18, issues related to the Persian Gulf and Arabia, and volumes 19–20 cover Turkey in the critical 1885–1914 period.

PERSONAL PAPERS

13:29   Hay, John, ed. *Letters of John Hay and Extracts from Diary.* Though Hay's letters are often a pleasure to read, they require good background to be used effectively. No index is provided, and proper names are represented throughout by the first letter of the name only. Volume 1 covers 1860–1870; volume 2, 1870–1895; and volume 3, 1896–1905. Originally compiled and edited (but only for private consumption) in 1908 by Henry Adams and Clara Louise Hay (11:22).

13:30   Brands, H. W., ed. *The Selected Letters of Theodore Roosevelt.* Although a single volume of Roosevelt letters cannot replace other, larger collections, Brands provides interesting and revealing selections covering personal matters as well as domestic and foreign policies. The volume's usefulness, however, is limited by an index restricted to names only (10:16).

13:31   Hagedorn, Hermann, ed. *Memorial Edition: Works of Theodore Roosevelt.* 24 vols. New York: Charles Scribner's Sons, 1923–1926. This collection is the place to begin research on Theodore Roosevelt, and includes much of what he wrote for publication or public consumption in the form of speeches. Volumes 14–16, 18, and 20 are most likely to be useful for U.S. foreign relations with Asia, Africa, and the Middle East, although the latter two topics are sparsely covered.

13:32   Lodge, Henry Cabot, Sr., and Charles F. Redmond. *Selections from the Correspondence of Theodore Roosevelt and Henry Cabot Lodge, 1884–1918.* These letters supplement other document collections on Theodore Roosevelt and contain some interesting perspectives on important issues, such as the Philippines. Index for both volumes in volume 2. Originally published in 1925 (9:86).

13:33   Hancock, W. K., and Jean van der Poel, eds. *Selections from the Smuts Papers.* 7 vols. Cambridge, UK: University Press, 1966–1973. This collection is most helpful for an understanding of Smuts's role at the Paris Peace Conference after World War I—especially his contributions to the formation of the League of Nations and the mandate system for German colonies—and for an assessment of South Africa's foreign policy from unification to the Nationalist triumph in 1945. Volumes 1–7 respectively cover 1886–1902, 1902–1910, 1910–1918, 1918–1919, 1918–1934, 1934–1945, and 1945–1950. Volume 7 also includes an index for the whole collection.

13:34   Link, Arthur S., et al., eds. *The Papers of Woodrow Wilson.* This invaluable collection of Woodrow Wilson's papers from 1856 to 1924 is a wonderful and comprehensive source. Index (11:33).

Bibliographies

13:35   Asada, Sadao, ed. *Japan and the World, 1853–1952: A Bibliographic Guide to Japanese Scholarship in Foreign Relations.* New York: Columbia University Press, 1989. Asada has provided a useful guide to Japanese-language materials, both primary and secondary sources. The first three chapters, respectively, cover published documents and reference works and the periods 1850–1905 and 1905–1931.

13:36   Buckingham, Peter H., ed. *Woodrow Wilson: A Bibliography of His Times and Presidency.* This annotated bibliography includes one chapter on Wilson and World War I, plus another on his foreign policy generally. It is easy to use, including helpful introductions to each chapter as well as author and subject indices. Works—articles, dissertations, and books—are categorized by both geographical area and personalities (12:20).

13:37   Clements, Frank, ed. *The Emergence of Arab Nationalism from the Nineteenth Century to 1921.* Wilmington, DE: Scholarly Resources, 1976. This is an excellent, well-annotated bibliography of books, articles, and pamphlets in English (including translations) arranged in three major sections, with a short introductory essay: 1) the struggle between the Arabs and the Turks; 2) the peace settlement and its consequences; 3) the "Fertile Crescent" under the mandate system.

13:38   Cordier, Henri, ed. *Bibliotheca Sinica: Dictionnaire bibliographique des ouvrages relatifs à* *l'Empire chinois [Bibliography of China: Bibliographical Dictionary of the Foreign Relations of the Chinese Empire].* 5 vols. Rev. ed. Paris: Guilmoto, 1904–1922. This classic work is the most extensive bibliography of China's foreign relations; while the first four volumes (published 1904–1907) contain minimal material on the twentieth century, the 1922 supplement has extensive coverage of western language materials regarding China's foreign relations, economics, and missionaries.

13:39   Gould, Lewis L., and Craig H. Roell, eds. *William McKinley: A Bibliography.* This useful bibliography provides a brief chapter on McKinley and his associates' unpublished papers and many nonannotated citations about his administration's foreign policy in a section that naturally focuses on the Spanish-American War (10:32).

13:40   Irick, Robert L., Ying-shih Yü, and Kwang-Ching Liu, eds. *American-Chinese Relations, 1784–1941: A Survey of Chinese-Language Materials at Harvard.* This listing includes entries on reference works, document collections, libraries and archives in the United States and East Asia, economic and cultural relations, Christian missions, education, social reform, immigration, and diplomatic relations (7:33).

13:41   Lust, John, with Werner Eichhorn, eds. *Index Sinicus: A Catalogue of Articles Relating to China in Periodicals and Other Collective Publications, 1920–1955.* Cambridge, UK: W. Heffer, 1964. This supplements Cordier's bibliography (*Bibliotheca Sinica: Dictionnaire bibliographiques des ouvrages relatifs à l'Empire chinois,* 1904–1922 [13:38]) and complements Yüan's list of monographs (*China in Western Literature: A Continuation of Cordier's Bibliotheca Sinica,* 1958 [13:44]). It lists 19,734 items from 830 periodicals and 137 collective works published from 1920 to 1955. Headings of interest include Sino-American Relations, Trade with USA, International Economic Relations—USA, and Missionary Field Work, among others. Author and subject index.

13:42   Shulman, Frank J. *Doctoral Dissertations on Japan and Korea, 1969–1979: A Classified Bibliographical Listing of International Research.* Microfilm. Ann Arbor: University Microfilms Interna-

tional, 1982. This is an update of Shulman's earlier compilation, *Japan and Korea: An Annotated Bibliography of Doctoral Dissertations in Western Languages, 1877–1969* (1970). It again covers both traditional topics in diplomatic history and studies of Korean and Japanese communities overseas and how these countries were viewed by others. Indices by author, subject, and institution.

13:43   _____, ed. *Japan and Korea: An Annotated Bibliography of Doctoral Dissertations in Western Languages, 1877–1969.* Chicago: American Library Association, 1970. This annotated bibliography includes dissertations on both traditional topics of Japanese and Korean foreign relations, listed by time period, and on Korean and Japanese communities overseas.

13:44   Yüan, Tung-li, ed. *China in Western Literature: A Continuation of Cordier's Bibliotheca Sinica.* New Haven: Yale University Press, 1958. This large volume lists about 15,000 books in English, French, and German published between 1921 and 1957. Around sixty pages are devoted to works on Chinese foreign relations, but other chapters also list books on trade, extraterritoriality, and missions, among other subjects.

Historiography

13:45   Cohen, Warren I., ed. *New Frontiers in American–East Asian Relations: Essays Presented to Dorothy Borg.* New York: Columbia University Press, 1983. Authors in this collection discuss the state of the field; twenty years later, some of the suggested research agenda remains unexplored. Relevant contributions are Akira Iriye, "Americanization of East Asia: Writings on Cultural Affairs since 1900" (45–75); Waldo H. Heinrichs, "The Middle Years, 1900–1945, and the Question of a Large U.S. Policy for East Asia" (77–106); and Ernest R. May, "Military and Naval Affairs since 1900" (107–27).

13:46   _____, ed. *Pacific Passage: The Study of American–East Asian Relations on the Eve of the Twenty-First Century.* New York: Columbia University Press, 1996. The essays in this volume both provide useful orientation to the vast historiography of U.S.-Asian relations and suggest many areas where fruitful research can still be done. For especially useful chapters, see entries for Charles W. Hayford, William C. Kirby, and Glenn Anthony May.

13:47   Coletta, Paolo E. "The Diplomacy of Theodore Roosevelt and William Howard Taft." In *American Foreign Relations, A Historiographical Review,* ed. Gerald K. Haines and J. Samuel Walker, 91–114. Coletta provides a balanced summary of scholarship from 1920 to 1980 on the foreign policies of Theodore Roosevelt and William Howard Taft (11:36).

13:48   Dingman, Roger V. "1917–1922." In *American–East Asian Relations: A Survey,* ed. Ernest R. May and James C. Thomson, Jr., 190–218. Cambridge, MA: Harvard University Press, 1972. Asking whether the years 1917–1922 make sense as a period, Dingman argues that while critically important, it lacks coherence in its mix of policies toward war, revolution, and the stirrings of Japanese expansion. His article also remains useful for its discussion of works by Japanese historians.

13:49   Hayford, Charles W. "The Open Door Raj: Chinese-American Cultural Relations 1900–1945." In *Pacific Passage: The Study of American–East Asian Relations on the Eve of the Twenty-first Century,* ed. Warren I. Cohen, 139–62. New York: Columbia University Press, 1996. Hayford takes a very broad, and welcome, view of the literature in his historiographical article on U.S.-China relations in the first half of the twentieth century, which enables him to explore the many exciting trends in the field.

13:50   Kirby, William C. "Chinese-American Relations in Comparative Perspective, 1900–1949." In *Pacific Passage: The Study of American–East Asian Relations on the Eve of the Twenty-first Century,* ed. Warren I. Cohen, 163–89. New York: Columbia University Press, 1996. Kirby provides a pointed reminder that placing U.S.-Chinese relations from 1900 to 1949 within the broader context of China's relations with other countries, both Asian and European, may change, even diminish, the importance of U.S. actions and policies.

13:51   May, Glenn Anthony. "The Unfathomable Other: Historical Studies of U.S.-Philippine Relations." In *Pacific Passage: The Study of American–East Asian Relations on the Eve of the Twenty-first Century,* ed. Warren I. Cohen, 279–312. New York: Columbia University Press, 1996. May finds that historians have paid too little attention to differences between the United States and the Philippines, stemming from the nearly fifty years of U.S. rule and written accounts that are one-sided and insufficiently attentive to Philippine history.

13:52   Ninkovich, Frank A. "Ideology, the Open Door, and Foreign Policy." *Diplomatic History* 6, no. 2 (Spring 1982): 185–208. Ninkovich argues that historians of the open door policy have not rigorously explored linkages between that policy and ideology. He then provides a sketch of how such linkages work.

13:53   Young, Marilyn B. "The Quest for Empire." In *American–East Asian Relations: A Survey,* ed. Ernest R. May and James C. Thomson, Jr., 131–42. Cambridge, MA: Harvard University Press, 1972. Young finds that the literature explaining U.S. expansionism falls into two interesting and compelling schools (typified by William Appleman Williams and Ernest May) that have failed to fully engage each other. She suggests more work needs to be done to understand the causes of U.S. expansion, a point that remains valid. Selected bibliography.

General Works

13:54   Bonsal, Stephen. *Suitors and Supplicants: The Little Nations at Versailles.* New York: Prentice-Hall, Inc., 1946. Bonsal was a translator and aid to Colonel Edward M. House at the Paris Peace Conference, with special responsibility for investigating the claims of "little nations." This is his chatty, often vivid memoir of the experiences such countries had while trying to be heard at the conference. Introduction by Arthur Krock.

13:55   Challener, Richard D. *Admirals, Generals, and American Foreign Policy, 1898–1914.* Challener's book explores how those in the United States navy and army envisioned the growing power of the United States in the early twentieth century, how they participated in increasing that power, and how military and diplomatic policies related. Approximately half the book covers Asian issues; the other half focuses on the Caribbean. Bibliography (11:101).

13:56   Cooper, John Milton, Jr. "Progressivism and American Foreign Policy: A Reconsideration." Elaborating on Leuchtenburg's thesis ("Progressivism and Imperialism: The Progressive Movement and American Foreign Policy, 1898–1916," 1952 [13:62]), Cooper finds a variety of opinions among progressives on such issues as imperialism and expansionism (10:89).

13:57   Curti, Merle E., and Kendall Birr. *Prelude to Point Four: American Technical Missions Overseas, 1838–1938.* Madison: University of Wisconsin Press, 1954. Curti's study of U.S. attempts to export knowledge during the nineteenth and early twentieth centuries remains useful for students of U.S. cultural or economic relations. Although broadly conceived, the book pays special attention to U.S. missions in Japan, Persia, Liberia, Cuba, the Dominican Republic, and Haiti. The bulk of the treatment is on 1900–1930.

13:58   Guttmann, Allen. *Games and Empires: Modern Sports and Cultural Imperialism.* New York: Columbia University Press, 1994. Guttmann surveys the global diffusion of cricket, soccer, baseball, basketball, American football, and the Olympic Games, then turns to an analysis of resistance to this spread, and to whether such global games are the result of cultural imperialism. This book contains many interesting anecdotes as well. Bibliography.

13:59   Headrick, Daniel R. *The Invisible Weapon: Telecommunications and International Politics, 1851–1945.* Headrick's interesting study of the interrelationships among politics, security, and quickly developing telecommunications during the late nineteenth and early twentieth centuries is helpful for scholars writing on a variety of topics. Chapters 5–7 ("Crises at the Turn of the Century, 1895–1901," "The Great Powers and the Cable Crisis, 1900–1913," and "The Beginnings of Radio 1895–1914") are most pertinent for this chapter (11:118).

13:60   Hinckley, Frank E. *American Consular Jurisdiction in the Orient.* Washington, DC: W. H. Loudermilk, 1906. Hinckley summarized treaty law as well as both historic and existing practice in the early twentieth century on the legal rights of Americans living in East Asia and the Middle East. His book is a useful reference for those studying missionaries, foreign investment, and a variety of other topics.

13:61   Lauren, Paul Gordon. "Entering the Twentieth Century: World Visions, War, and Revolutions." In *The Evolution of International Human Rights: Visions Seen,* ed. Paul Gordon Lauren, 72–104. Philadelphia: University of Pennsylvania Press, 1998. Since the pre-1945 concept of human rights is rarely studied, Lauren's chapter on various governmental and non-governmental efforts in the early twentieth century is valuable.

13:62   Leuchtenburg, William E. "Progressivism and Imperialism: The Progressive Movement and American Foreign Policy, 1898–1916." This landmark study argues that progressives, despite their primary concern for domestic reform, favored imperialism. This thesis has stimulated considerable historical controversy, and therefore remains critical to understandings of U.S. imperialism and dollar diplomacy (9:223).

13:63   Rosenberg, Emily S. *Financial Missionaries to the World: The Politics and Culture of Dollar Diplomacy, 1900–1930.* The political and strategic implications of dollar diplomacy have been extensively explored, but Rosenberg has done a great service in examining the financial aspects of that policy. Her book has a much broader scope, however, and provides intriguing insights into the ways rhetoric, financial strength, ideology, and political power combined to bring a coercive element to U.S. policy in the less developed parts of the world in the twentieth century before the Depression (11:91).

13:64   _____. *Spreading the American Dream: American Economic and Cultural Expansion, 1890–1945.* Rosenberg's classic study explores the linkages among U.S. economic, cultural, and political expansion, with welcome attention to continuities over the period 1890–1945 (9:151).

13:65   Rydell, Robert W., and Nancy E. Gwinn,

with contributions by James B. Gilbert, eds. *Fair Representations: World's Fairs and the Modern World.* Amsterdam: VU University Press, 1994. While many of these papers, mostly from a symposium organized by the Smithsonian Institution Libraries, could be of some interest to historians of foreign relations, two specifically treat interactions among different cultures in the context of various world's fairs: Burton Benedict's "Rituals of Representations: Ethnic Stereotypes and Colonized Peoples at World's Fairs" (28–61) and Aram A. Yengoyan's "Culture, Ideology and World's Fairs: Colonizer and Colonized in Comparative Perspective" (62–83).

13:66   Sklar, Martin J. *The United States as a Developing Country: Studies in U.S. History in the Progressive Era and the 1920s.* New York: Cambridge University Press, 1992. Although only one essay ("Dollar Diplomacy According to Dollar Diplomats: American Development and World Development") in this influential work is on a traditional topic of U.S. foreign relations, Sklar's work is critical both for the broad context of developments in U.S. politics and political institutions from the 1890s to 1920s and for understanding of U.S. history in a comparative context.

13:67   Taylor, Arnold H. *American Diplomacy and the Narcotics Traffic, 1900–1939: A Study in International Humanitarian Reform.* Durham, NC: Duke University Press, 1969. Taylor provides the only monograph to date exploring early-twentieth-century U.S. efforts to suppress trade in and use of narcotics overseas. His assessment that these efforts resulted from the relationship of "humanitarian and political influence" may now seem overly optimistic, but the only better analysis is Walker, *Opium and Foreign Policy: The Anglo-American Search for Order in Asia, 1912–1954* (1991) (13:182).

MISSIONARIES

13:68   Boyd, Nancy. *Emissaries: The Overseas Work of the American YWCA, 1895–1970.* Boyd explores the ways in which YWCA representatives overseas were emissaries for both Christianity and American womanhood. Part I covers 1895–1920; Part II covers 1920–1940; and Part III covers 1940–1970. Appendices (9:161).

13:69   Carpenter, Joel A., and Wilbert R. Shenk, eds. *Earthen Vessels: American Evangelicals and Foreign Missions, 1880–1980.* Grand Rapids, MI: Wm. B. Eerdmans Publishing Co., 1990. Although more focused on the dynamics of missions and theology than is usual in works on foreign relations, this collection includes several important essays on the role of missionaries in foreign relations, especially Andrew F. Walls, "The American Dimension in the History of the Missionary Movement" (1–25); Alvyn J. Austin, "Blessed Adversity: Henry W. Frost and the China Inland Mission" (29–70); and Ruth A. Tucker, "Women in Missions: Reaching Sisters in 'Heathen Darkness'" (251–80).

13:70   Hutchison, William R. *Errand to the World: American Protestant Thought and Foreign Missions.* Hutchison's thoughtful study explores the complex ways missionaries reflected, shaped, and rebelled against American culture while representing and sometimes spreading that culture along with Christianity. His book is must reading for those studying American missionaries or U.S. cultural relations. Bibliography (7:424).

RACE AND RACISM

13:71   Guterl, Matthew Pratt. "The New Race Consciousness: Race, Nation, and Empire in American Culture, 1910–1925." *Journal of World History* 10 (Fall 1999): 307–52. This article on the often contradictory relationships among anti-imperialist Irish-Americans and African-Americans in the early twentieth century investigates the way race and racism shaped anti-imperialist discourse and undermined alliances based on politics and class. The article is focused primarily on activities in the United States, with some attention to overseas conferences and movements.

13:72   Jacobson, Matthew Frye. *Barbarian Virtues: The United States Encounters Foreign Peoples at Home and Abroad, 1876–1917.* Jacobson's ambitious book works to link domestic attitudes about race and foreigners with U.S. foreign policy, especially trade policy but also immigration and imperialism. This work is particularly helpful in its careful attention to rhetoric about civilization and barbarians. Bibliography (9:174).

13:73   Krenn, Michael L., ed. *Race and U.S. Foreign Policy from 1900 through World War II. Vol. 3, Race and U.S. Foreign Policy from the Colonial Period to the Present: A Collection of Essays.* Krenn here reprints some of the best journal articles on the topic of U.S. foreign relations and race to have been published in the last forty years. That many of these were first published in the 1960s and 1970s suggests that this topic, and time period, are ripe for additional attention. See chapter 2 of this Guide for details (2:156).

13:74   Lauren, Paul Gordon. *Power and Prejudice: The Politics and Diplomacy of Racial Discrimination.* The connections between racism and policy are too often assumed. Lauren has systematically and insightfully examined them in this now classic work. Only one-third of the book treats the period to 1920, but this work remains important for any student of U.S. relations with Asia, Africa, or the Middle East in that period (2:159). First published in 1988.

13:75   McFerson, Hazel M. *The Racial Dimension of American Overseas Colonial Policy.* Westport, CT: Greenwood Press, 1997. McFerson explores the often noted but rarely examined relationship between the U.S. "racial tradition" and its colonial acquisitions and governance. Her book is primarily a theoretical treatment, but provides chapter-length case studies of the Virgin Islands and Puerto Rico. Bibliography.

13:76   Weston, Rubin Francis. *Racism in U.S. Imperialism: The Influence of Racial Assumptions on American Foreign Policy, 1893–1946.* Weston's pioneering study has inspired more nuanced and sophisticated treatments of race and U.S. foreign relations but remains worthwhile. He began by exploring the question of whether the Constitution followed the flag into U.S. overseas colonies, and found that racism influenced the answer, especially in the U.S. Congress. Bibliography (12:104).

ECONOMICS

13:77   DeNovo, John A. "The Movement for an Aggressive American Oil Policy Abroad, 1918–1920." *American Historical Review* 61 (July 1956): 854–76. DeNovo argues that wartime experiences

with oil shortages and supply difficulties convinced U.S. policymakers to change their attitude from "apathy to alarm" about the need to ensure foreign supplies of oil, especially for the U.S. navy.

13:78   Lake, David A. *Power, Protection, and Free Trade: International Sources of U.S. Commercial Strategy, 1887–1939.* Lake's book focuses on trade policy and ideology at a time the United States changed from a highly protectionist state to a leader in establishing free trade worldwide. This book is not the place to find information on trade with any particular country but rather the context in which such trade developed. Bibliography (9:208).

13:79   Rosenberg, Emily S. "Revisiting Dollar Diplomacy: Narratives of Money and Manliness." Rosenberg's provocative essay is critical to any understanding of the multiplicity of meanings of dollar diplomacy, as she explores the cultural narratives underlying such key terms as "loans" and "supervision" (9:197).

13:80   Wilkins, Mira. *The Emergence of Multinational Enterprise: American Business Abroad from the Colonial Era to 1914.* Although Wilkins devotes more space to North and South America in this volume than to Asia, Africa, and the Middle East, it remains a crucial starting point for all students of U.S. foreign economic relations. Bibliography (11:97).

13:81   Wolman, Paul. *Most Favored Nation: The Republican Revisionists and U.S. Tariff Policy, 1897–1912.* Although much of this study is devoted to the domestic wrangling over tariff issues in the late nineteenth and early twentieth centuries, Wolman argues that tariff revision was a key component of an increasingly global and imperial U.S. foreign policy in these years. Bibliography (9:214).

NAVAL POLICY

13:82   Bradford, James C., ed. *Admirals of the New Steel Navy: Makers of the American Naval Tradition, 1880–1930.* The authors in this collection provide biographical sketches of officers playing important roles in the transition from the old to the new navy. See chapter 9 of this Guide (9:240); see also

Bradford, "Henry T. Mayo: Last of the Independent Naval Diplomats" (253–81); David F. Trask, "William Snowden Sims: The Victory Ashore" (282–99); Mary Klachko, "William Shepherd Benson: Naval General Staff" (300–30); and William Reynolds Braisted, "Mark Lambert Bristol: Naval Diplomat Extraordinary of the Battleship Age" (331–73). Bibliography.

13:83 Braisted, William Reynolds. *The United States Navy in the Pacific, 1897–1909.* Austin: University of Texas Press, 1958. Braisted's work is particularly valuable for his attention to the relations between foreign and naval policies in this key period of U.S. expansion overseas. Bibliography.

13:84 _____. *The United States Navy in the Pacific, 1909–1922.* Austin: University of Texas Press, 1971. In this sequel to *The United States Navy in the Pacific, 1897–1909* (1958) (13:83), Braisted analyzes the interlocking of U.S. naval policy and East Asian diplomacy, treating the 1911 Orange Plan, the attempt to sell warships and provide naval personnel to China, the contradictions plaguing the Taft administration during the Chinese revolution of 1911–1912, conflicts with Japan in the Wilson administration, and both the Versailles and Washington conferences. Bibliography. The same press published an abridged version in 1977.

13:85 Brune, Lester H. *The Origins of American National Security Policy: Sea Power, Air Power, and Foreign Policy, 1900–1941.* Manhattan, KS: MA/AH Pub., 1981. Brune's balanced narrative provides a helpful overview of the relationship among foreign policy, military strategy, and planning in the years of growing U.S. power. Bibliography.

13:86 Dingman, Roger V. *Power in the Pacific: The Origins of Naval Arms Limitation, 1914–1922.* Chicago: University of Chicago Press, 1976. Dingman's important study explores how "the politics of national defense," or domestic political imperatives, in Britain, Japan, and the United States jointly and separately pushed all three countries to accept naval limitations in the early 1920s. Bibliography.

13:87 Reckner, James R. *Teddy Roosevelt's Great White Fleet.* Reckner's readable narrative concentrates on the cruise taken by the U.S. Atlantic Fleet,

which Reckner argues served to increase public awareness of the navy's role in defense of the United States. Bibliography (11:108).

13:88 Still, William N., Jr. *American Sea Power in the Old World: The United States Navy in European and Near Eastern Waters, 1865–1917.* This is mainly an "operational study" of U.S. naval developments in Europe and the Middle East during the transition from wooden to steel ships and from strategic emphasis on Europe to the Middle East and Asia. Bibliography (9:263).

13:89 Taylor, G. P. "New Zealand, the Anglo-Japanese Alliance and the 1908 Visit of the American Fleet." *Australian Journal of Politics and History* 15 (April 1969): 55–76. Taylor argues that the U.S. Atlantic Fleet was invited to New Zealand in order, first, to try to create the appearance of an Anglo-American alliance in warning to Japan, and second, because New Zealand officials thought it would be of some use in their changing relations with Britain. Though Roosevelt also saw the cruise as a warning to Japan, he was probably unaware of New Zealand's other purpose.

13:90 Turk, Richard W. "Defending the New Empire, 1900–1914." In *In Peace and War: Interpretations of American Naval History, 1775–1984,* 2d. ed, ed. Kenneth J. Hagan, 186–204. Westport, CT: Greenwood Press, 1984. Turk's essay argues that Navy Department officials were concerned throughout the period to build up the navy to meet the growing defense needs of the United States. In 1900–1905, strategists focused on the Caribbean, on Asia from 1905 to 1910, and on both areas in the 1910–1914 period. Although brief, the essay nicely integrates strategic and tactical issues. Bibliography.

Biographical Studies

WILLIAM MCKINLEY

13:91 Dobson, John M. *Reticent Expansionism: The Foreign Policy of William McKinley.* Although much of the book focuses on the Spanish-American

War and its consequences, Dobson endeavors to explore the broader context of U.S. expansion and growth in power at the turn of the century (9:78).

13:92   Gould, Lewis L. *The Presidency of William McKinley.* Gould's biography in the American Presidency series provides a good overview of the McKinley presidency, with much attention to his foreign policy (10:153).

WILLIAM W. ROCKHILL

13:93   Stanley, Peter W. "The Making of an American Sinologist: William W. Rockhill and the Open Door." *Perspectives in American History* 11 (1977–1978): 419–60. Stanley explores the career of Rockhill, author of the first Open Door Note and, Stanley argues, America's first "professional Sinologist."

13:94   Varg, Paul A. *Open Door Diplomat: The Life of W. W. Rockhill.* Urbana: University of Illinois Press, 1952. This biography relates the Rockhill story (1853–1914) primarily as it is revealed in the Rockhill Papers and the State Department archives. In addition to recounting his role as adviser to John Hay and later as minister at Beijing, the study tells much about him as an individual and a scholar.

THEODORE ROOSEVELT

13:95   Beale, Howard K. *Theodore Roosevelt and the Rise of America to World Power.* Beale's study remains a classic. About half the book is devoted to issues related to Asia (9:84).

13:96   Dyer, Thomas G. *Theodore Roosevelt and the Idea of Race.* Baton Rouge: Louisiana State University Press, 1980. Dyer explores how Theodore Roosevelt acquired his ideas about race, and how those ideas influenced both his domestic and foreign policies. This study is useful for understanding the intellectual underpinning of his approach to foreign policies for Asia, Africa, and the Middle East. Bibliography.

13:97   Gould, Lewis L. *The Presidency of Theodore Roosevelt.* Gould provides a useful narra-

tive of Theodore Roosevelt's presidency with some attention to the major foreign policy issues (11:468).

13:98   Morris, Edmund. *Theodore Rex.* This is an exciting read, which at key moments gives one the sense of actually being in the room—sometimes in Roosevelt's head. Although this is primarily a straightforward biography, Morris understands the importance of foreign policy for Roosevelt's approach to the presidency and power in general. Notes, bibliography (10:174).

13:99   Oyos, Matthew M. "Theodore Roosevelt and the Implements of War." *Journal of Military History* 60 (October 1996): 631–55. Oyos argues that Theodore Roosevelt was the first president to consider military technology and power in conjunction with foreign policy. He provides several examples of Roosevelt's interest in and involvement with decisions about military hardware and strategy and shows the influence of the Russo-Japanese War on Roosevelt's thinking.

13:100   Tilchin, William N. *Theodore Roosevelt and the British Empire: A Study in Presidential Statecraft.* In exploring Theodore Roosevelt's affinity for Britain, Tilchin discusses several neglected aspects of early-twentieth-century diplomacy, such as U.S. policy toward such British colonies or dominions as India, Jamaica, Canada, and South Africa (11:299).

WILLIAM HOWARD TAFT

13:101   Burton, David H. *William Howard Taft, in the Public Service.* Malabar, FL: R. F. Krieger Publishing Co., 1986. This brief biography is a useful overview of Taft's years of public service, with chapters on his years as governor in the Philippines and secretary of war as well as the foreign policy of his presidency.

13:102   Coletta, Paolo E. *The Presidency of William Howard Taft.* Coletta's biography in the American Presidency series is a good place to begin a study of Taft's presidency. He covers dollar diplomacy well, but provides little on U.S. policy toward Asia, Africa, or the Middle East, and—especially surprising—virtually nothing on the Philippines (11:479).

13:103 Minger, Ralph Eldin. *William Howard Taft and United States Foreign Policy: The Apprenticeship Years, 1900–1908.* Minger's study is a reminder of Taft's extensive pre-presidential foreign policy experience, especially in the Philippines and Japan, but also with Cuba, Panama, and China. Bibliography (11:480).

13:104 Pringle, Henry F. *The Life and Times of William Howard Taft: A Biography.* Although this biography is dated, both in style and to some extent in interpretation, it remains useful for its broad narrative coverage. The index is more helpful for locating particular events than are chapter titles (11:481).

13:105 Scholes, Walter V., and Marie V. Scholes. *The Foreign Policies of the Taft Administration.* More than half of this work is devoted to East Asian policy. Based on exhaustive research in U.S. and British records, it draws little on Japanese sources and none on Chinese. The authors see Taft's dollar diplomacy (1909–1913) as high-minded but inept. Bibliography (11:79).

COLLECTIVE

13:106 Graebner, Norman A., ed. *Traditions and Values: American Diplomacy, 1865–1945.* Lanham, MD: University Press of America, 1985. The essays in this collection tend to reflect the realist leanings of the editor and remain useful. Pertinent to this chapter are the essays by Richard E. Welch, Jr. ("William McKinley: Reluctant Warrior, Cautious Imperialist," 29–52), Frederick W. Marks, III ("Theodore Roosevelt and the Conservative Revival," 53–72), and Lloyd E. Ambrosius ("Woodrow Wilson and the Quest for Orderly Progress," 73–100).

OTHERS

13:107 Clements, Kendrick A. *William Jennings Bryan: Missionary Isolationist.* Clements's biography uses Bryan's foreign relations beliefs and policies as an anchor. Although more articulate, Bryan was representative of ordinary Americans in his thinking about foreign policy. Bibliography (12:108).

13:108 Griscom, Lloyd C. *Diplomatically Speaking.* Boston: Little, Brown and Company, 1940. Griscom's memoirs include four chapters on his year as U.S. chargé in Turkey, where he dealt with the Armenian indemnity issue; three on his time as minister in Persia, which focus on adventures rather than policy; and four as minister to Japan, the highlight of which are his conversations with Foreign Minister Komura before and during the Russo-Japanese War.

13:109 Widenor, William C. *Henry Cabot Lodge and the Search for an American Foreign Policy.* Widenor set out to write an "intellectual biography" of Lodge's thinking about foreign policy, and this work remains one of the few, and therefore indispensable, treatments of his important role in U.S. foreign policy. Bibliography (10:141).

13:110 Clymer, Kenton J. *John Hay: The Gentleman as Diplomat.* Still the classic work on John Hay, this book includes chapters on his views on race, the Spanish-American War, the Philippines, China, and his relationship with Theodore Roosevelt. Clymer explains effectively how Hay's understanding of U.S.-European relations helped shape his view of how to act in Asia (9:109).

13:111 Seager, Robert, II. *Alfred Thayer Mahan: The Man and His Letters.* Seager, editor of *Letters and Papers of Alfred Thayer Mahan* (1975) (9:6), provides a thorough narrative biography of Mahan (9:76).

13:112 Bacevich, A. J. *Diplomat in Khaki: Major General Frank Ross McCoy and American Foreign Policy, 1898–1949.* McCoy was Leonard Wood's aide when he was governor of Mindanao in the Philippines and later was a member of the post–World War I American military mission to Armenia. These episodes are covered at some length, but with little analysis, in this readable work (10:190).

13:113 Morgenthau, Henry, Sr., with French Strother. *All in a Life-Time.* Garden City, NY: Doubleday, Page and Company, 1922. Morgenthau's memoirs cover most of his involvement in foreign affairs during the Wilson presidency; the most interesting comments are about the status of Palestine.

13:114 Phillips, William. *Ventures in Diplomacy.* The diplomatic career of Phillips spanned the period from Theodore Roosevelt to Franklin Roosevelt. He served under Rockhill in China and was subsequently appointed first chief of the new Division of Far Eastern Affairs in 1908, then a low-status position (12:136).

13:115   Rauchway, Eric. "Willard Straight and the Paradox of Liberal Imperialism." *Pacific Historical Review* 66 (August 1997): 363–97. Rauchway argues that Straight's commitment to an "imperial mission" for the United States grew out of his liberal principles and resulted in a particular form of American empire as well as a racism directed at imperial competitors as much as colonial subjects.

13:116   Straus, Oscar S. *Under Four Administrations, from Cleveland to Taft: Recollections of Oscar S. Straus*. Boston: Houghton Mifflin Company, 1922. Straus was three times minister to Turkey (under Cleveland, McKinley, and Taft) and, according to his memoirs, involved in various other foreign policy issues of the late nineteenth and early twentieth centuries, including the Portsmouth Peace Conference, the Philippines, and the League of Nations.

13:117   Wilson, F. M. Huntington. *Memoirs of an Ex-Diplomat*. Huntington Wilson went to Tokyo in 1897 as second secretary of legation. His subsequent career on the State Department staff was devoted largely to East Asian affairs (he also served briefly in Turkey). His anti-Japanese inclinations had some impact on policy during the Roosevelt period but far more in the Taft administration. His memoirs are filled with candid information about people and events (11:512).

U.S. Foreign Relations with Other Countries and Regions

AFRICA

13:118   Contee, Clarence G. "Du Bois, the NAACP, and the Pan-African Congress of 1919."

Journal of Negro History 57 (January 1972): 13–28. Contee discusses the efforts of Du Bois and others on behalf of Pan-Africanism at Paris in 1919, and Du Bois's success in establishing the Pan-African conference. Du Bois encountered difficulties because of the reluctance of U.S. delegates to the Paris Peace Conference to support his actions.

13:119   Duignan, Peter, and L. H. Gann. *The United States and Africa: A History*. This comprehensive survey of American activities in Africa from earliest days to the 1980s includes a long chapter on 1900–1939. Emphasizing breadth rather than depth, the volume provides a useful introduction (2:255).

13:120   Geiss, Imanuel. *The Pan-African Movement: A History of Pan-Africanism in America, Europe, and Africa*. Translated by Ann Keep. New York: Africana Pub. Co., 1974. Geiss's work and attention to the global context of Pan-Africanism remains useful, even if some findings have been superseded. He demonstrates that Pan-Africanism became a political movement after 1900 but earlier was more religious and cultural in nature. Also published by Methuen (London) under the title *The Pan-African Movement* (1974). Bibliography.

13:121   Munene, G. Macharia. "The United States, Pressure Groups and Africa: 1885–1918." *Transafrican Journal of History* 23 (1994): 1–8. This brief article argues that pressure groups encouraged a change in official U.S. policy, from support for European colonialism in the late nineteenth and early twentieth centuries, to no longer encouraging colonialism by the end of World War I.

North Africa

13:122   Beer, George Louis. *African Questions at the Paris Peace Conference, with Papers on Egypt, Mesopotamia, and the Colonial Settlement*. New York: Macmillan Company, 1923. Beer prepared these essays for the American Commission of Inquiry for use at the Paris Peace Conference. This volume contains studies of Germany's African colonies, the economic and political aspects of the situation in "middle Africa," Egypt, and Mesopotamia as well as a chapter on "Colonial Problems" generally. Edited by Louis Herbert Gray, who also provided notes and an introduction.

13:123 Hall, Luella J. *The United States and Morocco, 1776–1956.* See chapter 2 of this Guide (2:260).

13:124 Larsen, Peter. "Theodore Roosevelt and the Moroccan Crisis, 1904–1906." Here multiarchival research allows a comprehensive study of what Larsen calls the two stages of the Moroccan crisis, the first being the abduction of Ion Perdicaris and the second the Algeciras conference. Bibliography (11:162).

13:125 Phillips, Dennis H. "The American Missionary in Morocco." *Muslim World* 65 (January 1975): 1–20. These early missionaries enjoyed little success in converting Moroccans, even though they had the support of American diplomats. To a greater degree than in many other countries, they focused on evangelization rather than medical work or getting involved in influencing U.S. foreign policy.

Southern Africa

13:126 Boisseau, T. J. "'They Called Me Bebe Bwana': A Critical Cultural Study of an Imperial Feminist." *Signs* 21 (Autumn 1995): 116–46. Boisseau uses the case of Mary French-Sheldon, the "first woman-explorer of Africa," to argue that the U.S. media and American women themselves used a rhetoric about progress, women's rights, and modernity to buttress the imperial project of the late nineteenth and early twentieth centuries.

13:127 Bowman, Larry W. "The United States and Mauritius, 1794–1994: A Bicentennial Retrospective." Primarily focused on the nineteenth century, this article explores the amiable but usually uneventful relations between the United States and Mauritius. Bowman mentions several U.S. travelers to the islands, including Mark Twain and Commodore Perry (9:377).

13:128 Fierce, Milfred C. *The Pan-African Idea in the United States, 1900–1919: African-American Interest in Africa and Interaction with West Africa.* New York: Garland Publishers, 1993. This study is valuable for providing in a single volume an exploration of the many ways African-Americans interacted with Africa in the early twentieth century. Fierce discusses intellectual engagement, missionaries, economic development, conferences, Back-to-Africa movements, and the special case of Liberia. The U.S. domestic context informs the entire discussion. Bibliography.

13:129 Harlan, Louis R. "Booker T. Washington and the White Man's Burden." *American Historical Review* 71 (January 1966): 441–67. Washington's major biographer tries to demonstrate that the black leader's involvement in African affairs was rather extensive. This interest, however, reflected his essential conservatism, since he felt that black people overseas should seek to better themselves within the existing political and racial order. This article explores the concrete efforts of the Tuskegee Institute in Togo, the Congo, Liberia, and South Africa.

13:130 Jacobs, Sylvia M. *The African Nexus: Black American Perspectives on the European Partitioning of Africa, 1880–1920.* Although several recent works have examined the views of African-Americans toward Africa during and after World War II, Jacobs's work remains virtually alone in exploring this earlier, from the late nineteenth century through World War I. African-Americans opposed European colonization, and those who actively opposed were often further politicized by the experience. Bibliography (9:284).

13:131 Louis, William Roger. "The United States and the African Peace Settlement of 1919: The Pilgrimage of George Louis Beer." *Journal of African History* 4, no. 3 (1963): 413–23. Louis demonstrates that European and American officials had very different ideas for the future of Africa and the meaning of mandates. Since Beer was virtually alone among U.S. representatives at Versailles in paying attention to the African mandate question, he failed both to get an American mandate and to block Belgium's claim to Ruanda and Urundi.

13:132 Pakenham, Thomas. *The Scramble for Africa: White Man's Conquest of the Dark Continent from 1876 to 1912.* Although the United States appears only rarely in this massive study, Pakenham provides a sweeping, extensive narrative of European efforts to carve up Africa during the late nineteenth and early twentieth centuries. Select bibliography (11:426). Paper editions used the title *The Scramble for Africa: White Man's Conquest of the Dark Continent from 1876 to 1912.*

13:133   Rainey, Timothy A. "Buffalo Soldiers in Africa: The U.S. Army and the Liberian Frontier Force, 1912–1927: An Overview." *Liberian Studies Journal* 21, no. 2 (1996): 203–38. Rainey explores the circumstances surrounding the decision to recruit black former U.S. army officers and noncommissioned officers to serve in the Liberian Frontier Force, the selection process, and the experiences of these soldiers in Liberia.

13:134   Shepperson, George, and Thomas Price. *Independent African: John Chilembwe and the Origins, Setting and Significance of the Nyasaland Native Rising of 1915.* Edinburgh: University Press, 1958. This massive study of a rare rebellion against European rule also investigates the activities of Joseph Booth, the African-American who baptized Chilembwe, carrying the story back to 1892. Shepperson and Price note the influence on Chilembwe of his time in the United States (1897–1900) and of African-American churches and missionaries. Bibliography.

13:135   Skinner, Elliott P. *African Americans and U.S. Policy toward Africa, 1850–1924: In Defense of Black Nationality.* Skinner, an anthropologist and former ambassador to the Republic of Upper Volta, wrote his book to demonstrate that African-Americans were active in attempting to "help their embattled homelands." The bulk of the book focuses on 1880–1920, with Liberia, Booker T. Washington, and Marcus Garvey receiving most coverage, although numerous other topics are touched upon. Bibliography (9:289).

13:136   Skinner, Robert P. *Abyssinia of To-day: An Account of the First Mission Sent by the American Government to the Court of the King of Kings (1903–1904).* New York: Longmans, Green, 1906. This is an account of the first mission sent by the U.S. government, led by the author, to the court of the king of Ethiopia. Firsthand accounts by diplomatic participants in American-African relations are a rarity, especially for these early years. Skinner's account is chatty and full of what he considered exotic.

13:137   Sternstein, Jerome L. "King Leopold II, Senator Nelson W. Aldrich, and the Strange Beginnings of American Economic Penetration of the Congo." *African Historical Studies* 2, no. 2 (1969): 189–204. Sternstein argues that King Leopold II of Belgium hoped to gain U.S. acquiescence in his rule over the Congo by granting a large rubber and mineral concession to an American syndicate led by Wall Street financier Thomas Fortune Ryan and Senator Nelson W. Aldrich.

South Africa

13:138   Hull, Richard W. *American Enterprise in South Africa: Historical Dimensions of Engagement and Disengagement.* Hull has used a broad definition of "enterprise"—covering investment, trade, missions, education, and development—in this fine overview of U.S. engagement with South Africa from the late eighteenth to the late twentieth centuries. Chapters 3–4 cover the period 1886–1929. Bibliography (2:265).

13:139   Noer, Thomas J. *Briton, Boer, and Yankee: The United States and South Africa, 1870–1914.* Noer argues that involved Americans came quickly to support continued British imperial rule in South Africa as most conducive to the kind of economic development they wanted and believed would be best for South Africans. Bibliography (10:577).

13:140   Page, Carol A. "Colonial Reaction to AME Missionaries in South Africa, 1898–1910." In *Black Americans and the Missionary Movement in Africa,* ed. Sylvia M. Jacobs, 177–96. Westport, CT: Greenwood Press, 1982. African-American missionaries in South Africa were viewed with suspicion by Europeans—both officials and other missionaries—because they were believed to be politically disruptive and likely to have an advantage in gaining converts. The U.S. government gave the AME little help in its difficult efforts to gain permission to work in South Africa.

Liberia

13:141   Lyon, Judson M. "Informal Imperialism: The United States in Liberia, 1897–1912." *Diplomatic History* 5 (Summer 1981): 221–44. In Liberia, as in such countries as China and Santo Domingo, the informal imperialism accompanying dollar diplomacy was the most important aspect of U.S. foreign policy. Although Lyon mentions the role of African-Americans, their involvement is not his central theme.

13:142 Rosenberg, Emily S. "The Invisible Protectorate: The United States, Liberia, and the Evolution of Neocolonialism, 1909–1940. American administration of Liberian customs collections and a U.S. financial adviser to the Liberian government created a relationship between the two countries analogous to those between the United States and countries in Central America (11:427).

MIDDLE EAST

13:143 Barton, James L. *Story of Near East Relief (1915–1930).* New York: Macmillan, 1930. Barton chaired the private Near East Relief Committee, and not surprisingly lauds its efforts and achievements in this book. He also, however, provides a wealth of detail that any scholar of the topic will find useful. Appendices include the charter and listings of personnel.

13:144 DeNovo, John A. *American Interests and Policies in the Middle East, 1900–1939.* Minneapolis: University of Minnesota Press, 1963. This remains the classic treatment of U.S.–Middle East relations during the interwar era, covering a wide range of problems in U.S.-Turkish negotiations, the quest for oil in Iraq, Saudi Arabia, Persia, and Bahrain, the rights of Americans in the mandates, trade expansion, and the problems of philanthropists and missionaries. Bibliography.

13:145 Grabill, Joseph L. *Protestant Diplomacy and the Near East: Missionary Influence on American Policy, 1810–1927.* While Grabill introduces the missionary lobby in early U.S.–Middle Eastern relations, his major focus is on its influence in the Wilson era. He is sympathetic to missionaries' goals and provides insight into their motives. Helpful bibliography (9:295).

13:146 Kark, Ruth. *American Consuls in the Holy Land, 1832–1914.* Kark's study is useful both for understanding the history of the professionalization of

the U.S. consular service through the early twentieth century and its treatment of U.S.–Middle East relations, especially regarding Palestine, in the nineteenth and early twentieth centuries. Its detail is sometimes overwhelming. Bibliography (9:296).

13:147 Nash, Gerald D. *United States Oil Policy, 1890–1964: Business and Government in Twentieth Century America.* Pittsburgh: University of Pittsburgh Press, 1968. Reprint 1976 (Greenwood Press). This study focuses on the relationship between the U.S. government and oil interests, and on the latter's quest for Middle East oil concessions. Nash asserts that from the Wilson era forward, the government supported Americans in Iraq, Bahrain, and Saudi Arabia. Bibliography.

13:148 Penrose, Stephen Beasley Linnard. *That They May Have Life: The Story of the American University of Beirut, 1866–1941.* Beirut: American University of Beirut, 1941. This narrative history focuses on the development of this important institution while also exploring its role in the changing politics and society of the Middle East.

13:149 Sabki, Hisham. "Woodrow Wilson and Self-Determination in the Arab Middle East." *Journal of Social and Political Studies* 4 (Winter 1979): 381–99. Sabki demonstrates how secret agreements among the Allies and power politics doomed Wilson's stated policy of self-determination for inhabitants of the Ottoman empire.

13:150 Sachar, Howard M. *The Emergence of the Middle East: 1914–1924.* New York: Alfred A. Knopf, 1969. This examination of the complex negotiations between the European powers that led to the partition of the Ottoman empire treats the postwar negotiations in the region at the time that Wilson was trying to impose his principles upon a Middle Eastern settlement at Versailles. His failure led to the Lausanne settlement. Bibliography.

Armenia

13:151 Blacher, Michael. "From the Tip of the Tongue to the Back of the Mind: The United States and the Armenian Question, 1917–1920." *Armenian Review* 44 (Autumn 1991): 1–21. Blacher explores why, since there was so much governmental and public support for Armenia during World War I, the United States failed to accept the mandate for Armenia afterward.

13:152 Bryson, Thomas A. "Mark Lambert Bristol, U.S. Navy, Admiral-Diplomat: His Influence on the Armenian Mandate Question." *Armenian Review* 21 (Winter 1968): 3–22. Bryson argues that Bristol, in his position as U.S. high commissioner to Turkey, used his influence to help defeat the proposed U.S. mandate for Armenia largely because he believed Britain had proposed the U.S. mandate to serve its own imperial and economic purposes in the region.

13:153 _____. "Woodrow Wilson and the Armenian Mandate: A Reassessment." *Armenian Review* 21 (Autumn 1968): 10–29. This essay appraises Wilson's handling of the Armenian question during and after the Paris Peace Conference and examines some conflicting historical interpretations.

13:154 Gidney, James B. *A Mandate for Armenia.* Kent, OH: Kent State University Press, 1967. This is a good one-volume treatment of the American involvement in the Armenian question from 1915 to 1927. It gives broad analytical treatment to American policy on the Armenian mandate question at the Paris Peace Conference and to the Senate's consideration of the matter in 1919–1920. Bibliography.

13:155 Grabill, Joseph L. "Missionary Influence on American Relations with the Near East, 1914–1923, Parts 1 and 2." *Muslim World* 58 (January, April 1968): 43–56, 141–54. Grabill argues that U.S. missionaries both indirectly encouraged Armenian nationalism and publicized the plight of Armenians, leading to sympathy for them in the United States. Despite missionary efforts to promote a U.S. mandate for Armenia after World War I, this proposal did not succeed. The lasting influence of U.S. missionaries in Turkey lies in the field of philanthropy.

13:156 Hovannisian, Richard G. *Armenia on the Road to Independence, 1918.* Berkeley: University of California Press, 1967. In this study, Hovannisian, author of a four-volume history of Armenian independence (*The Republic of Armenia* [Berkeley: University of California Press, 1971–1996]), analyzes the rise of the Armenian Republic, which played a

role in American-Turkish relations during and after the Paris Peace Conference. Bibliography.

13:157 Kazemzadeh, Firuz. *The Struggle for Transcaucasia, 1917–1921.* New York: Philosophical Library, 1951. Reprint 1981 (Hyperion Press). The writer discusses in detail the situation in the Transcaucasus during and after World War I. He describes the events that gave rise to the Armenian Republic and the Turkish and Russian reaction thereto. Bibliography.

Turkey

13:158 Bryson, Thomas A. "Admiral Mark Lambert Bristol: An Open Door Diplomat in Turkey." *International Journal of Middle East Studies* 5 (September 1974): 450–67. Bryson argues that Bristol worked to maintain an open door for U.S. trade and investment but not for the purpose of promoting U.S. economic expansion. Rather, he did so to reduce European economic power and provide fair opportunities for U.S. businesses.

13:159 Cohen, Naomi W. "Ambassador Straus in Turkey, 1909–1910: A Note on Dollar Diplomacy." *Mississippi Valley Historical Review* 45 (March 1959): 632–42. Oscar Straus did not conform to the pattern of other "dollar" diplomats. Viewing dollar diplomacy as a ploy that would involve the United States in the web of European intrigue in Turkey, he earned the displeasure of Secretary of State Knox, who recommended that he not be retained in the diplomatic service.

13:160 Evans, Laurence. *United States Policy and the Partition of Turkey, 1914–1924.* Baltimore: Johns Hopkins Press, 1965. Evans considers the multiplicity of problems associated with U.S.-Turkish relations, including questions related to Armenians, Palestinians, and American neutral rights. His work also traces the development of U.S. policy vis-à-vis Turkey at the Paris Peace Conference.

13:161 Helmreich, Paul C. *From Paris to Sèvres: The Partition of the Ottoman Empire at the Peace Conference of 1919–1920.* Columbus: Ohio State University Press, 1974. This comprehensive account examines the protracted negotiations leading to the partition of the Ottoman empire and the American efforts for a settlement that would accommodate the conflicting imperial aspirations of the powers and nationalistic aspirations of the subject peoples of the old Ottoman empire. Bibliography.

13:162   Howard, Harry N. *The Partition of Turkey: A Diplomatic History, 1913–1923.* Norman: University of Oklahoma Press, 1931. Howard's study usefully places the partition of Turkey in the broader context of developments in European history, providing helpful background to developments in U.S. policy during World War I and at Versailles. Bibliography.

13:163   Patrick, Mary Mills. *A Bosporus Adventure: Istanbul (Constantinople) Woman's College, 1871–1924.* Stanford, CA: Stanford University Press, 1934. Patrick discusses the growth and development of an important American educational institution in the Middle East in the context of the last years of the Ottoman empire and early years of the new state, Turkey.

13:164   _____. *Under Five Sultans.* New York: Century Co., 1929. This autobiographical account of fifty years of work with the Constantinople Woman's College provides the reader with numerous details relating to diplomatic efforts on behalf of an American educational institution, and is a lively companion to her more formal history of the college.

Palestine Question

13:165   Brecher, Frank W. "Woodrow Wilson and the Origins of the Arab-Israeli Conflict." *American Jewish Archives* 39 (April 1987): 23–47. Wilson failed to resolve these conflicts in his foreign policy, wanting both to support a Jewish homeland in Palestine, as stated in the Balfour Declaration, and encourage Arab self-determination, as U.S. missionaries in the region advocated.

13:166   Howard, Harry N. *The King-Crane Commission: An American Inquiry in the Middle East.* Beirut: Khayat, 1963. This study describes the investigation conducted in 1919 by the American section of the Inter-Allied Commission on the Middle East authorized by the peace conference. The report, officially published only in 1947, opposed establishment of a Zionist state in Palestine, warned against French control in Syria, favored a British mandate for Mesopotamia and Palestine, and proposed an American mandate for Armenia and the internationalizing of Constantinople. Bibliography.

13:167   Knee, Stuart E. "The King-Crane Commission of 1919: The Articulation of Political Anti-Zionism." *American Jewish Archives* 29 (April 1977): 22–52. Knee finds that members of the King-Crane Commission were more sympathetic to the goals of U.S. missionaries, which were to support Arab self-determination, than to Zionists' goals. This sympathy shaped their final report but did not, the author argues, reflect the views of Muslims in the region.

13:168   Lebow, Richard Ned. "Woodrow Wilson and the Balfour Declaration." *Journal of Modern History* 40 (December 1968): 500–23. Lebow argues that President Wilson delayed endorsement of the Balfour Declaration to avoid arousing Turkish antipathy toward American missionary interests.

13:169   Manuel, Frank E. *The Realities of American-Palestine Relations.* Washington, DC: Public Affairs Press, 1949. Although setting U.S. policy toward Palestine within a broader chronological sweep, Manuel primarily explores U.S. official reaction to the Jewish question during World War I, treats Zionist influence on Woodrow Wilson after the war, and shows that U.S. officials considered the Palestine question to be a British problem during the interwar years. Bibliography.

13:170   Stein, Leonard. *The Balfour Declaration.* New York: Simon and Schuster, 1961. Although primarily a study of European politics and the Balfour Declaration, several chapters address American involvement, particularly the Wilson administration's ultimate decision to support the declaration. Bibliography.

Persia

13:171   McDaniel, Robert A. *The Shuster Mission and the Persian Constitutional Revolution.* Minneapolis: Biblioteca Islamica, 1974. William Morgan Shuster was head of the first U.S. advisory mission to

Persia. Reviewing Persia's internal politics, Mc-Daniel finds that its politicians opposed the Shuster mission, which, coupled with Russian resistance, led to its ultimate termination. He is critical of Shuster's inability to maintain adequate communication with British and Russian diplomats. Bibliography.

13:172   Shuster, W. Morgan. *The Strangling of Persia: Story of the European Diplomacy and Oriental Intrigue That Resulted in the Denationalization of Twelve Million Mohammedans: A Personal Narrative.* Washington, DC: Mage Publishers, 1987. In a book first published in 1912, the leader of a U.S. financial mission to Persia sets forth the obstacles confronting his efforts to reform Persian finances. He concludes that political intrigue and the machinations of Britain and Russia prevented the completion of his objectives.

13:173   Yeselson, Abraham. *United States–Persian Diplomatic Relations, 1883–1921.* New Brunswick: Rutgers University Press, 1956. This overview based on U.S. sources emphasizes how early American interests in Persia centered on missionaries, although some nineteenth-century diplomats also sought to expand commercial connections. Washington had little interest in Persia and was reluctant to entangle itself in the Anglo-Russian power struggle. After World War I, the United States prevented ratification of the Anglo-Persian treaty that would have made Persia a client state of Britain. Bibliography.

Others

13:174   Hitti, Philip K. *The Syrians in America.* New York: George H. Doran Company, 1924. Hitti provides a detailed narrative study of why Syrians decided to come to the United States, their economic, political, and religious choices once arrived, and the course of their assimilation.

13:175   Wright, Lenoir Chambers. *United States Policy toward Egypt, 1831–1914.* This is the only extended treatment of American-Egyptian relations in the nineteenth and early twentieth centuries. It covers diplomatic, commercial, and cultural ties, and devotes considerable space to the American impact on Egypt during and after the Civil War. Part I covers 1830–1882; part II covers 1882–1914. Bibliography (6:282).

ASIA

East Asia

13:176   Dietrich, Ethel B. *Far Eastern Trade of the United States.* New York: International Secretariat, Institute of Pacific Relations, 1940. Based largely on publications from the U.S. Department of Commerce, Dietrich provides a useful summary as well as charts and statistics for U.S. trade with Asia from 1900, though with emphasis on 1919–1940. Japan, China, the Philippines, Malaysia, and Indonesia receive extended treatment.

13:177   Fifield, Russell H. *Woodrow Wilson and the Far East: The Diplomacy of the Shantung Question.* New York: Crowell, 1952. Fifield argues that Wilson supported the Chinese position on Shantung at the Paris Peace Conference for both idealistic and strategic reasons but in the end gave in to guarantee Japanese membership in the League. Bibliography.

13:178   Gallicchio, Marc S. *The African American Encounter with Japan and China: Black Internationalism in Asia, 1895–1945.* Chapel Hill: University of North Carolina Press, 2000. Scholars are paying increased attention to the important role played by African-Americans in U.S. foreign relations and to various groups' conceptions of U.S. foreign responsibilities. Gallicchio's work extends this trend in his attention to how African-Americans viewed U.S. relations toward non-African "nations of color," helping explain the variety of ways international and domestic racial politics were conceived before 1945. Bibliography.

13:179   Oehling, Richard A. "Hollywood and the Image of the Oriental, 1910–1950—Part I." *Film and History* 8 (May 1978): 33–41. Oehling argues that films reflected the general racism and concern about internal and external threats posed by Asians. He focuses on the years before World War II. Part I explores images of Japanese, and part II images of Chinese.

13:180   _____. "Hollywood and the Image of the Oriental, 1910–1950—Part II." *Film and History* 8 (September 1978): 59–67. See the reference to Part I, May 1978 (13:179).

13:181 Thomson, James C., Jr., Peter W. Stanley, and John Curtis Perry. *Sentimental Imperialists: The American Experience in East Asia.* This survey of U.S.–East Asian relations is the combined effort of a China expert, a Japan expert, and a Philippines expert, and so nicely demonstrates the complex interconnections in U.S. policy toward Asia's diverse peoples. Chapters 8–12 cover 1900–1920 (2:274).

13:182 Walker, William O., III. *Opium and Foreign Policy: The Anglo-American Search for Order in Asia, 1912–1954.* Chapel Hill: University of North Carolina Press, 1991. In this classic account, Walker makes two complementary arguments: opium control was a key issue of contention both between the British and Americans and between the two western powers and a revolutionary Asia, especially China. Bibliography.

China

13:183 Anschel, Eugene. *Homer Lea, Sun Yat-sen, and the Chinese Revolution.* New York: Praeger, 1984. This chatty biography of Sun Yat-sen's self-appointed American adviser sticks to narrative rather than analysis of the broader meaning of Lea's activities. Bibliography.

13:184 Buck, Peter. *American Science and Modern China, 1876–1936.* New York: Cambridge University Press, 1980. Buck's fascinating study explores how American missionaries and scientists, such as Rockefeller Foundation employees, attempted to introduce modern science to China. He also explores how Chinese students, especially those studying in the United States on Boxer indemnity scholarships, appropriated the "American science." Bibliography.

13:185 Campbell, Charles Soutter. *Special Business Interests and the Open Door Policy.* New Haven: Yale University Press, 1951. This brief study remains valuable for Campbell's careful attention to publications and organizations sponsored by American businesses interested in developing the China trade. It is focused on the formulation, not the implementation, of the open door policy.

13:186 Chong, Key Ray. *Americans and Chinese Reform and Revolution, 1898–1922: The Role of Pri-*

vate Citizens in Diplomacy. Lanham, MD: University Press of America, 1984. Chong's study sets Sun Yat-sen's efforts to get help for his reform movement in a broader context than Anschel, *Homer Lea, Sun Yat-sen, and the Chinese Revolution* (1984) (13:183), by discussing a wider group of both American and Chinese participants. Like Anschel, he is primarily concerned to report what happened, not why it happened. Bibliography.

13:187 Cochran, Sherman. *Big Business in China: Sino-Foreign Rivalry in the Cigarette Industry, 1890–1930.* Cambridge, MA: Harvard University Press, 1980. This study provides a detailed and welcome exploration of a neglected aspect of the China market by examining U.S. and British capital invested in China and its impact within China itself. Cochran also explores competition between Chinese and foreign companies and the latter's influence on local political and cultural developments.

13:188 Cohen, Warren I. *America's Response to China: A History of Sino-American Relations.* This is perhaps the best introduction to the full sweep of the history of U.S.-China relations. Chapters 2 and 3 cover the late nineteenth and early twentieth centuries. Bibliography (2:276). First published in 1971.

13:189 Crane, Daniel M., and Thomas A. Breslin. *An Ordinary Relationship: American Opposition to Republican Revolution in China.* Gainesville: University Presses of Florida, 1986. Through a close examination of U.S. policy during the Taft and Wilson administrations, the authors seek to undermine the notion that a "special relationship" ever existed between China and the United States, helping, they hope, to put U.S.-China relations on a "normal" and more stable basis. Bibliography.

13:190 Edwards, E. W. *British Diplomacy and Finance in China, 1895–1914.* New York: Oxford University Press, 1987. Although primarily focused on Britain's policy, and European and Japanese challenges to its aspirations, Edwards's study also provides useful context for the growing importance of U.S. activity in China after the turn of the century. Bibliography.

13:191 Fairbank, John K., ed. *The Missionary Enterprise in China and America.* Although often superseded by later scholarship, some of it their own, many of these essays remain useful. It is organized in three parts on Protestant Missions in American Expansion, which focuses on the experience of Americans; Christianity and the Transformation of China, concentrating on interactions between American missionaries and Chinese; and China Mission Images and American Policies, which explores the relationship between mission work and politics as traditionally understood. For details on the essays, see chapter 2 of this Guide (2:235).

13:192   Hu, Bin (Xinwei Zhang, trans.). "Contradictions and Conflicts among the Imperialist Powers in China at the Time of the Boxer Movement." *Chinese Studies in History* 20 (Spring-Summer 1987): 156–74. Hu demonstrates persuasively that sharp differences of interests and goals separated the foreign powers in China at the time of the Boxer Rebellion but not why they were able to unite anyway in suppressing the uprising.

13:193   Hunt, Michael H. *Frontier Defense and the Open Door: Manchuria in Chinese-American Relations, 1895–1911.* New Haven: Yale University Press, 1973. Hunt's study, based on Chinese and English-language sources, remains critical for a full understanding of the open door policy and Manchuria's important place in its execution. It is also a pleasure to read. Bibliography.

13:194   _____. *The Making of a Special Relationship: The United States and China to 1914.* The classic study of U.S.-China relations in the nineteenth and early twentieth centuries, it remains the best work to read first on this topic. Bibliography (2:279).

13:195   Hunter, Jane. *The Gospel of Gentility: American Women Missionaries in Turn-of-the-Century China.* Hunter is primarily interested in exploring the lives of Protestant women missionaries in China, but her study also addresses the important aspect of U.S.-Chinese relations carried out by missionaries. Bibliography (2:236).

13:196   Iriye, Akira. "Public Opinion and Foreign Policy: The Case of Late Chi'ing China." In *Approaches to Modern Chinese History,* ed. Albert Feuerwerker, Rhoads Murphey, and Mary C. Wright,

216–38. Berkeley: University of California Press, 1967. A significant part of this essay deals with the role of Chinese public opinion in the anti-American boycott of 1905. The author concludes that the boycott itself was far less important than the experience it gave the Chinese in asserting their right to influence policymaking.

13:197   Israel, Jerry. "'For God, China and for Yale'—The Open Door in Action." *American Historical Review* 75 (February 1970): 796–807. Israel's ability to show the interconnections among the goals and activities of U.S. businesspeople, missionaries, reformers, and diplomats in China demonstrates the far-reaching implications of the open door policy in the first decade of the twentieth century.

13:198   _____. *Progressivism and the Open Door: America and China, 1905–1921.* Pittsburgh: University of Pittsburgh Press, 1971. Israel's study is motivated by his desire to explain how progressivism in the United States shaped U.S.-China policy in the first two decades of the twentieth century. As the battle between proponents of laissez-faire and rationalized cooperation raged at home, U.S. foreign policy shifted as well. The open door policy reflected cultural as well as economic imperialism. Brief bibliography.

13:199   Latourette, Kenneth Scott. *A History of Christian Missions in China.* Although Latourette's learned survey covers the history of Christian missions in China from their first appearance, almost half the book is devoted to the period after 1890. It remains a useful source of information. Bibliography (7:448).

13:200   Li, Ting-I. *Zhongmei waijiao shi [The History of Sino-American Relations].* 4 vols. Taipei: Li xing shiju, 1960. Written by a Nationalist Chinese historian, this book stresses the friendship that characterized Sino-American relations from the beginning, a contrast to Maoist Chinese historians. This book is most valuable in its tracing of earliest Chinese awareness of America.

13:201   Lian, Xi. *The Conversion of Missionaries: Liberalism in American Protestant Missions in China, 1907–1932.* University Park: Penn State University Press, 1997. As a result of political and theological developments in the first three decades of the twentieth century, American missionaries in China became less certain of their superiority and correctness and more admiring of Chinese culture and religion. Based primarily on English-language sources but including some Chinese sources. Bibliography.

13:202 Lodwick, Kathleen L. *Crusaders against Opium: Protestant Missionaries in China, 1874–1917.* Lexington: University Press of Kentucky, 1996. Lodwick argues that American Protestant missionaries in China played an important role in initiating and sustaining the antiopium movement in its early years. Bibliography.

13:203 Matsuo, Kazuyuki. "American Propaganda in China: The U.S. Committee on Public Information, 1918–1919." *Journal of American and Canadian Studies* 14 (1996): 19–42. Based primarily on U.S. sources, this study demonstrates that Creel Committee efforts to "sell America" were not limited to Europe and the United States but extended to China as well. Bibliography.

13:204 May, Ernest R., and John K. Fairbank, eds. *America's China Trade in Historical Perspective: The Chinese and American Performance.* Cambridge, MA: Committee on American–East Asian Relations of the Dept. of History and the Council on East Asian Studies, Harvard University, 1986. Some of the premier historians of China have contributed to this important volume. Lillian Li wrote on silk ("The Silk Export Trade and Economic Modernization in China and Japan," 77–99); Kang Chao on cotton ("The Chinese-American Cotton-Textile Trade 1830–1930," 103–27); Bruce L. Reynolds on textiles ("The East Asian 'Textile Cluster' Trade 1868–1973," 129–50); Sherman Cochran on cigarettes ("Commercial Penetration and Economic Imperialism in China: An American Cigarette Company's Entrance into the Market," 151–203); Chu-Yuan Cheng on petroleum ("The United States Petroleum Trade with China, 1876–1949," 205–33); and both Peter Schran ("The Minor Significance of Commercial Relations between the United States and China, 1850–1931," 237–58) and Mira Wilkins ("The Impacts of American Multinational Enterprise on American-Chinese Economic Relations, 1786–1949," 259–92) on general trade and investments. Notes and bibliography are at the end of the book.

13:205 McCormick, Thomas J. *China Market: America's Quest for Informal Empire, 1893–1901.* One of the classic works on the open door policy, this work explores how the McKinley administration's commitment to marketplace expansionism reinforced a more activist foreign policy at the turn of the century. It is essential for students of U.S.-China policy (9:548).

13:206 McKee, Delber L. *Chinese Exclusion versus the Open Door Policy, 1900–1906: Clashes over China Policy in the Roosevelt Era.* Detroit: Wayne State University Press, 1977. McKee notes that the two China policies, open door and exclusion, seemed to work at cross-purposes. Bibliography.

13:207 Noble, Dennis L. *The Eagle and the Dragon: The United States Military in China, 1901–1937.* New York: Greenwood Press, 1990. Noble provides an in-depth, welcome study of a neglected topic, but he focuses almost exclusively on the experiences of U.S. military men serving in China rather than considering the broader context of either Chinese or U.S. history. Bibliography.

13:208 Rabe, Valentin H. *The Home Base of American China Missions, 1880–1920.* Cambridge, MA: Council on East Asian Studies, Harvard University, 1978. Although focused on the growth of home base boards, interdenominational societies, and the businesslike methods adopted to run them efficiently, this study is invaluable for understanding changes in how mission work was conceived during the late nineteenth and early twentieth centuries. Bibliography.

13:209 Reed, James. *The Missionary Mind and American East Asia Policy, 1911–1915.* Cambridge, MA: Council on East Asian Studies, Harvard University, 1983. Reed argues that U.S. policy and business relations with China in 1911–1915 were shaped by the "missionary mind," an attitude adopted from Protestant missionaries' paternalistic, emotional sense of responsibility for the Chinese people. As a study of American attitudes, it remains useful. Bibliography.

13:210 Reins, Thomas D. "Reform, Nationalism, and Internationalism: The Opium Suppression Movement in China and the Anglo-American Influence, 1900–1908." *Modern Asian Studies* 25 (February

1991): 101–42. The bulk of this article details the measures taken by the Chinese government to curb opium trade and consumption but also places the story within an international context, emphasizing both pressure on and support for China from Britain and the United States. Based on British, U.S., and Chinese sources.

13:211   Reinsch, Paul S. *An American Diplomat in China.* Garden City, NY: Doubleday, Page and Company, 1922. Reinsch was U.S. minister in China in the eventful 1913–1919 period. His memoir reflects his love of the country and people as well as his belief that the Chinese viewed the United States as a model for their republic.

13:212   Schmidt, Hans. "Democracy for China: American Propaganda and the May Fourth Movement." *Diplomatic History* 22 (Winter 1998): 1–28. Schmidt argues that the very success of U.S. propaganda efforts in China, especially compared to those of Europeans, helped contribute to the anti-foreign sentiment expressed by students in the May Fourth Movement, who were disappointed when Americans' actions did not live up to their rhetoric.

13:213   Scully, Eileen P. *Bargaining with the State from Afar: American Citizenship in Treaty Port China, 1844–1942.* New York: Columbia University Press, 2001. Scully explores the anomalous institution, the U.S. District Court for China, and its role both in relations between overseas Americans and the U.S. government and between the United States and China. The result is a complex, nuanced picture of the meanings and consequences of extraterritoriality in China. Based on U.S. and Chinese sources. Bibliography.

13:214   _____. "Taking the Low Road to Sino-American Relations: 'Open Door' Expansionists and the Two China Markets." *Journal of American History* 82 (June 1995): 62–83. Scully urges historians to explore both China markets, the one in legitimate trade goods, the other in illegal activities, particularly prostitution. The perceived need to control the latter market to promote the former led to establishment of a U.S. court for China.

13:215   Stross, Randall E. *The Stubborn Earth: American Agriculturalists on Chinese Soil, 1898–*

1937. Berkeley: University of California Press, 1986. Stross, using biographies of Americans who lived in China, finds that most of them believed application of technology alone could solve China's agricultural problems, ignored the impact of political upheaval, and were usually frustrated by their meager accomplishments. Bibliography.

13:216   Tsai, Shih-shan Henry. *China and the Overseas Chinese in the United States, 1868–1911.* Struggles over Chinese immigration to the United States played a key role in determining the nature of U.S.-Chinese relations generally, and helped prompt the growth of Chinese nationalism. Tsai relies on both U.S. and Chinese sources (9:555).

13:217   Uhalley, Stephen, Jr. "The Wai-wu-pu, the Chinese Foreign Office from 1901 to 1911." *Journal of the China Society* 5 (1967): 9–27. Uhalley provides a detailed narrative of the origin and structure of the Chinese Foreign Office. Despite its reputation for reactionary anti-foreign sentiment, he believes it had many informed, capable ministers but was plagued by lack of information and direction.

13:218   Wang, Qingjia Edward. "Guests from the Open Door: The Reception of Chinese Students into the United States, 1900s-1920s." *Journal of American–East Asian Relations* 3 (Spring 1994): 55–75. Wang argues effectively that although both Chinese and U.S. officials wanted to increase the number of Chinese students in the United States, their motivations were often conflicting. He also explores how American racism affected the experience of the Chinese students.

13:219   Wong, K. Scott. "The Transformation of Culture: Three Chinese Views of America." *American Quarterly* 48 (June 1996): 201–32. Wong elucidates his argument that Asian-American studies have suffered from neglect of Asian-Americans' ties to Asia by exploring Chinese understandings of George Washington, the travel diary of Liang Qichao's 1903 trip to the United States, and the memoirs of Yung Wing.

13:220   Young, Marilyn B. *The Rhetoric of Empire: American China Policy, 1895–1901.* Cambridge, MA: Harvard University Press, 1968. Young reminds us that fear, stemming from the 1893 Depression, reinforced America's newfound sense of power following the war with Spain and was a strong motivator of China policy at the turn of the century. Careful attention to the broad context of both the anxiety and the optimism behind U.S. China policy makes this a study of continuing critical interest. Bibliography.

Japan

13:221   Bailey, Thomas A. "The Lodge Corollary to the Monroe Doctrine." *Political Science Quarterly* 48 (June 1933): 220–39. Responding in 1912 to rumors that Japan was interested in Magdalena Bay in Baja California, the Senate passed the Lodge Resolution to express its concern about foreign control (governmental or private) of harbors critical to U.S. security. Bailey argues that there was no serious Japanese threat at the time, and that the Lodge Corollary was meant to be an addition to the Monroe Doctrine.

13:222   Beers, Burton F. *Vain Endeavor: Robert Lansing's Attempts to End the American-Japanese Rivalry.* Durham, NC: Duke University Press, 1962. Beers argues that some of the apparent contradictions and changes of course in Wilson's policy toward Asia can be explained by attention to Lansing's role in policy formulation, since Lansing had independent views, and the ability to influence policy. Bibliography.

13:223   Daniels, Roger. *The Politics of Prejudice: The Anti-Japanese Movement in California and the Struggle for Japanese Exclusion.* 2d ed. Berkeley: University of California Press, 1977. Daniels demonstrates the connections between anti-Japanese racism, political movements to exclude Japanese immigrants from California and the United States, and U.S. relations with an increasingly powerful Japan, although he focuses on the first two. Originally published in 1962. Bibliography.

13:224   Davidann, Jon Thares. *A World of Crisis and Progress: The American YMCA in Japan, 1890–1930.* Davidann's study, based on English- and Japanese-language sources, explores the interaction between American missionaries and Japanese Protestants, using their conflicts, compromises, and theological disputes to provide a more complex understanding of how cultural imperialism functioned in Japan in the early twentieth century. Bibliography (9:559).

13:225   Esthus, Raymond A. *Double Eagle and Rising Sun: The Russians and Japanese at Portsmouth in 1905.* Although focused primarily on Russian and Japanese personalities and their role at the peace conference, Esthus also explores the influence and activities of U.S. participants. Bibliography (11:380).

13:226   _____. *Theodore Roosevelt and Japan.* Esthus argues that despite the cordial nature of U.S.-Japanese relations during the Roosevelt administration, the interests of the two nations clashed more and more often. Bibliography (11:382).

13:227   Harris, Neil. "All the World a Melting Pot? Japan at American Fairs, 1874–1904." In *Mutual Images: Essays in American-Japanese Relations,* ed. Akira Iriye, 24–54. Cambridge, MA: Harvard University Press, 1975. Harris argues that the fair provided an important source of information about modern and traditional Japan to many interested and admiring visitors, but also that many American visitors were disappointed when the Japanese exhibits proved less exotic than they had hoped.

13:228   Hellwig, David J. "Afro-American Reactions to the Japanese and the Anti-Japanese Movement, 1906–1924." *Phylon* 38 (March 1977): 93–104. African-Americans did not welcome Japanese immigrants or perceive benefits in joining them in political organization but did believe that anti-Japanese policies and racism promoted a general atmosphere of racism hurtful to themselves as well.

13:229   Iriye, Akira. "Japan as a Competitor, 1895–1917." In *Mutual Images: Essays in American-Japanese Relations,* ed. Akira Iriye, 73–99. Cambridge, MA: Harvard University Press, 1975. Iriye's use of the term "competitor" provides a useful framework for connecting the various and often conflicting images that Americans had of Japan during the years 1895–1917. He especially stresses American fears of Japan's growing power.

13:230   _____. *Pacific Estrangement: Japanese and American Expansion, 1897–1911.* Cambridge, MA: Harvard University Press, 1972. Based on a wide range of materials—cultural, intellectual, diplomatic, and economic—this study examines the confrontation and interaction of American and Japanese expansionist ideas and policies. Close readings of works by contemporary Japanese politicians and intellectuals are particularly useful for American scholars. Bibliography.

13:231   Kaikoku, Hyakunen Kinen Bunka Jigyokai, ed. *Nichi-Bei Bunka Kosho Shi [History of Japanese-American Cultural Relations]*. 6 vols. Tokyo: Yoyosha, 1954–1956. In this series, volume 1 covers Japanese-American diplomatic relations; volume 2 covers Japan's trade and industry; volume 3 (by Kishimoto Hideo) covers religion and education; volume 4 covers literature, manners, and customs; volume 5 (by Nagai Matsuzo) covers immigration to the United States; and volume 6 is an index. Volumes 1, 2, and 4 have been translated into English and are also listed separately.

13:232   Kimura, Ki. *Japanese Literature: Manners and Customs in the Meiji-Taishō Era*. Translated by Philip Yampolsky. Tokyo: Obunsha, 1957. This is an informative, digressive, and rather subjective account of American-Japanese literary relations (1868–1926). It is one of the volumes of the *Nichi-Bei Bunka Kosho Shi [History of Japanese-American Cultural Relations]* (13:231).

13:233   Mehnert, Ute. "German *Weltpolitik* and the American Two-Front Dilemma: The 'Japanese Peril' in German-American Relations, 1904–1917." *Journal of American History* 82 (March 1996): 1452–77. Mehnert's interesting study demonstrates how German policymakers hoped to exploit U.S. fear of a Japanese "yellow peril" in the Pacific to undermine the growing strength of Anglo-American rapprochement in the Atlantic.

13:234   Miller, Edward S. *War Plan Orange: The U.S. Strategy to Defeat Japan, 1897–1945*. Annapolis: Naval Institute Press, 1991. Miller argues that the common perception of War Plan Orange as a failure does not take into account that its authors did not intend to defend the Philippines, but rather devised an offensive strategy to defeat Japan.

13:235   Neu, Charles E. *An Uncertain Friendship: Theodore Roosevelt and Japan, 1906–1909*. Cambridge, MA: Harvard University Press, 1967. This is a detailed study of the Japanese immigration issue and discrimination against the Japanese. It is particu-

larly strong on the relationship between the troubles with Japan and the development of Roosevelt's naval policy. Bibliography.

13:236   Nish, Ian. *Alliance in Decline: A Study in Anglo-Japanese Relations, 1908–23*. London: Athlone Press, 1972. In contrast to the argument of his earlier book covering the alliance to 1907 (*The Anglo-Japanese Alliance: The Diplomacy of Two Island Empires, 1894–1907*, 2d ed. [Dover, NH: Athlone Press, 1985]), Nish sees the later period as greatly shaped by the increasingly global interests of the United States and expanding interests of Japan.

13:237   _____. *Japanese Foreign Policy, 1869–1942: Kasumigaseki to Miyakezaka*. Nish's overview of Japanese foreign relations centers on the views, policies, and actions of twelve foreign ministers. Although the United States is rarely the focus of any particular chapter, this approach to the study of Japanese foreign relations provides useful insight. Bibliography (2:287).

13:238   Ohara, Keiji, ed. *Japanese Trade and Industry in the Meiji-Taisho Era*. Tokyo: Obunsha, 1957. Despite the general title, this volume deals only with U.S.-Japanese relations (1853–1926). It is volume 2 of *Nichi-Bei Bunka Kosho Shi [History of Japanese-American Cultural Relations]* (13:231), which covers financial relations, the introduction of American industrial and agricultural technology, and trade in tea, silk, and cotton goods. It includes a wealth of details, especially about particular industries, not easily found elsewhere. Translated and adapted by Okato Tamotsu.

13:239   Okamoto, Shumpei. *The Japanese Oligarchy and the Russo-Japanese War*. New York: Columbia University Press, 1970. Okamoto's careful, extensive study, based on both English- and Japanese-language sources, provides a valuable exploration of Japanese policymaking during these crucial years. Extensive quotations from Japanese sources are included. Bibliography.

13:240   Okihiro, Gary Y. *Cane Fires: The Anti-Japanese Movement in Hawaii, 1865–1945*. Okihiro's study argues that anti-Japanese sentiment built up during the late nineteenth and early twentieth centuries on Hawaii, as on the mainland, contrary to the generally held view that Hawaii was a bastion of tolerance (9:470).

13:241 Roden, Donald. "Baseball and the Quest for National Dignity in Meiji Japan." Roden argues that its embrace of baseball helped counter western images of Japan as a weak and effeminate nation (9:568).

13:242 Sacki, Shoichi. "Images of the United States as a Hypothetical Enemy." In *Mutual Images: Essays in American-Japanese Relations,* ed. Akira Iriye, 100–14. Cambridge, MA: Harvard University Press, 1975. Sacki provides a tantalizingly brief discussion of pre-1933 Japanese "war-scare books," which predicted a coming war between the United States and Japan.

13:243 Sawada, Mitziko. "Culprits and Gentlemen: Meiji Japan's Restrictions of Emigrants to the United States, 1891–1909." The Japanese government took extensive steps to control the types of Japanese emigrating to the United States, hoping to promote a positive image of its country and people and to counter American newspaper stories about Asian contract laborers and prostitutes entering the United States (9:570).

13:244 Scheiner, Irwin. *Christian Converts and Social Protest in Meiji Japan.* Berkeley: University of California Press, 1970. Scheiner recounts how young samurai (1868–1912) who were alienated by the Meiji restoration accepted Christianity, choosing a new value system and legitimizing the choice by finding in it parallels with the Confucian world order. The majority of missionaries, especially early, important ones, were American Protestants. Bibliography.

13:245 Schwantes, Robert S. *Japanese and Americans: A Century of Cultural Relations.* New York: Harper for the Council on Foreign Relations, 1955. Reprint 1976 (Greenwood Press). Produced as part of the Council on Foreign Relations study group on U.S.-Japanese relations, this work is primarily aimed at providing historical context for issues in U.S.-Japanese relations of the 1950s. It remains, however, an informed and often interesting exploration of cultural relations. Extensive bibliography of English- and Japanese-language sources. For a far more recent work that mostly concerns the late nineteenth cen-

tury, see Henning, *Outposts of Civilization: Race, Religion, and the Formative Years of American-Japanese Relations* (2000) (9:563).

13:246 Storry, Richard. *Japan and the Decline of the West in Asia, 1894–1943.* New York: St. Martin's Press, 1979. Storry, a well-known historian of Japan, characterizes its foreign policy during these years as reflecting a combination of confidence and fear. His study is especially useful for understanding the perception of Japanese diplomats observing U.S. and European activities.

Korea

13:247 Chay, Jongsuk. *Diplomacy of Asymmetry: Korean-American Relations to 1910.* Chay's narrative history provides a balanced, updated complement to Fred Harvey Harrington's classic *God, Mammon and the Japanese: Dr. Horace N. Allen and Korean-American Relations, 1884–1905* (1944) (13:248). He spends as much time on Korean as on U.S. actions, policies, and motivations (9:575).

13:248 Harrington, Fred H. *God, Mammon and the Japanese: Dr. Horace N. Allen and Korean-American Relations, 1884–1905.* This book centers on Horace N. Allen, an important figure in early U.S.-Korean relations, and remains a comprehensive and readable work on this relationship before World War I. It provides a balanced account of the diplomatic, commercial, and missionary relationships between the two nations. Extensive bibliography (9:579).

13:249 LaFeber, Walter. "Betrayal in Tokyo." *Constitution* 6 (Fall 1994): 4–11. LaFeber demonstrates that Taft made a secret agreement with Japan, nodding at its control over Korea. The historical importance of this event stems both from Korea's "betrayal" and Theodore Roosevelt's decision to make agreements with foreign powers without consulting the Senate.

13:250 Lee, Yur-Bok, and Wayne Patterson, eds. *One Hundred Years of Korean-American Relations, 1882–1982.* Three of the essays in this book are of interest to scholars of U.S.-Korean relations in the late nineteenth and early twentieth centuries. Yur-Bok Lee argues that Koreans consistently misunderstood U.S. policy statements on Korea. Fred Harvey Harrington demonstrates that Korean misunderstandings probably originated in U.S. duplicity, both intentional and unintentional. Wi Jo Kong shows that U.S. missionaries often favored Korean independence but had little political influence. Notes and bibliography are at the end of the book. See chapter 2 of this Guide for chapter titles and page numbers (2:291).

13:251 Patterson, Wayne. *The Korean Frontier in America: Immigration to Hawaii, 1896–1910.* Honolulu: University of Hawaii Press, 1988. Using Korean and American sources, Patterson places Korean immigration to Hawaii in the context of Korea's internal politics and diplomatic relations among the United States, Korea, and Japan. Bibliography.

13:252 Wiltz, John E. (John Edward Wilz). "Did the United States Betray Korea in 1905?" *Pacific Historical Review* 54 (August 1985): 243–70. A close reading of the U.S. diplomatic record shows that Washington had an obligation to assist Korea in resisting Japan in 1905 but failed to fulfill it in part to pursue its own interests and in part out of a belief that weak nations should not be propped up.

Pacific

13:253 Farrell, Don A. "The Partition of the Marianas: A Diplomatic History, 1898–1919." *Isla: A Journal of Micronesian Studies* 2 (Dry Season 1994): 273–301. Farrell is primarily interested in why the United States acquired only Guam, rather than all of the Marianas, after the Spanish-American War, and how the separation was maintained after both World War I and World War II.

13:254 Spennemann, Dirk H. R. "The United States Annexation of Wake Atoll, Central Pacific Ocean." *Journal of Pacific History* 33 (September 1998): 239–47. Spennemann clarifies the confusing history of U.S. attempts to annex Wake Atoll in the aftermath of the Spanish-American War and of the contested claims to sovereignty of the island.

South Asia

13:255 Bose, Arun Coomer. "Indian Nationalist Agitators in the U.S.A. and Canada till the Arrival of

Har Dayal in 1911." *Journal of Indian History* 43 (April 1965): 227–39. Bose provides a detailed narrative history of the founding years of the pro-India movement in the United States, especially the Society for the Advancement of India.

13:256 Dignan, Don K. "The Hindu Conspiracy in Anglo-American Relations during World War I." *Pacific Historical Review* 40 (February 1971): 57–76. Dignan argues that the British were extremely worried about the Indian revolutionary movement, and worked hard to convince U.S. officials to view it with the same concern. The 1917 trial in San Francisco of the "Hindu conspiracy" demonstrates British success.

13:257 Ejaz, Ahmad. "United States-Indo-Pakistan Subcontinent Relations: Historical Perspective 1800 to 1947." *Journal of the Research Society of Pakistan* 28 (July 1991): 61–76. Based on both U.S. and Indian sources, Ejaz provides an overview of educational, economic, and political contacts between India and the United States from 1800 to 1947.

13:258 Jensen, Joan M. "The 'Hindu Conspiracy': A Reassessment." *Pacific Historical Review* 48 (February 1979): 65–83. Jensen explores how the increasing convergence of U.S. and British interests in Europe in World War I made it easier for the United States to prosecute Indian revolutionaries in the United States.

13:259 Manchanda, Mohinder K. *India and America: Historical Links, 1776–1920.* Chandrigarh: Young Men Harmilap Association, 1976. This short, narrative history of Indo-America covers the late eighteenth through early twentieth centuries but mostly treats the last decade of the nineteenth and the first two decades of the twentieth century. The author emphasizes the nature of Indian migration to the United States, exclusion of Indian immigrants, anticolonial activities by Indians in the United States, and Indian views of Woodrow Wilson.

13:260 Mathur, L. P. *Indian Revolutionary Movement in the United States of America, by L. P. Mathur.* Delhi: S. Chand, 1970. This detailed narrative of the organization of Indian Nationalists living in the United States, primarily the Ghadar Party, argues that U.S. officials monitored but mostly did not disturb the group. Bibliography.

Southeast Asia

13:261 Foster, Anne L. "Prohibition as Superiority: Policing Opium in South-East Asia, 1898–1925." *International History Review* 22 (June 2000): 253–73. Foster explores the growing regime of opium prohibition during the early twentieth century and argues that U.S. insistence on prohibition rather than greater regulation, as preferred by European colonial officials, complicated everyone's efforts to suppress smuggling.

13:262 Fox, Thomas Darryl. "Diplomacy, Revolution, and Power: The United States, Great Britain, and the Destabilization of Southeast Asia, 1873–1948." Ph.D. dissertation, Ohio State University, 1994. This study is one of very few to consider U.S. foreign policy in Southeast Asia before 1945. Fox compares the effect of U.S. policy in the Philippines and British policy in Malaysia during the colonial and independence struggle periods. Bibliography.

13:263 McCoy, Alfred W. "Heroin as a Global Commodity: A History of Southeast Asia's Opium Trade." In *War on Drugs: Studies in the Failure of U.S. Narcotics Policy*, ed. Alfred W. McCoy and Alan A. Block, 237–79. Boulder: Westview Press, 1992. The United States entered the picture in the long history of the opium trade and attempted to control it when it acquired the Philippines. This overview begins to place post–World War II antinarcotics policies in a broader historical context.

13:264 Oblas, Peter. "Treaty Revision and the Role of the American Foreign Affairs Advisor, 1909–1925." *Journal of the Siam Society* 60 (January 1972): 171–86. This useful narrative of the Thai government's experience with Americans serving in the role of foreign affairs advisor shows that the Thais believed Americans would be more sympathetic to their interests than Europeans had been. Based on U.S. and Thai government sources.

Netherlands Indies

13:265 Gould, James W. *Americans in Sumatra*. Gould traces the development of American commercial, scientific, humanitarian, and political activities in Sumatra from the Atjeh War in 1873 to 1940. Of special interest is the discussion of the role of American

icans in the development of the oil and rubber industries. Bibliography (7:496).

13:266 Reed, Peter M. "Standard Oil in Indonesia, 1898–1928." *Business History Review* 32 (Autumn 1958): 311–37. Reed's principal focus is on the 1920s, when the Department of State vigorously supported Standard Oil in its efforts to expand its interests in the East Indies.

Philippines

13:267 Abelarde, Pedro E. *American Tariff Policy towards the Philippines, 1898–1946*. New York: King's Crown Press, 1947. Abelarde believes that because of its power to pass tariff legislation, the U.S. Congress was the most important institution influencing the development of the Philippines economy. This study sticks close to congressional sources. Bibliography.

13:268 Alvarez, David J. "Purely a Business Matter: The Taft Mission to the Vatican." One of the few studies to emphasize the diplomatic component to the friar land question in the colonial Philippines, this essay explores how Taft attempted to negotiate not only for sale of the lands but also departure of the friars. He did not succeed (11:349).

13:269 Anderson, Warwick. "Immunities of Empire: Race, Disease, and the New Tropical Medicine, 1900–1920." In the nineteenth century, colonial rulers tended to ascribe their poor health and the apparent good health of their subjects to a racial immunity to the diseases of a person's native land. Anderson demonstrates, using U.S. rule in the Philippines as his primary example, that more sophisticated understandings of the extent of disease among indigenous populations and the ways disease is spread did not end such racial assumptions. Rather, indigenous people were then believed to be uniquely dangerous transmitters of tropical disease (10:433).

13:270 Brands, H. W. *Bound to Empire: The United States and the Philippines*. Brands provides a highly readable introduction to the U.S.-Philippine relationship from the 1890s to the 1990s, with the first six chapters covering the years to 1920. More useful for narrative than analysis, this study is a good place to start (2:296).

13:271   Clymer, Kenton J. *Protestant Missionaries in the Philippines, 1898–1916: An Inquiry into the American Colonial Mentality.* Using Protestant American missionaries as a lens for examining the U.S. colonial project in the Philippines, Clymer has written an important, revealing account. Bibliography (10:457).

13:272   Giesecke, Leonard F. *History of American Economic Policy in the Philippines during the American Colonial Period, 1900–1935.* New York: Garland Publishers, 1987. This narrative study includes chapters on government involvement in business and tariff, monetary, land, and labor policy. Giesecke explores the nature of economic institutions established or influenced by U.S. policy.

13:273   Gleeck, Lewis E. *The American Half-Century, 1898–1946.* Manila: Historical Conservation Society, 1984. Gleeck, a prolific historian of U.S.-Philippines relations, provides a useful review that emphasizes narrative detail more than analysis. His attention to events within the Philippines is welcome. Appendices by R. John Pritchard, Thomas Carter, and Mercedes Sotelo de Carter.

13:274   Go, Julian. "Chains of Empire, Projects of State: Political Education and U.S. Colonial Rule in Puerto Rico and the Philippines." *Comparative Studies in Society and History* 42 (April 2000): 333–62. Rarely have scholars explored the influences flowing from one colony to another *among* U.S. colonies. Go finds that the various and changing nature of political education in the Philippines and Puerto Rico stemmed partly from relations among the United States, Philippines, and Puerto Rico. This essay is helpful in understanding the broader nature of the U.S. imperial project.

13:275   Golay, Frank H. *Face of Empire: United States–Philippine Relations, 1898–1946.* Madison: University of Wisconsin, Madison, Center for Southeast Asian Studies, 1998. Finished and published posthumously, this study represents Golay's lifetime concern with the political economy of the Philippines. Although using the structure of political history, the study's greatest contribution is careful attention to the intertwined nature of economic and political relations between the United States and the Philippines. Extensive notes.

13:276   Gowing, Peter G. *Mandate in Moroland: The American Government of Muslim Filipinos, 1899–1920.* Quezon City: Philippine Center for Advanced Studies, University of the Philippines, 1977. Gowing's classic study of U.S. rule in Mindanao treats a too often neglected subject, since U.S. intervention in this southern Philippine island was more sustained and substantial than in the rest of the colony. Bibliography.

13:277   Hutchcroft, Paul. "Colonial Masters, National Politicos, and Provincial Lords: Central Authority and Local Autonomy in the American Philippines, 1900–1913." *Journal of Asian Studies* 59 (May 2000): 277–306. Contrary to most scholarship, Hutchcroft argues that the primary legacy of U.S. colonial rule in the Philippines was a relatively decentralized state, with the strongest centralizing force stemming from patronage associated with the Philippine National Assembly. Taft era (1900–1913) policies have had a lasting impact.

13:278   Ileto, Reynaldo. "Cholera and the Origins of the American Sanitary Order in the Philippines." Although traditional historiography has separated the two events—Filipino nationalist resistance in 1899–1902 and U.S. attempts to end the 1902–1904 cholera epidemic—Ileto argues that similar issues of power, force, resistance, and even oppression link the two events analytically as well as in the eyes of Filipinos at the time (10:440).

13:279   Karnow, Stanley. *In Our Image: America's Empire in the Philippines.* Karnow writes with the attention to detail and drama one would expect from a journalist. He also provides an analytical overview of U.S. rule in the Philippines. Bibliography (10:441).

13:280   Kramer, Paul A. "Empires, Exceptions, and Anglo-Saxons: Race and Rule between the British and United States Empires, 1880–1910." Part of a growing trend to situate the American imperial project firmly within both the broader European imperial project and the context of a changing America at the turn of the century, Kramer's essay explores the myriad implications of Anglo-Saxonism, the various uses of exceptionalist rhetoric, and the interrelationships between empire and racial identities. Although focusing on intellectual history, the essay sketches the social and geopolitical situation effectively as well (10:478).

13:281 _____. "Making Concessions: Race and Empire Revisited at the Philippine Exposition, St. Louis, 1901–1905." Kramer examines the discourses and imaginings regarding U.S. colonial possessions as represented at the St. Louis Exposition, highlighting the fragmented, contested nature of both the colonial project and its representations (10:479).

13:282 Linn, Brian McAllister. *Guardians of Empire: The U.S. Army and the Pacific, 1902–1940.* Chapel Hill: University of North Carolina Press, 1997. Linn's careful study explores a neglected but puzzling aspect of U.S. colonial rule in the Philippines: why the U.S. army was unprepared to fight the one country, Japan, all U.S. policymakers viewed as the likely enemy. He explains that the lack of preparation did not stem from ignorance or racism, but rather from a complex interweaving of politics in the U.S. and Philippines as well as relations between them. Bibliography.

13:283 May, Glenn Anthony. *Social Engineering in the Philippines: The Aims, Execution, and Impact of American Colonial Policy, 1900–1913.* Westport, CT: Greenwood Press, 1980. May, one of the most important historians of the Philippines in the United States, argues that although U.S. policy aimed to prepare Filipinos for self-government, to provide basic education for all, and to develop the economy, it failed in all three areas.

13:284 McCoy, Alfred W. "Philippine-American Relations: A Problem of Perception." *Australasian Journal of American Studies* 6 (December 1987): 17–27. Partly a review of Raymond Bonner's *Waltzing with a Dictator: The Marcoses and the Making of American Policy* (1987) (27:126), this article is also a damning critique of how Americans have studied U.S.-Philippine relations, a critique mostly still relevant.

13:285 McCoy, Alfred W., and Alfredo Roces. *Philippine Cartoons: Political Caricature of the American Era, 1900–1941.* Quezon City: Vera-Reyes, Inc., 1985. The cartoons are amusing and revealing, while the introductory essays and accompanying explanations provide analytical context.

13:286 Owen, Norman G., ed. *Compadre Colonialism: Studies on the Philippines under American Rule.* Ann Arbor: Center for South and Southeast

Asian Studies, University of Michigan, 1971. This interesting collection of essays features the early work of some important scholars of the Philippines, including Norman G. Owen on U.S. economic policy (103–28), Michael Cullinane on Taft administration policy toward local government (13–76), and Frank Jenista on U.S. policy toward the Philippine Assembly, 1907–1913 (77–102).

13:287 Paredes, Ruby R., ed. *Philippine Colonial Democracy.* Vol. 32. New Haven: Yale University Southeast Asia Studies, Yale Center for International and Area Studies, 1988. A collection of four essays by prominent scholars of Philippine history sheds important light on the impact of U.S. attempts to structure how democracy was introduced into the Philippines. Relevant for this chapter are Paredes, "The Origins of National Politics: Taft and the Partido Federal" (41–69)"; Michael Cullinane, "Playing the Game: The Rise of Sergio Osmena, 1898–1907" (70–113); and Paredes's introductory essay, "The Paradox of Philippine Colonial Democracy" (1–12).

13:288 Rafael, Vicente L. *White Love and Other Events in Filipino History.* Durham, NC: Duke University Press, 2000. Rafael explores key components of the U.S. imperial project, particularly issues of race, gender, and imagery during colonialism and the legacies of the particularities of U.S. imperialism for the period during and after World War II. He also explores the important issue of Filipinos in the United States in the late twentieth century. A key work for understanding the full power of U.S. imperialism. Notes, bibliography.

13:289 Salamanca, Bonifacio S. *The Filipino Reaction to American Rule, 1901–1913.* Hamden, CT: Shoe String Press, 1968. Reprint 1984 (New Day). The conservative Filipino elite influenced and limited the United States in its choice of policy. The author concludes that the impact of American rule was "greatest in the educational and religious field, less in democratization of politics and weakest in economic and social aspects of Filipino life."

13:290 Stanley, Peter W. *A Nation in the Making: The Philippines and the United States, 1899–1921.* Stanley's classic study of U.S. rule in the Philippines remains the starting point, as demonstrated by the many subsequent works that have elaborated on or quarreled with his assessment of what he called the "imperialism of suasion." Bibliography (2:297).

13:291 _____, ed. *Reappraising an Empire: New Perspectives on Philippine-American History.* This collection includes essays by some of the most important scholars of U.S.-Philippines relations: Michael Cullinane, "The Politics of Collaboration in Tayabas Province: The Early Political Career of Manuel Luis Quezon, 1903–1906" (59–84); Reynaldo Ileto, "Orators and the Crowd: Philippine Independence Politics, 1910–1914" (85–113); Stanley, "'The Voice of Worcester Is the Voice of God': How One American Found Fulfillment in the Philippines" (117–41); Kenton J. Clymer, "Protestant Missionaries and American Colonialism in the Philippines, 1899–1916: Attitudes, Perceptions, Involvement" (143–70); Ronald K. Edgerton, "Americans, Cowboys, and Cattlemen on the Mindanao Frontier" (171–97); and Frank H. Golay, "The Search for Revenues" (231–60) (2:298).

13:292   Thompson, Winfred Lee. *The Introduction of American Law in the Philippines and Puerto Rico, 1898–1905.* Thompson's narrative account focuses on the project of transferring U.S. law to its colonies as well as on the legal basis of U.S. rule. The book concentrates primarily on the Philippines and uses U.S. rather than Spanish or Filipino sources (10:490).

13:293   Tuason, Julie A. "The Ideology of Empire in *National Geographic Magazine*'s Coverage of the Philippines, 1898–1908." Although firmly situated within the field of the history of geography, this article will nonetheless be useful to historians of U.S.-Philippine relations, and of imperialism generally. Tuason explores both how geographers portrayed the Philippines and Filipinos in ways that reinforced their image of the United States as a benevolent colonial power, and how that portrayal helped shape U.S. colonial policy. Bibliography (10:492).

14

The United States, World War I, and the Peace Settlement, 1914–1920

Contributing Editor

Thomas J. Knock
Southern Methodist University

With the Assistance of

Kurt W. Hanson
American University

Contents

Introduction

This chapter contains 626 entries. Its organization is fairly straightforward, if imperfect. Except for the sections on document collections, bibliographies, overviews, and biographies, the entries are basically arranged by subject (and subtopic) in chronological sequence, starting with the more comprehensive or broadly thematic studies and followed by the more specialized. Some of the 340 entries in the 1983 version of the chapter have been eliminated, many have been rewritten, and most relevant books on Latin America and Asia that had no direct bearing on World War I appear elsewhere in the new Guide.

In surveying the entire body of work described herein, two particularly striking aspects of it seem worthy of comment. First, this incalculably important field has been enriched by changes that have taken place not only in the practice of diplomatic history, but also in the historical profession in general, since 1983. Until then, it was somewhat unusual to encounter a work of diplomatic history about America and the Great War that tapped very deeply the domestic political roots of foreign policy (though some studies about the League of Nations and peace movements may seem an exception), and rarer still to encounter one that viewed the era through the lens of social and cultural history, or of gender, labor, or race. This is no longer the case. No single work can account for *all* of the foregoing, but a fair number of the more recent monographs (and a few of the older and overlooked) included here, by shedding such light on parts of it, have increased the sum of our comprehension of the whole.

The second striking thing, which was apparent in the literature twenty years ago but somehow seems almost palpable today, is that so many of the issues surrounding the role that the United States played in the war and the peace have remained hotly contested ground. In the beginning, there was revisionism in the 1920s and 1930s, a compound of lively journalism and excellent scholarship that questioned chiefly the quality of American neutrality and the soundness of the Treaty of Versailles. Even a cursory review of those impassioned writings conveys a sense of the epochal—that the proper understanding of the then immediate past was a high-stakes enterprise upon which the future of the nation and the world depended. Then came World War II and America's "second chance," which yielded a respectful reconsideration of Woodrow Wilson and his ephemeral apotheosis via the United Nations. Thus, the protean term, "Wilsonianism," gained enduring currency. Yet once the cold war began, a new school of historical and political thought, the "realists" argued that the salient tents of Wilson's own conception of internationalism actually had not well served American interests during World War I and that they were even less likely to do so in the new bipolar world. Largely denying kinship with Wilson, the realists counseled a foreign policy that was at once both globalist and unilateralist in nature. Meanwhile, as other historians revived and refined the debate over neutrality and intervention, some historians of the new left in the 1960s, with the Vietnam War as a reference point, argued that cold war realism represented the (logical) triumph of Wilsonianism. More lately, alongside the aforementioned socially and culturally oriented explorations, a surge of studies has demonstrated anew the transcendent importance of the great events of 1914–1919. Many of these varied works have revisited historical questions related to minorities and self-determination, great power imperialism, the League of Nations and world order, national sovereignty, and competing definitions of internationalism and isolationism—at least in part, the inevitable reflection of the dramatic transformations that have taken place in world politics and American foreign policy since 1989.

Document Collections

14:1   U.S. Department of State. *Foreign Relations of the United States.* 19 vols. Washington, DC: Government Printing Office, 1920–1936. Excluding the other, more specialized volumes and supplements in this vital series, separately listed, the general chronological volumes (including those covering the period of U.S. neutrality) and other supplementary volumes on World War I are essential for any researcher of the 1914–1920 period (1:93).

14:2   _____. *Foreign Relations of the United States: General Index, 1900–1918.* Washington, DC: Government Printing Office, 1941. This is an important aid to finding the documents assembled in this published collection or records. It does not cover *Foreign Relations of the United States: The Lansing Papers, 1914–1920* (1939–1940) (14:7).

14:3   _____. *Foreign Relations of the United States: The Paris Peace Conference, 1919.* 13 vols. Washington, DC: Government Printing Office, 1942–1947. This supplement on the Paris Peace Conference is notable for its publication of whole series of records rather than excerpts. It is a source of fundamental importance.

14:4   U.S. National Archives. *General Records of the American Commission to Negotiate Peace, 1918–1931.* Microfilm. Washington, DC: National Archives and Records Service, 1970. This collection of 563 rolls (Microfilm Publication M820) covers virtually all the U.S. documentation pertaining to the work of the American Commission to Negotiate Peace at the Paris Peace Conference.

14:5   Rangel, Sandra K., ed. *Records of the American Commission to Negotiate Peace: Inventory of Record Group 256.* Washington, DC: National Archives and Records Service, 1974. This is an indispensable finding aid to the collection of records of the American Commission to Negotiate Peace at the Paris Peace Conference of 1919. This aid will facilitate use of Record Group 256 at the National Archives and also of National Archives and Records Service Microfilm Publication M820. Unfortunately, it does not indicate which documents are available on microfilm.

14:6   U.S. National Archives and Records Service. *Records of the Department of State Relating to World War I and Its Termination, 1914–29.* Microfilm. Washington, DC: National Archives and Records Service, 1965. This vast collection (518 rolls, M367) consists of records from the Department of State concerning American participation in World War I but not the proceedings of the Paris Peace Conference or the wartime records of other government departments and bureaus.

14:7   U.S. Department of State. *Foreign Relations of the United States: The Lansing Papers, 1914–1920.* 2 vols. Washington, DC: Government Printing Office, 1939–1940. These volumes contain

important selections from the correspondence, memoranda, and other documents generated by Wilson's second secretary of state.

14:8   _____. *Foreign Relations of the United States, 1918. World War Supplement II: Russia.* 3 vols. Washington, DC: Government Printing Office, 1931–1932. This series, along with the companion volume for 1919 (14:9), provides a useful selection from the basic U.S. documents relevant to Russian affairs and the Russian civil war.

14:9   _____. *Foreign Relations of the United States, 1919: Russia.* Washington, DC: Government Printing Office, 1937. These documents are a supplement to the comparable volume for 1918 (14:8).

14:10   U.S. Department of the Army. Office of Military History. *United States Army in the World War, 1917–1919.* 17 vols. Washington, DC: Government Printing Office, 1948. This is a massive documentary history of the American Expeditionary Force.

14:11   U.S. Congress. Senate. Committee on Foreign Relations. *Treaty of Peace with Germany. Hearings before the Committee on Foreign Relations, United States Senate, Sixty-sixth Congress, First Session on the Treaty of Peace with Germany, Signed at Versailles on June 28, 1919, and Submitted to the Senate on July 10, 1919.* Washington, DC: Government Printing Office, 1919. This is a fascinating and essential source on the battle over ratification.

14:12   *The Treaties of Peace, 1919–1923.* 2 vols. New York: Carnegie Endowment for International Peace, 1924. This is a convenient compilation of the peace treaties concluded at the Paris Peace Conference.

14:13   Seymour, Charles, ed. *The Intimate Papers of Colonel House Arranged as a Narrative by Charles Seymour.* Although these documents are somewhat "doctored" and exaggerate House's influence, they remain one of the most important published primary sources on the colonel's activities and thoughts. Volumes 2–4 provide material on the war and the peace settlement (11:23).

14:14   Miller, David Hunter. *My Diary at the Con-*

ference at Paris, with Documents. 21 vols. New York: Appeal Printing Co., 1924. The diary and collected documents remain useful for historians, though perhaps not as much as when first published. Volume 21 contains an excellent index. Microfilm copies are available.

14:15   Baker, Ray Stannard, and William E. Dodd, eds. *The Public Papers of Woodrow Wilson*. A fairly substantial selection of addresses, messages, and public papers covering Wilson's presidency (12:16), these volumes have been superseded by the sixty-nine volumes of Link's *The Papers of Woodrow Wilson* (1966–1994) (14:16).

14:16   Link, Arthur S., et al., eds. *The Papers of Woodrow Wilson*. This is truly a monumental series of thousands of documents gathered by the project editors over a thirty-year period from countless archives in the United States and around the world. The war is covered, from the assassination of Franz Ferdinand to the end of the struggle over the ratification of the Treaty of Versailles, starting with Volume 30. Every thirteenth volume in the series is a superbly detailed index of the previous twelve (11:33).

14:17   Link, Arthur S., and Manfred F. Boemeke, eds. *The Deliberations of the Council of Four (March 24–June 28, 1919): Notes of the Official Interpreter, Paul Mantoux*. This is the definitive translation into English from the French of Mantoux's notes, the most complete record of the discussions of the Big Four available in any form. They are based on his personal notes and evening dictations during the most crucial period of the Paris Peace Conference. Link and Boemeke translated as well as edited (13:3).

14:18   Gooch, G. P., and Harold Temperley, eds. *British Documents on the Origins of the War, 1898–1914*. These eleven volumes remain possibly the most important collection of British documents on the origins of the war ever published; they begin with the Anglo-Japanese alliance and the Franco-British entente and end with the crisis of June-August 1914. The eleventh volume contains a fair number of materials pertaining to the United States (11:10).

Bibliographies and Reference Works

14:19   Almond, Nina, and Ralph Haswell Lutz, eds. *An Introduction to a Bibliography of the Paris Peace Conference: Collections of Sources, Archive Publications, and Source Books*. Stanford, CA: Stanford University Press, 1935. This early, thirty-two-page bibliography is especially concerned with materials housed at the Hoover Institution in Stanford, California, and remains a useful introduction to materials available before 1935.

14:20   Bayliss, Gwyn M., ed. *Bibliographical Guide to the Two World Wars: An Annotated Survey of English-Language Reference Materials*. New York: Bowker, 1977. This is a useful, sizable compilation (nearly 600 pages).

14:21   Braisted, William Reynolds. "The Navy in the Early Twentieth Century, 1890–1941." This essay and list of some 300 sources relate to the U.S. navy in World War I, the naval limitation treaties of the 1920s and 1930s, and navy activities generally in the interwar era (9:242).

14:22   Buckingham, Peter H., ed. *Woodrow Wilson: A Bibliography of His Times and Presidency*. Through the date of publication, this excellent volume covers most aspects of domestic and foreign affairs in the Wilson era in over 3,000 annotated entries (12:20).

14:23   Ellis, Richard N. "Civil-Military Relations, Operations, and the Army, 1865–1917." This is an eight-page bibliographical essay on civil-military relations that outlines the main issues in the topic, followed by a 286-item, unannotated bibliography (10:29).

14:24   Gilbert, Martin, ed. *First World War Atlas*. New York: Macmillan, 1971. This valuable atlas, though somewhat dated, is still a helpful tool for students of World War I.

14:25   Higham, Robin, ed. *Official Histories: Essays and Bibliographies from around the World.* Manhattan: Kansas State University Library, 1970. This compendium includes a country-by-country survey of World War I national histories.

14:26   Link, Arthur S., and William M. Leary, Jr., eds. *The Progressive Era and the Great War, 1896–1920.* Arlington Heights, IL: AHM Publishing, 1978. This work contains a substantial section on sources on American involvement in World War I and is still worth consulting. First issued in 1969.

14:27   Mulder, John M., Ernest M. White, and Ethel S. White, eds. *Woodrow Wilson: A Bibliography.* Westport, CT: Greenwood Press, 1997. Boasting some 4,216 annotated entries, this is the most comprehensive source of its kind and extremely useful for the war and the peace conference.

14:28   Schaffer, Ronald, ed. *The United States in World War I: A Selected Bibliography.* Santa Barbara, CA: ABC-CLIO, 1978. Although this bibliography does not emphasize foreign relations, it includes references to bureaucratic organization, military affairs, popular attitudes toward the war, demobilization, and postwar organization.

14:29   Toscano, Mario, ed. *The History of Treaties and International Politics: An Introduction to the History of Treaties and International Politics: The Documentary and Memoir Sources.* Baltimore: Johns Hopkins Press, 1966. An extensive listing of memoirs and documentary material relating to World War I is provided, along with insightful comments on the value of specific materials and collections.

14:30   Venzon, Anne Cipriano, ed. *The United States and the First World War, An Encyclopedia.* New York: Garland Publishing, 1995. At over 800 pages, this is undoubtedly the best reference work of its kind.

Historiography

14:31   Adler, Selig. "The War-Guilt Question and American Disillusionment, 1918–1928." *Journal of Modern History* 23 (March 1951): 1–28. This is an impressive, wide-ranging, and hard-hitting review essay on American revisionist writing during the first postwar decade, with a heavy stress on the controversy among academics and journalists over the war-guilt clause in the Treaty of Versailles. Adler uses the work of revisionist Harry Elmer Barnes as the pivot of his analysis of the debate over U.S. involvement in the war and what then seemed to be a vindictive settlement on Germany.

14:32   Ambrosius, Lloyd E. "The Orthodoxy of Revisionism: Woodrow Wilson and the New Left." *Diplomatic History* 1 (Summer 1977): 199–214. Ambrosius aptly discerns in the new left's revisionism a certain convergence of views with, if not quite an affinity for, many of the tenets of Wilson's liberal internationalism; thus, he argues that the new left fails to understand fully the president's progressive vision of a new world order.

14:33   Barnes, Harry Elmer. *The Genesis of the World War: An Introduction to the Problem of War Guilt.* New and rev. ed. New York: Alfred A. Knopf, 1929. Barnes was one of the first major revisionists (and perhaps the most influential) to argue that the causes behind the war lay at least as much with the Allies as with Germany; he thus contributed mightily to the interwar debate over whether the United States should have entered the war at all. First published in 1926 without the subtitle.

14:34   Binkley, Robert C. "Ten Years of Peace Conference History." *Journal of Modern History* 1 (December 1929): 607–29. In a superb retrospective assessment, one of the first in a decade marked by intense revising, Binkley reviews the works of Keynes, House, Seymour, Baker, Lansing, Temperley, Steed, and Churchill. He complains that some Americans tended to write in the language of melodrama and hang the issues "around personalities . . . and high-sounding generalities."

14:35   Birdsall, Paul. "The Second Decade of Peace Conference History." *Journal of Modern History* 11 (September 1939): 362–78. This important historiographical essay is a companion piece to Binkley's "Ten Years of Peace Conference History" (1929) (14:34), though not as extensive or incisive. Writers under review include Nicolson, Nevins,

Edith Bolling Wilson, Lloyd George, Shotwell, and Baker. Birdsall suggests that the published documents then available were making it increasingly possible for scholars to begin a serious examination.

14:36   Cohen, Warren I. *The American Revisionists: The Lessons of Intervention in World War I.* Chicago: University of Chicago Press, 1967. Cohen examines the writings and utterances of C. Hartley Grattan, Walter Millis, Charles Callan Tansill, Harry Elmer Barnes, and Charles A. Beard, who questioned whether Germany alone was responsible for the war and whether American interests were served by intervening in it. The author argues that the work of these revisionists contributed to isolationist sentiment in the 1930s.

14:37   Hill, Thomas M., and William H. Barclay. "Interests, Ideals and American Interventionism in World War I: An Historiographical Appraisal." *International Review of History and Political Science* 14 (February 1977): 1–24. This somewhat dated but still useful piece outlines historiographical schools on U.S. intervention in World War I: the traditionalists, the first wave, who accepted Wilson's position that Germany virtually forced war upon the United States; the revisionists, who saw market preservation and a conspiracy of moneyed interests driving intervention; the postrevisionists, mostly cold war realists, who saw national security–based intervention as inevitable while conceding some economic considerations; and the new left, who viewed foreign policy as an ideological struggle determined by systems of power within, rather than between states.

14:38   Kennan, George F. "Soviet Historiography and America's Role in the Intervention." *American Historical Review* 65 (January 1960): 302–22. Kennan denounces the lack of objectivity in Soviet historical writing and argues that such work contributes little to international scholarly debate.

14:39   Leopold, Richard W. "The Problem of American Intervention, 1917: An Historical Retrospect." *World Politics* 2 (April 1950): 404–25. The author surveys the issue by focusing on several important works written in the 1930s, noting that as of 1950 such subjects as the war Congress, strategic planning, and public opinion had been almost entirely neglected.

14:40   Lewis, Thomas T. "Alternative Psychological Interpretations of Woodrow Wilson." *Mid-America* 65 (April-July 1983): 71–85. Lewis reviews psychological interpretations of Wilson and cautions the reader that psychology, like history, is subject to theoretical and methodological pluralism. Freudian analysis (psychologism) tends toward simplistic and reductionist explanations, but more nuanced conclusions are available from more commonsensical "cognitive-affective" models. Any psychological interpretation that assumes a direct relationship between Wilson's policies and his character, he cautions, is inherently ahistorical.

14:41   Moses, John A. *The Politics of Illusion: The Fischer Controversy in German Historiography.* New York: Barnes and Noble, 1975. The author's intent is to present, for the benefit of American scholars, a detailed review of Fischer's controversial work combined with an overview of German historical scholarship on the origins of World War I.

14:42   Neilson, Keith. "Total War: Total History." *Military Affairs* 51 (January 1987): 17–21. This is a concise review essay, with extensive bibliographical references, mainly on works published between the early 1970s and 1986. The emphasis is on military matters.

14:43   Ostrower, Gary B. "Historical Studies in American Internationalism." *International Organization* 25 (Autumn 1971): 899–916. This is a review essay considering four works on internationalism, two of which (Kuehl, *Seeking World Order: The United States and International Organization to 1920* [2:214] and Herman, *Eleven against War: Studies in International Thought, 1898–1921* [11:133], both published in 1969) focus on the internationalist movement's relation to World War I. Ostrower includes a brief discussion of Wilson historiography to 1970.

14:44   Schmitt, Bernadotte E. "American Neutrality, 1914–1917." *Journal of Modern History* 8 (June 1936): 200–11. This early review essay focuses on volume 5 of Ray Stannard Baker's *Woodrow Wilson: Life and Letters* (1927–1939) (14:147), along with works by Charles Seymour, Walter Millis, Grattan, and others, to assess the strained quality of Wilson's neutrality policies. Schmitt leans toward Baker and

Seymour, who maintained that neutrality was an insoluble problem. His own major contribution to the historiography of World War I came in *The Coming of the War, 1914*, 2 vols. (New York: C. Scribner's Sons, 1930).

14:45   Smith, Daniel M. "National Interest and American Intervention, 1917: An Historiographical Appraisal." *Journal of American History* 52 (June 1965): 5–24. Smith reviews the works of Buehrig, Link, Osgood, May, and others on the issue of national interest and intervention in World War I. He emphasizes that those authors have stressed Wilson's practice of realistic diplomacy and balance-of-power politics as the primary motivations for his decision to intervene.

14:46   Steigerwald, David. "The Reclamation of Woodrow Wilson?" *Diplomatic History* 23 (Winter 1999): 79–99. This historiographical essay discusses major works published in the 1980s and 1990s, including those of Lloyd Gardner, Lloyd Ambrosius, Friedrich Katz, Tony Smith, Betty Miller Unterberger, Thomas Knock, and Mark Gilderhus. The author's thematic focus—on realism, new left revisionism, nationalism, and one worldism—is oriented toward post–cold war concerns.

14:47   Thompson, John A. "Woodrow Wilson and World War I: A Reappraisal." *Journal of American Studies* 19 (December 1985): 325–48. Thompson briefly reviews the historiography on Wilson's war aims, from John Maynard Keynes through the new left, and dismisses most of their criticisms. Wilson, he argues, was more pragmatic than generally considered (until the Senate debate on the peace treaty) as he sought to "shape a foreign policy that would both be effective abroad and command broad support at home."

14:48   Trachtenberg, Marc. "Versailles after Sixty Years." *Journal of Contemporary History* 17 (July 1982): 487–506. In reviewing several significant past works, the author argues that many historians sympathetic to Wilson (from Ray Stannard Baker to Arthur Link to Arno Mayer) overlooked his contribution to the punitive aspects of the treaty. While he resisted Allied territorial aggrandizement, he did not object to reparations in either principle or practice; as a form of retributive justice, they did not contradict his conception of a fair and just peace.

14:49   Watson, Richard L., Jr. "Woodrow Wilson and His Interpreters, 1947–1957." *Mississippi Valley Historical Review* 44 (Spring 1957): 207–36. This is an extremely useful review of the literature on Wilson published during the postwar decade and the centennial of his birth.

Overviews

14:50   Ambrosius, Lloyd E. *Wilsonian Statecraft: Theory and Practice of Liberal Internationalism during World War I.* Wilmington, DE: SR Books, 1991. As a variation on the realist critique that took root in the 1950s, this compact study synthesizes some of the ideas in the author's *Woodrow Wilson and the American Diplomatic Tradition: The Treaty Fight in Perspective* (1987) (14:585), and suggests that many problems inhered in Wilson's conception of collective security.

14:51   Anderson, George L., ed. *Issues and Conflicts: Studies in Twentieth Century American Diplomacy.* Lawrence: University of Kansas Press, 1959. This anthology contains three articles on crucial issues for the Wilson era: Roland N. Stromberg, "The Riddle of Collective Security" (147–70); Louis L. Gerson, "Immigrant Groups and American Foreign Policy" (171–92); and Robert H. Ferrell, "Woodrow Wilson and Open Door Diplomacy" (193–209).

14:52   Chambers, John Whiteclay, II. *The Tyranny of Change: America in the Progressive Era, 1900–1917.* New York: St. Martin's Press, 1980. Chambers's overview provides a good introduction to the war years; among other things, he emphasizes social problems born of industrial capitalism and the process of modernization, and how both individuals and institutions responded to them.

14:53   Duroselle, Jean-Baptiste. *From Wilson to Roosevelt: Foreign Policy of the United States, 1913–1945.* Translated by Nancy Lyman Roelker. Cambridge, MA: Harvard University Press, 1963. The first six chapters cover 1913 to 1921 and attempt to explain why the United States rejected the role of world leadership that the international situation seemed to require. One of the first French scholars to write on recent U.S. history, Duroselle takes the "internationalist" position but is not uncritical of Wilson.

14:54   Ferrell, Robert H. *Woodrow Wilson and World War I, 1917–1921.* New York: Harper and Row, 1985. Part of the New American Nations series, the first half of this lively synthesis provides an overview of the decision for war, the problems surrounding mobilization, and the sights and sounds of combat. The second half focuses on wartime politics and diplomacy, through the final Senate votes on the peace treaty. Ferrell's perspective on Wilson is fairly critical.

14:55   Fussell, Paul. *The Great War and Modern Memory.* New York: Oxford University Press, 1975. Declared by the Modern Library one of the twentieth century's 100 best nonfiction books, this analysis of literary works generated by the war (Sassoon, Robert Graves, Owen, etc.) yields greater insights into the origins and meaning of the terrible struggle than many studies in diplomacy.

14:56   Gardner, Lloyd C. "American Foreign Policy, 1900–1921: A Second Look at the Realist Critique of American Diplomacy." This essay is a new left revisionist critique of the *realists'* critique of Wilson, suggesting that Wilson and the realists have perhaps more in common than the latter might wish to acknowledge (11:52).

14:57   _____. *A Covenant with Power: America and World Order from Wilson to Reagan.* New York: Oxford University Press, 1984. In his opening chapter, the author has rethought Wilson and posits the idea that he had to grapple with more complex issues than any previous president and that he did not do as badly as his cold war critics argue.

14:58   _____. *Safe for Democracy: The Anglo-American Response to Revolution, 1913–1923.* The age of reform, Frederick Jackson Turner once remarked, was "also the age of socialistic inquiry." And thus, at the beginning of his first term, Woodrow Wilson had to contend with the Mexican revolution and, at the beginning of his second, with the Russian revolution—in the context of world war. In this study brimming with original insights, Gardner engages both Lloyd George and Wilson as they endeavored to understand a new kind of world poli-

tics (born of industrial capitalism and imperialism and in which there seemed scarcely any difference between revolution and war) and struggled to make the world, among other things, "safe for democracy" (12:41).

14:59   Hawley, Ellis W. *The Great War and the Search for a Modern Order: A History of the American People and Their Institutions, 1917–1933.* 2d ed. New York: St. Martin's Press, 1992. The author's theme is "the continued search for a modern managerial order geared to the realization of liberal ideas." The war, he says, was thus emblematic and in this way shaped the new era of the 1920s. First published in 1979.

14:60   James, D. Clayton, and Anne Sharp Wells. *America and the Great War, 1914–1920.* Arlington Heights, IL: Harlan Davidson, 1998. James and Wells present a concise survey (fewer than 100 pages) of American involvement in World War I: its strength lies in breadth of coverage rather than analysis. The book's four chapters cover the American and European roads to war, military efforts on land and sea, the American home-front, and Wilson's travails in Paris and Washington. It succeeds admirably as an undergraduate introduction to the major issues of the war.

14:61   Kennan, George F. *American Diplomacy, 1900–1950.* In this seminal realist critique, Kennan condemns Wilson for not leading the United States into the war before 1917, for his idealistic goals and rhetoric when he finally did so, and for his entire conception of international order. Reprinted often, including in an "expanded edition" in 1984 (2:65).

14:62   Link, Arthur S., ed. *Woodrow Wilson and a Revolutionary World, 1913–1921.* Chapel Hill: University of North Carolina Press, 1982. This volume, based on a 1979 Princeton conference, contains several important essays. Lloyd C. Gardner, "Woodrow Wilson and the Mexican Revolution" (3–48), offers many comparative insights into the Russian revolution and argues that in both instances Wilson hoped that fundamental changes might be effected by democratic political processes but came to the realization that the cause of revolutionary self-determination was rarely advanced by outside military intervention.

Synthesizing some of her own earlier work, Betty Miller Unterberger in "Woodrow Wilson and the Russian Revolution" (49–104) comes to more or less the same conclusion as Gardner. Kay Lundgreen-Nielsen, "Woodrow Wilson and the Rebirth of Poland" (105–26), outlines the problems the president faced in helping create the new Central European state, replete with access to the sea—including divergent opinion among the Allies, intense Polish nationalism and not a little antisemitism, and the question of frontiers (which ultimately were determined by the Polish-Soviet War of 1920). Inga Floto, "Woodrow Wilson: War Aims, Peace Strategy, and the European Left" (127–45), begins by praising Arno Mayer's work for setting the international debate over war aims within the various domestic political contexts in Europe but maintains that Mayer did not adequately analyze the American scene; she concludes that Wilson's ultimate weapon, the appeal to the Europeans over the head of their governments, was wielded primarily with domestic politics in mind. Kurt Wimer, "Woodrow Wilson and World Order" (146–73), provides a workmanlike overview of Wilson's quest, arguing that it fused elements of moral principles with Machiavelli, based on the proposition, as Wilson once remarked, of "What will stay put?" Herbert G. Nicholas, "Woodrow Wilson and Collective Security" (174–89), traces the evolution of the idea from the concept of bilateral alliance to the balance of power and beyond, with help from Aristotle and Gibbon as well as Wilson, concluding that the latter's model, though far from perfect, was reasonably serviceable. Whittle Johnston, "Reflections on Wilson and the Problems of World Peace" (190– 231), is a meditation on the realist-idealist construct, the old diplomacy and the new, the Fourteen Points, and Wilson's relationship with the peoples of Europe. In Wilson, Johnston says, motivation and strategy were the same and grew out of his perception "that in world politics the special interests are organized, but the common interest remains unorganized."

14:63 _____. *Woodrow Wilson and the Progressive Era, 1910–1917.* New York: Harper, 1954. The first volume published in the New American Nation series, Link's is a highly readable monograph (and a kind of outline to his five-volume biography of Wilson) that ends with Wilson standing before Congress on April 2, 1917.

14:64   Ninkovich, Frank A. *Modernity and Power: A History of the Domino Theory in the Twentieth Century.* Ninkovich offers a challenging and highly theoretical contemplation that posits the idea that interdependence among nations (i.e., modernity) had so transformed the world by the turn of the nineteenth century that conflict almost anywhere affected the United States (ergo, the domino theory). The catastrophe of World War I thus caused Americans to press for a new approach to international relations, supplied by Wilsonian internationalist thought, mutating over the decades into "world opinion," deterrence, credibility, "a world psychology of power," neo-Wilsonianism, etc. (11:57).

14:65   Osgood, Robert E. *Ideals and Self-Interest in America's Foreign Relations: The Great Transformation of the Twentieth Century.* In this famous and highly influential book, Osgood argues, from a cold war intellectual's perspective, that Wilson rarely made foreign policy decisions on the grounds of practicality or "realism" and that his idealism and moralistic preachments ill served American interests (2:72).

14:66   Paxson, Frederic L. *American Democracy and the World War.* 3 vols. Boston: Houghton Mifflin Company, 1936–1948. These volumes provide a comprehensive though somewhat historiographically outdated survey of the years 1913 to 1923. The author's contention is that American democracy adapted adequately to the crisis.

14:67   Seymour, Charles. *American Diplomacy during the World War.* 2d ed. Baltimore: Johns Hopkins Press, 1942. Although various aspects of Seymour's work have been revised, it holds up reasonably well, especially as it relates the president's position on neutrality and his reasons for intervention. Seymour's attitude toward Wilson is generally appreciative, though not uncritical. First published in 1934.

14:68   Smith, Daniel M. *The Great Departure: The United States and World War I, 1914–1920.* New York: J. Wiley, 1965. Smith aims mainly to answer two questions: why the United States repudiated its neutrality and went to war and why, once committed to war, the nation abandoned the product of victory by rejecting the Versailles Treaty. The book offers a good narrative, though some of the scholarship is outdated.

14:69   Smith, Tony. *America's Mission: The United States and the Worldwide Struggle for Democracy in the Twentieth Century.* Princeton: Princeton University Press, 1994. The end of the cold war sparked new interest in that struggle's ideological origins, going back to World War I. Historians and political scientists also began to look anew at Woodrow Wilson in the 1990s; thus, he becomes the pivot of Smith's sweeping account, which argues that the promotion of democracy was the central tenet of American foreign policy in the twentieth century. The volume may fairly be described as a vintage example of cold war "triumphalism," albeit moderate in tone.

14:70   Steigerwald, David. *Wilsonian Idealism in America.* Ithaca: Cornell University Press, 1994. Steigerwald examines Wilsonian idealism and its intellectual legacy in the twentieth century. After devoting the first three chapters to Wilson, he studies the philosophical struggles and questionable relevance of Wilsonian idealists from Newton Baker to Francis Fukuyama. He argues that Wilsonian idealism contained too many paradoxes (e.g., advocating global interdependence without surrendering U.S. independence) and too readily assumed the universal appeal of democracy and capitalism. John Dewey's less universalistic optimism, he concludes, would better accommodate the fragmentation of the modern world.

14:71   Stevenson, David. *The First World War and International Politics.* New York: Oxford University Press, 1988. This is a fairly comprehensive study, starting with the outbreak of war and ending with the peace conference; it emphasizes relations between the Allies and the United States once the latter became a belligerent and political strategy over economics all around.

14:72   Taylor, A. J. P. *The Struggle for Mastery in Europe, 1848–1918.* This is a brilliant, if eccentric, treatise (by a brilliant, if eccentric, historian) on the origins of World War I that examines the decline of the European balance of power and the lack of suitable alternatives for perpetuating peace (11:64).

14:73   Winter, Jay, and Blaine Baggett. *The Great War and the Shaping of the 20th Century.* New York: Penguin Studio, 1996. The companion volume to the eight-hour PBS documentary series of the same title in addition to a good text, this volume contains many evocative photos and personal stories from the diaries and letters of contemporaries. It makes for a fine teaching supplement for introducing undergraduates to the subject.

Origins of the War

14:74   Albertini, Luigi. *The Origins of the War of 1914.* Translated by Isabella M. Massey. 3 vols. New York: Oxford University Press, 1952–1957. Albertini was an Italian senator and Milan newspaper publisher before World War I. His prodigious work ("the best of the detailed studies," according to James Joll) had enormous influence on later interpretations, notably Fritz Fischer's. Albertini holds Germany primarily responsible for the outbreak of war because it did not try to discourage Austria-Hungary's demands. (Quite the contrary.) Similarly, he is hard on the British government (specifically Grey) for failing both to stand up to Germany from the start of the crisis and to keep the Russians in check. Originally published in 1942–1943 as *Le origini della guerra del 1914.*

14:75   Boemeke, Manfred F., Roger Chickering, and Stig Förster, eds. *Anticipating Total War: The German and American Experiences, 1871–1914.* Underwritten by the German Historical Institute, this collection focuses on the experience of war and its impact on society and culture in the United States and Germany. For details, see chapter 9 of this Guide (9:231). The chapter by John Whiteclay Chambers, II, "The American Debate over Modern War, 1870–1914" (241–79), explores the fascinating, but inconclusive, debate over the impact of new weaponry and industrialization on mass warfare, the implications for civil society and reform of a professional army establishment, and speculation over whether a great war would necessarily be long or short.

14:76   Fay, Sidney B. *The Origins of the World War.* 2 vols. in 1. 2d ed. New York: Macmillan, 1930. A renowned historian and colleague of Harry Elmer

Barnes at Smith College in the 1920s, Fay has been described as "a moderate revisionist." His massive study was the first work of scholarship to enumerate and tie together imperialism, militarism, the secret alliance system, and runaway nationalism as the broader causes of the war. At the same time, he argues that Germany neither wanted nor plotted the war, that Russia was just as blameworthy for egging Belgrade on, as was Britain for its maddening passivity at every turn until it was too late. "In view of the evidence now available," he argued, "the verdict of the Versailles Treaty . . . is historically unsound." First published in 1928.

14:77   Ferguson, Niall. *The Pity of War.* New York: Basic Books, 1999. In this highly controversial, partly counterfactual book, a politically conservative Scot argues that World War I ("the greatest error of modern history") was chiefly the consequence of Britain's decision to enter a struggle that otherwise might have remained continental in scope. Thus, Ferguson also argues, a more limited war, with Germany the easy victor, would have prevented the Bolshevik revolution, the rise of Hitler, and World War II. The British government's decision, alas, was motivated mainly by domestic concerns, and it set in motion a century-long tragedy.

14:78   Fischer, Fritz. *Germany's Aims in the First World War.* New York: W. W. Norton, 1967. In one of the most controversial revisionist works on the origins of World War I ever published, Fischer lays the blame for war squarely on Germany and its expansive territorial ambitions; he emphasizes Germany's relations with Austria on the eve of the struggle and its plans for a Prussian-dominated MittelEuropa. The book sparked numerous other studies intended either to sustain or refute Fischer's thesis.

14:79   Gordon, Michael R. "Domestic Conflict and the Origins of the First World War: The British and the German Cases." *Journal of Modern History* 46 (June 1974): 191–226. Gordon analyzes the effect of domestic conflict in Great Britain and France through the interpretations of Fritz Fischer, Arno Mayer, and Peter Lowenberg.

14:80   Joll, James. *The Origins of the First World War.* 2d ed. New York: Longman, 1992. Because of its concision, fine literary style, and balanced treat-

ment of the various causal factors, this work is often cited as the best one-volume study of its kind. In addition to his treatments of such topics as nationalism and imperialism, Joll's multidimensional interpretation is particularly impressive in re-creating the social and intellectual milieu (the "unspoken assumptions," as he put it in an earlier work) that underlay the more proximate causes. First published in 1984.

14:81   Kennan, George F. *The Decline of Bismarck's European Order: Franco-Russian Relations, 1875–1890.* Princeton: Princeton University Press, 1979. At the age of seventy-six, the former diplomat and author of the containment doctrine published the first volume of a projected trilogy on the causes of the Great War. His focus is on why Russia turned away from its quasi alliance with Germany and began to move toward a new relationship with France, which itself feared sudden attack from Germany. The rise of intense nationalism in Russia and the lack of accountability and restraint among its ruling classes were major factors.

14:82   _____. *The Fateful Alliance: France, Russia and the Coming of the First World War.* New York: Pantheon Books, 1984. As the sequel to *The Decline of Bismarck's European Order: Franco-Russian Relations, 1875–1890* (1979) (14:81), this volume laments the Franco-Russian union of 1894 as a kind of Rubicon that led ultimately to epochal disaster, partly because the mutual security pact contained an agreement allowing either party to mobilize "immediately and simultaneously . . . and without necessity for prior agreement." (Kennan's final volume in the series, intended to take the story through the war itself, has yet to be published.)

14:83   Lafore, Laurence. *The Long Fuse: An Interpretation of the Origins of World War I.* 2d ed. Philadelphia: Lippincott, 1971. This synthetic reinterpretation is especially strong in its coverage of Central and Eastern European political and social developments before August 1914. Lafore suggests that none of the belligerents envisaged a drawn-out catastrophic war, and that its principal cause was the threat Serbian nationalism posed to the future of Austria-Hungary. First published in 1965.

14:84   Lee, Dwight E. *Europe's Crucial Years: The Diplomatic Background of World War I, 1902–*

1914. Hanover, NH: University Press of New England, 1974. The author disparages revisionist interpretations and concludes that balance-of-power politics and an insoluble Serbian situation made war inevitable.

14:85   Massie, Robert Kinloch. *Dreadnought: Britain, Germany, and the Coming of the Great War.* New York: Random House, 1991. In this sizable, highly readable account, Massie focuses on the intense rivalry between the two great powers for dominance on the seas and the technology and strategic planning that fed it.

14:86   Mayer, Arno J. "Domestic Causes of the First World War." In *The Responsibility of Power: Historical Essays in Honor of Hajo Holborn,* ed. Leonard Krieger and Fritz Stern, 286–300. Garden City, NY: Doubleday, 1967. Mayer's is a controversial interpretation that argues that, in most of the incipient belligerent countries, domestic tensions characteristic of revolutionary situations were a central consideration in the ruling elites' decision for war—that they seized upon the crisis in the Balkans as a way to shore up the state and suppress the "forces of movement" (Democrats and socialists) at home.

Biographical Studies

AMERICAN

Diplomatic and Political

Jane Addams

14:87   Addams, Jane. *Peace and Bread in Time of War.* New York: Macmillan Company, 1922. Reprint 1983 (National Association of Social Workers). In certain ways, this is a more moving and significant work than *Twenty Years at Hull House* (New York: Macmillan, 1910). In it, Addams chronicles her extensive efforts on behalf of mediation, the creation of the Woman's Peace Party, her interviews with Wilson (including one just before the United States entered the war), and the dilemma that many progressive internationalists faced from April 1917 onward.

14:88   Davis, Allen F. *American Heroine: The Life and Legend of Jane Addams.* New York: Oxford University Press, 1973. In this analytical study of Addams as a symbol of her times, the author contrasts her highly positive prewar image with the assaults on her character after she assumed a leading role in the peace movement. (The American Legion declared her "un-American," while the Daughters of the American Revolution said she was out "to destroy civilization and Christianity." She was awarded the Nobel Peace Prize in 1931.)

Newton D. Baker

14:89   Baker, Newton D. *Why We Went to War.* New York: Harper for the Council on Foreign Relations, 1936. This work, part memoir, contains revealing comments by the wartime secretary of war; it is still worth reading.

14:90   Beaver, Daniel R. *Newton D. Baker and the American War Effort, 1917–1919.* Lincoln: University of Nebraska Press, 1966. This monograph describing the operations of the War Department includes valuable sections on how the armed forces of the United States grew from a few hundred thousand to 4 million troops in a little over a year and how Secretary Baker related to his high-ranking officers, particularly General Pershing.

Bernard Baruch

14:91   Baruch, Bernard M. *Baruch.* 2 vols. New York: Holt, Rinehart and Winston, 1957–1960. In the second volume, *The Public Years,* Baruch, a friend and great admirer of Wilson, discusses his own career in public service from World War I through the cold war.

14:92   Schwarz, Jordan A. *The Speculator, Bernard M. Baruch in Washington, 1917–1965.* Chapel Hill: University of North Carolina Press, 1981. Schwarz's shrewd and lively study is possibly the best ever written on the subject.

William E. Borah

14:93   Maddox, Robert James. *William E. Borah and American Foreign Policy.* Baton Rouge: Louisiana State University Press, 1970. Borah was a progressive isolationist, anti-imperialist, and ring-leader of the Irreconcilables. The first three chapters of this book describe his leadership of those senators opposed to U.S. membership in the League of Nations as well as his own opposition to the American intervention in Russia.

14:94 McKenna, Marian C. *Borah.* Ann Arbor: University of Michigan Press, 1961. This sympathetic biography concerns American participation in World War I and the League of Nations as well as Borah's influence on foreign policy in the interwar years. McKenna argues that both Borah and Wilson were idealists and that they differed not on principles but on "methods."

William Jennings Bryan

14:95 Ashby, LeRoy. *William Jennings Bryan: Champion of Democracy.* This is a good, short biography that aptly portrays the Great Commoner as the most neutral member of Wilson's cabinet. "He is absolutely sincere," Ashby quotes Wilson as saying upon Bryan's resignation over the submarine issue. "That is what makes him dangerous." The discussion about his doubts about the League is thought-provoking, too (10:115).

14:96 Clements, Kendrick A. *William Jennings Bryan: Missionary Isolationist.* Covering the period from the Spanish-American War through World War I, Clements elucidates Bryan's idealism as few have done before. At once critical and respectful of his subject, he considers Bryan, in his aversion to the use of force and his belief in the efficacy of moral example, as "unmatched as a prophet of American confusion, uncertainty, and basic optimism" (12:108).

14:97 Coletta, Paolo E. "Bryan Briefs Lansing." *Pacific Historical Review* 27 (November 1958): 383–96. This lengthy memorandum, written by Bryan after he submitted his resignation as secretary of state in reaction to Wilson's protests against German submarine warfare, was intended to inform his successor, Robert Lansing, of the status of U.S. foreign affairs, including such matters as the "cooling-off" treaties, conditions in Central America and the Caribbean, and Sino-Japanese relations.

14:98 _____. *William Jennings Bryan.* Vol-umes 2 and 3 (*Progressive Politician and Moral Statesman, 1909–1915* and *Political Puritan, 1915–1925*) chronicle in detail Bryan's tenure as secretary of state and his exertions to keep the United States out of war after he resigned from office (11:439).

William C. Bullitt

14:99 Farnsworth, Beatrice. *William C. Bullitt and the Soviet Union.* Bloomington: Indiana University Press, 1967. Farnsworth covers the mercurial Bullitt's career in the history of Soviet-American relations, highlighting his mission to Russia in 1919 (especially a famous interview with Lenin) and his subsequent disillusionment with Wilson and public denunciation of the Treaty of Versailles. (Later years bore witness to Samuel Gompers's description of Bullitt as "a faddist parlor socialist.")

14:100 Freud, Sigmund, and William C. Bullitt. *Thomas Woodrow Wilson, Twenty-eighth President of the United States: A Psychological Study.* Boston: Houghton Mifflin, 1967. Declared "a disastrously bad book" by none other than Erik Erikson, this infamous work of "psychobiography" posits the idea that Wilson thought himself the son of God; thus, perhaps predictably, it is more revealing of the embittered Bullitt than of Wilson. Allegedly coauthored in the late 1930s, Freud's family always maintained that he had little or nothing to do with writing it (though it is likely he encouraged Bullitt to proceed).

Josephus Daniels

14:101 Cronon, E. David, ed. *The Cabinet Diaries of Josephus Daniels, 1913–1921.* Although diaries for 1914 and 1916 are missing, this collection of the secretary of the navy's observations on strategic and diplomatic considerations provides an important record of the war and armistice periods (12:8).

14:102 Daniels, Josephus. *The Wilson Era: Years of Peace, 1910–1917.* Chapel Hill: University of North Carolina Press, 1944. Daniels, among Wilson's cabinet his most loyal lieutenant, offers insights into the first administration and the travails of neutrality. As might be expected, the sections on the development of the U.S. navy are of most value.

John Dewey

14:103   Farrell, John C. "John Dewey and World War I: Armageddon Tests a Liberal's Faith." *Perspectives in American History* 9 (1975): 299–340. At first, Dewey supported American intervention in World War I because he thought that by such means the Old Order could be made over by extending the American model of government. After the peace negotiations, he became a sort of isolationist.

14:104   Howlett, Charles F. *Troubled Philosopher: John Dewey and the Struggle for World Peace.* Port Washington, NY: Kennikat Press, 1977. This study examines Dewey's activism as a onetime pragmatic supporter of Wilson's war aims, his later disillusionment, and his efforts on behalf of peace education in the 1920s and 1930s.

Herbert C. Hoover

14:105   Burner, David. *Herbert Hoover, A Public Life.* New York: Alfred A. Knopf, 1979. In this fine one-volume biography, Burner devotes four chapters to Hoover's efforts to alleviate hunger in Belgium, his views on food as a diplomatic tool, and his role at the Paris Peace Conference and in the politics of the League of Nations at home.

14:106   Gelfand, Lawrence E., ed. *Herbert Hoover —The Great War and Its Aftermath, 1914–23.* Iowa City: University of Iowa Press, 1979. This is a collection of essays by Hoover on such topics as organizing the wartime government, international economics, and the use of food in diplomacy.

14:107   Hoover, Herbert. *An American Epic.* Vol. 3: *Famine in Forty-Five Nations: The Battle on the Front Line, 1914–1932.* Chicago: H. Regnery Co., 1961. Part memoir, part documentary history, this work depicts how the author and the American government attempted to cope with the international dilemma of hunger and privation.

14:108   _____. *Memoirs. Vol. 1: Years of Adventure, 1874–1920.* 3 vols. New York: Macmillan, 1951. This volume of Hoover's three-volume memoir covers his service as head of the U.S. Food Administration, director of the Belgian relief, and member of the American peace commission.

14:109   Nash, George H. *The Life of Herbert Hoover.* 2 vols. New York: W. W. Norton, 1983–1988. Volumes 2 and 3 (*The Humanitarian, 1914–1917* and *Master of Emergencies, 1917–1918*) provide full coverage of the reason behind Hoover's initial claim to fame as well as of the evolution of his working relationship with Wilson during the war.

14:110   O'Brien, Francis William, ed. *The Hoover-Wilson Wartime Correspondence, September 24, 1914, to November 11, 1918.* Ames, IA: Iowa State University Press, 1974. These documents focus mainly on the food situation throughout the war.

Edward M. House

14:111   Esposito, David M. "Imagined Power: The Secret Life of Colonel House." In this interesting article, the author describes essentially a "yes man" suffering from delusions of grandeur who in private virtually took credit for bringing down Nicholas II. As for his impact on Wilson, Esposito's evidence finds House guilty of "habitual dissimulation and calculated mendacity on a previously unrecognized scale" (12:131).

14:112   George, Alexander L., and Juliette L. George. *Woodrow Wilson and Colonel House: A Personality Study.* New York: J. Day Co., 1956. This is a pioneering psychological analysis of the famous relationship and far more successful than Freud and Bullitt, *Thomas Woodrow Wilson, Twenty-eighth President of the United States: A Psychological Study* (1967) (14:100). The Georges apply Freudian analysis to Wilson's personality to explain important decisions, particularly those pertaining to the peace conference and the League. (They do not emphasize Wilson's health as an explanatory device.) They also describe how House came to understand Wilson and how their relationship helped chart the direction of Wilsonian diplomacy. On the whole, the perspective is critical.

14:113   House, Edward M. *Philip Dru, Administrator: A Story of Tomorrow, 1920–1935.* New York: B. W. Huebsch, 1912. This grandiose work of futuristic fiction, published privately and anonymously, provides many curious clues about House's ambitions. In it, the protagonist leads a revolution against America's plutocrats, imposes the single tax, old-age pensions, and the eight-hour day, and nationalizes public utilities. He then persuades the great powers to eliminate trade barriers and armaments and establishes an international parliament, whereupon he relinquishes power.

14:114 Neu, Charles E. "Woodrow Wilson and Colonel House: The Early Years, 1911–1915." In *The Wilson Era: Essays in Honor of Arthur S. Link,* ed. John Milton Cooper, Jr. and Charles E. Neu, 248–78. Arlington Heights, IL: Harlan Davidson, 1991. Starting with the 1912 campaign and ending with Wilson's marriage to Edith Galt, Neu's thirty pages offer innumerable insights into the famous friendship.

Hiram W. Johnson

14:115 Burke, Robert E., ed. *The Diary Letters of Hiram Johnson, 1917–1945.* 7 vols. New York: Garland, 1983. This is a convenient compendium of primary materials about the progressive Californian.

14:116 DeWitt, Howard A. "Hiram W. Johnson and Economic Opposition to Wilsonian Diplomacy: A Note." *Pacific Historian* 19 (Spring 1975): 15–23. Johnson opposed Wilson's foreign policy, especially U.S. participation in the League of Nations, because he feared a conspiracy of bankers and businessmen whom he believed stood to profit from American international involvement.

14:117 Lower, Richard Coke. "Hiram Johnson: The Making of an Irreconcilable." *Pacific Historical Review* 41 (November 1972): 505–26. The author makes the case that Johnson's opposition to U.S. entrance into the League of Nations was based less on political ambition or isolationism than to adherence to the principles of democracy and progressive reform. (His intense anglophobia was a major factor, too.)

David Starr Jordan

14:118 Abrahamson, James L. "David Starr Jordan and American Antimilitarism." *Pacific Northwest Quarterly* 67 (April 1976): 76–87. This is in part a survey of the historiographical debate over American pacifist movements before World War I. In scrutinizing the work of David Starr Jordan, the author reveals that his manifold motivations included worries about draining the racial stock, because "always and everywhere, war means the reversal of natural selection."

14:119 Burns, Edward McNall. *David Starr Jordan: Prophet of Freedom.* Stanford, CA: Stanford University Press, 1953. Burns has written a perceptive, though rather uncritical, study of a leading internationalist and peace seeker and the first director of the World Peace Foundation.

Robert M. La Follette

14:120 La Follette, Belle Case, and Fola La Follette. *Robert M. La Follette, June 14, 1855–June 18, 1925.* 2 vols. New York: Macmillan, 1953. Several chapters of this official biography are devoted to exploring the reasons behind the Wisconsin senator's opposition to the war and Wilson's peace program.

14:121 Thelen, David P. *Robert M. La Follette and the Insurgent Spirit.* Boston: Little, Brown, 1976. The latter portion of this brief biography focuses on the war, emphasizing its subject's antipathy toward Wilson and his works, while noting La Follette's pariah status among Republicans for having voted against the war resolution. See also Bernard A. Weisberger, *The La Follettes of Wisconsin: Love and Politics in Progressive America* (Madison: University of Wisconsin Press, 1994).

Robert Lansing

14:122 Brands, H. W. "Unpremeditated Lansing: His 'Scraps.'" *Diplomatic History* 9 (Winter 1985): 25–33. Brands assesses Lansing's private notebooks, which contain interesting critical observations about several individuals, especially Wilson, during the war and the peace conference.

14:123 Lansing, Robert. *The Big Four and Others of the Peace Conference.* Boston: Houghton Mifflin Company, 1921. The secretary of state wrote a series of essays about the principals at the peace conference: Orlando, Lloyd George, Clemenceau, and Wilson as well as Venizelos, Feisal, Botha, and Paderewski.

14:124 _____. *The Peace Negotiations, A Personal Narrative.* Boston: Houghton Mifflin Company, 1921. Lansing provides justifications for his actions and opinions at the peace conference and attempts, by his lights, to set the record straight.

14:125 _____. *War Memoirs of Robert Lansing, Secretary of State.* Indianapolis: Bobbs-Merrill, 1935. This is Lansing's posthumously published evaluation of his activities as secretary of state during the war years.

14:126 Lazo, Dimitri D. "A Question of Loyalty: Robert Lansing and the Treaty of Versailles." *Diplomatic History* 9 (Winter 1985): 35–53. The author suggests that Lansing, though indiscreet, was not much more at odds with Wilson at Paris than were several other leading advisers, and that he did not plot with the Republicans to defeat the treaty; even so, he could hardly be described as loyal to the president.

14:127 Williams, Joyce G. "The Resignation of Secretary of State Robert Lansing." *Diplomatic History* 3 (Summer 1979): 337–44. A reprint of Rear Admiral James E. Helm's "Report of Conversations Concerning the Resignation of Secretary Lansing," dated February 18, 1920.

14:128 Zivojinovic, Dragan R. "Robert Lansing's Comments on the Pontifical Peace Note of August 1, 1917." *Journal of American History* 56 (December 1969): 556–71. The secretary of state recommended that the peace note of Pope Benedict XV be rejected as a basis for negotiation. He saw the papal pronouncement emanating from a fear that socialism might undermine respect for Catholicism.

Henry Cabot Lodge

14:129 Garraty, John A. *Henry Cabot Lodge: A Biography.* Garraty ably captures Lodge's personality as well as the contest between the senator and Wilson over the future of American foreign policy during the war and after. While he acknowledges that Lodge acted partly out of principle, he stresses heavily the personal and partisan as the stronger motives behind his resistance to "Wilson's League." The volume's final section features a running commentary, in the form of footnotes, by then ambassador to the United Nations, Henry Cabot Lodge, Jr., in defense of his grandfather (in the course of which he meticu-

lously makes the case that the UN Charter embraced virtually all of the salient "Lodge Reservations") (9:113).

14:130 Mervin, David. "Henry Cabot Lodge and the League of Nations." *Journal of American Studies* 4 (February 1971): 201–16. This is a concise overview of the evolution of Senator Lodge's opposition to the League of Nations.

14:131 Parsons, Edward B. "Some International Implications of the 1918 Roosevelt-Lodge Campaign against Wilson and a Democratic Congress." *Presidential Studies Quarterly* 19 (Winter 1989): 141–57. This essay stresses Lodge's concerns that Wilson's policies, if unchecked, might weaken Great Britain while strengthening Germany.

14:132 Widenor, William C. *Henry Cabot Lodge and the Search for an American Foreign Policy.* Widenor's impressive intellectual biography analyzes Lodge's public and private ruminations on how a democracy might conduct an effective foreign policy and the relationship between force and peace; in the process it demolishes outworn notions that Lodge was an isolationist and implies that he was an early founder of the "realist" school (10:141).

Walter Hines Page

14:133 Cooper, John Milton, Jr. *Walter Hines Page: The Southerner as American, 1855–1918.* Chapel Hill: University of North Carolina Press, 1977. The idea of reconciliation is a central theme in Cooper's elegantly written biography of Wilson's ambassador to London: as a boy, Page had to reconcile his parents' conflicting ambitions for him, and as a southerner transplanted to the north, he hoped his journalism would help close sectional wounds. Thus, his chief mission as ambassador was to foster enduring Anglo-American cooperation in the most difficult of circumstances.

14:134 Gregory, Ross. *Walter Hines Page: Ambassador to the Court of St. James's.* This biography of a dedicated Wilsonian illustrates how the president sometimes chose to ignore his diplomatic appointees and, in this case, caused considerable confusion at an important post. Gregory also characterizes Page as the "superfluous ambassador" (11:505).

14:135   Hendrick, Burton J. *The Life and Letters of Walter Hines Page.* 3 vols. Garden City, NY: Doubleday, Page, 1922–1926. These volumes contain many of Page's more important letters from London and extol the ambassador's rather naïve acceptance of Britain's point of view.

Paul S. Reinsch

14:136   Pugach, Noel H. "Making the Open Door Work: Paul S. Reinsch in China, 1913–1919." *Pacific Historical Review* 38 (May 1969): 157–75. This essay describes the efforts of Paul Samuel Reinsch, the American minister to China, to maintain the open door policy by promoting and strengthening economic ties between the United States and China.

14:137   Reinsch, Paul S. *An American Diplomat in China.* The American minister to China includes material on the U.S. response to Japan's Twenty-One Demands, the Lansing-Ishii notes, and the efforts of the United States to preserve Chinese territorial integrity (13:211).

Raymond Robins

14:138   Meiburger, Anne Vincent. *Efforts of Raymond Robins toward the Recognition of Soviet Russia and the Outlawry of War, 1917–1933.* Washington, DC: Catholic University of America Press, 1958. Robins led the American Red Cross mission to the provisional government in 1917 as part of the effort to keep Russia in the war; he subsequently served as the U.S. liaison to the Bolshevik regime. This study in part chronicles those activities as well as his work to secure diplomatic recognition of the Soviet Union.

14:139   Salzman, Neil V. *Reform and Revolution: The Life and Times of Raymond Robins.* Kent, OH: Kent State University Press, 1991. Robins was one of a few voices arguing that good relations with communist Russia would advance Allied interests. Salzman establishes his subject's claim as possibly the most astute American observer on the scene in the early Bolshevik period; this is likely to remain the definitive work on the subject.

Elihu Root

14:140   Hopkins, C. Howard, and John W. Long.

"American Jews and the Root Mission to Russia in 1917: Some New Evidence." *American Jewish History* 69 (March 1980): 342–54. The Wilson administration sent the Root mission to Russia to demonstrate U.S. support for Kerensky's provisional government; none of the principals thought to appoint any Jews to the delegation, however, despite the fact that the Americans would be depending on Russian Jews for a clear picture of the new regime's prospects.

14:141   Jessup, Philip C. *Elihu Root.* In volume 2, Jessup tracks his subject's collaboration with Lodge, who happily stood aside when Root proposed the idea of reservations (rather than amendments) to the League Covenant—the basic strategy of the "Mild Reservationists," of which Root was the key member, for making the League safe for the United States (11:475).

14:142   Leopold, Richard W. *Elihu Root and the Conservative Tradition.* Boston: Little, Brown, 1954. Leopold covers much ground in this one-volume biography. He devotes two chapters to the conservative legalist's concept of world peace (and stability) as primarily a function of the growth of international law and shows how it shaped Root's critical view of Wilson and the League of Nations.

Oswald Garrison Villard

14:143   Villard, Oswald Garrison. *Fighting Years: Memoirs of a Liberal Editor.* New York: Harcourt, Brace and Company, 1939. The "liberal's liberal," editor of *The Nation,* and erstwhile admirer of Wilson gives his scalding opinions of what he considered the president's attempts to subvert the American liberal tradition.

14:144   Wreszin, Michael. *Oswald Garrison Villard, Pacifist at War.* Bloomington: Indiana University Press, 1965. In 1915, Villard ran Wilson's portrait on the front page of the *New York Evening News* and praised him lavishly for refusing to go to war over the *Lusitania* and the *Arabic.* By March 1919, in *The Nation,* he was denouncing the president for having abandoned "the fourteen points and the league that he formerly preached." This is the story of Villard's struggle, as an editor and activist, to reconcile pacifism with liberalism.

Brand Whitlock

14:145 Davidson, John Wells. "Brand Whitlock and the Diplomacy of Belgian Relief." *Prologue* 2 (Winter 1970): 145–60. The essay describes the activities of the minister and ambassador to Belgium (1914–1921) regarding the relief operations in that country before and during the German occupation.

14:146 Nevins, Allan, ed. *The Letters and Journal of Brand Whitlock.* These volumes constitute a documentary record of Whitlock's assignment as ambassador to Belgium (11:31).

Woodrow Wilson

14:147 Baker, Ray Stannard, ed. *Woodrow Wilson: Life and Letters.* Baker, one of the great journalists of his day, won exclusive access to Wilson's papers because of his sympathetic reporting on the president's labors at Paris. The results were mixed. The beautifully produced volumes remain an essential source, but they are largely hagiography. Volumes 7 and 8 are a collection of documents, ending at the armistice, with very little narrative or analysis; yet, published upon the outbreak of World War II, they were awarded the Pulitzer Prize for biography (12:118).

14:148 Bell, Herbert C. F. *Woodrow Wilson and the People.* Garden City, NY: Doubleday, Doran and Company, 1945. This is one of several studies that appeared as part of the "second chance" revival of interest in Wilson during World War II. Fulsome and uncritical, Bell's book stresses Wilson's efforts to educate the public about new international responsibilities and obtain a popular mandate for his policies.

14:149 Blum, John Morton. *Woodrow Wilson and the Politics of Morality.* Boston: Little, Brown, 1956. Among several works published in the centenary of his birth, this short biography by a distinguished historian is a classic example of the realist critique of Wilson. Though sporadically sympathetic, Blum pronounces him "a nineteenth-century intelligence, obsolescing at a rapid rate."

14:150 Clements, Kendrick A. *The Presidency of Woodrow Wilson.* Among the finest of the American Presidency series, this wide-ranging assessment focuses on the impact of both Wilson's leadership and the war in increasing the power of the executive branch (12:67).

14:151 _____. *Woodrow Wilson, World Statesman.* Often cited as the best one-volume biography of Wilson to date (and deservedly so), Clements's work places Wilson's personal alongside his public life and addresses his accomplishments and legacies to contemporary America (12:119).

14:152 Cooper, John Milton, Jr. "'An Irony of Fate': Woodrow Wilson's Pre–World War I Diplomacy." *Diplomatic History* 3 (Fall 1979): 425–37. In a review of volumes 27–30 of *The Papers of Woodrow Wilson* (1966–1994) (11:33), Cooper concludes that Wilson had gained considerable experience and expertise in foreign affairs between March 1913 and September 1914, the Mexico imbroglio having served as something of a chastening apprenticeship.

14:153 _____. *The Warrior and the Priest: Woodrow Wilson and Theodore Roosevelt.* In this distinguished comparative biography, which emphasizes politics more than foreign policy, Cooper, in his summation, turns the table on the reader's expectations by casting Wilson in the role of warrior and Roosevelt in that of priest (11:467).

14:154 Cooper, John Milton, Jr., and Charles E. Neu, eds. *The Wilson Era: Essays in Honor of Arthur S. Link.* Arlington Heights, IL: Harlan Davidson, 1991. In addition to a foreword by George McGovern (his first dissertation student), this Festschrift for Link contains twelve essays, several of which are pertinent here: Ralph B. Levering, "Public Culture and Public Opinion: The League of Nations Controversy in New Jersey and North Carolina" (159–97); Cooper, "Fool's Errand or Finest Hour? Woodrow Wilson's Speaking Tour in September 1919" (198–220); Neu, "Woodrow Wilson and Colonel House: The Early Years" (248–78); Dewey W. Grantham, "*The Papers of Woodrow Wilson*: A Preliminary Appraisal" (281–301); Thomas J. Knock, "Kennan versus Wilson" (302–26); and George F. Kennan, "Comments on the Paper Entitled 'Kennan versus Wilson' by Professor Thomas J. Knock" (327–30). Cooper's own essay is treated separately in this chapter.

14:155 Diamond, William. *The Economic Thought of Woodrow Wilson.* Baltimore: Johns Hopkins Press, 1943. Reflecting the influence of Charles A. Beard, this early work on Wilson's economic philosophy devotes two chapters to Wilsonian foreign economic policy. The chapter entitled "The New World Order" anticipates some of the revisionist writing of the 1960s.

14:156 Heckscher, August. *Woodrow Wilson.* New York: Scribner, 1991. This is a substantial one-volume biography, very nicely written and highly favorable to its subject.

14:157 Hoover, Herbert. *The Ordeal of Woodrow Wilson.* New York: McGraw-Hill, 1958. Reprint 1992 (Johns Hopkins University Press). The only major study of a president ever written by a former president, this volume remains insightful and often quite moving. Hoover based it on his own notes and recollections as well as on some primary research; he portrays Wilson as a great but tragically flawed figure in his pursuit of a more progressive and stable world order.

14:158 Link, Arthur S. *The Higher Realism of Woodrow Wilson, and Other Essays.* In several of these twenty-four essays or addresses (1944–1969) covering various aspects of Wilson's character, philosophy, and politics, Link advances the notion that, in many salient respects, Wilson's idealism in politics and diplomacy constituted a "higher realism" (11:80).

14:159 _____. *Wilson.* 5 vols. Princeton: Princeton University Press, 1947–1965. Although it ends just as the United States declares war on Germany, this is a monumental biography. Characterized by massive, multinational archival research and a lively style, Link's volumes provide insights into Wilson the individual while explicating his role in the domestic reform movement as well as his foreign policies, in "a considerable admixture of history with biography." The second volume, *The New Freedom* (1956), and the third, *The Struggle for Neutrality, 1914–1915* (1960), in particular, are considered historiographical milestones, and both won the Bancroft Prize. The others are *The Road to the White House* (1947), *Confusions and Crises, 1915–1916* (1964), and *Campaigns for Progressivism and Peace, 1916–1917* (1965) (See 14:278 and 14:315 for the latter two). Link originally planned three additional volumes—one each on the war period,

the peace conference, and the fight for the League—but decided instead to put all of his energies into *The Papers of Woodrow Wilson* (1966–1994) (14:16), which he considered his own most significant achievement as a historian.

14:160 Mulder, John M. *Woodrow Wilson: The Years of Preparation.* Princeton: Princeton University Press, 1978. Wilson once told a British audience, during his grand tour of Europe prior to the peace conference, "The stern Covenanter tradition that is behind me sends many an echo down the years." Mulder takes this statement as his cue and argues that the key to understanding young Woodrow's "years of preparation"—and, by implication, many of his initiatives as president, including the *Covenant* of the League of Nations—is the Presbyterian covenantal religious tradition, the spiritual curriculum that the Reverend Joseph Ruggles Wilson imparted to his son.

14:161 Schulte Nordholt, Jan Willem. *Woodrow Wilson: A Life for World Peace.* Translated by Herbert H. Rowen. Berkeley: University of California Press, 1991. This biography offers a fundamentally hostile European perspective on Wilson, reminiscent of the critical writings of the interwar years; though occasionally marred by factual errors, it nonetheless makes for compelling reading.

14:162 Thorsen, Niels Aage. *The Political Thought of Woodrow Wilson, 1875–1910.* Princeton: Princeton University Press, 1988. Although this study by a Danish scholar opens with Wilson's college years and ends with his election as governor of New Jersey, it contains often brilliant prospective insights into Wilson the politician and diplomatist. A supplementary volume to *The Papers of Woodrow Wilson.*

14:163 Walworth, Arthur. *Woodrow Wilson.* 2 vols. 2d rev. ed. Boston: Houghton Mifflin, 1965. The second volume of this Pulitzer Prize–winning biography covers the period of the war and the peace settlement. Walworth's identification of Wilson as "the prophet" gives some idea of the mold in which he casts the president. (In subsequent works, Walworth would grow more skeptical of Wilson.) Originally published in 1958.

14:164 Weinstein, Edwin A. *Woodrow Wilson: A Medical and Psychological Biography.* Princeton:

Princeton University Press, 1981. Expanding on his earlier articles, Weinstein addresses a variety of topics on Wilson's personality and health, elaborating on his theory that he suffered from long-standing hypertension, carotid artery disease, and progressive cerebrovascular disease—all of which, he argues, had a palpable effect on the outcome of the battle over the League of Nations. He asserts categorically "that the cerebral dysfunction which resulted from Wilson's devastating strokes prevented the ratification of the treaty."

Others

14:165   Forcey, Charles. *The Crossroads of Liberalism: Croly, Weyl, Lippmann, and the Progressive Era, 1900–1925.* New York: Oxford University Press, 1961. Forcey analyzes the intertwined lives and political thought of three of the greatest journalists of the era and demonstrates that they wielded considerable influence on the affairs of state and Woodrow Wilson's foreign policies. As much a study in intellectual and political history as in biography, this engaging monograph was somewhat pioneering in its time and continues to reward.

14:166   Crane, Katharine Elizabeth. *Mr. Carr of State: Forty-Seven Years in the Department of State.* New York: St. Martin's Press, 1960. Chapters 18–25 treat the American consular service under the direction of Wilbur Carr. In addition to Carr's activities during the war, it details the relief of Americans stranded in Europe and prisoner of war management.

14:167   Coolidge, Harold Jefferson, and Robert Howard Lord. *Archibald Cary Coolidge: Life and Letters.* Boston: Houghton Mifflin Company, 1932. Reprint 1971 (Books for Libraries Press). This book about the editor of *Foreign Affairs* combines narrative with documents and tells the story of his missions in Archangel, Vienna, and the peace conference.

14:168   Smith, Daniel M. *Aftermath of War: Bainbridge Colby and Wilsonian Diplomacy, 1920–1921.* Philadelphia: American Philosophical Society, 1970. An ardent anti-Bolshevik and pro-Leaguer, Colby was Wilson's last secretary of state (1920–1921). In the circumstances (and as a Republican), his list of accomplishments was not long.

14:169   Creel, George. *The War, the World, and Wilson.* New York: Harper and Brothers, 1920. "What I seem to see—with all my heart I hope I am wrong—is a tragedy of disappointment," the president said to the author on the eve of the peace conference. And that is the central theme of this recollection of the war and the battle for an honorable peace, written by the director of the Committee on Public Information and irreconcilable Wilsonian.

14:170   Levy, David W. *Herbert Croly of the New Republic: The Life and Thought of an American Progressive.* Princeton: Princeton University Press, 1985. Herbert Croly and his magazine enjoyed a regular readership in the White House and even supplied Wilson with one of his most important phrases, "Peace Without Victory." Levy's is a splendid biography of the influential journalist.

14:171   Dawes, Charles G. *A Journal of the Great War.* 2 vols. Boston: Houghton Mifflin Company, 1921. A record of Dawes's activities as general purchasing agent for the American Expeditionary Force, this journal also has interesting comments on interallied cooperation (and the lack thereof), European politics, and military strategy.

14:172   Salvatore, Nick. *Eugene V. Debs: Citizen and Socialist.* Urbana: University of Illinois Press, 1982. Although Salvatore's stress is on the politics of American socialism, he demonstrates that Debs was one of the most incisive commentators on foreign policy of his times. The discussions of American intervention in the war, the Bolshevik revolution, and Debs's famous trial and imprisonment are very good. The book won the Bancroft Prize.

14:173   Ellis, Mark. "'Closing Ranks' and 'Seeking Honors': W. E. B. Du Bois in World War I." *Journal of American History* 79 (June 1992): 96–124. In July 1918, W. E. B. Du Bois told the readers of *The Crisis* (which he edited for the NAACP), "Let us, while this war lasts, forget our special grievances" and join the fight against German autocracy. "Close Ranks" proved to be the most controversial essay of his career; that he was then also seeking a captaincy in the Military Intelligence Branch of the U.S. Army General Staff only intensified questions about his motivation. Ellis argues that, while Du Bois sincerely believed manifold demonstrations of patriotism would help the cause of racial justice, he later deeply regretted the editorial.

14:174 Eastman, Max. *Enjoyment of Living.* New York: Harper, 1948. Although he had turned sharply right and became editor of the *Reader's Digest* in the 1950s, Eastman had been a prominent socialist in the 1910s who rather admired Wilson. He wrote many editorials praising his politics and foreign policy—until the peace conference. His autobiography offers many insights into those times.

14:175 Francis, David R. *Russia from the American Embassy, April, 1916–November, 1918.* New York: C. Scribner's Sons, 1921. Reprint 1970 (Arno Press). The American ambassador to Russia explains the Bolshevik revolution as the work of the Germans and tells of his efforts to depose Lenin's government.

14:176 Gerard, James W. *My Four Years in Germany.* The U.S. ambassador to Berlin in 1914–1917 describes the German military establishment and the futile negotiations preceding the American declaration of war (11:451).

14:177 Grew, Joseph C. *Turbulent Era: A Diplomatic Record of Forty Years, 1904–1945.* In the first volume of his memoir, Grew recounts his service as first secretary of the American embassy at Berlin during the neutrality period as well as his role as a member of the American Commission to Negotiate Peace. Edited by Walter Johnson, assisted by Nancy Harvison Hooker (11:21).

14:178 Briggs, Mitchell P. *George D. Herron and the European Settlement.* Stanford, CA: Stanford University Press, 1932. This monograph is a valuable account of Herron's mission in Switzerland to confer with various leaders of the Central Powers during and after the war.

14:179 Pusey, Merlo J. *Charles Evans Hughes.* 2 vols. New York: Macmillan, 1951. Volume 1 of this Pulitzer Prize–winning biography offers the most detailed account yet written of Hughes's 1916 campaign for president and his views on the war and the League of Nations. Although Theodore Roosevelt dubbed him "the bearded iceberg," Hughes was an intellectual and political force to be reckoned with, as Pusey ably demonstrates, as well as one of the era's most thoughtful conservative internationalists.

14:180 Arnett, Alex M. *Claude Kitchin and the Wilson War Policies.* Boston: Little, Brown and Company, 1937. Reprint 1971 (Russell and Russell). This is a very good biography of the irrepressible North Carolinian, chair of the House Ways and Means Committee, and House majority leader. Kitchin opposed Wilson's preparedness program and regarded the administration as un-neutral toward Germany (among other trespasses).

14:181 Lamont, Thomas W. *Across World Frontiers.* New York: Harcourt, Brace, 1951. Lamont, an informal political adviser to Wilson and partner in J. P. Morgan and Company, represented the U.S. Treasury Department at the Paris Peace Conference and was closely involved with reparations. His memoir includes discussion of American financial contributions to both the Allied war effort and the second China Consortium as well as an overview of debates on German economic problems.

14:182 Steel, Ronald. *Walter Lippmann and the American Century.* Boston: Little, Brown, 1980. Reprint 1999 (Transaction). The chapters covering the Great War in this Pulitzer Prize–winning biography highlight Lippmann's sense of urgency that the United States must enter the war on Wilson's terms, his contributions to the formulation of the Fourteen Points, and his change of heart during the Paris Peace Conference.

14:183 McAdoo, William G. *Crowded Years: The Reminiscences of William G. McAdoo.* Boston: Houghton Mifflin Company, 1931. Reprint 1971 (Kennikat Press). McAdoo was an unusually able member of Wilson's cabinet; he exerted an impact on events through his vigorous pursuit of foreign trade expansion during the neutrality period and his design for financing the war effort. Although he married the president's daughter, Eleanor, and served as secretary of the treasury, he and Wilson personally did not get on terribly well toward the end (which McAdoo leaves out of the story), partly because he was too transparent about his own presidential ambitions.

14:184 Morgenthau, Henry, Sr. *Ambassador Morgenthau's Story.* Garden City, NY: Doubleday, Page and Company, 1918. Morgenthau recounts the German subversion of and subsequent alliance with Turkey. He was the American ambassador to Turkey (1913–1916); his son, Henry, Jr., became secretary of the treasury under Franklin Roosevelt.

14:185 Mitchell, Kell F., Jr. "Frank L. Polk and Continued American Participation in the Paris Peace Conference, 1919." *North Dakota Quarterly* 41 (Spring 1973): 50–61. Frank Polk took charge of the American Commission to Negotiate Peace after Wilson's departure from Paris in the summer of 1919 and continued at the helm until the commission ended its activities at the end of the year.

14:186 Josephson, Hannah. *Jeannette Rankin, First Lady in Congress: A Biography.* Indianapolis: Bobbs-Merrill, 1974. This book remains the only full-scale biography of the first woman ever elected to Congress, whose dedication to pacifism caused her to vote against going to war on two notable occasions. The first was in April 1917, when fifty-five of her colleagues did likewise; for her courage she lost her seat in the House of Representatives in 1918; twenty-two years later, Montana returned her to Washington in time to vote against the war resolution in December 1941 — the only member to do so.

14:187 Rosenstone, Robert A. *Romantic Revolutionary: A Biography of John Reed.* New York: Alfred A. Knopf, 1975. Reprint 1990 (Harvard University Press). A leading member of the "lyrical left," John Reed rode with Villa, sat in the councils of Lenin, and in between campaigned for Wilson in 1916 because of the latter's progressivism and peace platform. Among his more remarkable essays is one about Wilson and the Mexican revolution, based on an extended White House interview. This book became the basis for Warren Beatty's altogether remarkable film, *Reds* (1981). See also Eric Homberger with John Biggart, eds., *John Reed and the Russian Revolution: Uncollected Articles, Letters, and Speeches on Russia, 1917–1920* (New York: St. Martin's Press, 1992).

14:188 Sharp, William G. *The War Memoirs of William Graves Sharp, American Ambassador to France, 1914–1919.* London: Constable and Co., 1931. In the absence of existing manuscript papers from Ambassador Sharp, this memoir portrays the activities of the lawyer from Elyria, Ohio, who assumed important responsibilities at the outset of the European war. Edited by Warrington Dawson.

14:189 Josephson, Harold. *James T. Shotwell and the Rise of Internationalism in America.* Rutherford, NJ: Fairleigh Dickinson University Press, 1974. Shotwell was a dedicated Wilsonian internationalist of sorts all his life. Although this study emphasizes the interwar years, it gives three chapters to the Columbia historian's work on The Inquiry during the war and at the peace conference.

14:190 Blum, John Morton. *Joe Tumulty and the Wilson Era.* Boston: Houghton Mifflin, 1951. This is the only major study of one of Wilson's most important advisers, who at times appeared almost pathetic in his devotion to his boss. Tumulty nonetheless possessed keen political instincts; more often than not he gave Wilson very good advice.

14:191 Fortenberry, Joseph E. "James Kimble Vardaman and American Foreign Policy, 1913–1919." *Journal of Mississippi History* 35 (May 1973): 127–40. A one-term senator from Mississippi (1913–1919), Vardaman was critical of the administration's "pro-British" neutrality, of preparedness, and especially of American intervention in the war.

14:192 Vopicka, Charles J. *Secrets of the Balkans.* Chicago: Rand, McNally and Company, 1921. This memoir of the U.S. minister to Rumania, Serbia, and Bulgaria (1913–1920) traces the impact of the war on the Balkan nations, particularly Rumania. One interesting emphasis is Vopicka's attention to Eastern European royalty.

14:193 Nevins, Allan. *Henry White: Thirty Years of American Diplomacy.* This is an authorized biography (and Pulitzer Prize awardee) by a soon-to-be famous historian of the Civil War; it tells the story of the sole Republican member of the American Commission to Negotiate Peace who played a creditable, if not terribly important, role in the nation's service (11:486).

Naval and Military

Tasker H. Bliss

14:194 Palmer, Frederick. *Bliss, Peacemaker: The Life and Letters of General Tasker Howard Bliss.* New York: Dodd, Mead and Company, 1934. The former army chief of staff and amateur classicist was Wilson's military adviser on the American peace commission; his letters reveal a critical view of the Paris negotiations, yet a favorable view of Wilson.

14:195 Trask, David F. *General Tasker Howard Bliss and the "Sessions of the World," 1919.* Philadelphia: American Philosophical Society, 1966. This brief monograph explains Bliss's role at the peace conference as well as his thoughts and frustrations, as reflected in the numerous letters he wrote to his wife and Secretary of War Newton Baker. Bliss's belief in the utter necessity of disarmament is emphasized.

John J. Pershing

14:196 Lowry, Bullitt. "Pershing and the Armistice." *Journal of American History* 55 (September 1968): 281–91. During the armistice negotiations, a controversy arose between General Pershing and the White House over the military terms to be imposed on Germany. Pershing's hard line toward Germany, the author explains, was effectively quashed by Wilson, but not before the general came perilously close to provoking a reprimand from the War Department.

14:197 Pershing, John J. *My Experiences in the World War.* 2 vols. New York: F. A. Stokes Co., 1931. The value of this best-selling memoir of the head of the American Expeditionary Force lies partly in its exposition of the difficulties of interallied military cooperation and in Pershing's interpretation of Wilson's policies. It sparked some controversy with Peyton March and won the Pulitzer in history.

14:198 Smythe, Donald. *Pershing, General of the Armies.* Bloomington: Indiana University Press, 1986. In this fairly critical biography, Pershing comes across as a military leader alternately possessed of the qualities of both McClellan and Grant, with the former's penchant for delay and meticulous planning and the latter's brutal willingness to sacrifice thousands of lives, as Pershing did at Belleau Wood.

14:199 Vandiver, Frank E. *Black Jack: The Life and Times of John J. Pershing.* 2 vols. College Station: Texas A&M University Press, 1977. As leader of the punitive expedition into Mexico (1916–1917) and commander of the American Expeditionary Forces (1917–1919), Pershing sometimes played the role of diplomat and maker of foreign policy as well as that of soldier. This is a fine biography, though one should also consult Smythe, *Pershing, General of the Armies* (1986) (14:198).

Peyton C. March

14:200 Coffman, Edward M. *The Hilt of the Sword: The Career of Peyton C. March.* Madison: University of Wisconsin Press, 1966. The army chief of staff during World War I is resurrected here as something of a curmudgeon, intolerant of bureaucratic indiscipline, but, in Coffman's hands, March also earns credit on a par with Pershing (with whom he was often at odds) for the success of the American Expeditionary Force.

William Sims

14:201 Morison, Elting E. *Admiral Sims and the Modern American Navy.* Boston: Houghton Mifflin Company, 1942. This is the fullest treatment of the chief officer in charge of America's naval operations during the war; Sims was constantly at odds with Secretary Daniels, whom the admiral regarded as incompetent.

Leonard Wood

14:202 Lane, Jack C. *Armed Progressive: General Leonard Wood.* This is the standard biography of Taft and Wilson's army chief of staff (1910–1914), Theodore Roosevelt's close friend, and would-be president, who helped to build the modern army but was denied a command in France by Pershing (10:178).

EUROPEAN

Count Johann H. von Bernstorff

14:203 Bernstorff, Johann H. von. *Memoirs of Count Bernstorff.* Translated by Eric Sutton. Bernstorff was appointed ambassador to the United States in 1908 and served until 1917. His memoirs are rather sad, a story about frustration and bitterness toward his own country and the United States (11:437).

14:204   Doerries, Reinhard R. *Imperial Challenge: Ambassador Count Bernstorff and German-American Relations, 1908–1917*. Translated by Christa D. Shannon. The author does his subject justice. He explains how Bernstorff earlier had urged that England would make a better ally than enemy and emphasizes how hard he worked to keep diplomatic channels open with the United States during the various submarine crises after the war broke out. For all of his labors, he was out of step with his own government; when he returned home in 1917, General Ludendorff denounced him as a "democrat" and the kaiser refused to see him (11:196). This is a revised, translated version of *Washington-Berlin, 1908/1917* (1975).

Lord Robert Cecil

14:205   Cecil, Robert. *A Great Experiment, an Autobiography*. New York: Oxford University Press, 1941. Lord Robert was one of the three chief architects (along with Wilson and Smuts) of the Covenant of the League of Nations as well as the president's most important ally on the British delegation, even though the two disliked each other. Cecil tells his own story well.

Georges Clemenceau

14:206   Duroselle, Jean-Baptiste. "Wilson and Clemenceau." In *Centenaire Woodrow Wilson, 1856–1956*, 75–94. Geneva: Centre Européen de la Dotation Carnegie, 1956. In this volume based on a conference at the Institut Universitaire de Hautes Etudes Internationale at Geneva, the French scholar juxtaposes the personal lives and politics of the two (sometimes friendly) antagonists and argues that Clemenceau actually took on the mantle of idealist from time to time while Wilson often played the realist.

14:207   Watson, David R. *Georges Clemenceau: A Political Biography*. New York: David McKay, 1976. Watson sees "the Tiger" as the only politician who could have brought France through the final year of

the war with its constitutional system intact. A "master of political tactics," at the Paris Peace Conference he prevailed in the final agreement in almost every area that mattered to him. Published in 1974 in the United Kingdom.

Lord Edward Grey

14:208   Boothe, Leon E. "A Fettered Envoy: Lord Grey's Mission to the United States, 1919–1920." *Review of Politics* 33 (January 1971): 78–94. As the distinguished former foreign secretary, Grey was dispatched to America in part to compose the controversy over the Treaty of Versailles. He never got to see Wilson after four months in Washington, and the mission otherwise ended in failure.

14:209   Grey, Edward. *Twenty-Five Years, 1892–1916*. The memoirs of Lord Grey, Great Britain's foreign secretary (1905–1916), convey a sense of the author's personality as well as his travails as his country's chief diplomatist. In discussing the United States and the war, he is mainly tactful (11:498).

14:210   Robbins, Keith. *Sir Edward Grey: A Biography of Lord Grey of Fallodon*. London: Cassell, 1971. In most respects, this sympathetic account is much more useful than Grey's own memoirs.

David Lloyd George

14:211   Egerton, George W. "The Lloyd George 'War Memoirs': A Study in the Politics of Memory." *Journal of Modern History* 60 (March 1988): 55–94. Egerton explores the genesis and repercussions of the prime minister's controversial, lucrative, 1-million-word-long endeavor to vindicate his wartime leadership.

14:212   Lentin, Anthony. *Lloyd George, Woodrow Wilson and the Guilt of Germany: An Essay in the Pre-History of Appeasement*. Baton Rouge: Louisiana State University Press, 1985. This fascinating study portrays Wilson as a tragic hero and Lloyd George as merely tragic, mainly because he did not have the stomach to uphold his own work, thus helping lay the foundation for the unraveling of the treaty in the interwar period.

14:213 Lloyd George, David. *The Truth about the Peace Treaties.* 2 vols. London: V. Gollancz, 1938. Reprint 1972 (H. Fertig). These volumes are a heated documentary account that tries in part to rebut the criticisms of British policies in André Tardieu's *La Paix* (Paris: Payot and Cie, 1921).

14:214 _____. *War Memoirs.* 6 vols. Boston: Little, Brown and Company, 1933–1937. At the time, these volumes were the commercially most success-ful memoirs in British history, but they contain many factual errors. Although there are generous references to diplomacy, the emphasis is on military events. (Lloyd George took pains, in particular, to excoriate Haig for Passchendaele.)

14:215 Rowland, Peter. *David Lloyd George: A Bi-ography.* New York: Macmillan, 1975. According to the author, the British leader, for all his faults, had ex-traordinary political skills and ably used them to set in motion Britain's welfare state, negotiate peace with Germany, and forge a settlement with Ireland.

14:216 Woodward, David R. "The Origins and In-tent of David Lloyd George's January 5 War Aims Speech." *Historian* 34 (November 1971): 22–39. This is a reliable account of the prime minister's notable speech to the British Trades Union League at Caxton Hall, in which he paid obeisance to the new diplomacy and tried to assuage British labor with a declaration of moderate terms at a critical juncture during the war.

Jan Smuts

14:217 Hancock, W. K. *Smuts.* 2 vols. Cambridge, UK: Cambridge University Press, 1962–1968. Smuts, the celebrated scholar-statesman of South Africa, was the author of an important pamphlet, *The League of Nations: A Practical Suggestion* (1918), which helped to shape the Covenant of the League. This is a lengthy, favorable biography of the South African leader.

14:218 Hancock, W. K., and Jean van der Poel, eds. *Selections from the Smuts Papers.* This collec-tion is especially useful for understanding Smuts's role at the Paris Peace Conference and his contribu-tions to the formation of the League of Nations and the mandate system (13:33).

George Buchanan

14:219 Buchanan, George. *My Mission to Russia and Other Diplomatic Memories.* 2 vols. Boston: Little, Brown and Company, 1923. Reprint 1970 (Arno Press). Sir George Buchanan, the British am-bassador to St. Petersburg from 1910 to 1917, has a few things to say about American attitudes toward the Russians.

James Bryce

14:220 Fisher, H. A. L. *James Bryce (Viscount Bryce of Dechmont, O.M.).* The second volume of this biography considers Bryce's attachments to the United States and his efforts on behalf of the League of Nations (11:442).

Winston Churchill

14:221 Churchill, Winston. *The World Crisis.* 4 vols. in 5. New York: Scribner, 1923–1929. Churchill's critical examination of the conduct of military operations (which, in light of Gallipoli, is somewhat galling) reveals the evolution of the idea he applied during World War II: the authority of the government must prevail over that of the military in the conduct of war. The work contains interesting re-marks about Wilson. Scribner in 1992 published a one-volume abridgement, *The World Crisis.*

Franz von Papen

14:222 Papen, Franz von. *Memoirs.* Translated by Brian Connell. New York: Dutton, 1953. Von Papen describes his activities as German military attaché in Washington.

William Wiseman

14:223 Fowler, W. B. *British-American Relations, 1917–1918: The Role of Sir William Wiseman.* Princeton: Princeton University Press, 1969. The strains in Anglo-American relations did not end with the American declaration of war. Wiseman, the head of British intelligence in America, worked hand in glove with Colonel House and sometimes at cross-purposes with Wilson. Fowler maintains that Wiseman became essential to Anglo-American cooperation during the war.

Wilsonian Foreign Policy: Thematic Studies on Diplomacy and War

14:224   *Wilson's Diplomacy: An International Symposium.* Cambridge, MA: Schenkman Pub. Co., 1973. This collection of essays discusses Wilson's conception of the role of the president in foreign affairs (Arthur Link); French responses to Wilsonian diplomacy (Jean-Baptiste Duroselle); the varieties of "German anti-Wilsonism" (Ernst Frankel); and Wilson's intentions at the Paris Peace Conference (Herbert G. Nicholas).

14:225   Buehrig, Edward H., ed. *Wilson's Foreign Policy in Perspective.* Bloomington: Indiana University Press, 1957. Reprint 1970 (Peter Smith). This collection of essays, part of the centennial observance of Wilson's birth, covers several subjects, including the way the British saw him, his relationship with his chief adviser, his East Asian and Latin American policies, and the League of Nations. Among the more interesting or otherwise notable contributions are Charles Seymour, "The Role of Colonel House in Wilson's Diplomacy" (11–33); Buehrig, "Woodrow Wilson and Collective Security" (34–60); Samuel Flagg Bemis, "Woodrow Wilson and Latin America" (105–40); and Sir Llewellyn Woodward, "A British View of Mr. Wilson's Foreign Policy" (141–76).

14:226   _____. *Woodrow Wilson and the Balance of Power.* Buehrig attempts to split the difference over the realists' critiques of Wilson by making the case that he sometimes practiced balance-of-power politics in pursuit of ostensibly idealistic goals, and that he was usually quite practical about America's security concerns (11:148).

14:227   Calhoun, Frederick S. *Power and Principle: Armed Intervention in Wilsonian Foreign Policy.* Calhoun examines seven cases of intervention (including Mexico and Russia) to test his argument that Wilson was the first president to use military force systematically to try to bring about certain kinds of political results in foreign policy without letting the military intervention get out of hand; thus, while he sometimes failed to achieve the desired ends, he nonetheless averted potential catastrophes by the measured use of force and by keeping his generals in check (12:65). (The same press published an abridgement, *Uses of Force and Wilsonian Foreign Policy,* in 1993.)

14:228   Esposito, David M. *The Legacy of Woodrow Wilson: American War Aims in World War I.* Westport, CT: Praeger, 1996. This brief volume covers some highlights of Wilson's foreign policy from the outbreak of war in 1914 through the armistice; a short postscript chapter follows.

14:229   Gelfand, Lawrence E. "The Mystique of Wilsonian Statecraft." *Diplomatic History* 7 (Spring 1983): 87–101. In this interesting meditation (his SHAFR presidential address), the author laments "the duality of Wilsonian ideas and Wilsonian management of foreign policy." While admiring the president's motives and goals, Gelfand stresses that the crush of business at Paris was bound to break down his overly centralized management of diplomacy.

14:230   Kennan, George F. "Comments on a Paper Entitled 'Kennan versus Wilson' by Professor Thomas J. Knock." In *The Wilson Era: Essays in Honor of Arthur S. Link,* ed. John Milton Cooper, Jr. and Charles E. Neu, 327–30. Arlington Heights, IL: Harlan Davidson, 1991. Forty years after the publication of *American Diplomacy, 1900–1950,* Kennan significantly modified his views, characterizing Wilson "as ahead of any other statesman of his time" and acknowledging the "great and commanding relevance many of his ideas would acquire before the century was out."

14:231   Kennedy, Ross A. "Woodrow Wilson, World War I, and an American Conception of National Security." *Diplomatic History* 25 (Winter 2001): 1–31. This essay aptly states that it was Wilson's great objective to forge "national security" in a world dominated by a complex alliance system, mutual suspicion, and preponderating armaments. In addition to a form of collective security, the author finds that Wilson laid a heavy stress on controlling German militarism and on dramatic reductions in armaments among the other great powers. He nonetheless concludes that America's cold war global commitments, the nuclear arms race, and the "military-industrial complex" could "in some measure" be blamed on "the enduring influence of Woodrow Wilson's conception of American national security." Kennedy sustains constant dialogue with other authors in the field.

14:232   Knock, Thomas J. "Kennan versus Wilson." In *The Wilson Era: Essays in Honor of Arthur S. Link,* ed. John Milton Cooper, Jr. and Charles E. Neu, 302–26. Arlington Heights, IL: Harlan Davidson, 1991. The author argues that Kennan's understanding of Wilson, in the 1950s and 1960s, was seriously flawed and that, by the 1980s, Kennan himself was advocating many of the same ideas associated with Wilsonian foreign policy that he had once scorned. Kennan's response (327–30) (14:230), following Knock's essay in the volume, is of some historiographical importance.

14:233   Levin, N. Gordon, Jr. *Woodrow Wilson and World Politics: America's Response to War and Revolution.* New York: Oxford University Press, 1968. Taking certain cues from Arno Mayer, William Appleman Williams, and Louis Hartz, Levin argues that Wilson's historic importance lies in his attempt to lead the nations of the world away from both socialist revolution and atavistic imperialism and toward the path of "liberal-capitalist-internationalism." This Bancroft Prize book remains historiographically significant.

14:234   Link, Arthur S. *Wilson the Diplomatist: A Look at His Major Foreign Policies.* Based on his Albert Shaw lectures at the Johns Hopkins University, Link's book concentrates on the main features of Wilsonian foreign policy, including problems of neutrality, the decision for war, the program for peace, and the struggle for the League of Nations (12:71).

14:235   _____. *Woodrow Wilson: Revolution, War, and Peace.* This is a revision of *Wilson the Diplomatist: A Look at His Major Foreign Policies*

(1957) (14:234), but partly because Link substantially softened his earlier balanced criticisms, it is not necessarily an improvement. Still, it is a good place to start, especially for undergraduates, and because the earlier version is out of print (12:72).

14:236   Lippmann, Walter. *The Stakes of Diplomacy.* 2d ed. New York: Henry Holt, 1917. Lippmann was arguably the brightest of all of Wilson's bright young men and later suffered disillusionment with the president; yet he sometimes exhibited inconsistencies and poor judgment himself—as when he collaborated with the "Battalion of Death" in 1919. This is an important contemporary treatise, written before that time (and first published in 1915), in which Lippmann made a strong case for Wilsonian idealism and its practical applications.

14:237   Martin, Laurence. *Peace without Victory: Wilson and the British Liberals.* New Haven: Yale University Press, 1958. Reprint 1973 (Kennikat Press). This monograph was one of the first studies to explicate and analyze Wilson's important relationship with leading liberals, radicals, and other public men and women who formed the vanguard of the new diplomacy in Britain.

14:238   Mayer, Arno J. *Political Origins of the New Diplomacy, 1917–1918.* New Haven: Yale University Press, 1959. Reprint 1970 (Vintage Books). In this extremely important book, Mayer places the war aims of the various belligerents in the context of their respective domestic political circumstances as a way of comprehending the emerging international debate between the advocates of the "old diplomacy" and those of the "new diplomacy." His two concluding chapters—"Wilson Issues a Counter Manifesto" and "Wilson vs. Lenin"—offered the first historical analysis of its kind since Baker's *Woodrow Wilson and the World Settlement, Written from His Unpublished and Personal Material* (1922) (14:467) and constitute one of the two or three most incisive commentaries ever written about the Fourteen Points.

14:239   Ninkovich, Frank A. *The Wilsonian Century: U.S. Foreign Policy since 1900.* A companion piece to the author's *Modernity and Power: A History of the Domino Theory in the Twentieth Century* (1994) (14:64), this study credits Wilson with having discovered a (or the) remedy to "modernity," or at least to its manifest potential for calamity. Before 1914, Ninkovich suggests, "normal internationalism" (relations marked by peaceful trade and proliferating liberalism) prevailed, but then, as the slaughter of the Great War strained human comprehension, Wilson, as "the first statesman to understand the self-destructive side of modern international relations," thought through and advanced "crisis internationalism," a notion never fully appreciated or understood in his own time. Yet it survived the century, permutated into cold war globalism. Readers may wish to engage this notable contribution to the historiography of the 1990s in tandem with one or two other studies that hold that cold war globalism was anti-Wilsonian in most of its essentials, or with those in the cold war triumphalist school (2:84).

14:240   Notter, Harley A. *The Origins of the Foreign Policy of Woodrow Wilson.* Baltimore: Johns Hopkins Press, 1937. This work contends that Wilson had formed the essential outlines of his foreign policy before he became president.

14:241   Parsons, Edward B. *Wilsonian Diplomacy: Allied-American Rivalries in War and Peace.* St. Louis: Forum Press, 1978. The author argues that Wilson's postwar economic and territorial objectives led him to overturn his earlier (1915–1916) proposals by the time of the peace conference.

14:242   Rosenberg, Emily S. *Spreading the American Dream: American Economic and Cultural Expansion, 1890–1945.* Three chapters of this widely acclaimed synthesis provide students with essential insights into the ideology of "liberal-developmentalism," which informed American foreign policy during World War I (9:151).

14:243   Tucker, Robert W. "The Triumph of Wilsonianism?" *World Policy Journal* 10 (Winter 1993–1994): 83–99. In this extremely interesting reconsideration, the distinguished political scientist composes a mixed legacy for the Wilsonian vision. Wilson's unbending commitment to multilateralism, though not utopian, must be judged harshly, according to Tucker, because in his aversion to the old diplomacy he refused to come to terms with the world as it was. Lodge and Root, in contrast, favored a limited commitment to Western Europe's security, which (in the

form of NATO) is what emerged after World War II—an internationalism based on the balance of power (or the old diplomacy reconstituted). Thus, to the extent that Wilsonian ends (a more peaceful, more democratic world) prevailed by the 1990s, they did so by highly un-Wilsonian means.

14:244   Wells, Samuel F., Jr. "New Perspectives of Wilsonian Diplomacy: The Secular Evangelism of American Political Economy: A Review Essay." *Perspectives in American History* 6 (1972): 389–419. In this review essay, Wells points out new areas of endeavor, concentrating on such themes as the continuity between the Wilson-Harding eras, the economic and strategic objectives of Wilsonian diplomacy, and the growing acceptance by historians of Wilson as a realistic diplomatist.

14:245   Williams, William Appleman. *The Tragedy of American Diplomacy.* In this classic study, among the most influential works of diplomatic history ever written, Williams devotes three chapters to Wilson's thought and foreign policy. The author casts him, as he does Herbert Hoover, as a highly sophisticated, generally well intentioned practitioner who attempted to reconcile democratic principles and capitalistic expansion in a revolutionary world. Originally published in 1959 (2:97).

Economic Policies in Response to War

14:246   Abrahams, Paul P. "American Bankers and the Economic Tactics of Peace, 1919." *Journal of American History* 56 (December 1969): 572–83. This study demonstrates that, under certain conditions, American bankers were willing to float loans for European reconstruction, but that the Treasury Department refused to provide guarantees or supervision. Hence, almost no American capital flowed to Europe until the Dawes Plan of 1924.

14:247   Burk, Kathleen. *Britain, America and the Sinews of War, 1914–1918.* Boston: G. Allen and Unwin, 1985. This is an excellent overview of the evolution of the changing economic relationship between the two countries wrought by the war. As the author observes, this was the great turning point, "the passing of hegemony from Britain to the United States . . . as the leading financial power." (Lord Northcliffe, the head of the British war mission to the United States in July 1917, put it somewhat more forlornly: "We are down on our knees to the Americans.") See also the author's "Great Britain in the United States, 1917–1918: The Turning Point," *International History Review* 1 (April 1979): 228–45.

14:248   Cooper, John Milton, Jr. "The Command of Gold Reversed: American Loans to Britain, 1915–1917." *Pacific Historical Review* 45 (May 1976): 209–30. Cooper challenges some of the revisionist interpretations of the causes behind American belligerency by arguing that Wilson and the Federal Reserve were making loans more and more difficult for the British to obtain, and that the Germans should have been able to figure out that they could win at least a partial victory simply by sitting tight and keeping the submarine faction in check. He also shows that, after the war, American bankers and the government used their swollen gold reserves to supplant the British as the world's leading financial power.

14:249   Cuff, Robert D. "Woodrow Wilson and Business-Government Relations during World War I." *Review of Politics* 31 (July 1969): 385–407. Wilson harbored doubts about close relations between business and government but put them aside to win the war and actively sought the assistance of business leaders in mobilizing the economy. Thus, he invited them to cooperate in Bernard M. Baruch's idea for a businessmen's commission to carry out that plan.

14:250   Dayer, Roberta Allbert. "Strange Bedfellows: J. P. Morgan & Co., Whitehall and the Wilson Administration during World War I." *Business History* 18 (July 1976): 127–51. At the beginning of World War I, U.S. Treasury Secretary William Gibbs McAdoo and others were suspicious of J. P. Morgan and Company's role as British purchasing and banking agent; when the United States entered the war, however, suspicion gave way to close collaboration.

14:251   DeNovo, John A. "The Movement for an Aggressive American Oil Policy Abroad, 1918–1920." Probably for the first time, policy planners, owing to World War I, made close connections

among diplomacy, national security, and access to adequate petroleum reserves. However, this new understanding did not immediately result in a coherent national petroleum policy (13:77).

14:252   Hogan, Michael J. *Informal Entente: The Private Structure of Cooperation in Anglo-American Economic Diplomacy, 1918–1928*. Columbia: University of Missouri Press, 1977. Reprint 1991 (Imprint Publications). The opening section of this important study explores the early cooperation between the Americans and British on various postwar economic concerns; Hogan stresses the continuity between the Wilson administration and those of Harding and Coolidge.

14:253   _____. "The United States and the Problem of International Economic Control: American Attitudes toward European Reconstruction, 1918–1920." *Pacific Historical Review* 44 (February 1975): 84–103. While President Wilson encouraged privately financed reconstruction, he rejected intergovernmental debt adjustment schemes (as well as treasury loans) mainly because he feared the Allies would use such formal economic structures as a way to keep Germany weak.

14:254   Kaufman, Burton I. *Efficiency and Expansion: Foreign Trade Organization in the Wilson Administration, 1913–1921*. During World War I, American opportunities in foreign trade expansion increased dramatically. In this important book, Kaufman describes how, to that end, the Wilson administration collaborated with business interests; the ensuing liaison marked the beginning of a new era in the nation's economic history (12:85).

14:255   _____. "Organization for Foreign Trade Expansion in the Mississippi Valley, 1900–1920." In this overview, the author explains how regional trade expansion within the United States shaped foreign trade expansion in general (12:86).

14:256   Parrini, Carl P. *Heir to Empire: United States Economic Diplomacy, 1916–1923*. Pittsburgh: University of Pittsburgh Press, 1969. Parrini's study remains one of the most significant of its kind; among his emphases are the vigorous efforts of the United States to open foreign markets and the way it was able to profit from the war and its aftermath, particularly with respect to its financial relations with the Allies.

14:257   Pugach, Noel H. "Standard Oil and Petroleum Development in Early Republican China." *Business History Review* 45 (Winter 1971): 452–73. In 1914, the Standard Oil Company of New York (Socony) attempted to enter an oil exploration partnership with the new republican government of China. Despite diplomatic support from the Wilson administration, the project was abandoned.

14:258   Rosenberg, Emily S. "Anglo-American Economic Rivalry in Brazil during World War I." In part because of its preoccupation with the war in Europe, Great Britain's position receded and thus American trade and capital made considerable inroads into Brazil's economy (12:331).

14:259   _____. "Economic Pressures in Anglo-American Diplomacy in Mexico, 1917–1918." The author argues that during the war Mexico was the object of unrelenting economic pressure from the United States, which hoped thereby to dampen the radicalism of the revolution (12:239).

14:260   _____. "The Exercise of Emergency Controls over Foreign Commerce: Economic Pressure on Latin America." Rosenberg surveys the growth of U.S. executive power over international trade and discusses its use in dealing with Ecuador, Mexico, Honduras, and Brazil during World War I (12:92).

14:261   Safford, Jeffrey J. "Edward Hurley and American Shipping Policy: An Elaboration on Wilsonian Diplomacy, 1918–1919." *Historian* 35 (August 1973): 568–86. Hurley, a self-made millionaire, headed the U.S. Shipping Board (1917–1919) and presided over the procurement of America's vast new merchant marine. At the peace conference, he and Wilson initially intended to use it as a lever against the British, but, according to the author, the effort was subordinated to the larger Wilsonian vision of a new international order.

14:262   _____. "Experiment in Containment: The United States Steel Embargo and Japan, 1917–1918." *Pacific Historical Review* 39 (November 1970): 439–51. As a means of curbing Japan's commercial and territorial expansion into the Far East during the Great War, the United States placed an embargo on steel. That policy, however, only tended to push Japan in the direction of imperialist expansion to meet its needs.

14:263   _____. *Wilsonian Maritime Diplomacy, 1913–1921.* Safford examines Wilson's merchant shipping policies and concludes that the administration's maritime goals during the neutrality and war years were shaped with the postwar foreign trade position of the United States clearly in mind (11:109).

14:264   Sklar, Martin J. "Woodrow Wilson and the Political Economy of Modern United States Liberalism." In *For a New America: Essays in History and Politics from Studies on the Left, 1959–1967,* ed. James Weinstein and David W. Eakins, 46–100. New York: Random House, 1970. This is an important left revisionist article connecting Wilson's fundamental views on capitalist economics to the sort of foreign policies he pursued. Sklar dismisses interpretations of "Wilson as moralist" as beside the point; what mattered was that he was a pragmatic capitalist reformer.

14:265   Van Alstyne, Richard W. "Private American Loans to the Allies, 1914–1916." *Pacific Historical Review* 2 (June 1933): 180–93. Van Alstyne stresses the importance to the Allied war effort of the loans Americans made to Britain and France in October 1915. An early study of wartime economic foreign policy, this essay should be supplemented by more recent work.

14:266   Weinstein, James. *The Corporate Ideal in the Liberal State, 1900–1918.* Boston: Beacon Press, 1968. The concluding chapter of this highly significant work, "War as Fulfillment," argues that the war gave progressive reformers the chance to show big business that liberalism could serve corporate interests as well as those of labor; in this they were largely successful, but in so doing they had (necessarily) abetted the power of the nation's financial and industrial leaders and thus cast the die for liberalism in the twentieth century.

American Neutrality, 1914–1917

GENERAL AND THEMATIC STUDIES

14:267   Adler, Selig. *The Isolationist Impulse: Its Twentieth-Century Reaction.* New York: Abelard-Schuman, 1957. Although Adler devotes several chapters to explicating the isolationist attitudes of Americans toward Europe both before and after they entered the war, most of this study is about the 1920s. It is a very good book, except for one significant shortcoming—the absence of an adequate conceptualization of both isolationism and internationalism.

14:268   Birdsall, Paul. "Neutrality and Economic Pressures, 1914–1917." *Science and Society* 3 (Spring 1939): 217–28. This early effort seeks to revise the historical consensus that German U-boat policy led the United States into war. Birdsall observes that "powerful economic forces [i.e., American economic ties to the Allies] almost at once began to undermine" neutrality; thus, it was only a matter of time before the United States would enter the war against Germany.

14:269   Bonadio, Felice A. "The Failure of German Propaganda in the United States, 1914–1917." *Mid-America* 41 (January 1959): 40–57. Bonadio argues that German propaganda failed to enlist American sympathy because of the conservative attachments of immigrants to basic American political institutions and because of the ability of growing numbers of immigrants either to assimilate into American society or to carve out an otherwise comparatively decent life for themselves.

14:270   Cooper, John Milton, Jr. *The Vanity of Power: American Isolationism and the First World War, 1914–1917.* Westport, CT: Greenwood Press, 1969. Cooper argues that isolationism evolved into a coherent (and rather enduring) outlook on foreign policy during World War I. A powerful bloc in Congress, some isolationists were ultranationalists and some were progressive idealists; among the latter,

isolation seemed quite practical when the alternative seemed to be war and an end to liberal reform.

14:271   Cuddy, Edward. "Pro-Germanism and American Catholicism, 1914–1917." *Catholic Historical Review* 54 (October 1968): 427–54. The article refutes the assertion of Arthur Link and others that the Catholic Church was practically uniform in its pro-German sympathy, and concludes that there was considerable diversity of opinion in the church between 1914 and 1917.

14:272   Devlin, Patrick. *Too Proud to Fight: Woodrow Wilson's Neutrality.* New York: Oxford University Press, 1975. Part biography, part diplomatic history, this book, while examining the full range of issues involved, treats the legal problems of neutrality extensively; it ends by arguing that, in the final analysis, the question of belligerency or continued neutrality lay with one person only.

14:273   Fenton, Charles A. "A Literary Fracture of World War I." *American Quarterly* 12 (Summer 1960): 119–32. This is an interesting story, somewhat reminiscent of Lyndon Johnson's problems in another time, about the American Academy of Arts and Letters and its criticisms of Wilson's neutrality policies.

14:274   Finnegan, John P. *Against the Specter of a Dragon: The Campaign for American Military Preparedness, 1914–1917.* Westport, CT: Greenwood Press, 1974. In this useful study of preparedness, one of the few monographs focusing solely on that topic, Finnegan explores the movement's implications both for military planning and the economy during wartime and finds that it laid the foundation for a successful war effort.

14:275   Katz, Friedrich. *The Secret War in Mexico: Europe, the United States, and the Mexican Revolution.* Translated by Loren Goldner. Katz's study enjoys an exalted position within the vast historiography on the Mexican revolution; among its innovative contributions is the notion of a secret war, of sorts—"the new strategy of exploiting social conflicts and anticolonial struggles"—practiced by American and European interests. In that context, midway into the story, he presents the German intrigue to bring on war between the United States and Mexico (12:165).

14:276 Kihl, Mary R. "A Failure in Ambassadorial Diplomacy." *Journal of American History* 57 (December 1970): 636–53. By the fall of 1916, neither Walter Hines Page, U.S. ambassador to Britain, nor Sir Cecil Arthur Spring-Rice, his British counterpart, was able to function effectively. Wilson regarded Page as hopelessly pro-British, while Colonel House considered Spring-Rice overly suspicious of German intrigue.

14:277 Link, Arthur S. *Wilson. Vol. 3: The Struggle for Neutrality, 1914–1915.* Distinguished by prodigious research in European archives, the third volume of Link's biography makes a strong case for the argument that, in his policies toward the belligerents, the president was as neutral as it was humanly possible to be (12:122).

14:278 _____. *Wilson. Vol. 4: Confusions and Crises, 1915–1916.* This installment of Link's biography picks up where *The Struggle for Neutrality, 1914–1915* (1960) (14:277) left off, beginning with the preparedness controversy and ending with the *Sussex* pledge, which Link characterizes as the diplomatic triumph of Wilson's first term (12:123).

14:279 Livermore, Seward W. "'Deserving Democrats': The Foreign Service under Woodrow Wilson." This article examines Bryan and Wilson's use of patronage (more often than not on behalf of southerners) in filling high-level appointments and much to the detriment of the foreign service (12:73).

14:280 May, Ernest R. *The World War and American Isolation, 1914–1917.* Cambridge, MA: Harvard University Press, 1959. In focusing on German and British decisions in tandem with the alternatives Wilson faced, May was among the first historians to achieve an international perspective for judging whether the administration's actions were properly directed. As for the decision for war, Wilson made it because German submarines jeopardized the credibility and prestige of both the administration and the nation.

14:281 Millis, Walter. *Road to War: America, 1914–1917.* Boston: Houghton Mifflin Company, 1935. This popular work of revisionism by a prominent journalist struck a chord among an isolationist-minded public during the Great Depression. The

original dust jacket captures the tone: "1914–1917 when . . . a peace-loving democracy, muddled but excited, misinformed and whipped to a frenzy, embarked upon its greatest foreign war . . . Read it and beware!" (Millis would later become a respected military historian.)

14:282 Morrissey, Alice M. *The American Defense of Neutral Rights, 1914–1917.* Cambridge, MA: Harvard University Press, 1939. The author (also known as Alice Magdalen Morrissey McDiarmid) looks at Wilson's efforts to balance public sensibilities and economic interests in formulating neutrality.

14:283 Peterson, H. C. *Propaganda for War: The Campaign against American Neutrality, 1914–1917.* Norman: University of Oklahoma Press, 1939. The author concludes that Britain, by adroitly advertising Anglo-American ties and exposing German duplicity, altered American consciousness and thereby helped push the United States into the war.

14:284 Rappaport, Armin. *The British Press and Wilsonian Neutrality.* Stanford, CA: Stanford University Press, 1951. Although the results are perhaps predictable in the main, this is a useful study that gets at British opinion toward American neutrality by taking soundings in a wide variety of contemporary British publications—dailies, weeklies, monthlies, and quarterlies.

14:285 Sanders, M. L. "Wellington House and British Propaganda during the First World War." *Historical Journal* 18 (March 1975): 119–46. This essay traces Britain's masterful attempt to counteract Germany's clumsy propaganda.

14:286 Sarkissian, Arshag Ohannes, ed. *Studies in Diplomatic History and Historiography in Honour of G. P. Gooch, C.H.* New York: Barnes and Noble, 1961. This Festschrift contains one important essay relating to American neutrality during World War I: Bernadotte E. Schmitt, "The Relation of Public Opinion and Foreign Affairs before and during the First World War."

14:287 Smith, Daniel M. *Robert Lansing and American Neutrality, 1914–1917.* Berkeley: University of California Press, 1958. Reprint 1972 (Da Capo Press). This major study argues that Lansing's outlook emanated from a blend of strategic and ideological factors leading him to believe that German-American differences were irreconcilable and that Britain and America had, within limits, important parallel interests.

14:288 _____. "Robert Lansing and the Formulation of American Neutrality Policies, 1914–1915." *Mississippi Valley Historical Review* 43 (June 1956): 59–81. Smith's essay is something of a preview of his *Robert Lansing and American Neutrality, 1914–1917* (1958) (14:287); the view that the benighted Lansing actually exerted influence on Wilson is pronounced.

14:289   West, Rachel. *The Department of State on the Eve of the First World War.* This book conveys a careful picture of the Department of State during the first two years of the Wilson administration, which was not a happy scene. Wilson and Bryan piled on too many patronage appointments, and, of course, they were all caught unawares in August 1914 (11:73).

MARITIME ISSUES: THE BRITISH BLOCKADE AND GERMAN SUBMARINE WARFARE

14:290   Bailey, Thomas A. "The United States and the Blacklist during the Great War." *Journal of Modern History* 6 (March 1934): 14–35. In the summer of 1916, Great Britain published a list of American and Latin American firms that were doing (or trying to do) business with the Central Powers. In one of his earliest articles, Bailey traces the highly negative impact of Britain's behavior on Wilson's attitude toward that country during a crucial interlude.

14:291   Bailey, Thomas A., and Paul B. Ryan. *The Lusitania Disaster: An Episode in Modern Warfare and Diplomacy.* New York: Free Press, 1975. This account of the sinking of the great passenger liner is generally regarded the most balanced. Bailey and Ryan rebut the conspiracy theories of authors such as Colin Simpson (*The Lusitania*, 1973) (14:303) and assess the highly consequential impact of the incident on public opinion and American neutrality.

14:292   Birnbaum, Karl E. *Peace Moves and U-Boat Warfare: A Study of Germany's Policy toward the United States, April 18, 1916–January 9, 1917.* Stockholm: Almqvist and Wiksell, 1958. Reprint 1970 (Archon Books). Beginning with the auspicious resolution of the *Sussex* crisis and ending with the start of the political struggle over whether to revert to unrestricted submarine warfare, this important monograph tracks Germany's wavering policy between peace moves and undersea war. A failure to communicate and understand one another's purposes, according to the author, led to the break between the United States and Germany.

14:293   Borchard, Edwin, and William Potter Lage. *Neutrality for the United States.* 2d ed. New Haven: Yale University Press, 1940. Reprint 1973 (AMS Press). Very much a revisionist work motivated by contemporary concerns, its authors argue that submarine warfare was but a symptom (or response) to a larger problem—that, from August 1914 onward, "the conduct of the American government was a negation of nearly all the requirements of neutrality both in thought and action." First published in 1937.

14:294   Coogan, John W. *The End of Neutrality: The United States, Britain, and Maritime Rights, 1899–1915.* In this fine study, Coogan traces the origins of the British blockade and makes a strong case for the argument that American neutrality was very much tilted in favor of the Allies (11:277).

14:295   Handlin, Oscar. "A Liner, a U-Boat . . . and History." *American Heritage* 6 (June 1955): 40–45, 105. Handlin argues that the *Lusitania* calamity was a major turning point for the United States—and a gigantic public relations disaster for Germany—regardless of Wilson's disinclination to go to war at the time of the sinking.

14:296   Herwig, Holger H. *Politics of Frustration: The United States in German Naval Planning, 1889–1941.* See chapter 9 of this Guide (9:337).

14:297   Hurt, R. Douglas. "The Settlement of Anglo-American Claims Resulting from World War I." *American Neptune* 34 (July 1974): 155–73. Although a formula was achieved to obtain compensation for Britain's seizure of American ships and property, the negotiations were impeded by London's fear of having both to make a large payment and modify its naval blockade policy.

14:298   Lundeberg, Philip K. "The German Naval Critique of the U-Boat Campaign, 1915–1918." *Military Affairs* 27, part 1 (January 1964): 105–18. German naval authorities disagreed on the importance of U-boat campaigns to the war effort. Lundeberg evaluates the arguments, notably those of Bauer, Tirpitz, and Spindler.

14:299   McDonald, Timothy G. "The Gore-McLemore Resolutions: Democratic Revolt against Wilson's Submarine Policy." *Historian* 26 (November 1963): 50–74. This article is about the abortive effort of primarily western Democrats in the spring of 1916 to discourage or prohibit Americans from traveling on armed belligerent vessels, in defiance of the administration's assertion of their right to do so.

14:300   Morrissey, Alice M. "The Neutrality Board and Armed Merchantmen, 1914–1917." *American Journal of International Law* 69 (April 1975): 374–81. After pondering the proper role of a neutral, the Joint State and Navy Neutrality Board affirmed the right of merchant ships to be armed for defensive purposes. Author also known as Alice Magdalen Morrissey McDiarmid.

14:301   Pratt, Julius W. "The British Blockade and American Precedent." *U.S. Naval Institute Proceedings* 46 (November 1920): 1789–1802. The author seeks to demonstrate that British blockade operations in World War I were "an almost inevitable outgrowth of earlier practice" and that Britain looked to and cited American Civil War examples to justify its own practice from 1914 to 1918, much to the annoyance of the Wilson administration.

14:302   Savage, Carlton. *Policy of the United States toward Maritime Commerce in War.* 2 vols. Washington, DC: Government Printing Office, 1934. In the second volume, Savage treats the issues of contraband, trade restrictions, loans and credits, control of exports, armed merchant ships, and enemy trading lists.

14:303   Simpson, Colin. *The Lusitania.* Boston: Little, Brown, 1973. Simpson agrees with German claims that a British conspiracy existed to have the *Lusitania* sunk. He also argues that the ship was armed and carrying dangerous contraband munitions (which of course it was—albeit a cache of inconsequential volume). The case is overstated all around.

14:304   Siney, Marion C. *The Allied Blockade of Germany, 1914–1916.* Ann Arbor: University of Michigan Press, 1957. This book is primarily concerned with Allied efforts to block northern European neutral trade with Germany; it also contains information about American business relationships with various European neutrals.

14:305   Smith, Gaddis. *Britain's Clandestine Submarines, 1914–1915.* New Haven: Yale University Press, 1964. Smith focuses on the Bethlehem Steel Corporation's construction of submarines for the British, raising interesting questions about American neutral rights.

WILSON'S MEDIATION EFFORTS

14:306   Cooper, John Milton, Jr. "The British Response to the House-Grey Memorandum: New Evidence and New Questions." *Journal of American History* 59 (March 1973): 958–71. In February 1916, Colonel House and Secretary Grey initialed their controversial memorandum, which in essence stated that soon President Wilson would call an international conference to mediate an end to war; if Germany refused to attend or proved otherwise obdurate, the United States would "probably" enter the war on the side of the Allies. From the time Seymour and House published the latter's *Intimate Papers* (1926–1928) (14:13), the House-Grey Memorandum became grist for the mills of the interwar revisionists, and it is discussed in many other works in this section. Not for fifty years though was its meaning clear. Cooper thus explicates then newly released documents that show that no one in the British government ever took the proposal seriously—neither Grey, nor Lloyd George, who unjustly had claimed Grey alone torpedoed it—except as possible insurance against abject defeat. (If House sensed this, he badly misinformed Wilson about the prospects; Wilson inserted the "probably," thinking that if that was all it took to get both the British and the Germans to the peace table, the gamble was worthwhile.)

14:307 Kernek, Sterling J. "The British Government's Reactions to President Wilson's 'Peace' Note of December 1916." *Historical Journal* 13 (December 1970): 721–66. The quotation marks around the word "Peace" say much about both the British government and the author's attitudes toward Wilson's penultimate interposition; Lloyd George never took the note seriously, and Kernek thinks the prime minister was right to view it as dangerous.

14:308 Patterson, David S. "Woodrow Wilson and the Mediation Movement, 1914–1917." *Historian* 33 (August 1971): 535–56. This article describes the efforts of various groups and prominent individuals in the American peace movement to gain Wilson's support for their mediation plans.

America's Decision to Intervene

14:309 Bridges, Lamar W. "Zimmermann Telegram: Reaction of Southern, Southwestern Newspapers." *Journalism Quarterly* 46 (Spring 1969): 81–86. Although the danger of a Mexican attack was remote and the plan itself ludicrous, the Zimmermann note made Germany appear out of control to the American people; thus, its effect was to solidify opinion on behalf of belligerency.

14:310 Buchanan, A. Russell. "American Editors Examine American War Aims and Plans in April, 1917." *Pacific Historical Review* 9 (August 1940): 253–65. Once considered a significant article employing the then latest techniques of public opinion sampling through textual analysis of newspaper editorials, this piece examines such questions as the assignment of guilt for the war, the reasons for American participation, and the plans America should make for the future.

14:311 Buehrig, Edward H. "Wilson's Neutrality Re-examined." *World Politics* 3 (October 1950): 1–19. In part a reflection of the cold war "realist school," Buehrig (who served at the UN conference in San Francisco in 1945) argues that the Wilson administration apprehended that a German victory might bode ill for the United States's more immedi-

ate security as well as its longer-term interests. Yet Wilson's call to arms was determined as much by his internationalist vision as by the need to respond to submarine warfare. Thus, the declaration of war, with regard to war aims, was lacking in real clarity.

14:312 Coletta, Paolo E. "A Question of Alternatives: Wilson, Bryan, Lansing, and America's Intervention in World War I." *Nebraska History* 63 (Spring 1982): 33–57. This comparative analysis considers Wilson and Lansing from the point of view of William Jennings Bryan.

14:313 Doerries, Reinhard R. "Imperial Berlin and Washington: New Light on Germany's Foreign Policy and America's Entry into World War I." *Central European History* 11 (March 1978): 23–49. The author is hard on Germany for its ill-conceived propaganda and sabotage in America. He concludes that the Germans refused mediation by the American president, even when it appeared highly improbable that they could win the war.

14:314 Gregory, Ross. *The Origins of American Intervention in the First World War.* New York: Norton, 1971. Written primarily for undergraduates, this book emphasizes Wilson's perception of the role of the United States as a world power and the requirements of an expanding American economy. Gregory says that, once Germany resumed unrestricted submarine warfare, Wilson decided for war "for both moral and practical reasons."

14:315 Link, Arthur S. *Wilson. Vol. 5: Campaigns for Progressivism and Peace, 1916–1917.* In the fifth and final volume of his uncompleted biography, Link suggests that the immediate factors behind Wilson's decision were unrestricted submarine warfare, the Zimmermann note, and Germany's negative response to his "peace without victory" appeal; together they caused him to lose faith in Germany's good intentions. The president still did not consider the Allied cause as altogether just, Link argues, but Wilson believed American participation would hasten the war's end and ensure his place at the peace conference, thus guaranteeing a liberal settlement (12:124).

14:316 Lippmann, Walter. "The Atlantic and America." *Life,* April 7, 1941, 85–92. Only weeks after the enactment of lend-lease, Lippmann published his essay about American security and events of the spring of 1917 with constant reference to those of the spring of 1941. "We intervened the first time when, and only when, a victorious Germany was threatening to conquer Britain and to become the master of the other shore of the Atlantic Ocean," he stated categorically. "We are intervening a second time at a similar point in the war and for exactly the same fundamental reason." He subsequently expanded his interpretation in *U.S. Foreign Policy: Shield of the Republic* (1943) (2:67), which was instrumental in setting in motion the "realist" school after World War II.

14:317   Seymour, Charles. *American Neutrality, 1914–1917: Essays on the Causes of American Intervention in the World War*. New Haven: Yale University Press, 1935. By the mid-1930s, revisionist writings were questioning just how neutral Wilson had been toward Germany, while members of Congress held hearings to demonstrate that the United States had gone to war "to save the skins of bankers" and other "merchants of death." It was Seymour's concern to refute them when he wrote this series of essays. Acknowledging that Wilson felt a vague sympathy for the Allies, he argues that he kept "a studied insistence not to permit that feeling to affect national policy." As for the influence of financial interests, he mounts a vigorous case on behalf of the submarine thesis and thus asks, "How could we have stayed out of the war?"

14:318   Small, Melvin. "Woodrow Wilson and U.S. Intervention in World War I." In *Modern American Diplomacy,* ed. John M. Carroll and George C. Herring, Jr., 21–34. Wilmington, DE: Scholarly Resources, 1986. Small argues that the main factor behind the unraveling of American neutrality can be located in the administration's decision, early in the war, to permit the trade in arms to the Allies.

14:319   Tansill, Charles Callan. *America Goes to War.* Boston: Little, Brown and Company, 1938. As Europe began its plunge, in 1938, into yet another terrible struggle, Tansill wrote a historical object lesson for contemporary Americans still dubious about their involvement in the Great War. He focuses on public opinion, domestic economic troubles, and Wilson's pro-British advisers to reveal why, in his view, war with Germany became inevitable for the United States.

14:320   Tuchman, Barbara W. *The Zimmermann Telegram*. Tuchman traces the progress of the Zimmermann telegram from Room 40 (the British Admiralty Intelligence Bureau) to President Wilson. The final chapter argues that the telegram both tipped the balance of American public opinion and confirmed Wilson's decision to intervene (12:229).

The Peace Movement and Other Dissenting Views

14:321   Alonso, Harriet Hyman. "Gender and Peace Politics in the First World War United States: The People's Council of America." *International History Review* 19 (February 1997): 83–102. "What happened when feminist peace activists teamed up with men in an anti-war effort?" is the chief question this essay asks. In the case of the People's Council of America, the answer is that feminist and pacifist women, on one hand, and socialist men, on the other, found it impossible to cooperate for long, owing to cross-purposes, mutual suspicions, and especially federal harassment.

14:322   _____. *Peace as a Women's Issue: A History of the U.S. Movement for World Peace and Women's Rights*. Written by a pioneer in women's peace history, this study focuses on the Women's International League for Peace and Freedom from its founding in 1915 through the cold war. Alonso demonstrates how activists in the women's rights movement found common cause in the peace movement in part by seeing connections "between institutional violence and violence against women." "Motherhood," too, became a useful rhetorical device in making their case as critics of war, as did the concept of responsible women being citizens of the world as well as of the local community (9:158).

14:323   Bolt, Ernest C., Jr. *Ballots before Bullets: The War Referendum Approach to Peace in America, 1914–1941*. Charlottesville: University Press of Virginia, 1977. Although the most famous example was the Ludlow Amendment of 1935, the author firmly locates the idea of referenda on war within the reform impulse of the early twentieth century, more particularly among progressive pacifists of 1915–1917. He observes that, whatever its shortcomings, the proposal was at least partly an experiment grounded in the democratic tradition.

14:324   Bourne, Randolph S. *War and the Intellectuals: Essays, 1915–1919.* New York: Harper and Row, 1964. This volume brings together many of the most trenchant essays by the brilliant radical (and disillusioned former disciple of John Dewey). It includes Bourne's most famous piece, "Twilight of Idols," in which he asked all pro-war liberals and socialists the haunting question: "If the war is too strong for you to prevent, how is it going to be weak enough for you to control and mould to your liberal purposes?" Edited with an introduction by Carl Resek.

14:325   Bussey, Gertrude, and Margaret Tims. *Women's International League for Peace and Freedom, 1915–1965: A Record of Fifty Years' Work.* London: Allen and Unwin, 1965. This organization, founded in Zurich as the Paris Peace Conference proceeded, was an outgrowth of the Woman's Peace Party. Beginning with the Treaty of Versailles and the League of Nations, through the Vietnam era and beyond, the WILPF took brave and controversial stands on any number of foreign policy issues. This is the standard history, up to the Vietnam War.

14:326   Cantor, Milton. "The Radical Confrontation with Foreign Policy: War and Revolution, 1914–1920." In *Dissent: Explorations in the History of American Radicalism,* ed. Alfred F. Young, 215–49. DeKalb: Northern Illinois University Press, 1968. Cantor reviews left-wing writings on the causes of the war (published, for example, in *The Masses* and the *International Socialist Review*). Because they alternately stressed commercial competition, militarism, feudalism versus capitalism, and autocracy versus democracy, he argues that leftist analysis "scarcely differed from that of [liberal] reformers."

14:327   Chambers, John Whiteclay, II, ed. *The Eagle and the Dove: The American Peace Movement and United States Foreign Policy, 1900–1922.* This is an excellent collection of eighty-five documents—essays, of sorts—that provide a cross-section of views among peace seekers; the author's eighty-

three-page monographic introduction is very helpful (11:131). First published in 1976.

14:328   Chatfield, Charles. *For Peace and Justice: Pacifism in America, 1914–1941.* Knoxville: University of Tennessee Press, 1971. Chatfield, a pioneer in the field of peace history, defines the place of pacifists, who refused to sanction any rationale for war in general, within the American peace movement. The first three chapters describe the activities of various pacifists and their organizations during World War I.

14:329   _____. "World War I and the Liberal Pacifist in the United States." *American Historical Review* 75 (December 1970): 1920–37. In this excellent article, Chatfield explores the dynamic relationships among pacifism, radicalism, internationalism, and progressive reform.

14:330   Cook, Blanche Wiesen. "Democracy in Wartime: Antimilitarism in England and the United States, 1914–1918." *American Studies* 13 (Spring 1972): 51–68. Cook scrutinizes the emergence of peace organizations in both countries and finds that they commonly sought to preserve and protect political and civil liberties in wartime.

14:331   _____. "The Woman's Peace Party: Collaboration and Non-Cooperation." *Peace and Change* 1 (Fall 1972): 36–42. Cook offers a brief overview of some of the dilemmas that the Woman's Peace Party had to contend with in advancing their cause.

14:332   _____. "Woodrow Wilson and the Antimilitarists, 1914–1917." Ph.D. dissertation, Johns Hopkins University, 1970. In this pioneering work, Cook brings to light the important role that organizations such as the American Union Against Militarism and the Woman's Peace Party played in shaping the national debate over preparedness and internationalism during the neutrality period.

14:333   Curti, Merle E. *Peace or War: The American Struggle, 1636–1936.* New York: W. W. Norton and Company, 1936. Reprint 1972 (Garland). Later monographs have expanded on many of the subjects Curti covers, but this monumental work remains a significant contribution to the history of the broad peace movement in the United States prior to 1936.

The focus is on pressure groups and their efforts to influence foreign policies. The reprint (Garland) contains a new introduction by Curti.

14:334   DeBenedetti, Charles. *Origins of the Modern American Peace Movement, 1915–1929.* Millwood, NY: KTO Press, 1978. This revisionist work traces the development of the modem American peace movement from its origins during World War I as a coalition of internationalists, legalists, and social progressives to its development as a middle-class movement.

14:335   _____, ed. *Peace Heroes in Twentieth-Century America.* Bloomington: Indiana University Press, 1986. This volume contains biographical essays by leading scholars in the field of peace studies—including Michael A. Lutzker on Jane Addams and Lawrence S. Wittner on Eugene V. Debs—and closes with an assessment by Merle Curti.

14:336   _____. *The Peace Reform in American History.* Bloomington: Indiana University Press, 1980. DeBenedetti's interpretation brings a considerable measure of sophisticated analysis to American peace movements through the years. Each chapter has an acute focus, those relating to the World War I era titled "Practical Reform" (1901–1914) and "Necessary Reform" (1914–1941).

14:337   Degen, Marie Louise. *The History of the Woman's Peace Party.* Baltimore: Johns Hopkins Press, 1939. Reprint 1972 (Garland Pub.). This is a very important early work in the field of peace studies that traces the efforts of the first organization of its kind in the United States to engage in direct political action; the Woman's Peace Party, in January 1915, produced the earliest and most comprehensive manifesto on peace and internationalism advanced by any American organization or political party through the entire war.

14:338   Duram, James C. "In Defense of Conscience: Norman Thomas as an Exponent of Christian Pacifism during World War I." *Journal of Presbyterian History* 52 (Spring 1974): 19–32. The author discusses early writings of Norman Thomas on conscientious objection (1915–1918) as a tenet of Christianity and pacifism in the face of universal conscription.

14:339   Filene, Peter G. "The World Peace Foundation and Progressivism: 1910–1918." *New England Quarterly* 36 (December 1963): 478–501. Filene sets peace activity within the context of progressivism and its characteristic assumptions.

14:340   Herman, Sondra R. *Eleven against War: Studies in American Internationalist Thought, 1898–1921.* This is an intellectual history that examines leading American thinkers who tried to formulate programmatic alternatives to war, although not all of them counseled staying out of the European war itself. The author divides them into such categories as "polity" advocates and "community" proponents. Some of those who fell into the latter classification opposed (at least initially) American intervention. Herman's "Eleven" are Elihu Root, Nicholas Murray Butler, Hamilton Holt, Josiah Royce, Jane Addams, Thorstein Veblen, Woodrow Wilson, Theodore Marburg, John Bates Clark, A. Lawrence Lowell, and Franklin H. Giddings (11:133).

14:341   Hoff, Joan. "'Peace Is a Woman's Job . . .': Jeannette Rankin and Foreign Policy: The Origins of Her Pacifism." *Montana Magazine of History* 30 (January 1980): 28–41. This article was followed by "'Peace Is a Woman's Job . . .': Jeannette Rankin and Foreign Policy: Her Life Work as a Pacifist," in the same journal (April 1980): 38–53. Hoff (then Hoff-Wilson) tells the story of the only member of Congress to vote against both war resolutions, in 1917 and 1941.

14:342   Jeffreys-Jones, Rhodri. *Changing Differences: Women and the Shaping of American Foreign Policy, 1917–1994.* New Brunswick: Rutgers University Press, 1995. The author's second chapter explores the relationship between the suffrage and peace movements and women's efforts to influence public opinion and the White House; thereon he elucidates the parallel divisions between "moderates" and "radicals" within the suffrage movement and supporters and opponents of intervention in the war.

14:343   Jordan, William. "'The Damnable Dilemma': African-American Accommodation and Protest during World War I." *Journal of American History* 81 (March 1995): 1562–83. Jordan challenges the findings of Mark Ellis and David Levering

Lewis (*W.E.B. DuBois. Vol. 1: Biography of a Race, 1868–1919* [New York: H. Holt, 1993]), among others, about Du Bois's exhortation to "close ranks." He points out that, in other instances, Du Bois acceded to accommodation; unlike William Monroe Trotter, he sanctioned segregated training camps for the opportunities they presented; and he accepted passage to Paris in an official capacity to cover the peace conference—in exchange for signing a pledge "to avoid criticism of all Allied Forces." Responding (1584–90), Ellis reiterates that Du Bois hoped to promote participation in the war effort by both the rank and file and the "Talented Tenth" but had made a "fatal miscalculation."

14:344 Kornweibel, Theodore, Jr. "Apathy and Dissent: Black America's Negative Responses to World War I." *South Atlantic Quarterly* 80 (Summer 1981): 322–38. Kornweibel suggests that although perhaps half of all African-Americans agreed with Du Bois and "closed ranks," about half did not. In July 1917, for instance, in the wake of the riot in East St. Louis, 5,000 black New Yorkers marched down Fifth Avenue carrying banners reading, "Bring Democracy to America before You Carry It to Europe." James Weldon Johnson overheard one black say in a barber shop, "the Germans ain't done nothin' to me, and if they have, I forgive 'em." Thus, apathy, indifference, and (far less often) antiwar sentiment were widespread. "It was something that didn't concern Negroes," former slave and Seattle journalist Horace Cayton wrote in his autobiography: "It was a white folks' war."

14:345 Kraft, Barbara S. *The Peace Ship: Henry Ford's Pacifist Adventure in the First World War.* New York: Macmillan, 1978. "We are going to try to get the boys out of the trenches and back to their homes by Christmas Day," Ford explained. Thus, in December 1915, began the most conspicuous attempt by peace seekers to bring about mediation among the belligerents, in the famous, abortive voyage to Europe of the *Oscar II* (dubbed "the Ship of Fools" by the *London Spectator*), whose passengers hoped to stop the war. Kraft tells the story well and respectfully.

14:346 Kuehl, Warren F. *Hamilton Holt: Journalist, Internationalist, Educator.* Gainesville: University of Florida Press, 1960. Kuehl's is a fine biography of an important journalist and publisher (of *The*

Independent), successively or simultaneously a liberal, pacifist, advocate of preparedness, and internationalist located somewhere between the movement's conservative and progressive wings.

14:347 Marchand, C. Roland. *The American Peace Movement and Social Reform, 1898–1918.* Decades after its publication, this remains one of the finest studies of its kind. Among other things, Marchand explains the important relationship between domestic politics and foreign policy, which was manifest in the reformist peace movement. He goes on to show that the peace movement was not dominated by pacifists but mostly individuals involved in a broad range of social reform organizations. The analyses of the impact of the war and of American belligerency on the movement are particularly valuable (11:139).

14:348 Martin, James P. "The American Peace Movement and the Progressive Era 1910–1917." 2 vols. Ph.D. dissertation, Rice University, 1975. This notable dissertation relates peace efforts to other contemporary reforms through a study of leaders and organizations. It traces the transformation of the peace movement during the neutrality period, as new groups opposed to both preparedness and intervention emerged, motivated by the fear that belligerency would destroy hard-won progressive reforms at home.

14:349 Peterson, H. C., and Gilbert C. Fite. *Opponents of War, 1917–1918.* Madison: University of Wisconsin Press, 1957. This is a gripping account of the travails of those who opposed America's involvement in World War I. The authors not only identify the most important dissident groups and individuals and analyze the reasons for their opposition, but also relate harrowing stories of the fate awaiting many of them.

14:350 Ryley, Thomas W. *A Little Group of Willful Men: A Study of Congressional-Presidential Authority.* Port Washington, NY: Kennikat Press, 1975. This is an interesting monograph about those antiwar senators who, a month before the United States entered the war, put Wilson's armed ship legislation to death by filibuster.

14:351 Weinstein, James. "Anti-War Sentiment and the Socialist Party, 1917–1918." *Political Science Quarterly* 74 (June 1959): 215–39. The article maintains that the Socialist Party represented the opinions of many Americans in its opposition to the war, which helps explain why the socialists did so well at the polls. (Although its share of the presidential vote fell, the turnout for socialist candidates at the local and state level in 1916 increased by 25 percent over Debs's historic high in 1912, and the party continued to do well in many major centers in 1917.)

American Belligerency, 1917–1918

THE HOME FRONT: ECONOMIC MOBILIZATION, POLITICS, AND PROPAGANDA

14:352   Adler, Selig. "The Congressional Election of 1918." *South Atlantic Quarterly* 36 (October 1937): 447–65. Mainly because of its impact on foreign policy, this midterm election remains one of the two or three most important such contests in American history. Adler places it within the context of the new Republican majority's supposed move to "splendid isolation," but he is not unmindful that regional economic issues contributed to the Democrats' reversal of fortunes.

14:353   Blakey, George T. *Historians on the Homefront: American Propagandists for the Great War.* Lexington: University Press of Kentucky, 1970. This book concerns pro-war historians in nonmilitary service who wrote propaganda for the U.S. government for domestic consumption. The endeavor to serve one's country and one's profession as a scholar did not, in this instance, bring much credit to those who tried.

14:354   Burner, David. *The Politics of Provincialism: The Democratic Party in Transition, 1918–1932.* New York: Alfred A. Knopf, 1968. Reprint 1986 (Harvard University Press). The first seventy-three pages of this study provide keen insights into the domestic political environment that helped shape American foreign policy during the latter stages of the war and the peacemaking. Burner presents a good

overview of the politics of the League as well.

14:355   Chafee, Zachariah, Jr. *Free Speech in the United States.* Cambridge, MA: Harvard University Press, 1941. Chafee is always quoted in studies of civil liberties in wartime, particularly regarding the most famous First Amendment cases—Schenck, Debs, and Abrams—triggered by the Espionage Act. The Supreme Court rendered all three decisions in 1919. This work superseded an earlier book, *Freedom of Speech* (New York: Harcourt, Brace and Howe, 1920).

14:356   Clarkson, Grosvenor B. *Industrial America in the World War: The Strategy behind the Line, 1917–1918.* Boston: Houghton Mifflin, 1923. Written by the official historian of the War Industries Board, this book is an important source of information about the personnel and policies of that organization.

14:357   Conner, Valerie Jean. *The National War Labor Board: Stability, Social Justice, and the Voluntary State in World War I.* Chapel Hill: University of North Carolina Press, 1983. This careful examination of the temporary partnership of labor and business under the aegis of the federal government ranks among the best studies of wartime industrial mobilization.

14:358   Creel, George. *How We Advertised America: The First Telling of the Amazing Story of the Committee on Public Information That Carried the Gospel of Americanism to Every Corner of the Globe.* New York: Harper and Brothers, 1920. In this instance, the title clearly sets the tone. Creel is audacious, exuberant, and fairly staggering as he frames and details his "amazing story." Hardly objective or self-critical, this is certainly not the last word on the subject.

14:359   Cuff, Robert D. *The War Industries Board: Business-Government Relations during World War I.* Baltimore: Johns Hopkins University Press, 1973. Among Cuff's more important themes are those pertaining to the development of a wartime planning structure that conjoined business, government, and the military, and an evaluation of the defense planning bureaucracy.

14:360   Dubofsky, Melvin. *We Shall Be All: A History of the Industrial Workers of the World.* 2d ed.

Urbana: University of Illinois Press, 1988. In this monumental history, Dubofsky details the efforts of members of the Wilson administration to harass and undermine the Wobblies, especially once the Russian revolution fused so many domestic and foreign policy issues together. Originally published in 1969.

14:361   Duff, John B. "German-Americans and the Peace, 1918–1920." *American Jewish Historical Quarterly* 59 (June 1970): 424–44. This article describes German-American opinion toward Wilson's peace initiatives as well as the denunciations of him during the presidential election of 1920.

14:362   Ellis, Mark. "Federal Surveillance of Black Americans during the First World War." *Immigrants and Minorities* 12 (March 1993): 1–20. Though their criticism of American racism rarely had anything to do with sedition, black leaders were closely watched by federal and state authorities after April 1917. As Ellis suggests in this engrossing piece, white northerners (from Newton D. Baker to William English Walling) seemed to think blacks were easy dupes of German intrigue in part because so few whites had ever read the black press and therefore had no basis for understanding black wartime protest. In the south, other forces were at work. After some years of decline, lynching now rose sharply as fears of insurrection were reborn ("Teutons Try Yankee Trick of Making Negroes Rise in Rebellion against Whites," ran a South Carolina headline), while white Texans expected a combined uprising of blacks, Indians, and Mexicans.

14:363   _____. "J. Edgar Hoover and the 'Red Summer' of 1919." *Journal of American Studies* 28 (April 1994): 39–59. Ellis reveals that the FBI's infamous phone tapping and harassment of Martin Luther King had a long historical context. As early as 1917, J. Edgar Hoover monitored the black press. He kept W. E. B. Du Bois, Marcus Garvey, and A. Phillip Randolph under surveillance for months after the armistice. And he suspected that "Bolshevist agitation" was behind all the "Negro agitation" following the riots of May-September 1919. Thereafter, Hoover saw to it that "Negro Activities" would become a permanent subject category in the files of the FBI.

14:364   Gerson, Louis L. *The Hyphenate in Recent American Politics and Diplomacy.* Four chapters ex-amine the influence of immigrant Americans on Wilsonian diplomacy and their response to its articulation of self-determination (2:154).

14:365   Gompers, Samuel. *American Labor and the War.* New York: G. H. Doran, 1919. The president of the American Federation of Labor assesses labor's contribution to the war and its opinion of Wilson's diplomatic objectives.

14:366   Gruber, Carol S. *Mars and Minerva: World War I and the Uses of the Higher Learning in America.* Baton Rouge: Louisiana State University Press, 1975. By focusing on the work of academics in such organizations as the Committee on Public Information and The Inquiry, Gruber reveals the various pressures on scholars who found themselves conflicted by a sense of loyalty to their country and their regard for the truth.

14:367   Hilderbrand, Robert C. *Power and the People: Executive Management of Public Opinion in Foreign Affairs, 1897–1921.* Hilderbrand considers the impact of public opinion on foreign policymakers, with an emphasis on the Wilson years (2:144).

14:368   Johnson, Donald Oscar. *The Challenge to American Freedoms: World War I and the Rise of the American Civil Liberties Union.* Lexington: University Press of Kentucky, 1963. This is an important work about the organization that came into being in the struggle over the right to oppose American participation in the war.

14:369   Kennedy, David M. *Over Here: The First World War and American Society.* New York: Oxford University Press, 1980. Essential reading for any student of the era, Kennedy's account re-creates and interprets the home-front war for the American mind, the task of economic mobilization, the doughboys' encounters with battle, and the politics of peacemaking. It ends with a moving evocation of Wilson's fate and the meaning of Armistice Day.

14:370   Koistinen, Paul A. C. "The 'Industrial Military Complex' in Historical Perspective: World War I." *Business History Review* 41 (Winter 1967): 378–403. This essay was among the first (in a now well-established literature) to portray World War I as a "watershed" in the organizational development of

American business and the emerging interdependence of modern business and the military.

14:371 Kornweibel, Theodore, Jr. *"Investigate Everything": Federal Efforts to Compel Black Loyalty during World War I.* Bloomington: Indiana University Press, 2002. Kornweibel has written one of the first comprehensive studies of its kind. Fitted neatly into the broader contexts of the quest for patriotic conformity and the preexisting antipathy toward African-American activism generally, his topics range from draft enforcement for the Jim Crow army to the federal government's scrutiny of *The Crisis* ("Every word is loaded with sedition") and its harassment of the *Chicago Defender* ("The most dangerous of all Negro journals").

14:372 Larson, Simeon. *Labor and Foreign Policy: Gompers, the AFL, and the First World War, 1914–1918.* Rutherford, NJ: Fairleigh Dickinson University Press, 1974. For the first time in a truly consequential way, union labor during World War I took a firm position on a crucial issue of foreign policy. This book examines how Samuel Gompers and the AFL came to favor military preparedness and belligerency.

14:373 Lasswell, Harold D. *Propaganda Technique in the World War.* New York: Alfred A. Knopf, 1927. Reprint 1972 (M.I.T. Press). Lasswell discusses several topics related to the manipulation of public opinion (and the demoralization of the enemy) through propaganda.

14:374 Livermore, Seward W. *Politics Is Adjourned: Woodrow Wilson and the War Congress, 1916–1918.* Middletown, CT: Wesleyan University Press, 1966. This is the most detailed such study ever written. It focuses on the bitter factional and partisan quarrels that accompanied virtually every significant piece of war-related legislation and the rancor that suffused the fateful congressional elections of 1918.

14:375 Luebke, Frederick C. *Bonds of Loyalty: German-Americans and World War I.* DeKalb: Northern Illinois University Press, 1974. This fine study focuses on those groups who embraced the slogan, "Germania our mother; Columbia our bride," and lived to regret it. During the neutrality period, German-Americans apparently did not realize that their unabashed support of the fatherland was viewed as disloyal by many other Americans. Their agitation, the author posits, paved the way for repression and violence after April 1917.

14:376 Mock, James R., and Cedric Larson. *Words That Won the War: The Story of the Committee on Public Information, 1917–1919.* Princeton: Princeton University Press, 1939. This is the earliest, more or less scholarly, study of the committee and its works in the schools, the workplace, the home, and popular entertainment.

14:377 Mullendore, William C. *History of the United States Food Administration, 1917–1919.* Stanford, CA: Stanford University Press, 1941. In this official history of the U.S. Food Administration, the author describes its organization, Herbert Hoover's role as director, and its contribution to winning the war.

14:378 Murphy, Paul L. *World War I and the Origin of Civil Liberties in the United States.* New York: Norton, 1979. This is the standard history on the subject, and it addresses, among other concerns, many of the problems—particularly for hyphenate groups, socialists, and civil libertarians—that arose as a result of the Committee on Public Information's quest for patriotic conformity.

14:379 Murray, Robert K. *Red Scare: A Study in National Hysteria, 1919–1920.* Minneapolis: University of Minnesota Press, 1955. A half century after its publication, this remains the standard account of the domestic postscript to America's involvement in the Great War. Murray appropriately emphasizes that the scare was driven by corporate and political hostility to organized labor, and that both journalists and Supreme Court justices fanned the flames. A very good narrative, it is shy on analysis and broad context: Murray calls it (in 1955, no less) "a story of a phenomenon."

14:380 Radosh, Ronald. *American Labor and Foreign Policy.* New York: Random House, 1969. Radosh offers many insights into the subject, from World War I to Vietnam, in a study that emphasizes but is not limited to centrist trade unions such as the AFL or the UMW.

14:381 Read, James M. *Atrocity Propaganda, 1914–1919.* New Haven: Yale University Press, 1941. According to Read, atrocity stories about the Germans published as propaganda fed the public's appetite for a Carthaginian peace and thereby limited the flexibility of negotiators at the peace conference.

14:382 Ross, Steven J. "Struggles for the Screen: Workers, Radicals, and the Political Uses of Silent Film." *American Historical Review* 96 (April 1991): 333–67. This pioneering study chronicles the rise and fall of successful, popular filmmaking by socialists and trade unionists during the era of World War I as well as the machinations of the established industry and the U.S. government to negate, and suppress, their productions by making films (in the words of Franklin K. Lane) "to spread anti-Red teachings all over the country."

14:383 Schaffer, Ronald. *America in the Great War: The Rise of the War Welfare State.* New York: Oxford University Press, 1991. Emphasizing the new roles the federal government took on in so many areas of national life, Schaffer makes the case that the war wrenched the United States out of the nineteenth century and thrust it into the modern age. Topical chapters deal with propaganda and dissent, motivating the AEF, the war's impact on African-Americans and women, and the origins of the concept of the welfare state.

14:384 Scheiber, Harry N. *The Wilson Administration and Civil Liberties, 1917–1921.* Ithaca: Cornell University Press, 1960. Scheiber's hard-hitting study chronicles the wartime assault on the First Amendment, in the form of the Sedition Act and the Espionage Act (used against socialists and left-leaning liberals in nearly all instances). While the estimable Postmaster General Albert Sidney Burleson and Attorney General Thomas Watt Gregory were the chief enforcers (and abusers) of the laws, Scheiber lays ultimate responsibility at Wilson's feet.

14:385 Stansell, Christine. *American Moderns: Bohemian New York and the Creation of a New Century.* New York: Metropolitan Books, 2000. Working on the premise that Greenwich Village of the 1910s was "a beacon of American possibility in the new age," Stansell re-creates New York's radical community during the Progressive era. This is a work of cul-

tural, intellectual, and social history, and many of Stansell's "moderns"—Bourne, Goldman, Eastman, Reed, and Lippmann, for example—had something at least as worthwhile to say about the war and the Mexican and Russian revolutions (not to mention civil liberties) as most of the policymakers about whom diplomatic historians usually write.

14:386 Thompson, John A. "American Progressive Publicists and the First World War, 1914–1917." *Journal of American History* 58 (September 1971): 364–83. Thompson analyzes the views of twenty prominent progressives (liberals and socialists alike) toward preparedness and the decision for war as those issues related to their concerns about the future of the reform movement.

14:387 _____. *Reformers and War: American Progressive Publicists and the First World War.* New York: Cambridge University Press, 1987. In this often brilliant book, Thompson expands his earlier work ("American Progressive Publicists and the First World War, 1914–1917," 1971 [14:386]) to cover American belligerency, the peacemaking, and its aftermath. Here the tension between belligerency and liberal (and socialist) values is all the more pronounced, in the high-stakes leap of faith that most pro-war progressives took in the hope that the struggle was worthwhile—that it could be molded to serve good purposes both at home and internationally.

14:388 Vaughn, Stephen. *Holding Fast the Inner Lines: Democracy, Nationalism, and the Committee on Public Information.* Chapel Hill: University of North Carolina Press, 1980. This is possibly the best history of the CPI and Creel, whose work ironically helped to create a political environment hostile to Wilsonian internationalism. A supplementary volume to *The Papers of Woodrow Wilson.*

14:389 Ward, Larry Wayne. *The Motion Picture Goes to War: The U.S. Government Film Effort during World War I.* Ann Arbor: UMI Research Press, 1985. This analysis is a good place to start for an understanding of film propaganda in its crucial early stages as it related to American popular conceptions of war and foreign policy.

14:390 Ward, Robert D. "The Origin and Activities of the National Security League, 1914–1919." *Mis-*

sissippi Valley Historical Review 47 (June 1960): 51–65. Ward describes how this organization became such a powerful political force in the United States in its emphasis on compulsory military training and promotion of intervention; the article also highlights the NSL's intense nationalism and antidemocratic tactics.

14:391   Wynn, Neil A. *From Progressivism to Prosperity: World War I and American Society.* New York: Holmes and Meier, 1986. This well-written short history underscores the expanding influence of the federal government on the lives of everyday Americans—women and blacks are highlighted—because of the war and the attendant acceleration of industrialization and modernization.

THE MILITARY AND NAVAL DIMENSION

14:392   Allard, Dean C. "Anglo-American Naval Differences during World War I." *Military Affairs* 44 (April 1980): 75–81. While most naval studies concentrate on cooperation between the two powers, Allard (a senior naval historian) identifies sometimes sharp differences in goals and expectations. The British, for instance, expected the U.S. navy to give unquestioning assistance to the Royal Navy's mercantile and antisubmarine operations. American naval policy was not unresponsive, but it was also focused on coastal defenses and Japanese expansion in the Pacific.

14:393   Bailey, Thomas A. *The Policy of the United States toward the Neutrals, 1917–1918.* Baltimore: Johns Hopkins Press, 1942. In this study of its policy after it became a belligerent, Bailey concludes that the United States recognized the rights of neutrals under international law in keeping with the principles to which it once appealed before entering the war.

14:394   Barbeau, Arthur E., and Florette Henri. *The Unknown Soldiers: Black American Troops in World War I.* Philadelphia: Temple University Press, 1974. Reprint 1996 (Da Capo Press). The first scholarly account of its kind, this study details how black manpower (or labor troops) and black officers were used, abused, and misused in the Great War for democracy. About half of the book is devoted to the exploits of

the two black divisions of the American Expeditionary Force.

14:395   Braim, Paul F. *The Test of Battle: The AEF in the Meuse-Argonne Campaign.* Newark: University of Delaware Press, 1987. This is a thorough account of the decisive campaign that helped to bring on Germany's military collapse. Beginning in late September 1918 and lasting until the armistice, it involved 500,000 American troops, 26,000 of whom lost their lives (half of all U.S. battle deaths in the war).

14:396   Braisted, William Reynolds. *The United States Navy in the Pacific, 1909–1922.* The author researched diplomatic records as well as Navy and War Department records to consider the relationship between American foreign and naval policies before, during, and immediately after World War I. The same press published an abridged version in 1977 (13:84).

14:397   Camfield, Thomas M. "'Will to Win'—The U.S. Army Troop Morale Program of World War I." *Military Affairs* 41 (October 1977): 125–28. This essay explains the evolution of the first systematic military morale program in American history, a perceived necessity owing to the army's consisting mainly of draftees, many of whom were illiterate, foreign born, or indifferent to (or uninformed about) the purposes behind the war for democracy.

14:398   Chambers, John Whiteclay, II. *To Raise an Army: The Draft Comes to Modern America.* New York: Free Press, 1987. Most Americans of the Civil War era regarded conscription as tyrannical; by 1917–1918, with the raising of the first full-scale draft army to fight a "foreign" war, most considered it legitimate. Chambers offers a thorough explication of this radical change brought on by World War I, set in the context of a controversy spanning two centuries.

14:399   Coffman, Edward M. "The American Military and Strategic Policy in World War I." In *War Aims and Strategic Policy in the Great War, 1914–1918: Papers,* ed. Adrian W. Preston and Barry D. Hunt, 67–84. Totowa, NJ: Rowman and Littlefield, 1977. Coffman makes the case that General Pershing cooperated with the Allied forces strictly on his own terms, exemplified in the case of his insistence that American units not be integrated with British and French units.

14:400 _____. *The War to End All Wars: The American Military Experience in World War I*. New York: Oxford University Press, 1968. Reprint 1998 (University Press of Kentucky). This solid military history details the organization, planning, administration, and deployment of the American Expeditionary Force in World War I. Coffman's account of the soldiers' training and the action they saw in combat is particularly effective.

14:401 Coletta, Paolo E. *Sea Power in the Atlantic and Mediterranean in World War I*. Lanham, MD: University Press of America, 1989. Although not its exclusive focus, this volume contains a fair amount on American naval strategy.

14:402 DeWeerd, Harvey A. *President Wilson Fights His War: World War I and the American Intervention*. New York: Macmillan, 1968. In this comprehensive military history, the author sees somewhat mixed results: on the one hand, the AEF and all that came with it was essential to boosting Allied morale and winning the war; on the other, because the United States had waited so long even to start getting prepared, those achievements were not as great as they otherwise might have been.

14:403 Dorwart, Jeffery M. *The Office of Naval Intelligence: The Birth of America's First Intelligence Agency, 1865–1918*. In his concise and authoritative study, Dorwart deals with the ONI's efforts to cooperate with its British counterpart as well as its various surveillance activities (9:246).

14:404 Eisenhower, John S. D., with Joanne Thompson Eisenhower. *Yanks: The Epic Story of the American Army in World War I*. New York: Free Press, 2001. With his wife and coauthor, the son of the thirty-fourth president has written a reliable account, starting with the task of raising an army—the numbers increased from 100,000 to over 4 million within a year—and getting it overseas, and then detailing the important campaigns in which the American military participated. Eisenhower is impressed with the achievement overall, but (taking a cue from Pershing) suggests that the victory was incomplete owing to a premature armistice.

14:405 Flammer, Philip M. *The Vivid Air, the Lafayette Escadrille*. Athens, GA: University of Georgia Press, 1981. The average World War I combat pilot's lifespan over enemy lines was fifteen hours. Only six out of thirty-eight of these American volunteer fliers survived the war, although the squadron nonetheless managed to shoot down 199 enemy planes. Flammer has written a well-researched history.

14:406 Freidel, Frank. *Over There: The Story of America's First Great Overseas Crusade*. Rev. ed. Philadelphia: Temple University Press, 1990. This is a reliable, vivid pictorial history, from boot camp to battleground. First published in 1964.

14:407 Hankey, Maurice P. A. *The Supreme Command, 1914–1918*. 2 vols. London: Allen and Unwin, 1961. Hankey, secretary to the Committee of Imperial Defense and later involved with the Supreme War Council and Paris Peace Conference, writes from the British insider's point of view. He is not uncritical of the late-arriving Yanks.

14:408 Healy, David F. "Admiral William B. Caperton and United States Naval Diplomacy in South America, 1917–1919." Caperton's attempts to get Brazil, Uruguay, and Argentina into World War I against Germany were impressive but not successful; only Brazil eventually declared war on Germany, Uruguay was already pro-Allied, and Argentina stayed neutral and ambivalent (12:321).

14:409 Laurie, Clayton D. "'The Chanting of Crusaders': Captain Heber Blankenhorn and AEF Combat Propaganda in World War I." *Journal of Military History* 59 (July 1995): 457–81. Laurie demonstrates the importance of the work of a former journalist whose distinctive military and diplomatic weapon probably shortened the war. Delivered by artillery shell, balloon, and airplane in the latter months of 1918, millions of Blankenhorn's leaflets listed the rations German POWs might expect, the numbers of AEF troops in France, and, finally, Woodrow Wilson's words (including his correspondence with the German government after October 6).

14:410 Link, Arthur S., and John Whiteclay Chambers, II. "Woodrow Wilson as Commander in Chief." In *The United States Military under the Constitution of the United States, 1789–1989*, ed. Richard H. Kohn, 317–75. New York: New York University Press, 1991. The authors look at Wilson's sensitivity to constitutional issues regarding his role both as the head of the armed forces and manager in chief of the nation's resources in wartime.

14:411   Mead, Gary. *The Doughboys: America and the First World War.* New York: Overlook Press, 2000. A journalist, Mead has mined a lode of primary sources (including interviews and questionnaires) generated by veterans and gathered by the army's Military History Institute. The result is a rich social history based on first-person accounts on a variety of topics—from tales of combat to what it was like to be black in a Jim Crow army.

14:412   Nenninger, Timothy K. "Tactical Dysfunction in the AEF, 1917–1918." *Military Affairs* 51 (October 1987): 177–81. This article describes Pershing's insistence on offensive tactics, in contrast to the other Allies' defensive attitude manifested in trench warfare. Yet the author finds that offensive tactical training of infantry was inadequate because circumstances compelled the large-scale commitment of the AEF a year sooner than expected, and because of weak combat support capabilities at the divisional level.

14:413   Parsons, Edward B. "Why the British Reduced the Flow of American Troops to Europe in August-October 1918." *Canadian Journal of History* 12 (December 1977): 173–92. Parsons argues that Great Britain reduced the flow of American troops to Europe to regain export markets it had lost to the United States during the war and to weaken the American challenge to British maritime supremacy as well as Wilson's potential to control peace terms.

14:414   Patton, Gerald W. *War and Race: The Black Officer in the American Military, 1915–1941.* Westport, CT: Greenwood Press, 1981. This book concentrates on the efforts of groups such as the Central Committee of Negro College Men to enter the army officers corps and to overcome various forms of discrimination. Patton also chronicles the army's deliberate distortion of hundreds of black officers' combat performance records.

14:415   Spector, Ronald H. "'You're Not Going to Send Soldiers over There Are You!': The American Search for an Alternative to the Western Front 1916–1917." *Military Affairs* 36 (February 1972): 1–4. For

decades the United States had planned for a war with Germany in the Western Hemisphere. (The idea was that the army would prevent an invasion of American soil, while the navy anticipated a decisive sea battle in the western Atlantic.) Yet well into 1917, military strategists planned for a second front by an invasion of, alternately, Holland (to attack the Germans from the rear), the Middle East, or Italy. Newton D. Baker was always dubious; ultimately he had his way.

14:416   Sprout, Harold, and Margaret Sprout. *The Rise of American Naval Power, 1776–1918.* In the discussion of American naval preparations during World War I, the authors focus (as they do throughout their sweeping study) on the intersection between civilian leadership and the navy's planners and strategists (7:56). First published in 1939.

14:417   _____. *Toward a New Order of Sea Power: American Naval Policy and the World Scene, 1918–1922.* 2d ed. Princeton: Princeton University Press, 1943. Chapter 5 is especially important, bearing on the relation between the League of Nations and naval power. First issued in 1940.

14:418   Stallings, Laurence. *The Doughboys: The Story of the AEF, 1917–1918.* New York: Harper and Row, 1963. Near the end of his life, Stallings, the coauthor of the play "What Price Glory?," decided to write a book about a subject near to his heart—the experiences of American soldiers in combat in France. The results are impressive.

14:419   Trask, David F. *Captains & Cabinets: Anglo-American Naval Relations, 1917–1918.* Columbia: University of Missouri Press, 1972. Trask blends a discussion of naval planning operations with that of British-American foreign policy; he emphasizes how both Britain and the United States, while cooperating against the Germans, also sought to protect their respective postwar positions.

14:420   _____. *The United States in the Supreme War Council: American War Aims and Inter-Allied Strategy, 1917–1918.* Middletown, CT: Wesleyan University Press, 1961. Focusing on military strategy in the French theater of war, Trask illuminates American war aims and the relationship between President Wilson's wartime preparations and his plans for the peace to come.

14:421 Williams, William J. "Josephus Daniels and the U.S. Navy's Shipbuilding Program during World War I." *Journal of Military History* 60 (January 1996): 7–38. In 1917, German submarines sank an average of 530,000 tons of Allied shipping per month. In this article, Williams praises the secretary of the navy for reversing construction priorities in light of that fact. "Destroyers first and battle cruisers last" became the order of the day. The lighter craft, along with the convoy system, helped to curb German success in 1918. Daniels's destroyers again proved valuable when FDR transferred fifty of them to the British in September 1940.

Relations with Revolutionary Russia and the Allied Intervention, 1917–1920

14:422 Bradley, John F. N. *Allied Intervention in Russia.* New York: Basic Books, 1968. A useful survey of the Allied intervention in Russia, this book is not as historiographically significant as some others in this section.

14:423 Davis, Donald E., and Eugene P. Trani. "The American YMCA and the Russian Revolution." *Slavic Review* 33 (September 1974): 469–91. As the communists tightened the screws of repression, YMCA personnel retaliated by aiding the regime's opponents, primarily in Siberia.

14:424 Dupuy, R. Ernest. *Perish by the Sword: The Czechoslovakian Anabasis and Our Supporting Campaigns in North Russia and Siberia, 1918–1920.* Harrisburg, PA: Military Service Publishing Co., 1939. In a severely critical work, the author describes how Allied and American military policy in north Russia and Siberia made for a disastrous campaign. Blame is laid upon the State Department.

14:425 Fic, Victor M. *The Collapse of American Policy in Russia and Siberia, 1918: Wilson's Decision Not to Intervene (March-October, 1918).* Boul-

der: East European Monographs, 1995. Based on research in American, British, French, Russian, and Czech archives, Fic contends that anti-Bolshevik views did not drive Wilson to intervene, and that his refusal to consent to a massive Allied intervention after September 1918 was a great mistake.

14:426 Fike, Claude E. "The United States and Russian Territorial Problems, 1917–1920." *Historian* 24 (May 1962): 331–46. President Wilson's vow to support national self-determination is analyzed in this article about the Ukraine, Georgia, and Turkestan.

14:427 Filene, Peter G. *Americans and the Soviet Experiment, 1917–1933.* Cambridge, MA: Harvard University Press, 1967. In the first two chapters, the author traces the abrupt shift from a favorable attitude toward the Russian revolution of March 1917 to a hostile attitude after the Bolsheviks came to power in November 1917.

14:428 Foglesong, David S. *America's Secret War against Bolshevism: U.S. Intervention in the Russian Civil War, 1917–1920.* Chapel Hill: University of North Carolina Press, 1995. Foglesong argues that ideological antipathy to Lenin's government fundamentally shaped Wilson's policies, including clandestine efforts to extend financial and material aid to groups fighting to overthrow the Bolsheviks.

14:429 Fry, Michael G. "Britain, the Allies, and the Problem of Russia, 1918–1919." *Canadian Journal of History* 2 (September 1967): 62–84. The author delineates the different British views on intervention in Russia and demonstrates how these differences contributed to the difficulties of Allied planning.

14:430 Graves, William S. *America's Siberian Adventure, 1918–1920.* New York: J. Cape and H. Smith, 1931. The commander of the American forces in Siberia criticizes the State Department and Allied military commanders for embroiling American forces in the Russian civil war—in his words, "a deliberate interference in the internal affairs of the Russian people."

14:431 Guins, George C. "The Siberian Intervention, 1918–1919." *Russian Review* 28 (October 1969): 428–40. This article provides an overview of the military and political situation in Siberia at the time of the Allied intervention. The description of the actual landing of troops, their activities, what the Czechs were doing, and so on, is quite interesting.

14:432   Kennan, George F. "Russia and the Versailles Conference." *American Scholar* 30 (Winter 1960–1961): 13–42. Kennan describes Wilson's illness, the Hoover relief program, and the consequences of leaving Russia out of the peace conference.

14:433   _____. *Russia and the West under Lenin and Stalin.* Boston: Little, Brown, 1961. The first 150 pages deal with Soviet-American relations under Wilson, Kerensky, and Lenin.

14:434   _____. *Soviet-American Relations, 1917–1920.* 2 vols. Princeton: Princeton University Press, 1956–1958. Various aspects of this monumental study have either been corrected, reinterpreted, or elaborated upon—in particular, the degree to which Wilson was truly knowledgeable about Russian affairs and the nature of his intentions regarding the Bolshevik regime. Even so, it remains the most comprehensive narrative of Soviet-American relations from 1917 to 1920. Vol. 1, *Russia Leaves the War* (1956), begins with the last days of the provisional government and ends with the Treaty of Brest-Litovsk. Vol. 2, *The Decision to Intervene* (1958), continues the story to the end of the Allied intervention, an enterprise Kennan condemns as futile and terribly counterproductive.

14:435   Killen, Linda R. *The Russian Bureau: A Case Study in Wilsonian Diplomacy.* Lexington: University Press of Kentucky, 1983. In October 1918, Wilson authorized the War Trade Board's creation of a Russian Bureau; its activities in Archangel and Vladivostok favored anti-Bolshevik factions.

14:436   _____. "The Search for a Democratic Russia: Bakhmetev and the United States." *Diplomatic History* 2 (Summer 1978): 237–56. The author tells the inconclusive story of the Russian ambassador to the United States under Kerensky whom the Wilson administration belatedly recognized and perhaps disingenuously encouraged.

14:437   Lasch, Christopher. "American Interven-

tion in Russia: A Reinterpretation." *Political Science Quarterly* 77 (June 1962): 205–23. Lasch makes the case that, rather than the spread of Bolshevism, American intervention was based on the fear that the Bolsheviks were the tools of Germany: "The whole business rested on an illusion of staggering proportions."

14:438   _____. *American Liberals and the Russian Revolution.* New York: Columbia University Press, 1962. Reprint 1972 (McGraw-Hill). This important work describes the impact of the Russian revolution on American politics and foreign policy, focusing on the differences in outlook between the "war liberals" and the "anti-imperialists." American foreign policy failed, according to Lasch, because the anti-imperialists failed effectively to challenge the assumptions and principles of the war liberals.

14:439   Long, John W. "American Intervention in Russia: The North Russian Expedition, 1918–19." *Diplomatic History* 6 (Winter 1982): 45–67. In reviewing the work of other scholars, Long also makes his own contribution to the literature, arguing that the chief factor behind Wilson's decision to undertake the expedition was the intense pressure the Allies put on him to do so.

14:440   Maddox, Robert James. *The Unknown War with Russia: Wilson's Siberian Intervention.* San Rafael, CA: Presidio Press, 1977. This work concludes that Wilson agreed to intervene in Siberia to assure the success of his plan for world peace, which he believed the Bolsheviks threatened.

14:441   McFadden, David W. *Alternative Paths: Soviets and Americans, 1917–1920.* New York: Oxford University Press, 1993. This important book, based on research in Soviet archives, is about paths not taken. In it, McFadden reevaluates the relationship, pointing to a number of areas of cooperation—uninterrupted activities of the American Red Cross in Russia, the Bolsheviks' exemption of several American corporations from nationalization decrees, and their sale of strategic raw materials to the United States.

14:442   Morley, James W. *The Japanese Thrust into Siberia, 1918.* New York: Columbia University Press, 1957. The author discusses the Japanese policymaking process, the split between Asia- and west-first cliques, and the importance that the Japanese attached to cooperative relations with Americans in East Asia.

14:443 Radosh, Ronald. "John Spargo and Wilson's Russian Policy, 1920." *Journal of American History* 52 (December 1965): 548–65. Spargo, a leading American socialist of the 1910s who supported the war, was also anti-Bolshevik; this essay traces his efforts to get the administration to support anti-Bolshevik forces in Russia.

14:444 Rhodes, Benjamin D. "The Anglo-American Intervention at Archangel, 1918–1919: The Role of the 339th Infantry." *International History Review* 8 (August 1986): 367–88. In this interesting account of the American infantry's experience with arctic conditions, the author pronounces the intervention a disaster in every way—even comparable to the worst blunders of the Crimean War. And, of course, the Soviets never forgot it. In 1959, Khrushchev said, "Never have any of our soldiers been on American soil, but your soldiers were on Russian soil."

14:445 _____. *The Anglo-American Winter War with Russia, 1918–1919: A Diplomatic and Military Tragicomedy.* Westport, CT: Greenwood Press, 1988. This is mainly a military history of the ill-conceived and badly managed Allied campaign against the Bolsheviks around Archangel, where ice closed down the port and snow incapacitated the railroads every winter. In his intelligent and interesting reconstruction of what he implies was an impossible undertaking, Rhodes credits Wilson for his reluctance to go in and his eagerness to get out at the first opportunity, but he takes no sides, except for his sympathy for all the suffering soldiers involved—be they British, American, Bolshevik, or White Russian.

14:446 Richard, Carl J. "'The Shadow of a Plan': The Rationale behind Wilson's 1918 Siberian Intervention." *Historian* 49 (November 1986): 64–84. The author defends Wilson's actions, suggesting he would never have intervened in the revolution to begin with had it not been for the European war.

14:447 Schild, Georg. *Between Ideology and Realpolitik: Woodrow Wilson and the Russian Revolution, 1917–1921.* Westport, CT: Greenwood Press, 1995. The author maintains that, while he had definite goals, uncertainty suffused Wilson's fluctuating

attitudes and policies toward revolutionary Russia; while his "heart was with the Bolsheviks, his mind had a contempt for them." An even more recent work, focusing less on the revolution and U.S. intervention than the two nations' (and peoples') relations, and based on remarkable multiarchival research, is Norman E. Saul, *War and Revolution: The United States and Russia, 1914–1921* (Lawrence: University Press of Kansas, 2001).

14:448 Somin, Ilya. *The Stillborn Crusade: The Tragic Failure of Western Intervention in the Russian Civil War, 1918–1920.* New Brunswick: Transaction Publishers, 1996. In a tone as compelling as it is tendentious, this wishful post–cold war polemic argues that the Allies could have smothered the Bolsheviks in their crib if only Wilson and Lloyd George had avoided half measures and paid more attention to Robert Lansing and Winston Churchill. Of his colleagues in the field, Somin states categorically, "virtually all of them are, broadly speaking, liberal or radical in political orientation," and none of them (whether realist or left revisionist) ever grasped the great lesson—"that totalitarian regimes must, as much as possible, be destroyed while they are still in their infancy."

14:449 Strakhovsky, Leonid I. *Intervention at Archangel: The Story of Allied Intervention and Russian Counter-Revolution in North Russia, 1918–1920.* Princeton: Princeton University Press, 1944. Reprint 1971 (New York: H. Fertig). This detailed study is somewhat dated but, partly because of the time in which the author wrote, still worth reading.

14:450 Thompson, John M. *Russia, Bolshevism, and the Versailles Peace.* Princeton: Princeton University Press, 1967. Among many other issues, this widely acclaimed study examines the plans of Allied and American policymakers on, alternately, the recognition or overthrow of Lenin's regime and their worries at the Paris Peace Conference about the possibilities of Bolshevik expansion.

14:451 Trani, Eugene P. "Woodrow Wilson and the Decision to Intervene in Russia: A Reconsideration." *Journal of Modern History* 48 (September 1976): 440–61. Trani cites numerous British documents, including Lloyd George's statement to the War Cabinet that the Americans "had always been very much against" intervention but had gone along "only on account of the pressure which had been brought to bear on President Wilson." This, he argues, was the key factor in the president's reluctant decision.

14:452 Ullman, Richard H. *Anglo-Soviet Relations, 1917–1921.* 3 vols. Princeton: Princeton University Press, 1961–1972. The three volumes—the most comprehensive work available on the subject—are subtitled *Intervention and the War, Britain and the Russian Civil War, Nov. 1918–Feb. 1920,* and *The Anglo-Soviet Accord.* Ullman treats American policy toward Russia as dependent on British aims and evaluations.

14:453 Unterberger, Betty Miller. *America's Siberian Expedition, 1918–1920: A Study of National Policy.* Durham, NC: Duke University Press, 1956. A good starting point for the historiography of the American intervention into north Russia and Siberia, this book by a leading authority argues that Wilson believed the Allies would go in with or without the United States. Thus, he decided reluctantly to participate so he could apply the brakes on the expedition (Japan being his main worry).

14:454 _____. "Woodrow Wilson and the Bolsheviks: The 'Acid Test' of Soviet-American Relations." *Diplomatic History* 11 (Spring 1987): 71–90. In this SHAFR presidential address, Unterberger makes the case on Wilson's behalf that the principle of self-determination guided his actions in going in (i.e., to restrain the Japanese) and in getting out (because by then he regarded the intervention an abject failure and could see no good coming of it).

14:455 White, John Albert. *The Siberian Intervention.* Princeton: Princeton University Press, 1950. Primary emphasis is given to the Russian-Japanese rivalry for control over Siberia. The American intervention, the author argues, was meant to block Japan from absorbing Siberia.

14:456 Williams, William Appleman. "The American Intervention in Russia, 1917–1920 (Part One)." *Studies on the Left* 3 (Fall 1963): 24–48. Williams scrutinizes the period before the actual decision to intervene in a reply to George Kennan and other postwar writers. His argument relies heavily on the pa-

pers of Robert Lansing, an extreme anti-Bolshevik, and therefore may be somewhat distorted. Williams asserts that Wilson's initial reluctance owed chiefly to a concern about offending various counterrevolutionary groups.

14:457 _____. "The American Intervention in Russia, 1917–1920 (Part Two)." *Studies on the Left* 4 (Winter 1964): 39–57. Resuming the story from "The American Intervention in Russia, 1917–1920 (Part One)" (1963) (14:456) in February 1918, Williams maintains that Wilson was searching for the most propitious circumstances to join the Allied intervention (not to stay out) and that the motive should not be an impenetrable mystery—Wilson's deeply held anti-Bolshevik sentiments.

14:458 Woodward, David R. "The British Government and Japanese Intervention in Russia during World War I." *Journal of Modern History* 46 (December 1974): 663–85. The new sources that Woodward brings to bear on the British point of view imply that some modification of Richard Ullman's *Anglo-Soviet Relations, 1917–1921* (1961–1972) (14:452) is needed.

War's End and the Paris Peace Conference

THE ARMISTICE

14:459 Lowry, Bullitt. *Armistice 1918.* Kent, OH: Kent State University Press, 1996. This well-researched study maintains that the Allies (not Wilson or the Fourteen Points) controlled the terms of the armistice with Germany; thus, because it was in fact a preliminary peace, the armistice fundamentally determined the contents of the Treaty of Versailles long before it was written.

14:460 Nelson, Keith L. "What Colonel House Overlooked in the Armistice." *Mid-America* 51 (April 1969): 75–91. The colonel's biggest job was to get the Fourteen Points accepted as the basis for the armistice, which he accomplished but for two Allied reservations—on freedom of the seas and reparations. However, House utterly caved in, Nelson demonstrates, on the question of Allied military occupation of the Rhineland; this concession, he argues, held grave implications for the peace conference, for it gave Lloyd George and Clemenceau a considerable advantage in dealing with Wilson.

14:461   Renouvin, Pierre. *L'Armistice de Rethondes, 11 novembre 1918.* Paris: Gallimard, 1968. This version of the story is the most important source on the French perspective; not surprisingly, it is critical of Wilson (and slightly less so of House).

14:462   Rudin, Harry R. *Armistice, 1918.* New Haven: Yale University Press, 1944. Although it was published prior to the opening of the archives of the belligerents, Rudin offers an excellent introduction to the subject. He argues that the Allies, because they took explicit exception to only two of the Fourteen Points, had thereby pretty much bound themselves to Wilson's program.

14:463   Walworth, Arthur. *America's Moment, 1918, American Diplomacy at the End of World War I.* New York: Norton, 1977. Focusing on the period between the armistice and the opening of the peace conference, Walworth explores the fleeting days of high expectation when it appeared that the United States (and Woodrow Wilson) stood at the threshold of supreme accomplishments.

14:464   Weintraub, Stanley. *A Stillness Heard round the World: The End of the Great War: November 1918.* New York: E. P. Dutton, 1985. Weintraub creates an evocative panorama that illuminates the diverse reactions, in all of the belligerent countries, to the closing days of the war to end all wars.

THE PEACE CONFERENCE

14:465   Bailey, Thomas A. *Woodrow Wilson and the Lost Peace.* New York: Macmillan Company, 1944. Bailey wrote this volume with his own generation in mind, and it remains the most vivid example of the "second chance" school of historical writing. With considerable dramatic flair, he outlines the dilemmas the president faced during the peace nego-

tiations and underscores his mistakes in the hope that the United States would avoid them when the time came to craft a new peace at the end of World War II.

14:466   Baker, Ray Stannard. *What Wilson Did at Paris.* New York: Doubleday, Page and Company, 1919. This brief volume was intended as an antidote to Keynes's unflattering portrait of Wilson in *The Economic Consequences of the Peace,* published the same year in London (14:545). Baker offers an interesting, quasi-journalistic account emphasizing the machinations of the president's adversaries at Paris and other obstacles he faced.

14:467   _____. *Woodrow Wilson and the World Settlement, Written from His Unpublished and Personal Material.* 3 vols. Garden City, NY: Doubleday, Page and Co., 1922. In the first extensive history of the peace conference written from the Wilsonian perspective, Baker is remarkable in his broad understanding of the profound effect of the Bolshevik revolution on the peace conference (e.g., "Paris cannot be understood without Moscow"), an insight that, amazingly, did not register with historians until the 1960s. The first two volumes contain a narrative account partly drawn from Baker's own materials; the third is a supplementary volume of documents. They deserve revisiting.

14:468   Benns, F. Lee. "The Two Paris Peace Conferences of the Twentieth Century." In *Essays in History and International Relations, in Honor of George Hubbard Blakeslee,* ed. Dwight E. Lee and George E. McReynolds, 153–70. Worcester, MA: Clark University, 1949. This essay comparing the two peace conferences following the two world wars may be of particular interest to students concerned with comparative history. Benns offers some provocative judgments.

14:469   Birdsall, Paul. *Versailles Twenty Years After.* New York: Reynal and Hitchcock, 1941. Written before both Pearl Harbor and the upturn of interest in Wilson, this book was perhaps the first in the new wave of "second chance" writing during World War II. Birdsall refers to Wilson as an "American Prophet," portraying his Paris exertions sympathetically if not entirely uncritically. It was important in explaining to a contemporary readership why the Versailles Treaty turned out as it did; today the book is mainly of historiographical interest.

14:470 Boemeke, Manfred F., Gerald D. Feldman, and Elisabeth Glaser, eds. *The Treaty of Versailles: A Reassessment after 75 Years.* New York: Cambridge University Press, 1998. The results of an international conference at the University of California at Berkeley, this large volume contains an outstanding collection of essays by leading scholars on a wide variety of significant topics, with an editors' introduction and a prologue by Ronald Steel. Because of their scope, depth, and relevance to American diplomatic history—the contributions on reparations by Marks, Glaser, and Ferguson are especially good—the essays all warrant listing: Klaus Schwabe, "Germany's Peace Aims and the Domestic and International Constraints" (37–67); David French, "'Had We Known How Bad Things Were in Germany, We Might Have Got Stiffer Terms': Great Britain and the German Alliance" (69–86); David Stevenson, French War Aims and Peace Planning" (87–109); Thomas J. Knock, "Wilsonian Concepts and International Realities at the End of the War" (111–29); Alan Sharp, "A Comment" (131–44); Erik Goldstein, "Great Britain: The Home Front" (147–66); Georges-Henri Soutou, "The French Peacemakers and Their Home Fronts" (167–88); Lawrence E. Gelfand, "The American Mission to Negotiate the Peace: An American Looks Back" (189–202); Fritz Klein, "Between Compiegne and Versailles: The Germans on the Way from a Misunderstood Defeat to an Unwanted Peace" (203–20); Anthony Lentin, "A Comment" (221–43); Carole Fink, "The Minorities Question at the Paris Peace Conference: The Polish Minority Treaty, June 28, 1919" (249–74); Stephen A. Schuker, "The Rhineland Question: West European Security at the Paris Peace Conference of 1919" (275–312); Piotr S. Wandycz, "The Polish Question" (313–35); Sally Marks, "Smoke and Mirrors: In Smoke-Filled Rooms and the Galerie Des Glaces" (337–70); Glaser, "The Making of the Economic Peace" (371–99); Niall Ferguson, "The Balance of Payments Question: Versailles and After" (401–40); Feldman, "A Comment" (441–47); Jon Jacobson, "The Soviet Union and Versailles" (451–68); William R. Keylor, "Versailles and International Diplomacy" (469–505); Antoine Fleury, "The League of Nations: Toward a New Appreciation of Its History" (507–22); Diane B. Kunz, "A Comment" (523–32); Wolfgang J. Mommsen, "Max Weber and the Peace Treaty of Versailles" (535–46); William C. Widenor, "The Construction of the American Interpretation: The Pro-Treaty Version" (547–64); Michael G. Fry, "British Revisionism" (565–601); Boemeke, "Woodrow Wilson's Image of Germany, the War-Guilt Question, and the Treaty of Versailles" (603–14); and Gordon Martel, "A Comment" (615–36).

14:471 Floto, Inga. *Colonel House in Paris: A Study of American Policy at the Paris Peace Conference 1919.* Translated by Pauline B. Katborg. Princeton: Princeton University Press, 1980. This critique of Colonel House's activities by a Danish historian, published as a supplementary volume to *The Papers of Woodrow Wilson,* is a valuable study of Wilsonian foreign policy and the peace negotiations of 1919. Floto sees House's loyalty to Wilson as less than complete. A corrected edition of the 1973 Aarhus University Press of Copenhagen edition.

14:472 Gelfand, Lawrence E. *The Inquiry: American Preparations for Peace, 1917–1919.* New Haven: Yale University Press, 1963. This is an administrative study of the independent bureau—a body of some 130 experts, mostly university professors—established by Wilson in September 1917 to help him formulate the American peace program. (Investigation by experts was an innovation that inhered in progressivism and seemed a most fitting agent to advance the new diplomacy.) Gelfand traces the creation of this first "Brain Trust" and compares its myriad recommendations with the final terms of the treaties.

14:473 Hankey, Maurice P. A. *The Supreme Control at the Paris Peace Conference 1919: A Commentary.* London: Allen and Unwin, 1963. This last substantial writing from Sir Maurice Hankey, British secretary of various commissions during and after World War I, is especially useful to scholars eager to understand the administrative procedures and organization of the peace conference.

14:474 House, Edward M., and Charles Seymour, eds. *What Really Happened at Paris: The Story of the Peace Conference, 1918–1919.* New York: C. Scribner's Sons, 1921. This collection of lectures delivered by former members of The Inquiry and the American mission at the peace conference endeavors to explain the evolution of important provisions of the treaties.

14:475 Lauren, Paul Gordon. "Human Rights in History: Diplomacy and Racial Equality at the Paris Peace Conference." *Diplomatic History* 2 (Summer 1978): 257–78. The European and American peacemakers not only refused to adopt the principle of racial equality in the face of Japanese pleading but also declined to acknowledge that this issue was of intense concern to many nations and peoples.

14:476 Mantoux, Paul. *Paris Peace Conference: Proceedings of the Council of Four, March 24–April 18.* Translated by John Boardman Whitton. Genève: Libraire Droz, 1964. An English translation of the minutes of the Council of Four meetings as recorded by the French secretary, Paul Mantoux, this volume contains material not found in the British minutes, but the definitive edition, edited by Link and Boemeke (*The Deliberations of the Council of Four [March 24–June 28, 1919]: Notes of the Official Interpreter, Paul Mantoux,* 1992) (14:17) and listed in "Document Collections," is more extensive and covers the subject to the signing of the treaty in the Hall of Mirrors.

14:477 Marston, F. S. *The Peace Conference of 1919, Organization and Procedure.* London: Oxford University Press, 1944. Reprint 1981 (Greenwood Press). This is a basic description of the organization and procedures used at the peace conference. Students will find Marston's work useful in understanding how the conference functioned.

14:478 Mayer, Arno J. *Politics and Diplomacy at Peacemaking: Containment and Counterrevolution at Versailles 1918–1919.* New York: Alfred A. Knopf, 1967. Among the two or three most significant books ever written on the subject, this massive study asserts a symbiotic connection between domestic and foreign policy and argues that the peacemakers were at least as concerned about containing revolutionary Russia and the spread of Bolshevism as with punishing the Germans. Among all the dramatis personae, only Wilson emerges as a statesman of truly broad vision, albeit one whose tragedy flowed from his own rationality and faith in the idea of progress in history. (The book boasts a superb bibliography, unusual among works in English for its extensive listings of foreign-language studies, country by country.)

14:479 Nicolson, Harold. *Peacemaking, 1919: Being Reminiscences of the Paris Peace Conference.*

Boston: Houghton Mifflin Company, 1933. This memoir by an able British diplomatist—the latter portion featuring extended excerpts from his diary—offers a good read as well as a valuable and often cynical vantage point on the atmosphere and goings-on of the peacemaking. It is laced with acerbic observations (e.g., "Wilson was leaking badly"; Clemenceau is described as "A crunched homunculus").

14:480 Nielson, Jonathan M. *American Historians in War and Peace: Patriotism, Diplomacy, and the Paris Peace Conference 1919.* Dubuque, IA: Kendall/Hunt Pub. Co., 1994. This excellent study elucidates the origins of modern "scholar experts" and their works in the Great War. Historians served as propagandists—on J. Franklin Jameson's National Board for Historical Service as well as on the Creel Committee—and, according to Harry Elmer Barnes, "prostituted their art in an effort to hamstring the Hun." Perhaps more crucially, they also served on The Inquiry and the peace commission at Paris; historians drew up, among countless others, some fourteen reports on Poland, nineteen on Russia, twenty-five on Austria-Hungary, eight on Italy, twenty on the Ottoman empire, and eighty on German colonies. "You are in truth, my advisers," Wilson told them. Not all believed him. Nielson maintains a fair balance of the good, the bad, and the ugly with regard to the results all around.

14:481 _____. "The Scholar as Diplomat: American Historians at the Paris Peace Conference of 1919." *International History Review* 14 (May 1992): 228–51. This is a much abridged version of a part of the author's *American Historians in War and Peace: Patriotism, Diplomacy, and the Paris Peace Conference 1919* (1994) (14:480), concentrating almost entirely on The Inquiry—its membership, attitudes toward Wilson (and vice versa), its moderating influences on the settlement, and its "didactic application of expertise to contemporary international problems."

14:482 Riddell, George Allardice. *Lord Riddell's Intimate Diary of the Paris Peace Conference and After, 1918–1923.* New York: Reynal and Hitchcock, 1934. As personal documents of secondary participants at Paris go, this seldom-cited volume occasionally rivals Nicolson's *Peacemaking* for both its incisiveness and acidity and, in these respects (like Nicolson's) it excels most of the accounts by the primary participants. Published in Britain the previous year.

14:483   Seymour, Charles. *Letters from the Paris Peace Conference.* New Haven: Yale University Press, 1965. These revealing letters written in 1919 by the young Charles Seymour to his wife provide a fascinating record of events at the peace conference; they convey the impression that Wilson, in the eyes of his peers, was undiminished by the 1918 congressional elections. Edited by Harold B. Whiteman, Jr.

14:484   _____. "The Paris Education of Woodrow Wilson." *Virginia Quarterly Review* 32 (Fall 1956): 578–93. Addressing certain unflattering accounts of Wilson's performance, Seymour characterizes the protagonist as "eminently educable" and fully the match of his peers at the conclave.

14:485   Startt, James D. "Wilson's Mission to Paris: The Making of a Decision." *Historian* 30 (August 1968): 599–616. The author traces the controversy—in the press, in Congress, and among his advisers—over the president's resolve personally to lead the American delegation and attend the peace conference.

14:486   Temperley, Harold, ed. *A History of the Peace Conference of Paris.* 6 vols. London: H. Frowde, and Hodder and Stoughton, 1920–1924. This massive work combines narrative description with selected documentary appendices. The many authors of individual chapters were participants in the British or American delegations.

14:487   Thompson, Charles T. *The Peace Conference Day by Day: A Presidential Pilgrimage Leading to the Discovery of Europe.* New York: Brentano's, 1920. This volume is a chronological guide to the activities of the peace conference.

14:488   Tillman, Seth P. *Anglo-American Relations at the Paris Peace Conference of 1919.* Princeton: Princeton University Press, 1961. Although subsequent scholarship has significantly modified some of his findings, Tillman's fine study remains the most comprehensive treatment of Anglo-American relations of its kind.

14:489   Walworth, Arthur. *Wilson and His Peace-makers: American Diplomacy and the Paris Peace Conference, 1919.* New York: Norton, 1986. The amazing Mr. Walworth published this huge book at the age of eighty-three. Its coverage is more or less encyclopedic, his research in both European and American archives is impressive, and the writing is felicitous. Yet, while it contains innumerable insights, the book advances no major new interpretations. What is new, for Walworth, is his highly critical perspective on Wilson, after having written his prize-winning hagiographic biography of the president some thirty years earlier.

The Irish Issue

14:490   Carroll, Francis M. "The American Commission on Irish Independence and the Paris Peace Conference of 1919." *Irish Studies in International Affairs* 2, no. 1 (1985): 103–18. Carroll scrutinizes the strivings of both Irish and Irish-American leaders on behalf of self-rule before and during the conference and their failure to bring Wilson to their point of view. See also the edited work by the same author, *The American Commission on Irish Independence, 1919: The Diary, Correspondence, and Report* (Dublin: Irish Manuscripts Commission, 1985).

14:491   Duff, John B. "The Versailles Treaty and the Irish-Americans." *Journal of American History* 55 (December 1968): 582–98. In 1917–1918, Irish-Americans supported President Wilson prior to his departure for Paris; by the summer of 1919, however, the president's relationship with influential Irish-American leaders had cooled mainly because he had not obtained Irish self-rule in the peace treaty.

14:492   Hopkinson, Michael. "President Woodrow Wilson and the Irish Question." *Studia Hibernica*, no. 32 (1993): 89–111. The author ably outlines Wilson's troubled relationship with the Irish over self-rule, but he also demonstrates that the president tried to persuade the British on the question, albeit to keep fences mended among Irish politicians within the Democratic Party.

14:493   Noer, Thomas J. "The American Government and the Irish Question during World War I." *South Atlantic Quarterly* 72 (Winter 1973): 95–114. Noer follows the efforts of Irish nationalists to exploit Wilson's rhetoric about self-determination and hold his feet to the fire as well as the latter's denunciations of the extremists of Sinn Fein.

France

14:494 Ambrosius, Lloyd E. "Wilson, the Republicans, and French Security after World War I." *Journal of American History* 59 (September 1972): 341–52. The French security treaty—which betokened Clemenceau's lack of confidence in the League, but which Wilson regarded as merely an amplification of Article X—was devised by Lloyd George to split the difference between his two antagonistic colleagues over the issue of French occupation of the Rhineland. Ambrosius capably lays out the details while seeing the pact as symbolic of the bigger problem: it was a limited, practical form of internationalism, and many leading Republicans (including Lodge) favored its ratification; alas, Wilson would not allow the security treaty to be considered apart from the peace settlement as a whole.

14:495 Andrew, Christopher M., and A. S. Kanya-Forstner. "The French Colonial Party and French Colonial War Aims, 1914–1918." *Historical Journal* 17 (March 1974): 79–106. The French colonialists claimed for France a zone from the Tarsus Mountains to the Sinai, but they got only the northern part, in the Sykes-Picot deal. Continuing to dominate French imperial policy, the colonialists won Cameroon in Africa and beat back Italian claims there and in Asia Minor.

14:496 Blumenthal, Henry. *Illusion and Reality in Franco-American Diplomacy, 1914–1945*. The first portion of this book covers relations during World War I and the peace conference; the author finds the antagonism and disagreements between Clemenceau and Wilson most unfortunate—perhaps even the taproot of the peace treaty's negative qualities (2:318).

14:497 McCrum, Robert. "French Rhineland Policy at the Paris Peace Conference, 1919." *Historical Journal* 21 (September 1978): 623–48. Foch and French military efforts to help separatists establish an independent Rhineland failed for lack of public support in the affected areas. Meanwhile, Clemenceau had a dubious view of the project and worried about

Allied opposition; he thus accepted Allied economic and strategic guarantees of French national security.

14:498 Noble, G. Bernard. *Policies and Opinions at Paris, 1919: Wilsonian Diplomacy, the Versailles Peace, and French Public Opinion*. New York: Macmillan Company, 1935. This work derives from Noble's assumption that the ills of the mid-1930s "can in large measure be ascribed to the devastation and dislocation of the World War and to the failure of the peace makers of 1919 to establish a viable international order."

14:499 Yates, Louis A. R. *The United States and French Security, 1917–1921: A Study in American Diplomatic History*. New York: Twayne Publishers, 1957. This study of the American guarantee treaty of French security remains valuable for its broad coverage of this important question.

Germany

14:500 Bane, Suda Lorena, and Ralph Haswell Lutz, eds. *The Blockade of Germany after the Armistice, 1918–1919: Selected Documents of the Supreme Economic Council, Superior Blockade Council, American Relief Administration, and Other Wartime Organizations*. Stanford, CA: Stanford University Press, 1942. Insofar as the United States is here treated, relevant topics among the many documents include the delivery methods and value of relief shipped from America to the Allies, neutrals, and Germany and the resumption of trade with Germany.

14:501 Kimmich, Christoph M. *Germany and the League of Nations*. Chicago: University of Chicago Press, 1976. The most authoritative monograph on the subject, among its chief concerns is Wilson's decision to exclude Germany, for the time being, from the League of Nations.

14:502 Nelson, Harold. *Land and Power: British and Allied Policy on Germany's Frontiers, 1916–19*. London: Routledge and Paul, 1963. This work examines the negotiations of the German territorial settlement at the Paris Peace Conference. The British viewpoint and Anglo-American cooperation are stressed.

14:503   Nelson, Keith L. *Victors Divided: America and the Allies in Germany, 1918–1923.* Berkeley: University of California Press, 1975. As part of the terms of the armistice, a small contingent of American troops (about 15,000) joined an Allied occupation force in Germany, mainly around Coblenz. At Paris, Wilson was not unhappy to initiate these arrangements to prevent Germany's fate from falling completely into the hands of the French.

14:504   Schwabe, Klaus. "Woodrow Wilson and Germany's Membership in the League of Nations, 1918–19." *Central European History* 8 (March 1975): 3–22. Wilson first believed Germany should become a member of the League; then that it should not; then that it should only be admitted after it was disarmed, had served a probation, and could offer assurances it would abide by the League's rules.

14:505   _____. *Woodrow Wilson, Revolutionary Germany, and Peacemaking, 1918–1919: Missionary Diplomacy and the Realities of Power.* Translated by Rita Kimber and Robert Kimber. Chapel Hill: University of North Carolina Press, 1985. This important study by a distinguished German scholar, based on German and American source materials, covers a wide range of concerns beginning with the armistice negotiations through the peace conference and offers insight into the American-German relationship and various negotiations. Published as a supplement to the *Papers of Woodrow Wilson.* Originally published in 1971 in German (Düsseldorf: Droste).

14:506   Snell, John L. "Wilson's Peace Program and German Socialism." *Mississippi Valley Historical Review* 38 (September 1951): 187–214. The author probes Wilson's exertions to dissuade German socialists from lending moral and material support to the Bolsheviks.

14:507   Spence, Robert B. "K. A. Jahnke and the German Sabotage Campaign in the United States and Mexico, 1914–1918." *Historian* 59 (Fall 1996): 89–112. The talented Mr. Jahnke was a German saboteur, British double agent, and a veteran of both the German army and the U.S. marine corps. His exploits included smuggling arms both to the Carranzistas and to Huerta, setting off the bomb that killed ten preparedness paraders in San Francisco in July 1916 (for which Tom Mooney

served twenty-two years in prison), and masterminding the gigantic explosion at Black Tom only a few days later. Spence points out that the Germans and British alike encouraged the rogue, though for quite different reasons.

Italy and Yugoslavia

14:508   Albrecht-Carrié, René. *Italy at the Peace Conference.* New York: Columbia University Press, 1938. In one of the earliest such scholarly works, the author assesses the problem of Italian ambitions and territorial claims at Paris; as a monograph primarily about negotiations at the peace conference, it remains a major study of Italy's collision with Woodrow Wilson's aspirations.

14:509   Kernek, Sterling J. "Woodrow Wilson and National Self-Determination along Italy's Frontier: A Study of the Manipulation of Principles in the Pursuit of Political Interests." *Proceedings of the American Philosophical Society* 126 (August 1982): 243–300. This is a very substantial essay about Wilson's inconsistency (of which the author is quite critical) in applying the principle of self-determination—in this case, his concession to Orlando's strategic claims along the Austrian-Italian border, which gave Italy jurisdiction over 200,000 Austrians.

14:510   Lederer, Ivo J. *Yugoslavia at the Paris Peace Conference: A Study in Frontiermaking.* New Haven: Yale University Press, 1963. This monograph offers a careful analysis of the controversies between the new Yugoslav state and Italy over the status of Fiume and Istria.

14:511   Page, Thomas Nelson. *Italy and the World War.* New York: C. Scribner's, 1920. The American ambassador to Italy (1913–1919) provides a very sympathetic history of Italy, Italian war aims, and the Italian people.

14:512   Rossini, Daniela. *Il mito american, nell'Italia della Grande Guerra [The American Myth in World War I Italy].* Rome: Gius, Laterza and Figli, 2000. This is an important, comprehensive study of mutual perceptions and misperceptions of Italians and Americans and of their diplomatic relations during the war and the peace conference—by a leading

Italian scholar of Italo-American relations whose erudition about both sides is extremely impressive.

14:513 _____. "World War One and Wilsonian Exceptionalism: The Dual Response of the Italian Masses and Leaders to the American Message." In *Reflections on American Exceptionalism,* ed. David K. Adams and Cornelis A. van Minnen, 129–47. Staffordshire, UK: Ryburn Pub., 1994. In this fascinating essay, the author argues that the Italian lower classes (the source of immigration) in many ways better understood America than political elites, and that their sympathetic attitude, abetted by the Committee on Public Information and about a thousand YMCA volunteers in Italy, contributed dramatically to the Wilsonian myth ("the only one capable of balancing the rising myth of Lenin"). Thus, during the peace conference, Wilson's advisers urged him to bypass the politicians and reach out to the masses. Successful propaganda, Rossini points out, did not necessarily make for keen political analysis or good diplomacy.

14:514 Schmitz, David F. "Woodrow Wilson and the Liberal Peace: The Problem of Italy and Imperialism." *Peace and Change* 12 (December 1987): 29–44. Schmitz sheds interpretative light on Wilson's refusal to indulge Italy's desire for the Yugoslav port city of Fiume and the Dalmatian coast, the famous contretemps that prompted Orlando to walk out of the peace conference and Wilson to appeal to the Italian people over his head.

14:515 Zivojinovic, Dragan R. *America, Italy, and the Birth of Yugoslavia (1917–1919).* New York: East European Monographs, 1972. This comprehensive history focuses on American-Italian relations during the war and the peace conference and maintains that Wilson was not as inflexible as others have argued.

14:516 _____. "The Emergence of American Policy in the Adriatic: December 1917–April 1919." *East European Quarterly* 1 (September 1967): 173–215. Zivojinovic traces the changing American policy in the Italian-Yugoslav territorial dispute and the controversy over its disposition; he also scores Wilson for pushing the Italians so hard on the issue of the League of Nations.

Czechoslovakia

14:517 Kelly, David. "Woodrow Wilson and the Creation of Czechoslovakia." *East European Quarterly* 26 (Summer 1992): 185–207. In this account of the event, Wilson is shorn of some of the credit that has accrued to him in other studies.

14:518 Unterberger, Betty Miller. *The United States, Revolutionary Russia, and the Rise of Czechoslovakia.* Chapel Hill: University of North Carolina Press, 1989. In this extensively researched volume, Unterberger elucidates Wilson's role in the breakup of the Hapsburg empire and the rise of the Czech state. She attributes considerable coherence and rationality to the president's thinking about self-determination in the face of mercurial circumstances throughout Central Europe and despite the skepticism or opposition of all the great powers.

Austria-Hungary

14:519 Dumin, Frederick. "Self-Determination: The United States and Austria in 1919." *Research Studies* 40, no. 3 (1972): 176–94. Dumin discusses the proposed Austro-German *Anschluss* of November 1918 and why the American delegation ultimately rejected the idea at the Paris Peace Conference.

14:520 Hopkins, George W. "The Politics of Food: United States and Soviet Hungary, March-August, 1919." *Mid-America* 55 (October 1973): 245–70. The Allies chose Herbert Hoover's food blockade policy rather than Marshal Foch's policy of force to bring down the coalition government of Hungary's Bolshevik leader Bela Kun.

14:521 Kann, Robert A., Bela K. Király, and Paula S. Fichtner, eds. *The Hapsburg Empire in World War I: Essays on the Intellectual, Military, Political, and Economic Aspects of the Hapsburg War Effort.* Boulder: East European Quarterly, 1977. This collection examines various institutions and sources of conflict that ultimately led to the dissolution of the Hapsburg empire. For American historians, perhaps the most relevant essay is by coeditor Fichtner, titled "Americans and the Disintegration of the Hapsburg Monarchy: The Shaping of a Historiographical Mode."

14:522   Mamatey, Victor S. *The United States and East Central Europe, 1914–1918.* Princeton: Princeton University Press, 1957. In this study of Wilsonian self-determination, Mamatey is critical of Wilson for what he describes as confusion in the president's thinking about and application of the principle, and for not appreciating its limitations in re-forming the Austro-Hungarian empire as it was being dismembered.

14:523   Pastor, Peter. "The Hungarian Revolution's Road from Wilsonianism to Leninism, 1918–19." *East Central Europe* 3 (June 1976): 210–19. Pastor challenges Arno Mayer's contention that the 1918 Károlyi government in Hungary had little or no ideological basis. He asserts that Mihály Károlyi embraced Wilsonianism as a revolutionary ideology because he felt it would radically change the country's antiquated social, political, and economic structure.

14:524   Smallwood, James M. "Banquo's Ghost at the Paris Peace Conference: The United States and the Hungarian Question." *East European Quarterly* 12 (Fall 1978): 289–307. The author describes the reactions of Wilson's advisers when Bela Kun took power in Hungary in March 1919. Neither Wilson nor Tasker Bliss was utterly hostile to the communist regime and opposed intervention to bring him down, but that goal was pursued by Lansing and Hoover once Wilson returned to America.

Bulgaria

14:525   Petkov, Petko M. *The United States and Bulgaria in World War I.* Boulder: East European Monographs, Columbia University Press, 1991. Written by the leading authority on the subject, this is a useful supplement to the monographic literature on American–East European relations.

Poland

14:526   Biskupski, M. B. "The Diplomacy of Wartime Relief: The United States and Poland, 1914–1918." *Diplomatic History* 19 (Summer 1995): 431–51. This essay indirectly explains the genesis of Wilson's Thirteenth Point by telling how Americans developed sympathy for the suffering Poles during the war and how Polish-Americans and the famous pianist-politician Paderewski skillfully used the relief issue to advance the cause of Polish statehood.

14:527   Fink, Carole. "The Paris Peace Conference and the Question of Minority Rights." *Peace and Change* 21 (July 1996): 273–88. In this excellent essay (about a historical problem with contemporary resonance), Fink explicates the origins of the Polish Minority Treaty (the provisions of which were also inserted into treaties with Czechoslovakia, Romania, Yugoslavia, Greece, Austria, Hungary, Bulgaria, and the Baltic states). Though related to the principle of self-determination, the protection of minorities came about in the wake of outrageous pogroms conducted by Poles against mainly Jews in 1918–1919. Thus, the peacemakers had no choice but to respond. At once pragmatic and idealistic, the model treaty guaranteed "life and liberty to all inhabitants . . . without distinction of birth, nationality, language, race, or religion." Fink suggests that part of the motivation was to keep minorities from turning to Bolshevism and to check Polish expansion. The document was far from perfect, she concludes, yet it "nevertheless revolutionized the history of minority rights."

14:528   Gerson, Louis L. *Woodrow Wilson and the Rebirth of Poland, 1914–1920: A Study in the Influence on American Policy of Minority Groups of Foreign Origin.* New Haven: Yale University Press, 1953. Reprint 1972 (Archon Books). This monograph emphasizes the activities of pressure groups in the United States on behalf of the formation of a postwar, independent Polish national state.

14:529   Kusielewicz, Eugene. "Wilson and the Polish Cause at Paris." *Polish Review* 1 (Winter 1956): 64–79. The author argues that Wilson was utterly sincere in espousing its independence in the thirteenth of the Fourteen Points but did not necessarily have a good understanding of other issues of concern to Poland.

14:530   Lundgreen-Nielsen, Kay. "The Mayer Thesis Reconsidered: The Poles and the Paris Peace Conference, 1919." *International History Review* 7 (February 1985): 68–102. The author says that Wilson's intentions for Poland were not to check Bolshevism, for he was troubled by the more extreme nationalist elements; what he wanted was a socially reformed, ethnic state living in peace with its neighbors so that it might help stabilize the region.

14:531 _____. *The Polish Problem at the Paris Peace Conference: A Study of the Policies of the Great Powers and the Poles, 1918–1919.* Translated by Alison Borch-Johansen. Odense, Denmark: Odense University Press. 1979. Based on research in British, French, American, and Polish archives, this study examines not only the deliberations of the great powers but also those of the Poles. The author's chief contribution, based on Polish sources, is demonstrating that Polish policymakers were equally concerned about pushing settlements as far east and west as was possible.

East Asia

14:532 Beers, Burton F. *Vain Endeavor: Robert Lansing's Attempts to End the American-Japanese Rivalry.* Beers demonstrates that Lansing took a fairly independent position on the subject of Japanese-American relations and shows how the secretary of state diverged from Wilson's intentions during important negotiations (13:222).

14:533 Craft, Stephen G. "John Bassett Moore, Robert Lansing, and the Shandong Question." *Pacific Historical Review* 66 (May 1997): 231–49. Ku Wei-chun (V. K. Wellington Koo) referred to Shandong (Shantung) as "the cradle of Chinese civilization, the birthplace of Confucius and Mencius, and a Holy Land for the Chinese." Thus, when the Big Four recognized the legality of Japanese claims on the peninsula, the Chinese declined to sign the Treaty of Versailles. Subsequently, they employed the services of Moore and then Lansing, who both proved ineffectual. In bilateral negotiations in 1922, Japan agreed to withdraw in exchange for monetary compensation from China, a deal financed by a Japanese loan. Craft tells the story well and succinctly.

14:534 Fifield, Russell H. *Woodrow Wilson and the Far East: The Diplomacy of the Shantung Question.* Henry Cabot Lodge may or may not have been sincere when he denounced the settlement as "one of the blackest things in the history of diplomacy." But Fifield, while explicating various factors that led Wilson to accede to Japan's claims against China, makes a pretty strong case for the significance of Shantung's role in the Senate's rejection of the Versailles Treaty (13:177).

14:535 Howlett, Charles F. "Democracy's Ambassador to the Far East: John Dewey's Quest for World Peace." *Pacific Historian* 20 (Winter 1976): 388–406. John Dewey's visit to East Asia at the conclusion of World War I had a twofold significance, says Howlett: he was the first major American intellectual to recognize the importance of East Asia in American policy, and he became the symbol of American democracy.

14:536 Kawamura, Noriko. "Wilsonian Idealism and Japanese Claims at the Paris Peace Conference." *Pacific Historical Review* 66 (November 1997): 503–26. The author explores the clash between Wilson and the Japanese over Shantung and the failed motion to include a statement about racial equality in the Covenant of the League of Nations. On the latter issue, Kawamura describes the Americans (who tacitly supported the proposal) as relieved when the British persisted in their decisive opposition; as for Shantung, the Japanese had secretly gained France and Britain's assent, and they considered Wilson's interposition an attempt to thwart their legitimate interests in the region. It was not entirely surprising then that Baron Makino should later characterize Wilson as "a politician best suited to a dictatorship."

14:537 King, Wunsz. *Woodrow Wilson, Wellington Koo, and the China Question at the Paris Peace Conference.* Leyden: A. W. Sythoff, 1959. When the issue of Shantung arose, Wilson caved in to the Japanese because he needed their support for the League's future: "They are not bluffers, & they will go home unless we give them what they should not have." V. K. Wellington Koo (Ku Wei-chun) served on the League of Nations Commission and worked reasonably well with Wilson. This brief study focuses on the roles the two played in the tortured Shantung Settlement.

14:538 Li, Tien-yi. *Woodrow Wilson's China Policy, 1913–1917.* Kansas City: University of Kansas City Press, 1952. This study omits consideration of the Shantung question but provides solid information on the American withdrawal from the China Consortium and Wilson's response to Japan's Twenty-One Demands, both of which helped shape Japanese-American relations at the Paris Peace Conference.

14:539 May, Ernest R. "American Policy and Japan's Entrance into World War I." *Mississippi Val-*

ley *Historical Review* 40 (September 1953): 279–90. May suggests that Bryan's attempt to revive former Secretary of State Hay's method of diplomacy and the reluctance of the State Department to assume new responsibilities allowed Japan to capitalize on the war.

14:540   Mazuzan, George T. "'Our New Gold Goes Adventuring': The American International Corporation in China." *Pacific Historical Review* 43 (May 1974): 212–32. U.S. business interests sought to penetrate the putative China market during World War I through the creation of the American International Corporation. But Chinese politics and the demands of the war combined to minimize the effectiveness of the AIC, and the open door remained as elusive as ever.

14:541   Trani, Eugene P. "Woodrow Wilson, China, and the Missionaries, 1913–1921." *Journal of Presbyterian History* 49 (Winter 1971): 328–51. Wilson viewed Christianity as a unifying force in the world and the Chinese revolution of 1911 as the first step toward the spread of Christianity and democracy for China.

REPARATIONS ISSUE

14:542   Baruch, Bernard M. *The Making of the Reparation and Economic Sections of the Treaty.* New York: Harper and Brothers, 1920. Baruch was economic adviser to the American Commission to Negotiate Peace and a member of every important economic and reparations committee at Paris. These recollections form an important part of the record on American intentions for reparations.

14:543   Bunselmeyer, Robert E. *The Cost of the War, 1914–1919: British Economic War Aims and the Origins of Reparation.* Hamden, CT: Archon Books, 1975. This is a reinterpretation of the concept and practice of assigning and assessing reparations as a part of the peace settlement.

14:544   Burnett, Philip M. *Reparation at the Paris Peace Conference from the Standpoint of the American Delegation.* 2 vols. New York: Columbia University Press, 1940. This work remains one of the most comprehensive treatments of the reparations question. The first volume consists of a narrative; the second is a valuable compilation of relevant documentation.

14:545   Keynes, John Maynard. *The Economic Consequences of the Peace.* London: Macmillan, 1919. Reprint 1988 (Penguin Books). This economic analysis of the settlement, particularly of reparations, by the famous economist who served on the delegation at Paris, has been pretty much refuted by diplomatic and economic historians alike, although he was certainly correct in predicting that the Versailles system would fail. Keynes's withering caricature of the "bamboozled" Wilson had a big impact in the United States.

14:546   Mantoux, Étiene. *The Carthaginian Peace: Or, the Economic Consequences of Mr. Keynes.* New York: Oxford University Press, 1946. In a spirited refutation of Keynes's *The Economic Consequences of the Peace* (1919) (14:545), Mantoux argues that the reparations forced upon defeated Germany were not that excessive. The French economist's view was no doubt shaped by Germany's ravaging of his country, but his argument is not without merit. The son of Paul Mantoux (who served as secretary to the Council of Four), Étiene died on the front lines in Germany in 1945 shortly after finishing this work.

14:547   Pruessen, Ronald W. "John Foster Dulles and Reparations at the Paris Peace Conference, 1919: Early Patterns of Life." *Perspectives in American History* 8 (1974): 381–410. Dulles played an important role at Paris as a member of the reparations commission as well as legal counsel to the American peace commission. Although he was able to convince the Allies to exclude actual war costs from the total bill, he still believed the magnitude of reparations (not only in the treaty but also in the terms of the Dawes and Young Plans to follow) far exceeded Germany's ability to finance.

14:548   Trachtenberg, Marc. *Reparation in World Politics: France and European Economic Diplomacy, 1916–1923.* New York: Columbia University Press, 1980. The author demonstrates that the French never truly desired exorbitant reparation (and never nearly as much as the British did). More than money, they wanted raw materials (especially coal), and their occasionally extreme demands were intended as a lever to get American credits. They remained rational and, in their relatively modest requirements, understood why Germany also would need to be repaired.

OTHER STUDIES RELATED TO WAR'S END AND THE PEACE CONFERENCE

14:549 Bonsal, Stephen. *Unfinished Business.* Garden City, NY: Doubleday, Doran and Company, 1944. Bonsal served as an assistant to and interpreter for both Wilson and Colonel House; based on his diary and personal notes from the peace conference, this is the account of a quasi insider.

14:550 Carr, James M. "A Sacred Trust of Civilization: Woodrow Wilson and the Genesis of the Mandate System." Senior Thesis, Princeton University, 1982. Though never published (and written by an undergraduate), this excellent monographic study may be the most comprehensive of its kind.

14:551 Fisch, Max H., ed. *Selected Papers [of Robert C. Binkley].* Cambridge, MA: Harvard University Press, 1948. Binkley was among America's first historians to write critically about the peace conference of 1919. The three articles reprinted here—"The Peace That Failed," "The Economy of Scholarship," and "Ideas and Institutions"—were first published in the 1920s and early 1930s, but their insights remain of value. Fisch also provides a biographical sketch and bibliography.

14:552 Haskins, Charles Homer, and Robert Howard Lord. *Some Problems of the Peace Conference.* Cambridge, MA: Harvard University Press, 1920. Haskins was chief of the Western European Division of The Inquiry, and Lord, who was instrumental in arrangements leading to the establishment of the new Polish state, was chief of the Eastern European Division. Both men were members of the American peace commission at Paris.

14:553 O'Grady, Joseph P., ed. *The Immigrants' Influence on Wilson's Peace Policies.* Lexington: University Press of Kentucky, 1967. This collection of essays focuses on the efforts of eleven immigrant groups to influence President Wilson's peace program. O'Grady himself writes about the Irish; A. J. App, the Germans; D. J. McCarthy, the British; John B. Duff, the Italians; George Bárány, the Magyars; George J. Prpic, the South Slavs; Otakar Odlozilik, the Czechs; Victor S. Mamatey, the Slovaks and Carpatho-Ruthenians; Arthur J. May, the "Mid-European Union"; Louis L. Gerson, the Poles; and M. Tenzer, the Jews.

14:554 Pomerance, Michla. "The United States and Self-Determination: Perspectives on the Wilsonian Conception." *American Journal of International Law* 70 (January 1976): 1–27. While idealists blame Woodrow Wilson for the failure of the principle of self-determination, realists consider the idea impractical and moralistic; when radicals hear the slogan uttered by capitalists (liberal or otherwise), they suspect it as a mask for imperialism. And so, the author concludes, the principle is mightily ambiguous.

14:555 Seymour, Charles. *Geography, Justice, and Politics at the Paris Conference of 1919.* New York: American Geographical Society, 1951. In this twenty-four-page lecture Seymour explains the relation of political geography to the European settlement, largely through the activities of Isaiah Bowman of the American Geographical Society. In both subtle and conclusive ways, he suggests, geography contributed to Wilson's failure.

14:556 Shaw, George Bernard. *Peace Conference Hints.* London: Constable, 1919. Shaw wrote an intensely interesting, epigraphically rich little pamphlet that deals with most of the major issues at Paris. (Though not uncritical of him, he observed of Wilson that "American democracy" had "accidentally produced a greater individual success than it is capable of appreciating.")

14:557 Shotwell, James T. *At the Paris Peace Conference.* New York: Macmillan Company, 1937. This diary of personal activities by an American adviser and a member of The Inquiry covers a multitude of subjects concerned with the peace negotiations. It is especially informative on the creation of the International Labor Organization.

14:558 Startt, James D. "The Uneasy Partnership: Wilson and the Press at Paris." *Mid-America* 52 (January 1970): 55–69. During the war, Wilson was rather distant in dealing with journalists, but on the eve of his departure for the peace conference he made efforts to cultivate better relations in order to build support for his policies—an effort that proved to be too little, too late.

The League of Nations

GENERAL AND THEMATIC STUDIES

14:559   Bartlett, Ruhl J. *The League to Enforce Peace.* Chapel Hill: University of North Carolina Press, 1944. This history of the League to Enforce Peace remains the only substantial study of the most influential American pro-League organization during the war. Bartlett ably describes the myriad activities of the LEP, especially its efforts to muster popular support for the League of Nations movement and, later, ratification of the peace treaty.

14:560   Egerton, George W. "Collective Security as Political Myth: Liberal Internationalism and the League of Nations in Politics and History." *International History Review* 5 (November 1983): 496–524. In this wide-ranging, insightful meditation, the author observes that at its inception, the League and collective security represented for its liberal advocates "a new international social contract in the ongoing, historical, progressive imposition of political and legal order upon social anarchy." During the cold war, this "myth" was adopted (or exploited) by Americans to legitimate their interventions "'in defence of freedom'" in such places as Vietnam, and by Russians to rationalize their own depredations in Eastern Europe.

14:561   _____. *Great Britain and the Creation of the League of Nations: Strategy, Politics, and International Organization, 1914–1919.* Chapel Hill: University of North Carolina Press, 1978. This is an extremely important examination of the birth and early life of the League idea in British politics and of the impact of the League's architects and supporters (both the ardent, like Cecil, and the lukewarm, like Lloyd George) on British foreign policy. Egerton is particularly good in explaining how, in embracing the League, the chief policymakers had felt their way toward a new understanding of the empire's strategic future in world politics with respect to the continent on one hand and the United States on the other.

14:562   _____. "The Lloyd George Government and the Creation of the League of Nations." *American Historical Review* 79 (April 1974): 419–44. Egerton explains that Lloyd George, though highly ambivalent, decided to go along with the League because he believed that the United States would surely join it as well and thus help shoulder the burden, and that a conservative construction would be placed on the Covenant in any event. The prime minister also saw Britain's future tied to an Atlantic, rather than a continental, strategy.

14:563   Fleming, Denna Frank. *The United States and the League of Nations, 1918–1920.* New York: G. P. Putnam's Sons, 1932. This study was once the standard work on the League of Nations controversy in the United States. It is still very much worth reading, at least for specialists.

14:564   Fosdick, Raymond B. *Letters on the League of Nations: From the Files of Raymond B. Fosdick.* Princeton: Princeton University Press, 1966. This is a collection of correspondence between Fosdick and other leading Wilsonians and internationalists of various stripes. Fosdick served as undersecretary-general of the League (1919–1920) and during World War II became a noted proponent of the United Nations.

14:565   Helbich, Wolfgang J. "American Liberals in the League of Nations Controversy." *Public Opinion Quarterly* 31 (Winter 1967–1968): 568–96. While charting liberals' growing disillusionment with Wilson during and after Paris, this essay's most important contribution is the light it sheds on the short-lived League of Free Nations Association, whose membership included Paul U. Kellogg, Jane Addams, Herbert Croly, Lillian Wald, Charles Beard, John Dewey, Felix Frankfurter, and Frederic C. Howe.

14:566   Knock, Thomas J. *To End All Wars: Woodrow Wilson and the Quest for a New World Order.* New York: Oxford University Press, 1992. Emphasizing Wilson's relationship with the American progressive left, this book maintains that two competing forms of internationalism developed during the neutrality period and that their adherents—"progressive" and "conservative" internationalists—differed strongly over major domestic issues as well, intensifying the ideological and partisan nature of the struggle over the treaty. The prospects for a *Wilsonian* league, Knock argues, were undermined as much by the unraveling of the progressive coalition (caused partly by Wilson's own acquiescence in the suppression of civil liberties) as by the opposition of Republican conservative internationalists. Drawing distinctions between "authentic Wilsonian internationalism" and unilateralist cold war globalism, the author concludes that "Lodgian, not Wilsonian, values" triumphed after 1945.

14:567   Kuehl, Warren F. *Seeking World Order: The United States and International Organization to 1920.* This pioneering study, the standard history of early American efforts to achieve a world organization, shows the interrelationships among peace and arbitration movements, international law, and diplomacy in the evolution of an idea that culminated in the League of Nations. The author also offers a concise overview of the ratification controversy (2:214).

14:568   Marburg, Theodore, and Horace E. Flack, eds. *Taft Papers on League of Nations.* New York: Macmillan Company, 1920. This is a useful collection on the president of the League to Enforce Peace, but they must be supplemented by Taft's own papers as well as those of Woodrow Wilson and Theodore Roosevelt to get the complete picture of the exertions of the second most important American advocate of a League of Nations.

14:569   Osgood, Robert E. "Woodrow Wilson, Collective Security, and the Lessons of History." *Confluence* 5 (Winter 1957): 341–54. Written as the cold war neared its hottest temperature, this essay seeks to demonstrate "how poorly [Wilson's] conception of collective security fits contemporary American practice and how badly the prevailing American conception of collective security is distorted by the efforts to reconcile the two." Among shorter pieces emanating from the "realist" school, Osgood's is a classic—a compelling statement that more than merely implies that, despite its role in creating the UN, the United States has conducted a fundamentally anti-Wilsonian foreign policy and correctly so. Reprinted in several 1950s collections, including Earl Latham, ed., *The Philosophy and Policies of Woodrow Wilson* (Chicago: University of Chicago Press, 1958).

14:570   Stromberg, Roland N. *Collective Security and American Foreign Policy: From the League of Nations to NATO.* New York: Praeger, 1963. Written at the height of the cold war, this is a classic example of the dim view of the "realist" school toward Wilson and collective security. Stromberg devotes the first fifty pages to the League and finds it wanting mainly for its failure, in his view, to take adequate account of power relationships in world politics.

14:571   Walters, F. P. *A History of the League of Nations.* 2 vols. New York: Oxford University Press, 1952. Walters served on Robert Cecil's staff in Paris and then as a member of the League Secretariat (1920–1940). His volumes are impassioned (grounded in what one scholar called the "Whig internationalist interpretation of history") and were once the preeminent work. Volume 1 *(The Making of the League)* covers the origins of the League idea through the drafting of the Covenant.

14:572   Winkler, Henry R. *The League of Nations Movement in Great Britain, 1914–1919.* New Brunswick: Rutgers University Press, 1952. Until the publication of Egerton's *Great Britain and the Creation of the League of Nations: Strategy, Politics, and International Organization, 1914–1919* (1978) (14:561), Winkler's was considered the standard study, and it is still a significant source on the movement in Britain as well as on Anglo-American relations thereon. His thesis is that the Covenant amounted to a limited League and that it could "safely be said to have reflected the official British position in many of its most important aspects."

ORIGINS OF THE LEAGUE IDEA

14:573   Boothe, Leon E. "Anglo-American Pro-League Groups Lead Wilson 1915–1918." *Mid-America* 51 (April 1969): 92–107. Boothe highlights the exasperation of League advocates in Britain because of Wilson's disinclination to discuss specifics before the peace conference convened. The author also argues that the president thus retarded public education on the subject in America, whereas, in England, public opinion had already been carefully marshaled in support of the general idea by late 1918.

14:574   Dubin, Martin D. "The Carnegie Endowment for International Peace and the Advocacy of a League of Nations, 1914–1918." *Proceedings of the American Philosophical Society* 123 (December 1979): 344–68. Dubin focuses on the endowment's leaders—Elihu Root, Nicholas Murray Butler, and James Brown Scott—to explicate the classic legalistic (alternately, "voluntarist") approach to international cooperation.

14:575   _____. "Elihu Root and the Advocacy of a League of Nations, 1914–1917." *Western Political Quarterly* 19 (September 1966): 439–55. This article explores Root's thinking on the subject during the neutrality period and also attempts to understand—though there is not much mystery here—how he could at once advocate the League and "mastermind the Republican attack on the covenant."

14:576   _____. "Toward the Concept of Collective Security: The Bryce Group's 'Proposals for the Avoidance of War,' 1914–1917." *International Organization* 24 (Spring 1970): 288–318. The author highlights those proposals advanced by the Bryce Groups that eventually found their way into the League Covenant in one form or another; these included chiefly the provisions for arbitration and conciliation and for the imposition of economic sanctions.

14:577   Latané, John H., ed. *Development of the League of Nations Idea: Documents and Correspondence of Theodore Marburg.* 2 vols. New York: Macmillan Company, 1932. Marburg, one of his generation's leading internationalists, was the League to Enforce Peace's main correspondent with President Wilson. The latter once referred unkindly to Marburg as a "woolgatherer." Happily, he also gathered important documents, and published them in these two illuminating volumes, which are also more comprehensive than the title suggests.

14:578   Olson, William C. "Theodore Roosevelt's Conception of an International League." Olson discusses Roosevelt's thoughtful essays about international organization written early in the war (1914–1915) as well as his subsequent views (1917–1919), which reflected a spheres-of-influence approach (11:472).

14:579   Patterson, David S. "The United States and

the Origins of the World Court." *Political Science Quarterly* 91 (Summer 1976): 259–77. After providing historical background (1890–1914), this essay concentrates on the war's impact on practitioners of international law who thought about a world court and what was "justiciable" and what was not. The author also examines Wilson's initial antipathy to the general notion and identifies how the Covenant of the League of Nations reflected a variety of views thereon.

DRAFTING THE COVENANT

14:580   Curry, George. "Woodrow Wilson, Jan Smuts, and the Versailles Settlement." *American Historical Review* 66 (July 1961): 968–86. The author's purpose is to establish the commanding importance of General Smuts's *The League of Nations: A Practical Suggestion* (1918) (14:583) on the peace conference and, especially, its impact on Wilson's thinking (although Curry misreads the latter's motives in touting the pamphlet and exaggerates the degree to which Smuts and Wilson were on the same wavelength).

14:581   Miller, David Hunter. *The Drafting of the Covenant.* 2 vols. New York: G. P. Putnam's Sons, 1928. A conservative internationalist, Miller was The Inquiry's chief consultant on international law and performed that function for Wilson at Paris. Volume 1 is a narrative history of the League commission's drafting process; volume 2 contains the corresponding documents.

14:582   Raffo, Peter. "The Anglo-American Preliminary Negotiations for a League of Nations." *Journal of Contemporary History* 9 (October 1974): 153–76. The author overemphasizes Smuts's impact on Wilson to the extent of claiming that the latter exerted "very little influence on the actual provisions and structure of the Covenant"; a close reading of Wilson's Paris Drafts, the minutes of the League commission, and the Covenant itself would suggest a very different conclusion.

14:583   Smuts, Jan. *The League of Nations: A Practical Suggestion.* New York: Hodder and Stoughton, 1918. This pamphlet, published in December 1918 by the celebrated scholar-soldier-statesman, was generally regarded as the single most important formulation of its kind advanced during the Paris Peace Conference. In particular, Smuts's recommendations for the so-called mandate system was considered highly original, though he pretty much abandoned the idea whenever it collided with British ambitions for captured colonies. Today the pamphlet is an extremely rare item; it is printed in full in Miller, *The Drafting of the Covenant* (1928) 2: 23–60 (14:581).

RATIFICATION CONTROVERSY

14:584 Abbott, Frank. "The Texas Press and the Covenant." *Red River Valley Historical Review* 4 (Winter 1979): 32–41. This survey of newspapers in a diehard Democratic state shows journalists generally praising Wilson and supporting American membership in the League, although the author notes a few nationalist, if not quite isolationist, viewpoints.

14:585 Ambrosius, Lloyd E. *Woodrow Wilson and the American Diplomatic Tradition: The Treaty Fight in Perspective.* New York: Cambridge University Press, 1987. About two-thirds of this important study is a highly detailed explication of the great parliamentary struggle. The author argues that the United States confronted a new dilemma born of World War I—global interdependence and pluralism. His thesis is that Wilson, in his conception of the League, "attempted to resolve the fundamental dilemma of American foreign relations through control over other nations," and that his failure epitomized the shortcomings of progressivism itself, which "furnished unrealistic guidance for the United States in the modern world."

14:586 Bagby, Wesley M. *The Road to Normalcy: The Presidential Campaign and Election of 1920.* Baltimore: Johns Hopkins Press, 1962. This is a comprehensive monograph that contains many interesting insights and observations pertaining to the League as a factor in the electoral contest from start to finish.

14:587 Bailey, Thomas A. *Woodrow Wilson and the Great Betrayal.* New York: Macmillan Company, 1945. Even though he was limited in his access to sources, no one else so far has ever told the *story* better than Bailey. The book's animating force—at once its greatest strength and shortcoming—is the immediacy he infuses into a work written chiefly to persuade Americans of 1945 that they must support the creation of a new League of Nations once the second awful war (which Wilson had prophesied) was over.

14:588 Cooper, John Milton, Jr. *Breaking the Heart of the World: Woodrow Wilson and the Fight for the League of Nations.* New York: Cambridge University Press, 2001. This is the most detailed and persuasive study thus far to argue that the outcome of the League fight was fundamentally determined by Wilson's health. In doing so, Cooper brings to bear medical information about the president available only since the 1990s as well as an enormous amount of research on the Senate's deliberations. Whether he settles the debate for all concerned, his book addresses many other issues and, in all, is an impressive achievement, brimming with innumerable smaller insights along with the more sweeping interpretation. In the end, for Cooper, two facts remain incontrovertible: "For all their decency and intelligence, Wilson's opponents were wrong. For all his flaws and missteps, Wilson was right. He should have won the League fight."

14:589 _____. "Fool's Errand or Finest Hour? Woodrow Wilson's Speaking Tour of September 1919." In *The Wilson Era: Essays in Honor of Arthur S. Link,* ed. John Milton Cooper, Jr. and Charles E. Neu, 198–220. Arlington Heights, IL: Harlan Davidson, 1991. In telling well this dramatic story, Cooper would like to split the difference on the question he poses, but he leans toward the "fool's errand" interpretation in arguing that Wilson might have better served his cause by staying in Washington and not wearing himself out on a whirlwind itinerary akin to a presidential campaign.

14:590 Egerton, George W. "Britain and the 'Great Betrayal': Anglo-American Relations and the Struggle for United States Ratification of the Treaty of Versailles, 1919–1920." *Historical Journal* 21 (December 1978): 885–911. Egerton focuses on debates within the British cabinet over whether to accommodate or stand firm against the Republican reservations to the League of Nations. He also highlights Viscount Grey's ultimately futile mission to the United States to try to move the ratification process along, in part by suggesting that some kinds of reservations would be acceptable to Great Britain. (His endeavors did not endear him to Wilson.)

14:591 _____. "Diplomacy, Scandal, and Military Intelligence: The Craufurd-Stuart Affair and Anglo-American Relations, 1918–1920." *Intelligence and National Security* 2 (October 1987): 110–34. This is a fascinating story about how a relatively minor fracas—over a critical remark about Wilson, an off-color joke about the second Mrs. Wilson, and gossip about a sexual impropriety of Bernard Baruch's—may have had a major impact on international relations.

14:592 Fleming, Denna Frank. *The Treaty Veto of the American Senate.* New York: G. P. Putnam's Sons, 1930. Reprint 1998 (Gaunt, Inc.). The book scrutinizes the Treaty of Versailles, but it examines the general issue and looks at other treaties as well. Fleming's basic conclusion might have been drawn from Wilson's observations, in *Congressional Government* (Boston: Houghton Mifflin, 1885) on the "treaty-marring power" of the upper house: "The Senate always has the last word."

14:593 Hewes, James E., Jr. "Henry Cabot Lodge and the League of Nations." *Proceedings of the American Philosophical Society* 114 (August 1970): 245–55. In a review of Lodge's changing position (1896–1920), the author finds the senator fairly consistent in opposing expansive, open-ended commitments and reasonable in seeking a more limited alternative during the treaty fight.

14:594 Holt, W. Stull. *Treaties Defeated by the Senate: A Study of the Struggle between President and Senate over the Conduct of Foreign Relations.* In this examination of the Senate and the Versailles Treaty, Holt undertakes what was a pioneering analysis of the votes taken on all the reservations and a similar breakdown of the attempts to obtain ratification without the reservations (2:182).

14:595 Johnson, Robert David. "Article XI in the Debate on the United States' Rejection of the League of Nations." *International History Review* 15 (August 1993): 502–24. Johnson points out that many progressives and "radicals" cited this part of the League Covenant as their main reason for opposing membership. "Any threat of war [was] . . . a matter of concern to the whole League," the article said, and Wilson thought it would help to shore up the right of self-determination and facilitate change. But Senators La Follette, Walsh, Norris, Gronna, and Borah considered it a potential tool of imperialism and an invasion of the right to revolution.

14:596 Kuehl, Warren F., and Lynne K. Dunn. *Keeping the Covenant: American Internationalists and the League of Nations, 1920–1939.* Kent, OH: Kent State University Press, 1997. This posthumously published sequel to Kuehl's 1969 work (14:567) is a critical appraisal of the internationalists and their efforts during the interwar period. Starting with efforts of Republican internationalists to contain their isolationist minority, Kuehl and Dunn assess other efforts such as the creation of nonpartisan educational programs, the divisions between internationalists over the League of Nations and the World Court, and legalist efforts to bring the United States into the latter organization. Excellent bibliography.

14:597 Lancaster, James L. "The Protestant Churches and the Fight for Ratification of the Versailles Treaty." *Public Opinion Quarterly* 31 (Winter 1967–1968): 597–619. As much concerned with their motivation as with their effect, the author chronicles the major pro-League activities of the Protestant churches, whose leaders generally embraced the cause as a moral crusade.

14:598 Lodge, Henry Cabot, Sr. *The Senate and the League of Nations.* New York: C. Scribner's Sons, 1925. Published the year after his death, this is the account of the sometimes brilliant politician who led the fight against American membership in the League of Nations.

14:599 Logan, Rayford W. *The Senate and the Versailles Mandate System.* Washington, DC: Minorities Publishers, 1945. In this rarely cited work, the Pan-Africanist and scholar-activist Logan offered a pioneering approach to political-diplomatic history and the Treaty of Versailles. By devoting his study to the Senate's consideration of mandates—Article XXII of the Covenant—he aired important issues of race and foreign policy and the relationship between the two. (The African and Armenian mandates receive special attention.)

14:600 Margulies, Herbert F. *The Mild Reservationists and the League of Nations Controversy in the Senate.* Columbia: University of Missouri Press, 1989. In this important study, the only detailed monograph on the subject, Margulies explicates the vain endeavor of a group of Republican senators to bridge the gap between the "strong reservationists" and Wilson. In part because of deep partisan feelings all around, the author maintains, the effort proved unavailing, but he chiefly blames what he characterizes as the extreme views of both the president and the Irreconcilables.

14:601 _____. "The Moderates in the League of Nations Battle: An Overlooked Faction." *Historian* 60 (Winter 1998): 273–87. To the list of categories of opponents of Wilson's League—the "irreconcilables, "strong reservationists," and "mild reservationists"— the author adds the "moderates," a group of about eight senators whose voting records on various amendments and reservations to the treaty suggest a little more flexibility on the issue than the others and thus a lengthier continuum of opinion.

14:602 Maxwell, Kenneth R. "Irish-Americans and the Fight for Treaty Ratification." *Public Opinion Quarterly* 31 (Winter 1967–1968): 620–41. The author demonstrates that, in part owing to their anger over Wilson's failure at Paris to fight for Irish home rule (i.e., self-determination), Irish-Americans became a potent force in marshaling public opinion against the treaty and the League.

14:603 McKillen, Elizabeth. "The Corporatist Model, World War I, and the Public Debate over the League of Nations." *Diplomatic History* 15 (Spring 1991): 171–97. This essay explicates the negative reactions to League membership of Irish-Americans and numerous local labor organizations (who defied Gompers and the AFL). Their opposition, according to the author, grew from their fear of "corporatism" on an international scale—of a continuation, in any form, of the various federal boards (the evil marriage between government and industry) that ran the wartime economy.

14:604 Merritt, Richard L. "Woodrow Wilson and the 'Great and Solemn Referendum,' 1920." *Review of Politics* 27 (January 1965): 78–104. Thomas Bailey once called Wilson's gambit to turn the election

into a referendum on the League "a great and solemn muddlement." Merritt notes that he had lost all influence by convention time, and that Cox's nomination (a loyalist but never an ardent League man) made that palpable. "The election returns tell their own story," House wrote in his diary. "Another Samson has pulled a temple down upon himself."

14:605 Redmond, Kent G. "Henry L. Stimson and the Question of League Membership." *Historian* 25 (February 1963): 200–12. This is a cursory survey of the thinking of the conservative internationalist Stimson from the 1920s to the 1940s.

14:606 Rosenberger, Homer T. "The American Peace Society's Reaction to the Covenant of the League of Nations." *World Affairs* 141 (Fall 1978): 139–52. Since its founding in Boston in 1828, the American Peace Society had had a considerable influence on the peace movement—though not necessarily on the American internationalist movement during the Progressive era. The author shows that the APS reaction to the treaty and the Covenant was decidedly mixed.

14:607 Stern, Sheldon M. "American Nationalism vs. the League of Nations: The Correspondence of Albert J. Beveridge and Louis A. Coolidge, 1918–1920." *Indiana Magazine of History* 72 (June 1976): 138–58. Stern presents some pertinent correspondence between Beveridge of Indiana and Coolidge of Massachusetts. The tone and substance are well represented in Beveridge's statement that "the Leaguers will try to honeyfruggle or bully or softsoap or frighten our men into . . . some sort of 'compromise.' They must not succeed."

14:608 Stone, Ralph. *The Irreconcilables: The Fight against the League of Nations.* Lexington: University Press of Kentucky, 1970. In this fine study, remarkable for both its brevity and incisiveness, Stone explores the politics (and tactics) of the sturdy knot of sixteen senators known as the Irreconcilables. Among its virtues, the book establishes a wide diversity of views among the group (several were progressives while only a few were isolationists, per se) notwithstanding their uniform resistance.

14:609 Trow, Clifford W. "'Something Desperate in His Face': Woodrow Wilson in Portland at the

'Very Crisis of His Career.'" *Oregon Historical Quarterly* 82 (Spring 1981): 40–64. A combination of political analysis (senatorial opposition) and high drama (the title is more than a hint), this essay recounts Wilson's visit to the American northwest during his "swing around the circle."

14:610　Vinson, J. Chal. *Referendum for Isolation: The Defeat of Article Ten of The League of Nations Covenant.* Athens, GA: University of Georgia Press, 1961. As many other historians have done, Vinson argues that the great debate boiled down to differences over Article X. He also maintains that the defeat of the treaty indicated the public's desire for an isolationist foreign policy, yet he does not entirely account for why the majority of Americans favored ratification early in the struggle or note that most of the opponents of Wilson's League were not really isolationists.

14:611　Wimer, Kurt. "Woodrow Wilson Tries Conciliation: An Effort That Failed." *Historian* 25 (August 1963): 419–38. Wimer argues that Wilson was at times more flexible in his relations with senators than some were with him.

14:612　_____. "Woodrow Wilson's Plan for a Vote of Confidence." *Pennsylvania History* 28 (July 1961): 279–93. In January 1920, Wilson sketched out an idea—never made public—to challenge his senatorial opponents to resign their seats and immediately seek reelection on the basis of their position on the League. This was the precursor to his call to make the 1920 election "a great and solemn referendum."

WOODROW WILSON'S HEALTH

14:613　Ambrosius, Lloyd E. "Woodrow Wilson's Health and the Treaty Fight, 1919–1920." *International History Review* 9 (February 1987): 73–84. While additional medical information became available after this article's publication, it is an otherwise excellent—thorough, fair, and concise—place to start. Ambrosius suggests that the ongoing debates—over whether it was Wilson's health or his personality and psychological makeup that determined the outcome of the treaty fight—have grown somewhat partisan and narrow in perspective, and that most, if not all, of these scholarly contenders (as of 1987)

have neglected the domestic political context (which had deep roots) as well as the realities of international politics.

14:614　George, Juliette L., and Alexander L. George. "*Woodrow Wilson and Colonel House:* A Reply to Weinstein, Anderson, and Link." *Political Science Quarterly* 96 (Winter 1981–1982): 641–65. The authors reassert the essential lines of argument of their book and point to the paucity of available medical evidence on which Weinstein, Anderson, and Link ("Woodrow Wilson's Political Personality: A Reappraisal," 1978–1979) (14:619) base their findings.

14:615　George, Juliette L., Michael F. Marmor, and Alexander L. George. "Issues in Wilsonian Scholarship: References to Early 'Strokes' in the *Papers of Woodrow Wilson.*" *Journal of American History* 70 (March 1984): 845–53. The authors raise serious questions about the nature of the evidence offered by Edwin Weinstein (whose work is cited in footnotes in the *Papers of Woodrow Wilson*); in particular, they challenge his thesis that Wilson suffered a series of smaller strokes prior to the fully debilitating one of October 1919. This article is featured as a "Research Note"; the reply of the editors of *The Papers of Woodrow Wilson* (of roughly equal length) appears as a letter to the editor (945–55) in the same issue.

14:616　Laukhoff, Perry. "The Price of Woodrow Wilson's Illness." *Virginia Quarterly Review* 32 (Fall 1956): 598–610. In contrasting Wilson's condition and behavior during the ratification fight with his earlier leadership in the passage of progressive legislation and superintending the war effort, the author argues that the absence of Wilson's leadership is what kept the United States out of the League, and thus "quite possibly our absence from the League made possible the Second World War."

14:617　Park, Bert Edward. "The Impact of Wilson's Neurologic Disease during the Paris Peace Conference." In *The Papers of Woodrow Wilson,* ed. Arthur S. Link et al., 58: 611–30. Princeton: Princeton University Press, 1988. Based on new evidence released by the family of Wilson's doctor (Cary Grayson), neurosurgeon Park diagnoses Wilson's brief illness during the peace conference as probably a minor stroke. He is also "reasonably certain" that Wilson's faltering during his meeting with the Senate

Foreign Relations Committee (August 19, 1919) was the result of yet another stroke on July 19, 1919.

14:618 Weinstein, Edwin A. "Woodrow Wilson's Neurological Illness." *Journal of American History* 57 (September 1970): 324–51. In this article, which set in motion a long-lived controversy, a professor of neurology first offered evidence that Wilson suffered from a series of undetected smaller strokes after 1896, and that therefore the devastating stroke of October 1919, rather than traits of personality, explains his behavior in the fight over ratification of the Versailles Treaty.

14:619 Weinstein, Edwin A., James William Anderson, and Arthur S. Link. "Woodrow Wilson's Political Personality: A Reappraisal." *Political Science Quarterly* 93 (Winter 1978–1979): 585–98. In this article, which set off a round of sometimes sharp published exchanges, the authors criticized the thesis in the George's *Woodrow Wilson and Colonel House: A Personality Study* (1956) (14:112), which was based on a Freudian analysis of the president's relationship with his father. Weinstein, Anderson, and Link cited a series of smaller strokes in Wilson's earlier life to account for instances of untoward behavior and argued that the massive stroke "produced mental attitudes and personality changes which were important factors in his failure to obtain ratification of the Treaty of Versailles."

14:620 Wimer, Kurt. "Woodrow Wilson and a Third Nomination." *Pennsylvania History* 29 (April 1962): 193–211. According to the author, Wilson was serious about pursuing a third term and intent on making his campaign a referendum on the League.

14:621 _____. "Woodrow Wilson's Plans to Enter the League of Nations through an Executive Agreement." *Western Political Quarterly* 11 (December 1958): 800–12. Wimer tells the story of Wilson's dubious plan—at least in part a reflection of his current mental and emotional state—to have the United States enter the League through an executive agreement; he relented when legal advisers declared the procedure unconstitutional.

Miscellaneous Studies

14:622 Crozier, Emmet. *American Reporters on the Western Front, 1914–1918.* New York: Oxford University Press, 1959. Crozier recounts the experiences of American reporters assigned to Europe during the war.

14:623 Curti, Merle E. *American Philanthropy Abroad: A History.* New Brunswick: Rutgers University Press, 1963. Reprint 1988 (Transaction Books). In this remarkable study (among the first in its field), Curti explores "the American self-conception of generosity" via nonofficial agencies, starting with Greece in the 1820s and ending with Taiwan in the 1960s. Two chapters on the Great War range widely—from Hoover's sacrifice of the presidency of Stanford to organize Belgian relief, to the pledge of 150,000 American school children to send $36 a year for two years to 150,000 French children who lost their fathers in the war.

14:624 Harris, Charles H., III, and Louis R. Sadler. "The Plan of San Diego and the Mexican–United States War Crisis of 1916: A Reexamination." The authors examine a plan that called for a Mexican-American rebellion and the establishment of an independent republic in the southwest. Guerrilla raids on Anglos in south Texas followed (February 1915–July 1916). The authors found no solid evidence of German involvement (12:164).

14:625 McKillen, Elizabeth. "Ethnicity, Class, and Wilsonian Internationalism Reconsidered: The Mexican-American and Irish-American Immigrant Left and U.S. Foreign Relations, 1914–1922." *Diplomatic History* 25 (Fall 2001): 553–87. In this innovative essay, McKillen examines the activities of Mexican-American and Irish-American leftist labor activists to explore both class and ethnic alignments regarding Wilsonian internationalism. Her focus is the radical Flores Magon brothers of the Partido Libera Mexicano (of Los Angeles) and the Chicago Federation of Labor, led by John Fitzpatrick; in the context of other concerns, these groups and individuals opposed the League of Nations idea because they believed it would become the tool of international finance and aid in the continued oppression of working people around the world.

14:626   Startt, James D. "American Propaganda in Britain during World War I." *Prologue* 28 (Spring 1996): 17–33. This essay chronicles the CPI's efforts—through pamphlet literature, films, etc.—to overcome British resentment toward the United States for having taken so long to get into the war and to counter the notion that it had finally done so mainly for material gain.

15

The United States, Latin America, and the Caribbean between the World Wars

Contributing Editor

STEPHEN M. STREETER
McMaster University

Contents

Introduction

This chapter covers works that discuss inter-American relations between World Wars I and II. Extra effort was made to include Latin American perspectives and studies of previously neglected topics in inter-American relations, such as cultural affairs and immigration. A comprehensive search was made for studies of U.S. relations with all individual Latin American nations during the interwar period, including the Caribbean, so the absence of certain countries (e.g., Paraguay) under the bilateral heading indicates lack of such studies. Dissertations were included only if they presented important primary documentation and did not appear later in published form. Excluded were accounts based on secondary sources that failed to offer significant or new interpretations, bibliographies whose entries are included in this chapter, foreign-language studies available in English translation, and works covering the 1940s that focus on strategic issues related to World War II.

Document Collections

15:1   U.S. Department of State. *Foreign Relations of the United States.* Washington, DC: Government Printing Office, 1936–1961. The *FRUS* series culls the most important primary sources on foreign affairs from U.S. government records. Unlike later volumes, whose reliability has been compromised by censorship, the 1920–1945 volumes are of high quality and contain valuable material on Latin America. Thirty-seven of the *FRUS* volumes published for the period 1921–1940 include material on the Western Hemisphere.

15:2   Rosenman, Samuel I., ed. *Public Papers and Addresses of Franklin Delano Roosevelt.* 13 vols. New York: Random House, 1938–1950. This collection of documents contains President Roosevelt's public addresses. Numerous references to Latin America can be found in the index.

15:3   Nixon, Edgar B., ed. *Franklin D. Roosevelt and Foreign Affairs.* 3 vols. Cambridge, MA: Belknap Press of Harvard University Press, 1969. This valuable series contains selected foreign policy documents from the Franklin D. Roosevelt administration, including the president's personal correspondence, letters, memos, telegrams, notes, speeches, and messages to Congress. The index lists various Latin American countries and the Good Neighbor Policy. For a continuation of the series, see the fourteen volumes (numbered 4–17) of Schewe, *Franklin D. Roosevelt and Foreign Affairs, January 1937–August 1939* (1979–1980) (17:6).

15:4   Roosevelt, Franklin D. *Development of United States Foreign Policy: Addresses and Messages of Franklin D. Roosevelt Compiled from Official Sources, Intended to Present the Chronological Development of the Foreign Policy of the United States from the Announcement of the Good Neighbor Policy in 1933, Including the War Declarations.* Washington, DC: Government Printing Office, 1942. This special collection of FDR's speeches begins with the 1933 address announcing what became known as the Good Neighbor Policy.

15:5   Rodríguez Ayçaguer, Ana María, ed. *Selección de Informes de Los Representantes Diplomaticos de los Estados Unidos en el Uruguay, Tomo I: 1930–1933 [Selected Reports of U.S. Diplomatic Representatives in Uruguay, Vol. 1: 1930–1933].* Montevideo: Facultad de Humanidades y Ciencias de la Educación, Universidad de la República, 1996. This book presents U.S. diplomatic correspondence relating to Uruguay from 1930 to 1933. The documents were culled from the U.S. State Department and translated into Spanish.

15:6   Myers, William Starr, ed. *The State Papers and Other Public Writings of Herbert Hoover.* 2 vols. Garden City, NY: Doubleday, Doran and Company, 1934. Reprint 1970 (Kraus). Material pertaining to Latin America is indexed in this two-volume collection of Herbert Hoover's official papers.

15:7   Scott, James Brown, ed. *The International Conferences of American States, 1889–1928: A Collection of the Conventions, Recommendations, Resolutions, Reports, and Motions Adopted by the First Six International Conferences of the American States, and Documents Relating to the Organization of the Conferences.* New York: Oxford University

Press, 1931. Reprint 2000 (Gaunt). This handy collection contains the recommendations, resolutions, and motions adopted by the first six Pan American conferences. *The International Conferences of American States, 1889–1928: First Supplement, 1933–1940* (Washington, DC: Carnegie Endowment for International Peace, 1940) added documents from the seventh and eighth conferences.

15:8 Burr, Robert N., ed. *Documents on Inter-American Cooperation. Vol. 2: 1881–1948.* Philadelphia: University of Pennsylvania Press, 1955. This documentary collection contains newspaper editorials, speeches, treaties, and official statements relating to the inter-American system. During the interwar period, the key issues discussed at inter-American conferences included boundary disputes, interventionism, and the organization of the Pan American Union.

15:9 Gantenbein, James Watson, ed. *The Evolution of Our Latin-American Policy: A Documentary Record.* New York: Octagon, 1950. This collection includes speeches about Latin America by American presidents and high-ranking State Department officials. Also important are U.S. government documents relating to the agrarian and oil controversies in Mexico as well as the U.S. interventions in Haiti, the Dominican Republic, and Nicaragua.

15:10 Long, David F., and Ruhl J. Bartlett, eds. *Documentary History of U.S. Foreign Relations: Selections from and Additions to Ruhl J. Bartlett's The Record of American Diplomacy. Vol. 2: The Mid-1890s to 1979.* Washington, DC: University Press of America, 1980. This volume of documents includes several of the more important statements of U.S. policy toward Latin America during the interwar period.

15:11 Kilpatrick, Carroll, ed. *Roosevelt and Daniels, A Friendship in Politics.* Chapel Hill: University of North Carolina Press, 1952. This documentary collection contains some of the correspondence between President Roosevelt and Josephus Daniels regarding Mexican affairs. Unfortunately, the editor eliminated some of Daniels's longer letters from Mexico, claiming they were of little general interest.

15:12 Cox, Isaac Joslin. *Nicaragua and the United States, 1909–1927.* Boston: World Peace Foundation, 1927. The appendices to this general account of the U.S. intervention in Nicaragua include British, American, and Nicaraguan documents.

15:13 Ramírez, Sergio, ed. *Sandino: The Testimony of a Nicaraguan Patriot, 1921–1934.* Princeton: Princeton University Press, 1990. This collection of Augusto Sandino's correspondence from 1921 to 1934 sheds light on the ideals and ambitions of Nicaragua's legendary guerrilla fighter. Translation and abridgement of the two-volume 1984 edition of *El pensamiento vivio de Sandino,* with an introduction by translator Robert Edgar Conrad.

15:14 Wagenheim, Kal, and Olga Jiménez de Wagenheim, eds. *The Puerto Ricans: A Documentary History.* New York: Praeger, 1973. Reprint 1994 (M. Wiener Publishers). This documentary collection includes material from the interwar period relating to the issue of Puerto Rican independence.

15:15 Hill, Robert A., ed. *The Marcus Garvey and Universal Negro Improvement Association Papers.* 3 vols. Berkeley: University of California Press, 1983. The index to this multivolume collection of historical documentation on Marcus Garvey includes numerous references to Jamaica.

TRAVEL ACCOUNTS

15:16 Beals, Carleton. *Banana Gold.* Philadelphia: J. B. Lippincott, 1932. Reprint 1983 (Editorial Nueva Nicaragua). Beals describes his travels through Central America and Mexico. Especially noteworthy is his description of his encounter with the Nicaraguan rebel Augusto César Sandino.

15:17 _____. *Brimstone and Chili: A Book of Personal Experiences in the Southwest and in Mexico.* New York: Alfred A. Knopf, 1927. This travel account by an American journalist contains a brief firsthand description of the transition of power between Carranza and Obregón in the final stages of the Mexican revolution.

15:18 Carpenter, Rhys. *The Land beyond Mexico.* Boston: Richard G. Badger, 1920. A U.S. archaeologist describes his travels through Guatemala, El Salvador, and Honduras, offering commentary on the landscape and the local population.

15:19   Cunningham, Eugene. *Gypsying through Central America.* New York: E. P. Dutton and Co., 1922. This travel narrative of a journey through the Central American countryside by an American adventurer reveals much about North American ethnocentrism and cultural prejudices.

15:20   Ruhl, Arthur Brown. *The Central Americans: Adventures and Impressions between Mexico and Panama.* New York: Charles Scribner's Sons, 1928. This account by an American travel writer describes the sights and sounds he experienced while traveling through Central America.

15:21   Thompson, Wallace. *Rainbow Countries of Central America.* New York: E. P. Dutton and Co., 1927. This travel account includes photographs of several American legations in Central America.

Bibliographies and Other Reference Works

BIBLIOGRAPHIES

15:22   Beede, Benjamin R., ed. *Intervention and Counterinsurgency: An Annotated Bibliography of the Small Wars of the United States, 1898–1984.* This annotated bibliography describes studies of U.S. military interventions in Latin America, including the American occupations of Cuba, Haiti, the Dominican Republic, and Nicaragua during the interwar period (12:18).

15:23   Britton, John A., ed. *The United States and Latin America: A Select Bibliography.* This annotated bibliography includes lengthy descriptions of scholarly works that cover the interwar period. The entries are arranged thematically and by nation (12:19).

15:24   Grieb, Kenneth J., ed. *Central America in the Nineteenth and Twentieth Centuries: An Annotated Bibliography.* Boston: G. K. Hall, 1988. Though now dated, this massive reference work remains by far the best annotated bibliography on Central America. Entries are arranged by country and include the names of libraries where the works are located.

15:25   Library of Congress. Hispanic Division, ed. *Handbook of Latin American Studies.* This bibliographical series contains annotated entries of selected scholarly works on Latin America. Volumes are published yearly, alternating between the social sciences and the humanities. The series can now be searched through the Library of Congress website at http://lcweb2.loc.gov/hlas/ (1:251).

15:26   Meyer, Michael C., ed. *Supplement to a Bibliography of United States–Latin American Relations since 1810.* See chapters 1 and 12 of this Guide (1:254; 12:23).

15:27   Sheinin, David. *The Organization of American States.* New Brunswick: Transaction Publishers, 1996. This valuable reference guide includes material on the inter-American system prior to the formation of the OAS in 1948.

15:28   Snarr, Neil, et al., eds. *Sandinista Nicaragua: An Annotated Bibliography with Analytical Introductions.* Ann Arbor: Pierian Press, 1992. This annotated bibliography lists works about the Nicaraguan rebel Augusto César Sandino.

15:29   Thorp, Rosemary. "Latin America and the International Economy, 1914–1929." In *The Cambridge History of Latin America. Vol. 11: Bibliographical Essays,* ed. Leslie Bethell, 326–31. New York: Cambridge University Press, 1995. This bibliographical essay includes works that discuss U.S. economic penetration of Latin America in the context of the international economy. For her essay on the subject, see "Latin America and the International Economy from the First World War to the World Depression," in Bethell, ed., *The Cambridge History of Latin America. Vol. 4: c. 1870 to 1930* (New York: Cambridge University Press, 1986): 57–81.

15:30   Trask, David F., Michael C. Meyer, and Roger R. Trask, eds. *A Bibliography of United States–Latin American Relations since 1810: A Selected List of Eleven Thousand Published References.* This bibliography, the most comprehensive of its kind, contains a chapter on the interwar period and the Good Neighbor Policy (1:257). See also Meyer,

Supplement to a Bibliography of United States–Latin American Relations since 1810 (1979) (15:26).

DICTIONARIES AND ENCYCLOPEDIAS

15:31 Atkins, G. Pope, ed. *Encyclopedia of the Inter-American System.* Westport, CT: Greenwood Press, 1997. Useful material on the interwar period can be found in this important reference work on the inter-American system.

15:32 Beede, Benjamin R., ed. *The War of 1898 and U.S. Interventions, 1898–1934: An Encyclopedia.* Although the encyclopedia concentrates on the war of 1898, many entries offer intriguing details about the U.S. military occupations of Latin America in the interwar period. Included are maps of the occupation zones and lists of naval operations (10:21).

15:33 Shavit, David, ed. *The United States in Latin America: A Historical Dictionary.* New York: Greenwood Press, 1992. This historical dictionary lists persons, institutions, and events that brought the United States into contact with Latin America. The appendix lists all chiefs of U.S. diplomatic missions in Latin America, but the main entries include only those diplomats who left some record of their service.

GUIDES AND HANDBOOKS

15:34 Bingaman, Joseph W., ed. *Latin America: A Survey of Holdings at the Hoover Institution on War, Revolution and Peace.* Stanford, CA: n.p., 1972. The Hoover Institution on War, Revolution, and Peace houses many books, pamphlets, and newspapers on Latin America. Special collections include the Colonel Charles Wellington Furlong Collection, which contains manuscripts related to the Tacna-Arica arbitration.

15:35 Dent, David W. *The Legacy of the Monroe Doctrine: A Reference Guide to U.S. Involvement in Latin America and the Caribbean.* This reference work contains concise chronological summaries of U.S. relations with twenty-four Latin American countries. Most of the chapters, which are organized by country, include a discussion of the Good Neighbor Policy (12:22).

15:36 Grieb, Kenneth J., with Ralph Lee Woodward, Jr., Graeme S. Mount, and Thomas Mathews, eds. *Research Guide to Central America and the Caribbean.* Madison: University of Wisconsin Press, 1985. The archival holdings described in this valuable reference guide include considerable material on inter-American relations. The most important essays are Grieb, "Materials Regarding Central America and the Caribbean in the National Archives of the United States" (3–8); and "Central American International Relations" (82–86); Neill Macaulay, "Central America: Military History and Guerrilla Warfare" (96–105); and Thomas L. Karnes, "Records of North American Firms Doing Business in Central America" (161–66).

15:37 Grow, Michael, and Craig VanGrasstek, eds. *Scholars' Guide to Washington, D.C., for Latin American and Caribbean Studies.* This guide is essential for finding sources on inter-American relations in the greater Washington, D.C., area. Collections described in the guide include libraries, archives, museums, and map and film collections (25:30). First published in 1979.

15:38 Keller, Gary D. *Hispanics and United States Film: An Overview and Handbook.* Tempe, AZ: Bilingual Press, 1994. According to this handbook, Hollywood gave halfhearted support to the Good Neighbor Policy by portraying Hispanics more favorably in American films.

15:39 Leonard, Thomas M., ed. *A Guide to Central American Collections in the United States.* Westport, CT: Greenwood Press, 1994. This reference guide lists by state miscellaneous archival materials relating to Central America. The guide is especially useful for locating nontraditional primary sources, such as firsthand accounts by American travelers and missionaries.

15:40 Macaulay, Neill. "Material on Latin America in the United States Marine Corps Archives." *Hispanic American Historical Review* 46 (May 1966): 179–81. This essay describes U.S. marine archival material related to U.S. interventions in the Dominican Republic, Nicaragua, and Haiti.

15:41 Richard, Alfred C. *Censorship and Hollywood's Hispanic Image: An Interpretive Filmogra-*

phy, 1936–1955. Westport, CT: Greenwood Press, 1993. This reference work lists feature films that have perpetuated stereotypes about Hispanics. The entries, arranged alphabetically by year of production, provide essential details about the film, including its Hispanic connection. During the era of the Good Neighbor Policy, various government and Hollywood agencies attempted to improve the Hispanic image in films, especially musicals.

15:42   _____. *The Hispanic Image on the Silver Screen: An Interpretive Filmography from Silents into Sound, 1898–1935*. New York: Greenwood Press, 1992. This reference work lists feature films that have perpetuated stereotypes about Hispanics. The entries, which are arranged alphabetically by year of production, provide essential details about the film, including its Hispanic connection. The compiler observes that despite Mexican protests and the voluntary adoption of production codes, the film industry continued to foster racist images of Latin Americans on the screen in the 1920s.

Historiography

15:43   Benjamin, Jules R. "The Framework of U.S. Relations with Latin America in the Twentieth Century: An Interpretive Essay." This historiographical essay explores the reform effort underlying American expansion into Latin America in the twentieth century. Early attempts to impose reform by force during the big stick era shifted in the 1930s to a more liberal policy of promoting change and stability internally (12:33).

15:44   Berger, Mark T. *Under Northern Eyes: Latin American Studies and U.S. Hegemony in the Americas, 1898–1990*. In this historiographical survey the author observes that during the 1920s most North American scholars tended to justify the expansion of U.S. hegemony in Latin America. By the advent of the Good Neighbor Policy of the 1930s, critics of imperialism began to shift the discourse toward more critical studies (12:26).

15:45   Connell-Smith, Gordon. "Latin America in

the Foreign Relations of the United States." *Journal of Latin American Studies* 8 (May 1976): 137–50. This dated but still useful historiographical essay explores different interpretations of rising American hegemony in Latin America between the wars.

15:46   Gilderhus, Mark T. "Founding Father: Samuel Flagg Bemis and the Study of U.S.–Latin American Relations." This SHAFR presidential address criticizes the writings of Samuel Flagg Bemis, an American pioneer in the study of inter-American relations. Gilderhus observes that Bemis failed to describe adequately U.S. economic interests and to account for Latin American resistance to American imperialism, faults that appear especially glaring in his treatment of the interwar period (2:8).

15:47   McKercher, Brian J. C. "Reaching for the Brass Ring: The Recent Historiography of Interwar American Foreign Relations." *Diplomatic History* 15 (Fall 1991): 565–98. This historiographical essay helps situate inter-American relations within the debate between traditionalists and revisionists over the origins and consequences of U.S. foreign policy in the interwar period.

15:48   Parker, James R., and Terry G. Summons. "The Rise and Fall of the Good Neighbor Policy: The North American View." *Maryland Historian* 1 (Spring 1970): 31–44. The authors of this essay assess the historical interpretations of the Good Neighbor Policy, emphasizing divergent viewpoints.

15:49   Pérez, Louis A., Jr. *Essays on Cuban History: Historiography and Research*. Gainesville: University Press of Florida, 1995. This reference work contains a historiographical essay on twentieth-century U.S.-Cuban relations that includes a section on the interwar period.

15:50   _____. "Intervention, Hegemony, and Dependency: The United States in the Circum-Caribbean, 1898–1980." *Pacific Historical Review* 51 (May 1982): 165–94. Pérez offers a sophisticated historiographical analysis of American interventions in the Caribbean. He notes that during the 1930s the United States could forgo direct military intervention because much of the Caribbean had already fallen under the control of U.S.-backed dictators who would protect American interests.

15:51 Salisbury, Richard V. "Good Neighbors? The United States and Latin America in the Twentieth Century." In *American Foreign Relations, A Historiographical Review,* ed. Gerald K. Haines and J. Samuel Walker, 311–33. Westport, CT: Greenwood Press, 1981. Since World War II scholars have varied widely in their interpretation of inter-American affairs. The author describes various realist and revisionist approaches, including dependency theory, while lamenting the lack of empirical case studies.

Overviews and Regional Studies

GENERAL INTERPRETATIONS

15:52 Adler, Selig. *The Uncertain Giant: 1921–1941: American Foreign Policy between the Wars.* New York: Macmillan, 1965. This survey of U.S. interwar foreign policy supports the view that the Good Neighbor Policy began under the Hoover administration. The author also praises Roosevelt's handling of Latin American affairs.

15:53 Aguilar Monteverde, Alonso. *Pan-Americanism from Monroe to the Present: A View from the Other Side.* Translated by Asa Zatz. The Latin American author of this survey describes the 1920s as a period of increasing American economic penetration. The author views the Good Neighbor Policy as a sham to promote U.S. foreign investment in Latin America and ensure a cheap supply of raw materials (2:344).

15:54 Beals, Carleton, Bryce Oliver, Herschel Brickell, and Samuel Guy Inman. *What the South Americans Think of Us, A Symposium.* New York: R. M. McBride and Company, 1945. This collection of essays by North American journalists and scholars presents South American views of the United States and its foreign policies. Although the authors draw mostly on elite sources and make paternalistic and racist judgments, their accounts offer a selected glimpse into the Latin American setting before World War II.

15:55 Bemis, Samuel Flagg. *The Latin American Policy of the United States: An Historical Interpretation.* This survey served as the standard account of U.S. policy toward Latin America until attacked by *dependistas* in the 1960s. Bemis alleges that during the interwar period the United States began to retreat from imperialism in Latin America, a trend that culminated in the Good Neighbor Policy (2:345).

15:56 Buell, Raymond Leslie. "Changes in Our Latin American Policy." *Annals of the American Academy of Political and Social Science* 156 (July 1931): 126–32. The director of the Foreign Policy Association of New York maintains that U.S. military intervention in Central America and the Caribbean can no longer be justified on the basis of national security. Since World War I, the United States has gained naval supremacy in the region and has become the greatest financial power in the world.

15:57 Callcott, Wilfrid Hardy. *The Western Hemisphere: Its Influence on United States Policies to the End of World War II.* Austin: University of Texas Press, 1968. This straightforward narrative of U.S.–Latin American relations during the interwar period is noteworthy largely because of the author's inclusion of British sources.

15:58 Connell-Smith, Gordon. *The United States and Latin America: An Historical Analysis of Inter-American Relations.* This study by a British scholar, although dated, remains one of the best surveys of inter-American relations up to World War II. Especially useful is the description of tensions within the inter-American system generated by U.S. interventionism (2:348).

15:59 Dennis, Lawrence. "Revolution, Recognition and Intervention." *Foreign Affairs* 9 (January 1931): 204–21. This former American diplomat views U.S. military intervention in Latin America as a violation of Wilsonian principles. He concludes that interventions are not necessary to protect American businesses and are too costly in American lives.

15:60 Drake, Paul W. "From Good Men to Good Neighbors, 1912–1932." In *Exporting Democracy: The United States and Latin America: Themes and Issues,* ed. Abraham F. Lowenthal, 3–40. According to Drake, U.S. presidential administrations from Wilson to Hoover sincerely tried to promote democracy in Latin America. These efforts failed because U.S. officials employed improper means, followed inconsistent policies, equated elections with democracy, and lacked sufficient allies (12:39).

15:61   Gil, Federico G. *Latin American–United States Relations.* New York: Harcourt Brace Jovanovich, 1971. This survey of inter-American relations identifies the 1920s as the crucial period when the United States began the transition from interventionism toward the Good Neighbor Policy.

15:62   Gilderhus, Mark T. *The Second Century: U.S.–Latin American Relations since 1889.* This concise survey, which contains several chapters on the interwar period, is one of the few studies of inter-American relations to include Latin American responses to U.S. policy (9:384).

15:63   Goldwert, Marvin. *The Constabulary in the Dominican Republic and Nicaragua: Progeny and Legacy of United States Intervention.* Gainesville: University of Florida Press, 1962. U.S. interventions in the Dominican Republic and Nicaragua failed to achieve stability because in the process of subduing rebels such as Sandino, Washington unified divided military establishments and empowered dictators.

15:64   Hoff, Joan. *American Business and Foreign Policy, 1920–1933.* Lexington: University Press of Kentucky, 1971. Hoff (formerly Hoff-Wilson) employs the concept of "independent internationalism" to describe apparent inconsistencies in U.S. foreign policy during the interwar period. According to this analysis, the United States continued to protect its own sphere of influence in Latin America while simultaneously promoting the open door policy in China.

15:65   Hopkins, J. A. H., and Melinda Alexander. *Machine-Gun Diplomacy.* New York: Lewis Copeland Company, 1928. This anti-imperialist tract blames U.S. military interventions in Central America and the Caribbean on American economic interests, especially the banking industry. The authors call for a redefinition of the Monroe Doctrine to support self-determination.

15:66   Langley, Lester D. *America and the Americas: The United States in the Western Hemisphere.*

According to this sweeping account of the Western Hemisphere idea, Latin American intellectuals of the 1920s rejected American materialism in favor of Latin America's spiritual values as expressed in the writings of Uruguayan writer José Enrique Rodó (2:350).

15:67   Leffler, Melvyn P. "Expansionist Impulses and Domestic Constraints, 1921–1932." In *Economics and World Power: An Assessment of American Diplomacy since 1789,* ed. William H. Becker and Samuel F. Wells, Jr., 225–76. New York: Columbia University Press, 1984. After World War I, American diplomats tried to promote a liberal capitalist order in Latin America and elsewhere. They failed because of the opposition of certain domestic groups and because of their own false assumptions about the benefits of the free enterprise system.

15:68   Mecham, J. Lloyd. *A Survey of United States–Latin American Relations.* Boston: Houghton Mifflin, 1965. During the interwar period U.S. officials, prodded by public opinion and troubled by their consciences, began to retreat from interventionism in Latin America. In addition to adopting the principle of nonintervention, the Good Neighbor Policy was noteworthy because U.S. policymakers tried for the first time to improve cultural relations with Latin America.

15:69   Nerval, Gaston. *Autopsy of the Monroe Doctrine: The Strange Story of Inter-American Relations.* New York: Macmillan Company, 1934. Based on the history of how the United States has applied the Monroe Doctrine to Latin America, the author predicts that the Good Neighbor Policy will founder upon Washington's traditional insistence that intervention is justified to protect American property and lives. True Pan-Americanism can be achieved only if the United States repudiates the Monroe Doctrine in all its forms. Gaston Nerval is a pseudonym for Raúl Díez de Medina.

15:70   Perkins, Dexter. *A History of the Monroe Doctrine.* According to this general history of the Monroe Doctrine, Latin American diplomats strained in the 1920s and 1930 to get the United States to repudiate interventionism (2:351). Originally published in 1941 as *Hands Off: A History of the Monroe Doctrine.*

15:71   Schoultz, Lars. *Beneath the United States: A History of U.S. Policy toward Latin America.* Chapters 13–15 of this survey cover the interwar years. The author decries American arrogance toward Latin America, which helped justify the pursuit of traditional economic and security interests (9:393).

15:72   Smith, Robert Freeman. "American Foreign Relations, 1920–1942." In *Towards a New Past: Dissenting Essays in American History,* ed. Barton J. Bernstein, 232–62. New York: Pantheon Books, 1968. This essay describes the American effort to maintain U.S. economic, military, and political hegemony in Latin America during the interwar period. The Good Neighbor Policy is viewed as a new tactic in dollar diplomacy that helped the U.S. economy recover from the Great Depression.

15:73   Smith, Tony. *America's Mission: The United States and the Worldwide Struggle for Democracy in the Twentieth Century.* The author of this study contends that U.S. policymakers sincerely wanted to spread democracy across the globe. The best illustration of this effort in Latin America was FDR's Good Neighbor Policy (14:69).

15:74   Tulchin, Joseph S. *The Aftermath of War: World War I and U.S. Policy toward Latin America.* With Europe in ruins after World War I, the United States was well positioned to establish its hegemony in Latin America. This book describes the transition from war to peace, as Americans strove to secure their economic, strategic, and political interests south of the border. The author praises Secretary of State Charles Evans Hughes for not extending U.S. military occupations in Central America and the Caribbean, thus pointing the way toward the Good Neighbor Policy (12:55).

15:75   Williams, William Appleman. "Latin America: Laboratory of American Foreign Policy in the Nineteen-Twenties." *Inter-American Economic Affairs* 11 (Autumn 1957): 3–30. One of the most prominent left revisionist historians of the cold war era argues in this essay that the historical record does not support the popular view of the 1920s as a period of American isolationism. To the contrary, Washington promoted U.S. private interests in Latin America but was unprepared for social unrest and nationalist resistance.

15:76   Wright, Theodore P., Jr. *American Support of Free Elections Abroad.* Washington, DC: Public Affairs Press, 1964. This study of American interference in Latin American elections from 1898 to 1933 concludes that U.S. officials were far more concerned with checking revolutions than promoting democracy. The author traces the roots of this counterrevolutionary policy to security concerns rather than economic interests.

15:77   _____. "Free Elections in the Latin American Policy of the United States." *Political Science Quarterly* 74 (March 1959): 89–112. Wright concludes that U.S. efforts to support free elections in the Caribbean and Central America failed in the early twentieth century because they were "backward" regions with illiterate populations that had never experienced democracy.

LATIN AMERICA IN THE INTERNATIONAL SYSTEM

15:78   Bailey, Norman A. *Latin America in World Politics.* New York: Walker, 1967. This volume provides a concise summary of the development of the inter-American system through the interwar period. A table lists the regular and special inter-American conferences and meetings of foreign ministers.

15:79   Díaz de Arce, Omar. "Contradicciones interimperialistas en América Latina entre las dos guerras mundiales [Imperialist Contradictions in Latin America between the Two World Wars]." *Santiago* 33 (March 1987): 23–86. This essay describes the rivalry of Great Britain, Germany, and the United States for control of Latin America's economic resources and markets during the interwar period.

15:80   Haglund, David G. "'Gray Areas' and Raw Materials: Latin American Resources and International Politics in the Pre–World War II Years." *Inter-American Economic Affairs* 36 (Winter 1982): 23–51. According to this essay, Latin America's raw materials reached an unprecedented level of importance to U.S. policymakers during the interwar period. The author offers a mix of political, economic, and strategic reasons, but he emphasizes that by the late 1930s U.S. officials especially feared that Latin America's strategic raw materials might fall into the hands of Germany.

15:81 Salisbury, Richard V. *Anti-Imperialism and International Competition in Central America, 1920–1929.* Wilmington, DE: SR Books, 1989. This study argues that isthmian anti-imperialists as well as the governments of Mexico and Spain combined to challenge U.S. hegemony in Central America during the 1920s. The author explores opposition to the U.S. intervention in Nicaragua to demonstrate that Washington did not enjoy total freedom of action in the region.

INTER-AMERICAN SYSTEM

15:82 Connell-Smith, Gordon. *The Inter-American System.* This institutional history of the inter-American system contains a valuable chapter on the Good Neighbor Policy emphasizing the system's failure to resolve inter-American disputes peacefully (2:347).

15:83 Fenwick, Charles G. *The Organization of American States: The Inter-American Regional System.* Washington, DC: Kaufman, 1963. This analysis and description of the inter-American regional system by a Pan American Union official contains material on the interwar years, including documentation related to border disputes, treaties, international law, the League of Nations, and inter-American conferences.

15:84 Grieb, Kenneth J. "The United States and the Fifth Pan American Conference." *Inter-American Review of Bibliography* 20 (April-June 1970): 157–68. Grieb praises President Harding for sending experienced career diplomats to the Fifth Pan American Conference (1923), where they supported an international treaty that required potential combatants to submit all disputes to an inquiry commission and refrain from war preparations for at least six months.

15:85 Inman, Samuel Guy, ed. *Inter-American Conferences, 1826–1954: History and Problems.* Washington, DC: University Press, 1965. This history of inter-American conferences by a U.S. missionary and advocate of Pan-Americanism contains useful nuggets of firsthand observations on inter-American conferences he attended in the 1920s and 1930s. Edited by Harold E. Davis.

15:86 Johnson, Robert David. "Transformation of Pan-Americanism." In *On Cultural Ground: Essays in International History,* ed. Robert David Johnson, 173–96. Chicago: Imprint Publications, 1994. This essay discusses how the onset of World War II shattered the shared vision of cultural Pan-Americanism held by a group of American missionaries and peace activists in the 1920s.

15:87 Kane, William Everett. *Civil Strife in Latin America: A Legal History of U.S. Involvement.* Baltimore: Johns Hopkins University Press, 1972. This book examines legal issues raised by U.S. interventions in Latin America. During the 1920s, the inter-American system forced Washington to replace big stick diplomacy with a nonintervention policy.

15:88 Lira, Alejandro. *Memorias.* Santiago: El Imparcial, 1950. This Chilean diplomat describes his attendance at the Sixth Pan American Conference in Havana (1928) and praises the U.S. role in helping to settle a boundary dispute between Peru and Chile.

15:89 Mecham, J. Lloyd. *The United States and Inter-American Security, 1889–1960.* Two of the chapters in this standard history of inter-American relations cover the interwar period. The defeat of Germany in World War I led to complacency among Latin American nations about threats emanating outside the hemisphere, as diplomats signed peace pacts having more to do with keeping Latin American nations from attacking each other than with providing a common defense (12:47).

15:90 Miller, Francesca. "The International Relations of Women in the Americas, 1890–1928." *Americas* 43 (October 1986): 171–82. This essay discusses the participation of women at inter-American meetings and scientific conferences as they helped shape Pan-Americanism through their discussions of such social issues as imperialism, suffrage, and women's rights.

15:91 Seidel, Robert Neal. "Progressive Pan Americanism: Development and United States Policy towards South America, 1906–1931." Ph.D. dissertation, Cornell University Press, 1973. Seidel explains how the United States tried to use Pan-Americanism to promote economic growth in South America during the 1920s. The author researched

State Department records and the personal papers of many U.S. officials but neglected Latin American sources.

15:92   Sheinin, David, ed. *Beyond the Ideal: Pan Americanism in Inter-American Affairs.* Westport, CT: Praeger, 2000. Several of the essays on Pan-Americanism in this collection intersect with the interwar period, covering such topics as interventionism, feminism, the environment, and hispanismo. See Sheinin, "Rethinking Pan Americanism: An Introduction"; David Barton Castle, "Leo Stanton Rowe and the Meaning of Pan Americanism"; Mark T. Berger, "A Greater America? Pan Americanism and the Professional Study of Latin America, 1890–1990"; Richard V. Salisbury, "Hispanismo versus Pan Americanism: Spanish Efforts to Counter U.S. Influence in Latin America before 1930"; K. Lynn Stoner, "In Four Languages but with One Voice: Division and Solidarity within Pan American Feminism, 1923–1933"; Thomas M. Leonard, "The New Pan Americanism in U.S.–Central American Relations, 1933–1954"; Sheinin, "'Its Most Destructive Agents': Pan American Environmentalism in the Early Twentieth Century"; W. Michael Weis, "Pan American Shift: Oswaldo Aranha and the Demise of the Brazilian-American Alliance"; and Earl E. Fitz, "The Theory and Practice of Inter-American Literature: An Historical Overview."

CARIBBEAN

15:93   Ayala, César J. *American Sugar Kingdom: The Plantation Economy of the Spanish Caribbean, 1898–1934.* Chapel Hill: University of North Carolina Press, 1999. Ayala argues that U.S. corporations transformed class relations in the Caribbean sugar plantation system by introducing wage labor and rationalizing the production system.

15:94   Fernandez, Ronald. *Cruising the Caribbean: U.S. Influence and Intervention in the Twentieth Century.* Monroe, ME: Common Courage Press, 1994. This book explores the cultural sources of U.S. Caribbean policy with the aim of exposing American prejudice, racism, and paternalism. Fernandez depicts the Good Neighbor Policy used as a sham by U.S. officials to prop up dictators.

15:95   Howland, Charles Prentice. *American Relations in the Caribbean: A Preliminary Issue of Section I of the Annual Survey of American Foreign Relations, 1929.* New Haven: American Council of the Institute of Pacific Relations, Yale University Press, 1929. Reprint 1970 (Arno Press). This study, prepared for the Council on Foreign Relations, describes economic and political affairs of various countries in Central America and the Caribbean, emphasizing their economic importance to the United States. It attributes U.S. difficulties in administering occupation governments to the political and cultural legacy of Latin American colonialism, while U.S. public opinion has prevented Washington from engaging in overt political imperialism.

15:96   Jones, Chester Lloyd, Henry Kittredge Norton, and Parker Thomas Moon. *The United States and the Caribbean.* Chicago: University of Chicago Press, 1929. The three authors offer a sample of the debate in the 1920s over American imperialism in the Caribbean. Norton, citing trade statistics, denies that U.S. policy has been driven by economic concerns. Moon maintains that the many military interventions in the Caribbean amount to imperialism, even if they were not wholly supported by the American public.

15:97   Langley, Lester D. *The Banana Wars: United States Intervention in the Caribbean, 1898–1934.* According to this survey of selected U.S. interventions in Mexico and the Caribbean, U.S. military officials were not conquerors, but well-intentioned rulers who mistakenly thought they could reform their subjects. Despite its title, the book does not discuss the banana industry in the region. Originally published in 1983 (10:107).

15:98   _____. *The United States and the Caribbean in the Twentieth Century.* This survey of U.S.-Caribbean relations puts the Good Neighbor Policy into historical context. According to Langley, the Roosevelt administration altered the means but not the objectives of U.S. policy toward the Caribbean (2:365). First published in 1980 as *The United States and the Caribbean, 1900–1970.*

15:99   Logan, Rayford W. *Haiti and the Dominican Republic.* This general history of the Dominican Republic and Haiti includes a fairly useful narrative of the U.S. military occupation of both countries (2:380).

15:100 Millett, Richard. "The State Department's Navy: A History of the Special Service Squadron, 1920–1940." *American Neptune* 35 (April 1975): 118–38. The Special Service Squadron, which the State Department organized after World War I, allowed U.S. naval forces to be deployed more efficiently in the Caribbean.

15:101 Munro, Dana G. *The United States and the Caribbean Republics, 1921–1933.* Princeton: Princeton University Press, 1974. This description of U.S. policy toward the Caribbean by a former American diplomat relies on State Department records and the author's personal recollections. Munro asserts that U.S. policy was not driven by economic interests but a genuine commitment to democratic principles that prevented Washington from opposing dictators.

15:102 Musicant, Ivan. *The Banana Wars: A History of United States Military Intervention in Latin America from the Spanish-American War to the Invasion of Panama.* This study of the banana wars by a former U.S. marine emphasizes the logistical complications of military intervention. Unfortunately, the author relied exclusively on English-language sources. Macmillan printed two editions of this book in 1990, the subtitle of the other concluding *to the Invasion of Panama* (12:101).

15:103 Perkins, Dexter. *The United States and the Caribbean.* According to this study, U.S. military interventions in the Caribbean were justified because of local political instability and the Bolshevik threat. The Roosevelt administration wisely adopted the Good Neighbor Policy in response to Latin American criticisms of U.S. interventionism (2:367). First published in 1947.

15:104 Perkins, Whitney T. *Constraint of Empire: The United States and Caribbean Interventions.* The author examines U.S. interventions in Cuba, Nicaragua, the Dominican Republic, and Haiti to explain the goals, processes, and limitations of American imperialism. He contends that U.S. officials sincerely tried to promote self-government in the Caribbean but had unrealistic expectations (10:110).

15:105 Thompson, Wallace. "The Doctrine of the 'Special Interest' of the United States in the Region of the Caribbean Sea." *Annals of the American Acad-*

emy of Political and Social Science 132 (July 1927): 153–59. The author describes American economic and security interests that have guided U.S. policy toward the Caribbean.

15:106 Yerxa, Donald A. *Admirals and Empire: The United States Navy and the Caribbean, 1898–1945.* In the 1930s, the U.S. navy replaced gunboat diplomacy with "goodwill cruising" in the Caribbean (with the important exceptions of Cuba and Nicaragua) to shed the image of the big stick while maintaining an informal empire in the region (12:256).

CENTRAL AMERICA

15:107 Buell, Raymond Leslie. *The Central Americas. I. Political Progress. II. Foreign Enterprise. III. Foreign Relations.* New York: Foreign Policy Association, 1930. In this thirty-page pamphlet, Buell, who toured Central America in 1930, claims that Central Americans have become alienated from the United States, not because of U.S. investments, but because of treaties that surrendered canal rights and gave Washington veto power over local elections.

15:108 _____. "Union or Disunion in Central America?" *Foreign Affairs* 11 (April 1933): 478–89. This essay discusses the issues surrounding U.S. policy toward the region in light of the 1923 Central American agreement stipulating that leaders coming to power by revolutionary force would not be given diplomatic recognition.

15:109 Grieb, Kenneth J. "The Myth of a Central American Dictators' League." *Journal of Latin American Studies* 10 (November 1978): 329–45. Grieb reveals that State Department officials did not believe in the existence of an alleged Central American Dictators' League, a fictional conspiracy created by the mass media in the 1930s.

15:110 LaFeber, Walter. *Inevitable Revolutions: The United States in Central America.* This prominent revisionist diplomatic historian maintains that because the United States created dependencies in Central America, it made revolution in the region inevitable. Much of the tinder for the revolutionary explosion of the 1970s and 1980s was created during the interwar period, when Washington established military dictatorships to protect U.S. economic interests, thereby blocking peaceful democratic change. Despite the deterministic-sounding title, LaFeber's book is well grounded in U.S. primary and secondary sources, and he demonstrates at least a passing knowledge of Central American history (2:355). First published in 1983.

15:111 Langley, Lester D., and Thomas D. Schoonover. *The Banana Men: American Mercenaries and Entrepreneurs in Central America, 1880–1930.* This book describes the efforts of U.S. entrepreneurs to create banana empires in Central America, especially Nicaragua and Honduras. According to the world systems analysis offered by the authors, the United States was ideally situated to exploit Central America after 1917 because World War I gravely weakened competing European powers (9:463).

15:112 Leonard, Thomas M. *Central America and the United States: The Search for Stability.* During the interwar period the United States abandoned intervention in Central America because of public opposition and local resistance. Washington was unable to prevent dictators such as Somoza from seizing power because of a commitment to noninterventionism (2:356).

15:113 Schoonover, Thomas D. *Germany in Central America: Competitive Imperialism, 1821–1929.* This study concludes that World War I disrupted nearly a hundred years of German expansion into Central America. Germany managed to regain much of its economic and cultural influence in Central America in the 1920s, however, because the local governments wanted to counter rising U.S. hegemony (9:464).

SOUTH AMERICA

15:114 Haring, Clarence H. "South America and Our Policy in the Caribbean." *Annals of the American Academy of Political and Social Science* 132 (July 1927): 146–52. Haring describes Latin American distrust of the United States, especially among students and intellectuals, as the consequence of U.S. interventionism.

15:115 _____. *South America Looks at the United States.* New York: Macmillan Company, 1928. A Harvard University professor who spent 1925–1926 in South America offers an optimistic assessment of inter-American relations. The author reluctantly admits that many Latin Americans distrust the United States, but he claims that mutual understanding is growing.

15:116 Pike, Fredrick B. *The United States and the Andean Republics: Peru, Bolivia, and Ecuador.* During the 1920s, the Andean countries became more authoritarian and dependent on foreign capital. Increasing American influence, as exemplified in the attempt to mediate the Tacna-Arica dispute, eventually provoked nationalist and leftist resistance (2:387).

15:117 Whitaker, Arthur Preston. *The United States and the Southern Cone: Argentina, Chile, and Uruguay.* The author employs the concept of corporatism to describe how the countries of the Southern Cone converged politically, economically, and culturally during the interwar years under the growing influence of the United States (2:388).

Chaco War, 1928–1935

15:118 Gillette, Michael L. "Huey Long and the Chaco War." *Louisiana History* 11 (Fall 1970): 293–311. Huey Long offered impressive arguments to implicate Standard Oil in the origins of the Chaco War, but the company was not the main cause of the war.

15:119 Hill, Chesney. "Recent Policies of Non-Recognition." *International Reconciliation* 293 (October 1933): 9–127. This essay by a member of the American Commission of Neutrals, which included representatives from Colombia, Uruguay, Cuba, and Mexico, argues that the nonrecognition policy failed to alleviate the conflict between Bolivia and Paraguay over the Chaco region.

15:120 Rout, Leslie B., Jr. *Politics of the Chaco Peace Conference, 1935–39.* Austin: University of Texas Press, for the Institute of Latin American Studies, 1970. This study of the negotiations that ended the Chaco War describes in passing how U.S. officials strove for a settlement to preserve inter-American solidarity as war threatened in Europe.

15:121 Wood, Bryce. *The United States and Latin American Wars, 1932–1942*. New York: Columbia University Press, 1966. This study by an expert on the Good Neighbor Policy assesses the Roosevelt administration's efforts to settle several Latin American boundary disputes, including the Chaco War.

Tacna-Arica Dispute

15:122 Alessandri, Arturo. *Recuerdos de gobierno [Government Memoirs]*. Santiago: Editorial Nascimento, 1952. Argentine President Arturo Alessandri offers his perspectives on diplomatic negotiations over the Tacna-Arica dispute.

15:123 Pike, Fredrick B. *Chile and the United States, 1880–1962: The Emergence of Chile's Social Crisis and the Challenge to United States Diplomacy*. According to this survey of Chilean relations with the United States, Chilean diplomats hoped that settling the Tacna-Arica boundary dispute would forestall an American invasion and allow Chile to become a leader in the hemisphere (2:394).

15:124 Wilson, Joe F. *The United States, Chile and Peru in the Tacna and Arica Plebiscite*. Washington, DC: University Press of America, 1979. This well-researched history of the Tacna-Arica dispute includes a description of the U.S. role in helping Bolivia, Peru, and Chile devise a plebiscite that would peacefully settle the conflict.

Presidential Administrations

HARDING ADMINISTRATION

15:125 Grieb, Kenneth J. *The Latin American Policy of Warren G. Harding*. Fort Worth: Texas Christian University Press, 1976. President Harding sought to promote American business interests in Latin America through conciliation rather than military intervention. Examples of his softer approach include efforts to settle border disputes, moderate the impact of U.S. troop presence in the Caribbean, promote rap-

prochement with Mexico after its revolution, and create goodwill at the Fifth Pan American Conference.

15:126 Hughes, Charles Evans. *Our Relations to the Nations of the Western Hemisphere*. Princeton: Princeton University Press, 1928. In these published lectures, U.S. Secretary of State Charles Evans Hughes defends U.S. policy toward Latin America. American interventions in countries such as Haiti, he argues, are necessary to establish governments that will honor their treaty obligations.

15:127 Trani, Eugene P., and David L. Wilson. *The Presidency of Warren G. Harding*. Lawrence: Regents Press of Kansas, 1977. Even though the U.S. Commerce Department helped promote U.S. investment in Latin America, the Harding administration's foreign policy toward Latin America was governed more by strategic than economic considerations.

COOLIDGE ADMINISTRATION

15:128 Cohen, Warren I. "America and the World in the 1920s." In *Calvin Coolidge and the Coolidge Era: Essays on the History of the 1920s,* ed. John Earl Haynes, 233–43. Washington, DC: Library of Congress, 1998. This brief essay on U.S. foreign policy in the 1920s rejects the "isolationist" label for the decade. To the contrary, America's willingness to intervene militarily to protect U.S. private investments in regions such as Latin America demonstrates that Washington played an active role in world affairs.

15:129 Ferrell, Robert H. *The Presidency of Calvin Coolidge*. Lawrence: University Press of Kansas, 1998. This study of Coolidge includes a chapter on Latin America, which is described as the area of greatest concern to American foreign policymakers during the 1920s. Using Mexico and Nicaragua as case studies, the author claims that Coolidge retreated from the imperialist policies of his predecessors.

15:130 McCoy, Donald R. *Calvin Coolidge: The Quiet President*. New York: Macmillan, 1967. Reprint 1988 (University Press of Kansas). McCoy praises the Coolidge administration for withdrawing the marines from Nicaragua and giving Mexico diplomatic recognition after its revolution.

HOOVER ADMINISTRATION

15:131 DeConde, Alexander. *Herbert Hoover's Latin-American Policy.* Stanford, CA: Stanford University Press, 1951. Reprint 1971 (Octagon Books). This dated work remains the only comprehensive history of the Hoover administration's Latin American policies. The author maintains that the Hoover administration began the retreat from U.S. imperialism in Latin America that culminated in the Good Neighbor Policy.

15:132 Ferrell, Robert H. "Repudiation of a Repudiation." *Journal of American History* 51 (March 1965): 669–73. In failing to implement the Clark Memorandum, which repudiated the Roosevelt Corollary of 1905, the Hoover administration missed an opportunity to salvage the Monroe Doctrine.

15:133 Myers, William Starr. *The Foreign Policies of Herbert Hoover, 1929–1933.* New York: C. Scribner's Sons, 1940. This survey of Hoover's foreign policies devotes one chapter to Latin American affairs. The author praises Hoover for repudiating dollar diplomacy and helping Latin American countries achieve autonomy, independence, and stability.

ROOSEVELT ADMINISTRATION

15:134 Dallek, Robert. *Franklin D. Roosevelt and American Foreign Policy, 1932–1945.* New York: Oxford University Press, 1979. This study is valuable for helping to put FDR's views on Latin America into the context of his foreign policy generally.

15:135 Haines, Gerald K. "The Roosevelt Administration Interprets the Monroe Doctrine." *Australian Journal of Politics and History* 24 (December 1978): 332–45. The Monroe Doctrine, which had traditionally been used by Washington to justify intervention in Latin American affairs, was redefined by FDR's administration to rally the hemisphere against the Axis. The author concludes that Roosevelt and his advisers used the doctrine more as a rhetorical device than as a master guide in formulating foreign policy.

15:136 _____. "Under the Eagle's Wing: The Franklin Roosevelt Administration Forges an American Hemisphere." *Diplomatic History* 1 (Fall 1977): 373–88. Haines, then a State Department historian, shows how the Roosevelt administration tried to court Latin American countries through propaganda and military and economic aid. Although U.S. officials were motivated primarily by fears of the Axis threat, American programs benefited Latin Americans while strengthening U.S. hegemony in the hemisphere.

15:137 Mathews, John M. "Roosevelt's Latin-American Policy." *American Political Science Review* 29 (October 1935): 805–20. The author asserts that the Roosevelt administration has been able to follow the Good Neighbor Policy because the European threat to the region has receded, Latin America has become more stable, the United States needs Latin American markets, and U.S. officials reject Manifest Destiny.

15:138 Roosevelt, Franklin D. "Our Foreign Policy: A Democratic View." *Foreign Affairs* 6 (April 1928): 573–86. In this overview of American foreign policy, New York governor Franklin Roosevelt criticizes dollar diplomacy and U.S. military interventionism in Latin America.

15:139 Young, Lowell T. "Franklin D. Roosevelt and the Expansion of the Monroe Doctrine." *North Dakota Quarterly* 42 (Winter 1974): 23–32. This article shows how FDR continually used the Monroe Doctrine as a vehicle for protecting American economic and security interests.

Good Neighbor Policy

15:140 Barclay, Wade Crawford. *Greater Good Neighbor Policy.* Chicago: Willett Clark and Company, 1945. This study explores a spiritual realm of the Good Neighbor Policy, urging that greater hemispheric unity can be obtained through more cooperation between Catholics and Protestants.

15:141 Black, George. *The Good Neighbor: How the U.S. Wrote the History of Central America and the Caribbean.* New York: Pantheon Books, 1988. Utilizing a wide variety of cultural materials, including cartoons, newspaper stories, advertisements, tourist accounts, and U.S. official records, Black offers a trenchant critique of the Good Neighbor Policy in Central America and the Caribbean.

15:142   Cuevas Cancino, Francisco M. *Roosevelt y la buena vecindad [Roosevelt and the Good Neighbor Policy].* 2d ed. México: Fondo de Cultura Económica, 1989. This study by a Mexican scholar offers an intellectual history of the Good Neighbor Policy based on Roosevelt's personal papers at Hyde Park. Originally published at substantially greater length in 1954.

15:143   Douglas, Donald G. "Cordell Hull and the Implementation of the 'Good Neighbor Policy.'" *Western Speech* 34 (Fall 1970): 288–99. Cordell Hull invoked the concept of "community" as a rhetorical device in his speeches to convince audiences of the sincerity of the United States in devising the Good Neighbor Policy.

15:144   Dozer, Donald M. *Are We Good Neighbors? Three Decades of Inter-American Relations, 1930–1960.* Gainesville: University of Florida Press, 1959. Reprint 1972 (Johnson Corp.). A former State Department official concedes that although Latin Americans initially welcomed the Good Neighbor Policy, they became disenchanted after Roosevelt embraced Latin American dictators to gain allies in World War II.

15:145   Duggan, Laurence. *The Americas: The Search for Hemispheric Security.* New York: Holt, 1949. According to this former State Department officer in the Roosevelt administration, the Good Neighbor Policy failed because of bureaucratic resistance within the foreign service, powerful domestic lobbies that interfered with free trade, poor administration of the U.S. economic aid program for Latin America, and a general lack of public interest in Latin American affairs.

15:146   Gellman, Irwin F. *Good Neighbor Diplomacy: United States Policies in Latin America, 1933–1945.* Baltimore: Johns Hopkins University Press, 1979. This diplomatic history of the Good Neighbor Policy emphasizes power struggles within the Roosevelt administration. The author also addresses the policy's strategic dimension as well as its legacies, such as the development of a U.S. foreign aid program for Latin America.

15:147   Green, David. *The Containment of Latin America: A History of the Myths and Realities of the Good Neighbor Policy.* Chicago: Quadrangle Books, 1971. This study of the Good Neighbor Policy traces the explosion of Latin American revolutionary nationalism after World War II to the Roosevelt administration's support for dictators who facilitated U.S. economic penetration.

15:148   Guerrant, Edward O. *Roosevelt's Good Neighbor Policy.* Albuquerque: University of New Mexico Press, 1950. The author praises the Good Neighbor Policy as an unqualified success but laments that Roosevelt's successors have neglected Latin America.

15:149   Johnson, Robert David. "Anti-Imperialism and the Good Neighbor Policy: Ernest Gruening and Puerto Rican Affairs, 1934–1939." *Journal of Latin American Studies* 29 (February 1997): 89–110. This essay describes the futile efforts of a Roosevelt administration official to implement the Good Neighbor Policy in Puerto Rico. Gruening, an anti-imperialist who directed the Division of Territories and Islands Possessions, was unable to enact reforms because Puerto Rican nationalists polarized relations between the island and the mainland. Gruening gradually lost Roosevelt's support as the president turned toward a more conservative policy to secure Puerto Rico as a strategic asset in World War II.

15:150   Kimball, Warren F. *The Juggler: Franklin Roosevelt as Wartime Statesman.* Princeton: Princeton University Press, 1991. This study of Roosevelt's foreign policy explains the Good Neighbor Policy as an effort to reformulate the Monroe Doctrine so that Latin America would accept American leadership in the hemisphere.

15:151   Meyer, Donald C. "Toscanini and the Good Neighbor Policy: The NBC Symphony Orchestra's 1940 South American Tour." *American Music* 18 (Fall 2000): 233–56. Italian conductor Arturo Toscanini's tour of South America in 1940 helped promote the Good Neighbor Policy as well as the long-term overseas interests of NBC even when the tour itself lost money.

15:152   Pike, Fredrick B. *FDR's Good Neighbor Policy: Sixty Years of Generally Gentle Chaos.*

Austin: University of Texas Press, 1995. This account of the Good Neighbor Policy emphasizes cultural relations and relies almost exclusively on secondary English-language sources.

15:153   Ramírez Necochea, Hernan. *Los Estados Unidos y América Latina, 1930–1965 [The United States and Latin America, 1930–1965].* Santiago: Editora Austral, 1965. This Marxist interpretation depicts the Good Neighbor Policy as a farcical policy designed solely to appease anti-imperialist critics.

15:154   Ramírez Novoa, Ezequiel. *La farsa del panamericanismo y la unidad indoamerica [The Farce of Pan-Americanism and the Unity of Indoamerica].* Buenos Aires: Editorial Indoamerica, 1955. This book ridicules the Good Neighbor Policy. The author, a Peruvian nationalist, observes that Washington replaced U.S. marines with Latin American dictators who would preserve U.S. hegemony under the facade of Pan-Americanism.

15:155   Roorda, Eric Paul. "Genocide Next Door: The Good Neighbor Policy, the Trujillo Regime, and the Haitian Massacre of 1937." *Diplomatic History* 20 (Summer 1996): 301–19. To preserve the facade of the Good Neighbor Policy, the Roosevelt administration tolerated the gruesome massacre of 16,000 Haitians in 1937 ordered by Rafael Trujillo, dictator of the Dominican Republic.

15:156   Schmitz, David F. *Thank God They're on Our Side: The United States and Right-Wing Dictatorships, 1921–1965.* Chapel Hill: University of North Carolina Press, 1999. This study places the Good Neighbor Policy in a global context, showing how American support for Latin American dictators in the 1930s reflected a general policy of favoritism toward authoritarian regimes that would maintain political stability and promote U.S. investment and trade.

15:157   Sealander, Judith. "In the Shadow of Good Neighbor Diplomacy: The Women's Bureau and Latin America." *Prologue* 11 (Winter 1979): 236–50. This article describes the role of the Woman's Bureau of the U.S. Labor Department in promoting the Good Neighbor Policy. The essay tracks the activities of Mary Cannon, the bureau's director, as she struggled to overcome bureaucratic and cultural resistance to her goodwill tours of Latin America.

15:158   Sessions, Gene A. "The Clark Memorandum Myth." *Americas* 34 (July 1977): 40–58. Sessions maintains that the Clark Memorandum, which originated during U.S. congressional deliberations over the Kellogg antiwar treaty, represented a manifestation rather than a cause of the transition from big stick diplomacy to the Good Neighbor Policy.

15:159   Smith, Daniel M. "Bainbridge Colby and the Good Neighbor Policy, 1920–1921." *Mississippi Valley Historical Review* 50 (June 1963): 56–78. This author traces the origins of the Good Neighbor Policy to President Wilson's appointment of Bainbridge Colby as secretary of state. Colby ordered the withdrawal of U.S. troops from Haiti and the Dominican Republic and made a goodwill tour of Latin America in late 1920.

15:160   Smith, Robert Freeman. "The Good Neighbor Policy: The Liberal Paradox in United States Relations with Latin America." In *Watershed of Empire: Essays on New Deal Foreign Policy,* ed. Leonard P. Liggio and James J. Martin, 65–94. Colorado Springs: Ralph Myles, 1976. The Roosevelt administration's pursuit of traditional U.S. economic and security interests in Latin America clashed with the Good Neighbor Policy, a futile attempt to create a friendly image of America.

15:161   _____, ed. *The United States and the Latin American Sphere of Influence. Vol. 2: Era of Good Neighbors, Cold Warriors, and Hairshirts, 1930–1982.* Malabar, FL: Krieger Pub. Co., 1983. This study describes the Good Neighbor Policy as a bungled attempt to integrate the entire hemisphere under economic liberalism. The policy, which the author traces back to the Wilson administration, unfolded in a chaotic manner and was undermined by ambiguities, paradoxes, and bureaucratic power politics.

15:162   Steward, Dick. *Trade and Hemisphere: The Good Neighbor Policy and Reciprocal Trade.* Columbia: University of Missouri Press, 1975. Cordell Hull's reciprocal trade program, which primarily benefited the United States during the interwar period, collapsed after the war because Latin America could not indefinitely withstand the impact of open door policies.

15:163   Wood, Bryce. *The Making of the Good*

Neighbor Policy. New York: Columbia University Press, 1961. According to this former State Department official, the Roosevelt administration renounced military intervention in Latin America because the occupation of countries such as Nicaragua was proving to be expensive and counterproductive. Washington also tried to accommodate Latin American nations to gain their support in the event of a world war.

15:164 Woods, Kenneth F. "'Imperialistic America': A Landmark in the Development of U.S. Policy toward Latin America." *Inter-American Economic Affairs* 21 (Winter 1967): 55–72. In the July 1924 issue of the *Atlantic Monthly,* American academic Samuel Guy Inman published an article condemning U.S. imperialism in Latin America. According to Woods, State Department officials tried unsuccessfully to suppress the article, which unleashed a public backlash that prodded Washington into adopting the Good Neighbor Policy.

Special Topics

AVIATION

15:165 Benson, Erik. "Flying Down to Rio: American Commercial Aviation, the Good Neighbor Policy, and World War Two, 1939–45." *Essays in Economic and Business History* 19 (2001): 61–73. U.S. security concerns overrode the Good Neighbor Policy when it came to U.S. commercial aviation policy toward Latin America in the early 1940s. As war approached, the Roosevelt administration increasingly tried to regulate Latin American airlines to defend the Panama Canal and weaken Axis influence in the Western Hemisphere.

15:166 Melzer, Richard. "The Lone Eagle in Mexico: Charles A. Lindbergh's Less Famous Record-Setting Flight of 1927." *Journal of the West* 30 (January 1991): 30–36. This essay describes Lindbergh's flight to Mexico City in 1927 and his subsequent visit to eleven Latin American nations.

15:167 Newton, Wesley Phillips. *The Perilous Sky:*

U.S. Aviation Diplomacy and Latin America, 1919–1931. Coral Gables: University of Miami Press, 1978. This book describes U.S. aviation diplomacy in Latin America during the interwar period, stressing both the commercial and strategic advantages sought by U.S. officials.

15:168 _____. "The Role of Aviation in Mexican–United States Relations, 1912–1929." In *Militarists, Merchants, and Missionaries: United States Expansion in Middle America,* ed. Eugene R. Huck and Edward H. Moseley, 107–30. University: University of Alabama Press, 1970. According to Newton, the 1927 flight to Mexico by Charles Lindbergh spread goodwill that helped accelerate the development of commercial airlines in Mexico.

15:169 _____. "The Role of the Army Air Arm in Latin America, 1922–1931." *Air University Review* 18 (September-October 1967): 76–90. U.S. Army Air Service began its operations in Latin America in the 1920s to protect the Panama Canal from Europe. Development of U.S. airpower continued for many reasons, including dollar diplomacy, the expansion of U.S. commercial airlines into Latin America, and the need to conduct goodwill tours to sell the Good Neighbor Policy.

15:170 Randall, Stephen J. "Colombia, the United States, and Interamerican Aviation Rivalry, 1927–1940." *Journal of Interamerican Studies and World Affairs* 14 (August 1972): 297–324. Randall traces the Americanization of commercial aviation in Latin America not to strategic imperatives of World War II but to the 1920s and 1930s, when the U.S. State Department practiced open door imperialism by actively championing the interests of U.S. airline companies such as Pan American Airways.

CULTURAL RELATIONS

15:171 Burton, Julianne. "Don (Juanito) Duck and the Imperial-Patriarchal Unconscious: Disney Studios, the Good Neighbor Policy, and the Packaging of Latin America." In *Nationalism & Sexualities,* ed. Andrew Parker et al., 21–41. New York: Routledge, 1992. Burton, a literary critic, analyzes Walt Disney cartoon films commissioned by the State Department to promote the Good Neighbor Policy.

15:172 Cortés, Carlos E. "To View a Neighbor: The Hollywood Textbook on Mexico." In *Images of Mexico in the United States,* ed. John H. Coatsworth and Carlos Rico, 91–118. San Diego: Center for U.S.-Mexican Studies, University of California, San Diego, 1989. After World War I the Mexican government objected to the plethora of American movies that portrayed Mexicans as "greasers." During the Good Neighbor era U.S. filmmakers tried to rectify some of the more grotesque caricatures, but many Hollywood productions of this period committed gross historical errors that fostered new racial stereotypes.

15:173 Cueto, Marcus, ed. *Missionaries of Science: The Rockefeller Foundation and Latin America.* Bloomington: Indiana University Press, 1994. These conference papers suggest that the Rockefeller Foundation's scientific and medical projects in Latin America attempted to impose cultural values on Latin America in much the same manner as religious missionary organizations. The first three essays discuss the Foundation's activities in the 1920s and 1930s: Cueto, "Visions of Science and Development: The Rockefeller Foundation's Latin American Surveys of the 1920s" (1–22); Steven C. Williams, "Nationalism and Public Health: The Convergence of Rockefeller Foundation Technique and Brazilian Federal Authority during the Time of Yellow Fever, 1925–1930" (23–51); and Armando Solorzano, "The Rockefeller Foundation in Revolutionary Mexico: Yellow Fever in Yucatan and Veracruz" (52–71).

15:174 Delpar, Helen. *Enormous Vogue of Things Mexican: Cultural Relations between the United States and Mexico, 1920–1935.* Tuscaloosa: University of Alabama Press, 1992. This innovative study explores the exchange of art, literature, and music between Mexico and the United States in the interwar period. This book enriches the study of cultural imperialism by showing how the American appropriation of Mexican culture distorted its production and fostered romantic stereotypes of Mexico's past.

15:175 Dunn, W. E. "The Postwar Attitude of Hispanic America toward the United States." *Hispanic American Historical Review* 3 (February 1920): 177–83. The North American author of this essay laments the continuing hostility of Latin Americans toward the United States after World War I, which he

traces to long-standing cultural prejudices that have been fanned by America's competitors in the region.

15:176 Espinosa, J. Manuel. *Inter-American Beginnings of U.S. Cultural Diplomacy, 1936–1948.* Washington, DC: Bureau of Educational and Cultural Affairs, U.S. Department of State, 1977. This official State Department history of its cultural affairs program in Latin America describes private and public efforts to foster better inter-American cultural understanding through art exhibits and student and teacher exchanges.

15:177 Fejes, Fred. *Imperialism, Media, and the Good Neighbor: New Deal Foreign Policy and United States Shortwave Broadcasting to Latin America.* Norwood, NJ: Ablex Publishing Corp., 1986. This book describes how the Roosevelt administration forged the shortwave broadcasting industry into a tool of U.S. cultural diplomacy aimed at promoting American private economic interests in Latin America.

15:178 Gamero, Roy. "La guerra de las ideas: la diplomacia cultural norteamericana y la imagen de América Latina en los Estados Unidos, 1938–1941 [The War of Ideas: North American Cultural Diplomacy and the Image of Latin America in the United States, 1938–1941]." *Revista de Ciencias Sociales* 32 (junio 1986): 37–56. The cultural component of the Good Neighbor Policy tried to shift the traditional image of Latin America as a tropical paradise marred by political instability to a view that emphasized Latin America's strategic importance to the United States.

15:179 Johnson, John J. *Latin America in Caricature.* Austin: University of Texas Press, 1980. This book presents political cartoons of Latin America from leading U.S. periodicals, arranged chronologically within themes. Cartoons from the interwar period reflect the prevailing stereotypes of Latin Americans as weak, immature, and racially inferior.

15:180 Joseph, Gilbert M., Catherine C. LeGrand, and Ricardo D. Salvatore, eds. *Close Encounters of Empire: Writing the Cultural History of U.S.–Latin American Relations.* Although the essays in this pioneering volume vary widely in chronological scope, there is important material here on the interwar period. For the interwar period, see also Michael J. Schroeder, "The Sandino Rebellion Revisited: Civil War, Imperialism, Popular Nationalism, and State Formation Muddied Up Together in the Segovias of Nicaragua, 1926–1934" (208–68); Eric Paul Roorda, "The Cult of the Airplane among U.S. Military Men and Dominicans during the U.S. Occupation and the Trujillo Regime" (269–310); and Catherine C. LeGrand, "Living in Macondo: Economy and Culture in a United Fruit Company Banana Enclave in Colombia" (333–68). See chapters 9 and 12 of this Guide for information on essays of general significance (9:385; 12:99).

15:181   Martínez, Oscar J. *Border Boom Town: Ciudad Juárez since 1848.* Austin: University of Texas Press, 1978. During Prohibition thousands of Americans flocked to Mexican border towns such as Ciudad Juárez to buy liquor. Temperance reforms enacted by the Mexican government, the end of Prohibition, and the Great Depression curtailed tourism in the 1930s.

15:182   Pike, Fredrick B. "Latin America and the Inversion of United States Stereotypes in the 1920s and 1930s: The Case of Culture and Nature." *Americas* 42 (October 1985): 131–62. Pike traces changing U.S. perceptions of Latin America to the American counterculture of the 1920s. The stereotypes of Latin Americans as black, Indian, feminine, poor, and childlike suddenly acquired positive connotations, as American intellectuals and artists began to romanticize Latin Americans as noble savages. The author speculates that these new stereotypes helped shaped the formation of the Good Neighbor Policy.

15:183   _____. *The United States and Latin America: Myths and Stereotypes of Civilization and Nature.* This book explains how North Americans came to view Latin Americans as primitive savages. The author traces cultural stereotypes after World War I to the nativist backlash against immigrants and American Indians. Racist imagery persisted through the 1930s as New Dealers romanticized Latin American culture (5:529).

15:184   Powell, Philip Wayne. *Tree of Hate: Propaganda and Prejudices Affecting United States Relations with the Hispanic World.* New York: Basic Books, 1971. This book explores the origins of the Black Legend, which blamed Latin America's alleged "backwardness" on the legacy of Spanish colonialism. In a chapter on foreign policy the author explains how the legend justified U.S. interventionism in Latin America and undermined the Good Neighbor Policy.

15:185   Reid, John T. *Spanish American Images of the United States, 1790–1960.* Gainesville: University Presses of Florida, 1977. This work offers selected insight into Latin American views of U.S. foreign policy, including in the interwar period. The author observes that many Latin American intellectuals had become so jaded by U.S. military interventions they remained skeptical of the Good Neighbor Policy.

15:186   Robin, Ron. *Enclaves of America: The Rhetoric of American Political Architecture Abroad, 1900–1965.* Princeton: Princeton University Press, 1992. This study analyzes the architecture of U.S. embassy buildings for their symbolic contribution to the American overseas empire. Embassies, which had been modeled in the 1920s on the basis of plantation houses, began in the 1930s to resemble colonial Spanish mansions, presumably because of a desire to accommodate Latin American sentiments under the Good Neighbor Policy.

15:187   Schulzinger, Robert D. *The Making of the Diplomatic Mind: The Training, Outlook, and Style of United States Foreign Service Officers, 1908–1931.* This study of U.S. foreign service officers in the early twentieth century makes a passing reference to Latin America. During the 1920s, U.S. foreign service officers received instructional training that reinforced prevailing cultural and racial prejudices about Latin Americans that helped justify American paternalism (2:198).

15:188   Schwoch, James. *The American Radio Industry and Its Latin American Activities, 1900–1939.* Urbana: University of Illinois Press, 1990. This monograph chronicles the rise of American commercial dominance of the radio industry in Latin America.

15:189   Sharbach, Sarah E. *Stereotypes of Latin America, Press Images, and U.S. Foreign Policy, 1920–1933.* New York: Garland Publishing, 1993.

This study describes three stereotypes of Latin America commonly found in the U.S. press during the 1920s: the political child, backward nation, and exotic temperament. These cultural stereotypes, which allegedly transcended racial conceptions, helped justify U.S. policy toward Latin America.

15:190   Stokes, William S. "Cultural Anti-Americanism in Latin America." In *Issues and Conflicts: Studies in Twentieth Century American Diplomacy,* ed. George L. Anderson, 315–38. Lawrence: University of Kansas Press, 1959. Stokes analyzes anti-American literature from Latin America before and after 1933 to show that the Good Neighbor Policy did not mitigate Latin American hostility on the cultural plane.

15:191   Velasco, Jesús. "Reading Mexico, Understanding the United States: American Transnational Intellectuals in the 1920s and 1930s." *Journal of American History* 86 (September 1999): 641–67. This essay comparing the impact of American intellectuals on U.S.-Mexican relations during the early 1920s and early 1930s finds that intellectuals were influential in shaping political and economic ideas in both periods, but think tanks played a much greater role in the transnational dialogue by the 1990s.

15:192   Weston, Rubin Francis. *Racism in U.S. Imperialism: The Influence of Racial Assumptions on American Foreign Policy, 1893–1946.* The author explores the much neglected racial dimension of U.S. imperialism in Latin America. He points out that in the United States most imperialists and anti-imperialists shared derogatory assumptions about foreign peoples (12:104).

15:193   Whisnant, David E. *Rascally Signs in Sacred Places: The Politics of Culture in Nicaragua.* Chapel Hill: University of North Carolina Press, 1995. This sophisticated cultural analysis of Nicaraguan politics contains a chapter describing how U.S. opponents of Sandino denigrated the rebel as a bandit.

15:194   Woll, Allen L. "Hollywood's Good Neighbor Policy: The Latin Image in American Film, 1939–1946." *Journal of Popular Film* 3 (Fall 1974): 278–93. This essay describes Hollywood's attempt to eliminate stereotypes of Latin Americans from its

films during the 1930s. The author attributes the effort to a variety of motives, including the Good Neighbor Policy, a perceived need to create hemispheric solidarity due to the Nazi threat, and a desire to expand into the Latin American film market.

15:195   Yaremko, Jason M. *U.S. Protestant Missions in Cuba: From Independence to Castro.* Gainesville: University Press of Florida, 2000. Protestant missions generally supported U.S. hegemony in Cuba until the 1930s, when they suffered a decline owing to limited resources and rising Cuban nationalism.

ECONOMIC RELATIONS

15:196   Adams, Frederick C. *Economic Diplomacy: The Export-Import Bank and American Foreign Policy, 1934–1939.* Columbia: University of Missouri Press, 1976. This study describes how the Roosevelt administration tried to use the Export-Import Bank to promote a liberal capitalist world order. In Latin America, U.S. officials eventually advocated a more lenient lending policy to implement the Good Neighbor Policy and stimulate inter-American trade.

15:197   Bulmer-Thomas, Victor. *The Economic History of Latin America since Independence.* Cambridge, UK: Cambridge University Press, 1994. This study by a British economic historian describes how U.S. economic influence surpassed European hegemony in Latin America after World War I.

15:198   _____. *The Political Economy of Central America since 1920.* New York: Cambridge University Press, 1987. This overview of Central American economic history describes the failure of export-led growth during the interwar period.

15:199   Díaz Fuentes, Daniel. "Latin America during the Interwar Period: The Rise and Fall of the Gold Standard in Argentina, Brazil, and Mexico." In *Latin America and the World Economy since 1800,* ed. John H. Coatsworth and Alan M. Taylor, 443–69. Cambridge, MA: Harvard University, David Rockefeller Center for Latin American Studies, 1998. This economic study maintains that the three largest Latin American countries did not follow the advice of foreign financial missions during the interwar period.

Domestic considerations governed decisions about whether to restore the gold standard or establish a central bank.

15:200   Drake, Paul W. *The Money Doctor in the Andes: The Kemmerer Missions, 1923–1933.* Durham, NC: Duke University Press, 1989. This study of financial diplomacy in Latin America describes the technical assistance missions undertaken by Princeton economist Edwin Walter Kemmerer in Colombia, Ecuador, Chile, Bolivia, and Peru. The author shows how Kemmerer's reforms benefited the local elite and increased the host countries' dependence on the United States, thus exacerbating the devastation caused by the Great Depression.

15:201   Eichengreen, Barry. "House Calls of the Money Doctor: The Kemmerer Missions to Latin America, 1917–1931." In *Debt, Stabilization, and Development: Essays in Memory of Carlos Díaz-Alejandro,* ed. Guillermo Calvo et al., 57–77. Cambridge, MA: B. Blackwell for WIDER, 1989. This 1986 conference paper by an economist concludes that the advice given by the Kemmerer financial missions to Latin American countries succeeded in securing access to the international capital market during the interwar period only in countries already experiencing rapid economic growth. When the Great Depression dampened trade, capital markets dried up regardless of whether a country followed Kemmerer's advice.

15:202   Gardner, Lloyd C. *Economic Aspects of New Deal Diplomacy.* Madison: University of Wisconsin Press, 1964. According to this overview of U.S. economic diplomacy during the Roosevelt administration, U.S. officials adopted the Good Neighbor Policy to protect American businesses from the swelling tide of Latin American nationalism that had been spawned by big stick diplomacy.

15:203   Harrison, Benjamin T. *Dollar Diplomat: Chandler Anderson and American Diplomacy in Mexico and Nicaragua, 1913–1928.* This author uses the failures of a prominent American business lobbyist in Nicaragua and Mexico to discredit the new left contention that economic considerations have played a primary role in determining U.S. foreign policy (12:266).

15:204   Krenn, Michael L. *U.S. Policy toward Economic Nationalism in Latin America, 1917–1929.* This study challenges the thesis of Seidel, "Progressive Pan Americanism: Development and United States Policy towards South America, 1906–1931" (1973) (15:91), that U.S. policies benefited Latin America economically in the 1920s. Krenn argues that racist and anticommunist ideologies justified the American effort to combat Latin American economic nationalism. Like Seidel, however, Krenn ignores Latin American sources (12:88).

15:205   Lebergott, Stanley. "The Returns to U.S. Imperialism, 1890–1929." *Journal of Economic History* 40 (June 1980): 229–52. This study draws on economic data and the history of the U.S. interventions in Cuba and Panama to argue that U.S. imperialism in Latin America benefited workers and peasants, while injuring local businesses by destroying monopoly profits.

15:206   Nearing, Scott, and Joseph Freeman. *Dollar Diplomacy: A Study in American Imperialism.* This classic work on dollar diplomacy explains U.S. military interventions in the Caribbean after World War I as driven primarily by U.S. economic interests, especially finance capital (2:87).

15:207   O'Brien, Thomas F. *The Century of U.S. Capitalism in Latin America.* Albuquerque: University of New Mexico Press, 1999. According to O'Brien, popular resistance to the U.S. corporate agenda in Latin America stiffened considerably during the interwar period, as economic nationalism flourished in response to the surge in foreign investment.

15:208   _____. *The Revolutionary Mission: American Enterprise in Latin America, 1900–1945.* The populist and revolutionary upheavals of the 1930s in Latin America emerged in response to the attempt by American business to promote a corporate culture south of the border. U.S. companies in turn sought protection from Washington as economic nationalists began to demand that Latin American governments adopt trade restrictions and expropriate foreign companies (12:91).

15:209   Park, James William. *Latin American Underdevelopment: A History of Perspectives in the*

United States, 1870–1965. This book charts changing American interpretations of Latin American development. In the 1920s, Americans began to challenge the prevailing view that Latin American underdevelopment resulted from culture, geography, and climate (9:390).

15:210   Rippy, J. Fred. "The Inter-American Highway." *Pacific Historical Review* 24 (August 1955): 287–98. Rippy criticizes the construction of the Inter-American Highway, which began in the 1920s, for bogging down due to poor planning, cost overruns, and bureaucratic red tape.

15:211   Rosenberg, Emily S. *Financial Missionaries to the World: The Politics and Culture of Dollar Diplomacy, 1900–1930.* This theoretically sophisticated study of dollar diplomacy describes the efforts by U.S. government officials, bankers, and technical experts to create an infrastructure that would promote the open door policy in Latin America and elsewhere. The author's narrative incorporates diplomatic, economic, and cultural history as well as the role of international actors (11:91).

15:212   _____. *Spreading the American Dream: American Economic and Cultural Expansion, 1890–1945.* This landmark study explores the ideology of "liberal developmentalism," the American effort to remake the world in its own mythical capitalist image. The book provides a good starting point for understanding how U.S. officials approached the issue of underdevelopment in Latin America between the wars (9:151).

15:213   Rosenberg, Emily S., and Norman L. Rosenberg. "From Colonialism to Professionalism: The Public-Private Dynamic in United States Foreign Financial Advising, 1898–1929." This essay explains how and why the U.S. State Department turned to private financial advisory missions to perpetuate U.S. economic hegemony in Latin America during the first three decades of the twentieth century. The key transition occurred in the 1920s, when financial missions became sufficiently professional that U.S. officials could play a less direct role in supervising the national economies of Latin America (9:198).

15:214   Samper Kutschbach, Mario. "In Difficult Times: Colombian and Costa Rican Coffee Growers

from Prosperity to Crisis, 1920–1936." In *Coffee, Society, and Power in Latin America,* ed. William Roseberry, Lowell Gudmundson, and Mario Samper Kutschbach, 151–80. Baltimore: Johns Hopkins University Press, 1995. The author compares peasant farmers and hacienda coffee production in Colombia and Costa Rica. Social struggles over land were as important as the boom-bust cycle of the world economy in shaping the pattern of coffee production in a particular country.

15:215   Seidel, Robert Neal. "American Reformers Abroad: The Kemmerer Missions in South America, 1921–1931." *Journal of Economic History* 32 (June 1972): 520–45. Seidel discusses the activities of Edwin Kemmerer, a prominent U.S. financial adviser ("money doctor"), in five Andean countries. The essay is mostly descriptive and raises questions for future research.

15:216   Stallings, Barbara. *Banker to the Third World: U.S. Portfolio Investment in Latin America, 1900–1986.* Berkeley: University of California Press, 1987. This study by a political scientist denies that the U.S. government assisted private bank lending to Latin America in the 1920s. Rather, U.S. banks expanded their operations in Latin America after World War I because they anticipated increased profits in the wake of diminished public sector lending. Private lending to Peru is analyzed as a case study.

15:217   Thorp, Rosemary, ed. *Latin America in the 1930s: The Role of the Periphery in World Crisis.* London: Macmillan in Association with St Antony's College, Oxford, 1984. This collection of essays describes the performance of Latin American economies during the 1930s in the context of growing U.S. economic hegemony in the region. Although the evidence is mixed, the findings suggest that Latin American economies recovered from the Great Depression relatively rapidly and, therefore, may have contributed to the U.S. recovery. Charles P. Kindleberger, "The 1929 World Depression in Latin America—from the Outside" (315–29), by a prominent economist with admittedly little knowledge of Latin America, ably summarizes the individual essays in this volume and offers technical commentary. Those essays also include Marcelo de Paiva Abreu, "Argentina and Brazil during the 1930s: The Impact of British and American International Economic Policies" (144–62), and Victor Bulmer-Thomas, "Central America in the Inter-War Period" (279–304).

15:218   Topik, Steven C., and Allen Wells, eds. *The Second Conquest of Latin America: Coffee, Henequen, and Oil during the Export Boom, 1850–1930.* Austin: Institute of Latin American Studies, University of Texas Press, 1997. Despite its title, the essays in this book argue that the Latin American export boom of the late nineteenth and early twentieth centuries did not represent the complete domination of Latin America by foreign capital. Businesses that exported oil, henequen, and coffee had to contend with local political and social resistance. Topik and Wells wrote most of the essays, but others are by Jonathan C. Brown and Peter S. Linder (oil) and Mira Wilkins.

15:219   Twomey, Michael J. "The 1930s Depression in Latin America: A Macro Analysis." *Explorations in Economic History* 20 (July 1983): 221–47. The performance of Latin American economies during the Great Depression more closely resembled Europe than the United States. The author, an economist, concludes that the central banks established by American financial missions did not greatly influence the impact of the depression in Latin America.

15:220   Varg, Paul A. "The Economic Side of the Good Neighbor Policy: The Reciprocal Trade Program and South America." *Pacific Historical Review* 45 (February 1976): 47–71. U.S. reciprocal trade programs failed to halt Latin American economic nationalism because Latin American leaders rejected most favored nation principles as contrary to their interests.

15:221   Wilkins, Mira. "Multinational Oil Companies in South America in the 1920's." *Business History Review* 48 (Autumn 1974): 414–46. The author found no evidence that the State Department offered to intervene militarily on behalf of U.S. corporations seeking to exploit South American oil.

IMMIGRATION

15:222   Balderrama, Francisco E. *In Defense of La Raza, the Los Angeles Mexican Consulate, and the Mexican Community, 1929 to 1936.* Tucson: University of Arizona Press, 1982. This book describes the efforts of the Mexican consulate in Los Angeles to protect the civil rights of Mexican immigrants, who faced discrimination and deportation during the Great Depression.

15:223   Balderrama, Francisco E., and Raymond Rodríguez. *Decade of Betrayal: Mexican Repatriation in the 1930s.* Albuquerque: University of New Mexico Press, 1995. The author of this book claims to provide the first comprehensive account of Mexican repatriation in the 1930s. The study, which is based on archival materials and oral interviews, sympathetically portrays Mexican immigrants and their struggle to cope with the rising tide of American nativism during the Great Depression.

15:224   Cardoso, Lawrence A. *Mexican Emigration to the United States, 1897–1931: Socio-Economic Patterns.* Tucson: University of Arizona Press, 1980. Cardoso describes "push" and "pull" factors governing Mexican migration to the United States between the end of the Porfiriato and the beginning of the Great Depression. Besides providing a bibliographical essay on the topic, the study explores official government policies, public opinion, and the lives of migrant workers.

15:225   Guerin-Gonzales, Camille. *Mexican Workers and American Dreams: Immigration, Repatriation, and California Farm Labor, 1900–1939.* New Brunswick: Rutgers University Press, 1994. This study explains how Mexicans were lured into the United States by the American Dream and then forced by white nativists to repatriate during the 1930s. This account is particularly valuable for discussing how Mexican government officials welcomed the return of Mexicans to their homeland.

15:226   Hoffman, Abraham. *Unwanted Mexican-Americans in the Great Depression: Repatriation Pressures, 1929–1939.* Tucson: University of Arizona Press, 1974. This book describes the repatriation of more than 400,000 Mexican-Americans during the 1930s. High unemployment in the United States created public pressure to curtail immigration from Mexico and forcibly deport Mexicans who would not repatriate voluntarily.

15:227   James, Winston. *Holding Aloft the Banner of Ethiopia: Caribbean Radicalism in Early Twentieth-*

Century America. New York: Verso, 1998. This book provides a wealth of information about Caribbean immigrants to the United States from the turn of the century to the Great Depression. The author is especially interested in explaining how they influenced American radicalism.

15:228 McWilliams, Carey, and Matt S. Meier. *North from Mexico: The Spanish-Speaking People of the United States.* New ed. New York: Greenwood Press, 1990. This book by a prominent American journalist represents one of the seminal works on Mexican immigration to the United States. First published by McWilliams in 1948.

15:229 Nodín Valdes, Dennis. "Mexican Revolutionary Nationalism and Repatriation during the Great Depression." *Mexican Studies* 4, no. 1 (1988): 1–23. This essay discusses Diego Rivera's visit to Detroit (1932–1933) to help organize Mexican repatriation.

LABOR

15:230 Calderón, Roberto R. *Mexican Coal Mining Labor in Texas and Coahuila, 1880–1930.* College Station: Texas A&M University Press, 2000. This transnational study explores the social history of Mexican coal miners who worked in American-owned mines along the Texas-Coahuila border.

15:231 Chomsky, Aviva. *West Indian Workers and the United Fruit Company of Costa Rica, 1870–1940.* This study explores the social history of United Fruit Company plantations in Costa Rica. The author describes the labor conditions and struggles of West Indian workers as well as their contribution to the anti-imperialist movement in the 1920s and 1930s (9:456).

15:232 González, Gilbert G. *Mexican Consuls and Labor Organizing: Imperial Politics in the American Southwest.* Austin: University of Texas Press, 1999. This book describes how Mexican consuls in the American southwest cooperated with labor unions to promote the interests of Mexican immigrant workers.

15:233 Kofas, Jon V. *The Struggle for Legitimacy: Latin American Labor and the United States, 1930–1960.* Tempe, AZ: Center for Latin American Studies, Arizona State University, 1992. The author

analyzes labor movements in Chile, Cuba, Guatemala, and Bolivia to illustrate how the Latin American labor movement pursued a reformist "Popular Front" strategy during the interwar period.

15:234 Levenstein, Harvey A. "The AFL and Mexican Immigration in the 1920s: An Experiment in Labor Diplomacy." *Hispanic American Historical Review* 48 (May 1968): 206–19. This essay describes the efforts of the American Federation of Labor to restrict immigration from Mexico during the 1920s.

15:235 _____. *Labor Organizations in the United States and Mexico: A History of Their Relations.* The death of Samuel Gompers in 1924, U.S. immigration restrictions enacted during the Great Depression, and the radicalization of the Mexican labor movement enabled the Congress of Industrial Organizations to replace the American Federation of Labor as the most influential American union south of the border (12:89).

15:236 Roberts, John W. *Putting Foreign Policy to Work: The Role of Organized Labor in American Foreign Relations, 1932–1941.* New York: Garland Publishing, 1995. Nativist and anticommunist elements within the AFL fought to prevent the union from assisting international labor organizations that were active in Latin America, especially the International Labor Organization, Pan American Federation of Labor, and the International Federation of Trade Unions. The CIO was more supportive of radical labor unions, especially in Mexico.

15:237 Snow, Sinclair. *The Pan-American Federation of Labor.* Durham, NC: Duke University Press, 1964. This well-researched history of the short-lived Pan American Federation of Labor traces its downfall primarily to the split between the American Federation of Labor's strategy of accommodationism and the Latin American trade unionists' strategy of direct confrontation with capitalism.

15:238 Toth, Charles W. "Samuel Gompers, Communism, and the Pan American Federation of Labor." *Americas* 23 (January 1967): 273–78. This essay describes how American labor leader Samuel Gompers tried to rid the Pan American Federation of Labor of Bolshevist and radical influences.

Biographical Studies

JOSEPHUS DANIELS

15:239   Daniels, Josephus. *Shirt-Sleeve Diplomat.* Chapel Hill: University of North Carolina Press, 1947. Reprint 1973 (Greenwood Press). This autobiography by the U.S. ambassador to Mexico from 1933 to 1942 offers a journalistic account of his efforts to implement the Good Neighbor Policy. In addition to being a valuable contemporary source that sheds light on diplomatic relations, the book also provides glimpses at the "American colony" in Mexico.

15:240   Morrison, Joseph L. "Josephus Daniels—'Simpatico.'" *Journal of Interamerican Studies and World Affairs* 5 (April 1963): 277–89. This essay, based on Josephus Daniels's memoirs and personal papers, praises FDR's emissary to Mexico for his skill in carrying out the Good Neighbor Policy.

CHARLES EVANS HUGHES

15:241   Perkins, Dexter. *Charles Evans Hughes and American Democratic Statesmanship.* Boston: Little, Brown, 1956. A brief section of this biography of Charles Evans Hughes praises the secretary of state for promoting the transition between big stick diplomacy and the Good Neighbor Policy.

15:242   Pusey, Merlo J. *Charles Evans Hughes.* The second volume of this biography of Charles Evans Hughes discusses the secretary of state's Latin American policy. Topics covered include the Monroe Doctrine, U.S. occupation of the Dominican Republic and Nicaragua, Hughes's trip to Rio, the Mexican oil controversy, Latin American border disputes, and the Fifth International Conference of American States (Havana). The author praises Hughes for retreating from big stick diplomacy (14:179).

15:243   Trani, Eugene P. "Charles Evans Hughes: The First Good Neighbor." *Northwest Ohio Quarterly* 40 (Fall 1968): 138–52. The author praises Secretary of State Charles Evans Hughes for trying to reinterpret the Monroe Doctrine as an instrument to promote Pan-Americanism rather than intervention. The analysis is based on published speeches and the secretary's personal papers.

CORDELL HULL

15:244   Hull, Cordell, with Andrew Berding. *The Memoirs of Cordell Hull.* 2 vols. New York: Macmillan Co., 1948. In the first volume Hull discusses his role in implementing the Good Neighbor Policy. He also offers commentary on inter-American conferences, boundary disputes, the Cuban revolution of 1933, and the Chaco War.

15:245   Pratt, Julius W. *Cordell Hull, 1933–44.* Vols. 12–13, *The American Secretaries of State and Their Diplomacy,* ed. Samuel Flagg Bemis and Robert H. Ferrell. New York: Cooper Square Publishers, 1964. This account of U.S. Secretary of State Cordell Hull's diplomacy discusses his role in implementing the Good Neighbor Policy and championing it at inter-American conferences.

FRANK B. KELLOGG

15:246   Bryn-Jones, David. *Frank B. Kellogg: A Biography.* New York: G. P. Putnam's Sons, 1937. This biography includes a brief description of Kellogg's participation in the U.S. delegation to the Fifth Pan American Conference in Santiago, Chile, in 1923. Several chapters are also devoted to discussing his Latin American policies as secretary of state.

15:247   Ellis, L. Ethan. *Frank B. Kellogg and American Foreign Relations, 1925–1929.* New Brunswick: Rutgers University Press, 1961. This biographical study maintains that U.S. Secretary of State Frank B. Kellogg guided but did not take a direct hand in shaping policy toward Mexico and Nicaragua. Ambassador Dwight D. Morrow deserves most of the credit for negotiating the oil controversy in Mexico, while emissary Henry L. Stimson skillfully arranged the Peace of Tipitapa in Nicaragua. Kellogg's role in attempting to settle the Tacna-Arica boundary dispute between Peru and Chile is also briefly discussed.

SUMNER WELLES

15:248 Hanson, Gail. "Ordered Liberty: Sumner Welles and the Crowder-Welles Connection in the Caribbean." *Diplomatic History* 28 (Summer 1994): 311–32. This essay portrays Welles as a liberal reformer whose ideas about the Caribbean reflected the general contours of American foreign policy in the twentieth century.

15:249 Welles, Benjamin. *Sumner Welles: FDR's Global Strategist: A Biography.* New York: St. Martin's Press, 1997. This biography praises Sumner Welles for engineering Grau's exodus from the Cuban presidency in 1934. The account is valuable primarily because the author (Welles's son) enjoyed unrestricted access to Sumner Welles's personal papers.

15:250 Welles, Sumner. *The Time for Decision.* New York: Harper and Brothers, 1944. In these memoirs, Sumner Welles describes how he tried to carry out the Good Neighbor Policy in Cuba. He also discusses Latin American issues during his tenure as assistant and undersecretary of state, including President Roosevelt's tour of Argentina, the renegotiation of the Panama Canal treaty, and the Nazi threat in Latin America.

OTHERS

15:251 Britton, John A. *Carleton Beals: A Radical Journalist in Latin America.* Albuquerque: University of New Mexico Press, 1987. This biography offers a sympathetic portrait of one of the few American journalists to visit Latin America during the interwar period. An especially important chapter describes Beals's reporting on the U.S. intervention in Nicaragua.

15:252 Beaulac, Willard L. *Career Ambassador.* New York: Macmillan, 1951. This diplomatic memoir contains observations about the author's posts in Mexico, Honduras, Chile, Haiti, and Nicaragua. Especially important are his reflections on the Tacna-Arica dispute and the U.S. marine occupations in Haiti and Nicaragua.

15:253 Braden, Spruille. *Diplomats and Demagogues: The Memoirs of Spruille Braden.* New Rochelle, NY: Arlington House, 1971. This memoir by a U.S. diplomat discusses his long career in Latin America. Most important for the interwar period is his account of his role in settling the Chaco War.

15:254 Cabot, John Moors. *First Line of Defense: Forty Years' Experiences of a Career Diplomat.* Washington, DC: School of Foreign Service, Georgetown University, 1979. In these memoirs a U.S. foreign service officer gives brief descriptions of his early posts in Latin America, which included Peru, the Dominican Republic, Brazil, and Guatemala.

15:255 Dur, Philip F. *Jefferson Caffery of Louisiana: Ambassador of Revolutions: An Outline of His Career.* Lafayette: University of Southwestern Louisiana Libraries, 1982. This biography of diplomat Jefferson Caffery briefly discusses his posts in El Salvador (1925–1928) and Colombia (1928–1931). In El Salvador, he advised the Department of State to recognize General Maximiliano Hernández Martínez, who came to power through a coup in December 1931. Caffery ignored calls by aggrieved American citizens for U.S. military intervention in Colombia, but he openly endorsed a liberal candidate for the presidency who promised to protect U.S. oil interests.

15:256 Carrillo, Justo. *Cuba 1933: Students, Yankees, and Soldiers.* Translated by Mario Llerena. New Brunswick: Transaction Publishers, 1994. In this historical memoir a former member of a Cuban student organization reflects on the failed 1933 revolution. The author exalts the role of the students and blames Welles for helping Batista launch the coup against Grau San Martín.

15:257 Lockmiller, David A. *Enoch H. Crowder: Soldier, Lawyer, and Statesman.* Columbia: University of Missouri Studies, 1955. Chapter 16 of this biography of General Enoch Crowder describes his mission to Cuba (1921–1924), which the author praises for its overseeing of two presidential elections and various economic, political, and social reforms.

15:258 La Botz, Dan. *Edward L. Doheny: Petroleum, Power, and Politics in the United States and Mexico.* This biographer claims that an extremely wealthy American oil baron enjoyed unparalleled influence over U.S. policies toward Mexico after 1917. The study draws on State Department records and Doheny's personal papers (12:129).

15:259   Hoover, Herbert. *The Memoirs of Herbert Hoover.* 3 vols. New York: Macmillan Co., 1951–1952. The second volume contains Hoover's account of his trip to Latin America as president-elect and a brief description of his foreign policy.

15:260   Ickes, Harold L. *The Secret Diary of Harold L. Ickes.* 3 vols. Vol. 3. New York: Simon and Schuster, 1953–1954. The third volume of these diaries of a high-ranking cabinet member of the Roosevelt administration contains scattered references relating to the political administration of the territory of Puerto Rico.

15:261   Lamont, Edward M. *The Ambassador from Wall Street: The Story of Thomas W. Lamont, J. P. Morgan's Chief Executive: A Biography.* Lanham, MD: Madison Books, 1994. In this biography Lamont's son explains his father's role in defending the interests of U.S. oil companies from Mexican nationalism.

15:262   Petrov, Vladimir. *A Study in Diplomacy: The Story of Arthur Bliss Lane.* Chicago: H. Regnery Co., 1971. This study describes U.S. diplomat Arthur Bliss Lane's service in Nicaragua from 1933 to 1936. According to the author, Lane opposed Somoza's rise to power but was prevented from intervening because of the Good Neighbor Policy.

15:263   Stiller, Jesse H. *George S. Messersmith, Diplomat of Democracy.* Chapel Hill: University of North Carolina Press, 1987. This biography of George S. Messersmith includes a brief discussion of his ambassadorship to Cuba from 1940 to 1942. Messersmith encouraged Cuba to honor a $15 million debt to American bondholders and advocated economic and military assistance to bolster the Fulgencio Batista regime.

15:264   Nicolson, Harold. *Dwight Morrow.* New York: Harcourt, Brace and Company, 1935. This undocumented biography of Dwight Morrow by an English author praises him for attempting to reach out to the Mexicans on a cultural level despite difficult diplomatic negotiations over agrarian reform, oil, and religion.

15:265   Millett, Allan R. *In Many a Strife: General Gerald C. Thomas and the U.S. Marine Corps, 1917–1956.* Annapolis: Naval Institute Press, 1993.

This account of the career of a U.S. marine leader includes a brief section on his role in the U.S. occupation of Haiti (1919–1921) and the suppression of the caco (named for a local bird of prey) rebellion.

15:266   Crassweller, Robert. *Trujillo: The Life and Times of a Caribbean Dictator.* New York: Macmillan, 1966. This biography of one of Latin America's most rapacious dictators touches upon Trujillo's early contacts with U.S. officials.

15:267   Grieb, Kenneth J. *Guatemalan Caudillo, the Regime of Jorge Ubico: Guatemala, 1931–1944.* Athens, OH: Ohio University Press, 1979. This book is the standard biography of Guatemalan dictator Jorge Ubico, who facilitated the rise of the United Fruit Company and accommodated Washington diplomatically until he was overthrown in 1944 by a middle-class revolution.

Bilateral Relations

ARGENTINA

15:268   Bernard, L. L. "What Our Latin-American Neighbors Think of Us." *Historical Outlook* 19 (December 1928): 363–67. This account by a Tulane University professor describes anti-American sentiments he encountered during a yearlong visit to South America.

15:269   Ciria, Alberto. *Estados Unidos nos mira [The United States Views Us].* Buenos Aires: Ediciones La Bastilla, 1973. In this critical study an Argentine scholar traces current North American stereotypes about Argentina to the writings of U.S. scholars and journalists from the Good Neighbor era.

15:270   Conil Paz, Alberto, and Gustavo Ferrari. *Argentina's Foreign Policy, 1930–1962.* Translated by John J. Kennedy. Notre Dame, IN: Notre Dame University Press, 1966. These Argentine scholars claim that although Argentina and the United States followed isolationist foreign policies after World War I, they both became more active in international affairs after 1930.

15:271 Peterson, Harold F. *Argentina and the United States, 1810–1960.* This survey of U.S.-Argentine relations charts the expansion of commerce between the two countries in the 1920s and 1930s despite strong differences over the Monroe Doctrine, commercial policies, and the League of Nations (2:389).

15:272 Sheinin, David. *Argentina and the United States at the Sixth Pan American Conference (Havana 1928).* London: Institute of Latin American Studies, 1991. This pamphlet describes Argentina's attempt at the Sixth Pan American Conference to challenge U.S. military intervention in Latin America. The author contends that the United States defeated Argentina's challenge, not through brilliant diplomacy, but underhanded hegemonic maneuvering that undermined the democratic functioning of the Pan American Union.

15:273 _____. *Searching for Authority: Pan Americanism, Diplomacy and Politics in United States–Argentine Relations, 1910–1930.* On the basis of exhaustive research in American and Argentine archives, this study explains how and why Argentina lost its bid to compete with the United States for influence in the hemisphere. Argentina succumbed to American hegemony due to the rapid pace of U.S. industrialization and the ability of U.S. diplomats to sell a free market version of Pan-Americanism (12:325).

15:274 Smith, O. Edmund. *Yankee Diplomacy: U.S. Intervention in Argentina.* Dallas: Southern Methodist University Press, 1953. Reprint 1980 (Greenwood Press). The second chapter of this study describes Argentina's challenges to U.S. definitions of Pan-Americanism prior to World War II. Argentina welcomed the Good Neighbor Policy but feared the United States would continue to invoke the Monroe Doctrine to intervene unilaterally in the affairs of Latin American nations.

15:275 Tulchin, Joseph S. *Argentina and the United States: A Conflicted Relationship.* Chapter 4 of this survey discusses the interwar years, when Argentina became more economically dependent on the United States even as the two countries began to clash diplomatically over the issue of American interventionism in Latin America (2:390).

15:276 Whitaker, Arthur Preston. *The United States and Argentina.* The foreign polices of the United States and Argentina clashed in the 1920s, as Argentina began to challenge big stick diplomacy at inter-American conferences. Even the Good Neighbor Policy could not check the growing chasm in U.S.-Argentine relations because of strong differences over neutrality policy as war in Europe heated up (2:391).

BOLIVIA

15:277 Klein, Herbert S. "American Oil Companies in Latin America: The Bolivian Experience." *Inter-American Economic Affairs* 18 (Autumn 1964): 47–72. This essay describes the nationalization of Standard Oil Company of Bolivia in 1937. The State Department initially fought the expropriation but eventually yielded to keep Bolivia on the side of the allies in World War II.

15:278 Lehman, Kenneth D. *Bolivia and the United States: A Limited Partnership.* Athens, GA: University of Georgia Press, 1999. This superb survey of U.S.-Bolivian relations describes the growth of U.S. economic hegemony in Bolivia after World War I. The Great Depression greatly accelerated this trend as Bolivia became dependent on U.S. economic aid and U.S. markets for tin, its major export.

15:279 Marsh, Margaret Alexander. *The Bankers in Bolivia: A Study in American Foreign Investment.* New York: Vanguard Press, 1928. Reprint 1970 (AMS Press). The author describes increasing control of Bolivia's economy by American bankers and investors, a trend she believes may necessitate military intervention to defend U.S. economic interests.

BRAZIL

15:280 Hilton, Stanley E. *Brazil and the Great Powers, 1930–1939: The Politics of Trade Rivalry.* Austin: University of Texas Press, 1975. This book describes the Brazilian response to international trade rivalries in the interwar period. The devastation of World War I enabled the United States to displace Great Britain and Germany temporarily as Brazil's leading trade partner. U.S. economic hegemony could not be easily maintained because the Brazilian military welcomed bilateral trading agreements with Germany during the Great Depression.

15:281   Repko, Allen F. "The Failure of Reciprocal Trade: United States–German Commercial Rivalry in Brazil, 1934–1940." *Mid-America* 60 (January 1978): 3–20. U.S. reciprocal trade programs failed to combat growing German trade with Brazil in the 1930s because Brazil welcomed German commercial ties, and U.S. tariff retaliation would have violated the spirit of the Good Neighbor Policy.

15:282   Smith, Joseph. *Unequal Giants: Diplomatic Relations between the United States and Brazil, 1889–1930.* This book describes friction between the United States and Brazil over naval armaments, reciprocity arrangements, coffee valorization, and Brazil's active participation in the League of Nations. By 1930, the growth of the American empire forced the Brazilian elite to acknowledge that their country was hardly on an equal footing with the United States (9:437).

15:283   Wirth, John D. *The Politics of Brazilian Development 1930–1954.* Stanford, CA: Stanford University Press, 1970. This book exploring development policy under the regime of Getúlio Vargas concludes that foreign interest groups, including U.S. oil companies, did not dominate decisionmaking. Brazil managed to industrialize with less interference from foreign control because of the rise of economic nationalism.

CHILE

15:284   Fermandois, Joaquín. *Abismo y Cimiento: Gustavo Ross y las relaciones entre Chile y Estados Unidos, 1932–1938 [Abyss and Foundation: Gustavo Ross and United States–Chilean Relations, 1932–1938].* Santiago: Ediciones Universidad Católica de Chile, 1997. A Chilean historian describes how the Arturo Alessandri administration defied Washington during the Great Depression by erecting tariff barriers and implementing import substitution policies.

15:285   Klubock, Thomas Miller. *Contested Communities: Class, Gender, and Politics in Chile's El Teniente Copper Mine, 1904–1951.* Durham, NC:

Duke University Press, 1998. This study of a U.S.-owned copper mine in Chile explores race, gender, labor, and class struggles within an enclave economy. The political opening created by popular-front governments of the 1930s enabled workers to form a union that challenged the company's discriminatory practices.

15:286   Monteón, Michael. *Chile in the Nitrate Era: The Evolution of Economic Dependence, 1880–1930.* Madison: University of Wisconsin Press, 1982. This neodependency interpretation traces Chile's economic dependence on the United States to World War I, when a decline in trade with Germany enabled American companies to increase their control over the nitrate industry.

15:287   Muñoz, Heraldo, and Carlos Portales. *Elusive Friendship: A Survey of U.S.-Chilean Relations.* Boulder: Lynne Rienner, 1991. The introductory chapter of this survey presents a succinct summary of U.S.-Chilean relations before World War II, emphasizing the rise of U.S. hegemony. Topics discussed include the Tacna-Arica boundary dispute, trade relations, and tensions between Washington and the short-lived socialist government of Marmaduke Grove.

15:288   Sater, William F. *Chile and the United States: Empires in Conflict.* Chile suffered economic decline after World War I owing to a reduction in the demand for nitrates, its main export. American companies and financial institutions then began to flood the country, buying up mines and banks at bargain rates. On the diplomatic front, U.S. officials antagonized Chileans by failing to resolve the Tacna-Arica dispute and by facilitating American economic expansion, especially in the copper industry. During the Great Depression Chilean nationalists formed the popular front to elect radical presidents who would challenge U.S. hegemony (2:395).

15:289   Snyder, J. Richard. "William S. Culbertson in Chile: Opening the Door to a Good Neighbor, 1928–1933." *Inter-American Economic Affairs* 26 (Summer 1972): 81–96. This essay describes how U.S. ambassador William S. Culbertson carried out the Good Neighbor Policy by helping to strengthen economic ties between Chile and the United States.

COLOMBIA

15:290 Abel, Christopher A. "External Philanthropy and Domestic Change in Colombian Health Care: The Role of the Rockefeller Foundation, ca. 1920–1950." *Hispanic American Historical Review* 75 (August 1995): 339–76. In the 1920s, the Rockefeller Foundation established a health mission in Colombia that successfully helped curtail such diseases as hookworm. The mission did not represent scientific or cultural imperialism during the interwar period because it was not imposed on the Colombians.

15:291 Bushnell, David. *Eduardo Santos and the Good Neighbor, 1938–1942.* Gainesville: University of Florida Press, 1967. This monograph discusses efforts by Colombian President Eduardo Santos (1938–1942) to obtain U.S. economic and military aid in exchange for breaking relations with Germany. Based on U.S. State Department records and Colombian newspapers and official documents.

15:292 Gellman, Irwin F. "Prelude to Reciprocity: The Abortive United States–Colombian Treaty of 1933." *Historian* 32 (November 1969): 52–68. U.S. congressional opposition blocked a reciprocal trade agreement between the United States and Colombia, but diplomatic negotiations were cordial and represented a step in the direction of the Good Neighbor Policy.

15:293 Randall, Stephen J. *Colombia and the United States: Hegemony and Interdependence.* This overview of Colombian-American relations includes a description of U.S. political, economic, and cultural penetration of Colombia in the 1920s, as U.S. officials sought to check rising economic nationalism. In the 1930s, relations between the two countries warmed because Colombian leaders sought to accommodate Washington while exercising some autonomy (2:397).

15:294 _____. *The Diplomacy of Modernization: Colombia-American Relations, 1920–1940.* Toronto: University of Toronto Press, 1977. Randall, a Canadian historian who sympathizes with Colombia's plight as a victim of U.S. hegemony, observes that U.S. officials employed economic rather than military pressure to defend American interests under the Good Neighbor Policy. This well-researched study includes a useful bibliographical essay.

15:295 Rippy, J. Fred. *The Capitalists and Colombia.* New York: Vanguard Press, 1931. This study describes the impact of rising American investments, especially in the oil industry, on Colombia up to 1930. The author concludes that despite labor unrest on American-owned plantations such as the United Fruit Company, U.S. trade and investment were helping Colombia develop into a modern industrial state.

COSTA RICA

15:296 Salisbury, Richard V. "Domestic Politics and Foreign Policy: Costa Rica's Stand on Recognition, 1923–1934." *Hispanic American Historical Review* 54 (August 1974): 453–78. This study traces Costa Rica's efforts to adhere to a 1923 international treaty which denied recognition from any isthmian government coming to power by force. By the 1930s, Costa Rica had abandoned the treaty as unworkable. The author stresses that Costa Rican diplomats were governed more by their perceptions of national interests than a perceived need to accommodate Washington.

15:297 _____. "La lucha anti-imperialista de Alejandro Alvarado Quirós [The Anti-Imperialist Struggle of Alejandro Alvarado Quirós]." *Anuario de Estudios Centroamericanos [Costa Rica]* 8 (1985): 85–98. This essay describes the opposition of a Costa Rican congressional official to the Bryan-Chamorro Treaty, U.S. marine occupation of Nicaragua, and the United Fruit Company.

15:298 _____. "Política interna y doctrina de relaciones internacionales: La postura de Costa Rica en el reconocimiento 1923–1934 [Internal Politics and Doctrines of International Relations: The Stand of Costa Rica Regarding Recognition 1923–1934]." *Anuario de Estudios Centroamericanos [Costa Rica]* 3 (1977): 267–93. Costa Rica acted independently of the United States by recognizing the Maximiliano Hernández Martínez regime of El Salvador.

CUBA

15:299 Aguilar, Luis E. *Cuba 1933: Prologue to Revolution.* Ithaca: Cornell University Press, 1972. This study of the failed 1933 revolution by a Cuban historian explains how Sumner Welles engineered the overthrow of the Grau government and encouraged Batista to seize power. The author complains that too many accounts of the 1959 Cuban revolution have overlooked this important period when Cuban nationalism took root.

15:300   Benjamin, Jules R. "The New Deal, Cuba, and the Rise of a Global Foreign Economic Policy." *Business History Review* 51 (Spring 1977): 57–78. This article describes the Roosevelt administration's efforts to shape Cuban economic affairs by revising trade treaties and creating fiscal policy. The New Dealers' willingness to use federal financial institutions such as the Export-Import Bank in Cuba belies descriptions of FDR's foreign policy as isolationist.

15:301   _____. *The United States & Cuba: Hegemony and Dependent Development, 1880–1934.* This book explores the many sides to American hegemony in Cuba. The author tries to explain revolutionary upheaval in 1933 as a consequence of internal tensions traceable to U.S. influence (9:415).

15:302   Buell, Raymond Leslie. *Problems of the New Cuba.* New York: Foreign Policy Association, 1935. This book is the product of the Commission on Cuban Affairs, a body of U.S. scholars, journalists, and government officials who toured Cuba for three months in 1934. In addition to recommending certain economic and social reforms, the commission chided Washington for interfering in Cuban politics.

15:303   Cronon, E. David. "Interpreting the New Good Neighbor Policy: The Cuban Crisis of 1933." *Hispanic American Historical Review* 39 (November 1959): 538–67. The author praises President Roosevelt for rejecting Sumner Welles's request for troops to quell the 1933 Cuban revolution.

15:304   Deere, Carmen Diana. "Here Come the Yankees! The Rise and Decline of the United States Colonies in Cuba, 1898–1930." This study describes the impact of the colonies of Americans in early-twentieth-century Cuba. After 1917, Americans began to leave Cuba because of political instability, environmental disturbances, and restrictive tariffs. The exodus after World War I ultimately doomed the annexationist movement (10:391).

15:305   Domínguez, Jorge I. "Seeking Permission to Build a Nation: Cuban Nationalism and U.S. Response under the First Machado Presidency." *Cuban Studies* 16 (1986): 33–48. By refusing to revise the Platt Amendment and negotiate trade regulations during the Machado regime, Washington stoked a more radical form of Cuban nationalism.

15:306   Fitzgibbon, Russell H. *Cuba and the United States: 1900–1935.* Menasha, WI: George Banta Publishing Company, 1935. The author of this book claims to offer a "unified, objective, and scientific study" of Cuban-American relations unencumbered by the framework of imperialism.

15:307   Gellman, Irwin F. *Roosevelt and Batista: Good Neighbor Diplomacy in Cuba, 1933–1945.* Albuquerque: University of New Mexico Press, 1973. In lieu of armed intervention, the United States supported dictators such as Fulgencio Batista to protect American interests in Cuba. The study is based almost entirely on U.S. diplomatic records and does not attempt to explore the Cuban side.

15:308   Jenks, Leland Hamilton. *Our Cuban Colony, a Study in Sugar.* New York: Vanguard Press, 1928. Reprint 1970 (Arno Press). This commissioned history describes the American business colony in Cuba and its rapid expansion after World War I.

15:309   O'Brien, Thomas F. "The Revolutionary Mission: American Enterprise in Cuba." *American Historical Review* 98 (June 1993): 765–85. This study of American and Foreign Power, a privately owned utility company, explores the impact of U.S. investment in Cuba. State Department and company records reveal that discriminatory hiring and promotion practices fostered worker resentment and fanned Cuban nationalism.

15:310   Pérez, Louis A., Jr. *Cuba and the United States: Ties of Singular Intimacy.* This unique study explores the cultural, economic, and political points of contact between Cuba and the United States since the eighteenth century. In chapter 7 Pérez explains how rising American hegemony in Cuba after World War I fomented Cuban nationalism and triggered the 1933 revolution (2:370). First published in 1990.

15:311   _____. *Cuba under the Platt Amend-*

ment, 1902–1934. Using the concept of hegemony the author describes how the United States used the Platt Amendment to build an empire in Cuba that inadvertently galvanized revolutionary nationalism (12:300).

15:312 _____. *Cuba: Between Reform and Revolution.* 2d ed. New York: Oxford University Press, 1995. In chapter 9 of this magisterial overview of Cuban history the author explains the background to the revolution of 1933 and the effort by Sumner Welles to replace Grau with Batista. First published in 1988.

15:313 _____. "In Defense of Hegemony: Sumner Welles and the Cuban Revolution of 1933." In *Ambassadors in Foreign Policy: The Influence of Individuals on U.S.–Latin American Policy,* ed. C. Neale Ronning and Albert P. Vannucci, 28–48. New York: Praeger, 1987. According to Pérez, U.S. ambassador Sumner Welles acted as an "active power-broker" who astutely grasped the Cuban setting and operated out of a hegemonic framework that enabled him to manipulate Cuban politics and empower Fulgencio Batista.

15:314 Smith, Robert Freeman. *The United States and Cuba: Business and Diplomacy, 1917–1960.* New York: Bookman Associates, 1960. Smith describes U.S. efforts to promote American investments in Cuba from 1917 to 1960. Several chapters focus on the sugar tariff battles of the 1920s and 1930s.

15:315 Whitney, Robert. *State and Revolution in Cuba: Mass Mobilization and Political Change, 1920–1940.* Chapel Hill: University of North Carolina Press, 2001. This study analyzes Cuban politics during the interwar period with attention to both local and foreign actors. The author argues that the revolution of 1933 failed not only because of U.S. opposition, but also because of divisions within the Cuban left. Batista emerges as a clever caudillo who established himself as a populist while simultaneously appeasing the State Department. Based primarily on research in Cuban and British archives.

15:316 Wright, Theodore P., Jr. "United States Electoral Intervention in Cuba." *Inter-American Economic Affairs* 13 (Winter 1959): 50–71. The author concludes that the failed American efforts to bring democracy to Cuba prior to 1930 suggest that Washington should not withhold aid to the Castro regime on the condition that he hold free elections.

DOMINICAN REPUBLIC

15:317 Atkins, G. Pope, and Larman C. Wilson. *The Dominican Republic and the United States: From Imperialism to Transnationalism.* This general survey of U.S.-Dominican relations admits that the U.S. marine occupation (1916–1924) helped prepare the way for Trujillo, but the authors maintain that Trujillo would likely have seized power anyway (2:376).

15:318 _____. *The United States and the Trujillo Regime.* This laudatory account of U.S. policy toward the Trujillo dictatorship (1930–1961) denies that the U.S. military occupation from 1916 to 1924 created the conditions for Trujillo's seizure of power. According to the authors, Washington had little choice but to recognize the new government, and U.S. officials could not reform the regime because of their commitment to the nonintervention principle under the Good Neighbor Policy (2:377).

15:319 Calder, Bruce J. *The Impact of Intervention: The Dominican Republic during the U.S. Occupation of 1916–1924.* This study, noteworthy for its detailed attention to the local setting, describes how the U.S. military intervention in the Dominican Republic bogged down. Calder blames the failure of the U.S. intervention on a lack of clear objectives, bureaucratic politics, and local resistance to American tutelage (12:309).

15:320 Curry, Earl R. *Hoover's Dominican Diplomacy and the Origins of the Good Neighbor Policy.* New York: Garland Publishing, 1979. This revised doctoral dissertation recounts the U.S. intervention in the Dominican Republic to dispute the contention that the Good Neighbor Policy actually began with the Hoover administration.

15:321 Grieb, Kenneth J. "Warren G. Harding and the Dominican Republic: U.S. Withdrawal, 1921–1923." *Journal of Interamerican Studies and World Affairs* 11 (July 1969): 425–40. This essay praises the Harding administration for withdrawing U.S. troops from the Dominican Republic, fostering goodwill, and taking the first steps toward the Good Neighbor Policy.

15:322   Juárez, Joseph Robert. "United States Withdrawal from Santo Domingo." *Hispanic American Historical Review* 42 (May 1962): 152–90. This essay attempts to explain why the United States withdrew from the Dominican Republic in 1924. Especially valuable is the description of the anti-intervention campaign led by Dominican nationalists and American anti-imperialists.

15:323   Knight, Melvin M. *The Americans in Santo Domingo.* New York: Vanguard Press, 1928. Reprint 1970 (Arno Press). This study, commissioned for a series on American imperialism, describes the U.S. occupation of the Dominican Republic as motivated by a desire to protect American investors.

15:324   Pulley, Raymond H. "The United States and the Trujillo Dictatorship, 1933–1940: The High Price of Caribbean Stability." *Caribbean Studies* 5 (October 1965): 22–31. Franklin D. Roosevelt supported Latin American dictators such as Rafael Trujillo of the Dominican Republic because they defended U.S. interests, thus making it possible to repudiate direct U.S. military intervention as part of the Good Neighbor Policy.

15:325   Roorda, Eric Paul. *The Dictator Next Door: The Good Neighbor Policy and the Trujillo Regime in the Dominican Republic, 1930–1945.* Durham, NC: Duke University Press, 1998. This study emphasizes the many historical actors that shaped U.S.-Dominican relations in the era of the Good Neighbor Policy, including dictators, diplomats, military officers, lobbyists, journalists, and bankers. The author contends that most U.S. officials tolerated dictators such as Rafael Trujillo to preserve the nonintervention principle of the Good Neighbor Policy and to gain hemispheric allies in the war against European and Asian fascism.

15:326   San Miguel, Pedro L. "Peasant Resistance to State Demands in the Cibao during the US Occupation." *Latin American Perspectives* 22 (Spring 1996): 41–62. This Puerto Rican historian concludes that local resistance to property taxes in the 1920s fostered an economic crisis that undermined the U.S.

occupation of the Dominican Republic. Although not based on original research, this essay is valuable for its analytical approach and the use of numerous Spanish-language sources.

15:327   Welles, Sumner. *Naboth's Vineyard: The Dominican Republic, 1844–1924.* This history of the Dominican Republic published by a prominent American diplomat in 1928 is surprisingly critical of the U.S. military occupation from 1916 to 1924 (9:431).

15:328   Zuleta Alvarez, Enrique. "Pedro Henriquez Urena y los Estados Unidos [Pedro Herniquez Urena and the United States]." *Cuadernos Hispanoamericanos,* no. 442 (abril 1987): 93–110. This essay discusses a Dominican journalist who valued American culture yet opposed the U.S. occupation of the Dominican Republic.

EL SALVADOR

15:329   Dur, Philip F. "American Diplomacy and the Rebellion of 1932 in El Salvador." *Journal of Latin American Studies* 30 (February 1998): 95–119. The Roosevelt administration decided to recognize the regime of General Maximiliano Hernández because U.S. officials feared the consequences of a "communist-tainted" peasant rebellion.

15:330   Grieb, Kenneth J. "The United States and the Rise of General Maximiliano Hernández Martínez." *Journal of Latin American Studies* 3 (November 1971): 151–72. This essay discusses Washington's deliberations over the granting of diplomatic recognition to the military regime of Maximiliano Hernández Martínez, who seized power in El Salvador in December 1931.

GUATEMALA

15:331   Dosal, Paul J. *Doing Business with the Dictators: A Political History of United Fruit in Guatemala, 1899–1944.* This well-documented study shows how the U.S. State Department supported the expansion of the United Fruit Company empire in Guatemala by propping up dictators and delaying antitrust suits until well after World War II (12:263).

15:332 Grieb, Kenneth J. "American Involvement in the Rise of Jorge Ubico." *Caribbean Studies* 10 (April 1970): 5–21. Grieb maintains that American policymakers unintentionally aided the rise to power of Jorge Ubico, one of Central America's most brutal dictators.

15:333 _____. "Negotiating a Reciprocal Trade Agreement with an Underdeveloped Country: Guatemala as a Case Study." *Prologue* 5 (Spring 1973): 22–29. Unequal trade patterns between Guatemala and the United States were so deeply entrenched and Guatemala's economic needs so great that attempts to establish a wide-ranging reciprocal trade agreement between Guatemala and the United States were doomed from the start.

15:334 Kemmerer, Donald L., and Bruce R. Dalgaard. "Inflation, Intrigue, and Monetary Reform in Guatemala, 1919–1926." *Historian* 46 (November 1983): 21–38. This study examines the attempt of an American private financial mission to implement fiscal reforms in Guatemala during the 1920s. The authors insist that the mission offered sound financial advice and should not be viewed as an attempt by the State Department to colonize Latin America.

15:335 Kit, Wade. "The Fall of Guatemalan Dictator, Manuel Estrada Cabrera: U.S. Pressure or National Opposition?" *Canadian Journal of Latin American and Caribbean Studies* 15, no. 29 (1990): 105–27. This study argues that the role of Guatemalan students, workers, professionals, and wealthy merchants was more important than the United States in the 1920 overthrow of Manuel Estrada Cabrera, Central America's longest reigning dictator.

15:336 Pitti, Joseph. "Jorge Ubico and Guatemalan Politics in the 1920s." Ph.D. dissertation, University of New Mexico, 1975. This unpublished dissertation remains the finest account of the origins of the Ubico dictatorship. The author shows that U.S. officials welcomed Ubico's seizure of power because they believed he would protect American economic interests, such as the United Fruit Company.

HAITI

15:337 Balch, Emily Greene, ed. *Occupied Haiti: Being the Report of a Committee of Six Disinterested Americans Representing Organizations Exclusively American, Who, Having Personally Studied Conditions in Haiti in 1926, Favor the Restoration of the Independence of the Negro Republic.* New York: Writers Publishing Company, 1927. Reprint 1972 (Garland Publishing). This edited book by a prominent member of the anti-imperialist movement offers firsthand observations of the U.S. marine occupation of Haiti based on the report of a six-member commission that toured Haiti in 1926.

15:338 Chapman, Charles E. "The Development of the Intervention in Haiti." *Hispanic American Historical Review* 7, no. 3 (1927): 299–319. A U.S. academic praises the U.S. occupation in Haiti on the basis of the high commissioner's report and his own personal observations.

15:339 Cooper, Donald B. "The Withdrawal of the United States from Haiti, 1928–1934." *Journal of Interamerican Studies and World Affairs* 5 (January 1963): 83–101. The Hoover administration withdrew U.S. troops from Haiti because European threats to the region had faded, a National Guard had been established to create stability, U.S. commercial stakes were minimal, and Haitian resistance was growing.

15:340 Dash, J. Michael. *Haiti and the United States: National Stereotypes and the Literary Imagination.* 2d ed. New York: St. Martin's Press, 1997. This study analyzes literary stereotypes in American and Haitian literature that fostered cultural myths that made each country seem less threatening to the other. Originally published in 1988.

15:341 Hauptman, Laurence M. "Utah Anti-Imperialist: Senator William H. King and Haiti, 1921–34." *Utah Historical Quarterly* 41 (Spring 1973): 116–27. Senator William H. King of Utah was an outspoken critic of the U.S. intervention in Haiti, arguing that U.S. military intervention in Haiti and elsewhere in Latin America was immoral, costly, and undermined the American commitment to democracy.

15:342 Heinl, Robert Debs, Jr., Nancy Gordon Heinl, and Michael Heinl. *Written in Blood: The*

Story of the Haitian People, 1492–1995. In a sweeping narrative history of Haiti marred by stereotypes and simplistic generalizations, the authors praise the U.S. marine occupation (1915–1934) for bringing order to a chaotic country (2:379). First published in 1978.

15:343   Holly, Burgess, and Alonzo Potter. "Our Future Relations with Haiti." *Annals of the American Academy of Political and Social Science* 156 (July 1931): 110–15. A former consul for Haiti criticizes U.S. policy toward it, calling for friendlier relations and greater respect for Haiti's territorial sovereignty.

15:344   McCrocklin, James H. *Garde d'Haiti, 1915–1934: Twenty Years of Organization and Training by the United States Marine Corps.* Annapolis: United States Naval Institute, 1956. This laudatory account of the U.S. occupation of Haiti is based largely on an official report written by a marine official in 1934.

15:345   Millspaugh, Arthur C. *Haiti under American Control, 1915–1930.* This narrative of the U.S. occupation of Haiti emphasizes economic and political affairs. The author, who served as the U.S. financial adviser to the American high commissioner, concludes that the occupation generally benefited Haitians by teaching them how to run an orderly government (12:312).

15:346   Montague, Ludwell Lee. *Haiti and the United States, 1714–1938.* This dated historical survey of U.S.-Haitian relations concludes with a discussion of the U.S. marine occupation of the early twentieth century. The author claims that the American occupation was a benign but fruitless attempt to impose democracy on a backward nation (5:523).

15:347   Nicholls, David. *From Dessalines to Duvalier: Race, Colour and National Independence in Haiti.* Rev. ed. New Brunswick: Rutgers University Press, 1996. This general history of Haiti contains a valuable chapter documenting the nationalist reaction to the U.S. marine occupation. First published in 1979.

15:348   Padgett, James A. "Diplomats to Haiti and Their Diplomacy." *Journal of Negro History* 25 (July 1940): 265–330. The author praises the diplomatic record of African-American ministers appointed to Haiti, while deploring how white American leaders tried to use these political appointments to buy the black vote in the United States.

15:349   Plummer, Brenda Gayle. *Haiti and the United States: The Psychological Moment.* This survey of U.S.-Haitian relations includes important and previously neglected cultural dimensions of the occupation, such as the rise of the tourist industry (9:429).

15:350   Renda, Mary A. *Taking Haiti: Military Occupation and the Culture of U.S. Imperialism, 1915–1940.* This study of the U.S. occupation of Haiti explores the cultural dimension of American paternalism through the writings of American activists, missionaries, intellectuals, marines, and politicians (12:316).

15:351   Rotberg, Robert I., and Christopher K. Clague. *Haiti: The Politics of Squalor.* Boston: Houghton Mifflin, 1971. This general history of Haiti contains a chapter on the American occupation that assesses its impact and the Haitian reaction to it.

15:352   Schmidt, Hans. *The United States Occupation of Haiti, 1915–1934.* The U.S. occupation of Haiti was motivated not by the open door policy but by racism and a missionary zeal to spread democracy among so-called inferior peoples. Although U.S. troops were eventually withdrawn from Haiti under the Good Neighbor Policy, Washington did not renounce interventionism in principle and continued to treat Haiti as a special American preserve (12:317).

15:353   Shannon, Magdaline W. *Jean Prince-Mars, the Haitian Elite and the American Occupation, 1915–1935.* New York: St. Martin's Press, 1996. This study of one of Haiti's most prominent intellectuals shows how the self-interested Haitian elite and the American occupation authorities resisted Prince-Mars's prescriptions for badly needed social reforms.

15:354   Spector, Robert M. *W. Cameron Forbes and the Hoover Commissions to Haiti, 1930.* Lanham, MD: University Press of America, 1985. This study evaluates the Forbes Commission, an American delegation sent to Haiti by the Hoover administration in early 1930 to determine whether the U.S.

military occupation should be terminated. Based on unpublished materials, including State Department records and Forbes's personal papers.

HONDURAS

15:355   Barahona, Marvin. *La hegemonia de los Estados Unidos en Honduras, 1907–1932 [United States Hegemony in Honduras, 1907–1932]*. Tegucigalpa: El Centro de Documentación de Honduras, 1989. The rising U.S. hegemony in Honduras continued unabated through the 1920s, as American investments, primarily in the banana industry, dominated the country's economic and political life.

15:356   Euraque, Dario A. *Reinterpreting the Banana Republic: Region and State in Honduras, 1870–1972*. Chapel Hill: University of North Carolina Press, 1997. Based on extensive research in Honduran archives, this book is one of the few sophisticated historical treatments of Honduras, a Central American country much neglected by scholars of inter-American relations. The work begins with a history of the Honduran North Coast prior to 1930 in a challenge to traditional views of the country as an undifferentiated banana republic.

JAMAICA

15:357   Lewis, Rupert. *Marcus Garvey, Anti-Colonial Champion*. Trenton, NJ: Africa World Press, 1988. This study of Marcus Garvey's struggle against racism and colonialism includes an account of his attempts to recruit black followers in Panama, Central America, and the Caribbean.

MEXICO

15:358   Beelen, George D. "The Harding Administration and Mexico: Diplomacy by Economic Persuasion." *Americas* 41 (October 1984): 177–89. This article explains how the Harding administration delayed recognition of the revolutionary Mexican government for several years, hoping to force the regime into signing a treaty protecting American oil and land interests. The State Department eventually recognized Mexico in 1923, according to the author,

only after American trading interests began to outweigh the oil lobby.

15:359   _____. *Harding and Mexico: Diplomacy by Economic Persuasion, 1920–1923*. New York: Garland, 1987. This published doctoral dissertation argues that domestic and foreign lobbies successfully pressed the Harding administration into recognizing the Mexican regime of Álvaro Obregón to promote trade between the two countries.

15:360   Blanco Fombona, Horacio. *Crímenes del imperialismo norteamericano [Crimes of North American Imperialism]*. México: Ediciones "Churubusco," 1927. This book, based on articles that the author first published in the Mexican newspaper *Excelsior*, denounces U.S. imperialism, especially the interventions in the Dominican Republic and Haiti.

15:361   Bodayla, Stephen D. *Financial Diplomacy: The United States and Mexico 1919–1933*. New York: Garland, 1987. This published dissertation describes the attempts by the Department of State to solve Mexicans' foreign debt problems following the Mexican revolution. Because U.S. officials rejected armed intervention to pursue a diplomatic solution, the author traces the origins of the Good Neighbor Policy to the Coolidge administration.

15:362   Britton, John A. "In Defense of Revolution: American Journalists in Mexico, 1920–1929." *Journalism History* 5 (Winter 1978–1979): 124–30, 136. This essay discusses how three prominent leftist American journalists successfully challenged the State Department's characterization of post-revolutionary Mexico as chaotic and irresponsible.

15:363   _____. *Revolution and Ideology: Images of the Mexican Revolution in the United States*. This study analyzes U.S. interpretations of the Mexican revolution and its legacy from the revolution's inception to the post–cold war era. Interpretative differences over the revolution emerged in the 1930s, when power in the Mexican government shifted from conservative dictatorships to the more radical regime of Lázaro Cárdenas (12:157).

15:364   Buchenau, Jürgen. *In the Shadow of the Giant: The Making of Mexico's Central American Policy, 1876–1930*. This study depicts Mexico as a "middle power" that attempted to challenge U.S. hegemony in Central America. The Mexican government offered limited support to liberals and radicals in Nicaragua in the 1920s, not out of revolutionary sympathy, but as a pragmatic tactic to weaken the U.S. military presence in Central America (12:141).

15:365   Cárdenas Noriega, Joaquín. *American Diplomacy in Mexico, 1929: According to the National Archives, Washington, D.C.* Cuernavaca: Centro de Estudios Históricos Americanos, 1988. This Mexican writer draws upon U.S. State Department records to describe the 1929 Mexican presidential election that followed the assassination of General Álvaro Obregón. Although the author acknowledges that Mexicans were largely to blame for corruption, he also faults Ambassador Dwight D. Morrow for acquiescing in the fraud that established the Partido Revolucionario Institucional as Mexico's ruling party.

15:366   Cline, Howard F. *The United States and Mexico.* This survey of U.S.-Mexican relations, originally published in 1953 as a volume in the *American Foreign Policy Library* series edited by Sumner Welles, describes the interwar period as a retreat from imperialism, as evidenced by Dwight Morrow's goodwill mission and Roosevelt's Good Neighbor Policy (2:382).

15:367   Dunn, Frederick Sherwood. *The Diplomatic Protection of Americans in Mexico.* New York: Columbia University Press, 1933. Dunn argues that international law hampered the efforts of U.S. diplomats to protect American property and lives in Mexico after the 1917 revolution.

15:368   Dwyer, John J. "Diplomatic Weapons of the Weak: Mexican Policymaking during the U.S.-Mexican Agrarian Dispute, 1934–1941." *Diplomatic History* 26 (Summer 2002): 375–95. The Cárdenas regime maneuvered diplomatically to delay awarding financial compensation to U.S. citizens whose property was expropriated under Mexico's agrarian reform. These tactics, which ranged from foot-dragging to deception and noncompliance, are presented as an illustration of subaltern resistance to U.S. hegemony.

15:369   _____. "The End of U.S. Intervention

in Mexico: Franklin Roosevelt and the Expropriation of American-Owned Agricultural Property." *Presidential Studies Quarterly* 28 (September 1998): 495–509. Because President Roosevelt and his key adviser on Mexico, Josephus Daniels, sympathized with the major goals of the Mexican revolution, the United States did not intervene directly to protect American property holders from Cárdenas's agrarian reform.

15:370   Fabela, Isidro. "Los Estados Unidos y América Latina [The United States and Latin America]." *Cuadernos Americanos [Mexico]* 79, no. 1 (1955): 7–80. This article reprints articles from Mexican newspapers that discuss U.S. relations with Mexico and Nicaragua and the Sixth Pan American Conference.

15:371   Hall, Linda B. *Oil, Banks, and Politics: The United States and Postrevolutionary Mexico, 1917–1924.* This nuanced study evaluates the impact of Article 27 of the 1917 Mexican Constitution on Mexico's economic development and its relations with the United States. The author concludes that the Mexican case supports *dependista* claims that foreign investments more often expand rather than contract the economic role of third world states (12:233).

15:372   Hart, John M. *Empire and Revolution: The Americans in Mexico since the Civil War.* This work traverses traditional diplomatic and military terrain, but Hart concentrates more on the "hidden but history-making interactions between Americans and Mexicans in Mexico." Part 3, which explores such diverse topics as cultural relations and immigration during the interwar period, is especially good at revealing the impact of the Mexican revolution on American property holders (2:383).

15:373   Horn, James J. "Did the United States Plan an Invasion of Mexico in 1927?" *Journal of Interamerican Studies and World Affairs* 15 (November 1973): 454–71. The author argues that Mexican foreknowledge of American plotting, the winding down of the Nicaraguan crisis, and mounting press and congressional criticism deterred the Coolidge administration from seriously considering a military invasion of Mexico in 1927.

15:374   _____. "U.S. Diplomacy and the

'Specter of Bolshevism' in Mexico (1924–1927)." *Americas* 32 (July 1975): 31–45. U.S. officials confused radical Mexican nationalism with Bolshevism, thus exacerbating the real conflict between the United States and Mexico over American property, anticlericalism, and the Nicaraguan revolution.

15:375 Ignasias, C. Dennis. "Propaganda and Public Opinion in Harding's Foreign Affairs: The Case for Mexican Recognition." *Journalism Quarterly* 48 (Spring 1971): 41–52. The author argues that Mexican officials waged a successful propaganda campaign in the United States that forced the Harding administration to recognize the Obregón regime.

15:376 Kane, N. Stephen. "American Businessmen and Foreign Policy: The Recognition of Mexico, 1920–1923." *Political Science Quarterly* 90 (Summer 1975): 293–313. According to this State Department historian, Washington's decision to recognize the Mexican regime of Álvaron Obregón resulted, not from pressure brought on diplomats by the American business community, but from concessions made by the revolution's leaders. The author concludes that his findings undermine the revisionist claim that business interests control American foreign policy.

15:377 _____. "Bankers and Diplomats: The Diplomacy of the Dollar in Mexico, 1921–1924." *Business History Review* 47 (Autumn 1973): 335–52. American investment bankers and State Department officials worked together in the 1920s to check radical Mexican nationalism by withholding loans and diplomatic recognition. Although successful at forcing the Mexican government to honor its financial debts, dollar diplomacy proved to be counterproductive in the long run because it pushed the Mexican government toward nationalizing the petroleum industry.

15:378 Knight, Alan. *U.S.-Mexican Relations, 1910–1940: An Interpretation.* This monograph by a prominent historian of the Mexican revolution disputes depictions of U.S.-Mexican relations as a contest between American economic imperialism and Mexican economic nationalism. According to Knight, Mexican counterrevolutionaries seeking to gain power fostered the myth of Mexican nationalism, which historians subsequently embraced despite the lack of supporting evidence. The author also

claims that many studies have exaggerated the influence of the U.S. oil lobby. By the 1920s, the U.S. State Department had decided to reject big stick and dollar diplomacy in Latin America (12:146).

15:379 _____. "The United States and the Mexican Peasantry, circa 1880–1940." In *Rural Revolt in Mexico: U.S. Intervention and the Domain of Subaltern Politics,* ed. Daniel Nugent, 25–63. 2d ed. Durham, NC: Duke University Press, 1998. Knight, a prominent scholar of the Mexican revolution, downplays the influence of American diplomacy and emphasizes how U.S. direct private investment altered class relations in post-revolutionary Mexico by accelerating the development of a proletariat.

15:380 Melzer, Richard. "The Ambassador *Simpático:* Dwight Morrow in Mexico 1927–30." In *Ambassadors in Foreign Policy: The Influence of Individuals on U.S.–Latin American Policy,* ed. C. Neale Ronning and Albert P. Vannucci, 1–27. New York: Praeger, 1987. Melzer rejects the view that U.S. ambassador Dwight D. Morrow duped President Plutarco Elías Calles into killing off the Mexican revolution by accommodating Washington on oil, religious, and agrarian issues. Calles used U.S. support to defeat his enemies, so Morrow's alleged successes have been overrated.

15:381 Raat, W. Dirk. *Mexico and the United States: Ambivalent Vistas.* This survey, first published in 1992, includes a discussion of the key issues in U.S.-Mexican relations in the 1920s and 1930s, including economic affairs, cultural exchanges, the oil controversy, agrarian reform, militarization, and religious riots. In this period the United States had to confront revolutionary Mexican nationalism while its influence in Europe began to wane due to the Great Depression (2:384).

15:382 _____. "US Intelligence Operations and Covert Action in Mexico, 1900–47." *Journal of Contemporary History* 22 (October 1987): 615–38. This essay provides a valuable discussion of the various U.S. federal agencies that spied on the Mexican government as well as the labor movement and its allies after World War I.

15:383 Ross, Stanley R. "Dwight D. Morrow, Ambassador to Mexico." *Americas* 14 (January 1958):

273–89. Ross praises Morrow's mission to Mexico (1927–1930) as generally successful, thus laying the groundwork for the Good Neighbor Policy. Morrow managed to settle disputes over petroleum and religion but failed to rehabilitate Mexico's finances and protect American real estate from expropriation.

15:384 _____. "Dwight Morrow and the Mexican Revolution." *Hispanic American Historical Review* 38 (November 1958): 506–28. Dwight Morrow's attempts to slow down the pace of change following the Mexican revolution actually strengthened the Mexican government and ensured its survival.

15:385 Salisbury, Richard V. "Mexico, the United States, and the 1926–1927 Nicaraguan Crisis." *Hispanic American Historical Review* 66 (May 1986): 319–40. Mexico's meddling in the 1926–1927 political crisis in Nicaragua enhanced the Coolidge administration's perception that Bolshevism was a real danger in Nicaragua. The U.S. marine intervention stymied Mexican attempts to establish its own hegemony in Nicaragua.

15:386 Schmitt, Karl M. *Mexico and the United States, 1821–1973: Conflict and Coexistence.* This broad survey of U.S.-Mexican relations describes how the two nations attempted to settle conflicts during the interwar period. Mexico established its sovereignty by expropriating land and oil, while the United States forced Mexico to provide financial compensation (2:385).

15:387 Schuler, Friedrich E. *Mexico between Hitler and Roosevelt: Mexican Foreign Relations in the Age of Lázaro Cárdenas, 1934–1940.* Albuquerque: University of New Mexico Press, 1998. This book emphasizes Mexico's ability to maneuver successfully among the great powers in the postrevolutionary period. The Cárdenas administration, while receptive to New Dealers, exploited Mexico's ties with other Latin American and European nations (primarily Spain, Germany, and Italy) to promote modernization.

15:388 Smith, Robert Freeman. "The Morrow Mission and the International Committee of Bankers on Mexico: The Interaction of Finance Diplomacy and the New Mexican Elite." *Journal of Latin American Studies* 1 (November 1969): 149–66. Smith as-sesses attempts by Dwight D. Morrow and the international banking community to combat revolutionary Mexican nationalism. He concludes that although U.S. negotiators failed to obtain their immediate goals, they did establish secure footing for future investments.

15:389 _____. *The United States and Revolutionary Nationalism in Mexico, 1916–1932.* This study describes the U.S. confrontation with economic nationalism in Mexico following the Mexican revolution, emphasizing the tactical differences among officials on both sides (12:172).

15:390 _____. "The United States and the Mexican Revolution, 1921–1950." In *Myths, Misdeeds, and Misunderstandings: The Roots of Conflict in U.S.-Mexican Relations,* ed. Jaime E. Rodríguez O. and Kathryn Vincent, 181–97. Wilmington, DE: SR Books, 1997. Smith explains how and why Mexico and the United States accommodated each other after 1917. The United States repudiated the use of armed force, while Mexico did not try to spread its revolution to other Latin American countries, pulled back from intervention in Nicaragua, and broke relations with the Soviet Union.

15:391 Spenser, Daniela. *The Impossible Triangle: Mexico, Soviet Russia, and the United States in the 1920s.* Durham, NC: Duke University Press, 1999. Mexican leaders officially recognized the Soviet Union in 1924, not out of any revolutionary affinity, but to counter U.S. hegemony. Mexico broke relations with the Soviet Union in 1930 because of U.S. diplomatic pressure and the Mexican left's disenchantment with the course of the Soviet regime.

15:392 Tannenbaum, Frank. "The Anvil of American Foreign Policy." *Political Science Quarterly* 63 (December 1948): 501–27. Tannenbaum asserts in this undocumented essay that the U.S. executive branch's commitment to democratic principles, especially in the administrations of Wilson and FDR as well as American public support for Mexican sovereignty, defeated calls for military intervention in Mexico.

15:393 _____. "Mexico's Internal Politics and American Diplomacy." *Annals of the American Academy of Political and Social Science* 132 (July

1927): 172–75. A prominent U.S. academic warns that U.S. military intervention in Mexico will lead to annexation, thus exacerbating racial tension within the United States.

15:394   Trani, Eugene P. "The Harding Administration and Recognition of Mexico." *Ohio History* 75 (Winter 1966): 137–48. Hughes wanted the recognition of the Obregón regime to be conditional upon its signing a treaty guaranteeing the rights of American property. Obregón could not be railroaded, however, so Harding overruled Hughes and recognized Mexico in exchange for an agreement to set up an arbitration commission to settle land claim disputes.

15:395   Vázquez, Josefina Zoraida, and Lorenzo Meyer. *The United States and Mexico.* This survey of U.S.-Mexican relations from a Mexican perspective describes the 1920–1940 period as a contest between U.S. economic imperialism and Mexican revolutionary nationalism (2:386).

15:396   Walker, William O., III. "Control across the Border: The United States, Mexico, and Narcotics Policy, 1936–1940." *Pacific Historical Review* 47 (February 1978): 91–106. This study shows how the Roosevelt administration managed to get the Mexican government to curtail drug smuggling across the border. The author views the success of this effort as an example of how the Good Neighbor Policy averted the need for overt U.S. military intervention.

15:397   Zorrilla, Luis G. *Historia de las relaciones entre México y los Estados Unidos de América 1800–1958 [History of Relations between Mexico and the United States of America 1800–1958].* Vol. 2. México: Editorial Porrúa, 1965–1966. The third part of volume 2 of this survey of U.S.-Mexican relations discusses the oil, religious, and agrarian controversies that followed the Mexican revolution. The account offers a moderate Mexican nationalist's view of the stormy interwar period.

Mexico: Oil Issue

15:398   Brown, Jonathan C. "Why Foreign Oil Companies Shifted Their Production from Mexico to Venezuela during the 1920s." *American Historical Review* 90 (April 1985): 362–85. According to oil com-

pany and British records reviewed by the author, the U.S. oil industry shifted its production from Mexico to Venezuela in the 1920s, not to escape revolutionary nationalism as widely believed, but because oil production in Mexico was becoming less competitive.

15:399   Brown, Jonathan C., and Alan Knight, eds. *The Mexican Petroleum Industry in the Twentieth Century.* Austin: University of Texas Press, 1992. Several of these essays from a 1988 academic conference touch on the oil expropriation issue following the Mexican revolution: Brown's "The Structure of the Foreign-Owned Petroleum Industry in Mexico, 1880–1938" (1–35); Knight's "The Politics of the Expropriation" (90–128); and Lorenzo Meyer's "The Expropriation and Great Britain" (154–72).

15:400   Cronon, E. David. *Josephus Daniels in Mexico.* Madison: University of Wisconsin Press, 1960. U.S. Ambassador Josephus Daniels held true to the spirit of the Good Neighbor Policy in Mexico by treating Mexicans with respect as he attempted to mediate the clash between Mexican nationalism and U.S. business interests.

15:401   Gómez Robledo, Antonio. *The Bucareli Agreements and International Law.* Translated by Salomón de la Selva. México: National University of Mexico Press, 1940. This book is a legal study of the Bucareli agreements that Mexico and the United States signed in 1923 to settle the oil dispute. The author, a Mexican legal scholar, accuses the United States of continuing to practice imperialism, which he traces to the Monroe Doctrine.

15:402   Gordon, Wendell C. *The Expropriation of Foreign-Owned Property in Mexico.* Washington, DC: American Council on Public Affairs, 1941. Reprint 1975 (Greenwood Press). This study faults the Mexican government for expropriating property from U.S. oil companies without providing adequate financial compensation as stipulated under international law.

15:403   Harrison, Benjamin T. "The Business of America Is Business—Except in Mexico: Chandler Anderson's Lobby Efforts in the 1920's." *Mid-America* 68 (April-July 1986): 79–97. This essay discusses the futile attempts by a Republican corporate executive to lobby the Harding and Coolidge administrations on behalf of U.S. oil companies suffering from economic restrictions imposed by the Mexican government after Mexico's revolution. The account is based on archival research and Anderson's diary.

15:404 Jayne, Catherine E. *Oil, War, and Anglo-American Relations: American and British Reactions to Mexico's Expropriation of Foreign Oil Properties, 1937–1941.* Westport, CT: Greenwood Press, 2001. London permitted the United States to take the lead in settling the Mexican oil dispute because it was more concerned about securing oil supplies for the war in Europe than about defending private British oil companies. Despite differences within the Roosevelt administration about how to respond to the oil expropriation, FDR and U.S. ambassador to Mexico Josephus Daniels finally made concessions to Mexico in hopes of dislodging British oil interests.

15:405 Kane, N. Stephen. "Corporate Power and Foreign Policy: Efforts of American Oil Companies to Influence United States Relations with Mexico, 1921–1928." *Diplomatic History* 1 (Spring 1977): 170–98. Kane concludes that U.S. oil companies failed to influence the State Department's Mexican policy because the two entities had different agendas.

15:406 Koppes, Clayton R. "The Good Neighbor Policy and the Nationalization of Mexican Oil: A Reinterpretation." *Journal of American History* 69 (June 1982): 62–81. This essay challenges the scholarly consensus that the Roosevelt administration turned its back on U.S. oil companies and accommodated Mexican nationalism to honor the Good Neighbor Policy and gain Mexican support in World War II. The 1942 compensation agreement concerned only immediate property interests and therefore did not interfere with Washington's long-term objective of reversing Mexican nationalization.

15:407 McConnell, Burt M. *Mexico at the Bar of Public Opinion: A Survey of Editorial Opinion in Newspapers of the Western Hemisphere.* New York: Mail and Express Publishing Company, 1939. This study, financed by Standard Oil Company, contains editorial excerpts and political cartoons from mostly American newspapers about Mexico's confiscation of American property. Despite claims of impartiality, the author obviously collected material from sources that were highly sympathetic to American oil companies.

15:408 Meyer, Lorenzo. *Mexico and the United States in the Oil Controversy, 1917–1942.* Translated by Muriel Vasconcellos. A Mexican scholar emphasizes the extraordinary pressure that the American government put on the Mexican government to appease U.S. oil companies after the Mexican revolution. He concludes that the Roosevelt administration never ruled out the possibility of using force against Mexico despite the Good Neighbor Policy. U.S. officials finally agreed to settle the conflict because of the need to gain allies against the Axis powers during World War II (12:234). First published, in Spanish, in 1968.

15:409 Philip, George D. E. *Oil and Politics in Latin America: Nationalist Movements and State Companies.* New York: Cambridge University Press, 1982. This book describes the development of the oil industry in Latin America as a conflict between private companies and economic nationalism. The Mexican case is discussed in depth.

15:410 Randall, Stephen J. *United States Foreign Oil Policy, 1919–1948: For Profits and Security.* Kingston, Ontario: McGill-Queen's University Press, 1985. This study of U.S. foreign oil policy includes a chapter on efforts to contest Mexico's expropriation of U.S. oil companies after the Mexican revolution. The author maintains that the U.S. policy was guided more by a desire to curtail Mexican nationalism than to defend particular U.S. economic interests.

15:411 Silva Herzog, Jesús. *Historia de la expropiación de las empresas petroleras [History of the Expropriation of Oil Companies].* 3d ed. México: Instituto Mexicano de Investigaciones Económicas, 1964. A Mexican author explains why the Mexican government expropriated the oil industry.

15:412 Stevens, Guy. "Protecting the Rights of Americans in Mexico." *Annals of the American Academy of Political and Social Science* 132 (July 1927): 164–67. An oil company representative complains that the nationalization proposals under consideration by the revolutionary Mexican government violate the rights of American citizens with investments in Mexico.

15:413 Strauss Neuman, Martha. *Reconocimiento de Álvaro Obregón: opinión americana y propa-*

ganda mexicana (1921–1923) [The Recognition of Álvaro Obregón: American Opinion and Mexican Propaganda (1921–1923)]. México: Universidad Nacional Autónoma de México, 1983. This study maintains that Harding and Hughes were so ignorant about Mexican affairs that the oil lobby could tilt public opinion against recognizing the Obregón regime.

15:414   Velasco Gil, Carlos M. *Nuestros buenos vecinos [Our Good Neighbors].* 8th ed. México: Azteca, 1972. This survey of U.S.-Mexican relations by a Mexican nationalist defends Cárdenas's expropriation of American oil companies as a necessary measure to combat Yankee imperialism and promote Mexican industrialization. First published in 1955 under the pseudonym Mario Gil.

Mexico: Religious Issue

15:415   Cronon, E. David. "American Catholics and Mexican Anticlericalism, 1933–1936." *Mississippi Valley Historical Review* 45 (September 1958): 201–30. The American Catholic community, because of its internal divisions, failed to press the Roosevelt administration into retaliating against Mexico for its anticlerical policies in the mid-1930s. President Roosevelt was willing to risk alienating American Catholics to preserve the Good Neighbor Policy.

15:416   Ellis, L. Ethan. "Dwight Morrow and the Church-State Controversy in Mexico." *Hispanic American Historical Review* 38 (November 1958): 482–505. Ellis praises U.S. diplomat Dwight Morrow for moderating the Mexican government's anticlerical policies through clever diplomacy.

15:417   Flynn, George Q. *American Catholics & the Roosevelt Presidency, 1932–1936.* Lexington: University Press of Kentucky, 1968. The American Catholic Church pressed the Roosevelt administration to recall Ambassador Josephus Daniels because he was not doing enough to stop anticlericalism in Mexico. The author maintains that although FDR was sympathetic to the Catholic Church, he refused to bend to the lobby.

15:418   Quirk, Robert E. *The Mexican Revolution and the Catholic Church, 1910–1929.* Bloomington:

Indiana University Press, 1973. This narrative of the clash between the Mexican revolution and the Catholic Church touches on U.S. Ambassador Dwight D. Morrow's efforts to mediate the dispute.

15:419   Rice, Elizabeth Ann. *The Diplomatic Relations between the United States and Mexico, as Affected by the Struggle for Religious Liberty in Mexico, 1925–1929.* Washington, DC: Catholic University of America Press, 1959. This revised doctoral dissertation casts Ambassador Morrow's attempts to mediate between the Calles regime and the Catholic Church as well intentioned but doomed, for he was bound by duty to defend secular American interests above all others. Based on State Department records and Morrow's personal papers.

NICARAGUA

15:420   Bacevich, A. J. *Diplomat in Khaki: Major General Frank Ross McCoy and American Foreign Policy, 1898–1949.* In 1927, the State Department dispatched Brigadier General Frank R. McCoy to Nicaragua to organize an election that would end the need for an increasingly embarrassing U.S. military occupation. His strong-arm measures produced an admired election, but his failure to eliminate the anti-American opposition led by August César Sandino doomed his mission. America neither established its authority nor withdrew its troops. It intervened to secure stability, deemed a vital interest, but the intervention actually generated instability and anti-Americanism (10:190).

15:421   Bermann, Karl. *Under the Big Stick: Nicaragua and the United States since 1848.* This study, which is highly critical of U.S. policy toward Nicaragua, contains a useful chapter on Sandino's resistance to the U.S. marine occupation (2:362).

15:422   Clark, Paul Coe, Jr. *The United States and Somoza, 1933–1956: A Revisionist Look.* Westport, CT: Praeger, 1992. This study challenges the prevailing view that Washington controlled the Somoza dynasty in Nicaragua. To the contrary, argues the author, Anastasio Somoza García enjoyed relative autonomy under the Good Neighbor Policy because the United States could no longer intervene militarily.

15:423   Dennis, Lawrence. "Nicaragua: In Again, Out Again." *Foreign Affairs* 9 (April 1931): 496–500. Dennis advocates withdrawing the marines from Nicaragua, with the winner of the civil war gaining diplomatic recognition.

15:424   Denny, Harold N. *Dollars for Bullets: The Story of American Rule in Nicaragua.* New York: Dial, 1929. Reprint 1980 (Greenwood Press). This ambivalent account of the U.S. intervention in Nicaragua was written by an American journalist who toured the country in 1927–1928. He claims that the United States had acted as both hero and villain in Nicaragua.

15:425   Dodd, Thomas J. *Managing Democracy in Central America: A Case Study, United States Election Supervision in Nicaragua, 1927–1933.* New Brunswick: Transaction Publishers, 1992. This study describes the effort by Henry L. Stimson to supervise Nicaraguan elections so that the marines could be withdrawn. The author does not question American motives—a sincere effort to promote democracy.

15:426   Dodds, H. W. "The United States and Nicaragua." *Annals of the American Academy of Political and Social Science* 132 (July 1927): 134–41. The author denies that the State Department sent the marines to Nicaragua to save American banking interests.

15:427   Dozier, Craig L. *Nicaragua's Mosquito Shore: The Years of British and American Presence.* This study of British and American influences in Nicaragua's east coast focuses mostly on the nineteenth century, but chapter 10 discusses the rise of the short-lived banana and gold-mining industries as well as the impact of the civil war and U.S. marine occupation (9:460).

15:428   Frazier, Charles E. "Colonel Henry L. Stimson's Peace Mission to Nicaragua, April-May, 1927." *Journal of the West* 2 (January 1963): 66–84. Frazier describes the Stimson mission to Nicaragua as an honest attempt to broker a peace between the Liberals and Conservatives. The U.S. marines were needed to ensure that the Peace of Tipitapa was honored by all sides.

15:429   Greer, Virginia L. "State Department Policy in Regard to the Nicaraguan Election of 1924." *Hispanic American Historical Review* 34 (November 1954): 445–67. This essay, based primarily on State Department records, discusses failed U.S. efforts to reform the Nicaraguan electoral system.

15:430   Hill, Roscoe R. *Fiscal Intervention in Nicaragua.* New York: Paul Maisel, 1933. This book describes the efforts of U.S. bankers to reform Nicaragua's fiscal structure. The author, who was personally involved in the negotiations, generally praises U.S. efforts and dismisses Nicaraguan critics as politically biased and "irresponsible."

15:431   Johnson, Robert David. *The Peace Progressives and American Foreign Relations.* This important study of U.S. "Peace Progressives" in the 1920s includes a discussion of congressional opposition to U.S. imperialism in Latin America, especially the marine occupation of Nicaragua (11:134).

15:432   Kamman, William. *A Search for Stability: United States Diplomacy toward Nicaragua 1925–1933.* Notre Dame, IN: University of Notre Dame Press, 1968. This detailed description of the U.S. intervention in Nicaragua (1925–1933) downplays dollar diplomacy and traces Washington's motivations to a variety of factors, including the Monroe Doctrine, a fear of Mexican radicalism, racism, and concern about Nicaragua's potential as a site for the construction of a second isthmian canal. The study includes a bibliographical essay slanted heavily toward English-language materials.

15:433   Millett, Richard. *Guardians of the Dynasty.* Maryknoll, NY: Orbis Books, 1977. This book describes U.S. efforts to build a National Guard in Nicaragua that could assume the policing responsibilities of the U.S. marines who departed in 1933.

15:434   Salisbury, Richard V. "United States Intervention in Nicaragua: The Costa Rican Role." This article describes how Costa Rican President Ricardo Jiménez accommodated U.S. intervention in Nicaragua to offset Mexican support for Nicaraguan liberals (12:258).

15:435   Stimson, Henry L. *American Policy in Nicaragua.* New York: Charles Scribner's Sons, 1927. Reprint 1970 (Arno Press). In this report,

Henry Stimson describes his negotiations with Nicaraguan leaders that led to the signing of the Peace of Tipitapa.

15:436   Walter, Knut. *The Regime of Anastasio Somoza, 1936–1956.* Chapel Hill: University of North Carolina Press, 1993. This account of the first Somoza regime in Nicaragua concentrates mostly on the dictatorship's innovative methods of control but also discusses U.S. attempts to influence Somoza.

Nicaragua: Sandino

15:437   Baylen, Joseph O. "Sandino: Death and Aftermath." *Mid-America* 36 (April 1954): 116–28. U.S. officials did not have a direct hand in Sandino's assassination, but Washington refused to deter Somoza from seizing power because the Good Neighbor Policy prevented U.S. interference in Nicaragua's internal affairs.

15:438   _____. "Sandino: Patriot or Bandit?" *Hispanic American Historical Review* 31 (August 1951): 394–419. While giving some credit to Sandino for organizing authentic resistance to the U.S. marine occupation of Nicaragua, this author observes that his attacks on American property gave his enemies the opportunity to denigrate him as a bandit.

15:439   Brooks, David C. "U.S. Marines, Miskitos and the Hunt for Sandino: The Río Coco Patrol in 1928." *Journal of Latin American Studies* 21 (May 1989): 311–42. This essay praises a U.S. marine for successfully recruiting the Miskito Indians in the campaign against Sandino, thus establishing the doctrine of "ethno-liberation" as a U.S. counterinsurgency strategy.

15:440   Frazier, Charles E. "Augusto César Sandino: 'Good Devil or Perverse God?'" *Journal of the West* 3 (October 1964): 517–38. The author harshly condemns Sandino and laments that a bandit rather than his assassin (Somoza) became enshrined as a national hero in Nicaragua.

15:441   Howlett, Charles F. "Neighborly Concern: John Nevin Sayre and the Mission of Peace and Goodwill to Nicaragua, 1927–28." *Americas* 45 (July 1988): 19–46. In 1927, Episcopal minister John

Nevin Sayre headed a peace mission to Central America for the Fellowship of Reconciliation, a pacifist Quaker organization. Sayre failed to broker a peace between the Nicaraguan rebels and the marines because U.S. diplomats opposed negotiations and because a marine ground offensive interfered with his attempt to contact Sandino in person. The account is based on Sayre's personal papers in the Swarthmore College Peace Collection.

15:442   Jennings, Kenneth A. "Sandino against the Marines: The Development of Air Power for Conducting Counterinsurgency Operations in Central America." *Air University Review* 37 (July-August 1986): 85–95. The central thesis of this essay, based on secondary sources and a few newspaper articles, is that U.S. airpower played "an important, if inconclusive role" against Sandino.

15:443   Macaulay, Neill. *The Sandino Affair.* Chicago: Quadrangle Books, 1967. Reprint 1985 (Duke University Press). The author, a former officer in Castro's army, recounts the guerrilla campaigns of Augusto César Sandino, the Nicaraguan rebel who eluded the U.S. marines in the countryside for more than six years.

15:444   Tierney, John J., Jr. "U.S. Intervention in Nicaragua, 1927–1933: Lessons for Today." *Orbis* 14 (Winter 1971): 1012–28. The author describes the failed U.S. military campaign against Sandino to show the futility of the Vietnam War.

PANAMA

15:445   Conniff, Michael L. *Panama and the United States: The Forced Alliance.* According to this survey of U.S.-Panamanian relations, Washington made minor concessions to Panamanian nationalism during the interwar period, while retaining control over the Canal because of its strategic importance (2:358). First published in 1992.

15:446   Ealy, Lawrence O. *The Republic of Panama in World Affairs, 1903–1950.* Philadelphia: University of Pennsylvania Press, 1951. Reprint 1970 (Greenwood Press). U.S. military intervention and dollar diplomacy in Latin America fostered anti-Americanism at inter-American conferences until the advent of the Good Neighbor Policy. Particularly irksome to Panamanian nationalists was the Hay-Bunau-Varilla Treaty, which the Franklin D. Roosevelt administration was forced to modify to grant Panama greater control over the Canal.

15:447   LaFeber, Walter. *The Panama Canal: The Crisis in Historical Perspective.* After World War I the State Department facilitated the penetration of American capital in Panama, which did little to alleviate poverty. In 1936, FDR renegotiated the Panama Canal treaty and granted minor economic concessions to lessen the danger of a nationalist backlash. First issued in 1978 (2:360).

15:448   Langley, Lester D. "Negotiating New Treaties with Panama: 1936." *Hispanic American Historical Review* 48 (May 1968): 220–33. Langley describes negotiations that led to a new Panama Canal treaty, which granted certain concessions to Panamanian nationalists, including a greater share of the Canal's profits.

15:449   _____. "The World Crisis and the Good Neighbor Policy in Panama, 1936–1941." *Americas* 24 (October 1967): 137–52. Langley describes how the overthrow of the nationalist regime of Harmodio Arias by his political foes fortuitously facilitated Washington's attempts to fortify military base sites in Panama.

15:450   Major, John. "F.D.R. and Panama." *Historical Journal* 28 (June 1985): 357–77. The author concludes that Roosevelt made limited concessions to Panamanian nationalists under the Good Neighbor Policy to secure American access to the Canal Zone.

15:451   _____. *Prize Possession: The United States and the Panama Canal, 1903–1979.* This well-researched account of U.S. policy toward Panama includes a scattered discussion of U.S. attempts to implement fiscal, military, and social reforms in Panama after World War I. According to the author, the United States was able to establish and maintain a protectorate in Panama because the local elite collaborated with Washington and failed to establish ties with other great powers that could have challenged U.S. hegemony (2:361).

15:452   McCain, William David. *The United States*

and the Republic of Panama. Durham, NC: Duke University Press, 1937. Reprint 1970 (Arno Press). The last two chapters of this general history of U.S.-Panamanian relations discusses diplomatic negotiations over treaties that did little to mitigate growing Panamanian resentment over American control of the Canal.

15:453   Pearcy, Thomas L. *We Answer Only to God: Politics and the Military in Panama, 1903–1947.* Albuquerque: University of New Mexico Press, 1998. This book downplays the role of the United States in shaping Panama's history but nonetheless provides essential background for understanding the development of the internal security forces. Chapter 3 discusses the Panama's revolutionary "Generation of '31," a group of dissidents who seized power in 1931 and attempted to modernize the police force.

PERU AND ECUADOR

15:454   Carey, James C. *Peru and the United States, 1900–1962.* This survey of U.S.-Peruvian relations describes American banking loans, U.S. naval missions, and boundary disputes during the interwar period (2:398).

15:455   Clayton, Lawrence A. *Peru and the United States: The Condor and the Eagle.* This general survey of U.S.-Peruvian relations since the nineteenth century describes the 1920s as the period of greatest cooperation between the two countries. President Augusto B. Leguía (1919–1930) facilitated the "Americanization" of Peru by appointing economic and military advisers to his government and promoting the expansion of U.S. investment in Peru, especially in the oil, mining, and shipping industries. The author maintains that U.S. diplomats helped defend Peruvian interests in the complex Tacna-Arica border dispute with Chile (9:448).

15:456   Quiroz, Alfonso W. *Domestic and Foreign Finance in Modern Peru, 1850–1950: Financing Visions of Development.* Pittsburgh: University of Pittsburgh Press, 1993. World War I disrupted European investments in Peru, thus benefiting agro exporters and strengthening the local market.

15:457 St. John, Ronald Bruce. "The End of Innocence: Peruvian Foreign Policy and the United States, 1919–1942." *Journal of Latin American Studies* 8 (November 1976): 325–44. This survey of its foreign policy in the interwar period describes how Peru's rising nationalism impeded the efforts of various officials to elicit Washington's assistance in settling Peru's boundary disputes with its neighbors.

15:458 Striffler, Steve. *In the Shadows of State and Capital: The United Fruit Company, Popular Struggle, and Agrarian Restructuring in Ecuador, 1900–1995.* Durham, NC: Duke University Press, 2002. The first chapter of this anthropological study relies on State Department records to show that the United Fruit Company penetrated Ecuador because the labor movement was weak, the land disease-free, and the government cooperative.

PUERTO RICO

15:459 Argüelles, María del Pilar. *Morality and Power: The U.S. Colonial Experience in Puerto Rico from 1898 to 1948.* Lanham, MD: University Press of America, 1996. In this work a Puerto Rican political scientist explains how Puerto Rican nationalists fought against U.S. neocolonialism.

15:460 Bhana, Surendra. *The United States and the Development of the Puerto Rican Status Question, 1936–1968.* Lawrence: University Press of Kansas, 1975. The initial chapters of this study describe the political struggles that raged in Puerto Rico during the 1930s over the island's uncertain political relationship to the United States.

15:461 Clark, Truman R. *Puerto Rico and the United States, 1917–1933.* Pittsburgh: University of Pittsburgh Press, 1975. Clark surveys Puerto Rico's relationship with the United States from the Jones Act of 1917 to the beginning of the Great Depression, emphasizing how the island stagnated because of its uncertain political status.

15:462 Diffie, Bailey W., and Justine Whitfield Diffie. *Porto Rico: A Broken Pledge.* New York: Vanguard Press, 1931. This study, one of a series on American imperialism, tries to show that the American occupation has not improved life for Puerto Ri-

cans, primarily because the wealth of the island has been extracted by absentee land owners.

15:463 Fernandez, Ronald. *The Disenchanted Island: Puerto Rico and the United States in the Twentieth Century.* This study is highly critical of the United States for its governance of Puerto Rico during the interwar period. The author, clearly sympathetic to the *independista* movement, highlights Puerto Rican resistance to U.S. neocolonialism (2:375). First published in 1992.

15:464 _____. *Prisoners of Colonialism: The Struggle for Justice in Puerto Rico.* Monroe, ME: Common Courage Press, 1994. This first chapter of this book about Puerto Rican political prisoners discusses the life of Pedro Albizu Campos, a prominent Puerto Rican nationalist who founded an independence party in the 1920s.

15:465 Goodsell, Charles T. *Administration of a Revolution: Executive Reform in Puerto Rico under Governor Tugwell, 1941–1946.* Cambridge, MA: Harvard University Press, 1965. This study assesses administrative reforms enacted by the governor of Puerto Rico in the early 1940s. The author praises Tugwell for laying the groundwork for the welfare state.

15:466 Johnson, Roberta Ann. *Puerto Rico: Commonwealth or Colony?* New York: Praeger, 1980. This history of Puerto Rico by a political scientist sympathetic to Puerto Rican nationalism contains a useful chronology of events that includes the interwar period.

15:467 Morales-Carrión, Arturo, ed. *Puerto Rico, a Political and Cultural History.* New York: W. W. Norton, 1983. This survey of Puerto Rican history includes several chapters on the interwar period. The author condemns Republican administrations of the 1920s for committing gaffes that inflamed Puerto Rican nationalism. Puerto Rico remained an American colony in the 1930s, but Roosevelt's New Deal brought important reforms that divided local politicians. Besides the editor, other authors, including María Teresa Babín, have contributed essays to this volume.

15:468 Perkins, Whitney T. *Denial of Empire: The United States and Its Dependencies.* This account of various American dependencies contains a lengthy chapter on U.S. tutelage of Puerto Rico. After the landmark Jones Act of 1917, which denied Puerto Rico statehood, the island sank into even greater dependence on the United States despite attempts to implement New Deal reforms (10:111).

15:469   Quintero-Rivera, Angel. "Puerto Rico, c. 1870–1940." In *The Cambridge History of Latin America. Vol. 5: c. 1870 to 1930,* ed. Leslie Bethell. New York: Cambridge University Press, 1986. This essay explores the transition between Spanish and American colonization of Puerto Rico, explaining how capitalist transformation shaped class relations.

15:470   Santiago-Valles, Kelvin A. *"Subject People" and Colonial Discourses: Economic Transformation and Social Disorder in Puerto Rico, 1898–1947.* Albany: State University of New York Press, 1994. The author uses a variety of theoretical approaches (hegemony, post-structuralism, feminism, and subaltern studies) to explain the relationship between colonialism and social unrest in Puerto Rico. Chapters 5–7 cover the interwar period.

VENEZUELA

15:471   Ewell, Judith. *Venezuela and the United States: From Monroe's Hemisphere to Petroleum's Empire.* During the interwar period Washington changed its view of Venezuelan President Juan Vicente Gómez from cunning scoundrel to sagacious good neighbor. This transformation is traced in part to the complicated array of a Venezuelan lobby, which included oil companies, missionaries, universities, labor organizations, and scientists. Gómez himself was an important factor in checking U.S. hegemony, as he courted European oil investors while red-baiting his domestic opposition (2:400).

15:472   Liss, Sheldon B. *Diplomacy & Dependency: Venezuela, the United States, and the Americas.* This narrative history of Venezuelan diplomacy toward the United States includes several chapters on the interwar years. Although the author relied solely on published materials, the study nonetheless provides a useful summary of the Gómez regime's policies (2:401).

15:473   Rabe, Stephen G. "Anglo-American Rivalry for Venezuelan Oil, 1919–1929." *Mid-America* 58 (April-July 1976): 97–110. This essay explains how the U.S. government helped the American oil industry displace British oil firms in Venezuela in the 1920s. U.S. officials arranged meetings between American oil company executives and Venezuelan politicians, discouraged Venezuela from allowing other foreign oil firms to expand there, and used diplomatic pressure to persuade its officials to adhere to open door policies.

15:474   _____. *The Road to OPEC: United States Relations with Venezuela, 1919–1976.* Austin: University of Texas Press, 1982. According to this survey of U.S.-Venezuelan relations, Venezuela became an important strategic and economic asset to the United States after World War I, when State Department officials decided to promote American investments, especially in the oil industry. Under the Good Neighbor Policy, Washington signed new reciprocal trade agreements and reluctantly tolerated Venezuelan efforts to regulate the oil industry.

15:475   Schwartzberg, Steven. "Rómulo Betancourt: From a Communist Anti-Imperialist to a Social Democrat with US Support." *Journal of Latin American Studies* 29 (October 1997): 613–55. This essay discusses a prominent Venezuelan leader's transformation from a communist anti-imperialist in the 1930s to an anticommunist social democrat who courted the United States after World War II. During the interwar period, Betancourt remained a critic of American monopolies, such as the United Fruit Company, but he admired Franklin D. Roosevelt's ideas about using the state to reform capitalism.

The United States, the Middle East, and Africa between the World Wars

Contributing Editor

JAMES F. GOODE

Grand Valley State University

Contents

Introduction

I have focused on books and articles published in English since 1980. The entries reflect the perspectives of scholars in African and Middle Eastern studies as well as those of foreign relations experts. I tried to avoid narrow compass; hence, in addition to works on traditional topics of American foreign relations, readers will find entries on such subjects as archaeology, education, and film that speak to the history of American foreign relations writ large. I have interpreted the chapter's chronological boundaries flexibly, deciding for example to include some works about developments in World War I if they also provided significant material on the Paris Peace Conference. The entries also reflect the fact that much of what took place in U.S. foreign relations with the Middle East and Africa in the 1920s was rooted in World War I. At the other end, I have usually not included works largely focused on World War II and beyond.

Published Primary Sources

DOCUMENT COLLECTIONS

16:1   U.S. Department of State. *Foreign Relations of the United States, 1921–1940*. Washington, DC: Government Printing Office, 1936–1958. This official compilation is the place to start in examining the official relations of the U.S. government with both the nations of the Middle East and Africa and, in some cases, their European colonial masters. Counting the latter, some forty-eight volumes covering the 1921–1940 period are likely to hold pertinent material (1:93).

16:2   Bein, Alex. "Resources for American Zionist History in the Jerusalem Archives." In *Early History of Zionism in America: Papers Presented at the Conference on the Early History of Zionism in America, Convened by the American Jewish Historical Society and the Theodor Herzl Foundation, in New York City, on December Twenty-sixth and Twenty-seventh,*

Nineteen Hundred and Fifty-five, ed. Isidore Meyer, 109–30. New York: American Jewish Historical Society, 1958. Reprint 1977 (Arno Press). Bein discusses some of the collections containing exchanges between Zionists in Palestine and in the United States in the interwar years.

16:3   Hill, Adelaide Cromwell, and Martin Kilson, eds. *Apropos of Africa: Sentiments of Negro American Leaders on Africa from the 1800s to the 1950s.* London: Cass, 1969. This document collection includes selections from Paul Cuffe, Martin Delany, Henry M. Turner, Marcus Garvey, Booker T. Washington, and W. E. B. Du Bois. Bibliography.

16:4   Hurewitz, J. C., ed. *The Middle East and North Africa in World Politics: A Documentary Record.* The documents are arranged chronologically. The second volume covers the period of British and French supremacy during the years 1914 to 1945. Extensive bibliography (13:24). First published in 1956.

Bibliographies and Other Reference Works

BIBLIOGRAPHIES

16:5   Littlefield, David W., ed. *The Islamic Near East and North Africa: An Annotated Guide to Books in English for Non-Specialists.* Littleton, CO: Libraries Unlimited, 1977. This is a selective bibliography with extensive annotation, covering the period from 1800 to the present. Chapters are devoted either to separate topics or to geographical areas. Littlefield includes as well a short list of bibliographies and reference works.

16:6   Silverburg, Sanford R., and Bernard Reich, eds. *U.S. Foreign Relations with the Middle East and North Africa: A Bibliography.* Reich and Silverburg list important books, articles, document collections, and bibliographies, without annotation. A majority of entries concern the post–World War II period but are useful for the interwar period as well (1:262).

16:7   _____. *U.S. Foreign Relations with the Middle East and North Africa: A Bibliography, Supplement 1998.* Lanham, MD: Scarecrow Press, 1999. In this supplement to their *U.S. Foreign Relations with the Middle East and North Africa: A Bibliography* (1994) (16:6), Reich and Silverburg list new dissertations, books, articles, document collections, and bibliographies, without annotation. Some foreign-language entries included.

16:8   Bryson, Thomas A., ed. *United States/Middle East Diplomatic Relations, 1784–1978: An Annotated Bibliography.* This work provides an annotated list of books, articles, dissertations, document collections, and treaty collections (1:259).

16:9   Clements, Frank, ed. *The Emergence of Arab Nationalism from the Nineteenth Century to 1921.* See chapter 13 of this Guide (13:37).

16:10   DeNovo, John A. "American Relations with the Middle East: Some Unfinished Business." In *Issues and Conflicts: Studies in Twentieth Century American Diplomacy,* ed. George L. Anderson, 63–98. Lawrence: University of Kansas Press, 1959. This essay introduces the reader to many of the American interest groups that have influenced the shaping of American Middle Eastern policy, with footnotes pointing to bibliographic guides and both primary and secondary sources.

16:11   Selim, George Dimitri, ed. *American Doctoral Dissertations on the Arab World, 1883–1974.* 2d ed. Washington, DC: Library of Congress, 1976. This collection includes dissertations on all aspects of the Arab world and Islam. Subject and keyword indices.

16:12   _____. *American Doctoral Dissertations on the Arab World. Supplement, 1975–1981.* Washington, DC: Library of Congress, 1983. Supplement compiled by George Dimitri Selim of the Near East Section, African and Middle Eastern Division, Library of Congress, using the same format as his earlier work.

16:13   _____. *American Doctoral Dissertations on the Arab World. Supplement, August 1981– December 1987.* Vol. 2. Washington, DC: Library of Congress, 1989. Supplement compiled by George Dimitri Selim of the Near East Section, African and Middle Eastern Division, Library of Congress, using the same format as his previous volumes.

16:14   Tamkoç, Metin, ed. *A Bibliography on the Foreign Relations of the Republic of Turkey, 1919– 1967: And Brief Biographies of Turkish Statesmen.* Ankara: Middle East Technical University, 1968. A bibliography prepared primarily for English speakers, this lists sources by Turkish officials and nationals in Turkish as well as other languages. A final section contains non-Turkish sources and reflects holdings in major western collections.

16:15   Duignan, Peter, with Helen Field Conover, eds. *Guide to Research and Reference Works on Sub-Saharan Africa.* Stanford, CA: Hoover Institution Press, 1971. This work will lead the serious researcher to materials that provide a background to U.S. activities in Africa. Particularly relevant are accounts of British and French colonial possessions.

16:16   Keto, C. Tsehloane, ed. *American–South African Relations, 1784–1980: Review and Select Bibliography.* Though not annotated, this bibliography includes articles, reports, books, and dissertations published up to 1983. These are arranged chronologically and thematically. It also contains a useful review essay and index (1:231).

16:17   Lulat, Y. G.-M., ed. *U.S. Relations with South Africa: An Annotated Bibliography.* This work includes books, documents, reports, and periodical literature from the beginning of the twentieth century, but the focus is on recent decades (1:232).

HISTORIOGRAPHY

16:18   Papazian, Dennis R. "The Changing American View of the Armenian Question: An Interpretation." *Armenian Review* 39 (Winter 1986): 47–72. The author provides some review of historiography and of divisions among historians. He explains why the Armenian question has become but a distant memory for most Americans.

16:19   Trask, Roger R. "United States Relations with the Middle East in the Twentieth Century: A Developing Area in Historical Literature." In *American Foreign Relations, A Historiographical Review,* ed.

Gerald K. Haines and J. Samuel Walker, 293–309. Westport, CT: Greenwood Press, 1981. Much of this chapter refers to the post–World War II period; Trask points out the dearth of studies on the pre-1941 era.

16:20 Zingg, Paul J. "America and North Africa: A Case in United States–Third World Relations." *History Teacher* 12 (February 1979): 253–70. Zingg discusses this relatively neglected area of study and surveys some of the available material. He believes that the field is on the threshold of expansion and suggests some areas where new work is needed.

OTHER RESEARCH AIDS

16:21 Witherell, Julian W., ed. *The Republic of Turkey: An American Perspective: A Guide to U.S. Official Documents and Government-Sponsored Publications.* Washington, DC: Library of Congress, 1988. This annotated and indexed compilation includes lists of documents on U.S.-Turkish relations (1919–1939), Armenian-Turkish relations, and the Lausanne conference.

16:22 _____. *The United States and Africa: Guide to U.S. Official Documents and Government-Sponsored Publications on Africa, 1785–1975.* Washington, DC: Library of Congress, 1978. This collection provides lists of documents for all of Africa. Indexed with some annotations.

16:23 Duignan, Peter, ed. *Handbook of American Resources for African Studies.* Stanford, CA: Hoover Institution on War, Revolution, and Peace, 1967. Duignan has prepared a valuable compilation of library and manuscript collections, with some discussion of the holdings. Indexed.

16:24 Shavit, David, ed. *The United States in Africa: A Historical Dictionary.* This collection contains brief entries on selected Americans in Africa from the eighteenth century with some references and a short bibliographical essay (1:233).

16:25 _____. *The United States in the Middle East: A Historical Dictionary.* Shavit presents brief entries for a selection of Americans active in the Middle East from the late eighteenth century. Some references and a short bibliographical essay (1:261).

16:26 Simon, Reeva S. *The Modern Middle East: A Guide to Research Tools in the Social Sciences.* Boulder: Westview Press, 1978. This volume emphasizes pertinent reference works. Its primary stress is on modern history, political science, sociology, and anthropology. Subject index.

Overviews

UNITED STATES AND AFRICA

16:27 Chester, Edward W. *Clash of Titans: Africa and U.S. Foreign Policy.* This is one of the few comprehensive surveys covering both North and South Africa, with the bulk of the narrative dealing with those years between the American revolution and World War II. It touches on economic, religious, and cultural contacts as well as political affairs, relying heavily on the Foreign Relations series (2:253).

16:28 Duignan, Peter, and L. H. Gann. *The United States and Africa: A History.* Duignan provides a comprehensive survey from the seventeenth century, focusing on American responses to Africa. Through most of the interwar period, Africa remained a backwater for Americans, with only limited official representation and a few thousand businessmen, missionaries, hunters, and photographers. The missionaries had perhaps the most significant impact, especially on the first generation of African nationalist leaders (2:255).

16:29 Howe, Russell Warren. *Along the Afric Shore: An Historic Review of Two Centuries of U.S.-African Relations.* New York: Barnes and Noble, 1975. Howe surveys African affairs with a critical eye, emphasizing the spasmodic nature of American relations with the continent and explaining that the interwar years saw a decline in these ties as trade between Europe and the continent revived. He limits his discussion for this period to developments in Liberia and Ethiopia.

16:30 McCarthy, Michael. *Dark Continent: Africa as Seen by Americans.* McCarthy discusses

American representations or images of Africa as a physical space in the late nineteenth and early twentieth centuries (2:257).

16:31   Rosenthal, Eric. *Stars and Stripes in Africa: Being a History of American Achievements in Africa by Explorers, Missionaries, Pirates, Adventurers, Hunters, Miners, Merchants, Scientists, Soldiers, Showmen, Engineers, and Others with Some Account of Africans Who Have Played a Part in American Affairs.* London: G. Routledge and Sons, 1938. A series of short chapters in this rather disorganized work concentrate on southern Africa but also cover Liberia and Ethiopia. Bibliography.

16:32   Skinner, Elliott P. *African Americans and U.S. Policy toward Africa, 1850–1924: In Defense of Black Nationality.* Skinner explains that although African-Americans were an embattled minority in their own land, they took an active part from the end of the nineteenth century in trying to influence U.S. policy in Africa, knowing that their fate in the United States was intimately linked to the position of Africa in the minds of their fellow citizens and the international community (9:289).

UNITED STATES, THE MIDDLE EAST, AND NORTH AFRICA

16:33   Bryson, Thomas A. *American Diplomatic Relations with the Middle East, 1784–1975: A Survey.* See chapter 2 of this Guide (2:403).

16:34   _____. *Tars, Turks, and Tankers: The Role of the United States Navy in the Middle East, 1800–1979.* See chapter 2 of this Guide (2:404).

16:35   DeNovo, John A. *American Interests and Policies in the Middle East, 1900–1939.* See chapter 13 of this Guide (13:144).

16:36   Gallagher, Charles F. *The United States and North Africa: Morocco, Algeria, and Tunisia.* See chapter 2 of this Guide (2:259).

16:37   Gordon, Leland James. *American Relations with Turkey, 1830–1930: An Economic Interpretation.* See chapter 9 of this Guide (9:294).

16:38   Said, Edward W. *Orientalism.* New York: Pantheon Books, 1978. Reprint 1994 (Vintage Books). This classic study describes how intellectual traditions are created and transmitted. Said criticizes western scholars who present the Orient as being mysterious, unchanging, and ultimately inferior. Although his study focuses more on European than American scholarship, his arguments provide an essential starting point for anyone studying the Middle East.

16:39   Thomas, Lewis V., and Richard N. Frye. *The United States and Turkey and Iran.* Cambridge, MA: Harvard University Press, 1951. This work concentrates on cultural and historical development in Turkey and Iran (1800–1950), with one brief chapter on U.S.-Turkish and U.S-Iranian relations.

16:40   Zingg, Paul J. "Sand, Camels and the U.S.A.: American Perceptions of North Africa." In *Through Foreign Eyes: Western Attitudes toward North Africa,* ed. Alf Andrew Heggoy, 93–140. Washington, DC: University Press of America, 1982. Zingg examines some of the twentieth-century roots of American misperceptions of North Africa. In the first half of the century, U.S. policies were generally influenced by the desire to maintain good relations with France.

U.S. MISSIONARIES AND ARAB NATIONALISM

16:41   Al-Sayegh, Fatma. "American Missionaries in the UAE Region in the Twentieth Century." *Middle Eastern Studies* 32 (January 1996): 120–39. The author argues that British officials were suspicious of American missionaries in the region and did what they could to restrict their activities.

16:42   Antonius, George. *The Arab Awakening: The Story of the Arab National Movement.* Philadelphia: J. B. Lippincott, 1939. Reprint 1979 (G. P. Putnam). This is a classic account of the Arab intellectual awakening, which the author traces to the influences of American missionaries. He reflects Arab resentment of secret Allied wartime treaties (and the assent of Woodrow Wilson), which divided the defunct Ottoman empire and undermined Arab nationalism. Recently, his conclusions have come in for considerable criticism, but the work remains an important starting point. Bibliography.

16:43   Bergman, Hermas J. "The Diplomatic Missionary: John Van Ess in Iraq." *Muslim World* 72 (July-October 1982): 180–96. Van Ess served as a missionary and consul in Iraq during the first half of the twentieth century. He established close ties with Iraqi leaders and State Department officials, often speaking on behalf of Arab and Iraqi interests.

16:44   Daniel, Robert L. *American Philanthropy in the Near East, 1820–1960.* Daniel concentrates on early efforts by American missionaries to educate Middle Eastern peoples through their schools and colleges and covers the activities of Near East Relief, which expended $100 million on relief in the aftermath of World War I (6:272).

16:45   Earle, Edward Mead. "American Missions in the Near East." *Foreign Affairs* 7 (April 1929): 398–417. Earle claims that the missionary activity in the Near East outstripped all other American activities up to the 1920s and asserts that the missionaries had an important role in arousing nationalism among the subject peoples of the Ottoman empire.

16:46   Grabill, Joseph L. *Protestant Diplomacy and the Near East: Missionary Influence on American Policy, 1810–1927.* See chapter 9 of this Guide (9:295).

16:47   Kaplan, Robert D. *The Arabists: The Romance of an American Elite.* New York: Free Press, 1993. The author presents a critical survey of twentieth-century Arabists, detailing ties between missionaries and diplomats. Kaplan attributes considerable influence to the Arabists in the formation of U.S. Middle Eastern policy.

Biographical Studies

JOSEPH GREW

16:48   Grew, Joseph C. *Turbulent Era: A Diplomatic Record of Forty Years, 1904–1945.* This Amer-

ican diplomat's memoirs give extensive treatment to U.S. participation at the Lausanne conference and to American relations with Turkey during his tenure as U.S. ambassador, 1927–1932. Edited by Walter Johnson, assisted by Nancy Harvison Hooker (14:177).

16:49   Heinrichs, Waldo H. *American Ambassador: Joseph C. Grew and the Development of the United States Diplomatic Tradition.* This work contains three chapters on American-Turkish relations during the time of Grew's tenure as U.S. ambassador to Turkey (1927–1932) and discusses his representation of missionary interests and his aid in laying the groundwork for better American-Turkish relations (11:497).

OTHERS

16:50   Bryson, Thomas A. "Admiral Mark Lambert Bristol: An Open Door Diplomat in Turkey." Bristol opposed the Armenian mandate and sought to achieve American economic parity with the British and French in post–World War I Turkey (13:158).

16:51   Childs, J. Rives. *Foreign Service Farewell: My Years in the Near East.* Charlottesville: University Press of Virginia for Randolph-Macon College, 1969. This is the memoir of a diplomat whose career in the Middle East began in 1923 and who held posts throughout the region. In the 1930s, while posted to Cairo, he did all he could to mix with local Egyptians. Childs was consistently outspoken, which caused him problems. He warned, for example, against establishing too close ties with Israel.

16:52   Gates, Caleb F. *Not to Me Only.* Princeton: Princeton University Press, 1940. This memoir by a former president of Robert College covers the World War I years in Istanbul and shows the influence that American missionary-educators had on the shaping of U.S. policy in the Middle East during and after the war.

16:53   Hare, Paul J. *Diplomatic Chronicles of the Middle East: A Biography of Ambassador Raymond A. Hare.* Lanham, MD: University Press of America, 1993. This work covers Hare's forty-year career, largely in the Middle East. It quotes extensively from an interview located at Georgetown University's Foreign Affairs Oral History Program. Hare was a practitioner of classical diplomacy, trying always to merge the desirable with the possible. A cautious man, he believed military force should only be used as a last resort. Describing the State Department as a bureaucratic minefield on Middle Eastern issues by the mid-1960s, he chose to retire in 1966.

16:54   Patrick, Mary Mills. *Under Five Sultans.* See chapter 13 of this Guide (13:164).

16:55   Hancock, W. K. *Smuts.* These volumes provide a detailed and favorable biography of the South African leader. Hancock discusses similarities between the views on peace of Smuts and Woodrow Wilson in 1918 and on relations between the South African and FDR in the years leading up to U.S. entry into World War II (14:217).

United States and the Middle East, 1919–1941

16:56   Baram, Philip J. *The Department of State in the Middle East, 1919–1945.* Philadelphia: University of Pennsylvania Press, 1978. Baram discusses in detail the various foreign service officers responsible for the shaping of American policy vis-à-vis the Middle East. He argues that the United States worked to dismantle the imperial structures in the region to further American commerce.

16:57   Curti, Merle E., and Kendall Birr. *Prelude to Point Four: American Technical Missions Overseas, 1838–1938.* This work touches on technical assistance efforts and the King-Crane and Harbord missions (13:57).

16:58   DeNovo, John A. "On the Sidelines: The United States and the Middle East between the Wars, 1919–1939." In *The Great Powers in the Middle East, 1919–1939,* ed. Uriel Dann, 225–37. New York: Holmes and Meier, 1988. Despite the official government retreat from a forward position in the Middle East, American cultural and economic interests continued to expand. On the eve of World War II, Washington remained, politically, very much on the sidelines in the region.

16:59   Fromkin, David. *A Peace to End All Peace: Creating the Modern Middle East, 1914–1922.* New York: H. Holt, 1989. Reprint 1990 (Avon Books). Included in this readable, detailed account of the final years of the Ottoman empire from 1908 are useful chapters on the early post–World War I period up to 1922, featuring European diplomacy but with some attention to U.S. policies as well. Bibliography. The 1990 reprint is titled *A Peace to End All Peace: The Fall of the Ottoman Empire and the Creation of the Modern Middle East.*

16:60   Rubin, Barry. "America as Junior Partner: Anglo-American Relations in the Middle East, 1919–1939." In *The Great Powers in the Middle East, 1919–1939,* ed. Uriel Dann, 238–51. New York: Holmes and Meier, 1988. Based on their experiences as junior partners to Great Britain during the interwar years, American officials concluded that British imperialism in the Middle East was doomed and destabilizing.

16:61   Sachar, Howard M. *The Emergence of the Middle East: 1914–1924.* Sachar examines the complex negotiations among the European powers that led to the partition of the Ottoman empire. He presents a bleak picture of the region, arguing that its revived importance after the war came not as a result of any new creativity or productivity on the part of its inhabitants but from its strategic location. Even local nationalists, he claims, recognized that much could be gained from the west after the long night of Ottoman rule. Bibliography (13:150).

16:62   _____. *Europe Leaves the Middle East, 1936–1954.* New York: Alfred A. Knopf, 1972. This book devotes considerable space to official U.S. reaction to the Zionist question. It provides a comprehensive study, drawing on some sources in Arabic and Hebrew as well as those in western languages. Sachar traces many of the problems of the post-1945 period—the growth of Arab xenophobia, for example—to the poorly developed policies of Britain and France during the mandate period. Extensive bibliography.

16:63   Sheean, Vincent. *Personal History.* New York: Literary Guild, 1935. Reprint 1986 (Citadel Press). Sheean presents fascinating essays from his experiences in the 1920s as a journalist in Iran, Morocco, and Palestine.

16:64   Stivers, William. "Woodrow Wilson and the Arab World: The Liberal Dilemma." In *The Prospects of Liberalism: Nine Essays,* ed. Timothy Fuller, 106–23. Colorado Springs: Colorado College, 1984. The dilemma for liberals like Wilson and his successors was that they supported self-determination but demanded that change be orderly. In the third world, change was anything but orderly; hence, Wilson usually endorsed continued control by western powers, minus the heavy-handedness of the nineteenth century. This proved to be the case especially in the Arab world. Liberalism, says Stivers, needed to reshape itself to remain relevant.

16:65   Stookey, Robert W. *America and the Arab States: An Uneasy Encounter.* New York: Wiley, 1975. Stookey briefly treats the advent of Protestant missionaries, the growth of American humanitarian and secular interests, and the U.S. role in obtaining a share of regional oil for American companies during the interwar period.

PARIS PEACE CONFERENCE

16:66   Buzanski, Peter M. "The Inter-Allied Investigation of the Greek Invasion of Smyrna, 1919." *Historian* 25 (May 1963): 325–43. This essay examines the role of an American naval officer serving on an interallied commission to investigate the Greek landings at Smyrna.

16:67   Helmreich, Paul C. *From Paris to Sèvres: The Partition of the Ottoman Empire at the Peace Conference of 1919–1920.* See chapter 13 of this Guide (13:161).

16:68   Howard, Harry N. *The Partition of Turkey: A Diplomatic History, 1913–1923.* The author discusses the partition of the Ottoman empire and provides a background to America's Turkish policy during the war and at the Paris Peace Conference. Extensive bibliography (13:162).

16:69   Rappaport, Joseph. "Zionism as a Factor in Allied Central Power Controversy (1914–1918)." In *Early History of Zionism in America: Papers Presented at the Conference on the Early History of Zionism in America, Convened by the American Jewish Historical Society and the Theodor Herzl Foun-*

dation, *in New York City, on December Twenty-sixth and Twenty-seventh, Nineteen Hundred and Fifty-five,* ed. Isidore Meyer, 297–35. New York: American Jewish Historical Society, 1958. Reprint 1977 (Arno Press). Although President Wilson came late to public support of the Balfour Declaration (1919–1920), Wilsonian idealism contributed to securing a privileged position for Zionists at Versailles.

ARMENIA

16:70   Bierstadt, Edward H. *The Great Betrayal: A Survey of the Near East Problem.* New York: R. M. McBride and Co., 1924. The author concludes that the United States compromised efforts to salvage an independent Armenia in deference to the aspirations of American commercial interests in Turkey.

16:71   Brown, Philip M. "The Mandate over Armenia." *American Journal of International Law* 14 (January 1920): 396–406. Senate opposition to the Armenian mandate was based on the premise that U.S. acceptance of this obligation was tantamount to adherence to the League of Nations Covenant.

16:72   Bryson, Thomas A. "The Armenia-America Society: A Factor in American-Turkish Relations, 1919–1924." *Records of the American Catholic Historical Society* 82 (June 1971): 83–105. This essay demonstrates the manner in which an ethnic lobby tried to shape U.S. policy on the Armenian question in the postwar era.

16:73   _____. "Mark Lambert Bristol, U.S. Navy, Admiral-Diplomat: His Influence on the Armenian Mandate Question." Bristol was influential in producing Senate rejection of President Wilson's proposed mandate for Armenia (13:152).

16:74   _____. *Walter George Smith.* Washington, DC: Catholic University of America Press, 1977. Smith was an Armenophile who worked to achieve Armenian goals at the Paris Peace Conference.

16:75   _____. "Woodrow Wilson and the Armenian Mandate: A Reassessment." See chapter 13 of this Guide (13:153). See also Bryson, "An American Mandate for Armenia: A Link in British Near Eastern Policy," *Armenian Review* 21 (Summer

1968): 23–41, and his "John Sharp Williams: An Advocate for the Armenian Mandate, 1919–1920," ibid. 26 (Autumn 1973): 23–42.

16:76   Daniel, Robert L. "The Armenian Question and American-Turkish Relations, 1914–1927." *Mississippi Valley Historical Review* 46 (September 1959): 252–75. Daniel contends that America's concern for Armenian rights and the question of self-determination aggravated relations between the United States and Turkey. Harsh treatment of Armenians by the Turks created an unstable diplomatic environment, but American policymakers never considered the Armenian question serious enough to warrant the use of force.

16:77   Gidney, James B. *A Mandate for Armenia.* See chapter 13 of this Guide (13:154).

16:78   Grabill, Joseph L. "Missionary Influence on American Relations with the Near East, 1914–1923, parts 1 and 2." The author assesses the influence that missionaries brought to bear on the course of U.S.-Turkish relations during the interwar years, particularly on the Armenian question (13:155).

16:79   Housepian, Marjorie. *The Smyrna Affair.* New York: Harcourt Brace Jovanovich, 1971. The author concentrates on the fire that destroyed Smyrna (Izmir) in 1922 at the end of the Greek-Turkish war. She criticizes American diplomacy for compromising Armenian goals in favor of the Turks. Housepian is highly critical of the U.S. high commissioner to Turkey, Admiral Mark Bristol. Bibliography.

16:80   Hovannisian, Richard G. *Armenia on the Road to Independence, 1918.* See chapter 13 of this Guide (13:156).

16:81   _____. *The Republic of Armenia. Vol. 1: The First Year, 1918–1919.* Berkeley: University of California Press, 1971. This volume provides further material on the Armenian Republic and continues the development of events in the Transcaucasus, which so concerned the U.S. government in the post–World War I era. Extensive bibliography.

16:82   Kazemzadeh, Firuz. *The Struggle for Transcaucasia, 1917–1921.* See chapter 13 of this Guide (13:157).

16:83   Malkasian, Mark. "The Disintegration of the Armenian Cause in the United States, 1918–1927." *International Journal of Middle East Studies* 16 (August 1984): 349–65. Malkasian examines the formation, activity, and gradual disintegration of the Armenian consensus in the United States. Inherent divisions within the Armenian cause led to complete disarray by 1927.

16:84   Nevins, Allan. *Henry White: Thirty Years of American Diplomacy.* Nevins provides correspondence between White and Senator Lodge, which is valuable in understanding the U.S. consideration of the Armenian question at the Paris Peace Conference, 1919 (11:486).

16:85   Westermann, William L. "The Armenian Problem and the Disruption of Turkey." In *What Really Happened at Paris: The Story of the Peace Conference, 1918–1919,* ed. Edward M. House and Charles Seymour, 176–203. New York: Charles Scribner's Sons, 1921. Westermann examines Wilson's consideration of the Armenian question and his qualified acceptance of the mandate at the Paris Peace Conference.

WORLD WAR I AND THE MANDATE ISSUE

16:86   Daniel, Robert L. "The Friendship of Woodrow Wilson and Cleveland Dodge." *Mid-America* 43 (July 1961): 182–96. Daniel describes the close relationship between these two men and details Dodge's considerable influence on the course of American foreign policy in the Near East during Wilson's administration.

16:87   Davis, M. Thomas. "The King-Crane Commission and the American Abandonment of Self-Determination." *American-Arab Affairs* 9 (Summer 1984): 55–66. Davis concludes that there is no evidence Wilson ever rejected findings of his commission that recommended self-determination for Palestine.

16:88   Evans, Laurence. *United States Policy and the Partition of Turkey, 1914–1924.* See chapter 13 of this Guide (13:160).

16:89   Howard, Harry N. *The King-Crane Commission: An American Inquiry in the Middle East.* See chapter 13 of this Guide (13:166).

MISSIONARIES AND PHILANTHROPY

16:90   Barton, James L. *Story of Near East Relief (1915–1930).* Barton discusses the inception of Near East Relief, its scope, history, and aims. He claims that the organization made no attempt to influence the formulation of U.S. Middle East policy (13:143).

16:91   Bryson, Thomas A. "A Note on Near East Relief: Walter George Smith, Cardinal Gibbons, and the Question of Discrimination against Catholics." *Muslim World* 61 (July 1971): 202–9. Smith persuaded Gibbons that no discrimination against Roman Catholics (especially Armenian Catholics) was being practiced (1919–1920) and that the cardinal and American Catholics should support Near East Relief.

16:92   Carter, B. L. "On Spreading the Gospel to Egyptians Sitting in Darkness: The Political Problem of Missionaries in Egypt in the 1930s." *Middle Eastern Studies* 20 (October 1984): 18–36. Carter presents a rather critical view of missionary (largely American) activity in Egypt, discussing problems created for British and American but most importantly Egyptian officials.

16:93   Curti, Merle E. *American Philanthropy Abroad: A History.* Curti claims American efforts reached a high point in the Middle East during and immediately after World War I (14:623).

16:94   Horton, George. *The Blight of Asia: An Account of the Systematic Extermination of Christian Populations by Mohammedans and of the Culpability of Certain Great Powers, with a True Story of the Burning of Smyrna.* New York: Bobbs-Merrill, 1926. A consular official who served in Turkey (1920–1927) asserts that the U.S. government did not assist the American missionaries in the post–World War I era but rather compromised their interests in favor of commercial activity.

THE PALESTINIAN QUESTION

The United States and the Palestinian Question: Overviews

16:95   Adler, Selig. "The United States and the Middle Eastern Dilemma, 1917–1939." *Maryland Historian* 7 (Spring 1976): 1–17. If FDR had put more pressure on Britain about Palestine, many Jews might have been saved from the Holocaust. However, several factors combined to inhibit the administration, including isolationism, anglophobia, the State Department's hostility to Zionism, Arab propaganda, and pressure from American oil companies concerned with maintaining friendly relations with the Arab majority in the Middle East.

16:96   Ahmed, Hisham H. "From the Balfour Declaration to World War II: The U.S. Stand on Palestinian Self-Determination." *Arab Studies Quarterly* 12 (Winter 1990–Spring 1991): 9–41. U.S. support for self-determination was selective; beyond the defeated Central Powers, it was applied only where it worked to American benefit. Wilson's Zionist advisers influenced him to support the Balfour Declaration, and later he kept the truth about Palestine from the American people and Congress. His pronouncements formed the basis on which subsequent policy was formulated, contributing to the denial of Palestinian rights.

16:97   _____. "Roots of Denial: American Stand on Palestinian Self-Determination from the Balfour Declaration to World War II." In *U.S. Policy on Palestine: From Wilson to Clinton,* ed. Michael W. Suleiman, 28–57. Normal, IL: Association for Arab-University, University Graduates, 1995. Focusing on events of the Wilson administration, Ahmed argues that the Anglo-American Convention of 1924 put the U.S. seal of approval on the British mandate in Palestine, including the Balfour Declaration. FDR continued the policy of ignoring the Palestinians. Bibliography.

16:98   Brecher, Frank W. *Reluctant Ally: United States Foreign Policy toward the Jews from Wilson to Roosevelt.* New York: Greenwood Press, 1991. The policy of the United States had been consistent since Wilson's administration: to keep the Palestine issue and the question of Jewish refugees in the background and let Britain deal with them. There were frequent warm statements of support, without any real policy change until the end of World War II. The Holocaust forced Truman, albeit reluctantly, to support a Jewish state.

16:99   Davidson, Lawrence. *America's Palestine: Popular and Official Perceptions from Balfour to Israeli Statehood.* Gainesville: University Press of Florida, 2001. In this revisionist study of U.S. relations with Palestine, Davidson argues that Americans came to see Zionism as a form of altruistic imperialism. American Zionists used this popular sentiment and effective lobbying techniques to outmaneuver the State Department. Thus, a powerful and determined interest group turned the U.S. political system to its own advantage and shaped foreign policy.

16:100   _____. "The State Department and Zionism, 1917–1945: A Reevaluation." *Middle East Policy* 7 (October 1999): 21–37. In a provocative essay, Davidson challenges the widely held view that State Department officials were unreasonably anti-Zionist, even antisemitic. He believes that historians making such claims have often been too involved emotionally in the subject and that much of what they have written is bad history. Actions of U.S. officials, he cautions, should be put into context; when that is done, it becomes apparent that they were guided by the prevailing traditions of American foreign policy.

16:101   Friedrich, Carl J. *American Policy toward Palestine.* Washington, DC: Public Affairs Press, 1944. Reprint 1971 (Greenwood Press). This summary of interwar governmental policies on Zionism also contains a collection of pertinent documents.

16:102   Khalidi, Walid, ed. *From Haven to Conquest: Readings in Zionism and the Palestine Problem until 1948.* Washington, DC: Institute for Palestine Studies, 1987. This collection of documents, selected to illustrate the process by which Zionism sought to wrest control of Palestine and its surroundings from the Arabs, is preceded by a lengthy introduction in which the editor details the unfolding of the Palestine tragedy. In addition to several documents from the Wilson years, there is a section titled "Green Light from the White House, 1939–1947." First published in 1971.

16:103   Knee, Stuart E. "Jewish Non-Zionism in

America and Palestine Commitment, 1917–1941." *Jewish Social Studies* 39 (Summer 1977): 209–26. Knee focuses on the non-Zionist Jews in the United States, who have been relatively neglected. By 1941, under wartime exigencies, they had moved so close to the Zionist position that they were absorbed.

16:104   Plesur, Milton. "The Relations between the United States and Palestine (1917–1945)." *Judaism* 3 (September 1954): 469–79. Plesur surveys American policy from Woodrow Wilson's reaction to the Balfour Declaration to President Roosevelt's handling of the Palestine question during World War II. He concludes that the U.S. government attempted to follow a neutral course on Palestine in the interwar years. Although official rhetoric might have supported a Jewish national home, it meant "absolutely nothing." Only its involvement in World War II drew the United States into the Middle East.

16:105   Rook, Robert E. "An American in Palestine: Elwood Mead and Zionist Water Resource Planning, 1923–1936." *Arab Studies Quarterly* 22 (Winter 2000): 71–89. Using his experience from the American west, Mead was the first American to advise Zionist leaders on water management issues and to lobby the British mandatory regime on behalf of the Zionist program. His recommendations, many based on Wyoming irrigation laws, ultimately became Israeli realities.

16:106   Urofsky, Melvin I. *American Zionism from Herzl to the Holocaust.* Garden City, NY: Anchor Press, 1975. Reprint 1995 (University of Nebraska Press). This comprehensive study argues that Zionism in the United States has been part of and reflective of larger trends in society, enjoying its greatest successes precisely when its goals and methods have coincided with the dominant trends in the broader society. Zionist leaders, especially during the Wilson years, enjoyed considerable success in matters related to the Palestine mandate.

The United States and the Balfour Declaration

16:107   Lebow, Richard Ned. "Woodrow Wilson and the Balfour Declaration." See chapter 13 of this Guide (13:168).

16:108 Parzen, Herbert. "Brandeis and the Balfour Declaration." *Herzl Year Book* 5 (1963): 309–50. Parzen believes that Wilson favorably considered the Balfour Declaration because of a growing pro-Zionist sentiment among his top advisers.

16:109 Stein, Leonard. *The Balfour Declaration.* Stein, an early convert to Zionism and later an official in mandate Palestine, has written an exhaustive study of the Balfour Declaration, showing how it was altered as it moved through the British bureaucracy. Although President Wilson was only mildly interested in the document and in Zionism generally, that was a great advance over thinking in the State Department. A chapter on American Jewry reveals their limited support of Zionism during World War I. Bibliography (13:170).

The 1920s

16:110 Cohen, Naomi W. *The Year after the Riots: American Responses to the Palestine Crisis of 1929–30.* Detroit: Wayne State University Press, 1988. Cohen sees the crisis as a turning point in Zionist history. Enemies of the movement, including many in the State Department, appeared to have won a victory in the aftermath of the riots, for the Jewish community had shown itself too fragmented to respond effectively. This failure, however, encouraged the Zionist community in Palestine toward greater self-reliance, which grew throughout the 1930s, facilitating the transition to statehood after World War II.

16:111 Davidson, Lawrence. "Zionism, Socialism and United States Support for the Jewish Colonization of Palestine in the 1920s." *Arab Studies Quarterly* 18 (Summer 1996): 1–16. The American image of Zionism in Palestine provided a strong enough illusion of capitalism and American values to generate ongoing support for what was in truth socialist development.

16:112 Knee, Stuart E. "Anglo-American Relations in Palestine, 1919–1925: An Experiment in *Realpolitik.*" *Journal of American Studies of Turkey* 5 (Spring 1997): 3–18. Knee analyzes the sharp change in U.S. policy from Wilson's humanitarian-collective concerns to the realpolitik of his Republican successors, which was especially apparent in Palestine. The new policy saw the submergence of idealism, belligerence toward Great Britain, and the preeminence of the business motive; this formula encouraged neither peace nor conciliation in the mandate and was abandoned after 1945.

16:113 _____. "The King-Crane Commission of 1919: The Articulation of Political Anti-Zionism." The author claims that the members of the King-Crane Commission were anti-Zionist; therefore, the commission's report opposed Zionist goals in Palestine (13:167).

The 1930s

16:114 Adler, Selig. "The Roosevelt Administration and Zionism: The Pre-War Years, 1933–1939." In *Essays in American Zionism, 1917–1948,* ed. Melvin I. Urofsky, 132–48. New York: Herzl Press, 1978. Although FDR was ultimately responsible for the failure to smooth the way for European Jews to emigrate to Palestine, Adler focuses on the so-called Arabists of the State Department, especially Wallace Murray, whose deeply entrenched anti-Zionism helped maintain the status quo in U.S. policy.

16:115 _____. "United States Policy on Palestine in the FDR Era." *American Jewish Historical Quarterly* 62 (September 1972): 11–29. This richly detailed excerpt from a colloquium on America and the Holy Land features Adler and several other experts discussing their research on FDR and Zionism. Adler concludes that the president was a master at hiding his personal views about the prospects of a Jewish state in Palestine.

16:116 Berman, Aaron. *Nazism, the Jews, and American Zionism, 1933–1948.* Detroit: Wayne State University Press, 1990. Berman studies the developing and changing worldview of American Zionists, including their view of Palestinian Arabs. Bibliography.

16:117 Medoff, Rafael. *Bakhsheesh Diplomacy: Secret Negotiations between American Jewish Leaders and Arab Officials on the Eve of World War II.* Lanham, MD: Lexington Books, 2001. Medoff writes of two unsuccessful attempts by American

Jewish millionaires, Felix Warburg and Edward Norman, to bribe Arab leaders of Iraq and Transjordan to accept Arab immigrants from Palestine in the 1930s.

16:118 _____. "Herbert Hoover's Plan for Palestine: A Forgotten Episode in American Middle East Diplomacy." *American Jewish History* 79 (Summer 1990): 449–76. In the late 1930s, Hoover became interested in the Palestine issue, suggesting that Jewish refugees be accommodated in central Africa. Later, at the end of World War II, he suggested that the valleys of the Tigris and Euphrates Rivers be irrigated to prepare for the resettlement there of the Palestinian Arabs. Neither of these plans came to fruition, says Medoff, because they did not fit with great power interests in the region.

16:119 Rosenblum, Chanoch. "The New Zionist Organization's Diplomatic Battle against Partition, 1936–1937." *Studies in Zionism* 11 (Autumn 1990): 157–81. Revisionists under Vladimir Jabotinsky tried to avoid the partition of Palestine and to increase the number of European Jews allowed to enter the mandate. They failed, however, to get the United States to pressure Britain on these two points because Americans feared the adverse reaction of the Arabs and also because the American Jewish community was badly split and therefore unable to influence the State Department.

Americans and Zionism: Jews and Others

16:120 Adler, Selig. "American Jewry and That Explosive Statehood Question, 1933–1945." In *A Bicentennial Festschrift for Jacob Rader Marcus,* ed. Bertram Wallace Korn, 5–21. New York: Ktav Pub. House, 1976. Adler elaborates on divisions within the Jewish community in the 1930s over the statehood question. Bickering was continual, not only between groups but within them as well. Adler suggests that a united community front at critical points might have gained more administration support.

16:121 Ariel, Yaakov S. *On Behalf of Israel: American Fundamentalist Attitudes toward Jews, Judaism, and Zionism, 1865–1945.* Brooklyn: Carlson Publishing, 1991. Ariel discusses the spread of dispensationalism in the United States during the late nineteenth and early twentieth centuries, with implications for American policy toward a Jewish state. This minority Christian belief holds that humans must respond in specific ways to show their obedience to God and that the current dispensation is to support the founding of a nation of Israel to help make ready for the second coming of Jesus. Ariel details the efforts of two prominent Christian Zionists, William E. Blackstone and Arno C. Gaebelein, in the early decades of the twentieth century.

16:122 Cohen, Naomi W. "The Specter of Zionism: American Opinions, 1917–1922." In *Essays in American Zionism, 1917–1948,* ed. Melvin I. Urofsky, 95–116. New York: Herzl Press, 1978. Cohen argues that wartime successes of Zionism spurred anti-semitism in the postwar United States, often concealed in the guise of anti-Zionism.

16:123 Gelvin, James J. "Zionism and Representation of 'Jewish Palestine' at the New York World's Fair, 1939–1940." *International History Review* 22 (March 2000): 37–64. This article details how the pavilion at the fair became a focal point for Zionist political agitation, transforming it into a symbolic site for the U.S. movement.

16:124 Goldstein, Yaacov. "American Jewish Socialists' Attitude to Zionism and Palestine in the 1920s." *YIVO Annual* 23 (1996): 419–44. Goldstein discusses early socialist disdain for Jewish nationalism and the changing views of Abraham Cahan, a leading socialist, after he visited Europe and Palestine in 1925.

16:125 Knee, Stuart E. *The Concept of Zionist Dissent in the American Mind, 1917–1941.* New York: R. Speller, 1979. Knee analyzes the several groups within the anti-Zionist coalition of the 1920s, which had fallen apart by 1941 because of varied interests and changed political circumstances abroad. Most importantly, there was no Jewish anti-Zionism in the United States by 1941 as there had been in the 1920s. It was only then, argues Knee, that the idea of an independent Jewish state was formulated.

16:126 _____. "Jewish Socialists in America: The Debate on Zionism." *Wiener Library Bulletin* 28, nos. 33–34 (1975): 13–24. Knee surveys the changing nature of the debate on Zionism among American

Jewish socialists from World War I to World War II, with particular reference to the issue of Palestine. He also discusses the anti-Zionist views of American communists.

16:127   Medoff, Rafael. *Zionism and the Arabs: An American-Jewish Dilemma, 1898–1948.* Westport, CT: Praeger, 1997. American Jews modified Zionism so that it would in no way pose a barrier to American Jewish acculturation, but they drew the line at accepting a binational, democratic state in Palestine.

16:128   Murphy, Bruce Allen. *The Brandeis/Frankfurter Connection: The Secret Political Activities of Two Supreme Court Justices.* New York: Oxford University Press, 1982. Murphy presents a brief but detailed account of Brandeis's activities. During the years 1917–1933, he often worked through intermediaries, such as then professor Felix Frankfurter, on behalf of Zionism.

16:129   Parzen, Herbert. "American Zionism and the Quest for a Jewish State, 1939–43." *Herzl Year Book* 4 (1962): 345–94. The American Jewish community, being the wealthiest and most secure by 1939, became the mainstay of Zionism, at least financially, once internal divisions had been resolved. Leading members exerted considerable pressure on American policymakers. By 1943, the community was ready for the statehood struggle.

16:130   Raider, Mark A. *The Emergence of American Zionism.* New York: New York University Press, 1998. Raider argues that Zionism had a major, positive effect in the American Jewish community long before the Biltmore conference (1942); it was central to the American Jewish experience.

The United States and "Israel"

16:131   Brown, Michael. "The American Element in the Rise of Golda Meir, 1906–1929." *Jewish History* 6, nos. 1–2 (1992): 35–50. Brown argues that Meir's American background was a crucial factor in her rise to power.

16:132   _____. *The Israeli-American Connection: Its Roots in the Yishuv, 1914–1945.* Detroit:

Wayne State University Press, 1996. In this study of six Jewish leaders in interwar Palestine, Brown argues that collectively they oriented the Zionist community toward the United States. The connections that they cultivated had much to do with the successful establishment of the state of Israel after World War II.

16:133   Gal, Allon. *David Ben-Gurion and the American Alignment for a Jewish State.* Translated by David S. Segal. Bloomington: Indiana University Press, 1991. Ben-Gurion understood the change in power relationships taking place in the late 1930s, and he built bridges to the United States in preparation for the future statehood struggle, while Weizmann and others continued to look to Britain.

16:134   _____. "Zionist Foreign Policy and Ben-Gurion's Visit to the United States in 1939." *Studies in Zionism* 7 (Spring 1986): 37–50. In the face of Britain's apparent determination to create an Arab state in Palestine rather than partition it, Ben-Gurion decided to turn to the United States to press Britain to alter its plans. Although he found American Jews badly divided, and unable or unwilling to bring effective pressure on the U.S. government, he continued this approach in succeeding years.

16:135   Grose, Peter. *Israel in the Mind of America.* New York: Alfred A. Knopf, 1983. Grose agues that the United States and Israel share a special relationship that goes back more than 150 years, and his study examines the entire period. In the interwar years, American Zionism was a mediocre endeavor, however, which allowed U.S. policy to be shaped by a handful of unremarkable professional diplomats at the State Department.

16:136   Medoff, Rafael. "Menachem Begin as George Washington: The Americanizing of the Jewish Revolt against the British." *American Jewish Archives* 46 (Fall-Winter 1994): 185–95. The Zionists tried to win public sympathy in the United States by presenting themselves as the founding fathers, the Palestinians as Indians, and the British as Redcoats.

The United States, Palestinians, and Other Arabs

16:137 Brecher, Frank W. "Charles R. Crane's Crusade for the Arabs, 1919–39." *Middle Eastern Studies* 24 (January 1988): 42–55. Brecher argues that Crane continued his efforts on behalf of Arabs throughout the interwar period and that his views became increasingly anti-Jewish.

16:138 Manuel, Frank E. *The Realities of American-Palestine Relations.* See chapter 13 of this Guide (13:169).

LAUSANNE (1923) AND MONTREUX (1936) CONFERENCES

16:139 Burns, Richard Dean. *Arms Control and Disarmament: A Bibliography.* This work lists books, essays, and dissertations relating to the conferences (1:136).

16:140 Davison, Roderic H. "Turkish Diplomacy from Mudros to Lausanne." In *The Diplomats, 1919–1939. Vol. 1: The Twenties,* ed. Gordon A. Craig and Felix Gilbert, 179–202. New York: Atheneum, 1965. In addition to dealing with postwar Turkish diplomacy, this essay treats the development of Turkish negotiations with the allies up to and including the Lausanne conference. First published in 1953.

16:141 DeLuca, Anthony R. "Montreux and Collective Security." *Historian* 38 (November 1975): 1–20. At the Montreux conference of 1936, the demilitarized zones at the Turkish Straits were abolished, new rules of passage were adopted, and the international administrative commission was eliminated.

16:142 Grew, Joseph C. "The Peace Conference of Lausanne, 1922–1923." *Proceedings of the American Philosophical Society* 98 (January 1954): 1–10. Although Grew goes into much greater detail in *Turbulent Era: A Diplomatic Record of Forty Years, 1904–1945* (1952) (16:48), this article is valuable for the "pen sketches" of such figures as Benito Mus-solini, Raymond Poincaré, Lord Curzon, Eleutherios Venizelos, Ismet Inonu, and George Chicherin.

16:143 Howard, Harry N. *Turkey, the Straits, and U.S. Policy.* Howard develops American-Turkish relations from the Treaty of 1830 through World War I, the Paris Peace Conference, and the Lausanne conference, when the initial postwar straits regime was adopted (2:426).

16:144 _____. "The United States and the Problem of the Turkish Straits." *Middle East Journal* 1 (January 1947): 59–72. This reference article briefly covers the Lausanne conference, the Montreux Convention, and the period immediately following World War II.

16:145 Nicolson, Harold. *Curzon: The Last Phase, 1919–1925: A Study in Post-War Diplomacy.* Boston: Houghton Mifflin, 1934. This biography focuses on the character and diplomacy of Britain's postwar foreign secretary, Lord Curzon, discussing weaknesses as well as strengths. The study builds slowly to the Lausanne conference, where, according to Nicolson, Curzon performed brilliantly. Anglo-French tensions in the Middle East receive considerable attention.

ECONOMIC INFLUENCES

16:146 Baram, Philip J. "Undermining the British: Department of State Policies in Egypt and the Suez Canal before and during World War II." *Historian* 40 (August 1978): 631–49. As Britain moved to adopt a more conciliatory policy toward Egypt following the Montreux conference, the State Department increased its competition with Britain, seeking power, prestige, and markets. The United States tried to show itself more sympathetic toward Egyptian nationalism than any other western power, believing that with the end of capitulations Egyptians would prefer American imports over those of France or Britain. This policy undermined Britain's attempts to strengthen its ties with Cairo and helped arouse Egyptian paranoia toward Britain.

16:147 Beard, Charles A., with G. H. E. Smith. *The Idea of National Interest: An Analytical Study in American Foreign Policy.* The authors describe Admiral Mark Bristol's efforts to achieve American parity with Britain in the Turkish economy (2:163).

16:148   Hogan, Michael J. *Informal Entente: The Private Structure of Cooperation in Anglo-American Economic Diplomacy, 1918–1928*. Hogan shows the limits of cooperation reached in negotiations over the rubber industry. The United States sought private and cooperative arrangements whereas Britain wanted government price-fixing schemes. Acrimony rather than harmony prevailed, though a useful chapter on Middle East oil details the institutionalizing of Anglo-American cooperation at the private level, which allowed American interests a share in Middle Eastern resources while avoiding state management and economic competition (14:252).

16:149   Issawi, Charles. "The Historical Development of US-Arab Economic Relations." *American-Arab Affairs* 3 (Winter 1982–1983): 14–21. Issawi presents a brief survey showing increasing interdependence.

16:150   Rosenberg, Emily S. *Financial Missionaries to the World: The Politics and Culture of Dollar Diplomacy, 1900–1930*. Rosenberg analyzes the efforts by government, bankers, and experts to integrate new and potentially risky areas into U.S. economic and strategic systems. She presents the history of dollar diplomacy as bridging the sub-disciplines of diplomatic, economic, and cultural history and includes brief studies of American financial missions to Liberia and Iran (11:91).

16:151   Trask, Roger R. "The United States and Turkish Nationalism: Investments and Technical Aid during the Ataturk Era." *Business History Review* 38 (Spring 1964): 58–77. Trask reviews American commercial and technical assistance activities in Turkey. He writes that the preponderance of economic influence gained by the United States after World War II had its roots in American policy of the interwar years. At that time Washington cemented good relations with Ankara by proving that it had no political objectives in the young republic and by supporting Ataturk's reforms.

16:152   Wilkins, Mira. *The Maturing of Multinational Enterprise: American Business Abroad from 1914 to 1970*. Cambridge, MA: Harvard University Press, 1974. U.S. companies invested heavily to gain foreign raw material supplies, especially oil and rubber, in the interwar period. Despite the hazards of the Depression, they became more multinational during the 1930s.

The Quest for Oil

16:153   Bilovich, Yossef. "The Quest for Oil in Bahrain, 1923–1930: A Study in British and American Policy." In *The Great Powers in the Middle East, 1919–1939*, ed. Uriel Dann, 252–73. New York: Holmes and Meier, 1988. The American oil concession in Bahrain, won with little assistance from the State Department and in the face of considerable British resistance, paved the way for the later concession in neighboring Saudi Arabia.

16:154   DeNovo, John A. "The Movement for an Aggressive American Oil Policy Abroad, 1918–1920." This essay treats the American anticipation of a postwar oil shortage and the aggressive effort of government and oil men to formulate a comprehensive policy to find new sources (13:77).

16:155   Earle, Edward Mead. "The Turkish Petroleum Company—A Study in Oleaginous Diplomacy." *Political Science Quarterly* 39 (June 1924): 265–77. This essay criticizes the State Department's effort (1920–1927) to assist American oil companies in their bid for new sources of petroleum in the Middle East and asserts that such action was inconsistent with the Monroe Doctrine. If the U.S. government expects European powers to recognize the economic implications of the Monroe Doctrine, it needs to recognize that they, too, have their particular spheres of interest.

16:156   Finnie, David H. *Desert Enterprise: Middle East Oil Industry in Its Local Environment*. Cambridge, MA: Harvard University Press, 1958. Finnie examines the origins of American oil concessions in the Middle East, the problems faced by the oil companies in dealing with the host countries and the U.S. government, and the impact of the companies on the peoples of the Middle East (1920–1939).

16:157   Fitzgerald, Edward Peter. "Business Diplomacy: Walter Teagle, Jersey Standard, and the Anglo-

French Pipeline Conflict in the Middle East, 1930–1931." *Business History Review* 67, no. 2 (Summer 1993): 207–45. International controversy arose over plans to build an oil pipeline from northern Iraq to the Mediterranean. Teagle devised a compromise, which the French and British accepted.

16:158 _____. "The Iraq Petroleum Company, Standard Oil of California, and the Contest for Eastern Arabia, 1930–1933." *International History Review* 13 (August 1991): 441–65. Fitzgerald relies on the archives of the Compagnie Française des Petroles (CFP) to refine our understanding of why the Iraq Petroleum Company lost the Saudi Arabian oil concession to Socal. Mainly, he argues, it lost because it showed less boldness than its competitor.

16:159 Gibb, George Sweet, and Evelyn H. Knowlton. *History of Standard Oil. Vol. 2: The Resurgent Years, 1911–1927.* New York: Harper, 1956. This work includes an excellent treatment of the State Department's use of the open door policy to support the effort of Standard Oil of New Jersey to gain access to Middle East oil in the 1920s.

16:160 Krasner, Stephen D. *Defending the National Interest: Raw Materials Investments and U.S. Foreign Policy.* Princeton: Princeton University Press, 1978. Where there were clear state interests as in Liberian rubber and Middle Eastern oil in the 1920s, the U.S. government was prepared to become actively engaged on behalf of American companies. Absent such interests, policymakers provided little support.

16:161 Lenczowski, George. *Oil and State in the Middle East.* Ithaca: Cornell University Press, 1960. This study considers the relations between American oil companies and their host countries in the Middle East (1920–1960), with special emphasis on the national aspirations of the latter and the legal rights of the former. Bibliography.

16:162 Mosley, Leonard. *Power Play: Oil in the Middle East.* New York: Random House, 1973. The author's readable account of the period 1920–1972 includes a discussion of U.S. governmental support for American oil men during the interwar period, concentrating on efforts in Iraq, Bahrain, and Saudi Arabia.

16:163 Nash, Gerald D. *United States Oil Policy, 1890–1964: Business and Government in Twentieth Century America.* See chapter 13 of this Guide (13:147).

16:164 Randall, Stephen J. *United States Foreign Oil Policy, 1919–1948: For Profits and Security.* U.S. policy developed to preserve and expand holdings overseas against emergent nationalism and competing great power interests. Oil companies were less dominant than many analysts have indicated. In the Middle East the American government used oil companies as an instrument of policy, thus furthering its own interests as well as those of the companies. On the eve of World War II, American interests were poised for a dramatic expansion in this traditional British sphere of influence (15:410).

16:165 Shwadran, Benjamin. *The Middle East, Oil, and the Great Powers.* 3d ed. New York: Wiley, 1974. Shwadran demonstrates the manner in which the U.S. government and the American oil industry worked during the interwar period to obtain oil concessions in the Middle East. First published in 1955.

16:166 Stivers, William. *Supremacy and Oil: Iraq, Turkey, and the Anglo-American World Order, 1918–1930.* Ithaca: Cornell University Press, 1982. Stivers details the early postwar economic crisis over oil. The United States moved in the wake of British power, achieving its objectives while avoiding the expenses incurred by Britain.

16:167 Stocking, George W. *Middle East Oil: A Study in Political and Economic Controversy.* Nashville: Vanderbilt University Press, 1970. This work surveys American oil diplomacy from the 1920s to 1970 and argues that the State Department initiated an aggressive Middle Eastern oil policy during the Wilson administration. This is a detailed treatment of the U.S. quest for Middle East oil in the period following World War I. Bibliography.

16:168 Venn, Fiona. "'A Futile Paper Chase': Anglo-American Relations and Middle East Oil, 1918–34." *Diplomacy & Statecraft* 1 (July 1990): 165–84. Expansion of U.S. oil concessions in the Middle East came as a result of active promotion by the American government. Britain gave way, reluctantly, to placate Washington and thereby gain its support on other issues such as the mandates. This development illustrated the power of the United States to accomplish its international objectives, even during the "isolationist" years.

16:169   Wall, Bennett H., and George Sweet Gibb. *Teagle of Jersey Standard.* New Orleans: Tulane University, 1974. This readable biography discusses Walter Teagle's efforts to secure Jersey Standard's entry into the Iraq international oil consortium in the 1920s. Bibliography.

16:170   Ward, Thomas Edward. *Negotiations for Oil Concessions in Bahrain, El Hasa (Saudi Arabia) the Neutral Zone, Qatar and Kuwait: A Story Dedicated to Those Who Worked with Heart, Hand, and Mind in Uncovering and Developing the Petroleum Resources of the Persian Gulf Area.* New York: Privately printed, 1965. Ward participated in the negotiations, kept notes, and provided many excellent details in this account.

16:171   Yergin, Daniel. *The Prize: The Epic Quest for Oil, Money, and Power.* Yergin provides a detailed account of the development of the oil industry worldwide, with particular attention to the Middle East. He argues that oil in the twentieth century has become central to the security and prosperity of nations and that it determined the very nature of civilization. He devotes over 200 pages to the interwar period, drawing on a variety of documents, published sources, and interviews in English (9:202).

16:172   Zahlan, Rosemarie Said. "Anglo-American Rivalry in Bahrain, 1918–1947." *Dilmun* 12 (1984): 41–56. Zahlan discusses British concerns at the advance of U.S. oil companies in Bahrain after World War I. U.S. firms acted expeditiously, without much assistance from Washington, whereas British firms, closely allied with London, moved sluggishly. World War II proved critical in leading the U.S. government to take a more active role in the Gulf. Pax Britannica temporarily prevailed in the region as Washington became more concerned about Soviet penetration.

Cultural Relations

16:173   Abt, Jeffrey. "Toward a Historian's Laboratory: The Breasted-Rockefeller Museum Projects in

Egypt, Palestine, and America." *Journal of the American Research Center Egypt* 33 (1996): 173–94. The author discusses James Breasted's proposal to use Rockefeller money to build Egypt a new museum for its treasures and an advanced research center, providing foreign supervision of antiquities. After much negotiation, Cairo rejected the offer, and Rockefeller built a museum in Jerusalem instead. Breasted also had grand plans for establishing his Oriental Institute in Chicago as the command center for archaeological study worldwide.

16:174   Breasted, Charles. *Pioneer to the Past: The Story of James Henry Breasted, Archaeologist.* New York: Charles Scribner's Sons, 1943. Reprint 1977 (University of Chicago Press). Breasted was an important American scholar and founder of the Oriental Institute. This biography by his son details the interwar expansion of archaeological activities throughout the Middle East with strong U.S. diplomatic support.

16:175   Dodge, Bayard. *The American University of Beirut: A Brief History of the University and the Lands Which It Serves.* Beirut: Khayat's, 1958. This is a history of an American university that has had a pervasive impact on Lebanon and the Middle East; AUB educated many students who later became prominent officials in their respective nations.

16:176   King, Philip J. *American Archaeology in the Mideast: A History of the American Schools of Oriental Research.* Philadelphia: American Society of Oriental Research, 1983. King presents a detailed account of ASOR activities in the Middle East from the late nineteenth century.

16:177   Kuklick, Bruce. *Puritans in Babylon: The Ancient Near East and American Intellectual Life, 1880–1930.* The author provides an intellectual history of the development of American archaeological research in the Middle East. Kuklick focuses on activities associated with the University of Pennsylvania, one of the first American institutions to undertake excavations in the region (9:297).

16:178   Lydon, Cindy Arkelyan. "American Images of the Arabs." *Mid East* 9 (May-June 1969): 3–14. Long-standing American stereotypes about the Arabs, rooted partly in literature and film, kept policymakers from decisions in the 1940s that would have benefited U.S. interests in the region.

16:179   Mousa, Issam Suleiman. *The Arab Image in the US Press.* New York: Peter Lang, 1984. Mousa presents a content analysis of the *New York Times, 1917–1947.* He found that the information on Arabs was generally limited and unbalanced.

16:180   Patrick, Mary Mills. *A Bosporus Adventure: Istanbul (Constantinople) Woman's College, 1871–1924.* See chapter 13 of this Guide (13:163).

16:181   Penrose, Stephen Beasley Linnard. *That They May Have Life: The Story of the American University of Beirut, 1866–1941.* This university, which had an important impact on the development of Syria and Lebanon, contributed to the modernization of the entire Middle East (13:148).

16:182   Said, Edward W. *Culture and Imperialism.* New York: Alfred A. Knopf, 1993. Continuing from his earlier *Orientalism* (1978) (16:38), Said looks not only at the worldwide pattern of imperial culture but also at the resistance to that culture throughout the colonial world. He moves beyond the Middle East, drawing on numerous third world literary examples and devoting much of his study to the postcolonial period.

16:183   Taylor, Arnold H. *American Diplomacy and the Narcotics Traffic, 1900–1939: A Study in International Humanitarian Reform.* Taylor focuses on international reform and control efforts, with special attention to Latin America and East Asia but with useful sections on Iran and Turkey as well (13:67).

16:184   Tibawi, A. L. "English and American Education for Arabs, 1900–1931." *Arab Studies Quarterly* 2 (Summer 1980): 203–12. Tibawi discusses the character and influence of educational activities conducted by missionaries of Great Britain and the United States in the Middle East.

Iran

16:185   Farman-Farmaian, Sattareh. *Daughter of Persia: A Woman's Journey from Her Father's Harem through the Islamic Revolution.* New York: Crown,

1992. The author provides a fascinating account of growing up in a traditional upper-class family in the interwar years under Riza Shah. She attended the American mission school, traveled to the United States for study during World War II, and worked for W. Alton Jones, a friend of President Eisenhower's, when Muhammad Musaddiq, her cousin, headed the Iranian government (1951–1953).

16:186   Millspaugh, Arthur C. *Americans in Persia.* Washington, DC: Brookings Institution, 1946. This account by the head of American financial missions to Iran (1922–1927, 1943–1945) focuses more on his second mission than on his first, but there is a useful chapter on the earlier one, including a critique of Riza Shah's regime (1925–1941). Writing after World War II, Millspaugh presents a rather pessimistic view of Iran's prospects for reform, barring an agreement to allow general great power supervision of policymaking.

16:187   _____. *The Financial and Economic Situation of Persia, 1926.* New York: Imperial Persian Government, 1926. A short handbook on conditions in Iran by the head of the American financial mission, it presents a relatively optimistic view of Iran's finances and economy and predicts future progress.

16:188   Ramazani, R. K. *The Foreign Policy of Iran: A Developing Nation in World Affairs, 1500–1941.* Ramazani treats the Millspaugh mission to Iran in the 1920s, when the Iranians sought to assert their nationalistic aspirations in the face of British and Russian opposition. He includes as well a brief treatment of the Shuster mission, an earlier attempt by American experts to bring order to Iran's finances (2:410).

16:189   Rubin, Michael A. "Stumbling through the 'Open Door': The U.S. in Persia and the Standard-Sinclair Oil Dispute, 1920–1925." *Iranian Studies* 28 (Summer-Fall 1995): 203–29. The American attempt to become a major player in Iran proved abortive as Britain showed the lengths it would go to defend its interests.

16:190   Smith, Douglas L. "The Millspaugh Mission and American Corporate Diplomacy in Persia, 1922–1927." *Southern Quarterly* 14 (January 1976): 151–72. Riza Shah Pahlavi appointed Millspaugh to be director-general of Iranian finances because he perceived the United States as a disinterested power with exportable capital and technology. This sort of activity appealed to the State Department, which hoped to secure concessions for private companies from Iran's anti-Soviet regime.

16:191   Yeselson, Abraham. *United States–Persian Diplomatic Relations, 1883–1921.* This is the only book-length treatment of U.S-Iranian relations for this period. Early American interests in Iran centered on the missionaries, although some nineteenth-century American diplomats did attempt to expand U.S. commercial interests. The United States had little interest in Iran and was reluctant to become entangled in the Anglo-Russian power struggle. After World War I, the United States prevented ratification of the Anglo-Iranian treaty, which would have made Iran a client state of Britain. Extensive bibliography (13:173).

16:192   Zirinsky, Michael P. "Blood, Power, and Hypocrisy: The Murder of Robert Imbrie and American Relations with Pahlavi Iran, 1924." *International Journal of Middle East Studies* 18 (August 1986): 275–92. Zirinsky details the murder of the American consul in Tehran, perhaps with the connivance of Iranian authorities, contributing to an unfortunate pattern of future bilateral relations.

16:193   _____. "A Panacea for the Ills of the Country: American Presbyterian Education in Inter-War Iran." *Iranian Studies* 26 (Winter-Spring 1993): 119–37. Missionaries represented the United States to Iran, in response to which many Iranians developed a favorable if sometimes unrealistic view of America. Alumni of mission schools, rather than serving as a bridge, became alienated from traditional Iranian society.

Morocco

16:194   Hall, Luella J. *The United States and Morocco, 1776–1956.* See chapter 2 of this Guide (2:260).

16:195   Kenbib, Mohammed. "L'impact Americain sur le Nationalisme Marocain (1930–1947) [The American Impact on Moroccan Nationalism (1930–

1947)]." *Hesperis-Tamuda* 26–27 (1988– 1989): 207–23. Kenbib discusses commercial and capitulatory issues that arose between the United States and France. Some nationalists found protection from French restrictions through the agency of the capitulatory powers.

Saudi Arabia

16:196   Casillas, Rex J. *Oil and Diplomacy: The Evolution of American Foreign Policy in Saudi Arabia, 1933–1945.* New York: Garland Publishing, 1987. Expansion of relations with Saudi Arabia resulted from mutuality of interests between ARAMCO and the State Department's Near Eastern Affairs office. The oil company was the principal American beneficiary. Bibliography.

16:197   Twitchell, Karl S., with Edward J. Jurji and R. Bayly Winder. *Saudi Arabia, with an Account of the Development of Its Natural Resources.* 3d ed. Princeton: Princeton University Press, 1958. This book treats the author's early efforts to find oil in Saudi Arabia and his success in interesting an American oil company in developing the rich petroleum resources in that country. He brings the story down to the postwar era, when Saudi oil assumed a larger role in American diplomacy. First published in 1947.

16:198   Watt, Donald Cameron. "The Foreign Policy of Ibn Saud, 1936–39." *Journal of the Royal Central Asian Society* 50 (April 1963): 152–60. Watt gives only limited attention to relations with the United States but presents an analysis of Ibn Saud's successful maneuvering among the great powers as World War II approached.

Turkey

16:199   Daniel, Robert L. "The United States and the Turkish Republic before World War II: The Cultural Dimension." *Middle East Journal* 21 (Winter 1967): 52–63. This essay argues that the missionary lobby created the "terrible Turk" image in the United States at a time when the Armenian question was paramount in U.S.-Turkish relations.

16:200   Kinross, John P. D. B. *Atatürk: A Biography of Mustafa Kemal, Father of Modern Turkey.* New York: Morrow, 1965. This is a fine biography of Kemal Ataturk, the key figure in modern Turkish history who consolidated the Muslim "sick man of Europe" into a viable secular republic. Kinross sees Ataturk as a flawed visionary determined to save his country from European and Russian domination while presiding over an ambitious program of social and economic modernization. Bibliography.

16:201   Kuran, Ercumand. "The Turkish National War of Independence and Admiral Bristol, the U.S. High Commissioner in Istanbul (1919–1923)." *Cultura Turcica* 11, nos. 1–2 (1987): 89–100. This short article gives high praise to Bristol, who opposed the U.S. mandate in Armenia and supported the idea of a Turkish republic from the beginning of his tenure.

16:202   Mango, Andrew. *Atatürk.* Woodstock, NY: Overlook Press, 2000. Mango's is the first full-length biography of the Turkish leader in English in many years. He draws on Turkish as well as English sources and is more critical in his analysis of Ataturk's career than were many earlier biographers.

16:203   Sherrill, Charles H. *A Year's Embassy to Mustafa Kemal.* New York: Charles Scribner's Sons, 1934. Ambassador Sherrill provides interesting details of his experiences in Turkey, 1932–1933, and presents a positive view of the Turkish leader and the republic he established.

16:204   Trask, Roger R. "The Terrible Turk and Turkish-American Relations in the Interwar Period." *Historian* 33 (November 1970): 40–53. Trask discusses the rise of the "terrible Turk" image in the United States during the 1920s as well as other Americans' efforts to correct this image, paving the way for Turkish-American rapprochement in later years.

16:205   _____. "Turco-American Rapprochement, 1927–1932." In *Studies on Asia,* ed. Sidney D. Brown, 139–70. Lincoln: University of Nebraska Press, 1967. American diplomats were finally able to persuade the various American interest groups in Turkey to accommodate Turkish nationalism, thus establishing goodwill toward the United States and paving the way for closer relations. Bibliography.

16:206   _____. *The United States Response to Turkish Nationalism and Reform, 1914–1939.* Minneapolis: University of Minnesota Press, 1971. Trask examines U.S. interests in Turkey and Washington's response to Turkish nationalism. He gives considerable space to missionary work, trade expansion, and the negotiation of the treaty that normalized relations between the two countries. He argues that the United States was concerned about Turkey and that post–World War II relations were rooted in developments of the interwar years. Relations were generally amicable, partly the result of the high quality of American diplomatic representation there. Bibliography.

16:207   _____. "Unnamed Christianity in Turkey during the Ataturk Era." *Muslim World* 55 (January, April 1965): 66–76, 101–11. Turkish authorities curtailed the teaching of Christian ethics in American schools, and the missionaries responded with a program of "unnamed Christianity" designed to replace the formal Christian teachings removed from the curricula.

United States and Sub-Saharan Africa, 1919–1941

16:208   Albion, Robert G., with Jennie Barnes Pope. *Seaports South of Sahara: The Achievements of an American Steamship Service.* New York: Appleton-Century-Crofts, 1959. The Farrell Lines (1914–1959) had commercial contacts with South, East, and West Africa. They cooperated with Albion by making their archives available and granting interviews, resulting in an objective study.

16:209   McKinley, Edward H. *The Lure of Africa: American Interests in Tropical Africa, 1919–1939.* Indianapolis: Bobbs-Merrill, 1974. McKinley provides an extensive study of a range of American interests, including missionaries, tourism, and trade. Americans paid little attention to Africa, looking upon it only as a landscape, not as a place of political complexities. He presents Africa not as it was, but as it appeared to Americans.

16:210 Plummer, Brenda Gayle. "Evolution of the Black Foreign Policy Constituency." *Transafrica Forum* 6 (Spring-Summer 1989): 67–81. Plummer discusses the development of African-American involvement with and influence on foreign policy from the 1930s, describing groups of activists and the organizations that spoke to and for them. She uses the Italo-Ethiopian War as a brief case study.

16:211 _____. *Rising Wind: Black Americans and U.S. Foreign Affairs, 1935–1960.* Chapel Hill: University of North Carolina Press, 1996. Plummer presents a corrective to the view that African-Americans of this era were apathetic and indifferent to the world beyond U.S. borders. She argues that they reacted strongly, especially to Africa-related questions. They frequently deserted their white, liberal allies in the foreign policy arena when prescribed policies conflicted with their perception of group interest, as in U.S. neutrality during the Italo-Ethiopian War of 1935 and entry into World War II. Such differences of opinion occurred with considerable regularity. Bibliography.

UNITED STATES, AFRICA, AND PEACE CONFERENCE, 1919

16:212 Beer, George Louis. *African Questions at the Paris Peace Conference, with Papers on Egypt, Mesopotamia, and the Colonial Settlement.* Beer provides lucid, thoughtful essays on the German colonies in Africa, which were written when he was a member of The Inquiry. The views expressed reflect his analysis of the colonial problems that would confront the peace conference. He also reviews some of the problems in the mandated territories awarded to Britain and France at Versailles. Edited by Louis Herbert Gray (13:122).

16:213 Contee, Clarence G. "Du Bois, the NAACP, and the Pan-African Congress of 1919." See chapter 13 of this Guide (13:118).

16:214 Louis, William Roger. "The United States and the African Peace Settlement of 1919: The Pilgrimage of George Louis Beer." Louis presents an exhaustive but narrow analysis of the mandate controversy. Not only did Beer fail to acquire a mandate for the United States, he was powerless to block the Ruanda-Urundi agreement (13:131).

PAN-AFRICANISM AND BACK-TO-AFRICA MOVEMENTS

16:215 American Society of African Culture, ed. *Pan-Africanism Reconsidered.* Berkeley: University of California Press, 1962. In this report of the third annual conference of the American Society of African Culture (1960), the most significant paper for pre-1945 historical background is by Rayford Logan. Unfortunately, neither a bibliography nor an index is included.

16:216 Clarke, John Henrik, with Amy Jacques Garvey, eds. *Marcus Garvey and the Vision of Africa.* New York: Random House, 1974. Clarke provides a collection of speeches and writings by and about Garvey and his work, with extended, chiefly favorable, commentaries by the editors. Relevant selections include W. E. B. Du Bois, "Back to Africa" (105–19); A. F. Elmes, "Garvey and Garveyism: An Estimate" (120–26); Cyril Briggs, "The Decline of the Garvey Movement" (174–79); Garvey, "The Political Activities of Marcus Garvey in Jamaica" (276–83); Edwin S. Redkey, "The Flowering of Black Nationalism: Henry McNeal Turner and Marcus Garvey" (388–401); Jabez Ayodele Langley, "Marcus Garvey and African Nationalism" (402–13); and Robert G. Weisbord, "Marcus Garvey, Pan-Negroists: The View from Whitehall" (421–27).

16:217 Cronon, E. David. *Black Moses: The Story of Marcus Garvey and the Universal Negro Improvement Association.* 2d ed. Madison: University of Wisconsin Press, 1972. In this first full-length biography of Garvey (1887–1940), Cronon is "sympathetic without being adulatory or patronizing." He marvels at the renewed interest in Garvey, a figure who had been largely forgotten by his death, and praises him for his legacy of race consciousness and pride. Extensive bibliography. First published in 1969.

16:218 Duberman, Martin B. *Paul Robeson.* New York: Alfred A. Knopf, 1988. Reprint 1996 (New

Press). Robeson came to appreciate fully his African cultural roots only in the early 1930s. He did not agree with the view that African-Americans would save Africa, but he supported the preservation of traditional African institutions and values from western encroachment.

16:219   Ejimofor, Cornelius. "Black American Contribution to African Nationalism and African Influence on U.S. Civil Rights." *Journal of Afro-American Issues* 2 (Fall 1974): 332–47. Ejimofor assesses the role of black Americans in rousing national consciousness among the elite of black Africa, which led eventually to the demand for African independence.

16:220   Geiss, Imanuel. *The Pan-African Movement: A History of Pan-Africanism in America, Europe, and Africa.* Translated by Ann Keep. Geiss states that "Pan-Africanism is probably one of the most complex phenomena in modern history." In tracing its development, he demonstrates that it became less a religious and cultural matter and more a political movement after 1900. Extensive bibliography (13:120).

16:221   Howard, Thomas C. "West Africa and the American South: Notes on James E. K. Aggrey and the Idea of a University for West Africa." *Journal of African Studies* 2 (Winter 1975–1976): 445–66. Howard has written a critical study of the idea of a university for Africans as promoted by Aggrey of the Gold Coast and North Carolina, foremost African educator and founder in 1924 of the Prince of Wales College at Achimota in the Gold Coast.

16:222   King, Kenneth J. "Africa and the Southern States of the U.S.A.: Notes on J. H. Oldham and American Negro Education for Africans." *Journal of African History* 10, no. 4 (1969): 659–77. King examines the conflict between the philosophy of W. E. B. Du Bois and that of J. H. Oldham and T. Jesse Jones, disciples of Booker T. Washington. The conflict represented an extension to Africa of fundamental New World conflicts over black education and political status. Du Bois lobbied for an assertive political platform; Washington—and his disciples— pursued a more accommodationist policy.

16:223   Legum, Colin. *Pan-Africanism: A Short Political Guide.* Rev. ed. New York: Frederick A.

Praeger, 1962. The first half of this volume is a narrative, the second a collection of documents. The period from 1900 through World War II is covered in the first two chapters.

16:224   Lemelle, Sidney J., and Robin D. G. Kelley, eds. *Imagining Home: Class, Culture and Nationalism in the African Diaspora.* New York: Verso, 1994. This collection of edited papers from the Seventh Pan-African Congress in 1988 is an effort to rethink the history of Pan-Africanism and document historically the many ways in which people of the African diaspora have continually reinvented and reimagined the home of their ancestors. Those likely to be of greatest interest to historians of foreign relations in the interwar period include the editors' introduction, "Imagining Home: Pan-Africanism Revisited" (1–16), and "'Afric's Sons with Banner Red': African-American Communists and the Politics of Culture, 1919–1934" (35–54).

16:225   Lynch, Hollis R. *Black American Radicals and the Liberation of Africa: The Council on African Affairs, 1937–1955.* Ithaca: Africana Studies and Research Center, Cornell University, 1978. Lynch, a committed Pan-Africanist, wrote this short introduction to provide a fair hearing for the Council on African Affairs, which, he argues, died because of its association with international Marxist politics.

16:226   Magubane, Bernard Makhosezwe. *The Ties That Bind: African-American Consciousness of Africa.* Trenton, NJ: Africa World Press, 1987. African-American views of Africa and Africans were ambiguous until the early decades of the twentieth century because they had internalized stereotypes put forth by the white power structure to keep them subordinate. Only with development of the Pan-African movement in the 1920s did they begin to appreciate and foster cultural ties with Africa.

16:227   Martin, Tony. *The Pan-African Connection: From Slavery to Garvey and Beyond.* Cambridge, MA: Schenkman Pub. Co., 1983. Much of this book focuses on Garvey's work in the Caribbean, but Martin includes two chapters on links between African-Americans and Africa. One discusses the impact of black missionaries in colonial Africa, the other effect of the Universal Negro Improvement Association in South Africa, which the author argues had a profound influence as a nursery for organizational skills, especially for the African National Congress.

16:228 Mboukou, Alexandre. "The Pan-African Movement, 1900–1945: A Study in Leadership Conflicts among the Disciples of Pan Africanism." *Journal of Black Studies* 13 (March 1983): 275–87. Mboukou examines the conflicts arising out of the claims and counterclaims of three sets of Pan-Africans (African-Americans, Afro-West Indians, and Continental Africans).

16:229 Moses, Wilson Jeremiah. *The Golden Age of Black Nationalism, 1850–1925.* Hamden, CT: Archon Books, 1978. Reprint 1988 (Oxford University Press). In the opinion of Moses, black nationalism is practically indistinguishable as an intellectual movement from Pan-Africanism. The author treats his subject as a conservative rather than a radical ideology. Chapter 3 deals with the "civilizing missionary," Alexander Crummell, while chapter 10 discusses Pan-Africanism at the turn of the twentieth century. Extensive bibliography.

16:230 Okonkwo, R. L. "The Garvey Movement in British West Africa." *Journal of African History* 21, no. 1 (1980): 105–17. The Garvey movement was important in this region, but it has been little studied because of the paucity of sources. It was viewed as an extension of earlier pan-African ideas. In some areas, however, there was resistance to cooperation with American blacks.

16:231 Rogers, Ben F. "William E. B. Du Bois, Marcus Garvey, and Pan-Africa." *Journal of Negro History* 40 (April 1955): 154–65. Rogers concludes that in the 1920s, Du Bois had intellect and ability but lacked appeal in the eyes of American blacks. Though charismatic, Garvey was a poor organizer and perhaps even an outright charlatan.

16:232 Scruggs, Otey M. "Carter G. Woodson, the Negro History Movement, and Africa." *Pan-African Journal* 7 (Spring 1974): 39–50. Scruggs begins his account in 1916, when Woodson began publishing *The Journal of Negro History.* In Woodson's opinion, the task of the black scholar was "to 'prove' the humanity of black people and to instill in them a healthy race pride by presenting the truth of the African

American past." He believed, along with Melville Herskovits, that African cultural elements survived among New World blacks.

16:233 Shepperson, George. "The American Negro and Africa." *British Association for American Studies Bulletin* 8 (June 1964): 3–20. This paper investigates the interaction of American blacks and African nationalists. Shepperson finds four perspectives in the 1880–1918 period: Africans in America, the ideas of Booker T. Washington, Pan-Africanism, and the black history movement. Finally, he discusses developments of the interwar years and post–World War II period, focusing on the rise of a new generation of African national leaders and their connections with black leaders and movements in the United States.

16:234 _____. "Notes on Negro American Influences on the Emergence of African Nationalism." *Journal of African History* 1, no. 2 (1960): 299–312. Shepperson concludes that African-American leaders such as Marcus Garvey, W. E. B. Du Bois, and Booker T. Washington helped to shape African nationalism.

16:235 Weisbord, Robert G. "The Back-to-Africa Idea." *History Today* 18 (January 1968): 30–37. This brief popular account discusses such figures as Paul Cuffe, Henry Highland Garnet, Martin R. Delany, Benjamin Singleton, Henry M. Turner, J. Albert Thorne, Alfred Charles Sam, and Marcus Garvey.

16:236 _____. *Ebony Kinship: Africa, Africans, and the Afro-American.* Westport, CT: Greenwood Press, 1973. This work extends from the founding of the American Colonization Society in 1816 to the 1970s. There are chapters on Marcus Garvey, the Italo-Ethiopian War, "The View from Africa," and "Afro-American's African Renaissance." Extensive bibliography.

CULTURAL RELATIONS

16:237 Berman, Edward H. "Educational Colonialism in Africa: The Role of American Foundations, 1910–1945." In *Philanthropy and Cultural Imperialism: The Foundations at Home and Abroad,* ed. Robert F. Arnove, 179–201. Boston: G. K. Hall,

1980. American philanthropists advocated an educational policy for colonial Africa that was both pedagogically questionable and racist.

16:238   Boyd, Nancy. *Emissaries: The Overseas Work of the American YWCA, 1895–1970.* This book contains a short chapter on Nigerian activities in the 1930s, using YWCA archives in New York (9:161).

16:239   Davis, Peter. *In Darkest Hollywood: Exploring the Jungles of Cinema's South Africa.* Athens, OH: Ohio University Press, 1996. Davis presents analyses of selected films, showing how Hollywood manipulated views of South Africa and Africans from the early years of the twentieth century.

16:240   Davis, Richard Hunt, Jr. "Producing the 'Good African': South Carolina's Penn School as a Guide for African Education in South Africa." In *Independence without Freedom: The Political Economy of Colonial Education in Southern Africa,* ed. Agrippah T. Mugomba and Mougo Nyaggah, 83–112. Santa Barbara, CA: ABC-CLIO, 1980. After World War I white South Africans involved in educating Africans were concerned with providing the necessary level of schooling while maintaining social control. They found their model in rural South Carolina's Penn School. The attempt to adapt this model to South Africa failed, however, because it was unsuited in important ways to the local environment, and more importantly because Africans opposed it, realizing that it represented an educational philosophy that asserted black subordination.

16:241   De Lombard, Jeannine. "Sisters, Servants or Saviors? National Baptist Women Missionaries in Liberia in the 1920s." *International Journal of African Historical Studies* 24, no. 2 (1991): 323–47. De Lombard analyzes writings of African-American missionary women to show their ambivalence toward Africa and Africans. They simultaneously informed and misinformed people at home about Africa. In limited measure they aided the imperialists of the day.

16:242   Glotzer, Richard. "The Career of Mabel Carney: The Study of Race and Rural Development in the United States and South Africa." *International Journal of African Historical Studies* 29, no. 2 (1996): 309–36. Carney was an African-American educator who spent her career working to improve educational opportunities in the U.S. south and South Africa. As she gained experience, she moved beyond comfortable limits of paternalistic "negro" education but never escaped them completely.

16:243   Hickey, Dennis, and Kenneth Wylie. *An Enchanting Darkness: The American Vision of Africa in the Twentieth Century.* East Lansing: Michigan State University Press, 1993. Hickey and Wylie discuss sources of and reasons for continuing stereotypes about Africa, despite decades of scholarly reappraisal. Bibliography.

16:244   Hooker, J. R. "The Negro American Press and Africa in the Nineteen Thirties." *Canadian Journal of African Studies* 1 (March 1967): 43–50. Hooker found little evidence of positive views of Africa in leading black newspapers, although interest appeared to increase late in the decade.

16:245   Jacobs, Sylvia M., ed. *Black Americans and the Missionary Movement in Africa.* These essays discuss the role of black Americans in the American Protestant mission movement in Africa in the nineteenth and early twentieth centuries. Although their impact on Africa was somewhat illusive, they helped to dispel negative stereotypes about the continent and to encourage a stronger African-American identity with the region. See especially Jacobs, "The Historical Role of Afro-Americans in American Missionary Efforts in Africa" (5–30); Manning Marable, "Ambiguous Legacy: Tuskegee's 'Missionary' Impulse and Africa during the Moton Administration, 1915–1935" (77–94); Thomas C. Howard, "Black American Missionary Influence on the Origins of University Education in West Africa" (95–127); and three additional essays by Jacobs, including "Their 'Special Mission': Afro-American Women as Missionaries to the Congo, 1894–1937" (155–76). See also chapter 9 of this Guide (9:285).

16:246   _____. "James Emman Kwegyir Aggrey: An African Intellectual in the United States." *Journal of Negro History* 81 (Fall 1996): 47–61. Aggrey applied the ideas of Booker T. Washington in Africa after his education in the United States. His life was full of contradictions; his education set him apart, yet he was determined to use it in the vindication of his race.

16:247 Kemp, Amanda D., and Robert Trent Vinson. "'Poking Holes in the Sky': Professor James Thaele, American Negroes and Modernity in 1920s Segregationist South Africa." *African Studies Review* 43 (April 2000): 141–59. James Thaele, president of the African National Congress in the Cape Western Province, had been educated in the United States, where he became enamored of Marcus Garvey's Universal Negro Improvement Association. Returning home, Thaele used evidence of African-American progress to dismiss white charges demeaning blacks. He adopted flamboyant dress and hyperbolic language as tools to subvert, mock, and reverse their categorizations of black South Africans.

16:248 King, Kenneth J. *Pan-Africanism and Education: A Study of Race Philanthropy and Education in the Southern States of America and East Africa.* Oxford: Clarendon Press, 1971. This is a study of the American-based Phelps-Stokes Fund, which for twenty years (1920–1940) supported the introduction of Tuskegee methods into African education with mixed results. King focuses here on its work in Kenya.

16:249 Meyer, Lysle E. *The Farther Frontier: Six Case Studies of Americans and Africa, 1848–1936.* In one of the book's case studies, Meyer discusses the career of Carl Akeley, famous hunter, author, taxidermist, and naturalist, who made repeated trips to Africa for specimens to fill the exhibition halls of major American museums of natural history. He commends Akeley, however, for his role in creating the first wildlife preserve in Africa (9:287).

16:250 Spivey, Donald. "The African Crusade for Black Industrial Schooling." *Journal of Negro History* 63 (January 1978): 1–17. Industrial education for Africans, modeled on Hampton and Tuskegee Institutes, was warmly embraced by colonial powers and their officials as an effective means of maintaining black subordination and white control. Thomas Jesse Jones, with support from the Phelps-Stokes Fund and Rockefeller International Education Board, introduced the concept into Liberia in the form of the Booker Washington Institute in cooperation with the Firestone Company. Local Africans came to despise the school, and it had disappeared by the late 1930s.

16:251 Thomas, Samuel S. "Transforming the Gospel of Domesticity: Luhya Girls and the Friends Africa Mission, 1917–1926." *African Studies Review* 43 (September 2000): 1–27. Thomas studies the attempts by Quaker missionaries to remake African womanhood in Western Province, Kenya. Their limited success was due in part to the female missionary in charge of the school and in part to the schoolgirls, who manipulated the missionaries and their institutions.

16:252 West, Michael O. "The Tuskegee Model of Development in Africa: Another Dimension of the African/African-American Connection." *Diplomatic History* 16 (Summer 1992): 371–87. The Tuskegee model in Africa has generally been ignored by Pan-Africanists because it does not conform to the standard conception of this movement, but West argues that the model must be regarded as an expression of pan-Africanism.

ETHIOPIA

16:253 Chukumba, Stephen U. *The Big Powers against Ethiopia: Anglo-Franco-American Diplomatic Maneuvers during the Italo-Ethiopian Dispute, 1934–1938.* Washington, DC: University Press of America, 1977. Chukumba provides a comparative study of the role of the three powers in the dispute. Writing from an "African perspective," the author concludes that the three powers effectively cooperated to ensure Italy's triumph over Ethiopia.

16:254 Collum, Danny Duncan. *African Americans in the Spanish Civil War: "This Ain't Ethiopia, But It'll Do."* New York: G. K. Hall, 1992. In addition to the documentary evidence, this project of the Abraham Lincoln Brigade Archives contains an excellent introduction by Robin Kelley, which discusses how black volunteers saw the relationship between the wars in Ethiopia and Spain.

16:255 Harris, Brice, Jr. *The United States and the Italo-Ethiopian Crisis.* Stanford, CA: Stanford University Press, 1964. Roosevelt sought ways to indicate to the British and French that the United States would not sabotage effective League action. The League's failure to act reinforced isolationist sentiment in the United States even as FDR became increasingly aware of international responsibilities.

16:256 Harris, Joseph E. *African-American Reactions to War in Ethiopia, 1936–1941.* Baton Rouge: Louisiana State University Press, 1994. Harris focuses on the African diaspora and the role of the Ethiopian crisis in accelerating the mobilization of African peoples worldwide.

16:257 _____. "Race and Misperceptions in the Origins of United States–Ethiopian Diplomatic Relations." *TransAfrica Forum* 3 (Winter 1986): 9–23. Americans knew little of Ethiopia in the 1920s. Harris explains how relations developed during the interwar years, especially between African-Americans and Africans. He underscores the seriousness with which the United States should pursue relations with nonwhite governments.

16:258 Scott, William R. "Black Nationalism and the Italo-Ethiopian Conflict, 1934–1936." *Journal of Negro History* 63 (April 1978): 118–34. The response to Italy's invasion was particularly strong among African-Americans, who had long drawn inspiration from Ethiopia as a symbol of black power and pride. Scott challenges the view that black nationalist fervor died with the Depression; it remained an influential and dynamic force in black life. News from the war zone led to increasing tensions and some violence between blacks and Italian-Americans on the east coast.

16:259 _____. "Colonel John C. Robinson: The Condor of Ethiopia." *Pan-African Journal* 5 (Spring 1972): 59–69. In addition to detailing the career of Robinson, Scott argues that the Ethiopian elite did not bear any deep-seated animosity toward African-Americans, an idea that had been fostered, he claimed, by some white editors and academics.

16:260 _____. *The Sons of Sheba's Race: African-Americans and the Italo-Ethiopian War, 1935–1941.* Bloomington: Indiana University Press, 1993. Diverse groups of African-Americans showed considerable interest in the plight of Ethiopia. Although unable to translate their feelings into effective action in the war, their concern strengthened unity within the African-American community, marking a sharp intensification of racial spirit.

16:261 Simmons, Thomas E. *The Brown Condor: The True Adventures of John C. Robinson.* Silver Spring, MD: Bartleby Press, 1988. This is a popular account of the adventures of John Robinson, an African-American pilot who served Emperor Haile Selassie in the Italo-Ethiopian War of 1935–1936 and returned to a hero's welcome in Chicago.

16:262 Ventresco, Fiorello B. "Italian-Americans and the Ethiopian Crisis." *Italian Americana* 6 (Autumn-Winter 1980): 4–27. Ventresco focuses on problems in the United States among profascist and antifascist Italian-Americans and on strained relations between blacks and Italian-Americans after the invasion of Ethiopia.

16:263 Weisbord, Robert G. "Black America and the Italian-Ethiopian Crisis: An Episode in Pan-Negroism." *Historian* 34 (February 1972): 230–41. Weisbord's article treats not only the Italo-Ethiopian War itself, but black American interest in Ethiopia. He concludes that "it is abundantly clear that Afro-Americans at a critical moment made a strong racial identification with their beleaguered 'brothers' in Ethiopia."

LIBERIA

16:264 Anderson, Robert Earle. *Liberia: America's African Friend.* Chapel Hill: University of North Carolina Press, 1952. The author visited Liberia, toured the Firestone rubber plantation, and interviewed several former presidents of the republic. Anderson feels that America has neglected Liberia at times, but that the ties between the two nations nevertheless have grown stronger over the years.

16:265 Bixler, Raymond W. *The Foreign Policy of the United States in Liberia.* New York: Pageant Press, 1957. This short volume portrays the American government as the great protector of Liberia against British and European imperialism, providing diplomatic, financial, military, and technical assistance to that nation. Over two-thirds of the book deals with the period after World War I. Bibliography.

16:266 Buell, Raymond Leslie. *The Native Problem in Africa.* 2 vols. New York: Macmillan, 1928. This account is based upon Buell's trip to Africa in 1925–1926. It emphasizes French, British, and Belgian Africa. Two chapters stress American activities in Liberia: "The Firestone Agreement" and "The Loan That Succeeded." Bibliography.

16:267 Chalk, Frank R. "The Anatomy of an Investment: Firestone's 1927 Loan to Liberia." *Canadian Journal of African Studies* 1 (March 1967): 12–32. Chalk presents a detailed analysis of the three-way negotiations for the 1927 loan and subsequent developments related to it.

16:268 _____. "Du Bois and Garvey Confront Liberia: Two Incidents of the Coolidge Years." *Canadian Journal of African Studies* 2 (November 1967): 135–42. Chalk discusses their experiences in the Coolidge years, bringing into sharper focus their conflict and the values they disputed, especially in the debate over an African-American strategy for advancement.

16:269 Gershoni, Yekutiel. *Black Colonialism: The Americo-Liberian Scramble for the Hinterland.* Boulder: Westview Press, 1985. Gershoni presents the history of Liberia as a tale of persistent domination of an Americo-Liberian elite over indigenous peoples. The book also treats the role of U.S. diplomats.

16:270 Johnston, Louise. "Tuskegee in Liberia: The Politics of Industrial Education, 1927–1935." *Liberian Studies Journal* 9, no. 2 (1980–1981): 61–68. Development of Booker Washington Industrial and Agricultural Institute by various foreign philanthropic groups failed because of the school's identification with the Firestone Company.

16:271 Knoll, Arthur J. "Firestone's Labor Policy, 1924–1939." *Liberian Studies Journal* 16, no. 2 (1991): 49–75. Knoll examines the labor policy of American industrialist Harvey S. Firestone on his Liberian rubber plantations, his relationship with the Liberian elite, and his influence on U.S.-Liberian relations.

16:272 McBride, David. "Solomon Porter Hood, 1853–1943: Black Missionary, Educator and Minister to Liberia." *Journal of the Lancaster County Historical Society* 84, no. 1 (1980): 2–9. McBride relates the career of this little-known missionary and educator. The article lauds his role as U.S. minister in facilitating the Firestone rubber agreement with the government in Monrovia.

16:273 Padgett, James A. "Ministers to Liberia and Their Diplomacy." *Journal of Negro History* 22 (January 1937): 50–92. This long essay includes a considerable amount of biographical material for the years from 1863 to 1931. Padgett concludes: "Perhaps in no small country, especially in an out of the way backward country, has the ministerial and consular work been carried on in a more satisfactory manner than in this little Republic."

16:274 Robinson, Cedric. "DuBois and Black Sovereignty: The Case of Liberia." *Race and Class* 32 (October-December 1990): 39–50. Robinson examines the activities of Du Bois on behalf of Liberia, noting how he supported the capitalist and elitist aspirations of the Americo-Liberians.

16:275 Rosenberg, Emily S. "The Invisible Protectorate: The United States, Liberia, and the Evolution of Neocolonialism, 1909–1940." Rosenberg argues that U.S. policy toward Liberia strongly resembled that in Central America between the wars. Liberia served as the precursor of the neocolonialism that would come to other African states after independence (11:427).

16:276 Sisay, Hassan B. "United States–Liberian Relations: A Reappraisal." *Journal of Afro-American Issues* 1 (Summer-Fall 1973): 340–49. Sisay challenges the view that the United States acted toward Liberia solely out of its own self-interest. He describes a policy that changed over time and that was influenced by a variety of factors.

16:277 Sundiata, I. K. *Black Scandal, America and the Liberian Labor Crisis, 1929–1936.* Philadelphia: Institute for the Study of Human Issues, 1980. The labor crisis of 1929–1936 tested control of the Americo-Liberian elite, which emerged from the period having established a symbiotic relationship with Firestone after the U.S. government adopted a policy of nonintervention.

LEAGUE AND SLAVERY ISSUE, 1929–1935

16:278 Du Bois, William E. B. "Liberia, the League and the United States." *Foreign Affairs* 11 (July 1933): 682–95. The author focuses on the

League of Nations investigation of alleged slave trading. Du Bois concludes that Liberia's "chief crime" was being "black and poor in a rich, white world."

16:279 Jones, R. L. "American Opposition to Slavery in Africa." *Journal of Negro History* 16 (July 1931): 266–86. This historical study (1876–1931) demonstrates that U.S. opposition to slavery in Liberia was merely a continuation of a long-established policy.

16:280 Normandy, Elizabeth L. "African-Americans and U.S. Policy towards Liberia, 1929–1935." *Liberian Studies Journal* 18, no. 2 (1993): 203–30. Normandy analyzes the role of African-Americans in the resolution of the international controversy over the use of forced labor in Liberia.

SOUTH AFRICA

16:281 Cell, John W. *The Highest Stage of White Supremacy: The Origins of Segregation in South Africa and the American South.* New York: Cambridge University Press, 1982. Cell addresses briefly the influence of African-Americans on African students studying in the United States. Concerned white South Africans advocated developing an African educational institution at home. South African whites were keen observers of developments in the American south. Although they admired much about segregation there, they concluded that white southern control was doomed and determined not to let this happen to them.

16:282 Cooper, Allan D. *U.S. Economic Power and Political Influence in Namibia, 1700–1982.* This work contains a short section on U.S. policy in Namibia between the wars, arguing that Washington consistently supported South African control because its policies reflected American policies toward blacks at home and also because important U.S. policymakers had personal and financial ties to South Africa (2:269).

16:283 Davis, Richard Hunt, Jr. "Charles T. Loram and the American Model for African Education in South Africa, 1910–1953." In *Apartheid and Education: The Education of Black South Africans,* ed. Peter Kallaway, 108–26. Johannesburg: Ravan Press, 1984. Loram, an influential South African official and educator, who spent many years studying and

working in the United States, proposed an American model of education for Africans that would maintain the existing system of subordination. It would be unwise, he thought, to educate blacks to have higher expectations than their position in society warranted.

16:284 Edgar, Robert. "African Educational Protest in South Africa: The American School Movement in the Transkei in the 1920s." In *Apartheid and Education: The Education of Black South Africans,* ed. Peter Kallaway, 184–91. Johannesburg: Ravan Press, 1984. The American School Movement, started in the 1920s by Elias Wellington Butelezi, a Garvey disciple and agent, was intended to free African education from European control. After a brief success, decline quickly followed, with Butelezi being forced out of the Transkei by the authorities. Edgar compares this movement with protests against white domination in the 1970s.

16:285 Fierce, Milfred C. "Selected Black American Leaders and Organizations and South Africa, 1900–1977: Some Notes." *Journal of Black Studies* 17 (March 1987): 305–26. Fierce discusses some of the black American leaders who joined in the campaign for African liberation in the 1920s and 1930s.

16:286 Gish, Steven. *Alfred B. Xuma: African, American, South African.* New York: New York University Press, 2000. Gish has written a political biography of Alfred Xuma. He explores the impact of African-American ideas on Xuma's political thought and the degree to which Xuma reshaped these ideas to fit the South African political climate.

16:287 Hill, Robert A., and Gregory A. Pirio. "Africa for the Africans: The Garvey Movement in South Africa, 1920–1940." In *The Politics of Race, Class, and Nationalism in Twentieth-Century South Africa,* ed. Shula Marks and Stanley Trapido, 209–53. New York: Longman, 1987. After World War I the Garvey movement developed in South Africa into a potent expression of mass-based African nationalism. South African historiography has downplayed the significance of Garveyism and failed to account for the potency of its appeal. It undermined loyalty to imperial Britain in positing Africa for the Africans.

16:288 Hull, Richard W. *American Enterprise in*

South Africa: Historical Dimensions of Engagement and Disengagement. Hull covers the full range of American activities in South Africa. The American involvement extends deeply into the past and has been marked by cycles of engagement and disengagement, related as much to developments in the United States as to those in South Africa or Great Britain. He concludes that in many complex and contradictory ways U.S. enterprise both strengthened and weakened the forces of apartheid. During the interwar years, U.S. business interests expanded rapidly, with little attention to the harsh realities of racial domination. Extensive bibliography (2:265).

16:289 Ngubo, Anthony. "Contributions of the Black American Church to the Development of African Independence Movements in South Africa." In *For Better or Worse: The American Influence in the World,* ed. Allen F. Davis, 145–56. Westport, CT: Greenwood Press, 1981. Black South Africans broke with white-dominated missions and merged with black American churches in part because whites denied them a role in policymaking. The relationship with African-American churches promoted the organizational skills of black South Africans, contributing to their advancement in South Africa.

16:290 Ralston, Richard D. "American Episodes in the Making of an African Leader: A Case Study of Alfred B. Xuma (1893–1962)." *International Journal of African Historical Studies* 6, no. 1 (1973): 72–93. Alfred B. Xuma of South Africa spent 1914 to 1926 acquiring a comprehensive education in the United States. The author compares Xuma's historical importance with that of James Aggrey and Nnamdi Azikiwe, while admitting that his experiences in the United States were not typical of the average African student.

16:291 Walshe, A. P. "Black American Thought and African Political Attitudes in South Africa." *Review of Politics* 32 (January 1970): 51–77. This study examines the impact of a number of key American blacks on South Africa, including Booker T. Washington, W. E. B. Du Bois, and Marcus Garvey. Walshe concludes that African leaders drew upon the examples of Du Bois and Washington to press for civil rights and equality of opportunity. The more radical ideas of Garvey became moderated in the South African context to produce a more assertive, but reformist, African nationalism. In the final section Walshe investigates Pan-Africanism.

16:292 Wolf, James B. "A Grand Tour: South Africa and American Tourists between the Wars." *Journal of Popular Culture* 25 (Fall 1991): 99–116. The South African government tried to promote tourism, hoping to attract American dollars. Authorities tried to provide unique experiences for the travelers, even if these had to be manufactured.

17

The United States, Europe, and Asia between the World Wars and the Prelude to World War II

Contributing Editor

JUSTUS D. DOENECKE
New College of Florida

With the Assistance of

JEREMI SURI
University of Wisconsin, Madison

JOHN M. BELOHLAVEK
University of South Florida

Contents

Introduction

This section begins with the advent of the Harding administration and ends with the Japanese attack on Pearl Harbor. In covering U.S. policy toward the Pacific and East Asia, I include material on such areas of Asia and the Pacific as French Indochina, Thailand, and Australia but not India or Ceylon. Certain works dealing primarily with military and economic history are cited, including biographies of generals and admirals, provided they have a strong diplomatic dimension. The same holds true for the peace and missionary movements, agents of public opinion, religious and ethnic groups, and labor and business pressure. Among the special topics are Prohibition, Jewish refugees, intelligence, the narcotics trade, and domestic policies with international ramifications. Major works on those British leaders whose diplomacy obviously impinges upon that of the United States (e.g., Winston Churchill and Anthony Eden) are covered. I do not limit biographical entries to those from the world of diplomacy but cover as well opinion leaders from the worlds of publishing, academic life, and even occasionally from literature (e.g., Pearl Buck) and aviation (e.g., Charles A. Lindbergh).

I have deemed certain contemporary works worthy of listing, including some by journalists, particularly when an author's thought is as seminal as Charles A. Beard (e.g., *The Open Door at Home*), Reinhold Niebuhr (e.g., *Christianity and Power Politics*), and Frederick L. Schuman (e.g., *Europe on the Eve*). Occasionally a French- or German-language work is cited as are sources published in Canada, Britain, Germany, India, Australia, and Japan. When they cover events and issues otherwise only thinly studied by published historians, I have also included dissertations. Major bibliographies, documentary collections, and congressional hearings are also noted.

Resources and Research Aids

DOCUMENT COLLECTIONS

17:1   U.S. Department of State. *Foreign Relations of the United States*. Washington, DC: Government Printing Office, 1936–1962. This is the essential compilation of official documentation of U.S. foreign relations. For the Harding, Coolidge, Hoover, and pre–Pearl Harbor Roosevelt administrations, there are 4, 14, 16, and 47 volumes, respectively (1:93).

17:2   _____. *Peace and War: United States Foreign Policy, 1931–1941*. Washington, DC: Government Printing Office, 1942. This volume contains in chronological order a large number of diplomatic messages, speeches, and official documents relating to warnings of German and Japanese aggressive intentions.

17:3   U.S. Congress. Senate. Committee on Foreign Relations. *The Legislative Origins of American Foreign Policy: Proceedings of the Committee on Foreign Relations, United States Senate, from December 3, 1923 to March 3, 1933*. Vol. 2. New York: Garland, 1979. This volume covers the period from Wilson's inauguration to the end of the Hoover administration. Some of the material had long been classified. Hearings on the Versailles Treaty are included. Introduction by Richard D. Challener.

17:4   Rosenman, Samuel I., ed. *Public Papers and Addresses of Franklin Delano Roosevelt*. A compilation by a close adviser of FDR, this collection is equivalent to the public papers of later presidents printed by the Government Printing Office. The reader should know that some addresses underwent editing before publication (15:2).

17:5   Nixon, Edgar B., ed. *Franklin D. Roosevelt and Foreign Affairs*. A massive documentary record of the international correspondence of Roosevelt (1933–1937), the collection is arranged chronologically and indexed (15:3).

17:6   Schewe, Donald B., ed. *Franklin D. Roosevelt and Foreign Affairs, January 1937–August 1939.* 11 vols. New York: Garland, 1979–1980. Ten volumes of documents, reproduced in facsimile, continue the set begun in Nixon, *Franklin D. Roosevelt and Foreign Affairs* (1969) (17:5). The eleventh volume contains a name and subject index.

17:7   Kimball, Warren F., ed. *Churchill & Roosevelt: The Complete Correspondence.* 3 vols. Princeton: Princeton University Press, 1984. Kimball offers the most comprehensive and scrupulously edited collection of the correspondence in existence.

17:8   Loewenheim, Francis L., Harold D. Langley, and Manfred Jonas, eds. *Roosevelt and Churchill: Their Secret Wartime Correspondence.* New York: Saturday Review Press, 1975. Despite the publication of Kimball's more thorough *Churchill & Roosevelt: The Complete Correspondence* (1984) (17:7), this volume remains helpful, possessing a particularly insightful introduction.

17:9   Roosevelt, Franklin D. *Complete Presidential Press Conferences of Franklin D. Roosevelt.* 25 vols. New York: Da Capo Press, 1972. Roosevelt's press conferences provide an excellent illustration of how FDR dealt with foreign policy subjects on and off the record. They are sometimes most valuable for the things he did not say in response to questions from hostile reporters.

17:10   Buhite, Russell D., and David W. Levy, eds. *FDR's Fireside Chats.* Norman: University of Oklahoma Press, 1992. This volume includes eight foreign policy fireside chats, delivered from September 3, 1939, to January 6, 1945. The editors offer general introductions to both foreign and domestic policies and indicate where the spoken word differs from the printed text.

17:11   Roosevelt, Elliott, ed. *F.D.R.: His Personal Letters.* 4 vols. New York: Duell, Sloan and Pearce, 1947–1950. Reprint 1970 (Kraut Reprint Co.). Volume 3 is the most relevant for foreign affairs.

17:12   Bullitt, Orville H., ed. *For the President, Personal and Secret: Correspondence between Franklin D. Roosevelt and William C. Bullitt.* Boston: Houghton Mifflin, 1972. These communiqués, edited by Bullitt's brother, reveal the view of Roosevelt's ambassador to the Soviet Union (1933–1936) and France (1936–1940). In his introduction, George F. Kennan defends Bullitt's suspicion of the Soviets and empathetically treats his growing disillusion with appeasement of Germany. One sees the vacillation between commitments and inaction that bedeviled American policy.

17:13   Quint, Howard H., and Robert H. Ferrell, eds. *The Talkative President: The Off-the-Record Press Conferences of Calvin Coolidge.* Amherst: University of Massachusetts Press, 1964. Topics include national defense, war debts and reparations, the World Court, the Kellogg-Briand pact, Mexico, Nicaragua, China, and the Soviet Union.

17:14   Lerski, George J., ed. *Herbert Hoover and Poland: A Documentary History of a Friendship.* Stanford, CA: Hoover Institution Press, 1977. This collection, which features a fifty-four-page introductory essay, traces Hoover's relief effort from World War I through the early cold war.

17:15   Myers, William Starr, ed. *The State Papers and Other Public Writings of Herbert Hoover.* The documents are in chronological order, with brief introductions. This collection is the equivalent of later collections, beginning with the papers of President Truman, published by the Government Printing Office (15:6).

17:16   Doenecke, Justus D., ed. *In Danger Undaunted: The Anti-Interventionist Movement of 1940–1941 as Revealed in the Papers of the America First Committee.* Stanford, CA: Hoover Institution Press, 1990. Doenecke first presents a seventy-eight-page introduction describing the leading anti-interventionist organization established to fight such measures as lend-lease, convoys, and the occupation of Iceland. The volume then reproduces 149 documents concerning the committee's work and policies.

17:17   Howlett, Charles F., ed. *The American Peace Movement: References and Resources.* This book briefly describes over 1,600 articles, books, and unpublished theses (11:34).

17:18   Great Britain. Foreign Office, and Ernest Llewellyn Woodward, eds. *Documents on British*

Foreign Policy, 1919–1939. First Series, 1919–1929. Series 1A, 1925–1929. Second Series, 1930–1938. Third Series, 1938–1939. 62 vols. London: H. M. Stationery Office, 1946–1985. This collection is of enormous value to the student of diplomacy not only for coverage of Anglo-American relations but also for documents on such matters as disarmament and East Asia.

17:19   Hachey, Thomas E., ed. *Confidential Dispatches: Analyses of America by the British Ambassador, 1939–1945.* Evanston, IL: New University Press, 1974. After his introductory essay, Hachey presents detailed dispatches written either by Ambassador Halifax or under his personal direction.

17:20   Swanson, Roger Frank, ed. *Canadian-American Summit Diplomacy, 1923–1973: Selected Speeches and Documents.* Toronto: McClelland and Stewart, 1975. Included are speeches of Herbert Hoover, Franklin D. Roosevelt, and prime ministers R. B. Bennett and MacKenzie King.

17:21   Goldberg, Harold J., ed. *Documents of Soviet-American Relations. Vol. 1: Intervention, Famine Relief, International Affairs, 1917–1933 (1993). Vol. 2: Propaganda, Economic Affairs, Recognition, 1917–1933. Vol. 3: Diplomatic Relations, Economic Relations, Propaganda, International Affairs, Neutrality, 1933–1941.* Vol. 3. Gulf Breeze, FL: Academic International Press, 1993–1998. These volumes not only offer official documents (e.g., formal communications, treaties, diplomatic reports) but also press interviews and Soviet press articles reflecting official policy.

17:22   Soviet Union. Ministerstvo Inostrannykh Del., and Andrei Gromyko, eds. *Soviet Peace Efforts on the Eve of World War II (September 1938–August 1939): Documents and Records.* 2 vols. Moscow: Novosti Press Agency Publishing House, 1973. This collection of 449 documents (September 29, 1938, to September 1, 1939) includes items from official American, British, German, Italian, and Polish publications available elsewhere, but most of the material from the Soviet archives is new.

BIBLIOGRAPHIES

17:23   Burns, Richard Dean, ed. *Herbert Hoover: A Bibliography of His Times and Presidency.* Wilmington, DE: Scholarly Resources, 1991. This annotated bibliographical guide has 2,452 entries.

17:24   Doenecke, Justus D., ed. *Anti-Intervention: A Bibliographical Introduction to Isolationism and Pacifism from World War I to the Early Cold War.* This work summarizes over 1,500 books, articles, and doctoral theses (1:201).

17:25   Frederick, Richard G., ed. *Warren G. Harding: A Bibliography.* Westport, CT: Greenwood Press, 1992. This book lists 3,386 entries, all having exceptionally brief annotations. The foreign affairs section is subdivided by regions and at times by countries; it also includes separate entries for such matters as war debts and the Washington conference of 1921–1922.

17:26   Lincove, David A., and Gary R. Treadway, eds. *The Anglo-American Relationship: An Annotated Bibliography of Scholarship, 1945–1985.* This volume shows earlier scholarship emphasizing convergence and community of interest; later scholarship stresses diversity and discord (1:244).

17:27   O'Brien, Patrick G., ed. *Herbert Hoover: A Bibliography.* Westport, CT: Greenwood Press, 1993. This book contains 2,643 entries, all of which are annotated. Much attention is given to foreign policy.

17:28   Smith, Myron J., Jr., ed. *Pearl Harbor, 1941: A Bibliography.* New York: Greenwood Press, 1991. The author lists over 1,500 entries, many of which are annotated. Although the collection is somewhat indiscriminate and the entries at times too terse, the sheer scope of this volume must give it a place in any listing.

17:29   Stewart, William J., with Jeanne Schauble, eds. *The Era of Franklin D. Roosevelt: A Selected Bibliography of Periodical, Essay, and Dissertation Literature, 1945–1971.* 2d ed. Hyde Park, NY: Franklin D. Roosevelt Library, 1974. Though obviously dated, this book still offers a handy reference to 1,339 articles and dissertations on aspects of the Roosevelt presidency. There is much material on foreign policy.

17:30   Tracey, Kathleen, ed. *Herbert Hoover, A Bibliography: His Writings and Addresses.* Stanford, CA: Hoover Institution Press, 1977. The material listed here covers the period from Hoover's engineering career at the turn of the century to his postpresidential years, excluding most presidential papers available elsewhere.

HISTORIOGRAPHY

17:31   Barnhart, Michael A. "The Origins of the Second World War in Asia and the Pacific: Synthesis Impossible?" *Diplomatic History* 20 (Spring 1996): 241–60. Barnhart offers a thorough bibliographical essay on the coming of the Pacific war, giving particular attention to internal Japanese decisionmaking. For an updated version, see Hogan, *Paths to Power: The Historiography of American Foreign Relations to 1941* (New York: Cambridge University Press, 2000).

17:32   Bolt, Ernest C., Jr. "Isolation, Expansion, and Peace: American Foreign Policy between the Wars." In *American Foreign Relations, A Historiographical Review,* ed. Gerald K. Haines and J. Samuel Walker, 133–57. Westport, CT: Greenwood Press, 1981. The essay ably traces historiography of the interwar period through publications appearing in 1980.

17:33   Braeman, John. "American Foreign Policy in the Age of Normalcy: Three Historiographical Traditions." *Amerikastudien/American Studies (Stuttgart)* 26 (November 1981): 125–58. Despite substantive differences, the major historiographical schools —Wilsonian internationalist, realist, and new left— are all guilty of presentism in evaluating American policies in terms of contemporary concerns. Crucial to American policy is the overwhelming sense of security enjoyed by the United States in the 1920s.

17:34   _____. "The New Left and American Foreign Policy during the Age of Normalcy: A Reexamination." *Business History Review* 57 (Spring 1983): 73–104. The author uses a host of recent studies and monographs to claim that the new left exaggerated how much American business leaders needed or wanted government support for their overseas activities. Government officials acted less as agents of corporate interests than as policymakers trying to harness private capital for national policy objectives.

17:35   _____. "Power and Diplomacy: The 1920s Reappraised." *Review of Politics* 44 (July 1982): 342–69. Braeman indicts the "realist" school, claiming that in the 1921–1933 period American policies were neither naïve nor unwise. During this period, the United States enjoyed unmatched security, explaining policies condemned by the realists.

17:36   Butow, Robert J. C. "How Roosevelt Attacked Japan at Pearl Harbor: Myth Masquerading as History." *Prologue* 28 (Fall 1996): 209–21. Butow accuses Pearl Harbor revisionists of disregarding the rules of scholarship and of glossing over the complexities of the historical record.

17:37   Clifford, J. Garry. "Both Ends of the Telescope: New Perspectives on FDR and American Entry into World War II." *Diplomatic History* 13 (Spring 1989): 213–30. In critiquing recent scholarly literature, Clifford advances the argument that Roosevelt failed to define common ground with his opponents and played down his own capacity to lead.

17:38   Cohen, Warren I. "Introduction." In *New Frontiers in American–East Asian Relations: Essays Presented to Dorothy Borg,* ed. Warren I. Cohen, xix–xxiv. New York: Columbia University Press, 1983. The author discusses the work of historians Tyler Dennett, A. Whitney Griswold, and Dorothy Borg.

17:39   Cole, Wayne S. "American Entry into World War II: A Historiographical Appraisal." *Mississippi Valley Historical Review* 43 (March 1957): 595–617. Cole provides a summary of the internationalist and revisionist perspectives, with attention given to the climate of opinion in which they developed, the problem of "court history," and certain historiographical deficiencies.

17:40   Craig, Campbell. "The Not-So-Strange Career of Charles Beard." In an article highly critical of a leading historian, Craig sees Beard in the late 1940s abandoning his economic analysis and adherence to national self-sufficiency to concentrate on the narrower political issue of presidential power, a shift prompted by Beard's realization that his belief in U.S. invulnerability was no longer valid (2:92).

17:41   Doenecke, Justus D. "Beyond Polemics: An Historiographical Re-appraisal of American Entry into World War II." *History Teacher* 12 (February 1979): 217–51. This survey supplements but does not replace older bibliographical essays. The author finds a newer breed of revisionists possibly exaggerating impersonal forces but helping to terminate an increasingly sterile quarrel over the "culpability" of Franklin Roosevelt.

17:42   _____. "U.S. Policy and the European War, 1939–1941." *Diplomatic History* 19 (Fall 1995): 669–98. This historiographical essay focuses on policymakers and pressure groups, emphasizing works published since 1981. For an updated version, see Hogan, *Paths to Power: The Historiography of American Foreign Relations to 1941* (New York: Cambridge University Press, 2000).

17:43   Dunne, Michael. "Isolationism of a Kind: Two Generations of World Court Historiography in the United States." *Journal of American Studies* 21 (December 1987): 327–51. The author suggests that the court's American opponents were correct in being wary about universalist claims made on its behalf. Furthermore, the campaign for adherence was subordinate to the larger goal of American membership, or at least alignment with, the League of Nations.

17:44   Gardner, Lloyd C. "Isolation and Appeasement: An American View of Taylor's Origins." In *The Origins of the Second World War Reconsidered: The A. J. P. Taylor Debate after Twenty-Five Years,* ed. Gordon Martel, 210–26. Boston: Allen and Unwin, 1986. Taylor's effort to portray "appeasement" as a rational response to the Anglo-French predicament required him incorrectly to show the United States as a totally isolationist nation.

17:45   Haines, Gerald K. "Roads to War: United States Foreign Policy, 1931–1941." In *American Foreign Relations, A Historiographical Review,* ed. Gerald K. Haines and J. Samuel Walker, 159–85. Westport, CT: Greenwood Press, 1981. The essay offers a fine summary of the literature through 1980.

17:46   Hata, Ikuhiko. "Japanese Historical Writing on the Origins and Progress of the Pacific War." In *Papers on Modern Japan 1968,* ed. David Carlisle Stanley Sissons, and Australian National University, Dept. of International Relations, 79–90. Canberra: Dept. of International Relations, Research School of Pacific Studies, Australian National University, 1968. Although this article takes note of Japan's friendly reception to American revisionist studies of the war's origins, it describes in a relatively objective manner the Japanese documents that escaped wholesale burning during the surrender.

17:47   Heinrichs, Waldo H. "The Middle Years, 1900–1945, and the Question of a Large U.S. Policy for East Asia." In *New Frontiers in American–East Asian Relations: Essays Presented to Dorothy Borg,* ed. Warren I. Cohen, 77–106. New York: Columbia University Press, 1983. In a bibliographical essay, the author finds American–East Asian policy tending to be cautious, conservative, and founded on the view that U.S. interests in Asia, considered alone, were marginal.

17:48   Jacobson, Jon. "Is There a New International History of the 1920s?" *American Historical Review* 88 (June 1983): 617–45. Jacobson sees a new international history that bypasses "tired debates" over the primacy of domestic or foreign policy. This article integrates military and political relations to financial and economic concerns and examines the interpenetration of the private and public sectors of the international political economy.

17:49   Loewenheim, Francis L. "An Illusion That Shaped History: New Light on the History and Historiography of American Peace Efforts before Munich." In *Some Pathways in Twentieth-Century History: Essays in Honor of Reginald Charles McGrane,* ed. Daniel R. Beaver, 177–220. Detroit: Wayne State University Press, 1969. This essay traces the exploratory efforts and soundings of diplomats of foreign countries, inspired mainly by Roosevelt and Undersecretary of State Welles, to set up an international peacemaking conference. It failed because of domestic politics, Anglo-American distrust, hostile feelings between Welles and Secretary of State Hull, and indifference in foreign capitals, especially Berlin.

17:50   Maddox, Robert James. "Another Look at the Legend of Isolationism in the 1920's." *Mid-America* 53 (January 1971): 35–43. Maddox is critical of the thesis of the Wisconsin school that the U.S. government was deeply involved economically in international affairs.

17:51 McKercher, Brian J. C. "Reaching for the Brass Ring: The Recent Historiography of Interwar American Foreign Relations." In a historiographical essay that pays particular attention to non-American historians, McKercher goes beyond older debates engendered by traditionalists and the Williams school of revisionists (15:47). For an updated version, see Hogan, *Paths to Power: The Historiography of American Foreign Relations to 1941* (New York: Cambridge University Press, 2000).

17:52 Schröder, Hans-Jürgen. "Twentieth-Century German-American Relations: Historiography and Research Perspectives." In *America and the Germans: An Assessment of a Three-Hundred-Year History. Vol. 2: The Relationship in the Twentieth Century,* ed. Frank Trommler and Joseph McVeigh, 147–67. Philadelphia: University of Pennsylvania Press, 1985. The author calls for more attention to the political dimensions of economic factors and to a multilateral approach, by which he means examining other powers.

Overviews

17:53 Adler, Selig. *The Uncertain Giant: 1921–1941: American Foreign Policy between the Wars.* This synthesis of secondary works on the interwar era focuses on policy hesitations that resulted from the public's uncertain response to Hitler. The author gives considerable attention to the effects of domestic problems on foreign policy (15:52).

17:54 Barnes, Harry Elmer, ed. *Perpetual War for Perpetual Peace: A Critical Examination of the Foreign Policy of Franklin Delano Roosevelt and Its Aftermath.* Caldwell, ID: Caxton Printers, 1953. This book is an anthology of the early revisionist case against FDR. Contributors range from such strident writers as Charles Callan Tansill, George Morgenstern, and Barnes himself to the more moderate William L. Neumann, William Henry Chamberlin, and George Lundberg. For the best treatment of Barnes's own revisionism, see Roy Carroll Turnbaugh, Jr., "Harry Elmer Barnes: The Quest for Truth and Justice" (Ph.D. diss., University of Illinois, 1977).

17:55 Beard, Charles A., with G. H. E. Smith.

The Idea of National Interest: An Analytical Study in American Foreign Policy. Rather than debunk the idea of national interest, Beard reapplied it to show that the United States could avoid war through national autarchy and geographic isolation (2:163).

17:56 Carr, Edward H. *The Twenty Years Crisis, 1919–1939: An Introduction to the Study of International Relations.* 2d ed. London: Macmillan and Co., 1946. Critical of the "harmony of interests" assumption that underlay Wilsonian thinking, a noted British scholar calls for orderly rectification of the status quo. Originally published in 1939.

17:57 Cohen, Warren I. *Empire without Tears: America's Foreign Relations, 1921–1933.* Philadelphia: Temple University Press, 1987. This account shows Republican statesmen worked closely with business leaders to create a stable order in which U.S. strategic and economic interests would survive.

17:58 Cole, Wayne S. *Determinism and American Foreign Relations during the Franklin D. Roosevelt Era.* Lanham, MD: University Press of America, 1995. This series of essays covers aspects of FDR's leadership and isolationism. The author shows skepticism concerning the "great man" and "devil" theories of history.

17:59 Current, Richard N. "The United States and 'Collective Security': Notes on the History of an Idea." In *Isolation and Security: Ideas and Interests in Twentieth-Century American Foreign Policy,* ed. Alexander DeConde, 33–55. Durham, NC: Duke University Press, 1957. In this thoughtful and critical review of pre-1930s ideas and their effect on foreign policy, Current most noteworthily comments on the origin of the phrase "collective security."

17:60 Doenecke, Justus D., and John E. (John Edward Wilz) Wiltz. *From Isolation to War, 1931–1941.* 2d. ed. Arlington Heights, IL: Harlan Davidson, 1991. In a major revision of then Wiltz's volume of the same name (1968), which is still valuable on earlier historiographical debates, the authors integrate over two decades of scholarship in an account that combines historiography and narrative.

17:61 Edmonds, Robin. *The Big Three: Churchill, Roosevelt, and Stalin in Peace & War.* New York: Norton, 1991. The author notes the dichotomy in Washington between U.S. strategic requirements in the Pacific, which would involve air support to the Philippines and a balanced British fleet at Singapore, and the conduct of American policy, which would make anything more than a brief respite unattainable.

17:62   Egan, Clifford L., and Alexander W. Knott, eds. *Essays in Twentieth-Century American Diplomatic History Dedicated to Professor Daniel M. Smith.* Washington, DC: University Press of America, 1982. Within this collection, Stephen John Kneeshaw notes opposition within Japan to the Kellogg-Briand pact in "The Japanese Reaction to the Kellogg-Briand Pact, 1928–1929: The View from the United States" (42–60); Benjamin D. Rhodes in "Sir Ronald Lindsay and the British View from Washington" (62–89) describes his skill in smoothing relations between the two countries; Michael Holcomb in "Sir John Simon's War with Henry L. Stimson" (90–110) traces tensions between the men over Manchuria policy; and Judith Papachristou discusses why FDR failed to collaborate with the Soviets over East Asia in "Soviet-American Relations and the East-Asian Imbroglio, 1933–1941" (111–36). Also included is Brooks Van Everen, "Franklin D. Roosevelt and the Problem of Nazi Germany."

17:63   Ellis, L. Ethan. *Republican Foreign Policy, 1921–1933.* New Brunswick: Rutgers University Press, 1968. This broad survey, with its brisk style, is friendly to Secretary of State Hughes, less so to Secretary Kellogg.

17:64   Ferrell, Robert H. *American Diplomacy in the Great Depression: Hoover-Stimson Foreign Policy, 1929–1933.* New Haven: Yale University Press, 1957. Reprint 1970 (Norton). Ferrell offers lively accounts of such crises as Manchuria, Shanghai, and the London Naval Conference of 1930 while offering harsh views of Secretary Stimson and President Hoover. See also Ferrell, *Henry L. Stimson* in Vol. 2, New Series, Bemis, ed., *The American Secretaries of State and Their Diplomacy* (New York: Cooper Square Publishers, 1963).

17:65   Gardner, Lloyd C. "New Deal Diplomacy: A View from the Seventies." In *Watershed of Empire: Essays on New Deal Foreign Policy,* ed. Leonard P. Liggio and James J. Martin, 95–131. Colorado Springs: Ralph Myles, 1976. Gardner sees New Deal policy centering on a liberal capitalist world order, one that would function with a minimum of international and intranational control.

17:66   Graebner, Norman A. "The Retreat to Utopia." In *America as a World Power: A Realist Appraisal from Wilson to Reagan: Essays,* ed. Norman A. Graebner, 1–30. Wilmington, DE: Scholarly Resources, 1984. The author finds that collective security of the interwar period offered no defense against aggression nor did it solve the problem of peaceful change.

17:67   Iriye, Akira. *The Globalizing of America, 1913–1945.* Although political and economic matters are given full play, Iriye makes an especially strong contribution in his discussion of frequently ignored cultural concerns (2:37).

17:68   _____. *The Origins of the Second World War in Asia and the Pacific.* New York: Longman, 1987. Steeped in Japanese and American sources, this work presents Japan as finding itself increasingly confined by the international system established during the Washington conference of 1921–1922 and feeling forced to challenge the western powers.

17:69   Jonas, Manfred. "The United States and the Failure of Collective Security in the 1930s." In *Twentieth-Century American Foreign Policy,* ed. John Braeman, Robert H. Bremner, and David Brody, 241–93. Columbus: Ohio State University Press, 1971. The author offers a succinct account of American isolationism in the 1930s, noting that the public mood changed only when the United States saw its own security at stake.

17:70   Junker, Detlef. *Der unteilbare Weltmarckt: Das ökonomische Interesse in der Aussenpolitik der USA, 1933–1941 [The Indivisible Market: Economic Interests in the Foreign Policy of the USA, 1933–1941].* Stuttgart: E. Klett, 1975. The author finds Roosevelt defining American self-interest globally, insisting that political freedom, international security, and economic markets were indivisible and must be safeguarded on a world scale.

17:71   Langer, William L., and S. Everett Gleason. *The World Crisis of 1937–1940 and American*

Foreign Policy. Vol. 1: The Challenge to Isolation. Vol. 2: The Undeclared War, 1940–1941. New York: Harper and Row, 1952–1953. Reprint 1970 (Peter Smith). The authors offer a pioneering and exhaustive study in the assessment of American foreign policy during the Roosevelt administration's struggle to escape from isolationism, based on original sources made available to the authors long before other researchers had such access. For Langer's account of the origins of these volumes, see his *In and Out of the Ivory Tower: The Autobiography of William L. Langer* (1977) (18:636).

17:72   Little, Douglas. "Antibolshevism and American Foreign Policy, 1919–1939: The Diplomacy of Self-Delusion." *American Quarterly* 35 (Fall 1983): 376–90. The State Department through the interwar years feared that replicas of the Bolshevik revolution might occur in Mexico, Nicaragua, El Salvador, Greece, and Spain.

17:73   Louria, Margot. *Triumph and Downfall: America's Pursuit of Peace and Prosperity, 1921–1933.* Westport, CT: Greenwood Press, 2001. The author focuses on the tenures as secretary of state of Hughes, Kellogg, and Stimson, finding all three acting responsibly amid difficult circumstances.

17:74   Maddux, Thomas R. "Red Fascism, Brown Bolshevism: American Image of Totalitarianism in the 1930's." *Historian* 40 (May 1977): 85–103. Maddux reevaluates the origins of the idea of "red fascism" as described in Adler and Paterson, "Red Fascism: The Merger of Nazi Germany and Soviet Russia in the American Image of Totalitarianism, 1930's–1950's" (1970) (17:500). He disputes their contention that such an identification between the two regimes came primarily in the 1939–1941 period, arguing instead that the American press had much earlier reached a widespread consensus on the essential similarities.

17:75   O'Connor, Raymond G. *Force & Diplomacy: Essays Military and Diplomatic.* Coral Gables: University of Miami Press, 1972. These essays cover disarmament, naval strategy, nonrecognition, and use of sanctions. See also O'Connor's *War, Diplomacy, and History: Papers and Reviews* (Lanham, MD: University Press of America, 1979), in which he claims FDR sought war in 1941.

17:76   Offner, Arnold A. *The Origins of the Second World War: American Foreign Policy and World Politics, 1917–1941.* New York: Praeger, 1975. Reprint 1986 (Krieger). Offner sets the scene of American foreign policy at the beginning of World War II in the broader ideological context of the European and Asian struggle for power.

17:77   Payne, Howard C., Raymond A. Callahan, and Edward M. Bennett. *As the Storm Clouds Gathered: European Perceptions of American Foreign Policy in the 1930s.* Durham, NC: Moore Publishing Co., 1979. Payne focuses on French-British-American "triangular tensions" as France contemplated its security dilemma after the collapse of the Anglo-American guarantee. Callahan explores the lack of substance behind the supposed Anglo-American special relationship. Bennett examines the Soviet Union's frustrating attempt to discover the "real" American attitude toward Germany and Japan. France, Russia, and to a lesser degree Britain all hoped that an aroused United States would forestall a devastating European war.

17:78   Reynolds, David. *From Munich to Pearl Harbor: Roosevelt's America and the Origins of the Second World War.* Chicago: Ivan R. Dee, 2001. This interpretive overview shows how FDR led Americans into a new global perception of international relations, suggesting also how some essentials of a later cold war worldview were also formed in this period.

17:79   Rhodes, Benjamin D. *United States Foreign Policy in the Interwar Period, 1918–1941: The Golden Age of American Diplomatic and Military Complacency.* Westport, CT: Praeger, 2001. This general survey presents the traditional picture of U.S. diplomacy toward Europe as far too selfish and sullen, though Rhodes praises the Good Neighbor Policy in Latin America. He finds cheapness and blind naïveté leading to a dangerous neglect of U.S. armed forces and sees FDR as weak in fighting isolationism and relying excessively on economic sanctions in attempting to restrain Japan.

17:80   Russett, Bruce M. *No Clear and Present Danger: A Skeptical View of the United States Entry into World War II.* Rev. ed. New York: Harper and Row, 1972. Reprint 1997 (Westview Press). A prominent political scientist denies that either Germany or Japan ever threatened American security. By the end of 1941, American lend-lease and naval convoys assured Britain's survival, and Germany was totally bogged down on the Russian steppes. Japan, he declared, opted for war when the United States raised the diplomatic ante by foolishly insisting on its evacuation of China.

17:81 Schmitz, David F., and Richard D. Challener, eds. *Appeasement in Europe: A Reassessment of U.S. Policies.* Westport, CT: Greenwood Press, 1990. Contributors include Wayne S. Cole, who denies that FDR was ever an appeaser (1–20); Douglas Little, who sees British and American policymakers so concerned with the specter of communist subversion that they ignored the danger of fascist aggression (21–50); Jane Karoline Vieth, who finds in Munich a turning point in British and American appeasement (51–74); Schmitz, who asserts that Italy's invasion of Ethiopia failed to shake FDR and the State Department's favorable analysis of Mussolini and fascism (75–102); and Richard A. Harrison, who traces FDR's efforts to develop alternatives to appeasement (103–43).

17:82 Smith, Robert Freeman. "American Foreign Relations, 1920–1942." Rejecting both the realist and traditionalist schools of diplomatic history, the author emphasizes the primacy of economics. Smith views the period from 1920 to 1942 as an era when American leaders experimented with neocolonialism (15:72).

17:83 _____. "Republican Policy and the Pax Americana, 1921–1932." In *From Colony to Empire: Essays in the History of American Foreign Relations,* ed. William Appleman Williams, 253–92. New York: John Wiley, 1972. The author sees Hughes and Kellogg as sober realists who believed that international flexibility could prevent the world conflagration that could destroy civilization. Republican objectives of stability and market expansion were to be accomplished by disarmament, the reentry of Germany into the world economy, and expansion of open door principles throughout Europe.

17:84 Tansill, Charles Callan. *Back Door to War: The Roosevelt Foreign Policy, 1933–1941.* Chicago: H. Regnery Co., 1952. In this major revisionist work, Tansill accuses FDR of foolishly thrusting the Poland guarantee on Chamberlain and of resisting accom-

modation with the Japanese so he could open his "back door to war."

17:85 Taylor, A. J. P. *The Origins of the Second World War.* New York: Atheneum, 1962. Taylor sees Hitler as a traditional European statesman merely defending legitimate German interests and regaining territories either vital to German security or belonging to Germany culturally and ethnically. He blames Great Britain for the war, with a reluctant France tied to her policy. In his preface to the American edition, Taylor sees the United States never more active or more effective in Europe than in the 1920s, as it played the major role in settling reparations, restoring stable finances, and pacifying Europe.

17:86 Weinberg, Gerhard L. *A World at Arms: A Global History of World War II.* New York: Cambridge University Press, 1994. This comprehensive multiarchival work argues that Hitler welcomed war with the United States, feeling confident about the Japanese navy and his own U-boats. Once the Russian campaign ended, he would attack the United States. See also Weinberg, "From Confrontation to Cooperation: Germany and the United States, 1933–1949," in Trommler and McVeigh, *America and the Germans: An Assessment of a Three-Hundred-Year History. Vol. 2: The Relationship in the Twentieth Century* (Philadelphia: University of Pennsylvania Press, 1985).

17:87 Williams, William Appleman. *The Tragedy of American Diplomacy.* Finding World War II "the war for the American frontier," Williams sees U.S. resistance to European and Asian challenges rooted in its quest for open door empire (2:97). This book was first published in 1959.

Biographical Studies

COLLECTIVE

17:88 Gellman, Irwin F. *Secret Affairs: Franklin Roosevelt, Cordell Hull, and Sumner Welles.* Baltimore: Johns Hopkins University Press, 1995. Reprint 2002 (Enigma Books). This collective biography of

Hull, Welles, and FDR shows Hull as ailing absentee secretary, Welles as troubled homosexual, and a confident FDR continually undercutting his aides.

17:89   Harper, John Lamberton. *American Visions of Europe: Franklin D. Roosevelt, George F. Kennan, and Dean G. Acheson.* New York: Cambridge University Press, 1994. Harper portrays Roosevelt finding U.S. entry into World War II necessary but also adhering to a vision of a morally superior United States redeeming a corrupt Europe. He divides the foreign policy establishment into "Hullian" liberals, a pro-British party, advocates of Soviet "protocontainment," and those espousing "Europhobic hemispherism."

17:90   Josephson, Harold, with Sandi E. Cooper, Solomon Wank, and Lawrence S. Wittner, eds. *Biographical Dictionary of Modern Peace Leaders.* This volume is particularly good on figures of the interwar period, both Americans and those from other nations (1:204).

17:91   Kuehl, Warren F., ed. *Biographical Dictionary of Internationalists.* Westport, CT: Greenwood Press, 1983. This work is particularly helpful on figures of the interwar period, both Americans and foreigners.

17:92   Merli, Frank J., and Theodore A. Wilson, eds. *Makers of American Diplomacy. Vol. 2: From Theodore Roosevelt to Henry Kissinger.* Contributions include biographical articles by Charles DeBenedetti on James T. Shotwell (385–405), William Kamman on Henry L. Stimson (407–30), Russell D. Buhite on Stanley K. Hornbeck (431–57), and Wilson and Richard D. McKinzie on Franklin D. Roosevelt (459–91) (2:195). This is the second of two volumes; also published in a single volume.

AMERICAN

William E. Borah

17:93   Maddox, Robert James. *William E. Borah and American Foreign Policy.* Maddox argues that Borah had a far more practical comprehension of for-

eign affairs than his often grotesque rhetoric and utopian peace plans would indicate (14:93).

17:94   McKenna, Marian C. *Borah.* In the best complete life of the powerful isolationist, McKenna argues that Borah did not seek withdrawal from world affairs but wanted to exercise the nation's influence at the most opportune times in the most advantageous locations (14:94).

John Dewey

17:95   Diggins, John P. "John Dewey in Peace and War." *American Scholar* 50 (Spring 1981): 213–30. Diggins shows how America's leading philosopher embraced nonintervention by 1939.

17:96   Howlett, Charles F. *Troubled Philosopher: John Dewey and the Struggle for World Peace.* This account shows how the prominent educator and philosopher converted to pacifism soon after World War I. Dewey found the League too coercive, backed the effort to outlaw war, and opposed most of FDR's foreign and domestic policies (14:104). See also Howlett, "John Dewey and the Crusade to Outlaw War," *World Affairs* 138 (Spring 1976): 336–55.

Calvin Coolidge

17:97   Ferrell, Robert H. *The Presidency of Calvin Coolidge.* Ferrell faults Coolidge for not taking more interest in the internal confusion of China and Japan and for ignoring the precarious nature of Germany's Weimar Republic (15:129).

17:98   McCoy, Donald R. *Calvin Coolidge: The Quiet President.* McCoy provides a generally sympathetic account of Coolidge and the problems of the White House between 1923 and 1929. In this carefully researched volume, the author analyzes in particular Coolidge's diplomacy toward Europe, Latin America, the World Court, and the movement for the outlawry of war (15:130).

John Foster Dulles

17:99   Dulles, John Foster. *War, Peace and*

Change. New York: Harper and Brothers, 1939. The prominent international lawyer argues for recognizing the needs of "have-not" nations. No effort at collective security could work that did not permit peaceful alteration of the status quo.

17:100 Keim, Albert N. "John Foster Dulles and the Protestant World Order Movement on the Eve of World War II." *Journal of Church and State* 21 (Winter 1979): 73–89. Conveying far more than the title suggests, the article shows how Dulles saw the outset of World War II as reflecting little more than a conflict between rival imperialisms.

17:101 Pruessen, Ronald W. *John Foster Dulles: The Road to Power.* New York: Free Press, 1982. At this date still the most balanced and thorough study of Dulles's early years, this book offers full coverage of his role in the Paris Peace Conference, the reparations issue of the 1920s, and the type of internationalism represented by the Federal Council of Churches.

17:102 Toulouse, Mark G. *The Transformation of John Foster Dulles: From Prophet of Realism to Priest of Nationalism.* Macon, GA: Mercer University Press, 1985. This biography defends Dulles against charges of narrow isolationism in the interwar period and shows how he long opposed dividing the world into "good" and "bad" nations.

William Randolph Hearst

17:103 Carlisle, Rodney P. *Hearst and the New Deal—The Progressive as Reactionary.* New York: Garland Publishing, 1979. Hearst's views were not based on simple opposition to war or a desire that the United States remain aloof from foreign affairs. Rather he worked from a militant nationalism, anti-communism, and long-held suspicion of the British, French, Japanese, and Russians. See also Swanberg, *Citizen Hearst: A Biography of William Randolph Hearst* (1961) (10:136).

17:104 Mugridge, Ian. *The View from Xanadu: William Randolph Hearst and United States Foreign Policy.* Mugridge finds the foreign policy of the leading publisher not based on a blind belief in a self-sufficient Fortress America but in a general attitude of friendly relations with others (10:133).

Warren G. Harding

17:105 DeWitt, Howard A. "The 'New' Harding and American Foreign Policy: Warren G. Harding, Hiram W. Johnson, and Pragmatic Diplomacy." *Ohio History* 86 (Summer 1977): 96–114. DeWitt shows how Harding pandered to Johnson to neutralize possible opposition from the Republican Party's progressive-isolationist wing.

17:106 Murray, Robert K. *The Harding Era: Warren G. Harding and His Administration.* Minneapolis: University of Minnesota Press, 1969. Murray, reinterpreting the era, argues that Harding was not the do-nothing of legend. Rather he played a significant part in events between 1921 and 1923. If the "new Harding" is possibly overdrawn, the work devotes needed attention to American diplomacy.

17:107 Trani, Eugene P., and David L. Wilson. *The Presidency of Warren G. Harding.* This volume analyzes the diplomacy of the Harding administration in detail, with emphasis on the powerful role of Secretary of Commerce Hoover in the making of Harding's diplomacy (15:127).

Herbert Hoover

17:108 *Herbert Hoover Reassessed: Essays Commemorating the Fiftieth Anniversary of the Inauguration of Our Thirty-first President.* Washington, DC: Government Printing Office, 1981. This volume includes many scholarly articles on Hoover's foreign policy, including those by Benjamin D. Rhodes on British perceptions (30–41), Alexander DeConde on presidential foreign policy (313–34), Carl Q. Christol on the League and the World Court (335–79), Joseph Brandes on economic diplomacy (380–89), Benjamin M. Weissman on the Soviet famine (390–97), George J. Lerski on aid to Poland (397–400), and Donald R. McCoy on foreign policy in the 1939–1941 period (401–25).

17:109 Best, Gary Dean. *Herbert Hoover: The Postpresidential Years, 1933–1964.* 2 vols. Stanford, CA: Hoover Institution Press, 1983. Best offers an extremely detailed discussion of Hoover's views, including foreign policy, after he left the White House. In the process, he shows Hoover as more moderate than many isolationists. See also Best, "Totalitarianism or Peace: Herbert Hoover and the Road to War, 1939–1941," *Annals of Iowa* 44 (Winter 1979): 516–29.

17:110   Christol, Carl Q. "Herbert Hoover: The League of Nations and the World Court." In *Herbert Hoover Reassessed: Essays Commemorating the Fiftieth Anniversary of the Inauguration of Our Thirty-first President*, 335–79 (17:108). The author traces Hoover's support for both institutions.

17:111   DeConde, Alexander. "Herbert Hoover and Foreign Policy: A Retrospective Assessment." In *Herbert Hoover Reassessed: Essays Commemorating the Fiftieth Anniversary of the Inauguration of Our Thirty-first President*, 313–34 (17:108). Though DeConde questions Hoover's "ethnocentric isolationism," he praises the president's aversion to ideological crusades overseas.

17:112   Fausold, Martin L., with George T. Mazuzan, eds. *The Hoover Presidency: A Reappraisal.* Albany: State University of New York Press, 1974. In this anthology, Selig Adler contributes an article on Hoover's foreign policy, in which he criticizes new left interpretations, accusing left historians of rehabilitating Hoover to detract from FDR (153–63). Joan Hoff (formerly Hoff-Wilson) offers an appreciative treatment of Hoover's foreign policy views (163–86).

17:113   Fausold, Martin L. *The Presidency of Herbert C. Hoover.* Lawrence: University Press of Kansas, 1985. This general study of the Hoover presidency portrays the president as an "independent internationalist."

17:114   Hearden, Patrick J. "Herbert C. Hoover and the Dream of Capitalism in One Country." In *Redefining the Past: Essays in Diplomatic History in Honor of William Appleman Williams*, ed. Lloyd C. Gardner, 143–55. Corvallis, OR: Oregon State University Press, 1986. Hoover perceived an American system that would function successfully as a self-contained economic unit.

17:115   Hoff, Joan. *Herbert Hoover, Forgotten Progressive.* Boston: Little, Brown, 1975. Reprint 1992 (Waveland Press). Highly respectful of Hoover, Hoff

relates his anti-interventionism to his domestic vision of a decentralized but corporatist society.

17:116   Hoover, Herbert. *Addresses upon the American Road, 1933–1938.* New York: Scribner's, 1938. This collection includes ex-President Hoover's speeches on increasing difficulties in foreign relations, especially with Europe.

17:117   _____. *Addresses upon the American Road, 1940–1941.* New York: C. Scribner's Sons, 1941. Hoover calls for moderate aid to Britain and China and pushes his plan to feed occupied Europe.

17:118   _____. *An American Epic. Vol. 4: The Guns Cease Killing and the Saving of Life from Famine Begins, 1939–1963.* Chicago: Regnery, 1964. The former president describes his efforts to promote relief for Poland and Finland and his sponsorship of the National Committee on Food for the Small Democracies.

17:119   _____. *Further Addresses upon the American Road, 1938–1940.* New York: C. Scribner's Sons, 1940. These speeches show Hoover's increasing anti-interventionism as war approached.

17:120   _____. *The Memoirs of Herbert Hoover.* The first volume is *The Years of Adventure* (1874–1920); the second, *The Cabinet and the Presidency* (1920–1933); the third, *The Great Depression* (1929–1941). The author's bitterness intrudes—a bitterness both against his successor, Roosevelt, and against the nations of Europe that, Hoover believed, caused the Great Depression (15:259).

17:121   Levin, Clifford R. "Herbert Hoover, Internationalist, 1919–1923." *Prologue* 20 (Winter 1988): 249–67. Denying that Hoover's internationalism was simply a personal phase or a political ploy, the author sees Hoover as a man fervently in favor of such international cooperation as the League. Though he joined more nationalist administrations, he did so in hopes of accomplishing his goals in the most efficient fashion.

17:122   Myers, William Starr. *The Foreign Policies of Herbert Hoover, 1929–1933.* The author offers a sympathetic survey of the Hoover policies (15:133).

17:123　Smith, Richard Norton. *An Uncommon Man: The Triumph of Herbert Hoover.* New York: Simon and Schuster, 1984. This book is especially good on his post-presidential career, including foreign policy matters.

Hiram Johnson

17:124　Boyle, Peter G. "The Roots of Isolationism: A Case Study." *Journal of American Studies* 6 (April 1972): 41–50. Boyle finds reasoned conviction, not merely nationalism and emotion, playing an important role in framing the isolationism of Hiram Johnson. Johnson saw all foreign policy in terms of World War I, a conflict in which his son's health was broken from gassing.

17:125　Burke, Robert E., ed. *The Diary Letters of Hiram Johnson, 1917–1945.* Reproduced are highly opinionated and colorful letters to relatives covering a Senate career lasting from 1917 to 1945. The editor supplies a lengthy introduction (14:115).

17:126　DeWitt, Howard A. "Hiram Johnson and Early New Deal Diplomacy, 1933–1934." *California Historical Quarterly* 53 (Winter 1974): 377–86. Johnson sponsored legislation banning loans to nations that defaulted on their war debts and pressed for an arms embargo that would apply impartially to all belligerents.

17:127　Lower, Richard Coke. *A Bloc of One: The Politics and Career of Hiram W. Johnson.* Stanford, CA: Stanford University Press, 1993. This is the most thorough biography of an arch anti-interventionist.

Charles A. and Anne Morrow Lindbergh

17:128　Berg, A. Scott. *Lindbergh.* New York: G. P. Putnam's, 1998. In the most comprehensive life of Lindbergh, Berg uses hitherto unpublished material in describing the aviator's isolationist crusade.

17:129　Cole, Wayne S. *Charles A. Lindbergh and the Battle against American Intervention in World War II.* New York: Harcourt Brace Jovanovich, 1974. Cole elucidates Lindbergh's general isolationism and

describes the Lone Eagle's evaluation of German aviation, attitudes toward Nazi Germany, and role in the America First Committee.

17:130　Fredette, Raymond H. "Lindbergh and Munich: A Myth Revived." *Missouri Historical Society Bulletin* 30 (April 1977): 197–202. Fredette effectively challenges the myth that Lindbergh's reports on German strength helped foster the Munich pact. He also critiques Berg's *Lindbergh* (1998) (17:128).

17:131　Hixson, Walter L. *Charles A. Lindbergh, Lone Eagle.* New York: HarperCollins, 1996. Hixson offers a balanced and succinct study that includes coverage of his isolationism.

17:132　Lindbergh, Anne Morrow. *The Flower and the Nettle: Diaries and Letters of Anne Morrow Lindbergh, 1936–1939.* New York: Harcourt Brace Jovanovich, 1976. A poet and woman of letters, the wife of Charles A. Lindbergh presents Charles's position on such matters as the strength of German aviation, the air decoration given her husband by Hermann Goering, and the rise of Soviet communism. According to Berg, *Lindbergh* (1998) (17:128), she purged enthusiastic comments about Germany from the published text while keeping those that were critical.

17:133　_____. *War Within and Without: Diaries and Letters of Anne Morrow Lindbergh, 1939–1944.* New York: Harcourt Brace Jovanovich, 1980. Here the wife of Charles Lindbergh offers an unmatched insight into the personalities of the isolationist movement, in the process showing her abhorrence of Nazism and the meaning of her phrase "the wave of the future."

17:134　_____. *The Wave of the Future: A Confession of Faith.* New York: Harcourt, Brace and Company, 1940. Examined carefully, this book urges the United States to face the new world of dictatorships not by promoting destructive war but by fostering domestic reform. The wave of the future was not totalitarianism but a scientific, mechanized, material era of civilization. For further defense of her thesis, see her "Reaffirmation," *Atlantic* 167 (June 1941): 681–86.

17:135　Lindbergh, Charles A. *The Wartime Journals of Charles A. Lindbergh.* New York: Harcourt

Brace Jovanovich, 1970. Amid his account of visits to Britain, France, Germany, and the Soviet Union, Lindbergh gives his reasons for admiration of the German people, hostility toward Soviet Russia, suspicion of "Jewish interests," and desire for a negotiated peace. Berg, in *Lindbergh* (1998) (17:128), notes that despite the publisher's disclaimer, there were several substantive omissions from Lindbergh's journal, primarily referring to Jews.

Walter Lippmann

17:136   Blum, D. Steven. *Walter Lippmann, Cosmopolitanism in the Century of Total War.* Ithaca: Cornell University Press, 1984. The author portrays the noted columnist as an advocate of realpolitik, breaking with the parochialism and dogmatic posture he found in Wilsonianism.

17:137   Blum, John Morton, ed. *Public Philosopher: Selected Letters of Walter Lippmann.* New York: Ticknor and Fields, 1985. This correspondence shows the noted columnist's evolution from a defender of the neutrality acts to a partisan of collective security.

17:138   Steel, Ronald. *Walter Lippmann and the American Century.* This book is undoubtedly the best study available of the prominent interventionist political analyst, as it is the most detailed and analytical (14:182).

George C. Marshall

17:139   Bland, Larry I., and Sharon R. Ritenour, eds. *The Papers of George Catlett Marshall. Vol. 2: "We Cannot Delay," July 1, 1939–December 6, 1941.* Baltimore: Johns Hopkins University Press, 1986. This volume covers the period from Marshall's accession as acting chief of staff of the army until the eve of Pearl Harbor. It reveals Marshall's caution on U.S. commitments to Britain and overly optimistic views on defending the Philippines. For the period December 1880 through June 1939, see *Vol. 1: The Soldierly Spirit* (1981).

17:140   Pogue, Forrest C. *George C. Marshall. Vol. 1: Education of a General, 1880–1939. Vol. 2: Or-*

deal and Hope, 1939–1942. New York: Viking Press, 1963–1966. Volume 1 covers Marshall's career in the Philippines during the Spanish-American War, France during World War I, and China in the time of the war lords. Volume 2 centers on prewar planning and American entry into World War II. See also Stoler, *George C. Marshall: Soldier-Statesman of the American Century* (1989) (18:415), and Cray, *General of the Army: George C. Marshall, Soldier and Statesman* (1990) (18:412).

Billy Mitchell

17:141   Brune, Lester H. "Foreign Policy and the Air Power Dispute, 1919–1932." *Historian* 23 (August 1961): 449–64. Brune first discusses such navalists as writer William Gardiner, historian Dudley W. Knox, and admirals Harold Yarnell and William V. Pratt, all of whom stressed economic expansion in the Pacific. He then turns to air advocate General William ("Billy") Mitchell, who, despite the interservice rivalry with the navy, also adopted a confrontationalist posture in Asia.

17:142   Hurley, Alfred F. *Billy Mitchell, Crusader for Air Power.* New ed. Bloomington: Indiana University Press, 1975. General Mitchell remained the principal source of the American conception of airpower. Hurley offers a balanced picture of the nation's leading advocate of airpower, a man both prophetic and self-destructive. Originally published in 1964.

Henry Morgenthau, Jr

17:143   Blum, John Morton, ed. *From the Morgenthau Diaries. Vol. 1: Years of Crisis, 1928–1938.* Boston: Houghton Mifflin, 1959. The first in a three-volume political biography of FDR's secretary of the treasury, this work emphasizes Morgenthau's activities at the Treasury and unique relationship with the president. Chapter 10 deals with loans to Chiang Kai-shek, aid to France, trade with the Soviet Union, relations with Mexico, and disagreements with Secretary of State Hull.

17:144   _____. *From the Morgenthau Diaries. Vol. 2: Years of Urgency, 1938–1941.* Boston:

Houghton Mifflin, 1965. This volume finds the treasury secretary and personal friend of Roosevelt leading the advocacy of economic assistance to the anti-Nazi powers, condoning aid to China despite the corruption of its government, and ardently proposing sanctions against the Japanese.

Douglas MacArthur

17:145   James, D. Clayton. *The Years of MacArthur. Vol. 1: 1880–1941.* Boston: Houghton Mifflin, 1970. In this definitive life of MacArthur, James covers his role as chief of staff and military adviser to the Philippines.

17:146   Petillo, Carol Morris. *Douglas MacArthur: The Philippine Years.* Bloomington: Indiana University Press, 1981. Significantly adding to the still definitive biography, James, *The Years of MacArthur* (1970–1985) (18:403), this book does much with MacArthur's role as military adviser from 1937 to 1941.

Reinhold Niebuhr

17:147   Doenecke, Justus D. "Reinhold Niebuhr and His Critics: The Interventionist Controversy in World War II." *Anglican and Episcopal History* 64 (December 1995): 459–81. This essay reveals the bitterness of a debate that rent American Protestantism, showing Niebuhr's strong dispute with Charles Clayton Morrison, editor of the *Christian Century.*

17:148   Fox, Richard Wightman. *Reinhold Niebuhr: A Biography.* New York: Pantheon Books, 1985. This biography, often critical of its subject, shows the intellectual odyssey of America's leading and most articulate interventionist among Protestant theologians.

17:149   Niebuhr, Reinhold. *Christianity and Power Politics.* New York: C. Scribner's Sons, 1940. Offering a highly influential attack on Christian pacifism, Niebuhr claims that its perfectionism sentimentalizes the Christian faith and betrays its deepest insights.

17:150   _____. *Moral Man and Immoral Society.* New York: C. Scribner's Sons, 1932. In a path-

breaking work, a major Protestant theologian points out the prominence of power and self-interest in all human affairs, including international relations.

Key Pittman

17:151   Cole, Wayne S. "Senator Key Pittman and American Neutrality Policies, 1933–1940." *Mississippi Valley Historical Review* 46 (March 1960): 644–62. Pittman, as the Democratic chairman of the Senate Foreign Relations Committee, generally sought a middle course between isolationists and interventionists. He was far more willing to take an aggressive stand against Japan than against Germany and, like Hull, was frightened of public opinion.

17:152   Glad, Betty. *Key Pittman: The Tragedy of a Senate Insider.* New York: Columbia University Press, 1986. The book slightly upgrades the reputation of the Nevada senator who served as chairman of the Senate Foreign Relations Committee in the 1930s and who shared the ambivalence of the Roosevelt administration toward overseas commitments.

17:153   Israel, Fred L. *Nevada's Key Pittman.* Lincoln: University of Nebraska Press, 1963. Israel offers a careful account of the chairman of the Senate Foreign Relations Committee from 1933 to 1940. A hard-drinking man, Pittman's conduct and views frequently embarrassed Roosevelt.

17:154   Libby, Justin H. "The Irreconcilable Conflict: Key Pittman and Japan during the Interwar Years." *Nevada Historical Society Quarterly* 18 (Fall 1975): 128–39. Libby analyzes the anti-Japanese views of Pittman, who worked unsuccessfully during the 1930s for stronger American resistance to Japanese aggression.

Franklin D. Roosevelt

17:155   Burns, James MacGregor. *Roosevelt: The Lion and the Fox.* New York: Harcourt, Brace, 1956. This volume, covering FDR's leadership through the election of 1940, finds that in facing the dictators, he was "unwilling to throw his weight into the balance" and thereby confined his policy to "pinpricks and righteous protest."

17:156 _____. *Roosevelt: The Soldier of Freedom.* New York: Harcourt Brace Jovanovich, 1970. In describing the period between the passage of lend-lease and the attack on Pearl Harbor, Burns stresses that FDR's only strategy was one of "no strategy." His main policy involved waiting on events.

17:157 Christman, Calvin L. "Franklin D. Roosevelt and the Craft of Strategic Assessment." In *Calculations: Net Assessment and the Coming of World War II,* ed. Murray Williamson and Allan R. Millett, 216–57. New York: Free Press, 1992. Quite early FDR saw the Axis as a threat and never doubted his ability to lead his nation. The president did, however, overestimate Germany's military strength and underestimate that of Japan.

17:158 Dallek, Robert. *Franklin D. Roosevelt and American Foreign Policy, 1932–1945.* This major study of FDR's foreign policy, based upon prodigious research in manuscript sources, finds Roosevelt farseeing and purposeful. Dallek continually interprets FDR's cautious foreign policy in light of his domestic priorities (15:134).

17:159 Freidel, Frank. *Franklin D. Roosevelt. Vol. 2: The Ordeal.* Boston: Little, Brown, 1954. The author finds Roosevelt "a rather realistic Wilsonian," remaining silent about U.S. membership in the League but promoting the study of international organization, U.S. membership in the World Court, and détente with Japan.

17:160 _____. *Franklin D. Roosevelt. Vol. 3: The Triumph.* Boston: Little, Brown, 1956. In examining the 1932 presidential race, the author develops FDR's advocacy of reciprocal trade and opposition to U.S. membership in the League.

17:161 _____. *Franklin D. Roosevelt. Vol. 4: Launching the New Deal.* Boston: Little, Brown, 1973. Freidel offers a comprehensive account of Roosevelt's actions from the time of his election to July 1933, presenting a most thorough picture of FDR's foreign policies. In discussing Roosevelt's role in "torpedoing" the London Economic Conference of 1933, he finds that it would have been difficult for him to have implemented national and world programs simultaneously.

17:162 _____. *Franklin D. Roosevelt: A Rendezvous with Destiny.* Boston: Little, Brown, 1990. A major FDR scholar sees Roosevelt in the 1930s attempting to move the United States toward collective security while still hoping his nation could stay out of war. Even as December 1941 approached, he hoped a limited conflict would suffice. See also Freidel, "FDR vs. Hitler: American Foreign Policy, 1933–1941," *Proceedings of the Massachusetts Historical Society* 99 (1987): 25–43.

17:163 Graham, Otis L., Jr., and Meghan Robinson Wander, eds. *Franklin D. Roosevelt, His Life and Times: An Encyclopedic View.* Boston: G. K. Hall, 1985. This volume contains superior entries on FDR's life and career, including his foreign policy.

17:164 Kimball, Warren F. *The Juggler: Franklin Roosevelt as Wartime Statesman.* In a series of essays, Kimball sees Roosevelt as manipulator or "juggler" par excellence. At the same time, he stresses FDR's desire for containment of Hitler, survival of Britain, and elimination of any need for large-scale American intervention (15:150).

17:165 Kinsella, William E., Jr. *Leadership in Isolation: FDR and the Origins of the Second World War.* Boston: G. K. Hall, 1978. Kinsella finds FDR the supreme realist, intensely interested in world affairs from the moment he took office. The president wisely foresaw the inevitability of war with the Axis powers. On the claim that FDR feared Hitler would first attempt economic control of Latin America, then use the area as a military launching pad upon the United States, see his "The Prescience of a Statesman: FDR's Assessment of Adolf Hitler before the World War, 1933–1941," in Herbert D. Rosenbaum and Elizabeth Bartelme, eds., *Franklin D. Roosevelt: The Man, the Myth, the Era, 1882–1945* (New York: Greenwood Press, 1987), 73–84.

17:166 Leuchtenburg, William E. *Franklin D. Roosevelt and the New Deal, 1932–1940.* New York: Harper and Row, 1963. This book remains the best general survey of political attitudes and policies in the 1930s. The volume suggests why foreign problems were secondary to domestic economic concerns, at least until 1938. The author is damning on FDR's role in the London Economic Conference of 1933 but less so on his increasing anti-Axis posture.

17:167   Marks, Frederick W., III. "Franklin Roosevelt's Diplomatic Debut: The Myth of the Hundred Days." *South Atlantic Quarterly* 84 (Summer 1985): 245–63. Marks finds Roosevelt's initial diplomacy as frantic as it was ineffectual, reducing his standing in the eyes of a jealous Senate and undermining his nation's credibility.

17:168   _____. *Wind over Sand: The Diplomacy of Franklin Roosevelt.* Athens, GA: University of Georgia Press, 1988. The author portrays FDR as accumulating "the largest overseas credibility gap of any president on record" while refusing to build American armaments "to a level commensurate with the nation's national defense." Marks accuses the president of promoting appeasement toward Hitler while failing to work toward an accommodation with Japan.

17:169   Minnen, Cornelis A. van, and John F. Sears, eds. *FDR and His Contemporaries: Foreign Perceptions of an American President.* For details, see chapter 18 of this Guide (18:289).

17:170   Range, Willard. *Franklin D. Roosevelt's World Order.* Athens, GA: University of Georgia Press, 1959. Looking beyond League of Nations and World Court involvement, Range examines Roosevelt's broader internationalist outlook from the perspective of the Good Neighbor Policy, disarmament, world economic policy, and collective security. He finds Roosevelt generally consistent in his assumptions but unable to fit the world into them.

17:171   Schlesinger, Arthur M., Jr. *The Age of Roosevelt. Vol. 1: The Crisis of the Old Order: 1919–1933. Vol. 2: The Coming of the New Deal. Vol. 3: The Politics of Upheaval.* Boston: Houghton Mifflin, 1957–1960. All volumes, which take FDR's public career down to the election of 1936, are marked by broad research, a lively style, and strong sympathy for the president. In volume 2, Schlesinger claims that it was the rigidity of the gold-standard proponents at the 1933 London Economic Conference, not FDR, that assured its failure.

17:172   Sherwood, Robert E. *Roosevelt and Hopkins, An Intimate History.* Rev. ed. New York: Harper, 1950. This book is a classic account written by a famous playwright, FDR speechwriter, and frequent presidential emissary overseas. Particularly significant were missions to Britain and Russia in 1941. Originally published in 1948. See also Adams, *Harry Hopkins: A Biography* (1977) (18:261); McJimsey, *Harry Hopkins: Ally of the Poor and Defender of Democracy* (1987) (18:262); and Wills, *Wartime Missions of Harry L. Hopkins* (1996) (18:265).

Anna Louise Strong

17:173   Duke, David C. "Anna Louise Strong and the Search for a Good Cause." *Pacific Northwest Quarterly* 66 (July 1975): 123–37. This essay pictures Strong as a social activist who found in the Russian and Chinese communist revolutions causes equal to her energy and enthusiasm.

17:174   Strong, Tracy B., and Helene Keyssar. *Right in Her Soul: The Life of Anna Louise Strong.* New York: Random House, 1983. The authors offer the biography of a journalist whose enthusiasm for Stalinism reached such a high point that she defended the forced labor camps, the Moscow show trials, and the Molotov-Ribbentrop pact of 1939. Later in life she was an ardent defender of Mao's cultural revolution.

James T. Shotwell

17:175   DeBenedetti, Charles. "James T. Shotwell and the Science of International Politics." *Political Science Quarterly* 89 (June 1974): 379–95. The author sees Shotwell strengthening the cause of world order by establishing a tradition of independent experts and agencies to devise, rationalize, and administer multinational agencies that could absorb the strains of global change.

17:176   Josephson, Harold. *James T. Shotwell and the Rise of Internationalism in America.* From 1924 to 1948, Shotwell directed the Division of Economics and History of the Carnegie Endowment for International Peace and from 1935 to 1939 was president of the League of Nations Association. He promoted the Kellogg-Briand pact as well as U.S. membership in the League, World Court, and International Labor Organization (14:189).

17:177   Shotwell, James T. *Autobiography*. Indianapolis: Bobbs-Merrill, 1961. This autobiography of a leading internationalist and advocate of collective security covers his prominent role in negotiating the Kellogg-Briand pact.

Robert A. Taft

17:178   Matthews, Geoffrey. "Robert A. Taft, the Constitution, and American Foreign Policy, 1939–53." *Journal of Contemporary History* 17 (July 1982): 507–20. Though claiming that Taft would have provided inadequate world leadership, the author finds many of his constitutional reservations about the use of presidential power justified.

17:179   Patterson, James T. *Mr. Republican: A Biography of Robert A. Taft*. Boston: Houghton Mifflin, 1972. The author finds Taft, who sought the presidency in 1940, objecting to FDR's expansive interpretation of presidential powers in foreign policy that even the president's fondest admirers would later find difficult to ignore. See also Patterson's "Alternatives to Globalism: Robert A. Taft and American Foreign Policy, 1939–1945," *Historian* 36 (August 1974): 670–88, and "Robert A. Taft and American Foreign Policy, 1939–1945," in Liggio and Martin, *Watershed of Empire: Essays on New Deal Foreign Policy* (1976), 183–207 (18:188).

Owen D. Young

17:180   Case, Josephine Young, and Everett Needham Case. *Owen D. Young and American Enterprise: A Biography*. Boston: D. R. Godine, 1982. This book, the biography of a leading financier, tells in detail of Young's role in drafting the Dawes plan in 1924 and his own Young plan in 1929.

17:181   Hughes, Brady A. "Owen D. Young and American Foreign Policy, 1919–1929." Ph.D. dissertation, University of Wisconsin Press, 1969. Owen D. Young, president of the Radio Corporation of America and General Electric, helped to shape U.S. policy on two key economic questions: control of overseas wireless communications and the financial reconstruction of Europe. This study analyzes Young's role

in creating an international wireless consortium and efforts to stabilize the German economy.

Others

17:182   Armstrong, Hamilton Fish. *Peace and Counterpeace: From Wilson to Hitler: Memoirs of Hamilton Fish Armstrong*. New York: Harper and Row, 1971. Armstrong served as a military attaché in Berlin and correspondent for the *New York Evening Post* before becoming editor of *Foreign Affairs* (1928–1972). This book tells of his life during the 1920s, when he made detailed observations on Central Europe and the Balkans.

17:183   Randall, Mercedes M. *Improper Bostonian: Emily Greene Balch, Nobel Peace Laureate, 1946*. New York: Twayne Publishers, 1964. Awarded the Nobel Peace prize in 1946, Balch was an outstanding leader of the peace movement. This biography traces her lengthy career in the Women's International League for Peace and Freedom, noting her moderation, as compared to strict pacifism, as the United States approached World War II.

17:184   Bowers, Claude G. *My Mission to Spain: Watching the Rehearsal for World War II*. New York: Simon and Schuster, 1954. American ambassador to Spain from 1933 to 1939, Bowers argued that the Spanish Republic was basically democratic. Its socialist leanings would have dropped away if it had been given a chance to evolve peacefully.

17:185   Warner, Hoyt Landon. *The Life of Mr. Justice Clarke: A Testament to the Power of Liberal Dissent in America*. Cleveland: Western Reserve University Press, 1959. Clarke's presidency of the League of Nations Non-Partisan Association and his internationalist convictions are fully portrayed in this biography, which also provides insight into ideas, movements, and strains among pro-League advocates in the 1920s.

17:186   Jones, Alfred Haworth. "The Making of an Interventionist on the Air: Elmer Davis and CBS News, 1939–1941." *Pacific Historical Review* 42 (February 1973): 74–93. This article shows the conversion of a prominent broadcaster with isolationist leanings when war first broke out and how interventionists came to dominate radio.

17:187   Detzer, Dorothy. *Appointment on the Hill.* New York: H. Holt, 1948. Twenty years executive secretary and lobbyist for the Women's International League for Peace and Freedom, Detzer helped persuade legislators to withdraw U.S. marines from Nicaragua and promoted the Nye inquiry into the munitions industry.

17:188   Taylor, S. J. *Stalin's Apologist: Walter Duranty, The New York Times's Man in Moscow.* New York: Oxford University Press, 1990. Taylor portrays the *New York Times* correspondent as an amoral pragmatist who consciously whitewashed Stalin's crimes.

17:189   Taylor, Sandra C. *Advocate of Understanding: Sidney Gulick and the Search for Peace with Japan.* Kent, OH: Kent State University Press, 1984. The book covers the life of the Congregationalist missionary who served as "Japan expert" of the Federal Council of Churches and who continually and futilely advocated conciliation. See also Taylor's "Japan's Missionary to the Americans: Sidney L. Gulick and America's Interwar Relationship with the Japanese," *Diplomatic History* 4 (Fall 1980): 387–407.

17:190   Leutze, James R. *A Different Kind of Victory: A Biography of Admiral Thomas C. Hart.* Annapolis: Naval Institute Press, 1981. A major naval historian offers a biography of the commander of the U.S. Asiatic Fleet at the time of the Pearl Harbor attack.

17:191   Ickes, Harold L. *The Secret Diary of Harold L. Ickes. Vol. 1: The First Thousand Days, 1933–1936. Vol. 2: The Inside Struggle, 1936–1939. Vol. 3: The Lowering Clouds, 1939–1941.* New York: Simon and Schuster, 1953–1954. Ickes, secretary of the interior and curmudgeon of the Roosevelt cabinet, is acerbic in his comments on political leaders. An isolationist until Hitler's aggressive design became obvious, he became a vocal supporter of aiding the allies. See also Graham J. White and John Maze, *Harold Ickes of the New Deal: His Private Life and Public Career* (Cambridge, MA: Harvard University Press, 1985), and T. H. Watkins, *Righteous Pilgrim: The Life and Times of Harold Ickes, 1874–1952* (New York: H. Holt, 1990).

17:192   Mark, Steven MacDonald. "An American Interventionist: Frank Knox and United States Foreign Relations." Ph.D. dissertation, University of Maryland, 1977. Mark offers a thorough account of the former Rough Rider and Republican leader whom FDR appointed secretary of the navy in 1940. He sees Knox pushing FDR to more interventionist positions. At times Knox would release trial balloons to test public reaction to interventionist moves being considered by the administration.

17:193   Lamont, Edward M. *The Ambassador from Wall Street: The Story of Thomas W. Lamont, J. P. Morgan's Chief Executive: A Biography.* This book shows the far-flung activities of a J. P. Morgan partner who was involved at the Paris Peace Conference and carried out operations in China, Mexico, and Japan (15:261).

17:194   Stoner, John Edgar. *S. O. Levinson and the Pact of Paris: A Study in the Techniques of Influence.* Chicago: University of Chicago Press, 1943. This biography of Salmon O. Levinson, the champion of the outlawry of war, shows why the Chicago publicist believed that "Outlawry" (Levinson always began the word with a capital "O") must be the starting point for all efforts at permanent peace.

17:195   Carroll, John M. "Henry Cabot Lodge's Contributions to the Shaping of Republican European Diplomacy, 1920–1924." *Capitol Studies* 3 (Fall 1975): 153–65. Lodge may have led the fight against Wilsonian internationalism, but he played a key role in constructing a new policy of cooperation with Europe under Harding. The Senate majority leader also defended executive prerogatives in foreign affairs against attacks from such "irreconcilables" as Borah and Johnson.

17:196   Herzstein, Robert Edwin. *Henry R. Luce: A Political Portrait of the Man Who Created the American Century.* New York: Charles Scribner's Sons, 1993. Herzstein traces Luce's evolution into a militant interventionist, whose famous "American Century" *Life* editorial of February 17, 1941, outlined his views of a new postwar order. His *Time* and *Life* waxed hot, then cold, on European fascism while continually supporting Chiang Kai-shek. See also W. A. Swanberg, *Luce and His Empire* (New York: Scribner, 1972).

17:197   Smith, Richard Norton. *The Colonel: The Life and Legend of Robert R. McCormick, 1880–*

1955. Boston: Houghton Mifflin Company, 1997. This book is a balanced and thorough biography of the colorful isolationist publisher of the *Chicago Tribune.* See also Joseph Gies, *The Colonel of Chicago* (New York: Dutton, 1979); Frank C. Waldrop, *Mc-Cormick: An Unconventional Portrait of a Controversial Figure* (Englewood Cliffs, NJ: Prentice-Hall, 1966); and Lloyd Wendt, *Chicago Tribune: The Rise of a Great American Newspaper* (Chicago: Rand McNally, 1979).

17:198   Robinson, Jo Ann Ooiman. *Abraham Went Out: A Biography of A. J. Muste.* Philadelphia: Temple University Press, 1981. Robinson offers the definitive work on the man whose name was synonymous with the Fellowship of Reconciliation and who was the nation's leading pacifist from the 1920s through the 1960s. See also Robinson, "A. J. Muste and Ways to Peace," in Charles Chatfield, ed., *Peace Movements in America* (New York: Schocken, 1973), 81–94.

17:199   Guinsburg, Thomas N. "The George W. Norris 'Conversion' to Internationalism, 1939–1941." *Nebraska History* 53 (Winter 1972): 477–90. Norris always retained his repugnance toward war, as seen by his opposition to conscription in 1940, but found Axis aggression a greater threat to freedom than increased presidential power.

17:200   Bacon, Margaret Hope. *One Woman's Passion for Peace and Freedom: The Life of Mildred Scott Olmsted.* Syracuse: Syracuse University Press, 1993. Bacon covers the life of a prominent leader of the Women's International League for Peace and Freedom.

17:201   Page, Kirby. *Kirby Page, Social Evangelist: The Autobiography of a 20th Century Prophet for Peace.* New York: Fellowship Press, 1975. A prolific writer, Page was a most influential American pacifist, especially during the interwar period. Edited by Harold Edward Fay.

17:202   Wheeler, Gerald E. *Admiral William Veazie Pratt, U.S. Navy: A Sailor's Life.* Washington, DC: Naval History Division, Dept. of the Navy, 1974. Wheeler covers the life of a leading admiral who was assistant chief of naval operations in World War I, president of the Naval War College, naval adviser at both the Washington naval conference of 1921–1922 and the London conference of 1930, and chief of naval operations from 1930 to 1933.

17:203   Hoff, Joan. "'Peace Is a Woman's Job . . .': Jeannette Rankin and Foreign Policy: The Origins of Her Pacifism." The author notes how Rankin, the only member of Congress to vote against a declaration of war against Japan, articulated a modified Pearl Harbor revisionism and accused the British of conspiring to bring the United States into World War II (14:341). Of the several biographies of Rankin, the most able is Ted Carlton Harris, "Jeannette Rankin: Suffragist, First Woman Elected to Congress, and Pacifist" (Ph.D. diss., University of Georgia, 1972).

17:204   MacKinnon, Janice R., and Stephen R. MacKinnon. *Agnes Smedley, The Life and Times of an American Radical.* Berkeley: University of California Press, 1988. The MacKinnons offer a biography of a journalist who always remained close to Chinese communist leaders.

17:205   Hamilton, John Maxwell. *Edgar Snow, a Biography.* Bloomington: Indiana University Press, 1988. The author of *Red Star over China* (New York: Random House, 1938) always believed that the Chinese communists would remain faithful to Marxism-Leninism while never allowing themselves to be dominated by Moscow.

17:206   Ferrell, Henry C., Jr. *Claude E. Swanson of Virginia: A Political Biography.* Lexington: University Press of Kentucky, 1985. The book covers the life of the Virginia politician who served as FDR's secretary of the navy from 1933 until his death in 1939.

17:207   Johnpoll, Bernard K. *Pacifist's Progress: Norman Thomas and the Decline of American Socialism.* Chicago: Quadrangle Books, 1970. The author greatly admires the socialist leader's integrity and courage, but finds that Thomas's anti-interventionism contributed to the downfall of his party. For other (appreciative) treatments of Thomas, see Harry Fleischman, *Norman Thomas: A Biography* (New York: Norton, 1964); Murray B. Seidler, *Norman Thomas: Respectable Rebel* (Syracuse: Syracuse University Press, 1961); and W. A. Swanberg, *Norman Thomas: The Last Idealist* (New York: Scribner, 1976).

17:208 Tompkins, C. David. *Senator Arthur H. Vandenberg: The Evolution of a Modern Republican, 1884–1945.* Lansing: Michigan State University Press, 1970. Written before all relevant papers were available, this book is primarily an account of Vandenberg's prewar career. It stresses the role of the Nye Committee in converting him to isolationism. For a summary see Tompkins, "Senator Arthur Hendrick Vandenberg: Middle Western Isolationist," *Michigan History* 44 (March 1960): 39–58. See also Wayne S. Cole, "And Then There Were None! How Arthur H. Vandenberg and Gerald P. Nye Separately Departed Isolationist Leadership Roles," in McCormick and LaFeber, *Behind the Throne: Servants of Power to Imperial Presidents, 1898–1968* (1993), 232–53.

17:209 Kleinman, Mark L. "Foreign Policy for the 'New Age': The Sources of Henry A. Wallace's Early Internationalism, 1920–1942." *Peace and Change* 19 (April 1994): 180–207. The article finds the internationalism of FDR's secretary of agriculture rooted in his scientific expertise and spiritualistic inclinations.

17:210 McFarland, Keith D. *Harry H. Woodring: A Political Biography of FDR's Controversial Secretary of War.* Lawrence: University of Kansas Press, 1975. Woodring's dismissal as secretary of war is marked as the point when FDR determined to go forward with all-out aid to the allies. Woodring found himself caught between his devotion to Roosevelt and his sincere belief that the chief executive's program would endanger national security.

EUROPEAN

Winston Churchill

17:211 Charmley, John. *Churchill, The End of Glory: A Political Biography.* New York: Harcourt Brace, 1993. The author attacks Churchill for being so obsessed with defeating Hitler that he declined a needed truce and sacrificed his nation to American and Soviet dominance. See also Charmley, *Churchill's Grand Alliance: The Anglo-American Special Relationship, 1940–57* (1995) (18:345).

17:212 Gilbert, Martin. *Winston S. Churchill. Vol. 5: The Prophet of Truth, 1922–1939.* Boston: Houghton

Mifflin, 1977. This volume of Gilbert's massive biography covers Churchill's five years as chancellor of the exchequer in the 1920s and the "wilderness years" of the 1930s. Gilbert quotes at length from letters, diaries, recollections, and speeches.

17:213 _____. *Winston S. Churchill. Vol. 6: Finest Hour, 1939–1941.* Boston: Houghton Mifflin, 1983. This volume, part of the definitive life of Churchill, offers an exhaustive account, often hour by hour, of his activities in over 1,300 pages. For supplementary firsthand accounts, see Dilks, *The Diaries of Sir Alexander Cadogan, O.M., 1939–1945* (1972) (18:74), and Colville, *The Fringes of Power: 10 Downing Street Diaries, 1939–1955* (1985) (18:75).

Others

17:214 Feiling, Keith. *The Life of Neville Chamberlain.* London: Macmillan and Co., 1946. Reprint 1970 (Archon Books). This account includes a description of the prime minister's attitude toward Roosevelt and American policy.

17:215 Naftali, Timothy. "Intrepid's Last Deception: Documenting the Career of Sir William Stephenson." *Intelligence and National Security* 8 (July 1993): 72–99. While conceding many of the exploits ascribed to Sir William Stephenson, Naftali finds that the major accounts of the principal representative of British intelligence in the United States have been highly exaggerated.

17:216 Berg, Manfred. *Gustav Stresemann und die Vereinigten Staaten von Amerika: Weltwirtschaftliche Verflechtung und Revisionspolitik, 1907–1929 [Gustav Stresemann and the United States of America: International Economic Ties and the Policy of Revisionism, 1907–1929].* This broad study of German-American relations during the first three decades of the twentieth century focuses on Gustav Stresemann and emphasizes the "consensus" on trade, financial stability, and economic expansion influencing German-American diplomacy, especially in the 1920s. Berg's German perspective provides an excellent complement to works by American historians, including Melvyn P. Leffler, Frank C. Costigliola, Michael J. Hogan, and Charles S. Maier (11:259).

ASIAN

17:217 Butow, Robert J. C. *Tojo and the Coming of the War.* Princeton: Princeton University Press, 1961. Although Tojo was a leading general, in this biography of Japan's premier at the time of Pearl Harbor, Butow focuses on political and diplomatic issues. See also Courtney Browne, *Tojo: The Last Banzai* (New York: Holt, Rinehart and Winston, 1967).

DIPLOMATIC OFFICIALS

Collective

17:218 Burns, Richard Dean, and Edward M. Bennett, eds. *Diplomats in Crisis: United States–Chinese-Japanese Relations, 1919–1941.* Santa Barbara, CA: ABC-CLIO, 1974. Among the chapters on Americans are Herbert J. Wood on Nelson T. Johnson (7–26), Thomas H. Buckley on John Van Antwerp MacMurray (27–48), Gary Ross on W. Cameron Forbes (49–64), Bennett on Joseph C. Grew (65–90), and Burns on Stanley K. Hornbeck (91–117).

17:219 Craig, Gordon A., and Felix Gilbert, eds. *The Diplomats, 1919–1939.* Princeton: Princeton University Press, 1953. This is an extraordinarily able analysis of mostly European diplomats of the interwar years. Although dated, the 1953 edition contains still helpful appraisals. Included is Dexter Perkins, "The Department of State and American Public Opinion" (282–308), and William W. Kaufmann, "Two American Ambassadors: Bullitt and Kennedy" (649–81).

17:220 Hulen, Bertram D. *Inside the Department of State.* New York: McGraw-Hill Book Company, 1939. A State Department correspondent describes the workings of the department and its personnel on the eve of World War II.

17:221 Jablon, Howard. *Crossroads of Decision: The State Department and Foreign Policy, 1933–1937.* Lexington: University Press of Kentucky, 1983. The author indicts the State Department for allowing abstract moral principles to govern foreign policy decisions.

17:222 Jones, Kenneth Paul, ed. *U.S. Diplomats in Europe, 1919–1941.* Santa Barbara, CA: Clio Press, 1981. These original essays are useful for examining second-level American diplomats. Covered are Thomas W. Lamont (Michael J. Hogan), Alanson B. Houghton (Jones), Owen D. Young (John M. Carroll), John B. Stetson, Jr. (Frank C. Costigliola), Hugh S. Gibson (Ronald E. Swerczek), Prentiss Gilbert (J. B. Donnelly), George S. Messersmith (Kenneth Moss), Claude Bowers (Douglas Little), Loy Henderson (Thomas R. Maddux), and Joseph P. Kennedy (Jane Karoline Vieth).

17:223 Pacy, James S. "British Views of American Diplomats in China." *Asian Affairs: An American Review* 8 (March-April 1981): 251–61. The British offered positive evaluations of such diplomats as Charles Richard Crane, Jacob Gould Schurman, John Van Antwerp MacMurray, Nelson T. Johnson, and Clarence Gauss.

American

William C. Bullitt

17:224 Brownell, Will, and Richard N. Billings. *So Close to Greatness: A Biography of William C. Bullitt.* New York: Macmillan, 1987. This book shows FDR's ambassador to France as an anti-interventionist until the Munich conference and a strong foe of German expansion afterward.

17:225 Farnsworth, Beatrice. *William C. Bullitt and the Soviet Union.* With wit, sympathy, and insight, this exemplary diplomatic biography discusses Bullitt's long involvement in Soviet-American affairs, especially in 1919 at Paris and in the mid-1930s in Moscow and Washington. Bullitt favored recognition in the early 1930s, quickly became disillusioned, and spent the rest of his years warning of Soviet imperialism (14:99).

17:226 Wright, Gordon. "Ambassador Bullitt and the Fall of France." *World Politics* 10 (October 1957): 63–90. The author sees Bullitt as biased, impetuous, and inconsistent but credits his awareness of the threat to American security posed by totalitarian regimes.

Joseph E. Davies

17:227 Davies, Joseph E. *Mission to Moscow, by Joseph E. Davies, United States Ambassador to the Soviet Union from 1936–1938. A Record of Confidential Dispatches to the State Department, Official and Personal Correspondence, Current Diary and Journal Entries, Including Notes and Comment up to October, 1941.* New York: Simon and Schuster, 1941. FDR's ambassador to the Soviet Union offers an almost roseate view of the Soviet Union, written in the glow of the rapprochement that occurred in its year of publication.

17:228 Eagles, Keith David. *Ambassador Joseph E. Davies and American-Soviet Relations, 1937–1941.* New York: Garland Publishing, 1985. The author finds Davies naïve in analyzing the Soviet Union.

17:229 MacLean, Elizabeth Kimball. *Joseph E. Davies: Envoy to the Soviets.* Westport, CT: Praeger, 1992. The author finds Davies perceptive on the reserve strength and staying power of the Soviet army, dictatorship, and economy. The U.S. ambassador, however, accepted the government's case in the Moscow show trials and grossly underestimated Stalin's personal desire for power.

17:230 Mayers, David. "Ambassador Joseph Davies Reconsidered." *Society for Historians of American Foreign Relations Newsletter* 23 (September 1992): 1–16. The author finds that some of Davies's private correspondence suggests a person alive to the "grim realities" of Stalinism, including the purges, as well as to the dangers posed by Hitler's Germany.

Charles G. Dawes

17:231 Dawes, Charles G. *Journal as Ambassador to Great Britain.* New York: Macmillan Company, 1939. Reprint 1970 (Greenwood Press). Dawes's diary of his tenure as ambassador (1929–1931) is the only such embassy diary on Anglo-American relations published during the interwar years. Colorful, colloquial, often candid, the diary is nonetheless bowdlerized from the manuscript version deposited in the Northwestern University library. Foreword by Herbert Hoover.

17:232 _____. *A Journal of Reparations.* London: Macmillan, 1939. Dawes chaired one of two committees assigned to recommend revisions in the German reparations settlement. In this book, not always faithful to his diary, he makes clear the large part played by fellow committeeman Owen D. Young and Secretary of State Hughes in creating the Dawes Plan. Appendices include various documents related to the issue.

William E. Dodd

17:233 Bailey, Fred Arthur. "A Virginia Scholar in Chancellor Hitler's Court: The Tragic Ambassadorship of William Edward Dodd." *Virginia Magazine of History and Biography* 100 (July 1992): 323–42. The author portrays Dodd as a Wilsonian idealist who saw the Third Reich's leaders as German counterparts to the antebellum planters of his native south he had treated so critically in his histories. From this perspective he extrapolated that German Junkers had assaulted Europe in 1914, that American entrepreneurs had sold out their countrymen for a profit, and that Hitler's Nazis endangered world peace.

17:234 Dallek, Robert. *Democrat and Diplomat: The Life of William E. Dodd.* New York: Oxford University Press, 1968. This careful account of the University of Chicago historian and ambassador to Germany from 1933 to 1937 examines Dodd's service in detail, showing perceptive predictions about Hitler and Nazi Germany. See also Dallek's "Beyond Tradition: The Diplomatic Careers of William E. Dodd and George S. Messersmith, 1933–1938," *South Atlantic Quarterly* 66 (Spring 1967): 233–44.

17:235 Dodd, Martha. *Through Embassy Eyes.* New York: Harcourt, Brace and Company, 1939. The daughter of Ambassador William E. Dodd offers a firsthand account of life in Germany.

17:236 Dodd, William E., Jr., and Martha Dodd. *Ambassador Dodd's Diary, 1933–1938.* New York: Harcourt, Brace and Company, 1941. One of FDR's shrewdest diplomatic observers, Dodd loathed Nazism in general and Hitler in particular. He continually warned that an unchecked Germany would act aggressively. Introduction by Charles A. Beard.

17:237 Offner, Arnold A. "William E. Dodd: Romantic Historian and Diplomatic Cassandra." *Histo-*

rian 24 (August 1962): 451–69. Offner argues that Dodd was quicker than most diplomats to see the strengths and weaknesses of National Socialism and the way Hitler used German grievances to support an expansive policy. Dodd urged Roosevelt to align the United States with Britain and France.

Herbert Feis

17:238   Feis, Herbert. *Seen from E. A.: Three International Episodes.* New York: Alfred A. Knopf, 1947. Feis deals with episodes in which he played a part and that focus on the search for national security prior to World War II: 1) stockpiling of rubber prior to Pearl Harbor; 2) the search for oil in the Middle East; and 3) the debate over embargoing oil to Italy during the Ethiopian crisis.

17:239   Healey, Maryanne F. "Witness, Participant, and Chronicler: The Role of Herbert Feis as Economic Adviser to the State Department, 1931–1943." Ph.D. dissertation, Georgetown University, 1973. Healey praises Feis for his clear perception of the crises facing the nation. Despite his formal assignments, he was not limited by a narrow specialized economic focus.

17:240   Yergler, Dennis Keith. *Herbert Feis, Wilsonian Internationalism, and America's Technological-Democracy.* New York: Peter Lang, 1993. This book portrays the economic adviser to the State Department from 1931 to 1943 as an advocate of a classical international system based on the free exchange of goods.

Joseph C. Grew

17:241   Grew, Joseph C. *Ten Years in Japan: A Contemporary Record Drawn from the Diaries and Private and Official Papers of Joseph C. Grew, United States Ambassador to Japan, 1932–1942.* New York: Simon and Schuster, 1944. Reprint 1973 (Greenwood Press). This work is an important contemporary record, notable for conveying the tenacity of Grew's efforts toward peace.

17:242   _____. *Turbulent Era: A Diplomatic Record of Forty Years, 1904–1945.* Grew covers his decade as ambassador. Volume 2 recounts events on the eve of Pearl Harbor. The work includes his "cer-

tainties" about prewar courses of action, particularly his abortive recommendation of summitry as a means of avoiding war. Edited by Walter Johnson, with Nancy Harvison Hooker (11:21).

17:243   Heinrichs, Waldo H. *American Ambassador: Joseph C. Grew and the Development of the United States Diplomatic Tradition.* A majestic treatment of Grew and his role in the U.S. diplomatic tradition, Heinrichs's account covers Grew's ambassadorships in Turkey (1927–1932) and Japan (1932–1941) (11:497).

Loy Henderson

17:244   Brands, H. W. *Inside the Cold War: Loy Henderson and the Rise of the American Empire, 1918–1961.* New York: Oxford University Press, 1991. This biography of an American diplomat covers Henderson's early career in Riga and Moscow, where he reported on Soviet collectivization, witnessed the purge trials, and expressed extreme skepticism about Soviet motives.

17:245   Henderson, Loy W. *A Question of Trust: The Origins of U.S.-Soviet Diplomatic Relations: The Memoirs of Loy W. Henderson.* Stanford, CA: Hoover Institution Press, 1986. Henderson was a State Department official stationed first in Riga, then in Moscow, who held strong suspicions of Soviet rule. Edited by George W. Baer.

Stanley K. Hornbeck

17:246   Doenecke, Justus D., ed. *The Diplomacy of Frustration: The Manchurian Crisis of 1931–1933 as Revealed in the Papers of Stanley K. Hornbeck.* Stanford, CA: Hoover Institution Press, 1981. The documents show that Hornbeck, long perceived as confrontational toward the Japanese, responded most cautiously to the Manchurian and Shanghai crises, favoring economic sanctions against Japan but warning against unilateral nonrecognition.

17:247   Hu, Shizhang. *Stanley K. Hornbeck and the Open Door Policy, 1919–1937.* Westport, CT: Greenwood Press, 1995. The author denies that Hornbeck ever gave blanket assent to China's national aspirations or chased after the Asian market. During much of the 1920s and 1930s, his China policy was passive and negative.

Charles Evans Hughes

17:248   Danelski, David J., and Joseph S. Tulchin, eds. *The Autobiographical Notes of Charles Evans Hughes*. Cambridge, MA: Harvard University Press, 1973. In the preface, Hughes described his efforts as "a body of facts for reference" and not an autobiography. The editors have supplemented Hughes's notes with material from the *Foreign Relations of the United States* series, the Hughes Papers, and other sources. In their introduction, the editors describe a man with a sophisticated understanding of American power and the limits imposed upon his office.

17:249   Glad, Betty. *Charles Evans Hughes and the Illusions of Innocence: A Study in American Diplomacy*. Urbana: University of Illinois Press, 1966. In a detailed treatment of Hughes as secretary of state, Glad argues that Hughes's background as a lawyer limited his vision. For a brief treatment of Hughes, see J. Chal Vinson, "Charles Evans Hughes," in Graebner, *An Uncertain Tradition: American Secretaries of State in the Twentieth Century* (1961), 128–48 (2:192).

17:250   _____. "Charles Evans Hughes, Rationalism, and Foreign Affairs." In *Traditions and Values: American Diplomacy, 1865–1945. Vol. 8: American Values Projected Abroad,* ed. Norman A. Graebner, 101–36. Lanham, MD: University Press of America, 1985. Hughes biographer Glad sees Hughes so committed to reason and perceived common interests that he contributed to an arrogant U.S. posture toward the rest of the world.

17:251   Hyde, Charles C. "Charles Evans Hughes." In *The American Secretaries of State and Their Diplomacy,* 10: 221–463. New York: Alfred A. Knopf, 1928. This semiofficial biography of Hughes, written by a former State Department official, is still valuable.

17:252   Perkins, Dexter. *Charles Evans Hughes and American Democratic Statesmanship*. Perkins finds Hughes "clearly one of the very most eminent Secretaries," combining technical skill, wide imagi-

nation, executive force, and genuine idealism. It was not his fault that such notable achievements as the Washington treaties did not last (15:241).

17:253   Pusey, Merlo J. *Charles Evans Hughes*. Traditional in approach, this biography praises its subject's diplomacy on all fronts (14:179).

Cordell Hull

17:254   Burns, Richard Dean. "Cordell Hull and American Interwar Internationalism." In *Traditions and Values: American Diplomacy, 1865–1945. Vol. 8: American Values Projected Abroad,* ed. Norman A. Graebner, 137–59. Lanham, MD: University Press of America, 1985. Burns criticizes Hull for moralistically responding to aggression in a way that enabled him to avoid fundamental issues of war and peace.

17:255   Hull, Cordell, with Andrew Berding. *The Memoirs of Cordell Hull*. The memoirs (ghostwritten by journalist Andrew Berding) are a lawyer's brief, often exaggerating his role but revealing on his views (15:244).

17:256   Pratt, Julius W. *Cordell Hull, 1933–44*. This book is an indispensable supplement to Hull's own memoirs, covering such material as the Good Neighbor Policy, the London Economic Conference of 1933, reciprocal trade, and the Spanish civil war. Although Pratt sympathizes with the secretary (acknowledging, for example, the eclipse of the State Department during his tenure), he rebukes the inflexible moralism that perhaps caused the breakdown of relations with Japan (15:245). Part of the series, *The American Secretaries of State and Their Diplomacy* (1:48). See also Donald F. Drummond, "Cordell Hull," in Graebner, ed., *An Uncertain Tradition: American Secretaries of State in the Twentieth Century* (1961), 184–209 (2:192).

17:257   _____. "The Ordeal of Cordell Hull." *Review of Politics* 28 (January 1966): 76–98. Hull's biographer praises FDR for pitting "gadflies" Harold Ickes and Henry Morgenthau, Jr. against the slow-moving Hull. Roosevelt benefited from Hull's salutary caution while others prodded him toward action against the Axis.

George F. Kennan

17:258 Kennan, George F. *From Prague after Munich: Diplomatic Papers, 1938–1940.* Princeton: Princeton University Press, 1968. Kennan wrote this series of thirty-six documents as secretary of legation and then caretaker of the Prague legation. They are valuable not only for what they reveal about young Kennan's thought processes, but for a remarkably objective portrait of the dismemberment of Czechoslovakia.

17:259 _____. *Memoirs. Vol. 1: 1925–1950.* Boston: Little, Brown, 1967. One of the nation's leading diplomats tells of his service during the interwar period in Riga, Prague, Moscow, and Berlin.

17:260 Mayers, David. *George Kennan and the Dilemmas of US Foreign Policy.* New York: Oxford University Press, 1988. The first chapters of this book describe how the underlying assumptions of Kennan's formulation of containment—the incompatibility of Soviet and U.S. political commitments, divergent security interests, the importance of patience and steady purpose in dealing with the Russians—can be traced to Kennan's early diplomatic career in Riga and Moscow. During his tenure in Prague and Berlin, Kennan opposed the fragmentation of the Hapsburg empire, expressed skepticism about Czech democracy and political viability, criticized the German occupation of Bohemia and Moravia, and saw in Hitler's Reich the seeds of its own destruction. See also Mayers, "George Kennan and the Soviet Union, 1933–1938: Perceptions of a Young Diplomat," *International History Review* 5 (November 1983): 525–49; "Nazi Germany and the Future of Europe: George Kennan's Views, 1939–1945" (1986); and Harper, *American Visions of Europe: Franklin D. Roosevelt, George F. Kennan, and Dean G. Acheson* (1994) (17:89).

Joseph P. Kennedy

17:261 Beschloss, Michael. *Kennedy and Roosevelt: The Uneasy Alliance.* New York: Norton, 1980. The most scholarly of the major biographies of Kennedy, this work draws upon unreleased material in the John F. Kennedy Presidential Library, Boston. The author claims that Kennedy was never secure in his social or financial position and hence sought international stability where he could find it.

17:262 de Bedts, Ralph F. *Ambassador Joseph Kennedy 1938–1940: An Anatomy of Appeasement.* New York: Peter Lang, 1985. This work shows how Kennedy often pushed his anti-interventionism as U.S. policy, thereby becoming an albatross to the Roosevelt administration.

17:263 Koskoff, David E. *Joseph P. Kennedy: A Life and Times.* Englewood Cliffs, NJ: Prentice-Hall, 1974. The most hostile of the biographies, it holds that Kennedy did not understand that Hitler sought world domination. For far friendlier treatment, see Richard J. Whalen, *The Founding Father: The Story of Joseph P. Kennedy* (New York: New American Library, 1964).

17:264 Smith, Amanda, ed. *Hostage to Fortune: The Letters of Joseph P. Kennedy.* New York: Viking, 2001. Included in this compilation is much correspondence dealing with Kennedy's stint as U.S. ambassador to the United Kingdom, 1938–1940.

George S. Messersmith

17:265 Adams, David K. "Messersmith's Appointment to Vienna in 1934: Presidential Patronage or Career Promotion?" *Delaware History* 18 (Spring-Summer 1978): 17–27. The records indicate that both factors played a role in his promotion.

17:266 Moss, Kenneth. "George S. Messersmith: An American Diplomat and Nazi Germany." *Delaware History* 17 (Fall 1977): 236–49. Particularly in the period 1933–1940, Messersmith helped shape American attitudes toward Nazi Germany. He believed in the balance of power, an international economy, and open trade, and sought economic pressure against Nazi Germany.

17:267 Shafir, Shlomo. "George S. Messersmith: An Anti-Nazi Diplomat's View of the German-Jewish Crisis." *Jewish Social Studies* 35 (January 1973): 32–41. Messersmith (1883–1960) was an early, resolute opponent of Hitler's antisemitic policies. He never, however, suggested any proposals for the rescue of Jews, for he considered the humanitarian issue secondary.

17:268 Stiller, Jesse H. *George S. Messersmith, Diplomat of Democracy.* This is a biography of a diplomat who was U.S. consul-general in Berlin,

1930–1934, minister to Austria from 1934 to 1937, and assistant secretary of state from 1937 to 1940 (15:263). See also Stiller's "Messersmith's Big Fight," *Foreign Service Journal* 64 (September 1987): 36–43, centering on State Department reorganization in 1937, and Robert Dallek's "Beyond Tradition: The Diplomatic Careers of William E. Dodd and George S. Messersmith, 1933–1938," *South Atlantic Quarterly* 66 (Spring 1967): 233–44.

Henry L. Stimson

17:269 Current, Richard N. *Secretary Stimson, A Study in Statecraft.* New Brunswick: Rutgers University Press, 1954. Reprint 1970 (Archon Books). Current believes that Stimson misread the future during his service in both the Hoover and Roosevelt administrations. Especially critical concerning Stimson's management of Japanese-American affairs, Current finds him both volatile and truculent. See also Current's "Henry L. Stimson," in Norman A. Graebner, ed., *An Uncertain Tradition: American Secretaries of State in the Twentieth Century* (1961), 168–83 (2:192).

17:270 Hodgson, Godfrey. *The Colonel: The Life and Wars of Henry Stimson, 1867–1950.* New York: Alfred A. Knopf, 1990. While somewhat helpful on Stimson's career, the author overstates his prominence in the interwar period. The publication of this book should not discourage other would-be biographers.

17:271 Morison, Elting E. *Turmoil and Tradition: A Study of the Life and Times of Henry L. Stimson.* Boston: Houghton Mifflin, 1960. This beautifully written "official" biography is strong on the years before 1940. It has shrewd, sympathetic analyses of Stimson's attitudes toward naval limitation, war debts, the Manchurian crisis, and Anglo-American relations.

17:272 Stimson, Henry L., and McGeorge Bundy. *On Active Service in Peace and War.* New York: Harper, 1948. Stimson combines autobiography with excerpts from the diary.

Myron C. Taylor

17:273 Conway, John S. "Myron C. Taylor's Mission to the Vatican 1940–1950." *Church History* 44 (March 1975): 85–99. The author finds Taylor able to gain the confidence of his hosts while firmly defending American interests.

17:274 Flynn, George Q. "Franklin Roosevelt and the Vatican: The Myron Taylor Appointment." *Catholic Historical Review* 58 (July 1972): 171–94. After tracing Protestant opposition to the appointment, Flynn finds FDR's naming Taylor to represent the United States at the Vatican connected to hopes of achieving a settlement of the European war, keeping Italy out of the conflict, and strengthening the Roman Catholic vote in the 1940 election.

Sumner Welles

17:275 Graff, Frank Warren. *Strategy of Involvement: A Diplomatic Biography of Sumner Welles.* New York: Garland, 1988. Welles's biographer sees him as pursuing expedient policy toward the Soviets, remaining suspicious of Vichy France, lacking enthusiasm for international cooperation, and sharing much of Hull's economic vision. Welles believed his mission of February 1940 could end the European war. See also Gellman, *Secret Affairs: Franklin D. Roosevelt, Cordell Hull, and Sumner Welles* (1995) (17:88).

17:276 Welles, Benjamin. *Sumner Welles: FDR's Global Strategist: A Biography.* The diplomat's son offers an appreciative account, portraying his father as a tragic figure (15:249).

17:277 Welles, Sumner. *Seven Decisions That Shaped History.* New York: Harper, 1951. This book is a thinly disguised attempt to justify Welles's actions in light of the publication of the Hull memoirs.

17:278 _____. *The Time for Decision.* Here Undersecretary of State Welles, closer to FDR than Secretary Hull, stresses the prominence of his role (15:250).

Hugh R. Wilson

17:279 Downing, Marvin L. "Hugh R. Wilson and American Relations with the League of Nations, 1927–1937." Ph.D. dissertation, University of Oklahoma, 1970. Wilson is portrayed as a capable if colorless diplomat who served as the U.S. observer at a number of League conferences while he was minister to Switzerland. These conferences were primarily concerned with disarmament questions, although they covered a number of other issues as well.

17:280   Wilson, Hugh R. *A Career Diplomat, the Third Chapter: The Third Reich.* New York: Vantage Press, 1960. Reprint 1973 (Greenwood Press). Hugh R. Wilson, Jr., the son of the last prewar American ambassador to Berlin, edited his father's unpublished reports to Washington along with excerpts from Wilson's diary.

17:281   _____. *Diplomat between Wars.* New York: Longmans, Green, 1941. This account is especially valuable for Wilson's recollections of the Geneva disarmament conference of 1932–1934.

John Gilbert Winant

17:282   Howland, Nina Davis. "Ambassador John Gilbert Winant: Friend of an Embattled Britain, 1941–1946." Ph.D. dissertation, University of Maryland, 1983. The author finds Winant performing invaluable service to Anglo-American friendship and helping to win the war. See also Bert R. Whittemore, "A Quiet Triumph: The Mission of John Gilbert Winant to London, 1941," *Historical New Hampshire* 30 (Spring): 1–11.

17:283   Reynolds, David. "Roosevelt, the British Left, and the Appointment of John G. Winant as United States Ambassador to Britain in 1941." *International History Review* 4 (August 1982): 393–413. British Labor Party leaders, such as Minister of Labor Ernest Bevin and political theorist Harold Laski, made direct requests for Winant's appointment, which helped determined FDR's selection.

17:284   Winant, John Gilbert. *Letter from Grosvenor Square: An Account of a Stewardship.* Boston: Houghton Mifflin, 1947. Despite its title, these memoirs are limited to events before Pearl Harbor and even here the material can be thin.

Others

17:285   Schwarz, Jordan A. *Liberal: Adolf A. Berle and the Vision of an American Era.* New York: Free Press, 1987. This biography ably conveys the anti-

British outlook and hemispheric focus of a powerful assistant secretary of state.

17:286   Cannistraro, Philip V., Edward D. Wynot, Jr., and Theodore P. Kovaleff, eds. *Poland and the Coming of the Second World War: The Diplomatic Papers of A. J. Drexel Biddle, Jr., United States Ambassador to Poland, 1937–1939.* Columbus: Ohio State University Press, 1976. After a thirty-eight-page introduction, the book includes the ambassador's lengthy report on the fall of Poland as well as representative selections of his diplomatic correspondence with FDR and the State Department.

17:287   Crane, Katharine Elizabeth. *Mr. Carr of State: Forty-Seven Years in the Department of State.* In her thorough biography of State Department official Wilbur John Carr, Crane notes his crucial role in drafting the Rogers Act of 1924, which united the consular and diplomatic services into one foreign service. Carr played the decisive role in developing a professional U.S. diplomatic corps, removing it from the influence of domestic politics. From 1937 to 1939, he was American minister to Czechoslovakia (14:166).

17:288   Castle, Alfred L. *Diplomatic Realism: William R. Castle, Jr., and American Foreign Policy, 1919–1953.* Honolulu: Samuel L. and Mary Castle Foundation, 1998. Castle was chief of the State Department's division of Western European Affairs (1921–1927), assistant secretary of state (1927–1929), ambassador to Japan (1930–1931), and undersecretary of state (1931–1933). His lively diary has been a major source for historians. See also the author's "William R. Castle and Opposition to U.S. Involvement in an Asian War, 1939–1941," *Pacific Historical Review* 54 (August 1985): 337–51.

17:289   Child, Richard Washburn. *A Diplomat Looks at Europe.* These reminiscences impart the depth of the U.S. disillusionment with the politics of Europe in the 1920s. Child served as chief American observer at the Geneva and Lausanne conferences as well as being ambassador to Italy (11:150).

17:290   Coolidge, Harold Jefferson, and Robert Howard Lord. *Archibald Cary Coolidge: Life and Letters.* This is a biography of a diplomat, Harvard historian, and editor of *Foreign Affairs* (14:167).

17:291   Hearden, Patrick J. "John Cudahy and the Pursuit of Peace." *Mid-America* (April-June 1986): 99–114. Until 1941, FDR's ambassador to Ireland and Belgium combined his belief in German access to world markets with calls for U.S. preparedness.

17:292   Davis, Julia, and Dolores A. Fleming, eds. *The Ambassadorial Diary of John W. Davis: The Court of St. James's, 1918–1921.* Morgantown: West Virginia University Press, 1993. The U.S. ambassador to Britain gives his perspective on such matters as the aftermath of the Russian revolution, control of Middle Eastern oil, problems in Yugoslavia and Ireland, and the Versailles Treaty. See also William H. Harbaugh, *Lawyer's Lawyer: The Life of John W. Davis* (New York: Oxford University Press, 1990).

17:293   Buhite, Russell D. *Nelson T. Johnson and American Policy toward China, 1925–1941.* East Lansing: Michigan State University Press, 1968. Chief of the Division of Far Eastern Affairs, assistant secretary, and minister and ambassador to China, Johnson exerted a considerable influence on China policy. Though lacking profundity and imagination, he was a firm advocate of China's cause and sought increasingly firm steps against Japan. See also Buhite, "Nelson Johnson and American Policy toward China, 1925–1928," *Pacific Historical Review* 35 (November 1966): 451–65.

17:294   Ellis, L. Ethan. *Frank B. Kellogg and American Foreign Relations, 1925–1929.* Ellis notes that Kellogg lost control of Mexican policy to Dwight Morrow and of Nicaraguan policy to Henry L. Stimson, although he remained in control of policy toward China and of the negotiations that resulted in the Kellogg-Briand pact (15:247). See also Ellis's "Frank B. Kellogg," in Graebner, *An Uncertain Tradition: American Secretaries of State in the Twentieth Century* (1961), 149–67 (2:192).

17:295   Israel, Fred L., ed. *The War Diary of Breckinridge Long: Selections from the Years 1939–1944.* Lincoln: University of Nebraska Press, 1966. On September 1, 1939, FDR appointed Long to head a special State Department division to handle emergency matters arising out of the European war. The following January, he became assistant secretary of state, a post he held until December 1944. These

beautifully edited diaries offer an intimate portrait of State Department personnel and perceptions.

17:296   Carroll, John M. "A Pennsylvanian in Paris: James A. Logan, Jr., Unofficial Diplomat 1919–1925." *Pennsylvania History* 45 (December 1978): 3–18. From 1923 to 1925, Logan was the chief unofficial observer on the reparations commission and did much to make the Dawes plan possible.

17:297   Hooker, Nancy Harvison, ed. *The Moffat Papers: Selections from the Diplomatic Journals of Jay Pierrepont Moffat, 1919–1943.* Cambridge, MA: Harvard University Press, 1956. This compilation covers Moffat's service as first secretary of the U.S. legation in Bern (1927–1931) and as chief of the State Department's Division of Western European Affairs (1932–1935) and Division of European Affairs (1937–1940). The diaries are an excellent source on the League of Nations and on the early diplomacy of the New Deal, especially the London Economic Conference. Foreword by Sumner Welles.

17:298   Burke, Bernard V. *Ambassador Frederic Sackett and the Collapse of the Weimar Republic, 1930–1933: The United States and Hitler's Rise to Power.* New York: Cambridge University Press, 1994. In a thorough study of Hoover's ambassador to Germany, the author notes Sackett's suspicion of American bankers, faith in German Chancellor Heinrich Brüning, enthusiasm for the Hoover moratorium, and belief that Germany's salvation lay with organized labor and the Social Democrats.

17:299   Rubin, Barry. "Ambassador Laurence A. Steinhardt: The Perils of a Jewish Diplomat, 1940–1945." *American Jewish History* 70 (March 1981): 331–46. The author finds Steinhardt, America's first Jewish "career" diplomat and U.S. ambassador to the USSR from 1939 to 1941, taking a hard line on granting visas to fleeing Polish Jews. Later, as ambassador to Turkey, he played a major role in saving tens of thousands of Balkan Jewish refugees. See also Joseph O'Connor, "Laurence A. Steinhardt and American Policy toward the Soviet Union" (Ph.D. diss., University of Virginia, 1968), and Ralph R. Stackman, "Laurence A. Steinhardt: New Deal Diplomat, 1933–1945" (Ph.D. diss., Michigan State University, 1967).

17:300 Halstead, Charles R. "Diligent Diplomat: Alexander W. Weddell as American Ambassador to Spain, 1939–1942." *Virginia Magazine of History and Biography* 82 (January 1974): 3–38. Weddell, laboring in a difficult environment, gained more than he lost for the U.S. government.

17:301 Mulcahy, Richard P. "Ambassador from Greensburg: The Tenure of Cyrus E. Woods in Japan, 1923–1924." *Western Pennsylvania Historical Magazine* 68 (January 1985): 25–42. This article shows how Woods, as American ambassador, opposed the Lodge-Johnson Immigration Act of 1924. He found Japan the only viable nation in East Asia and warned his countrymen against antagonizing it.

European

Anthony Eden

17:302 Carlton, David. *Anthony Eden, a Biography.* London: Allen Lane, 1981. Eden was foreign minister in 1935–1938 and 1940–1945. Carlton shows his futile efforts to promote Anglo-American cooperation in the late 1930s. For other biographies, see James, *Anthony Eden* (1986) (18:356), commissioned by his widow, and Victor Rothwell, *Anthony Eden* (New York: Manchester University Press, 1992).

17:303 Eden, Anthony. *Facing the Dictators: The Memoirs of Anthony Eden, Earl of Avon.* Boston: Houghton Mifflin, 1962. The British foreign secretary in the Baldwin and Chamberlain cabinets expresses his frustration with Prime Minister Chamberlain in January 1938 for failing to accept FDR's overtures for parallel action.

Hans Heinrich Dieckhoff

17:304 Jonas, Manfred. "Prophet without Honor: Hans Heinrich Dieckhoff's Reports from Washington." *Mid-America* 47 (May 1965): 222–33. Its ambassador warned Germany not to count on future American neutrality. Dieckhoff's recall to Germany in late 1938 deprived the Reich of a most prescient observer.

17:305 Kimball, Warren F. "Dieckhoff and America: A German's View of German-American Relations, 1937–1941." *Historian* 27 (February 1965): 218–43. Keenly aware of American sensitivity about foreign interference in U.S. domestic affairs, Dieckhoff urged his government to distance itself from the German-American Bund. He did not, however, speak out emphatically against the antisemitic and anti–Roman Catholic measures of the Hitler government.

17:306 Remak, Joachim. "Two German Views of the United States: Hitler and His Diplomats." *World Affairs Quarterly* 28 (April 1957): 25–35. Dieckhoff, German ambassador in Washington after 1937, warned repeatedly and unmistakably that the United States would not remain neutral. The warnings were accepted by the German Foreign Office, especially Baron Ernst von Weizsacker, but not by Hitler.

Lord Lothian

17:307 Jeffreys-Jones, Rhodri. "Lord Lothian and American Democracy: An Illusion in Pursuit of an Illusion." *Canadian Review of American Studies* 17 (Winter 1986): 411–22. The author stress Lothian's ineptitude as ambassador. See also his "The Inestimable Advantage of Not Being English: Lord Lothian's American Ambassadorship, 1939–1940," *Scottish Historical Review* 63 (April 1984): 105–10.

17:308 Reynolds, David. *Lord Lothian and Anglo-American Relations, 1939–1940.* Vol. 73, Transactions of the American Philosophical Society. Philadelphia: American Philosophical Society, 1983. Reynolds finds Lothian a skillful ambassador though neglectful of details and overly anxious to please the United States.

Others

17:309 Bonnet, Georges. *Defense de la Paix. Vol. 1: De Washington au Quai d'Orsay. Vol. 2: Fin d'une Europe de Munich a la guerre [Defending Peace. Vol. 1: From Washington to the Quai d'Orsay. Vol. 2: The End of One Europe from Munich to the War].* Geneva: Éditions du Cheval ailé, 1946–1948. In these memoirs of the French ambassador to Washington (1937) and minister of foreign affairs (April 1938–September 1939), Bonnet is not above distorting key events and even documents to make his case stronger; the book must be used with caution. The second volume was republished, with additions, in 1967 (Paris: Plon) as *De Munich à la guerre, défense de la paix.*

17:310 Roberts, Andrew. *The Holy Fox: A Biography of Lord Halifax.* London: Weidenfeld and Nicolson, 1991. Roberts sees Halifax as an inept ambassador to the United States before December 1941 but able afterward. For an earlier account of Halifax's career, see Birkenhead, *Halifax: The Life of Lord Halifax* (1966) (18:357).

17:311 Phillips, Hugh D. *Between the Revolution and the West: A Political Biography of Maxim M. Litvinov.* Boulder: Westview Press, 1992. Phillips offers a favorable account of the Soviet diplomat who negotiated the recognition treaty with the United States in 1933 and was ambassador to the United States in 1941–1942.

Asian

17:312 Conroy, Hilary. "The Strange Career of Admiral Nomura." *Proceedings of the American Philosophical Society* 114 (June 1970): 205–16. Conroy notes the anti-German stance of the Japanese ambassador to the United States, Nomura Kichisaburo, as well as his belief in a Japanese "Monroe Doctrine" that included suppression of communism in China.

17:313 Potter, John D. *Yamamoto: The Man Who Menaced America.* New York: Viking Press, 1965. Potter offers a general biography of the man who planned the Pearl Harbor attack but who later failed to capture Midway Island. See also Hiroyuki Agawa, *The Reluctant Admiral: Yamamoto and the Imperial Navy* (Tokyo: Kodansha International, 1979), and Edwin P. Hoyt, *Yamamoto: The Man Who Planned Pearl Harbor* (New York: McGraw-Hill, 1990).

Internationalism

LEAGUE OF NATIONS AND INTERNATIONAL ORGANIZATIONS

17:314 Accinelli, Robert D. "Militant Internationalists: The League of Nations Association, the Peace Movement, and U.S. Foreign Policy, 1934–38." *Diplomatic History* 4 (Winter 1980): 19–38. In an analysis of leaders, groups, and programs, the author notes the difficulties encountered in seeking agreement on relations with the League of Nations and the World Court, on isolationist sentiment, and on neutrality.

17:315 Fleming, Denna Frank. *The United States and World Organization: 1920–1933.* New York: Columbia University Press, 1938. Fleming offers a pioneering account valuable for its contemporary perspective.

17:316 Fosdick, Raymond B. *Letters on the League of Nations: From the Files of Raymond B. Fosdick.* As the first undersecretary general of the League, Fosdick had extensive contacts with European and American internationalists that are revealed in his letters. The work is especially full on the creation of the League, the first International Labor Organization meeting in Washington in 1919, and European responses to American refusals to join the League (14:564).

17:317 Jennings, David H. "President Harding and International Organization." *Ohio History* 75 (Spring-Summer 1966): 149–65, 192–95. Reassessing Harding, Jennings finds him more manipulative than previously assumed. Harding hedged on the League of Nations and World Court issues, assuaging both internationalist and isolationist factions to maintain party harmony.

17:318 Kenny, James T. "Manley O. Hudson and the Harvard Research in International Law." *International Lawyer* 11 (Spring 1977): 319–29. The article describes the work of Harvard scholar Hudson, who skillfully argued for an effective system of international organization buttressed by a coherent body of international law.

17:319 Kuehl, Warren F., and Lynne K. Dunn. *Keeping the Covenant: American Internationalists and the League of Nations, 1920–1939.* This book examines efforts to secure U.S. membership in the League of Nations and the World Court as well as various attempts to promote informal friendship societies, an international language, and world government (14:596).

17:320 Ostrower, Gary B. *Collective Insecurity: The United States and the League of Nations during* *the Early Thirties.* Lewisburg, PA: Bucknell University Press, 1979. After a brief review of 1920s isolationism and internationalism, Ostrower focuses on the Manchurian crisis, its origins, responses, and U.S. involvement in League discussions. Growing contacts with the League, resulting in membership in the International Labor Organization, represented erratic U.S. behavior that helped render the League a less effective agency. See also the author's "American Ambassador to the League of Nations—1933: A Proposal Postponed," *International Organization* 25 (Winter 1971): 46–58, and "The American Decision to Join the International Labor Organization," *Labor History* 16 (September 1975): 495–504.

17:321 _____. "Secretary of State Stimson and the League." *Historian* 41 (May 1979): 467–82. Ostrower sees Stimson as an important transition figure in the interwar period, moving from a position of supporting international cooperation and a reluctance to become involved during the Manchurian crisis to a later espousal of collective security.

17:322 Redmond, Kent G. "Henry L. Stimson and the Question of League Membership." In surveying Stimson's opinions from the 1920s to the 1940s, the author finds him advocating U.S. membership in the League of Nations despite some reservations about the Covenant (14:605).

17:323 Wimer, Kurt. "The Harding Administration, the League of Nations, and the Separate Peace Treaty." *Review of Politics* 29 (January 1967): 13–24. Wimer examines Harding's ambivalent position toward the League, his views on an association of nations, and developments in the early twenties that led to the separate treaty with Germany.

WORLD COURT

17:324 Accinelli, Robert D. "The Hoover Administration and the World Court." *Peace and Change* 4 (Fall 1977): 28–36. Accinelli weaves together popular interest in membership, congressional attitudes, and the ideas of Hoover and Stimson, especially Stimson. Reasons for failure can be traced not only to anticourt efforts but to the vacillation of the administration and the effect of the Depression.

17:325 _____. "Peace through Law: The United States and the World Court, 1923–1935." *Canadian Historical Association—Historical Papers, 1972* (1972): 249–61. The defeat of FDR's World Court proposal helped shatter the policy of voluntary cooperation he had pursued upon taking office. This setback made the administration more cautious in seeking further international involvements.

17:326 _____. "The Roosevelt Administration and the World Court Defeat, 1935." *Historian* 40 (May 1978): 463–78. On January 29, 1935, the Senate voted against joining the World Court. The Roosevelt administration failed to present a strong case in favor of U.S. membership.

17:327 _____. "Was There a 'New' Harding? Warren G. Harding and the World Court Issue." *Ohio History* 84 (Autumn 1975): 168–81. Harding, who personally took charge of the proposal for U.S. membership in the World Court, evidently would have made major concessions to the anticourt faction to keep the Republican Party together. The author finds the "old Harding" at work, displaying little of the initiative and determination that revisionist writers have seen.

17:328 Dunne, Michael. *The United States and the World Court, 1920–1935.* New York: St. Martin's Press, 1988. The author sees the majority of League powers seeking to mold the World Court to their individual and collective interests. Finding Congress already leaning against ratification, he challenges the claim that Senate rejection was based on violent, unscrupulous, and vicious propaganda.

17:329 Fleming, Denna Frank. *The United States and the World Court, 1920–1966.* Rev. ed. New York: Russell and Russell, 1968. Although this study concentrates on American participation in the World Court after 1920, it finds the League of Nations' failure in the Senate an important precedent. Originally issued in 1945.

17:330 Jessup, Philip C. *The United States and the World Court.* New ed. New York: Garland Publishing, 1972. This reprint of a work originally published in 1929 also includes newer essays by Jessup and European international law scholars, Wolfgang Friedmann and Hans Kelsen. Jessup wrote a new introduction for this 1972 edition, too. His original presentation, made shortly after his return with Elihu Root from a European meeting to arrange a formula for U.S. membership, is valuable for its review of developments in the 1920s.

17:331   Kahn, Gilbert N. "Presidential Passivity on a Nonsalient Issue: President Franklin D. Roosevelt and the 1935 World Court Fight." *Diplomatic History* 4 (Spring 1980): 137–60. The author analyzes the reasons why Roosevelt did not press the Senate for consent.

17:332   Margulies, Herbert F. "The Senate and the World Court." *Capitol Studies* 4 (Fall 1976): 37–52. The article traces Coolidge's failure to develop sufficient Senate support for American membership in the World Court in the years 1923–1924.

KELLOGG-BRIAND PACT

17:333   Current, Richard N. "Consequences of the Kellogg Pact." In *Issues and Conflicts: Studies in Twentieth Century American Diplomacy,* ed. George L. Anderson, 210–29. Lawrence: University of Kansas Press, 1959. This study offers material on interwar responses to the Pact of Paris and consultative pacts, appeals, embargoes, and pronouncements.

17:334   DeBenedetti, Charles. "Borah and the Kellogg-Briand Pact." *Pacific Northwest Quarterly* 73 (January 1972): 22–29. This article contends that Borah used the idea of the outlawry of war and the 1928 Kellogg-Briand pact to undercut those internationalists interested in tying the United States to the League of Nations and the Versailles Treaty.

17:335   DeBoe, David C. "Secretary Stimson and the Kellogg-Briand Pact." In *Essays on American Foreign Policy,* ed. Margaret F. Morris and Sandra L. Myres, 31–53. Austin: University of Texas Press for the University of Texas at Arlington, 1974. Stimson construed the Kellogg pact as implying consultation among its signatories in the event of the pact's breach, thereby hoping to promote collective security.

17:336   Ferrell, Robert H. *Peace in Their Time: The Origins of the Kellogg-Briand Pact.* New Haven:

Yale University Press, 1952. Ferrell discusses the American peace movement and the purposes of French diplomacy in Europe, which resulted in a grand démarche in 1927 that Secretary Kellogg skillfully turned into a largely useless multilateral treaty. See also Ferrell, *Frank B. Kellogg,* in Vol. 2, New Series, Bemis, ed., *The American Secretaries of State and Their Diplomacy* (1963).

17:337   Hefley, J. Theodore. "War Outlawed: 'The Christian Century' and the Kellogg Peace Pact." *Journalism Quarterly* 48 (Spring 1971): 26–32. Through the *Christian Century,* Charles Clayton Morrison spoke for the movement to outlaw war that resulted in the Kellogg-Briand pact of 1928. Morrison supported the movement from 1924 until 1933, when he realized the pact was dead. For Morrison's own vision, see his *The Outlawry of War: A Constructive Policy for World Peace* (Chicago: Willett, Clark and Colby, 1927).

17:338   Josephson, Harold. "Outlawing War: Internationalism and the Pact of Paris." *Diplomatic History* 3 (Fall 1979): 377–90. Josephson finds the internationalists viewing the Kellogg pact as the wedge to much wider involvements.

17:339   Kneeshaw, Stephen John. "Borah and the Outlawry of War: Another Look." *Idaho Yesterdays* 27 (Spring 1983): 2–9. The author notes that the isolationist Borah was an unlikely candidate for the outlawry movement of the 1920s. The Idaho senator steered the Kellogg-Briand pact through the Senate, preventing its becoming a partisan issue in the 1928 presidential race.

17:340   _____. "The Kellogg-Briand Pact and American Recognition of the Soviet Union." *Mid-America* 56 (January 1974): 16–31. Kellogg contended that the pact did not extend recognition to the Soviet government, while the Soviets hoped that the pact might smooth the way for a rapprochement.

17:341   Vinson, J. Chal. *William E. Borah and the Outlawry of War.* Athens, GA: University of Georgia Press, 1957. This study analyzes Borah's influence on the peace movement between 1917 and 1931. Especially detailed on the Kellogg-Briand pact, it demonstrates the political base the peace movement was able to build in the 1920s.

Disarmament and Arms Control

GENERAL

17:342   Burns, Richard Dean. "International Arms Inspection Policies between World Wars, 1919–1934." *Historian* 31 (August 1969): 583–603. This essay seeks to identify the policies of the major powers negotiating at League-sponsored conferences. It notes that the United States at first opposed inspection, while the Soviet Union endorsed it.

17:343   Burns, Richard Dean, and Donald Urquidi, with the assistance of Arthur L. Smith, Jr. and Seymour Chapin. *Disarmament in Perspective: An Analysis of Selected Arms Control and Disarmament Agreements between the World Wars, 1919–1939.* 4 vols. Los Angeles: Prepared for the U.S. Arms Control and Disarmament Agency by California State College at Los Angeles Foundation, 1968. The authors identify the characteristics of success and failure of seventeen interwar treaties: vol. 1, Disarmament and the Peace Conference; vol. 2, Demilitarization of Frontiers, Islands and Straits; vol. 3, Limitation of Sea Power; vol. 4, Conclusions.

17:344   McKercher, Brian J. C., ed. *Arms Limitation and Disarmament: Restraints on War, 1899–1939.* Westport, CT: Praeger, 1992. Among the articles in this collection are those of Malcolm H. Murfett, who sees the Washington conference of 1921–1922 conferring far more concessions on Japan than Britain (83–103); Richard W. Fanning, who finds the 1927 Geneva naval conference falling victim to bureaucratic infighting and strategic and technical differences (105–27); Marc Epstein, who faults historians for neglecting the 1927 Geneva naval conference (129–48); George C. Kennedy, who denies that the 1930 London naval conference marked any "perilous equilibrium" between Britain and the United States (149–71); McKercher, who explains the failure of the 1934 Geneva disarmament conference (173–201); and Meredith William Berg, who examines the consequences of the second London naval conference of 1935–1936 (203–27).

17:345   Winkler, Fred H. "The War Department and Disarmament, 1926–1935." *Historian* 28 (Autumn 1966): 426–46. Winkler finds that the War Department would only cooperate in disarmament as long as restrictions would apply solely to tangible forces and equipment, not to the nation's potential for mobilization.

NAVAL LIMITATION

17:346   Andrade, Ernest, Jr. "The Cruiser Controversy in Naval Limitations Negotiations, 1922–1936." *Military Affairs* 48 (July 1984): 113–20. The author argues that the Five Power Treaty of 1922 and London Naval Treaty of 1930 showed the subordination of military considerations to political needs. The abortive 1927 disarmament meeting manifested just the reverse.

17:347   Burns, Richard Dean. "Origins of the United States' Inspection Policies, 1926–46." *Disarmament and Arms Control (London)* 2 (Spring 1964): 157–69. Although Coolidge opposed international inspection in principle, Stimson and Hoover cautiously accepted on-the-spot verification to ensure compliance with arms limitation treaties.

17:348   _____. "Regulating Submarine Warfare, 1921–41: A Case Study in Arms Control and Limited War." *Military Affairs* 35 (April 1971): 56–62. This article discusses efforts to regulate submarine warfare, culminating in the submarine protocol of 1926, which was modified in the 1930 London naval conference. Its failure, obvious as soon as hostilities resumed in 1939, resulted from a utopian effort to outlaw submarine use under all conditions, thereby ignoring the proclivity of all major sea powers to use such a weapon whenever possible.

17:349   Dingman, Roger V. *Power in the Pacific: The Origins of Naval Arms Limitation, 1914–1922.* Historians have attributed the desire to disarm to mutual understandings of respective strategic and economic capabilities, but Dingman stresses domestic political factors and the desire of statesmen to shine at home. He offers a perceptive comparison of bureaucratic politics in London, Washington, and Tokyo (13:86).

17:350 Doyle, Michael K. "The United States Navy—Strategy and Far Eastern Foreign Policy, 1931–1941." *Naval War College Review* 29 (March 1977): 52–60. Between the two world wars, the interests of the United States in East Asia exceeded the capacity to defend them by force of arms. Navy officers disagreed with the assumptions underlying the Washington agreements of 1921–1922, which did not survive Japanese naval expansion in the 1930s.

17:351 Fanning, Richard W. *Peace and Disarmament: Naval Rivalry and Arms Control, 1922–1933.* Lexington: University Press of Kentucky, 1995. Using British, Japanese, and American sources, Fanning explores the effect of public opinion on policymaking. He traces how the failure of the 1927 Geneva conference led to the success of the one held in London in 1930.

17:352 Gibbs, Norman. "The Naval Conferences of the Interwar Years: A Study in Anglo-American Relations." *Naval War College Review* 30 (Summer 1977): 50–63. After years of argument, two major naval powers realized that common interests and realities called for plans for united action against enemies. This article traces the first steps in building an alliance.

17:353 Goldman, Emily O. *Sunken Treaties: Naval Arms Control between the Wars.* University Park: Pennsylvania State University Press, 1994. Finding naval arms control a limited success, Goldman claims that the failures of the 1930s should not discredit the successes of the 1920s.

17:354 Hall, Christopher. *Britain, America and Arms Control, 1921–37.* New York: St. Martin's Press, 1987. The author argues that the Washington naval system, launched in 1921–1922, eliminated the possibility of conflict between the Far Eastern "superpowers," thus providing Britain with the means to surrender gracefully the naval supremacy she had gone to war in 1914 to preserve.

17:355 Hone, Thomas C. "The Effectiveness of the 'Washington Treaty' Navy." *Naval War College Review* 32 (November-December 1979): 35–59. The ships of the "treaty navy" were effective, if not optimal, military units capable of performing their fundamental defensive strategic function.

17:356 Kaufman, Robert Gordon. *Arms Control during the Pre-Nuclear Era: The United States and Naval Limitation between the World Wars.* New York: Columbia University Press, 1990. Examining the naval conferences of the 1920s and 1930s, the author finds the varied agreements resting on fallacious assumptions about new technologies, the dynamics of Japanese politics, and Japan's strategic intentions.

17:357 O'Connor, Raymond G. "The 'Yardstick' and Naval Disarmament in the 1920s." *Mississippi Valley Historical Review* 45 (December 1958): 441–63. O'Connor traces the efforts of American negotiators to expedite naval disarmament by making various proposals for a "yardstick" that would evaluate the strength of the major powers. The concept spurred the London conference of 1930, as it caught the popular imagination and helped dispel an aura of disillusionment.

17:358 Rappaport, Armin. *The Navy League of the United States.* Detroit: Wayne State University Press, 1962. The book asserts that the League had little influence during most of its existence. When legislation that it backed was passed, outside factors—not its own propaganda—were responsible. Rappaport demolishes the myth that the League served as a front for munitions and shipbuilding lobbies.

17:359 Rosen, Philip T. "The Treaty Navy, 1919–1937." In *In Peace and War: Interpretations of American Naval History, 1775–1978*, 2d ed., ed. Kenneth J. Hagan, 221–36. Westport, CT: Greenwood Press, 1984. During this period the U.S. navy adjusted itself remarkably well to treaty limitations, even benefiting from them. It relied on a balanced fleet, controlled internal factionalism, and incorporated new weapons systems. First published in 1978.

17:360 Walter, John C. "Franklin D. Roosevelt and Naval Rearmament, 1932–1938." In *Franklin D. Roosevelt: The Man, the Myth, the Era, 1882–1945*, ed. Herbert D. Rosenbaum and Elizabeth Bartelme, 203–18. New York: Greenwood Press, 1987. The author finds no evidence of the popular thesis that FDR was predisposed toward a navy "second to none." The navy was simply his "personal plaything" until late 1938, when he considered another world war possible.

17:361 Williams, Benjamin H. *The United States and Disarmament.* New York: McGraw-Hill Book Co., 1931. This classic account, still helpful to the scholar, contains the text of both the Washington Naval Treaty (1922) and the London Naval Treaty (1930).

17:362 Winkler, Fred H. "Disarmament and Security: The American Policy at Geneva, 1926–1935." *North Dakota Quarterly* 39 (Autumn 1971): 21–33. The Geneva disarmament conference of 1932 to 1937 marked the high point of America's cooperation in international security during the interwar years. Yet even here Washington attempted to block any proposal that might interfere with its military affairs or entangle it in European matters.

WASHINGTON CONFERENCE, 1921–1922

17:363 Andrade, Ernest, Jr. "The United States Navy and the Washington Conference." *Historian* 31 (May 1969): 345–63. American naval power declined following the conference because auxiliary warships had not been restricted. This omission turned out to be crucial, for a stingy Congress, supported by public opinion, refused to provide funds to build cruisers, destroyers, and submarines in nearly the numbers constructed by the Japanese.

17:364 Birn, Donald S. "Open Diplomacy at the Washington Conference of 1921–2: The British and French Experience." *Comparative Studies in Society and History* 12 (July 1970): 297–319. The Washington conference, Birn claims, came as close to open diplomacy as any conference of the interwar era. Public opinion not only helped determine the policy of each nation but played a more direct role in day-to-day tactics. For a critique, see J. David Singer, "Popular Diplomacy and Policy Effectiveness: A Note on the Mechanisms and Consequences," ibid., 320–26.

17:365 Buckley, Thomas H. *The United States and the Washington Conference, 1921–1922.* Knoxville: University of Tennessee Press, 1970. In his thorough account, Buckley finds the Five Power Treaty, the Four Power Treaty, the Nine Power Treaty, and the other results of the conference all satisfactory to American diplomats.

17:366 Fry, Michael G. "The North Atlantic Triangle and the Abrogation of the Anglo-Japanese Alliance." *Journal of Modern History* 39 (March 1967): 46–64. The author finds the calling of the Washington conference a Canadian triumph, as it brought the United States back into world affairs and substituted the Four Power Pact for the Anglo-Japanese alliance. Subsequently, however, no entente was created.

17:367 Goldstein, Erik, and John Maurer, eds. *The Washington Conference, 1921–22: Naval Rivalry, East Asian Stability and the Road to Pearl Harbor.* Portland, OR: Frank Cass, 1994. Among the articles in this collection are those by William Reynolds Braisted, who presents the varied revisions of War Plan Orange (102–23); Thomas H. Buckley, who sees in the decade and a half of stability following the Washington conference a missed opportunity for lasting peace (124–46); and Maurer, who notes that the arms control created by the Washington conference could not survive in a political vacuum (267–93). These first appeared in a special issue of *Diplomacy & Statecraft* 4 (November 1993).

17:368 Guinsburg, Thomas N. "Victory in Defeat: The Senatorial Isolationists and the Four-Power Treaty." *Capitol Studies* 2 (Spring 1973): 23–38. With the Four Power Treaty, veteran Senate isolationists picked up some surprising allies, particularly among southern Wilsonians, but not enough to defeat a treaty they had already emasculated.

17:369 Hoag, C. Leonard. *Preface to Preparedness: The Washington Disarmament Conference and Public Opinion.* Washington, DC: American Council on Public Affairs, 1941. This book offers a detailed study of the public opinion campaign waged in the United States, often by women's groups, on behalf of disarmament.

17:370 McDonald, J. Kenneth. "The Washington Conference and the Naval Balance of Power, 1921–22." In *Maritime Strategy and the Balance of Power: Britain and America in the Twentieth Century,* ed. John B. Hattendorf and Robert S. Jordan, 189–213. New York: St. Martin's Press, 1989. McDonald stresses the stabilizing effect of the Washington conference.

17:371 Pugach, Noel H. "American Friendship for

China and the Shantung Question at the Washington Conference." *Journal of American History* 64 (June 1977): 67–86. Pugach assesses the role of American mediation in the Shantung dispute, which resulted from the 1914 Japanese occupation of that area.

17:372   Sales, Peter M. "American-Australian Relations and the Washington Disarmament Conference." *Australian Outlook* 27 (December 1973): 329–38. The author traces how the conference fostered U.S.-Australian friendship after a period of bitter tension.

17:373   Van Meter, Robert H., Jr. "The Washington Conference of 1921–1922: A New Look." *Pacific Historical Review* 46 (November 1977): 603–24. Harding, Hoover, and other leading U.S. officials were convinced that international disarmament would promote financial stabilization and economic recovery in Europe, which in turn would stimulate overseas demand for surplus American products and thereby help restore prosperity at home.

17:374   Vinson, J. Chal. "The Drafting of the Four Power Treaty of the Washington Conference." *Journal of Modern History* 25 (March 1953): 40–47. Vinson sees the Four Power Pact resulting from Secretary Hughes's consummate diplomatic skill, though he acknowledges the agreement could not fend off the impending international discord.

17:375   _____. *The Parchment Peace: The United States Senate and the Washington Conference, 1921–1922.* Athens, GA: University of Georgia Press, 1955. Vinson traces the role of the Senate in fostering the Washington naval conference, analyzes views of members toward disarmament and East Asian policy, and discusses the ratification debate, concentrating on the Senate's reaction to the Four Power Pact.

17:376   _____. "The Problems of Australian Representation at the Washington Conference for the Limitation of Naval Armament." *Australian Journal of Politics and History* 4 (November 1958): 155–64. The author notes how Secretary Hughes blocked Australia's desire for direct representation at the Washington conference. Australia feared Japanese naval power and sought national prestige.

COOLIDGE CONFERENCE, 1927

17:377   Carlton, David. "Great Britain and the Coolidge Naval Disarmament Conference of 1927." *Political Science Quarterly* 83 (December 1968): 573–98. The conference failed because the statesmen were unable to overrule pessimists among their naval advisers. Anglo-American relations suffered as a result.

17:378   Dubay, Robert W. "The Geneva Naval Conference of 1927: A Study of Battleship Diplomacy." *Southern Quarterly* 8 (January 1970): 177–99. Although the Washington conference had established an international ratio for capital ship construction among the leading world naval powers, lesser categories of vessels were not regulated. In 1927, President Coolidge called for a conference to negotiate a treaty to limit ships of less than 10,000 tons displacement.

LONDON NAVAL CONFERENCES, 1930, 1935–1936

17:379   Berg, Meredith William. "Admiral William H. Standley and the Second London Naval Treaty, 1934–1936." *Historian* 33 (February 1971): 215–36. As chief of naval operations and a representative on the U.S. delegation to the conference, Standley kept alive the idea of naval limitation.

17:380   Fagan, George V. "Edward Price Bell: The Journalist as Diplomat." *Newberry Library Bulletin* 4 (November 1955): 24–27. A correspondent for the *Chicago Daily News* served as Hoover's unofficial emissary in 1929 in negotiations with the British on naval disarmament.

17:381   Harada, Kumao. *Fragile Victory: Prince Saionji and the 1930 London Treaty Issue, from the Memoirs of Baron Harada Kumao.* Translated by Thomas Francis Mayer-Oakes. Detroit: Wayne State University Press, 1968. This view of the Japanese side of the 1930 London naval negotiations consists of an extended introduction and a translation of the first volume of Baron Harada Kumao's memoirs.

Mayer-Oakes provided annotations as well as a translation.

17:382 O'Connor, Raymond G. *Perilous Equilibrium: The United States and the London Disarmament Conference of 1930*. Lawrence: University of Kansas Press, 1962. The 1930 treaty extended the Washington treaty by restricting ships under 10,000 tons, revising ratios, and including an escalator clause. O'Connor finds the London conference both strengthening and weakening the disarmament system.

17:383 Pelz, Stephen E. *Race to Pearl Harbor: The Failure of the Second London Naval Conference and the Onset of World War II*. Cambridge, MA: Harvard University Press, 1974. This study of naval limitation concentrates on the general staff of the Japanese navy. It offers detailed commentary on both American and Japanese strategists as they adjusted their planning to rules produced by the disarmament conferences. Pelz shows how Japanese naval factions sought parity either to force changes in the limitation system or destroy it.

17:384 Wheeler, Gerald E. "Naval Diplomacy in the Interwar Years." In *Versatile Guardian: Research in Naval History*, ed. Richard A. Von Doenhoff, 35–51. Washington, DC: Howard University Press, 1979. Wheeler stresses the role of Admirals Hilary P. Jones and William V. Pratt at the London naval conference of 1930.

Prohibition and Narcotics Traffic

17:385 Holsinger, M. Paul. "The *I'm Alone* Controversy, 1929–1935." *Mid-America* 50 (October 1968): 305–13. In 1929, the U.S. coast guard, acting in international waters, sank a Canadian-registered ship carrying illegal alcoholic beverages. The author describes the subsequent negotiations.

17:386 Kottman, Richard N. "Volstead Violated: Prohibition as a Factor in Canadian-American Relations." *Canadian Historical Review* 43 (June 1962): 106–26. Kottman shows the divisive impact of Prohibition on domestic Canadian politics and U.S.-Canadian relations.

17:387 Spinelli, Lawrence. *Dry Diplomacy: The United States, Great Britain, and Prohibition*. Wilmington, DE: SR Books, 1989. The author describes the suspicions engendered by American Prohibition legislation, an antagonism not really solved when a 1924 treaty reduced the emotionalism of the issue. Problems arose again in 1929, when the United States attacked a Canadian vessel involved in smuggling, though by 1933 repercussions were minimized.

17:388 Taylor, Arnold H. *American Diplomacy and the Narcotics Traffic, 1900–1939: A Study in International Humanitarian Reform*. In the 1920s, the U.S. remained aloof from League of Nations efforts to abolish drug trafficking; in the 1930s, it took the lead in such efforts (13:67).

17:389 Tyrrell, Ian. "Prohibition, American Cultural Expansion, and the New Hegemony in the 1920s: An Interpretation." *Histoire Sociale/Social History* 27 (November 1994): 413–45. The author notes how American Prohibitionists, acting through the World League Against Alcoholism, failed in their effort to extend their war on liquor overseas due to anti-American sentiment, the negative American example, and complex class and cultural opposition to their cause.

17:390 Walker, William O., III. *Opium and Foreign Policy: The Anglo-American Search for Order in Asia, 1912–1954*. Included are differences between the United States and Britain over opium control, the social role of opium in helping shape China policy, Chiang Kai-shek's political use of opium to tighten his power, and Japan's involvement in China's narcotic trade (13:182).

Domestic Views and Groups

ISOLATION AND INTERVENTION

17:391 Barron, Gloria J. *Leadership in Crisis: FDR and the Path to Intervention*. Port Washington, NY: Kennikat Press, 1973. This study analyzes the restraints of public opinion on Roosevelt and documents his strategy, consistent except for the quarantine speech, of leading public opinion by lagging behind it. FDR encouraged others to speak out to goad him into action.

17:392   Bolt, Ernest C., Jr. *Ballots before Bullets: The War Referendum Approach to Peace in America, 1914–1941.* This book covers the efforts to secure a popular vote from the time of World War I through the movement for the Ludlow Amendment during the 1930s (14:323).

17:393   Bucklin, Stephen J. "Quincy Wright's Blueprint for a Durable Peace." *Mid-America* 76 (Fall 1994): 227–40. Quincy Wright, who taught international law at the University of Chicago from 1923 to 1956, established a reputation as the U.S. premier scholar in the field of international politics. This article traces the evolution of his schemes for world order, which centered increasingly on an effective international police force.

17:394   Butler, Harold T. "Partisan Positions on Isolationism vs. Internationalism, 1918–1933." Ph.D. dissertation, Syracuse University, 1963. This analysis of congressional votes, political campaigns, party platforms, press, and the partisanship of pressure groups concludes that neither party was more isolationist than the other. It affirms recent scholarship that sees the midwest as not peculiarly isolationist.

17:395   Chadwin, Mark L. *The Hawks of World War II.* Chapel Hill: University of North Carolina Press, 1968. Chadwin offers the history of the Fight for Freedom Committee, a more militant group than William Allen White's Committee to Defend America by Aiding the Allies. Reissued in 1970 by W. W. Norton as *The Warhawks: American Interventionists before Pearl Harbor.*

17:396   Divine, Robert A. *Foreign Policy and U.S. Presidential Elections. Vol. 1: 1940–1948. Vol. 2: 1952–1960.* Divine argues that the distressing European situation aided FDR in election seasons (2:147).

17:397   _____. *The Illusion of Neutrality.* Chicago: University of Chicago Press, 1962. Divine considers public attitudes as responsible for the dubious neutrality acts as any other factor but also finds

FDR negligent in leadership. Especially useful is his careful identification of three distinct groups: traditionalists, internationalists, and isolationists.

17:398   Engelbracht, H. C., and F. Cleary Hanighen. *Merchants of Death: A Study of the International Armament Industry.* New York: Dodd, Mead and Company, 1934. Reprint 1972 (Garland Publishing). The authors offer a popular account that helped prompt the Nye Committee's investigation into the activities of armament manufacturers. Foreword by Harry Elmer Barnes.

17:399   Feinman, Ronald L. *Twilight of Progressivism: The Western Republican Senators and the New Deal.* Baltimore: Johns Hopkins University Press, 1981. This volume shows the increasing divisions within progressive ranks over foreign policy.

17:400   Friedman, Donald J. *The Road from Isolation: The Campaign of the American Committee for Non-Participation in Japanese Aggression, 1938–1941.* Cambridge, MA: East Asian Research Center, Harvard University, 1968. Friedman traces the efforts of the committee to convince the American public that the United States ought to take stronger measures, such as economic sanctions, to halt Japanese expansion.

17:401   Guinsburg, Thomas N. "The Triumph of Isolation." In *American Foreign Relations Reconsidered, 1890–1993,* ed. Gordon Martel, 90–105. New York: Routledge, 1994. Guinsburg finds Roosevelt failing to educate the American public from 1933 to 1935.

17:402   Jablon, Howard. "The State Department and Collective Security." *Historian* 33 (February 1971): 248–63. Jablon disagrees with Divine in *The Illusion of Neutrality* (1962) (17:397) that Secretary of State Hull and Norman Davis were strong advocates of collective action during the arms embargo dispute in 1933.

17:403   Jessup, Philip C. *Neutrality, Its History, Economics and Law. Vol. 4: Today and Tomorrow.* New York: Columbia University Press, 1936. This fourth volume of a remarkable series was occasioned by the Nye Committee investigation of the mid-1930s and general interest in neutral rights prior to

World War II. Jessup, an outstanding legal scholar, finds a partial biographer in Marshall Kuehl, "Philip C. Jessup from America First to Cold War Interventionist" (Ph.D. diss., Kent State, 1985).

17:404 Johnson, Walter. *The Battle against Isolation.* Chicago: University of Chicago Press, 1944. Reprint 1973 (Da Capo Press). This book embodies an early and partisan effort to examine the struggle between the isolationist and interventionist forces. William Allen White's role in forming the Committee to Defend America by Aiding the Allies, as well as the battle between this group and the America First Committee, provide the framework for the debate.

17:405 Kuehl, Warren F. "Midwestern Newspapers and Isolationist Sentiment." *Diplomatic History* 3 (Summer 1979): 283–306. In a thorough examination of the editorial views of thirty newspapers in the heart of the midwest, the author notes more internationalism than isolationism between 1919 and 1935. Tables show the commitment to isolationism or internationalism.

17:406 Mazuzan, George T. "The Failure of Neutrality Revision in Mid-Summer, 1939: Warren R. Austin's Memorandum of the White House Conference of July 18." *Vermont History* 42 (Summer 1974): 239–45. Here is reproduced the text of the Vermont senator's memorandum on FDR's decision not to pursue revision of neutrality acts.

17:407 Muresianu, John M. *War of Ideas: American Intellectuals and the World Crisis, 1938–1945.* New York: Garland Publishing, 1988. While treating interventionist and anti-interventionist reactions to the Nazi conquest of Europe, the author discusses Walter Lippmann, Dorothy Thompson, Henry R. Luce, Lewis Mumford, Dwight Macdonald, William Henry Chamberlin, Reinhold Niebuhr, Max Lerner, Bruce Bliven, and the *New York Times.*

17:408 Namikas, Lise. "The Committee to Defend America and the Debate between Internationalists and Interventionists, 1939–1941." *Historian (London)* 61 (Summer 1999): 843–63. The author offers further detail on the evolution of the Committee to Defend America by Aiding the Allies, showing how the more militant interventionists increasingly dominated the committee.

17:409 Olsson, Christer. *Congress and the Executive: The Making of United States Foreign Policy, 1933–1940.* Solna, Sweden: Esselte Studium, 1982. The author covers the conflict over trade agreements, the World Court contest, and the debate over the arms embargo in 1939.

17:410 Papachristou, Judith. "An Exercise in Anti-Imperialism: The Thirties." *American Studies* 15 (Spring 1974): 61–77. The author sees certain critics of FDR, including editor Bruce Bliven and peace lobbyist Frederick J. Libby, as neither isolationist nor pacifist but as fundamentally anti-imperialist.

17:411 Patterson, James T. "Eating Humble Pie: A Note on Roosevelt, Congress, and Neutrality Revision in 1939." *Historian* 31 (May 1968): 407–14. As he approached the coming of World War II, Roosevelt successfully won over certain major senatorial foes of the New Deal, convincing them to support revision of the neutrality acts.

17:412 Platt, Rorin Morse. *Virginia in Foreign Affairs, 1933–1941.* Lanham, MD: University Press of America, 1991. Platt sees the state's militant interventionism rooted in concerns over democracy, security, trade, and a shared British heritage. See also Platt's "The Triumph of Interventionism: Virginia's Political Elite and Aid to Britain, 1933–1941," *Virginia Magazine of History and Biography* 100 (July 1992): 343–64.

17:413 Porter, David L. *The Seventy-Sixth Congress and World War II, 1939–1940.* Columbia: University of Missouri Press, 1979. This book offers a thorough treatment of the battles over cash-and-carry, aid to Finland, and the selective service bill of 1940.

17:414 Rossini, Daniela, ed. *From Theodore Roosevelt to FDR: Internationalism and Isolationism in American Foreign Policy.* Staffordshire, UK: Ryburn Publishing, Keele University Press, 1995. Included are essays by David K. Adams finding FDR an internationalist in the 1930s (113–20), Tibor Frank seeing the United States promoting a non-Hapsburg and anti-Nazi Hungary (131–36), and Hans Bak describing the shift of *The New Republic* to interventionism (147–84).

17:415 Schneider, James C. *Should America Go to War? The Debate over Foreign Policy in Chicago,*

1939–1941. Chapel Hill: University of North Carolina Press, 1989. Schneider finds the debate involving some shadowboxing. While Chicago interventionists were concentrating on discrediting their opponents, they also could not accept the need for outright war.

17:416   Sniegoski, Stephen J. "Unified Democracy: An Aspect of American World War II Interventionist Thought, 1939–1941." *Maryland Historian* 9 (Spring 1978): 33–48. This essay describes the arguments introduced by interventionists such as Lewis Mumford, Harold Ickes, Max Lerner, and Dorothy Thompson.

17:417   Steele, Richard W. "Franklin D. Roosevelt and His Foreign Policy Critics." *Political Science Quarterly* 44 (Spring 1979): 15–32. The author finds FDR involved in continued attempts to silence his opponents, including use of the FBI and Federal Communications Commission. Arthur M. Schlesinger, Jr. offers a rebuttal (33–35).

17:418   _____. "The Great Debate: Roosevelt, the Media, and the Coming of the War, 1940–1941." *Journal of American History* 71 (June 1984): 69–92. Roosevelt, finding the issue of war and peace too important for national debate, chose not to explore issues but to raise morale, an enterprise in which he was willingly supported by the great bulk of the press, radio, and motion picture industry. The effort effectively minimized public access to the anti-interventionist perspective.

17:419   _____. *Propaganda in an Open Society: The Roosevelt Administration and the Media, 1933–1941*. Westport, CT: Greenwood Press, 1985. The book describes Roosevelt's efforts at media control. See also Steele, "Preparing the Public for War: Efforts to Establish a National Propaganda Agency, 1940–1941," *American Historical Review* 85 (October 1970): 1640–53.

17:420   Stromberg, Roland N. "American Business and the Approach of War, 1935–1941." *Journal of Economic History* 13 (Winter 1953): 58–78. Based on his examination of its press, the author finds business as divided as any other segment of the American public.

17:421   Tuttle, William M., Jr. "Aid to the Allies Short-of-War versus American Intervention, 1940: A Reappraisal of William Allen White's Leadership." *Journal of American History* 56 (March 1970): 840–58. Tuttle shows the infighting between the two major interventionist groups launched in 1940 — the Committee to Defend America by Aiding the Allies and the Century Club group that organized Fight for Freedom.

17:422   Wala, Michael. "Advocating Belligerency: Organized Internationalism, 1939–1941." *Amerikastudien/American Studies (Stuttgart)* 38, no. 1 (1993): 49–59. Although internationalist organizations reflected much diversity of opinion, they possessed interlocking officers and overlapping membership. They were led by the same figures, most notably Morgan partner Thomas W. Lamont and organization leader Clark M. Eichelberger, and worked closely with the Roosevelt administration.

17:423   Wilburn, Mark Steven. "Keeping the Powder Dry: Senator Harry S. Truman and Democratic Interventionism, 1935–1941." *Missouri Historical Review* 84 (April 1990): 311–37. The article finds the future president always a loyal supporter of FDR's evolving internationalism.

ISOLATIONISM

17:424   Adler, Selig. *The Isolationist Impulse: Its Twentieth-Century Reaction.* Though in general the book is sharply critical of the isolationist movement and was written long before many crucial archives were open, it offers many helpful leads, particularly about the 1920s (14:267).

17:425   Barrow, Clyde W. "The Diversionary Thesis and the Dialectic of Imperialism: Charles A. Beard's Theory of American Foreign Policy Revisited." *Studies in American Political Development* 11 (Fall 1997): 248–91. Barrow offers an able exposition of Beard's foreign policy views.

17:426   Beard, Charles A. *American Foreign Policy in the Making, 1932–1940: A Study in Responsibilities.* New Haven: Yale University Press, 1946. Beard offers a revisionist work that used available documents to "prove" that Roosevelt deserted the liberal tradition and deliberately led the nation into war.

17:427 _____. *The Devil Theory of War: An Inquiry into the Nature of History and the Possibility of Keeping out of War.* New York: Vanguard Press, 1936. Beard, in calling for mandatory neutrality legislation, wrote that in the period 1914–1917, "the country faced an economic smash at home or intervention." The United States, he claims, entered World War I because it saw its newfound prosperity at stake.

17:428 Beard, Charles A., with G. H. E. Smith. *The Open Door at Home: A Trial Philosophy of National Interest.* New York: Macmillan, 1934. Beard and Smith called for a system of national autarchy calculated to minimize its dependence upon external trade.

17:429 Billington, Ray Allen. "The Origins of Middle Western Isolationism." The author finds midwestern isolationism rooted in Populism, Republican Party partisanship, a German and Scandinavian ethnic base, and the illusion of economic self-sufficiency (2:217).

17:430 Borchard, Edwin, and William Potter Lage. *Neutrality for the United States.* Borchard, a prominent professor of international law at Yale, and Lage, an attorney, combine traditional arguments for neutrality and denunciations of collective security with accusations that the Wilson administration had made American entry into World War I inevitable. First published in 1937 (14:293).

17:431 Carleton, William G. "Isolationism and the Middle West." *Mississippi Valley Historical Review* 33 (December 1946): 377–90. While isolationism may be stronger in the midwest than elsewhere, its strength is often exaggerated. In the middle and late 1930s, isolationism was often partisan rather than sectional.

17:432 Carlisle, Rodney P. "The Foreign Policy Views of an Isolationist Press Lord: W. R. Hearst and the International Crisis, 1936–41." *Journal of Contemporary History* 9 (July 1974): 217–27. During the mid-1930s, Hearst's readership represented 12–14 percent of the total for daily newspapers in the United States. Hearst believed the United States should establish a deterrent armed force, give no encouragement to Britain or France, and keep a wary eye on Japan and the Soviet Union. His isolationism was

never based on support for fascism, though he was willing to cooperate with Germany in opposition to Russia. See also the author's "William Randolph Hearst: A Fascist Reputation Reconsidered," *Journalism Quarterly* 50 (Spring 1973): 125–33.

17:433 Charles, Douglas M. "Informing FDR: FBI Political Surveillance and the Isolationist-Interventionist Foreign Policy Debate, 1939–1945." *Diplomatic History* 24 (Spring 2000): 211–32. While FDR had a low regard for the civil liberties of his opponents and was apt to use surreptitious means to monitor them, Hoover initiated political surveillance of administration critics.

17:434 Charles, Douglas M., and John P. Rossi. "FBI Political Surveillance and the Charles Lindbergh Investigation, 1939–1944." *Historian* 59 (Summer 1997): 831–47. This article shows Roosevelt's extensive political use of the FBI.

17:435 Clifford, J. Garry. "A Note on Chester Bowles's Secret Plan to End World War II." *Peace and Change* 14 (January 1989): 106–22. This article includes a profile of a leading advertising executive and liberal Democrat who served on the America First Committee. It includes verbatim his peace plan of November 1941.

17:436 Cohen, Warren I. *The American Revisionists: The Lessons of Intervention in World War I.* See chapter 14 of this Guide (14:36).

17:437 Cole, Wayne S. "America First and the South, 1940–1941." *Journal of Southern History* 22 (February 1956): 36–47. Noting the almost total failure of the America First Committee to organize in the south, the author points to traditional southern pride in the military, pro-British sentiment based upon Anglo-Saxon stock, political loyalty to the Democratic Party, and the role of defense spending in aiding the region's depressed economy.

17:438 _____. *America First: The Battle against Intervention, 1940–41.* Madison: University of Wisconsin Press, 1953. Reprint 1971 (Octagon Books). In this careful, analytical, and balanced account of the major anti-interventionist organization established to fight such measures as lend-lease and convoys to Britain, Cole shows how the America

First Committee seriously affected the debate over FDR's interventionist measures, both in maximizing congressional and public opposition and in forcing the president to be much more circumspect in what he advocated publicly.

17:439 Croog, Charles E. "FBI Surveillance and the Isolationist-Interventionist Debate, 1931–1941." *Historian* 54 (Spring 1992): 441–58. This article shows the political use of the FBI to intimidate isolationists.

17:440 DeConde, Alexander. "The South and Isolationism." *Journal of Southern History* 24 (August 1958): 332–46. Much of the south was isolationist during World War I. When issues do not center on aid to Britain, bolstering the southern economy, and appealing to party ties, the region might become more isolationist again.

17:441 Dennis, Lawrence. *The Dynamics of War and Revolution.* New York: Weekly Foreign Letter, 1940. Dennis, later indicted (but not convicted) for sedition, argues for isolation on the grounds of realpolitik. Finding aggression rooted in man's nature and the world's unequal distribution of goods and resources, he envisions division of the world into American, Japanese, Russian, German, and British spheres. For analysis of Dennis, see Justus D. Doenecke, "The Isolationist as Collectivist: Lawrence Dennis and the Coming of World War II," *Journal of Libertarian Studies* 3 (Summer 1979): 191–207.

17:442 Doenecke, Justus D. *The Battle against Intervention, 1939–1941.* Malabar, FL: Krieger Publishing Co., 1997. Combining narrative and documents, the volume reveals the varieties of anti-interventionism prevalent as the United States approached war. Strategic and economic arguments are stressed. See also Doenecke, "Power, Markets, and Ideology: The Isolationist Response to Roosevelt Policy, 1940–41," in Liggio and Martin, *Watershed of Empire: Essays on New Deal Foreign Policy* (1976), 132–61 (18:188).

17:443 _____. "Edwin M. Borchard, John Bassett Moore, and Opposition to American Intervention in World War II." *Journal of Libertarian Studies* 6 (Winter 1986): 1–34. This article shows why two major scholars of international law were so doggedly

isolationist. For specialized studies, see Richard H. Kendall, "Edwin M. Borchard and the Defense of Traditional Neutrality Policy" (Ph.D. diss., Yale University, 1964), and Richard Megargee, "The Diplomacy of John Bassett Moore: Realism in American Foreign Policy" (Ph.D. diss., Northwestern University, 1963).

17:444 _____. "Germany in Isolationist Ideology: The Issue of a Negotiated Peace." In *Germany and America: Essays on Problems of International Relations and Immigration,* ed. Hans L. Trefousse, 215–26. New York: Brooklyn College Press, 1980. This article stresses major isolationist sentiment for a negotiated peace.

17:445 _____. "Non-Intervention of the Left: The Keep America Out of the War Congress, 1938–41." *Journal of Contemporary History* 12 (April 1977): 221–36. In his account of the Keep America Out of War Congress, founded in New York in March 1938 and terminated just after Pearl Harbor, Doenecke finds socialists and pacifists sustaining their coalition amid defections from their ranks.

17:446 _____. "Rehearsal for Cold War: United States Anti-Interventionists and the Soviet Union, 1939–1941." *International Journal of Politics, Culture and Society* 7 (Spring 1994): 375–92. This article shows how strongly anti-Soviet sentiment permeated the isolationist movement.

17:447 _____. *Storm on the Horizon: The Challenge to American Intervention, 1939–1941.* Lanham, MD: Rowman and Littlefield Publishers, 2000. The author examines the opponents of FDR's foreign policy in light of the ever-changing military picture. Doenecke emphasizes military and economic arguments advanced by a rich variety of isolationists and pacifists.

17:448 _____. "Verne Marshall's Leadership of the No Foreign War Committee, 1940." *Annals of Iowa* 41 (Winter 1973): 1153–73. In his treatment of the short-lived action group established late in 1940, the author finds a prominent Iowa editor playing a destructive role within the anti-interventionist movement.

17:449 Edwards, Jerome E. *The Foreign Policy of Col. McCormick's Tribune, 1929–1941.* Reno: University of Nevada Press, 1971. Edwards examines the views on foreign policy of the publisher of the leading isolationist newspaper in the midwest in the 1920s and 1930s, Robert R. McCormick of the *Chicago Tribune*. The work includes a thorough account of McCormick's opposition to FDR's diplomacy between 1937 and 1941.

17:450   Griffin, Walter R. "Louis Ludlow and the War Referendum Crusade, 1935–1941." *Indiana Magazine of History* 64 (December 1968): 267–88. The Indiana congressman was nearly successful in amending the Constitution to provide for a national referendum before any declaration of war.

17:451   Jeansonne, Glen. *Women of the Far Right: The Mothers' Movement and World War II*. Chicago: University of Chicago Press, 1996. This book studies such rightist fringe leaders as Catherine Curtis and Elizabeth Dilling, showing the vehemence of their opposition to FDR. See also the author's "Furies: Women Isolationists in the Era of FDR," *Journal of History and Politics* (1990): 67–96. For a look at the opposite tendencies, women who urged intervention against the Axis powers on FDR (including journalist Dorothy Thompson), see Margaret Paton-Walsh, *Our War Too: American Women against the Axis* (Lawrence: University Press of Kansas, 2002).

17:452   Johnson, Robert David. *The Peace Progressives and American Foreign Relations*. The author finds certain "isolationists" in reality "peace progressives," hoping to achieve a more peaceful world order by directing American foreign policy along anti-imperialist lines. Such figures sought worldwide disarmament, backed the Weimar Republic, and supported democratic revolutions in Mexico, Nicaragua, and China. Among those covered are Borah, Nye, the La Follettes, George Norris, and Hiram Johnson (11:134).

17:453   Jonas, Manfred. *Isolationism in America, 1935–1941*. Ithaca: Cornell University Press, 1966. Jonas makes a careful distinction between the more aggressive isolationists, who called for full neutral rights, and those willing to forego traditional privileges. If the isolationist perspective could not be elevated to "political philosophy," it could not be dismissed as "simply obstructionism based on ignorance and folly." By including pacifists in his study, he shows how varied the anti-interventionist movement was.

17:454   _____. "Pro-Axis Sentiment and American Isolationism." *Historian* 29 (February 1967): 221–37. Jonas notes that many congressional anti-interventionists sympathized with the Ethiopians in 1935, the Spanish loyalists in 1936, the Chinese in 1937, and the British in 1940.

17:455   Kennedy, Thomas C. *Charles A. Beard and American Foreign Policy*. This study of Beard severely criticizes his opposition to intervention as World War II approached (2:93).

17:456   Nore, Ellen. *Charles A. Beard, An Intellectual Biography*. Carbondale: Southern Illinois University Press, 1983. Nore presents a thorough study that involves some appreciation of Beard's militant anti-interventionism.

17:457   Schacht, John N., ed. *Three Faces of Midwestern Isolationism: Gerald P. Nye, Robert E. Wood, John L. Lewis*. Iowa City: Center for the Study of the Recent History of the United States, 1981. Three congressional, business, and labor manifestations of isolationism are covered respectively by Wayne S. Cole, "Gerald P. Nye and Agrarian Bases for the Rise and Fall of American Isolationism" (1–10); Justus D. Doenecke, "The Isolationism of General Robert E. Wood" (11–22); and Melvyn Dubofsky, "John L. Lewis and American Isolationism" (23–33).

17:458   Smuckler, Ralph. "The Region of Isolationism." *American Political Science Review* 47 (June 1953): 365–401. The author finds isolationism predominant in a northern band of states, beginning in Ohio and ending in Idaho. Isolationists were more to be found in rural than urban states and in Republican rather than Democratic districts.

17:459   Stenehjem, Michele Flynn. *An American First: John T. Flynn and the America First Committee*. New Rochelle, NY: Arlington House Publishers, 1976. Stenehjem offers thorough coverage of the muckraking journalist who headed the semiautonomous New York chapter of the America First Committee.

17:460   Williams, William Appleman. "The Legend of Isolationism in the 1920s." *Science and Society* 18 (Winter 1954): 1–20. Claiming that the foreign policy of the 1920s was never isolationist, Williams asserts that Americans simply continued their economic expansion without binding political alliances. Lodge and Borah believed in "no entangling alliances," as they wanted to gain greater freedom to maneuver. Hughes, Hoover, and Stimson were apostles of a new corporatism designed to expand American power through the internationalization of business.

Congressional Isolationism

17:461   Anderson, John T. "Senator Burton K. Wheeler and United States Foreign Relations." Ph.D. dissertation, University of Virginia, 1982. Anderson offers a thorough treatment of one of FDR's major foreign policy foes. He argues that Wheeler's lifelong anti-interventionism proceeded logically from his progressive convictions.

17:462   Burns, Richard Dean, and W. Addams Dixon. "Foreign Policy and the 'Democratic Myth': The Debate on the Ludlow Amendment." *Mid-America* 47 (November 1965): 288–306. The authors analyze the arguments used in the House during the crucial debate on the Ludlow Amendment. Members staged a considerable discussion of the comparative merits of "pure" democracy and a representative form of government.

17:463   Cole, Wayne S. *Roosevelt & the Isolationists, 1932–45*. Lincoln: University of Nebraska Press, 1983. This book offers a definitive account of anti-interventionist activity, with emphasis on the activities of congressional leaders. Cole finds many such isolationists at first friendly toward the New Deal but later fearing that war would ruin the United States by dissipating its resources.

17:464   _____. *Senator Gerald P. Nye and American Foreign Relations*. Minneapolis: University of Minnesota Press, 1962. Speaking for a region that—broadly speaking—included Chicago manufacturing as well as Oklahoma dirt farmers, Nye believed that urban and financial powers were bleeding the agrarian sector to finance ruinous wars. In his analysis Cole offers a major explanation for much American isolationism. See also Wayne S. Cole, "And Then There Were None! How Arthur H. Vandenberg and Gerald P. Nye Separately Departed Isolationist Leadership Roles," in Thomas J. McCormick and Walter

LaFeber, *Behind the Throne: Servants of Power to Imperial Presidents, 1898–1968* (Madison: University of Wisconsin Press, 1993), 232–53.

17:465   Coulter, Matthew Ware. *The Senate Munitions Inquiry of the 1930s: Beyond the Merchants of Death*. Westport, CT: Greenwood Press, 1997. This study finds leaders of the munitions investigation often mistaken but deserving credit for providing the first critical examination of the nation's modern military establishment. Challenging conventional views, Coulter argues that the inquiry did not block a realistic U.S. response to aggression; rather, it held culpable American businesses that sold to aggressors.

17:466   Donovan, John C. "Congressional Isolationists and the Roosevelt Foreign Policy." *World Politics* 3 (April 1951): 299–316. In a pioneering essay, the author distinguishes between the more militant isolationists—such as Hamilton Fish, Jr. and William E. Borah—and such cautious figures as Gerald P. Nye and Arthur Vandenberg.

17:467   Guinsburg, Thomas N. "Ebb Tide of American Isolationism: The Senate Debate on the Arms Embargo, 1937–1939." *Canadian Historical Association—Historical Papers, 1972* (1972): 313–34. Guinsburg notes how the repeal of the arms embargo severely damaged the isolationist cause. Though all Americans dreaded entanglement in war, a large proportion also feared the possible consequences of allied defeat.

17:468   _____. *The Pursuit of Isolationism in the United States Senate from Versailles to Pearl Harbor*. New York: Garland Publishing, 1982. Guinsburg covers debates over the League of Nations, the Four Power Pact, the World Court, the Kellogg-Briand Pact, the neutrality acts of 1935–1937, repeal of the arms embargo, and the lend-lease bill. He warns of exaggerating the isolationism of either the American people or the Congress and opposes associating isolationism with the midwest.

17:469   Meijer, Hank. "Arthur Vandenberg and the Fight for Neutrality, 1939." *Michigan Historical Review* 16 (Fall 1990): 1–21. The author finds Vandenberg an absolutist on the neutrality issue.

17:470   Porter, David L. "Ohio Representative John M. Vorys and the Arms Embargo in 1939." *Ohio*

History 83 (Spring 1974): 103–13. Freshman representative Vorys assisted in preventing the repeal of the arms embargo in 1939, rallying bipartisan support for an amendment to the Bloom bill restoring the arms embargo.

17:471 Scherr, Arthur. "Louis Ludlow's War Referendum of 1938: A Reappraisal." *Mid-America* 76 (Spring-Summer 1994): 133–55. The author sees proponents of the Ludlow Amendment not as diehard isolationists, as usually depicted, but idealists who sought to set in motion a world revolution against war and dictatorship.

17:472 Shapiro, Edward S. "The Approach of War: Congressional Isolationism and Anti-Semitism, 1939–1941." *American Jewish History* 74 (September 1984): 45–65. The author finds most members of Congress who expressed antisemitic sentiments not intrinsically anti-Jewish but fearful that the Jews would push the United States into war with Germany.

17:473 Troncone, Anthony C. "Hamilton Fish, Sr. and the Politics of American Nationalism, 1912–1945." Ph.D. dissertation, Rutgers University, 1993. So far only doctoral theses cover the New York congressman who led the House isolationist forces in the debates of 1939–1941. Troncone offers a critical treatment. See also Richard Kay Hanks, "Hamilton Fish and American Isolationism, 1920–1944" (Ph.D. diss., University of California at Riverside, 1921). For Fish's autobiography see *Memoir of an American Patriot* (Washington, DC: Regnery Gateway, 1991).

17:474 Vinson, J. Chal. "War Debts and Peace Legislation: The Johnson Act of 1934." *Mid-America* 50 (July 1968): 206–22. Beginning in 1932, Senator Hiram Johnson led a congressional attack against war debts defaulters.

17:475 Weiss, Stuart L. "American Foreign Policy and Presidential Power: The Neutrality Act of 1935." *Journal of Politics* 30 (August 1968): 672–95. The author claims that Roosevelt could have avoided the restrictions of the 1935 act had he taken the initiative two years earlier.

17:476 Wiltz, John E. (John Edward Wilz). *In Search of Peace: The Senate Munitions Inquiry, 1934–36.* Baton Rouge: Louisiana State University Press, 1963. Offering a revisionist interpretation, Wiltz relates that the Nye Committee investigation in reality debunked the "merchants of death" thesis, established the National Munitions Control Board, and provided information that the government found useful during World War II. He explains that the investigation probably bore only minor responsibility in the passage of the neutrality acts of the latter 1930s. See also Wiltz, "The Nye Committee Revisited," *Historian* 23 (February 1961): 211–33.

PEACE GROUPS

17:477 Alonso, Harriet Hyman. "Jeannette Rankin and the Women's Peace Union." *Montana: The Magazine of Western History* 39 (Spring 1989): 34–49. Alonzo shows how Rankin's turbulent six-month service in 1929 as executive and legislative secretary of the WPU, an interwar organization centering on elimination of war through constitutional amendment, had a lasting impact on her antiwar ideology.

17:478 _____. "Suffragists for Peace during the Interwar Years, 1919–1941." *Peace and Change* 14 (July 1989): 243–62. The article offers a succinct study of four major women's peace groups: the Women's International League for Peace and Freedom–American Section, the National Committee on the Cause and Cure of War, the Women's Peace Society, and the Women's Peace Union. For the life of the NCCCW's leader, see Jacqueline Van Voris, *Carrie Chapman Catt: A Public Life* (New York: Feminist Press at the City University of New York, 1987).

17:479 _____. *The Women's Peace Union and the Outlawry of War, 1921–1942.* Knoxville: University of Tennessee Press, 1989. Reprint 1997 (Syracuse University Press). This book covers a small but militant pacifist organization formed by a group of suffragists in 1921 and based upon total nonresistance.

17:480 Brax, Ralph S. "When Students First Organized against War: Student Protest during the 1930s." *New York Historical Society Quarterly* 63 (July 1979): 228–55. The author describes the socialist and communist base of vocal student activism. He acknowledges that most American students never took part in the protests.

17:481   Chambers, John Whiteclay, II, ed. *The Eagle and the Dove: The American Peace Movement and United States Foreign Policy, 1900–1922.* This volume is a collection of contemporary documents and statements related to the peace movement's response to events from the First Hague Conference to the Five Power Pact of 1922 (11:131). The second edition (the first published in 1976) is virtually a new book.

17:482   Chatfield, Charles. *For Peace and Justice: Pacifism in America, 1914–1941.* This book describes pacifism's involvement in intense antiwar propaganda, efforts to secure arms limitation and end military training in the schools, relationship to radical politics, advancement of neutrality legislation, and wrestling with nonviolence. Because of the author's unmatched grasp of this topic, all scholars of the interwar peace movement must begin here (14:328).

17:483   Cohen, Robert. *When the Old Left Was Young: Student Radicals and America's First Mass Student Movement, 1929–1941.* New York: Oxford University Press, 1993. This study examines the activities of the American Student Union and the American Youth Congress and their foes. It contains much material on antiwar and Popular Front attitudes.

17:484   DeBenedetti, Charles. "The $100,000 American Peace Award of 1924." *Pennsylvania Magazine of History and Biography* 98 (April 1974): 224–49. Edward W. Bok's offer of a $100,000 prize for the best plan for connecting America to the maintenance of world peace attracted an outpouring of plans. This essay reviews the plans and the controversial process of selection.

17:485   _____. "Alternative Strategies in the American Peace Movement in the 1920's." *American Studies* 13 (Spring 1972): 69–79. In redefining America's role in European affairs, three strategies emerged: legalist, reformist, and functionalist.

17:486   _____. "The American Peace Movement and the State Department in the Era of Locarno." In *Doves and Diplomats: Foreign Offices and Peace Movements in Europe and America in the Twentieth Century,* ed. Solomon Wank, 201–16. Westport, CT: Greenwood Press, 1978. In the 1920s,

the State Department deferred to the conservative legalist peace leaders (such as Elihu Root), avoided pro–League of Nations internationalists (such as James T. Shotwell), and ignored the great majority of clergy, women, and pacifists who supported post-1918 peace activism.

17:487   _____. *Origins of the Modern American Peace Movement, 1915–1929.* This book offers extensive coverage of sentiment favoring the League of Nations, the World Court, outlawry of war, and the arbitration movement. In the process, DeBenedetti distinguishes among internationalists, legalists, and social progressives (14:334).

17:488   Eagan, Eileen. *Class, Culture, and the Classroom: The Student Peace Movement of the 1930s.* Philadelphia: Temple University Press, 1981. The author's discussion is particularly rich on the left-wing American Student Union.

17:489   Ferrell, Robert H. "The Peace Movement." In *Isolation and Security: Ideas and Interests in Twentieth-Century American Foreign Policy,* ed. Alexander DeConde, 82–106. Durham, NC: Duke University Press, 1957. Ferrell analyzes the movement for peace between the two world wars, dividing peace groups into conservative and liberal, and concludes that neither group understood international affairs during the era.

17:490   Foster, Carrie A. *The Women and the Warriors: The U.S. Section of the Women's International League for Peace and Freedom, 1915–1946.* Syracuse: Syracuse University Press, 1995. In a thorough treatment of the U.S. branch of the WIL, Foster does much with the personalities and activities of the interwar years, noting major internal divisions and membership losses as the nation approached war.

17:491   Jones, Mary H. *Swords into Plowshares: An Account of the American Friends Service Committee, 1917–1937.* New York: Macmillan, 1937. Reprint 1971 (Greenwood Press). Jones offers a history of the Quakers in times of crisis at home and abroad. A lengthy appendix lists their activities month by month.

17:492   Lynch, Cecelia. *Beyond Appeasement: Interpreting Interwar Peace Movements in World Poli-*

tics. Ithaca: Cornell University Press, 1999. In her general account of British and American peace movements between 1919 and 1939, Lynch offers a revisionist view, as she finds these bodies far less naïve than the "realists" have claimed.

17:493 Macfarland, Charles S. *Pioneers for Peace through Religion, Based on the Records of the Church Peace Union (Founded by Andrew Carnegie) 1914–1945.* New York: Fleming H. Revell Company, 1946. This book focuses on organized religion's peace activity and particularly on the World Alliance for International Friendship Through the Churches.

17:494 Orser, Edward W. "World War II and the Pacifist Controversy in the Major Protestant Churches." *American Studies* 14 (Fall 1973): 5–24. Given the unprecedented unity with which American public opinion faced World War II, the strength of the persistent pacifist controversy was remarkable.

17:495 Pois, Anne Marie. "The U.S. Women's International League for Peace and Freedom and American Neutrality, 1935–1939." *Peace and Change* 14 (July 1989): 263–84. The article shows the split within the WIL between neutrality and collective security advocates.

17:496 Rainbolt, Rosemary. "Women and War in the United States: The Case of Dorothy Detzer, National Secretary, Women's International League for Peace and Freedom." *Peace and Change* 4 (Fall 1977): 18–22. Rainbolt offers an appreciative treatment of Detzer's role in the WIL from 1920 to 1934.

17:497 Schott, Linda K. *Reconstructing Women's Thoughts: The Women's International League for Peace and Freedom before World War II.* Stanford, CA: Stanford University Press, 1997. Schott examines the intellectual roots of such WIL leaders as Jane Addams, Emily Greene Balch, Dorothy Detzer, and Mildred Scott Olmsted. Topics covered include nonviolence, feminism, social justice, and opposition to racism.

17:498 Zeiger, Susan. "Finding a Cure for War: Women's Politics and the Peace Movement in the 1920s." *Journal of Social History* 24 (Fall 1990): 69–86. In focusing on the Kellogg pact, the author

examines the role of the Conference on the Cause and Cure of War and the Women's Christian Temperance Union.

17:499 Zeitzer, Glen. "The Fellowship of Reconciliation on the Eve of the Second World War." *Peace and Change* 3 (Summer-Fall 1975): 45–51. Zeitzer shows that the Fellowship of Reconciliation had the ideological flexibility and strong leadership needed to coexist with a wartime government. In deciding how to demonstrate its resistance to war, it focused on nonviolence.

PUBLIC OPINION

17:500 Adler, Les K., and Thomas G. Paterson. "Red Fascism: The Merger of Nazi Germany and Soviet Russia in the American Image of Totalitarianism, 1930's–1950's." *American Historical Review* 75 (April 1970): 1046–64. Beginning in the 1930s, many Americans found similarities between Nazi Germany and Soviet Russia: their ideology, foreign policy, authoritarian and dictatorial governments, and trade practices.

17:501 Adler, Selig. "The War-Guilt Question and American Disillusionment, 1918–1928." By 1929, the war guilt question had made a deep impression upon the American mind, Germany enjoyed "a decent respect in the opinion of mankind," and Americans pledged not to be "taken in" again (14:31).

17:502 Cantril, Hadley, and Mildred Strunk, eds. *Public Opinion, 1935–1946.* Princeton: Princeton University Press, 1951. This collection is a crucial source, containing all major opinion polls, including those dealing with foreign policy. Polls from Gallup, Roper, and *Fortune* are among those offered from twenty-three organizations in sixteen countries.

17:503 Culbert, David. *News for Everyman: Radio and Foreign Affairs in Thirties America.* Westport, CT: Greenwood Press, 1976. This volume focuses on Boake Carter, Elmer Davis, H. V. Kaltenborn, Fulton Lewis, Jr., Edward R. Murrow, and Raymond Gram Swing, all of whom addressed foreign policy issues.

17:504 Gallup, George H. *The Gallup Poll: Public Opinion, 1935–1971.* 3 vols. New York: Random

House, 1972. Here one finds leading polls covering all matters concerning intervention.

17:505   Leigh, Michael. *Mobilizing Consent: Public Opinion and American Foreign Policy, 1937–1947*. Westport, CT: Greenwood Press, 1976. As World War II approached, FDR exaggerated the recalcitrance of public opinion. Only with the repeal of the arms embargo did he become an opinion maker in world affairs.

17:506   Thorson, Winston B. "The American Press and the Munich Crisis in 1938." *Research Studies of the State College of Washington* 18 (March 1950): 40–68. In this study of fifty newspapers and twelve periodicals, Thorson concludes that Munich made the public more aware of the dangers to peace, although the editorials reveal uncertainty about America's role in the growing world crisis.

17:507   _____. "The American Press and the Rhineland Crisis of 1936." *Research Studies of the State College of Washington* 15 (March 1947): 233–57. Public opinion, as reflected in the editorials of leading newspapers and magazines, did not view the Rhineland crisis as a threat to America. Many people, especially in the south and midwest, became more cynical about European diplomacy and pessimistic about the prospects for peace.

RELIGIOUS OPINION

17:508   Bauer, Yehuda. *American Jewry and the Holocaust: The American Jewish Joint Distribution Committee, 1939–1945*. Detroit: Wayne State University Press, 1981. The book thoroughly describes the activities of the body established by American Jewry to assist Jews persecuted overseas.

17:509   Cohen, Henry. "Crisis and Reaction: A Study in Jewish Group Attitudes." *American Jewish Archives* 5 (June 1953): 71–113. Cohen describes the response of major social groups within the American Jewish community toward Hitlerism, the Great Depression, and the New Deal.

17:510   Flynn, George Q. *American Catholics & the Roosevelt Presidency, 1932–1936*. The author notes the opposition of the Roman Catholic hierarchy

to the Cardenas regime in Mexico and American recognition of the Soviet Union (15:417).

17:511   _____. *Roosevelt and Romanism: Catholics and American Diplomacy, 1937–1945*. Westport, CT: Greenwood Press, 1976. Flynn covers such topics as the neutrality acts, the Spanish civil war, and aid to the Soviet Union. By the summer of 1941, Roman Catholic opinion, hitherto isolationist, was shifting toward intervention.

17:512   Hero, Alfred O., Jr. *American Religious Groups View Foreign Policy: Trends in Rank-and-File Opinion, 1937–1969*. By his analysis of public opinion polls, Hero shows the views of Protestants, Roman Catholics, and Jews on isolationist-interventionist issues (2:142).

17:513   Kanawada, Leo V. *Franklin D. Roosevelt's Diplomacy and American Catholics, Italians, and Jews*. Ann Arbor: UMI Research Press, 1982. Kanawada finds Roman Catholic pressure the crucial factor in retaining the Spanish embargo, Italian-American pressure sufficiently strong to influence FDR during the Ethiopian crisis, and Jewish-American pressure leading to considerable rescue efforts.

17:514   Miller, Robert M. "The Attitudes of the Major Protestant Churches in America toward War and Peace, 1919–1929." *Historian* 19 (November 1956): 13–38. This study offers a detailed account of the responses of Protestant denominations and their leaders to campaigns for League of Nations membership or cooperation, disarmament, and other international goals. See also Miller's *American Protestantism and Social Issues, 1919–1939* (Chapel Hill: University of North Carolina Press, 1958) and Donald B. Meyer, *The Protestant Search for Political Realism, 1919–1941* (Berkeley: University of California Press, 1960).

17:515   Nawyn, William E. *American Protestantism's Response to Germany's Jews and Refugees, 1933–1941*. Ann Arbor: UMI Research Press, 1981. This book shows the varied responses of thirteen denominations and several interdenominational bodies to Hitler's antisemitic policies.

17:516   Ribuffo, Leo P. *The Old Christian Right: The Protestant Far Right from the Great Depression* *to the Cold War.* Philadelphia: Temple University Press, 1983. Ribuffo offers a detailed study of antisemitic rightists and isolationists William Dudley Pelley, Gerald B. Winrod, and Gerald L. K. Smith. He shows how a "Brown Scare" undermined the left's commitment to civil liberties. See also Ribuffo, "Fascists, Nazis and American Minds: Perceptions and Preconceptions," *American Quarterly* 26 (October 1974): 417–32.

17:517   Sittser, Gerald L. *A Cautious Patriotism: The American Churches & the Second World War.* Chapel Hill: University of North Carolina Press, 1997. Before the war, pacifism made major inroads into the nation's Protestant establishment. Once the United States entered the conflict, however, the nation's churches manifested a chastened patriotism.

17:518   Thompson, Dean K. "World War II, Interventionism, and Henry Pitney Van Dusen." *Journal of Presbyterian History* 55 (Winter 1977): 327–45. Henry Pitney Van Dusen (1897–1975), a major theologian at New York's Union Theological Seminary, helped lead those Protestant clergy who backed FDR's foreign policy.

17:519   Valaik, J. David. "American Catholics and the Second Spanish Republic, 1911–1936." *Journal of Church and State* 10 (Winter 1968): 13–28. American Catholics had been well prepared to accept Franco as the savior from communism and atheism. The more liberal Catholic publications and leaders, however, correctly assessed the Spanish church's reactionary past and regressive social policies.

17:520   _____. "Catholics, Neutrality and the Spanish Embargo, 1937–1939." *Journal of American History* 54 (June 1967): 73–85. The author argues that American Roman Catholics did not act as blind followers of their clergy and the various organizations under its control. Hence, FDR would not have suffered dire political consequences had he lifted the arms embargo on the Spanish Republic. For a more specialized study, see Donald F. Crosby, "Boston's Catholics and the Spanish Civil War, 1936–1939," *New England Quarterly* 44 (March 1971): 82–100.

17:521   Wentz, Frederick K. "American Protestant Journals and the Nazi Religious Assault." *Church History* 23 (December 1954): 321–38. Drawing on

seventeen representative Protestant publications, Wentz finds Social Gospel journals stressing an aggressive fight against Nazism, mainline periodicals seeking personal and spiritual change within the existing institutional framework, and fundamentalist organs finding Nazism only a minor example of the "apostasy" prevalent in a host of modern developments. For a similar study but using only three journals, see Wentz's "American Catholic Periodicals React to Nazism," *Church History* 31 (December 1962): 400–20.

DOMESTIC VIEWS AND GROUPS: OTHER

17:522   Draper, Theodore. *American Communism and Soviet Russia: The Formative Period.* New York: Viking Press, 1960. Reprint 1986 (Vintage Books). Based on confidential minutes of top party committees, interviews with party leaders, and public records, this study shows how far-reaching and complete was Comintern influence in dictating party policy and leadership.

17:523   _____. *The Roots of American Communism.* New York: Viking Press, 1957. The author shows how the infant U.S. Communist Party was transformed from a new expression of American radicalism into an appendage of a Russian revolutionary power.

17:524   Dyson, Lowell K. "The Red Peasant International in America." *Journal of American History* 58 (March 1972): 958–73. Dyson describes the effort of the Communist International in the 1920s to organize American farmers by backing a coalition of noncommunist progressive and racial organizations.

17:525   Klehr, Harvey, John Earl Haynes, and Fridrikh Igorevich Firsov. *The Secret World of American Communism.* Translated by Timothy D. Sergay (for Russian documents). New Haven: Yale University Press, 1995. This collection of recently opened Soviet archives documents Soviet funding of the American Communist Party and links between party leaders and the Soviet espionage apparatus. Half the volume focuses on the interwar period.

17:526   Bell, Leland V. *In Hitler's Shadow: The*

Anatomy of American Nazism. Port Washington, NY: Kennikat Press, 1973. This work shows that the German-American Bund never received its direct orders from Hitler, had far from the half million members it claimed, and never prepared for the violent overthrow of the American government. The German Foreign Ministry severely frowned on its activities, and by the time it was suppressed in December 1941, it was a hollow shell. See also Bell, "The Failure of Nazism in America: The German-American Bund, 1936–1941," *Political Science Quarterly* 85 (December 1970): 585–99.

17:527 Brantz, Rennie W. "German-American Friendship: The Carl Schurz Vereinung, 1926–1942." *International History Review* 11 (May 1989): 229–51. Despite the dream of its promoters, the Carl Schurz Foundation failed to strengthen American sympathies for Germany, in part because of its narrow revisionist agenda, in part its obsequious subordination to the Third Reich.

17:528 Diamond, Sander A. *The Nazi Movement in the United States, 1924–1941.* Ithaca: Cornell University Press, 1974. This study shows that the German-American Bund was never a threat to American democracy as, from the outset, it was riddled with factionalism, recruited few German-Americans, and drew little support from the Nazi Party. See also Diamond, "The Years of Waiting: National Socialism in the United States, 1922–1933," *American Jewish Historical Quarterly* 59 (March 1970): 256–71, and "The Bund Movement in the United States: An Overview," in Hans L Trefousse, ed., *Germany and America: Essays on Problems of International Relations and Immigration* (New York: Brooklyn College Press, 1980), 183–98.

17:529 Johnson, Niel M. *George Sylvester Viereck, German-American Propagandist.* Urbana: University of Illinois, 1972. The author finds Viereck, who was a leading German-American propagandist in both world wars, a man who possessed dual national loyalties but who always maintained primary commitment to the United States.

17:530 Johnson, Ronald W. "The German-American Bund and Nazi Germany, 1936–1941." *Studies in History and Society* 6 (February 1975): 31–45. The German-American Bund, directed by Fritz Kuhn, at-tempted to organize support for Hitler's government. Kuhn's leadership embarrassed the German foreign ministry as well as German-Americans who opposed the Nazi regime.

17:531 Kipphan, Klaus. *Deutsche Propaganda in den Vereinigten Staaten, 1933–1941 [German Propaganda in the United States, 1933–1941].* Heidelberg: Carl Winter, 1971. Kipphan discusses the Volksbund für das Deutschtum im Ausland, founded in 1880; the Deutsches Ausland-Institut, founded in 1917; and the Freunde des Neuen Deutschland (the German-American Bund), founded in 1933. Although all sought favorable American responses to German policy, their propaganda efforts failed.

17:532 MacDonnell, Francis. *Insidious Foes: The Axis Fifth Column and the American Home Front.* New York: Oxford University Press, 1995. The author sees a fifth-column panic rooted in paranoid attitudes.

17:533 Remak, Joachim. "Friends of the New Germany: The Bund and German-American Relations." *Journal of Modern History* 29 (March 1957): 38–41. Fritz Kuhn, leader of the German-American Bund, and a few Nazi Party officials hoped to influence Americans, but State Department protests led Hitler to prohibit party members from propagandizing. Bund membership never exceeded about 6,000.

17:534 Walker, J. Samuel. "Communists and Isolationism: The American Peace Mobilization, 1940–1941." *Maryland Historian* 4 (Spring 1973): 1–12. Walker tells the story of the leading front of the Communist Party, U.S.A., at a time when the party was opposing the "imperialist war."

17:535 Heald, Morrell. *Transatlantic Vistas: American Journalists in Europe, 1900–1940.* In this treatment of the "Golden Age" of American foreign correspondents, the author covers such interwar figures as William L. Shirer, Dorothy Thompson, and Vincent Sheean (11:119). For Shirer's autobiography, see *20th Century Journey* (3 vols., Boston: Little, Brown, 1976–90). For Thompson, see Marion K. Sanders, *Dorothy Thompson: Legend in Her Own Time* (Boston: Houghton Mifflin, 1973), and Peter Kurth, *American Cassandra: The Life of Dorothy Thompson* (Boston, Little, Brown, 1990). For Sheean's autobiographical volumes, see *Personal History* (1935); *Not*

Peace but a Sword (New York: Doubleday, Doran and Company, 1939); and *Bird of the Wilderness* (New York: Random House, 1941).

17:536 Jeffreys-Jones, Rhodri. *Changing Differences: Women and the Shaping of American Foreign Policy, 1917–1994.* Included are chapters devoted to trade in the 1920s, support for Hoover in 1932, and peace activist Dorothy Detzer (14:342).

17:537 McKillen, Elizabeth. *Chicago Labor and the Quest for a Democratic Diplomacy, 1914–1924.* Ithaca: Cornell University Press, 1996. This study argues that the Chicago Federation of Labor and Chicago leaders of the Farmer-Labor Party backed the Soviet, Indian, and Irish revolutions, much to the dislike of the American Federation of Labor.

17:538 Miller, James Edward. "A Question of Loyalty: American Liberals, Propaganda, and the Italian-American Community, 1939–1940." *Maryland Historian* 9 (Spring 1978): 49–71. Miller examines the Roosevelt administration's efforts to counter fascist support among Italian-Americans. While conservative Italian-Americans nonetheless remained in control of the ethnic media and Italian fraternal organization, fears of fifth-column activity were baseless.

17:539 O'Reilly, Kenneth. "A New Deal for the FBI: The Roosevelt Administration, Crime Control, and National Security." *Journal of American History* 69 (December 1982): 638–58. The author shows FDR's use of the FBI against left-wing opponents and such domestic isolationists as Herbert Hoover.

17:540 Pencak, William. *For God & Country: The American Legion, 1919–1941.* Boston: Northeastern University Press, 1989. This study of the leading veterans' organization shows its ambivalence over whether aiding the allies in 1939–1941 would lead to war. See also Roscoe Baker, *The American Legion and Foreign Policy* (New York: Bookman Associates, 1954), and Richard Seelye Jones, *A History of the American Legion* (Indianapolis: Bobbs-Merrill Company, 1946).

17:541 Raucher, Alan R. "American Anti-Imperialists and the Pro-India Movement, 1900–1932." *Pacific Historical Review* 43 (February 1974):

83–110. American liberals, naïvely optimistic about India's problems, were unable to resolve the conflict between their alienation from destructive individualism and excessive materialism and their own belief in modernization.

17:542 Roberts, John W. *Putting Foreign Policy to Work: The Role of Organized Labor in American Foreign Relations, 1932–1941.* Roberts shows how American labor, never purely isolationist, became transformed into a powerful internationalist force (15:236).

17:543 Schulzinger, Robert D. *The Wise Men of Foreign Affairs: The History of the Council on Foreign Relations.* New York: Columbia University Press, 1984. During the interwar years, the CFR, far from being the primary policy planning apparatus of legend, was only modestly effective. The organization did not anticipate the success of revolution in Russia, the rise of Nazism, or the outbreak of World War II.

17:544 Smith, Geoffrey S. *To Save a Nation: American Extremism, the New Deal, and the Coming of World War II.* Rev. ed. Chicago: I. R. Dee, 1992. Originally published in 1973 under the title, *To Save a Nation: American Countersubversives, the New Deal, and the Coming of World War II.* The author argues that interventionists wantonly exaggerated the threat of domestic fascism, deliberately linking sincere and responsible isolationists with homegrown "fifth columnists." See also his "Isolationism, the Devil, and the Advent of the Second World War: Variations on a Theme," *International History Review* 4 (February 1982): 55–89.

Economic Policies

GENERAL

17:545 Adams, Frederick C. *Economic Diplomacy: The Export-Import Bank and American Foreign Policy, 1934–1939.* The author describes how the Export-Import Bank, by supplying foreign exchange assistance and aiding development programs, sought to stem the international currents that jeopardized the post–World War I world economy. Focusing on Latin America and East Asia, Adams maintains that policymakers were influenced, but not controlled, by economic interest groups seeking immediate export outlets (15:196).

17:546   Allen, James B. "The Great Protectionist, Sen. Reed Smoot of Utah." *Utah Historical Quarterly* 45 (Fall 1977): 325–45. The author of the ill-timed Smoot-Hawley tariff of 1930 was an ardent spokesman for protection, on which—he believed—American prosperity and self-sufficiency depended. See also Harvard S. Heath, ed., *In the World: The Diaries of Reed Smoot* (Salt Lake City: Signature Books, 1997).

17:547   Allen, William R. "Cordell Hull and the Defense of the Trade Agreements Program, 1934–1940." In *Isolation and Security: Ideas and Interests in Twentieth-Century American Foreign Policy,* ed. Alexander DeConde, 107–32. Durham, NC: Duke University Press, 1957. Allen examines Hull's trade philosophy, elucidating some of the deficiencies in his thinking. Yet he emphasizes the important transition that the reciprocity program represented in commercial policy.

17:548   _____. "The International Trade Philosophy of Cordell Hull, 1907–1933." *American Economic Review* 43 (March 1953): 106–16. The author finds Hull's intuition sound but his analysis weak.

17:549   Brandes, Joseph. *Herbert Hoover and Economic Diplomacy: Department of Commerce Policy 1921–1928.* Pittsburgh: University of Pittsburgh Press, 1962. This book covers Hoover's tenure as secretary of commerce, when he played a significant international role.

17:550   Butler, Michael A. *Cautious Visionary: Cordell Hull and Trade Reform, 1933–1937.* Kent, OH: Kent State University Press, 1998. At a time when the United States shrunk from political and military involvements in the wider world, Hull's trade policy offered the most effective American diplomacy to counter Hitler's Germany. At the same time, Hull's liberalism was ill-suited to a world in which military power predominated.

17:551   Clarke, Stephen V. O. *The Reconstruction of the International Monetary System: The Attempts of 1922 and 1933.* Princeton: International Finance Section, Princeton University, 1973. The debacle of the early 1930s led such nations as the United States to search for techniques that would satisfactorily reconcile the needs of both domestic prosperity and external stability. A forty-eight-page report.

17:552   Costigliola, Frank C. "The Other Side of Isolationism: The Establishment of the First World Bank, 1929–1930." *Journal of American History* 59 (December 1972): 602–20. The Bank for International Settlements was established by a group of prominent New York bankers who believed that settlement of exchange rates and payment of reparations out of expanded German exports was essential to U.S. economic expansion.

17:553   Dollar, Charles M. "The South and the Fordney-McCumber Tariff of 1922: A Study in Regional Politics." *Journal of Southern History* 39 (February 1973): 45–67. This article maintains that southern congressional sentiment for tariff protection is not a recent phenomenon, for as early as 1922 there was support for a high tariff among southerners in both houses of Congress.

17:554   Eckes, Alfred E., Jr. *Opening America's Market: U.S. Foreign Trade Policy since 1776.* In some major demythologizing, Eckes denies that the Smoot-Hawley tariff obstructed the bulk of American trade, precipitated the stock market crash, or worsened the Depression (7:49).

17:555   Falkus, M. E. "United States Economic Policy and the 'Dollar Gap' of the 1920's." *Economic History Review* 24 (November 1971): 599–623. It is doubtful whether American tariff adjustments could have produced the desired effect on the U.S. balance.

17:556   Feis, Herbert. *The Diplomacy of the Dollar: First Era, 1919–1932.* Baltimore: Johns Hopkins Press, 1950. The little book explores the effects of American investment bankers' underwriting of foreign securities.

17:557   Frieden, Jeffry A. "Sectoral Conflict and U.S. Foreign Economic Policy, 1914–1940." *International Organization* 42 (Winter 1985): 59–90.

Frieden finds two foreign policy camps produced in the wake of World War I: major U.S. banks and corporations seeking more political involvement in world affairs and domestically oriented economic groups hoping to preserve national isolation. The result was a standoff until the crisis of the 1930s.

17:558   Gardner, Lloyd C. *Economic Aspects of New Deal Diplomacy.* In a broadly conceived analysis of FDR's international economic policies that centers on reciprocal trade, Gardner notes the president's continued efforts to create an open world economy. In pursuit of such objectives, the United States invariably clashed with the Axis (15:202).

17:559   Hoff, Joan. *American Business & Foreign Policy, 1920–1933.* Hoff sketches a complex relationship between business and government. She argues that business opinion was too divided to allow for business management of foreign policy (15:64).

17:560   Kenkel, Joseph F. *Progressives and Protection: The Search for a Tariff Policy, 1866–1936.* The book shows how American progressives sought a tariff that was both competitive and scientific but failed to see that duties should equal foreign and domestic costs of production (9:207).

17:561   Kindleberger, Charles P. *The World in Depression, 1929–1939.* Rev. enl. ed. Berkeley: University of California Press, 1986. Challenging the new left claim that the United States took a leading world role in the 1930s, the author sees the nation acting most hesitantly. He opposes the position that it was poor American monetary policy that escalated the financial crisis into a world depression. First published in 1973.

17:562   Leffler, Melvyn P. "1921–1932: Expansionist Impulses and Domestic Constraints." In *Economics and World Power: An Assessment of American Diplomacy since 1789,* ed. William H. Becker and Samuel F. Wells, Jr., 225–75. New York: Columbia University Press, 1984. The article challenges the claim that American officials believed capitalism's survival at home depended on the open door abroad. Protecting the domestic market was more important than encouraging foreign trade.

17:563   Lewis, Cleona, with Karl T. Schlotterbeck. *America's Stake in International Investments.* Wash-

ington, DC: Brookings Institution, 1938. This classic remains indispensable to an understanding of international finance.

17:564   McHale, James M. "National Planning and Reciprocal Trade: The New Deal Origins of Government Guarantees for Private Exporters." *Prologue* 6 (Fall 1974): 189–99. In describing the relationship between the National Recovery Administration and the Export-Import Bank, McHale shows how planners publicly underwrote the risk of some foreign buyers' insolvency while the State Department sought worldwide markets.

17:565   Moley, Raymond, with the assistance of Elliot A. Rosen. *The First New Deal.* New York: Harcourt, Brace and World, 1966. In these recollections, Moley offers his views on the debt controversy and the London Economic Conference of 1933. Foreword by Frank Freidel.

17:566   Moore, James R. "Sources of New Deal Economic Policy: The International Dimension." *Journal of American History* 61 (December 1974): 728–44. Roosevelt and his advisers advocated schemes for global public works backed by American loans, stabilization of currency exchange rates at devalued levels, a tariff "truce," and settlement of the war debts issue. Britain and France failed to cooperate. Congress, bent on inflationary policies, turned FDR toward a nationalistic economic policy.

17:567   Rosen, Elliot A. "Intranationalism vs. Internationalism: The Interregnum Struggle for the Sanctity of the New Deal." *Political Science Quarterly* 81 (June 1966): 274–97. Rosen demonstrates that President Roosevelt sought domestic economic recovery without attempting to cooperate with other industrial states, thus implicitly seeking recovery at the expense of other nations.

17:568   Rosenberg, Emily S. *Financial Missionaries to the World: The Politics and Culture of Dollar Diplomacy, 1900–1930.* By focusing on international lending and advising in the early twentieth century, this study has represented the diverse traditions about money lending that framed a major foreign policy debate. The author puts such activities of private banking within broad historical and cultural contexts (11:91).

17:569 _____. *Spreading the American Dream: American Economic and Cultural Expansion, 1890–1945.* Rosenberg shows how private and public figures share a commitment to "liberal developmentalism," merging the lessons of the United States' own economic development with traditional market economics tenets. The year 1929 marked the shift from Hoover's stress on private voluntary efforts to more direct government activity in spreading America's economic and cultural influence worldwide (9:151).

17:570 Rothbard, Murray N. "The New Deal and the International Monetary System." In *Watershed of Empire: Essays on New Deal Foreign Policy,* ed. Leonard P. Liggio and James J. Martin, 19–64. Colorado Springs: Ralph Myles, 1976. An economic historian, writing from a free market perspective, accuses FDR of dollar nationalism and dollar imperialism.

17:571 Schatz, Arthur W. "The Reciprocal Trade Agreements Program and the 'Farm Vote,' 1934–1940." *Agricultural History* 46 (October 1972): 498–514. From 1934 to 1936, farm states tolerated Hull's program, but opposition soon increased, based on traditional protectionist attitudes, fear of eastern exploitation, and concern over the agreements' apparently undemocratic nature.

17:572 Snyder, J. Richard. "William S. Culbertson and the Formation of Modern American Commercial Policy, 1917–1925." *Kansas Historical Quarterly* 35 (Winter 1969): 396–410. A member of the U.S. Tariff Commission from 1917 to 1925, Culbertson sought to adapt America's commercial policy to its changed role in the world economy as a major creditor and exporter of manufactured goods.

17:573 Wicker, Elmus R. "Roosevelt's 1933 Monetary Experiment." *Journal of American History* 57 (March 1971): 864–79. Wicker demonstrates how FDR came into increasing conflict with financial advisers who sympathized with his domestic problems but who also stressed the need for international monetary cooperation.

17:574 Williams, Benjamin H. *Economic Foreign Policy of the United States.* New York: McGraw-Hill Book Co., 1929. This classic volume focuses on the

expansion of trade and investment as the United States began to assume its role in the world economy.

EUROPE AND THE SOVIET UNION

17:575 Abrahams, Paul P. "American Bankers and the Economic Tactics of Peace, 1919." The U.S. Treasury Department prevented public or public-guaranteed loans for European reconstruction, despite a more sympathetic view by bankers. For this reason, American capital was not available to Europe until the Dawes plan in 1924 (14:246).

17:576 Bennett, Edward W. *Germany and the Diplomacy of the Financial Crisis, 1931.* Cambridge, MA: Harvard University Press, 1962. Bennett systematically describes the efforts of European and American statesmen to deal with the great financial crisis of 1931. He criticizes America's failure to assume greater political responsibility to preserve the peace.

17:577 Burke, Bernard V. "American Economic Diplomacy and the Weimar Republic." *Mid-America* 54 (October 1972): 211–33. Although the Weimar Republic was in deep trouble because of the Great Depression and the gains of the Nazis in the elections of 1930, the Hoover administration virtually ignored Ambassador Frederic M. Sackett's plea for loans to Germany and a conference to resolve the war debts-reparations tangle.

17:578 Chandler, Lester Vernon. *Benjamin Strong, Central Banker.* Washington, DC: Brookings Institution, 1958. This account of Strong's career as governor of the Federal Reserve Bank of New York focuses on his efforts to restore European monetary and financial stability after World War I. The author also depicts Strong's conflicts with the Federal Reserve Board as the banker endeavored by new mechanisms to avoid inflation at home while contributing to monetary stability abroad.

17:579 Clarke, Stephen V. O. *Central Bank Cooperation, 1914–31.* New York: Federal Reserve Bank of New York, 1967. This book analyzes the efforts of the New York Federal Reserve Bank to cooperate with European central banks in an effort to restore monetary stability after World War I. In the process, he describes the successes of the mid-1920s and the domestic and international pressures that undermined central bank cooperation after 1927.

17:580 _____. *Exchange-Rate Stabilization in the Mid-1930s: Negotiating the Tripartite Agreement.* Princeton: International Finance Section, Dept. of Economics, Princeton University, 1977. This short report describes attempts to reestablish monetary cooperation among the democracies in the mid-1930s. Though FDR was suspicious of any effort to restore the gold standard, he realized that advantages might ensue from exchange rate stabilization. Hence, he agreed to open negotiations with the French and British so long as control over policy remained in the hands of Treasury Secretary Morgenthau.

17:581 Clavin, Patricia. *The Failure of Economic Diplomacy: Britain, Germany, France, and the United States, 1931–36.* New York: St. Martin's Press, 1996. This book covers the collapse of Central Europe's banking system, the German bank moratorium, Britain's decision to leave the gold standard, the crisis of 1932, and the abortive World Economic Conference of 1933.

17:582 Costigliola, Frank C. "Anglo-American Financial Rivalry in the 1920s." *Journal of Economic History* 37 (December 1977): 911–34. Both the United States and Britain sought to rebuild a viable capitalist world economy, yet their visions of how the international monetary system should function differed. The Americans, who desired a market-regulated gold standard that would give full vent to U.S. economic predominance, triumphed over the British, who wanted a flexible gold exchange.

17:583 Feis, Herbert. *1933: Characters in Crisis.* Boston: Little, Brown, 1966. The State Department's economic adviser describes the London economic conference and other efforts at international economic stabilization.

17:584 Flesig, Heywood. "War-Related Debts and the Great Depression." *American Economic Review* 66 (May 1976): 52–58. Because history is an uncontrolled experiment, it is questionable what would have happened to the war-related debts without the Depression. In any event, they were destined for default.

17:585 Gillette, Philip S. "American Capital in the Contest for Soviet Oil, 1920–23." *Soviet Studies* 24 (April 1973): 477–90. During these years there was a possibility of U.S. companies acquiring concessionary rights to Russian oil. Gillette reviews the oil situation before 1917 and analyzes the relationships among the Soviet government, the American government, and American oil companies from 1920 to 1923.

17:586 _____. "Armand Hammer, Lenin, and the First American Concession in Soviet Russia." *Slavic Review* 40 (Fall 1981): 355–65. This article stresses American businessman Hammer's personal ties to Lenin, which made him an "insider" in comparison to his American rivals.

17:587 Goldberg, Michael D. "Anglo-American Economic Competition 1920–1930." *Economy and History* 16 (1973): 15–36. Goldberg examines the factors that enabled the United States to enjoy prosperity in the decade after World War I while Britain suffered depression. He focuses on the role of Hoover as secretary of commerce in building overseas trade.

17:588 Hogan, Michael J. *Informal Entente: The Private Structure of Cooperation in Anglo-American Economic Diplomacy, 1918–1928.* In focusing on Anglo-American economic programs for the postwar order, Hogan emphasizes cooperation rather than rivalry. He sees continuity between the Wilsonian and Harding-Coolidge leadership. The book is organized around such topics as petroleum, European reconstruction, cables, and radio (14:252).

17:589 James, Harold. "Financial Flows across Frontiers during the Interwar Depression." *Economic History Review* 45 (August 1992): 594–613. The author denies the frequently made claim that too much international capital movement existed during the interwar period. The problem, instead, was a changed debt structure that made it difficult to accommodate international capital movements, even in such major centers as Washington, London, and Paris.

17:590 Kent, Bruce. *The Spoils of War: The Politics, Economics, and Diplomacy of Reparations, 1918–1932.* New York: Oxford University Press, 1989. Concentrating on American, British, German, and French policies, Kent rejects the view that the intractability of reparations and the war debt problem stemmed from systematic attempts of former belligerents to punish, emasculate, or impoverish each other. Instead, political leaders of all involved countries sought to evade the domestic financial consequences of the war.

17:591 Kottman, Richard N. *Reciprocity and the North Atlantic Triangle, 1932–1938.* Ithaca: Cornell University Press, 1968. Kottman balances the primacy of economics in the international perceptions of Hull with the realpolitik views manifested in Britain and the dominions during the 1930s. He focuses on the negotiations for the reciprocal trade agreement with Canada in 1935 and the British-American agreement of 1938. Until 1938, Kottman sees slight cooperation between London and Washington.

17:592 Leffler, Melvyn P. "The Origins of Republican War Debt Policy, 1921–1923: A Case Study in the Applicability of the Open Door Interpretation." *Journal of American History* 59 (December 1972): 585–601. Although a significant segment of American business, farm, and political leadership urged partial cancellation of Europe's war debts, congressional pressure resulted in pressing France to reduce reparations and in lowering the interest rate on the British debt.

17:593 McNeil, William C. *American Money and the Weimar Republic: Economics and Politics on the Eve of the Great Depression.* New York: Columbia University Press, 1986. Given the fragmentation of German politics, the United States found it difficult to alter German policy along American lines. Moreover, competition and division among American bankers left the Germans free to use loans as they saw fit.

17:594 Meyer, Richard Hemmig. *Bankers' Diplomacy: Monetary Stabilization in the Twenties.* New York: Columbia University Press, 1970. This monograph describes central bank efforts to stabilize the currencies of Belgium, Italy, Poland, and Rumania in the mid-1920s. Meyer ably analyzes relationships among French, British, and American central bankers but skirts those between central bankers and government officials in the United States, Britain, and France.

17:595 Moulton, Harold G., and Leo Pasvolsky. *War Debts and World Prosperity.* Washington, DC:

Century Co. for the Brookings Institution, 1932. This volume summarizes the evolution of most war debt and reparation agreements in the 1920s. The authors ably trace the breakdown of the settlements during the early years of the Depression. Appendices provide statistical data on war debt borrowing and postwar payments.

17:596 Nichols, Jeannette P. "Roosevelt's Monetary Diplomacy in 1933." *American Historical Review* 56 (January 1951): 295–317. Nichols studies the developments that led to Roosevelt's famous "bombshell address" breaking up the London conference. She emphasizes FDR's uncertain course in the months before the conference, noting his increasing desire for maximum flexibility in pursuing internal recovery and a rise in domestic prices.

17:597 Offner, Arnold A. "Appeasement Revisited: The United States, Great Britain, and Germany, 1933–1940." *Journal of American History* 64 (September 1977): 373–93. Offner attacks the view that the United States fought Nazi Germany because the German autarchic policy challenged the open door in Eastern Europe and Latin America and because of the American conception of a world political economy. This view, he contends, failed to take into account American efforts to appease Germany from 1933 to 1940. From 1936 to 1940, German-American trade increased, as did U.S. investment in the Reich. See also Offner, "The United States and National Socialist Germany," in Mommsen and Kettenacker, *The Fascist Challenge and the Policy of Appeasement* (1983), 413–27 (17:755).

17:598 Oye, Kenneth A. "The Sterling-Dollar-Franc Triangle: Monetary Diplomacy, 1929–1937." *World Politics* 38 (October 1985): 173–99. The author shows how the U.S., British, and French governments sought together to resolve problems inherent in gold exchange and floating monetary systems.

17:599 Pullen, William G. "World War Debts and United States Foreign Policy." Ph.D. dissertation, University of Georgia, 1972. This account explores the political and economic realities and misunderstandings that eventually led to an impasse in financial relations.

17:600 Repko, Allen F. "The Failure of Reciprocal

Trade: United States–German Commercial Rivalry in Brazil, 1934–1940." The reciprocal trade program sought to block German economic and political penetration of Latin America, especially of Brazil, its proponents believing that tariff reduction and unconditional most-favored-nation status for American-Brazilian trade would reverse the gains of the Germans. When this policy failed to curb the competitive Reich, the Americans turned to a more aggressive technique, Export-Import Bank credits (15:281).

17:601 Rhodes, Benjamin D. "Herbert Hoover and the War Debts, 1919–33." *Prologue* 6 (Summer 1974): 130–44. Settlement of World War I war debts revolved about the person of Herbert Hoover, who first favored a conciliatory approach but was forced by political considerations to change course.

17:602 _____. "Reassessing 'Uncle Shylock': The United States and the French War Debt, 1917–1929." *Journal of American History* 55 (March 1969): 787–803. The United States deserved the reputation of "Uncle Shylock" for its insistence on payment of the World War I debt. Policy, however, was more shortsighted than grasping.

17:603 Schatz, Arthur W. "The Anglo-American Trade Agreement and Cordell Hull's Search for Peace, 1936–1938." *Journal of American History* 57 (June 1970): 85–103. The author describes Hull's effort to force an Anglo-American commercial alliance that bore fruit in the trade agreement of 1938. Though Schatz finds the secretary naïve in his belief that such agreements would slow the drift toward war, he had few other options, as the democracies were divided and the United States isolationist.

17:604 Schröder, Hans-Jürgen. "The Ambiguities of Appeasement: Great Britain, the United States and Germany, 1937–39." In *The Fascist Challenge and the Policy of Appeasement,* ed. Wolfgang J. Mommsen and Lothar Kettenacker, 391–99. Boston: G. Allen and Unwin, 1983. Schröder denies that the United States and Britain followed a uniform economic policy on Germany. See also the author's "Economic Appeasement: Zur Britischen und Amerikanischen Deutschlandpolitik vor dem Zweiten Weltkrieg [The Origins of British and American Policy in Germany before the Second World War]," *Vierteljahrshefte für Zeitgeschichte* 30, no. 2 (1982): 82–92.

17:605 Schuker, Stephen A. *American "Repatriations" to Germany, 1919–33: Implications for the Third-World Debt Crisis.* Princeton: International Finance Section, Dept. of Economics, Princeton University, 1988. The author finds Germany not only avoiding the payment of net reparations to its wartime opponents but actually extracting the equivalent of reparations from the allied powers, principally the United States. The net capital flow ran toward Germany during both the inflation and stabilization phases of the Weimar Republic. See also Schuker's "Origins of American Stabilization Policy in Europe: The Financial Dimension, 1918–1924," in Schröder, *Confrontation and Cooperation: Germany and the United States in the Era of World War I, 1900–1924* (Providence, RI: Berg Publishers, 1993), 377–407, and responses by Manfred Berg and Michael Behlen, 408–18.

17:606 _____. *The End of French Predominance in Europe: The Financial Crisis of 1924 and the Adoption of the Dawes Plan.* Chapel Hill: University of North Carolina Press, 1976. Schuker demonstrates how French financial weakness compelled French leaders to make concessions to Germany that assured Germany's rise to preeminence. Focusing on the firm of J. P. Morgan, this study develops the central mediating role of American diplomats at the London reparations conference of July 1924, where France alone remained committed to a rigid Versailles structure.

17:607 Silverman, Dan P. *Reconstructing Europe after the Great War.* Cambridge, MA: Harvard University Press, 1982. The book offers a major description of the problems created by budget deficits, massive internal debts, interallied debts, and German reparations. Considering that the Anglo-Saxon nations sought to impose their diplomatic and financial hegemony on Europe, French resistance was completely rational.

17:608 Trachtenberg, Marc. *Reparation in World Politics: France and European Economic Diplomacy, 1916–1923.* An interpretative study of European diplomacy that sealed the fate of the Versailles system, this book supplies useful background on U.S. reparations policies (14:548).

ASIA

17:609   Anderson, Irvine H. *The Standard-Vacuum Oil Company and United States East Asian Policy, 1933–1941.* Princeton: Princeton University Press, 1975. Finding its aims increasingly frustrated by the eve of Pearl Harbor, Stanvac actively supported Roosevelt's oil embargo.

17:610   Cochran, Sherman. *Big Business in China: Sino-Foreign Rivalry in the Cigarette Industry, 1890–1930.* This work shows the competition between the British-American Tobacco Company and China's Nanyang Tobacco Company (13:187).

17:611   Cohen, Warren I. "America's New Order for East Asia: The Four Power Financial Consortium and China, 1919–1946." In *Essays in the History of China and Chinese-American Relations,* ed. Kwan Wai So and Warren I. Cohen, 41–74. East Lansing: Asian Studies Center, Michigan State University, 1982. Cohen notes that the consortium, the product of an American initiative designed to roll back Japanese expansion in China, failed because of Chinese nationalism, world depression, and the Japanese invasion of Manchuria.

17:612   Ghosh, Partha Sarathy. "Passage of the Silver Purchase Act of 1934: The China Lobby and the Issue of China Trade." *Indian Journal of American Studies* 6 (November 1976): 18–29. The China lobby pushed through this act over the opposition of Roosevelt and Secretary of the Treasury Morgenthau. The silver purchase program enriched the act's promoters but neither stabilized the Chinese currency nor revitalized U.S.-Chinese trade.

17:613   Grover, David H. *American Merchant Ships on the Yangtze, 1920–1941.* New York: Praeger, 1992. This account details operations of American shipping firms, describing such hazards as wrecks, piracy, the opium trade, and confrontation with Japanese and communist forces.

17:614   Hunt, Michael H. "Americans in the China Market: Economic Opportunities and Economic Nationalism, 1890s-1931." *Business History Review* 51 (Autumn 1977): 277–307. In examining the leading U.S. enterprises in China, Hunt finds Standard Oil and American Tobacco Company eminently success-ful in penetrating its market. Cotton goods first flourished, then faltered. American financiers, particularly in the 1920s, were reluctant to make long-term loans to a defaulting China. U.S. government support to business was of little value, as successful companies accommodated themselves to Chinese nationalism and business practices.

17:615   Liling, Xiang. "From Silver Agreement to Tung Oil Loan: The Origins of United States Aid to China in the Triangular Relations between China, Japan and the United States during the 1930's." In *Sino-American Relations since 1900,* ed. Priscilla Roberts, 238–55. Hong Kong: Centre of Asian Studies, University of Hong Kong, 1991. In tracing the growing commitment to the Chinese cause, the author denies that the United States ever connived with Japan over any matter.

17:616   Masland, John W. "Commercial Influence upon Far Eastern Policy, 1937–1941." *Pacific Historical Review* 11 (September 1942): 281–99. In a significant early analysis of East Asian trade groups in America, Masland concludes that their influence was nominal. Pursuing business as usual even while decrying Japan's political ambitions, they opposed any restrictions on Tokyo until 1941.

17:617   Mason, Mark. *American Multinationals and Japan: The Political Economy of Japanese Capital Controls, 1899–1980.* Cambridge, MA: Council on East Asian Studies, Harvard University, 1992. This work notes the increasing restrictions during the 1930s on such firms as Ford and General Motors. As a result of new regulations, U.S. direct investment in Japan sharply declined.

17:618   Moore, Jamie W. "Economic Interests and American-Japanese Relations: The Petroleum Controversy." *Historian* 35 (August 1973): 551–67. In March 1934, the Japanese Diet took the nation's oil industry out of the hands of foreigners. During the years of diplomatic controversy, the United States avoided deference to a single corporate interest while defending the right of Americans to trade in East Asia.

17:619   Pugach, Noel H. *Same Bed, Different Dreams: A History of the Chinese American Bank of Commerce, 1919–1937.* Hong Kong: Centre of Asian

Studies, University of Hong Kong, 1997. In the 1920s, neither Americans nor Chinese were psychologically ready for such an extensive joint venture. Differing cultural values and business methods, Chinese nationalism, and American arrogance created a gulf too wide to be bridged. See also Pugach's "The Sinicization of the Chinese American Bank of Commerce: Causes and Consequences" in Priscilla Roberts, ed., *Sino-American Relations since 1900* (Hong Kong: Center of Asian Studies, University of Hong Kong, 1991), and "Keeping an Idea Alive: The Establishment of a Sino-American Bank, 1910–1920," *Business History Review* 56 (Summer 1982): 265–93.

17:620   Rossi, John P. "Broad Principles of Cooperation? The Open Door and Western Electric in China, 1917–1925." *Essays in Economic and Business History* 13 (1995): 231–46. Challenging the corporatist thrust of business-government relations, the article shows that in the area of telecommunications, the U.S. government upheld the principle of the open door against its own nationals.

17:621   _____. "A 'Silent Partnership'? The U.S. Government, RCA, and Radio Communications with East Asia, 1919–1928." *Radical History Review* 33 (September 1985): 32–52. Rossi finds the U.S. government refusing to sanction monopoly; rather, it sought to ensure domestic competition between radio communications and manufacturing firms and worked to promote competition between American and foreign radio firms in China.

17:622   Sewall, Arthur F. "Key Pittman and the Quest for the China Market, 1933–1940." *Pacific Historical Review* 44 (August 1975): 351–71. Senator Pittman, believing that overseas economic expansion could raise the domestic price of silver, saw his position triumph at the World Economic and Monetary Conference in 1933 and in the Silver Purchase Act of 1934.

17:623   Wilkins, Mira. "The Role of U.S. Business." In *Pearl Harbor as History: Japanese-American Relations, 1931–1941*, ed. Dorothy Borg and Shumpei Okamoto, with Dale K. A. Finlayson, 341–76. New York: Columbia University Press, 1973. American businessmen's thoughts and action concerning Japanese-American relations are presented through the

study of six different types of businesses. All six disdained the East Asian war, influenced the course of events only minimally, and lost profits even before Pearl Harbor.

17:624   Wilson, David A. "Principles and Profits: Standard Oil Responds to Chinese Nationalism, 1925–1927." *Pacific Historical Review* 46 (November 1977): 625–47. In March 1925, the Kuomintang government in Kwantung imposed a tax on imported kerosene to which the oil companies responded with an embargo. Support from workers in Kwantung and Hong Kong and oil from the Soviet Union circumvented the embargo.

STRATEGIC RESOURCES

17:625   Chalk, Frank R. "The United States and the International Struggle for Rubber, 1914–1941." Ph.D. dissertation, University of Wisconsin, 1970. During the 1920s, U.S. dependence upon rubber as a raw material for industrialization markedly increased. Chalk shows how Great Britain tried to combat American economic power by restricting production early in the 1920s. The endeavor merely delayed greater American control of world rubber supplies.

17:626   Eckes, Alfred E., Jr. *The United States and the Global Struggle for Minerals.* Austin: University of Texas Press, 1979. This study shows the American inclination to secure low-cost, high-quality materials from abroad rather than seek self-sufficiency through tariffs, tax inducements, and other devices.

17:627   Erdmann, Andrew P. N. "Mining for the Corporatist Synthesis: Gold in American Foreign Economic Policy, 1931–1936." *Diplomatic History* 17 (Spring 1993): 171–200. The Great Depression led to a state-centralized system of formulating monetary stabilization.

17:628   Marshall, Jonathan. *To Have and Have Not: Southeast Asian Raw Materials and the Origins of the Pacific War.* Berkeley: University of California Press, 1995. This book advances the thesis that the raw materials of Southeast Asia made the region crucial to the thinking of American policymakers, an argument that could well be overstated.

17:629 Randall, Stephen J. *United States Foreign Oil Policy, 1919–1948: For Profits and Security.* During the 1920s, due to fears over a rapidly developing shortage of domestic oil, government and corporate officials developed a petroleum policy consistently oriented toward expanding American oil holdings throughout the world (15:410).

U.S. Relations with Europe

GENERAL

17:630 Baer, George W. *Test Case: Italy, Ethiopia, and the League of Nations.* Stanford, CA: Hoover Institution Press, 1976. While focusing on Italy, Germany, Britain, and France, Baer does not neglect the United States. Ethiopia became a test case that discredited collective security, convinced British and French leaders that appeasement worked, and showed Hitler that the west was indecisive.

17:631 Baptiste, Fitzroy André. *War, Cooperation, and Conflict: The European Possessions in the Caribbean, 1939–1945.* New York: Greenwood Press, 1988. The book notes the increasing prominence of the Caribbean in American strategic thinking. In the end, both Britain and the Netherlands had to acknowledge U.S. strategic prominence in the area.

17:632 Buckingham, Peter H. *International Normalcy: The Open Door Peace with the Former Central Powers, 1921–29.* Wilmington, DE: Scholarly Resources, 1983. The book covers such controversies as Yap, the mandate problem, American claims, and European reparations.

17:633 Burks, David D. "The United States and the Geneva Protocol of 1924: 'A New Holy Alliance'?" *American Historical Review* 64 (July 1959): 891–905. Americans feared the Geneva protocol, by which states would bind themselves to submit disputes either to the World Court or to arbitration. If ratified, the protocol might bring a European concert for intervention in Western Hemisphere affairs. This

anxiety reinforced the British opposition to the protocol that ultimately killed it.

17:634 Costigliola, Frank C. *Awkward Dominion: American Political, Economic, and Cultural Relations with Europe, 1919–1933.* Ithaca: Cornell University Press, 1984. This book stresses the unofficial diplomacy fostered by government officials, central bankers, and private promoters all cooperating to advance the U.S. creditor position and open the world to Americanizing influences. The material is placed within the context of American cultural expansion.

17:635 DeBenedetti, Charles. "The Origins of Neutrality Revision: The American Plan of 1924." *Historian* 25 (November 1972): 75–89. A draft treaty designed by a handful of internationalists, who formed the American Committee on Disarmament and Security, combined disarmament, the outlawry of war, and use of the World Court. It fell prey to domestic indifference and European skepticism.

17:636 Divine, Robert A. "Franklin D. Roosevelt and Collective Security, 1933." *Mississippi Valley Historical Review* 48 (June 1961): 42–59. Divine suggests that the 1933 controversy over the arms embargo showed Roosevelt had not yet been converted to collective security, although Secretary of State Cordell Hull and Ambassador Norman Davis advocated such a policy.

17:637 Gellman, Irwin F. "The *St. Louis* Tragedy." *American Jewish Historical Quarterly* 5 (December 1971): 144–56. In June 1939, more than 900 Jewish refugees aboard the Hamburg-American Liner *St. Louis* sought to obtain entry into Cuba but were barred. The United States turned the refugees away though its State Department unsuccessfully asked Cuba and European governments to admit them.

17:638 George, James H., Jr. "Another Chance: Herbert Hoover and World War II Relief." *Diplomatic History* 16 (Summer 1992): 389–407. This article covers Hoover's plan to feed occupied Europe.

17:639 Graebner, Norman A. "The American Road to Munich." In *The David A. Sayre History Symposium: Collected Lectures, 1985–1989,* ed. F. Kevin Simon, 169–94. Lexington, KY: Sayre School, 1991.

Graebner sees the United States as little affecting the conference outcome.

17:640   Haight, John McVickar, Jr. "France, the United States, and the Munich Crisis." *Journal of Modern History* 32 (December 1960): 340–58. American rhetoric led the French to think that Roosevelt would back the democracies against Hitler. Yet FDR's cautious statements only convinced the Daladier government that France could not count on the Americans. In essence, Washington helped to push Foreign Minister Georges Bonnet toward concessions.

17:641   Hilton, Stanley E. "The Welles Mission to Europe, February-March 1940: Illusion or Realism?" *Journal of American History* 58 (June 1971): 93–120. This article challenges the assumption in Langer and Gleason, *The World Crisis of 1937–1940 and American Foreign Policy* (1952–1953) (17:71), that illusion persisted in Washington about allied war aims. FDR realistically foresaw peril for the allies and attempted to stall the Nazi offensive.

17:642   Leffler, Melvyn P. *The Elusive Quest: America's Pursuit of European Stability and French Security, 1919–1933.* Chapel Hill: University of North Carolina Press, 1979. To promote American exports while reconstructing Germany and stabilizing Europe, policymakers recognized the need for involvement in European affairs, although domestic matters usually took priority. In an era of isolationism, Republican leaders used bankers whenever possible while making the Europeans bear the burden of stabilization. See also Leffler's "American Policy Making and European Stability, 1921–1933," *Pacific Historical Review* 46 (May 1977): 207–28.

17:643   _____. "Political Isolationism, Economic Expansionism, or Diplomatic Realism: American Policy toward Western Europe, 1921–1933." *Perspectives in American History* 8 (1974): 413–61. In the 1920s, Americans sought to bring Germany into the international order by achieving a reparations agreement, stabilizing the mark, and deterring French military adventures. The United States, more than the France, believed the German government conciliatory. It supported German claims to equality of rights under the Treaty of Versailles as well as claims to territorial adjustments in the east.

17:644   Lifka, Thomas E. *The Concept of "Totalitarianism" and American Foreign Policy, 1933–1949.* New York: Garland Publishing, 1988. The first part of this study shows how the term "totalitarianism" emerged in the 1930s as a common description for the regimes of Germany, Italy, and the Soviet Union and the implications of this term for policymaking.

17:645   McDougall, Walter A. *France's Rhineland Diplomacy, 1914–1924: The Last Bid for a Balance of Power in Europe.* Princeton: Princeton University Press, 1978. The Anglo-Americans did not seize upon new forms of international organization in seeking to resolve the Rhineland crisis but hearkened back to traditional models of national self-determination and free international economic competition. Indeed both nations "spent the interwar years looking for excuses to do nothing."

17:646   Roi, Michael L. "'A Completely Immoral and Cowardly Attitude': The British Foreign Office, American Neutrality, and the Hoare-Laval Plan." *Canadian Journal of History/Annales canadiennes d'histoire* 29 (August 1994): 334–51. Because the British were uncertain about American material and financial support, they sought a diplomatic solution to end the Abyssinian crisis, an effort that in turn played a significant role in fostering the Hoare-Laval agreement of December 1935.

17:647   Schmidt, Royal J. *Versailles and the Ruhr: Seedbed of World War II.* The Hague: Martinus Nijhoff, 1968. Schmidt examines the Ruhr controversy and the Dawes plan from the French, British, German, and American viewpoints. Chapters on Wilson and Hughes provide an overview of U.S. policy.

17:648   Schmitz, David F. *Thank God They're on Our Side: The United States and Right-Wing Dictatorships, 1921–1965.* From the end of World War I though the 1960s, argues Schmitz, American policymakers supported authoritarian regimes that promoted stability, anticommunism, and investment opportunities. At times, American diplomats backed Mussolini's Italy, Franco's Spain, and Metaxas's Greece (15:156).

17:649   Wert, Hal Elliott. "The Specter of Starvation: Hoover, Roosevelt, and Aid to Europe." Ph.D.

dissertation, University of Kansas, 1991. Wert finds Hoover fighting German duplicity, British hostility, and the growing apathy of the American people in his efforts to feed occupied Europe. He claims Hoover exaggerated the extent of starvation in 1940–1941.

17:650　Wilson, Hugh R. *Disarmament and the Cold War in the Thirties.* New York: Vantage Press, 1963. Based on the Hugh Wilson files, this brief book blames the failure of Hoover's diplomacy on the intransigence of French and British leaders.

U.S. RELATIONS WITH PARTICULAR COUNTRIES

Great Britain

17:651　Cull, Nicholas John. *Selling War: The British Propaganda Campaign against American "Neutrality" in World War II.* New York: Oxford University Press, 1994. This book shows how Britain made every effort to entice the United States into the war as an equal fighting partner. See also Cull's "Radio Propaganda and the Art of Understatement: British Broadcasting and American Neutrality, 1939–1941," *Historical Journal of Film, Radio and Television* 13, no. 4 (1993): 403–31.

17:652　Dayer, Roberta Allbert. "The British War Debts to the United States and the Anglo-Japanese Alliance, 1920–1923." *Pacific Historical Review* 45 (November 1976): 569–95. Recently opened British records show the relation between war debts and East Asian issues in British postwar policy. Whitehall believed that cooperation with Washington in East Asia might lead either to outright cancellation or, at least, to a scaling down of war debts to the United States.

17:653　Fry, Michael G. *Illusions of Security: North Atlantic Diplomacy, 1918–22.* Toronto: University of Toronto Press, 1972. The book notes the optimism of elite British advocates of "Atlanticism"—such as Lord Milner, Arthur Balfour, and Philip Kerr—through the Washington conference of 1922. Optimism faded thereafter, when cooperation over Europe, the Middle East, and financial issues failed to materialize.

17:654　Grace, Richard J. "Whitehall and the Ghost of Appeasement." *Diplomatic History* 3 (Spring 1979): 173–91. The author is critical of the British foreign office for failing to support Hull's desire for a modus vivendi with Japan. He finds the British obsessed with memories of Munich rather than seeking to postpone war with Japan by temporary agreement.

17:655　Graebner, Norman A. "Roosevelt, Chamberlain, and the Coming of War." In *America as a World Power: A Realist Appraisal from Wilson to Reagan: Essays,* ed. Norman A. Graebner, 31–63. Wilmington, DE: Scholarly Resources, 1984. In his Harmsworth Inaugural Lecture delivered at the University of Oxford in 1979, Graebner finds FDR's internationalism embracing everything but coming to grips with nothing. Throughout the crisis of 1939 Roosevelt avoided any commitments to European contestants. The lecture is published separately as *Roosevelt and the Search for a European Policy, 1937–1939* (New York: Oxford University Press, 1980).

17:656　Hachey, Thomas E. "Winning Friends and Influencing Policy: British Strategy to Woo America in 1937." *Wisconsin Magazine of History* 55 (Winter 1971–1972): 120–29. Hachey edits a dispatch of Sir Ronald Lindsay, dated March 22, 1937, in which the British ambassador calls for opening British markets to American farm produce in exchange for U.S. political cooperation.

17:657　Harrison, Richard A. "A Neutralization Plan for the Pacific: Roosevelt and Anglo-American Cooperation, 1934–1937." *Pacific Historical Review* 57 (February 1988): 47–72. The author sees FDR constantly striving for a transatlantic connection that might deter aggression. Although the Pacific could not have been neutralized, as Roosevelt proposed, Anglo-American cooperation might have affected the more important situation in Europe.

17:658　_____. "A Presidential Démarche: President Roosevelt's Personal Diplomacy and Great Britain, 1936–1937." *Diplomatic History* 5 (Summer 1981): 245–72. The author finds FDR making vague and often erratic efforts to secure a partnership with Britain, only to be stymied by Neville Chamberlain.

17:659　_____. "The Runciman Visit to Washington in January 1937: Presidential Diplomacy and the Non-Commercial Implications of Anglo-American Trade Negotiations." *Canadian Journal of History* 19 (August 1984): 217–39. Harrison notes that the mission of Walter Runciman, president of the British board of trade, was in itself inconclusive but created some British confidence that cooperation with the United States was attainable.

17:660 _____. "Testing the Water: A Secret Probe toward Anglo-American Military Co-operation in 1936." *International History Review* 7 (May 1985): 214–34. Harrison describes FDR's little-known efforts to exchange armament information with the British.

17:661 Hurt, R. Douglas. "The Settlement of Anglo-American Claims Resulting from World War I." The author describes the resolution of legal claims arising from Britain's seizure of American goods before the United States entered World War I (14:297).

17:662 Hyde, H. Montgomery. *Room 3603: The Story of the British Intelligence Center in New York during World War II.* New York: Farrar, Straus, 1962. Hyde, a British intelligence operative, offers a eulogistic biography of his boss, Sir William Stephenson, a Canadian-born industrialist who ran British intelligence operations in the Western Hemisphere. The book shows Stephenson's intimate ties to the Roosevelt administration. The British edition is entitled *The Quiet Canadian*.

17:663 Kimball, Warren F. "Lend-Lease and the Open Door: The Temptation of British Opulence, 1937–1942." *Political Science Quarterly* 86 (June 1971): 232–59. Kimball discusses the negotiation of the Lend-Lease Consideration agreement (1941–1942) against the background of earlier U.S. foreign economic policy. He argues that the agreement represented the triumph of Hull's plans for peace and prosperity, including the abandonment of British Imperial Preference.

17:664 Kimball, Warren F., and Bruce Bartlett. "Roosevelt and Prewar Commitments to Churchill: The Tyler Kent Affair." *Diplomatic History* 5 (Fall 1981): 291–311. In presenting the story of the State Department clerk imprisoned by Britain for attempting to leak FDR-Churchill correspondence, the authors find little substance in the "exposés" Kent

claimed he possessed. See also Ray Bearse and Anthony Read, *Conspirator: The Untold Story of Tyler Kent* (New York: Doubleday, 1991).

17:665 Klein, Ira. "Whitehall, Washington, and the Anglo-Japanese Alliance, 1919–1921." *Pacific Historical Review* 46 (September 1972): 460–83. Contrary to myth, the dominion leaders did not determine British foreign policy at the imperial conference. London decided to strengthen the North Atlantic triangle at the expense of the Anglo-Japanese alliance.

17:666 Leahy, Stephen M. "Even the Irish Kept Quiet: The British Foreign Office and the 1939 Royal Visit to the United States." *New York History* (October 1990): 435–50. The article shows the behind-the-scenes participation of the British Foreign Office in the visit of George VI to the United States in 1939. The office sought not only to improve Britain's general standing but to secure favorable neutrality legislation.

17:667 Leutze, James R. "The Secret of the Churchill-Roosevelt Correspondence September 1939–May 1940." *Journal of Contemporary History* 10 (July 1975): 465–91. A careful examination of the Roosevelt-Churchill file discloses no U.S. plot to enter the war, contrary to the claims of Tyler Gatewood Kent, code clerk in the American embassy in London, who illegally possessed hundreds of classified documents when he was arrested and convicted in 1940.

17:668 MacDonald, Callum A. *The United States, Britain and Appeasement, 1936–1939.* New York: St. Martin's Press, 1981. Beginning in 1936, the United States sought to foster European peace by means of restoring world trade. The British opposed any Anglo-American commercial treaty, however, and only in March 1939, with Hitler's conquest of Prague, did the two countries find their vital interests coinciding. See also MacDonald, "The United States, Appeasement and the Open Door," in Mommsen and Kettenacker, *The Fascist Challenge and the Policy of Appeasement* (1983), 400–12 (17:755).

17:669 Mahl, Thomas E. *Desperate Deception: British Covert Operations in the United States, 1939–44.* Washington, DC: Brassey's, 1998. The book shows covert British cooperation with the Roosevelt administration and interventionist lobbies. By overstating his case and failing to distinguish between interventionist moves plotted by the British and those fostered by Americans on their own, Mahl somewhat mars what could have been a superb study.

17:670 Matson, Robert W. *Neutrality and Navicerts: Britain, the United States, and Economic Warfare, 1939–1940.* New York: Garland, 1994. This work shows how severe U.S. protests forced Ambassador Lothian, Foreign Secretary Halifax, and Prime Minister Churchill to make alterations in their economic blockade. See also Matson's "The British Naval Blockade and U.S. Trade, 1939–40," *Historian* 53 (Summer 1991): 743–64.

17:671 McKercher, Brian J. C., ed. *Anglo-American Relations in the 1920s: The Struggle for Supremacy.* Edmonton: University of Alberta Press, 1991. Articles in this collection include McKercher's own introduction, which stresses that the 1920s are far more than a backdrop to the 1930s (1–16); George W. Egerton's description of tensions over League of Nations proposals (17–54); John R. Ferris's claim that the Washington treaty of 1922 maintained Britain's maritime security (55–80); McKercher's observation that Mackenzie King exercised skillful diplomacy in the 1927 Geneva conference (81–124); Kathleen Burk's description of the House of Morgan (125–57); Roberta Albert Dayer's narration of Anglo-American rivalry in Europe and Asia (158–86); Benjamin D. Rhodes's coverage of Britain's image in the United States (187–208); and McKercher's analysis of British officialdom's deep suspicion of the United States (209–38). Foreword by Donald Cameron Watt.

17:672 _____. "A British View of American Foreign Policy: The Settlement of Blockade Claims, 1924–1927." *International History Review* 3 (July 1981): 358–84. The article shows the success of British Foreign Minister Austen Chamberlain in negotiating the thorny issue of blockade claims. The issue was raised by a large number of American shippers and industrialists whose goods had been seized by the British between August 1914 and April 1917.

17:673 _____. "'Our Most Dangerous Enemy': Great Britain Pre-eminent in the 1930s." *International History Review* 13 (November 1991): 751–83. Although U.S. wealth gave it the potential in the 1930s to be a major player, until the summer of 1940 Britain was correctly seen as the world's lead-

ing power, for it expressed its national strength far more vigorously. See also the author's *Transition of Power: Britain's Loss of Global Pre-eminence to the United States, 1930–1945* (New York: Cambridge University Press, 1999).

17:674 _____. *The Second Baldwin Government and the United States, 1924–1929: Attitudes and Diplomacy.* New York: Cambridge University Press, 1984. After the failure of the 1927 naval conference, Anglo-American relations fell to the lowest point in the twentieth century. Arbitration, belligerent rights, and naval limitation all remained sore points, not fully resolved until Ramsay MacDonald resumed the prime ministership in 1929.

17:675 _____. "Wealth, Power, and the New International Order: Britain and the American Challenge in the 1920s." *Diplomatic History* 12 (Fall 1988): 411–41. The author challenges widely held assumptions about British decline and the corresponding American rise. To the contrary, so long as the United States remained politically isolationist, Britain was able to protect its interests and resist any challenge to its global status.

17:676 Medlicott, W. N. *The Economic Blockade.* 2 vols. London: Her Majesty's Stationery Office, 1952–1959. This work, long definitive on the topic, covers the British blockade imposed in 1939, which drew American protest.

17:677 Moser, John E. *Twisting the Lion's Tail: American Anglophobia between the World Wars.* New York: New York University Press, 1999. In tracing American antagonism toward Britain in the interwar period, the author finds anglophobia involving far more than traditional isolationism or Irish- or German-American sentiments. Also highly important were anxieties over British naval expansion, commercial competition, global imperialism, and rivalry for world leadership.

17:678 Orde, Anne. *The Eclipse of Great Britain: The United States and British Imperial Decline, 1895–1956.* Although during the interwar period Britain was experiencing relative economic decline, the United States did not attempt to translate its massive economic resources into military power and thus was unable to exert its full, potential power (9:315).

17:679 Ray, Deborah Wing. "The Takoradi Route: Roosevelt's Prewar Venture beyond the Western Hemisphere." *Journal of American History* 62 (September 1975): 340–58. The author notes how FDR surreptitiously sought to rescue threatened British operations in the Middle East. FDR used Pan American Airways to operate a primitive route extending from the coast of West Africa to Cairo.

17:680 Reynolds, David. *The Creation of the Anglo-American Alliance 1937–41: A Study in Competitive Co-operation.* Chapel Hill: University of North Carolina Press, 1982. Reynolds offers a pioneering multiarchival study stressing the tentative nature of the alliance. He finds that lend-lease, when first passed, was not particularly novel, attractive, or important. Even after the Newfoundland summit meeting of August 1941, Roosevelt was not committed to all-out hostilities.

17:681 _____. "FDR's Foreign Policy and the British Royal Visit to the USA, 1939." *Historian* 45 (August 1983): 461–72. FDR sought to use the visit to strengthen ties to Canada, toughen British policy, and symbolize Anglo-American amity for his countrymen, the British, and the dictators.

17:682 Rhodes, Benjamin D. "British Diplomacy and the Congressional Circus, 1929–1939." *South Atlantic Quarterly* 82 (Summer 1983): 300–13. This article stresses the strong criticism of Congress made by British Ambassador Ronald Lindsay, who found himself frustrated by war debts policy and Nye Committee rhetoric. For further criticism, see Rhodes on Francis D'Arcy Godolphin, Britain's number two diplomat in Washington, in "Confessionals of a British Diplomat in Washington," *Society for Historians of American Foreign Relations Newsletter* 14 (September 1983): 11–19.

17:683 _____. "British Diplomacy and the Silent Oracle of Vermont, 1923–1929." *Vermont History* 50 (Spring 1982): 69–79. The article notes the high respect accorded President Coolidge by British Ambassador Sir Esme Howard.

17:684 _____. "The British Royal Visit of 1939 and the 'Psychological Approach' to the United States." *Diplomatic History* 2 (Spring 1978): 197–211. There was much more to the royal visit with

FDR than the famed hot dogs and strawberry shortcake picnic. The trip, which began as purely social, strengthened American goodwill toward Britain on the eve of World War II.

17:685 _____. "The Election of 1932 as Viewed from the British Embassy at Washington." *Presidential Studies Quarterly* 13 (Summer 1983): 453–57. Rhodes notes that the British embassy predicted Hoover's defeat, reported the presidential campaign in a partisan way, and was not displeased by the outcome. At the same time, it had serious reservations about FDR's abilities as statesman.

17:686 Richards, David A. "America Conquers Britain: Anglo-American Conflict in Popular Media during the 1920s." *Journal of American Culture* 3 (Spring 1981): 95–103. Richards finds the United States seeing Britain as its chief economic rival, with only the threat from the Axis ending the mutual rivalry.

17:687 Roberts, Priscilla. "The Anglo-American Theme: American Visions of an Atlantic Alliance, 1914–1933." *Diplomatic History* 21 (Summer 1997): 333–64. Roberts notes the role of a host of "Atlanticists," including Elihu Root and Henry L. Stimson. These figures saw the keystone to international organization lying in an allied-American alliance, based ultimately on military force and domination of the world by a few great powers.

17:688 Rock, William R. *Chamberlain and Roosevelt: British Foreign Policy and the United States, 1937–1940.* Columbus: Ohio State University Press, 1988. In covering events from May 1937 to May 1940, the author sees FDR retaining suspicions of the British empire while exaggerating its ability to restrain Germany.

17:689 Stevenson, William. *A Man Called Intrepid: The Secret War.* New York: Harcourt Brace Jovanovich, 1976. This book combines description of British intelligence operation in the United States with sweeping claims concerning the accomplishments of its leader William Stephenson. For a critique, see Mark M. Lowenthal, "INTREPID and the History of World War II," *Military Affairs* 41 (April 1977): 88–90.

17:690 Vieth, Jane Karoline. "The Donkey and the Lion: The Ambassadorship of Joseph P. Kennedy at the Court of St. James, 1938–1940." *Michigan Academician* 10 (Winter 1978): 273–82. The author sees Kennedy hoping to preserve capitalism by avoiding war. She notes that the ambassador favored rapid American rearmament and the destroyer-bases deal along with limited financial and military aid to Britain and repeal of the neutrality act. But he also sought a negotiated peace and opposed U.S. entry into the conflict.

17:691 Watt, Donald Cameron. *Personalities and Policies: Studies in the Formation of British Foreign Policy in the Twentieth Century.* Notre Dame, IN: Notre Dame University Press, 1965. In his essay "America and the British Foreign-Policy-Making Élite, from Joseph Chamberlain to Anthony Eden, 1895–1956" (19–52), Watt notes that in the 1930s, British and American policymakers engaged in "back-stage debates" about how much their policies should intertwine. In "Britain, the United States, and Japan in 1934" (83–99), he notes the split between a pro-Japanese group, led by permanent Secretary to Treasury Warren Fisher and Chancellor of the Exchequer Neville Chamberlain, and a pro-American one, represented by Prime Minister Ramsay MacDonald and foreign secretary John Simon.

17:692 _____. "Roosevelt and Chamberlain: Two Appeasers." *International Journal* 28 (Spring 1972–1973): 185–204. Watt finds surprising similarities between the two leaders, including antipathy to the 1919 settlement, suspicion of official machinery, a preference for personal diplomacy, and a liberal belief in the economic origin of war and healing qualities of international trade.

17:693 _____. *Succeeding John Bull: America in Britain's Place, 1900–1975: A Study of the Anglo-American Relationship and World Politics in the Context of British and American Foreign-Policy-Making in the Twentieth Century.* This book finds Roosevelt policymaking involving procrastination, indiscretion, an inability to handle Congress, and choosing "the worst possible man" for diplomatic appointments (2:328).

17:694 Weinberger, James W. "The British on Borah: Foreign Office and Embassy Attitudes toward Idaho's Senior Senator, 1935–1940." *Idaho Yesterdays* 25 (Fall 1981): 2–14. The article shows British diplomats taking careful note of Borah's isolationism and presidential ambitions.

17:695 Whitham, Charlie. "On Dealing with Gangsters: The Limits of British 'Generosity' in the Leasing of Bases to the United States, 1940–41." *Diplomacy & Statecraft* 7 (November 1996): 589–630. Early in 1941 the British government came periously close to a serious diplomatic fracture with the United States over the terms of the leases in the destroyer-bases deal.

British Commonwealth and Empire

17:696 Baldwin, Raymond James. "David Gray, the Aiken Mission, and Irish Neutrality, 1940–41." *Diplomatic History* 9 (Winter 1985): 55–71. Baldwin offers an account of U.S. minister to Ireland, David Gray, special Irish emissary to Washington, Frank Aiken, and an abortive mission to secure American arms.

17:697 Barclay, Glen St. J. "Australia Looks to America: The Wartime Relationship, 1939–1942." *Pacific Historical Review* 46 (May 1977): 251–71. Australian expectations of U.S. support in the first critical months of the Pacific war were based on a serious misunderstanding of American strategic occupations, for which neither Washington nor Canberra was to blame. Until Pearl Harbor, Australia incorrectly assumed that the United States had assigned strategic priority to the Pacific. Though Prime Minister John Curtin expected massive American aid, the United States was committed to an Atlantic-first strategy.

17:698 Bridge, Carl. "R. G. Casey, Australia's First Washington Legation, and the Origins of the Pacific War, 1940–42." *Australian Journal of Politics and History* 28 (1982): 181–89. Based on recently opened files of the Australian war cabinet secretary, this article shows that, contrary to myth, Australia was not ill-informed about the British-American "Europe-First" strategy. Richard Gardiner Casey, Australian ambassador to the United States, sought last-minute negotiations not to appease Japan but to gain time.

17:699 Carroll, Francis M. "The American Committee for Relief in Ireland, 1920–1922." *Irish His-*

torical Studies 23 (May 1982): 30–49. In examining the creation of relief operations in Ireland to ease the burden of destruction created by the Anglo-Irish war, Carroll finds the committee surprisingly successful in financing reconstruction. By the same author, see "'All Standards of Human Conduct': The American Commission on Conditions in Ireland, 1920–21," *Eire-Ireland* 16 (Winter 1981): 598–74, and "Protocol and International Politics, 1928: The Secretary of State Goes to Ireland," *Eire-Ireland* 26 (Winter 1992): 45–57.

17:700 Drummond, Ian M., and Norman Hillmer. *Negotiating Freer Trade: The United Kingdom, the United States, Canada, and the Trade Agreements of 1938.* Waterloo, Ontario: Wilfrid Laurier University Press, 1989. The authors describe the process leading to the British-Canadian-American treaties of November 17, 1938. Because of the growing international crisis that soon culminated in war, the treaties had only marginal effect. Besides, neither side won concessions of real substance.

17:701 Dwyer, T. Ryle. *Irish Neutrality and the USA, 1939–47.* Totowa, NJ: Rowman and Littlefield, 1977. Challenging the claim of American minister David Gray, who claimed Eamon De Valera sought a German victory in World War II, Dwyer finds the prime minister and his people genuinely neutral.

17:702 Edwards, Peter G. "R. G. Menzies's Appeal to the United States, May-June 1940." *Australian Outlook* 28 (April 1974): 64–70. The article notes that the pleas of Australia's prime minister to the United States, including requests for volunteer airmen, served as a benchmark in his nation's increasing reliance on the United States and decreasing dependence on Britain.

17:703 English, John Alan. "Not an Equilateral Triangle: Canada's Strategic Relationship with the United States and Britain, 1939–1945." In *The North Atlantic Triangle in a Changing World: Anglo-American-Canadian Relations, 1902–1956,* ed. Brian J. C. McKercher and Lawrence Aronsen, 147–83. Toronto: University of Toronto Press, 1996. Although Canada sought to be "linchpin" between the United States and Britain, it found itself pushed aside by the more powerful United States.

17:704 Fogelson, Nancy. *Arctic Exploration & International Relations: 1900–1932.* Fairbanks: University of Alaska Press, 1992. Fogelson notes how competing interests in the Arctic produced tension between the United States and Canada and how this tension was reduced in the 1930s as the United States turned to the Antarctic for exploration. To see how, later, U.S.-Chilean relations were affected by interest in Antarctica, consult Jason Kendall Moore, "Maritime Rivalry, Political Intervention, and the Race to Antarctica: US-Chilean Relations, 1939–1949," *Journal of Latin American Studies* 33 (November 2001): 713–38.

17:705 Galbraith, John S. "The United States, Britain, and the Creation of the Irish Free State." *South Atlantic Quarterly* 48 (October 1949): 566–74. The United States played a prominent role in the Irish fight for freedom but once the Irish Free State was created, the issue lost its political potency.

17:706 Granatstein, J. L. "Getting on with the Americans: Changing Canadian Perceptions of the U.S., 1939–1945." *Canadian Review of American Studies* 5 (Spring 1974): 3–17. Granatstein shows the shift in 1940–1941 from Canada being perceived by the United States as a vital link in hemispheric defense to being an appendage of limited importance.

17:707 Granatstein, J. L., and Robert D. Cuff. "The Hyde Park Declaration 1941: Origins and Significance." *Canadian Historical Review* 55 (March 1974): 59–80. The economic agreement between FDR and Mackenzie King revealed how Canada successfully gained benefits in an economic order dominated by the United States.

17:708 Jha, Manoranjan. "Britain and Pro-India Activities in the U.S.A." *Political Science Review* 12 (Spring 1973): 1–34. Jha notes how the British officials, concerned over Indian nationalism and its supporters in the United States, sought to organize their own propaganda through press, lectures, university forums, and films.

17:709 Johnson, Gregory A., and David A. Lenarcic. "The Decade of Transition: The North Atlantic Triangle during the 1920s." In *The North Atlantic Triangle in a Changing World: Anglo-American-Canadian Relations, 1902–1956,* ed. Brian J. C.

McKercher and Lawrence Aronsen, 81–109. Toronto: University of Toronto Press, 1996. The article notes how the Anglo-American naval rivalry demonstrated the precarious nature of the triangular relationship during the 1920s, with Canada in particular suffering when Anglo-American relations soured.

17:710 Kottman, Richard N. "Herbert Hoover and the Smoot-Hawley Tariff: Canada, a Case Study." *Journal of American History* 62 (December 1975): 609–35. By his support of the high Smoot-Hawley tariff, Hoover alienated Canadian producers and disrupted American markets. His indifference to the U.S. best customer assured the electoral success of R. B. Bennett's Conservative Party in Canada.

17:711 _____. "Herbert Hoover and the St. Lawrence Seaway Treaty of 1932." *New York History* 56 (July 1975): 314–46. The article notes Hoover's political ineptitude, vindictiveness, irascibility, and sensitivity while nonetheless giving him credit for political courage and a positive vision.

17:712 _____. "Hoover and Canada: Diplomatic Appointments." *Canadian Historical Review* 51 (September 1970): 292–309. Hoover had little interest in Canada, except for fostering the St. Lawrence Seaway. His diplomatic appointments reflected this indifference.

17:713 _____. "The Hoover-Bennett Meeting of 1931: Mismanaged Summitry." *Annals of Iowa* 42 (Winter 1974): 205–21. Kottman finds the failure of Canadian Prime Minister Richard Bennett's informal visit to the White House in January 1931 rooted in poor planning. Hoover could not gain cooperation in his effort to advance the St. Lawrence Seaway. Bennett in turn could not secure alleviation of Canada's wheat surplus.

17:714 Maga, Timothy P. "Staying Neutral: John Cudahy in Ireland." *Milwaukee History* 7 (Summer 1984): 46–61. The article shows how a wealthy Wisconsin Democrat, whom FDR appointed minister to the Irish Free State, sought in vain to persuade the Roosevelt administration to support Irish neutrality amid Britain's growing tensions with Germany.

17:715 McKercher, Brian J. C. "World Power and Isolationism: The North Atlantic Triangle and the

Crises of the 1930s." In *The North Atlantic Triangle in a Changing World: Anglo-American-Canadian Relations, 1902–1956,* ed. Brian J. C. McKercher and Lawrence Aronsen, 110–46. Toronto: University of Toronto Press, 1996. The author notes the unease of both British-American and British-Canadian relations in the 1930s, for Britain confronted strong isolationism in both powers.

17:716 Megaw, M. Ruth. "Australia and the Anglo-American Trade Agreement, 1938." *Journal of Imperial and Commonwealth History* 3 (January 1975): 191–211. Australia wanted mutually open trade relations with the United States. However, lack of direct diplomatic ties and U.S. friendliness with Britain caused Australia to forfeit favorable possibilities in the 1935–1938 negotiations.

17:717 Ovendale, Ritchie. *"Appeasement" and the English Speaking World: Britain, the United States, the Dominions, and the Policy of "Appeasement" 1937–1939.* Cardiff: University of Wales Press, 1975. Ovendale argues that British policy was limited by U.S. and dominion opinion, both of which were unlikely to give even qualified support for British involvement in a continental war.

17:718 Perras, Galen Roger. *Franklin Roosevelt and the Origins of the Canadian-American Security Alliance, 1933–1945: Necessary, but Not Necessary Enough.* Westport, CT: Praeger, 1998. Until 1939, Prime Minister King and the Canadian military resisted FDR's strategic overtures and sought only modest rearmament, fearing American diplomatic domination.

17:719 Pollock, Fred E. "Roosevelt, the Ogdensburg Agreement, and the British Fleet: All Done with Mirrors." *Diplomatic History* 5 (Summer 1981): 203–19. The article shows how skillfully FDR linked the Ogdensburg defense agreement with Canada to U.S. control of any remnants of a British fleet seeking refuge in Canadian waters.

17:720 Raymond, Raymond James. "American Public Opinion and Irish Neutrality, 1939–1945." *Eire-Ireland* 18 (Spring 1983): 20–45. The author finds American official opinion indifferent and mass opinion hostile to Irish neutrality.

17:721 Rosenberg, Joseph L. "The 1941 Mission of

Frank Aiken to the United States: An American Perspective." *Irish Historical Studies* 86 (September 1980): 162–77. The article shows why Aiken, minister for Co-ordination of Defensive Measures for the Irish Republic, was unable to purchase American food and weapons. Aiken's open criticism of Britain and his encouragement of American anti-interventionists only irritated U.S. officials.

17:722   Rowland, Benjamin M. *Commercial Conflict and Foreign Policy: A Study in Anglo-American Relations, 1932–1938.* New York: Garland, 1987. Both modeling itself upon American policy and defending itself in opposition to it, the Ottawa commercial system continued through the late 1930s. Canada capitulated to Cordell Hull in the Anglo-American trade agreement of 1938 from a need to appease its more powerful neighbor.

France

17:723   Blumenthal, Henry. *Illusion and Reality in Franco-American Diplomacy, 1914–1945.* In the interwar period, France oscillated between staying close to the United States and maintaining merely peripheral contacts. This work also stresses the naïveté of French leaders about receiving American aid when war first broke out. It defends U.S. dealings with Vichy as a valid effort to temper French collaboration with Nazi Germany (2:318).

17:724   Grant, Philip A., Jr. "Naval Disarmament, Reparations, War Debts, and Franco-American Relations, 1921–1928." *Mid-America* 60 (suppl., April 1978): 37–44. The author notes that the United States placed primary emphasis on naval disarmament and resolving the German reparation crisis, while France focused on a meaningful reduction of its burdensome war debt to the Americans.

17:725   Haight, John McVickar, Jr. "France and the Aftermath of Roosevelt's 'Quarantine' Speech." *World Politics* 14 (January 1962): 283–306. Such French leaders as Léon Blum and Yvon Delbos, who advocated resistance to the dictators, welcomed FDR's speech although they found American inertness at the Brussels conference of November 1937 disappointing.

17:726   _____. "France's Search for American

Military Aircraft: Before the Munich Crisis." *Aerospace Historian* 25 (Fall 1978): 141–52. Baron Amaury de la Grange, an old friend of President Roosevelt's, and Air Minister Guy la Chambre spearheaded a drive to make up for France's aerial deficiency with purchases from America. La Grange and la Chambre faced significant domestic opposition as well as an isolationist American public. See also Haight, "Franklin D. Roosevelt, l'Aviation Européen, et la Crise de Munich," in *Revue d'Histoire de la Deuxieme Guerre Mondiale* 33 (1983): 23–40.

17:727   Hurstfield, Julian G. *America and the French Nation, 1939–1945.* Chapel Hill: University of North Carolina Press, 1986. The author denies that FDR ever saw his French policy, including recognition of the Vichy government, as either morally awkward or inconsistent.

17:728   Maga, Timothy P. *America, France, and the European Refugee Problem, 1933–1947.* New York: Garland, 1985. The study stresses the fear of "subversion" in explaining why both countries increasingly closed their doors. Each nation was too preoccupied with national survival to aid refugees significantly. See also Maga, "The United States, France, and the European Refugee Problem, 1933–1940," *Historian* 46 (August 1981): 29–37.

17:729   Rossi, Mario. *Roosevelt and the French.* Westport, CT: Praeger, 1993. The book notes Roosevelt's deep disappointment with the French surrender and his exaggeration of Vichy's independence from Germany.

17:730   Schrecker, Ellen W. *The Hired Money: The French Debt to the United States, 1917–1929.* New York: Arno Press, 1979. The author finds the debt issue impossible to resolve as long as both France and the United States treated it as a moral issue. Challenging claims that the United States was lenient toward France to facilitate foreign trade, she finds the United States driving a hard bargain.

17:731   Strauss, David. *Menace in the West: The Rise of French Anti-Americanism in Modern Times.* Westport, CT: Greenwood Press, 1978. The author identifies the sources of modern anti-Americanism in France. Concentrating on 1917 to 1932, he highlights intellectual differences.

17:732 Zahniser, Marvin R. *Uncertain Friendship: American-French Diplomatic Relations through the Cold War.* Zahniser observes that the United States "sowed a harvest of resentments," first by allowing Germany to escape retribution after the Great War and then by refusing to confront the dictators in the 1930s (2:321).

Germany

17:733 Costigliola, Frank C. "The United States and the Reconstruction of Germany in the 1920's." *Business History Review* 50 (Winter 1976): 477–502. U.S. officials and businessmen sought to maximize American economic expansion and minimize political commitment by furthering a prosperous and peaceful European order, which in turn meant bringing the German economy into that of the capitalist west.

17:734 Drechsler, Karl. "German-Japanese Relations and Pearl Harbor: The American Factor in Germany's Policy toward Japan, 1940–1942." *Amerikastudien/American Studies (Stuttgart)* 38, no. 1 (1993): 37–47. In describing Germany's policy toward the United States and Japan, Drechsler focuses on leading German corporations, banks, and economic associations, all of which wanted the United States to give up its global principle of the indivisible world market.

17:735 Eisen, George. "The Voice of Sanity: American Diplomatic Reports from the 1936 Berlin Olympiad." *Journal of Sport History* 11 (Winter 1984): 56–78. The article shows how American diplomats accurately reported on Nazi propaganda manipulation of the 1936 Berlin Olympics, in the process uncovering the sordid reality behind Germany's glittering facade.

17:736 Etzold, Thomas H. "The (F)utility Factor: German Information Gathering in the United States, 1933–1941." *Military Affairs* 39 (April 1975): 77–82. The author challenges Ladislas Farago's *The Game of the Foxes* (New York: D. McKay Co., 1971) by claiming that German intelligence operations in the U.S. were of limited effectiveness and ignored in Berlin.

17:737 Evans, Ellen L., and Joseph O. Baylen. "History as Propaganda: The German Foreign Office and the 'Enlightenment' of American Historians on the War Guilt Question, 1930–1933." *Canadian Journal of History* 10 (August 1975): 185–208. The authors examine the campaign of the Kriegsschuldreferat, a subdivision of the German Foreign Office, and especially the work of the editor of the office's journal, Alfred Von Wegerer, in publicizing the writings of American revisionist historians.

17:738 Frye, Alton. *Nazi Germany and the American Hemisphere, 1933–1941.* New Haven: Yale University Press, 1967. The Germans spent a good deal on propaganda, concluded profitable barter agreements with Latin American countries and a few exchanges of military personnel, sought to persuade Argentina, Brazil, and Chile to join the Anti-Comintern pact, and funneled money to political opponents of President Roosevelt.

17:739 Gassert, Philipp. *Amerika im Dritten Reich: Ideologie, Propaganda und Volksmeinung, 1933–1945 [America and the Third Reich: Ideology, Propaganda, and Public Opinion, 1933–1945].* Stuttgart: Franz Steiner Verlag, 1997. This book, which helps elucidate connections between popular culture and power politics, examines German public perceptions of America in the decades after World War I, concentrating on the years of Nazi rule. Gassert argues that German public opinion wavered between a profound respect for America's "modern" technology and a deep antipathy toward U.S. cultural decadence. Roosevelt's opposition to Nazi expansion after 1937 became a pretext for Hitler to emphasize the anti-American tendencies in German thought.

17:740 Goda, Norman J. W. *Tomorrow the World: Hitler, Northwest Africa, and the Path toward America.* College Station: Texas A&M University Press, 1998. The author retraces the documentary evidence to demonstrate that Germany's long-term strategy, developed early in the war, pointed toward assault on the United States after victory in Europe. Goda focuses on secret German efforts to gain base sites for transcontinental bombers and a massive surface navy in French North and West Africa, Spain's Canary Islands and West Africa, and Portugal's Azores and Cape Verde Islands.

17:741 Gottlieb, Moshe R. *American Anti-Nazi Resistance, 1933–1941: An Historical Analysis.* New York: Ktav Publishing House, 1982. The book focuses primarily on a boycott organized by American Jews in 1933, which they continued until 1941. It failed because of their lack of unity and inability to make their purpose appear universalistic and humanitarian. See also Gottlieb, "In the Shadow of War: The American Jewish Anti-Nazi Boycott Movement in 1939–1941," *American Jewish Historical Quarterly* 62 (December 1972): 146–61, and "The Anti-Nazi Boycott Movement in the United States: An Ideological and Sociological Appreciation," *Jewish Social Studies* 35 (October 1973): 198–227.

17:742 _____. "The American Controversy over the Olympic Games." *American Jewish Historical Quarterly* 61 (March 1972): 181–213. Although the Olympics reflected a less brutal case of Nazi persecution of Jews than many others, the persecution formed a rallying point for those hoping to combat the Hitler menace.

17:743 Haglund, David G. *Latin America and the Transformation of U.S. Strategic Thought, 1936–1940.* Albuquerque: University of New Mexico Press, 1984. Haglund finds FDR opposed to intervention in Europe until the mid-1930s, when he started to see German designs on Latin America.

17:744 Herwig, Holger H. *Politics of Frustration: The United States in German Naval Planning, 1889–1941.* The author finds Hitler's Germany envisioning an inevitable naval war with the United States (9:337).

17:745 _____. "Prelude to Weltblitzkrieg: Germany's Naval Policy toward the United States of America, 1939–41." *Journal of Modern History* 43 (December 1971): 649–68. By late fall 1941, German naval planners expected war with the United States though Hitler was completely surprised by the Pearl Harbor attack. He declared war against the United States to split American forces between Europe and the Pacific so he could concentrate on quickly defeating Russia.

17:746 Herzstein, Robert Edwin. *Roosevelt & Hitler: Prelude to War.* New York: Paragon House, 1989. In a much contested work, the author finds FDR the virtual architect of German defeat by pressuring London, Paris, and Warsaw to stand up to Hitler. He sees FDR abandoning prospective Jewish

refugees at home to aid Jews overseas. For a challenge to the book's thesis see Arnold A. Offner's essay, "Misperception and Reality: Roosevelt, Hitler, and the Search for a New Order in Europe," *Diplomatic History* 15 (Fall 1991): 607–19.

17:747 Hessen, Robert, ed. *Berlin Alert: The Memoirs and Reports of Truman Smith.* Stanford, CA: Hoover Institution Press, 1984. This volume deals with the U.S. military attaché to Nazi Germany between 1935 and 1939. It reproduces Smith's biographical memoir, 1922 interviews with German leaders, including Hitler, narrative commentary on Charles Lindbergh's visits to Germany, and reports to army headquarters in Washington.

17:748 Junker, Detlef. "Hitler's Perception of Franklin D. Roosevelt and the United States of America." *Amerikastudien/American Studies (Stuttgart)* 38, no. 1 (1993): 25–36. Alternating between admiration and contempt, Hitler's view never coalesced into a realistic or permanent picture of the United States. He regarded it as a major power when it was actually or potentially involved in world affairs (1919–1930, 1940–1945) but a negligible quantity when it was not (1933–1939).

17:749 _____. *Kampf um die Weltmacht: Die USA und das Dritte Reich, 1933–1945* [*Struggle for World Superiority: The USA and the Third Reich, 1933–1945*]. Düsseldorf: Schwann-Bagel, 1988. The author finds Nazi Germany primarily seeking to keep the United States out of Europe and sees Hitler lacking the resources to attack the United States. Although covering a much wider span, the author concentrates on the years 1939–1941.

17:750 _____. "Roosevelt and the National Socialist Threat to the United States." In *America and the Germans: An Assessment of a Three-Hundred-Year History. Vol. 2: The Relationship in the Twentieth Century,* ed. Frank Trommler and Joseph McVeigh, 30–44. Philadelphia: University of Pennsylvania Press, 1985. FDR smeared his opponents as disloyal citizens, and the isolationists misrepresented the president's motives. In the process both sides obscured serious issues in the major debate over the future position of the United States in the world.

17:751 Kolko, Gabriel. "American Business and

Germany, 1930–1941." *Western Political Quarterly* 15 (December 1962): 713–28. Relying on corporation records that reveal cooperation with Axis cartels, Kolko argues that business, wanting stability and predictability in the world economy, was willing to share existing markets with the Axis rather than pursue the chimerical open door.

17:752 MacDonald, Callum A. "Deterrent Diplomacy: Roosevelt and the Containment of Germany, 1938–1940." In *Paths to War: New Essays on the Origins of the Second World War,* ed. Robert Boyce and Esmonde M. Robertson, 297–329. New York: St. Martin's Press, 1989. The author sees FDR remaining reluctant to enter into a European land war. Until the Pearl Harbor attack, he sought to defeat Hitler by means of lend-lease and the deployment of naval power.

17:753 Marks, Frederick W., III. "Six between Roosevelt and Hitler: America's Role in the Appeasement of Germany." *Historical Journal* 28 (December 1985): 969–82. Marks finds FDR more intimately involved with appeasing Germany than anyone supposed.

17:754 McKale, Donald M. *The Swastika outside Germany.* Kent, OH: Kent State University Press, 1977. This account details the activities of the Nazi Foreign Organization and its efforts to spread Nazi doctrine among groups abroad.

17:755 Mommsen, Wolfgang J., and Lothar Kettenacker, eds. *The Fascist Challenge and the Policy of Appeasement.* London: G. Allen and Unwin, 1983. Hans-Jürgen Schröder denies that the United States and Britain followed a uniform economic policy toward Germany (389–99); Callum A. MacDonald stresses the U.S. effort to contain the threat of Nazi expansion and reintegrate both London and Berlin into an open door world economy (400–12); Arnold A. Offner emphasizes American appeasement from 1933 until the spring of 1940 (413–27).

17:756 Moss, Kenneth. "The United States, the Open Door, and Nazi Germany: 1933–1938." *South Atlantic Quarterly* 78 (Autumn 1979): 489–506. The Roosevelt administration never escaped from a major dilemma. Pushing the open door to the letter would invite stern retaliation from Berlin, thereby risking

political relations. Acquiescence in German economic demands suggested that the open door was a worthless doctrine.

17:757 Offner, Arnold A. *American Appeasement: United States Foreign Policy and Germany, 1933–1938.* Cambridge, MA: Belknap Press of Harvard University Press, 1969. Offner is mindful of foreign and domestic constraints on American diplomats but critical of the Roosevelt administration's failure to cooperate in efforts to contain Germany. Examples of "American appeasement" include approval of the Anglo-German naval agreement of 1935 and indifference to Ethiopian and Spanish crises.

17:758 Schröder, Hans-Jürgen. *Deutschland und die Vereinigten Staaten, 1933–1939: Wirtschaft und Politik in der Entwicklung des Deutsch-Amerikanischen Gegensatzes [Germany and the United States, 1933–1939: Economics and Politics in the Development of German-American Hostility].* Wiesbaden: Franz Steiner, 1970. The conflict between America's economic open door and Germany's policy of autarchy set the steadily deteriorating course of American-German relations. U.S. officials saw Germany's blocked currencies, bilateral trade policies and barter agreements, inroads into Latin American markets, and the economic domination of the Balkans as threats to the sort of free economic relations they desired. Economic conflict underlay the coming war.

17:759 Smith, Arthur L., Jr. *The Deutschtum of Nazi Germany and the United States.* The Hague: M. Nijhoff, 1965. Smith offers a history of the relationship of German-Americans to the rise of Nazism in Germany and of the efforts by Hitler to win their support. See also his "The Kamaradshaft USA," *Journal of Modern History* 34 (December 1962): 398–408, and "The Foreign Organization of the Nazi Party and the United States, 1931–39," in Hans L Trefousse, ed., *Germany and America: Essays on Problems of International Relations and Immigration* (New York: Brooklyn College Press, 1980), 173–82.

17:760 von Klemperer, Klemens. *German Resistance against Hitler: The Search for Allies Abroad, 1938–1945.* New York: Oxford University Press, 1992. This account includes the mission of German resister Adam von Trott to the United States in the winter of 1940–1941. See also Hans Rothfels, "The

German Resistance in Its International Aspects," *International Affairs* 34 (October 1958): 477–89, and his "Adam von Trott und das State Department," *Vierteljahrshefte für Zeitgeschichte* 7 (July 1959): 318–32.

17:761   Weinberg, Gerhard L. *The Foreign Policy of Hitler's Germany. Vol. 1: Diplomatic Revolution in Germany, 1933–36. Vol. 2: Starting World War II, 1937–1939.* Chicago: University of Chicago Press, 1970–1980. Reprint 1994 (Humanities Press). Weinberg offers traditional, archive-based history of the highest order. Volume 1 suggests that Hitler did not consider the proposed 1935 trade treaty with the United States essential to his purposes. Volume 2 finds Hitler envisioning an eventual war against a weak United States.

17:762   _____. "Hitler's Image of the United States." *American Historical Review* 69 (July 1964): 1006–21. Hitler's contradictory racial and sociopolitical ideas led him in the 1920s to admire American productive, technical, and financial capabilities but in the 1930s to see America as politically and economically effete. These failings, combined with the neutrality acts, led the Führer to disregard the United States as an effective military force. See also Weinberg, *World in the Balance: Behind the Scenes of World War II* (1981), 53–74 (18:179).

17:763   _____. "Schachts Besuch in den USA im Jahre 1933 [Schacht's visit to the United States of America in 1933]." *Vierteljahrshefte für Zeitgeschichte* 11 (April 1963): 166–80. When Roosevelt invited Hitler to Washington for economic talks, the Führer sent in his place Hjalmar Schacht, president of the Reichsbank, who demanded equality of arms and revision of debts and a moratorium on transfer of interest and amortization payments. The trip led only to an impasse and to continued American-German disagreement about finance, trade, and disarmament.

The Weimar Period

17:764   Falkus, M. E. "The German Business Cycle in the 1920's." *Economic History Review* 28 (August 1975): 451–65. Falkus argues that "exogenous" declines in foreign investment, for the most part by American capital, preceded the 1929 downturn in the German business cycle, and hence, as President Hoover maintained, helped cause the stock market collapse on Wall Street.

17:765   Faulkner, Ronnie W. "American Reaction to Hindenburg of the Weimar Republic, 1925–1934." *Historian* 51 (May 1989): 402–22. The article shows that by skilled mythmaking, American opinion makers turned the monarchist into a republican, the militarist into a peacemaker, the rightist into a moderate. Naïve expectations attached themselves to "the mythical Wotan," although the real flesh-and-blood man let them down.

17:766   Feingold, Henry L. *The Politics of Rescue: The Roosevelt Administration and the Holocaust, 1938–1945.* Expanded and updated ed. New York: Holocaust Library, 1980. Insensitivity, apathy, and fear of domestic and foreign reactions contributed to the U.S. failure to help rescue Europe's Jews. Many Americans, including the personnel of the State Department, refused to believe the antisemitic activities of the Third Reich were taking place. Originally published in 1970; see also Feingold, "Roosevelt and the Holocaust: Reflections on New Deal Humanitarianism," *Judaism* 18 (Summer 1969): 259–76.

17:767   Friedman, Saul S. *No Haven for the Oppressed: United States Policy toward Jewish Refugees, 1938–1945.* Detroit: Wayne State University Press, 1973. The author blames American indifference on a distracted Hull, an evasive Roosevelt, a divided and timid American Jewry, and above all the American people, who in 1938 were too preoccupied with their own jobs.

17:768   Girard, Jolyon P. "Congress and Presidential Military Policy: The Occupation of Germany, 1919–1923." *Mid-America* 56 (October 1974): 211–20. Although Congress was unwilling to cut off funds for the U.S. Army of Occupation in Germany after World War I, it exerted pressure on Presidents Wilson and Harding to withdraw the troops.

17:769   Glaser-Schmidt, Elisabeth. "German and American Concepts to Restore a Liberal World Trading System after World War I." In *Confrontation and Cooperation: Germany and the United States in the Era of World War I, 1900–1924,* ed. Hans-Jürgen Schröder, 353–76. Providence, RI: Berg Publishers, 1993. Although Germany and the United States showed a common interest in the ideal of nondiscriminatory and liberal commercial policies, the practical protectionism of both nations impaired this vision of commercial liberalism.

17:770   Gottwald, Robert. *Die Deutsch-Amerikanischen Beziehungen in der Ära Stresemann [German-American Relations in the Stresemann Era]*. Berlin-Dahlem: Colloquium Verlag, 1965. German diplomats encouraged Americans to mediate the reparations tangle and invest in their nation. They persuaded American opinion that fear of militarism was unfounded and that the Weimar Republic was a stable, liberal, middle-class polity. German-American friendship was at its height when Stresemann died in 1929.

17:771   Jonas, Manfred. "Mutualism in the Relations between the United States and the Early Weimar Republic." In *Germany and America: Essays on Problems of International Relations and Immigration*, ed. Hans L. Trefousse, 41–53. New York: Brooklyn College Press, 1980. In presenting the background to the Dawes plan, Jonas sees mutual interest between the United States and Germany overcoming German resentment over America's wartime role and Wilson's much misunderstood actions at Versailles.

17:772   Jones, Kenneth Paul. "Discord and Collaboration: Choosing an Agent General for Reparations." *Diplomatic History* 1 (Spring 1977): 118–39. This study covers disputes between the Coolidge administration, J. P. Morgan and Company, and the Bank of England over choosing an agent general to administer German reparations under the Dawes plan. It reveals the discord between government officials and private financiers on how to guarantee repayment of loans to American creditors and to depoliticize reparations.

17:773   Link, Werner. *Die amerikanische Stabilisierungspolitik in Deutschland 1921–32 [America's Policy of Stabilization in Germany, 1921–32]*. Düsseldorf: Droste Verlag, 1970. Link offers a massive study of American-German relations, which considers the connection between political ideology and economic interests as well as foreign and domestic politics. He argues that Americans, public and private, sought to maintain moderate governments, foster trade, help improve relations between Germany

and its erstwhile enemies, and weaken German-Russian relations.

17:774   Marks, Sally. "The Myths of Reparations." *Central European History* 11 (September 1978): 231–55. The amount of reparations required of Germany and its Allies after World War I was not the 132 billion marks cited in the London Schedule of 1921 but the 50 million marks stipulated in the A and B bonds. Germany paid very little, and most of that was out of loans from western bankers.

17:775   Nelson, Keith L. *Victors Divided: America and the Allies in Germany, 1918–1923*. In an exhaustive and detailed account of U.S. policy toward the occupation of Germany, this book finds that President Harding and Secretary Hughes gave more attention to European affairs than previously believed (14:503).

17:776   Rupieper, Hermann-Josef. *The Cuno Government and Reparations, 1921–1923: Politics and Economics*. Boston: M. Nijhoff, 1979. The book notes mediation efforts of John Foster Dulles in the wake of the Rhineland crisis.

17:777   Schwabe, Klaus. "The United States and the Weimar Republic: A 'Special Relationship' That Failed." In *America and the Germans: An Assessment of a Three-Hundred-Year History. Vol. 2: The Relationship in the Twentieth Century*, ed. Frank Trommler and Joseph McVeigh, 18–29. Philadelphia: University of Pennsylvania Press, 1985. The author is critical of American policymakers for assuming that economic measures, as exemplified by its reparations policies, could solve any political problem in Europe.

17:778   Singer, David G. "The Prelude to Nazism: The German-American Press and the Jews, 1919–1933." *American Jewish Historical Quarterly* 61 (March 1977): 417–31. Singer analyzes the German-American press, particularly that of the midwest, from 1919 to 1933. He finds attitudes toward Jews changing from support to unfriendliness.

17:779   Spencer, Frank. "The United States and Germany in the Aftermath of War, 1918–1929." *International Affairs* 43 (October 1967): 693–703. The United States came to the financial rescue of Europe twice, first with the Dawes and then the Young plan. Germany used the American loans to reorganize heavy industry, the basis for eventual rearmament.

17:780 Wandel, Eckhard. *Die Bedeutung der Vereinigten Staaten von Amerika für das Deutsche Reparationsproblem, 1924–1929 [The Influence of the United States on the German Reparations Problem, 1924–1929].* Tübingen: Mohr, Paul Siebeck, 1971. Americans saw that a solution to reparations was essential for Allied war debt repayment and for producing a European economy able to absorb American capital and manufactures. However, they failed to recognize formally the essential link between reparations and war debts, indeed between American and European affairs.

Persecution of Jews and Jewish Immigration

17:781 Breitman, Richard D., and Alan M. Kraut. *American Refugee Policy and European Jewry, 1933–1945.* Bloomington: Indiana University Press, 1987. The authors examine restrictive immigration laws, the State Department bureaucracy, American public opinion, and Roosevelt's own caution, in the process finding that antisemitism was not central to the shaping of a refugee policy.

17:782 Brody, David. "American Jewry, the Refugees and Immigration Restriction (1932–1942)." *Publications of the American Jewish Historical Society* 45 (Winter 1955–1956): 219–47. When the Immigration Act of 1924 effectively restricted the inflow of additional immigrants, American Jewry agreed with this policy. This position underwent a decisive change after 1933, when Nazi persecutions in Europe forced an increased exodus of European Jews.

17:783 Gottlieb, Moshe R. "The Berlin Riots of 1935 and Their Repercussions in America." *American Jewish Historical Quarterly* 59 (March 1970): 302–31. The Berlin riots of 1935, which culminated in the Nuremberg laws, dramatized the helplessness of German Jewry as well as the disinclination of the U.S. government to get involved.

17:784 Kraut, Alan M., Richard D. Breitman, and Thomas W. Imhoof. "The State Department, the Labor Department, and German Jewish Immigration,

1930–1940." *Journal of American Ethnic History* 3 (Spring 1984): 5–38. The authors describe the futile bureaucratic effort made by Labor Secretary Francis Perkins and her department to modify immigration restrictions that were maintained and even tightened by the State Department.

17:785 Lazin, Frederick. "The Response of the American Jewish Committee to the Crisis of German Jewry, 1933–1939." *American Jewish History* 68 (March 1979): 283–304. The author finds the committee relying on informal diplomacy, facilitation of immigration, and predominantly non-Jewish media outlets to aid fellow Jews. He sees the AJC limited by aging leadership and conflicting personal and professional demands.

17:786 Neuringer, Sheldon. "Franklin D. Roosevelt and Refuge for Victims of Nazism, 1933–1941." In *Franklin D. Roosevelt: The Man, the Myth, the Era, 1882–1945,* ed. Herbert D. Rosenbaum and Elizabeth Bartelme, 85–100. New York: Greenwood Press, 1987. The author notes that FDR took steps to aid refugees in 1938–1941 amid a hostile political climate. In the period mid-1940 to the end of 1941, however, he permitted zealous State Department officeholders to create administrative barriers.

17:787 Schmitt, Hans A. *Quakers and Nazis: Inner Light in Outer Darkness.* Columbia: University of Missouri Press, 1997. This book traces Quaker efforts to relieve the sufferings of Jews, Christians, socialists, and communists persecuted by the Nazi regime.

17:788 Spear, Sheldon. "The United States and the Persecution of the Jews in Germany: 1933–1939." *Jewish Social Studies* 30 (October 1968): 215–42. Roosevelt and the State Department refused to protest German persecution of the Jews, urged Congress to avoid condemnatory resolutions, and remained aloof from private trade boycotts. The author stresses the failure of FDR's informal diplomacy and the tight U.S. immigration policies, which must, Spear claims, be seen in the context of American isolationism and fear of a glutted labor market.

17:789 Stewart, Barbara McDonald. *United States Government Policy on Refugees from Nazism, 1933–1940.* New York: Garland Publishing, 1982. The U.S. government gave little aid to refugees although it did as much as most Americans desired and more than many governments. American Jews feared arousing antagonism, most Gentiles looked on refugees as a Jewish problem, and FDR, preoccupied with more urgent matters, allowed the State Department to chart its own timid course.

17:790 Szajkowski, Zosa. "The Attitude of American Jews to Refugees from Germany in the 1930's." *American Jewish Historical Quarterly* 51 (December 1971): 101–43. Against the background of American reluctance to admit additional immigrants, the attitude of American Jews toward refugees from Germany was ambiguous.

17:791 Wyman, David S. *Paper Walls: America and the Refugee Crisis, 1938–1941.* Amherst: University of Massachusetts Press, 1968. Reprint 1985 (Pantheon Books). The author traces the combination of fear and cupidity that marred refugee assistance, stressing the role of Breckinridge Long, who headed the refugee section of the State Department.

17:792 Zucker, Bat-Ami. *In Search of Refuge: Jews and US Consuls in Nazi Germany, 1933–1941.* Portland, OR: Vallentine Mitchell, 2001. The author shows how bureaucratic prerogative can thwart broader humanitarian concerns.

Italy

17:793 Braddick, Henderson B. "A New Look at American Policy during the Italo-Ethiopian Crisis, 1935–1936." *Journal of Modern History* 34 (March 1962): 64–73. Braddick argues that Hull supported the British against Italy in hope of promoting their cooperation in East Asia.

17:794 Cannistraro, Philip V., and Theodore P. Kovaleff. "Father Coughlin and Mussolini: Impossible Allies." *Journal of Church and State* 13 (Autumn 1971): 427–43. Mussolini was aware that American public opinion must be cultivated. Coughlin's policies were in agreement with those of Il Duce, but Mussolini hesitated to press such extreme views on Americans.

17:795 Diggins, John P. *Mussolini and Fascism: The View from America.* Princeton: Princeton University Press, 1972. Diggins analyzes American attitudes toward Italian fascism from the early 1920s through World War II. In the 1920s, many Americans backed Il Duce's corporatism and believed that Mussolini's regime would become more democratic once the Italian economy improved. After the Ethiopian War, Americans began to link Mussolini with Hitler as predatory aggressors. See also Diggins's "Mussolini and America: Hero-Worship, Charisma, and the 'Vulgar Talent,'" *Historian* 28 (August 1966): 559–85; "Flirtation with Fascism: American Pragmatic Liberals and Mussolini's Italy," *American Historical Review* 71 (January 1966): 487–506; and "The Italo-American Antifascist Opposition," *Journal of American History* 54 (December 1967): 579–88.

17:796 Friedlander, Robert A. "New Light on the Anglo-American Reaction to the Ethiopian War, 1935–1936." *Mid-America* 45 (April 1963): 115–25. The author argues that Ambassador Breckinridge Long's opposition to a stand against Italy greatly influenced American policy. Long feared Italy might go to war with the United States.

17:797 Harris, Brice, Jr. *The United States and the Italo-Ethiopian Crisis.* Harris assigns blame to Britain and France for allowing Mussolini to conquer Ethiopia. He portrays FDR and Hull as prisoners of isolationist public opinion and preoccupied with domestic concerns (16:255).

17:798 Luconi, Stefano. *La "diplomazia parallela": il regime fascista e la mobilitazione politica degli italo-americani ["Parallel Diplomacy": The Fascist Regime and the Political Mobilization of Italian Americans.* Milan: Franco-Angeli, 2000. Using Italian immigrant organizations, including newspapers, churches, and veterans' groups, Mussolini's government had significant success influencing the opinion of Italian-Americans, who in turn successfully lobbied the federal government on issues ranging from Italy's World War I debt to the mid-1930s arms embargo.

17:799 Norman, John. "Influence of Pro-Fascist Propaganda on American Neutrality, 1935–1936." In *Essays in History and International Relations, in Honor of George Hubbard Blakeslee,* ed. Dwight E. Lee and George E. McReynolds, 193–214. Worcester, MA: Clark University, 1949. This is an early effort to gauge the propaganda appeal of Italian-American publications during the Ethiopian War.

17:800   Salvemini, Gaetano. *Italian Fascist Activities in the United States.* New York: Center for Migration Studies, 1977. Based on a wartime report written in 1944, the book begins with an account of various front organizations, then moves to coverage of riots between fascists and their opponents, support for Italy's regime by Roman Catholic clergy and the Italo-American press, and the relationships of profascists with Tammany politicians. Edited with introduction by Philip V. Cannistraro.

17:801   Schmitz, David F. *The United States and Fascist Italy, 1922–1940.* Chapel Hill: University of North Carolina Press, 1988. The author argues that fear of Bolshevism and social change first led the United States to welcome Mussolini's regime as an acceptable member of the world community. FDR's Italy policy shows he opposed Nazi Germany's economic nationalism and military aggression but not fascism as a system. See also the author's "'A Fine Young Revolution': The United States and the Fascist Revolution in Italy, 1919–1925," *Radical History Review* 33 (September 1985): 117–38.

Soviet Union

17:802   Bacino, Leo J. *Reconstructing Russia: U.S. Policy in Revolutionary Russia, 1917–1922.* Kent, OH: Kent State University Press, 1999. American efforts to promote reconstruction in Siberia between 1917 and 1922 confronted insurmountable obstacles, ranging from widespread social and economic instability to irreconcilable conflicts with the Allies.

17:803   Bennett, Edward M. *Franklin D. Roosevelt and the Search for Victory: American-Soviet Relations, 1939–1945.* Wilmington, DE: SR Books, 1990. The author claims FDR recognized the repressive nature of the Soviet regime. He finds Roosevelt pursuing "crisis-to-crisis" diplomacy, continually shifting between short- and long-range goals.

17:804   _____. "Soviet-American Relations, 1939–1942: Searching for Allies in a Threatening World." In *Soviet-U.S. Relations, 1933–1942,* ed. G. N. Sevost'ianov and Warren F. Kimball, 29–39.

Moscow: Progress Publishers, 1989. This article stresses Roosevelt's efforts to use the Soviets as a counterweight against the Axis.

17:805   Clauss, Errol MacGregor. "'Pink in Appearance, but Red at Heart': The United States and the Far Eastern Republic, 1920–1922." *Journal of American–East Asian Relations* 1 (Fall 1992): 327–57. Clauss argues that through skillful cooperation with the Soviet-sponsored Far Eastern Republic, created in April 1920 to help edge Japanese forces from Siberia, Washington was able to stabilize Northeast Asia without either recognizing Moscow or precipitating conflict with Tokyo.

17:806   Condoide, Mikhail V. *Russian-American Trade: A Study of the Soviet Foreign-Trade Monopoly.* Columbus: Bureau of Business Research, College of Commerce and Administration, Ohio State University, 1946. This careful study of the "Soviet foreign trade monopoly," one of the first postwar efforts to assess the history of Soviet-American economic relations, contains much information on trade before World War II.

17:807   De Santis, Hugh. *The Diplomacy of Silence: The American Foreign Service, the Soviet Union, and the Cold War, 1933–1947.* This book examines the assumptions about the Soviet Union held by thirty major career diplomats during the 1930s and 1940s. The study concludes that those who served in Moscow and in Eastern and southern Europe developed a much harsher view of the USSR than those who did not (2:189).

17:808   Dunn, Dennis J. *Caught between Roosevelt & Stalin: America's Ambassadors to Moscow.* Lexington: University Press of Kentucky, 1998. The book criticizes FDR for failing to use his power to reduce the expansionism of Stalin. Of the pre-1941 ambassadors, Dunn sees Bullitt and Steinhardt as the most able, Davies as the most destructive.

17:809   Filene, Peter G. *Americans and the Soviet Experiment, 1917–1933.* Filene covers businessmen, educators, labor leaders, and representatives of the extreme right and left. Many Americans favored the 1917 revolution, differed among themselves when Russia left World War I, felt reassured by the New Economic Policy, and experienced new interest when the Great Depression forced them to focus on planning and trade (14:427).

17:810   Fisher, Harold H. *The Famine in Soviet Russia, 1919–1923: The Operations of the American Relief Administration.* New York: Macmillan, 1927. Fisher offers a thorough contemporary account of the American effort, led by Herbert Hoover, to alleviate the Russian famine.

17:811   Fithian, Floyd J. "Dollars without the Flag: The Case of Sinclair and Sakalin Oil." *Pacific Historical Review* 1970 (May): 205–22. In 1922, oil magnate Harry F. Sinclair signed a contract with the Far Eastern Republic, a Soviet satellite, but due to the lack of State Department support was never able to exploit his concession.

17:812   Grant, Natalie. "The Russian Section: A Window on the Soviet Union." *Diplomatic History* 2 (Winter 1978): 107–15. After the Russian revolution, American contacts with the USSR were limited. To remedy the situation, the State Department established a center for the study of Soviet affairs in the office of the Commissioner of the United States for the Baltic Provinces of Russia, located in Riga, Latvia.

17:813   Herndon, James S., and Joseph O. Baylen. "Col. Philip R. Faymonville and the Red Army, 1934–43." *Slavic Review* 34 (September 1975): 483–505. Faymonville, the first military attaché the United States ever assigned to the Soviet Union, gave uncritical reports concerning the nation, Stalin's rule, and the Red Army. He did, however, correctly predict that the Red Army would stave off the Wehrmacht.

17:814   Jacobs, Travis Beal. *America and the Winter War, 1939–1940.* New York: Garland Publishing, 1981. This book criticizes FDR for procrastinating in aiding the Finns though Jacobs denies that U.S. arms sales could have altered the war's outcome.

17:815   Kagedan, Allan L. "American Jews and the Soviet Experiment: The Agro-Joint Project, 1924–1937." *Jewish Social Studies* 43 (Spring 1981): 153–64. The article describes the efforts of the American Jewish Joint Distribution Committee to sponsor a corporation that would eventually resettle more than 100,000 urban Jews on farming communities in Crimea and the Ukraine.

17:816   Langer, John D. "The 'Red General: Philip R. Faymonville and the Soviet Union, 1917–52." *Prologue* 8 (Winter 1976): 209–21. Brigadier General Faymonville's long absorption in Soviet affairs brought him into a position of influence when the United States granted diplomatic recognition to the USSR in 1933. As military attaché in Moscow (1933–1938), he gained a reputation as a pro-Soviet observer despite his often unfavorable opinion of Soviet actions.

17:817   Larson, Simeon. "Opposition to AFL Foreign Policy: A Labor Mission to Russia, 1927." *Historian* 43 (May 1981): 345–64. This article shows the failure of the American Trade Union Delegation to the Soviet Union to change anti-Soviet policies of the American Federation of Labor.

17:818   Libbey, James K. "The American-Russian Chamber of Commerce." *Diplomatic History* 9 (Summer 1985): 233–48. Libbey sees the organization playing a more crucial role than scholars had previously assigned it. Predating the Bolshevik revolution, it was reactivated in the 1920s.

17:819   _____. "Liberal Journals and the Moscow Trials of 1936–38." *Journalism Quarterly* 52 (Spring 1975): 85–92. American liberals were disenchanted with the USSR prior to the Nazi-Soviet pact of 1939. Commentary in the *Nation* and *The New Republic* shows that liberals were progressively disturbed by the Moscow trials.

17:820   Lukas, Richard C. "The Impact of 'Barbarossa' on the Soviet Air Force and the Resulting Commitment of the United States Aircraft, June-October, 1941." *Historian* 29 (November 1966): 60–80. U.S. efforts to meet Soviet requests for military aircraft reveal the disagreement between the president, who favored a stopgap shipment, and War Department officials, who thought U.S. security needs precluded such a shipment.

17:821   Maddux, Thomas R. "American Diplomats and the Soviet Experiment: The View from the Moscow Embassy, 1934–1939." *South Atlantic Quarterly* 74 (Autumn 1975): 468–87. Despite differences of views, the embassy representatives understood Stalin and the USSR rather well, being candid about such matters as the purges, the new constitution, war preparations, and economic advances.

17:822 _____. "American News Media and Soviet Diplomacy." *Journalism Quarterly* 58 (Spring 1981): 29–57. Maddux sees the prewar press divided between conservatives, who stressed Stalin's desire to expand communism, and moderates, who saw the dictator's policies rooted in national defense.

17:823 _____. "United States–Soviet Naval Relations in the 1930's: The Soviet Union's Efforts to Purchase Naval Vessels." *Naval War College Review* 29 (Fall 1976): 28–37. Stalin's decision in 1936 to purchase American naval vessels coincided with FDR's desire to cooperate with the Soviets in Europe and East Asia. Senior American naval officers, opposed to doing business with the Soviet Union on ideological and national security grounds, obstructed the sales.

17:824 _____. "Watching Stalin Maneuver between Hitler and the West: American Diplomats and Soviet Diplomacy, 1934–1939." *Diplomatic History* 1 (Spring 1977): 140–54. American diplomats George Kennan, Charles Bohlen, and Loy Henderson underestimated Stalin's overtures to the west. Consequently, the State Department discouraged FDR from making efforts at even limited cooperation.

17:825 _____. *Years of Estrangement: America's Relations with the Soviet Union, 1933–1941.* Tallahassee: University Presses of Florida, 1980. The study finds FDR ignoring the State Department's Soviet specialists, who sought a quid pro quo in any bargaining with the USSR.

17:826 Mayers, David. *The Ambassadors and America's Soviet Policy.* New York: Oxford University Press, 1995. In the half of the book devoted to the pre-1942 period, the author finds Bullitt and Steinhardt correct in challenging Soviet activities but more myopic than Davies, who correctly saw the need for a U.S.-British-Soviet alliance against Hitler.

17:827 Morris, M. Wayne. "Stalin's Famine and the American Journalists." *Continuity* 18 (Spring-Fall 1994): 69–78. This article notes how such American journalists as Walter Duranty deliberately concealed news of the Soviet famine.

17:828 Naleszkiewicz, Wladimir. "Technical Assistance of the American Enterprises to the Growth of the Soviet Union." *Russian Review* 25 (January 1966): 54–76. The study examines the extended and strategic significance of U.S. private technological aid. See also Robert A. Clawson, "An American Businessman in the Soviet Union: The Reimer Report," *Business History Review* 50 (July 1976): 203–18, and Dana G. Dalrymple, "American Technology and Soviet Agricultural Development, 1924–1933," *Agricultural History* 40 (July 1966): 187–206.

17:829 Parks, J. D. *Culture, Conflict, and Coexistence: American-Soviet Cultural Relations, 1917–1958.* Jefferson, NC: McFarland, 1983. Cultural contacts between the nations remained surprisingly free until the early 1930s, when Stalin consolidated his power.

17:830 Rodis, Themistocles Clayton. "Russo-American Contacts during the Hoover Administration." *South Atlantic Quarterly* 51 (April 1952): 235–45. The author notes that the Hoover administration engaged in comparatively extensive unofficial trade relations with the Soviets, who simultaneously were successfully promoting their art, music, and drama within the United States.

17:831 Seppain, Hélène. *Contrasting US and German Attitudes to Soviet Trade, 1917–91: Politics by Economic Means.* New York: St. Martin's Press, 1992. The work argues that the U.S. government sought to "cure" the Bolshevik revolution by its use of food relief in 1921–1923, thereby steering it along a path of capitalist development. Conversely, Germany in the 1920s sought peace with the Soviets by not interfering in their internal affairs.

17:832 [Sevost'ianov, G. N., and Warren F. Kimball], eds. *Soviet-U.S. Relations, 1933–1942.* Moscow: Progress Publishers, 1989. Among the authors are Hugh Phillips, who finds both nations estranged in the 1930s over relatively small debts and ineffective communist propaganda (9–17); Charles Alexander, who finds the "Red Romance" of 1930s intellectuals a temporary infatuation (18–28); Edward M. Bennett, who notes that just before Pearl Harbor both nations sought the participation of the other in their own battles (29–39); J. Garry Clifford, who sees FDR retaining certain essential tenets of the isolationist credo until Pearl Harbor (52); Kimball, who portrays FDR as governed by Wilsonian liberalism (53–71);

and Theodore A. Wilson, who describes initial lend-lease aid (121–39).

17:833   Siegel, Katherine A. S. *Loans and Legitimacy: The Evolution of Soviet-American Relations, 1919–1933.* Lexington: University Press of Kentucky, 1996. The Soviet search for trade and financing in the United States was a success not only in the acquisition of needed goods but in increasing the prominence and legitimacy of the regime.

17:834   _____. "Technology and Trade: Russia's Pursuit of American Investment, 1917–1929." *Diplomatic History* 17 (Summer 1993): 375–98. Although Washington limited credits and banned loans, it did not prevent a growing commercial relationship. Contrarily, Moscow strictly defined conditions for American firms, including high demands for investment and output, limits on repatriation of profits, and high requirements for pay and benefits.

17:835   Sutton, Antony C. *Western Technology and Soviet Economic Development. Vol. 1: 1917 to 1930. Vol. 2: 1930 to 1945. Vol. 3: 1945 to 1965.* Stanford, CA: Hoover Institution on War, Revolution and Peace, Stanford University, 1968–1973. Sutton offers a detailed, sophisticated work essential to understanding Soviet development. He argues that western aid was the sine qua non of Soviet progress.

17:836   Ullman, Richard H. "The Davies Mission and United States–Soviet Relations, 1937–1941." *World Politics* 9 (January 1957): 220–39. Davies constantly misread Soviet affairs during his tenure as American ambassador. However, he proved to be correct in his prediction that the Russians could withstand the Hitler juggernaut.

17:837   Weissman, Benjamin. *Herbert Hoover and Famine Relief to Soviet Russia, 1921–1923.* Stanford, CA: Hoover Institution Press, 1974. Weissman offers a detailed treatment of the American Relief Administration, headed by Secretary of Commerce Hoover, analyzing the apparent contradiction of the staunch anticommunist assisting the Soviet government. See also Weissman's "Herbert Hoover's 'Treaty' with Soviet Russia: August 20, 1921," *Slavic Review* 28 (June 1969): 276–88. An account just published is Bertrand M. Patenaude, *The Big Show in Bololand: The American Relief Expedition to Soviet Russia in the Famine of 1921* (Stanford, CA: Stanford University Press, 2002).

17:838   White, Christine A. *British and American Commercial Relations with Soviet Russia, 1918–1924.* Chapel Hill: University of North Carolina Press, 1992. From the outset of the Bolshevik revolution, both the United States and Great Britain showed substantial interest in capturing Russia's lucrative postwar markets. Without this early concern, the trade boom in the latter part of the 1920s could scarcely have occurred.

Diplomatic Recognition

17:839   Bennett, Edward M. *Franklin D. Roosevelt and the Search for Security: American-Soviet Relations, 1933–1939.* Wilmington, DE: Scholarly Resources, 1985. The author traces the interrelationship of Soviet and American expectations and disappointments, in the process showing that each side found collaboration possible only on its own terms.

17:840   _____. *Recognition of Russia: An American Foreign Policy Dilemma.* Waltham, MA: Blaisdell Publishing Co., 1970. Bennett argues that FDR decided to recognize the Soviet Union because he found nonrecognition ineffective. By inflating American expectations, however, he severely injured Soviet-American relations.

17:841   Bishop, Donald G. *The Roosevelt-Litvinov Agreements: The American View.* Syracuse: Syracuse University Press, 1965. Despite shortcomings in carrying out the Roosevelt-Litvinov agreements, recognition was advantageous to the United States. No other government exceeded the United States in compelling the Russians to honor their promises.

17:842   Bowers, Robert E. "American Diplomacy, the 1933 Wheat Conference, and Recognition of the Soviet Union." *Agricultural History* 11 (January 1966): 39–52. This article discusses the lowering of commodity prices, particularly important in time of depression, and its impact on the recognition issue. U.S. officials concerned with agricultural prices came to favor relations with the Soviet Union, which may have influenced Roosevelt.

17:843   _____. "Hull, Russian Subversion in

Cuba, and Recognition of the USSR." *Journal of American History* 53 (December 1966): 524–54. Bowers suggests that Hull's opposition to recognition derived partly from concern over communist efforts in Cuba, an anxiety not shared by FDR.

17:844 Browder, Robert Paul. *The Origins of Soviet-American Diplomacy.* Princeton: Princeton University Press, 1953. In the late 1920s, Soviet leaders sought recognition because of economic need, prestige, and fear of Japan. The delay in recognition from 1917 to 1933 led to exaggerated hopes on both sides, virtually ensuring disappointment.

17:845 _____. "Soviet Far Eastern Policy and American Recognition, 1932–1934." *Pacific Historical Review* 21 (August 1952): 25–39. Browder describes Russia's failure to interest the United States in a collaborative effort to police the Pacific.

17:846 Hoff, Joan. *Ideology and Economics: U.S. Relations with the Soviet Union, 1918–1933.* Columbia: University of Missouri Press, 1974. Hoff argues that nonrecognition led to a lack of coordination between American economic foreign policy and "political" foreign policy, for the growing foreign affairs bureaucracy became strong ideological opponents of recognition. To see how business was divided, note also her, "American Business and Recognition of the Soviet Union," *Social Science Quarterly* 52 (September 1971): 349–68.

17:847 Libbey, James K. *Alexander Gumberg & Soviet-American Relations, 1917–1933.* Lexington: University Press of Kentucky, 1977. A Russian-born American businessman with sympathy for the Soviet experiment, Gumberg worked for recognition and good U.S.-Soviet relations. Libbey sees people-to-people contacts as dominating relations between the two countries.

17:848 Morris, M. Wayne. *Stalin's Famine and Roosevelt's Recognition of Russia.* Lanham, MD: University Press of America, 1994. Morris sees the State Department so anxious to secure recognition of the Soviet Union that it ignored all reports concerning a forced famine.

17:849 Morris, Robert L. "A Reassessment of Russian Recognition." *Historian* 24 (August 1953):

470–82. The author finds international considerations primary in granting recognition. Economic factors, he says, have been greatly overrated.

17:850 Phillips, Hugh D. "Rapprochement and Estrangement: The United States in Soviet Foreign Policy in the 1930s." In *Soviet-U.S. Relations, 1933–1942,* ed. G. N. Sevost'ianov and Warren F. Kimball, 9–17. Moscow: Progress Publishers, 1989. The author finds Moscow seeking better relations with Washington merely to offset the growing threat posed by Japan. Little wonder that soon after diplomatic relations were established, a period of estrangement set in.

17:851 Propas, Frederic L. "Creating a Hard Line toward Russia: The Training of State Department Soviet Experts, 1927–1937." *Diplomatic History* 8 (Summer 1984): 209–26. The article shows that under the tutelage of Robert F. Kelley, its chief, the State Department's Eastern European Division sought to isolate as well as study the Soviet Union. Until 1933, Kelley was successful in blocking recognition.

17:852 Richman, John. *The United States & the Soviet Union: The Decision to Recognize.* Raleigh, NC: Camberleigh and Hall, 1980. The recognition of the USSR accentuated the differences between FDR and his State Department, creating a duality of policy that lasted throughout the 1930s.

17:853 Welch, Richard E., Jr. "United States Recognition of the Soviet Union: The Influence of Wishful Thinking." *Mid-America* 67 (April-July 1985): 83–92. Welch finds FDR never establishing a clear set of priorities in approaching the Soviet Union or understanding the Russians' own long-term interests. Hence his policies were doomed to frustration.

17:854 Williams, Andrew J. *Trading with the Bolsheviks: The Politics of East-West Trade, 1920–1939.* New York: Manchester University Press, 1992. In covering American, British, and French commerce with the Soviets, the author focuses on the political rather than economic background. He notes that the United States began to act favorably only in 1928–1929, when American firms felt the first squeeze of the oncoming recession. He is critical of how the powers recognized the Soviet Union, dispensed piecemeal in a way that revealed division and weakness.

Other European Areas

17:855   Lane, Peter B. *The United States and the Balkan Crisis of 1940–1941.* New York: Garland, 1988. This work shows increasing American political, economic, and military involvement, though it denies that the United States fostered anti-German underground activities in Yugoslavia. America played only a limited role in the events surrounding the 1941 Yugoslav coup.

17:856   Peselj, Branko M. "Serbo-Croatian Agreement of 1939 and American Foreign Policy." *Journal of Croatian Studies* 11–12 (Winter 1970–1971): 3–82. This essay examines the political and constitutional character of the agreement of August 26, 1939, and demonstrates the posture of the United States toward the agreement.

17:857   Crowe, David. "American Foreign Policy and the Baltic State Question, 1940–1941." *East European Quarterly* 17 (Winter 1983): 401–15. The author discusses the process by which the United States refused to recognize the Soviet seizure of the Baltic states while still keeping diplomatic relations with the USSR open and not enforcing the neutrality act against the Russians.

17:858   Tarulis, Albert N. *American-Baltic Relations, 1918–1922: The Struggle over Recognition.* Washington, DC: Catholic University of America Press, 1965. This study reviews the attitudes of the Wilson and Harding administrations toward the Baltic states and describes those states' efforts to obtain *de jure* recognition from Washington.

17:859   Lewandowski, Richard B. "The Phantom Government: The United States and the Recognition of the Czechoslovak Republic, 1939–1943." *Southern Quarterly* 11 (July 1973): 369–88. The decision by the United States not to recognize the Munich agreement and the occupation of Czechoslovakia led to the creation of a Czech government-in-exile.

17:860   Paasivirta, Juhani. *The Victors of World War I and Finland: Finland's Relations with the British, French, and United States Governments in 1918–1919.* Translated by Paul Sjöblom. Helsinki: Finnish Historical Society, 1965. In examining Finland's relations with Britain, France, and the United States during the closing stages of World War I and the period immediately afterward, the author covers such matters as recognition for Finnish independence, the Aland Islands, East Karelia, and intervention in Russia.

17:861   Rhodes, Benjamin D. "The Origins of Finnish-American Friendship, 1919–1941." *Mid-America* 54 (January 1972): 3–19. Rhodes provides details of the funding of the Finnish war debt from the agreement of May 1922 to August 1949, when Congress, recognizing the cold war implications of the debt, authorized that remaining payments fund a joint educational program.

17:862   Schwartz, Andrew J. *America and the Russo-Finnish War.* Washington, DC: Public Affairs Press, 1960. Reprint 1975 (Greenwood Press). Schwartz credits American friendship with assisting Finnish efforts during the Winter War. Introduction by Quincy Wright.

17:863   Wert, Hal Elliott. "Hoover, Roosevelt and the Politics of American Aid to Finland, 1939–1940." In *World War II: A Fifty Year Perspective on 1939: Selected Papers,* ed. Richard W. Hoeffner, 89–112. Albany: Siena College Research Institute Press, 1992. Wert finds Finland the ultimate beneficiary of the intensely political rivalry between Roosevelt and Hoover.

17:864   Cassimatis, Louis P. *American Influence in Greece, 1917–1929.* Kent, OH: Kent State University Press, 1988. After 1922, when Greece lay prostrate after a decade of crisis, American relief, technical knowledge, and capital investment contributed heavily to its rehabilitation.

17:865   Morgenthau, Henry, Sr., with French Strother. *I Was Sent to Athens.* Garden City, NY: Doubleday, Doran and Company, 1929. The chairman of the League of Nations Resettlement Commission in 1923 describes his efforts to aid the many Greek refugees fleeing from Turkey.

17:866   Costigliola, Frank C. "American Foreign Policy in the 'Nutcracker': The United States and Poland in the 1920's." *Pacific Historical Review* 48 (February 1979): 85–105. American efforts to stabilize the Polish economy failed because of massive and intertwined economic and political problems.

U.S. policy had sought to rebuild postwar European economies to protect its markets, prevent the spread of communism, and reduce the possibility of war and revolution.

17:867   Pease, Neal. *Poland, the United States, and the Stabilization of Europe, 1919–1933.* New York: Oxford University Press, 1986. Pease recounts varied attempts of Polish governments to secure substantial loans from Wall Street financiers as the foundation for a secure geopolitical and economic future. Nearly all these failed as American investors, who considered Poland unstable and insecure, found greater opportunities in Latin America and Western Europe. See also Pease's study of a prominent Chicago banker: "Charles Dewey as the United States Financial Adviser to Poland, 1927–1930," *International History Review* 9 (February 1987): 85–94.

17:868   Wert, Hal Elliott. "U.S. Aid to Poles under Nazi Domination, 1939–1940." *Historian* 57 (Spring 1995): 511–24. This article notes the abortive efforts of the American Red Cross and Herbert Hoover's commission to aid Poland in the fall of 1939. See also Wert's "Flight and Survival: American and British Aid to Polish Refugees in the Fall of 1939," *Polish Review* 24 (Fall 1989): 227–48.

17:869   Carroll, Peter N. *The Odyssey of the Abraham Lincoln Brigade: Americans in the Spanish Civil War.* Stanford, CA: Stanford University Press, 1994. Carroll not only narrates experiences in Spain but the lives of the volunteers before and afterward. He challenges the view that the Comintern and U.S. Communist Party managed the brigade and its men.

17:870   Eby, Cecil. *Between the Bullet and the Lie: American Volunteers in the Spanish Civil War.* New York: Holt, Rinehart and Winston, 1969. In his account of the Lincoln Battalion, the author argues that communist support was surreptitious. Some Americans fought out of motivations alien to communist purposes.

17:871   Guttmann, Allen. *The Wound in the Heart: America and the Spanish Civil War.* New York: Free Press of Glencoe, 1962. Very much in the "American Studies" genre, this book draws upon literature as well as history to capture the symbolic nature of the struggle.

17:872   Landis, Arthur H. *Death in the Olive Groves: American Volunteers in the Spanish Civil War, 1936–1939.* New York: Paragon House, 1989. The book offers a friendly treatment of the Abraham Lincoln Brigades.

17:873   Little, Douglas. "Architects of Appeasement: Franklin Roosevelt, the State Department, and the Spanish Civil War." In *Appeasing Fascism: Articles from the Wayne State University Conference on Munich after Fifty Years,* ed. Melvin Small and Otto Feinstein, 73–88. Lanham, MD: University Press of America, 1991. FDR's love of peace and the perils of election-year politics outweighed his commitment to democratic principles, attitudes that cost the Spanish Republic dearly. Only in 1937 did he start to second-guess the State Department, which feared the radicalism of the Spanish Republic.

17:874   _____. *Malevolent Neutrality: The United States, Great Britain, and the Origins of the Spanish Civil War.* Ithaca: Cornell University Press, 1985. The author finds the Spanish civil war sharpening the Anglo-Saxons' long-standing distaste for the Spanish Republic's leftist policies, trade policies, and treatment of foreign investments.

17:875   _____. "Twenty Years of Turmoil: ITT, the State Department, and Spain, 1924–1944." *Business History Review* 53 (Winter 1979): 449–72. Although managerial and mechanical ingenuity contributed to the success of the International Telephone and Telegraph Company, it was State Department support that largely determined its ability to survive Spain's political upheavals from 1931 to 1939.

17:876   Rosenstone, Robert A. *Crusade of the Left: The Lincoln Battalion in the Spanish Civil War.* New York: Pegasus, 1969. Reprint 1980 (University Press of America). In this narrative, the author denies that the Lincoln volunteers were dupes of the Kremlin but, instead, honest, sensitive individuals responding to malfunctions in America's socioeconomic system. See also Rosenstone, "The Men of the Abraham Lincoln Battalion," *Journal of American History* 54 (September 1967): 327–38, and "American Commissars in Spain," *South Atlantic Quarterly* 67 (Autumn 1968): 688–702. For more material, see Alvah Bessie and Albert Prago, *Our Fight: Writings by Veterans of the Abraham Lincoln Brigade, 1936–1939* (New

York: Monthly Review Press, 1987), and John Carver Edwards, *Airmen without Portfolio: U.S. Mercenaries in Civil War Spain* (Westport, CT: Praeger, 1997).

17:877 Singerman, Robert. "American-Jewish Reactions to the Spanish Civil War." *Journal of Church and State* 19 (Spring 1977): 261–78. Americans Jews saw the Spanish civil war as the last chance to check the spread of fascism though most Jewish organizations played no active role, not considering the war a religious concern.

17:878 Taylor, Foster Jay. *The United States and the Spanish Civil War.* New York: Bookman Associates, 1956. This work describes the major role played by the Spanish civil war in the struggle over revision of the American neutrality laws. Accepting a fait accompli in 1939 was difficult for FDR, but the politically cautious Hull convinced the president to acknowledge Franco's victory.

17:879 Traina, Richard P. *American Diplomacy and the Spanish Civil War.* Bloomington: Indiana University Press, 1968. Traina sees FDR subjugating sympathies for the loyalists to the dictates of perceived internal political pressures. Although both he and Hull thought the crisis might lead to general war, administration response was halting.

17:880 Whealey, Robert H. "Anglo-American Oil Confronts Spanish Nationalism, 1927–31: A Study of Economic Imperialism." *Diplomatic History* 12 (September 1988): 111–26. Whealey notes how Anglo-American oil companies sought to maintain their domination of Spain's oil imports at the very time Spain sought self-sufficiency.

17:881 Jakub, Jay. *Spies and Saboteurs: Anglo-American Collaboration and Rivalry in Human Intelligence Collection and Special Operations, 1940–45.* New York: St. Martin's Press, 1999. Using the mass declassification of OSS documents, the author covers Donovan's missions to Europe in 1940 and 1941. He attributes the 1941 anti-German coup in Yugoslavia less to Donovan's visit of January 1941 than to British activity and internal Yugoslav politics.

U.S. Relations with Asia

GENERAL

17:882 Borg, Dorothy. *The United States and the Far Eastern Crisis of 1933–1938: From the Manchurian Incident through the Initial Stage of the Undeclared Sino-Japanese War.* Cambridge, MA: Harvard University Press, 1964. Because of the Manchurian episode and the breakdown of naval disarmament in 1935, Congress, the press, and public opinion generally disapproved of Japanese policy. Far more influential on U.S. attitudes, however, were the Great Depression, the Nye investigation, and fear of war, which saw expression in the neutrality acts.

17:883 Clauss, Errol MacGregor. "The Roosevelt Administration and Manchukuo, 1933–1941." *Historian* 32 (August 1970): 595–611. The fact that Roosevelt inherited both the Japanese fait accompli in Manchuria and the Hoover-Stimson policy did not forestall accommodation. The United States restrained its diplomatic representatives and yet at the same time urged them to seek fair treatment of business concerns.

17:884 Clifford, Nicholas R. "Britain, America, and the Far East, 1937–1940: A Failure in Cooperation." *Journal of British Studies* 3 (November 1963): 137–54. The United States, by rejecting Chamberlain's proposal for joint action against Japan, undermined Britain's effort to secure American protection of the empire.

17:885 _____. *Retreat from China: British Policy in the Far East, 1937–1941.* Seattle: University of Washington Press, 1967. The author finds Britain and the United States unwilling either to form an alliance that might stop Japan or to make concrete proposals that would meet Japan's needs and thus defect her from her imperialism.

17:886 Coox, Alvin D. *Year of the Tiger.* Philadelphia: Orient/West, 1964. This is a journalistic reconstruction of Japanese domestic and foreign episodes in 1937–1938, especially in China. In Coox's analysis of the *Panay* crisis, he concludes that the Japanese government bore no responsibility and the navy little guilt, given the intelligence equipment that was part of the American ship's cargo.

17:887   Craft, Stephen G. "Peacemakers in China: American Missionaries and the Sino-Japanese War, 1937–1941." *Journal of Church and State* 41 (Summer 1999): 575–91. Craft finds missionaries playing a crucial role in transforming American opinion from indifference to outrage over the Japanese invasion of China. In advocating an economic boycott of Japan and the severing of U.S. war supplies to Japan, missionaries stressed the immorality of Japan's activity and its threat to American religious, economic, and security interests.

17:888   Current, Richard N. "The Stimson Doctrine and the Hoover Doctrine." *American Historical Review* 59 (April 1954): 513–42. Hoover was content with nonrecognition as a simple statement of American disapproval, whereas Stimson wanted to use the policy as a first step toward stronger statements and perhaps sanctions.

17:889   Doenecke, Justus D. *When the Wicked Rise: American Opinion-Makers and the Manchurian Crisis of 1931–1933.* Cranbury, NJ: Associated University Presses, 1984. Despite the stereotype of an aloof and apathetic United States, most opinion makers were outraged by Japan's actions in Manchuria and Shanghai. Many endorsed U.S. cooperation with the League, Stimson's nonrecognition policy, and the Lytton report, though they were divided over economic coercion. See also Doenecke, "The Debate over Coercion: The Dilemma of American Pacifists and the Manchurian Crisis," *Peace and Change* 2 (Spring 1974): 47–52.

17:890   Donnelly, J. B. "Prentiss Gilbert's Mission to the League of Nations Council, October 1931." *Diplomatic History* 4 (Fall 1978): 373–87. As American consul in Geneva, Gilbert took his seat at the League table at the outset of the Manchurian crisis although he contributed little to the discussions. Decisions by Stimson, Dawes, and Hoover fluctuated, thus limiting Gilbert's effectiveness.

17:891   Fifield, Russell H. "Secretary Hughes and the Shantung Question." *Pacific Historical Review* 23 (November 1954): 375–85. Secretary of State Hughes skillfully conducted informal negotiations with British, Japanese, and Chinese representatives. The question was resolved primarily because there existed no desire to embarrass Japan.

17:892   Hecht, Robert A. "Great Britain and the Stimson Note of January 7, 1932." *Pacific Historical Review* 38 (February 1969): 177–91. Foreign Secretary Sir John Simon rejected Stimson's nonrecognition strategy during the Manchurian crisis in the belief that for economic, political, and strategic reasons his government could not afford to antagonize Japan.

17:893   Iriye, Akira. *After Imperialism: The Search for a New Order in the Far East, 1921–1931.* Cambridge, MA: Harvard University Press, 1965. With the breakdown of earlier imperialist models, both Japan and the west unsuccessfully sought a cooperative approach to China. This volume has long been a standard account.

17:894   Iriye, Akira, and Warren I. Cohen, eds. *American, Chinese, and Japanese Perspectives on Wartime Asia, 1931–1949.* Wilmington, DE: SR Books, 1990. Included among the book's chapters are: Cohen on FDR, who centered less on China than the Axis threat to an American-led global order (1–27); Wang Xi on U.S. silver policy helping force a Chinese economic collapse (29–71); Chihiro Hosoya on the indifference to East Asia shown in American wheat policy in 1933 (73–91); and Katsumi Usui on splits within the Japanese policymaking elite over cooperation with the western powers; Sherman Cochran challenges stereotypes of business-government collusion among major powers. Waldo H. Heinrichs writes on the 1939–1941 linkages in U.S. policy between the Pacific and European theaters (147–78); and Gary R. Hess considers U.S. trade with Southeast Asia (179–211).

17:895   Koginos, Manny T. *The Panay Incident: Prelude to War.* Lafayette, IN: Purdue University Studies, 1967. More analytical than Perry, *The Panay Incident: Prelude to Pearl Harbor* (1969) (17:902), this volume moves beyond the episode's details—including questions of context, motive, and responsibility—to its overall significance as the driving force behind Roosevelt's program of naval expansion and as a factor in the denouement of pacifism.

17:896   Langer, Robert. *Seizure of Territory: The Stimson Doctrine and Related Principles in Legal Theory and Diplomatic Practice.* Princeton: Princeton University Press, 1947. This book offer extensive material on historical background and the details of 1930s conferences.

17:897   Louis, William Roger. *British Strategy in the Far East, 1919–1939.* Oxford: Clarendon Press, 1971. Louis offers a subtle overview of British foreign policy toward East Asia in the interwar period, especially 1919 to 1935. Foreign Office distrust of American motives runs throughout.

17:898   McCarty, Kenneth G., Jr. "Stanley K. Hornbeck and the Manchurian Crisis." *Southern Quarterly* 10 (July 1972): 305–24. Hornbeck, chief of the Division of Far Eastern Affairs in the State Department, advised Secretary Stimson to let the League handle the Manchurian problem, arguing that invocation of the Kellogg-Briand Pact would be ineffective. He advocated legal action against Japan, not moralistic condemnation.

17:899   Ogata, Sadako. *Defiance in Manchuria: The Making of Japanese Foreign Policy, 1931–1932.* Berkeley: University of California Press, 1964. Although many Japanese resented U.S. policies on immigration, trade, and China, defiance of Washington was only incidental to the purposes of Japanese nationalists, who, through action in Manchuria, sought to defy the presumed timidity of their own government.

17:900   Okumiya, Masatake. "How the *Panay* was Sunk." *U.S. Naval Institute Proceedings* 79 (June 1953): 587–96. Okumiya led the dive bomber squadron that attacked the *Panay* while pursuing the Chinese. He emphasizes, as the Japanese government did, the unintentional guilt of his country and attributes mistakes to explainable delays in announcing the victim's change of location.

17:901   Pearson, Alden B., Jr. "A Christian Moralist Responds to War: Charles C. Morrison, *The Christian Century* and the Manchurian Crisis, 1931–33." *World Affairs* 139 (Spring 1977): 296–307. Morrison and his Protestant weekly were forced to wrestle with

the issue of coercion after having maintained that the Kellogg pact had ended all global conflict.

17:902   Perry, Hamilton D. *The Panay Incident: Prelude to Pearl Harbor.* New York: Macmillan, 1969. Based in part on the author's discussions with crew members of the vessel as well as interviews conducted in Japan, this book covers Tokyo's subsequent apologies, payments, scapegoating, and rationalizing.

17:903   Rappaport, Armin. *Henry L. Stimson and Japan, 1931–33.* Chicago: University of Chicago Press, 1963. In his thorough account of the entire crisis, Rappaport voices strong criticism of Stimson. By brandishing an "unloaded pistol" in the form of the Stimson Doctrine, the secretary had "placed his own country in jeopardy."

17:904   Smith, Sara R. *The Manchurian Crisis, 1931–1932: A Tragedy in International Relations.* New York: Columbia University Press, 1948. Reprint 1970 (Greenwood Press). Smith sees Manchuria as one of many tragedies that resulted from failure of the United States to join the League of Nations, cooperate with Britain, and live up to the obligations of the Washington treaties and the Kellogg-Briand pact.

17:905   Sternsher, Bernard. "The Stimson Doctrine: FDR 'versus' Moley and Tugwell." *Pacific Historical Review* 31 (August 1962): 281–89. These key members of FDR's "brain trust" tried unsuccessfully to convince the president-elect to break with the Hoover-Stimson East Asian policies.

17:906   Stimson, Henry L. *The Far Eastern Crisis: Recollections and Observations.* New York: Harper for the Council on Foreign Relations, 1936. Reprint 1974 (H. Fertig). Stimson does not regret so much his mistakes or the rise of Japanese militarism as he does the inability of peace-seeking nations to work together. Aggression succeeded because of failures in international law, the League of Nations, systems of mutual security, and Anglo-American relations.

17:907   Swanson, Harlan J. "The *Panay* Incident: Prelude to Pearl Harbor." *U.S. Naval Institute Proceedings* 93 (December 1967): 26–37. Swanson confronts the disappearance of the incident from American consciousness, explaining the matter with reference to an isolationist mood that precluded strong action.

17:908 Thorne, Christopher. *The Limits of Foreign Policy: The West, the League and the Far Eastern Crisis of 1931–1933.* New York: Putnam, 1972. In a multiarchival study, Thorne criticizes both British and American diplomacy during the Manchurian affair and after, although—contrary to others—he does not see the affair as the beginning of World War II. He denies that the United States or Britain could have coerced Japan without high risks. Even had the American people endorsed sanctions, it would have been most difficult to impose them with sufficient speed and power to bring Japan to terms.

17:909 Waldron, Arthur, ed. *How the Peace Was Lost: The 1935 Memorandum Developments Affecting American Foreign Policy in the Far East, Prepared for the State Department by John Van Antwerp MacMurray.* Stanford, CA: Hoover Institution Press, 1992. MacMurray, U.S. minister in Peking from 1925 to 1929, drafted a major memorandum that sought to preserve the balance of power by promoting moderation toward Japan and restraint toward China.

17:910 Williams, William Appleman. "China and Japan: A Challenge and a Choice of the 1920s." *Pacific Historical Review* 26 (August 1957): 259–79. American diplomats sought economic expansion in China while wishing to avoid military involvement. Such goals were threatened by both the Chinese revolution and the increasing intervention of Japan.

JAPAN

17:911 Asada, Sadao. "The Japanese Navy and the United States." In *Pearl Harbor as History: Japanese-American Relations, 1931–1941,* ed. Dorothy Borg and Shumpei Okamoto, with Dale K. A. Finlayson, 225–60. New York: Columbia University Press, 1973. In describing the demise of the Washington-London treaty system and the reopening of the armament race, the author finds the Japanese navy greatly underestimating the war potential of the United States while overestimating that of Germany.

17:912 _____. "Japan's 'Special Interests' and the Washington Conference, 1921–22." *American*

Historical Review 67 (October 1961): 62–70. In consenting to cancel the Lansing-Ishii agreement, the Japanese government believed that it reserved freedom of action in Manchuria. The ambiguity of the agreement was perpetuated in the "security" clause of the Nine-Power Pact.

17:913 Borg, Dorothy. "Notes on Roosevelt's 'Quarantine' Speech." *Political Science Quarterly* 72 (September 1957): 405–33. Borg suggests that the speech was not meant to be a drastic departure from previous foreign policy but reflected FDR's own groping.

17:914 Daniels, Roger. *The Politics of Prejudice: The Anti-Japanese Movement in California and the Struggle for Japanese Exclusion.* Daniels reinforces the argument that the 1924 legislation was a blow to Japanese pride and therefore one of several factors that led to hostilities. Originally published in 1962; the second edition includes a supplementary bibliography (13:223).

17:915 Davidann, Jon Thares. "'Colossal Illusions': U.S.-Japanese Relations in the Institute of Pacific Relations." *Journal of World History* 12 (Spring 2001): 155–82. The author notes that nationalism, growing U.S. power, and U.S.-Japanese rivalry all undermined the internationalist goals of the IPR. While Japanese delegates sought a rational calculation of national interests, Americans, often strong Wilsonians, thought nationalism itself was irrational.

17:916 Dingman, Roger V. "Farewell to Friendship: The USS *Astoria*'s Visit to Japan, April 1939." *Diplomatic History* 10 (Spring 1986): 121–39. After outlining the career of Saito Hiroshi, Japanese ambassador to the United States, the author tells of the botched effort to advance détente by ceremoniously transporting his body home.

17:917 Gardner, Lloyd C. "The Role of the Commerce and Treasury Departments." In *Pearl Harbor as History: Japanese-American Relations, 1931–1941,* ed. Dorothy Borg and Shumpei Okamoto, with Dale K. A. Finlayson, 261–85. New York: Columbia University Press, 1973. Gardner emphasizes the Commerce and Treasury Departments' fears of Japanese attempts to integrate additional areas in East Asia into their "state-trading system." The author focuses on Secretary of the Treasury Henry Morgenthau's efforts to use silver policy and American credits to combat Japanese expansion.

17:918 Graebner, Norman A. "Hoover, Roosevelt, and the Japanese." In *Pearl Harbor as History: Japanese-American Relations, 1931–1941,* ed. Dorothy Borg and Shumpei Okamoto, with Dale K. A. Finlayson, 25–52. New York: Columbia University Press, 1973. Hoover's nonrecognition doctrine "successfully avoided the obligation to create a policy." FDR was never able to establish goals that reflected U.S. limited interests, its lack of available strength, and its desire to avoid war. See also Graebner, "Japan: Unanswered Challenge," in his *America as a World Power: A Realist Appraisal from Wilson to Reagan: Essays* (1984), 64–84 (24:36).

17:919 Haight, John McVickar, Jr. "Franklin D. Roosevelt and a Naval Quarantine of Japan." *Pacific Historical Review* 40 (May 1971): 203–26. Haight challenges the claim that FDR backed down from his firm stand against aggression when isolationists protested his quarantine speech. Spurred by the *Panay* outrage a few weeks later, he explored more intensely the plans already in existence for a naval blockade against Japan.

17:920 _____. "Roosevelt and the Aftermath of the Quarantine Speech." *Review of Politics* 24 (April 1962): 233–59. Haight attempts to clarify the uncertainty about how Roosevelt meant to implement his quarantine speech by demonstrating the president's regard for the Nine Power conference at Brussels as an opportunity for initiating positive action in East Asia.

17:921 Haines, Gerald K. "American Myopia and the Japanese Monroe Doctrine, 1931–41." *Prologue* 13 (Summer 1981): 101–14. The author argues that U.S. policies had more in common with Japanese declarations in Asia than American officials cared to admit. Both the United States and Japan were highly industrialized, capitalist powers attempting to create, preserve, justify, and protect a regional system within which their vital interests would be secured and their predominance maintained. By refusing to recognize Japan's regional claims, the Roosevelt administration helped harden positions on both sides.

17:922 Heinrichs, Waldo H. "1931–1937." In *American–East Asian Relations: A Survey,* ed. Ernest R. May and James C. Thomson, Jr., 243–59. Cambridge, MA: Harvard University Press, 1972. Heinrichs notes that the multilateralism and universalism of the 1920s did not end abruptly with the Manchurian crisis but lingered from year to year.

17:923 Herzberg, James R. *A Broken Bond: American Economic Policies toward Japan, 1931–1941.* New York: Garland, 1988. In covering the span of economic relations from the Manchurian crisis through the freezing orders of July 1941, the author claims that the United States could hardly tolerate Japan's ambitions. From a global perspective, latter-day Japanese mercantilism would severely impair the liberal international order the United States sought to establish.

17:924 Herzog, James H. *Closing the Open Door: American-Japanese Diplomatic Relations, 1936–1941.* Annapolis: Naval Institute Press, 1973. In his account, Herzog notes that Admiral Harold Stark refused to condone naval reinforcements and embargoes against Japan while Admiral Harry E. Yarnell sought these sanctions.

17:925 _____. "Influence of the United States Navy in the Embargo of Oil to Japan, 1940–1941." *Pacific Historical Review* 35 (August 1966): 317–28. Ironically, the Japanese aircraft and carriers that attacked Pearl Harbor operated on imported American fuel. Such high-ranking navy personnel as Admiral Harold Stark, feeling unprepared for the war in the Pacific, had counseled against embargoes.

17:926 Hirobe, Izumi. "American Attitudes toward the Japanese Immigration Question, 1924–1931." *Journal of American–East Asian Relations* 2 (Fall 1993): 275–301. The author shows how both clergy and businessmen sought to modify the 1924 immigration law and were partially able to influence Congress. Had there been more time and more favorable U.S.-Japan relations over China, they might have succeeded in modifying the act.

17:927 _____. *Japanese Pride, American Prejudice: Modifying the Exclusion Clause of the 1924 Immigration Act.* Stanford, CA: Stanford University Press, 2001. Hirobe shows how American internationalists sought more cordial relations with Japan by opening America's door at least a crack to Japanese immigration. He examines such ameliorative groups as clergy, peace activists, and business leaders as well as more conservative trade unions and west coast politicians and newspapers.

17:928   Hoffer, Peter C. "American Businessmen and the Japan Trade, 1931–1941: A Case Study of Attitude Formation." *Pacific Historical Review* 41 (May 1972): 189–205. Until well into 1941, economic leaders and business journals supported U.S. neutrality, arguing that the maintenance of contact with Japanese businessmen contributed to both future peace and the American economy.

17:929   Hosoya, Chihiro. "Britain and the United States in Japan's View of the International System, 1919–37." In *Anglo-Japanese Alienation, 1919–1952: Papers of the Anglo-Japanese Conference on the History of the Second World War,* ed. Ian Nish, 3–26. New York: Cambridge University Press, 1982. The article sees Japan viewing the United States separately from Britain until the latter half of the 1930s, when it perceived both nations as stumbling blocks to Japan's new order.

17:930   _____. "Miscalculations in Deterrent Policy: Japanese-U.S. Relations, 1938–1941." *Journal of Peace Research* 5 (1968): 97–115. U.S. warnings and actual imposition of economic sanctions accelerated the Japanese southern advance, thereby leading to war.

17:931   Ienaga, Saburo. *The Pacific War: World War II and the Japanese, 1931–1945.* Translated by Frank Baldwin. New York: Pantheon, 1978. The author, an aggrieved but astute Japanese civil libertarian, indicts himself, his country, and the economic expansionism of the United States. If the book is idiosyncratic, it does not lack insights.

17:932   Iguchi, Haruo. "A Quest for Peace: Ayukawa Yoshisuke and U.S.-Japan Relations, 1940." *Journal of American–East Asian Relations* 5 (Spring 1996): 15–36. The article notes efforts of Japanese industrialist Ayukawa Yoshisuke, who founded the Nissan business conglomerate, to improve Japanese-U.S. relations and attract American investments to Manchukuo. Iguchi also describes the mission of lawyer and businessman, Major General John F. Ryan, in the summer of 1940.

17:933   Jablon, Howard. "Cordell Hull, His 'Associates,' and Relations with Japan, 1933–1936." *Mid-America* 56 (July 1974): 160–74. Hull followed Stimson's demonstrably bankrupt policy because of an excessive reliance on advisers, especially Hornbeck, who believed in the nonrecognition doctrine and the open door.

17:934   Jacobs, Travis Beal. "Roosevelt's 'Quarantine Speech.'" *Historian* 24 (August 1962): 483–502. This article shows that public reaction was mixed if not slightly favorable toward the speech. Unfortunately, Roosevelt was caught without a specific plan.

17:935   Kase, Toshikazu. *Journey to the Missouri.* New Haven: Yale University Press, 1950. This memoir reaches back before Pearl Harbor and includes materials on wartime Japanese peace efforts. It absolves the emperor of war guilt, identifies prominent antiwar elements before 1941, and traces the rise of militarism back to the Meiji Constitution. Edited by David Nelson Rowe.

17:936   LaFeber, Walter. *The Clash: A History of U.S.-Japan Relations.* The author finds U.S. policy driven by Hull and Hornbeck's growing anger over Japanese intentions to use military force to cordon off large parts of Asia to secure its own economic self-sufficiency (2:284).

17:937   Libby, Justin H. "Anti-Japanese Sentiment in the Pacific Northwest: Senator Schwellenbach and Congressman Coffee Attempt to Embargo Japan." *Mid-America* 58 (October 1976): 167–74. Libby analyzes the efforts in the 1930s of Lewis B. Schwellenbach and John M. Coffee to enact an American embargo of Japan they believed would protect the fishing interests of Washington State and keep the United States out of a war with Japan.

17:938   Mitchell, Kell F., Jr. "Diplomacy and Prejudice: The Morris-Shidehara Negotiations, 1920–1921." *Pacific Historical Review* 39 (February 1970): 85–104. The United States sought to coerce Japan under the guise of solving the difficulties plaguing Japanese immigration, discrimination, and restriction, problems that were secondary to a larger East Asian policy.

17:939   Miwa, Kimitada. "Japanese Images of War

with the United States." In *Mutual Images: Essays in American-Japanese Relations,* ed. Akira Iriye, 115–37. Cambridge, MA: Harvard University Press, 1975. The author finds the Japanese navy confident about a confrontation with the United States; the army saw Japan unprepared for war.

17:940   Morley, James W., ed. *Japan's Road to the Pacific War: Japan Erupts: The London Naval Conference and the Manchurian Incident, 1928–1932 (1984); The China Quagmire: Japan's Expansion on the Asian Continent, 1933–1941 (1983); Deterrent Diplomacy: Japan, Germany, and the USSR, 1935–1940 (1976); The Fateful Choice: Japan's Advance into Southeast Asia, 1939–1941 (1980); The Final Confrontation: Japan's Negotiations with the United States, 1941 (1994).* New York: Columbia University Press, 1976–1994. Fourteen Japanese historians using sources not hitherto available have recounted the foreign policies of Japan and the Japanese policies of other powers, with emphasis on military affairs and decisionmaking. They are published in seven volumes by Asahi Shimbun Sha in Tokyo under the title *Taiheiyo senso e no michi: kaisen gaiko-shi* [*The Road to the Pacific War: A Diplomatic History before the War*]. Excerpts from these volumes have been selected and translated under Morley's editorship.

17:941   Neumann, William L. "Franklin D. Roosevelt and Japan, 1913–1933." *Pacific Historical Review* 22 (May 1953): 143–53. Neumann suggests that Roosevelt's family commercial ties to China made him pro-Chinese and anti-Japanese, notwithstanding his efforts to recognize Japan's role in East Asia in the 1920s.

17:942   _____. *The Genesis of Pearl Harbor.* Philadelphia: Pacifist Research Bureau, 1945. Neumann, then a conscientious objector, offered the first critique of FDR's Pacific diplomacy ever made by a professional historian in this pamphlet. He claims that intelligent American conciliation could have avoided war.

17:943   Nish, Ian. *Alliance in Decline: A Study in Anglo-Japanese Relations, 1908–23.* The author denies any U.S.-British collusion over the termination of the Japanese-British alliance, but its demise opened the possibility of a fresh approach in Asia, deemed particularly crucial in light of China's growing nationalism (13:236).

17:944   Okihiro, Gary Y. *Cane Fires: The Anti-Japanese Movement in Hawaii, 1865–1945.* The author finds the seeds of Hawaii's martial law and suppression of the Japanese during World War II in a long-maintained exploitation of Japanese labor (9:470).

17:945   Paul, Rodman W. *The Abrogation of the Gentlemen's Agreement, Being the Harvard Phi Beta Kappa Prize Essay for 1936.* Cambridge, MA: The Society, 1936. The Immigration Act of 1924 was a turning point in Japanese-American relations, for it challenged Japanese self-esteem and produced long-remembered bitterness. Had there been no "grand disillusionment," Japanese officials might have been in a stronger position to resist antidemocratic pressures.

17:946   Sacki, Shoichi. "Images of the United States as a Hypothetical Enemy." The author finds Japanese writing about the United States becoming increasingly confrontational by the 1930s. Japan's authors saw the United States as gigantic but feeble, huge but fragile (13:242).

17:947   Smith, M. J. J. "F.D.R. and the Brussels Conference, 1937." *Michigan Academician* 14 (Fall 1981): 109–22. The author finds that FDR, confronted by Chamberlain's opposition to Japanese sanctions, acquiesced in the torpedoing of the Brussels conference, although he personally had sought collective action against Japan.

17:948   Spinks, C. N. "The Termination of the Anglo-Japanese Alliance." *Pacific Historical Review* 6 (December 1937): 321–40. The abrogation in 1921 of a treaty that had existed since 1902 resulted from assorted motives: American opposition to the alliance, strong Canadian support of the American position, and the postwar British desire to cut commitments.

17:949   Taylor, Sandra C. "The Ineffectual Voice: Japanese Missionaries and American Foreign Policy, 1870–1941." American domestic racism and Japanese aggression in Manchuria and China ruled out any missionary attempts to present an image of a peaceful, friendly Japan (9:573).

17:950   Toland, John. *The Rising Sun: The Decline and Fall of the Japanese Empire, 1936–1945.* New

York: Random House, 1970. Volume 1 is a most successful reconstruction of the enemy's mentality as disclosed in interviews with 500 Japanese military and civilian leaders. Pro-Japanese postures and exaggerated faultfinding with America are offset by an impressive philological analysis of Magic intercepts.

17:951   Utley, Jonathan G. "Japanese Exclusion for American Fisheries." *Pacific Northwest Quarterly* 65 (January 1974): 8–126. Utley shows how the State Department successfully thwarted pressures from domestic salmon fishermen to reach an accommodation with Japan.

17:952   Wheeler, Gerald E. "Isolated Japan: Anglo-American Diplomatic Cooperation, 1927–1936." *Pacific Historical Review* 20 (May 1961): 165–78. Wheeler examines Anglo-American diplomatic cooperation, first with the idea of preventing Japanese naval parity and then, after Japan in 1934 abrogated the Washington naval treaty, of drawing the English-speaking nations together on Asian affairs.

CHINA

17:953   Abend, Hallett. *My Life in China: 1926–1941.* New York: Harcourt, Brace and Company, 1943. These reminiscences of a *New York Times* correspondent portray the gradual development of the Chinese Nationalist regime and the expansion of Japanese power at China's expense.

17:954   Borg, Dorothy. *American Policy and the Chinese Revolution, 1925–1928.* New York: Macmillan Company, 1947. Kellogg's positive responses to Chiang Kai-shek (Jiang Jieshi) abetted the victory of the Nationalist Party. The secretary's diplomacy encouraged the Nationalists to avoid political extremes.

17:955   Breslin, Thomas A. *China, American Catholicism, and the Missionary.* University Park: Pennsylvania State University Press, 1980. Breslin sees the Roman Catholic Church in China long experiencing disintegration although World War II was the immediate cause of its collapse.

17:956   Butterfield, Fox. "A Missionary View of the Chinese Communists (1936–1939)." In *American Missionaries in China: Papers from Harvard Semi-*

nars, ed. Kwang-Ching Liu, 249–301. Cambridge, MA: East Asian Research Center, Harvard University, 1966. Focusing on Congregationalist missionaries, the author notes how they perceived the communists as coworkers in efforts to save the Chinese masses from poverty and oppression.

17:957   Clifford, Nicholas R. *Spoilt Children of Empire: Westerners in Shanghai and the Chinese Revolution of the 1920s.* Hanover, NH: Middlebury College Press, 1991. This work gives full coverage to American participation in Shanghai's international community, showing how Secretary Kellogg ignored U.S. minister John Van Antwerp MacMurray's pleas in 1927 that the United States match Britain in defending the area.

17:958   Clubb, O. Edmund. *Communism in China, as Reported from Hankow in 1932.* New York: Columbia University Press, 1968. This is a reprint of a report Clubb wrote while serving as vice-consul at Hankow. It is still most helpful on the origins of the communist movement from its split with the Kuomintang in 1927.

17:959   Cohen, Warren I. "America and the May Fourth Movement: The Response to Chinese Nationalism, 1917–1921." *Pacific Historical Review* 35 (Fall 1966): 83–100. Cohen shows the United States unsuccessful in its effort to befriend the burgeoning Chinese Nationalist movement, thereby inadvertently encouraging China to turn to the revolutionary Soviets for guidance.

17:960   _____. *The Chinese Connection: Roger S. Greene, Thomas W. Lamont, George E. Sokolsky and American–East Asian Relations.* New York: Columbia University Press, 1978. Cohen covers the activities of philanthropist Greene, banker Lamont, and journalist Sokolsky to show the intensification of the U.S. relationship with East Asia.

17:961   _____. "The Development of Chinese Communist Policy toward the United States, 1922–1933." *Orbis* 11 (Spring 1967): 219–37. The Chinese Communist Party concentrated its propaganda against Japan and England, the two powers with the greatest political, economic, and military stakes in China, rather than the United States. In late 1932, the CCP began to separate the United States from the other foreign powers as part of Stalin's search for allies against Japan.

17:962   Cole, Bernard D. *Gunboats and Marines: The United States Navy in China, 1925–1928.* Newark: University of Delaware Press, 1983. The Asiatic Fleet was responsible for protecting U.S. citizens and property in China. Despite limited resources and contradictory guidance, it performed ably during the most turbulent years of the Chinese revolution.

17:963   Dayer, Roberta Allbert. *Bankers and Diplomats in China, 1917–1925: The Anglo-American Relationship.* Totowa, NJ: F. Cass, 1981. Denying that the United States served as a beneficent protector of China during the 1920s, the author finds American leaders seeking to expand the nineteenth-century system of international control that had reduced China to semicolonial status.

17:964   Fairbank, John K., ed. *The Missionary Enterprise in China and America.* See chapter 2 of this Guide (2:235). See also Hutchison, *Errand to the World: American Protestant Thought and Foreign Missions* (1987) (7:424).

17:965   Flynt, Wayne, and Gerald W. Berkley. *Taking Christianity to China: Alabama Missionaries in the Middle Kingdom, 1850–1950.* As the missionaries found themselves increasingly secure, they abjured gunboat protection and supported Chiang's Nationalist political movement (9:539).

17:966   George, Brian T. "The State Department and Sun Yat-sen: American Policy and the Revolutionary Disintegration of China, 1920–1924." *Pacific Historical Review* 46 (August 1977): 387–408. Makers of American foreign policy came to see Sun not as a revolutionary and a nationalist, but as a troublemaker who retarded China's peaceful unification and political reform.

17:967   Graham, Gael. *Gender, Culture, and Christianity: American Protestant Mission Schools in China, 1880–1930.* New York: Peter Lang, 1995. The author shows how Americans used mission schools to alter the customs and gender beliefs of the Chinese.

17:968   Hoyt, Frederick B. "Americans in China and the Formation of American Policy, 1925–1937."

Ph.D. dissertation, University of Wisconsin, 1971. Hoyt covers the reaction of businessmen and missionaries, both Protestant and Roman Catholic, to the Chinese revolution. By 1937, missionaries were generally satisfied with new informal arrangements that bypassed older privileges. Diplomats considered bargaining away vestiges of extraterritoriality in return for placing U.S. traders in a more favorable economic position. For a sample of Hoyt's findings, see "The Open Door Leads to Reluctant Intervention: The Case of the Yangtse Rapid Steamship Company," *Diplomatic History* 1 (Spring 1977): 155–69.

17:969   _____. "Protection Implies Intervention: The U.S. Catholic Mission at Kanchow." *Historian* 38 (August 1976): 709–27. In 1928, as the communists advanced on Kanchow, the missionaries remained, seeking American diplomatic help, a move that forced the Nationalists to protect them.

17:970   _____. "The Summer of '30: American Policy and Chinese Communism." *Pacific Historical Review* 46 (May 1977): 229–49. During the summer the Chinese communists attacked major cities, threatening the lives and property of Americans. Hoyt argues that these events convinced American diplomats that the communists were "organized brigands."

17:971   Hunt, Michael H. "Pearl Buck—Popular Expert on China, 1931–1949." *Modern China* (January 1977): 33–64. Hunt finds the author of *The Good Earth* (New York: John Day Company, 1931) advancing a reductionist, sentimental picture of China that inadvertently reinforced American ethnocentrism. The article includes a full listing of Buck's writings on China.

17:972   Huskey, James L. "The Cosmopolitan Connection: Americans and Chinese in Shanghai during the Interwar Years." *Diplomatic History* 11 (Summer 1987): 227–42. Huskey shows how American businessmen and American-trained Chinese coordinated efforts to develop social, commercial, and intellectual bonds. For additional commentary by Charles R. Lilly and Michael H. Hunt, see 243–50.

17:973   Israel, Jerry. "Carl Crow, Edgar Snow, and Shifting American Journalistic Perceptions of China." In *America Views China: American Images of China Then and Now,* ed. Jonathan Goldstein,

Jerry Israel, and Hilary Conroy, 148–68. Bethlehem, PA: Lehigh University Press, 1991. Israel compares the left-leaning Snow to fellow midwestern journalist Carl Crow, who described a "treaty-port" China full of entrepreneurial people anxious for American goods.

17:974 _____. "Mao's 'Mr. America': Edgar Snow's Images of China." *Pacific Historical Review* 47 (February 1978): 107–22. Journalist Snow hoped to see America's democratic doctrines spread in China through aid, trade, and education. He feared Japanese domination of China and searched for an alternative, one that led him to see the communists in an increasingly sympathetic light.

17:975 Jespersen, T. Christopher. *American Images of China, 1931–1949.* Stanford, CA: Stanford University Press, 1996. Earlier parts of this book note the positive images of China conveyed by publisher Henry Luce and United China Relief. The UCR and Time, Inc. manipulated instruments of mass culture to serve American political and diplomatic ends by reinforcing notions about unique American opportunities in Asia. See also Jespersen's "'Spreading the American Dream' of China: United China Relief, the Luce Family, and the Creation of American Conceptions of China before Pearl Harbor," *Journal of American–East Asian Relations* 1 (Fall 1992): 269–94.

17:976 Keenan, Barry. *The Dewey Experiment in China: Educational Reform and Political Power in the Early Republic.* Cambridge, MA: Council on East Asian Studies, Harvard University, 1977. The study shows how educator John Dewey, who visited China in 1919–1921, exercised a temporary influence there.

17:977 Kessler, Lawrence D. *The Jiangyin Mission Station: An American Missionary Community in China, 1895–1951.* The author examines Jiangyin station in Shanghai, a project sponsored by First Presbyterian Church of Wilmington, North Carolina. Using the station to examine Chinese-American cultural interaction in the first half of the twentieth century, the author concludes that Chinese welcomed the Protestant missionary movement not because of its religious message but the secular benefits redounding from its presence (9:546).

17:978 Leary, William M., Jr. "Wings for China: The Jouett Mission, 1932–1935." *Pacific Historical*

Review 38 (November 1969): 447–62. Japanese bombing of China's cities in 1932 prompted the Chinese to seek aid in training its air force. While State and War Departments would not help, Commerce sent Colonel John H. Jouett, who trained 300 cadets and provided China with the nucleus of a modern air force.

17:979 Lian, Xi. *The Conversion of Missionaries: Liberalism in American Protestant Missions in China, 1907–1932.* In covering such missionaries as Edward H. Hume, Frank J. Rawlinson, and Pearl S. Buck, the author finds such liberal Protestants downplaying the uniqueness of Christianity (13:201).

17:980 Neils, Patricia, ed. *United States Attitudes and Policies toward China: The Impact of American Missionaries.* The book includes articles on editor Frank Rawlinson by John Rawlinson (111–32), social worker Ida Pruitt by Marjorie King (133–48), and the Maryknoll religious order by Jean-Paul Wiest (171–92) (9:550).

17:981 Pugach, Noel H. "Anglo-American Aircraft Competition and the China Arms Embargo, 1919–1921." *Diplomatic History* 2 (Summer 1978): 351–72. Pugach finds U.S.-British competition over aircraft sales only one of the many challenges to a well-intentioned embargo.

17:982 Rand, Peter. *China Hands: The Adventures and Ordeals of the American Journalists Who Joined Forces with the Great Chinese Revolution.* New York: Simon and Schuster, 1995. This book covers such journalists in China as Harold R. Isaacs, Edgar Snow, and Agnes Smedley, all of whom were sympathetic to the communists.

17:983 Schaller, Michael. "American Air Strategy in China, 1939–1941: The Origins of Clandestine Air Warfare." *American Quarterly* 28 (Spring 1976): 3–19. This article shows how influential American officials worked with quasi-private individuals and special interest groups to assist the Chinese Nationalists in their war against Japan. While seeking to create a deterrent, they in fact escalated the Japanese-American confrontation.

17:984 _____. *The U.S. Crusade in China, 1938–1945.* New York: Columbia University Press,

1979. In the pre–Pearl Harbor sections of this book, Schaller covers the economics of containing Japan, the relationship between U.S. aid and Chinese politics, and the clandestine air war involving U.S. fliers.

17:985   Shewmaker, Kenneth E. *Americans and Chinese Communists, 1927–1945: A Persuading Encounter.* Ithaca: Cornell University Press, 1971. This book traces the favorable views of Chinese communists presented by such travelers as Edgar and Helen Snow, Agnes Smedley, Evans F. Carlson, Anna Louise Strong, and Theodore H. White.

17:986   Smylie, Robert F. "John Leighton Stuart: A Missionary in the Sino-Japanese Conflict, 1937–1941." *Journal of Presbyterian History* 53 (Fall-Autumn 1975): 256–76. President of Yenching University, John Leighton Stuart possessed a unique outlook on China that made him an intermediary among the varying forces striving for dominance there. Because he was not a diplomat, however, Roosevelt paid little attention to him.

17:987   Stross, Randall E. *The Stubborn Earth: American Agriculturalists on Chinese Soil, 1898–1937.* The author notes how Americans were captivated by the vision that China could undergo a technological revolution in agriculture without making more fundamental political, social, and economic changes (13:215).

17:988   Sun, Youli. "Chinese Military Resistance and Changing American Perceptions, 1937–1938." In *On Cultural Ground: Essays in International History,* ed. Robert David Johnson, 81–96. Chicago: Imprint Publications, 1994. China's decision to fight Japan, "a world-class power," caused the United States to see China as fighting its own battle, abandoning acquiescence for confrontation.

17:989   Thomas, S. Bernard. *Season of High Adventure: Edgar Snow in China.* Berkeley: University of California Press, 1996. Thomas offers a detailed account of the American journalist whose *Red Star over China* (New York: Random House, 1938) did so much to publicize the Chinese communist movement.

17:990   Thomson, James C., Jr. *While China Faced West: American Responses in Nationalist China, 1928–1937.* Cambridge, MA: Harvard University Press, 1969. When Nanking announced the need for "relevant reforms," the call was answered by American specialists in education, monetary policy, bureaucratic management, flood control, and bridge construction. While certain improvements resulted, cultural differences led to many failures.

17:991   Tolley, Kemp. *Yangtze Patrol: The U.S. Navy in China.* Annapolis: Naval Institute Press, 1971. A prominent rear admiral ably captures the flavor of the most unconventional sea duty in the U.S. navy.

17:992   Valone, Stephen J. *"A Policy Calculated to Benefit China": The United States and the China Arms Embargo, 1919–1929.* Westport, CT: Greenwood Press, 1991. The multilateral arms embargo on China of May 1919 benefited the United States by thwarting Japan's hegemonic ambitions there. Washington's commitment to this cooperative policy waned as enforcement proved frustrating and as Americans returned to their policy of aloofness in international affairs.

17:993   Varg, Paul A. *Missionaries, Chinese, and Diplomats: The American Protestant Missionary Movement in China, 1890–1952.* Varg traces the Protestant missionary movement from the time of the Boxer Rebellion to the communist era. He finds it playing little role in determining U.S. policy (2:239).

17:994   Vincent, John Carter. *The Extraterritorial System in China: Final Phase.* Cambridge, MA: East Asian Research Center, Harvard University, 1970. A former State Department official describes the extent of the extraterritorial system. Topics include missionaries, taxation, education, and the foreign press.

17:995   Zhang, Xiaoming. "For China's Internal Stability: U.S. Arms Sales Policy, 1929–1936." *Journal of American–East Asian Relations* 2 (Fall 1993): 243–73. When the American government limited arms exports to the Chinese central government, it enabled the Nanjing regime to extend more effectively its control over the remaining portions of China.

SOUTHEAST ASIA

17:996   Aldrich, Richard J. *The Key to the South: Britain, the United States, and Thailand during the*

Approach of the Pacific War, 1929–1942. New York: Oxford University Press, 1993. The book notes how Thailand emerged as a crucial factor in the calculations of the United States, Britain, and France. Thailand itself was surprisingly influential, exploiting the value of its strategic location and its supposed ability to shape the policies of the powers.

17:997 Barclay, Glen St. J. "Singapore Strategy: The Role of the United States in Imperial Defense." *Military Affairs* 39 (April 1975): 54–59. The author notes that the British did not have a policy, much less a strategy, for defending the Pacific dominions. Hence, as war approached, they stressed the supposed protective power of the United States.

17:998 Hess, Gary R. *The United States' Emergence as a Southeast Asian Power, 1940–1950*. New York: Columbia University Press, 1987. Hess argues that Southeast Asia became crucial to the United States in 1940, for the Japanese movement to Indochina threatened to sever British access to resources to the south and west when they were just becoming essential to the European struggle.

17:999 Miller, Robert Hopkins. *The United States and Vietnam, 1787–1941*. Washington, DC: National Defense University Press, 1990. The author, an American diplomat, devotes a fourth of the book to the 1937–1941 crisis with Japan. Quoting extensively from diplomatic dispatches, he sees Indochina's progressive subjugation by Japan as triggering a major shift in Washington's strategic assessment.

17:1000 Reed, Peter M. "Standard Oil in Indonesia, 1898–1928." The activities of Standard Oil were unsuccessful until the State Department in the 1920s encouraged revision of Dutch petroleum policies (13:266).

PHILIPPINES

17:1001 Friend, Theodore. *Between Two Empires: The Ordeal of the Philippines, 1929–1946*. New Haven: Yale University Press, 1965. The author focuses on political independence for the Filipinos. Nevertheless, he gives attention to the commonwealth status between the wars and to the excitement caused by this short-term arrangement among Japan-

ese and Southeast Asian nationalists. See also Friend, "The Philippine Sugar Industry and the Politics of Independence, 1929–1935," *Journal of Asian Studies* 22 (February 1963): 179–82.

17:1002 Hayden, Joseph Ralston. *The Philippines: A Study in National Development*. New York: Macmillan Company, 1942. Here is a careful analysis of conditions, promising and discouraging, concerning Filipino capabilities for self-rule at the time of the Tydings-McDuffie Act of 1934. Hayden was vice-governor of the islands from 1933 to 1935.

17:1003 Kirk, Grayson L. *Philippine Independence: Motives, Problems, and Prospects*. New York: Farrar and Rinehart, 1936. Kirk claims that the islands were not ready for independence. The author was spokesman for a Filipino faction that included Manuel Quezon, who sought to delay American retirement from the islands.

17:1004 Smith, M. J. J. "Henry L. Stimson and the Philippines: American Withdrawal from Empire, 1931–1935." *Michigan Academician* 5 (Winter 1973): 335–48. This article stresses Stimson's persistent belief that the United States must retain the Philippines, which he saw as essential to preserving the open door in China and deterring Japanese aggression.

17:1005 Wheeler, Gerald E. "The Movement to Reverse Philippine Independence." *Pacific Historical Review* 33 (May 1964): 167–81. Wheeler shows President Quezon publicly pushing for accelerated independence while privately seeking dominion status.

17:1006 _____. "Republican Philippine Policy." *Pacific Historical Review* 28 (November 1959): 377–90. Wheeler shows the lack of harmony between Congress and the executive over the fate of the Philippines, as seen by Congress's overriding of Hoover's veto of the independence bill.

PACIFIC ISLANDS

17:1007 Ballendorf, Dirk Anthony. "Secrets without Substance: U.S. Intelligence in the Japanese Mandates, 1915–1935." *Journal of Pacific History* 19 (April 1984): 83–99. The article shows that the Office of Naval Intelligence could find no evidence of Japanese fortifications in Micronesia. The Japanese appeared secretive precisely because they had nothing to hide.

17:1008 Burns, Richard Dean. "Inspection of the Mandates, 1919–1941." *Pacific Historical Review* 37 (November 1968): 445–62. As a result of the peace settlement of 1919, the Japanese received the former German island groups—the Marianas, the Carolines, and the Marshalls. U.S. authorities were long convinced that the Japanese were violating their promise not to construct military installations, although Japan did not begin outright military construction until 1940.

17:1009 Maga, Timothy P. *Defending Paradise: The United States and Guam, 1898–1950.* New York: Garland Publishing, 1988. Both FDR and the U.S. navy saw Guam, considered indefensible, as expendable.

17:1010 _____. "Prelude to War? The United States, Japan, and the Yap Crisis, 1918–22." *Diplomatic History* 9 (Summer 1985): 215–31. Maga shows how a remote tropical island of little economic worth became a matter of intense controversy, as it could serve as a communications center, and how the conflict was resolved.

17:1011 McPoil, William D. "The Development and Defense of Wake Island, 1934–1941." *Prologue* 23 (Winter 1991): 360–66. From 1934 on, the navy saw Wake as expendable. To sustain attack, it needed three to four times the defense force and aircraft it was allotted.

17:1012 Megaw, M. Ruth. "The Scramble for the Pacific: Anglo–United States Rivalry in the 1930s." *Historical Studies* 17 (October 1977): 458–73. In tracing disputes over Canton and Enderbury Islands, Megaw finds the United States continually attempting to push Britain out of commercial opportunities. The islands had acquired a strategic importance in view of Pan American Airways' attempt to open routes between Hawaii and Australia and New Zealand. Agreement was finally reached in 1938 for fifty years of joint sovereignty over Canton and Enderbury.

17:1013 Young, Lowell T. "Franklin D. Roosevelt

and America's Islets: Acquisition of Territory in the Caribbean and in the Pacific." *Historian* 35 (February 1973): 205–20. FDR sought such islands and chains as Canton, Enderbury, Baker, Howland, Johnson, and Swan not because he coveted additional territory but because he sought naval bases and refueling stations.

Crises of the 1930s and Early 1940s

GENERAL

17:1014 Beard, Charles A. *President Roosevelt and the Coming of the War, 1941: A Study in Appearances and Realities.* New Haven: Yale University Press, 1948. In a highly publicized work, Beard finds the president vitiating democracy and violating his own pledges when he "maneuvered" the nation into the conflict. For a spirited defense of FDR, see Howard K. Beale, "The Professional Historian: His Theory and His Practice," *Pacific Historical Review* 22 (August 1953): 227–55.

17:1015 Carr, William. *Poland to Pearl Harbor: The Making of the Second World War.* Baltimore: Edward Arnold, 1985. The book gives more attention than most accounts of the coming of the war to American diplomacy. Carr argues that in the summer of 1941, a modus vivendi with Japan would have made excellent strategic sense but would have been politically suicidal and demoralized the allies.

17:1016 Churchill, Winston. *The Second World War. Vol. 1: The Gathering Storm. Vol. 2: Their Finest Hour. Vol. 3: The Grand Alliance.* 6 vols. Boston: Houghton Mifflin, 1948–1950. In the first three volumes of his six-volume war history, Churchill offers eloquent detail on British policy, including his increasing rapport with FDR. Caution is needed, however, for the author's recollections are colored by Britain's contemporary need, as he saw it, of a renewed U.S. alliance in the cold war.

17:1017 Cole, Wayne S. "What Might Have Been." *Chronicles: A Magazine of American Culture* 15 (December 1991): 20–22. Cole covers varied alternatives open to the United States in 1940–1941.

17:1018 Divine, Robert A. *The Reluctant Belligerent: American Entry into World War II.* 2d ed. New York: Wiley, 1979. Without condemning Roosevelt, Divine claims that his surrender of the initiative to Germany and Japan nearly permitted an Axis victory. First published in 1965. See also the first part of Divine's *Roosevelt and World War II* (1969) (18:280).

17:1019 Gregory, Ross. *America 1941: A Nation at the Crossroads.* New York: Free Press, 1988. Gregory shows the impact of the international crisis on wider American society.

17:1020 Heinrichs, Waldo H. "The United States Prepares for War." In *The Secrets of War: The Office of Strategic Services in World War II,* ed. George C. Chalou, 8–18. Washington, DC: National Archives and Records Administration, 1992. Heinrichs argues that the United States could hardly urge such allies as the Soviets to stand firm in Europe while it pursued appeasement in East Asia. At the same time, FDR sought to avoid war as long as possible, fearing the United States would be overextended.

17:1021 Ikle, Frank William. *German-Japanese Relations, 1936–1940.* New York: Bookman Associates, 1956. Though taking the dated view that anti-Americanism motivated the Japanese, the book remains useful for showing how internal and international realities contributed to, and in turn were affected by, the alliance.

17:1022 Kimball, Warren F. *Forged in War: Roosevelt, Churchill, and the Second World War.* New York: William Morrow, 1997. Kimball denied that in 1941 FDR sought full-scale participation in the European war, that is, commitment of ground troops. Nor did he want to fight the Japanese. Rather, he wanted "to gain victory and global political influence without paying the price."

17:1023 Meskill, Johanna Menzel. *Hitler & Japan: The Hollow Alliance.* New York: Atherton Press, 1966. Until this book's appearance, historians had slighted the content and significance of secret addenda to the Tripartite pact that diluted its automatic character, rendering it hollow from the beginning.

17:1024 Presseisen, Ernst L. *Germany and Japan: A Study in Totalitarian Diplomacy, 1933–1941.* The Hague: M. Nijhoff, 1958. A major study of the pact's origins, this book links the agreement to the origins of the contemporary destroyer-bases deal. It portrays Japan as motivated by fears of both Russia and America.

EUROPE

17:1025 Asher, Harvey. "Hitler's Decision to Declare War on the United States Revisited." *Society for Historians of American Foreign Relations Newsletter* 31 (September 2000): 2–20. Through thorough coverage of the secondary literature, the author speculates that Hitler's decision was based on psychological considerations—the belief that his destiny was in the hands of providence and that he needed to maintain feelings of invisibility.

17:1026 Bailey, Thomas A., and Paul B. Ryan. *Hitler vs. Roosevelt: The Undeclared Naval War.* New York: Free Press, 1979. This account of quasi hostilities (1939–1941) focuses on Roosevelt's efforts to assist the British in the delivery of supplies through the Nazi submarine blockade.

17:1027 Boyce, Robert. "World Depression, World War: Some Economic Origins of the Second World War." In *Paths to War: New Essays on the Origins of the Second World War,* ed. Robert Boyce and Esmonde M. Robertson, 55–95. New York: St. Martin's Press, 1989. The author claims that the increasing prosperity of the 1920s was not matched by increasing harmony among the powers. At best a kind of armed truce developed, which in the period 1929–1934 developed into a state of virtual war.

17:1028 Bratzel, John F., and Leslie B. Rout, Jr. "FDR and the 'Secret Map.'" *Wilson Quarterly* 9 (New Year's 1985): 167–73. The authors posit that the British doctored the "secret" German map flourished by FDR in October 1941 to prove Hitler's designs on the Western Hemisphere.

17:1029 Brinkley, Douglas, and David R. Facey-Crowther, eds. *The Atlantic Charter.* New York: St. Martin's Press, 1994. This collection contains the charter itself; Brinkley and Facey-Crowther, "Introduction: The Making of a Commemoration: The Atlantic Charter Fifty Years Later"; Theodore A. Wilson, "Commemorative Remarks at Placentia Bay, Newfoundland: The First Summit: FDR and the Riddle of Personal Diplomacy"; Gaddis Smith, "Roosevelt, the Sea, and International Security"; Lloyd C. Gardner, "The Atlantic Charter: Idea and Reality, 1942–1945"; Warren F. Kimball, "The Atlantic Charter: 'With All Deliberate Speed'"; J. L. Granatstein, "The Man Who Wasn't There: Mackenzie King, Canada, and the Atlantic Charter"; David Reynolds, "British Foreign Policy and the Churchill-Roosevelt Meeting of August 1941"; James Eayrs, "The Atlantic Charter and Its Charter: A Canadian's Reflections"; David Robinson, "An Eyewitness Account of the Atlantic Charter Meeting."

17:1030 Chester, Edward W. *The United States and Six Atlantic Outposts: The Military and Economic Considerations.* After describing the destroyer-bases deal, the author covers in turn the Bahamas, Jamaica, Iceland, the Azores, and Greenland (2:333).

17:1031 Clifford, J. Garry. "The Isolationist Context of American Foreign Policy toward the Soviet Union in 1940–1941." In *Soviet-U.S. Relations, 1933–1942*, ed. G. N. Sevost'ianov and Warren F. Kimball, 40–52. Moscow: Progress Publishers, 1989. The author finds FDR's cautious decision to aid the Soviet militarily in June 1941 rooted in his efforts to gain time for an American buildup.

17:1032 _____. "The Odyssey of the *City of Flint*." *American Neptune* 32 (April 1972): 100–16. Clifford tells of the German capture of an American merchant ship in October 1939, an event that created an international incident.

17:1033 Compton, James V. *The Swastika and the Eagle: Hitler, the United States, and the Origins of World War II.* Boston: Houghton Mifflin, 1967. Compton concludes that German views of the United States were contradictory and confused. Only some professional German diplomats took it seriously. The author denies Hitler had a plan to invade the United States when the war began though his ambitions would have led to aggression.

17:1034 Dawson, Raymond H. *The Decision to Aid Russia, 1941: Foreign Policy and Domestic Politics.*

Chapel Hill: University of North Carolina Press, 1959. Roosevelt believed that the existing military situation warranted support for the Russians. Dawson examines the tactics used by the administration to gain approval from Congress and the public.

17:1035 Dobson, Alan P. *US Wartime Aid to Britain, 1940–1946.* New York: St. Martin's Press, 1986. This study finds lend-lease more magnanimous in conception than in execution.

17:1036 Douglas, Roy. *New Alliances, 1940–41.* New York: St. Martin's Press, 1982. In tracing what would soon be called the Grand Alliance, the author sees the British and Americans offering the Soviets too many concessions.

17:1037 Farnham, Barbara Rearden. *Roosevelt and the Munich Crisis: A Study of Political Decision-Making.* Princeton: Princeton University Press, 1997. This book challenges claims that FDR was either a tacit isolationist or a drifting opportunist. The president long sought to restrain aggressor nations by mutual disarmament, economic boycott, and—at the time of Munich—a defensive blockade.

17:1038 Friedländer, Saul. *Prelude to Downfall: Hitler and the United States, 1939–41.* Translated by Aline B. Werth and Alexander Werth. New York: Alfred A. Knopf, 1967. Friedländer denies that Hitler was so blinded by his hatred of the United States not to fear its intervention. The whole of Hitler's policy points to his full awareness of America's importance in the event of a long war.

17:1039 Goodhart, Philip. *Fifty Ships That Saved the World: The Foundation of the Anglo-American Alliance.* Garden City, NY: Doubleday, 1965. FDR transferred fifty aging destroyers to Britain in return for the lease of bases in the Caribbean and Newfoundland. Churchill overestimated the importance of the ships and Roosevelt oversold the significance of the bases. See also Daniel S. Greenberg, "U.S. Destroyers for British Bases—Fifty Old Ships Go to War," *U.S. Naval Institute Proceedings* 88 (November 1962): 70–83, and William H. Langenberg, "Destroyers for Naval Bases: Highlights of an Unprecedented Trade," *Naval War College Review* 22 (September 1970): 80–92.

17:1040 Haglund, David G. "George C. Marshall and the Question of Military Aid to England, May-June 1940." *Journal of Contemporary History* 15 (October 1980): 745–60. In May-June 1940, the Roosevelt administration saw Britain as finished.

17:1041 Haight, John McVickar, Jr. *American Aid to France, 1938–1940.* New York: Atheneum, 1970. This study shows how the Roosevelt-Morgenthau policy helped to prepare the American aircraft industry for later years. See also Haight's "France's First War Mission to the United States," *Airpower History* 11 (January 1964): 11–15, and "Roosevelt as Friend of France," *Foreign Affairs* 44 (April 1966): 518–26.

17:1042 Hearden, Patrick J. *Roosevelt Confronts Hitler: America's Entry into World War II.* DeKalb: Northern Illinois University Press, 1987. Hearden sees U.S. involvement rooted in fears that American leaders were primarily concerned about the menace a triumphant Germany would present to the U.S. free enterprise system.

17:1043 Heinrichs, Waldo H. "FDR and the Entry into World War II." *Prologue* 26 (Fall 1994): 719–35. This article traces the options facing FDR, including the dilemma he faced in spring and early summer of 1941.

17:1044 _____. "President Franklin D. Roosevelt's Intervention in the Battle of the Atlantic, 1941." *Diplomatic History* 10 (Fall 1986): 311–32. Heinrichs sees Roosevelt as a cautious, stubborn nationalist, responding to what he perceived as immediate, powerful threats to America's physical safety.

17:1045 _____. *Threshold of War: Franklin D. Roosevelt and American Entry into World War II.* New York: Oxford University Press, 1988. Challenging those historians who find FDR too vacillating, the author portrays him as an active and purposeful policymaker. Roosevelt's concern with maintaining the Russian front lay at the center of a world strategy bent on preventing Hitler from world domination.

17:1046 Herwig, Holger H. "Miscalculated Risks: The German Declaration of War against the United States, 1917 and 1941." *Naval War College Review* 3 (August 1986): 88–100. A German historian finds Hitler's declaration of war defying all tenets of realpolitik.

17:1047 Hillgruber, Andreas. *Germany and the Two World Wars.* Translated by William C. Kirby. Cambridge, MA: Harvard University Press, 1981. A prominent German historian finds Hitler's declaration of war on the United States a tacit admission that he no longer controlled the direction of the war.

17:1048 Kimball, Warren F. *The Most Unsordid Act: Lend-Lease, 1939–1941.* Baltimore: Johns Hopkins Press, 1969. This first-rate account of the origins of lend-lease shows FDR at his best as politician and diplomatist but does not spare criticism of the president's tactics. The United States imposed its own terms in framing its alliance with the British, who were forced to come "hat in hand" to the Americans for goods needed to continue the war effort. See also Kimball, "'Beggar My Neighbor': America and the British Interim Finance Crisis, 1940–1941," *Journal of Economic History* 29 (December 1969): 758–72.

17:1049 Langenberg, William H. "Destroyers for Naval Bases: Highlights of an Unprecedented Trade." *Naval War College Review* 22 (September 1970): 80–92. Langenberg traces the maneuvers of Roosevelt and Churchill during the summer of 1940.

17:1050 Langer, John D. "The Harriman-Beaverbrook Mission and the Debate over Unconditional Aid for the Soviet Union, 1941." *Journal of Contemporary History* 14 (July 1979): 463–82. The article offers a tacit defense of American and British aid to the Soviets.

17:1051 Lash, Joseph P. *Roosevelt and Churchill, 1939–1941: The Partnership That Saved the West.* New York: Norton, 1976. Lash puts together a fascinating if not altogether convincing picture of the president consciously leading the nation to intervention, in the process tracing the evolution of Anglo-American cooperation from hesitant beginnings to firm alliance.

17:1052 Leutze, James R., ed. *The London Journal of General Raymond E. Lee, 1940–1941.* Boston: Little, Brown, 1971. The book offers an unmatched view of Britain under siege as seen by a high-ranking U.S. military attaché. Foreword by Dean Acheson.

17:1053 Lindley, William R. "The Atlantic Charter: Press Release or Historic Document?" *Journalism Quarterly* 41 (Summer 1964): 375–79, 394. This essay explores how a press release became one of the important declarations of modern political history.

17:1054 Offner, Arnold A. "Influence without Responsibility: American Statecraft and the Munich Conference." In *Appeasing Fascism: Articles from the Wayne State University Conference on Munich after Fifty Years,* ed. Melvin Small and Otto Feinstein, 51–72. Lanham, MD: University Press of America, 1991. The author finds FDR weak and vacillating, being surrounded by anticommunist conservatives in the State Department.

17:1055 Reynolds, David. "Churchill and the British 'Decision' to Fight On in 1940: Right Policy, Wrong Reasons." In *Diplomacy and Intelligence during the Second World War: Essays in Honor of F. H. Hinsley,* ed. Richard Langhorne, 147–67. New York: Cambridge University Press, 1985. Churchill was not only mistaken in believing the German economy possessed no slack; he assumed imminent American belligerency when the United States showed no apparent readiness to declare war.

17:1056 Shogan, Robert. *Hard Bargain: How FDR Twisted Churchill's Arm, Evaded the Law, and Changed the Role of the American Presidency.* New York: Scribner, 1995. This book argues that American policy elites skirted the law to cement a bargain that shortchanged the British while setting the United States on the road to war.

17:1057 Small, Melvin. *Was War Necessary? National Security and U.S. Entry into War.* The author finds Germany lacking technical capacity in 1941 to invade the Western Hemisphere. He concedes that a victorious Axis would have developed adequate attack facilities within twenty years (2:251).

17:1058 Smith, Kevin. *Conflict over Convoys: Anglo-American Logistics Diplomacy in the Second World War.* New York: Cambridge University Press, 1996. As the British were logistically dependent upon U.S. allocations of merchantmen, Churchill placed the British war effort at the mercy of American decisions concerning shipbuilding and allocations.

17:1059 Sobel, Robert. *The Origins of Interventionism: The United States and the Russo-Finnish War.* New York: Bookman Associates, 1961. Sobel notes

how the Russo-Finnish war undermined many isolationist arguments, including the claim that the origin of modern war was basically economic and that the United States could stay aloof if it severed trade with belligerents.

17:1060 Thompson, John A. "Another Look at the Downfall of 'Fortress America.'" *Journal of American Studies* 26 (December 1992): 393–408. Thompson denies that the United States was forced into war out of the need for self-defense. Rather, it was motivated by the belief that it alone stood between Hitler and victory.

17:1061 Trefousse, Hans L. *Germany and American Neutrality, 1939–1941.* New York: Bookman Associates, 1951. Hitler sought to keep Germany "neutral" in relations with the United States, at least until the end of the Russian campaign, constraining his navy's hopes to confront the ever more belligerent American patrol policies. By the time American negotiations with Japan reached an impasse, he realized that he had to support Japan or lose it as an ally. See also Trefousse's "Germany and Pearl Harbor," *Far Eastern Quarterly* 11 (February 1951): 35–50.

17:1062 Troy, Thomas F. *Wild Bill and Intrepid: Donovan, Stephenson, and the Origin of the CIA.* New Haven: Yale University Press, 1996. The author finds U.S. and British intelligence working in tandem.

17:1063 Watt, Donald Cameron. *How War Came: The Immediate Origins of the Second World War, 1938–1939.* New York: Pantheon Books, 1989. In a major multiarchival work, Watt portrays Roosevelt continually falling victim to his own secretiveness, distrust, and a self-confidence bordering on arrogance.

17:1064 Weinberg, Gerhard L. "Why Hitler Declared War on the United States." *MHQ: The Quarterly Journal of Military History* 4 (Spring 1992): 18–23. Weinberg argues that Germany was eager to fight the United States provided only that Japan took the plunge. For an update, see Weinberg, "Pearl Harbor: The German Perspective," in his *Germany, Hitler, and World War II: Essays in Modern German and World History* (1995), 195–204. See also Weinberg's "Germany's Declaration of War on the United States: A New Look," in Hans L. Trefousse, ed., *Germany and America: Essays on Problems of Interna-*

tional Relations and Immigration (New York: Brooklyn College Press, 1980), 54–70.

17:1065 Wilson, Theodore A. *The First Summit: Roosevelt and Churchill at Placentia Bay, 1941.* Lawrence: University Press of Kansas, 1991. Wilson uses materials recently released from the Public Record Office to shatter what he calls "the Churchillian paradigm," that is, the assertion that the prime minister and the president shared a unique friendship devoid of all differences. The informal meeting's significance transcended any concrete agreements made, which were of limited importance and soon modified by the demands of war. In an extensively rewritten account, Wilson offers fresh material on the British decision to reinforce the Middle East, FDR's belief in "the strategic bombing arsenal of democracy" role for the United States, the president's apathy toward production priorities, and bureaucratic rivalries in the State and War Departments. First published in 1969.

17:1066 Zahniser, Marvin R. "Rethinking the Significance of Disaster: The United States and the Fall of France in 1940." *International History Review* 14 (May 1992): 252–76. The author calls on historians to stress the radical shift in global power relations engendered by France's fall.

ASIA AND THE PACIFIC

17:1067 Adams, Frederick C. "The Road to Pearl Harbor: A Reexamination of American Far Eastern Policy, July 1937–December 1938." *Journal of American History* 58 (June 1971): 73–92. America's initial response to the China incident is shown to have anticipated subsequent policies toward Japan, particularly after July 1941. The United States moved for the first time to preserve the open door; the Export-Import Bank provided credit to China; armed intervention was contemplated.

17:1068 Anderson, Irvine H. "The 1941 de Facto Embargo on Oil to Japan: A Bureaucratic Reflex." *Pacific Historical Review* 44 (May 1975): 201–31. Notable for its insights into the background of Pearl Harbor and the dynamics of federal bureaucracy, this article finds the U.S. freeze of Japanese assets in July 1941 compatible with continued oil shipments until a monthlong administrative tangle turned the freeze into a total embargo.

17:1069 Barnhart, Michael A. *Japan Prepares for Total War: The Search for Economic Security, 1919–1941.* Ithaca: Cornell University Press, 1987. Japan's drive for autarchy in continental Asia ironically increased its dependence upon the United States for scrap iron, copper, machine tools, and oil. The U.S. freezing orders of July 25, 1941, backfired on the United States, for Japan had not yet resolved its debate over advancing into Southeast Asia, and the U.S. action pushed it further toward aggression.

17:1070 _____. "Japanese Intelligence before the Second World War: 'Best Case' Analysis." In *Knowing One's Enemies: Intelligence Assessment before the Two World Wars,* ed. Ernest R. May, 424–55. Princeton: Princeton University Press, 1984. The article describes the woeful state of Japanese intelligence. In 1941, Japan assumed Germany would not be defeated, Britain would surrender or sue for peace terms, the Soviets would be crushed or badly drained, and American public opinion would force its leaders to give up.

17:1071 Ben-Zvi, Abraham. *The Illusion of Deterrence: The Roosevelt Presidency and the Origins of the Pacific War.* Boulder: Westview Press, 1987. This book, departing from revisionist-internationalist simplicities, offers a typology of policymakers based on three belief systems: globalist-realists (Stimson, Morgenthau, Hornbeck), globalist-idealists (Hull), and nationalist-pragmatists (Roosevelt, Grew, and the military). See also Ben-Zvi's "American Preconceptions and Policies toward Japan, 1940–1941: A Case Study in Misperception," *International Studies Quarterly* 19 (June 1975): 228–48.

17:1072 Borg, Dorothy, and Shumpei Okamoto, with Dale K. A. Finlayson, eds. *Pearl Harbor as History: Japanese-American Relations, 1931–1941.* New York: Columbia University Press, 1973. These essays, written by twenty-seven Japanese and American scholars who met in Lake Kawaguchu, Japan, in 1969, focus on decisionmaking processes within the respective foreign policy elites and on other comparable institutions, such as the press and private agencies. Several of the essays are separately annotated in this chapter.

17:1073 Boyle, John H. "The Drought-Walsh Mission to Japan." *Pacific Historical Review* 34 (May 1965): 141–61. This intriguing essay recounts amateur diplomatic efforts made in late 1940 and early 1941 by two American Roman Catholic priests. The attempt was briefly taken seriously in Roosevelt's circles, who misinterpreted Japan's official policies.

17:1074 Brune, Lester H. "Considerations of Force in Cordell Hull's Diplomacy, July 26 to November 26, 1941." *Diplomatic History* 2 (Fall 1978): 389–405. By rejecting proposal B on November 26, Hull assumed a hard line against Japan that contradicted the U.S. hesitation in rearming and preparing to defend the Philippines.

17:1075 Butow, Robert J. C. "Backdoor Diplomacy in the Pacific: The Proposal for a Konoye-Roosevelt Meeting, 1941." *Journal of American History* 59 (June 1972): 48–72. Long said to have foundered through bad timing and the realities of Japanese militarism; the controversial idea of a Japanese-American summit also collapsed because of the activities—unbeknown to Grew and Konoye—of amateur diplomats.

17:1076 _____. "The Hull-Nomura Conversations: A Fundamental Misconception." *American Historical Review* 65 (July 1960): 822–36. This article focuses on the quiet diplomatic dialogue in Washington initiated by two Roman Catholic priests of the Maryknoll order. They conveyed informal proposals that misled the Americans on how much Japan was ready to compromise with the United States, thereby contributing to further mistrust between the two nations.

17:1077 _____. *The John Doe Associates: Backdoor Diplomacy for Peace, 1941.* Stanford, CA: Stanford University Press, 1974. This book tells the story of the secret, and in the end, damaging efforts of Father James Drought and James E. Walsh, banker Wikawa Tadeo, and Colonel Iwakuro Hideo to avert a Pacific war in the spring of 1941.

17:1078 Conroy, Hilary, and Harry Wray, eds. *Pearl Harbor Reexamined: Prologue to the Pacific War.* Honolulu: University of Hawaii Press, 1990. Seventeen contributors offer sometimes quite brief chapters on various subjects, including Wray, "Japanese-American Relations and Perceptions, 1900–1940";

Akira Iriye, "U.S. Policy toward Japan before World War II"; Gary Dean Best, "Franklin Delano Roosevelt, the New Deal, and Japan"; Hosoya Chihiro, "Miscalculations in Deterrent Policy: U.S.-Japanese Relations, 1938–1941"; Jonathan G. Utley, "Cordell Hull and the Diplomacy of Inflexibility"; Tsunoda Jun, "On the So-Called Hull-Nomura Negotiations"; Conroy, "Ambassador Nomura and His 'John Doe Associates': Pre–Pearl Harbor Diplomacy Revisited"; Norman A. Graebner, "Nomura in Washington: Conversations in Lieu of Diplomacy"; Alvin D. Coox, "Repulsing the Pearl Harbor Revisionists: The State of Present Literature on the Debacle"; David Klein and Conroy, "Churchill, Roosevelt, and the Chinese Question in Pre–Pearl Harbor Diplomacy"; and Waldo H. Heinrichs, "The Russian Factor in Japanese-American Relations, 1941."

17:1079 Current, Richard N. "How Stimson Meant to 'Maneuver' the Japanese." *Mississippi Valley Historical Review* 40 (June 1953): 67–74. Stimson's troublesome diary entry of November 25, 1941 ("the question was how we should maneuver them into the position of firing the first shot"), is placed in the context of marshaling American support for resistance to Japanese moves in Southeast Asia.

17:1080 Eismeier, Dana L. "U.S. Oil Policy, Japan, and the Coming of War in the Pacific, 1940–1941." *Michigan Academician* 14 (Spring 1982): 359–67. The author finds oil diplomacy allowing FDR to control the degree of U.S. involvement in the war until it could make a viable military commitment to the allied cause.

17:1081 Esthus, Raymond A. "President Roosevelt's Commitment to Britain to Intervene in a Pacific War." *Mississippi Valley Historical Review* 50 (June 1963): 28–38. This article clarifies American assurances to Britain, given on December 1, 1941, regarding joint military action against Japan in cases not involving American territory. Roosevelt's generosity hedged on preventive moves by Britain and assumed the necessity of prior congressional consent.

17:1082 Feis, Herbert. *The Road to Pearl Harbor: The Coming of the War between the United States and Japan.* Princeton: Princeton University Press, 1950. This moderately pro-Roosevelt volume perceives a progression of separation, hostility, enmity, and war; delineates the motives of Japan's Southeast Asia program; and argues that the abortive summit, not subsequent "demands," terminated an era of negotiation.

17:1083 _____. "War Came at Pearl Harbor: Suspicions Considered." *Yale Review* 45 (Spring 1956): 378–90. A former State Department official defends the Roosevelt administration for entering into the ABC1 agreement of March 1941, levying economic sanctions on Japan, rejecting Premier Konoye's bid for a summit, and turning down Japanese proposals of that November.

17:1084 Hill, Norman. "Was There an Ultimatum before Pearl Harbor?" *American Journal of International Law* 42 (April 1948): 355–67. The Japanese note of November 20, 1941, and the American note of November 26, 1941, are compared to other historic ultimata. Neither constituted an ultimatum as defined in international law, as neither was a communication threatening war.

17:1085 Hsü, Immanuel C. Y. "Kurusu's Mission to the United States and the Abortive Modus Vivendi." *Journal of Modern History* 24 (September 1952): 301–7. This article repudiates the popular view of the special envoy's last-minute dispatch to Washington as a camouflage for military preparations, for these had already been completed.

17:1086 Iguchi, Haruo. "An Unfinished Dream: Yoshisuke Ayukawa's Economic Diplomacy toward the U.S., 1937–1940." *Journal of American and Canadian Studies (Tokyo)* 16 (1998): 21–47. This article shows the efforts of Ayukawa, president of the Manchurian Industrial Development Corporation and founder of the Nissan conglomerate, to bring American capital into Manchukuo. Ayukawa negotiated through intermediaries with American financiers and industrialists, only to find his efforts often frustrated by the increasing international tension.

17:1087 Ike, Nobutaka, ed. *Japan's Decision for War: Records of the 1941 Policy Conferences.* Stanford, CA: Stanford University Press, 1967. This translation of Japanese Liaison and Imperial Conference notes by the Japanese army's chief of staff discloses extreme rigidity, unanimity about the New Order, and the risk taking that thwarted deterrence strategies.

17:1088 Lowe, Peter. *Great Britain and the Origins of the Pacific War: A Study of British Policy in East Asia, 1937–1941.* Oxford: Clarendon Press, 1977. This study examines British policy toward the approach of war in the Pacific, contains much information about the common Anglo-American underestimation of Japan and preoccupation with Europe, and notes Britain's reliance on the United States, except where appeasement of Japan seemed likely to save its empire.

17:1089 Lu, David J. *From the Marco Polo Bridge to Pearl Harbor: Japan's Entry into World War II.* Washington, DC: Public Affairs Press, 1961. This older work on Japanese expansionism is important for portraying Matsuoka as a consistent moderate. It also anticipates the more recent focus on the anti-Soviet rather than anti-American nature of the Tripartite pact. Foreword by Herbert Feis.

17:1090 Marks, Frederick W., III. "Facade and Failure: The Hull-Nomura Talks of 1941." *Presidential Studies Quarterly* 15 (Winter 1985): 99–112. Marks defends the Walsh-Drought mission and is critical of Hull. FDR's diplomatic methods at best frustrated the normal process of communication and at worst violated fair dealing.

17:1091 _____. "The Origin of FDR's Promise to Support Britain Militarily in the Far East—A New Look." *Pacific Historical Review* 53 (November 1984): 447–62. Under pressure from Churchill, FDR made the equivalent of a formal military guarantee to Britain in the fall of 1940, just after the British reopening of the Burma Road. Otherwise, he feared, the British could capitulate to Japan's New Order.

17:1092 Moore, Frederick. *With Japan's Leaders: An Intimate Record of Fourteen Years as Counselor to the Japanese Government, Ending December 7, 1941.* New York: C. Scribner's Sons, 1942. An adviser on international affairs in the Japanese Foreign Office and in the Japanese embassy in Washington, the author describes chronologically and anecdotally the diplomacy that failed. He vigorously defends the diplomacy of Ambassador Nomura.

17:1093 Morley, James W., ed. *Deterrent Diplomacy: Japan, Germany, and the USSR, 1935–1940.* New York: Columbia University Press, 1976. These excerpts from *Taiheiyo senso e no michi* [*The Road to* the Pacific War] deal with Japan's use of alliance diplomacy (1935–1940), particularly toward Germany and the Soviet Union. Chihiro Hosoya, "The Tripartite Pact, 1939–1940," sees the Japanese desiring to deter war but mistakenly strengthening the forces for aggression and stiffening the resolve of the Americans. The other translated essays are T. Ohata, "The Anti-Comintern Pact, 1935–1939," and I. Hata, "The Japanese-Soviet Confrontation, 1935–1939" (17:940).

17:1094 Morton, Louis. "The Japanese Decision for War." *U.S. Naval Institute Proceedings* 80 (December 1954): 1325–35. Morton carefully reconstructs the Japanese rationale for decisions made in the fall of 1941. He portrays Japanese leaders as assuming that the United States would negotiate for peace rather than pursue a long and costly war in East Asia. See also Morton, "Japan's Decision for War," in Greenfield, *Command Decisions* (1960), 63–88.

17:1095 Richardson, James L. *Crisis Diplomacy: The Great Powers since the Mid-Nineteenth Century.* The author faults the United States in 1941 for not exploiting Japan's fears of a Pacific war or making sufficient efforts to avert it (9:150).

17:1096 Sagan, Scott D. "The Origins of the Pacific War." *Journal of Interdisciplinary History* 18 (Spring 1988): 893–922. The author sees the Pacific war originating from two sources: Japan's desire to expand in Southeast Asia while deterring U.S. support of the European colonial powers and the U.S. attempt to deter this expansion without provoking a war. He is critical of FDR's total embargo against Japan, warning that a desperate nation can launch a disastrous war. See also Sagan's article by the same title in Robert I. Rotberg and Theodore K. Rabb, eds., *The Origin and Prevention of Major Wars* (New York: Cambridge University Press, 1989), 323–52.

17:1097 Schroeder, Paul W. *The Axis Alliance and Japanese-American Relations, 1941.* Ithaca: Cornell University Press, 1958. Schroeder examines the role played by the Tripartite Alliance in Japanese-American negotiations, including the misunderstood "fact" that Japan hoped the agreement would prevent war while giving her a free hand in Asia. U.S. diplomats are indicted for being obstinate in their demands for Japanese evacuation from China.

17:1098 Smith, Bradley F. *The Ultra-Magic Deals and the Most Secret Special Relationship, 1940–1946.* Novato, CA: Presidio, 1993. The book traces the growing cryptanalytic partnership between the United States and Britain.

17:1099 Smith, M. J. J. "'Renovationists' and 'Warhawks': The Japanese-American Diplomatic Crisis of 1940." *Michigan Academician* 16 (Winter 1984): 145–56. Smith finds both Japanese and American diplomats avoiding a candid analysis of motive and substituting force for reason. The Tripartite pact destroyed the last best chance for limiting the conflict to Europe, containing the dual menace of Nazi and Soviet imperialism, and averting the Great East Asia war.

17:1100 Sun, Youli. *China and the Origins of the Pacific War, 1931–1941.* New York: St. Martin's Press, 1993. This work traces the increasing U.S. involvement in the Sino-Japanese war, which the author finds rooted in the American desire to preserve the open door.

17:1101 Togo, Shigenori. *The Cause of Japan.* Translated by Teogeo Fumihiko and Ben Bruce Blakeney. New York: Simon and Schuster, 1956. In a prison memoir, the foreign minister of Japan at the time of Pearl Harbor chronicles the negotiations of the Tojo cabinet with America, including his own efforts. He argues that military officers, not civilian officials, initiated and supervised the war.

17:1102 Utley, Jonathan G. *Going to War with Japan, 1937–1941.* Knoxville: University of Tennessee Press, 1985. The author finds American policy increasingly determined by a powerful bureaucracy that eventually brought about the economic warfare that led to hostilities. This bureaucracy was less concerned with defending China or preserving treaties than promoting a "liberal commercial" world order. See also Utley's "Upstairs, Downstairs at Foggy Bottom: Oil Exports and Japan, 1940–41," *Prologue* 8 (Spring 1976): 17–28, and "Diplomacy in a Democracy: The United States and Japan, 1937–1941," *World Affairs* 193 (Fall 1976): 130–40.

17:1103 Worth, Roland H., Jr. *Secret Allies in the Pacific: Covert Intelligence and Code Breaking Cooperation between the United States, Great Britain,* and *Other Nations prior to the Attack on Pearl Harbor.* Jefferson, NC: McFarland, 2001. This book covers the nature of British-American intelligence cooperation, dealing with the creation and evolution of the relationship and finding the level of cooperation much greater than had been thought.

Pearl Harbor

17:1104 Barnhart, Michael A. "Planning the Pearl Harbor Attack: A Study in Military Politics." *Aerospace Historian* 29 (December 1982): 246–52. When the Japanese army demanded that its southward advance begin with an assault on Malaya, the Japanese navy insisted that a simultaneous attack could wipe out the American fleet at Pearl Harbor.

17:1105 Beach, Edward L. *Scapegoats: A Defense of Kimmel and Short at Pearl Harbor.* Annapolis: Naval Institute Press, 1995. A prominent naval writer denies Roosevelt engineered the Pearl Harbor attack but also argues that the military commanders in Hawaii were not derelict in their duty.

17:1106 Bratzel, John F., and Leslie B. Rout, Jr. "Pearl Harbor, Microdots, and J. Edgar Hoover." *American Historical Review* 87 (December 1982): 1342–51. Because of bureaucratic rivalries, FBI chief J. Edgar Hoover did not transmit vital military information to military intelligence. Involved was the full text of intelligence data secured from German double agent Dusko Popov about enemy interest in Pearl Harbor.

17:1107 Burtness, Paul S., and Warren U. Ober. "Secretary Stimson and the First Pearl Harbor Investigation." *Australian Journal of Politics and History* 14 (April 1968): 24–36. This article reviews the activities of Stimson before, during, and after the Roberts Commission's hearings. It sees him influencing findings to minimize army responsibility.

17:1108 Butow, Robert J. C. "Marching off to War on the Wrong Foot: The Final Note Tokyo Did Not Send to Washington." *Pacific Historical Review* 63 (February 1994): 67–79. Butow notes the discovery of an unsent Japanese message to the United States dated December 7 that clearly specified that a state of war existed between the two nations.

17:1109 Clausen, Henry C., and Bruce Lee. *Pearl Harbor: Final Judgment.* New York: Crown, 1992. Clausen, a prosecutor in the Pearl Harbor case, offers the traditional view that Kimmel and Short were derelict in their duty.

17:1110 Coox, Alvin D. "The Pearl Harbor Raid Revisited." *Journal of American–East Asian Relations* 3 (Fall 1994): 211–27. A prominent military historian draws on personal interviews in reconstructing Admiral Yamamoto's attack plans.

17:1111 Farago, Ladislas. *The Broken Seal: The Story of Operation Magic and the Pearl Harbor Disaster.* New York: Random House, 1967. The book is a necessary if overdramatized account of American and Japanese codebreaking operations between 1921 and 1941.

17:1112 Ferrell, Robert H. "Pearl Harbor and the Revisionists." *Historian* 17 (Spring 1955): 215–33. This is a considered response to revisionism as summarized in Barnes, *Perpetual War for Perpetual Peace: A Critical Examination of the Foreign Policy of Franklin Delano Roosevelt and Its Aftermath* (1953) (17:54). Ferrell concludes that military errors, while not matters of deliberate diplomatic planning, abounded at Pearl Harbor.

17:1113 Harris, James Russell. "Admiral Kimmel and Pearl Harbor: Heritage, Perception, and the Perils of Calculation." *Filson Club Historical Quarterly* 68 (July 1994): 379–417. The author finds Kimmel a dedicated, aggressive naval officer eager to confront Japan but victim to ambivalent warnings from Washington and to his own tactical orthodoxy.

17:1114 Harris, Ruth R. "The 'Magic' Leak of 1941 and Japanese-American Relations." *Pacific Historical Review* 50 (February 1981): 77–96. In the spring of 1941, the Axis learned that the United States had penetrated Japan's diplomatic codes. Hence, by that fall, the United States was unaware of subsequent shifts in Japanese policy.

17:1115 Hata, Ikuhiko. "Going to War: Who Delayed the Final Note?" *Journal of American–East Asian Relations* 3 (Fall 1994): 229–47. Hata finds the Japanese foreign ministry itself bearing some responsibility, for the United States did not receive Japan's announcement that diplomatic relations were broken off until after the Pearl Harbor attack.

17:1116 Herde, Peter. *Pearl Harbor, 7 December 1941: Der Ausbruch des Krieges zwischen Japan und den Vereinigten Staaten und die Ausweitung des europaischen Krieges zum Zweiten Weltkrieg [Pearl Harbor, December 7, 1941: The Outbreak of the War between Japan and the United States and the Widening of the European War into the Second World War].* Darmstadt: Wissenschaftliche Buchgesellschaft, 1980. Drawing on exhaustive multiarchival research, this book traces in painstaking detail the global developments that led to the outbreak of war in the Pacific.

17:1117 Kimmel, Husband Edward. *Admiral Kimmel's Story.* Chicago: H. Regnery Co., 1955. This self-exoneration, written in the vogue of revisionist literature, emphasizes the administration's withholding of Magic intercepts from the area commanders.

17:1118 Komatsu, Keiichiro. *Origins of the Pacific War and the Importance of "Magic."* New York: St. Martin's Press, 1999. This book focuses on Magic, the system the United States used in decoding Japanese diplomatic messages in the months before the Pearl Harbor attack. Because of mistranslations, the United States could well have based crucial decisions on incorrect assumptions. Similarly, Japanese policymakers consistently misinterpreted American policies.

17:1119 Layton, Edwin T., with Roger Pineau and John Costello. *"And I Was There": Pearl Harbor and Midway—Breaking the Secrets.* New York: William Morrow, 1985. Admiral Layton, the staff officer responsible for keeping Admiral Kimmel informed about Japanese potential and objectives, points to incompetence in Washington.

17:1120 Lewin, Ronald. *The American Magic: Codes, Ciphers, and the Defeat of Japan.* New York: Farrar Straus Giroux, 1982. Lewin shows how American intelligence succeeded in penetrating Japanese codes. He finds blind inefficiency on the part of all American leaders concerned with protecting Pearl Harbor.

17:1121 Love, Robert W., Jr., ed. *Pearl Harbor Revisited.* New York: St. Martin's Press, 1995. Among the articles in this anthology are essays by Donald

Cameron Watt showing the relationship between the Asian and European wars (1–12), Frederick W. Marks, III, faulting FDR for adopting Stimson's moralistic policies toward Japan while failing to build his navy to treaty strength (37–59), Stephen E. Ambrose portraying Roosevelt as taking great risks with national security because of his unwillingness or inability to rouse the nation to an all-out effort against Germany (93–102), Waldo H. Heinrichs connecting the Pacific and Russian situations (103–9), Jon Bridgman describing Roosevelt's moves the day before Pearl Harbor (143–71), and Robert W. Love, Jr. critiquing FDR's failures as commander in chief (173–91).

17:1122 Melosi, Martin V. *The Shadow of Pearl Harbor: Political Controversy over the Surprise Attack, 1941–1946.* College Station: Texas A&M University Press, 1977. This study analyzes the domestic political repercussions of the Pearl Harbor attack during and immediately after World War II. The issue became the focus of excessive partisanship by both parties, with the Democratic administration attempting a "mutated cover-up." See also the author's "National Security Misused: The Aftermath of Pearl Harbor," *Prologue* 9 (Summer 1977): 75–89.

17:1123 Mueller, John E. "Pearl Harbor: Military Inconvenience, Political Disaster." *International Security* 16 (Winter 1991–1992): 172–203. Japanese torpedoes did little military damage, as many of the destroyed ships and planes were obsolete and others quickly repaired or replaced. Politically the attack was a disaster, for the United States was forced into a long Asian war when a less costly policy of containment might have been more successful.

17:1124 Prange, Gordon W., with Donald M. Goldstein and Katherine V. Dillon. *At Dawn We Slept: The Untold Story of Pearl Harbor.* New York: McGraw-Hill, 1981. Based on lifelong research into the Pearl Harbor controversy by the chief of the Historical Section under General MacArthur, this book exhaustively covers the preparations for the attack and the failure of the United States to prevent it. Prange strongly blames Japanese militarism for the aggression in China, expansion into Southeast Asia, and decision to fight the United States.

17:1125 _____. *Dec. 7, 1941: The Day the Japanese Attacked Pearl Harbor.* New York: McGraw-

Hill, 1988. This book presents a moment-by-moment account of the "day that will live in infamy."

17:1126 _____. *Pearl Harbor: The Verdict of History.* New York: McGraw-Hill Book Co., 1986. This book, a sequel to *At Dawn We Slept: The Untold Story of Pearl Harbor* (1981) (17:1124), systematically covers the culpability of the American people, the Congress, and the nation's civilian and military leadership.

17:1127 Richardson, James O. *On the Treadmill to Pearl Harbor: The Memoirs of Admiral James O. Richardson as Told to George C. Dyer.* Washington, DC: Naval History Division, Dept. of the Navy, 1973. The man who was commander in chief, Pacific Fleet, at the outset of 1941 devotes considerable attention to the disagreement with FDR that caused him to be relieved. Richardson argued that, for practical rather than strategic reasons, the fleet should be retained on the Pacific coast rather than deployed to Pearl Harbor.

17:1128 Rusbridger, James, and Eric Nave. *Betrayal at Pearl Harbor: How Churchill Lured Roosevelt into World War II.* New York: Summit Books, 1991. The authors advance the highly debatable thesis that Churchill, who—they claim—possessed foreknowledge of the Pearl Harbor attack, deliberately kept the United States in the dark to drag it into a war to defend Britain's Asian interests.

17:1129 Slackman, Michael. *Target—Pearl Harbor.* Honolulu: University of Hawaii Press, 1990. This book covers the prelude to the attack, the status of Japanese-Americans in Hawaii, American efforts to find the Japanese strike force, repair of the sunken ships, and the intensive scholarly debate over ultimate responsibility.

17:1130 Stephan, John J. *Hawaii under the Rising Sun: Japan's Plans for Conquest after Pearl Harbor.* Honolulu: University Press of Hawaii, 1984. The author shows how the Japanese military prepared for invasion while civilians focused on restructuring the Hawaiian economy, reforming its society, and laying the basis for a new political administration.

17:1131 Theobald, Robert A. *The Final Secret of Pearl Harbor: The Washington Contribution to the Japanese Attack.* New York: Devin-Adair, 1954. This memoir of a senior officer at Pearl Harbor emphasizes Washington's failure to disclose to area commanders full data about the hardening of U.S. relations with Japan. Forewords by Husband E. Kimmel and William F. Halsey.

17:1132 Toland, John. *Infamy: Pearl Harbor and Its Aftermath.* Garden City, NY: Doubleday, 1982. In a much publicized work, the author advances the dubious claim that Roosevelt and his inner circle possessed foreknowledge of the Pearl Harbor attack.

17:1133 Trefousse, Hans L. *Pearl Harbor, The Continuing Controversy.* Malabar, FL: Krieger, 1982. Trefousse offers an able defense of the Roosevelt administration together with selected documents. One should also see his *What Happened at Pearl Harbor: Documents Pertaining to the Japanese Attack of December 7, 1941, and Its Aftermath* (New York: Twayne Publishers, 1958).

17:1134 U.S. Congress, 79th Cong., 1st Sess. Joint Committee on the Investigation of the Pearl Harbor Attack. *Investigation of the Pearl Harbor Attack.* Washington, DC: Government Printing Office, 1946. This one-volume summary of thirty-nine parts includes both the report of the Democratic majority, which placed primary responsibility on the Japanese and the Hawaiian commanders, and the minority Republican report, which allocates far more responsibility to Washington officialdom.

17:1135 _____. *Pearl Harbor Attack: Hearings before the Joint Committee on the Investigation of the Pearl Harbor Attack.* 39 vols. Washington, DC: Government Printing Office, 1946. This massive compilation of documents and testimony includes not only the congressional hearings held from November 15, 1945, through May 23, 1946, but the wartime investigations of the Roberts Commission, Hart inquiry, Navy Board of Inquiry, Clarke investigation, Clausen investigation, and the Hewitt inquiry.

17:1136 Wohlstetter, Roberta. *Pearl Harbor: Warning and Decision.* Stanford, CA: Stanford University Press, 1962. This examination of the American failure to predict the Pearl Harbor attack emphasizes the limits of intelligence operations in terms of perception and communication. This work remains definitive on the limitations of intelligence operations at Pearl Harbor.

U.S. Armed Forces and Strategy

GENERAL

17:1137 Brune, Lester H. *The Origins of American National Security Policy: Sea Power, Air Power, and Foreign Policy, 1900–1941*. The author focuses on the evolution of naval and air doctrines. Because of inadequate military and political cooperation in the interwar years, the nation lacked national security plans integrating elements of force and diplomacy (13:85).

17:1138 Clodfelter, Mark. "Pinpointing Devastation: American Air Campaign Planning before Pearl Harbor." *Journal of Military History* 58 (January 1994): 75–101. All air planners believed that airpower could singlehandedly achieve victory by destroying the enemy's will to resist. They therefore stressed strategic bombing over tactical support for land and sea forces.

17:1139 Coletta, Paolo E. "Prelude to War: Japan, the United States, and the Aircraft Carrier, 1919–1945." *Prologue* 23 (Winter 1991): 342–59. Until the Pearl Harbor attack, both the United States and Japan saw carriers as merely supportive weapons; battleships would be the crucial instrument in engagements that would resemble Jutland.

17:1140 Conn, Stetson. "Changing Concepts of National Defense in the United States, 1937–1947." *Military Affairs* 28 (July 1964): 1–7. Conn traces the evolution of American policy from defending U.S. territory only to waging limited war.

17:1141 Dorwart, Jeffery M. *Conflict of Duty: The U.S. Navy's Intelligence Dilemma, 1919–1945*. Annapolis: Naval Institute Press, 1983. The author notes the twin missions of providing intelligence on foreign naval capabilities and domestic political surveillance.

17:1142 Fagan, George V. "F.D.R. and Naval Limitation." *U.S. Naval Institute Proceedings* 81 (April 1955): 411–18. Fagan sees FDR as championing naval preparedness as he backed the Vinson Trammel Act of 1934 and the Vinson Naval Act of 1938.

17:1143 Greene, Fred. "The Military View of National Policy, 1904–1940." *American Historical Review* 66 (January 1961): 354–77. The article finds military leaders lacking guidance from civilian policymakers on national policy and having to make policies on their own. During the interwar period U.S. army planners sought complete withdrawal from the western Pacific while their naval counterparts wanted a strong American presence.

17:1144 Griffith, Robert K. *Men Wanted for the U.S. Army: America's Experience with an All-Volunteer Army between the World Wars*. Westport, CT: Greenwood Press, 1982. The author shows the huge impoverishment endured by the U.S. army in the 1920s and 1930s. Though the National Defense Act of 1920 allowed for an all-volunteer army, congressional budget cutting hampered the military at every turn.

17:1145 Hammond, Paul Y. *Organizing for Defense: The American Military Establishment in the Twentieth Century*. Princeton: Princeton University Press, 1961. The book includes material on the Senate naval affairs investigation of 1920, the origins of airpower unification, and relations between the secretary of war and the Joint Chiefs of Staff.

17:1146 Kennedy, Greg C. "Depression and Security: Aspects Influencing the United States Navy during the Hoover Administration." *Diplomacy & Statecraft* 6 (July 1995): 342–72. Challenging accusations that President Hoover failed to give the U.S. navy necessary support, Kennedy argues that, though well aware of the realities of military power, he was limited in what he could do by technological change, budgetary restraints, and the lack of national will.

17:1147 Koistinen, Paul A. C. "The 'Industrial-Military Complex' in Historical Perspective: The Interwar Years." *Journal of American History* 56 (March 1970): 819–39. The author argues that the postwar military-industry complex originated in the close relations between the military and their suppliers in the interwar period, to which FDR's War Resources Board gave additional impetus.

17:1148 Leutze, James R. *Bargaining for Supremacy: Anglo-American Naval Collaboration, 1937–1941.* Chapel Hill: University of North Carolina Press, 1977. Leutze finds the Europe-first strategy of FDR aiming at supplanting Britain as the major Atlantic power. Roosevelt sought a U.S. navy "second to none."

17:1149 _____. "Technology and Bargaining in Anglo-American Naval Relations, 1938–1946." *U.S. Naval Institute Proceedings* 103 (June 1977): 50–66. Between 1938 and 1946, the United States and Britain exchanged a great deal of technical information, although there were people on both sides who did not fully accept the arrangements. It was not until early 1941, when President Roosevelt signed the Lend-Lease Act, that a more open and extensive exchange began.

17:1150 Levine, Robert H. *The Politics of American Naval Rearmament, 1930–1938.* New York: Garland Publishing, 1988. Until 1937, the navy sought to justify rearmament as a mechanism for relief from the Great Depression. After that date it could take advantage of an increasingly ominous situation overseas.

17:1151 Major, John. "The Navy Plans for War, 1937–1941." In *In Peace and War: Interpretations of American Naval History, 1775–1978,* 2d ed., ed. Kenneth J. Hagan, 237–62. Westport, CT: Greenwood Press, 1984. As World War II broke out, the navy was increasingly bold in the Atlantic, cautious in the Pacific.

17:1152 McKercher, Brian J. C. "No Eternal Friends or Enemies: British Defence Policy and the Problem of the United States, 1919–1939." *Canadian Journal of History/Annales canadiennes d'histoire* 28 (April 1993): 258–93. During the 1920s, Britain saw the United States as a potential naval rival but in the 1930s as an important adjunct to its own defense planning.

17:1153 Meilinger, Philip S. "Proselytiser and Prophet: Alexander P. de Seversky and American Airpower." *Journal of Strategic Studies* 18 (March 1995): 7–36. Meilinger traces the career of the Rus-

sian-born aviator, industrialist, and major in the U.S. air corps reserve who, contrary to legend, was less a military theorist than popularizer and synthesizer. See also Meilinger, "Alexander P. de Seversky," in Meilinger, ed., *The Paths of Heaven: The Evolution of Airpower Theory* (Maxwell Air Force Base, AL: Air University Press, 1997), 239–78.

17:1154 Murfett, Malcolm H. "'Are We Ready?' The Development of American and British Naval Strategy, 1922–39." In *Maritime Strategy and the Balance of Power: Britain and America in the Twentieth Century,* ed. John B. Hattendorf and Robert S. Jordan, 214–42. New York: St. Martin's Press, 1989. Compared to ad hoc British plans, those of the United States were more centralized, detailed, and systematic.

17:1155 _____. *Fool-Proof Relations: The Search for Anglo-American Naval Cooperation during the Chamberlain Years, 1937–1940.* Singapore: Singapore University Press, 1984. This study shows how British-American naval cooperation took place even before Churchill's rise to the prime ministership.

17:1156 O'Brien, Phillips Payson. *British and American Naval Power: Politics and Policy, 1900–1936.* Realizing that the United States could not be bluffed into accepting inferiority, Britain between 1919 and 1939 recognized the Americans as naval equals (11:107).

17:1157 Roskill, Stephen. *Naval Policy between the Wars.* 2 vols. New York: Walker, 1968–1976. The official historian for British naval policy during World War II offers much material on Anglo-American rivalry in the 1920s, including details on the hesitant efforts at cooperation under Franklin D. Roosevelt and on the timidity of British naval planners in Europe and the Mediterranean.

17:1158 Rossi, John P. "'World Wide Wireless': The U.S. Navy, Big Business, Technology, and Radio Communications, 1919–22." In *Naval History: The Seventh Symposium of the U.S. Naval Academy,* ed. William B. Cogar, with Patricia Sine, 170–85. Wilmington, DE: Scholarly Resources, 1988. To develop a global radio communications system to serve security and commercial needs, the Navy Department cooperated closely with corporate interests, as manifested by the formation of the Radio Corporation of America.

17:1159 Schaffer, Ronald. "General Stanley D. Embick: Military Dissenter." *Military Affairs* 37 (October 1973): 89–95. Although almost unknown outside the military establishment, in the 1920s and 1930s Embick was the foremost advocate of limiting the U.S. defense perimeter.

17:1160 Sherry, Michael S. *The Rise of American Air Power: The Creation of Armageddon.* New Haven: Yale University Press, 1987. This book shows the emergence of the doctrine of strategic bombing, indicating its popularity among both isolationists and interventionists before the United States entered the war.

17:1161 Spector, Ronald H. "The Military Effectiveness of the US Armed Forces, 1919–39." In *Military Effectiveness. Vol. 2: The Interwar Period,* ed. Allan R. Millett and Williamson Murray, 70–77. Boston: Allen and Unwin, 1988. Spector finds the U.S. armed forces obligated to function in a hostile political environment and hence lacking the financial, industrial, and human resources needed to carry out anticipated wartime missions.

17:1162 Stoler, Mark A. "From Continentalism to Globalism: General Stanley D. Embick, the Joint Strategic Survey Committee, and the Military View of American National Policy during the Second World War." *Diplomatic History* 6 (Summer 1982): 303–21. Stoler shows how a top aide of General Marshall could remain a strong isolationist.

17:1163 Underwood, Jeffery S. *The Wings of Democracy: The Influence of Air Power on the Roosevelt Administration, 1933–1941.* College Station: Texas A&M University Press, 1991. The book stresses how the army air corps, by abandoning the confrontational tactics of General William ("Billy") Mitchell, convinced FDR and the General Staff to back airpower strongly.

17:1164 Watson, Mark Skinner. *Chief of Staff: Prewar Plans and Preparations.* Washington, DC: Historical Division, Department of the Army, 1950. One of the volumes in the series United States Army in World War II, this book treats General Marshall's response to America's unreadiness for war during the

1930s to 1941. It covers changes in American policy on the defense of the Philippines and the appointment of MacArthur to the Far Eastern command.

17:1165 Weigley, Russell F. "The Interwar Army, 1919–1941." In *Against All Enemies: Interpretations of American Military History from Colonial Times to the Present,* ed. Kenneth J. Hagan and William R. Roberts, 257–77. Westport, CT: Greenwood Press, 1986. The author sees the U.S. army partially prepared for full mobilization during the interwar years.

17:1166 Wilson, John. "The Quaker and the Sword: Herbert Hoover's Relations with the Military." *Military Affairs* 38 (April 1974): 41–47. The author sees Hoover as hindering the development of a stronger, more modernized national defense.

EUROPE AND ASIA

17:1167 Braisted, William Reynolds. "On the American Red and Red-Orange Plans, 1919–1939." In *Naval Warfare in the Twentieth Century, 1900–1945: Essays in Honor of Arthur Marder,* ed. Gerald Jordan, 167–85. New York: Crane Russak, 1977. After outlining the Red and Orange Plans, which present Britain and Japan, respectively, as enemies, the author notes the increasing U.S. naval concentration on Orange and sees the strategic thinking put to valuable use in World War II.

17:1168 Kahn, David. "The United States Views Germany and Japan in 1941." In *Knowing One's Enemies: Intelligence Assessment before the Two World Wars,* ed. Ernest R. May, 476–501. Princeton: Princeton University Press, 1985. Kahn finds the United States overestimating Japan's strength and underrating that of Japan, a failure rooted in a widespread disregard for military intelligence.

EUROPE

17:1169 Bell, Christopher M. "Thinking the Unthinkable: British and American Naval Strategies for an Anglo-American War, 1918–1931." *International History Review* 19 (November 1997): 789–808. According to contingency plans concerning a British-American war, the United States based its strategy on an overland invasion of Canada. In turn, the British would send a battle fleet across the ocean.

17:1170 Manson, Janet M. *Diplomatic Ramifications of Unrestricted Submarine Warfare, 1939–1941.* New York: Greenwood Press, 1990. The author sees similarities in the decisions by Britain, Germany, and the United States to implement unrestricted submarine warfare.

17:1171 Morton, Louis. "Germany First: The Basic Concept of Allied Strategy in World War II." In *Command Decisions,* ed. U.S. Department of the Army, Office of Military History, 3–38. New York: Harcourt, Brace, 1959. Morton traces the development of war plans Rainbow 5 and ABC-1.

ASIA AND THE PACIFIC

17:1172 Doyle, Michael K. "The U.S. Navy and War Plan Orange, 1933–1940: Making Necessity a Virtue." *Naval War College Review* 33 (May-June 1980): 49–63. The article argues that the Orange Plan was a device to preserve as many alternatives as possible in an uncertain world, not a document rigidly prescribing behavior in a given situation.

17:1173 LaPlante, John B. "The Evolution of Pacific Policy and Strategic Planning: June 1940–July 1941." *Naval War College Review* 25 (May 1973): 57–72. The author finds careful integration of political and military processes lacking.

17:1174 Linn, Brian McAllister. *Guardians of Empire: The U.S. Army and the Pacific, 1902–1940.* Contrary to the popular view, the U.S. army early recognized the danger from Japan, some officers foreseeing the events of 1941 with uncanny accuracy. Preparations, however, were stymied by inadequate manpower and resources, changes in weaponry and tactics, low budgets, public and political indifference, and professional rivalries (13:282).

17:1175 Miller, Edward S. *War Plan Orange: The U.S. Strategy to Defeat Japan, 1897–1945.* This work, challenging the claim that the pre–World War II navy was obsessed with battleships and defensive thinking, stresses the vision of farsighted leaders who devised an offensive strategy to defeat Japan (13:234).

17:1176 Morison, Samuel Eliot. *The Rising Sun in the Pacific, 1931–April 1942.* Boston: Little, Brown, 1948. This volume of the well-known multivolume *History of United States Naval Operations in World War II* (1947–1962) (18:207) provides general information about the American-Japanese naval rivalry before December 7, 1941.

17:1177 Morton, Louis. "Army and Marines on the China Station: A Study in Military and Political Rivalry." *Pacific Historical Review* 29 (February 1960): 51–73. Morton describes the futile efforts of the American army in China to bring the marines under its command and to shake State Department control.

17:1178 _____. "War Plan Orange: Evolution of a Strategy." *World Politics* 11 (January 1959): 221–50. The U.S. navy maintained a contingency plan for war until the late 1930s, the Orange Plan, which envisioned fleet battles in the western Pacific. Such a plan was considered necessary for defense of the Philippines.

17:1179 Noble, Dennis L. *The Eagle and the Dragon: The United States Military in China, 1901–1937.* This book describes the social conditions under which American armed forces served in China from the Boxer Rebellion to the China Incident of 1937. The author denies that these forces were continually engaged in landings under fire; usually a display of flag and force sufficed (13:207).

17:1180 Pratt, Lawrence. "The Anglo-American Naval Conversations on the Far East of January 1938." *International Affairs* 47 (October 1971): 745–63. Although unwilling to make general commitments to Britain for joint action against Japan, FDR saw the need for joint planning with the British navy in the event of a two-ocean war.

17:1181 Roberts, Stephen S. "The Decline of the Overseas Station Fleets: The United States Asiatic Fleet and the Shanghai Crisis, 1932." *American Neptune* 37 (July 1977): 185–202. The Japanese assault on Shanghai in January 1932 demonstrated the weakness of western station fleets in the face of a major naval conflagration. Roberts notes the disagreements between the U.S. Asiatic Fleet commander, Admiral Montgomery Meigs Taylor, and Secretary Stimson.

17:1182 Tuleja, Thaddeus V. *Statesmen and Admirals: Quest for a Far Eastern Naval Policy.* New York: Norton, 1963. In this account of American naval policy in the Pacific in the Hoover and Roosevelt administrations, Tuleja shows conflicting positions within the naval service. Disarmament policies in the 1920s reduced the possibility of using the navy to support East Asian policy.

17:1183 Wheeler, Gerald E. *Prelude to Pearl Harbor: The United States Navy and the Far East, 1921–1931.* Columbia: University of Missouri Press, 1963. Wheeler carries forward the themes of Braisted's *The United States Navy in the Pacific, 1897–1909* (1958) (13:83) and *The United States Navy in the Pacific, 1909–1922* (1971) (13:84). Wheeler's book is less detailed in exploring the intricacies of naval policy where policy meets diplomacy but has greater details on ships and naval organization.

17:1184 _____. "The United States Navy and War in the Pacific, 1919–1941." *World Affairs Quarterly* 30 (October 1959): 199–225. This article reviews the vicissitudes of American naval construction between the wars. The article's main contributions, however, lie in the elaboration of naval strategy toward the Philippines and Hawaii and estimate of naval influence upon American East Asian policy.

Preparation for War

17:1185 Clifford, J. Garry. "A Connecticut Colonel's Candid Conversation with the Wrong Commander-in-Chief." *Connecticut History* 28 (November 1988): 25–38. This article shows the pessimism of intelligence staffer Colonel Truman Smith as U.S. entry into World War II approached.

17:1186 Clifford, J. Garry, and Samuel R. Spencer, Jr. *The First Peacetime Draft.* Lawrence: University Press of Kansas, 1986. The study finds conscription the result of the "Plattsburger" group within the "Eastern Establishment." FDR kept hands off while the army preoccupied itself with hemispheric defense.

17:1187 Dunne, Gerald T. *Grenville Clark, Public Citizen.* New York: Farrar, Straus, Giroux, 1986. This book offers the biography of the figure most instrumental in framing the Selective Training and Service Act of 1940.

17:1188 Flynn, George Q. *Lewis B. Hershey, Mr. Selective Service.* Chapel Hill: University of North Carolina Press, 1985. The author finds surprising isolationism in the selective service director.

17:1189 Gough, Terrence J. "Soldiers, Businessmen, and U.S. Industrial Mobilization Planning between the World Wars." *War & Society* 9 (May 1991): 68–98. Despite two decades of planning that involved businessmen, the army was not fully prepared to work in harmony with industry as the United States began World War II mobilization. Officers distrusted the commercial ethic, which industrialists felt army men did not comprehend.

17:1190 Harrington, Daniel F. "A Careless Hope: American Air Power and Japan, 1941." *Pacific Historical Review* 48 (May 1979): 217–38. In the four months before Japan declared war, the administration exhibited quixotic hopes about the acceleration of U.S. airpower in the Philippines.

17:1191 Kirkpatrick, Charles Edward. *An Unknown Future and a Doubtful Present: Writing the Victory Plan of 1941.* Washington, DC: Center of Military History, United States Army, 1990. Drafted by Major Albert C. Wedemeyer, the plan embodied an acute meshing of political and military aims and an appreciation of U.S. economic power.

17:1192 Koistinen, Paul A. C. *The Hammer and the Sword.* New York: Arno Press, 1979. This reprint of the author's 1965 thesis, focusing on the development of American planning for economic mobilization in war, finds that FDR never created the powerful mobilization agency necessary to direct such vital matters as procurement, production, labor relations, and civilian and military manpower. In such vital concerns as munitions production, business would remain in control.

17:1193 _____. *Planning War, Pursuing Peace: The Political Economy of American Warfare, 1920–1939.* Lawrence: University Press of Kansas, 1998. Koistinen examines preparations for economic mobilization by military and industrial elites, then covers congressional investigations that focused on the emerging military-business partnership.

17:1194 Lowenthal, Mark M. *Leadership and Indecision: American War Planning and Policy Process, 1937–1942.* 2 vols. New York: Garland Publishing, 1988. The author finds FDR unwilling to make the precise, definite decisions needed to execute fundamental policy, making life difficult for anyone trying to plan grand strategy. See also the author's "Roosevelt and the Coming of the Second World War: The Search for United States Policy, 1937–42," *Journal of Contemporary History* 16 (July 1981): 413–40.

17:1195 O'Sullivan, John. *From Voluntarism to Conscription: Congress and Selective Service, 1940–1945.* New York: Garland Publishing, 1982. The book focuses on the debates of 1940–1941.

17:1196 Ross, Steven T., ed. *American War Plans, 1919–1941. Vol. 1: Peacetime War Plans, 1919–* *1935. Vol. 2: Plans for War against the British Empire and Japan: The Red, Orange, and Red-Orange Plans, 1923–1938. Vol. 3: Plans to Meet the Axis Threat, 1939–1940. Vol. 4: Coalition War Plans and Hemispheric Defense Plans, 1940–1941. Vol. 5: Plans for Global War: Rainbow-5 and the Victory Program, 1941.* New York: Garland Publishing, 1992. Ross offers facsimiles of the major U.S. war plans, including Plan Dog, contingency plans for the occupation of Martinique and Guadeloupe, and Rainbow 5. A shortened version is found in his *American War Plans, 1939–1945* (Portland, OR: Frank Cass, 1995). See also Maurice Matloff, "Prewar Military Plans and Preparations, 1939–1941," *U.S. Naval Institute Proceedings* 79 (July 1953): 741–48.

17:1197 Watson, Mark Skinner. "First Vigorous Steps in Re-arming, 1938–39." *Military Affairs* 12 (Summer 1948): 65–78. Watson describes FDR's initial steps in his national rearmament program.

18

The United States and Wartime Diplomacy, 1941–1945

Contributing Editor

MARK A. STOLER
University of Vermont

Contributor

STEPHEN LOFGREN
Center for Military History

With the Assistance of

JAMES HEINES
University of Vermont

Contents

933

The United States and Wartime Diplomacy, 1941–1945

Introduction

The first problem facing the editor in compiling this chapter was the sheer volume of World War II literature. It was already enormous when the first edition of this guide appeared in 1983. Since then it has increased prodigiously, fueled by the fiftieth anniversary of the war, the aging and passing of the World War II generation, contemporary controversies over specific wartime events, and continuing documentary revelations—most notably but far from exclusively in the intelligence field, where the resulting literature is large enough to fill this entire chapter. So is the enormous recent literature in the fields of social and cultural history for the World War II years.

Another and related problem is the unavoidable overlap between diplomatic, domestic, and military events and issues during the war years. World War II was a total war in which these components were not neatly segregated. It was also a war the United States fought as a member of a coalition, to which it contributed material supplies as well as military personnel. Consequently, such aspects of the war as industrial productivity, strategy making, and coalition military operations have to be included in any chapter on wartime diplomacy.

Including all of the vast literature on these subjects published in the last two decades would not have been possible even if all the material from the relevant first edition chapters could have been deleted. But most of that material remains important enough to be retained, especially the numerous official histories, document collections, and memoirs of key individuals.

Consequently, the contents of this chapter only scratch the surface of the material now available, especially in regard to domestic issues, and do not include many foreign-language sources. For this very reason, the chapter does include a large number of the numerous published bibliographies now available; these are listed in the bibliographic, historiographic, and specific topical sections of the chapter, and should be consulted for additional citations. It also contains special sections on strategy and operations, allied interactions, major wartime and postwar issues, U.S. and allied relations with other countries, and the Axis surrender. Each of these has been divided into subsections, some of which overlap in terms of coverage. The reader is advised to consult more than one of them as appropriate.

The guiding principle in all selections has been to include both classic and recent important works on each aspect of a broadly defined U.S. wartime diplomacy, to the extent possible given space limitations.

Published Primary Materials

GUIDES

18:1 *The Cumulated Index to the U.S. Department of State Papers Relating to the Foreign Relations of the United States, 1939–1945.* 2 vols. Millwood, NY: Kraus International Publications, 1980. These volumes organize the separate indexes in the fifty-seven annual volumes of this series into one alphabetical arrangement.

18:2 *Diplomatic Records: A Select Catalogue of National Archives Microfilm Publications.* Washington, DC: National Archives Trust Fund Board, National Archives and Records Administration, 1986. The microfilm publications are listed in four categories: by record group, decimal file (1910–1963), country or area, and numerically. The record group category also contains a subheading for records of the World War II and postwar periods. These microfilm publications are distributed by Scholarly Resources, which also issues periodic announcements of new collections that have been added to the available list since 1986.

18:3 Blanc, Brigitte, Henry Rousso, and Chantal de Tourtier-Bonazzi, eds. *La Seconde Guerre Mondiale, Guide des sources conservées en France 1939–1945 [The Second World War: Guide to Sources Preserved in France, 1939–1945].* Paris: Direction des Archives de France, Archives Nationales, 1994. This guide catalogs the official collections of government ministries held in the National Archives in Paris, the French Overseas Archives, and other important holdings. Although the descriptions of the collections are not detailed, this will be an essential starting point for those planning archival research about France in World War II.

18:4   Cantwell, John D., ed. *The Second World War: A Guide to Documents in the Public Record Office.* London: Her Majesty's Stationery Office, 1993. This guide when first published (1972) was prepared to accompany the 1970 release of previously closed papers relating to World War II. It consists largely of lists of documents and brief summaries of the wartime responsibilities of various ministries. It is an invaluable work for those beginning work in the British archives.

OFFICIAL DOCUMENTS

18:5   U.S. Department of State. *Foreign Relations of the United States, 1941–1945.* 37 vols. Washington, DC: Government Printing Office, 1956–1972. The regular chronological Foreign Relations series, including several annual volumes on China not designated by volume number, runs to thirty-seven volumes. In addition, the State Department has published a special set of six volumes for the wartime summit conferences: Washington, 1941–1942, and Casablanca, 1943; Washington and Quebec, 1943; Cairo and Tehran, 1943; Quebec, 1944; Malta and Yalta, 1945; and Berlin (Potsdam). These invaluable volumes include documents from many non–State Department sources, including the Joint Chiefs of Staff, and are remarkably extensive. Postwar as well as wartime issues were a major topic of conversation at the conferences. Each volume is cited and described separately within its appropriate category under "Summit Conferences" (1:93).

18:6   _____. *A Decade of American Foreign Policy: Basic Documents 1941–1949.* Washington, DC: Department of State, 1985. This collection of 313 items reproduces public documents, treaties, reports, etc., dealing with allies' negotiations. Originally printed in 1950.

18:7   *Map Room Messages of President Roosevelt (1939–1945).* Microfilm. Bethesda, MD: Lexis-Nexis Academic and Library Solutions, 1981. The documents on the nine reels of microfilm in this collection are taken from the files of the president's wartime map room and include high-level correspondence with allied leaders and military officials.

18:8   *Map Room Messages of President Truman (1945–1946).* Microfilm. Bethesda, MD: LexisNexis Academic and Library Solutions, 1980. The five reels of microfilm in this high-level collection at the Truman Library contain correspondence on a wide range of diplomatic as well as military issues in 1945 and 1946.

18:9   *President Franklin D. Roosevelt's Office Files, 1933–1945.* Microfilm. Bethesda, MD: Lexis-Nexis Academic and Library Solutions, 1990. This collection of microfilmed documents (twenty-two reels) is taken from the Roosevelt Library at Hyde Park, New York, and is broken down into four parts: "Safe" and Confidential Files, Diplomatic Correspondence File, Departmental Correspondence File, and Subject Files. Part 1 is particularly valuable.

18:10   National Archives and Records Administration. *The U.S. Department of State Decimal File Relating to World War II, 1939–1945.* Microfilm. Wilmington, DE: Scholarly Resources, 1981. The 252 rolls of microfilm in this collection are taken from the State Department's huge central file. The Purport List briefly describing each document and listing them in the order in which they appear is also available on microfilm. Numerous additional State Department files covering the World War II years are also available; see *Diplomatic Records: A Select Catalogue of National Archives Microfilm Publications* (1986) (18:2).

18:11   *The MAGIC Documents: Summaries and Transcripts of the Top-Secret Diplomatic Communications of Japan, 1938–1945.* Microfilm. Bethesda, MD: LexisNexis Academic and Library Solutions, 1980. These fourteen reels of microfilm contain the transcripts and intelligence summaries of deciphered radio messages between the Tokyo Foreign Office and Japanese officials overseas, including material from Baron Oshia in Berlin that provides valuable information on Hitler's intentions. A subject and name index is also available.

18:12   *OSS/State Department Intelligence and Research Reports.* Microfilm. Bethesda, MD: LexisNexis Academic and Library Solutions, 1977–1980. The 3,774 reports reproduced in this collection cover the years 1941–1961 and are arranged in 14 geographic parts and 124 reels.

18:13   *Potsdam Conference Documents.* Microfilm. Bethesda, MD: LexisNexis Academic and Library Solutions, 1980. The documents on these two reels of microfilm are taken from the Truman Library files on the Potsdam conference.

18:14 *Post World War II Foreign Policy Planning.* Microfiche. Bethesda, MD: LexisNexis Academic and Library Solutions, 1987. Harley Notter played a major role in the State Department's extensive wartime planning for the postwar world. This huge collection (5,313 microfiche covering a quarter of a million pages) from his National Archives files provides extensive documentation on that effort. It includes Notter's *Postwar Foreign Policy Preparation, 1939–1945* (1949) (18:191). A two-volume cloth-bound index is also available.

18:15 Iokibe, Makoto. *The Occupation of Japan. Part 1: U.S. Planning Documents, 1942–1945.* Microfiche. Bethesda, MD: Congressional Information Service, 1987. Nearly 1,000 documents in this microfiche collection have been taken from numerous U.S. archives and libraries and cover all U.S. wartime planning for the postwar occupation of Japan. A reprinted index is also available.

18:16 Combined Chiefs of Staff (United States and Great Britain). *Wartime Conferences of the Combined Chiefs of Staff. Reel 1: Arcadia; Casablanca, vols. 1–2; Trident (Dec. 1941–May 1943). Reel 2: Quadrant; Sextant; Eureka (Aug. 1943–Nov. 1943). Reel 3: Octagon; Argonaut; Terminal (Sept. 1944– 1945).* Microfilm. Wilmington, DE: Scholarly Resources, 1982. These three rolls of microfilm contain the proceedings of the meetings of the Anglo-American Combined Chiefs of Staff, who were responsible for the strategic direction of the Anglo-American war effort, during the major allied summit conferences. Also included are their meetings at some conferences with their Chinese and Soviet counterparts.

18:17 *Records of the Joint Chiefs of Staff. Part 1: 1942–1945.* Microfilm. Bethesda, MD: LexisNexis Academic and Library Solutions, 1980. The fifty rolls of microfilm in this collection cover an enormous number of diplomatic as well as military issues that concerned the Joint Chiefs during World War II. They are divided into five categories: European Theater, Meetings of the JCS and the CCS (Combined Chiefs of Staff), Pacific Theater, The Soviet Union, and Strategic Issues.

18:18 Marshall, George C., Henry H. Arnold, and Ernest J. King. *The War Reports of General of the Army George C. Marshall, Chief of Staff, General of the Army H. H. Arnold, Commanding General, Army Air Forces [and] Fleet Admiral Ernest J. King, Commander-in-Chief, United States Fleet and Chief of Naval Operations.* Philadelphia: Lippincott, 1947. These official war reports of the three service members of the Joint Chiefs of Staff offer a wealth of detailed information on the planning, logistics, and execution of global war. The volume is enhanced by a detailed index. Previously published separately by the Government Printing Office; foreword by Walter Millis.

18:19 Mountbatten, Louis. *Report to the Combined Chiefs of Staff of the Supreme Allied Commander South East Asia, 1941–1945.* London: Her Majesty's Stationery Office, 1951. This is an official report on strategy, command, and operations in the South East Asia Command (1943–1945).

18:20 Kimball, Warren F., ed. *Churchill & Roosevelt: The Complete Correspondence.* These award-winning volumes constitute a complete compilation of the extensive Churchill-Roosevelt correspondence from 1933 to 1945 and include an introductory essay on the Churchill-Roosevelt relationship and correspondence, a digest of each document, extensive headnotes, and numerous editorial commentaries on the major issues discussed in the documents (17:7).

18:21 Loewenheim, Francis L., Harold D. Langley, and Manfred Jonas, eds. *Roosevelt and Churchill: Their Secret Wartime Correspondence.* This is a useful collection of wartime correspondence between Roosevelt and Churchill, supplemented by a lengthy introductory essay that provides context. Reproduced are 548 of the nearly 2,000 pieces of correspondence exchanged by Churchill and Roosevelt. The messages are arranged chronologically in four parts, with introductions for each and three introductory essays on the personal, military, and diplomatic-political relationship between the two leaders (17:8). For the complete correspondence, see the three volumes of Kimball, *Churchill & Roosevelt: The Complete Correspondence* (1984) (18:20).

18:22 Richardson, Stewart, ed. *The Secret History of World War II: The Ultra-Secret Wartime Let-*

ters and Cables of Roosevelt, Stalin and Churchill. New York: Richardson and Steirman, 1986. Published in cooperation with Novosti Publishing House, this volume consists of reproductions of Stalin's correspondence with Churchill and Roosevelt as originally published by the Soviet Ministry of Foreign Affairs in 1957. It is neither complete nor "the first time" these cables have been published, as the editor incorrectly asserts. Some of the messages are out of chronological order. The reader should therefore consult the original 1957 volumes instead if they are available: U.S.S.R. Ministry of Foreign Affairs, *Correspondence between the Chairman of the Council of Ministers of the U.S.S.R. and the Presidents of the U.S.A. and the Prime Ministers of Great Britain during the Great Patriotic War of 1941–1945* (1957) (18:30).

18:23   Taylor, Myron C. *Wartime Correspondence between President Roosevelt and Pope Pius XII.* New York: Macmillan Company, 1947. Reprint 1975 (Da Capo Press). The notes by Taylor, President Roosevelt's personal representative to the Vatican, often tell more than the letters.

18:24   Esherick, Joseph W., ed. *Lost Chance in China: The World War II Despatches of John S. Service.* New York: Random House, 1974. While these selected dispatches (1941–1945) by Service from China do not replace the official files, they offer a useful and handy compendium. Service's criticisms of the Nationalist regime would get him in trouble after the war.

18:25   Petersen, Neal H., ed. *From Hitler's Doorstep: The Wartime Intelligence Reports of Allen Dulles, 1942–1945.* University Park: Pennsylvania State University Press, 1996. Dulles was wartime mission chief of the Office of Strategic Services in Switzerland and as such a pivotal intelligence figure. Most of the chronologically organized documents here are from the operational records of the OSS at the National Archives. Petersen provides introductory commentaries as well as a general introduction and epilogue.

18:26   Spector, Ronald H., ed. *Listening to the Enemy: Key Documents on the Role of Communications Intelligence in the War with Japan.* Wilmington, DE: Scholarly Resources, 1988. This volume consists of twenty-one U.S. intelligence monographs, reports,

and studies based on intercepted and decrypted Japanese communications, along with a general introduction and brief introductions to each document. The documents are organized into five topical chapters covering prewar communications intelligence, examples of Ultra in action, maintaining the secret of U.S. codebreaking, U.S. analysis of Japanese codebreaking, and intelligence information on the Japanese surrender.

18:27   Hachey, Thomas E., ed. *Confidential Dispatches: Analyses of America by the British Ambassador, 1939–1945.* This volume contains the fourteen annual and quarterly wartime political reviews of the United States by British ambassadors in Washington (Lords Lothian and Halifax), along with an introduction by the editor. As Hachey notes, the reports "are more revealing of British views and attitudes than they are of any particular aspect of American life"; read in sequence, they constitute a virtual diplomatic diary of events in the United States during the war years as seen through British eyes (17:19).

18:28   Nicholas, H. G., ed. *Washington Despatches 1941–1945: Weekly Political Reports from the British Embassy.* Chicago: University of Chicago Press, 1981. Sent as lengthy telegrams and widely circulated within the British war cabinet, these weekly cables provide extensive information on U.S. attitudes toward a host of wartime and postwar issues. The volume is arranged chronologically and includes an introduction by Sir Isaiah Berlin, who prepared the first draft of many reports.

18:29   Ross, Graham, ed. *The Foreign Office and the Kremlin: British Documents on Anglo-American Relations, 1941–45.* New York: Cambridge University Press, 1984. This volume consists of forty-six previously unpublished documents from the Public Records Office on relations with the Soviet Union, along with a lengthy introduction by Ross. Taken primarily but not exclusively from Foreign Office files, the documents have been selected to illustrate the evolution of Foreign Office attitudes toward the USSR from 1941 through the December 1945 Moscow conference.

18:30   U.S.S.R. Ministry of Foreign Affairs. *Correspondence between the Chairman of the Council of Ministers of the U.S.S.R. and the Presidents of the*

U.S.A. and the Prime Ministers of Great Britain during the Great Patriotic War of 1941–1945. 2 vols. Moscow: Foreign Languages Publishing House, 1957. This early cold war collection contains Stalin's complete and unedited correspondence with Roosevelt, Churchill, Truman, and Attlee, with one volume devoted to correspondence with the British prime ministers and the second to correspondence with the U.S. presidents. Differences will be found between some messages in these volumes and versions published elsewhere.

18:31 _____. *The Teheran, Yalta and Potsdam Conferences.* Moscow: Progress Publishers, 1969. This book contains the Soviet records of these big three conferences.

18:32 Molotov, Vyacheslav. *Problems of Foreign Policy: Speeches and Statements, April 1945– November 1948.* Moscow: Foreign Languages Publishing House, 1949. The first few documents in this volume pertain to Soviet postwar plans as the war in Europe ended.

18:33 Pechatnov, Vladimir O. *The Big Three after World War II: New Documents on Soviet Thinking about Post War Relations with the United States and Great Britain.* Woodrow Wilson Center for International Scholars, June 1995. These are planning memoranda written for Molotov in 1944–1945 by former foreign minister and ambassador to Washington, Maxim Litvinov; his successor in Washington, Andrei Gromyko; and former ambassador to London, Ivan Maisky. They emphasize postwar cooperation, geopolitical considerations, and probable Anglo-American conflict.

18:34 Rzheshevsky, Oleg A., ed. *War and Diplomacy: The Making of the Grand Alliance: Documents from Stalin's Archives.* 2 vols. Amsterdam: Harwood Academic Publishers, 1996. This volume consists of 130 Soviet documents from Stalin's personal files in the Russian presidential archives, with commentaries by the editor. They include the Soviet minutes, draft agreements, and telegrams relating to Anthony Eden's visit to Moscow in December 1941 and Molotov's three visits to London and Washington in May-June 1942. Translated by Tatiana Sorokina.

18:35 Detwiler, Donald S., Charles Burton Bur-

dick, and Jürgen Rohwer, eds. *World War II German Military Studies: A Collection of 213 Special Reports on the Second World War Prepared by Former Officers of the Wehrmacht for the United States Army.* 10 vols. New York: Garland, 1980. These facsimile reproductions include 213 special reports prepared for the U.S. army by former officers of the Wehrmacht.

18:36 Leiss, Amelia C., with Raymond Dennett, eds. *European Peace Treaties after World War II: Negotiations and Texts of Treaties with Italy, Bulgaria, Hungary, Rumania, and Finland.* Boston: World Peace Foundation, 1954. This is a convenient collection of negotiations and texts of treaties with Italy, Bulgaria, Hungary, Rumania, and Finland.

18:37 Jacobsen, Hans-Adolf, and Arthur L. Smith, Jr., eds. *World War II: Policy and Strategy: Selected Documents with Commentary.* Santa Barbara, CA: Clio Books, 1979. These well-organized documents cover broad issues of strategy and policy for both the Axis and the allied powers. They are divided into seven chronological sections composed of seventeen topical chapters.

18:38 Detwiler, Donald S., and Charles Burton Burdick, eds. *War in Asia and the Pacific, 1937– 1949: A Fifteen Volume Collection.* 15 vols. New York: Garland Publishing, 1980. The volumes contain sixty-six contemporary documents reproduced in facsimile from a large number of studies located at the army's Center for Military History, the Library of Congress, or the National Archives.

UNOFFICIAL DOCUMENTS

18:39 Buchanan, A. Russell, ed. *The United States and World War II: Military and Diplomatic Documents.* Columbia: University of South Carolina Press, 1972. This is an uneven collection of documents, intended to give the reader a taste of diplomatic cable traffic, war planning, policy planning, and combat accounts.

18:40 Flower, Desmond, and James Reeves, eds. *The Taste of Courage: The War, 1939–1945.* New York: Harper, 1960. Reprint 1997 (Da Capo Press). This large volume of over 1,100 pages consists of contemporary documents and later recollections by participants, along with occasional historical and reliable fictional accounts to fill in gaps in the documentary record. The chapters are organized chronologically and topically and attempt to cover all aspects of the war, with selections ranging from the statements of national leaders to the experiences of everyday men and women, civilian as well as military, from all the major powers. The 1997 reprint is titled *The War, 1939–1945: A Documentary History* and contains a new introduction by John S. D. Eisenhower.

18:41 Langsam, Walter Consuelo, ed. *Historic Documents of World War II.* Princeton: Van Nostrand, 1958. This is a useful collection of forty-seven military and political documents dating from 1938. Each is preceded by a short paragraph placing it in historical context.

18:42 Litoff, Judy Barrett, and David C. Smith, eds. *What Kind of World Do We Want? American Women Plan for Peace.* Wilmington, DE: SR Books, 2000. This volume contains sixty-three primary source documents on women's interest and involvement in postwar planning, many from the umbrella Committee on the Participation of Women in Post War Planning, along with a highly informative general introduction and brief introductions.

18:43 Polenberg, Richard. *The Era of Franklin D. Roosevelt: A Brief History with Documents.* Boston: Bedford/St. Martin's, 2000. This volume is designed for undergraduate courses. It consists of a brief introductory essay, followed by forty-seven documents in nine topical chapters, a chronology, questions for consideration, and a selected bibliography. As befits a volume by Polenberg, the emphasis is on domestic issues.

18:44 Royal Institute of International Affairs. *Review of the Foreign Press, 1939–1945.* 27 vols. Munich: Kraus International Publications, 1980. This work reprints in facsimile form articles published in the foreign press, first issued every week or two by London's Royal Institute of International Affairs.

18:45 Werth, Alexander. *Russia at War, 1941–1945.* 2d ed. New York: Carroll and Graf, 2000. Written by a journalist living in Moscow, this volume offers numerous insights into the Russian wartime experience, including how the Soviets regarded their allies. Originally published in 1964.

18:46 Wilson, Theodore A., ed. *WW 2: Readings on Critical Issues.* New York: Charles Scribner's Sons, 1974. This collection provides an excellent introduction to the variety of primary and secondary material available on World War II. Topics covered include causes and legacies of the war, grand strategy, wartime diplomacy, strategic bombing, total war, and war crimes. Historians and other writers are represented by excerpts from works published elsewhere, including Arthur Bryant, Trumbull Higgins, Kent Roberts Greenfield, and Wilson himself.

18:47 Wyman, David S., ed. *America and the Holocaust: A Thirteen-Volume Set Documenting the Acclaimed Book The Abandonment of the Jews.* 13 vols. New York: Garland Publishing, 1989–1991. These volumes contain photocopies of a wide variety of primary sources dealing with different aspects of the U.S. response to the Holocaust.

18:48 Berle, Beatrice Bishop, and Travis Beal Jacobs, eds. *Navigating the Rapids, 1918–1971: From the Papers of Adolf A. Berle.* New York: Harcourt Brace Jovanovich, 1973. This compilation of Berle papers, drawn primarily from his "diary file" for the post-1937 period, provides a good starting point for understanding his wartime actions, political beliefs, and personal relationships with other policymakers. Three chapters cover his service during the war years as assistant secretary of state.

18:49 Butcher, Harry C. *My Three Years with Eisenhower: The Personal Diary of Captain Harry C. Butcher, USNR, Naval Aide to General Eisenhower, 1942 to 1945.* New York: Simon and Schuster, 1946. Butcher, Eisenhower's naval aide, was directed to keep a diary of the general's activities. The actual diary is detailed, but must be used carefully, as it is chatty and opinionated about personalities and military operations and strategy, where Butcher was often out of his depth. (The complete diary with supporting papers is in the Eisenhower Library.)

18:50 Davies, Joseph E. *Our Soviet Ally in War and Peace.* New York: National Council of American-Soviet Friendship, 1944. This late 1944 pamphlet by the former U.S. ambassador to the Soviet Union is a public call for greater wartime and postwar cooperation with the Soviet Union as well as an attack on critics of the USSR.

18:51 Chandler, Alfred D., ed. *The Papers of Dwight David Eisenhower. Vols. 1–5: The War Years.* 5 vols. Baltimore: Johns Hopkins University Press, 1970. This superbly edited collection consists of previously classified memoranda, notes, telegrams, and letters written or dictated by Eisenhower as a member of General Marshall's planning staff in Washington (1941–1942) and as American and allied commander in North Africa and Europe (1942–1945).

18:52 Hobbs, Joseph Patrick, ed. *Dear General: Eisenhower's Wartime Letters to Marshall.* Baltimore: Johns Hopkins Press, 1971. This collection is enhanced by Hobbs's introductory chapters, which highlight recurring themes. The letters and commentary help place in perspective Eisenhower's problems and growth as supreme commander as well as his relationship with Marshall.

18:53 Millis, Walter, with E. S. Duffield, eds. *The Forrestal Diaries.* New York: Viking Press, 1951. While primarily of value for the early cold war years, this volume reproduces many of Forrestal's 1944–1945 diary entries, when he was wartime secretary of the navy.

18:54 Hoff, Joan. "Herbert Hoover's Plan for Ending the Second World War." *International History Review* 1 (January 1979): 84–102. This presents two May 1945 memoranda by Herbert Hoover on America's position in the postwar world and how to terminate the war with Japan, and a third memo that summarizes his May 1945 meeting with President Truman. The author provides a thorough introduction to the documents.

18:55 *The Papers of Cordell Hull.* Microfilm. Washington, DC: Library of Congress Photoduplication Service, 1975. The documents on these 118 reels are taken from the Hull papers at the Library of Congress. They are divided into seven categories plus an index.

18:56 Buhite, Russell D. "Patrick J. Hurley and American Policy toward China." *Chronicles of Oklahoma* 45 (Winter 1967–1968): 376–92. Buhite reproduces with introduction and annotations a long letter of January 11, 1950, from Hurley to Herbert Hoover. Officially a reply to Hoover's request for some facts and opinions, Hurley provided an extended defense

of his actions while in China and repeated his charges of a procommunist conspiracy within the State Department to subvert both Roosevelt's policy and his mission in support of that policy.

18:57 Iatrides, John O., ed. *Ambassador Mac-Veagh Reports: Greece, 1933–1947.* Princeton: Princeton University Press, 1980. This volume contains letters and telegrams to President Roosevelt from Lincoln MacVeagh, the U.S. ambassador to the Greek government in Cairo and then in Athens. A large portion of the correspondence relates to Anglo-American arguments and policy regarding postwar Greece.

18:58 Bland, Larry I., with Sharon R. Ritenour, eds. *The Papers of George Catlett Marshall.* 4 vols. Baltimore: Johns Hopkins University Press, 1981–1996. Four volumes have so far been published, with three more projected. Volumes 3 and 4 cover December 7, 1941, through the end of 1944, while volume 5, when published, will cover 1945–1946. As army chief of staff through the war (1939–1945), Marshall was a pivotal figure whose contacts included virtually every high-ranking allied official, civilian as well as military. This fact and superb editing make these volumes an invaluable source for wartime strategy and diplomacy.

18:59 DeWeerd, Harvey A., ed. *Selected Speeches and Statements of General of the Army George C. Marshall.* Washington, DC: Infantry Journal, 1945. Reprint 1973 (Da Capo Press). Fourteen of the forty-eight speeches reproduced here were given by the wartime army chief of staff after Pearl Harbor and before Japan's surrender. They cover a host of diplomatic as well as military issues.

18:60 *The Morgenthau Diaries, 1933–1945.* Microfilm. Bethesda, MD: LexisNexis Academic and Library Solutions, 1981. The documents on these thirty-five reels of microfilm are taken from the papers of Roosevelt's Treasury secretary at the Roosevelt Library in Hyde Park, New York, and contain much information on wartime foreign affairs. A supplement of two reels titled *The Presidential Diaries of Henry Morgenthau, Jr. (1938–1945)* was issued the same year.

18:61 Perry, Glen C. H. *"Dear Bart": Washington Views of World War II.* Westport, CT: Greenwood

Press, 1982. This volume consists of confidential wartime memoranda that Perry and fellow journalist Phelps Adams sent to their editor after often confidential conversations with high-ranking Washington officials—most notably army and navy chiefs General George C. Marshall and Admiral Ernest J. King.

18:62 Buhite, Russell D., and David W. Levy, eds. *FDR's Fireside Chats.* This volume consists of Roosevelt's thirty-one radio addresses to the American people (and Congress) from 1933 to 1945, along with introductions to each and a general introduction. Part 2 contains the eighteen foreign policy addresses, thirteen delivered after Pearl Harbor (17:10).

18:63 Bullitt, Orville H., ed. *For the President, Personal and Secret: Correspondence between Franklin D. Roosevelt and William C. Bullitt.* In addition to the letters he sent Roosevelt as ambassador to the Soviet Union (1933–1936) and France (1939–1940), this compilation includes Bullitt's wartime letters to FDR on numerous diplomatic and military issues. Most notable are his support for a Mediterranean strategy, warnings not to trust Stalin, and calls for a Balkan invasion to halt Soviet expansion. Introduction by George F. Kennan (17:12).

18:64 Hassett, William D. *Off the Record with F.D.R., 1942–1945.* New Brunswick: Rutgers University Press, 1958. Hassett was a confidential White House secretary during the war who accompanied Roosevelt on more than forty of his trips out of Washington. The diary that he kept throughout the war provides interesting information on the individuals FDR met as well as the president himself.

18:65 Roosevelt, Elliott, ed. *F.D.R.: His Personal Letters.* Volumes 3 and 4 cover 1928–1945, with approximately 330 of 1,581 pages devoted to the period after Pearl Harbor (17:11).

18:66 Ward, Geoffrey C., ed. *Closest Companion: The Unknown Story of the Intimate Friendship between Franklin Roosevelt and Margaret Suckley.* Boston: Houghton Mifflin, 1995. "Daisy" Suckley was Roosevelt's distant cousin and, according to Ward, his closest companion during the last years of his life. This volume contains letters and journal entries from her recently discovered papers as edited and annotated by Ward, including thirty-eight letters

FDR sent her, which cover the gamut, from domestic trivia to matters of state.

18:67 Campbell, Thomas M., and George C. Herring, Jr., eds. *The Diaries of Edward R. Stettinius, Jr., 1943–1946.* New York: New Viewpoints, 1975. Stettinius served during these years first as undersecretary of state and then as secretary of state and first U.S. representative to the United Nations. These excerpts from his diaries, calendar notes, and memoranda of conversations are quite informative on a host of issues, most notably the postwar international organization planning at the Dumbarton Oaks, Yalta, and San Francisco conferences.

18:68 Sunderland, Riley, and Charles F. Romanus, eds. *Stilwell's Personal File: China, Burma, India, 1942–1944.* 5 vols. Wilmington, DE: Scholarly Resources, 1976. This collection documents the diplomatic and military organizational plans and controversies surrounding Stilwell's Asian mission. It includes letters and documents as well as Stilwell's own abridged version of the report of his CBI operation, which he submitted to the War Department.

18:69 White, Theodore H., ed. *The Stilwell Papers.* New York: W. Sloan Associates, 1948. This volume reproduces selections from General Stilwell's personal command journal, longer essays and analyses, and letters to his wife (December 1941–October 1944). The result is a colorful and caustic firsthand account of the major characters and issues in the China-Burma-India theater and high-level strategic planning at the conferences Stilwell attended.

18:70 *The Papers of Henry Lewis Stimson.* Microfilm. Wilmington, DE: Scholarly Resources, 1973. Reproduced from the Yale University Library, these 169 rolls of microfilm of the wartime war secretary bear on a series of crucial wartime and immediate postwar issues, including various diplomatic-military issues, Anglo-American strategic disagreements, and the use of the atomic bomb in 1945. The date of publication refers to Yale's microfilming of the records. Nine additional rolls cover *The Diaries of Henry Lewis Stimson,* issued the same year.

18:71 Ferrell, Robert H., ed. *Harry S. Truman and the Bomb: A Documentary History.* Worland, WY: High Plains Pub., 1996. This is a small collection of primary sources related to the atomic bombing of Japan, probably intended for classroom use. Most interesting are the excerpts from Truman's Potsdam diary.

18:72   Blum, John Morton, ed. *The Price of Vision: The Diary of Henry A. Wallace, 1942–1946.* Boston: Houghton Mifflin, 1973. This highly informative volume consists of approximately a fourth of the orally dictated diary of FDR's secretary of commerce and second vice-president, along with an introductory essay by Blum. Major issues include relations with Britain, China, and the Soviet Union; assessments of Roosevelt and Truman; economic warfare; trade; and atomic energy.

18:73   Eiler, Keith E., ed. *Wedemeyer on War and Peace.* Stanford, CA: Hoover Institution Press, 1987. This is a collection of the most important papers of the general who served as one of Marshall's chief strategic planners from 1941 to 1943, then in Southeast Asia and as Stilwell's replacement in China; after the war he headed an important and controversial mission to China.

18:74   Dilks, David, ed. *The Diaries of Sir Alexander Cadogan, O.M., 1939–1945.* New York: Putnam, 1972. This is one of the best inside looks at the British Foreign Office during World War II. As permanent undersecretary of the Foreign Office, Cadogan could see and judge events. The diaries contain much valuable information about decisions, people, and the passing scene.

18:75   Colville, John. *The Fringes of Power: 10 Downing Street Diaries, 1939–1955.* New York: Norton, 1985. Colville was Churchill's wartime private secretary. His published diaries are quite informative on a host of diplomatic issues as well as personal relations.

18:76   Simpson, Michael. *The Cunningham Papers: Selections from the Private and Official Correspondence of Admiral of the Fleet Viscount Cunningham of Hyndhope. Vol. 1: The Mediterranean Fleet, 1939–1942.* Brookfield, VT: Ashgate for the Navy Records Society, 1999. This first volume of Cunningham's papers covers only his command of the Mediterranean Fleet up to March 1942. An ensuing volume will cover his 1942 service as head of the

naval section of the British Joint Staff Mission in Washington and naval commander of the North African landings, and his 1943–1945 work as first sea lord and member of the Combined Chiefs of Staff—subjects of great interest to diplomatic historians who deal with allied relations during the war.

18:77   Danchev, Alex, ed. *Establishing the Anglo-American Alliance: The Second World War Diaries of Brigadier Vivian Dykes.* Washington, DC: Brassey's, 1990. Dykes was British secretary to the Anglo-American Combined Chiefs of Staff until his death in early 1943. His diary and letters provide exceptional insights into the early organization and functioning of this pivotal wartime body, and into both U.S. interservice and Anglo-American wartime relations.

18:78   Macmillan, Harold. *War Diaries: Politics and War in the Mediterranean, January 1943–May 1945.* New York: St. Martin's Press, 1984. These diaries of the key British diplomat in the Mediterranean, 1943–1945, and the future British prime minister are an excellent primary source for allied relations in French North Africa, Italy, and Greece. Macmillan used these diaries in writing his memoir, *The Blast of War, 1939–45* (1968) (18:372), but in so doing created unwarranted clarity and coherency. The original diaries reveal the overlapping and chaotic nature of the events in this theater.

18:79   Moran, Charles McMoran Wilson. *Churchill: Taken from the Diaries of Lord Moran: The Struggle for Survival, 1940–1965.* Boston: Houghton Mifflin, 1966. The prime minister's physician was present at many historic moments during and after the war and privy to many state and private secrets. Churchill appears here in his strength and his weakness.

18:80   Nicolson, Nigel, ed. *Diaries and Letters [by] Harold Nicolson. Vol. 2: The War Years: 1939–1945.* New York: Atheneum, 1967. This volume contains numerous comments by a noted British diplomat on political and military leaders and developments during the war.

18:81   King, William Lyon Mackenzie. *The Mackenzie King Diaries, 1932–1949.* Microfiche. Toronto: University of Toronto Press, 1973. This microfiche edition (492 microfiche) of the Canadian prime minister's original diaries is perhaps the single most important source for Canadian external policy during the 1930s and 1940s. The diaries detail their author's relationship with Roosevelt and describe the spy scandals of 1945–1946.

18:82   Pickersgill, J. W., ed. *The Mackenzie King Record.* 4 vols. Toronto: University of Toronto Press, 1960–1970. These are the wartime and postwar diaries of Canada's prime minister from 1935 to 1948. The first volume, covering 1939–1944, was heavily edited; the remaining three faithfully represent the original diaries. Of particular interest is discussion of King's meetings with Roosevelt, Churchill, Attlee, and Truman; the two Quebec conferences; and the founding of the United Nations.

Bibliographies and Other Reference Works

18:83   ABC-CLIO Information Services. *World War II from an American Perspective: An Annotated Bibliography.* Santa Barbara, CA: ABC-CLIO, 1983. This highly useful annotated bibliography consists of 1,107 citations, arranged alphabetically by author, for articles that appeared in scholarly journals between 1971 and 1981. They were compiled from the periodicals database of the American Bibliographical Center by editors at ABC-CLIO Information Services.

18:84   Adamczyk, Richard D., and Morris J. MacGregor, eds. *United States Army in World War II: Reader's Guide.* Washington, DC: Government Printing Office, 1992. This volume lists the table of contents and provides brief analytical descriptions for each of the volumes in the United States Army in World War II series (the "Green Books").

18:85   Ancell, R. Manning, and Christine Marie Miller, eds. *The Biographical Dictionary of World War II Generals and Flag Officers: The U.S. Armed Forces.* Westport, CT: Greenwood Press, 1996. This volume contains brief entries on 2,400 wartime officers who held star rank between December 7, 1941, and September 2, 1945. They are divided into army,

army air forces, national guard, navy, marine corps, and coast guard officers.

18:86   Baudot, Marcel, with Alvin D. Coox and Thomas R. H. Havens, eds. *The Historical Encyclopedia of World War II.* New York: Facts on File, 1980. In addition to nearly 900 alphabetical listings, this volume includes photographs, an introduction on the origins of the war, a chronology of events from 1931 to 1946, a concluding essay that seeks to describe the immediate and long-term effects of the war, and a brief bibliography. Translated by Jesse Dilson from the original French and noticeably European in outlook.

18:87   Bayliss, Gwyn M., ed. *Guide to the Two World Wars: An Annotated Survey of English-Language Reference Materials.* New York: Bowker, 1977. Works included in this annotated guide were published before 1976 and are divided into seven sections: general guides; bibliographies; directories and library catalogs; dictionaries and encyclopedias; periodicals; biographies; and other. Each section begins with an introductory survey of the literature.

18:88   Blewett, Daniel K., ed. *American Military History: A Guide to Reference and Information Sources.* Englewood, CO: Libraries Unlimited, 1995. The topically organized chapter 10 of this annotated bibliography covers over 100 World War II reference works.

18:89   Bloomberg, Marty, and Hans H. Weber, eds. *World War II and Its Origins: A Selected Annotated Bibliography of Books in English.* Littleton, CO: Libraries Unlimited, 1975. This annotated bibliography of books remains a valuable if somewhat dated guide for diplomatic historians. It actually begins with the 1920s and 1930s and emphasizes the political dimension.

18:90   Boatner, Mark M., III, ed. *Biographical Dictionary of World War II.* Novato, CA: Presidio Press, 1996. Designed for general readers as well as researchers, this reference work consists of approximately 1,000 biographical sketches ranging from 250 to 1,000 words in length and arranged alphabetically, along with a lengthy glossary and a bibliography. It updates Christopher Tunney, *A Biographical Dictionary of World War II* (New York: St. Martin's Press,

1972), and complements Dear, *The Oxford Companion to World War II* (1995) (18:93).

18:91 Chant, Christopher, ed. *The Encyclopedia of Codenames of World War II*. London: Routledge and Kegan Paul, 1986. This description and explanation of numerous code names for operations such as OVERLORD used during the war is of particular value to researchers interested in operational-strategic issues and the high command in the war.

18:92 Coletta, Paolo E., ed. *A Selected and Annotated Bibliography of American Naval History*. Lanham, MD: University Press of America, 1988. This updated version of an earlier (1981) bibliography of American naval history devotes six of twenty-eight chapters to the World War II years. Annotations are brief and used only for some of the entries.

18:93 Dear, I. C. B., ed. *The Oxford Companion to World War II*. New York: Oxford University Press, 1995. This is generally considered the most comprehensive and best written of the numerous World War II encyclopedias to be published during the fiftieth anniversary years of the war. It contains 1,700 alphabetically arranged entries by 140 international historians, many if not most of them notable World War II scholars. It also includes numerous maps, charts, photographs, and tables, and the longer entries include brief bibliographies.

18:94 Ellis, John. *World War II: A Statistical Survey: The Essential Facts and Figures for All the Combatants*. New York: Facts on File, 1993. This comprehensive and valuable reference work is divided into eight sections: maps; command structures; orders of battle; tables of organization and equipment; army, armored, air, and naval forces; casualties and losses; production; and hardware. The author has made a special effort to include full statistics for all belligerents in an effort to overcome the parochialism of many Anglo-American studies.

18:95 Enser, A. G. S., ed. *A Subject Bibliography of the Second World War, and Aftermath: Books in English, 1975–1987*. Brookfield, VT: Gower, 1990. This work updates the 1985 edition of this work *(A Subject Bibliography of the Second World War, and Aftermath: Books in English, 1975–1983)*, which covered publications appearing 1975 to 1983, by

adding some 1,600 titles appearing between 1984 and 1987, together with books on the war's aftermath. Organization remains alphabetical by topic and within each topic.

18:96 _____. *A Subject Bibliography of the Second World War: Books in English, 1939–1974*. Boulder: Westview Press, 1977. This is an extensive list of books on World War II published before 1975. Organization is alphabetical by topic and within each topic. The volume includes author and subject indexes. See also Enser's updates for the years 1975–1987 (18:95).

18:97 Funk, Arthur L., ed. *The Second World War: A Select Bibliography of Books in English Published since 1975*. Claremont, CA: Regina Books, 1985. This volume updates Funk's *A Select Bibliography of Books on the Second World War in English, Published in the United States, 1966–1975* (1975) (18:98) and is substantially larger. See also the quarterly newsletter of the World War Two Studies Association for more recent updates.

18:98 Funk, Arthur L., et al., eds. *A Select Bibliography of Books on the Second World War in English, Published in the United States, 1966–1975*. Gainesville, FL: American Committee on the History of the Second World War, 1975. This brief bibliography partially updates Ziegler, *World War II: Books in English, 1945–65* (1971) (18:124). See also Funk, *The Second World War: A Select Bibliography of Books in English Published since 1975* (1985) (18:97) and the quarterly newsletter of the World War Two Studies Association.

18:99 Goralski, Robert, ed. *World War II Almanac, 1931–1945: A Political and Military Record*. New York: Putnam, 1981. Designed for the general reader, this chronology includes a chapter for each year covered, numerous photographs and maps, statistical appendices on men and arms, and a topical bibliography.

18:100 Gutman, Israel, ed. *Encyclopedia of the Holocaust*. 4 vols. New York: Macmillan, 1990. Each entry in this comprehensive reference work is followed by a brief bibliography. Numerous entries by the most notable historians in the field deal with key U.S. individuals, organizations, and policies.

18:101   Higham, Robin, ed. *A Guide to the Sources of United States Military History.* The original guide was published in 1975, with supplements in 1981, 1986, 1993, and 1998. The key chapters for World War II scholars in the original guide were by Robert Coakley on the U.S. army in World War II, Dean Allard on the U.S. navy from 1941 to 1973, and Robert Futrell on the army air corps and U.S. air forces from 1909 to 1973. Coakley updated the army chapter in 1981 and 1986, Christopher Gabel in 1993 and 1998. Allard updated the navy chapter in 1981, 1986, and 1993, while John Hattendorf did so in 1998. The air chapter was updated by Robert Finney in 1981 and 1986, Warren Trest in 1993, and Daniel Haulman in 1998. The 1981 and 1986 supplements also added an important chapter on U.S. government documentation by Timothy Nenninger and Dale Floyd, which Nenninger updated in 1998 (1:188).

18:102   _____. *Official Histories: Essays and Bibliographies from around the World.* This country-by-country survey covering both world wars is uneven but introduces most of the important national series as of 1970 (14:25).

18:103   Keegan, John, ed. *Rand McNally Encyclopedia of World War II.* Chicago: Rand McNally, 1977. Designed for the general reader, this volume contains numerous illustrations, maps, and photographs as well as more than 1,000 entries.

18:104   _____. *Who's Who in World War II.* New York: Oxford University Press, 1995. This brief volume contains over 300 entries. The same text with extensive photographs was published by Crowell in 1978 under the title *Who Was Who in World War II.*

18:105   Mason, David. *Who's Who in World War II.* Boston: Little, Brown, 1978. This illustrated biographical guide contains approximately 350 entries of varying length, arranged alphabetically, along with a large number of photographs.

18:106   O'Neill, James E., and Robert W. Krauskopf, eds. *World War II: An Account of Its Documents.* Washington, DC: Howard University Press, 1976. In addition to papers by U.S. historians and archivists about collections in the United States, representatives from Great Britain, France, and the Soviet Union report on documents in their countries.

18:107   Parrish, Michael, ed. *The U.S.S.R. in World War II: An Annotated Bibliography of Books Published in the Soviet Union, 1945–1975: With an Addenda for the Years 1975–1980.* 2 vols. New York: Garland Publishing, 1981. This two-volume bibliography is divided into five sections: military campaigns, the Soviet armed forces, geographic areas of the USSR, subject divisions, and economic divisions. A subdivision for Soviet wartime diplomacy is in volume 2 in the subject section.

18:108   Parrish, Thomas, ed. *The Simon and Schuster Encyclopedia of World War II.* New York: Simon and Schuster, 1978. Although designed via its prose, photographs, and maps for casual reading, this alphabetically arranged collection of 4,000 entries has been authored by 47 well-known scholars and is a solid reference work. It includes a chronology from 1931 through 1945 and a selected bibliography.

18:109   Petersen, Neal H., ed. *American Intelligence, 1775–1990: A Bibliographical Guide.* Chapter 3 of this chronologically organized guide is devoted to works on World War II intelligence, with the term broadly defined to include related subjects. The entire volume encompasses more than 6,000 entries. Although no annotations are provided, critical works have been highlighted by asterisks and within introductory paragraphs (1:194).

18:110   Rasor, Eugene L. *Winston S. Churchill, 1874–1965: A Comprehensive Historiography and Annotated Bibliography.* Westport, CT: Greenwood Press, 2000. This is the most comprehensive and recent bibliography of works by and about Churchill. Its detail, description, and judgments as well as its comprehensiveness make it a vital reference for any research on him.

18:111   Royal Institute of International Affairs. *Chronology and Index of the Second World War, 1938–1945.* Westport, CT: Meckler, 1990. Originally published in parts throughout the war itself and then as a whole in 1947, this extensive and detailed chronology was republished in 1975 with a full index and then again in 1990.

18:112   Sandler, Stanley, ed. *World War II in the Pacific: An Encyclopedia.* New York: Garland Publishing, 2001. The more than 250 alphabetically arranged entries (with a brief bibliography after each) cover social, cultural, diplomatic, political, and military aspects of the Pacific war. Many are quite lengthy and attempt to provide Japanese as well as American perspectives. Also included in the volume are a brief introduction and an epilogue on the results of the Pacific war.

18:113 Sbrega, John J., ed. *The War against Japan, 1941–1945: An Annotated Bibliography.* New York: Garland Publishing, 1989. This massive annotated bibliography contains over 5,200 entries within its 1,050 pages, divided into six major and clearly subdivided sections: general, diplomatic and political, economic and legal, military, religious, and social and cultural. These are followed by appendices listing periodicals, abbreviations, Japanese-American relocation centers, a chronology, and separate author and subject indexes. The entries cover books, articles, documents, novels, etc., published through December 1987.

18:114 Sexton, Donal, J., Jr., ed. *Signals Intelligence in World War II: A Research Guide.* Westport, CT: Greenwood Press, 1996. The bulk of this work consists of an annotated bibliography of more than 800 citations published (most in English) from the 1930s to 1995. They are divided into four sections: reference works and research guides, general and introductory works, general and theoretical works, and works on strategy and operations. Sexton also provides a list of abbreviations, a signals intelligence chronology, an introductory historiographical review of the major works in the field, and separate author and subject indexes. This work is invaluable given the flood of studies in the field and should be consulted before beginning any research into World War II signals intelligence.

18:115 Smith, Myron J., Jr., ed. *World War II at Sea: A Bibliography of Sources in English.* 3 vols. Metuchen, NJ: Scarecrow Press, 1976. The original three-volume set (volume 3 is in two parts) provides comprehensive coverage of the sea forces of all nations engaged in World War II. The approximately 10,500 entries cover materials published between 1939 and December 1973—books, essays, documents, dissertations, etc. The edition includes interpretive essays by Donald Macintyre, Benjamin Franklin Cooling, Edwin H. Simmons, Edward L.

Beach, F. S. Washington, Kinley J. Brauer, Ernest M. Eller, and Dean C. Allard. A 1990 supplement, titled *World War II at Sea: A Bibliography of Sources in English, 1974–1989* (also Scarecrow Press), has 3,600 entries published between 1974 and 1989 as well as a number of titles omitted in the original volumes.

18:116 _____. *World War II, The European and Mediterranean Theaters: An Annotated Bibliography.* New York: Garland Publishing, 1984. This annotated bibliography contains over 2,800 items organized into six categories: reference works, special studies, the air war, the land war, the war at sea, and documentary films. Each category begins with an introduction and is subdivided.

18:117 Snyder, Louis L. *Louis L. Snyder's Guide to World War II.* Westport, CT: Greenwood Press, 1982. The mostly brief references in this guide cover key wartime events and personalities. They are arranged alphabetically, with emphasis placed on the nonmilitary aspects of the war. Also included is a brief chronology covering 1939–1945.

18:118 U.S. Army Military History Institute. *The Era of World War II.* 4 vols. Carlisle Barracks, PA: Government Printing Office, 1977–1979. This four-volume reference aid in the U.S. Army's Military History Institute's Special Bibliographic series lists the institute's published World War II holdings. Volume 1 (compiled by Roy Barnard et al.) contains general works, references, biographies, and personal accounts. Volume 2 (Duane Ryan) deals with the Pacific war, volume 3 (Laszlo Alfoldi) with the Eastern and Balkan fronts, and volume 4 (Louise Arnold) with Western Europe. Also of value among such bibliographies is series 6 on the institute's manuscript collections (by Richard Sommers) and 13 on its oral histories (by Roy Barnard).

18:119 U.S. National Archives and Records Service. *Federal Records of World War II.* 2 vols. Washington, DC: Government Printing Office, 1950–1951. Reprint 1982 Gale Research Co.). This was the initial effort to describe the archival materials created by civilian and military agencies during World War II. Volume 1 contains fifty-four pages on the Department of State, while volume 2 deals with military agencies.

18:120   Wells, Anne Sharp, ed. *Historical Dictionary of World War II: The War against Japan.* Lanham, MD: Scarecrow Press, 1999. In addition to 280 pages of alphabetically arranged entries, this includes a chronology and introductory essay on the causes, conduct, and consequences of the Far Eastern war, appendices of coded names and selected statistics, a brief bibliographic essay, and an extensive, well-organized bibliography.

18:121   Wheal, Elizabeth-Anne, Stephen Pope, and James Taylor, eds. *A Dictionary of the Second World War.* New York: Peter Bedrick Books, 1990. This is an alphabetically arranged encyclopedia of the war, with longer entries and separate chronological appendices for each theater as well as maps and photographs.

18:122   World War Two Studies Association. *World War Two Studies Association Newsletter* (1981–). Formerly the American Committee on the History of the Second World War, the World War Two Studies Association since 1981 has provided within its semi-annual *Newsletter* periodic bibliographies of, and bibliographic essays about, recently published works on all aspects of World War II.

18:123   Zabecki, David T., with Carl O. Schuster, Paul J. Rose, and William H. Van Husen, eds. *World War II in Europe: An Encyclopedia.* 2 vols. New York: Garland Publishing, 1999. Contributors to this massive work (1,920 pages) number 155, providing 1,400 entries covering prewar and postwar as well as wartime people and events, with a brief bibliography after each entry. The entries are divided into six alphabetically arranged sections on social and political issues and events; leaders and individuals; units and organizations; weapons and equipment; strategy, tactics and operational techniques; and battles, campaigns, and operations. Appendices provide a chronology, tables of comparative ranks, a glossary of acronyms, abbreviations, a list of code names, and a selected bibliography.

18:124   Ziegler, Janet, ed. *World War II: Books in English, 1945–65.* Stanford, CA: Hoover Institution Press, 1971. This extensive list of books (4,519 titles) on the war at all levels is still of considerable value despite its age. It also has a valuable introduction on bibliographies of foreign sources. Ziegler updated

part of this collection in Funk, *A Select Bibliography of Books on the Second World War in English, Published in the United States, 1966–1975* (1975) (18:98), and it has served as the basis for updates by the World War Two Studies Association.

Historiography

18:125   "The Future of World War II Studies: A Roundtable." *Diplomatic History* 25 (Summer 2001): 347–499. This roundtable consists of essays on the present state and the future of World War II scholarship by Warren F. Kimball, Loyd E. Lee, Mark A. Stoler, Anders Stephanson, Omer Bartov, Yukiko Koshiro, Amir Weiner, David Reynolds, and Alex Danchev, along with a commentary by Gerhard Weinberg.

18:126   Alperovitz, Gar. "Hiroshima: Historians Reassess." *Foreign Policy,* no. 99 (Summer 1995): 15–34. In this essay, Alperovitz notes the dichotomy between scholarly and popular knowledge about the atomic bomb decision, argues that the bomb was used to influence the Soviet Union, and points out that several military leaders opposed its use.

18:127   Baxter, Colin F., ed. *The Normandy Campaign: A Selected Bibliography.* Westport, CT: Greenwood Press, 1992. Approximately two-thirds of this volume is a series of historiographical essays on different aspects of the Normandy campaign, with each work mentioned cross-referenced by number to its bibliographic citation.

18:128   _____. *The War in North Africa, 1940–1943: A Selected Bibliography.* Westport, CT: Greenwood Press, 1996. As with Baxter's Normandy campaign volume in this series, approximately two-thirds of this volume is a series of historiographical essays on different aspects of the North African campaign, with each work mentioned cross-referenced by number to its bibliographic citation.

18:129   Draper, Theodore. "Neoconservative History." *New York Review of Books,* January 16, 1986, 5–15. This is a review of and response to an article in the September 1985 issue of *Commentary* by John Colville, Churchill's private secretary, and to ensuing responses in the November issue by Lionel Abel, Jeane Kirkpatrick, Irving Kristol, and Robert Nisbet, all sharply criticizing Roosevelt for naïveté on the Soviet Union in general and Yalta in particular. Draper in turn critiqued all of them for abusing history in an effort to discredit liberal internationalism and replace it with "global unilateralism"—a new and extremist fusion of isolationism and interventionism. Abel and Nisbet's acid rejoinders, and Draper's equally acid reply, can be found in the ensuing April 24 issue ("Neoconservative History: An Exchange"); Paul Seabury responds in the August 1986 issue of *Commentary* (47–49). Draper's original essay is reprinted in *A Present of Things Past: Selected Essays* (1990).

18:130 Keegan, John. *The Battle for History: Refighting World War II.* New York: Vintage Books, 1996. This brief volume by a noted British military historian is actually an extended bibliographic essay, with a focus on the British war effort and European ground war.

18:131 Kohn, Richard H. "The Scholarship on World War II: Its Present Condition and Future Possibilities." *Journal of Military History* 55 (July 1991): 365–93. This is an edited version of a panel discussion on the state of World War II scholarship that took place at the 1990 meeting of the American Military Institute. It includes comments by panelists Stephen Ambrose, Ronald Spector, Gerhard Weinberg, and Michael Howard as well as members of the audience.

18:132 Lee, Loyd E., ed. *World War II in Asia and the Pacific and the War's Aftermath, with General Themes: A Handbook of Literature and Research.* Westport, CT: Greenwood Press, 1998. This volume, along with its companion, *World War II in Europe, Africa, and the Americas, with General Sources: A Handbook of Literature and Research* (1997) (18:133), provide comprehensive and up-to-date essays, often of historiographical emphasis, on different aspects of the war and its literature. Bibliographies are included. Among the more pertinent for scholarly readers are Michael A. Barnhart, "International Relations and the Origins of the War in Asia and the Pacific War"; Jeffrey G. Barlow,

"American and Allied Strategy and Campaigns in the Pacific War, 1941–1945"; Conrad C. Crane, "The Air War against Japan and the End of the War in the Pacific"; Lee, "Propaganda, Public Opinion, and Censorship during the Second World War"; Stephen Curley, "War and Film in the United States and Britain"; Judith E. Doneson, "Holocaust and Film"; Ruth Elwell, "Popular Culture and World War II"; Gerald L. Sittser, "American Christianity on the Home Front during the Second World War"; Donald J. Mrozek, "Cultural Background to the War"; Mark A. Stoler, "Allied Summit Diplomacy"; Georg Schild, "Planning for the Postwar World Economy and the United Nations"; Lawrence Aronsen, "Breakdown of the Grand Alliance and the Origins of the Cold War"; and R. John Pritchard, "War Crimes, International Criminal Law, and the Postwar Trials in Europe and Asia."

18:133 _____. *World War II in Europe, Africa, and the Americas, with General Sources: A Handbook of Literature and Research.* Westport, CT: Greenwood Press, 1997. Along with *World War II in Asia and the Pacific and the War's Aftermath, with General Themes: A Handbook of Literature and Research* (1998) (18:132), this work offers updated coverage of many World War II issues, with most of the essays having a historiographical bent and including attached bibliographies. Of particular interest are Donald G. Schilling, "General Histories of the War in Europe and the Pacific"; Eugene L. Rasor and Lee, "Reference Works: Bibliographies, Encyclopedias, Dictionaries, Atlases, and Chronologies"; Rasor and Lee, "Primary Published Sources and Published Documents"; Lee, "Personal Narratives of War Leaders"; Brian P. Farrell, "Grand Strategy and the 'Second Front' Debate"; D. K. R. Crosswell, "Anglo-American Strategy and Command in Northwest Europe, 1944–1945"; John M. Shaw, "Intelligence: Code Breaking, Espionage, Deception, and Special Operations"; Richard Libowitz, "The Holocaust"; Geofrey T. Mills, "Comparative Economic Mobilization in World War II"; Greta Bucher, "Women in World War II"; Otto B. Burianek, "Refugees, Displaced Persons, and Migration as a Consequence of World War II"; Errol D. Jones, "World War II and Latin America"; John M. Vander Lippe, "World War II and the Middle East"; Ritchie Ovendale, "The War and the British Commonwealth"; and Thomas Ofcansky, "Sub-Saharan Africa."

18:134　Morton, Louis. *Writings on World War II.* Washington, DC: Service Center for Teachers of History, 1967. This pamphlet contains a long bibliographical essay analyzing interpretations and significant writings on World War II and a selected bibliography. Both the essay and the bibliography are topically organized and remain quite valuable. They should be supplemented, however, with Morton's "World War II: A Survey of Recent Writings," *American Historical Review* 75 (December 1970): 1987–2008 as well as more recent works.

18:135　Murray, G. E. Patrick. *Eisenhower versus Montgomery: The Continuing Debate.* Westport, CT: Praeger, 1996. This work is a valuable historiographical analysis of the debates over allied strategy and command in Europe that took place between 1945 and 1968. It illustrates the enormous impact of postwar events on the different participants in the debate.

18:136　Neumann, William L. "Allied Diplomacy in World War II: A Bibliographical Survey." *U.S. Naval Institute Proceedings* 81 (July 1955): 829–34. This essay offers an early appraisal of the emerging historical controversies on the issues involved as well as a solid review of the documents, memoirs, and histories then available.

18:137　Rasor, Eugene L. *The China-Burma-India Campaign, 1931–1945: Historiography and Annotated Bibliography.* Westport, CT: Greenwood Press, 1998. The first part of this volume contains ten separate historiographical essays covering a broad range of topics, many diplomatic, in addition to military operations. The second is an alphabetically arranged bibliography, with works cited in the essays cross-referenced by number to their full citations within the bibliography.

18:138　_____. *General Douglas MacArthur: Historiography and Annotated Bibliography.* Westport, CT: Greenwood Press, 1994. This volume includes a series of historiographical essays on different aspects of MacArthur's career, with one chapter devoted to the World War II campaigns as well as an alphabetically organized bibliography. Works cited in the essays are cross-referenced by number to their full citations within the bibliography.

18:139　_____. *The Southwest Pacific Campaign, 1941–1945: Historiography and Annotated Bibliography.* Westport, CT: Greenwood Press, 1996. The first part of this volume contains eleven separate historiographical essays covering a broad range of topics (including diplomacy, personalities, and intelligence) as well as operations. The second part is the alphabetically arranged bibliography, with works cited in the essays cross-referenced by number to their full citations within the bibliography. See also in this series Rasor's *The Solomon Islands Campaign, Guadalcanal to Rabaul: Historiography and Annotated Bibliography* (Westport, CT: Greenwood Press, 1997).

18:140　Roberts, Jeffrey J. "Peering through Different Bombsights: Military Historians, Diplomatic Historians, and the Decision to Drop the Bomb." *Airpower Journal* 12 (Spring 1998): 66–78. This thoughtful examination of the historiography of the atomic bomb decision finds that diplomatic and military historians approach the issue from different perspectives, with different assumptions, and with different agendas.

18:141　Stoler, Mark A. "A Half Century of Conflict: Interpretations of U.S. World War II Diplomacy." *Diplomatic History* 18 (Summer 1994): 375–403. This essay covers the literature produced in the 1980s and early nineties on U.S. wartime diplomacy (see his "World War II Diplomacy in Historical Writing: Prelude to Cold War" [1981] for pre-1981 works [18:142]). While many of the works focus at least implicitly on the origins of the cold war, there are growing signs of a historiographical trend to examine the period on its own terms rather than as a "seed time." Reprinted in Hogan, *America in the World: The Historiography of American Foreign Relations since 1941* (1995) (2:10).

18:142　_____. "World War II Diplomacy in Historical Writing: Prelude to Cold War." In *American Foreign Relations, A Historiographical Review,* ed. Gerald K. Haines and J. Samuel Walker, 187–206. Westport, CT: Greenwood Press, 1981. This essay, which critiques diplomatic historians for writing about World War II as the preface to the cold war rather than on its own terms, remains a useful overview of the first three decades of conflicting interpretations of U.S. World War II diplomacy. See his "A Half Century of Conflict: Interpretations of U.S.

World War II Diplomacy" (1994) (18:141) for more recent interpretations.

18:143   Walker, J. Samuel. "The Decision to Use the Bomb: A Historiographical Update." *Diplomatic History* 14 (Winter 1990): 97–114. This excellent historiographical essay focuses on works published since 1974. Walker notes that the 1980s reexamination resulted partly from the availability of new evidence, but the evidence itself was unclear, inconclusive, and contradictory. He concludes that the 1970s consensus on military motives as primary and diplomatic motives as secondary still prevails, but that there is now general historical agreement that the bomb was not needed to avoid invasion and end the war. The essay is reproduced in revised and updated form in Hogan's *America in the World: The Historiography of American Foreign Relations since 1941* (1995) (2:10) and *Hiroshima in History and Memory* (1996) (18:1282).

18:144   _____. "History, Collective Memory, and the Decision to Use the Bomb." *Diplomatic History* 19 (Spring 1995): 319–28. Popular opinion about President Truman's decision to drop atomic bombs on Japan has not been affected by important changes in scholarly consensus on this topic. Surveying a number of high school and college history texts, Walker finds that they give outdated explanations even as they perpetuate an overly simplified collective memory.

18:145   Watt, Donald Cameron. "Britain and the Historiography of the Yalta Conference and the Cold War." *Diplomatic History* 13 (Winter 1989): 67–98. Watt develops a six-stage pattern for historical interpretations before an event ceases to be "contemporary history" and applies this pattern to British and American histories of Yalta and the origins of the cold war.

18:146   Weinberg, Gerhard L. "Some Thoughts on World War II." *Journal of Military History* 56 (October 1992): 659–68. Originally a 1991 Society for Military History address, Weinberg's essay discusses numerous issues about the war requiring "further discussion and examination." These include the distortions contained within numerous wartime German and British memoirs, the willingness of Vichy French officers to resist allied but not Axis forces, newly

opening Soviet sources, Nationalist Chinese resistance before 1944, Japanese failure to translate military victories into anything lasting, third world Nationalists who sided with Japan, the relationship of the U.S. war effort to that of its allies, British military failures, the atomic bomb decision, and the significance of personality conflicts.

18:147   _____. "World War II Scholarship, Now and in the Future." *Journal of Military History* 61 (April 1997): 335–45. In this essay, the dean of World War II historians discusses how much recent scholarship has taken advantage of newly available sources, the likely direction of future scholarship on the war, wartime records that still remain classified, and the need to preserve the fast-deteriorating paper record.

Overviews and General Works

GENERAL

18:148   Adams, Michael C. C. *The Best War Ever: America and World War II.* Baltimore: Johns Hopkins University Press, 1994. This iconoclastic volume challenges the "good war" of popular memory, labeling it a distortion and examining the numerous negative but seldom mentioned aspects of the conflict.

18:149   Baldwin, Hanson W. *Great Mistakes of the War.* New York: Harper, 1949. A leading military journalist of the World War II and cold war eras, the author attacks U.S. officials for failure to keep political objectives in mind. Aside from suggesting that U.S. grand strategy was flawed, he argues against the unconditional surrender doctrine and the dropping of the atomic bomb. Although simplistic and dated, this work remains a classic early indictment of U.S. policies and strategies.

18:150   Butler, James R. M., ed. *Grand Strategy.* 6 vols. in 7. London: Her Majesty's Stationery Office, 1956–1976. Volume 1 (by Norman Gibbs) of this official history covers British military planning and policies during the interwar years. Volume 2 (by

J. R. M. Butler) covers British and allied strategic planning from the outbreak of the war to the German invasion of Russia, including sections on the exploratory staff talks with the United States (1940–1941), combined policy in the Atlantic, and strategy in the Pacific. Volume 3 (J. M. A. Gwyer and J. R. M. Butler) covers British and allied strategic planning from Germany's attack on Russia through the decision to invade North Africa. It emphasizes the formation of the Grand Alliance, aid to Russia, the cross-channel versus North Africa controversy of 1942, and the numerous conferences associated with these issues. Volume 4 (Michael Howard) covers the period of critical Anglo-American conferences, debates, and decisions on cross-channel versus Mediterranean strategy and a host of related issues. It contains an extended introduction that summarizes and updates available information on the Anglo-American strategic debate prior to August 1942. Volume 5 (John Patrick William Ehrman) analyzes the strategic debates of 1943–1944, most notably over the invasions of northern and southern France, and the numerous conferences that determined final strategy, the most important at Cairo and Teheran. Volume 6 (John Ehrman) analyzes allied planning and conferences from the second Quebec conference of 1944 through the Japanese surrender and deals with the numerous diplomatic as well as military issues that arose at this time.

18:151 Calvocoressi, Peter, Guy Wint, and John Pritchard. *Total War: The Causes and Courses of the Second World War.* 2 vols. 2d rev. ed. New York: Pantheon Books, 1989. Reprint 2001 (Penguin Books). This outstanding general history of the war was originally published in 1972 as *Total War: The Story of World War II* (by Calvocoressi and Wint). It remains an excellent, comprehensive, and highly readable work on the background to the war, its strategy and operations, and its meaning. The 2001 reprint is titled *The Penguin History of the Second World War.*

18:152 Coles, Harry L., ed. *Total War and Cold War: Problems in Civilian Control of the Military.* Columbus: Ohio State University Press, 1962. This volume includes numerous chapters on civilian-military relations in numerous countries before, during, and after World War II. Most relevant for the United States during the war are the essays by Maurice Matloff, "Franklin Delano Roosevelt as War

Leader" (42–65), and Forrest C. Pogue, "Political Problems of a Coalition Command" (108–28).

18:153 Draper, Theodore. *A Present of Things Past: Selected Essays.* New York: Hill and Wang, 1990. Included in this collection are two of Draper's World War II essays for the *New York Review of Books:* "Eisenhower's War" (September 25, October 9 and 23, 1986), and "Neoconservative History" (April 24, 1986), each of which is cited separately in this chapter.

18:154 Graebner, Norman A. "The Limits of Victory." *Studies in Modern European History and Culture* 3 (1977): 75–93. The United States entered World War II with high-minded goals, but during the war cooperation with a Soviet Union that did not share these goals was necessary to defeat Germany. Alternative military strategies to limit the Soviets might have turned out even worse than what resulted in 1945.

18:155 Hess, Gary R. *The United States at War, 1941–1945.* 2d ed. Arlington Heights, IL: Harlan Davidson, 2000. Designed for undergraduate class use, this brief survey is a solid and useful introduction to the diplomatic and military aspects of the U.S. war effort. It also contains a useful and up-to-date bibliography. First published in 1986.

18:156 Iriye, Akira. *Power and Culture: The Japanese-American War, 1941–1945.* Cambridge, MA: Harvard University Press, 1981. In this pathbreaking work in cultural history, Iriye maintains that U.S. and Japanese cultures were not inherently contradictory and that the war was a subversion rather than an expression of Japanese cultural aspirations.

18:157 Kennedy, David M. *Freedom from Fear: The American People in Depression and War, 1929–1945.* New York: Oxford University Press, 1999. Approximately 300 of the 850 pages of text in this Pulitzer prize volume cover the period after Pearl Harbor. In six chapters Kennedy offers a superb, up-to-date, and beautifully written analysis of the diplomatic and military as well as home-front events and issues of the war years.

18:158 Kimball, Warren F., ed. *America Unbound: World War II and the Making of a Superpower.* New

York: St. Martin's Press, 1992. The essays in this volume analyze the war's impact on America's role in the world, U.S. economic and military strategies, intelligence gathering and espionage, and other issues. Contents include David Reynolds, "Power and Superpower: The Impact of Two World Wars on America's International Role" (13–36); Donald Cameron Watt, "U.S. Globalism: The End of the Concert of Europe" (37–54); Walter LaFeber, "American Empire, American Raj" (55–72); Kimball "U.S. Economic Strategy in World War II: Wartime Goals, Peacetime Plans" (139–58); and William Korey, "Genocide Treaty Ratification: Ending an American Embarrassment" (159–80).

18:159   Kitchen, Martin. *A World in Flames: A Short History of the Second World War in Europe and Asia, 1939–1945.* New York: Longman, 1990. Designed for college courses, this volume provides a comprehensive yet relatively brief (344 pages) overview of the war from the German invasion of Poland through Japan's surrender. It includes maps and bibliography and for the most part is organized chronologically.

18:160   Laqueur, Walter, ed. *The Second World War: Essays in Military and Political History.* Beverly Hills, CA: Sage Publications, 1982. Reproduced in this volume are twenty-two scholarly articles on different aspects of World War II that originally appeared in volume 16 (January-July 1981) of the *Journal of Contemporary History.* More than half concern U.S. wartime policies, allied diplomacy, and wartime intelligence. Contents include: Mark M. Lowenthal, "Roosevelt and the Coming of the War: The Search for United States Policy, 1937–42" (50–77); David G. Haglund, "George C. Marshall and the Question of Military Aid to England, May-June 1940" (142–58); Ronald Lewin, "A Signal-Intelligence War" (184–94); Paul Kramer, "Nelson Rockefeller and British Security Coordination" (202–17); Graham Ross, "Foreign Office Attitudes to the Soviet Union, 1941–45" (255–74); and John D. Langer, "The Harriman-Beaverbrook Mission and the Debate over Unconditional Aid for the Soviet Union, 1941" (300–19).

18:161   Leckie, Robert. *Delivered from Evil: The Saga of World War II.* New York: Harper and Row, 1987. Although primarily a military history of the war, this large volume also discusses its causes, diplomacy, home-fronts, and key personalities. It is designed for a general audience and tries to mix high command decisions and operational discussions with accounts based on the memoirs of Axis and allied soldiers.

18:162   Lee, Loyd E. *World War II.* Westport, CT: Greenwood Press, 1999. Designed primarily for high school and college audiences, this volume provides an excellent introduction to the war via six topical essays, biographical sketches of major figures, and seventeen key documents as well as a chronology, list of casualty figures, glossary of terms, and annotated bibliography. The topical essays cover the Grand Alliance as well as home-fronts, European resistance movements, the changing nature of military power, the continuing significance of the war, and an overview.

18:163   Leopard, Donald D. *World War II: A Concise History.* 2d ed. Prospect Heights, IL: Waveland Press, 1992. This brief overview of the causes and conduct of the war is designed for college courses. Its 200 pages include maps and a summary and brief bibliography at the end of each chapter.

18:164   MacDougall, Robert. "Red, Brown, and Yellow Perils: Images of the American Enemy in the 1940s and 1950s." *Journal of Popular Culture* 32 (Spring 1999): 59–75. The author compares popular images of Japan and Germany during World War II and of the Soviet Union during the cold war, and concludes that there were similarities, but that the perception of racial threat to American security was gradually replaced by the perception of ideological threat.

18:165   Maddox, Robert James. *The United States and World War II.* Boulder: Westview Press, 1992. Despite the title and ensuing emphasis on the United States, this volume provides a comprehensive overview of the entire war. Maddox analyzes the causes and consequences as well as the conduct of the war, and its domestic and diplomatic as well as its military aspects. Each chapter contains a selected bibliography.

18:166   Michel, Henri. *The Second World War.* Translated by Douglas Parmee. 2 vols. New York: Praeger, 1975. This general history of World War II gives special attention to German occupation and national resistance movements and emphasizes global strategy and diplomatic planning. First published in French in 1968.

18:167   Moskin, J. Robert. *Mr. Truman's War: The Final Victories of World War II and the Birth of the Postwar World.* New York: Random House, 1996. This popular history of the final five months of war in 1945 focuses on allied leaders and is based on secondary sources only.

18:168   Ninkovich, Frank A. *The Diplomacy of Ideas: U.S. Foreign Policy and Cultural Relations, 1938–1950.* New York: Cambridge University Press, 1981. This is a pathbreaking work that follows the fate of the State Department's Division of Cultural Relations and the U.S. transition from voluntary and private cultural interchange to state-dominated programs with political purposes. Avoiding simplistic answers, Ninkovich shows that American culture was reflected in both the State Department's cultural program and its processes.

18:169   O'Neill, William L. *A Democracy at War: America's Fight at Home and Abroad in World War II.* New York: Free Press, 1993. O'Neill is both highly critical and laudatory (and often provocative and revisionist) in this readable analysis of numerous aspects of the U.S. war effort.

18:170   Overy, Richard J. *Why the Allies Won.* New York: W. W. Norton, 1996. This outstanding volume rejects the idea that allied victory over the Axis powers was preordained and provides an excellent analysis of the key factors enabling the allies to win. Overy focuses not only on the prominent air, ground, and naval campaigns, but also on economics, technology, allied relations and leaders, and moral factors.

18:171   Parker, R. A. C. *The Second World War: A Short History.* Rev. ed. New York: Oxford University Press, 1997. Originally published in 1989 as *Struggle for Survival,* this work analyzes the causes and consequences as well as the conduct of the war. It focuses on major episodes and issues rather than attempting to provide a comprehensive narrative.

18:172   Parkinson, Roger. *Blood, Toil, Tears and Sweat: The War History from Dunkirk to Alamein,* *Based on the War Cabinet Papers of 1940 to 1942.* New York: D. McKay and Co., 1973. The is the second volume of a narrative history based on the British War Cabinet papers and further fleshed out with diaries and official histories. It is useful on how Britain organized for and dealt with the war and how the war was perceived in London.

18:173   Purdue, A. W. *The Second World War.* New York: St. Martin's Press, 1999. Designed for students and general readers, this brief volume provides a succinct account of the war and an introduction to its major interpretive controversies. In the process the author also attempts to provide a long-range, post–cold war perspective on World War II, emphasizing historic national rivalries over ideological factors. Separate chapters and chapter sections cover the origins of the European and Far Eastern wars, early German victories, economic factors, Nazi occupation policies, the Holocaust, the air, naval, and ground wars, and allied victory and conflicts.

18:174   Stokesbury, James L. *A Short History of World War II.* New York: Morrow, 1980. This is a well-written history of the war suitable for the general reader or college student. Although it is essentially a military history, it also covers the causes and consequences of the war.

18:175   Thorne, Christopher. *Allies of a Kind: The United States, Britain and the War against Japan, 1941–1945.* New York: Oxford University Press, 1978. This detailed and comprehensive volume is a major synthesis and reinterpretation of Anglo-American relations in the war against Japan. It covers political as well as military issues and postwar planning for East Asia, emphasizing the sharp differences marking the Anglo-American alliance.

18:176   _____. *The Issue of War: States, Societies, and the Far Eastern Conflict of 1941–1945.* New York: Oxford University Press, 1985. Thorne designed this volume as a complement to his *Allies of a Kind: The United States, Britain and the War against Japan, 1941–1945* (1978) (18:175) in an effort to fuse western with nonwestern history and diplomatic history with sociology, social psychology, and economic and intellectual history. As such it represents the new "international" and cultural history emerging in the 1980s. Organization is thematic rather than chronological with heavy use of theory, especially those propounded by Kuhn and Braudel. Thorne argues that the U.S. conviction of the need to create "fundamental change" in Asia was a significant element in the course of international relations.

18:177   Weinberg, Gerhard L. *The Place of World War II in History.* Vol. 38, The Harmon Memorial Lectures in Military History. Colorado Springs: United States Air Force Academy, 1995. In this sweeping lecture, the dean of World War II historians attempts to assess the long-term consequences of the war.

18:178   _____. *A World at Arms: A Global History of World War II.* This magisterial work by one of the world's leading World War II scholars covers the entire diplomatic and military history of the war. It is both comprehensive in its coverage and provocative in its conclusions and is currently the most up-to-date and best politico-military history of the war available in a single volume (17:86).

18:179   _____. *World in the Balance: Behind the Scenes of World War II.* Hanover, NH: University Press of New England for Brandeis University Press, 1981. This work consists of two 1980 lectures on the Axis and allied coalitions followed by four specialized and previously published articles on Hitler's image of the United States, the German declaration of war against the United States, German colonial plans and policies, and the July 20, 1944, attempt to assassinate Hitler.

18:180   Willmott, H. P. *The Great Crusade: A New Complete History of the Second World War.* New York: Free Press, 1990. Although primarily concerned with strategy and operations, this is a balanced and comprehensive general history of the war that also covers its causes and diplomacy. It is also one of the few to give equal attention to the Asia-Pacific conflict.

18:181   Wilmot, Chester. *The Struggle for Europe.* New York: Harper, 1952. This early military and diplomatic history of the war in Europe is sharply critical of Roosevelt and his advisers for naïvely subordinating political ends to military means and for thereby making extension of Soviet power inevitable.

18:182   Wright, Gordon. *The Ordeal of Total War,*

1939–1945. New York: Harper, 1968. Although somewhat dated, this volume remains a brilliant analysis of the history and impact of World War II in Europe. The author emphasizes the economic, psychological, scientific, and cultural as well as the more traditional military, political, and diplomatic aspects of the war.

DIPLOMATIC AND POLITICAL

18:183   Chamberlin, William Henry. *America's Second Crusade.* Chicago: Regnery, 1950. Written from the prewar anti-interventionist point of view, this volume is highly critical of Roosevelt for manipulating the United States into a needless war, for appeasing Stalin during the conflict, and for thereby creating a new Soviet menace at least as dangerous as the defeated Axis. Although dated, it constitutes an excellent example of the immediate postwar revisionist critique of FDR.

18:184   Cole, Wayne S. *Roosevelt & the Isolationists, 1932–45.* This prodigiously researched work remains the best examination of Roosevelt's relations with congressional proponents of isolationism, despite its emphasis on the western progressive Republicans. Cole argues that changes in Roosevelt's stance on foreign policy stemmed from shifts in power between Roosevelt and the isolationists (17:463).

18:185   Dougall, Richardson. "The U.S. Department of State from Hull to Acheson." In *The Diplomats, 1939–1979,* ed. Gordon A. Craig and Francis L. Loewenheim, 38–64. Princeton: Princeton University Press, 1994. This is a useful overview of the U.S. State Department from 1933 to 1945, particularly strong on organizational changes within the agency, but also covering major policies and problems.

18:186   Fleming, Thomas. *The New Dealers' War: Franklin D. Roosevelt and the War within World War II.* New York: Basic Books, 2001. This popular history indicts Roosevelt for manipulating the United States into World War II and for his wartime policies, most notably in regard to unconditional surrender and Soviet-American relations. Although these have long been traditional points of attack for revisionist critics of Roosevelt, Fleming provides some new conspiratorial twists.

18:187   Kolko, Gabriel. *The Politics of War: The World and United States Foreign Policy, 1943–1945.* New York: Random House, 1968. This major revisionist work maintains that American foreign policy had three basic goals: suppression of the left wherever it appeared, the maintenance of the open door for American trade and influence in Eastern Europe, and economic expansion at the expense of the British empire. The Soviet Union's policies were essentially conservative, trying to control or suppress the left.

18:188   Liggio, Leonard P., and James J. Martin, eds. *Watershed of Empire: Essays on New Deal Foreign Policy.* Colorado Springs: Ralph Myles, 1976. Although most of the essays in this revisionist collection focus on events before Pearl Harbor, two have a bearing on the war years themselves: William L. Neumann's highly critical "Roosevelt's Options and Evasions in Foreign Policy Decisions, 1940–1945" (162–82), and James T. Patterson's "Robert A. Taft and American Foreign Policy, 1939–1945" (183–205).

18:189   Messer, Robert L. "World War II and the Coming of the Cold War." In *Modern American Diplomacy,* ed. John M. Carroll and George C. Herring, Jr., 117–35. Wilmington, DE: Scholarly Resources, 1996. Messer's contribution to this volume introducing students to major issues in twentieth-century American diplomacy explores how and why the wartime Grand Alliance formed and then collapsed, resulting in the cold war. He finds the two wars "inextricably linked" and emphasizes the shift in U.S. policy from Roosevelt to Truman as one of the key factors in the change from a cooperative to an adversarial relationship.

18:190   Misse, F. B. "Roosevelt et le Departement d'Etat [Roosevelt and the Department of State]." *Revue d'histoire de la deuxième guerre mondiale* 21 (avril 1971): 1–26. The inconsequential role assigned the State Department in World War II is attributed to attitudes FDR developed years before the war.

18:191   Notter, Harley A. *Postwar Foreign Policy Preparation, 1939–1945.* Washington, DC: Department of State, 1949. This is an indispensable source on mid-level State Department thinking during the war about almost every conceivable postwar issue. Although much of the book is concerned with bu-

reaucratic and organization matters, it offers valuable insights by a participant into the development of department thinking, even though the recommendations of the various committees were rarely implemented.

18:192   Packard, Jerrold M. *Neither Friend nor Foe: The European Neutrals in World War II.* New York: Scribner, 1992. Based upon secondary research, the volume is a useful introduction to the wartime policies of the five European nations that maintained their neutrality throughout the war: Eire, Portugal, Spain, Sweden, and Switzerland. The author also provides brief discussions of other European nations that tried but failed to maintain their neutrality. He concludes that the key factors in successful neutrality included geographic location and ability and willingness to defend oneself while simultaneously accommodating Germany or the allies sufficiently to command respect for their official neutrality.

18:193   Rubin, Barry. *Secrets of State: The State Department and the Struggle over U.S. Foreign Policy.* New York: Oxford University Press, 1985. Chapter 2 of this study of the State Department deals with the Roosevelt administration. Rubin surveys the major personalities and issues of the department during this period.

18:194   Schulzinger, Robert D. *The Wise Men of Foreign Affairs: The History of the Council on Foreign Relations.* Three chapters examine the actions of the council during the war and start of the cold war. In particular, chapter 4 reviews its planning for the postwar period and recommendations on peace settlements (17:543).

18:195   Smith, Gaddis. *American Diplomacy during the Second World War, 1941–1945.* 2d ed. New York: McGraw-Hill, 1985. Designed primarily for undergraduate classes, this succinct survey offers a comprehensive overview of U.S. diplomacy during the war. The second edition is less critical of Roosevelt than the first (1965) and offers substantially more information on decolonization and U.S. relations with the third world in general.

18:196   Snell, John L. *Illusion and Necessity: The Diplomacy of Global War, 1939–1945.* Boston: Houghton Mifflin, 1963. This is an excellent, compact, and well-rounded overview of global diplomacy between the outbreak and close of World War II. Snell finds allied diplomacy as successful as Axis diplomacy was unsuccessful.

18:197   Weinberg, Gerhard L. *Germany, Hitler, and World War II: Essays in Modern German and World History.* New York: Cambridge University Press, 1995. The twenty-three essays in this volume are revised versions of earlier articles and talks. Of particular interest to historians interested in U.S. wartime diplomacy are the essays on the interaction between the European and Pacific theaters, the Normandy invasion, and the comparative assessment of allied and Axis government leaders.

18:198   Woodward, Ernest Llewellyn. *British Foreign Policy in the Second World War.* 5 vols. London: Her Majesty's Stationery Office, 1970–1976. Part of the series History of the Second World War, this is a straightforward, chronologically ordered narration of British foreign policy conducted by the Foreign Office. Woodward selected his evidence mainly from previously closed Foreign Office records and produced an invaluable work. Although it rigorously avoids criticism of British policy, it is the starting point for research in the British records on Anglo-American relations and postwar planning. Woodward previewed his full, five-volume account with a one-volume version, *British Foreign Policy in the Second World War* (London: Her Majesty's Stationery Office, 1962).

MILITARY

18:199   *United States Army in World War II.* Washington, DC: Government Printing Office, 1947–1998. This massive official history, published in seventy-nine volumes (including works on technical services and revised editions), covers virtually every aspect of the U.S. army war effort. Volumes of particular value to the diplomatic historian are cited separately in this bibliography by individual author. A reader's guide summarizing the contents of each volume is also available and is listed separately (18:84): Adamczyk and MacGregor, *United States Army in World War II: Reader's Guide* (1992). For the marines, see U.S. Marine Corps Historical Division, *History of U.S. Marine Corps Operations in World War II* (5 vols., Washington, DC: Government Print-

ing Office, 1958–1971). For the navy, see Morison, *History of United States Naval Operations in World War II* (1947–1962), separately listed (18:207). And for the air force, also separately listed in this chapter (18:202), see Craven and Cate, *The Army Air Forces in World War II* (1948–1958).

18:200   Bellafaire, Judith Lawrence, ed. *The U.S. Army and World War II: Selected Papers from the Army's Commemorative Conferences.* Washington, DC: Center of Military History, United States Army, 1998. These papers from the army's commemorative international conferences of 1990, 1992, and 1994 are divided into four sections: prewar planning, the home-front, the war in Europe, and the war in the Pacific. The latter two contain papers of interest to World War II diplomatic as well as military historians, covering such issues as the OSS, combined operations, the U.S. army effort in China, and the atomic bomb. Individual chapters of most interest are Henry G. Gole, "War Planning at the U.S. Army War College, 1934–1940: The Road to Rainbow" (7–32); Theodore A. Wilson, "'Through the Looking Glass': Bradford G. Chynoweth as United States Military Attache in Britain, 1939" (47–72); Keir B. Sterling, "American Geographers and the OSS during World War II" (217–34); Monroe M. Horn, "Everything Old Is New Again: The American Military Effort in China, 1941–1945" (325–52); Marc S. Gallicchio, "Army Advisers and Liaison Officers and the 'Lessons' of America's Wartime Experience in China" (353–70); and Robert James Maddox, "Generals, Admirals, and Atomic Bombs: Ending the War with Japan" (405–18).

18:201   Coates, Kenneth, and W. R. Morrison. "The American Rampant: Reflections on the Impact of United States Troops in Allied Countries during World War II." *Journal of World History* 2, no. 2 (1991): 201–21. The authors sketch in broad topical strokes the enormous impact of the presence of millions of American troops in allied countries during World War II and call for a global, comparative approach to the subject. In the process they also provide within their footnotes an introductory bibliography of existing works in the field.

18:202   Craven, Wesley Frank, and James Lea Cate, eds. *The Army Air Forces in World War II.* 7 vols. Chicago: University of Chicago Press, 1948–1958.

Reprint 1983 (Office of Air Force History). This multivolume official history covers both the organizational and operational aspects of the U.S. army air forces during World War II. Separate volumes deal with early plans and operations (1939 to mid-1942), the European theater, the Pacific theater, the homefront, and worldwide services.

18:203 Ellis, John. *Brute Force: Allied Strategy and Tactics in the Second World War.* New York: Viking, 1990. Ellis maintains that the allies defeated the Axis in World War II through strength of their materiel superiority, a superiority that often was used, without skill, to bludgeon the enemy into submission. While providing many industrial production statistics to support this view, he focuses more on the war against Germany than Japan, where this argument does not fit as neatly.

18:204 Huntington, Samuel P. *The Soldier and the State: The Theory and Politics of Civil-Military Relations.* Cambridge, MA: Belknap Press of Harvard University Press, 1957. This highly influential general work on U.S. civil-military relations sharply criticizes the World War II Joint Chiefs of Staff for accepting unrealistic civilian views of appropriate policies in place of their own previous balance-of-power views.

18:205 Keegan, John. *The Second World War.* New York: Penguin Books, 1990. This is one of the more notable of the best-selling popular histories of the war published during the fiftieth anniversary years. Written by one of Britain's foremost military historians, it is divided into six geographic and chronological sections (West, East, and Pacific for 1940–1943 and 1943–1945). Each section is arranged topically, beginning with a strategic analysis, followed by a narrative and a relevant "theme of war," and each concludes with a battle piece chosen to illustrate the nature of a particular form of warfare. It is written in Keegan's engaging style and contains numerous photographs and a brief bibliographic essay.

18:206 Liddell Hart, B. H. *History of the Second World War.* New York: Putnam, 1970. Reprint 1982 (Perigee Books). A famous twentieth-century military theoretician and historian, the author emphasizes British and Anglo-American operations, supports British strategic concepts, and criticizes American

wartime ideas and decisions. Although primarily concerned with military affairs, the work includes diplomatic-strategic issues.

18:207 Morison, Samuel Eliot. *History of United States Naval Operations in World War II.* 15 vols. Boston: Little, Brown, 1947–1962. Written by one of the most prominent historians of his generation, this series constitutes the navy's official history of the war. It combines details on naval strategy, high-level planning, and operations throughout the world. Morison's *The Two Ocean War: A Short History of the United States Navy in the Second World War* (Boston: Little, Brown, 1963) is a one-volume summary.

18:208 Murray, Williamson, and Allan R. Millett. *A War to Be Won: Fighting the Second World War.* Cambridge, MA: The Belknap Press of Harvard University Press, 2000. This well-written volume is the most comprehensive and up-to-date operational history of the war. It provides an excellent introduction to current military history scholarship regarding the conflict.

18:209 Roskill, Stephen. *The War at Sea, 1939–1945.* 3 vols. London: Her Majesty's Stationery Office, 1954–1961. These official British volumes deal mostly with operations but are also valuable for the development of British maritime strategy in the 1939 to 1945 period.

18:210 Spector, Ronald H. "The Pacific War and the Fourth Dimension of Strategy." In *The Pacific War Revisited,* ed. Günter Bischof and Robert L. Dupont, 141–56. Baton Rouge: Louisiana State University Press, 1997. Spector outlines how the "social dimension" of the Pacific war influenced the war's conduct. Rival Japanese and American attitudes, hopes, and fears profoundly affected the nature of the war and how it was waged, from combat atrocities to strategic decisionmaking.

DOMESTIC (HOME-FRONT)

18:211 Alonso, Harriet Hyman. *Peace as a Women's Issue: A History of the U.S. Movement for World Peace and Women's Rights.* Chapter 5 surveys the efforts and fates of activist women's peace movements, 1935–1945, emphasizing how removed most groups were from mainstream public sentiment in America (9:158).

18:212   Anderson, Michael J. "McCarthyism before McCarthy: Anti-Communism in Cincinnati and the Nation during the Election of 1944." *Ohio History* 99 (Winter-Spring 1990): 5–28. In this suggestive work, Anderson examines campaign rhetoric in the 1944 presidential election to show that communism was a prominent issue and that Republican strategy regularly resorted to anticommunism as part of its campaign appeals.

18:213   Blum, John Morton. *V Was for Victory: Politics and Culture during World War II.* New York: Harcourt Brace Jovanovich, 1976. Blum provides a most useful if now somewhat dated analysis of factors affecting domestic life during the war.

18:214   Brinkley, David. *Washington Goes to War.* New York: Alfred A. Knopf, 1988. This well-written popular history by the famous television newscaster provides useful information on, as well as a feel for, the dramatic transformation of the national capital and government that took place during the war. It is based on personal memories and interviews as well as published and unpublished sources, but it contains no notes or index.

18:215   Darilek, Richard E. *A Loyal Opposition in Time of War: The Republican Party and the Politics of Foreign Policy from Pearl Harbor to Yalta.* Westport, CT: Greenwood Press, 1976. This volume analyzes the origins and evolution of Republican Party attitudes toward foreign policy during World War II. It finds the Republican "loyal opposition" and bipartisan approach part of a strategy designed to maintain party unity, rather than any "conversion" in foreign policy beliefs.

18:216   Dion, Susan. "Pacifism Treated as Subversion: The FBI and the War Resisters League." *Peace and Change* 9 (Spring 1983): 43–54. This short article covers the FBI's campaign against the War Resister's League, a pacifist organization the FBI viewed as subversive precisely and solely because it espoused pacifism. Dion argues that the FBI exceeded its charge in suppressing the legitimate dissent of the WRL.

18:217   Fox, Richard Wightman, et al. "A Round Table: The Living and Reliving of World War II." *Journal of American History* 77 (September 1990): 553–93. This roundtable explores the continuing, enormous impact of the war on historians who lived through it.

18:218   Goodwin, Doris Kearns. *No Ordinary Time: Franklin and Eleanor Roosevelt: The Home Front in World War II.* New York: Simon and Schuster, 1994. This Pulitzer prize winner and best-seller examines the wartime home-front through the lens of the Roosevelts and their White House. The organization is chronological.

18:219   Jeffries, John W. *Wartime America: The World War II Home Front.* Chicago: Ivan R. Dee, 1996. This brief volume assesses the enormous domestic impact of the war. It is topically organized and includes a valuable note on sources.

18:220   Leff, Mark H. "The Politics of Sacrifice on the American Home Front in World War II." *Journal of American History* 77 (March 1991): 1296–1318. Leff explores how Americans tried to reconcile the issues of personal sacrifice and capitalistic cultural values. He examines Roosevelt's unsuccessful attempt to cap wartime salaries and the War Advertising Council's successful coordination of a private advertising campaign to promote personal sacrifice, and provides a brief comparison with the British experience.

18:221   Lingeman, Richard R. *Don't You Know There's a War On? The American Home Front, 1941–1945.* New York: Putnam, 1970. Reprint 1976 (Capricorn Books). This early popular history recounts the frustrations at home emerging from social, economic, and political events.

18:222   Melosi, Martin V. *The Shadow of Pearl Harbor: Political Controversy over the Surprise Attack, 1941–1946.* See chapter 17 of this Guide (17: 1122).

18:223   Moore, John Robert. "The Conservative Coalition in the United States Senate, 1942–1945." *Journal of Southern History* 33 (August 1967): 368–76. Through an examination of roll-call voting records, Moore shows that a southern Democrat-

Republican coalition existed in the Senate in 1942–1945 and notes some of the legislation and issues that caused the coalition to operate.

18:224 Orser, Edward W. "World War II and the Pacifist Controversy in the Major Protestant Churches." Despite the general belief that unity over war existed after Pearl Harbor, the author maintains that debates over pacifism—previously a major line of belief among American Protestants—continued to play a major role in the Protestant churches (17:494).

18:225 Perret, Geoffrey. *Days of Sadness, Years of Triumph: The American People 1939–1945*. New York: Coward, McCann and Geoghegan, 1973. Reprint 1985 (University of Wisconsin Press). This is an older but still valuable and readable popular history of the home-front during the World War II years.

18:226 Polenberg, Richard. *War and Society: The United States, 1941–1945*. Philadelphia: Lippincott, 1972. Reprint 1980 (Greenwood Press). This early study delineates the changes that took place in American society, focusing on the modernization and concentration of agriculture, industry, and government.

18:227 Robin, Ron. *The Barbed-Wire College: Reeducating German POWs in the United States during World War II*. Princeton: Princeton University Press, 1995. This volume analyzes a little-known effort by the Special Projects Division of the Office of the Provost Marshal General to reeducate German prisoners of war in the United States. The author maintains that liberal arts academics in charge of the program, who faced a decline in status compared to the social sciences, were primarily concerned with illustrating that the humanities were not irrelevant to the postwar world.

18:228 Ross, Davis R. B. *Preparing for Ulysses: Politics and Veterans during World War II*. New York: Columbia University Press, 1969. Ross analyzes the origins, enactment, and implementation of legislation (GI Bill) designed to ease the burdens of the returning veterans.

18:229 Shulman, Holly Cowan. *The Voice of America: Propaganda and Democracy, 1941–1945*. Madison: University of Wisconsin Press, 1990. Shulman analyzes the wartime radio propaganda of the French desk of the Voice of America and the bureaucratic and ideological struggle within the U.S. government over the nature and control of overseas propaganda. In the process she traces the shifting nature of that propaganda as the war progressed and the eventual defeat of the New Deal liberals and their ideas.

18:230 Sibley, Mulford Q., and Philip E. Jacob. *Conscription of Conscience: The American State and the Conscientious Objector, 1940–1947*. Ithaca: Cornell University Press, 1952. This study of conscientious objectors during World War II is particularly useful for clarifying the history of the provisions for conscientious objection in the Selective Service Act of 1940 and describing the broad range of activities engaged in by pacifists during and immediately after the war.

18:231 Warren, Frank A. *Noble Abstractions: American Liberal Intellectuals and World War II*. Columbus: Ohio State University Press, 1999. Warren analyzes the liberal vision of World War II as a democratic revolution domestically and globally, and the conflict between that vision and the reality of Roosevelt's wartime actions. Two chapters focus on liberal views of Britain and the Soviet Union.

18:232 Winfield, Betty Houchin. *FDR and the News Media*. Urbana: University of Illinois Press, 1990. Reprint 1994 (Columbia University Press). Advantageously using the papers of his press secretary, Stephen T. Early, this is an account of President Roosevelt's style and methods of dealing with the American press.

18:233 Winkler, Allan M. *Home Front U.S.A.: America during World War II*. 2d ed. Wheeling, IL: Harlan Davidson, 2000. This edition successfully updates the first edition, published in 1986. It remains the best brief introduction to the now extensive literature on the American wartime home-front. Separate chapters cover mobilization, societal issues, women and ethnic groups, and politics, followed by a valuable bibliographic essay.

18:234 Wittner, Lawrence S. *Rebels against War: The American Peace Movement, 1933–1983*. Rev. ed. Philadelphia: Temple University Press, 1984. Beginning with the heyday of American pacifism in the 1930s, this work elucidates the peace movement's wartime and postwar difficulties as well as its gradual revival after the mid-1950s. Four chapters cover the World War II years. First published in 1969.

Biographical Studies

COLLECTIVE

18:235 Barker, Elisabeth. *Churchill and Eden at War.* New York: St. Martin's Press, 1978. Barker examines the Churchill-Eden relationship during the war in three main contexts: their differences over De Gaulle; their differences over Roosevelt as exhibited in connection with Spain, Portugal, Italy, and Greece; and their efforts to deal with Stalin as illustrated by the issues of Soviet frontiers, Poland, Czechoslovakia, and the Balkans. She finds Eden disagreeing with Churchill quite often and playing a major role in British decisionmaking.

18:236 De Santis, Hugh. *The Diplomacy of Silence: The American Foreign Service, the Soviet Union, and the Cold War, 1933–1947.* See chapter 2 of this Guide (2:189).

18:237 Fromkin, David. *In the Time of the Americans: FDR, Truman, Eisenhower, Marshall, MacArthur—The Generation That Changed America's Role in the World.* New York: Alfred A. Knopf, 1995. This best-seller is a collective biography of five of the most important U.S. political and military leaders in World War II. Very few of its 552 pages of text actually deal with the years 1942–1945, however. Instead, the author attempts to trace the experiences of all five and the development of their thoughts about America's place in the world.

18:238 Gardner, Lloyd C. *Architects of Illusion: Men and Ideas in American Foreign Policy, 1941–1949.* Chicago: Quadrangle Books, 1970. Gardner argues that the cold war was shaped by American officials who, in determined adherence to their "illusions" about the nature of the postwar world, missed

opportunities for accommodation with the Soviet Union.

18:239 Gellman, Irwin F. *Secret Affairs: Franklin Roosevelt, Cordell Hull, and Sumner Welles.* Gellman analyzes U.S. diplomacy from 1933 to 1945 through the lens of the complex and often secretive personal lives—and the complex and often poisonous interactions—of Roosevelt, Hull, and Welles. Much of the volume focuses on the years before Pearl Harbor, but the last third covers 1942–1945 (17:88).

18:240 Harper, John Lamberton. *American Visions of Europe: Franklin D. Roosevelt, George F. Kennan, and Dean G. Acheson.* The essays in this intriguing, award-winning work plumb the attitudes toward Europe as well as the foreign policy preferences of three significant Americans: President Franklin Roosevelt ("partial internationalism" aimed at retiring Europe from world politics while avoiding entanglement), George F. Kennan ("partial isolationism" with temporary engagement to restore Europe's centrality and autonomy), and Dean Acheson ("accommodating interventionism" on a permanent basis to maintain U.S. and European interests). For each, Harper speculates intelligently on what shaped his views, from the psychological to the experiential (17:89).

18:241 Kimball, Warren F. "Churchill and Roosevelt: The Personal Equation." *Prologue* 6 (Fall 1974): 169–82. Kimball in this early assessment reviews the personal correspondence between President Roosevelt and Prime Minister Churchill. Their relations were generally amicable, but their few disagreements were fundamental.

18:242 _____. *Forged in War: Roosevelt, Churchill, and the Second World War.* Kimball distills his unsurpassed knowledge of the Roosevelt-Churchill relationship to provide a comprehensive, nuanced, and entertaining study of both the personalities and issues involved in grand strategy and Grand Alliance diplomacy in World War II. Overall he defends both leaders against their critics, though not without his own criticisms of their behavior. He also makes clear that their admittedly special relationship was never as special as they would have had the world believe (17:1022).

18:243 Muir, Malcolm, Jr., ed. *The Human Tradi-*

tion in the World War II Era. Wilmington, DE: SR Books, 2000. Designed to introduce students to the variety of wartime experiences through biography, this volume of sixteen brief biographies and memoirs includes two pertinent chapters: Dewey A. Browder, "Henry Morgenthau Jr: American Statesman and German American Jew" (101–19), and Charles F. Brower, IV, "George A. Lincoln: The Evolution of a National Strategist" (261–78).

18:244   Sainsbury, Keith. *Churchill and Roosevelt at War: The War They Fought and the Peace They Hoped to Make.* Washington Square: New York University Press, 1994. This judicious analysis of the wartime Churchill-Roosevelt relationship is organized topically rather than chronologically, with separate chapters on grand strategy, Russia, Eastern Europe, France, Germany, and China. Sainsbury concludes that the two leaders were more successful in forging a common and successful military strategy than in forging common political policies for the postwar world, though he questions the wisdom of that strategy and whether any common political policy could have worked.

AMERICAN

Dean Acheson

18:245   Acheson, Dean. *Present at the Creation: My Years in the State Department.* New York: Norton, 1969. Although most of this memoir focuses on Acheson's later tenure as secretary of state, the first 115 pages cover his work as assistant secretary of state during the war.

18:246   _____. *Sketches from Life of Men I Have Known.* New York: Harper, 1961. This lively, informal series of portraits includes those statesmen Acheson dealt with during as well as after the war, including Churchill, Molotov, Marshall, Bevin, and Vandenberg.

18:247   Perlmutter, Oscar William. "Acheson and the Diplomacy of World War II." *Western Political Quarterly* 14 (December 1961): 896–911. This essay dismisses as "fanciful legend" the notion, politically popular in right-wing circles in the early 1950s, that

Acheson was the architect of American wartime policy. It rebuts the charge that he was the leader of a pro-Russian clique, that he protected Alger Hiss, and that he was responsible for controversial China and Yalta policies.

Charles E. Bohlen

18:248   Bohlen, Charles E. *Witness to History, 1929–1969.* New York: Norton, 1973. Bohlen served as interpreter for Roosevelt and Truman at wartime summit conferences with Stalin. This memoir contains separate chapters on each of those conferences.

18:249   Ruddy, T. Michael. *The Cautious Diplomat: Charles E. Bohlen and the Soviet Union, 1929–1969.* Kent, OH: Kent State University Press, 1986. This is a brief intellectual study of a diplomat who generally wielded influence behind the scenes. Ruddy emphasizes Bohlen's nuanced view of the Soviet Union and continued support for negotiations rather than confrontations in dealing with it.

Joseph E. Davies

18:250   MacLean, Elizabeth Kimball. "Joseph E. Davies and Soviet-American Relations, 1941–1943." *Diplomatic History* 4 (Winter 1980): 73–93. This is an account of Davies's mission to Moscow in 1943 to persuade Stalin to meet with Roosevelt (minus Churchill) as well as an overview of his role as Roosevelt's personal liaison with the Soviets in 1941–1942. MacLean argues that Davies and Roosevelt held similar views about the desirability of a close relationship with the USSR, and that Roosevelt's death and the Truman presidency upset the delicate balance in Soviet-American relations. See also her *Joseph E. Davies: Envoy to the Soviets* (1992) (18:251).

18:251   _____. *Joseph E. Davies: Envoy to the Soviets.* This sympathetic biography covers not only Davies's ambassadorship to the Soviet Union in the 1930s but also his views on the Soviet war effort and the importance of close wartime and postwar Soviet-American relations as well as his efforts to ensure such close relations (17:229).

James Forrestal

18:252 Albion, Robert G., and Robert Howe Connery. *Forrestal and the Navy*. New York: Columbia University Press, 1962. This early biography covers Forrestal's wartime service as assistant secretary of the navy under Secretary Frank Knox and then as secretary after Knox's 1944 death.

18:253 Hoopes, Townsend, and Douglas Brinkley. *Driven Patriot: The Life and Times of James Forrestal*. New York: Alfred A. Knopf, 1992. This is the first full biography of Forrestal in thirty years. Approximately a fourth of the book is devoted to his World War II service as undersecretary and secretary of the navy.

18:254 Rogow, Arnold A. *James Forrestal, A Study of Personality, Politics, and Policy*. New York: Macmillan, 1963. This early but still valuable biography of Forrestal probes the subject psychologically.

W. Averell Harriman

18:255 Abramson, Rudy. *Spanning the Century: The Life of W. Averell Harriman, 1891–1986*. New York: William Morrow, 1992. This first full-length biography of Harriman was researched and written with his cooperation. Approximately one-quarter of the volume analyzes his World War II service as presidential envoy to London and Moscow. It is a sympathetic account that is well researched, if not overly burdened with critical analysis.

18:256 Harriman, W. Averell, and Elie Abel. *Special Envoy to Churchill and Stalin, 1941–1946*. New York: Random House, 1975. Harriman was Roosevelt's lend-lease representative in London from 1941 to 1943 and ambassador to the Soviet Union from 1943 to 1946. This book is part memoir, part biography; while containing some fresh material, it rarely offers insights into policymaking.

Carlton J. H. Hayes

18:257 Halstead, Charles R. "Historians in Politics: Carlton J. H. Hayes as American Ambassador to Spain, 1942–45." *Journal of Contemporary History*

10 (July 1975): 383–405. Hayes, an eminent historian, was instructed to keep Spain from allying with the Axis powers, dissuade Spanish authorities from cooperating with the enemy against the allies, and try to obtain facilities for the American war effort. Halstead carefully notes his strengths and weaknesses as an ambassador, concluding that his knowledge of history gave him no advantages as a diplomat.

18:258 Hayes, Carlton J. H. *Wartime Mission in Spain, 1942–1945*. New York: Macmillan, 1945. Hayes stresses the nonbelligerent status of Spain and notes that Franco moved in the direction of benevolent neutrality toward the United States before the allies had made significant gains in northwest Europe.

Loy W. Henderson

18:259 Brands, H. W. *Inside the Cold War: Loy Henderson and the Rise of the American Empire, 1918–1961*. This biography covers the entire career of foreign service officer and Russian specialist Henderson, including his World War II service in Washington, Moscow, and the Near East (17:244).

18:260 Henderson, Loy W. *A Question of Trust: The Origins of U.S.-Soviet Diplomatic Relations: The Memoirs of Loy W. Henderson*. Although most of this memoir deals with events before Pearl Harbor, the last section covers institutions and individuals with whom Henderson as head of the East European area of the State Department's European Affairs Division had frequent dealings between October 1938 and August 1942. Edited by George W. Baer (17:245).

Harry Hopkins

18:261 Adams, Henry H. *Harry Hopkins: A Biography*. New York: Putnam, 1977. Drawing on memoirs that have appeared and papers opened after Sherwood's *Roosevelt and Hopkins, An Intimate History* (1950) (18:263), Adams provided a sympathetic and more complete picture of Hopkins's personal contribution to the winning of the war than had hitherto appeared. His work has largely been superseded, however, by the more recent volumes by McJimsey (*Harry Hopkins: Ally of the Poor and Defender of Democracy,* 1987 [18:262]) and Tuttle (*Harry L.*

Hopkins and Anglo-American-Soviet Relations, 1941–1945, 1983 [18:264]). Foreword by W. Averell Harriman.

18:262   McJimsey, George T. *Harry Hopkins: Ally of the Poor and Defender of Democracy.* Cambridge, MA: Harvard University Press, 1987. This excellent study is presently the most comprehensive and up-to-date biography of Roosevelt's closest adviser.

18:263   Sherwood, Robert E. *Roosevelt and Hopkins, An Intimate History.* Although dated and superseded by the more recent biographical studies of Hopkins, this remains a classic work by one of America's foremost writers. In addition to its literary merits and insights, it contains all or parts of numerous important World War II documents (17:172). First published in 1948.

18:264   Tuttle, Dwight William. *Harry L. Hopkins and Anglo-American-Soviet Relations, 1941–1945.* New York: Garland Publishing, 1983. Tuttle in this revised dissertation explores Hopkins's role in the formation and functioning of the Grand Alliance during the war.

18:265   Wills, Matthew B. *Wartime Missions of Harry L. Hopkins.* Raleigh, NC: Pentland Press, 1996. This brief volume analyzes Hopkins's major overseas missions during the war—England in early 1941 and July 1942, the Soviet Union in July 1941 and May 1945. The missions were important in the decisions to aid Britain and Russia and invade North Africa in 1942 and in lessening Soviet-American tensions in the spring of 1945.

Cordell Hull

18:266   Hull, Cordell, with Andrew Berding. *The Memoirs of Cordell Hull.* Although Roosevelt made most of the wartime policy decisions without Hull's advice, this memoir by the 1933–1944 secretary of state is essential for understanding wartime policies toward specific countries and areas (such as Vichy France, Spain, and Latin America) as well as postwar planning efforts by the State Department (15:244).

18:267   Pratt, Julius W. *Cordell Hull, 1933–44.* Despite its age, this remains the only book-length study

of Hull's entire 1933–1944 tenure as secretary of state. Pratt is sympathetic to yet often critical of his subject (15:245).

Patrick J. Hurley

18:268   Buhite, Russell D. *Patrick J. Hurley and American Foreign Policy.* Ithaca: Cornell University Press, 1973. This balanced work notes Hurley's strong points but also spells out his failures as a diplomat. The author points to Hurley's making Chiang Kai-shek's case his own, his role in the recall of General Stilwell, and his confusing testimony before the congressional hearings on the Far Eastern crisis. Extensive bibliography.

18:269   Lohbeck, Don. *Patrick J. Hurley.* Chicago: H. Regnery Co., 1956. This authorized biography reflects the extremely unfriendly view Hurley had developed toward Stilwell. This volume, like Stilwell's, should be checked carefully against other sources.

George F. Kennan

18:270   Kennan, George F. *Memoirs. Vol. 1: 1925–1950.* Six chapters cover Kennan's wartime service (far more than in any Kennan biographies), three dealing with his posting and internment in Germany, Lisbon assignment and the Azores controversy, and work on the European Advisory Commission. The others concern his reassignment to and work in the Moscow embassy in 1944–1945. Reprinted in their entirety are two of his most important wartime papers: "Russia—Seven Years Later" (September 1944), and "Russia's International Position at the Close of the War with Germany" (May 1945) (17:259).

18:271   Mayers, David. "Nazi Germany and the Future of Europe: George Kennan's Views, 1939–1945." *International History Review* 8 (November 1986): 550–72. This article examines Kennan's views on Nazi Germany and Europe's future during his European postings immediately before and during the war. These views, Mayers finds, reflected and reinforced his assessments of communist Russia, his distrust of modern politics and belief that it led to totalitarianism, and his desire for both a nonpunitive peace and a return to federated, aristocratic rule in postwar Europe.

Henry Morgenthau, Jr.

18:272   Blum, John Morton, ed. *From the Morgenthau Diaries. Vol. 3: Years of War, 1941–1945.* Boston: Houghton Mifflin, 1967. This account gives valuable material on administration policy as seen by Secretary of Treasury Morgenthau, a close personal friend and neighbor of President Roosevelt, who relied heavily on him for advice on many issues besides Treasury matters.

18:273   _____. *Roosevelt and Morgenthau.* Boston: Houghton Mifflin, 1970. About a third of this revision and condensation of *From the Morgenthau Diaries* (1959–1967) is devoted to the years 1941–1945.

Franklin D. Roosevelt

18:274   Bishop, Jim. *FDR's Last Year, April 1944–April 1945.* New York: William Morrow, 1974. This popular biography is based on oral history interviews as well as published sources but contains no footnotes. It is organized chronologically, with a focus on Roosevelt's health problems and personal life but with a good deal of information on the numerous diplomatic conferences and issues of this period.

18:275   Burns, James MacGregor. *Roosevelt: The Soldier of Freedom.* This second volume of Burns's biography of FDR centers on the war. As in the first volume, the central theme is the gap between Roosevelt as the courageous lion in the realm of ideas and the cautious and wily fox in the realm of implementation. FDR's refusal to match ends and means led to serious negative repercussions (17:156).

18:276   Crispell, Kenneth R., and Carlos F. Gomez. *Hidden Illness in the White House.* Durham, NC: Duke University Press, 1988. One of the authors of this volume is a professor of law and medicine, the other a public policy fellow. Two of the four chapters on specific presidents deal with Roosevelt (the others treat Wilson and Kennedy). They summarize previous accounts of Roosevelt's health problems and the efforts to hide them from the press and public.

18:277   Dallek, Robert. *Franklin D. Roosevelt and American Foreign Policy, 1932–1945.* This 1979 work remains the most comprehensive and extensive study of Roosevelt's foreign policies. Overall Dallek defends FDR against attacks from his early critics, most notably in regard to the Russians, and emphasizes both his accomplishments and the constraints under which he had to work. He does criticize him, however, for "unnecessary and destructive compromises of legal and moral principles" (15:134).

18:278   _____. "Franklin Roosevelt as World Leader: A Review Article." *American Historical Review* 76 (December 1971): 1503–13. This assessment uses Burns's *Roosevelt: The Soldier of Freedom* (1970) (18:275) and Feingold's *The Politics of Rescue: The Roosevelt Administration and the Holocaust, 1938–1945* (1970) (18:859) as backdrops to examine the evolution of American scholarship on FDR as a foreign policy leader since the revisionist and "court" histories of the 1940s and 1950s. It presages many of Dallek's conclusions in *Franklin D. Roosevelt and American Foreign Policy, 1932–1945* (1979) (18:277).

18:279   Davis, Kenneth S. *FDR, the War President, 1940–1943: A History.* New York: Random House, 2000. Published posthumously, this fifth volume of Davis's prize-winning biography covers Roosevelt from his November 1940 reelection to the end of 1942, with a strong focus on the latter year. It emphasizes both the complexity of the issues FDR faced and the personalities with whom he dealt. While quite laudatory, Davis criticizes FDR for numerous actions and inactions.

18:280   Divine, Robert A. *Roosevelt and World War II.* Baltimore: Johns Hopkins University Press, 1969. This major reinterpretation of World War II diplomacy challenges the traditional view of Roosevelt as an idealistic internationalist and emphasizes instead the isolationism, pragmatism, and realism that characterized his foreign policies from 1933 through 1945.

18:281   Emerson, William. "Franklin D. Roosevelt as Commander-in-Chief in World War II." *Military*

Affairs 22 (Winter 1958–1959): 181–207. This re-assessment of Roosevelt as military leader argues that he was acutely sensitive to the political aspects of war, that he controlled his military advisers rather than vice versa, and that he planned wartime strategy on the basis of political, albeit negative, motives. The article is reproduced in Ernest R. May, ed., *The Ultimate Decision: The President as Commander-in-Chief* (New York: George Braziller, 1960).

18:282 Ferrell, Robert H. *Ill-Advised: Presidential Health and Public Trust*. Columbia: University of Missouri Press, 1992. Ferrell devotes one chapter to Roosevelt's health problems, focusing on how they affected the 1944 selection of Truman as his vice-presidential running mate.

18:283 Freidel, Frank. *Franklin D. Roosevelt: A Rendezvous with Destiny*. This final volume by one of Roosevelt's most notable biographers offers a traditional analysis and defense of his wartime diplomacy (17:162).

18:284 Kimball, Warren F. "Franklin D. Roosevelt: 'Dr. Win-the-War.'" In *Commanders in Chief: Presidential Leadership in Modern Wars*, ed. Joseph G. Dawson, III, 87–105. Lawrence: University Press of Kansas, 1993. Roosevelt's performance as a commander in chief must be seen as part of a broader picture of presidential leadership whose aim was reform of the international system. See Kimball, *The Juggler: Franklin Roosevelt as Wartime Statesman* (1991) (18:285) for greater detail on this interpretation.

18:285 _____. *The Juggler: Franklin Roosevelt as Wartime Statesman*. This volume consists of two previously published articles and six unpublished papers on different aspects of Roosevelt's wartime foreign policies as well as extensive historiographical notes. Kimball's overall theme is that Roosevelt did have a consistent foreign policy during the war: creation of a postwar world based on liberal American values as well as U.S. power, continued cooperation among wartime allies, recognition and integration of Soviet power, and a gradual dismantling of European colonial empires (15:150).

18:286 Maney, Patrick J. *The Roosevelt Presence: A Biography of Franklin Delano Roosevelt*. New York: Twayne Publishers, 1992. This brief and read-able biography is highly critical of Roosevelt for his procrastination and inability to consider the long-term consequences of his actions. It was reprinted in 1998 by the University of California Press with the subtitle *The Life and Legacy of FDR*.

18:287 Marks, Frederick W., III. *Wind over Sand: The Diplomacy of Franklin Roosevelt*. Marks is highly critical of Roosevelt as a parochial and provincial American who never understood international affairs. The one chapter focusing on 1941–1945 insists he was not the prisoner of wartime events but never understood the need for an alternative policy toward the Soviet Union (17:168).

18:288 Matloff, Maurice. "Franklin Delano Roosevelt as War Leader." In *Total War and Cold War: Problems in Civilian Control of the Military*, ed. Harry L. Coles, 42–65. Columbus: Ohio State University Press, 1962. This essay by a noted army historian defends most of Roosevelt's policies, most notably unconditional surrender, but criticizes the president for holding rigidly to policies after they had outlived their usefulness, for underestimating Soviet ambitions, and for ignoring the postwar repercussions of wartime military actions.

18:289 Minnen, Cornelis A. van, and John F. Sears, eds. *FDR and His Contemporaries: Foreign Perceptions of an American President*. New York: St. Martin's Press, 1992. The fifteen essays in this volume originated in a 1990 conference in the Netherlands. They are divided into four sections: an introduction by Arthur M. Schlesinger, Jr.; Roosevelt's relationships with his allies; his relationships with his foes; and the legacy of his internationalism: Schlesinger, "Franklin D. Roosevelt's Internationalism" (1–15); David K. Adams, "Churchill and Franklin D. Roosevelt: A Marriage of Convenience" (17–32); Claude Fohlen, "De Gaulle and Franklin D. Roosevelt" (33–44); Valentin Berezhkov, "Stalin and Franklin D. Roosevelt" (45–62); Lubomir W. Zyblikiewicz, "Sikorski, Mikolajczyk, and Franklin D. Roosevelt, 1939–1945" (63–74); Ivan Cizmic, "Review of American-Yugoslav Relations in World War II" (75–84); Albert E. Kersten, "Wilhemina and Franklin D. Roosevelt: A Wartime Relationship" (85–96); Ger van Roon, "The Oslo States and Franklin D. Roosevelt" (97–110); Henry Raymont, "Latin America and Franklin D. Roosevelt"

(111–26); Hsi-sheng Ch'i, "Chiang Kai-shek and Franklin D. Roosevelt" (127–41); Detlef Junker, "Hitler's Perception of Franklin D. Roosevelt and the United States of America" (143–56); Maurizio Vaudagna, "Mussolini and Franklin D. Roosevelt" (157–70); Javier Tussell, "Franco and Franklin D. Roosevelt" (171–84); Akira Iriye, "Emperor Hirohito and Franklin D. Roosevelt" (185–94); and Leon Gordenker, "The Legacy of Franklin D. Roosevelt's Internationalism" (195–210).

18:290 Neumann, William L. "Franklin Delano Roosevelt: A Disciple of Admiral Mahan." *U.S. Naval Institute Proceedings* 78 (July 1952): 713–19. Neumann analyzes Mahan's extensive but little-known influence on Roosevelt.

18:291 Park, Bert Edward. *The Impact of Illness on World Leaders.* Philadelphia: University of Pennsylvania Press, 1986. One of the six chapters in this volume analyzes Roosevelt's illness and its impact on his behavior. Park judiciously concludes that while illness affected his behavior, its impact on his diplomacy, especially at Yalta, has been overstated.

18:292 Range, Willard. *Franklin D. Roosevelt's World Order.* Range in this early study sees Roosevelt as a deep-thinking internationalist, a global Mahanite geopolitician, and a practical idealist (17:170).

18:293 Roosevelt, Elliott. *As He Saw It.* New York: Duell, Sloan and Pearce, 1946. This is a highly personal memoir by the president's son, who was present at all of the wartime conferences except Yalta. Roosevelt claims his father was very interested in economic postwar planning and believed that the European colonial powers threatened the future peace of the world more than the Soviet Union. There appear to be a number of historical inaccuracies here, but the book is a useful source for FDR's postwar aims.

18:294 Sbrega, John J. "The Anticolonial Politics of Franklin D. Roosevelt: A Reappraisal." *Political Science Quarterly* 101 (Spring 1986): 65–84. Roosevelt was generally constant in his anticolonialism, but his buoyant optimism fostered overconfidence that he could achieve objectives on issues beyond American power to influence. Although he felt constrained by his belief that many Americans remained isolationist at heart, Sbrega argues that through passivity

he forfeited his diplomatic leverage by waiting until the end of the war to engage the complicated issue of colonialism.

18:295 Smith, Gaddis. "Forty Months: Franklin D. Roosevelt as War Leader, 1941–1945." *Prologue* 26 (Fall 1994): 131–39. Based on a talk at the National Archives, Smith in this essay admits he had previously underrated Roosevelt and uses the metaphor of wise seamanship to analyze and praise his wartime performance.

Henry L. Stimson

18:296 Current, Richard N. *Secretary Stimson, A Study in Statecraft.* See chapter 17 of this Guide (17:269).

18:297 Hodgson, Godfrey. *The Colonel: The Life and Wars of Henry Stimson, 1867–1950.* This is one of the most recent full-length biographies of Stimson. Only two chapters cover his 1940–1945 tenure as secretary of war; however, one focused solely on the atomic bomb (17:270).

18:298 Morison, Elting E. *Turmoil and Tradition: A Study of the Life and Times of Henry L. Stimson.* Although it is more than forty years old, this award-winning, semiofficial biography remains quite valuable and informative as well as a joy to read. Morison focuses on the years before 1940 but devotes over a hundred pages to Stimson's wartime service as secretary of war (17:271).

18:299 Schmitz, David F. *Henry L. Stimson: The First Wise Man.* Wilmington, DE: SR Books, 2001. Designed for use in undergraduate courses, this brief and well-written biography portrays Stimson as a key individual in America's movement from traditional imperialism and isolationism to internationalism as well as an exemplar of the bipartisan foreign policy establishment. Approximately one-third of its pages deal with Stimson's work as secretary of war during World War II.

18:300 Stimson, Henry L., and McGeorge Bundy. *On Active Service in Peace and War.* This combination memoir and biography covers the years 1905 to 1945, with over half devoted to Stimson's experiences as secretary of war from 1940 to 1945. Diary excerpts provide an excellent, firsthand account of the War Department during these years, with special emphasis on wartime mobilization, grand strategy, postwar planning, and the atomic bomb decision (17:272).

Robert A. Taft

18:301   Patterson, James T. "Alternatives to Globalism: Robert A. Taft and American Foreign Policy, 1939–1945." *Historian* 36 (August 1974): 670–88. Taft never made it clear how he reconciled his faith in a powerful World Court with his insistence on the preservation of national sovereignty, nor how a World Court could operate without an international police force.

18:302   _____. *Mr. Republican: A Biography of Robert A. Taft.* Eight chapters of this authorized biography cover Taft in the 1939–1945 period, but only one deals with foreign policy issues after Pearl Harbor (17:179).

Myron C. Taylor

18:303   Conway, John S. "Myron C. Taylor's Mission to the Vatican 1940–1950." The mission of Taylor, personal representative of Roosevelt and Truman to Pope Pius XII, remains an anomaly in U.S. foreign relations. Since the United States maintained no formal mission to the Vatican, Taylor was the main link between the papacy and Washington (17:273).

18:304   Flynn, George Q. "Franklin Roosevelt and the Vatican: The Myron Taylor Appointment." Roosevelt appointed Taylor as a special representative to the Vatican on December 24, 1939, culminating years of negotiating with leading American Catholics (17:274).

Arthur Vandenberg

18:305   Gazell, James A. "Arthur H. Vandenberg, Internationalism, and the United Nations." *Political Science Quarterly* 88 (September 1973): 375–94. The author perceptively traces the evolution of Vanden-

berg's views from the late 1920s to his participation at the San Francisco conference in 1945. Vandenberg's conversion owed much to his belief that modern technology had rendered isolationism obsolete.

18:306   Gregg, Richard G. "A Rhetorical Re-examination of Arthur Vandenberg's 'Dramatic Conversion,' January 10, 1945." *Quarterly Journal of Speech* 61 (April 1975): 154–68. Gregg argues that Vandenberg's speech announcing his conversion to internationalism was designed to induce Franklin D. Roosevelt to delineate his foreign policy more clearly.

Henry A. Wallace

18:307   Culver, John C., and John Hyde. *American Dreamer: The Life and Times of Henry A. Wallace.* New York: Norton, 2000. This biography uses previously closed family and personal papers to cover Wallace's political and professional careers and his private life. The World War II chapters emphasize his responsibilities for economic mobilization and efforts to shape postwar political economies both at home and abroad.

18:308   Markowitz, Norman D. *The Rise and Fall of the People's Century: Henry A. Wallace and American Liberalism, 1941–1948.* New York: Free Press, 1973. This is a sympathetic account of Wallace's public career during World War II and the early cold war years with an emphasis on the latter.

18:309   Schapsmeier, Edward L., and Frederick H. Schapsmeier. *Prophet in Politics: Henry A. Wallace and the War Years, 1940–1965.* Ames, IA: Iowa State University Press, 1971. This second volume of an early full-length biography is sympathetic and emphasizes his religious faith. Approximately half the chapters deal with the war years and are topically organized.

18:310   Walker, J. Samuel. *Henry A. Wallace and American Foreign Policy.* Westport, CT: Greenwood Press, 1976. This is a brief but balanced account of Wallace's foreign policy views, with more attention than usual paid to the pre-1941 period. Three of fourteen chapters concern the war years.

18:311   White, Graham J., and John Maze. *Henry A. Wallace: His Search for a New World Order.*

Chapel Hill: University of North Carolina Press, 1995. This study makes extensive use of Wallace's 5,000-page oral history transcript as well as his papers in attempting to analyze the relationship between his spiritual and political ideas. Two chapters focus on the World War II years.

Sumner Welles

18:312   Graff, Frank Warren. *Strategy of Involvement: A Diplomatic Biography of Sumner Welles.* This revised dissertation is extensively researched even though written before the opening of the Welles papers. It contains two chapters on his diplomatic activities and views during the war, one covering Latin America, France, and the Soviet Union, the other postwar planning, relations with Hull, and his 1943 resignation (17:275).

18:313   Welles, Benjamin. *Sumner Welles: FDR's Global Strategist: A Biography.* This long-awaited and graceful biography of Welles by his son focuses on the years before Pearl Harbor but contains informative chapters on Welles and De Gaulle, the 1942 Rio conference, the Holocaust, and postwar planning (including his opposition to Soviet territorial demands and work on the UN Charter) (15:249).

18:314   Welles, Sumner. *Seven Decisions That Shaped History.* This volume is simultaneously a memoir, an explanation, and overall a strong defense of seven of Roosevelt's major foreign policies before and during the war. Most relevant for the post–Pearl Harbor years are the chapters on the decision to preserve hemispheric unity, the postponement until after the war of various political and territorial issues, wartime Far Eastern policies, and the creation of the United Nations (17:277).

18:315   _____. *Where Are We Heading?* New York: Harper, 1946. Welles assesses various American officials and their actions during World War II and provides an insider's view of the Atlantic Charter meeting. Welles advocates strong support for the infant United Nations. He states that Roosevelt, prior to his death, had taken the first steps in seeking a cooperative relationship with the system of Russian communism.

John G. Winant

18:316   Bellush, Bernard. *He Walked Alone: A Biography of John Gilbert Winant.* The Hague: Mouton, 1968. Winant was wartime ambassador to Great Britain as well as governor of New Hampshire, New Deal administrator, and the first American director of the International Labor Organization. Bellush presents a sympathetic portrait.

18:317   Winant, John Gilbert. *Letter from Grosvenor Square: An Account of a Stewardship.* Winant was the U.S. ambassador to Great Britain during the war, but this memoir is quite limited in scope and content (17:284).

Others

18:318   Almquist, Leann Grabavoy. *Joseph Alsop and American Foreign Policy: The Journalist as Advocate.* Lanham, MD: University Press of America, 1993. This biography covers Alsop's career as a journalist-advocate from the 1930s through his 1974 retirement. One of its seven chapters focuses on his World War II efforts to convince Roosevelt to support Chennault and dismiss Stilwell.

18:319   Schwarz, Jordan A. *Liberal: Adolf A. Berle and the Vision of an American Era.* This biography contains substantial information on Berle's expansive foreign policy ideas and ideology as well as his wartime activities as assistant secretary of state and, in 1945, ambassador to Brazil. Separate chapters are devoted to that ambassadorship and to Berle's extensive negotiations on postwar commercial aviation as well as his other wartime activities (17:285).

18:320   Brownell, Will, and Richard N. Billings. *So Close to Greatness: A Biography of William C. Bullitt.* This first full biography of Bullitt portrays him, often in overstated terms, as a brilliant and prescient but tragically flawed individual. The World War II sections are brief but cover his wartime assignments, memoranda to Roosevelt, and break with FDR over the Sumner Welles affair (17:224).

18:321   Hershberg, James G. *James B. Conant: Harvard to Hiroshima and the Making of the Nuclear Age.* New York: Alfred A. Knopf, 1993. This full biography of Conant gives considerable attention to his work on the atomic bomb project and allied relations during World War II.

18:322　Davies, John Paton, Jr. *Dragon by the Tail: American, British, Japanese, and Russian Encounters with China and One Another.* New York: Norton, 1972. Davies's book is both a memoir of his years as a foreign service officer in China (1937–1945) and an analysis of American and Soviet confrontations with Chinese nationalism. His account of political infighting in China and Washington makes compelling reading.

18:323　Grose, Peter. *Gentleman Spy: The Life of Allen Dulles.* Boston: Houghton Mifflin, 1994. Although this extensive biography focuses on Dulles's postwar career as head of the CIA, four chapters are devoted to his important wartime intelligence work with the OSS in Europe.

18:324　Eggleston, George T. *Roosevelt, Churchill, and the World War II Opposition: A Revisionist Autobiography.* Old Greenwich, CT: Devin-Adair, 1979. The second half of this memoir by a former leader of the America First Committee details what he considers a government vendetta to prosecute him during and after U.S. entry into the war.

18:325　Eichelberger, Clark M. *Organizing for Peace: A Personal History of the Founding of the United Nations.* New York: Harper and Row, 1977. The author, director of the League of Nations Association and its successor, the United Nations Association, describes his personal role in the formation of the UN. Especially informative are chapters on his organization's role in mobilizing public opinion during World War II and on his conversations with Sumner Welles and FDR.

18:326　Elsey, George M. "Some White House Recollections, 1942–53." *Diplomatic History* 12 (Summer 1988): 357–64. Assigned in April 1942 to Roosevelt's map room as naval intelligence officer, Elsey was one of eight individuals who served in what was effectively FDR's secretariat for communication with allied leaders as well as his generals and admirals. These recollections provide interesting details on both how this crucial room operated and the individuals involved.

18:327　Emmerson, John K. *The Japanese Thread:*

A Life in the U.S. Foreign Service. New York: Holt, Rinehart and Winston, 1978. The earlier chapters of this carefully crafted memoir by a distinguished American diplomat offer valuable commentary on the makers of U.S. East Asian policy. Chapters 7–9 are of special interest for their discussions of the author's wartime experiences in Washington and the China-Burma-India theater (including Yenan).

18:328　Gildersleeve, Virginia Crocheron. *Many A Good Crusade: Memoirs.* New York: Macmillan, 1954. These memoirs recount Gildersleeve's long-time interest in the movement for U.S. participation in an international organization. There is valuable material on her role as a delegate at the UN Conference on International Organization in 1945, particularly her interest in human rights.

18:329　Heinrichs, Waldo H. *American Ambassador: Joseph C. Grew and the Development of the United States Diplomatic Tradition.* This critical assessment, although dated on some issues such as Japan's surrender, remains the best biography of Grew as well as a thoughtful critique of American diplomats and the State Department (11:497).

18:330　Israel, Fred L., ed. *The War Diary of Breckinridge Long: Selections from the Years 1939–1944.* This edited diary provides a glimpse inside the Roosevelt administration as well as Long's notorious role in the U.S. response to the Holocaust. Long had special entree into two camps, the conservative southern Democratic group and the official State Department organization. Both had their differences with the president and his advisers, and in candidly recounting his views and reactions Long makes a significant contribution. Edited by Fred L. Israel (17:295).

18:331　Bird, Kai. *The Chairman: John J. McCloy, The Making of the American Establishment.* New York: Simon and Schuster, 1992. In this detailed biography of the "ultimate power-broker," Bird is critical of McCloy's performance as assistant secretary of war during World War II. He examines McCloy's concern with domestic sabotage and his role in the internment of Japanese-Americans as well as his opposition to bombing the rail lines to Auschwitz.

18:332　Murphy, Robert D. *Diplomat among Warriors.* Garden City, NY: Doubleday, 1964. As a representative of Roosevelt in North Africa (1942–1943) and political adviser to Eisenhower in the Mediterranean and northwest Europe, Murphy was involved in many momentous, sometimes controversial, events during World War II.

18:333 Eiler, Keith E. *Mobilizing America: Robert P. Paterson and the War Effort, 1940–1945.* Ithaca: Cornell University Press, 1997. This well-researched and -written study focuses on the critical role of Patterson, the former judge and wartime assistant secretary of war, in the fields of industrial and manpower mobilization. The organization is topical, albeit within a three-part chronological framework of pre–Pearl Harbor, the war years, and aftermath (1945–1947).

18:334 Berger, Jason. *A New Deal for the World: Eleanor Roosevelt and American Foreign Policy.* New York: Columbia University Press, 1981. Berger provides a general treatment of Eleanor Roosevelt's beliefs and activities regarding foreign affairs. Although willing to voice opinions on selected issues, she was careful to stay within the president's policies and had limited effect on foreign policy in general.

18:335 Standley, William H., and Arthur A. Ageton. *Admiral Ambassador to Russia.* Chicago: H. Regnery Co., 1955. Admiral Standley, ambassador to the Soviet Union in 1942–1943, was critical of Roosevelt's policy of giving aid to Moscow without demanding a quid pro quo. He particularly faults the lend-lease activities of Harry Hopkins and Brigadier General Faymonville and visits to Russian officials by such FDR representatives as former Ambassador Joseph Davies and Wendell Willkie.

18:336 Rubin, Barry. "Ambassador Laurence A. Steinhardt: The Perils of a Jewish Diplomat, 1940–1945." This brief account of Ambassador Steinhardt's wartime activities, particularly in Turkey, focuses on how being Jewish may have influenced his behavior (17:299).

18:337 Walker, Richard L. "E. R. Stettinius, Jr." In *The American Secretaries of State and Their Diplomacy,* ed. Samuel Flagg Bemis and Robert H. Ferrell, 14, 1–83, 318–40, 397–404. New York: Cooper Square, 1965. A brief but workmanlike biography, it should be supplemented with Campbell and Herring, *The Diaries of Edward R. Stettinius, Jr., 1943–1946* (1975) (18:67).

18:338 Miscamble, Wilson D. "The Evolution of an Internationalist: Harry S. Truman and American Foreign Policy." *Australian Journal of Politics and History* 23 (August 1977): 268–83. This review of Truman's thinking examines impressions and ideas that evolved from his extensive reading and experiences as a World War I soldier and senator. His internationalist views as president had thus been set long before 1945.

OTHERS (FOREIGN)

Valentin Berezhkov

18:339 Berezhkov, Valentin M. *At Stalin's Side: His Interpreter's Memoirs from the October Revolution to the Fall of the Dictator's Empire.* Translated by Sergei M. Mikheyev. Seacaucus, NJ: Carol Publishing Group, 1994. Written after the fall of the Soviet Union and published in the United States, this autobiography by Stalin's wartime interpreter is much more personal and revealing than his *History in the Making: Memoirs of World War II Diplomacy* (1983) (18:340).

18:340 _____. *History in the Making: Memoirs of World War II Diplomacy.* Translated by Dudley Hagen and Barry Jones. Moscow: Progress Publishers, 1983. Berezhkov served as Stalin's interpreter during his World War II conferences with Churchill and Roosevelt. These memoirs were written while the Soviet Union was still in existence and in the Soviet style. See also his more personal and informal 1994 autobiography, *At Stalin's Side: His Interpreter's Memoirs from the October Revolution to the Fall of the Dictator's Empire* (18:339).

Winston Churchill

18:341 Ben-Moshe, Tuvia. *Churchill, Strategy and History.* Boulder: Lynne Rienner Publishers, 1992. The author is sharply critical of Churchill, arguing that he did not have a coherent strategy or policy during the war, that he divorced the two, and that the British were as optimistic and incoherent about the Soviet Union as they claim the Americans were.

18:342 Blake, Robert, and William Roger Louis, eds. *Churchill.* New York: W. W. Norton, 1993. This important collection includes several significant chapters, including Warren F. Kimball, "Wheel within a Wheel: Churchill, Roosevelt, and the Special Relationship" (275–90); Robin Edmonds, "Churchill and Stalin" (291–308); John Keegan, "Churchill's Strategy" (309–26); and Stephen E. Ambrose, "Churchill and Eisenhower in the Second World War" (397–406).

18:343 Callahan, Raymond A. *Churchill: Retreat from Empire.* Wilmington, DE: Scholarly Resources, 1984. Callahan deftly synthesizes the mass of material now available on Churchill to analyze his role in the loss of the British empire from 1940 to 1955. One of the four content chapters in this volume focuses on the period from Pearl Harbor to Germany's surrender.

18:344 Charmley, John. *Churchill, The End of Glory: A Political Biography.* This highly revisionist and controversial biography is deeply critical of Churchill's foreign policies, particularly his refusal to negotiate with Hitler and his later actions that resulted in American and Soviet dominance. Although most of the volume focuses on the years before official U.S. entry into the war, the last fourteen of its fifty-five chapters cover the wartime Grand Alliance (17:211). For an even more detailed account of Churchill's faith in an Anglo-American alliance, see his *Churchill's Grand Alliance: The Anglo-American Special Relationship, 1940–57* (1995) (18:345).

18:345 _____. *Churchill's Grand Alliance: The Anglo-American Special Relationship, 1940–57.* New York: Harcourt Brace and Co., 1995. Continuing his revisionist assault begun in *Churchill, The End of Glory: A Political Biography* (1993) (18:344), Charmley in this volume argues that Churchill's misconceived faith in a "special relationship" with the United States was disastrous for Britain. The only one of the Big Three not to have a thoughtful and workable long-range policy and grand strategy, he never recognized that U.S. goals were antithetical to his and would result in the disintegration of Britain's empire and power. Better, Charmley argues, to have reached postwar accord with Stalin as recommended by Eden in 1941 than to have relied upon the United States. Approximately half of this volume focuses on the World War II years.

18:346 Churchill, Winston. *The Second World War.* 6 vols. Boston: Houghton Mifflin, 1948–1953. For many years these volumes (*The Gathering Storm, Their Finest Hour, The Grand Alliance, The Hinge of Fate, Closing the Ring,* and *Triumph and Tragedy*) constituted an essential source for anyone interested in allied strategy and diplomacy during World War II. They remain a significant source and the finest memoir by any major World War II figure, but they must be used with caution and recognition that Churchill is presenting his case.

18:347 Cohen, Eliot A. "Churchill and Coalition Strategy in World War II." In *Grand Strategies in War and Peace,* ed. Paul Kennedy, 43–67. New Haven: Yale University Press, 1991. Churchill made close Anglo-American relations the core of his grand strategy and succeeded in obtaining what he wanted from the United States until June 1944, something Cohen finds remarkable given his weak bargaining position. Unlike Tuvia Ben-Moshe in *Churchill, Strategy and History* (1992) (18:341), Charmley in *Churchill's Grand Alliance: The Anglo-American Special Relationship, 1940–57* (1995) (18:345), and other recent critics, Cohen concludes that Churchill's grand strategy was excellent and consistent.

18:348 Gilbert, Martin. *Road to Victory: Winston S. Churchill, 1941–1945.* Boston: Houghton Mifflin, 1986. This seventh volume of the official biography covers the entire period of the wartime alliance with the United States and the Soviet Union, providing virtually a daily account of Churchill's activities.

18:349 Parker, R. A. C., ed. *Winston Churchill: Studies in Statesmanship.* Washington, DC: Brassey's, 1995. Of these conference essays, the most valuable to World War II scholars are Anita Prazmowska, "Churchill and Poland" (110–23); François Kersaudy, "Churchill and de Gaulle" (124–34); and Warren F. Kimball, "Churchill, Roosevelt and Postwar Europe" (135–49).

18:350 Reynolds, David. "Churchill the Appeaser? Between Hitler, Roosevelt and Stalin in World War II." In *Diplomacy and World Power: Studies in British Foreign Policy, 1890–1950,* ed. Michael Dockrill and Brian J. C. McKercher, 197–220. New York: Cambridge University Press, 1996. Reynolds largely dismisses criticism of Churchill as an "appeaser" of other allies' wartime demands, noting his often limited bargaining leverage. His strategic dilemma was that the Commonwealth could not win the war against Germany alone and could not dispense with Soviet and American military power.

18:351 Taylor, A. J. P., et al. *Churchill Revised: A Critical Assessment.* New York: Dial Press, 1969. The five essays in this book examine Churchill as a statesman, politician, author, military leader, and as a private individual. These are thoughtful studies presenting Churchill's view of the world in which he lived and of the world he hoped to create in the postwar era: Taylor, "The Statesman"; Robert Rhodes James, "The Politician"; J. H. Plumb, "The Historian"; B. H. Liddell Hart, "The Military Strategist"; and A. Storr, "The Man."

18:352 Thompson, Kenneth W. *Winston Churchill's World View: Statesmanship and Power.* Baton Rouge: Louisiana State University Press, 1983. This topically organized work of political science provides a detailed and insightful analysis of Churchill's views on international relations. It focuses on his emphasis on both military strength and negotiation as the road to peace.

Charles de Gaulle

18:353 De Gaulle, Charles. *The Complete War Memoirs of Charles De Gaulle.* Translated by J. Griffin and R. Howard. 3 vols. New York: Simon and Schuster, 1972. The three volumes, *The Call to Honour, 1940–1942; Unity, 1942–1944;* and *Salvation, 1944–1946,* range from de Gaulle's call for resistance to the enemy after the fall of France to his establishment of a provisional government in liberated France and relations with the allies after the war. Originally published 1955–1960.

18:354 Funk, Arthur L. *Charles de Gaulle: The Crucial Years, 1943–1944.* Norman: University of Oklahoma Press, 1959. This volume, which clarifies his role at the Casablanca conference, shows de Gaulle's efforts to establish France's position on Great Britain, the Soviet Union, and the United States.

Anthony Eden

18:355 Eden, Anthony. *The Reckoning: The Memoirs of Anthony Eden, Earl of Avon.* Boston: Houghton Mifflin Co., 1965. Although beginning with his resignation from the Chamberlain cabinet in 1938, most of this memoir deals with Eden's experiences as British foreign secretary (1941 to mid-1945) and offers exceptional insights into and explanations of the men and events dominating allied diplomacy during the war.

18:356 James, Robert Rhodes. *Anthony Eden.* London: Weidenfeld and Nicolson, 1986. This authorized biography devotes relatively few pages to Eden's work as wartime foreign secretary.

Lord Halifax

18:357 Birkenhead, Frederick W. F. Smith. *Halifax: The Life of Lord Halifax.* Boston: Houghton Mifflin, 1966. Halifax was British foreign secretary (1938–1940) and ambassador to the United States (1940–1946). This biography devotes more than half its pages to his career before he became foreign secretary in 1938. It is valuable for the description of his service as ambassador to the United States.

18:358 Halifax, Edward Frederick Lindley Wood. *Fulness of Days.* London: Collins, 1957. The volume is disappointingly thin with the author offering little information on foreign relations.

Mackenzie King

18:359 Henderson, George F., ed. *W. L. Mackenzie King: A Bibliography and Research Guide.* Toronto: University of Toronto Press, 1998. This bibliography is divided into two major sections concerning Canada's wartime prime minister: works by him and works about him, the latter divided by type and organized alphabetically within each section. It also contains a chronology and numerous appendices.

18:360 Stacey, Charles P. *Mackenzie King and the Atlantic Triangle.* Toronto: Macmillan of Canada, 1976. A series of lectures delivered at the University of Western Ontario in 1976, this small book concisely describes Mackenzie King's relations with the United States and Britain before, during, and after World War II.

Joseph Stalin

18:361 Deutscher, Isaac. *Stalin: A Political Biography.* 2d ed. New York: Oxford University Press, 1966. This comprehensive study remains an insightful, valuable work, despite its age. Deutscher writes that traditional and revolutionary elements intertwined in Stalin's postwar foreign policies, with the former holding sway over the latter. First published in 1949.

18:362 Tucker, Robert C. *The Soviet Political Mind: Stalinism and Post-Stalin Change.* New York: Norton, 1971. This work elaborates how the psychopathological aspects of Stalin's personality shaped his domestic and foreign policies.

18:363 Volkogonov, Dmitri A. *Stalin: Triumph and Tragedy.* Translated by Harold Shukman. New York: Grove Weidenfeld, 1991. Based on Stalin's papers and written by the head of Soviet military history, this highly critical biography was a milestone in the Gorbachev-era development of Soviet historiography.

Others

18:364 Attlee, Clement. *As It Happened.* New York: Viking Press, 1954. Though an unusually candid memoir by the leader of the Opposition, lord privy seal, and deputy prime minister during the war, the main revelations here are about Attlee's own reactions to events.

18:365 Birse, A. H. *Memoirs of an Interpreter.* New York: Coward-McCann, 1967. Birse was the British translator at the wartime Teheran, Yalta, Potsdam, San Francisco, and two Moscow conferences of 1942 and 1944. His memoir provides interesting insights into these conferences beyond the official minutes.

18:366 Casey, Richard Gardiner. *Personal Experience, 1939–1946.* London: Constable, 1962. Casey was the first Australian minister to the United States (1940–1942) and subsequently British minister of

state for the Middle East and governor of Bengal. This volume is a narrative based on, and with excerpts from, his diary. Somewhat scattered, it tends to minimize Casey's role in Anglo-American collaboration prior to U.S. entry into the war.

18:367 Ciechanowski, Jan. *Defeat in Victory.* Garden City, NY: Doubleday and Company, 1947. Ciechanowski was the ambassador to the United States from the Polish government-in-exile in London (1941–1945). These memoirs, while highly biased and critical of Roosevelt, offer numerous insights into Polish-American relations during the war.

18:368 Dalton, Hugh. *Memoirs. Vol. 2: The Fateful Years, 1931–1945.* London: Frederick Muller, 1957. The most important sections of this sometimes indiscreet memoir of a Labour Party leader who became a senior British official during the war and in the Attlee government concern the party's approach to the war and Dalton's service as minister of economic warfare and director of the Special Operations Executive. See also Ben Pimlott, ed., *The Second World War Diary of Hugh Dalton 1940–45* (London: Cape and the London School of Economics and Political Science, 1986).

18:369 Jebb, Gladwyn. *The Memoirs of Lord Gladwyn.* New York: Weybright and Talley, 1972. Jebb was a major British Foreign Office official who played a pivotal role in postwar planning, most notably but far from exclusively in regard to the occupation of Germany and the establishment of the United Nations.

18:370 Gromyko, Andrei. *Memoirs.* Translated by Harold Shukman. New York: Doubleday, 1989. The then young and little-known Gromyko served as wartime Soviet ambassador to the United States following the 1943 recall of Maxim Litvinov. Foreword by Henry Kissinger.

18:371 Bix, Herbert P. *Hirohito and the Making of Modern Japan.* New York: HarperCollins Publishers, 2000. This prize-winning book will stand as the revisionist view of Hirohito as an active war leader. As culpable for the Pacific war as his military leaders, he eluded blame for the war through a combination of luck, calculation, and MacArthur's political needs. Bix draws on many Japanese-language sources published since Hirohito's death.

18:372 Macmillan, Harold. *The Blast of War, 1939–45.* New York: Harper and Row, 1968. This memoir of Britain's chief political adviser in the Mediterranean area provides important information on decisions and actions from Africa to Italy. Naturally defending British policy and most of Churchill's views, Macmillan takes the Americans to task for supporting Giraud, Operation Anvil, and opposition to the monarchy in Greece. The volume should be supplemented with Macmillan, *War Diaries: Politics and War in the Mediterranean, January 1943–May 1945* (1984) (18:78).

18:373 Maisky, Ivan M. *Memoirs of a Soviet Ambassador: The War, 1939–43.* Translated by Andrew Rothstein. New York: Scribner, 1968. These memoirs by the Soviet ambassador to Britain in 1939–1943 offer numerous insights into Anglo-Soviet relations during the war and are highly critical of Churchill for delaying a second front. First published in 1967 in the United Kingdom.

18:374 Resis, Albert, ed. *Molotov Remembers: Inside Kremlin Politics: Conversations with Felix Chuev.* Chicago: Ivan R. Dee, 1993. This is a translation and reorganization of portions of *One Hundred Forty Conversations with Stalin, From the Diary of F. Chuev,* which itself constituted 700 of the more than 5,000 typewritten pages resulting from Chuev's sessions with the wartime and postwar Soviet foreign minister. Resis has organized the material into four sections: international affairs, with Lenin, with Stalin, and after Stalin. At times Molotov recalls trying to restrain the more aggressive Stalin.

18:375 Strang, William. *Home and Abroad.* London: Deutsch, 1956. Lord Strang was the permanent undersecretary of state for foreign affairs. Of special interest to scholars working on postwar planning is Strang's chapter on his role as Britain's representative on the European Advisory Commission.

MILITARY

Collective

18:376 Blumenson, Martin. "America's World War II Leaders in Europe: Some Thoughts." *Parameters* 19 (December 1989): 2–13. Blumenson favorably contrasts the senior military leaders of the allies, and particularly the Americans, against their German opponents. He argues that the Americans were equipped intellectually to deal with the strategic aspects of waging war, while the Germans produced virtually no strategists.

18:377 Danchev, Alex. *Very Special Relationship: Field-Marshal Sir John Dill and the Anglo-American Alliance, 1941–44.* Washington, DC: Brassey's Defence Publishers, 1986. Danchev uses Dill's heading of the British Joint Staff Mission in Washington and ensuing friendship with Marshall from early 1942 to his death in 1944 to explore previously neglected aspects of the Anglo-American alliance.

18:378 James, D. Clayton, with Anne Sharp Wells. *A Time for Giants: Politics of the American High Command in World War II.* New York: Franklin Watts, 1987. Designed as an introductory volume for the general reader, this work analyzes eighteen U.S. World War II admirals and generals, including all members of the wartime Joint Chiefs of Staff, all the main theater commanders, and all those who rose to five-star rank, and in so doing addresses major issues of coalition warfare.

18:379 Keegan, John, ed. *Churchill's Generals.* New York: G. Weidenfeld, 1991. The essays in this volume cover eighteen British generals. Most useful to diplomatic historians are those on Sir John Dill by Alex Danchev and Alanbrooke by David Fraser, both of which address Anglo-American military diplomacy.

18:380 Larrabee, Eric. *Commander in Chief: Franklin Delano Roosevelt, His Lieutenants, and Their War.* New York: Harper and Row, 1987. Based on secondary sources, this eloquent and well-argued account consists of extensive biographical studies of Roosevelt and nine of his key military advisers and commanders (Marshall, King, Arnold, Vandegrift, MacArthur, Nimitz, Eisenhower, Stilwell, and LeMay). The author focuses on FDR's relationship with each, portraying him as both an activist commander in chief of the U.S. war effort and a capable strategist who ensured that military operations meshed with political objectives.

18:381   Marolda, Edward J., ed. *FDR and the U.S. Navy.* New York: St. Martin's Press, 1998. While mostly dealing with prewar years, several of these papers from a 1996 conference explore pertinent wartime issues: Harold D. Langley, "Roosevelt and Churchill and the Fight for Victory and Stability" (115–30); Paul Miles, "Roosevelt and Leahy: The Orchestration of Global Strategy" (147–62); Thomas B. Buell, "Roosevelt and Strategy in the Pacific" (163–72); and Jeffrey G. Barlow, "Roosevelt and King: The War in the Atlantic and European Theaters" (173–92).

18:382   Parrish, Thomas. *Roosevelt and Marshall: Partners in Politics and War.* New York: William Morrow, 1989. This dual biography analyzes the extraordinary wartime relationship between Roosevelt and his army chief of staff. Parrish finds their relationship based not simply on mutual candor and respect but on a partial role reversal in which the politician Roosevelt became one of the strongest commanders in chief while the soldier Marshall became one of the nation's most effective politicians.

American

Henry H. Arnold

18:383   Arnold, Henry H. *Global Mission.* New York: Harper, 1949. Although a memoir covering his entire military career and the early history of army airpower, over half of this work deals with Arnold's experiences as chief of staff of the U.S. army air forces and member of the Joint Chiefs of Staff (1942–1945). He offers valuable insights into the issues, individuals, and conferences involved in the formulation of allied strategy, with special emphasis placed on the wartime development of airpower. He is sometimes unreliable on dates and the sequence of events.

18:384   Coffey, Thomas M. *HAP: Military Aviator: The Story of the U.S. Air Force and the Man Who Built It, General Henry H. "Hap" Arnold.* New York: Viking Press, 1982. This popular biography provides little if any information for the serious scholar about the wartime chief of the army air forces but remains one of the few works available on a significant figure.

18:385   Daso, Dik Alan. *Hap Arnold and the Evolution of American Airpower.* Washington, DC:

Smithsonian Institution Press, 2000. This is the best and most recent biography of Arnold, U.S. air chief and member of the Joint and Combined Chiefs of Staff. Unfortunately, however, only about forty pages deal with the World War II years.

Omar N. Bradley

18:386   Bradley, Omar N. *A Soldier's Story.* New York: Holt, 1951. In these modest memoirs written soon after the war, General Bradley, one of the most successful allied commanders, provides interesting insights on other leaders. More acerbic and critical are his later recollections in *A General's Life: An Autobiography* (1983) (18:387).

18:387   Bradley, Omar N., and Clay Blair. *A General's Life: An Autobiography.* New York: Simon and Schuster, 1983. This sequel to *A Soldier's Story* (1951) (18:386) is not a true autobiography. While informative, it should be used with care. It is far more critical of the people with whom Bradley worked during the war and of the decisions reached.

Mark Clark

18:388   Blumenson, Martin. *Mark Clark.* New York: Congdon and Weed, 1984. This first full biography of General Clark focuses on his World War II experiences in the Mediterranean, where he played major diplomatic as well as military roles in the North African and Italian campaigns.

18:389   Clark, Mark. *Calculated Risk.* New York: Harper, 1950. This memoir of the commander of the Fifth Army and 15th Army Group focuses primarily on the Italian theater, defending the concept of using Italy as a magnet to draw German troops from the French and Russian fronts. He also argues that the attack should have been continued into the Balkans, thus saving them from communist domination.

Dwight D. Eisenhower

18:390   Ambrose, Stephen E. *Eisenhower. Vol. 1: Soldier, General of the Army, President-Elect, 1890–1952.* New York: Simon and Schuster, 1983. The first of two volumes, and the best available biography of Eisenhower, this is a solid narrative of his life until his election as president. Relying heavily on

Chandler, *The Papers of Dwight David Eisenhower: Vols. 1–5: The War Years* (1970) (18:51) and secondary works for World War II, Ambrose examines Eisenhower's wartime rise to prominence and the political and military challenges he faced as supreme commander of the allied forces in Europe. Eisenhower's successes resulted from innate talents, nourished by his mentors, combined with an emphasis on action over thought and team over individual effort.

18:391   _____. *The Supreme Commander: The War Years of General Dwight D. Eisenhower.* Garden City, NY: Doubleday, 1970. Reprint 1999 (University Press of Mississippi). This biography covers Eisenhower from his assignment to the War Plans Division of the Army General Staff (December 1941) through his acceptance of German surrender as commander of SHAEF (May 1945). The author relies on the wartime Eisenhower papers he was helping edit. He defends Eisenhower's decisions in the numerous political-military conflicts in which he was involved. See also his *Eisenhower. Vol. 1: Soldier, General of the Army, President-Elect, 1890–1952* (1983) (18:390).

18:392   Bischof, Günter, and Stephen E. Ambrose, eds. *Eisenhower: A Centenary Assessment.* Baton Rouge: Louisiana State University Press, 1995. This collection of lectures delivered at the Eisenhower Center at the University of New Orleans focuses on Eisenhower's presidency rather than the World War II years but contains interesting pieces by Forrest C. Pogue on his experiences with Eisenhower in writing the official history of SHAEF ("The Genesis of the Supreme Command: Personal Impressions of Eisenhower the General," 19–39) and by M. R. D. Foot on "Eisenhower and the British" (40–54). In addition to a foreword by General Andrew J. Goodpaster, see also Thomas Alan Schwartz, "Eisenhower and the Germans" (206–21), and Stephen E. Ambrose, "Epilogue: Eisenhower's Legacy" (246–55).

18:393   Brendon, Piers. *Ike, His Life and Times.* New York: Harper and Row, 1986. Approximately one-quarter of this full biography of Eisenhower is devoted to the World War II years.

18:394   Draper, Theodore. "Eisenhower's War." *New York Review of Books* (September 25, October 9, and October 23, 1986): 30–38, 33–40, 61–67. This

three-part review of David Eisenhower's *Eisenhower at War, 1943–1945* (1986) (18:395) includes extensive analyses and commentaries by Draper on numerous diplomatic as well as military aspects of the war in Europe. The three essays are titled "Eisenhower's War," "Eisenhower's War-II," and "Eisenhower's War: The Final Crisis." They are reprinted in Draper's *A Present of Things Past: Selected Essays* (1990) (18:153).

18:395   Eisenhower, David. *Eisenhower at War, 1943–1945.* New York: Random House, 1986. Written by Eisenhower's grandson, this large volume focuses on the complex interaction between military and political factors in Eisenhower's wartime decisions. Particularly noteworthy is the emphasis on the impact of the eastern front and Soviet-American relations on his thinking and actions as well as his better-known emphasis on maintaining good Anglo-American relations.

18:396   Eisenhower, Dwight D. *At Ease: Stories I Tell to Friends.* Garden City, NY: Doubleday, 1967. Far more relaxed in tone and informative than his *Crusade in Europe* (1948) (18:397), here Eisenhower offers rich personal anecdotes and observations about a host of issues and individuals with whom he dealt before, during, and after the war.

18:397   _____. *Crusade in Europe.* Garden City, NY: Doubleday, 1948. Reprint 1988 (Da Capo Press). Eisenhower's memoirs of his wartime experiences from army General Staff planner to commander of SHAEF cover a host of important diplomatic as well as military issues and offer some valuable insights. Overall, however, the volume is bland.

Ernest J. King

18:398   Buell, Thomas B. *Master of Sea Power: A Biography of Fleet Admiral Ernest J. King.* Boston: Little, Brown, 1980. This biography is the most complete study of Admiral King as chief of naval operations during World War II. It emphasizes his role in U.S. strategic planning and naval operations.

18:399   King, Ernest J., and Walter Muir Whitehill. *Fleet Admiral King, a Naval Record.* New York: W. W. Norton, 1952. This volume is a combination memoir and biography of the chief of naval operations and commander in chief of the U.S. fleet during World War II. Less than half of the book deals with his World War II experiences.

William D. Leahy

18:400   Adams, Henry H. *Witness to Power: The Life of Fleet Admiral William D. Leahy.* Annapolis: Naval Institute Press, 1985. This is a very sympathetic narrative of the lengthy military career of Leahy, who was chief of naval operations in the 1930s, ambassador to Vichy France, and wartime chairman of the Joint Chiefs of Staff. It will be of limited use to serious scholars.

18:401   Leahy, William D. *I Was There: The Personal Story of the Chief of Staff to Presidents Roosevelt and Truman, Based on His Notes and Diaries Made at the Time.* New York: Whittlesey House, 1950. A retired chief of naval operations and former ambassador to Vichy France, Leahy then served as chief of staff to the commander in chief, the precursor to the present-day chairman of the Joint Chiefs of Staff. As such these memoirs and diary entries offer important insights into U.S. and allied strategic discussions at the highest levels.

Douglas MacArthur

18:402   Forbes, Joseph. "General Douglas MacArthur and the Implementation of American and Australian Civilian Policy Decisions in 1944 and 1945." *Military Affairs* 49 (January 1985): 1–4. The author disagrees splenetically with James (*The Years of MacArthur. Vol. 2: 1941–1945,* 1975 [18:403]) and others that MacArthur might have exceeded his authority in liberating the Philippines. He argues that MacArthur's authority came from President Roosevelt and that throughout the war MacArthur was a "loyal and conscientious implementer" of FDR's policies.

18:403   James, D. Clayton. *The Years of MacArthur.* 3 vols. Boston: Houghton Mifflin, 1970–1985. This is the definitive biography of MacArthur. Volume 2 covers the war years and is particularly good on the clash between MacArthur and his superiors in Washington, his bitter fight against the Europe-first strategy, his disputes with the navy, and his plans for island hopping.

18:404   Manchester, William. *American Caesar, Douglas MacArthur, 1880–1964.* Boston: Little, Brown, 1978. Although superior to previous popular biographies of MacArthur, this best-seller is marred by questionable research and conclusions. Serious scholars should consult D. Clayton James's three-volume *The Years of MacArthur* (1970–1985) (18:403), while general readers will be better served by Geoffrey Perret's one-volume *Old Soldiers Never Die: The Life of Douglas MacArthur* (1996) (18:405).

18:405   Perret, Geoffrey. *Old Soldiers Never Die: The Life of Douglas MacArthur.* New York: Random House, 1996. While not a substitute for D. Clayton James's three-volume biography (18:403), this popular work is the best single-volume biography of MacArthur available. A little more than a third of it is devoted to MacArthur's World War II campaigns. Some of the author's military judgments, such as his apportionment of blame for the conduct of operations in the Philippines in 1941–1942, have not gone unchallenged.

18:406   Petillo, Carol Morris. *Douglas MacArthur: The Philippine Years.* This penetrating psychological analysis of MacArthur focuses on his experiences in the Philippines before Pearl Harbor, but the final content chapter analyzes his return to the Philippines in 1944–1945 (17:146).

18:407   Rogers, Paul P. *The Bitter Years: MacArthur and Sutherland.* Westport, CT: Greenwood Press, 1990. This is the second of two volumes recounting the author's personal history of MacArthur's headquarters, and particularly the relationship between MacArthur and his chief of staff, Lieutenant General Richard K. Sutherland. This volume covers the period January 1943 through the end of the war.

18:408   _____. *The Good Years: MacArthur and Sutherland.* New York: Praeger, 1990. The author was stenographer and chief clerk in General MacArthur's office and served with him throughout the war. His personal account of the wartime relationship between MacArthur and his chief of staff, Lieutenant General Richard K. Sutherland, provides a unique perspective. Part 1 of a two-volume set, this volume covers the period through December 1942.

18:409 Schaller, Michael. *Douglas MacArthur: The Far Eastern General.* New York: Oxford University Press, 1989. Schaller offers a devastating, iconoclastic portrait of MacArthur in the Far East from 1935 to 1951, challenging virtually every previous positive assessment of the controversial general's personality, intelligence, motivations, policies, and behavior. Three chapters cover his activities during the war itself, with a heavy emphasis on his political motivations.

18:410 _____. "General Douglas MacArthur and the Politics of the Pacific War." In *The Pacific War Revisited,* ed. Günter Bischof and Robert L. Dupont, 17–40. Baton Rouge: Louisiana State University Press, 1997. Schaller attributes much of MacArthur's career success to his domestic political strength, which he honed with his "public relations abilities." He also suggests that FDR supported MacArthur's plan to retake the Philippines for political reasons.

George C. Marshall

18:411 Bland, Larry I., ed. *George C. Marshall Interviews and Reminiscences for Forrest C. Pogue.* Lexington, VA: George C. Marshall Research Foundation, 1991. This volume is a compilation of the transcripts and notes made by official biographer Pogue during his late 1956 to early 1957 oral history interviews with Marshall, who as army chief of staff was one of the most important U.S. officials throughout the war. Although the questions and answers cover Marshall's entire career, heavy emphasis is placed on the World War II years. This revised edition includes an introduction by Pogue, illustrations, and annotations.

18:412 Cray, Ed. *General of the Army: George C. Marshall, Soldier and Statesman.* New York: W. W. Norton, 1990. More than half of this solid popular biography of Marshall deals with his tenure as army chief of staff from 1939 to 1945.

18:413 Pogue, Forrest C. *George C. Marshall.* 4 vols. New York: Viking, 1963–1987. These four volumes constitute the definitive biography of the World War II army chief of staff and postwar secretary of state and defense. Volume 2 covers September 1939 through the North African invasion of November 1942, and volume 3 from the January 1943 Casablanca conference to German surrender in May 1945, with the opening chapter of volume 4 covering the final months of the war against Japan. The volumes are useful for an understanding of allied and U.S. strategy, decisionmaking, and civil-military relations as well as Marshall's central role in all of these issues.

18:414 _____. "George C. Marshall on Civil-Military Relationships in the United States." In *The United States Military under the Constitution of the United States, 1789–1989,* ed. Richard H. Kohn, 193–222. New York: New York University Press, 1991. Marshall's official biographer emphasizes Marshall's reluctance to make political decisions even as he was always aware of political factors in military decisions. In this he was typical of his generation of army officers. Marshall's fear of a repetition of the civil-military clashes occurring during the Civil War led him to insist upon a position of nonpartisanship during the war.

18:415 Stoler, Mark A. *George C. Marshall: Soldier-Statesman of the American Century.* Boston: Twayne Publishers, 1989. This carefully researched biography of Marshall covers all the important issues of his life, with appropriate attention to World War II. Though succinct, complexity and nuance are given their due, and readers will find in it an especially useful introduction to wartime grand strategy and Anglo-American relations.

Joseph Stilwell

18:416 Tuchman, Barbara W. *Stilwell and the American Experience in China, 1911–45.* New York: Macmillan, 1970. Reprint 2001 (Grove Press). This highly readable biography, and Pulitzer prize awardee, examines Sino-American relations, with heavy emphasis on 1942 to 1944, through the career of General Stilwell. While highly favorable to Stilwell, the work emphasizes American misconceptions of and inability to achieve objectives in Asia.

18:417 Young, Kenneth Ray. "The Stilwell Controversy: A Bibliographical Review." *Military Affairs* 39 (April 1975): 66–68. Young reviews Stilwell's career in Asia and examines the controversy over his effectiveness as the China-India-Burma theater commander (1942–1944). He concludes that Stilwell's mission to China was doomed from the start.

Albert C. Wedemeyer

18:418   Eiler, Keith E. "The Man Who Planned the Victory: An Interview with Gen. Albert C. Wedemeyer." *American Heritage* 34 (October-November 1983): 36–47. This is a biographical portrait of General Albert C. Wedemeyer by his former aide. It covers Wedemeyer's authorship of the Victory Program and role in the second front controversy as a strategic planner, his deputy command of the Southeast Asia theater in 1943, and his command in the China theater in 1944–1945 as well as postwar issues regarding China.

18:419   Wedemeyer, Albert C. *Wedemeyer Reports!* New York: Holt, 1958. The general takes the position that the politicians had imprecise war aims, underestimated the communists in Europe and in Asia, and squandered the hard-won peace. He holds that a 1943 cross-channel attack would have succeeded. Although he praises Marshall for his advocacy of the cross-channel attack, he is sharply critical of the postwar mission to China.

Others

18:420   Chennault, Claire Lee. *Way of a Fighter: The Memoirs of Claire Lee Chennault.* New York: G. P. Putnam's Sons, 1949. This volume consists of a bitter attack on General Stilwell and to some extent on Marshall and others in the War Department who supported Stilwell. Chennault's views are highly colored by the Generalissimo's views and by strong disagreements with Stilwell on air strategy. Edited by Robert Hotz.

18:421   Deane, John R. *The Strange Alliance: The Story of Our Efforts at Wartime Cooperation with Russia.* New York: Viking Press, 1947. Deane was the secretary of the Joint Chiefs of Staff, U.S. secretary of the Combined Chiefs of Staff in 1942–1943, and then head of the U.S. military mission to Moscow from late 1943 to 1945. He contends that the Soviets never intended to cooperate in the postwar world and that Roosevelt was duped by them into believing otherwise.

18:422   Brown, Anthony Cave. *The Last Hero: Wild Bill Donovan: The Biography and Political Experience of Major General William J. Donovan, Founder of the OSS and "Father" of the CIA, from His Personal and Secret Papers and the Diaries of Ruth Donovan.* New York: Times Books, 1982. This popular biography of the head of the wartime OSS is fascinating but should be used with care and checked against more scholarly sources.

18:423   Stoler, Mark A. "From Continentalism to Globalism: General Stanley D. Embick, the Joint Strategic Survey Committee, and the Military View of American National Policy during the Second World War." The author uses the career and ideas of Embick, a major and controversial army officer and global strategist throughout the 1930s and World War II, to illustrate the movement among army officers from an isolationist to a global view of U.S. national security (17:1162). See also Stoler, *Allies and Adversaries: The Joint Chiefs of Staff, the Grand Alliance, and U.S. Strategy in World War II* (2000) (18:477), for more on Embick and these issues.

18:424   Lawren, William. *The General and the Bomb: A Biography of General Leslie R. Groves, Director of the Manhattan Project.* New York: Dodd, Mead, 1988. Not a full-scale biography, this work focuses on Groves's responsibilities as director of the Manhattan Engineering District. The author argues that Groves was indispensable to the project's success. Citations are scarce.

18:425   Crosswell, D. K. R. *The Chief of Staff: The Military Career of General Walter Bedell Smith.* New York: Greenwood Press, 1991. The is the only biographical study of Smith, who headed the army and Joint and Combined Chiefs of Staff secretariats in 1941–1942 before serving as Eisenhower's chief of staff in 1942–1945.

18:426   Davis, Richard G. *Carl A. Spaatz and the Air War in Europe.* Washington, DC: Office of Air Force History, 1993. This is a detailed biography of the senior army air forces commander in Europe during World War II. As such, Spaatz was integrally involved in many of the allied debates over military strategy and prosecution of the war. Davis merges biography with operational history and concludes with a judicious assessment of the air war in Europe.

18:427 Simpson, B. Mitchell, III. *Admiral Harold R. Stark: Architect of Victory, 1939–1945*. Columbia: University of South Carolina Press, 1989. This is the first full-length biography of the chief of naval operations from 1939 through March 1942 and commander of U.S. naval forces in Europe after that date. As naval chief Stark played a major role in the formulation of the "Germany first" strategy and the initiation of ensuing staff talks with the British in 1940–1941.

18:428 Dyer, George Carroll. *The Amphibians Came to Conquer: The Story of Admiral Richmond Kelly Turner*. 2 vols. Washington, DC: Government Printing Office, 1972. Turner played a major role in U.S. and Anglo-American strategic planning before his assignment to the Pacific.

Others (Foreign)

Lord Alanbrooke

18:429 Bryant, Arthur. *Triumph in the West: A History of the War Years Based on the Diaries of Field-Marshal Lord Alanbrooke, Chief of the Imperial General Staff*. 2 vols. Garden City, NY: Doubleday, 1959. This second volume of Bryant's two-volume study clearly shows the declining British ability to direct or influence allied strategy.

18:430 _____. *The Turn of the Tide: A History of the War Years Based on the Diaries of Field Marshal Lord Alanbrooke, Chief of the Imperial General Staff*. Garden City, NY: Doubleday, 1957. This, and its sequel, *Triumph in the West* (1959) (18:429), combine excerpts from Alanbrooke's unpublished diaries with his reminiscences and Bryant's narrative to provide an important British view of the war. They reveal British and allied strategic differences and planning and are highly critical of Churchill as well as the Americans.

18:431 Danchev, Alex, and Daniel Todman, eds. *War Diaries, 1939–1945: Field Marshal Lord Alanbrooke*. Berkeley: University of California Press, 2001. These complete diaries of the wartime chief of the British Imperial General Staff are far more revealing than the expurgated versions reproduced in Bryant, *The Turn of the Tide: A History of the War Years Based on the Diaries of Field Marshal Lord* *Alanbrooke, Chief of the Imperial General Staff* (1957) (18:430) and *Triumph in the West: A History of the War Years Based on the Diaries of Field-Marshal Lord Alanbrooke, Chief of the Imperial General Staff* (1959) (18:429).

18:432 Fraser, David. *Alanbrooke*. New York: Atheneum, 1982. This is a full biography, with 300 of its 563 pages devoted to Brooke's 1941–1945 activities as chief of the Imperial General Staff. Making use of numerous unpublished sources, Fraser revises the picture of the British army chief presented in the 1950s in Sir Arthur Bryant's two-volume study, based on Alanbrooke's wartime diaries. Bryant himself provides a prologue and epilogue for this work.

Louis Mountbatten

18:433 Villa, Brian Loring. "Mountbatten, the British Chiefs of Staff, and Approval of the Dieppe Raid." *Journal of Military History* 54 (April 1990): 201–26. Villa in this article disagrees with Mountbatten's official biographer, Philip Ziegler, on whether Mountbatten ever received approval by the British Chiefs for the Dieppe raid. The article includes a rejoinder by Ziegler and a reply by Villa. For greater detail, see Villa's *Unauthorized Action: Mountbatten and the Dieppe Raid* (1989) (18:847) and Ziegler's *Mountbatten* (1985) (18:434).

18:434 Ziegler, Philip. *Mountbatten*. New York: Alfred A. Knopf, 1985. This is the official biography of Admiral Mountbatten, who was the wartime head of British Combined Operations and, from 1943 to 1945, the Southeast Asia Command.

Others

18:435 Cunningham, Andrew Browne. *A Sailor's Odyssey: The Autobiography of Admiral of the Fleet, Viscount Cunningham of Hyndhope*. New York: Dutton, 1951. Since Cunningham was central to the naval war in the Mediterranean from 1940 to 1943, this autobiography is essential reading for anyone interested in those actions; because he succeeded Dudley Pound as first sea lord, there is much on allied strategy making here as well.

18:436 De Guingand, Francis Wilfred. *Operation Victory*. New York: Charles Scribner's Sons, 1947.

De Guingand, Montgomery's chief of staff, largely supports Montgomery's positions in the major controversies over allied strategy, with the notable exception of the single thrust versus broad front issue. These memoirs are more judiciously phrased than Montgomery's.

18:437 Leasor, James, and Leslie Hollis. *War at the Top: Based on the Experiences of General Sir Leslie Hollis.* London: Michael Joseph, 1959. Hollis was assistant secretary for the British War Cabinet and Chiefs of Staff Committee and thus in attendance at numerous Anglo-American meetings.

18:438 Ismay, Hastings Lionel. *The Memoirs of General Lord Ismay.* New York: Viking Press, 1960. Although these memoirs cover Ismay's entire career, over half are devoted to his experiences as Churchill's chief of staff and personal representative on the British Chiefs of Staff Committee during World War II. Like Alanbrooke, Ismay offers an excellent firsthand account of British and allied strategic planning, conferences, and disputes, with emphasis on the disagreements that separated Churchill from his military advisers.

18:439 Richardson, Charles. *From Churchill's Secret Circle to the BBC: The Biography of Lieutenant General Sir Ian Jacob.* Washington, DC: Brassey's, 1991. These memoirs by a key member of Churchill's military staff are particularly valuable for their accounts of the numerous Anglo-American and Anglo-Soviet-American conferences Jacob attended.

18:440 Morgan, Frederick Edgworth. *Overture to Overlord.* Garden City, NY: Doubleday, 1950. Morgan headed the Anglo-American planning staff for cross-channel operations and became deputy chief of staff under Eisenhower in SHAEF. His memoirs offer valuable insights into the original planning for an invasion of Europe and the development of plans for military occupation of, and civil affairs in, Germany and the rest of Europe.

18:441 Kennedy, John, ed. *The Business of War: The War Narrative of John Kennedy.* New York: Morrow, 1958. As director of military operations, Kennedy was one of Alanbrooke and England's chief strategic planners during the war. These memoirs, drawn from his wartime notes, emphasize the numerous clashes between Churchill and his military advisers.

18:442 Montgomery, Bernard Law. *The Memoirs of Field-Marshal the Viscount Montgomery of Alamein.* Cleveland: World Publishing Co., 1958. Montgomery continues to argue strongly in favor of positions he took during the war and on his overall role. This book makes heavy use of contemporary messages, speeches, and the like, reprinted in full, but offers less detail and analysis of major operations. It should be used with care.

18:443 Slessor, John. *The Central Blue: Autobiography.* New York: Praeger, 1957. Slessor's numerous high-level wartime assignments included director of plans and assistant chief of the British Air Staff, British air commander in the Mediterranean and Middle East, and deputy allied air commander in chief for the Mediterranean. As such he was deeply involved in a host of Anglo-American conferences and conflicts, including the 1941 combined staff conversations, the 1942 debate over European strategy, the 1943 Casablanca conference, and discussions of Mediterranean strategy in 1943–1944.

18:444 Slim, William J. *Defeat into Victory.* New York: D. McKay, 1961. This volume, one of the best personal accounts by a high-level commander in World War II, recounts how victory in Burma was brought out of earlier defeat. It is valuable for depicting command problems involving Chinese, Indian, and British forces and, especially, General Stilwell as commander of Chinese forces owing allegiance to Mountbatten and Jiang Jieshi.

18:445 Strong, Kenneth. *Intelligence at the Top: The Recollections of an Intelligence Officer.* Garden City, NY: Doubleday, 1969. The memoirs of Eisenhower's (British) chief of intelligence, while largely a narrative, provide useful insights into the operations of Supreme Headquarters, Anglo-American coordination, the role and use of intelligence, and especially the disputes between Eisenhower and Montgomery.

18:446 Tedder, Arthur William. *With Prejudice: The War Memoirs of Marshal of the Royal Air Force, Lord Tedder.* Boston: Little, Brown, 1967. Tedder was British air chief in the Middle East, vice-chief of the British air staff, and deputy supreme commander of SHAEF from late 1943 to the German surrender. These memoirs are particularly valuable for his work on and insights into the functioning of Eisenhower's Anglo-American coalition command in Europe. Published in the United Kingdom in 1966.

18:447   Wilson, Henry Maitland. *Eight Years Overseas, 1939–1947.* New York: Hutchinson, 1950. These memoirs are useful for the years Wilson spent as British commander in chief in the Middle East, as supreme allied commander in the Mediterranean, and as head of the British staff mission to Washington after the death of Sir John Dill in 1944. He gives valuable background on allied planning and disagreements.

Strategy and Operations

GLOBAL STRATEGY

18:448   Ambrose, Stephen E. "Applied Strategy of World War II." *Naval War College Review* 22 (May 1970): 62–70. Ambrose attacks the myth of a purely military and nonpolitical strategy by the United States as compared to Britain, pointing out that at war's end America occupied, controlled, or exerted the major influence in four of the five major industrial areas of the world.

18:449   Cline, Ray S. *United States Army in World War II: The War Department: Washington Command Post: The Operations Division.* Washington, DC: Government Printing Office, 1951. Established as part of the major administrative reorganization of early 1942, the Operations Division of the Army General Staff was the central army planning agency for the global war effort. As such it dealt extensively with numerous allied strategic issues and conflicts. This volume is the official history of the division during the war.

18:450   Cohen, Eliot A. "The Strategy of Innocence? The United States, 1920–1945." In *The Making of Strategy: Rulers, States, and War,* ed.

Williamson Murray, MacGregor Knox, and Alvin Bernstein, 428–65. New York: Cambridge University Press, 1994. Cohen focuses on the elements of U.S. strategies and strategic decisionmaking in World War II. He analyzes their strengths and weaknesses, concludes that they were highly effective, and notes that "if innocence gave birth to those strategies, it was a particularly providential brand of innocence."

18:451   Conn, Stetson. "Changing Concepts of National Defense in the United States, 1937–1947." The former chief historian of the army traces the evolution of U.S. defense policies from continentalism to globalism (17:1140).

18:452   Davis, Vernon E. *The History of the Joint Chiefs of Staff in World War II: Organizational Development.* 2 vols. Washington, DC: Historical Division, Joint Secretariat, Joint Chiefs of Staff, 1972. Written in 1953, this two-volume official history was declassified in 1972. Volume 1, *Origin of the Joint and Combined Chiefs of Staff,* is an extremely useful history of the formation of the Joint Chiefs of Staff and early allied planning and coordination through mid-1942, including two excellent chapters on U.S. and British defense organizational development prior to the war. It is particularly useful on the relationship between the growth and development of JCS and collaboration with Britain and the overall course of the war. Volume 2, *Development of the JCS Committee Structure,* concentrates on the internal development of the Joint Chiefs as it carried out its role in U.S. and allied planning.

18:453   Farrell, Brian P. *The Basis and Making of British Grand Strategy, 1940–1943: Was There a Plan?* 2 vols. Studies in British History. Lewiston, NY: Edwin Mellen Press, 1998. This two-volume work is based upon extensive research in British unpublished records as well as secondary works. Farrell defends British grand strategy against recent detractors. He argues that Britain genuinely had a strategy and a consensus supporting it, and that it was generally successful. The introduction contains a brief but comprehensive historiographical essay.

18:454   Freedman, Lawrence, Paul Hayes, and Robert O'Neill, eds. *War, Strategy, and International Politics: Essays in Honour of Sir Michael Howard.* New York: Oxford University Press, 1992. This collection includes three World War II essays: John Gooch, "'Hidden in the Rock': American Military Perceptions of Great Britain, 1919–1940" (155–74); Brian Bond, "Alanbrooke and Britain's Mediterranean Strategy, 1942–44" (175–94); and Alex Danchev, "Being Friends: The Combined Chiefs of Staff and the Making of Allied Strategy in the Second World War" (195–210).

18:455   Fuller, J. F. C. *The Second World War, 1939–1945.* 3d impression with revisions. New York: Duell, Sloan and Pearce, 1962. A major British military theorist, Fuller originally published this work in 1949. He is bitterly critical of allied leaders, especially Churchill, for the political and moral bankruptcy he believes inherent in their waging of total war without limitations or consideration to real political objectives. His distrust of civilian leadership and near sympathy for a nonmaterialistic fascistic philosophy taints many valuable judgments.

18:456   Graham, Dominick, and Shelford Bidwell. *Coalitions, Politicians & Generals: Some Aspects of Command in Two World Wars.* New York: Brassey's, 1993. This provocative set of collaboratively written essays covers Anglo-American coalition strategy and politics in both world wars, with about half the work devoted to the workings of the alliance of Britons and Americans in World War II.

18:457   Greenfield, Kent Roberts. *American Strategy in World War II: A Reconsideration.* Baltimore: Johns Hopkins Press, 1963. Reprint 1982 (Krieger Pub. Co.). The former chief historian of the U.S. army summarizes some of the controversies over American World War II strategy. He discusses and reinterprets the basic elements of U.S-allied strategy, Anglo-American strategic disputes, Roosevelt's role as commander in chief, and the role of airpower.

18:458   _____, ed. *Command Decisions.* Washington, DC: Government Printing Office, 1960. These twenty-three essays by historians working on the official army history of World War II analyze decisions at various levels on both allied and Axis sides of the war, covering many types of decisions: diplomatic, political, logistical, and strategic. Among the more pertinent are Louis Morton, "Germany First: The Basic Concept of Allied Strategy in World War II" and "The Decision to Withdraw to Bataan

(1941)"; Leo J. Meyer, "The Decision to Invade North Africa (TORCH) (1942)"; Robert W. Coakley, "The Persian Corridor as a Route for Aid to the U.S.S.R. (1942)"; Richard M. Leighton, "OVERLORD versus the Mediterranean at the Cairo-Tehran Conferences (1943)"; Sidney T. Mathews, "General Clark's Decision to Drive on Rome (1944)"; Maurice Matloff, "The ANVIL Decision: Crossroads of Strategy (1944)"; Robert Ross Smith, "Luzon versus Formosa (1944)"; Forrest C. Pogue, "The Decision to Halt at the Elbe (1945)"; and Morton, "The Decision to Use the Atomic Bomb." A briefer, commercial edition appeared in 1959 (Harcourt Brace).

18:459   Henrikson, Alan K. "The Map as an 'Idea': The Role of Cartographic Imagery during the Second World War." *American Cartographer* 2 (April 1975): 19–53. The author maintains that a "revolution" of perceptions occurred during World War II involving a shift from the sea-land Mercator view of the world to the air view of a North Pole–centered azimuthal projection. The change helped promote a new global outlook that played a major role in shaping American conduct of the war and planning for the peace.

18:460   Kingston-McLoughry, Edgar James. *The Direction of War: A Critique of the Political Direction and High Command in War.* New York: F. A. Praeger, 1955. This is an early attempt to show the lessons taught by World Wars I and II and the great need to unite military and political command. Written by a high-ranking British air officer who was a participant in much of what he describes, it provides a valuable and provocative reappraisal of both British and allied politico-military decisions and structures.

18:461   Leighton, Richard M., and Robert W. Coakley. *United States Army in World War II: The War Department: Global Logistics and Strategy.* 2 vols. Washington, DC: Government Printing Office, 1955–1968. These two volumes in the official army history of the war provide a very important and detailed analysis of the link between global logistics and military strategies during the war.

18:462   Lippmann, Walter. *U.S. Foreign Policy: Shield of the Republic.* This wartime volume played a major role in popularizing geopolitical, balance-of-power thought in the United States (2:67).

18:463 Love, Robert W., Jr. "Fighting a Global War, 1941–1945." In *In Peace and War: Interpretations of American Naval History, 1775–1984*, ed. Kenneth J. Hagan, 263–89. Westport, CT: Greenwood Press, 1984. Love provides an excellent summary and analysis of U.S. naval strategy in the war, including U.S.-British debates on that strategy.

18:464 Lowenthal, Mark M. *Leadership and Indecision: American War Planning and Policy Process, 1937–1942*. Volume 2 is especially valuable for its analysis of the 1942 debate over Anglo-American strategy. Lowenthal is highly critical of Roosevelt for refusing to provide his military advisers with guidance or support (17:1194). For a summary of this work, see Lowenthal's article as reproduced in Laqueur, *The Second World War: Essays in Military and Political History* (1982) (18:160).

18:465 Matloff, Maurice. "The American Approach to War, 1919–1945." In *The Theory and Practice of War: Essays Presented to Captain B. H. Liddell Hart on His Seventieth Birthday*, ed. Michael Howard, 213–43. New York: F. A. Praeger, 1966. Only the last few pages of this older work directly address U.S. wartime strategy, but the essay as a whole still provides an excellent historical explanation and introduction to the development of that strategy and to the evolution of U.S. strategic thinking within the different services.

18:466 _____. *United States Army in World War II: The War Department: Strategic Planning for Coalition Warfare, 1943–1944*. Washington, DC: Government Printing Office, 1959. See Matloff and Snell, *United States Army in World War II: The War Department: Strategic Planning for Coalition Warfare, 1941–1942* (1953) (18:467).

18:467 Matloff, Maurice, and Edwin M. Snell. *United States Army in World War II: The War Department: Strategic Planning for Coalition Warfare, 1941–1942*. Washington, DC: Government Printing Office, 1953. This and Matloff's *United States Army in World War II: The War Department: Strategic Planning for Coalition Warfare, 1943–1944* (1959) (18:466) in the official army history trace U.S. strategic planning within the context of the Grand Alliance and the numerous allied wartime conferences. Both are rich in detail, well organized, and indexed.

18:468 McCloy, John J. "Turning Points of the War: The Great Military Decisions." *Foreign Affairs* 26 (October 1947): 52–72. This is an early assessment of the most important U.S. and allied politico-military decisions, written by an important and experienced War Department official.

18:469 Moon, John Ellis van Courtland. "Chemical Weapons and Deterrence: The World War II Experience." *International Security* 8 (Spring 1984): 3–35. Chemical weapons were not used during World War II because political and military policymakers in each country were convinced that the risks of initiation were simply too great. Deterrence thus worked, Moon concludes, but it probably would have broken down had the Pacific war continued into 1946.

18:470 _____. "United States Chemical Warfare Policy in World War II: A Captive of Coalition Policy?" *Journal of Military History* 60 (July 1996): 495–511. The author provides a brief overview of allied policy on the use of chemical weapons, notes exceptions to declared policy, and generally asserts that the coalition politics influenced policy.

18:471 Morison, Samuel Eliot. *Strategy and Compromise*. Boston: Little, Brown, 1958. This is a brisk, older review of allied strategy during the war by the renowned historian who authored the navy's official history of the war. Morison tends to stress strategic differences, with Churchill and Alanbrooke emerging as the main villains.

18:472 Pearlman, Michael D. *Warmaking and American Democracy: The Struggle over Military Strategy, 1700 to the Present*. Lawrence: University Press of Kansas, 1999. This remarkable synthesis, which includes an extended chapter devoted to politico-military issues during World War II, emphasizes the impact of democratic politics on military policymaking and the general paucity of impressive American strategic thinking and action. Though Pearlman offers a major, original reinterpretation of military strategy and its relationship to the political system, his biting wit and irony occasionally push him to dubious conclusions.

18:473 Pogue, Forrest C. "The Wartime Chiefs of Staff and the President." In *Soldiers and Statesmen: The Proceedings of the 4th Military History Sympo-*

sium, United States Air Force Academy, 22–23 October 1970, ed. Monte D. Wright and Lawrence J. Paszek, 67–117. Washington, DC: Office of the Air Force History Headquarters USAF and U.S. Air Force Academy, 1973. Marshall's official biographer analyzes the relationship between Roosevelt and the World War II members of the Joint Chiefs of Staff, the Anglo-American strategic debate, and the relationship between U.S. strategy and political goals. Also included in this session are comments on Pogue's paper by Gaddis Smith, Maurice Matloff, and Richard M. Leighton.

18:474   Ross, Steven T. *American War Plans, 1941–1945: The Test of Battle.* New York: Garland Publishing, 1988. Reprint 1997 (Frank Cass). Ross compares U.S. war plans with what actually occurred and analyzes the numerous politico-military reasons for the differences between the two.

18:475   Spykman, Nicholas J. *America's Strategy in World Politics: The United States and the Balance of Power.* The publication of this volume by Yale geopolitician Spykman was a milestone in the wartime development of geopolitical, balance-of-power thought in the United States (2:233).

18:476   _____. *The Geography of the Peace.* New York: Harcourt, Brace and Company, 1944. Spykman had planned a follow-up volume to *America's Strategy in World Politics: The United States and the Balance of Power* (1942) (18:475) but died before he could write it. This brief volume, prepared by his Yale colleagues (edited by Helen R. Nicholl), consists of the 1942 lecture that was to be the basis of the new book along with his maps, notes, and correspondence. These continue his focus on geopolitical balance-of-power concepts but develop his focus on the "rimlands" of Europe and Asia as more important than the Mackinder-Haushofer "heartland" or "inner crescent."

18:477   Stoler, Mark A. *Allies and Adversaries: The Joint Chiefs of Staff, the Grand Alliance, and U.S. Strategy in World War II.* Chapel Hill: University of North Carolina Press, 2000. Stoler analyzes the wartime views of the U.S. military chiefs of staff and their subordinates regarding their British and Soviet allies, the impact of those views on U.S. strategic proposals, civil-military relations, and the wartime

growth of military influence on U.S. foreign policy. In the process he demonstrates the centrality of the JCS to political policymaking, showing both how the military gained unprecedented influence in policy formulation and the wartime processes by which U.S. security interests expanded. He also highlights the 1945 paradigm shift in strategic thought, the core of which was a global view of U.S. national security and acceptance of a Soviet threat.

18:478   _____. "The 'Pacific First' Alternative in American World War II Strategy." *International History Review* 2 (July 1980): 432–52. Stoler argues that the U.S. Chiefs of Staff seriously considered turning American forces to the Pacific theater in 1942 unless the British agreed to cross-channel operations for that year. A strong stand by Roosevelt prevented this action.

18:479   Weinberg, Gerhard L. "Who Won World War II and How?" *Journal of Mississippi History* 57 (Winter 1995): 275–87. This brief essay defends U.S. and allied strategies and policies against critics from the left and right in analyses of unconditional surrender, Germany-first, the cross-channel approach in Europe, the dual advance in the Pacific, and the atomic bomb. Overall, Weinberg concludes, the allies won not because of any material abundance, but because their strategies were superior to those of their Axis enemies.

EUROPEAN STRATEGY AND OPERATIONS

General

18:480   Auty, Phyllis, and Richard Clogg, eds. *British Policy towards Wartime Resistance in Yugoslavia and Greece.* New York: Barnes and Noble, 1975. This series of papers and recollections reconsiders British policy toward Yugoslav and Greek resistance movements. Specific topics covered include the activities of the Special Operations Executive and the "myth" of British plans for an allied invasion of the Balkans.

18:481   Blumenson, Martin. "A Deaf Ear to Clausewitz: Allied Operational Objectives in World

War II." *Parameters* 23 (Summer 1993): 16–27. Blumenson incisively critiques the allies' prosecution of the war against Germany, arguing that they mistook movement for progress.

18:482 Eisenhower, John S. D. *Allies: Pearl Harbor to D-Day.* Garden City, NY: Doubleday, 1982. In this popular history Eisenhower's son traces the numerous strategic conflicts and compromises within the Anglo-American alliance from late 1941 to mid-1944. Primary focus is given to such key personalities as Churchill, Eisenhower, Marshall, and Roosevelt.

18:483 Higgins, Trumbull. "The Anglo-American Historians' War in the Mediterranean, 1942–1945." *Military Affairs* 34 (October 1970): 84–88. This historiographical essay examines the dispute between British and American historians, and among historians within each country, over the wisdom of the British Mediterranean approach to victory as opposed to the American cross-channel concept. The author offers a balanced and comprehensive overview of the debate as of 1970.

18:484 Jones, Matthew. *Britain, the United States and the Mediterranean War, 1942–44.* New York: St. Martin's Press, 1996. This revised doctoral dissertation focuses on Anglo-American conflicts in the Mediterranean theater command from 1942 through late 1944 and their links to Anglo-American political and military disagreements at higher levels.

18:485 Leighton, Richard M. "OVERLORD Revisited: An Interpretation of American Strategy in the European War, 1942–1944." *American Historical Review* 68 (July 1963): 919–37. This major reinterpretation of U.S. World War II strategy in Europe argues that the American approach was not fundamentally different from Britain's. Despite perceptions to the contrary, both national strategies were pragmatic, flexible, and peripheral.

18:486 MacDonald, Charles Brown. *The Mighty Endeavor: The American War in Europe.* 2d ed. New York: Quill, 1986. First published in 1969 (as *The Mighty Endeavor: American Armed Forces in the European Theater in World War II*), this remains a highly readable but now dated general work on American forces in Europe in World War II by an official army historian of the war. The 1986 edition

added only an eleven-page addendum assessing the impact of Ultra.

18:487 Runyan, Timothy J., and Jan M. Copes, eds. *To Die Gallantly: The Battle of the Atlantic.* Boulder: Westview Press, 1994. Most of the essays in this collection originated in a 1992 conference marking the fiftieth anniversary of the Battle of the Atlantic. They cover strategic, intelligence, and diplomatic as well as military aspects of the campaign and include: Werner Rahn, "The Atlantic in the Strategic Perspective of Hitler and Roosevelt, 1940–1941" (3–21); Jeffrey G. Barlow, "The Views of Stimson and Knox on Atlantic Strategy and Planning" (22–37); Theresa L. Kraus, "Planning the Defense of the South Atlantic, 1939–1941: Securing Brazil" (55–67); John F. Bratzel, "Brazil, Espionage, and Dönitz's Dream" (67–74); R. A. Bowling, "Mahan's Principles and the Battle of the Atlantic" (231–50); and Lawrence H. Suid, "The Battle of the Atlantic in Feature Films" (311–22).

18:488 Smith, Kevin. *Conflict over Convoys: Anglo-American Logistics Diplomacy in the Second World War.* This volume analyzes the 1942–1943 crisis in British merchant shipping, the Anglo-American effort to resolve that crisis, and the relationship between such "logistics diplomacy" and allied strategy (17:1058).

18:489 Steele, Richard W. *The First Offensive 1942: Roosevelt, Marshall and the Making of American Strategy.* Bloomington: Indiana University Press, 1973. Steele examines the 1942 allied debate over European strategy within American ranks as well as between the United States and Britain. He argues that all participants were motivated by political rather than strategic factors, and finds Marshall's 1942 cross-channel plan a militarily unsound attempt to accommodate Roosevelt's politico-military demands.

18:490 _____. "Political Aspects of American Military Planning, 1941–1942." *Military Affairs* 35 (April 1971): 68–74. Army anxieties in the early months of the war over its lack of influence in allied policymaking, combined with suspicion of British manipulation, played a significant role in the development of cross-channel plans in early 1942. For greater detail, see Steele's *The First Offensive 1942: Roosevelt, Marshall and the Making of American Strategy* (1973) (18:489).

18:491 Weiss, Steve. *Allies in Conflict: Anglo-American Strategic Negotiations, 1938–44.* New York: St. Martin's Press, 1996. Weiss examines the Anglo-American wartime debates and compromises over European strategy through the mid-1944 invasion of southern France, focusing on major strategic summit conferences and finding the "special relationship" to have been "a public relations myth." The coalition worked, he concludes, primarily because the external threat was greater than the internal discord.

North Africa

18:492 Funk, Arthur L. "Negotiating the 'Deal with Darlan.'" *Journal of Contemporary History* 8 (April 1973): 81–117. French cooperation with the allies' invasion of North Africa in November 1942 was obtained at the price of recognizing Admiral Jean Darlan as high commissioner in Morocco and Algeria, despite his earlier pro-German record.

18:493 _____. *The Politics of TORCH: The Allied Landings and the Algiers Putsch, 1942.* Lawrence: University Press of Kansas, 1974. This is the first study to examine the political aspects of the Anglo-American invasion and occupation of North Africa from the French as well as the American and British points of view. The result is an excellent synthesis, with emphasis on Algiers and the Darlan affair.

18:494 Gelb, Norman. *Desperate Venture: The Story of Operation Torch, the Allied Invasion of North Africa.* New York: William Morrow, 1992. This popular history of the North African campaign focuses on the preinvasion Anglo-American strategic debate, the negotiations with French officers that would culminate in the Darlan affair, the actual invasion and ensuing campaign, and the Darlan assassination and its aftermath. The author emphasizes the importance of political factors and concludes that, despite numerous gains, the campaign was a mistake.

18:495 Goda, Norman J. W. *Tomorrow the World: Hitler, Northwest Africa, and the Path toward America.* Goda analyzes Hitler's efforts to obtain bases in Northwest Africa in 1940–1941, which he sees as part of a strategy to obtain control of the eastern Atlantic for war against the United States (17:740).

18:496 Howe, George F. *United States Army in World War II: The Mediterranean Theater of Operations: Northwest Africa: Seizing the Initiative in the West.* Washington, DC: Government Printing Office, 1957. This volume in the official army history of the war covers Anglo-American planning and operations in North Africa from 1941 through 1943, with major emphasis on the period from the Torch landings (November 1942) to the German surrender in Tunisia (May 1943). It includes detailed information also on the diplomatic negotiations and political issues that arose in this theater regarding French military forces, government, and leadership.

18:497 Sainsbury, Keith. *The North African Landings, 1942: A Strategic Decision.* Newark: University of Delaware Press, 1979. Originally published in the United Kingdom in 1976 (Davis-Poynter), this volume analyzes both the 1942 allied strategic debate over cross-channel versus Mediterranean operations and the ensuing North African invasion and Darlan affair. For the most part the author supports the British position in these disputes.

18:498 Walker, David A. "OSS and Operation Torch." *Journal of Contemporary History* 22 (October 1987): 667–79. This is a balanced brief assessment of the OSS role and performance in the North African invasion. The author concludes that OSS personnel made important contributions to military intelligence but badly misjudged how the Vichy French army would respond to the invasion.

Italy and the Mediterranean

18:499 Barker, Thomas M. "The Ljubljana Gap Strategy: Alternative to Anvil/Dragoon or Fantasy?" *Journal of Military History* 56 (January 1992): 57–85. Barker maintains that the key factor in Churchill's original support for this strategic option was national prestige and support of his Mediterranean commander, not fear of the Soviet Union. The latter emerged as a key factor only after the August 1944 invasion of southern France. The author also concludes that the option was not militarily viable.

18:500 Blumenson, Martin. *United States Army in World War II: The Mediterranean Theater of Operations: Salerno to Cassino.* Washington, DC: Government Printing Office, 1969. This volume in the official U.S. army history of the war provides detailed coverage of allied and U.S. military planning for and operations in Italy from September 1943 through March 1944.

18:501   Botjer, George F. *The Sideshow War: The Italian Campaign, 1943–1945.* College Station: Texas A&M University Press, 1996. The author analyzes the interplay between nonmilitary and military factors in the theater. His revisionist and ironic conclusion is that both the allies and the Axis achieved their objectives in this campaign and that neither lost—but primarily because the theater was not militarily important and did not warrant the attention given to it by both sides.

18:502   Fisher, Ernest F., Jr. *United States Army in World War II: The Mediterranean Theater of Operations: Cassino to the Alps.* Washington, DC: Government Printing Office, 1977. This volume in the official army history covers military operations from the spring of 1944 through the spring of 1945, including the German surrender.

18:503   Garland, Albert N., and Howard M. Smyth, with Martin Blumenson. *United States Army in World War II: The Mediterranean Theater of Operations: Sicily and the Surrender of Italy.* Washington, DC: Government Printing Office, 1965. This volume in the official U.S. army history of the war provides detailed information on the 1943 surrender of Italy as well as military operations in Sicily.

18:504   Higgins, Trumbull. *Soft Underbelly: The Anglo-American Controversy over the Italian Campaign, 1939–1945.* New York: Macmillan, 1968. Higgins evaluates British aims and methods in the Italian campaign and the strategic disputes over the Mediterranean versus cross-channel approach to victory in Europe. The work extends the intense criticism of Churchill and the British approach found in his *Winston Churchill and the Second Front, 1940–1943* (1957) (18:843).

18:505   Holland, Jeffrey. *The Aegean Mission: Allied Operations in the Dodecanese, 1943.* New York: Greenwood Press, 1988. This study, based primarily upon research in British archives, analyzes the Anglo-American dispute in the summer and fall of

1943 over operations in the eastern Mediterranean, most notably an invasion of Rhodes to bring Turkey into the war and the ensuing British military defeats on the islands of Kos and Leros.

18:506   Howard, Michael. *The Mediterranean Strategy in the Second World War.* New York: Praeger, 1968. Howard in this brief work sees the Mediterranean strategy not as fundamentally conflicting with U.S. strategies, but as the opportunistic exploitation of an available theater when the allies were unready to do anything else and could not afford to sit idle.

18:507   _____. *Studies in War and Peace.* New York: Viking Press, 1971. This contains a chapter on "The Mediterranean in British Strategy in the Second World War," providing in brief form his thesis as fully explored in his *The Mediterranean Strategy in the Second World War* (1968) (18:506).

18:508   Parish, Michael W. *Aegean Adventures 1940–43: And the End of Churchill's Dream.* Sussex, UK: Book Guild, 1993. This memoir by a British officer deeply involved in special operations in the Mediterranean is sharply critical of U.S. wartime policies he believes lengthened the war and led to both the demise of the British empire and Soviet domination of Eastern Europe. He is particularly critical of U.S. opposition to Churchill's strategy in the eastern Mediterranean.

18:509   Wilkinson, Peter. *Foreign Fields: The Story of an SOE Operative.* New York: I. B. Taurus Publishers, 1997. The author, a wartime intelligence officer in Britain's Special Operations Executive (SOE), provides an insider's description of the organization's foundation and structure as well as recounts his personal experiences, most notably his activities in the Balkans and Central Europe.

Cross-Channel Attack and European Operations

18:510   Ambrose, Stephen E. *Citizen Soldiers: The U.S. Army from the Normandy Beaches to the Bulge to the Surrender of Germany, June 7, 1944–May 7, 1945.* New York: Simon and Schuster, 1997. This best-selling history was written as a sequel to Ambrose's 1994 *D-Day, June 6, 1944: The Climactic Battle of World War II* (Simon and Schuster). It covers strategy, operations, tactics, and army life in Europe.

18:511   _____. *Eisenhower and Berlin, 1945: The Decision to Halt at the Elbe.* New York: W. W. Norton, 1967. This brief volume by Eisenhower's foremost biographer explains and defends his controversial decision not to attempt to capture Berlin before the Russians, despite British entreaties that he do so. Ambrose clearly analyzes the numerous military and political factors that influenced Eisenhower.

18:512   Brower, Charles F., IV, ed. *World War II in Europe: The Final Year.* New York: St. Martin's Press, 1998. From a 1994 symposium on the war's last year at the Roosevelt Study Center in Middelburg, the Netherlands, this collection of papers and commentaries is grouped into sections on grand strategy, military operations, the liberation of the Netherlands, and the human side of the war. As such the collection is of value to diplomatic as well as military, social, and cultural historians. See particularly Warren F. Kimball, "FDR and Allied Grand Strategy, 1944–1945: The Juggler's Last Act"; David Reynolds, "Churchill and Allied Grand Strategy in Europe, 1944–1945: The Erosion of British Influence"; and Mark A. Stoler, "Strategy, Grand and Otherwise: A Commentary."

18:513   de Lattre, Jean. *The History of the First French Army.* Translated by Malcolm Barnes. London: Allen and Unwin, 1952. This operational story of the French army in France and Germany (1944–1945), by its commander, covers the landings in the south, drive up the Rhone Valley, the fight in the Vosges, the crossing of the Rhine, and the drive into Germany, but also includes important information about U.S.-French strategic differences.

18:514   Harrison, Gordon A. *United States Army in World War II: The European Theatre of Operations: Cross-Channel Attack.* Washington, DC: Office of the Chief of Military History, Dept. of the Army, 1951. This volume in the official U.S. army history of the war covers planning for the cross-channel attack and the operations in Normandy until the beachhead was established. Approximately one-half of the book discusses strategy and allied preparations for the invasion, including all the allies' debates and arguments.

18:515   Naftali, Timothy. "Creating the Myth of the *Alpenfestung*: Allied Intelligence and the Collapse of the Nazi Police State." In *Austrian Historical Memory & National Identity,* ed. Günter Bischof and Anton Pelinka, 203–46. New Brunswick: Transaction Publishers, 1997. Behind Eisenhower's controversial strategic decisions in April 1945 stood not simply the well-known fears of a Nazi alpine redoubt, but more importantly the longer-standing fear, drawn from U.S. intelligence, of an ideologically driven underground resistance or guerrilla movement. Late intelligence reports on Bavaria provided a geographic focus for these alarms. Naftali carefully analyzes their origins and development and explains the numerous reasons for these incorrect intelligence assessments. *Austrian Historical Memory* is volume 5 of *Contemporary Austrian Studies.*

18:516   Pogue, Forrest C. "Political Problems of a Coalition Command." In *Total War and Cold War: Problems in Civilian Control of the Military,* ed. Harry L. Coles, 108–28. Columbus: Ohio State University Press, 1962. Eisenhower's contribution as supreme commander has been underestimated. His job was complicated by conflicting allied political interests and national pride.

18:517   _____. *United States Army in World War II: The European Theater of Operations: The Supreme Command.* Washington, DC: Government Printing Office, 1954. This volume in the official U.S. army history of the war is a detailed study of the organization and activities of Supreme Headquarters, Allied Expeditionary Forces. One-third of the volume is devoted to planning and organization prior to the Normandy invasion; the remainder covers events and issues through the German surrender.

18:518   Powers, Stephen T. "The Battle of Normandy: The Lingering Controversy." *Journal of Military History* 56 (July 1992): 455–71. This article traces the continuing controversy in recent historical literature over Anglo-American conflict during the European campaign of 1944–1945. British leaders' anger was due not to Eisenhower's supposed incompetence, Powers concludes, but to their frustration over their loss of power within the coalition.

18:519   Shepardson, Donald E. "The Fall of Berlin and the Rise of a Myth." *Journal of Military History*

62 (January 1998): 135–53. Based on published sources, this article attempts to re-create the full diplomatic and military context of Eisenhower's decision not to try taking Berlin in the spring of 1945. The author concludes that the decision was appropriate, and he labels as myth the continued belief that Eisenhower could and should have taken the German capital.

18:520   Weigley, Russell F. *Eisenhower's Lieutenants: The Campaign of France and Germany, 1944–1945.* Bloomington: Indiana University Press, 1981. Although primarily a detailed military history of the 1944–1945 campaign in Europe, this volume deals with Anglo-American conflicts that erupted during that campaign. It is highly critical of Montgomery but also of U.S. military doctrine, leadership, and performance.

18:521   Weingartner, Steven, ed. *The Greatest Thing We Have Ever Attempted: Historical Perspectives on the Normandy Campaign.* Wheaton, IL: Cantigny First Division Foundation, 1998. These published proceedings of a 1994 commemorative conference at the Cantigny First Division Museum focus on the military aspects of the Normandy invasion but include numerous brief papers and discussions about the coalition aspects of the operation and its impact on other nations.

18:522   Wilson, Theodore A., ed. *D-Day 1944.* Lawrence: University Press of Kansas, 1994. This collection of papers, many prepared for an Eisenhower Library commemoration of the fiftieth anniversary of the Normandy invasion, updates the twenty-fifth anniversary volume, published by the same press in 1971 under the title *D-Day: The Normandy Invasion in Retrospect.* Essays include Maurice Matloff, "Wilmot Revisited: Myth and Reality in Anglo-American Strategy for the Second Front" (3–34); Alex Danchev, "Biffing: The Saga of the Second Front" (35–41); Kevin Smith, "Constraining Overlord: Civilian Logistics, Torch, and the Second Front" (42–62); Mark A. Stoler, "Dwight D. Eisenhower: Architect of Victory" (298–318); and Gerhard L. Weinberg, "D-Day: Analysis of Costs and Benefits" (318–37).

The Eastern Front

18:523   Erickson, John. *Stalin's War with Germany.* 2 vols. London: Weidenfeld and Nicolson, 1975–1983. Reprint 1999 (Yale University Press). These two monumental volumes, separately titled *The Road to Stalingrad* and *The Road to Berlin,* are considered the outstanding history of the Russo-German war in the English language. They are based on extraordinary research in Soviet as well as German documents and published materials, along with East European memoirs and monographs.

18:524   Glantz, David M. "Soviet Military Strategy during the Second Period of War (November 1942–December 1943): A Reappraisal." *Journal of Military History* 60 (January 1996): 115–50. Glantz is the foremost U.S. authority on the World War II Red Army. In this article he maintains that despite their stupendous victories at Stalingrad and Kursk, the Soviets attempted to achieve far more than they actually did during this period and suffered major military failures in their unsuccessful efforts to destroy the German Army Group Center. These failures explain Stalin's continued demands for an Anglo-American second front. Among his numerous books on the Red Army during the war, see especially his overview, written with Jonathan M. House, *When Titans Clashed: How the Red Army Stopped Hitler* (Lawrence: University Press of Kansas, 1995).

18:525   Kimball, Warren F. "Stalingrad: A Chance for Choices." *Journal of Military History* 60 (January 1996): 89–114. This article analyzes the impact of this decisive eastern front battle on U.S. policy toward the Soviet Union.

FAR EASTERN STRATEGY AND OPERATIONS

General

18:526   Dockrill, Saki, ed. *From Pearl Harbor to Hiroshima: The Second World War in Asia and the Pacific, 1941–1945.* New York: St. Martin's Press, 1994. This collection consists of conference papers commemorating the fiftieth anniversary of the Pearl Harbor attack and ensuing globalization of the European and Far Eastern wars. Key topics include British policies, U.S. strategy and codebreaking, and the war on the Asian mainland. Among the more pertinent chapters are John Pritchard, "Winston Churchill, the Military, and Imperial Defence in East Asia" (11–25); Ronald H. Spector, "American Seizure of Japan's Strategic Points, Summer 1942–44" (75–87); Peter Lowe, "Britain, the Commonwealth and Pacific Security" (174–90); Lawrence Freedman and Dockrill, "Hiroshima: A Strategy of Shock" (191–214); and Dockrill, "The Legacy of the 'Pacific War' as Seen from Europe" (215–24).

18:527　Dower, John W. "Race, Language, and War in Two Cultures: World War II in Asia." In *The War in American Culture: Society and Consciousness during World War II*, ed. Lewis A. Erenberg and Susan E. Hirsch, 169–201. Chicago: University of Chicago Press, 1996. Highlighting the intense race hatred of the Pacific war, Dower surveys the racial imagery and stereotyping used by each side and suggests how such sentiment influenced the course of the war. He also suggests how stereotypes helped smooth the transition to peace at the end of the war.

18:528　_____. *War without Mercy: Race and Power in the Pacific War.* New York: Pantheon Books, 1986. This important work explores the racial images and propaganda in both Japan and the United States during the Pacific war, and finds them key components of the ferocity of that conflict.

18:529　Hayes, Grace Person. *The History of the Joint Chiefs of Staff in World War II: The War against Japan.* Annapolis: Naval Institute Press, 1982. This official history of the World War II JCS and the Far Eastern war was written by a navy member of the JCS Historical Section and completed in 1953. Naval Institute Press published the typescript in 1982. It provides great detail on strategic disputes and decisions in the war against Japan.

18:530　Iriye, Akira, and Warren I. Cohen, eds. *American, Chinese, and Japanese Perspectives on Wartime Asia, 1931–1949.* This "experiment in multinational historical writing" (based on meetings in 1982–1985) consists of ten essays written by historians from all three countries. Most deal with prewar issues, but wartime concerns appear in Sherman Cochran, "Businesses, Governments, and War in

China, 1931–1949" (117–46); Gary R. Hess, "The Emergence of U.S. Influence in Southeast Asia" (179–222); Iriye, "Japan against the ABCD Powers" (223–42); and Luo Rongqu, "China and East Asia in America's Global Strategy, 1931–1949" (269–92) (17:894).

18:531　Kirby, S. Woodburn, with C. T. Addis et al. *The War against Japan.* 5 vols. London: Her Majesty's Stationery Office, 1957–1969. The official account of British operations in the war against Japan combines a narrative of operations with valuable material on high-level planning and cooperation with American political and military leaders.

18:532　Levine, Alan J. *The Pacific War: Japan versus the Allies.* Westport, CT: Praeger, 1995. This brief volume offers a concise and at times provocative summary of the war against Japan, including strategies and polices as well as operations.

18:533　Spector, Ronald H. *Eagle against the Sun: The American War with Japan.* New York: Free Press, 1985. This remains the best single volume on the U.S. war against Japan.

18:534　Weinberg, Gerhard L. "Grand Strategy in the Pacific War." *Air Power History* 43 (Spring 1996): 4–13. Weinberg links pre– to post–Pearl Harbor U.S. policies and strategies in the war against Japan and explains their evolution from 1941 to 1945. He focuses on the reasons for the three-pronged advance on Japan from China and the southwest and central Pacific, the expanded emphasis on the two Pacific theaters after 1944 failures in China, and the final 1945 strategy for Japanese defeat. As with all Weinberg scholarship, the article is well reasoned and filled with numerous surprises and attacks on conventional wisdom.

18:535　Willmott, H. P. *Empires in the Balance: Japanese and Allied Strategies to April 1942.* Annapolis: Naval Institute Press, 1982. In this volume a British military historian offers a comprehensive, comparative analysis of Japanese, British, and U.S. strategies and policies from World War I through the Doolittle raid in April of 1942. See also his *The Barrier and the Javelin: Japanese and Allied Strategies, February to June 1942* (Annapolis: Naval Institute Press, 1983).

Pacific Strategy and Operations

18:536   Bartlett, Merrill L., and Robert W. Love, Jr. "Anglo-American Naval Diplomacy and the British Pacific Fleet, 1942–1945." *American Neptune* 42 (July 1982): 203–16. The article traces British naval opposition to complementary naval operations in the war against Japan in 1942–1943 and U.S. naval objections to any combined Pacific operations in 1944, until forced by Roosevelt to agree to them.

18:537   Bischof, Günter, and Robert L. Dupont, eds. *The Pacific War Revisited.* Baton Rouge: Louisiana State University Press, 1997. The eight essays in this volume originated in a 1991 conference of the Eisenhower Center at the University of New Orleans. They explicitly focus on relatively unfamiliar topics in military, diplomatic, and social history and are preceded by an introductory historiographical essay by D. Clayton James, "Introduction: Rethinking the Pacific War" (1–16). Of particular interest to diplomatic historians are: Michael Schaller, "General Douglas MacArthur and the Politics of the Pacific War" (17–40); Ronald H. Spector, "The Pacific War and the Fourth Dimension of Strategy" (41–56), emphasizing American hatred of the Japanese as a key strategic factor; and Stephen Ambrose and Brian Loring Villa on the ironic role of the atomic bomb in breaking down Japanese-American racial hatred in "Racism, the Atomic Bomb, and the Transformation of Japanese-American Relations" (179–98).

18:538   Kimball, Warren F. "Roosevelt and the Southwest Pacific: 'Merely a Facade'?" *Journal of American–East Asian Relations* 3 (Summer 1994): 103–26. Kimball explores Roosevelt's attitudes toward global strategy, colonialism, and the postwar southwest Pacific via analysis of his comments to the Pacific War Council from 1942 to 1944, with a special focus on U.S.-Australian relations. This article is reprinted in David Day, ed., *Brave New World: Dr. H. C. Evatt and Australian Foreign Policy, 1941–1949* (St. Lucia, Australia: Queensland University Press, 1996), but the article is more accessible for most than the book.

18:539   Milner, Samuel. *United States Army in World War II: War in the Pacific: Victory in Papua.* Washington, DC: Government Printing Office, 1957.

This account of the New Guinea campaign in the U.S. army's official history provides an interesting comparison with the Australian official version by Dudley McCarthy (*South-west Pacific Area: First Year: Kokoda to Wau* [Canberra: Australian War Memorial, 1959]).

18:540   Morton, Louis. *United States Army in World War II: The War in the Pacific: Strategy and Command: The First Two Years.* Washington, DC: Government Printing Office, 1962. This volume in the official U.S. army history of the war concentrates on allied and Japanese grand strategy in the Pacific from antecedents and prewar plans to the end of 1943. Appendices include a number of useful primary documents from both sides.

18:541   Perras, Galen Roger. "We Have Opened the Door to Tokyo: United States Plans to Seize the Kurile Islands, 1943–1945." *Journal of Military History* 61 (January 1997): 65–91. Perras makes extensive use of military records in the National Archives to trace and analyze not only plans to attack and occupy the Kurile Islands as part of a North Pacific offensive, but also the military debates over such plans and the reasons they were proposed and rejected. He includes military assessments of the Soviet Union and concludes that Roosevelt at Yalta rejected the wishes of his military leaders to occupy the islands.

18:542   Renzi, William A., and Mark D. Roehrs. *Never Look Back: A History of World War II in the Pacific.* Armonk, NY: M. E. Sharpe, 1991. This brief volume concentrates on the Japanese-American war in the Pacific (albeit with one chapter on the China-Burma-India theater) and as such is a useful introduction to that conflict. It attempts to provide the reader with Japanese as well as American viewpoints and is based on published primary and secondary sources. It contains no footnotes or general bibliography but does provide suggestions for further reading at the end of each chapter.

China-Burma-India

18:543   Barrett, David D. *Dixie Mission: The United States Army Observer Group in Yenan, 1944.* Berkeley: Center for Chinese Studies, University of California, 1970. Barrett headed the U.S. army observer group to Mao's communists in Yenan in 1944–1945. This account is rich in anecdote and revealing of the personalities involved.

18:544   Elsey, George M. *Roosevelt and China: The White House Story: "The President and U.S. Aid to China—1944."* Wilmington, DE: Michael Glazier, 1979. This volume contains a facsimile reproduction of a previously unavailable November 1944 White House staff report on FDR and U.S. wartime aid to China, declassified in 1972, that Elsey authored as a map room officer; covering memos by Elsey and Roosevelt; and a commentary by Riley Sunderland, coauthor of the army's three-volume official history of the China-Burma-India theater.

18:545   Gordon, Leonard H. D. "American Planning for Taiwan, 1942–1945." *Pacific Historical Review* 37 (May 1968): 201–28. This article deals with Taiwan in U.S. wartime strategy in the Pacific and with plans for postwar occupation. American officials resisted Chinese Nationalists' claims to control the island, so, despite statements at the Cairo conference, Taiwan's legal status was still unresolved at the war's end.

18:546   Hsiung, James C., and Steven I. Levine, eds. *China's Bitter Victory: The War with Japan, 1937–1945.* Armonk, NY: M. E. Sharpe, 1992. The chapters in this edited collection, each by a noted scholar of China, analyze the political, diplomatic, military, economic, and cultural dimensions of China's eight-year war against Japan. John W. Garver writes on the foreign policy of the Chinese Nationalists, and Jonathan Goldstein on that of the CCP.

18:547   Romanus, Charles F., and Riley Sunderland. *United States Army in World War II: China-Burma-India Theater: Stilwell's Command Problems.* Washington, DC: Government Printing Office, 1956. Covering 1943–1944, this second volume on the China-Burma-India theater in the official army history of the war deals with the complicated command structure in that area, preparations for a Burma campaign, and controversies among the British, Americans, and Chinese on priorities. It is informative on the Stilwell effort to put pressure on Jiang Jieshi to move against the Japanese.

18:548   _____. *United States Army in World War II: China-Burma-India Theater: Stilwell's Mission to China.* Washington, DC: Government Printing Office, 1953. This volume in the official army history of the war deals with the establishment of the Stilwell mission to China, the defeat in Burma, Stilwell's role as a trainer of troops, his clash with Chennault, and the beginnings of trouble with Jiang Jieshi in 1942–1943.

18:549   _____. *United States Army in World War II: China-Burma-India Theater: Time Runs Out in CBI.* Washington, DC: Government Printing Office, 1959. This third and final volume of the official army history on the China-Burma-India theaters deals with the 1944–1945 reorganization of the China theater under General Wedemeyer, plans for air attacks from China, completion of communications begun by Stilwell, serious Japanese threats against allied air bases, and the end of Japanese control in China.

18:550   Schaller, Michael. "The Command Crisis in China, 1944: A Road Not Taken." *Diplomatic History* 4 (Summer 1980): 327–31. Schaller reproduces in full the unsent message Marshall drafted for Roosevelt to send Chiang threatening an end to aid and support. The author does not believe it was a bluff and that it constitutes a policy contrary to the one FDR took.

18:551   Sunderland, Riley. "The Secret Embargo." *Pacific Historical Review* 29 (February 1960): 75–80. This brief essay is a perceptive comment on Jiang Jieshi's wartime practice of conserving his own forces while sacrificing the troops of rival commanders within his own Nationalist ranks and blaming the losses on General Stilwell. Warren I. Cohen provides more evidence on this same point in "Who Fought the Japanese in Hunan? Some Views of China's War Effort," *Journal of Asian Studies* 27 (November 1967): 111–15.

HEMISPHERIC DEFENSE

18:552   Baptiste, Fitzroy André. *War, Cooperation, and Conflict: The European Possessions in the Caribbean, 1939–1945.* This is a solid overview of Caribbean issues from 1938 through 1943. The author covers such topics as U.S. hemispheric defense, the details of the destroyers-for-bases deal, military operations in the region, and the wartime fates of such European possessions as France's Guadeloupe and Martinique (17:631).

18:553   Coates, Kenneth, ed. *The Alaska Highway: Papers of the 40th Anniversary Symposium.* Vancouver: University of British Columbia Press, 1985. Many of the fourteen papers in this collection focus on Canadian-American relations regarding this wartime project. Most pertinent for historians of foreign relations are David Remley, "The Latent Fear: Canadian-American Relations and Early Proposals for a Highway to Alaska" (1–8); M. V. Bezeau, "The Realities of Strategic Planning: The Decision to Build the Alaska Highway" (25–35); and Richard J. Diubaldo, "The Alaska Highway in Canada–United States Relations" (102–15). See also Heath Twichell, *Northwest Epic: The Building of the Alaska Highway* (New York: St. Martin's Press, 1992).

18:554   Coates, Kenneth, and W. R. Morrison. *The Alaska Highway in World War II: The U.S. Army of Occupation in Canada's Northwest.* Norman: University of Oklahoma Press, 1992. The authors focus on the social and economic impact on the Canadian northwest of what they label a friendly occupation by the U.S. army in this wartime construction project. That army profoundly affected the area by bringing with it American culture, racial tensions, economic system, political agenda, and military values. Canadian officials exposed to this impact became more protective of the area.

18:555   Conn, Stetson, Rose C. Engelman, and Byron Fairchild. *United States Army in World War II: The Western Hemisphere: Guarding the United States and Its Outposts.* Washington, DC: Government Printing Office, 1964. This study describes the army's "basic and primary concern"—the defense of the continental United States and its principal outposts: Hawaii, the Caribbean, Alaska, Greenland, and Iceland.

18:556   Conn, Stetson, and Byron Fairchild. *United States Army in World War II: The Western Hemisphere: The Framework of Hemispheric Defense.* Washington, DC: Government Printing Office, 1960. This volume analyzes American military planning (1939–1942) for and with other nations in the hemisphere, and includes much information on diplomatic

as well as military relations with those nations, including Brazil, Mexico, and Canada.

18:557   Dziuban, Stanley W. *United States Army in World War II: Special Studies: Military Relations between the United States and Canada, 1939–1945.* Washington, DC: Government Printing Office, 1959. This volume in the official U.S. army history of the war analyzes military-related political issues and agreements between the United States and Canada. Diplomatic discussions and negotiations figure prominently.

18:558   Keenleyside, Hugh L. "The Canadian–United States Permanent Joint Board on Defence, 1940–1945." *International Journal* 16 (Winter 1960–1961): 50–77. A well-informed account of the first five years of the board, this is based on the author's personal experience as Canadian secretary. The essay is especially valuable for its perceptions of personalities and the details of the board's functioning.

18:559   Palmer, Annette. "The United States in the British Caribbean, 1940–1945: Rum and Coca Cola." *Americas* 43 (April 1987): 441–52. The racial attitudes of American troops in the British Caribbean destroyed prewar sentiment for an American takeover of the islands and led instead to aggressive nationalist demands for self-government.

STRATEGIC BOMBING

18:560   Beaumont, Roger. "The Bomber Offensive as a Second Front." *Journal of Contemporary History* 22 (January 1987): 3–19. Beaumont argues that the politico-military need to show the Soviets military action in the absence of a 1942 cross-channel invasion played a role in the high priority given to the strategic bombing campaign against Germany, and that the campaign did constitute an effective "second front."

18:561   Biddle, Tami Davis. "British and American Approaches to Strategic Bombing: Their Origins and Implementation in the World War II Combined Bomber Offensive." *Journal of Strategic Studies* 18 (March 1995): 91–144. Biddle analyzes the development of British and American thinking about strategic bombing from the end of World War I through the combined bomber offensive against Germany to understand why the two allies adopted different operational practices.

18:562   Crane, Conrad C. *Bombs, Cities, and Civilians: American Airpower Strategy in World War II.* Lawrence: University Press of Kansas, 1993. Arguing that with selected exceptions American airmen remained committed to the concept of precision bombing, Crane traces the evolution of U.S. strategic bombing doctrine, its practice, and the role of technology. He emphasizes how the subtle interactions of established doctrine and wartime realities, technological innovation, public opinion, and AAF leaders' belief in "Victory through Air Power" affected military policy and the conduct of operations.

18:563   _____. "Evolution of U.S. Strategic Bombing of Urban Areas." *Historian* 50 (November 1987): 14–39. Responding to Schaffer ("American Military Ethics in World War II: The Bombing of German Civilians," 1980 [18:576], *Wings of Judgment: American Bombing in World War II,* 1985 [18:577]) and Sherry (*The Rise of American Air Power: The Creation of Armageddon,* 1987 [18: 578]), Crane addresses the issue of American indiscriminate bombing of enemy civilians with a study of operations over Germany and Japan. Although army air force leaders opposed terror bombing and sought tactical restraint, he finds their declared intentions eroded in practice by technological limitations, the belief that bombing offered the swiftest end to war at the lowest cost, and an absence of American popular opposition to bombing.

18:564   Helmreich, Jonathan E. "The Diplomacy of Apology: U.S. Bombings of Switzerland during World War II." *Air University Review* 28 (May-June 1977): 19–37. This essay discusses the problems caused by the inadvertent bombing of Swiss territory in 1943, 1944, and 1945 by elements of the Eighth Air Force. The most serious damage was inflicted in the cities of Schaffhausen, Zurich, and Basel. Helmreich examines U.S. efforts to solve the problem and handle the diplomatic situation in detail.

18:565   Hopkins, George E. "Bombing and the American Conscience during World War II." *Historian* 28 (May 1966): 451–73. The consensus favored the strategic bombing of German and Japanese cities.

Americans ignored ethical distinctions between weapons because they were constantly reminded that they were engaged in "a total war."

18:566   Huston, John W. "The Impact of Strategic Bombing in the Pacific." *Journal of American–East Asian Relations* 4 (Summer 1995): 169–79. Huston examines the changes in strategic bombing practices against Japan in 1945. The crucial change was legitimating enemy population centers as military targets, and Huston argues that acceptance of the new tactics "paved the way" for dropping the atomic bombs.

18:567   Jacobs, William A. "Strategic Bombing and American National Strategy, 1941–1943." *Military Affairs* 50 (July 1986): 133–39. Jacobs examines the origin and development of the strategic bombing offensive against Germany from the start of war until its acceptance at the Casablanca conference. He emphasizes the influence exerted on strategic policy by American success in the Pacific, Anglo-American military antagonism over strategic direction of the war, and General Henry A. Arnold's championing of the bomber offensive.

18:568   Julian, Thomas A. "Operations at the Margin: Soviet Bases and Shuttle-Bombing." *Journal of Military History* 57 (October 1993): 627–52. This overview of Operation FRANTIC examines its origins, the differing allied and Soviet perspectives on the operation, and the problems encountered in U.S.-Soviet cooperation.

18:569   Levine, Alan J. *The Strategic Bombing of Germany, 1940–1945.* New York: Praeger, 1992. This is a concise introduction to the strategic bombing campaign waged against Germany. Although useful for novices, the author relies on secondary sources and the U.S. Strategic Bombing Survey.

18:570   MacIsaac, David. *Strategic Bombing in World War Two: The Story of the United States Strategic Bombing Survey.* New York: Garland Publishing, 1976. This study provides an account of the organization and operation of the USSBS and of its findings and conclusions. MacIsaac also reviews the development of strategic bombing doctrine.

18:571   _____, ed. *The United States Strategic Bombing Survey.* 10 vols. New York: Garland Publishing, 1976. The Strategic Bombing Survey staff produced 321 reports on various aspects of strategic bombing during World War II. Thirty of the more important reports are included in these volumes, eleven for the first time.

18:572   Markusen, Eric, and David Kopf. *The Holocaust and Strategic Bombing: Genocide and Total War in the Twentieth Century.* Boulder: Westview Press, 1995. Viewing mass death as a defining characteristic of modernity, the authors conduct a comparative analysis of the Holocaust and the allied strategic bombing campaign. Although paying attention to the dramatic differences between these events, they ultimately conclude they were more alike than different— and both "genocide."

18:573   Overy, Richard J. *The Air War, 1939–1945.* New York: Stein and Day, 1980. Overy provides a thorough yet succinct overview of World War II as fought in the air. He covers the research, technology, and economies behind the air forces as well as the strategic and political issues and personalities central to the air war. He presents a judicious argument for the importance of airpower to the allied victory.

18:574   Parrish, N. F. "Hap Arnold and the Historians." *Aerospace Historian* 20 (September 1973): 113–15. This brief article relates a little-known 1943–1944 episode in which General Arnold, skeptical of statistical analyses, sought the aid of a committee of distinguished historians (including Carl Becker, Henry S. Commager, Edward Mead Earle, and Dumas Malone) to assess whether the air campaign alone, without invasion, could lead to a German collapse similar to that in 1918. The committee judiciously and correctly concluded that the situations were not analogous, that bombing was and would continue to be vital to the allied war effort, but that it could not alone cause a German collapse in 1944. A land attack would be necessary.

18:575   Rumpf, Hans. *The Bombing of Germany.* Translated by Edward Fitzgerald. New York: Holt, Rinehart and Winston, 1963. This German view is critical of allied bombing of Germany and especially of Douhet's theories. Rumpf holds that bombing strengthens the victims' will and does not remove the necessity of ground efforts.

18:576   Schaffer, Ronald. "American Military Ethics in World War II: The Bombing of German Civilians." *Journal of American History* 67 (September 1980): 318–34. Schaffer argues that the air force's declared wartime policy of avoiding indiscriminate bombing of German civilians was not followed in practice. When some AAF leaders questioned actual practices, they did so on pragmatic, operational grounds or out of concern for the service's public reputation. For rejoinders by Alfred C. Mierzejewski and Kenneth P. Werrell, and a response by Schaffer, see "American Military Ethics in World War II: An Exchange," *Journal of American History* 68 (June 1981): 85–92.

18:577   _____. *Wings of Judgment: American Bombing in World War II.* New York: Oxford University Press, 1985. Schaffer analyzes the strategic bombing campaigns against Germany and Japan with particular attention to the morality of operations that targeted civilians, either directly or indirectly. Noting that throughout the war American planners never lost sight of "moral concerns," he nevertheless concludes that their distinctions between their "precision" bombing and British area bombing in the European theater tended to disappear in practice.

18:578   Sherry, Michael S. *The Rise of American Air Power: The Creation of Armageddon.* Sherry makes a compelling and provocative case that the cultural allure of technology, specifically airplanes and airpower, contributed significantly to the brutal military doctrine of strategic bombing. Air leaders, he holds, single-mindedly pursued dictates of doctrine rather than contingent solutions when confronted with operational problems (17:1160).

18:579   Webster, C. K., and Noble Frankland. *The Strategic Air Offensive against Germany, 1939–1945.* 4 vols. London: Her Majesty's Stationery Office, 1961. This official British history of the air war against Germany focuses on such topics as early planning and operations, the combined bomber offensive, disagreement between British and American commanders on types of bombing, and preparations for OVERLORD. The last volume consists of appendices, documents, and statistics.

18:580   Werrell, Kenneth P. "The Strategic Bombing of Germany in World War II: Costs and Accomplishments." *Journal of American History* 73 (December 1986): 702–13. Werrell offers a summary assessment of the costs and achievements of strategic bombing in Europe during World War II, pointedly excluding moral criteria.

INTELLIGENCE: GENERAL

18:581   Aldrich, Richard J. *Intelligence and the War against Japan: Britain, America and the Politics of Secret Service.* New York: Cambridge University Press, 2000. This book details the administrative development of the British secret service and its institutional relations with its American counterparts. Aldrich argues that the British never abandoned long-term intelligence gathering even during wartime, and he sees the secret service as an "essential catalyst" for the more acrimonious interallied disputes about the future of Asia.

18:582   Alexander, Martin S., ed. *Knowing Your Friends: Intelligence inside Alliances and Coalitions from 1914 to the Cold War.* Portland, OR: Frank Cass, 1998. Two of the eleven essays in this collection, which first appeared in the Spring 1998 issue (vol. 13) of the *Journal of Intelligence and National Security,* deal closely with the World War II alliance: Kathryn E. Brown on the role of signals intelligence on U.S. Indochina policy during the war ("The Interplay of Information and Mind in Decision-Making: Signals Intelligence and Franklin D. Roosevelt's Policy-Shift on Indochina") and Richard J. Aldrich on the OSS and India, 1942–1947 ("American Intelligence and the British Raj: The OSS, the SSU and India, 1942–1947"). Particularly notable is the OSS-British preoccupation with the competition for postwar influence in Asia as analyzed by Aldrich and Brown's conclusion that signals intelligence did not affect Roosevelt's worldview or policy while he was healthy, but that it did affect his advisers and played a role in the policy shift of 1945 as his health declined.

18:583   Ambrose, Stephen E., with Richard H. Immerman. *Ike's Spies: Eisenhower and the Espionage Establishment.* Garden City, NY: Doubleday, 1981. Ambrose traces and analyzes Eisenhower's presidential fondness for using the CIA and for espionage to his positive wartime experiences with Ultra, decep-

tion plans, and resistance movements. Nearly half of the book is devoted to the World War II years.

18:584   Andrew, Christopher M. *For the President's Eyes Only: Secret Intelligence and the American Presidency from Washington to Bush.* New York: HarperCollins Publishers, 1995. Andrew devotes two of his thirteen chapters in this extensive history to Roosevelt and one to Truman. He criticizes FDR for not understanding the crucial importance of codebreaking as opposed to more traditional spying and covert operations.

18:585   Andrew, Christopher M., and David Dilks, eds. *The Missing Dimension: Governments and Intelligence Communities in the Twentieth Century.* Urbana: University of Illinois Press, 1984. Although most of the eleven scholarly essays in this collection focus on Great Britain and the pre–Pearl Harbor years, three are of interest to U.S. World War II diplomatic and military historians: David Kahn on the successes and failures of codebreaking during the two world wars, Jürgen Rohwer on the role of radio intelligence in the Battle of the Atlantic, and Robert Cecil on wartime Soviet spies in Great Britain. Also of interest is Christopher M. Andrew, "Codebreakers and Foreign Offices: the French, British, and American Experience."

18:586   Annan, Noel. *Changing Enemies: The Defeat and Regeneration of Germany.* New York: W. W. Norton and Co., 1996. The author served on both British and Anglo-American intelligence staffs during the war and as a political adviser in postwar occupied Germany. This volume is part memoir and part scholarly analysis of the transformation of British policy toward Germany between 1941 and 1946. The chapters on the war years offer valuable insights into and assessments of the allied intelligence effort.

18:587   Bath, Alan Harris. *Tracking the Axis Enemy: The Triumph of Anglo-American Naval Intelligence.* Lawrence: University Press of Kansas, 1998. Based upon research in recently declassified records of Australia, Canada, and New Zealand as well as Britain and the United States, this volume analyzes Anglo-American cooperation and conflict in the field of naval intelligence during the war. The author finds dissimilar patterns of cooperation and conflict in the

Atlantic and Pacific theaters, with cooperation much greater in the former theater. He also finds the periods of cooperation in both theaters to have resulted from British initiatives but limited by political and bureaucratic factors as well as specific personalities.

18:588   Brown, Anthony Cave. *Bodyguard of Lies.* New York: Harper and Row, 1975. Although this work refers as well to OSS activities, it mainly emphasizes British intelligence services, focusing on preparation for D-Day. It is a popular history and should be checked against later and more scholarly works based on declassified sources as well as the official history of British intelligence by Hinsley, *British Intelligence in the Second World War* (1979–1990) (18:596).

18:589   Casey, Steven. "Franklin D. Roosevelt, Ernst 'Putzi' Hanfstaengl and the 'S-Project,' June 1942–June 1944." *Journal of Contemporary History* 35 (July 2000): 339–59. Casey analyzes and explains Roosevelt's bizarre insistence upon using a high-ranking and thoroughly unreliable former Nazi official as an intelligence operative and psychological warfare adviser, despite strong British objections. He sees the episode as illustrative of Roosevelt's attitudes toward both Germany and intelligence as well as an example of wartime Anglo-American conflict.

18:590   Gaddis, John Lewis. "Intelligence, Espionage, and Cold War Origins." *Diplomatic History* 13 (Spring 1989): 191–212. Although primarily concerned with the cold war, this article contains substantial information on World War II intelligence and espionage and an excellent summary of work in the field as of 1989. See also Donald Cameron Watt's extensive comment on this article in *Diplomatic History* 14 (Spring 1990): 199–204.

18:591   Handel, Michael I., ed. *Intelligence and Military Operations.* Portland, OR: Frank Cass, 1990. This is the third volume in a series by Handel on military intelligence. It consists of eleven essays by notable intelligence scholars originally presented at various international conferences on intelligence and military operations held in the 1980s at the U.S. Army War College. Most pertinent to this chapter is Ralph F. Bennett, "Intelligence and Strategy: Some Observations on the War in the Mediterranean, 1941–45" (444–64).

18:592   _____. *Leaders and Intelligence.* London: Frank Cass, 1989. Of particular interest to World War II scholars in this collection are Christopher M. Andrew, "Churchill and Intelligence" (181–93); Harold C. Deutsch, "Commanding Generals and the Uses of Intelligence" (194–260); and R. V. Jones, "Intelligence and Command" (288–98).

18:593   _____. *Strategic and Operational Deception in the Second World War.* Totowa, NJ: Frank Cass, 1987. The six essays in this volume were first presented at a 1986 international conference at the U.S. Army War College on intelligence and military operations and originally published in a special issue of the *Journal of Intelligence and National Security* (volume 2). Though little related to foreign relations, researchers might wish to consult these essays written by Handel, John P. Campbell, T. L. Cubbage, David M. Glantz, Katherine L. Herbig, Klaus-Jürgen Müller, and T. L. Cubbage.

18:594   Hartgrove, J. Dane, ed. *The OSS-NKVD Relationship, 1943–1945.* New York: Garland, 1989. Reproduced in this volume are 133 National Archives documents detailing the wartime relationship between the forerunners of the American CIA and Soviet KGB, from late 1943 through August 1945. The editor relied heavily on Bradley Smith, *The Shadow Warriors: O.S.S. and the Origins of the C.I.A.* (1983) (18:641), in compiling these documents.

18:595   Hilton, Stanley E. *Hitler's Secret War in South America, 1939–1945: German Military Espionage and Allied Counterespionage in Brazil.* Baton Rouge: Louisiana State University Press, 1981. This is a revised version of his *Suástica sobre o Brasil* (1977). Hilton provides a detailed account of wartime German espionage efforts in Latin America and the Brazilian, British, and American responses.

18:596   Hinsley, F. H., with E. E. Thomas, C. F. G. Ransom, and R. C. Knight. *British Intelligence in the Second World War.* 5 vols. in 6. New York: Cambridge University Press, 1979–1990. This is the official and, currently, definitive history of British intelligence operations during World War II. It is also the single most important work for any scholar dealing with allied intelligence during the war. Vols. 1–3 carried the subtitle *Its Influence on Strategy and Operations;* vol. 4, *Security and Counter-Intelligence;* and vol. 5, written by Michael Howard, *Strategic Deception.* Part 2 of vol. 3 was written by C. A. G. Simkins. Howard's *Strategic Deception* was published by Norton as a paperback in 1995. An abridged, single-volume version of the entire series was published in 1993 by Cambridge University Press.

18:597   Hitchcock, Walter Theodore, ed. *The Intelligence Revolution: A Historical Perspective: Proceedings of the Thirteenth Military History Symposium, U.S. Air Force Academy, Colorado Springs, Colorado, October 12–14, 1988.* Washington, DC: U.S. Air Force Academy, Office of Air Force History, United States Air Force, 1991. Included in this symposium collection are works on allied intelligence collaboration, the impact of the intelligence revolution on postwar diplomacy, and other matters. Among the individual contributions are F. H. Hinsley, "World War II: An Intelligence Revolution" (3–11), and Christopher M. Andrew, "Intelligence Collaboration between Britain, the United States, and the Commonwealth during World War II" (111–21).

18:598   Hyde, H. Montgomery. *Room 3603: The Story of the British Intelligence Center in New York during World War II.* New York: Farrar, Straus, 1963. This is a narrative account of the sub-rosa activities of William Stephenson (Intrepid) and his British Security Coordination office in the United States during the war by a member of his staff. While marred by incoherent organization, this should be used in preference to Stevenson, *A Man Called Intrepid: The Secret War* (1976) (18:608).

18:599   Persico, Joseph E. *Roosevelt's Secret War: FDR and World War II Espionage.* New York: Random House, 2001. Persico focuses in this broad history on Roosevelt's attitudes toward American wartime intelligence gathering and espionage activities. FDR was deeply attracted to such activities and critical in effecting the wartime creation of the U.S. intelligence establishment, but too focused on human sources over signals intelligence.

18:600   Richelson, Jeffrey T., and Desmond Ball. *The Ties That Bind: Intelligence Cooperation between the UKUSA Countries, the United Kingdom, the United States of America, Canada, Australia, and New Zealand.* 2d ed. Boston: Unwin Hyman, 1990. This broad survey examines intelligence cooperation

among the United States, Britain, and three members of the British Commonwealth from World War II to the present. It shows how Washington replaced London as the dominant partner and how this multinational security bureaucracy is held together. First published in 1985.

18:601   Smith, Bradley F. "Anglo-Soviet Intelligence Co-operation and Roads to the Cold War." In *British Intelligence, Strategy, and the Cold War, 1945–51,* ed. Richard J. Aldrich, 50–64. New York: Routledge, 1992. Smith concludes that Anglo-Soviet wartime intelligence cooperation was more circumspect and less successful than Anglo-American intelligence cooperation. See also his *Sharing Secrets with Stalin: How the Allies Traded Intelligence, 1941–1945* (1996) (18:602).

18:602   _____. *Sharing Secrets with Stalin: How the Allies Traded Intelligence, 1941–1945.* Lawrence: University Press of Kansas, 1996. Using recently declassified Anglo-American documents, Smith maintains that a substantial level of intelligence sharing existed between the two western powers and the Soviet Union during the war.

18:603   Stafford, David. *Camp X.* New York: Dodd, Mead, 1986. This work illuminates the Anglo-American-Canadian wartime intelligence alliance as it operated and corrects much of the mythology in Stevenson, *A Man Called Intrepid: The Secret War* (1976) (18:608).

18:604   _____. "'Intrepid': Myth and Reality." *Journal of Contemporary History* 22, no. 2 (April 1987): 303–17. Stafford summarizes and seconds the numerous attacks on Stevenson, *A Man Called Intrepid: The Secret War* (1976) (18:608), and then attempts to construct an accurate portrait of Stevenson and his contributions.

18:605   _____. *Roosevelt and Churchill: Men of Secrets.* Woodstock, NY: Overlook Press, 2000. Stafford maintains that Churchill and Roosevelt shared a fascination with intelligence information and used it to forge their wartime alliance. He also notes the limits of their cooperation in this realm as in others, primarily the result of conflicting national interests and policies.

18:606　Stafford, David, and Rhodri Jeffreys-Jones, eds. *American-British-Canadian Intelligence Relations, 1939–2000.* Portland, OR: Frank Cass, 2000. These essays originated in a 1999 colloquium and a special issue of *Intelligence and National Security* 15 (Summer 2000). Most relevant for the history of World War II are Jeffreys-Jones, "The Role of British Intelligence in the Mythologies Underpinning the OSS and Early CIA" (5–19); Roderick Baily, "OSS-SOE Relations, Albania, 1943–44" (20–35); Stafford, "Roosevelt, Churchill and Anglo-American Intelligence: The Strange Case of Juan March" (36–48); Stephen Budiansky, "The Difficult Beginnings of US-British Codebreaking Co-operation" (49–73); and Douglas M. Charles, "American, British and Canadian Intelligence Links: A Critical Annotated Bibliography" (259–69).

18:607　Stephenson, William Samuel, ed. *British Security Coordination: The Secret History of British Intelligence in the Americas, 1940–1945.* New York: Fromm International, 1999. This official 1945 history was commissioned by Sir William Stephenson, the head of British Security Coordination in the Americas during the war, but not released until the nineties. It was written by numerous individuals identified in Nigel West's informative introduction, and both used and misused in studies of Stephenson by Hyde (*Room 3603: The Story of the British Intelligence Center in New York during World War II,* 1963 [18:598]) and Stevenson (*A Man Called Intrepid: The Secret War,* 1976 [18:608]), both of which helped to popularize numerous myths. It is topically organized and contains a wealth of information on British intelligence activities in the Western Hemisphere.

18:608　Stevenson, William. *A Man Called Intrepid: The Secret War.* This best-selling and sensational account popularized numerous myths about British Security Coordination and its head during World War II. It contains numerous inaccuracies and should be used only with great caution and in conjunction with more recent and scholarly works (17:689).

18:609　Trefousse, Hans L. "The Failure of German Intelligence in the United States, 1935–1945." *Mississippi Valley Historical Review* 42 (June 1955): 84–100. This early essay documents the ineptness of German espionage efforts and shows how intelligence was rejected or misused by Hitler and his staff.

18:610　Wires, Richard. *The Cicero Spy Affair: German Access to British Secrets in World War II.* Westport, CT: Praeger, 1999. This is the most comprehensive and up-to-date analysis and assessment of one of the most notorious spy cases during the war, pulled off by the valet to Britain's ambassador to Turkey.

ULTRA, SIGNALS INTELLIGENCE, AND CODEBREAKING

18:611　Alvarez, David J., ed. *Allied and Axis Signals Intelligence in World War II.* Portland, OR: Frank Cass, 1999. The essays in this collection examine numerous facets of signals intelligence; two bearing on diplomatic history are Alvarez's "Axis Sigint Collaboration: A Limited Partnership" and Lee A. Gladwin, "Cautious Collaborators: The Struggle for Anglo-American Cryptanalytic Co-operation, 1940–43."

18:612　_____. *Secret Messages: Codebreaking and American Diplomacy, 1930–1945.* Lawrence: University Press of Kansas, 2000. Alvarez describes the army's interwar intelligence efforts and then focuses on the subsequent evolution of the Signals Intelligence Service during World War II. He covers the scope of SIS operations in a readable and well-researched organizational history of the army's pre-eminent wartime codebreaking agency and U.S. efforts to intercept and decrypt the secret diplomatic as well as military communications of foreign governments. He cautiously concludes that for numerous reasons signals intelligence had a limited impact on U.S. diplomacy during these years.

18:613　Bennett, Ralph F. *Ultra and Mediterranean Strategy.* New York: William Morrow, 1989. This is the second of Bennett's two outstanding studies of Ultra's use in the European war. It is based upon then just-declassified Ultra material and interviews with surviving participants and shows how Ultra's importance came to be recognized and used in the Mediterranean. As with *Ultra in the West: The Normandy Campaign* (1979) (18:615), Bennett provides meticulous scholarship and eschews simplistic conclusions.

18:614 _____. "Ultra and Some Command Decisions." *Journal of Contemporary History* 16 (January 1981): 131–51. This admittedly "partial and provisional" early estimate by a member of the Bletchley Park group and historian of Ultra, made only six years after the public learned of Ultra, argues that to date it has been overrated as a factor in allied victory and that a balanced assessment of its impact must await the full release and study of all pertinent Ultra materials. Bennett's ensuing analysis of specific operations suggests the material was important but not decisive—and occasionally ignored with serious consequences. He is particularly critical of Winterbotham's inflated claims (*The Ultra Secret*, 1974 [18:629]). This article appeared soon after publication of his detailed and highly regarded *Ultra in the West: The Normandy Campaign 1944–45* (1979) (18:615) but before his *Ultra and Mediterranean Strategy* (1989) (18:613).

18:615 _____. *Ultra in the West: The Normandy Campaign 1944–45.* New York: Charles Scribner, 1979. This is a highly detailed and balanced early assessment of Ultra's importance by a historian who was also a wartime cryptographer at Bletchley Park.

18:616 Boyd, Carl. *Hitler's Japanese Confidant: General Oshima Hiroshi and Magic Intelligence, 1941–1945.* Lawrence: University Press of Kansas, 1993. Based upon the communications from Japan's wartime ambassador in Berlin decoded by American Magic cryptographers, this volume provides important information not only on Nazi wartime activities and attitudes, but on the use allied strategists made of that information.

18:617 Budiansky, Stephen. *Battle of Wits: The Complete Story of Codebreaking in World War II.* New York: Free Press, 2000. Budiansky uses recently declassified NSA records to provide a well-written overview and assessment of the role of communications intelligence in the defeat of the Axis in World War II. His ability to explain succinctly and clearly the mathematics of codebreaking offers a needed perspective on the subject.

18:618 Calvocoressi, Peter. *Top Secret Ultra.* New York: Pantheon Books, 1980. The author, a historian and wartime member of the British team deciphering Ultra intercepts at Bletchley Park, recalls his experiences in this brief volume; he also uses recently declassified documents in this exceptionally clear explanation and assessment of Ultra's early history and importance.

18:619 Cochran, Alexander S., Jr. *The MAGIC Diplomatic Summaries: A Chronological Finding Aid.* New York: Garland Publishing, 1982. This finding aid is based on the 1942–1945 diplomatic and military summaries of cryptographic intercepts, as deposited with the National Archives in sanitized form by the National Security Agency between 1978 and 1980.

18:620 _____. "'MAGIC,' 'ULTRA,' and the Second World War: Literature, Sources, and Outlook." *Military Affairs* 46 (April 1982): 88–92. Although now dated, this early article provides a clear and brief analysis of the first generation of works to deal with World War II signal intelligence. Cochran concludes that the historiography had not yet progressed "past the initial stage of superficial amazement."

18:621 Drea, Edward J. *MacArthur's ULTRA: Codebreaking and the War against Japan, 1942–1945.* Lawrence: University Press of Kansas, 1992. This is the most comprehensive and balanced assessment of cryptography's role in the southwest Pacific, and it clearly fulfills U.S. army historian Drea's intent to "do for ULTRA in the Pacific what Ralph Bennett did for ULTRA in Europe—to analyze its significance for military operations." Using Japanese as well as U.S. sources, he finds that significance to have been less than in Europe, partially because of a paucity of cryptographic intelligence before 1944 and partially because of MacArthur's consistent rejection of Ultra information when it did not fit his preconceptions. Nevertheless, Ultra played a pivotal role in the U.S. air and submarine campaigns as well as a few ground operations.

18:622 Gardner, W. J. R. *Decoding History: The Battle of the Atlantic and Ultra.* Annapolis: Naval Institute Press, 1999. The author concludes in this detailed analysis of the Battle of the Atlantic that, although important, Ultra's role in allied victory has been overrated.

18:623 Hinsley, F. H., and Alan Stripp, eds. *Codebreakers: The Inside Story of Bletchley Park.* New York: Oxford University Press, 1993. This edited collection consists of thirty essays and recollections on different aspects of wartime codebreaking by individuals working at Bletchley Park during the war. They include diplomatic considerations.

18:624 Kahn, David. *The Codebreakers: The Story of Secret Writing.* Rev. ed. New York: Scribner, 1996. Although first written before revelation of the Ultra secret, this extensive and comprehensive history of codebreaking contains much useful and readable information on World War II cryptology and has now been revised to accommodate newly available information. First published in 1967.

18:625 Lewin, Ronald. *The American Magic: Codes, Ciphers, and the Defeat of Japan.* This sequel to Lewin's study of the then newly released Ultra secret—*Ultra Goes to War: The First Account of World War II's Greatest Secret Based on Official Documents* (1978) (18:626)—focuses on the relationship between that codebreaking operation and similar U.S. operations against Japan (17:1120).

18:626 _____. *Ultra Goes to War: The First Account of World War II's Greatest Secret Based on Official Documents.* New York: McGraw-Hill, 1978. Lewin discusses how the allies intercepted and decoded German cryptographic messages and attempts to show how this information influenced combat decisions. Written soon after the first release of Ultra information in 1974, this book has been largely superseded by more detailed and recent accounts but still provides a readable introduction to the topic.

18:627 Smith, Bradley F. "Sharing Ultra in World War II." *International Journal of Intelligence and Counterintelligence* 2 (Spring 1988): 59–72. Smith surveys what is known about sharing "special intelligence" at the time of writing, notes that the Soviet Union received Ultra-derived intelligence before the United States did, and recounts the establishment of sharing agreements. More sharing with the Soviet Union took place, he concludes, than has previously been thought. For more detail, see his *Sharing Secrets with Stalin: How the Allies Traded Intelligence, 1941–1945* (1996) (18:602).

18:628 _____. *The Ultra-Magic Deals and the Most Secret Special Relationship, 1940–1946.* Smith traces the halting evolution of Anglo-American agreements to share "most secret" cryptoanalytic intelligence during World War II, showing how the process was beset by bureaucratic rivalries and suspicions both within and between Washington and London. He also argues for greater attention to the long-term importance of the decision to continue postwar intelligence cooperation (17:1098).

18:629 Winterbotham, F. W. *The Ultra Secret.* New York: Harper and Row, 1974. This memoir by a British intelligence officer was the first to reveal the existence of the Enigma machine and Ultra secret project. It explains many of the essentials but unfortunately contains misinformation and should be used only in conjunction with more up-to-date and reliable sources.

THE OSS

18:630 Chalou, George C., ed. *The Secrets War: The Office of Strategic Services in World War II.* Washington, DC: National Archives and Records Administration, 1992. These conference proceedings include both historical analyses and recollections by members of the wartime OSS. Contents include: Waldo H. Heinrichs, "The United States Prepares for War" (8–18); Robin W. Winks, "Getting the Right Stuff: FDR, Donovan, and the Quest for Professional Intelligence" (19–42); Barry M. Katz, "The OSS and the Development of the Research and Analysis Branch" (43–48); Walt W. Rostow, "The London Operation: Recollections of an Economist" (48–60); Arthur Schlesinger, Jr., "The London Operation: Recollections of a Historian" (61–68); Lawrence H. McDonald, "The OSS and Its Records" (78–102); Richard D. Breitman, "Research in OSS Records: One Historian's Concerns" (103–8); George C. Constantinides, "The OSS: A Brief Review of Literature" (109–20); Helene Deschamps-Adams, "Behind Enemy Lines in France" (140–65); Arthur L. Funk, "The OSS in Algiers" (166–82); Max Corvo, "The OSS and the Italian Campaign" (183–93); Dusan Biber, "Failure of a Mission: Robert McDowell in Yugoslavia, 1944" (194–217); Timothy Naftali, "Artifice: James Angleton and X-2 Operations in Italy" (218–45); Fabrizio Calvi, "The OSS in France"

(247–72); Neal H. Petersen, "From Hitler's Doorstep: Allen Dulles and the Penetration of Germany" (273–94); M. R. D. Foot, "OSS and SOE: An Equal Partnership?" (295–301); Carolle J. Carter, "Mission to Yenan: The OSS and the Dixie Mission" (302–17); James R. Ward, "The Activities of Detachment 101 of the OSS" (318–53); and Bradley F. Smith, "The OSS and Record Group 266: Some Perspectives and Prospects" (359–68).

18:631   Cline, Ray S. *Secrets, Spies and Scholars: Blueprint of the Essential CIA.* Washington, DC: Acropolis Books, 1976. The author was a member of the wartime OSS as well as deputy director of the CIA and director of State Department intelligence in the decades after the war. He draws from his personal experiences to explain how the CIA evolved from the OSS's wartime experiences.

18:632   Heideking, Jürgen, and Christof Mauch, with Marc Frey, eds. *American Intelligence and the German Resistance to Hitler: A Documentary History.* Boulder: Westview Press, 1996. This volume consists of 102 OSS intelligence documents regarding the German resistance, arranged chronologically, along with an editorial introduction, a bibliography, and name and subject indexes. Among other activities, the OSS was probing anything that resembled German peace feelers.

18:633   Hymoff, Edward. *The OSS in World War II.* Rev. and updated ed. New York: Richardson and Steirman, 1986. This is an early popular history of the wartime OSS by one of its former members, originally published in 1972. It focuses on operations and is mostly based on secondary research and interviews with former OSS members.

18:634   Jakub, Jay. *Spies and Saboteurs: Anglo-American Collaboration and Rivalry in Human Intelligence Collection and Special Operations, 1940–45.* This work of multiarchival research examines both the wartime cooperation and competition between the Office of Strategic Services and its British counterparts in the Secret Intelligence Service and Special Operations Executive (17:881).

18:635   Katz, Barry M. *Foreign Intelligence: Research and Analysis in the Office of Strategic Services, 1942–1945.* Cambridge, MA: Harvard University Press, 1989. Katz provides a detailed analysis of this key research branch of the OSS, including its scholars and the ideas they enunciated.

18:636   Langer, William L. *In and Out of the Ivory Tower: The Autobiography of William L. Langer.* New York: Neale Watson Academic Publications, 1977. Historian Langer headed the Research and Analysis Branch of the Office of Strategic Services during the war. This memoir provides some interesting information on the work of that branch, its academic members, and its relationship to other government organizations during the war.

18:637   Laurie, Clayton D. *The Propaganda Warriors: America's Crusade against Nazi Germany.* Lawrence: University Press of Kansas, 1996. The author analyzes the anti-Nazi propaganda of, and bureaucratic conflicts among, the Office of Strategic Services, the Office of War Information, and U.S. army. Using archival records and manuscript collections as well as published sources, he portrays the OSS as dominated by conservative and realist notions, the OWI by liberal ideology, and the army by pragmatic assessments of propaganda most likely to help win the war. He concludes that the U.S. propaganda effort was generally highly effective and that in the bureaucratic struggle the OWI lost out to the OSS and the army.

18:638   Mauch, Christof. "Dream of a Miracle War: The OSS and Germany, 1942–1945." *Prologue* 27 (Summer 1995): 135–43. This article provides a general overview of OSS operations against Germany, emphasizing the desire to foment internal German resistance and also the limitations within which the OSS had to operate.

18:639   McDonald, Lawrence H. "The Office of Strategic Services: America's First National Intelligence Agency." *Prologue* 23 (Spring 1991): 6–22. Written at the time of completion of the National Archives accessioning of the records of the OSS, this article discusses the organization's origins, branches, wartime activities, membership, and leadership. As such it is a useful, brief introduction to the OSS and its records.

18:640   Rudgers, David F. *Creating the Secret State: The Origins of the Central Intelligence*

Agency, 1943–1947. Lawrence: University Press of Kansas, 2000. Rudgers locates the origins of the CIA in the government-wide reassessment of American security needs beginning during World War II. Downplaying the role of OSS chief William Donovan, he emphasizes the role of other people and agencies in shaping the outcome, such as Dean Acheson and the Bureau of the Budget.

18:641 Smith, Bradley F. *The Shadow Warriors: O.S.S. and the Origins of the C.I.A.* New York: Basic Books, 1983. This revisionist work challenges the standard, hagiographic view of OSS director Donovan. It sees the development of the OSS and then the CIA to have been primarily the result of his promotional efforts rather than actual accomplishments or any master plan.

18:642 Smith, R. Harris. *OSS: The Secret History of America's First Central Intelligence Agency.* Berkeley: University of California Press, 1972. This remains a valuable guide to the organization, bureaucratic struggles, and operations of the OSS during World War II, though in many areas it has been superseded by more recent works.

18:643 Troy, Thomas F. *Donovan and the CIA: A History of the Establishment of the Central Intelligence Agency.* Frederick, MD: University Publications of America, 1981. This is a declassified and slightly revised version of an internal 1975 CIA history of the agency's origins. Twenty-five percent of the text deals with U.S. intelligence before Pearl Harbor and another 50 percent with the wartime OSS. Numerous key official documents dealing with wartime and postwar intelligence services are reproduced as appendices.

18:644 _____. *Wild Bill and Intrepid: Donovan, Stephenson, and the Origin of CIA.* The core of this volume is a formerly classified 1970 CIA study, first released in 1987, analyzing the British contribution to the wartime establishment of Donovan's Coordinator of Information Office and its OSS-CIA successors. This study and a series of brief additional essays assess and reject as myths several interpretations regarding Anglo-American intelligence relations (17:1062).

18:645 Winks, Robin W. *Cloak & Gown: Scholars in the Secret War, 1939–1961.* 2d ed. New Haven: Yale University Press, 1996. This study focuses on the role of university personnel, especially but far from exclusively at Winks's own Yale University, in the origins and development of U.S. intelligence services from 1939 to 1961. It is based on interviews with over 200 former OSS and CIA agents as well as manuscript collections, archival documents, and secondary accounts. The volume is organized around individuals rather than years, with separate chapters providing biographical sketches of key individuals and their accomplishments. First published in 1987.

SOVIET ESPIONAGE

18:646 Albright, Joseph, and Marcia Kunstel. *Bombshell: The Secret Story of America's Unknown Atomic Spy Conspiracy.* New York: Times Books, 1997. This is an examination of the Soviet spy network that infiltrated the Manhattan Project and passed atomic secrets to the Soviet Union; it doubles as a biography of the never prosecuted chief spy, Theodore Hall ("Mlad"). The authors used information from the Venona decryptions.

18:647 Andrew, Christopher M., and Oleg Gordievsky. *KGB: The Inside Story of Its Foreign Operations from Lenin to Gorbachev.* New York: Harper-Collins Publishers, 1990. This history draws on information from western archives as well as secret KGB files provided by Gordievsky and his long experience in the foreign intelligence arm of the KGB. One long chapter of seventy pages is devoted to Soviet espionage against its allies as well as its enemies during World War II, while an ensuing chapter covers the takeover of Eastern Europe, 1944–1948.

18:648 Andrew, Christopher M., and Vasili Mitrokhin. *The Sword and the Shield: The Mitrokhin Archive and the Secret History of the KGB.* New York: Basic Books, 1999. This history is based on the extensive notes from the files of the KGB Foreign Office intelligence archives Mitrokhin assembled and smuggled out of Russia in 1996. Two chapters deal with the World War II years.

18:649 Benson, Robert Louis, and Michael Warner, eds. *Venona: Soviet Espionage and the American Response, 1939–1957.* Laguna Hills, CA:

Aegean Park Press, 1996. In 1995, the National Security and Central Intelligence Agencies began declassification of the files of Venona, the code name for the interception, decryption, and translation of some 3,000 messages between Moscow and Soviet intelligence stations during the 1940s. This volume was published in conjunction with the conference on Venona that the two agencies and the Center for Democracy sponsored in 1996 and as a handbook for scholars interested in the project. It includes an explanatory preface, documents outlining the U.S. response to Soviet espionage, and ninety-nine Venona messages, all but four of World War II vintage. This edition includes several monographs by Benson not included in the original CIA staff edition.

18:650   Haynes, John Earl. "The Cold War Debate Continues: A Traditionalist View of Historical Writing on Domestic Communism and Anti-Communism." *Journal of Cold War Studies* 2 (Winter 2000): 76–115. Although this historiographical article focuses on interpretive disputes about the history of American communism (as perceived by one of the scholarly protagonists), it also contains a section on the impact of recently declassified Soviet and U.S. intelligence records on recent scholarship concerning the 1940s.

18:651   Haynes, John Earl, and Harvey Klehr. *Venona: Decoding Soviet Espionage in America.* New Haven: Yale University Press, 1999. This volume by two historians of the American Communist Party analyzes Soviet intelligence activities within the United States as revealed in the National Security Agency's Venona files, which were declassified in 1995. The organization of the volume is topical rather than chronological, with a focus on specific spies and their activities as revealed by the Venona documents. The authors conclude that these documents show espionage to have been far more central to the American Communist Party than they had previously concluded.

18:652   Weinstein, Allen, and Alexander Vassiliev. *The Haunted Wood: Soviet Espionage in America— The Stalin Era.* New York: Random House, 1999. This best-selling analysis of Soviet espionage activities in the United States is based on research in the Soviet KGB archives as well as the recently declassified U.S. Venona files. One section describes those

espionage activities as well as the key individuals involved during the World War II years. See also Harvey Klehr, John Earl Haynes, and Fridrikh Igorevich Firsov, *The Secret World of American Communism* (New Haven: Yale University Press, 1995), and Klehr, Haynes, and Kyrill M. Anderson, *The Soviet World of American Communism* (New Haven: Yale University Press, 1998).

Interaction of Allies

GENERAL

18:653   Beardsley, E. H. "No Help Wanted: Medical Research Exchange between Russia and the West during the Second World War." *Medical History* 22, no. 4 (1978): 365–77. For the most part Moscow rebuffed wartime Anglo-American efforts to establish a medical research exchange, which would have benefited both sides. This caused Anglo-American conflict as well as ill feelings in the west.

18:654   _____. "Secrets between Friends: Applied Science Exchange between the Western Allies and the Soviet Union during World War II." *Social Studies of Science* 7 (November 1977): 447–74. Beardsley describes the inability of the United States and Britain to agree at the same time to scientific information exchange with the Soviet Union during World War II. At first the British supported while the United States opposed such an exchange, but by 1944 the two had reversed positions.

18:655   Beitzell, Robert. *The Uneasy Alliance: America, Britain, and Russia, 1941–1943.* New York: Alfred A. Knopf, 1972. The author describes the tensions between the Big Three during the first two years of the Grand Alliance through an examination of their numerous conferences during this period. He relies primarily on the published official records of those conferences as well as memoirs.

18:656   Berthon, Simon. *Allies at War: The Bitter Rivalry among Churchill, Roosevelt, and de Gaulle.* New York: Carroll and Graf, 2001. This is a breezy, popular account, by the creator of the public television series, of the stormy wartime relationship among Churchill, Roosevelt, and de Gaulle. It focuses on the years 1940–1943.

18:657   Brinkley, Douglas, and David R. Facey-Crowther, eds. *The Atlantic Charter.* Most of this work consists of papers first prepared for and delivered at the fiftieth anniversary commemoration of the charter in 1991. See chapter 17 of this Guide (17: 1029).

18:658   Bullitt, William C. "How We Won the War and Lost the Peace." *Life* (August 30, 1948): 82–97. In this important magazine article, Bullitt drew on his personal experiences as ambassador to the Soviet Union and former Roosevelt confidant to popularize the idea that the United States "lost" the peace because of FDR's naïveté regarding Stalin.

18:659   Chan, K. C. "The Abrogation of British Extraterritoriality in China, 1942–43: A Study of Anglo-American-Chinese Relations." *Modern Asian Studies* 11 (April 1977): 257–91. The Nationalist government announced in 1929 its intention of terminating extraterritoriality in China. Anglo-American negotiations with China during the war resulted in both countries agreeing to new treaty relationships.

18:660   Costigliola, Frank C. "'Mixed Up' and 'Contact': Culture and Emotion among the Allies in the Second World War." *International History Review* 20 (December 1998): 791–805. Cultural expectations about contact with foreigners affected British and American analysts posted to the Soviet Union and colored their subsequent representations of the Soviet regime. Costigliola offers "contact" between peoples as a category of historical analysis.

18:661   Dockrill, Michael, and Brian J. C. McKercher, eds. *Diplomacy and World Power: Studies in British Foreign Policy, 1890–1950.* New York: Cambridge University Press, 1996. Two essays in this tribute to Zara Steiner focus on British diplomacy during World War II: David Reynolds's defense of Churchill's wartime policies against critics such as Charmley ("Churchill the Appeaser? Between Hitler, Roosevelt and Stalin in World War Two") and Geoffrey Warner's analysis of Anglo-Soviet relations ("From Ally to Enemy: Britain's Relations with the Soviet Union, 1941–1948").

18:662   Edmonds, Robin. *The Big Three: Churchill, Roosevelt, and Stalin in Peace & War.* This history of allied relations through the wartime Big Three begins in 1933 rather than the conventional 1941, with only half of the volume covering the actual wartime alliance. It makes use of Soviet sources published in the 1980s as well as Anglo-American archives and French, German, and Polish sources. Edmonds emphasizes the achievements of the alliance rather than its failures and concludes that 1989 provides a "second chance" to create an enduring peace (17:61).

18:663   Feis, Herbert. *Churchill, Roosevelt, Stalin: The War They Waged and the Peace They Sought.* Princeton: Princeton University Press, 1957. This early study of World War II diplomacy was long the standard work. Because it focuses on the three leaders, it remains a useful source of information on their thoughts, particularly as they expressed themselves during the major wartime conferences. Although it has in many ways been superseded by new sources and ideas, it still provides a good summary of tripartite wartime diplomacy.

18:664   Gardner, Lloyd C. *Spheres of Influence: The Great Powers Partition Europe, from Munich to Yalta.* Chicago: Ivan R. Dee, 1993. Gardner organizes this diplomatic history of the war years around the theme of allied views of and actions regarding spheres of influence, analyzing how U.S. views of the matter changed over time.

18:665   Gorodetsky, Gabriel, ed. *Soviet Foreign Policy, 1917–1991: A Retrospective.* Portland, OR: Frank Cass, 1994. The twenty brief essays in this collection were originally delivered by Russian and western scholars at a 1992 scholarly conference in Moscow. Among the most pertinent for this chapter are Anita J. Prazmowska, "Poland between East and West: The Politics of a Government-in-Exile," and Alexei Filitov, "The Soviet Union and the Grand Alliance: The Internal Dimension of Foreign Policy."

18:666   King, F. P. *The New Internationalism: Allied Policy and the European Peace, 1939–1945.* Hamden, CT: Archon Books, 1973. In this survey the author views the war as an opportunity for internationalism, i.e., international cooperation as opposed to the isolationist sentiments of the 1930s. King claims that as long as the war mandated cooperation, the allies continued to work together—through the Yalta conference.

18:667 Lane, Ann, and Howard Temperley, eds. *The Rise and Fall of the Grand Alliance, 1941–45.* New York: St. Martin's Press, 1995. These essays, originating in a September 1993 conference, examine the three powers' war aims and military strategies, economic policies, intelligence relations, and issues surrounding Japan, Yalta, Potsdam, and the atomic bomb. Contents include Warren F. Kimball, "Anglo-American War Aims, 1941–43, 'The First Review': Eden's Mission to Washington" (1–21); Jonathan Haslam, "Soviet War-Aims" (22–42); Kathleen Burk, "American Foreign Economic Policy and Lend-Lease" (43–68); Mark Harrison, "The Soviet Economy and Relations with the United States and Britain, 1941–45" (69–89); John Charmley, "Churchill's Roosevelt" (90–107); Christopher M. Andrew, "Anglo-American-Soviet Intelligence Relations" (108–35); John Erickson, "Stalin, Soviet Strategy and the Grand Alliance" (136–73); Correlli Barnett, "Anglo-American Strategy in Europe" (174–89); Peter Lowe, "The War against Japan and Allied Relations" (190–206); David Holloway, "The Atomic Bomb and the End of the Wartime Alliance" (207–25); and Norman A. Graebner, "Yalta, Potsdam and Beyond: The British and American Perspectives" (226–54).

18:668 Langer, William L. "Turning Points of the War: Political Problems of a Coalition." *Foreign Affairs* 26 (October 1947): 73–89. Langer in this very early assessment of allied diplomacy defends Roosevelt's decision to aid Russia as the only alternative to a Hitler-ordered peace and thus the lesser of two evils but criticizes some of his ensuing Soviet policies.

18:669 Mastny, Vojtech. *Russia's Road to the Cold War: Diplomacy, Warfare, and the Politics of Communism, 1941–1945.* New York: Columbia University Press, 1979. This book is a thorough, scholarly account of Russian war aims, postwar aims, and allied diplomatic interaction from the Soviet perspective. It is based on extensive research in Soviet and East European documents available in 1979 and sees Stalin's policies as flexible and pragmatic within the context of minimal and maximum goals established early in the war.

18:670 McNeill, William H. *America, Britain and Russia: Their Cooperation and Conflict, 1941– 946.* New York: Oxford University Press, 1953. Reprint 1970 (Johnson Corp.). This pioneering work remains in many ways an excellent general history of the Grand Alliance. Placing that alliance in the broad context of world history, McNeill explains the conflicting aims, methods, and worldviews of each member, which, while successfully compromised during the war, ultimately led to the alliance's dissolution.

18:671 Nadeau, Remi. *Stalin, Churchill, and Roosevelt Divide Europe.* New York: Praeger, 1990. Nadeau castigates Roosevelt for misplaced idealism and innocence regarding Stalin and holds him responsible for losing the peace by allowing Europe to be divided.

18:672 Neumann, William L. *After Victory: Churchill, Roosevelt, Stalin and the Making of the Peace.* New York: Harper and Row, 1967. This early history of the Grand Alliance is a balanced analysis of the conflicting war aims of its major members. The author argues that how the war was waged, rather than diplomatic blunders, fundamentally dictated the shape of the peace.

18:673 Offner, Arnold A. "Uncommon Ground: Anglo-American-Soviet Diplomacy, 1941–1942." *Soviet Union. Union Sovietique* 18, no. 1–3 (1992): 237–57. Offner attacks the conclusion of critics holding that Anglo-American appeasement of the Soviet Union at this time invited later Russian expansion. Instead he sees Roosevelt and Churchill crafting their diplomatic and military strategies to meet both domestic political concerns and long-term national security interests. Reprinted in Joseph Wieczynski, ed, *Operation Barbarossa: The German Attack on the Soviet Union, June 22, 1941* (Salt Lake City: Charles Schlacks, Pub., 1993).

18:674 Raack, R. C. *Stalin's Drive to the West, 1938–1945: The Origins of the Cold War.* Stanford, CA: Stanford University Press, 1995. This revisionist work argues that Stalin's policies throughout the war were highly aggressive rather than defensive. They were based on the belief that another general war would lead to an overthrow of existing governments and enormous expansion of Soviet influence.

France's sudden and unexpected collapse in 1940 upset these plans and left Stalin unprepared for Hitler's 1941 invasion, but naïve British and American diplomacy from 1941 to 1945 enabled him to retain his 1939 conquests and extend his control in Eastern Europe.

18:675   Resis, Albert. "Spheres of Influence in Soviet Wartime Diplomacy." *Journal of Modern History* 53 (September 1981): 417–39. Resis sees Stalin as a "conservative nationalist" seeking spheres-of-influence understanding within a framework of great power cooperation to keep Germany under control.

18:676   Reynolds, David, Warren F. Kimball, and A. O. Chubarian, eds. *Allies at War: The Soviet, American, and British Experience, 1939–1945.* New York: St. Martin's Press, 1994. The sixteen chapters in this volume were written by World War II historians from all three countries and are divided into four sections: strategy, economics, home-front, and foreign policy. Each section consists of three essays on each nation's individual experience, followed by a fourth essay on the allied experience as a whole in each sphere. The most pertinent chapters are Alex Danchev, "Great Britain: The Indirect Strategy"; Oleg A. Rzheshevsky, "The Soviet Union: The Direct Strategy"; Mark A. Stoler, "The United States: The Global Strategy"; Theodore A. Wilson et al., "Coalition: Structure, Strategy, and Statecraft"; Richard J. Overy et al., "Co-operation: Trade, Aid, and Technology"; Mikhail N. Narinsky, Lydia V. Pozdeeva et al., "Mutual Perceptions: Images, Ideals, and Illusions"; Reynolds, "Great Britain: Imperial Diplomacy"; Pozdeeva, "The Soviet Union: Territorial Diplomacy"; Lloyd C. Gardner and Kimball, "The United States: Democratic Diplomacy"; and Reynolds et al., "Legacies: Allies, Enemies, and Posterity."

18:677   Toynbee, Arnold J., and Veronica M. Toynbee, eds. *The Realignment of Europe.* New York: Oxford University Press, 1955. This volume in the Survey of International Affairs series for the war years (1939–1946) deals with events in Europe following the collapse of German power: the first steps toward economic rehabilitation under UNRRA, the expansion of Soviet control in the states of Eastern Europe, and the hectic resurrection of political life in Greece, Italy, and Western Europe. Authors represented include the editors R. G. Hawtrey, F. Ashton-Gwatkin,

Sidney Lowery, Hugh Seton-Watson, Elizabeth Wiskemann, William H. McNeill, Katharine Duff, Margaret Carlyle, and Viscount Chilston.

18:678   Wheeler-Bennett, John, and Anthony Nicholls. *The Semblance of Peace: The Political Settlement after the Second World War.* New York: St. Martin's Press, 1972. Reprint 1974 (Norton). This general study, though dated by the opening of the British archives, spans the entire wartime era with the emphasis on planning for the peace. The authors place the blame for the breakdown in wartime cooperation and the subsequent cold war on Russia's ambitions for European and Asian expansion and U.S. appeasement of the Soviet Union.

SUMMIT CONFERENCES

Cairo-Teheran

18:679   U.S. Department of State. *Foreign Relations of the United States. The Conferences at Cairo and Teheran, 1943.* Washington, DC: Government Printing Office, 1961. This volume of documents covers the three continuous yet separate conferences of November-December 1943: the first Cairo conference involving Churchill, Roosevelt, and Jiang Jieshi; the Teheran conference among the Big Three; and the second Cairo conference between Churchill and Roosevelt. Strategic arguments and agreements dominated all three conferences, although numerous postwar political issues were also discussed.

18:680   Berezhkov, Valentin M. "The Teheran Meeting." *New Times* (November 29, December 6, and December 13, 1967): 16–21; (November 29): 27–32; (December 6): 30–34; (December 13). The author served as translator for Stalin during the Teheran conference. These recollections offer interesting information, descriptions, and insights but must be used with care. See also his *At Stalin's Side: His Interpreter's Memoirs from the October Revolution to the Fall of the Dictator's Empire* (1994) (18:339) and *History in the Making: Memoirs of World War II Diplomacy* (1983) (18:340).

18:681   Eubank, Keith. *Summit at Teheran.* New York: William Morrow, 1985. Eubank is highly critical of Roosevelt for his general diplomatic naïveté and pro-Soviet behavior at this conference.

18:682 Franklin, William M. "Yalta Viewed from Tehran." In *Some Pathways in Twentieth-Century History: Essays in Honor of Reginald Charles Mc-Grane,* ed. Daniel R. Beaver, 253–61. Detroit: Wayne State University Press, 1969. Franklin argues that many of the most important decisions spelled out at Yalta were actually reached in general fashion at Tehran. He recommends that Tehran be studied more extensively.

18:683 Mastny, Vojtech. "Soviet War Aims at the Moscow and Teheran Conferences of 1943." *Journal of Modern History* 47 (September 1975): 481–504. Mastny believes Stalin incorrectly concluded during these conferences that a second front would not be forthcoming but that his allies would acquiesce in his postwar plans for Poland and the rest of Eastern Europe. He blames the carelessness of Churchill and Roosevelt for encouraging him to embark upon these policies.

18:684 Mayle, Paul D. *Eureka Summit: Agreement in Principle and the Big Three at Tehran, 1943.* Newark: University of Delaware Press, 1987. This solid and relatively brief history of the first Big Three summit meeting is organized chronologically. The author concludes that the leaders only reached agreements "in principle," and therefore subject to differing interpretations, which may have been the best that could have been expected.

18:685 Misse, M. "Le rôle des États-Unis dans les conférences du Caire et de Téhéran [The role of the United States in the Cairo and Teheran Conferences]." *Revue d'histoire de la deuxième guerre mondiale* 18 (juil 1968): 13–30. Misse examines the policy followed by the American delegation at the Cairo and Teheran summit conferences (November-December 1943), focusing on the Roosevelt-Stalin relationship and concluding, as have others more recently, that the decisions made at Teheran had greater effects on postwar Europe than those at Yalta.

18:686 Sainsbury, Keith. *The Turning Point: Roosevelt, Stalin, Churchill, and Chiang-Kai-Shek, 1943: The Moscow, Cairo, and Teheran Conferences.* Oxford: Oxford University Press, 1985. This volume

is the most comprehensive and scholarly account of the Moscow-Cairo-Tehran conferences of late 1943. The author is judicious in his conclusions but remains highly critical of the U.S. decision to form a closer relationship with the Soviet Union at the expense of the Anglo-American relationship.

18:687 Sharp, Tony. "The Origins of the 'Teheran Formula' on Polish Frontiers." *Journal of Contemporary History* 12 (April 1977): 381–93. Sharp traces the history of the formula for moving the Polish boundary along the Oder River–Curzon Line, proposed by Churchill just before the Tehran conference. Stalin agreed as long as Russia got the Königsberg area of East Prussia. This "Teheran formula" was accepted on the premise that British and American influence in the negotiated area would not be great.

Yalta

18:688 U.S. Department of State. *Foreign Relations of the United States. The Conferences at Malta and Yalta, 1945.* Washington, DC: Government Printing Office, 1955. This was the first of the special documentary volumes on the World War II summit conferences to be published by the State Department. Major issues discussed at this second Big Three meeting include plans for the military defeat of Germany, the future of Poland, European occupation policies, the United Nations, and Soviet entry into the war against Japan.

18:689 Buhite, Russell D. *Decisions at Yalta: An Appraisal of Summit Diplomacy.* Wilmington, DE: Scholarly Resources, 1986. Designed as a college text, this volume is highly critical of both Roosevelt's diplomacy at Yalta and summit conferences in general. The author claims Roosevelt had great strengths he failed to exploit at the conference and offers numerous comparisons between Yalta and 1970s détente—including the ensuing collapse of both sets of accords.

18:690 _____. "Patrick J. Hurley and the Yalta Far Eastern Agreement." *Pacific Historical Review* 37 (August 1968): 343–53. Using Hurley's own papers, Buhite refutes his 1951 Senate testimony on his reaction to the Yalta accords on China, discussions with Roosevelt, and right-wing conspiracy theories.

Buhite sees Hurley's distortions as tarnishing an otherwise admirable record and blames them on his egocentric personality. See also Buhite's *Patrick J. Hurley and American Foreign Policy* (1973) (18:268).

18:691 Clemens, Diane Shaver. *Yalta*. New York: Oxford University Press, 1970. According to Clemens, Yalta was marked by compromise by all parties rather than a Soviet triumph or western retreat. The author analyzes the advantages held by each of the major participants and concludes that reasonable adjustments were made in the face of differing national interests. Instead of the start or a prelude to the cold war, Yalta was an alternative.

18:692 Hammersmith, Jack L. "In Defense of Yalta: Edward R. Stettinius's *Roosevelt and the Russians.*" *Virginia Magazine of History* 100 (July 1992): 429–54. Making extensive use of the unpublished Stettinius papers, the author explores Stettinius's motives as well as the process by which his strong defense of Roosevelt at Yalta was drafted, revised, and published in 1949. Of particular interest is Stettinius's correspondence with historian Walter Johnson, who collaborated in the writing of the book, and the comments and suggestions for revision by former aides and State Department officials.

18:693 Laloy, Jean. *Yalta: Yesterday, Today, Tomorrow*. Translated by William R. Tyler. New York: Harper and Row, 1990. This brief volume deals more with the causes and consequences—as of 1988, when published in French as *Yalta: hier, aujourd'hui, demain*—of Yalta than it does with the conference itself. Nearly half of it is devoted to allied relations before the Crimean meeting, with only one chapter focusing on the actual negotiations and agreements.

18:694 Leffler, Melvyn P. "Adherence to Agreements: Yalta and the Experiences of the Early Cold War." *International Security* 11 (Summer 1986): 88–123. Contrary to U.S. claims originating in the Truman presidency and revived by the Reagan administration, Leffler contends that the Soviet Union adhered to the Yalta accords as much as the United States, and Washington broke them as often as the Soviets. In effect, both sides complied with some of the accords and disregarded others. The United States also used supposed Soviet violations to excuse its own. The author offers a security interpretation of

why this occurred and concludes that Americans remain guilty of self-deception in their views of the conference.

18:695 Olla, Paola Brundu, ed. *Yalta: Un mito che resiste: relazione e comunicazione presentate al convegno internazionale organizzato dalla Provincia di Cagliari, 23–26 aprile 1987* [*Yalta: A Stubborn Myth: Papers Presented at the International Conference, Cagliari Province, 23–26 April 1987*]. Rome: Edizioni dell'Ateneo Provincia di Cagliari, 1988. These published proceedings from a 1987 conference in Cagliari, Italy, on the significance of the Yalta conference, contain more than thirty presentations of greatly varying length. Among those writing in English are Diane S. Clemens, "Yalta: Conference of Victory and Peace," which places the conference in historical context and outlines major themes and agreements; David N. Dilks, "Churchill as Negotiator at Yalta," analyzing Churchill's temporary optimism about the summit; Arthur M. Schlesinger, Jr., "Roosevelt's Diplomacy at Yalta," noting the domestic and alliance pressures on FDR and holding that he achieved his objectives, except in Eastern Europe; Geir Lundestad, "The United States, Great Britain, and Eastern Europe: The Period from Yalta to Potsdam," seeing Eastern Europe's fate settled by the Red Army and the western allies' efforts to protect interests of greater priority; and Melvyn P. Leffler, "From Accommodation to Containment: The United States and the Far East Provisions of the Yalta Agreements," who contends that while FDR prudently pursued American interests at Yalta and generally achieved his objectives, American policymakers would soon reassess their policy toward the Far East and initiate a policy of containment. Other contributors include Robert James Maddox, "American Diplomacy before the Conference in the Crimea"; James Edward Miller, "Things Left Undone: The United States, Italy, and the Yalta Conference"; Peter Lowe, "Yalta and the Problems of Terminating the Pacific War, 1945"; Marion Einhorn, "The Declaration on Liberated Europe: Guiding Principles of British and American Foreign Policy? Pretensions and Reality"; James L. Gormly, "The Yalta Myths and American Politics"; and D. Cameron Watt, "Britain and the Historiography of the Yalta Conference and the Cold War."

18:696 Rodine, Floyd H. *Yalta: Responsibility and Response, January-March 1945*. Lawrence: Coronado Press, 1974. This otherwise thin and basic work on the conference contains an interesting section on press and legislative reactions.

18:697 Schulzinger, Robert D. "Yalta by Diane Shaver Clemens and the Yalta Myths: An Issue in U.S. Politics, 1945–1955 by Athan G. Theoharis." *History and Theory* 12 (February 1973): 146–62. This review essay points out the shortcomings of these (18:691; 18:703) and other then recent works on U.S. World War II diplomacy. Specifically, the author believes that more emphasis is needed on Yalta as an important issue in the battle between the advocates of the "new" and the defenders of the "old" diplomacy.

18:698 Senarclens, Pierre de. *Yalta.* Translated by Jasmer Singh. New Brunswick: Transaction Books, 1988. While critical of Churchill and Roosevelt on specifics, this brief volume defends their overall behavior at the conference and the resulting agreements.

18:699 Snell, John L., et al. *The Meaning of Yalta: Big Three Diplomacy and the Balance of Power.* Baton Rouge: Louisiana State University Press, 1956. This is an early, collaborative study of the Yalta conference, written in the aftermath of the publication of the conference proceedings, with different scholars addressing key Yalta issues: Germany, Central–Eastern Europe, the Far East, and the United Nations: Forrest C. Pogue, "The Struggle for a New Order"; Snell, "What to Do with Germany?"; Charles F. Delzell, "Russian Power in Central–Eastern Europe"; George A. Lensen, "Yalta and the Far East"; Pogue, "The Big Three and the United Nations"; and Pogue, "Yalta in Retrospect."

18:700 Stettinius, Edward R., Jr. *Roosevelt and the Russians: The Yalta Conference.* Garden City, NY: Doubleday, 1949. As Roosevelt's secretary of state, Stettinius took meticulous notes of each day's events at Yalta. These provide a chronological account of the meeting and the basis of this book. Stettinius defends Roosevelt's actions at Yalta. Edited by Walter Johnson.

18:701 Theoharis, Athan G. "The Origins of the Cold War: A Revisionist Interpretation." *Peace and Change* 4 (Fall 1976): 3–11. This essay considers FDR's vagueness at the Yalta conference a source of the cold war.

18:702 _____. "Roosevelt and Truman on Yalta: The Origins of the Cold War." *Political Science Quarterly* 87 (June 1972): 210–41. Inexperienced in foreign affairs and receiving advice from State Department hardliners, Truman attempted to "undo" FDR's Yalta commitments. This manifestation of Truman's presidential leadership contributed to the deterioration in U.S.-Soviet relations.

18:703 _____. *The Yalta Myths: An Issue in U.S. Politics, 1945–1955.* Columbia: University of Missouri Press, 1970. This study examines conservative attacks on Roosevelt's diplomacy and the Democrats' defense.

18:704 Vloyantes, John P. "The Significance of Pre-Yalta Policies Regarding Liberated Countries in Europe." *Western Political Quarterly* 11 (June 1958): 209–28. This early account concludes that Big Three policies in the period before Yalta combined with military developments to determine the fate of the liberated countries, particularly those in the Balkans and East-Central Europe.

Potsdam

18:705 U.S. Department of State. *Foreign Relations of the United States. The Conference of Berlin, 1945.* 2 vols. Washington, DC: Government Printing Office, 1960. This is the official U.S. documentary record of the 1945 Potsdam conference as prepared by the Department of State. It includes major U.S. preparatory papers as well as the conference minutes and agreements, and it covers military issues regarding the ongoing war against Japan as well as numerous postwar issues.

18:706 Feis, Herbert. *Between War and Peace: The Potsdam Conference.* Princeton: Princeton University Press, 1960. This narrative of allied diplomacy in the period between the German and Japanese surrenders focuses on the intricate negotiations at Potsdam. Feis places his highly detailed account of Big Three discussions within the broader context of the mutual distrust and suspicion eroding the wartime coalition.

18:707 Mark, Eduard M. "'Today Has Been a Historical One': Harry S Truman's Diary of the Potsdam Conference." *Diplomatic History* 4 (Summer 1980):

317–26. Mark reprints Truman's July 1945 handwritten impressions, only discovered and made available to researchers thirty-five years later, of persons and events at Potsdam. These notes are also reproduced in Ferrell, *Off the Record: The Private Papers of Harry S. Truman* (1980) (19:54).

18:708   Mee, Charles L., Jr. *Meeting at Potsdam.* New York: M. Evans, 1975. Mee blames the cold war on all sides: the United States, Britain, and the Soviet Union were distrustful, aggressive, and provocative. All three leaders appear as opportunists in this work. The loss of the common foe led to an inevitable clash of victors holding conflicting political and economic objectives.

18:709   Paterson, Thomas G. "Potsdam, the Atomic Bomb, and the Cold War: A Discussion with James F. Byrnes." *Pacific Historical Review* 41 (May 1972): 225–30. Paterson presents and comments on a memorandum by Senator Warren R. Austin on a conversation with Secretary of State James F. Byrnes (August 20, 1945). The document sheds light on Soviet-American diplomacy at the Potsdam conference and includes information about the relationship between the dropping of the atomic bomb and Russian participation in the war against Japan.

18:710   Strang, William, et al. "Potsdam after Twenty-Five Years." *International Affairs* 46 (July 1970): 441–89. Lord Strang assesses the diplomatic background to the Potsdam conference; Robert Cecil ("Potsdam and Its Legends") examines the Potsdam decisions and how the conference became a part of Soviet and American cold war mythology; André Fontaine ("Potsdam: A French View") analyzes French objections to a united Germany; and Walter C. Clemens, Jr. ("The Soviet World Faces West: 1945–1970") sees the failure to reach agreement on Germany as a constant factor and the central problem in the Soviet relations with the west.

OTHER MAJOR CONFERENCES

18:711   U.S. Department of State. *Foreign Relations of the United States. The Conference at Quebec, 1944.* Washington, DC: Government Printing Office, 1972. This volume of documents covers the second Anglo-American summit conference held in Quebec during the war. Major topics include both wartime strategy and postwar issues, including atomic energy and the "Morgenthau Plan" for postwar Germany.

18:712   _____. *Foreign Relations of the United States. The Conferences at Washington and Quebec, 1943.* Washington, DC: Government Printing Office, 1970. Although the emphasis at both conferences was on Anglo-American strategic plans and disputes, much documentation is included on the Italian surrender, atomic energy, and numerous postwar issues.

18:713   _____. *Foreign Relations of the United States. The Conferences at Washington, 1941–1942, and Casablanca, 1943.* Washington, DC: Government Printing Office, 1968. Major issues at these three conferences included the formation of the United Nations alliance and the Combined Chiefs of Staff, Anglo-American strategic planning and arguments, North Africa and French leadership, and the unconditional surrender formula.

18:714   United Nations Conference on International Organization. *Documents of the United Nations Conference on International Organization, San Francisco, 1945.* 22 vols. New York: United Nations Information Organization, 1945–1955. Reprint 1998 (W. S. Hein). This is the full documentary record with background introductions. Volumes 1–16 were originally published in 1945–1946, volumes 17–22 in 1954–1955. In English and French. The 1998 reprint includes four microfiche.

18:715   Acheson, A. L. K., J. F. Chant, and M. F. J. Prachowny. *Bretton Woods Revisited: Evaluations of the International Monetary Fund and the International Bank for Reconstruction and Development. Papers Delivered at a Conference at Queen's University, Kingston, Canada.* Toronto: University of Toronto Press, 1972. This account, coming on the twenty-fifth anniversary of Bretton Woods, includes reflections of the surviving Canadian participants.

18:716   Knight, Jonathan. "Russia's Search for Peace: The London Council of Foreign Ministers, 1945." *Journal of Contemporary History* 13 (January 1978): 137–63. Russian foreign policy in 1945 hoped to refurbish the ideological armory of communism, to bring friendly governments into power on the Soviet periphery, and to resume a central role in European politics. At the London meeting, the Soviets unsuccessfully pursued a trusteeship over an Italian colony, especially one on the Mediterranean.

18:717   Resis, Albert. "The Churchill-Stalin Secret 'Percentages' Agreement on the Balkans, Moscow, October 1944." *American Historical Review* 83 (April 1978): 368–87. Working from memoirs and British documents, particularly the British records of the Moscow conference (code-named TOLSTOY), Resis concludes that the spheres of influence doctrine in the Balkans was only part of the British and Soviet agreement: the larger plan of Britain regarding her empire in the Far East and Soviet aspirations of territorial gains in Eastern Europe were silently acknowledged.

18:718   Ross, Graham. "Operation Bracelet: Churchill in Moscow, 1942." In *Retreat from Power: Studies in Britain's Foreign Policy of the Twentieth Century. Vol. 2: After 1939,* ed. David Dilks, 101–19. London: Macmillan, 1981. This analysis of the first Churchill-Stalin summit conference is based on then recently declassified Foreign Office records, including Clark-Kerr's diary. Ross concludes that although nothing positive was accomplished at the conference, an open break between the two powers over the second front was avoided.

18:719   Schild, Georg. *Bretton Woods and Dumbarton Oaks: American Economic and Political Postwar Planning in the Summer of 1944.* New York: St. Martin's Press, 1995. Based on extensive research in unpublished as well as published primary sources, this volume focuses on the intra- and interdepartmental decisionmaking processes within the State and Treasury Departments before and during these two key wartime conferences as well as the conference deliberations themselves.

18:720   Siracusa, Joseph M. "The Meaning of Tolstoy: Churchill, Stalin, and the Balkans: Moscow, October 1944." *Diplomatic History* 3 (Fall 1979): 443–63. The author reproduces the British record of the October 1944 meetings at the Kremlin between Churchill and Stalin (and Eden and Molotov) with little comment on or interpretation of those highly important discussions on the makeup of postwar Eastern Europe. See his "The Night Stalin and

Churchill Divided Europe" (1981) (18:721) for his interpretation.

18:721   _____. "The Night Stalin and Churchill Divided Europe." *Review of Politics* 43 (July 1981): 381–409. The author makes use of recently opened British files as well as other sources to trace Anglo-Soviet-American diplomacy over spheres of influence in Eastern Europe from the May 1944 negotiations through the October Moscow conference. Roosevelt, torn between a realistic acceptance of the Anglo-Soviet agreements and idealistic State Department opposition, consequently pursued seemingly contradictory policies.

18:722   Villa, Brian Loring. "The Atomic Bomb and the Normandy Invasion." *Perspectives in American History* 11 (1977–1978): 461–502. The author maintains that Roosevelt during the first Quebec conference in August 1943 exploited Churchill's desire for an Anglo-American partnership in atomic energy to obtain British agreement to a 1944 cross-channel attack with a U.S. commander.

18:723   Wilt, Alan F. "The Significance of the Casablanca Decisions, January 1943." *Journal of Military History* 55 (October 1991): 517–29. Wilt sees Casablanca as the decisive conference in the formation of Anglo-American strategy, emphasizing cooperation rather than conflict.

18:724   Woolner, David B., ed. *The Second Quebec Conference Revisited: Waging War, Formulating Peace: Canada, Great Britain, and the United States in 1944–1945.* New York: St. Martin's Press, 1998. This collection commemorates the fiftieth anniversary of the 1944 Quebec conference, including six papers on Canada's participation. Contents include: Warren F. Kimball, "The Two-Sided Octagon: Roosevelt and Churchill at Quebec, September 1944" (3–16); Brian J. C. McKercher, "Toward the Postwar Settlement: Winston Churchill and the Second Quebec Conference" (17–48); J. L. Granatstein, "Happily on the Margins: Mackenzie King and Canada at the Quebec Conferences" (49–64); Woolner, "Coming to Grips with the 'German Problem': Roosevelt, Churchill, and the Morgenthau Plan at the Second Quebec Conference" (65–104); John Alan English, "Atlanticism at High Tide: The Quebec Conference, 1944" (105–18); and Hector Mackenzie, "Finance and 'Functionalism': Canada and the Combined Boards in World War II" (171–94).

ANGLO-AMERICAN RELATIONS

18:725   Anderson, Terry H. *The United States, Great Britain, and the Cold War, 1944–1947*. Columbia: University of Missouri Press, 1981. Anderson focuses on British efforts to influence U.S. foreign policy toward the Soviet Union and Eastern Europe. Contrary to both traditional and revisionist scholarship, he argues that Truman in May 1945 reverted to an independent mediatory role between Great Britain and the Soviet Union abandoned in March by Roosevelt, and that had FDR lived longer he would have moved against the Soviets even earlier than Truman.

18:726   Beloff, Max. "The Special Relationship: An Anglo-American Myth." In *A Century of Conflict, 1850–1950: Essays in Honor of A. J. P. Taylor*, ed. Martin Gilbert, 148–71. New York: Atheneum, 1967. Beloff was one of the first to attack this Churchill-inspired myth of a harmonious "special relationship" during the war.

18:727   Clarke, Richard. *Anglo-American Economic Collaboration in War and Peace, 1942–1949*. New York: Oxford University Press, 1982. This volume consists of the unfinished memoirs of a major British wartime and postwar Treasury official, as edited by Sir Alec Cairncross, along with a large collection of economic documents pertaining to wartime issues in which Clarke was involved. These included Anglo-American wartime economic collaboration, negotiations for a postwar U.S. loan, the Marshall Plan, and associated European economic issues.

18:728   Danchev, Alex. *On Specialness: Essays on Anglo-American Relations*. New York: St. Martin's Press, 1998. The nine chapters in this volume reproduce revised scholarly papers by Danchev originally published as journal articles or book chapters. They cover both wartime and postwar issues, with the former including the Combined Chiefs of Staff, the second-front controversy, civil-military relations with allies, and Field Marshal Sir John Dill.

18:729   Davis, Simon. "Keeping the Americans in

Line? Britain, the United States and Saudi Arabia, 1939–45: Inter-Allied Rivalry in the Middle East Revisited." *Diplomacy & Statecraft* 8 (March 1997): 96–136. Davis uses the case of Saudi Arabia as a microcosm for examining the clash of American and British economic systems—and styles of pursuing their interests. He agrees with Reynolds (*The Creation of the Anglo-American Alliance 1937–41: A Study in Competitive Co-operation*, 1982 [17:680]) that the British vastly underestimated American anti-imperialist sentiment, which ultimately drove American policy and ended British hopes of basing their postwar great power rehabilitation on Middle East oil.

18:730   Dimbleby, David, and David Reynolds. *An Ocean Apart: The Relationship between Britain and America in the Twentieth Century*. This book is based on the television series of the same name that Dimbleby presented, with Reynolds the principal historical adviser. One chapter provides a solid if brief overview of wartime Anglo-American relations after Pearl Harbor (2:325).

18:731   Dobson, Alan P. "'A Mess of Potage for Your Economic Birthright?' The 1941–42 Wheat Negotiations and Anglo-American Economic Diplomacy." *Historical Journal* 28 (September 1985): 739–50. Dobson examines the 1941 American pressure on the United Kingdom, sponsored by Cordell Hull, to adopt free trade after the war. The issue of wheat, however, exposed the limitations of U.S. support for free trade. Heavy-handed tactics, such as using lend-lease to club the British, significantly eroded goodwill between the two countries and set the stage for future acrimonious discussions of economic issues.

18:732   _____. "The Other Air Battle: The American Pursuit of Post-War Civil Aviation Rights." *Historical Journal* 28 (June 1985): 429–39. Even as they fought the Axis, the United States and the United Kingdom skirmished over postwar civil air aviation supremacy. The British resisted heavy-handed American tactics and managed after the war to prevent a U.S. economic victory. Dobson provides good coverage of both the business issues and the diplomatic strategies. See also his *Peaceful Air Warfare: The United States, Britain, and the Politics of International Aviation* (1991) (18:733).

18:733   _____. *Peaceful Air Warfare: The*

United States, Britain, and the Politics of International Aviation. New York: Oxford University Press, 1991. This volume includes important information on wartime Anglo-American conflict over postwar civil aviation, including the 1944 International Aviation conference in Chicago and its aftermath.

18:734 _____. *The Politics of the Anglo-American Economic Special Relationship, 1940–1987.* New York: St. Martin's Press, 1988. Dobson covers economic relations during and immediately after the war, with a focus on both the conflict and cooperation that marked this as well as other aspects of the wartime Anglo-American relationship.

18:735 Hachey, Thomas E. "American Profiles on Capitol Hill: A Confidential Study for the British Foreign Office in 1943." *Wisconsin Magazine of History* 57 (Winter 1973–1974): 141–53. This is a reproduction of, and commentary on, an April 1943 memorandum written by Isaiah Berlin of the British embassy in Washington, concerning the Senate and House committees on foreign affairs. It analyzes the beliefs and personalities of each member.

18:736 Harbutt, Fraser J. "Churchill, Hopkins, and the 'Other' Americans: An Alternative Perspective on Anglo-American Relations, 1941–1945." *International History Review* 8 (May 1986): 236–62. Anglo-American cooperation during the war depended too much, Harbutt concludes, on Harry Hopkins. This led to the "atrophy of conventional diplomacy" and the breakdown of good relations due to Hopkins's illness and his late 1944 shift on Anglo-American relations as postwar imperial issues began to outweigh wartime issues.

18:737 _____. *The Iron Curtain: Churchill, America, and the Origins of the Cold War.* New York: Oxford University Press, 1986. Harbutt portrays Churchill as an old anti-Bolshevik who tried throughout the war to enlist the United States in an anti-Soviet crusade but failed as long as the war was in progress. Not until early 1946 would his efforts meet with success.

18:738 Hathaway, Robert M. *Ambiguous Partnership: Britain and America, 1944–1947.* New York: Columbia University Press, 1981. Hathaway focuses on the numerous conflicts that marked Anglo-Amer-

ican relations during and immediately after the war. In the process he questions how much of a partnership existed.

18:739 Herring, George C., Jr. "The United States and British Bankruptcy, 1944–1945: Responsibilities Deferred." *Political Science Quarterly* 86 (June 1971): 260–80. The author places the blame for British financial problems at the close of the war on the fact that Americans had not understood how much it had drained British power. They were suspicious and antagonistic toward the British, considering them dangerous postwar competitors.

18:740 Johnson, Howard. "The Anglo-American Caribbean Commission and the Extension of American Influence in the British Caribbean, 1942–1945." *Journal of Commonwealth and Comparative Politics* 22 (July 1984): 180–203. Johnson explores the American use of the AACC to further American economic and strategic interests and to influence colonial policy in the British Caribbean while avoiding the need to assume formal financial or administrative responsibilities.

18:741 Kelly, Thomas O., II, ed. *World War II: Variants and Visions.* Collingdale, PA: Diane Publishing Co., 1999. This volume reproduces fourteen of the papers delivered since 1986 at Siena College's annual multidisciplinary conference on World War II. Of particular interest to diplomatic historians are two on Anglo-American wartime relations, one by Gerhard Weinberg on the conflicting postwar visions of Churchill and Roosevelt, the other by Raymond Callahan on the Burma campaign of 1945.

18:742 Kimball, Warren F. "Lend Lease and the Open Door: The Temptation of British Opulence, 1937–1942." *Political Science Quarterly* 86 (June 1971): 232–59. At first the United States did not use lend-lease as economic leverage against the British, Kimball concludes, but when Hull took control of policy in June 1941 he decided to use it as a tool to force Britain to abandon the imperial preference system.

18:743 Mahl, Thomas E. *Desperate Deception: British Covert Operations in the United States, 1939–44.* This volume focuses on covert British efforts to support interventionists and discredit isolationists from 1939 to 1944. It is weakened by over-statement and a conspiratorial tone (17:669).

18:744   Morley, Patrick. *"This Is the American Force Network": The Anglo-American Battle of the Air Waves in World War II.* Westport, CT: Praeger, 2001. This history of the American Forces Radio Network analyzes BBC opposition to and Anglo-American conflict over its establishment.

18:745   Moser, John E. *Twisting the Lion's Tail: American Anglophobia between the World Wars.* Despite the subtitle, this volume also covers the continuation of anglophobia into World War II (17:677).

18:746   Orde, Anne. *The Eclipse of Great Britain: The United States and British Imperial Decline, 1895–1956.* One chapter in the broad study covers the World War II years (9:315).

18:747   Parmar, Inderjeet. *Special Interests, the State and the Anglo-American Alliance, 1939–1945.* Portland, OR: Frank Cass, 1995. This dense work of political science examines the roles and influence of British special interest groups and political parties in five major events in the Anglo-American wartime alliance: the 1940 destroyer-bases agreement, Atlantic Charter, 1942 lend-lease agreement, Bretton Woods accords, and 1945 $5 billion loan agreement. The author concludes that the British state acted independently of and was more powerful than these groups, mobilized those supporting its pro-alliance policies, and defeated or excluded those that were pro-empire or pro-Soviet.

18:748   Paul, Septimus H. *Nuclear Rivals: Anglo-American Atomic Relations, 1941–1952.* Columbus: Ohio State University Press, 2000. Several chapters deal with Anglo-American atomic relations during the war, the author emphasizing the conflict over collaboration between Roosevelt and his advisers (Bush, Conant, and Groves) and the ability of the latter to subvert his preference for collaboration with Britain. On Britain's having to accept the junior role in the allied nuclear partnership, see also Margaret Gowing, *Britain and Atomic Energy, 1939–1945* (New York: St. Martin's Press, 1964), and Andrew J. Pierre, *Nuclear Politics: The British Experience with an Independent Strategic Force, 1939–1970* (London: Oxford University Press, 1972).

18:749   Renwick, Robin. *Fighting with Allies: America and Britain in Peace and at War.* New York: Times Books, 1996. This narrative history of twentieth-century Anglo-American relations was written by the British ambassador to the United States in the 1990s. Approximately one-quarter of the text is devoted to the World War II years.

18:750   Reynolds, David. "Competitive Cooperation: Anglo-American Relations in World War Two." *Historical Journal* 23 (March 1980): 233–45. In a review article dealing with six recently published books on Anglo-American wartime relations, Reynolds argues that opposition to Hitler's Germany never made British and U.S. policymakers forget other, more national objectives.

18:751   _____. *Rich Relations: The American Occupation of Britain, 1942–1945.* New York: Random House, 1995. A distinguished diplomatic historian explores the "hidden side" of the "special relationship"—the history and impact of the approximately 3 million U.S. service personnel who visited England during the war. In doing so he moves beyond traditional disciplinary subdivisions in adopting the "new" international history, encompassing cultural, social, political, diplomatic, and military history.

18:752   _____. "Roosevelt, Churchill, and the Wartime Anglo-American Alliance, 1939–1945." In *The "Special Relationship": Anglo-American Relations since 1945,* ed. William Roger Louis and Hedley Bull, 17–41. New York: Oxford University Press, 1986. Reynolds finds the alliance "neither natural nor inevitable" and far from what Churchill claimed for it. Rather, it was a "marriage of necessity" marred by numerous arguments reflecting major divergences of interests and ideals. Nevertheless, it was still "less imperfect than most" coalitions and "probably the most remarkable alliance in modern history."

18:753   Rose, Sonya O. "The 'Sex Question' in Anglo-American Relations in the Second World War." *International History Review* 20 (December 1998): 884–903. Exploring American and British attitudes toward prostitution, Rose shows how different cultural values and customs created vexing diplomatic issues in the context of the vast deployment of U.S. military personnel to Great Britain.

18:754   Ryan, Henry Butterfield. *The Vision of Anglo-America: The US-UK Alliance and the Emerging Cold War, 1943–1946.* New York: Cambridge University Press, 1987. After analyzing British efforts to create an Anglo-American bloc, which the United States resisted, Ryan develops case histories of the Greek and Polish crises in which Britain sought American power to support its diplomacy.

18:755   Safford, Jeffrey J. "Anglo-American Maritime Relations during the Two World Wars: A Comparative Analysis." *American Neptune* 41 (October 1981): 262–79. Safford compares the maritime relations between the two allies during the world wars. He finds the greater success of World War II came from the determined efforts of individuals, particularly Americans, to avoid the mutual distrust of the past.

18:756   Stevens, Donald G. "World War II Economic Warfare: The United States, Britain, and Portuguese Wolfram." *Historian* 61 (Spring 1999): 539–55. Making use of both Foreign Office and State Department files, the author analyzes Anglo-American wartime conflicts over appropriate ways to stop Portugal from selling wolfram ore, used to make tungsten, to Germany. At first the United States deferred to Britain's flexible economic warfare policy, but in 1944 Britain acquiesced in the much harsher and more coercive U.S. policy.

18:757   Watt, Donald Cameron. *Succeeding John Bull: America in Britain's Place, 1900–1975: A Study of the Anglo-American Relationship and World Politics in the Context of British and American Foreign-Policy-Making in the Twentieth Century.* Based on 1981 lectures at the Queen's University of Belfast, this volume deals with different aspects of how the United States in the twentieth century assumed Britain's nineteenth-century role in the international arena, focusing on how foreign policy elites in each country conceived and perceived the shift. One chapter covers the years 1941–1947, with additional case studies covering Anglo-American policies toward Indochina, 1942–1945, and the role of U.S. anticolonial policies in the demise of the European colonial empires from 1941 to 1962 (2:328).

18:758   Woods, Randall B. *A Changing of the Guard: Anglo-American Relations, 1941–1946.*

Chapel Hill: University of North Carolina Press, 1990. Based on extensive research in U.S. and British archives and manuscript collections, this volume analyzes the Anglo-American wartime effort to create a new international economic order and interdependent world economy. The effort, Woods argues, was so modified by forces of isolationism and economic nationalism as well as bureaucratic politics that it failed to achieve its goals. What emerged instead was the U.S. replacement of Britain as world economic hegemon and a modified multilateralism that hampered fulfillment of the original economic and political goals.

ANGLO-SOVIET RELATIONS

18:759   Carlton, David. *Churchill and the Soviet Union.* New York: Manchester University Press, 2000. Carlton analyzes Churchill's views on the Soviet Union from 1917 to 1955, including one chapter on the war years, concluding that "ideologically-based anti-Sovietism and anti-Communism" were his "most abiding obsession," the wartime alliance notwithstanding.

18:760   Folly, Martin H. *Churchill, Whitehall and the Soviet Union, 1940–45.* New York: St. Martin's Press, 2000. Based on extensive research in archival and manuscript sources, this volume analyzes the images of the Soviet Union and its likely postwar policies existing in the British government during the war. The author, concluding that the dominant image was of a cooperative postwar Soviet government, rejects the view that this image was window dressing masking an anti-Soviet policy or a false image planted by Soviet spies.

18:761   Gorodetsky, Gabriel. "The Origins of the Cold War: Stalin, Churchill and the Formation of the Grand Alliance." *Russian Review* 47 (April 1988): 145–70. Contrary to the version of events given in his memoirs, Churchill made no effort to alter Britain's anti-Soviet policies or his military strategy after the German invasion of Russia. The seeds of the cold war were planted in these 1941–1942 decisions.

18:762   _____. *Stafford Cripps' Mission to Moscow, 1940–42.* New York: Cambridge University Press, 1984. In this revisionist analysis Gorodetsky defends Cripps and his mission—Britain had no policy for true alliance with the Soviets but Cripps, his reputation victimized by Churchill's memoirs, did.

18:763   Holdich, P. G. H. "A Policy of Percentages? British Policy and the Balkans after the Moscow Conference of October 1944." *International History Review* 9 (February 1987): 28–47. This article focuses on British interests and activities in the Balkans, and British views of Anglo-Soviet relations, in the aftermath of the Churchill-Stalin "percentages" deal.

18:764   Kitchen, Martin. *British Policy towards the Soviet Union during the Second World War.* New York: St. Martin's Press, 1986. Based primarily on British archival research, this volume analyzes Anglo-Soviet relations during the war and the divisions within the British government over proper wartime and postwar policy. It concludes that the foundations for cooperation and conflict were laid before the German invasion of Russia, and that the cold war was not in progress at war's end.

18:765   Miner, Steven Merritt. *Between Churchill and Stalin: The Soviet Union, Great Britain, and the Origins of the Grand Alliance.* Chapel Hill: University of North Carolina Press, 1988. Miner is highly critical of the Churchill government for not strongly opposing Stalin's territorial demands.

18:766   Ross, Graham. "Foreign Office Attitudes to the Soviet Union 1941–45." *Journal of Contemporary History* 16 (July 1981): 521–40. Ross traces and explains Foreign Office insistence throughout the war on a cooperative approach toward the Soviets, and the resulting conflict with the more pessimistic British military chiefs of staff. See also Ross's document collection, *The Foreign Office and the Kremlin: British Documents on Anglo-American Relations, 1941–45* (1984) (18:29).

SOVIET-AMERICAN RELATIONS

18:767   Bennett, Edward M. *Franklin D. Roosevelt and the Search for Victory: American-Soviet Relations, 1939–1945.* As with his *Franklin D. Roosevelt and the Search for Security: American-Soviet Relations, 1933–1939* (1985) (17:839), Bennett maintains that Russia was always a key element in FDR's plans.

But while before 1939 he wanted to use Moscow to help preserve the peace, afterward the aim of his Soviet policy was to ensure military victory. Soviet ideology, history, and culture as well as Stalin's personality probably made genuinely friendly relations impossible, but military necessity dictated FDR's efforts to woo Stalin during the war (17:803).

18:768   Bennett, Todd. "Culture, Power, and *Mission to Moscow:* Film and Soviet-American Relations during World War II." *Journal of American History* 88 (September 2001): 489–518. The author analyzes the wartime movie *Mission to Moscow* both as an example of corporatist business-government cooperation and as an integral component of Roosevelt's wartime policies toward the Soviet Union. He concludes that the movie failed to build a popular consensus for a pro-Soviet foreign policy but did have a positive influence on Stalin and solidified the alliance at a tenuous moment. It also facilitated the reintroduction of American movies into the USSR, subverting Stalin's rule at the same time it helped legitimate it.

18:769   Buhite, Russell D. "Soviet-American Relations and the Repatriation of Prisoners of War." *Historian* 35 (May 1973): 384–97. The author summarizes the 1945 prisoner of war issue, seeing it as a major factor in the breakdown of Soviet-American relations. This work documents the lack of planning on the POW issue and the serious consequences that arose as a result.

18:770   Clemens, Diane Shaver. "Averell Harriman, John Deane, the Joint Chiefs of Staff, and the 'Reversal of Co-operation' with the Soviet Union in 1945." *International History Review* 14 (May 1992): 277–306. As ambassador to the Soviet Union and head of the U.S. military mission to Moscow, Harriman and Deane pressed in late 1944 and early 1945 for a tougher policy toward the Soviets. Roosevelt rejected their proposals, but with his death in April, Clemens argues in this careful reconstruction of policy discussions in Washington, they won the support of President Truman as well as the Joint Chiefs of Staff. The result was a reversal of FDR's pro-Soviet wartime policies.

18:771   Conversino, Mark J. *Fighting with the Soviets: The Failure of Operation FRANTIC, 1944–*

1945. Lawrence: University Press of Kansas, 1997. Based on interviews with participants and both published and unpublished records, this volume provides a detailed history of the Soviet-American 1944–1945 "shuttle bombing" project, the army air forces' effort to bomb targets deep in Germany by shuttling bombers between western and Soviet bases in the Ukraine. The author considers this one of the most significant attempts at Soviet-American military cooperation during the war. His coverage ranges from the experiences of airmen to the differences in culture and strategic priorities that inhibited genuine cooperation. He concludes that the project was largely a failure because of these differences and because allied military successes in 1944 negated the need for such an operation.

18:772   Culbert, David. "Our Awkward Ally: Mission to Moscow." In *American History/American Film,* ed. John E. O'Connor and Martin A. Jackson, 121–45. New York: Frederick Ungar, 1979. Culbert analyzes this 1943 film as "the most significant example," albeit not necessarily a successful one, "of official attempts to promote wartime unity through manipulating the content of an entertainment medium." See also his introductory essay to the screenplay published by the University of Wisconsin Press in 1980.

18:773   Davis, Lynn Etheridge. *The Cold War Begins: Soviet-American Conflict over Eastern Europe.* Princeton: Princeton University Press, 1974. Davis considers Soviet-American differences over Eastern Europe the single most important cause of the cold war. Focusing on the State Department, she concludes that American policies were neither devious nor especially coherent, but rather unrealistic in that they sought to implement the principles of the Atlantic Charter while failing to take into account how that might threaten vital Soviet security interests.

18:774   Dennett, Raymond, and Joseph E. Johnson, eds. *Negotiating with the Russians.* Boston: World Peace Foundation, 1951. Included in this older volume are John R. Deane, "Negotiating on Military Assistance, 1943–1945" (3–30); John N. Hazard, "Negotiating under Lend-Lease, 1942–1945" (31–48); Sidney S. Alderman, "Negotiating the Nuremberg Trial Agreements, 1945" (49–100); Raymond F. Mikesell, "Negotiating at Bretton Woods, 1944"

(101–18); and George H. Blakeslee, "Negotiating to Establish the Far Eastern Commission, 1945" (119–38). Philip E. Mosely, "Some Soviet Techniques of Negotiation" (271–304), sums up the basic problems as perceived by the diplomats of the era of World War II.

18:775   Dunn, Dennis J. *Caught between Roosevelt & Stalin: America's Ambassadors to Moscow.* Dunn examines the relationships between President Roosevelt and his ambassadors to the Soviet Union and their evolving views, assessments, and recommendations. Overall he favors the ambassadorial viewpoints and their calls for a tougher stance against the USSR. Consequently, he condemns Roosevelt's cooperative Soviet policy, which, he believes, squandered opportunities to prevent Soviet domination of Eastern Europe (17:808).

18:776   Elliott, Mark R. *Pawns of Yalta: Soviet Refugees and America's Role in Their Repatriation.* Urbana: University of Illinois Press, 1981. This is a broad-ranging and well-documented account of the forced repatriation of Soviet refugees and prisoners of war at the conclusion of World War II. The affair was one of the war's "cruel by-products," and Elliott argues that the Americans acquiesced from concern for their own captives in Soviet custody, British pressure, and inept diplomacy combined with a desire to maintain Soviet goodwill.

18:777   _____. "The United States and Forced Repatriation of Soviet Citizens, 1944–47." *Political Science Quarterly* 88 (June 1973): 253–75. British and American concern for the welfare of their captured countrymen liberated by the Soviet Union was the overriding motive behind the odious repatriation agreement. Elliott cites this episode as an example of western diplomatic ineptitude and evidence of the diminished role of the State Department in the making of American foreign policy. See his *Pawns of Yalta: Soviet Refugees and America's Role in Their Repatriation* (1981) (18:776).

18:778   Gaddis, John Lewis. *Strategies of Containment: A Critical Appraisal of Postwar American National Security Policy.* New York: Oxford University Press, 1982. Although Gaddis's focus in this volume is clearly on postwar Soviet-American relations, his opening chapter credits Roosevelt with a highly realistic though flawed strategy of "containment by integration" of the Soviet Union into his proposed postwar order. He also concludes that had he lived longer, FDR would probably have shifted to a tougher Soviet strategy after the defeat of the Axis.

18:779 _____. *The United States and the Origins of the Cold War, 1941–1947.* New ed. New York: Columbia University Press, 2000. This monograph, first published in 1972, deals exclusively with the origins of the cold war and excludes other aspects of tripartite diplomacy during the war. It traces the development of wartime and early postwar Soviet-American relations, finding that the responsibility for the cold war lies primarily with the Soviets, although Roosevelt's policies frequently contributed to the growing tension. Gaddis emphasizes the role played by American public opinion.

18:780 Herz, Martin F. *Beginnings of the Cold War.* Bloomington: Indiana University Press, 1966. A long-time foreign service officer, the author examines issues such as Poland, spheres of influence, and lend-lease and shows their roles in beginning the cold war. Aiming primarily at students, he gives a balanced account without attempting any conclusions.

18:781 Holloway, David. *Stalin and the Bomb: The Soviet Union and Atomic Energy, 1939–1956.* New Haven: Yale University Press, 1994. Several chapters of this history of the Soviet nuclear program deal with wartime events, particularly the impact that the American bombing of Hiroshima had on the Soviet Union's nuclear program and diplomacy. There is much, too, on the benefits to the Soviet atomic program of espionage against the Manhattan Project.

18:782 Infield, Glenn B. *The Poltava Affair: A Russian Warning, An American Tragedy.* New York: Macmillan, 1973. Infield describes a little-known story of the establishment of three American airfields in Russia destroyed by German air strikes. The Russians cooperated with the Germans, Infield believes, making this one of the first incidents of the cold war.

18:783 Linz, Susan J., ed. *The Impact of World War II on the Soviet Union.* Totowa, NJ: Rowman and Allanheld, 1985. While most of the essays in this collection deal with the domestic impact of the war on the Soviet Union, two are pertinent to foreign relations

scholars: Robert M. Slusser, "Soviet Policy and the Division of Germany, 1941–1945" (107–21), and Jerry F. Hough, "Debates about the Postwar World" (253–81).

18:784 Lukas, Richard C. *Eagles East: The Army Air Forces and the Soviet Union, 1941–1945.* Tallahassee: Florida State University Press, 1970. Special attention is given to the issues of lend-lease, attempted military collaboration, and the ill-fated 1942 plan to send an Anglo-American air force to the eastern front; see also his "The Velvet Project: Hope and Frustration" (1964) (18:785).

18:785 _____. "The Velvet Project: Hope and Frustration." *Military Affairs* 28 (Winter 1964): 145–62. This article analyzes the 1942 proposal to send an American air force to the eastern front. See also Lukas, *Eagles East: The Army Air Forces and the Soviet Union, 1941–1945* (1970) (18:784), for additional information on this project.

18:786 Mark, Eduard M. "American Policy toward Eastern Europe and the Origins of the Cold War, 1941–1946: An Alternative Interpretation." *Journal of American History* 68 (September 1981): 313–36. This is a historiographically significant article demonstrating that U.S. opposition to a Soviet sphere of influence in Eastern Europe was conditional rather than categorical. Policymakers understood the Soviet Union would dominate the region and actively sought to appease its security concerns in the hope that Eastern Europe would become an "open"—rather than a "closed"—sphere.

18:787 _____. "October or Thermidor? Interpretations of Stalinism and the Perception of Soviet Foreign Policy in the United States, 1927–1947." *American Historical Review* 94 (October 1989): 937–62. By the early 1930s, Mark argues, Americans had constructed four competing interpretations of Soviet behavior and Stalinism, reflecting divergent American ideological preconceptions and political interests. Although the interpretations remained generally unchanged and influenced American perceptions of the Soviet Union during World War II and after, the relative support each interpretation enjoyed varied. Tracing this process, Mark believes, illuminates both wartime optimism and the postwar fears about Soviet behavior and intentions that laid the groundwork for public support of containment.

18:788 McNeal, Robert H. "Roosevelt through Stalin's Spectacles." *International Journal* 18 (Spring 1963): 194–206. Stalin's Marxist-Leninist preconceptions of imperialist behavior led him to interpret Roosevelt's actions and efforts to build a personal bond in a negative light, and actually to heighten his suspicions of U.S. wrongdoing at every turn in regard to China, the disposition of colonies, the United Nations, and the revival of Germany.

18:789 Nisbet, Robert. *Roosevelt and Stalin: The Failed Courtship.* Washington, DC: Regnery Gateway, 1988. An outgrowth of a 1986 article in *Modern Age,* this brief volume is sharply critical of Roosevelt for appeasing Stalin and is representative of the neoconservative assault on FDR in the 1980s, with Tehran replacing Yalta as the nadir of Rooseveltian appeasement. See also Theodore Draper's critique (as reprinted from the *New York Review of Books*) in *A Present of Things Past: Selected Essays* (1990) (18:153).

18:790 Perlmutter, Amos. *FDR & Stalin: A Not So Grand Alliance, 1943–1945.* Columbia: University of Missouri Press, 1993. This polemic attacks Roosevelt for overall "diplomatic and strategic failure" in his conduct of the war. His dealings with Stalin are treated scornfully, with Roosevelt portrayed as both naïve and a betrayer of Eastern Europe and American national interests. This work should be used with care.

18:791 Phillips, Hugh D. "Mission to America: Maksim M. Litvinov in the United States, 1941–43." *Diplomatic History* 12 (Summer 1988): 261–75. This is a useful account of Litvinov's tenure as Soviet ambassador to the United States and of high-level dealings between the allies in Washington during the first period of war. Phillips shows that by the spring of 1942 Stalin believed the Americans had agreed to the retention of the Soviet Union's 1941 borders.

18:792 Riste, Olav. "Free Ports in North Norway: A Contribution to the Study of FDR's Wartime Policy toward the USSR." *Journal of Contemporary History* 5 (October 1970): 77–95. Riste investigates the origins of and response to FDR's 1941 proposal that a postwar network of free ports under international trusteeship would help foster peace. The president reasoned that easy access to several internationalized warm water ports might serve to slake Russia's territorial appetite.

18:793 [Sevost'ianov, G. N., and Warren F.] Kimball, eds. *Soviet-U.S. Relations, 1933–1942.* This Soviet publication reproduces nineteen papers from the first Soviet-American colloquium on World War II history, held in Moscow in 1986. These papers cover numerous aspects of Soviet-American relations from 1933 to 1942. Individual writers and their subject matter include Kimball (crisis diplomacy in 1941), Steven Merritt Miner (Stalin's conditions for the alliance), Mark A. Stoler (second-front planning), Lloyd C. Gardner (tripartite diplomacy), Theodore A. Wilson (lend-lease), David M. Glantz (U.S. views of the eastern front), Boris Gilenson (cultural relations), Valentin Berezhkov (the international position of the USSR), Vladimir Pozniakov (U.S. public opinion in 1941), Oleg A. Rzheshevsky (the anti-Hitler coalition), Georgy Kumanev and Leonid Chuzavkov (military-economic relations), Georgy Baidukov (Soviet mission to the United States in 1941), and Zinovy Sheinis (Maxim Litvinov and FDR). Translations of chapters in Russian by Kim Pilarski (17:832).

18:794 Taubman, William. *Stalin's American Policy: From Entente to Detente to Cold War.* New York: Norton, 1982. Taubman agrees with others that Stalin had no foreign policy "blueprint" and did want postwar as well as wartime cooperation with the United States, but on his terms: U.S. credits and acceptance of expanded Soviet influence everywhere.

SINO-AMERICAN RELATIONS

18:795 Bagby, Wesley M. *The Eagle-Dragon Alliance: America's Relations with China in World War II.* Newark: University of Delaware Press, 1992. This is an up-to-date general history of U.S.-Chinese relations from Pearl Harbor to Japan's surrender based on research in Chinese as well as U.S. sources. It finds U.S. policies based on a series of faulty military and political assumptions.

18:796 Carter, Carolle J. *Mission to Yenan: American Liaison with the Chinese Communists, 1944–1947.* Lexington: University Press of Kentucky, 1997. This is the first book-length, scholarly study of the Dixie mission to communist Yenan during and immediately after the war. It is based on numerous interviews by the author with participants as well as extensive archival research.

18:797 Chern, Kenneth S. *Dilemma in China: America's Policy Debate, 1945.* Hamden, CT: Archon Books, 1980. Chern argues in this revised dissertation that the critical turning point in U.S. China policy came with the vigorous China debate of 1945 rather than later. He focuses on the formation of attitudes, legislative-executive relations, pressure groups, and public opinion.

18:798 Cohen, Warren I. "The Development of Chinese Communist Policy toward the United States, 1934–1945." *Orbis* 11 (Summer 1967): 551–69. This second of a two-part study of Chinese communist policy toward the United States between 1922 and 1945 is based on communist sources. Cohen argues that the Hurley mission was pivotal in arousing communist mistrust of the United States.

18:799 Denning, Margaret B. *The Sino-American Alliance in World War II: Cooperation and Dispute among Nationalists, Communists, and Americans.* Bern: Peter Lang, 1986. This University of Zurich Ph.D. dissertation is based on research in published Chinese as well as U.S. sources. It concludes that the Sino-American wartime alliance was one of convenience that achieved the basic war aims of both partners, but nothing else.

18:800 Feis, Herbert. *The China Tangle: The American Effort in China from Pearl Harbor to the Marshall Mission.* Princeton: Princeton University Press, 1953. A former State Department official with access to then closed official records, Feis in this early study of U.S. China policy during and immediately after World War II defends that policy and blames its failure on the incompetence of the Guomindang and the malevolence of the communists.

18:801 Gallicchio, Marc S. "Colouring the Nationalists: The African-American Construction of China in the Second World War." *International History Review* 20 (September 1998): 571–96. Gallicchio examines the wartime experiences of African-American soldiers and the disappointment of blacks at home when the soldiers posted to China encountered Chinese racial prejudice.

18:802 _____. "The Other China Hands: U.S. Army Officers and America's Failure in China, 1941–1950." *Journal of American–East Asian Relations* 4 (Spring 1995): 49–72. A combination of faith in Nationalist junior officers and military successes in the final weeks of the war led U.S. army officers in China to be optimistic and recommend postwar support of the Guomindang. This placed them at odds with foreign service officers in China.

18:803 Kubek, Anthony. *How the Far East Was Lost: American Policy and the Creation of Communist China, 1941–1949.* Chicago: H. Regnery Co., 1963. Kubek was the principal scholarly spokesperson for the thesis that the United States "lost" China to the communists through a combination of incompetence by Democratic officials and treason by professional bureaucrats. For a variant on this McCarthyite attack, see Fred Utley, *The China Story* (Chicago: Regnery, 1951).

18:804 Liu, Xiaoyuan. *A Partnership for Disorder: China, the United States, and Their Policies for the Postwar Disposition of the Japanese Empire, 1941–1945.* New York: Cambridge University Press, 1996. Detailing the Chinese actions in unprecedented detail, Liu examines differing Chinese and American policies over the postwar future of the Japanese empire and Jiang's growing disaffection as Roosevelt discarded Chinese goals in favor of closer Soviet-American ties.

18:805 _____. "Sino-American Diplomacy over Korea during World War II." *Journal of American–East Asian Relations* 1 (Summer 1992): 223–64. Making use of Chinese as well as U.S. sources, Liu provides a detailed analysis of Sino-American wartime differences and negotiations on Korean independence. Behind their rhetoric stood sharply different policies: while the Chinese saw Korea in geostrategic terms, the Americans saw it as a testing ground for their concept of postwar great power cooperation.

18:806 Ma, Xiaohua. "The Sino-American Alliance during World War II and the Lifting of the Chinese Exclusion Acts." *American Studies International* 38 (June 2000): 39–61. The author shows how World War II, and American strategic needs, set in motion a transformation of the popular American image of China. One tangible manifestation of the new "strong" and "independent" China was the campaign to repeal the 1882 act prohibiting Chinese immigration. The author notes that U.S. policymakers were cognizant of the symbolic value of the action.

18:807　Miles, Milton E. *A Different Kind of War: The Little-Known Story of the Combined Guerrilla Forces Created in China by the U.S. Navy and the Chinese during World War II.* Garden City, NY: Doubleday, 1967. Miles presents one side of a bitter controversy about a naval mission's attempt to train guerrillas in China. The OSS, War Department, General Wedemeyer, and the State Department each found reasons for opposing this venture, part of the wartime story of U.S.-Chinese relations. Prepared by Hawthorne Daniel from Miles's original manuscript.

18:808　Ninkovich, Frank A. "Cultural Relations and American China Policy, 1942–1945." *Pacific Historical Review* 49 (August 1980): 471–98. Examining the State Department's wartime cultural relations program with China, Ninkovich argues that it tried to promote democratic and halt authoritarian tendencies within the Kuomintang and reflected a liberal cultural vision of Sino-American relations, including in the more visible political program, which was based on false premises about the relationship between the Chinese and U.S. cultures.

18:809　Reardon-Anderson, James. *Yenan and the Great Powers: The Origins of Chinese Communist Foreign Policy, 1944–1946.* New York: Columbia University Press, 1980. This was the first complete study of Chinese communist policy toward the United States and the Soviet Union at the close of World War II. It relates that policy to domestic and interparty politics and the changing situation on the battlefield.

18:810　Schaller, Michael. *The U.S. Crusade in China, 1938–1945.* Schaller examines in great detail and criticizes U.S. support of Chiang during the war (17:984).

18:811　Sheng, Michael M. "America's Lost Chance in China? A Reappraisal of Chinese Communist Policy toward the United States before 1945." *Australian Journal of Chinese Affairs* 29 (January 1993): 135–57. Making use of recently released documents, Sheng argues that Chinese Communist Party

pragmatism was limited to tactics and did not extend to any possible modification of its anticapitalist and anti-imperialist ideology. Consequently, there was no "lost chance" for the United States to win over the party in 1944–1945.

18:812　Shyu, Larry N. "The Chinese Communist Party's Relations with the United States during the Sino-Japanese War: Ideology and Pragmatism." *Tamkang Journal of American Studies* 7 (Winter 1990): 17–33. Shyu argues that Mao's changing relations with the United States during and immediately after the war resulted from a fusion of ideology and tactical pragmatism, not one or the other. See also Shewmaker, *Americans and Chinese Communists, 1927–1945: A Persuading Encounter* (1971) (17:985).

18:813　Tsou, Tang. *America's Failure in China, 1941–50.* 2 vols. Chicago: University of Chicago Press, 1963. This cold war–era study focuses on the mismatch between the ends of U.S. policy in China and the means Washington was willing to use in pursuit of those ends during and after World War II. The author harshly condemns U.S. policymakers for this mismatch and for naïveté about communism.

18:814　Varg, Paul A. *Closing of the Door: Sino-American Relations, 1936–1946.* East Lansing: Michigan State University Press, 1973. This chronicle of U.S. policy toward China during and immediately after the World War II years focuses on the conflict between U.S. goals and perceptions on the one hand and Chinese realities on the other. Varg concludes that U.S. efforts to reform China's government and prevent civil war were beyond attainment and created lasting ill will and distrust.

18:815　White, Theodore H. *In Search of History: A Personal Adventure.* New York: Harper and Row, 1978. These recollections by an outstanding journalist are of value to historians for informed comments on wartime China and descriptions of General Stilwell, Jiang Jieshi, Mao Tse-tung, and Chou En-lai.

18:816　Young, Arthur N. *China and the Helping Hand, 1937–1945.* Cambridge, MA: Harvard University Press, 1963. Young, an American financial adviser to China (1929–1947), attempts to give a balanced picture of foreign aid—particularly American—to Nationalist China. While stressing the positive side of

Nationalist China's efforts, he points to factors within China that interfered with reform efforts.

18:817 Yu, Maochun. *OSS in China: Prelude to Cold War.* New Haven: Yale University Press, 1996. The author makes extensive use of OSS documents and communist Chinese materials on World War II intelligence, all of which became available during the 1980s, to reinterpret the reasons for the failure of U.S. policies in China. Yu emphasizes the fierce competition in China between the OSS and other intelligence agencies, the infighting between high-ranking U.S. officials in China, Anglo-American-Chinese conflicts, and the lack of strong central command from Washington as key factors in explaining both the U.S. failure and how China policy became a partisan tool after the war. The ultimate winners in the ensuing bureaucratic struggle, he argues, were the Chinese communists, whose intelligence penetration of the OSS and other agencies was stunningly successful.

FRANCO-AMERICAN RELATIONS

18:818 Aglion, Raoul. *Roosevelt and de Gaulle: Allies in Conflict: A Personal Memoir.* New York: Free Press, 1988. Aglion was one of de Gaulle's first representatives to the United States. This is a translation and expansion of the memoir he published in France in 1984.

18:819 Anglin, Douglas G. *The St. Pierre and Miquelon Affaire of 1941: A Study in Diplomacy in the North Atlantic Quadrangle.* Toronto: University of Toronto Press, 1966. Cordell Hull's careful policy toward Vichy France caused him to be circumspect in the disposition of these tiny French islands near the entrance to the Gulf of St. Lawrence and to be infuriated by de Gaulle's "invasion" of them. This volume reveals much about the Hull-Roosevelt relationship, the administration's "hemispheric" preparation for World War II, and its mistrust of de Gaulle.

18:820 Gottschalk, Louis R. "Our Vichy Fumble." *Journal of Modern History* 20 (March 1948): 47–56. This extended review is deeply critical of Langer, *Our Vichy Gamble* (1947) (18:822) and the State Department's pro-Vichy and anti–de Gaulle policies

from mid-1940 through the North African invasion and Darlan deal of late 1942.

18:821 Hurstfield, Julian G. *America and the French Nation, 1939–1945.* This is a detailed examination of American attitudes and policies toward France during World War II. Hurstfield shows that Roosevelt's French policy unsurprisingly accorded with his affinity for "court diplomacy" and for giving primacy to military strategy and goals and their immediate requirements. Troublesome political decisions were postponed, and this generally suited the American public (17:727).

18:822 Langer, William L. *Our Vichy Gamble.* New York: Alfred A. Knopf, 1947. The author was granted early access to classified records to explain why the Roosevelt administration pursued its opportunistic policy toward the collaborationist Vichy government. The explanation is persuasive but the examination of alternatives is neither exhaustive nor totally convincing.

18:823 Maga, Timothy P. *America, France, and the European Refugee Problem, 1933–1947.* Maga assesses the "refugee relations" between France and the United States, concluding that refugee policies failed because both countries had more pressing problems, and refugees lacked a political constituency (17:728).

18:824 Maguire, G. E. *Anglo-American Policy towards the Free French.* New York: St. Martin's Press, 1995. Extensively researched in French, British, and U.S. archives, this work analyzes the complex relationships and conflicts among de Gaulle's Free France, Washington, and London. The chapters are organized topically and cover a host of wartime issues.

18:825 Rossi, Mario. *Roosevelt and the French.* Rossi explores Roosevelt's perceptions of and attitudes toward France, particularly the deep ambivalence that stemmed from his fundamental misunderstanding of the differences between French and Anglo-American culture. He covers the course of wartime relations between Roosevelt and various French leaders, particularly de Gaulle (17:729).

18:826 _____. "United States Military Authorities and Free France, 1942–1944." *Journal of Mili-*

tary History 61 (January 1997): 49–64. Rossi examines the role General Eisenhower played in U.S. dealings with the Free and Vichy French factions, arguing convincingly that his diplomatic skill with both Americans and French yielded significant success in securing support for de Gaulle and reestablishing legitimate French civil authority after the liberation.

18:827   Vigneras, Marcel. *United States Army in World War II: Special Studies: Rearming the French.* Washington, DC: Government Printing Office, 1957. Vigneras outlines the discussions between Roosevelt and Giraud at Casablanca concerning arms and the later negotiations between French representatives and the War Department.

18:828   Viorst, Milton. *Hostile Allies: FDR and Charles de Gaulle.* New York: Macmillan, 1965. This is a sympathetic treatment of de Gaulle in his disagreements with Roosevelt and Churchill during World War II. Viorst is careful to note that the Roosevelt–de Gaulle incompatibility rested on differing national interests of the United States and France more than on personal characteristics.

18:829   White, Dorothy Shipley. *Seeds of Discord: De Gaulle, Free France, and the Allies.* Syracuse: Syracuse University Press, 1964. This book is primarily a synthesis of the complex diplomatic developments that occurred while de Gaulle was trying to establish his legitimacy as leader of the non-Vichy French. He comes off far better than blundering U.S. officials.

Major Wartime and Postwar Issues

LEND-LEASE

18:830   Dobson, Alan P. *US Wartime Aid to Britain, 1940–1946.* Dobson recounts the politics of Anglo-American economic cooperation and conflict within the context of lend-lease. Because preexisting economic rivalry conditioned American policymakers to suspect British motives, as U.S. economic and military power grew, policymakers increasingly exploited British weakness to make agreements to the postwar economic disadvantage of the United Kingdom (17:1035).

18:831   Dougherty, James J. *The Politics of Wartime Aid: American Economic Assistance to France and French Northwest Africa, 1940–1946.* Westport, CT: Greenwood Press, 1978. Dougherty provides a thorough treatment of the wartime U.S. economic assistance to France and its North African territories, where lend-lease was employed to provide large-scale civilian assistance. He accurately summarizes the tale as "one of frustration, controversy, and limited success," as competing French and Arab interests and American missteps caused U.S. intentions to outpace achievements.

18:832   Herring, George C., Jr. *Aid to Russia, 1941–1946: Strategy, Diplomacy, the Origins of the Cold War.* New York: Columbia University Press, 1973. Herring describes Roosevelt's policy of unconditional aid to the Soviet Union, which had virtually no limitations as FDR sought to reassure Stalin of Anglo-American intentions. As the war drew to a close, Roosevelt refused to modify the program, while Truman accepted the advice of Harriman and others by taking a tougher stand. He did not intend to use lend-lease as an instrument of coercion but did assume the Soviets would accept political compromises in return for postwar aid.

18:833   _____. "Lend-Lease to Russia and the Origins of the Cold War, 1944–1945." *Journal of American History* 56 (June 1969): 93–114. The abrupt reduction of lend-lease assistance to Russia in May 1945 was not an attempt to coerce the Soviet Union. Lend-lease to all countries was being reduced, but termination of Roosevelt's liberal policy of aid to Russia and an initially overzealous interpretation of the new policy hurt the Russians economically.

18:834   Jones, Robert H. *The Roads to Russia: United States Lend-Lease to the Soviet Union.* Norman: University of Oklahoma Press, 1969. Designed to correct the Soviet Union's cold war assertions about the insignificance of lend-lease, this volume demonstrates just how substantial and vital American aid was to the Soviet war effort. Focusing on lend-lease aid to the Soviet Union, Jones covers policymaking, the difficulties of shipment, and the aid itself.

18:835 Jordan, George Racey, with Richard L. Stokes. *From Major Jordan's Diaries.* New York: Harcourt, Brace, 1952. Jordan was a businessman who served in the army as a lend-lease "expediter" and liaison officer with the Soviets in the United States. In this memoir he relates, and strives to document, the existence of lend-lease shipments of a "non-military nature," such as U.S. money plates that were used for nefarious purposes by the Soviets. Suspicious that Harry Hopkins among others was underhandedly assisting Moscow, Jordan later become something of a cult figure on the American right.

18:836 Langer, John D. "The Harriman-Beaverbrook Mission and the Debate over Unconditional Aid for the Soviet Union, 1941." Three months after German armies invaded the Soviet Union, British and American delegations in Moscow promised Stalin a long-range, large-scale aid program, "the First Soviet Supply Protocol." This generous unilateral commitment provoked high-level dissent within both British and American governments and touched off an ongoing debate (17:1050). This article is reprinted in Laqueur, *The Second World War: Essays in Military and Political History* (1982) (18:160).

18:837 Leighton, Richard M. "The American Arsenal Policy in World War II: A Retrospective View." In *Some Pathways in Twentieth-Century History: Essays in Honor of Reginald Charles McGrane,* ed. Daniel R. Beaver, 221–52. Detroit: Wayne State University Press, 1969. Leighton provides a highly detailed and informative analysis of U.S. industrial strategy for itself and its allies during the war, including its relationship to the size of the armed forces and military strategy, the alternative available strategies, conflicts with the allies, and ensuing compromises.

18:838 Martel, Leon. *Lend-Lease, Loans, and the Coming of the Cold War: A Study of the Implementation of Foreign Policy.* Boulder: Westview Press, 1979. Primarily concerned with decisionmaking within the U.S. government, the book concentrates on four economic decisions made near the end of the war relating to U.S.-Soviet relations: the curtailment of lend-lease, the cessation of lend-lease to the USSR, and U.S. responses to two Soviet loan requests.

18:839 Motter, Thomas Hubbard Vail. *United States Army in World War II: The Middle East The-* ater: The Persian Corridor and Aid to Russia.* Washington, DC: Government Printing Office, 1952. This is an official account of the development of a lend-lease supply route to Russia (1941–1945) and is replete with the difficulties the allies had in cooperating with one another.

18:840 Stettinius, Edward R., Jr. *Lend Lease, Weapon for Victory.* New York: Macmillan Company, 1944. This is a firsthand account of the lend-lease program by its administrator and soon-to-be secretary of state. It is interesting primarily for the attitudes and motivations of one of the program's primary advocates, who contended that its value must be monetarily balanced against the U.S. allies' contribution in the front lines.

THE SECOND FRONT

18:841 Dunn, Walter Scott, Jr. *Second Front Now, 1943.* University: University of Alabama Press, 1980. Dunn argues that a 1943 second front was possible and should have been launched instead of invading Italy.

18:842 Grigg, John. *1943, the Victory That Never Was.* New York: Hill and Wang, 1980. This journalistic account argues that a cross-channel invasion was possible in 1943, that Alanbrooke rather than Churchill blocked it, and that such an invasion would have shortened the war and placed the western powers in a better bargaining position with the Soviet Union. Though based on limited research in secondary works, it serves as a useful introduction to this thesis. Much greater detail and analysis is provided in Dunn, *Second Front Now, 1943* (1980) (18:841).

18:843 Higgins, Trumbull. *Winston Churchill and the Second Front, 1940–1943.* New York: Oxford University Press, 1957. This early work examines British strategic concepts for the European theater and the ensuing Anglo-American strategic debate over cross-channel versus North African–Mediterranean operations (1939 to early 1943). It is highly critical of Churchill and the entire British approach as well as of the compromise strategy that emerged. See also his *Soft Underbelly: The Anglo-American Controversy over the Italian Campaign, 1939–1945* (1968) (18:504).

18:844   Stoler, Mark A. *The Politics of the Second Front: American Military Planning and Diplomacy in Coalition Warfare, 1941–1943.* Westport, CT: Greenwood Press, 1977. The dispute dividing the United States, Britain, and the Soviet Union over when and where to establish a second front, according to Stoler, stemmed from the differing political and military necessities of each country. Although the dispute was settled in late 1943, it increased interallied suspicions enormously.

18:845   _____. "The 'Second Front' and American Fear of Soviet Expansion, 1941–1943." *Military Affairs* 39 (October 1975): 136–41. American political and military leaders considered the danger of Soviet expansion in planning their cross-channel strategy for victory over Germany. In 1943, Washington acted to preclude postwar Soviet domination of Europe by developing both the OVERLORD plan and three "Rankin" plans for an occupation of Germany in the event of German weakening or collapse before OVERLORD could be launched.

18:846   Strange, Joseph L. "The British Rejection of Operation SLEDGEHAMMER, an Alternative Motive." *Military Affairs* 46 (February 1982): 6–13. The author concludes that Britain rejected a 1942 second front for fear of yet another disgraceful defeat for the British army. The history of such defeats in 1940 and 1941 had convinced Churchill that his forces simply could not stand up to the Germans.

18:847   Villa, Brian Loring. *Unauthorized Action: Mountbatten and the Dieppe Raid.* New York: Oxford University Press, 1989. Villa argues in this fascinating revisionist account that the disastrous Canadian raid on Dieppe resulted from a combination of pressure for a second front, public opinion, Admiral Mountbatten's ambition, and political maneuvering within the British high command and government.

SEPARATE-PEACE THREATS

18:848   Breitman, Richard D. "A Deal with the Nazi Dictatorship? Himmler's Alleged Peace Emissaries in Autumn 1943." *Journal of Contemporary History* 30 (July 1995): 411–30. Breitman intelligently probes the available evidence about Heinrich Himmler's alleged peace overtures to the allies in

1943, concluding both that he was not the driving force behind the action and that an opportunity to end the war earlier was not lost.

18:849   Koch, H. W. "The Spectre of a Separate Peace in the East: Russo-German 'Peace Feelers,' 1942–1944." *Journal of Contemporary History* 10 (July 1975): 531–49. Koch analyzes a series of meetings that took place in 1942–1944 involving Germany's Dr. Peter Kleist, a specialist in international law and honorary member of the SS, and a certain Edgar Clauss, a middleman for the USSR.

18:850   Mastny, Vojtech. "Stalin and the Prospects of a Separate Peace in World War II." *American Historical Review* 77 (December 1972): 1365–88. Mastny uses German documents to suggest that Stalin was ready to conclude a separate peace in 1943 but was unable to obtain a satisfactory territorial settlement from Germany. His desire for more ambitious territorial gains was stimulated by British and American efforts to placate the Soviet Union for the failure to provide a second front.

18:851   Steele, Richard W. "American Popular Opinion and the War against Germany: The Issue of a Negotiated Peace, 1942." *Journal of American History* 65 (December 1978): 704–23. The author emphasizes administration fears of a negotiated peace movement led by prewar isolationist opponents of Roosevelt and the president's efforts to counter this threat.

RESPONSES TO THE HOLOCAUST

18:852   Abzug, Robert H. *Inside the Vicious Heart: Americans and the Liberation of Nazi Concentration Camps.* New York: Oxford University Press, 1985. This volume combines historical narrative and analysis with first-person accounts and numerous photographs, from both official and private collections, in an effort to understand the impact of the April-May 1945 discoveries on the camp liberators, other eyewitnesses, and the general public.

18:853   Adler, Selig. "The United States and the Holocaust." *American Jewish Historical Quarterly* 64 (September 1974): 14–23. Adler argues that the

U.S. government did less to mitigate the catastrophe that befell European Jews than it could have because it initially made incorrect assumptions concerning the extent of the Holocaust, because possible responses fell too low in wartime priorities, and because measures that were taken came too late to save many victims.

18:854   Bauer, Yehuda. *American Jewry and the Holocaust: The American Jewish Joint Distribution Committee, 1939–1945.* Bauer covers the efforts of the primary agency of American Jews for overseas relief, the American Jewish Joint Distribution Committee, to respond to the overwhelming challenge of Nazi policies and the Holocaust. He addresses the purported "Jews for trucks" ransom offer (17:508).

18:855   Breitman, Richard D. "The Allied War Effort and the Jews, 1942–1943." *Journal of Contemporary History* 20 (January 1985): 135–56. Examining the claim that the demands of war precluded giving significant aid to European Jews, Breitman concludes that the extraordinary latitude with which "war effort" was defined effectively provided justification for opposing virtually any action. Moreover, European Jews were not popular, Washington saw little to be gained from assistance, and in London and Washington personal disinclination both to help and to take risks justified inaction.

18:856   _____. *Official Secrets: What the Nazis Planned, What the British and Americans Knew.* New York: Hill and Wang, 1998. Using previously classified British intelligence sources, Breitman reveals the extensive wartime knowledge the allies possessed about German implementation of genocide against the Jews, presents new information on German activities and behavior, and, through the weight of evidence, provides a dispassionate indictment of allied inaction.

18:857   Breitman, Richard D., and Alan M. Kraut. *American Refugee Policy and European Jewry, 1933–1945.* This is the most thorough examination of American refugee policy toward European Jews in this period. The authors find American policy to be the result of State Department bureaucratic interests, existing immigration laws, public opposition to immigration, and President Roosevelt's unwillingness to accept political risk (17:781).

18:858   Feingold, Henry L. *Bearing Witness: How America and Its Jews Responded to the Holocaust.* Syracuse: Syracuse University Press, 1995. In this collection of essays, Feingold examines many U.S.-related issues surrounding the Holocaust including rescue and relief efforts, President Roosevelt's role, government policy, public opinion, the impact of foreign policy, and the divided nature of the U.S. Jewish community.

18:859   _____. *The Politics of Rescue: The Roosevelt Administration and the Holocaust, 1938–1945.* See chapter 17 of this Guide (17:766).

18:860   Foregger, Richard. "The Bombing of Auschwitz." *Aerospace Historian* 34 (June 1987): 98–110. This was one of the first efforts to rebut the charge made by Wyman (*The Abandonment of the Jews: America and the Holocaust, 1941–1945,* 1984 [18:881]) that the allies could and should have bombed the Auschwitz extermination camp. The author concludes that the task was not feasible.

18:861   _____. "Two Sketch Maps of the Auschwitz-Birkenau Extermination Camps." *Journal of Military History* 59 (October 1995): 687–96. The author notes that the allies received two maps of the extermination camp in 1944, but they were insufficient sources on which to base bombing raids. The article contains reproductions of the maps.

18:862   Friedman, Saul S. *No Haven for the Oppressed: United States Policy toward Jewish Refugees, 1938–1945.* Friedman argues that anti-semitism within the State Department was not the reason for tepid willingness to help European Jews; more important were resistance to bargaining with the Nazis and general preoccupation of Americans with the war. He also criticizes the American Jewish leadership for not applying greater pressure to government leaders (17:767).

18:863   Gilbert, Martin. *Auschwitz and the Allies.* New York: Holt, Rinehart and Winston, 1981. This account of what, how, and when the allies learned of the Holocaust contains significant information but has been dated by new information and analysis. For a more accurate account, see Breitman, *Official Secrets: What the Nazis Planned, What the British and Americans Knew* (1998) (18:856).

18:864   Kitchens, James H., III. "The Bombing of Auschwitz Re-examined." *Journal of Military History* 58 (April 1994): 233–66. Kitchens critiques the charge made in Wyman, *The Abandonment of the Jews: America and the Holocaust, 1941–1945* (1984) (18:881), that the allies could and should have bombed the Auschwitz extermination camp. After examining possible military scenarios and technical aircraft capabilities, he concludes that the bombing option was "illusory."

18:865   Laqueur, Walter. "No Exit?" *Commentary* (October 1997): 59–62. This is a useful review of Rubinstein's *The Myth of Rescue: Why the Democracies Could Not Have Saved More Jews from the Nazis* (1997) (18:876), summarizing the major problems of that book.

18:866   _____. *The Terrible Secret: Suppression of the Truth about Hitler's "Final Solution."* Boston: Little, Brown, 1980. This important book, which examines the spread of knowledge about the Final Solution, focuses on the period June 1941–December 1942. Laqueur asks: when did information reach the west, through what channels did it flow, and what was the reaction of the recipients? He shows that the information was widely disseminated, if not always believed, by the end of 1942. See Breitman, *Official Secrets: What the Nazis Planned, What the British and Americans Knew* (1998) (18:856), for an updated assessment.

18:867   Lipstadt, Deborah. *Beyond Belief: The American Press and the Coming of the Holocaust, 1933–1945*. New York: Free Press, 1986. Lipstadt's well-researched volume makes clear that the American press knew about and reported the German destruction of European Jewry but did so in a way allowing them and the American public to ignore it.

18:868   Marrus, Michael R. *The Holocaust in History*. Hanover, NH: University Press of New England for Brandeis University Press, 1987. The last two of the nine chapters in this outstanding synthesis and assessment of the existing literature concern the responses to the Holocaust of the allies, including the United States, and other "bystanders."

18:869   Mashberg, Michael. "Documents Concerning the American State Department and the Stateless European Jews, 1942–1944." *Jewish Social Studies* 39 (Winter-Spring 1977): 163–82. This collection of documents from the papers of Secretary of the Treasury Morgenthau shows the efforts of his department to bring to FDR's attention the negation by the State Department of tangible efforts to rescue European Jewry.

18:870   Morse, Arthur D. *While Six Million Died: A Chronicle of American Apathy*. New York: Random House, 1968. Reprint 1998 (Overlook Press). This is a journalist's early indictment of U.S. and British bureaucratic lethargy toward the Holocaust.

18:871   Neufeld, Michael J., and Michael Berenbaum, eds. *The Bombing of Auschwitz: Should the Allies Have Attempted It?* New York: St. Martin's Press, 2000. This comprehensive volume on what has become one of the most controversial topics in World War II historiography originated in a 1993 symposium. Different sections of the published collection cover allied knowledge and capabilities, arguments for and against the bombing of Auschwitz, and new perspectives on the controversy. Contents include: Gerhard L. Weinberg, "The Allies and the Holocaust" (15–26); Richard D. Breitman, "Auschwitz Partially Decoded" (27–34); Tami Davis Biddle, "Allied Air Power: Objectives and Capabilities" (35–51); Martin Gilbert, "The Contemporary Case for the Feasibility of Bombing Auschwitz" (65–75); Gerhard M. Riegner, "The Allies and Auschwitz: A Participant's View" (76–79); James H. Kitchens, III, "The Bombing of Auschwitz Re-examined" (80–100); Richard H. Levy, "The Bombing of Auschwitz Revisited: A Critical Analysis" (101–26); Walter Laqueur, "Auschwitz" (181–85); Henry L. Feingold, "Bombing Auschwitz and the Politics of the Jewish Question during World War II" (193–203); Williamson Murray, "Monday-Morning Quarterbacking and the Bombing of Auschwitz" (204–13); Richard G. Davis, "The Bombing of Auschwitz: Comments on a Historical Speculation" (214–26); and Deborah E. Lipstadt, "The Failure to Rescue and Contemporary American Jewish Historiography of the Holocaust: Judging from a Distance" (227–36).

18:872   Newton, Verne W., ed. *FDR and the Holocaust*. New York: St. Martin's Press, 1996. This volume consists of a summary of participants' remarks at a 1993 Roosevelt Library conference on U.S. government responses to the Holocaust ("Transcript of the Summary of the Conference on 'Policies and Responses of the American Government toward the Holocaust,' 11–12 November 1993," 3–28), submissions by participants after the conference, and relevant submissions by historians who did not attend. The overall result is primarily a response to and critique of Wyman, *The Abandonment of the Jews: America and the Holocaust, 1941–1945* (1984) (18:881). Individual essays of note include Karen J. Greenberg, "The Burden of Being Human: An Essay on Selected Scholarship of the Holocaust" (29–39); Robert Dallek, "Roosevelt as a Foreign Policy Leader" (41–50); Henry L. Feingold, "'Courage First and Intelligence Second': The American Jewish Secular Elite, Roosevelt, and the Failure to Rescue" (51–87); Feingold, "Was There Communal Failure? Some Thoughts on the American Jewish Response to the Holocaust" (89–108); Richard D. Breitman, "Roosevelt and the Holocaust" (109–27); Breitman, "The Failure to Provide a Safe Haven for European Jewry" (129–43); Feingold, "Review of David Wyman's *The Abandonment of the Jews: America and the Holocaust, 1941–1945*" (145–49); Michael R. Marrus, "Bystanders to the Holocaust (Review of Monty Penkower's *The Jews Were Expendable: Free World Diplomacy and the Holocaust* and David Wyman's *The Abandonment of the Jews: America and the Holocaust, 1941–1945*)" (151–58); Arthur Schlesinger, Jr., "Did FDR Betray the Jews? Or Did He Do More than Anyone Else to Save Them?" (159–61); Breitman, "Allied Knowledge of Auschwitz-Birkenau in 1943–1944" (175–82); James H. Kitchens, III, "The Bombing of Auschwitz Reexamined" (183– 217); and Richard H. Levy, "The Bombing of Auschwitz Revisited: A Critical Analysis" (219–72).

18:873   Penkower, Monty Noam. "American Jewry and the Holocaust: From Biltmore to the American Jewish Conference." *Jewish Social Studies* 47 (Spring 1985): 95–114. The author traces the views, attitudes, and internal divisions of American Jews toward allied wartime policies, efforts to promote the rescue of European Jews, and the goal of creating a postwar Jewish national homeland.

18:874   _____. "The Bermuda Conference and Its Aftermath: The Allied Quest for 'Refuge' during the Holocaust." *Prologue* 13 (Fall 1981): 145–73.

This is a critical and condemnatory assessment of the U.S. and British failure to help European Jews following the United Nations Declaration of 1943.

18:875   _____. *The Jews Were Expendable: Free World Diplomacy and the Holocaust.* Urbana: University of Illinois Press, 1983. Penkower examines the failures of the United States and the United Kingdom to take concerted action to save Jews from the Nazi Holocaust, emphasizing that a psychology of disbelief inhibited a stronger response.

18:876   Rubinstein, William D. *The Myth of Rescue: Why the Democracies Could Not Have Saved More Jews from the Nazis.* New York: Routledge, 1997. This controversial and polemical revisionist work attacks the standard interpretations, most notably but far from exclusively the works of David Wyman, condemning allied inaction during the Holocaust. Rubinstein labels these condemnations "inaccurate and misleading" and their arguments "illogical and ahistorical." Instead, he maintains that no Jews who perished could have been saved by any action the allies could have taken at the time given what was known about the Holocaust, what was actually proposed, and what was "realistically possible." For a succinct critique, see Laqueur, "No Exit?" (1997) (18:865).

18:877   Schechtman, Joseph B. *The United States and the Jewish State Movement: The Crucial Decade, 1939–1949.* New York: Herzl Press, 1966. This is a study of the U.S. position and policies on the establishment of a Jewish state in Palestine. Two chapters deal with the war years.

18:878   Slany, William Z. *U.S. and Allied Efforts to Recover and Restore Gold and Other Assets Stolen or Hidden by Germany during World War II: Preliminary Study.* Washington, DC: Department of State, 1997. This is an interagency preliminary study on this subject, which became a major international issue in the 1990s. An appendix prepared by Greg Bradsher is a finding aid to records on the subject at the National Archives, College Park. See also *U.S. and Allied Wartime and Postwar Relations and Negotiations with Argentina, Portugal, Spain, Sweden and Turkey on Looted Gold and German External Assets and U.S. Concerns about the Fate of the Wartime Ustasha Treasury: Supplement to Preliminary Study on U.S.*

and Allied Efforts to Recover and Restore Gold and Other Assets Stolen or Hidden by Germany during World War II, a 1998 supplement covering the diplomacy described in the title. The project leading to these publications was overseen by Stuart Eizenstat.

18:879   Szajkowski, Zosa. "Relief for German Jewry: Problems of American Involvement." *American Jewish Historical Quarterly* 62 (December 1972): 111–45. This essay illustrates Jewish disunity (Zionists versus anti-Zionists) and governmental foot-dragging, which together made consistent, massive assistance impossible.

18:880   Willson, John P. "Carlton J. H. Hayes, Spain, and the Refugee Crisis, 1942–1945." *American Jewish Historical Quarterly* 62 (December 1972): 99–110. Willson describes the efforts of Hayes, wartime U.S. ambassador to Spain, to organize and expedite relief efforts for Jewish refugees moving through Spain and analyzes his conflict with the U.S. War Refugee Board.

18:881   Wyman, David S. *The Abandonment of the Jews: America and the Holocaust, 1941–1945.* New York: Pantheon Books, 1984. Reprint 1998 (New Press). In this well-researched analysis, Wyman argues that antisemitism played an influential role in determining the reproachable U.S. responses to the plight of European Jews and to news of the Holocaust. He is also critical of the media, American Jewish groups, and others for failure to generate pressure for action. One chapter is a revised version of "Why Auschwitz Was Never Bombed" (1978) (18:882).

18:882   _____. "Why Auschwitz Was Never Bombed." *Commentary* (May 1978): 37–46. Wyman examines the American response to repeated requests to bomb the Auschwitz death camp and surrounding railroads in 1944. These requests were rejected on the grounds that they would divert resources needed to prosecute the war effort, although, as Wyman notes, American bombers were striking targets in the same area. Wyman examines what might have been done and concludes the attempt should have been made.

POSTWAR INTERNATIONAL ORGANIZATION

18:883   *The United Nations Conference on International Organization, San Francisco, California, April 25 to June 26, 1945: Selected Documents.* Washington, DC: Government Printing Office, 1946. This volume provides documentary material on U.S. positions and the U.S. role at the San Francisco conference.

18:884   Anderson, Carol. "From Hope to Disillusion: African Americans, the United Nations, and the Struggle for Human Rights, 1944–1947." *Diplomatic History* 20 (Fall 1996): 531–63. Anderson's article is part of a symposium in this issue of *Diplomatic History* on African-Americans and the cold war. The first part of the article deals with failed African-American efforts to promote inclusion of strong human rights and anticolonial planks in the United Nations Charter at the San Francisco conference, their efforts foundering on American national security concerns in the early cold war, the communist affiliations of some African-American organizations, and the concerns of policymakers and politicians that domestic American practices would be held up for international scrutiny.

18:885   Briggs, Philip J. "Senator Vandenberg, Bipartisanship and the Origins of United Nations' Article 51." *Mid-America* 60 (October 1978): 163–69. Vandenberg played a key role in the decision to incorporate Article 51 into the Charter. This provision allowing regional defensive alliances was considered vital to Western Hemisphere accords, and Briggs argues that it opened the way for the NATO treaty.

18:886   Campbell, Thomas M. *Masquerade Peace: America's UN Policy, 1944–1945.* Tallahassee: Florida State University Press, 1973. Campbell focuses on efforts by policy leaders to develop a UN reflecting U.S. traditions and aspirations, showing how American actions contributed to the origins of the cold war.

18:887   _____. "Nationalism in America's UN Policy, 1944–1945." *International Organization* 27 (Winter 1973): 25–44. Using apprehension about the Soviet Union, the armed forces successfully subverted Hull's universalist approach, despite the fact that Roosevelt supported it. See also Campbell, *Mas-*

querade Peace: America's UN Policy, 1944–1945 (1973) (18:886).

18:888   Capello, H. H. Krill de. "The Creation of the United Nations Educational, Scientific and Cultural Organization." *International Organization* 24 (Winter 1970): 1–30. This article examines the Conference of Ministers of Education of the Allied Governments (1942–1945), and the 1945 Conference of the United Nations for the Establishment of an International Organization for Education and Culture. The author provides an informative account of the way in which American negotiators modified the proposals of their British and French counterparts.

18:889   Culbertson, Ely. *Total Peace: What Makes Wars and How to Organize Peace.* Garden City, NY: Doubleday, Doran and Company, 1943. This widely discussed book helped develop favorable attitudes toward international organizations during the war and the world federation movement in the late 1940s.

18:890   Divine, Robert A. *Second Chance: The Triumph of Internationalism in America during World War II.* New York: Atheneum, 1967. Divine analyzes the numerous individuals and groups who kept Wilsonianism alive during the interwar years, their struggles and triumph during the war years, and their conflicts with Roosevelt as well as with isolationists.

18:891   Gross, Leo. "The Charter of the United Nations and the Lodge Reservations." *American Journal of International Law* 41 (July 1947): 531–54. Recalling the Lodge Reservations and the fear that the British empire would get six votes in the League of Nations compared to one for the United States, Gross finds no parallel concern over unequal voting strength for the USSR in the UN in this comparison of the League and the UN.

18:892   Hilderbrand, Robert C. *Dumbarton Oaks: The Origins of the United Nations and the Search for Postwar Security.* Chapel Hill: University of North Carolina Press, 1990. The author analyzes in detail the conference that established the basis for the postwar United Nations organization. He argues that its shortcomings were built into the organization, which was designed not as a genuinely internationalist body but to institutionalize the international power structure existing at the end of the war.

18:893   Hoopes, Townsend, and Douglas Brinkley. *FDR and the Creation of the U.N.* New Haven: Yale University Press, 1997. Based on previously published works, this popular account provides a basic description and analysis of Roosevelt's views and actions regarding the creation of the UN.

18:894   Riggs, Robert E. "Overselling the UN Charter—Fact and Myth." *International Organization* 14 (Spring 1960): 277–90. This analysis of the propaganda campaign (1944–1945) to persuade the American people to accept the UN dispels the myth that the promises and descriptions were starry-eyed. A realistic awareness pervaded speeches and literature.

18:895   Robins, Dorothy B. *Experiment in Democracy: The Story of U.S. Citizens Organizations in Forging the Charter of the United Nations.* New York: Parkside Press, 1971. Despite this study's drawbacks, it contains useful information about the citizen organizations and, perhaps most important, includes an excellent eighty-two-page appendix containing scores of documents bearing on the public campaign for the United Nations.

18:896   Russell, Ruth B., with Jeannette E. Muther. *A History of the United Nations Charter: The Role of the United States, 1940–1945.* Washington, DC: Brookings Institution, 1958. This massive study of U.S. government planning for the UN during World War II is based on then classified State Department records. It traces the major role played by U.S. officials in shaping the UN Charter to come, with nearly half of the 1,110-page volume devoted to its final drafting in San Francisco.

18:897   Schild, Georg. "The Roosevelt Administration and the United Nations: Re-creation or Rejection of the League Experience?" *World Affairs* 158 (Summer 1995): 26–34. Schild examines Roosevelt's thoughts about a postwar international collective security organization and his efforts to avoid President Wilson's mistakes. He argues that State Department pressure, domestic opposition, and changing views of the Soviet Union led to a solution that more resembled the League of Nations than the "four policemen" Roosevelt had wanted.

18:898   Schlesinger, Stephen. "FDR's Five Policemen: Creating the United Nations." *World Policy*

Journal 11 (Fall 1994): 88–93. Intelligence documents released under the Freedom of Information Act reveal that the United States intercepted the diplomatic messages of other nations before the San Francisco conference to ensure the adoption of the U.S. agenda, especially on the Security Council and veto power. Unfortunately, no footnotes are included.

18:899 Tillapaugh, J. "Closed Hemisphere and Open World? The Dispute over Regional Security at the U.N. Conference, 1945." *Diplomatic History* 2 (Winter 1978): 25–42. The author emphasizes the misunderstandings and mismanagement at the San Francisco conference regarding the potential conflict between U.S. proposals for an open world and hemispheric security concerns.

18:900 Tiwari, Shreesh Chandra. *Genesis of the United Nations: A Study of the Development of the Policy of the United States of America in Respect of the Establishment of a General International Organization for the Maintenance of International Peace and Security, 1941–1945.* Varanasi, India: Naivedya Niketan, 1968. This study of U.S. involvement in the creation of the UN by an Indian scholar is of special interest because its perspective allows unusual insights into political attitudes and the internal formulation of policies.

18:901 U.S. Congress. Senate. Committee on Foreign Relations. *The Charter of the United Nations. Hearings before the Committee on Foreign Relations, United States Senate, Seventy-ninth Congress, First Session, on the Charter of the United Nations for the Maintenance of International Peace and Security, Submitted by the President of the United States on July 2, 1945 [Revised] July 9, 10, 11, 12, and 13, 1945.* Washington, DC: Government Printing Office, 1945. These hearings were held July 9–13, 1945. The volume is indexed and includes documents as well as the hearings themselves.

18:902 U.S. Department of State. *Charter of the United Nations. Report to the President on the Results of the San Francisco Conference by the Chairman of the United States Delegation, the Secretary of State.* Washington, DC: Government Printing Office, 1945. This is the report of the U.S. delegation on the founding conference of the United Nations.

18:903 _____. *The International Court of Justice: Selected Documents Relating to the Drafting of the Statute.* Washington, DC: Government Printing Office, 1946. This report contains the deliberations of a committee of jurists in Washington in April 1945 that drafted the statute for the court.

18:904 Widenor, William C. "American Planning for the United Nations: Have We Been Asking the Right Questions?" *Diplomatic History* 6 (Summer 1982): 245–65. Widenor suggests that the debate over whether FDR was an idealist or a realist is not relevant to an understanding of his UN policy: the key instead was domestic politics. Roosevelt shifted and made the UN a high priority in late 1943 because the public and the Republican Party had come to favor it and because he needed the support of internationalist Republicans in the 1944 election. He succeeded but in the process misled both the public and the Soviets.

18:905 Wilson, Craig Alan. "Rehearsal for a United Nations: The Hot Springs Conference." *Diplomatic History* 4 (Summer 1980): 263–81. This May-June 1943 conference to discuss postwar food and agricultural problems was conceived by the administration as a rehearsal for future meetings leading to a postwar UN and to promote public favor for internationalism. Ironically, however, FDR's decision to limit press coverage and run the conference in his own way led to congressional and press bitterness and a revival of isolationism until FDR reversed his policies.

18:906 Woods, Randall B. "Conflict or Community? The United States and Argentina's Admission to the United Nations." *Pacific Historical Review* 46 (August 1977): 361–86. The author does not accept the revisionist view of U.S. support for Argentina's membership in the United Nations. Rather than seeking to build anticommunist strength in the UN, policymakers were motivated by a commitment to principles of nonintervention, internationalism, and respect for the sovereignty of all nations.

POSTWAR ECONOMIC POLICY

18:907 Balogh, Thomas. *Unequal Partners.* 2 vols. Oxford: Blackwell, 1963. This memoir-analysis of war economics and postwar economic planning is written by an economist who was involved with J. M. Keynes in that planning. Balogh, who opposed the Bretton Woods agreement, views the problems of the peace as caused by the failure of postwar economic planning.

18:908   Black, Stanley W. *A Levite among the Priests: Edward M. Bernstein and the Origins of the Bretton Woods System.* Boulder: Westview Press, 1991. A key economist in the wartime Treasury Department, Bernstein played a major role in U.S. preparations for and participation in the Bretton Woods conference. He also helped guide the ensuing agreement through Congress and after the war served as the first director of research of the International Monetary Fund. This volume consists of a series of oral history interviews with him conducted at the Brookings Institution in 1983.

18:909   Dormael, Armand van. *Bretton Woods: Birth of a Monetary System.* New York: Holmes and Meier, 1978. Complementing Gardner, *Sterling-Dollar Diplomacy in Current Perspective: The Origins and Prospects of Our International Economic Order* (1980) (18:912), this work examines official British and U.S. plans for a postwar monetary system, centering on the Bretton Woods conference and the implementation of the agreements reached there.

18:910   Eckes, Alfred E., Jr. "Open Door Expansionism Reconsidered: The World War II Experience." *Journal of American History* 59 (March 1973): 909–24. Eckes criticizes the analyses of Williams and Kolko of U.S. postwar economic planning and argues that the domestic market generally was seen as more important than foreign trade. He also maintains that multilateralism was framed to include the USSR and was generally welcomed abroad, for example by Britain, as beneficial economic internationalism.

18:911   _____. *A Search for Solvency: Bretton Woods and the International Monetary System, 1941–1971.* Austin: University of Texas Press, 1975. Although this volume covers events to 1971, most of it is devoted to an analysis of U.S. wartime planning to restructure the postwar international monetary system. Focusing on the efforts of Treasury Department officials, especially Henry Morgenthau and Harry

Dexter White, Eckes demonstrates how U.S. policymakers sought to create a postwar economic order that would be conducive to peace and prosperity.

18:912   Gardner, Richard N. *Sterling-Dollar Diplomacy in Current Perspective: The Origins and Prospects of Our International Economic Order.* New expanded ed. New York: Columbia University Press, 1980. Gardner's study depicts American efforts to reconstruct the international monetary system and revive world commerce along multilateral lines. He focuses on the Bretton Woods accords, the Anglo-American Financial agreement, and the General Agreement on Tariffs and Trade. Originally published in 1956 as *Sterling-Dollar Diplomacy: Anglo-American Collaboration in the Reconstruction of Multilateral Trade.*

18:913   Maddox, Robert Franklin. *The War within World War II: The United States and International Cartels.* Westport, CT: Praeger, 2001. This topically organized volume analyzes three broad issues on German and Japanese cartels: their use against U.S. interests before and during World War II; American wartime investigations and responses; and the development, implementation, and cold war reversal of postwar anticartel U.S. policies.

18:914   Oliver, Robert W. *International Economic Co-operation and the World Bank.* New York: Holmes and Meier, 1975. Tracing the development of the World Bank, Oliver examines U.S. foreign economic policy in the interwar era to explain the origins and purposes of the new institution. Focusing on Harry Dexter White's role, he analyzes American plans for the International Bank for Reconstruction and Development.

18:915   Opie, Redvers. "Anglo-American Economic Relations in War-Time." *Oxford Economic Papers* 9 (February-October 1957): 115–51. Economic adviser to the British embassy in Washington during the war, Opie draws on his own experiences to survey negotiations to formulate and then implement Article 7 of the Lend-Lease Consideration agreement, which committed the United States and Britain to agree on steps leading to the elimination of economic discrimination.

18:916   Paterson, Thomas G. "The Abortive Loan

to Russia and the Origins of the Cold War, 1943–1946." *Journal of American History* 56 (June 1969): 70–92. Paterson traces the evolution of U.S. policy and diplomacy with respect to postwar reconstruction aid to the Soviet Union. From 1944 to 1946, he argues, the United States used the possibility of a postwar loan to Russia as a bargaining lever with which to influence its behavior. The failure to arrange a loan exacerbated tensions between the two countries.

18:917 Penrose, E. F. *Economic Planning for the Peace.* Princeton: Princeton University Press, 1953. In this book, which is part memoir and part economic theory, Penrose, economic adviser to ambassador to Great Britain, John Gilbert Winant, traces the development of postwar economic plans from 1941 through 1946. Penrose contends that errors of the peace were caused by faulty planning in the areas of postwar international economic recovery and permanent international economic stability.

18:918 Pollard, Robert A. "Economic Security and the Origins of the Cold War: Bretton Woods, the Marshall Plan, and American Rearmament, 1944–50." *Diplomatic History* 9 (Summer 1985): 271–89. Wartime planners did not anticipate postwar conflict with the Soviets on economic matters, according to Pollard, and sought to include them at the Bretton Woods conference. The later European Recovery Program was perceived as the alternative to yet another war or a huge arms buildup and would have occurred even without a perceived Soviet threat.

18:919 Rowland, Benjamin M. "Preparing the American Ascendancy: The Transfer of Economic Power from Britain to the United States, 1933–1944." In *Balance of Power or Hegemony: The Interwar Monetary System,* ed. Benjamin M. Rowland, 193–224. New York: New York University Press, 1976. Rowland examines the origins of the Bretton Woods system, arguing that substantial dollar hegemony was an accident of war and that Britain had an alternative in the form of the sterling area. But, hoping for U.S. political and military support, Britain accepted the covert nationalism of Washington's multilateral trade and monetary policies.

18:920 Sayers, R. S. *Financial Policy, 1939–45.* London: Her Majesty's Stationery Office, 1956. This volume in the official British History of the Second

World War (Civil Series) deals learnedly and extensively with wartime planning for finance in the postwar world. It is the starting point for any study of Anglo-American financial relations.

PUBLIC OPINION

18:921 Boyle, Peter G. "Reversion to Isolationism? The British Foreign Office View of American Attitudes to Isolationism and Internationalism during World War II." *Diplomacy & Statecraft* 8 (March 1997): 168–83. Boyle in this article analyzes the wartime Weekly Political Reports of the British Embassy in Washington, Foreign Office files on postwar trends in U.S. public opinion, and the records of the Interdepartmental Committee on American Opinion and the British empire, finding British observers and analysts consistently fearful of both a public reversion to isolationism and support for an internationalism divorced from reality.

18:922 Brewer, Susan A. *To Win the Peace: British Propaganda in the United States during World War II.* Ithaca: Cornell University Press, 1997. Brewer analyzes both the wartime British effort to build a public consensus for postwar Anglo-American cooperation and American responses to that effort. The volume is organized topically, with separate chapters on the legacies of 1914–1917 and 1939–1941; British organization, methods, and themes; India; British imperialism in general; and lend-lease. The author concludes that the British effort was a "qualified success" in that it ensured postwar cooperation, but not on the equal terms desired.

18:923 Buckley, Gary J. "American Public Opinion and the Origins of the Cold War: A Speculative Assessment." *Mid-America* 60 (January 1978): 35–42. This case study of American public opinion on the USSR during and shortly after World War II shows supportive attitudes rarely running above 50 percent.

18:924 Campbell, Thomas M. "The Resurgence of Isolationism at the End of World War II." *West Georgia College Studies in the Social Sciences* 13 (June 1974): 41–56. Campbell argues that isolationism remained a potent and influential force in blocking U.S. commitment to the internationalism espoused by Willkie and Wallace during the war.

18:925 Casey, Steven. *Cautious Crusade: Franklin D. Roosevelt, American Public Opinion, and the War against Nazi Germany.* New York: Oxford University Press, 2001. Casey challenges standard views of wartime public opinion and government propaganda, emphasizing the restrained and "soft" nature of public support for the war and its limiting effect on both propaganda and Roosevelt's plans for postwar Germany.

18:926 Foster, H. Schuyler. *Activism Replaces Isolationism: U.S. Public Attitudes, 1940–1975.* Washington, DC: Foxhall Press, 1983. Written by a former American opinion analyst in the State Department, this work provides a detailed analysis of public attitudes as expressed in public opinion polls. It is organized topically as well as chronologically, with the first four chapters covering the wartime shift to internationalism, opinions on U.S. aid policies 1941– 1950, security issues 1945–1949, and attitudes toward the State Department between 1944 and 1950.

18:927 Gallicchio, Marc S. *The African American Encounter with Japan and China: Black Internationalism in Asia, 1895–1945.* Gallicchio analyzes the rise of a new form of internationalism among African-Americans during the age of imperialism, based on the primacy of race and racism in world affairs, which placed their own plight in a global context. Along with this worldview came an affinity for Japan as the champion of the nonwhite races. Gallicchio also analyzes the challenge to this worldview and affinity brought on by the war with Japan and the ensuing ineffective replacement of Japan with China as the champion against colonialism and racism (13:178).

18:928 Isserman, Maurice. *Which Side Were You On? The American Communist Party during the Second World War.* Middletown, CT: Wesleyan University Press, 1982. This revisionist work emphasizes the "Americanization" of, rather than the Soviet control over, the U.S. Communist Party during the war.

18:929 Kearney, Reginald. *African American Views of the Japanese: Solidarity or Sedition?* Albany: State University of New York Press, 1998. Most of this well-researched volume focuses on the pro-Japanese views African-Americans developed during the early decades of the twentieth century, primarily resulting from the Japanese challenge to western racial stereotypes. One chapter analyzes the ensuing reluctance of black leaders and their constituents to give wholehearted support to the war against Japan.

18:930 Koppes, Clayton R., and Gregory D. Black. *Hollywood Goes to War: How Politics, Profits, and Propaganda Shaped World War II Movies.* New York: Free Press, 1987. Reprint 1990 (University of California Press). As in their "What to Show the World: The Office of War Information and Hollywood, 1942–1945" (1977) (18:931), Koppes and Black emphasize the substantial censorship powers OWI used over the movie industry. They also emphasize the industry's self-censorship both before and during the war. Separate chapters analyze the Hollywood wartime portrayal of the Russians, British, and Chinese as well as the Germans and Japanese.

18:931 _____. "What to Show the World: The Office of War Information and Hollywood, 1942–1945." *Journal of American History* 64 (June 1977): 87–105. This revisionist article emphasizes the substantial censorship powers OWI exercised over the movie industry, as opposed to the industry's self-regulation during the war. OWI's power derived from its ability to block overseas distribution of films not conforming to approved ideology about the war. See also the authors' *Hollywood Goes to War: How Politics, Profits, and Propaganda Shaped World War II Movies* (1987) (18:930).

18:932 Leigh, Michael. *Mobilizing Consent: Public Opinion and American Foreign Policy, 1937–1947.* This work of political science as well as history rejects notions of both public opinion controlling foreign policy and policymakers manipulating that opinion. Instead Leigh maintains that between 1937 and 1947, the relationship between pubic opinion and policymakers was transformed as the president learned to use mass public opinion to counter the previous countervailing power of Congress. Such use, however, can easily become a later restraint (17:505).

18:933 Levering, Ralph B. *American Opinion and the Russian Alliance, 1939–1945.* Chapel Hill: University of North Carolina, 1976. The author explores the wartime climate of public opinion, which he perceives as being schizophrenic: friendliness for the Soviet Union grew but so did fear of communism. Levering finds no intense animosity present during the war, but public opinion opposed to the Soviet Union increased sharply following the war's end.

18:934   Meriwether, James H. *Proudly We Can Be Africans: Black Americans and Africa, 1935–1961.* Chapel Hill: University of North Carolina Press, 2002. This study, whose main focus lies outside World War II, nonetheless offers important findings on African-Americans' interest in Africa generally and the possibility that decolonization would follow the war.

18:935   Plummer, Brenda Gayle. *Rising Wind: Black Americans and U.S. Foreign Affairs, 1935– 1960.* One of the seven chapters in this major reinterpretation of the Afro-American response to foreign affairs focuses on the World War II years. The author rejects previous interpretations of general black indifference to international affairs and argues instead for a strong interest that paralleled and intersected with both domestic issues and American globalism (16:211).

18:936   Rossi, Joseph S. *American Catholics and the Formation of the United Nations.* Lanham, MD: University Press of America, 1993. Rossi focuses on three consultants appointed by national Catholic organizations to attend the San Francisco conference in 1945 and sheds light on the diversity of Catholic opinions about the direction of American foreign policy.

18:937   Schrijvers, Peter. *The Crash of Ruin: American Combat Soldiers in Europe during World War II.* New York: New York University Press, 1998. Schrijvers analyzes the perceptions American combat soldiers developed during the war toward Europe and Europeans. Emphasizing destruction and ruin, they reinforced preexisting notions of American superiority and European decadence and decline.

18:938   Sirgiovanni, George. *An Undercurrent of Suspicion: Anti-Communism in America during World War II.* New Brunswick: Transaction Publishers, 1990. While anticommunists were a small minority during the war and Russia was perceived as a valiant ally, public opinion was never procommunist or pro-Soviet.

18:939   Small, Melvin. "Buffoons and Brave Hearts: Hollywood Portrays the Russians, 1939– 1944." *California Historical Quarterly* 52 (Winter 1973): 326–37. Before the German invasion of the USSR, films caricatured Russians as buffoons (as in "Ninotchka"), but after the USSR (and the United States) joined the fight against the Nazis, Hollywood portrayed the Russian people as defenders of freedom against tyranny ("Mission to Moscow," "North Star").

18:940   _____. "How We Learned to Love the Russians: American Media and the Soviet Union during World War II." *Historian* 36 (May 1974): 455–78. Public opinion polls reveal that people changed their minds about the USSR during World War II, reflecting a favorable shift in media presentations and interpretations. The rapidity with which Americans would later return to anticommunist views suggests doubts about the media's permanent effectiveness.

18:941   Von Eschen, Penny M. *Race against Empire: Black Americans and Anticolonialism, 1937– 1957.* Ithaca: Cornell University Press, 1997. Von Eschen examines the ideology and activities of anticolonial and anticapitalist black activists of the 1940s, such as Paul Robeson and W. E. B. Du Bois, who tried to link the struggle for civil rights at home with anticolonialism abroad but who were eventually defeated by cold war liberalism.

18:942   Willkie, Wendell L. *One World.* New York: Simon and Schuster, 1943. This ghostwritten account by the 1940 presidential candidate of a wartime trip to Russia, China, and the Middle East became an instantaneous best-seller. Its popularity demonstrated the public's receptiveness to the vague, idealistic internationalism Willkie preached.

18:943   Winkler, Allan M. *The Politics of Propaganda: The Office of War Information, 1942–1945.* New Haven: Yale University Press, 1978. This administrative history of the Office of War Information covers its overseas as well as its domestic propaganda operations. The author concludes that American propaganda matured during the war as OWI shifted from an ideological to a military orientation, and that it played a role in achieving victory—albeit not the huge role its early proponents had prophesied or with the insidious consequences its opponents had feared.

18:944　Woods, Randall B. "F.D.R. and the Triumph of American Nationalism." *Presidential Studies Quarterly* 19 (Summer 1989): 567–81. A public undercurrent of political and military isolationism, economic nationalism, and anglophobia existed throughout the war, according to Woods. This undercurrent dictated rather than circumscribed Roosevelt's foreign policies. Unable to confront and defeat these forces, he became their willing or unwilling servant.

SOVIET ENTRY INTO THE WAR AGAINST JAPAN

18:945　Lensen, George Alexander. *The Strange Neutrality: Soviet-Japanese Relations during the Second World War, 1941–1945.* Tallahassee: Diplomatic Press, 1972. While the volume concentrates on Soviet-Japanese wartime relations, it necessarily deals with how Moscow's attempts to maintain neutrality affected its relations with the United States. A special appendix on Soviet treatment of U.S. fliers and the entry of the Soviet Union into the war against Japan are important parts of this work.

18:946　May, Ernest R. "The United States, the Soviet Union and the Far Eastern War, 1941–1945." *Pacific Historical Review* 24 (May 1955): 153–74. This early article traces U.S. interest in Soviet entry into the war against Japan from is inception immediately after Pearl Harbor through the end of World War II as well as Roosevelt's efforts to obtain that entry.

18:947　Morton, Louis. "Soviet Intervention in the War with Japan." *Foreign Affairs* 40 (July 1962): 653–62. Tracing the history of U.S. policy toward Soviet intervention in the Pacific war, Morton concludes that it was based on the subordination of political to military considerations and caused the United States to pay too high a price for Soviet entry.

18:948　U.S. Department of Defense. *The Entry of the Soviet Union into the War against Japan: Military Plans, 1941–1945.* Washington, DC: Government Printing Office, 1955. This is a straightforward and convenient collection of documents, accompanied by narrative, concerning U.S. military advice on the question of Soviet participation in the war against Japan from 1941 to 1945.

DECOLONIZATION: GENERAL

18:949　Gifford, Prosser, and William Roger Louis, eds. *The Transfer of Power in Africa: Decolonization, 1940–1960.* New Haven: Yale University Press, 1982. Some of the nineteen topical chapters in this collection deal with the United States during the World War II years as well as the postwar era. Particularly noteworthy are Louis and Ronald Robinson, "The United States and the Liquidation of the British Empire in Tropical Africa, 1941–1951" (31–56); Hollis R. Lynch, "Pan-African Responses in the United States to British Colonial Rule in Africa in the 1940s" (57–86); John D. Hargreaves, "Toward the Transfer of Power in British West Africa" (117–40); David E. Gardinier, "Decolonization in French, Belgian, and Portuguese Africa: A Bibliographical Essay" (515–66); and A. H. M. Kirk-Greene, "A Historiographical Perspective on the Transfer of Power in British Colonial Africa: A Bibliographical Essay" (567–602).

18:950　Jensdóttir Hardarson, Sólrún B. "'Republic of Iceland' 1940–44: Anglo-American Attitudes and Influences." *Journal of Contemporary History* 9 (October 1974): 27–56. This study examines how Iceland's planned independence from Denmark was complicated by British and American occupation. Neither ally had Danish-Icelandic relations in mind when undertaking to guarantee the independence of Iceland, although the Icelanders adopted that interpretation.

18:951　Kimball, Warren F. "'A Victorian Tory': Churchill, the Americans, and Self-Determination." In *More Adventures with Britannia: Personalities, Politics and Culture in Britain,* ed. William Roger Louis, 221–39. Austin: University of Texas Press, 1998. In this 1996 lecture Kimball explores the Churchill-Roosevelt clash over decolonization and its link to the president's overall views and plans for the postwar world.

18:952　Louis, William Roger. "American Anti-Colonialism and the Dissolution of the British Empire." *International Affairs* 61 (Summer 1985): 395–420. This article examines the ideology of American anticolonialism and its conflicts with the "special relationship" with Britain via three case studies taken from the Roosevelt, Truman, and Eisenhower administrations. The Roosevelt-era case study is India during World War II.

18:953 _____. *Imperialism at Bay: The United States and the Decolonization of the British Empire, 1941–1945.* New York: Oxford University Press, 1978. This informative work deals with British and American wartime planning for the future of the colonial world. Louis explores the historic and wartime antagonism between Britain's imperial colonial system and America's informal, liberal, democratic vision of empire-as-trusteeship. He also explores the differences within each government over colonial issues.

18:954 Watt, Donald Cameron. "American Anti-Colonial Policies and the End of the European Colonial Empire 1941–1962." In *Contagious Conflict,* ed. Arie Nicolaas Jan den Hollander, 93–125. Leiden: Brill, 1973. The author claims that the anticolonial policies of the United States failed not because the United States abandoned them to gain European support to counterbalance Soviet influence, but because they reflected narrow and rigid American political thought.

18:955 Williams, John E. "The Joint Declaration on the Colonies: An Issue in Anglo-American Relations, 1942–1944." *British Journal of International Studies* 2 (October 1976): 267–92. Williams compares British and American attitudes toward colonialism and imperialism in regard to British colonies in Southeast Asia and examines the Roosevelt administration's unsuccessful attempt to form a joint declaration toward the colonies.

Asia

18:956 Habibuddin, S. M. "Franklin D. Roosevelt's Anti-Colonial Policy toward Asia: Its Implications for India, Indo-China, and Indonesia (1941–45)." *Journal of Indian History* 53 (December 1975): 497–522. Habibuddin argues that the shock of war combined with the decline of European influence in Asia required a new American policy toward colonialism. Insufficient political determination and numerous obstacles, such as British opposition, American military hostility toward trusteeship, and Roosevelt's death, served to prevent the United States from following a new course of action.

18:957 Sbrega, John J. *Anglo-American Relations*

and Colonialism in East Asia, 1941–1945. New York: Garland Publishing, 1983. Sbrega analyzes the role of colonies and colonialism in the Anglo-American alliance and in postwar security planning. He finds the colonial issue leading to great suspicion and splitting the allies. Roosevelt's use of platitudes and expediency in place of confrontation, he argues, ensured the reimposition of colonialism at war's end.

India

18:958 Clymer, Kenton J. "The Education of William Phillips: Self-Determination and American Policy toward India, 1942–1945." *Diplomatic History* 8 (Winter 1984): 13–36. Clymer traces and analyzes Phillips's surprising shift from a pro-British position to one favoring Indian independence during his wartime mission as Roosevelt's personal representative to India.

18:959 Hess, Gary R. *America Encounters India, 1941–1947.* Baltimore: Johns Hopkins Press, 1971. This study traces the American official and popular response to Indian nationalism during the political upheavals of 1941–1947 and includes material on British and Indian propaganda activities in the United States. It is critical of the Roosevelt administration's handling of the Indian question during the war.

18:960 Hope, A. Guy. *America and Swaraj: The U.S. Role in Indian Independence.* Washington, DC: Public Affairs Press, 1968. This study, concentrating on the years 1941 to 1947, is wholly favorable in its assessment of the American response to Indian nationalism.

18:961 Jauhri, R. C. *American Diplomacy and Independence for India.* Bombay: Vora, 1970. This book detailing the 1941 to 1947 period of Indo-American relations is critical of the Roosevelt administration's policy during the war.

18:962 Muzumdar, Haridas T. *America's Contributions to India's Freedom.* New York: Universal Publishing Co. for World-in-Brief, 1962. Based on secondary sources as well as memory, this brief study by one of the major Indian political activists in the United States from 1930 to 1947 contains useful information on the operations of and rivalries among Indian nationalists in America.

18:963 Prasad, Yuvaraj Deva. "American Reaction to Gandhi's Arrest in 1942: The Conflict of Ideology and Necessity." *Journal of Indian History* 50, no. 149 (1972): 611–18. In August 1942, when the Indian National Congress demanded that the British immediately "quit India," Gandhi and other Indian leaders were arrested. The need to preserve British-American cooperation in the war against Germany and Japan forestalled any official U.S. support for Indian independence.

18:964 Venkataramani, M. S. "The Roosevelt Administration and the Great Indian Famine." *International Studies (Delhi)* 4 (January 1963): 241–64. This article explains why the United States refused to provide economic assistance when a disastrous famine struck Bengal. The author also notes British opposition to both official and private aid efforts.

18:965 Venkataramani, M. S., and B. K. Shrivastava. "America and the Indian Political Crisis, July-August 1942." *International Studies (Delhi)* 6 (July 1964): 1–48. Examining American attitudes toward events in India in the three weeks after the Wardha Congress in July 1942, the authors explain Roosevelt's "hands-off" policy toward India as a result of U.S. deference to the British for the sake of good relations, growing prejudice against Indian nationals, and a narrow focus on military operations.

18:966 _____. *Quit India: The American Response to the 1942 Struggle.* New Delhi: Vikas Publishing House, 1979. Summarizing and expanding on their scholarly articles of 1963–1964, the authors analyze and criticize the U.S. response to Gandhi's 1942 demand for freedom from British imperial rule, offering a detailed description of the American response. Coming in the midst of wartime crisis, however, the Indian struggle could be seen as threatening to allied success. See also their companion volume, *Roosevelt, Gandhi, Churchill: America and the Last Phase of India's Freedom Struggle* (1983) (18:967).

18:967 _____. *Roosevelt, Gandhi, Churchill: America and the Last Phase of India's Freedom Struggle.* New Delhi: Radiant Publishers, 1983. This companion volume to the authors' *Quit India: The*

American Response to the 1942 Struggle (1979) (18:966) continues their analysis of U.S. policies toward Indian independence from the late 1942 inception of William Phillips's mission through 1945. They remain highly critical of those policies, and of Roosevelt in particular, for not supporting immediate Indian freedom. They again analyze British efforts to influence the American government and people and conclude that Roosevelt and America's support for independence movements have been greatly overstated.

18:968 _____. "The U.S. and the Cripps Mission." *India Quarterly* 19 (July-September 1963): 214–65. This article focuses on April 1942 when leaders of the Indian National Congress met with a representative of the U.S. government (Louis Johnson) at the same time they negotiated for their wartime cooperation with the British. The authors critique the view that Roosevelt actively supported Indian interests.

18:969 _____. "The United States and the 'Quit India' Demand." *India Quarterly* 20 (April-June 1964): 101–39. This is an examination of how American sentiment turned against Indian nationalism during the weeks in 1942 between the Cripps mission and the Wardha Congress.

Indonesia

18:970 Homan, Gerlof D. "The United States and the Indonesian Question, December 1941–December 1946." *Tijdschrift voor Geschiedenis* 93 (1980): 35–56. Homan argues that the United States largely followed a hands-off policy on the Netherlands East Indies. American desire to preserve a strong Dutch presence in the region precluded more than tepid support for Indonesian independence.

18:971 _____. "The United States and the Netherlands East Indies: The Evolution of American Anticolonialism." *Pacific Historical Review* 53 (November 1984): 423–46. Homan examines American perceptions of Dutch Asian colonialism in the East Indies, going into detail about differing opinions within the State Department, and concludes that wartime pro-Dutch sympathies, U.S. economic interests, and vague Dutch statements about improving postwar governance largely muted any significant American action.

18:972   McMahon, Robert J. "Anglo-American Diplomacy and the Reoccupation of the Netherlands East Indies." *Diplomatic History* 2 (Winter 1978): 1–24. Although primarily concerned with postwar events, McMahon devotes the first few pages of this article to the shift in U.S. policies toward Britain and the Netherlands in 1944–1945, especially at the Potsdam conference, regarding responsibility for this area and military reoccupation. See also the opening chapters of his *Colonialism and the Cold War: The United States and the Struggle for Indonesian Independence, 1945–49* (1981) (18:973).

18:973   _____. *Colonialism and Cold War: The United States and the Struggle for Indonesian Independence, 1945–49.* Ithaca: Cornell University Press, 1981. Chapter 2 of this volume and the first few pages of the next analyze the history of prewar and wartime U.S. interest in the area, with an emphasis on decolonization plans and reoccupation issues.

Korea

18:974   Cumings, Bruce, ed. *Child of Conflict: The Korean-American Relationship, 1943–1953.* Seattle: University of Washington Press, 1983. The essays and commentaries in this volume originated in two conferences on Korean-American relations held at the University of Washington in 1978 and 1980. Although most of the essays focus on the cold war and the Korean War, three are of interest to World War II scholars: Cumings, "Introduction: The Course of Korean-American Relations, 1943–1953" (3–56) (commentary by Lloyd C. Gardner, 57–66); Mark Paul, "Diplomacy Delayed: The Atomic Bomb and the Division of Korea, 1945" (67–92); and Stephen E. Pelz, "U.S. Decisions on Korean Policy, 1943–1950: Some Hypotheses" (93–132).

18:975   Matray, James I. "An End to Indifference: America's Korean Policy during World War II." *Diplomatic History* 2 (Spring 1978): 181–96. Roosevelt's plan for Korean trusteeship was designed to preclude Chinese more than Soviet efforts to dominate the area and caused tension with allies.

18:976   _____. *The Reluctant Crusade: American Foreign Policy in Korea, 1941–1950.* Honolulu: University of Hawaii Press, 1985. The first two chapters of this volume deal with U.S. interest in Korea during World War II.

18:977   Park, Hong-Kyu. "From Pearl Harbor to Cairo: America's Korean Diplomacy, 1941–43." *Diplomatic History* 13 (Summer 1989): 343–58. Park traces the evolution of American wartime planning for Korea up to the December 1943 Cairo Declaration, which called for Korean independence after international trusteeship. Focusing on efforts of exile Korean nationalist groups to influence American policy, he argues that apparent U.S. indifference to Korean independence stemmed from both appreciation of the international ramifications surrounding the issue and beliefs that the exile groups were not representative of the Korean people.

PLANS AND POLICIES FOR THE OCCUPATION OF GERMANY

18:978   Allen, Diane Manchester. "Development of Postwar Policy in Germany." *Western Political Quarterly* 17 (March 1964): 109–16. Hull and Stimson offered a moderate postwar policy for Germany, the author concludes, while Morgenthau's projected program was harshly vindictive. A "hasty compromise" was reached with Truman's endorsement of JCS 1067, a supposedly definitive directive. Truman did not approve Morgenthau's ideas but was unable to prevent their inclusion in the later discarded JCS 1067.

18:979   Chase, John L. "The Development of the Morgenthau Plan through the Quebec Conference." *Journal of Politics* 16 (May 1954): 324–59. This is an early but highly detailed analysis, based on materials then available, of the origins and development of the Morgenthau Plan for Germany as an alternative to State and War Department plans. The author analyzes the internal U.S. government disagreements over the issue, the Anglo-American discussions at the 1944 Quebec conference, and their relationship to the questions of continued aid to Britain, trade concessions, and zones of occupation in Germany.

18:980   Dorn, Walter L. "The Debate over American Occupation Policy in Germany in 1944–1945." *Political Science Quarterly* 72 (December 1957): 481–501. This is an early, detailed study of the background of JCS 1067, the Joint Chiefs of Staff directive guiding initial American occupation policy in Germany.

18:981   Eisenberg, Carolyn Woods. *Drawing the Line: The American Decision to Divide Germany, 1944–1949.* New York: Cambridge University Press, 1996. This important revisionist volume focuses on the postwar years, but the first two chapters cover U.S. wartime planning for postwar Germany and allied negotiations in 1945. A work of a different character appeared as this Guide neared publication: Michael Beschloss, *The Conquerors: Roosevelt, Truman and the Destruction of Germany* (New York: Simon and Schuster, 2002).

18:982   Franklin, William M. "Zonal Boundaries and Access to Berlin." *World Politics* 16 (October 1963): 1–31. This painstaking early study of allied plans deals with the political-military problem of the occupation of Berlin. Franklin emphasizes the deep divisions between Roosevelt and the State Department and the Americans and the British rather than any Anglo-American-Soviet problem. He argues that a right of access to Berlin for the allies was understood by all sides.

18:983   Kimball, Warren F. "The Ghost in the Attic: The Soviet Union as a Factor in Anglo-American Wartime Postwar Planning for Postwar Germany, 1943–1945." In *Politics and Strategy in the Second World War: Germany, Great Britain, Japan, the Soviet Union and the United States: Papers Presented under the Auspices of the International Committee for the History of the Second World War, San Francisco, August 26, 1975,* ed. Arthur L. Funk, 88–112. Manhattan, KS: Military Affairs/Aerospace Historian Publishers, 1976. Kimball argues that fear of the Soviet Union did not play a major role in the Anglo-American postwar plans for Germany.

18:984   _____. *Swords or Ploughshares? The Morgenthau Plan for Defeated Nazi Germany, 1943–1946.* New York: Lippincott, 1976. In a long essay, combined with documents, on the Morgenthau plan for Germany, Kimball argues that in throwing

out the plan, the United States also surrendered the possibility of a neutral, disengaged Germany that might have eliminated a major source of cold war tension.

18:985   Kochavi, Arieh J. "Discord within the Roosevelt Administration over a Policy toward War Criminals." *Diplomatic History* 19 (Fall 1995): 617–39. Kochavi traces the wartime development of two strands of U.S. thought on war crimes that pitted the State, War, and Navy Departments against the UN War Crimes Commission. He focuses on the key role of the commission's American representative, Herbert C. Pell, in the ensuing struggle over a war crimes policy. See also his *Prelude to Nuremberg: Allied War Crimes Policy and the Question of Punishment* (1998) (18:986).

18:986   _____. *Prelude to Nuremberg: Allied War Crimes Policy and the Question of Punishment.* Chapel Hill: University of North Carolina Press, 1998. Based on extensive multiarchival research, this work traces the complex wartime development of allied policies on Nazi war crimes that culminated in the 1945–1946 Nuremberg trials. It examines the roles of the European governments-in-exile and the UN War Crimes Commission as well as the major powers in this process and the numerous conflicts among them that precluded agreement while the war was in progress.

18:987   Kuklick, Bruce. *American Policy and the Division of Germany: The Clash with Russia over Reparations.* Ithaca: Cornell University Press, 1972. This is a carefully reasoned account of the German reparations issue and its role in the coming of the cold war. The book also offers an excellent early analysis of multilateralism as the key to the economic origins of American-Soviet antagonisms in the mid-1940s, and of the internecine struggle among the State, War, and Treasury Departments that contributed to the partition of Germany and the subsequent hostile division of Europe.

18:988   _____. "The Genesis of the European Advisory Commission." *Journal of Contemporary History* 4 (October 1969): 189–201. The EAC was established in 1943 to provide planning for the last phases of the war and thereafter. This study is important because negotiations for the EAC's organization revealed the distrust between Russia and the west and bared the long-range objectives of each of the Big Three.

18:989 _____. "A Historian's Perspective: American Appeasement of Germany, 1944–1945." *Prologue* 8 (Winter 1976): 237–40. U.S. policy had long been to integrate Germany into the European economic community, on the premise that an economically strong Germany was vital to the good health of the continent. This policy, begun during the Weimar Republic, was continued following World War II.

18:990 Mosely, Philip E. "Dismemberment of Germany: The Allied Negotiations from Yalta to Potsdam." *Foreign Affairs* 28 (April 1950): 487–98. An early account of allied discussions on the dismemberment of Germany, it is still valuable because the author served on a State Department planning staff and then with the U.S. delegation on the European Advisory Commission (1944–1945).

18:991 _____. *The Kremlin and World Politics: Studies in Soviet Policy and Action.* New York: Vintage Books, 1960. This volume contains an inside account of the European Advisory Commission and remains useful for that reason.

18:992 _____. "The Occupation of Germany: New Light on How the Zones Were Drawn." *Foreign Affairs* 28 (July 1950): 580–604. Mosely gives a valuable account, with personal insight, on the drawing of lines of occupation: he was a member of the working Security Committee, an interdepartmental committee of the State, War and Navy Departments established to coordinate U.S. members of the European Advisory Commission and, later, as political adviser designated by the State Department to be U.S. member of the European Advisory Commission.

18:993 Nelson, Daniel J. *Wartime Origins of the Berlin Dilemma.* University: University of Alabama Press, 1978. This important book traces the wartime negotiations that led to situations resulting in the series of confrontations over Berlin in later years. Basically a history of the European Advisory Commission, it demonstrates that the Big Four shackled the commission's work.

18:994 Schlauch, Wolfgang. "American Policy towards Germany, 1945." *Journal of Contemporary History* 5 (October 1970): 113–28. Certain American leaders concluded during the war that restoring a stable Europe, potent enough to prevent communism from spreading into Western Europe, depended largely on the rapid rehabilitation of Germany.

18:995 Sharp, Tony. *The Wartime Alliance and the Zonal Division of Germany.* Oxford: Clarendon Press, 1975. Sharp claims that current military strategy and western and Soviet images of the other side's postwar power and intentions affected discussions of the German zonal issues. He brings British sources to bear on his analysis.

18:996 Smith, Bradley F. *The Road to Nuremberg.* New York: Basic Books, 1981. Smith focuses on the origins and evolution of U.S. plans in 1944–1945 for German war crimes trials, which he labels a "conspiracy-criminal organization" model that emerged as an alternative to the Morgenthau Plan. See also his companion volume of primary sources, *The American Road to Nuremberg: The Documentary Record, 1944–1945* (Stanford, CA: Hoover Institution Press, 1982).

18:997 Snell, John L. *Wartime Origins of the East-West Dilemma over Germany.* New Orleans: Hauser Press, 1959. Snell views the international dilemma over Germany in the late 1950s as stemming from the wartime policy of postponement. Germany became the focal point of several nonrelated problems, including nationalism versus internationalism and Soviet territorial expansion versus American economic and cultural expansion.

18:998 Stein, Harold, ed. *American Civil-Military Decisions: A Book of Case Studies.* University: University of Alabama Press, 1963. Numerous essays in this collection deal with specific civil-military issues before, during, and after World War II. For the war years, see especially Robert J. Quinlan, "The Italian Armistice" (203–310), and Paul Y. Hammond, "Directives for the Occupation of Germany: The Washington Controversy" (311–464). Also pertinent are Marvin D. Bernstein and Francis L. Loewenheim, "Aid to Russia: The First Year" (97–152), and Quinlan, "The United States Fleet: Diplomacy, Strategy and the Allocation of Ships (1940–1941)" (153–202).

COLD WAR ORIGINS

18:999   Aga Rossi, Elena. "Roosevelt's European Policy and the Origins of the Cold War: A Reevaluation." *Telos* 96 (Summer 1993): 65–85. The author maintains that both orthodox and revisionist historians incorrectly overemphasize Soviet-American relations and the last months of the war, ignoring Roosevelt's views and behavior toward Europe throughout the war. Nevertheless, her conclusions echo those of orthodox critics: that Roosevelt never understood the true nature of the Soviet Union and the resultant impossibility of the U.S.-Soviet collaboration so central to his postwar plans.

18:1000   Aronsen, Lawrence, and Martin Kitchen. *The Origins of the Cold War in Comparative Perspective: American, British, and Canadian Relations with the Soviet Union, 1941–48.* New York: St. Martin's Press, 1988. In separate chapters, the authors analyze and compare U.S., British, and Canadian relations with the Soviet Union from the inception of the Grand Alliance to the formation of NATO, concluding that the cold war was not inevitable and that the policies of all three nations toward the Soviets were "tentative, uncertain, contradictory, ideologically blinkered, and frequently selfish."

18:1001   Backer, John H. *The Decision to Divide Germany: American Foreign Policy in Transition.* Durham, NC: Duke University Press, 1978. American-Soviet cooperation in Germany failed not because of Soviet aggression or American capitalist imperialism, Backer maintains, but because of a multiplicity of factors: failure of leadership, American public desire to end the war and leave Europe, and mistrust and intransigence on both sides.

18:1002   Bland, Larry I. "Averell Harriman, the Russians and the Origins of the Cold War in Europe, 1943–45." *Australian Journal of Politics and History* 23 (December 1977): 403–16. This is an insightful analysis of Harriman's views of Stalin and how to deal with the Soviets, which were generally ignored by Roosevelt and the State Department. Bland emphasizes how wartime events modified Harriman's attitudes toward the end of the war when his advice was more likely to be accepted in Washington.

18:1003   Chandler, Harriette L. "The Transition to

Cold Warrior: The Evolution of W. Averell Harriman's Assessment of the U.S.S.R.'s Polish Policy, October 1943 — Warsaw Uprising." *East European Quarterly* 10 (Summer 1976): 229–46. Although Harriman helped develop the philosophical foundations of the containment policy, he approached his job as ambassador to the USSR with considerable understanding and acceptance of Soviet foreign policy goals. His position was generally conciliatory until the Soviet refusal to aid the beleaguered Poles in the Warsaw uprising.

18:1004   Deighton, Anne, ed. *Britain and the First Cold War.* New York: St. Martin's Press, 1990. Many of the fifteen articles in this collection deal with British planning and policies during as well as after World War II.

18:1005   Douglas, Roy. *From War to Cold War, 1942–48.* New York: St. Martin's Press, 1981. Douglas blames Churchill more than Roosevelt for refusing to recognize Stalin as a cynical opportunist or use the bargaining power they possessed against him.

18:1006   Gallicchio, Marc S. *The Cold War Begins in Asia: American East Asian Policy and the Fall of the Japanese Empire.* New York: Columbia University Press, 1988. Gallicchio offers a detailed and incisive analysis of U.S. policies in 1945 for Asia in this brief but important study. Major topics addressed include civilian-military disagreements over the U.S. postwar role in Asia, the Truman transition and the Potsdam conference, the atomic bomb, and postwar occupation of Indochina, Korea, and north China.

18:1007   Hammond, Thomas T., ed. *Witnesses to the Origins of the Cold War.* Seattle: University of Washington Press, 1982. This collection consists of recollections of U.S. diplomats and other officials stationed in Eastern or Central European countries in the last years of World War II and first years of the cold war, along with editor Hammond's introduction and conclusions. Represented are George F. Kennan (Soviet Union), Michael B. Petrovich (Yugoslavia), Cyril E. Black (Bulgaria), William H. McNeill (Greece), Cortlandt V. R. Schuyler (Romania), Martin F. Herz (Austria), Louis Mark, Jr. (Hungary), John A. Armitage (Czechoslovakia), Karl Mautner (Germany), and Richard T. Davies (Poland).

18:1008 Kuniholm, Bruce R. *The Origins of the Cold War in the Near East: Great Power Conflict and Diplomacy in Iran, Turkey, and Greece.* Princeton: Princeton University Press, 1980. This important study of cold war origins in the Near East contains substantial information on great power conflict in the area during the war.

18:1009 Larson, Deborah Welch. *Origins of Containment: A Psychological Explanation.* Princeton: Princeton University Press, 1985. Although primarily a work of political science and social psychology for the years 1945–1947, this work contains much valuable information on wartime Soviet-American relations and their deterioration in 1944–1945.

18:1010 Lewis, Julian. *Changing Direction: British Military Planning for Post-War Strategic Defence, 1942–1947.* London: Sherwood, 1988. Based on extensive archival research, this important study analyzes British postwar military planning during and immediately after World War II.

18:1011 Maddox, Robert James. "Truman, Poland, and the Origins of the Cold War." *Presidential Studies Quarterly* 17 (Winter 1987): 27–41. Maddox argues that Truman, like Roosevelt, was willing to accept almost any compromise on Poland that would be acceptable domestically. This absence of American intransigence was best evidenced by Truman's acceptance of a thinly disguised version of a Soviet-backed Warsaw government. Maddox criticizes Kimball ("Naked Reverse Right: Roosevelt, Churchill, and Eastern Europe from TOLSTOY to Yalta—and a Little Beyond," 1985 [18:1080]) for failing to acknowledge FDR's change to a more hardline position toward the Soviet Union in the weeks prior to his death.

18:1012 McCagg, William O. *Stalin Embattled, 1943–1948.* Detroit: Wayne State University Press, 1978. McCagg argues in this highly revisionist and controversial work that Stalin desired postwar cooperation with his wartime allies but that domestic restraints and conflicts within the Communist Party and movement distorted his foreign policy at war's end.

18:1013 Messer, Robert L. *The End of an Alliance: James F. Byrnes, Roosevelt, Truman, and the Origins of the Cold War.* Chapel Hill: University of North Carolina Press, 1982. Messer makes use of then newly discovered and recently declassified documents to clarify the complex relationships among Byrnes, Roosevelt, and Truman and their impact on Soviet-American relations. Approximately half of the volume focuses on the period from Yalta through Potsdam.

18:1014 Miscamble, Wilson D. "Anthony Eden and the Truman-Molotov Conversations, April 1945." *Diplomatic History* 2 (Spring 1978): 167–80. The Truman-Molotov conversation of April 23, 1945, did not indicate a reversal of America's wartime policy of cooperation with the USSR. At Eden's instigation, President Truman, who had discussed questions of general policy with Molotov in the scheduled meeting the previous day, intended the famous "dressing down" to refer to the Polish question only.

18:1015 Poole, Walter S. "From Conciliation to Containment: The Joint Chiefs of Staff and the Coming of the Cold War, 1945–1946." *Military Affairs* 42 (February 1978): 12–16. At first the JCS saw the United States simply mediating Anglo-Soviet quarrels but gradually came to see it as the prime mover in stopping Soviet aggression. By late 1945, the author argues, the JCS had turned anti-Soviet, but their recommendations then remained defensive in nature, in reaction to perceived Soviet threats.

18:1016 Reynolds, David. "The 'Big Three' and the Division of Europe, 1945–48: An Overview." *Diplomacy & Statecraft* 1 (July 1990): 111–36. This extended review of new works focuses on all three allies' hope for postwar cooperation and why each interpreted, or misinterpreted, the actions of the others as hostile. Reynolds emphasizes the roles of ideology and the "lessons" each drew from recent history as well as the intractability of the German problem and the new U.S. concern with the European balance of power.

18:1017 Rose, Lisle A. *After Yalta.* New York: Scribner, 1973. This monograph maintains that U.S. foreign policy in Truman's first months was marked by vacillation and confusion on the part of American policymakers in the face of Soviet belligerence. Rose sees the atomic bomb, especially, as the primary cause of the Soviet-American break, but denies that Washington officials devised a coherent strategy of atomic diplomacy for the purpose of challenging the Russians.

18:1018 _____. *The Coming of the American Age, 1945–1946. Vol. 1: Dubious Victory: The United States and the End of World War II.* Kent, OH: Kent State University Press, 1973. A narrative of Soviet-American relations from Truman's succession to Hiroshima, this book elaborates certain points put forth in the author's *After Yalta* (1973) (18:1017). He focuses on the influence of Congress and public opinion on policy, the administration's diplomatic and military calculations on Europe, its preoccupation with the war in the Far East, and how acquisition and use of the atomic bomb dissipated what little trust existed between the United States and the Soviet Union. (A volume 2 has never been published.)

18:1019 Rothwell, Victor. *Britain and the Cold War, 1941–1947.* London: Jonathan Cape, 1982. Rothwell examines the British role in the origins of the cold war on the basis of detailed research in Foreign Office records. Approximately half of the volume covers the World War II years, during which, the author maintains, British fears of a resurgent Germany led to a strong desire for postwar cooperation rather than conflict with the Soviets.

18:1020 Smith, Arthur L., Jr. *Churchill's German Army: Wartime Strategy and Cold War Politics, 1943–1947.* Beverly Hills, CA: Sage Publications, 1977. Smith contends that Britain initiated the cold war against the Soviet Union and did so before World War II ended. Churchill allowed German army units that should have surrendered to the Soviets to surrender instead to the British and to keep their units intact in the event of a confrontation with the Soviets. Furthermore, the British kept a sizable portion of the units long after the war was over.

18:1021 Smith, Denis. *Diplomacy of Fear: Canada and the Cold War, 1941–1948.* Toronto: University of Toronto Press, 1988. Nearly half of this volume deals with the World War II years. The author sees the 1946 revelation of Soviet espionage as pivotal in the anti-Soviet transformation of Canadian attitudes toward its wartime ally.

18:1022 Warner, Geoffrey. "The United States and the Origins of the Cold War." *International Affairs* 46 (July 1970): 529–44. This review of 1945 volumes of *Foreign Relations of the United States* provides a useful introduction to the series. It examines the beginnings of Russo-American antagonism over policy, primarily in Europe, but also in Asia and Latin America.

18:1023 Westad, Odd Arne. *Cold War and Revolution: Soviet-American Rivalry and the Origins of the Chinese Civil War, 1944–1946.* New York: Columbia University Press, 1993. Making extensive use of Chinese as well as U.S. archival material, Westad focuses on both the impact of Chinese political developments on the Soviet-American rivalry and the impact of that rivalry on the struggle for political power in China. Approximately half of this volume deals with events before Japan's surrender.

18:1024 Zubok, Vladislav M., and Constantine Pleshakov. *Inside the Kremlin's Cold War: From Stalin to Khrushchev.* Cambridge, MA: Harvard University Press, 1996. Making use of recently released Soviet documents, these two Russian historians reinterpret Soviet foreign policy. They maintain that Stalin fused ideology with power politics to create a "revolutionary-imperial paradigm" that was at odds with a wartime desire for pragmatic cooperation with his allies. The choice of policies depended on events and personalities.

POSTWAR NATIONAL SECURITY

18:1025 Davis, Vincent. *Postwar Defense Policy and the U.S. Navy, 1943–1946.* Chapel Hill: University of North Carolina Press, 1966. Davis analyzes navy plans for the postwar world and finds intra- as well as interservice rivalry focusing on the wartime rise of naval airpower.

18:1026 Foltos, Lester J. "The New Pacific Barrier: America's Search for Security in the Pacific, 1945–47." *Diplomatic History* 13 (Summer 1989): 317–42. This article analyzes the genesis and development of plans for a series of U.S. air and naval bases to guarantee the United States postwar control of the Pacific.

18:1027 Sherry, Michael S. *Preparing for the Next War: American Plans for Postwar Defense, 1941–45.* New Haven: Yale University Press, 1977. With a focus on the army, Sherry carefully examines wartime planning for postwar military and national security policies. He argues that the sense of national insecurity created by the Axis threat generated a strong preparedness movement and a preoccupation with military strength that antedated the cold war.

18:1028 Smith, Perry McCoy. *The Air Force Plans for Peace, 1943–1945*. Baltimore: Johns Hopkins Press, 1970. Smith traces wartime planning within the army air forces for the postwar world. As expected, such planning noted numerous potential threats, including the Soviet Union, and emphasized strong airpower through an independent air force as the solution.

18:1029 Watt, Donald Cameron. "Every War Must End: War-Time Planning for Post-War Security, in Britain and America in the Wars of 1914–18 and 1939–45: The Roles of Historical Example and of Professional Historians." *Transactions of the Royal Historical Society* 5th ser. 28 (1978): 159–73. Watt in this 1977 conference paper compares the World War I and World War II British and American use of historians and historical examples in planning the postwar peace. He concludes that the British were far more sophisticated and successful.

U.S. and Allied Relations with Other Countries and Areas

POLAND

18:1030 Abarinov, Vladimir. *The Murderers of Katy'n.* New York: Hippocrene Books, 1993. A special correspondent for the weekly *Literaturnaya Gazeta,* the author was quite active in researching and exposing this infamous "blank spot" in Soviet history. This volume is a collection of his findings and experiences and was first published in Russia in early 1991. Foreword and chronology by Iwo Cyprian Pogonowski.

18:1031 Cable, John N. "Vandenberg: The Polish Question and Polish Americans, 1944–1948." *Michigan History* 57 (Winter 1973): 296–310. Michigan's

Republican senator Arthur H. Vandenberg, best remembered for his strong bipartisanship as World War II ended and the cold war began, was only moderately bipartisan on the Polish issue. Responding sympathetically to his anticommunist, Polish-American constituency, he articulated and championed the Polish cause at the national level.

18:1032 Garrett, Crister S. "Death and Politics: The Katyn Forest Massacre and American Foreign Policy." *East European Quarterly* 20 (Winter 1986): 429–46. The Roosevelt administration consistently downplayed the significance of the event in the interest of maintaining the alliance with the Soviet Union and avoiding domestic political controversy; the administration also took extraordinary steps to ensure that any discussion of Katyn sympathetic to the Polish position was excluded from the public domain.

18:1033 Hammersmith, Jack L. "Franklin Roosevelt, the Polish Question, and the Election of 1944." *Mid-America* 59 (January 1977): 5–17. Since the Republicans made major gains in the 1942 congressional elections, in part by concentrating on ethnic minorities, FDR and the Democrats took special care in 1944 to woo Polish-Americans. Roosevelt avoided the Polish-Russian question and successfully appealed to Polish-Americans' special interests.

18:1034 _____. "The U.S. Office of War Information (OWI) and the Polish Question, 1943–1945." *Polish Review* 19 (February 1974): 67–76. This essay shows how the Office of War Information's overseas branch disseminated propaganda while trying to avoid creating friction between Poland and the USSR.

18:1035 Kacewicz, George V. *Great Britain, the Soviet Union, and the Polish Government in Exile (1939–1945).* Boston: Martinus Nijhoff, 1979. The author is sharply critical of what he considers Anglo-American ignorance and inappropriate diplomacy vis-à-vis Poland and the Soviet Union during World War II, to Poland's disadvantage. For a wider scope, see also J. Lee Ready, *Forgotten Allies: The Military Contribution of the Colonies, Exiled Governments, and Lesser Powers to the Allied Victory in World War II,* 2 vols. (Jefferson, NC: McFarland, 1985).

18:1036 King, F. P. "British Policy and the Warsaw

Rising." *Journal of European Studies* 4 (March 1974): 1–18. King surveys the changes in interallied relations occasioned by the Warsaw uprising in the autumn of 1944.

18:1037 Lebedeva, Nataliya. "The Katyn Tragedy." *International Affairs (Moscow)* 6 (June 1990): 98–115, 144. Based on previously classified Soviet documents, this article by a Soviet scholar first made clear that Stalin's secret police had indeed been responsible for the wartime massacres of Polish officers.

18:1038 Lukas, Richard C. "The Big Three and the Warsaw Uprising." *Military Affairs* 39 (October 1975): 129–34. Lukas discusses the impact of the 1944 Warsaw uprising on the Big Three and analyzes the policies each power pursued during the crisis. It nearly ruptured the alliance and may well have been the starting point of the cold war.

18:1039 _____. *The Strange Allies, the United States and Poland, 1941–1945.* Knoxville: University of Tennessee Press, 1978. This volume is better researched and less biased than its predecessor, Rozek, *Allied Wartime Diplomacy: A Pattern in Poland* (1958) (18:1046), but still highly sympathetic toward the Polish government-in-exile and condemnatory of U.S. behavior vis-à-vis Poland and the Soviet Union. In addition to the standard diplomatic history, it includes a detailed study of Polish-American reactions to U.S. policy and analyzes the relationships among policy, public opinion, and the press.

18:1040 Mikolajczyk, Stanislaw. *The Rape of Poland: Pattern of Soviet Aggression.* New York: Whittlesey House, 1948. Reprint 1972 (Greenwood Press). The prime minister of the Polish government in London (1943–1945) gives his view of the Polish problem in the last years of the war. Mikolajczyk criticizes Roosevelt for misleading Polish leaders and praises Churchill for attempting to aid them. He believes the western allies sold out Poland at Yalta.

18:1041 Orzell, Laurence J. "A 'Painful Problem': Poland in Allied Diplomacy, February-July, 1945." *Mid-America* 59 (October 1977): 147–70. The future of Poland seriously affected allied diplomacy in the winter and spring of 1945; differences among the United States, Britain, and the USSR "created and maintained an atmosphere of distrust and suspicion" that eventually led to the cold war.

18:1042 _____. "Poland and Russia, July 1941–April 1943: The 'Impossible' Alliance." *Polish Review* 21 (November 1976): 35–58. Orzell examines wartime foreign relations between the Polish exile government in London and the USSR (1941–1943), their tenuous diplomatic ties, and acts of Soviet aggression, which led to the termination of diplomatic relations in 1943.

18:1043 Paul, Allen. *Katy'n: The Untold Story of Stalin's Polish Massacre.* New York: Charles Scribner's Sons, 1991. This volume was published soon after the 1990 Soviet admission of responsibility for the Katyn Forest massacre. It focuses not only on the event itself but the broader Stalinist effort to Sovietize Poland and Anglo-American acquiescence. Paul makes use of extensive personal interviews with surviving Polish family members as well as recently released records of the 1951–1952 congressional committee investigating the episode.

18:1044 Polonsky, Antony, ed. *The Great Powers and the Polish Question, 1941–45: A Documentary Study in Cold War Origins.* London: Orbis Books, 1976. This compilation consists of 149 documents, taken from unpublished as well as published collections and covering August 1939 to August 1945, along with a lengthy editorial introduction.

18:1045 Prazmowska, Anita J. *Britain and Poland, 1939–1943: The Betrayed Ally.* New York: Cambridge University Press, 1995. This detailed study focuses on why the Polish government-in-exile failed to obtain a British commitment to Poland's prewar boundaries, concluding that this resulted from incorrect Polish diplomatic and military perceptions as well as British wartime priorities vis-à-vis the Soviet Union.

18:1046 Rozek, Edward J. *Allied Wartime Diplomacy: A Pattern in Poland.* New York: Wiley, 1958. This early work examines British and American diplomatic maneuvering (1939–1947) and subsequent agreements with the Soviet Union concerning postwar Poland. Rozek is highly critical of the allies, claiming that their unwillingness to look beyond the defeat of Germany and general diplomatic bungling led to the sacrifice of Poland.

18:1047 Ryan, Henry Butterfield. "Anglo-American Relations during the Polish Crisis in 1945: A Study of British Efforts to Shape American Policy toward the Soviet Union." *Australian Journal of Politics and History* 30 (March 1984): 69–84. Ryan makes extensive use of British archival documents in tracing British efforts, motivated in part by pending elections in the United Kingdom, to toughen U.S. policy toward the Soviet Union over Poland between the Yalta and Potsdam conferences. He concludes that London did succeed in prodding Washington into a tougher stance than it would have otherwise taken, but not nearly enough to satisfy Churchill and his associates.

18:1048 Sadler, Charles. "'Pro-Soviet Polish-Americans': Oskar Lange and Russia's Friends in the Polonia, 1941–1945." *Polish Review* 22 (December 1977): 25–39. Lange emerged from the pro-Soviet faction of American Poles to become an articulate statesman of its beliefs. Later he renounced the U.S. citizenship he had received in 1943 to become the first ambassador to the United States from the postwar Polish government.

18:1049 Terry, Sarah Meiklejohn. "The Oder-Neisse Line Revisited: Sikorski's Program for Poland's Postwar Western Boundary, 1939–42." *East Central Europe* 5, no. 1 (1978): 39–68. General Wladyslaw Sikorski's memorandum of December 4, 1942, to President Roosevelt, giving his views about postwar Poland, refutes the conventional wisdom that the Oder-Neisse line was the invention of the Soviets.

18:1050 _____. *Poland's Place in Europe: General Sikorski and the Origin of the Oder-Neisse Line, 1939–1943.* Princeton: Princeton University Press, 1983. Terry refutes the conventional wisdom on the Anglo-Soviet-American origins of Poland's postwar western boundary, arguing that the concept originated with the London Poles and that Prime Minister Sikorski proposed it within the framework of an overall reorientation of Poland's international posture based on Polish-Soviet reconciliation and creation of a Central European federation.

18:1051 Thackrah, John Richard. "Aspects of American and British Policy towards Poland from the Yalta to the Potsdam Conferences, 1945." *Polish Review* 21 (November 1976): 3–34. Examining U.S. and British policy toward Poland in the first half of 1945, Thack-

rah concludes that Churchill, Roosevelt, and their advisers encouraged Stalin's uncompromising behavior by acquiescing in his acts and holding negative attitudes toward the Polish government-in-exile.

18:1052 White, Mark J. "Harry Truman, the Polish Question, and the Significance of FDR's Death for American Diplomacy." *Maryland Historian* 23 (Fall-Winter 1992): 29–48. White examines the allied controversy over the Polish government in early 1945 to assess the contention that Roosevelt's death resulted in a dramatic shift in U.S. policy from cooperation to confrontation with the Soviet Union. He concludes that Truman did not completely reverse or continue Roosevelt's policy but vacillated between the two alternatives.

ITALY

18:1053 Alvarez, David J. "The Vatican and the War in the Far East, 1941–1943." *Historian* 40 (May 1978): 508–23. This essay examines the role of papal diplomacy in East Asia and analyzes the U.S. and British responses to the diplomatic meetings between the Holy See and Japan.

18:1054 Miller, James Edward. "The Politics of Relief: The Roosevelt Administration and the Reconstruction of Italy, 1943–44." *Prologue* 13 (Fall 1981): 193– 208. In 1944, Roosevelt courted Italian-American voters with promises of concessions to Italy. These led to clashes with Britain and "decisively restructured" domestic Italian-American politics. The article reveals internal political divisions within the Italian-American community and shows the effects of the relationship between domestic and foreign policies.

18:1055 _____. "The Search for Stability: An Interpretation of American Foreign Policy in Italy: 1943–1946." *Journal of Italian History* 1 (Autumn 1978): 246–86. U.S. policy toward Italy was "remarkably constant": political democratization, diminution of British and Soviet influence, and stopgap economic aid. By 1947, the United States had achieved its political goals, but deep-rooted Italian economic problems demanded that long-term economic support have a higher priority.

18:1056 _____. *The United States and Italy,*

1940–1950: The Politics and Diplomacy of Stabilization. Chapel Hill: University of North Carolina Press, 1986. More than one-half of this volume covers U.S.-Italian relations in the war years. Miller reconstructs the evolution of U.S. policy from its origins in dialogues involving Italian-Americans, antifascist exiles, the U.S. government, the Vatican, and the British government. The result was a distinctively American political and economic reconstruction effort that hinged on creating a middle-class democracy in Italy.

SPAIN

18:1057 Beaulac, Willard L. *Franco: Silent Ally in World War II.* Carbondale: Southern Illinois University Press, 1986. Beaulac, counselor at the U.S. embassy in Spain from May 1941 to June 1944, focuses on such issues and personalities as Spanish foreign policy, Franco, and Sir Samuel Hoare. The author generally praises allied policy for adapting to Franco's precarious position and enabling him to stay out of the war.

18:1058 Cortada, James W. "Spain and the Second World War: The Laurel Incident." *Journal of Contemporary History* 5 (October 1970): 65–75. This article focuses on U.S. anger at Madrid for recognizing the collaborationist Philippine government of Jose P. Laurel and the Anglo-U.S. efforts in 1943–1944 to persuade Franco to embargo the sale of wolfram to Germany.

18:1059 _____. *United States–Spanish Relations, Wolfram and World War II.* Barcelona: Manuel Pareja, 1971. This volume expands the analysis Cortada first provided in his 1970 article ("Spain and the Second World War: The Laurel Incident" [18:1058]) on Anglo-American efforts to halt Spanish sales of tungsten ore (wolfram) to Germany, where it was needed by the munitions industry. He emphasizes successful Spanish exploitation of Anglo-American differences, criticizes Washington's diplomatic insensitivity, and praises the more subtle approach of the British. Written before the opening of significant archival records, the work is based primarily on published U.S., British, and Spanish primary sources.

18:1060 Feis, Herbert. *The Spanish Story: Franco and the Nations at War.* New York: Alfred A. Knopf, 1948. Feis's interpretive narration of the U.S. relationship to Franco's Spain (1939–1941) emphasizes how crucial the dealings with Spain were in keeping Hitler from access to the Mediterranean Sea at Gibraltar.

GREECE

18:1061 Frazier, Robert. *Anglo-American Relations with Greece: The Coming of the Cold War, 1942–47.* New York: St. Martin's Press, 1991. Frazier examines the competing policies toward Greece pursued by the United States and the United Kingdom during World War II, noting the problems created by both Churchill and Roosevelt. Half of the book focuses on the postwar period, assessing the reasons behind the Anglo-American policy changes announced in the Truman Doctrine, which Frazier argues marked the start of the cold war.

18:1062 Iatrides, John O. *Revolt in Athens: The Greek Communist "Second Round," 1944–1945.* Princeton: Princeton University Press, 1972. This book provides a balanced account of the bloody military conflict that flared up between the Greek resistance forces and British troops in the winter of 1944–1945. The fighting did not result from an attempted communist coup, but from the disagreements and suspicions that emerged in the crucible of wartime unrest. The book provides a background to the American 1947 decision to intervene.

18:1063 Karalekas, Anne. *Britain, the United States, and Greece, 1942–1945.* New York: Garland Publishing, 1988. This published dissertation emphasizes the internal bureaucratic conflicts within the British and U.S. governments over appropriate policies as well as the conflicts among different Greek factions.

18:1064 Wittner, Lawrence S. *American Intervention in Greece, 1943–1949.* New York: Columbia University Press, 1982. Only the first chapter of this critique of U.S. policy in Greece covers the war years. Wittner concludes that Roosevelt shared Churchill's attachment to the Greek monarchy, that the State Department and OSS were more critical of British policy, but that behind Anglo-American tactical differences stood the shared goal of containing the Greek left. See also the author's "American Policy toward Greece during World War II" (1979) (18:1065).

18:1065 _____. "American Policy toward Greece during World War II." *Diplomatic History* 3 (Spring 1979): 129–49. In this overview of America's wartime Greek policy, the author contends that, despite State Department protests, Roosevelt supported Britain's policy of containing the Greek left and maintaining the status quo.

18:1066 Woodhouse, C. M. *The Struggle for Greece, 1941–1949.* London: Hart-Davis, MacGibbon, 1976. Reprint 1979 (Beckman/Esanau). A distillation of much scholarship in the 1970s as well as the author's personal experience as the top British agent in wartime Greece, this work marked the emergence of a new and important synthesis on the Greek civil war and its international dimensions.

18:1067 Xydis, Stephen G. "America, Britain and the USSR in the Greek Arena, 1944–1947." *Political Science Quarterly* 78 (December 1963): 581–96. This early work examines the progression of events during and after World War II that led the United States toward the decision to assist the Greek government in 1947. The author states that Greece served as a testing ground for allied cooperation and experiments.

YUGOSLAVIA

18:1068 De Santis, Hugh. "In Search of Yugoslavia: Anglo-American Policy and Policy-Making, 1943–45." *Journal of Contemporary History* 16 (July 1981): 541–63. De Santis cogently surveys the dynamic and complex American and British attitudes and policies toward Yugoslav partisans during World War II and the process by which Tito rose to prominence. Anglo-American priorities diverged throughout the war until concerns about the Soviet Union brought the two countries together in confronting communism in Yugoslavia.

18:1069 Dinardo, Richard S. "Glimpse of an Old World Order? Reconsidering the Trieste Crisis of 1945." *Diplomatic History* 21 (Summer 1997):

365–81. The Trieste crisis did not originate in the early cold war. British and U.S. aims differed, the Soviets refused to back Tito, and the crisis was resolved by traditional great power diplomacy.

18:1070 Ford, Kirk, Jr. *OSS and the Yugoslav Resistance, 1943–1945.* College Station: Texas A&M University Press, 1992. This volume focuses on the operational aspects of OSS work in Yugoslavia and in the process covers conflicts with the British SOE over political issues, with the different Yugoslav resistance groups, and with the Soviets. It is based on OSS field intelligence reports as well as correspondence and interviews with participants and relevant published sources. The author rejects the standard, polarized view of Mihailovich as collaborator and Tito as liberator.

18:1071 Rabel, Roberto G. *Between East and West: Trieste, the United States, and the Cold War, 1941–1954.* Durham, NC: Duke University Press, 1988. This volume constitutes the most detailed and comprehensive examination of the Trieste issue and its role in the origins and development of the cold war.

18:1072 _____. "Prologue to Containment: The Truman Administration's Response to the Trieste Crisis of May 1945." *Diplomatic History* 10 (Spring 1986): 141–60. Rabel's thesis is in his title. See also his *Between East and West: Trieste, the United States, and the Cold War, 1941–1954* (1988) (18:1071).

18:1073 Roberts, Walter R. *Tito, Mihailovic and the Allies, 1941–1945.* New Brunswick: Rutgers University Press, 1973. This volume shows British and American differences toward Yugoslav warring factions and the ultimate decisions to aid Tito. Tito's independent attitude toward the USSR was based in part on his cordial relations with western liaison officers.

18:1074 Wheeler, Mark C. *Britain and the War for Yugoslavia, 1940–1943.* Boulder: East European Monographs, 1980. Using then recently declassified British documents, Wheeler provides a clear development of British wartime policy.

EASTERN EUROPE
IN GENERAL

18:1075 Barker, Elisabeth. *British Policy in South-East Europe in the Second World War.* New York: Barnes and Noble, 1976. Although this volume concentrates on British policy, it outlines the differences in Anglo-American attitudes and policies during the war.

18:1076 Boll, Michael M. "U.S. Plans for a Postwar Pro-Western Bulgaria: A Little-Known Wartime Initiative in Eastern Europe." *Diplomatic History* 7 (Spring 1983): 117–38. Boll counters the view of American wartime policy toward Eastern Europe as largely passive with a detailed examination of a wartime plan to detach Bulgaria from the Axis.

18:1077 Deakin, William, Elisabeth Barker, and Jonathan Chadwick, eds. *British Political and Military Strategy in Central, Eastern, and Southern Europe in 1944.* New York: St. Martin's Press, 1988. This volume originated in a 1984 scholarly conference on World War II. Emphasizing British and allied politico-military issues, the 1944 Quebec and Moscow conferences, resistance movements, and individual countries in the area, its most pertinent essays for U.S. diplomatic historians are Barker, "Problems of the Alliance: Misconceptions and Misunderstandings" (40–53); Keith Sainsbury, "Central and Eastern Europe at the Quebec Conference" (54–66); and K. G. M. Ross, "The Moscow Conference of October 1944 (Tolstoy)" (67–77).

18:1078 Garson, Robert A. "The Atlantic Alliance, Eastern Europe and the Origins of the Cold War." In *Contrast and Connection: Bicentennial Essays in Anglo-American History,* ed. H. C. Allen and Roger Thompson, 296–320. Athens, OH: Ohio University Press, 1976. Fundamentally different British and American ideas about the postwar world, the nature of the Soviet Union, and the importance of Eastern Europe precluded a coherent Anglo-American approach to Soviet territorial demands. This encouraged Stalin to inflate and extend his demands, thereby bringing about disillusionment and confrontation.

18:1079 Keyserlingk, Robert H. *Austria in World War II: An Anglo-American Dilemma.* Kingston, Ontario: McGill-Queen's University Press, 1988. Based on multiarchival research, this work rejects the wartime and postwar Anglo-American public statements on Austria as World War II and cold war propaganda not reflecting actual beliefs or policies. The Anglo-American allies did not view Austria as a victim of Nazi aggression and were not committed to reestablishing what they considered a fragile and unstable Austrian independence. They hoped instead to fit postwar Austria into a larger, federative structure of Danubian states. Appendices reproduce numerous 1938–1945 British and U.S. documents on the issue.

18:1080 Kimball, Warren F. "Naked Reverse Right: Roosevelt, Churchill, and Eastern Europe from TOLSTOY to Yalta—and a Little Beyond." *Diplomatic History* 9 (Winter 1985): 1–24. The 1944 Churchill-Stalin summit meeting in Moscow established an implicit spheres-of-influence deal for all of Eastern Europe, including Poland, which Roosevelt accepted. Churchill later reversed himself to protect his public image.

18:1081 Kovrig, Bennett. *The Myth of Liberation: East-Central Europe in U.S. Diplomacy and Politics since 1941.* Baltimore: Johns Hopkins University Press, 1973. From 1941 to 1973, U.S. policies toward East-Central Europe had as a common denominator an interest in (but not necessarily a commitment to) the area's liberation. At no time, though, was the United States able to translate its declarations in favor of liberation into operational policies.

18:1082 Lundestad, Geir. *The American Non-Policy towards Eastern Europe, 1943–1947: Universalism in an Area Not of Essential Interest to the United States.* New York: Humanities Press, 1975. Eastern Europe was never a high priority for the United States, Lundestad maintains, and Washington never developed a real policy toward it.

18:1083 Mark, Eduard M. "Charles E. Bohlen and the Acceptable Limits of Soviet Hegemony in Eastern Europe: A Memorandum of 18 October 1945." *Diplomatic History* 3 (Spring 1979): 201–13. As outlined by Bohlen and proclaimed by Secretary of State Byrnes in October 1945, the United States did not categorically oppose spheres of influence in Eastern Europe at the end of the war. Officials distinguished between wholly closed or "exclusive" spheres, which they did oppose, and "open" spheres that limited great power control to foreign affairs, which they did not. The key distinction was whether great power intervention extended to the internal affairs of nations within the sphere.

18:1084 Saiu, Liliana. *The Great Powers and Rumania, 1944–1946: A Study of the Early Cold War Era.* New York: Columbia University Press for Eastern European Monographs, 1992. Saiu analyzes the complex interactions of allied and German policies toward Romania and their Romanian context for the dynamic period between August 1944 and February 1947. She thinks the "extraordinary self-confidence" of American policymakers and their lack of urgency contributed to Soviet success in dominating Romania.

SOUTHEAST ASIA

18:1085 Aldrich, Richard J. "A Question of Expediency: Britain, the United States and Thailand, 1941–42." *Journal of Southeast Asian Studies* 19 (September 1988): 209–44. Most of this article concerns the opportunist and expedient attempts of the United States and the United Kingdom to maneuver Thailand and its prime minister, Field Marshal Luang Phibun Songkhram, to meet the Japanese threat as well as Phibun's own counterefforts.

18:1086 Benda, Harry J. *The Crescent and the Rising Sun: Indonesian Islam under the Japanese Occupation, 1942–1945.* The Hague: W. Van Hoeve, 1958. Benda in this early work sees Japanese occupation as stimulating Indonesian nationalism, an issue in postwar affairs.

18:1087 Drachman, Edward R. *United States Policy toward Vietnam, 1940–1945.* Rutherford, NJ: Fairleigh Dickinson University Press, 1970. Written in the midst of the war in Vietnam and before major document declassification, this early volume looks to the World War II years for the roots of U.S. interest in the area. It finds those roots to lie in 1940–1941 in the strategic significance of Vietnam, then from 1942 to 1945 in Roosevelt's decolonization plans. Drachman's central thesis, however, is that U.S. policy on Vietnam's postwar status was ultimately determined by events in Europe.

18:1088 Gardner, Lloyd C. *Approaching Vietnam: From World War II through Dienbienphu, 1941–*

1954. New York: W. W. Norton and Co., 1988. The first chapter of this volume covers Roosevelt's wartime thinking on French Indochina.

18:1089 Hammer, Ellen J. *The Struggle for Indochina, 1940–1955.* Rev. ed. Stanford, CA: Stanford University Press, 1966. Hammer's detailed account, combining political and military analysis, puts the war in broad international context. The early chapters contain substantial information on the World War II years. Early chapters were published in 1954 as *The Struggle for Indochina* and the last chapter in 1955 as *The Struggle for Indochina Continues.*

18:1090 Hess, Gary R. "Franklin Roosevelt and Indochina." *Journal of American History* 59 (September 1972): 353–68. Hess suggests that Roosevelt's trusteeship plan offered a possible alternative to the thirty years of conflict that followed the war and that it "deserved more thoughtful consideration by the allies and more vigorous advocacy by Roosevelt than it received."

18:1091 _____. *The United States' Emergence as a Southeast Asian Power, 1940–1950.* This useful examination of American policy toward Southeast Asia notes a continuum of U.S. interest in the area but argues that American policymakers generally constructed country policies in the context of their perceptions of the more important needs of Europe and, in the postwar period, Japan, thereby limiting their ability to cope successfully with emergent nationalism in the region. The World War II chapters focus on U.S. plans for decolonization; ensuing conflicts with its British, French, and Dutch allies; and U.S. accommodation to their wishes by war's end (17:998).

18:1092 LaFeber, Walter. "Roosevelt, Churchill, and Indochina: 1942–1945." *American Historical Review* 80 (December 1975): 1277–95. The 1945 reversal of wartime U.S. policy on independence for French Indochina was the work of Roosevelt himself, not Truman. FDR's shift resulted from Chiang Kaishek's weakness and open defiance in late 1944 as well as Churchill's entreaties, de Gaulle's success, and fear of the Soviets. Furthermore, the Joint Chiefs and State Department had never agreed with FDR's plans, and Roosevelt himself had always favored trusteeship, not immediate independence.

18:1093 Liu, Xiaoyuan. "China and the Issue of Postwar Indochina in the Second World War." *Modern Asian Studies* 33 (May 1999): 445–82. The author challenges the conventional view that China did not have an Indochina policy during the war and that it followed U.S. policy. Chiang rejected Roosevelt's trusteeship plans as paternalistic and called instead for unilateral Chinese responsibility in the area as part of his assertion of great power status for China. By late 1944 to early 1945, Chinese military and diplomatic weakness forced him to drop this policy and accept American plans, which at that moment were shifting toward acceptance of French control.

18:1094 Sbrega, John J. "'First Catch Your Hare': Anglo-American Perspectives on Indochina during the Second World War." *Journal of Southeast Asian Studies* 14 (March 1983): 63–78. Sbrega examines the different British and American attitudes toward the postwar status of French Indochina. He notes that the wartime positions of the countries varied and were internally inconsistent, and he criticizes Roosevelt's policy of delaying any decisions until after the war.

18:1095 Thorne, Christopher. "Indochina and Anglo-American Relations, 1942–1945." *Pacific Historical Review* 45 (February 1976): 73–96. Thorne emphasizes the lack of clarity and coherency in both British and U.S. policies.

18:1096 Tønnesson, Stein. *The Vietnamese Revolution of 1945: Roosevelt, Ho Chi Minh, and De Gaulle in a World at War.* Newbury Park, CA: Sage Publications, 1991. Tønnesson argues that allied wartime policy in Indochina created a political power vacuum, which the communist-dominated Vietminh front successfully exploited.

18:1097 Williams, John E. "Siam: A Bone of Contention between Britain and the United States, 1942–46." *Review of International Studies* 8 (July 1982): 187–202. Based primarily on research in British Foreign Office records, this article explores the wartime and immediate postwar Anglo-American difference about whether Thailand should be treated as a Japanese ally (United Kingdom) or an occupied country (United States). The debate reflected conflicting interests and policies in the area and illustrated the ability of Thai diplomats to exploit these differences to gain more lenient peace terms.

BRITISH COMMONWEALTH

Australia

18:1098 Barclay, Glen St. J. "Australia Looks to America: The Wartime Relationship, 1939–1942." Canberra's shocked discovery in mid-1942 that U.S. strategic conceptions differed from its own was intense if not necessarily damaging in its effects. See chapter 17 of this Guide (17:697).

18:1099 Bell, Roger J. "Australian-American Disagreement over the Peace Settlement with Japan, 1944–1946." *Australian Outlook* 30 (August 1976): 238–62. Australian-American disagreements were essentially a continuation of wartime frictions over strategic priorities and consultative relationships. As Japan's defeat grew nearer, Australia's complaints over its marginalized role grew stronger as the United States resisted its desires to participate in the occupation of Japan.

18:1100 _____. "Australian-American Discord: Negotiations for Post-War Bases and Security Arrangements in the Pacific, 1944–1946." *Australian Outlook* 27 (April 1973): 12–33. Bell recounts Australian diplomatic strategy and efforts during the latter part of the war and the early peacetime to maximize its political and military influence in the South Pacific, while simultaneously seeking a regional security relationship with the United States even as it sought to limit its influence in the region. Special attention is given to the negotiations for American basing rights on Manus Island.

18:1101 _____. "Australian-American Relations and Reciprocal Wartime Economic Assistance, 1941–6: An Ambivalent Association." *Australian Economic History Review* 16 (March 1976): 23–49. Although Australia and the United States provided each other with high levels of reciprocal economic aid during the war, they simultaneously attempted to exploit their wartime arrangements for their own national postwar trade and economic benefit.

18:1102 _____. *Unequal Allies: Australian-American Relations and the Pacific War.* Carlton, Victoria: Melbourne University Press, 1977. Bell examines the political, military, and economic relations between Australia and the United States during the war and shows the extent to which the United States treated Australia as a subordinate, rather than an allied, nation.

18:1103 Edwards, Peter G., ed. *Australia through American Eyes, 1935–1945: Observations by American Diplomats.* St. Lucia: University of Queensland Press, 1979. A slim collection of ten documents—ranging from the views of J. Pierrepont Moffat to Nelson T. Johnson—this particular compendium examines how Australia appeared to a significant and highly trained group of U.S. diplomats in a most critical period. This is a good source on the subject.

18:1104 Evatt, Herbert Vere. *Foreign Policy of Australia: Speeches by the Rt. Hon. H. V. Evatt.* Sydney: Angus and Robertson, 1945. In this volume are the foreign policy thoughts of Evatt, minister for external affairs in the Labor Party's federal administration under Prime Ministers John Curtin and Ben Chifley (1941–1949). It is impossible to appreciate the nature of Australian-American wartime relations without first coming to grips with Evatt's policies.

18:1105 Potts, E. Daniel, and Annette Potts. *Yanks Down Under 1941–45: The American Impact on Australia.* New York: Oxford University Press, 1985. Although short on analysis, this useful study of the impact and influence of American military personnel on Australia is studded with information and anecdotes.

18:1106 Robertson, John. *Australia at War, 1939–1945.* Melbourne: Heinemann, 1981. Numerous chapters in this brief survey of Australia's war effort, designed for the general reader and student, contain information on U.S.-Australian relations and collaboration during the war.

18:1107 Thorne, Christopher. "MacArthur, Australia and the British, 1942–1943: The Secret Journal of MacArthur's Liaison Officer. Parts I and II." *Australian Outlook* 29 (April-August 1975): 53–67, 197–210. The entries in the journal suggest that while future relations between Britain and the dominions were unclear, the United States had clearly established itself as an important factor in future Australian affairs.

Canada

18:1108 Cuff, Robert D., and J. L. Granatstein. *The Ties That Bind: Canadian-American Relations in Wartime from the Great War to the Cold War.* 2d ed. Toronto: A. M. Hakkert, 1977. Two of the eight chapters in this volume focus on World War II, one on the 1941 Hyde Park Declaration, the other on Canadian perceptions of the United States during the war. Both originally appeared in Canadian journals. First published in 1975 as *Canadian-American Relations in Wartime.*

18:1109 Diubaldo, Richard J. "The Canol Project in Canadian-American Relations." *Canadian Historical Association Historical Papers* (1977): 178–95. This essay concerns U.S. army plans to construct an impractical and expensive oil pipeline in the Canadian north during the war and ensuing Canadian sovereignty fears and opposition.

18:1110 Douglas, W. A. B. "Democratic Spirit and Purpose: Problems in Canadian-American Relations, 1939–1945." In *Fifty Years of Canada–United States Defense Cooperation: The Road from Ogdensburg,* ed. Joel J. Sokolsky and Joseph T. Jockel, 31–57. Lewiston, NY: Edwin Mellen Press, 1992. Douglas addresses the various wartime debates over Canadian-American military policy (especially unity of command), the Permanent Joint Board on Defense, and the effects of dramatically reduced urgency to North American security concerns after 1942.

18:1111 English, John Alan. "Not an Equilateral Triangle: Canada's Strategic Relationship with the United States and Britain, 1939–1945." In this solid overview of the problems Canada encountered trying to play the "linchpin" between the Americans and the British, English highlights its lack of participation in high-level allied planning, both political and military, and faults Mackenzie King for not establishing a "strategic voice" for Canada before the Arcadia conference (17:703).

18:1112 Granatstein, J. L. *Canada's War: The Politics of the Mackenzie King Government, 1939–1945.* Toronto: Oxford University Press, 1975. In addition to the civilian side of the Canadian war effort, this volume covers Canadian-American relations in considerable detail and is useful for its examples and conclusions.

18:1113 _____. *How Britain's Weakness Forced Canada into the Arms of the United States.* In these 1988 Joanne Goodman lectures, Granatstein disputes the view that the Liberals sold out Canada to the United States. Revising "one of the hoary myths" of Canadian history and historiography, he argues instead that British economic and military weakness and failures forced Canada to turn to its southern neighbor (11:315).

18:1114 Holmes, John W. *The Shaping of Peace: Canada and the Search for World Order, 1943–1957.* Toronto: University of Toronto Press, 1979. This work by a former Canadian diplomat focuses on Canadian wartime planning for the postwar era, most notably but far from exclusively about the United Nations and Anglo-American-Canadian relations.

18:1115 James, R. Warren. *Wartime Economic Cooperation: A Study of Relations between Canada and the United States.* Toronto: Ryerson, 1949. James's comprehensive account of Canadian-American economic relations is solid and reliable, though difficult to read.

18:1116 Perras, Galen Roger. "Canada as a Military Partner: Alliance Politics and the Campaign to Recapture the Aleutian Island of Kiska." *Journal of Military History* 56 (July 1992): 423–54. Perras outlines the workings of alliance politics in this detailed account of how Canadian ground forces came to participate in the recapture of Kiska in the Aleutian Islands—the first time a Canadian unit served under American command.

18:1117 _____. *Franklin Roosevelt and the Origins of the Canadian-American Security Alliance, 1933–1945: Necessary, but Not Necessary Enough.* Perras emphasizes Roosevelt's "pivotal role" in the formation of the Canadian-American alliance. Although the title suggests coverage of the entire war, Perras focuses on 1940–1941, when Roosevelt paid most attention to relations with Canada. Perras covers the debates over unity of command for continental defense and participation in military strategy committees (17:718).

18:1118 Plumptre, Arthur FitzWalter Wynne. *Three Decades of Decision: Canada and the World Monetary System, 1944–75.* Toronto: McClelland and Stewart, 1977. Despite its title, the book gives considerable space to the wartime background of postwar economic arrangements.

18:1119 Stacey, Charles P. *Arms, Men and Governments: The War Policies of Canada, 1939–1945.* Ottawa: Queen's Printer, 1970. Although more than thirty years old, Stacey's book remains one of the fullest accounts of the Canadian war effort in general and Anglo-Canadian-American relations in particular. It relies on American and British as well as Canadian documents, with one part covering Canada and the allied direction of the war and another the wartime military cooperation with the United States.

18:1120 _____. *Canada and the Age of Conflict: A History of Canadian External Policies. Vol. 2: 1921–1948, The Mackenzie King Era.* Toronto: University of Toronto Press, 1981. This volume is particularly useful for Canadian diplomacy during World War II and for the relationship between King and Roosevelt.

Ireland

18:1121 Dwyer, T. Ryle. *Irish Neutrality and the USA, 1939–47.* Dwyer examines the complex interaction among the British, Irish, and American governments and people over wartime Irish neutrality, showing how and why Dublin intervened in U.S. domestic politics. He also defends de Valera's neutrality policy against U.S. Minister David Gray's wartime and postwar charges (17:701). See also his *Strained Relations: Ireland at Peace and the USA at War, 1941–45* (1988) (18:1122).

18:1122 _____. *Strained Relations: Ireland at Peace and the USA at War, 1941–45.* Totowa, NJ: Barnes and Noble, 1988. This account of American-Irish wartime relations—or, more accurately, the lack thereof—is most useful for providing the Irish perspective of events to balance the perceptions of the American ambassador, David Gray. Making use of recently declassified intelligence documents as well as manuscript and archival collections, the author continues the strong defense of de Valera's neutrality policies begun in his *Irish Neutrality and the USA, 1939–47* (1977) (18:1121). Here he emphasizes how pro-allied in general and pro–United States in particular those policies actually were.

18:1123 O'Grady, Joseph P. "A Troubled Triangle: Great Britain, Ireland, the United States, and Civil Aviation, 1944–45." *Journal of Transport History* 15 (September 1994): 179–96. O'Grady examines the Anglo-American disagreements over postwar civil aviation and how Ireland exploited them for its own benefit.

LATIN AMERICA

18:1124 Benson, Erik. "Flying Down to Rio: American Commercial Aviation, the Good Neighbor Policy, and World War Two, 1939–45." In the early years of the war, U.S. commercial air policy helped promote hemispheric unity. As the war progressed, however, it became a catalyst for conflict and an indicator of the demise of the Good Neighbor Policy (15:165).

18:1125 Blasier, Cole. "The United States, Germany, and the Bolivian Revolutionaries (1941–1946)." *Hispanic American Historical Review* 52 (February 1972): 26–54. Blasier examines the American wartime belief, which the British actively encouraged, that a dangerous Nazi-fascist movement existed in Bolivia and covers the resultant policy and pressure applied to Bolivia during the war. He focuses on three related episodes: the Nazi putsch of 1941, the initial refusal of the United States to recognize the Villarroel government in 1944, and the 1946 publication of the blue book against Argentina's Juan Perón.

18:1126 Callcott, Wilfrid Hardy. *The Western Hemisphere: Its Influence on United States Policies to the End of World War II.* Although this older volume covers the entire chronology of U.S. history to 1945, nearly 40 percent focuses on Roosevelt's policies. The author lauds his hemispheric diplomacy as a success and concludes that it succeeded in guaranteeing the whole hemisphere against European aggression. As a result, American nations developed an essential unity in outlook and objectives (15:57).

18:1127 Francis, Michael J. "The United States and Chile during the Second World War: The Diplomacy

of Misunderstanding." *Journal of Latin American Studies* 9 (May 1977): 91–113. The U.S. government felt that all American nations were morally obligated to fight the Axis, but the Chilean government considered the war beyond its influence.

18:1128 _____. "The United States at Rio, 1942: The Strains of Pan Americanism." *Journal of Latin American Studies* 6 (May 1974): 77–95. Focusing on the domestic and foreign policy aims of the representatives from Chile, Argentina, and Brazil, this article explains why a rupture of diplomatic relations with the Axis powers at the Rio conference (1942), rather than a joint declaration of war with the Axis, was recommended.

18:1129 Friedman, Max Paul. "Specter of a Nazi Threat: United States–Colombian Relations, 1939–1945." *Americas* 56 (April 2000): 563–89. This article analyzes the complex interaction among Nazi efforts in Colombia, the German and Jewish refugee communities in that country, and the U.S. and Colombian governments. U.S. officials were motivated by a lack of faith in Colombia's ability to manage its own affairs as well as inflated fears of a Nazi threat, while Colombian fears of the United States led its officials to downplay the threat.

18:1130 Gellman, Irwin F. *Good Neighbor Diplomacy: United States Policies in Latin America, 1933–1945.* This study examines the relationship of FDR's Latin American diplomacy to his global strategies. Gellman concludes that Good Neighbor diplomacy was as much the product of personality as policy (15:146).

18:1131 _____. *Roosevelt and Batista: Good Neighbor Diplomacy in Cuba, 1933–1945.* FDR's avoidance of military intervention brought praise for the administration's success in hemispheric relations, but stability and expanded commercial relations between the island and its northern neighbor continued to be the goals; only the tactics changed (15:307).

18:1132 Grow, Michael. *The Good Neighbor Policy and Authoritarianism in Paraguay: United States Economic Expansion and Great-Power Rivalry in Latin America during World War II.* Lawrence: Regents Press of Kansas, 1981. This monograph traces wartime relations between the United States and

Paraguay through the latter's 1947 civil war. Grow views the discordant wartime relationship as stemming from tumultuous domestic Paraguayan politics, competition for markets and competing economic interests, and dramatically differing definitions of national security requirements. He characterizes U.S. policy as "liberal imperialism."

18:1133 Haines, Gerald K. "Under the Eagle's Wing: The Franklin Roosevelt Administration Forges an American Hemisphere." During the late 1930s and early 1940s, the Roosevelt administration desired stable political conditions in its own "backyard." Involved in a worldwide struggle, U.S. policymakers sought to create a stable, orderly hemisphere (15:136).

18:1134 Humphreys, R. A. *Latin America and the Second World War. Vol. 1: 1939–1942.* Atlantic Highlands, NJ: Humanities Press, 1981. The first half of a short narrative survey of the impact of World War II on the countries of Latin America, this volume covers the period 1939 to the Rio de Janeiro conference in January 1942.

18:1135 _____. *Latin America and the Second World War. Vol. 2: 1942–1945.* Atlantic Highlands, NJ: Humanities Press, 1982. In this volume, Humphreys covers the years 1942–1945 with individual chapters on the Caribbean, Mexico, Bolivia, Uruguay and Paraguay, and Argentina. He concludes with a chapter covering the various arrangements of the emergent inter-American system.

18:1136 Knape, John. "British Foreign Policy in the Caribbean Basin, 1938–1945: Oil, Nationalism and Relations with the United States." *Journal of Latin American Studies* 19 (November 1987): 279–94. Using the case study of access to Venezuelan oil, Knape analyzes how British "ad hoc" policy fared in the face of declining British power, growing American influence, and burgeoning Venezuelan nationalism.

18:1137 Pena, Luis. "Fighting the Invisible Enemy and Enhancing the United States Image in Venezuela, 1941–1945." *Maryland Historian* 15 (Fall-Winter 1984): 11–22. This article examines U.S. efforts, in conjunction with the Venezuelan government, to combat malaria and other diseases in Venezuela dur-

ing the war. Caracas supported the program to satisfy nationalistic demands for improvement in the standard of living, while Washington saw it as a way to protect U.S. troops in the area, aid in the procurement of vital raw materials, and further postwar economic ties. Overall the program was highly successful.

18:1138 Rout, Leslie B., Jr., and John F. Bratzel. *The Shadow War: German Espionage and United States Counterespionage in Latin America during World War II.* Frederick, MD: University Publications of America, 1986. This volume is based on extensive research in the archives of the major Latin American nations as well as Germany, Great Britain, and the United States; published works; and personal interviews and correspondence with key individuals. Separate chapters cover the espionage war in Argentina, Brazil, Chile, and Mexico.

18:1139 Taylor, Graham D. "The Axis Replacement Program: Economic Warfare and the Chemical Industry in Latin America, 1942–44." *Diplomatic History* 8 (Spring 1984): 145–64. New government-business links were forged during the war in an effort to displace Axis trade in Latin America. The primary aim was to dislodge the Axis, the secondary goal to promote Latin American industrial development, which would increase U.S. trade opportunities and promote better relations. Although this policy was successful in airlines, radio, and telephones, it failed in the chemical-pharmaceutical industry because of nationalist resentment and struggles between the corporations and the State Department.

18:1140 Whitaker, Arthur Preston, ed. *Inter-American Affairs: An Annual Survey.* 5 vols. New York: Columbia University Press, 1941–1945. These annual volumes are a gold mine of information on politics, diplomacy, economics and finance, cultural relations, and developments in social welfare, public health, and labor during the war. In addition to appendices incorporating a great variety of statistics, each volume concludes with an annotated chronology.

18:1141 Woods, Randall B. "Decision-Making in Diplomacy: The Rio Conference of 1942." *Social Science Quarterly* 55 (March 1975): 901–18. After forming a construct to measure the motives and behavior of diplomats in policymaking situations, the author tests it in the specific historical context of the

1942 Rio de Janeiro conference. This method sheds new light on the U.S-Argentine confrontation immediately following U.S. entry into World War II.

Argentina

18:1142 di Tella, Guido, and Donald Cameron Watt, eds. *Argentina between the Great Powers, 1939–46.* Pittsburgh: University of Pittsburgh Press, 1990. The conference papers in this collection assess intersections of American, Argentine, and British policies. Individual chapters include Alexander E. Campbell, "Anglo-American Relations, 1939–46: A British View" (1–17); Warren F. Kimball, "'The Juggler': Franklin D. Roosevelt and Anglo-American Competition in Latin America" (18–33); Joseph S. Tulchin, "The Origins of Misunderstanding: United States–Argentine Relations, 1900–40" (34–55); Carlos Escudé, "US Political Destabilisation and Economic Boycott of Argentina during the 1940s" (56–76); Ronald C. Newton, "Disorderly Succession: Great Britain, the United States and the 'Nazi Menace' in Argentina, 1938–47" (111–34); Stanley E. Hilton, "The United States and Argentina in Brazil's Wartime Foreign Policy, 1939–45" (158–80); di Tella, "Argentina between the Great Powers, 1939–46: A Revisionist Summing-up" (181–98); and John Major, "A Northern Summing-up" (199–206).

18:1143 Francis, Michael J. *The Limits of Hegemony: United States Relations with Argentina and Chile during World War II.* Notre Dame, IN: University of Notre Dame Press, 1977. This volume is valuable in relating diplomatic exchanges to internal political developments in Argentina and Chile. The author concludes that U.S. efforts to achieve its goals through public condemnations and experiments in economic deprivations accomplished far less than quiet, secret diplomacy.

18:1144 MacDonald, Callum A. "The Politics of Intervention: The United States and Argentina, 1941–1946." *Journal of Latin American Studies* 12 (November 1980): 365–96. In this strong overview of wartime relations, MacDonald traces the growth of U.S. intervention in Argentine politics and internal affairs. He characterizes increasing American hostility to Perón as "hysterical," unrealistic, and based on a complete misunderstanding of Argentine attitudes.

In a lengthy postscript, MacDonald critiques Woods, *The Roosevelt Foreign-Policy Establishment and the "Good Neighbor": The United States and Argentina, 1941–1945* (1979) (18:1148).

18:1145 Newton, Ronald C. *The "Nazi Menace" in Argentina, 1931–1947.* Stanford, CA: Stanford University Press, 1992. Newton rates the supposed Nazi menace in Argentina as largely "nonsense." In reality, he maintains, German blunders and Argentine countermeasures destroyed any possibility of such a menace becoming a reality. Nevertheless, it became a U.S. obsession during the war, fanned by British propaganda. About half of the book focuses on German-Argentine relations before 1939, the other half on wartime and immediate postwar events.

18:1146 _____. "The United States, the German-Argentines, and the Myth of the Fourth Reich, 1943–1947." *Hispanic American Historical Review* 64 (February 1984): 81–103. This article examines German activities in Argentina from 1933 to 1942, U.S. fears about them and the possible establishment of a new German government in that nation, and Washington's consequent pressure on Buenos Aires to destroy German institutions and the German economic base within the country. Such fears, the author finds, were fantasies, but administration officials continued exploiting them, seeking revenge for Argentine neutrality and U.S. commercial expansion.

18:1147 Woods, Randall B. "Hull and Argentina: Wilsonian Diplomacy in the Age of Roosevelt." *Journal of Interamerican Studies and World Affairs* 16 (August 1974): 350–71. Cordell Hull's paradoxical 1943–1944 policy toward Argentina's government of General Pedro Ramirez can be understood better in the context of the Wilsonian tradition. Like Wilson, Hull viewed foreign policy matters in terms of right and wrong, "sin" and "salvation." As a result, he abetted the rise of an even more intransigent regime, that of Juan Perón.

18:1148 _____. *The Roosevelt Foreign-Policy Establishment and the "Good Neighbor": The United States and Argentina, 1941–1945.* Lawrence: Regents Press of Kansas, 1979. Woods demonstrates how wartime U.S.-Argentine relations undermined the Good Neighbor Policy. He takes issue with both orthodox and revisionist historians by focusing on the impact of bureaucratic conflicts within the U.S. government on the making of U.S. policy.

Brazil

18:1149 Hilton, Stanley E. "Brazilian Diplomacy and the Washington–Rio de Janeiro 'Axis' during the World War II Era." *Hispanic American Historical Review* 59 (May 1979): 201–31. This well-researched account disputes the thesis in McCann, "Brazil, the United States, and World War II: A Commentary" (1979) (18:1150), of Brazilian passivity and American domination in wartime relations. Hilton emphasizes the diplomatic skill and "Machiavellian opportunism" of Brazilian leaders in exploiting U.S. strategic exigencies and Washington's perception of Brazil as an important ally from which it could gain valuable concessions and favorable policies.

18:1150 McCann, Frank D., Jr. "Brazil, the United States, and World War II: A Commentary." *Diplomatic History* 3 (Winter 1979): 59–76. McCann finds three distinct periods in Brazilian foreign policy from 1935 to 1945. Five years of diplomatic flexibility were followed by wartime uncertainty and narrowing Brazilian options (1940–1942), and then by a period of acquiescence in American requests that ultimately facilitated expanded American predominance in Brazil.

18:1151 _____. *The Brazilian-American Alliance, 1937–1945.* Princeton: Princeton University Press, 1974. McCann analyzes the events during the Vargas regime that brought about a close alliance between Brazil and the United States and resulted in Brazil's dependence upon its new ally. He emphasizes the internal dynamics of Brazilian politics.

Mexico

18:1152 Paz Salinas, María Emilia. *Strategy, Security, and Spies: Mexico and the U.S. as Allies in World War II.* University Park: Pennsylvania State University Press, 1997. This work assesses the multifaceted "security dimension" of U.S.-Mexican relations, beginning when the United States felt compelled to respond to the potential threat the Axis powers posed to the Western Hemisphere. The au-

thor covers such topics as differing security perceptions, strategic resources, Mexican resistance to American initiatives, and Axis and American intelligence efforts.

18:1153 Schuler, Friedrich E. "Germany, Mexico and the United States during the Second World War." *Jahrbuch für Geschichte von Staat, Wirtschaft und Gesellschaft Lateinamerikas [Yearbook for the History of State, Economy, and Society in Latin America]* 22 (1985): 457–76. Schuler shows that a Mexican-German wartime diplomatic relationship based solely on economic interests was bound to break down given tone-deaf German statecraft and an ever-present U.S. presence that constrained Mexican policy options.

MIDDLE EAST AND AFRICA

18:1154 Baram, Philip J. *The Department of State in the Middle East, 1919–1945.* This is a detailed analysis of State Department policies in the Middle East (defined as Iraq, Syria, Lebanon, Egypt, Palestine-Transjordan, and Saudi Arabia), with special emphasis on 1939–1945. Baram argues that the homogeneity of the department's middle-level management led it to support principles that were self-serving, contradictory, and shortsighted (16:56).

18:1155 Blair, Leon Borden. "Amateurs in Diplomacy: The American Vice Consuls in North Africa, 1941–1943." *Historian* 35 (August 1973): 607–20. Blair examines the work of Robert Murphy and the twelve businessmen appointed U.S. vice-consuls in North Africa in 1941. He praises their military intelligence reports, which were useful in planning the North African invasion, but criticizes their political planning for a coup as amateurish and ineffective. His harshest criticism is reserved for Murphy's "uncritical support" of French colonialism in North Africa.

18:1156 _____. "The Impact of Franco-American Military Agreements on Moroccan Nationalism, 1940–1956." *Rocky Mountain Social Science Journal* 9 (January 1972): 61–68. This short work seeks to determine the impact of the U.S. presence in North Africa on Moroccan nationalism.

18:1157 Bryson, Thomas A. *Seeds of Mideast Crisis: The United States Diplomatic Role in the Middle*

East during World War II. Jefferson, NC: McFarland, 1981. This is a short narrative overview of U.S. wartime policy toward the countries of the Middle East. The author argues that ad hoc country-by-country policies gave way to a broader regional approach by the end of the war, laying the foundation for postwar U.S. policies in the area, most notably in elevating dominant strategic-national security interests above specific commercial, missionary, and philanthropic interests previously dominant in U.S. policymaking for the area.

18:1158 DeNovo, John A. "The Culbertson Economic Mission and Anglo-American Tension in the Middle East, 1944–1945." *Journal of American History* 63 (March 1977): 913–36. William S. Culbertson's special 1944 economic mission to the Middle East to survey postwar business prospects illustrates a deep-rooted American emphasis on free enterprise as a stabilizing political force.

18:1159 Dougherty, James J. "Lend-Lease and the Opening of French North and West Africa to Private Trade." *Cahiers d' Études Africaines* 15, no. 3 (1975): 481–500. Focusing on French North and West Africa, Dougherty examines the inherent conflicts between lend-lease policy and commercial interests, and between competing French and private American economic interests. The latter importuned the State Department to secure access to formerly restricted markets. French recalcitrance battled with American opportunism through 1945 with American officials achieving significant gains.

18:1160 Dumett, Raymond. "Africa's Strategic Minerals during the Second World War." *Journal of African History* 26, no. 4 (1985): 381–408. Dumett analyzes how allied wartime efforts to secure important strategic mineral resources caused economic changes in several African countries and notes that the war strengthened the position of multinational corporations in Africa.

18:1161 Painter, David S. *Oil and the American Century: The Political Economy of U.S. Foreign Oil Policy, 1941–1954.* Baltimore: Johns Hopkins University Press, 1986. Using a corporatist approach, Painter analyzes the conflicts within and between the oil companies and the government as well as their cooperation in the creation of a foreign oil policy be-

tween 1941 and 1954. Approximately half of the volume deals with the World War II years.

18:1162 Randall, Stephen J. *United States Foreign Oil Policy, 1919–1948: For Profits and Security.* Randall traces the evolution of U.S. policy toward foreign oil after World War I. He argues that public and private interests supported expanding influence over oil supplies overseas and offers a nuanced view of the interactions of U.S. corporations and government (15:410).

18:1163 Rubin, Barry. *The Great Powers in the Middle East, 1941–1947: The Road to the Cold War.* London: Frank Cass, 1980. Rubin explores the role that great power relations in the Middle East played in the breakdown of the wartime alliance and, as U.S. suspicion about British intentions was replaced by concern over the potential Soviet threat to Middle East oil, in the origins of the cold war. Wartime chapters focus on Anglo-American relations, Turkey, Iran, and Saudi Arabia.

18:1164 Stoff, Michael B. *Oil, War, and American Security: The Search for a National Policy on Foreign Oil, 1941–1947.* New Haven: Yale University Press, 1980. Published during the 1973 oil crisis, this volume analyzes the unsuccessful U.S. effort during and immediately after World War II to create a national policy on foreign oil. Stoff focuses on the Middle East and on disputes within and between the U.S. government and the oil industry.

18:1165 Wilmington, Martin W. *The Middle East Supply Centre.* Albany: State University of New York Press, 1971. An account of the American role in the British-originated mechanism for wartime civilian supply in the Middle East, this work reveals a lack of direct American interests in the Middle East beyond the common war aims of the allies and the secondary and supporting role played by the United States in the project. Edited by Laurence Evans.

Egypt

18:1166 Baram, Philip J. "Undermining the British: Department of State Policies in Egypt and the Suez Canal before and during World War II." Baram traces the course of State Department policy toward Egypt, contending that the "engine" of American policy was competition with the British for influence and access to markets, not for control of the Suez Canal (16:146).

18:1167 Vitalis, Robert. "The 'New Deal' in Egypt: The Rise of Anglo-American Commercial Competition in World War II and the Fall of Neocolonialism." *Diplomatic History* 20 (Spring 1996): 211–39. Vitalis cites the decisive period of Anglo-American commercial competition in Egypt in the war years, when American New Dealers—typified by James Landis—and multinationals forged bonds with a reform-minded, pro-capitalist Egyptian social coalition whose investment choices and strategies, reinforced by U.S. investors, ultimately undermined the British neocolonialist position. He presents a cogent argument for delving beneath great power national security concerns to local politics and society to better understand outcomes.

Iran

18:1168 Lenczowski, George. *Russia and the West in Iran, 1918–1948: A Study in Big-Power Rivalry.* Ithaca: Cornell University Press, 1949. The contribution of this early volume lies in its treatment of the role of the great powers in Iran during World War II and the early postwar period. It is also a valuable account of Iran's domestic politics (1942–1945). A 1953 reprint carried events through 1952.

18:1169 Lytle, Mark H. *The Origins of the Iranian-American Alliance, 1941–1953.* New York: Holmes and Meier, 1987. Lytle focuses on the years 1941–1947 and sees the key to U.S. postwar policy as the wartime perception by State Department policy-makers of a Soviet threat to Iran.

18:1170 McFarland, Stephen L. "A Peripheral View of the Origins of the Cold War: The Crises in Iran, 1941–1947." *Diplomatic History* 4 (Fall 1980): 333–52. During World War II the Iranians tried to intensify first Anglo-Soviet and then Anglo-American differences as a means of maintaining their independence amidst an allied military occupation. The resulting crises of 1944 and 1945 were thus initiated by the Iranians, not the United States or the Soviet Union.

Liberia

18:1171 Akingbade, Harrison. "U.S. Liberian Relations during World War II." *Phylon* 46 (March 1985): 25–36. This article surveys the revival of U.S. interest in Liberia, primarily for strategic reasons, and the ensuing course of wartime relations and accords between the two. It emphasizes how perceived exigencies led to closer relations between the countries with, in the author's opinion, substantial benefits for each.

18:1172 Beecher, Lloyd N., Jr. "The Second World War and U.S. Politico-Military Expansionism: The Case of Liberia, 1938–45." *Diplomatic History* 3 (Fall 1979): 391–412. The armed forces had no desire to assume full military responsibility for Liberia, but Roosevelt, the State Department, other civilian officials, and private companies combined to overcome JCS reluctance.

Palestine

18:1173 Halperin, Samuel, and Irwin Oder. "The United States in Search of a Policy: Franklin D. Roosevelt and Palestine." *Review of Politics* 24 (July 1962): 320–41. This early article makes use of then recently released documents in the Roosevelt Library and the Central Zionist Archives in Jerusalem to trace the development of official U.S. attitudes toward Palestine during the war. Despite Zionist hopes for U.S. support, Roosevelt and the State Department throughout the war refused to challenge British policies and practiced a policy of postponement in hopes of mollifying both Jews and Arabs.

18:1174 Parzen, Herbert. "The Roosevelt Palestine Policy, 1943–1945." *American Jewish Archives* 26 (April 1974): 31–65. Parzen examines wartime American policy toward the creation of a Jewish state in Palestine, highlighting the inherent difficulty of setting a policy acceptable to both Jews and Arabs. He criticizes Roosevelt and the State Department for their pro-Arab biases.

Saudi Arabia

18:1175 Anderson, Irvine H. *Aramco, the United States, and Saudi Arabia: A Study in the Dynamics of*

Foreign Oil Policy, 1933–1950. Princeton: Princeton University Press, 1981. Using ARAMCO as a case study, Anderson details the change in official attitudes after the discovery that the United States would become a net importer of oil in the postwar world, the ensuing unsuccessful efforts to establish a federal petroleum reserves corporation with a controlling interest in ARAMCO, the failure to accomplish the same ends through an Anglo-American oil agreement, and the eventual turn to private enterprise to achieve government goals.

18:1176 _____. "Lend-Lease for Saudi Arabia: A Comment on Alternative Conceptualizations." *Diplomatic History* 3 (Fall 1979): 413–24. Anderson challenges the then standard view that giving lend-lease to Saudi Arabia resulted from the pressure of U.S. oil companies fearful of the British. Instead he notes new concern by the State Department and the armed forces for future oil reserves as U.S. reserves declined. Which interpretation one selects, he further argues, depends upon one's conceptualization of international relations.

18:1177 Casillas, Rex J. *Oil and Diplomacy: The Evolution of American Foreign Policy in Saudi Arabia, 1933–1945.* Examining the wartime transformation of American foreign policy toward Saudi Arabia, Casillas argues that heightened strategic concerns of policymakers about oil supplies meshed with private oil interests to generate a vigorous campaign to advance U.S. influence in Saudi Arabia. The U.S. oil company ARAMCO was "instrumental" in pushing State Department policymakers into decisive action (16:196).

18:1178 Gormly, James L. "Keeping the Door Open in Saudi Arabia: The United States and the Dhahran Airfield, 1945–46." *Diplomatic History* 4 (Spring 1980): 189–205. The author focuses on this particular issue as illustrative of Anglo-American wartime rivalry over influence in Saudi Arabia.

18:1179 Miller, Aaron David. *Search for Security: Saudi Arabian Oil and American Foreign Policy, 1939–1949.* Chapel Hill: University of North Carolina Press, 1980. Miller looks at the origins of the U.S.-Saudi "special relationship," focusing on the development of Saudi oil during World War II and the immediate postwar years.

18:1180 Rubin, Barry. "Anglo-American Relations in Saudi Arabia, 1941–1945." *Journal of Contemporary History* 14 (April 1979): 253–68. By mid-1943, American officials were suspicious of the British over postwar competition for oil. Rubin argues that this was due to general State Department hostility to British imperialism, especially in the Near East Affairs Division, concerns expressed by American oil companies, and successful Saudi efforts to play the Americans against the British in pursuit of foreign aid.

Turkey

18:1181 Alvarez, David J. *Bureaucracy and Cold War Diplomacy: The United States and Turkey, 1943–1946.* Thessaloniki: Institute for Balkan Studies, 1980. The reversal of U.S. policies toward Turkey and the Soviet Union between 1943 and 1946 resulted not from monolithic administrative decisions but from the bureaucratic goals of and interactions between different middle-level agencies and officials within the State, Navy, and War Departments.

18:1182 _____. "The Embassy of Laurence A. Steinhardt: Aspects of Allied-Turkish Relations, 1942–1945." *East European Quarterly* 9 (Spring 1975): 39–52. Steinhardt acted to restrain the United States from following Britain's attempts to force Turkey into the war. He argued that Turkey's fear of the Soviet Union as well as its domestic problems and military and economic weaknesses made it reluctant to join the allies. He recommended substantial assistance to the Turks and opposed any policy designed to threaten or pressure them.

18:1183 Weisband, Edward. *Turkish Foreign Policy, 1943–1945: Small State Diplomacy and Great Power Politics.* Princeton: Princeton University Press, 1973. Focusing first on the domestic sources of it policies, the author provides an incisive analysis of Turkey's foreign policy during a critical period in World War II. The author had access to private papers unavailable to the general public.

Axis Surrender

UNCONDITIONAL SURRENDER

18:1184 Armstrong, Anne. *Unconditional Surrender: The Impact of the Casablanca Policy upon World War.* New Brunswick: Rutgers University Press, 1961. The author concludes in this early work that the unconditional surrender formula arose because of a failure to separate means from ends or military from political strategy. The decision undoubtedly reflected the U.S. view of war as a crusade, but its effects were far from salutary.

18:1185 Balfour, Michael. "Another Look at 'Unconditional Surrender.'" *International Affairs* 46 (October 1970): 719–36. In this speculative essay Balfour argues that unconditional surrender was appropriate if one assumes the Germans were a greater menace than the Soviets.

18:1186 _____. "The Origin of the Formula: 'Unconditional Surrender' in World War II." *Armed Forces & Society* 5 (Winter 1979): 281–301. Balfour attacks both the Churchill-Roosevelt claims that FDR's unconditional surrender announcement was unpremeditated and the critics who called it a blunder. He traces 1942 U.S. and British government discussions and recommendations on the policy as well as the Churchill-Roosevelt discussions before the Casablanca announcement, defends the policy as appropriate, and concludes that modifying it for Germany would have been unwise.

18:1187 Campbell, Alexander E. "Franklin Roosevelt and Unconditional Surrender." In *Diplomacy and Intelligence during the Second World War: Essays in Honor of F. H. Hinsley,* ed. Richard Langhorne, 219–41. New York: Cambridge University Press, 1985. Campbell concludes that Roosevelt enunciated unconditional surrender in early 1943 primarily to reassure U.S. public opinion over the Darlan affair, that it was not new and did not lengthen the war or determine its outcome, that the circumstances of the Axis surrenders were so various that the doctrine did not provide any basis for treating them alike, and that those circumstances determined the terms of each surrender.

18:1188 Chase, John L. "Unconditional Surrender Reconsidered." *Political Science Quarterly* 70 (June 1955): 258–79. Defending the doctrine against its numerous early critics, Chase argues in this early article that it reinforced the ban on premature discussion of postwar territorial issues and reassured Stalin despite delays in launching the second front.

18:1189 Glennon, John P. "'This Time Germany Is a Defeated Nation': The Doctrine of Unconditional Surrender and Some Unsuccessful Attempts to Alter It, 1934–1944." In *Statesmen and Statecraft of the Modern West: Essays in Honor of Dwight E. Lee and H. Donaldson Jordan,* ed. Gerald N. Grob, 109–51. Barre, MA: Barre Publishers, 1967. This is a valuable summary of the background of the unconditional surrender formula.

18:1190 Kecskemeti, Paul. *Strategic Surrender: The Politics of Victory and Defeat.* Stanford, CA: Stanford University Press, 1958. The author undertook four case studies—the surrender of France, Italy, Germany, and Japan—to find the point at which it was clear that the war had been lost.

18:1191 O'Connor, Raymond G. *Diplomacy for Victory: FDR and Unconditional Surrender.* New York: Norton, 1971. O'Connor examines, and ultimately rejects, the leading criticisms of unconditional surrender. He traces the origins of the doctrine to Roosevelt's World War I experience and sees it as a convenient way to avoid internal and allied disharmony over political issues while successfully prosecuting the war.

ITALIAN SURRENDER

18:1192 Aga Rossi, Elena. *A Nation Collapses: The Italian Surrender of September 1943.* Translated by Harvey Fergusson, II. New York: Cambridge University Press, 2000. Based on extensive research in Italian, British, and U.S. archives, this brief volume analyzes the secret negotiations between Italy and the western allies culminating in Italy's September 1943 surrender. The author focuses on and is sharply critical of the Italian government's behavior.

GERMAN SURRENDER

18:1193 Bacque, James. *Other Losses: The Shocking Truth behind the Mass Deaths of Disarmed German Soldiers and Civilians under General Eisenhower's Command.* Rocklin, CA: Prima Pub., 1991. This unreliable book accuses General Eisenhower of vengefully engineering the deaths of some 1 million German prisoners of war at the end of the war and the early postwar months. Bacque believes Eisenhower ordered a policy of deliberate neglect, which included the systematic withholding of food and supplies, throughout the POW camps. As has been shown by other historians (Bischof and Ambrose, *Eisenhower and the German POWs: Facts against Falsehood,* 1992 [18:1194]), Bacque badly—and willfully—misunderstood the documents on which he based his claim. Originally published in 1989 with the subtitle *An Investigation into the Mass Deaths of German Prisoners at the Hands of the French and Americans after World War II.*

18:1194 Bischof, Günter, and Stephen E. Ambrose, eds. *Eisenhower and the German POWs: Facts against Falsehood.* Baton Rouge: Louisiana State University Press, 1992. This collection of essays refutes the thesis in Bacque, *Other Losses: The Shocking Truth behind the Mass Deaths of Disarmed German Soldiers and Civilians under General Eisenhower's Command* (1991) (18:1193). In doing so, the authors provide substantial information on the treatment of German POWs and the 1945 food shortage in Europe. Contents include: Ambrose, "Eisenhower and the Germans" (29–51); Brian Loring Villa, "The Diplomatic and Political Context of the POW Camps Tragedy" (52–77); Albert E. Cowdrey, "A Question of Numbers" (78–94); James F. Tent, "Food Shortages in Germany and Europe, 1945–1948" (95–126); Rüdiger Overmans, "German Historiography, the War Losses, and the Prisoners of War" (127–69); Rolf Steininger, "Some Reflections on the Maschke Commission" (170–82); Thomas M. Barker, "A British Variety of Pseudohistory" (183–98); and Bischof, "Bacque and Historical Evidence" (199–234).

18:1195 Chandler, Harriette L. "Another View of Operation Crossword: A Revision of Kolko." *Military Affairs* 42 (April 1978): 68–74. Operation Crossword was the preliminary effort to secure a surrender on the northern Italian front in the spring of 1945.

The Anglo-American decision to deny Soviet participation in the negotiations prompted historian Gabriel Kolko (*The Politics of War: The World and United States Foreign Policy, 1943–1945,* 1968 [18:187]) to suggest that the move was politically motivated. The author maintains, however, that the decision was based solely on military considerations.

18:1196 Dulles, Allen. *The Secret Surrender.* New York: Harper and Row, 1966. This is a personal account by the future head of the CIA of the negotiations that led to the surrender of German forces in northern Italy before the final capitulation in Germany.

18:1197 Frohn, Axel. "Das Schicksal deutscher Kriegsgefangener in amerikanischen Lagern nach dem Zweiten Weltkrieg: Eine Auseinandersetzung mit den Thesen von James Bacque [The Fate of German Prisoners-of-War in American Camps after the Second World War: An Argument with the Thesis of James Bacque]." *Historisches Jahrbuch* 111, no. 3, pt. 2 (1991): 466–92. This article highlights several of the problems inherent in Bacque, *Other Losses: The Shocking Truth behind the Mass Deaths of Disarmed German Soldiers and Civilians under General Eisenhower's Command* (1991) (18:1193).

18:1198 MacKenzie, S. P. "Essay and Reflection: On the *Other Losses* Debate." *International History Review* 14 (November 1992): 717–31. This is an even-handed treatment of Bacque, *Other Losses: The Shocking Truth behind the Mass Deaths of Disarmed German Soldiers and Civilians under General Eisenhower's Command* (1991) (18:1193), and the subsequent literature that demolished Bacque's argument.

18:1199 Offner, Arnold A., and Theodore A. Wilson, eds. *Victory in Europe 1945: From World War to Cold War.* Lawrence: University Press of Kansas, 2000. Most of the essays in this collection originated in a 1995 symposium at the University of Kansas commemorating the fiftieth anniversary of the end of the war in Europe. The central focus is the relatively unexplored issue of war termination, the transition from war to uneasy peace, and the view from 1945. Contents include: Wilson, "Endgames: V-E Day and War Termination" (11–46); Anna M. Cienciala, "The View from Poland" (47–76); David Hogan, "Berlin Revisited—and Revised: Eisenhower's Decision to

Halt at the Elbe" (77–102); Ronan Fanning, "Dublin: The View from a Neutral Capital" (103–16); Hal Elliott Wert, "Military Expediency, the 'Hunger Winter,' and Holland's Belated Liberation" (117–44); Mark A. Stoler, "Allies or Adversaries? The Joint Chiefs of Staff and Soviet-American Relations, Spring 1945" (145–66); Randall B. Woods, "Congress and the Roots of Postwar American Foreign Policy" (167–82); Vladimir V. Pozniakov, "Commoners, Commissars, and Spies: Soviet Policies and Society, 1945" (183–212); Warren F. Kimball, "Churchill, the Americans, and Self-Determination" (213–32); Offner, "From Reims to Potsdam: Victory, Atomic Diplomacy, and the Origins of the Cold War" (233–56); and J. Garry Clifford, "Endings and Beginnings" (257–82).

18:1200 Smith, Bradley F., and Elena Aga Rossi. *Operation Sunrise: The Secret Surrender.* New York: Basic Books, 1979. This is a comprehensive study of the negotiations leading to the 1945 surrender of German forces in Italy.

18:1201 Steinert, Marlis G. *23 Days: The Final Collapse of Nazi Germany.* Translated by Richard Barry. New York: Walker, 1969. This is the story of the Doenitz government, its capitulation, and the immediate postsurrender period. Primary value derives from the uniquely German perspective and good portraits of Doenitz, Jodl, and von Krosigk.

THE ATOMIC BOMB AND JAPANESE SURRENDER

Overviews

18:1202 "The End of the War with Japan." *MHQ: The Quarterly Journal of Military History* 7 (Spring 1995). This special issue of a popular military history publication, containing brief articles by experts summarizing material and arguments presented elsewhere, focuses on the termination of the Pacific war. Authors include Williamson Murray ("Armageddon Revisited," 6–11), Haruko Taya Cook ("The Myth of the Japan Suicides," 12–19), Stanley L. Falk ("'A Nation Reduced to Ashes,'" 54–61), Bruce Gudmundsson ("Okinawa," 64–73), Edward J. Drea

("Previews of Hell," 74–81), Stanley Weintraub ("The Three Week War," 86–95), and Peter Maslowski ("Truman, the Bomb, and the Numbers Game," 103–7).

18:1203 Alperovitz, Gar. *Atomic Diplomacy: Hiroshima and Potsdam: The Use of the Atomic Bomb and the American Confrontation with Soviet Power.* 2d expanded ed. Boulder: Pluto Press, 1994. This revised and expanded version of the original 1965 edition maintains the argument that U.S. use of the atomic bomb against Japan was designed to gain political influence over the Soviet Union.

18:1204 Alperovitz, Gar, with Sanho Tree et al. *The Decision to Use the Atomic Bomb and the Architecture of the American Myth.* New York: Alfred A. Knopf, 1995. This work is best described as the brief for the prosecution—a lengthy, one-sided compilation of evidence organized to prove the Alperovitz thesis (best summarized in "Why the United States Dropped the Bomb," 1990 [18:1206]).

18:1205 Alperovitz, Gar. "More on Atomic Diplomacy." *Bulletin of the Atomic Scientists* 41 (December 1985): 35–39. Alperovitz argues that there was opposition to dropping the atomic bombs, that the issue of President Truman inheriting the assumption of use from Roosevelt is debatable, and that James F. Byrnes steadfastly resisted efforts to avoid dropping the bomb.

18:1206 _____. "Why the United States Dropped the Bomb." *Technology Review* 93 (August-September 1990): 22–34. This is a useful summary of the Alperovitz thesis that the atomic bombing of Japan was not needed either to end the war or to avoid an invasion of Japan, and that the strongest motive for using the bomb was to influence the postwar balance of power with the Soviet Union.

18:1207 Bernstein, Barton J. "Roosevelt, Truman, and the Atomic Bomb, 1941–1945: A Reinterpretation." *Political Science Quarterly* 90 (Spring 1975): 23–69. This major reinterpretation, along with Sherwin's "The Atomic Bomb and the Origins of the Cold War: U.S. Atomic Energy Policy and Diplomacy, 1941–45" (1973) (18:1218), argues that Roosevelt originally defined the relationship between the atomic bomb and American diplomacy. When Truman became president, he was restricted politically, psychologically, and institutionally from critically reassessing this legacy. He accepted the bomb as a legitimate weapon of war and fully appreciated that its power would be a factor in U.S. diplomacy. It was used to obtain Japan's surrender and, as a "diplomatic bonus," to impress the Soviets. Possession of the bomb reduced the incentives for compromise and stiffened American demands vis-à-vis the Soviet Union, and thus contributed to the onset of the cold war.

18:1208 _____. "Shatterer of Worlds: Hiroshima and Nagasaki." *Bulletin of the Atomic Scientists* 31 (December 1975): 12–22. U.S. policymakers in the Roosevelt and Truman administrations had little doubt about the desirability of using atomic weapons both for ending the war in the Pacific and for intimidating the Soviet Union.

18:1209 _____. "The Uneasy Alliance: Roosevelt, Churchill, and the Atomic Bomb, 1940–1945." *Western Political Quarterly* 29 (June 1976): 202–30. Bernstein reinterprets the wartime Anglo-American relationship on atomic energy, defined primarily by Roosevelt and Churchill. A postwar Anglo-American entente could be constructed on the atomic bomb.

18:1210 Feis, Herbert. *The Atomic Bomb and the End of World War II.* Rev. ed. Princeton: Princeton University Press, 1966. The volume is partly a rebuttal of the charge that the atomic bomb was dropped to influence the Soviets. Feis notes that use of the bomb may have spared both the United States and Japan heavy casualties. The original 1961 edition was entitled *Japan Subdued: The Atomic Bomb and the End of the War in the Pacific.*

18:1211 Frank, Richard B. *Downfall: The End of the Imperial Japanese Empire.* New York: Random House, 1999. Based on extensive research in Japanese and American sources, Frank analyzes military operations, strategy, diplomacy, and politics, and the links among them, during the spring and summer of 1945. The result is one of the most balanced, accurate, and comprehensive accounts in English of the end of the Pacific war.

18:1212 Hammond, Thomas T. "'Atomic Diplomacy' Revisited." *Orbis* 19 (Winter 1976): 1403–28. The theses of Gar Alperovitz in his *Atomic Diplo-*

macy (1994) (18:1203), Hammond argues, "are either implausible, exaggerated, or unsupported by the evidence" and do not stand up under careful analysis.

18:1213 Maddox, Robert James. "'Atomic Diplomacy': A Study in Creative Writing." *Journal of American History* 59 (March 1973): 925–34. Maddox criticizes the original 1965 edition of Alperovitz's *Atomic Diplomacy: Hiroshima and Potsdam: The Use of the Atomic Bomb and the American Confrontation with Soviet Power* (18:1203) for distortions and misrepresentations of the evidence, and the historical profession in general for its uncritical acceptance of this work. For a more detailed and comprehensive critique by Maddox of new left histories in general, see his *The New Left and the Origins of the Cold War* (1973) (19:105).

18:1214 _____. "The Biggest Decision: Why We Had to Drop the Atomic Bomb." *American Heritage* 46 (May-June 1995): 70–77. In this brief survey of the atomic bomb decision, Maddox rebuts several criticisms of the decision that are common in the historiography.

18:1215 _____. *Weapons for Victory: The Hiroshima Decision Fifty Years Later.* Columbia: University of Missouri Press, 1995. This somewhat strident defense of the atomic bomb decision is designed to refute a variety of historical judgments, involving issues from Truman's purported desire to influence the Soviets to projected casualties of an invasion of Japan. Maddox ultimately insists that use of the bomb was the logical step for ending the war.

18:1216 Newman, Robert P. *Truman and the Hiroshima Cult.* East Lansing: Michigan State University Press, 1995. Newman vigorously defends Truman's decision to use atomic bombs as motivated by military factors. He maintains that critics are incorrect in their conclusions to the contrary and in stating that Japan was ready to surrender before the bombs were dropped. He also labels their approach and followers a "cult" that has emerged as a result of 1960s disillusionment with the United States, one that has incorrectly come to view Hiroshima as America's original sin.

18:1217 Schoenberger, Walter Smith. *Decision of Destiny.* Athens, OH: Ohio University Press, 1969.

This detailed, older examination of the development of the atomic bomb and the thinking about its use, which changed as the war and the bomb progressed, shows that Truman's Hiroshima-Nagasaki decisions grew logically from the earliest assumptions about its use.

18:1218 Sherwin, Martin J. "The Atomic Bomb and the Origins of the Cold War: U.S. Atomic Energy Policy and Diplomacy, 1941–45." *American Historical Review* 78 (October 1973): 945–68. President Roosevelt left no definitive statement on the postwar role of the atomic bomb. Among the alternatives he considered were international control, advocated by his science advisers, and an Anglo-American postwar monopoly, urged by Churchill. This indicates that the potential postwar diplomatic value of the bomb began to shape his atomic energy policies as early as 1943.

18:1219 _____. *A World Destroyed: Hiroshima and Its Legacies.* 3d ed. Stanford, CA: Stanford University Press, 2000. In this important analysis of U.S. nuclear policy during World War II, Sherwin portrays President Truman as constrained by decisions made by his predecessor Roosevelt, who originated "atomic diplomacy" as one of many factors in U.S. atomic policy. Originally published in 1975 as *A World Destroyed: The Atomic Bomb and the Grand Alliance.*

18:1220 Wainstock, Dennis D. *The Decision to Drop the Atomic Bomb.* New York: Praeger, 1996. This is a general history of the Japanese and American efforts to end the war from April to August 1945 that contains little analysis. Wainstock believes that modification of the surrender terms would have brought a prompt surrender.

18:1221 Walker, J. Samuel. *Prompt and Utter Destruction: Truman and the Use of the Atomic Bombs against Japan.* Chapel Hill: University of North Carolina Press, 1997. Walker has produced an admirably brief and even-handed discussion of why the atomic bomb was used against Japan and the resultant historiography that deserves reading. He believes Emperor Hirohito would have ended the war before Japan was invaded.

18:1222 Wolk, Herman S. "General Arnold, the Atomic Bomb, and the Surrender of Japan." In *The*

Pacific War Revisited, ed. Günter Bischof and Robert L. Dupont, 163–78. Baton Rouge: Louisiana State University Press, 1997. Wolk describes the "obsession" of General Henry H. Arnold, commander of the U.S. army air forces, with the B-29 strategic bombing campaign against Japan, his belief that it could end the war, and its importance for an independent postwar air force.

Developing a Nuclear Weapon

18:1223 Bernstein, Barton J. "An Analysis of 'Two Cultures': Writing about the Making and the Using of the Atomic Bombs." *Public Historian* 12 (Spring 1990): 83–107. This is a wide-ranging, thoughtful, useful (and scathing) review essay of Rhodes, *The Making of the Atomic Bomb* (1986) (18:1227).

18:1224 Groves, Leslie R. *Now It Can Be Told: The Story of the Manhattan Project.* New York: Harper, 1962. Reprint 1975 (Da Capo Press). This personal story of General Groves, who supervised the building of the first atomic bombs, is in some sense an administrative history of the problems and triumphs of this ambitious project. The developments are described against a background of anxiety about security, the German program, and progress of the war. Valuable information is also included about military-civilian and allied technological cooperation.

18:1225 Harper, John Lamberton. "Henry Stimson and the Origin of America's Attachment to Atomic Weapons." *SAIS Review* 5 (Summer-Fall 1985): 17–28. Harper uses the example of Stimson to explore the thinking of American officials about the atomic bomb and emphasizes the emotional allure the bomb had for Americans who felt anxious about the future.

18:1226 Helmreich, Jonathan E. *Gathering Rare Ores: The Diplomacy of Uranium Acquisition, 1943–1954.* Princeton: Princeton University Press, 1986. This is a thorough account of the allied initiative to gain a monopoly of the world's thorium and uranium, elements considered both scarce and vital to the production of atomic bombs. The effort ultimately failed because of the relative abundance of both elements.

18:1227 Rhodes, Richard. *The Making of the Atomic Bomb*. New York: Simon and Schuster, 1986. This is a detailed, prize-winning, narrative account of the people and challenges involved in designing and building the atomic bomb, yet it would have benefited from wider research and greater analysis.

18:1228 Steiner, Arthur. "Baptism of the Atomic Scientists." *Bulletin of the Atomic Scientists* 31 (February 1975): 21–28. Steiner traces the fate of the June 11, 1945, Franck Report, calling for a "non-lethal demonstration of the soon-to-be-ready atomic bomb," to illuminate one aspect of scientists' participation in national policymaking.

Invasion, Surrender Terms, Alternatives

18:1229 Allen, Thomas B., and Norman Polmar. *Code-Name Downfall: The Secret Plan to Invade Japan and Why Truman Dropped the Bomb*. New York: Simon and Schuster, 1995. This is a concise and useful account that places invasion planning within the context of ongoing military operations in the Pacific. The authors give detailed attention to U.S. casualty estimates and the probable nature of ground operations in the Japanese home islands.

18:1230 Bernstein, Barton J. "The Alarming Japanese Buildup on Southern Kyushu, Growing U.S. Fears, and Counterfactual Analysis: Would the Planned November 1945 Invasion of Southern Kyushu Have Occurred?" *Pacific Historical Review* 68 (November 1999): 561–609. Bernstein concludes in this well-researched counterfactual analysis that had Japan not surrendered in August 1945, its military buildup on southern Kyushu as revealed by Ultra might very well have led to cancellation of the planned November invasion of the island out of the fear of incurring heavy U.S. casualties.

18:1231 _____. "Compelling Japan's Surrender without the A-bomb, Soviet Entry, or Invasion: Reconsidering the US Bombing Survey's Early-Surrender Conclusions." *Journal of Strategic Studies* 18 (June 1995): 101–48. Bernstein thoughtfully investigates the postwar counterfactual claim of the U.S. Strategic Bombing Survey that Japan would have surrendered by November 1, 1945, if the atomic

bomb had not been used. Examining the survey members' biases, evidence, and arguments, he finds that their contentions should not be accepted as authoritative and that, using the survey's own stipulated conditions (which excluded consideration of Soviet entry into the war), Japanese surrender would likely have occurred at a later date. Bernstein notes, however, that the combination of continued bombing and Soviet entry probably would have brought surrender by November 1.

18:1232 _____. "Eclipsed by Hiroshima and Nagasaki: Early Thinking about Tactical Nuclear Weapons." *International Security* 15 (Spring 1991): 149–73. Bernstein demonstrates a growing, albeit numerically limited, military desire to use atomic bombs against military targets in conjunction with an invasion rather than continue to bomb cities and civilians. He uses Marshall's thinking about the need for invasion to engage Gar Alperovitz on American motivation for using the atomic bombs. Marshall had been interested since early 1945 in possible tactical use of nuclear weapons to support an invasion of the Japanese home islands, and after Nagasaki he considered substituting such tactical use for destruction of a third Japanese city on the grounds that strategic use of the weapon had failed to produce the desired result and that destroying a third city would be both senseless and immoral. Correspondence on this and related issues among Alperovitz, Robert L. Messer, and Bernstein is in the Winter 1991–1992 issue of this journal, 204–221. See also Gallicchio, "After Nagasaki: General Marshall's Plan for Tactical Nuclear Weapons in Japan" (1991) (18:1241).

18:1233 _____. "A Postwar Myth: 500,000 Lives Saved." *Bulletin of the Atomic Scientists* 42 (June-July 1986): 38–40. Bernstein uses wartime plans—particularly those of the Joint War Plans Committee—to show that contemporary casualty estimates for the invasion of Japan were significantly lower than was subsequently reported in postwar writings and memoirs.

18:1234 _____. "Reconsidering Truman's Claim of 'Half a Million American Lives Saved' by the Atomic Bomb: The Construction and Deconstruction of a Myth." *Journal of Strategic Studies* 22 (March 1999): 54–95. This article revisits and expands upon the conclusions in Bernstein, "A Postwar Myth:

500,000 Lives Saved" (1986) (18:1233) and Miles, "Hiroshima: The Strange Myth of Half a Million American Lives Saved" (1985) (18:1245), which first attacked Truman's postwar memoir claim that the atomic bombs saved 500,000 U.S. lives. The revisit was occasioned by recent disclosure of a major mid-1945 Japanese buildup on Kyushu and the ensuing resurrection of Truman's claim by Giangreco ("Casualty Projections for the U.S. Invasion of Japan, 1945–1946: Planning and Policy Implications," 1997 [18:1242]), Maddox (*Weapons for Victory: The Hiroshima Decision Fifty Years Later,* 1995 [18:1215]), Newman (*Truman and the Hiroshima Cult,* 1995 [18:1216]), and McCullough (*Truman,* 1992 [19:231]). Bernstein concludes that no reliable archival evidence exists that before Hiroshima Truman received such an estimate of U.S. deaths in an invasion, or that he or Marshall believed such a number. He also cautions against reliance on any memoir claims unsupported by archival evidence.

18:1235 _____. "Understanding the Atomic Bomb and the Japanese Surrender: Missed Opportunities, Little-Known Near Disasters, and Modern Memory." *Diplomatic History* 19 (Spring 1995): 227–73. In this thoughtful essay Bernstein summarizes his views on a variety of issues that surround historical debate over the use of the atomic bomb against Japan, including the ethics and necessity of its use, the American decisionmaking climate, and possible alternative means of gaining Japan's surrender. He also dismantles the claim of Alperovitz and Messer, "Marshall, Truman, and the Decision to Drop the Bomb" (1991–1992) (18:1249), that intimidating the Soviet Union was the key consideration in its use.

18:1236 Brower, Charles F., IV. "Assault or Siege? The Debate over Final Strategy for the Defeat of Japan, 1943–1945." *Joint Perspectives* 2 (Spring 1982): 72–83. Brower maintains that army insistence on invasion of Japan instead of the siege strategy advocated by the air force and navy was based on political factors as well as interservice issues. Most notable in this regard was army recognition that the siege strategy could not obtain quick and unconditional Japanese surrender. For greater depth, see his "Sophisticated Strategist: General George A. Lincoln and the Defeat of Japan, 1944–45" (1991) (18:1237).

18:1237 _____. "Sophisticated Strategist: General George A. Lincoln and the Defeat of Japan, 1944–45." *Diplomatic History* 15 (Summer 1991): 317–37. A West Point graduate and Rhodes scholar, Lincoln was one of General Marshall's key strategic planners in the latter years of the war and a leading figure in the postwar army's "brain trust." Brower focuses on him to illustrate the complex and sophisticated strategic thinking in the armed forces about how to obtain Japanese surrender.

18:1238 Chappell, John D. *Before the Bomb: How America Approached the End of the Pacific War.* Lexington: University Press of Kentucky, 1997. This is an informative study of American public opinion and home-front discourse in 1945 about the war with Japan. Chappell notes the existence of contradictory impulses and spirited debate and suggests that unimaginative leadership failed to grasp the public's willingness to support modified peace terms that would end the war.

18:1239 Coox, Alvin D. "Needless Fear: The Compromise of U.S. Plans to Invade Japan in 1945." *Journal of Military History* 64 (April 2000): 411–38. Coox explores revelations by a former U.S. officer of serious breaches in the security of invasion plans for Kyushu located in MacArthur's headquarters in Manila. He concludes, however, that these breaches were not damaging and did not cause the mid-1945 Japanese buildup on Kyushu.

18:1240 Drea, Edward J. *In the Service of the Emperor: Essays on the Imperial Japanese Army.* Lincoln: University of Nebraska Press, 1998. This volume of essays is based on extensive Japanese sources and focuses primarily on the Imperial Japanese army. The final three chapters—addressing Japanese preparations for homeland defense in 1945, what Americans learned of those preparations from signal intelligence, and the wartime role of the emperor—provide important insights into the process of war termination in the Pacific.

18:1241 Gallicchio, Marc S. "After Nagasaki: General Marshall's Plan for Tactical Nuclear Weapons in Japan." *Prologue* 23 (Winter 1991): 396–404. Using newly declassified documents, Gallicchio concludes that Army Chief of Staff General Marshall, concerned about Japanese defenses on Kyushu, seriously considered tactical use of nuclear weapons in support of an invasion if Tokyo did not surrender after the bombing of Nagasaki. Radiation dangers to U.S. troops were neither known nor considered. See also Bernstein's simultaneous article on this subject, "Eclipsed by Hiroshima and Nagasaki: Early Thinking about Tactical Nuclear Weapons" (1991) (18:1232).

18:1242 Giangreco, D. M. "Casualty Projections for the U.S. Invasion of Japan, 1945–1946: Planning and Policy Implications." *Journal of Military History* 61 (July 1997): 521–81. Analyzing casualty estimates for the invasion of Japan, the author argues for the "existence and complete acceptance" by the War Department and the army of casualty projections of 1 million or more as the cost of conquering Japan. He does not, however, muster direct evidence to support this position.

18:1243 Hikins, James W. "The Rhetoric of 'Unconditional Surrender' and the Decision to Drop the Atomic Bomb." *Quarterly Journal of Speech* 69 (November 1983): 379–400. Hikins argues perceptively that the term "unconditional surrender" metamorphosed from a tool to unify the allies into a "social reality" that, once accepted by the American public as a war aim, constrained policymakers seeking to conclude the war with Japan. Their unwillingness to risk possible domestic political damage by modifying "unconditional surrender," therefore, was an important causal factor for use of the atomic bombs.

18:1244 MacEachin, Douglas J. *The Final Months of the War with Japan: Signals Intelligence, U.S. Invasion Planning, and the Atomic-Bomb Decision.* Washington, DC: Center for the Study of Intelligence, Central Intelligence Agency, 1998. This volume examines the intelligence available to American policymakers during the final months of the war with Japan and considers how it might have influenced deliberations about invading Japan. The work contains a useful and even-handed discussion of the deliberations, including casualty estimates, and reprints twenty-five significant documents.

18:1245 Miles, Rufus E., Jr. "Hiroshima: The Strange Myth of Half a Million American Lives Saved." *International Security* 10 (Fall 1985):

121–40. This is one of the early skeptical works highlighting discrepancies between wartime casualty estimates for the invasion of Japan and those put forward after the war. Miles concludes that the decision to drop atomic bombs was not based on casualty considerations.

18:1246 Newman, Robert P. "Ending the War with Japan: Paul Nitze's 'Early Surrender' Counterfactual." *Pacific Historical Review* 64 (May 1995): 167–94. In this important article, Newman investigates the claims of the U.S. Strategic Bombing Survey that Japan was close to surrender in the summer of 1945 and shows that there is little evidence to support this contention.

18:1247 Pearlman, Michael D. *Unconditional Surrender, Demobilization, and the Atomic Bomb.* Fort Leavenworth, KS: Combat Studies Institute, U.S. Army Command and General Staff College, 1996. In its 1945 strategic and policy recommendations, the War Department expressed fear of a decline in public morale and support for the war against Japan should it not end soon after Germany's surrender or in the event of high combat casualties.

18:1248 Skates, John Ray. *The Invasion of Japan: Alternative to the Bomb.* Columbia: University of South Carolina Press, 1994. Skates provides a sober and detailed assessment and analysis of U.S. plans for the invasion of Japan as well as planned Japanese countermeasures. He also offers an even-handed appraisal of the probable outcome of ground operations. See also Timothy P. Maga, *America Attacks Japan: The Invasion That Never Was* (Lexington: University Press of Kentucky, 2002).

Truman Uses the Atomic Bomb

18:1249 Alperovitz, Gar, and Robert L. Messer. "Marshall, Truman, and the Decision to Drop the Bomb." *International Security* 16 (Winter 1991–1992): 204–14. Responding to Bernstein, "Eclipsed by Hiroshima and Nagasaki: Early Thinking about Tactical Nuclear Weapons" (1991) (18:1232), the authors criticize his suggestion that desire to influence the Soviet Union might not have been a primary consideration in dropping the atomic bombs, arguing that efforts to avoid Soviet intervention against Japan gained momentum in the late summer of 1945. Countering (214–21), Bernstein notes how much these accounts rely on interpretations of President Truman's writings in July 1945 and states that preempting Soviet intervention was a "confirming but not essential reason" for using the bomb.

18:1250 Bernstein, Barton J. "The Atomic Bombings Reconsidered." *Foreign Affairs* 74 (January-February 1995): 135–52. Bernstein emphasizes that use of the atomic bomb did not raise "profound moral issues" for policymakers. Nor did they seek to avoid its use; rather, the assumption of use prevailed. In his conclusion, however, Bernstein suggests that pursuing alternative tactics would have permitted them to avoid the invasion and still achieve Japan's surrender by the end of November 1945.

18:1251 _____. "Seizing the Contested Terrain of Early Nuclear History: Stimson, Conant, and Their Allies Explain the Decision to Use the Atomic Bomb." *Diplomatic History* 17 (Winter 1993): 35–72. Bernstein shows that articles written by Karl T. Compton ("If the Atomic Bomb Had Not Been Used," *Atlantic Monthly,* December 1946) and Henry L. Stimson ("The Decision to Use the Atomic Bomb," 1947 [18:1262]) were calculated efforts to shape both public opinion and historical interpretation of the decision to drop atomic bombs on Japan. See also Hershberg, *James B. Conant: Harvard to Hiroshima and the Making of the Nuclear Age* (1993) (18:321).

18:1252 _____. "Truman and the A-Bomb: Targeting Noncombatants, Using the Bomb, and Defending the 'Decision.'" *Journal of Military History* 62 (July 1998): 547–70. In this essay, Bernstein uses a review of Ferrell, *Harry S. Truman and the Bomb: A Documentary History* (1996) (18:71), as a takeoff to discuss a variety of issues central to atomic bomb historiography, including casualty estimates, Roosevelt-era momentum for use of the bomb, and Truman's postwar writings, self-contradictions, and self-deceptions. He concludes that any other nation would have used the bomb and that the war could have ended before November 1945 without its use had the Soviets entered as scheduled, the United States modified unconditional surrender to guarantee retention of the emperor, and both the naval blockade and conventional bombing continued.

18:1253 _____. "Writing, Righting, or Wronging the Historical Record: President Truman's Letter on His Atomic-Bomb Decision." *Diplomatic History* 16 (Winter 1992): 163–73. Bernstein traces the development of President Truman's 1952 response to questions posed by air force historians to illustrate how sources must be examined critically and how historical "facts" can be inadvertently created.

18:1254 Burnham, Alexander. "Okinawa, Harry Truman, and the Atomic Bomb." *Virginia Quarterly Review* 71 (Summer 1995): 377–92. Burnham asserts that the carnage of fighting on Okinawa, especially the American casualties, was an important factor in Truman's justifiable decision to use the atomic bombs against Japan.

18:1255 Cary, Otis. "The Sparing of Kyoto: Mr. Stimson's 'Pet City.'" *Japan Quarterly* 22 (October-December 1975): 337–47. Cary examines the stories about why the city of Kyoto was not heavily bombed by U.S. air forces during the war and was also spared from nuclear attack.

18:1256 Freedman, Lawrence, and Saki Dockrill. "Hiroshima: A Strategy of Shock." In *From Pearl Harbor to Hiroshima: The Second World War in Asia and the Pacific, 1941–1945,* ed. Saki Dockrill, 191–212. New York: St. Martin's Press, 1994. The authors contend that use of the atomic bomb against Japan reflected a coherent "shock" strategy that proved effective in hastening the Japanese surrender.

18:1257 Goldberg, Stanley. "Racing to the Finish: The Decision to Bomb Hiroshima and Nagasaki." *Journal of American–East Asian Relations* 4 (Summer 1995): 117–28. The author asserts that General Leslie Groves and the War Department feared that the war against Japan might end before the atomic bomb was used and took "all steps possible" to ensure that it was used. In reaching this judgment, he emphasizes the factors of momentum, reputation protection, and personal ambition.

18:1258 Messer, Robert L. "New Evidence on Truman's Decision." *Bulletin of the Atomic Scientists* 41 (August 1985): 50–56. Messer evaluates Truman's newly discovered diary and letters from the Potsdam conference. While seeming to clarify Truman's thoughts on some issues—that the bomb was not needed to end the war, that Truman wanted the Soviets to enter the war—the papers are inconclusive by themselves and can support contradictory interpretations.

18:1259 Morton, Louis. "The Decision to Use the Atom Bomb." *Foreign Affairs* 35 (January 1957): 334–53. The author disagrees in this early work with the notion that the bomb was used to forestall Russian intervention, though there were undoubtedly some people who favored this course.

18:1260 Newman, Robert P. "Hiroshima and the Trashing of Henry Stimson." *New England Quarterly* 71 (March 1998): 5–32. This is an insightful analysis of Stimson's 1947 article, "The Decision to Use the Atomic Bomb" (18:1262), the resultant historiography that has grown around it, and the major criticisms leveled against the article. Newman argues that Stimson's greatest fault was in framing the atomic bomb decision as an "either/or decision," which skewed perceptions of the decisionmaking process.

18:1261 Sigal, Leon V. "Bureaucratic Politics and Tactical Use of Committees: The Interim Committee and the Decision to Drop the Atomic Bomb." *Polity* 10 (Spring 1978): 326–64. Working within the bureaucratic politics framework, Sigal shows how various types of committees forged interagency agreement on and secured compliance by governmental agencies to drop the atomic bomb. See also his *Fighting to a Finish: The Politics of War Termination in the United States and Japan, 1945* (1988) (18:1275).

18:1262 Stimson, Henry L. "The Decision to Use the Atomic Bomb." *Harper's Magazine* (February 1947): 97–107. Stimson wrote this article with the assistance of McGeorge Bundy in a largely successful effort to control public debate over dropping the atomic bombs on Japan. He argued that, following Japan's rejection of the Potsdam ultimatum, the bombs were used to compel the surrender of Japan as quickly as possible. For his own account, see Truman, *Memoirs. Vol. 1: Year of Decisions* (1955) (19:234).

Race and Rage

18:1263 Ambrose, Stephen E., and Brian Loring Villa. "Racism, the Atomic Bomb, and the Transfor-

mation of Japanese-American Relations." In *The Pacific War Revisited*, ed. Günter Bischof and Robert L. Dupont, 179–98. Baton Rouge: Louisiana State University Press, 1997. The authors examine the racism and barbarism of the Pacific war and argue that the use of the atomic bomb actually paved the way for cultural reconciliation and reduced racial hatred. They also criticize Alperovitz's arguments presented in *Atomic Diplomacy: Hiroshima and Potsdam: The Use of the Atomic Bomb and the American Confrontation with Soviet Power* (1994) (18:1203) and elsewhere.

18:1264 Cameron, Craig M. *American Samurai: Myth, Imagination, and the Conduct of Battle in the First Marine Division, 1941–1951*. New York: Cambridge University Press, 1994. Focusing on the case of the First Marine Division, Cameron has produced an insightful study of cultural and organizational beliefs, values and norms, the changes that occurred in them during the Pacific war, and the effects those changes had on how the division and its men fought the Japanese. Cameron's work provides an interesting complement to Dower, *War without Mercy: Race and Power in the Pacific War* (1986) (18:528). Both indirectly help explain the decision to bomb Hiroshima and Nagasaki. For similar reasons, see George Feifer, *Tennozan: The Battle of Okinawa and the Atomic Bomb* (New York: Ticknor and Fields, 1992). For further consideration of the impact of American dehumanization of its enemies, especially the Japanese, see two unusual works by Edmund P. Russell, III: "'Speaking of Annihilation': Mobilizing for War against Human and Insect Enemies, 1941–1945," *Journal of American History* 82 (March 1996): 1505–29, and *War and Nature: Fighting Humans and Insects with Chemicals from World War I to Silent Spring* (New York: Cambridge University Press, 2001).

18:1265 Takaki, Ronald T. *Hiroshima: Why America Dropped the Atomic Bomb*. Boston: Little, Brown and Co., 1995. Takaki suggests that racism was the root cause of the atomic bombing of Japan.

Japan Surrenders

18:1266 Asada, Sadao. "The Shock of the Atomic Bomb and Japan's Decision to Surrender—A Reconsideration." *Pacific Historical Review* 67 (November 1998): 477–512. This important article draws on extensive Japanese sources to examine Japanese decisionmaking during the final days of the Pacific war. Asada argues that the atomic bomb, not the Soviet entry into the war, proved decisive; in particular, the "peace party" viewed the bomb as a "gift from Heaven" for providing necessary leverage to compel military leaders to accept surrender. Asada also reviews recent historiography.

18:1267 Bernstein, Barton J. "The Perils and Politics of Surrender: Ending the War with Japan and Avoiding the Third Atomic Bomb." *Pacific Historical Review* 46 (February 1977): 1–27. The ambiguous American response to Japan's August 10, 1945, surrender offer strengthened the militarists in Japan and nearly prolonged the war. Americans were concerned about domestic political effects if the emperor were retained; therefore, they were considering either a third atomic bomb or a costly invasion.

18:1268 Bix, Herbert P. "Japan's Delayed Surrender: A Reinterpretation." *Diplomatic History* 19 (Spring 1995): 197–225. This is an important reinterpretation, based on extensive use of Japanese sources, of the decisionmaking process that led to surrender. Bix places "heavy responsibility" on Japanese leaders for prolonging the war (with callous disregard for the suffering of the Japanese people), and, correcting the view that the military dominated the political process, emphasizes the pivotal role played by Emperor Hirohito at every stage. Noting the inept reliance on the vague hope of Soviet mediation, Bix argues that Japanese leaders let slip several opportunities to end the war because of their preoccupation with maintaining the political integrity of the Imperial monarchy.

18:1269 _____. "The Showa Emperor's 'Monologue' and the Problem of War Responsibility." *Journal of Japanese Studies* 18 (Summer 1992): 295–363. Bix completely revises the traditional interpretation of Hirohito as a passive or powerless emperor, arguing that he was an active and "well-informed belligerent leader." He relies heavily on the *Showa tenno dokuhakuroku (The Showa Emperor's Monologue)* to demonstrate Hirohito's activism, using the emperor's own words.

18:1270 Butow, Robert J. C. *Japan's Decision to Surrender.* Stanford, CA: Stanford University Press, 1954. Despite its age, this early study remains an excellent account of the factors leading to Japanese surrender. Butow writes with great knowledge and appreciation of the subtleties and intricacies of the Japanese political process. The focus throughout is on the situation in and as seen from Tokyo.

18:1271 Coox, Alvin D. "The *Enola Gay* and Japan's Struggle to Surrender." *Journal of American–East Asian Relations* 4 (Summer 1995): 161–67. Coox criticizes revisionist accounts of American motivation in dropping the atomic bomb for framing arguments in a strictly western context and surveys Japanese military preparations to counter an invasion as well as the military's unwillingness to surrender. He argues that the decision to employ the atomic bomb was based on "preponderantly military considerations."

18:1272 Iokibe, Makoto. "American Policy towards Japan's Unconditional Surrender." *Japanese Journal of American Studies,* no. 1 (1981): 19–54. The author traces the history of the unconditional surrender concept, its different definitions, and its applications to Germany and Japan during the war. He emphasizes the modification of the formula for Japan within the Potsdam Declaration, which he credits to lower-level staff initiatives by "Japan Hands" within the State Department and the Council on Foreign Relations as well as Joseph Grew and those favoring a shift in Soviet policy.

18:1273 Munro-Leighton, Judith. "The Tokyo Surrender: A Diplomatic Marathon in Washington, August 10–14, 1945." *Pacific Historical Review* 65 (August 1996): 455–73. This article examines the role of the State-War-Navy Coordinating Committee in the days after the initial Japanese surrender offer and blames the hastily made, subsequent policy decisions for adding to growing Soviet mistrust of the United States.

18:1274 Pape, Robert A., Jr. "Why Japan Surrendered." *International Security* 18 (Fall 1993): 154–201. Viewing Japan's surrender as the most successful example of "military coercion" in modern history, Pape argues that its timing was not the result of conventional or atomic bombing or Washington's agreement to Japanese retention of the emperor. It came instead from Japanese recognition of their extreme military vulnerability due primarily to the successful U.S. naval blockade but also to the fall of Okinawa and rapid collapse of Japanese forces in Manchuria under Soviet attack. This article is reprinted as chapter 4 of the author's *Bombing to Win: Air Power and Coercion in War* (Ithaca: Cornell University Press, 1996).

18:1275 Sigal, Leon V. *Fighting to a Finish: The Politics of War Termination in the United States and Japan, 1945.* Ithaca: Cornell University Press, 1988. Sigal questions historians' reliance on a rational actor model to explain the process of war termination in Japan and the United States. In its place, he presents an organizational conflict model that gives primacy to bureaucratic and domestic politics in determining the final outcome.

18:1276 Villa, Brian Loring. "The U.S. Army, Unconditional Surrender, and the Potsdam Declaration." *Journal of American History* 63 (June 1976): 66–92. This administrative study analyzes the debate over possible modification of the unconditional surrender formula, most notably in regard to Japan, which took place within and between the War and State Departments.

Contemporary Reactions

18:1277 Bernstein, Barton J. "Ike and Hiroshima: Did He Oppose It?" *Journal of Strategic Studies* 10 (September 1987): 377–89. Bernstein challenges the claim of Eisenhower in his memoirs that he had openly disagreed with those thinking it necessary to drop the atomic bomb on Japan. The circumstantial evidence suggests he never expressed such an opinion at the time.

18:1278 Boller, Paul, Jr. "Hiroshima and the American Left: August 1945." *International Social Science Review* 57 (Winter 1982): 13–28. Boller examines attitudes on the American left in 1945 and argues that the strongest defenders of the atomic bombings were also those groups friendliest to Stalin, which did not interpret use of the bomb as an effort to intimidate the Soviet Union. The strongest critics of the bomb were anti-Stalin liberals.

18:1279 Fussell, Paul. *Thank God for the Atom Bomb, and Other Essays.* New York: Summit Books, 1988. Literary critic and iconoclast Fussell offers a spirited defense of the decision to drop the atomic bomb on Japan from his 1945 perspective as an American G.I. fearfully anticipating a bloody invasion of the Japanese home islands. He originally wrote and published this as "Hiroshima: A Soldier's View," in *The New Republic* of August 22 and 29, 1981. Also reproduced from the September 23, 1981, issue of that magazine is the ensuing exchange between Fussell and Michael Walzer.

Memory and History

18:1280 Bird, Kai, and Lawrence Lifschultz, eds. *Hiroshima's Shadow: Writings on the Denial of History & the Smithsonian Controversy.* Stony Creek, CT: Pamphleteer's Press, 1998. This is a hefty compilation of contemporary and historians' revisionist critiques of the atomic bomb decision. Many have been previously published, but educators will find the aggregation useful. Accounts of survivors' experiences, essays about the 1995 Smithsonian exhibit, and reproductions of a selection of significant documents are also included. Those of greatest scholarly pertinence not separately listed in this chapter in their original form are Lifschultz and Bird, "The Legend of Hiroshima"; Uday Mohan and Sanho Tree, "The Construction of Conventional Wisdom"; Martin J. Sherwin, "Hiroshima and Modern Memory"; John W. Dower, "Unconditional Surrender at the Smithsonian"; Sherwin, "Memory, Myth and History"; Martin Harwit, "The *Enola Gay:* A Nation's, and a Museum's, Dilemma"; and Bird, "The Curators Cave In."

18:1281 Boyer, Paul. "Exotic Resonances: Hiroshima in American Memory." *Diplomatic History* 19 (Spring 1995): 297–318. This is a thoughtful analysis of the complex role Hiroshima has played in influencing postwar American culture and thought.

18:1282 Hogan, Michael J., ed. *Hiroshima in History and Memory.* Cambridge, UK: Cambridge University Press, 1996. This is a collection of reedited essays originally published in *Diplomatic History* (6 in the Summer 1995 issue), plus introductory and concluding essays by editor Hogan on the 1995

Smithsonian *Enola Gay* exhibit. Other contributors include J. Samuel Walker, "The Decision to Use the Bomb: A Historiographical Update" (11–37) and "History, Collective Memory, and the Decision to Use the Bomb" (187–99); Barton J. Bernstein, "Understanding the Atomic Bomb and the Japanese Surrender: Missed Opportunities, Little-Known Near Disasters, and Modern Memory" (38–79); Herbert P. Bix, "Japan's Delayed Surrender: A Reinterpretation" (80–115); John W. Dower "Bombed: Hiroshimas and Nagasakis in Japanese Memory"(116–42); and Paul Boyer "Exotic Resonances: Hiroshima in American Memory" (143–67).

18:1283 Lifton, Robert Jay, and Greg Mitchell. *Hiroshima in America: Fifty Years of Denial.* New York: Putnam's Sons, 1995. This work examines the long-term impact of the atomic bombing of Japan on the American psyche. One section is devoted to psychoanalyzing President Truman's decision to authorize using the bomb and his postwar struggle with, in the authors' words, "unrealized guilt."

18:1284 Linenthal, Edward Tabor, and Tom Engelhardt, eds. *History Wars: The Enola Gay and Other Battles for the American Past.* New York: Metropolitan Books, 1996. This is a collection of essays on various aspects of the controversy surrounding the 1995 Smithsonian *Enola Gay* exhibit. With the exceptions of Dower and Boyer's contributions, the essays contain little about American foreign relations, but offer a variety of insights into the politicization and turmoil of late-twentieth-century American culture. Contents include: Engelhardt and Linenthal, "Introduction: History under Siege" (1–8); Linenthal, "Anatomy of a Controversy" (9–62); John W. Dower, "Three Narratives of Our Humanity" (63–96); Michael S. Sherry, "Patriotic Orthodoxy and American Decline" (97–114); Paul Boyer, "Whose History Is It Anyway? Memory, Politics, and Historical

Scholarship" (115–39); Richard H. Kohn, "History at Risk: The Case of the *Enola Gay*" (140–70); Mike Wallace, "Culture War, History Front" (171–98); Marilyn B. Young, "Dangerous History: Vietnam and the 'Good War'" (199–209); and Engelhardt, "The Victors and the Vanquished" (210–50). See also Thelen, "History and the Public: What Can We Handle? A Round Table about History after the *Enola Gay* Controversy" (1995) (18:1285).

18:1285 Thelen, David P., ed. "History and the Public: What Can We Handle? A Round Table about History after the *Enola Gay* Controversy." *Journal of American History* 82 (December 1995): 1029–1135. Published in the wake of the Smithsonian controversy over the fiftieth anniversary of the atomic bombings (and some reproduced in Linenthal and Engelhardt, *History Wars: The Enola Gay and Other Battles for the American Past,* 1996 [18:1284]), this fascinating probe into history and memory begins with Thelen's introduction, "History after the *Enola Gay* Controversy: An Introduction" (1029–35). Following are Richard H. Kohn, "History and the Culture Wars: The Case of the Smithsonian Institution's *Enola Gay* Exhibition" (1036–63); Martin Harwit, "Academic Freedom in the 'Last Act'" (1064–84); Martin J. Sherwin, "Hiroshima as Politics and History (1085–93); Edward T. Linenthal, "Struggling with History and Memory" (1094–1101); Neil Harris, "Museums and Controversy: Some Introductory Reflections" (1102–10); Thomas A. Woods, "Museums and the Public: Doing History Together" (1111–15); Rinjiro Sodei, "Hiroshima/Nagasaki as History and Politics" (1118–23); and John W. Dower, "Triumphal and Tragic Narratives of the War in Asia" (1124–35). In addition are a few comments made at an OAH session that originated this panel (1116–17) and a section of reproduced documents (1136–44), including Senate Resolution 257, a speech by Senator Nancy Kassenbaum, and excerpts from Senate hearings.